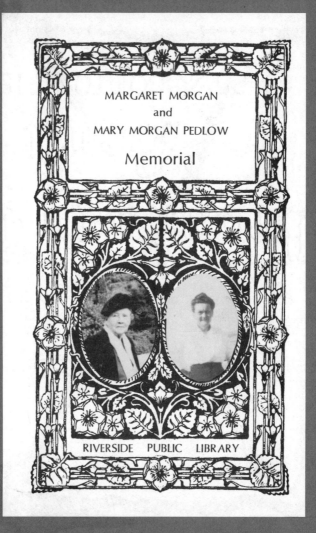

MARGARET MORGAN
and
MARY MORGAN PEDLOW

Memorial

RIVERSIDE PUBLIC LIBRARY

HISTORICAL TIMES
ILLUSTRATED ENCYCLOPEDIA
OF THE CIVIL WAR

Historical Times Illustrated Encyclopedia of the Civil War

PATRICIA L. FAUST

EDITOR

NORMAN C. DELANEY
EDWARD G. LONGACRE
JOHN E. STANCHAK
JEFFRY D. WERT

ASSOCIATE EDITORS

MARSHA L. LARSEN

EDITORIAL ASSISTANT

1817

HARPER & ROW, PUBLISHERS, New York
*Cambridge, Philadelphia, San Francisco, Washington
London, Mexico City, São Paulo, Singapore, Sydney*

FIRST EDITION

Designer: Sidney Feinberg
Copy editor: William C. Reynolds
Maps by Mark H. Pfoutz

Library of Congress Cataloging-in-Publication Data

Historical times illustrated encyclopedia of the Civil
    War.
1. United States—History—Civil War, 1861–1865—
Dictionaries. 2. United States—History—Civil War,
1861–1865—Pictorial works. I. Faust, Patricia L.
E468.H57 1986   973.7   86-45095
ISBN 0-06-181261-7

---

86 87 88 89 90 RRD 10 9 8 7 6 5 4 3 2 1

To Patricia L. Faust
1948–1984
the editor of this work

Contents

Contributors

ECB   Edwin C. Bearss, chief historian of the National Park Service, has done extensive research for the Park Service, including research on Civil War parks. He found and helped with the salvage of the Civil War gunboat *Cairo* and has edited 13 books and more than 100 scholarly articles in this field.

LJB   Lawrence J. Bopp, a teacher for the Baltimore County school system, has been a Civil War reenactor and lecturer for 18 years. He is a member of the Company of Military Historians and has been engaged in living-history programs at home and abroad.

WRB   William R. Brooksher, brigadier general, USAF (ret.), and manager, safeguards and security, Westinghouse Hanford Company, is the co-author of a number of articles on Confederate cavalry raids. His work has appeared in *Civil War Times Illustrated, Military History,* and *Military Review.*

AC   Albert Castel, professor of history at Western Michigan University, Kalamazoo, Mich., has written, among other works, *A Frontier State at War: Kansas, 1861–1865* and *General Sterling Price and the Civil War in the West,* and presently is writing a history of the Atlanta Campaign.

MTC   Michael T. Cochran has written reviews and articles for *Civil War Times* and *American History Illustrated.*

JPC   Joseph P. Cullen, retired historian, National Park Service, is the author of *The Peninsula Campaign 1862* and *A Concise Illustrated History of the American Revolution,* in addition to several historical handbooks for the National Park Service and numerous articles in *Civil War Times Illustrated, American History Illustrated,* and other journals.

WCD   William C. (Jack) Davis is editorial director of Historical Times Inc. He was editor of the 6-volume series The Image of War as well as the author or editor of a dozen other books on the Civil War, including a prize-winning biography of John C. Breckinridge.

NCD   Norman C. Delaney, professor of history at Del Mar College, Corpus Christi, Tex., and an adjunct professor for the Naval War College, Carlisle, Pa., is the author of *John McIntosh Kell of the Raider Alabama.* His chapter on the Confederate commerce destroyers appears in The Image of War series.

PLF   Patricia L. Faust, at the time of her death in November 1984, was editor of *Virginia Cavalcade.* Previously she had been managing editor, then editor, of *American History Illustrated.*

DEF   Dale E. Floyd, an archivist in the National Archives' Navy and Old Army Branch for over a decade, has been a historian with the Historical Division, Office, Chief of (Army) Engineers, for more than 6 years. He has written articles in scholarly journals, including "Army Engineers in the Civil War" and "Paper in the Confederacy; or, the Soldier's Search for Stationery," and *The Southeast During the Civil War: Selected War Department Records in the National Archives . . . ; National Archives Reference Information Paper No. 69* (1973). In addition, he edited *"Dear Friends at Home . . .": The Letters and Diary of Thomas James Owen, Fiftieth New York Volunteer Engineer Regiment in the Civil War,* published by the Government Printing Office in 1985, and is presently writing a volume on Union Army engineer activities during the Civil War.

RHF   Robert H. Fowler founded the magazines *Civil War Times* and *American History Illustrated.* He now serves as chairman of the board of Historical Times Inc. Fowler holds a master's degree in journalism from Columbia University. Formerly a Harrisburg, Pa., newspaper editorial writer, he has written 3 historical novels.

LG   Larry Gara, professor of history and chairman of the history department at Wilmington College (Ohio), is the author of articles on the antislavery movement and *The Liberty Line: The Legend of the Underground Railroad.*

AG   Arnold Gates, secretary, Civil War Round Table of New York, and its editor of publications (1954–67), was literary editor of *Lincoln Herald* (1956–77); wrote The Gates Report: The Civil War Today for *Civil War Times* (1978–82); and contributed to *Abraham Lincoln, A New Portrait* (Putnam 1959) and *Lincoln for the Ages* (Doubleday 1960). He is a member of the Society of American Historians and the National Book Critics Circle.

ACG   Allen C. Guelzo, assistant professor of church history at the Theological Seminary of the Reformed Episcopal Church in Philadelphia, is also lecturer in American history at Drexel University/University College. He is the author of several studies of American religion and culture from 1750 to 1860. He is a member of the American Society of Church History, the Conference on Faith and History, and the Union League of Philadelphia, and is a staff book reviewer for *Civil War Book Exchange.*

JOH   James O. Hall is a Lincoln scholar who writes and lectures extensively on various aspects of the Civil War, particularly on intelligence operations and the assassination of Abraham Lincoln.

LHH   Lowell H. Harrison, professor of history at Western Kentucky University, is the author of *The Civil War in Kentucky* and numerous articles on that conflict, and is a frequent speaker at Civil War round tables.

HH   Herman Hattaway, professor of history at the University of Missouri–Kansas City, is the author of nearly 100 articles and encyclopedia entries on Civil War topics, and of *General Stephen D. Lee* (1976), for which he won the Museum of the Confederacy's Jefferson Davis Award, and is co-author of *How the North Won* (1983), which won the National Historical Society's Bell I. Wiley Award. He is a member of the Civil War Research Society and of the Society of Civil War Historians.

RDH   Robert D. Hoffsommer, at the time of his death in January 1985, was associate editor of *Civil War Times Illustrated.* He was co-founder in 1959 of the Civil War Round Table of Harrisburg, Pennsylvania, today one of the strongest such groups in the nation, and he also helped found the Gettysburg Battlefield Preservation Association, an organization that purchased Gettysburg battlefield lands threatened by commercialization.

JTH   John T. Hubbell, professor of history and director of The Kent State University Press, has been the editor of *Civil War History* and is the author of *Battles Lost and Won: Essays from Civil War History.*

LDJ   Les D. Jensen, director of the 2nd Armored Division Museum at Fort Hood, Tex., was formerly curator of collections at the Museum of the Confederacy in Richmond, Va. He is a contributor to The Image of War series and is the author of numerous articles and studies. He has served as a consultant to a number of museums and historical organizations. He specializes in the material culture of the Civil War, with emphasis on the Confederate military.

VCJ   Virgil Carrington (Pat) Jones is the author of *Ranger Mosby, The Hatfields and the McCoys, Gray Ghosts and Rebel Raiders, Eight Hours Before Richmond, The Civil War at Sea* (3 vols.), *Birth of Liberty, Roosevelt's Rough Riders,* and *Log of Apollo 11,* the first official government account of the moon landing, as well as *First Manassas,* a 12,000-word special account for *Civil War Times Illustrated.* He was one of the founders of the Civil War Round Table of the District of Columbia, served as liaison officer for the Civil War Centennial Commission, and lives in Centreville, Va., on the edge of the Manassas battlefield.

JDK   John D. Kallmann is publisher and co-founder, along with his wife, Diane, of South Mountain Press in Carlisle, Pa., where he resides. He was until recently the head of the book-publishing division of Historical Times Inc., where he developed the business plan for this volume. He has had over 20 years' experience in publishing with various houses, including R. R. Bowker, Praeger Publishers, and Reader's Digest Press.

KAK   Kimberly A. Keefer, a free-lance writer and photographer specializing in articles on American and local history and historic sites, is presently the assistant editor of *Mercer Mosaic,* the Bucks County Historical Society journal, and is a correspondent for *The Wayfarer* of Bucks County, Pa. She was assistant editor of *American History Illustrated* and editorial assistant of *Civil War Times Illustrated,* to both of which she contributed articles, and also served as project coordinator for the Civil War Action Cards series published by Historical Times Inc.

DPK   Dennis P. Kelly, historian at Kennesaw Mountain National Battlefield Park, Ga., was formerly a National Park Service historian at Manassas National Battlefield Park, Va.

FSK   Frederic S. Klein, professor of American history at Franklin and Marshall College, Lancaster, Pa., is the author of *Just South of Gettysburg* (1963) and various contributions to *Civil War Times Illustrated* (1960–70). He was associate editor of *American History Illustrated* from 1968 to 1972 and was director of the television series *The Great Centennial* (1960–61). From 1964 to 1972, he was director of Civil War Times Battlefield Tours.

MK   Maury Klein, professor of history at the University of Rhode Island, is the author of 4 books and of forthcoming volumes on Jay Gould and the Union Pacific Railroad.

RKK   Robert K. Krick, a historian with the National Park Service at the Fredericksburg National Military Park, Va., is the author of several books on the Confederate army, including *Lee's Colonels, A Biographical Register of the Field Officers of the Army of Northern Virginia,* and *Parker's Virginia Battery.* He is a noted bibliographer of the Civil War as well.

DL   David Lindsey, professor of history, California State University, Los Angeles, and a director of the Institute for Civil War Studies, is the author of numerous articles and 7 books on American history, among the latter *Americans in Conflict: The Civil War and Reconstruction.*

EGL   Edward G. Longacre, a staff historian at the Headquarters of the Strategic Air Command, USAF, is the author of 4 books on the Civil War and the editor of a fifth. His most recent book, published in 1986, is *The Cavalry at Gettysburg: A Tactical Study of Mounted Operations During the Civil War's Pivotal Campaign, 9 June–14 July 1863.*

PMM   Patrick M. McCoy received an M.A. at Southern Illinois University, Carbondale, where he worked as a research assistant on *The Papers of Ulysses S.*

dale, where he worked as a research assistant on *The Papers of Ulysses S. Grant.* He is currently pursuing a Ph.D. at the University of Tennessee with the proposed dissertation title "The Cultural Origins of Confederate Military Leadership, 1861–1863."

BMcG Brian McGinty is an attorney and frequent contributor to scholarly journals and popular magazines in the fields of law and American history. He is the author of *Haraszthy at the Mint* (1975), *The Palace Inns: A Connoisseur's Guide to Historic American Hotels* (1978), and more than 100 articles that have appeared in such journals and magazines as *Americana, American Artist, American Bar Association Journal, American History Illustrated, American West, California History, California Lawyer, Catholic Digest, Civil War Times Illustrated, Early American Life,* and *Liberty, The Magazine of Religious Freedom.*

RMcM Richard M. McMurry teaches at North Carolina State University and is the author of *John Bell Hood and the War for Southern Independence.* He is currently working on a history of the Virginia Military Institute during the Civil War.

RJM Robert J. Maddox, professor of history at The Pennsylvania State University, has written 3 books and more than 40 articles, many of which deal with military affairs.

TMM Tamara Moser Melia, historian, Research Branch, Naval Historical Center, Washington, D.C., is also associate editor of volume two of *The Naval War of 1812: A Documentary History* and teaches Civil War history at Georgetown University. She did her graduate work at Southern Illinois University, Carbondale, where she assisted in editing *The Papers of Ulysses S. Grant.*

MM Maurice Melton, formerly an instructor in history at Clemson University, Greenville, S.C., writes about Confederate industry and the Union and Confederate navies. He is author of *The Confederate Ironclads,* published in 1968.

MMul Michael A. Mullins is the book-review editor of the *Civil War Book Exchange* and is the author of *The Union Bookshelf.* He is president of the Civil War Round Table of New Jersey.

MPM Michael P. Musick, archivist at the Navy and Old Army Branch of the National Archives, has contributed to *Prologue, The Military Collector and Historian, North-South Trader, Civil War Times Illustrated,* and other periodicals.

BNO Broeck N. Oder, chairman of the history department at the Santa Catalina School for Girls, Monterey, Calif., pursued extensive postgraduate training on the Civil War era and has contributed articles on that period to *Civil War*

MJO'D Michael J. O'Donnell, a graduate of Washington and Lee University with a B.A. in history, is associate editor of *North-South Trader* magazine. With Stephen W. Sylvia, he founded Moss Publications and co-authored 5 books for military collectors, the first of which was the acclaimed *Illustrated History of American Civil War Relics* (1978).

JTP J. Tracy Power received his B.A. from Emory University and his M.A. from the University of South Carolina. He plans to pursue his Ph.D. in history at the University of North Carolina. He has written an article and several book reviews for *Civil War Times Illustrated* and has contributed sketches to the *Dictionary of Literary Biography*.

RAP Russ A. Pritchard, director of the War Library and Museum of the Military Order of the Loyal Legion of the United States, in Philadelphia, has written articles for the *Journal of the Company of Military Historians,* the *Bugle of the Pennsylvania Antique Gun Collectors' Association,* the *Loyal Legion Historical Journal* and the *Maine Antique Digest.*

FR Frederic Ray, founder and former art director for the Tomahawk Comic Book series and former art director for the magazines *American History Illustrated, British Heritage Illustrated,* and *Civil War Times Illustrated,* is a foremost authority on historical art and a noted authority on military uniforms and equipment.

PR Peggy Robbins has been a free-lance writer for more than 3 decades. Her articles, many of which have been either about the Civil War or related to the Civil War era, have appeared in *Civil War Times Illustrated, American History Illustrated, American Heritage, Smithsonian, Early American Life, Southern Review, Delta Review, San Francisco Magazine, Southwest Art,* and several educational publications and state history journals.

JIR James I. Robertson, C. P. Miles Professor of History at Virginia Polytechnic Institute and State University, is the author of *The Stonewall Brigade, Civil War Sites in Virginia, Civil War Books: A Critical Bibliography,* and the editor of more than 15 volumes of Civil War history.

JWR John W. Rowell, retired editor, is the author of *Yankee Cavalrymen: Through the Civil War with the Ninth Pennsylvania Cavalry* and *Yankee Artillerymen: Through the Civil War with Eli Lilly's Indiana Battery,* and of several articles in *Civil War Times Illustrated.*

PRR Phillip R. Rutherford, professor of English at the University of Southern Maine, is the author of numerous articles on the Civil War and the history of weapons, and of *The Dictionary of Maine Place Names, Dissertations in Linguistics,* and *Fifty Years in Texas.*

DBS   David B. Sabine, retired research microbiologist, has written more than 50 articles on the Civil War and other phases of American history. He was a member of the Civil War Round Table of New York and has contributed articles to *Civil War Times Illustrated, American History Illustrated,* and *Early American Life.*

FLS   Fred L. Schultz, assistant editor of *Civil War Times Illustrated,* was formerly a member of the Gettysburg National Military Park Restoration Crew and is currently serving on the board of directors of the Gettysburg Battlefield Preservation Association. He is also a member of the Pennsylvania Memorial Preservation Fund Committee. His work has appeared in *American History Illustrated, British Heritage,* and *Chevron USA* magazines.

JYS   John Y. Simon, executive director and managing editor of the Ulysses S. Grant Association and professor of history at Southern Illinois University, Carbondale, edits *The Papers of Ulysses S. Grant,* of which 14 volumes have been published as of 1985.

DS   Dean E. Smith, executive vice-president, Arizona Historical Foundation, is a lifelong student of the Civil War in the Far West. He has been a contributor to *American History Illustrated, Civil War Times Illustrated,* and *Arizona Highways,* and is the author of a biography of former senator Barry Goldwater and 3 other biographical books.

DKS   David K. Snider, lieutenant colonel, USAF, is currently assigned to the Space Shuttle Project at Vandenberg Air Force Base, Calif. With co-author William R. Brooksher, he is a frequent contributor to *Civil War Times Illustrated* and other periodicals. His specialty is the Confederate cavalry.

RJS   Richard J. Sommers, chief archivist–historian at the U.S. Army Military History Institute, Carlisle, Pa., is the author of *Richmond Redeemed: the Siege at Petersburg* and also of "Petersburg Besieged" in The Image of War series. *Richmond Redeemed* was the first recipient of the National Historical Society's Bell I. Wiley Prize as the best Civil War book published in the 2 preceding years.

CMS   Charles M. Spearman, chief ranger at Fort Union National Monument, Watrous, N.M., has presented papers on Nathan G. "Shanks" Evans, German-Americans in the Civil War, and the Star Fort at Fort Union. He is a member of several Civil War round tables.

JES   John E. Stanchak has been editor of *Civil War Times Illustrated* since 1981.

WNS   William N. Still, Jr., professor of history and director of the Program in Maritime History and Underwater Research, East Carolina University, has written extensively on the naval side of the Civil War. Among his publications are *Iron Afloat: The Story of the Confederate Armorclads; Confederate Shipbuilding;* "The New Ironclads," in *Guns of 61,* as well as numerous articles. He is co-author of the forthcoming book *Why the South Lost the Civil War.*

WS   Wiley Sword is the author of *Shiloh: Bloody April* and *President Washington's Indian War,* and is a prominent collector of historical American weapons.

SWS   Stephen W. Sylvia, co-publisher of Moss Publications and publisher and editor of *North-South Trader* magazine, is an American military collector, historian, and author. He has co-authored *The Illustrated History of American Civil War Relics, Civil War Canteens, Civil War Reenactments, World War II G.I.,* and *The Guns of Grenada.* He has been a contributor to, and publisher of, a number of other books on the American military experience.

EMT   Emory M. Thomas, professor of history at the University of Georgia, has written a number of books, chapters in books, and articles on the American Civil War, including *The Confederate State of Richmond: A Biography of the Capital; The Confederacy As a Revolutionary Experience; The American War and Peace, 1860–1877;* and *The Confederate Nation, 1861–1865.*

JDW   Jeffry D. Wert, instructor of history at The Pennsylvania State University, has written dozens of articles on the Civil War and military history for such publications as *American History Illustrated, Civil War Times Illustrated, Blue & Gray, Virginia Cavalcade,* and *Military History.* He is the author of *Kernstown to Cedar Creek: The Shenandoah Valley Campaign, July–August 1864.*

BIW   Bell I. Wiley was senior consulting editor of the 6-volume series The Image of War, and wrote or edited over 50 books on the Civil War, particularly on its common soldiers. After a long and distinguished career, he died in 1979.

FDW   Frederick D. Williams, professor and chairman, department of history, Michigan State University, has written and edited books and articles on the Civil War. His writings include *The Wild Life of the Army: Civil War Letters of James A. Garfield* and a 4-volume study, *The Diary of James A. Garfield,* of which he was co-editor.

DLW   David L. Wilson, associate editor of *The Papers of Ulysses S. Grant* and adjunct associate professor of history at Southern Illinois University, Carbondale, has co-authored *The Presidency of Warren G. Harding* and edited *Ulysses S. Grant: Essays and Documents.*

Foreword

Americans have not been able to forget their Civil War. The enormity of the struggle
is one reason: More of our people died in the Civil War than during all of our wars,
from the Revolution through the Korean War, combined. This encyclopedia's entry
on the cost of the war estimates the total casualties at more than one million human
beings and the financial price at more than $8 billion. Americans could not forget a
conflict that produced death, suffering, and destruction in these quantities. It is also
true that millions of our citizens have recognized, in widely varying ways, that the Civil
War is a fundamental event in their past. The understanding that northerners and
southerners, black and white, have of Reconstruction, the civil rights movement of the
1960s, indeed, of any of their history, depends in some measure on their perception
of the events that occurred between 1861 and 1865. The military history of the war,
with its drama, human interest, immense scale, and blending of old and new warfare,
holds a fascination of its own. Americans today are interested in two of their wars
above all others: the Second World War and the Civil War.

Here is an encyclopedia that thousands of Civil War students will find a useful
reference, particularly commendable for the diversity of its entries. A work like this
is founded on its biographies, and the *Historical Times Illustrated Encyclopedia of the
Civil War* goes beyond the usual collection of high-ranking military leaders. The
generals are here, but so too are political figures such as William Porcher Miles, James
Harlan, Andrew Jackson Hamilton, and Harris Flanagin; correspondents and editors
George Smalley, Joseph Howard, Jr., Benjamin F. Dill, and William Howard Russell;
and artists and photographers Alfred R. Waud, Winslow Homer, Timothy O'Sullivan,
Mathew Brady, and Alexander Gardner. Women, Indians, foreign soldiers, and parti-
sans also are well represented. There is solid treatment of the war's campaigns, battles,
and famous units, with fair attention given to naval actions and the Trans-Mississippi.
The surveys of the political parties, elections, and congresses are matched by the
entries on social and economic topics, including the draft riots, taxes, and greenbacks.
The volume also introduces the New York *Tribune,* Richmond *Examiner,* Charleston
Mercury, and other important newspapers of the 1860s. Its maps, and several entries,
are helpful on the military geography of the war. There are discussions of the three
capitals, key locations such as City Point and Hampton Roads, and the major railroads.

New students of the Civil War often have been frustrated to find that many authors assume their readers don't need explanations of basic subjects. This encyclopedia addresses that problem, supplying clearly written introductions to strategy and tactics, cotton diplomacy, wartime medicine, ordnance, music, and other broad topics. Several entries help take the mystery out of the terminology of Civil War army life, with straightforward explanations of commutation, parole, the company fund, and other vagaries.

Beyond its utility, this encyclopedia offers impressive scholarship. Patricia Faust, her staff, and dozens of contributors have produced a volume that, in addition to names and dates, provides analysis, synthesis, and interpretation. The "industry" entry is a balanced essay on Thomas C. Cochran's thesis that the Civil War retarded industrialization. Controversial topics, such as the Fort Pillow massacre, the Spring Hill episode, and the Lincoln assassination, are treated judiciously. The entries on important Civil War books are an especially pleasant surprise. Here are descriptions and evaluations of the *Official Records,* Livermore, Fox, Miller, and other essential sources. The volume makes for enjoyable browsing, because it offers the satisfaction of finding an odd fact here and there, and of appreciating the research that has been invested in this project. Earl Weaver, the manager of the Baltimore Orioles, once contended: "It's what you learn after you know it all that counts." This volume reminds us that the Civil War is an enormous and interesting subject, and, yes, there is more to be learned about it.

Three days after the Battle of Gettysburg, an enlisted man in the 2d New Hampshire sent a letter to his family in Cheshire County. "You will want me to tell you of the battle," he wrote. "It was awful. Language will not convey an idea." Groping for words, the infantryman related that his regiment was under a "heavy fire that made the earth tremble and the air shook and was so full of smoke you could not see." War, this young soldier was trying to explain to his relatives, produces a confusion that overwhelms the senses. We try to understand war by making sense of its turmoil. In this volume, Patricia Faust and her associates have imposed order on the four tumultuous years of the American Civil War. They have created a beautiful illusion, the appearance that the confusion can be mastered, that the chaos of a vast conflict can be sorted out into twenty-two hundred compact entries. It is an illusion, of course, but it is one that gives us a better understanding of our worst national tragedy.

—PERRY D. JAMIESON

History Office,
USAF Space Command

Preface

Books about the Civil War began appearing long before the conflict ended in 1865. As early as 1862, E. A. Pollard, editor of the Richmond *Examiner,* published a review titled *The First Year of the War,* in which he summarized events since Fort Sumter and editorialized about the strengths and weaknesses of Confederate generals. (He gave low marks to Robert E. Lee.)

Although there have been peaks and valleys in the output, not a year has gone by since Appomattox without a fresh lot of books about the war in general, some aspect thereof, or biographies of war leaders. The number, including Pollard's work, totals approximately 100,000.

Each generation seems to require a retelling of the war. Each new wave of books both feeds the appetites of Civil War buffs and creates a taste for more. And, curiously, by their very number, it may be that so many books confuse, rather than enlighten, some persons who have a genuine interest in that crucial period of American history but lack the time to keep abreast of all the newly published material.

Thus far, however, there has been no single, well-illustrated omnibus volume on which students of the war could rely as a reference work and still enjoy as recreational reading. We offer this book as the end to that long wait.

The conception of our *Historical Times Illustrated Encyclopedia of the Civil War* sprang from a suggestion by Harper & Row in 1982 that our company, Historical Times Inc., join them in some sort of encyclopedia of the Civil War. During subsequent conferences, we considered and ultimately rejected several options, including a very extensive, multivolume work, as well as a single, nonillustrated volume. Finally we settled on the concept reflected herein: a one-volume, richly illustrated encyclopedia that would be equally at home on one's desk or bedside table.

The Civil War lasted four years, and it has taken about that long to produce this *Historical Times Illustrated Encyclopedia of the Civil War.* It has been a challenging project, involving both careful planning and, at times, exhausting execution.

This volume reflects the work of five editors and sixty-two authors. Besides their two thousand written entries, we have included nearly a thousand photographs and other illustrations, plus sixty-seven maps.

Naturally, at the outset guidelines had to be established for what to put in and what to leave out. Our editors decided to emphasize biographical entries, but about whom? After all, some three million men served in one uniform or the other, and many other persons of both sexes were involved in war-related activities. The line had to be drawn somewhere. Accordingly, while all Confederate general officers are profiled, we omitted a few Union brigadiers who were never in the field. This left more room for some persons of lesser rank who made significant contributions, persons such as Marie Tebe, sutler and mascot of the 114th Pennsylvania Volunteers, and Lt. Dick Dowling, the Confederate hero of Sabine Pass.

Likewise, it was out of the question to include an entry on each of the 6,500 recorded clashes between Federal and Confederate forces from 1861 to 1865. So, very few skirmishes or minor affairs have found their way into our pages. We have saved our space for major campaigns and the more important battles.

Choices had to be made as to what to call those engagements of sufficient size and significance to be included. As is well known, Federals tended to name a battle after some natural feature while the more bucolic Confederates used the name of the nearest settlement or church. In general, our editors have chosen what they felt to be the most popular current usage, as Shiloh rather than Pittsburg Landing and Antietam rather than Sharpsburg.

Although this work deals mainly with military events and leaders, we have reserved a generous allotment of space for political and diplomatic events, art and artists of the time, popular music and musicians, photography and photographers, newspapers and journalists—indeed, activities and personalities of all sorts. And we have not over-looked technical aspects, such as the use of telegraphy, railroads, and modern weaponry.

And in writing about technical matters such as fortifications and tactics, we have taken pains to define terms such as *cheveaux-de-frise* and *vidette.*

In compiling army strengths and casualties, we have relied on William F. Fox's *Regimental Losses in the American Civil War 1861–65, War of the Rebellion Official Records,* and other standard works. We do not pretend to have based our entries on primary sources.

Historical Times Inc. has published the magazine *Civil War Times Illustrated* ten times every year since its inception in 1959. Throughout the magazine's history, its various editors have struggled with the problem of balancing the content, but not—as most would think—between North and South. The more difficult task has been to balance the various theaters of the war or the branches of service. Many is the time some reader from Oklahoma or Kansas has written to remind us that there was a lot of fighting west of the Mississippi, or someone from the Deep South has complained that Lee and his Virginians have been getting too much of our attention. So, too, are navy buffs offended when they think the war at sea has been neglected.

The editors of *Historical Times Illustrated Encyclopedia of the Civil War* have drawn upon our long experience in publishing *Civil War Times Illustrated* in both their selection of subjects to be covered and their writing and editing of the entries, and in recruiting our contributors. The authors of entries range from young but talented historians to some who are household names, at least in the households of Civil War knowledgeables. Their initials follow their entries; brief biographies can be found under Contributors, p. ix.

Under our agreement with Harper & Row to produce this work, it fell to Historical Times Inc. to arrange for the writing and editing of the entries. The late Patricia Faust, then editor of HTI's *American History Illustrated,* agreed to take on the chief editorship, with the assistance of Jeffry Wert and Norman Delaney, both teachers and writers; Edward Longacre, historian for the U.S. Air Force; and John Stanchak, editor of *Civil War Times Illustrated.*

While work on this encyclopedia was in progress, Pat accepted the post of editor of the prestigious *Virginia Cavalcade,* which is published in Richmond by the Virginia State Library. But she was so caught up in this project that she eagerly agreed to continue as editor from her new base in the capital of the old Confederacy.

In November 1984, Pat was returning to her home in Richmond from a convention of the Southern Historical Association held in Louisville, Kentucky. While leaving the Richmond airport, the car in which she was riding was struck by another and she was killed. To catch the colors and carry on the advance, Marsha Larsen was hired as a member of the HTI staff. Marsha's exceptional organizational abilities made possible the completion of this project.

The editors of the *Historical Times Illustrated Encyclopedia of the Civil War* owe special thanks to William C. Reynolds, the project's copy editor, who shaped the manuscript, assured consistency of tone and style, and helped to check, recheck, then check again for factual accuracy. Bill's thoroughness and demand for excellence established in great part the editorial quality of this volume.

But Pat Faust was the real heroine of the struggle to produce a reference work of lasting value. It is fitting that her name should be given a special place of remembrance in this volume to which she devoted so much of her time and energy. Neither she nor the fruits of her labor will be soon forgotten.

—Robert H. Fowler
Founder and Chairman,
Historical Times Inc.

To the User

This encyclopedia is arranged alphabetically by subject, with cross-references at appropriate points. In the text of an essay, certain names and terms have been printed in SMALL CAPITAL LETTERS to indicate that an entry exists for those subjects. Individual corps are found under the general entry Corps. Entries for specific regiments and brigades whose designations begin with a number follow the entry for the state they are from and are presented in numerical order; e.g., the entry for Pennsylvania is followed by entries for the 6th Pennsylvania Cavalry, the 11th Pennsylvania Reserves, the 83d Pennsylvania, etc.

Biographical Designations

CSA   Confederate States Army
USA   United States Army
CSN   Confederate States Navy
USN   United States Navy
CSP   Confederate States political figure
USP   United States political figure

Illustration Sources

AC	Architect of the Capitol, Washington, D.C.
AHI	*American History Illustrated,* Historical Times Inc., Publisher, Harrisburg, Pa.
CHS	Chicago Historical Society, Chicago, Ill.
CMH	Confederate Memorial Hall, New Orleans, La.
CV	*Confederate Veteran,* Sons of Confederate Veterans, Publisher, Murfreesboro, Tenn.
CWTI	*Civil War Times Illustrated,* Historical Times Inc., Publisher, Harrisburg, Pa.
DAM/LSU	Department of Archives and Manuscripts, Louisiana State University, Baton Rouge, La.

GB	*Generals in Blue,* Ezra J. Warner (Louisiana State Univ. Press: Baton Rouge, 1964)
GG	*Generals in Gray,* Ezra J. Warner (Louisiana State Univ. Press: Baton Rouge, 1959)
HTIC	Historical Times Inc. Collection, Harrisburg, Pa.
KA	Kean Archives, Philadelphia, Pa.
LC	Library of Congress, Washington, D.C.
MC	Museum of the Confederacy, Richmond, Va.
NA	National Archives, Washington, D.C.
OHS	Ohio Historical Society, Columbus, Ohio
OR	*War of the Rebellion Official Records of the Union and Confederate Armies* (United States War Department: Washington, D.C.)
PHCW	*The Photographic History of the Civil War,* Francis Trevelyan Miller, ed. (Thomas Yoseloff: New York, 1957)
TU	Tulane University Library, Special Collections Division, New Orleans, La.
USA	United States Army, Department of Defense, Washington, D.C.
USMHI	United States Army Military History Institute, Carlisle, Pa.
USMHI/MA	United States Army Military History Institute/Meade Album, Carlisle, Pa.
USN	United States Navy, Department of Defense, Washington, D.C.
VM	Valentine Museum, Richmond, Va.
WPC	West Point Collections, U.S. Military Academy, West Point, N.Y.

HISTORICAL TIMES
ILLUSTRATED ENCYCLOPEDIA
OF THE CIVIL WAR

A

abatis. One of the oldest forms of defense for fortifications, the abatis is an arrangement of felled trees, with branches facing outward from the defending position to impede the charging enemy. —PLF

USMHI

abolition. In colonial America antislavery sentiment was grounded in the belief that slavery was incompatible with the rights of man, and in 1688 Quakers in Germantown, Pa., became the first to issue an abolitionary protest. Until the 19th century reformers were moderate and optimistic that slavery would gradually disappear. But it did not, and in 1831 William Lloyd Garrison began publishing *The Liberator,* an abolitionary newspaper. Garrison's objection to slavery was religious and moral, and he soon became the symbol of militant abolition, with agitation and "moral suasion" his main weapons. Garrison helped found the New England Antislavery Society, demanded the immediate abolition of slavery, and demolished the argument that African colonization would disrupt that institution.

The abolitionists' efforts met with violence and repression, but as civil liberties were violated, others converted to the cause. Elijah Lovejoy, an antislavery editor who died defending his press from a mob in Alton, Ill., in 1837, was the movement's first martyr. The South's support of slavery and its demand for the return of all fugitive slaves helped convince Northerners that their own interests were threatened by the institution.

Some former slaves added authenticity to the crusade by joining it, among them Frederick Douglass and William Wells Brown, who proved that ex-slaves could be educated and function effectively outside slavery. Former slaves and free blacks also helped others escape by the Underground Railroad.

The Liberty party, the first antislavery political organization, appeared in 1840, followed in 1848 by the FREE SOIL PARTY, and by 1854 Northern opinion would no longer accept any new slave states. Reaction to the KANSAS-NEBRASKA ACT created the REPUBLICAN PARTY in 1854, with free soil part of its platform. Party policy was a far cry from Garrisonian abolition, but the election of Abraham Lincoln as president sparked the chain of events that brought on the Civil War and, with it, abolition as a war measure. The 13TH AMENDMENT, effective 18 Dec. 1865, formally ended chattel slavery. *See also* AMERICAN ANTISLAVERY SOCIETY. —LG

acoustic shadow. Several times during the war, observers watching a battle only a few miles away reported hearing no battle sounds, while people 10 or 20 mi away clearly heard the booming of artillery. This phenomenon, referred to as an acoustic shadow, was attributed to abnormal atmospheric conditions that prevented normal transmission of sound, resulting in a pocket of silence.

Several veterans of the Civil War described these "silent battles." Confederate Brig. Gen. Raleigh E. Colston witnessed the engagement between the USS *Congress* and the CSS *Virginia* at HAMPTON ROADS, Va., 8 Mar. 1862; though only a few hundred yards distant, he heard no report from the guns. A Union soldier had a similar experience as he watched the Battle of PORT ROYAL from a transport ship not more than 2 mi off the South Carolina coast. But the classic incidence occurred at GAINES' MILL, 27 June 1862. Confederates stationed on the Richmond side of the Chickahominy River saw troops fighting about a mile and a half across the valley. Smoke from muskets and artillery was visible, but for 2 hours during the battle, which involved 50,000 men and an estimated 100 pieces of artillery, the Confederates heard no sound of fighting.

—PLF

Adams, Charles Francis, Sr. diplomat b. Boston, Mass., 18 Aug. 1807. Adams began his political career as a moderate Whig in 1841. Opposing both slavery and hard-line abolitionism, he quickly became a leader of the troubled party's antislavery faction. When the party split in 1848, the Free-Soil Whigs nominated Adams vice-president on their own ticket, giving the election to the Democrats. Adams subsequently joined the emerging REPUBLICAN PARTY.

Though Adams had supported WILLIAM H. SEWARD for the

presidential nomination in 1860, Lincoln appointed Adams minister to England early in 1861. He arrived in London in May, just after Britain had recognized the Confederacy as a belligerent. With European sentiment favoring the South, the situation threatened to culminate in war with the North. Adams' mission was to keep England from recognizing the South as a legally constituted independent nation and thereby, under international law, prevent

KA

the Confederacy from seeking military alliances abroad. He was also to convince English officials that selling arms to Confederate agents violated England's neutrality.

Tactful and unimpassioned, Adams was hindered by Europeans' distrust of Seward, then secretary of state, but impressed English officials as a reasonable, thorough diplomat. He convinced British Foreign Minister Lord John Russell that the U.S. would regard continued interviews with Southern agents as hostile and thus end formal meetings between British and Confederate officials. During the *TRENT* AFFAIR, he influenced Seward in releasing Confederate commissioners JAMES MASON and JOHN SLIDELL, whose detention had inflamed British public opinion against the U.S. Though he was unable to prevent the cruiser CSS *ALABAMA* from leaving the Laird shipyards, in Sept. 1863 he skillfully blocked Confederate purchase of 2 rams, cutting off the South's access to foreign-built warships. These diplomatic successes, coupled with Northern victories on the battlefield, cooled English sympathy for the South.

Adams remained in his post until June 1868, producing the diplomatic correspondence that supported postwar U.S. claims for damages inflicted on American shipping by English-built Confederate cruisers. When the *ALABAMA* CLAIMS were referred to arbitration by the Treaty of Washington, Adams came out of retirement to negotiate U.S. interests, which he skillfully concluded in 1872.

Adams spent his later years editing the diary of his father, John Quincy Adams. d. Boston, 21 Nov. 1886.   —PLF

Adams, Daniel Weisiger. CSA b. Frankfort, Ky., 1821. While Adams was a child, he moved to Mississippi with his family, which included a brother, WILLIAM WIRT ADAMS, who became a prominent Mississippi secessionist and a Confederate general; there he read law and was admitted to the bar. Relocating in Louisiana, in 1861 he was appointed by Gov. THOMAS O. MOORE to a military board organizing the state for war.

Adams entered military service as a lieutenant colonel of the 1st Louisiana Regulars and was advanced to colonel after the regiment was ordered to Pensacola, Fla. Early in 1862 he and his men were transferred to the West, where he remained for the duration of the war.

GG

Adams distinguished himself by leading a successful attack on Brig. Gen. Benjamin M. Prentiss' division at SHILOH, where he lost his right eye. On 23 May 1862 he was commissioned brigadier general and that year led the Louisiana Brigade at PERRYVILLE, Ky., 8 Oct., and at STONE'S RIVER, Tenn., 31 Dec. Wounded again in the latter battle, he returned to the field in time to command at CHICKAMAUGA, Sept. 1863. On the second day of battle, his men broke through Union lines but were driven back by reinforcements. Adams was wounded a third time and captured.

After his exchange and recovery, he briefly commanded a cavalry brigade in Alabama. During the last month of the war, he was given command of the DEPARTMENT OF THE GULF, taking part in the defense of Selma, Ala., and in resisting the final Union advances, Apr. 1865. Adams was paroled at Meridian, Miss., 9 May.

After spending some time in England, he resumed practicing law in New Orleans, where he died 13 June 1872.   —PLF

Adams, John. CSA b. Nashville, Tenn., 1 July 1825. The son of Irish immigrants, Adams entered the U.S. Military Academy in 1841, graduating 25th in his class. Commissioned 2d lieutenant in the 1st Dragoons/ U.S. Regular Army, Adams served under Capt. Philip Kearny in the Mexican War. On 16 Mar. 1848 he was brevetted for gallantry and meritorious conduct at the Battle of Santa Cruz de Rosales and in 1851 was commissioned 1st lieutenant; promotion to captain followed in 1856. Except for 2 years as a recruiting officer, Adams completed his U.S. Army career on frontier duty at Fort Crook, Calif., resigning 31 May 1861.

CV

Adams traveled to New York City, where he learned that Gen. Winfield Scott had ordered the arrest of Regular Army officers suspected of resigning to join the Confederacy. Evading capture, he went to Tennessee, enlisted in the Confederate army as a captain of cavalry, and was placed in command at Memphis. By May 1862 he had advanced to colonel and by December to brigadier general, assuming command of Brig. Gen. Lloyd Tilghman's Mississippi infantry brigade after Tilghman's death in May 1863. Adams served under Gen. Joseph E. Johnston during the campaign to relieve Vicksburg, then joined Lt. Gen. Leonidas Polk in Mississippi, marching with him to Resaca, Ga., where he was transferred to the ARMY OF TENNESSEE. His brigade served in the advance during most of Gen. John B. Hood's campaign to force Maj. Gen. William T. Sherman northward after the fall of Atlanta, and Adams received commendation for his valiant service.

Adams remained with Hood during the FRANKLIN AND NASHVILLE CAMPAIGN, serving briefly under Maj. Gen. Nathan B. Forrest. He was severely wounded in the right arm early in the Battle of FRANKLIN, 30 Nov. 1864, but refused to leave the field. Later that day he was killed leading his regiment in a determined but unsuccessful assault on the Union lines.   —PLF

Adams, William Wirt. CSA b. Frankfort, Ky., 22 Mar. 1819. In 1825 Adams moved to Mississippi with his family, which included a brother, future Confederate Brig. Gen. DAN-IEL W. ADAMS. Educated in Bardstown, Ky., Adams graduated from college in 1839, then became a private in the Army of the Republic of Texas. By autumn of that year he had returned to Mississippi, where he entered business and served 2 terms in the state legislature before the war. When Mississippi seceded, Adams was appointed commissioner to Louisiana to encourage that state to leave the Union.

Refusing the cabinet position of postmaster general offered by Jefferson Davis, Adams instead raised the 1st Mississippi Cavalry and was commissioned its colonel 15 Oct. 1861. Adams' regiment served as rear guard for Gen. ALBERT SIDNEY JOHNSTON during the retreat from Kentucky to Nashville and was then detached for picket and scouting duty until spring 1862. The command fought at SHILOH and distinguished itself that summer by stopping a Federal advance on Chattanooga.

Assigned to outpost duty in Mississippi during the Corinth Campaign, Adams led 4 companies to rout a Federal regiment commanded by Maj. Gen. PHILIP H. SHERIDAN near Booneville. A regiment of Arkansas troops was added to his command, which he led at Iuka, Miss., under Maj. Gen. STERLING PRICE.

During the Second Vicksburg Campaign Adams' men were commended for harassing Maj. Gen. William T. Sherman's troops when they advanced against Jackson, Miss., after Vicksburg was surrendered. As a result of his effective skirmishing, Adams was promoted to brigadier general as of 28 Sept. 1863 and given command of a brigade. Ordered to meet Sherman's forces as they advanced on Meridian, Miss., Feb. 1864, he was again commended for his success.

For the rest of the war Adams operated in north Alabama, Mississippi, and West Tennessee as part of Maj. Gen. Nathan B. Forrest's cavalry corps. He was surrendered with Forrest near Ramsey Station in Alabama 4 May 1865.

After the war, Adams lived in Vicksburg and later in Jackson, Miss. In 1880 he became state revenue agent and in 1885 Pres. Grover Cleveland appointed him postmaster in Jackson. He died there 1 Mar. 1888 in a street brawl with a local newspaper editor who had severely criticized him in print.
                                                                                                                                —PLF

aide-de-camp. A confidential *ex officio* officer appointed by general officers to their staffs, an aide-de-camp reported directly to his commander and took orders only from him. In a position of great responsibility, an aide was required to write orders, deliver them personally if necessary, and be thoroughly knowledgeable about troop positions, maneuvers, columns, orders of corps, routes, and the locations of officers' quarters. An aide also had to understand TACTICS and operations thoroughly enough to modify orders on the battlefield if new orders could not be issued by the commanding general. In wartime, a lieutenant general was permitted to appoint 4 aides, a major general 2, and a brigadier general 1.   —PLF

Alabama. On 11 Jan. 1861 Alabama became the fourth state to leave the Union, its secession convention calling for a meeting of delegates from all Southern states in Montgomery, the state capital, on 4 Feb. At this meeting the new provisional government of the Confederate States of America was organized, with Montgomery selected as its temporary seat and JEFFERSON DAVIS elected president. The Confederacy went to war financed largely by a $500,000 loan from the state of Alabama.

In one section of northern Alabama, where antislavery feeling was strong, there was a movement to form a pro-Union state. State Rep. Hugh Lawson Clay feared that an attempt would be made "to excite the people of N. Ala. to rebellion vs. the State and we will have a civil war in our midst," but the movement failed.

At the beginning of hostilities Alabama state troops seized forts at the entrance to Mobile Bay and the Union arsenal at Mount Vernon. There was no fighting in the state early in the war, but in 1862 invading Federal forces held sizable areas. To resist the invasion, almost every white Alabamian old enough to carry a gun enlisted in the Confederate forces. Some 2,500 white men and 10,000 blacks had already enlisted in the Union army.

Alabama supplied most of the iron used by the Confederacy, with an average annual output of 40,000 tons during the 4 years of war. Not only did its 16 ironworks steadily produce iron for shot and shell, but the state's munitions plants manufactured the products.

There are no statistics on Alabama's contributions to the Confederate army, but estimates vary between 75,000 and 125,000 fighting men from a population of just above 500,000 whites. Estimates of losses range from 25,000 to 70,000. The state furnished the Confederacy with 60–65 regiments of infantry, 12–15 regiments of cavalry, and over 20 batteries of artillery.   —PR

Alabama, CSS. The CSS *Alabama* was constructed at the Laird Shipyards in Liverpool, England, and christened the *Enrica* on its launching 15 May 1862. Also known as the "290," being the 290th vessel launched at the shipyards, this screw sloop was 211 ft 6 in. in length, 31 ft 8 in. in beam, with a 14-ft draft, and displaced 1,050 tons. As a Confederate warship, the *Alabama* would carry a battery of 1 110-pounder, 1 68-pounder, and 6 32-pounder cannon. The ship left Liverpool 29 July, successfully eluding the USS *Tuscarora,* stationed in wait, and arrived 12 days later at Porta Praya in the Azores. There it received its armaments and was commissioned with Capt. RAPHAEL SEMMES in command.

After a brief shakedown cruise, the *Alabama* captured and burned several whaling vessels in the mid-Atlantic, took vessels off the Newfoundland banks, sailed for the Caribbean, where coal and provisions were taken on, then sank the USS *HATTERAS* in a brisk action off Galveston, Tex. After drifting down the Brazil coast, the *Alabama* spent summer 1863 cruising the South Atlantic, passing 2 months in the vicinity of Capetown, South Africa, with negligible results, before an extended cruise through the Indian Ocean.

Returning to the South Atlantic, the cruiser arrived at Cherbourg, France, 11 June 1864. Since its commissioning, the *Alabama* had cruised for approximately 21 months over nearly 75,000 mi and had taken 64 prizes worth more than $6.5 million. The ship never entered a Confederate port but was replenished and refueled in such spots as Bahia in Brazil, Capetown, Singapore, and Cherbourg. 3 days after the Confederate warship anchored in the French harbor, the USS *KEAR-SARGE* took up station off the port.

Despite *Alabama's* poor condition Semmes decided to fight the Union vessel. On Sunday, 19 June, the 2 warships engaged each other outside the 3-mi limit, exchanging fire for just over an hour as they steamed in slowly narrowing circles. At the beginning of the eighth circle, when the ships were approximately 400 yd apart, the *Alabama* sank. The *Kearsarge* took 63 prisoners. Semmes, 14 officers, and 24 crew were rescued by the English yacht *Deerhound* and taken to England.

—WNS

Alabama, Union Department of. Formed 27 June 1865, the department comprised the state of Alabama and was commanded by Maj. Gen. CHARLES R. WOODS, with headquarters at Mobile throughout its 9-month existence. It was merged with the Department of the South 19 May 1866. —PLF

Alabama and West Florida, Confederate Department of. On 14 Oct. 1861 Maj. Gen. BRAXTON BRAGG assumed command of this newly established department, which included the state of Alabama and western Florida. Bragg's responsibility focused on defending the coast and preventing Federal forces from capturing the Pensacola Navy Yard and taking Mobile, the Confederacy's major Western port.

Bragg retained Brig. Gen. JONES M. WITHERS in command of the District of Alabama at Mobile. The department was enlarged 12 Dec. 1861 to include Pascagoula Bay and the section of Mississippi east of the Pascagoula River, and Withers was ordered to strengthen Forts Morgan and Gaines as "best he could" with the 5,000 men assigned to him.

Establishing his headquarters at Pensacola, Bragg traveled frequently to Mobile to oversee Withers' operations. Shortly after the heavy bombardment of Forts McRee and Barrancas from Fort Pickens, 22–24 Nov. 1861, he placed Brig. Gen. SAMUEL JONES in command of the army at Pensacola and turned his attention to administering the far-flung region assigned to him. But Bragg was hindered by the murky status of his authority over navy personnel and by a lack of arms.

Early in 1862, Pres. Jefferson Davis offered Bragg command of the TRANS-MISSISSIPPI DEPARTMENT, which he refused in anticipation of a heavy Union assault on Pensacola. But in February, when Brig. Gen. ULYSSES S. GRANT invaded Tennessee, Bragg was ordered to send most of the approximately 18,200 men serving under him to Gen. ALBERT SIDNEY JOHNSTON'S aid. He immediately began preparations to abandon Pensacola, commanding Jones to dismantle as much artillery as possible, ship it by rail to Tennessee via Mobile and Montgomery, and destroy any equipment or buildings that Union troops might find useful. Bragg turned over command of the department to Jones 27 Feb.

Placing Mobile under martial law, protected by garrisons stationed at Forts Morgan and Gaines, Jones concentrated on holding Pensacola with about 5,000 Florida state troops and a few artillery pieces.

During the disruption caused by Federal troops in Tennessee, command of the department changed hands 6 times 5 Feb.–28 Apr., finally falling to Brig. Gen. JOHN H. FORNEY. After the Confederates evacuated Pensacola, the department was discontinued, 27 June 1862, and absorbed into Confederate DEPARTMENT NO. 2. —PLF

***Alabama* Claims.** The most serious international problem Ulysses S. Grant inherited with the presidency in 1868 was the demand that the U.S. be compensated for losses inflicted on its shipping by CONFEDERATE CRUISERS built and outfitted in England during the Civil War.

Little headway was made in early negotiations overseen by Sec. of State WILLIAM H. SEWARD. The bulk of U.S. claims hinged on charges levied against the *ALABAMA*, the most notorious of the Confederate cruisers, and British officials would agree to consider the case only in terms of already existing correspondence regarding the ship's activities, terms the U.S. Congress rejected. In a revised treaty the British dropped the prohibition against new evidence and amended one clause, originally referring the case to binding arbitration by a neutral head of state, to require the approval of both British and U.S. governments.

These negotiations nearly failed because of CHARLES SUMNER, head of the Senate Committee on Foreign Relations and a foe of the Grant administration. Sumner's demands included indirect claims that covered losses in ship registries to foreign governments, high insurance rates, and the cost of pursuing Confederate cruisers—demands many thought preposterous. He also sought indemnity on the grounds that the war had been prolonged because Britain did not strictly enforce its neutrality laws. As just compensation, Sumner proposed complete British withdrawal from North America, turning the issue of wartime liability into a contest for continental supremacy.

In Mar. 1869 Hamilton Fish succeeded Seward, and under his moderating influence the excessive claims were dropped. Renewed negotiation in the U.S. capital resulted in the Treaty of Washington, ratified 24 May 1871.

The case was placed before a tribunal of arbitration in Geneva, Switzerland, and CHARLES FRANCIS ADAMS was called from retirement to represent the U.S. The British commissioner, the king of Italy, the president of the Swiss Confederation, and the emperor of Brazil completed the tribunal. The trial was held 15 Dec. 1871–14 Sept. 1872, and after extensive deliberation, balancing the national pride of 2 powerful countries, the "indirect claims" were discarded and Britain was ruled liable for failing to apply "due diligence" in enforcing its neutrality acts. The tribunal awarded the U.S. $15.5 million in gold, and Great Britain received $1,929,819 for wartime losses to its subjects. Both nations escaped with dignity and embarked on an era of friendlier relations. —PLF

Alabama, Mississippi, and East Louisiana, Confederate Department of. Created 9 May 1864, this department was an enlarged successor to the Department of Mississippi and East Louisiana, which had been commanded by Lt. Gen. LEONIDAS POLK. Maj. Gen. STEPHEN D. LEE had assumed temporary command 5 May as Polk prepared to depart with troops from the old department to join Gen. JOSEPH E. JOHNSTON in the ATLANTA CAMPAIGN. With the death of Polk, Lee continued in command until late July, when he was called to take over a corps in the Army of Tennessee. Maj. Gen. DABNEY H. MAURY briefly took charge of the department, and 15 August Lt. Gen. RICHARD TAYLOR succeeded him, remaining until the end of the war.

With headquarters at Meridian, Miss., the department commander had to coordinate fragmented forces over a far-flung region of responsibility: the grain-producing prairies of northeastern Mississippi and the industrial region in south-central Alabama—especially the machinery and ships in Selma and Montgomery, the railroads, and the important port city of Mobile. At the outset Lee was to have had 35,676 men, but with huge numbers absent and others debilitated, he had only 15,758 effectives. When Taylor surrendered the department 2 May 1865, he yielded 12,000 troops.

The major clashes within the department included the Confederate triumph in the Battle of BRICE'S CROSS ROADS, the repulse of Maj. Gen. Andrew J. Smith's raid in the Battle of TUPELO, that part of the Atlanta Campaign involving Maj. Gen. NATHAN B. FORREST, Federal operations against the forts in Mobile Bay and the Mobile Campaign, and Brig. Gen. JAMES H. WILSON's devastating 2-month raid through Alabama and into Georgia, which brought about the fall of Selma and Montgomery.   —HH

Albemarle, CSS. The CSS _Albemarle_ was built near Edwards' Ferry, N.C., on the Roanoke River by contractors Gilbert Elliott and William P. Martin. Its naval supervisor was Comdr. James W. Cooke, who also became the ironclad's first commander. Designed by naval constructor John Porter for operation in the shoal waters of the North Carolina sounds, the ship was 152 ft in length, 34 ft in beam, had a 9-foot draft, and carried 2 6.4-in. Brooke guns. Its casemate and part of its hull were covered with 4 in. of wrought-iron plate.

OR

The ship was commissioned 17 Apr. 1864 and 2 days later participated in an attack on Plymouth, N.C., during which it rammed and sank the Union gunboat _Southfield_ and forced the _Miami, Ceres,_ and _Whitehead_ to withdraw down the Roanoke. The following day Plymouth surrendered to Confederate forces.

On 5 May the _Albemarle,_ supported by the steamers _Bombshell_ and _Cotton Plant,_ engaged a Union squadron of wooden gunboats near the mouth of the Roanoke. The _Bombshell_ was captured and the _Albemarle_ damaged, limping back to Plymouth, where efforts were made to repair it.

6 months later the Confederate armorclad was sunk in a daring attack by a small Union raiding party. On the night of 28 Oct. 1864, Lt. WILLIAM B. CUSHING, with 14 volunteers in a small steam launch, successfully placed a spar TORPEDO beneath the hull of the ironclad while under heavy fire. Though the _Albemarle_ sank to the bottom, the water was so shallow that the ship's casemate remained above the surface.

The _Albemarle_ was raised after Union forces recaptured Plymouth. Stripped of armor and guns, the ship was towed to the Norfolk Navy Yard, condemned as a prize, and sold for scrap in 1867.   —WNS

Alcott, Louisa May. nurse/author b. Germantown, Pa., 29 Nov. 1832. Best known as an author, Alcott published her first book during the war, a result of her experiences as a

volunteer nurse in Washington, D.C., at Georgetown's Union Hospital. During several months of efficient service, Alcott wrote detailed letters to her family describing the "cold, damp, dirty" conditions in the military hospital, focusing on the appalling lack of ventilation and sanitary systems and portraying the hospital as a "perfect pestilence box."

As disheartening were her characterizations of the indifferent nurses and surgeons she encountered, and of the type she criticized as the "funereal lady"—a woman temperamentally unsuited to hospital work. The letters, published in book form as _Hospital Sketches_ (1863), attracted attention and remain one of the most vivid portrayals of Civil War hospital life.

Alcott became known as the "Nurse with the Bottle" because she sprinkled herself and her surroundings with lavender water to combat the smells of poor sanitation and sickness. She left the nursing corps in 1862 because of ill health, devoting the rest of her life to writing. d. Boston, Mass., 6 Mar. 1888.   —PLF

Alden, James. USN b. Portland, Maine, 31 March 1810. Appointed midshipman in the U.S. Navy in 1828, Alden was assigned to the naval station at Boston for 2 years. He spent the early part of his career at sea in the Mediterranean and on 2 world tours, receiving appointments as passed midshipman 14 June 1834 and as lieutenant 25 Feb. 1841. Attached to the home squadron 1846–47, Alden served in the Mexican War and in the 1855 Indian War at Puget Sound. He was promoted to commander 14 Sept. of that year.

In 1861 Alden commanded the steamer _South Carolina,_ which reinforced FORT PICKENS, Fla. From there he was trans-

USN

ferred to blockade duty off Galveston, Tex., capturing 13 schooners. He commanded the sloop of war _Richmond_ when the Union fleet passed FORTS JACKSON AND ST. PHILIP, during the capture of New Orleans, and at PORT HUDSON.

Advanced to captain 2 Jan. 1863, Alden commanded under Rear Adm. DAVID G. FARRAGUT at the Battle of MOBILE BAY, Aug. 1864, and in December of that year fought conspicuously during both attacks on FORT FISHER, N.C.

Few officers fought at sea more often or harder during the Civil War than James Alden. His superiors repeatedly commended his personal bravery and effectiveness as a commander. He remained in the navy after the war, in 1871 earning his commission as rear admiral and command of the European Squadron. Alden retired to California, where he died, in San Francisco, 6 Feb. 1877.   —PLF

Aldie, Va., eng. at. 17 June 1863 When Gen. ROBERT E. LEE began his movement away from Fredericksburg, into the SHENANDOAH VALLEY and north toward Pennsylvania, a major problem for Union Maj. Gen. JOSEPH HOOKER was to ascertain Lee's whereabouts and direction. On 17 June 1863 this task was entrusted to Federal cavalry under Brig. Gen. ALFRED PLEASONTON, who ordered a movement from Manassas Junction to Aldie, a village located at the junction of roads through the Blue Ridge Mts. to Winchester, an excellent base for reconnaissance into the valley.

When Confederate Col. Thomas T. Munford made a stand, Federal cavalry under Brig. Gen. H. JUDSON KILPATRICK drove the small force from the town to the west. In an afternoon of sharp fighting Munford was pressed back, but the Federals were severely bloodied in scattered actions.

Pleasonton learned that none of Lee's Confederate infantry was east of the mountains, but his report of an easy victory was far from the mark.   —JTH

Alexander, Edward Porter. CSA b. Washington, Ga., 26 May 1835. Known to his friends as "Porter," Alexander, a talented engineer and artillerist, graduated 3d in the West Point class of 1857, receiving his commission as 2d lieutenant 10 Oct. 1858. His routine postings and a teaching assignment at the academy were broken up by brief participation in the army's 1858 Utah Expedition and, in 1859, historic work with Albert J. Myer, with whom he developed the WIGWAG *(semaphore)* communications system.

Resigning from the U.S. Army May 1861, Alexander entered Confederate army service as a captain attached to Brig. Gen. P. G. T. BEAUREGARD's staff as signal officer. With Beauregard at the FIRST BATTLE OF BULL RUN, serving opposite his old friend Myer, a major in the Union army, he used the wig-wag system they had developed to warn Confederate troops of a potentially fatal Union flanking movement, warding off possible early disaster for the Southern forces.

For his Bull Run service, he was made chief of ordnance for the ARMY OF NORTHERN VIRGINIA and promoted to major, then lieutenant colonel, beginning his long association with that army's artillery arm; service in almost all its battles and campaigns followed.

Alexander advanced to colonel late in 1862. Through May 1863, when he took part in Lt. Gen. Thomas J. "Stonewall" Jackson's CHANCELLORSVILLE operations, he was listed as Lt. Gen. JAMES LONGSTREET's chief of artillery. In July 1863 he participated in the Battle of GETTYSBURG, and on the third day of fighting commanded 140 Confederate cannon in the sustained 2-hour bombardment of the center of the Union lines. The Federals replied with 100 guns, and at the end of the duel, Alexander had almost completely expended his corps' supply of artillery ammunition.

That summer Alexander and his cannon accompanied Longstreet on detached service from the Army of Northern Virginia, participating in Tennessee campaigning and in the Siege of KNOXVILLE. He returned to Virginia early in 1864, and 26 Feb. was promoted to brigadier general, one of only 3 Confederates to hold that rank in the artillery service. Alexander then took part in the Battles of SPOTSYLVANIA and COLD HARBOR.

The last months of the war found the brigadier general with the Army of Northern Virginia resisting the Federal investment of Petersburg. Even before the Battle of the CRATER, Alexander saw possibilities for Union mining operations against the Confederate defenses and urged that countermines be tried.

Shortly after the battle he was seriously wounded and, on his return from recuperative leave, was involved in operations at Chaffin's Farm and Drewry's Bluff along the James River before joining the remaining Virginia troops for their final march to Appomattox. He was surrendered and paroled there with the rest of Gen. Robert E. Lee's army.

Following the war, Alexander's engineering skill brought him prominence in the railroad industry, the academic community, and in minor public offices before he died in Savannah, Ga., 28 April 1910.   —JES

Alexandria, Va. A busy Potomac River port and the terminus of 3 Virginia railroads, Alexandria, with over 12,000 residents, was already a major trade center by 1861. Separated from Washington, D.C., by the Potomac, it became a vulnerable target with the advent of the war, when its location caused the city to pay a terrible price.

Shortly after the Virginia convention approved secession, 17 Apr. 1861, a small force of 481 untrained Confederate volunteers occupied Alexandria, commanded by Lt. Col. A. S. Taylor. Alexandrians greeted the secession and occupation with enthusiasm and ultimately contributed an artillery battery and 5 companies of infantry to the Confederacy.

Taylor evacuated Alexandria 5 May, citing a lack of guns, ammunition, and discipline among his troops, while across the river thousands of Federal volunteers occupied Washington, D.C. None moved immediately on the Virginia city as the North waited for Virginians to vote on a referendum on secession. When the citizens of the Old Dominion overwhelmingly approved the ordinance 23 May, Federal authorities reacted swiftly.

Before daylight on 24 May, 2 Union regiments, supported by additional units and a Federal gunboat, seized control of Alexandria. Col. ELMER E. ELLSWORTH, a favorite of Pres. Abraham Lincoln, led one of the regiments, the gaily attired New York Fire Zouaves. On entering the city, Ellsworth saw a Confederate flag flying defiantly from atop the Marshall House hotel and bolted to the roof to tear it down. While descending the stairs, the fervently patriotic colonel encountered the proprietor, James T. Jackson, who blasted Ellsworth with a shotgun-load of slugs. A fire zouave, Pvt. FRANCIS BROWNELL, killed Jackson, and the North and South each mourned a martyr early in the war.

From its initial occupation until the end of the war, Alexandria remained in Federal hands. Entrenchments and works rimmed its edges while the city simultaneously served as a Union supply depot, naval base, hospital center, and rendezvous and training camp for Union armies. During the war, few Southern communities suffered more.   —JDW

Alexandria, Confederate Department of. Created 24 Apr. 1861, with the secession of Virginia, the Confederate Department of Alexandria encompassed much of the northern part of the state, following the course of the Potomac River from the Blue Ridge Mts. east to Alexandria, then south to Chesapeake Bay.

Col. PHILIP ST. GEORGE COCKE initially assumed command of the department but was replaced a month later by Brig. Gen. MILLEDGE L. BONHAM, who moved department headquarters from Culpeper to Manassas Junction. On 2 June Brig. Gen. P.G.T. BEAUREGARD assumed command. Since Southern authorities reckoned, correctly, that the initial Federal offensive would pass through the department, thousands of Confederate volunteers poured in.

Beauregard withdrew his forces to a main defensive position behind Bull Run, and on 21 July 1861 the FIRST BATTLE OF BULL RUN was fought within the department. Gen. JOSEPH E. JOHNSTON replaced Beauregard in departmental command after the battle. On 22 Oct. Confederate authorities created the DEPARTMENT OF NORTHERN VIRGINIA, which included the Department of Alexandria.   —JDW

Alexandria line. With the mobilization of Virginia after it seceded in Apr. 1861, the state's volunteers occupied the Alexandria line, a long front along the Potomac River, running from the Blue Ridge Mts. east to Alexandria, then south to Chesapeake Bay. It was basically this Alexandria line that the Confederates defended during the FIRST BULL RUN CAMPAIGN. *See also* ALEXANDRIA, CONFEDERATE DEPARTMENT OF.   —JDW

Allatoona, Ga., eng. at. 5 Oct. 1864 In late Sept. 1864, a month after the fall of Atlanta, Confederate Gen. JOHN B. HOOD crossed the Chattahoochee River and marched north to threaten the Western & Atlantic, the railroad that supplied Maj. Gen. WILLIAM T. SHERMAN's Federal forces in the captured city. Hood hoped to lure Sherman north, to fight on ground more favorable to the Confederates.

2–6 Oct. Hood's army struck at the railroad between the Chattahoochee and Etowah rivers, capturing small garrisons and damaging the track. Allatoona Pass, where the railroad pierced the hills south of the Etowah and served a Federal supply base, quickly became the focus. Sherman, by signal flag, ordered Brig. Gen. JOHN M. CORSE from Rome, Ga., to reinforce the 900 men who garrisoned the post; Corse reached Allatoona with about 1,100 men early 5 Oct.

That morning, Maj. Gen. SAMUEL G. FRENCH, whose division had been sent by Hood to capture Allatoona, examined the position and decided to attack from the west and north. After Corse refused a demand to surrender, the Confederates assaulted. In several hours of vicious fighting, the Southerners often came close to breaking through the Federal positions, but always the Northerners rallied and held. By early afternoon French concluded that he could not take the position and drew off to rejoin Hood. Federal casualties in the battle were reported at 706; French reported a loss of about 800.

The battle gave rise to several legends, the most famous of which concerned a Federal message sent over the Confederates by signal flag, from Sherman to Corse. This message was quoted by journalists as "Hold the fort; I am coming" and in that form became the basis for the 19th-century revival hymn "Hold the Fort."   —RMcM

Allen, Henry Watkins. CSA/war governor b. Prince Edward Cty., Va., 29 Apr. 1820. Of the few outstanding state politicians to emerge in the Confederacy, Allen was one of the best. Largely through his efforts to reorganize the system of supply and to industrialize Louisiana after taking office as governor in Jan. 1864, the western section of the state remained firmly under Confederate control. Much admired by his constituents, Allen encouraged cooperation with Gen. E. KIRBY SMITH, the military authority in the TRANS-MISSISSIPPI DEPARTMENT, of which Louisiana was a part.

Allen disliked and quit the position in business his father obtained for him when the family moved to Missouri in 1833.

DAM/LSU

In Missouri he attended Marion College briefly, then found work as a teacher in Gulfport, Miss. But the idea of soldiering seemed appealing, so Allen volunteered in the War for Texas Independence. Though his military career lasted only 6 months, he displayed a talent for military affairs that served him well during the Civil War.

Allen moved to West Baton Rouge in 1852, studied law at Harvard the next year, then returned to Louisiana for what appeared to be a successful career in politics; but the war interrupted his plans. He enlisted in Confederate service as a private and was soon elected lieutenant colonel of the 4th Louisiana Infantry.

Assigned to Ship Island off the Mississippi coast, Allen quelled a threatened mutiny and proceeded to drill his recruits into reliable soldiers. By the time he joined Gen. P.G.T. BEAUREGARD in Tennessee in 1862 he was colonel of the regiment.

Despite being wounded in the face at SHILOH, he refused to leave the field. With the same determination, he refused amputation of his leg, shattered by a shell fragment during Maj. Gen. JOHN C. BRECKINRIDGE's Aug. 1862 attack on Federal troops at BATON ROUGE. Though no longer fit for field duty, in Sept. 1863 Allen was promoted to brigadier general and transferred to the Trans-Mississippi. The citizens of Louisiana met him with a hero's welcome, electing him governor soon after his arrival at Shreveport.

Here Allen began his most valuable service to the Confederacy. By the time of his inauguration, the state west of the Mississippi had been effectively severed from communication with the government in Richmond; the economy had collapsed and morale was at its lowest since 1861. Allen immediately began collecting sugar and cotton for export to Mexico in exchange for desperately needed ordnance, munitions, dry goods, and machinery. These he distributed through a system of state-controlled stores, and he enacted extensive welfare measures to relieve the hardpressed civilian population. By allowing the people to pay for the goods with Louisiana or Confederate currency, he reestablished an economic stability almost nonexistent elsewhere in the South.

With supplies Allen imported from Mexico, Kirby Smith was relatively well equipped when Gen. ROBERT E. LEE surrendered in the East. Initially Allen supported Kirby Smith's decision to continue fighting, but by mid-May 1865 he had recognized the hopelessness of holding out and encouraged disbanding the army. Fearing for his safety, he fled to Mexico with a small band of Confederate exiles.

For a while Allen published an English-language newspaper in Mexico City, but he had never fully recovered from his wounds. His health deteriorated rapidly until his death 22 Apr. 1866. He is remembered as a man whose energy and commitment to the Confederacy played a critical role in strengthening the government's tenuous claim to the Trans-Mississippi.

                                                                    —PLF

Allen, Robert. USA b. West Point, Ohio, 15 Mar. 1811. Little is known of Allen's early life except that he was appointed to the U.S. Military Academy at West Point from Indiana, graduating in the bottom third of its 1836 class with rank as 2d lieutenant in the 2d U.S. Artillery. In 1847, midway through the Mexican War, the lifelong professional soldier was advanced to captain. After being brevetted major for gallant and meritorious service at the Battle of Cerro Gordo, he joined the Quartermaster's Department. In 1851 Allen was made a full major in the Regular

NA

service and was assigned as chief quartermaster for the Pacific Department. During the Civil War he advanced to colonel in the Regular service and won brevets as brigadier and major general in both the volunteer and Regular services.

With the reestablishment of the Union DEPARTMENT OF THE MISSOURI, 19 Sept. 1862, Allen became its chief quartermaster and was faced with achieving a difficult goal: reinstating efficiency, competence, and confidence in a departmental supply system scandalized by theft, profiteering, and the cashiering of its former supply chief, Brig. Gen. JUSTUS MCKINSTRY.

Such was Allen's honesty and efficiency that soon his duties were expanded to encompass the entire Mississippi Valley. In the next few years he supplied all major and secondary operations in that sphere, including Maj. Gen. ULYSSES S. GRANT's campaigns against Vicksburg and Maj. Gen. WILLIAM T. SHERMAN's campaign for Atlanta. His duties were expanded again to include all areas west of the Mississippi, except California. Troops in the New Mexico Territory, the Plains states, and the Northwest all counted on Allen to supply their needs.

Ranking only behind Q.M. Gen. MONTGOMERY C. MEIGS in the extent and weight of his responsibility, Allen, following the war, stayed in army service until retirement in 1878. During his years of quartermaster service, he was estimated to have expended over $111 million in discharging his duties. He died 5 Aug. 1886 while traveling abroad and was buried in Switzerland. —JES

Allen, William Wirt. CSA b. New York, N.Y., 11 Sept. 1835. Though born in the North, Allen was raised in Montgomery, Ala., a polished Southern gentleman. He traveled north late in his youth to attend the College of New Jersey and study law, graduating in 1854 and returning south to become an Alabama planter.

At the outbreak of civil war he joined a local volunteer regiment, the Montgomery Mounted Rifles, as a 1st lieutenant and early in 1862 was elected major of the 1st Alabama Cavalry, beginning a career with the mounted arm of the Army of Tennessee that lasted until that organization's surrender.

USMHI

Allen traveled with the army to its first great test at the Battle of SHILOH, where he saw combat and was made colonel of his regiment. He served under Gen. BRAXTON BRAGG during the invasion of Kentucky, fighting in the Battles of PERRYVILLE and STONE'S RIVER and receiving wounds in both engagements.

Skillful soldiering and the rapid attrition of officers gained Allen a brigadier general's commission in Feb. 1864, at the end of Bragg's winter campaign in East Tennessee, which had badly depleted the Army of Tennessee's cavalry. As spring approached, Allen's was the only full brigade available to Confederate Maj. Gen. JOSEPH WHEELER in his attempt to probe Maj. Gen. WILLIAM T. SHERMAN's front and screen possible Union invasion routes as Sherman began his ATLANTA CAMPAIGN. Allen's period of heavy responsibility with Wheeler's II Corps was brief but included the battles and holding actions that culminated in the fall of Atlanta.

When the Confederates evacuated the city, Allen remained with Wheeler, from Atlanta to the sea and during the CAROLINAS CAMPAIGN. He exercised divisional command without commensurate commission until 4 Mar. 1865, when he became the last major general appointed by Confederate Pres. Jefferson Davis. But the Confederate civil government was in rapid dissolution, and Allen's appointment was never confirmed by the Confederate Senate; when he was surrendered in North Carolina, his parole papers listed him as a brigadier general.

After the war, Allen returned to farming and dabbling in the railroad business and Democratic politics. He served as Alabama's state adjutant general and was briefly a U.S. marshal before dying in Sheffield, Ala., 24 Nov. 1894.   —JES

Allen's Farm (Peach Orchard), Va., eng. at. 29 June 1862 The Union defeat at GAINES' MILL 27 June resulted in Maj. Gen. GEORGE B. MCCLELLAN's abandonment of his supply base at White House on the Pamunkey River; that night the Northern commander ordered a withdrawal of his army down the Virginia peninsula to a new base on the James River.

The retreat began about noon the next day, 2 corps marching while 3 remained posted on the army's western flank until nightfall. With a herd of cattle and an immense wagon train, the Federals angled southeast across the marshy bottomlands of the peninsula. At White House enormous amounts of supplies, railroad cars, locomotives, and barges lay smoldering in a blistered heap.

Gen. ROBERT E. LEE reacted cautiously to the situation on the 28th. Uncertain of McClellan's movements, the Confederate general dispatched his cavalry and probed with infantry to gather intelligence. By nightfall Lee had devised plans to trap the fleeing Federals.

Operations shifted from north of the Chickahominy River to the south, with Lee ordering a complicated advance on 4 roads. As the Federals slogged through White Oak Swamp, Lee intended to converge his 4 segments and cripple or destroy the Union army.

Lee assigned to Maj. Gen. JOHN B. MAGRUDER the important task of slowing the retreat and inflicting as much damage as possible. For the past 3 days, while Lee assumed the offensive north of the Chickahominy, Magruder had demonstrated against the bulk of the Union army, a trying ordeal that the general had handled skillfully.

Early on the 29th Magruder led his 11,000 men eastward on the Williamsburg Road, paralleling the York River Railroad.

The Confederates advanced cautiously but at 9 o'clock made contact with the Federals. Instead of a retreating army, Magruder encountered 2 Union infantry corps, supported by 40 cannon a mile east of Fair Oaks at Allen's Farm.

Magruder probed the woods with a solitary regiment, rifle and artillery fire erupting among the trees. The Confederates hesitated, and Magruder wisely decided to deploy his command, waiting for the arrival of Maj. Gen. THOMAS J. "STONE-WALL" JACKSON's troops from the north and Maj. Gen. BENJA-MIN HUGER's from the south. As the Southerners aligned in the woodland, Union gunners sent shells into the trees. The only general officer killed in the engagement was Richard Griffith, a brigadier.

Maj. Gen. EDWIN V. SUMNER, the Union corps commander directly in front of Magruder, withdrew at 11 o'clock to SAV-AGE'S STATION, where a new Union line was being erected. The engagement at Allen's Farm ended with little resolution. Magruder followed, and 5 hours later a fiercer battle ensued at Savage's Station.   —JDW

Alligator, USS. In Nov. 1861 the U.S. Navy Department commissioned Philadelphia contractor Martin Thomas to build a submarine-type vessel; the result was the USS *Alligator.* Although considered for use against the South's IRONCLAD *VIR-GINIA,* the *Alligator* was not ready in time to engage it.

The second effort of French engineer Brutus de Villeroi, whose earlier experimental submarine had impressed naval authorities, the *Alligator* was 45 ft long, 66 in. from keel to deck, and was propelled underwater by 16 folding oars attached to a hull that resembled a steamship boiler. Each oar was to be manned by a sailor who, along with 2 helmsmen and 2 divers, would be commanded by an officer. The divers were expected to leave the submerged submarine and attach to enemy vessels mines that would be detonated electronically.

In June 1862 the *Alligator* was thought to be ready for use against the Confederate James River defenses. The submarine was expected to remove enemy obstructions near Fort Darling and help destroy the strategic James River Bridge. But the *Alligator* was found to be completely unsuited to such an operation. The ship required 7.5 ft to operate totally submerged, and the James, a tidal river, was not consistently deep enough for the submarine to move undetected; with a speed of less than 4 knots and no protection, the *Alligator* would be an easy target. Both Flag Officer LOUIS M. GOLDSBOROUGH and Comdr. JOHN RODGERS concluded that the ship was useless, and it was sent away.

At the Washington Navy Yard, the *Alligator* had its oars replaced with a hand-operated screw propeller that increased its speed slightly. On 2 Apr. 1863, while being towed south for action against Charleston, S.C., the *Alligator* encountered a gale and was cast loose by its tow ship. Helpless, it foundered and sank.   —NCD

Alton Prison. The first Illinois state penitentiary was located in Alton, a city on the Mississippi River. Too near the river and in an undrained area, the prison aroused so much criticism in the 1850s from reformer DOROTHEA DIX that there was an investigation, resulting in a decision to abandon the operation as soon as a new prison could be completed at Joliet. With the Joliet facilities in use just before the Civil War, the abandoned Alton Prison was taken over by authorities early in 1862 for use as a "military detention camp."

Severe overcrowding and bad sanitation produced a smallpox epidemic that raged for weeks, with 6–10 prisoners dying daily. Alton's citizens demanded that ill prisoners be removed from the city area, and many were taken to an uninhabited island in the Mississippi, where a deserted building had been converted to a hospital. There is no record showing any stricken captives returned to Alton, nor were records kept of deaths at the prison or on the island; but it was estimated that several thousand Confederates were buried on the island 1863–64, and many were buried in the Confederate Soldiers' Cemetery in North Alton.

There were constant escape attempts from the prison, some successful. Setting a fire, one group got over the wall during the confusion. On a July night in 1862, 36 prisoners, led by Col. Ebenezer Magoffin of Missouri, crawled into a tunnel they had cut through 8 ft of masonry and excavated for 50 ft; then they cut through the 3-ft-thick limestone foundation of the outer prison wall. Only 8 were recaptured.

As the war closed, the prison was evacuated; later it was demolished.   —PR

ambulance corps. Americans entered their civil war with no experience in dealing with large numbers of battle casualties and few examples to follow. While the Union Medical Department eventually built a well-supplied, remarkably efficient ambulance corps, supported by the U.S. SANITARY COM-MISSION, the Confederate soldier's plight grew more difficult with each year of war—not from lack of concern but from rapidly diminishing resources. With no equivalent to the Sanitary Commission, Confederate doctors relied for help on local soldiers' relief societies and ambulance committees. Whether a physician wore gray or blue, he learned quickly that the fate of the wounded depended on which army held the field when the slaughter ended.

USMHI

For several days after the debacle at FIRST BULL RUN, Washington residents witnessed desperately wounded men walking or crawling into the city for help. Horrified, they insisted that the government do something to keep this from happening again; pressure, in turn, shifted to the army.

Surgeon General Charles S. Tripler, commanding the Army of the Potomac Medical Department, initiated a series of reforms for evacuating casualties from the battlefield. Though unable to transfer responsibility for ambulances from the Quartermaster's Department, he insisted they be employed only as transport for wounded men, not as officers' pleasure vehicles or supply wagons. And since the civilian drivers had fled in panic at Bull Run, he designated line troops to be assigned as ambulance crew. Tripler also discarded the 2-wheel ambulances designed to carry seriously wounded men (and called "avalanches" because they were dangerously unsafe) in favor of the 4-wheel model, drilled stretchermen, and established that 250 ambulances were necessary to accompany an army of 100,000 men. Each ambulance carried 5 litter patients or up to 8 sitting wounded; the prescribed crew included the driver and 2 stretcher-bearers.

Though conditions improved, soldier-attendants remained untrained, and severe shortages of equipment hampered operations. Only 177 ambulances accompanied Maj. Gen. GEORGE B. MCCLELLAN's troops during the PENINSULA CAMPAIGN, and large numbers of wounded were left behind. At SECOND BULL RUN vehicles broke down repeatedly because they were fragile, and were abandoned. Again drivers bolted, and those hired as replacements in Washington broke open the supplies to pillage the whiskey. The few who arrived at the battlefield arrived drunk and once there handled the wounded roughly, sometimes refusing to give them water or robbing the helpless men and the dead. Owing to the system's inadequacy and the deplorable performance of attendants, the last wounded lay on the field for nearly a week, suffering through thunderstorms and blistering heat before being removed.

Civilians were enraged, and on 4 July 1862 Tripler was replaced by Jonathan Letterman, who persuaded McClellan that a distinct ambulance corps was needed; early in August the commander issued an order establishing such a unit for the ARMY OF THE POTOMAC.

Letterman organized ambulance service into corps and division units staffed by soldiers chosen by Medical Department officers and also intensified the drills. In the few weeks before ANTIETAM, performance improved significantly, and by the night after the battle the wounded had been removed. Stretcher-bearers carried them first to "primary stations," then loaded them into ambulances. The 8,350 who could be transported were taken to improvised hospitals in Frederick, Md., on a fixed schedule, with regular rest stops along the route.

In Feb. 1863 a bill was put before Congress to increase the corps army-wide to 10,000–12,000 trained enlisted men and 400–500 noncombatant officers, but the disapproval of both Maj. Gen. HENRY W. HALLECK and Sec. of War EDWIN M. STANTON killed the bill in committee; an earlier proposal in Oct. 1861 had suffered a similar fate. Nonetheless, at GETTYSBURG Letterman had 650 medical officers, 1,000 ambulances, and 3,000 attendants on the field, and they completed the orderly removal of 14,000 Union wounded by 4 July.

The Ambulance Corps Act was finally passed 11 Mar. 1864, establishing the corps as a regular army unit and giving the Medical Department the right to train and examine men for duty and to reject any who were unfit. Those chosen for the service wore an inverted green chevron, which helped create an *esprit de corps.* The act also included a measure that prohibited combat soldiers from leaving the field to assist wounded comrades, restricting that responsibility to trained personnel.

Increasing numbers of casualties and the armies' heightened mobility continued to tax the system, especially in the Western theater, but by the end of the war an ambulance organization had been developed that remained the model

for most armies through World War I.   —PLF

American Antislavery Society. Alarmed by the growing radicalism of William Lloyd Garrison's New England Antislavery Society, a group of abolitionists led by Theodore D. Weld, James G. Birney, and brothers Lewis and Arthur Tappan met in Philadelphia in 1833 to form the American Antislavery Society. National headquarters were soon moved to New York City.

Despite their disaffection for extremists, the new leadership was hardly moderate, and for half a decade proponents of the South's "peculiar institution" lashed out against this "dangerous association" engaged in a holy crusade to abolish SLAVERY. During that time the efficient, highly organized professional staff operated as a prolific propaganda machine, disseminating books, pamphlets, and lecturers to encourage recruits to form local antislavery societies intent on immediate abolition accompanied by total equality for blacks. Official records for 1838 show an impressive 1,350 auxiliaries with an active membership totaling 250,000, principally in the Northern states.

But millions feared antislavery militancy. In the South, rewards as high as $100,000 were offered for some high-placed leaders of the society, and antiabolitionist rioting erupted in many localities. Violence peaked when a mob attacked the office of the abolitionist newspaper *The Observer* in Alton, Ill., 7 Nov. 1837, and murdered its editor, Elijah Lovejoy, a prominent society member.

By the end of the decade, the society had begun to decline, partly from internal bickering and curtailed funding, but to a large extent because opposition to antislavery waned in the 1840s as the movement gained respectability. The national organization gradually lost ground to the increasing number of local antislavery societies.   —PLF

American Colonization Society. Envisioned as a national organization, in 1817 the American Colonization Society was begun and subscribed to almost entirely by Southerners, with such prominent men as Bushrod Washington, Henry Clay, James Monroe, and John Marshall among its early supporters. Eventually local chapters existed in all Southern states except South Carolina and Arkansas, and professionally staffed headquarters were established in Washington, D.C.

The politically active ACS members lobbied for passage of the 1819 Antislave Trade Act but directed most of their efforts toward raising funds to establish a colony of free blacks in Africa. Their motives varied. Some saw colonization as a first step toward ending SLAVERY, as a way to Christianize Africa, or as a chance for blacks to build their own republic. Others wanted to eliminate the "bad influence" of free blacks in order to strengthen slavery. Manumission laws banishing freed slaves also encouraged some owners to favor colonization, with the Federal government and several state legislatures appropriating funds to aid the venture. Approximately 1,400 free blacks were settled in Liberia by 1830, with only moderate success. Many blacks vigorously protested the colonization movement, fearing they might be forced to leave the country they considered their home.

After a dozen active years the ACS faltered through internal dissension. Northern abolitionist members dominated the society after 1830, and the Southern contingent lost interest in the face of mounting criticism. The society became insolvent in

1834, though it continued to exist until the 1850s. *See also* ÎLE À VACHE.   —PLF

American Flag Dispatch. By mid-Jan. 1861, 4 Southern states had seceded, seized Federal property, and threatened to acquire more. To head off seizures of U.S. Treasury interests in Southern states of doubtful loyalty, on 18 Jan. outgoing U.S. Pres. James Buchanan's secretary of the treasury, JOHN A. DIX, sent department official W. Hemphill Jones to Louisiana. There Jones was to ensure that the department's REVENUE CUTTERS were turned over to reliable Federal military authorities in the ports of New Orleans, Mobile, and Galveston, and not surrendered to state officers sympathetic to secession.

On 26 Jan. Louisiana seceded from the Union, and 29 Jan. Jones wired Dix from New Orleans that the captain of the cutter USS *McClelland,* waiting in port, refused to follow the secretary's directive. Dix dispatched a reply the same day.

> Tell Lieutenant Caldwell [USN] to arrest Captain Breshwood [commanding the *McClelland*], assume command of the cutter, and obey the order I gave through you. If Captain Breshwood, after arrest, undertakes to interfere with the command of the cutter, tell Lieutenant Caldwell to consider him as a mutineer, and treat him accordingly. If anyone attempts to haul down the American flag, shoot him on the spot.

Dix's warlike "shoot-him-on-the-spot" statement, made while efforts at conciliation were still being put forth by the Buchanan administration, made a stir in the Northern press and galvanized hostile public opinion toward the South.   —JES

American Letter Express Co. The Confederate postal service, under Postmaster General JOHN H. REAGAN, was the most efficient and dependable department of the Southern government during the Civil War. But this did not help many Southerners who had family and friends living beyond Confederate lines. Until June 1861 the Southern Express Co. took mail from customers in Confederate states to Louisville, Ky., at that time in neutral territory. It was then turned over to the Adams Express Company, a Northern business, for delivery. From its Southern point of origin to its arrival at its intended Northern destination, a letter moved through 2 companies for 25 cents.

The American Letter Express Co. was founded at that time and by special dispensation kept offices in both Louisville and Nashville, delivering mail in both directions at a reduced fee. After several months the service was interrupted by Union and Confederate military operations on its route and operations ceased.   —JES

Ames, Adelbert. USA b. Rockland, Maine, 31 Oct. 1835. Few if any officers, considering their age and experience, contributed more to the Union war effort than did Ames, who served in the artillery as a battery commander and in the infantry as a regiment, brigade, division, and temporary corps commander. His outstanding record included 6 brevet ranks and the MEDAL OF HONOR.

As a young man Ames went to sea on a clipper ship, first as a sailor, then as a mate. He graduated 5th in the West Point class of 1861, was commissioned a lieutenant of artillery, and commanded a section of Battery D/5th U.S. Artillery at FIRST BULL RUN, where he was badly wounded in the thigh. Refusing to leave the field, he issued orders until he was too weak to remain in command. For his bravery Ames was brevetted

major in the Regular Army and eventually awarded the Medal of Honor 1 Sept. 1893.

Ames returned to duty after several weeks, assigned to the Washington defenses. In the PENINSULA CAMPAIGN he commanded Battery A/5th U.S. Artillery, winning the rank of brevet lieutenant colonel for his conduct at MALVERN HILL. On 20 Aug. 1862 Ames was appointed colonel of the 20TH MAINE, leading this infantry regiment in the ANTIETAM CAMPAIGN and at FRED-

NA

ERICKSBURG, Va. During the Battle of CHANCELLORSVILLE, the Maine officer served as an aide to Maj. Gen. GEORGE G. MEADE.

On 20 May 1863 Ames received his commission as brigadier general of volunteers with the command of a brigade in the 1st Division/XI Corps. During the second and third days' battle at GETTYSBURG, Pa., he commanded the division, for which service he added the brevet of colonel.

For the final 15 months of the war Ames served in various commands and capacities, participating in operations of the X Corps around Charleston, S.C., before leading a division of the XVIII Corps at COLD HARBOR and PETERSBURG. He returned to the X Corps in the fall, temporarily commanding it Nov. 1864, and 2 Dec. assumed command of a division in the XXIV Corps, participating with it in the subsequent capture of FORT FISHER, N.C. For gallantry in this operation Ames was brevetted major general of volunteers and brigadier and major general in the Regular Army.

His postwar career, however, tarnished his war record. Involved in the murky Reconstruction politics of Mississippi, Ames served for 8 years as, successively, the state's provisional governor, U.S. senator, then elected governor, resigning in 1876 while facing impeachment proceedings. He briefly served as brigadier general of volunteers during the Spanish-American War. The last surviving full-rank Civil War general, Ames died in Ormand, Fla., 13 Apr. 1933 at 97.   —JDW

Ammen, Daniel. USN b. Ohio, 16 May 1819. Ammen entered the U.S. Navy as midshipman 7 July 1836 and by 1861 had risen to the rank of commander with a reputation as a solid and responsible officer. His special interest was in new types of ordnance.

On 7 Nov. 1861 Ammen commanded the gunboat *Seneca* in the attack on PORT ROYAL, S.C., and after the Federal landing personally raised the U.S. flag over Fort Beauregard. In operations on Florida's St. John's River, Ammen was commended by his commanding officer, Adm. SAMUEL F. DU PONT.

In Mar. 1863 Ammen commanded the monitor *Patapsco* during the successful attack on Fort McAllister, Ga., and the next month participated in the unsuccessful attack on Charles-

LC

ton, S.C. As commander of the steam sloop *Mohican,* he took part in the final attacks on FORT FISHER, N.C., 1864–65.

Ammen demonstrated courage and coolness whether in action or faced with mutinous conduct. In May 1864 he was placed in charge of 220 naval recruits aboard the merchant vessel *Ocean Queen.* While at sea between New York and Panama, a mutiny occurred, which Ammen suppressed by shooting 2 of the ringleaders.

Much of Ammen's reputation rests on his postwar career as writer, inventor, and outspoken advocate of an isthmian canal. He contributed *The Atlantic Coast* (1885) to the *Navy in the Civil War* series. d. at his estate 13 mi north of Washington, D.C., 11 July 1898. —NCD

amnesty proclamations, Confederate. Faced with an alarming number of DESERTIONS early in 1862, Confederate officials took steps to draw absentees back into the army. Special Order No. 107, 9 May 1862, ordered all unauthorized absentees to return to their command; though no pardon was offered, neither was disciplinary action threatened. With government permission various generals did promise amnesty, issuing proclamations clearly betraying the military's hesitance to prosecute absenteeism severely since the scarcity of military-age men made them too valuable to execute. Couched in flowery prose, worded to restore delinquent patriotism, amnesty offers were accompanied by assurances of duty near home or of furlough. The transparently phrased amnesty extended by Gen. BRAXTON BRAGG to his command Nov. 1862 reflected the frustration of many top-ranking Confederates: "If you come voluntarily, I will be proud to receive you. I will not have you, and you need not expect to join me, if brought as prisoners." Lt. Gen. THEOPHILUS H. HOLMES's offer of pardon in the Trans-Mississippi Department, Jan. 1863, brought a large number of deserters back into the ranks, but a similar offer by Lt. Gen. LEONIDAS POLK yielded few returns.

When JEFFERSON DAVIS decided to appeal to deserters personally, Gen. ROBERT E. LEE, usually a strict disciplinarian, advised the president that only pardon would induce deserters and stragglers to rejoin their units. Thus, on 1 Aug. 1863, Davis issued a proclamation of pardon and general amnesty to all absentees except twice-convicted deserters, giving them 20 days to return without fear of punishment. He anticipated good response, but leniency had the opposite effect, encouraging men to stay at home or join the more loosely disciplined partisan units. Lee hardened his position, and amnesty offers in 1864 ceased to spare offenders from prosecution. But even increased harshness failed to discourage desertion because so few convicted offenders were executed.

Though individual generals continued the practice, Davis refused to issue a second amnesty proclamation in 1864. Finally, in Feb. 1865, Lee, as general-in-chief, tried to lure deserters back with a fervent appeal to patriotism and victory, accompanied by the Confederacy's last general amnesty for all but second offenders and soldiers guilty of deserting to the enemy. The desperate plea accomplished nothing. Lee's terms did not appear in some Western newspapers until mid-March, and by then the army had begun to disintegrate rapidly as defeat seemed imminent in the closing weeks of war. —PLF

amnesty proclamations, Federal. Of the 2 general amnesties issued by Pres. ABRAHAM LINCOLN in an effort to stem DESERTIONS, the first, 10 Mar. 1863, promised to restore to their units without punishment all soldiers "improperly absent," provided they returned by 1 Apr. Failure to respond would incur forfeiture of citizenship rights and the possibility of being court-martialed for desertion; 12,000–15,000 men rejoined their units.

Commanding officers sometimes issued amnesty proclamations effective within their jurisdiction, and these enjoyed some success. Northern leaders phrased amnesty offers as threats, with serious consequences if not accepted, and were consistently less hesitant than Confederate authorities to prosecute offenders. Still, few deserters faced firing squads, increasing the temptation to disregard amnesty when it was offered. Further, Lincoln's presidential act of clemency of Feb. 1864 reduced the sentences of deserters condemned to death to imprisonment at Dry Tortugas, Fla., for the duration of the war. Lincoln's second general amnesty offer, 11 Mar. 1865, extended similar terms to deserters who would return to their companies within 60 days.

Prior to Gen. Robert E. Lee's surrender, Lincoln made several limited amnesty offers to encourage loyalty among Confederates in border states and in occupied territory, and to pave the way for RECONSTRUCTION. The CONFISCATION ACT OF 1862 authorized the president to pardon at his discretion anyone involved in the rebellion, and his 8 Dec. 1863 Amnesty Proclamation extended limited pardon contingent on swearing an oath of allegiance, excluding all Confederates who had held civil office and anyone guilty of mistreating prisoners. Another restrictive amnesty aimed at civilians followed 26 May 1864.

Pres. ANDREW JOHNSON's amnesty provisions of 29 May 1865 broadened eligibility to include former soldiers under the rank of colonel, sailors under the rank of lieutenant, and persons whose taxable property did not exceed $20,000; former Confederates in these categories could apply for individual pardons. Thousands did, and Johnson's liberal policy of granting them goaded Congress into limiting the power of presidential pardons in the 15TH AMENDMENT, ratified 30 Mar. 1870.

An unconditional pardon of all war participants except high-ranking civil and military officials was granted by Johnson 25 Dec. 1868. —PLF

Anaconda Plan. The first military strategy offered to Pres. ABRAHAM LINCOLN for crushing the rebellion of Southern states was devised by Union Gen.-in-Chief WINFIELD SCOTT. From 1 Apr. through early May 1861 Scott briefed the president daily, often in person, on the national military situation; the results of these briefings were used by Scott to work out Union military aims.

About 3 May Scott told his protégé, Maj. Gen. GEORGE B. MCCLELLAN, that he believed an effective BLOCKADE of Southern ports, a strong thrust down the Mississippi Valley with a large force, and the establishment of a line of strong Federal positions there would isolate the disorganized Confederate nation "and bring it to terms." Contemporary sources said McClellan called it Scott's "boa-constrictor" plan. Scott then presented it to the president, in greater detail, proposing that 60,000 troops move down the Mississippi with gunboats until they had secured the river from Cairo, Ill., to the Gulf, which, in concert with an effective blockade, would seal off the South. Then, he believed, Federal troops should stop, waiting for Southern Union sympathizers to turn on their Confederate governors and compel them to surrender. It was his belief that sympathy for secession was not as strong as it appeared and that isolation and pressure would make the "fire-eaters" back down and allow calmer heads to take control.

But the war-fevered nation wanted combat, not armed diplomacy, and the passive features of Scott's plan were ridiculed as a proposal "to squeeze the South to military death." The press, recalling McClellan's alleged "boa-constrictor" remark, named the plan after a different constricting snake, the anaconda. The plan was not adopted, but in 1864 it reappeared in aggressive form. Lt. Gen. ULYSSES S. GRANT's 2-front war, fought in Virginia and Tennessee, pressed the Confederates, while Maj. Gen. WILLIAM T. SHERMAN's march through Georgia to the sea helped "squeeze the South to military death." —JES

Anderson, George Burgwyn.

CSA b. Hillsborough, N.C., 12 Apr. 1831. Remembered for intellect as well as bravery, Anderson matriculated at the University of North Carolina while quite young, leaving at 17 on receiving an appointment to West Point. Graduating 10th in the class of 1852, he accepted an appointment as a brevet 2d lieutenant of dragoons and served on the frontier and in Kansas until the Civil War.

Detached for recruiting service when secession came, Anderson sided with his home state, resigned from the U.S. Army 25 Apr. 1861, and shortly afterward was commissioned colonel of the 4th North Carolina Infantry. His men reached

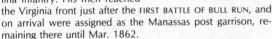

LC

the Virginia front just after the FIRST BATTLE OF BULL RUN, and on arrival were assigned as the Manassas post garrison, remaining there until Mar. 1862.

Anderson's troops were ordered south to take part in rearguard action during the Union's offensive on the Virginia peninsula. At Williamsburg, Confederate Pres. Jefferson Davis was on hand to watch the fighting and during the 5 May battle witnessed a furious charge against Union troops led by Anderson. Impressed by his nerve and leadership, Davis promoted Anderson to brigadier general on the spot; Anderson received his commission 9 June. In the interim he and the 4th North Carolina distinguished themselves at the Battle of SEVEN PINES and in the SEVEN DAYS' CAMPAIGN. In the latter, at MALVERN HILL, Anderson led another awesome charge against Union lines, receiving a severe wound in one hand and further commendations from his superiors.

Because of his wound Anderson was withheld from the SECOND BULL RUN CAMPAIGN in late summer 1862, but that autumn, as a part of Maj. Gen. Daniel H. Hill's division, he took part in Gen. Robert E. Lee's invasion of Maryland and one of its first major actions, the 14 Sept. Battle of SOUTH MOUNTAIN.

3 days later, at the Battle of ANTIETAM, Anderson, fighting on Hill's left, found himself in an unsupported and exposed position on a rise along the Confederate's "BLOODY LANE" front. 2 Union attacks on his line were thrown back, but in the second Anderson received a wound in one foot. At first "pronounced severe, but not serious," it received rudimentary treatment, but on Anderson's evacuation to Virginia it developed complica-

tions, and he was moved again, to Raleigh, N.C. Nearly a month after being wounded, an unsuccessful amputation was performed, and the general died in Raleigh 16 Oct. 1862. —JES

Anderson, George Thomas.

CSA b. Covington, Ga., 3 Feb. 1824. Anderson went into service when he left Georgia's Emory College in 1847 and entered the Georgia Mounted Volunteers as a 1st lieutenant during the Mexican War. Though he was mustered out the following year, his taste for the military lingered, and in 1855 he was commissioned in the Regular Army, serving until 1858, when he was mustered out as a captain in the 1st U.S. Cavalry.

Known as "Tige," short for "Tiger," Anderson was elected a colonel of the 11th Georgia Infantry when his state organized for civil war. He led this unit in combat during the SEVEN

USMHI

DAYS' CAMPAIGN, was given brigade-level command, then fought on through the SECOND BULL RUN and ANTIETAM campaigns before receiving a brigadier general's commission 1 Nov. 1862. In these last 2 campaigns, as part of Maj. Gen. JAMES LONGSTREET's command, he often performed strategically important, if not glamorous, assignments that ensured the success of Confederate maneuvers—particularly in the Second Bull Run fighting, where he was severely wounded.

In December, at the Battle of FREDERICKSBURG, Anderson fought for the first time with full brigade authority. Then, early Apr.–early May 1863, as part of Longstreet's Corps, he participated in the strategic investment of the Federal garrison at Suffolk, Va., an unsuccessful move intended to divert Federal attention from Confederate preparations for the CHANCELLORSVILLE CAMPAIGN.

As in the past, Anderson's fortunes were intertwined with Longstreet's for much of the rest of the war. With his commander, he missed the Battle of Chancellorsville, campaigned into Pennsylvania, where he was badly wounded in the DEVIL'S DEN fighting at GETTYSBURG, then went on detached service, participating at CHICKAMAUGA and KNOXVILLE in Tennessee. He returned to Virginia in summer 1864 to take part in the defense against Lt. Gen. Ulysses S. Grant's OVERLAND CAMPAIGN. "Tige" Anderson's service followed the rest of the Army of Northern Virginia's, and on its surrender at Appomattox he was paroled as a member of Maj. Gen. Charles W. Field's division.

Finally done with soldiering, Anderson pursued a career as a peace officer and was chief of police of Atlanta, Ga., and later Anniston, Ala., where he died 4 Apr. 1901. —JES

Anderson, James Patton.

CSA b. Franklin Cty., Tenn., 16 Feb. 1822. Anderson was reared in Mississippi and briefly attended college in southwest Pennsylvania. Family financial reverses forced him to return home before graduation, so as an apprentice he took up the study and practice of practical medicine in De Soto Cty., Miss. A popular man, known to associates as "Patton," Anderson followed many careers. As a lieutenant colonel he helped raise and command the 1st Battalion of

Mississippi Rifles in the Mexican War, sat in the Mississippi legislature, was appointed U.S. marshal for Washington Territory by Pres. Franklin Pierce, and in 1855 was elected the territory's delegate to the U.S. Congress. Two years later he moved to Florida, establishing a plantation near Monticello and taking part in that state's secession convention.

USMHI

Anderson's military and political experience impressed influential Floridians, who appointed him colonel of the 1st Florida Infantry and sent him to serve under Gen. BRAXTON BRAGG at Pensacola. He was commissioned brigadier general 10 Feb. 1862 and that April led his brigade at the Battle of SHILOH. Then, without promotion, he assumed divisional command in the Army of Tennessee for Bragg's Kentucky Campaign and the subsequent Battle of PERRYVILLE, performing credibly there. In the following Battle of STONE'S RIVER he distinguished himself by leading Col. Edward C. Walthall's brigade in an awesome charge on Federal artillery that ended in the capture of several enemy guns.

Anderson held divisional command again during the fighting around Chickamauga and Chattanooga. On 17 Feb. 1864 he was finally promoted to major general, a rank commensurate with his duties, and was transferred from the Western theater for the first time since early in the war. Shortly after his promotion he commanded the small Confederate District of Florida.

Anderson was recalled to the Army of Tennessee in July 1864, serving in Georgia little more than a month. He fought in the Battle of EZRA CHURCH, in a small combat at Utoy Creek, and in the Battle of JONESBOROUGH, 31 Aug.–1 Sept. 1864, where he sustained a severe chest wound that removed him from command. Army physicians were prepared to muster him from service on medical grounds.

Patriotic, Anderson was upset by his army's reverses and against doctors' orders rejoined his troops for their last desperate battles in the Carolinas. He was surrendered and paroled with his men at Greensborough, N.C., spring 1865.

Following the war he lived in Memphis, Tenn., where his old wound kept him from active employment. There he edited a small agricultural newspaper and existed in genteel poverty until his death 20 Sept. 1872.   —JES

Anderson, Joseph Reid. CSA b. Botetourt Cty., Va., 16 Feb. 1813. Few men contributed more to the Confederate war effort than Anderson, who graduated from West Point 4th in his class in 1836 and was commissioned a 2d lieutenant in the artillery. Though he served primarily on engineering duty, he felt that his engineering talents would be better rewarded outside the military and left the army in 1837, working for the next 5 years as an engineer in his native state. By 1841 he had begun an association with Richmond's Tredegar Iron Co. that would make him the premier industrialist of the South. Intelligent, innovative, and ambitious, Anderson built up Tredegar to be one of the nation's leading foundries. In 1860 the TREDEGAR IRON WORKS was producing locomotives, boilers, cables, naval hardware, and cannon.

Anderson supported the secession movement and, when the Confederate government was formed, offered himself as a man educated to lead troops. He became a brigadier general 3 Sept. 1861 and commanded on the North Carolina coast until his brigade was transferred to Virginia to counter Maj. Gen. George B. McClellan's thrust toward the capital. Anderson's performance in the field was creditable, including action at MECHANICSVILLE and GAINES' MILL and culminating at WHITE OAK SWAMP 30 June 1862, when he was wounded.

USMHI

Anderson knew his administrative skills were more needed at Tredegar than in the army and resigned his commission 19 July 1862 to resume supervising the crucial factory. Tredegar's war output was astonishingly high, including not only cannon but also munitions, iron plate for IRONCLADS, and artillery carriages. Perhaps Anderson's greatest handicap was one over which he had no control: the South's failure to develop an adequate system of exploiting her rich deposits of natural resources. That problem was even greater than the drain of skilled labor to an insensitive CONSCRIPTION and the problems of an inferior transportation network. Under Anderson's supervision Tredegar was the bulwark of ordnance production, and there was no comparable operation anywhere in the Confederacy.

After the fall of Richmond, Tredegar was confiscated by Federal authorities, but by 1867 it had been released and Anderson was back at the helm, continuing as a prominent and respected member of the Richmond business community. d. Isles of Shoals, N.H., 7 Sept. 1892.   —MPM

Anderson, Richard Heron. CSA b. Sumter Cty., S.C., 7 Oct. 1821. Gen. Richard "Fightin' Dick" Heron Anderson was one of Gen. Robert E. Lee's most trusted generals. Once, after Anderson's command beat off several assaults by far larger forces, Lee shook his friend's hand, exclaiming, "My noble soldier, I thank you from the bottom of my heart!"

Anderson, grandson of Revolutionary War hero Richard Anderson, was "born with a taste for the military." An 1842 U.S. Military Academy graduate, 40th in his class, he attended cavalry school at Carlisle, Pa., and served with the dragoons in the West and in the Mexican War, where he was brevetted

USMHI

1st lieutenant "for gallant and meritorious conduct in combat."

When South Carolina seceded, Dec. 1860, Anderson resigned his commission to become colonel of the 1st South Carolina Infantry. He served during the Siege of FORT SUMTER and July 1861 succeeded Brig. Gen. P.G.T. Beauregard in command at Charleston. On 18 July he was made brigadier general and in August went to Pensacola, Fla., as Gen. BRAXTON BRAGG's top assistant.

During the PENINSULA CAMPAIGN in 1862 Anderson fought in the Battles of SEVEN PINES, GAINES' MILL, and MALVERN HILL. Of the Battle of Seven Pines near Richmond, Maj. Gen. JAMES LONGSTREET reported: "The attack of the two brigades under General R. H. Anderson was made with such spirit and regularity as to have driven back the most determined foe. This decided the day in our favor." Anderson, promoted major general July 1862, distinguished himself at SECOND BULL RUN, ANTIETAM, and FREDERICKSBURG that year, in the Battles of CHANCELLORSVILLE and GETTYSBURG in 1863, and at SPOTSYLVANIA and COLD HARBOR in 1864. He was promoted lieutenant general May 1864. After the Battle of Chancellorsville, General Lee reported that Anderson, who held the Confederate right wing, was "distinguished for the promptness, courage, and skill with which he and his division executed every order."

Anderson's command was scattered after fighting in the battle at SAYLER'S CREEK, 6 Apr. 1865, and Anderson himself barely escaped capture. He returned to Richmond, but with no command appropriate to his rank he was relieved as supernumerary the day before Lee surrendered.

Like so many of his fellow Confederates, Anderson passed his postwar years in poverty. d. Beaufort, S.C., 26 June 1879.   —PR

Anderson, Robert. USA b. near Louisville, Ky., 14 June 1805. Anderson was 56 when he became the first Union hero of the Civil War. A deeply religious man, he was cautious and motivated more by reflection than impulse. But nobody questioned his courage when he bowed to the inevitable and surrendered FORT SUMTER to attacking Confederates.

Anderson graduated from West Point in 1825, 15th in his class; fought in the Black Hawk and Seminole Indian wars; served with Gen. WINFIELD SCOTT in Mexico; and translated important military texts from French into English before Sec. of War JOHN B. FLOYD ordered him in Nov. 1860 to take command of the Federal garrison at Charleston harbor, S.C. Of Virginian ancestry, married to a Georgian, Anderson was sympathetic to SLAVERY and unconvinced that military force could prevent secession. But his loyalty to the Union was unquestioned and his devotion to duty unswerving.

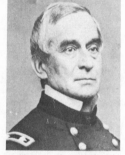
USMHI

In Apr. 1861, confronted with a formal demand for the surrender of Fort Sumter, Anderson stood firm. Only after the fort had been bombarded continuously for 34 hours, the main gates destroyed, the walls breached, and the magazine surrounded by flames did he surrender his post to Confederate Brig. Gen. P.G.T. BEAUREGARD. The following day Anderson marched out of the badly damaged fort "with colors flying and drums beating . . . and saluting my flag with fifty guns."

President Lincoln honored the hero of Fort Sumter by elevating him to the rank of brigadier general 15 May 1861 and giving him command first of the Department of Kentucky, later of the DEPARTMENT OF THE CUMBERLAND. Ill health led to Anderson's retirement in 1863, but he was able to return to Sumter 14 Apr. 1865, the fourth anniversary of his surrender, to raise the Stars and Stripes over the newly recaptured stronghold and acknowledge the acclaim of the gathered crowd—who remembered that Sumter was the symbol of the war's beginning and Anderson of the Union's resolve to win it. d. Charleston, S.C., 26 Oct. 1871.   —BMcG

Anderson, Robert Houston. CSA b. Savannah, Ga., 1 Oct. 1835. An 1857 graduate of West Point, Anderson graduated 35th in his class, then served at a New York state garrison and at Fort Walla Walla in Washington Territory as a lieutenant of infantry. At the time of the secession crisis, Anderson accepted a commission as a Confederate lieutenant of artillery and was listed as "absent without leave" from the U.S. Army until 17 May 1861, when his resignation was received.

Promoted to major Sept. 1861, Anderson assumed the administrative post of assistant adjutant general to W.H.T. Walker, major general of Georgia state troops, commanding on the Georgia coast. In Jan. 1863 he was transferred to line duty but not before finally seeing action in coastal Georgia at FORT McALLISTER, where he helped repel assaults by Federal IRONCLADS testing the strength of the Confederate works.

His transfer came with a promotion to colonel of the 5th Georgia Cavalry, a part of Col. WILLIAM WIRT ALLEN'S brigade serving in the Army of Tennessee. A few months later, on Allen's promotion, Anderson was raised to brigade command and made brigadier general, 26 July 1864. As a cavalryman in the Army of Tennessee he was commanded by Maj. Gen. JOSEPH WHEELER and took part in all of Wheeler's operations during the ATLANTA CAMPAIGN. During one of these, a raid on Federal communications near Franklin, Tenn., Brig. Gen. John H. Kelly, a division commander, was killed and Anderson was temporarily placed in divisional command.

Following the fall of Atlanta and his reversion to brigade command, Anderson fought on through the MARCH TO THE SEA and the CAROLINAS CAMPAIGN and was surrendered with the rest of the army by Gen. Joseph E. Johnston. With the peace, he returned to Savannah and was that city's chief of police from 1867 until his death there 8 Feb. 1888.   —JES

Anderson, Samuel Read. CSA b. Bedford Cty., Va., 17 Feb. 1804. Anderson moved to Kentucky, then Tennessee, when they were little more than frontier, and grew up in this region as it developed. By the 1840s he had become a prominent citizen of Davidson Cty., Tenn., and was the 1st Tennessee Infantry's lieutenant colonel in the Mexican War. Later he worked for the Bank of Tennessee and on the eve of civil war was Nashville's postmaster.

In appreciation of his military experience and political connections, Gov. ISHAM G. HARRIS appointed him major general of Tennessee state troops 9 May 1861. He was then commissioned a brigadier general in Confederate service 9 July 1861 and attached to Gen. Robert E. Lee's first Civil War field command for action in western Virginia.

USMHI

Lee's campaign was unsuccessful, but Anderson committed himself honorably in these maneuvers and played a strategic role in the Battle of CHEAT MOUNTAIN, where he successfully led his brigade in an enveloping move to cut off the Federals' retreat. Following the campaign's end and Lee's transfer to the Carolinas, he was placed under Maj. Gen. WILLIAM WING LORING's command for winter duty in the western Virginia mountains. But his stay with Loring was brief and he was transferred to Maj. Gen. JOHN B. MAGRUDER's forces at Yorktown. There foul weather, the exertions of the past few months, and age combined to break his health and cause his resignation 10 May 1862, after the Yorktown line was abandoned.

On 7 Nov. 1864 Confederate Pres. Jefferson Davis reappointed 60-year-old Anderson a brigadier general in a position closer to his abilities, running the Confederate Bureau of Conscription for Tennessee. But because of extensive Federal seizures in the state, Anderson was compelled to execute his office from headquarters in Selma, Ala. This ended his Confederate service.

Following the war, he returned to Nashville, became a businessman, and died there 2 Jan. 1883.   —JES

Andersonville Prison. In 1863 Confederates recognized the need to move Richmond's crowded military prison to a location more isolated from warfare. The concentration of war prisoners in the Confederate capital had drained local food supplies and attached soldiers for guard duty who were needed elsewhere. Further, as Gen. Robert E. Lee pointed out, prisoners would cause more problems if Yankees attacked RICHMOND.

A new prison site was selected in Sumter County, southwestern Georgia, and construction begun on a stockade to enclose 16.5 (later enlarged to 26) acres. An Augusta newspaper reported the site was near Andersonville, "on the Southwestern railroad, about half way between Oglethorpe and Americus, in a fine agricultural region where supplies are abundant." But with the devastation caused by Maj. Gen. WILLIAM T. SHERMAN's invasion of Georgia, the region could not produce adequate supplies for the number of prisoners that arrived, or for the defending Confederate army.

Late in Feb. 1864 about 500 prisoners came to Andersonville, and by July about 32,000 Union enlisted men were crowded in the stockade. Inadequate shelter, bad sanitation, food shortages, and lack of medicines made living conditions hellish. Most Confederate guards were old men or young boys incapable of properly policing the crowded facility, and criminals—called "raiders"—terrorized their fellow prisoners. The stream flowing through the stockade became polluted, most of the prisoners grew sick, and by war's end Andersonville had 12,912 graves. Estimates of the total number of deaths at the prison have been much higher.

The publicity about Andersonville's human misery and horror made a lasting impression on America's consciousness. The South was condemned for the "notorious Hell Hole," though in fact prisoners had the same rations as prison guards and Confederate soldiers, and had all the medical care possible in the impoverished Confederacy. Further, Lt. Gen. ULYSSES S.

USMHI

GRANT's refusal to exchange Confederate for Union prisoners was a major factor in the suffering of Northern captives.

—PR

Andrew, John Albion. war governor b. Windham, Maine, 31 May 1818. From a liberal and progressive family, Andrew was reared, tutored, and schooled in the state of his birth. Impressed with abolitionist philosophy in his youth, he studied at Bowdoin College, then left Maine in 1837 to take up residence and a law career in Boston; thereafter he was associated with the state of MASSA-CHUSETTS.

NA

In 1848 Andrew's interests in abolition and politics merged when he took part in organizing the FREE SOIL PARTY. When most of its adherents were absorbed by the new REPUBLICAN PARTY a few years later, Andrew worked among Republicans to ensure their election.

In 1857 Andrew won a seat in the Massachusetts state legislature on the Republican ticket and the next year, through legislative and public-speaking skill, took a position in the state party leadership, which he retained in preference to reelection. During this period, Andrew's abolitionist connections pulled him into controversy. He helped raise defense funds for radical JOHN BROWN, accused of treason against the commonwealth of Virginia in the 1859 raid on the HARPERS FERRY, Va., Federal arsenal. And on Brown's conviction, he raised funds for the man's family, which brought him under the scrutiny of a U.S. Senate investigating committee probing the background of the raid and those connected to it. Committee hearings could prove nothing against Andrew, and the publicity they generated pushed him into prominence.

He was a delegate and supporter of ABRAHAM LINCOLN at the Republicans' 1860 Chicago convention, and later that summer, when Massachusetts Gov. NATHANIEL P. BANKS declined reelection, Andrew was the party's dark-horse choice for that office. Elected when he was only 42, he had just 2 years' experience in government.

Governor until 1866, Andrew survived 2 reelection bids, was among the strongest Union supporters, and goaded the Lincoln administration into "vigorous prosecution of the war" and the advancement of black rights. But his greatest national service may have been the level at which he kept the Massachusetts Militia prepared for war. At the start of hostilities with the South, he was the first loyal governor able to respond to Lincoln's call for troops. With Confederate forces closing in on the national capital, Andrew dispatched the 6th Massachusetts Regiment to Washington. Its few men could have done little to stop a forceful Confederate attack, but its presence provided moral support for the week Washington was without any real defenses.

In Andrew's other war activities he attended the 1862 Altoona, Pa., governors' conference (where war and emancipation aims were debated), filled state volunteer quotas, raised black regiments, and looked to the defense of the state itself. In these last 2 areas his most notable achievements were raising the state's first black regiment, the martyred and distin-

guished 54TH MASSACHUSETTS, and maintaining a voluminous and cranky correspondence with Sec. of War EDWIN M. STANTON about his state's vulnerability to assaults and invasions from Confederate sympathizers he believed were waiting in the Canadian maritime provinces.

With the end of the war and the death of Lincoln, Andrew backed Pres. ANDREW JOHNSON's approach to RECONSTRUCTION and urged a lenient attitude toward the South. Then in 1866 he left public office for his private law practice, dying suddenly in Boston, Mass., 30 Oct. the following year.   —JES

Andrews, James J. spy b. Hancock Cty., Va., 1829. Shortly before the Civil War Andrews lived near Flemingsburg, Ky., where he was a house painter and singing coach. But the requirements of his Civil War career have kept the rest of his background a mystery: Andrews was a spy.

He remained a civilian; his secrets were for sale. However, a patriotic Union man, he worked exclusively for the Federal army. Brig. Gen. DON CARLOS BUELL was one of his first major Union employers, using him during the campaign for FORTS HENRY AND DONELSON in Tennessee. Andrews penetrated Southern lines "under the guise of a merchant of contraband materials for Southern customers."

Before the campaign that ended in the Battle of SHILOH, Andrews graduated from spy to saboteur. At Buell's instigation, Andrews took a small group of men into Georgia to destroy Western & Atlantic Railroad bridges, but the scheme was never realized. In Atlanta a locomotive engineer would help in the plot, but the contact was never made. Nervous, Andrews called off the plan, returning to Union lines in Tennessee.

Andrews' next outing was his last. Federal Brig. Gen. ORMSBY M. MITCHEL came up with an assignment similar to the one that had just failed. Andrews was to take a bigger party of men and sabotage the railroad bridges between Atlanta and Chattanooga. Instead of civilian accomplices, the spy would lead Union Army volunteers in civilian clothes.

In Apr. 1862 the plan was put into action. ANDREWS' RAID, remembered in history as the "Great Locomotive Chase," was a failure. The Union spy was captured, tried in a summary Confederate court-martial, caught in an escape attempt, and in conflicting Confederate and Union accounts "was hanged on nearly every street corner north of Five Points in Atlanta." In truth, Andrews was hanged at the corner of 3rd and Juniper streets in Atlanta, 7 June 1862.   —JES

Andrews' Raid. 12 Apr. 1862 Brig. Gen. ORMSBY M. MITCHEL asked one of Maj. Gen. DON CARLOS BUELL's best spies, JAMES J. ANDREWS, to take some men, capture a train, and isolate Chattanooga by burning bridges on the northern section of the Georgia State Railroad and the East Tennessee Railroad near the Georgia state line. Andrews recruited 24 Union Army volunteers with no difficulty, and 12 Apr. 1862, out of uniform, they broke up into small groups to make their separate ways to Marietta, Ga. Heavy rains, swollen streams, and muddy roads delayed them. The men planned to board the train at Marietta and ride to Big Shanty (now Kennesaw), Ga., a meal stop without telegraph communications.

Unknown to Andrews, the Confederates had established a camp at Big Shanty, and his mission—to seize the train and drive 100–200 mi burning bridges, destroying railbeds, and cutting telegraph lines—was now complicated by the presence of hundreds of Confederate soldiers. At Big Shanty, all the

passengers went into the station for breakfast except Andrews and his men, who left the train from the side opposite the station, dashed to the engine (called *The General*), uncoupled it, its tender, and 3 boxcars, and took off with wheels screeching. William A. Fuller, the conductor, and Anthony Murphy, foreman of the railway shop at Atlanta, realized instantly what had happened and started in pursuit—first on foot, then in a handcar, and finally in an engine they found with its steam up.

Andrews discovered that bridges soaked by rain did not take fire easily. The best his men could do was to cut telegraph lines and throw obstacles on the tracks, but Fuller and Murphy were gaining rapidly. Finally, out of fuel 18 mi south of Chattanooga, they abandoned the train and took to the woods, but all were captured within a week. Being out of uniform, they were held to be spies. Within 2 months of the raid, Andrews and 7 of his men were court-martialed and executed—Andrews 7 June, the others 18 June 1862. The fate of the rest had to be postponed because Union forces were advancing rapidly. 8 escaped but the rest were held as prisoners of war until they were exchanged through a special arrangement with Sec. of War EDWIN M. STANTON.   —DBS

"Angel of Cairo." *See* SAFFORD, MARY JANE.

"Angel of Marye's Heights." Wave after wave of Federal units charged the Confederate position at the foot of Marye's Heights outside FREDERICKSBURG, Va., 13 Dec. 1862. The Confederates, impregnable behind a stone wall along a sunken road, repulsed each attack, with appalling casualties. When the fighting ceased, the frozen ground before the wall appeared blue—thousands of Yankees, dead and wounded, littered the field.

The wounded Federals cried for help throughout the bitterly cold night and into the next morning. Behind the stone wall, a South Carolina soldier could bear their pitiful pleas no longer. Richard Rowland Kirkland, a 19-year-old sergeant, asked permission to give his enemies water. His brigade commander acquiesced, and Kirkland, carrying several canteens, climbed over the wall. He walked to the first suffering Yankee, knelt down, held the man's head, and gave the thankful Yankee a drink. Amazed soldiers on both sides watched in silence until the Federals cheered the compassionate man. For over an hour Kirkland walked among the maimed men, providing water and comfort. He covered one Federal with his own overcoat. He was killed at CHICKAMAUGA, 20 Sept. 1863. A fountain in Camden, S.C., memorializes the "Angel of Marye's Heights."
—JDW

Annapolis, Union Department of. Constituted 27 Apr. 1861, the Union Department of Annapolis included Maryland counties within 20 mi of either side of the railroad running from Annapolis to Washington, D.C., as far as Bladensburg, Md.

Brig. Gen. BENJAMIN F. BUTLER assumed initial command.

The creation of this department resulted from the powder-keg situation in Baltimore following the surrender of FORT SUMTER and Pres. Abraham Lincoln's call for 75,000 volunteers. Baltimore was a hotbed of Southern sympathizers who openly espoused secession, and when the 6th Massachusetts detrained in the city 19 Apr. 1861, a mob descended on them. A riot ensued and before the police could restore order at least 4 soldiers and 9 Baltimoreans lay dead or wounded. For the next 5 days secessionists ruled the city, hunting Federal soldiers and Northern sympathizers while driving thousands of Unionists into the countryside. (*See* BALTIMORE RIOTS.)

The nation's capital faced imminent isolation: Virginia had seceded 17 Apr., and if Maryland followed its secessionist sentiments, the capital would be surrounded by enemy territory. But Butler, leading more volunteers south to Washington, cleverly bypassed Baltimore, steaming across the Chesapeake to Annapolis, where the troops repaired a railroad engine and the track to Washington. Butler's route soon became the major avenue from the North into the capital, and thousands of Union volunteers rolled into Washington on the refurbished railroad line.

Unionists soon regained control in Baltimore, but Federal authorities created the department to protect the lifeline, and Butler's initiative resulted in his assignment to the command. The department became the DEPARTMENT OF MARYLAND 19 July and 6 days later was merged into the DEPARTMENT OF PENNSYLVANIA. Maj. Gens. George Cadwalader, NATHANIEL P. BANKS, and JOHN A. DIX also commanded the department during its brief existence.   —JDW

Antietam (Sharpsburg), Md., Battle of. 17 Sept. 1862 The bloodiest single day in the Civil War began with an attack at dawn, and for the next 12 hours soldiers of the ARMY OF THE POTOMAC and the ARMY OF NORTHERN VIRGINIA fought with a "fighting madness." Before the battle ended, 4,710 lay dead, 18,440 wounded, and another 3,043 were missing.

Confederate Gen. ROBERT E. LEE, determined to salvage his Maryland invasion with a decisive battle, regrouped his army around Sharpsburg 15–16 Sept. Union Maj. Gen. GEORGE B. MCCLELLAN reached the field on the 16th, formulated his battle scheme, and pushed 2 corps across Antietam Creek. McClellan proposed to strike both Confederate flanks while maintaining a reserve to crush the center. With 75,000 men, the Union general enjoyed an advantage of nearly 2 to 1 over Lee's 40,000-man army, which had been badly reduced through straggling.

At dawn Maj. Gen. JOSEPH HOOKER's Union I Corps launched the battle with a battering assault against Lee's left on the northern edge of the field. Emerging from the North Woods and around Miller's farm buildings, the Federals surged into a 40-acre cornfield. Musketry and artillery fire mowed down Union soldiers and Maj. Gen. THOMAS J. "STONEWALL" JACKSON's Confederate troops. Hooker's men wrenched the cornfield from its defenders, flailed at Confederates behind the Hagerstown Pike, and lapped toward the small, whitewashed DUNKARD CHURCH. Suddenly Confederate Maj. Gen. JOHN B. HOOD's division hammered into Hooker's spent veterans, who raced back through the leveled cornstalks.

The furious combat did not diminish. Maj. Gen. JOSEPH MANSFIELD's Union XII Corps, passing through the East Woods, swept across the cornfield and into the West Woods. The

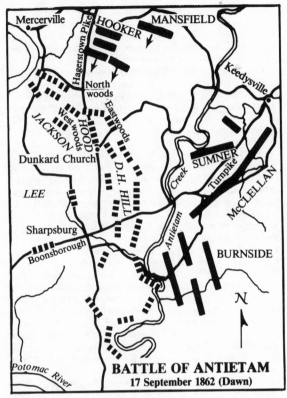

BATTLE OF ANTIETAM
17 September 1862 (Dawn)

ing the Federals reeling back to the creek. Lee's stretched lines held because of tenacious fighting, Union command errors, McClellan's timidity, and plain luck.

Neither army seemed capable of resuming the struggle the next day. The suffering and carnage numbed the participants. During the night Lee recrossed the Potomac, his campaign ended.
                                                                    —JDW

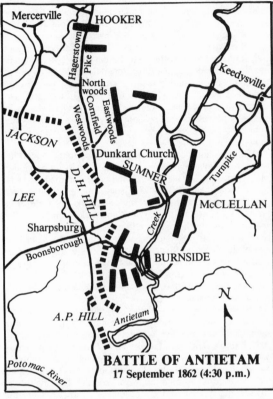

BATTLE OF ANTIETAM
17 September 1862 (4:30 p.m.)

ravaged ranks of Jackson's 3 divisions clung to the ground. Hundreds more fell, including Mansfield dead and Hooker wounded. A third Union corps, the II, under Maj. Gen. EDWIN V. SUMNER, soon entered the fury on the Confederate left. The leading Union division knifed into the West Woods, penetrating deep into the trees. 2 fresh Confederate divisions, sent by Lee from his right, and Jackson's remnants raked the Federals on 3 sides. In 20 minutes of horror, 2,200 Yankees fell and Sumner withdrew. Jackson counterattacked across the cornfield only to be repulsed with even heavier losses.

The battle shifted south along the Confederate center, where Maj. Gen. DANIEL H. HILL's tough veterans manned a sunken farm lane. While Sumner lost 1 division in the West Woods, he watched his 2 other divisions assault Hill's line. For 3 hours furious Union attacks stormed toward the Southern troops in the sunken road, thereafter called "BLOODY LANE," until a misunderstood order opened a gap for the Federals, who dislodged the Confederates. Lee's center lay open, undefended by infantry, but McClellan refused pleas from subordinates to attack with part of his reserve.

McClellan looked to his left, where Maj. Gen. AMBROSE E. BURNSIDE's IX Corps was finally moving against Lee's weakened right. Though McClellan repeatedly sent him orders throughout the morning, Burnside delayed crossing Antietam Creek by the stone-arched Rohrback Bridge (known derisively thereafter as "Burnside Bridge"). He finally forced a crossing, slowly deployed, and at 3 p.m. rolled toward Sharpsburg and Union victory. Suddenly, from the south, Confederate Maj. Gen. AMBROSE P. HILL's troops smashed Burnside's flank, send-

Antietam Campaign. 4–22 Sept. 1862   On 4 Sept. 1862 the Army of Northern Virginia forded the Potomac River in an invasion of Union territory. Confident after their smashing victory at SECOND BULL RUN, the ragged Confederates, many of whom were barefoot, spilled into western Maryland, concentrating 3 days later at Frederick. Gen. ROBERT E. LEE proposed with this bold movement to relieve war-ravaged Virginia during the fall harvest, acquire thousands of Maryland recruits, earn European diplomatic recognition for the Confederacy, and perhaps force the Union to sue for peace.

At Frederick, Lee formulated the details of his audacious campaign. In Special Order No. 191 the Confederate general divided his army for the third time in as many campaigns. Shielded by South Mountain, Lee planned to move his army north into Pennsylvania. To open a supply line into the SHENANDOAH VALLEY, he sent Maj. Gen. THOMAS J. "STONEWALL" JACKSON against the Union garrison at Harpers Ferry. After capturing this force Jackson was to reunite with Maj. Gen. JAMES LONGSTREET's 3 divisions for the thrust northward. Lee believed he could combine his divided command before his troops could be overtaken by the pursuing reunited ARMY OF THE POTOMAC.

Restored to full command in Virginia 2 Sept. by a doubting Abraham Lincoln, the popular Maj. Gen. GEORGE B. MCCLELLAN had reorganized his army, his presence electrifying the demoralized ranks. "Little Mac" advanced from Washington, D.C., on the 7th, the day the Confederates poured into Frederick. Uncertain of Lee's whereabouts or plans, covering the capital and Baltimore, the cautious McClellan marched slowly northwestward. For 5 days the Union army filled the Maryland roads, its cavalry probing the horizon for the elusive Confederates. On the 10th McClellan learned that the Southern troops had abandoned Frederick, and the march quickened.

2 days later the Federals entered the city, 48 hours behind the Confederates, and the next morning, the 13th, 2 Union infantrymen, lounging in an abandoned Confederate campsite, found a paper wrapped around 3 cigars. That paper, a copy of Lee's Special Order No. 191 (see LEE'S LOST ORDER), was immediately forwarded through channels to McClellan, who suddenly possessed a great opportunity to destroy his divided opponent. "Little Mac," however, waited 16 hours before moving.

Within 24 hours Lee learned of the misfortune—which has never been fully explained—from his cavalry commander, Maj. Gen. J.E.B. STUART. The Confederate commander faced the abandonment of his invasion and, more important, the piecemeal destruction of his army. Since the departure from Frederick on the 10th, the various Confederate commands had scattered toward their assigned goals. 2 of Longstreet's divisions were near Hagerstown, while 30 mi to the south and across the Potomac River Jackson's troops were moving on Harpers Ferry. 2 additional divisions were closing the trap on the Union garrison. Lee had at hand only 1 infantry division at Boonsborough and Stuart's horsemen to hold the vital gap of the South Mountain.

On the morning of 14 Sept. the Confederate defenders in the mountain defiles watched the blue columns, stretching out of sight, fill the valley below. By 9 o'clock the leading division of the Union IX Corps had entered Fox's Gap, where musketry opened the action. The Confederate defenders, commanded by Maj. Gen. DANIEL H. HILL, fought stubbornly all day, against mounting odds. A mile north, where the National Road crossed the mountain at Boonsborough (Turner's) Gap, the Union I Corps assaulted. Hill shifted his 5 brigades against the mounting Federal numbers. Only the late-afternoon arrival of elements of Longstreet's other 2 divisions salvaged a disaster for the South. The Confederates lost 2,700 men, the Federals 1,800. But Lee's supply trains were secured and he had an extra day to regroup.

While this fighting raged, 5 mi to the south Maj. Gen. WILLIAM B. FRANKLIN'S Union VI Corps marched into CRAMPTON'S GAP. The timid Federal advance stalled before a small force of Southern troops. During the afternoon the struggle intensified until the weak Confederate center broke. Franklin, however, halted, instead of obeying McClellan's orders to relieve Harpers Ferry.

With his invasion plans wrecked, Lee prepared orders for a retreat to Virginia, but on the morning of the 15th Jackson captured Harpers Ferry. The garrison commander, Col. Dixon S. Miles, who was killed in the battle's final moments, was subsequently charged with drunkenness and ineptitude; even treason has been proposed to explain his unskillful defense. Over 10,000 men, 13,000 small arms, and 73 cannon fell into Confederate hands.

Jackson's success altered Lee's plans, and he ordered a concentration at Sharpsburg, Md. Unwilling to retreat without a showdown, the Confederate commander gambled once more. Throughout the 16th Lee gathered his separate wings along Antietam Creek. Jackson arrived after an all-night forced march, leaving a division behind to count the seizures and parole the prisoners. McClellan characteristically moved cautiously onto the field, perhaps frittering away another opportunity. "Little Mac" developed his plans for an assault the next day while pushing 2 corps westward across Antietam Creek. A nighttime rain fell on 75,000 Federals and slightly over 40,-000 Confederates as they slept.

The Battle of ANTIETAM, or Sharpsburg, began soon after dawn on a field shrouded in fog. McClellan's sound battle plan of assaults on both Confederate flanks soon faltered in a series of uncoordinated, piecemeal attacks. In some of the most savage fighting of the war the opponents bloodied each other across the farmlands and in the woods. Hammering Federal assaults were met with howling Confederate counterattacks. Artillerists on both sides scorched the field with shells and waves of canister. Lee parried the thrusts by shifting troops from his right to the left and center. Union Maj. Gen. AMBROSE E. BURNSIDE'S inexcusable failure to assault the Confederate right until afternoon permitted Lee to juggle his units. But the arrival of Jackson's absent division finally saved the Confederate army when it repulsed Burnside's tardy assault. In a bloody war, the conflict's bloodiest day ended.

The exhausted armies rested the next day, and during the night of the 18th–19th Lee retreated across the Potomac. On the 20th McClellan sent a force in pursuit, which Jackson repulsed. Lee's bold campaign ended without Maryland recruits or European recognition. A turning point had been reached. 5 days after the battle, 22 Sept. 1862, Lincoln issued the EMANCIPATION PROCLAMATION; the Union armies now had another goal—human freedom.   —JDW

Apache Canyon, New Mexico Territory, Battle of.

26–28 Mar. 1862 *See* LA GLORIETA PASS, NEW MEXICO TERRITORY, BATTLE OF.

Appomattox Campaign, Va.

25 Mar.–9 Apr. 1865 The final campaign of the ARMY OF NORTHERN VIRGINIA began 25 Mar. 1865, when Gen. ROBERT E. LEE sought to break Gen. ULYSSES S. GRANT'S ever-tightening stranglehold at PETERSBURG, Va., by attacking the Federal position at FORT STEDMAN. The assault failed, and when Grant counterattacked a week later at FIVE FORKS, 1–2 Apr., the thin Confederate line snapped, and Lee's skeleton forces abandoned Richmond and Petersburg. The Confederate retreat began southwestward as Lee sought to use the still-operational Richmond & Danville Railroad. At its western terminus at Danville he would unite with Gen. JOSEPH E. JOHNSTON's army, which was retiring up through North Carolina. Taking maximum advantage of Danville's hilly terrain, the 2 Southern forces would make a determined stand against the converging armies of Grant and Maj. Gen. WILLIAM T. SHERMAN.

But Grant moved too fast for the plan to materialize, and Lee waited 24 hours in vain at Amelia Court House for trains to arrive with badly needed supplies. Federal cavalry, meanwhile, sped forward and cut the Richmond & Danville at Jetersville. Lee had to abandon the railroad, and his army stumbled across rolling country in an effort to reach Lynchburg, another supply base that could be defended. Union horsemen seized

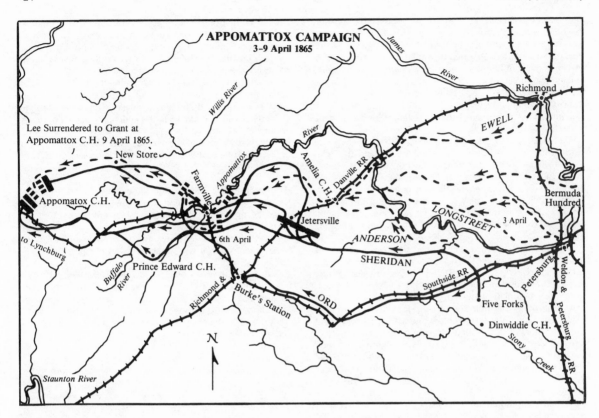

APPOMATTOX CAMPAIGN
3–9 April 1865

Lee Surrendered to Grant at
Appomattox C.H. 9 April 1865.

New Store

Appomatox C.H.

to Lynchburg

6th April

Prince Edward C.H.

Burke's Station

Staunton River

N

Farmville

Jetersville

ANDERSON

SHERIDAN

ORD

Five Forks

Dinwiddie C.H.

Amelia C.H.

Danville RR

LONGSTREET

3 April

Southside RR

Richmond

EWELL

Bermuda
Hundred

Petersburg

Weldon &
Petersburg RR

Stony Creek

Willis River

Buffalo River

Richmond &

James River

the vital rail junction at Burkeville as Federal infantry continued to dog the Confederates.

On 6 Apr. almost one-fourth of Lee's army was trapped and captured at SAYLER'S CREEK. Lee, at Farmville when he received news of the disaster, led his remaining 30,000 men in a north-by-west arc across the Appomattox River and toward Lynchburg. In the meantime, Grant, with 4 times as many men, sent Maj. Gen. PHILIP H. SHERIDAN's cavalry and most of 2 infantry corps on a hard, due-west march from Farmville to Appomattox Station. Reaching the railroad first the Federals blocked Lee's only line of advance.

On the morning of 9 Apr. Confederate probes tested the Union lines and found them to be too strong. Lee's options were now gone. That afternoon—Palm Sunday—Lee met Grant in the front parlor of WILMER MCLEAN's home to discuss peace terms.

The actual surrender of the Confederate Army occurred 12 Apr., an overcast Wednesday. As Southern troops marched past silent lines of Federals, a Union general noted "an awed stillness, and breath-holding, as if it were the passing of the dead."   —JIR

Archer, James Jay. CSA   b. Bel Air, Md., 19 Dec. 1817. Archer practiced as a lawyer, volunteered during the Mexican War, was cited for gallantry at Chapultepec, then temporarily resumed his legal practice before entering the Regular Army as a captain of the 9th Infantry in 1855.

With the advent of war, Archer resigned his commission,

mustering into Confederate service as colonel of the 5th Texas. His regiment, along with 2 other Texas units and 2 from Georgia, were merged into a brigade under former Texas Sen. LOUIS T. WIGFALL. Brig. Gen. JOHN BELL HOOD replaced Wigfall Mar. 1862, leading the brigade in the PENINSULA CAMPAIGN. In action at ELTHAM'S LANDING and SEVEN PINES, Archer performed capably under the aggressive Hood.

On 3 June 1862 Archer was promoted to brigadier general, succeeding Brig. Gen. Robert Hatton in command of 3 Tennessee regiments. In a reorganization of the army later that month, Archer's and 5 other brigades combined to form the historic LIGHT DIVISION led by Maj. Gen. AMBROSE P. HILL, under whose brilliant leadership Archer distinguished himself that year.

Through the SEVEN DAYS' CAMPAIGN, Cedar Mountain, and SECOND BULL RUN Archer led his brigade, then numbering 5 regiments. At Cedar Mountain, in the final Confederate attack, his men assisted in breaking the Union line. Less than a month later, at Second Bull Run, his horse was killed under him.

Late on the afternoon of 17 Sept. 1862, when the Light Division arrived at ANTIETAM to save Gen. Robert E. Lee's beleaguered army, Archer delivered

USMHI

a crunching assault. Too sick to ride, the Marylander directed his brigade from an ambulance as his veterans, with a defiant scream, pitched into the charging Federals, who were driving toward Sharpsburg. Supported by the fire of 2 other brigades, Archer's men crushed the Union flank, driving them rearward while recapturing a Confederate battery. 3 days later, at the Battle of SHEPHERDSTOWN, Archer and Brig. Gen. WILLIAM D. PENDER, in another riveting attack, dismembered a Union pursuit force and sent it reeling into the Potomac River, ending the ANTIETAM CAMPAIGN.

On 13 Dec. 1862, at FREDERICKSBURG, Archer again served with distinction. His brigade was positioned behind a railroad embankment, but between him and the brigade on his left was a gap of several hundred yards. In the massive Union assault against Lee's right, a Federal division poured into the hole. Archer, still physically unwell, refused his left and his command clung stubbornly to their line. Finally a stunning Confederate countersurge blunted the Yankee attack and secured the position.

A proven, solid brigadier, Archer seemed destined for higher command when the battles resumed in spring 1863. At CHANCELLORSVILLE, 3 May, Archer's brigade singlehandedly captured a Federal battery, seizing Hazel Grove, a strategically important hill commanding the battlefield. Confederate batteries soon rolled onto the plateau, providing decisive artillery fire during the final Confederate assaults. Less than 2 months later, at GETTYSBURG, 1 July, Archer, now in Maj. Gen. HENRY HETH's new division, led the Southern attack. In a clash with Northerners west of the town, the brigadier and most of his thin brigade were routed and captured. Archer became the first general officer to be taken since Lee commanded the army.

A year's imprisonment at JOHNSON'S ISLAND in Ohio shattered Archer's feeble health. Exchanged in late summer, the Marylander assumed command of 2 brigades for only a short time. d. Richmond, Va., 24 Oct. 1864.   —JDW

Arkansas.   As tension over SLAVERY and STATES RIGHTS grew, Arkansas aligned itself with the South, and Feb. 1861 state officers took over the Federal arsenal at Little Rock. However, a convention in Mar. 1861 voted against secession, hoping the differences between North and South might be resolved without bloodshed but vehemently opposing coercion of the seceding states.

Then, 12–14 Apr., FORT SUMTER was bombarded and captured by Confederates, Lincoln asked for 75,000 volunteers to put down the rebellion, and Arkansas called a second convention. On 6 May they passed, with only one adverse vote, a secession ordinance joining the state to the Confederacy.

Arkansas Gov. HENRY M. RECTOR had already replied to Lincoln's call for volunteers:

> In answer to your requisition of troops from Arkansas to subjugate the Southern States, I have to say that none will be furnished. The demand is only adding insult to injury. The people of this commonwealth are freemen, not slaves, and will defend to the last extremity their honor, lives, and property against Northern mendacity and usurpation.

Arkansas troops fought in Virginia, Kentucky, and Missouri, as well as in their home state; in northwest Arkansas Confederates were defeated in the bloody Battle of PEA RIDGE, Mar. 1862.

In 1863 the Confederate state government was forced from Little Rock southwest to Washington, Ark., and early the next year Union sympathizers from 23 counties met in Little Rock, wrote a Unionist constitution, and set up their own government. For the remainder of the war Arkansas had 2 civil governments, one giving allegiance to the North, the other to the South; the dividing line roughly followed the Arkansas River.

Arkansas furnished 70 separate military organizations to the Confederate armies and 17 to the Federals. Records of losses are incomplete, but at least 3,080 Arkansans in Confederate service were killed in action or died of wounds and 3,780 died of disease. Total deaths of Arkansans in Union service from all causes numbered 1,713.   —PR

Arkansas, CSS.   Built by John Shirley, the CSS *Arkansas* was laid down at Memphis, Tenn., Oct. 1861. But before the ship could be completed, Memphis was threatened by Federals descending the Mississippi River, and the unfinished Confederate IRONCLAD was towed down that river and up the Yazoo. At Yazoo City, Miss., it was completed and commissioned July 1862.

The *Arkansas* was a twin-screw ram, 165 ft long, 35 ft in beam, with a draft of 11–12 ft. Unlike those of other Confederate armored vessels, the sides of its casemate were perpendicular, although the 2 ends were slanted; and the casemate itself was covered with railway T-rails. It carried a battery of 10 guns and a crew of 200 officers and men.

OR

Descending the Yazoo River 15 July 1862, the *Arkansas* encountered 3 Union vessels, the *CARONDELET, TYLER,* and *QUEEN OF THE WEST.* In the engagement that followed, the *Carondelet* was disabled and the other 2 Union vessels retired downstream with the *Arkansas* in pursuit. The chase continued into the Mississippi River, where the Confederate ironclad found at anchor the combined naval forces of Cmdr. CHARLES H. DAVIS and Rear Adm. DAVID G. FARRAGUT, 30 warships in all. The *Arkansas,* then commanded by Lt. Henry K. Stevens, steamed slowly through the Union force, hit repeatedly by shot and shell. Several of the Union vessels were struck by the *Arkansas'* guns but only the *Lancaster* was seriously damaged.

The *Arkansas* reached Vicksburg and on the night of the 15th came under attack a second time by Farragut's vessels as they ran the Southern batteries and headed back downstream. The Confederate ironclad, already damaged from the early morning engagement, was hit several times. On 3 Aug. the

Arkansas, repairs completed, left Vicksburg to cooperate in a land/sea attack on BATON ROUGE. 24 hours after leaving Vicksburg the ironclad's engines began giving trouble, and the ship anchored while its engineers worked on them. The *Arkansas* got under way again for Baton Rouge the following morning, but within sight of the port, the engines broke down completely. With a Union naval force approaching, led by the ironclad *Essex,* the Confederates abandoned the *Arkansas* after setting it on fire. It drifted downstream before sinking.
—WNS

Arkansas, Union Department of. This Federal geographical designation was created 6 Jan. 1864 and applied to all the territory within the state of Arkansas except FORT SMITH, which was not included until 17 Apr. 1864. The department in turn was part of the MILITARY DIVISION OF WEST MISSISSIPPI 7 May 1864–17 May 1865. With headquarters at Little Rock, the state capital, the department was to clear Arkansas, which had some indigenous Union sympathy, of organized Confederates who might aid the South's operations east of the Mississippi.

Federal troops within the geographical area were designated as the VII Corps, initially under the command of Maj. Gen. FREDERICK STEELE, until 22 Dec. 1864, at which time Maj. Gen. JOSEPH J. REYNOLDS took over, commanding through 1 Aug. 1865, when the department was discontinued.

Primary military activities consisted of the Arkansas Campaign of 1864, also known as the Expedition to Camden, or Steele's CAMDEN EXPEDITION, which was supposed to be the diversionary movement of Gen. NATHANIEL P. BANKS's ill-fated RED RIVER CAMPAIGN but itself was a dismal failure.   —RAP

Arkansas Post, Ark., eng. at. 10–11 Jan. 1863 Fort Hindman at Arkansas Post, Ark., was one of the strongest bastions Southerners had built, sitting high on a hill overlooking a bend in the Arkansas River, 50 mi above its mouth and 117 mi below Little Rock, the state capital. It was particularly useful to the Confederates in obstructing the navigation of the Mississippi River, but Union officers were divided over the wisdom of capturing it. Maj. Gen. ULYSSES S. GRANT, for one, looked on its capture as a "wild-goose chase." But Maj. Gen. JOHN A. MCCLERNAND, commanding the Army of the Mississippi, thought otherwise, and he and Lt. DAVID D. PORTER, heading naval forces in the area, planned an expedition against the fort.

An army of 32,000 men set sail up the river in transports, accompanied by 3 IRONCLADS and 6 gunboats, arriving within a short distance of the fort late on 9 Jan. 1863 and landing the next day. The fort was defended by 3 brigades, 1 commanded by Col. John W. Dunnington, in charge of the fort, and the others, spread out in mile-long trenches on the off-river side, by Brig. Gen. THOMAS J. CHURCHILL.

Late on the 10th, ironclads moved up the river, shelling the fort for about 2 hours, then withdrew. It was nearly noon the next day before Union troops got in position. At 1 p.m., Porter's fleet moved up again and began shelling, and within 3 hours all but one of the Southerners' cannon had been silenced.

Meanwhile, Federals on land were having less success, with each attack they made on the Confederate trenches repulsed. Then, about 4:30 p.m., the end came quickly, following a fierce bombardment by the fleet. White flags began appearing along the left on the Confederate line, and the surrender was soon executed.

The North captured about 5,000 men, the greatest number of prisoners since the capture of ISLAND NO. 10, as well as large stores of guns and commissary and quartermaster supplies. The importance of the victory was great: coming at a time when Union arms had been unsuccessful on several battlefields, the success caused Northern sympathizers throughout the nation to rejoice.   —VCJ

Armistead, Lewis Addison. CSA b. New Berne, N.C., 18 Feb. 1817. In 1834 young Armistead, the son of a high-ranking U.S. Army officer, entered West Point. 2 years later he was dismissed from the academy for breaking a mess-hall plate over the head of fellow cadet (and future Confederate general) JUBAL A. EARLY.

Armistead entered the army in 1839 as a lieutenant in the 6th U.S. Infantry, seeing service in the Seminole War and being brevetted 3 times for heroism in the Mexican War. Noted for his casual manner and friendly disposition, Armistead was nevertheless a disciplinarian to whom "obedience to duty" was "the first qualification of a soldier."

LC

When he resigned from the army 26 May 1861 to cast his lot with the Confederacy, Armistead, a widower with a son who later served as his aide, was older than most of his compatriots. He served as colonel of the 57th Virginia Infantry until 1 Apr. 1862, when he was promoted to brigadier general. Armistead first took his brigade into action at SEVEN PINES, where he promptly distinguished himself.

Armistead's promising career ended in PICKETT'S CHARGE at GETTYSBURG, where his brigade was in the climactic assault against the Union center. He and 150 men scaled the stone wall on CEMETERY RIDGE and momentarily drove Federal cannoneers from their pieces. "Give them the cold steel!" Armistead shouted as he put his hand on one of the cannon barrels. A moment later he slumped to the ground, mortally wounded. He died 5 July 1863 in a Federal field hospital. Friends later claimed his body, which was interred in St. Paul's Churchyard, Baltimore.

Of the 6 Confederate generals killed at Gettysburg, Armistead is generally regarded as the one with the most potential for advancement to higher command.   —JIR

Armstrong, Frank Crawford. CSA b. Choctaw Agency, Indian Territory, 22 Nov. 1835. Armstrong grew up indoctrinated in military life: his father was a Regular Army officer assigned as agent to the Choctaws at the time of his son's birth and his stepfather was the Mexican War hero, Gen. Persifor Frazer Smith. After graduating from Holy Cross Academy in Massachusetts, Armstrong in 1854 accompanied Smith on a military expedition to New Mexico. Because of conspicuous bravery in an Indian engagement, the following June he was offered and accepted a commission as 2d lieutenant in the Regular Army, advancing to captain by June 1861.

At FIRST BULL RUN Armstrong commanded a company of dragoons for the Union, but his sympathies lay with the Confederacy. 3 days before his resignation was accepted, the cavalryman was serving as a volunteer aide-de-camp to Brig. Gen. BEN MCCULLOCH at WILSON'S CREEK. He officially entered Confederate service as a lieutenant but was soon elected colonel of the 3d Louisiana Infantry.

CMH

Armstrong showed himself to be an accomplished professional soldier, always ready to fight. In July 1862, Maj. Gen. Sterling Price detailed him as acting brigadier general in command of cavalry for the Army of the West. He fought conspicuously in the operations around CORINTH and covered Price's retreat from IUKA, Miss. Thereafter he headed brigades under Maj. Gen. Joseph Wheeler, Brig. Gen. James R. Chalmers, and Lt. Gens. Stephen D. Lee and Nathan B. Forrest, continuing to fight admirably in all the major Western campaigns. Repeated commendations from superiors, notably for raids on Courtland, Ala., 25 July, and into West Tennessee the next month, prompted Armstrong's advancement to brigadier general 20 Jan. 1863. Except during Gen. JOHN B. HOOD's campaign from Dalton to Atlanta during summer 1864, Armstrong remained in the Trans-Mississippi. He was with Forrest at Selma, Ala., when the city surrendered 2 Apr. 1865.

Armstrong settled in the Southwest after the war, working in the Texas Overland Mail Service, then serving successively as U.S. Indian inspector and assistant commissioner of Indian affairs. d. Bar Harbor, Maine, 8 Sept. 1909.   —PLF

Armstrong, James F. USN b. N.J., 20 Nov. 1817. Armstrong was appointed acting midshipman 7 Mar. 1832. His promotion to passed midshipman came in 1838, to lieutenant in 1842, and to commander in 1861. Armstrong was commandant of the Pensacola Navy Yard when Florida seceded and was compelled to surrender the yard to state forces 12 Apr. 1861. During 1862–63 he commanded the *State of Georgia* of the NORTH ATLANTIC BLOCKADING SQUADRON. In addition to capturing several BLOCKADE RUNNERS off the Carolina coast, Armstrong participated in the joint army/navy attack on FORT MACON, N.C., 25 Apr. 1862, which resulted in the surrender of the fort the same day.

In 1864 Armstrong commanded the *San Jacinto* of the East Gulf Blockading Squadron, then returned to the command of the Pensacola Navy Yard. Promoted to captain in 1867, he continued at the yard until 1868. Armstrong's last tour of duty was at the Mare Island Navy Yard. d. New Haven, Conn., 19 Apr. 1873.   —NCD

Armstrong gun. Among those rapidly advancing artillery technology in mid-19th-century Europe was England's Lord Armstrong, who in 1855 developed a revolutionary cannon and projectile. Available as a breech- or muzzle-loader, this weapon enjoyed long range and accuracy and was used by the British army 1858–1900.

Constructed with built-up rings of wrought iron, the tube of the gun withstood greater pressure than most of its contemporaries. Armstrong perfected a balanced projectile that doubled as canister, exploding as it was fired, and shrapnel, bursting over the enemy. 3 rows of brass studs (shunts) ensured that the

USMHI

shell adhered to the twist of the rifling. A variety of this projectile without studs was sheathed in lead, which expanded to fit the 40 bands and grooves within the barrel.

Following the outbreak of hostilities in America, the English made their weaponry available to the South. Despite the Armstrong's proven capabilities, these guns were used less often than those of rival British manufacturers WHITWORTH and BLAKELY, since apparently the Confederate Ordnance Department considered them unsatisfactory in combat. Replacing spent ammunition posed a problem that forced the Southerners to fashion their own, in some instances by reworking 3-in. Parrott shells.

Several specimens of large-caliber siege guns were imported in addition to field artillery. Fort Fisher, near Wilmington, N.C., kept the Union fleet at bay with the aid of a deadly 8-in. Armstrong, as did several other Confederate coastal fortifications. Excavated projectiles indicate that the 3-in. field gun saw service with the Army of Northern Virginia as early as 1862. Similar shells have been recovered from the earthworks at Petersburg, Va., but the only documented battery of Armstrongs was captured on the road to Appomattox without ever having fired a shot.   —MJO'D

Armstrong's Mill, Va., Battle of. 5–7 Feb. 1865 *See* HATCHER'S RUN, VA., BATTLE OF.

army. In 1861 the U.S. Regular Army consisted of 1,108 officers and 15,259 enlisted men. With South Carolina already out of the Union and 12 more states on the verge of secession, the outlook for the North was far from favorable. In the Northern states the white population was 18,936,579; Southern whites numbered 5,449,646, but 3,521,111 slaves contributed materially to the Confederacy's ability to wage war. Moreover, in the South a military career was an honored profession, a view not widely held in the North. When nearly one-third of the West Point–trained officers on active duty resigned to join the Confederacy (among them a very few of Northern birth), the question of leadership became acute.

In the U.S. Regular Army, the primary unit was the company: 10 companies made a regiment, 5 regiments a brigade, 3 brigades a division, and 3 divisions a corps. These figures were more often mythical than real. Battle losses frequently destroyed units—at times a division was hardly as large as a regiment. The Regular Army was kept intact, not scattered through volunteer units. As losses mandated additional recruits, these formed new units, rather than being used as replacements.

The Southern army was formed similarly.

Armies were the largest operational organizations and were usually named for the department in which they were found, departments in turn being named, in the Union, for rivers and in the Confederacy for states or regions. There were 16 Union and 23 Confederate armies. The North raised the equivalent of 2,040 regiments, of which 1,696 were infantry, 272 cavalry, and 72 artillery. Reliable figures for the Confederacy are not available but it is known that at least 600,000 and perhaps as many as 900,000 men served in the Confederate Army.

Appointment of officers in both armies was too often influenced by politics, frequently resulting in inadequate leadership with ghastly errors and unnecessary deaths. The practice was more prevalent in the North but did occur in the South. *See also* REGULAR ARMY, UNITED STATES and REGULAR ARMY, CONFEDERATE STATES.   —DBS

art. Before news photography, *FRANK LESLIE'S ILLUSTRATED NEWSPAPER, HARPER'S WEEKLY,* and other illustrated newspapers produced the bulk of art informing the public about the Civil War. *Leslie's* employed such artists as EDWIN FORBES, William Waud, and James E. Taylor to produce battlefield sketches from which woodblock engravings were made. *Harper's* hired ALFRED R. WAUD and Theodore Davis to do the same and provided training for WINSLOW HOMER, one of the few artists of the war whose work has remained popular in the 20th century. The foreign press also made contributions through such men as FRANK VIZETELLY, news artist for the *Illustrated London News,* who covered the Confederate side of the war. But the individuality and style of most news artists' work was usually lost in the uniformity imposed by the woodblock engraving process, and the best of their battlefield sketchwork is found today only in the originals, in government or private repositories.

Art that inspired the Union and Confederate public came from both amateurs and professionals. Among the latter, Missourian George Caleb Bingham, an established genre artist before the war, painted *Order No. 11* (c. 1868), a political canvas he hoped would render the order "infamous in history." The scene, depicting residents of Missouri counties being driven from their homes by Union troops, successfully inspired among the Union public contempt for their army's draconian measures in the West.

Confederate artist William Washington, a professor of fine arts at the Virginia Military Institute, painted *The Burial of Latané* (1864), which memorialized an incident of 1862 involving Capt. William Latané, who was killed during Confederate Brig. Gen. J.E.B. STUART'S "RIDE AROUND MCCLELLAN" and left to be buried by strangers. The scene of a collection of women and slaves gathered to read the burial service for a man they did not know touched Southern sensibilities and symbolized the lonely state of the Confederate cause.

Professional artist Francis B. Carpenter executed *The Proclamation of Emancipation* (1864), securing photographs of and sittings with President Lincoln and prominent members of his cabinet to create a 14.5 × 9-ft painting both accurate and allegorical in its depiction of the document's approval. Today it hangs in the Capitol in Washington, D.C., one of the most successful of the inspirational genre.

But perhaps the best artists of the Civil War served in the

LC

Union and Confederate armies. Julian Scott and Charles W. Reed both saw action in Federal service and memorialized Union soldier life after the war—Scott in his painting *The Drummer Boy* (undated), among many others, and Reed in a series of humorous illustrations for a popular postwar book, *Hardtack and Coffee* (1887). The life of Confederate soldiers, infrequently and poorly portrayed during the war, benefited postbellum by the work of Southern veterans ALLEN C. REDWOOD, CONRAD W. CHAPMAN, and William L. Shepherd. Shepherd worked in postwar decades illustrating books and articles, as did many other soldier artists. A veteran of Virginia's Richmond Howitzers, he trained in commercial art before the war and, following the conflict, studied in Europe. Though he turned his training to Confederate memorial sculpture in the late 19th century, through such paintings as *Equipment* and *Newspapers in Camp* (both undated) he communicated some of the war's more pacific moments.

James Walker, an English-born artist whose reputation was gained through his battle panoramas of the Mexican War, typified the public artist of the war period in his large canvases, such as *The Battle of Lookout Mountain* (1863–64), which both inspired and informed. The Civil War also touched the European art community when French impressionist Édouard Manet, an eyewitness to the battle of the CSS *ALABAMA* and the USS *KEARSARGE* in Cherbourg Harbor, recorded that fight in an oil painting that now hangs in the Philadelphia Museum of Art.

Today the National Portrait Gallery in Washington, D.C., the Museum of the Confederacy in Richmond, Va., and Illinois' Chicago Historical Society have large collections of powerful Civil War–era work.   —JES

LC

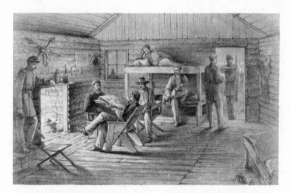

CHICKAMAUGA.
LC

Ashby, Turner. CSA b. Fauquier Cty., Va., 23 Oct. 1828. Ashby was one of many Civil War generals who fell in battle too early for their full potential to be realized. He received a rudimentary education from tutors and his widowed mother, then joined his brothers in managing the family farm, "Rose Hill." In 1859, following John Brown's Raid, Ashby raised a volunteer company of cavalry to patrol the Potomac River crossings against further incursions. After Virginia seceded, that company became part of the 7th Virginia Cavalry Regiment, and Ashby rose from captain to colonel in months.

GG

The June 1861 murder of his brother by a Union patrol filled Ashby with vengeance, and he rapidly gained a reputation for personal bravery equaled by few participants in the Civil War. But in spite of his devotion to the Southern cause, he was a quiet, soft-spoken leader whose commands were often criticized for lack of sufficient discipline.

Ashby performed a variety of scouting duties until spring 1862, when Maj. Gen. THOMAS J. "STONEWALL" JACKSON placed him in command of all Confederate cavalry in the SHENANDOAH VALLEY. Promotion to brigadier came 23 May, but Ashby's tenure as a general was tragically short. Near sundown, 6 June, 2 mi southeast of Harrisonburg, Va., Ashby took part in a rearguard action by dismounting and leading a column of infantry in a counterassault. He had just shouted, "Forward, my brave men!" when he was struck by a bullet and killed instantly. Jackson, a man of few words, was shaken by Ashby's death and wrote: "As a partisan officer I never knew his superior."

Ashby never married. He wrote but a handful of letters during his lifetime; and after his death few could recall anything he had said. One historian has observed: "He spoke best with his sword." The cavalryman's remains iie today in Stonewall Cemetery, Winchester, Va.   —JIR

Associated Press. To facilitate the fullest coverage of daily news, in 1848 7 New York City morning newspapers banded together as the New York Associated Press to collect news, swap features, and sell their efforts to other papers. In the years before the Civil War the association became popular, building up a national subscription and establishing several regional associations divided into loose geographic groups. Collectively, they became known colloquially as the Associated Press (AP).

By the time of the firing on FORT SUMTER, a national network of APs had existed for many years. In 1861 its president was New York *Journal of Commerce* publisher Gerard Hallock. AP writers, called "agents," were stationed in all the news capitals of the country. Their chief was General Agent Daniel Craig, with national policy set by AP board members Frederic Hudson of the New York *Herald* and Henry Raymond of the New York *Times.*

But the Civil War brought problems. The Southern AP was lost to national subscription, and in a squabble over his opposition to the war, President Hallock was forced out of office by AP executives. In 1862, unhappy with the national news given it by the parent New York AP, the Western AP fomented its own rebellion and incorporated as an association.

In the field, developments were more satisfactory but no smoother. The AP had more agents covering the war than any single paper and pulled some journalistic coups. One agent reported the bombardment of Fort Sumter firsthand from his shipboard post just outside the range of hostilities. AP Baltimore agent Charles C. Fulton, also editor of the Baltimore *American,* cultivated White House sources and became a steady, reliable conduit of political news. And in Louisville, Ky., AP agent George W. Tyler formed a professional friendship with the archenemy of correspondents, Brig. Gen. WILLIAM T. SHERMAN.

In covering FIRST BULL RUN, the local AP agent left the field before the fight had finished, prepared to file a story claiming Union victory, and when told of the outcome was forced to piece together his report from civilian refugees' eyewitness accounts. Then in 1862 agent Fulton was jailed in Baltimore's Fort McHenry for supposed violation of a presidential confidence in PENINSULA CAMPAIGN reportage. Problems with CENSORSHIP continued throughout the war, but the AP's inaccuracies were rarely as serious as at Bull Run. In a day when standards of journalistic writing were low and policies of attribution rare, the AP began efforts to build a reputation for trust.

Correspondents complained that the New York *Herald,* the New York *Times,* and a few other newspapers were favored by receiving government news releases before others. To quash the argument government spokesmen thereafter gave all releases to the AP agent first. He then cleared and passed on relevant releases to all newspapers simultaneously, even those out of town. This helped form a tradition that continues today: at presidential news conferences, the chief executive recognizes the questions of the AP correspondent before any others.

—JES

Atlanta, Ga., Battle of.   22 July 1864 Despite his decisive defeat at PEACHTREE CREEK, Confederate Gen. JOHN B. HOOD planned a second sortie against the armies investing Atlanta under Maj. Gen. WILLIAM T. SHERMAN. Hood was determined to recover ground lost in the 20 July 1864 battle and restore morale to his Army of Tennessee. He felt that under his predecessor, Gen. JOSEPH E. JOHNSTON, the army had lost the will and ability to fight anywhere except behind breastworks. This per-

nicious influence Hood hoped to eradicate through an openground assault on the 22d, east of the city.

His plan of attack was bold but enterprising and promising. The corps of Lt. Gen. A. P. STEWART would occupy the Union armies north and northeast of Atlanta. Hood would send the rest of his main army, the corps of Lt. Gen. WILLIAM J. HARDEE and Maj. Gen. BENJAMIN F. CHEATHAM, to strike the most vulnerable enemy force, Maj. Gen. JAMES B. MCPHERSON'S Army of the Tennessee, then moving westward from Decatur toward Atlanta. Cheatham would strike McPherson frontally, while Hardee would make a 15-mi night march to the south and east, coming up beyond McPherson's left flank and rear. This plan not only exploited McPherson's relative isolation but also his lack of a cavalry screen, which might allow Hardee's approach to go unnoticed until too late to prevent it.

On the evening of 21 July, Hood began his offensive by withdrawing from his outer works, slipping into the defenses of the city proper. Thinking Atlanta evacuated, McPherson's advance moved confidently along the Decatur Road on the morning of the 22d until struck by Confederate skirmishers about 2.5 mi from Atlanta. The attackers, 2 of Hardee's divisions under Maj. Gens. W. H. T. WALKER and WILLIAM B. BATE, came on with great energy. But because of errors by Hardee and Walker, they had not marched far enough eastward to clear the Union line and had struck McPherson's left, held by Maj. Gen. GRENVILLE M. DODGE'S XVI Corps. Dodge and his men were also hard fighters, as they proved by repulsing 2 attacks, during which General Walker was killed. Soon another casualty occurred: riding up to plug a gap between Dodge and

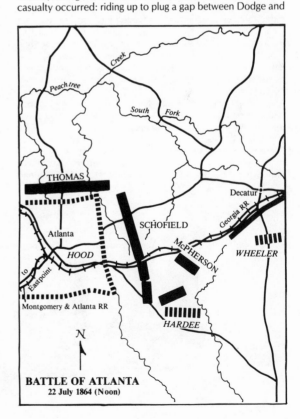

BATTLE OF ATLANTA
22 July 1864 (Noon)

Maj. Gen. FRANCIS P. BLAIR, JR.'s XVII Corps, on Dodge's right, McPherson exposed troops to enemy skirmishers and he was killed.

But his loss did not ensure Confederate success. Hardee committed his 2 other divisions, Brig. Gen. GEORGE E. MANEY'S and Maj. Gen. PATRICK R. CLEBURNE'S, to a furious, coordinated assault against Blair. Thanks largely to a heavy cannonade, they pushed back Blair's left flank, then moved toward the gap between Blair and Dodge. At the last minute, however, a reserve brigade ordered into the breach by McPherson shortly before his death slammed the Confederates backward. Hardee's offensive was snuffed out when part of the XVI Corps re-formed and reestablished the line.

Only at this point—in midafternoon—did Hood commit Cheatham's corps against the Union front, bolstered by 5,000 Georgia militia under Maj. Gen. GUSTAVUS W. SMITH. Had this strike been timed to coincide with Hardee's, the Army of the Tennessee might have been destroyed. But with Hardee stalled, Maj. Gen. JOHN A. LOGAN, who had temporarily replaced McPherson, secured the front with his own XV Corps and part of Blair's command. Cheatham and Smith penetrated below the line of the Georgia Railroad but were quickly repulsed by units shifted from the left. Toward evening the fighting died out. By then over 8,000 Confederates and 3,700 Federals had been killed or wounded, and Hood's second sortie had failed. —EGL

Atlanta, CSS. The screw steamer *Fingal,* built in Scotland in 1861, operated as a BLOCKADE RUNNER until taken by the Confederate Navy in 1862 and converted into the ironclad ram *Atlanta* by N. and A. F. Tift at Savannah, Ga. Edward C. Anderson, a Savannahian and a former naval officer, described how the *Fingal* was converted: "Her bulwarks were cut down, a heavy deck 3 feet in thickness laid over her own, and a shield of heavy timber plated with Rail Road iron erected." When completed it was 204 ft long, 41 ft in beam, with a draft of 15–17 ft. Unlike other Confederate IRONCLADS, the *Atlanta* had an iron hull; it could also reach greater speed (about 6 mph) than the others. Its armament consisted of 4 guns (2 7-in. and 2 6.4-in. BROOKE RIFLES), a spar TORPEDO, and a ram.

From the vessel's commissioning 22 Nov. 1862 until early June 1863, the *Atlanta* remained in the river near Savannah, only twice venturing below obstructions across the Savannah

River. On 16 June it passed through the obstructions and steamed down the river. The ironclad's commander, William A. Webb, planned to clear Wassaw Sound of Union vessels, "raise the blockade between here and Charleston, attack Fort Royal, and then blockade Fort Pulaski." Before carrying out this ambitious plan the *Atlanta* had to slip by the 2 Union monitors *Weehawken* and *Nahant.*

Webb entered the sound by way of the Wilmington River, where he encountered the monitors. As the *Atlanta* neared them, it ran aground. The *Weehawken* approached to 300 yd and fired its 11- and 15-in. DAHLGRENS only 5 times, but 4 shots scored with devastating results. Although none of the shots penetrated, fragments of iron and splinters from the wood backing spewed across the gundeck and wounded a number of men. The *Atlanta* gradually listed, and none of the 7 shots that it fired hit the monitors. Webb surrendered.

The *Atlanta* was taken into Union service, used in the James River until the end of the war, and was then scrapped.

—WNS

Atlanta Campaign. 1 May–2 Sept. 1864 By the first week in May 1864, Federal forces from lower Tennessee to the Virginia coast were in motion—participants in a coordinated offensive devised by General-in-Chief ULYSSES S. GRANT. One of the most strategically significant of these operations involved a movement south from Chattanooga, Tenn., by the armies of the Military Division of the Mississippi, under Maj. Gen. WILLIAM T. SHERMAN. These 98,000 men and 254 cannon —divided among Maj. Gen. GEORGE H. THOMAS' Army of the Cumberland, Maj. Gen. JAMES B. MCPHERSON'S Army of the Tennessee, the Army of the Ohio under Maj. Gen. JOHN M. SCHOFIELD, and 4 cavalry divisions—constituted, Sherman felt, "one of the best armies in the world." Their main objective was Gen. JOSEPH E. JOHNSTON'S Army of Tennessee, composed of 2 corps under Lt. Gens. JOHN B. HOOD and WILLIAM J. HARDEE (a third, under Lt. Gen. LEONIDAS POLK, was en route from Mississippi), plus attached artillery, and a cavalry corps under Maj. Gen. JOSEPH WHEELER—an aggregate force of 53,000. Grant had ordered Sherman, his most trusted subordinate, "to move against Johnston's army, to break it up, and to get into the interior of the enemy's country as far as you can, inflicting all the damage you can against their war resources. . . ."

Sherman looked beyond the enemy's present position near

NA

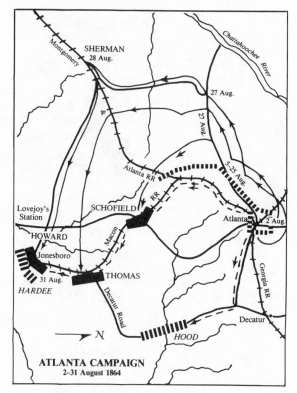

ATLANTA CAMPAIGN
2–31 August 1864

flanks with McPherson and Schofield, prompting another Confederate retreat, to the Cassville-Kingston area.

This time, when the Federals pursued, Johnston lashed out at Sherman's separated columns near Cassville. Only tactical errors and the uncharacteristic timidity of Hood, who shied from making the main attack on the 19th, saved the Federals from heavy loss. On the advice of his lieutenants, Johnston again fell back, this time crossing the Etowah River to AL-LATOONA PASS and then, threatened by another flanking movement, proceeded toward Dallas, Ga., via NEW HOPE CHURCH. At this last site, the Army of Tennessee repulsed several assaults by Thomas 25 May, and precipitated vicious fighting at Mount Zion Church and Pickett's Mills on the 27th. On the 28th, near Dallas, McPherson threw back a reconnaissance in force by Hardee.

Johnston abandoned New Hope Church 4 June, when the Federals shifted northeastward around his now vulnerable position. The Army of Tennessee then filled entrenchments atop Lost, Pine, and Brush mountains, in front of Marietta. During the next 2 weeks, fierce fighting swept each peak, General Polk meeting death on Pine Mountain 14 June. Still another movement against Johnston's right finally compelled him to drop down to KENNESAW MOUNTAIN, whose steep, rocky slopes furnished him with his most formidable position to date. On the 27th, it proved its worth when Sherman, tired of flanking movements, tried a frontal assault against the high ground. His men were met by a wall of rifle and cannon fire that inflicted 2,000 casualties, against one-fourth as many Confederate losses.

The Union commander resumed his sidestepping, forcing his enemy to move below Marietta 2 July. Further flank drives sent the Confederates to the upper bank of the CHATTAHOOCHEE RIVER, within 7 mi of Atlanta, on the 4th. And when Schofield's troops made a crossing on the Confederate right, 8 July, Johnston withdrew south of the river, removing the last great natural barrier between Sherman and the Gate City. This was too much for Jefferson Davis, who had long been skeptical of Johnston's defensive strategy, and on the 17th the Confederate president replaced him with the more aggressive Hood.

Only 3 days after assuming command, the former corps leader tried to repay Davis' confidence. North of Atlanta he attacked Thomas' army along PEACHTREE CREEK—and was sent reeling into the city's defenses, having suffered 4,800 casualties. Undeterred, Hood regrouped and launched a second sortie east of the city on the 22d, this time striking the left and front of McPherson's isolated army in the Battle of ATLANTA. Despite a promising attack that killed McPherson and rocked his column, the offensive fell short due to tactical and logistical mistakes by Hood and Hardee.

Subsequently Sherman concentrated on the vital railroad lines south of the city, attempting to reach them through cavalry raids under Maj. Gen. GEORGE STONEMAN and Brig. Gens. Edward M. McCook and H. JUDSON KILPATRICK (Kilpatrick's raids including engagements at JUG TAVERN, 3 Aug., and LOVE-JOY'S STATION, 18–20 Aug.). None of these, however, inflicted great damage, confirming Sherman's generally low opinion of his horsemen. By the middle of July he had sent his infantry toward the same objective, circling around the west side of Atlanta. Hood tried to stop the move by a third sortie near EZRA CHURCH on the 28th, but failed once again, retaliating by sending his cavalry on a month-long campaign against Sherman's lines of communications. But WHEELER'S RAID, 10 Aug.–10

Dalton, Ga., some 25 mi below Chattanooga. His intended route would carry him another 80 mi into the Confederacy, to the industrial, supply, and communications center of Atlanta. An advocate of total war—aggression directed against not only an enemy's army but its civilian population as well—Sherman realized that from Atlanta he could destroy crucial segments of the Confederate military, economic, and social structure. Then, too, the psychological impact of the Gate City's capture would devastate Southern morale, perhaps ensuring Abraham Lincoln's reelection in November and quashing efforts in some quarters toward a negotiated peace.

Although preliminary skirmishing began near Chattanooga 1 May, the campaign, and Sherman's march, did not get under way till the 7th. By 9 May, Sherman had reached Johnston's advance positions and moved to circumvent them. Using the armies of Thomas and Schofield to hold the enemy in place at Buzzard Roost and Rocky Face Gap, he sent McPherson to the west and south to cut the railroad in Johnston's rear and block his line of retreat. After passing through SNAKE CREEK GAP, however, McPherson pulled back in the face of unexpected resistance, disappointing his commander and allowing the enemy to slip the trap by a quick fallback on the 12th.

Sherman quickly pursued, and the result was a battle at RESACA, 14–15 May, in which part of Thomas' command repulsed an advance by Hood. Sherman wished to follow up the success but, finding the enemy position too strong to attack head-on, sent cavalry and infantry to flank it below the Oostenaula River. The wily Johnston, however, withdrew toward Calhoun and Adairsville on the 17th. There Sherman pressed his front with Thomas' army while menacing both Confederate

Sept., failed to halt the Federals' inexorable advance.

Having failed to reach the railroads early in August (being halted at Utoy Creek on the 6th), Sherman made a lodgment on the Montgomery & Atlanta line on the 28th. Concerned for his lifeline of supply, Hood struck the Union flank at JONESBOROUGH, 31 Aug.–1 Sept. There he lost a battle he could not afford to lose, dooming the city. Late on the 1st the rear guard of the Army of Tennessee filed out of the city, and the next day the Federal advance marched in. Word of Atlanta's fall soon swept the divided nation. Millions in the North rejoiced, hailing Sherman as the war's greatest hero; the South, as Sherman had predicted, began to despair. —EGL

Atlantic, Union Military Division of the.

A postwar and RECONSTRUCTION command, this division, established 27 June 1865, comprised the Eastern Seaboard from Maine to South Carolina. Embracing the Middle Department and the Departments of the East, Virginia, North Carolina, and South Carolina, it was commanded from Philadelphia by Maj. Gen. GEORGE G. MEADE. On 19 May 1866 the Carolinas were combined into a single department, the rest of the division's organizational structure remaining intact; 3 months later the division was discontinued.

Reconstituted 12 Feb. 1868, it consisted of the New England states, New York, New Jersey, Pennsylvania, Ohio, Michigan, Indiana, Illinois, Wisconsin, Delaware, the whole of Maryland (part of which had been excluded from divisional jurisdiction in 1865), and the District of Columbia. The new division was composed of the Departments of the East, the Lakes, and Washington. Offered to and rejected by Lt. Gen. WILLIAM T. SHERMAN, the post was taken by Maj. Gen. WINFIELD SCOTT HANCOCK 31 Mar. 1868. Originally in Washington, D.C., division headquarters was moved to New York City in October.

In Mar. 1869 the division was again reorganized and returned to General Meade's command. It now consisted of the Department of the East (which included the former Department of Washington), the Department of the Lakes (minus Illinois, transferred to another division), and the 1st Military District, consisting solely of Virginia. In Jan. 1870 the 1st Military District became the Department of Virginia and also received jurisdiction over North Carolina, Maryland, and West Virginia. That April this district merged with the Department of the East and adopted the latter's designation.

In Dec. 1872 Hancock again replaced Meade in command of the division, whose subsidiary departments were abolished 10 months later. No further changes were made until June 1876, when the division acquired territory formerly within the Department of the South: the Carolinas, Georgia, Florida, and parts of Tennessee and Kentucky. Except for the loss of jurisdiction over West Point, N.Y., this was the status of the division when Military Reconstruction ended early in 1877. —EGL

Augur, Christopher Columbus.

USA b. Kendall, N.Y., 10 July 1821, Maj. Christopher C. Augur was commandant of cadets at West Point when the Civil War erupted in early summer 1861. Augur grew up in Michigan, from which state he was appointed to West Point, graduating 16th of 39 in the class of 1843 and serving in the Mexican War and on frontier duty before returning to West Point as commandant.

Ordered to Washington on the outbreak of war, he helped organize the defenses of the national capital, earning promotion to brigadier general, U.S. Volunteers, Nov. 1861. He

served as a brigade commander on the Rappahannock in early 1862 and led a force that captured Fredericksburg 21 Apr. of that year. Augur was given command of a division in Maj. Gen. NATHANIEL P. BANKS'S II Corps and served under him in Virginia and on the Mississippi.

USMHI

He was wounded severely at CEDAR MOUNTAIN, 9 Aug. 1862, just before Second Bull Run. Despite the defeat of Banks's corps by Maj. Gen. Thomas J. "Stonewall" Jackson in the bloody Cedar Mountain fighting, Augur was cited for gallantry and promoted to major general. When he had recovered from his wounds in Nov. 1862, he was ordered to New Orleans, where Banks had asked for him as his second-in-command.

Augur saw his last field service in the Mississippi River campaigns of 1862–63. He commanded the District of Baton Rouge in early 1863, then led the left wing of Banks's force, which besieged and captured PORT HUDSON after the fall of Vicksburg.

Augur, noted for his sound administrative ability, commanded the XXII Corps and the DEPARTMENT OF WASHINGTON, D.C., from Oct. 1863 until the end of the war. He remained in the Regular Army until 1885, when he was retired with the rank of brigadier general. d. Washington, D.C., 16 Jan. 1898. —DS

Augusta Arsenal.

The arsenal at Augusta, Ga., was one of the first Federal installations to fall into Confederate hands. On 24 Jan. 1861, only 5 days after the state's secession, Gov. JOSEPH E. BROWN, backed by 800 state militia, overawed its commander, Capt. ARNOLD ELZEY, and took possession of its shops, equipment, and property. Thereafter it became one of 5 Confederate arsenals in the state.

Originally a storehouse for 22,000 rifles, the arsenal was so quickly expanded by Maj. JOSIAH GORGAS, Confederate chief of ordnance, that by May 1861 it held 27,714 small arms and 29,000 lb of gunpowder. Under Gorgas' energetic supervision, its facilities were directed to the production of ammunition and other matériel, and soon it was turning out 20,000–30,000 rounds of rifle cartridges and 125–150 rounds of field ammunition daily. Plagued throughout the war by raw materials of undesirable quality and in inadequate supply, the arsenal occasionally produced defective ordnance, such as rifle cartridges of irregular size. On the whole, however, it kept up a steady, high-quality production of critically needed war goods until the Confederacy's collapse in spring 1865. —EGL

Augusta Powder Works.

Early in the war, the South faced a critical shortage of gunpowder and the means to manufacture it. In Apr. 1861 Confederate officials were able to collect at various points 491,111 lb of cannon, rifle, and musket powder, enough to supply 30 rounds of ammunition per man in the armies then projected. Prewar ordnance manuals, however, specified 200 rounds per man as a desirable standard. Since the Confederacy could not produce more with its present facilities and because the North's shipping BLOCKADE would prevent large-scale importation, the South faced the herculean task of developing, under wartime conditions, facilities to rectify the deficiency.

The man who, virtually alone, shouldered this burden was Col. GEORGE W. RAINS, a West Point–trained engineer who had operated an ironworks in the North. Though he had only designed steam engines, Rains at once set about creating an ammunition works from scratch. After months of scouting locations, planning the factory layout, and designing the equipment and architecture, he began to erect a powder works near the Savannah River just west of Augusta, Ga. This spot, formerly the site of a U.S. arsenal, was far enough inland to be secure from enemy attack and near enough to forests to make vital raw materials available.

Working from his own designs, Rains, Sept. 1861–May 1863, erected a 2-mi long factory complex, including offices, a refinery, laboratory, cooling magazine, press house, granulating building, drying house, magazine and, central to the whole, a mixing house where a dozen incorporating mills ground charcoal, sulfur, and saltpeter (potassium nitrate) into gunpowder. Rains laid out each building in a pattern that ensured the processing of components in logical sequence and made maximum use of the nearby Augusta Canal to transport materials from one building to another. His layout also reduced to the minimum the chance of detonating gunpowder by accident.

Despite his stress on safety, 4 explosions occurred in the powder works but did not stop the facilities from producing as much as 5,000 lbs of gunpowder per day, for a total of 2,750,000 lbs of cannon and small-arms powder by the war's close. A monument to the inventive and mechanical genius of George Rains, the Augusta Works closed a matériel gap that, if left open, would have ended the Confederacy long before Appomattox.   —EGL

Averasborough, N.C., Battle of. 16 Mar. 1865 The confrontation at Averasborough was the next-to-last sizable engagement of the CAROLINAS CAMPAIGN. The Federals of Maj. Gen. WILLIAM T. SHERMAN had occupied Fayetteville 11 Mar. Sherman's next objective was Goldsborough, where he planned to meet another Federal force that had come inland from the coast. The Confederates, realizing that a junction of the 2 Union columns would make further Southern resistance hopeless, sought to block the Northern advance.

Sherman marched from Fayetteville in 2 columns, one threatening Raleigh, the other advancing toward Goldsborough. Sherman's left wing, Maj. Gen. HENRY W. SLOCUM'S Army of Georgia (XIV and XX corps), moved north toward Averasborough while the right wing, Maj. Gen. OLIVER O. HOWARD'S Army of the Tennessee, struck northeast toward Goldsborough.

When Slocum's column, accompanied by Sherman, approached Averasborough 16 Mar., his cavalry, followed by the XX Corps, ran into some 6,000 entrenched Confederates, under Lt. Gen. WILLIAM J. HARDEE, posted on a narrow ridge with the Black River on one side and a swamp on the other. 2 divisions of the XX Corps moved against Hardee's front while a brigade was sent (by Sherman's personal order) to try to envelop the Confederate right. The flanking force pushed the Confederates back while heavy fighting raged along the main line, but darkness soon fell, ending fighting for the day. The

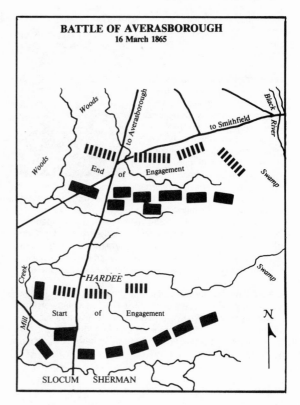

BATTLE OF AVERASBOROUGH
16 March 1865

Northerners went into camp in front of the Confederate position.

Hardee withdrew his men during the night and marched northeast toward Smithfield to unite with the other Southern forces in the area. He had lost about 865 men and a 3-gun battery. Slocum, who lost 678 men, continued his march northeast toward BENTONVILLE.

The chief result of the fight was that Sherman's left column was delayed, increasing the distance between the wings of the Federal force. The Confederates hoped to cripple the isolated left wing as it approached Bentonville 19 Mar.   —RMcM

Averell, William Woods. USA b. Cameron, N.Y., 5 Nov. 1832. After graduating from West Point in 1855, 26th in his class, Averell fought Indians in the Southwest and when civil war began was recuperating from wounds inflicted by Navajos. Early in 1861 he carried secret dispatches to army installations in Arkansas and Indian Territory and at FIRST BULL RUN served as a staff officer, later doing provost duty in Washington, D.C.

Averell, one of the most prominent Union cavalry officers of the early war period, gained field command Aug. 1861 when named colonel of the 3d Pennsylvania Cavalry. The next year, during the PENINSULA CAMPAIGN, he led a mounted brigade and won notice as commander of the rear guard during the Army of the Potomac's retreat to the James River. Promoted to brigadier general of volunteers, he served less conspicuously at Antietam and Fredericksburg. In Mar. 1863, however, he received credit for KELLY'S FORD, the Union cavalry's first large-scale victory over its Confederate counterpart.

2 months later Averell lost his command through dilatory leadership during the CHANCELLORSVILLE CAMPAIGN. Transferred to West Virginia, he was denied the publicity bestowed on him while in the ARMY OF THE POTOMAC. Nevertheless, he led several successful expeditions against Confederate communications, often over treacherous terrain and through bitter

LC

weather. During one he reported having "marched, climbed, slid and swum 355 miles."

Through the first half of 1864 Averell performed capably in division command but that summer clashed with Maj. Gen. PHILIP H. SHERIDAN, commander of the Army of the Shenandoah. When Averell's dilatoriness resurfaced during his pursuit of Confederates routed at FISHER'S HILL, 22 Sept., Sheridan relieved him from duty.

Averell held no further command, though by war's close he had received the brevets of major general of volunteers and brigadier general of Regulars. In postwar life he was a successful inventor, the U.S. counsel general in Montreal, and the inspector general of the Soldiers' Home at Bath, N.Y., where he died 3 Feb. 1900.   —EGL

Ayres, Romeyn Beck. USA b. Montgomery Cty., N.Y., 20 Dec. 1825, Ayres graduated from the U.S. Military Academy in 1847, ranking 22d in his class. First assigned to the occupation forces in Puebla and Mexico City at the end of the Mexican War, he was then sent to various frontier posts and Eastern garrisons. On 14 May 1861 he was promoted to captain of the 5th Artillery, serving under Brig. Gen. IRVIN MCDOWELL at FIRST BULL RUN and subsequently remained with the Army of the Potomac through the war. A respected, competent career soldier, Ayres was promoted to brigadier general 29 Nov. 1862 and assigned to the V Corps after distinguished leadership as an artillerist at ANTIETAM. Brigade and divisional command followed, from CHANCELLORSVILLE until the Confederate surrender. At GETTYSBURG he commanded the 1st Division, then led the 2d Division June 1864–Jan. 1865 in the fighting around Petersburg. Wounded in the fighting, he ended the war with brevets for gallantry as brigadier and major general in both the volunteer and Regular armies.

Ayres returned to the Regular Army 30 Aug. 1866, following a year as commander of the Reconstruction District of the Shenandoah. His rank reverted to lieutenant colonel, 28th Infantry, and he served in garrison duty in the South during the 1870s. On 15 July 1879 he was promoted to colonel of the 2d Artillery and posted to Florida. He died on active duty at Fort Hamilton in New York harbor 4 Dec. 1888.   —PLF

B

badges. *See* CORPS BADGES.

Bailey, Joseph. USA b. near Pennsville, Ohio, 6 May 1825. Bailey was taken as a child to Illinois, where he studied civil engineering. After becoming a lumberman in Wisconsin in 1847, he was mustered into Federal service as a captain in the 4th Wisconsin Infantry 2 July 1861 and spent most of his wartime service under Maj. Gen. BENJAMIN F. BUTLER and Maj. Gen. NATHANIEL P. BANKS in the DEPARTMENT OF THE GULF.

NA

Bailey played an active role in the defense of New Orleans in 1862 and in the capture of PORT HUDSON after the fall of Vicksburg, July 1863, but he is best remembered as the adept engineer who rescued the Union fleet and army during the RED RIVER CAMPAIGN, May 1864.

Banks and Rear Adm. DAVID D. PORTER led a combined land and naval force up the Red River of Louisiana in a bold drive into Texas. When the campaign stalled short of Shreveport, they were forced to retreat, but the rapidly falling water level left some 30 navy gunboats, transports, and auxiliary craft stranded above the Alexandria rapids.

Bailey, chief engineer of Brig. Gen. William B. Franklin's XIX Corps, designed a series of wing dams, built of felled trees and stonefilled cribs, to raise the level of the river (760 ft wide at that point) by 7 ft, long enough to permit the fleet's escape over the rapids. A short time later, near the mouth of the Red River, Bailey was again called on to improvise a bridge of steamers over which Banks's wagon trains could cross the Atchafalaya River to safety.

In recognition of these engineering feats, Bailey was brevetted brigadier general 7 June 1864 and awarded the THANKS OF CONGRESS citation. After the Red River Campaign he distinguished himself in the reduction of MOBILE, Apr. 1865, and was rewarded with a brevet promotion to major general.

Bailey became sheriff of Vernon Cty., Mo., after the war and 21 Mar. 1867 was killed near Nevada, Mo., by 2 bushwhackers he had arrested. —DS

Bailey, Theodorus. USN b. Chateaugay, N.Y., 12 Apr. 1805. Bailey was educated at Plattsburg Academy in that state and entered the U.S. Navy as a midshipman in 1818, serving off the African coast and in the Pacific before being promoted to lieutenant 3 Mar. 1827. After 2 world cruises, Bailey commanded the storeship *Lexington,* serving conspicuously off the California coast during the Mexican War. He advanced to commander 6 Mar. 1849 and to captain 15 Dec. 1855, on completing a second tour in the Pacific. Bailey was ordered to Panama to protect Americans during the uprising of Apr. 1856 and was praised for accomplishing the assignment with firmness and discretion.

In 1861 he took command of the steamer *Colorado* on BLOCKADE duty at Pensacola, Fla., aiding in operations against that city and commanding the expedition to destroy the Confederate privateer *Judah.*

Appointed second in command to Capt. DAVID G. FARRAGUT, Bailey was prominent in the capture of New Orleans. After transferring to the *Cayuga,* a gunboat small enough to navigate the Mississippi River, he led the right column of Farragut's fleet past FORTS JACKSON AND ST. PHILIP during the attack on New Orleans. At his suggestion the attack was made at night. Despite poor health, Bailey insisted on leading the first assault against the Confederate river fleet, initially engaging the defenders alone in a fierce battle that resulted in the capture of the Chalmette batteries, part of the river defense system. His report to the secretary of the navy 7 May 1862 contained his widely quoted description of the battle "as a contest between iron hearts in wooden vessels and ironclads with iron beaks—and the iron hearts won."

When Farragut reached New Orleans, he sent Bailey and Lt. George H. Perkins to demand the city's surrender. The 2 men walked unarmed through a hostile crowd to city hall, which, an observer, author George Washington Cable, later recalled, was "one of the bravest deeds I ever saw done." Bailey then carried dispatches announcing the victory to Washington, D.C.

Bailey took command of the East Gulf Blockading Squadron 4 Nov. 1862 and captured 150 vessels over the next 18 months. He volunteered to join Farragut for the attack on Mobile, but an outbreak of yellow fever prevented the fleets from being combined.

Bailey was commissioned admiral 25 July 1866 and placed on the retired list in October of that year. He died in Washington, D.C., 14 Feb. 1877, praised as one of the ablest wartime naval commanders. —PLF

Baird, Absalom. USA b. Washington, Pa., 20 Aug. 1824, into a traditionally military family, Baird entered West Point in 1845, graduating 9th in his class in 1849. During the 12 years until the war started, he married, became a father, fought the Seminoles in Florida, spent 3 months' sick leave in Europe, taught for 6 years at West Point, served on the Texas frontier, and was stationed at FORT MONROE when war began. He saw action at FIRST BULL RUN and earned presidential gratitude when he and several other officers protected Confederate prisoners from a threatening Washington mob.

In the PENINSULA CAMPAIGN Baird served as IV Corps chief of staff and was subsequently promoted to brigadier general. Soon after, he was sent west to command a brigade in the Army of the Ohio, followed by a division in the Army of Kentucky, a division in the Army of the Cumberland's Reserve Corps, and finally the 1st Division of Maj. Gen. George H. Thomas' XIV Corps. Shortly thereafter he dis-

NA

tinguished himself at CHICKAMAUGA, then in the assault on MISSIONARY RIDGE. From this time till the end of the war, his commanders repeatedly—but unavailingly—recommended him for promotion.

Baird's division fought through the ATLANTA CAMPAIGN, the MARCH TO THE SEA, and the CAROLINAS CAMPAIGN, but Baird's greatest glory came at JONESBOROUGH, Ga., 1 Sept. 1864, when he won the MEDAL OF HONOR by leading the brigade that broke the Confederate position. Military historian George Fielding Eliot has described Baird as one of the outstanding division commanders of the Civil War.

Baird returned to the Regular Army after the war. As its inspector general he was sent to France in 1887 as a military observer; a year later Congress authorized his acceptance of the French Legion of Honor. He died 14 June 1905 near Relay, Md., and was buried in Arlington National Cemetery.   —RDH

Baker, Alpheus. CSA b. Abbeville District, S.C., 28 May 1828. Baker taught school in South Carolina and Georgia before he read law and moved to Eufaula, Ala., in 1848. The next year he was admitted to the Alabama state bar.

In 1861 Baker was elected to represent Barbour County at the Alabama constitutional convention but resigned to enlist in the Eufaula Rifles, of which he was elected captain. As part of the 1st Alabama Infantry, Baker's men were assigned to Pensacola, Fla., and in Nov. 1861 he went to Tennessee, where he was elected colonel of a regiment of Tennessee, Mississippi, and Alabama troops. He participated in the Battle of NEW

LC

MADRID and was captured at ISLAND NO. 10, Apr. 1862.

After being exchanged in September, Baker became colonel of the reorganized 54th Alabama, which he led during the VICKSBURG CAMPAIGN. Seriously wounded at CHAMPION'S HILL, May 1863, Baker recovered to take command of an Alabama brigade and was promoted to brigadier general to rank from 5 Mar. 1864. He kept this command through the ATLANTA CAMPAIGN, distinguishing himself at RESACA, Ga.

Baker was wounded again at EZRA CHURCH, 28 July 1864, and reassigned to the DEPARTMENT OF THE GULF. His brigade returned east Jan. 1865 to participate in the CAROLINAS CAM-

PAIGN. At BENTONVILLE, N.C., shortly before Gen. Robert E. Lee's surrender, his brigade captured 204 of the enemy.

After the war, Baker resumed his law practice in Alabama, then moved to Louisville, Ky., in 1878, where he died 2 Oct. 1891.   —PLF

Baker, Edward Dickinson. USP/USA b. London, England, 24 Feb. 1811. Baker took his seat as U.S. Senator from Oregon in Dec. 1860 after a remarkable career that had carried

the English-born lawyer-politician to seats in the U.S. House of Representatives from Illinois, to leadership of the Republican party in California, then to a similar role in Oregon. Famed for his spread-eagle oratory, he strongly impressed fellow Illinois Whig ABRAHAM LINCOLN, who named one of his sons after Baker. His lengthy patriotic speeches in the Senate soon brought him national attention.

Baker served as a colonel in the Mexican War and in spring

LC

1861 declined an appointment as brigadier general, for which he would have had to give up his Senate seat. He did, however, raise a regiment in Pennsylvania and 21 Oct. 1861 led a brigade across the Potomac River to attack a Confederate camp at Leesburg, Va. Baker had inadequate means of retreat, was misinformed about the position and strength of his opponents and knew little of STRATEGY or TACTICS. But he held a commission as major general—which he had neither accepted nor declined—from his old friend Lincoln and hoped for a quick dramatic victory that would enhance his career.

Baker's death, 21 Oct. 1861, at the resulting Battle of BALL'S BLUFF transformed an inept commander, but a popular politician, into a national hero. Though the Union suffered heavy losses, the COMMITTEE ON THE CONDUCT OF THE WAR, unwilling to blame the fallen Baker, instead ruined the career of Brig. Gen. CHARLES P. STONE, the talented professional soldier in command who had only ordered a demonstration. Ball's Bluff cost many lives for no greater purpose than the advancement of Baker's career; his death may have saved many more.   —JYS

Baker, Lafayette Curry. espionage agent b. Stafford, N.Y., 13 Oct. 1826. Baker, head of the Federal Secret Service, became one of the most feared and hated men in the country. As a young man, he went to California shortly before the war and served on the infamous Vigilance Committee of San Francisco, a citizens' law-and-order organization. Finding he had a natural talent for spying and informing, Baker hurried east, offering his services to the Union at the outbreak of hostilities.

To ingratiate himself with the government, Baker offered to supply intelligence on Confederate troop concentrations at Manassas. Heading south, he was captured but managed to convince Pres. JEFFERSON DAVIS and Gen. P.G.T. BEAUREGARD of his Southern sympathies. Released, Baker was sent north as a double agent, but he betrayed the South, bringing back valuable information on the position of the Confederate army and the plans of its leaders.

As a reward Baker became a special agent with a "roving

commission'' from Sec. of War
EDWIN M. STANTON. Working
outside regular army channels
and in conjunction with Supt.
William Wood of the OLD CAPI-
TOL PRISON, Baker inaugurated a
reign of terror against Southern
sympathizers, spies, and anyone else in the North who
seemed suspicious. Citizens
were secretly arrested, thrown
into isolation, and coerced into
giving confessions.

NA

When Maj. Gen. GEORGE B.
MCCLELLAN fell out of favor so
did the Pinkerton Detective Agency, the source of army intelligence. In the administrative shake-up that followed, Baker was
appointed head of a secret police force called the National
Detectives and answerable only to Stanton. Invested with almost unlimited authority, Baker began examining all sorts of
irregularities, investigating fraudulent practices of contractors,
chasing counterfeiters and bounty jumpers, and suppressing
other "vicious citizens"; he also headed the pursuit of Lincoln's assassins. At war's end Baker's power waned, and he
was subsequently charged with corruption and dismissed by
Pres. ANDREW JOHNSON for conducting espionage activities in
the White House. Nothing was proved, however, and the
scourge of Confederate spies passed into obscurity after he
produced falsified documents in testimony against Johnson
during the president's impeachment trial. d. Philadelphia, 3
July 1868.   —MTC

Baker, Laurence Simmons. CSA b. Gates Cty., N.C., 15
May 1830. Baker graduated from West Point 42d in the class of
1851 and was commissioned 2d lieutenant in the Mounted
Riflemen. He spent most of his
10 years in the Regular Army on
frontier duty, attaining the rank
of captain before he resigned 10
May 1861. Though he opposed
secession, he remained loyal to
his state. A strict disciplinarian,
he was commissioned lieutenant
colonel in the Confederate army
to date from 16 Mar. 1861 and
given command of the 1st North
Carolina Cavalry. In spring 1862
Baker was elected colonel and
his regiment transferred to the
ARMY OF NORTHERN VIRGINIA.

USMHI

He and his men participated
in the PENINSULA CAMPAIGN, and 29 June, during the SEVEN DAYS'
CAMPAIGN, drove Federal cavalry back from the Charles City
road until infantry reinforcements arrived. Baker was then assigned to Brig. Gen. Wade Hampton's brigade, and his regiment
was praised for its bravery at SECOND BULL RUN and ANTIETAM.

Baker assumed brigade command after Hampton was
wounded at GETTYSBURG 3 July 1863. He engaged in rearguard
action, including fighting at Hagerstown and Falling Waters,
Md., covering the Confederate retreat from Pennsylvania.
Baker was promoted to brigadier general 23 July. On 31 July
the brigade resisted a Federal cavalry advance across the Rap-

pahannock toward Brandy Station, at which time Baker was
severely wounded in the right arm. Gen. ROBERT E. LEE personally commended him for this action.

Baker was assigned to departmental command in North Carolina, June 1864. After recovering from a second wound, he
briefly commanded a brigade of reserves in South Carolina
before returning to North Carolina to lead his old brigade in the
CAROLINAS CAMPAIGN and at BENTONVILLE. Baker's command
was detached from Gen. JOSEPH E. JOHNSTON's army when
word of Lee's surrender reached him, and since Federal troops
prevented him from rejoining Johnston, he disbanded his men.

Baker was paroled in Raleigh, May 1865. He engaged in
several careers after the war, in 1878 becoming a railroad-
station agent in Suffolk, Va., where he died 10 Apr. 1907.
                                                              —PLF

Baker's Creek, Miss., Battle of. 16 May 1863 *See*
CHAMPION'S HILL, MISS., BATTLE OF.

Baldwin, William Edwin. CSA b. Statesburg, S.C., 28
July 1827. As a child Baldwin moved to Mississippi, where he
eventually operated a book and stationery store in Columbus.
With several years of training in
the local militia, he joined the
Confederate army early in 1861
and was commissioned colonel
of the 14th Mississippi Infantry.
He and his men were ordered to
Pensacola, Fla., but soon returned to the West. Brig. Gen.
FELIX ZOLLICOFFER sent him to
East Tennessee, Aug. 1861, to
quiet Unionists, and from there
he was attached to the army in
central Kentucky.

USMHI

In Feb. 1862 Brig. Gen.
GIDEON J. PILLOW commended
Baldwin for his men's bravery
during the initial attack on FORT DONELSON, Tenn., where Baldwin was taken prisoner and held at FORT WARREN in Boston
harbor. After being exchanged in August, he was commissioned
brigadier general and given command of a brigade of Mississippi and Tennessee regiments in the Army of West Tennessee.

He was again commended for gallantry at the engagement
at COFFEEVILLE, Miss., 5 Dec. 1862 and led his men effectively
at PORT GIBSON, CHAMPION'S HILL, and through the VICKSBURG
CAMPAIGN. Captured a second time, he was paroled and ordered to the District of Mobile.

Baldwin died near Dog River Factory, Ala., 19 Feb. 1864,
when a broken stirrup caused him to fall from his horse.
                                                              —PLF

balloons. Both Union and Confederate governments experimented with using balloons for aerial reconnaissance. With
his flamboyant demonstrations, aeronaut THADDEUS S. C. LOWE
convinced Washington army and government officials of the
advantage balloon ascensions would give the military. Lowe
was officially attached to the army Aug. 1861 and awarded a
contract to deliver 7 observation balloons by June 1862. His
balloons varied in size. The largest measured 45 ft from the
neck of the bag (envelope) to the valve at the top of the inflated
bulb and held 32,000 cu ft of gas. Completed the same month

USMHI

he received his contract, it required 1,200 yd of silk and the labor of 5 seamstresses, and cost about $1,500 to construct.

The outside of a new envelope was treated with 4 coats of boiled linseed oil, benzine, and japan drier, then was turned inside out and treated with neat's-foot oil to keep the fabric pliable. Linen cord woven into a diamond-mesh net fit over the envelope and attached below the neck to the basket. The smallest balloons held about 15,000 cu ft of gas, carrying 1–5 men and about 100 lb of sand ballast. Lowe used manila rope for the 3 or 4 cables he needed to tow his balloons and to anchor them for captive ascensions.

Quickly abandoning hot-air balloons for those filled with more dependable gas, Lowe developed a mobile field generator to fit a regular army wagon frame and employed a sulfuric-acid-and-iron process to produce hydrogen gas in the field. Lowe received government funding for his program but was repeatedly tangled in red tape. Technical problems in the field kept the Union balloon corps busy making repairs and recoating weather-battered envelopes.

The Confederacy lacked the resources, financial and technical, to sustain a significant aeronautics program but did have balloons available for reconnaissance intermittently through spring 1863, 2 of which were built within the private sector.

Northern newspapers first reported sighting Southern balloonists June 1861. Capt. E. PORTER ALEXANDER was placed in charge of the programs in Virginia, assisted by John R. Bryan, an aide on Brig. Gen. JOHN B. MAGRUDER's staff, who volunteered to make the first ascension. Aerial observation missions were carried out extensively during the PENINSULA and SEVEN DAYS' campaigns.

Because gas-filled balloons could only be inflated at the Richmond Gas Works, their range was limited. The South's famous "silk dress" balloon (actually made of new fabric bought for the purpose, not from dresses contributed by Confederate women) was transported from Richmond by rail, then transferred down the James River aboard the CSS Teaser. It made daily ascensions from 27 June until a few days after

MALVERN HILL, 1 July 1862, when the Teaser went aground and ship and balloon were captured. In spring 1863 a second multicolored silk balloon was built in Charleston by Charles Cevor, the only civilian aeronaut paid by the Confederate government; it floated off in a high wind, ending the Confederacy's use of balloons.

Aeronauts quickly learned the hazards as well as the tactical benefits of their missions. They had to be men with courage who knew the countryside and understood troop deployments sufficiently to make maps of what they saw from the air. Getting critical information to the ground, especially during a battle, was haphazard at best. Lowe experimented with using a telegraph to transmit messages, but the wires frequently failed to withstand the ride. Attempts at tying messages to rocks and dropping them from the basket proved little more efficient. But the aeronauts were able to gather information, guard against surprise movements by the enemy, and to a limited extent direct artillery fire.

They also learned to fear the "danger zone," the height at which they could be hit by artillery fire and a regular concern on descents, because the enemy by then had had time to train its sights on the balloon's path. Sometimes a team of horses was hitched to the windlass in an effort to speed the descent.

Balloons imposed a need for innovation upon artillerists, who increased the height of their firing range by dropping a cannon's tail into a ditch, creating a kind of antiballoon gun. Commanders also ordered tents to be pitched in thickly wooded areas to shield them from view, and lights to be screened after dark in case the enemy decided to make a nighttime ascension.

Despite its many flaws, aeronautics excited the imagination of many high-ranking officers who had the vision to recognize the possibilities of aerial reconnaissance.   —PLF

Ball's Bluff (Conrad's Ferry; Harrison's Island; Leesburg), Va., Battle of.

21 Oct. 1861   On the eve of the Battle of Ball's Bluff, Brig. Gen. CHARLES P. STONE commanded a Union division headquartered near Poolesville, Md. His assignment was to protect upper Potomac River fords and ferries between Great Falls and Point of Rocks and keep watch on Brig. Gen. NATHAN G. EVANS' small Confederate force at Leesburg, Va.

Union Brig. Gen. George A. McCall's division was at Dranesville, Va., south of Leesburg, trying to maneuver the Confederates out of position and back toward Snicker's Gap. Maj. Gen. GEORGE B. MCCLELLAN, Army of the Potomac commander, sought to give McCall help, so on 20 Oct. 1861 he telegraphed Stone, ". . . perhaps a slight demonstration on your part would have the effect to move them." The 21 Oct. "demonstration" became the Battle of Ball's Bluff.

Col. EDWARD D. BAKER (technically a U.S. Senator from Oregon) commanded 1 brigade of Stone's division. On 21 Oct. Stone ordered him to "push" the Leesburg Confederates, giving him the option of withdrawing a small Ball's Bluff detachment, on the Virginia side of the Potomac (opposite Harrison's Island), or of sending his brigade to reinforce it. Electing to reinforce, Baker immediately had his brigade cross the river by way of Harrison's Island and scale the 70-ft bluff on the Virginia side—without having scouted the enemy and without enough boats to move his command over the river.

Evans, aware of Union plans, quietly withdrew most of his men from Edward's Ferry, where they faced another of Stone's

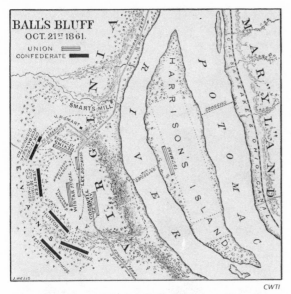

BALL'S BLUFF
OCT. 21st 1861.
UNION
CONFEDERATE

CWTI

brigades, commanded by Col. Willis A. Gorman. These troops were concentrated in woods near where Baker's brigade was still making the difficult crossing. The attack caught the Union force in open ground, half organized and with their backs to the river. In the disaster that followed, of the 1,700 men in Baker's brigade, 49 were killed, 158 wounded, and 714 missing, Colonel Baker was shot dead by a SHARPSHOOTER.

The blame fell on General Stone, who was arrested 9 Feb. 1862 on charges that insinuated treason and was imprisoned in Forts Lafayette and Hamilton in New York for 189 days without trial. This shabby treatment by President Lincoln and his new secretary of war, EDWIN M. STANTON, came at the urging of the legislative COMMITTEE ON THE CONDUCT OF THE WAR and other Radicals who needed a scapegoat and who considered Stone "unsound on the question of slavery."   —JOH

Baltimore & Ohio Railroad.

The potential importance of the B&O Railroad became evident during the BALTIMORE RIOTS Apr. 1861, when pro-Southern sentiment in the border state interfered with the transport of Federal recruits from Philadelphia to Washington, D.C. With Maryland remaining in the Union, B&O Pres. John W. Garrett and Master of Transportation William P. Smith used the railroad to help the Federal government move troops and supplies. This commitment proved costly to the railroad, which throughout the war assumed responsibility for rebuilding or replacing destroyed facilities and equipment.

Early in 1861 the Confederate government of JEFFERSON DAVIS threatened retaliation against Garrett if he operated his trains in Confederate territory. In all, about 188 mi of B&O track ran through Virginia, most of which comprised the critical road from Harpers Ferry to Wheeling via Grafton and the trunk line from Grafton to Parkersburg in the western section of the state.

Confederate officials believed that to hold the Unionist counties in western Virginia they had to control the B&O line, which provided access to the strategically important SHENANDOAH VALLEY. Confederate raiders repeatedly attacked railroad

property, destroying bridges and stations, tearing up track, and burning any rolling stock they could not take south to replace deteriorating Southern equipment. Destruction was so great in Maryland during the ANTIETAM CAMPAIGN, when Confederate forces destroyed 35 mi of track, that rail transportation between Baltimore and Washington had to be extensively rebuilt.

The Federal government seized 22 mi of B&O track for use as a military route 23 Apr. 1861, but at that time field commanders made no organized use of the railroad. Though Maj. Gen. GEORGE B. McCLELLAN's advance on Grafton and victory at PHILIPPI in northwestern Virginia had resulted from using the railroad for troop transport, the first significant experiment with the B&O came Aug. 1862, when Brig. Gen. JACOB D. COX was ordered to take his men from the Great Kanawha Valley in western Virginia to join Maj. Gen. JOHN POPE's army for an attack on Richmond. Cox marched his men to the B&O line at Parkersburg, loaded them into boxcars, and sent them east. The operation was tedious but far more efficient than an overland march. Some of the troops arrived in time to participate in the Second Battle of Bull Run.   —PLF

Baltimore Riots.

After ABRAHAM LINCOLN was inaugurated, Baltimore secessionists decided to prevent Northern troops from passing through the city to reinforce Washington. The clash came 19 Apr. 1861.

At 10:30 a.m. a train from Philadelphia arrived at Baltimore's President St. Station carrying the 6th Massachusetts Infantry. The regiment was to march to the Calvert St. Station to board a BALTIMORE & OHIO train for Washington, but an angry crowd began to gather. To avoid confrontation, the loaded cars were drawn by horses over a connecting line between stations. The first 8 cars passed, but the ninth was stoned, with windows broken and some occupants injured; the tenth car was forced back by debris on the tracks. Some regimental units were stranded with no way to join the others except by marching through the streets, now lined with hostile citizens. The troops were instructed to ready their weapons and told orders would be given to fire if fired on.

As they progressed, brickbats flew into the ranks and firing broke out, which continued along part of the march. Marshal of Police George Kane and Mayor George Brown tried protecting harassed troops, but the situation was out of control and the regiment had to be gotten out of Baltimore quickly. The train pulled out at 12:45 p.m., leaving some equipment, the killed and wounded, and the regimental band.

The first serious bloodshed of the war had occurred on Baltimore's streets. Col. Edward Jones reported his command suffered 3 killed (later raised to 4) and 39 wounded; Mayor Brown wrote that 12 civilians were killed and dozens wounded, but the exact number of civilian casualties is uncertain.

That night Baltimore police and militia detachments burned railroad bridges north of the city to prevent other troops from coming in. On 20 Apr. Lincoln suspended troop movements through Baltimore and for the next few days conditions in the city were chaotic. Secessionists consolidated their control and appeared to have achieved their objective—the isolation of Washington so the city could be picked off at will.

On the evening of 13 May, during a heavy thunderstorm, Brig. Gen. BENJAMIN F. BUTLER brought the 6th Massachusetts Infantry back to Baltimore, digging in on Federal Hill above the harbor. Until the end of the war, Baltimore was treated as an occupied city.   —JOH

AHI

Banks, Nathaniel Prentiss. USA b. Waltham, Mass., 30 Jan. 1816. Banks was a self-made man who rose from poverty to become a leader in the DEMOCRATIC PARTY. Because of his opposition to the KANSAS-NEBRASKA ACT, he left the Democrats and joined the newly created REPUBLICAN PARTY, becoming governor of Massachusetts 1858–61. Like others in the Union Army, he attained high rank not because of military experience but from political muscle.

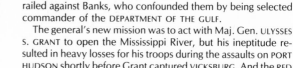

USMHI

At the outbreak of war, when Pres. Abraham Lincoln appointed Banks major general of volunteers, the officer quickly ran into trouble. The general's first encounter with the enemy was in summer 1861 while commanding troops in the SHENANDOAH VALLEY, where Brig. Gen. THOMAS J. "STONEWALL" JACKSON was harassing Union forces. Beset by conflicting orders from Lincoln and Maj. Gen. GEORGE B. MCCLELLAN, Banks tried to trap the Confederates, but his forces were outmaneuvered and routed. Though the defeat created an uproar, the general, through Lincoln's support, was cleared of wrongdoing.

Some months later Banks, commanding the vanguard of Maj. Gen. John Pope's army, clashed with Jackson at CEDAR MOUNTAIN. The battle favored the North, but at a critical moment Maj. Gen. AMBROSE P. HILL's Confederates arrived, driving the surprised Federal troops from the field. Critics again

railed against Banks, who confounded them by being selected commander of the DEPARTMENT OF THE GULF.

The general's new mission was to act with Maj. Gen. ULYSSES S. GRANT to open the Mississippi River, but his ineptitude resulted in heavy losses for his troops during the assaults on PORT HUDSON shortly before Grant captured VICKSBURG. And the RED RIVER CAMPAIGN he commanded in 1864 to occupy northwestern Louisiana turned into a fiasco. The navy's gunboats were almost captured, and Banks, after some minor fighting, returned to the Mississippi with little gained. At this point even Lincoln could not save the general from the clamor that followed. Removed from effective military command, Banks subsequently left the army. Returning to Massachusetts Aug. 1865, he served 6 terms in the U.S. House of Representatives. d. Waltham, 1 Sept. 1894.   —MTC

barbette. Usually found only in permanent or semiperma-

USMHI

nent fortifications, a barbette was a raised wooden bed or platform that allowed an artillery piece to be fired over a protective wall or parapet without exposing its gun crew to the enemy. During a long siege, the besieging army often set up elaborate but temporary fortifications for their artillery pieces, in which case a large mound of earth was often used as a substitute for a formal wooden barbette platform.   —JES

Barhamsville, Va., eng. at. 7 May 1862 *See* ELTHAM'S LANDING, VA., ENG. AT.

Barksdale, William. CSA b. Rutherford Cty., Tenn., 21 Aug. 1821. As a youth Barksdale moved to Columbus, Miss., where he practiced law and edited the proslavery Columbus *Democrat*. During the Mexican War he enlisted in the 2d Mississippi and was promoted to captain Jan. 1847. After leaving the army Barksdale entered politics, resigning his seat in Congress when Mississippi passed the secession ordinance. He served the state as quartermaster general in spring 1861, then joined the army as a colonel in the 13th Mississippi.

His command was ordered east, fighting in all the major early battles except SECOND BULL RUN, and Barksdale was considered a competent and respected regimental commander. Brig. Gen. Richard Griffith recommended his promotion to brigadier general Apr. 1862, citing his bravery under fire and attributing to him "the highest qualities of the soldier." Barksdale led his regiment through the PENINSULA CAMPAIGN, assuming brigade command when Griffith was wounded at SAVAGE'S STATION, and received his promotion to brigadier general to rank from 12 Aug.

Barksdale's command consisted of his own and 3 other Mississippi regiments, a hard-fighting unit that became known as Barksdale's Mississippi Brigade. An aggressive officer, he earned praise as an obstinate defender of his line regardless of the odds and as a commander eager to take the offensive. In a defending position, he deployed his troops efficiently: ordered to hold Marye's Heights at FREDERICKSBURG, 2 May 1863, he delayed the Federal advance until midday on the 3d, buying Gen. ROBERT E. LEE several hours to prepare for battle at CHANCELLORSVILLE. Maj. Gen. Lafayette McLaws recalled him as a "radiant wild joy" who was always far ahead of his men in a charge. He fell mortally wounded leading the Confederate assault on the Round Tops at GETTYSBURG 2 July, was taken prisoner, and died the next day within enemy lines.   —PLF

Barlow, Francis Channing. USA b. Brooklyn, N.Y., 19 Oct. 1834. In an army with a predominance of commanders devoted to the cultivation of facial foliage, Barlow was known as one of the "boy generals," not because of extreme youth but because he went clean-shaven. Frail-looking, pale, unsoldierly in appearance, he nevertheless was a driving fighter and disciplinarian. Barlow's contemporary, zoologist Theodore Lyman, wrote that he carried "a huge saber, which he says he likes, because when he hits a straggler he wants to hurt him."

Barlow graduated from Harvard in 1855, practicing law in New York City until war came, when he enlisted as a private in the 12th New York, a 3-month regiment. He reenlisted in August, rose from lieutenant colonel to colonel of the 61st New York in the PENINSULA CAMPAIGN, was severely wounded at ANTIETAM, and was made brigadier general 19 Sept. 1862. He commanded a brigade in the XI Corps when Lt. Gen. THOMAS J. "STONEWALL" JACKSON routed it at CHANCELLORSVILLE,

and at GETTYSBURG, temporarily paralyzed by a bullet and left for dead, he was cared for by Confederate Brig. Gen. JOHN B. GORDON. He rejoined the army to command a division in the II Corps as Gen. ULYSSES S. GRANT began his drive for Richmond May 1864.

USMHI

Barlow reached the high point of his career in the rainy dawn of 12 May, when his and Maj. Gen. DAVID B. BIRNEY's divisions charged the "MULE SHOE" at SPOTSYLVANIA, fought all day at the "BLOODY ANGLE," and captured 3,000 Confederates, 2 generals (George H. "Maryland" Steuart and Edward "Old Allegheny" Johnson), 20 guns, and 30 regimental colors. Shortly after Petersburg was besieged, his health broke, but he returned to lead a division at SAYLER'S CREEK and Farmville before Gen. ROBERT E. LEE surrendered. He was commissioned major general 25 May 1865.

Barlow returned to his law practice after the war. A founder of the American Bar Association, as New York State attorney general he initiated prosecution of the Tweed ring, a corrupt faction of Tammany Hall politicians. d. New York City, 11 Jan. 1896.   —RDH

Barnard, George N. photographer b. Conn., 1819, Barnard opened his first daguerreotype gallery in Oswego, N.Y., in 1843. After years of practice with portraiture and landscapes, in 1853 he took 2 landmark images, shots of a gigantic Oswego mill fire, that were among the world's first news photographs. After moving his studios to Syracuse in 1854, Barnard switched to collodion wet-plate photography and took his darkroom on the road until 1862, when he joined photographic entrepreneur MATHEW BRADY and his "photographic corps" to record the Civil War.

KA

For Brady he shot an historic series of images of the battlefields from the FIRST BULL RUN CAMPAIGN and also took pictures of ruins in the Virginia countryside, of soldiers in camp and of the aftermath of the Union's Siege of YORKTOWN. In these views individuals, buildings, trees, shattered cannon, and ruins were incorporated into broad composites implying the action that had taken place. Barnard's compositions required imagination from the viewer, a quality that became his trademark.

His stay with Brady was brief, and in 1863 he was in Tennessee working independently on breathtaking shots of the river valleys and mountain country of the border South. Much of this scenery, never photographed before, was impressive to Eastern viewers and included the sites of the Battle of LOOKOUT MOUNTAIN, CHATTANOOGA, and other Tennessee fights, vistas that incorporated great natural beauty with historic interest.

When Maj. Gen. WILLIAM T. SHERMAN's campaign for AT-

LANTA began, Barnard reportedly followed the army and, immediately after the war, started his best-remembered work. He made plates of almost all the Army of the Tennessee's battlefields, from the Volunteer State to the Atlanta city limits, was contracted by the U.S. government to photograph the Confederates' Atlanta defenses and fortifications, then continued to Savannah and the Carolinas.

Barnard next went to New York City, where in 1866 he produced *Photographic Views of Sherman's Campaign,* a $100 book made up of 61 full-size contact prints of his best work from previous years, which established his reputation as photographic historian and artist.

Barnard's remaining years were spent in Chicago (where he shot the destruction caused by the great fire), the Deep South, and elsewhere in the Midwest, keeping at the photographer's art and working briefly with photographic pioneer George Eastman. d. Cedarville, Ohio, 1902.   —JES

Barnard, John Gross. USA b. Sheffield, Mass., 19 May, 1815, Barnard graduated from West Point at 18, 2d in the class of 1833. He began his 48 years' service with the Corps of Engineers by supervising construction of fortifications and harbor improvements on the Atlantic and Pacific coasts, the Gulf of Mexico, and the Great Lakes. During the Mexican War he built the defenses of Tampico and surveyed the battlefields around Mexico City, and in 1855–56 he served a term as superintendent of West Point, achieving through numerous publications recognition as an engineer and scientist.

In Apr. 1861, assigned as chief engineer of the Depart-

USMHI/MA

ment of Washington, Barnard began the construction of the defenses of the capital, a frustrating, underappreciated task that on completion stood as a major engineering feat. He directed the reconnaissance preceding the FIRST BATTLE OF BULL RUN and in Maj. Gen. GEORGE B. MCCLELLAN'S PENINSULA CAMPAIGN conducted the Siege of YORKTOWN, directing engineering operations before Richmond. When McClellan ran for president in 1864, Barnard, encouraged by Sec. of War EDWIN M. STANTON, wrote a scathing attack on the general's actions on the peninsula.

Barnard spent 2 more years in command of the DEFENSES OF WASHINGTON, then in June 1864 was reassigned as chief engineer of the armies in the field on the staff of Lt. Gen. Ulysses S. Grant, commanding engineering operations in the PETERSBURG CAMPAIGN. He was also present during the pursuit and at the surrender of the Army of Northern Virginia at Appomattox. For distinguished services in the war he received brevets up to the rank of major general, U.S. Army, and promotion to colonel, Corps of Engineers.

Barnard's postwar studies of European harbors led to modifications in American coastal defenses. A prolific writer, he contributed to science, mathematics, and history and was one of the 50 incorporators of the National Academy of Sciences. Because Barnard was an engineer, he is not so well remembered as Civil War field commanders, yet his achievement in

protecting the capital made field operations possible. d. Detroit, Mich., 14 May 1882.   —TMM

Barnes, Joseph K. USA b. Philadelphia, Pa., 21 July 1817. Barnes was a Harvard alumnus, an 1838 graduate of the University of Pennsylvania's Medical School, and a U.S. Army Medical Corps veteran of the Seminole and Mexican wars. He became the Union army's surgeon general during the Civil War.

Joining the army in 1840, Barnes was promoted from assistant surgeon to surgeon and spent most of his years on frontier duty. In 1861, posted in the Pacific Northwest, he was suddenly recalled for duty in the East when Civil War combat commenced and his surgery skills were needed in hospitals around Washington, D.C.

NA

At this time the army's Medical Corps was commanded by Brig. Gen. WILLIAM A. HAMMOND, a progressive professional active in military medical reform and a supporter of Maj. Gen. GEORGE B. MCCLELLAN. Hammond's calls for reform and his involvement in the feuds concerning McClellan made him unpopular with the administration. Impressed with Major Barnes's length of service and pleased with his apolitical appearance, Sec. of War EDWIN M. STANTON appointed Barnes "acting surgeon general" in 1862.

Charges of unlawfully awarding contracts for hospital supplies were brought against Hammond, who was still surgeon general, by members of the Lincoln administration, whom Hammond countercharged with obstructing reform. After an acrimonious court-martial, Hammond left the army.

During the court-martial and the controversy that followed, Barnes was made medical inspector and promoted to lieutenant colonel, then colonel, though he was still listed as "acting surgeon general." On 22 Aug. 1864 he received his brigadier general's commission and surgeon general's appointment. But infighting between Hammond's partisans and old army Medical Corps regulars had done much to hurt Barnes personally. Few in the War Department took serious notice that he was quietly continuing many of Hammond's reforms.

In his Civil War tenure as surgeon general, Barnes's annual appropriations for medicines and supplies ballooned from $9 million in 1863–64 to $20.5 million the next year—money used not only to cure the growing number of casualties but to provide quality treatment. The surgeon general also lured many talented doctors from civilian practice to medical service in the volunteer army, and the medical payroll jumped from $437,000 to $949,000 in little more than a year.

At the end of the conflict, the effectiveness of his reforms surprised many, and he was brevetted major general in the Regulars 13 Mar. 1865.

In the postwar years, before retiring in 1882, he supervised the publication of several volumes of the *Medical and Surgical History of the War of the Rebellion.* His saddest army duties were attending mortally wounded Presidents Abraham Lincoln and James A. Garfield. d. Washington, D.C., 5 Apr. 1883.

—JES

Barnwell, Robert Woodward.

Barnwell, Robert Woodward. CSP b. near Beaufort, S.C., 10 Aug., 1801. Barnwell stands out as one of the more adept Confederate politicians. From a prominent family, he received his early education in his native state, then graduated from Harvard with honors in 1821, becoming a respected educator in the antebellum years. Barnwell embarked on his public career in 1826 as a member of the state house of representatives, was elected to Congress in 1829, signed the Ordinance of Nullification in 1832, and was appointed by South Carolina's governor to succeed JOHN C. CALHOUN in the Senate June 1850.

As a politician Barnwell advocated a moderate position for Southerners, though he favored secession, participating in the South Carolina secession convention and serving on the committee that drew up the DECLARATION OF IMMEDIATE CAUSES. As a delegate to the Provisional Confederate Congress in Montgomery, Ala., Feb. 1861, Barnwell used his influence to gain the presidency for JEFFERSON DAVIS. He was also one of the signers of the CONFEDERATE CONSTITUTION.

Barnwell was one of the few who staunchly supported the Davis administration throughout the war, though he declined Davis's proposal that he become secretary of state in favor of serving as senator from South Carolina. He held seats in each of the Confederate Congresses and headed the Senate Finance Committee throughout the war. He was also a member of the Territories Committee during the second congressional session.

With his property destroyed during the war, Barnwell moved to Greenville, S.C., early in 1865. That December, the governor named him faculty chairman of the University of South Carolina, a position he held until 1873. He then served as the university's librarian until his death at Columbia 5 Nov. 1882. —PLF

***Baron De Kalb*, USS.** See *ST. LOUIS*, USS.

Barringer, Rufus. CSA b. "Poplar Grove," Cabarrus Cty., N.C., 2 Dec. 1821. Barringer ranks among the finest cavalry officers to emerge from North Carolina during the war years.

Described by an officer who served under him as "prudent, methodical and cautious," he impressed his superiors as an aggressive leader who could be relied on to hold his line without taking foolish risks.

There is no indication that Barringer had any military experience before his Civil War service. He became a lawyer after graduating from North Carolina University in 1842 and established a practice in Concord. A politically moderate Whig and staunch Unionist, he was

USMHI

elected to the state assembly twice, in 1848 and 1850, and served as a presidential elector in 1860.

Barringer abandoned his antisecessionist stance when his state withdrew from the Union 20 May 1861. He soon joined Confederate service as captain of the 1st North Carolina Cavalry, and during the war his troops fought in all battles involving the ARMY OF NORTHERN VIRGINIA. Many years after the war Gen. Wade Hampton recalled the officer's cool, efficient conduct at

BRANDY STATION, June 1863, where Barringer was seriously wounded in the face. He fell again twice before the war ended.

Despite his excellent military record, Barringer had so far been promoted slowly. Though still a major in Aug. 1863, he soon was advanced to colonel, and when Maj. Gen. James B. Gordon died May 1864, after the engagement at YELLOW TAVERN, Barringer became brigadier general with command of Gordon's brigade (the 1st, 2d, 3d, and 5th North Carolina Infantry regiments), Maj. Gen. W. H. F. LEE's division.

W. H. F. Lee relied on him heavily in the battles around Richmond 1864–65, ordering him to cover Gen. ROBERT E. LEE's withdrawal from the city in the last weeks before the surrender. His command was destroyed by the Union advance 3 Apr. 1865, and Barringer was captured by Union cavalry scouts and held at FORT DELAWARE until July.

In the postwar years Barringer allied himself with former Confederates supporting Presidential Reconstruction, eventually joining the Republican party and advocating black suffrage. He passed the 12 years before his death, 3 Feb. 1895, in retirement at Poplar Grove, where he wrote, often about history, usually about the war. —PLF

Barron, Samuel. CSN b. Hampton, Va., 28 Nov. 1809. Barron was appointed midshipman 1 Jan. 1812, when he was only 2—a tribute to his father, a commodore of the same name who died in 1810. The younger Barron began active service in 1820 and rose to captain by 1855. There is evidence that he was actively working to take control of the Navy Department from Sec. GIDEON WELLES during the first weeks after Abraham Lincoln was inaugurated in 1861. Dismissed by Welles, who refused to accept his resignation of 22 Apr. 1861, Barron became a captain in Virginia service and head of his state's Office of Naval Detail and Equipment. When the Virginia navy was incorporated into the Confederate navy, he was appointed head of the Office of Orders and Detail until 20 July 1861.

CHS

Barron was anxious for an active command and convinced Confederate Navy Sec. STEPHEN R. MALLORY to place him in charge of the naval defenses of Virginia and North Carolina. He commanded the 2 forts at HATTERAS INLET when they were surrendered 29 Aug. 1861, and for the next 11 months he remained a prisoner of the Federals.

Following his exchange, Barron again commanded naval forces in Virginia waters, but Mallory had another assignment for the man once called "Navy Diplomat" by his colleagues in Washington. In summer 1863 Barron arrived in England to take charge of the 2 RAMS near completion at the Laird Shipyards. Working closely with Confederate agent JAMES D. BULLOCH, he had the responsibility of assigning officers to the rams and was also authorized to inspect other vessels being prepared in England for the Confederacy. To appease Northern demands that Britain strictly adhere to its neutrality laws, the British government seized the rams, and Barron left for France, where he set up an office in Paris as "flag officer commanding naval forces in Europe." Here Barron met the same growing resistance to the Confederacy that he had found in England. Increasingly frustrated, he had little to do except tend to the numerous Southern naval officers awaiting assignment to Confederate CRUISERS. Barron finally resigned his position 28 Feb. 1865, after receiving orders to return to the Confederacy.

After the war, Barron went back to his home in Essex Cty., Va., where he died 26 Feb. 1888. —NCD

Barry, John Decatur. CSA b. Wilmington, N.C., 21 June 1839. Barry was a recent graduate of the University of North Carolina when in 1861 he enlisted as a private in the 8th North Carolina Volunteer's 1st Company. After redesignation as the 18th North Carolina Infantry and a year of civil war, Barry's regiment was reorganized and the young man was elected its captain.

As part of the Army of Northern Virginia's II Corps, Barry and his men fought through some of the toughest campaigns of the next year: the SEVEN DAYS' battles for Richmond, SECOND BULL RUN, and ANTIETAM. For his action in the last battle he won praise from his superiors and a commission as major.

LC

At CHANCELLORSVILLE, 3 May 1863, Barry's 4th Brigade was so heavily engaged it lost 3 colonels, 3 lieutenant colonels, and 2 majors to wounds, and in the heat of the action broad command and responsibility devolved on him. His ability to rise to crisis and command drew commendation in Brig. Gen. JAMES H. LANE's battle reports, and he was appointed colonel.

Within 60 days of Chancellorsville, Barry took part in PICKETT'S CHARGE in the Battle of GETTYSBURG; leading his regiment in this desperate assault, he fought under Lane in the third rank on the Confederate left. Then Barry's fortunes followed the Army of Northern Virginia's until the fight at COLD HARBOR in summer 1864, where Lane was wounded, and Barry advanced to brigadier general, to date from 3 Aug.

Later that month Barry was badly wounded by a Union SHARPSHOOTER. While he was away on recuperative leave, Lane returned to duty, and Barry's promotion, which had not been confirmed by the Confederate Congress, was canceled. He never fully recovered from his wound and was reported to be in command of his regiment, though nominally, only Jan.–Feb. 1865. He may have been detached for duty in North Carolina, but records do not agree on where he was at the end of the war.

His postbellum career as the editor of a Wilmington, N.C., newspaper was short. 24 Mar. 1867, he died, at 27, of complications from his wound. —JES

Barry, William Farquhar. USA b. New York, N.Y., 18 Aug. 1818. Barry began his military career as a lieutenant of artillery on the Canadian border after he graduated from the U.S. Military Academy, 17th in the class of 1838. In the next 23 years he fought in the Mexican, Seminole, and Kansas-Missouri border wars, rising to captain of the 2d U.S. Artillery.

At the beginning of the Civil War he was promoted to major of the 5th U.S. Artillery, posted to FORT PICKENS, Fla., then sent north to Brig. Gen. Irvin McDowell's Washington command as

NA

chief of artillery for the FIRST BULL RUN CAMPAIGN. This first major clash of the war was nearly Barry's last. At the height of the action he led 2 infantry regiments to support Capts. Charles Griffin's and James B. Rickett's batteries on the slope of Henry Hill. His command mistook flanking Confederate troops for more Union units coming to their support, and Barry and the other Federals were blasted from their position by the enemy's flank fire.

Despite this error, Barry displayed his bravery and organizational skills and 20 Aug. 1861 was made brigadier general of volunteers. Maj. Gen. GEORGE B. MCCLELLAN then appointed him his chief of artillery and had him organize the ordnance arm of the ARMY OF THE POTOMAC.

During the PENINSULA CAMPAIGN he supervised and saw combat at the Siege of YORKTOWN, MECHANICSVILLE, GAINES' MILL, WHITE OAK SWAMP, and MALVERN HILL. But following action at Harrison's Landing, he asked to be relieved for duty elsewhere. Until 4 Mar. 1864 Barry supervised the ring of forts and batteries surrounding Washington, D.C., and served on various ordnance boards. He advanced to lieutenant colonel in the Regular service 1 Aug. 1863.

At the outset of the ATLANTA CAMPAIGN, Barry was sent west as Maj. Gen. WILLIAM T. SHERMAN's chief of artillery. He fought in all the campaign's battles and for his service in the contest for Atlanta was brevetted a colonel in the Regulars and major general of volunteers 1 Sept. 1864. He then fought in the campaign against Gen. JOHN B. HOOD's Tennessee invasion and in Sherman's campaign from Savannah through the Carolinas. On 13 Mar. 1865 he was brevetted brigadier and major general in the Regulars for his war service.

After the war, Barry was made a colonel in the Regulars, oversaw troops on the Canadian border during diplomatic troubles, and ran the army's Fort Monroe, Va., artillery school for 10 years. He died on active duty at Baltimore's Fort McHenry 18 July 1879. —JES

bar shot. See CHAIN SHOT; BAR SHOT.

Bartlett, Joseph Jackson. USA b. Binghamton, N.Y., 21 Nov. 1834. When the Civil War began Bartlett was a young attorney living in Elmira, N.Y., and had only been in practice 3 years. On 21 May 1861 he enlisted in a company of the 27th New York Infantry and was elected its captain; shortly afterward, the regiment chose its field officers and Bartlett was made major.

With only a few weeks' training, the 27th New York was shipped to Washington, D.C., and 21 July found itself on the field at FIRST BULL RUN. Bartlett demonstrated there the calm that would become his trademark. After an attack on a 6-gun enemy battery, Col. HENRY W. SLOCUM was wounded, and command of the regiment fell to Bartlett. Wisely withholding his men from a piecemeal attack that had been ordered on an enemy position, he began moving his unit from the field in an orderly manner. Around him Federal troops were fleeing, with the Confederates in pursuit. Bartlett pulled his men into a line of battle in the middle of the Union rout and held off the Confederates behind them. Then he resumed the retreat until it was necessary to form another firing line. He did this 3 times, helping to keep the enemy at bay and bringing himself to the attention of Federal commander Maj. Gen. IRVIN MC-DOWELL. On 21 Sept. 1861 Bartlett was promoted to colonel.

He fought in almost every battle remaining to the ARMY OF THE POTOMAC, handling himself well at GAINES' MILL, and winning

praise at CRAMPTON'S GAP and in the ANTIETAM CAMPAIGN; he was commissioned brigadier general 4 Oct. 1862. In May the next year he used his troops to strategic effect in the fighting of FREDERICKSBURG and SALEM CHURCH and maintained order despite losing over a third of his men.

In Apr. 1865, at APPOMATTOX, he was selected to receive the ceremonial surrender of the arms of Gen. Robert E. Lee's ARMY OF NORTHERN VIRGINIA. Then, for his service throughout the war, he was brevetted major general of volunteers before being mustered out in 1866.

In peacetime Bartlett served as U.S. minister to Sweden 1867–69, was a deputy pension commissioner under Pres. Grover Cleveland, and pursued his law career. d. Baltimore, Md., 14 Jan. 1893.   —JES

Barton, Clara Harlowe. nurse b. Oxford, Mass., 25 Dec. 1821. The youngest of 5 children born to a middle-class family, Barton was educated at home, and at 15 started teaching school. Her most notable antebellum achievement was the establishment of a free public school in Bordentown, N.J. Though she is remembered as the founder of the American Red Cross, her only prewar medical experience came when for 2 years she nursed an invalid brother.

In 1861 Barton was living in Washington, D.C., working at the U.S. Patent Office. When the 6th Massachusetts Regiment arrived in the city after the BALTIMORE RIOTS, she organized a relief program for the soldiers, beginning a lifetime of philanthropy.

When Barton learned that many of the wounded from FIRST BULL RUN had suffered, not from want of attention but from need of medical supplies, she advertised for donations in the Worcester, Mass., *Spy* and began an independent organization to distribute goods. The relief operation was successful, and the following year U.S. Surgeon General WILLIAM A. HAMMOND granted her a general pass to travel with army ambulances "for the purpose of distributing comforts for the sick and wounded, and nursing them."

For 3 years she followed army operations throughout the Virginia theater and in the Charleston, S.C., area. Her work in Fredericksburg, Va., hospitals, caring for the casualties from the Battle of the WILDERNESS, and nursing work at BERMUDA HUNDRED attracted national notice. At this time she formed her only formal Civil War connection with any organization when she served as superintendent of nurses in Maj. Gen. Benjamin F. Butler's command.

She also expanded her concept of soldier aid, traveling to Camp Parole, Md., to organize a program for locating men

listed as missing in action. Through interviews with Federals returning from Southern prisons, she was often able to determine the status of some of the missing and notify families.

By the end of the war Barton had performed most of the services that would later be associated with the American Red Cross, which she founded in 1881. In 1904 she resigned as head of that organization, retiring to her home at Glen Echo, outside Washington, D.C., where she died 12 Apr. 1912.

—JES

Barton, Seth Maxwell. CSA b. Fredericksburg, Va., 8 Sept. 1829, Barton entered West Point at 15, graduating 28th in his class in 1849. After a brief posting outside New York City, he served on frontier duty, and by the time the war started he had advanced to captain.

Barton resigned from the U.S. Army June 1861 and was appointed lieutenant colonel of the 3d Arkansas Infantry. He first campaigned under Gen. ROBERT E. LEE in western Virginia, where he took part in the CHEAT MOUNTAIN and GREENBRIER RIVER fights, then spent the winter as Maj. Gen. THOMAS J. "STONEWALL" JACKSON's chief engineer in the 1862 SHENANDOAH VALLEY CAM-

PAIGN. The Confederacy needed experienced general officers, but for some reason, when Barton was nominated for brigadier general, Pres. Jefferson Davis pulled his name from the confirmation list. He was renominated 11 Mar. 1862 and confirmed by the Confederate Senate.

Until December Barton held brigade command in East Tennessee, then was transferred to the VICKSBURG theater. Along the Vicksburg perimeter that month he displayed the bravery to which other officers would later testify. First sent to Grenada, Miss., Barton and his men were moved quickly into Vicksburg, then marched out to the CHICKASAW BLUFFS front to meet an attack by Maj. Gen. WILLIAM T. SHERMAN. Positioned in the center of the Confederate line between Brig. Gens. John Vaughn and Stephen D. Lee, Barton reinforced S. D. Lee's troops and repulsed 5 Union charges.

When Vicksburg fell Barton was taken prisoner and after his exchange returned east to lead a brigade in Maj. Gen. GEORGE E. PICKETT's command. His performance disappointed Pickett, who claimed Barton had fumbled his part in the campaign to take NEW BERNE, N.C., Feb. 1864. Pickett entered his complaint in the official record and had Barton censured "for want of cooperation." Barton was then posted to Drewry's Bluff under Maj. Gen. ROBERT RANSOM, who endorsed Pickett's criticism and relieved Barton from duty.

Spending several months without an assignment, Barton was given command of a brigade assigned to the Richmond defenses after his fellow officers circulated a petition attesting to his patriotism and bravery. He was ordered to the front when Gen. Robert E. Lee made his desperate march toward Appomattox but was captured as he moved toward the fighting at SAYLER'S CREEK 6 Apr. 1865 and was imprisoned at Boston harbor's FORT WARREN. Barton was released in July after taking the Union loyalty oath and lived in Fredericksburg until his death 11 Apr. 1900.   —JES

Bartow, Francis Stebbins.

Bartow, Francis Stebbins. CSA b. Savannah, Ga., 6 Sept. 1816. After the Confederate Congress prohibited men from holding both political and military positions, one citizen, lamenting the drain on political talent, included Bartow among the losses. From a distinguished Georgia family, Bartow, a planter and slaveowner, graduated from Yale Law School. After supporting the Whig party, he was defeated in his bid for a congressional seat on the Know-Nothing ticket in 1854; with both Whigs and Know-Nothings moribund in 1860, Bartow became a Democrat. Wholeheartedly supporting the secessionist movement, he was a delegate to the Georgia secession convention, where he spoke out forcefully in favor of withdrawing from the Union; as a result, his constituents elected him to the Provisional Confederate Congress. He served on the Engrossment, Flag and Seal, and Military Affairs committees, and as chairman of the last devoted his energy to preparing the country for war.

Bartow believed the South would be allowed to secede peacefully, but Pres. JEFFERSON DAVIS convinced him to support 24-month rather than 60-day volunteer enlistments in the army. He acquired his own limited military experience as a captain in the Oglethorpe Light Infantry, a home-guard unit made up of the sons of Savannah's leading families, and when the time came to choose between soldiering and politicking, he opted for the former. The Oglethorpes, which had been part of the detachment that seized Fort Pulaski Jan. 1861, were transferred to the 8th Georgia Infantry, and with Bartow they reported to Gen. JOSEPH E. JOHNSTON in the Shenandoah Valley shortly before the FIRST BATTLE OF BULL RUN. When orders came for Bartow to move to the front, he could only find rail transportation for 2 regiments in his brigade; thus half his force arrived too late to fight.

Once on the field, 21 July 1861, his Georgians fought valiantly during some of the heavier fighting to stem the Union advance. Bartow proved himself a competent, aggressive commander, rallying his men when they fell back in confusion from Matthews Hill. Taking the forward position, he led his troops in a charge down Henry Hill but fell mortally wounded by a rifle ball. By several accounts his last words were, "They have killed me, boys, but never give up the field." Bartow died a few minutes later. —PLF

Bate, William Brimage.

Bate, William Brimage. CSA b. Bledsoe's Lick, Tenn., 7 Oct. 1826. Little formal education was open to Bate in the rural area in which he was born. He left home at 16 to be a clerk on the steamboat *Saladier* and in turn became a Mexican War officer, a journalist, a law-school graduate and attorney, the attorney general for the Nashville district, a state legislator, and a presidential elector for John Breckinridge in 1860.

Bate had enlisted in the Mexican War as a private and come out a lieutenant. At the start of the Civil War he again enlisted as a private and was soon elected colonel of the 2d Tennessee Infantry, which he led at SHILOH, receiving a leg

USMHI

wound that kept him out of action for several months.

On 3 Oct. 1862 he was commissioned brigadier general and fought in all the Army of Tennessee's campaigns from TULLAHOMA to CHATTANOOGA. During his assignment to Wartrace, Tenn., state politicians offered to nominate him governor, but he declined, saying, "I would feel dishonored in this hour of trial to quit the field." Voters remembered his commitment to duty favorably years later when he returned to his political career.

Bate was promoted major general to rank from 23 Feb. 1864 at the end of operations in East Tennessee. He then fought at Dalton, Ga., and in the battles for ATLANTA, and joined Gen. JOHN BELL HOOD's Tennessee expedition for the Battles of FRANKLIN and NASHVILLE. At the end of the war he was surrendered with the Army of Tennessee in North Carolina. During his military career, Bate, an excellent soldier, was wounded 3 times and had 6 horses killed under him.

After the war he reestablished his law offices in Nashville and was twice elected governor, first in 1882. On the expiration of his last term in 1886, Tennesseans sent him to the U.S. Senate, where he held a seat until his death in Washington, D.C., 9 Mar. 1905. —JES

Bates, Edward.

Bates, Edward. USP b. Belmont, Va., 4 Sept. 1793, Bates moved from his widowed mother's Virginia home in 1814 and 2 years later passed his bar examination. His brother secured for him the post of prosecuting attorney for St. Louis, where Bates practiced law and eventually became a political power.

During the Civil War he was called "colorless," but as a youth he had derived pleasure from politics, holding local offices until 1826, when his constituents elected him to Congress on the Whig ticket. He served one term, then filled many state posts in the legislature. Through speeches, articles, and his growing influence in the Whig and REPUBLICAN parties, he gained national recognition. Pres. Millard Fillmore offered to appoint him secretary of war, but he declined the post.

NA

A staunch antisecessionist, Bates was nominated president at the 1860 Republican national convention in Chicago. After garnering only 48 votes on the first ballot, he asked that his name be withdrawn and threw his support behind ABRAHAM LINCOLN. Once elected, Lincoln appointed Bates attorney general.

The cabinet post was the peak of Bates's career. In office, his inconsistency won him no allies in either party, making his tenure difficult. Some colleagues called him an anomaly. He disagreed with Lincoln's efforts to have western Virginia admitted to the Union as a separate state, disliked Sec. of State WILLIAM H. SEWARD, distrusted Sec. of the Treasury SALMON P. CHASE and Sec. of War EDWIN M. STANTON, supported Lincoln's legal positions on the BLOCKADE of Southern ports and suspension of *HABEAS CORPUS*, believed legal claims in the *TRENT* AFFAIR should be disregarded to avoid war with Britain, and opposed emancipation. Sometimes he favored strict constitutional application of law; other times he was willing to sidestep. Though he worked tirelessly in his office and was noted for his strong sense of justice, his inconsistency created difficulties for the administration. With the rise of the RADICAL REPUBLICANS, Bates was cut from Lincoln's inner circle of advisers and resigned his post 24 Nov. 1864.

Returning to Missouri, Bates quarreled with Radical Republicans in state office and involved himself once again in local politics until his death in St. Louis, 25 Mar. 1869.　　—JES

Baton Rouge, La., eng. at.　5 Aug. 1862　Returning south after a failed naval assault on Vicksburg, Miss., late July 1862, Union Navy Rear Adm. DAVID G. FARRAGUT's Mississippi River flotilla landed 3,200 Federal troops in Baton Rouge to serve as the city's garrison. Their commander, Brig. Gen. THOMAS WILLIAMS, tried shoring up defenses north of the city while confining his camps and the garrison's defensive lines to a small area on Baton Rouge's eastern outskirts. Several Union gunboats moored at the city's docks covered the Federals' western river front and in an emergency could provide artillery support for Williams.

Vicksburg's temporary Confederate commander, Maj. Gen. EARL VAN DORN, pleased at the failure of Farragut's earlier assault, believed that the occupation of PORT HUDSON, a high spot on the Mississippi's banks between Vicksburg and Baton Rouge, would secure his command's southern river flank. He authorized an attack on Baton Rouge by Maj. Gen. JOHN C. BRECKINRIDGE and 4,000 of the Vicksburg garrison. Even temporary seizure of the city would allow Confederates time to occupy Port Hudson and reinforce it with heavy artillery. The ironclad ARKANSAS was dispatched to support the attack and eliminate the Union gunboats at Baton Rouge.

On 4 Aug. Union scouts reported Confederates preparing for attack northeast of the city. Williams deployed 3 regiments in a line running from the intersection of the Clinton and Bayou Sara–Jackson roads northeast of the city to the intersection of Perkins and Clay Cut roads to the southwest. 4 regiments were ordered to form an interior defensive line and 4 artillery batteries to support both interior and exterior lines; Williams alerted the gunboats to protect his rear. Nearly half the garrison was incapacitated by fever, but many left their sickbeds to join the defense, bringing Williams' strength to 2,400–2,700 men.

From a camp on the Comite River, 10 mi northeast of Baton Rouge, Breckinridge's force marched on the city at 11 p.m., 4 Aug. After his 4,000 men had joined a small command at Camp Moore, 60 mi northeast of Baton Rouge, half the group came down with fever, and he had only 2,600 troops to attack the Federals. Cut into 2 small divisions, they were led by Brig. Gens. DANIEL RUGGLES and CHARLES CLARK. On the Mississippi, Confederate Navy Lt. Henry K. Stevens was having trouble with the Arkansas' engines. The ironclad was pulled into shore 8 mi above Baton Rouge and was undergoing repairs when the engagement's first shots were fired at 4:30 a.m., 5 Aug.

In a morning fog so heavy that one Confederate said, "we could not see more than twenty steps," Confederate and Union pickets skirmished all along Williams' eastern defense line, some troops mistakenly firing on their comrades. A small Confederate detachment with artillery marched around to the north and hit the Federals' left flank. Repulsed, they were fired on in the fog by troops coming to their support under Clark. Clark's men charged on, routed a regiment of left-flank Federals, and drove them headlong at their comrades on the Federal right, interrupting Ruggles' attack on the Federal right flank. Fog, charging and retreating troops, and the small area of combat created confusion. Union troops broke, running west

into the city. Confederates followed, and street and house-to-house fighting began. Some armed Baton Rouge civilians joined attacking Confederates and turned on the retreating Federals; others streamed out of town, refugees in their night-clothes.

As Union troops fell back toward the river, Williams was killed while haranguing his men to counterattack: leaderless, the Federals ran for the safety of the gunboats. Shellfire from the Union vessels covered the infantry's flight, and Breckinridge's men could not pursue them. After a fruitless wait for the Arkansas to drive away the Union boats, Breckinridge withdrew his force from the city. The fight was effectively over by 10 a.m.

Col. Thomas W. Cahill assumed temporary Union command, confining his demoralized troops to their defensive perimeter for several days. Breckinridge used this time to have Ruggles' troops occupy Port Hudson and cover its bluffs with heavy cannon. Union casualties were 84 dead and 299 wounded and missing; Confederates lost 372 wounded and missing and 84 dead. Clark, his legs shattered during a charge on a Union battery, was left crippled on the field and taken prisoner. The Arkansas was scuttled by Lieutenant Stevens when, still inoperable, it was threatened by gunboats advancing from Baton Rouge.

16 days after the engagement the Federals evacuated the Louisiana capital and returned to New Orleans.　　—JES

battery.　Ideally, a Civil War field battery mustered 6 guns of the same caliber, each attached to a limber (a 2-wheel ammunition chest) drawn by 3 pairs of horses in tandem (called lead, swing, and wheel pairs), and supplied by 6 or more caissons (2 or 3 ammunition chests mounted on 4-wheel carts) each also drawn by 6 horses. Guns, limbers, and caissons were serviced by a traveling forge. A battery's standard strength was 155 men: a captain, 4 lieutenants, 2 staff sergeants, 6 sergeants, 12 corporals, 6 artificers, 2 buglers, 52 drivers, and 70 cannoneers. A standard supply of ammunition—a mixture of

LC

solid shot, spherical case, and CANISTER—varied from 1,218 to 1,344 rounds.

Actual war conditions forced changes. Battery strength, especially in the Confederate army, often dropped to 4 or 5 guns (frequently of mixed caliber) and fewer horses and caissons; casualties obliged drivers and cannoneers to do double duty.

In battle a lieutenant commanded a section of 2 guns, each usually under a sergeant (chief of caisson). Beside the gunner (usually a corporal), who sighted the gun, 7 men served the piece. No. 1, at the right of the muzzle, sponged and rammed; No. 2, at the left, inserted either fixed ammunition or powder bag and projectile; No. 3, at right of breech, kept his left thumb (in a leather thumbstall) over the vent during sponging and loading, and pricked the cartridge through the vent; No. 4, at the left of the breech, inserted friction primer in the vent, hooked his lanyard to it, and jerked the lanyard on command to fire; No. 5 carried ammunition from the limber, 5 yd behind the gun, to No. 2; No. 6, at the limber, cut fuses when necessary and issued ammunition to No. 7, who passed it to No. 5.

Although the standard firing rate was 1 shot in 2 minutes, normally a smoothbore gun crew got off 2 aimed shots (FIXED AMMUNITION) per minute. With canister, the rate was doubled.
—RDH

Battery Wagner, S.C., Siege and evacuation of. 10 July–6 Sept. 1863 When he relieved Maj. Gen. DAVID HUNTER outside Charleston, S.C., June 1863, Maj. Gen. QUINCY A. GILLMORE planned an offensive against that Confederate stronghold from the southeast, via Morris Island. To secure the latter, Gillmore realized, he must first seize Battery Wagner, near its northern tip, about 1.5 mi below FORT SUMTER. Defended by 1,200 troops and several heavy guns, the earthen REDOUBT was a formidable obstacle, despite its relatively small size and isolated position.

By 10 July Gillmore was ready to test his strategy. That morning, one brigade of his X Corps, under Brig. Gen. GEORGE C. STRONG, moved toward Morris from the army base of operations on Folly Island, 400 yd to the southwest. Under a heavy shelling from Folly and from Adm. JOHN A. DAHLGREN's fleet, Confederates on the southern end of Morris Island fled toward the fort, allowing Strong to establish a beachhead without difficulty.

Strong's success may have made him overconfident. As Battery Wagner lay barely 1,300 yd north of his position, the general planned a quick strike with only two and a half regiments. He did not know that the garrison had recently been reinforced and underestimated the number and firepower of its cannon.

At dawn on the 11th, 4 companies of Strong's 7th Connecticut Infantry braved a storm of rifle and cannon fire, some of the men mounting Wagner's parapets. But their supports—the 9th Maine and 76th Pennsylvania—melted under the barrage, isolating the companies. Finally forced to retreat, the Connecticut men lost 108 of 196 engaged; the Confederates suffered only 12 casualties.

Frustrated but undeterred, Gillmore spent the following week emplacing below the fort 40 long-range cannon and siege mortars. With these he pounded away at the garrison, which now consisted of 1,300 troops under Brig. Gen. WILLIAM B. TALIAFERRO. On the 18th, supposing the fort softened up, Gillmore launched a second offensive.

This time 2 attacks were made under Brig. Gen. TRUMAN

SEYMOUR, but the added weight—a total of 6,000 infantry—failed to overcome the fort's defenses. During the first assault, Seymour was wounded severely and General Strong mortally. Though some of Strong's men entered the fort, all were eventually shot down, captured, or repulsed, and most of his regimental leaders were killed, including Col. ROBERT G. SHAW, whose black troops of the 54TH MASSACHUSETTS spearheaded the effort. The second assault fared no better, and its leader, Col. H. S. Putnam, was also killed. Some of Putnam's men entered the fort's left salient but withdrew when a planned third attack, under Brig. Gen. Thomas G. Stevenson, failed to materialize.

Afterward, Union dead, many hideously mutilated, littered the beach in front of Wagner. Viewing the spectacle, a Charleston journalist wrote that "probably no battlefield in the country has ever presented such an array of mangled bodies in a small compass."

Sobered by the carnage (1,515 Union and 174 Confederate casualties), Gillmore returned to shelling the redoubt with his guns and those of Admiral Dahlgren. For the next 7 weeks, under this barrage, his troops dug zigzag trenches toward the fort, protected by SAP ROLLERS and other defenses. By 6 Sept. they had reached the ditch of the redoubt—close enough to ensure a successful assault. Gillmore planned an attack for the next morning. Late on the 6th, however, the garrison was evacuated by boat across the harbor, ending what one disgusted Federal called the "most fatal and fruitless campaign of the entire war."
—EGL

Battle, Cullen Andrews. CSA b. Powelton, Ga., 1 June 1829. Battle was a natural leader who, without formal military training, became an accomplished, capable combat officer. He learned warfare with his men, in the ordeal of battle, distinguishing himself as a regimental commander and then a brigade commander in one of the best divisions in the Army of Northern Virginia.

As a young boy, Battle moved with his family to Eufaula, Ala., matriculating in the state university, studying law, and becoming an attorney in 1852. An ardent secessionist, he was a member of a militia company, offering his services immediately after Alabama seceded, Jan. 1861. Com-

LC

missioned lieutenant colonel of the 3d Alabama, Battle saw initial action at SEVEN PINES, May 1862, following which he was promoted to colonel and the regiment shifted into the brigade of Brig. Gen. Robert E. Rodes. With this command of Alabama regiments Battle served until his career ended.

At SOUTH MOUNTAIN, Md., 14 Sept. 1862, Battle faced 3 veteran Federal brigades as the Alabamians doggedly defended a barren hill north of the gap. In the vicious mountainside combat, the 3d Alabama broke before one massive charge, but Battle reacted coolly and efficiently. 3 days later at ANTIETAM, his men again fought courageously, defending the "BLOODY LANE."

The Alabama brigade, held in reserve, saw limited action at FREDERICKSBURG, but at CHANCELLORSVILLE, 2 May 1863, Battle participated in his division's surprise attack against the Union right flank. His performance at GETTYSBURG, praised in reports, earned him promotion to brigadier general. On 25 Aug., to date from the 20th, this rugged, self-taught soldier received his commission and command of the Alabama brigade.

During the furious combat of 1864, Battle's Alabamians suffered heavy casualties at WILDERNESS, SPOTSYLVANIA, and in the SHENANDOAH VALLEY. In this last campaign he led his brigade in a brilliant counterattack at THIRD WINCHESTER before being severely wounded in the knee at CEDAR CREEK 19 Oct. 1864. The debilitating wound incapacitated him for the rest of the war.

After the war Battle resumed his law practice in Alabama. Elected to Congress in 1868, he refused to take the IRONCLAD OATH, required before he could take his seat. He eventually moved to New Berne, N.C., where he edited a newspaper. d. Greensborough, N.C., 8 Apr. 1905.   —JDW

"Battle Above the Clouds." 24 Nov. 1863 *See* LOOKOUT MOUNTAIN, TENN., BATTLE OF.

Baxter Springs, Kans., Massacre at. 6 Oct. 1863 In late Sept. 1863, fresh from sacking LAWRENCE, Kans., Col. WILLIAM C. QUANTRILL led his band of bushwhackers south from Blue Springs. With the coming of cold weather, the raider realized that profitable operations in Kansas were over for the year. His force augmented by guerrilla units under William C. "Bloody Bill" Anderson and Col. John Holt, Quantrill headed toward Indian Territory, where he planned to winter.

By 6 Oct. his 400 bushwhackers were heading south on the Fort Scott Road when their advance, under Quantrill's subordinate, Dave Poole, captured 2 Union teamsters. Before killing the hated Yankees, the raiders ascertained their destination: a small garrison at Baxter Springs, some miles farther south. Hitherto ignorant of the post's location, Quantrill decided to attack and loot it. While Poole's band continued down the main road, Quantrill led his men north of the fort's reported location to mount a 2-pronged assault.

Arriving at his destination, Dave Poole led his men against the small dirt-and-log fort they found there. Their opponents, some 90 Union soldiers, most of them black, were under Lt. James B. Pond, 3d Wisconsin Cavalry. Experienced in fighting guerrillas, Pond prepared to defend his post, although his men, most of whom had assembled for a midday meal at a mess station some distance from the fort, were at a great disadvantage. Caught unarmed, they broke and fled from Poole's men, who, shouting and shooting, ran them down. Many of the soldiers were overtaken and gunned down at close range. Only quick action by Pond, who trundled out a small HOWITZER and blasted the terrorists into retreat, prevented a massacre of the entire garrison.

At the same time, Quantrill's main force was also heavily engaged. Leading his troops out of a neck of woods above the outpost, the guerrilla chief had spied the approach of a line of wagons, escorted by Union cavalry. The wagons turned out to be the personal retine of Maj. Gen. JAMES G. BLUNT, who was transferring the headquarters of his ARMY OF THE FRONTIER from Fort Scott to FORT SMITH, Indian Territory. The 100 or so men in this column carried equipment and weapons of value to the bushwhackers and were too few to make much resistance. Accordingly, Quantrill forgot about the fort and prepared his men for a charge.

Noting the captured blue uniforms worn by many of the guerrillas, Blunt took the strangers to be an honor guard from Baxter Springs and approached them incautiously. Only when George Todd, one of Quantrill's lieutenants, led a screaming band of raiders against him, did Blunt realize his error. Though he managed to reach safety on a swift horse, as did some of his mounted men, those in the wagons—including a military band—were overtaken and dispatched without mercy. Most were found shot in the head, some stripped, burned, and mutilated. Among them was an artist-correspondent for *FRANK LESLIE'S* and Maj. Henry Z. Curtis, son of Maj. Gen. SAMUEL R. CURTIS, Blunt's colleague.

The massacre took 90 Union lives, with only 3 bushwhackers killed. Survivors made their way to Fort Scott, where General Blunt, for his negligence in failing to protect his column, was relieved of command. Meanwhile, at Baxter Springs, as his men looted corpses, a drunken Quantrill was invoking the names of 2 prominent Confederate generals, exclaiming: "By God, Shelby could not whip Blunt, neither could Marmaduke, but I whipped him!"   —EGL

Bayard, George Dashiell. USA b. Seneca Falls, N.Y., 18 Dec. 1835. Bayard was reared in Iowa Territory by his pioneering family. He secured an appointment to West Point, graduating 11th in the class of 1856 with a commission as 2d lieutenant of cavalry. For the next 5 years he fought Indians on the Kansas and Colorado frontiers.

Bayard was on temporary duty as a captain teaching cavalry tactics at West Point when he received a commission as colonel of the 1st Pennsylvania Cavalry 14 Sept. 1861. Assigned to duty in the WASHINGTON DEFENSES, he used scouting details in the countryside to discipline his volunteers into good soldiers.

On 28 Apr. 1862 Bayard was appointed chief of cavalry of the III Corps and commissioned brigadier general of volunteers. The promotion came as a result of a routine probe of enemy bridge defenses outside Falmouth, Va., where his men were caught in a trap and had to fight their way out. During the engagement Bayard's horse was hit 3 times by rifle fire, but Bayard continued in command and came away from the fighting unharmed. In the Shenandoah Valley fighting that followed, he led 1,000 cavalrymen in the advance of Maj. Gen. Irvin McDowell's force at Strasburg and Woodstock, and under Maj. Gen. John C. Frémont fought in the reserve at PORT REPUBLIC.

In Aug. 1862 he commanded the Union advance at CEDAR MOUNTAIN, and in autumn, when the ARMY OF THE POTOMAC was restructured by its new commander, Maj. Gen. AMBROSE E. BURNSIDE, Bayard advanced to cavalry commander for the Left Grand Division. At Maj. Gen. William B. Franklin's headquarters that December, during the battle at FREDERICKSBURG, he was badly wounded by an enemy artillery round and died the next day, 14 Dec. 1862.   —JES

Baylor, John Robert. CSA b. Paris, Ky., 20 July 1822. Baylor lived up to every image his contemporaries had of a tough, individualistic Texan. Born into an army family, he spent most of his childhood at his father's various duty stations in Indian Territory. At 17 he went to Texas to fight Indians, quickly winning the reputation of a brave and impetuous frontiersman.

His colorful personality rather than experience assured his

election to the state legislature in 1853 and soon after an appointment as agent to the Comanches. Baylor, however, hated Indians, and his opinions about dealing with them harshly soon resulted in his dismissal. In May 1859, without government approval, he led some 350 fellow ranchers in an attempt to force removal of Texas Indians from the Brazos reservation to Indian Territory.

As a delegate to the state secession convention, Baylor urged Texas' withdrawal from the Union, and when the secession ordinance passed he rode furiously day and night through the small towns around San Antonio collecting a large party to "hunt buffalo on the plains." By 1 May 1861 he had recruited about 1,000 men for BAYLOR'S "BUFFALO HUNT," organized them into the 2d Texas Mounted Rifles with himself as lieutenant colonel, and launched the first Confederate invasion of NEW MEXICO TERRITORY. The invasion was moderately successful, with Baylor capturing the large Union force left to hold Fort Fillmore and 1 Aug. pronouncing himself military governor of the Confederate Territory of New Mexico. Baylor established himself at Mesilla until his plans to entrap and exterminate the Apache Indians resulted in his dismissal by the government in Richmond.

Back in Texas in 1863 he handily defeated pro-administration representative Malcolm D. Graham for a seat in the Second Regular Congress, but Baylor was too much the soldier to become a politician. While he took little part in debate, his congressional voting record consistently supported all legislation to resist peace and keep the Confederacy at war. Convinced that he could regain the Southwest, he passed the rest of the war in Richmond lobbying for permission to invade New Mexico again; but with serious defeats in the East, Sec. of War JAMES A. SEDDON rejected the plan.

Baylor's behavior as a maverick continued to provide copy for journalists after the war. He lived in San Antonio for a brief time, then settled in Montell, Tex., as a rancher and local politician. In 1881 he was described as "a man who does not seek a fight, but is always ready to defend himself." He died 8 Feb. 1894. The old Indian fighter was related to Robert Baylor, a founder of Baylor University in Waco.   —PLF

Baylor's "buffalo hunt."   In late spring 1861 the colorful Indian fighter and ardent Confederate JOHN ROBERT BAYLOR raised a force of about 1,000 Texas frontiersmen to join a "buffalo hunt" on the Southwestern plains. The hunt was actually a clumsy, well-publicized ruse to launch the first small-scale invasion of NEW MEXICO TERRITORY.

By 1 May Lt. Col. Baylor's men, styled the 2d Texas Mounted Rifles and supplied with their own horses, guns, and ammunition, left San Antonio for the arduous 700-mi journey to Confederate-held Fort Bliss, near El Paso. The recruits' early enthusiasm waned quickly, and desertion had reduced the ranks to about 400 by the time the column arrived 1 July. On 23 July scarcely 250 men started out on an offensive against the Federal troops holding Fort Fillmore. Riding north, they crossed the Rio Grande at San Tomás and in less than 24 hours camped 600 yd outside the Union garrison while Baylor planned a morning attack.

The Federal territorial military commander, Maj. E. R. S. CANBY, had received word of a Confederate assault late in May and had sent Maj. Isaac Lynde to protect the fort with 700 soldiers and sufficient supplies to hold it. Reluctant to take the offensive, Lynde promptly wrote Canby, insisting the country

was too dry to sustain his men, the livestock, and his officers' families. Baylor's presence, however, forced him to act.

On 25 July Lynde descended on nearby Mesilla, where Baylor had deployed his men. Lynde demanded the Texans' surrender, fired a couple of shots from his HOWITZER, and ordered a charge on the Confederate line. In the brief skirmish, Baylor's men repulsed the halfhearted attack, killing 3 Union soldiers. Lynde retreated and, without consulting his staff, decided to abandon the fort that night, striking out for Fort Stanton, 154 mi to the northeast.

At daylight Baylor saw the dust clouds raised by the retiring troops. Leaving a small force at Mesilla, he force-marched his men to a pass (known since as Baylor's Pass) 4 mi south of San Augustine Springs, Lynde's first destination. He easily captured several hundred stragglers who had foolishly filled their canteens with whiskey from the abandoned hospital stores and were by then parched enough to surrender for the promise of a long drink of water. The Confederates caught up with the main body 27 July, when Lynde, his men in no condition to offer resistance, surrendered.

Baylor, who had pursued Lynde with about 200 soldiers, took an estimated 500–600 prisoners. When word of the capture reached Fort Stanton, it too was evacuated. Lynde came under severe censure for deserting his post and was dismissed from the army for neglect of duty.

On 1 Aug. Baylor ended his "buffalo hunt" by declaring New Mexico south of the 34th parallel the Confederate Territory of New Mexico and himself military governor with his capital at Mesilla. In mid-December Confederate Brig. Gen. HENRY H. SIBLEY arrived for an official invasion of New Mexico Territory.   —PLF

bayonet.   The Civil War was the beginning of the end for the bayonet as a major weapon of war. When the conflict started, musketry fire was still used to weaken or confuse the enemy, but the battle itself was decided by a bayonet charge. The widespread use of the rifle musket, however, resulted in heavy casualties for troops attempting traditional charges; often the charges were repulsed long before troops could close to a range where the bayonet would be effective. The spread of the use of skirmishers, the relatively rare instances of true hand-to-hand combat, and the troops' realization of the bayonet's ineffectiveness resulted in many men discarding their bayonets or using them as candlesticks or tent pegs.

Generally there were 2 styles of Civil War bayonets: sword and angular. The sword bayonet was a relatively new development, used by French troops serving in Africa in the 1830s and 1840s. It was first used in this country with the 1841 Mississippi rifle. Most of the relatively short rifles used during the Civil War—including the U.S. Model 1855, the English Brunswick and 2-band pattern 1853 ENFIELD, the Plymouth Navy rifle, the SHARPS, the HENRY, and the SPENCER, and such Confederate-made arms as the Fayetteville, the Cook and Brother, and the Georgia Armory rifles—were equipped with sword bayonets. They were heavy and cumbersome to carry, and as use of the bayonet declined, they went out of favor. The Confederacy stopped the manufacture of all sword bayonets early in 1864, and though the Federal government continued to accept them, troops much preferred the angular bayonets.

The angular was the traditional form used with muskets, rifle muskets, and most full-length arms, and some rifles were equipped to use them. The SPRINGFIELD 1861 rifle musket and its subsequent models, as well as the 1853 Enfield and many of the European arms, used the angular bayonet. —LDJ

Bayou Bourbeau, La., eng. at. 3 Nov. 1863 His inglorious repulse at SABINE PASS, 8 Sept. 1863, forced Union Maj. Gen. NATHANIEL P. BANKS to give up his plan of an amphibious invasion of Texas. From his headquarters in New Orleans, the commander of the ARMY OF THE GULF eventually decided on a land movement as a prelude to invasion. He would send his subordinate, Maj. Gen. WILLIAM B. FRANKLIN, with the majority of the XIII and XIX corps, from southern Louisiana up Bayou Teche to Lafayette (Vermillionville) and from there westward into Texas.

The drive got under way early in October, when Franklin led 2 divisions of his own XIX Corps out of Fort Bisland, on the lower Teche, toward the village of Opelousas. Simultaneously, Maj. Gen. CADWALLADER C. WASHBURN, with the XIII Corps divisions of Maj. Gens. Michael K. Lawler and George F. McGinnis and Brig Gen. Stephen G. Burbridge, left Berwick, La., southeast of Bisland, and also marched north. Washburn joined Franklin on the 14th at Bayou Carrion Crow, giving the expedition 19,500 troops with which to oppose the local enemy, about half as many Confederates under Maj. Gen. RICHARD TAYLOR, commander of the District of Western Louisiana.

With his numerical advantage, it was no chore for Franklin to push the Confederates before him as he moved toward the upper Teche. But after occupying the Opelousas vicinity, the Union leader found local bayous too treacherous to cross, forage for his troops too difficult to obtain, and rain-drenched roads too muddy to travel. By 26 Oct. he had given up the offensive, retracing his steps toward New Iberia. Taylor's small army pressed him, but Franklin worried so little about his enemy's intentions that he allowed his divisions to march and encamp far from each other. By 3 Nov. they were scattered over a wide area, with part of the XIII Corps holding a rearguard position near Grand Coteau, on Bayou Bourbeau.

Here was the opening Taylor had sought. Just before noon, his advance echelon, 2 divisions of cavalry and 3 infantry regiments under Brig. Gen. THOMAS GREEN, attacked the camp of Burbridge's division, the most exposed command. Federal sentinels were so lax that the Confederates charged out of a ravine into Burbridge's front and flanks before he could deploy. From his position in the rear, General Washburn rode to the scene, only to discover that "many of the troops had broken and were scattered over the field, and the utter destruction or capture of the whole force seemed imminent."

Burbridge tried to fight his way out. Directing his attention to the single cavalry brigade and the foot troops assailing his front and right, he entrusted the defense of his other flank—threatened by the rest of Green's horsemen—to Lt. Col. Theodore Buehler, the commander of his 67th Indiana. Through what Washburn later called "incompetency or cowardice," Buehler failed to take action till too late; eventually surrounded, he surrendered his regiment en masse to the cavalry. Finding his left "totally gone," Burbridge ordered a retreat. Many of his men had started without him, fleeing 3 mi to the safety of General McGinnis' camp.

With the assistance of that division, Burbridge re-formed and stood firm. Fighting vigorously but making no further headway, Green finally drew off, having killed 25, wounded 129, and captured 562 men and 1 10-pounder cannon. The day

after this galling defeat, the Federals resumed their withdrawal, but with more caution and a healthier regard for Confederate strength, savvy, and opportunism. —EGL

Bayou De Glaize, La., eng. at. 18 May 1864 See YELLOW BAYOU, LA., ENG. AT.

Bayou La Fourche, La., eng. at. 13 July 1863 Following the surrender of PORT HUDSON early in July 1863, the XIX Corps divisions of Union Brig. Gens. GODFREY WEITZEL and CUVIER GROVER were transported to Donaldsonville, La. From there they could operate along either side of Bayou La Fourche, below Donaldsonville, a haven for Confederate Regulars and guerrillas. On the 11th and 12th skirmishing broke out between the pickets of both divisions and Confederate cavalry under Brig. Gen. THOMAS GREEN. On the 13th, Weitzel and Grover each sent out a brigade, down opposite sides of the bayou, to neutralize their opposition.

Instead of awaiting their arrival, Green decided to land the first blow. Up the west side of the bayou he led 3 Texas cavalry regiments and a 2-gun artillery section of his own brigade—some 750 effectives in all—against Weitzel's 3d Brigade. The latter, under Col. Nathan A. M. Dudley, consisted of 1 Massachusetts and 2 New York infantry regiments, with 2 artillery sections and a cavalry troop attached. Positioned some miles in Dudley's rear a supporting brigade led by Col. CHARLES J. PAINE comprised 5 infantry regiments—1 each from Louisiana, Maine, and New York, and 2 from Massachusetts.

Undeterred by the size of the opposition, Green advanced briskly through a cornfield that stretched from the bayou to a dense swamp farther west. 2 detachments of his 5th and 7th Texas led the attack, striking Dudley's front and left flank simultaneously near Cox's Plantation. The flanking troops broke up Dudley's horsemen and captured 3 of his cannon. Meanwhile, Green's 4th Texas Cavalry cut between the cornfield and swamp to strike the Union right. The timing and strength of the attack were such that Dudley's men rushed north in haste, several times attempting without success to re-form. Not till they had reached Paine's position could they make a stand, forcing their opponents to pull back.

At the same time, on the east bank of the bayou, the Federals suffered an even more ignominious repulse. Grover's southward-marching 1st Brigade, under Col. Joseph S. Morgan of the 90th New York, consisted of Morgan's regiment plus the 91st and 131st New York, the 1st Louisiana, and the 22d Maine infantry regiments. With such numbers, it should have overwhelmed the 400 opposing effectives under Green's subordinate, Col. W. P. Lane. Unaccountably, Morgan panicked on first contact, and his men seemed to assimilate his fear, throwing down their guns in the face of a limited assault by mounted and dismounted troopers and fleeing north through plowed fields and thickets. Many were picked up as prisoners, without offering resistance. His opposition having melted away, Colonel Lane pointed his cannon across the bayou and helped complete the rout of the Federals on the west bank.

After the Union forces reached the safety of fortifications near Donaldsonville, their superiors sought the reasons for their disgraceful performance. A brief investigation determined that Colonel Morgan (who at Port Hudson had been accused of dereliction of duty through alcoholism) had been drinking heavily on the morning of the fight. On these grounds, he was court-martialed and sentenced to dismissal from the army.

Only the vanquished, however, were interested in fault-finding. To General Green and his hard-fighting Texans, it was enough to know that they had "completely paralyzed" the Yankees who had come to run them out of southeastern Louisiana. —EGL

Beale, Richard Lee Turberville. CSA b. Westmoreland Cty., Va., 22 May 1819. Beale was an 1837 University of Virginia graduate and an attorney in his home county. Elected to a term in Congress in 1846, he also served in his state's 1851 constitutional convention and in its legislature.

He was commissioned 1st lieutenant of cavalry May 1861 and served in a provisional unit, Lee's Light Horse, later organized into the 9th Virginia Cavalry. Commissioned captain in July, major in October, and lieutenant colonel the following April, Beale fought on the Virginia peninsula in early 1862, then served under Maj. Gen. J. E. B. STUART in the SECOND BULL RUN and ANTIETAM campaigns.

In Oct. 1862 Beale was promoted to colonel of the 9th after 3 times offering his resignation from the service. Annoyed with the minutiae of regular duty, he asked for a guerrilla command or for the opportunity to return to the ranks as a private. Superiors dissuaded him from following either course, convincing him to retain his regular rank and command. That December he fought at FREDERICKSBURG and the following spring and summer served in the cavalry's campaigns through GETTYSBURG.

After 3 months' recuperative leave for a wound received in a September skirmish, Beale returned to duty Jan. 1864 as a part of Maj. Gen. W. H. F. LEE's division. At this time some of his command took part in the pursuit and capture of Union cavalry involved in the KILPATRICK-DAHLGREN RAID. Late in the year a shortage of general officers boosted him to brigade command without a commission. On 6 Jan. the next year, his appointment came through and he was made brigadier general.

Beale reestablished his law practice in Hague, Va., in Westmoreland County, after his army's surrender, and in 1879 was elected to a term in the U.S. House of Representatives. He died in Hague 21 Apr. 1893. —JES

Beall, Lloyd James. CSA b. R.I., 19 Oct. 1808. Not much is known of Beall's early life except that he was appointed to the U.S. Military Academy at West Point from Maryland, graduated 25th in the class of 1830, and was appointed a 2d lieutenant in the 1st U.S. Infantry 1 July that year.

Beall served as the CONFEDERATE STATES MARINE CORPS' first and only commandant. At the time of his appointment by Confederate Sec. of the Navy STEPHEN R. MALLORY, 23 May 1861, he was commissioned colonel. His selection was based on a hard-bitten 30-year career with both the infantry and the 2d U.S. Dragoons that saw him rise to the rank of major and fight in both the Seminole and Mexican wars. Since Beall was an administrator during the Civil War, his combat and field experience was not put to good use.

His correspondence Dec. 1861 reveals an argument with the Confederate States Navy Department. "This Corps, being, as it were, isolated from the other military branches of the service, should be complete within itself," he wrote. But to Beall's misfortune this point was often lost on his superiors, and he repeatedly had to argue for more noncommissioned officers, more musicians, better recruitment, and even better shelter for Marines at permanent duty stations.

Beall's accomplishments matched his complaints, and at the end of the war he could boast of having maintained a separate Marine training camp in Charleston, S.C., several permanent stations along the Mississippi River and Atlantic Coast (and one atop Virginia's Drewry's Bluff named Camp Beall in his honor), and of Marines distinguishing themselves in combat on the sea and on every front, including the Battle of SAYLER'S CREEK.

In the postwar years he lived quietly in Richmond, Va., and kept most of the old Confederate States Marine Corps records in his home. Unfortunately, a fire destroyed these, and much of the Confederate Marines' and Beall's personal history was lost. d. Richmond, 10 Nov. 1887. —JES

Beall, William Nelson Rector. CSA b. Bardstown, Ky., 20 Mar. 1825. In 1844 Beall was appointed to the U.S. Military Academy from Arkansas, where his family had been living for several years. 30th in the class of 1848, he received rank as brevet 2d lieutenant on graduating and his commission 9 months later. Beall drew assignments in frontier duty, in the Northwest until early Mar. 1855, then in Indian Territory, after which he transferred to the cavalry, engaging in several skirmishes with the Plains Indians.

Beall entered the Confederate service in late summer 1861 with the rank he had last held in the U.S. Army, captain of cavalry, to rank from 16 Mar. Sent

NA

first to Arkansas, he impressed Maj. Gen. Earl Van Dorn as a man born to military life, handling his command well and being quick to press his advantage in combat. Twice Van Dorn recommended Beall for a colonelcy; instead Congress confirmed him as a brigadier general 11 Apr. 1862. Less than 2 weeks later he assumed cavalry command of Gen. P.G.T. Beauregard's mounted troops around CORINTH.

Later that year Beall was transferred to PORT HUDSON, where his troops defended the center during the Union siege until Maj. Gen. FRANKLIN GARDNER surrendered the command 8 July 1863. After Beall's capture, he was sent to JOHNSON'S ISLAND until 1864.

The last months of his army career may have been the most challenging. By special agreement between officials in Richmond and Washington, Beall, paroled, was appointed Confederate agent to purchase supplies for prisoners of war. The Federal government arranged for him to open an office in New York, and Beall set up a cotton brokerage; his ships were permitted to pass through the Federal BLOCKADE with stores of Southern cotton. With the profits, he bought food, clothing, and blankets for distribution among Confederates held in Union prison camps. He was finally released 2 Aug. 1865, after most of the Confederate soldiers had been paroled and sent home.

Beall stayed in business as a commission merchant in St. Louis, Mo., after the war. d. McMinnville, Tenn., 25 July 1883. —PLF

Bean's Station, Tenn., eng. at. 14 Dec. 1863 Confederate Lt. Gen. JAMES LONGSTREET broke off the Siege of Knoxville the night of 4 Dec. 1863, and his troops began a 5-day retreat north to Rogersville in East Tennessee. A timid pursuit column commanded by Union Maj. Gen. JOHN G. PARKE set out from the city shortly afterward, following in Longstreet's path but always remaining a few days behind. The Federal pursuit and the fight at Bean's Station concluded the KNOXVILLE CAMPAIGN.

Traveling northeast, paralleling the East Tennessee & Virginia Railroad line, Longstreet's men reached the community of Rutledge 6 Dec., then pressed on. On 9 Dec. Parke reached Rutledge with the body of his column. Union Brig. Gen. JAMES M. SHACKELFORD, with 4,000 cavalry and infantry, stayed in Parke's advance, searching his front for Longstreet. The Confederates reached Rogersville, several miles northeast of Rutledge, 9 Dec.

Shackelford's probing went on through the 13th. His presence at Bean's Station, hard by the banks of the Holston River, tempted Longstreet, who ordered a force of Confederates to backtrack along the retreat route and take the hamlet. Longstreet planned a 3-pronged attack. A division of infantry under Brig. Gen. BUSHROD R. JOHNSON would make a direct march to the village from Rogersville. Maj. Gen. WILLIAM T. MARTIN would take 4 cavalry brigades by a circuitous mountain route to the banks of the Holston, cross the river south of the Federals, and attack them in flank. Brig. Gen. WILLIAM E. JONES would take an even longer route to the far side of the Federal rear, descend the north side of the Clinch Mts. with 2 cavalry brigades, and seal the pass, Bean's Gap. The Federals' escape route would be cut off. Batteries from Col. E. PORTER ALEXANDER's artillery would lend support.

Late on the night of the 13th Johnson's men and an advance of 100 cavalry left camp and by 2 a.m. 14 Dec. were driving in Union pickets 3 mi from Bean's Station. Federals twice tried making a stand and sent an alarm back to Shackelford. The Union commander deployed his men in the village, positioning his available artillery on 2 hills to the northwest behind the hamlet and on a southwestern rise beyond the fields.

As Confederate skirmishers came over foothills east of the village, Shackelford's artillery opened fire. Johnson's men splashed across the Holston and tried turning the Federals' left, then hit their right. Confederate artillery dueled with Union cannon from positions on hills in front of the village. Union troops in the village hotel opened up a hot fire on flanking Confederates, beginning a fight that lasted all day.

Elsewhere on the field Confederate flanking moves were slow and inconclusive. Martin's cavalry, expected to ride in from the south, never appeared that day. Longstreet personally commanded the assaults and ordered more troops from Rogersville to tip the balance, finally driving the Union command out of Bean's Station. At nightfall Shackelford's men were retreating through Bean's Gap to Blain's Cross Roads 3 mi away, most escaping before Jones's cavalry were in place to stop them. Confederates captured only a few trailing wagons from the retreating force.

The next morning Longstreet sent Brig. Gen. JOSEPH B. KERSHAW and his division after them, but when the major general approached the crossroads he found Shackelford's men dug in behind rail breastworks, in a stronger position than the day before. The Federals were allowed to retreat without further incident.

Though inconclusive, casualty figures for this engagement are, for the intensity of the fighting, remarkably low—no more than two hundred on either side.   —JES

Beardslee Telegraph. Perfected by George W. Beardslee, the Beardslee Patent Magneto-Electric Field Telegraph Machine eliminated the standard telegraphing sets, which required heavy cable, a compact but fairly powerful electric battery, and a knowledge of Morse code. Beardslee's cables were light, insulated with gutta-percha, and strong for their weight. His receiving and sending sets featured pointers on dials showing the alphabet; the sender directed the dial's pointer at a letter and the pointer on the receiver's dial indicated the same letter. His system replaced the battery of a standard set with a hand-cranked magneto.

Many of the system's portable features were later used on all military telegraphs, particularly the light wire spools carried by 2 runners who were followed by "lance" or pole carriers, allowing telegraph line to be quickly strung under battlefield conditions. The entire Beardslee system was usually transported by FLYING TELEGRAPH TRAIN.

First favored by Union Signal Officer ALBERT J. MYER, the Beardslee system was introduced during the 1862 PENINSULA CAMPAIGN. Its popularity rose and waned, and by Nov. 1863 it was discontinued. The magneto power system was its great failing, limiting the telegraph's effective range to 5 mi; when used 5–10 mi the magneto current easily became erratic.

Only about 70 sets were produced. With the advent of the Military Telegraph Service, they were scrapped, and commercial lines and standard telegraphing systems were used exclusively.   —JES

Beauregard, Pierre Gustave Toutant. CSA b. St. Bernard Parish, La., 28 May 1818. Perhaps no other Southern general was involved in so many pivotal military events as P.G.T. Beauregard. Beginning his Confederate service by directing the bombardment of Fort Sumter, he served as second in command to Gen. JOSEPH E. JOHNSTON at First Bull Run and to Gen. ALBERT SIDNEY JOHNSTON during the first major battle in the West, Shiloh, directed the defense of Charleston 1863–64, and supported Gen. ROBERT E. LEE south of Richmond toward the end of the war.

Of Creole parentage, Beauregard spoke French before he learned English, a background

USMHI

that served him well at West Point, where he read the classics on the art of war, in his mother tongue. He graduated from the academy in 1838, ranking 2d in his class of 45; among his classmates was IRVIN MCDOWELL, whom Beauregard would later defeat in 1861 at First Bull Run. Commissioned a 2d lieutenant in the Corps of Engineers, Beauregard was assigned to Fort Adams near Newport, R.I. In June 1839 he was advanced to 1st lieutenant, then transferred to Pensacola, Fla., to construct coastal defenses, and to Batavia Bay on the Louisiana Gulf.

In the Mexican War he served as an engineer under Gen. WINFIELD SCOTT, receiving 2 wounds and 2 brevets for gallantry. Over the next several years Beauregard supervised the building of coastal fortifications. From 1858 to 1861 he was chief engineer in charge of the draining of New Orleans and directed the construction of the Federal customs house there. Appointed superintendent of West Point Jan. 1861, he held the position for only a few days before being relieved because of his outspoken Southern sympathies.

Beauregard resigned his commission 20 Feb. 1861 and 1 Mar. accepted a position as brigadier general in the Confederate States Army. On 12 Apr. he commanded the bombardment of FORT SUMTER in Charleston harbor, where U.S. Army forces had retreated for greater safety and defense. By the 14th, Union forces under Maj. Robert Anderson surrendered Sumter, giving the South its first victory and making Beauregard a hero.

Following a triumphal trip to Richmond, Beauregard received orders to direct Confederate forces in the vicinity of Manassas Junction during the FIRST BATTLE OF BULL RUN, where he was in command of the line directly under Joseph E. Johnston. Beauregard was promoted to general in the Confederate Regular Army 31 Aug. 1861. Almost immediately he clashed with the War Department and, to get him away from Richmond, Pres. Jefferson Davis transferred him to the Western theater where, in early 1862, he served under Gen. Albert Sidney Johnston. Together they planned the assault on Maj. Gen. U.S. Grant's Federal army at Pittsburg Landing; when Johnston was killed during the resulting Battle of SHILOH, Beauregard assumed command. Although he had already wired of victory to Richmond, his tired and dispirited forces were unable to crush the Union troops and were forced to retreat. Davis blamed Beauregard for failing to pursue total victory and, unfairly, began questioning his fitness for field command; his misgivings seemed confirmed by Beauregard's subsequent evacuation of CORINTH.

In June 1862, Beauregard became ill and relinquished his command to Gen. BRAXTON BRAGG for what he believed would be a brief period. Davis took this opportunity to make a permanent change.

When Beauregard recovered he was placed in command of the Carolina and Georgia coastal defenses, reporting to Gen. Joseph E. Johnston, and until spring 1864 conducted a skillful defense against repeated Federal assaults. In April he was recalled to Virginia, where he assisted Gen. Robert E. Lee by defending the southern approach to Richmond, bottling up Maj. Gen. Benjamin F. Butler's force at BERMUDA HUNDRED and defeating his army at SECOND DREWRY'S BLUFF.

Beauregard, vain and egotistical, was more competent as an engineer than a military tactician. Though he was an able field commander, his tremendous popularity as the hero of Sumter exceeded his abilities as a combat leader, and his excessively critical remarks, textbook strategies, and excitable Gallic temperament kept him in disfavor with the Confederate high command. Toward the end of the war he was assigned to command the Military Division of the West, an administrative position that carried no military power and little prestige. During the last weeks of the war, he was once again in the Carolinas with Johnston, trying to halt Maj. Gen. WILLIAM T. SHERMAN's advance.

After Johnston surrendered, Beauregard returned to New Orleans. His postwar career included a railroad presidency, an appointment as a supervisor of the Louisiana State Lottery, and several years as state adjutant general. He refused offers to command the armies of several foreign governments. d. New Orleans 20 Feb. 1893.   —JDK

Beaver Dam Creek, Va., Battle of. 26 June 1862 See MECHANICSVILLE, VA., BATTLE OF.

Bee, Barnard Elliott. CSA b. Charleston, S.C., 8 Feb. 1824. Bee's family moved to Texas while he was a boy. Because Texas was not yet part of the U.S., he received his appointment to West Point under a special arrangement, graduating 33d in the class of 1845 and serving with distinction in the Mexican War, during which he was brevetted twice for gallantry. He remained in the Regular Army until 3 Mar. 1861, when he resigned as a captain in the 10th Infantry, and was immediately appointed lieutenant colonel of the 1st South Carolina Regulars, an artillery regiment organized for Confederate service.

On 17 June 1861 Bee was assigned command of a brigade of recruits in the Confederate army that was being mobilized at Manassas Junction. Bee's brigade and that of Col. FRANCIS S. BARTOW were in the path of the initial attack of the Federal army at FIRST BULL RUN, 21 July. While rallying his troops, Bee was mortally wounded. Before he died the next day, he became the first to call Confederate Brig. Gen. THOMAS J. JACKSON "Stonewall." Some say he bitterly remarked that while his and Bartow's brigades were being annihilated, Jackson "stood like a stone wall" with his own brigade and failed to support the hard-pressed units.

Bee died in a cabin near the Bull Run battlefield 22 July and was buried at Pendleton, S.C. His rank of brigadier general was confirmed posthumously by the Provisional Confederate Congress.   —JWR

Bee, Hamilton Prioleau. CSA b. Charleston, S.C., 22 July 1822. Bee is probably best remembered for his courageous performance in the Confederate repulse of Maj. Gen. Nathaniel P. Banks's Federals in the RED RIVER CAMPAIGN of 1864. He was also the older brother of Gen. BARNARD E. BEE, who coined the nickname "Stonewall" for Brig. Gen. THOMAS J. JACKSON at FIRST BULL RUN.

From the time his family moved west to Texas in 1835 Bee was interested in public service, which he entered in 1839 as secretary to the U.S.-Texas (then a republic) Boundary Commission. In 1846 Bee, a Democrat, was secretary of the first Texas senate. He subsequently served as a clerk for the republic's comptroller, future governor FRANCIS R. LUBBOCK, then in the state house of representatives where he was its speaker for 1 term.

TU

He fought in the Mexican war with the Texas Rangers, attaining rank of 1st lieutenant with Capt. BEN MCCULLOCH's cavalry. In 1861 he enlisted in the Texas Militia as brigadier general in the state provisional army at Brownsville. In 1862 Bee was commissioned brigadier general in the Confederate Army, administering the cotton-munitions trade with European countries. In Nov. 1863 his hopelessly outnumbered command at Brownsville saved $1 million in stores and ammunition from the Federals under General Banks.

Bee soon met Banks again in Louisiana. In Apr. 1864, 3 of

his Texas cavalry regiments participated in halting Banks's Red River Campaign at MANSFIELD and PLEASANT HILL. Though he had 2 horses shot under him and suffered a wound to the face, he was later censured by Lt. Gen. RICHARD TAYLOR for allowing Banks to escape at CANE RIVER CROSSING, 23 Apr. Taylor remarked that Bee "displayed great personal gallantry, but no generalship."

Bee later served with Maj. Gens. SAMUEL B. MAXEY and JOHN A. WHARTON, both veterans of fighting in Louisiana. He lived in Mexico after the war but returned to San Antonio, Tex., in 1876, dying there 3 Oct. 1897.   —FLS

Beecher, Henry Ward. minister b. Litchfield, Conn., 24 June 1813. Few of Reverend Beecher's contemporaries mastered his knack for attracting public attention or his enthusiasm for enjoying it. Sharing the limelight with his father, Lyman, and his sister, HARRIET BEECHER STOWE, author of *Uncle Tom's Cabin,* he was, like them, an outspoken opponent of SLAVERY, although he abhorred the fanaticism of radical abolitionists. Beecher was passionate, opinionated, steeped in New England moralism, and prone to use his pulpit as an antislavery platform. He epitomized those qualities Southerners despised in many of the more vocal critics of their society.

Beecher studied for the ministry at Lane Theological Seminary in Cincinnati, Ohio, which turned out several radical social reformers. Though not much of an intellectual, he was extremely well read, with a powerful speaking style characterized by wit, audacity, and the ability to address his audiences with an air of intimacy.

By 1847, newspapers were printing his sermons, and he became a great favorite on the lecture circuit. From the podium and as a regular contributor to the reformist magazine *The Independent,* he opposed the COMPROMISE OF 1850, promoted disobedience to the FUGITIVE SLAVE ACT, and urged free-soilers to settle in Kansas to keep it from becoming a slave state. Never one to shun theatrics, Beecher staged a "slave auction" at Plymouth Church in Boston in an emotional fundraising appeal to buy freedom for 2 mulatto girls. But his humanitarian objections to slavery extended only to limiting its growth and to decrying its evils until the institution died out, as he believed it would; unlike extremists, he believed abolishing slavery unconstitutional.

Beecher distrusted Abraham Lincoln's moderate position on slavery and his delay in issuing an EMANCIPATION PROCLAMATION once the war started. But in 1862 he traveled through England as a self-appointed antislavery propagandist, capitalizing on the popularity of his sister's book. In the postwar years he advocated black suffrage but also favored readmitting the Southern states to the Union quickly, with leniency.

Beecher remained an influential public figure until his death in New York City, 8 Mar. 1887. His life radiated controversy as he continuously involved himself in such unpopular causes as woman suffrage and the theory of evolution.   —PLF

Beech Grove, Ky., Battle of. 19 Jan. 1862 *See* MILL SPRINGS, KY., BATTLE OF.

Belknap, William Worth. USA b. Newburgh, N.Y., 22 Sept. 1829. Belknap attended the College of New Jersey, practiced law in the District of Columbia, then moved west. In 1857 he was elected to the Iowa legislature as a Democrat but 4 years later supported Lincoln's war effort.

On 7 Dec. 1861 Belknap was commissioned major of the 15th Iowa Volunteers, in which he served with distinction, being wounded the following April at SHILOH. As lieutenant colonel of the regiment he also performed with merit at CORINTH, winning promotion to colonel June 1863. During the VICKSBURG CAMPAIGN he led the 15th Iowa in several engagements and was promoted brigadier general of volunteers the following summer. Given command of the 3d Brigade/4th

LC

Division/XVII Corps, he was conspicuous throughout the ATLANTA CAMPAIGN, particularly in repulsing Gen. JOHN B. HOOD'S second sortie, 22 July 1864. On that field, according to his division commander, Belknap "displayed all the qualifications of an accomplished soldier." Six days later, at EZRA CHURCH, he provided timely support to an embattled XV Corps division. By July 1865, following participation in Maj. Gen. William T. Sherman's MARCH TO THE SEA and the CAROLINAS CAMPAIGN, he led the XVII Corps as a brevet major general.

Returning to civilian life, Belknap became a collector of internal revenue in Iowa, allied himself with the Republican party, and in 1869 was named Pres. ULYSSES S. GRANT's secretary of war. In Mar. 1876 he was accused of malfeasance in office for accepting over $24,000 in bribes from a post trader seeking immunity from removal. It is not clear whether Belknap was aware of the bargain or whether his wife had made the arrangement and received the payoffs. Nevertheless, he was impeached by unanimous vote of the U.S. Senate, though at his trial the Senate fell short of the number of votes required to convict; by then Belknap had resigned, which doubtless accounted for his acquittal.

In later years he resided in Philadelphia, then practiced law in Washington, D.C. He died in the capital 13 Oct. 1890 and was buried in Arlington National Cemetery.   —EGL

Bell, Tyree Harris. CSA b. Covington, Ky., 5 Sept. 1815, Bell was reared on his family's Tennessee plantation and, some years before the Civil War, began one of his own in the same state. Early in 1861 he recruited a company for the 12th Tennessee Infantry and was elected its captain 4 June.

An enthusiastic Confederate and a fighter, Bell quickly advanced to lieutenant colonel of the 12th before leading the regiment at the Battles of BELMONT, Mo., and SHILOH. In July 1862 he was commissioned colonel and in August participated in the Battle of RICHMOND, Ky. He then transferred to cavalry command, taking part in operations at the Battles of PERRYVILLE and STONE'S RIVER.

USMHI

When Maj. Gen. NATHAN B. FORREST was given authority to organize an independent command in West Tennessee and northern Mississippi in late 1863, he recruited Bell, who served with the famous commander until the end of the war. Under Forrest, Bell was first a recruiting and conscript officer, then was given command of a brigade of Tennessee regiments, though it was not until 28 Feb. 1865 that he received his commission as brigadier general for recognition of action in the Tennessee campaigns, the Battle of BRICE'S CROSS ROADS, and combat in Mississippi. Following the defeats around SELMA, Ala., he was surrendered with the rest of Forrest's force.

In the postwar years he migrated to Fresno, Calif., and became a farmer. He died while traveling through New Orleans, 1 Sept. 1902. —JES

Belle Grove, Va., Battle of. 19 Oct. 1864 *See* CEDAR CREEK, VA., BATTLE OF.

Belle Isle Prison. After First Bull Run, beautiful Belle Isle in the James River near Richmond, Va., became a Confederate prison for confining Union noncommissioned officers and enlisted men; by the end of 1863 it held over 7,000 prisoners. Its location in the rapids of the river made escape unlikely— which did not keep prisoners from trying, and drowning.

Belle Isle in distance USMHI

Accounts of living conditions at this tent camp vary: one witness claimed "drainage was good. . . . There were enough tents . . . and rations sufficient to preserve strength"; correspondents for the London *Times* and Richmond *Index* found "not one emaciated man" and "no truth in the statements of the Northern press as to the starving conditions of the prisoners"; and *The Illustrated London News* correspondent reported Apr. 1864 that conditions were remarkably good: "On the day I visited the island, out of 7,000 of these 'cruelly-used captives,' there were only thirteen in the hospital."

Other accounts claim there were never enough tents on the "unhealthy" island, that prisoners slept outside on "damp, boggy ground," and on one occasion several froze to death. There is little doubt that, as shortages of food and supplies almost paralyzed the Confederacy and the number of prisoners grew, the captives suffered. At one time there were about 10,000 on Belle Isle. A committee sent to the island by the U.S. SANITARY COMMISSION reported being told the men were fed "mule meat and wormy, buggy soup" and some were so near starving as to "devour a dog." A Union doctor who treated exchanged prisoners confined at Belle Isle wrote that "every case wore upon it the visage of hunger, the expression of de-

spair. . . . Their frames were, in the most cases, all that was left of them." After the war, a prisoner recalled Belle Isle as a "nightmare of starvation, disease, and suffering from cold." —PR

Belmont, Mo., Battle of. 7 Nov. 1861 On this day Pres. Abraham Lincoln's recent decision to give a brigadier general's command to ULYSSES S. GRANT began bearing fruit. Acting under orders from Maj. Gen. JOHN C. FRÉMONT, Grant, with over 3,000 troops, steamed down the Mississippi River from Cairo, Ill., with an escort of 2 makeshift, timberclad gunboats, the *Tyler* and *Lexington*, hastily converted from river transports.

Grant landed his troops on the Mississippi shore just north of the hamlet of Belmont, opposite the bluffs at Columbus, Ky., a key Confederate stronghold defended by heavy guns and a huge garrison. The Federals advanced to Belmont, captured it, but had to retreat when Confederate Maj. Gen. LEONIDAS POLK sent troops on boats from Columbus to counter them.

Though only a large raid and reconnaissance, the battle produced high casualties: 607 Unionists and 641 of the 5,000 secessionists who saw action. Grant accomplished little, for he could easily have confirmed what he in fact already knew: the great strength of Columbus. But the battle delighted Lincoln, who desperately desired action and had grown impatient with other slow-to-act generals, and it gave Grant and his men valuable operational and combat experience.

Afterward officers from both sides met to decide such procedures as prisoner exchange. The light and friendly mood was characteristic of this early stage in the war. At one of the conferences Confederate Brig. Gen. BENJAMIN F. CHEATHAM and Grant had a lively discussion of horse racing, which interested both. Cheatham playfully suggested that they have a horse race to decide the war; Grant said he wished they could, but had to decline. —HH

Benjamin, Judah Philip. CSP b. Christiansted, Virgin Islands, 6 Aug. 1811. Of English-Jewish parents and perhaps the most brilliant member of Pres. JEFFERSON DAVIS' cabinet, Benjamin excelled in each of the 3 careers he pursued. He received preliminary education in Fayetteville, N.C., and Charleston, S.C., and entered Yale College at 14, leaving before graduating and at 17 moving to New Orleans. In 6 years he was admitted to the bar and by 1840 was a highly successful lawyer. Elected to the U.S. Senate from Louisiana in 1852, he soon gained a reputation as an eloquent and persuasive speaker.

NA

A second career began in early Feb. 1861 when he resigned his seat in the Senate; late that month Davis appointed him attorney general in the new Confederacy. On 17 Sept. he replaced the ineffectual LEROY POPE WALKER as secretary of war, but his impatience with stiff military protocol made his term a brief and stormy one. In Mar. 1862 GEORGE W. RANDOLPH was made secretary of war and Davis named Benjamin secretary of state.

A third career began 3 May 1865, when, to avoid capture, he separated from the fleeing Confederate president's party at the

Savannah River in Georgia. Disguised, he went on to Florida, sailed to the West Indies, and eventually arrived to enroll at Lincoln's Inn, London, as a barrister in 1866. He quickly rose to Queen's Counsel for Lancashire County, becoming so successful that by 1877 he would accept no case for a fee of less than 300 guineas ($1,500). When he retired in 1883, the Bar of England honored him with a farewell dinner.

Benjamin was an enigma to those who knew him. His habitual half-smile and ironical comments led people to question whether he took his responsibilities seriously, but few men were more industrious. Though brilliant, he never allowed his quick grasp of ideas or affairs to substitute for a solid background of facts. In retrospect, Jefferson Davis called him "a master of law, and the most accomplished statesman I have ever known." d. Paris, France, 6 May 1884.   —RDH

Bennett House, N.C. *See* SURRENDERS: Johnston.

Benning, Henry Lewis. CSA b. Columbia, Ga., 2 Apr. 1814. After graduating from Georgia's Franklin College in 1834, Benning moved to Columbus, Ga., where he excelled in law and in STATES-RIGHTS politics, rising to associate justice of the Georgia supreme court and serving as a delegate in the 1860 Democratic conventions. A vocal secessionist, he argued vigorously for the state's supremacy in almost all government matters, and while on the state bench he endorsed that court's authority over Federal court decisions and claimed the state and Federal judiciary were "co-equals."

Benning served as a delegate in the Georgia state secession convention and as a Georgia delegate in the Virginia convention that followed. But he preferred military service to politics and was commissioned colonel of the 17th Georgia Infantry Aug. 1861.

After service with his regiment in the SEVEN DAYS' CAMPAIGN and the SECOND BATTLE OF BULL RUN, he acquitted himself with distinction at ANTIETAM, where, serving in Brig. Gen. Robert A. Toombs's brigade, he fought in the vicious Confederate holding action at "Burnside Bridge." Toombs was badly wounded and the brigade's command fell to Benning, who led it through the rest of the battle and at the head of his troops drove the Federals from the town of Sharpsburg. He credited Toombs, an old political associate, with the brigade's success that day, but the honors belonged to Benning.

Benning led Toombs's brigade again at FREDERICKSBURG in his superior's absence. Then, after squabbles with the Confederate administration, Toombs resigned his commission Mar. 1863 and Benning was appointed brigadier general on the 23d of that month, to rank from 17 Jan.

Attached to Maj. Gen. John B. Hood's division in the army's I Corps, Benning fought with it through the Battle of GETTYS-BURG. Along with Lt. Gen. James Longstreet's men, he was detached from Eastern field service for campaigning in Tennessee. At the Battle of CHICKAMAUGA, with several of Longstreet's other brigades, he and his men were sent into a large gap that had developed in the Federal line, and fell into fierce fighting. After saving Brig. Gen. Evander M. Law's brigade from a Union flank attack, capturing 8 cannon, and losing 510 men, he received commendation in official reports.

Benning served in the Battle of KNOXVILLE and the fight for FORT SANDERS, then was transferred back to Virginia for the Battle of the WILDERNESS. There, serving in Maj. Gen. Charles W. Field's division, he was wounded and unable to rejoin

his command until the Siege of Petersburg.

With his men he sat out the siege, then campaigned on to APPOMATTOX. Though he never rose to high command, his tough war service won him his troops' esteem and the army nickname "Old Rock." He took this tenacity back with him to civilian life and remade his law career in Georgia, where he died, in Columbus, 10 July 1875. The U.S. Army's Fort Benning, Ga., was named in his memory.   —JES

Benton, Samuel. CSA b. Williamson Cty., Tenn., 18 Oct. 1820. In 1861 Benton attended the Mississippi state secession convention and voted to take his state out of the Union. He was a state legislator, attorney, and one-time schoolmaster with no military experience—which did not keep him from being appointed captain of the 9th Mississippi Infantry in 1861.

USMHI

Although the 9th, a local unit, was dissolved after a year's service, during that time Benton learned the soldier's craft. In early 1862 he obtained a commission as colonel of the 37th Mississippi Infantry, a unit later reorganized and redesignated the 34th Mississippi, and led these men at the Battle of SHILOH.

Benton saw service in northern Mississippi until 1864. In the spring of that year he briefly commanded the 24th and the 27th Mississippi but at the start of Maj. Gen. WILLIAM T. SHERMAN's march on Atlanta, he resumed command of the 34th. Benton was given charge of Edward C. Walthall's brigade when Walthall advanced to major general. Several days later, 22 July, Benton was struck by shell fragments during the Battle of ATLANTA. A piece of iron was lodged over his heart and part of one foot was blown away. The mangled foot was amputated, but he died of his wounds in Griffin, Ga., 28 July 1864. Shortly afterward, his brigadier general's commission arrived, dated 26 July.   —JES

Benton, USS. An armored gunboat, the *Benton* was built by civilian contractor James B. Eads at St. Louis. 2 figures are given for her tonnage: 633 and 1,033.

On 15 Jan. 1862 the *Benton* was delivered to Adm. ANDREW H. FOOTE and, as the largest and most powerful of the IRON-

LC

CLADS, became his flagship, contributing greatly to Federal success in the river war against FORTS HENRY AND DONELSON and ISLAND NO. 10. Despite the protection of its iron plates, the *Benton* was vulnerable due to slowness and difficult steering. Foote found the ship "wanting in steam power" and refused additional plating, which he feared would reduce its speed further. During his attack on Island No. 10, Foote had the *Benton* lashed between 2 vessels with more powerful engines.

In Dec. 1862 Rear Adm. DAVID D. PORTER directed Lt. William Gwin, commanding the *Benton,* to proceed up the Yazoo River to aid in securing a landing for troops of Maj. Gen. WILLIAM T. SHERMAN. While tied to the bank of the Yazoo during high winds, the *Benton* came under enemy fire and was hit repeatedly. Gwin was killed and 9 others were killed or wounded. Although badly damaged, the *Benton* was repaired and ready for action in time for final operations against VICKSBURG in 1863.

The *Benton's* last major action was during the RED RIVER CAMPAIGN, Mar. 1864, and it was still operating at war's end. In Nov. 1865 the ship was stripped of plating and sold for scrap.   —NCD

Bentonville, N.C., Battle of.   19–21 Mar. 1865   In mid-Mar. 1865 Maj. Gen. WILLIAM T. SHERMAN's Union force reached Fayetteville, N.C. From Fayetteville Sherman moved in 2 columns. His right, Maj. Gen. OLIVER O. HOWARD's Army of the Tennessee, marched northeast toward Goldsborough, where it was to join another Federal column that had come inland from the coast. Sherman's left, Maj. Gen. HENRY W. SLOCUM's Army of Georgia (XIV and XX corps), moved north to threaten Raleigh.

On 16 Mar. Slocum briefly engaged the Confederates near AVERASBOROUGH, turning east toward Goldsborough after the Southerners fell back.

By that time the Confederate commander, Gen. JOSEPH E. JOHNSTON, with about 21,000 men, had decided to strike at Slocum while he was separated from the other Federals, in the hope of delaying or preventing the Union concentration at Goldsborough.

Early on 19 Mar. Slocum's leading units met a force of Confederate cavalry south of Bentonville. The Federals forced the Southern horsemen back, Johnston soon counterattacked, then Slocum quickly pulled his forces together to beat off additional Southern attacks. When Johnston found that he could not dislodge Slocum, he drew back and took up a strong defensive position.

On 20 Mar. there was little fighting. Sherman was bringing up more troops to attack Johnston; the Confederate commander was content to hold his ground.

With all his troops on the scene, Sherman moved to attack 21 Mar. While some Northerners struck Johnston's front, a division of the XVII Corps tried to get around the Confederate left to cut off its retreat. Johnston was able to block the flanking maneuver and hold his position, but that night he fell back toward Smithfield. His battle had been well planned and executed, but he had too few men to achieve any decisive results. Realizing the hopelessness of further resistance, Johnston soon opened negotiations that led to his surrender.

Federal losses in the 3 days have been put at 1,645; Confederate casualties numbered 2,606.   —RMcM

Berdan, Hiram G.   USA b. N.Y., c. 1823. A mechanical engineer living in New York City at the start of the war, Berdan had been ranked the top amateur rifle shot in the nation since 1846. Eager to promote himself, several ideas for inventions, and his views on weapons development, he organized BERDAN'S SHARPSHOOTERS, which led to the formation of 2 regiments of U.S. Sharpshooters. Berdan was commissioned colonel of the 1st Regiment 30 Nov. 1861.

The regiment did valuable service throughout the PENINSULA CAMPAIGN and at MALVERN HILL and was heavily engaged at CHANCELLORSVILLE. Though Berdan personally commanded a scout of the Confederates' position on the second day of battle at GETTYSBURG, he was often busy with affairs away from the front, involving himself in controversies over the superiority of certain rifles and pursuing government contracts for inventions; he was more often found in a parlor than in a rifle pit. Military and civilian Civil War contemporaries independently formed an opinion of him as "unscrupulous"—one called him "totally unfit for command" —and he was believed to be a great liar.

Before the war he patented a repeating rifle and rifle ball; postbellum he worked on inventing "a submarine gunboat," a

USMHI

SLOCUM
3:00 P.M.

N

Woods

Woods

4:00 P.M.

JOHNSTON
Positions at
2:30 P.M.

Positions at 2:30 P.M.

Swamp

Woods

Swamp

Driven out at 11:30 A.M.

Noon   Skirmish   Line

Swamp

Goldsborough Road

Woods

Rebel Works

Rebel Works

Rebel Works

BATTLE OF BENTONVILLE
19 March 1865

range finder, an artillery fuse, and a torpedo boat. He was brevetted brigadier general for service at Chancellorsville and major general after the battle at Gettysburg. These brevets were truly honorary, did not come with appointment to full rank, and did not allow the exercise of command above the level of colonel. He resigned his commission 2 Jan. 1864 to pursue other interests and died in 1893. —JES

Berdan's Sharpshooters. In summer 1861 HIRAM G. BERDAN, a well-known New Yorker, proposed the organization of a corps of picked marksmen to be selected from the Northern states and armed with the best rifles. Such troops, he argued, would be invaluable as SHARPSHOOTERS and skirmishers. The proposal was approved by Sec. of War EDWIN M. STANTON; eventually 2 regiments were organized, and Berdan became colonel of the 1st U.S. Sharpshooters.

Armed with .52-caliber SHARPS RIFLES (some of which had telescopic sights), the sharpshooters wore a distinctive uniform consisting of a green cap with a black plume, a green coat, and light blue trousers (later changed to green). The 1st Sharpshooter Regiment was assigned to the V Corps 1862–63, the III Corps in 1863, and the II Corps in 1864. Berdan led the regiment until he took command of a brigade; Col. George C. Hastings succeeded him. The Sharpshooters played an important role in the fighting on the Federal left at GETTYSBURG, 2 July 1863, helping slow the Confederate attack, thus giving the Northerners a chance to organize their defenses.

The 2d Sharpshooters, led by Col. Henry A. V. Post, then by Col. Homer R. Stoughton, served with the I, III, and II corps and had only 8 companies; the 1st Sharpshooters had the usual 10 companies.

The 2 regiments were consolidated 31 Dec. 1864, then Feb. 1865 were broken up and the companies distributed to other regiments.

The Sharpshooters performed well, sometimes silencing artillery batteries with their accurate fire. They claimed to have inflicted more casualties on the Confederates than any other unit of comparable size. The Sharpshooter regiments lost 1,008 of their 2,570 men killed and wounded during the war. —RMcM

Bermuda Hundred, Va. A large neck of land between the James and Appomattox rivers, Bermuda Hundred lay 15 mi south of Richmond, capital of the Confederacy, and 7 mi north of the vital railroad junction of Petersburg. Across its western base ran the RICHMOND & PETERSBURG RAILROAD, the lifeline connecting Richmond to points south. Though sparsely defended by the Confederates, Bermuda Hundred was strategically important to the authorities in Richmond.

The war finally came in earnest to Bermuda Hundred 5 May 1864, when the leading elements of Maj. Gen. BENJAMIN F. BUTLER's 39,000-man ARMY OF THE JAMES spilled off Union transports at the Bermuda Hundred plantation on the James River. Butler and his imposing force occupied the peninsula with orders to operate against Richmond. On the day the Federals disembarked, Gen. P.G.T. BEAUREGARD assumed command of the Confederate defenses at Petersburg. Ill, Beauregard gave control to Maj. Gen. GEORGE E. PICKETT, who reacted swiftly to the threat by rushing reinforcements to the railroad junction.

From 6–11 May Butler pressed westward against Pickett's beleaguered Confederates. The Union politician-turned-gen-

Entrenchments on left of Bermuda Hundred lines

eral built a line of entrenchments as a secure base across the peninsula's narrowest point. Skirmishes and minor engagements flared at Port Walthall Junction and SWIFT CREEK. Content to destroy the railroad, Butler returned to his works on the 11th. The next day he resumed the advance northward against Confederate defenses at DREWRY'S BLUFF, 5 mi from Richmond. Beauregard, back in command, had bolstered the garrison there with 7 brigades on the 11th. Butler canceled an attack planned for the 15th and on the next day Beauregard assumed the offensive; in a dense fog, the Confederates achieved some early successes before losing cohesion and force. Butler withdrew in a heavy rain to his line of works. Beauregard followed, rimmed the base of the peninsula with his own works and, as Lt. Gen. Ulysses S. Grant said, "bottled up" Butler.

Butler had failed and Bermuda Hundred was corked for the rest of the war. During the PETERSBURG CAMPAIGN, June 1864–Apr. 1865, the Confederate lines across the peninsula were an integral part of its defense. The Confederates abandoned their works in Bermuda Hundred when Petersburg fell during the war's final week in Virginia.   —JDW

Bethel Church, Va., Battle of. 10 June 1861 See BIG BETHEL, VA., BATTLE OF.

Bickerdyke, Mary Anne Ball. nurse b. Knox Cty., Ohio, 19 July 1817. With "a bend toward nursing" from an early age, Bickerdyke was one of the most noted—and certainly the most resourceful and colorful—of the women who served in Union hospitals during the Civil War. In 1847, living in Cincinnati, she married Robert Bickerdyke, musician and sign painter. In 1856 the Bickerdykes moved to Galesburg, Ill., where, 3 years later, Robert died, leaving Mary Anne to support herself and her 2 half-grown sons by practicing as a "botanic physician."

AHI

She was described by Benjamin Woodward, a young Galesburg doctor and Union volunteer, as "a woman rough, uncultivated, even ignorant, but a diamond in the rough." Woodward wrote home about the filthy, ill-equipped hospitals at the Cairo camp where he was stationed; the citizens of Galesburg gathered together $500 worth of supplies and selected the 44-year-old Widow Bickerdyke to deliver them. She went, returning during the war years only to visit her sons.

"Mother" Bickerdyke became noted in Union camps, particularly in field hospitals as near the fighting as she could get, for ignoring regulations, cutting through red tape, resourcefully acquiring supplies, and making "cyclone clean-ups" of dirty hospitals; for the last she was given the name "Cyclone in Calico." She directed the operation of diet kitchens, introduced and managed army laundries, and in general fought for the welfare of enlisted men. She was with Maj. Gen. ULYSSES S. GRANT's army en route to Vicksburg, and, at Maj. Gen. WILLIAM T. SHERMAN's request, with his army throughout the ATLANTA CAMPAIGN as the U.S. SANITARY COMMISSION's field agent.

During later life Mother Bickerdyke was often asked for an account of her war service, and she always replied: "I served in our Civil War from June 9, 1861, to March 20, 1865. I was in nineteen hard-fought battles in the Departments of Ohio, Tennessee, and Cumberland Armies. I did the work of one, and I tried to do it well." d. Bunker Hill, Kans., 8 Nov. 1901.   —PR

Bickley, George Washington Lamb. CSP b. Bickley's Mills, Va., 18 July 1823. The founder and first leader of the KNIGHTS OF THE GOLDEN CIRCLE, a secret order of militant Southerners and Northern subversives, Bickley was, in the words of historian Frank L. Klement, a "charlatan" with a "glib tongue and facile pen," whose penchant for hyperbole and self-promotion magnified the size of and the threat posed by his organization.

Born into an old Virginia family, Bickley moved to Cincinnati in the late 1840s; there he established a medical practice and a reputation as a political orator. From 1852 to 1859 he served on the faculty of the Eclectic Medical Institute of Ohio but after 1854 spent much of his time forming "castles" (chapters) of his secret society in Ohio and, later, throughout the South.

Originally the Knights were devoted to furthering Manifest Destiny, seeking the colonization and Americanization of the northern provinces of Mexico, which would then enter the Union as slave states. By late 1860 a few members had assembled above Mexico, but when the Civil War became imminent, Texas officials blocked their effort at invasion and broke up their camps.

Sensing that the order, by now largely Southern in membership, could foster support for secession, Confederate authorities revamped the KGC into an anti-Federal organization. Bickley could not oppose this change, for in 1860 he had been ousted from command by members who considered him long on oratory but short on practical leadership. By 1 Mar. 1861 the headquarters of the organization had moved to Montgomery, Ala., and Confederate officials had assumed positions of power. Soon after FORT SUMTER, however, support for secession became so strong in the South that the new hierarchy considered the KGC's job done and disbanded the order.

The Knights remained active in some parts of the Northwest but were so few that they posed no threat to the Union. Nevertheless, Gov. OLIVER P. MORTON of Indiana and other Northern political and military officials exploited the order's reputation to justify strict suppression of anti-Unionist sentiment in their region. Their work was made easier July 1863, when "General" Bickley was arrested in Indiana after a stint as a Confederate army surgeon and an ill-advised effort to cross enemy lines. He was refused a trial when his captors realized that a public hearing would explode the myths they had concocted about the KGC and expose them as alarmists or liars.

The luckless Bickley was not released until late in 1865, after which he made an unsuccessful speaking tour of England. Returning to the U.S. destitute, he died in obscurity in Baltimore, 10 Aug. 1867.   —EGL

Bierce, Ambrose Gwinnett. USA/author b. Meigs Cty., Ohio, 24 June 1842. A contemporary of Samuel "Mark Twain" Clemens, William Dean Howells, and other late-19th-century American literary notables, Bierce made his reputation after the Civil War, much of it founded on his experiences as a member of the Union army.

In 1848 the Bierce family moved to Indiana, where Ambrose was reared and in 1861 worked in a store in Elkhart. He joined Company C of the 9th Indiana Volunteers in April of that year, then fought in Maj. Gen. GEORGE B. MCCLELLAN's western Virginia campaign and under Maj. Gen. WILLIAM B. HAZEN in all the army's major battles from SHILOH to the CAROLINAS CAMPAIGN. In that time he rose from private to 1st lieutenant, became a staff topographical engineer, was wounded in the head at KENNESAW MOUNTAIN, became a personal friend of Hazen's, and saw enough violence to change his perception of the human condition.

In the postwar years, largely through the efforts of news magnate William Randolph Hearst, Bierce became a nationally known satirist. His best remembered work is *The Devil's Dictionary* (1906), a compendium of caustic definitions. Published in *Tales of Soldiers and Civilians* (1891), his short stories "An Occurrence at Owl Creek Bridge" and "One of the Missing," dealing with the dark side of war, are frequently reprinted and have been adapted by modern media.

Bierce disappeared in 1913 while working as a correspondent covering Pancho Villa's Mexican insurrection. The exact place and date of his death are unknown.   —JES

Big Bethel (Bethel Church; Great Bethel), Va., Battle of

. 10 June 1861   This early engagement in southeastern Virginia was one of 3 during June 1861 in which the Union army cautiously felt out Confederate positions. Big Bethel caused some embarrassment for the North, ended the life of Union Maj. Theodore Winthrop—a brilliant young author—and brought Confederate Maj. GEORGE W. RANDOLPH, commanding an artillery battalion, to the attention of his superiors, who marked him for advancement; Randolph became a brigadier general and Confederate secretary of war.

Union Col. Joseph B. Carr, later a major general, called it "the disastrous *fight* at Big Bethel—battle we scarce may term it." The Federals proved too green, especially against the Confederate earthworks toward which they blundered during the night, even dragging one cannon by hand. Some of the Northern regiments had gray uniforms; thus the 3d New York drew fire from the 7th New York, whose commander, Col. John Bendix, had not been given the watchword. The attacked Federals continually shouted the watchword "Boston," but Bendix, unaware of its significance, assaulted. After a short retreat the error was discovered, but meanwhile the 2 Federal regiments in the vanguard, hearing the firing, concluded that the Confederates had reached their rear and immediately retired. Now, with hopes of any surprise gone, the Northern commanders regrouped piecemeal.

One Union colonel recalled that "for at least one mile from the scene of the action the men and officers were scattered singly and in groups, without form or organization, looking far more like men enjoying a huge picnic than soldiers awaiting battle." The Confederates fired at first inaccurately but soon found the range. After an hour's hesitant and confused attack, the Union troops retired, having engaged over 2,500 men and lost 18 killed, 53 wounded, 5 missing. The Confederates had engaged 1,200 with only 1 killed and 7 wounded. Elated and encouraged, Southerners displayed trophies of the fight in Richmond store windows.   —HH

Big Black River Bridge, Miss., Battle of.

17 May 1863 The 2 Confederate divisions mauled at CHAMPION'S HILL reached Big Black River Bridge on the night of 16 May. Lt. Gen. JOHN C. PEMBERTON, expecting Maj. Gen. WILLIAM WING LORING's division to rejoin him, told Brig. Gen. JOHN S. BOWEN,

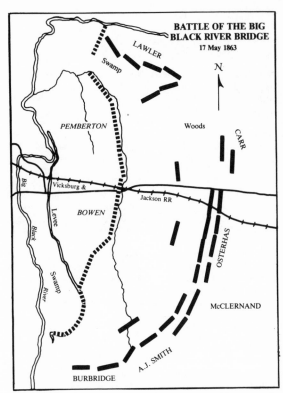

BATTLE OF THE BIG
BLACK RIVER BRIDGE
17 May 1863

with 3 brigades and 18 cannon, to hold the line of breastworks on the east side of the Big Black.

On the morning of the 17th the Army of the Tennessee resumed its advance from Champion's Hill. Union Maj. Gen. JOHN A. MCCLERNAND's XIII Corps took the lead as columns tramped through Edward's Station. Miles beyond the village, Union Brig. Gen. PETER J. OSTERHAUS' vanguard emerged from a woods and saw earthworks to their front. Skirmishers were thrown forward, artillery called up, and Osterhaus deployed his division south of the road. As the Federals took position, the Confederate artillery opened fire.

Union Brig. Gen. EUGENE A. CARR's division came up, and McClernand posted Carr's brigades on Osterhaus' right. Brig. Gen. STEPHEN G. BURBRIDGE's brigade of Brig. Gen. ANDREW J. SMITH's division then occupied the ground on Osterhaus' left.

Maj. Gen. ULYSSES S. GRANT determined to employ his other corps to turn the Confederate position. Maj. Gen. JAMES B. MCPHERSON's corps was to bridge the Big Black at Amsterdam and Maj. Gen. WILLIAM T. SHERMAN's at Bridgeport, while McClernand's men kept the Confederates pinned behind their fortifications.

More than 6 hours before Union PIONEERS bridged the Big Black, Brig. Gen. MICHAEL K. LAWLER, whose brigade was on the right near the river, massed his regiments into a column. With Lawler in front, the brigade surged out of a shallow trench, passing across the front of Brig. Gen. MARTIN E. GREEN's Missouri-Arkansas brigade; seeing a number of their comrades cut down, the men closed on breastworks defended by a brigade of panicked Federal East Tennesseans. There was a wild fight across the Big Black. To delay pursuit by McClernand's corps,

Confederates fired the bridges. It was a mob rather than an army with which Pemberton retreated into Vicksburg that day. Federal casualties numbered 39 killed, 237 wounded, 3 missing; 1,700 Confederates were captured. —ECB

Big Round Top, at Gettysburg, Pa. 2 July 1863 The twin peaks of Little and Big Round Tops towered above the southern portion of the battlefield at GETTYSBURG. Rockstrewn, boulder-studded, Big Round Top rose 785 ft above the surrounding farmland. A 500-yd saddle or trough connected the 2 hills. Big Round Top was the steeper, more heavily wooded eminence, more than 100 ft higher than the lower hill. The army that occupied their summits controlled the southern half of the battlefield.

When the Confederate attack 2 July finally burst across the farmlands, no significant Union force occupied either Round Top. The fierce action soon flared across the PEACH ORCHARD, into the WHEATFIELD, and through DEVIL'S DEN. The final struggle for the peaks eventually spilled up the slopes of LITTLE ROUND TOP.

The Confederate troops assigned to this sector of the field belonged to Maj. Gen. JOHN B. HOOD's division. 5 Alabama regiments of Brig. Gen. EVANDER M. LAW anchored the right of Hood's charging soldiers, the unit nearest the Round Tops. As the Confederate assault knifed into Maj. Gen. DANIEL E. SICKLES' Union III Corps, Law dispatched the 47th and 15th Alabama, under Col. William C. Oates, toward the saddle between the Round Tops.

The 2 Alabama regiments entered the heavy woods in front of Big Round Top, where a contingent of Federal SHARPSHOOT-ERS opened fire. Oates replied, shoving the Federals up the hillside. Swinging farther right, the Alabamians ascended the sheer southern face of Big Round Top. Clutching bushes and trees and clinging to rocks, the Confederates scaled the precipitous, wooded eminence, and from the summit Oates could see the Union lines trailing northward toward Gettysburg.

2 understrength Confederate regiments held the highest ground on the field. If they could have hauled guns up the sheer slope and planted them on the peak, Little Round Top would have been untenable by the Federals, as would the center of the Union line on CEMETERY RIDGE. But no guns were hauled. Hood fell wounded, Law replaced him; Oates received orders to attack Little Round Top. The Southerners stormed up its slopes, only to be repulsed by a valiant Union defense.

That evening the Union command recognized the importance of Big Round Top, and 3 regiments climbed to the summit, securing the crucial position. The Confederates were forced to assault the Union center. —JDW

Big Shanty, Ga. 12 Apr. 1862 See ANDREWS' RAID.

Bird Creek (Chusto-Talasah; High Shoal), Indian Territory, eng. at. 9 Dec. 1861 Troops of Federal and Confederate Indians met in battle infrequently during the war, but one of the more notable confrontations occurred at Bird Creek. With the coming of war, many Creeks and Seminoles adhered to the Union, and one of the Confederacy's prime objectives, once it had organized in Indian Territory, was the dispersal or elimination of these "tories." Led by Opothleyahola and Halleck Tustenuggee, the pro-Union Creeks and Seminoles, numbering about 1,000 able-bodied men, clustered on the Canadian River in the heart of Creek country.

As early as 15 Nov. Col. DOUGLAS H. COOPER led some 1,400 Southern soldiers against the Indians but found them gone. Pursuing, he met and defeated them at Round Mountain on the 19th but was forced to allow them to escape. By 8 Dec. Opothleyahola and his band were camped at Bird Creek in the heart of the Cherokee Nation. Fearing that the Unionist Indians would attack, Cooper decided to take the offensive himself.

Believing the Indians to number 2,000 or more, Cooper marched in 2 columns, arriving late on 8 Dec. Opothleyahola had sent a message saying that he wanted peace, not a fight, and Cooper responded that "we did not desire the shedding of blood among the Indians." A conference for the next day was proposed, and Cooper began bedding down his men for the night. But apparently many of Opothleyahola's warriors were tired of running and bargaining; they had painted themselves for war and even prevented Cooper's peace emissary from reaching the chief. Worse, word of their intent to attack had panicked most of Cooper's regiment of CONFEDERATE INDIANS, the 1st Cherokee Mounted Rifles, who dispersed into the countryside.

At once Cooper formed his command to defend itself, but the threatened attack did not come. Instead, at dawn on 9 Dec. Cooper began drawing together his scattered Indians and prepared to take the offensive. Forming his Choctaws and Chickasaws on the right, his Texas cavalry in the center with the shaky Cherokees and Creeks on the left, Cooper ordered all to advance at the gallop.

Opothleyahola's men formed along Bird Creek and in a nearby ravine, then fell back to a strong position. But Cooper's Creeks attacked on the left and in a vicious hand-to-hand struggle drove back the enemy's flank in confusion, while Confederate Choctaws and Chickasaws did the same on the right. As the Texans moved by detachments around those flanks, the Union Indians had little choice but to abandon their position and fall back. The battle continued for another hour or more, however, as Opothleyahola's men fiercely contested their ground. The outcome was still somewhat in doubt, as both sides fought themselves near to exhaustion, when a fresh detachment of Confederate Creeks came up on Cooper's right, attacked, and finally forced the enemy to retreat, ending the battle. Cooper lost 15 killed and 37 wounded, but his estimate of 500 or more enemy losses is almost certainly an exaggeration.

While Cooper did gain a marginal victory, he was unable to exploit it because of the supply problems that always haunted him and the ever-present threat of dissolution among his Cherokees. As for Opothleyahola, he continued to resist being driven out of the territory, but by the end of the year, after a defeat at Chustenahlah, he was forced to take his followers to Kansas, leaving Indian Territory to Cooper and his Confederate Indian allies. —WCD

Birdsong Ferry, Miss., eng. at. 5 July 1863 Maj. Gen. WILLIAM T. SHERMAN's IX, XIII, and IV corps set out from Oak Ridge, Miss., within hours of the Confederate surrender of VICKSBURG, 4 July. From positions northeast of the city, they marched southeast from Oak Ridge to the Big Black River and Birdsong Ferry, 5 July, 2 divisions of the XVI Corps under Maj. Gen. John G. Parke taking the advance. So began the campaign against Gen. JOSEPH E. JOHNSTON's army at Jackson.

Johnston's advance held the Big Black's east bank at Birdsong Ferry; the west bank was hit by elements of Parke's division after 7 a.m., 5 July, beginning an all-day small-arms fight with Confederates on the east bank. Under fire Federals could not test the Big Black's depth; the ferryboat they had expected to find was scuttled. Ohio, Illinois, and Indiana troops sent scouting parties north and south searching for fords after deploying skirmish companies.

At dark the water at Birdsong was tested and found "swimming deep." A Major Willison of the 103d Illinois and a Pvt. Joseph Weston swam to the ferry, were fired on, and returned, the fire concealing operations to raise the ferryboat. Fords found north and south were also contested. The next day the ferryboat was raised, bridges were constructed at fords above and below, the Confederates retired, and the Federals advanced southeast to their first objective, the Vicksburg & Jackson Railroad. A second skirmish followed on the railroad at Bolton Station, east of Jackson, 8 July. Casualties at Birdsong Ferry were insignificant. —JES

Birney, David Bell. USA b. Huntsville, Ala., 29 May 1825. Though a Southerner, Birney became famous as one of the most ardent enemies of SLAVERY among Union army generals. His father, James G. Birney,
hated Southern slavery so much that he had moved his family North and once ran for president as an antislavery candidate. His brother, WILLIAM, also became a Union general. The outbreak of civil war found David Birney practicing law in Philadelphia; he promptly closed his practice, organized the 23d Pennsylvania Volunteers, dressed them in ZOUAVE uniforms, and marched off to war at their head as colonel 31 Aug. 1861.

USMHI

Birney's antislavery connections resulted in his promotion to brigadier general, 17 Feb. 1862, in the division commanded by the colorful Brig. Gen. PHILIP KEARNY. Although Birney and Kearny became close friends, Birney's political clout aroused jealousy among his older, Regular Army superiors. Twice in 1862, after battles at WILLIAMSBURG and FREDERICKSBURG, Birney was accused of disobeying orders from Regular generals SAMUEL P. HEINTZELMAN and GEORGE G. MEADE. Nevertheless, Birney was exonerated of all charges, and when Kearny was killed at CHANTILLY in 1862, Birney took over his famous division.

Birney had a new, and friendlier, superior officer when Maj. Gen. DANIEL E. SICKLES was given command of the II Corps, to which Birney's division was attached. Sickles was a politician who made no secret of the political influence he had used to obtain his rank, and Birney became the right-hand man of the rollicking officer. At CHANCELLORSVILLE Birney tried to save Sickles' corps from cracking under Confederate attack, an effort that resulted in Birney's promotion to major general. At GETTYSBURG Birney was the first of Sickles' division commanders to open fire against the Confederates attacking the III Corps in the PEACH ORCHARD, and he took command of the corps when Sickles was wounded.

In Mar. 1864 the III Corps was broken up by Gen. ULYSSES S. GRANT, who kept Birney to command the X Corps. In Octo-

ber Birney fell ill and went home to Philadelphia, where he died suddenly 18 Oct., crying deliriously, "Keep your eyes on that flag, boys." —ACG

Birney, William. USA b. Madison Cty., Ala., 28 May 1819. Birney began work as a lawyer in Cincinnati, then spent 5 years in Europe, where he was involved in the French revolution of 1848. In 1853 he returned to establish a newspaper in Philadelphia.

When war broke out, Birney became a captain with the 1st New Jersey Infantry and participated at FIRST BULL RUN. On 27 Sept. 1861 he rose to major with the 4th New Jersey Infantry, with which he served through the CHANCELLORSVILLE CAMPAIGN, becoming a colonel 13 Jan. 1863.

The son of an abolitionist from Alabama and a brother of Union Maj. Gen. DAVID B. BIRNEY, William helped expedite emancipation in Maryland by recruiting slaves into 7 black regiments. In 1863 he became recruiting officer for black troops in that state with a commission as brigadier general, effective 22 May. In Feb. 1864 Birney and his newly raised regiments reported to the commander of the DEPARTMENT OF THE SOUTH at Hilton Head, S.C. Birney's command served poorly in South Carolina but did well in Florida, restoring Union prestige after the defeat at OLUSTEE.

Also serving under Maj. Gen. BENJAMIN F. BUTLER in Virginia, Birney's brigade was joined by more black regiments to form the 3d Division of the X Corps. On 28 Sept. 1864 the new division secretly moved across the James River to surprise the defenders of Richmond. The next day, at Deep Bottom, Birney lost 430 men in the Battle of CHAFFIN'S FARM, where the unsuccessful assault of the men on Fort Gilmer, an almost impregnable position, was especially disastrous.

Birney's division continued to fight on the Richmond line, participating in 2 battles along the DARBYTOWN ROAD. In Dec. 1864 the black regiments of the X and XVIII corps were combined into the all-black XXV Corps under Maj. Gen. GODFREY WEITZEL; Birney's command became the 2d Division and in late March was secretly moved to the Hatcher's Run area of the Petersburg line, where it took part in the last assaults on those defenses. During the APPOMATTOX CAMPAIGN the division followed the army but saw little action.

Birney was brevetted major general 13 Mar. 1865 and left the service in August. In later years he served as U.S. attorney for the District of Columbia, dying at his home in Forest Glen, Md., 14 Aug. 1907. —CMS

bivouac. Civil War armies did not always provide temporary shelter for their men on the move. The 2-man shelter (dog tent) was widely issued in Northern armies but not always carried. In active operations men were expected to bivouac, to sleep in the open. The U.S. Army defined the term in 1861: "When an army passes the night without shelter, except such as can be hastily made of plants, branches, & c., it is said to bivouac." —JES

Blackburn's Ford, Va., eng. at. 18 July 1861 The advance elements of Brig. Gen. IRVIN MCDOWELL's Union troops cautiously entered Centreville about 9 a.m., 18 July. The Federals found no Confederates, only abandoned earthworks, trenches, and a signal tower. Brig. Gen. Daniel Tyler, commanding the Northern troops, ordered a halt, asked for further instructions, and gathered local citizens for information.

Bivouac   LC

Tyler learned that the Confederates had withdrawn during the night to a stone bridge over Bull Run Creek and toward Blackburn's Ford. Directed by McDowell not to bring on an engagement but to observe the roads toward the creek, Tyler sent Col. ISRAEL B. RICHARDSON's brigade south toward the ford; sometime after noon the Northerners found it.

Tyler and Richardson examined the crossing, where the Bull Run bent southward in a loop. From the Union position in a woodland, a cleared field sloped down to the stream's bank, which was heavily covered in underbrush and trees. The 2 officers located a section of a Confederate battery but no infantry in any strength at Blackburn's or Mitchell's Ford farther upstream. Tyler decided to test the Confederate position and strength.

2 Union cannon opened the engagement, which soon escalated into a brief artillery duel. Another Union battery added its firepower, while Richardson sent forward 2 infantry companies as skirmishers. The novice soldiers of the 1st Massachusetts swept down the hillside, shoving aside a few Confederates, who fired a round and pulled back across the creek. The Federals closed on the ford, then suddenly a volley of musketry erupted from the trees. The Northerners took cover but volley after volley sliced into them.

Richardson's men had encountered Col. JAMES LONGSTREET's brigade of 3 Virginia regiments. Some of the Confederates broke at their first taste of battle, but Longstreet steadied them with drawn sword. The fire fight lasted for nearly an hour until the Federals withdrew.

Tyler, however, ordered 2 cannon forward, supported by Richardson's brigade. The Union artillerists unlimbered before the ford and seared the woods with several charges of canister. Confederate volleys quickly silenced one piece and the other withdrew. Tyler, having exceeded McDowell's orders not to bring on an engagement, finally decided to cease his attacks; for one of Richardson's regiments the order came too late.

The 12th New York advanced down the slope only to be met by another galling volley from the Virginians. The New Yorkers dove to the ground and fired lying down. Once more the concealed Southerners had the best of the battle. The

Union regiment began a slow withdrawal that rapidly accelerated into a stampede. Longstreet, now supported by Col. JUBAL A. EARLY's brigade, counterattacked, but the assault quickly dissolved in the confusion of his untrained troops.

For the rest of the action Richardson's brigade clung to the crest of the hill, subjected to artillery and musketry fire from across the stream. Upset, McDowell arrived, ordering Tyler to disengage but remain in position; but after McDowell departed, Tyler again disobeyed orders, withdrawing to Centreville.

The engagement cost few men: Tyler reported losses of 83, while Confederate casualties reached 68. McDowell learned little more than that the Confederates would contest a crossing of Bull Run. For the men engaged, however, it was an initiation into combat.   —JDW

black codes. Passed by Southern politicians in the former Confederate states 1865–66, these codes were meant to regulate the life and labor of newly freed slaves. Constitutional clauses and statutes written into state Reconstruction governments replaced prewar slave codes as a means of racial control. For the postwar South, the codes provided a way of dealing with the problems of freedmen, which the Northern Congress had attempted to do by establishing the FREEDMEN'S BUREAU in Mar. 1865.

The codes varied in severity but basically specified blacks' rights to due process in a court of law; to buy, own, sell, and bequeath land and personal property; to make legally binding contracts, including marriage; to parental rights; and to have their freedom of mobility and personal liberty protected. But legislators denied more rights than they granted by closing certain trades and professions to blacks without special license; prohibiting ownership of weapons; restricting assembly; requiring travel passes and proof of residence; imposing residence restrictions; and establishing a deferential code of behavior toward whites. They also withheld the franchise and excluded blacks from holding political office and serving on juries. Though the old planter class regarded the concessions as liberal, former slaves were given little more status than free blacks had been allowed before the war.

During the same period some Northern state legislatures passed antiblack laws to keep blacks out of the region; nonetheless legislators railed against the Southern black codes as an arrogant, nonpenitent attempt to circumvent the 13TH AMENDMENT and return blacks to some form of slavery. RADICAL REPUBLICANS responded by forcing passage of the 14TH AMENDMENT to guarantee civil rights and impose harsher RECONSTRUCTION measures. Once Republican governments were installed in the Southern states, most of the codes were repealed or modified.   —PLF

Black Hat Brigade. *See* IRON BRIGADE OF THE WEST.

***Black Hawk,* USS.** Formerly a powerful sidewheel steamer, the *Black Hawk* was bought by the Federal government 24 Nov. 1862 at Cairo, Ill., for $36,000. A 260-ft vessel with a 45-ft beam, it was put in commission early in December and its name changed from *New Uncle Sam.*

Rear Adm. DAVID D. PORTER, who commanded the Mississippi Squadron, asked the Navy Department for more vessels, and the *Black Hawk* was one of those sent him. He immediately made it his flagship, taking on board, among other things, his saddle horses; tales of his riding a horse over the gangplank for a gallop ashore became legendary.

Armed with 8 cannon, the ship saw its first action at ARKANSAS POST, 11 Jan. 1863, where it helped bring the affair to a close by shelling the fort with its 2 30-pounder rifled guns fastened to the upper deck. During the following spring, the ship took part in a feigned attack on fortifications along the Yazoo River. When VICKSBURG fell, 4 July 1863, the *Black Hawk* swept up to the levee there and took on board Gen. ULYSSES S. GRANT and other officers.

USMHI

In Mar. 1864 it was one of 7 gunboats assembled with 13 IRONCLADS—the most formidable force ever pulled together in Western waters—for the RED RIVER CAMPAIGN. Its objectives were to advance into Louisiana and Texas as a threat to French troops in Mexico and to open up sugar and cotton lands of the 2 states. But nature did not cooperate. The floods along the river, usually occurring in March, did not develop, and the vessels ran into trouble at the start. They finally got up to Grand Ecore, La., then had to return, bringing the war's last river campaign to a dismal close. The *Black Hawk,* though shot up by Confederate defense batteries, had managed to stay afloat.

On 22 Apr. 1865 the ship burned and sank in the Ohio River 3 mi above Cairo. 2 years later it was raised by a wrecking company and sold at St. Louis; the government received $389.05—one-fourth of the proceeds.   —VCJ

black Republicans. From 1854, when the REPUBLICAN PARTY was founded, Democrats labeled its adherents "black" Republicans to identify them as proponents of black equality. During the 1860 elections Southern Democrats used the term derisively to press their belief that Abraham Lincoln's victory would incite slave rebellions in the South and lead to widespread miscegenation. The image the term conveyed became more hated in the South during RECONSTRUCTION as RADICAL REPUBLICANS forced legislation repugnant to Southerners and installed Northern Republicans or Unionists in the governments of the former Confederate states.   —PLF

black soldiers. When the Civil War broke out, thousands of black men tried to enlist but were turned away by the Lincoln administration, which was influenced by race prejudice and concern that the loyal BORDER STATES would rebel if black soldiers were enlisted. But in 1861 Maj. Gen. BENJAMIN F. BUTLER used fugitive slaves as laborers, as did several other Union commanders; in July 1862 Congress authorized the president to use blacks in the army; and after the EMANCIPATION PROCLAMATION, 1 Jan. 1863, large numbers of black soldiers were recruited in the North and those parts of the South occupied by Union forces, serving in segregated units known as U.S. Colored Troops, mostly commanded by white officers.

Eventually almost 200,000 blacks served in the Union army and navy, about half of whom were freedmen from the South; some performed valuable service as spies and scouts. They fought in 449 engagements in every theater of the war and suffered 35% greater losses than white troops, partly because some Confederate commanders refused to take black prisoners. At FORT PILLOW, Tenn., Gen. Nathan B. Forrest's men massacred more than 100 black soldiers who had surrendered.

While military service became a source of pride for free blacks and former slaves, and sometimes provided opportunity for elementary education, there was also much discrimination. Until 1865 black soldiers were paid less than whites, and many were used exclusively in heavy labor and other duties. White officers humiliated and abused them and only a small number were promoted to officers. By 1865 blacks provided nearly two-thirds of the troops in the Mississippi Valley. Lincoln said that black soldiers had been decisive in bringing the Union victory.

In the Confederacy blacks were used for military labor as well as in agricultural and industrial production. Some blacks supported the Confederate military cause, but many more fled to Union lines whenever possible.   —LG

black troops, Confederacy approves use of. Winter 1864–65 saw the climax of a bitter debate over enlisting slaves in the Confederate army. Pres. JEFFERSON DAVIS, an early advocate of using slaves in any way necessary to win the war, appealed for enlisting blacks as soldiers. His 7 Nov. 1864 presidential message called for radical revision in Southern legal theory—one acknowledging the slave as a person whose military service would lead to gradual compensated emancipation.

Protest flared, some opponents decrying the policy as unconstitutional and insisting it destroyed the basis for Southern resistance to the North. Others feared Europe would interpret the move as weakness and continue to withhold formal recognition of the Confederacy or that the agricultural labor force would be drained. Diehards argued bondage as the blacks' natural state, insisting that arming slaves violated property rights and natural law.

Only militarily hard-pressed Virginia showed signs of softening. Sensing hope, Davis sent a secret envoy to Europe to discuss emancipation in exchange for political recognition and military aid. Word leaked to state leaders, who violently protested arming freed slaves as a "suicidal policy." Compromise seemed impossible.

The 3 Feb. 1865 HAMPTON ROADS CONFERENCE so devastated morale that politicians heeded desperate pleas to deliver every possible resource, including slaves, to the Confederacy, though they still recoiled from emancipation. On 13 Mar. the Confederate Congress passed an act to enlist blacks, though only after the public intervention of Gen. ROBERT E. LEE, who saw no way to stall Federal advances except by enlisting black soldiers.

Grudgingly Southern leaders yielded. Virginia placed its black population at the Confederacy's disposal, still hedging on emancipation; but the War Department insisted that slaves fight as free men. On 15 Mar. Richmond papers carried notices authorizing recruitment of blacks. North Carolina followed, and on 15 Apr. a Georgia paper published an encouraging note: "Negroes are now being enlisted . . . for service in the Confederate army."

But acceptance came too late. Lee had surrendered 6 days earlier.   —PLF

Blaine, James Gillespie. USP b. West Brownsville, Pa., 31 Jan. 1830. Blaine was raised in western Pennsylvania, schooled at Washington College, and, after a period as a schoolteacher and law student, entered the newspaper business in Maine, where he edited the Kennebec *Journal* in 1854 and established himself as a political power. Through his newspaper he successfully urged Maine voters to abandon the Whigs and adopt the infant Republican party, for which in 1856 he served as delegate and secretary to its first national convention. He was appointed chairman of the state Republican committee and functioned as Maine's political "boss" for the next 32 years, serving consecutive terms 1858–63 in the state legislature and as speaker of the house during his last 2 years in office.

His Civil War career began with his 1863 election to the U.S. House of Representatives. Unallied with the Radical Republicans, Blaine, just prior to his election, adopted Abraham Lincoln's term *Unionism,* urging cooperation with WAR DEMOCRATS and others interested in the success of the Union cause. He was a strong supporter of Lincoln, but his conciliatory stance won him enemies on his own side of the aisle.

After the war Blaine urged leniency toward former Confederates and their states. Because he advocated returning the vote to disenfranchised ex-Confederates and giving it to blacks, Radical Republicans charged him with favoring "universal amnesty." This was not so, but he used publicity from the controversy to become prominent on the Congressional Committee on Military Affairs and to form an alliance with future president James A. Garfield.

Blaine's constituents sent him to the Senate in 1876 and in

1881 he became Garfield's secretary of state. In the interim he was involved in a railroad kickback scandal and, though becoming a rich man without visible means of support, denied his guilt. A contender for his party's presidential candidacy many times and in 1884 its standard-bearer against Grover Cleveland, his tag "Blaine, the Liar from the State of Maine" kept him from the highest office. Benjamin Harrison appointed him secretary of state again in 1889, but he retained his reputation as a notoriously bad diplomat and foreign-policy strategist. d. Washington, D.C., 27 Jan. 1893.   —JES

Blair, Austin. war governor b. Caroline, N.Y., 8 Feb. 1818. Blair attended Hamilton and Union colleges, graduating from the latter in 1837, was admitted to the bar 4 years later, then migrated to Jackson, Mich. There he became a Whig, joined the state legislature 1845–49, and helped to secure the abolition of capital punishment.

After leaving the Whigs for the FREE SOIL PARTY, in 1854 Blair helped found the REPUBLICAN PARTY. He was defeated in an 1857 bid for the U.S. Senate on the Republican ticket but was elected governor of Michigan in 1860.

Blair made defiant statements on the secession movement, and Unionist sentiment was

LC

strong in Michigan. But on Pres. Abraham Lincoln's first call for troops, following the fall of FORT SUMTER, Michigan's empty coffers (the result of theft) prevented Blair's immediate dispatch of so much as a company. Typical of his support for Lincoln and enthusiasm for the Union cause, Blair helped raise the funds through donations, formed and equipped units, and had a Michigan regiment inside the Washington city limits ahead of schedule. Throughout the war he strove to keep up the troop quotas of his sparsely populated state. Having (unsuccessfully) promoted black suffrage in his state before the war, he continued to back emancipation measures.

Blair left office Jan. 1865 and continued his political career in the U.S. Congress during RECONSTRUCTION. He was unsuccessful in a second bid for election to the U.S. Senate in 1871, joined the Independent Republican movement, then left Congress in 1873. He died in Jackson 6 Aug. 1894, having served 2 terms as a regent of the University of Michigan.   —JES

Blair, Francis Preston, Jr. USA/USP b. Lexington, Ky., 19 Feb. 1821. From secession to Reconstruction, Frank Blair of Missouri made an unbroken series of major contributions to the Union cause: no man did more to block Missouri's bolt to the Confederacy in 1861; as a U.S. Congressman he battled for President Lincoln's early war programs; and he was a distinguished divisional and corps commander in the FIRST VICKSBURG and ATLANTA campaigns; finally, as a postwar senator, he battled the RADICAL REPUBLICANS in an attempt to bring reconciliation to a shattered nation.

Blair was the son of an adviser to presidents and the brother of MONTGOMERY BLAIR, Lincoln's first postmaster general. He attended the College of New Jersey, took his law degree at Transylvania College in Kentucky, and served briefly as attorney general of New Mexico Territory in 1847. In a trial there he first clashed with military governor STERLING PRICE, who was to be one of Blair's major foes in the fight for Missouri loyalty. As a Missouri congressman in May 1861, Blair teamed with Brig. Gen. NATHANIEL LYON to wrest the St. Louis arsenal from Confederate hands in the Camp Jackson affair.

USMHI

He recruited 7 regiments during summer 1862 and was commissioned a Union brigadier general 7 Aug. By Nov. 1862 he was a major general, leading a division in the Yazoo Expedition and earning plaudits from Maj. Gen. WILLIAM T. SHERMAN for his leadership at CHICKASAW BLUFFS early in the VICKSBURG CAMPAIGN. Blair was commanding the Union line north of Vicksburg when Lt. Gen. JOHN C. PEMBERTON surrendered the city to Maj. Gen. ULYSSES S. GRANT 4 July 1863. At CHATTANOOGA he led the XV Corps, and during Sherman's drive toward Atlanta Blair commanded the XVII Corps in bloody fighting. After Atlanta fell, Blair led his corps in the MARCH TO THE SEA. He was at Goldsborough, N.C., when word came that Gen. ROBERT E. LEE had surrendered.

Both Grant and Sherman, highly critical of most "political" generals, rated Blair one of the most competent military leaders of the war. Blair became the Democratic nominee for vice-president in 1868 and was appointed to the Senate in 1871 to fill an unexpired term. d. St. Louis, 9 July 1875.

—DS

Blair, Francis Preston, Sr. editor b. Abingdon, Va., 12 Apr. 1791. Though Blair never held elected office through the antebellum years, he considerably influenced national politics as a close friend of ANDREW JACKSON and as editor of the Washington *Globe,* a Democratic newspaper powerful 1830–54. Reared in Kentucky, Blair owned slaves but stringently believed the Union took precedence over sectional interests. During the NULLIFICATION Crisis of 1832, he vigorously opposed JOHN C. CALHOUN over STATES RIGHTS, editorializing as he did throughout his career on the sacredness of the Constitution.

Believing his party had betrayed the principles of Jacksonian Democracy with the controversial KANSAS-NEBRASKA ACT, Blair aligned himself with the emerging Republicans. At the Chicago convention in 1860, he threw his support behind ABRAHAM LINCOLN for the presidential nomination and after the election offered advice on the selection of cabinet members. 2 of his sons held influential political positions through the war: Montgomery, as postmaster general, and Francis Preston, Jr., who was a senator from Missouri as well as a brigadier general.

Blair backed Lincoln on emancipation and encouraged his colonization efforts, but disagreed with the president's decision to replace GEORGE B. MCCLELLAN as general-in-chief of the army. Like the combat-shy McClellan, he believed the war should be won with as little bloodshed as possible.

His desire to bring peace spurred him to arrange an unofficial meeting with Pres. JEFFERSON DAVIS, Dec. 1864. Though Lincoln was aware of the visit beforehand, Blair carried no

message from Washington to the Confederate capital. The aged intermediary proposed a truce between the 2 warring governments, to be secured by joint military operations against the monarchy Maximilian had established in Mexico. Theoretically, the shared interest in enforcing Manifest Destiny would draw the seceded states back into the Union or at least restore domestic peace. As a result of his conversations with Davis and subsequent reports to Lincoln, the HAMPTON ROADS CONFERENCE was held 3 Feb. 1865. His effort failed, but the attempt represented Blair's dream of playing a leading role in restoring the Union.

When peace finally came, Blair returned to the Democratic party because he could not coexist with the RADICAL REPUBLICANS. Though not an extraordinarily wealthy man, he did all he could to help ease individual Southerners through their postwar hardships, as he had during the hostilities. He died in Silver Spring, Md., 18 Oct. 1876, still professing faith in Jacksonian Democracy.

—PLF

Blair, Montgomery. USP b. Franklin Cty., Ky., 10 May 1813. Soon after his famous father, FRANCIS P. BLAIR, SR., became Pres. Andrew Jackson's close political adviser and editor of the administration newspaper in Washington, eldest son Montgomery went off to West Point. Emerging a 2d lieutenant, he served briefly in the Seminole War but soon resigned to study law at Kentucky's Transylvania College. In 1837 he moved to St. Louis and entered law practice under the aegis of Sen. Thomas H. Benton. Blair became U.S. district attorney, mayor of St. Louis 1842–43, and judge of common pleas court 1845–49. In 1853 he moved to Maryland and developed an active law practice. By this time his free-soil views on SLAVERY edged him out of the Democratic party, and shortly he was an active Republican. When he argued the case for Dred Scott's freedom before the Supreme Court, he became widely known (*see DRED SCOTT CASE*).

In 1860 he presided at Maryland's Republican state convention and served as a delegate to the Chicago convention that nominated ABRAHAM LINCOLN president. As postmaster general in Lincoln's administration, he argued strongly for holding Federal forts in the South. Although a staunch Lincoln man, he befriended Maj. Gen. GEORGE B. MCCLELLAN and held to be illegal the seizure of Confederate agents JAMES MASON and JOHN SLIDELL. In the Post Office Department he organized postal service to the army, introduced compulsory payment of postage by the sender and free mail delivery in cities, improved mail registry, worked out the postal draft (money-order) system that his successor, WILLIAM DENNISON, put into full effect, and helped convene the Paris International Postal Union convention.

In 1864 RADICAL REPUBLICANS maneuvered him out of the cabinet. On Lincoln's death Blair supported Pres. ANDREW JOHNSON's moderate policy toward the South and deplored disfranchising ex-Confederates and black suffrage. Increasingly at odds with Radicals, he resumed his Democratic allegiance. When beaten in a bid for Congress in 1882, he continued working on a biography of Andrew Jackson until his death in Silver Spring, Md., 27 July 1883.

—DL

Blair's Landing (Pleasant Hill Landing), La., eng. at. 12 April 1864 The engagement occurred during the RED RIVER CAMPAIGN. Following the Battle of PLEASANT HILL, La., 9 April, a detachment of Confederate cavalry under Brig. Gen. THOMAS

GREEN arrived at Pleasant Hill's port. There they discovered several Federal transports and gunboats either grounded or severely damaged. Men of Union Brig. Gen. Thomas Kilby Smith's XVII Corps moved guns from 3 of the transports to shore, where they opened fire on the Confederates. Emboldened by liquor, Green led a cavalry charge against the gunboats. The Federals on board protected themselves behind cotton bales, hay, and sacks of oats. Green was among the first to fall. As many as 300 other Confederate cavalrymen fell, as the USS gunboats *Neosho, Lexington, Hindman,* and *No. 13* poured GRAPE and canister into them. Following the action, all but 5 of the transports were able to proceed upriver.   —NCD

Blakely gun. The Blakely rifled cannon, invented by Capt. Alexander T. Blakely of the British army, was used extensively during the Civil War, primarily in the Southern armies.

Blakely was a recognized pioneer in the banding of cannon, but in England he met difficulties because he lacked his own foundry and had to compete with the designs of William G. A. Armstrong and Sir Joseph Whitworth. Constant experiments with his designs resulted in at least 5 and perhaps as many as 10 distinct types of Blakely guns, firing projectiles 10–470 lb. Externally, Blakelys are difficult to identify, and confirmation of their authenticity must be based on an evaluation of outward configuration, markings, and the distinctive Blakely hookslant rifling.

Blakely guns were used in both field and garrison. The first rifled cannon fired in battle in this country was a 12-pounder Blakely, presented to South Carolina early in 1861 by Charlestonian Charles K. Prioleau. It was mounted on Morris Island and sent its projectiles across 1,250 yd of water against FORT SUMTER with unerring accuracy. The 2 largest guns in the Confederacy were a pair of 12.75 in. Blakelys mounted at Charleston, S.C., in 1863.

Col. E. PORTER ALEXANDER, chief of artillery of the I Corps of the Army of Northern Virginia, considered the 12-pounder Blakely a good muzzle-loading rifle when used with English ammunition but felt the use of Confederate-made shells diminished its accuracy. Alexander also considered the gun too light and its recoil too great for the carriage. His men were constantly splitting trails or otherwise damaging even specially made carriages. Despite these drawbacks, the widespread use of the gun was a tribute to its accuracy.   —LDJ

Blanchard, Albert Gallatin. CSA b. Charlestown, Mass., 10 Sept. 1810. A classmate of Robert E. Lee and Joseph E. Johnston, Blanchard graduated from West Point in 1829, 26th in his class, and served on frontier and recruiting duty as a lieutenant with the 3d Infantry until resigning from the Regular Army Oct. 1840. After settling in New Orleans, Blanchard entered business and taught school. He returned briefly to the army as a captain of Louisiana volunteers during the Mexican War, taking part in the battles at Monterrey and Cuernavaca and in the Siege of Vera Cruz.

Early in 1861 Blanchard left civilian life to enter Confederate service as a colonel of the 1st Louisiana Infantry. In May his regiment was assigned to Brig. Gen. BENJAMIN HUGER's division at Norfolk, Va. Blanchard advanced to brigadier general 21 Sept. 1861, remaining in brigade command through spring 1862, when AMBROSE R. WRIGHT replaced him.

Blanchard did not impress his superiors as an effective commander and was given a series of secondary assignments in

Virginia and North Carolina, usually on conscript or training duty. In Feb. 1863 he was ordered to report to Lt. Gen. E. KIRBY SMITH in Louisiana. Within a few months he was again without a command and did not receive one before the war ended. Blanchard complained of being overlooked by the War Department, though at the time of his correspondence with Confederate Sec. of War JAMES A. SEDDON, Maj. Gen. RICHARD TAYLOR was branding him incompetent.

LC

Blanchard returned to New Orleans to become a surveyor and civil engineer for the city until his death there 21 July 1891.   —PLF

Blazer's Scouts. The purpose of this force, organized by Union Maj. Gen. GEORGE CROOK, was to destroy Confederate Lt. Col. JOHN S. MOSBY's PARTISAN RANGERS operating in Virginia's Loudoun, Prince William, Fauquier, and Fairfax counties. Made up of 100 men outfitted with SPENCER repeating carbines, the force was formed Aug. 1864 and designated the Independent Scouts, though it was informally called Blazer's Scouts, after its commander, Union Capt. Richard Blazer of Ohio.

The unit met with some success against Mosby's men, engaging the Rangers at Myer's Ford, Myerstown, and near Berry's Ferry. But until November conflict was largely limited to running fights and chance encounters.

After a particularly galling encounter with Blazer's men in early November, Mosby determined to bring the issue to a close, dispatching 100 men from his Companies A and B under the command of Maj. A. E. Richards and ordering them to "wipe Blazer out"—which they did 18 Nov. in a second affair at Myerstown.

There Blazer, at the head of 62 men, was lured from a wooded position to an open field, attacked in flank, and forced into fierce hand-to-hand combat. After taking many casualties, the Federal unit began to scatter, ignoring Blazer's efforts to rally it. The Rangers pursued the Scouts through the streets of the village of Myerstown; Blazer himself was overtaken on a road west of the community, clubbed from his horse, and taken prisoner. 29 Scouts escaped death, wounding, or capture and returned to Union lines. The unit was disbanded. Blazer was sent to LIBBY PRISON and not released until late in the war.   —JES

"Bleeding Kansas." With the passage of the KANSAS-NEBRASKA ACT in 1854, Kansas, a pawn in the festering sectional conflict, moved toward internal civil war. For several years Northern abolitionist societies had encouraged settlers to populate the territory in anticipation of a struggle for statehood there between pro-slavery and free-soil factions. With the repeal of the MISSOURI COMPROMISE, the contest exploded into a bloodletting that included the pro-slavery attack on Lawrence 21 May 1856 and, two days later, the massacre at Pottawatomie of 5 pro-slavery men by fanatic abolitionist JOHN BROWN and his sons.

Mob rule, vindictive property destruction, and murder induced Pres. Franklin Pierce to send federal troops to the territory to calm the insurrection and oversee elections, which in the past had been marred by fraud and manipulation. A measure of peace returned to Kansas after the U.S. Congress subjected the controversial pro-slavery Lecompton constitution to a popular vote; Kansans defeated it decisively 2 Aug. 1858. Ultimately 5 constitutions (4 of which were rejected) were drafted before Kansas was admitted to the Union as a free state in 1861. By the time the nation entered the Civil War "Bleeding Kansas" had lost more than 50 men to border warfare over the slavery issue. —PLF

Blenker, Louis. USA b. Worms, Germany, 12 May 1812. One of the largest groups to form volunteer units early in 1861 were newly arrived German immigrants. Prominent among the

early organizers of these men was Louis Blenker, who, like many German immigrant leaders, had led troops in the German revolution of 1848. After the revolution failed, he fled to the U.S. where he went into business in New York City.

In 1861, as colonel, he led the 8th New York to war and by July 1861 his reputation had gained him the command of a German brigade, which, on 21 July at FIRST BULL RUN, repulsed a Confederate cavalry attack in a rearguard action. Blenker was

USMHI/MA

given an appointment as brigadier general 9 Aug. By Oct. 1861 he had gathered enough German regiments for the War Department to organize Blenker's Division.

In Mar. 1862, when most of the army was sent to the Virginia peninsula, Blenker was assigned to the MOUNTAIN DEPARTMENT under Maj. Gen. JOHN C. FRÉMONT. Leaving for western Virginia 6 Apr., Blenker ran into a foot of snow and rain that ruined the health of his men, who had been ordered to leave their tents behind. In addition, confusion followed Blenker's injury in a fall from his horse at Warrenton, and insufficient rations prompted his starving troops to raid farms.

The War Department finally sent Maj. Gen. WILLIAM S. ROSECRANS with orders to find the division and escort it to Frémont. When Rosecrans discovered the troops were demoralized by insufficient food and equipment, he resupplied them and rushed them to Frémont at PETERSBURG 11 May.

After little rest Frémont pushed on with Blenker's exhausted men to catch Maj. Gen. THOMAS J. "STONEWALL" JACKSON in the Shenandoah Valley. On 7 June 1862 Frémont caught up with Jackson at CROSS KEYS, Va., and the next day Blenker's division was repulsed with heavy losses in an attempt to turn the Confederate left flank.

Shortly after this action Blenker was relieved, although there were no charges against him. He saw no more action and was discharged 31 Mar. 1863. He died 31 Oct. of that year at his farm in Rockland Cty., N.Y., from the injuries received in the fall from his horse. —CMS

blockade. 13 Apr. 1861 was an important date in Civil War history: FORT SUMTER fell and, down at Pensacola, Fla., the USS *Sabine* became the first ship to blockade a Southern port.

The *Sabine* was acting on its own; 4 days passed before Pres. Abraham Lincoln issued a proclamation establishing a blockade, specifying that vessels attempting to enter or leave Southern ports would be warned first, then, if further attempts were made, captured and confiscated. Lincoln's action drew ridicule from many sources. England derided the idea of trying to blockade 3,549 mi of coast, a waterfront pierced by 180 openings for commerce—bays, channels, rivers, lagoons, swamps—the largest blockade ever attempted by any nation.

At first it was only a paper blockade—the North had just 3 ships in port—but efforts were tightened rapidly. When the Federal Congress met in December, the navy reported that 136 vessels had been bought, 34 had been repaired and put in commission, and 52 were under construction. Within 6 months 4 squadrons had been organized to guard the coast from Virginia to Texas—2 along the Atlantic and 2 in the Gulf of Mexico. The Mississippi River, with its 5 separate passes, was the hardest stream to blockade.

The effectiveness of the blockade gradually increased, and during 1861 1 out of every 9 vessels was captured in or out of port; by 1862 the rate had increased to 1 out of 7.

FORT FISHER, opening the approach to Wilmington, N.C., was kept busy until mid-Jan. 1865, when it was finally captured, the last port to fall.

Historians generally agree that the blockade, with more than 600 ships, not the force of Union arms, finally brought about the downfall of the Confederacy; 1,504 vessels, valued at more than $30 million, were captured. —VCJ

blockade runners. Beginning early in the war, the blockade-running business was highly profitable and brought a rush of participants, some of whom made millions of dollars while prices soared. Salt worth $6.50 a ton in NASSAU, Bahamas, brought $1,700 in the South, and coffee selling for $249 per ton in Nassau commanded $5,500 Confederate on the Southern market. Freight rates ranged from $300 to $1,000 a ton, and the wages of blockade runners were also high. A successful ship's captain might make as much as $5,000 on a single run, against the prevailing rate of $150 in the merchant service.

All sorts of ploys were used to stop the runners. In England a reward of £30 was offered to anyone who could supply reliable information concerning vessels leaving for blockaded ports. When the North learned blockade-running ships used anthracite coal because it burned without smoke, all shipments of this fuel to foreign ports were banned.

The runners themselves adopted ruses: drums ostensibly filled with fish, for instance, were found to contain kegs of powder. And in time the runners began to use ships built especially for the business: long, low, rakish craft, they were lead-colored, with short masts and convex forecastle decks, and were designed to go through instead of over rough seas.

Runners resorted to a new trick once they were warned, by friendly consuls abroad, of Federal ships waiting to seize them or of new Confederate prohibitions on luxury goods, which took space otherwise available for war materials. Instead of coming directly to Confederate ports, they went to intermediary points, such as Nassau and Bermuda, and there transferred their cargoes to smaller craft that could be sneaked into points along the Southern coast.

The Confederate government itself was forced to go into the business since private enterprise, concentrating on light cargoes that brought the best profit, shied from transporting such heavy items as steel, copper, iron, and munitions of war, all urgently needed by the Confederacy. No blockade runner commanded by an officer of the Confederate Navy was ever captured.

Blockade running was a continuous activity throughout the war, and some ships sneaked into port even after the South had surrendered.   —VCJ

"Bloody Angle," at Spotsylvania, Va.   12 May 1864

On this date, shielded by darkness, fog, and a drenching rain, 4 Union divisions of Maj. Gen. WINFIELD S. HANCOCK's II Corps charged the center of the Confederate line at the apex of the MULE SHOE salient in an attack planned and led by Col. EMORY UPTON. What followed was 20 hours of unrelenting combat, some of the most vicious of the war.

The Federal divisions, in close-packed ranks, stormed over the earthworks, capturing most of the STONEWALL BRIGADE of Maj. Gen. EDWARD JOHNSON's division, then surged deeper into the salient, trying to sever Southern lines. Maj. Gen. JOHN B. GORDON's Confederates, however, stemmed the penetration in a riveting counterattack, and another Southern division bolstered the line while the Union VI Corps poured across the salient's western face. All together, 24 Federal brigades plunged into the few hundred yards of works.

The 2 armies fought murderously throughout the day and into the night. With the lines in some places only a few yards apart and with rain pouring, soldiers tried to save their lives and sanity. The fighting ended after midnight when the Confederates withdrew to a new line along the base.

In a square mile of terrain 12,000 men lay as casualties. One particularly sanguinary area became known as the "Bloody Angle." A Federal soldier described the ordeal as "the most terrible day I have ever lived."   —JDW

"Bloody Lane," at Antietam, Md.   17 Sept. 1862

A farm lane, worn by use, zigzagged from the Hagerstown Pike to the Boonsborough Pike in the center of the Confederate battle at ANTIETAM. As the day's combat shifted southward, this sunken road became the focus of the struggle for 3 hours.

Around noon Union Brig. Gen. WILLIAM H. FRENCH led his division across the open farmlands toward the road. In serried ranks, the Federals advanced, only to be engulfed by a rippling flame of Confederate musketry; regrouping, they came again. The 2 brigades of Alabamians and North Carolinians under Maj. Gen. DANIEL H. HILL turned them back, and a handful of Confederates counterattacked. Smoke covered the ground as Maj. Gen. ISRAEL B. RICHARDSON's Union division of fresh veterans replaced French's bloodied ranks and surged down the hill. The fury intensified but Hill's Confederates, suffering appalling casualties, would not budge. Finally, along the blazing lane a Confederate officer mistakenly withdrew a regiment and the Federals poured in, delivering a raking, enfilading fire. Bodies of Southerners, piled several men deep as they fell, lay in the roadbed. From the carnage there, this road earned a new name: "Bloody Lane."   —JDW

"Bloody Pond," at Shiloh, Tenn.   6 Apr. 1862

This small pond, slightly north of the Peach Orchard, on the Union left, was in the vicinity of heavy fighting on the Battle of SHILOH's first day. Late on 6 Apr., wounded troops of both armies dragged themselves to it, drank its water, and washed their wounds; many died there. Survivors remembered enemies lying side by side, trying to care for themselves. The water was

spattered with battle debris and colored red with blood. The sight of "the bodies of soldiers and horses intermingled with broken gun carriages . . . half-submerged in blood-tinted water" had a profound effect on anyone who saw it. The next day "Bloody Pond" lay in the rear of Union artillery positions, and some care could be tendered to the wounded still hanging on to life there.   —JES

Blountsville, Tenn., eng. at.   22 Sept. 1863

Confederate Maj. Gen. SAMUEL JONES's small force descended on the East Tennessee & Virginia Railroad from the north in mid-Sept. 1863 to counter Union Maj. Gen. AMBROSE E. BURNSIDE's pacification efforts in northeast Tennessee. Jones wanted the railroad for supply lines north to Virginia; Burnside wanted it for communication lines south to Knoxville. The hamlet of Blountsville, just west of the railroad and north of the Watauga River, and Carter's Depot, southeast of Blountsville on the rail line, had been passed back and forth between the enemies for several days. These moves were preliminaries to the KNOXVILLE CAMPAIGN.

On 20 Sept. Jones's troops, holding the village of Zollicoffer, 6 mi west of Blountsville, lured Federals west from the hamlet for a fight. When the skirmishing broke off, the enemy retreated through Blountsville and Carter's Depot, and Confederates occupied both. Jones believed that in days ahead Burnside would try to divert him at Zollicoffer or Blountsville while trying to retake Carter's Depot and secure the railroad. Burnside sent a letter through the lines on 22 Sept. asking that villages near the railroad north of the Watauga be evacuated by 5 p.m. He also wrote Jones that he expected to use artillery on the hamlets; later Jones noted he received the message at 4:30 p.m.

Union Col. John W. Foster led the 2d Cavalry Brigade/4th Division/XXIII Corps, to the banks of the Watauga and skirmished across at 9 a.m. on the 22d, heading north for Blountsville. Confederates commanded by the 1st Tennessee Cavalry's Col. James E. Carter withdrew, fighting to the edge of town. Foster's men stumbled into a prepared Confederate position and 4 cannon, and a 4-hour fight ensued through late afternoon. 3 Union regiments charged the Confederate position near nightfall and pushed them from the town. Foster reported 6 killed, 14 wounded, the capture of 50 Confederates and 1 cannon, and wrote that "the shells of the enemy set fire to the town and a great portion of it was consumed."

Jones forwarded no casualty figures to headquarters but wrote that "the enemy had, in an artillery duel with one of my batteries at Blountsville, fired upon and burned the best part of that village." This began a small controversy over the integrity of Foster's report and Burnside's warning letter. Confederates, too few to man Zollicoffer and Carter's Depot with the enemy between, consolidated at Zollicoffer, and Burnside temporarily took the railroad.   —JES

Blue Springs, Tenn., engs. at.   5, 7, 10 Oct. 1863

Brig. Gen. JOHN S. WILLIAMS' 1,500-man cavalry drove Federal horsemen from Jonesborough, Tenn., 29 Sept., occupied the town, then received word to wait. Ordered southwest from Blountsville by District Commander Maj. Gen. SAMUEL JONES, Williams screened a large troop movement, the last independent attempt to push Maj. Gen. AMBROSE E. BURNSIDE's Federals out of East Tennessee before the KNOXVILLE CAMPAIGN.

Confederate Maj. Gen. ROBERT RANSOM and infantry arrived

in Jonesborough 1 Oct. Williams, given an additional detachment of 200 troops, was instructed to march southwest near Bull's Gap on the East Tennessee & Virginia Railroad and demonstrate strength; then Ransom's troops were to push northwest and retake Cumberland Gap, which Confederates had surrendered to Burnside 9 Sept.

On 3 Oct., 9 mi east-southeast of Bull's Gap, Williams' force collided with Brig. Gen. SAMUEL P. CARTER's Union cavalry at Blue Springs along the railroad. Uncertain of the Confederates' intent, Carter withdrew, Williams deployed his force west of Blue Springs, and the two jostled each other until 5 Oct. With infantry in supporting distance at Bull's Gap, Carter dared an evening attack, skirmished heavily for 2 hours over rolling terrain, broke off the right, and retired west. Meanwhile, Williams received unsettling word from Ransom: Williams had overstepped his advance. Ransom had intended him to move no farther than Greeneville, 8 mi in the rear. Because Williams' operations would cut communication, Ransom also conferred on him command of all remaining troops in East Tennessee.

Anxious for Ransom's success at Cumberland Gap, the brigadier general decided against retiring to Greeneville as ordered, which would have exposed his actual strength and intent. Brig. Gen. ALFRED E. JACKSON, somewhere north, commanded 400 infantry and home guards, the only other Confederates within 80 mi. Williams sent back scouts to find him, then employed ruses to show strength: extra campfires were lighted, and drummers and buglers sounded rolls and calls for large numbers of nonexistent troops.

Carter probed the Confederate front again around the 7th, skirmished, and withdrew; at 10 a.m., 10 Oct., he returned in force. From Bull's Gap, Burnside advanced a Union cavalry brigade, then followed with an infantry division. The cavalry covered the field throughout the day while Williams retired east of Blue Springs, deploying his battle line in front of a ridge and positioning a battery of 4 cannon and a battery of WILLIAMS RAPID-FIRE GUNS in the rear. Federals were reinforced steadily, persistently attacking and extending their lines, forcing Confederates to extend theirs. At 5 p.m. Burnside's infantry division rushed Williams' thin center over undulating and wooded ground. The Confederate right and left folded back, Federals rushed within 250 yd of their rear, then canister and Rapid-Fire Guns opened on them. Burnside's column crumpled, ran for woods on the Confederate left, and dissolved under infantry fire. Survivors retreated as night fell, and Confederates resumed defensive positions.

Williams raced to the Greeneville telegraph to wire Major General Jones about his predicament. There he learned the Cumberland Gap expedition had been canceled; the Blue Springs fight had been unnecessary. Subordinates organized the withdrawal as Brig. Gen. ALFRED E. JACKSON's troops marched into Greeneville. Together the 2 Confederate forces hiked north the way they had come. At daybreak they clashed with Federal cavalry astride the retreat line, then at Rheatown hit a larger force in the afternoon, fighting their way through. Confederates had a last brush with Union cavalry 13 Oct. at BLOUNTSVILLE, then marched north across the Virginia state line to Jones at Abingdon. In the Blue Springs fighting they suffered 216 killed, wounded, and captured; Burnside recorded 100 killed and wounded in the fight and pursuit.

Repercussions from Williams' sacrificial march to Blue Springs are unrecorded, but 4 Nov. the brigadier general requested relief from command, later transferring to

Maj. Gen. JOSEPH WHEELER's cavalry.   —JES

Blunt, James Gillpatrick. USA b. Trenton, Maine, 21 July 1826. Blunt had a colorful early career, serving as a seaman in his youth and earning a medical degree in Ohio, where he practiced medicine before migrating to the Kansas frontier. There he continued his practice and became known as one of the most ardent abolitionist leaders of "BLEEDING KANSAS," assisting JOHN BROWN in helping escaped slaves reach Canada.

USMHI

During the first year of civil war Blunt commanded a cavalry regiment in Brig. Gen. JAMES H. LANE's Kansas Brigade, which was not mustered into Federal service until 8 Apr. 1862, the same day Blunt was promoted to brigadier general. Appointed commander of the DEPARTMENT OF KANSAS 5 May–19 Sept. he then defeated Col. DOUGLAS H. COOPER's Indian troops at Old Fort Wayne, Indian Territory, Oct. 1862. On 29 Nov. he was promoted to major general, subsequently leading the 1st Division/ARMY OF THE FRONTIER in the capture of Van Buren, Ark., and to victories at Cane Hill and PRAIRIE GROVE. Blunt served as commander of the District of the Frontier June–Oct. 1863. On 6 Oct., as he was transferring his headquarters from Fort Scott to Fort Smith, a band of William C. Quantrill's guerrillas attacked the wagon train, massacring 90 of his Federal soldiers, most of them black. Subsequently dismissed from command, he was kept in the army because of his popularity and reassigned by Pres. Abraham Lincoln to recruit blacks along the frontier. Blunt was restored to the field when Confederate Maj. Gen. STERLING PRICE led his final desperate raid to recapture Missouri Sept.– Oct. 1864, and was one of the Federal generals whose troops repulsed him in more than a score of bloody engagements, at last driving Price out of Missouri permanently. In the final year of war, Blunt commanded the District of Upper Arkansas and the District of South Kansas.

Returning to civilian life July 1865, Blunt settled in Leavenworth, Kans., where he resumed practicing medicine. 4 years later, he moved to Washington, D.C., working first as a claims agent, then in a government hospital for the insane. He died in the nation's capital 27 July 1881.   —DS

Bocock, Thomas Stanhope. CSP b. Buckingham Cty., Va., 18 May 1815. Bocock received his early education and prelaw training from his brother Willis. He passed the Virginia state bar after graduating from Hampden-Sydney College in 1838, then entered public life, completing his political apprenticeship in the Virginia General Assembly in 1845. At that time he began a 2-year term as commonwealth attorney for Appomattox County (formerly Buckingham County).

Beginning in 1847 Bocock was elected 7 times to the U.S. House of Representatives as a Democrat; generally a political moderate, he voted in favor of the KANSAS-NEBRASKA ACT and the Lecompton constitution. When Virginia seceded Apr. 1861, Bocock resigned his House seat to represent the state in the Provisional Confederate Congress and subsequently in both regular sessions. Acknowledging his reputation as a skilled parliamentarian, his colleagues unanimously elected him Speaker of the House 18 Feb. 1862. He held the position until the government dissolved, which limited his participation in debate but did not affect his pro-administration bias. On several occasions he defended Pres. JEFFERSON DAVIS against tirades from radicals LOUIS T. WIGFALL and HENRY S. FOOTE and broke with the president only on the issue of arming slaves and when taxation and impressment fell heavily on his constituents.

When dissatisfaction with Davis' administration reached one of its recurring peaks Jan. 1865, the Virginia delegation assigned Bocock to recommend a cabinet reorganization in order to restore confidence among the Confederate public. Davis characteristically responded to the advice as "a warning if not a threat" and rebuffed the Virginians for questioning his executive prerogatives.

As a moderate conservative in the postwar years Bocock assumed leadership in the "readjuster movement," advancing compromise between repudiation of the Confederate debt and dollar-for-dollar repayment. After nurturing a thriving law practice, his popularity as a speaker, and a life-long love for books, he died at his estate, "Wildway," near Appomattox Court House, 5 Aug. 1891, leaving one of the largest private libraries in Virginia.   —PLF

Boggs, William Robertson. CSA b. Augusta, Ga., 18 Mar. 1829. Boggs was, above all, an engineer. Attending Augusta Academy and eventually winning an appointment to the U.S. Military Academy at West Point, he graduated 4th in his class of 1853 and was brev- etted 2d lieutenant in the Corps of Topographical Engineers, transferring to ordnance the fol- lowing year. In 1856 he won a promotion to 1st lieutenant of ordnance in Louisiana.

Boggs served with Juan Cor- tina's Mexican marauders in combat near Fort Broome in 1859 and Feb. 1861 accepted an appointment as captain in the Confederate Corps of Engi- neers, transferring immediately   *TU*
to Charleston, S.C., under Provisional Army Brig. Gen. P.G.T. BEAUREGARD. He then joined Maj. Gen. BRAXTON BRAGG in Pensacola, Fla., commanding all engineers and artillery there. His efforts as an army engineer were praised by both Bragg and Beauregard, and in 1862 he was assigned as chief engineer of the state of Georgia.

After duty under Maj. Gen. JOHN C. PEMBERTON in Georgia and Florida, Boggs was promoted brigadier general, 4 Nov. 1862, and served as Gen. E. KIRBY SMITH's chief of staff in the TRANS-MISSISSIPPI DEPARTMENT through the final months of the war.

In his postwar years Boggs was an architect, a railroad con- struction engineer, and a civil and mining engineer in St. Louis, Mo., until 1875. He ended his professional career as a me- chanics and drawing professor at Virginia Polytechnic Institute, dying in retirement at his home in Winston-Salem, N.C., 11 Sept. 1911.   —FLS

Bohemian Brigade. *See* WAR CORRESPONDENTS.

Bonham, Milledge Luke. CSA/war governor b. Red Bank, S.C., 25 Dec. 1813. Graduating from South Carolina College in 1834, Bonham practiced law, served as adjutant of the South Carolina Brigade in the Seminole War, and 1840–44 represented his district in the state legislature. During the Mexican War he was lieutenant colonel of the 12th U.S. Infantry and by the start of the Civil War was both a U.S. congressman and a major general of militia.

USMHI

Shortly before the conflict began, Bonham commanded all troops in Charleston harbor. In the weeks prior to FIRST BULL RUN, as a Confederate brigadier, he controlled a force in advance of Brig. Gen. P.G.T. BEAURE- GARD's position near Manassas Junction, Va. On 21 July 1861 he held the center of Beauregard's line during the war's first major battle.

After the fight, Bonham quarreled with the professional sol- diers in Confederate ranks, which was indicative of the strengths and weaknesses of the typical political general. Though brave and energetic, he conspired with other officials, including South Carolina Gov. FRANCIS PICKENS, against peers and superiors. One of his aides characterized him as "too excitable & dictatorial," the victim of ambition and an uncon- trollable temper.

In Jan. 1862 Bonham resigned his commission in a dispute over seniority and became a Confederate congressman, in which role he strove to pass legislation giving states greater power over military matters such as CONSCRIPTION. That De- cember, elected governor of South Carolina, he continued to seek expanded STATES RIGHTS and to battle Pres. JEFFERSON DAVIS, whose administration he distrusted. Occasionally he sided with the government—for example, over the tightening of draft exemptions for plantation overseers—but more often fought Davis, especially the president's policy of confiscating state supplies for army use.

In other matters, Bonham moved swiftly against disaffected portions of his state, especially hill-country districts where des- erters congregated; impressed thousands of slaves for labor on coastal defenses, penalizing recalcitrant owners; tried (with mixed success) to raise a permanent state volunteer force; and favored sending South Carolina's militia to aid neighboring states under invasion, such as Georgia.

Replaced in office Dec. 1864 by ANDREW G. MAGRATH, Bon- ham spent the last months of the war as a brigadier general of cavalry. In postbellum years he was a lawyer, planter, insur- ance agent, legislator, and state railroad commissioner. d. Sul- phur Springs, N.C., 27 Aug. 1890.   —EGL

"Bonnie Blue Flag, The." Popular as an expression of Confederate nationalism and sung often in the first Confeder- ate capital at Montgomery, Ala., "The Bonnie Blue Flag" was a patriotic tune written by Harry McCarthy, who had immi- grated from England in 1845 at 15 and toured the South prior to the Civil War as a variety entertainer called the "Arkansas Comedian." He penned "The Bonnie Blue Flag" in spring 1861 and included it in his act for the first time at a Jackson,

Miss., performance. With the author's encouragement it rivaled "DIXIE" for a time as the Confederate standard. By the end of the war, 11 editions of the song had been printed.

The lyrics noted how 1 star on the flag (South Carolina) had grown to 11 and in some versions expressed the hope Missouri would join the Confederacy and add a 12th star. Upon Federal occupation of New Orleans, Union authorities tried to keep the song from being printed.

"The Bonnie Blue Flag" lost some of its appeal late in the war when McCarthy abandoned the Confederate cause and "skedaddled" to Philadelphia.   —JES

Booneville, Miss., action at.   1 July 1862   Following the Battle of SHILOH, Apr. 1862, and before the Confederate evacuation of CORINTH that October, Southern forces concentrated at Tupelo, about 50 mi south of Booneville. To protect the movement of Confederate infantry to that city, Brig. Gen. JAMES R. CHALMERS feinted, clashing with 2 cavalry regiments under Union Col. PHILIP H. SHERIDAN a few miles west of Booneville.

When Sheridan's advance guard made contact, he immediately supported it, sending 4 companies to hit the Confederate rear. Stubborn but indecisive fighting continued all day, until Chalmers' superior force retired unmolested. At 5 p.m. Sheridan requested a battery of artillery, with which he thought he "might then be able to follow up the enemy," but at 9:30 the next morning he reported that "the enemy have 'skedaddled.' "

Sheridan then wrote a report that made him look masterly, resulting in his first publicity. His men had fought doggedly, in hand-to-hand combat, "in some cases using the butts of their guns," and this "so much disconcerted the enemy that they commenced falling back, leaving a large number of their dead and wounded officers and men on the field. . . ." Sheridan reported his losses at 1 killed, 24 wounded, and 16 missing, and he asserted that "the loss of the enemy must have been severe," later estimating the number of dead Confederates at 65.

Maj. Gen. WILLIAM S. ROSECRANS immediately recommended that "Sheridan ought to be made a brigadier. *He* would not be a stampeding general!" Brig. Gen. Alexander S. Asboth telegraphed to Washington that "he is worth his weight in gold," while Brig. Gen. GORDON GRANGER praised "the excellent management of the troops by Col. Sheridan. . . ." 10 weeks later Sheridan got the promotion, backdated to the day of the fighting at Booneville.

No official Confederate report of the affair survived, and veterans later claimed that no Southerners had been killed and only 1 was wounded. In 1916 Chalmers' aide-de-camp wrote that "Napoleon, in defining history, said it was 'fable agreed upon.' Apply that . . . to Sheridan's report of this insignificant skirmish . . . and we realize how much fiction there is in recorded incidents of the War." Apparently Chalmers never contested Sheridan's account because of the former's postwar Republican political aspirations. Whatever the truth, the encounter gave the Union one of its most relentless and effective cavalry generals.   —HH

Booth, John Wilkes.   actor   b. Bel Air, Md., 26 Apr. 1838. At 17 Booth debuted at Baltimore's St. Charles Theater and until the Civil War grew in skill as an actor while touring the South, Midwest, and Northwest. During this period his naïve outlook on secession and slavery grew into a monomania in

which he saw the South as an oppressed nation. While other Southerners to some degree shared this view, they found Booth's advocacy strange, violent, and frightening.

LC

As a member of Virginia's Richmond Grays, in 1859 Booth was called to duty during JOHN BROWN'S HARPERS FERRY RAID and was present at Brown's hanging.

In the next few years Booth received the best reviews of his career, but Confederate military reverses during the war upset him and those close to him were concerned for his emotional health. In 1864 Booth suddenly stopped acting, made several visits to Washington, D.C., and formulated a plan to kidnap Pres. ABRAHAM LINCOLN.

Booth began frequenting the Washington boardinghouse of widow MARY SURRATT and her son John, a Confederate agent. The actor recruited John and several others for his plot to ambush the president's coach on Washington's 7th St. extension, while Lincoln made one of his frequent visits to the Soldiers' Home outside the city. Booth planned to take Lincoln south and ransom him for the release of thousands of Confederate prisoners of war, but an attempt on 17 Mar. 1865 failed.

The rest of Booth's story is well known. By 14 Apr., after the surrender of the Army of Northern Virginia, he had revived his gang for a different purpose. That evening he entered FORD'S THEATER, shot Lincoln, who was attending a play, then broke his left leg during his escape. On 26 Apr., in a burning tobacco shed on the Virginia farm of Richard Garrett, Booth was shot while surrounded by Federal troops. Exactly what he had hoped to gain for the Southern cause by Lincoln's murder has never really been understood.   —JES

border states.   The Lincoln administration regarded Delaware, Maryland, Kentucky, and Missouri as border states, critical because of their geographical positions and questionable in loyalty because of their strong ties to both South and North. Slavery existed in all 4 states, though its importance had diminished in Delaware and Maryland as their prewar economies became increasingly interwoven with the North's.

DELAWARE rejected an invitation to join the Confederacy early in 1861, and through the war remained loyal to the North, mobilizing its industries to provide supplies for the Union Army; despite some Southern sentiments, it never seriously threatened to leave the Union.

MARYLANDers were much more divided in their sympathies, being distinctly Southern in character and attached to the South by strong blood ties. They resented radical secessionists and abolitionists alike as the cause of hostilities, urging recognition of the Confederacy. The first blood was spilled during the BALTIMORE RIOTS Mar. 1861, and though the state contributed substantially to the war effort with men and matériel, the Federal government garrisoned troops in the state as a precautionary measure.

Believing KENTUCKY to be a buffer zone, Gov. BERIAH MAGOFFIN refused the call for troops and formally declared the state's neutrality. But the attempt proved futile: both Union and Confederate recruiters operated in the state, with Kentuckians serving on both sides. When Confederate troops moved into western Kentucky Sept. 1861, and Brig. Gen. U.S. Grant occupied Paducah, the legislature officially endorsed the Union. Pro-South Magoffin established a provisional government at Russellville, ratified the Confederate Constitution, and Kentucky was admitted to the Confederacy in December. The state, like Missouri, suffered the tragedy of a war that pitted father against son, brother against brother.

MISSOURI attempted neutrality after delegates to a secession convention in Feb. 1861 refused to secede, but Federal invasion in May pushed many Unionists into the Confederate camp. As in Kentucky, pro-Union and pro-Confederate governments were established, the latter run in exile by Gov. CLAIBORNE F. JACKSON. Missouri became a Confederate state Nov. 1861. Its thriving prewar economy was devastated, its people terrorized by brutal guerrilla warfare.

The border states represented a serious dilemma for President Lincoln. Convinced they were the key to victory, he could not afford to alienate them with his emancipation policies, thus incurred the scorn of Radicals by failing to abolish border-state slavery until the 13TH AMENDMENT, passed in 1865. And in the Western border states Federal troops had to be kept from the front to hold the occupied territory from Confederate invaders. Soldiers also policed the polls to protect loyal Unionists during wartime elections. Though the border states remained pro-Union, even severely divided Kentucky and Missouri, the effort to nurture their loyalty in the face of bitter internal struggles weighed heavily on Lincoln's overall plan to win the war.
—PLF

Bormann fuse. With a 5-second limit for use with smoothbore cannon shells, this simple time fuse was developed before the war by a Belgian captain named Bormann, was used frequently by both Union and Confederate artillerists, and was considered 75% effective.

The top of the fuse looked like a crude watch face and was marked in quarter-seconds. The base was a threaded cylinder that screwed in the nose of a shell. A small square hole in the watch face allowed a key to be inserted and used to tighten the fuse in the shell. The fuse itself was made entirely of pewter or some other soft white metal.

The interior of the top of the fuse was a hollow ring filled with powder that sat beneath the thin soft surface of the watch face. The cylindrical lower portion was hollow, filled with powder, and sealed at the bottom with a very thin plate. After an artilleryman screwed and tightened the fuse into the shell, he used a knife to cut or puncture the top at the point showing the number of seconds desired. When his cannon was fired, flame from the discharge would hit the hole he had made, burn powder in the interior ring for the number of seconds he desired, then set off the powder in the cylinder fixed in the shell's nose. Exploding powder in the cylinder blew off the thin bottom plate and set off the bursting charge inside the shell.
—JES

Boudinot, Elias Cornelius. CSP b. in the Cherokee Nation near present-day Rome, Ga., 1 Aug. 1835. Boudinot, an accomplished Indian lawyer, represented the Cherokee Nation as territorial delegate in the First and Second Confederate Congresses. He was raised by an aunt in Manchester, Vt., where his Connecticut-born mother had sent him to live when his father was murdered by political enemies in 1839. Searching

LC

for a career, Boudinot tried engineering for an Ohio railroad but quit after a year and moved to Fayetteville, Ark., where he read law, passed the state bar in 1856, and established a thriving practice.

Over the next few years he built a reputation as a forceful speaker and local politician, going to Little Rock in 1860 as chairman of the Democratic State Central Committee. The Arkansas secession convention elected him its secretary in 1861. After the state seceded 6 May, Boudinot traveled into Indian Territory to help his uncle, STAND WATIE, a Cherokee chief, organize a Cherokee regiment for the Confederacy, and served briefly as its lieutenant colonel. The Cherokees then elected him to the Confederate Congress.

There was debate in Richmond over whether his credentials would be accepted, but under recent treaty terms the representatives ruled his election constitutional. Boudinot took his seat 9 Oct. 1862 and was active on the Cherokees' behalf throughout 1863. Speaker of the House THOMAS S. BOCOCK appointed him to the Indian Affairs Committee 10 Dec. 1863, permitting him to introduce but not vote on measures for the Indians.

Boudinot's motives were questioned during his 2 terms in office. While he agitated to procure food and supplies for Indian refugees suffering pitifully because of the war, he also allied himself with the unscrupulous Brig. Gen. DOUGLAS H. COOPER, a former Indian agent who saw the war as a means of extending his hold over the tribes. The two conspired to secure for Cooper a brigadier general's rank with full military jurisdiction over Indian Territory, thus undermining Confederate departmental commands. Apparently Boudinot was also involved in an unsuccessful shady proposal concerning a military land-grant system that would have opened the territory to white settlers in violation of the Cherokee-Confederate treaty.

After the Confederates were defeated, Boudinot was prominent in the negotiating to restore peace between the Cherokees and the Federal government. Many tribal members resented his efforts to promote land ownership in severalty but most respected his efforts to press their claims in Washington, D.C.

In 1885 he married, and the couple settled in Fort Smith, Ark., where Boudinot died 27 Sept. 1890.   —PLF

bounties. Begun in part as an expression of citizens' gratitude to soldiers for their wartime service, the bounty system, a program of monetary incentive to attract recruits, was quickly riddled with corruption.

While the South also offered bounties, the system flourished in the North, particularly in seaboard cities crowded with immigrants. Bounties were offered to encourage ENLISTMENT since CONSCRIPTION was unpopular, and local governments added monetary incentives to attract enough volunteers to meet their quotas. Amounts varied with each locale but had to be high enough to draw men who could easily find employment at high wartime salaries. In 1863 New York County offered $677 to new recruits ($777 to veterans) and some rural Midwestern counties offered as much as $1,500 for a 3-year enlistment—

tempting figures to privates earning $11–$16 a month.

Unscrupulous men turned the system into a business, sometimes operating as organized rings: they enlisted, collected the bounty, deserted at the first opportunity, and enlisted again in another district under a different name. Bounty-jumping led to a vicious brokerage trade in which opportunists known as "crimps" or "runners" supplied for a price recruits of questionable character or with physical disabilities. Scores of them ended up deserters.

Poor administration and the ease of getting lost in a big country made detecting bounty jumpers difficult, but those discovered were imprisoned or marched to the front lines as prisoners. One convicted offender admitted to having jumped 32 times before being caught.

The cost of administering the bounty system was high. Throughout the war nearly $600 million was paid, half by the Federal government, half by state and local governments. Besides the expense of the bounty, each recruit received full military gear, adding $300 in equipment costs for every bounty jumper that had to be tracked down.

To an extent bounties did accomplish their purpose, but never enough to eliminate the draft or counter the resentment of soldiers and their families over the system's injustices.
—PLF

Boutwell, George Sewall. USP b. Brookline, Mass., 28 Jan. 1818. In his teens Boutwell contributed to the support of his family by working as a mercantile clerk. Though his schooling was limited, to advance himself he left his home in Lunenburg, Mass., to work in a store in Groton. There he began a program of self-education and wrote political articles for newspapers.

Boutwell was an antislavery Democrat in the Massachusetts state legislature, where his humble beginnings and acumen in journalism helped him gain popularity with the FREE SOIL PARTY and much of the liberal Massachusetts public. 7 terms in the state house and a Free Soil– Democratic coalition won him the governorship in 1851.

His part in the Civil War was played out in the halls of the Federal bureaucracy and Congress.

Embracing the young REPUBLICAN PARTY, Boutwell won a Federal appointment on ABRAHAM LINCOLN's election to the presidency: on 17 July 1862 he was made commissioner of internal revenue. Boutwell invented an internal revenue service (not the one known today) and wrote *A Manual of the Direct and Excise Tax System of the United States* (1863). He was one of the more practical men among the RADICAL REPUBLICANS then beginning to influence national government and, along with Treasury Sec. SALMON P. CHASE, knew Radical war aims would never be fully realized without adequate financing.

His success in upholding this position won him recognition and election to Congress from Massachusetts in 1863. In the House of Representatives he worked with the Radical wing of his party for war and RECONSTRUCTION legislation that was punitive to former slave states slowly being brought back under Federal control. At the end of the war, a member of the Joint Committee on Reconstruction, he opposed Pres. ANDREW JOHNSON over postwar policy toward the South.

Boutwell's long postbellum career was memorable for his part in Johnson's impeachment hearings (where he was one of 7 managers of the prosecution's case); his tenure as Pres. ULYSSES S. GRANT's secretary of the treasury, Mar. 1869–Mar. 1873; his term as senator from Massachusetts, 1873–77; his revision and codification of U.S. statutes; and his divorce from the Republican party in 1898 over its position on annexation of the Philippine Islands. When he died in Washington, D.C., 27 Feb. 1905, he was president of the Anti-Imperialist League, an organization opposed to the U.S. handling of recent Spanish territorial gains.
—JES

Bowen, John Stevens. CSA b. Savannah, Ga., 30 Oct. 1830, Bowen received his early education in Milledgeville, Ga., then graduated 13th in the U.S. Military Academy class of 1853. He was assigned to the cavalry school at Carlisle, Pa., as a brevet 2d lieutenant in the Mounted Rifles before serving on frontier duty. In May 1856, less than 2 years after being commissioned 2d lieutenant, Bowen resigned from the army to establish himself as an architect in St. Louis, Mo.

At the outbreak of civil war he held rank as captain in the Missouri State Militia, with an appointment as chief of staff to Brig. Gen. DANIEL M. FROST. Bowen was among the Missouri recruits taken prisoner May 1861 when Brig. Gen. NATHANIEL LYON seized Camp Jackson. On his release Bowen organized the 1st Missouri Infantry and was elected colonel of the unit 11 June 1861. The Confederate War Department promoted him to brigadier general as of 14 Mar. 1862, following a brief tour of duty under Maj. Gen. LEONIDAS POLK at Columbus, Ky. He then fought at SHILOH attached to Maj. Gen. JOHN C. BRECKINRIDGE's command. Though wounded in the battle, Bowen returned to the field in time to participate in all the battles leading to the Siege of VICKSBURG. His divisions valiantly but unsuccessfully opposed Maj. Gen. JOHN A. MCCLERNAND at PORT GIBSON 1 May 1863, and in recognition of his gallant service, Bowen was advanced to major general to rank from 25 May.

Maj. Gen. ULYSSES S. GRANT credited Bowen with influencing his commanding officer, Lt. Gen. JOHN C. PEMBERTON, to surrender the Confederate army besieged at Vicksburg. The Northern-born Pemberton sent Bowen to Grant with an armistice proposal 3 July, and Bowen returned carrying Grant's terms stipulating unconditional surrender. Along with the remnants of Pemberton's army Bowen was paroled, but he died 13 July on a farm near Raymond, Miss., the result of severe dysentery contracted during the siege. Though he was initially buried on the property, in July 1887 his remains were reinterred in the Confederate Cemetery at Vicksburg.   —PLF

Bowie knife. The era of the Bowie knife coincided with the most sanguinary period of 19th-century American history. Designed for close combat, the Bowie gained notoriety far exceeding its actual use. Numerous manufacturers and black-smiths made their own versions of this popular weapon, resulting in a potpourri of sizes and shapes of knives carrying the name *Bowie.*

The fame of the knife began with a deadly brawl involving Texas frontiersman Jim Bowie, but his brother, Rezin, was responsible for the development of the weapon. Both brothers were wealthy planters in Louisiana. Although no one knows the exact dimensions of the first Bowie, Rezin loosely patterned the knife after a Spanish dagger. The blade was 5–8 in. long and shaped like an elongated triangle. The blade edge was sharpened, as was a short section of the back edge near the point for cutting on the backswing.

Jim Bowie's knife first received national attention following a backwoods duel in which he served as a second. Apparently, the gentleman's code of ethics was cast aside and a free-for-all ensued, causing several deaths. Bowie was both shot and cut up, but after the newspaper embellished the story, he became a national celebrity, and copies of his knife appeared across the country.

The period between the Mexican and Civil wars marked the heyday of the Bowie knife. With the outbreak of fighting in 1861 the Bowie became a badge of ferocity, particularly among the Confederates. Although the knives were not required by regulations, soldiers in the North and South carried them. There is no doubt they were used in combat, yet the Bowie served more often as a camp implement for cutting wood and cooking.

The most common Bowie of the war was the D-guard style, which, differing considerably from the original, resembled a cutlass or butcher knife more than a fighting knife. Many of these cumbersome weapons were fashioned from worn-out files and wagon springs. Equipped with a 12–18-in. blade, clipped point, and rectangular iron or brass handguard, the D-guard frequently appeared in period photographs. —MJO'D

Boyd, Belle. spy b. Martinsburg, Va., 9 May 1843. French war correspondents called her "La Belle Rebelle"; New York newspapers labeled her "That Secesh Cleopatra." Vivacious, outspoken Belle Boyd basked in the attention. Her career as a Confederate spy began soon after the war broke out, and she became the most colorful and most famous of Southern agents.

Belle had a knack for spying, using her keen eyes and her charms to coax military secrets from Union officers. She seemed to thrive on dramatic night rides to pass intelligence on to Gens. THOMAS J. "STONE-WALL" JACKSON and J.E.B. STUART, recklessly neglecting to disguise her handwriting or cipher her messages until a sharp reprimand from Union Brig. Gen. JAMES SHIELDS, who suspected her activities, frightened Belle into more discretion. From Port Royal, Va., she once rode 30 mi in one night to report a major offensive planned by Shields, in command there, and returned before daylight to keep Federals from discovering her absence.

LC

Even imprisonment did not daunt the South's sauciest agent.

By the time she turned 21, Belle had been imprisoned twice, reported about 30 times, and arrested 6 or 7. During her stay in Washington, D.C.'s OLD CAPITOL PRISON she managed to carry out espionage by putting messages in India rubber balls and tossing them through the bars on the window to an accomplice known to her only as "C.H." Twice union authorities sent Belle back behind Confederate lines with warnings to stay there. In 1863, she accepted a mission to carry diplomatic dispatches to England for Pres. JEFFERSON DAVIS.

Despite her popularity, not even Belle's staunch patriotism could compensate for behavior that scandalized well-bred Confederate ladies. She liked to travel alone, striking up acquaintances with soldiers whether they wore blue or gray, and visiting officers in their tents, leaving herself open to claims of fraternizing with the enemy.

When the war ended, Belle turned actress, a role suited to her flamboyant personality, and lectured audiences on her wartime escapades. In 1865 she published a dramatic account of her exploits, *Belle Boyd in Camp and Prison.* Wherever she traveled, North or South, people loved "La Belle Rebelle," the lady who was the Confederacy's most notorious spy. Boyd died from a heart attack in Kilbourne, Wis., 11 June 1900.

—PLF

Boydton Plank Road, Va., Battle of. 5–7 Feb. 1865
See HATCHER'S RUN, VA., BATTLE OF.

Boydton Plank Road, Va., eng. at. 27 Oct. 1864 *See* BURGESS' MILL, VA., ENG. AT.

Brady, Mathew. photographer b. Warren Cty., N.Y., about 1823. Early in life, Brady, pioneer photographer of the Civil War, became an accomplished practitioner of the new art of the daguerreotype. By the 1850s he was the most fashionable photographer in the country, and in his portrait studios in New York and Washington his camera recorded the famous personages of the day.

USMHI

With the outbreak of war in 1861 Brady, clad in linen duster and straw hat, set off with camera and darkroom wagon following Brig. Gen. IRVIN MCDO-WELL's Union army marching on Richmond. "I felt I had to go," he said later. "A spirit in my feet said 'go' and I went." Caught up in the Federal rout at FIRST BULL RUN, he managed to salvage the plates he had exposed on the battlefield. After that, with a staff of field photographers including TIMOTHY O'SULLIVAN and ALEXANDER GARDNER, he "covered" the operations of the Union armies throughout the war, himself coming under fire at Fredericksburg and Petersburg.

Because of the time exposures required to photograph an image on wet collodion glass plates, action pictures could not be taken; instead, action sketches were made by newspaper artists. The cameras were cumbersome and the plates had to be developed immediately after exposure, in the confines of a darkroom, which, in the field, was outfitted in the wagon in which the photographer traveled.

After the war Brady added to his collection of war pictures, and in 1875, financially ruined by his efforts, he sold this historic collection of 5,712 negatives to the U.S. government for $25,000. Plagued by illness and near-poverty in his later years, Brady died in a charity hospital in New York City 16 Jan. 1896.

Today the Brady Collection, preserved in the Library of Congress, is one of this country's national treasures. —FR

Bragg, Braxton. CSA b. Warrenton, N.C., 22 Mar. 1817. Graduated 5th in the West Point class of 1837, Bragg served in the Mexican War and rose to lieutenant colonel before leaving the army in 1856 to become a Louisiana planter. In Mar. 1861, after being appointed a brigadier general in the Confederate service, he took command of the Pensacola-Mobile area. A year later, as a major general, he joined Gen. ALBERT SIDNEY JOHNSTON's army and commanded a corps at the Battle of SHILOH and during the Siege of CORINTH. In June 1862 Pres. Jefferson Davis, a friend, raised Bragg's rank to full general and placed him in command of the Army of Tennessee.

USMHI

In late summer 1862 Bragg skillfully outflanked Union forces in Tennessee and invaded Kentucky, but a superior Federal army forced him back to Tennessee following the standoff at the Battle of PERRYVILLE 8 Oct. On 31 Dec. 1862 and 2 Jan. 1863 he attacked Maj. Gen. WILLIAM S. ROSECRANS' army at STONE'S RIVER and after initial success was heavily defeated. Early in Sept. 1863 Rosecrans maneuvered him out of CHATTANOOGA; Bragg counterattacked at CHICKAMAUGA 12–20 Sept. and drove the Federals back into the city. His failure to follow up this victory and his personal unpopularity caused most of Davis' generals to urge the president in vain to relieve Bragg of command. On 25 Nov. Bragg's army suffered a humiliating rout at MISSIONARY RIDGE, and shortly thereafter he resigned his command.

Davis sought to ease Bragg's chagrin by making him chief of staff. In Mar. 1865, after ROBERT E. LEE became commanding general of the Confederate army, Bragg commanded a division in Gen. JOSEPH E. JOHNSTON's Army of Tennessee and participated in the Battle of BENTONVILLE.

Bragg displayed talent as an organizer and strategist, qualities negated by serious defects of personality and intellect. The story of his military operations is a dismal one of blunders, wasted opportunities, useless slaughters, and ultimate disaster. d. Galveston, Tex., 27 Sept. 1876. —AC

Bragg, Thomas. CSP b. Warrenton, N.C., 9 Nov. 1810. Bragg's reserved demeanor contrasted sharply with the abrasive personality of his younger brother, Confederate Gen. BRAXTON BRAGG. Aloofness and loyalty to Jeffersonian Democracy in a Whig county delayed Bragg's entry into politics but gave him time to build a reputation as a diligent, highly respected lawyer. He won his first elected office as a candidate for county attorney; followed with a term in the state legisla-

ture, 1842–43; attended the Democratic national convention 3 times as a delegate, 1844, 1848, and 1852; and served 2 terms as governor, 1850–58, encouraging internal improvements and the expansion of North Carolina's railroads.

Politically conservative, Bragg urged other Southern leaders to be cautious before severing the Union. He had been serving as a U.S. senator for 2 years when the secession crisis began, and though convinced the Southern states had just cause, he believed secession impractical. When the time came to choose sides, Bragg resigned his seat; honor, the reluctant secessionist recorded in his diary, had inspired the Southerners to resign so quickly after ABRAHAM LINCOLN's election. The Senate formally expelled him 11 July 1861.

Pres. JEFFERSON DAVIS appointed Bragg Confederate attorney general in November. Dissatisfied with his role in the CONFEDERATE CABINET, he ended his service a few months later, resigning April 1862. In his diary Bragg expressed disappointment that Davis sought his counsel so infrequently. Bragg returned to North Carolina determined to mediate between the state and central governments and deserves considerable credit for ensuring Gov. ZEBULON B. VANCE's loyalty to Richmond.

Once the war ended, Bragg resumed his law practice in Raleigh and became active in rebuilding the state government under RECONSTRUCTION. Though not a great politician, he was a reliable, pragmatic man who chose the moderate path in all his endeavors. d. Raleigh, 19 Jan. 1872. —PLF

Branch, Lawrence O'Bryan. CSA b. Enfield, N.C., 28 Nov. 1828. In a varied and distinguished prewar career, Branch was tutored by future Union Sec. of the Treasury SALMON P. CHASE, was a graduate of the College of New Jersey, a newspaperman, a Florida lawyer, veteran of the Seminole War, and a Democratic congressman from his native state for 3 terms beginning in 1854.

When North Carolina seceded, Branch accepted an appointment as quartermaster and paymaster of state troops; he subsequently resigned, accepting the colonelcy of the 33d North Carolina. On 16 Nov. 1861 he was promoted to brigadier general and assumed command of troops in the New Berne, N.C., area. In this command, Branch opposed a Union expedition under Maj. Gen. AMBROSE E. BURNSIDE in late winter 1862. Burnside captured New Berne 14 Mar. and the town remained in Federal hands for the rest of the war. (*See* NEW BERNE, N.C., RAID ON.)

Confederate authorities then ordered Branch and his brigade to Virginia, where they became a part of Maj. Gen. AMBROSE P. HILL'S LIGHT DIVISION. Hill soon came to regard Branch highly as a commander, though the North Carolinian was not a professional soldier. Branch also respected Hill greatly, believing him to be more fit for command of the corps than Maj. Gen. THOMAS J. "STONEWALL" JACKSON. The brigadier considered "Old Jack" a great battle commander but an officer who allowed his men too little rest.

The SEVEN DAYS' CAMPAIGN was the first test for Branch and his men under Hill, and his soldiers fought and charged bravely, suffering more casualties than any brigade except one. In mid-July the Light Division, now part of Jackson's command, marched to Gordonsville. 3 weeks later, at CEDAR MOUNTAIN, Branch's Confederates led the division onto the field to save a hard-pressed Jackson. The SECOND BULL RUN CAMPAIGN followed, with 8 consecutive days of combat and exhausting marches. Branch might have complained of Stonewall's tireless generalship but never failed him.

In the Confederate invasion of Maryland in September 1862, Branch participated in the capture of HARPERS FERRY, Va., on the 15th. 2 days later, while the Battle of ANTIETAM raged, Hill drove his Light Division to the field. Branch's brigade and 2 others arrived in time to repulse the final Union assault of the day. A short time later, Hill conferred with his 3 brigadiers. A Federal sharpshooter, seeing the group, fired a shot that hit Branch in the right cheek and exited behind his left ear, killing him instantly. He was buried in Raleigh, N.C.   —JDW

Brandon, William Lindsay. CSA b. Adams Cty., Miss., about 1801. When the Civil War began Brandon was nearly 60. Since family records were destroyed by fire, his exact birthdate is uncertain, but it is known that he was a planter and state legislator educated at the College of New Jersey, and he is believed to have studied medicine.

When the 21st Mississippi was organized, Brandon's age was ignored and he was appointed lieutenant colonel. The regiment was sent to the Virginia Peninsula and fought in the Battle of MALVERN HILL, where Brandon lost a leg. He refused to be invalided from service and after almost a year of recuperation rejoined the 21st. At the Battle of GETTYSBURG his brigade commander, Brig. Gen. WILLIAM BARKSDALE, was killed. Col. BENJAMIN G. HUMPHREYS, the regiment's commander, was promoted to brigadier to replace him, and Brandon was commissioned colonel of the 21st in his stead. Under Humphreys, he served on detached service from the Army of Northern Virginia (see CORPS) and fought in the CHICKAMAUGA and KNOXVILLE campaigns.

In spring 1864 he was returned to the East with Lt. Gen. JAMES LONGSTREET's corps, was promoted brigadier general, and sent home to Mississippi. His commission promoted him to rank from 18 June 1864, and with that authority he was made head of the state's Confederate Bureau of Conscription. This new command offered little reward, since Brandon spent his time dispatching state troops to capture deserters and round up what few able-bodied men remained in his district. The bureau was closed shortly before the end of the war.

Following the Confederate surrender, Brandon returned to planting and a life of semiretirement at "Arcole," his plantation in Wilkinson Cty., Miss. d. 8 Oct. 1890.   —JES

Brandy Station, Va., Battle of. 9 June 1863 The Battle of Brandy Station, the largest cavalry engagement of the war, resulted from the initial movements of the GETTYSBURG CAMPAIGN. Maj. Gen. JOSEPH HOOKER, commander of the ARMY OF THE POTOMAC, sorely needed solid evidence of a rumored major Confederate offensive. A reconnaissance in force by the Union VI Corps 5 June, at FRANKLIN'S CROSSING on the Rappahannock River, failed to verify the suspicions, so Hooker assigned the task to his cavalry corps, supported by 2 infantry brigades and 6 light batteries.

The 11,000-man force, commanded by Maj. Gen. ALFRED PLEASONTON, left Falmouth 8 June. Angling up the Rappahannock, the troopers and infantrymen moved toward Culpeper, where, unknown to the Federals, most of Gen. ROBERT E. LEE's Confederate army was located. Pleasonton planned to strike, in 2 columns, across the Rappahannock at dawn 9 June. On the opposite bank Maj. Gen. J.E.B. STUART's Confederate horsemen patrolled the fords.

Screened by an early morning mist, the Union troopers

splashed across the river at about 4 o'clock. Brig. Gen. JOHN BUFORD's division, crossing at Beverly Ford, surprised the pickets of Brig. Gen. WILLIAM E. "GRUMBLE" JONES's Confederate brigade, overrunning its camp and capturing 150 prisoners. Jones's startled troopers quickly regrouped and fiercely contested the ground as they withdrew toward Brandy Station. 4 mi downstream at Kelly's Ford, Brig. Gen. DAVID M. GREGG's Union cavalrymen pushed aside Brig. Gen. BEVERLY H. ROBERTSON's pickets and moved to connect with Buford. The 2d Division, under Union Col. Alfred N. A. Duffié, was late, trailing Gregg's troopers.

Meanwhile, Stuart, learning of the Union attacks, hurriedly ordered a concentration of his scattered brigades. Brig. Gen. WADE HAMPTON soon galloped up in support of Jones, but both had a tough time with Buford's troops. The Union general eventually turned the Confederate right, thundering up Fleetwood Hill, where Stuart had his headquarters.

The oncoming 12th Virginia Cavalry crashed into the Federal horsemen in a savage counterattack. Other units arriving on both sides added to the fury. It was a classic cavalry fight —saber-wielding horsemen galloping into pistol-firing horsemen. Charge and countercharge, engulfed in clouds of dust, flowed back and forth. One Union regiment claimed it made 6 distinct charges. Horse artillery units added thunder to the flashes.

The Confederate horsemen finally shoved Buford's troopers back, but Gregg appeared from the south, renewing the battle. Hampton counterattacked, securing Fleetwood Hill. Meanwhile, 5.5 mi to the south at Stevensburg, Duffié's tardy division was engaging 2 Confederate regiments in a confusing, spreading fight, capturing nearly half of the 4th Virginia.

When Pleasonton saw the dust clouds of approaching Confederate infantry, he ordered a withdrawal. His losses totaled 936, with Brig. Gen. Benjamin F. "Grimes" Davis, an excellent officer, killed in a charge. Stuart lost 523.

Though Stuart could claim a victory, for he held the field, the Battle of Brandy Station, said a Confederate, "made the Federal cavalry." In the past, Stuart's superb horsemen had consistently defeated and embarrassed the Union cavalrymen, but no more. With the confidence they earned at Brandy Station, Federal cavalry became a fierce antagonist. The sensitive, ambitious Stuart, however, suffered public humiliation over the surprise and near-defeat. As the Confederates moved north, the flamboyant general eagerly sought to erase the stain; his attitude would have grave consequences for Lee at GETTYSBURG.   —JDW

Brannan, John Milton. USA b. District of Columbia, 1 July 1819. At 18 Brannan worked as a messenger in Congress, so impressing Indiana Congressman Ratliff Boon that Boon raised a petition among other representatives to have young Brannan admitted to West Point; his appointment thus reads "from Indiana." He graduated 23d in the class of 1841 and went into a lifelong artillery career, winning citations for his fighting in the Mexican War and rising to captain in the Regular Army before 1861.

On 28 Sept. 1861 he was made brigadier general of volunteers and sent to the tropical outpost of Key West, Fla., the next spring. He distinguished himself on the Florida mainland in a combat sometimes called the Battle of Jacksonville, which began as an assault on heavy gun emplacements on Florida's St. John's River. It was Brannan's first real combat experience leading infantry and, in a time of few Federal successes, it brought him notice and a brevet to lieutenant colonel in the Regular service. Later, in Port Royal, S.C., he won attention in expeditions against Confederates at Pocotaligo. By the end of the war he had received Regular Army brevets through every rank to major general.

USMHI

Brannan was next assigned to the Army of the Ohio and commanded an infantry division under Maj. Gen. WILLIAM S. ROSECRANS. He served through the TULLAHOMA CAMPAIGN to CHICKAMAUGA, and in the latter battle saw the fiercest combat of his life. On the morning of 19 Sept. 1863 he was dispatched on an aggressive reconnaissance of the Confederate right, which started an intense shoving match with Confederates in his front. The afternoon of the following day found him along the last Union defense line at HORSESHOE RIDGE with Maj. Gen. GEORGE H. THOMAS, and with most of his army routed behind him. He survived the fight and went on to CHATTANOOGA.

In the repercussions following the Chickamauga debacle, and despite another Regular Army brevet for bravery, he was relieved from infantry command and appointed chief of artillery for the ARMY OF THE CUMBERLAND. In that post he fought through the Georgia battles to ATLANTA and oversaw the construction of the Union defenses there. He spent the rest of the war in administrative work, and 23 Jan. 1865 he was brevetted major general of volunteers.

As an acknowledgment of his gallantry in the fighting to Atlanta and for all services rendered during the war, he was brevetted major general in the Regulars 13 Mar. 1865. He served on in the artillery until he was retired at the mandatory age of 62. d. New York City, 10 Dec. 1892.   —JES

Brantley, William Felix. CSA b. Greene Cty., Ala., 12 Mar. 1830. After migrating to Mississippi with his family, Brantley became an attorney, pursuing the profession 1852–61, when he became a delegate to Mississippi's secession convention.

When a local company, the Wigfall Rifles, was organized for the Civil War, Brantley was elected its captain. He was later commissioned colonel of the 29th Mississippi, a unit incorporating his old company, and fought with them through the Civil War at STONE'S RIVER, CHICKAMAUGA, CHATTANOOGA, and in the battle for ATLANTA.

In the Atlanta fighting, Brig. Gen. EDWARD C. WALTHALL was promoted to major general and Col. SAMUEL BENTON was given the brigade command. On 22 July 1864 Benton was severely wounded and died on the 28th, thrusting command on Brantley, who received a brigadier general's commission to rank from 26 July 1864. Brantley led this brigade into Tennessee as a part of Lt. Gen. STEPHEN D. LEE's corps and fought in the FRANKLIN AND NASHVILLE campaigning. Then he returned to the rest of the ARMY OF TENNESSEE in the Carolinas and was surrendered with it there Apr. 1865.

Postwar Brantley practiced law in Mississippi. On 2 Nov. 1870, near the town of Winona, he was murdered as a result of his involvement in an old local feud.   —JES

Bratton, John. CSA b. Winnsboro, S.C., 7 Mar. 1831. After attending Mount Zion College and graduating from South Carolina College, in 1853 Bratton received a diploma from the Medical College of Charleston, achieving moderate success as a physician until his state went to war.

GG

Entering the 6th South Carolina Infantry as a private, Bratton was immediately promoted to captain, serving in his regiment throughout the FORT SUMTER crisis and reaching Virginia shortly after FIRST BULL RUN. In spring 1862, he was elected colonel of the 6th. Though concerned about his lack of military experience (he wrote his wife that "my first drill will be on the battlefield"), he served well in the field, performing conspicuously at SEVEN PINES, where he was wounded and taken prisoner. Exchanged several months later, he returned to the ARMY OF NORTHERN VIRGINIA to play a supporting role at FREDERICKSBURG.

In spring 1863, the 6th South Carolina was part of Lt. Gen. JAMES LONGSTREET's command during the Siege of Suffolk, Va.; for part of that period, Bratton led the brigade of Brig. Gen. MICAH JENKINS. His regiment was sent to Richmond in June, and he remained on duty there till after GETTYSBURG. That fall it went to Georgia under Longstreet but failed to reach its destination in time to participate at CHICKAMAUGA.

Throughout 1863–64 Bratton was bothered by chronic illness, homesickness, and the heavy burden of command ("it has been one protracted, head-cracking job for me," he lamented Jan. 1864). Nevertheless, when he received Jenkins' brigade permanently following the latter's death at the WILDERNESS, Bratton led it so well that he won the nickname "Old Reliable" and was appointed a brigadier general, to rank from 6 May 1864. Late that year a superior described him as "the best commander of the best brigade in the Army of Northern Virginia."

At Appomattox, his brigade was the most completely manned in Gen. Robert E. Lee's army—the only one to quit the war as an organized unit. With the return of peace, Bratton became a farmer and a politician, serving in the South Carolina legislature 1865–66 and the U.S. House of Representatives 1884–85. He died in Winnsboro 12 Jan. 1898, 8 years after being defeated for the governorship of his state.   —EGL

Brawner's Farm, Va., Battle of. 28 Aug. 1862 *See* GROVETON, VA., BATTLE OF.

"Breadbasket of the Confederacy." *See* SHENANDOAH VALLEY.

Bread Riot, Richmond, Va.

Bread Riot, Richmond, Va. 2 Apr. 1863 On this date a crowd of several hundred women, boys, and a few men began an orderly march from Richmond's Capitol Square to the city's business district. They were going, one woman told an onlooker, to the bakeries to get bread. The crowd, quickly swelling to more than 1,000, engaged in widespread, indiscriminate looting. When Pres. JEFFERSON DAVIS learned of the unrest, he went to the scene and urged the crowd to stop its lawlessness. Reason failing, the president ordered the rioters to disperse within 5 minutes, after which time a military company would be prepared to fire on them. Realizing the men might be forced to shoot, the crowd scattered. By 13 Apr. several participants had been arrested and either released or held for trial; eventually the principals were convicted and given sentences of varying severity.

Wishing the North to have no further knowledge of conditions in Richmond, the government requested that newspapers refrain from reporting the event at all; instead, they printed exaggerated accounts. The RICHMOND *EXAMINER* blamed the trouble on Yankee agents. Davis, along with other observers, believed the rioters merely wanted an excuse to pillage. The needy, meanwhile, were no better off than before their protest. —PLF

Breckinridge, John Cabell. CSA/CSP b. Lexington, Ky., 15 Jan. 1821. Few 19th-century men rose so meteorically as Breckinridge. He studied law, practiced for several years, then in 1849 won a seat in his state legislature, followed by 2 terms in the U.S. House of Representatives, 1851–55. In 1856, against his wishes, the Democratic party nominated him to run with James Buchanan in the presidential contest; at 35, he became the youngest vice-president in U.S. history.

USMHI

Though never a secessionist and always inclined to compromise on volatile issues, Breckinridge became identified with Southern extremists, who in 1860 helped nominate him president when the Democrats split. He intended to decline but was persuaded that his acceptance would force STEPHEN A. DOUGLAS to withdraw and open the way for a compromise Democratic candidate who could defeat ABRAHAM LINCOLN. Douglas did not withdraw, and both Southern and Northern factions ran presidential candidates in the 1860 ELECTIONS.

Though he had committed no treasonous act, Breckinridge was suspected of being a Confederate sympathizer and was ordered arrested in Washington, D.C., Sept. 1861 while he was still serving as a U.S. senator. Escaping before he could be taken into custody, he went south and embraced the Confederacy, though he confided to friends he knew the South could not win. Promoted from brigadier to major general 14 Apr. 1862, he commanded a corps at SHILOH, led the attack on BATON ROUGE in August, and played a significant role at STONE'S RIVER in December. From this battle arose a controversy with Gen. BRAXTON BRAGG, over the treatment of Kentucky troops, that lasted more than a year. Breckinridge later fought at JACKSON, Miss., and at CHICKAMAUGA; commanded a corps at MIS-

SIONARY RIDGE; then went east to command the DEPARTMENT OF SOUTHWESTERN VIRGINIA. At NEW MARKET, 15 May 1864, he won perhaps the most important small battle of the war, following it with service at COLD HARBOR, in Lt. Gen. Jubal A. EARLY'S WASHINGTON RAID, and against Maj. Gen. PHILIP H. SHERIDAN in the SHENANDOAH VALLEY CAMPAIGN of 1864.

In Feb. 1865 Pres. JEFFERSON DAVIS appointed Breckinridge secretary of war, and in his new position he strove to bring about honorable surrender. He organized Richmond's evacuation, accompanied the cabinet in its flight to North Carolina, and took part in the negotiations for surrender between Maj. Gen. WILLIAM T. SHERMAN and Gen. JOSEPH E. JOHNSTON. Escaping to Cuba in May, he spent 3 years in exile, then returned to Kentucky in 1869 to take up law again. Exhausted by the war, he died at home in Lexington 17 May 1875, aged 54. —WCD

Breckinridge, Margaret E. nurse b. Philadelphia, Pa., 24 Mar. 1832, Breckinridge, a Union Civil War nurse and U.S. SANITARY COMMISSION agent, was a cousin of former U.S. Vice-President and Confederate Maj. Gen. JOHN C. BRECKINRIDGE. At 6, following her mother's death, she was reared in her grandparents' home in Princeton, N.J. In 1862, unmarried, living with family, and possessing independent means, she traveled alone to Lexington, Ky., and took up nursing. Her tenure in Lexington's Union Hospital was enlivened in September when Confederates occupied the town for several weeks and she stayed on to nurse Federal wounded. After the Confederates' evacuation, she worked for the Sanitary Commission on a relief boat carrying wounded between VICKSBURG and St. Louis during the 1863 siege in Mississippi.

Breckinridge made only 2 relief-boat trips while working in St. Louis hospitals and, conforming to mores of the day, stayed with her brother, a St. Louis attorney. But in a campaign capturing Northern news headlines, Breckinridge's exposure to danger on relief-boat duty and her Confederate family connection brought her recognition.

In Mar. 1863, suffering from exhaustion and an unnamed ailment contracted in the line of duty, she returned east. After more than a year of convalescence and a turn at surgical-nursing training in Philadelphia's Episcopal Hospital, she suffered a relapse and died in Niagara Falls, N.Y., 27 July 1864. Her prominent social position, the sociological daring of her independent work in a place of danger, and her death from war causes made her a heroine of the war period. —JES

Brevard, Theodore Washington. CSA b. Tuskegee, Ala., 26 Aug. 1835. Moving to Florida as a youth, Brevard later studied law at the University of Virginia in Charlottesville and in 1858 opened a legal practice in Florida, while serving in the state assembly.

When the war commenced, he resigned the positions of Florida adjutant general and inspector general to raise a unit known as Brevard's Partisan Rangers. For the first 3 years of the conflict Brevard served exclusively in his adopted state, taking part in numerous engagements and SKIRMISHES. His command formed part of a large force of irregulars who, Mar. 1863, invaded a Unionist enclave near Jacksonville, burned dwellings and businesses, and killed or arrested citizens suspected of aiding the enemy.

The following February, at OLUSTEE, Fla., Brevard temporarily commanded the 28th Georgia of Brig. Gen. ALFRED H. COLQUITT's brigade. A month later, a lieutenant colonel, he led another Georgia regiment on a sweep of the Fort Meade vicinity, seeking to disperse bands of deserters terrorizing the citizenry. When the deserters failed to appear in groups large enough to warrant a fight, the campaign ended in failure. Later in 1864 Brevard took over the 2d Florida Battalion before being promoted to colonel and given command of the 11th Florida infantry.

A member of Brig. Gen. JOSEPH FINEGAN's brigade, he was sent to join the ARMY OF NORTHERN VIRGINIA. In Gen. R. E. Lee's army the 11th Florida participated in many of the battles around PETERSBURG. Brevard was named a brigadier general 28 Mar. 1865, less than a week before the Confederate government fled Richmond. During that brief period he led the Florida Brigade before being captured prior to or in the Battle of SAYLER'S CREEK, during the APPOMATTOX CAMPAIGN.

After being imprisoned on JOHNSON'S ISLAND, Brevard was allowed to return to Florida. There he resumed his legal career, which soon flourished. He died in Tallahassee 20 June 1882 and was buried in a local cemetery.   —EGL

brevet rank. Brevet rank, usually an honor, was borrowed from the British and introduced into the American army during the Revolutionary War. Over the years Congress, in legislation, specified reasons for granting brevet ranks and gave the Senate the right to approve or reject them after they were recommended by the president. *Army Regulations,* published periodically, stipulated that an officer functioned at his brevet rank on special assignment of the president in commands composed of different corps and when in detachments or on courts-martial composed of different corps. In these instances the officers ordinarily received pay based on their brevet rank.

In early 1861 some recent graduates of the U.S. Military Academy at West Point were named brevet 2d lieutenants because there were not enough vacancies in the Regular Army to give them commissions as 2d lieutenants. Many officers held brevet commissions higher than their ordinary rank, usually for gallant actions or meritorious service in combat or to allow them to serve in a staff position.

The Civil War encouraged the granting of hundreds of brevet commissions to both Regular and volunteer army officers and to at least one enlisted man, Pvt. Frederick W. Stowe, who was brevetted a 2d lieutenant. About 1,700 Union officers held brevet rank as brigadier or major general.

The awarding of numerous new brevets often created confusion, such as in the case of GEORGE ARMSTRONG CUSTER. In addition to holding rank as major general of volunteers in the Civil War, Custer was a lieutenant colonel in the Regular Army when in 1876 he was killed at the Little Big Horn, and also held brevet commissions as major general of volunteers and major general in the Regular Army. For a long time after the war, the army had to determine the official title of many an officer and the rank he should show on his uniform.

Although brevet commissions were provided for in Confederate Army regulations, evidence indicates that officers were not awarded them.

In the years after the Civil War these commissions were issued to some U.S. Army officers for various reasons, but few were awarded after the Spanish-American War. In 1918 Tasker H. Bliss received the last brevet commission.
                                                                            —DEF

Brice's Cross Roads (Guntown, Tishomingo Creek),

Miss., Battle of. 10 June 1864   Early in May 1864 Union Maj. Gen. WILLIAM T. SHERMAN took the offensive in northwest Georgia. His mission was to destroy Gen. JOSEPH E. JOHNSTON's ARMY OF TENNESSEE and occupy Atlanta. By employing his superior numbers to threaten Johnston's flanks, Sherman compelled the Confederates to retire south of the Etowah River. But as Sherman advanced, he became increasingly concerned about the security of the single-track railroad over which he supplied his more than 100,000 men from Nashville and Chattanooga depots.

To forestall the possibility of raids on the Nashville & Chattanooga Railroad by Maj. Gen. NATHAN B. FORREST, then based in northeast Mississippi, Sherman ordered Brig. Gen. SAMUEL D. STURGIS to seek and destroy Forrest's corps. On 2 June 1864 Sturgis left Memphis at the head of 8,100 infantry and cavalry and 22 cannon manned by 400 artillerists. Slowed by heavy rains, the Federals did not reach Ripley until the 7th. Sturgis' advance came at an inopportune time for the South, because Forrest, in accordance with orders from his immediate superior, Maj. Gen. STEPHEN D. LEE, had left Tupelo 1 June to raid the railroad. On 6 June, before he crossed the Tennessee River, Forrest was recalled when Lee learned of Sturgis' advance.

To counter Sturgis, Forrest posted his brigades at Rienzi, Booneville, and Baldwyn, with patrols thrown out toward the west. By sundown on the 9th, Sturgis had advanced from Ripley and camped 9 mi northwest of Brice's Cross Roads. The plan outlined to Forrest by S. D. Lee called for a Confederate concentration and a battle near Okolona. But when Forrest rode on the 10th, he planned to meet the foe at Brice's Cross Roads, and issued orders for his 3 columns to meet there.

Brig. Gen. BENJAMIN H. GRIERSON, commanding Sturgis' 3,300-man cavalry, had the lead as the Federals moved out. It had rained on and off since 3 June and the roads were muddy, but at daybreak the clouds cleared and the day promised to be hot and muggy. Grierson's cavalry routed a Confederate patrol, crossed Tishomingo Creek, and by 9:45 was at Brice's. The Confederates were pursued down the Baldwyn Road about a mile. Here the Union horsemen encountered Forrest with a brigade and were checked; although outnumbered 3-to-1, the Confederates held their own until reinforced.

Forrest boldly seized the initiative, intending to defeat Grierson's cavalry before Sturgis could bring up his infantry. The hard-pressed horse soldiers called for help, and the blue-clad infantry brigades hurried forward.

Though outnumbered, Forrest had beaten Grierson by noon. Coming up on the double, exhausted Union infantry took position covering the crossroads. Forrest was joined by Col. TYREE H. BELL's brigade, and a slashing frontal attack, coordinated with a dash at the Federals' left and right, sent the Union troops recoiling across Tishomingo Creek. Fording the rain-swollen stream, the Confederates hammered Sturgis' rear guard. On the evening of the 10th, as the battered Union column threaded its way across the Hatchie Bottom, its teamsters and a number of soldiers panicked. Most of the artillery and wagons were abandoned, and the next day Forrest and his men pursued the fleeing Federals beyond Ripley.

At Brice's Cross Roads, Forrest scored a brilliant tactical success. Union casualties in the battle were 223 killed, 394 wounded, and 1,623 missing, while Forrest captured 192 wagons and ambulances, 16 cannon, and 1,500 stands of small arms. Forrest's corps counted 96 killed and 396 wounded.
                                                                            —ECB

brigade. The common tactical infantry and cavalry unit of the Civil War, the brigade generally consisted of 4–6 REGIMENTS. However, it could have as few as 2 and, later in the war, when consolidation of Confederate regiments became common, some brigades contained remnants of as many as 15 regiments. There were 3 or 4 brigades to a DIVISION and several divisions to a CORPS.

By definition, a brigadier general commanded a brigade. But colonels were often in charge of brigades too small to justify a brigadier, and if the brigadier was absent, the senior colonel would act in his stead; on occasion, temporary brigades organized for special purposes were commanded by colonels. The brigade's staff usually comprised the brigadier general, his aide, the quartermaster, ordnance and commissary officers, an inspector, and one or more clerks.

The brigade's effectiveness depended on regimental and company commanders instructing their 1,000–1,500 men in the complicated maneuvers of the period, and on each regiment coordinating its movements with the others under the brigade commander. A poor commander might watch his brigade's actions dissolve into regimental or company-level conflicts coordinated loosely, if at all, by the brigadier.

Some brigades became justly famous during the war. The STONEWALL BRIGADE was one of Gen. R. E. Lee's best units, as was HOOD'S TEXAS BRIGADE. Western Confederate brigades included the ORPHAN BRIGADE of Kentucky and the 1st Missouri Brigade. On the Union side, the IRON BRIGADE earned fame in the Army of the Potomac, as did the PHILADELPHIA BRIGADE. WILDER'S LIGHTNING BRIGADE of mounted infantry combined infantry and cavalry tactics to become one of the best Union units. —LDJ

Bristoe Campaign, Va. 9–22 Oct. 1863 The lull in fighting in the East after the GETTYSBURG CAMPAIGN stretched for nearly 3 months as the Confederate ARMY OF NORTHERN VIRGINIA and the Union ARMY OF THE POTOMAC, both ravaged by the campaign, recuperated. Gen. ROBERT E. LEE concentrated his Confederates east of the Blue Ridge Mts. near Culpeper, Va., while Maj. Gen. GEORGE G. MEADE's Federals deployed across the Rappahannock River.

Both commanders detached troops for temporary duty elsewhere, contributing to the relative inactivity. In September Lee sent Lt. Gen. JAMES LONGSTREET with 2 divisions west to join Gen. BRAXTON BRAGG at CHICKAMAUGA. When Meade learned of Longstreet's movement, he advanced on Culpeper while Lee withdrew beyond the Rapidan River. But early in October Meade lost the XI and XII corps, ordered west to CHATTANOOGA.

Lee seized this opportunity by attempting to turn Meade's right flank and advance on Washington, D.C. On 9 Oct. 1863, screened by Maj. Gen. J.E.B. STUART's cavalry, the Confederate corps of Lt. Gens. AMBROSE P. HILL and RICHARD S. EWELL marched west and north toward Federal lines at Culpeper. For the next 2 days the armies skirmished extensively as Lee advanced and Meade withdrew. On the 11th the Confederates entered Culpeper.

Lee, following a strategy similar to his SECOND BULL RUN CAMPAIGN in 1862, sent Hill on a wide circuitous swing to the west while Ewell followed the Federals along the line of the ORANGE & ALEXANDRIA RAILROAD. Throughout the 12th and 13th, Union rear guards fought with the oncoming Confederates. Although outnumbering Lee, Meade continued his retreat, conducting it with great skill.

Early on 14 Oct. Hill's leading corps approached New Baltimore, 5 mi north of Warrenton, where the corps commander learned that the Federals were marching northward, almost parallel to him; Hill hurriedly angled his division eastward toward BRISTOE STATION. Approaching the railroad stop, Hill saw the retreating blue column and, without reconnoitering, attacked with his leading division. The resulting battle, which cost the impetuous Hill dearly, was the major action of the campaign.

Hill's repulse at Bristoe Station permitted Meade to solidify his lines around Centreville. For the next 2 days the armies probed each other's positions on the familiar terrain along Bull Run. Lee, unable to attack the entrenched Northerners or remain near Manassas, began his retreat on the 17th.

For the next 3 days, reversing roles, the retreating Confederates protected their rear against pursuing Federals. Skirmishing flared at numerous points along the route. On the 19th, at BUCKLAND MILLS, Stuart's horsemen routed Brig. Gen. H. JUDSON KILPATRICK's Union cavalry division, an engagement marking the last significant action of the campaign. By the following day most of Lee's army had recrossed the Rappahannock.

The Bristoe Campaign had been one of maneuver, with several opportunities lost on both sides. Confederate casualties amounted to 1,381, of which 1,300 occurred at Bristoe Station; Meade placed his losses at 2,292. Lee had failed to intercept the Union retreat, and the campaign had no significant strategic result; but his brilliant maneuver succeeded in pushing Meade back 40 mi and denying him the use of the railroad for over a month. The campaign illustrated the principle of the offensive that made the Confederate commander a great general. —JDW

Bristoe Station, Va., eng. at. 14 Oct. 1863 Bristoe Station was the scene of Confederate Lt. Gen. AMBROSE P. HILL's first defeat by a comparable Union force. A remarkable combat officer, commander of Gen. ROBERT E. LEE's III Corps, Hill stumbled into a sharp, bloody defeat because of his impetuosity and failure to reconnoiter; 2 Confederate brigades were slaughtered by his poor generalship.

During Lee's BRISTOE CAMPAIGN Hill had drawn the assignment of trying to outflank Union Maj. Gen. GEORGE G. MEADE's retreating army. During the initial 5 days of the Southern offensive, Hill's soldiers marched hard and skirmished constantly. By the morning of 14 Oct. Hill's corps and Lt. Gen. RICHARD S. EWELL's corps were encamped at Warrenton, Va., west of Meade's line of march along the ORANGE & ALEXANDRIA RAILROAD.

Hill learned early that day that the Federals were marching hastily northward, strung out along the tracks. Excited at the prospect of inflicting heavy losses, Hill galloped ahead of his corps to locate the Federals. From a hill overlooking Bristoe Station, the corps commander saw the Union III Corps rapidly crossing Broad Run, east of the station. Hill quickly dispatched aides to hurry forward his infantry.

Arriving on the field was the division of Maj. Gen. HENRY HETH, whose 2 leading brigades, those of Brig. Gens. JOHN R. COOKE and WILLIAM W. KIRKLAND, deployed rapidly as Hill bristled with impatience. The corps commander sent them straight ahead into an obtuse angle formed by the railroad and the stream, and the Confederates charged down the hillside.

Suddenly a furious burst of rifle fire erupted along the railroad embankment: concealed behind the tracks were the divisions of Union Maj. Gen. GOUVERNEUR K. WARREN's II Corps, carefully hidden by Warren to protect the Federal march. Hill's impetuous attack had hurled the Confederates into Warren's trap.

Cooke and Kirkland, their flanks exposed, turned toward the embankment and charged. The Federal fire destroyed the Confederate ranks; both brigadiers fell wounded. Hill's failure to reconnoiter cost the Confederates 1,300 casualties, while Warren lost 548. —JDW

Brooke, John Mercer. CSN b. at an army base near Tampa, Fla., 18 Dec. 1826. Brooke entered the U.S. Navy as midshipman in 1841 and graduated from the U.S. Naval Academy in 1847. As a result of his surveying work, he invented a deep-sea sounding apparatus for mapping the ocean bottom. Promoted to lieutenant in 1855, Brooke was using his invention to survey North Pacific waters when the Civil War began.

LC

Resigning his commission 20 Apr. 1861, Brooke entered the Virginia state navy, then the Confederate navy, as a lieutenant. Early in June, he met with Sec. of the Navy STEPHEN R. MALLORY to discuss the possible use of IRONCLADS. After Brooke assured Mallory that the South was capable of building its own, the secretary appointed him his inspecting officer for the conversion of the USS *Merrimack* into an armored ship. Assisted by Lt. CATESBY AP R. JONES, Brooke, responsible for the vessel's armor and guns, found that armor placed at an angle of about 38° from the horizontal offered good protection against projectiles traveling along a flat trajectory. With this discovery, the *Merrimack* could become the CSS *VIRGINIA,* the South's first ironclad. During the project friction developed when the ship's constructor, JOHN L. PORTER, claimed credit for the *Virginia*'s design. Though Mallory interceded to credit Brooke, the fracas contributed to Brooke's loss of interest in the ironclad program.

Promoted to commander 13 Sept. 1862, Brooke became chief of the Bureau of Ordnance and Hydrography Mar. 1863, an office he held until war's end. After the war, Brooke was professor of physics and astronomy at the VIRGINIA MILITARY INSTITUTE until 1899. He also designed the BROOKE RIFLE, a heavy weapon strengthened by single, double, or triple banding of the breech rings. d. Lexington, Va., 14 Dec. 1906. —NCD

Brooke rifle. An excellent heavy artillery piece, Confederate-invented and -manufactured, the Brooke rifle saw service both on IRONCLADS and in seacoast fortifications.

The rifle was invented by JOHN MERCER BROOKE, an Annapolis graduate and former U.S. Navy officer who helped plan the conversion of the USS *Merrimack* into the ironclad ram CSS *VIRGINIA.* From Mar. 1863 until the close of the war, Brooke was chief of the Confederate Navy's Bureau of Ordnance and Hydrography. His guns were manufactured at the TREDEGAR IRON WORKS in Richmond and the Confederate Naval Ordnance Works in Selma, Ala.

The Brooke was a cast-iron weapon with a wrought-iron reinforcing band at the breech. It had a heavy, tapered tube

USMHI

and could be single-, double-, or triple-banded. The band consisted of 6-in.-wide rings, which were not welded together. The gun was rifled with 7 bands and grooves and had a simplified form of hookslant rifling. These guns were made in a number of calibers, including 6.4-, 7-, 8-, and 11-in. There were also a few smoothbores of 10- and 11-in. caliber made for use on ironclads.

The Confederates regarded the triple-banded Brooke highly. During one test, a 140-lb bolt with a 16-lb powder charge was fired 260 yd and penetrated 8 in. of iron and 18 in. of wood. A Confederate product from start to finish, the Brooke was a source of pride to the South. —LDJ

Brooks, William Thomas Harbaugh. USA b. New Lisbon, Ohio, 28 Jan. 1821. Brooks entered the U.S. Military Academy at 16, graduating 46th in 1841 in a class with 20 future Civil War generals. After serving against the Seminoles in Florida and in the Mexican war, where he was brevetted captain and major for gallantry, Captain Brooks served as a staff officer and on frontier duty until the Civil War.

NA

On 28 Sept. 1861 Brooks received an appointment as brigadier general of volunteers, assuming command of a division a few days later. In Mar. 1862 he commanded a brigade in Brig. Gen. WILLIAM F. SMITH's division of the IV Corps, leading it in action at WILLIAMSBURG before the division was transferred to the VI Corps. Brooks led a brigade of Vermont regiments during the SEVEN DAYS' CAMPAIGN. At ALLEN'S FARM, 29 June, his Vermonters counterattacked on the Union left, suffering heavy casualties. Brooks received a leg wound but remained on the field.

During the ANTIETAM CAMPAIGN Brooks and his Vermonters

saw limited action at CRAMPTON'S GAP and ANTIETAM. In the latter battle, he was again wounded, as his brigade repulsed a brief Confederate counterattack late in the day. Promoted to command of a division, Brooks led it through FREDERICKSBURG and CHANCELLORSVILLE.

The most controversial aspect of Brooks's military career occurred between these 2 Union defeats. In the wake of the decisive loss at Fredericksburg, the Union commander, Maj. Gen. AMBROSE E. BURNSIDE, held several officers, including Brooks, responsible for the debacle. Burnside accused Brooks of complaining about government policy and using language that tended to demoralize his command. The commanding general tried to dismiss Brooks from the service but lacked the authority. Brooks stayed, but his career suffered.

On 10 June 1863 he was promoted to major general, commanding the DEPARTMENT OF THE MONONGAHELA, headquartered in Pittsburgh. His association with the anti-Burnside clique, however, resulted in the revocation of his commission 6 Apr. 1864. Apr.–July 1864 he commanded a division in the XVIII Corps and then one in the X Corps in operations at COLD HARBOR and PETERSBURG. Throughout his career he was plagued by poor health and, with his condition worsening, he resigned 14 July 1864.

After the war he bought a farm near Huntsville, Ala. He soon won the respect of his former enemies and died among them 19 July 1870. His grave bears a Confederate emblem.   —JDW

Brough, John. war governor b. Marietta, Ohio, 17 Sept. 1811. Brough, an orphaned tavern keeper's son, supported himself early in life by working as a printer's devil. Between typesetting jobs, he attended Ohio University at Athens and perfected his newspaper business skills, which ultimately resulted in his owning 3 profitable newspapers. A Democrat, he was clerk of the state senate 1835–37; elected to the legislature 1837; and state auditor 1839–45. From 1848 to 1863 he became president of 3 railroad companies successively.

Brough made his contribution to Civil War history when in 1863 he ran against CLEMENT L. VALLANDIGHAM for the governorship of Ohio in one of the most irregular and, possibly, flagrantly illegal gubernatorial elections in American history. Vallandigham, a PEACE DEMOCRAT, threatened the Lincoln administration with pulling Ohio out of the war if elected, and during the campaign he was arrested, tried by a military court, and banished to the Confederacy. Unhappy and unwanted there, he traveled by ship to Canada, where he tried to keep his campaign alive.

Brough had entered the war years as a WAR DEMOCRAT, then switched to the REPUBLICAN PARTY, largely to win this election. Rough and unpolished, he sauntered through the motions of electioneering. A passionate (though not a very good) speaker, Brough found it both difficult and inexpedient to answer tough questions on many aspects of state government and instead campaigned on a platform of support for the national war effort. As publisher of the pro-Lincoln Cincinnati *Enquirer,* Brough had done his best to back the president in the past. On being told of Brough's victory by a 140,000-vote margin, Lincoln is reputed to have wired the new governor, "Thank God, Ohio has saved the nation."

As governor, Brough busied himself with financial matters, raising relief for the families of Ohio veterans and obtaining a 34,000-troop levy for 100 days to relieve the Army of the Potomac veterans for duty at the front. But because of his

unappealing personality and inability to represent Ohio interests well, the public turned from him. In a June 1865 address he sadly withdrew his candidacy for reelection, saying he owed "the people of Ohio too much to embarrass their future action for the gratification of my own ambition."

In a freak complication from a sprained ankle, he contracted gangrene and died in Cleveland 29 Aug., failing to complete his term in office.   —JES

Brown, Egbert Benson. USA b. Brownsville, N.Y., 4 Oct. 1816. Although born in New York, Brown loved his adopted state of Missouri. Soon after he moved to St. Louis and started in the railroad business in 1852, he became a staunch Unionist spokesman against Missouri's secessionist faction.

After the war began, Brown accepted a commission as a lieutenant colonel in the state's 7th Infantry Regiment but resigned 1 May 1862; 10 days later he was appointed brigadier general of the state militia, commanding the District of Southwest Missouri, and by November he had become a brigadier general of U.S. Volunteers.

Although Brown received 2

NA

disabling wounds, in the shoulder and in the hip, his performance was never considered more than adequate. In fact, his reluctance and caution allowed Brig. Gen. JOSEPH O. SHELBY'S brigade to escape into the Arkansas frontier. "Like a black cloud from Jefferson City," Brown's 1,600 Federal troopers pinned Shelby's Confederates against Brig. Gen. THOMAS EWING's command of 11,000 between Booneville and Marshall. But Shelby took advantage of Brown's timidity and slipped away. In an engagement at WESTPORT, Oct. 1864, Brown again held back, and Maj. Gen. ALFRED PLEASONTON arrested him for failure to attack; there is no evidence Brown was ever convicted. Brown finished the war in command of the District of Rolla, also in Missouri.

A year after the war he became a pension agent in St. Louis, later taking up farming and becoming a member of the state board of equalization. He died 11 Feb. 1902 in West Plains and was buried in Cuba, Mo.   —FLS

Brown, John. abolitionist b. Torrington, Conn., 9 May 1800. The son of a wandering New Englander, Brown spent much of his youth in Ohio, where he was taught in local schools to resent compulsory education and by his parents to revere the Bible and hate slavery. As a boy he herded cattle for Gen. William Hull's army during the War of 1812; later he served as foreman of his family's tannery. In 1820 he married Dianthe Lusk, who bore him 7 children; 5 years later they moved to Pennsylvania to operate a tannery of their own. Within a year after Dianthe's death in 1831, Brown wed 16-year-old Mary Anne Day, by whom he fathered 13 more children.

During the next 24 years Brown built and sold several tanneries, speculated in land sales, raised sheep, and established a brokerage for wool growers. Every venture failed, for he was too much a visionary, not enough a businessman. As his financial burdens multiplied, his thinking became increasingly metaphysical and he began to brood over the plight of the weak and oppressed. He frequently sought the company of blacks, for 2 years living in a freedmen's community in North Elba, N.Y. In time he became a militant abolitionist, a "conductor" on the Underground Railroad, and the organizer of a self-protection league for free blacks and fugitive slaves.

By the time he was 50, Brown was entranced by visions of slave uprisings, during which racists paid horribly for their sins, and he came to regard himself as commissioned by God to make that vision a reality. In Aug. 1855 he followed 5 of his sons to Kansas to help make the state a haven for antislavery settlers. The following year, his hostility toward slave-staters exploded after they burned and pillaged the free-state community of Lawrence. Having organized a militia unit within his Osawatomie River colony, Brown led it on a mission of revenge. On the evening of 23 May 1856, he and 6 followers, including 4 of his sons, visited the homes of pro-slavery men along Pottawatomie Creek, dragged their unarmed inhabitants into the night, and hacked them to death with long-edged swords. At once, "Old Brown of Osawatomie" became a feared and hated target of slave-staters.

In autumn 1856, temporarily defeated but still committed to his vision of a slave insurrection, Brown returned to Ohio. There and during 2 subsequent trips to Kansas, he developed a grandiose plan to free slaves throughout the South. Provided with moral and financial support from prominent New England abolitionists, Brown began by raiding plantations in Missouri but accomplished little. In summer 1859 he transferred his operations to western Virginia, collected an army of 21 men, including 5 blacks, and on the night of 16 Oct. raided the government armory and arsenal at Harpers Ferry (see HARPERS FERRY, WESTERN VA., JOHN BROWN'S RAID). From there he planned to arm the thousands of chattels who, learning of his crusade, would flock to his side. Instead, numerous bands of militia and a company of U.S. Marines under Bvt. Col. ROBERT E. LEE hastened to the river village, where they trapped the raiders inside the fire-engine house and on the 18th stormed the building. The fighting ended with 10 of Brown's people killed and 7 captured, Brown among them.

After a sensational trial, he was found guilty of treason against Virginia and was hanged at Charlestown, amid much fanfare, 2 Dec. 1859. The stately, fearless, unrepentant manner in which he comported himself in court and on the gallows made him a martyr in parts of the North.   —EGL

Brown, John Calvin. CSA b. Giles Cty., Tenn., 6 Jan. 1827. A successful attorney when the Civil War began, Brown, active in conservative Whig-Unionist politics, took part in the 1860 electoral college before going on a long European tour. While abroad, he heard about the divisions in his home state and returned to enlist as a Confederate army private. On 16 May 1861 Brown was made colonel of the 3d Tennessee Infantry and was captured 9 months later in the fall of Confederate FORT DONELSON.

Brown's Confederate career seemed more promising after he was exchanged Aug. 1862. Commissioned brigadier general 30 Aug., he was assigned to the ARMY OF TENNESSEE and embarked on a string of battles and campaigns that lasted more than a year and a half. He fought and was wounded in the Battle of PERRYVILLE, marched in the TULLAHOMA CAMPAIGN, fought at the Battles of STONE'S RIVER and CHICKAMAUGA, and took part in the siege of CHATTANOOGA.

GG

Following the end of Gen. BRAXTON BRAGG's command of the Army of Tennessee and a short tour of duty in Georgia, Brown was promoted to major general 4 Aug. 1864. Under Lt. Gen. JOHN B. HOOD's command he returned to Tennessee and took part in the Battle of FRANKLIN, during which, at the head of the 3d Division, he fought on the Confederate left and, with Maj. Gen. PATRICK R. CLEBURNE, headed the attack on Maj. Gen. JOHN M. SCHOFIELD's entrenched troops. Instead of directing the attack from the rear, Brown went in with his men, crossing Union trenches and making the deepest hole in the Federal defenses. But he had outrun his flank support and was hit with a counterattack. Forced back to just inside the Union's last outer works, Brown and his men were hit by a 3-way crossfire and held down for much of the rest of the battle. Heavy hand-to-hand fighting finished the contest before he could remove his troops to safety.

Brown's losses were horrific, with 2 of his brigade commanders killed, 1 wounded, and another captured. Brown himself was so badly mangled in the crossfire that his field career was ended. In the last month of the war, out of a sense of duty, he joined what remained of the Army of Tennessee for its surrender in North Carolina.

In the peace that followed, Brown resumed his law practice, was twice elected governor of Tennessee, 1870 and 1872, and was the president of both a railroad and a coal and iron company. d. Red Boiling Springs, Tenn., 17 Aug. 1889.   —JES

Brown, Joseph Emerson. war governor b. Pickens District, S.C., 15 Apr. 1821. Moving to Union Cty., Ga., Brown spent his early years as a laborer, intermittently attending rural schools and receiving a strict Baptist upbringing. In youth he was attracted to the politics and public figures of his age, especially admiring the egalitarianism and strong leadership of Andrew Jackson and the states-rights creed of JOHN C. CALHOUN, both of whom became lifelong influences.

As a young man, Brown taught school, then studied law. After being admitted to the bar, he attended Yale Law School, graduating in 1846. While practicing law in the village of Canton, Ga., he entered political life, campaigning in 1849 as a Jacksonian and winning a seat in the Georgia senate, where he became a power in the state Democratic party. After a single term, however, he retired from the legislature, being elected a circuit court judge in 1855. 2 years later he was the compromise choice for the Democratic gubernatorial candidate when the state convention deadlocked. Though not widely known, he possessed an image that inspired respect and trust and he won the election; in office he established a reputation for

LC

independence, shrewdness, and intelligence impressive even to experienced political observers.

As governor, Brown reformed and expanded the militia and promoted state education and agricultural interests, frequently clashing on these issues with the legislature and vetoing bills he felt insufficiently provincial. In time, his principal antagonist became the Confederate government.

When war approached, Brown, an avid secessionist and slaveholder, seemed a model Confederate official. Before the shooting started, he took possession of Federal property in his state, including Fort Pulaski, below Savannah, and the AUGUSTA ARSENAL. He also worked diligently to organize military units. But he soon became a foe of Pres. JEFFERSON DAVIS' war measures, which he believed gave the Confederate government too much power. An absolutist in a period that demanded pragmatism and flexibility, Brown cherished a view of STATES RIGHTS that was extreme even in a society modeled on that governmental philosophy. Thus he lashed out at the government in Richmond over every piece of legislation or matter of policy that even remotely threatened the power of its constituent parts. He fought its practice of forming state militia and volunteers into regiments and larger organizations and appointing their officers, which Brown considered a usurpation of gubernatorial prerogatives. He opposed Confederate CON-SCRIPTION policies, especially as they applied to Georgia, and challenged government-imposed tax laws, which he thought were apportioned unevenly among the states. He objected to the employment of Georgia's troops far from their home state, continually buffeting Richmond with demands that his regiments on duty elsewhere be returned to guard the state's coastline and interior. He and Davis feuded bitterly over the administration's suspension of HABEAS CORPUS, which Brown saw as a violation of a basic tenet of personal liberty.

To the end of his term, Brown never perceived—at least, never acknowledged—that his actions and utterances harmed the Confederacy, or that the exigencies of wartime required the moderation of internal dissent and criticism. He believed his opposition would ensure that the sort of government established under Davis would not prevail after the South had won its independence, undermining the principles on which the Confederacy had been erected.

Late in 1864, Brown fled the state capital at Milledgeville on the approach of Maj. Gen. WILLIAM T. SHERMAN, but at war's end he was captured and for a time imprisoned in Washington, D.C. Returning home after his release, he shocked and enraged his former constituents by advising them to accept the outcome of the war and submit to RECONSTRUCTION rule. Soon, in fact, he joined the Republicans and flirted with Radicalism. Ostracized by Georgians as a renegade opportunist, he nevertheless was successful in a postwar business career that included mining, railroad, and real-estate interests. By these and other means, he worked to rebuild the ravaged economy of his state. Gradually, Southerners came to accept, many to embrace, his views. In 1868 Brown became chief justice of the state supreme court, mended old fences, and in 1880 was appointed by a Democratic governor to the U.S. Senate; later that year he was elected in his own right, and twice reelected. Retiring from politics in 1891, he died in Atlanta 30 Nov. 1894.   —EGL

Browne, William Montague. CSP b. Cty. Mayo, Ireland, 7 July 1827. Son of the Right Hon. D. Geoffrey Browne, MP, William was educated at Rugby and at Trinity College,

Dublin. He served in the Crimean War, then joined the British diplomatic service before moving to New York City in 1851 to become political editor of the *Journal of Commerce.* At the request of Pres. James Buchanan, Browne moved to Washington, D.C., in 1857 to become editor-in-chief of the *Constitution,* an administration organ. While in Washington he became sympathetic to the Southern way of life and friendly with HOWELL COBB, Buchanan's secretary of the treasury. Ultimately, he accompanied Cobb to Georgia and resided in Athens.

LC

In Feb. 1861, as the Confederacy organized, Browne met JEFFERSON DAVIS, establishing a lifelong intimacy. At once he became the Confederate president's aide-de-camp, with the rank of colonel of cavalry. As one biographer noted, Browne's "remarkably attractive personal appearance and his wide information on public affairs proved invaluable." After serving in Davis' Department of Organization, Browne was the Confederate secretary of state *ad interim,* 17 Feb.–18 Mar. 1862.

He held other political and military posts in Virginia until Apr. 1864, when he became commandant of conscripts for Georgia. Thereafter he was appointed a brigadier general with temporary rank from 11 Nov. 1864, though the Confederate Senate later rejected the nomination. Nonetheless, at the initiative of Gen. BRAXTON BRAGG, military adviser to the Confederate president, Browne was assigned an infantry brigade in Georgia and was sent to Savannah to serve under Brig. Gen. HUGH W. MERCER in opposing Sherman's advance.

After the Confederate surrender, Browne was paroled as a brigadier general and returned to Athens. In 1866 he graduated from the state university with a law degree, practiced that profession briefly, then edited an agricultural journal and the Macon *Star,* meanwhile writing a biography of Confederate Vice-Pres. ALEXANDER H. STEPHENS. In 1874 he was named a professor of law, history, and political science at the University of Georgia in Athens, teaching there until his death 28 Apr. 1883.   —EGL

Brownell, Francis Edwin. USA On 24 May 1861 Union troops in Alexandria, Va., took exception to a Confederate flag that flew over the roof of the Marshall House hotel, and ELMER E. ELLSWORTH, colonel of New York City's 11th Fire Zouaves, decided to pull it down. He marched into the hotel and up the stairs to the roof, taking with him Pvt. Francis Brownell to stand guard. Having removed the Confederate banner, Ellsworth, preceded by Brownell, started down the stairs, rolling the flag in a bundle as he went. Brownell said, "As I reached the first landing and turned, with a half dozen steps between me and the floor, there stood a man with a double-barreled shotgun pointing at my breast."

Hotel owner James T. Jackson started to fire his shotgun, and as he did so Brownell jumped at him, knocking aside the weapon with his musket. Jackson fired and hit Ellsworth in the chest. Brownell went for him again and in a short struggle shot and bayoneted the hotel owner.

Ellsworth had been a friend of Pres. Abraham Lincoln's and

was the first Union officer fatality of the war. In the national attention and grief that followed his death, Brownell was made a hero for avenging him and was feted in his home city and elsewhere. He had only been with his regiment since 20 Apr. but was immediately commissioned a 2d lieutenant and in Oct. 1861 was promoted to 1st lieutenant of U.S. Volunteers.

NA

After national publicity faded, Brownell retired from the army in 1863. Years later the former private tried twice to have himself nominated for the MEDAL OF HONOR; succeeding on a third attempt with help from his congressman, he was decorated in 1877. d. 1894. ——JES

Brownell, Kady. nurse b. 1842, Africa. Unlike many of the women who became known for their Civil War exploits, Brownell did not write a memoir or become prominent in the postwar years. Yet she is remembered as a heroine, a "staunch danger-sharer," who followed her husband into battle and selflessly nursed the wounded when her services were needed.

Brownell was the daughter of a Scottish soldier in the British army and the wife of an orderly sergeant in the 5th Rhode Island Infantry. Familiar with the rigors of military life, she marched off to war as the color-bearer of her husband's regiment, carrying the flag at FIRST BULL RUN. Unlike so many young women, called VIVANDIÈRES, whose enthusiasm for wartime adventure died from boredom in camp or disgust on the battlefield, Kady stayed with the army. Although no longer enjoying any official position, she advanced with Maj. Gen. AMBROSE E. BURNSIDE's expedition to New Berne, N.C., Jan. 1862. Some contemporary accounts claim she begged permission to carry the colors during a charge against the enemy breastworks and, having received it, saved the regiment by rushing forward when another Union force mistakenly opened fire as the 5th Rhode Island advanced unexpectedly from a wooded area.

Kady's husband Robert was seriously wounded in the capture of NEW BERNE, 14 Mar. She nursed him along with several others, including Confederates, until he could be moved to New York. After 18 months an army doctor discharged Sgt. Brownell as unfit for duty. Kady returned with him to Rhode Island, ending her career with the military. Date of death unknown. ——PLF

Brownlow, William Gannaway. journalist/politician b. Wythe Cty., Va., 29 Aug. 1805. After immigrating to Tennessee with his family, Brownlow was orphaned and grew up around Knoxville with little formal education. Self-taught in literature and religion, in 1826 he took up the Methodist ministry, developing speaking and writing skills and political opinions. Describing himself as a "national man," he took the Federal government's part in the early tariff and STATES-RIGHTS controversies, and, after years as an itinerant preacher, successively assumed the editorship of 3 Whig newspapers.

As editor of the Knoxville *Whig* Brownlow became notorious during the Civil War. Known to enemies and adherents as "Parson" Brownlow, he editorialized often on the national-sectional debates and, though a white supremacist, said he

would follow the Federal government's position on slavery. The controversies he and the *Whig* aroused kept its circulation the highest in East Tennessee and brought it some measure of influence and protection after the rise of the Confederate government. But Brownlow's incessant Union advocacy, which included taunting the Davis government, brought on the *Whig*'s suppression 24 Oct. 1861. Brownlow would not pledge loyalty to the Confederacy, insisted on flying the Union flag over his home, and in his last editorial wrote that he did not "see the hand of God" in what secessionists had brought about, and would rather be in prison than agree to it. Confederates acquiesced and ordered his arrest.

USMHI

Brownlow fled to North Carolina, was caught, returned to Knoxville, and found his presses wrecked by secessionists. He was jailed 6 Dec. 1861 for treason and suspicion of sabotage (an erroneous charge); then, after a period of house arrest, in poor health, he was banished to Federal territory.

The "Parson" became popular in the North, wrote a tract, *Sketches of the Rise, Progress, and Decline of Secession* (1862), and went on a lecture tour. When Maj. Gen. AMBROSE E. BURNSIDE occupied Knoxville, Brownlow returned and reopened his newspaper, calling it the Knoxville *Whig and Rebel Ventilator*. With other Tennessee Unionists he urged elections and the return of a "loyal" civilian government. In the meantime he participated in the occupation government's Union Central Committee.

Earlier he had vied with ANDREW JOHNSON for a congressional nomination to the House of Representatives. With the end of the war he finally had his turn in government, being elected governor by acclamation in 1865, then reelected in 1867 and serving as U.S. Senator from Tennessee 1869–75. d. Knoxville, 29 April 1877. ——JES

Bryan, Goode. CSA b. Hancock Cty., Ga., 31 Aug. 1811. In 1834 Bryan graduated 25th in his West Point class and was brevetted a 2d lieutenant in the 5th Infantry. Resigning his commission after only 10 months' service, he was back in Georgia looking into the prospects of becoming a planter.

Bryant followed agricultural pursuits, worked land in Georgia and Alabama, served 11 months as major of the 1st Alabama Volunteers in the Mexican War, and was a delegate to the Georgia secession convention in 1861. With the coming of war he joined the 16th Georgia Infantry as a captain and this time found himself under arms for an extended period. He was elected regimental colonel the next February.

CWTI

The 16th Georgia first saw service in the Virginia peninsula fighting and in the SEVEN DAYS' CAMPAIGN. Later it fought in the Maryland invasion at FREDERICKSBURG, and in the CHANCELLORS-VILLE and GETTYSBURG campaigns. Bryan was appointed brigadier general 29 Aug. 1863 and assigned to Lt. Gen. JAMES LONGSTREET's command in Tennessee, which took him to CHICKAMAUGA and KNOXVILLE. In the latter operation he saw his old comrades from the 16th charge Knoxville's FORT SANDERS with bayonets and, after planting their flag on the Union parapets, be cut down in such numbers that even their brigade commander was shocked.

In Virginia again in spring 1864, Bryan led his brigade into the Battle of the WILDERNESS, fighting until its ammunition was nearly exhausted and its depleted numbers absorbed another 133 casualties. Shortly afterward, while taking part in the ARMY OF NORTHERN VIRGINIA's other operations, Bryan's health began to fail, and he resigned his commission 20 Sept. 1864.

In the postwar period he lived quietly in Georgia. d. Augusta, 16 Aug. 1885.

—JES

Buchanan, Franklin. CSN b. Baltimore, Md., 17 Sept. 1800. Buchanan became a midshipman 28 Jan. 1815 and was promoted to lieutenant in 1825. During his impressive naval career he was selected as the first superintendent of the U.S. Naval Academy and commanded the *Susquehanna* during the Perry Expedition to Japan; he became a captain in 1855.

LC

On 22 Apr. 1861 Buchanan resigned his commission, believing that Maryland would soon secede from the Union. When it became apparent that he was mistaken, he wrote to Navy Sec. GIDEON WELLES requesting that his resignation be withdrawn; Welles refused and had Buchanan dismissed from the service. After an attempt to be neutral in the war, Buchanan joined the Confederate navy with the rank of captain, becoming chief of the Bureau of Orders and Detail until 24 Feb. 1862. However, Buchanan was more fighter than administrator, and his seniority allowed him to command the CSS *VIRGINIA (Merrimack)*. On 8 Mar. 1862 the *Virginia* surprised the Federal squadron at HAMPTON ROADS, destroying the wooden warships *Congress* and *Cumberland*, and 3 steamers. A bullet wound prevented Buchanan from commanding the *Virginia* in its duel with the *MONITOR* the next day.

On 26 Aug. 1862 Buchanan was promoted admiral and made commander of naval forces at Mobile. For almost 2 years he prepared for the Federal attack, which finally came Aug. 1864. Again, during the Battle of MOBILE BAY, 5 Aug., Buchanan showed his courage, defending Mobile with the ram *TENNESSEE* and 3 small wooden gunboats. Finally, with his gunboats out of action, he took on the entire Federal fleet until, seriously wounded and with the *Tennessee* unmanageable, he was forced to surrender. Buchanan was a prisoner until exchanged Feb. 1865. His final assignment was again Mobile, and he arrived in time to surrender the city.

After the war Buchanan became president of the Maryland Agricultural College, 1868–69, and was an insurance execu-

tive in Mobile. He died at his home in Talbot Cty., Md., 11 May 1874.

—NCD

Buchanan, Robert Christie. USA b. Baltimore, Md., 1 Mar. 1811. Buchanan was a nephew, by marriage, of Pres. John Quincy Adams, from whose administration he received an appointment to the U.S. Military Academy, graduating 31st in his class in 1830. He saw service in the Black Hawk, Seminole, and Mexican wars, in the last as a captain of the 4th Infantry.

LC

At the outbreak of the Civil War, his regiment transferred to the DEFENSES OF WASHINGTON, D.C., where it remained for nearly a year. With the brevets of major and lieutenant colonel, Buchanan was appointed commander of the "Regulars," a tough brigade of old army troops in Brig. Gen. George Sykes's division of the V Corps. Called "Old Buck" by his men, Buchanan led his 4 regiments of veterans with distinction during the SEVEN DAYS' CAMPAIGN. The brigade fought stubbornly at GAINES' MILL, captured a Confederate flag at MALVERN HILL, and covered the retreat to Harrison's Landing. Buchanan was brevetted twice for his performance.

At SECOND BULL RUN Buchanan and the Regulars charged the Union left 30 Aug. but were repulsed with the rest of the army in the massive Confederate counterattack. At ANTIETAM, 17 Sept., the V Corps remained in reserve. The Regulars suffered minor casualties 3 months later at FREDERICKSBURG.

Buchanan was promoted to brigadier general of volunteers, to date from 29 Nov. 1862. The Senate, however, failed to act on his appointment—probably because of his close association with discredited Maj. Gen. FITZ JOHN PORTER—and, with the next session of Congress, 4 Mar. 1863, Buchanan's commission expired. He then assumed command of the defenses at FORT DELAWARE and served on several investigative commissions. In 1864, with his seniority, "Old Buck" became colonel of the 1st Infantry, a unit he commanded until the end of the war. In recognition of his services, he was brevetted brigadier and major general, U.S. Army.

Buchanan remained in the army for 5 years. Experienced, with a high sense of discipline and duty, he served as commander of the Department of Louisiana. Retiring in 1870, he lived in the nation's capital until his death there 29 Nov. 1878.

—JDW

buck and ball. This musket load, to be relied on in a defensive situation, was made up of 3 large buckshot bound on top of a .69-caliber, smoothbore musket ball and was encased in a paper cartridge like those used with the MINIÉ BULLET. The .69-caliber musket (most often found in Confederate ranks, but not preferred) was an inaccurate weapon that could be converted to good use at close range with this load. The use of buck and ball was not common.

—JES

buck and gag. Corporal punishment was permitted in both Union and Confederate armies and could be handed out summarily for minor offenses committed by noncommissioned officers and enlisted men. Among the most common and least physically damaging punishment was the buck and gag. The offending soldier was seated on the ground; his hands and feet were bound; his knees were drawn up between his arms and a rod inserted so that it ran under the knees and over the arms. A stick was thrust sideways into the offender's mouth and bound there. In this uncomfortable and humiliating trussed-up position the shirker, straggler, or drunkard was compelled to sit for hours, or longer, in full view of his company or regiment while it went about its daily business. As much as half a company was known to have been bucked and gagged at one time for straggling on a march. —JES

Buck Head Creek, Ga., eng. at. 28 Nov. 1864 While Maj. Gen. WILLIAM T. SHERMAN's infantry marched east from Milledgeville 24 Nov. 1864, his cavalry, under Brig. Gen. H. JUDSON KILPATRICK, ranged northeastward. At Sherman's orders, Kilpatrick prepared to feint toward Augusta, then move eastward to burn the trestle over Briar Creek, near Waynesborough, severing the railroad midway between Augusta and Millen. Before rejoining the main army, the troopers were to attempt to release Union prisoners being held at Millen.

Kilpatrick's counterpart in gray, Maj. Gen. JOSEPH "FIGHTIN' JOE" WHEELER, learned of the Federal movement toward Augusta and concentrated his cavalry there. Only when his enemy failed to appear did Wheeler realize he had been cozened, and, pounding after Kilpatrick, he spoiled for revenge.

His opportunity came on the 26th, when 2 Union regiments, the 8th Indiana and 2d U.S., lagged behind Kilpatrick's main force. Attacking their camp at Sylvian Grove by night, Wheeler chased them to their main column, which he also harassed, preventing Kilpatrick from destroying the bridge at Briar Creek. To compound the Union leader's discomfiture, he soon learned that the prisoners at Millen had been removed to points unknown. Easing his frustration, Kilpatrick wrecked more than a mile of railroad before turning to the southwest to rejoin Sherman near Louisville.

On the night of the 27th, Kilpatrick encamped a short distance from Buck Head Creek, for some reason pitching his tent far from the main bivouac. Due to his carelessness, he was almost captured when Wheeler's persistent troopers surprised him early the next morning. Riding to safety just ahead of his pursuers, the Union general led his men to Buck Head Creek, with Wheeler close behind.

While Kilpatrick's main force crossed the swampy creek, his rear guard, the 5th Ohio, with a section of howitzers, waited to greet the Confederates. On their appearance, the regiment opened with carbines and cannon. As its colonel reported: "When the smoke . . . cleared away the rebels who were crowded on the causeways of the bridge were not seen."

The Ohioans then burned the bridge over the creek, buying enough time for Col. Smith D. Atkins' brigade to dismount and form line of battle a few miles farther south, at Reynolds' Plantation. There, protected by barricades, it repulsed 2 columns of charging Confederates "quickly and easily." Wheeler then withdrew, and Kilpatrick marched toward Louisville without further difficulty. —EGL

Buckingham, William Alfred. war governor b. East Hartford, Conn., 28 May 1804. During the Civil War CONNECTICUT had a population of only 461,000. From that tiny number Gov. William Buckingham was able to raise 54,882 volunteers

for Union military service. In a state with only 80,000 registered voters, this speaks much for Buckingham's organizing ability and loyalty to the Lincoln administration.

Buckingham was a prosperous businessman who made his money first with a dry goods business and a carpet company, then as an officer and investor in the Hayward Rubber Co. Aside from his business prominence, he was active in reform politics, was twice mayor of Norwich, and was an enthusiastic Republican. In Mar. 1860, when ABRAHAM LINCOLN was preparing to seek the party's presidential nomination, he visited Buckingham for counsel since the governor had already been successful running on what was then the new Republican ticket. Elected in 1858, when the party itself was only a few years old, Buckingham remained governor for 8 years, the second longest stint any Connecticut governor had served.

Lincoln made a good impression on Buckingham and received his support. On Lincoln's ascendance to the presidency and first call for volunteers, Buckingham's eagerness to please ended in a slight embarrassment. Because of his state's size, the governor was only expected to field 1 regiment but ordered equipment for 5 times that many men and called for volunteers. But neither men nor equipment could be authorized because the legislature was not in session. Thus the first Connecticut men were unable to reach Washington until mid-May 1861, weeks behind other states.

Buckingham was consistent in his loyalty to Union war aims and was numbered among the "War Governors," those state executives who kept Lincoln's local support strong and dissenting party men in line.

His last gubernatorial term expired at the end of 1866. He spent 2 years pursuing his business interests, won a U.S. Senate seat in 1868, and died in Norwich, Conn., 5 Feb. 1875, shortly before this term ended. —JES

Buckland Mills, Va., eng. at. 19 Oct. 1863 Cavalry operations during the BRISTOE CAMPAIGN were generally confined to the traditional role prescribed for the mounted arm. Confederate Maj. Gen. J.E.B. STUART's 2 divisions of horsemen screened the Southern infantry, demonstrated against Union forces, and probed for weaknesses. As the Federals retreated before the Confederate flanking movement, Union Maj. Gen. ALFRED PLEASONTON's troopers shielded the rear, protecting wagons and infantry columns.

For 8 days, as the armies moved north toward Washington, Stuart and Pleasonton dueled inconclusively. The Southerners often dashed on Union detachments, creating the impression of a full-scale attack. The Federals usually counterattacked and brief, running gunfights ensued. On 11 Oct., near their old battleground of BRANDY STATION, the 2 antagonists fought furiously for some time with no resolution. 2 days later Stuart was caught between wings of the Federal army, eluding capture by concealing his division in a little valley. From 14–17 Oct. Stuart harassed the still-retreating Federals.

When Gen. ROBERT E. LEE abandoned his advance on BRISTOE STATION on the 17th, after Lt. Gen. AMBROSE P. HILL's defeat, Stuart, personally commanding Maj. Gen. WADE HAMPTON's division, retreated through Gainesville and Haymarket. His other division, under Maj. Gen. FITZHUGH LEE, withdrew via Manassas Junction and Bristoe Station. On the evening of the 18th, Stuart, vigorously attacked by some of Pleasonton's troopers, fell back to the south bank of Broad Run at Buckland, a good position to defend while waiting for Fitzhugh Lee's arrival.

The next morning the Federal cavalry, Brig. Gen. H. JUDSON KILPATRICK's division, advanced on Stuart, but the Confederates repulsed the feeble demonstrations. A courier from Fitzhugh Lee told Stuart that the former's division was en route and, if Stuart lured the Federals south, Lee would attack their flank.

Stuart immediately withdrew to Chestnut Hill, about 2.5 mi northeast of Warrenton. Deploying his troopers behind the crest, the flamboyant cavalry commander waited. Kilpatrick's troopers soon approached, marching to within 200 yd of the crest. Suddenly a lone cannon boomed, the prearranged signal of Fitzhugh Lee's arrival.

From front and flank Confederate horsemen galloped from concealment. Kilpatrick's startled troopers abruptly drew rein and immediately fled in confusion. For 5 mi across the open country, the Southerners chased the Federals, capturing over 150 of them. The "Buckland Races," thought some Confederates, were like a glorious fox hunt. The last significant encounter in the Bristoe Campaign was a minor affair but pleased Stuart immensely.

—JDW

"Buckland Races." *See* BUCKLAND MILLS, VA., ENG. AT.

Buckner, Simon Bolivar. CSA b. Hart Cty., Ky., 1 Apr. 1823. After graduating from the U.S. Military Academy 11th in the class of 1844, Buckner served with Gen. Winfield Scott's army in Mexico. Following several routine postings, the handsome, courtly Kentuckian left the army in 1855 to pursue business interests.

In 1860 Buckner became head of the Kentucky State Guard. A nonslaveholder, he saw slavery as a state concern. Supporting Kentucky's neutrality in 1861, he refused a commission in the Union army. In July he resigned from the guard and in September fled south to avoid arrest as a suspected traitor. Commissioned brigadier

USMHI

general in Confederate service 14 Sept. 1861, Buckner occupied Bowling Green at the center of Gen. ALBERT SIDNEY JOHNSTON's line. On 16 Feb. 1862, after his superiors had fled, Buckner surrendered FORT DONELSON and its troops to his former classmate at West Point, Brig. Gen. ULYSSES S. GRANT.

Exchanged during the summer, Major General Buckner led the 3d Division in Maj. Gen. William J. Hardee's corps during Gen. BRAXTON BRAGG's 1862 invasion of Kentucky. At PERRYVILLE, 8 Oct., Buckner lost heavily in an afternoon assault before breaking the Union line. He was sent to the District of the Gulf, Department No. 2, Dec. 1862, to improve coastal defenses. Given command of the DEPARTMENT OF EAST TENNESSEE April–August 1863, he was transferred back to Bragg's Army of Tennessee in September. Though he commanded the left wing corps at CHICKAMAUGA, he did not play a major role. A leader in the efforts to have Bragg removed, Buckner was promoted to lieutenant general 20 Sept. 1864 and shifted to the TRANS-MISSISSIPPI DEPARTMENT, where he served as chief of staff to Gen. E. Kirby Smith.

When Buckner was allowed to return home in 1867 he engaged in profitable business enterprises, wrote, and was

active in Confederate veterans' groups. Elected Democratic governor in 1887, Buckner gave Kentucky 4 years of honest, efficient government. In 1896 he ran for vice-president on the Gold Democrat ticket. When he died at his home near Munfordville 8 Jan. 1914, Buckner was the last survivor of the top 3 Confederate ranks.

—LHH

Buell, Don Carlos. USA b. Lowell, Ohio, 23 Mar. 1818. Buell seemed likely to become one of the Union's great generals at the start of the Civil War. Graduating 32d in the West Point class of 1841, he was a Mexican War hero, a talented strategist, a man of great bravery, and a military professional with friends in high places. Yet, 18 months after the war began, he was removed from command of an army, investigated by a military commission, and left "awaiting orders" until being mustered out May 1864.

Commissioned a brigadier general 17 May 1861, Buell helped organize the DEFENSES OF WASHINGTON, D.C., until August, when he was given com-

USMHI

mand of a division in the ARMY OF THE POTOMAC. In November he succeeded Brig. Gen. William T. Sherman as commander of the DEPARTMENT OF THE OHIO and was promoted to major general 22 Mar. 1862. The arrival of Buell's army at the Battle of SHILOH, 6–7 Apr. 1862, on the evening of the first day, came just in time to prevent a catastrophic Union defeat.

Then Buell's fortunes shifted dramatically. His operations in Kentucky and Tennessee were marked by delays and missed opportunities, and his evacuation of central Tennessee Sept. 1862 brought him public condemnation. On 30 Sept. he was notified that Maj. Gen. GEORGE H. THOMAS had been chosen to replace him in the critical campaign to repel the invasion of Kentucky by Confederate Gen. BRAXTON BRAGG and Maj. Gen. E. KIRBY SMITH. But Thomas protested that Buell was ready to attack, so the order was canceled. On 8 Oct. 1862 Buell clashed with Bragg in the bloody Battle of PERRYVILLE. Though Bragg retreated from Kentucky, Buell's failure to pursue him disappointed his superiors and enraged the public. Buell was removed from command 24 Oct. and never led troops again.

Buell's failure as a field general is generally attributed to his overly cautious approach to combat and his uninspiring personality. After the war he became president of a Kentucky ironworks and later served as a Federal pension agent in Louisville. d. Paradise, Ky., 19 Nov. 1898.

—DS

"buffalo hunt." *See* BAYLOR's "BUFFALO HUNT."

Buford, Abraham. CSA b. Woodford Cty., Ky., 18 Jan. 1820, Buford studied with tutors and attended Centre College before entering West Point in 1837. Graduating 51st in his class 4 years later, he was assigned to the 1st Dragoons as a brevet 2d lieutenant and received his commission in 1842. He was brevetted for gallantry at Buena Vista during the Mexican War, then served on frontier duty until resigning from the army Oct. 1854 with rank of captain.

Before the Civil War Buford raised cattle and thoroughbred

horses on his farm near Versailles, Ky. Politically he advocated STATES RIGHTS but opposed secession. He stayed out of the fighting until Gen. BRAXTON BRAGG'S KENTUCKY CAMPAIGN in 1862, when he joined the Confederate army. Commissioned brigadier general to rank from 2 Sept., he led 3 Kentucky infantry regiments in Maj. Gen. WILLIAM WING LORING's division through the SECOND VICKSBURG CAMPAIGN and into spring 1864.

In Mar. 1864 Buford's regiments were mounted and attached to Maj. Gen. NATHAN B. FORREST's cavalry corps, and Buford was promoted to divisional command. On 29 Nov. 1864, his force was the first to encounter Union troops at Spring Hill, where his men fought dismounted. During the Battle of Nashville 2 weeks later he was sent with Forrest to raid near Murfreesboro, but returned to the Army of Tennessee to serve in the rear guard during its retreat. Buford was wounded in skirmishing at Richland Creek, Tenn., 24 Dec., and went on recuperative leave until early in 1865. On 18 Feb. Forrest placed him in command of all cavalry forces in Alabama. Through the latter months of the war he operated in that state, fighting in the defense of Selma.

Buford returned to his farm after the surrender. There he became a prominent breeder of thoroughbreds and in 1879 was elected to a term in the Kentucky legislature. Depressed by business reverses and the loss of his home early in the 1880s, he committed suicide in Danville, Ind., 9 June 1884. His body was returned to Kentucky for burial.   —PLF

Buford, John. USA b. Woodford Cty., Ky., 4 Mar. 1826. Buford immigrated with his family to Rock Island, Ill., while he was a child. He followed his older half-brother, Napoleon Bonaparte Buford, to West Point, graduating 16th in the class of 1848, then served in the dragoons, fighting the Sioux, keeping peace in Kansas, taking part in the abortive Utah Expedition, and finally marching with his regiment from Kansas to Washington, D.C., at the onset of civil war.

When Maj. Gen. JOHN POPE reached Washington in 1862 to take command of the army assigned to defend the capital, he was shocked to learn that Buford, one of the most talented and experienced cavalry officers

USMHI

in the Regular Army, held a trivial assignment as inspector. Soon Buford was appointed a brigadier general and given a major role as a cavalry commander.

As a dragoon officer Buford had learned the technique of using cavalry as mounted infantry, employing horses to get the men where they were needed, then dismounting to fight. In addition, he recognized that the chief value of cavalry lay in scouting. Through scouting, Buford's active brigade captured both the famous plumed hat of Confederate Maj. Gen. J.E.B. STUART and a copy of Gen. ROBERT E. LEE's orders to mass the Army of Northern Virginia against Pope. After skirmishing with Lt. Gen. JAMES LONGSTREET's troops at Thoroughfare Gap, Buford sent Pope information about Confederate strength and position that might have prevented the disaster of SECOND BULL RUN had it been acted on properly.

On 30 June 1863 Buford led his division into GETTYSBURG,

where it pushed to the west to skirmish. When Confederates arrived in force the next day, Buford's dismounted men delayed the enemy long enough for Federals to occupy the position southeast of town that Buford had selected as best suited for defense.

Campaigning through fall 1863 weakened Buford's health, and he went on sick leave in November. His appointment as major general, backdated to the first day of the Battle of Gettysburg, was confirmed after his death in Virginia from typhoid fever 16 Dec.   —JYS

bugle calls.   Musicians were used by the Union and Confederate armies to call out directions for duty and maneuvers in battle. In the infantry, cavalry, and artillery buglers directed men in daily camp duties; on the field, infantry relied more on drummers for this service, while buglers continued to direct cavalry and artillerymen.

In camp a soldier responded to a minimum of 19 calls each day. If he was a cavalryman or an artilleryman the number could exceed 25.

Each day the first call, at 5 a.m., was "Assembly of Buglers," followed by "Reveille," "Assembly," "Stable Call," and "Breakfast Call." These called the men, respectively, to wake up, gather on the grounds for roll call, feed and care for horses, and eat. "Sick Call," "Water Call," "Fatigue Call," and "Guard Mount" followed these, directing men to report to the doctor's tent, then water the horses, clean up camp, and take guard assignments for the day, the last being called at 9 a.m. "Drill Call," "Recall," "Dinner Call," and "Assembly for Regimental Drill" were called next, through 4 p.m., and directed men to company drill, then retire from company drill, eat, and return for drill with the regiment. "Assembly for Dress Parade," another "Stable Call" and "Water Call," "Supper Call," and "Roll Call" were followed by "Taps," which concluded the day at 10 p.m., requiring lights out.

In the cavalry, special calls on the march directed the regiment's pace: walk, canter, trot. "Boots and Saddles" called troopers to the ready for march or combat. The "Charge" call directed the final rush into combat. In infantry and artillery services, "Officers' Call" or "Sergeants' Call" brought men to meetings, and other calls assembled them for everything from honor parades to worship services. The contending armies used almost identical calls.   —JES

Bulloch, James Dunwody. CSN b. near Savannah, Ga., 25 June 1823, Bulloch entered the U.S. Navy as midshipman in 1839, was promoted to lieutenant in 1853, and resigned from the navy that year. For the next 8 years Bulloch captained commercial vessels carrying mail for the government. When Georgia seceded 19 Jan. 1861, he was commanding the steamer *Bienville,* operating between New York and Southern ports. Despite his decision to support the Confederacy, Bulloch felt morally bound to return the steamer to its owners in New York.

After delivering the ship, Bulloch went South and offered his services to Confederate Navy

CWTI

Sec. STEPHEN R. MALLORY. Impressed with Bulloch, Mallory appointed him civilian agent for the navy and instructed him to secure steamers and military equipment abroad. Both men were anxious to initiate cruiser warfare against the North's merchant navy as soon as possible.

In Liverpool, England, Bulloch established himself with the banking house of FRASER, TRENHOLM & CO. Working secretly, he arranged with separate contractors to build 2 ships he would specially design as CONFEDERATE CRUISERS. Despite the obstacles created by Federal agents in England, Bulloch succeeded in getting both vessels—the *FLORIDA* and the *ALABAMA*—to sea in 1862. He also succeeded in manning and equipping the 2 ships without technically violating England's neutrality laws. While the cruisers were being built, Bulloch took command of the steamer *Fingal* and brought a large cargo of arms through the BLOCKADE and into Savannah harbor.

Delighted at Bulloch's resourcefulness and initiative, Mallory appointed him commander and promised him the captaincy of one of the cruisers being built in England. However, Mallory realized that Bulloch's work in England made him indispensable there, and command of the *Florida* and *Alabama* went instead to Lt. JOHN N. MAFFITT and Capt. RAPHAEL SEMMES respectively.

In addition to the cruisers, Bulloch secured in England several BLOCKADE RUNNERS and contracted for the building of 2 powerful ironclads—the LAIRD RAMS—intended to break the North's blockade. He also arranged for the building of cruisers and ironclads in France but was frustrated in securing possession of these vessels after they were completed. Because of the obstacles Napoleon III created over releasing ships built for the Confederacy, only one of the French-built ships reached Confederate hands—the *STONEWALL,* which did not arrive in American waters in time to see action.

In 1864 Bulloch scored yet another success by purchasing the British merchant ship *Sea King,* which became the *SHENANDOAH.* Commanded by Lt. JAMES I. WADDELL, it cruised to the North Pacific, eventually reaching the Arctic Ocean. There, its captain and crew destroyed a large part of the North's whaling fleet, unaware that the war had ended. The *Shenandoah* returned to England and was surrendered Nov. 1865.

Excluded from Pres. ANDREW JOHNSON's general amnesty, Bulloch remained in England, where he engaged in the cotton mercantile trade. He died in Liverpool 7 Jan. 1901, the year his nephew Theodore Roosevelt became president of the U.S.
—NCD

Bullock, Robert. CSA b. Greenville, N.C., 8 Dec. 1828. Receiving his education in local schools, Bullock moved at 16 to Fort King, near Ocala, Fla. He taught in the first school built in Sumter County and at 21 was elected clerk of the Marion County circuit court, an office he held for 6 years.

In 1856 the governor of Florida commissioned Bullock to raise a mounted company to suppress renewed violence by the Seminoles; the unit served under Federal authority for 18 months. In 1859 he was admitted to the bar but 2 years later left his law practice to enter Confederate service as a captain in the 7th Florida Infantry. In 1862 he was jumped to lieutenant colonel and sent to eastern Tennessee. That winter he was severely wounded at STONE'S RIVER.

The following year, having recuperated, he became colonel of the 7th Florida and led the outfit at CHICKAMAUGA, where the regiment suffered heavy losses but captured 150 prisoners

_LC_

while supporting embattled comrades. The promptness of this support gained Bullock widespread praise. He also distinguished himself at MISSIONARY RIDGE and during part of the ATLANTA CAMPAIGN. In the Georgia operations, he was most noted for participating in a spirited attack 28 May 1864 against Union works near Dallas. He was not with his regiment for much of the latter part of the campaign but that November rose to command Brig. Gen. Jesse J. Finley's brigade/Army of Tennessee, as a brigadier general.

During Gen. John Bell Hood's FRANKLIN AND NASHVILLE CAMPAIGN, Bullock's brigade supported the left flank of Maj. Gen. William B. Bate's division at SPRING HILL, then covered Bate's rear and left during a fierce but unsuccessful assault at FRANKLIN. On 4 Dec. 1864, during the Confederate advance from Franklin to Nashville, Bullock led 3 of his 4 regiments against an enemy outpost near Murfreesboro and during a Union counterattack was severely wounded.

Finished as a field commander, he returned to his law practice in Florida, where in 1866 he was elected a probate court judge in Marion County and in 1879 a member of the state legislature. Later he was again Marion County court clerk, then served 2 terms in the U.S. House of Representatives, 1889–93. d. Ocala, 27 July 1905, while a county judge. —EGL

Bull Run, Va., First Battle of. 21 July 1861 By early summer, the war-fevered citizenry of the Union and of the newly established Confederacy were clamoring for the fighting to begin. Pressured by public opinion, opposing presidents Jefferson Davis and Abraham Lincoln urged their respective armies to begin offensive operations. On Lincoln's order, 16 July, Federal troops under Brig. Gen. IRVIN MCDOWELL left Washington to attack Confederate forces commanded by Brig. Gen. P.G.T. BEAUREGARD and drive them from Manassas Junction, a vital railroad center about 29 mi southwest of the Northern capital. (*See* BULL RUN, FIRST CAMPAIGN.)

The commander of each inexperienced army planned an ENVELOPMENT of the other's left flank. Inadequate orders delayed the Confederate advance, but by 2 a.m., 21 July, McDowell had his 12,000-man flanking column marching down the Warrenton Pike from Centreville, where they had been camped since the 18th. His plan to attack Beauregard near Bull Run, a meandering stream to the east of Manassas, was sound, but it was too much for the raw Federals to execute, and he did not know that spies had reported his advance, giving Gen. JOSEPH E. JOHNSTON time to reinforce Beauregard.

Shortly after 5 o'clock Union artillery north of Bull Run opened fire, while Federal infantrymen feinted against the 8-mi-long Confederate line. The flanking column forded the stream at Sudley Springs and deployed 3 hours behind schedule. Confederate signalmen had already detected the movement, and Confederate troops were rushing north to meet the threat.

The battle began in earnest in midmorning when Col. NATHAN G. EVANS' Confederates opposed the Union attack force.

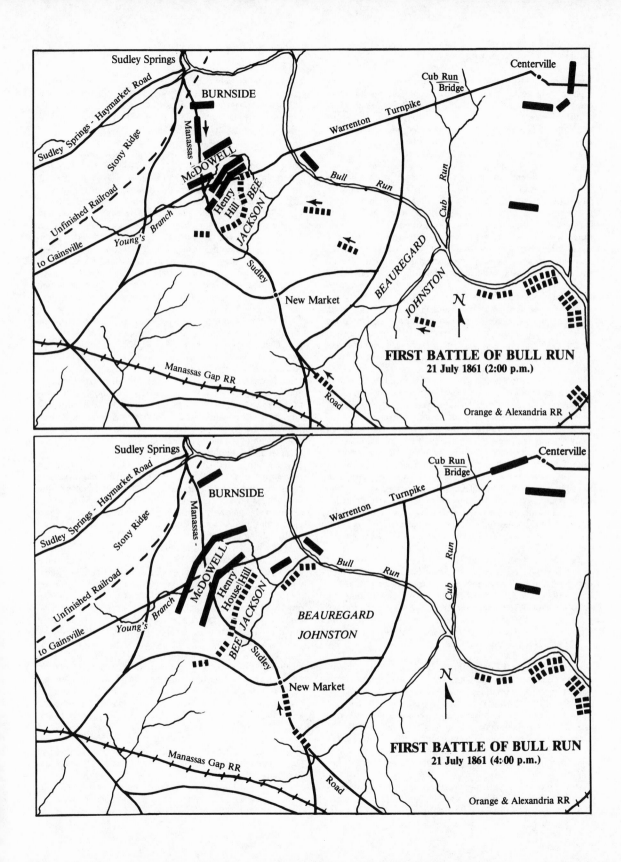

FIRST BATTLE OF BULL RUN
21 July 1861 (2:00 p.m.)

FIRST BATTLE OF BULL RUN
21 July 1861 (4:00 p.m.)

Evans urgently asked for reinforcements, which came piece-meal, slowly being drawn from the Confederate right, miles downstream. The troops of Evans, Brig. Gen. BARNARD E. BEE and Col. FRANCIS S. BARTOW held until early noon against the disjointed Union attacks. Finally the outnumbered Confederates cracked under the assaults, racing back across Young's Branch and the Warrenton Road. McDowell bolstered his attack force by funneling other units across Bull Run.

Beauregard and Johnston likewise sent reinforcements scrambling toward their crumbling left flank. One unit of these fresh troops was a brigade of 5 Virginia regiments commanded by an eccentric former college professor, Brig. Gen. THOMAS J. JACKSON. Jackson took a defensive position on Henry Hill, down whose slope the remnants of Evans' and Bee's troops were streaming. Bee, trying to rally his shattered brigade, pointed to Jackson's line and shouted: "Look! There is Jackson standing like a stone wall! Rally behind the Virginians!" Bee soon fell mortally wounded, but he had given Jackson his immortal nickname, "Stonewall."

In the meantime, the disorganized Federals regrouped. About 2 p.m. the Yankees surged up the slope against the stone wall of Virginians. For the next 2 hours the battle blazed up and down the hillside. Beauregard and Johnston arrived to direct the defense personally. Since, in the first months of the war, neither side had standard uniforms, the confusion and casualties were compounded. 2 Union batteries, mistaking a Confederate regiment for one of their own, were ravaged by a point-blank volley. Charges and countercharges swirled back and forth as the soldiers on both sides fought bravely.

Throughout the struggle, Confederate commanders kept bringing up reinforcements. Shortly before 4 p.m., with the last of Johnston's brigades now on the field, the Confederates ripped into McDowell's right flank, and rolled up the Yankee line. The exhausted Federals at first retreated slowly across Bull Run, but a Confederate artillery shell hit a wagon on Cub Run Bridge, jamming the main avenue of retreat to Centreville. Some panicked, and the withdrawal turned into a rout. Caught up in the unexpected rush were numerous civilian spectators who had come from Washington, D.C., to enjoy war from a safe distance.

Throughout the night the frightened Federals filled the road to Washington. The Confederates meanwhile celebrated their decisive tactical victory, now even more convinced that one of them could whip 10 Yankees. The battle cost the Southerners 387 killed, 1,582 wounded, and 13 missing, for a total of 1,982. The attacking Federals lost 2,896—460 killed, 1,124 wounded, and 1,312 missing. The number was low compared to the battles yet to be fought.   —JDW

Bull Run, Va., First Campaign 16–22 July 1861. Americans of both the North and South greeted the outbreak of war with an outburst of patriotism and visions of a quick, romantic struggle. In the North, politicians, newspapermen, and the public clamored for an immediate invasion to crush the rebellious South. Northern politicians insisted the Confederate Congress must not be allowed to convene in their new capital, Richmond, Va., 20 July, and Northern newspapers printed headlines and editorials urging the Federal army "On to Richmond."

While professional officers urged patience, Pres. Abraham Lincoln, bowing to public opinion, ordered a premature advance. He assigned the task to Brig. Gen. IRVIN MCDOWELL,

commander of the principal Union army encircling Washington, D.C. While McDowell advanced across northern Virginia, Maj. Gen. ROBERT PATTERSON, with 18,000 men, was directed to prevent Confederates in the Shenandoah Valley from reinforcing the army facing McDowell.

On 16 July, with a regiment of colorful ZOUAVES in front, McDowell's 35,000-man army marched out of Washington. 2 days of confusion, straggling, and a snail-like pace followed before the Federals entered Centreville, a village directly north and east of Bull Run. Behind this muddy, sluggish stream lay Gen. P.G.T. BEAUREGARD's Army of the Potomac, 22,000 Confederates, protecting the strategically vital railroad intersection of Manassas Junction.

When McDowell arrived at Centreville, he ordered a reconnaissance in force that same day. This probe by Brig. Gen. Daniel Tyler's division resulted in a brief, sharp engagement with 2 Confederate brigades at BLACKBURN'S FORD. McDowell spent 2 more crucial days reconnoitering, reissuing ammunition and rations lost or consumed by his ill-disciplined troops, and preparing a battle plan.

These delays also permitted the Confederates to combine their forces. In the Shenandoah Valley opposing Patterson was Brig. Gen. JOSEPH E. JOHNSTON and 12,000 Southerners. When Confederate authorities learned through spies of McDowell's advance, they had ordered Johnston east to reinforce Beauregard. Screened by a cavalry brigade, Johnston abandoned his lines early on the 18th and marched to Piedmont, where his troops boarded cars of the Manassas Gap Railroad—the first time in military history that a railroad was used to achieve strategic mobility. A befuddled Patterson did not learn of Johnston's departure until the 20th, and by then all but one of the brigades had joined Beauregard.

The long-awaited showdown finally occurred Sunday, 21 July. In a battle fought basically between 2 armed mobs of green soldiers, the Confederates, on the defensive, had the best of it, and the day ended in a Union rout. Confederate Pres. Jefferson Davis arrived at the climax, urging a pursuit to Washington, but the victorious Confederates were as disorganized as the fleeing Federals.

The campaign had a profound impact on the country. Southerners became overconfident, while Northerners became grimly determined. The battle, which brought carriages filled with festive spectators from Washington, confirmed realists' insistence that this war would be neither romantic nor brief. 6 days after the defeat Lincoln replaced McDowell with Maj. Gen. GEORGE B. MCCLELLAN, a popular career soldier he believed could lead the Union to victories on the battlefield.   —JDW

Bull Run, Va., Second Battle of. 29–30 Aug. 1862 During the initial days of the SECOND BULL RUN CAMPAIGN Confederate strategy succeeded as Maj. Gen. THOMAS J. "STONEWALL" JACKSON's FOOT CAVALRY marched around the Union right flank, pouncing on its supply base at Manassas Junction and leveling it with a torch. To meet this disaster in his rear, Union Maj. Gen. JOHN POPE sent his Army of Virginia northward against Jackson's troops, locating the Southerners 28 Aug. when Jackson lashed into a Union division at GROVETON. The Union commander ordered a concentration on the old Bull Run battlefield.

Pope fought the ensuing battle with great energy but with defective tactics and judgment. As his divisions filtered onto the field on the 29th, he hurled them, piecemeal, against Jack-

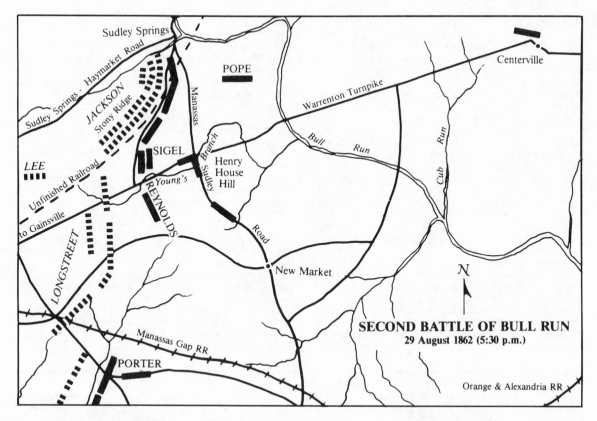

SECOND BATTLE OF BULL RUN
29 August 1862 (5:30 p.m.)

son. The Confederates manned a concealed position behind an abandoned railroad embankment in a wooded area running from the Warrenton Pike to Sudley Springs on Bull Run.

First to come against the strong Southern line, Brig. Gen. FRANZ SIGEL's command of Germans was stopped by Confederate artillery and musketry. Maj. Gen. JOSEPH HOOKER's division followed, driving for the Southern center. One of Hooker's brigades momentarily held the top of the embankment, only to be pushed off in hand-to-hand fighting. Maj. Gen. PHILIP KEARNY then charged Jackson's left, manned by Maj. Gen. AMBROSE P. HILL's Light Division. Hill's veterans, bolstered by reinforcements, repulsed the attack and sent another Federal command reeling. Finally, Brig. Gen. JOHN F. REYNOLDS, leading his division of Pennsylvanians across the open ground, was smothered in artillery fire.

On the Union left, meanwhile, Maj. Gen. FITZ JOHN PORTER and his V Corps arrived. Pope believed Porter had a clear avenue of attack on Jackson's right flank and ordered him forward. But Porter stumbled into Maj. Gen. JAMES LONGSTREET's 30,000-man wing of the Confederate army, which had reached the field about noon. Porter informed Pope, who refused to believe the troops were present. The Union commander renewed his attack order, but it was never carried out. Though Porter's decision ruined his career, it probably saved the army.

During the night the Confederates compacted their lines, a move Pope mistakenly interpreted as a retreat. The myopic Union general informed Washington of his great victory and

ordered a pursuit. On the 30th Porter drew the assignment, and his men, in massed lines, advanced. Artillery fire greeted the Union attack, and from the woods Jackson's veterans stepped forward. Musketry, in long crashing rolls, engulfed the field. Twice Porter's men crumbled before the searing fire, only to come on a third time. Once more hand-to-hand combat flared along the railroad bed. In one place the Confederates, out of ammunition, threw rocks to beat back an attack. Other Union commands added their weight, but Jackson held.

As the Union attack climaxed, Longstreet ordered his soldiers forward. A mighty Rebel yell reverberated across the field from the south, and the Confederates surged from their concealment. The attack was unrelenting; Federal units dissolved before the onslaught. Jackson charged, and Pope's army fled in retreat. Only a stubborn defense by Yankees on Henry House Hill prevented a disaster. Nightfall ended the battle with the Union army in full retreat to Centreville.

Gen. Robert E. Lee's tactical scheme to halt Maj. Gen. George B. McClellan's advance toward Richmond, Jackson's stalwart defense, and Longstreet's timely attack resulted in a complete Confederate victory, and Pope was justifiably discredited as a general. His army suffered 16,000 casualties out of its 60,000-man force while inflicting only 9,200 casualties on Lee's 50,000. Pope blamed the officers of the Army of the Potomac for conspiring against him, but he saw Rebels where they were not and refused to see them where they were. The Confederate victory at Second Bull Run cleared the way for an invasion of the North.　　　　　　　　　　　　　—JDW

Bull Run, Va., Second Campaign.   26 Aug.–1 Sept. 1862

During July and Aug. 1862, Gen. ROBERT E. LEE, with Richmond secure after his victorious SEVEN DAYS' CAMPAIGN, shifted operations to north-central Virginia, shuttling his army in stages northwestward against the newly created Union Army of Virginia under Maj. Gen. JOHN POPE. During the last week of August the Confederate commander decided on a bold gamble against Pope, whose 75,000 men were located on the north side of the Rappahannock River.

Lee, in what became a pattern of his brilliant generalship, split his army. On 25 Aug. Maj. Gen. THOMAS J. "STONEWALL" JACKSON, with half the army, began a wide flanking march around Pope's right to sever his communication and supply lines. In one of the war's great marches, Jackson's rugged FOOT CAVALRY covered 50 mi, falling on the huge Union supply depot at Manassas Junction. While Jackson's hungry, footsore veterans burned and feasted on the 27th, Pope abandoned his position, fanning his units northward. Lee, with Maj. Gen. JAMES LONGSTREET's corps, also left the Rappahannock, arcing northward to join Jackson.

The elusive Jackson left the smoldering depot during the night, marching to a wooded ridge north of the Warrenton Pike on the old Bull Run battlefield. Throughout the 28th the Federals, marching and countermarching, under confusing and contradictory orders, searched for the Confederates. At sunset Brig. Gen. JOHN GIBBON's brigade, marching on the Warrenton Pike, crossed Jackson's concealed front. The general seized the

opportunity and attacked. In this Battle of GROVETON, the 2 foes fought fiercely until dark.

Pope ordered a concentration against Jackson, neglecting Longstreet, who had entered Thoroughfare Gap to the west during the evening of the 28th. As Union divisions—some of which belonged to Maj. Gen. GEORGE B. MCCLELLAN's Army of the Potomac—reached the field on the 29th, Pope hurled them by detail against Jackson's veterans, located behind an abandoned railroad embankment. The Southerners repulsed 6 bloody assaults by the right half of the Union army. On Pope's left Maj. Gen. FITZ JOHN PORTER failed to attack Jackson's flank, arguing that he could not because of Longstreet's arrival.

During the night Lee pulled back some units to buttress his lines. Pope misinterpreted the Confederate retrenchment as a retreat and on the 30th advanced to cut it off. But Jackson's men were waiting and once more battered the charging Federals. Finally, Lee sent Longstreet's 30,000 soldiers forward in a furious counterattack. The entire Union line crumbled under the assault, withdrawing a mile before a stubborn rear guard halted the Confederates.

Pope regrouped his defeated army on the heights near Centreville on the 31st. 2 corps from McClellan's command arrived, belatedly, to bolster Pope's ranks. Lee, meanwhile, sought another opportunity to turn the Union right, ordering Jackson to a position west of Chantilly. The next day Stonewall advanced, which resulted in the Battle of CHANTILLY. Pope

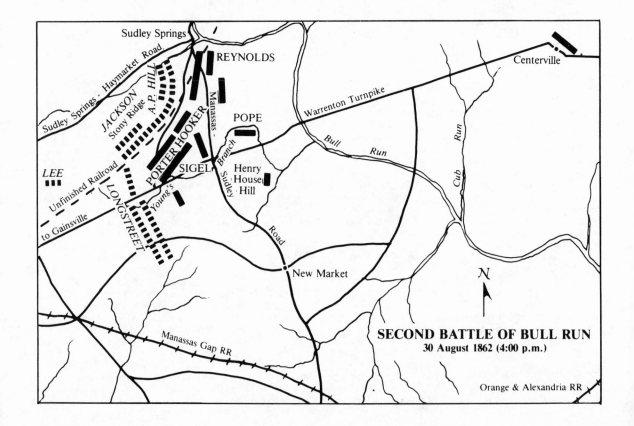

SECOND BATTLE OF BULL RUN
30 August 1862 (4:00 p.m.)

withdrew closer to Washington, D.C., and the campaign ended.

Recriminations followed this humiliating Union defeat. The boastful Pope, thoroughly outgeneraled by Lee and Jackson, blamed McClellan and his clique of officers for not reinforcing him promptly and adequately. As for the late arrival of McClellan's corps and his egotistical criticism of Pope, Pres. Abraham Lincoln considered "Little Mac's" evident lack of cooperation "unpardonable." Some cabinet members thought he should be court-martialed, while one wanted him shot. But Lincoln knew that only the popular McClellan could reorganize the demoralized army, and the general resumed command as Lee marched northward into Maryland.   —JDW

bummers. The origin of this term, applied to Maj. Gen. WILLIAM T. SHERMAN's foragers during the MARCH TO THE SEA and the CAROLINAS CAMPAIGN, is obscure but was common army parlance by 1864. Possibly deriving from the German *Bummler,* meaning "idler" or "wastrel," the name was embraced by many soldiers, who believed it struck terror in the hearts of Southern people.

The soldiers of the ARMY OF GEORGIA were authorized to live off the land, since it was Sherman's intent to "make Georgia howl" and to lay just as heavy a hand on South Carolina, which many Federals considered a "hellhole of secession." On the road from Atlanta to the sea and then north, Sherman's columns left their supply bases far behind, and their wagons could not carry provisions sufficient for all. Nevertheless, the Union commander sought to regulate and limit foraging, keeping it within accepted rules of warfare. Each brigade leader was to organize a foraging detail under "discreet officers." The details were empowered to gather rations and forage of any sort and quantity useful to their commands and could appropriate animals and conveyances without limit. Soldiers, however, were not to trespass on any private dwelling, were to avoid abusive or threatening language, and, when possible, were to leave each family "a reasonable portion [of provisions] for their maintenance." In regions where the army moved unmolested, no destruction of property was permitted. But where bushwhackers or guerrillas impeded the march, corps commanders were enjoined to "enforce a devastation more or less relentless, according to the measure of hostility."

Many who marched through Georgia and the Carolinas disregarded these prohibitions. Too often, foraging parties became bands of marauders answering to no authority. One conscientious bummer wrote to his sister about the depredations inflicted on South Carolina:

> How would you like it, do you think, Ab, to have troops passing your house constantly . . . ransacking and plundering and carrying off everything that could be of any use to them? There is considerable excitement in foraging, but it is [a] disagreeable business in some respects to go into people's houses and take their provisions and have the women begging and entreating you to leave a little when you are necessitated to take all. But I feel some degree of consolation in the knowledge I have that I never went beyond my duty to pillage.   —EGL

Burbridge, Stephen Gano. USA b. Scott Cty., Ky., 19 Aug 1831. A lawyer when war erupted, Burbridge raised the 26th Kentucky Infantry and was commissioned its colonel. As part of the Union Army of the Ohio, the regiment took part in the Battle of SHILOH, Apr. 1862. Promoted to brigadier general of volunteers as of 9 June 1862, Burbridge commanded a brigade in the XIII (Maj. Gen. JOHN A. MCCLERNAND's) Corps during the ARKANSAS POST and VICKSBURG campaigns. Assigned, temporarily at first, to command the District of Kentucky, Burbridge relieved Brig. Gen. Jeremiah Boyle in Feb. 1864. As civil administrator, he incensed the

USMHI

people of Kentucky and was charged with interference in the general election of Nov. 1864; he was removed Jan. 1865.

As part of Lt. Gen. ULYSSES S. GRANT's 1864 spring offensive, Burbridge was ordered to mount a raid into southwest Virginia aimed at saltworks and lead mines near SALTVILLE, Va. To forestall such a raid, Confederate Brig. Gen. JOHN HUNT MORGAN staged his own into Kentucky from Virginia in June 1864, so Burbridge abandoned his plan in order to follow Morgan. After a forced march of 90 mi in 24 hours, Burbridge caught the dismounted portion of Morgan's command at Mount Sterling and dispersed it. Unable to prevent the taking of Lexington and then Cynthiana, Burbridge did keep Morgan from fully exploiting the situation by staying as close as possible to his rear guard. At Cynthiana, 12 June 1864, Burbridge caught Morgan again and delivered a crushing defeat, capturing or scattering Morgan's entire command. In recognition of his success, Burbridge was brevetted major general of volunteers and congratulated by Pres. Abraham Lincoln among others. Burbridge also led 2 raids against SALTVILLE in the fall and winter of 1864, the first repulsed, the second only partly successful.

Because Burbridge had joined the Federal army, he found he was unwelcome in Kentucky after the war. d. Brooklyn, N.Y., 2 Dec. 1894.   —PMMC

Burgess' Mill, Va., eng. at. 27 Oct. 1864 The fighting of trench warfare had been the daily, deadly tedium along the miles of front encircling Petersburg since the beginning of Oct. 1864. During the last week of the month, Lt. Gen. ULYSSES S. GRANT ordered a movement to the left against the Boydton Plank Road and the South Side Railroad, and to sever these vital Confederate arteries Grant assigned 43,000 men of the 57,000 available.

Parts or all of 3 infantry corps and a cavalry division abandoned their positions at 7:30 on the rainy morning of 27 Oct. Maj. Gen. WINFIELD S. HANCOCK with 2 divisions of his II Corps moved on the force's left, directed to cross Hatcher's Run on the Vaughan Road and move north to the Boydton Road. Maj. Gen. JOHN G. PARKE's IX Corps, supported by Maj. Gen. GOUVERNEUR K. WARREN's V Corps, was ordered to attack Confederate lines north of Hatcher's Run. If Parke succeeded, Warren would extend the penetration.

By noon Hancock and Maj. Gen. DAVID M. GREGG's cavalry had reached the Boydton Road near Burgess' Mill, 12 mi southwest of Petersburg. Hancock waited while Parke and Warren advanced on the right, but the 2 corps floundered, unable to coordinate their commands. Maj. Gen. CADMUS M. WILCOX's Confederate division repulsed Parke's sorties north of

Hatcher's Run. Warren then sent Brig. Gen. SAMUEL W. CRAW-FORD's Pennsylvania Reserves in an attack along the south bank, but the charge lost cohesion in the dense foliage and failed to crack Wilcox's line.

Confederate Lt. Gen. AMBROSE P. HILL meanwhile abandoned his trenches to counterattack Hancock and Gregg. Maj. Gens. WILLIAM MAHONE's and HENRY HETH's infantry divisions and Maj. Gen. WADE HAMPTON's cavalry division momentarily rolled back the Union flanks, but a Federal charge finally stabilized the line. Hampton's horsemen fought particularly well, but for Hampton it was a tragic day: in the midst of the fighting he found his 2 sons—one dying and the other badly wounded.

Since Hancock could not be resupplied or reinforced, the Federals withdrew, returning to the trenches the next day. The operation cost Grant 166 killed, 1,028 wounded, and 564 missing. Confederate losses are unknown, but Lee's thinning ranks held once more, and another month of relative quiet followed. —JDW

Burns, John L. b. Pa., 1789. A veteran of the War of 1812 and a former constable of Gettysburg, Pa., Burns was a cobbler there in 1863. On 1 July, when the Battle of GETTYSBURG began, he picked up his flintlock musket, hiked to the field, and asked the 150th Pennsylvania's Col. Langhorne Wister where to fight. For safety, the officer directed the old man to the woods, but Burns took a place in the open on the battle line beside Wister's troops. Later, he also fought with the IRON BRIGADE, was wounded 3 times, and briefly held prisoner. "The Old Hero of Gettysburg" met Abraham Lincoln on the president's Nov. 1863 visit to the town and became a national folk hero. He died 4 Feb. 1872, and in 1903 his statue was erected on the Gettysburg battlefield. —JES

USMHI

Burns, William Wallace. USA b. Coshocton, Ohio, 3 Sept. 1825. Following graduation from West Point, ranking 28th in the class of 1847, Burns was commissioned a lieutenant in the 3d U.S. Infantry. On recruiting duty during the Mexican War, he spent the next 10 years on garrison duty in the Far West and the Southwest. In 1858 he became a captain in the Commissary of Subsistence and continued in that branch of service into the first months of the Civil War.

On 28 Sept. 1861, after serving as Maj. Gen. GEORGE B. MCCLELLAN's chief of commissary in the Western Virginia campaigning, Burns was appointed a brigadier general of volunteers. During the 1862 PENINSULA CAMPAIGN, he led a II Corps brigade in the Army of the Potomac. At SAVAGE'S STA-

LC

TION 29 June, his command was split by charging Confederates. Although hit in the face by a MINIÉ BULLET, he remained on the front line, repulsing the attack and causing enemy batteries to withdraw. Afterward, as Burns wrote, "I was prostrated with my wound, malaria, and twenty-eight days of constant strain."

He went on sick leave, returning to duty in time to lead the 1st Division of the IX Corps at FREDERICKSBURG, where his 4,000 men were attached to the Left Grand Division, under Brig. Gen. WILLIAM B. FRANKLIN. Held mostly in reserve, guarding bridges and other points on the Rappahannock River south of the city, Burns was praised by his corps commander for his "promptness, coolness, and good judgment" during the battle.

Apparently the field command was not his preference: 20 Mar. 1863 he resigned his volunteer commission to return to his Regular rank of major in the Commissary of Subsistence, holding a staff position through the remainder of the war and serving as the chief commissary of, successively, the Departments of the NORTHWEST, the Carolinas, GEORGIA, FLORIDA, and the SOUTH.

In postwar years he was on duty in Washington Territory, being promoted to lieutenant colonel in 1874 and to colonel 10 years later. He was retired as a brevet brigadier general (dating from his Civil War service) on his 64th birthday. Burns died in Beaufort, S.C., 19 April 1892, and was buried in Arlington National Cemetery. —EGL

Burnside, Ambrose Everett. USA b. Liberty, Ind., 23 May 1824. Burnside, the son of a South Carolina slaveowner, was reared in Indiana, where his father had moved after freeing his slaves. At 19, Burnside accepted an appointment to West Point, graduating 18th in the class of 1847 as a brevet 2d lieutenant, 2d Artillery, and serving in garrison duty during the Mexican War. Later, when stationed along the Southwestern frontier, he was slightly wounded in a skirmish with Apaches.

The easy-going officer got along well with people, and had an attitude toward life that was almost cavalier. He also liked to gamble, which sometimes resulted in poor judgment. Burnside resigned his army commission in 1853 to open a factory in Rhode Island to manufacture a breech-loading rifle of his own design. The enterprise depended on a government contract that the hapless businessman did not receive, so he was forced into bankruptcy. Creditors assumed control of the patents and during the war produced more than 55,000 BURNSIDE CARBINES and millions of rounds of ammunition for army use. Meanwhile, Burnside worked for his friend GEORGE B. MCCLELLAN, who was chief engineer of the Illinois Central Railroad, survived being jilted at the altar by a Kentucky belle, and accepted an appointment as major general of the Rhode Island Militia.

When war erupted Burnside rejoined the army as a colonel in the 1st Rhode Island Volunteers, a unit he had helped organize and one of the first 90-day regiments to reach Washington when the capital was threatened. At FIRST BULL RUN he com-

USMHI

manded a brigade, accepting on 6 Aug. the brigadier generalship offered by an admiring President Lincoln. Early in 1862
Burnside showed promise in coastal campaigns in North Carolina, destroying a small Confederate fleet in Albemarle and
Pamlico sounds. He also captured Roanoke Island, taking
2,600 prisoners and 32 guns, then proceeded to take NEW
BERNE, Beaufort, and Fort Macon, for which he was promoted
to major general 18 Mar. 1862.

Burnside commanded the IX Corps and Maj. Gen. Joseph
Hooker's I Corps under Maj. Gen. George B. McClellan at
ANTIETAM, where, like his superior, he displayed signs of hesitancy when speed was critical to victory: as a result of Burnside's single-minded determination to construct a bridge over
Antietam Creek—subsequently called "Burnside Bridge"—his
arrival in the field was delayed, which cost him the opportunity
to overrun the weak enemy position opposite the site. Eventually his men crossed the stream at a ford a mile distant but too
late to crush the Confederates on the other side.

Though an able subordinate, Burnside doubted his ability as a
commander. Twice, after Lincoln became disillusioned with
McClellan, he offered Burnside command of the ARMY OF THE
POTOMAC, and twice Burnside declined it. Finally, on orders
from Washington, 7 Nov. 1862, he reluctantly accepted the
assignment. Keenly aware of the need to exploit the Union
success at Antietam, Burnside decided to attack Gen. ROBERT E.
LEE's army at FREDERICKSBURG, Va., halfway between Washington and Richmond. As at Antietam, irresolution and the inability
to see beyond Marye's Heights, his immediate objective, cost
him the battle and Lincoln's confidence, and further damaged
the army's sagging morale. His attempt to cross the Rappahannock in Jan. 1863 ended in the disastrous "BURNSIDE'S MUD
MARCH" and ultimately his removal from command.

In March Burnside was given command of the DEPARTMENT
OF THE OHIO, where he presided over the arrest and military
trial of former Congressman CLEMENT L. VALLANDIGHAM for alleged sedition and captured Confederate cavalryman JOHN
HUNT MORGAN and several of his men. That fall Burnside acquitted himself well by defending KNOXVILLE against an assault
by Confederate troops under Lt. Gen. JAMES LONGSTREET.

Burnside returned east in spring 1864 to take command of
his old IX Corps, leading it at the WILDERNESS, SPOTSYLVANIA,
NORTH ANNA, Totopotomoy, and Bethesda Church. Finally, at
Petersburg, Burnside's failure to move quickly resulted in the
slaughter of his men at the Battle of the CRATER. He was relieved of his command for improper handling of troops and
resigned his commission 15 Apr. 1865.

After the war, Burnside was elected governor of Rhode
Island 3 times, 1866, 1867, and 1868, and returned to his
business activities. In 1874 he was elected to the U.S. Senate
and served there until his death at Bristol, R.I., 13 Sept. 1881.
—JDK

Burnside carbine. After the SPENCER and SHARPS, the Burnside, a first-class carbine, was purchased by the Federal government in larger numbers than any other. Patented 25 Mar.
1856 by AMBROSE E. BURNSIDE, later commander of the Army
of the Potomac, it was produced in 4 types or models and was
the first U.S. military arm to use a metallic cartridge.

The Type 1 carbine was produced by the Bristol Firearms
Co. of Bristol, R.I., a firm organized by Burnside to produce the
weapon. It was a somewhat delicate arm, with no forestock
and a tape priming device similar to that of the Maynard, a

USMHI

breechloader also popular during the war. Only about 250
carbines were produced, and at least 200 had been purchased
by the army by 1858.

The Type 2 carbine was produced first by the Bristol firm
and after 1860 by the Burnside Rifle Co. of Providence, R.I. It
too lacked a forestock, but the primer mechanism was eliminated and a spring catch was installed on the breech block to
keep it from dropping loose from its bed. It was the first of the
carbines to be produced in quantity, and 800 were purchased
by the Federal government, 48 by the state of Indiana, and 640
by Rhode Island.

Produced about Mar.–Oct. 1862, the Type 3 carbine was
the first to use the forestock, as called for in an Ordnance
Department order for 7,500 carbines 27 Aug. 1861. By now
the arm was fairly well developed and only a short step from
Type 4, the pattern produced in the greatest quantity. Among
Type 4's improvements was a hinged, double-pivoting breech
block patented by Isaac Hartshorn 31 Mar. 1864. While exact
production figures of this model are vague, a total of 55,567
carbines of Types 2, 3, and 4 were delivered during the war,
along with 22 million distinctive cone-based cartridges. All of
these guns were produced in .54-caliber. Numerous cavalry
units used the Burnside, and apparently it was also issued to
some infantry.   —LDJ

Burnside's "Mud March." 19–24 Jan. 1863 After the
major Union defeat at FREDERICKSBURG, Dec. 1862, the ARMY
OF THE POTOMAC was demoralized, having lost faith in its commander, Maj. Gen. AMBROSE E. BURNSIDE. In an ill-conceived
attempt to redeem himself, Burnside planned to march the
army several miles above Fredericksburg, cross the Rappahannock River at Banks' Ford, and fall on the Confederate rear. On
19 Jan. 1863 he ordered the lead elements to move out, despite strong objections from his corps commanders. As one
officer wrote, "The general demoralization that had come
upon us made two or three months of rest a necessity." He
also admitted sadly that he "came to the conclusion that Burnside was fast losing his mind."

No sooner had the movement begun than a pelting rain with
high winds set in for 48 hours. By the end of the day the march
was completely disorganized and bogged down. "An inde-
scribable chaos of pontoons, vehicles, and artillery encumbered all the roads," one Union officer noted, "supply wagons
upset by the roadside, guns stalled in the mud, ammunition
trains ruined by the war, and hundreds of horses and mules
buried in the liquid mud. The army, in fact, was embargoed;
it was no longer a question of how to go forward—it was a
question of how to get back." And the morale of the bedrag-
gled Federals was not helped when their Confederate counterparts on the other side of the river erected signs with such
messages as: "Yanks, If You Can't Place Your Pontoons Your-
self, We Will Send Help."

Finally admitting the hopelessness of the situation, Burnside canceled the movement 23 Jan., and the army began its struggle back to its old camp at Stafford Heights opposite Fredericksburg. Later one Confederate general frankly admitted that he had "looked upon the rain . . . as almost a providential interference in our behalf." 2 days later Burnside was relieved of command, replaced by Maj. Gen. JOSEPH HOOKER.

—JPC

Burnside's North Carolina Expedition. Jan.–Mar. 1862 *See* NEW BERNE, N.C., CAPTURE OF. 14 Mar. 1862

Bushnell, Cornelius Scranton. businessman b. Madison, Conn., 18 July 1828. The coasting trade—the business of shuttling wholesale goods up and down the New England seaboard by boat—offered Bushnell his first commercial opportunity. At 15 he went into the business and after a year was captaining a 60-ton schooner. By the time he was 21 he had established Bushnell & Co., a New Haven, Conn., wholesale food distributorship. Turning his attention to transportation industries, he invested his money in Connecticut's Shore Line Railroad and dabbled in iron construction.

At the start of the Civil War he became a partner in the construction of the ironclad USS *GALENA,* which brought him into contact with Swedish immigrant inventor JOHN ERICSSON, who became the consulting engineer on the project. During a business meeting with the engineer, Bushnell heard about Ericsson's old plan for an ironclad of his own and was shown a small scale model. He became enthusiastic over its potential and urged Ericsson to submit the plan to Washington officials in Aug. 1861. At a 9 Sept. meeting with Ericsson he was distressed to hear the government had made no response to the new ironclad proposal and he personally undertook a series of railroad shuttle trips between New York, Connecticut (to visit Sec. of the Navy GIDEON WELLES), and Washington; by 15 Sept. he had helped secure contracts for construction and financial partners for the enterprise. Along with iron industrialists Cornelius H. Delameter and Thomas F. Rowland, he undertook the construction of the ship that became known as the *MONITOR.*

Bushnell's involvement with the *Monitor* is his best-known war contribution, but in 1862 he was also elected to the Connecticut state legislature, worked with Connecticut Gov. WILLIAM BUCKINGHAM in drafting war legislation, and briefly served with Connecticut militia in the DEFENSES OF WASHINGTON, D.C., in the war's early days.

In the postwar years he shifted his attention back to the railroad industry and, as one of its incorporators, became the largest single stockholder in the Union Pacific Railroad. d. 6 May 1896. —JES

Bussey, Cyrus. USA b. Hubbard, Ohio, 5 Oct. 1833. Having moved to Indiana when he was 4, Bussey took a position as clerk in a dry goods store in 1847, and with 2 years' experience opened his own business in Dupont, settling with his wife in Bloomfield, Iowa, a decade later. There Bussey entered local politics, was elected to the state senate in 1858, and supported STEPHEN A. DOUGLAS for the presidency at the 1860 Democratic convention.

He may have had some prewar militia experience, because the governor placed him in command of militia in southeastern Iowa early in 1861. He was involved in skirmishing with Missouri secessionists before being mustered into Federal service

as colonel of the 3d Iowa Cavalry.

GB

Bussey's soldiering abilities were adequate, though he won neither great praise nor high command during his military career. At PEA RIDGE, 6–7 Mar. 1862, his men, plus an additional small force and 3 guns, fought bravely but were repulsed by Confederate Brig. Gen. ALBERT PIKE's Indian troops. During Maj. Gen. FREDERICK STEELE's successful winter 1862–63 expedition against ARKANSAS POST, Bussey had command of a full cavalry brigade, which he retained through the VICKSBURG CAMPAIGN. He was appointed brigadier general 5 Jan. 1864 and spent the rest of his career on garrison duty and in minor operations in the Southwest. After briefly commanding the District of Eastern Arkansas, he was ordered to FORT SMITH in Feb. 1865. His last few months of service were uneventful, though he was advanced to brevet major general and directed the victory celebration at Fort Smith when Charleston surrendered.

After the war Bussey resumed business as a commission merchant in, successively, St. Louis, New Orleans, and New York City. He reentered politics as a delegate to the Republican national conventions in 1868 and 1884. Pres. Benjamin Harrison appointed him assistant secretary of the interior in 1889, and over the next 4 years Bussey generously distributed pensions to Union veterans. He practiced law in Washington, D.C., from 1893 until his death there 2 Mar. 1915. —PLF

Butler, Benjamin Franklin. USA/USP b. Deerfield, N.H., 5 Nov. 1818. A criminal lawyer and powerful state legislator from Massachusetts, Butler was a delegate to the Democratic convention in Charleston, S.C., in 1860. Believing that only a moderate Southerner could hold the Union together, he voted to nominate JEFFERSON DAVIS from Mississippi for the presidency, not once but 57 consecutive times. For similar reasons Butler joined secessionists from the Democratic rump convention in Baltimore to support JOHN C. BRECKINRIDGE for the presidential candidacy. Nonetheless, when war erupted Butler unhesitatingly offered his services to the Union.

USMHI

7 days after the bombardment of FORT SUMTER, Butler made his first military contribution to the war, securing free movement of military personnel and equipment in and out of Washington, D.C., when he quelled the riots that ensued in Baltimore as he transported his regiment to the capital (*see* BALTIMORE RIOTS). Butler was the first major general of volunteers appointed by Pres. Abraham Lincoln, to rank from 16 May 1861, but proved to be one of the most incompetent of the president's many political generals. While Butler was in

command of FORT MONROE on the Virginia peninsula, his men were humiliated in a skirmish at nearby BIG BETHEL, boosting Southern confidence: the newspapers reported that the Union troops had discarded valuable equipment while retreating and noted other examples of inept conduct. The skirmish almost cost Butler his commission.

As Southern slaves fled northward through Fort Monroe, Butler declared the refugees "CONTRABANDS of war." This policy, initiated for want of any government directive dealing with the problem, caused great concern among Southern slaveholders, who regarded the action as confiscation of their rightful property.

To improve his image, Butler weeded out his weaker officers and prepared for a dramatic victory at HATTERAS INLET. On 27 Aug. 1861 Butler and Capt. SILAS H. STRINGHAM entered Pamlico Sound with 6 naval ships and 800 troops, overcoming 2 partially constructed Confederate forts and taking 615 prisoners. A grateful President Lincoln granted Butler a leave of absence to return to Massachusetts to raise new recruits throughout New England for further coastal engagements.

In May 1862 Butler was sent with troops to New Orleans when the city surrendered to the fleet of Capt. DAVID G. FARRAGUT. Appointed military governor of Louisiana, Butler was considered an effective administrator by his friends, but detractors accused him of corrupt practices, even of stealing the household silverware from the residence where he was headquartered. His enemies contemptuously dubbed him "Spoons" Butler, and Confederate Pres. Jefferson Davis went so far as to declare him an outlaw. Known also as "Beast" Butler, he created a national controversy by issuing his infamous "WOMAN'S ORDER," a decree designed to stop the women of New Orleans from insulting Union occupation troops. Extremely effective in stifling criticism and derision, the order did nothing to enhance his tarnished image in the community. Butler was removed in December 1862.

In 1863 Butler was given command of the ARMY OF THE JAMES, made up of 2 corps that were being held in readiness for Maj. Gen. ULYSSES S. GRANT's intended 1864 campaigns, but Butler allowed his entire force to be bottled up at BERMUDA HUNDRED by Gen. P.G.T. Beauregard and his men. As a result of this ineptitude, Butler's forces were reduced and he was transferred briefly to New York City Nov. 1864, after which Grant sent him home to await further orders. That month, when Butler learned of Grant's plans to mount a campaign against Fort Fisher, N.C., which guarded Wilmington, the last Confederate East Coast port still open, he demanded and through seniority received command of the operation. From its onset Butler mismanaged the assignment, the last he was ever given (*see* BUTLER'S NORTH CAROLINA EXPEDITION). He finally resigned his commission 30 Nov. 1865.

In 1868, as a Republican congressman, Butler played a significant role in the impeachment of ANDREW JOHNSON. From 1871 he ran for governor of Massachusetts consistently until 1882, when he was finally elected. In 1878 he was again elected to the House of Representatives, this time as a Greenbacker—yet another political transformation. As a Greenbacker he also ran unsuccessfully for the presidency in 1884. d. Washington, D.C., 11 Jan. 1893.   —JDK

Butler, Matthew Calbraith. CSA b. Greenville, S.C., 8 Mar. 1836. A nephew of naval heroes Oliver Hazard and Matthew Calbraith Perry, Butler attended a local academy

USMHI

then moved to Indian Territory with his father, an agent to the Cherokee Nation. On his parents' death, young Butler resided in Edgefield, S.C., with another uncle, Sen. Andrew P. Butler. He attended South Carolina College, was admitted to the bar, and in 1857 married the daughter of South Carolina Gov. FRANCIS PICKENS.

In 1861 Butler resigned a seat in the state legislature to become captain of a local cavalry unit. By FIRST BULL RUN, he was commanding a mounted unit in the HAMPTON LEGION, after which he was promoted to major and in Aug. 1862 became colonel of the 2d South Carolina Cavalry. He led the regiment with skill and enterprise in the ANTIETAM and FREDERICKSBURG campaigns.

At BRANDY STATION, 9 June 1863, Butler guarded the rear of Gen. J.E.B. STUART's cavalry division against a Union flanking movement. Though outnumbered, his tenacious cavalrymen were able to neutralize an enemy column, but in doing so the young colonel lost his right foot to an artillery shell.

Returning to the field on crutches early the next year, he was appointed a brigadier general and was conspicuous in many of the cavalry battles of 1864, especially Haw's Shop and TREVILIAN STATION. A major general from 19 Sept., at war's end he was fighting energetically but fruitlessly against the invaders of his native state.

After the war, Butler returned to law and politics. As a fusion candidate, he worked to integrate blacks into South Carolina politics. After failing in a bid to become lieutenant governor, he joined the Democratic party and when WADE HAMPTON became governor in 1876 was named a U.S. senator. He served 3 terms in Washington, being defeated in 1892 by Ben Tillman. Butler then practiced law in the capital, was a major general of volunteers during the Spanish-American War, and served on the commission that oversaw the Spanish evacuation of Cuba. Later he was an officer in a Mexican mining company and vice-president of the Southern Historical Association. He died in Washington, D.C., 14 Apr. 1909, and was buried at Edgefield, S.C.   —EGL

Butler Medal. In May 1865, as Union Maj. Gen. BENJAMIN F. BUTLER prepared to run for Congress, the first of these Civil War decorations were presented to black troops of the Federal XXV Corps for their assault on the Petersburg siege lines at NEW MARKET HEIGHTS and CHAFFIN'S FARM 28–30 Sept. 1864.

Tiffany's of New York designed the medals, of which 200 were struck, bearing the inscriptions *Ferro iis libertas prevenient* and *Distinguished for Courage* and hanging from a red, white, and blue ribbon. Many were presented to veterans of Brig. Gen. WILLIAM BIRNEY's 1st brigade/2d Division.   —JES

Butler's North Carolina Expedition. 7–27 Dec. 1864 By late 1864, Wilmington, N.C., was the last open Confederate seaport. To sever the South's only link to the outside world, and to stop a flow of BLOCKADE RUNNERS' goods estimated at $70 million yearly, Lt. Gen. ULYSSES S. GRANT planned an October army-navy expedition against the city. He postponed the project, however, when he feared the Wilmington defenses had been strengthened, and not until December, when he learned that troops had been sent from the city to oppose Maj. Gen. WILLIAM T. SHERMAN in Georgia, did he revive the plan.

The expedition was to be conducted by 6,500 troops of Maj. Gen. BENJAMIN F. BUTLER's Army of the James, aided by a fleet of almost 60 warships—mostly IRONCLADS, including 30 monitors —under Rear Adm. DAVID D. PORTER. Grant chose one of Butler's subordinates, Maj. Gen. GODFREY WEITZEL, to command the land troops, but at the eleventh hour Butler demanded the position. Though an incompetent field leader, the former Massachusetts legislator was a political power to be reckoned with. Displeased by Butler's determination to go, Grant nevertheless upheld his authority and hoped for good luck.

Butler needed it. To capture Wilmington he had to secure Confederate Point, a peninsula below the city, bordered on the east by the Atlantic Ocean and on the west by the Cape Fear River. And to secure Confederate Point, he had to capture Fort Fisher, a formidable earthwork near its southern tip. Called the "Gibraltar of the Confederacy," the fort was garrisoned by some 1,400 troops under Col. William Lamb and was protected by an awesome array of defenses along its 480-yd-long land-face and down its eastward looking sea-face, which ran for three-quarters of a mile along the Atlantic shore. These defenses embraced almost 50 cannon (including 15 heavy COLUMBIADS and a 150-pounder ARMSTRONG GUN); a cone-shaped mass of earth, 60 ft high, at the lower end of the sea-face, known as the Mound Battery; a detached 4-gun work, Battery Buchanan, situated a mile west of the Mound Battery and commanding the Cape Fear; a series of bombproof traverses within the fort's 14,500 sq ft of interior space, many rising more than 20 ft above the 10-ft-high parapets; plus ditches, palisades, and fields of approach strewn with battery-activated land mines ("TORPEDOES").

Even so, Butler appeared confident he could surmount these obstacles as well as a supporting force under Gen. BRAXTON BRAGG, commander of the Confederate Department of North Carolina, at Sugar Loaf, a sand hill 4 mi above the garrison. The Federal leader hoped to reach North Carolina so quickly that Gen. ROBERT E. LEE would be unable to send down reinforcements. Moreover, Butler had faith in the explosive effect of a barge filled with 235 tons of powder, to be beached near the fort and detonated by time fuses.

From the outset, however, his plans went awry. He was so secretive about his objectives and so unwilling to cooperate with the navy that he and Admiral Porter failed to reach a clear understanding as to the place and time of their rendezvous. Butler's troops massed at his headquarters at FORT MONROE, Va., 7 Dec., left aboard transports on the 14th, arrived off the North Carolina coast on the 15th, and waited in vain for Porter, who had gone to Beaufort for fuel and provisions. The delay made Butler's soldiers restive and seasick and so drained their coal and drinking water that the army too had to refit at Beaufort. Bad weather then held the troops for 6 days in that harbor, 90 mi north of Fort Fisher.

At last joining Porter near the fort 24 Dec., Butler learned that a division under Maj. Gen. ROBERT F. HOKE had come down from Virginia to bolster Bragg at Sugar Loaf. The delay at Beaufort had also prompted Admiral Porter to launch the "powder-boat" in Butler's absence. The weapon had proved a flop: grounded 800 yd from the fort, the barge, when touched off, had produced only a deafening explosion and a

brilliant flash of light. Hardly a particle of sand at Fort Fisher had been displaced.

Confronted by the unexpected, Butler nervously prepared to make a landing. Porter's ships spent 12 hours bombarding the fort, until the admiral felt the enemy's guns had been silenced. But when the first 2,200 of Butler's troops landed north of Fisher at 2 p.m. on Christmas Day, the garrison let loose with cannon and small arms, keeping the attackers 50 yd above the land-face. The Union advance contingent, under Col. Newton M. Curtis, trapped 300 teen-age Junior Reserves outside the fort, and one of Curtis' officers crawled through a hole in the palisade to seize the fort's colors, shot away by the navy. Pinned down by the garrison's fire, Butler's men could accomplish little more.

Late in the afternoon, Butler boarded a ship and reconnoitered the sea-face to determine if an attack could be renewed. On Weitzel's recommendation, he aborted the movement, pulling his transports out to sea so quickly that 700 of the troops ashore were stranded beneath the fort's guns until rescued 2 days later by Porter's sailors.

Returning to Fort Monroe on the 27th, Butler informed an astonished Grant that he had used proper discretion in withdrawing, after determining an assault impossible. Grant, who had ordered his subordinate to besiege the fort if unable to carry it, was so enraged that he relieved Butler of command and sent him home to Massachusetts. The general-in-chief then readied a second expedition against the Confederacy's last port, under Maj. Gen. ALFRED H. TERRY, a more determined and tenacious leader. (*See* FORT FISHER, N.C., EXPEDITION TO.) —EGL

Butt, Walter R. CSN b. Va., date unknown. Butt was appointed to the U.S. Naval Academy from Washington Territory 20 Sept. 1855. After he graduated from the academy in 1859, he was warranted midshipman, promoted to lieutenant 31 Aug. 1861, then dismissed from service 5 Oct. 1861 for refusing to take the oath of allegiance. Imprisoned at Fort Lafayette, then at Fort Warren, and later aboard the USS *Congress* at Newport News, Va., Butt was paroled 21 Dec. 1861. On 8 Jan. 1862 he was appointed lieutenant in the Confederate navy and on the 15th of that month was exchanged.

On 24 Jan. 1862 Butt received orders to report to the CSS *Virginia* and her commander, Capt. FRANKLIN BUCHANAN, serving aboard the ship as it dueled with the *Monitor* during the Battle of HAMPTON ROADS, 8–9 Mar. 1862.

In Feb. 1863 Lt. William H. Murdaugh selected Butt to accompany him on a daring raid on the Great Lakes to capture the USS *Michigan*. But the plan was canceled due to Pres. Jefferson Davis' concern that England might retaliate against this violation of her neutrality laws. Butt spent 16 months in Europe, Mar. 1863–July 1864, awaiting assignment to a CONFEDERATE CRUISER; disappointed at not receiving a command, he returned to the Confederacy. During Feb. and Mar. 1865, Butt commanded the *Nansemond* of the James River Squadron. After the evacuation of Richmond 3 Apr., Adm. RAPHAEL SEMMES organized his sailors into a naval brigade, with Butt named assistant adjutant general, and burned his ships.

Butt was with Gen. JOSEPH E. JOHNSTON's army when it was surrendered in North Carolina and was paroled 28 Apr. 1865. d. California, 1885. —NCD

Butterfield, Daniel. USA b. Utica, N.Y., 31 Oct. 1831. Butterfield graduated from Union College and became a New

York City businessman before the war. Despite his lack of Regular Army experience, he enjoyed one of the most meteoric careers in the Union ranks. In mid-1861 he was appointed colonel of the 12th New York Militia, which he commanded in the SHENANDOAH VALLEY during the FIRST BULL RUN CAMPAIGN. That September he was named a brigadier general of volunteers, to rank from the 7th, and led a brigade in the V Corps/Army of the Potomac.

USMHI

During the 1862 PENINSULA CAMPAIGN, Butterfield served prominently at GAINES' MILL, where his heroism won him (30 years later) the MEDAL OF HONOR. Following MALVERN HILL, he won renown by transforming a bugle call into the haunting lights-out refrain "Taps." He also designed the Federal army system of CORPS BADGES.

In Nov. 1862 Butterfield's political connections and talent for military administration gained him, successively, a DIVISION, a CORPS, and a major generalship (from 29 Nov.). Though few officers, including Regulars, had risen so quickly, his career soon declined. After the FREDERICKSBURG CAMPAIGN, in which he demonstrated indifferent ability, he reverted to divisional command.

In Jan. 1863, when Maj. Gen. JOSEPH HOOKER took over the Army of the Potomac, he named his friend Butterfield chief of staff. Through excessive officiousness and a bad temper, Butterfield gained many enemies and the nickname "Little Napoleon." When Hooker was relieved after CHANCELLORSVILLE, Butterfield retained his position under Maj. Gen. GEORGE G. MEADE till wounded during the third day at GETTYSBURG.

After recuperating, he returned to the army, again serving under Hooker at CHATTANOOGA. During the ATLANTA CAMPAIGN he led a division in the XX Corps, winning the brevets of brigadier and major general. Invalided home by sickness before Atlanta, Butterfield closed out the war on special service. Until 1870 he was superintendent of the army recruiting service and colonel of the 5th Infantry. When he died at Cold Spring, N.Y., 17 July 1901, he was buried by special order at West Point, an institution he had not attended.   —EGL

butternut. This synonym for a Confederate soldier was used late in the war, when many Southerners wore uniforms colored a yellowish-brown by dye made of copperas and walnut hulls. The term was also sometimes applied to PEACE DEMOCRATS.   —PLF

Buzzard's Roost, Ga., eng. at. 24–25 Feb. 1864 *See* TUNNEL HILL, GA., ENG. AT.

C

Cabell, William Lewis. CSA b. Danville, Va., 1 Jan. 1827. The man that cavalryman BASIL W. DUKE later praised for "élan and chivalrous bearing" began his Confederate service as a staff officer in the Quarter-master's Department. Graduat-ing 33d in the West Point class of 1850, Cabell performed simi-lar duty during most of his ca-reer in the U.S. Regular Army. After his resignation from that army in spring 1861, the Con-federate War Department as-signed him to Gen. P.G.T. BEAUREGARD's staff as chief quartermaster with the rank of major. He subsequently served under Gen. JOSEPH E. JOHNSTON until Jan. 1862, when he was ordered to join Maj. Gen. EARL VAN DORN's cavalry in Arkansas.

LC

Cabell remained in the West as a field commander, gaining distinction in leading troops and as an organizer. His first com-mand consisted of the troops stationed along the White River. There he distracted Union forces until after the battle at PEA RIDGE, then transferred Van Dorn's entire army to the east bank of the Mississippi within a week's time. When Van Dorn ad-vanced toward CORINTH, Cabell was given charge of a brigade, leading his men in several engagements around Corinth and covering the army's retreat to Tupelo.

After the fighting at IUKA in September, Cabell returned to Corinth, where he was slightly wounded leading a charge on the Union breastworks. He was wounded again, this time seri-ously, during a brief but severe skirmish along the Hatchie River when Union Maj. Gen. E.O.C. ORD intercepted the re-treating Confederates 5 Oct.

Cabell was sent to the Trans-Mississippi to recover. 20 Jan. 1863 he was advanced to brigadier general and given cavalry command of northwest Arkansas, with orders to recruit within the state. Over the next few months he organized one of the largest cavalry brigades in the Trans-Mississippi, but it was made up mostly of about 1,250 guerrillas, nightriders, PARTISAN RANGERS, and conscripts of questionable reliability.

Brig. Gen. WILLIAM STEELE ordered Cabell to hold FORT SMITH with these men in Aug. 1863, by which time desertion had seriously depleted his ranks. Vastly outnumbered, he loaded all available wagons with supplies and abandoned the garrison to Federal troops.

Cabell's Arkansas Brigade redeemed itself by fighting admi-rably in a skirmish at Marks' Mills, 5 Apr. 1864, but on 18 Apr. the unit participated in a grisly massacre at POISON SPRING,

which it ended by driving supply wagons over several hundred predominantly black wounded soldiers left on the battlefield.

Cabell was captured during Maj. Gen. STERLING PRICE's raid into Missouri Oct. 1864. First taken to JOHNSON'S ISLAND, he was transferred to FORT WARREN and held until Aug. 1865.

After his release Cabell returned to Fort Smith and became a lawyer. In 1872 he and his wife moved to Dallas, Tex., where he enjoyed a moderately successful career in politics. For sev-eral years he served as commander of the Trans-Mississippi Department of the United Confederate Veterans. d. Dallas, 11 Feb. 1916. —PLF

Cabinet, Confederate States. The CONFEDERATE CONSTI-TUTION did not provide for a cabinet but for the appointment of 6 heads of executive departments who functioned as and be-came known as the cabinet. During the 4 years of Southern nationhood, 14 secretaries served JEFFERSON DAVIS in the De-partments of Treasury, State, War, and Navy and as postmaster general and attorney general. 3 of them (JUDAH P. BENJAMIN, JOHN H. REAGAN, STEPHEN R. MALLORY) held continuous office; 2 (CHRISTOPHER G. MEMMINGER, JAMES A. SEDDON) resigned as a result of severe criticism by Congress; 6 (ROBERT A. TOOMBS, ROBERT M. T. HUNTER, LEROY POPE WALKER, GEORGE W. RANDOLPH, THOMAS BRAGG, THOMAS H. WATTS) resigned for personal rea-sons; 3 (GEORGE DAVIS, GEORGE A. TRENHOLM, JOHN C. BRECKIN-RIDGE) were appointed to fill vacancies in 1864 and 1865.

Though the cabinet was marked by frequent changes and the secretaries were accused of incompetence, Davis selected men of talent who performed capably with the limited re-sources of money, men, and material at their disposal. Con-gress objected strenuously only to the appointments of Benja-min (Treasury, State, and War Departments successively) and Mallory (Navy Department), but ultimately confirmed all of Davis' nominations quickly and consistently. Davis selected his secretaries prudently, consulting influential state leaders before naming a candidate. He looked first for men of ability, recog-nizing at the same time the importance of heeding political factions and of having the various states represented in his cabinet. Eventually men from 9 of the 11 Confederate states held secretaryships, Tennessee and Arkansas being the excep-tions. All had political experience, all were well educated, all had owned slaves, and most had earned rather than inherited some degree of financial affluence.

Davis nurtured good relations with his secretaries, held for-mal and informal meetings regularly to form policy, and gener-ally refrained from interfering with departmental administra-tion. He upheld the cabinet members despite a steady outcry of dissatisfaction from Congress, which expected more than any administrator could deliver in the Confederacy. The oppo-sition accused the president of manipulating the department heads and of showing favoritism by appointing men from the cotton states or from among those who had been radical secessionists before the war.

Within months after the Confederacy was formed, its congressmen were locked into a power play with the administration over the cabinet. Initially the provisional congress granted member secretaries (those who had been elected to represent their states) the right to participate in debate on any matters relating to their departments and considered restricting cabinet appointments to those holding a congressional seat. Davis favored the first proposal as a means of speeding legislation and dispelling misunderstanding between the executive and legislative branches, but neither provision was passed by the regular congresses for fear the secretaries would get credit due the congressmen for legislation. In Dec. 1863, 21 months after the cabinet of the permanent government was announced, Sen. Robert W. Johnston (Ark.) introduced a bill to limit cabinet appointments to 2-year terms, but the measure was dropped.

Beginning in winter 1861, Congress repeatedly called for Davis to reform his cabinet, never successfully. Representing the Virginia delegation, Speaker of the House THOMAS S. BOCOCK issued the final, desperate plea as a friend of the administration in Feb. 1865. Claiming pronounced public disapproval of the department heads, Bocock warned Davis to expect a congressional vote of censure if he refused to replace them. The president angrily defended executive privilege of appointment and the issue died after a heated exchange.

On Gen. Robert E. Lee's advice, the cabinet members fled Richmond with Davis the night of 2 Apr. They traveled together, attempting to run a government in exile until 2 May, when the administration party, realizing the futility of their efforts, began to disperse. Of the 14 men who had held cabinet positions, 6 (Hunter, Mallory, Reagan, Trenholm, G. Davis, and Seddon) were imprisoned by Federal authorities; 4 were never arrested (Bragg, Walker, Watts, and Memminger); 3 (Toombs, Breckinridge, Benjamin) escaped the country; and 1 (Randolph) was abroad at the time of surrender.   —PLF

Cabinet, United States. Faced with the formidable responsibility of uniting under his leadership the new, untried REPUBLICAN PARTY, made up of refugees from the Whig, American, Free Soil, and Democratic parties, ABRAHAM LINCOLN appointed to his cabinet men of power from each faction. He hoped a coalition cabinet in which each of the dominant interests was represented would work to overcome ideological differences. Those Lincoln selected were veteran politicians he

LC

had defeated for the Republican nomination in 1860. Each was more experienced in national politics than Lincoln. Most possessed considerable ability and ably supported the president's war policy, yet never before had a chief executive been subjected to such abusive criticism and deceitful maneuvering as was Lincoln.

13 men served as cabinet officers during Lincoln's administration: SIMON CAMERON and EDWIN M. STANTON (secretaries of war); SALMON P. CHASE, WILLIAM P. FESSENDEN, and HUGH MCCULLOCH (secretaries of the treasury); EDWARD BATES and JAMES SPEED (attorneys general); CALEB B. SMITH and JOHN P. USHER (secretaries of the interior); WILLIAM H. SEWARD (secretary of state); GIDEON WELLES (secretary of the navy); and MONTGOMERY BLAIR and WILLIAM DENNISON (postmasters general). Cameron's corruption and irresponsible use of patronage allowed Lincoln to replace him with Stanton 13 Jan. 1862. Smith and Usher, who succeeded Smith 8 Jan. 1863, exerted little influence on administration policies because the interior department did not play a prominent role in the war effort. Dennison succeeded Blair 24 Sept. 1864; by the end of 1864 Speed had replaced Bates, who resigned 24 Nov.; Fessenden replaced Chase 1 July 1864 and McCulloch succeeded Fessenden 6 Mar. 1865—all too late to influence the wartime cabinet substantially.

Lincoln respected the aged Bates, a competent constitutionalist and the first cabinet officer from west of the Mississippi River, but thought his advice too conservative for the times. Welles enjoyed the president's confidence; he in turn gave Lincoln complete loyalty and admiration. Seward proved to be exactly the man Lincoln needed to run the State Department, but his arrogant, abrasive personality engendered the distrust of congressmen, as did the false rumors he spread in summer 1861 accusing the Kentucky-born Lincoln of reluctance to preserve the Union by force. Few of his contemporaries failed to recognize the ploy as an attempt to usurp executive powers for himself. Seward, Welles, Blair, and Bates provided the most consistent support for Lincoln's war policies and for lenient Reconstruction. Chase and Stanton were Radicals who pushed for immediate emancipation and harsh treatment of the Southern states; to these 2 belongs the responsibility for most of the backstairs politics and internal dissension that marked Lincoln's administration.

Gossip in Washington predicted the reorganization of the cabinet whenever the success of the war effort seemed bleak, but only on 2 occasions did Lincoln's coalition come dangerously close to falling apart. The first threat climaxed in summer 1862 when Stanton and Chase, both abolitionists, tried to force the dismissal of Maj. Gen. GEORGE B. MCCLELLAN, who had repeatedly assured Confederates that he was not fighting a war for emancipation. The secretaries counted on 3 of their 5 colleagues to sign an ultimatum carefully modified by Bates; but Welles, who stubbornly refused to go along with the scheme, ended the palace revolution before the document was presented to the president.

The second challenge came on 16 Dec. 1862 when Congress attempted to take control of the executive powers by passing a resolution that would partially reorganize the cabinet. Initially aimed at Seward, the secretary closest to Lincoln, the campaign was fueled by Chase's indignant complaints that Lincoln did not solicit his secretaries' advice on war policies. 31 of the 32 Republican senators voted for the resolution, which called for the appointment of a new cabinet fully in agreement with the president, for congressional approval of each prospective secretary, and for a cabinet vote on all policy issues before they became effective. But under the Constitution the cabinet—designated heads of executive departments—held office at the president's discretion and had only whatever authority he permitted. Lincoln ended the challenge to his executive prerogative by arranging a meeting with the cabinet and Radical Republicans spearheading the movement. When asked along with the other secretaries to comment on the matter of consultation, Chase demurred. Having lost face, he resigned, which was precisely what Lincoln wanted since Seward had submitted his resignation earlier. Lincoln accepted neither resignation, assuring Congress of both men's exceptional qualifications to head their departments.

The coalition cabinet Lincoln had kept together for 3 years finally dissolved in 1864, and Chase figured prominently in its demise. At issue was a circular distributed Dec. 1863 that described Lincoln as a military despot and promoted Chase, a longtime presidential aspirant, as the only candidate with sufficient ability and principles to replace Lincoln in the fall election (*see* POMEROY CIRCULAR). In spring 1864 Blair, a moderate on slavery whom Radicals had earlier tried to oust from the cabinet, marshaled his powerful family in an investigation into Chase's dispersal of trade permits (licenses to buy cotton from Confederates in occupied territory) in Mississippi. Though Chase, with Lincoln's support, was cleared of the charges, the damage to his reputation destroyed his chances for the presidency and left the treasury secretary no choice but to resign. On at least 4 previous occasions Lincoln had refused to accept resignations from Chase, but that June he welcomed the opportunity to replace him. Knowing the Radicals would have to be appeased, Blair also offered to resign, an offer Lincoln accepted with regret in September. He safely disposed of Chase by appointing him chief justice of the Supreme Court 6 Dec.

Lincoln's coalition had held together until Radical Republicans began to dominate Congress. Notwithstanding the dissension caused by ambition and the desire of Radicals to turn the war prematurely into a war for emancipation and equal rights, the cabinet performed effectively under difficult circumstances. Under Seward diplomats in the State Department avoided war with England and prevented European nations from formally recognizing the Confederate government; Stanton purged the War Department of blatant corruption; Chase succeeded admirably in financing the war; and Blair, Bates, Welles, and Usher managed their departments effectively, providing the political balance Lincoln sought to keep the party from being splintered by factionalism until it gained strength. —PLF

Cairo, USS. The USS *Cairo* was one of 7 IRONCLAD river gunboats called "POOK TURTLES" after their designer, Samuel M. Pook. Built by James B. Eads at Mound City, Ill., for the War Department and commissioned 25 Jan. 1862, the *Cairo* was a flat-bottomed, light-draft stern-wheeler, tonnage 512, measuring 175 ft in length, 51 ft 2 in. in beam, with a 6-ft draft. Its original battery consisted of 3 8-in. guns, 6 32-pounders, 4 42-pounders, and 1 12-pounder HOWITZER.

From its commissioning until 1 Oct. 1862, the gunboat was a unit of the army's Western Gunboat Fleet. During this period it operated on the Mississippi River and its tributaries. After the capture of FORT HENRY Feb. 1862, the *Cairo* steamed down the Tennessee River and participated in the advance that led to the occupation of Clarksville and Nashville, Tenn. In April it escorted mortar boats down the Mississippi to begin operations against FORT PILLOW. In early May, while the Fort Pillow siege progressed, the CONFEDERATE RIVER DEFENSE FLEET attacked Union naval forces at PLUM RUN BEND, a few miles above Fort Pillow; although the *Cairo* was involved in the battle, it was not significantly damaged.

On 6 June the *Cairo,* with 6 additional Union warships, again fought the Confederate River Defense Fleet, off Memphis, Tenn. All the Confederate vessels but one were captured, sunk, or grounded.

For the rest of the summer it patrolled the Mississippi River from Memphis to Fort Pillow and in September was taken out of operations for overhaul and extensive modifications to its armor. In early December, once again operational, it was ordered to participate in a naval demonstration up the Yazoo River in Mississippi, prior to an attack on Vicksburg by a Union force under the command of Maj. Gen. WILLIAM T. SHERMAN. On 12 Dec. 5 gunboats including the *Cairo* started up the Yazoo. Shortly afterward the ship struck 2 TORPEDOES and within 12 minutes sank to the bottom, with no loss of life.

In summer 1956 the *Cairo's* remains were rediscovered. The gunboat was later raised and is being restored at the Vicksburg National Park.   —WNS

Calhoun, John Caldwell. politician b. Abbeville District, S.C., 18 Mar. 1782. Of the voices raised in defense of Southern rights during the mid-19th century, none sounded so forcefully as Calhoun's. The brilliant political theorist devoted more than 20 years to developing the STATES-RIGHTS doctrine and the secession argument advanced by radical Southerners to justify severing the Union in 1860. Foreseeing the day when war would hold the only solution to festering sectionalism characterized by the erosion of Southern dominance in Congress, he warned his Northern colleagues that the South would never tolerate interference with slavery, advanced his theory of

NA

concurrent majorities to equalize power between the sections, and labored aggressively to build Southern unity against an armed conflict he feared would be "irrepressible."

The South Carolina slaveowner was a lawyer by training and a statesman by choice. In 1810, after 2 years in the state legislature, he was elected to the House of Representatives as a War Democrat and achieved national fame for an eloquent speech urging the declaration of war against Great Britain. As secretary of war Dec. 1817–Mar. 1825 and as vice-president under John Quincy Adams, Calhoun followed a vigorous nationalistic course, but his early enthusiasm waned with reelection to the vice-presidency under Andrew Jackson. Once a proponent of federally funded internal improvements, a national bank, and the protective tariff, he broke with Jackson to assume the leadership in South Carolina's antitariff controversy, which resulted in the Nullification Crisis of 1832 (*see* NULLIFICATION). Except for a brief appointment as secretary of state, Mar. 1844–Mar. 1845, Calhoun thereafter represented his state in the Senate, becoming the champion of the radical states-rights faction.

The fiery orator's last great effort on the South's behalf was his opposition to the COMPROMISE OF 1850, which he believed would ultimately betray his region's interests and lead to war. Too ill and feeble to read his own speech denouncing the legislation, he listened silently as a colleague delivered to the congressmen his warning of the South's growing desperation. He was then carried from the Senate chamber to his home in the city, where his health deteriorated until his death 31 May 1850. He rarely spoke during his final 3 weeks, but among the few phrases he uttered was an anguished prophecy: "The South, the poor South."   —PLF

California. Although Abraham Lincoln carried the state by only a slim margin in the 1860 presidential contest, Civil War California remained staunchly loyal to the Union. Southern natives formed only 7% of the state's population but were extremely vocal, supporting a separate "Pacific Republic" 1860–61, whose flag was raised in Stockton Jan. 1861. Some U.S. Army career officers of Southern birth, notably Col. ALBERT SIDNEY JOHNSTON, commanding San Francisco's presidio, objected to the Federal government "coercing" states to remain in the Union and resigned their commissions, later joining the Confederacy. But when war came, California's legislature denounced secession, May 1861, pledging full support for "the Constitution and the Union in the hour of trial and peril."

Pro-Confederate efforts brought swift, effective response. The legislature outlawed "display [of] the rebel flag" and barred Confederate sympathizers from seeking redress in the courts. A small schooner sailed from Sacramento to San Francisco to hijack a large Pacific mail steamer for use as a Confederate PRIVATEER; the ship was seized by Federal authorities, and instigators of the plot were punished. Pro-Southern newspapers were shut down or barred from using the mails. San Francisco's Rev. Thomas Starr King stumped the state for the Union and to raise funds for the U.S. SANITARY COMMISSION. Republicans captured the legislature, elected Leland Stanford governor, and under the Union party label dominated politics for years.

California played little military part in the war, since the draft never went into effect there. But some 16,000 volunteers were assigned mainly to local home-guard duty; 500 Californians sailed east as the "California Battalion" and served in the 2d Massachusetts Cavalry; and a CALIFORNIA COLUMN also marched to New Mexico. More important, gold, wheat, wool, and other products from the state strongly helped the Union war effort. And war speeded congressional passage of the Pacific RAILROAD ACT in 1862, which eventually linked California to the rest of the Union.   —DL

California, Union Department of. This sparsely populated department existed as a military area of responsibility of the U.S. Regular Army prior to the beginning of overt hostilities in the Civil War. The area comprised the present state of California, the southwest corner of the present state of Oregon, the entire present state of Arizona, and that portion of the present state of Nevada west of 117° west longitude.

Headquartered in San Francisco, the department included Benecia Arsenal, a national mint, and the major West Coast seaport—all in San Francisco—and one of the country's primary sources of silver bullion, Nevada. Thus its loss to the Union would have been devastating.

The department ceased to exist 1 Jan. 1861, more than 3

months before the firing on FORT SUMTER, when it became part of the DEPARTMENT OF THE PACIFIC.   —BMcG

California Column.   Late in July 1861 the War Department requisitioned from California Gov. John G. Downy an infantry regiment (the 1st California Infantry) and 5 cavalry companies, under command of Maj. JAMES H. CARLETON, to guard the overland mail route in Nevada and Utah. The next month, Brig. Gen. EDWIN V. SUMNER, commanding Department of the Pacific, learned of Lt. Col. JOHN R. BAYLOR's Confederate invasion of New Mexico Territory. Though the information was fragmentary, he immediately ordered Carleton from departmental headquarters in San Francisco to southern California to prevent the Confederates from moving into the state's pro-secessionist stronghold there.

Carleton, a career officer in the Regular Army and now a colonel, dispatched a company of cavalry to guard the defile through which passed the road to Fort Yuma, the one weakly held garrison between the Confederates and California. For several months he drilled his men relentlessly and collected enough supplies to launch a 3-stage expedition to the Rio Grande to drive the Confederates out of New Mexico Territory.

Heavy rains early in Feb. 1862 delayed the departure but allowed Carleton time to learn that Col. E.R.S. CANBY had been defeated at VALVERDE by Brig. Gen. HENRY HOPKINS SIBLEY's Confederates and that 100 Confederate cavalrymen had occupied Tucson. Added to Carleton's command in light of this information were the 5th California Infantry, 1 company from the 2d California Cavalry, and Company A of the 3d U.S. Light Artillery. Finally, in early April, the 2,000-man force and 200 supply wagons left the coast on the first leg of a brutal 859-mi march across the mountains and through the desert.

Months of careful planning paid off as small detachments staggered their departures, reaching water holes at intervals to prevent overuse by men and stock. By 2 May all the troops had reached Fort Yuma with no losses. There Carleton officially named the expedition "The Column from California" and began moving toward Tucson. On 20 May an advance cavalry company entered the town to find that the Confederates had evacuated 48 hours earlier. Carleton secured Tucson, on 8 June declared himself military governor of Arizona Territory, and established martial law to restore order.

He rested the men for a month, then started toward the Rio Grande, meeting little opposition. By late August they had reoccupied Forts Thorn, Bliss, Quitman, and Davis, securing the territory for the Union and ending any Confederate hopes of recapturing the Southwest or recruiting in California.

On 21 Aug. Carleton, promoted to brigadier general, received orders to go to Santa Fe and assume command of the DEPARTMENT OF NEW MEXICO. After his departure, the California Column merged with other troops. They had never engaged Confederate forces in heavy fighting, skirmishing with them only occasionally; yet their heroic march had so disorganized the Southerners that they never recovered. The column had fought Indians and defeated the odds against a large body of men crossing the desert. The units in which they served were among the last Federal troops mustered out of service, remaining on active duty until late 1866.   —PLF

Camden Expedition, Ark.   23 Mar.–3 May 1864   Federal Maj. Gen. FREDERICK STEELE enjoyed a distinguished war record

until spring 1864, when, as commander of all Union forces in Arkansas, he was ordered by the War Department to cooperate with Maj. Gen. NATHANIEL P. BANKS in the latter's RED RIVER CAMPAIGN—the goal: the capture of Shreveport, La. Steele opposed the plan, for the roads were bad in that wet season, the country was stripped of forage, and his flanks would be susceptible to enemy raiders. But the government ordered him to move out of Little Rock, and Steele complied.

On 23 Mar. 1864, 3 weeks later than intended because of poor supply and organization, Steele led the 3d Division/VII Corps and 2 cavalry brigades south toward the Red. Brig. Gen. JOHN M. THAYER was to join him at Arkadelphia, making a combined army of 10,400. All along the way Steele skirmished with Confederate cavalry, slowing his march, but when he reached Arkadelphia 29 Mar., Thayer was not there, nor did he arrive for several days, by which time Steele had decided that he had to push on despite shortages of supplies. It was 9 Apr. before the 2 columns united in the vicinity of Elkin's Ferry on the Little Missouri, and already the campaign was in serious trouble.

Steele's role in the campaign was to draw enemy cavalry away from Shreveport, so that Banks could take the city with a minimum of opposition. The plan was working after a fashion, for 3 of the 5 available brigades of Confederate cavalry in the region were moving toward Steele. Confederate Brig. Gen. JOHN S. MARMADUKE, commanding the brigades of Brig. Gen. JOSEPH O. SHELBY, Col. Colton Greene, and Brig. Gen. WILLIAM L. CABELL, had set about harassing Steele's advance and began serious skirmishing with him 1 Apr. as the Federals left Arkadelphia. During the next several days additional skirmishes impeded Steele's advance at Wolf Creek and Okolona near Antoine, and at Elkin's Ferry. And on 10 Apr., when Steele and Thayer moved out into Prairie D'Ane, they engaged in a small-scale battle with foes that by now numbered more than 5,000, a battle that continued intermittently for 4 days. Confederates in the region were commanded by Maj. Gen. STERLING PRICE, and they believed that Steele's goal was Washington, Ark., some 10 mi west of Prairie D'Ane. But Steele only made a demonstration in that direction, then turned east and marched toward Camden, his original goal. Still short of supplies, he intended to make Camden his base for any further campaigning. His men had been on half-rations for almost 3 weeks, and the situation was made worse when word came of Banks's defeat at MANSFIELD, and his subsequent abandonment of the Red River Campaign. Now Steele was on his own, deep in enemy territory.

Thanks to the Washington feint, Steele reached Camden one step ahead of the Confederates. On 15 Apr., after a sharp skirmish with Marmaduke, Steele occupied the town with his exhausted, starving army. 3 days later further disaster loomed when a supply train sent out to forage was overwhelmed at POISON SPRING. On 20 Apr. Steele had confirmation of Banks's withdrawal when Confederate Maj. Gen. E. KIRBY SMITH arrived in front of him with 3 divisions. Smith ordered diversions made against Camden to cover the movement of other troops attempting to get behind Steele, and between Steele and Little Rock. Control of the campaign had gone over to the Southerners, and they completed Steele's discomfiture 25 Apr., when Price's troops captured a train of 211 wagons sent from Camden with a 2,000-man escort to get supplies. Only 300 men escaped. Out of supplies, outnumbered in the field, and in danger of being surrounded and isolated, Steele ordered a withdrawal to Little Rock.

Moving due north, by way of Princeton, Steele was harassed all the way and finally forced to battle 29–30 Apr. at JENKINS' FERRY on the Saline River. Leaving behind his seriously wounded, and abandoning or destroying the PONTOON BRIDGE he had constructed, Steele successfully defended himself and ended the pursuit. Still there were 3 more days of dreary march, often in the dark, the way lit by fires set by advance cavalry. On 3 May the Federals returned to Little Rock, thoroughly worn out, disgusted, and discouraged.

The whole campaign had been a failure, due chiefly to Steele's constant shortage of supplies and Banks's predictable failure on the Red River. Steele had suffered a total of 2,750 casualties—400 more than the Confederates—and lost 9 field pieces and well over 650 wagons. Worse, Smith and Price were now free to turn on the retreating Banks. Had they done so successfully, there might have been a major Union catastrophe in Louisiana. —WCD

Cameron, Robert Alexander. USA b. Brooklyn, N.Y., 22 Feb. 1828. Reared in Valparaiso, Ind., Cameron mustered into the Union army Apr. 1861 as captain of the 9th Indiana.

He had already had political experience as an 1860 Republican convention delegate and business experience as owner and publisher of the Valparaiso *Republican;* he had also studied medicine in Indiana and at Rush Medical College in Chicago. When the 9th completed its 3-month enlistment after the 1861 campaigning in western Virginia, he helped induce it to reenlist, almost to a man, for the duration of the war—a feat that won him appointment as lieutenant colonel of the 19th In-

LC

diana, then lieutenant colonel and colonel of the 34th Indiana. With these men he saw service under Maj. Gen. John Pope at NEW MADRID, Mo., and ISLAND NO. 10 on the Mississippi River. On 11 Aug. 1863, after the occupation of Memphis, Tenn., and trench duty during the Siege of VICKSBURG, Cameron was appointed brigadier general.

Transferred to the Union's Department of the Gulf for Maj. Gen. Nathaniel P. Banks's RED RIVER CAMPAIGN in 1864, Cameron and Brig. Gen. THOMAS E. G. RANSOM were given command of the XIII Corps' 3d and 4th divisions, respectively, both of which saw combat on Banks's failed Federal foray into the Louisiana bayou country. On 27 Apr. 1864, during one of this corps' frequent reorganizations and changes of command, Cameron was its commanding general for the day, his briefest and highest position of responsibility.

After Banks's campaign Cameron oversaw the occupation of Thibodeaux, La., as district commander, until the end of the war. He was brevetted major general 13 Mar. 1865 for his war service, and 22 June he resigned from the army.

Cameron spent the rest of his life in the Far West, pioneering in Colorado and living briefly in San Francisco. Before his death at Canon City, Colo., 10 Mar. 1894, he could number among his accomplishments the founding of the city of Greeley, Colo. —JES

Cameron, Simon. USP b. Lancaster Cty., Pa., 8 Mar. 1799. Cameron's contemporaries claimed that the Pennsylvania politician never forgot a friend or forgave an enemy. A printer by trade, he bought the Harrisburg *Republican* in 1826, using it to influence state and national affairs. A shrewd businessman, Cameron dominated state politics, maneuvering Democrat James Buchanan into the Senate in 1833 in exchange for appointment as Indian claims adjuster.

USMHI

His reputation for corruption grew with his power, and his first Senate term, 1845, resulted from compromise coalitions for which he was notorious. Cameron's bargaining cost him reelection consistently until 1858, when he returned to the Senate as a Republican. He delivered the state to ABRAHAM LINCOLN in 1860, expecting the president to make him secretary of war. Lincoln fulfilled his obligation reluctantly and with embarrassing results.

Faced with protecting a capital surrounded by Confederate sympathizers, provisioning the city, keeping communications open to the North, coping with excess volunteer troops, and replacing pro-Southern army officers, Cameron met only limited success and received sharp criticism for his efforts. In addition to manipulating Gen. WINFIELD SCOTT's resignation, he was accused of buying outdated carbines and overpriced Kentucky mules and of staffing the department with Pennsylvanians.

Cameron dispensed patronage so flagrantly that demands for his removal were incessant. Opponents interpreted his insistence on arming black troops as an attempt to gain public favor—charges Cameron denied, emphasizing his good intentions by endorsing JOHN C. FRÉMONT's aborted emancipation proclamation (*see* FRÉMONT'S EMANCIPATION ORDER). His order supporting Maj. Gen. BENJAMIN F. BUTLER's designation of refugee slaves as "CONTRABANDS" presaged the CONFISCATION ACT OF 1862.

Lincoln deposed Cameron Jan. 1862 by naming him minister to Russia, but the "Czar of Pennsylvania" returned to the U.S. to lose a bid for the Senate in 1863. Reelected in 1864, he remained in power for a decade. When he retired from public life, he succeeded in having his son appointed in his place. d. Lancaster Cty., Pa., 26 June 1889. —PLF

camouflet. To combat enemy miners tunneling under their siege works or trenches, Confederates and Federals sometimes used a simple explosive device called a camouflet. The explosive charge was planted in front of the defenses so that as enemy miners tunneled forward, the camouflet would rest in their path. When the enemy struck the device with a pick or shovel he would have to retreat hastily or the shaft would collapse on him. If planted skillfully, the camouflet would explode downward leaving the earth above intact so as not to reveal the mine's location.

Probably as old as the history of siege warfare and gunpowder, these countermining devices were rarely used during the Civil War but were tried by Confederates at Vicksburg. An 18th-century military dictionary stated that when miners struck camouflets, "stinking combustibles" would fly into their faces. *Camouflet,* from the Old French, means a whiff of smoke puffed into someone's face. —JES

camp. A camp was loosely defined as anywhere a regiment was "established in tents, huts, or in bivouac." It was set up roughly as the unit would be drawn up in line of battle, with each company tented in rank, perpendicular to a color line, the line of company guidons, and flags. Regimental cooking facilities were placed behind the rank of company tents; provost guards, noncommissioned officers, and SUTLERS in a horizontal line behind them; subalterns and lower officers lined up behind them; the regimental staff lined up next; then the baggage train positioned in a long file. A regiment's standard was raised in front of its colonel's tent, at the center of the staff officers' tent line, and the distance of all tent positions was strictly prescribed by a certain number of paces.

When larger units went into camp, these regimental formations stayed the same, but the regiments themselves were arranged with some flexibility to allow for the lay of the land and availability of wood and water. Cavalry was always camped at the rear. —JES

Campbell, Alexander William. CSA b. Nashville, Tenn., 4 June 1828. After enlisting in the Confederate Army as a private, Campbell spent most of his army service on staff duty, rising to brigadier general of cavalry late in the war. In civilian life the able administrator had been a noted attorney and a law partner of future U.S. Supreme Court Justice Howell E. Jackson.

Shortly after his enlistment he was made major, then colonel of the 33d Tennessee. At SHILOH with his regiment, he was badly wounded and sent on convalescent leave, returning to duty as Lt. Gen. LEONIDAS POLK's assistant adjutant and inspector general. Later Campbell was an

LC

officer of the Tennessee State Volunteer and Conscript Bureau, during which assignment he was captured near Lexington, Tenn., midsummer 1863, while traveling on department business, and was held prisoner until Feb. 1865, when he was exchanged. Early that month he was attached to Lt. Gen. NATHAN B. FORREST's new cavalry corps and given command of a brigade in the corps' Tennessee division.

Though Campbell was new to front-line soldiering, one corps veteran remembered him as an officer who brought something different to the command: "He carried his good breeding into camp, and even in the woods there was an air of refinement in all his ways." On 1 Mar. 1865 he was commissioned brigadier general and led his unit with dignity until its surrender.

Following the war he returned to law and dabbled in politics, making an unsuccessful bid for the Tennessee governorship in 1880. d. Jackson, Tenn., 13 June 1893. —JES

Campbell, John Archibald. CSP b. Washington, Ga., 24 June 1811. Campbell spent most of the Civil War as an assistant Confederate secretary of war. In antebellum years he was a prominent Alabama attorney and, by Pres. Franklin Pierce's Mar. 1853 appointment, an associate justice of the U.S. Supreme Court, where his decisions marked him a strict constitutionalist and STATES-RIGHTS advocate. Despite adherence to majority court opinion in the *DRED SCOTT* CASE, he was a moderate on SLAVERY and emancipated his own slaves on his appointment to the bench. Taking a conciliatory position, he validated the legal feasibility of state secession but advised Southern friends against it. His conservatism and ability to compromise won him national recognition and consideration as an 1860 Democratic presidential candidate.

Campbell's national stature involved him in the FORT SUMTER crisis. According to Associate Justice Samuel Nelson, new Sec. of State WILLIAM H. SEWARD claimed that Confederate demands for U.S. recognition made it impossible for the Lincoln administration to withdraw Fort Sumter's garrison. Campbell volunteered to intercede with Southern peace commissioners trying to avert war, repeatedly convincing them to accept Seward's intimations that no attempt would be made to reinforce Sumter. After the USS *STAR OF THE WEST* tried to sail into Charleston harbor to reprovision the fort, Southerners charged Campbell with treachery. Campbell believed Seward might have used him; the secretary's intent was never clear.

Feeling deceived, Campbell resigned his seat on the Supreme Court bench and withdrew to his home in Alabama. Several months of war obscured Southern prejudice toward him. In Oct. 1862 Confederate Sec. of War GEORGE W. RANDOLPH secured his appointment as assistant secretary and assigned him to duty overseeing CONSCRIPTION. His participation as a representative in the 1865 HAMPTON ROADS CONFERENCE was Campbell's only respite from office. On Richmond's fall in April, his last Confederate service involved approaching visiting President Lincoln to request that the Virginia state legislature be allowed to convene and consider Union Reconstruction orders. Lincoln tentatively agreed, but days later permission was withdrawn, the Federal government claiming its position was misunderstood. After Lincoln's assassination, Campbell was arrested, charged with misrepresenting the president's agreement to Richmond's military governor, Brig. Gen. GODFREY WEITZEL, and imprisoned for 4 months in Fort Pulaski. His release was effected by U.S. Justices Nelson and Benjamin Curtis.

Following his release he moved to New Orleans, established a successful law practice, and, pursuing several prominent cases, represented clients before old Supreme Court associates. d. New Orleans, 12 Mar. 1889. —JES

Campbell's Station, Tenn., eng. at. 16 Nov. 1863 Confederate Gen. BRAXTON BRAGG dispatched Lt. Gen. JAMES LONGSTREET, 2 infantry divisions, and 2 artillery battalions from the Chattanooga area 4 Nov. 1863 with license to crush Union Maj. Gen. AMBROSE E. BURNSIDE's force in East Tennessee. Thus began the KNOXVILLE CAMPAIGN.

Longstreet sent Brig. Gen. JOSEPH WHEELER's cavalry ahead, probing the defenses of Knoxville, where Burnside had his headquarters. On 14 Nov. the remaining Confederates marched northeast, up the Tennessee River banks, crossing the stream west of Loudon on the East Tennessee & Georgia Railroad. On the same day Burnside rushed southwest from Knoxville to evacuate Federal troops from Loudon, believing Longstreet's numbers overwhelmed his and that retreat to

Knoxville's fortifications offered the only chance of survival.

On 15 Nov. at 4 a.m., elements of the Federal IX and XXIII corps, separated from Longstreet's men by only 1 mi and a bend in the Tennessee, headed northeast for Knoxville along the rail line. Longstreet's 12,000 infantry raced along a parallel route, the Hotchkiss Valley Road, until night, when both forces stopped near Lenoir. If Burnside lost the race to Knoxville, his force could be trapped outside the city's defenses with its back to the Holston River. Both he and Longstreet realized that the first to reach Campbell's Station, 10 mi ahead on the Kingston Road, might fend off or capture the other.

At 2 a.m., 16 Nov., Federals and Confederates started off in a heavy rain for Campbell's Station. Col. JOHN F. HARTRANFT's IX Corps were ordered to run ahead of the main Union column to Concord, on the rail line, and clear the Concord Road northeast to Campbell's Station. Longstreet did the same, dispatching South Carolina cavalry and an artillery battery forward on the Kingston Road to beat Hartranft to the town. Brig. Gen. MICAH JENKINS' Confederate division veered from the main Kingston Road column and squeezed close to shadow Burnside's route. 2 mi now separated the 2 main columns.

Rain and mud slowed both forces as they hauled wagons and artillery, but Longstreet had a slight lead. Burnside ordered wagons and extra artillery caissons abandoned. Under Col. William Humphrey 3 Union regiments veered north, hit Jenkins' shadowing column, and skirmished northeast. The Union pace stepped up, and Burnside's troops inched in front. Longstreet's kept a normal step. Hartranft's men ran to the intersection of Concord and Kingston roads at Campbell's Station. Burnside's main column arrived at noon; Longstreet's advance appeared 15 minutes later.

While Hartranft's troops skirmished with the Confederate advance, the Federal retreat continued down the Kingston Road, and Brig. Gen. ROBERT B. POTTER, given 3 units to fight a holding action, deployed them across and to the rear of the intersection of the Kingston and Concord roads. The IX Corps' 1st and 2d divisions under Brig. Gen. EDWARD FERRERO and Hartranft covered the right and left flanks. Brig. Gen. JULIUS WHITE's elements of the XXIII Corps sat behind on the Kingston Road. Longstreet scattered his gathering column across their front, then troops under Brig. Gen. EVANDER M. LAW were sent circuitously around the Federal left to assault it in the rear. Law fumbled the maneuver, ended in front of the Federal left, and drew fire. Burnside and Potter, observing from a plateau in the rear, saw Longstreet's flanking plan and ordered Union defenders back about two-thirds of a mile. Before this could happen, Maj. Gen. LAFAYETTE MCLAWS' Confederates, rushing head-on at Ferrero's troops on the Federal right, were repulsed. A second attack on the Federal right-center failed.

In their new rearward position, right-flank Federals also repelled a flanking move by McLaws' men through woods on their line's end. Pulling in and wheeling their line to face the threat, they retreated, fighting, to the cover of artillery at their backs.

Night fell with Longstreet expecting additional combat in the morning. In the dark, Burnside's retreat continued, the Campbell's Station defenders retired, and cavalry called up from Tennessee River maneuvers took their place. At daylight, Confederates began skirmishes with 700 Federal horsemen that lasted through the 17th, allowing Burnside's force time to prepare trenches for Knoxville's coming siege. The Federals lost 318 killed and wounded from the 5,000 engaged at Camp-

bell's Station. Confederates, with 174 killed and wounded, suffered more by losing the race for the town.   —JES

Camp Chase. Until Nov. 1861, Camp Chase, named for Sec. of the Treasury and former Ohio governor SALMON P. CHASE, was a training camp for Union volunteers, housing a few political and military prisoners from Kentucky and western Virginia. Built on the western outskirts of Columbus, Ohio, the camp received its first large influx of captured Confederates from western campaigns, including enlisted men, officers, and a few of the latter's black servants. On oath of honor, Confederate officers were permitted to wander through Columbus, register in hotels, and receive gifts of money and food; a few attended sessions of the state senate. The public paid for camp tours, and Chase became a tourist attraction. Complaints over such lax discipline and the camp's state administration provoked investigation, and the situation changed.

OHS

Food supplies of poor quality resulted in the commissary officer's dismissal from service. After an influx of captured officers from ISLAND NO. 10, officers' privileges were cut, then officers were transferred to the JOHNSON'S ISLAND prison on Lake Erie. The camp's state volunteers and the camp commander were found to have "scant acquaintance" with military practice and were transferred, the camp passing into Federal government control. Under the new administration, rules were tightened, visitors prohibited, and mail censored. Prisoners were allowed limited amounts of money to supplement supplies with purchases from approved vendors and SUT-LERS, the latter further restricted when they were discovered to be smuggling liquor to the inmates.

As the war wore on, conditions became worse. Shoddy barracks, low muddy ground, open latrines, aboveground open cisterns, and a brief smallpox outbreak excited U.S. SANITARY COMMISSION agents who were already demanding reform. Original facilities for 3,500–4,000 men were jammed with close to 7,000. Since parole strictures prohibited service against the Confederacy, many Federals had surrendered believing they would be paroled and sent home. Some parolees, assigned to guard duty at Federal prison camps, were bitter, and rumors increased of maltreatment of prisoners at Camp Chase and elsewhere.

Before the end of hostilities, Union parolee guards were transferred to service in the Indian Wars, some sewage modifications were made, and prisoners were put to work improving barracks and facilities. Prisoner laborers also built larger, stronger fences for their own confinement, a questionable assignment under international law governing prisoners of war. Barracks rebuilt for 7,000 soon overflowed, and crowding and health conditions were never resolved. As many as 10,000 prisoners were reputedly confined there by the time of the Confederate surrender. —JES

camp follower. The broad term *camp follower* can be applied to any civilian who follows armies for profit and employment. During the Civil War these included contract laborers, SUTLERS, laundresses, VIVANDIÈRES, private servants, slaves, CONTRABANDS, bakers, barbers, and occasionally, private physicians. All were in some way recognized and dealt with in the official regulations of the Union and Confederate armies and were found in some numbers on all fronts.

And there were others: prostitutes, cardsharps, black marketeers, and illegal whiskey dealers. Large armies on the move, particularly if they set out from a large urban area, could attract hundreds. When Maj. Gen. WILLIAM T. SHERMAN marched from Atlanta to the sea he complained of thousands, almost all contrabands, following the army to freedom and willing to do any chores for little money.

With the exception of laundresses and some contract laborers, neither army was expected to provide for the needs of camp followers beyond their wages. The term *hooker,* then a slang phrase used for prostitutes, did not, as commonly believed, originally apply to the women who followed Maj. Gen. Joseph Hooker's army. The term, used in the Baltimore area, predated the Civil War. —JES

Camp Ford. The largest Confederate military prison in Texas, Camp Ford was established Aug. 1863, 4 mi northwest of Tyler. The prison population ranged from fewer than 100 to about 4,900 in July 1864, with most inmates arriving in spring of that year during Maj. Gen. Nathaniel P. Banks's disastrous RED RIVER CAMPAIGN. Both officers and enlisted men were held at the facility.

Like most Southern prisons, Camp Ford was an open stockade, its enclosure built by black laborers Nov. 1863. Confederate authorities provided no shelters, but the prisoners constructed a variety of enclosures, according to the resources available—sturdy log buildings, half-buried shanties, and caves dug into the ground. Generally shelter was adequate, and toward the end of 1864 incoming prisoners reported finding satisfactory quarters among those vacated by exchanged comrades.

Fortunately, Camp Ford enjoyed an abundant supply of good water from a stream that flowed through the compound. The prisoners collected the water in wooden reservoirs, keeping it relatively healthful. Though reports of half-rations occasionally surfaced, there seemed to be sufficient supplies of fresh beef, cornmeal, and some bacon and baked beans. In 1864 local farmers were permitted to sell their produce to inmates, and flour could be purchased for about $1 a pound. Prisoners prepared their meals over wood fires, gathering their fuel from outside the stockade. A variety of supplies was available from SUTLERS' stores, of which 2 were open for business during part of 1864, probably managed by officers of the 42d Massachusetts. Some of the men were able to keep money or personal possessions, which they sold or traded for goods, but most earned cash by manufacturing items to sell: during the camp's existence prisoners offered more than 40 different items for sale to townspeople. Connecticut Capt. William H.

May published at least 3 editions of a camp newspaper, *The Old Flag,* hand-printed at a subscription price, payable in advance, of $5 a year or the equivalent in coffee, tea, spices, tobacco, wine, liquors, or "seegars."

3 known major escape attempts were planned at Ford, but only 1, involving more than 50 men late in 1864, approached success; most prisoners were recaptured quickly. One deterrent may have been the rugged Western terrain to be crossed before reaching the North and the fact that much of it stretched through Indian country. A young German-born soldier escaped with 2 companions late in 1864, dodged Confederate scouting parties and fought the elements for nearly 3 months, only to be captured by some of Brig. Gen. DOUGLAS H. COOPER's Choctaw troops and returned to Ford barefooted and dressed in a barrel a few weeks before Gen. E. KIRBY SMITH surrendered the Confederacy's TRANS-MISSISSIPPI DEPARTMENT.

Through most of its 21-month existence, good health prevailed at Camp Ford. Deaths were estimated at 232–286, with 4 reasonably well substantiated cases of prisoners being shot by guards without provocation. The last prisoners left Camp Ford 17 May 1865, and 2 months later the stockade was burned by Federal occupation forces. Today the site is marked by a sign. —PLF

Camp Morton. The 1860 Indiana State Fair Grounds, 35 acres on the north side of Indianapolis, became Camp Morton in 1861, a recruitment and training depot for Indiana volunteers, named for Indiana governor OLIVER P. MORTON. Between the Feb. 1862 capture of FORT DONELSON and August of that year, it became a prison for 3,000 Confederates taken at the fort and was personally administered by Governor Morton. The first prisoners complained of being housed in old state-fair exhibit halls and stalls and stables with dirt floors. Although barracks were quickly built, like the old halls they were cheap and drafty.

USMHI

Following a general prisoner exchange, Aug. 1862, Camp Morton reverted to a troop facility until early 1863, when it was reestablished as a prison and placed under army administration, commanded by Col. William Hoffman, Union commissary general of prisoners. Remembered as a model of parsimony and reform, Hoffman instituted a system similar to the Union Army's COMPANY FUND: money saved from tightened rations was put in a camp fund and the proceeds, instead of being used to buy bread for prisoners, were used to buy an oven to bake it. Large boilers were bought from farmers to replace camp kettles for cooking meals in economic quantities. Stamps, stationery, cooking utensils, and tobacco bought for prisoners with the camp fund had a brief positive effect on morale. Prisoners were also permitted to speak to visitors. But continued Confederate reverses crowded Morton, and individual complaints of mal-treatment by guards surfaced. Several tunnels were discovered and collapsed as escape attempts began; during one attempt, 35 Confederates escaped but were recaptured.

In 1864 Hoffman's economies won him administrative rec-ognition, and the colonel cut rations again for greater savings. Prisoners grew restless, and the number of guards had to be increased. U.S. SANITARY COMMISSION agents recommended installing a sewage system to replace the open ditch in use and suggested feeding the prisoners more vegetables to combat an outbreak of scurvy. The advice was taken, within narrow lim-its: coffee, rice, hominy, sugar, and other foods were given only to the sick; those better off did without. Clothing was replaced in extreme cases, and then only if Confederate fami-lies did not send replacements. Deaths at Morton totaled 1,763 at the end of the war, including 7 reported killed in escape attempts and altercations. Still, Morton's mortality figures were lower than those of other open Northern prison compounds. Though the number of inmates is not certain, it ranged upward from 3,500.   —JES

Canby, Edward Richard Sprigg. USA b. Platt's Land-ing, Ky., 9 Nov. 1817. One of the Union's ablest generals in the Far West, Canby is best known as the commander who drove the invading Confederate army from NEW MEXICO TERRITORY in 1862 and, as commander of Federal forces in the Gulf states, the major general who received the surrender of the last South-ern army, more than 6 weeks after Gen. ROBERT E. LEE's surren-der.

USMHI

Canby moved with his par-ents from Kentucky to Indiana and was appointed to West Point from that state. After grad-uating 30th in the class of 1835, he served in the Florida Indian wars and led several major en-gagements in the Mexican War, during which he was twice cited for gallantry in action. When the Civil War erupted, Canby, on Indian-fighting duty at Fort Defiance, New Mexico Territory, was appointed commander of the DEPARTMENT OF NEW MEXICO.

Canby directed the campaign against Confederate invaders under Brig. Gen. HENRY HOPKINS SIBLEY, who beat the Federals at VALVERDE in New Mexico Territory. But with the help of newly arrived Colorado volunteers, Canby's force broke the Confederates' back at the Battle of GLORIETA PASS, often called the "Gettysburg of the West." Promoted to brigadier general within a week after Glorieta, Canby served 2 years as assistant adjutant general in Washington, D.C., and in July 1863 com-manded troops in New York City during the DRAFT RIOTS. 7 May 1864 he was made major general and given command of the MILITARY DIVISION OF WEST MISSISSIPPI.

Canby captured MOBILE 12 Apr. 1865, after a hard-fought campaign, and 26 May 1865 he accepted the surrender of the last Confederate army in the field, then under the command of Lt. Gen. E. KIRBY SMITH.

Given postwar permanent rank of brigadier general, Canby became commander of the Department of the Columbia on the Pacific Coast in 1870. He was murdered by hostile Modoc Indians while leading a peace mission at Siskiyou, Calif., 11 Apr. 1873.   —DS

Cane River Crossing (Monett's Ferry), La., eng. at. 23 Apr. 1864 The engagement at Cane River Crossing occurred during the final week of the RED RIVER CAMPAIGN. On 21 Apr. 1864 Federal Maj. Gen. NATHANIEL P. BANKS evacuated his army from Grand Ecore, La., and was moving toward Alex-andria, La., pursued by the Confederate forces of Maj. Gen. RICHARD TAYLOR. On the morning of 23 Apr., an advance party under Union Brig. Gen. WILLIAM H. EMORY surprised cavalry commanded by Confederate Brig. Gen. HAMILTON P. BEE. Real-izing the importance of holding the crossing, Bee took a posi-tion at Monett's Ferry, the only fordable point in the vicinity. The Confederates were protected by a high bank on one side and by swamps, lakes, and ravines on the other. Reluctant to attack their strong position, Emory feigned a demonstration while sending 2 brigades in search of another crossing. One brigade finally crossed the river and located the enemy by late afternoon. Federal Col. FRANCIS FESSENDEN led an attack against the enemy front and, after he was wounded, Lt. Col. Justus W. Blanchard continued the assault. The Confederates, outnum-bered and already demoralized from enemy shelling, fell back to a second hill until Bee ordered a general retreat, enabling Banks's men to lay a PONTOON BRIDGE; by early afternoon on the 24th, all had crossed the river. The devastation of the country begun at Grand Ecore continued to Alexandria. Taylor was highly critical of Bee for losing Monett's Ferry and allow-ing Banks to escape, faulting him for not having constructed breastworks and for having concentrated his force in the cen-ter. Federal casualties at Cane River Crossing are estimated at about 300 and Confederate losses at about 50.   —NCD

canister. *See* GRAPE SHOT; CANISTER.

cannon. Weaponry was revolutionized during the Civil War, and cannon received much attention from inventors—guns with names like Dahlgren, Parrott, and Rodman attest to this. Cannon models were referred to by the number of inches in their bore diameter (a 3-in. gun, an 8-in. gun, a 10-in. gun, etc.) or by the weight of their projectile (a 12-pounder, a 24-pounder, a 32-pounder, etc.). For all their variety, cannon fell into 2 basic types: rifled and smoothbore.

Smoothbore cannon reached the peak of their popularity and development during the war. They could be loaded, fired, and cared for with relative ease. The NAPOLEON, or Model 1857, was the most popular field piece of the conflict and epitomized the advantages of this type of cannon. Comparatively light and portable, adaptable to shells or such antipersonnel loads as CANISTER, it could be used equally well as an offensive or defen-sive weapon. Other popular smoothbore field cannon were HOWITZERS and the heavier pieces cast by individual foundries, simply classified as "guns." Howitzers—short, squat pieces with a tapered breech interior—lobbed a heavy shell a short distance with a light charge. Field guns, those pieces often distinguished by a bulbous muzzle, ranged from models taking 6-pounder loads to those accommodating 24-pounder loads.

The gun class ranged to the highest weight limits but beyond 24-pounders were ponderous or impossible in field use.

Rifled cannon were the most accurate field pieces, and the 3-INCH ORDNANCE GUN was preeminent among them. Unlike many field smoothbores, made of bronze, it and most other rifled cannon were made of iron. Its shells fit grooves in the tube interior (or, when fired, expanded to fit the grooves), and its loads spiraled on a straight, narrow trajectory to their targets. Like Napoleons, they were light, portable, useful in offense, and some, with modifications, could handle canister. PARROTT RIFLES were the second most popular rifled field piece. But they, the 3-in. ordnance gun, some imported English BLAKE-LYS, and all other common field pieces were muzzle loaders.

Awkward and undependable, breech-loading cannon were a Civil War rarity, though in the immediate postwar era they became the rule worldwide. The British ARMSTRONG and WHIT-WORTH firms both made breech-loading 12-pounder rifled field cannon, and both models were imported by Confederates for trial, though they were found unsatisfactory.

The smallest common field cannon were the 6-pounder and 12-pounder mountain howitzers. Since they could be broken down and transported on the backs of horses or mules, they were used mostly in mountainous regions. Among the largest were such seacoast, naval, and siege cannon as DAHLGRENS, RODMAN SMOOTHBORES, the Confederate-made BROOKE RIFLE, English-made ARMSTRONG GUNS, and antebellum COLUMBIADS. Depending on their caliber, some accommodated powder charges of over 25 lb. One Rodman smoothbore with a 20-in. bore took a 100-lb charge, sending a 1,080-lb shell approximately 3.5 mi. Most common heavy guns, however, had bores between 4.5 and 15 in. and took shells weighing from 24 to over 100 lb, with siege, garrison, and naval cannon tending to be smaller than seacoast guns. —JES

Cantey, James. CSA b. Camden, S.C., 30 Dec. 1818. After receiving a degree from South Carolina College, Cantey studied law in Charleston and was admitted to the bar about 1834. He spent 2 terms in the state legislature, departing to enlist in the Palmetto Regiment during the Mexican War. Below the border he rose to captain and was wounded in action, returning to settle on a plantation in Russell Cty., Ala.

When his state seceded, Cantey was again in uniform, this time as colonel of the 15th Alabama Infantry. The regiment was dispatched to Virginia, where it served under Maj. Gen. THOMAS J. "STONEWALL" JACKSON during the 1862 SHENAN-

LC

DOAH VALLEY CAMPAIGN. At FIRST WINCHESTER, 25 May, the Alabamians helped repel a Federal advance and 8 June, at CROSS KEYS, the last engagement of the campaign, Cantey and his regiment, part of Brig. Gen. ISAAC TRIMBLE's brigade, held a position so advanced that Maj. Gen. JOHN C. FRÉMONT's Federals nearly cut off the regiment from Trimble's main force. Later in the day, Cantey's men won praise for flanking Frémont's left, striking his rear, rolling up his line, and chasing his men westward.

On 8 Jan. 1863 Cantey was appointed brigadier general. Transferred to Mobile, he organized a brigade of 3 Alabama regiments and 1 from Mississippi, leading this command with much success early in the ATLANTA CAMPAIGN of 1864. That May his 5,300 effectives defended strategic RESACA, Ga., against some 15,000 members of the Army of the Tennessee, under Maj. Gen. JAMES B. MCPHERSON. For a time that summer, Cantey led a division, then reverted to brigade command in the Army of Mississippi.

He was absent for much of the fighting around Atlanta but returned to the field to serve under Gen. JOHN B. HOOD during the latter's foray into Tennessee. Early in 1865 Cantey aided Gen. JOSEPH E. JOHNSTON in opposing Sherman's invasion of the Carolinas. He saw his final battle at BENTONVILLE, 19 Mar., surrendering with Johnston 5 weeks later at Durham Station, N.C. Returning to his plantation, he resided in the Alabama hill country until his death at Fort Mitchell, 30 June 1874.

—EGL

Capers, Ellison. CSA b. Charleston, S.C., 14 Oct. 1837. The son of a Methodist bishop, Capers was graduated from the South Carolina Military Academy but entered into civilian professions, first as a lawyer, then as a teacher. After serving as principal of a college preparatory department, he returned to his alma mater and by 1860 was a full professor there, teaching mathematics and rhetoric.

When civil war neared, Capers enlisted in the South Carolina Rifles, rising to major. During the bombardment of FORT SUMTER, he commanded artillery on nearby Sullivan's Island and later helped recruit the 24th South Carolina Infantry, of which he was elected lieutenant colonel.

LC

Till mid-1863 Capers' regiment served around Charleston, seeing its heaviest service 16 June 1862 during the Union assault on SECESSIONVILLE, south of the city. There he won praise for his coolness and skill in directing an infantry/artillery defense of the Confederate position that resulted in the enemy's repulse. Only 2 weeks earlier he had accomplished a similar feat on a smaller scale—so ably commanding 4 companies of the 24th South Carolina near Secessionville that 3 regiments of Federals were foiled in an attack on the detachment.

In May 1863 Capers' regiment was sent west to help relieve the Siege of VICKSBURG. He was wounded in that forlorn effort, as he was again 4 months later while serving "nobly" and in "intrepid" fashion at CHICKAMAUGA. He recovered in time to lead Brig. Gen. STATES RIGHTS GIST's brigade in the Army of Tennessee during part of the ATLANTA CAMPAIGN, though his own promotion to brigadier general did not take place until early 1865. In the interim, he was wounded yet again, this time at FRANKLIN, 30 Nov. 1864. Sent home to Charleston to recuperate, he retook the field in time to oppose Maj. Gen. WILLIAM T. SHERMAN's invasion of his state.

He remained in Charleston after peace was declared, serving 1866–68 as secretary of state for South Carolina. During this period he entered the Episcopal ministry and in July 1893 was consecrated assistant bishop of South Carolina; a year later he became bishop. Elected chancellor of the University of the South, Sewanee, Tenn., in 1904, he served in that capacity—and also as chaplain general of the UNITED CONFEDERATE VETERANS—until shortly before his death in Columbia, S.C., 22 Apr. 1908. —EGL

Carleton, James Henry. USA b. Lubec, Maine, 27 Dec. 1814. Carleton was as colorful a character as the Old West ever knew—dragoon, frontiersman, Indian fighter, author, military governor—and controversy swirled about him throughout his stormy career.

As a youth, Carleton dreamed of becoming an author and as a teen-ager corresponded with Charles Dickens about his literary ambitions. His voluminous military writings of later years bear witness that Carleton never abandoned those ambitions.

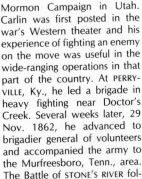

USMHI

After participating with the Maine Militia in the brief Aroostook War of 1838, Carleton was commissioned in the Regular Army in 1839. He went west with Brig. Gen. Stephen W. Kearny on the Rocky Mountain Expedition of 1846, then served in the Mexican War, earning a brevet as major for gallantry at Buena Vista.

A captain when the Civil War erupted, Carleton was promoted to colonel of the 1st California Infantry Regiment Aug. 1861. Most of the action he saw during the war was packed into the spring and summer of 1862. Brig. Gen. GEORGE WRIGHT, commander of the Department of the Pacific, chose Carleton to lead the CALIFORNIA COLUMN of more than 2,000 men on an epic march to recapture Federal forts and frontier settlements from the invading Confederates and sweep the enemy from Arizona, New Mexico, and West Texas.

With admirable foresight, Carleton planned the march across poorly mapped deserts, reoccupied Tucson May 1862, then moved eastward through blistering summer heat to New Mexico. When they learned of the column's approach, Brig. Gen. HENRY HOPKINS SIBLEY's Texans, whom Union Brig. Gen. E.R.S. CANBY had defeated in earlier New Mexico clashes, abandoned their Far West adventure and retreated to San Antonio.

Carleton was promoted to brigadier general from 28 Apr. 1862 and succeeded Canby as commander of the DEPARTMENT OF NEW MEXICO in Sept. of that year, holding the unruly territory under harsh martial law. Controversy marked his early disciplinary actions, his arrest of wealthy Southern sympathizer Sylvester Mowry in Tucson, his martial regime and his feud with New Mexico Judge Joseph Knapp.

Carleton remained in the army after the war and died in San Antonio, Tex., 7 Jan. 1873. —DS

Carlin, William Passmore. USA b. Richwoods, Ill., 24 Nov. 1829. Carlin was reared outside Carrollton, Ill., and entered the West Point class of 1850, ranking 20th academically on graduation.

On 15 Aug. 1861 he became colonel of the 38th Illinois after having spent a little more than 10 years in the Regulars fighting the Sioux and Cheyenne and taking part in the 1857

Mormon Campaign in Utah. Carlin was first posted in the war's Western theater and his experience of fighting an enemy on the move was useful in the wide-ranging operations in that part of the country. At PERRYVILLE, Ky., he led a brigade in heavy fighting near Doctor's Creek. Several weeks later, 29 Nov. 1862, he advanced to brigadier general of volunteers and accompanied the army to the Murfreesboro, Tenn., area. The Battle of STONE'S RIVER fol-

NA

lowed at the turn of the new year, and there Carlin and his brigade fought in the main battle line and along a Union salient fronting the grove of trees remembered as "Hell's Half-Acre."

Carlin's service followed that of the western armies for the rest of the war. He fought in the TULLAHOMA CAMPAIGN, at CHICKAMAUGA and CHATTANOOGA, in the ATLANTA CAMPAIGN, the MARCH TO THE SEA, the CAROLINAS CAMPAIGN, and at the Battle of BENTONVILLE where he commanded the 1st Division of Maj. Gen. William T. Sherman's XIV Corps, the advance troops who made the first contact with Gen. JOSEPH E. JOHNSTON's army on the last leg of the Carolinas Campaign.

On 13 Mar. 1865 he was brevetted major general in the Regulars and to the same rank in the volunteer service on the 19th. Carlin returned to the Regular Army as an infantry major. By 1893, before being retired, he had been commissioned a brigadier general and until his death near Whitehall, Mont., 4 Oct. 1903, traveled in the U.S. and abroad. —JES

Carnifix Ferry, western Va., Battle of. 10 Sept. 1861 After the rout of the Confederate Army in western Virginia July 1861, Union troops had no trouble occupying the pro-Union counties in the mountainous regions of the state. The occupation was made easier by a quarrel between the commanders of what remained of the Confederate forces in western Virginia. Brig. Gen. HENRY A. WISE had outfitted his own "Legion" of 4,500 men and was assigned to the southern Kanawha Valley. Meanwhile, Brig. Gen. JOHN B. FLOYD had raised a separate army, also in the Kanawha. Neither officer would take the other's advice and each was determined to win the western Virginia war by himself.

Floyd moved first, marching northwest up the Kanawha and crossing the Gauley River at Carnifix Ferry Aug. 1861. He planned to strike several isolated Union garrisons there but by September had failed to do much. Worse, he was threatened at Carnifix Ferry by the presence of a large Union force under Brig. Gen. WILLIAM S. ROSECRANS. Wise, camped 12 mi from the ferry, warned Floyd against being trapped with his back to the Gauley River. Floyd ignored him, was pinned against the river, and Wise refused to send him reinforcements.

On 10 Sept. Rosecrans struck Floyd's camps at Carnifix Ferry with 3 Ohio brigades. Rosecrans' men easily pushed in the Confederate pickets and captured Floyd's supplies. A seizure of the ferry seemed likely until Rosecrans discovered Floyd had withdrawn into a large fortified camp at the ferry and was prepared to fight it out. Rosecrans planned to storm the camp, but the fatigue of his men and the approach of night persuaded him to delay assault until morning. Floyd, with only

2,600 men, decided not to wait for the attack, slipping his command back across the ferry during the night. Rosecrans discovered Floyd's escape the next morning, but since Floyd's men had destroyed the ferry, he could not pursue them.

Ironically, it was Wise, not Floyd, who was blamed for the embarrassment of Carnifix Ferry. Responsibility for saving western Virginia for the Confederacy fell to Gen. ROBERT E. LEE.

—ACG

Carolinas Campaign. Feb.–Apr. 1865 As Maj. Gen. WILLIAM T. SHERMAN neared the end of his MARCH TO THE SEA, mid-Dec. 1864, Union General-in-Chief ULYSSES S. GRANT considered having Sherman's armies in Georgia bypass their objective, Savannah. Instead, he would place them in transports and ship them directly to the Virginia front, where they could aid local forces in crushing Gen. ROBERT E. LEE's weakened but still defiant army. Sherman acquiesced in this plan, but without enthusiasm.

Soon afterward, however, with Sherman's march completed, Grant reconsidered and gave the conqueror of Georgia his choice of a route north. Immediately Sherman opted for an overland march through South and North Carolina, believing that by occupying those states his army could permanently sever supply lines connecting Richmond and Petersburg with the Confederate heartland. This would constitute "as much a direct attack upon Lee's army as though we were operating within the sound of his artillery." Sherman had another, perhaps more compelling motive for choosing the overland route. A proponent of total war, he wished to bring destruction, terror, and suffering to unscathed parts of the "cradle of secession"; by turning north from Savannah, he wrote Grant, "we can punish South Carolina as she deserves."

Sherman was prepared to start northward by the middle of Jan. 1865, but rain, high rivers, and other logistical problems kept him from leading his main army into South Carolina until 1 Feb., when he forged ahead, leading his 62,000 veterans. His command still consisted of the XV and XVII corps of the Army of the Tennessee, under Maj. Gen. OLIVER O. HOWARD; the XIV and XX corps of Maj. Gen. HENRY W. SLOCUM's Army of Georgia; 2 cavalry brigades under Brig. Gen. H. JUDSON KILPATRICK; and a 64-gun artillery brigade. The troops were confident, even cocky: they had met little significant opposition in Georgia, and they doubted that the Confederacy would make life any tougher for them in South Carolina. Fearing no repercussions, many roamed far from the route of march, looting and destroying. Kilpatrick's troopers carried boxes of matches in their saddlebags, ready for use whenever they saw an appealing target; the BUMMERS in the infantry columns allowed few chicken coops and smokehouses to escape their attention.

One reason for their freedom of movement was Sherman's ability to outmaneuver his enemy. By the second week in February the invaders were moving up the Charleston & Augusta Railroad from Midway to Johnson's Station, a route that split the few Confederates in the state, under Gen. P.G.T. BEAUREGARD. The railroad carried them between forces along the coast and would-be pursuers near Aiken, S.C., and Augusta, Ga. This route also allowed Sherman to cut off Charleston from the interior of the state, forcing the evacuation of its garrison, under Maj. Gen. WILLIAM J. HARDEE. Beauregard ordered Hardee's troops to Cheraw, near the North Carolina border, where he hoped to make a stand against Sherman at last.

Before reaching Cheraw, Sherman's 2-column march—

Howard forming the right or eastward wing, Slocum and Kilpatrick the left flank—passed through several towns memorable ever afterward for the destruction wrought there. The greatest devastation occurred 17 Feb. with the capture of COLUMBIA, much of which went up in flames. Though Southerners blamed Sherman for deliberately causing a "perfect reign of terror" in the capital, most of the damage occurred before his arrival, when local Confederates torched bales of cotton piled in the streets.

Reaching Cheraw 3 Mar., Sherman still had no enemy to fight. Hardee—now subordinate to Gen. JOSEPH E. JOHNSTON, recently brought back into the field, superseding Beauregard—had fled north to Fayetteville N.C., on the Federals' approach. He fell back yet again, once the invaders left scarred and battered South Carolina for the Tarheel State, completing the occupation of FAYETTEVILLE on the 11th. After a 5-day stopover, Sherman led his troops northeastward, planning to link at Goldsborough with forces recently sent to support him—2 corps, fresh from capturing Wilmington and reoccupying New Berne under Maj. Gen. JOHN M. SCHOFIELD.

Foreseeing this junction, Johnston finally forced a showdown. Desperate to strike one of Sherman's columns short of Goldsborough, he sent Hardee to block the path of Slocum's wing below AVERASBOROUGH, which led to a spirited encounter on the 16th, ending with a beaten Hardee retiring toward Smithfield to regroup and a victorious Slocum curving eastward toward Bentonville. Wishing to strike again while time remained, Johnston collected every force available to him, including Hardee's; troops under Gen. BRAXTON BRAGG, recently bested by Schofield near KINSTON; cavalry led by Lt. Gen. WADE HAMPTON; and the remnants of the Army of Tennessee, now under Lt. Gen. A. P. STEWART—a total of some 21,000 effectives.

At BENTONVILLE, on the 19th, Johnston hurled these troops at Slocum. The wing leader, however, withstood every blow, even after his left flank collapsed, until Sherman could rush the rest of the army to his assistance, whereupon Johnston drew off, having suffered 2,600 casualties against Slocum's 1,500. Refusing to strike Sherman's reunited command, he dejectedly headed north, allowing the Federals to reach Goldsborough without further difficulty. En route, Sherman met a part of Schofield's force, under Maj. Gen. ALFRED H. TERRY, and, on his arrival in the city on the 23d, linked with the rest.

The junction effectively quashed Sherman's opposition. After trying to assemble a coherent force near Smithfield, Johnston decided that further resistance to the Union command, now 80,000 strong, would be futile. By mid-April he was sending out peace feelers. Sherman was receptive, and on the 26th Johnston surrendered his remaining forces at Durham Station, near Raleigh.

—EGL

Carondelet, USS. One of 7 armored gunboats referred to as "POOK TURTLES" and built for the War Department in 1861, the *Carondelet* was designed by naval constructor Samuel M. Pook and engine designer Thomas Merritt. Built near St. Louis, Mo., by contractor James B. Eads, the *Carondelet* was launched 12 Oct. 1861. The vessel weighed 512 tons, had a draft of 6 ft, and was operated by 5 boilers and 2 engines. Its casement showed 13 ports: 3 in the bow, 4 well forward on each beam, and 2 aft in narrow galleries on each side of the wheelrace. The ship was armed with 13 guns, including rifled 42-pounders. Later, its battery was altered to 3 9-in. DAHL-

USN

GRENS forward, 2 8-in. navies, 1 100-pounder PARROTT rifle on each beam, and 2 lighter Parrotts aft. Its crew consisted of regular navy men, volunteers, detailed army personnel, and contract civilians.

On 10 Jan. 1862 the *Carondelet* joined the Union fleet, commanded by Rear Adm. HENRY WALKE, at Cairo. During that year, the ship was involved in the combined military/naval operations against FORT HENRY, FORT DONELSON, ISLAND NO. 10, and VICKSBURG. Although slow, clumsy, and dangerous to its crew, the *Carondelet* proved invaluable in the RIVER WAR. However, the ship met its match in the Confederate ironclad *ARKANSAS*. As a result of their encounter, 15 July 1862, the *Carondelet* was disabled and grounded. Repaired, it was used in other operations and finally in the RED RIVER CAMPAIGN Mar. 1864. After the war, the *Carondelet* was stripped of its plating and sold for scrap. —NCD

carpetbagger. A term of contempt used in the South as early as 1846 to describe any suspicious stranger, during RECONSTRUCTION *carpetbagger* came to mean any Northerner still in the South. Though carpetbaggers included disreputable opportunists and corruptionists, the crafty and unscrupulous, most were involved in personal activities that in many instances benefited the South.

The ones despised by Southerners were unprincipled Northern radical political adventurers who gained control of state governments with the aid of the black vote. As a small minority these willful men devoted great energy to sponsoring appropriations that staggeringly increased state debts. Some of that breed who swarmed into Mississippi—the only Southern state where their number was disproportionately large—were finally run out by the Ku Klux Klan.

But few came south to be active in politics. Most were Union army veterans who had been to the South during the war and found the country pleasing. Some came to engage in trade, buy cotton lands, build factories, promote railroads, enter legitimate businesses, develop natural resources, or represent insurance companies. Others came as clergy, FREEDMEN'S BUREAU officers, or teachers. But carpetbaggers dedicated to worthy purposes—such as Albion W. Tourgee, who spent 14 years fighting for civil rights; S.C. Millet, who ably managed the new Port Royal, S.C., railroad; and ADELBERT AMES, Mississippi military governor, later elected its U.S. senator, then governor—found that their labors were not always appreciated.

Regardless of such demonstrations of good intentions, to many Southern whites all Northerners came south to join forces with Southern SCALAWAGS, and so, regardless of their business, were suspect. Even former slaves, usually flattered and patronized for their votes, grew suspicious of strangers. Many believed that "good men don't come South—they have business at home." —AG

Carr, Eugene Asa. USA b. Concord, N.Y., 20 Mar. 1830. Carr entered the U.S. Military Academy in 1846, graduated 19th in his class in 1850, and was commissioned in the Regiment of Mounted Riflemen, beginning a service that spanned 43 years.

For the next decade Carr's service was chiefly on the Western frontier, where he was involved in a number of skirmishes with hostile Indians. In 1854, near Limpia, Tex., he was severely wounded by an arrow. When the Civil War began, Carr was a cavalry captain at Fort Washita, Indian Territory. He soon joined Brig. Gen. NATHANIEL LYON's forces in Missouri and participated in the Battle of WIL-

USMHI

SON'S CREEK, 10 Aug. 1861; 6 days later he was commissioned colonel of the 3d Illinois Cavalry.

Over the next months Carr was active in the maneuvers that forced the Confederates out of Missouri. In the Battle of PEA RIDGE, Ark., 7–8 Mar. 1862, he was wounded 3 times but refused to leave the field; later he received the MEDAL OF HONOR for gallantry in this engagement. Effective 7 Mar. 1862 he was made brigadier general of volunteers. Carr commanded a division during the SECOND VICKSBURG CAMPAIGN, after which he was sent to Arkansas, where he saw only limited action. Early in 1865 he joined Maj. Gen. E.R.S. CANBY in the Siege of MOBILE.

Carr's military reputation rests mostly on his exploits as an Indian fighter after the war. He served with the 5th and 6th cavalry at various frontier posts 1868–91 and was described by another officer as "perhaps the most famous and experienced Indian fighter . . . following the Civil War." Artist Frederic Remington was quoted as saying that Carr "would rather be a colonel of cavalry than Czar of Russia."

Carr retired as a brigadier general 15 Feb. 1893. He died in Washington, D.C., 2 Dec. 1910, and was buried at West Point. —JOH

Carrick's Ford, western Va., action at. 13 July 1861
See CORRICK'S FORD, WESTERN VA., ACTION AT.

Carrington, Henry Beebee. USA b. Wallingford, Conn., 2 Mar. 1824. Carrington, though a Civil War army officer, is best remembered for his civilian pursuits as a writer, historian, and academic. He graduated from Yale in 1845 and in the next 3 years taught in Tarrytown, N.Y., and in New Haven, Conn., and went to Yale Law School. He also became known as a strong abolitionist.

Carrington settled in Ohio as an attorney, entering state politics. Over the next 13 years he became an intimate of FREE SOIL and REPUBLICAN politicians and served as state adjutant general of Ohio's militia beginning in 1857. Carrington had his troops well organized when the Civil war began and with little advance notice was able to dispatch 9 regiments for Union operations in western Virginia. As a reward, he was appointed a colonel in the U.S. Army Regulars 14 May 1861, and from then served on the Union's Midwestern homefront.

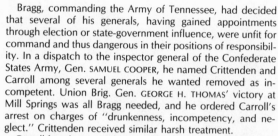

GB

Carrington energetically suppressed various PEACE DEMOCRAT (Copperhead) organizations, commanded the 18th U.S. Infantry at its Columbus, Ohio, camp, and organized Ohio and Indiana volunteers for Federal service, while maintaining his office as Ohio's adjutant general. He was promoted to brigadier general of volunteers 29 Nov. 1862.

The general aroused controversy in Indiana and Ohio, where he held for military trials civilians suspected of copperhead activities. The trials drew national attention when the U.S. Supreme Court overturned Carrington's actions, ruling that military courts held no sway in either state, since neither was in rebellion. He finished out the Civil War overseeing the trials of accused guerrillas in Tennessee.

After the war he was sent west to Fort Phil Kearny, where he proved to be an inept Indian fighter and was partially responsible for the U.S. Army's disastrous Fetterman Massacre in 1866. After facing an investigation into his role in the massacre, he went on inactive duty, resigning from the army in 1870. Until his death 26 Oct. 1912, he pursued a career as a college professor, a treaty negotiator with the Flathead tribe of Montana, and an author of 5 history books, among them *Battles of the American Revolution* (1876). —JES

Carroll, William Henry. CSA b. Nashville, Tenn., 1810. Carroll was one of many officers in the Confederate army who ran afoul of Gen. BRAXTON BRAGG. From a distinguished Tennessee family (his father was a 6-term governor of the state), he owned a plantation in Mississippi and for a time before the Civil War served as postmaster of Nashville.

He is believed to have been active in the Tennessee Militia at the start of the war. On Tennessee's fracture with the Union he entered the Confederate service as colonel of the 37th Tennessee Infantry, advancing to brigadier general 26 Oct. 1861, both appointment and promotion reflecting some political consideration.

LC

Carroll was sent to Knoxville as military commander and placed the city under martial law, an act not entirely unjustified since many residents had openly expressed Union sympathy. Under Maj. Gen. GEORGE B. CRITTENDEN, he was then dispatched to fight at MILL SPRINGS, Ky., 19 Jan. 1862. This ended his Confederate career.

Bragg, commanding the Army of Tennessee, had decided that several of his generals, having gained appointments through election or state-government influence, were unfit for command and thus dangerous in their positions of responsibility. In a dispatch to the inspector general of the Confederate States Army, Gen. SAMUEL COOPER, he named Crittenden and Carroll among several generals he wanted removed as incompetent. Union Brig. Gen. GEORGE H. THOMAS' victory at Mill Springs was all Bragg needed, and he ordered Carroll's arrest on charges of "drunkenness, incompetency, and neglect." Crittenden received similar harsh treatment.

Carroll faced a court of inquiry, then resigned from the army 1 Feb. 1863. Of the charges, incompetency may have been the most valid; the others appear to have been thrown in for good measure.

The one-time general lived in Canada with his family until 1868, when he died in Montreal 3 May. —JES

Carson, Christopher. USA b. Madison Cty., Ky., 1809, Carson is remembered in history as "Kit" Carson. Taken by his family to Missouri and apprenticed to a saddler, he ran away in 1826 and joined an expedition to what is now New Mexico, making his permanent home in Taos. Until the Mexican War he was a fur trapper, mountain man, and guide to explorer JOHN C. FRÉMONT on 3 expeditions. Heroism in California during his Mexican War service brought him national recognition, and in the remaining antebellum years he was a herder and an agent to the Ute Indians.

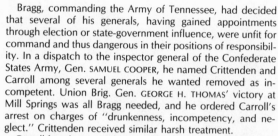

LC

Carson's fame in the Far West won him a commission as lieutenant colonel, then colonel, of the 1st New Mexico Infantry in 1861. He said he joined the service to fight Confederates, but following participation in the Battle of GLORIETA PASS, he spent the rest of the war fighting Indians in the Southwest. Union Brig. Gen. JAMES H. CARLETON, commander of NEW MEXICO TERRITORY, planned to confine the region's Indian population on reservations and put Carson in charge of the military operation.

In autumn 1862 Carson pursued the Mescalero Apaches, confining about 400 on the Bosque Redondo Reserve in eastern New Mexico Territory. On 7 July 1863 he began a 6-month campaign to round up the Navajos. With 736 hard-bitten volunteers, he captured 6,000 and helped force the surrender of another 6,000. But Carson protested the harsh pacification methods Carleton urged and rebelled at orders to shoot on sight Indians who resisted. He met greatest success through parley and persuasion, and after trapping the largest remaining group of Navajos in the Jan. 1864 Canyon de Chelly campaigning, he talked 200 into surrendering. (See NAVAJO, REMOVAL OF THE.)

That July, Carson was made superintendent of the Bosque Redondo Reservation, a post he held until autumn, when he was transferred to another Indian-fighting command. On 25 Nov. 1864, with 400 troops and 2 cannon, he assaulted a body of Comanches, 8 to 12 times larger than his own force, at Adobe Wells, Tex. Compelled to retreat after an all-day battle, he withdrew his men with few casualties. His Civil War service was ended, but 13 Mar. 1865 he was brevetted brigadier general of volunteers for gallantry at Glorieta Pass and in his Indian campaigns.

Carson continued in the army on frontier duty until 1867, then served briefly as an Indian agent, dying in New Mexico 23 May 1868. An autobiography, *Kit Carson's Own Story of His Life,* was first published in 1926.   —JES

Carter, John Carpenter. CSA b. Waynesborough, Ga., 19 Dec. 1837.

Before the Civil War, Carter taught law at Cumberland University in Lebanon, Tenn., where he had been a student before attending the University of Virginia. Shortly before the war he left teaching and established a law practice in Memphis. He entered Confederate service early in 1861 as a captain in the 38th Tennessee Infantry.

LC

Carter led his men at SHILOH, where he fought with a coolness and bravery praised by his commanding officer, Col. R. F. Looney, and thereafter enjoyed rapid promotion, attaining the rank of colonel by fall 1862. At PERRYVILLE and STONE'S RIVER, Carter again won commendations, in the latter battle for his part in a determined attack on the Federal right. After the fighting at CHICKAMAUGA, he and his Tennesseans were on detached duty and thus did not take part in the CHATTANOOGA CAMPAIGN. In summer 1864 he replaced Brig. Gen. MARCUS J. WRIGHT as brigade commander and led the troops during the ATLANTA CAMPAIGN. He received his commission as brigadier general to rank from 7 July.

Carter held temporary command of Maj. Gen. BENJAMIN F. CHEATHAM's division at the Battle of JONESBOROUGH, 1 Sept., then returned to Tennessee to take part in Lt. Gen. JOHN B. HOOD's invasion of that state. He fell mortally wounded in a charge on the enemy breastworks at FRANKLIN, 30 Nov., dying 10 Dec. 1864.   —JES

Carter, Samuel Powhatan. USA b. Elizabethton, Tenn., 6 Aug. 1819,

Carter, both a rear admiral and a major general, was educated at Washington College in Virginia and at the College of New Jersey. On 14 Feb. 1840 he received an appointment as a navy midshipman, seeing service aboard ships of the Pacific squadron, the Great Lakes, and the home squadron until 1845, when he was ordered to the Naval Academy at Annapolis. Carter graduated with the class of 1846 and returned to sea duty, serving on the ship of the line *Ohio* and witnessing the fall of Vera Cruz. He also served with the Naval Observatory and then shipped out with the Mediterranean squadron. Tours as an assistant professor at the Naval Academy and with the East India squadron brought him promotion to lieutenant. When the Civil War started he was at sea with the Brazil squadron.

Impressed by Carter's declaration for the Union, Tennessee Sen. ANDREW JOHNSON and others were influential in having him detailed to "special duty" with the War Department. He was sent to Tennessee to organize and train Union volunteers and within a month had readied more than a regiment of the first troops to come from that state. A month later he commanded a Tennessee brigade and 1 May 1862 received his commission as brigadier general of the volunteer army.

That same year Carter was in command of a Union cavalry raid that defeated the Confederates at Holston, Carter's Station, and Jonesville, actions that eased pressure on Maj. Gen. WILLIAM S. ROSECRANS at Murfreesboro. Carter commanded the left wing of the Union forces in the Battle of KINSTON, N.C., Mar. 1865, and later that month was brevetted major general of volunteers.

While performing with the army Carter was promoted to lieutenant commander in the navy in 1863 and to commander in 1865. After the war he continued in naval service, advancing to rear admiral before retirement in 1882. He died in Washington, D.C., 26 May 1891, and was remembered by his fellow officers as "tall, handsome and dignified, graceful in carriage and very affable . . . [a] soldierly Christian of sincere piety and undoubted courage."   —AG

carte de visite.

A small photographic image, the *carte de visite* first appeared in 1857 when the Italian Duke of Parma began gluing small paper images of himself onto the back of his calling cards. The practice quickly spread through Europe and America, and the cards were universally called by their French name.

USMHI

A card measured 2.5 in. by 4 in. and could be produced cheaply; in 1860 one New York firm advertised 25 for $1. For thousands of men leaving home for the army, this was the perfect memento to exchange with their families. Oliver Wendell Holmes once referred to *cartes de visite* as "the sentimental greenbacks of civilization."

Photographers produced millions of them 1861–65. Studio-made images frequently showed the proud soldier in full military regalia posed in front of a classical background or a painted landscape. Camp photographers' settings were necessarily less elaborate. Both featured props such as guns, swords, and embellishments for uniforms to enhance their customer's image as a belligerent. Portrait vignettes appeared as a variation to hold public interest once the fad peaked in the latter war years.

A brisk trade also existed in *cartes de visite* of famous people, which the public collected diligently, and some amputee veterans supplemented their meager pensions by selling images of themselves to a sympathetic audience.

The Federal government also recognized the revenue potential in the *cartes,* levying a tax of 2 or 3 cents on each image sold after 1 Sept. 1864. Interest fell off with the added expense, and the fad passed when families were reunited by peace and when a new, larger 5-by-7 in. cabinet photograph was introduced in 1870. —PLF

Carthage, Mo., eng. at. 5 July 1861 The situation in Missouri in early summer 1861 was chaotic. Gov. CLAIBORNE JACKSON and his prosecession legislature had been driven out of the state capital and were trying to stay ahead of pursuing Federals, led chiefly by Brig. Gen. NATHANIEL LYON. Jackson withdrew to the southwest of the state, rallying secessionists as he went. At Lamar, Jackson was joined by Brig. Gen. James S. Rains and about 4,000 ill-equipped militia; together they continued their retreat.

Meanwhile, Union Col. FRANZ SIGEL commanded a party of about 1,100 who searched for the secessionists. By 4 July Sigel had reached Carthage, the Jasper County seat, and there bivouacked for the night. When Jackson learned this, he immediately took command of the small army—even though he held no military commission and there were several generals present—and announced that they would attack.

The Confederates approached Sigel the next morning with not much of a battle plan; Sigel himself was little better prepared. Jackson drew up his army on a ridge, awaiting a Federal attack, and Sigel obliged, even though he knew he was outnumbered and had no cavalry to protect his flanks. He opened fire first with his artillery and sent enough metal into Jackson's line to shake it a bit but did not have enough antipersonnel charges to do real damage. Jackson, meanwhile, ordered 2,000 of his unarmed state-guard cavalry toward the shelter of woods on his right. Sigel misinterpreted this move as an attempt to turn his flank, decided that he had done enough fighting, and began to retreat.

After a desultory pursuit, halted frequently by able rearguard actions from Sigel's artillery, the Federals held Carthage that evening. In darkness they continued the retreat, having suffered 13 killed and 31 wounded. Jackson had lost just 10 killed and 64 wounded, and by any measure it was not much of a battle. Yet it meant a great deal to pro-Confederates, who, having been driven from the capital as well as having been handed a humiliating defeat at Boonville a few weeks earlier, now had a "victory" to their credit, renewing hope that they could still lead Missouri out of the Union. —WCD

Caruthers, Robert Looney. war governor b. Smith Cty., Tenn., 31 July 1800. Numbered among the South's "reluctant Confederates" was Judge Robert Caruthers. In Feb. 1861 he went to the WASHINGTON PEACE CONFERENCE, haggling over the Union's future for 23 days; when the effort failed, he returned home resolved to Southern nationhood.

A lifelong Tennessean, Caruthers was a store clerk, a newspaper editor, a state-court clerk, an attorney, a state legislator, a presidential elector for Henry Clay, a U.S. congressman on the Whig ticket, and a Tennessee supreme court judge. He also helped found Cumberland University and later its law school.

In 1861 Caruthers, one of the state's largest slave- and landholders, believed neither he nor his state could benefit from disunion, but when Tennessee seceded in May he accepted his election to the Provisional Confederate Congress. Caruthers contributed little to debate there but generally supported the Davis administration, opposing only one minor piece of legislation. Though the Congress met May–December, he attended

not at all in its last weeks. Standing for election to the First Regular Congress, he was defeated by Landon C. Haynes.

At the urging of Gov. ISHAM G. HARRIS, Caruthers made efforts to raise morale among Tennessee secessionists. State law prohibited Harris from succeeding himself, and in 1863 the secessionists' votes gained Caruthers the governorship. But with Federal armies occupying Nashville, the state capital, Caruthers was not inaugurated and never fulfilled the duties of the office.

After the Confederate surrender and the ascension of pro-Unionist Tennesseans to state office, Caruthers suffered verbal abuse from unforgiving Reconstructionists like WILLIAM G. "PARSON" BROWNLOW. He avoided public life in the 1870s and took a faculty post at Cumberland University, teaching there until his death 2 Oct. 1882. —JES

cascabel. The large round knob at the base of a cannon breech is called a cascabel. In gun-casting it was intended to turn something similar to a bottle's pontil mark into a useful feature for the hoisting and manipulation of the gun tube. It has a short neck and a base called a "fillet." —JES

case shot. Properly, case shot refers to grape shot, canister, or spherical case shot, an artillery round that purposely breaks apart on firing and is used as an antipersonnel load. Most often in Civil War literature, references to case shot imply spherical case, a round invented in 1784 by English artilleryman Lt. Henry Shrapnel. It was an iron sphere filled with bits or balls of iron and a bursting charge intended to break apart shortly after firing. Its effective range was 500–1,500 yd. —JES

Casey, Silas. USA b. East Greenwich, R.I., 12 July 1807. Despite an aptitude for higher mathematics, Casey graduated 39th in the 41-man class of 1826 at West Point. As a lieutenant in the 2d U.S. Infantry he served at stations along the Great Lakes and on the frontier and was in Florida to oppose the Seminoles 1836–45. He fought under Gen. WINFIELD SCOTT in Mexico, won 2 brevets for gallantry, and was severely wounded while leading a "forlorn hope" assault during the storming of Chapultepec.

During the decade preceding the Civil War, Casey served mostly on the Pacific Coast. He was also a member of an officers' board that revised the manual of TACTICS for foot

NA

troops and subsequently prepared the 3-volume *System of Infantry Tactics* officially adopted by the War Department and published in 1862. Casey's work was derivative, almost indistinguishable from the 2-volume manual first published by WILLIAM J. HARDEE in 1855. Both sought to adapt ages-old battle formations to mid-19th-century weaponry, whose long-range accuracy had revolutionized warfare. The major difference between the two was Casey's expansion of Hardee's company- and battalion-level tactics to fit the BRIGADE and DIVISION formations prevalent during the Civil War. The appearance of Casey's work early in the conflict made it a useful aid to thousands of volunteer officers coming into the Union army. To some extent his manual also influenced Confederate tactics, though most Southern officers preferred Hardee's. Casey's companion work, *Infantry Tactics for Colored Troops,* was published in 1863.

Casey's field service during the war was confined to the PENINSULA CAMPAIGN, where his division of the II Corps/Army of the Potomac was overrun by the initial Confederate attack at SEVEN PINES, 31 May 1862. Despite this, he attained high rank, being promoted from lieutenant colonel of the 9th Infantry to brigadier general of volunteers 31 Aug. 1861 and to major general as of the date of Seven Pines.

For the balance of the war he was on administrative duty, for a time commanding a provisional brigade in the DEFENSES OF WASHINGTON, D.C. Mustered out of the volunteer service July 1865, he served as colonel of the 4th Infantry until his retirement from the Regular army in 1868. He died in Brooklyn, N.Y., 22 Jan. 1882 and was buried at the family farm in North Kingstown, R.I.   —EGL

Cashier, Albert D. J. (*née* Jennie Hodgers) USA b. Belfast, Ireland, 25 Dec. 1844, Hodgers arrived in the U.S. as a shipboard stowaway and at the time of the Civil War was living in Belvidere, Ill. Dressed as a man and calling herself Albert D. J. Cashier, she enlisted as a private in Company G/95th Illinois Volunteer Infantry 6 Aug. 1862. Her regiment was mustered into Federal service at Camp Fuller 4 Sept. and a month later departed for Grand Junction, Tenn., where the 95th was assigned to the Army of the Tennessee.

Cashier's regiment participated in the VICKSBURG CAMPAIGN during 1863 and in the RED RIVER CAMPAIGN the following spring. Through the remainder of 1864 the 95th operated against Maj. Gen. NATHAN B. FORREST's cavalry in northern Mississippi, was heavily engaged at BRICE'S CROSS ROADS 10 June, pursued Maj. Gen. STERLING PRICE during his Missouri Raid, and fought at Nashville, Tenn. (*see* FRANKLIN AND NASHVILLE CAMPAIGN). Sent to the Gulf Feb. 1865, Cashier's unit ended its military service by taking part in the investment of Spanish Fort and FORT BLAKELY in front of Mobile.

In August Cashier returned with the 95th to Camp Butler, where the regiment was discharged after nearly 3 years of hard service. With her comrades, she received a hero's welcome in Belvidere. She lived in several towns in Illinois through 1869, finally settling in Saunemin to support herself by working as a farmhand and handyman.

She kept her sex a secret until 1911, when her leg was fractured in a minor automobile accident and the doctor called in to treat her discovered she was a woman. Realizing that the 66-year-old Cashier was too crippled by the infirmities of age to live alone any longer, her employer arranged to have her admitted to the Soldiers' and Sailors' Home in Quincy. For several years authorities there kept Cashier's secret, until her failing memory and increasingly erratic behavior induced them to transfer her to the insane asylum at Watertown Mar. 1913.

During her later years Cashier collected an invalid soldier's pension of $70 each month. Through the GRAND ARMY OF THE REPUBLIC she stayed in touch with her old army comrades, who never suspected her disguise until authorities at the asylum forced her to discard it. They recalled the slight, 5'3" veteran as an amiable loner and a good soldier who despite her diminutiveness had kept up on the hardest marches, handled a rifle with skill equal to any infantryman, and never shirked duty.

That she was the same person who had served with the 95th

under the name Albert Cashier was challenged when her secret identity became public late in 1913, but a special examining board at the Bureau of Pensions in Washington, D.C., upheld her veteran's claim. When Cashier died at Watertown, 11 Oct. 1915, members of the local GAR chapter saw that she was buried in uniform with full military honors at the cemetery in Saunemin.

Instances of women serving as soldiers in the ranks appear occasionally in Union and Confederate literature. Those who were discovered or who confessed their sex were discharged and sent home, usually with their motives questioned and with their reputations or sanity in doubt. Since women disguised themselves to enlist and carefully concealed their identities to avoid censure, evidence of their military service is fragmentary at best. Cashier's is the only documented case of a woman fulfilling an army enlistment.   —PLF

Castle Pinckney. Named for Revolutionary patriot Gen. Charles C. Pinckney, this fort was built late in the 18th century on a shoal in the harbor at Charleston, S.C. When South Carolina seceded at 3 o'clock, 20 Dec. 1860, Pinckney was garrisoned by the Charleston Zouave Cadets, a group of young soldiers, organized in summer 1860, who came to be noted for their effective operation of the fort. By 4 o'clock the young company, under the command of Capt. C. E. Chichester, was "securing Pinckney."

NA

After the FIRST BATTLE OF BULL RUN, 21 July 1861, some of the first Federal prisoners of the Civil War were sent to Castle Pinckney, the fort's casemates having been fitted with bunks and doors and turned into prisoners' sleeping quarters. Prisoners were from the 79th New York Regiment, the 69th New York Regiment, the 8th Michigan Infantry, and the 11th Fire Zouaves, the last recruited from New York City's Fire Department. The prisoners were an exceptionally intelligent lot, and the Charleston Zouaves, while maintaining strict discipline, treated them as such. The association of captives and keepers was remarkably agreeable. In September 156 prisoners were moved from Richmond to Pinckney, and even though these captives were some "of the most insubordinate disposition," the fort-prison remained peaceful, and the prisoners kept their quarters in excellent condition. When Captain Chichester engaged a photographer to take pictures of both the Charleston Zouaves and the prisoners, the 11th New York Zouaves had theirs taken in front of their quarters, over which they had

Union prisoners, captured at Bull Run. Castle Pinckney, Charleston, S.C.

placed a big sign, "Hotel de Zouave."

The prisoners did volunteer work of various kinds, shared the same food as their guards, and taught the Charleston Zouaves the preferred army method of softening HARDTACK. They created the "Castle Pinckney Brotherhood," which established a pattern for living, including rules for cleanliness and provisions for entertainment, and the Charleston Zouaves helped in the brotherhood's activities.

There is no record of escape from Castle Pinckney.

—PR

Castle Thunder. The Confederacy had 2 prisons called Castle Thunder, one in Richmond and one in Petersburg, Va.; both were converted tobacco warehouses. The more important, Castle Thunder in Richmond, the Confederate capital, was used to confine political prisoners who were described in one early account as "the murderer, the robber, the deserter, the substitute deserter, the pickpocket, and worst of all the

skulker—the man who by his skulking endangers his comrades, therefore worse than the murderer—the spy, the reconstructionist, the disloyal." Also among the prisoners were "semi-Yankees" being held "to answer charges of running off Negroes to the Yankees."

A newspaper correspondent wrote that the inmates of Castle Thunder in Richmond were so tough they laughed when death struck one of their number, saddened "no more than if it had never occurred. One simply stretched out the man's limbs with an 'I'll be damned if he ain't dead!' Another placed a billet of wood under his head, and notified the guard with the jocose remark, 'There's a fellow here got his discharge and wants to get out.' "

The many held in the prison as spies and criminals charged with treason were said to have been treated with unnecessary brutality by the guards. The unsavory reputation of the prison obliged the Confederate House of Representatives in 1863 to order an investigation of the commandant, Capt. George W. Alexander, who had been accused of "harshness, inhumanity, tyranny, and dishonesty." Alexander, by a majority report, was cleared by the investigation. During its course he said that the most difficult of the prisoners were "the plug-uglies of Baltimore and the wharf-rats of New Orleans." After Richmond fell, the Federals used the prison to confine Confederates accused of war crimes.

Castle Thunder in Petersburg was so named by Union prisoners confined there during the last siege of the city, when the sound of artillery fire was thunderous. —PR

Catlett's Station, Va., Raid, Stuart's. 22–23 Aug. 1862 Maj. Gen. JOHN POPE's Union Army of Virginia and Gen. ROBERT E. LEE's Army of Northern Virginia pursued each other across the Rappahannock River in mid-Aug. 1862. Pope had only to protect the fords and await the arrival of the leading elements of the Army of the Potomac. Lee had to act to prevent this juncture. Wherever the Confederates probed for a crossing, Federals barred the way. Maj. Gen. J.E.B. STUART, Lee's cavalry commander, proposed a raid to sever the ORANGE & ALEXANDRIA RAILROAD, the Union army's main supply line. Lee approved.

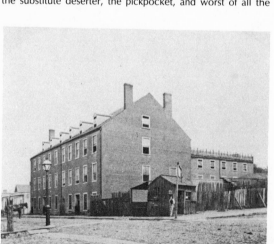

Stuart, with about 1,500 horsemen and 2 cannon, crossed the Rappahannock at Waterloo Bridge 22 Aug. Skirting Pope's

right, the Confederate cavalrymen entered Warrenton, Va., where they learned that no Federals had been seen for days. Stuart continued, angling his column toward Catlett's Station and the railroad bridge over Cub Run. As the Confederates rode, a violent thunderstorm erupted, with drenching rain and gusting winds.

Halting short of Catlett's in the evening, the Confederates quietly captured Union sentinels. From the Federals, Stuart learned that Catlett's was Pope's headquarters. A captured black CONTRABAND agreed to lead the Southerners to Pope's tent. Stuart hurriedly deployed his troopers, ordering them to scream the "Rebel yell" when the bugle sounded charge.

Through the lashing storm came the pistol-firing Confederates. Most of the Federals, completely surprised, surrendered immediately. A handful of Pennsylvania infantry fired from the depot until the charging Southerners vaulted their horses onto the platform and crashed into the building. Within minutes Stuart's troopers had seized hundreds of horses and mules, 300 prisoners, and Pope's hat, cloak, one of his dress uniforms, his dispatch book, and the army's money chests. A detachment of Confederates endeavored to burn the railroad trestle, but the rain and winds prevented it.

Stuart finally withdrew shortly before dawn, his elated men returning unmolested to the south side of the Rappahannock. His seizure of Pope's papers provided Lee with valuable information; the Union general's uniform was placed on public display in Richmond. On the 24th, Lee, with the intelligence gained, conferred with Maj. Gen. Thomas J. "Stonewall" Jackson, outlining his plans for what would become the SECOND BULL RUN CAMPAIGN.   —JDW

***Catskill*, USS.** One of a fleet of monitors constructed by JOHN ERICSSON, the *Catskill* was launched in New York City 16 Dec. 1862. Its first and only assignment came Mar. 1862, when it was sent to strengthen the BLOCKADE of Charleston, S.C.

Charleston, one of the 2 busiest blockade-running centers in the South, was showing complete defiance; only a month or so before the *Catskill* arrived, 2 vessels had come out from its harbor and driven off the besieging Union fleet, thereby temporarily lifting the blockade.

The city was defended by a series of fortifications, including Forts Sumter and Moultrie, Castle Pinckney, and Batteries Wagner and Beauregard, as well as guns on James, Sullivan's, and Morris islands. In the North leaders were determined that Charleston should fall by using against it a combination of land and sea forces. Newspapers announced that preparations were being made for an attack on the city that would "prove irresistible." Part of this build-up, the *Catskill* reached Charleston 5 Apr. and 2 days later took part in attacks on Fort Sumter and, 5 days later, on Battery Wagner and Morris Island. For months the monitor participated in an almost daily assault on the forts, sometimes serving as flagship and aiding in destroying BLOCKADE RUNNERS.

On 17 Aug. 1864 the vessel's commander, Capt. George W. Rodgers, was killed by a shell that damaged the ship's pilothouse. Repaired and back into service, the *Catskill* continued to aid in the attack on CHARLESTON until the city finally was evacuated 18 Feb. 1865. During that time the ship had 6 other commanders.

Ordered to FORT MONROE about a month later, the *Catskill* continued in Union naval service, for a brief period under the name *Goliath*.   —VCJ

Cedar Creek, Va., Battle of. 19 Oct. 1864   Union Maj. Gen. Philip H. Sheridan's SHENANDOAH VALLEY CAMPAIGN appeared concluded by mid-October. Union victories at WINCHESTER, FISHER'S HILL, and Tom's Brook had seriously reduced Lt. Gen. JUBAL A. EARLY's command, and the systematic destruction of the upper valley had made the region "a barren waste." Sheridan, consequently, journeyed to Washington, D.C., for a STRATEGY conference as his army rested securely in their camps behind Cedar Creek.

Early, an indomitable fighter, approved an elaborate and brilliant plan developed by Maj. Gen. JOHN B. GORDON and Maj. JEDEDIAH HOTCHKISS. Just before daybreak on 19 Oct., Early's 5 infantry divisions, charging through a thick fog, struck the sleeping Federal camps, the surprise assault spewing across the plain south of Middletown and wrecking 2 of Sheridan's 3 infantry corps. Clusters of Union soldiers resisted valiantly before being swept away. The VI Corps of Maj. Gen. HORATIO G. WRIGHT, who commanded in Sheridan's absence, and the Union cavalry retained their organizations and repulsed some Confederate charges before retreating. By 10 o'clock the Federals regrouped in a position over 3 mi from their camps.

Early's failure to press his advantage has since caused controversy. Many Confederates, hungry and fatigued from an all-night march, stopped to enjoy the fruits of their victory; also, the Confederate divisions required time to regroup. Early finally formed a line north of Middletown, a splendid victory seemingly assured.

Sheridan, who was at Winchester and heard the rumblings of battle, returned to his battered army about 10:30 a.m. "Little Phil" rode along his front, inspiring his men. At 4 p.m. the Federals counterattacked, breached Early's left front, and crushed the Confederate troops, who fled southward. Early's gamble had failed, costing him 2,900 men; Sheridan suffered 5,665 casualties.   —JDW

Cedar Mountain, Va., Battle of. 9 Aug. 1862   While the fighting raged on the Virginia Peninsula during the SEVEN DAYS' CAMPAIGN, Maj. Gen. JOHN POPE assumed command of the newly created Union Army of Virginia. Summoned from the West, Pope was given an amalgam of 3 Union commands. The general, assigned to protect Washington, D.C., and to guard the SHENANDOAH VALLEY, advanced to the area near Culpeper, Va., east of the Blue Ridge Mts.

After the Confederate victory on the outskirts of Richmond, Gen. ROBERT E. LEE moved to meet the threat posed by Pope. In mid-July 1862 he sent Maj. Gen. THOMAS J. "STONEWALL" JACKSON northwestward to protect the rail junction at Gordonsville and to watch the Federals. A fortnight of little activity followed; then, 7 Aug., Jackson started north for Orange Court House, which he reached that night. The march resumed the next day but, because Jackson modified his orders without informing Maj. Gen. AMBROSE P. HILL, the Confederates covered a mere 8 mi.

Pope, meanwhile, also planned an advance toward the Rapidan River, in a demonstration against Charlottesville. When on the 8th he learned of the Confederate movement, Pope deployed on a wide front to cover both Madison Court House and Culpeper. Early on 9 Aug., Federal cavalry rimmed the front; in support at Cedar Run, 8 mi south of Culpeper, was a brigade of Maj. Gen. NATHANIEL P. BANKS' II Corps, the remainder being stationed 3 mi farther back with another Union division nearby.

Informed of the presence of Federal cavalry and infantry of unknown strength, Jackson hurried his 3 divisions northward. By midmorning the van of the 24,000-man Confederate force was making contact with Pope's cavalrymen, followed soon by Jackson, whose deployment consumed most of the afternoon. When the Confederates finally went forward at 4 p.m., there were gaps in their line and no one knew what lay in the woods on their left.

The 2 Confederate divisions, under Maj. Gen. RICHARD S. EWELL and Brig. Gen. CHARLES S. WINDER, swept forward, meeting little initial opposition. But Winder, commanding the left, fell mortally wounded, mangled by a Union shell. Soon afterward, Banks, Jackson's antagonist in the Shenandoah Valley, launched a massive assault on the exposed Confederate left; Winder's Confederates buckled, then broke under the onslaught. When Jackson saw his left crushed, he rode into the woods to rally his shattered units.

Though Banks had thrown nearly all of his 9,000 soldiers into the charge, Ewell's men, on the right, bent back but held. Slowly the Confederate line mended the break, reinforced by the leading brigades of Hill's oncoming division. In the twilight of the early evening, the Confederates counterattacked. The Federals still fought stubbornly, withdrawing grudgingly from the field. Jackson ordered Hill forward in pursuit, which Union artillery and darkness cut short.

Jackson could claim a victory at Cedar Mountain, for he held the field. But the Confederate commander had miscalculated, nearly suffering a humiliating defeat from an opponent less than half his strength. Banks erred by neither leaving a reserve when he attacked nor requesting reinforcements from Pope. The Union corps commander lost nearly 2,400 men, while Jackson suffered nearly 1,350 casualties. The loss of the capable Winder diminished the value of this hard-fought Confederate victory. —JDW

Cemetery Hill, at Gettysburg, Pa.

Cemetery Hill, at Gettysburg, Pa. 1–2 July 1863 The broken remnants of 2 Union corps spilled onto Cemetery Hill late on the afternoon of 1 July 1863. Routed by 4 Confederate divisions, the Federals rallied on the hill at the southeastern edge of GETTYSBURG. Union Maj. Gen. WINFIELD S. HANCOCK restored order and prepared a defensive position. Cemetery Hill anchored the northern end of CEMETERY RIDGE, the center of the Union line.

Throughout 2 July the Federals on the hill anticipated a Confederate charge, which finally came in the twilight as the fighting on the southern part of the field was flickering out. 2 brigades, under Brig. Gen. HARRY T. HAYS and Col. Isaac E. Avery, stormed up the east face of the hill about 7:30 p.m. 16 Federal guns on Cemetery Hill and 6 more on CULP'S HILL blasted the charging Southerners. The Confederates fell in clumps, and Avery received a mortal wound; but on they came, taking nearly an hour to reach the crest. A Union brigade crumbled before them and the conflict raged in the darkness around the guns, which now belonged to the Confederates. The attackers, however, were spent; a Confederate division ordered to attack did not. When a Union brigade counterattacked, the Southerners broke and streamed down the hillside. The rifle flashes ceased in the darkness and Cemetery Hill remained in Union hands. —JDW

Cemetery Ridge, at Gettysburg, Pa. 1–3 July 1863 During the night of 1–2 July 1863, and on into the daylight

hours of the 2d, Union troops poured onto Cemetery Ridge south of Gettysburg. Over 2 mi long, flanked by CEMETERY HILL on the north and the Round Tops on the south, the crest was the center of the Union line. To the west, across 1,200 yd of cultivated fields and orchards, lay Seminary Ridge, the main position of the Confederate army. In the shallow valley between, much of the searing drama of the battle at GETTYSBURG occurred.

When the full-scale Confederate assault erupted late 2 July on the southern portion of the field, Federal units on the ridge were shifted into the combat. The Southerners, attacking *en echelon* to the north, soon moved against the Union center. Brig. Gen. AMBROSE R. WRIGHT's brigade of Georgians stormed through the fury, seizing a section of the crest before being repulsed. Wright's temporary lodgment convinced Gen. ROBERT E. LEE that a massive charge could crush the Union center. It came about 3 p.m., 3 July, when on the order of Maj. Gen. GEORGE E. PICKETT, 15,000 Confederates charged toward a clump of trees on the ridge. The stalwart Federal defenders halted PICKETT'S CHARGE with artillery and rifle fire; the Union ranks on Cemetery Ridge held. —JDW

censorship. Neither the Union nor Confederate government had uniform or effective press censorship; instead, Washington and Richmond officials, appealing to patriotism, asked the press to censor itself. But at some time during the war, both Northern and Southern newspapers were suppressed and closed by government officials. Northern reporters were on rare occasion imprisoned; Southern battlefield correspondents, often members of the army, were threatened with military justice.

Commanding generals imposed their own censorship. 2 weeks before the July 1861 FIRST BATTLE OF BULL RUN, Union Lt. Gen. WINFIELD SCOTT forbade wiring news of military movements from any Washington telegraph office unless he personally inspected the reporter's dispatch. Briefly loosened, censorship was again tightened in the hours following the Union defeat at Manassas, though an enterprising reporter found a loophole in the rule and was able to wire out news the following day.

As reporters sought to evade censorship, stricter controls were enforced 10 Aug. 1861, when Union War Department orders forbade reporters to telegraph from the capital anything referring to past, present, or future army operations; in addition, any information on army operations anywhere in the country could not be disseminated unless authorized by the major general commanding. However, this rule was freely abused by all parties and eyewitness coverage of battles was often telegraphed on the day fighting occurred. In 1865 a petition was placed before Congress to remove the War Department orders because administration officials showed favoritism to some newspapers through dispensations.

Union Maj. Gen. WILLIAM T. SHERMAN habitually expelled reporters from his camp, and in June 1864 Union Maj. Gen. GEORGE G. MEADE made no news by expelling Philadelphia *Inquirer* reporter Edward Crapsey from the Army of the Potomac. As a gesture of support for Crapsey, other Union reporters agreed to omit Meade's name from all future stories and ascribe all future army successes or moves to Lt. Gen. ULYSSES S. GRANT.

Confederate censorship was similar. The Provisional Confederate Congress imposed censorship of the telegraph May

1861 and allowed placement of government agents in telegraph offices to monitor transmissions; those using the telegraph for uncensored news transmissions were liable to fine or imprisonment. In June Confederate postmasters were ordered to censor the mail. But self-censorship by the press was the most effective. The Confederate Press Association instructed its agents to omit crucial military details from their battle and campaign coverage and reporters frequently sent war accounts to their newspapers with instructions not to publish them until after a certain date. Self-restraint avoided heavier measures such as those proposed in an 1862 bill to the Confederate Congress that would have punished any newspaper printing a story giving details threatening the success of Confederate military operations. The bill did not pass but was proposed on legitimate grounds: it was well known that Gen. ROBERT E. LEE preferred the battle reportage in the Philadelphia *Inquirer* and often gleaned from it Union troop strengths and movements; the situation could be easily reversed.   —JES

Centralia, Mo., massacre at.

27 Sept. 1864 On the night of 26 Sept. Confederate guerrilla leader William "Bloody Bill" Anderson camped with 225 men at the Singleton farm, 4 mi south of Centralia, Mo. Early the next morning he and 30 men rode into the town. For 3 hours they terrorized the residents, shooting wildly and looting the homes and businesses of Unionists. Several were drunk by the time the stage from Columbia arrived about noon. They forced the passengers into the street and robbed them, moving toward the railroad depot as the westbound train approached from St. Charles.

Quickly the guerrillas tore up a stretch of track, and when the train stopped, they surrounded it, unloaded the passengers, and robbed them. On board were 25 unarmed Federal soldiers, most on furlough. Half of Anderson's men formed a guard and marched the line of soldiers down the platform. "Bloody Bill" questioned them, then ordered them to strip and give their uniforms to his men. When Anderson asked if there were officers or noncommissioned officers among them, one Federal, Sgt. Thomas Goodman of the Missouri Engineers, stepped forward expecting to be shot. Someone pushed Goodman aside and set fire to the train. On Anderson's order, his men shot the soldiers in cold blood, tied Goodman on a horse, and returned to Singleton's farm. There, to Goodman's amazement, Anderson's men congratulated him for his courage and released him.

That afternoon Union Maj. A.V.E. Johnson, with 158 men of the 39th Missouri Infantry, reached Centralia. Though the frantic residents warned him of more guerrillas nearby, the officer divided his force, leaving half to restore order; the rest of the company took off in pursuit of the murderers. A short distance out of town they spotted 10 horsemen, who led the Federals into a deadly ambush. Unable to escape, Johnson ordered his men, nearly all of them inexperienced recruits, to dismount and form a battle line. Anderson's men charged, killing most of the Federals, including Johnson, then rode back to Centralia, attacking and brutally murdering the remainder of Johnson's command. In little over an hour, the 39th lost 116 men killed, 2 wounded, and 6 missing.   —PLF

Central Kentucky, Confederate Army of.

On 10 Sept. 1861 Gen. ALBERT SIDNEY JOHNSTON took command of Confederate DEPARTMENT NO. 2, stretching from the Appalachians to Indian Territory. He devoted most of his attention to the Ken-

tucky sector, which he saw as 3 main areas centered on Cumberland Gap, Bowling Green, and Columbus. When Brig. Gen. SIMON B. BUCKNER occupied Bowling Green 18 Sept., he began to refer to that region as the Central Division of Kentucky. On 28 Oct., 2 weeks after he arrived in Bowling Green, Johnston organized the troops in those areas into the Army of Central Kentucky. Maj. Gen. WILLIAM J. HARDEE, commander of the 1st Division, also headed the army; Buckner commanded the 2d Division.

Expecting the main Union thrust along the Louisville–Bowling Green–Nashville line, Johnston prepared strong defensive positions at Bowling Green. He longed to take the offensive but was disappointed in the small number of Kentucky volunteers and in the insufficient reinforcements and supplies from the Confederate government. Johnston's eastern Kentucky army was defeated at MILL SPRINGS 19 Jan. 1862, and FORT HENRY fell to Flag Officer ANDREW H. FOOTE's gunboats 6 Feb. The next day Johnston decided to withdraw south to the Tennessee River, ordering troops to FORT DONELSON to protect his retreat. But overcome by a land/sea assault, Donelson surrendered 16 Feb.

On 31 Dec. 1861 Hardee reported an aggregate troop strength of 22,272 men in his 1st Division, Buckner's 2d Division, Col. JOHN S. BOWEN's understrength 4th Division, and the unattached brigades of Brig. Gen. CHARLES CLARK and Col. Reuben Davis. On 23 Feb. 1862, when the army reached Murfreesboro on its retreat, Johnston reorganized it, assuming personal command. With Buckner a prisoner, the divisional commanders were Hardee, Maj. Gen. GEORGE B. CRITTENDEN, and Brig. Gen. GIDEON J. PILLOW. Brig. Gen. JOHN C. BRECKINRIDGE and the cavalry units of Cols. NATHAN B. FORREST and JOHN A. WHARTON were unattached.

When Johnston reached Corinth, Miss., he reunited the Central Army with the troops from Columbus. On 23 Mar. 1862 the 2 were combined in a new ARMY OF MISSISSIPPI, and the Army of Central Kentucky ceased to exist.   —LHH

Chaffin's Farm, Va., Battle of.

29–30 Sept. 1864 To bolster Confederate forces in the Shenandoah Valley, Gen. ROBERT E. LEE decided mid-Sept. 1864 to detach troops from the Petersburg front. Learning this, Lt. Gen. ULYSSES S. GRANT readied attacks against both ends of the Confederate line. The details of the main offensive were worked out by Maj. Gen. BENJAMIN F. BUTLER and involved a 2-pronged movement by his Army of the James across its namesake river toward Richmond. Some 800 infantry under Maj. Gen. E.O.C. ORD would cross a PONTOON BRIDGE opposite Varina Landing and strike the Confederate capital's southern defenses near Chaffin's Farm. Meanwhile, 18,000 infantry and cavalry under Brig. Gen. WILLIAM BIRNEY would cross another bridge at Deep Bottom, 18 mi downstream, and strike the easternmost Confederate works atop New Market Heights.

Butler's columns moved across before daylight 29 Sept. and fell on their startled enemy with great force. Charging across a cleared space of 1,400 yd under heavy fire, Ord's forces seized Fort Harrison, which protected Confederate bridges, camps, and batteries along the James. In the effort hundreds fell dead, including Brig. Gen. Hiram Burnham, commander of the first attack wave. The Federals then moved north against the smaller but more heavily defended Fort Gilmer, the key to the Chaffin's Farm complex. Meeting spirited resistance, Ord was wounded and his assault bogged down. Farther east, meanwhile, Birney took the outer works along New Market Heights but failed to expand his gains despite 3 successive assaults. In these his several brigades of black infantry demonstrated conspicuous gallantry and suffered dreadfully.

Fearing the collapse of his northern flank, Lee rushed reinforcements to the scene and personally supervised 3 attempts to regain Fort Harrison 30 Sept. From hastily improvised trenches the Federals repulsed each, thanks especially to the leadership of Brig. Gen. George J. Stannard, seriously wounded in the final assault. The 2 days of fighting closed with Butler holding positions within sight of Richmond but having suffered 3,300 casualties against Lee's 2,000.   —EGL

chain shot; bar shot. Chain shot and bar shot were both obsolete forms of artillery ammunition by the Civil War, although they appear to have been used in isolated instances.

According to ordnance manuals of the day, chain shot consisted of 2 hollow hemispheres connected by a short length of chain, with the chain folded inside and the hemispheres closed together into a ball for loading. When fired, the shot whirled toward the enemy. In some early chain shot, and a few wartime examples, 2 round solid shots were connected by a length of chain and loaded down the barrel one after the other. Chain shot was used in the famous Confederate double-barreled cannon made in Athens, Ga., during the war, but because the firing of the 2 barrels could not be synchronized, the chain snapped and the balls flew in different directions.

Bar shot was similar to chain shot but consisted of solid iron hemispheres connected by an iron bar. It too was loaded down the barrel as if it were one shot. On firing it reacted much the same as chain shot, flying in an erratic, whirling motion toward the enemy.

Both chain and bar shot were originally developed to be used against the rigging of sailing vessels, where the whirling motion would wreak havoc on masts, yards, and lines, which were more difficult to hit with standard solid shot. The few examples of Civil War vintage known to exist come from weapons as heavy as 32-pounders and as light as 9-pounders. Examples located at Fort Sumter reflect the Confederates' fear of a naval attack against Charleston. Yet the development of the IRONCLAD vessel rendered bar and chain shot even less useful, and the discovery of these devices in a Civil War context can be seen as evidence of some desperation in the allotment of artillery ammunition.   —LDJ

Chalmers, James Ronald. CSA b. Halifax Cty., Va., 11 Jan. 1831. When Chalmers was appointed colonel of the 9th Mississippi at the outset of the Civil War, he had no military experience. Despite this, in the next few years he succeeded in both infantry and cavalry command. A graduate of South Carolina College in 1851, he moved to Holly Springs, Miss., and opened a law practice in the antebellum years. Exhibiting a feisty, independent temperament, he became an aggressive district attorney there and later a member of the Mississippi state secession convention.

After becoming colonel of the 9th, Chalmers was sent to Pensacola, Fla., where, under Gen. BRAXTON BRAGG, he had the unusual experience of being liked by the fussy and fault-finding Bragg. Though Chalmers had no real command experience, Bragg thought he had potential and made him head of his 1st Brigade. Chalmers threw himself and his men into the heavy drill and training Bragg prescribed for his troops. His

attention to soldiering brought him promotion to brigadier general 13 Feb. 1862 and a position of responsibility in the Battle of SHILOH the next April.

At Shiloh Chalmers fought on the Confederate right under Bragg and during the first day's fighting took his command into 6 separate combats. Only the last failed, an assault on a Federal battery driven back to the Tennessee River. Exhausted, Chalmers' men were unable to press the Union cannoneers further. That evening, Chalmers won a compliment from a man he would come to know better, Confederate cavalry commander NATHAN B. FORREST. After a day of chaotic combat, when Forrest asked Chalmers the whereabouts of the latter's troops, Chalmers answered that they were right in front of him sleeping on their arms. Forrest replied, "You are the first general I have found tonight who knows where his men are!"

After Shiloh, Chalmers followed Bragg on his KENTUCKY CAMPAIGN and into the Battle of STONE'S RIVER, where he led his troops on the Union SALIENT at the grove of trees called the "Round Forest," or "Hell's Half-Acre." Chalmers' men were badly cut up, and he himself was wounded in the attack, thus ending his infantry career. After convalescing he transferred to the cavalry and through 1863 was given command of the District of Mississippi and East Louisiana. In Jan. 1864 his command was joined to Forrest's.

While Chalmers charmed the cavalrymen of Forrest's force (they affectionately called him "Little 'Un"), his relationship with his major general was stormy. Not only were the two from different social classes, but Forrest had been required to take away some of Chalmers' authority (as part of consolidating command) and, as a last insult, Chalmers claimed Forrest "took my only tent from me and gave it to his brother." A court of inquiry and a period of reassignment followed, but Chalmers was back with Forrest, resolved to his new station, by late spring 1864 and fought with him through all his battles and campaigns to the end of the war. In several of these last fights, particularly on duty during Lt. Gen. JOHN B. HOOD's invasion of Tennessee, Chalmers was said to have played "a brilliant part."

Following the surrender of Forrest's forces, Chalmers went home to Mississippi, where he practiced law and ran for the U.S. House of Representatives 6 times, each one a contested election, winning 3 of those campaigns in 1876, 1878 and 1882. In 1888 he moved to Memphis, where he practiced law until he died 9 Apr. 1898.   —JES

Chamberlain, Joshua Lawrence. USA b. Brewer, Maine, 8 Sept. 1828. In summer 1862 34-year-old Prof. Joshua L. Chamberlain of Bowdoin College secured a sabbatical, supposedly to study in Europe; instead of traveling abroad, however, Chamberlain became lieutenant colonel of the 20TH MAINE Infantry.

As part of the V Corps, Chamberlain and the 20th Maine were with the ARMY OF THE POTOMAC through most of its engagements from Antietam to Appomattox. At FREDERICKSBURG, Chamberlain and his men lay under relentless Confederate fire for hours, well into the cold night of 13 Dec. 1862. Chamberlain's most heroic moment, though, awaited him at GETTYSBURG.

On 2 July 1863 Chamberlain, now colonel of the 20th Maine, received orders to hold a small wooded hill on the extreme left of the Union line. Chamberlain recognized LITTLE ROUND TOP to be vital to the Federal position, and late into the hot afternoon he and his men repulsed repeated Confederate attacks. As the Southerners formed for a final attempt, Chamberlain realized his men had exhausted their ammunition. Refusing to retreat, at the crucial moment he led a furious bayonet charge that broke the Confederate onslaught and held Little Round Top for the Union. Although wounded, Chamberlain continued to lead until the Confederates retreated from Gettysburg. 30 years later, in Aug. 1893, the nation recognized his valor by awarding him the MEDAL OF HONOR.

USMHI

Still commanding the 20th Maine, Chamberlain suffered his fourth wound during the Petersburg assaults of June 1864. His gallantry so impressed Ulysses S. Grant that the general-in-chief promoted him to brigadier general on the field.

Against all expectations, Chamberlain recovered and returned to the army, and 12 Apr. 1865 Bvt. Maj. Gen. Chamberlain received the formal surrender of Gen. ROBERT E. LEE'S veterans. As the shattered remnants of the Confederate army stacked arms, Chamberlain, in a conciliatory gesture, snapped his men to attention in a salute to the late foe.

Refusing a commission in the Regular army when he was mustered out of the service Jan. 1866, Chamberlain subsequently served 4 terms as governor of Maine, 1866–70, and as president of Bowdoin College, 1870–83. He spent his later years as a businessman, writing extensively about his wartime experiences. d. Portland, 24 Feb. 1914.   —BNO

Chambersburg, Pa., burning of. 30–31 July 1864
Nearly 2,600 Confederate cavalrymen halted on the outskirts of Chambersburg about 3 a.m., Saturday, 30 July 1864. Their commander, Brig. Gen. JOHN MCCAUSLAND, carried written orders from Lt. Gen. JUBAL A. EARLY demanding from the citizens of this southern Pennsylvania town $100,000 in gold or $500,-000 in GREENBACKS as compensation for 3 Virginia houses burned by Maj. Gen. DAVID HUNTER's Union troops. According to the orders, if the payment was not made, the town would be "laid in ashes in retaliation."

3 cannon shots signaled the Confederates' presence and by 6 a.m. some 500 Southerners occupied the town; 100 Union troops had already fled. McCausland had the proclamation read and gave citizens 6 hours to pay the ransom. While the commander waited, his men plundered the stores, including some liquor businesses; soon drunken Confederates began looting private homes, taking jewelry, silverware, and money. The citizens refused to pay the ransom and McCausland ordered the town fired.

The Confederates torched a warehouse first, then the courthouse and town hall, and within 10 minutes the flames enveloped the main part of Chambersburg. The terrified residents, seizing a few possessions, fled to a cemetery and fields around the village. Some citizens who had paid money to have their homes spared saw them burned anyway. One elderly woman thrashed a soldier with a broom, driving him away and saving her house. A cavalry officer isolated from his men was shot and killed by a mob of townspeople. Those Confederates who disapproved of the burning did save several houses.

The Confederates departed by 1 p.m. Behind them 400 buildings, 274 of them homes, smoldered in ruins. Damages amounted to nearly $1.5 million. To Early it was just retribution.   —JDW

Chambersburg, Pa., Raid, Stuart's. 10–11 Oct. 1862
On 8 Oct. 1862 Gen. Robert E. Lee ordered Maj. Gen. J.E.B. STUART to take his cavalry on a raid into Maryland, and even as far as Chambersburg, Pa., to cut the Cumberland Valley Railroad supplying Maj. Gen. George B. McClellan's army at Hagerstown. Further, Stuart was to gather intelligence on enemy numbers, supplies, and intentions. It was a typical cavalry operation, the sort of independent lark that Stuart loved.

On 10 Oct. Stuart led 1,800 troopers north from their Virginia camps toward the Potomac River. They rode to McCoy's Ford several miles above Harpers Ferry, sliced across the narrow Maryland panhandle, and rode into Pennsylvania that same day. Already a Federal pursuit was mounting.

By nightfall the horsemen reached Chambersburg. The startled citizens surrendered the town, and Stuart commenced at once its capture and destruction. By dawn the next morning he was ready to leave, his mission only partly fulfilled, for the railroad was still intact. Guessing that McClellan would have cut off a return by way of the upper Potomac, Stuart led the command east to Cashtown, then south to Emmitsburg, Md., continuing on past Frederick to recross the Potomac finally at White's Ferry. In effect, he had ridden completely around McClellan yet again (see STUART'S RIDE AROUND MCCLELLAN). Only at the final river crossing did Federal cavalrymen catch him in an ineffectual attempt to cut off escape.

Stuart had covered more than 100 mi in 2 days, destroyed some stores, captured more, and severely disorganized the Federal cavalry for weeks to come. Against a better opponent Stuart's Chambersburg Raid would not have been significant; against McClellan, however, it made an already timid general even more fearful.   —WCD

Chambliss, John Randolph, Jr. CSA b. Hicksford, Va., 23 Jan. 1833. After graduating from West Point 31st in his class in 1853 and spending a year in a unit of mounted riflemen, Chambliss resigned from the army and returned to Virginia, where he managed the family plantation, commanded a militia regiment, and 1856–61 was an aide to the governor.

USMHI

When his state joined the Confederacy (his father becoming a member of the First Confederate Congress), Chambliss' military and social connections gained him command of the 41st Virginia Infantry. Preferring mounted service, he obtained the colonelcy of the 13th Virginia Cavalry, which eventually joined Maj. Gen. J.E.B. STUART's division of the Army of Northern Virginia. For a time Chambliss served below the James River, then along the Rappahannock during the ANTIETAM CAMPAIGN, winning praise for his diligence in reconnaissance.

In Nov. 1862 the 13th Virginia, as part of Brig. Gen. W.H.F. LEE's brigade of Stuart's cavalry, participated in the FREDERICKS-

BURG CAMPAIGN and in an expedition into the Dumfries-Occoquan area during which Stuart attacked outposts near the Federal capital. The following May, during the CHANCELLORS-VILLE CAMPAIGN, Chambliss operated apart from his regiment, fighting dismounted in the Virginia Wilderness at the head of the 5th Virginia Cavalry.

He rejoined the 13th Virginia in time for the mounted clash at BRANDY STATION, 9 June 1863, succeeding to the command of W.H.F. Lee's brigade after the latter was severely wounded late in the day. He led the brigade throughout the GETTYSBURG CAMPAIGN, seeing action at ALDIE (where he captured a mob of Union troopers), Middleburg, and Hanover (where his charge nearly routed a Federal cavalry brigade). East of Gettysburg, 3 July, from his position on Stuart's left flank, he launched a less successful attack, being repulsed with heavy losses. In Jan. 1864, after fighting at BRISTOE STATION and again at Brandy Station, he was promoted to brigadier general.

Chambliss continued in command of Lee's brigade at the WILDERNESS, YELLOW TAVERN, Haw's Shop, TREVILIAN STATION, and in the opening engagements in the PETERSBURG CAMPAIGN. On 16 Aug. 1864, countering a Union infantry/cavalry offensive along the Charles City Road outside Richmond, he was shot by a member of the 16th Pennsylvania Cavalry. Captured, he died of his wounds later that day.   —EGL

Chameleon, CSS. *See* TALLAHASSEE, CSS.

Champion's Hill, Miss., Battle of. 16 May 1863 Confederate Gen. JOSEPH E. JOHNSTON, reaching Jackson, Miss., ordered Lt. Gen. JOHN C. PEMBERTON, 14 May 1863, to march east and assail the Union army near Clinton. By the time Pemberton joined his 22,000-man army at Edward's Station, Miss., he had decided it would be "extremely hazardous" to implement his superior's instructions. A council of war determined that Pemberton would march southeast and attack Union supply trains and reinforcements en route from Grand Gulf to Raymond, Miss. On 15 May the army moved out, slowed by delays for which Pemberton was responsible; by nightfall the column had moved less than 5 mi.

Maj. Gen. U. S. GRANT, apprised of Johnston's plans, moved to intercept Pemberton, employing the corps of Maj. Gen. JAMES B. MCPHERSON and JOHN A. MCCLERNAND. Maj. Gen. WILLIAM T. SHERMAN's corps remained in Jackson. When Union troops bivouacked on the 15th, 3 divisions were near Bolton on the Jackson Road, 2 on the Middle Road, and 2 on the Raymond Road.

On the morning of the 16th Pemberton's pickets clashed with Grant's approaching columns, and a message came from Johnston reiterating an order to concentrate north of the Southern Railroad. Pemberton issued orders to countermarch through Edward's and out the Brownsville Road.

He was too late. McPherson had advanced from Bolton and was nearing Champion's Hill, a commanding elevation. To meet this threat, Pemberton deployed 3 brigades of Maj. Gen. CARTER L. STEVENSON's division, while the divisions of Brig. Gen. JOHN S. BOWEN and Maj. Gen. WILLIAM WING LORING fronted to the southeast to counter McClernand's columns. At 10:30 Grant mounted an attack on Stevenson. During the fighting, Champion's Hill and the crossroads changed hands 3 times. Out-generaled, the Confederates by 5 p.m. were fleeing across Baker's Creek, leaving 27 cannon and hundreds of prisoners on the field. In the retreat to the Big Black River, Loring's division was cut off but eventually joined Johnston.   —ECB

Chancellorsville, Va., Battle of. 1–4 May 1863 By the evening of 30 Apr. 1863 Gen. ROBERT E. LEE was grappling with the gravest strategic situation of his 11-month command of the Army of Northern Virginia. Maj. Gen. JOSEPH HOOKER, commander of the Army of the Potomac, had enveloped the Confederate left flank, interposing 75,000 men 10 mi behind Lee's lines at Fredericksburg. Opposite the Confederate works, across the Rappahannock River, an additional 40,000 Federals lay poised to strike. With only 60,000 effectives, Lee could either retreat or offer battle. The aggressive Confederate, leaving 10,000 soldiers behind at Fredericksburg, advanced against Hooker's wing in the Wilderness, a large demonic landscape of scrub brush and oak trees.

Swinging into columns, 50,000 Confederates marched westward 1 May. The Federals, whose officers were jubilant over the prospects of success, abandoned the Wilderness, tramping into the open country. About 2 mi from the woodland, they encountered Lt. Gen. THOMAS J. "STONEWALL" JACKSON's oncoming veterans, and skirmishing erupted along the lines. Hooker, who admitted later that he lost his nerve, ordered a sudden withdrawal into the dense foliage; over the protest of his corps commanders, he abandoned the initiative to Lee. By deciding to make a stand in the Wilderness, Hooker neutralized the superiority of both his numbers and his artillery. The Federals withdrew into a line encircling the crossroads of Chancellorsville.

Lee reacted cautiously to this sudden retreat. But when Maj. Gen. J.E.B. STUART's cavalry discovered that Hooker's right flank was unsupported, Lee decided to attack. That night he and Jackson, sitting on cracker boxes, devised one of the most daring plans in military history. Defying accepted strategic and tactical laws, Lee again split his army, ordering Jackson, with 26,000 men, to march beyond Hooker's vulnerable flank and attack while Lee, with nearly 20,000, demonstrated along the Federal works.

Jackson's 14-mi march took nearly all of 2 May to complete. Federal scouts had discovered it and notified Hooker, who warned his flank commander, Maj. Gen. OLIVER O. HOWARD, XI Corps commander; Howard dismissed the vital intelligence. As twilight enveloped the woodland, Jackson's veterans stormed into Howard's unsuspecting troops, Howard's line collapsing under the lightning assault and his men fleeing 2 mi to the rear. Darkness and the combined Confederate commands prevented a full-scale pursuit.

While reconnoitering between the lines, Jackson was mistakenly shot by members of the 18th North Carolina. Stuart assumed command of the infantry and at daylight on the 3d launched another assault on Hooker's contracted lines. When the Federals abandoned Hazel Grove, Stuart moved 50 cannon onto the commanding hill. Supported by this massed artillery fire, Stuart's and Lee's wings wrenched the Chancellorsville crossroads from the Federals. Hooker withdrew to a new line, its flanks firmly secured by the Rapidan and Rappahannock rivers.

Lee, meanwhile, prepared to charge this new line, when he learned that his force at FREDERICKSBURG had been dislodged by Maj. Gen. JOHN SEDGWICK's Federals, who were marching against Lee's rear. The Confederate commander detached part of his command to SALEM CHURCH, a good defensive position across Sedgwick's line of advance. The next day, 4 May, Sedgwick, threatened on front, flank, and rear, held on until nightfall, when he withdrew across the Rappahannock at Banks' Ford.

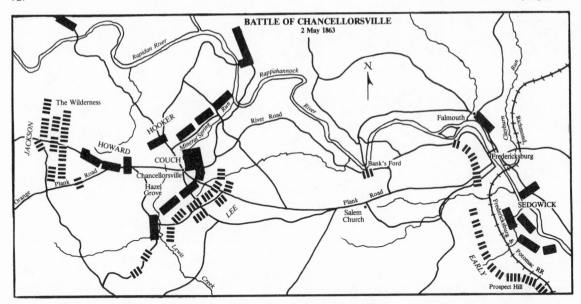

Hooker's army withdrew across the Rapidan during the night of 5–6 May. The general's earlier boasts of a great victory lay in ashes in the woods surrounding Chancellorsville. He lost 1,606 killed, 9,762 wounded, and 5,919 missing, totaling 17,287. Lee suffered a greater percentage of casualties—1,665 killed, 9,081 wounded, and 2,018 missing, for a total of 12,764. But the death of Jackson perhaps cost Lee more than his brilliant generalship had achieved.   —JDW

Chancellorsville Campaign, Va. Apr.–May 1863 Morale in the ARMY OF THE POTOMAC reached a low point during

winter 1863. Plagued by bad luck, sacrificed by incompetent commanders, the veterans despaired. The staggering defeat at FREDERICKSBURG Dec. 1862 and the "Mud March" (*see* BURNSIDE'S MUD MARCH) fiasco in Jan. 1863 had destroyed the soldiers' and officers' faith in the well-intentioned but inept Maj. Gen. AMBROSE E. BURNSIDE. When top-ranking commanders urged Pres. Abraham Lincoln to remove Burnside, the furious army commander cashiered this coterie of generals, demanding that Lincoln approve his actions or accept his resignation.

The overburdened president replaced Burnside 25 Jan. with one of the general's most outspoken critics, Maj. Gen. JOSEPH

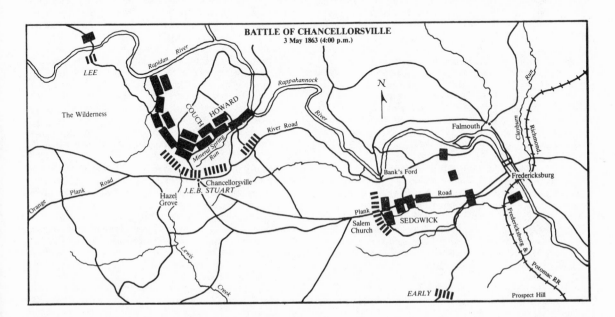

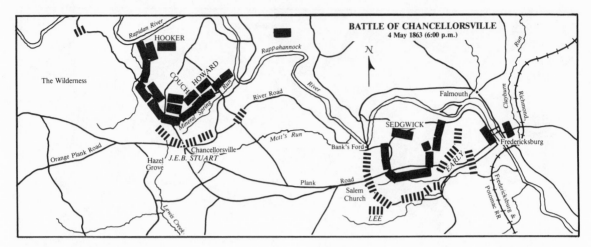

HOOKER, who had long coveted the position. Aggressive and boastful, "Fighting Joe" was popular with the troops and the public and had alluded to the possibility of a postwar dictatorship under the winning general. When Lincoln appointed Hooker, he wrote him: "What I now ask of you is military success, and I will risk the dictatorship."

Hooker immediately demonstrated his ability as an administrator, abolishing Burnside's bulky 4 grand divisions and uniting the cavalry into a corps. He developed distinctive badges for each corps, instilling pride and helping to restore morale, and also looked after the men's needs. By spring 1863, "Fighting Joe" was bragging that he had created "the finest army on the planet."

In April Lincoln visited "the finest army," admonishing its commander to commit all his troops in the next battle. Hooker developed a brilliant strategic plan to utilize his overwhelming strength. Wisely unwilling to repeat the Fredericksburg disaster, he evolved a wide strategic ENVELOPMENT of Gen. ROBERT E. LEE's entrenched troops behind Fredericksburg. With approximately one-third of his 134,000-man army, Hooker would march up the Rappahannock River, cross it and the Rapidan River, and assault Lee's left and rear. Maj. Gen. JOHN SEDGWICK, with another third, was directed to make a diversionary attack across the Rappahannock at Fredericksburg, holding the Confederates in their works. The remaining third would act as a reserve, to reinforce either wing. Hooker would also dispatch his rejuvenated cavalry, under Maj. Gen. GEORGE STONEMAN, to precede the infantry advance by moving on a raid against Lee's communications.

On 27 Apr. Union infantry abandoned their winter quarters at Falmouth, marching upriver. A confident Hooker had told Lincoln during the latter's visit that the question was not if he would capture Richmond, but when; the army's initial advance reinforced Hooker's boast. By the 29th the Federal infantry were crossing the Rappahannock, while Stoneman's cavalry, delayed 2 weeks by swollen rivers, were cantering southward on their raid. On the 30th Hooker's veterans entered the Wilderness, a forbidding landscape 10 mi from Fredericksburg. By nightfall a Federal force by now numbering 75,000 lay in the Confederate rear at Chancellorsville, a crossroads hostelry in the Wilderness, while Sedgwick's 40,000 threatened the

Southern works at FREDERICKSBURG.

Hooker's brilliant maneuver endangered Lee's entire army. The Confederate commander could either withdraw toward Richmond or give battle at an enormous disadvantage. When his cavalry confirmed the Federals' presence near CHANCELLORSVILLE, Lee reacted with an audacious plan. The general had only 60,000 underfed, ragged veterans, having earlier dispatched Lt. Gen. JAMES LONGSTREET with 2 divisions on a foraging expedition to southeastern Virginia. Outnumbered nearly 2-to-1, the bold Lee divided his army. Leaving Maj. Gen. JUBAL A. EARLY with 10,000 men to oppose Sedgwick, Lee marched against Hooker. Lee the gambler had never taken such a risk.

Lee's seasoned troops, led by Lt. Gen. THOMAS J. "STONEWALL" JACKSON's II Corps, marched westward on the beautiful spring day of 1 May. Leading elements of the Northern army resumed their advance, abandoning the confining Wilderness for the open farmlands. The 2 forces collided, and a vicious fire fight ensued. Hooker, at this critical moment, over the vigorous protests of his corps commanders, abandoned the initiative, ordering a withdrawal into the Wilderness. Suddenly facing the redoubtable Lee directly, Hooker lost his nerve, becoming "a whipped man," as one of his subordinates later admitted.

Jackson's infantry filed into battle lines and skirmished with the Federals. Lee's cavalry commander, Maj. Gen. J.E.B. STUART, learned later in the day that Hooker's right flank was "in the air." That night Lee and Jackson conferred; the Confederate commander divided his army once more, ordering Jackson with 28,000 men on a circuitous 14-mi march beyond the Union flank.

Jackson's march consumed most of 2 May, while Lee's remaining troops demonstrated against the Federals, and about 5:30 p.m. the Confederates burst on the Union XI Corps, whose members were cooking their suppers. The surprise assault crushed Hooker's flank, rolling it back 2 mi. In the darkness Jackson rode beyond his lines to reconnoiter for another attack. As he returned, he fell wounded, shot by his own troops, who mistook his party for the Union cavalry. Surgeons amputated Jackson's left arm, but the great "Stonewall" developed pneumonia, dying 8 days later, May 10.

Stuart replaced Jackson, resuming the offensive on the 3d with fierce attacks that constricted the Federal lines. During the action a Confederate shell struck a column of the Chancellor house on which Hooker was leaning, stunning the Union commander. The Federals withdrew to a new line closer to the river, and the heavy fighting around Chancellorsville ended.

While the Confederates bent Hooker back on the 3d, Sedgwick's troops dislodged early from the Fredericksburg heights. Leaving 25,000 men to confront a defeated Hooker, Lee marched against Sedgwick. At SALEM CHURCH, the Southerners halted Sedgwick's advance 4 May. 2 days later Hooker retreated across the river.

The Chancellorsville Campaign, according to some military historians, was Lee's masterpiece, an achievement perhaps unequalled by any other American general. The Confederate commander gambled audaciously, recovered the initiative, and executed a flawless offensive. Hooker, conversely, displayed the worst battlefield generalship of the war when he abandoned his advance 1 May. Stoneman's detachment, which proved fruitless, eliminated the flank protection that cavalry provided (see STONEMAN'S RAID, CHANCELLORSVILLE CAMPAIGN).

The brilliant Confederate victory resulted in the loss of nearly 13,000 men while inflicting over 17,000 Federal casualties. But the fatal wounding of Jackson cost Lee perhaps more than he had gained: the Army of Northern Virginia was never the same without "Stonewall." —JDW

Chandler, Zachariah. USP b. Bedford, N.H., 10 Dec. 1813. Descended from English immigrants who settled in Massachusetts early in the 17th century, Chandler was educated in his native village and neighboring academies, then moved to Detroit in 1833. Successful in the dry goods business, he purchased real estate and in time amassed great wealth. By 1848 he had become active in politics, speaking locally on behalf of presidential candidate Zachary Taylor. In 1851, a Whig, Chandler won a term as mayor of Detroit and made a bid the next year for the state's governorship; despite an energetic race, he was defeated.

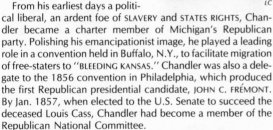

LC

From his earliest days a political liberal, an ardent foe of SLAVERY and STATES RIGHTS, Chandler became a charter member of Michigan's Republican party. Polishing his emancipationist image, he played a leading role in a convention held in Buffalo, N.Y., to facilitate migration of free-staters to "BLEEDING KANSAS." Chandler was also a delegate to the 1856 convention in Philadelphia, which produced the first Republican presidential candidate, JOHN C. FRÉMONT. By Jan. 1857, when elected to the U.S. Senate to succeed the deceased Louis Cass, Chandler had become a member of the Republican National Committee.

In the Senate he quickly rose to prominence in his party as a "radical among radicals." A tough, blunt politician of sometimes immoderate temperament, Chandler was also idealistic and incorruptible. Beyond the freedom and social advancement of blacks, he promoted internal improvements to develop the nation's commerce, especially within the Midwest, furthering this interest through his 14-year chairmanship of the

Senate Committee on Commerce, which enabled him to dispense appropriations for river and harbor improvement. Chandler also had a keen interest in military affairs and, when the Civil War began, stirred the martial spirit of his constituents to raise and equip state units. Late in 1861 he became a member of the COMMITTEE ON THE CONDUCT OF THE WAR, a Radical-oriented panel that held frequent inquests into the military prosecution, and the political orientation, of the conflict.

An outspoken enemy of the Confederacy, Chandler initiated legislation aimed at confiscating Southerners' property, prepared plans for ruling a conquered South (laying the basis for Congressional RECONSTRUCTION), and opposed political and military leaders he considered "soft" on slavery or secession, a prime target being Maj. Gen. GEORGE B. MCCLELLAN. During his Senate career he supported a national bank, a high tariff, and GREENBACK currency and censured those foreign nations, especially Great Britain, friendly with the Confederacy. In 1864 he almost singlehandedly persuaded Frémont to drop his third-party candidacy in favor of ABRAHAM LINCOLN, which not only helped Chandler's party retain the White House at a crucial period but helped force the resignation from Lincoln's cabinet of Postmaster General MONTGOMERY BLAIR, a friend of Frémont's and an enemy of RADICAL REPUBLICANS.

After the war, Chandler fought to impeach Pres. ANDREW JOHNSON and served as chairman of the Republican National Executive Committee during the presidential campaigns of 1868 and 1876. In 1874 he was defeated for reelection to the Senate but late the next year was appointed secretary of the interior by Pres. ULYSSES S. GRANT, retaining the post until early 1877. Returning to the Senate Feb. 1879, he served only a few months, dying 1 Nov. in Chicago during a speaking tour. —EGL

Chantilly (Ox Hill), Va., Battle of. 1 Sept. 1862 The resounding Confederate victory at SECOND BULL RUN, 29–30 Aug. 1862, spurred Gen. ROBERT E. LEE to renew his offensive to destroy the demoralized Union Army of Virginia. On the day after the battle, Lee ordered flanking movement around Maj. Gen. JOHN POPE's position on the heights near Centreville. If Lee's plan succeeded, the Federals might be struck a fatal blow before they could find shelter in the defenses rimming the Union capital.

Maj. Gen. THOMAS J. "STONEWALL" JACKSON's weary FOOT CAVALRY drew the assignment. Jackson's route on the 31st took him across Bull Run at Sudley Ford, then to the Little River Turnpike and down that road toward Fairfax Court House. A nighttime rain turned the roundabout roads into troughs of mud, and the Confederates made little progress. By nightfall Jackson's veterans were slogging into Pleasant Valley, camping along the turnpike. With their wagon train far to the rear, the Southerners went to sleep without food.

Hungry and exhausted, Jackson's troops crawled eastward on the turnpike on the morning of 1 Sept. Dark, lowering clouds portended more rains as the Confederates reached the country mansion of Chantilly. Early in the afternoon the Confederate van encountered Federals, who were deployed in numbers and ready. Pope's cavalry had detected Lee's flank movement, and the Union commander recalled some retreating units to meet the threat.

Jackson deployed his 3 divisions south of the turnpike, with his artillery across the road. Confederate Maj. Gen. AMBROSE P. HILL, on the right, sent in 2 brigades. A thunderstorm suddenly broke over the fields, its winds driving sheets of rain into the faces of the charging Confederates. The 2 brigades crossed a field and entered a stand of woods. 2 Federal divisions, under Maj. Gen. PHILIP KEARNY and Brig. Gen. ISAAC I. STEVENS, responded with a hot volley. The 2 Confederate brigades clung to their woodline position as the combat intensified.

Hill threw another brigade forward, then 2 more. The torrential downpour only added to the confusion and misery as musketry lashed up and down the opposing lines. Jackson then committed his left division, commanded by Brig. Gen. WILLIAM E. STARKE, but the Federals repulsed this attack directly south of the turnpike. The fighting had twisted Jackson's line into an arc of a circle facing southward.

Attacks and counterattacks flared across the soaked woodlands and fields. Neither side gained much of an advantage until Stevens was killed, and the popular Kearny fell dead after riding unaware into the midst of some Confederate skirmishers. In the gathering darkness, the Federals withdrew and the action ended.

The battle was a vicious little fire fight that cost Jackson about 500 men, while the Federals sustained probably 1,000 casualties. The driving rainstorm perhaps saved Jackson from a serious defeat, for the weather delayed Pope from sending into the battle 2 nearby Union corps. Nevertheless, Pope's men held, thwarting Lee's offensive. This stalemated battle concluded the SECOND BULL RUN CAMPAIGN.   —JDW

chaplains. At the outbreak of war, neither the Confederate nor the U.S. War Department had a policy regarding chaplains. Their rank, pay, and duties were poorly defined, their services often little appreciated. The quality of men seeking the appointments was uneven, especially after the 60- and 90-day ENLISTMENTS ended. The best of them soon learned that a good preacher had less place in the field than a good Samaritan. The worst—drunkards, slackers, and failures in civilian ministry—were generally removed.

Difficulties arose when unreligious superiors refused to take clergymen seriously, but at the heart of the problem lay the uncertainty of the chaplain's role in war. Rev. James J. Marks of the 63d Pennsylvania suspected the Union chaplaincy of being a "concession made to the religious sentiment of the country—one of those formless, shapeless things thrown in to fill up a vacuum." Union regimental commanders held authority to appoint chaplains, with no guidance other than a stipulation requiring the applicant to be an ordained minister in one of the Christian sects.

Though initially most chaplains were Protestant or Catholic, in Sept. 1862, after nearly a year of debate in Congress, Lincoln appointed the first Jewish chaplain. Union chaplains were paid $100 a month, the same as a captain of cavalry, but served without command. Officially the Federal Congress required chaplains to do no more than report on the moral and religious state of the troops and make suggestions for improving social conditions among them. Not until a congressional bill passed Apr. 1864 were regular church services added to their duties, but by then many chaplains were so busy administering to the soldiers' practical needs that they preached only as circumstances permitted. Many preferred to expend their energies where they were more appreciated: foraging, defending enlisted men at courts-martial, procuring supplies from home congregations, serving as correspondents to home newspapers, operating regimental libraries, escorting wounded offi-

cers home, sending pay to families, and frequently acting as mail orderlies. Chaplains usually served with regiments from their own communities and thus knew the families of many of the men in the unit, providing the link between family and soldier. To them came letters asking news of a negligent letter writer, and to them fell the responsibility of writing condolence letters when a soldier died. They comforted the dying, forwarded mementos to relatives, buried the dead, and often served as regimental historians.

Though some chaplains worked in field hospitals or as ambulance drivers during battle, many believed they belonged with their men at the front. Some did fight, but more were captured when they stayed on the field to aid the wounded. Because chaplains were eligible for pay only when fulfilling their duties, paymasters sometimes refused to pay them for absences resulting from illness, wounds, or capture, until legislation passed by the U.S. Congress in 1864 added them to regimental rosters, after surgeons. Though their situation improved, some still transferred to combat duty to avoid discrimination; others resigned.

By Jan. 1863 half the Union regiments lacked chaplains, sometimes for want of a good man to fill the position. In all, at least 2,300 chaplains served in the Union armies; at least 66 died in service and 3 received the MEDAL OF HONOR.

Confederate chaplains suffered the same discriminations in pay and status, but Southern commanders showed more sympathy toward their services, making special efforts to recruit them. Congress authorized JEFFERSON DAVIS to appoint chaplains, but he deferred to the recommendations of the commanders to avoid assigning chaplains of one denomination to regiments composed principally of another. Jews were not excluded from the Confederate chaplaincy, but there is no record of any serving. Shortages of chaplains plagued the army throughout the war, partly because of low pay—a stipend of $85 a month approved May 1861 was cut 3 weeks later to $50—and partly because Southern preachers preferred to serve in the ranks. About 600 ministers joined the Confederate armies as chaplains; 25 died in service, 14 were killed in battle.

Before the surge of revivalism late in the war, chaplains serving with the Union army often complained of being without an audience for their sermons, but Southern soldiers judged a chaplain's worth by his vigorous and regular preaching. Some units raised their chaplain's salary by subscription, criticizing him only if he let too much time pass without visiting the trenches. Southern churches also supported ministers in the field: in Feb. 1864 the Baptist *Religious Herald* reported 80 Presbyterian-supported ministers serving the troops at a cost of $9,000 per month. And chaplains' associations formed throughout the Southern armies to discuss the problems of the calling, find ministers for units without them, and petition Congress to prohibit inspections, reviews, and parades on Sundays. Gen. ROBERT E. LEE encouraged organization of a chapter of the association in the ARMY OF THE POTOMAC and frequently attended its meetings.

The Confederate Congress never specified uniforms for chaplains, but those in the ARMY OF TENNESSEE wore a gold or brass Maltese Cross on either side of the collar, and similar distinguishing symbols were adopted in other armies.

North or South, the chaplain walked a narrow line. He could not press too hard against drinking, swearing, and gambling, nor could he neglect his charges' spiritual needs. Severely

criticized as often as heartily praised, he endured the war like some kind of indispensable appendage, rarely given full credit for his contributions, yet expected to serve wherever needed.
—PLF

Chaplin Hills, Ky., Battle of. 8 Oct. 1862 *See* PERRYVILLE, KY., BATTLE OF.

Chapman, Conrad Wise. CSA/artist b. Washington, D.C., 14 Feb. 1842. The mid-19th-century American artist John Gadsby Chapman moved his family to Rome in the late 1840s. There his son Conrad studied under him, achieving recognition for his own artistic talents by the time civil war disrupted the U.S. Virginia-born John Chapman nurtured in his family a deep sentimental patriotism for the state, and when the fighting began Conrad left Italy for New York City, determined to join the Old Dominion's defenders. Unable to reach Richmond, he went to Kentucky, enlisting in the 3d Kentucky Infantry.

For all his enthusiasm, Chapman remained an artist at heart. John S. Wise, son of Brig. Gen. HENRY A. WISE (a close friend of the family), described him as a good and energetic soldier who nonetheless "had not the slightest idea of how to take care of himself . . . he lost, gave away, or forgot everything that belonged to him." His comrades called him "Old Rome" and encouraged his sketching of camp activities.

The regiment saw its first combat at SHILOH, where Chapman was seriously wounded. After several months' convalescence in Memphis, he was ordered to Virginia and attached to the 46th Regular Virginia Volunteers at the request of General Wise. Through winter 1862–63 Chapman filled his time by drawing. Wise arranged his appointment as ordnance sergeant, partly as a favor to Chapman's father and partly to keep the likable soldier-artist away from combat. In fall 1863, following the unit's transfer to Charleston, Wise urged Gen. P.G.T. BEAUREGARD to have Chapman make a series of sketches of the city's defenses to accompany a set of maps then being drawn. Eagerly accepting the assignment, Chapman often worked under fire of Union bombardment, contemptuously disregarding the danger.

Chapman was granted a leave to Rome in spring 1864 to visit his mother, who was seriously ill, and over the next few months painted a series of pictures based on the Charleston sketches, rich in descriptive detail of Confederate camp life. He completed most of his wartime canvases that winter, the remainder during 1866. John Chapman contributed 6 of his own paintings to the collection, based on his son's account of the war.

Conrad's parents attempted to arrange his discharge, and when he learned of this he once again sailed for the Confederacy, arriving in Galveston, Tex., in 1865, about the time Gen. ROBERT E. LEE surrendered. Discouraged, he accompanied Maj. Gen. JOHN B. MAGRUDER's band of exiles to Mexico, remaining there a year before he traveled through the U.S. and Europe.

Illness, poverty, unhappiness, and a 3-year period of insanity marked Chapman's postwar years. He finally settled in Hampton, Va., where he continued to paint until his death 10 Dec. 1910, but never repeated the artistic success of his wartime endeavors. Those 31 small paintings, which are in the collections of the Valentine Museum in Richmond, represent the finest work produced by a Confederate artist during the war.
—PLF

Charles City Cross Roads, Va., Battle of. 30 June 1862 *See* WHITE OAK SWAMP, VA., BATTLE OF.

Charleston, S.C., Du Pont's attack on. 7 Apr. 1863 Determined to capture Charleston in Apr. 1863, Rear Adm. SAMUEL F. DU PONT assembled a flotilla of 7 monitors—the most powerful, irresistible warships afloat—plus the ironclads *Keokuk* and *NEW IRONSIDES*. Each packed a punch as heavy as anything then seen in American warfare, with 1 11-in. and 1 15-in. cannon.

Du Pont launched his attack at noon, 7 Apr., and was met by 77 Confederate guns opening fire as the ships ran afoul of the harbor's TORPEDOES (mines) and obstructions. The monitors' guns brought great chunks of Fort Sumter's masonry sliding into the harbor, but the return fire from the batteries was even more destructive. "Such a fire I never saw," said one naval officer. "Nothing could be heard but the whistling of shot." Confederate gunners struck the little ships over 400 times, and when a solid shot hit true, it jarred the entire vessel, shaking turrets from their tracks and jamming them. Decks were pierced, armor ripped up, smokestacks shredded, and guns knocked out of commission. The *Keokuk* was shot to pieces with over 90 hits; the *Weehawken* was hit 53 times; the *Nahant* 51. The entire flotilla hit Fort Sumter with only 55 shots in return.

As evening came, Du Pont signaled a withdrawal. Though he intended to renew the battle the next morning, a look at his ships and reports from his captains dissuaded him. The *Keokuk* sank during the night, and the rest of the monitors were heavily damaged. The guns of Charleston had proved a match for the feared monitors. Du Pont lost his command for the failure, and the Union army and navy turned to other means to try to take Charleston.
—MM

Charleston, S.C., evacuation of. 17 Feb. 1865 Early in 1865 Charleston was endangered from the land side as Union Maj. Gen. WILLIAM T. SHERMAN marched northward from Georgia. Though Sherman passed west of the city, he cut its communications with the interior, leaving the garrison there isolated and useless. On 2 Feb. Confederate authorities determined to evacuate Charleston to prevent the loss of the garrison. On 14 Feb. Gen. P.G.T. BEAUREGARD, Confederate commander in the Carolinas, issued instructions for the evacuation of the city, and Lt. Gen. WILLIAM J. HARDEE, commanding at Charleston, prepared to abandon it.

Meanwhile, to assist Sherman, the Federals along the coast began demonstrations on James Island south of Charleston and at Bull's Bay 20 mi to the north, but their efforts accomplished little against Charleston's strong coastal fortifications.

The evacuation was delayed by Hardee's illness, but by 17 Feb. the preparations were complete. That night the Confederates left Charleston, retreating north via Florence and Cheraw to join the force assembling to oppose Sherman's march. There was confusion in the city as cotton was burned and several military installations were blown up. The Federals occupied Charleston on the 18th, capturing 250 heavy cannon. On 14 Apr. Union Brig. Gen. ROBERT ANDERSON, who had commanded FORT SUMTER in 1861, returned to Charleston to raise over the fort the flag that he had hauled down 4 years earlier. *See also* CAROLINAS CAMPAIGN.
—RMcM

Charleston, S.C., Siege of. July 1863 Situated on a narrow peninsula between 2 rivers, Charleston was 7 mi from the bar stretching across the entrance to the harbor, formed by Sullivan's Island on the north and Morris Island on the south. It was protected by several forts, the chief of which was Sumter, scene of the first rebellious firing against the U.S. flag. An early target of the Union, Charleston withstood several naval assaults during the first months of the war, and after another attack by water failed in Apr. 1863, Washington decided that a joint attack by land and naval forces was necessary.

The Union plan of assault called for land forces to attack Morris Island from the south, capture Batteries Wagner and Gregg at the north end of the island, and bombard Fort Sumter into submission. Then channel obstructions in the harbor would be removed and the final advance on the city made.

Preparations started in June under the direction of Brig. Gen. QUINCY A. GILLMORE, a skillful military engineer. Working secretly and mostly at night, troops were assembled for the assault and ready by 6 July. Heavy rains delayed the attack until the 10th, when the south end of Morris Island was occupied. But the Southerners put up such a determined defense that Batteries Wagner and Gregg were not captured until 7 Sept.

Meanwhile, bombardment of Fort Sumter continued relentlessly both from land and sea—5,643 shots in 7 days, according to the Confederate commander, Gen. P.G.T. BEAUREGARD. Sumter was finally reported to be "a shapeless and harmless mass of ruins," but the attack of July 1863 had still failed to capture Charleston. The city was effectively blockaded, but fire from forts other than Sumter was so hot that not until Charleston was evacuated by the Southerners in Feb. 1865 was the North able to occupy it. *See also* BATTERY (FORT) WAGNER.   —VCJ

Charleston *Mercury*. From its founding in 1822 the *Mercury* led Southern newspapers in speaking for SLAVERY and radical secessionist opinion. The wartime editor, ROBERT BARNWELL RHETT, JR., turned the *Mercury* into one of the 2 most vitriolically antiadministration newspapers in the Confederacy, in the long run harming more than helping the cause of independence. The "ultra views" he printed railed against the "imbecility" of JEFFERSON DAVIS and his cabinet, condemned the suspension of *HABEAS CORPUS,* and berated the quality of Southern military leadership. Too often the editorials anticipated what might happen instead of reporting hard news.

Insisting on complete freedom of the press, Rhett decried Confederate Sec. of War LEROY P. WALKER'S 1 July 1861 open letter asking newspapers to refrain from printing information on troop strengths and movements. The public, Rhett claimed, had the right to any war-related news. He countered as invalid charges of leaking information to the North, arguing that any news of value would have reached the free states long before any Southern publication could print it.

It was probably fortunate that the shortage of paper caused by the BLOCKADE reduced the *Mercury* to a single 2-page sheet early in the war. Rhett heralded each day Charleston lay under siege with a numeral in his newspaper's headline, hurting attempts to raise morale in the city.   —PLF

chase. The chase is that part of an artillery piece sitting over the gun carriage's axle or center of gravity. In Civil War cannon a reinforced breech was popular; the chase was that part running from the front of the breech to the point where the gun's

muzzle was flared or became bulbous.   —JES

Chase, Salmon Portland. USP   b. Cornish, N.H., 13 Jan. 1808. Chase pursued a legal career in Ohio and became involved with first the Liberty, then the FREE SOIL PARTY, both espousing abolition of slavery.

NA

Radical abolitionist to some, moderate to others, he went to the U.S. Senate in 1848 backed by an independent Democrat/ Free Soil coalition to oppose the COMPROMISE OF 1850 and the KANSAS-NEBRASKA ACT. Then, writing an article for the New York *Times,* he at once laid out the bedrock gospel of the fledgling REPUBLICAN PARTY, assuring his political rise. Elected governor of Ohio in 1855, then competing with ABRAHAM LINCOLN for the 1860 Republican presidential nomination, Chase soon found himself, without a professional background in finance, Lincoln's secretary of the treasury.

His tenure, marked by internecine warfare, ironically threw him in most often with Lincoln, who exasperated him, and with Sec. of State WILLIAM H. SEWARD, whom he distrusted. However, Lincoln valued his competence and the political savvy that enabled him to get financial measures passed. But while he held Lincoln's trust, for the president often preferred Chase's military opinions to those of his army and navy secretaries, and shared in the social prominence of his daughter— famous hostess KATE CHASE SPRAGUE—he was lured into another attempt at the presidency.

A member of a faction increasingly resisting Lincoln's RECONSTRUCTION aims, Chase secretly acquiesced in making a bid for the 1864 Republican nomination. In an anti-Lincoln letter circulated by Kansas Sen. Samuel Pomeroy, dubbed the "POMEROY CIRCULAR," Chase was touted as the man for president. Embarrassed when the letter was made public, the secretary offered his resignation. Lincoln refused the offer, but the damage was done. Though Chase campaigned for Lincoln, their relationship was ruined. When he offered his resignation again late in 1864, it was accepted. But Lincoln still valued Chase and in December appointed him Chief Justice of the Supreme Court. d. New York City, 7 May 1873.   —JES

Chattahoochee River, Ga. 3–9 July 1864 By 1 July 1864 rains slowing the armies of Maj. Gen. WILLIAM T. SHERMAN above Atlanta had ended and the Federals were again on the move. That day Sherman renewed his tried-and-true strategy of threatening the left flank of Gen. JOSEPH E. JOHNSTON's Army of Tennessee, compelling the Confederates to fall back south, ever closer to Atlanta. By early on the 3d, Johnston had withdrawn from his position near Marietta to works previously constructed astride the Western & Atlantic Railroad near Smyrna.

Pursuing doggedly, Sherman probed the new position, then celebrated Independence Day by striking the same flank he had threatened 3 days before. Fire fights broke out north and west of Smyrna, then south of the town near the rail depot of VINING'S STATION. The force of Confederate resistance somewhat surprised the Union leader: he had not expected Johnston to make a stand north of the nearby Chattahoochee River but to cross that stream and dig in near Atlanta. Late that day, Johnston retreated farther, sending his wagons and rear guard across the river and building bridges on which to cross his main body. The latter, however, he placed behind another strong line of works along the north bank of the river and appeared ready for another confrontation. If Sherman wanted the Confederates to pass over the Chattahoochee he would have to persuade them violently.

This placed the Union commander in a dilemma. His disastrous decision to attack frontally against Johnston at KENNESAW MOUNTAIN, 27 June, had left him wary of direct offensives, especially against strong, fixed positions. But he hesitated only briefly and early on the 5th moved Maj. Gen. GEORGE H. THOMAS' Army of the Cumberland into place opposite Johnston's bridgehead, holding the Confederates in place. Meanwhile, he sent the cavalry of the Army of the Ohio, under Maj. Gen. GEORGE STONEMAN, and Maj. Gen. JAMES B. MCPHERSON's Army of the Tennessee once more toward the enemy's left, as though to cross the river at Turner's Ferry, a half-dozen miles downstream from Johnston's main body. At the same time, part of Maj. Gen. JOHN M. SCHOFIELD's XXIII Corps—his 3d Division, under Brig. Gen. JACOB D. COX—readied a surprise crossing an equal distance upstream near Phillips' Ferry, by the mouth of Soap Creek.

At midafternoon 8 July, as McPherson and Stoneman demonstrated near Turner's Ferry, one of Schofield's regiments paddled across the Chattahoochee in pontoons. The crossing was covered so well that a small force of Confederate cavalry, with 1 cannon, which provided the only opposition, was easily repulsed. Another of Cox's brigades then forded the stream a mile above the first crossing, occupied a high ridge on the other side, and established a foothold along the Confederate right. Later the pontoons were used to construct a bridge over which the whole of Schofield's corps crossed. The next morning the cavalry division of Brig. Gen. KENNER GARRARD splashed across farther upriver, near Roswell, supported by one of McPherson's corps and a division detached from Thomas' army.

These several dispositions had the desired effect: on the evening of the 9th, the Army of Tennessee evacuated its defenses and crossed the Chattahoochee, removing the last great natural barrier between Sherman and Atlanta. The crossing had another valuable benefit for Sherman: distressed by Johnston's Fabian policies, the Confederate War Department soon relieved him from command. By removing an opponent he considered wily and stubborn, Sherman felt the authorities in Richmond had "rendered us most valuable service."   —EGL

Chattanooga, Tenn., battles for.

23–25 Nov. 1863 At Chattanooga in Oct. 1863 Maj. Gen. ULYSSES S. GRANT faced an effective siege by Gen. BRAXTON BRAGG's 50,000 Confederates entrenched on Missionary Ridge, located northeast-to-southwest of the town, and Lookout Mountain, on the southwest edge of town. The month-long siege broke 30 Oct., supplies were available on the CRACKER LINE OPERATION, and Union communications were open through Lookout Valley and secured at Wauhatchie (see WAUHATCHIE NIGHT ATTACK). Chattanooga, reinforced twice, held nearly 70,000 Federals. Inexplicably, Bragg dispatched quarrelsome Lt. Gen. JAMES LONGSTREET to Knoxville 4 Nov. with 2 divisions and 2 artillery battalions. Outnumbered, Bragg sat for no reason other than

to distract Grant during Longstreet's operations against the Federals at Knoxville.

Out of patience, Grant and Maj. Gens. WILLIAM T. SHERMAN, JOSEPH HOOKER, and GEORGE H. THOMAS formulated rough battle plans to clear the Confederates from the heights. Orchard Knob, a foothill far front and center of the Confederate line on Missionary Ridge, was the closest target. If it was taken, the Federals could advance from town, extend their lines with some safety, and gain maneuvering room. On 23 Nov. 2 divisions uniformed as if for dress parade marched out toward the hill. A subterfuge for a reconnaissance in force, it developed into the pitched Battle of ORCHARD KNOB. Confederates on the knob watched the divisions approach without artillery and expected an entertaining display. Encouraged by a close look at defenses and enemy passivity, the Federals rushed and took the hill. Thomas ordered up more troops for support, extended the lines, and began maneuvers.

Grant made Orchard Knob headquarters for the fight ahead. Thomas, at his side, would command the Union center facing Missionary Ridge; Sherman's 4 divisions, positioned behind the town north and west of the Tennessee River, would cross to the river on the Confederate right and assault the north end of Missionary Ridge; Hooker's 2 divisions would take Lookout Mountain on the Confederate left, maneuvering in Bragg's left rear as a diversion. As Sherman's assault carried the north crest, Thomas would hit the center or reinforce either flank.

On the 24th one of Sherman's divisions, separated from the general at Moccasin Point on the Tennessee, was absorbed by Hooker. With 3 divisions he fought the Battle of LOOKOUT MOUNTAIN under cover of an all-day blanket of mist and fog. On the Confederate right Bragg observed Sherman's moves and placed Maj. Gen. PATRICK R. CLEBURNE's division on the fortified ridge line. Sherman forced a PONTOON BRIDGE crossing and by day's end had taken low ground. Hooker won on Lookout and began flanking maneuvers.

Many Federals at the center were unaware of Hooker's success. As the Battle of MISSIONARY RIDGE began on the bright morning of 25 Nov., they cheered a Union flag waving from Lookout's summit. Then Sherman's cannon shelled Cleburne's force, backed by troops under Maj. Gen. CARTER L. STEVENSON and Brig. Gen. STATES RIGHTS GIST. At 11 a.m. Sherman's men ran into stiff resistance at low-lying Tunnel Hill in front of the north face of Missionary Ridge. By 3 p.m. Federals on the Union left had not pushed back Cleburne's troops; the first of the Confederates' 3 trench lines on the ridge itself was unassaulted. At Grant's suggestion, Thomas' men rushed the first Confederate center-line trench 3–4 p.m., and without orders, continued on, routing the enemy from the second and third trench lines and pushing them over the crest.

The final charge and a day's pursuit ended the battles for Chattanooga. Bragg's losses were 361 dead, 2,160 wounded, and 4,146 missing (most captured) in 3 days' fighting; Grant lost 753 dead, 4,722 wounded, and 349 captured. It taught the Confederacy a belated lesson: Bragg was no longer suited to major field command.   —JES

Chattanooga Campaign, Tenn.

Oct.–Nov. 1863 Late on 20 Sept. 1863, Federal survivors of the Battle of CHICK-AMAUGA started filing through Rossville Gap to refuge in Chattanooga. Days later Gen. BRAXTON BRAGG's Confederates perched on hills around the town and waited for Maj. Gen. WILLIAM S. ROSECRANS' Union Army of the Cumberland to evac-

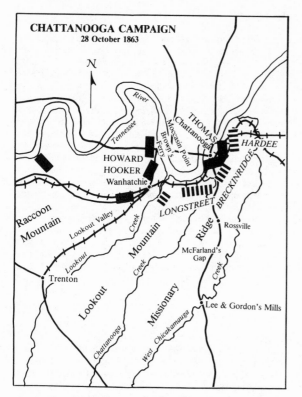

CHATTANOOGA CAMPAIGN
28 October 1863

uate. With the Tennessee River at its back, fearing annihilation if it left the safety of Chattanooga, the Union army covered its front with trenches and rifle pits and waited for relief.

In Washington, Pres. Abraham Lincoln was despondent over his crushed Army of the Cumberland and 25 Sept. dispatched Maj. Gen. JOSEPH HOOKER and 2 Virginia corps to its aid. With his cabinet he discussed removing Rosecrans from command.

Bragg's patience was exhausted by 1 Oct. If Rosecrans would not march out of Chattanooga, he would starve him out. Confederates held Missionary Ridge along the town's northeast-southwest front, Lookout Mountain on the southwest, and Raccoon Mountain and Lookout Valley on the west. All rail lines were cut, all river traffic stopped. Bragg ordered Brig. Gen. JOSEPH WHEELER's cavalry to mangle remaining Union supply lines. WHEELER'S RAID, 1–9 Oct., destroyed wagon trains bringing supplies to Chattanooga by the only open route, 60 twisting miles of bad road leading northwest from Bridgeport, Ala., a town only 26 linear miles from the Federals. The Army of the Cumberland went on reduced rations and settled in for the Siege of Chattanooga.

On 16 Oct. the Union Military Division of the Mississippi was created and Maj. Gen. ULYSSES S. GRANT was named its commander. Lincoln and Sec. of War EDWIN M. STANTON left Rosecrans' future to Grant, who relieved him, appointed Maj. Gen. GEORGE H. THOMAS commander of the Army of the Cumberland, then traveled to Chattanooga, arriving 23 Oct. After consulting with Thomas and Chief Engineer Maj. Gen. WILLIAM F. SMITH, and finding an inventory showing only a few car-

tridges for each Federal, Grant agreed to a bold plan to break the siege. Smith proposed throwing infantry over a neck of land called Moccasin Point, on the river west of town. Other troops would travel on the Tennessee to Brown's Ferry, a point opposite the Federals at Moccasin Point. Together they would assault Confederates on the east bank, establish a bridgehead, and hold on.

Hooker's men arrived at Bridgeport in mid-October and awaited orders. By Smith's proposal they would move up Lookout Valley, meet the Union bridgehead, and drive Confederates from Raccoon Mountain in their front. Supplies would travel the shorter water route from Bridgeport to Brown's Ferry, then be hauled across Moccasin Point to hungry Chattanooga troops. The system was named the "Cracker Line."

Grant approved the plan. CRACKER LINE OPERATION went into effect 26 Oct. The bridgehead was made the 27th, Hooker linked up on the 28th, and the first steamboat arrived 1 Nov. A bloody, indecisive engagement resulted: Hooker left a division in his rear at Wauhatchie on his march to Moccasin Point. Confederates assaulted it in the WAUHATCHIE NIGHT ATTACK 28–29 Oct. Though they were resupplied, the fight at Wauhatchie reminded Federals they were not secure.

Wanting action, the Confederates surrounding them were unhappy with Bragg's tactics. Dissenting commanders Lt. Gen. LEONIDAS POLK, DANIEL H. HILL, and THOMAS C. HINDMAN were relieved. Lt. Gen. JAMES LONGSTREET, 2 divisions, and 35 cannon were sent to invest Maj. Gen. AMBROSE E. BURNSIDE's Knoxville garrison 4 Nov., reducing Confederate numbers even as Federals prepared for battle.

Maj. Gen. WILLIAM T. SHERMAN arrived in Chattanooga 14 Nov.; his 17,000-man column from the Memphis and Vicksburg garrisons waited at Bridgeport, having traveled by rail and foot from Memphis. They had been assigned by general-in-chief Maj. Gen. HENRY W. HALLECK to relieve Chattanooga and repair damaged rail lines as they approached. Grant, impatient to attack, canceled Halleck's order, telling Sherman to rush ahead. In Chattanooga, Sherman reconnoitered the north end of Missionary Ridge, received battle plans from Grant, returned to Bridgeport, then marched his column up Lookout Valley to Brown's Ferry.

Earlier that month Grant had ordered an attack on the Confederates holding Missionary Ridge, but Thomas had declined, claiming his 40,000 troops were insufficient to hold the town and attack simultaneously. Sherman's fresh troops made attack possible 23 Nov. when 2 Union divisions marched out of town dressed as for military parade. Confederates on a foothill below Missionary Ridge came out to look at the pageant. The divisions rushed them, beating the Confederates from their forward position on ORCHARD KNOB. Thomas sent more troops to support the victors, and the entire army moved ahead to dig a new trench line.

On 24 Nov. contenders fought the day-long battle for LOOKOUT MOUNTAIN. Hooker's 3 divisions assaulted the stronghold in the morning, and by 10 a.m. heavy fighting had begun in fog and mist that covered the battle scene all day. 3 of Sherman's divisions crossed the Tennessee River at Brown's Ferry and marched behind Chattanooga to the Confederate right at the north end of Missionary Ridge. Thomas' remaining troops held the Union center. Once Hooker took Lookout, his men were to march south and approach Bragg's left rear on Missionary Ridge. Sherman would assault the Confederate right, Hooker would move on Confederates from the south end of the ridge, and Thomas would either hit the center or reinforce wherever the Union lines might falter.

The day was a qualified Union success. By evening Sherman had won foothill positions on the north face of Missionary Ridge and Hooker was moving toward Bragg's left. The day-long fog kept many guessing about results on Lookout Mountain, but on the morning of 25 Nov. the Battle of MISSIONARY RIDGE began with a Union flag flying from the summit of Lookout Mountain.

Grant's fight for Missionary Ridge ended past 4 p.m., after an all-day struggle for the slopes by Sherman's force and a final, unplanned rush on the last Confederate line by Thomas' troops at the Union center. Bragg's men were routed from the ridge and forced to retreat southeast toward Dalton, Ga. Through 26 Nov. Federals pursued them to Chickamauga Creek. Hooker caught some elements near Rossville but could not bring them to a stand. The Confederates had been pushed out of south Tennessee, giving Sherman a base from which to launch his ATLANTA CAMPAIGN the next spring. The Chattanooga Campaign ended with Federals believing in the prospect of a final victory in 1864.   —JES

Cheatham, Benjamin Franklin. CSA b. Nashville, Tenn., 20 Oct. 1820. Cheatham was a farmer with strong military inclinations and considerable ability as a commander in battle; he was highly regarded for his boldness and hard fighting. During the Mexican War he served as a captain and later as a colonel of Tennessee volunteers, attaining notice for distinguished service at Monterrey and Cerro Gordo. Cheatham later became a major general in the Tennessee State Militia, leaving that state to participate in the 1849 gold rush to California, then returning in 1853. During the early days of the Civil War his close friend, Tennessee Gov. ISHAM G. HARRIS, made him a brigadier general and later a major general in the Provisional Army of Tennessee. On 9 July 1861 he received a commission as brigadier general in the Confederate Army, and 10 Mar. 1862 was promoted to major general.

USMHI

His reputation grew as a gifted brigade, division, and corps commander, but he was also controversial. Cheatham saw action in the battles of BELMONT, SHILOH, PERRYVILLE, STONE'S RIVER, CHICKAMAUGA, MISSIONARY RIDGE, KENNESAW MOUNTAIN, ATLANTA, and Nashville (see FRANKLIN AND NASHVILLE CAMPAIGN). Pres. JEFFERSON DAVIS briefly considered, though rejected, the possibility of elevating him to army command. After the Confederate fiasco at SPRING HILL, Gen. JOHN B. HOOD accused Cheatham of culpable errors, but a military court cleared him of all charges. Cheatham then rejoined the army in North Carolina and surrendered with it there Apr. 1865.

After the war Cheatham farmed in Tennessee and ran unsuccessfully for the U.S. House of Representatives in 1872. In 1881 he wrote an account of the Spring Hill affair, which he later published; it was reprinted in *Battles and Leaders of the Civil War* (1877–88). For 4 years he served as superintendent of Tennessee's state prison and from 1885 held the position as

postmaster in Nashville, where he died 4 Sept. 1886.   —HH

Cheat Mountain, western Va., Battle of. 11–13 Sept. 1861 The Battle of Cheat Mountain, a relatively minor action, was Gen. ROBERT E. LEE's first operation of the Civil War. Union victories at PHILIPPI in June of that year and RICH MOUNTAIN a month later secured for the Federals much of pro-Union western Virginia. The twin victories elevated Maj. Gen. GEORGE B. McCLELLAN to command of Union armies in the East and brought Lee west from Richmond to recover the territory lost to the Northern forces.

In September, after a period of inactivity, Lee decided on an advance against the Federals at Cheat Mountain, the key position in central western Virginia controlling several mountain passes and the Staunton-Parkersburg Turnpike. The Union command—6 regiments numbering 2,000 men under Brig. Gen. JOSEPH J. REYNOLDS—was divided: Col. Nathan Kimball and the 14th Indiana occupied the vital Cheat Summit; Reynolds, with the other 5 regiments, covered the turnpike at Elkwater in the Tygart Valley to the west of Kimball. The 2 Union wings were separated by 7 mi of mountain trail, 18 mi by a wagon road.

Lee assumed personal direction of Brig. Gen. WILLIAM WING LORING's 15,000 Confederates, dividing the force into 5 separate columns after Col. Albert Rust discovered a concealed route to Kimball's formidable position. While Rust surprised Kimball's right, Brig. Gen. SAMUEL R. ANDERSON's brigade would cut the wagon road in the rear of Cheat Summit. Brig. Gen. HENRY R. JACKSON was ordered to occupy the mountain peak once Rust opened the way. Against Reynolds, Lee assigned his 3 remaining brigades, 2 of which Loring personally led, and prepared a complicated plan requiring coordination and initiative on the part of Rust.

The Confederates marched into the rugged country 10 Sept., with heavy seasonal rains drenching the gray columns and hampering operations. On the 11th Reynolds contested Loring's advance at Conrad's Mill before withdrawing to Elkwater. The Confederate operation went smoothly early the next day as Loring pressed Reynolds at Elkwater and Anderson severed the wagon road behind Kimball. The Confederates waited for the sound of Rust's surprise attack on the summit, but it never came: Rust faltered at the crucial moment, believing he was plunging into a Union trap. Captured Federals convinced the Southern officer he was outnumbered 2-to-1, while he actually faced only 300 against his 2,000.

Early on the 13th Reynolds hurried 3 regiments to Kimball's aid. Lee ordered a reconnaissance at Elkwater, probing for an opening; his aide, Col. John A. Washington, was killed while examining Union lines. With the element of surprise gone and because of the incessant rains, Lee withdrew on the 15th.

Casualties for the campaign totaled slightly over 200. Lee's failure brought severe criticism from newspapers and the people. "Granny" Lee, as he was dubbed, was recalled by Jefferson Davis and sent to South Carolina to supervise fortifications.   —JDW

Chesnut, James, Jr. CSA/CSP b. Camden, S.C., 18 Jan. 1815. A descendant of Irish immigrants who originally settled in Virginia, Chesnut came from a family that owned 5 sq mi of plantation land. The youngest of 13 children, he graduated with honors in 1835 from the College of New Jersey. After reading law in Charleston under the tutelage of James L. Petigru, he was admitted to the bar in 1837 and opened a practice in Camden.

NA

In Apr. 1840 Chesnut married Mary Boykin Miller, daughter of a former governor of South Carolina, who was to become the most celebrated diarist of the Confederacy. Chesnut served in the state assembly 1840–46 and again 1850–52, and in South Carolina's upper house 1854–58, when named to fill a seat in the U.S. Senate. When war drew near, Chesnut, an ardent secessionist and a defender of SLAVERY, resigned his Senate seat and returned home. He was a delegate to his state's secession convention and a member of the committee that drafted the ordinance taking South Carolina out of the Union 20 Dec. 1860. When the Confederacy formed a provisional Congress early the next year, Chesnut helped draft the nation's permanent constitution. He was also a member of congressional committees dealing with naval affairs and territorial matters and advocated the reopening of the African slave trade.

When war appeared certain, Chesnut was appointed a colonel in the Confederate army and served on the staff of Brig. Gen. P.G.T. BEAUREGARD at FORT SUMTER. There, along with Capt. STEPHEN D. LEE, he relayed to the U.S. Army garrison Beauregard's demand that the fort be evacuated. That summer Chesnut served as Beauregard's aide during FIRST BULL RUN, afterward filling a similar post on the staff of JEFFERSON DAVIS. In 1862 he was a member of the executive council of South Carolina and chief of the state militia, which post he resigned that autumn to serve again on Davis' staff.

Yearning for field service, he was appointed brigadier general 23 Apr. 1864 and led the reserve forces of South Carolina till war's end. In postbellum years, he took an active part in RECONSTRUCTION in his state and in the Democratic party. He died on his plantation near Camden 1 Feb. 1885. —EGL

Chesnut, Mary Boykin Miller. diarist b. Statesburg, S.C., 31 Mar. 1823. Of the many diaries kept by women during the Civil War, Chesnut's stands as the cleverest and most detailed; it clearly, warmly—sometimes bluntly—reveals social, economic, political, and military status in the South during the 4 years of hostility and is considered an important source on the life of the Confederacy.

Chesnut, well educated and articulate, could hardly have been better qualified to record the feelings, beliefs, and actions of the South. Daughter of distinguished South Carolinian Stephen Decatur Miller—lawyer, governor, congressman—she was born into the life of wealthy Southern planters. An intelligent observer of all classes of people, including black slaves, at 17 she married JAMES CHESNUT, JR., and was his confidante as he distinguished himself in the U.S. Senate, resigned that seat, was active as a member of South Carolina's secession convention, rose in the Confederate army to brigadier general, and served as an aide to Pres. JEFFERSON DAVIS. Mary Chesnut was a close friend of VARINA DAVIS, the Confederate president's wife, and knew the leaders of the Confederate government and the Confederate army, many of them quite well. She shrewdly evaluated them all in her diary.

Of the FIRST BATTLE OF BULL RUN, Chesnut wrote, "We lacked the will to push on. . . . We stopped to plunder. . . . It sent us off in a fool's paradise of conceit." Of Gen. BRAXTON BRAGG she wrote, "He has a winning way of earning everybody's detestation." Of the defeat of the South she said, "The Confederacy has been done to death by the politicians."

After the war Chesnut rewrote and condensed her diary, some 400,000 words, to about 150,000. She had no children, and when she died 22 Nov. 1886, she left it to a friend. *A Diary from Dixie* was first published in 1905. In it Mary Chesnut said she hoped the diary would "at some future day afford facts about these times and prove useful to more important people than I am." The most reliable edition is *Mary Chesnut's Civil War,* ed. by C. Van Woodward, published in 1981.

—PR

chevaux-de-frise. Designed for "stopping a breach or for obstructing a ditch," chevaux-de-frise, like ABATIS, were field obstructions used to defend Civil War fortifications or positions. Each angle of this square "timber or iron, six to nine feet long," was studded with long pointed stakes, anticipating the military need for barbed wire. Charging infantry were often stopped by chevaux-de-frise and fired on with ease by defenders. —JES

USMHI

Chicago Conspiracy. *See* NORTHWEST CONSPIRACY.

Chickahominy River, Va., Battle of the. 27 June 1862 *See* GAINES' MILL, VA., BATTLE OF.

Chickamauga, Ga., Battle of. 19–20 Sept. 1863 Between 13–17 Sept. 1863 Union Major Gen. WILLIAM S. ROSECRANS concentrated divisions of his Army of the Cumberland that were scattered between Chattanooga, Tenn., and northwest Georgia. After prying Confederate Gen. BRAXTON BRAGG's army out of Chattanooga, Rosecrans' troops followed it south, jockeyed with it at Dug Gap, then pulled back near Lee and Gordon's Mills.

Nightfall of the 17th found Union Maj. Gen. THOMAS L. CRITTENDEN's XXI Corps at Lee and Gordon's Mills, Maj. Gen. GEORGE H. THOMAS' XIV Corps nearby, and Maj. Gen. ALEXANDER M. MCCOOK's XX Corps in McLemore's Cove. Maj. Gen. GORDON GRANGER's reserve corps, called up from near Bridge-

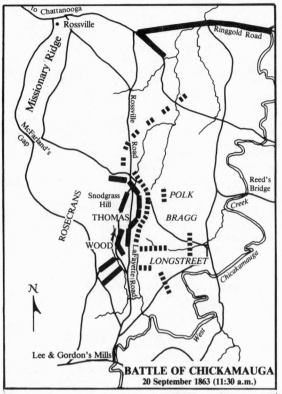

BATTLE OF CHICKAMAUGA
20 September 1863 (11:30 a.m.)

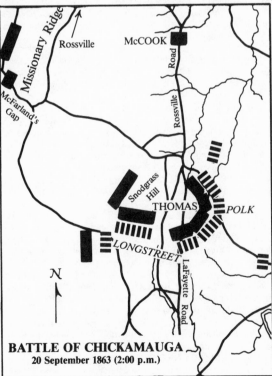

BATTLE OF CHICKAMAUGA
20 September 1863 (2:00 p.m.)

port, Ala., went north to Rossville to guard the road to Chattanooga. Since Thomas and Crittenden had had close brushes with Bragg days earlier, Rosecrans was apprehensive; facing south, he looked for the enemy.

Bragg marched his columns northward on the east side of Chickamauga Creek, planning to cross it north of Lee and Gordon's Mills, block the road to Chattanooga, and either crush Crittenden's corps or hurl it back on Thomas'. By mauling Rosecrans' left (Crittenden and Thomas' positions west of the north-south La Fayette Road), Bragg could reoccupy Chattanooga and possibly destroy the Union army before it entered Tennessee. On the 18th Bragg was reinforced by Lt. Gen. JAMES LONGSTREET and 5 brigades of Virginians, bringing his strength to over 66,000. As Confederates felt their way toward the La Fayette Road on the afternoon of the 18th, cavalry clashed northwest of Crittenden and Thomas near Reed's Bridge.

On the morning of the 19th fighting began between Reed's Bridge and the La Fayette Road, Federals on the west, Confederates on the east. A vicious day-long struggle in dense woods and scattered clearings, it was characterized by attacks and counterattacks along a 4-mi front between the La Fayette Road and Chickamauga Creek on the east. While the Federals' northern line took a beating, there was no apparent victor.

On the 20th, Bragg resumed sledgehammer blows to the Union left. Near 11 a.m., Rosecrans was told a gap existed in his line. Unable to see a unit in position shielded by trees, he ordered Brig. Gen. THOMAS J. WOOD to move his men from their location on the right to fill the supposed hole. Wood protested, said there was no gap, then obeyed. Where Wood had been, Longstreet's Confederate column surged through. Rosecrans and half his army were swept from the field. Thomas, the senior Union officer present, redeployed brigades along the crest of Snodgrass Hill in the rear. In the face of savage attacks, these soldiers held ground until dusk, when Thomas withdrew most troops, leaving the field to the Confederates.

Rosecrans and many survivors began a march for Tennessee that afternoon. Thomas set up a rear guard at Rossville Gap, holding through the 21st, then followed the rest of the army into Chattanooga, where it was besieged.

Chickamauga was Bragg's greatest victory. To the frustration of many, he failed to follow it up, and losses were staggering. Bragg listed 2,312 dead, 14,674 wounded, and 1,468 missing; Rosecrans reported 1,657 Union dead, 9,756 wounded, and 4,757 missing. —JES

Chickamauga Campaign. Aug.–Sept. 1863 After the TULLAHOMA CAMPAIGN, Union Maj. Gen. WILLIAM S. ROSECRANS' Army of the Cumberland regrouped and by Aug. 1863 was ready to resume the offensive. His immediate objective was to maneuver the Confederates out of their stronghold in Chattanooga, the Gateway City.

On 16 Aug. Rosecrans' columns crossed the Cumberland Plateau and approached the Tennessee River from the west. Maj. Gen. THOMAS L. CRITTENDEN'S XXI Corps, on the left, crossed Walden's Ridge and advanced on Chattanooga. Maj. Gen. GEORGE H. THOMAS' and ALEXANDER M. MCCOOK'S XIV and XX corps neared the river on a broad front, about 50 mi downstream from the city.

Needing reinforcements to deal with Crittenden's columns, Confederate Gen. BRAXTON BRAGG massed troops in and around Chattanooga. Crittenden's artillery, north of the river, fired on the town. To counter this threat Bragg recalled most of his troops guarding downstream crossings, and Rosecrans ordered Thomas' and McCook's troops to cross the Tennessee. Pressing rapidly forward, the 2 corps entered mountainous northwest Georgia. By 10 Sept. McCook's corps was at Alpine, Thomas' vanguard in McLemore's Cove, and Crittenden's in Chattanooga; 45 mi of rugged country separated the army's wings.

Meanwhile Bragg had been reinforced. Maj. Gen. SIMON B. BUCKNER's 8,000-man corps, threatened by the advance of Union Maj. Gen. AMBROSE E. BURNSIDE's columns, evacuated Knoxville and came west to Bragg's Army of Tennessee; then some 11,500 troops arrived from central Mississippi. On 6 Sept. Bragg evacuated Chattanooga and massed his army near La Fayette, Ga., planning to take advantage of Rosecrans' nearsightedness and defeat the Federals in detail as they emerged from the mountain passes. On 10 Sept. he moved to crush Thomas' advance at Dug Gap, Pigeon Mountain, but plans were frustrated by principal subordinates. Bragg then turned to assail Crittenden near Lee and Gordon's Mills, south of Chattanooga and north of La Fayette and Pigeon Mountain. Once again, a senior corps commander failed and Bragg's plans misfired. Squabbling with subordinates continued through the campaign.

Rosecrans, realizing his army's peril, recalled all his corps to Lee and Gordon's Mills. Roughly 4 mi northwest, late on the 18th, fighting opened at Reed's Bridge on twisting Chickamauga Creek. The 2-day battle began the next morning, bringing Federals north from Lee and Gordon's Mills and the

CHICKAMAUGA CAMPAIGN
Night of 9–10 September 1863

action west from Reed's Bridge. In 48 hours battle lines drawn up roughly along the north-south La Fayette Road, with Federals on the west, Confederates on the east, curled. Thomas commanded a tattered Union line around Snodgrass Hill, west of the La Fayette Road; behind him Rosecrans' army streamed through McFarland's Gap in the southern Missionary Ridge.

From late on the 20th, the Army of the Cumberland raced for Rossville Gap and Chattanooga. To the disappointment of subordinates, Bragg's slow pursuit allowed Rosecrans to reach the Gateway City. On the 23d, from atop Missionary Ridge, a Confederate cannon fired a shell over those below. The Chickamauga Campaign ended where it began, at Chattanooga.

—JES

Chickasaw Bluffs, Miss., Battle of.   27–29 Dec. 1862
In Dec. 1862, when Maj. Gen. ULYSSES S. GRANT's advance south down the line of the Mississippi Central Railroad stalled, he decided to use naval power to outflank the Confederates around VICKSBURG. Maj. Gen. WILLIAM T. SHERMAN was to return from Oxford, Miss., to Memphis with 1 division, assume command of troops being assembled there by Maj. Gen. JOHN A. MCCLERNAND, and descend the Mississippi to the mouth of the Yazoo River, north of Vicksburg. (See YAZOO PASS EXPEDITION.)

Supported by Rear Adm. DAVID D. PORTER's gunboats, he was to ascend the Yazoo a short distance, disembark his 32,000-man army, and seize the high ground northeast of Vicksburg. To keep Lt. Gen. JOHN C. PEMBERTON from reinforcing Vicksburg defenders with his 6,000 men from Grenada, Grant would press him along entrenchments behind the Yalobusha River, northeast of the city. But cavalry raids led by Maj. Gen. EARL VAN DORN and Brig. Gen. NATHAN B. FORREST cut his supply lines at HOLLY SPRINGS and in West Tennessee, and Grant was compelled to yield and pull back.

Sherman's transports entered the Yazoo on the 26th, and before nightfall 3 divisions had landed at Johnson's plantation. But Confederate reinforcements had already arrived: Pemberton's 2 brigades from north Mississippi and a third sent from middle Tennessee bolstered the 6,000 defenders already stationed on bluffs overlooking the scene.

News that the invasion convoy was approaching the Yazoo had sent Confederates into rifle pits covering approaches to Walnut Hills, also known as Chickasaw Bluffs. As Sherman's men disembarked facing these distant bluffs, Porter's gunboats moved up the river shelling Confederate batteries on Haynes' Bluff on the Federal left. Union troops deployed on rough ground with an enormous swamp in their front and the bluffs beyond.

On the 27th, after a heavy artillery bombardment of the Confederates, the Federals pressed forward through swampland until they reached water barriers fronting the Confederate defenses. Officers complained they found only 4 approaches to the bluffs not barred by water, and those were swept by enemy artillery.

Union Brig. Gen. FREDERICK STEELE's division sought to reach the bluffs on the 28th, crossing Blake's Levee, but was checked by Confederate ABATIS and cannon. Sherman decided to assault the center. At noon on the 29th 2 brigades charged across Chickasaw Bayou causeway to the foot of the bluffs and were savaged by Confederate fire from high ground. The twisted swampland forbade Federals from bringing up artillery support. Confederate positions gave them a clear field of fire.

Thrusts to keep Southerners pinned down were unsuccessful, and Sherman recalled his troops.

Advised that more reinforcements had joined Pemberton from Gen. BRAXTON BRAGG's Army of Tennessee, Sherman withdrew his men from the Yazoo 2 Jan. 1863. At that time Confederate defenders numbered 14,000; their losses were 63 dead, 134 wounded, and 10 missing. The number of Union losses assesses Sherman's failure at Chickasaw Bluffs: 208 dead, 1,005 wounded, 563 missing out of 31,000 effectives. —JES

Chicora, CSS. The Confederate ironclad ram *Chicora* was vital to the South's defense of Charleston, S.C., during much of the war. Commissioned Sept. 1862, the 150-ft ship, commanded by JOHN R. TUCKER, had an iron shield 4 in. thick, backed by 22 in. of wood, with 2-in. armor at her ends. Its battery consisted of 2 9-in. guns and 4 32-pounders. The ram's major difficulty was its slowness: its engine, taken from a small steamer, limited speed to 5 mi an hour in calm water. And, like all RAMS, the *Chicora* was top-heavy and difficult to steer.

Despite these deficiencies, on 31 Jan. 1863 the *Chicora,* along with its sister ram *PALMETTO STATE,* surprised ships of the Federal blockading squadron outside Charleston harbor by attacking in a thick predawn fog. The attack was a limited success, but Confederate Gen. P.G.T. BEAUREGARD was overly optimistic in declaring the BLOCKADE lifted as a result of the action. One Federal steamer rammed by the *Palmetto State* surrendered, while another, the *Keystone State,* was disabled by the *Chicora* and escaped destruction only because the USS *Memphis* towed it to safety; 20 crewmen on the ship were killed and another 20 wounded. The *Chicora* suffered no damage or casualties from enemy fire at any time during the war.

On other occasions, 1863–64, the *Chicora* played a defensive role as Federal naval forces attacked Charleston harbor. By early 1864, however, the poor condition of its boiler severely limited the *Chicora*'s usefulness. Finally, in mid-Feb. 1865 officers and crew were detached to assist in the defense of Wilmington, N.C. Then, 18 Feb., as CHARLESTON was being evacuated, the *Chicora,* with the other Charleston rams, was blown up to prevent capture by the Federals.

The history of the *Chicora* includes 2 notable facts about its crew: 3 were free blacks, and in Aug. 1863 5 other crewmen became the first volunteers to man the ill-fated Confederate torpedo boat *H.L. HUNLEY.* —NCD

Chilton, Robert Hall. CSA b. Loudoun Cty., Va., 25 Feb. 1815. Graduating from the U.S. Military Academy in 1837, Chilton ranked 48th in his 57-man class. Posted to a dragoon outfit, he served in Kansas, Texas, and Indian Territory, and during the Mexican War he won the brevet of major at Buena Vista, where he carried to safety the wounded JEFFERSON DAVIS, then a colonel of Mississippi volunteers. From 1854 until the Civil War, he was a paymaster in Washington, D.C., New York, Michigan, and Texas.

On 29 Apr. 1861 Chilton resigned his commission to join the Confederate army as an adjutant general with the rank of lieutenant colonel. During the rest of that year he served as chief of staff to an old friend, Gen. ROBERT E. LEE, and later held a similar position in the ARMY OF NORTHERN VIRGINIA. It was Chilton who, during the ANTIETAM CAMPAIGN, penned LEE'S LOST ORDER of 9 Sept. 1862.

The next month, Chilton was appointed a brigadier general, but in part because of clashes with field commanders, including Brig. Gen. JOHN B. MAGRUDER, his nomination was rejected by the Confederate Senate, which did not confirm his reappointment until early in 1864. That April he was relieved from the field at his own request, thereafter operating out of Richmond as inspector general of Lee's army.

LC

In May 1864 Chilton held his first and only combat command, during a Union movement against the capital. To help oppose an offensive by the ARMY OF THE JAMES, he was appointed by Maj. Gen. ROBERT RANSOM, commander of the Department of Richmond, to lead a Virginia infantry regiment and attached cavalry. On the 10th he rendered valuable service by helping rout the enemy column along the RICHMOND & PETERSBURG RAILROAD.

Despite winning praise for his tactical ability, Chilton immediately returned to his inspector's post and held it through the rest of the war. After Lee's surrender, he returned to civil life as president of a manufacturing concern in Columbus, Ga., dying there 18 Feb. 1879. —EGL

Chivington, John Milton. USA b. Lebanon, Ohio, 27 Jan. 1821. On 26 Aug. 1861 the Rev. John M. Chivington was commissioned major in the 1st Colorado Volunteers. He had migrated to Denver the previous year, begun a church, organized a Sunday school, become presiding elder of the Rocky Mountain Methodist District, and gotten interested in politics. With the invasion of NEW MEXICO TERRITORY by Confederates in summer 1861, the "Fighting Parson" anticipated a chance at the military glory and public advancement enjoyed by several Union officers in the East as a result of the greater attention they received from the press.

As a major with the 1st Colorado he met with some success. Commanded by Brig. Gen. E.R.S. CANBY and Col. John P. Slough, Chivington made a name for himself in the Battle of GLORIETA PASS, New Mexico Territory, turning it into a Federal victory by leading a charge on the Confederate supply train and destroying it.

When the colonel of the reorganized Colorado Volunteers resigned, spring 1862, Chivington replaced him. About this time the first great push began to bring Colorado into the Union as a state. John Evans, appointed territorial governor of Colorado, hoped with statehood to be elected governor; Chivington the territorial hero envisioned himself as a congressman from the state. The political ambitions of these 2 men led to their exaggeration of Indian troubles in the territory in a ploy to win attention from the Federal government.

After Sec. of War EDWIN M. STANTON denied a request for troops for Colorado service, Evans asked to raise another regiment of volunteers to fight hostile Indians "before we are cut off and destroyed." He hoped that if it appeared he, Chivington, and others put down the overblown Indian war with only a few extra recruits, they would receive greater Federal favor.

The raising of the regiment was approved and placed under Chivington's command along with elements of the 1st Colorado. The new unit was to be called the 3d Colorado. (There was a 2d Colorado, on duty in Kansas.) However, unlike most of the volunteers in the 1st Regiment, many of the recruits for the 3d turned out to be "street toughs, claim jumpers, and assorted riffraff."

Chivington led these men in an attack on a Cheyenne village 29 Nov. 1864. Under Chief Black Kettle, the Cheyennes were butchered while camped, they believed, under the protection of the Union Army. The scandal of this SAND CREEK MASSACRE was investigated in Congress and Colonel Chivington, revealed as a frightening, pathological racist, resigned his commission in early 1865 to avoid court-martial.

After the Civil War Chivington's political ambitions and clerical future were ruined, and he traveled through California, Nebraska, and Colorado until his death in Denver, 4 Oct. 1894. —JES

Choctaw, USS. A sidewheel steamer acquired by the Federal government in 1862 and converted into an IRONCLAD fitted with a ram, the *Choctaw* was recognized as the most powerful gunboat on the Western waters. Built in St. Louis, the ship had a draft of 8 ft when heavily laden and a speed of 2 knots moving upstream. On its deck at launching were 3 9-in. DAHLGREN guns, 2 30-pounder PARROTT rifles, and 2 24-pounder smoothbores. The *Choctaw* received its baptism of fire during the SECOND VICKSBURG CAMPAIGN.

USMHI

Commanded by Lt. Cmdr. F.H. Ramsay, it went up the Yazoo River with other vessels to Chickasaw Bayou 29 Apr. 1863. The next day the fleet attacked the enemy's batteries on Drumgould's Bluffs. The *Choctaw,* the only ship under heavy fire, was struck 53 times, but without substantial damage and with no one hurt. On 21 May 1863 it accompanied the expedition that captured Yazoo City and, alone, destroyed more than $2 million in Confederate property.

The *Choctaw's* next action came 7 June 1863 at Milliken's Bend, where Union army stores were kept under guard. Learning that the Confederates were planning an attack there, the Federals sent 2 gunboats, the *Choctaw* and *LEXINGTON.* Even before dawn, while the ships were still en route, the attack began, and Union forces were overpowered. But when the gunboats arrived and began shelling the riverbank, the Southern troops fled in confusion.

During the RED RIVER CAMPAIGN of 1864, essentially a movement of the Army of the Gulf to more thoroughly control Louisiana and eastern Texas, the *Choctaw* and other ironclads, as well as gunboats—the most formidable naval force

collected in Western waters—were called to cooperate. It seemed like an easy assignment, for it was planned to begin in March, when the river was usually swelled by the spring rise. But that year the rise did not occur. During the weeks ahead, the ships were kept busy forcing a passage and building dams to aid transportation. The venture, during which 5 ships were lost, was one of the North's most humiliating and disastrous.

After the war, the *Choctaw* was dismantled at New Orleans and sold there 30 Mar. 1866 for $9,272. —VCJ

Choctaw Resolutions. On 7 Feb. 1861, the General Council of the Choctaw Nation passed resolutions stating that, while they hoped political differences could be resolved between North and South, in the event they were not, the chiefs would be

left to follow the natural affections, education, institutions, and interests of our people, which indissolubly bind us in every way to the destiny of our neighbors and brethren of the Southern states.

Strongly influenced by Indian agent DOUGLAS H. COOPER, the Choctaws were the first tribe to declare for the Confederate cause. Eager to let their loyalty be known, the council sent copies of the resolutions to the governors of each Southern state and a delegation to MONTGOMERY seeking formal alliance with the Confederacy. The emissaries were sent home with a rejoinder to be patient. Anticipating some kind of treaty, George Hudson, principal chief of the Choctaws, appointed a committee to await Confederate Commissioner ALBERT PIKE'S arrival and ordered compulsory draft of all Choctaw men 18–35 and the formation of home guards in response to Cooper's request for a mounted regiment. The Chickasaw legislature passed similar resolutions 25 May. On 12 Jan. 1863 Indian Commissioner S. S. Scott reported (not entirely accurately) to Sec. of War JAMES A. SEDDON that of the CONFEDERATE INDIANS allies, only the Choctaws remained thoroughly loyal to the Southern nation, with the Chickasaws following close behind. —PLF

Christian Commission, United States. The U.S. Christian Commission was organized in New York City 14 Nov. 1861 by the Young Men's Christian Association. The idea was suggested by Vincent Colyer, an influential artist who would become president of the YMCA.

As it expanded throughout the North in the early war years, the commission worked in conjunction with the U.S. SANITARY COMMISSION for the relief of soldiers at the front. Free box lunches and coffee wagons were sent to compete with SUTLERS selling whiskey, and special diet kitchens were provided for the sick and wounded. Ladies affiliated with the commission volunteered their nursing skills in hospitals.

Its members felt it their duty to provide more than physical comforts; consequently, they attempted to uplift soldiers' moral and religious spirit. In the more permanent camps, reading rooms were established and stocked with Bibles, magazines, and newspapers from home. The commission encouraged men to write their families and provided free writing material and stamps.

The government was grateful for all the benefits provided by the Christian Commission and estimated that over $6 million was raised and spent for soldiers' aid. The commission held its final meeting 11 Feb. 1866. —MTC

Chrysler, Morgan Henry. USA b. Columbia Cty., N.Y., 30 Sept. 1822. It was widely believed at the time of the Civil War that native intelligence and drive could compensate for any lack of training; generals could be appointed from civilian life and be expected to excel. Morgan Chrysler proved this theory. A farmer from New York State, he entered the 30th New York Infantry as a private in spring 1861 and left the service 15 Jan. 1866 as a full brigadier general of volunteers and with a brevet of major general of volunteers.

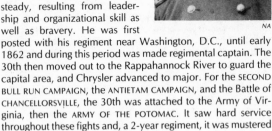

His service and rise were steady, resulting from leadership and organizational skill as well as bravery. He was first posted with his regiment near Washington, D.C., until early 1862 and during this period was made regimental captain. The 30th then moved out to the Rappahannock River to guard the capital area, and Chrysler advanced to major. For the SECOND BULL RUN CAMPAIGN, the ANTIETAM CAMPAIGN, and the Battle of CHANCELLORSVILLE, the 30th was attached to the Army of Virginia, then the ARMY OF THE POTOMAC. It saw hard service throughout these fights and, a 2-year regiment, it was mustered out of service at the end of its term.

Chrysler showed his powers of persuasion after he received authorization to raise a regiment of cavalry and was given a lieutenant colonel's commission. Before they received mustering-out pay, the 30th's veterans were approached by their old major and reenlisted into the 2d New York Veteran Cavalry, agreeing to fight on for the duration of the war after their veterans' furloughs.

In Dec. 1863 Chrysler was made colonel of the regiment while it went through winter training and organization. In spring they set out for Louisiana and the Department of the Gulf for Maj. Gen. Nathaniel P. Banks's RED RIVER CAMPAIGN. Until the end of the war Chrysler and his men stayed in the Deep South fighting through the Red River battles and the Siege of MOBILE. On 11 Nov. 1865 Chrysler won his brigadier general's commission. This appointment and his brevet to major general on mustering out were for his war service and his last military duty, serving as military governor for the District of Northern Alabama.

In the postwar period, Chrysler resumed farming in New York State until his death at Kinderhook, 24 Aug. 1890. —JES

Churchill, Thomas James. CSA b. Jefferson Cty., Ky., 10 Mar. 1824. Churchill studied law at Transylvania College, then served as a lieutenant with a volunteer regiment of mounted riflemen during the Mexican War. Following his release as a prisoner of war, he settled in Little Rock, Ark., and became a farmer. When the state seceded, he was elected colonel of the 1st Arkansas Mounted Rifles, establishing himself as one of the more competent commanders in the Western theater. His skillful leadership at WILSON'S CREEK, 10 Aug. 1861, aided his promotion to brigadier general 4 Mar. 1862, and he served conspicuously at PEA RIDGE that same month. Churchill went on to gather more laurels in the battle at RICHMOND, Ky., when he rallied his wavering line to repulse a severe Federal charge.

Late in 1862 Churchill was placed in command of ARKANSAS POST at the mouth of the Arkansas River approach to Little Rock. The Confederates planned to use the fort as a base from which to attack Union transports on the Mississippi River, but Churchill's 4,900-man force could not withstand the overwhelming land/sea assault mounted by Maj. Gen. JOHN A. McCLERNAND and Lt. DAVID D. PORTER Jan. 1863. Hopelessly outnumbered, he was surrendered with the fort on the 11th and taken prisoner with his men.

CV

After his exchange he was transferred to Gen. E. KIRBY SMITH'S command in the Trans-Mississippi, where he participated in the RED RIVER CAMPAIGN as commander of an Arkansas infantry division at BLAIR'S LANDING and JENKINS' FERRY. On 18 Mar. 1865 he received his commission as major general.

After the Western troops were surrendered 26 May 1865, Churchill joined the band of exiles Smith led to Mexico but soon returned to Arkansas. His career in postwar politics was marred when he was held liable for shortages in the accounts during his tenure as state treasurer. Apparently the discrepancy resulted from poor bookkeeping rather than from dishonorable motives, and he repaid the loss. d. Little Rock, 14 May 1905. —PLF

Chusto-Talasah, Indian Territory, eng. at. 9 Dec. 1861 *See* BIRD CREEK, INDIAN TERRITORY, ENG. AT.

City Point, Va. During the final 10 months of the Civil War, the nerve center of Union operations was located at City Point, Va. From a bluff above the confluence of the James and Appomattox rivers, Lt. Gen. ULYSSES S. GRANT directed operations of all Union armies. When Grant established his headquarters there, 15 June 1864, this small Virginia community was destined to become the scene of memorable events of the war.

Grant chose City Point because of its location: 7 mi east of Petersburg, on the south side of the James River, City Point was easily reached by water from FORT MONROE, Va., and Washington, D.C. From his headquarters the Union general-in-chief could oversee the campaign against PETERSBURG while remaining in contact with the War Department and the farflung Union armies. It remained Grant's headquarters until the final week of the war, when the Union army pursued the ARMY OF NORTHERN VIRGINIA from Five Forks to Appomattox.

City Point was thus largely a Union creation. When Grant arrived, the transformation began. In a short period of hectic building, a new wharf to handle the river traffic, a series of warehouses to store rations, and a new hospital to care for 6,000 patients were all erected. Union railroad crews repaired the City Point Railroad, which ran west to Confederate-held Petersburg, and laid new spurs behind the Union lines for easy distribution of matériel. A line of earthworks, manned by an assigned garrison and running from river to river south of the town, protected the headquarters and depot. The Federals also laid a telegraph cable to Fort Monroe, where a direct line connected it to Washington.

In Grant's busy headquarters the Union commander, from his tents on the lawn of a large house, telegraphed orders, suggestions, and plans while receiving reports and current intelligence. Thousands of Federal soldiers embarked from the wharf, en route to other fronts. Twice Pres. Lincoln visited City Point; on the latter occasion he, Grant, and Maj. Gen. WILLIAM T. SHERMAN conferred on peace terms for the Confederates.

The South did not overlook such a vital area. On 9 Aug. 1864 Grant narrowly escaped death when 2 Confederate agents sabotaged an ammunition barge, killing 43 and injuring 126 in the explosion.

The fall of Petersburg and Richmond and the surrender at Appomattox ended the city's importance. The headquarters of the Union armies and the immense supply depot soon vanished. As with so many other places, it was only the war that gave City Point historic significance.   —JDW

Clanton, James Holt. CSA b. Columbia Cty., Ga., 8 Jan. 1827. The grandson of a soldier in the Revolutionary War, Clanton moved with his family to Alabama in 1835, attending local schools, then entering the University of Georgia. Before his freshman year was over he left college to fight in the Mexican War; afterward, he studied law under Judge Robert Chilton and was admitted to the bar. He was elected to the Alabama legislature as a Democrat in 1855, and 5 years later was a presidential elector for John Bell.

When war came, Clanton cast his lot with Alabama and enthusiastically supported the Confederacy. He entered military service as a captain of mounted troops before being sent to Florida as an aide to Gen. BRAXTON BRAGG. While there he was elected colonel of the 1st Alabama Cavalry. Transferred to Tennessee, he led his regiment during the opening phase of the Battle of SHILOH and in the engagements of Farmington and BOONEVILLE.

PHCW

Thereafter he served on the staff of Lt. Gen. LEONIDAS POLK while raising 3 additional cavalry regiments, which brought him a promotion to brigadier general, to rank from 16 Nov. 1863. In that grade he participated in the ATLANTA CAMPAIGN and was active in the DEPARTMENT OF ALABAMA, MISSISSIPPI, AND EAST LOUISIANA.

By July 1864 he was commanding a small mounted brigade near Blue Mountain, Ala., a region raided by a large force of Union cavalry. On the 14th Clanton led 200 troopers against 10 times as many Federals under Maj. Gen. LOVELL H. ROUSSEAU. Near Ten Island Ford on the Coosa River the defenders were decimated and forced to retreat, permitting Rousseau to destroy a strategic rail line between Montgomery, Ala., and West Point, Ga.

8 months later, at Bluff Springs, Fla., Clanton was severely wounded and captured. Paroled at Mobile, Ala., May 1865, he returned to his law practice and became a mover in the Democratic party in his adopted state. In the late 1860s he was state's attorney for Alabama. On 27 Sept. 1871, in Knoxville, Tenn., he quarreled with the drunken son of a justice of the Tennessee supreme court, who shot Clanton to death.   —EGL

Clark, Charles. CSA/war governor b. Warren Cty., Ohio, 24 May 1811. Educated in Kentucky, Clark moved to Mississippi when he was about 21 and became a schoolteacher there. Before the Civil War he was twice a state legislator—first as a Whig, then as a Democrat—served as colonel of the 2d Mississippi Regiment in the Mexican War, was defeated in a bid for a U.S. congressional seat, and was a delegate to the Democratic state and national conventions in 1860. He made his living as a planter.

At the start of the war he was appointed brigadier, then major general of state troops; on their absorption by the Confederate army he was made brigadier general 22 May 1861. He first fought at SHILOH, where he was wounded, and on returning to command, he took part in Maj. Gen. JOHN C. BRECKINRIDGE's Aug. 1862 assault on BATON ROUGE. While leading a charge on batteries of the 6th Michigan, one of their shells exploded near him, crippling him for life. Left on the field when the Confederates evacuated the city, he was taken prisoner. The Federals shipped Clark to New Orleans, and his wife was allowed through Confederate lines to go to him. Considered no military threat, he was paroled and sent home to live out his days.

Clark ignored his handicap, moved about with crutches, and became active in politics again. In 1863 he was elected governor of Mississippi over frail opposition. During his tenure Clark urged state residents to support the war effort and look to home defense; he was quoted as saying Mississippians should "repel raids, not make them." The state's ravished economy also commanded his attention, and he encouraged home industry and domestic use of Mississippi's agricultural products.

A moderate secessionist, Clark encouraged reconciliation as the war was ending. In May 1865, on learning that Lt. Gen. RICHARD TAYLOR had surrendered, he called the state legislature into a special session. Addressing the body, he spoke of "the profound sentiment of detestation" over the murder of ABRAHAM LINCOLN and voiced concern for Mississippi's future. As he spoke, Federal troops approached the legislature with orders to arrest all its members. Clark was taken into custody and shipped to Fort Pulaski, Ga., where he was held prisoner pending Federal authorities' decision on the disposition of former Confederate civil leaders.

After his release Clark returned to his plantation, "Doro," under parole and began a law career. Planting and law served him well until 1876, when he was given a minor administrative office in state government. d. at Doro 18 Dec. 1877.

—JES

Clark, Edward. war governor b. Wilkes Cty., Ga., 1 Apr. 1815. Clark moved with his mother to Montgomery, Ala., shortly after his father died in 1832. There he attended local schools and worked as a store clerk while he studied law, opening a practice in Marshall, Tex., in 1842. During the Mexican War he served as a volunteer on the staff of Gen. James P. Henderson.

Clark established himself as a prominent politician and a competent executive in the Republic of Texas, becoming a member of the Texas constitutional convention in 1845, serving as secretary in the first house of representatives, and winning election to the second Texas senate. In 1853 Gov. Elisha M. Pease appointed him secretary of state, an office he held for 4 years. After a year as state commissioner of claims, 1858, he was elected lieutenant governor on the Democratic ticket, 1859–61.

When Gov. Sam Houston refused to swear an oath of allegiance to the Confederate government, the secession convention removed him from office and 16 Mar. 1861 inaugurated Clark to fill the vacancy. Immediately the enthusiastic Confederate began preparing the state for war by recruiting and opening camps of instruction in each of 11 newly established military districts. Anticipating increased Indian hostilities in western Texas once U.S. Regulars were withdrawn, he had in February sent a delegation to court allies among the Five Civilized Tribes and corresponded with JEFFERSON DAVIS about making treaties with them and the other tribes (see INDIANS, CONFEDERATE). He became involved in raising the 14th Texas Infantry, and 8 June issued a formal proclamation declaring a state of war in Texas.

Defeated for election in his own right in November, Clark served as governor for only 8 months. Though he did not again hold a prominent political position, he continued to support the war effort as a colonel of Texas troops. When Gen. E. KIRBY SMITH surrendered, Clark traveled to San Antonio with several other former Confederate officials and 15 June joined Brig. Gen. JOSEPH O. SHELBY's band of exiles to Mexico. For a while he lived at the Confederate settlement at Carlota, then returned to Marshall to resume practicing law until his death there 4 May 1880.   —PLF

Clark, Henry Toole. war governor b. Tarborough, N.C., 7 Feb. 1808. Receiving an M.A. from the University of North Carolina in 1832, Clark went on to study law and, though admitted to the bar, turned to farming in his mid-twenties. In 1849 he was elected to the North Carolina legislature, where he remained until after the outbreak of civil war, for the last 3 years as speaker of the state senate.

When Clark became governor on the death of JOHN W. ELLIS in July 1861, one of his first acts was to seek additional appropriations to strengthen the state's war footing; an initial outlay of $5 million had already been consumed. He also presided over the transfer of North Carolina's military and naval forces to Virginia as part of the Confederate establishment, an act that put Clark in political jeopardy and his state in military danger. With North Carolina's Atlantic coast stripped of most of its defense force, Union army/navy expeditions captured Fort Hatteras (see HATTERAS INLET) and supporting works, below Roanoke Island, in August; from this base they moved inland, occupying other parts of the state.

Soon citizens of eastern North Carolina were petitioning Clark for protection. He could do little: though he asked that troops be returned from Virginia, JEFFERSON DAVIS thought this move would be "highly inexpedient" because of the upper Confederacy's vulnerability. Most promises of aid Clark received remained promises. In Oct. 1861 he restated his dilemma in more plaintive tones: "my resources are now restricted almost to Militia—and they are unarmed, undrilled, and some not yet organized. We feel very defenseless here without arms . . . [a plight] effected by our generosity to others"—a reference to the 13,000 STANDS OF ARMS North Carolina had sent to Richmond. Still, the Confederate government sat on its hands.

The result was the capture of ROANOKE ISLAND, key to the North Carolina interior, by troops under Maj. Gen. AMBROSE E. BURNSIDE on 8 Feb. 1862. Much unmerited criticism of

Clark followed, unleashed by politicians, editors, and citizens who considered him incompetent or traitorous. A convention of state officials meeting in Raleigh protested the "total incapacity" of the governor, and the Confederate Congress empaneled a committee to investigate the debacle at Roanoke. When the Federals raided far from their foothold position, wails of anxiety went up from residents of northern and western North Carolina. When Clark attempted to shift to those parts of the state some of the regiments stationed along the eastern coast, he was excoriated by seaboard residents.

In this impossible situation, the governor had no chance to be reelected. One of his most vocal critics, the influential editor William W. Holden, finished him off by denouncing him for waging a "rich man's war and a poor man's fight," a label that stuck to Clark. At Holden's urging, the popular ZEBULON B. VANCE, colonel of the 26th North Carolina Infantry, became a gubernatorial candidate in late 1862 and succeeded Clark in office.

Clark returned to private life till war's close. In 1865 he was elected to the state legislature but could not serve because Holden, the new governor, refused to pardon him. He never again sought public office, dying in Tarborough 14 Apr. 1874.   —EGL

Clark, John Bullock, Jr. CSA b. Fayette, Mo., 14 Jan. 1831. Choosing to follow his father's civic and military careers, Clark attended local schools in Missouri, entered the Fayette Academy, and began his studies at the University of Missouri when he was 15. After 2 years there he entered Harvard Law School, graduating in 1854 and opening a law practice in Fayette, where the senior Clark had begun his own law career in 1824.

In 1861 Clark left his successful practice for the Confederate army, where he was appointed lieutenant, soon rose to captain of the 6th Missouri Infantry, "acted a gallant part" in the Battles of CARTHAGE and WILSON'S

GG

CREEK as a major, and received a commendation from Maj. Gen. THOMAS C. HINDMAN after leading a brigade at the Battle of PEA RIDGE as a colonel. He was commissioned brigadier general, 6 Mar. 1864.

Clark spent the rest of the war with Brig. Gen. JOHN S. MARMADUKE's Missouri division, commanding a brigade of cavalrymen who were a major part of the "expeditionary force" in Maj. Gen. STERLING PRICE's raid into Missouri in 1864. After the war Clark went home to Fayette and his law practice, traveling to Washington, D.C., in 1873 after his home state elected him to Congress; he remained in office for 10 years, ending his congressional career as clerk of the House of Representatives. Clark maintained a law office in Washington from 1889 until his death there 7 Sept. 1903.   —FLS

Clay, Cassius Marcellus. USA b. "White Hall," Madison Cty., Ky., 19 Oct. 1810. Clay was educated at the best state schools in Kentucky and at Yale, where he graduated in

1832; though he studied law at Transylvania College, he never practiced. Elected to the state legislature as a Whig in 1835, 1837, and 1840, he was defeated in 1841 on the SLAVERY issue; son of a wealthy slaveholder, Clay had nevertheless become an emancipationist. In 1845 he established the antislavery *True American* in Lexington, but his press was shipped to Cincinnati by a proslavery committee determined to keep the paper from being published. Though in the 1850s Clay helped establish Kentucky's antislavery Berea College, abolitionists denounced him because his main objection to slavery was its detrimental effect on nonslaveholding whites.

LC

Opposing the annexation of Texas, Clay nevertheless went to Mexico with the 1st Kentucky Cavalry, but he and his men were soon captured. After helping to form the REPUBLICAN PARTY, in 1860 Clay ran a strong second for the Republican vice-presidential nomination; campaigning actively for ABRAHAM LINCOLN, he anticipated a cabinet post but accepted the ministry to Russia, delaying his departure to raise an irregular force that helped protect Washington, D.C., until troops arrived.

Clay returned to the U.S. in 1862 and was commissioned major general of volunteers on 11 Apr. His services were not in demand, and he rejected offers he deemed unsuitable. Lincoln sent him to Kentucky to gauge attitudes toward slavery; Clay later claimed considerable credit for the EMANCIPATION PROCLAMATION. Disgruntled with his inactivity, he resigned 11 Mar. 1863 without seeing active service of consequence.

He returned to Russia as minister, 1863–69, then came home to dabble in politics; a Liberal Republican since the party organized, he became a Democrat in 1876, then returned to the Republican party in 1880. Tall and physically powerful, Clay during his life participated in a number of duels and bloody personal encounters; the BOWIE KNIFE was his favorite weapon. His behavior became increasingly erratic before his death at White Hall 22 July 1903. —LHH

Clay, Clement Claiborne. CSP b. near Huntsville, Ala., 13 Dec. 1816. Clay graduated from the University of Alabama in 1834, worked as private secretary to his father, Gov. Clement Comer Clay, briefly edited the Huntsville *Democrat,* then entered law school at the University of Virginia. Though he received his degree in 1839, Clay spent the next 9 years in public service as a representative in the state legislature and as a county court judge.

Clay withdrew from politics to practice law in 1848, but in 1853, the year he lost his bid for a seat in the U.S. House of Representatives, he was elected to the Senate as a Democrat. His firm STATES-RIGHTS stand appealed to his Alabama constitu-

NA

ents, who returned him to office in 1859. Once ABRAHAM LINCOLN won the presidency, Clay endorsed secession, resigning his Senate seat in Feb. 1861, shortly after his state seceded to join the Confederacy.

Clay lobbied arduously for JEFFERSON DAVIS' presidency but turned down a cabinet position as secretary of war, recommending fellow Alabamian LEROY P. WALKER for the post. In Nov. 1861 Clay was elected to the First Regular Congress; an expert in finance, he chaired the Committee on Commerce, was a member of the Indian Affairs, Rules, and Military Affairs committees, and participated in an investigation of the Navy Department.

The Richmond community recognized Clay as a wholehearted defender of the administration, but as a man known for his high principles he also maintained good relations with the opposition. While he supported Davis' war measures, he frequently voted against the president's political appointments. The observant diarist MARY CHESNUT called Clay the one personal friend who remained loyal to the president, a loyalty that contributed to Clay's defeat at the polls in 1863.

In Apr. 1864 Davis appointed Clay and JACOB THOMPSON agents to Canada, with instructions to unofficially seek peace through whatever channels became open. The secretive nature of the mission involved plans to encourage peace movements in the midwestern states and to arrange the escape of Confederate prisoners held at Johnson's Island, a short distance from Sandusky, Ohio (*see also* NORTHWEST CONSPIRACY). After a year without success, Clay returned home just as Gen. ROBERT E. LEE surrendered. On hearing that a warrant for his arrest had been issued charging him with complicity in LINCOLN'S ASSASSINATION and plotting against the government from Canada, Clay rode 170 mi to Macon, Ga., where he surrendered. He was held with Davis at Fort Monroe for almost a year before his wife and friends arranged his release 17 Apr. 1866. Since the case did not come to trial, Clay never had the chance to defend himself against the charges. Discouraged and in ill health, he resumed his law practice without returning to public life. d. Madison Cty., Ala., 3 Jan. 1882. —PLF

Clayton, Henry DeLamar. CSA b. Pulaski Cty., Ga., 7 Mar. 1827. The son of a planter and legislator, Clayton attended an academy near Macon before graduating from Emory and Henry College in 1848. After reading law in Eufaula, Ala., he practiced in neighboring Clayton. From 1857–61 he sat in the Alabama house of representatives, leaving it to enlist in a local military unit. Soon, however, Gov. ANDREW B. MOORE commissioned him a colonel in charge of all Alabama troops.

Clayton resigned that post Mar. 1861, when elected commander of the 1st Alabama Infantry, leaving at once for Pensacola, Fla., to reorganize the

GC

unit. After 10 months of irregular duty, he returned to his own state and recruited the 39th Alabama, which he led during Gen. Braxton Bragg's 1862 KENTUCKY CAMPAIGN. He was severely wounded that winter at STONE'S RIVER and was promoted to brigadier general on his recovery Apr. 1863. Commanding 5 Alabama regiments and an Arkansas battery, he served notably at CHICKAMAUGA, where he was again wounded and where his command absorbed losses of almost 45%. That November the brigade suffered even more severely at MISSIONARY RIDGE. The next year, Clayton fought under Gen. Joseph E. Johnston in the ATLANTA CAMPAIGN, seeing action at Dalton, NEW HOPE CHURCH, and the engagements outside Atlanta.

On 7 July 1864 Clayton won a major generalship and command of Lt. Gen. A.P. STEWART's old division, fighting at JONESBOROUGH and during Gen. JOHN BELL HOOD's unsuccessful foray into Tennessee. In Dec. 1864, during the retreat from Nashville, his command formed a part of the rear guard of the Army of Tennessee, Hood commending him for "admirable coolness and courage" in fending off pursuers. After Hood's relief, Clayton guided 2 brigades to North Carolina, helping to stop Sherman's invasion. When this failed, he surrendered with Johnston at Durham Station, 26 Apr. 1865.

Clayton returned to Alabama, where he was elected a circuit court judge in 1866 but was barred by RECONSTRUCTION law from serving until 1874. After 2 terms, he retired from the bench in 1886 to become president of his state's university. He died in Tuscaloosa 13 Oct. 1889, and was buried in Clayton.   —EGL

Cleburne, Patrick Ronayne. CSA b. County Cork, Ireland, 17 Mar. 1828. A naturalized American citizen and an adopted Arkansan, Cleburne grew up in Ireland, where his father was a well-known physician in Cork. After being tutored at home and receiving an Episcopal church-school education, Cleburne apprenticed himself to a pharmacist to prepare for a medical career. But he failed the examinations and in shame joined Her Majesty's 41st Regiment of Foot. After serving 3 years with the unit he purchased his discharge and emigrated to the U.S. in 1849. He worked as a pharmacist in Cincinnati, Ohio, then moved to Helena, Ark., where he became a partner in a drugstore.

LC

At the urging of friends Cleburne studied law and became an affluent attorney. In 1861 he enlisted as a private in a company being raised for the 15th Arkansas, and his old friends elected him captain, which marked the beginning of a meteoric military career that won him praise as one of the South's best infantry commanders.

Cleburne was soon made colonel of the regiment and under Maj. Gen. WILLIAM J. HARDEE spent the fall and winter of 1861 in the vicinity of Bowling Green, Ky. His British military training, discipline, and charm earned him the loyalty of his men, Hardee's friendship, and a temporary brigade command; on 4 Mar. 1862 the post became permanent when Cleburne received his brigadier's commission.

The next month he participated in his first battle, at SHILOH, where he fought in the advance on the far left of the Confederate line. After an initial repulse, Cleburne rallied the brigade and shoved the Federals through their camps to the Tennessee River. Though the fighting had reduced his command to only

800 men, on the next day he personally stemmed a Confederate rout, led a counterattack, then fought rearguard action while the bulk of his army retreated.

Cleburne was rewarded for his performance with lavish praise and increased command authority. In August, at the Battle of RICHMOND, Ky., he oversaw 2 brigades. However, on the morning of the 30th, while readying his men for the second day's fight, he was shot in the left cheek, the bullet carrying away several teeth before it exited; unable to speak, he relinquished command. Congress rewarded him with a vote of appreciation and, 13 Dec. 1862, a brigadier general's commission.

He reaffirmed his reputation as an outstanding combat officer in most of the major 1864 campaigns, organized a band of SHARPSHOOTERS, and strengthened his command. Under Gen. John B. Hood at the Battle of FRANKLIN, 30 Nov., Cleburne's division headed the charge on the Federal entrenchments. After Cleburne's horse was shot under him, he mounted another, and it too was killed. He then raised his KEPI on his sword and led his men forward on foot until he was shot and killed 50 yd from the Union lines.

His death set off mourning in most Confederate quarters, though his foreign birth had annoyed some aristocrats in high command and his proposal to use blacks as combat troops had shocked and angered others. Cleburne, who had never owned slaves, mistakenly believed the promise of freedom would encourage blacks to fight for Southern nationhood, but his convictions had only blocked his promotion to lieutenant general. Confederate fighting men grieved over his death, and Pres. Jefferson Davis elegized: "a vacancy was created which will never be filled."   —JES

Clem, John Lincoln "Johnny." USA b. Newark, Ohio, 13 Aug. 1851. Clem ran away from home in May 1861 to join the army and found the army was not interested in 9-year-old boys. When he applied to the commander of the 3d Ohio Regiment, the officer said he "wasn't enlisting infants," and turned him down. Clem tried the 22d Michigan next, and its commander said roughly the same. Determined, Clem tagged after the regiment, acted "just the same as a drummer boy," and wore down resistance. Though still not regularly enrolled, he performed camp duties and received a soldier's pay, $13 a month, a sum donated by the officers.

The next April, at SHILOH, Clem's drum was smashed by an artillery round and he became a minor news item as "Johnny Shiloh," the smallest drummer. More than a year later, at the Battle of CHICKAMAUGA, he rode an artillery caisson to the front and wielded a musket trimmed to his size. In one of the Union retreats a Confederate officer ran after the cannon Clem rode with, and before the drummer killed him, said, "Surrender you damned little Yankee!" This pluck won for Clem national attention and the name "Drummer Boy of Chickamauga."

Clem stayed with the army through the war, served as a courier, and was wounded twice. Between Shiloh and Chickamauga he was regularly enrolled in the service and thereafter received his own pay. After the Civil War he tried to enter West Point but was turned down because of his slim education. A personal appeal to Pres. U.S. GRANT, his general at Shiloh, won him a 2d lieutenant's appointment in the Regular army 18 Dec. 1871, and in 1903 he became colonel and assistant quartermaster general. He retired from the army as a major general in 1916. d. San Antonio, Tex., 13 May 1937.   —JES

Clingman, Thomas Lanier.

CSA b. Huntersville, N.C., 27 July 1812. After an in-home education, Clingman graduated at the head of the class of 1832 at the University of North Carolina. He entered law and in 1834 was admitted to the bar. A year later Clingman represented Surry County in the North Carolina legislature, afterward moving to Buncombe County, where he resided for 60 years. In 1840 he was elected to the state senate from North Carolina's mountain country, which he also represented in the U.S. House of Representatives, 1843–45 and 1847–58. He was then appointed to fill an unexpired term in the Senate, winning a full term in 1861.

MC

At first a staunch Whig, Clingman engaged in numerous controversies with Democrats and fought a duel with WILLIAM L. YANCEY of Alabama, in which neither party was injured. As the nation moved toward civil war, he voted against compromise measures that might have further delayed the conflict. Increasingly protective toward slavery and suspicious of Northern Whigs, he joined the Democratic party in the early 1850s.

When war broke out, Clingman was appointed colonel of the 25th North Carolina Infantry, serving principally in the Carolinas—including Charleston and NEW BERNE—through early 1864, when he was sent to Virginia. As a brigadier general, commissioned 17 May 1862, he led a brigade at DREWRY'S BLUFF, COLD HARBOR, and in many battles of the PETERSBURG siege. In August he was badly wounded in the WELDON RAILROAD OPERATIONS, fighting to preserve the link between Virginia and the interior of the Confederacy. After a long recuperation, he rejoined his command shortly before his army's surrender.

After the war Clingman returned home, attempting to retake his U.S. Senate seat, from which he had been expelled early in the conflict, but he was prevented from doing so under the conditions of his parole. Practicing law again, he also explored the peaks of the Allegheny Mountains, one of which was named after him. In 1875 he was a member of the convention that drafted North Carolina's postwar constitution. He died 3 Nov. 1897 in Morgantown, N.C., in the western region of the state whose natural resources he had devoted himself to developing.   —EGL

Cloyd's Mountain, Va., eng. at.

9 May 1864   In spring 1864 the grand Union offensive of the war began. In Georgia a massive Union army prepared to crush the Confederacy's heartland; in Virginia, Federal thrusts against Richmond and up the SHENANDOAH VALLEY were planned. As a final element of the strategy, General-in-Chief ULYSSES S. GRANT ordered Brig. Gen. GEORGE CROOK on a raid toward southwestern Virginia to destroy the vital VIRGINIA & TENNESSEE RAILROAD.

On 29 Apr. 1864 Crook's 6,155-man army of 3 brigades advanced into the rugged Allegheny Mountains. For over a week the Federal raiders, drenched by rain and snowstorms, slithered through the difficult, forbidding terrain. The poor roads turned into oozing troughs of mud, but Crook pushed the column. On the morning of 9 May the Union command encountered at Cloyd's Mountain a patchwork Confederate line composed of veteran troops and home-guard novices under Brig. Gen. ALBERT G. JENKINS.

The Confederate commander had selected a defensive position on high, wooded bluffs within sight of Cloyd's Mountain and 5 mi north of Dublin Depot. With 2,400 soldiers and 10 cannon, Jenkins contested Crook's advance with artillery fire as the Federals deployed. Crook maneuvered leftward his 1 brigade, under Col. Carr B. White, to turn the Confederate right. His remaining brigades, under Cols. RUTHERFORD B. HAYES and Horatio G. Sickel, meanwhile deployed for a frontal assault across a creek and a large meadow.

About 11 a.m. White's unsuspected attack on Jenkins' right flank initiated the vicious battle. A sheet of flame erupted from the Confederate line; volley after volley soon pealed upward from the trees. Crook, dismounting, personally led Sickel and Hayes toward the ridge. A galling fire from the Southerners crumbled Sickel's ranks, which fled back toward the mountain. The Union brigade quickly reformed and, with Hayes's command, delivered a riveting attack on the Confederate center. A furious battle raged at the rail breastworks. Southern counterattacks temporarily bolstered the Confederates' crumbling front but Crook, recklessly exposing himself, parried these bloody thrusts. The hand-to-hand combat soon flowed rearward to a second ridge, where White's Federals came in on Crook's left, and the Confederate line collapsed.

Jenkins lay wounded and in Federal hands; his casualties amounted to 538, nearly 23% of his command. The Federals lost 688 men, or almost 10%. In this minor, though extremely vicious, engagement, the Union victory enabled Crook to burn New River Bridge, a major objective of the raid. But the Union general, learning of Grant's repulse at the WILDERNESS, abandoned the raid 11 May.   —JDW

Cobb, Howell.

CSA/CSP b. Jefferson Cty., Ga., 17 Sept. 1815. As a child, Cobb moved to Athens, Ga., with his family (including brother THOMAS R. R. COBB, a future lawyer and Confederate army officer), graduating from the University of Georgia in 1834. Admitted to the bar in 1836, Cobb became a congressman, 1843–51, 1855–57; Speaker of the House, 1849–51; and governor of Georgia, 1851–53. He was also a close friend of James Buchanan, in whose nomination and election as the 15th president he played an important role; in 1857 Buchanan named Cobb secretary of the treasury. An advocate of compromise until the election of Abraham

USMHI

Lincoln to the presidency, Cobb in early Dec. 1860 addressed a letter to the people of Georgia urging immediate secession. In Feb. 1861, when delegates from the seceding states met in Montgomery, Ala., to organize the Confederacy, Cobb chaired the convention and enjoyed some support for the presidency.

While serving as speaker of the Provisional Congress, Cobb organized the 16th Georgia Infantry, accompanying it to Yorktown as its colonel. He was named a brigadier general 12 Feb. 1862 and led his brigade creditably on the retreat up the PENINSULA and in the SEVEN DAYS' CAMPAIGN. After fighting with the brigade at CRAMPTON'S GAP, 14 Sept., and ANTIETAM, 17 Sept., Cobb was detached from the ARMY OF NORTHERN VIRGINIA in October and returned to the Deep South.

On 9 Sept. 1863 Cobb became a major general and was placed in command of the District of Georgia and Florida. In this role he was responsible for the suggestion that led to the establishment of the prison at ANDERSONVILLE, and in the 1864 Georgia campaigning he commanded the Georgia reserve corps.

After the collapse of the Confederacy Cobb resumed his law practice and vigorously opposed the RECONSTRUCTION policies of the RADICAL REPUBLICANS. On 9 Oct. 1868 he died in New York City and was buried in Athens' Oconee Hill cemetery.
—ECB

Cobb, Thomas Reade Rootes. CSA/CSP b. Jefferson Cty., Ga., 10 Apr. 1823. In 1842 Cobb was admitted to the bar, having graduated from the University of Georgia 1st in his class. He was assistant secretary to the state senate during the late 1840s and 1849–57 was a state supreme court reporter.

Early in his career Cobb developed a reputation as a talented constitutional lawyer with a great capacity for work, qualities that were demonstrated in the 20 volumes of Georgia supreme court reports he edited and in the digest of Georgia laws he published in 1851. The latter has been described as "unique in America" for its methodology and comprehensiveness.

LC

During the late 1850s, while his brother, former Georgia governor HOWELL COBB, urged loyalty to the Union and compromise on SLAVERY, Thomas crusaded for secession, his speeches strongly influencing the Georgia general assembly and the state's citizenry. At the state secession convention of 1861, he advocated formation of the Confederacy. Politically, he felt that the South could "make better terms out of the Union than in it." In time, he was appointed to the Provisional Confederate Congress and helped write the new nation's constitution.

Soon after war broke out, Cobb surprised many colleagues by rejecting further political posts to recruit a military unit in Georgia. Though lacking military experience, he received a colonelcy and command of a force of mixed arms afterward known as COBB'S LEGION. He served diligently if awkwardly in North Carolina, on the Virginia peninsula, and in the James River fortifications. His lack of military training was a handicap ("I have to study hard, utterly inexperienced as I am, to maintain myself in the drill," he wrote to his wife), but he soon became a proficient soldier. His political skills served him well in command, for the infantrymen and troopers in his legion often feuded: "It requires all of my tact and patience to keep them all harmonious."

In Sept. 1862, Cobb's men suffered heavily at ANTIETAM, costing him "the flower of my battalion." 6 weeks later he had to leave this remnant when given a brigade in Maj. Gen. LAFAYETTE MCLAWS' division/Army of Northern Virginia. On 13 Dec. his command held a stone wall at the base of Marye's Heights at FREDERICKSBURG. Late in the day, while Cobb's troops repulsed one of 6 attacks on their position, his thigh was shattered by a musket ball. Despite medical aid, he bled to death in a house on the battlefield.
—EGL

Cobb's Legion. In June 1861 Confederate Congressman THOMAS R. R. COBB of Georgia set out to raise a regiment of cavalry. Learning that Gov. JOSEPH E. BROWN could make available only 300 carbines, Cobb decided to form instead a 10-company outfit of mixed arms: 300 troopers, 600 infantrymen, and 100 artillerists. Soon after being recruited, organized, and sent to Virginia, Cobb's Legion lost its artillery company, which was left behind to defend Georgia.

At the outset, the military inexperience of Cobb and his men, and friction between the infantry and cavalry units, hobbled the legion. But in time Cobb became an able field commander and his troops some of the hardest fighters in the Confederacy. The legion began its field service Sept. 1861 on the Virginia peninsula, then briefly saw duty along the North Carolina coast in early 1862. It suffered heavy losses at ANTIETAM, lost its commander to a mortal wound while holding a strategic position at FIRST FREDERICKSBURG, and shortly before CHANCELLORSVILLE was permanently divided into 2 units, one of horsemen, the other of foot soldiers. Prodded by the Confederate War Department, which had come to view a legion as an unwieldy organization, Gen. ROBERT E. LEE ordered both units recruited to regimental strength. He then placed the cavalry, led by Col. PIERCE M. B. YOUNG, in Brig. Gen. WADE HAMPTON's brigade of Maj. Gen. J.E.B. STUART's mounted division, and he assigned the infantry, under Lt. Col. Luther J. Glenn, to Brig. Gen. WILLIAM T. WOFFORD's brigade/I Corps/Army of Northern Virginia.

Both regiments established distinguished combat records. Each saw heavy action during Lee's summer 1863 offensive, the cavalry making what Stuart called a "brilliant" charge to turn the tide at BRANDY STATION and again clashing with Union horsemen at Hunterstown and GETTYSBURG; and the infantry helping decimate the Union III Corps near the PEACH ORCHARD and WHEATFIELD at Gettysburg, 2 July. 3 months later the foot troops accompanied Lt. Gen. JAMES LONGSTREET to Georgia and Tennessee, arriving too late to participate at CHICKAMAUGA, then making a spirited but costly assault at KNOXVILLE, under Maj. William D. Conyers.

Returning to Virginia for the 1864 campaign, the Cobb's Legion infantry fought from the WILDERNESS to APPOMATTOX, winning distinction on several fields. Meanwhile, the cavalry, under Young and his successor, Col. Gilbert J. Wright, participated in most of Stuart's and Hampton's battles, notably at TREVILIAN STATION and along the railroad south of PETERSBURG. Early in 1865 the troopers accompanied Hampton to South Carolina, finishing the war by opposing an enemy that had recently invaded their home state.
—EGL

Coburn, Abner. war governor b. Canaan, Maine, 22 Mar. 1803. The son of a wealthy timber magnate and state legislator, Coburn spent most of his youth farming, attending a local academy, and teaching school. He became a surveyor and in 1830 joined his father's land-purchase and lumber business, which became the largest landowner in Maine, later expanding into other states.

By 1854 Coburn and his younger brother had become railroad developers, Abner as president of the Maine Central. Prior to the war, he also served 3 terms in the state legislature as a Whig (1838, 1840, 1844), before helping to establish the REPUBLICAN PARTY in Maine. In 1860 he ran for governor but, despite support from prominent officials, failed to win his party's nomination. In 1863 he received the nomination without difficulty and won at the polls, though the sluggishness of the war effort produced a strong Democratic challenge and provided him only a small majority.

It has been said that "as governor Coburn gave Maine a clean, honest, business-like administration, making appointments and awarding contracts with regard to the interest of the state rather than that of the politicians." He was an eager if unspectacular supporter of the Lincoln administration and did much to bolster his state's ardor for the war. However, his relatively unsophisticated approach to politics and the still uncertain course of the war in late 1863 combined to deprive him of a second term. Seeking to broaden party support, Republican officials passed over him in favor of a WAR DEMOCRAT, SAMUEL CONY, who succeeded Coburn.

After leaving the governor's chair, Coburn held no major political office but devoted himself to his businesses, to charity work, and to state education, bequeathing heavily to the University of Maine and Colby College. He died in Skowhegan, Maine, following a long illness, 4 Jan. 1885. —EGL

Cocke, Philip St. George. CSA b. "Bremo Bluff," Fluvanna Cty., Va., 17 Apr. 1809. "Shattered in health and mind" is the documented reason given for Cocke's suicide after only 8 months' service in the Confederate Army.

Graduating 6th in the class of 1832 at the U.S. Military Academy as a brevet 2d lieutenant, Cocke maintained that rank with the artillery at Charleston, S.C. On 13 July 1833 he became adjutant of the 2d Artillery but resigned in favor of farming in 1834. As an agriculturist, Cocke wrote *Plantation and Farm Instruction* (1852) and was voted president of the Virginia Agricultural Society 1853–56. He also served on the board of visitors at the VIRGINIA MILITARY INSTITUTE for 9 years.

LC

After serving on the Advisory Council of the State of Virginia in the state's secession process, he accepted an appointment as brigadier general in command of the frontier district at the Potomac River. He was later commended by Gen. Robert E. Lee for his defensive policies and by Gen. P.G.T. Beauregard for his actions as a colonel at BLACKBURN'S FORD. The Battle of Centreville was Cocke's last before he took his own life in Powhatan Cty., Va., 26 Dec. 1861. —FLS

Cockrell, Francis Marion. CSA b. Johnson Cty., Mo., 1 Oct. 1834. Reared on a farm, Cockrell attended log-cabin schools and at 20 graduated with honors from Missouri's Chapel Hill College. He took up law and was admitted to the bar in 1855, thereafter practicing in Warrensburg. An avid secessionist, in 1861 he enlisted as a private in the pro-Confederate Missouri State Guard of Gen. STERLING PRICE. Rising quickly to captain, he served in the 3d Missouri at CARTHAGE, WILSON'S CREEK (where he was cited for his "discretion and soldierly bearing"), and PEA RIDGE.

During the SECOND VICKSBURG CAMPAIGN Cockrell was con-

spicuous at Grand Gulf as colonel of the 1st Missouri Infantry. Captured at Vicksburg and later paroled, he was appointed a brigadier general to rank from 18 July 1863. Under his tutelage, his 1st Missouri Brigade became one of the best-drilled and most effective commands in the Army of Tennessee. In May 1864 Cockrell and his troops won the THANKS OF THE CONFEDERATE CONGRESS for their publicly renewed "pledges of fidelity to the cause of Southern independence."

LC

During the ATLANTA CAMPAIGN the brigade served in the division of Maj. Gen. SAMUEL G. FRENCH, often with distinction. At KENNESAW MOUNTAIN, for example, it sturdily resisted an attack on its trench line, repulsing numerous Federal regiments. It accompanied Gen. JOHN BELL HOOD into Tennessee late in 1864, Cockrell being severely wounded at FRANKLIN (by war's close he had accumulated 5 wounds). Having recovered, he led a division under Lt. Gen. RICHARD TAYLOR in the Siege of MOBILE.

After Taylor's surrender, May 1865, Cockrell returned to Warrensburg, resumed his law practice, then charged into politics. As a Democrat he served 5 consecutive terms in the U.S. Senate, beginning in 1875. When he left Congress in 1905, he was appointed by Pres. Theodore Roosevelt as a member of the Interstate Commerce Commission. The pinnacle of his political career came during the Democratic national convention of 1905, when he was nominated for the presidency by Democratic politicians James Beauchamp, "Champ" Clark and William Jennings Bryan. Later, he served as a civilian member of the Board of Ordnance and Fortifications until his death in Washington, D.C., 13 Dec. 1915. —EGL

coehorn mortar. See MORTAR.

Coffeeville, Miss., eng. at. 5 Dec. 1862 Maj. Gen. U.S. GRANT's first march to Vicksburg followed the Mississippi Central Railroad out of southwest Tennessee. On 1 Dec. resisting Mississippi Confederates, close by the railroad north of Abbeville, pulled out of south-bank entrenchments along the Tallahatchie River and moved south. Union XIII Corps' cavalry commander, Col. T. Lyle Dickey, ordered to pursue, gathered his troops near Abbeville 2 Dec. and skirmished with Confederate Maj. Gen. EARL VAN DORN's rear guard through town, down the railroad, and through Oxford.

On 3 Dec. Dickey divided his force in 4: 1 regiment secured Oxford; Col. John K. Mizner's men, dispatched west, roved the right flank looking for the enemy; Cols. Albert L. Lee and Edward Hatch headed up 2 columns, Hatch's traveling the Coffeeville Road south and Lee's moving down a parallel route on the east. Grant sent Dickey encouragement to press the Southerners as far as possible. Hatch hit stout resistance on the Yocknapatalfa River. Following behind his columns, Dickey sent word forward ordering Lee to ride to Hatch's support, cross the river, and then press on for Coffeeville.

Dickey caught up with his force the next day below the Yocknapatalfa at Water Valley and found that rough terrain and resistance had kept Lee and Hatch from receiving orders.

They met at Water Valley by accident after Hatch was driven from the hamlet by superior numbers. At Dickey's direction, Mizner also arrived shortly.

Federal units, some scattered below the Confederates at Grenada, others to the west, composed the nearest support. Dickey, unsure of enemy numbers behind or in front, decided to press pursuit one more day, perhaps making contact with other Federal forces.

Dickey's men crossed the Otuckalofa River south of Water Valley the morning of 5 Dec., pressing down the Coffeeville Road as one column. They hit Van Dorn's skirmishers at 2 p.m., fanned out forming a broad front, and moved within a mile of Coffeeville. Resistance briefly cooled. Having hauled 2 cannon with them, they probed the enemy's front with artillery fire. From a screened front Confederates answered with 6 cannon and sent an infantry battle line forward.

Maj. Gen. MANSFIELD LOVELL and Brig. Gen. LLOYD TILGHMAN, Van Dorn's subordinates, commanded the defense. Federals, reeling under superior fire, organized a fighting retreat and withdrew, alternating defensive lines. Tilghman admitted that "the tactics of the enemy did them great credit," but volunteered pursuit. With Col. WILLIAM H. JACKSON's 700 cavalry and about 600 infantry, he pressed Dickey's force until nightfall, when the Federals secured a superior position opposite a large open field. The engagement broke off.

Dickey's cavalry returned to Grant's lines unmolested. The pursuit from the Tallahatchie netted them 750 prisoners, 200 horses, 4 wagons, and $7,000 in Confederate money. Losses at Coffeeville were 10 killed, 63 wounded, and 43 captured. Lovell reported 7 killed and 43 wounded. Van Dorn summed up the engagement in a 2-sentence report, saying Federals had learned a lesson about pursuit. —JES

Coffin, Charles. journalist b. Boscawen, N.H., 26 July 1823. In summer 1861 Coffin was visiting Washington, D.C., when the FIRST BATTLE OF BULL RUN broke out. Recently laid off from the Boston *Journal*'s reportorial staff, he raced off to cover the battle anyway, hoping to sell his story to the paper as a freelance reporter. His coverage of the fight was timely and complete and won him reinstatement on the paper's staff, beginning his career as a WAR CORRESPONDENT. According to many sources he was the only reporter to cover all 4 years of the Civil War.

A farmer and surveyor, Coffin had an elementary and some secondary schooling, helped install Boston's first electric fire-alarm system, then took up newspaper work in 1853. After being an assistant editor on the Boston *Atlas* 1856–57, he was associated with the Boston *Journal*. Following his coverage of First Bull Run, Coffin was one of few reporters who traveled between the Eastern and Western war theaters, assuming the pen name "Carleton."

Coffin was known for "scooping" his competitors and was the first Union correspondent to report Brig. Gen. Ulysses S. Grant's victory at FORT DONELSON, Tenn. His stories included the battles at ANTIETAM, GETTYSBURG, and the WILDERNESS, the 1863 bombardment of CHARLESTON by Adm. Samuel Du Pont's fleet, Lincoln's GETTYSBURG ADDRESS, the fall of FORT FISHER, and the capture of Richmond and Lincoln's triumphal visit there. Human-interest pieces like those dispatched from his tour of conquered Atlanta, as well as his battle reports, won him a national following. At the end of the war he filed the first story on the Union flag-raising ceremonies at Fort Sumter.

In the postwar decades he turned his war experiences into 8 books; toured Europe, Asia, and the American West; wrote 11 children's books and travel books; penned 2 novels; and gave over 2,000 lectures. He was elected to the Massachusetts state assembly in 1884 and to 1 term in the state senate in 1890. Coffin made his home in Boston, where he died 2 Mar. 1896. —JES

Cold Harbor, Va., First Battle of. 27 June 1862 *See* GAINES' MILL, VA., BATTLE OF.

Cold Harbor, Va., Second Battle of. 1–3 June 1864 The Battle of Cold Harbor was the final major engagement of the OVERLAND CAMPAIGN of 1864. Throughout May 1864 the armies of Maj. Gen. GEORGE G. MEADE and Gen. ROBERT E. LEE were stalemated: 3 times the combatants collided, at the WILDERNESS, SPOTSYLVANIA, and NORTH ANNA, and 3 times Lee's veterans foiled Federal plans in deadly fighting. A pattern emerged—the Northerners sidled leftward, closer to Richmond, with the Confederates always there first, blocking the path.

On the night of 26 May, from behind the North Anna River, the Union army initiated another movement beyond the Confederate right flank. Lt. Gen. ULYSSES S. GRANT, personally directing operations of Meade's army, ordered Maj. Gen. PHILIP H. SHERIDAN with 2 cavalry divisions southeastward. The cavalrymen rode throughout the night in a pelting rainstorm, and by 9 the next morning had secured a vital crossing on the Pamunkey River.

For the next 2 days the 4 Union infantry corps shuffled toward the river. By the end of the 28th Grant had 3 corps across the stream, rimming Hanover Town, on the road to Richmond. During this second day Union Brig. Gen. DAVID M. GREGG's cavalry division, reconnoitering to the west, struck 3 brigades of Confederate cavalry on a similar mission. For 6 hours the 2 forces, fighting dismounted, contested the ground around Haw's Shop.

Since Grant's departure from the North Anna, Lee had cautiously begun moving toward the Confederate capital. The wily general believed correctly that Grant would cross near Hanover Town; with the intelligence gathered at Haw's Shop, Lee's 3 infantry corps were covering the roads between the Federals and Richmond by darkness of the 28th. The artery of approach still open passed through New and Old Cold Harbor.

Throughout the 29th and 30th, little movement occurred, though skirmishes flared periodically along the front. The 2 armies had now become so interlocked that each could readily discover the other's movements. Grant received reinforcements from Bermuda Hundred—the XVIII and part of the X corps, numbering 16,000. Lee, likewise, secured Maj. Gen. ROBERT F. HOKE's 6,000-man division from the defenses south of Richmond.

By the morning of 31 May, the crossroads village of Cold Harbor had assumed an importance it had not known for 2 years. Grant ordered Sheridan to seize the town and the intersecting roads. Approaching the village by 2 roads, the Union troopers encountered Brig. Gen. FITZHUGH LEE's horsemen. The Federals, in a spirited attack, drove the Confederates from the crossroads. When the Northern advance struck Southern infantry, Sheridan withdrew after dark. On the way back to his former camp, the cavalry commander received orders to hold the crossroads at all hazards. The Federals retraced their route, built a line of breastworks, and slept.

When Lee learned late on the 31st of Sheridan's movement, he ordered Lt. Gen. RICHARD H. ANDERSON, commander of the I Corps, to retake the crossroads early 1 June. At dawn Anderson's troops advanced on the blue-clad cavalrymen. 2 brigades of Maj. Gen. JOSEPH B. KERSHAW's division led the charge. Advancing across an open field in serried ranks, the Confederates stormed forward. Sheridan's troopers, armed with SPENCER repeaters, riddled the Southerners' lines, killing a brigade commander. The Confederates reformed and came again, only to be swept back by a withering fire.

About noon Union Maj. Gen. HORATIO G. WRIGHT's VI Corps replaced the cavalrymen. Wright, ordered to attack when Maj. Gen. WILLIAM F. SMITH's XVIII Corps arrived, waited the entire afternoon. Smith had been ordered to the wrong place, not arriving until 4 o'clock. Finally, an hour later, 6 Union divisions charged against Anderson and Hoke. The Federals momentarily broke through on one part of the line, but a Confederate counterattack dislodged the Northerners. In this brief, furious assault Union losses amounted to 2,650, while the Confederate casualties were probably slightly less.

The news of Wright's and Smith's repulse concluded a difficult day for Grant, one of disjointed operations and missed opportunities. Rightly believing that an early morning, coordinated attack at Cold Harbor could secure the field, Grant ordered Maj. Gen. WINFIELD S. HANCOCK's II Corps on an all-night march to the crossroads. What Grant asked for, however, the army could not deliver. The torpid heat, suffocating dust, and bone-weary fatigue slowed Hancock's march to a crawl. Not until 6:30 a.m., 2 June, did the exhausted leading elements of the corps reach Cold Harbor. Grant held the assault till 5 p.m., but additional delays and the condition of Hancock's men finally canceled the attack until the next morning. The best opportunity of the entire 30-day campaign had slipped by.

This failure provided Lee and his army all the time they required. Throughout the 2d, the Confederate general funneled his units toward Cold Harbor. By late afternoon the entire army was filing into their positions along the front, which extended for 7 mi, from Pole Green Church on the north to Grapevine Bridge on the south. The expert Confederates blended their line with all the natural features of the land. With interlocking sectors and overlapping fields of fire, the position was probably the best the Army of Northern Virginia ever defended.

Precisely at 4:30 a.m., 3 June, the Army of the Potomac, in double lines along a 6-mi front, charged the nearly impregnable position. Many in the 40,000-man attack force, expecting to be killed, had earlier pinned to their blouses papers with their names on them. The concealed Confederates waited patiently; with the precision of veterans, the earthworks suddenly bristled with thousands of rifles. Seconds later, in a volcanic blast of sound and flame, the Confederate line erupted. Then, as a Southerner said, the "inexplicable and incredible butchery" began.

Along the entire Federal line, the Northerners crumpled in heaps from sheets of lethal flame; men fell on top of men. Wright in the center and Smith on the right made little headway in the raking crossfire. Only on the Union left did 2 brigades of Hancock's corps penetrate the Confederate line. Momentarily the Federals stood on the breastworks before being blown away by rifle and canister fire. The assault along the entire front had been completely repulsed in less than a half-hour.

Nearly 7,000 Federal soldiers had been killed or wounded in the charge, while fewer than 1,500 Confederates were casualties. Grant always regretted this frontal assault, though he had believed Lee's back had been to the wall and one more assault might have crushed the Confederate army and ended the war. Instead, Cold Harbor became perhaps the most terrible of all Civil War names.   —JDW

Cold Spring Foundry. *See* WEST POINT FOUNDRY AT COLD SPRING, N.Y.

Colfax, Schuyler. USP b. New York City, N.Y., 23 Mar. 1823, Colfax, the son of a Revolutionary War general, left school at age 10 to help support his widowed mother. In 1836, 2 years after she remarried, the family moved to New Carlisle, Ind. There Colfax clerked in his stepfather's store until 1841, when the latter relocated in South Bend. That year his stepfather, active in local Whig politics, arranged to have Colfax appointed deputy auditor of St. Joseph County, which subsequently elected the younger man to the U.S. House of Representatives, 1854–69. During his early years in South Bend, Colfax became a journalist, contributing articles on political issues to HORACE GREELEY's New York *Tribune.* As editor of the South Bend *Free Press,* he purchased the newspaper in 1845, renaming it the St. Joseph *Valley Register.* The newspaper became an influential Whig organ while Colfax gained stature as a Midwestern politician and the nickname the "Little Greeley of the West."

A moderate on slavery, Colfax opposed the COMPROMISE OF 1850 and later the KANSAS-NEBRASKA ACT. When the Whigs dissolved, he joined the Know Nothing party until his election as a Republican congressman in 1854. Described as a liberal by colleagues, he promoted the establishment of an overland mail route and a transcontinental telegraph to link the East with the Western territories, and lobbied for passage of the homestead and land-grant college bills (*see* HOMESTEAD ACT; MORRILL ACT).

Colfax urged President-elect ABRAHAM LINCOLN to stand firm against "the heresy of peaceable secession" Nov. 1860, but also supported Republican efforts to make any honorable concessions necessary to appease the South. Though willing to restore the MISSOURI COMPROMISE, he voted against the CRITTENDEN COMPROMISE because it would have extended the 36° 30' line to the Pacific Ocean. Anticipating that the war would last longer than a few months, Colfax energetically worked to organize and equip Indiana troops for the field, though he himself did not enlist. Throughout the war he supported programs aimed at improving soldiers' welfare.

Many Republicans considered the industrious Indianan a strong candidate for a cabinet appointment, but Lincoln chose Missourian EDWARD BATES to represent the Midwest in his administration. Colfax nonetheless continued to support the president's war aims, including income tax, emancipation, conscription, and passage of the 13th Amendment. In Dec. 1863 he was elected Speaker of the House, an office he retained for 6 years.

As a Radical Republican who wanted Southerners to behave penitently after their defeat, Colfax in Nov. 1865 delivered a speech that became the basis for Congressional RECONSTRUCTION. He helped pass the Civil Rights Act over Pres. ANDREW JOHNSON's veto and threw his support behind passage of the 14th Amendment. When every Southern state except Tennessee refused to ratify the amendment, Colfax became a proponent of Military Reconstruction and a powerful figure in bringing impeachment charges against Johnson.

Colfax's radical stance and his years of experience in government resulted in his election to the vice-presidency on the ticket with ULYSSES S. GRANT in 1868. Called "Smiler" Colfax by his detractors, his emotionally charged campaign speeches defended Congressional Reconstruction, called for just treatment of veterans, and played heavily on the war prejudices Northerners felt toward the defeated South.

The Republicans did not nominate Colfax for reelection in 1872, partly because of his premature decision to retire, and partly because of Grant's dissatisfaction with him. Colfax was charged with accepting bribes to vote in favor of awarding the Union Pacific Railroad contract to Crédit Mobilier of America; though the charges were not substantiated, they sealed his retirement in 1873.

Colfax returned to South Bend, remaining an influential political force without again holding elective office. A popular speaker, he traveled widely during his later years to lecture on political topics. On 13 Jan. 1885 he died from a heart attack at the Mankato, Minn., railroad station as he was coming home from a lecture tour. His body was returned to South Bend for burial.   —PLF

Collins, Napoleon. USN b. Pa., 4 Mar. 1814. Collins, one of the most colorful and maligned Civil War naval personalities, received his midshipman's appointment from Iowa in June 1834. 6 years later he was promoted to lieutenant, serving aboard the sloop *Decatur* in the Mexican War. Through spring 1862 of the Civil War, he was assigned to the SOUTH ATLANTIC BLOCKADING SQUADRON, taking part in the capture of PORT ROYAL, S.C.

Promoted to commander 16 July and given command of the *Octorara,* Collins took 12 prizes off the Bahamas Nov. 1862–June 1863, during which time his capture of the British schooner *Mont Blanc* created a minor international incident. The court at Key West decided in favor of the U.S., citing that Collins had "probable cause" to detain the vessel, but the government demurred publicly, reprimanding Collins for "inconsiderate conduct," over the disapproval of Navy Sec. GIDEON WELLES.

Rather than remove the controversial commander from active duty, the secretary rewarded Collins by giving him command of the USS *WACHUSETT,* with orders to patrol the coast of Brazil in search of CONFEDERATE CRUISERS. That October he located the CSS *FLORIDA* at anchor for repairs in the port of Bahia. Prohibited by Brazilian authorities from battling the *Florida* in neutral waters, Collins waited until a large contingent of enemy officers and crew went on shore leave, took the cruiser in tow in the middle of the night, and hauled it to Hampton Roads, Va. This time Collins faced a court of inquiry when the *Florida* sank under questionable circumstances as the commander was returning it to Bahia under orders. Privately U.S. authorities approved the capture; publicly, amends had to be made for violating international neutrality laws. Collins was sentenced to dismissal, but Welles refused to approve the window-dressing censure, instead promoting Collins to captain in July 1866.

The next year he faced charges of negligence when his ship *Sacramento* wrecked in the Bay of Bengal. Welles suspended him until Mar. 1869 and assigned him to a tour of duty inspecting lighthouses. In Aug. 1874 the Navy Department advanced Collins to rear admiral with command of the South Pacific Squadron. Well regarded by South Americans during his year-long tour, he died at Callao, Peru, 9 Aug. 1875.   —PLF

Colorado Territory. Organized as a territory in 1861, Colorado was not actively involved in the Civil War until the following year. Its settlers had come from both North and South and during the war served in both the Federal and Confederate armies, though its governor pledged support to the Union. Colorado contributed 3 regiments of cavalry, 1 light artillery battery, and 2 infantry companies, for a total of 4,903 men for the Union. About the same number went to other areas to join Confederate units.

There were no major battles in the territory, but Colorado soldiers served in Kansas, New Mexico, Oklahoma, and Missouri, suppressing Indian raids and guerrilla attacks or protecting stage lines and army forts. One military engagement in 1862 was significant in halting a Confederate invasion of NEW MEXICO TERRITORY. In February Colorado volunteers joined with Col. CHRISTOPHER "KIT" CARSON and Federal troops at VALVERDE, New Mexico Territory, hoping to stop Brig. Gen. HENRY H. SIBLEY, who was moving north along the Rio Grande with a brigade of Texas troops to claim the Western lands for the South. The Confederates swept on to occupy Albuquerque and Santa Fe. In March Sibley's force was defeated at Apache Canyon and GLORIETA PASS by troops under Col. JOHN M. CHIVINGTON, Colorado's "Fighting Parson," and the Confederates fell back, ending hopes of invading the Southwest.

Unfortunately for Chivington's reputation as a model officer, he became notorious after 29 Nov. 1864 when he led Colorado volunteer troops in a bloody massacre of 300 Cheyenne and Arapahoe Indians camped peaceably at Sand Creek, near Fort Lyon, where they had been promised protection by the army. (*See* SAND CREEK MASSACRE.) The brutal attack provoked a great wave of Indian outbreaks throughout the West, beginning with a massive raid at Julesburg 7 Jan. 1865 and continuing with attacks on railroad lines, stage stops, army garrisons, and ranches.   —FSK

Colquitt, Alfred Holt. CSA b. Walton Cty., Ga., 20 Apr. 1824. The son of a Democratic senator, Colquitt, who became an ardent secessionist, was educated in local schools and in 1844 graduated from the College of New Jersey. After studying law, he was admitted to the Georgia bar in 1846 and a year later entered the army to fight in the Mexican War, leaving the service as a major and staff officer.

Returning to law, Colquitt practiced in Macon until named assistant secretary of the Georgia senate in 1849 and elected to the U.S. House of Representatives in 1852. In 1854, because of the poor health of his wife, he temporarily left politics,

LC

returning after her death the next year. In 1859 he served in the Georgia legislature and in the campaign of 1860 was a presidential elector for JOHN C. BRECKINRIDGE of Kentucky. Colquitt was a delegate to the Georgia secession convention of 1861 and did not hesitate to follow his state when it left the Union.

In May 1861 he was elected colonel of the 6th Georgia Infantry, having been promoted from captain, and served throughout the PENINSULA CAMPAIGN, seeing action at WILLIAMS-BURG and in the SEVEN DAYS' CAMPAIGN, so distinguishing himself that he attained brigade command under Maj. Gen. DANIEL H. HILL at ANTIETAM. He was appointed a brigadier general to rank from 1 Sept. 1862 and served in that grade at FREDERICKS-BURG and CHANCELLORSVILLE. In 1863 he accompanied Hill to North Carolina, where he served until being transferred to Florida early the next year.

The high point of Colquitt's career occurred at OLUSTEE, 20 Feb. 1864, where his handling of one of Brig. Gen. JOSEPH FINEGAN's brigades helped ensure a Confederate victory. He participated less conspicuously at DREWRY'S BLUFF, during a Union attack on the Richmond defenses 16 May 1864. After taking part in the siege of PETERSBURG, he surrendered in North Carolina 1 May 1865.

With the return of peace, Colquitt was licensed as a Methodist preacher but elected not to serve in the ministry. He resumed law and farming, fought bitterly against Congressional RECONSTRUCTION, and in 1876 was elected governor of Georgia by the largest majority in state history until that time. After serving 6 years, he entered the U.S. Senate, where he remained until his death in Washington, D.C., 26 Mar. 1894.
—EGL

Colston, Raleigh Edward.

CSA b. Paris, France, 31 Oct. 1825. The adopted son of a Virginia physician, Colston came to the U.S. in 1842. Entering the VIRGINIA MILITARY INSTITUTE, he graduated 4 years later, at which time he joined the faculty of his alma mater as a professor of French, remaining there until 1861.

When the war began, Colston was appointed colonel of the 16th Virginia and 24 Dec. 1861 received promotion to brigadier general and command of a brigade of 3 regiments. During the PENINSULA CAMPAIGN he served in Maj. Gen. JAMES LONGSTREET's command. For his service at WILLIAMSBURG, he received a mild commendation in the reports,

USMHI

but for his disputed role at SEVEN PINES, 31 May–1 June 1862, he was mildly rebuked. After the latter battle he was stricken with a long and obscure illness, leaving the army until December.

In spring 1863 Maj. Gen. THOMAS J. "STONEWALL" JACKSON chose his old VMI colleague to command Brig. Gen. WILLIAM B. TALIAFERRO's brigade. Colston was the senior brigadier of the Stonewall Division and, when its commander, Maj. Gen. ISAAC R. TRIMBLE, could not return to command because of a crippling wound, he assumed divisional leadership. With limited combat experience, and having been with the division less than a month, Colston led it at CHANCELLORSVILLE. Because of his performance there, for reasons not fully clear, Colston was relieved of his command 20 May 1863. In the early morning Confederate assault on 3 May, Colston apparently lost control of his

troops. The blame was not entirely his, for the division was sadly depleted of officers. More importantly, perhaps, Colston, ordered to advance that afternoon, reported that he could not; his superiors may have judged this a failure, a crucial flaw that meant he could never regain his soldiers' confidence.

Assigned to Gen. P.G.T. BEAUREGARD at PETERSBURG, Va., Colston served under him during the operations there in 1864. When the war ended, he commanded Confederate forces at Lynchburg.

After the war, Colston joined the Egyptian army as a colonel. Badly crippled in a fall from a camel, Colston returned to the U.S. in 1879. He died impoverished in the Confederate Soldiers' Home in Richmond 29 July 1896.
—JDW

Colt Army and Navy revolvers. Of all the handguns used during the Civil War, the Colt Army and Navy models were by far the most popular. The major difference between the 2 models lay in their caliber; the model designation, however, was not necessarily indicative of their use, for Navies were used by the army and Armies by the navy.

The Model 1860 Army revolver was a 6-shot weapon in .44-caliber that fired a cartridge loaded from the front of the cylinder, which had to be capped before the weapon could be fired. Although an awkward system, it was one of the most advanced of its time. Some Army revolvers were fitted with shoulder stocks, and some had fluted cylinders, but the majority were plain holster revolvers. The gun weighed 2 lb, 11 oz. All together, about 200,000 of these guns were made 1860–72, of which 127,156 were purchased by the U.S. government, and about 4,800 by the Navy; an additional 2,219 were purchased on the open market. The final delivery date for the weapons under government contract was Nov. 1863. Apparently because Colt was charging $13.75 per gun while other contractors, such as REMINGTON and STARR, were producing weapons at lower prices, no more orders were placed.

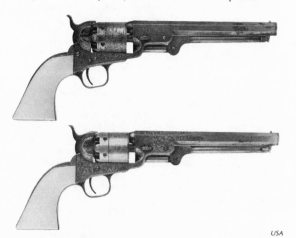

USA

Colt Navy revolvers

The Colt Model 1861 Navy revolver was similar in most respects to the Army model, except for its .36 caliber. Although some of the parts were scaled down, the weight of the gun was the same as the Army model, and, while designated the Navy model, of the 38,000 revolvers produced, only about

4,000 were bought by the U.S. Army and only 650 by the Navy. A fine weapon, the revolver was handicapped by Colt's excessive pricing, which resulted in the termination of government contracts in 1863. Production was curtailed by the burning of the factory in 1864. Most Navy revolvers appear to have been privately purchased. —LDJ

Colt repeating rifle. The Colt rifle, more properly known as the Colt-Root Model 1855 percussion repeating rifle, saw service with a number of well-known Civil War units, the most illustrious being BERDAN'S SHARPSHOOTERS. It came in a bewildering variety of models, in calibers ranging from .40 through .64 (.44, .50, and .56 were the most common), in a number of barrel lengths, and with cylinders holding either 5 or 6 shots. There were civilian as well as military models, both of which were purchased by Northern and Southern states, before and during the Civil War.

The Colt-Root rifle was essentially a large version of the Colt-Root revolving pistol. The dominant features of the rifle were its side hammer, patented by Elisha Root, Colt's armory superintendent, 25 Dec. 1855; the solid frame of the cylinder, also Root's contribution; and the revolving cylinder itself, which was Colt's invention. The first U.S. government order for these rifles was received Oct. 1856, when 100 rifles were purchased. Between this initial delivery and 1859, Colt supplied 765 of these rifles to the government. With the war, increased orders were placed, and Jan. 1861–mid-1866, 4,712 additional rifles were delivered.

The fairly small number of rifles ordered was probably a result of their greatest handicap, the tendency of one round to set off all the cylinders at once. Because Berdan's men complained about this deficiency and also because they had initially been promised SHARPS rifles, they were resupplied with Sharps. Their old rifles went to several Michigan regiments, who carried them during the PENINSULA CAMPAIGN. In the West the 21st Ohio Volunteer Infantry was instrumental in stopping Lt. Gen. JAMES LONGSTREET's breakthrough at CHICKAMAUGA with their Colt-Root rifles. A number of Confederate companies, including some Mississippi units and part of the 1st Virginia Battalion, also had Colt-Roots at the beginning of the war. In general, however, while the Colt-Root seemed to be a promising weapon, in practice it proved complicated and dangerous and was therefore not popular. —LDJ

Columbia, S.C., capture of. 17 Feb. 1865 In Feb. 1865 Maj. Gen. WILLIAM T. SHERMAN moved through South Carolina on his way north from Savannah, Ga., to Virginia. Sherman's right wing was Maj. Gen. OLIVER O. HOWARD's Army of the Tennessee (XV and XVII corps), which moved by sea from Savannah to Port Royal Sound and then marched inland, threatening both Charleston on the right and Columbia on the left. Meanwhile, Sherman's left wing, under Maj. Gen. HENRY W. SLOCUM, marched into South Carolina above Savannah, threatening both Augusta to the left and Columbia to the right.

Confederate defense forces were scattered—at Augusta, near Port Royal Sound, and at Charleston. The Confederates were unsure of Sherman's objective and unable to unite to oppose his advance. On 7 Feb. the Federals cut the Augusta-Charleston railroad near Blackville. The Confederates were forced back across the Edisto River. Gen. P.G.T. BEAUREGARD, commanding the Southern forces opposing Sherman, ordered his troops to concentrate at Chester and Cheraw, thus aban-

NA

doning the central part of the state to Sherman with only token opposition.

Slocum and Howard continued their advance, the former marching toward Lexington and the latter on Columbia. On 16 Feb. a division of the XV Corps reached Columbia, and the city was formally surrendered.

On 17 Feb., as the Federals entered the city, retreating Confederates set fire to bales of cotton that had been piled in the streets. High winds and drunken soldiers spread the blaze, and over half the city was destroyed before the flames were brought under control. Each side blamed the other.

The Federals remained in Columbia until 20 Feb. before they continued their northward march. —RMcM

Columbiad. The Columbiad was a smoothbore heavy-artillery piece capable of firing both shot and shell with a heavy charge at a high angle of elevation. Ideally suited for defending narrow channels, it was the mainstay of American coastal fortifications prior to and during the Civil War.

The 50-pounder Columbiad was invented in 1811 by Col. George Bomford but saw only limited service and was obsolete by the Civil War. In 1844 the Columbiad was revived, this time in both 8- and 10-in. models, and eventually in a 12-in. that proved too weak for service. The Model 1858 Columbiad was a streamlined version of the 1844, with a strengthened breech. The previous models had had chambers in the breeches, which were eliminated in the 1858 and later models. The 1861 Model, manufactured in 8-, 10-, 13-, 15- and 20-in. calibers, was cast by the Rodman process (see RODMAN SMOOTHBORE) in which the bore was integral with the gun.

The Confederate Columbiads were generally manufactured to the 1861 specifications, but instead of being cast by the Rodman method, they were cast solid and then bored out. This weapon is sometimes rather confusingly known as a "Confederate Rodman," even though it had nothing to do with Rodman's process. Some Confederate Columbiads are distinguishable from their Union counterparts by their rather long trunnions. The Confederates attempted to band and rifle some of their Columbiads, which proved capable of firing 225-lb bolts a distance of 1,100–1,800 yd.

The Civil War marked the end for the Columbiad. Heavier rifled artillery developed during the war rendered these guns obsolete, but while they held sway, Columbiads proved to be formidable weapons. —LDJ

Columbus Iron Works Co. Next to Atlanta, Columbus was Georgia's busiest industrial center during the war; following Atlanta's capture by Sherman, Sept. 1864, Columbus almost singlehandedly carried the state's contribution to Confederate industry. The number and size of its war factories, plus its centralized location and the quality of its transportation facilities, prompted JOSIAH GORGAS, chief of Confederate ordnance, to term Columbus "the nucleus of our Ordnance establishment."

One of the city's largest and most productive firms was the Columbus Iron Works Co. Founded in 1853, the 5-building complex was taken over at the outset of the war by the Confederate navy, becoming the Confederate States Naval Iron Works. In this capacity, it produced a variety of equipment for the Southern fleet, principally engines, machinery, ordnance, and ammunition.

Early in 1862 a visitor there observed in operation "twelve or fifteen large and small lathes and customary machinery, also a large foundry." The foundry boasted an air furnace capable of melting 20 tons of pig iron "at a heat" to make brass field pieces, shot and shell, and equipment for warships of all types. Perhaps the foundry's most notable product was a rare item of ordnance, a 2.75-in. breechloading rifle, made of wrought iron. How many were produced is unknown; only 1 survives today, displayed in Columbus adjacent to a marker noting that it was bored in 1863 from the shaft wheel of a river steamer.

On 16 Apr. 1865 the foundry's life came to an end when Federal cavalry under Brig. Gen. JAMES H. WILSON captured Columbus while raiding from Gravelly Springs, Ala., to Macon, Ga. As his objective was the economic and military destruction of the Lower South, Wilson had one of his subordinates, Col. Edward F. Winslow, torch and blow up every building of the works, rendering the complex inoperable. —EGL

Committee of Thirteen. On 20 Dec. 1860, the day South Carolina seceded, the U.S. Senate appointed 8 Democratic and 5 Republican legislators to investigate measures to avert the disunion crisis. To ensure representation of the dominant interests, the committee was composed of 3 border-state Democrats (ROBERT M. T. HUNTER, Virginia, and Lazarus W. Powell and JOHN J. CRITTENDEN, Kentucky); 2 Lower South Democrats (JEFFERSON DAVIS, Mississippi, and ROBERT A. TOOMBS, Georgia); 3 Northern Democrats (STEPHEN A. DOUGLAS, Illinois, William M. Bigler, Pennsylvania, and Henry M. Rice, Minnesota); 2 Republican moderates (WILLIAM H. SEWARD, New York, and Jacob Collamer, Vermont); and 3 Radical Republicans (BENJAMIN F. WADE, Ohio, James W. Grimes, Iowa, and James R. Doolittle, Wisconsin).

The committee met 22 Dec. with Crittenden as chairman, and immediately agreed that any recommendations placed before the Senate must first have the support of both Democratic and Republican majorities in the committee. Crittenden, a longtime admirer of Henry Clay, presented an outline for 6 constitutional amendments to safeguard Southern slave interests. The proposals, which were based on Clay's COMPROMISE OF 1850, offered a moderate course of action known as the CRITTENDEN COMPROMISE.

Toombs, speaking for Southern extremists, submitted inflammatory demands calling for slavery to be protected in all the territories, the surrender of all escaped slaves without a writ of *habeas corpus,* and a stipulation that no laws pertaining to slavery be passed without a majority approval by the Southern

states. To these Davis added a resolution assigning to slave property the same constitutional guarantees as any other property. The concessions, obviously unacceptable to Republicans, would have restored to the South the political power it had been losing over the preceding 3 decades.

After consulting with President-elect Lincoln, who refused to retreat from his commitment to prevent the spread of slavery, Seward introduced 3 resolutions as repugnant to the Southerners as Toombs's demands were to the Republicans and the Northern Democrats. Advancing Lincoln's hard-line position, he advocated enforcing the fugitive slave laws but wanted the repeal of all state laws in conflict with Federal law and unopposed submission to congressional legislation. The final resolution stated bluntly and emphatically "that the Federal Union must be preserved."

After 7 hours of discussion, Crittenden called for a vote on his compromise, the only one with any chance of passing. But the measures were defeated when all of the 5 Republicans voted no because they would not agree to reestablishing the MISSOURI COMPROMISE line. Without a display of "sincere assent" from the opposition party, Toombs and Davis also cast negative votes, killing the proposals before they reached the Senate floor.

Had the Republicans relented, the war might have been delayed, but in Lincoln's mind delay would have betrayed his Northern constituents and destroyed Republican credibility by abandoning the party's commitment to contain slavery.

—PLF

Committee of Thirty-three. When the secession crisis peaked, the U.S. House of Representatives appointed 1 representative from each state to discuss compromise solutions to end the movement toward disunion. This counterpart to the U.S. Senate's COMMITTEE OF THIRTEEN was formed at the suggestion of Virginia Congressman Alexander R. Boteler and began meeting mid-Dec. 1860.

2 proposals reached the floor, the first from Maryland Republican HENRY W. DAVIS, who introduced a plan to admit New Mexico as a slave state since it was a slave territory. The concession would have permitted slavery in a large block of land above the MISSOURI COMPROMISE line. Moderate Republicans expected to lose little by the arrangement, since they believed slavery could not survive within the region.

The second compromise attempt called for an inalterable amendment to the Constitution guaranteeing no interference with slavery in the existing states, and was meant to reassure Southerners of an honest Republican conciliatory effort; it also included provisions to repeal the North's personal liberty laws and to enforce the FUGITIVE SLAVE ACT.

These proposals might have passed as a constitutional amendment had not events moved so quickly. Both houses of Congress approved them as a bill, submitting it to the states as the first Thirteenth Amendment, and 3 states ratified the measure before it was rendered moot by circumstances.

Though the Committee of Thirty-three failed, hampered by radicals in both camps, it came closer than any other body to delaying the war. —PLF

Committee on the Conduct of the War. On 31 Jan. 1862 Brig. Gen. CHARLES P. STONE of the Army of the Potomac appeared before the Committee on the Conduct of the War to defend himself against charges of disloyalty and incompetence. Stone had been overall commander of the force defeated at BALL'S BLUFF, Va., 21 Oct. 1861. He was forced to appear alone in a secret session before the committee, without the right of counsel or a chance to face his accusers. Stone was subsequently arrested on Sec. of War EDWIN M. STANTON'S orders and placed in solitary at Fort Lafayette, N.Y., his military career ruined. He had become the first victim of the committee and of civilian interference in the war effort.

Originally proposed Dec. 1861 to inquire into the Union disasters at BALL'S BLUFF and FIRST BULL RUN, the committee became a body with broad powers of investigation over the entire war effort. Under the leadership of RADICAL REPUBLICANS "Bluff" BENJAMIN WADE, ZACHARIAH CHANDLER, and GEORGE W. JULIAN, it became a threat to all conservative and Democratic generals in the Union army. The committee directed its main attack against GEORGE B. MCCLELLAN, whom they considered soft on slavery, and tried to strike at him through his subordinate generals, Stone and FITZ JOHN PORTER. The committee also did its best to support Radical and abolitionist generals, throwing its support to BENJAMIN F. BUTLER, JOHN C. FRÉMONT, and JOSEPH HOOKER long after these generals had proved their incompetence. Congress enlarged the committee's powers in 1864, and committee members delved into the Battle of FORT PILLOW and the treatment of Union prisoners, exaggerating both as propaganda issues to stir the public demand for vengeance.

Although the committee was able to sway President Lincoln on such issues as emancipation and the dismissal of McClellan, which he partially favored, it had little effect when he disagreed. Powerless without the cooperation of the executive branch, the committee was unable to dispose of Gens. GEORGE G. MEADE and ULYSSES S. GRANT and Sec. of War WILLIAM H. SEWARD. It continued to push the Radical cause and a harsh RECONSTRUCTION policy until June 1865, when it was disbanded. —CMS

Commodore Perry, USS.

A wooden steamboat only 143 ft long, the *Commodore Perry* was developed by the Federal government into a war vessel that earned an impressive record along the sounds of North Carolina and Virginia.

The ship was equipped with 4 heavy guns, later increased to 6. Its ferry-boat pilothouse was armored, and a casemate of iron plates was added to protect the gunners. The *Commodore Perry* was placed under command of Lt. Cmdr. Charles W. Flusser, an officer recognized for his bravery and, toward the end of the war, killed on board the USS *Miami* in its fight with the CSS *ALBEMARLE.*

The *Commodore Perry* was headed southward Nov. 1861 when it ran into a gale below Cape Hatteras. Badly damaged, it was sent to Baltimore for repairs.

The ship's first action came 7 Feb. 1862 off North Carolina, when it aided in capturing the Confederate battery on Roanoke Island. On the 10th it destroyed the Southern flagship *Sea Bird* at New Berne and a few days later led a fleet to attack and destroy the town of Winston, an enemy stronghold. Throughout spring and summer 1862 the vessel made several captures and in October, despite an outbreak of typhoid fever on board, aided in attacks on Plymouth, N.C., and Franklin, Va.

The ship was as busy the following year, but in Feb. and Apr. 1864 it participated in failed expeditions up the Nansemond River from Hampton Roads. Moreover, in the James River it was unable to gain a foothold leading to Richmond.

By late July its boiler was so badly damaged that it was sent

USMHI

to Norfolk for repairs. Though it came back into service, its action was over, and it lay as a part of the NORTH ATLANTIC BLOCKADING SQUADRON until the war ended.

Originally purchased in New York for $38,000, with repairs totaling $56,431.12, the *Commodore Perry* was eventually sold at auction to the New York and Brooklyn Ferry Co. for $16,200. The investment of $78,231.12 was vastly offset by the ship's many captures. —VCJ

commutation.

Written into both Union and Confederate draft laws was a provision allowing draftees to pay a commutation fee to escape military service. Though defended as a way to keep skilled labor out of the army, it quickly became little more than a legalized form of draft evasion.

The Confederacy kept commutation to a minimum only because the Southern Congress approved an extensive exemption list 5 days after it approved the Conscription Acts of 16 Apr. 1862. For the most part, the $500 commutation clause applied to pacifist religious sects—Dunkards, Mennonites, and Quakers. Overseers or slaveowners in charge of 20 (later 15) or more slaves were initially exempted as well, but when Congress revised the draft laws, May 1863, they too became subject to the $500 provision. Overseers were also required to prove that they had been employed before the act went into effect. (*See* TWENTY-NEGRO LAW.)

Few hired plantation managers used the loophole—at the end of 1863, 200 were listed as excused in Virginia, 120 in North Carolina, 301 in South Carolina, and 201 in Georgia—but its existence nurtured the increasingly bitter belief that draft legislation favored the rich. Strict limits on commutation did not prevent Confederate men from evading military service with ingenious ploys: some hired substitutes, moved to states where they were ineligible for the draft as temporary residents, or took prolonged "vacations" outside the Confederacy.

The Federal Congress provided for few exemptions in its Draft Act of 3 Mar. 1863, but the vast number of Northern men available to the draft permitted promiscuous use of the commutation clause, which was based on precedents set by old militia acts and on practice followed by foreign governments. Of the 292,441 men whose names were drawn in the first draft in August, 52,000 paid the $300 commutation fee for total exemption, and many could afford to do so every time their names came up. During the war 4 out of every 10 draftees were found eligible for military service, and 2 of the 4 paid the commutation. Postwar records show 86,724 draftees buying their way out of service, exclusive of those who hired substitutes.

To the Northern public, commutation appeared to raise more money than men, with the poor and immigrants supplying the men. In the South, commutation implied upper-class favoritism, with the army ranks being filled by the poor. One class-conscious journalist predicted that the Union army would soon be made up of "not one man able to pay $300. Not one!" —PLF

company. North and South, a company was considered any unit of 50–100 soldiers commanded by a captain. Generally, 10 of these made up a REGIMENT, though regiments of artillery and cavalry sometimes contained more. Each company was to be subdivided into 4 squads commanded by a sergeant or corporal, and each company in a regiment was required to have an official letter (or number) designation for purposes of record: e.g., Company B/4th Ohio Volunteers. Many also had colorful local names such as the Clinch Rifles, the Davis Guard, and the Rankin Grays. —JES

company fund. The company fund was made up from the savings of the post fund, which was derived from a tax on SUTLERS and savings from the post bakery and stores. The savings were distributed to each company and, under strict regulations, were available for the purchase of supplemental food or minor items for use and distribution through the entire company. The governing rules were identical in both Union and Confederate armies. —JES

Compromise of 1850. When the SLAVERY issue threatened to dissolve the Union in 1850, 72-year-old Kentucky Sen. Henry Clay placed before Congress several provisions that he hoped would placate sectional antagonisms. After 10 weeks of intense debate, the bill, which STEPHEN A. DOUGLAS of Illinois shepherded through the legislative process, reached the Senate floor as a modified but politically brilliant compromise measure, calling for California to be admitted as a free state; for the passage of a strict FUGITIVE SLAVE LAW; for new territories in the Southwest to be allowed to organize without restrictions on slavery; for protecting slavery in the District of Columbia while abolishing domestic slave trade there; and for a settlement of $10 million to Texas if the state would relinquish claims to certain lands in NEW MEXICO TERRITORY.

The leading statesmen addressed their colleagues and a crowded gallery on the importance of subverting sectional interests to solve the nation's great dilemma and restore the balance of power. Clay argued that the North had little to lose by giving the Southern states what they wanted—laws ensuring the protection of slavery. Virginian JAMES M. MASON read JOHN C. CALHOUN's carefully prepared speech to the audience: the old STATES RIGHTS theorist was too ill and frail to deliver it himself. Calhoun eloquently reiterated the Southern position: if the South could not be made secure on the slavery issue, it would never remain within the Union. The words had a powerful effect on Congress, which passed Clay's compromise in Sept. 1850. The people and their representatives were lulled

into believing the nation's problems had been solved, but the statesmen had bought a fragile peace that lasted scarcely a decade. —PLF

Comrades of the Southern Cross. In Aug. 1863, after attending meetings of the Chattanooga, Tenn., Masonic Lodge (and perhaps being inspired by them), Confederate Maj. Gen. PATRICK R. CLEBURNE conceived and urged organization of the Comrades of the Southern Cross, a fraternal organization within the Confederate army binding soldiers in "exalted oneness of action." Cleburne, Chaplain Charles T. Quintard, and Brig. Gens. ST. JOHN R. LIDDELL and JOHN C. BROWN met 28 Aug., adopted a constitution and the name Comrades of the Southern Cross, and planned to disseminate the organization throughout the army. Campaigns through early 1864 limited its growth, but the comrades' ritual, in part, was adopted by the UNITED CONFEDERATE VETERANS after the war. —JES

***Conestoga,* USS.** The *Conestoga* was one of 3 wooden steamers purchased by the U.S. Navy in Cincinnati, June 1861. Comdr. JOHN RODGERS had the steamers converted into gunboats and sent to Cairo, Ill., where the *Conestoga,* 572 tons burden, under Lt. Comdr. Samuel L. Phelps, was assigned to protect the Federal positions, in addition to scouting Western rivers for enemy batteries and troops. During 1861 the ship captured 2 Confederate steamers on the Cumberland River and helped break up an enemy force at Canton, Ky.

NA

In Jan. 1862 the *Conestoga* became part of the combined army/navy task force that attacked FORT HENRY, Tenn. Following the capture of the strategic post, it participated in operations against FORT DONELSON and ISLAND NO. 10.

Early in 1863, under Lt. Comdr. THOMAS O. SELFRIDGE, the ship joined another army/navy force that opened up communications on the White River, control of which was assured after the capture of Confederate batteries at St. Charles, Ark., 14 Jan. 1863. Thereafter, Selfridge and his men continued to capture enemy vessels and break up guerrilla stations.

In Mar. 1864 the *Conestoga* was part of a naval squadron reconnoitering the Ouachita River in Louisiana preliminary to the RED RIVER CAMPAIGN. On 8 Mar. the USS *General Price* accidentally struck the *Conestoga,* causing it to sink in only 4 minutes, with the loss of 2 of its crew. —NCD

Confederate River Defense Fleet. Confederate Maj.

Gen. MANSFIELD LOVELL impressed 14 river steamers at New Orleans 15 Jan. 1862. At the suggestion of riverboat captain James E. Montgomery and others, Lovell and Confederate Sec. of War JUDAH P. BENJAMIN obtained funds to compensate owners and outfit the boats as a river defense fleet. On Benjamin's instructions they were not to be organized under the navy; their captains were to be selected from experienced river men and commissioned into the army. Their crews were to be lightly armed with cutlasses, their sterns to carry 1 heavy cannon, and their prows heavily armored and fitted out as RAMS. The armored Union gunboat fleet at Cairo, Ill., on the Mississippi River, was to be their first objective.

Nothing ever worked well for the river defense fleet. The Confederate treasury could not afford the cost of maintaining the ships. Montgomery was commissioned as a fleet commander, but 3 of the captains he selected were denied commissions because of questionable Confederate loyalty. Confederates evacuated Columbus, Ky., the proposed base for the attack on Cairo, and the assault had to be canceled. The arrival of Union Navy Capt. DAVID G. FARRAGUT's fleet at New Orleans caused a public outcry and the recall to that port of 6 boats in Montgomery's fleet.

The remaining portion of the defense fleet had its first engagement at PLUM RUN BEND, near Fort Pillow, Tenn. At the urging of Fort Pillow's Confederate commander, Col. M. JEFF THOMPSON, 10 May 1862, Montgomery took his ships against the Union IRONCLADS *Mound City, Cincinnati, BENTON, CARONDELET,* and *Pittsburg.* To the Confederates' amazement, though badly battered, they won the Battle of Plum Run Bend, sinking the *Cincinnati* and *Mound City* in ramming attacks. Despite success, the defense fleet's crews, Confederate infantrymen, were unhappy with their duty and asked Thompson and other commanders for relief.

The Battle of MEMPHIS, 6 June, was the defense fleet's last. In a spectacular engagement they took on the more sophisticated Union ram fleet commanded by Col. CHARLES R. ELLET and were badly cut up. Only 2 of Montgomery's boats, the *General Van Dorn* and the *GENERAL STERLING PRICE,* escaped with little damage. Thompson removed some men from the crews, dispatched the surviving boats to different assignments, and the defense fleet was disbanded.   —JES

Confederate Veteran. This magazine was established Jan. 1893 by journalist Sumner A. Cunningham, a former sergeant major in the 41st Tennessee Infantry, publishing biographies and memoirs of Southern soldiers and articles about reunions, monument dedications, and Confederate army life in general. After Cunningham's death in 1913, Edith Pope took over the publication, which continued till Dec. 1932. Complete 40-year runs of *Confederate Veteran* in its original format are located at Newberry Library, Chicago; University of South Carolina, Columbia; Tennessee State Library, Nashville; State Department of Archives and History, Jackson, Miss.; Princeton University, Princeton, N.J.; Cleveland Public Library, Ohio;

CV

North Carolina State Library, Raleigh; College of William and Mary, Williamsburg, Va.; University of Texas, Austin; Nashville Public Library, Tenn.; George Peabody College, Nashville, Tenn.; Cossett Reference Library, Memphis, Tenn.; Washington and Lee University, Lexington, Va.; North Texas State College, Denton; Western Kentucky State College, Bowling Green; and U.S. Army Military History Institute, Carlisle, Pa.   —PLF

Confiscation Act of 1862. The Second Confiscation Act, approved by Congress 16 July 1862, contained the first definite provisions for emancipating slaves in the rebellious states.

Under the act, Confederates who did not surrender within 60 days of the act's passage were to be punished by having their slaves freed. The act also dealt with a problem that plagued field commanders occupying Southern territory. As troops advanced, slaves sought refuge in Union camps, and Federal commanders were confused over their obligations to the refugees. Some freed the slaves, others sent them back to their masters for lack of means to care for them. The Confiscation Act of 1862 declared all slaves taking refuge behind Union lines captives of war who were to be set free.

Though the act implied a willingness to emancipate, at the convenience of the government, it offered blacks no guarantee of civil rights. Instead, it incorporated provisions for transporting and colonizing any black consenting to emigrate to some tropical country that was prepared to guarantee them the rights and privileges of free men. A clause requiring the consent of the freedmen to be colonized was approved after much controversy in Congress. (*See also* ÎLE À VACHE.)

RADICAL REPUBLICANS, who envisioned distributing confiscated lands to former slaves, succeeded in passing the bill only after agreeing to President Lincoln's demand to limit seizure of Confederate estates to the lifetime of the offender.

Lincoln's limited emancipation gesture applied only to states in open rebellion. The same act granting freedom to Confederate slaves guaranteed the return of fugitives from the BORDER STATES to any owner who could prove loyalty to the Union. Lincoln could not risk alienating these states, and he hoped that one part of the bill, calling for gradual, compensated emancipation, would draw Virginia and Tennessee back into the Union.

Essentially, the Confiscation Act of 1862 prepared the way for the EMANCIPATION PROCLAMATION and solved the immediate dilemma facing the army concerning the status of slaves within its jurisdiction.   —PLF

Congress, Confederate States. The Provisional Confederate Congress, the first of 3 congresses to convene during the 4 years of Southern nationhood, met in Montgomery, Ala., 4 Feb. 1861 for the first of 5 sessions. Patriotic enthusiasm ran high among delegates from the 7 states already seceded. None of the representatives held elective office; rather, each arrived as an appointee of a secession convention or of his state government. Delegates immediately assumed legislative function of government and within 6 weeks drafted a constitution, elected JEFFERSON F. DAVIS president and ALEXANDER H. STEPHENS vice-president, authorized raising an army, and established a financial basis to support the new nation. Though divided on many issues, their "Great Debate" concerned the admission of nonslave states into the Confederacy, which radicals feared would in time lead to a second sectional conflict.

The men engaged in this taxing work represented the South's

best political talent, well-educated, experienced legislators drawn mainly from the propertied class. Ironically, the fire-eaters among them, the radical secessionist leaders, were pushed into the background as the government took shape. While their impassioned rhetoric had served the purpose of SOUTHERN NATIONALISM, the cooler-headed moderates now assumed power. As the hesitant states joined the Confederacy, the Provisional Congress, a unicameral body, swelled to 106 members before ELECTIONS were held later in the year. On the whole members endorsed Davis' emergency war measures during his early months in office, approving 3-year ENLISTMENTS, suspension of *HABEAS CORPUS,* and appropriations requests. Congress did challenge several of Davis' cabinet appointments but confirmed his choices quickly when they came to a vote. (*See also* CABINET, CONFEDERATE STATES.)

Before the end of the year the relationship between Congress and the executive began to deteriorate rapidly and would continue to do so with dreadful intensity until the government collapsed. Davis' dictatorial attitude toward the infringement of presidential power aggravated the conflict, but at its heart lay the inconsistency between the insistence on STATES RIGHTS and the wartime need for strong central government controls. Bitter opposition delayed or weakened critical legislation on CONSCRIPTION, taxation, IMPRESSMENT, martial law, and control over the military. The bicameral First Regular Congress (18 Feb. 1862–7 Dec. 1863) passed a series of stringent acts to keep and provision an army in the field by measures Davis or one of his cabinet members initiated; congressmen were generally compelled to support administration programs because they had none better to propose. They debated but failed to renew the suspension of *Habeas Corpus,* never enacted the constitutional provision for a supreme court, approved but never created a badly needed general staff for the military, and delayed passing critical impressment and income-tax legislation until spring 1863. By fall 1862 a desperate, openly hostile Congress had lost faith in Davis' conduct of the war, launching several unnecessarily vindictive investigations into various government departments, alienating the press with a policy of secret, closed-door sessions, and spending too much energy waging personal battles with the president.

War-weary voters expressed dissatisfaction with the administration and their representatives in fall 1863 by electing a startling number of "peace" men to office. Idealistically, the Confederate founding fathers had hoped to nurture a 1-party system to avoid tainting their patriotism with partisan politics, but what began as vigorous pro- and anti-secessionism now evolved into factions arguing either for peace at the bargaining table or peace on the battlefield. Between the internecine struggles the Second Regular Congress (2 May 1864–18 Mar. 1865) finally did renew suspension of *habeas corpus* in cases of treason, DESERTION, and aid to the enemy, and passed a strict conscription act and an extensive if thoroughly inadequate funding act. To their credit, they debated and in desperation approved limited emancipation for Southern blacks and their enlistment in the army. (*See* BLACK TROOPS, CONFEDERACY APPROVES USE OF.) All these measures came too late to save the Confederacy.

Among the most vitriolic critics of the administration were LOUIS T. WIGFALL, a senator from Texas who in disgust resigned his seat to join the army; Sen. ROBERT M. T. HUNTER, a persistent states rights Virginian; Vice-President Stephens, a prominent peace advocate; and Rep. HENRY S. FOOTE of Tennessee, who was censured by his Congressional colleagues for his trea-

sonous overtures to Washington early in 1865. Nor was the administration entirely bereft of supporters in the legislature. Georgia Sen. BENJAMIN H. HILL, South Carolina Sen. ROBERT W. BARNWELL, Virginia Rep. and Speaker of the House THOMAS S. BOCOCK, and Mississippi Rep. Ethelbert Barksdale backed Davis consistently. And despite a serious lack of nationalistic vision, when the final votes were called, the Confederate politicians as a whole displayed a remarkable willingness to support, "for the good of the country," measures they opposed, even when those measures violated the states rights doctrine. (*See also* CONSTITUTION, CONFEDERATE.)   —PLF

Congress, United States. In spring 1861, as Southerners organized a government in MONTGOMERY, ALA., Northern congressmen held "Union" or "war" meetings across the country. With the Southern legislators gone, declared newly elected Rep. Isaac N. Arnold of Illinois, Congress at last constituted "a unit against treason and rebellion."

With the exception of a few still hoping for compromise, he was correct. The politicians staged the rallies to stir war fever, demonstrate unified support for ABRAHAM LINCOLN, and urge the president to pursue an aggressive war policy. Moderate Northern Democrats prudently muffled their opposition; War Democrats could be counted among the most ardent administration supporters. The loss of the Southerners weakened the Democratic party to ineffectiveness, but when the special session of the 37th Congress met 4 July, just over one-fourth of the members were Democrats. Though they were disorganized and no longer in control of the majority, their influence would be felt increasingly over the next 4 years.

During the special session Lincoln called for 4 July, the president asked for and received congressional approval of several emergency war measures already in force, establishing a pattern characteristic of the relationship that would emerge between the executive and legislative branches, one that frequently involved bitter criticism of Lincoln's policies, particularly on the issues of confiscation, *HABEAS CORPUS,* emancipation (*see* EMANCIPATION PROCLAMATION), and RECONSTRUCTION; but Congress ultimately supported the president's broad vision of executive wartime powers, and only once did Lincoln seriously consider vetoing a legislative act (the CONFISCATION ACT of 1862). Before adjourning, the war session formally declared the existence of a state of insurrection and issued a call for 500,000 3-year volunteers.

The initial cordiality between Lincoln and Congress had waned by 1862 as public dissatisfaction with the war's progress inspired legislators to aggressive opposition in anticipation of the fall elections. Though Congress remained firmly in Republican control, several discordant factions emerged. WAR DEMOCRATS demanded reunion with no other conditions attached to peace. Moderate Republicans lined up behind the president in favor of Union, emancipation, and mild Reconstruction; but the increasingly vocal RADICAL REPUBLICANS lashed out against his proposed leniency toward Southerners in conquered territory and condemned his slowness in effecting emancipation. By 1864 a contingent of PEACE DEMOCRATS had organized in response to the nation's war-weariness, favoring conciliatory negotiations with the Davis administration even at the expense of reestablishing the old Union. More disruptive than threatening, the congressional doves clashed with their hawkish colleagues over the former's willingness to make "peace with traitors."

Nevertheless, the Democrats did not attempt to undermine majority will, generally allying with moderate Republicans to block Radical demands for harsh Reconstruction and total emancipation. Civil and military appropriations usually passed both houses with little division, and there was, surprisingly, minimal opposition to Lincoln's insistence that constitutional restraints apply more to Congress than to the president during a state of war. In the face of criticism from state leaders, the legislators consistently voted to strengthen the power of the Federal government by endorsing national controls over the military, direct taxation to fund the war, government aid to industry, and an aggressive program of federally funded internal improvements. Among the major nonwar legislation passed were the MORRILL, HOMESTEAD, and Pacific RAILROAD acts, and the LEGAL TENDER ACTS. Of the government agencies created during the war, the Department of Agriculture stands as a tribute to congressional concern for the nation's economic future.

Not all congressional legislation proved wise, though at the time most of it was directed toward hastening a satisfactory end to the war. Some of the investigatory activities of the powerful Radical-dominated COMMITTEE ON THE CONDUCT OF THE WAR interfered with the war effort more than they helped. And as a body the wartime congressmen were not a particularly distinctive lot, most of them being new to national politics and drawn largely from the rising industrialist class. Yet they were overwhelmingly nationalistic and, beyond their goal of preserving the Union, helped prepare the U.S. to take its place among the world powers.   —PLF

***Congress,* USS.** *See* HAMPTON ROADS, VA., BATTLE OF. 8–9 Mar. 1862.

Conkling, Roscoe. USP b. Albany, N.Y., 30 Oct. 1829. Among RADICAL REPUBLICANS Conkling was known as one of the most vigorous partisans. His career is most often associated with the post–Civil War period, but during the war years he served in the House of Representatives 1859–63 and was a close ally of THADDEUS STEVENS, one of the most prominent Radical Republicans.

When Conkling entered Congress he represented Utica, N.Y. Though raised in Auburn, N.Y., he lived most of his life in Utica, had briefly been the city's mayor before entering Congress, and had also been district attorney in Albany. The sentiments of the district he represented in Congress were strongly pro-war, reflecting Conkling's own feelings, and he took the hardest Republican line on the conduct of the war and on the treatment of slave states conquered by Union armies. His extreme stance brought him into conflict with Congressman JAMES G. BLAINE, a conciliatory Republican, beginning a feud that lasted for most of the rest of the century.

During RECONSTRUCTION, Conkling became the leader of New York State Radical Republicans opposed to Pres. ANDREW JOHNSON's lenient policies toward the conquered South. He was elected to the U.S. Senate in 1867, remaining there till

1881, after which he pursued a profitable law career until his death in New York City, 18 Apr. 1888.   —JES

Connecticut. From its beginning in the mid-1850s the RE-PUBLICAN PARTY, with its opposition to the spread of SLAVERY into the territories, won a wide following in Connecticut under the stimulus of such leaders as the old Jacksonian GIDEON WELLES and Hartford lawyer Joseph R. Hawley.

In 1858 Republicans elected WILLIAM A. BUCKINGHAM governor, a position he held through the Civil War, pursuing an effective policy of supporting the war and the Lincoln administration and urging a rapid end to slavery. In 1863 he was challenged by veteran Democrat and former governor Thomas H. Seymour, who denounced in an active campaign the arbitrary actions of the Lincoln administration, violations of civil liberties, incompetent military leadership, and the excessive cost and waste of the war. But Buckingham rallied the Unionist, antislavery forces to rout the Democrats in the election. With Maj. Gen. WILLIAM T. SHERMAN sweeping through the Lower South and Lt. Gen. ULYSSES S. GRANT moving toward Richmond by the time of the 1864 elections, the Republicans remained firmly in control in Connecticut, which again gave Lincoln a landslide vote.

In military and economic terms Connecticut played a large part in the Union victory. Within 3 days after FORT SUMTER surrendered, volunteers formed 1 military regiment, and in another 3 weeks there were 5 more. All together Connecticut sent more than 50,000 men in 30 infantry units, 1 of cavalry, and 2 of heavy artillery, plus 3 battalions of light artillery, and contributed 250 officers and 2,500 men to the U.S. Navy. Connecticut units took part in every major campaign and battle of the war, notably at ANTIETAM and GETTYSBURG, where losses ran high. By war's end some 20,000 of about 55,000 Connecticut participants were casualties. Connecticut firms and factories turned out 1,000 rifles a month early in the war and doubled that figure by 1864. Powder, cartridges, clothing, and wagons were turned out in quantity, while private civilian groups gave aid and supplies to men at the front and in hospitals.   —DL

Conner, James. CSA b. Charleston, S.C., 1 Sept. 1829. One of the best officers that South Carolina furnished the Confederacy, Conner, a graduate of South Carolina College, became a distinguished lawyer and a U.S. district attorney before the outbreak of civil war.

Captain of the Montgomery Guards, a local militia company, Conner participated in the bombardment of FORT SUMTER, entering Confederate service May 1861 as a captain in the HAMPTON LEGION, a mixed command of cavalry, infantry, and artillery. At FIRST BULL RUN, when Col. WADE HAMPTON fell wounded, Conner led the legion, earning promotion to major, and fought with the unit during the PENINSULA CAMPAIGN through the Battle of SEVEN PINES. In June 1862 Conner became colonel of the 22d North Carolina, serving as its commander for 2 years. A disci-

LC

plinarian, he never earned the volunteer soldiers' affection, but his courage and skill won their respect. At GAINES' MILL, during the SEVEN DAYS' CAMPAIGN, a rifle ball shattered his leg, disabling him for 2 months.

Returning to his regiment, the South Carolinian led his men at CHANCELLORSVILLE and GETTYSBURG, and 1 June 1864 received his promotion to brigadier general. Conner temporarily commanded 2 brigades in succession, seeing action in the PETERSBURG CAMPAIGN, and in late summer 1864 was permanently assigned command of Maj. Gen. JOSEPH B. KERSHAW's old brigade of South Carolinians. On 13 Oct., in a skirmish near CEDAR CREEK, Conner lost the leg that had been broken at Gaines' Mill, but resumed command of the brigade until the war's end.

Returning to his native state after the war, Conner took up his law practice and entered politics, allying himself with his old commander, Hampton, and was elected state's attorney general. d. Richmond, Va., 26 June 1883.   —JDW

Conrad's Ferry, Md., Battle of. 21 Oct. 1861 *See* BALL'S BLUFF, VA., BATTLE OF.

conscientious objectors. Members of several pacifist religious groups conflicted with Union and Confederate officials to defend their conscientious scruples against bearing arms. They tended to suffer most severely in the South, where manpower shortages, a martial spirit, and invading armies left little sympathy for men unwilling to fight. But under each of the opposing governments they sometimes endured violent persecution by civilians, brutal punishment by military authorities, and death by firing squad.

The membership of smaller sects such as Dunkards, Amanists, and Schwenkfelders varied between 800 and 1,200. The largest politically active sects, the Society of Friends (Quakers) and the Mennonites, counted well over 200,000 members in 1860; most lived in the North. Shaker and Quaker leaders sought blanket exemptions for their draft-age men, but most cases throughout the war were resolved individually. Often draftees reported voluntarily to instruction camps, then either refused to serve in any military capacity or requested assignments in hospitals; others expressed willingness to support the war effort by furnishing supplies to the army. Lincoln accepted these alternatives and encouraged objectors to apply for exemptions, thus delaying any legislative attempt to address the problem until the draft became an issue in Aug. 1863.

After passing the South's first CONSCRIPTION act, 16 Apr. 1862, which made no provision for pacifist exemptions, Confederate politicians were prodded into finding solutions acceptable to dissenting religious groups. Some states tried to deal with the problem locally: North Carolina accepted objectors for hospital duty or substitute work in salt mines. But the revised Confederate Exemption Act of Oct. 1862 included a national solution, exempting Quakers, Nazarenes, Mennonites, and Dunkards, provided they furnished substitutes or paid a $500 exemption tax. Some pacifists objected to supplying either men or money to support the fighting, but most complied until the increasing scarcity of both made the alternatives nearly impossible. The difficulty of collecting the exemption fee finally forced the government to abandon the attempt. The October act placed pursuit of conscientious objectors under army control, where pacifists found unexpected sympathy from military leaders who believed using force against

them to be a wasted effort. Lt. Gen. THOMAS J. "STONEWALL" JACKSON recommended allowing pacifists to produce supplies or serve as NONCOMBATANTS.

Pacifists in combat-torn regions such as the SHENANDOAH VALLEY hid or fled with their families to escape being hunted by home guards. By war's end Kentucky Shakers at Pleasant Hill reported having fed at least 50,000 soldiers from both armies and estimated losses in supplies, stock, and buildings at $100,-000. Some Southern pacifists did enlist voluntarily for combat positions, among them a few Shakers and 6–20 Quakers; 2 companies of Moravian men from Forsyth Cty., N.C., were also mustered into the army in June 1861. Most were expelled from their sects during the war but were readmitted afterward.

Greater manpower resources and more tolerant attitudes in general eased the pressures on Northern pacifists. Congress objected to exempting specific religious sects for fear of missing the smaller ones, and a blanket exemption for all conscientious objectors would have invited abuse. Yet the compromise, providing a substitute or paying a $300 commutation fee, violated the principles of men who considered either alternative a contribution to the bloodshed. The Militia Act of 1862 made no provision for conscientious objectors; though the Draft Act of 1863 did, it failed to define "conscientious objector," again resulting in a flood of individual petitions from draftees. In December 1863 Sec. of War EDWIN M. STANTON eased the situation by paroling all conscientious objectors held in custody and ordering no more to be called.

143 Quakers reportedly enlisted as Union soldiers, but the majority of their brethren and of all pacifists served in hospitals, cared for sick soldiers in their homes, or worked among the CONTRABANDS. Finally, in Feb. 1864, Congress dealt with the question by ruling pacifists subject to the draft but assuring noncombatant assignments to members of those religious groups whose articles of faith clearly expressed opposition to bearing arms. They were also given the option of paying $300 for the relief of sick and wounded soldiers.

Though neither government solved the problem of how to deal with conscientious objectors, officials for the first time debated the issue at the national level, offering the option of noncombatant service which remained in effect through World War I.   —PLF

conscription. There was no general military draft in America until the Civil War. The Confederacy passed its first of 3 conscription acts 16 Apr. 1862, and scarcely a year later the Union began conscripting men. Government officials plagued with manpower shortages regarded drafting as the only means of sustaining an effective army and hoped it would spur voluntary enlistments.

But compulsory service embittered the public, who considered it an infringement on individual free will and personal liberty and feared it would concentrate arbitrary power in the military. Believing with some justification that unwilling soldiers made poor fighting men, volunteer soldiers despised conscripts. Conscription also undercut morale, as soldiers complained that it compromised voluntary enlistments and appeared as an act of desperation in the face of repeated military defeats.

Conscription nurtured SUBSTITUTES, bounty-jumping (*see* BOUNTIES), and DESERTION. Charges of class discrimination were leveled against both Confederate and Union draft laws since exemption and COMMUTATION clauses allowed propertied men to avoid service, thus laying the burden on immigrants and men with few resources. Occupational, only-son, and medical exemptions created many loopholes in the laws. Doctors certified healthy men unfit for duty, while some physically or mentally deficient conscripts went to the front after sham examinations. Enforcement presented obstacles of its own; many conscripts simply failed to report for duty. Several states challenged the draft's legality, trying to block it and arguing over the quota system. Unpopular, unwieldy, and unfair, conscription raised more discontent than soldiers.

Under the Union draft act men faced the possibility of conscription in July 1863 and in Mar., July, and Dec. 1864. DRAFT RIOTS ensued, notably in New York in 1863. Of the 249,259 18-to-35-year-old men whose names were drawn, only about 6% served, the rest paying commutation or hiring a substitute.

The first Confederate conscription law also applied to men between 18 and 35, providing for substitution (repealed Dec. 1863) and exemptions. A revision, approved 27 Sept. 1862, raised the age to 45; 5 days later the legislators passed the expanded Exemption Act. The Conscription Act of Feb. 1864 called all men between 17 and 50. Conscripts accounted for one-fourth to one-third of the Confederate armies east of the Mississippi between Apr. 1864 and early 1865.   —PLF

Constitution, Confederate. On 4 Feb. 1861, delegates from the 6 Lower South states meeting in Montgomery, Ala., to form a confederacy, appointed a committee of 12 to frame a constitution. Under Chairman CHRISTOPHER G. MEMMINGER, the representatives worked diligently, and on the 9th submitted to the Provisional Confederate Congress a first draft modeled on the U.S. Constitution, with variations to safeguard STATES RIGHTS and SLAVERY. ALEXANDER H. STEPHENS, the greatest constitutionalist among them, described their objectives as "not to tear down so much as to build up [a government] with greater security and permanency." After debating the document, the delegates ratified the provisional constitution at about midnight on the 8th, then appointed a new committee to frame a permanent constitution.

During the next 5 weeks, after Congress adjourned each day, the committee members met to refine the Constitution to address their accumulated dissatisfactions and create a government under which Southerners could live free of threats to their domestic institutions. Though they adopted verbatim large sections of the U.S. Constitution, including the first 12 amendments, significant differences emerged in the relationship between the executive and legislative branches, and between the states and the central government. The committee provided for a president more powerful than the United States' chief executive, giving him control over appropriations with item veto and the authority to remove political appointees at his discretion.

These prerogatives, however, were counterbalanced by severe restrictions on the power of the central government, establishing the basis for much of the devastating opposition to JEFFERSON DAVIS' wartime measures. To protect and give legitimacy to the states rights' doctrine, the framers abolished federal review of state courts, eliminated protective tariffs, prohibited the federal government from undertaking internal improvements, permitted states to enter into agreements among themselves and maintain armies (though not wage war), required the agreement of only 3 state legislatures to initiate constitutional amendments, and limited the president to 1 6-year term.

Significantly, the framers failed to address secession or NULLIFICATION, fully aware of the danger both could pose to their "permanent federal government." They did, however, guarantee slavery in 3 clauses, prohibit the importation of slaves, reluctantly provide for new states to be admitted with the consent of a two-thirds majority in each house of Congress, and restrict voting rights to Confederate citizens. The federal treasury was to be funded by an export tax on cotton and tobacco, in keeping with Confederate agrarianism.

Designed to preserve the existing order rather than establish a new one, the Constitution reflected conservative, not revolutionary, intentions. Moderate politicians prevailed over the fire-eaters, who had served the purpose of SOUTHERN NATIONALISM and were pushed into the background. The Provisional Congress unanimously approved the Constitution 11 Mar., then sent it to the various state secession conventions and legislatures for ratification. Each accepted it with varying degrees of enthusiasm. None submitted it to the people for a vote.

Though the insistence on states rights ultimately destroyed the infant Confederate nation, its constitution did encompass important improvements in government. Budgetary procedures, the power to remove cabinet officers, the establishment of a civil service, and a limit to the number of presidential terms one person could serve anticipated postwar U.S. constitutional reforms.   —PLF

contrabands. Wherever Federal troops invaded Southern territory, fugitive slaves sought protection behind Union lines. Since the government had no policy for dealing with the runaways, military commanders used their own discretion, according to circumstances. Union political general and abolitionist BENJAMIN F. BUTLER first applied the term *contrabands of war* to fugitives at FORT MONROE when he learned they had been building fortifications for the Confederates. These slaves he did

USMHI

not return to their owners, but later, under different circumstances in Louisiana, he did order fugitives back to Unionist masters.

In summer 1861 several officers recommended returning all fugitives because they had no system of caring for them, a policy generally adopted in the West. The House of Representatives addressed the problem 9 July by passing a resolution absolving the army from any responsibility to capture and return fugitives, but a few weeks later Lincoln interceded on behalf of some Virginia slaveowners seeking to cross the Potomac River to recover their property. The Confiscation Act of Aug. 1861 established the first official policy: any fugitive slave used with his master's knowledge to advance Confederate victory was to be considered a prize of war and set free.

Using these criteria, several commanders set up contraband camps where they provided as best they could for the fugitives' welfare. Lacking funds to carry out extensive relief programs, they provisioned their charges variously, sometimes leasing them to loyal planters or hiring them as laborers for the army. Finally, in Dec. 1862, Brig. Gen. RUFUS SAXTON, then commanding the Department of the South, ordered the refugees under his jurisdiction settled on abandoned lands, issued each laborer 2 acres of land, and gave them tools to plant crops for their own consumption; in exchange, they produced a portion of cotton for government use. Some commanders appointed superintendents to oversee the blacks' welfare, and private relief associations quickly organized to provide additional supplies, supervision, and education.

Despite efforts to care for the contrabands, many were crowded into unhealthy camps, where they died from disease, exposure, or, occasionally, starvation. An official in one camp reported a 25% mortality rate over a 2-year period. Some contrabands returned voluntarily to former masters and many men joined the Union army when permitted to enlist in 1863.

Regardless of relief measures taken, commanders complained chronically of the trouble caused by hordes of contrabands following the army. Congress finally established the FREEDMEN'S BUREAU in Mar. 1865 to provide a formal structure for helping former slaves adapt to their new status.   —PLF

Convention of Rebel States. *See* MONTGOMERY CONVENTION.

Cony, Samuel. war governor b. Augusta, Maine, 27 Feb. 1811. Cony graduated from Brown University in 1829, and was active in the DEMOCRATIC PARTY in the 1830s, becoming an attorney and Maine state legislator. Till 1861 he remained a loyal party man and was, successively, state legislator, a member of the governor's council, a probate judge, and state treasurer.

With the secession crisis, Cony split with party peace advocates, becoming a WAR DEMOCRAT. His loyal support of Lincoln's prosecution of the war won him election to the Maine state legislature again in 1862 after an absence of 23 years. Cony built statewide support for his war-advocacy platform, then gained the governor's office in 1864. In contrast to other Democratic candidates for state executive office, Cony was unopposed by the Lincoln administration, which welcomed his support—most of which, by this late period in the conflict, needed only to be verbal.

Reelected twice by a sound majority, Cony remained in office until 1867. He declined further service because of poor health, and died in Augusta, 5 Oct. 1870.   —JES

Cook, George Smith. photographer b. Stratford, Conn., 1819. At 14, Cook traveled down the Mississippi River to New Orleans, learning the art of daguerreotype photography. By 1849 he had settled in Charleston, S.C. MATHEW BRADY recog-

VM

nized Cook's skill as a master daguerreotypist and in 1851 hired him to manage his New York gallery while Brady traveled to Europe. Over the next few years Cook opened galleries of his own in several Northern cities but turned his attention to Charleston as the South prepared for war.

He made his first wartime photographs of Union Maj. ROBERT ANDERSON and his staff at FORT SUMTER in Feb. 1861; these images quickly became famous, with a ready market in the North. During the early months of war Cook took pictures of soldiers and military installations. Brig. Gen. P.G.T. BEAUREGARD, in command of Charleston's defenses, hired him to make photographic copies of maps and drawings, but Cook's reputation as "the photographer of the Confederacy" rested on the exceptional series of pictures taken of Sumter over the course of the war. 2 of the most dramatic images were made 8 Sept. 1863, from atop a high point on Sumter's fortifications. The first shows Federal monitors firing on Fort Moultrie; when Union troops began firing at Cook as well, he was ordered to a safer location, but not before achieving one of the first pictures of IRONCLADS in action. The second photograph records one of the rare occasions when a photographer was able to capture the image of an exploding shell.

In postwar years Cook moved his operations to Richmond, maintaining studios in several major cities. Though Cook died in Richmond in 1902, his sons operated the studio there until the 1950s. The Cook collection of over 10,000 photographs (more than 500 of these portraits of wartime personalities) is maintained by the Valentine Museum in Richmond. In photographic quality and historical importance, Cook's work rivals the Brady collection at the Library of Congress.   —PLF

Cook, Philip. CSA b. Twiggs Cty., Ga., 31 July 1817. The son of transplanted Virginians, Cook was educated at Oglethorpe University, near Milledgeville, and later at the University of Virginia, from whose law school he graduated in 1841. He led an uneventful life in Madison Cty., Ga., until early 1861, when he volunteered as a private in the 4th Georgia Infantry, whose adjutant he became after being sent with the regiment to Portsmouth, Va.

Cook's military experience in the Seminole War stood him in good stead during the 4th Georgia's early campaigning on the Virginia peninsula in 1862. By the close of the SEVEN DAYS' CAMPAIGN, he had sufficiently

USMHI

distinguished himself to win the lieutenant colonelcy of the regiment. Present for SECOND BULL RUN and ANTIETAM, Cook was promoted to colonel 1 Nov. 1862. He led the 4th Georgia at SECOND FREDERICKSBURG and CHANCELLORSVILLE, being wounded in the leg and cited for gallantry during the latter engagement. After 3 months' convalescence, he retook the field, then secured leave to sit in a session of the Georgia legislature.

When his brigade commander, Brig. Gen. GEORGE P. DOLES, was killed at COLD HARBOR, June 1864, Cook succeeded him. In the Siege of PETERSBURG he was again wounded, then went to the Shenandoah Valley, fighting under Maj. Gen. STEPHEN D. RAMSEUR at CEDAR CREEK. Returning to Petersburg, Cook was wounded again, in the arm, during the aborted Confederate assault on FORT STEDMAN, 25 Mar. 1865. He spent the final weeks of the war in a local hospital and was captured when the city was evacuated, 3 Apr.

Following Gen. ROBERT E. LEE's surrender, Cook settled in Americus, Ga., practicing law and remaining active in politics. From 1873 to 1883 he represented his district in Congress and in 1890 became Georgia's secretary of state, meanwhile serving on the commission that erected the new state capitol in Atlanta. After his death there, 21 May 1894, it was said that "no man in Georgia was more entirely beloved by the people of the state." —EGL

Cooke, Jay. financier b. Brookville, Ohio, 10 Aug. 1821. The scion of a politically powerful family, Cooke made his mark through finance. He left home at 14 to seek his fortune and by 1858 retired a wealthy man through his association with bankers and investors E. W. Clark & Co. of Philadelphia. In his time with them he worked with security sales, railroad finance and development, and in arranging loans to the government to finance the Mexican War. He also made a number of influential contacts in the Northern investment community.

KA

Cooke's family was closely associated with Sec. of Treasury SALMON P. CHASE and the Ohio state Republican party. By summer 1861 the Federal government had an $80 million deficit and only $3 million on hand. Cooke approached Chase with a proposal to sell government bonds on a commission basis. The secretary accepted, and Jay Cooke & Co. successfully pursued sales, helping to introduce "GREENBACKS," Union paper money.

Before the end of the war, Cooke helped secure a $3 million loan for Pennsylvania, promoted Sen. JOHN SHERMAN's Omnibus Revenue Act, and uncovered a scheme by Ketchum, Son & Co. of New York to manipulate government bond sales. During the war Cooke was often accused of profiting immensely by the bond sales and government associations; once, his appointment to sell floating bond issues for the U.S. government was revoked because of congressional suspicions, though it was later reinstated.

At the end of the war it was estimated that Cooke's agency had sold more than $853 million in bonds just between Jan. and July 1865. At times during the war Cooke moved more than $9.5 million in government bonds a day, an effort praised as contributing greatly to Union success in the field. The financier's government associations slackened slightly in the postwar period and Cooke pursued other financial interests until his death in Ogontz, Pa., 16 Feb. 1905. —JES

Cooke, John Esten. author/CSA b. Winchester, Va., 3 Nov. 1830. For an impressionable young writer already steeped in romanticism, the Civil War offered enough exciting experiences to fuel a lifetime of literary endeavor. Cooke, a dashing Virginian self-styled in the Cavalier tradition, greeted the war as a welcome interruption from routine. He had abandoned his law practice early in the 1850s, soon after discovering he could earn a living by his pen with less effort, and by 1861 the nation knew him not as a great author, but as one who created literary pictures of a gracious antebellum Southern society.

An impassioned secessionist, he enlisted as an artillerist in the Confederate army soon after Virginia withdrew from the Union, and fought through to Appomattox. Cooke served as ordnance officer on the staff of flamboyant Maj. Gen. J.E.B. STUART, a close friend and a relative, and had many opportunities to observe first-hand Gen. ROBERT E. LEE and Lt. Gen. THOMAS J. "STONEWALL" JACKSON. From this personal contact he characterized each in his wartime columns for the *Southern Illustrated News.*

His experiences led to *A Life of Stonewall Jackson,* published opportunistically a few months after the hero's death in 1863, and to 5 war-related books written shortly after the surrender. They include 2 novels, *Surry of Eagle's Nest* (1866) and *Mohun* (1870); 2 collections of essays, *Wearing of the Gray* (1867) and *Hammer and Rapier* (1870); and *A Life of Robert E. Lee* (1871), a military biography. His 4 nonfiction works are of uneven quality and must be read with caution because Cooke tended to blend fact and fiction indiscriminately. Though of little historical value, they offer an intriguing vision of the war through the eyes of a soldier-writer who ignored the terrible suffering to see only a grand, swashbuckling adventure. Cooke is supposed to have buried his silver spurs on the surrender field at Appomattox.

After 1871 Cooke turned to other topics, nearly all of them treated nostalgically, idealizing Virginia's past. He died 27 Sept. 1886 from typhoid fever. —PLF

Cooke, John Rogers. CSA b. Jefferson Barracks, Md., 9 June 1833. In the ARMY OF NORTHERN VIRGINIA no brigadier general served more capably or with greater distinction than John Rogers Cooke. Wounded 7 times, he performed with such gallantry and prowess that he received frequent commendation from superiors and subordinates alike and as a regimental and brigade commander had few rivals in an army blessed with many superb officers.

The son of Union Bvt. Maj. Gen. PHILIP ST. GEORGE COOKE and the future brother-in-law of Confederate Maj. Gen. J.E.B. STUART, Cooke was educated at Harvard as an engineer. He entered the Regular Army in 1855 and was directly commissioned a 2d lieutenant, 8th Infantry. When Virginia seceded, he and Stuart went with the Confederacy, while his father remained loyal to the Union, a family breach that would not be healed until long after the war.

Commissioned a 1st lieutenant, he fought at FIRST BULL RUN,

LC

and was promoted to major in Feb. 1862 and chief of artillery of the DEPARTMENT OF NORTH CAROLINA. On 16 Apr. 1862 Cooke assumed command of the 27th North Carolina, and the new colonel led the regiment at SEVEN PINES, where he was wounded. Recovered, Cooke and his regiment distinguished themselves at ANTIETAM. When a Federal attack crushed the Confederate center at "BLOODY LANE," the Southerners faced imminent defeat. Cooke, commanding his regiment and the 3d Arkansas, advanced. The 2 regiments blunted the Federal thrust with withering volleys and then charged. The Northern line wavered and finally broke. Cooke's gallant charge possibly saved the day.

On 1 Nov. 1862 Cooke was promoted to brigadier general, commanding the same brigade until the war's end. At FREDER-ICKSBURG his men held Marye's Heights, repulsing, with other units, the massive Union assaults. At BRISTOE STATION he was ordered into a trap and saw his brigade slaughtered. Cooke suffered a severe wound, as he did later at the WILDERNESS. When the army surrendered at Appomattox, Cooke stood in the ranks with the remainder of his brigade.

He became a merchant in Richmond, Va., after the war and was prominent in civic affairs, co-founding the Confederate Soldiers' Home. He died in Richmond 10 Apr. 1891, and was buried beside his comrades in Hollywood Cemetery.
                                                                                   —JDW

Cooke, Philip St. George. USA b. Leesburg, Va., 13 June 1809. The U.S. Army was Cooke's life for 50 years. Graduating 23d in the West Point class of 1827, he was a veteran of frontier service and the Black Hawk and Mexican wars. He became a dragoon officer, a cavalry tactician, and an explorer in the Far West; in the late 1850s he was also a U.S. observer in the Crimean War.

When the Civil War began he was a colonel, but 12 Nov. 1861 he was commissioned a brigadier general in the Regular Army and given command of the cavalry forces in Washington, D.C. Cooke's sole combat service followed the next spring when he took part in Maj. Gen. George B.

NA

McClellan's PENINSULA CAMPAIGN. He led a cavalry division in front of YORKTOWN and in the battles at WILLIAMSBURG, GAINES' MILL, and WHITE OAK SWAMP. The rest of his war service was administrative: he served on courts-martial until Aug. 1863, commanded the District of Baton Rouge until May 1864, then headed the Union's recruiting service until the Confederate surrender. He is remembered not so much for what he did during the Civil War but for what became of his family.

Cooke had 3 daughters and a son, JOHN R. COOKE, who became a Confederate general. Like her father, one daughter held to the Union cause. The other 2 daughters, one of whom was married to Confederate cavalry commander J.E.B. STUART, allied with the South. This political split estranged the family members for most of their lives and became the subject of national gossip.

The older soldier was brevetted major general for his war service 13 Mar. 1865, and after more administrative duty he

was retired 29 Oct. 1873, a little more than half a century after he had entered West Point. In retirement he wrote books about his army life, dying in Detroit, Mich., 20 Mar. 1895.   —JES

Cooper, Douglas Hancock. CSA b. probably Amite Cty., Miss., 1 Nov. 1815. More than any other Confederate military leader, Cooper represented the South's hope of holding Indian Territory. As U.S. agent to the Choctaw and Chickasaw tribes from 1853 until the war, he exerted tremendous influence over those tribes and over the entire disputed area.

The Confederate War Department authorized Cooper to secure military alliances with several tribes early in 1861. Before ALBERT PIKE, who was appointed Commissioner of Indian Affairs, concluded official treaties, Cooper had raised the 1st Choctaw and Chickasaw Mounted Rifles and was commissioned its colo-

LC

nel. He commanded the Indian troops at PEA RIDGE, where they fought well but were justly accused of scalping and mutilating the dead on the battlefield. Cooper led his men in the fighting against Federal Indian troops at NEWTONIA, Mo., 30 Sept. 1862, which ended in a Confederate victory and temporarily forestalled Federal reoccupation of the territory. Less than a year later, 17 July 1863, his forces were defeated at HONEY SPRINGS, the largest cavalry engagement fought in Indian Territory.

Cooper's Indian troops had a reputation for being undisciplined and undependable. He preferred they fight along with white troops as a means of keeping them under control and resisted attempts to segregate them. His men were usually and most effectively deployed as scouts and skirmishers, and occasionally to track escaped prisoners. Because of their success as raiders, Cooper recommended using his Indians as guerrillas in Missouri, but the plan was never approved because his superiors feared the troops would commit atrocities the North would use as propaganda.

Though an effective leader, Cooper was dominated by ambition. He was promoted to brigadier general to rank from 2 May 1863 but wanted to be named superintendent of Indian affairs with full military jurisdiction over the territory. Special orders were issued to that effect Sept. 1862, but the appointment was withheld pending charges of Cooper's excessive drunkenness. When placed in positions subordinate to Brig. Gens. WILLIAM STEELE and SAMUEL B. MAXEY, he used his influence among the Indians to undermine the officers' authority. He finally received district command of Indian Territory July 1864, and the superintendency Feb. 1865, but never with the independent authority he coveted.

Whatever his motives, Cooper apparently felt some genuine concern for the Indians' interests. He remained in the territory after the war, pressing prewar Choctaw and Chickasaw claims against the Federal government. He died impoverished at Old Fort Washita, Indian Territory, 29 Apr. 1879.   —PLF

Cooper, James. USA b. Frederick Cty., Md., 8 May 1810, Cooper received his education at St. Mary's College and Washington College in Pennsylvania, graduating from the latter in 1832. He studied law under THADDEUS STEVENS in Gettysburg, and passed his bar examinations in 1834. An active member of the Whig party, he was elected twice to the U.S. House of Representatives beginning in 1838. Thereafter he served 4 terms in the Pennsylvania legislature, including 1 term as speaker of the house; as state attorney general in 1848; and as U.S. senator, 1849–55. His participation on the Committee of Thirteen, which drafted the COMPROMISE OF 1850, and his opposition to the KANSAS-NEBRASKA ACT led Abraham Lincoln to appoint him brigadier general as of 17 May 1861. A solid supporter of the administration's policies, he was assigned by Lincoln to recruit troops in Maryland in hopes that he would attract enlistments in his home state.

Cooper served briefly in the field as commander of the 1st Brigade in Maj. Gen. FRANZ SIGEL's division during the 1862 campaigning in the Shenandoah Valley (*see* SHENANDOAH VALLEY CAMPAIGN, JACKSON'S). That September he was placed in charge of Camp Wallace, a facility near Columbus, Ohio, for paroled prisoners of war, and was later reassigned as commander of CAMP CHASE, also in Columbus. He died at his post 28 Mar. 1863. —PLF

Cooper, Joseph Alexander. USA b. Whitley Cty., Ky., 25 Nov. 1823. As a boy Cooper moved to Campbell Cty., Tenn., where he grew up a strong Unionist and farmer. He was a veteran of brief service in the Mexican War and in 1861 was involved in antisecessionist political activity. On Tennessee's secession, he secretly began recruiting Union sympathizers, and months later moved them to Kentucky to be sworn into Federal service as the Union's 1st Tennessee Infantry. Cooper was elected one of its captains.

After combat service in some engagements in Tennessee and at MILL SPRINGS, in Mar. 1862 Cooper received his commission as colonel of the 6th Tennessee, at which rank he saw considerable combat: he was driven from Cumberland Gap with the rest of the Union army, fought in the Battles of STONE'S RIVER and CHICKAMAUGA, participated in the CHATTANOOGA CAMPAIGN, and set out with Maj. Gen. WILLIAM T. SHERMAN's army on the campaign from Tennessee to Atlanta. On 30 July 1864 he was promoted to brigadier general.

Though he had command of a brigade until the end of the war, 3 times between summer 1864 and spring 1865 he had charge of a division: after the battle at JONESBOROUGH, during the FRANKLIN AND NASHVILLE campaigning, and during the advance on BENTONVILLE.

For his war service and gallant conduct at the Battle of Nashville, Cooper was brevetted major general of volunteers on his mustering out of service 15 Jan. 1866. Subsequently he lost a bid for the U.S. Senate in 1868, was collector of Internal Revenue in Knoxville for a decade, continued farming, and at 57 moved his family to Kansas to try his luck at agriculture. d. Stafford, Kans., 20 May 1910. —JES

Cooper, Samuel. CSA b. Hackensack, N.J., 12 June 1798. Northern-born, Cooper was the highest-ranking general in the Southern armies. Graduating from West Point in 1815, he spent 3 decades in the artillery before becoming adept at administrative detail. In 1852 Cooper was appointed adjutant general of the U.S. Army, a position that led to a close friendship with then Secretary of War JEFFERSON DAVIS.

This attachment, the influence of a Virginia wife (the great-granddaughter of Revolutionary-era statesman George Mason), and a home in the Old Dominion were paramount to Cooper's decision to cast his lot with the Confederacy. On 7 Mar. 1861 he resigned from the army. He was promptly appointed Confederate adjutant general—a post he held for the duration of the war—and his name headed the first list of full generals submitted to the Congress for confirmation.

LC

Cooper's duties were to promulgate orders and regulations, maintain communication with generals in the field, and oversee the keeping of records. Disagreement exists over Cooper's effectiveness. Some historians praise him as "clear-headed and without prejudice," a man who handled organizational matters and routine procedures with "a calmness and a cultivated mind." Other writers assert that Cooper was "a slave to red tape," totally uninformed of the military state of affairs anywhere, and repeatedly unable to keep orderly records. His Northern background and a nervous habit of tugging at his shirt collar created suspicions about both his loyalty and his ability.

At the Confederacy's downfall, Cooper turned over all of his records intact to Federal authorities. That he did so has enabled generations of historians to study Confederate military history in greater depth than would otherwise have been possible. Cooper died 3 Dec. 1876 and is buried in Christ Church Cemetery, Alexandria, Va. —JIR

Copperheads. *See* PEACE DEMOCRATS.

Corcoran, Michael. USA b. Cty. Donegal, Ireland, 21 Sept. 1827. Corcoran, whose father was an officer in the British army, emigrated to America in 1849 and in 1859 became colonel of the 69th New York Militia. The next year, however, he lost his position for refusing to parade the regiment before the visiting Prince of Wales, escaping court-martial only because the outbreak of the war made him invaluable for raising Irish volunteers.

USMHI

A hero at FIRST BULL RUN, the captured Corcoran soon became involved in a fresh controversy. Union naval forces had seized the merchant schooner *Enchantress,* manned by a prize crew from the Confederate PRIVATEER *Jefferson Davis.* The Federal government tried the prize master of the *Enchantress,* among others, on charges of piracy, and threatened capital punishment. In retaliation, acting Confederate Sec. of War JUDAH P. BENJAMIN ordered that a high-ranking Federal prisoner be chosen to share whatever fate might befall the *Enchantress's* prize master. Through drawing lots, Corcoran won the dubious honor of being this hostage. Faced by Benjamin's determination, the Federal government wisely moderated its stance on Confederate naval prisoners. (*See also* ENCHANTRESS AFFAIR.)

Steadfastly refusing a parole, Corcoran was finally exchanged in Aug. 1862 and promptly received a brigadier general's commission and an invitation to dine with President Lincoln. As enthusiastic as ever, Corcoran continued to rally Irish support for the Union by raising the CORCORAN LEGION. He served as a divisional commander in the VII Corps/Army of Virginia, most notably at Suffolk, Va., Apr. 1863, and later exercised divisional command in the XXII Corps Defenses of Washington. On 22 Dec. 1863, near Fairfax Court House, Va., Corcoran suffered a fall while riding and was crushed to death beneath his horse. —BNO

Corcoran Legion. Also called the Irish Legion, this unit was raised by MICHAEL CORCORAN, an Irish-American hero of the FIRST BATTLE OF BULL RUN who, after being held prisoner and threatened with execution for a year, was released by Confederates and made a brigadier general by the Union as a reward. With no command available, Corcoran went to New York City, his home, and raised the 155th, 164th, 170th, and 184th New York regiments, constituting the brigade called the Corcoran Legion and mostly made up of Irish immigrants.

The Legion's first post was at winter quarters in Virginia, late 1862–spring 1863. There they skirmished in front of their southeast Virginia camps, then defended Suffolk, Va., during a spring siege by Lt. Gen. JAMES LONGSTREET's Confederates. From July 1863 to May they were billeted in the Washington, D.C., area, losing their commander in a riding accident 22 Dec. 1863. After Corcoran's death the Legion was assigned to Maj. Gen. Winfield S. Hancock's II Corps of the Army of the Potomac for the severest fighting of the war: the WILDERNESS, SPOTSYLVANIA, and COLD HARBOR. At the last of these, the Legion suffered terribly. A dawn charge on the entrenched Confederate position was almost suicidal, but one of the Legion's colonels, James McMahon of the 164th New York, managed to plant his regiment's flag on the enemy works before he was riddled by rifle fire.

The Corcoran Legion was destroyed, but its members served to the end of the war with the Army of the Potomac's 2d Division/II Corps. —JES

Corinth, Miss., Battle of. 3–4 Oct. 1862 Confederate Maj. Gen. EARL VAN DORN's 22,000 men left Chewalla, Tenn., at dawn, 3 Oct. 1862. Marching 10 mi south to Corinth, Miss., they assaulted Maj. Gen. WILLIAM S. ROSECRANS' 23,000 Federals in their works. The Confederates, a combined command of Van Dorn's and Maj. Gen. STERLING PRICE's troops, intended to take the town, control the Mobile & Ohio and Memphis & Charleston railroads, and organize an invasion of Tennessee. At least, Federals would be diverted from Gen. BRAXTON BRAGG's preparations to invade Kentucky.

Van Dorn believed Rosecrans thought Confederates were moving against Northern railroad lines. Rosecrans, unsure of Confederate intent, recalled all his troops within the Corinth lines. Van Dorn's attack, calculated as a surprise, depended on 3 divisions, under Brig. Gens. DABNEY H. MAURY and LOUIS HÉBERT and Maj. Gen. MANSFIELD LOVELL, rushing the town's western works on a broad front and carrying them by shock.

Driving in Union pickets, Confederate lines were formed with Lovell's division on the right and Maury's and Hébert's on the left. As the Federals approached the pickets, 3 earthquake tremors occurred, frightening the troops. Van Dorn, conscious

of his men's morale, urged commanders to show firmness in the assault.

Federals manned a chain of field forts on Corinth's western perimeter. A 400-yd expanse of felled timber surrounded them. Corinth sat over a half-mile behind, surrounded by a second fortification line. Rosecrans posted only half his troops in the works. When a brigade of skirmishers rushed into the lines on 3 Oct. crying that Confederates were about to attack, defenders were not prepared for the numbers that did.

Confederates dressed ranks in the fallen timber, rushed forward, carried the works, and drove Federals toward their interior lines. Van Dorn's troops pursued, but 90° heat, fatigue, and water shortages slowed them. An hour's halt, called for rest, allowed Federals to reinforce a second line outside interior fortifications. Renewed Confederate assault failed. Rosecrans' men, holding a compact front, gave stiffer resistance. Daylight faded. Van Dorn consulted Price, and the battle was stopped. Lovell had performed poorly in the 3 Oct. fighting. Price claimed that a reliable performance from him might have made a last assault successful.

Battle would resume at dawn, with Hébert attacking and flanking the Union right at the same time Maury rushed on the center. Lovell would advance from the southwest to roll up the Union left. 3 artillery batteries on high ground west of town would soften up Federals at 4 a.m.

But at 4 o'clock Confederate cannon were smothered by heavier Union guns. Hébert reported sick after his advance was delayed, and replacement Brig. Gen. MARTIN E. GREEN lost an hour fumbling with instructions. Maury's unsupported

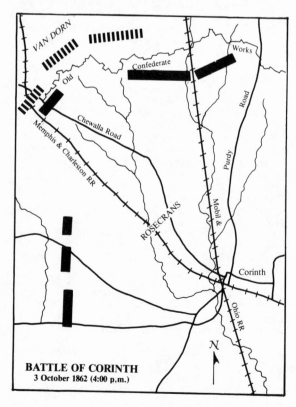

BATTLE OF CORINTH
3 October 1862 (4:00 p.m.)

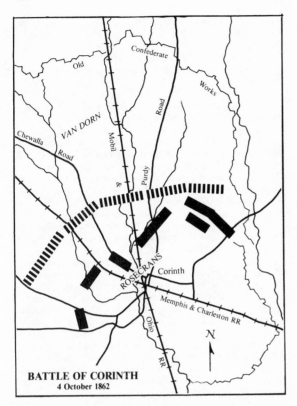

BATTLE OF CORINTH
4 October 1862

troops escalated skirmishing with Federals to pitched proportions, bringing enemy artillery fire down on Confederate positions. The Southerners' center advanced and Green's division followed.

At 9:30 Lovell's troops skirmished but did not move. He never appeared at the front or ordered attack. Maury's and Green's men fought into Federal lines, Maury's piercing them and charging into Corinth itself. Without Lovell's support on the south, the breakthrough was thrown back, and Confederates caught in Corinth were cut up by crossfire. On the Confederate right-center Col. William P. Rogers assaulted Union Battery Robinett, and the Southern troops briefly took possession of the work. Rogers was killed, and a counterattack by 4 regiments retook the battery.

By noon the Confederates had withdrawn toward the road north to Chewalla. Nearly a third of those engaged in the 4 Oct. fighting were casualties. Lovell's division reported few. Rosecrans' troops, badly shaken, did not pursue. A 2-day Confederate retreat took Van Dorn's troops to Ripley.

Rosecrans lost nearly 2,500 killed and wounded in the 2-day fight. Confederates lost 2,470 dead and wounded, and another 1,763 missing in battle or deserted during retreat to Ripley. Hébert and Lovell were relieved of command weeks later.

—JES

corps. Military units during the Civil War were, in ascending order of size, company, (occasionally) battalion, regiment, brigade, division, corps, and army. The term *corps* comes from the French phrase *corps d'armée*. Although *corps d'armée*

existed in the French army before Napoleon, he revamped them and popularized the phrase. A corps was composed of 2 or more divisions and, except for cavalry corps, included all arms of service.

Corps were established in the Union army in Mar. 1862 by Maj. Gen. George B. McClellan. A major general commanded each of the 43 corps that were established in the Union army before the end of the war. Each corps was designated by a number, I to XXV. CORPS BADGES such as triangles, crescents, arrows, and acorns were adopted by most corps and worn by officers and enlisted men. Of the Union corps, 2 were noted for their failures: the XI Corps, which took flight after a surprise attack by Lt. Gen. Thomas J. "Stonewall" Jackson's men at CHANCELLORSVILLE, and the IX Corps, which bungled the opportunity of the CRATER at Petersburg. More successful corps included the I and II/Army of the Potomac, known for their bravery; the XXV, composed entirely of black troops; and the XXII, which garrisoned the fortifications around Washington, D.C., during most of the war and guarded the Union capital.

Corps were organized in the Confederate army Nov. 1862 and were commanded by lieutenant generals. Confederate corps were designated by numbers duplicated in the East and West but were often referred to by the name of their commander. Thus, the II Corps in the East was called Jackson's Corps, even after he was killed. This corps endured some of the hardest marching and heaviest fighting of the war.

After their initial trial in the Civil War, corps became an integral part of the organization of the U.S. Army in wartime.

Individual Confederate and Union corps follow.   —DEF

Confederate Corps

I Corps/Army of Northern Virginia

Until Sept. 1862 Confederate law recognized no units larger than divisions. Commanders, however, often grouped divisions into informal organizations called "wings" or "commands." In the fighting around Richmond May–June 1862, JAMES LONGSTREET led a command consisting of all or part of 3 divisions. In the Second Bull Run and Antietam campaigns, "Longstreet's Wing" contained 5 divisions.

On 6 Nov. 1862 the Army of Northern Virginia was organized into 2 infantry corps, and Longstreet was promoted to lieutenant general to command the I (Longstreet's) Corps. The corps consisted of divisions led by LAFAYETTE MCLAWS, RICHARD H. ANDERSON, JOHN B. HOOD, GEORGE E. PICKETT, and ROBERT RANSOM, and fought at FREDERICKSBURG with these officers.

Ransom's division was sent to North Carolina early in 1863, and Longstreet went with Pickett and Hood on the expedition against Suffolk. Anderson and McLaws remained with the army and fought at CHANCELLORSVILLE, after which the army was reorganized into 3 corps, each of 3 divisions. Hood, McLaws, and Pickett led Longstreet's divisions in the GETTYSBURG CAMPAIGN. Longstreet took Hood's and McLaws' divisions and a brigade of Pickett's to CHICKAMAUGA (Pickett and his 4 remaining brigades stayed in Virginia), where he commanded a wing of the Confederate army, with Hood leading the corps.

In November Longstreet was sent with 2 divisions to besiege KNOXVILLE and, in spring 1864, he returned to Virginia. The division commanders were then JOSEPH B. KERSHAW and CHARLES W. FIELD. Pickett rejoined the corps 1 June 1864. Longstreet was wounded 6 May, and Richard H. Anderson commanded the corps until Longstreet returned in October. The I Corps held the left of the Confederate line during the Siege of PETERSBURG and fought in the retreat to APPOMATTOX.

Longstreet's Corps was distinguished in all the major battles in Virginia and at Chickamauga. It contained some of the Confederacy's best troops—HOOD'S TEXAS BRIGADE, the 1st Virginia Regiment, Kershaw's South Carolinians, the WASHINGTON ARTILLERY of New Orleans—and some of its finest brigade and regimental leaders. Longstreet's administration of the corps was usually good, but sometimes he played favorites among his subordinates and allowed their rivalries to get out of hand.

—RMcM

I Corps/Army of Tennessee; Army of Mississippi

The I Corps/Army of Tennessee began in LEONIDAS POLK'S 1st Division of the Western Department. For a short time, 5–29 Mar. 1862, it was called the 1st Grand Division in P.G.T. Beauregard's ARMY OF MISSISSIPPI. When Albert Sidney Johnston took command of the Army of Mississippi 29 Mar., the unit, still commanded by Polk, was designated the I Corps, and as such it fought at SHILOH.

When the Army of Tennessee was organized Nov. 1862, the I Corps was officially born. Immediately thereafter, it fought in the STONE'S RIVER campaign, its divisions led by BENJAMIN F. CHEATHAM and JONES M. WITHERS.

At CHICKAMAUGA the corps was split. Polk, commanding the right wing of the army, had DANIEL H. HILL'S corps under him, along with Cheatham's division of the I Corps. THOMAS C. HINDMAN's division of the corps fought as part of JAMES LONGSTREET'S left wing. After Chickamauga, Polk was relieved from duty by BRAXTON BRAGG for not attacking when ordered and never again commanded the corps. Though Polk was to face a court-martial, his friend Pres. Jefferson Davis interceded for him. On Polk's dismissal, the command passed to WILLIAM J. HARDEE in July 1863.

Hardee led the corps at CHATTANOOGA with divisions under JOHN K. JACKSON, PATRICK R. CLEBURNE, WILLIAM WALKER, EDWARD C. WALTHALL, and CARTER L. STEVENSON. In the ATLANTA CAMPAIGN the corps had the same composition, except that Stevenson's division was replaced by WILLIAM B. BATE's. When the corps covered John B. Hood's retreat from JONESBOROUGH, Ga., in 1864, Cleburne commanded for a short time.

In Oct. 1864, with Cheatham commanding, the corps consisted of the infantry divisions of Cleburne, Bate, and JOHN C. BROWN and the cavalry division of JAMES R. CHALMERS. Under this leadership it fought the disastrous FRANKLIN AND NASHVILLE CAMPAIGN.

The I Corps, called variously Polk's Corps, Hardee's Corps, and Cheatham's Corps, earned a good fighting reputation, though most of the campaigns in which it participated were marginally successful at best.

—PRR

II Corps/Army of Northern Virginia

THOMAS J. "STONEWALL" JACKSON's left wing—descended from the Army of the Valley—became the II Corps/Army of Northern Virginia 6 Nov. 1862, with Jackson commanding it until his death at CHANCELLORSVILLE. His successors were RICHARD S. EWELL, JUBAL A. EARLY, and JOHN B. GORDON; temporary commanders included AMBROSE P. HILL, J.E.B. STUART, and ROBERT E. RODES. The corps is also called Jackson's Corps, Ewell's Corps, and Early's Corps.

Throughout, the corps contained the Stonewall Division, the

Ewell-Early Division, and the D.H. Hill-Rodes Division. Ambrose P. Hill's LIGHT DIVISION also belonged through Chancellorsville.

The II Corps initially enjoyed great successes at FREDERICKSBURG, CHANCELLORSVILLE, SECOND WINCHESTER, and during GETTYSBURG's first day. 2–3 July at Gettysburg, Rappahannock Bridge, and Kelly's Ford, however, brought unexpected reverses. The corps at least ended 1863 well under Early in blunting George G. Meade's offensive at Mine Run.

Ever aggressive, the II Corps effectively attacked U. S. Grant in the WILDERNESS, 5–6 May 1864. But at SPOTSYLVANIA, 12 May, disaster struck: Federals, overrunning the "MULE SHOE," captured most of the Stonewall Division. Staggering losses, 5–12 May, caused the corps to be consolidated from 13 brigades to 10 (the smallest of Robert E. Lee's 3 main corps). Through Cold Harbor, the weakened corps fared well defensively but repeatedly saw its counterattacks parried.

Strategic counterstrokes, however, remained possible. Detached in mid-June to relieve Lynchburg, it carried the war to Washington's outskirts, 11–12 July. Thereafter, its divisions—Early's Army of the Valley's main elements—won handsomely at Snicker's Ferry and SECOND KERNSTOWN but lost disastrously at THIRD WINCHESTER, FISHER'S HILL, and CEDAR CREEK.

Foiled in the Valley, the corps rejoined Lee in December, Gordon's 2 divisions going to Petersburg, Bryan Grimes reuniting with them in February after bolstering James Longstreet. Gordon, repulsed at Hatcher's Run and Fort Stedman, did hold the main Petersburg works, 2 Apr., allowing Lee to escape. Gordon suffered severely at SAYLER'S CREEK but broke away. At Appomattox Court House, however, he could not cut through to Lynchburg—the reverse that spelled doom. At the surrender the II Corps contained barely 6,000 men.   —RJS

II Corps/Army of Tennessee; Army of Mississippi

The II Corps/ARMY OF TENNESSEE had its genesis in Mar. 1862, when BRAXTON BRAGG with his Florida and Alabama men joined P.G.T. BEAUREGARD's newly formed ARMY OF MISSISSIPPI. When ALBERT SIDNEY JOHNSTON reorganized the Army of Mississippi later that month, Bragg was put in command of its II Corps, composed of the divisions of JONES M. WITHERS and DANIEL RUGGLES. In this form it fought at SHILOH.

SAMUEL JONES took over the corps during July and August, when Bragg was given command of the army after Johnston's death. WILLIAM J. HARDEE succeeded Jones and led the corps when it was designated II Corps/Army of Tennessee in November. In July 1863 Hardee relinquished command of the corps when appointed commander of the I Corps. DANIEL H. HILL then became the new commander.

At CHATTANOOGA the II Corps was under JOHN C. BRECKINRIDGE with divisions commanded by THOMAS C. HINDMAN, WILLIAM B. BATE, and ALEXANDER P. STEWART. In the ATLANTA CAMPAIGN a series of commanders appeared: JOHN B. HOOD, CARTER L. STEVENSON, BENJAMIN F. CHEATHAM, and STEPHEN D. LEE. Its divisions fought under Hindman and Stewart. S. D. Lee retained command during the FRANKLIN AND NASHVILLE CAMPAIGN with divisions under EDWARD JOHNSON, Stevenson, and HENRY D. CLAYTON.

In its last campaign, in the CAROLINAS, the II Corps was headed again by D. H. Hill with divisions under Stevenson, Clayton, and JOHN G. COLTART. On its last organization, 9 Apr. 1865, it was again under S. D. Lee with divisions under Hill and Stevenson.

The II Corps fought bravely in all its engagements, but its effectiveness was diminished due to the constant rotation of commanders. Other than the "II Corps," the organization was known as Bragg's Corps, Hardee's Corps, D. H. Hill's Corps, Hood's Corps, and S. D. Lee's Corps. Since there was no continuity of leadership, the troops had little opportunity to develop the kind of *esprit* that characterized other units.   —PRR

III Corps/Army of Northern Virginia

Thomas J. "Stonewall" Jackson's death led Robert E. Lee to create a third corps, 30 May 1863, to increase flexibility, accommodate deserving officers, and reduce new corps commanders' burdens. This III Corps consisted of a I Corps division under RICHARD H. ANDERSON and WILLIAM MAHONE; the II Corps Light Division under AMBROSE P. HILL, WILLIAM D. PENDER, and CADMUS M. WILCOX; and HENRY HETH's new division. Hill was the only official corps commander, but JUBAL A. EARLY and Heth also led it temporarily. The unit is sometimes called A. P. Hill's Corps.

Formerly hard-hitting Hill proved disappointing. His inability to coordinate forces repeatedly aborted victory in his corps' early battles: GETTYSBURG, Second Bristoe Station, and the WILDERNESS. Under Early at SPOTSYLVANIA, the corps fared better, but again under Hill at the NORTH ANNA, it failed to overrun the isolated V Corps.

At PETERSBURG, however, the corps consistently performed well; a year's service had helped it coalesce. Some III Corps brigades secured BERMUDA HUNDRED, covered Deep Bottom, and recaptured the CRATER. The corps' most important service was battling, often successfully, every thrust at Petersburg's vital supply lines.

But the end eventually came. On 2 Apr. 1865, Federals pierced Wilcox's works and cut the last communications. Hill —Lee's principal subordinate at Petersburg after mid-September 1864 and whose troops had so often saved that city—was killed during this fighting. With him fell Petersburg and Richmond. On the retreat to Appomattox, the III Corps, nominally under Heth, was attached to JAMES LONGSTREET's command. Mahone failed to secure the High Bridge crossings, but all 3 divisions formed the final battlelines at Cumberland Church and Appomattox Court House. At the surrender, the III Corps numbered 8,600 men, the largest command in Lee's army.
    —RJS

III Corps/Army of Tennessee; Army of Mississippi

The III Corps/Army of Tennessee never formally used that designation. Only after the war was "III Corps" coined to facilitate understanding.

When ALBERT SIDNEY JOHNSTON reorganized the Army of Mississippi, 29 Mar. 1862, the III Corps, commanded by WILLIAM J. HARDEE, came into being. At SHILOH it fought as Hardee's Corps, although it was only a single division composed of 3 brigades under THOMAS C. HINDMAN, PATRICK R. CLEBURNE, and STERLING A. M. WOOD.

In Nov. 1862, when the Army of Tennessee was founded, it comprised only 2 infantry corps, I and II. Though eventually 3 corps existed, the III Corps was referred to by the names of its various commanders.

When LEONIDAS POLK rejoined the Army of Tennessee in May 1864, having been dismissed by BRAXTON BRAGG as commander of the I Corps for not obeying orders at CHICKAMAUGA, he took command of the III Corps, now called Polk's Corps.

He was killed 14 June 1864 in the ATLANTA CAMPAIGN, and ALEXANDER P. STEWART succeeded him. During that campaign the corps was composed of infantry divisions under WILLIAM WING LORING, SAMUEL G. FRENCH, and JAMES CANTEY and a cavalry division commanded by WILLIAM H. JACKSON. Later in 1864, during the Franklin and Nashville Campaign, the corps contained the same infantry divisions, but by then Jackson's cavalry had become part of NATHAN B. FORREST's cavalry corps.

From 16 Mar. to 9 Apr. 1865, while Stewart was detached, EDWARD C. WALTHALL commanded. When the final organization of the corps took place, 9 Apr., Stewart was again the commander, with divisions under Loring, Walthall, and J. PATTON ANDERSON.

The III Corps fought valiantly throughout its existence, but like the I Corps, II Corps, and the Army of Tennessee itself, it suffered from a lack of stable leadership due to its constant parade of new commanders.   —PRR

IV Corps/Army of Northern Virginia

With P.G.T. Beauregard reassigned from Petersburg to the West, the Department of Northern Virginia absorbed his former department 3 Oct. 1864. On 19 Oct. the recuperated James Longstreet displaced RICHARD H. ANDERSON as commander, I Corps/Army of Northern Virginia. To accommodate Anderson, Robert E. Lee gave him a new IV Corps, also called Anderson's Corps.

Unlike other corps, the IV Corps was largely administrative, not tactical. It never served as a unit. ROBERT F. HOKE's division remained under Longstreet on the Virginia peninsula until leaving for Wilmington in December. Anderson's direct command thus consisted of BUSHROD R. JOHNSON's infantry division and Hilary P. Jones's artillery brigade east of Petersburg, plus Edward L. Thomas' temporarily attached infantry brigade in Chesterfield County.

From its creation until mid-March 1865, the IV Corps' unglamorous but vital mission was securing PETERSBURG against direct assault. When other, more mobile forces were away (e.g., at Burgess' Mill in Oct. 1864), Anderson often temporarily commanded all troops at Petersburg.

In mid-March, though, roles changed. The II Corps assumed Petersburg's defense, and Anderson shifted to the far right. 2 of his brigades returned to share John B. Gordon's debacle at FORT STEDMAN, 25 Mar. A week later, those brigades endured worse defeat under George E. Pickett at FIVE FORKS. Meanwhile, Anderson, with his other 2 brigades plus Eppa Hunton's and Samuel McGowan's, successfully defended the WHITE OAK ROAD but repeatedly failed to drive off increasing Northern forces. Even worse, his futile marchings, 1–2 Apr., cost Lee his services anywhere during those final, fatal days.

During the retreat, most of Anderson's artillery escaped to Lynchburg, but his infantry—Johnson's and Pickett's divisions —met disaster at SAYLER'S CREEK and most were captured. Anderson, Johnson, and Pickett themselves escaped, only to be relieved by Lee, 8 Apr., ostensibly because their commands no longer existed. The 2,300 remaining infantry constituted HENRY A. WISE's brigade and was transferred to Gordon's corps.
    —RJS

Anderson's Corps.

See IV CORPS/Army of Northern Virginia.

Bragg's Corps.

See II CORPS/Army of Tennessee; Army of Mississippi.

Breckinridge's Corps.

See RESERVE CORPS/Army of Tennessee; Army of Mississippi.

Buckner's Corps/Army of Tennessee; Army of Mississippi

In Apr. 1863 SIMON B. BUCKNER was given command of the pro-Unionist Department of East Tennessee and its small army of questionable loyalty. BRAXTON BRAGG, 6 Aug., assumed command of the Department of Tennessee, which effectively eliminated Buckner's department, and designated Buckner's old command II Corps/Army of Tennessee. Buckner, however, retained command of his troops, which became known as Buckner's Corps.

In late August Ambrose E. Burnside, with a vastly superior Union army, began to approach Buckner's 2 divisions of 5,000 men at Knoxville. Buckner appealed to Bragg for reinforcements, but Bragg, threatened at CHATTANOOGA by William S. Rosecrans, could not aid him; instead, he ordered Buckner to withdraw toward Chattanooga. The controversial retreat was precipitous; Buckner abandoned mountains of supplies.

By mid-September Buckner's Corps had linked up with Bragg's army in preparation for the coming Battle of CHICKAMAUGA. On the first day of the battle, 19 Sept., the 3 divisions composing the corps—ALEXANDER P. STEWART'S, WILLIAM PRESTON'S, and BUSHROD R. JOHNSON'S—were in the bloodiest part of the fight, on Chickamauga Creek below Lee and Gordon's Mills. The Union force that Buckner faced was commanded by Thomas J. Wood, a childhood friend and West Point classmate. The next day, when JAMES LONGSTREET came up, Buckner's Corps was placed under Longstreet's command in the left wing of Bragg's army. The corps sustained heavy casualties, especially in the successful storming of log breastworks when the famous gap in the Union lines occurred.

After the battle Buckner joined numerous other Confederate officers in their condemnation of Bragg for squandering their victory by not pursuing Rosecrans and his broken army. An acrimonious debate between Bragg and Buckner followed. Bragg, under the pretext that the Department of East Tennessee no longer existed, relieved Buckner of command of his army 28 Oct. 1863. Buckner's Corps, as such, ceased to exist.

Buckner's Corps was essentially a temporary organization that fought its only major engagement at Chickamauga. There it laid to rest the question of its loyalty when it contributed materially to the Confederate victory. —PRR

Cheatham's Corps.

See I CORPS/Army of Tennessee; Army of Mississippi.

Early's Corps.

See II CORPS/Army of Northern Virginia.

Ewell's Corps.

See II CORPS/Army of Northern Virginia.

Forrest's Cavalry Corps/Army of Tennessee; Army of Mississippi

NATHAN B. FORREST's Cavalry Corps had its genesis in a volunteer battalion formed in mid-1861. Consisting at various times of troops from Tennessee, Kentucky, Alabama, Georgia, Texas, and Arkansas, it grew from this modest beginning to an independent command late in 1863. The organization first saw action Nov. 1861 and remained almost continuously in action

until it surrendered at Gainesville, Ala., 9 May 1865.

In the corps' early days, units assigned to it were constantly shuffled; as a result, it frequently went into battle filled with untrained personnel. The situation was aggravated throughout the war by a chronic shortage of material, often forcing Forrest's troops to fight with what they could capture from Union sources. They compensated remarkably well for these deficiencies by employing unorthodox tactics and sheer fighting determination to achieve their objectives. Led by commanders such as A. A. Russell, Tyree H. Bell, Abraham Buford, Edward W. Rucker, J. W. Starnes, and C. R. Barteau, the corps established one of the world's premier cavalry records.

The corps' service encompassed combat in all its forms. As raiders they consistently frustrated Union plans by diverting troops in an attempt to stall the Federal advance, and by destroying critical stocks of supplies. As regular cavalry, they performed superbly in support of Confederate forces when the main armies clashed in battles such as SHILOH and CHICKAMAUGA. Forrest's cavalry displayed the same skill and indomitable will when they provided rearguard services to the Army of Tennessee as it withdrew before the inexorable Union advance. Finally, in perhaps its finest hour, the corps demonstrated its ability to fight a set-piece battle when it humiliated the U.S. Army by crushing a force twice its size in the Battle of BRICE'S CROSS ROADS. —WRB/DKS

Hampton's Cavalry Corps.

See STUART'S CAVALRY CORPS/Army of Northern Virginia.

Hardee's Corps.

See I CORPS; II CORPS; III CORPS/Army of Tennessee; Army of Mississippi.

A. P. Hill's Corps.

See III CORPS/Army of Northern Virginia.

D. H. Hill's Corps.

See II CORPS/Army of Tennessee; Army of Mississippi.

Hood's Corps.

See II CORPS/Army of Tennessee; Army of Mississippi.

Jackson's Corps.

See II CORPS/Army of Northern Virginia.

Lee's Cavalry Corps.

See STUART'S CAVALRY CORPS/Army of Northern Virginia.

S. D. Lee's Corps.

See II CORPS/Army of Tennessee; Army of Mississippi.

Longstreet's Corps.

See I CORPS/Army of Northern Virginia.

Pemberton's Corps/Army of Vicksburg

The Confederate force generally referred to as Pemberton's Corps/Department of Mississippi fought several major battles in Mississippi, Dec. 1862–May 1863, against Ulysses S. Grant's Union army.

Joseph E. Johnston had been sent 24 Nov. 1862 to command a "super headquarters" known as the Division of the West, including, among others, a department commanded by

JOHN C. PEMBERTON. Pemberton's Corps had primary responsibility for the defense of the vital Vicksburg, Miss., stronghold.

During the Battle of CHICKASAW BLUFFS, just north of Vicksburg, Pemberton's Corps consisted of 25,000 men, who repulsed William T. Sherman's invading XIII Corps, which had 32,000.

At Chickasaw Bluffs the corps included these units: 1) Defenses of Vicksburg, under MARTIN L. SMITH and CARTER L. STEVENSON; brigades of SETH BARTON, JOHN C. VAUGHN, JOHN GREGG, and EDWARD D. TRACY (Barton, Vaughn, and Tracy had just joined Pemberton after seeing action at Grenada, Miss.); and 2) Provisional Division, under STEPHEN D. LEE and DABNEY H. MAURY; brigades of William T. Withers and ALLEN THOMAS.

Pemberton deployed his force skillfully, positioning his artillery on high ground and taking advantage of swamps and bayous blocking the Northern advance. Federal brigades under George W. Morgan moved up the west bank of Chickasaw Bayou and attacked 28 and 29 Dec., suffering heavy losses before withdrawing. Pemberton cited these regiments for outstanding gallantry: the 40th, 42d, and 52d Georgia; the 17th, 26th, and 28th Louisiana; and the 3d, 30th, and 80th Tennessee.

Pemberton's success was only temporary. Grant continued to close his vise on Vicksburg—at Steele's Bayou, PORT GIBSON, JACKSON, CHAMPION'S HILL, BIG BLACK RIVER BRIDGE—and by 19 May 1863 had Pemberton's forces trapped in the city itself.
—DS

Polk's Corps.

See I CORPS; III CORPS/Army of Tennessee; Army of Mississippi.

Reserve Corps/Army of Tennessee; Army of Mississippi

Usually known as Breckinridge's Corps, this outfit was organized 5 Mar. 1862 under the command of GEORGE B. CRITTENDEN. Crittenden was under severe criticism for poor conduct in January at the Battle of MILL SPRINGS, and now, within a month, was relieved for drunkenness. On 31 Mar. JOHN C. BRECKINRIDGE took over the corps. With 6,439 men, a sizable reserve for an army 40,000 strong, the corps was organized into 3 brigades under Robert P. Traube, JOHN S. BOWEN, and W. S. Stratham.

The green corps fought hard at SHILOH, 6–7 Apr. 1862. Pressed into combat almost from the start, it served not at all as a reserve but constituted instead the right of the main assault line. Although some of the regiments moved sluggishly, the corps hurled many vicious assaults on the enemy's powerful position at the "HORNETS' NEST." During the night the corps shifted its position toward the center; it gradually gave ground the next day, but finished the battle as the covering force behind which the remainder of the Confederate army withdrew.

The corps helped hold off the Siege of CORINTH, then moved from Tupelo into Louisiana, where the men cooperated in a scheme ordered by Earl Van Dorn to try taking BATON ROUGE. On 6 Aug. 1862 they reached the suburbs, but the ensuing all-day struggle ended with Breckinridge unable to hold the city because he could get no river support. The campaign did bear some fruit when a fragment of the corps under Daniel Ruggles took PORT HUDSON.

The rest of the Reserve Corps moved to support the invasion of Kentucky. Near Murfreesboro, Tenn., the corps combined with a cavalry force under NATHAN B. FORREST to constitute the ARMY OF MIDDLE TENNESSEE. In Nov. 1862, when the Army of Tennessee reorganized, Breckinridge's enlarged force became the 1st Division of William J. Hardee's II Corps.   —HH

Kirby Smith's Corps/Army of East Tennessee; Army of Kentucky; Army of Tennessee

This corps was created when E. KIRBY SMITH assumed command of the Army of East Tennessee in Feb. 1862. It was an army in name only, mainly undisciplined, widely dispersed units of doubtful loyalty primarily raised from heavily pro-Union East Tennessee.

By the time Smith invaded Kentucky with his commander, Braxton Bragg, he had whipped his unruly mob into an acceptable fighting force. The corps, soon to be called the Army of Kentucky, left Tennessee with its divisions commanded by HENRY HETH, PATRICK R. CLEBURNE, and THOMAS J. CHURCHILL. Another division under CARTER L. STEVENSON stayed behind to maintain pressure on a small Union army at Cumberland Gap. On 24 Aug. the corps met and destroyed 2 Federal brigades under Mahlon D. Manson and Charles Cruft at Richmond. After much maneuvering in southern Kentucky, the corps fought no more major battles. It missed Bragg's inconclusive battle at Perryville, where it might have turned the tide against Don Carlos Buell. When Bragg later refused repeated requests by Smith to attack Buell's army and force a major battle, the relationship between the 2 commanders was ruptured. In the end, the corps, no more than mildly bloodied, retreated with Bragg from Kentucky back into Tennessee.

In Nov. 1862 the Army of Tennessee, commanded by Bragg, was formed, and Smith's Army of Kentucky formally became Kirby Smith's Corps in that army. The full corps never fought under Bragg but became an independent entity under Smith in East Tennessee. In December the corps was reduced to 6,000 men when Pres. Jefferson Davis sent Stevenson's division to reinforce John C. Pemberton at VICKSBURG, and JOHN P. MCCOWN's division was detached to Bragg at Murfreesboro.

Kirby Smith's Corps ceased to exist when Smith left Tennessee to take command of the Southwestern Army 14 Jan. 1863 and thereafter the command of the Trans-Mississippi Department. Though fighting creditably in its few engagements, the corps never realized its potential, primarily due to Bragg's excessive caution in Kentucky and eastern Tennessee.
—PRR

Stewart's Corps.

See III CORPS/Army of Tennessee; Army of Mississippi.

Stuart's Cavalry Corps/Army of Northern Virginia

The Confederate cavalrymen of the Army of Northern Virginia for 2 years embodied the ideal of Southern chivalry, matchless horse soldiers who somehow maintained the romantic conception of warfare. Led by a brilliant officer in a plumed hat and red-lined cape, who was accompanied by a banjo player, these gray-clad troopers consistently bloodied and battled their more numerous Union opponents. But by mid-1863 their antagonists—with better mounts, better arms, and experienced officers—ended the supremacy of the Confederates. Even as they were being organized into a corps, these Southern cavalrymen were being surpassed.

The man responsible for forging this successful command

was J.E.B. STUART. A natural leader with West Point training, Stuart had so impressed J. E. Johnston at FIRST BULL RUN that the latter helped secure Stuart's promotion to brigadier general and gave him command of all the army's cavalry. Then in June 1862, after Stuart's brilliant ride around the Union army on the Virginia peninsula (See STUART'S RIDE AROUND MCCLELLAN) and his performance in the SEVEN DAYS' CAMPAIGN, Robert E. Lee gave him 2 cavalry brigades, while promoting him to major general. In August the cavalry command was augmented by the addition of Thomas J. "Stonewall" Jackson's cavalry and another brigade. One more brigade was added after Antietam, and such able officers as WADE HAMPTON, FITZHUGH LEE, WILLIAM E. "GRUMBLE" JONES, and W.H.F. "ROONEY" LEE commanded them.

In the reorganization of the army after Chancellorsville, R. E. Lee grouped all his cavalry units under Stuart in a large division, though it was frequently termed a "corps." But the Confederacy's dwindling resources were seriously crippling the cavalry's effectiveness. Further hampered by a shortage of troopers and horses, and by the increasing prowess of Union horsemen, Stuart faced setbacks during the year. At Kelly's Ford in March, at Brandy Station in June and at GETTYSBURG in July, Federal cavalry dueled evenly or defeated the Confederate troopers. After Gettysburg, Hampton and Fitzhugh Lee, both promoted to major general, assumed command of divisions, and the cavalry command became a true corps.

When Stuart was mortally wounded in May 1864, Fitzhugh Lee temporarily assumed control of the corps until Hampton proved his capability. Hampton commanded the corps until transferred to South Carolina Jan. 1865. Fitzhugh Lee led the reduced command until Appomattox. As was often the case in the Confederate army, the corps was closely identified with its commanders, and is sometimes referred to as Hampton's Cavalry Corps or as Lee's Cavalry Corps.

Like most of the Confederacy, Stuart's legions were surpassed by superior Union matériel and numbers, in a war in which relentlessness counted for more than the spectacular.

—JDW

Wheeler's Cavalry Corps/Army of Tennessee; Army of Mississippi

"I'll tell you, Joe Wheeler was the gamest little banty I ever seen. He wasn't afeered of nuthin' or nobody!" This comment by one of JOSEPH WHEELER's former troopers some years after the Civil War aptly describes the man and the cavalry he led. Operating in the Western theater, and normally composed of some 4,200 horsemen, Wheeler's Confederate cavalry enjoyed prestige as a competent, dependable fighting force in the Army of Tennessee. Its exploits were a direct reflection of the ability of the youthful West Pointer who commanded them. Characterized by a fighting quality and eagerness to close with an enemy, Wheeler's corps is perhaps best known for its accomplishments at STONE'S RIVER and in Tennessee's Sequatchie Valley.

In Dec. 1862 Wheeler's cavalry delayed a full Union army for 4 days before the mutually destructive standoff at Stone's River near Murfreesboro, Tenn. His raid against Union supply lines in the Sequatchie Valley in fall 1863 destroyed over 1,000 loaded wagons, killed 2,000 Federals, and destroyed millions of dollars' worth of Union property and supplies. Within 2 weeks the Union's William S. Rosecrans was relieved of command.

—WRB/DKS

Union Corps

I Corps/Army of the Potomac

WILLIAM B. FRANKLIN's, George A. McCall's, and RUFUS KING's divisions of the Army of the Potomac became IRVIN MCDOWELL's I Corps 8 Mar. 1862. The corps left that army to form McDowell's Department of the Rappahannock–III Corps/Army of Virginia 4 Apr.–12 Sept. 1862, but thereafter resumed its original number. By mid-September those 4 generals and Franklin's division were gone. JOSEPH HOOKER and later JOHN F. REYNOLDS and JOHN NEWTON were the corps' official commanders; GEORGE G. MEADE and ABNER DOUBLEDAY led it briefly. Senior subordinates eventually included Doubleday, JAMES S. WADSWORTH, LYSANDER CUTLER, JAMES B. RICKETTS, JOHN GIBBON, JOHN C. ROBINSON, Meade, and JOHN R. KENLY.

The I Corps rejoined the Army of the Potomac as Hooker outflanked the secessionists at SOUTH MOUNTAIN, with Meade's Pennsylvania Reserves prominent. Meade also fought heavily in the ANTIETAM preliminaries; in the main battle all 3 divisions overran Thomas J. "Stonewall" Jackson in the Cornfield, only to be thrown back by John B. Hood's counturcharge. Hooker himself fell wounded. Meade's division again distinguished itself at Fredericksburg. The Pennsylvania Reserves left Reynolds Feb. 1863, but reinforcements created Doubleday's new 3d Division.

The corps performed much marching but little fighting at Chancellorsville. Still its manpower shrank considerably, as 11 short-term regiments left service that spring. It entered the GETTYSBURG CAMPAIGN with just 6 brigades; 2 others joined 2 and 10 July. Thus only 6 brigades were available at Gettysburg for the corps' greatest day, 1 July 1863. Reynolds, commanding the Northern left wing, was killed right away; Doubleday directed the corps until night. Heavily attacked in the front and right flank, outflanked from the east and south, the little corps absorbed staggering casualties but repeatedly stopped and drove the Confederates before being pushed back. Its valiant stand gave Meade time to secure his main defense line. Under Newton the corps was engaged 2–3 July; George J. Stannard's new brigade helped repel PICKETT'S CHARGE.

The corps subsequently served at MINE RUN and secured Meade's railroads, but its Gettysburg casualties had fatally weakened it. Discontinued 23 Mar. 1864, it became the 2d and 4th divisions (ultimately the 3d) of the V Corps.

Devastating in attack, unshakable in defense, well led, the I Corps was destroyed by its own achievements.   —RJS

I Corps/Army of Virginia

Mountain Department troops entered the Army of Virginia 26 June 1862 and became its I Corps; their commander, JOHN C. FRÉMONT, was the senior subordinate. He proved more senior than subordinate. Refusing to serve under new army commander JOHN POPE, whom he outranked, he resigned 28 June. FRANZ SIGEL succeeded Frémont, with senior division commander ROBERT C. SCHENCK occasionally leading the corps. Schenck, later JULIUS STAHEL, headed the 1st Division. ADOLPH VON STEINWEHR, CARL SCHURZ, ROBERT H. MILROY, and John Beardsley led the 2d and 3d divisions, the Independent Brigade, and the cavalry brigade, respectively. During late August IRVIN MCDOWELL oversaw the I Corps in addition to his own III Corps/Army of Virginia.

Many I Corps commanders, like their men, were Central European immigrants or Americans of German descent. Ardent Republicans and abolitionists, these men represented constituencies important to the Lincoln administration, so their unit was the most politicized corps of the Union Army. Good politics, however, did not necessarily make good warfare; except for professional soldier von Steinwehr, the corps and division commanders were inept generals, often defeated earlier in the war.

This unfortunate pattern was evident in August, when the I Corps failed to aid Nathaniel P. Banks at CEDAR MOUNTAIN. The corps subsequently occupied Pope's right along the Rapidan, then along the Rappahannock. Its sortie at Freeman's Ford was disastrously repulsed; Brig. Gen. Henry Bohlen was killed. Two days later the corps failed to trap Jubal A. Early near Warranton, White Sulphur Springs.

Nor did Sigel's slow, impeded, misdirected marchings subsequently snare Thomas J. "Stonewall" Jackson near Manassas Junction. At SECOND BULL RUN, 29 Aug., Schurz, von Steinwehr, and Milroy were repeatedly repulsed. The corps initially remained in reserve on 30 Aug., but the 1st Division, then several brigades, became embroiled in the valiant but vain effort to stay James Longstreet's counterattack. In that resistance Schenck was wounded.

Thereafter, Sigel briefly held the left center at Centreville, then retired into Washington's southern fortifications. There his force was absorbed into the Army of the Potomac as the XI Corps, 12 Sept. 1862.   —RJS

II Corps/Army of the Potomac

On 8 Mar. 1862, ISRAEL B. RICHARDSON'S, JOHN SEDGWICK'S, and LOUIS BLENKER's divisions of the Army of the Potomac constituted EDWIN V. SUMNER's II Corps. Blenker's men left immediately to reinforce JOHN C. FRÉMONT in western Virginia. The 1st Division subsequently served under WINFIELD S. HANCOCK, John C. Caldwell, FRANCIS C. BARLOW, and NELSON A. MILES; and the 2d under OLIVER O. HOWARD, JOHN GIBBON, THOMAS A. SMYTH, THOMAS W. EGAN, WILLIAM HAYS, and Barlow. WILLIAM H. FRENCH and ALEXANDER HAYS led the 3d Division, Sept. 1862–Mar. 1864, until the other divisions absorbed it. The III Corps joined as the 3d and 4th divisions (later the 3d) under DAVID B. BIRNEY and Gershom Mott 24 Mar. 1864. DARIUS N. COUCH, Hancock, and ANDREW A. HUMPHREYS, officially, and William Hays, GOUVERNEUR K. WARREN, and Birney, unofficially, commanded the corps.

After northern Virginia forays and Yorktown, the II Corps crossed the rain-swollen Chickahominy River to fight at SEVEN PINES and were repeatedly engaged during the SEVEN DAYS' CAMPAIGN.

Committed piecemeal at ANTIETAM, the corps incurred frightful casualties as Sedgwick was blasted from the West Woods, French was repulsed, and mortally wounded Richardson stormed "BLOODY LANE." Such success eluded the 3 divisions' gallant but futile charges at FREDERICKSBURG. At CHANCELLORSVILLE, though, Hancock and French repulsed Southern onslaughts before withdrawing 3 May.

In the corps' greatest battle, GETTYSBURG, Caldwell gained, then lost the WHEATFIELD 2 July. Hancock secured George G. Meade's left center the same day and with Gibbon and Alexander Hays repulsed PICKETT'S CHARGE 3 July. With Hancock wounded, Warren temporarily led the corps at BRISTOE STATION and MINE RUN.

Under Hancock again, the mighty 4-division corps hammered Ambrose P. Hill in the WILDERNESS, 5–6 May 1864, only to be overthrown by James Longstreet. Checked on the Ni River, it overran Spotsylvania's "MULE SHOE." Success at NORTH ANNA, a stalemate at Totopotomoy River, and a setback at COLD HARBOR completed a month's inferno.

Casualties sustained 5 May–3 June vitiated the once-powerful corps. By Petersburg it had met mixed success (First and Second Deep Bottom), defeat (PETERSBURG), and disaster (WELDON RAILROAD OPERATIONS, Second REAMS' STATION). However, in Hancock's final engagement, at BURGESS' MILL, Oct. 1864, he skillfully repulsed assaults from 4 sides before withdrawing. That winter the corps' strength returned. In 1865, under Humphreys, it won at HATCHER'S RUN, Watkins' Farm, Sutherland's Station, Sayler's Creek, and High Bridge. The corps was discontinued 28 June 1865.   —RJS

II Corps/Army of Virginia

When the Army of Virginia was created 26 June 1862, forces formerly in the Department of the Shenandoah became its II Corps, still under NATHANIEL P. BANKS. Alpheus S. Williams, FRANZ SIGEL, and JOHN P. HATCH led the 1st and 2d divisions and cavalry brigade, respectively. Soon James Cooper, then CHRISTOPHER C. AUGUR replaced Sigel, and JOHN BUFORD succeeded Hatch, who was relieved for twice failing to cut the Gordonsville railroad network in mid-July.

His superior was bolder. After marching from Middletown to Culpeper County, Banks attacked the Confederates at CEDAR MOUNTAIN, 9 Aug. He had rashly joined battle before reinforcements reached him, save for GEORGE D. BAYARD's cavalry brigade, and the absence of Buford offset its presence. By late afternoon Thomas J. "Stonewall" Jackson's counterblows had driven the Unionists from the field. Only then did Federal supports arrive, too late to do anything but cover the retreat. In the heavy fighting Augur and John W. Geary were wounded, and HENRY PRINCE was captured. The 2d Division finally devolved on George S. Greene.

Cedar Mountain was the oft-battered II Corps' first battle—and its last. It remained in reserve until the army abandoned Culpeper County, thereafter helping cover the left-center along the Rappahannock, then moving upriver to support futile attempts to attack Robert E. Lee. Except for crossriver shelling, its main body saw no action. One of its battalions, though, uncovered Catlett's Station to J.E.B. Stuart's raiders, and Buford was active in reconnoitering Confederate moves.

Even when the Army of Virginia left the Rappahannock, Banks did no fighting but guarded the army's trains at Manassas Junction and Bristoe Station. Following Second Bull Run, he destroyed the railroad trains, some wagons, and many supplies, bringing the remaining supplies via Blackburn's Ford and Centreville to Washington. From there the corps moved to Rockville, Md. Williams, who had often exercised its operational control, succeeded Banks 4 Sept., and the 1st Division passed to SAMUEL W. CRAWFORD. The II Corps joined the Army of the Potomac as the XII Corps 12 Sept. 1862.

Brave, hard-fighting, but unsuccessful, the II Corps/Army of Virginia received such a pummeling in early campaigning that army commander JOHN POPE never committed it again.

                                                                     —RJS

III Corps/Army of the Potomac

SAMUEL P. HEINTZELMAN, GEORGE STONEMAN, DANIEL E. SICKLES,

and WILLIAM H. FRENCH, officially, and DAVID B. BIRNEY, temporarily, eventually commanded the III Corps, created from 3 Army of the Potomac divisions 8 Mar. 1862. The corps contained the 1st Division, that of CHARLES S. HAMILTON, PHILIP KEARNY, Stoneman, and Birney; and the 2d Division, that of JOSEPH HOOKER, Sickles, Hiram G. Berry, ANDREW A. HUMPHREYS, and HENRY PRINCE. It briefly contained 3 other divisions: those of FITZ JOHN PORTER, Mar.–May 1862; Amiel W. Whipple and Charles K. Graham, Nov. 1862–June 1863; and WASHINGTON L. ELLIOT and Joseph B. Carr, July 1863–Mar. 1864.

The corps fought heavily throughout the PENINSULA CAMPAIGN, especially at WILLIAMSBURG, SEVEN PINES, and Frayser's Farm. Though sometimes repulsed, Heintzelman repeatedly contained Confederate onslaughts. He then joined JOHN POPE's command Aug. 1862. Hooker drove the Confederates at First BRISTOE STATION, but neither division made headway against Thomas J. "Stonewall" Jackson at SECOND BULL RUN. Then at CHANTILLY, Kearny, accidentally riding into enemy lines, was killed.

The corps remained around Washington during the ANTIETAM CAMPAIGN. Stoneman and Whipple, rejoining the Army of the Potomac Oct.–Nov. 1862, briefly served with the IX and XII corps, respectively, then with AMBROSE E. BURNSIDE's wing. When Sickles joined Nov. 1862, the corps was reestablished. Though it fought at Fredericksburg, it saw little action.

Under Sickles the corps was heavily engaged at CHANCELLORSVILLE and GETTYSBURG. His 1st and 3d divisions briefly harried Jackson's rear 2 May 1863, then occupied Hazel Grove. Army headquarters ordered Sickles from that commanding height 3 May. On lower ground, he repeatedly repulsed J.E.B. Stuart's onslaughts before finally being pushed back; Berry and Whipple were both killed there. Sickles would not concede the heights to the secessionists at Gettysburg, 2 July. On his initiative he advanced the army's left to the Emmitsburg road. In the ensuing fighting he lost a leg; Birney was crushed; and Humphreys was compelled to withdraw. Sickles' controversial move absorbed James Longstreet's blow but jeopardized the army.

In the subsequent pursuit, French, adding Elliot's division, took over the corps. He succeeded at Second Kelly's Ford but badly failed at MANASSAS GAP and MINE RUN. The corps was discontinued 23 Mar. 1864. Its divisions became the 3d and 4th divisions of the II Corps and the 3d Division of the VI Corps.   —RJS

III Corps/Army of Virginia

Most of IRVIN MCDOWELL's Department of the Rappahannock brigades became his III Corps/Army of Virginia 26 June 1862. RUFUS KING, JAMES B. RICKETTS, and GEORGE D. BAYARD, respectively, led its 1st and 2d divisions and cavalry brigade. JOHN F. REYNOLDS' 3d Division rejoined 26 Aug.

Ricketts and Bayard initially held Manassas Junction early in the Second Bull Run Campaign, and King occupied Falmouth to cover reinforcements. Bayard fought at CEDAR MOUNTAIN, but Ricketts protected only the withdrawal, and King arrived too late. The III Corps subsequently occupied JOHN POPE's center along the Rapidan, then along the Rappahannock; its Rappahannock Station bridgehead resisted heavy secessionist skirmishing. McDowell also supported Union operations upriver 23–26 Aug.

He subsequently led the I and III corps/Army of Virginia seeking Thomas J. "Stonewall" Jackson near Manassas Junction, but the groping pursuers became the pursued 28 Aug. When Jackson counterattacked 2 1st Division brigades at GROVETON, in a brave stand-up fire fight the Federals repulsed him. The 2d Division fared worse as James Longstreet overcame its defense of Thoroughfare Gap. Disengaging, both divisions withdrew southeastward overnight.

In the ensuing SECOND BATTLE OF BULL RUN, Reynolds, who had remained with Franz Sigel, became engaged with Longstreet while covering Pope's left 29 Aug. The 1st Division (now under John P. Hatch) and Ricketts arrived late because of difficulty in getting orders to McDowell. Once there, however, Hatch became embroiled with Longstreet near sundown.

All 3 divisions saw severe action 30 Aug. as McDowell directed the army's "pursuit" of the supposedly fleeing foe. Far from retreating, Robert E. Lee's reunited army bloodily repulsed the charge of Hatch's division. Longstreet's counterattack crushed Reynolds' 3d Brigade, then forced back 2 reinforcing brigades from the 2d Division. Jackson's onslaught meanwhile drove Ricketts' other brigades, however—along with other forces McDowell was coordinating—slowed Confederate pursuit sufficiently for Pope to withdraw.

McDowell thereafter covered the army's right rear beyond Centreville and supported Northerners at CHANTILLY. He then moved into the Washington works. On 5 Sept. that unpopular general was replaced, briefly by Ricketts, then by Joseph Hooker. Hooker's troops, again designated the I Corps, rejoined the Army of the Potomac 12 Sept. 1862.   —RJS

IV Corps/Army of the Cumberland

The IV Corps/Army and Department of the Cumberland was re-created by General Order No. 322, Adjutant General's Office, 28 Sept. 1863, after the dissolution of the corps bearing the same designation in the Army of the Potomac. Organized to comply with the order 9 Oct., the corps was composed of troops from Illinois, Indiana, Kansas, Kentucky, Michigan, Missouri, Ohio, Pennsylvania, Wisconsin, and a few U.S. Regulars drawn from the old XX and XXI corps/Army and Department of the Cumberland. It was organized into 3 divisions of 3 brigades each and attached artillery units. A separate artillery brigade was formed 26 July 1864. The corps adopted as its badge the triangle insignia of its predecessor. The first commander was GORDON GRANGER.

Its army commander, WILLIAM S. ROSECRANS, was replaced by GEORGE H. THOMAS 19 Oct. 1863. The IV Corps saw most of its service under him, sustaining the highest battle casualties of any Western command of comparable size.

Granger led the corps at MISSIONARY RIDGE and during the KNOXVILLE CAMPAIGN, but failed to live up to the promise he had shown at CHICKAMAUGA. On 10 Apr. 1864 he was relieved by OLIVER O. HOWARD, under whom the corps fought hard throughout the ATLANTA CAMPAIGN. Howard, promoted to command the Army of the Tennessee, was succeeded by DAVID S. STANLEY. Under Stanley the corps fought against John B. Hood's Army of Tennessee. Wounded at the Battle of Franklin, Stanley was replaced by THOMAS J. WOOD, who commanded the unit for 2 months, through the Battle of Nashville (see FRANKLIN AND NASHVILLE CAMPAIGN), which was the IV Corps' last major engagement. The corps remained in Tennessee until June 1865, when it was ordered to Texas to serve as occupation troops under PHILIP H. SHERIDAN. Most of the regiments were mustered out in December.   —RAP

IV Corps/Army of the Potomac; Department of Virginia

DARIUS N. COUCH's, WILLIAM F. SMITH's, and SILAS CASEY's divisions of the Army of the Potomac constituted ERASMUS D. KEYES's IV Corps 8 Mar. 1862. On the Virginia peninsula Smith failed at Lee's Mill but succeeded at WILLIAMSBURG. His 2d Division joined the VI Corps 18 May 1862. Casey's 3d Division was redesignated the 2d Division 6 June 1862.

By then Casey and Couch had been bloodily defeated at SEVEN PINES. After its staggering fighting 31 May, the IV Corps was never committed again. During the SEVEN DAYS' CAMPAIGN, Keyes simply escorted wagons to the James River. Couch, though, did bolster Fitz John Porter at MALVERN HILL.

When GEORGE B. MCCLELLAN subsequently transferred north, Couch served with the VI Corps until formally joining it 26 Sept. 1862. Plans for Keyes and the 2d Division to follow were changed, however, and they remained at Yorktown. JOHN J. PECK, who succeeded the discredited Casey 24 June 1862, took one old and one new brigade to Suffolk in September. He stayed there until June 1863, but his 2 brigades plus the 1st Brigade/2d Division went to North Carolina Dec. 1862.

Keyes's command thus shrank to his headquarters, 1 cavalry regiment, and the IV Corps artillery. It gradually resumed corps size, initially with Richard Busteed's Yorktown brigade (subsequently expanded into RUFUS KING's 1st Division), then with Robert M. West's Williamsburg brigade and GEORGE W. GORDON's 2d Division from the VII Corps at Suffolk. Gordon briefly occupied West Point, May 1863, but Keyes proved less bold in the 1863 GETTYSBURG CAMPAIGN toward Richmond. Using only West's and Burr Porter's brigades plus Henry D. Terry's VII Corps brigade, he advanced hesitantly and retreated promptly. Unhindered, the Richmond garrison attacked his rear guard at Baltimore Cross Roads.

Keyes's troops then rushed northward to save Pennsylvania, but when Keyes accompanied them, the War Department refused to let him command there, nor would John Dix receive him back, so he was relieved 15 July. Most of his troops (including his division commanders) were distributed through the XI and XXII corps. The XVIII Corps absorbed the remaining outfits when the IV Corps was abolished 1 Aug. 1863.

—RJS

V Corps/Army of the Potomac

NATHANIEL P. BANKS's V Corps, 8 Mar.–4 Apr. 1862, was transferred with Banks to the Department of the Shenandoah, and later became the II Corps/Army of Virginia, then the XII Corps. GEORGE B. MCCLELLAN combined the 1st Division/III Corps and the largely Regular Reserve Infantry Division/Army of the Potomac to create what became the permanent V Corps for his friend FITZ JOHN PORTER 18 May 1862. Subsequent commanders were DANIEL BUTTERFIELD, GEORGE G. MEADE, GEORGE SYKES, GOUVERNEUR K. WARREN, and CHARLES GRIFFIN. Division commanders included George W. Morell, Butterfield, Griffin, JOSEPH J. BARTLETT, Sykes, ROMEYN B. AYRES. The corps contained George A. McCall's (later SAMUEL W. CRAWFORD's) Pennsylvania Reserves, June–Aug. 1862 and June 1863–June 1864. ANDREW A. HUMPHREYS' 3d Division belonged Sept. 1862–May 1863. Griffin absorbed Ayres 24 Mar. 1864 as JOHN C. ROBINSON's and JAMES S. WADSWORTH's (later LYSANDER CUTLER's) I Corps divisions joined Warren. By Sept. 1864 all I Corps regiments formed Crawford's 3d Division; Griffin and Ayres led the other divisions.

On the Virginia peninsula Porter fought well in victory (Hanover Court House, MECHANICSVILLE, MALVERN HILL) and defeat (GAINES' MILL). At SECOND BULL RUN his corps suffered heavily, and he was cashiered in 1863 for alleged noncooperation with John Pope.

The corps saw little action at Antietam, Fredericksburg, and Chancellorsville except for its Shepherdstown rebuff and Humphreys' valiant but vanquished assault on Marye's Heights. At Gettysburg 4 V Corps brigades saved the ROUND TOPS, while 4 others were chewed up farther west. RAPPAHANNOCK STATION and MINE RUN closed 1863.

Warren opened 1864 fighting in the WILDERNESS. First successful, he was eventually driven back on the Orange Turnpike; Wadsworth was killed 6 May. Warren made little headway at SPOTSYLVANIA, but at NORTH ANNA and Bethesda Church initial setbacks became successes. Crawford, covering the army's right, fared badly at Second Riddell's Shop.

After initial fighting at Petersburg, the corps was not engaged until its costly Globe Tavern victory cut the crucial WELDON RAILROAD OPERATIONS. Warren punched through the next Southern defenses at Poplar Spring Church, then saved the IX Corps there. Second Squirrel Level Road, Burgess' Mill, and the Hicksford Raid were followed by defeat at Hatcher's Run. The corps fared unevenly in the Mar. 1865 battles but did storm FIVE FORKS—too late, though, to save Warren from being relieved for noncooperation.

Griffin intercepted and doomed R. E. Lee at Appomattox Court House. The corps was discontinued 28 June 1865.

—RJS

VI Corps/Army of the Potomac; Army of the Shenandoah

GEORGE B. MCCLELLAN united the 1st Division/I Corps and 2d Division/IV Corps to give his friend WILLIAM B. FRANKLIN a VI Corps 18 May 1862. WILLIAM F. SMITH, JOHN SEDGWICK, and HORATIO G. WRIGHT later commanded. Divisions were under HENRY W. SLOCUM, WILLIAM T. H. BROOKS, Wright, DAVID A. RUSSELL, and Frank Wheaton (1st Division); and Albion P. Howe and GEORGE W. GETTY (2d Division). DARIUS N. COUCH's (eventually JOHN NEWTON's, JOSEPH J. BARTLETT's, and HENRY D. TERRY's) 1st Division/IV Corps constituted the 3d Division/VI Corps 26 Sept. 1862 until disbanded 10 Jan. 1864. Joseph B. Carr's 3d Division/III Corps (subsequently under JAMES B. RICKETTS and TRUMAN SEYMOUR) became the 3d Division/VI Corps 24 Mar. 1864. The Light Division, usually under Calvin Pratt, lasted only 26 Jan.–11 May 1863.

The corps initially fought only by brigades and divisions in the SEVEN DAYS' CAMPAIGN and at Bull Run Bridge during the SECOND BULL RUN CAMPAIGN. Accused of moving too slowly to save John Pope and Harpers Ferry, Franklin at least had a sizable battle at CRAMPTON's GAP; at Antietam and Fredericksburg, though, the corps did little.

But in 1863, during CHANCELLORSVILLE, the corps stormed supposedly impregnable Marye's Heights. Repulsed at SALEM CHURCH, Sedgwick skillfully extricated his isolated, imperiled command. After a prodigious 19-hour, 34-mi march, the corps reached GETTYSBURG 2 July, though it did little fighting there. Its handsomest success of the year came at RAPPAHANNOCK STATION. MINE RUN closed 1863.

In the Wilderness the corps was routed 6 May. Sedgwick's death, 9 May, and EMORY UPTON's brilliant temporary penetration of the "MULE SHOE," 10 May, highlighted SPOTSYLVANIA. Wright's fortunes varied at Spotsylvania, NORTH ANNA, COLD

HARBOR, Bethesda Church, PETERSBURG, and WELDON RAIL-ROAD. Rushed northward July 1864, the 3d Division sufficiently delayed Jubal A. Early at MONOCACY for Wright to save Washington. Unsuccessful at Snicker's Gap, the corps, temporarily part of the Army of the Shenandoah, served in Sheridan's SHENANDOAH VALLEY CAMPAIGN, fighting at Third Winchester, Fisher's Hill, and Cedar Creek.

Returning to George G. Meade's Army of the Potomac Dec. 1864, the corps saw limited action during the Hicksford Raid and Hatcher's Run. On 2 Apr., its massive breakthrough doomed Petersburg, and it later destroyed Richard S. Ewell at Sayler's Creek. After briefly threatening Joseph E. Johnston from Danville, Va., the corps was discontinued 28 June 1865.
—RJS

VII Corps/Department of Arkansas

The VII Corps, like the IV Corps, was given its designation after another unit so designated in the Eastern theater had been discontinued. The second, Western VII Corps was composed of all Federal troops within the geographical boundaries of the state of Arkansas, the Union Department of Arkansas, and was organized 6 Jan. 1864. Thus it was the military unit responsible for territorial integrity within the state.

The corps, initially commanded by FREDERICK STEELE, comprised Friedrich Salomon's division, JOHN M. THAYER's division, and EUGENE A. CARR's cavalry division. In addition to performing the basic mission of occupying the state, the command of about 12,000 men conducted the CAMDEN EXPEDITION of 1864. Also known as Steele's Expedition, it was supposed to be the diversionary phase of Nathaniel P. Banks's RED RIVER CAMPAIGN. Unfortunately, Steele was more than 3 weeks late in beginning his advance from Little Rock. Actions at Mt. Elba, Terre Noir Creek (or Antoine), Okolona, Elkin's Ferry, Prairie D'Ane, and Marks' Mills culminated in a fight at Jenkins' Ferry, 30 Apr. 1864, from which Steele barely managed to withdraw the remainder of his corps. He and his roughly handled command thereafter returned to Little Rock.

Steele was replaced by Joseph J. Reynolds, a classmate at West Point. The corps saw little activity until it was discontinued 1 Aug. 1865.
—RAP

VII Corps/Department of Virginia

JOHN A. DIX's Department of Virginia became his VII Corps 22 July 1862. Never mobile, the corps controlled southeastern Virginia garrisons from Fort Monroe headquarters. The principal posts—Yorktown, Norfolk, and Suffolk—were under ERASMUS D. KEYES (IV Corps), Egbert L. Viele, JOSEPH K. F. MANSFIELD, and later JOHN J. PECK, respectively.

The corps' initial 3 brigades soon dropped to 2. Peck's 2d Division/IV Corps, however, bolstered Dix. The IX Corps, moreover, passed through his department Feb.–Mar. 1863, and its 3d Division (George W. Getty's) became the 2d Division/VII Corps 21 Mar. Besides these veterans, many new 9-month and 3-year regiments, including William Gurney's (later GEORGE W. GORDON's) division, joined Dix Sept. 1862–Apr. 1863. Though the experienced IV Corps brigades and Francis B. Spinola's brigade transferred to North Carolina, Dec. 1862–Jan. 1863, and 4 brigades joined Keyes, May 1863, the VII Corps could still form 2 divisions and 5 brigades.

Most VII Corps troops constituted the exposed Suffolk outpost. Mansfield, joining the Army of the Potomac Sept. 1862,

reduced its garrison. Mounting Confederate threats led Dix to reinforce the town with 2 of Peck's brigades. When they departed, Michael Corcoran's 1st Division was formed there; Getty and Gurney subsequently joined it. Peck thus led a corps equivalent at Suffolk.

Heavy skirmishing flared around Suffolk for months, especially at Deserted House. With spring, James Longstreet's reinforced secessionists besieged Suffolk. Though confining Peck to town and gathering supplies, they could not capture the garrison. The Federals particularly thwarted their efforts to close the Nansemond River. In May Longstreet withdrew.

Dix then transferred most of Peck's troops north of the James River; Gordon's division to join the IV Corps, HENRY D. TERRY's brigade to aid it; Getty's brigades to the Pamunkey. Dix remained, but his operations against Richmond and its railroads accomplished little. Half the VII Corps rushed north to confront Robert E. Lee, transferred to South Carolina, or mustered out after their 9 months. Entrusting corps command to Henry M. Naglee, then Getty, Dix left 16 July to suppress DRAFT RIOTS in New York City. The VII, IV, and XVIII corps remnants merged as the XVIII Corps/Department of Virginia and North Carolina 1 Aug. 1863, when the VII Corps was discontinued. In that new corps, most former VII Corps troops became Getty's division at Portsmouth or Isaac J. Wistar's brigade at Yorktown.

A garrison, the VII Corps could defend territory but could not conquer more.
—RJS

VIII Corps/Middle Department

When the Union Middle Department was created 22 Mar. 1862, troops within the area were organized into the VIII Corps and were commanded by the elderly JOHN E. WOOL. The corps was composed of the Railroad District, the Railroad Brigade, District Eastern Shore, Defenses of Baltimore, the Maryland Brigade, Robert H. Milroy's division, and a number of "separate brigades" and smaller commands. With geographic security its mission, the VIII Corps did no fighting as a unit, but some of the integral forces were involved in several severe engagements.

ROBERT C. SCHENCK succeeded Wool and led the corps until 5 Dec. 1863, except during 12–22 Mar., 10–31 Aug., and 22–29 Sept., when William W. Morris commanded, and 28 Sept.–10 Oct., when Erastus B. Tyler commanded.

During the preliminary Gettysburg Campaign movements, Milroy's forces were roughly handled at Berryville and Martinsburg and then virtually destroyed at Winchester, 14 June 1863, by Confederate Richard S. Ewell's command. On 9 July 1864 the 1st Separate Brigade under Tyler was engaged at the Union defeat on the Monocacy River during Confederate Jubal A. Early's raid. At the time the VIII Corps was under the command of LEWIS WALLACE, who had succeeded HENRY H. LOCKWOOD 22 Mar. 1864. Wallace continued to command until the VIII Corps was discontinued 1 Aug. 1865, except for a brief period when Morris again temporarily was in command, 1 Feb.–19 Apr. 1865.

Throughout its existence the VIII Corps saw little action since it was deployed in what was more a geographic area than a combat command and thus had no freedom of maneuverability. It was, in fact, a garrison force that engaged any opponents who happened to traverse its area of responsibility.
—RAP

IX Corps/Army of the Potomac; Army of the Ohio; Department of Washington, D.C.

3 Carolinas divisions, rushed to Fort Monroe to help GEORGE B. McCLELLAN, constituted the IX Corps 22 July 1862. Its 3d Division became the 2d Division/VII Corps Mar. 1863. The 1st Division, redesignated the 3d Division Apr.–Sept. 1864, resumed its former title when the new 1st Division disbanded. The black 4th Division, joining Apr. 1864, became the 3d Division Sept. 1864 and was traded to the Army of the James for a white 3d Division Nov. 1864. The Kanawha Division was with the corps Sept.–Oct. 1862. AMBROSE E. BURNSIDE, JESSE L. RENO, WILLIAM F. SMITH, and JOHN G. PARKE (officially) and JACOB D. COX, ORLANDO B. WILLCOX, and ROBERT B. POTTER (temporarily) led the corps. Other prominent division commanders included ISAAC I. STEVENS, EDWARD FERRERO, THOMAS L. CRITTENDEN, JULIUS WHITE, SAMUEL D. STURGIS, JOHN F. HARTRANFT, Isaac P. Rodman, and GEORGE W. GETTY.

Burnside initially moved to Fredericksburg. Reno's 1st and 2d divisions fought at SECOND BULL RUN and CHANTILLY, where Stevens died. In Maryland Reno perished at SOUTH MOUNTAIN, and Rodman fell at ANTIETAM, where Burnside and Sturgis stalled at "Burnside Bridge." Sturgis again failed at Marye's Heights.

Early in 1863 the corps returned to Fort Monroe, where its 3d Division stayed. The other divisions went west, Mar. 1863–Mar. 1864, to garrison Kentucky, take Vicksburg and Jackson, and defend East Tennessee at the engagement at CAMPBELL'S STATION and the fighting at KNOXVILLE.

The IX Corps transferred to Annapolis, Mar.–Apr. 1864, where divisions under Thomas G. Stevenson and Ferrero joined and Burnside resumed command. First cooperating with—and, after 24 May, part of—the Army of the Potomac, the corps fought from the Wilderness to Petersburg.

Poor planning, inept leadership, and the blacks' poor combat debut ended in disaster at the Crater 30 July. Burnside's mine cost him his command; Parke thereafter had charge. The corps battled superbly at Globe Tavern, disastrously at Peebles' Farm, pointlessly at Second Squirrel Level Road and Burgess' Mill. It fought no more until FORT STEDMAN, where it defeated John B. Gordon's attempted breakthrough. Gordon, in turn, repelled Parke's assaults on PETERSBURG 2 April, but Parke occupied the city unopposed 3 April.

The IX Corps covered U. S. Grant's rear in the APPOMATTOX CAMPAIGN. It joined the Department of Washington until discontinued 1 Aug. 1865. Mediocre in leadership, ineffective in battle, the IX Corps had 2 distinctions: losing more senior generals and traveling farther than any Northern corps.
—RJS

X Corps/Department of the South; Army of the James; Department of North Carolina

In Apr. 1864, after 20 months of campaigning against Charleston, S.C., the X Corps joined the Army of the James. Its permanent Virginia commanders were QUINCY A. GILLMORE, WILLIAM T.H. BROOKS, and DAVID B. BIRNEY. ALFRED H. TERRY often led it temporarily.

The corps initially feinted up the York River, then joined Benjamin F. Butler's James River dash to BERMUDA HUNDRED. In May it fought at Port Walthall Junction, Swift Creek, First and Second Ware Bottom Church, Wooldridge's Hill, Second Drewry's Bluff, and Bermuda Hundred. Butler's failure at the last caused the XVIII Corps, reinforced by the 2d and 3d Divi-

sions/X Corps, to transfer to Cold Harbor. Gillmore meantime commanded all forces remaining at Bermuda Hundred. He repulsed P.G.T. Beauregard's attack there 2 June, but with August V. Kautz failed to take Petersburg 9 June. For this failure Gillmore's constant adversary, Butler, relieved him.

Now temporarily under Terry, the corps on 15 June seized the Howlett line (the Confederate defense line across Bermuda Hundred Neck) and the Richmond & Petersburg Railroad but withdrew to Bermuda Hundred under pressure 16–17 June. There it remained until late August, first under Brooks, then Birney. A X Corps brigade established the Deep Bottom bridgehead 20 June. In heavily reinforcing Winfield S. Hancock's 2 sorties from Deep Bottom, 27–29 July and 14–20 Aug., the X Corps overran Southern advanced lines near NEW MARKET HEIGHTS and at Fussell's Mill but could exploit neither victory.

Birney's troops thereafter served a month in the trenches east of Petersburg. On 29 Sept. they returned to the Virginia peninsula only to be checked at New Market Heights and repulsed at Fort Gilmer. Though fatally ill, Birney won the X Corps' greatest victory in repelling Robert E. Lee's counterattack at Darbytown Road 7 Oct. Again under Terry, the corps got nowhere at Darbytown Road and Fair Oaks 13, 27 Oct. It held Butler's right on the peninsula until discontinued 3 Dec. 1864, when its white infantry joined the XXIV Corps and its artillery, black infantry, and corps staff entered the XXV Corps.

On 27 Mar. 1865, Terry's Provisional Corps, captors of Fort Fisher and Wilmington, became the re-created X Corps/Army of the Ohio. After Joseph E. Johnston's surrender, it garrisoned mid–North Carolina until discontinued 1 Aug. 1865. —RJS

XI Corps/Army of the Potomac; Army of the Cumberland

The I Corps/Army of Virginia became the XI Corps 12 Sept. 1862. Its official commanders were FRANZ SIGEL, Sept. 1862–Feb. 1863, and OLIVER O. HOWARD, Apr. 1863–Apr. 1864. Temporary commanders included JULIUS STAHEL, ADOLPH VON STEINWEHR, and CARL SCHURZ, initially leading its 1st, 2d, and 3d divisions, respectively. CHARLES DEVENS, FRANCIS C. BARLOW, and GEORGE W. GORDON subsequently directed the 1st Division, and numerous brigadiers briefly headed each division. The corps was made up largely of regiments of German birth or descent. Their American-born fellow soldiers suspected and often disliked these men of foreign language, foreign ways, and pro-black sentiments.

The battered XI Corps' service only reinforced such distrust. After sitting out the Antietam and Loudoun campaigns near Washington, it joined the Army of the Potomac too late for Fredericksburg but in time for Ambrose E. Burnside's "Mud March." By then Schurz headed the corps in Sigel's Reserve Grand Division.

Howard had charge when campaigning resumed April 1863. Ahead lay the XI Corps' 2 big battles—each a disaster. Robert E. Lee and Thomas J. "Stonewall" Jackson won their greatest victory, CHANCELLORSVILLE, at Howard's expense. The 1st Division and 3 other XI Corps brigades again fled before the II Corps/Army of Northern Virginia at GETTYSBURG 1 July. Howard that day directed the Union left wing and Schurz commanded the routed corps. Their last fresh brigade atop CEMETERY HILL went unchallenged 1 July, but even that eminence could not protect the 1st Division 2 July. Only a counterattack by non–XI Corps troops saved the key salient.

After such debacles, the Army of the Potomac understandably rid itself of the XI Corps when troops were required elsewhere. Gordon's 1st Division transferred to Charleston harbor, S. C., Aug. 1863; then Howard's remaining forces went to the Army of the Cumberland in Tennessee, Sept.–Nov. 1863, where they served at Wauhatchie (see WAUHATCHIE NIGHT ATTACK), MISSIONARY RIDGE, and the fatiguing relief of KNOXVILLE. While wintering near Chattanooga, Howard received William T. Ward's new 1st Division, only part of which actually joined from Middle Tennessee garrisons. The XI Corps lost its identity in the XII Corps when both merged as the reconstituted XX Corps 14 Apr. 1864.   —RJS

XII Corps/Army of the Potomac; Army of the Cumberland

The tiny, 5-brigade II Corps/Army of Virginia became the XII Corps 12 Sept. 1862. JOSEPH K. F. MANSFIELD led it until 17 Sept.; HENRY W. SLOCUM became his permanent successor 20 Oct. 1862. In the interim, and later, Alpheus S. Williams often temporarily headed the corps. He and JOHN W. GEARY were the regular commanders of the 1st and 2d divisions, respectively.

At ANTIETAM, the troops' first battle since Cedar Mountain, Mansfield was killed immediately. Under Williams, SAMUEL W. CRAWFORD's and George S. Greene's divisions fought heavily around the East Woods and Dunkard Church. The corps did not accompany GEORGE B. MCCLELLAN back into Virginia that fall but, true to its origin, held the upper Potomac around Harpers Ferry. Slocum shifted to Fairfax County during the FREDERICKSBURG CAMPAIGN and rejoined the Army of the Potomac during Ambrose E. BURNSIDE's "MUD MARCH."

In spring 1863 he led the army's right wing to CHANCELLORSVILLE, where, 3 May, the corps redeemed its many earlier defeats. Though first Williams, then Geary eventually had to withdraw from increasingly untenable positions, their steadfast defense blunted Southern attacks sufficiently to prevent defeat from becoming disaster. The corps performed even greater service on the night of 2–3 July at GETTYSBURG, where Greene's brigade almost singlehandedly held CULP'S HILL against the reinforced Stonewall Division. After daybreak, Slocum drove off the secessionists and secured George G. Meade's right.

That fall the XII Corps went west to help at CHICKAMAUGA. Refusing to serve there under Joseph Hooker, Slocum was left to guard the Nashville-Chattanooga Railroad with Williams' division. The 2d Division remained with Hooker; after valiantly repulsing James Longstreet's surprise night attack at WAUHATCHIE, it helped storm LOOKOUT MOUNTAIN and MISSIONARY RIDGE but was checked at Ringgold Gap.

The 1st and 2d divisions wintered around Tullahoma and Bridgeport. Lovell H. Rousseau's new 3d Division, containing other Middle Tennessee garrisons, reported to Slocum 2 January. On 14 Apr. 1864 the XII Corps absorbed the XI Corps to become the reconstituted XX Corps. In commanders, structure, tone, and emblem, the XII predominated in the new corps; only the number was different.   —RJS

XIII Corps/Army of the Tennessee; Army of the Gulf

The original Union XIII Corps was established by General Order No. 168, Adjutant General's Office, 24 Oct. 1862, whereby all troops in the Department of the Tennessee, created 16 Oct. 1862, were assigned to it. Widely separated and scattered over Kentucky, Mississippi, and Tennessee, they technically composed the XIII Corps commanded by ULYSSES S. GRANT. General Order No. 210, Adjutant General's Office, 18 Dec. 1862, created 4 corps (the new XIII, and the XV, XVI, and XVII) out of what formerly had been one.

The new XIII Corps, made up of the old 9th and 10th divisions of the Army of the Tennessee and all the Union troops operating on the Mississippi River below Memphis not included in the XV Corps, was not actually organized as such until Jan. 1863; 18 Dec. 1862–12 Jan. 1863 the troops that were to comprise the corps were part of WILLIAM T. SHERMAN's unsuccessful YAZOO EXPEDITION.

On 28 July 1863, following the investment and capture of Vicksburg, the corps was again reorganized, and 7 Aug. transferred south to the Department of the Gulf, where it served until 11 June 1864, when the corps was deactivated and most of its units were reassigned to the Reserve Corps of the Department of the Gulf.

A new XIII Corps was formed 18 Feb. 1865 from the same units that had been transferred to the Reserve Corps. On 20 July the XIII Corps was discontinued permanently and dismantled at Galveston, Tex.

The corps' battle record while a part of the Army of the Tennessee was commendable during the Yazoo Expedition and the VICKSBURG CAMPAIGN. Its work was not spectacular while attached to the Department of the Gulf during the Texas coast operations late 1863–early 1864 and the RED RIVER CAMPAIGN. One peculiarity was the turnover in commanding officers; during its nearly 3 years of service the corps had 14 commanders, including Grant, Sherman, JOHN A. MCCLERNAND, and E.O.C. ORD.   —RAP

XIV Corps/Army of the Cumberland; Army of Georgia

The XIV Corps was created by General Order No. 168, Adjutant General's Office, 24 Oct. 1862, with the organization of the Department of the Cumberland, and was actually the original Army of the Ohio that had marched from Louisville, fought the Battle of PERRYVILLE, and moved on to Nashville. Redesignated the Army of the Cumberland and placed under the command of WILLIAM S. ROSECRANS, it fought the Battle of STONE'S RIVER, 31 Dec. 1862–2 Jan. 1863.

With the reorganization of the Army of the Cumberland 9 Jan. 1863, the XIV Corps came under the command of GEORGE H. THOMAS. In June, the corps was first to break through the Confederate defenses south of Murfreesboro at the start of the CHATTANOOGA CAMPAIGN. By holding the left of the Union line at the Battle of CHICKAMAUGA, 12–20 Sept., the XIV Corps won for Thomas the sobriquet "The Rock of Chickamauga." When Thomas replaced Rosecrans as commander of the Army of the Cumberland in October, JOHN M. PALMER took command of the XIV Corps. On 25 Nov. the XIV was the principal force in the storming of MISSIONARY RIDGE at Chattanooga and the rout of the Confederate Army of Tennessee.

As the largest corps in William T. Sherman's Army of Georgia, the XIV had a major role in the ATLANTA CAMPAIGN in spring and summer 1864. In August, during the campaign, Palmer resigned and JEFFERSON C. DAVIS took command of the corps. It was one of the 4 corps that made Sherman's MARCH TO THE SEA, Nov.–Dec. 1864.

During winter 1865, the XIV Corps was part of Sherman's army in his CAROLINAS CAMPAIGN and marched from Savannah to North Carolina. After Joseph E. Johnston's surrender, 26 Apr., the XIV Corps marched on to Washington to take part in the Grand Review.   —JWR

XV Corps/Army of the Tennessee

The XV Corps was established by General Order No. 210,

Adjutant General's Office, 18 Dec. 1862, which also formed the new XIII and the XVI and XVII corps. Union troops used to make up the unit had previously served in the old 5th Division/District of Memphis and Frederick Steele's division from Helena, Ark., in the old XIII Corps/Army of the Tennessee. The actual regiments were Western troops primarily from Illinois, Iowa, Missouri, and Ohio.

From 18 Dec. 1862 to 12 Jan. 1863, the units were part of WILLIAM T. SHERMAN's unsuccessful YAZOO EXPEDITION and JOHN A. MCCLERNAND's briefly extant Army of the Mississippi. Confusion sometimes arises because the I and II corps of McClernand's army were being used by Sherman between the date the new XIII Corps and XV Corps were organized and the date the Army of the Mississippi ceased to exist, 12 Jan. 1863. Thus, the XV Corps held a joint identity for a short while.

After their return to the Army of the Tennessee, the XV Corps was commanded by Sherman until 29 Oct. 1863. During that time the corps was heavily engaged in the investment and capture of VICKSBURG. FRANCIS P. BLAIR, JR., Sherman's successor, commanded the corps during the CHATTANOOGA CAMPAIGN, 29 Oct.–11 Dec. 1863.

The XV Corps participated in the ATLANTA CAMPAIGN and the MARCH TO THE SEA in 1864, and the CAROLINAS CAMPAIGN in 1865 under JOHN A. LOGAN, then Morgan L. Smith, Logan again, PETER J. OSTERHAUS, Logan, and finally WILLIAM B. HAZEN until 1 Aug. 1865.

Invariably in the thick of action, the XV Corps adopted a distinctive badge, a square surmounted by a cartridge box with the numeral *40* on it and the motto *40 Rounds,* which could be translated today as "Always Ready."

Throughout its existence the XV Corps had an excellent battle record and was a unit that could be relied on under almost any circumstances; all of its commanders performed admirably during their respective tours of duty. —RAP

XVI Corps/Army of the Tennessee; Army of the Gulf

Formed by General Order No. 210, Adjutant General's Office, 18 Dec. 1862, the XVI Corps initially consisted of troops drawn from the old 6th, 7th, and 8th divisions, and of troops from the Districts of Memphis, Jackson, and Columbia of the old XIII Corps/Army of the Tennessee. Then, 20 Jan. 1863, the old 6th and 7th divisions were transferred to the newly created XVII Corps, even before assimilation, in exchange for the old 1st and 4th divisions and the District of Corinth. Such changes set the trend for the corps, and it never operated as a unit, being used primarily as a source of reinforcement for other commands.

The XVI Corps was composed of 4 divisions, commanded by WILLIAM SOOY SMITH, GRENVILLE M. DODGE, NATHAN KIMBALL, and JACOB G. LAUMAN and stationed in the vicinities of Memphis and La Grange, Tenn., and Corinth, Miss., until June 1863. At that time 3 divisions, excluding Dodge's, were sent to assist in the investment of Vicksburg but did no heavy fighting during the campaign.

In Sept. 1863, Smith's 1st Division was transferred to the XV Corps and replaced by James M. Tuttle's division from that corps; Lauman's division went to the XVII Corps. The following year, 10–16 July 1864, at Jackson, Lauman's division, farmed out to the new XIII Corps, and Smith's division, attached to the IX Corps, suffered heavy casualties. During March–May 1864 2 divisions designated Detachment/Army of the Tennessee participated in the RED RIVER CAMPAIGN.

The corps was ordered deactivated 7 Nov. 1864, but 15 Dec. ANDREW J. SMITH's division fought actively at NASHVILLE, still with its "detachment" designation. On 18 Feb. 1865 the corps was officially re-created, commanded by Sooy Smith but with only 3 divisions, and transferred to the Army of the Gulf, where it took part in the Siege of MOBILE. The corps was permanently discontinued 20 July 1865. —RAP

XVII Corps/Army of the Tennessee; Army of the Gulf

Established by General Order No. 210, Adjutant General's Office, 18 Dec. 1862—along with the new XIII and the XV and XVI corps—the XVII Corps was taken from the old 1st, 3d, and 4th divisions, the 1st Cavalry Brigade, and the District of Corinth. Then, 20 Jan. 1863, the 1st and 4th divisions and District of Corinth went to the XVI Corps in exchange for that corps' 6th and 7th divisions.

With divisions consisting of 3 brigades and attached artillery, and under its first commander, JAMES B. MCPHERSON, the corps fought with distinction during the siege and capture of VICKSBURG in summer 1863—its only campaign as an intact unit.

During the remainder of its service the corps was divided and fragmented, much like the XVI Corps, with half its forces in the Mississippi Valley with the Army of the Gulf and the rest with WILLIAM T. SHERMAN in the ATLANTA CAMPAIGN.

Part of the corps, with units of the XVI Corps (also called Detachment/Army of the Tennessee) and other miscellaneous elements, was formed into a detached unit called the Provisional Division (or the Red River Division) and took part in Nathaniel P. Banks's RED RIVER CAMPAIGN Apr. 1864, the YAZOO EXPEDITION of May 1864, the expedition to Jackson, Miss., the Battle of BRICE'S CROSS ROADS, and the expedition to TUPELO; finally it went with ANDREW J. SMITH's forces to Nashville (*see* FRANKLIN AND NASHVILLE CAMPAIGN).

The detachments that went under Sherman to Atlanta fought at Big Shanty and KENNESAW MOUNTAIN, Ga., June 1864. McPherson was killed in front of ATLANTA 22 July 1864. FRANCIS P. BLAIR, JR., having succeeded McPherson 23 Apr., commanded the corps through the Atlanta Campaign—during which it saw more hard marches than hard fighting—and through the Carolinas. Blair was relieved by THOMAS E.G. RANSOM, MORTIMER D. LEGGETT, and JOSEPH A. MOWER for some 6 weeks in September and October.

The corps was present at Joseph E. Johnston's surrender in North Carolina and was later commanded by WILLIAM W. BELKNAP until officially discharged 1 Aug. 1865. —RAP

XVIII Corps/Army of the James

Federal troops in North Carolina became the XVIII Corps 24 Dec. 1862, absorbing the Department of Virginia 15 July 1863. Though its immediate predecessor, troops operating in the Department of North Carolina, had conducted JOHN G. FOSTER's expedition to Goldsborough, the corps did not take the field until the fighting at BERMUDA HUNDRED in May 1864. Under William F. Smith, WILLIAM T. H. BROOKS's and GODFREY WEITZEL's white divisions fought at Port Walthall Junction, Swift Creek, and SECOND DREWRY'S BLUFF. Meantime, EDWARD W. HINCKS's black 3d Division manned garrisons.

Smith subsequently reinforced U. S. Grant with Brooks's and JOHN H. MARTINDALE's divisions plus Charles Devens' attached X Corps division. At COLD HARBOR, the XVIII Corps succeeded 1 June 1864, but shared the bloody repulse of 3 June. In midmonth it spearheaded Grant's bold strike against Petersburg. Brooks, Martindale, and Hincks overran the city's outer defenses 15 June, but Smith's hesitancy and Confederate bravery saved the communications center itself. The XVIII Corps held the right of the siege line just east of town, within easy sniping range. In late August it transferred to quieter Bermuda Hundred, with small garrisons at Dutch Gap, Deep Bottom, and downriver. By then, Smith was gone, victim of his own plot to overthrow army commander BENJAMIN F. BUTLER. Martindale temporarily succeeded Smith, but on 21 July E.O.C. ORD became permanent corps commander.

Under him its farflung garrisons reunited for field duty and their greatest victory, CHAFFIN'S FARM, 29 Sept. Though CHARLES J. PAINE's blacks repeatedly failed at NEW MARKET HEIGHTS, George J. Stannard's 1st Division stormed Fort Harrison and threw Richmond into mortal peril. But Ord's wounding, successor CHARLES A. HECKMAN's blunders, and Southern skill and valor limited Federal gains.

Under Weitzel, who succeeded Heckman, the corps repulsed counterattacks against Fort Harrison 30 Sept. Weitzel also secured the Northern left while the X Corps fought heavily at First and Second Darbytown Road. But the last independent foray, under unsure Weitzel, failed at Fair Oaks 27 Oct. 1864.

The corps was discontinued 3 Dec. 1864. Its white troops entered the XXIV Corps, and Paine's blacks joined the XXV Corps.   —RJS

XIX Corps/Army of the Gulf; Army of the Shenandoah

This corps, generally associated with the Army of the Gulf, was officially organized under General Order No. 5, 5 Jan. 1863, retroactively to 14 Dec. 1862. It consisted of all troops within the area designated Department of the Gulf and troops en route there by sea. Composed primarily of personnel from New York, Massachusetts, and Maine, the force was the first Federal unit to recruit and employ local Louisiana blacks as troops.

The unit participated at FORT BISLAND and IRISH BEND, Apr. 1863, and suffered over 4,300 casualties in the Siege of PORT HUDSON and its capture 9 July 1863. From July 1863 until Mar. 1864 the corps, based in New Orleans, performed garrison duty in territory occupied by Federal forces. On 15 Mar. 1864 the corps was fragmented, with the 1st Division under WILLIAM H. EMORY and the 2d Division under CUVIER GROVER becoming part of the ill-fated RED RIVER CAMPAIGN, while the remaining troops continued garrison duty at New Orleans. In July 1864, after the Red River debacle, the 1st Division, led by WILLIAM DWIGHT, and the 2d Division, led by Grover, were transferred under Emory's command to northern Virginia and designated Detachment/XIX Corps to serve in the Army of the Shenandoah under PHILIP H. SHERIDAN against Jubal A. Early's Confederate troops. On 7 Nov. 1864, the remainder of the corps was merged into the Gulf Reserve Corps, and the XIX Corps ceased to exist in the Department of the Gulf.

Meanwhile, in Virginia, the Detachment/XIX Corps was again transferred. Grover's 2d Division was sent south to Savannah Jan. 1865, and the 1st Division followed in April. Selected units of these 2 divisions remained on duty in Savannah well into 1866.

Those units serving in the Gulf Reserve Corps performed admirably under E.R.S. CANBY at Fort Blakely, Spanish Fort, and the capture of MOBILE in spring 1865.

The commanders of the corps as an integral unit were NATHANIEL P. BANKS, 16 Dec. 1862–20 Aug. 1863, and WILLIAM

B. FRANKLIN, until 2 May 1864, after which date the command structure of the fragmented corps evolved into other armies or departments.   —RAP

XX Corps/Army of the Cumberland

The XX Corps was created when the Army of the Cumberland was organized 9 Jan. 1863. Commanded by ALEXANDER M. MCCOOK, it was made up of troops that had formed the right wing of the Army of the Ohio at the Battle of PERRYVILLE and the right wing of the XIV Corps at the Battle of STONE'S RIVER. Later that year the XX Corps participated in the CHATTANOOGA CAMPAIGN, and 19–20 Sept. was routed with heavy losses during the Battle of CHICKAMAUGA. On 9 Oct. the XX and the XXI corps were consolidated to form the IV Corps.

On 4 Apr. 1864 a new XX Corps, commanded by JOSEPH HOOKER, was created through the consolidation of the XI and XII corps, originally from the Army of the Potomac. These units had been shipped to the West Oct. 1863 to relieve Chattanooga, where the Army of the Cumberland was besieged, and had captured LOOKOUT MOUNTAIN 24 Nov. Under Hooker, the XX Corps/Army of the Cumberland participated in Sherman's ATLANTA CAMPAIGN in spring and summer 1864. On 27 Aug. Hooker resigned the command and was replaced by HENRY W. SLOCUM. The XX was one of the 4 corps to make the MARCH TO THE SEA Nov.–Dec. 1864. With Slocum commanding the Federal left wing, Alpheus S. Williams assumed command of the XX Corps.

During winter 1865, the XX was part of the army that made the march from Savannah through the Carolinas. After the surrender of the Confederate army at Durham Station, N. C., 26 Apr. 1865, the corps, commanded by JOSEPH A. MOWER as of 2 Apr., marched on to Washington for the Grand Review before being disbanded.   —JWR

XXI Corps/Army of the Cumberland

The XXI Corps was created when the Army of the Cumberland was organized 9 Jan. 1863. The troops making up the corps had formed the left wing of the Army of the Ohio at the Battle of PERRYVILLE and the left wing of the XIV Corps at the Battle of STONE'S RIVER. The XXI Corps was commanded by THOMAS L. CRITTENDEN.

Later that year the corps was engaged in the CHATTANOOGA CAMPAIGN and occupied the city 9 Sept. At the Battle of CHICKAMAUGA, 19–20 Sept., the Confederate army broke through the XXI's sector and routed both the XXI and XX corps. Some units of the XXI, however, joined the XIV Corps and helped to hold the left of the Union position.

On 9 Oct. 1863 the XXI Corps was consolidated with the XX to form the IV Corps/Army of the Cumberland.   —JWR

XXII Corps/Department of Washington, D.C.

As a permanent garrison for the Federal capital and a ready force for service in the Union Department and District of Washington, the XXII Corps was begun 2 Feb. 1863 and placed under command of SAMUEL P. HEINTZELMAN.

First composed of the 1st and 2d divisions under John J. Abercrombie and SILAS CASEY, 4 infantry and 2 artillery regiments in the District of Alexandria, Va., an artillery brigade for service south of the Potomac River, and Horatio G. Sickel's division of Pennsylvania Reserves, the corps maintained modest strength even during the capital's reversion to district status. Shortly after its organization the corps' strength was augmented with a light artillery camp, a cavalry division, a division-sized force for service north of the Potomac, and several regiments to be quartered inside the city proper.

The size of the XXII Corps expanded and contracted with need and military crises in the Washington area. Among its members were troops of the 1st, 3d, 6th, 7th, 9th, 10th, 12th, 14th, 18th, 19th, 21st, 22d, and 24th regiments of the VETERAN RESERVE CORPS. All were wounded Union veterans, disabled for active campaigning; several of their regiments saw action again during Confederate Jubal A. Early's 1864 raid on Washington.

CHRISTOPHER C. AUGUR replaced Heintzelman in corps command 13 Oct. 1863 and served with but one interruption until the corps' dissolution 11 June 1866. JOHN G. PARKE briefly relieved Augur June 1865.   —JES

XXIII Corps/Army of the Ohio; Department of North Carolina

Most non–IX Corps Union troops in Kentucky became the XXIII Corps 27 April 1863. GEORGE L. HARTSUFF, Mahlon W. Manson, JACOB D. COX, and GEORGE STONEMAN successively had charge during its first year. The Army of the Ohio's commander, JOHN M. SCHOFIELD, exercised direct command of the corps Apr. 1864–Feb. 1865. During those times when Schofield commanded more than 1 corps—briefly before Feb. 1865, permanently thereafter—Cox or DARIUS N. COUCH led the XXIII. Until Jan. 1865, when the corps was transferred east, it remained responsible for garrisoning Kentucky and East Tennessee. The latter region came under its control when overrun by Hartsuff's mobile force Aug.–Sept. 1863. That November its cavalry became the Cavalry Corps/Army of the Ohio. Then purely infantry, it served under Manson at CAMPBELL'S STATION and KNOXVILLE and under Cox and Stoneman in John G. Foster's and Schofield's campaigns in East Tennessee, where the cold, poorly supplied foot soldiers wintered.

In spring 1864 the 2 veteran divisions under HENRY M. JUDAH (later MILO S. HASCALL) and Cox, and ALVIN P. HOVEY's new Indiana division joined William T. Sherman to threaten Rocky Face Ridge, Ga., then fight heavily at RESACA and NEW HOPE CHURCH. Reduced in size in June, the corps consisted of 2 divisions under Hascall and Cox. This tiny "corps/army" battled at Kolb's Farm and Utoy Creek.

Its day of glory came 30 Nov. 1864, when, under Cox at FRANKLIN, Tenn., it repeatedly repelled John B. Hood's charges. Then on 15–16 Dec. the XXIII—again under Schofield—helped rout Hood at Nashville.

With the Western theater secured, Schofield took his 2 mobile divisions and THOMAS H. RUGER's new division to North Carolina. Cox then led 4 XXIII Corps brigades and three X Corps brigades in capturing WILMINGTON, after which he returned to New Berne to command Ruger and local forces in Cox's provisional corps. Stiff opposition at KINSTON led Couch's 2 veteran divisions to join him from Wilmington. Both corps reached Goldsborough and 31 Mar. merged as Cox's XXIII Corps for Sherman's final drive. The corps garrisoned western North Carolina until 1 Aug. 1865, when the corps was discontinued.   —RJS

XXIV Corps/Army of the James

Most white regiments of the Army of the James were combined to form the new XXIV Corps 3 Dec. 1864. ALFRED H. TERRY's (later ROBERT S. FOSTER's) 1st Division, ADELBERT AMES's 2d Division, and CHARLES DEVENS' 3d Division had es-

sentially been the 1st and 2d Divisions/X Corps and 1st Division/XVIII Corps, respectively. The XVIII Corps distributed 9 other regiments between Terry and Devens and also contributed the artillery brigade and corps staff. On 24 Dec. THOMAS M. HARRIS' (later JOHN W. TURNER's) 1st Division/VIII Corps joined as the Independent Division/XXIV Corps. E.O.C. ORD, then JOHN GIBBON, were the permanent corps commanders. Interim replacements included Terry, Devens, and Turner.

The corps initially held the Army of the James's right on the Virginia peninsula. After easily checking James Longstreet's demonstration against NEW MARKET HEIGHTS, 10 Dec., it spent a quiet winter except for a foray to Fredericksburg in March. Ames, too, struck the coast, first in Benjamin F. Butler's Fort Fisher fiasco (*see* BUTLER'S NORTH CAROLINA EXPEDITION), then in Terry's expedition to Cape Fear. Ames and Joseph C. Abbott's 2d Brigade/1st Division/XXIV Corps stormed FORT FISHER 15 Jan. 1865 and helped capture Wilmington 22 Feb. Abbott garrisoned that city, and Ames marched to Goldsborough. There, 27 Mar., Terry's Provisional Corps became the X Corps, thus severing his, Ames's, and Abbott's nominal connection with the XXIV Corps.

By then Virginia was erupting into action. For the final, decisive onslaught Gibbon's 1st and Independent divisions and 3 batteries crossed the James River 27–28 Mar. to strike PETERSBURG. During ensuing operations he and his subordinates frequently directed the accompanying 2d Division/XXV Corps. They skirmished heavily along Hatcher's Run, 31 Mar.–1 Apr. Then in the XXIV Corps' one great battle, 2 Apr., they finally overwhelmed FORT GREGG's determined defenders. The next day Richmond and Petersburg fell; Devens, who had remained under Godfrey Weitzel on the peninsula, helped occupy the capital.

Gibbon meantime pursued westward along the Southside Railroad. 2 of his regiments suffered in the High Bridge disaster before the main body reached Farmville. On 8–9 Apr., however, his forced march to Appomattox Court House provided the infantry support that headed off and doomed R. E. Lee's army. Gibbon was a commissioner for Lee's surrender. His corps also occupied Lynchburg and garrisoned southern Virginia until the unit was discontinued 1 Aug. 1865.   —RJS

XXV Corps/Army of the James

Black soldiers' real and supposed successes, May–Sept. 1864, made Benjamin F. Butler favor concentrating into a corps all black troops besieging PETERSBURG. His Army of the James eventually contained the black 3d Division/X Corps and 3d Division/XVIII Corps. In mid-November, he traded 6 white regiments to the Army of the Potomac for the black 3d Division/IX Corps.

The X and XVIII corps were discontinued 3 Dec.; all black outfits plus the X Corps' white staff and artillery brigade constituted the XXV Corps. Butler reshuffled regiments and brigades into 3 new divisions: CHARLES J. PAINE's 1st (later 3d), WILLIAM BIRNEY's 2d, and CHARLES A. HECKMAN's (later EDWARD A. WILD's, then AUGUST V. KAUTZ's) 3d (later 1st). Butler's protégé, GODFREY WEITZEL, led the corps.

Its 1 cavalry and 9 infantry brigades were the largest black force assembled in the Civil War. The corps manned the Army of the James's left on the Virginia peninsula but never fought as a unit. Paine's division returned to North Carolina to support the white troops that took FORT FISHER and WILMINGTON. At

Goldsborough, 27 Mar., it became the 3d Division/X Corps.

Weitzel meantime resumed command from Heckman, who had temporarily led the corps Dec. 1864–Feb. 1865. At the end of the Petersburg Campaign, Weitzel occupied the peninsula–Bermuda Hundred backwater with Kautz, the artillery, and 2 white divisions. Only Birney's 9 regiments—sometimes reporting to E.O.C. Ord, sometimes under XXIV Corps control —moved to the Southside, where they did little until their important show of strength at Appomattox Court House. By then Birney had been relieved, and his brigades served with XXIV Corps divisions.

The 2d Division was reestablished 10 Apr. under RICHARD H. JACKSON. Weitzel had entered Richmond 3 Apr. His efforts to carry out Pres. Abraham Lincoln's conciliatory policies displeased the War Department, which transferred him to Chesterfield County. His corps sailed to southern Texas May–July 1865, to confront Confederates, overawe the French rulers in Mexico, and occupy the state. GILES A. SMITH and Jackson led his 2 divisions; Alonzo Draper commanded a new 3d Division until killed 30 Aug. When discontinued 8 Jan. 1866, the XXV was the last remaining Federal corps. —RJS

Cavalry Corps/Army of the Potomac

The Cavalry Corps of the Army of the Potomac developed over the 4 years of war from a small, underutilized scouting force to a major combat arm with a significant role in Union victory.

Early in the war numerous volunteer cavalry regiments were raised to supplement the Regulars, but until spring 1863 both bodies were poorly trained and used, serving mainly as guards, couriers, and orderlies. More than once they were humiliated in engagements with J.E.B. Stuart's Confederates; their combat record was so meager that the Union army jibe was "Whoever saw a dead cavalryman?"

In spring 1863 Joseph Hooker began ordering the use of cavalry as a body. GEORGE STONEMAN launched the first full-scale cavalry raid on Richmond during the Chancellorsville Campaign (see STONEMAN'S RAID, Apr.–May 1863). On 9 June Stoneman's successor, ALFRED PLEASANTON, sent 10,000 Union troopers to attack an equal number of Confederates at BRANDY STATION. It was the first true cavalry battle of the war, and though the Federals retired after the fight, their newfound audacity and skill shook Confederate confidence.

On 1 July, at Gettysburg, John Buford's 2 brigades demonstrated that cavalry could hold off infantry as his troopers fought dismounted until reinforced by Union infantry. On 3 July the cavalry clashed with Stuart's troopers east of Gettysburg in a mounted engagement and emerged victorious.

Through 1864–65 the role of the cavalry increased greatly. Under the overall command of PHILIP H. SHERIDAN, and with young leaders like GEORGE A. CUSTER, WESLEY MERRITT, H. JUDSON KILPATRICK, and JAMES H. WILSON, the Cavalry Corps destroyed railroads, barns, ships, factories, granaries, and anything else of use to the Confederates. The individual campaigns were almost continuous, and Union troopers ranged over Virginia. Armed with repeating carbines, they not only bested Confederate cavalry but prevailed over Confederate infantry. In the last days of the war they broke Lee's last supply line, harried his retreating army, and finally forced their way ahead to block his march. Appomattox was to a great extent a result of their work. —LDJ

Cavalry Corps/Military Division of the Mississippi

The Army of the Tennessee was one of the few major Union field armies that never maintained a true cavalry corps like those of the Army of the Potomac and, later, the Military Division of the Mississippi, where many of the Army of the Tennessee's cavalry troops were assigned. One reason is that in the Western theater some of the Army of the Tennessee's operations took place in areas inhospitable to cavalry. Another, more important, reason is that many of this army's operations were launched in cooperation with other Federal armies that either supplied the cavalry or shared the services of an independent cavalry corps.

Thus, during the Battle of Shiloh only 6 battalions and 13 additional companies were assigned to the army and were scattered throughout the various infantry divisions with differing degrees of strength. The 1st Division had only 1 cavalry company assigned; the 4th, 5th, and 6th divisions each had 2 battalions. During the Vicksburg Campaign most of the infantry divisions had 1 cavalry company assigned as escorts; an additional 15 companies were assigned to the 9th Division of the XIII Corps, and 3 unassigned regiments attended to the organizational charts. During the Chattanooga Campaign no cavalry was attached to the army; cavalry duties were carried out by horsemen of the Army of the Cumberland. Finally, during the Atlanta Campaign, the old system was revived of assigning a company or sometimes a regiment to the various corps headquarters, but the general duties were carried out by an independent cavalry corps shared by the 3 Federal armies.

On 24 Oct. 1864 James H. Wilson was announced as chief of cavalry of all horsemen from Sherman's armies. The new organization, Cavalry Corps of the Military Division of the Mississippi, gained fame in the Selma and Columbus raids. —LDJ

Reserve Corps/Army of the Cumberland

The Reserve Corps/Army and Department of the Cumberland, also known popularly as the Army of Kentucky, was a portion of the second army formed under that name, created by General Order No. 168, Adjutant General's Office, 24 Oct. 1862, and previously known as the Army of the Ohio. This army was reorganized by General Order No. 9, Adjutant General's Office, 9 Jan. 1863, and was to consist of troops in Tennessee and such parts of Alabama and Georgia in the possession of Federal forces. At this time, on his own initiative, the army commander, WILLIAM S. ROSECRANS, organized a reserve corps under GORDON GRANGER, to date from 8 June 1863.

During its existence, the Reserve Corps consisted of 3 divisions, each composed of 3 brigades and attached artillery units from Illinois, Indiana, Kentucky, Michigan, Ohio, Tennessee, and Wisconsin. Initially based at Murfreesboro, Tenn., the corps participated in the advance on TULLAHOMA, particularly in the Battles of Shelbyville and Guy's Gap, and played a decisive part in the second day of the Battle of CHICKAMAUGA. There JAMES B. STEEDMAN's 1st Division of the Reserve Corps saved the beaten and fleeing Union army from total disaster after Braxton Bragg's Confederate forces routed most of Rosecrans' troops. Their timely arrival on Snodgrass Hill stopped James Longstreet's assault and assisted GEORGE H. THOMAS, Granger's immediate superior, in winning the name "The Rock of Chickamauga."

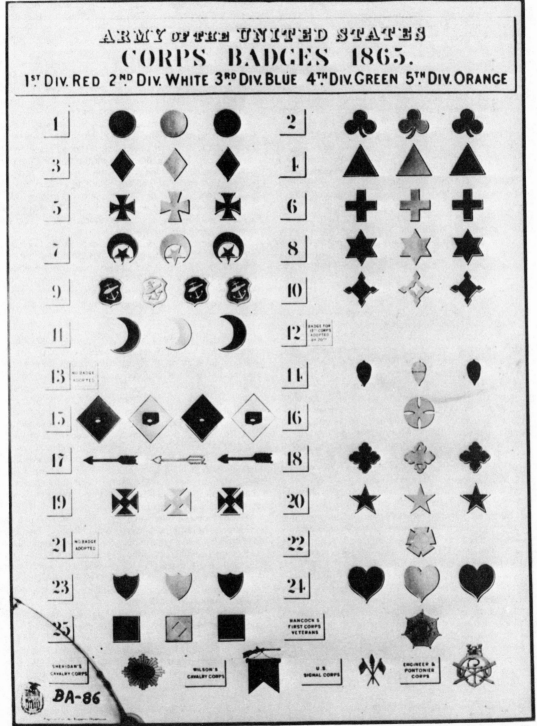

Corps badges

This was the corps' zenith. After it was discontinued 9 Oct. 1863, the troops merged into the reorganized IV and XIV corps/Army and Department of the Cumberland, after Rosecrans' relief from command. The corps had existed only 4 months, but it helped save the day for the Union at the crucial Battle of Chickamauga. —RAP

Terry's Provisional Corps

In Dec. 1864 a Union force under BENJAMIN F. BUTLER made an unsuccessful attempt to capture Fort Fisher at the mouth of the Cape Fear River in North Carolina (*see* BUTLER'S NORTH CAROLINA EXPEDITION). The purpose was to close Wilmington, N.C., the Confederacy's last important Atlantic port.

Dissatisfied with Butler's failure, Union commander ULYSSES S. GRANT, 2 Jan. 1865, ordered ALFRED H. TERRY, commander of the XXIV Corps/Army of the James, to organize a second expedition against the fort. This force, which became Terry's Provisional Corps, consisted of the 2d Division/XXIV Corps, under ADELBERT AMES; the 3d Division/XXV Corps, under CHARLES J. PAINE; the 2d Brigade/1st Division/XXIV Corps, under Joseph C. Abbott (which was attached to Ames's division); and 2 artillery batteries (10 guns). The corps had a strength of about 9,000 officers and men. A siege train (heavy artillery and mortars) and an engineer company were also assigned to Terry's command to be used if necessary to besiege the fort.

The corps left Virginia by boat 5 Jan. Joined by vessels of the North Atlantic Blockading Squadron, the expedition arrived off FORT FISHER 12 Jan. The troops were put ashore on the peninsula above the fort on the 13th. Terry's men established their beachhead on the 14th, and on the following day they assaulted and captured Fort Fisher.

In February Terry's command advanced up the river to Wilmington, which the Confederates evacuated during the night of 21–22 Feb. From Wilmington, Terry moved toward Goldsborough in cooperation with a column from New Berne, to open communication with the Federal armies under William T. Sherman, which were marching from Savannah, Ga., toward Virginia. This mission was accomplished in late March.

On 27 Mar. 1865, its assignment completed, Terry's Provisional Corps was merged into the reorganized X Corps. —RMcM

corps badges. Initially corps badges were distinctive shapes of colored cloth sewn onto combat soldiers' uniforms or hats as an indication of the men's unit. Badges of various kinds were seen before 1861, but their use beyond the regimental level evolved during the Civil War.

Corps badges first appeared in the 3d Division/III Corps of the Union Army by order of Maj. Gen. PHILIP KEARNY, who mistakenly reprimanded officers from another command on the battlefield. To avoid repeating the error, he ordered each of his officers to sew a 2-in. square patch of red flannel onto the top of his hat. The distinctive patch became a mark of pride among Kearny's troops, and enlisted men soon began wearing the Kearny badge as well. After Kearny's death at Chantilly, Va., 1 Sept. 1862, his successor, Brig. Gen. DAVID BIRNEY, continued the practice out of respect for the popular commander.

Shortly after Maj. Gen. JOSEPH HOOKER assumed command of the Army of the Potomac, corps badges were officially assigned on a wide scale. To bolster the sagging morale of his men Hooker assigned Maj. Gen. DANIEL BUTTERFIELD to develop the shapes for badges on the corps level. Butterfield distinguished different divisions within a corps by the color of their patch: 1st Division, red; 2d Division, white; 3d Division, blue; 4th Division, green; 5th Division, orange.

Orders authorizing most of the corps badges were issued 21 Mar. 1863, and the idea rapidly gained acceptance among the fighting men: an estimated two-thirds of the front-line troops wore corps badges by 1864. The badges became more elaborate, those worn by officers frequently being embroidered or made of various metals, with some of the latter enameled. Generally the regimental number in metal was pinned in the center of cloth badges. The badges were worn on the left shirt front, sometimes on the side or front of the hat, or frequently at the top of the hat, where they were easily visible. Some of the more elaborate versions were suspended from a metal pin. Many continued to be produced after the war, making it difficult to distinguish between those actually worn in the service and those made as keepsakes after the surrender.

No system of corps badges developed in the Confederate army, though Gen. P.G.T. BEAUREGARD considered the use of wing badges (a strip of red cloth worn above the elbow) in combat before FIRST BULL RUN, and in the Valley of Virginia Maj. Gen. THOMAS J. "STONEWALL" JACKSON ordered his men to tie strips of white cloth around their hats to distinguish them from the enemy. —PLF

Corpus Christi, Tex., Siege of. 16–18 Aug. 1862 In mid-July 1862 Union Capt. John W. Kittredge, on blockade duty off the coast of Texas, planned to attack Corpus Christi. Though his 100-man force could not hold the town, he hoped a victory would strengthen the Unionist mayor's position. Word of Kittredge's plans reached the town, where pro-Confederates immediately prepared to defend themselves. In the absence of an experienced military leader, Provost Marshal Col. Charles G. Lovenskiold assumed command of the few resident volunteer companies, sent cotton and tobacco stores inland to prevent their capture, and sank 3 cement-laden schooners in the channel to block entrance to Corpus Christi Bay. When Confederate Maj. Alfred Hobby arrived with 300 men from the 8th Texas Infantry, 20 July, Lovenskiold willingly turned over command.

Hobby would be commanding his first battle with untrained volunteers. At his disposal were 3 smoothbore cannon, 1 18-pounder and 2 old 12-pounders, the latter abandoned by the U.S. Army several years earlier. The Seacoast Defense Battery also had 2 6-pounder artillery pieces, which the gun crews had not learned to use properly for lack of gunpowder with which to practice. With no experienced artillerists to handle the ordnance, Hobby willingly accepted help from Mexican War veteran Felix Blucher and from Billy Mann, a disabled Confederate soldier recently returned from the fighting at Island No. 10.

On 12 Aug. Kittredge cleared the bay by using the steam power of the recently arrived *Sachem*. Early the next day and again in the afternoon he landed at Corpus Christi under a truce flag. His parley with Hobby resulted in a 48-hour truce during which civilians were to be evacuated from the city. After he departed, Hobby unwisely ordered the cannon placed in the abandoned Kinney Fort on a bluff overlooking the bay. Mann advised the commander to move the cannon from the bluff to existing fortifications along the water at the city's northern end, but it was too late to reposition the ordnance before the truce expired. When Kittredge failed to attack once the truce ended on the 16th, Hobby feverishly hauled the ordnance to the beach. The work was finished about 2 a.m., and the troops hid behind the earthworks and in nearby ravines.

At daybreak on the 17th, either Mann or Blucher shouted the order to fire, taking Kittredge's men by surprise. Shells hit the *Sachem* and the *Carypheus,* both of which returned the fire ineffectively. Of the 5 small vessels in Kittredge's fleet, 2, the *Reindeer* and the *Bella Italia,* sat becalmed too far out of artillery range, and the *Breaker* stood in reserve as a hospital ship. The return shelling inflicted only superficial damage on several buildings.

On the Confederate side, Mann directed the men from atop the earthworks, encouraging and warning them of incoming shells. The battle continued for 4 hours before Kittredge withdrew his ships. He reopened the fighting briefly, but ended the battle for the day after expending 300 shells against the Texans. Certain Kittredge intended to attack again, the defenders, reinforced with volunteers from nearby communities, prepared for another assault.

On the morning of the 18th Kittredge sailed to a position about a mile south of Hobby's battery to launch a land/sea attack. The *Bella Italia* landed 30 men and a 12-lb howitzer. The troopers rushed toward the battery, firing rapidly, while the ships, 400 yd offshore, bombarded the Confederates with grape and shrapnel. Unable to turn his cannon, Hobby ordered a company of cavalry to stand in reserve and with 25 volunteers advanced on the enemy, by now only 600 yd from his works. Outfought, Kittredge's men retreated under cover of heavy fire from the ships. The cavalry joined the rout before Hobby ended the counterattack. 1 Confederate had been killed, and a few men on both sides slightly wounded. Kittredge shelled those buildings he thought hid Confederates, then withdrew to nearby Shell Bank to make repairs.

2 days later Brig. Gen. HAMILTON P. BEE arrived in Corpus Christi to reinforce the city's defenses. Though the defenders were highly praised and Corpus Christi was proclaimed the "Vicksburg of Texas" by a local newspaper, from then until the end of the war the town languished. In the 7 months before Kittredge was captured by Confederates in Sept. 1862, he effectively ended the coastal trade in the area, and a garrison stationed on Mustang Island in 1863 harassed the townspeople frequently. Federal troops under Maj. Gen. NATHANIEL P. BANKS occupied Corpus Christi 16 Nov. 1863.   —PLF

Corrick's Ford, western Va., action at.   13 July 1861

The mountainous western counties of Virginia, defying Confederate authorities in Richmond, seceded from Virginia 11 July 1861 to rejoin the Union. With 20,000 Federal soldiers, Union Maj. Gen. GEORGE B. MCCLELLAN, commander of the Department of the Ohio, had moved into the Allegheny Mountains region in late May to support the counties. Against this army, Virginia authorities dispatched Brig. Gen. ROBERT S. GARNETT and 4,500 men.

Garnett's Virginia and Georgia troops occupied Beverly, a vital crossroads village in the Tygart River Valley, 50 mi west of the Shenandoah Valley. The Confederate general divided his command to cover the northern and western approaches. 5 mi west of the town, on the crest of Rich Mountain, Garnett stationed 1,300 men and 4 cannon, under Lt. Col. JOHN PEGRAM. The remaining Confederates and 4 guns, which Garnett

commanded personally, occupied Laurel Mountain, 16 mi north of Beverly, which served as the supply depot. The Southerners entrenched both positions with log breastworks.

Garnett harassed Union supply lines but could do little more against McClellan's overwhelming numbers. The Northern commander, angered by the raids, decided to destroy the Confederates. With 4 brigades numbering 15,000 men, McClellan arrived opposite the Southern positions 9 July. He spent the 10th reconnoitering, deciding on an attack against Pegram.

On 11 July, in a lashing rainstorm, Brig. Gen. WILLIAM S. ROSECRANS' Union brigade scrambled up Rich Mountain beyond the Confederate left flank. The Federal assault forced Pegram to divide his force. After 2 or 3 hours of skirmishing, part of the Union brigade broke the Southerners' line. Pegram, losing 2 cannon, abandoned the crest and retreated to Beverly.

Garnett learned that evening of Pegram's defeat and evacuated his position about midnight. He marched toward Beverly only to receive false intelligence that McClellan's soldiers occupied the town. The Confederates then retraced their march, abandoning the turnpike at Leadsville, and crossed Cheat Mountain into the Cheat River Valley. Union Brig. Gen. Thomas A. Morris, with his Indiana brigade, pursued them.

About noon, 13 July, Morris overtook Garnett's rear guard at Corrick's (often spelled Carrick's) Ford, and the Hoosiers pitched into the retreating Virginians. Garnett personally directed the Confederate skirmishers, soon withdrawing to another ford a mile or two farther away, where the running skirmish resumed briefly. As Garnett prepared again to retreat, a Federal volley killed him instantly. The Southerners fled, abandoning their dead commander, 1 cannon, and nearly 40 wagons.

The Confederates lost an estimated 20 killed and wounded and some 50 captured in the engagement; reports of Federal wounded vary from 10 to 53. Pegram, whose retreat had been cut off by McClellan, surrendered an additional 555 men that day. McClellan had won a victory that resulted in instant fame and a summons from Washington, D.C., to come east. For Confederate authorities the disaster called for a new commander in western Virginia. 2 weeks after Corrick's Ford, Gen. ROBERT E. LEE came west to coordinate the Confederate operations.   —JDW

Corse, John Murray.   USA b. Pittsburgh, Pa., 27 Apr. 1835.

At 7 Corse moved with his parents to Burlington, Iowa Territory, where his father became a 6-term mayor and owner of a book and stationery business in which young Corse eventually became a partner. Corse studied law and was admitted to the bar but also attended West Point 1853–55.

In June 1861 Corse was named major of the 6th Iowa Infantry and early in 1862 served on the staff of Maj. Gen. JOHN POPE during the operations against NEW MADRID and ISLAND NO. 10. That May he returned to his regiment as its lieutenant colonel, after distinguishing himself at Corinth and Farmington. The next spring and summer, as a colonel, he was conspicuous for gallantry at VICKSBURG, where his regiment maintained a position above the Confederate stronghold.

In Aug. 1863 he was promoted to brigadier general of volunteers, receiving command of the 4th Brigade/4th Division/XV Corps/Army of the Tennessee, leading that brigade in the CHATTANOOGA CAMPAIGN, during which he was knocked unconscious by a rifle ball at MISSIONARY RIDGE. After recuperating in Iowa, he returned to staff duty as inspector general to Maj. Gen. WILLIAM T. SHERMAN, remaining with him until July 1864, when assigned a XVI Corps division.

After the fall of Atlanta, as Sherman's main army prepared for its MARCH TO THE SEA, Gen. JOHN BELL HOOD moved north to sever communications in the Union rear. Before the enemy could strike, Sherman set the trusted Corse to secure strategic ALLATOONA Pass, which Corse did, 5 Oct., commanding a force of 2,000 against a Confederate division under Maj. Gen. SAMUEL G. FRENCH. During some of the war's bloodiest fighting, Corse lost a third of his command and was again wounded. Still, he "held the fort" as ordered, until the approach of reinforcements late in the day forced French to withdraw.

Later, Corse accompanied Sherman on his march through Georgia, leading a division of the XV Corps at the Siege of SAVANNAH and in the CAROLINAS CAMPAIGN as a brevet major general. He was mustered out of the volunteers 30 Apr. 1866, declining a lieutenant colonelcy in a Regular regiment.

In civilian life, he was collector of internal revenue for Chicago, built railroads and bridges, then moved to Massachusetts, where he became chairman of the state Democratic committee and postmaster of Boston. d. Winchester, Mass., 27 Apr. 1893, on his 58th birthday. —EGL

Corse, Montgomery Dent.

CSA b. Alexandria, Va., 14 Mar. 1816, Corse served as a captain of Virginia volunteers in the Mexican War, sought gold in California, and at 40 entered the banking business in his hometown. An ardent militiaman, in 1860 Corse organized the Old Dominion Rifles, subsequently commanding a battalion of several companies.

When Virginia seceded, Corse readily volunteered. Appointed assistant adjutant general in Alexandria, he remained on duty until the Confederates evacuated the city. With his militia service and war experience, Corse was commissioned colonel of the 17th Virginia, initially as part of Brig. Gen. JAMES LONG-

USMHI

STREET's brigade and later Brig. Gen. JAMES L. KEMPER's brigade. Corse and his regiment fought at BLACKBURN'S FORD, FIRST BULL RUN, and in the PENINSULA and SEVEN DAYS' campaigns. At SECOND BULL RUN he temporarily led the brigade, suffering a slight wound. 2 weeks later, at Boonsborough, he received another wound. With his regiment reduced to 56 men, Corse and the remnant fought valiantly at ANTIETAM, capturing 2 battle flags but emerging with only 7 left in the ranks. Longstreet praised him highly in his report, considering Corse one of the best officers in the army.

Appointed brigadier general 1 Nov. 1862, Corse received a brigade in Maj. Gen. GEORGE E. PICKETT's all-Virginia division. He led his new command at Fredericksburg, but the brigade was on detached duty when the division made its famous charge at GETTYSBURG. The brigade went west with the I Corps in autumn 1863, fighting at CHICKAMAUGA and KNOXVILLE. During the war's final year Corse and his Virginians saw action at the WILDERNESS; DREWRY'S BLUFF; NEW BERNE, N.C.; PETERSBURG; DINWIDDIE COURT HOUSE; and FIVE FORKS, where the brigade

performed magnificently in the Confederate rout. 5 days later, 6 Apr. 1865, at SAYLER'S CREEK, Corse was captured. The Federals confined him in Fort Warren, Mass., until August.

Corse resumed his banking business in Alexandria after the war. Blind during his final years, the Confederate brigadier died in Alexandria 11 Feb. 1895. —JDW

Cosby, George Blake.

CSA b. Louisville, Ky., 19 Jan. 1830. On 9 May 1861, Cosby was promoted to captain of the 2d U.S. Cavalry. On 10 May he resigned to join the Confederacy. Cosby had been in the army since West Point, graduating 17th in the class of 1852 and spending the next 9 years fighting Comanches in Texas. Except for a brief stay in St. Louis and duty teaching cavalry tactics at the academy, he had not often been out of the Lone Star State in a decade. But as a Confederate staff officer, on 15 Feb. 1862 he found himself in Tennessee walking out across Confederate lines to ask Brig. Gen. U.S. GRANT for surrender terms.

USMHI

Cosby had received his Confederate army appointment as a staff major assigned successively to forces under Brig. Gens. GIDEON J. PILLOW, JOHN B. FLOYD, and LLOYD TILGHMAN in Tennessee. After the fall of Confederate FORT HENRY and Tilghman's capture, Grant's forces converged on FORT DONELSON, where Pillow passed command to Floyd, then escaped. Floyd in turn passed command to Brig. Gen. SIMON B. BUCKNER, then escaped. And Buckner gave Major Cosby a note to carry to Grant offering surrender. Cosby was exchanged after a brief period as a prisoner of war.

On Gen. JOSEPH E. JOHNSTON's recommendation he was given a brigadier general's commission, to rank from 20 Jan. 1863, and assumed command of cavalry under Maj. Gen. EARL VAN DORN, who had been Cosby's major in the old U.S. Cavalry. Cosby saw action in the engagement at Thompson's Station, Tenn., in spring 1863, then moved to Johnston's command for operations around VICKSBURG. His next and last transfer was to the Confederate Department of West Virginia and East Tennessee, where he served as cavalry commander of a body of men that varied from 2,000 to 4,000 and was briefly led by Brig. Gen. JOHN HUNT MORGAN after his escape from the Ohio State Penitentiary. In this theater of the war Cosby dueled with troops led by his old West Point classmate Brig. Gen. GEORGE CROOK.

When he heard of Gen. ROBERT E. LEE's surrender of the Army of Northern Virginia, Cosby was still in the field, commanding Kentucky horsemen and led by a senior brigadier general, John Echols. Echols wanted to join forces with Johnston's army in North Carolina, but Cosby believed resistance useless and disbanded his men, advising them to go home as quietly and as safely as possible, ending his part in the Civil War.

Later Cosby farmed in California and served as secretary of the state board of engineers. He committed suicide 29 June 1909, apparently because of poor health caused by old war injuries. —JES

cost of the war. The approximately 10,455 military engagements, some devastating to human life and some nearly bloodless, plus naval clashes, accidents, suicides, sicknesses, murders, and executions resulted in total casualties of 1,094,-453 during the Civil War. The Federals lost 110,100 killed in action and mortally wounded, and another 224,580 to disease. The Confederates lost approximately 94,000 as a result of battle and another 164,000 to disease. Even if one survived a wound, any projectile that hit bone in either an arm or a leg almost invariably necessitated amputation. The best estimate of Federal army personnel wounded is 275,175; naval personnel wounded, 2,226. Surviving Confederate records indicate 194,026 wounded.

In dollars and cents, the U.S. government estimated Jan. 1863 that the war was costing $2.5 million daily. A final official estimate in 1879 totaled $6,190,000,000. The Confederacy spent perhaps $2,099,808,707. By 1906 another $3.3 billion already had been spent by the U.S. government on Northerners' pensions and other veterans' benefits for former Federal soldiers. Southern states and private philanthropy provided benefits to the Confederate veterans. The amount spent on benefits eventually well exceeded the war's original cost.

Inflation affected both Northern and Southern assets but hit those of the Confederacy harder. Northern currency fluctuated in value, and at its lowest point $2.59 in Federal paper money equaled $1 in gold. The Confederate currency so declined in purchasing power that eventually $60–$70 equaled a gold dollar.

The physical devastation, almost all of it in the South, was enormous: burned or plundered homes, pillaged countryside, untold losses in crops and farm animals, ruined buildings and bridges, devastated college campuses, and neglected roads all left the South in ruins.

Detailed studies of Union and Confederate military casualties are found in *Numbers and Losses in the Civil War in America 1861–65* by Thomas L. Livermore (1901) and *Regimental Losses in the American Civil War, 1861–1865* by William F. Fox (1889).   —HH

Cotton Diplomacy. Almost unanimously, Southerners believed they could use cotton to lure England and France into recognizing the Confederacy. Since the administration of JEFFERSON DAVIS wanted to avoid any appearance of international "blackmail," the Confederate Congress never formally approved an embargo, but state governments and private citizens voluntarily withheld the crop from the market in hopes of causing a "cotton famine" overseas. Theoretically, widespread shortages would shut down European mills, forcing governments to recognize and perhaps come to the military aid of the Confederacy, or to declare the Union blockade ineffective and disregard or break it in order to reopen Southern ports.

The "King Cotton" mentality was seriously flawed, not the least in overestimating the value of "white gold." First, a bumper crop in 1860 had glutted the marketplace, lowering prices and allowing mill owners to stockpile. Cotton prices did rise sharply late in 1861, but workers, not owners, suffered from the effects of unemployment. Producers, drawing from their reserves, did not feel the pinch until late in 1862, and within a year imports from India, Egypt, and Brazil sufficiently replaced Southern cotton. Second, Davis, never an astute diplomat, failed to recognize how much Europe feared the possibility of war with the U.S. Private European citizens and industrialists invested in speculative ventures tenuously backed by Southern cotton securities, but their governments would not antagonize the North by recognizing the Confederacy for the sake of guaranteeing those investments or increasing supplies of the staple. Further, Southern society tied cotton inseparably to slavery, and England, the example Napoleon III would follow, led the abolitionist movement in the world community.

Europe's wait-and-see attitude hardened into unassailable neutrality after the Southern armies suffered reverses beginning at Gettysburg, and Davis and his supporters realized the cotton strategy had failed as a diplomatic tool. They had unwisely hoarded their one great asset and undermined their best chance of financing the war.   —PLF

Couch, Darius Nash. USA b. Putnam Cty., N.Y., 23 July 1822, Couch graduated from West Point 13th out of 59 in the class of 1846, along with Thomas J. "Stonewall" Jackson and George B. McClellan. As an artillerist he saw action in both the Mexican and Seminole wars, and he also showed ability as a naturalist with a Smithsonian Institution expedition in Mexico during a leave of absence in 1853. 2 years later he resigned his commission to enter a copper goods manufacturing business.

NA

Slight and rather frail, his health impaired during the Mexican War, Couch was nevertheless a good professional soldier. He was impatient with incompetence and his comments could be blunt and caustic. A brief dispatch to a subordinate during the GETTYSBURG CAMPAIGN is characteristic: "An order was given to take rations last night. Do troops want me to tell them to breathe? Always have rations in your haversacks. . . . Now is the time to aid your country. Let trifles go; march."

Starting the war as colonel of the 7th Massachusetts, June 1861, by August Couch was a brigadier general and the next year so efficiently led a division of Keyes's IV Corps in the PENINSULA CAMPAIGN that he was promoted to major general 4 July 1862. Still commanding a division, he was at SECOND BULL RUN and at CRAMPTON'S GAP during the Antietam Campaign. At FREDERICKSBURG and CHANCELLORSVILLE he led the II Corps. Disgusted with Maj. Gen. JOSEPH HOOKER after his defeat in the latter battle, he requested transfer and 11 June 1863 was made commander of the newly formed Department of the Susquehanna. From headquarters in Harrisburg he directed Pennsylvania home-guard units for defense of the state during Gen. ROBERT E. LEE's invasion. In Dec. 1864 he led a division of the XXIII Corps in the decisive Battle of Nashville and in operations in North Carolina. He resigned his commission 26 May 1865. d. 12 Feb. 1897, in Norwalk, Conn.   —RDH

coup de main. One of many French military terms adapted by Union and Confederate services, *coup de main* is a quick vigorous attack that surprises the enemy.   —JES

Covode, John. USP b. Westmoreland Cty., Pa., 18 Mar. 1808. After a childhood as a farmboy and apprenticeship to a blacksmith, Covode worked in woolen mills, first in New York, then in Lockport, Pa. Speculating in the coal business, he also became owner of a woolen mill, invested in the Pennsylvania Canal and the Pennsylvania Central Railroad, and was a justice of the peace and a state legislator.

At the start of the Civil War Covode was known nationally as "Honest John" Covode, a 3-term Republican congressman from the Lockport district. In 1860 he opened an investigation into Pres. James Buchanan's political practices, claiming that 2 House members had been offered bribes and coerced by Buchanan into voting for passage of the Lecompton resolution. Some speculated that Covode opened his investigation because of Buchanan's charges that through bribery the 1858 congressional elections in Pennsylvania had been fixed, elections that had returned Covode to the House. Others speculated that Covode pursued the investigation only to get favorable press coverage for Republicans running in the 1860 elections, or that Covode was just vindictive. Whatever his motives, the investigation resulted in Covode's appointment to the joint COMMITTEE ON THE CONDUCT OF THE WAR, a body with a reputation for vindictiveness.

On 10 Dec. 1861 the U.S. House of Representatives voted unanimously to establish the committee and appointed 3 senators and 4 congressmen members, Covode among them. Until 1863 he helped look into the Union defeats at BALL'S BLUFF and SECOND BULL RUN, Va.; Lexington, Ky.; and WILSON'S CREEK, Mo. He took part in the inquisition and ruin of Brig. Gen. CHARLES P. STONE, supported the possibilities of having Maj. Gen. GEORGE B. MCCLELLAN relieved, and helped absolve former Republican presidential candidate Maj. Gen. JOHN C. FRÉMONT of charges of incompetence.

In other legislative areas Covode, a Radical Republican, stuck by that wing of his party, favoring vigorous prosecution of the war, all abolition measures, and a hard hand with former Confederates.

In 1863 Covode ended his Civil War congressional career, declining to run for reelection. He professed to be tired after having served in Congress since 1854. But following the Confederate surrender he toured the South at Pres. Andrew Johnson's request to report on the progress of Reconstruction, a report that displeased Johnson. In 1866 Covode won his seat in Congress again, and later in his term introduced the resolution calling for Johnson's impeachment. Covode served 1 more term, then left Congress in 1870. d. Harrisburg, Pa., 11 Jan. 1871.   —JES

Cox, Jacob Dolson. USA b. Montreal, Canada, 27 Oct. 1828, where the future general's father, a New York contractor, was roofing a church. Cox entered Oberlin College, graduating in 1851. After serving 2 years as superintendent of schools in Warren, Ohio, he opened a law practice. A free-soil Whig, Cox was elected a state senator in 1858 and, on taking his seat Jan. 1859, helped form a radical antislavery group.

On 23 Apr. 1861, after Pres. ABRAHAM LINCOLN's call for 75,000 volunteers, Cox entered service as a brigadier general of Ohio state troops and was subsequently named a brigadier general of volunteers to rank from 17 May 1861. He participated in the western Virginia campaign of 1861, first under Maj. Gen. GEORGE B. MCCLELLAN, then under Brig. Gen. WILLIAM S. ROSECRANS.

In Aug. 1862 Cox and his Kanawha division were assigned to Maj. Gen. JOHN POPE's Army of Virginia and joined the Army of

USMHI

the Potomac for the ANTIETAM CAMPAIGN. At SOUTH MOUNTAIN, 14 Sept., Cox temporarily succeeded to command of the IX Corps on the death of Maj. Gen. JESSE L. RENO and led it at Antietam 17 Sept. He was advanced to the rank of major general 6 Oct. 1862, but Mar. 1863 was reduced to his former rank because the number of major generals permitted by law had been exceeded. He was reappointed and confirmed as major general by the U.S. Senate 7 Dec. 1864.

During winter 1862–63, Cox commanded forces in western Virginia and from April to mid-December 1863 was responsible for the District of Ohio. He was then assigned to the XXIII Corps.

Cox returned to Middle Tennessee Oct. 1864, and he and his troops played a key role in turning back the Confederate surge at Franklin, 30 Nov. At Nashville he fought on the right of the Union line as it rolled back the Confederates.

In late winter 1865 Cox finished the war, accompanying the XXIII Corps to North Carolina, where, 8–10 Mar., he defeated Gen. BRAXTON BRAGG's Confederates at KINSTON, and at Goldsborough on the 23d rendezvoused with Maj. Gen. WILLIAM T. SHERMAN's army.

Cox was elected governor of Ohio before being mustered out of the service. He served in that office 1866–67, but as a moderate on the black suffrage issue he failed to win reelection. Pres. U. S. Grant appointed Cox secretary of the interior in 1868, and in this position he was an active proponent of civil service reforms. He resigned the cabinet post in 1870 after difficulties with the president, returning to his law practice and working as an educator; he wrote extensively on military topics during his last 30 years. d. near Gloucester, Mass., 4 Aug. 1900.   —ECB

Cox, William Ruffin. CSA b. Halifax Cty., N.C., 11 Mar. 1832, Cox was the grandson of a British naval officer who settled in the Carolinas in the early 19th century. In his youth he moved with his widowed mother to Tennessee, graduating from Franklin College in 1853 and from Lebanon College Law School 2 years later. Admitted to the bar, he practiced in Nashville before returning to his native state to run a plantation.

A militant secessionist, Cox raised a volunteer company before war broke out. When his state joined the Confederacy, he was appointed major of the 2d North Carolina Infantry and was sent to Virginia. During the

LC

Peninsula Campaign, he fought at MECHANICSVILLE and MALVERN HILL, displaying a boldness and courage that endangered his life. At CHANCELLORSVILLE, May 1863, he was 5 times wounded and was lost to his army for many months.

Cox was not again conspicuous in battle until May 1864, when he led his regiment at SPOTSYLVANIA. There, on the 12th, he guarded the right center of Maj. Gen. STEPHEN D. RAMSEUR'S brigade, driving 2 lines of Union infantry into retreat, despite an enfilading fire that cost Cox's men dearly. Early the next month, shortly after COLD HARBOR, he received Ramseur's command and the rank of brigadier general.

In late summer 1864 Cox followed Ramseur to the Shenandoah Valley, where he commanded 6 North Carolina regiments during Lt. Gen. JUBAL A. EARLY'S campaign against Maj. Gen. PHILIP H. SHERIDAN. He returned to the main fighting front in time to accompany Gen. ROBERT E. LEE on the road to Appomattox. Near the courthouse village on the morning of 9 Apr. 1865, Cox led the last organized attack launched by the Army of Northern Virginia. Within hours of its failure, Lee surrendered to Lt. Gen. ULYSSES S. GRANT.

Though almost disabled by his 11 wounds, Cox led a varied and successful postwar life in North Carolina as a lawyer; railroad president; district solicitor; chairman of the state Democratic party; superior court judge; agricultural society president; university trustee; and U.S. congressman, serving 3 consecutive terms beginning in 1880. One of the last surviving Confederate generals, he died in Richmond, Va., 26 Dec. 1919. —EGL

Coxetter, Louis Mitchell. CSN b. Nova Scotia, Canada, 10 Dec. 1818. Settling in Charleston, S.C., Coxetter entered the merchant service there and commanded sailing ships and steam packets plying between Charleston and St. Augustine, Fla.

Soon after the outbreak of Civil War, Confederate Pres. JEFFERSON DAVIS issued a letter of marque, which gave official encouragement to privateering. As a consequence, Coxetter and other private citizens of Charleston purchased and outfitted the brig *Putnam* (earlier called the *Echo,* a slave ship) and renamed it *Jefferson Davis,* which was armed with 5 60-year-old British cannon. Coxetter became captain of the *Jefferson Davis,* and a crew of 70 was recruited. In only 7 weeks, operating off northern waters, the privateers captured 9 U.S. merchant ships and created a panic among coastal residents and shippers from Delaware to New England. However, because of the North's BLOCKADE, only 2 of the prizes reached the Southern port of Savannah; 2 others were recaptured by their crews, 2 were burned, and the remaining vessels released. Then, when the *Jefferson Davis* ran aground while attempting to enter the port of St. Augustine, 18 Aug. 1861, Coxetter ended his service as a privateer.

Coxetter next became a blockade runner for the banking house of John Fraser & Co. of Charleston and FRASER, TRENHOLM & CO. of Liverpool, England. Coxetter's final effort for the South was an attempt to mine the Savannah River during the last weeks of the war.

With war over, Coxetter returned to the merchant service on the Charleston-Palatka shipping line. d. Charleston, 10 July 1873. —NCD

Cracker Line Operation, Bridgeport, Ala. 24 Oct.–1 Nov. 1863 On 23 Oct., Maj. Gen. ULYSSES S. GRANT took command of Federal troops besieged at Chattanooga, and on the 24th Chattanooga's chief engineer, Maj. Gen. WILLIAM F. SMITH, submitted plans for opening a water supply route from Bridgeport, Ala. Chattanooga's garrison, on reduced rations, received its few staples by wagon trains traveling over 60 mi of bad road from Bridgeport, through the Sequatchie Valley, and over Walden's Ridge in the Cumberland Mts. The wagons were subject to frequent attack, arrivals were uncertain, and the trip took twice as long as the water route Smith proposed. If Federal troops secured Tennessee River frontage below Confederate-held Raccoon Mountain west of town, supplies could be transported by boat.

Grant approved the plan, and on 26 Oct., at 3 a.m., 24 pontoon boats carried Brig. Gen. WILLIAM B. HAZEN'S brigade and a detachment of the 1st Michigan Engineers on the Tennessee's current around Moccasin Point, a dry neck of land opposite Raccoon Mountain. Brig. Gen. JOHN BASIL TURCHIN'S brigade marched west across Moccasin Point in the dark and met Hazen's men at Brown's Ferry, a point beyond the range of Confederate artillery on the southern slope of Lookout Mountain. Contested by 1,000 Confederates and 3 cannon, they thrust a pontoon bridge to the west bank, erecting a bridgehead on the 27th. Maj. Gen. JOSEPH HOOKER'S reinforcing divisions, sent from Virginia weeks before and awaiting orders in north Alabama, finally received instructions to march up Lookout Valley from Bridgeport to link up with the battered engineers on the 28th. Hooker's men cleaned the Confederates from Raccoon Mountain, and on 1 Nov. the first steamboat arrived at Brown's Ferry, breaking the siege.

Water-borne supplies were landed at Brown's Ferry and shuttled overland out of artillery range on Moccasin Point. Chattanooga's hungry garrison, happy for hardtack, named this route the "Cracker Line." —JES

Crampton's Gap, Md., Battle of. 14 Sept. 1862 On this day of the ANTIETAM CAMPAIGN, battles were fought at 3 crucial passes through South Mountain (*see also* Battle of SOUTH MOUNTAIN). The southernmost defile, Crampton's Gap, was a few miles northeast of Harpers Ferry, where a Union garrison lay besieged by 3 Confederate forces. To relieve the surrounded Federals, Maj. Gen. GEORGE B. MCCLELLAN committed his 12,000-man VI Corps under Maj. Gen. WILLIAM B. FRANKLIN.

The Union corps arrived at the foot of the mountain about noon; 2 Confederate cavalry regiments and 3 of infantry, Virginians all, defended the pass. The defending force, commanded by Col. William A. Parham, was probably only one-tenth the number opposing it. Behind the Confederates lay Pleasant Valley and direct access to Maryland Heights, where Maj. Gen. LAFAYETTE MCLAWS' command was attacking to seal the fate of the Union garrison at the ferry. A successful Federal assault up Pleasant Valley could result in the destruction of McLaws' force.

Maj. Gen. HENRY W. SLOCUM'S division initiated Franklin's attack on the mountain gap. Scaling the wooded mountainside, the Federals charged the Confederate line. Parham's Confederates clung to their position, repulsing Slocum's thrusts for several hours. Franklin finally sent in Maj. Gen. WILLIAM F. "BALDY" SMITH'S division on Slocum's left. Parham's ranks began cracking under the mounting Union numbers.

At this crucial moment Brig. Gen. HOWELL COBB, with 4 Confederate regiments, arrived from the south. Cobb's soldiers rapidly filed into line but could not stem the relentless Union assault. The Southern center collapsed under the onslaught. Hammered for hours, Parham's Confederates broke wildly, running down the western side of the mountain. Cobb and

Parham vainly tried to rally the panicked fugitives. Cobb delayed the pursuing Federals with a battery and 2 regiments of Brig. Gen. PAUL J. SEMMES' brigade, which had arrived as reinforcements.

McLaws, when he learned of the disaster in his rear, immediately withdrew 2 brigades and 2 cannon from Maryland Heights. These reinforcements formed a line of battle about a mile and a half below Crampton's Gap, where the remnants of the defenders finally rallied.

Franklin, under orders to relieve the Union garrison, pushed into Pleasant Valley, halting short of this new Confederate line. Overestimating McLaws' strength, the VI Corps commander lost his nerve, and nightfall soon ended the action. Franklin's hesitation doomed the garrison, which surrendered the next day. The battle in the gap had cost him only 533 men, while inflicting nearly 1,000 casualties. But Franklin had missed an opportunity to alter the course of the Antietam Campaign.

—JDW

Crapo, Henry Howland. war governor b. Dartmouth, Mass., 22 May 1804. Reared and self-educated in Bristol Cty., Mass., Crapo became a schoolteacher, then a surveyor, and, on moving to New Bedford, Mass., in 1832, an insurance-company secretary, land speculator, and colonel in the state militia. While speculating in land in Western states, he gained government experience in New Bedford city offices. His civic and business career in that city spanned 22 years.

Growing lumber and sawmill investments in the Flint area compelled his move in 1858 to Michigan, where financial influence and his civic experience in the East won him the office of mayor of Flint in 1860 and, as a Republican supporter of Gov. AUSTIN BLAIR, a seat in the state senate, 1863–64. Pledging to carry on Blair's Republican Civil War and fiscal policies, Crapo was elected Michigan's governor in 1864.

A Radical Republican, Crapo organized the state's congressional delegation in support of the 13TH AMENDMENT and at war's end urged private relief efforts for families of Michigan's 87,000 returning volunteers. His performance in office as the war was ending won him reelection in 1866. He committed his second term to opposing Pres. Andrew Johnson's Reconstruction policies and addressing Michigan's continuing postwar fiscal problems.

Shortly after his second term ended, Crapo died in Flint, 22 July 1869.

—JES

Crater, Battle of the (Petersburg, Va.). 30 July 1864 Union army engineers dismissed the idea as "claptrap and nonsense." The army commander, Maj. Gen. GEORGE G. MEADE, initially opposed it, while the general in chief, ULYSSES S. GRANT, greeted it with skepticism. Meade's engineers argued that no one could dig—undetected—a mineshaft over 500 ft long to a point under the Confederate trenches at PETERSBURG, fill a chamber with gunpowder, and detonate it.

Lt. Col. Henry Pleasants, a civil engineer and commander of the 48th Pennsylvania, thought otherwise. In Pleasants' regiment were many coal miners from Schuylkill County, and Pleasants overheard one of them claim that they could blow away a Confederate artillery salient by tunneling underneath it. The Pennsylvania officer liked the idea, convinced his IX Corps commander, Maj. Gen. AMBROSE E. BURNSIDE, of the plan's feasibility, and ultimately secured Grant's approval.

The coal miners began digging 25 June 1864, with Pleasants

USMHI

devising an ingenious and invisible ventilation system. The tunnel was completed 23 July; 4 additional days were required to place the powder charge. The shaft measured 586 ft in length, 5 ft in height, 4.5 ft in width at the bottom, and 2 ft at the top. 2 lateral galleries, totaling 75 ft in length, ran underneath Confederate trenches. The Pennsylvanians placed 320 kegs of powder, 8,000 lb, in the galleries. Sealing the shaft for 38 ft, the miners improvised a fuse.

Burnside, meanwhile, trained Brig. Gen. EDWARD FERRERO's division of black troops to spearhead the assault. On 29 July, the day before the scheduled detonation, Meade and Grant ordered Burnside to substitute a division of white troops for Ferrero's men. The 2 Union commanders did not want to be accused of using black volunteers as cannon fodder if the charge failed. Burnside had his 3 white division commanders draw straws; Brig. Gen. JAMES H. LEDLIE picked the short one.

The explosion was set for 3:30 a.m. on the 30th, but the fuse failed. 2 volunteers of the 48th crawled into the shaft and relit it at the splice. At 4:45 the 4 tons of powder exploded in the most awesome spectacle of the war. 9 companies of the 19th and 22d South Carolina were hurled high into the air; nearly 300 of them were killed or maimed. The blast rent the Confederate lines with a hole 170 ft long, 60–80 ft wide, and 30 ft deep. Stunned Confederates on both sides of the chasm fled in fear.

Ledlie's division charged, while their commander, drinking liquor, remained behind in a bombproof. Instead of forming around the crater, many Federals plunged into it. Burnside then sent in his 2 other divisions of white soldiers; but the Confederates had regrouped and counterattacked. Southern artillerymen scorched the huddled Northern masses in the crater. About 8 o'clock Maj. Gen. WILLIAM MAHONE's Confederate division sealed the breach in their lines. The Southerners rimmed the crater, shooting the nearly helpless Federals, who floundered about in their huge, earthen barrel. Burnside ordered in Ferrero's black troops, but it was too late. Enraged Southerners shot many of the blacks after they had surrendered. By 1 p.m. the Federals had been pushed back to their lines.

Union casualties amounted to 3,798; Confederate losses were about 1,500. The spectacular explosion created an excellent opportunity to sever Confederate lines but Grant described the assault as a "stupendous failure." A subsequent court of inquiry found Burnside, Ledlie, and Ferrero primarily responsible for the bungled affair.

—JDW

Craven, Thomas Tinsey. USN b. District of Columbia, 20 Dec. 1808. Older brother of TUNIS A. M. CRAVEN, Thomas was appointed midshipman in 1822, rising to lieutenant in 1830 and commander in 1852. At the beginning of the Civil War, he commanded the Potomac River flotilla and in 1862, as captain of the *Brooklyn,* served under Rear Adm. DAVID G. FARRAGUT on the Mississippi. Having proven himself a competent and reliable officer, Craven was promoted to commodore in 1863 and assigned to the *Iroquois* to search for CONFEDERATE CRUISERS in European waters; there he discovered the former Confederate cruiser *Georgia* off Portugal and seized it, despite its recent transfer to an English merchant. Then, in Mar. 1865, the *Iroquois* and the USS *Sacramento,* commanded by Capt. HENRY WALKE, discovered the formidable CSS *STONEWALL* at Ferrol, Spain. Confederate Capt. Thomas J. Page sent a challenge to fight both ships, but Craven declined, believing his and Walke's wooden ships were no match for the ironclad and its heavier guns. A naval court-martial followed, which included as members Farragut and Capt. JOHN A. WINSLOW of the USS *KEARSARGE.* Craven, found guilty of having failed to fight, was sentenced to be suspended from the navy for 2 years with leave pay. The verdict was overruled by Sec. of the Navy GIDEON WELLES, who considered it inappropriate to the offense and restored Craven to duty.

Despite this blot Craven's naval career was otherwise distinguished, and he was promoted to rear admiral in 1866. He retired 3 years later and died in Boston, Mass., 23 Aug. 1887.
—NCD

Craven, Tunis Augustus MacDonough. USN b. 11 Jan. 1813, Portsmouth, N.H. Craven, a younger brother of Rear Adm. THOMAS T. CRAVEN, entered the navy as a midshipman in 1829, was promoted to passed midshipman in 1835, and to lieutenant in 1841. Craven became one of the navy's leading surveyors and hydrographers and spent more than 20 years with the U.S. Coast Survey. In 1861, while commanding the *Crusader,* he helped save Key West for the Union. Promoted to commander the same year, he was ordered to the *Tuscarora,* which cruised European waters in search of the elusive Confederate commerce destroyers. One, the *SUMTER,* was found at Gibraltar, and Craven kept it blockaded there until the cruiser finally ended its career as a raider and was sold in spring 1862.

LC

In April 1864 Craven took command of the *TECUMSEH,* a new monitor of the James River flotilla. On 24 June the *Tecumseh* exchanged fire with enemy batteries at Howlett's Bluff, on the James. Then Craven received orders to join the squadron of Rear Adm. DAVID G. FARRAGUT off Mobile. The *Tecumseh* arrived there under tow 4 Aug. 1864. The next day the attack began, and the monitors led the advance toward Fort Morgan. The *Tecumseh,* the lead vessel, struck an enemy TORPEDO and sank within minutes. Before it sank, Craven and pilot John Collins reached the ladder leading to the top of the turret at the same time. Craven held back to allow the pilot to go first. This act cost Craven his life, and he drowned with most of the *Te-*

*cumseh'*s officers and crew; Collins' life was saved.   —NCD

Cravens' Farm, Tenn., Battle of. 24 Nov. 1863 *See* LOOKOUT MOUNTAIN, TENN., BATTLE OF.

Crawford, Samuel Wylie. USA b. Franklin Cty., Pa., 8 Nov. 1829. Crawford graduated from the University of Pennsylvania in 1846 and from its medical school in 1850. A year later he joined the army as an assistant surgeon and served on the Western frontier until Apr. 1861, when he had command of a battery during the attack on FORT SUMTER. Once hostilities began Crawford surrendered his staff position and was appointed major of the newly created 13th U.S. Infantry. In Apr. 1862 he was promoted to brigadier general of volunteers and earned praise as a brigade commander at WINCHESTER, CEDAR MOUNTAIN, and ANTIETAM. His unit suffered 50% casualties at Cedar Mountain; at Antietam he took command of a division until he was severely wounded.

LC

After convalescence Crawford in May 1863 was assigned command of the Pennsylvania Reserve Corps, which he led at GETTYSBURG as the 3d Division of Sykes's V Corps. At the Battles of the WILDERNESS, SPOTSYLVANIA, and FIVE FORKS, and at the Siege of PETERSBURG, he was brevetted for gallantry, and by war's end received brevet rank for all grades through major general in both the Regular and volunteer services. He had also been commissioned to lieutenant colonel of the 2d Infantry (Regulars) 17 Feb. 1864.

Crawford saw duty in the South until 1866, when he was mustered out of volunteer service. He retired from the army in 1873 and was promoted on the retirement list to brigadier general 2 years later. He lived in Philadelphia until his death there 3 Nov. 1892.   —MK

Crew's Farm, Va., Battle of. 1 July 1862 *See* MALVERN HILL, VA., BATTLE OF.

Crittenden, George Bibb. CSA b. Russellville, Ky., 20 Mar. 1812. While both his father, Sen. JOHN J. CRITTENDEN of Kentucky, and his younger brother THOMAS L. CRITTENDEN worked to save the Union, George joined the Confederacy. Graduating from West Point 26th in his class in 1832, he quit the army after a year and went to Texas, serving in the Texas Army. In 1843 he was captured by the Mexicans as part of the Mier Expedition, but was released from prison through the influence of his father's friend, Andrew Jackson. Reenlisting for the Mexican War, George continued in the Regular Army, rising to lieutenant colonel.

DAM/LSU

When the Civil War broke out, Crittenden came south to join the Confederate army. In Oct. 1861 JEFFERSON DAVIS made him a major general and sent him to lead an army of invasion into his native Kentucky. He was to concentrate on the Kentucky border with the troops of Brig. Gens. FELIX ZOLLICOFFER and WILLIAM H. CARROLL. Early in 1862 Crittenden joined his small command, which had crossed the rain-swollen Cumberland River to Beech Grove, Ky.

As his troops attempted to defeat one of 2 Union armies before they united into one force, Crittenden ran into Union pickets near MILL SPRINGS in the rain on the morning of 19 Jan.; this proved to be his first and last major battle. By late morning the Union commander, Brig. Gen. GEORGE H. THOMAS, had outflanked Crittenden's defeated army, which retreated to Beech Grove. The public demanded that Crittenden be replaced and many claimed he was drunk at the time of the battle. However, ALBERT SIDNEY JOHNSTON, Confederate commander in the West, gave him command of the reserve corps in the army he was building in northern Mississippi to regain Tennessee. But Crittenden lost his chance to salvage his career 1 Apr. 1862, when Maj. Gen. WILLIAM J. HARDEE came into Iuka, Miss., and found Crittenden and Carroll drunk and their commands in a "wretched state of discipline." Crittenden was arrested and court-martialed. He resigned 23 Oct. 1862 but continued to serve in a subordinate role under the various commanders in western Virginia. After the war he lived in Danville, Ky., where he died 27 Nov. 1880. —CMS

Crittenden, John Jordan. USP b. Woodford Cty., Ky., 10 Sept. 1787. On the eve of civil war, no man devoted himself more completely to compromise than Crittenden. His failure turned into personal tragedy when 2 of his sons became major generals in the armies of opposing governments.

Crittenden graduated from the law course at William and Mary College in 1807 and established himself in western Kentucky as a skillful defense attorney in murder cases. In more than 50 years as a politician, from 1809, he served his state in the legislature; as secretary of state; in the U.S. Senate, 1817–19; and as U.S. district attorney, moving again into national poli-

LC

tics in 1835 when reelected to the U.S. Senate. There he stayed, except for an appointment as attorney general under Pres. William H. Harrison, Mar.–Sept. 1841; a term as governor of Kentucky, 1848–50; and a second appointment as attorney general under Pres. Millard Fillmore, July 1850–Mar. 1853.

As a Whig and staunch Union man, Crittenden esteemed Henry Clay for his efforts at compromise, sharing Clay's broad vision for the country if not his genius as a legislator. No abolitionist, he nonetheless hoped slavery would die out, knowing the South could never support any Federal legislation that threatened the institution.

When the Whigs fell apart in the 1850s, Crittenden joined the short-lived Know-Nothing party, and when it too disintegrated, he became a Democrat. He opposed the KANSAS-NEBRASKA ACT, 1854, because it repealed the MISSOURI COM-

PROMISE line, and took instead a noninterventionist stand on slavery in the territories, in opposition to STEPHEN A. DOUGLAS' call for a policy of POPULAR SOVEREIGNTY.

Abraham Lincoln's election pushed Crittenden into the forefront of compromise politics. In Dec. 1860 he placed before the Senate a series of resolutions he hoped would receive enough support to halt the movement toward disunion and war. On the 18th, the Senate appointed a COMMITTEE OF THIRTEEN, with Crittenden as chairman, to consider the proposals, but after a week of intense debate committee members voted down the CRITTENDEN COMPROMISE.

With hopes of averting war destroyed, Crittenden returned to Kentucky in an effort to keep his state from seceding. The arguments he advanced to the legislature 16 Mar. eventually became the basis of the neutrality position adopted by the state in April. The next month, as chairman of the Border Slave State Convention in Frankfort, he presided over a debate that urged the seceded states to reconsider their actions and the national government to follow a moderate course.

Finally accepting the inevitability of war, Crittenden redirected his energy toward defining the war goals as a struggle to preserve the Union. But as the conflict gained momentum he increasingly disagreed with the administration on such issues as independent statehood for western Virginia, black enlistments into the army, and confiscation of Confederate property. Discouraged but unwilling to admit defeat, the 76-year-old warrior died in Frankfort, Ky., 26 July 1863, in the midst of his campaign for reelection. —PLF

Crittenden, Thomas Leonidas. USA b. Russellville, Ky., 15 May 1819. The son of Kentucky statesman JOHN J. CRITTENDEN and younger brother of Confederate Maj. Gen. GEORGE B. CRITTENDEN, Thomas studied law with his father, began practicing in 1840, and in 1842 was elected state attorney for his district. During the Mexican War he served as Gen. Zachary Taylor's aide at Buena Vista, then became colonel of the 3d Kentucky Infantry. Appointed consul at Liverpool, England, by President Taylor, he returned home in 1853 and opened a law practice in Frankfort before going into business in Louisville.

Crittenden became a major general in the state guard in 1860 and assumed command in 1861 after Gen. SIMON B. BUCKNER joined the Confederate forces. Commissioned brigadier general in the Union army Sept. 1861, Crittenden commanded the 5th Division in Brig. Gen. DON CARLOS BUELL's army at SHILOH and was promoted to major general 17 July 1862. He performed well at STONE'S RIVER, where he led the left wing, and in the TULLAHOMA CAMPAIGN. At CHICKAMAUGA his XXI Corps was overrun 20 Sept. 1863. Maj. Gen. WILLIAM S. ROSECRANS removed him from command, but Crittenden demanded a court of inquiry, which acquitted him of all charges. His career was blighted, however, and he was transferred to the Army of the Potomac, where he led the 1st Division/IX Corps for a brief time in spring 1864. He requested to be relieved 9 June, claiming that the command was not equal to his rank, and he resigned from the army in December.

In Jan. 1866 Crittenden was appointed Kentucky state treasurer, but he resigned Nov. 1867 to accept Pres. Andrew Johnson's offer of a colonelcy in the Regular Army. Much of his postwar service was with the 17th Infantry. After retiring in 1881, he lived on Staten Island, N.Y., until his death there 23 Oct. 1893. He was buried in Frankfort, Ky.   —LHH

Crittenden Compromise. In Dec. 1860 Kentucky Sen. JOHN J. CRITTENDEN, whose compromise efforts had helped postpone war for nearly a decade, proposed a set of resolutions that became known as the Crittenden Compromise. They were referred for discussion to the COMMITTEE OF THIRTEEN 18 Dec.

The statesman advocated passage of 6 constitutional amendments: the first prohibited slavery north of 36° 30' (the MISSOURI COMPROMISE line) but extended protection by the Federal government to slavery existing below the line, and permitted the citizens of future states to decide for themselves whether they would enter the Union slave or free; the second prohibited Congress from abolishing slavery in any territory under national jurisdiction; the third forbade emancipation in the District of Columbia as long as Maryland or Virginia had slavery, or until a majority of citizens wanted it, and required compensation should it be demanded; the fourth protected interstate transportation of slaves; the fifth provided compensation by the U.S. government for any "rescued" slave, with reimbursement to the national treasury by the county where the rescue took place; and the sixth stipulated that no future amendments could render these guarantees null and void.

The measures might have been passed had not President-elect ABRAHAM LINCOLN let it be known through committeeman WILLIAM H. SEWARD that he refused to bend on the issue of containing slavery, though he was willing to make concessions on several other points. Since the compromise could only succeed if the 36° 30' line was reinstated, it was voted down in committee.

On 3 Jan. 1861 Crittenden delivered a forceful speech before Congress, seeking approval for a public referendum on the issue and directing attention to the flood of memorials and petitions thousands had signed in support of his compromise. But when the critical vote was called on the 16th, the Senate rejected the appeal 25–23, effectively ending all hopes of avoiding war by congressional action.   —PLF

Crocker, Marcellus Monroe. USA b. Franklin, Ind., 6 Feb. 1830, Crocker attended West Point, and though he did not graduate, he had great military ability and was later praised by Lt. Gen. U. S. GRANT as one of the army's best division commanders. Beginning his military career in Iowa, where he had lived for most of the preceding decade while practicing law in Des Moines, Crocker enlisted when the 2d Iowa Infantry was being raised for the Civil War. Elected one of its company captains 27 May 1861, he was made regimental major 4 days later, during organization.

Crocker was promoted to lieutenant colonel, then colonel,

USMHI

and fought in the Battles of SHILOH and CORINTH. In the latter battle he commanded the Iowa Brigade without commensurate rank and performed well. This so impressed his superiors that he was given command of a division, again without commensurate rank. Late in 1862 Crocker was promoted to brigadier general, to rank from 29 Nov. Through the VICKSBURG fighting he commanded the 7th Division of Maj. Gen. JAMES B. MCPHERSON's XVII Corps; in late summer he briefly led the XIII Corps' 4th Division; then until May 1864 he was back with his old XVII Corps, leading its 4th Division. In this last post, as in all the others, he was popular with his men. They performed well for him, and when they were engaged in fighting in north Georgia on Maj. Gen. WILLIAM T. SHERMAN's ATLANTA CAMPAIGN, they became known as "Crocker's Greyhounds" for the pace they kept.

Crocker was tubercular and in May 1864, before he could be commissioned major general, he tendered his resignation. Neither McPherson nor Sherman would accept it and instead arranged for his transfer to New Mexico, where, it was thought, the climate would help his condition. There he responded well and by December was back in Tennessee under Maj. Gen. GEORGE H. THOMAS. But in less than 3 months he was sent to Washington, D.C., and there relapsed, dying 26 Aug. 1865.   —JES

Crook, George. USA b. near Dayton, Ohio, 8 Sept. 1828. Though Crook earned fame as an Indian fighter and pacifier in the 1870s and 1880s, he was also an effective combat leader in the Civil War. Commanding divisions at ANTIETAM and CHICKAMAUGA and leading the Army of Western Virginia through the 1864 SHENANDOAH VALLEY CAMPAIGN, Crook was wounded, captured, and in 4 different battles was cited for gallantry.

An 1852 West Point graduate, ranking 38th in his class, Crook was stationed in the Pacific Northwest when the war began. He was made colonel of the 36th Ohio Infantry Sept. 1861 and conducted operations in western Virginia. Wounded at Lewisburg, Va., 23 May 1862, he was promoted to brigadier general 3 months later.

At SOUTH MOUNTAIN and Antietam he commanded the Kanawha Division, and early in 1863 was prominent in eastern Tennessee operations. In July 1863 he was placed in command of the 2d Cavalry Division of Maj. Gen. GEORGE H. THOMAS' Army of the Cumberland, leading troops in heavy fighting up to and including Chickamauga.

In Feb. 1864 Crook took command of the Kanawha District and led a series of actions designed to interrupt Confederate rail communications between Lynchburg, Va., and East Tennessee. After the repulse of Lt. Gen. JUBAL A. EARLY's raid on Washington during summer 1864, Crook succeeded Maj. Gen. DAVID HUNTER as commander of the Department of Western Virginia and led the Army of Western Virginia during Maj. Gen. PHILIP H. SHERIDAN's Shenandoah Valley Campaign against Early. Successes at Winchester, Fisher's Hill, and Cedar Creek enhanced the reputation of "Uncle George" Crook. His citation for Fisher's Hill was added to previous honors at Lewisburg, Antietam, and Farmington.

Crook was promoted to major general 21 Oct. 1864 and commanded the Department of Western Virginia from headquarters at Cumberland, Md. There, 21 Feb. 1865, he and Brig. Gen. BENJAMIN F. KELLEY were captured in a daring raid by Southern PARTISANS. Crook was exchanged just in time to command a cavalry division in the Army of the Potomac during the final weeks of the war.

Sent west after the war to protect settlers from Indian depredations, he remained in the army until his death in Chicago, 21 Mar. 1890. —DS

Cross Keys, Va., Battle of. 8 June 1862 Fought back-to-back with the Battle of PORT REPUBLIC, this battle was the third engagement of Maj. Gen. Thomas J. "Stonewall" Jackson's SHENANDOAH VALLEY CAMPAIGN and resulted in a Confederate victory against Maj. Gen. JOHN C. FRÉMONT's Union army.

Confronting Frémont near the village of Cross Keys 7 June 1862, Confederate Brig. Gen. RICHARD S. EWELL established good defensive positions: his troops were posted on a ridge with several hundred acres of open fields in front, and woods protected both flanks. Ewell had 3 brigades, about 5,000 men, in the line, along with several batteries. He considered the center his weak point and posted 4 batteries there, with Brig. Gen. ARNOLD ELZEY's infantry brigade as a reserve. Jackson's own division, along with Brig. Gen. EDWARD JOHNSON's and the Louisiana Brigade of Brig. Gen. RICHARD TAYLOR, came up on the morning of 8 June and were posted north of Port Republic, within supporting distance of Ewell but not actually in the line.

That morning the 18th Alabama Infantry of Brig. Gen. ISAAC R. TRIMBLE's brigade, posted in advance, was pushed back by Frémont's infantry. The Federals then moved against Trimble's brigade, posted on the Confederate right. Trimble's men held their fire until the Federals were close, fired 3 volleys, and repulsed the attack. The action, which had commenced with artillery, shifted back to the guns, but ammunition shortages reduced the rate of fire on both sides. Impatient for action, Trimble moved his troops forward to take a Federal battery, which escaped before he could reach it. Trimble moved a mile in advance, and Taylor's brigade was brought up to reinforce the left and center. The Federal reaction was slight, and by nightfall Ewell's troops had occupied the former Federal positions.

During the night, all the Confederate troops except Trimble's brigade, the 42d Virginia Infantry, and 1st Virginia Battalion went to reinforce Jackson's Port Republic positions. On 9 June the remaining Confederates fell back. —LDJ

cruisers, Confederate. On 10 May 1861 the Confederate Congress voted to approve Sec. of the Navy STEPHEN R. MALLORY's recommendation that the government immediately begin ordering ships to be built abroad for its navy. Influenced by what he believed to have been the success of American commerce destroyers during the Revolution and the War of 1812, Mallory felt that a serious blow to the North's merchant fleet would help win the war. The South's cruisers were also

LC

expected to spread terror among the population of the northeast seaboard and divert ships from the Federal BLOCKADE. JAMES D. BULLOCH, an able and experienced officer, was given the important task of securing the cruisers. In England he had private contractors build the first 2 foreign-constructed cruisers—the *FLORIDA* and the *ALABAMA*. He got both ships to sea by eluding British authorities, securing men and arms for them at neutral ports and on the high seas. During the next 2 years these vessels became the most formidable of the Confederate cruisers, crisscrossing the ocean lanes at will and destroying Northern whalers and merchantmen while evading all pursuers.

The captain of the *Alabama*, RAPHAEL SEMMES, had already gained experience as commander of the *SUMTER*, a screw steamer purchased by the Confederacy in spring 1861 to be its first cruiser. Converted at New Orleans, the *Sumter* proved inadequate and was laid up and sold at Gibraltar in 1862. Also unsuited was the second ship bought and converted, the *Nashville*. It operated as a cruiser only long enough to reach England; Bulloch thought it had been sent there to demonstrate the ineffectiveness of the Federal blockade and to give the Confederate flag visibility abroad.

Other Confederate agents arrived in England to secure cruisers, but only Cmdr. MATTHEW F. MAURY succeeded in getting to sea the 2 he purchased—the *GEORGIA* and the *RAPPAHANNOCK*. Neither vessel was suited as a cruiser, although the *Georgia* took 9 prizes during 6 months at sea. The *Rappahannock* developed engine trouble on its maiden voyage and was detained at Calais, France, after pulling into that port for repairs.

Prevented by the blockade from bringing captured ships into a home port, cruiser captains saw their prizes customarily condemned and burned if found to be owned by a U.S. citizen. If the ship carried a U.S. registry but transported neutral cargo, it was bonded by the owners, the value of the ship to be paid to the Confederacy after the war. Semmes and Lt. JOHN N. MAFFITT of the *Florida* both converted prizes into "satellite cruisers" for limited operations. Maffitt allowed Lt. Charles W. Read to take the prize *Clarence* as a cruiser and, until he was captured, Read caused near-panic along the northeast coast.

For as long as the South appeared to be winning, cruisers were usually welcome at foreign ports, but by 1864 the tide had turned. At Calais the *Rappahannock* was prevented from putting to sea by order of Napoleon III, who was being pressured by the British government to deny port facilities to the Confederates. In October the *Florida* was rammed and captured by the *WACHUSETT* at Bahia harbor, Brazil. In June of the same year the *Alabama* had been sunk by the *KEARSARGE* off Cherbourg, France. To make up for these losses, Mallory secured 2 BLOCKADE RUNNERS at Wilmington, N.C., and had them converted into cruisers. Both vessels, the *TALLAHASSEE* and the *Chickamauga,* eluded the blockaders but, unable to secure coal, were soon forced to return to Wilmington. The surprising success of the *Tallahassee* was due largely to its resourceful commander, Lt. JOHN TAYLOR WOOD. After a debate between army officials and the Navy Department concerning the effectiveness of the *Tallahassee,* the ship was renamed the *Olustee* and made 1 cruise along the Atlantic coast.

In England, Bulloch purchased and got to sea 1 more ship, the *SHENANDOAH*, the last of the cruisers. Commanded by Lt. JAMES I. WADDELL, the *Shenandoah* reached arctic waters, where it destroyed a large part of the U.S. whaling fleet. Learning that the war was over, Waddell returned to England

and surrendered his ship Nov. 1865.

Although both officers and crew of the cruisers were condemned by Northerners as "pirates," none was ever tried on this charge. Semmes was imprisoned for 3 months after the war but was released without a trial. The cruisers they manned accounted for over 200 U.S. vessels destroyed, at a loss of millions of dollars. Fear caused hundreds of other owners to transfer their ships' registries to English agents. Despite this, the cruisers had no appreciable effect on the war except to raise Southern expectations. In 1872 the *ALABAMA* CLAIMS were settled when England agreed to pay the U.S. $15.5 million for losses inflicted by the *Alabama, Florida,* and *Shenandoah,* and by their satellite cruisers.   —NCD

Cullum, George Washington. USA b. New York City, N.Y., 25 Feb. 1809. Moving with his family to Meadville, Pa., Cullum entered West Point, graduating 3d in the 43-man class of 1833. His high academic ranking gained him a position in the construction engineers, where he helped build harbor fortifications in his native city as well as in Boston, Newport, New London, Annapolis, and Charleston. When the corps was expanded in 1838, Cullum was promoted to captain, a grade he held for the next 23 years. During that period he also taught engineering at his alma mater and for 2 years was on inactive duty due to poor health.

LC

Early in the Civil War, Cullum served as aide-de-camp to WINFIELD SCOTT, commanding general of the army, then took a position with the U.S. SANITARY COMMISSION. Promoted to brigadier general of volunteers 1 Nov. 1861, he became chief of staff and chief engineer to Maj. Gen. HENRY W. HALLECK, then commanding the Department of the Missouri and later the Department of the Mississippi. After serving in the advance on CORINTH, Cullum accompanied Halleck to Washington when the latter replaced Maj. Gen. GEORGE B. MCCLELLAN in army command. Retaining the rank of engineer, Cullum was promoted to lieutenant colonel of Regulars 3 Mar. 1863.

In Sept. 1864 Cullum left Halleck's staff and spent the next 2 years as the superintendent of the U.S. Military Academy. Later he held posts on engineering boards and engaged in other assignments with his corps until he retired, with the rank of colonel and brevet major general, 13 Jan. 1874.

In civilian life Cullum resided in New York City, married the widow of General Halleck (the granddaughter of Alexander Hamilton), and pursued scientific and philanthropic endeavors. From 1877 till his death he was vice-president of the American Geographical Society of New York, and wrote and translated monographs on engineering. In retirement he also wrote histories of the Revolution and the War of 1812, and updated a work originally published in 1850: *Biographical Register of the Officers and Graduates of the United States Military Academy.* A 3d edition of this major reference work was released a year before Cullum's death in New York City, 28 Feb. 1892. In accordance with his will, supplements were added to the set in 1900, 1910, and 1920.   —EGL

Culp's Hill, at Gettysburg, Pa. 1–3 July 1863 The tip of the so-called Union "fishhook" line at GETTYSBURG, Culp's Hill towered above CEMETERY HILL and CEMETERY RIDGE, anchoring the northeastern end of the Union position. If the Confederates seized the wooded eminence, the Federal line on the lower hill and ridge would be untenable.

Union Maj. Gen. WINFIELD S. HANCOCK immediately recognized its tactical importance on the afternoon of 1 July 1863, ordering a battered Union division to occupy it. But the next day, as the battle shifted to the southern portion of the field, Union commands holding the hill were sent as reinforcements to the endangered left flank. When Maj. Gen. EDWARD JOHNSON's Confederate division finally attacked Culp's Hill late in the day, only Brig. Gen. George S. Greene's brigade held it. Greene's thin line, however, repulsed the 3 Confederate brigades.

During the night the Union XII Corps reoccupied the vital crest, and before daylight at 4 a.m. on 3 July, the struggle for Culp's Hill resumed. For 7 hours the fighting raged as the Confederates hurled themselves against the Federals. The sheets of musketry destroyed one of the area's finest oak forests, ruining the favorite picnic grounds of Gettysburg residents. The Federals could not be dislodged from their strong position and before noon the fighting ceased. The battle then shifted to a climax on Cemetery Ridge.   —JDW

Cumberland, Union Army of the. The army began with the creation of the second Department of the Cumberland 24 Oct. 1862 by General Order No. 168, Adjutant General's Office. Commanded by Maj. Gen. WILLIAM S. ROSECRANS from 30 Oct., it was responsible for all of Tennessee east of the Tennessee River, northern Alabama, and northern Georgia. At the time of its organization, the army consisted of the soldiers of the Army of the Ohio. Originally designated the XIV Corps, the Army of the Cumberland fought the Battle of STONE'S RIVER, 31 Dec. 1862–3 Jan. 1863, after which it was reorganized into the XIV Corps, under Maj. Gen. GEORGE H. THOMAS; XX Corps, Maj. Gen. ALEXANDER M. MCCOOK; XXI Corps, Maj. Gen. THOMAS L. CRITTENDEN; Reserve Corps, Maj. Gen. GORDON GRANGER; and Cavalry Corps, Maj. Gen. David S. Stanley.

In June 1863 the Army of the Cumberland broke the Confederate lines south of Murfreesboro, Tenn., and occupied CHATTANOOGA 9 Sept. It was defeated at the Battle of CHICKAMAUGA, 19–20 Sept., then was besieged in Chattanooga. Removed from command 19 Oct., Rosecrans was replaced by Thomas, and 25 Nov. the army broke the Siege of Chattanooga by storming MISSIONARY RIDGE, routing the Confederates and driving them into Georgia.

In 1864, numbering over 70,000 and still commanded by Thomas, the army made up more than half of Maj. Gen. WILLIAM T. SHERMAN's forces during the ATLANTA CAMPAIGN, at which time it included the IV Corps, under Maj. Gen. OLIVER O. HOWARD; XIV Corps, Maj. Gens. JOHN M. PALMER and JEFFERSON C. DAVIS; XX Corps, Maj. Gens. JOSEPH HOOKER and HENRY W. SLOCUM; and Cavalry Corps, Maj. Gen. Washington L. Elliott. The army was engaged in most actions of the campaign, including KENNESAW MOUNTAIN and PEACHTREE CREEK. After the occupation of Atlanta, it was broken up, the XIV and XX corps joining Sherman on the MARCH TO THE SEA and the remainder returning to Middle Tennessee with General Thomas.   —JWR

Cumberland, Union Department of the. There were 2 Departments of the Cumberland, the first comprising all of Tennessee and Kentucky, except for a portion of the latter state bordering Cincinnati, Ohio, and an area of West Tennessee along the Mississippi, which were the responsibility of the Union's Departments of the Ohio and the West. Its commanders were, first, Brig. Gen. ROBERT ANDERSON, then Brig. Gen. WILLIAM T. SHERMAN. Its bureaucratic lifespan dated from Anderson's 15 Aug. 1861 appointment as commander until 8 Oct. that same year, when it was assimilated by the Union's Department of the Ohio.

After Confederate Gen. BRAXTON BRAGG began his invasion of Kentucky, tried to set up a Confederate state government, and was defeated by Union Maj. Gen. DON CARLOS BUELL at the Battle of PERRYVILLE, Federals saw the need of reorganization and reinstated the Department of the Cumberland 24 Oct. 1862, by General Order No. 168, Adjutant General's Office. Its area was to include Kentucky and all of Tennessee east of the Tennessee River, and whatever parts of northern Alabama and Georgia Union troops might occupy. On 30 Oct. Maj. Gen. WILLIAM S. ROSECRANS was given the command.

Following Rosecrans' defeat at CHICKAMAUGA and flight to CHATTANOOGA, and Maj. Gen. U.S. GRANT's victory at VICKSBURG, the Military Division of the Mississippi was created 16 Oct. 1863, and Grant was made commander of all Union forces in the West. This new division incorporated under his authority the Department of the Cumberland and the Departments of the Ohio and Tennessee. However, the Department of the Cumberland continued to exist on paper until the end of the war. Maj. Gen. GEORGE H. THOMAS was given geographic responsibility and command of the department 19 Oct. 1863, and on Grant's elevation to command of all Union armies, Sherman was given charge of the Military Division of the Mississippi 12 Mar. 1864. For organizational purposes, as Sherman made conquests in northern Georgia, he added these to the Department of the Cumberland's geographic area of responsibility.

Early in 1865 Sherman was in the Carolinas. Because of his distance from the division he commanded and the secure state of affairs in Tennessee and Kentucky, on 10 Feb. 1865 the Department of Kentucky was created, for purposes of political Reconstruction. Thomas was given command of all that department's troops, as well as those occupying the now halved Department of the Cumberland. This was merely a bureaucratic change, and organization remained stable until the Confederate armies surrendered.   —JES

***Cumberland*, USS.** *See* HAMPTON ROADS, VA., BATTLE OF. 8–9 Mar. 1862.

Cumming, Alfred. CSA b. Augusta, Ga., 30 Jan. 1829, Cumming was the son of a cotton magnate and the nephew of a governor of the Utah Territory. At 20 he graduated from West Point, ranking 35th in his 43-man class. In the prewar army he served mainly in the West, including 2 years in Louisiana as an aide to Brig. Gen. DAVID E. TWIGGS. Later he accompanied ALBERT SIDNEY JOHNSTON's expedition to Utah, where he aided his uncle in suppressing Mormon violence.

In Jan. 1861 Cumming resigned a captaincy in the 10th U.S. Infantry to accept the lieutenant colonelcy of the Augusta Volunteer Battalion. He soon resigned that position to become major of the 1st Georgia Infantry; by June he was lieutenant colonel of the 10th Georgia and 4 months later its colonel, succeeding LAFAYETTE MCLAWS. He served with such distinction during the PENINSULA CAMPAIGN of 1862—including YORKTOWN, SAVAGE'S STATION, and MALVERN HILL, where he was wounded—that he received an Alabama brigade prior to ANTIETAM. On 14 Sept. 1862 Cumming's command came up quickly to support troops under Brig. Gen. HOWELL COBB, forced back from CRAMPTON'S GAP by an enemy

LC

offensive. His promptness helped keep the Union advance from its objective, Harpers Ferry; 6 weeks later he was awarded a brigadier's star. Afterward, he went west: first to Mobile, then in Apr. 1863 to Mississippi as a subordinate to Lt. Gen. JOHN C. PEMBERTON. Cumming led a brigade in Maj. Gen. CARTER L. STEVENSON's division at CHAMPION'S HILL and in the actions outside VICKSBURG. Captured and paroled with the city's garrison, he reorganized Stevenson's old brigade at Decatur, Ga., in fall 1863, and led it gallantly at MISSIONARY RIDGE.

Cumming was conspicuous in many actions during the AT-LANTA CAMPAIGN. At SNAKE CREEK GAP, 9 May 1864, his troops repulsed several Federal advances, and on the 14th, at RESACA, he wheeled his brigade out of a position exposed to enfilading fire, leaving his division leader "much gratified by the gallantry" of the maneuver. He also won praise for an unsuccessful but spirited attack 22 June at Mount Zion Church, and 31 Aug., at JONESBOROUGH, he was in the forefront of an attack against Federal works, being disabled by another wound.

In postbellum years, Cumming farmed in Floyd Cty., Ga., before moving to Rome, then to his native city. He pursued a minor public career, including service on the American Military Commission to Korea in 1888. d. Rome, Ga., 5 Dec. 1910.   —EGL

Cumming, Kate. nurse b. Edinburgh, Scotland, 1835. The Cumming family moved to Montreal, Canada, then settled permanently in Mobile, Ala., while Kate was still young enough to become thoroughly Southern. Intelligent and courageous, she did not believe in the right to secede, yet she became an impassioned Confederate, blaming Abraham Lincoln for the war, condemning Yankees for being Yankees, and lashing out against her own people for anything less than wholehearted patriotism and at the soldiers for not fighting as often as she thought they should.

During the war Cumming ignored those of her family who opposed hospital work as un-

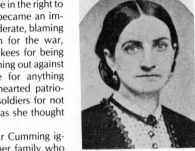

LC

ladylike and became one of the best-known nurses in the Western Confederacy. Through 1861, illness and reluctance to displease her brother restricted her service to collecting supplies and distributing them to convalescents. But in Apr. 1862

she nursed the wounded at SHILOH, worked that summer at CORINTH, OKOLONA, and CHATTANOOGA, and in the fall enlisted in the army's medical department as a hospital matron. Opinionated and assertive, Cumming worked under Dr. S. H. Staub, a progressive military physician committed to the employment of women in hospitals. Cumming applied her energy and organizational ability to running efficient, clean wards and adequate kitchens, and to making the wounded as comfortable as possible as the army retreated before Sherman through Alabama, Tennessee, and Georgia.

Back in Mobile in 1866 she published *A Journal of Hospital Life in the Confederate Army of Tennessee,* one of the most accurate and vivid accounts of life in Southern wartime hospitals. In the preface she challenged Southern women to attend unselfishly to the needs of the maimed and disabled soldiers. A later, revised edition, titled *Gleanings from the Southland* (1895), is weakened by the passage of time and by a chastened Cumming's conciliatory tone toward the North.

Cumming never married, supporting herself by teaching school and music. During her later years she was active in the United Daughters of the Confederacy and the United Confederate Veterans. d. Birmingham, Ala., 5 June 1909.   —PLF

currency, Confederate. Confederate money was printed in every denomination found in the states of the Union, and individual Southern states and even corporations were allowed to print scrip, resulting in additional denominations. The style of printing on all currency varied widely, and because there was no Confederate coinage in circulation, Confederate fractional currency ("paper coins") added to the profusion and confusion of Southern currency. (Illustration p. 201)

In 1862 Sec. of the Treasury CHRISTOPHER G. MEMMINGER secured congressional approval for a new currency issue. The increase raised the notes in circulation to $250 million at a time when Charleston financier GEORGE A. TRENHOLM believed $120 million would have supported the economy. In addition, South Carolina, for example, printed paper in such odd denominations as 75 cents; notes of $1 and more were printed by Georgia's Augusta Insurance & Banking Co. and other corporations; and 4% Confederate Cotton Bonds were often passed as money.

Some of the first Confederate currency was printed by a New York City firm when Pres. JEFFERSON DAVIS maintained the Southern national capital in MONTGOMERY, ALA.; the printing contract was made before the Apr. 1861 firing on FORT SUMTER and was abruptly canceled afterward. From then the South's money was manufactured within its borders, often by the Archer & Daly firm in Richmond, Va., and Keating & Ball of Columbia, S.C. Confederate national scrip after 1861 bore a portrait of a Confederate notable in the lower right corner (Confederate Sec. of State JUDAH P. BENJAMIN was on the $2 bill, Treasury Secretary Memminger was on the five), and had a band running down the left of the note declaring the denomination. All Confederate national currency bore the legend "will pay the bearer" or "will pay the bearer on demand," with the qualifier "six months or two years after the ratification of a treaty of peace between the Confederate States and the United States." Confederate Treasury officials presumed that, on peace, a free Confederate nation would return to a gold standard.

Presumably, Confederate citizens were able to offer only national currency in payment for goods or services, notwithstanding issues of scrip by individual states and banking houses. Secretary of the Treasury Memminger had canceled specie payments on the outbreak of hostilities and all precious mint medals had been secured. But near the end of the war Confederate citizens' confidence in the national currency eroded completely. Over $1 billion in national paper was already circulating or stored in warehouses. The Southern public began to rely on barter or on U.S. currency obtained through a black market. (*See also* GREENBACKS and LEGAL TENDER ACTS.)

—JES

Curry, Jabez Lamar Monroe. CSP b. Lincoln Cty., Ga., 5 June 1825. One of the more capable Confederate statesmen, Curry was among the few staunch supporters of the Davis administration, serving in the Provisional and First Confederate congresses as a representative from Alabama, where his family had lived since 1838. This ardent supporter of JOHN C. CALHOUN and states rights was educated at Franklin College and at Harvard College Law School. He abandoned his legal practice in Talladega for a brief stint as a private in the Texas Rangers during the Mexican War but resigned because of ill health.

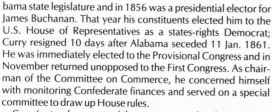

LC

Between 1847 and 1855 Curry served 3 terms in the Alabama state legislature and in 1856 was a presidential elector for James Buchanan. That year his constituents elected him to the U.S. House of Representatives as a states-rights Democrat; Curry resigned 10 days after Alabama seceded 11 Jan. 1861. He was immediately elected to the Provisional Congress and in November returned unopposed to the First Congress. As chairman of the Committee on Commerce, he concerned himself with monitoring Confederate finances and served on a special committee to draw up House rules.

Curry's stand on states rights gave way to his desire for the triumph of Confederate nationalism. He drifted from the administration's position only on CONSCRIPTION, which he feared would drain the manufacturing sector of too many essential workers. Curry's voice was one of those raised in favor of Davis' ambition to be general-in-chief of the Confederate armies. His insistent support of the administration cost him reelection Aug. 1863. He then secured a lieutenant colonelcy and was assigned in the last 2 years of war as aide-de-camp to Gens. JOSEPH E. JOHNSTON and JOSEPH WHEELER.

Curry turned to religion after the war and was ordained a Baptist minister, but his greatest achievements for the South resulted from his devotion to educational reform. He became president of Howard College, Washington, D.C., in 1865, and 3 years later a professor at Richmond College. His work as an advocate of public schools for blacks and whites led in 1881 to his appointment as agent for the Peabody Fund, established in 1866 by philanthropist George S. Peabody for the development of schools in the South. The next year he accepted a similar position with the Slater Fund.

In 1885 and again in 1902 Curry interrupted his work to serve as minister to Spain. d. near Asheville, N.C., 12 Feb. 1903; at his request, he was buried in Richmond's Hollywood Cemetery.

—PLF

Curtin, Andrew Gregg. war governor b. Bellefonte, Pa., 1817. Called "the greatest of the Northern war governors," Curtin began political life as Whig campaign manager in James Pollock's victorious 1854 gubernatorial race and as Pennsylvania's secretary of state. Elected governor Oct. 1860, the first Republican to hold the office, he was registered on the ballot under the anomalous People's Party, with a platform addressing "low tariff, free homesteads, and the well being of the laboring man." Others had recommended the odd registration and the planks unrelated to war because of past poor Republican showings in the state. His inaugural address, denying

KA

the legality of secession, at once addressed the war issue and declared him in the Republican camp.

Curtin became a national political figure. Handling a state-budget deficit half the size of the Federal government's, he secured an additional $3 million appropriation in 1861 for pay and outfitting of state troops. He personally raised regiments, his state contributing 427,000 enlistments during the war. In the 1862 political gloom following the Battle of ANTIETAM, Curtin organized the Union governors' conference at Altoona, Pa., where he engineered a declaration of support for Abraham Lincoln's administration; many of those who signed placed themselves in political jeopardy.

Curtin disliked Lincoln's first secretary of war, SIMON CAMERON, only slightly less than he disliked Confederates. Cameron, called the "Czar of Pennsylvania," was the state Republican boss. The governor refused recognition of the "Czar's" system and power, and their feud, begun in the 1850s, lasted Cameron's lifetime, costing Curtin important appointments and support.

Like other Northern governors, Curtin organized relief for soldiers' families, suppressed dissent, and urged industry in war production. Temporarily in poor health and declining reelection in 1864, he was nevertheless drafted that year for a second run by the Republicans, who successfully touted him as "the soldier's friend." In both terms he was also a friend to business, repealing an unpopular railroad tonnage tax and permitting industrialists to hire private police forces for suppression of labor organizations. These "Coal and Iron Police" were used to put down dissenters during coal-field draft riots late in the war. Curtin tried to minimize his involvement to prevent harming the Republicans' image with the working man.

In postwar years Curtin lost U.S. Senate, vice-presidential, and presidential nominations because of Cameron's influence, briefly served as U.S. minister to Russia, switched parties, and was a failed Democratic candidate for Congress. In 1880 he was elected to Congress as a Democrat, served 3 terms, then retired in 1887. d. Bellefonte, Pa., 7 Oct. 1894.

—JES

Curtis, Samuel Ryan. USA b. Clinton Cty., N.Y., 3 Feb. 1805. An army veteran when he was mustered back in as a colonel in 1861, Curtis had to resign his seat in the 37th U.S. Congress to become a soldier again.

Growing up in Ohio, Curtis went to the public schools in Licking County before his appointment to the U.S. Military

Academy in 1827; in 1831 he graduated 27th in his class as a brevet 2d lieutenant in the 7th Infantry. After a year of garrison duty in Indian Territory he resigned to become a civil engineer and study law in Ohio. While maintaining a law practice he served as chief engineer for improvements on the Muskingum River.

NA

Curtis then fought in the war with Mexico as adjutant general of Ohio, colonel of the 2d Ohio Infantry, and assistant adjutant general to Brig. Gen. JOHN E. WOOL. After being discharged June 1847 he moved to Keokuk, Iowa, and opened a law office, which he maintained during 3 years' employment as city engineer of St. Louis, Mo., 1850–53. Curtis returned to Keokuk and in spring 1856 was elected mayor, an office he held until fall, when voters sent him to the U.S. House of Representatives for the first of 3 consecutive terms.

In 1861 he entered the service as a colonel in the 2d Iowa, and resigned his congressional seat in August to accept an appointment as brigadier general of volunteers as of 17 May. Curtis acquitted himself admirably commanding the Federal forces at the Battle of PEA RIDGE, 7–8 Mar. 1862. The victory won for Curtis a promotion to major general 21 Mar. Later that year he commanded the Department of the Missouri, but was reappointed to the Department of Kansas after clashing with Missouri Gov. HAMILTON R. GAMBLE. He finished the war in the Department of the Northwest.

Curtis accepted an appointment as U.S. peace commissioner to the Indians in 1865 and served as commissioner for the Union Pacific Railroad until 8 months before his death in Council Bluffs, Iowa, 26 Dec. 1866.   —FLS

Cushing, Alonzo Hersford. USA b. Waukesha Cty., Wis., 1841. Brother of naval hero WILLIAM B. CUSHING, Alonzo was appointed to West Point from New York, graduating 12th in the class of 1861. His only promotion in the Regular Army was from 2d lieutenant to 1st lieutenant of artillery, appointments that both came on 24 June 1861, the academy's graduation day, at which time Cushing was assigned to the 4th U.S. Artillery. In the months after his graduation he trained volunteers in Washington, D.C., then fought at FIRST BULL RUN, the Siege of YORKTOWN, and in the PENINSULA CAMPAIGN. Though offered a transfer to a less hazardous assignment with the Corps of Engineers July 1862, he declined it to stay with his batteries. During the ANTIETAM and FREDERICKSBURG campaigns, he was assigned temporarily to engineer duty and later fought at Chancellorsville and Thoroughfare Gap. He was brevetted captain 13 Dec. 1862 and major 2 May 1863 for gallant service at FREDERICKS-BURG and during the CHANCELLORSVILLE CAMPAIGN.

USA

At GETTYSBURG, 3 July 1863, Cushing's 4th Artillery sat at the center of the Union line that would face PICKETT'S CHARGE. In the enormous artillery duel that preceded the Confederates' assault, he did his best to answer enemy fire and consequently had his batteries blasted apart: 3 cannon limbers were destroyed, several wheels were shot off his guns and replaced, all his officers were killed or wounded, and he was wounded in both thighs. With all the Federal artillerymen already on the line, there was no one to relieve him, and he fought for over an hour while wounded. Seeing the Confederates preparing for their charge, he and his remaining cannoneers pushed by hand their only remaining workable 3-gun section down to a rail fence where the assault was expected to hit. When the charge came, Cushing started firing canister, and kept firing while his men were being hit around him. Reportedly, just as the Confederates swarmed over his guns, he pulled his lanyard to give them a last round and was killed beside the cannon.

Cushing was only 22 when he died, and his bravery in the face of certain death made him a national hero. He was posthumously awarded a brevet of lieutenant colonel for his performance at Gettysburg.   —JES

Cushing, William Barker. USN b. Delafield, Wis., 4 Nov. 1842, Cushing, younger brother of 1st Lt. ALONZO H. CUSHING, was appointed to the U.S. Naval Academy in 1857, but his lack of application forced him to resign before graduation. When war began, the navy gave him another chance by appointing him acting master's mate. Aboard the *Minnesota,* Cushing helped capture a BLOCKADE RUNNER and bring it to New York City, resulting in his appointment as acting midshipman. Assigned to the NORTH ATLANTIC BLOCKADING SQUADRON, he was promoted to lieutenant July 1862.

USMHI

In Oct. 1862 Cushing, commanding the *Ellet,* entered New Topsail Inlet, N.C., and destroyed a large Confederate saltworks. A few weeks later he led a raid on Jacksonville, N.C., but was forced to destroy the *Ellet* to prevent its capture. Cushing's reputation as a daredevil earned praise from his superiors; Sec. of the Navy GIDEON WELLES praised his "brilliant example of courage and enterprise," and Adm. DAVID D. PORTER admired his willingness to perform daring deeds.

After commanding the *Commodore Barney* and the *Shokokon,* Cushing was assigned the *Monticello* 5 Sept. 1863. Twice, in Feb. and in June 1864, he led night missions behind enemy lines and returned with prisoners and important information. Then, in October, Cushing volunteered for his most difficult and dangerous assignment: the capture or destruction of the powerful Confederate ram *ALBEMARLE* at Plymouth, N.C. With 15 volunteers aboard an improvised torpedo boat, Cushing approached the *Albemarle* and, under heavy fire, lowered his torpedo boom and drove its torpedo under her. During the confusion that followed the explosion and sinking of the ram, Cushing swam ashore and eventually reached the safety of the fleet; 2 of his men drowned, and only 1 other managed to avoid capture. The sinking of the *Albemarle* made possible the recapture of Plymouth and brought Cushing promotion to lieutenant commander; he also received the THANKS OF CONGRESS.

On 15 Jan. 1865 Cushing led sailors and marines of the squadron in the assault against the sea face of FORT FISHER. Although the force was repulsed, it distracted the defending Confederates, enabling the Federal infantry to capture the land face; the fort was surrendered that evening. Cushing spent the last weeks of the war in the hazardous removal of enemy mines from river waters.

After the war Cushing continued in active service and in 1872 was promoted to commander. While commanding the *Wyoming* in 1873 he intervened with the Spanish governor of Cuba to prevent the killing of American sailors detained at Santiago. The following year, Cushing suffered a physical and mental collapse, dying in Washington, D.C., 8 Dec. 1874.   —NCD

Cushman, Pauline. spy b. New Orleans, La., 10 June 1833. Fact and fiction are difficult to separate in Cushman's life, since much of what is known about her comes from memoirs written to exploit her brief career as a Union spy. Her family moved from New Orleans to the frontier community of Grand Rapids, Mich., and at 18 Pauline ran off to New York to begin a career as a mediocre actress.

A few years later she was working in New Orleans, where she married fellow performer Charles Dickenson, who enlisted as a musician in the Union army soon after the war started, but died ingloriously of dysentery sometime in 1862. Returning to the stage to earn a living, Cushman appeared in Union-held Louisville, where 2 paroled Confederate officers bribed her to toast JEFFERSON DAVIS during her performance. She did, but not before reporting the incident to the Federal provost marshal, who recognized the entrée into Confederate camps such an expression of secessionist loyalty would give Cushman.

Her performance was successful, and in Mar. 1863 she began following the Confederate army through Kentucky and Tennessee and was the darling of the Southern troops, gathering information of value to the advancing Federal army. Once Confederate suspicions were aroused, a search easily revealed secreted papers. Gen. BRAXTON BRAGG ordered her tried, and the court sentenced her to hang.

Before the execution could be carried out, Union troops invaded the region and the Confederates abandoned Cushman. She passed the information on to the Federal commander, then traveled north to praise and an honorary major's commission from ABRAHAM LINCOLN, and to acclaim from the public. Too well known to be of further use as a spy, she dressed in uniform to lecture about her experiences, embellishing them with each talk and subsequently in the book *Life of Pauline Cushman,* written from her notes by Ferdinand Sarmiento in 1865.

Cushman tried acting again, then retired to San Francisco, where she worked for a while as a seamstress. Widowed by a second husband and permanently separated from a third, she slipped into obscurity. Eventually her first husband's military service won her a small pension from the Federal government, but she had started taking opium for an illness and 2 Dec. 1893 died of an intentional overdose. The San Francisco GRAND ARMY OF THE REPUBLIC buried her with military honors in its cemetery.   —PLF

Custer, George Armstrong. USA b. Harrison Cty., Ohio, 5 Dec. 1839. American folklore has immortalized him

for his storied "last stand" at the Battle of the Little Big Horn, but Custer had achieved lasting fame more than a decade earlier in a score of major Civil War engagements.

USMHI

3 days after his graduation from West Point in 1861, last in his class, Lieutenant Custer was immersed in the FIRST BATTLE OF BULL RUN. From Bull Run to Appomattox, nearly 4 years later, he took part in virtually every important battle of the Army of the Potomac.

Headstrong, contemptuous of army regulations, and everthirsty for glory, Custer made many enemies but was idolized by millions for his unquestioned courage and his audacity in conducting cavalry operations. Fearless under fire, he had 11 horses shot under him, yet was wounded only once. In 1862 he was one of the first Union officers to make observations in combat from a BALLOON.

His reckless bravery attracted the attention of his senior commanders—Maj. Gens. Philip Kearny, William F. Smith, George B. McClellan, and Alfred Pleasonton—and after Custer's heroic charge during the June 1863 Battle of ALDIE, Va., Pleasonton recommended him for promotion from captain to brigadier general by 29 June. At 23 Custer became the youngest general in the Union army, assuming command of the 2d Brigade of the 3d Cavalry Division just in time to lead his men to new glories at GETTYSBURG.

In Oct. 1864 he took command of the 3d Cavalry, becoming one of Maj. Gen. PHILIP H. SHERIDAN's favorite commanders in the Shenandoah Valley Campaign. Custer was brevetted for gallantry at Gettysburg, YELLOW TAVERN (where he led the charge in which Lt. Gen. J.E.B. STUART was killed), THIRD WINCHESTER, FISHER'S HILL, and FIVE FORKS. He was promoted to major general, U.S. Volunteers, 15 Apr. 1865.

By war's end he was a national hero, his long golden ringlets and unorthodox attire as well known as his erratic brilliance on the battlefield. Surviving an 1867 court-martial conviction for unauthorized absence from his Fort Wallace, Kans., command, he was reinstated in 1868 at Sheridan's urging and went on to greater glories as an Indian fighter. Custer and his command were massacred by a superior force of Sioux at the Little Big Horn, 25 June 1876, and he was buried with honors at West Point. (See also CUSTER'S CAVALRY BRIGADE.)   —DS

Custer's Cavalry Brigade. In June 1863 GEORGE A. CUSTER was promoted to brigadier general and given charge of the 2d Brigade in Brig. Gen. H. JUDSON KILPATRICK's 3d Cavalry Division in the Army of the Potomac. His new command was made up of the 1st, 5th, 6th, and 7th Michigan cavalry regiments, men organized in Detroit and Grand Rapids. And though 3 of the regiments had already seen much active service, they had no nickname. Custer supplied it, dubbing them the "Wolverines," and led them in the fighting at GETTYSBURG.

The brigade's first fighting under Custer was ferocious, setting the standard for the remainder of its service. After Gettysburg came 16 months of almost unremittent combat at Boonsborough, Snicker's Gap, Culpeper Court House, Orange Court House, Bethesda Church, the WILDERNESS, YELLOW TAVERN, TRE-

VILIAN STATION, and in Maj. Gen. Philip H. Sheridan's SHENAN-DOAH VALLEY CAMPAIGN. And in Feb. 1864, while Custer was on leave for his wedding, division commander Kilpatrick drafted 200 men from the 6th Regiment, 100 from the 7th, and some from the 5th to join in his most famous personal escapade, the KILPATRICK-DAHLGREN RAID to Richmond, Va.

No other Union cavalry brigade had so high a percentage of men killed; during the war it lost 524 troopers. And perhaps no other Union cavalry brigade had so much spirit. The men "perfectly idolized Custer," and all adopted his flashy red necktie as their symbol.

On 30 Sept. 1864 Custer succeeded Brig. Gen. JAMES H. WILSON as commander of the 3d Cavalry Division. Though many of his old troopers from the Wolverines demanded transfers to his new command, none was forthcoming. But the men continued to distinguish their unit until the Confederate surrender, playing a part in Sheridan's actions and in the pursuit of the Army of Northern Virginia from Petersburg to Appomattox.
—JES

Cutler, Lysander. USA b. Worcester Cty., Mass., 16 Feb. 1804. A farmer's son, Cutler attended local schools and stud-

ied surveying on his own. He moved to Dexter, Maine, in 1828 to teach, then became a successful businessman, state senator, and militia colonel. When the depression of 1857 ruined him financially Cutler relocated to Milwaukee, Wis., working there as a grain broker.

Cutler joined the army in summer 1861, on 16 July becoming colonel of the 6th Wisconsin, later part of the famous IRON BRIGADE. Wounded at SECOND BULL RUN, his first major battle, Cutler recovered sufficiently to hold temporary brigade command in Brig. Gen. ABNER DOUBLEDAY's division at FREDERICKS-BURG. Promoted to brigadier general 29 Nov. 1862, he commanded the 4th Brigade/1st Division/I Corps until the army was reorganized in spring 1864 and he was given a brigade in the V Corps. On the death of Brig. Gen. JAMES S. WADSWORTH, Cutler succeeded to command of the 4th Division/V Corps.

Shortly after the promotion Cutler's health failed as a result of exposure and the effects of 2 wounds, causing him to be relieved at his own request in June. He was assigned to duty overseeing the draft in Jackson, Mich., resigning from the army 30 June 1865. His health ruined, Cutler returned to Milwaukee, dying there 30 July 1866.
—PLF

CWTI

Confederate currency

D

Dabney's Mill, Va., Battle of. 5–7 Feb. 1865 *See* HATCHER'S RUN, VA., BATTLE OF.

Dahlgren, John Adolph Bernard. USN b. Philadelphia, Pa., 13 Nov. 1809, Dahlgren was the son of the Swedish consul in Philadelphia. Initially denied a midshipman's commission in the navy, Dahlgren shipped before the mast to gain experience; in 1842 he started his naval career as an acting midshipman. In 1847 he began a tour of duty at the Washington Navy Yard, where he established and directed the U.S. Navy's ordnance department. Among his many contributions to naval ordnance was the DAHLGREN GUN, which became one of the standard weapons of the Civil War navies.

USMHI

At the outbreak of the Civil War, Dahlgren commanded the Washington Navy Yard and in July 1862 also became chief of the Bureau of Ordnance. Promoted to captain in summer 1862 and rear admiral the following year, he applied for sea duty and received command of the SOUTH ATLANTIC BLOCKADING SQUADRON July 1863. He spent most of his time at sea off Charleston, attempting to seal that harbor, and contributed to the capture of both Charleston and Savannah by assisting the army and directing an expedition up the St. John's River into Florida.

After the war he served for a time in the Pacific before returning to the Bureau of Ordnance. When he died, 12 July 1870, Washington, D.C., Dahlgren still commanded the Washington Navy Yard.   —EMT

Dahlgren, Ulric. USA b. Neshaminy, Pa., 3 Apr. 1842. After studying law and civil engineering, Dahlgren entered the Civil War as an officer on the staff of Maj. Gen. FRANZ SIGEL, commander of the XI Corps/Army of the Potomac. After serving as Sigel's artillery chief at SECOND BULL RUN, he was an aide to Maj. Gens. AMBROSE E. BURNSIDE at FREDERICKSBURG, JOSEPH HOOKER at CHANCELLORSVILLE, and GEORGE G. MEADE at GETTYSBURG.

A born adventurer, Dahlgren often volunteered for hazardous duty; in the early stages of the Chancellorsville Campaign, he perched in treetops for many hours, counting Confederates passing beneath. In May 1863 he unsuccessfully sought Hooker's permission to raid Richmond with a small contingent of Regular cavalry. The following month, ranging far from Meade's main army, at Greencastle, Pa., he seized a Confeder-

USMHI/MA

ate courier who was bringing Gen. ROBERT E. LEE word that he could expect no reinforcements from Richmond for his invasion of the North. Relayed to army headquarters, the news supposedly stiffened Meade's resolve to remain at Gettysburg instead of falling back into Maryland.

Following Lee's defeat at Gettysburg, Captain Dahlgren led a small band that dogged the Confederates' heels. At Hagerstown, Md., 6 July, he fell in with the cavalry division of Brig. Gen. H. JUDSON KILPATRICK, blocking the enemy's retreat. In street fighting, Dahlgren was severely wounded, losing a leg to amputation.

After recuperation and promotion to colonel, he rejoined Kilpatrick for a Feb. 1864 raid on lightly held Richmond, a venture the glory-hunting "Kill-cavalry" approved in the belief that Dahlgren's social credentials would lend the expedition favorable publicity. The operation, however, ended in disaster. While Kilpatrick led 3,500 troopers against the capital from the north, Dahlgren's satellite force of 500 failed to strike from the west at the appointed hour 1 Mar. Stymied by unfordable streams, snow, sleet, and bushwhackers, Dahlgren retreated from Richmond late that day and on the 2d was surrounded and killed.

Papers found on his body, apparently dictated by him, revealed the raiders' intention to destroy parts of the capital and to kill Confederate officials including JEFFERSON DAVIS. During the controversy that erupted, the dead colonel was branded a war criminal by the Southern press and public (*see* DAHLGREN PAPERS). Buried in an unmarked grave near Richmond, his remains were unearthed by local Unionists and reinterred in a Philadelphia cemetery.   —EGL

Dahlgren gun. Adm. JOHN A. DAHLGREN was responsible for the invention of 3 types of ordnance used by both the U.S. and (through capture) the Confederate navies during the Civil War: bronze boat howitzers and rifles, iron smoothbore shellguns, and iron rifles.

Dahlgren's boat howitzers and rifles were the result of the U.S. Navy's experiences in the Mexican War, where much service involved patrol work on inland rivers and close inshore. The bronze pieces were designed with a number of variations in 12- and 24-pounder size and were intended for use on launches and in amphibious assaults. Most U.S. naval vessels during the Civil War had these bronze guns aboard,

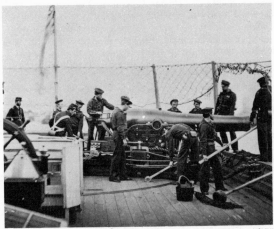

and they proved particularly useful in the river operations of the Western theater and in actions on inland sounds and waterways.

Dahlgren's iron shellguns were developed in 1850 with the production of the 9-in. gun, followed the next year by an 11-in. model. These guns were smoothbores, intended to fire shell against the wooden ships of the 1850s, but they proved strong enough to fire shot as well and thus saw service on many of the new IRONCLADS. The USS *Monitor* carried 2 11-in. Dahlgrens in its turret. In addition, Dahlgren designed a 10-in. model, but it was never popular and only a few were produced. In Mar. 1862 Dahlgren was asked to design both 15- and 20-in. guns. The 15-in. pieces saw service on some monitors, but apparently only 1 20-in. was ever made, and it did not see service.

Dahlgren's rifles were designed by 1860 and were produced in 50-, 80-, and 150-pounder sizes. The 80-pounder had a tendency to burst, and only a few 150-pounders were made; the 50-pounder, however, did see some service.   —LDJ

Dahlgren papers. During the retreat from Richmond after the ill-fated Dahlgren-Kilpatrick raid, Feb.–Mar. 1864, Col. ULRIC DAHLGREN was killed near King and Queen Court House in an ambush by Maj. Gen. FITZHUGH LEE'S cavalry. On his body were found 3 documents: the rough draft of an address to his men, a set of instructions, and a memorandum book. The first 2 papers described plans to penetrate the Richmond defenses and release 15,000 prisoners, who were to take the city and hold it until a larger body of Federal troops arrived. They further instructed the men to burn Richmond and murder JEFFERSON DAVIS and his cabinet.

Southerners were outraged by the plot to commit arson and assassinate civilian officials. The Richmond *Examiner* called for reprisal, claiming the North had turned the conflict into "a war for extermination." Confederate Sec. of War JAMES A. SEDDON favored executing at least some of the captured raiders, and Chief of Ordnance JOSIAH GORGAS suggested killing all prisoners. Gen. ROBERT E. LEE opposed any violent retribution, fearing a series of retaliatory hangings, and sent a formal letter of inquiry to Maj. Gen. GEORGE G. MEADE, commanding the Army of the Potomac. Meade promptly sent for Brig. Gen. H.

JUDSON KILPATRICK, who had planned and led the raid. In a formal written statement Kilpatrick repudiated the papers and cleared the names of everyone holding higher rank than Dahlgren, thus leaving the dead man to bear the blame.

Meade cited Kilpatrick's questionable reputation as fair reason to doubt his story, but because of the serious political implications in the charges, he was not in a position to challenge the cavalryman. Though Meade took no part in planning the raid, he may have known more than he could admit publicly; privately, he alluded to possessing certain "collateral evidence" that cast doubt on Kilpatrick's story. Nonetheless, he forwarded Kilpatrick's statement to R. E. Lee with assurances the plan had no official sanction.

Regardless of who was responsible for the burning and murder plot, in the aftermath Southern bitterness against the North hardened, rekindling the South's fighting spirit.

Claims that the Dahlgren papers may have been forged stirred a controversy that lingered until historian Virgil C. Jones laid the matter to rest through tests in the National Archives laboratory establishing the authenticity of Dahlgren's signature.   —PLF

Dakota Territory. Among the most active lobbyists in Washington to create Dakota Territory were 2 West Pointers, DANIEL M. FROST and John B. S. Todd, who resigned their army commissions in the late 1850s to form the Frost-Todd Co., trading with the Dakota settlers and establishing townsites. On 2 Mar. 1861, 2 days before he turned over the presidency to ABRAHAM LINCOLN, James Buchanan signed into law the bill creating the territory. That vast area, with a white population of less than 900, according to a special 1860 census, comprised the present states of North and South Dakota and most of Montana and Wyoming.

Yankton, Todd's hometown of 300 settlers, was made the first capital of the territory. Dr. William Jayne, Lincoln's family physician in Springfield, Ill., was appointed its first governor and ordered the formation of a Dakota company for Union service. However, the company was kept at home to protect Dakota settlements against the Sioux uprising that spread westward from Minnesota, 1862–63. Dakota Territory also recruited the Frontier Rangers, the Yankton Home Guard, and the Vermillion Home Guard in 1861; all were kept at home. But many young Dakotans joined Iowa and Nebraska units and fought in several major Civil War campaigns.

There were 2 Federal army posts in Dakota Territory at the outbreak of the Civil War, Fort Randall and Fort Abercrombie. 6 of the 22 Fort Randall officers resigned to join the Confederacy, as did a small group at Fort Abercrombie. The remaining men were called east for Union service in 1861, and the forts were manned by Dakota volunteers. Forts Rice, Sully, Thompson, and Dakota also were established in the territory.

Dakota Territory was placed under the Union District of Kansas Nov. 1861. Brig. Gen. Alfred Sully was made commanding general of the Dakota District May 1863 and directed Indian fighting in the territory until 1866.   —DS

Daniel, Junius. CSA b. Halifax, N.C., 27 June 1828, Daniel belonged to that group of professionally trained North Carolinians who became excellent combat officers. Men like GEORGE B. ANDERSON, WILLIAM D. PENDER, STEPHEN D. RAMSEUR, JAMES H. LANE, and Daniel rose to brigade and divisional commands in the II Corps/Army of Northern Virginia.

An 1851 West Point cadet graduating 33d in his class, Daniel served on garrison and frontier duty, resigning in 1858 to assume operation of his father's Louisiana plantation.

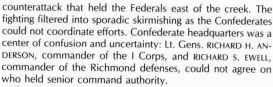

When his native state seceded in 1861, Daniel was elected colonel of the 14th North Carolina, his commission dated 3 June, and in Apr. 1862 he assumed command of the 45th North Carolina. During the SEVEN DAYS' CAMPAIGN, Daniel commanded a brigade in Maj.

LC

Gen. THEOPHILUS H. HOLMES's division, having a horse shot under him at MALVERN HILL. Promoted to brigadier general to rank from 1 Sept. 1862, Daniel spent the winter of 1862–63 with his brigade in North Carolina.

In May 1863 Daniel and his command returned to Virginia, assigned to the division of Maj. Gen. ROBERT E. RODES. On the first day at GETTYSBURG, Daniel's North Carolinians suffered the greatest losses of any brigade in the corps. Daniel performed with distinguished gallantry, and was commended in the reports. At the WILDERNESS, 5–6 May 1864, he again handled his brigade with skill, and a week later at SPOTSYLVANIA, when the Federals crushed the "MULE SHOE," Daniel's brigade counterattacked into the maelstrom. While guiding his men, Daniel fell mortally wounded, dying the next day, 13 May. His remains were interred in Halifax.   —JDW

Darbytown (Deep Bottom; New Market Road; Strawberry Plains), Va., eng. at.

27 July 1864 As a diversionary operation to assist the scheduled 30 July detonation of the Petersburg mine at the Battle of the CRATER, Union Lt. Gen. ULYSSES S. GRANT ordered a surprise attack north of the James River, committing to the secret movement Maj. Gen. WINFIELD S. HANCOCK's II Corps and 2 cavalry divisions under Maj. Gen. PHILIP H. SHERIDAN. The Union commander intended to divert Confederates from the Petersburg lines to the north side of the James; if the operation succeeded, Sheridan was to enter Richmond or raid the Virginia Central Railroad. Rumors of this Federal thrust north of the James forced Gen. ROBERT E. LEE to send Maj. Gen. JOSEPH B. KERSHAW north on the 23d.

During the night of 26–27 July, Hancock's infantry filed across the James while Sheridan's horsemen trailed. The Union corps moved into a bridgehead held by a division of the X Corps. On the morning of the 27th, Hancock's veterans advanced on the New Market and other roads toward Chaffin's Bluff. Leading the march was the brigade of Brig. Gen. NELSON A. MILES, Brig. Gen. FRANCIS C. BARLOW's division. Near Bailey's Creek, Miles charged advanced Confederate outposts, routing the Southern infantry and capturing 4 20-pounder Parrott cannon.

The Federal soldiers pursued to where the New Market Road crossed Deep Bottom Run. Suddenly the Confederate lines west of the creek erupted in rifle fire; the intensity and amount of the Southerners' resistance was unexpected. 2 solid, veteran Confederate divisions manned the works, under Maj. Gens. CADMUS M. WILCOX and Kershaw. When Hancock's attack exploded that morning, the Confederates were ready.

When Barlow's advance stalled, Kershaw launched a counterattack that held the Federals east of the creek. The fighting filtered into sporadic skirmishing as the Confederates could not coordinate efforts. Confederate headquarters was a center of confusion and uncertainty: Lt. Gens. RICHARD H. ANDERSON, commander of the I Corps, and RICHARD S. EWELL, commander of the Richmond defenses, could not agree on who held senior command authority.

Sheridan, meanwhile, moved his 2 cavalry divisions northward behind Hancock's front. Supported by a cavalry division from the Army of the James, Sheridan probed the Confederate lines on the Darbytown road. Hancock shifted 2 infantry divisions to Sheridan's front. The cavalrymen charged, securing some ground, but could not advance farther. Maj. Gen. HENRY HETH's Confederate division arrived to bolster the works before Sheridan.

Grant arrived during the afternoon and was also surprised by the numbers of Southern defenders. The Union commander ordered for the next day an envelopment of the Confederate northern flank to disengage the cavalry for its raid. About 10 a.m. on the 28th, however, Kershaw attacked Sheridan's troopers. The dismounted horsemen, armed with repeaters, repulsed the charge, counterattacked, and captured 300 Southerners and 2 battle flags. An infantry division replaced the cavalrymen, who withdrew to the New Market Road, where the Confederates again assailed the troopers. With the Confederates sealing the avenues of advance, Sheridan's raid was abandoned.

On 29 July the Federals recrossed the river, back to the Petersburg trenches. Northern casualties were 334 killed and wounded, while Southern losses are unknown. Grant succeeded in drawing Confederate forces from the besieged city, but little else. Lee's swift reaction prevented Sheridan's raid, an operation that could have damaged the Confederacy.   —JDW

Darbytown Road, Va., engs. at.

7 and 27 Oct. 1864 On 29 Sept. the Federal capture of FORT HARRISON, Va., and the Confederate exterior line above it forced Gen. ROBERT E. LEE to respond. The Confederate commander could either attempt to recover the losses or build a retrenchment between the Federals and his lines to the west. Lee characteristically chose the offensive, manning his works with local defense troops, thus freeing combat veterans for the assault.

Lee shifted the divisions of Maj. Gens. CHARLES W. FIELD and ROBERT F. HOKE into position for a frontal attack. Brig. Gen. MARTIN W. GARY's cavalry brigade and Brig. Gen. EDWARD A. PERRY's depleted brigade of Florida infantry were moved north of the Federal works. Lee planned for Gary and Perry to sweep down in the rear of the Federals while Field charged from the west. Hoke was ordered to advance as support on Field's right.

The Confederate attack began sometime after dawn 7 Oct. Gary's dismounted troopers and Perry's Floridians turned Brig. Gen. AUGUST V. KAUTZ's Union cavalry division, driving the Northern horsemen from their advanced position. Brig. Gen. JOHN GREGG's brigade of Texans, Field's division, cleared the front. Kautz fell back on the main works, where Union X Corps infantry and artillery were firmly entrenched. Gregg charged this strong line and Federal artillery battered the Texans' ranks. Field attacked again with his entire division but the Federal guns repulsed the charge. Gregg, an excellent officer, fell dead. When Hoke failed to advance, Lee halted the operation.

The Confederate offensive along the Darbytown Road cost 1,350 men; the Federals reported only 399 casualties. 4 days later the Southerners constructed a retrenchment, sealing off Fort Harrison and securing their front.

Against these new Confederate works the Federals assumed the offensive 27 Oct. Lt. Gen. ULYSSES S. GRANT, endeavoring to turn Lee's Petersburg lines, ordered this diversionary attack north of the James River, and Maj. Gen. BENJAMIN F. BUTLER's Army of the James accordingly attacked vigorously on the entire front.

Lt. Gen. JAMES LONGSTREET deftly shifted Confederate troops to meet Butler's assaults. In the area along the Darbytown road, Field and Hoke bloodied the Federal ranks, repulsing them easily. Farther north other Confederates also held firm. In a few hours of fighting Longstreet completely repulsed Butler's thrusts, capturing some 600 Federals and 11 flags. No Union offensive north of the James River had been so easily stopped. —JDW

David, CSS. This 50-ft long, cigar-shaped steamer, an iron torpedo boat, was built at Charleston, S.C., in 1863. Operated by a crew of 4, it was capable of a maximum speed of 7 knots. Its armament consisted of a TORPEDO, with up to 100 lb of explosives, connected to a 10-ft spar at the bow. During the war, the Federals used the term *David* to identify other Confederate torpedo boats, but these "Davids" remain unidentified by name.

USN

The CSS *David* was involved in at least 3 attempts to break the Federal blockade of Charleston harbor. On the night of 5 Oct. 1863 Lt. William T. Glassell, commanding the *David,* launched a surprise attack on the *NEW IRONSIDES* by approaching unseen until 50 yd from the target and setting off his explosives under the Federal ship's starboard quarter. The *New Ironsides* suffered severe damage but remained afloat, directing its fire at the *David,* now helpless in the water with the boiler fires extinguished. Glassell, Asst. Eng. James H. Tomb, and 1 crewman abandoned the *David,* but Tomb swam back and relighted the *David*'s fires. Through the efforts of Tomb and the ship's pilot, a nonswimmer who had stayed aboard, the ship was brought up channel to safety. Glassell and the crew member were captured by the Federals.

On 6 Mar. 1864 the *David,* now commanded by Tomb, struck the blockader *Memphis.* Despite 2 hits with a 95-lb load of explosives, no detonation occurred, and the *David* with-

drew under heavy fire. On 18 Apr. Tomb attacked the *Wabash* but was forced to withdraw after being detected and fired on.

The fate of the *David* is unknown; it was probably one of the several "David"-type vessels that fell into Federal hands after the capture of Charleston. As a result of Federal concern over these ships, Rear Adm. JOHN A. DAHLGREN, early in 1864, proposed that a reward of up to $30,000 be offered for the capture or destruction of every "David." —NCD

Davidson, Henry Brevard. CSA b. Shelbyville, Tenn., 28 Jan. 1831. At 15 Davidson served in Mexico as a sergeant in the 1st Tennessee Volunteers, distinguishing himself at Monterrey and winning an appointment to West Point. Graduating 33d in the class of 1853, he became a dragoon officer, and during service in Missouri, New Mexico Territory, and Oregon participated in numerous Indian skirmishes, shifting to the Quartermaster's Department in 1858.

GG

In July 1861 Davidson went on leave, never rejoining his regiment. Accepting an appointment as major in the Confederate Adjutant and Inspector General's Department, he subsequently served on the staffs of several Western commanders, attaining a colonelcy in 1862. That April, as part of the force under Brig. Gen. WILLIAM W. MACKALL, he was captured on Island No. 10. Soon released, he was promoted to brigadier general 18 Aug. 1863 and was assigned a brigade in the corps of Maj. Gen. JOSEPH WHEELER, cavalry commander of the Army of Tennessee.

Under Wheeler, Davidson's career varied. At Rome, Ga., mid-May 1864, he drove in a large band of approaching Union cavalry, thereby protecting an infantry force, and early in October he performed well during the initial phase of Wheeler's Sequatchie Valley expedition, capturing the outer defenses of McMinnville, Tenn., and compelling the surrender of that Union supply base. But 4 days later his failure to obey orders resulted in his brigade being overrun and stampeded by pursuing Federals near Farmington, compounding the poor showing he had turned in the month before at CHICKAMAUGA. On that occasion, charging Federals had caved in his brigade's flank and his troopers failed to rally as ordered.

To some extent, Davidson made up for these errors by competent service later that year in the Shenandoah Valley, where he served in the division of Brig. Gen. LUNSFORD L. LOMAX. Later he headed south, joined Gen. JOSEPH E. JOHNSTON, and finished the war opposing Maj. Gen. WILLIAM T. SHERMAN in North Carolina.

After surrendering with Johnston, Davidson lived for a time in New Orleans, where he was a deputy sheriff, 1866–67, then moved to California, serving as state inspector of public works 1878–86. In later years he was deputy secretary of state for California and an agent of the Southern Pacific Railroad. d. near Livermore, Calif., 4 Mar. 1899. —EGL

Davidson, Hunter. CSN b. District of Columbia, 20 Sept. 1826, Davidson was appointed midshipman from Fairfax Cty., Va., 29 Oct. 1841 and was promoted to lieutenant in 1855.

While an instructor at the Naval Academy in 1859, he invented a device for lowering boats at sea that was adopted by the navy. After Virginia seceded, Davidson resigned from the navy, 23 Apr. 1861, but Sec. of the Navy GIDEON WELLES ordered him dismissed from the service.

In June 1861 Davidson was appointed lieutenant in the Confederate navy and assigned to the school ship *PATRICK HENRY* on the James River. He served aboard the *VIRGINIA* during the

USN

Battle of HAMPTON ROADS, Va., 8–9 Mar. 1862, then, because of his special aptitude, was assigned to work under Comdr. MATTHEW F. MAURY in the Torpedo Division of the Office of Ordnance and Hydrography. Their top-secret work was performed aboard the CSS *Torpedo,* a converted tugboat. After Maury went abroad June 1862, Davidson became head of the the division. His electrical torpedoes sunk 2 enemy vessels: the *Commodore Barney* and the *Commodore Jones.*

In 1864 Davidson, promoted to commander, joined Maury in England for further experiments with torpedoes. Finally, as captain of the blockade runner *City of Richmond,* Jan. 1865, Davidson delivered sailors and stores to the CSS *STONEWALL* at Quiberon Bay, France.

After the war, Davidson settled in Maryland, joining the Argentine navy in 1873 and organizing a division of torpedoes for that service. During 1879 he headed a scientific expedition that explored and charted the Upper Paraná to the Paraguay River. Davidson resigned from the Argentine navy in 1885, settling in Paraguay, where he died 16 Feb. 1913.   —NCD

Davies, Henry Eugene. USA b. New York City, N.Y., 2 July 1836. Like many Civil War officers, Davies lacked professional training but, with the ability to lead, courage, and combat experience, rose to high rank with commensurate responsibility. Educated at Harvard, Williams, and Columbia, where he graduated in 1857, Davies practiced law before the war.

On 5 May 1861, Davies was commissioned a captain in the 5th New York. The infantry regiment fought in the Union defeat at BIG BETHEL, Va., 10 June. On 1 Aug., Davies joined the 2d New York Cavalry as a major; the unit served in the Washington, D.C., defenses and on the Rappahannock River during the

LC

PENINSULA CAMPAIGN with Maj. Gen. IRVIN MCDOWELL's corps. Davies and the regiment saw their initial major action at SECOND BULL RUN.

Promoted to lieutenant colonel 2 Dec. 1862 Davies served with the 2d New York Cavalry through most of 1863, assuming command of the regiment 16 June with the rank of colonel. During the Union march to Pennsylvania in the GETTYSBURG CAMPAIGN, the New Yorkers suffered heavy casualties in the

cavalry actions at Beverly Ford and ALDIE, Va. On 16 Sept. 1863 Davies received his commission as brigadier general.

During the war's final 18 months, Davies held brigade and divisional command in the Cavalry Corps of the Army of the Potomac, distinguishing himself in the corps' operations. His brigade participated in the 2 separate raids on Richmond under Brig. Gen. H. JUDSON KILPATRICK and Maj. Gen. PHILIP H. SHERIDAN. During the PETERSBURG CAMPAIGN, Davies was brevetted major general, 1 Oct. 1864, and suffered a wound in the action at HATCHER'S RUN, 6 Feb. 1865. Promoted to full rank of major general, 4 May, Davies commanded the Middle District of Alabama until his resignation from the army Jan. 1866.

Davies resumed his law practice after the war, serving as New York City public administrator, then as an assistant district attorney, and wrote a biography of Sheridan and several other books. d. Middleboro, Mass., 7 Sept. 1894.   —JDW

Davis, Charles Henry. USN b. Boston, Mass., 16 Jan. 1807, Davis was appointed midshipman in 1824, but because of his intelligence and an education that included 2 years at Harvard he qualified for a lieutenancy after only 3 years. He later completed his degree at Harvard, and for much of his naval career devoted himself to scientific work important to the navy. He was promoted commander in 1854.

When the Civil War began, Davis was head of the Bureau of Detail in Washington, helping to plan and organize the South Atlantic blockade and the expeditions against HATTERAS INLET and PORT ROYAL. During the Port Royal expedition, Davis served

USMHI

as chief of staff and fleet officer to Flag Officer SAMUEL F. DU PONT, contributing much to the successful attack of 7 Nov. 1861.

Though Davis officially replaced ANDREW H. FOOTE as flag officer of the Mississippi flotilla 17 June 1862, he had been in command since Foote's departure in May. On 6 June Davis's flotilla, along with the rams of Col. CHARLES ELLET, destroyed or captured all but 1 vessel of the CONFEDERATE RIVER DEFENSE FLEET during the Battle of MEMPHIS, resulting in the surrender of the city to Davis.

Joining Rear Adm. DAVID G. FARRAGUT's force before Vicksburg, Davis took a cautious approach to the Confederate ram *Arkansas,* which had passed through the Union fleet and reached the city. Farragut wanted a more aggressive flag officer, as did Sec. of the Navy GIDEON WELLES, who regarded Davis as "more of a scholar than a sailor." On 1 Oct. 1862 Comdr. DAVID D. PORTER was promoted to head a reorganized Mississippi Squadron.

Assigned once again to Washington, Davis resumed his scientific studies. At the time of his death, in Washington, D.C., 18 Feb. 1877, he was superintendent of the Naval Observatory.   —NCD

Davis, George. CSP b. Porter's Neck, N.C., 1 Mar. 1820. Davis, fourth and last of the Confederacy's attorneys general, was educated by private tutors before he graduated from the

University of North Carolina in 1838. He practiced law in Wilmington and became an active Whig, although he never sought public office. A "Union man" in 1860–61, Davis was a delegate to the WASHINGTON PEACE CONFERENCE and after its failure concluded that only secession could protect the South.

Davis was named an at-large delegate to the Provisional Confederate Congress and then to a 2-year term in the Confederate Senate, where he chaired the Senate Claims Committee and served on the Buildings, Finance, Naval Affairs, and Claims committees. Conservative in fiscal matters, he generally supported increased powers for the Confederate government and was one of North Carolina's staunchest Confederate nationalists. Davis was 1 of only 4 senators to favor granting to a proposed SUPREME COURT appellate jurisdiction over the state courts.

Davis' nationalism was unpopular in North Carolina, and he was not reelected. In Jan. 1864, Pres. JEFFERSON DAVIS named him attorney general, an appointment that owed much to the president's need for support in North Carolina. Most of Davis' duties were routine—supervision of the Justice Department bureaus, directing the prosecution of court cases, and providing legal advice for other officials. Davis' nationalism was apparent when, for example, he held some state laws unconstitutional because they conflicted with Confederate law.

Davis fled Richmond with the administration in 1865 and accompanied the government into North Carolina. Ascertaining that he could no longer be of service, he resigned to look after personal matters. He attempted to flee to Europe but was arrested in Key West, Fla.

After brief imprisonment, Davis returned to Wilmington and resumed his legal practice. He died there 23 Feb. 1896.
—RMcM

Davis, Henry Winter. USP b. Annapolis, Md., 16 Aug. 1817, Davis was the son of the Rev. Henry L. Davis, who was president of St. John's College at Annapolis, and the cousin of Judge David Davis, a political adviser of Pres. ABRAHAM LINCOLN's. Henry attended Ohio's Kenyon College and the University of Virginia Law School, became an accomplished attorney in Alexandria, Va., then moved to Baltimore in 1849, where he became a political power.

During the complicated series of feuds, alliances, and interparty rivalries that marked the border states in the late antebellum period, Davis emerged a strongman. At one time he was a leader of the reactionary Know Nothing party and one of its representatives in Congress, and in one party or another was in the House of Representatives from 1855. A spoiler in the young REPUBLICAN PARTY, Davis also used his vote and influence in Congress to make Republican William Pennington Speaker of the House in 1860. He was eager to become a power in the Republican cabinet when Lincoln was elected and toward this end made sure Unionist THOMAS H. HICKS was nominated governor of Maryland during the secession crisis. Aside from his own ambition and capricious character, his worst enemy in gaining a post in Lincoln's cabinet was MONTGOMERY BLAIR, leader of a rival Unionist faction in Maryland.

In spite of cousin David Davis's lobbying efforts, Blair was chosen over Henry Davis for postmaster general, then largely an advisory position. Blair also had strong family and political connections in Missouri, another crucial state, and so seemed the logical choice to the new president.

To Davis this was almost a personal affront, and thereafter he rarely took Lincoln's part in Republican party warfare, becoming an ardent Radical Republican. Although he lost his congressional seat in 1861 to a Southern sympathizer, he regained it in 1863 and allied himself with Radical leader BENJAMIN F. WADE. Opposing Lincoln's lenient Reconstruction proposals, he cosponsored the harsh WADE-DAVIS BILL, forcing the president to exercise the pocket veto. Lincoln's action angered him so much that he wrote the Wade-Davis Manifesto, a tirade against "soft" Lincoln policy, mocking the president's plans. Davis toyed with urging former failed Republican candidate JOHN C. FRÉMONT to run against Lincoln for the party's 1864 presidential nomination and as chairman of the House Foreign Relations Committee goaded the administration on its diplomatic policies.

Davis lost his next bid for reelection in 1864. He planned a comeback in the next campaign but died suddenly in Baltimore, Md., 30 Dec. 1865.
—JES

Davis, Jefferson Columbus. USA b. Clark Cty., Ind., 2 Mar. 1828. Raised on a farm, Davis enlisted at 18 in a state regiment, fighting in the Mexican War. In 1848 he was commissioned directly into the 1st U.S. Artillery and as a lieutenant was present at FORT SUMTER for the war's opening blow. Soon afterward he was promoted to captain, but in summer 1861 he accepted the colonelcy of the 22d Indiana Volunteers, a position tendered him by his friend Gov. OLIVER P. MORTON.

USMHI

Davis repaid Morton's trust so well that he soon commanded a brigade in the Army of the Southwest, handling it skillfully at WILSON'S CREEK; accordingly, he was advanced to brigadier general that December. Davis won additional laurels at PEA RIDGE and CORINTH, commanding a division in the Army of the Mississippi. That July he fell ill and was sent to Cincinnati to recuperate but soon was restive. Late in August, he rose from his sickbed to help defend neighboring Louisville, threatened by Gen. BRAXTON BRAGG's invasion of Kentucky. Maj. Gen. WILLIAM NELSON, a former naval officer who commanded there, appointed him to form a local defense battalion. But the 2 men failed to get along, and a few days later, in strong language, Nelson criticized Davis' efforts. When Davis replied with equal heat, Nelson relieved him, ordering him out of the city.

Angered and distraught, Davis left Louisville for a post where his services were more appreciated. He did not return to the city till late September, after learning that Nelson had been superseded by Maj. Gen. DON CARLOS BUELL. However, Nelson was still at his office at the Galt House hotel, and when Davis went there to report to Buell on the morning of the 29th, the pair met again. Pricked by the memory of their earlier confrontation, Davis cornered Nelson in the lobby, demanding a belated apology. When Nelson curtly refused, the brigadier crumpled up a hotel visiting card and flung it in the senior officer's face. Nelson retaliated by slapping Davis with the flat of his hand, then turned and left the room. Enraged, Davis borrowed a pistol from a friend, stalked his antagonist through the hotel, and shot him to death at point-blank range.

The murder of the unarmed general was witnessed by many

officers and civilians, some of whom called for Davis' hanging. Others, including the departmental commander, Brig. Gen. HORATIO G. WRIGHT, defended Davis as an aggrieved party in an affair of honor. Though imprisoned by General Buell, Davis was never tried: Bragg's invasion consumed too much time and attention. Finally, with the backing of Governor Morton and other influential authorities, Wright set him free.

Davis returned to the field as if nothing unusual had occurred. Regaining division command, he fought ably at STONE'S RIVER and CHICKAMAUGA and by Aug. 1864 was leading Maj. Gen. WILLIAM T. SHERMAN's XIV Corps in Georgia, having won the army leader's trust and respect. After the war, Sherman wrote of Davis: "He threw his whole soul into the contest, and wherever fighting was hardest . . . we found him at the front."

But his murder of Nelson did hinder his advancement and, though recommended for a major generalship, he failed to attain it except by brevet. After the war Davis commanded the 23d U.S. Infantry, serving for some time in Alaska, then helped to quell the Modoc Indian War. He died in Chicago 30 Nov. 1879, without ever publicly expressing regret over taking the life of a brother officer.   —EGL

Davis, Jefferson Finis. CSP b. Christian Cty., Ky., 3 June 1808. Few men of any nation, of any time, faced challenges as great as those confronting this man. The fate of the Confederacy was so intimately intertwined with his that the two are
inseparable and in both their
strengths and weaknesses must
be judged almost as one.

Davis was only a second-gen-
eration Southerner. His grandfather was a Pennsylvanian who
moved to Georgia, where
Davis' father was born. Though
not members of the true planter
aristocracy, the Davises early
adopted its manners and beliefs,
becoming as "Southern" as the
oldest families.

A Baptist, young Davis at-   CMH
tended a Catholic school in Kentucky, went to Jefferson College near Natchez, then to Transylvania College in Lexington, Ky. A year before graduation, he accepted an appointment at the Military Academy at West Point, and after a lackluster career as a cadet, graduated in June 1828, 23d in a class of 32. He spent the next 7 years in the army, rising to 1st lieutenant in a dragoon regiment before he resigned his commission to take up planting in Mississippi. That same year, 1835, he married Sarah Knox Taylor, daughter of Gen. and future president Zachary Taylor; just 3 months later she died of malaria. In 1845, Davis married Varina Howell of Natchez, whose influence on him while he was living, and on his memory after his death, was enormous (*see* DAVIS, VARINA HOWELL).

In 1845 Davis, a Democrat, also entered politics, winning election to Congress, and except for service during the Mexican War, he remained in public life almost continuously. In his first year in the House he attracted some attention as a champion of Southern rights, a position he would never abandon. Fervently in favor of the war with Mexico, he resigned his seat in 1846 and accepted appointment as colonel of the 1st Mississippi Rifles. There followed a victorious campaign in Mexico, capped

by Davis' part in the Battle of Buena Vista, where his regiment stopped an enemy cavalry charge and he was wounded in the foot. Though his wound put him out of the war, his regiment's success made him a hero; apparently it also helped convince Davis that he possessed considerable military finesse.

With the war over, he was appointed to represent Mississippi in the Senate, then resigned when he ran for the governorship (unsuccessfully) in 1851. Yet he was not out of politics for long, for when Franklin Pierce assumed the presidency in 1853, he called on Davis to serve as secretary of war, a position Davis filled with distinction. Davis took steps to improve and modernize the army, protect and defend the farflung frontier, and explore routes for a transcontinental railroad. Indeed, his influence spread beyond his department: he was influential in passing the KANSAS-NEBRASKA ACT, which exacerbated already heated sectional feelings, and many believed that he was really the "power behind the throne" in the administration.

Davis returned to the Senate in 1857, remaining there until 1861, when Mississippi seceded. Despite his increasingly militant support of Southern rights and slavery, Davis tried to effect a compromise in the divided Democratic party in 1860, a compromise that might have averted secession. He was unsuccessful, and with the election of ABRAHAM LINCOLN, Mississippi left the Union 9 Jan. 1861. On 21 Jan. he made his farewell speech in the Senate and left for home, expecting to be offered high military command in the new Confederacy then forming. Instead, with some shock and regret, he was informed in February that the MONTGOMERY, Ala., convention had elected him provisional president.

Davis was not the ideal man for the presidency. Prideful, stubborn, doctrinaire, and often narrow-minded, he was rarely willing to compromise to achieve greater goals, which prevented him from becoming a great chief executive. "He did not know the arts of the politician and would not practice them if understood," wrote his wife, and she was right. But his loyalty to the South was unquestioned, an unswerving devotion to the cause espoused, and he was willing to work himself almost to death for it. And, for all his faults, he was the best man available in Feb. 1861, a time when the South was suffering from a dearth of good statesmen.

Inaugurated 18 Feb. Davis became president of the permanent government 22 Feb. 1862, after the capital had been moved to RICHMOND, Va. He announced from the outset that he wanted only peace, that the Confederacy asked only to be "left alone." Nevertheless, the Confederacy prepared for war from the moment of its birth. While the selection of his cabinet ministers was largely dictated by political debts owed, he rarely interfered in most of the executive departments and generally listened to the counsel of his ministers in cabinet session. Only in the War Department did he interfere, so substantially that his war secretaries came to be regarded as pawns. As a result, Davis went through 6 secretaries of war in 4 years.

Davis also tended toward cronyism in in his appointments. Those who had been friends of his in Mexico and those who had served him well during Pierce's administration were all too often placed—and kept—in responsible positions long after they had demonstrated their unfitness. Thus LUCIUS B. NORTHROP remained commissary general until public pressure forced Davis to replace him, and thus Gen. BRAXTON BRAGG retained army command in the face of glaring inadequacy.

Davis' failings in office were many. He squabbled endlessly with his leading generals—except ROBERT E. LEE—and tended to lecture everyone based on his presumed superior knowledge of military affairs. Like so many of his generals, he was overly preoccupied with Richmond's and Virginia's defense, often failing to give proper attention to the Western commands; thus New Orleans was lost. His choice of foreign diplomats was often poor, and his understanding of European attitudes toward the South and slavery was deeply flawed. And Davis unwisely established a rigid system of departmental commands and districts throughout the South that set up local commanders more concerned with their parochial needs than with cooperation in greater matters; thus threatened points frequently went ill defended when help was only a department away.

Yet Davis had his strengths and no one could deny his wholehearted involvement in the cause. He worked himself unsparingly, to the neglect of his health, and even showed a measure of flexibility during the ATLANTA CAMPAIGN. Certainly he overcame the localism that hampered Congress and the governors' mansions by espousing a true nationalistic stance, the only hope at all for the Confederacy. And if he was too much attached to incompetent old friends, still he was perceptive enough to recognize real talent when he saw it: his constant support of Lee stands among his noblest efforts.

Certainly the fall of the Confederacy cannot entirely be blamed on Davis, though much of the internal dissension that plagued it can. With no formal political parties in the South, the Confederacy quickly became divided into pro- and anti-Davis factions, thus making him a major issue in its divided counsels. Unfortunately he was never able to see in opposition anything other than error or worse; few men in history have ever been so firmly convinced of their own infallible rightness.

With the fall of Richmond Apr. 1865, Davis and his cabinet attempted to flee. Even after the surrender of Lee's and Gen. JOSEPH E. JOHNSTON's armies, Davis still refused to believe it was all over, and only the united opposition of his remaining cabinet and generals forced him to accept defeat. He was captured near Irwinville, Ga., 10 May 1865, and was sent to prison for 2 years at Fort Monroe, Va. The Federal government was never sure what to do with him, and though a treason trial was intended, passions cooled, Davis won release on bail, and finally the case was dropped without prosecution.

Davis returned to the South after traveling in Canada and abroad, and in 1877 finally settled at "Beauvoir," near Biloxi, Miss., where he wrote his grand apologia, *The Rise and Fall of the Confederate Government* (1881). This work reveals all the weaknesses that hampered Davis as president—intolerance, dogmatism, and narrow vision—telling little of the inside story of the Confederacy but a great deal about Davis himself, which is perhaps appropriate, for in his own mind, Jefferson Davis and the Confederacy were inseparable. 8 years later, 9 Dec. 1889, he died. Few in the South truly loved him, but many revered the man who had made himself the symbol of the LOST CAUSE, remaining proud, defiant, and unrepentant to the end. —WCD

Davis, Jefferson Finis, capture of. By late Mar. 1865 Union troops were advancing on Richmond, Va., capital of the Confederate States of America. The city's defenders repeatedly warned Pres. JEFFERSON DAVIS that he and the rest of the government should evacuate before it was too late. At last, on 2 Apr., Davis and most of his cabinet boarded a train bearing what was left of the Confederate treasury: about half a million dollars in gold and silver, and boxes and sacks of coins in every denomination. The destination was Danville, Va., near the

North Carolina border. Davis and his "government on wheels," as he called it, were to hook up with retreating Confederate forces in hopes of reinvigorating the war effort. In fact, the South was beaten by this time, and Davis' journey soon turned into a headlong flight to evade capture.

A week after arriving in Danville, Davis had to move south again, this time to Greensborough, N.C. Even though Gen. ROBERT E. LEE had surrendered and Northern troops were occupying major Southern cities, Davis still hoped to fight on. His next stop was Charlotte, where he had sent his wife some weeks before. The treasure train had already gotten through, but Davis had to make this leg of the journey on horse since Northern raiders had destroyed portions of the railway. By the time he arrived in Charlotte his wife had gone, and even Davis now had to admit that all was lost. His "government" was dispersed, as was the treasury, to avoid capture.

With only 20 men and 3 wagons, Davis finally caught up with his family in Georgia, only 70 mi from the Florida border. Their reunion was short-lived. Northern cavalry units, tipped off to Davis' whereabouts, raided the camp the night of 10 May. Davis tried to flee but, quickly surrounded by Northern troops, he said simply, "God's will be done," and sat down by the campfire. —RJM

Davis, Joseph Robert. CSA b. Woodville, Maine, 12 Jan. 1825, this nephew of Confederate Pres. JEFFERSON DAVIS was educated at Miami University in Ohio, practiced law, and served in the Mississippi senate during the antebellum years.

Davis entered the Confederate army as captain of a company from Madison Cty., Miss. In Apr. 1861 he was commissioned lieutenant colonel of the 10th Mississippi, and 31 Aug. the Confederate president appointed his nephew to his staff in Richmond, Va., with the rank of colonel. For a year Davis served in the Confederate capital. On 15 Sept. 1862, after his nomination had been rejected on charges of nepotism, Davis received his brigadiership.

USMHI

With neither formal military training nor combat experience, Davis assumed command of a Mississippi brigade. Subsequently assigned to Maj. Gen. HENRY HETH's division, Davis led his brigade when the division marched to GETTYSBURG, 1 July 1863. In the ensuing Confederate attack Davis lost nearly 2 entire regiments, captured in a railroad cut; 2 days later his depleted command supported PICKETT'S CHARGE. He then contracted a fever and temporarily was relieved of his duties.

Davis returned to the army to participate in the Battles of the WILDERNESS, SPOTSYLVANIA, COLD HARBOR, PETERSBURG, and APPOMATTOX. He stood in the ranks 9 Apr. 1865 when the army surrendered.

Davis went back to Mississippi and resumed his legal career, spending most of his remaining years in Biloxi, where he died, 15 Sept. 1896. —JDW

Davis, Sam. CSA b. Rutherford Cty., Tenn., 6 Oct. 1842, Davis, an unsuccessful Southern courier, is remembered as a

Confederate martyr. His background has been highly romanticized and only the barest facts of his Civil War contributions are reliable. Born to a Tennessee farming family, Davis enlisted as a private in the 1st Tennessee 30 Apr. 1861, serving with this regiment in western Virginia and in the Shenandoah Valley. The regiment returned to Tennessee and in 1862 saw combat at SHILOH, where Davis was wounded.

On recovering, Davis enlisted in Capt. H. B. Shaw's company of scouts, also known as Coleman's Scouts. In Nov. 1863, while carrying intelligence on Union troop movements, he was apprehended by members of the 7th Kansas Cavalry and jailed in Pulaski, Tenn. During the next few days he was questioned for information on his command and the sources of intelligence on Union troop movements. At least once he was interrogated by Union Brig. Gen. GRENVILLE M. DODGE and at each interrogation was made to understand that if the information was not forthcoming the Federals would be obliged to hang him as a spy. Davis consistently refused, claiming he was a courier, not a spy.

He was swiftly tried, in proceedings that have caused some historical argument over legality, and hanged, 27 Nov. 1863. Before his execution his stoic behavior and youth moved several Federals as well as Confederate Tennesseans. The execution was widely reported and the condemned's "manly deportment" on the gallows made good newspaper copy. From there the story of Sam Davis' service began to travel and he became a martyred Southern hero, serving the same purpose ALONZO H. CUSHING and ELMER E. ELLSWORTH did in the North. In the 20th century, Davis' family home in Smyrna, Tenn., was made into a museum, and such items as his farewell letter to his mother were preserved there. —JES

Davis, Varina Howell. b. "The Briars," near Natchez, Miss., 7 May 1826. Had JEFFERSON DAVIS known at the time of his marriage in 1845 of the future awaiting him as president of a Southern confederacy, he could not have chosen a better wife than Varina Howell. In time she abandoned her Whig convictions, deferred to Davis' politics, and became the guardian of his beleaguered reputation.

Howell was an intelligent, deeply religious woman educated by a private tutor and close family friend, later attending a finishing school to polish her considerable social graces. Her mother at first objected to the marriage with Davis, who was 18 years older than her

LC

daughter, but the union turned out to be a long, happy one.

An accomplished hostess and lively conversationalist with a serious interest in politics, Varina adjusted well to life as the wife of a politician in Washington. In her own way, she shared her husband's ambitious temperament, though not his extreme sensitivity to criticism. The latter trait, coupled with the tendency to be aggressively critical of others, would help sustain her through the difficult years as First Lady of the Confederacy.

As living conditions in Richmond deteriorated during the second year of war, Varina found herself increasingly under public scrutiny. Some decried her as insensitive to the hardships endured by the city's residents because she entertained at the White House of the Confederacy; others complained that she did not entertain too lavishly enough. There were those who considered her influence on the president too great, challenged her loyalty to the cause because of her father's Northern roots, or called her ill-bred and unrefined. The last may have been justified by her heated retorts to gossip denigrating Davis' ability as a politician.

Of Varina's 6 children, 1 was born during these frantic years, and another died tragically. Yet through all the family's public and private trials, Varina provided Davis with loyalty, companionship, and a great reserve of strength.

Varina was with Davis when he was arrested in Georgia. After his capture and confinement the children were sent to Canada in the charge of their maternal grandmother. Varina was prohibited from leaving Georgia without permission from Federal authorities, but she lobbied incessantly to secure her husband's release from prison, succeeding May 1867.

The Davises lived in near-poverty until the early 1870s, when a friend arranged for them to purchase "Beauvoir," the Mississippi estate to which they retired. Varina stayed on to write her memoirs after Davis' death in 1889. She then gave Beauvoir to the state as a Confederate veterans' home and moved to New York City to support herself by writing articles for magazines and periodicals. She died there 16 Oct. 1905, survived by only 1 of her children. —PLF

Davis, William George Mackey. CSA b. Portsmouth, Va., 9 May 1812. Hoping to follow in the steps of his father, a naval officer, Davis ran away to sea at 17. Returning to pursuits on land, he settled in Eufaula, Ala., learned the basics of journalism, and edited a local newspaper. Later he moved to Franklin Cty., Fla., where he studied and practiced law, and speculated in cotton.

In 1844 Davis was elected judge of Franklin County but moved to the village of St. Joseph 2 years later and to Tallahassee in 1848. When the Civil War drew near he represented Leon County at the Florida secession convention, where, despite his Whig origins, he voted

LC

to pull his state out of the Union. He demonstrated his support for the Confederacy by donating $50,000 to its treasury and by recruiting and equipping the 1st Florida Cavalry, of which he became colonel.

Although elected to the Confederate Congress, Davis remained in the field, at first commanding provisional troops in eastern Florida. With these he operated against the Federal outpost at Jacksonville, which was forced to evacuate in spring 1862. He then arranged for the city's occupation, ensuring that its many pro-Union residents were not victimized by vengeful Confederates. Soon after he was transferred to Tennessee, despite the poor condition of his regiment's horses and over the protests of Gov. JOHN MILTON, who wished the 1st Cavalry to replace other troops stripped from Florida's coastal defenses.

In Tennessee, Davis served under Gen. JOSEPH E. JOHNSTON and was named a brigadier general 4 Nov. 1862; 6 months later, after commanding the Department of East Tennessee, he resigned his commission and retired to Virginia. In the war's closing months he resided in Wilmington, N.C., where, by arrangement with his close friend JEFFERSON DAVIS, he operated a fleet of BLOCKADE RUNNERS to Nassau. In postwar life, he practiced law in Jacksonville and later in Washington, D.C. d. Alexandria, Va., 11 Mar. 1898.   —EGL

Davis boot. Named for JEFFERSON DAVIS, at the time secretary of war under Pres. Franklin Pierce, this shoe was worn by both Confederate and Union infantry soldiers. It had a top that came slightly above the ankle and was tied at the front with a short lace run through 2 pair of eyes. It was found that "a few standard sizes fit most men," which eased standardization in production and prompted battles among Union manufacturers for government contracts. Feuds, swindles, an enormous end-of-war surplus, and a few personal fortunes resulted. This humble boot, along with the KEPI, became one of the most identifiable items of clothing from the Civil War period. The production of both broke ground for the mass-manufacture of clothing in the postwar era.   —JES

Davis Guard Medal. The Davis Guards, a militia company raised in Houston, Tex., in summer 1860, was mustered into the 1st Texas Regiment, Heavy Artillery, CSA, in fall 1861. Most if not all of them were Irish Americans. They fought bravely at the recapture of GALVESTON early in Jan. 1863 and in a naval engagement at the outlet of Sabine Lake later that month. But the gunners had their greatest glory at SABINE PASS that September when Lt. RICHARD W. DOWLING, his 43 artillerists, and their 6 guns (4 32-pounders and 2 24-pounders) captured 2 Federal gunboats and their crews, damaged 3 other craft, and sent 6 more, carrying 6,000 troops, on a quick retreat to New Orleans. The battle resulted in the most brilliant Confederate victory in Texas during the war.

In gratitude the residents of nearby Sabine City arranged to present each man with a medal—the only military medal ever awarded in the Confederacy. Charles Gottchalk made the medals of shaved silver dollars and suspended them from green ribbons. On one side he engraved a Maltese cross and the letters *DG*; on the other side he inscribed *Battle of Sabine Pass, September 8, 1863.*

A few weeks after the battle the men received their decorations. One was also sent to JEFFERSON DAVIS, who carried it until it was taken away at Fort Monroe after his capture. On 15 May 1875, at the 6th Texas State Fair, a second Davis Guard medal was given to him by the unit's 3 survivors.   —PLF

Dawes, Henry Laurens. USP b. Cummington, Mass., 30 Oct. 1816, Dawes was an 1839 Yale graduate, an editorial writer, attorney, and Massachusetts state legislator who became a financial power in the U.S. House of Representatives. But when the Civil War began he was little more than a freshman congressman, elected in 1859, and eager to be noticed.

Late the next year and early in 1861 war loomed and charges of treason were thrown at outgoing members of Pres. James Buchanan's cabinet. Early in Jan. 1861 it was revealed Buchanan's Sec. of War JOHN B. FLOYD had been sending military supplies south into secessionist hands; then, on the verge of arrest, Floyd resigned to take a Confederate army commission. A House investigating committee was formed to hunt for more officials like Floyd, and Dawes was placed on it. The

Massachusetts congressman was able to shock capital dwellers almost daily in committee hearings by revealing hints of further treachery, hints that came in "secret memoranda" supplied, Dawes later believed, by powerful Unionist attorney EDWIN M. STANTON—all of which brought Dawes recognition. His cross-examination techniques in the House were called "theatrical"; in investigation he was said to be a prober.

Late in 1861, another investigation by Dawes shattered the new Sec. of War, Pennsylvania's SIMON CAMERON. The congressman dug into Cameron's methods of awarding supply contracts and unearthed what some termed wholesale fraud and theft. Going beyond acceptable limits of patronage, the secretary had awarded contracts to political cronies that were rarely honestly filled. Horse and beef contracts were the examples most often cited. By late 1861 and early 1862 Dawes was making concrete accusations, which ultimately contributed to Cameron's departure from the cabinet.

With his expertise in government finance, following the war Dawes was named chairman of the House Appropriations Committee and the Ways and Means Committee. In 1875 he was elected to the Senate, made head of the Indian Affairs Committee, and served until his 1892 retirement. d. Pittsfield, Mass., 5 Feb. 1903.   —JES

Dayton, William Lewis. U.S. diplomat b. Basking Ridge, N.J., 17 Feb. 1807. After a distinguished career as an attorney and U.S. senator, Dayton became a founder of the REPUBLICAN PARTY and served the Union in the Civil War as U.S. minister to France. An 1825 graduate of the College of New Jersey, Dayton became an attorney in 1830, and until the 1850s was an active Whig. During this period he made the acquaintance of French heir Louis Napoleon, in exile in the U.S. In 1842 he was appointed to a U.S. Senate seat by the governor of New Jersey, then was elected to it in 1851.

LC

In his terms as senator, Dayton expressed independent opinions, protesting the Mexican War and opposing the admission of more slave states to the Union. His views predisposed him to break with his old party and join the Republicans. In 1856 he was chosen as JOHN C. FRÉMONT's running mate on the first Republican presidential ticket and thereafter became a minor policy maker in the party hierarchy. While Frémont's fortunes declined, Dayton built a strong party following in the East and in 1860 was nominated as the Republican presidential candidate. His candidacy lasted through the first 3 ballots. When it looked as though ABRAHAM LINCOLN would receive the party's nomination, Dayton withdrew, offering Lincoln his support. On Lincoln's election Dayton was rewarded with the post of U.S. minister to France.

Patronage appointments to U.S. foreign ministries were often considered harmless expressions of esteem, and after Lincoln's inauguration, with national attention centered on political rifts at home, they were still doled out without much regard for the appointee's qualifications. Few politicians believed the civil disturbance would have immediate foreign repercussions, but soon Dayton found himself in France without any diplomatic training or knowledge of the language, and facing a series of international crises.

Dayton's performance was admirable. In Louis Napoleon's court, he relied on his charm and Republican political skills and, renewing his acquaintance with the emperor, used them to great advantage. He skillfully guided the French away from intervening on the side of the Confederacy by appealing to their self-interest. In the delicate matters involving the French occupation of Mexico he carried out and interpreted instructions from Sec. of State WILLIAM H. SEWARD that, while not invoking the Monroe Doctrine, implied the extreme displeasure and danger the American people perceived in the French military presence in their hemisphere. He was also able to stop Confederate purchasing agents from operating in France, halt French manufacture of Confederate warships, and prevent French ports from giving sanctuary to Confederate sea raiders.

He died at his post in Paris, 1 Dec. 1864.   —JES

Dearing, James. CSA b. Campbell Cty., Va., 25 Apr. 1840, Dearing fell mortally wounded 3 days before the war ended, the last Confederate general officer to die of wounds received in battle; only 24, he had served with distinction as an artillery and cavalry officer.

A graduate of Hanover Academy, Va., Dearing entered West Point in 1858, resigning 22 Apr. 1861, after his native state seceded. He entered Confederate service as a lieutenant of the WASHINGTON ARTILLERY of New Orleans, serving with this battery for nearly a year. In spring 1862, Dearing, promoted to captain, commanded a battery attached to the brigade of Brig. Gen. GEORGE E. PICKETT, which

USMHI

saw action on the PENINSULA, at FREDERICKSBURG, and at CHANCELLORSVILLE. In May 1863 he was promoted to major and commanded an 18-gun battalion in the artillery reserve of Lt. Gen. JAMES LONGSTREET's I Corps. At GETTYSBURG, his battalion participated in the Confederate bombardment preceding PICKETT'S CHARGE on the third day's battle.

During winter 1863–64 Dearing commanded Pickett's cavalry in the District of North Carolina. He received command of the HORSE ARTILLERY of the Army of Northern Virginia early in Apr. 1864 with the rank of lieutenant colonel. On 29 Apr. 1864 he was promoted to brigadier and assigned to a cavalry brigade, leading it with distinction in the New Berne, N.C., expedition. He and his brigade transferred to Virginia, participating in the PETERSBURG CAMPAIGN. Dearing subsequently was assigned to Maj. Gen. W.H.F. LEE's cavalry division, where he fought until his death.

On 6 Apr. 1865, during the Confederate retreat to Appomattox, Dearing's brigade encountered Federals at High Bridge over the Appomattox River. Dearing rode to the brigade's front, where he engaged in a pistol duel with Union Lt. Col. Theodore Read. Read died instantly in the exchange, while the Southern officer fell mortally wounded. Dearing lingered until 23 Apr., 2 weeks after his army's surrender, dying in Lynchburg, Va.   —JDW

Deas, Zachariah Cantey. CSA b. Camden, S.C., 25 Oct. 1819. In 1861 Deas was a prosperous Mobile, Ala., cotton broker. He had moved to Mobile with his family when he was still a boy, then was sent to Columbia, S.C., and France for a quality education. As a young man he was a Mexican War volunteer; with the coming of civil war he fell back on this experience and briefly served as Gen. ALBERT SIDNEY JOHNSTON's aide-de-camp.

LC

With the help of Maj. Robert B. Armistead, Deas raised and financed his own regiment, the 22d Alabama, and was commissioned a Confederate colonel Sept. 1861. Deas outfitted his men with Enfield rifles at a cost to himself of $28,000, then they were brigaded into the Confederacy's western army for training.

The following spring Deas and the 22d had their baptism in combat at the Battle of SHILOH. Although the Confederates were successful on the first day of battle, by evening many officers had become separated from their commands. Also on this first day Deas's immediate superior, Brig. Gen. ADLEY H. GLADDEN, and the brigade's senior colonel, DANIEL W. ADAMS, were wounded. At nightfall, 6 Apr. 1862, Deas had command of the brigade but could not find most of his troops. At daybreak, 7 Apr., when the Federals counterattacked, the colonel was still looking for 2 of his regiments and his own 2d Division headquarters. He responded as best he could by throwing what men he had in on the left of the 1st Brigade in his corps' 1st Division and trying to organize resistance.

Deas was badly wounded the second day at Shiloh, but he recuperated in time to rejoin the Army of Tennessee for its invasion of Kentucky. On 13 Dec. 1862 he was promoted to brigadier general in preparation for the Murfreesboro campaigning and the Battle of STONE'S RIVER. At the head of the 1st Brigade in Maj. Gen. JONES M. WITHERS' 2d Division, he performed well at Stone's River and on through all of the Army of Tennessee's battles to its surrender in North Carolina. He and his brigade distinguished themselves at CHICKAMAUGA by capturing 17 Federal cannon, and performed sturdy service in the Battles of FRANKLIN and NASHVILLE.

In the Reconstruction era, Deas returned to the cotton business, this time in New York City as a member of the stock exchange. d. New York City, 6 Mar. 1882.   —JES

DeBow's Review. J.D.B. DeBow began publishing his *Review* in New Orleans Jan. 1846. He had come away from the Southern Commercial Convention the previous year with the idea of issuing a monthly journal devoted to the economic concerns of the South and the West. DeBow covered a broad range of topics pertinent to the regions: agriculture, commerce, urbanization, expansionism, and external improvements. He also editorialized against Northern industrialism, heatedly defended slavery, and advanced his belief that the South would inevitably seek independence from the North. Outspoken, sometimes vitriolic, clearly prosecessionist, DeBow built the *Review* into one of the most influential Southern periodicals of the antebellum years.

The *Review* moved to Washington for 6 years, 1853–59, during DeBow's tenure there as superintendent of the census. Once again publishing from New Orleans, at the time the city fell, Apr. 1862, the editor turned Confederate purchasing agent moved his magazine to the offices of the *South Carolinian* in Columbia, S.C. But only 1 issue (May-August 1864) was published thereafter; its pages stoutly defended the Davis administration.

No further issue appeared until 1866, when DeBow assumed a reserved editorial position in favor of Presidential Reconstruction. The *Review,* however, never regained its prewar eminence. It was published sporadically after DeBow died in 1867, and finally ceased altogether in 1880.   —PLF

Declaration of Immediate Causes.

Drafted by CHRISTO-PHER G. MEMMINGER during the South Carolina secession convention Dec. 1860, the declaration justified the state's right to secede on the grounds that the North had violated the Constitution. The Founding Fathers, argued Memminger, had intended the Constitution to be a compact between sovereign states to form a common federal government. The Union, however, was not perpetually binding. Any state choosing to withdraw if its rights were violated was at liberty to do so. By encouraging abolitionism and attempting to limit slavery, the Northern states had violated the Constitution, rendering it null and void.

Memminger, a capable lawyer, based his defense on the STATES-RIGHTS doctrine drafted meticulously by JOHN C. CAL-HOUN and touted by a succession of radical South Carolina politicians over the preceding 30 years. But the document was more than a justification for the Ordinance of Secession. The delegates at the convention consciously called for the establishment of an independent Southern nation. Their declaration openly invited other Southern states to join the movement.
—PLF

Declaration of Paris.

At the end of the Crimean War in 1856, 7 European nations agreed to the Declaration of Paris, which abolished privateering (the arming of private vessels) and the seizure of neutral goods on the high seas and established that an effective blockade had to prevent entirely access by neutrals to the enemy coast.

The U.S. did not at that time become a signatory because, as a small-navy nation, it relied on privateering for wartime defense. In spring 1861 Sec. of War WILLIAM H. SEWARD learned through captured letters that at Britain's invitation the Confederacy had acceded to the declaration and agreed to abide by all its principles but the ban on privateering. The Southern Congress issued letters of marque against the U.S. because it had not abandoned the right of privateering, and the Confederacy claimed the same right. Seward had rebuffed English and French diplomats bearing similar invitations because, in not accepting the Federal government's interpretation of the civil war as a domestic insurrection, their governments recognized the Confederacy as a responsible government conducting war. But now Seward realized the critical importance of U.S. participation in order to enforce the blockade of Southern ports and bring sanctions against Confederate PRIVATEERS.

Seward's recent hostility thwarted diplomatic attempts to secure the U.S. as a subscriber to the declaration in summer 1860. Nonetheless, the U.S. pressured Britain into interpreting the declaration in terms unfavorable to the Confederacy. Real-

izing that the Federal government intended to prosecute the war by whatever means necessary to defeat the South and that the Royal Navy could profit by cooperating indirectly with Washington, British officials redefined the word *effective* to make it fit the Union blockade of Southern ports: now, to be effective, a blockade needed only to present heightened threat to neutrals attempting to trade with the enemy.

The results caused a severe blow to the Confederacy. By mid-1863 most European ports were closed to Confederate raiders and few foreign ships would risk challenging the Federal fleet to run the blockade.   —PLF

decorations.

Medals were not issued to either Union or Confederate forces at the start of the Civil War. Recognition of exceptional service by soldiers or sailors was confined to brevet promotions or praise in superiors' reports. Federal General-in-Chief WINFIELD SCOTT and many other veterans, North and South, believed awarding medals and decorations was "contrary to the spirit of American Institutions." In a volunteer army or navy, to set a man apart with a medal was thought to detract from a presumed democratic spirit in the ranks. But many in service, particularly the foreign-born, did not agree. Elsewhere in the world medals were goals to be striven for and were believed to have a good effect on fighting spirit.

Though many in the Confederate government and officers' corps never accepted this, some Southerners encouraged medals and badges for bravery and provided for awards. None were made because the Confederacy lacked the materials to produce them. In Oct. 1862 the Confederate Congress passed a law calling for the publication of a Roll of Honor after each battle, which would contain the names of soldiers who had distinguished themselves. It would be read to the men at dress parade, included in official records, and printed in newspapers. This practice was not always followed regularly, but along with votes of the official THANKS OF THE CONFEDERATE CONGRESS, it was the only government-sponsored recognition for bravery and duty. There was only 1 Confederate medal awarded, the DAVIS GUARD MEDAL, given by the grateful citizens of Sabine City, Tex., not by the military.

Pressures from the public and the service ranks finally induced the U.S. government to come up with an award late in 1861. On 21 Dec. the U.S. Navy was permitted to give out a MEDAL OF HONOR; the next summer army personnel became eligible for the medal, known today as the Congressional Medal of Honor. This was the Union government's only individual decoration for bravery and service during the Civil War, aside from votes of the THANKS OF THE U.S. CONGRESS (as in the Confederacy, usually directed to army or navy commanders). All other medals and decorations came from individual commanders or communities. Among these were the FORT SUMTER AND FORT PICKENS MEDALS, the KEARNY MEDAL AND KEARNY CROSS, the GILLMORE MEDAL, the XVII CORPS MEDAL, and the BUTLER MEDAL. Of these, the XVII Corps Medal was available to the largest body of troops, and was conceived and ordered by corps commander JAMES B. MCPHERSON 2 Oct. 1863 for "gallantry in action and other soldier-like qualities." Made by Tiffany's of New York it came in 2 types, silver and gold, and was pinned over a red, white, and blue ribbon. Reportedly a gold medal was given to the soldier who ran to McPherson's aid when he fell mortally wounded in the Battle of Atlanta. The smallest unit to award a medal was the 2d Connecticut Regiment. Its colonel gave gold medals to Color Sgt. Austin Kirkham and Sgt. Robert Leggett "for bravery on the field."

To boost morale, both Union and Confederate services allowed units to inscribe on their flags the names of battles they had fought in; such inscriptions denoted brave and able service. In several instances units or ships' companies who performed poorly during a particular battle were ordered to strike from their flag the name of that battle.   —JES

Deep Bottom, Va.   27 July 1864   *See* DARBYTOWN, VA.

Deep Run, Va.   *See* FRANKLIN'S CROSSING, VA.

defeat in detail.   In Civil War literature the term *defeat in detail* is often misconstrued to mean complete destruction of a force. It actually meant to defeat a force unit by unit, usually because the individual regiments or companies were not within supporting distance of one another.   —JES

de Lagnel, Julius Adolph.   CSA   b. near Newark, N.J., 24 July 1827, de Lagnel entered the U.S. Army as a 2d lieutenant of artillery in 1847. He served nearly 14 years before resigning in 1861 with the outbreak of the war. A Northerner, he joined the Confederate cause when his adopted state of Virginia seceded.

LC

De Lagnel received a commission as captain and an appointment to the staff of Brig. Gen. Robert S. Garnett as chief of artillery. Garnett's command was ordered to western Virginia, where, 11 July 1861, at RICH MOUNTAIN, it battled a Union army. Attacked by a superior force, de Lagnel, with only a few infantry companies and a single cannon, opposed 4 Union infantry regiments and a cavalry unit. In the overwhelming Federal assault de Lagnel, manning his artillery piece alone, fell seriously wounded, eluding capture by hiding in a thicket. After recovering in a local residence the artillery officer, disguised as a herdsman, attempted to reach Confederate lines but was captured.

De Lagnel was exchanged nearly a year later and promoted to major of the 20th Battalion of Virginia Artillery. He declined his commission of brigadier general, dated 15 Apr. 1862, soon accepting a post in the Ordnance Bureau in Richmond. Promoted to lieutenant colonel, de Lagnel was second in command to Brig. Gen. Josiah Gorgas, head of the bureau. For the rest of the war, he oversaw operations at headquarters and inspected arsenals in various states.

During the postwar years, de Lagnel was a businessman in the Pacific steamship service. d. Washington, D.C., 3 June 1912.   —JDW

Delaware.   One of the border states of the Union at the beginning of the Civil War, Delaware was not so divided in its loyalties as Kentucky, Maryland, or Missouri. The majority of Delawareans disapproved of the secession of their state but also disapproved of any military coercion of Southern states back into the Union.

In the presidential election of 1860, the state gave John C.

Breckinridge, the Democratic candidate, 7,320 votes to Constitutional Unionist John Bell's 3,830 and Republican Abraham Lincoln's 3,810. With only 1,800 slaves, Delaware was nevertheless officially a slave state in 1860, and a proposal by Lincoln to compensate owners for the emancipation of their slaves failed to pass in the state legislature. The slaves were not technically freed until the adoption of the 13th Amendment Dec. 1865. Although there was some scattered support for the South, Delaware remained loyal to the Union throughout the war, proud of its distinction as the first state to ratify the Constitution in 1787.

Delaware furnished about 12,000 soldiers to the Union armies, in 9 infantry regiments and 1 cavalry regiment, most of the units serving with the Army of the Potomac. Among prominent Delawareans were Maj. Gen. GEORGE SYKES, commander of the V Corps/Army of the Potomac, and Brig. Gen. ALFRED T. A. TORBERT, commander of a division of Federal cavalry with Maj. Gen. Philip H. Sheridan in 1864. Flag Officer SAMUEL F. DU PONT commanded the Philadelphia Navy Yard in 1861 and was promoted to rear admiral in the Union navy in 1862 after his victory at PORT ROYAL, S.C.

The home front of Delaware made its own contributions to the Federal war effort, with much of the gunpowder produced by the North coming from the state's Du Pont mills. Many ships, including some ironclad monitors, were built at Wilmington and elsewhere. Fort Delaware, on Pea Patch Island in the Delaware River, was converted into a prisoner of war camp, and many Confederates captured at GETTYSBURG were sent to the barracks there.   —JTP

de Leon, Edwin.   propagandist   b. Columbia, S.C., 4 May 1818. In 1840, 3 years after his graduation from South Carolina College, de Leon was admitted to the bar. Rather than practice law, he became a journalist, editing the Savannah (Ga.) *Republican,* the Columbia *Telegraph,* and, 1850–54, the Democratic *The Southern Press* in Washington, D.C. In the capital he became acquainted with James Buchanan, who after his election to the presidency appointed de Leon consul general to Egypt.

Early in 1861 de Leon returned to the country to offer his services to the Confederacy. His old friend JEFFERSON DAVIS sent him to France early in 1862 with $25,000 and instructions to sway French public opinion by using the press to publish articles favorable to the Confederacy. He produced a tract, *La vérité sur des États Confédérés,* idealizing Southern slavery, and placed in print several articles touting Confederate successes on the battlefield, but de Leon never lived up to Davis' expectations of him as a propagandist. Instead of cultivating influence in the French press, he tried to present himself as a special diplomatic envoy of Davis', spoke so disparagingly of the French that he was unwelcome among them, and quarreled constantly with Confederate diplomat JOHN SLIDELL. Late in 1863 de Leon erred by criticizing Slidell in an official dispatch that was intercepted by U.S. agents and published in the New York *Daily Tribune.* Sec. of State JUDAH P. BENJAMIN, who did not approve of de Leon, took advantage of the opportunity to dismiss him for embarrassing the government. Official notice reached de Leon early in Feb. 1864, and the more talented HENRY HOTZE expanded his propaganda efforts in England to include France.

De Leon stayed abroad until 1879, returned to the U.S. for 2 years, then traveled to Egypt to organize telephone service in that nation's major cities. He wrote several books after returning permanently to the U.S. d. New York City, 1 Dec. 1891.   —PLF

Democratic party. Until the 1850s, when sectional strains, above all slavery, began tearing them apart, the 2 major political parties were the Whig and the Democratic. The Whigs went under first, replaced by the Northern-oriented Republican party. The Democratic party split in 1860, at which time the Southern wing bolted and nominated its own presidential candidate, JOHN C. BRECKINRIDGE. ABRAHAM LINCOLN failed to secure a popular majority in the election, but the electoral votes were so distributed that he would have won even if the regular Democratic candidate, STEPHEN A. DOUGLAS, had also received the Breckinridge vote.

Most Democrats tended to support the administration in the days following FORT SUMTER, but the consensus broke down when the FIRST BATTLE OF BULL RUN made it obvious that a bloody struggle lay ahead. The party then divided into 2 factions: War Democrats, who backed the struggle though not the administration's conduct, and Peace Democrats, who would accept an independent Confederacy.

Democratic political fortunes thereafter depended heavily on the course of the war. In 1862, when Northern spring offensives had bogged down along with hopes of a speedy victory, the Democrats picked up strength. Their prospects appeared even better in 1864, since Northern advances had foundered by the time the nominating conventions met. Contending Democratic factions compromised by balancing the nomination of GEORGE B. MCCLELLAN for the presidency with a Peace Democrat as his running mate and a peace plank in the platform. Although McClellan subsequently repudiated the peace plank, the capture of ATLANTA and other Union victories ensured Lincoln's reelection. Within the context of an impending Northern triumph, the Democratic party was seen by many as divisive, if not actually disloyal.   —RJM

demonstration. In this strategic maneuver, used frequently during the Civil War, a detached unit from the main force made a show of strength on a portion of the enemy's line not actually targeted for attack, distracting the enemy while an attack was made elsewhere. Demonstrations were useful to large bodies of troops as well as small ones. The largest in the Civil War involved a corps under Confederate Lt. Gen. Jubal A. Early in his Washington Raid, in which he brought 10,000 men early in front of the Washington, D.C., defenses and made a demonstration to distract Federals from Gen. Robert E. Lee's front. As in all other demonstrations, no attack was actually made. *See also* FEINT.   —JES

Dennison, William. war governor b. Cincinnati, Ohio, 23 Nov. 1815. Born into a family with roots in New England and New Jersey, Dennison was educated in Cincinnati before graduating from Miami University, Ohio. He then studied law in his native city and began a practice in Columbus. In 1848 he was elected to the state senate as a Whig, barely losing a contest for the post of presiding officer.

In the legislature Dennison worked to repeal the notorious "Black Laws" and other quasi-slavery measures, and in 1852 helped organize the state chapter of the REPUBLICAN PARTY. In June 1856 he was acting chairman of the national convention at which JOHN C. FRÉMONT became the party's first presidential

candidate. 3 years later Dennison ran a surprisingly effective race for the governorship, defeating an older, more prominent opponent. Despite his popular majority, he failed to win the esteem of the people, who considered him aristocratic and pompous. He also lacked administrative ability: when war came in 1861, he proved unable to arm, equip, train, and transport to the front the great number of citizens eager to defend the Union.

His inefficiency cost him the respect of the War Department, though ABRAHAM LINCOLN applauded his pro-war enthusiasm and loyalty. Dennison ably defended Ohio's borders, found competent leaders for its regiments, and supported Unionism in neighboring slave states such as Kentucky and Virginia. Since this last effort was politically indelicate—especially given Lincoln's wish to maintain Kentucky's neutrality—Dennison embarrassed the administration, as did his imperious assumption of authority over communications and transportation agencies and his sometimes unwise handling of state funds.

In 1864 Dennison's growing unpopularity and his party's need to widen its base resulted in his loss of the nomination to a War Democrat, DAVID TOD, who succeeded him in office. That year Lincoln appointed Dennison postmaster general, a position in which he served for 2 years. Defeated by JAMES A. GARFIELD in the 1880 senatorial race, Dennison made no further bid for elective office. d. Columbus, Ohio, 15 June 1882, after a long period of invalidism.   —EGL

Dent, Frederick Tracy. USA b. near St. Louis, Mo., 17 Dec. 1820, Dent was a friend of U. S. Grant's and a fellow cadet in the West Point class of 1843, Dent graduating 33d. By introducing Grant to his sister, Julia, Dent provided a wife for the future commanding general of the army.

For much of his military career Dent served in the shadow of his brother-in-law, but he accumulated a formidable record in the years preceding the war. As a lieutenant in the 6th U.S. Infantry, he served in Indian Territory, then at Baton Rouge, La., prior to participating in the Mexican War. Twice brevetted for gallantry, he fought at Vera Cruz, San Antonio, Contreras,

LC

Churubusco, and Molino del Rey, being wounded in the last battle. After recovering, he served again on the frontier, along the Pacific Coast, and in the Southeast during the removal of the Seminoles.

When the Civil War came, Dent was stationed in San Francisco as a captain in the 9th U.S. Infantry and Mar. 1863 was appointed major of the 4th Infantry, a regiment sent east and attached to the Army of the Potomac. Dent was present for the Battles of CHANCELLORSVILLE and GETTYSBURG, where his Regulars were lightly engaged, before going to New York City as a civil-military administrator. There he oversaw conscription and served on a commission to try prisoners of state.

When Grant came to Virginia early in 1864 to assume command of all Union forces, Dent secured a position on his staff, with the rank of lieutenant colonel of volunteers. He was at Grant's side throughout the last year of the war, being named a brigadier general 5 Apr. 1865, 4 days before Gen. Robert E. Lee's surrender at Appomattox Court House. After the fall of Richmond, Dent served briefly as the city's military governor, then commanded in the defenses of Washington.

As a brevet brigadier general of Regulars, Dent served during part of Grant's presidency as his military secretary, leaving the White House staff May 1873 to command Fort Trumbull, Conn. 10 years later he retired from active duty, at his own request, as colonel of the 3d U.S. Artillery. In retirement he lived in the capital, then moved to Denver, Colo., where he died 23 Dec. 1892.   —EGL

department. Subordinate to the geopolitical Military Division was the department, the basic geographical and political division of Northern and Southern territory. Particularly in Union-held territory, once designated, departments were frequently redefined or eliminated according to military or political expedience. As in the naming of armies and battles, Federals often named their departments after rivers: e.g., the Departments of the James, the Mississippi, the Cumberland, and the Missouri. Confederate departments were usually named for states or territories: e.g., Department of Southern Virginia, Tennessee, and Texas.

Individual departments are addressed under separate headings.   —JES

Department No. 1, Confederate. In spring 1861, when the Confederacy formed military-geographical divisions, Maj. Gen. DAVID E. TWIGGS was named to command Department No. 1, which comprised Louisiana, except for a portion of the northeastern corner of the state along the Mississippi River (then considered part of Confederate DEPARTMENT NO. 2); a portion of southern Mississippi; and southwestern Alabama, including Mobile.

By the close of the year, Maj. Gen. MANSFIELD LOVELL had succeeded Twiggs in command of the department's 10,300 troops and 173 cannon, and the military area now encompassed all of Louisiana; still included part of southern Mississippi, except its extreme southeastern edge; and excluded southwestern Alabama. Those portions of the latter 2 states no longer in the department were now part of the Department of Alabama and West Florida.

On 25 June 1862, Department No. 1 was discontinued, its New Orleans headquarters being under Union occupation. Within the Union military-geographical network, its territory had become part of the Department of the Gulf. The Confederacy considered most of Louisiana part of its TRANS-MISSISSIPPI DEPARTMENT and that portion of the old department east of the Mississippi River a part of Department No. 2.

For the rest of the war, most of Louisiana remained, on paper, a part of the Confederate Trans-Mississippi. The rest of the state went into the Confederate DEPARTMENT OF MISSISSIPPI AND EAST LOUISIANA, later expanded and renamed the DEPARTMENT OF ALABAMA, MISSISSIPPI, AND EAST LOUISIANA. At various times from late 1862 until the end of the conflict, the latter department was also considered a part of the more extensive Department No. 2 and an even larger domain, the Confederate DEPARTMENT OF THE WEST.   —EGL

Department No. 2, Confederate. By July 1861 this military administrative domain, commanded by Maj. Gen. LEONIDAS POLK, consisted of slices of eastern Arkansas, West Tennessee, northeastern Louisiana, and western Mississippi. Its northernmost section was bordered on the west by the White River and on the east by the Tennessee; its lower section was split by the Mississippi River. Jutting eastward along the lower boundary of Tennessee, the department also took in portions of northeastern Mississippi and northern Alabama. 6 months later, its jurisdiction was extended to include all of Tennessee and Arkansas, the western half of Mississippi, and "all military operations in the State of Missouri." The entire state of Louisiana was now part of CONFEDERATE DEPARTMENT NO. 1, while the whole of Alabama was in the DEPARTMENT OF ALABAMA AND WEST FLORIDA. At this time, Department No. 2 was commanded by Gen. ALBERT SIDNEY JOHNSTON.

On Johnston's death at SHILOH, 6 Apr. 1862, Gen. P.G.T. BEAUREGARD took over the department; later that spring his authority was extended to the southern half of Mississippi as well as to that part of Louisiana west of the Mississippi River. On 25 June, following the fall of New Orleans, Department No. 1 was discontinued, its territory being added to Department No. 2. A further expansion of the latter, 18 July, gave its new commander, Gen. BRAXTON BRAGG, jurisdiction over Mississippi, Alabama, southeastern Louisiana, the far western part of the Florida panhandle, West and Middle Tennessee, and a section of northwestern Georgia lying west of a line from Dalton to Decatur to La Grange and including Atlanta. Arkansas became part of the new TRANS-MISSISSIPPI DEPARTMENT.

On 1 Oct. 1862 Department No. 2 was reduced to Alabama, West and Middle Tennessee, and northwestern Florida. At the same time, a larger territorial unit, the CONFEDERATE DEPARTMENT OF THE WEST, was created to encompass Department No. 2 as well as the newly formed Departments of MISSISSIPPI AND EAST LOUISIANA, and EAST TENNESSEE. The Department of the West also included the portion of northwestern Georgia previously within Department No. 2.

Department No. 2 passed out of existence 25 July 1863 on the creation of the DEPARTMENT OF TENNESSEE, which absorbed most of its territory as well as parts of other states, including North and South Carolina and Virginia. See also WESTERN DEPARTMENT, CONFEDERATE.   —EGL

desertion. Desertion weakened Northern and Southern armies throughout the war. Homesickness, boredom, disillusionment, and infrequent pay contributed, but depression—especially following defeat—led soldiers to violate their oaths in staggering numbers. At the end of 1864 nearly half the Confederate fighting force was absent from the army and estimates of Union absenteeism ran as high as one-third. Not all absences were unauthorized, but many were, seriously affecting morale and effectiveness in the field.

Union desertions decreased as punishment became more severe, but an average of 5,500 Federals fled the army each month between 1863 and 1865. An initial reward of $5 for returning a deserter was raised to $30 to encourage arrests. While desertion wasn't confined to a single group, FOREIGN-BORN SOLDIERS from the East, recruits receiving BOUNTIES, and substitutes were likely candidates.

Gen. Robert E. Lee, desperately short of manpower, dealt with deserters leniently, preferring offers of AMNESTY to draw them back. His ill-clad, starving soldiers struggled between responsibility to the Confederacy and concern for families in territory occupied by the enemy. Letters from kin often begged men to come home, and some troops simply went; the farther away his home, the less likely was a soldier to return to his unit. Even Lee's appeals to patriotism had little effect on men torn by regional and family loyalties and who had lost faith in the Confederacy.

Authorities thought deserters were less guilty of cowardice than of fierce individualism and ignorance of military regulations. Many returned to duty in their own time; others joined partisan bands or took refuge in mountains or forests; some deserted to enemy lines.

If caught, deserters were subject to court-martial and were fined, flogged, imprisoned, thrown into solitary confinement, or sentenced to make up time lost. But few were executed. The one-time offender frequently faced humiliation from his comrades, then fought alongside them for the duration. Over the course of the war, more than 105,000 Confederate and 278,-000 Union desertions were recorded.   —PLF

Deshler, James. CSA b. Tuscumbia, Ala., 18 Feb. 1833. Graduating 7th in the West Point class of 1854, Deshler spent the years before the Civil War on cavalry duty in the Far West.

In spring 1861, having just completed a tour of service in Colorado, he was given a leave. Deshler never went back to the U.S. Army. He was dropped from the army rolls in July and, when next heard of, was a captain in the Confederate artillery.

LC

Deshler's Confederate service was made up of a string of hard luck. First a brigade adjutant under Brig. Gen. HENRY R. JACKSON in western Virginia, Deshler was shot through the thighs in a skirmish at Alleghany Summit, 13 Dec. 1861, and went on convalescent leave. On recovery he was made an artillery colonel and placed on the staff of Maj. Gen. THEOPHILUS H. HOLMES, who was widely regarded in army command as underqualified and unmotivated. With Holmes he served through the SEVEN DAYS' CAMPAIGN in Virginia, and, after Holmes's poor performance at the Battle of MALVERN HILL, was transferred with him to Arkansas in the Trans-Mississippi Department.

While Holmes was posted at Little Rock, Deshler was sent to Fort Hindman on the Arkansas River, where he commanded infantry on the Confederate lines the day Maj. Gens. JOHN A. MCCLERNAND and WILLIAM T. SHERMAN decided to attack with infantry and gunboats. In the one-sided battle of ARKANSAS POST, Deshler was surrendered against his will by Col. Robert Garland. While Garland and Confederate commander Brig. Gen. THOMAS J. CHURCHILL argued over who had ordered the surrender, Union troops swarmed in with Sherman. The argument continued in front of Sherman, and Deshler said, for his part, he was not ready to surrender. Sherman pointed out that his men were already disarmed.

After a brief period as a prisoner, Deshler was exchanged, then made a brigadier general 28 July 1863 and assigned a command under Maj. Gen. PATRICK R. CLEBURNE. With Cleburne, a winning general, he went to the Battle of CHICKAMAUGA. There, 20 Sept., while inspecting his men before they entered the fight, an artillery round flew into the ranks and killed him.   —JES

de Trobriand, Philippe Régis Dénis de Keredern. USA b. near Tours, France, 4 June 1816, at his wealthy father's Loire château, de Trobriand went to school in Paris, graduated from the Collège de Tours and in 1837 from Poitiers in law. 4 years later he went to America, where, during an extensive tour, he became engaged to New York heiress Mary Mason Jones. In Jan. 1843 the couple married in Paris, settled in Venice, then moved to New York in 1847. There de Trobriand served as editor of the *Revue de nouveau monde,* 1849–50, and contributed regularly to *Le courrier des États Unis.*

LC

In summer 1861 he volunteered, became colonel of the Gardes Lafayette, a Franco-American unit of the New York Militia, and marched off to subdue the Southern rebellion. He proved a brave, resourceful officer, participating in the campaigns of the Army of the Potomac. Fighting first during the PENINSULA CAMPAIGN, he headed brigades at FREDERICKSBURG, CHANCELLORSVILLE, and GETTYSBURG, where he held the center of Maj. Gen. GEORGE E. PICKETT's line at the PEACH ORCHARD. De Trobriand was present when the Army of Northern Virginia was surrendered at Appomattox Court House and received brevet rank of major general as of that date. In July 1866 he was commissioned a colonel in the Regular Army, but by then he was in Paris, where he remained to complete his book, *Quatre ans à l'armée du Potomac* (2 vol., 1867–68), which won praise and was later translated into English. After his return to America he served on army duty in the Dakotas, Montana, Wyoming, and Utah, a duty interspersed with frequent sojourns in France. In 1874, on the death of a cousin, he succeeded to the title of count. During the last days of RECONSTRUCTION he held military command in Louisiana, where he won respect from all factions. After retiring in 1879, he made his home in Louisiana, until his death in Bayport, N.Y., 15 July 1897.   —DL

Devens, Charles, Jr. USA b. Charlestown, Mass., 4 Apr. 1820, Devens had a distinguished civilian career. A graduate of Harvard's law school, Devens was an attorney, Massachusetts state senator 1848–49, U.S. marshal, outspoken critic of slavery, and a general in the state militia.

With the outbreak of civil war, Devens immediately volunteered, mustering into Federal service as major of the 3d Battalion of Massachusetts Rifles. The Rifles, a 90-day unit, was stationed at Baltimore until its term of enlistment expired July 1861. Within days, on 24 July, Devens received a commission as colonel of the 15th Massachusetts. The new colonel led his regiment at the Battle of BALL'S BLUFF, Va., where one of his uniform

NA

buttons deflected a rifle ball, saving his life. On 15 Apr. 1862 Devens was promoted to brigadier general and given a brigade of the IV Corps. The brigade fought at SEVEN PINES, where its commander was again wounded.

In autumn 1862 Devens transferred to the VI Corps, leading a brigade at FREDERICKSBURG, then assumed command of a division in Maj. Gen. OLIVER O. HOWARD's XI Corps. At CHAN-CELLORSVILLE, 2 May 1863, Devens' division held the corps' right flank. Near dusk, Lt. Gen. THOMAS J. "STONEWALL" JACK-SON's Confederates launched their surprise attack against Howard's lines. The furious assault virtually destroyed Devens' division as a fighting unit, while Devens suffered his third combat wound. The rather inept division commander was brevetted major general, apparently holding the proper political beliefs and connections.

Devens returned to active duty May 1864 as a division commander in the XVIII Corps and at COLD HARBOR commanded from a stretcher, being crippled with inflammatory rheumatism. Devens transferred again, to the XXIV Corps, temporarily commanding in Jan. 1865. Following the Confederate surrender, he was placed in charge of the District of Charleston, S.C.

In 1867 Devens was appointed judge of Massachusetts' superior court and 6 years later was named a justice of the state's supreme court. Pres. Rutherford B. Hayes selected the veteran as his attorney general in 1877. Universally esteemed, Devens died in Boston, 7 Jan. 1891. Camp Devens was named in his honor and a statue of him was placed on the state-house lawn.   —JDW

Devil's Den, at Gettysburg, Pa.   2 July 1863   The name Devil's Den has been applied to the demonic mass of rocks

that rise into a hill on the battlefield at Gettysburg. Boulders, from the size of a small house to that of a barrel, cover the rise. Separated from LITTLE ROUND TOP by the valley of Plum Run, Devil's Den was the left-flank anchor of the Union III Corps' line at Gettysburg 2 July 1863.

When the Confederate attack erupted against the III Corps at 4 o'clock in the afternoon, Brig. Gen. J. H. Hobart Ward's brigade and a 6-gun battery manned the boulders. Ward's regiments were little engaged until the 1st Texas and 3d Arkansas regiments of Brig. Gen. Jerome B. Robertson's brigade charged. The tough Confederates stormed toward the rise, suffering heavy casualties. About 5:30 p.m. Brig. Gen. Henry L. Benning's Georgia brigade came in against Ward's left. The Federals still clung to the boulders. One Union regiment lost over half its numbers in 25 minutes. Bent back, the Union line finally broke. The Texans and Georgians held Devil's Den until the Battle of Gettysburg ended.   —JDW

Devin, Thomas Casimer.   USA   b. New York City, N.Y., 10 Dec. 1822. A house painter by trade, Devin rose to lieutenant colonel of the 1st New York Militia Cavalry. At 38, he was considerably older than many of his fellow volunteer officers in the Union army. When the war broke out, Devin and 1 company of his militia regiment volunteered, and 18 Nov. 1861 Devin became colonel of the 6th New York Cavalry.

The Union cavalry, however, was so poorly organized that Devin's new regiment was not put into action with the Army of the Potomac until Sept. 1862. The following year the cavalry was reorganized; in the reshuffling Devin was given command of a brigade but, to his great irritation, not the rank of brigadier. Unhappily, the reorganization saved neither the cavalry nor Devin from a humiliating defeat at CHANCELLORSVILLE, May

A fallen sharpshooter at Devil's Den.

1863, and his brigade in particular suffered heavy losses.

At GETTYSBURG Devin and his men revenged themselves. Under the command of Brig. Gen. JOHN BUFORD, Devin's and another brigade held the Confederates out of Gettysburg long enough for the Union army to reach the scene of battle and force a showdown with Gen. ROBERT E. LEE's army. Devin distinguished himself again the next year under the Army of the Potomac's new cavalry com-

LC

mander, Maj. Gen. PHILIP H. SHERIDAN, with whom he raided Richmond and the SHENANDOAH VALLEY. Devin was finally promoted to brigadier general 19 Oct. 1864 and Mar. 1865 was given command of the 1st Cavalry Division. His promotion came just in time for him to lead the division in breaking the Confederate defenses of Richmond at the Battle of FIVE FORKS, and then on to Appomattox.

Devin never returned to civilian life. Unlike many other volunteers, he patiently mastered the art of soldiering, which included quietly enduring being passed over in promotion. He also learned to adopt new tactics, such as fighting his cavalrymen on foot and using carbines rather than sabers. After the war he commanded the 8th and then the 3rd cavalry. d. New York City, 4 Apr. 1878.   —ACG

Dibrell, George Gibbs. CSA b. Sparta, Tenn., 12 Apr. 1822. As a youth Dibrell worked on his father's farm, occasionally attending local schools and then East Tennessee College. At 18 he clerked in a branch office of the Bank of Tennessee and at 24 became a justice of the peace and a court clerk. Until the Civil War he was a successful merchant and state legislator.

A Whig, Dibrell originally opposed secession but finally cast his lot with the Confederacy, enlisting as a private in the 25th Tennessee Infantry and rising to lieutenant colonel by Aug. 1861. With the regiment he fought in such early battles in the West as MILL SPRINGS and Farmington.

NA

When the Army of Tennessee was reorganized after CORINTH, Dibrell failed to regain his former rank. Undaunted, he hastened to Richmond and received authority to raise a regiment of his own. Returning to his hometown, he organized the 8th Tennessee Cavalry, training it as a partisan unit. The regiment, however, became a regular Confederate outfit under Brig. Gen. NATHAN B. FORREST. As a colonel Dibrell fought under the "Wizard of the Saddle" at STONE'S RIVER, and 1 July 1863 succeeded to the command of Forrest's original brigade. Still, he did not become a brigadier until 28 Jan. 1865.

In spring 1863 Dibrell saw action at Tuscumbia and Florence, Ala., then during the TULLAHOMA CAMPAIGN. In May 1864, soon after joining the corps of Maj. Gen. JOSEPH "FIGHT-

IN' JOE" WHEELER for the ATLANTA CAMPAIGN, his troopers repulsed a Union attack at Varnell's Station and stampeded enemy cavalry at Rocky Face Gap. In these and other engagements, Dibrell fought well enough to prove his worthiness to succeed Forrest.

Under Wheeler, he also served prominently in the Siege of SAVANNAH, his horse being shot under him in one battle. Early in 1865, during the CAROLINAS CAMPAIGN, he skirmished incessantly with the Union troopers of Brig. Gen. H. JUDSON KILPATRICK. By now a division leader, Dibrell was warmly recommended for promotion, Wheeler calling him "a most excellent officer upon the field. You can hardly find a better or more reliable man."

In the waning days of the Confederacy, Dibrell joined the fugitive Jefferson Davis, who entrusted to his care the Confederate archives. After the president's escort disbanded, Dibrell returned to Tennessee and resumed his business career with much success. Until his death in Sparta, 9 May 1888, he was a financier, a coal-mine developer, a railroad president, and a U. S. congressman, 1874–84.   —EGL

"Dictator." *See* MORTAR.

Dill, Benjamin F. journalist b. Augusta, Ga., 1814. Among Confederate newspapers the MEMPHIS *APPEAL* is the most famous, and of its 2 Civil War–era editors, John R. McClanahan and Benjamin Dill, Dill is better remembered.

After coming to Memphis in 1837, Dill worked as an attorney and an editor for an Oxford, Miss., newspaper. He joined the *Appeal* as a writer in 1854 and by 1855 was an editor and part owner.

On the South's secession, Dill and company gracefully made the transition to a more patriotic Confederate editorial position, and with the war became strident secessionists. With Memphis likely to be captured by the Federals, the *Appeal* vowed to move rather than change its strong Confederate editorial stance. True to its word, it kept ahead of Union advances, publishing in Grenada, Jackson, and Meridian, Miss.; Atlanta, Ga.; Montgomery, Ala.; then Columbus, Ga. Throughout these moves Dill was ever-present in a wide-brimmed wool hat and carrying a silver-headed cane. Resembling "a portly Dutch burgher," he became a fixture in Atlanta during the year the *Appeal* was published there. During its Atlanta stay he was selected to sit on the new Confederate Press Association's board of directors.

On 16 Apr. 1865 Union Maj. Gen. JAMES H. WILSON captured Columbus, the *Appeal*'s last Civil War stop. Dill was taken into custody and Wilson forced him to sign a seriocomic pledge to give up his wool hat, silver cane, his spendable silver, and swear "[he], his heirs and assigns . . . not only to abjure and recant the fake doctrines he had professed, but thereafter" live as loyal Union men.

Dill swallowed his pride, then returned to Memphis and relaunched a chastened *Appeal.* McClanahan died July 1865. Dill followed January 1866 after the *Appeal* had returned to press.   —JES

Dinwiddie Court House, Va., eng. at. 31 Mar. 1865 On 29 Mar. 1865 the Union Army of the Potomac and the Army of the James advanced in the decisive movement against the extensive Confederate lines around Richmond and Petersburg, Va. With nearly 125,000 men, the Federals opposed less than half that number. Lt. Gen. Ulysses S. Grant intended to force Gen. Robert E. Lee out of the latter's entrenchments by turning the weakly held Confederate right flank.

Maj. Gen. PHILIP H. SHERIDAN, commanding 3 divisions of nearly 13,000 cavalrymen, led the Union turning movement. The Union V and II corps, under Maj. Gens. GOUVERNEUR K. WARREN and ANDREW A. HUMPHREYS, respectively, marched in support of the Federal cavalry. Lee, expecting Grant's leftward sidle, sent Maj. Gens. GEORGE E. PICKETT and FITZHUGH LEE with 19,000 infantry and cavalry toward FIVE FORKS, Va., a vital crossroads.

Skirmishing flared along the avenues of the Union advance. At Lewis' Farm near Gravelly Run, and on the Vaughan road near Hatcher's Run, the Southerners grudgingly contested the ground. Near the junction of the Boydton and Quaker roads, Warren's infantry, in a sharply contested engagement, pushed back Pickett's lines. Sheridan's horsemen reached Dinwiddie Court House, 5 mi south of Five Forks. A heavy rain in the evening halted the Union march.

The drenching rain continued on the 30th, churning the roads into bogs. Part of Sheridan's cavalry pressed north from Dinwiddie Court House but Fitz Lee's troopers repulsed the attack. Humphreys' II Corps slogged forward, probing the Confederate lines behind Hatcher's Run. Warren closed toward Gravelly Run to within 3 mi of Dinwiddie Court House. The mounting Federal numbers gravely threatened Lee's right and the vital Southside Railroad.

When the rains ended the morning of 31 Mar., the aggressive Sheridan immediately renewed his advance toward Five Forks. The Federals reached a point about 3 mi from Dinwiddie Court House when Pickett charged from the west into their left. The Confederates slowly shoved the Northerners south across the saturated ground. The tough cavalrymen withdrew but maintained a secure line. A flurry of Union orders and counterorders were issued for reinforcements in the mistaken notion that Sheridan faced imminent destruction.

Warren, meanwhile, also recoiled from another Confederate attack, near Gravelly Run. The V Corps likewise held firm, and at about 5 p.m. Warren dispatched a brigade to Dinwiddie Court House. By nightfall the thin Confederate ranks were in more danger than the Federals. Pickett, who had won a tactical victory, realized his precarious situation and withdrew to Five Forks in the darkness. This engagement at Dinwiddie Court House simply laid the scene for the next day's decisive action at Five Forks. —JDW

discipline. The Articles of War and civil laws covering military discipline were written and enacted before the Civil War to govern a small, self-contained professional military service. The military maintained order with a caste system and disciplined with shame and pain. With the mustering of great armies and navies, this way of life was revealed to vast numbers of civilian volunteers for the first time. Trouble resulted.

The Union and Confederate armies were led by small cadres of professionals who found that the war they were to fight required the coordinated movement of enormous bodies of men. The drill discipline this required was to be supplied by manuals such as HARDEE'S *TACTICS* and the vigorous efforts of noncommissioned and junior officers. But many of these were friends or relatives of the men in the hometown companies in which they served. The local origin and makeup of most volunteer units had a poor effect on discipline; the men had elected

their leaders, so volunteer officers were often wary of being strict with their troops. Early in the war this necessitated the removal or transfer of many volunteer officers, and in a few cases, the punishment of entire regiments.

Nor was the independent nature of volunteers and old loyalties easily overcome by discipline from Regular officers. Confederate Brig. Gen. CHARLES S. WINDER had been an officer in the antebellum U.S. Army and was an officer in the Confederate army, leading 5 volunteer regiments. During the Second Bull Run Campaign he had 30 men from his brigade bucked and gagged at one time for straggling on the march. They took the corporal punishment badly: half of them deserted that night, the rest "swore Winder's next battle would be his last." They never had a chance to carry out their threat: Federals killed Winder during the next battle.

Mutiny and threats of murder were not usual discipline problems. Straggling, drunkenness, fighting, dereliction of duty, theft, desertion, malingering, cowardice, bounty jumping, and insubordination were the common fare at courts-martial. Both Union and Confederate services made provisions for military courts and prescribed specific punishments for some offenses. But often, because of pressures of time, courts were not called in noncapital cases and commanding officers dispensed justice on the spot with some form of minor or corporal punishment. These included the BUCK AND GAG, walking guard duty carrying a heavy log instead of a rifle, being tied up by the thumbs, riding the "wooden mule" (a soldier was forced to sit for hours atop a narrow rail set high enough so his feet did not touch the ground), extra duty, fines, time in the guardhouse, and reduction in rank.

Cowardice, desertion, theft, sleeping on guard duty, treating with the enemy, spying, murder, and bounty jumping brought the hardest punishments. Execution by firing squad or hanging could be applied to all of these, but frequently cowards, thieves, and some deserters were branded (either on the face or the hip) and drummed out of camp in disgrace. In the artillery or cavalry, being tied for hours spread-eagled on a gun carriage wheel was common, and sometimes, when the culprit was hung horizontally, crippling. In both the army and navy, flogging had been outlawed several years before the war.

The hardest punishments could only be ordered by a court-martial (a select board of 3 or more officers), and in the case of a decision for execution, its vote had to show a 2-to-1 majority in agreement. Only the commanding general ordering the court or the U.S. or C.S. president could award a pardon.

At sea, limits of space and personnel prohibited some of the more curious corporal punishments and full court-martial boards. The ship's captain dispensed justice in the forms of fines, extra duty, time in the brig, confinement in single or double irons, confinement on bread and water, solitary confinement, or reduction in rank.

Officers could be, and frequently were, arrested and tried for any number of offenses, but most often their punishments amounted to fines, confinement to quarters, or assignment to an undesirable command. In those instances where a field officer was convicted of cowardice, his fate was nearly as ugly as an enlisted man's: he was publicly "read out of the army," his sword broken, his buttons stripped from his uniform; then he was drummed out of camp, often with a sign around his neck that read "Coward." Usually, in cases involving high disgrace, officers were expected to resign.

Combat discipline was imposed with force. In land assaults "file closers" with bayoneted rifles kept men in line and moving forward. Officers of the provost marshal waited in the rear to seize unwounded men leaving the field. At sea, marines kept shipboard peace and, if ordered to, kept men at their battle stations.

In the postwar years, amendments to service and enlistment regulations and revisions in the code of military justice were prompted by the disciplinary difficulties during the Civil War, and the bulk of the code was rewritten.   —JES

District Emancipation Act.   The presence of slavery in the U.S. capital embarrassed government officials sensitive to criticism from Northern abolitionists and from European governments opposed to the institution. The 1860 census numbered 3,185 slaves living in the District of Columbia, owned by 2% of the white population and valued at about $2 million. Efforts either to emancipate them or to guarantee their servitude appeared in most of the major compromise measures placed before Congress during the secession crisis but were in each case voted down. Once Southern congressmen resigned to go home, opposition to emancipation fell sharply, as did the number of slaves in the city.

Early in 1862 Massachusetts Republican Sen. HENRY WILSON introduced a bill to emancipate District slaves and appropriate $1 million to compensate loyal slaveowners for their losses. He argued the Radical opinion that freedom was a basic human right that Christians were duty-bound to provide. As expected, moderate border-state spokesmen, led by Sen. JOHN J. CRITTENDEN, objected to the legislation, largely because compensation would average $300 per slave, considerably less than market price. Many Washington residents disliked the prospect of having several thousand newly freed blacks living among them, and the Board of Aldermen urged Congress to make provisions for policing the city should the bill pass. The matter was partially resolved by a rider providing for the freedmen to be colonized abroad with their consent.

Both houses of Congress passed the bill with two-thirds majorities and sent it to Abraham Lincoln 14 Apr. Some doubted the president would sign the legislation if he thought any of the provisions would interfere with his broader plans for wartime emancipation measures, but he added his signature on the 16th. Within a short time Congress granted to District blacks full civil rights except for jury duty.

In all, about 1,000 people presented claims for compensation to the commission established for that purpose. Only a few applicants were denied reimbursement, usually because of faulty property titles or questionable loyalties. See also EMANCIPATION PROCLAMATION.   —PLF

District of Columbia.   Washington still presented a raw impression when ABRAHAM LINCOLN took office: streets were unpaved; Pennsylvania Avenue was lined with hotels, shops, and restaurants on the north side and with shabby buildings, sheds, and saloons on the south. With work only half done on the Capitol dome, parts strewn about the base of the unfinished Washington Monument, and canals turned into open sewers, the capital city looked like the symbol of a wrecked nation. Lord Lyons, British ambassador, regarded his assignment there as an early installment of purgatory.

Fear-ridden days followed FORT SUMTER's fall before troops restored order. First arrivals were quartered in the Capitol basement, the Treasury, and other public buildings. The Bull Run disaster produced near-panic, but Maj. Gen. GEORGE B. MCCLEL-

LAN's building of the ARMY OF THE POTOMAC engendered a sense of security. Washington became the symbol of the nation's power, to be defended at all costs. A vast encircling line of entrenchments anchored by 161 earthen forts and batteries was dug and manned. Thereafter Washington's morale and economic prosperity roughly paralleled the fortunes of the Army of the Potomac. Business and public opinion ran high while anticipating victory but slumped drastically following defeats.

With the growth of the army came city growth. Contractors, vendors, inventors, laborers, soldiers on furlough, runaway slaves, thieves, thugs, and prostitutes all flocked to Washington, the population swelling from 41,000 in 1860 to a wartime high of 160,000. As many as 50,000 wounded at a time recovered in Washington hospitals. Prices skyrocketed, lodging was scarce, and crime increased. The boomtown atmosphere was deflated by the death of young Willie Lincoln, President Lincoln's son. The great social event of the war years was the marriage of Sec. of the Treasury SALMON P. CHASE's daughter Kate (see SPRAGUE, KATE CHASE) to Gov. WILLIAM SPRAGUE of Rhode Island.

By 1864, with Gens. Thomas J. "Stonewall" Jackson's and Robert E. Lee's threats long past, Washington was immune to panic when Lt. Gen. Jubal A. Early probed the northern defenses at Fort Stevens. Home guards manned the forts until Lt. Gen. U.S. Grant's veterans arrived. Celebrations but no wild hysteria followed Richmond's fall and Lee's surrender. Washingtonians were gripped with horror at Lincoln's assassination, and trial and execution of the conspirators was swift. All Washington turned out to witness the GRAND REVIEW of Maj. Gen. George G. Meade's army 23 May 1865, followed the next day by Sherman's veterans.   —DPK

Ditch Bayou, Ark., eng. at.   6 June 1864   See LAKE CHICOT, ARK., ENG. AT.

Divers, Bridget.   nurse   b. Ireland, date unknown. Divers, whose real name was Deaver, attached herself to the 1st Michigan Cavalry when her husband enlisted as a private early in the war. Robust and fearless, she stayed with the army for the duration. Some accounts inaccurately refer to "Michigan" Bridget as a vivandière, but her dedicated work as a nurse attracted the attention and admiration of MARY LIVERMORE, a respected leader of the U.S. SANITARY COMMISSION. Much of the praise centered on her bravery in removing wounded men from the battlefield under fire.

Divers' regiment was assigned to Maj. Gen. PHILIP H. SHERIDAN's command for part of the war, during which time she became known as "Irish Biddy." Twice she is said to have rallied retreating soldiers and, by convincing them to return to the lines, helped prevent defeat. On occasion she is credited with having picked up a fallen soldier's gun and fought alongside the men.

Divers accompanied the regiment to Texas as part of the army of occupation, then returned to Michigan. Apparently peacetime did not suit her, and she rejoined the Regular Army as a laundress in the Far West. d. place and date unknown.
                                    —PLF

division.   In field armies on both sides in the Civil War, the division was the second largest unit. In ascending order of size, units were: company, regiment, brigade, division, corps. Theoretically, company strength was 100; regiment, 1,000;

brigade, 4,000; and division, 12,000. Occasionally, more often in the Confederate army, battalions of 2 to 10 companies were accepted into the ranks. In the Union army, the actual numbers, by the attrition of war, were only 40–50% of those figures by 1863; the percentage was higher in the Confederate army, thanks to its system of assigning recruits to existing regiments instead of creating new regiments.

In the Union armies the number of divisions in a corps varied from 2 to 4, though usually there were 3. In spring 1863, Maj. Gen. Joseph "Fighting Joe" Hooker ordered the Army of the Potomac to wear CORPS BADGES, which led to designating divisions by badges and by flags in red, white, and blue, for 1st, 2d, and 3d divisions, respectively; the few 4th divisions had green badges and flags; 5th divisions, orange. Without uniform badges and flags, the Confederates used a less complicated system. Though they began by numbering their divisions, in a short time divisions, as well as other army units, came to be known by their commanders' name.

Union divisions were commanded by brigadier or major generals, and the frontage of an average 1863 Union division, drawn up in double-rank line of battle with no skirmishers deployed, would have been just short of a mile. The Confederates were more logical: with rare exceptions, brigadiers commanded brigades and major generals led divisions, and these units were usually numerically superior to their Union counterparts. An extreme example: at one time Confederate Maj. Gen. Ambrose P. Hill's famous Light Division had 7 brigades, giving it a strength of about 17,000.   —RDH

Dix, Dorothea Lynde. nurse/hospital reformer b. Hampden, Maine, 4 Apr. 1802. To Dix, her Civil War career as the Federal government's superintendent of women nurses was only "an episode" in her life as a crusader for hospital reform. She left an unhappy home at age 10 to live with a grandmother in Boston, taught school, wrote several now-forgotten books, and by the war had become prominent for her pioneering work in providing humane care for the mentally ill.

5 days after FORT SUMTER was surrendered, Dix volunteered her services to the government and 10 June received her appointment from the secretary of war. She was given total authority over the selection and management of all women nurses employed by the armies, under the "control and direction" of the medical officers in charge at each hospital. Slight and generally soft-spoken, trying to organize a staff of nurses, with no precedents to follow, Dix developed an efficient operation despite the resentment and petty jealousy shown her by many army doctors. Some of the male opposition to the opinionated Dix was because of her sex, but some she invited with her high-handed, arbitrary methods.

Dix's rigid standards and strict rules for applicants provoked bitter criticism among the would-be nurses she turned away because they were too young or because she looked for those "plain to almost homeliness in dress, and by no means liberally endowed with personal attractions." One woman labeled her

NA

"Dragon Dix," but the many who overcame their fear of her occasional brusqueness learned to understand and appreciate her insistence on practical considerations.

In addition to personnel, large quantities of hospital supplies were allocated through Dix's Washington office. When the government did not provide the stores she wanted, she procured them as donations from private citizens. She tirelessly conducted tours of hospitals, interceded for her nurses when they needed help with uncooperative doctors, and operated a house where the women could rest during their infrequent leaves from duty.

Dix held her position without pay for the 4 years of war. Afterward she resumed her crusade to improve care for the insane. Dix, who never married, died 17 July 1887 in the living quarters set aside for her at the hospital she founded in Trenton, N.J.   —PLF

Dix, John Adams. USA   b. Boscawen, N.H., 24 July 1798, Dix first saw action as an ensign at 14, serving under his father, Lt. Col. Timothy Dix, Jr., in the War of 1812. Resigning from the service in 1828, he pursued commercial interests in Cooperstown, N.Y., and entered politics as a Jacksonian Democrat. He soon became a power in the party, state adjutant general, state school superintendent, and a member of the Albany Regency, the controlling political "machine" in the state. In 1845 Dix went to the U.S. Senate to fill an unexpired term, remaining there till 1850.

During the next 10 years Dix served as president of 2 different railroads while practicing law in

USMHI

New York City. In 1859 Pres. James Buchanan appointed him postmaster of that city. Then in the last days of Buchanan's administration, with civil war nearly certain, Dix was made secretary of the treasury, assuming his duties 15 Jan. 1861. Shortly afterward he telegraphed his famous AMERICAN FLAG DISPATCH to harried Treasury officers in New Orleans: "If anyone attempts to haul down the American flag, shoot him on the spot." Dix then received the first commission from Pres. Abraham Lincoln as major general of volunteers, dated 16 May 1861, outranking all other volunteer officers until the end of the Civil War.

Dix commanded the Department of Annapolis, 15–19 July 1861; the Department of Pennsylvania, 25 July–24 Aug. 1861; the Middle Department, 22 Mar.–9 June 1862; the Department of Virginia, 17 June 1862–15 July 1863; then the Department of the East until the war's end. His most important military contribution was the forceful suppression of the New York DRAFT RIOTS in 1863.

Resigning 30 Nov. 1865, he returned briefly to private life but served as minister to France, 1866–69, and governor of New York, 1872–74. Not reelected, he spent his remaining years in retirement. He died in New York City, N.Y., 21 Apr. 1879. The army installation in southern New Jersey now designated Fort Dix attests to his memory.   —RAP

"Dixie."   The unofficial anthem of the Confederacy, "Dixie"

was written by DANIEL DECATUR EMMETT, a noted minstrel performer who claimed to have written it while staying in New York City and first titled it "I Wish I Was in Dixie's Land." The song was copyrighted in 1860, and that year a New Orleans publisher printed it under the name of another writer, with Emmett's publisher bringing suit. The song fast became popular, and after it was played at Confederate Pres. Jefferson Davis' Montgomery, Ala., inauguration it became the theme song of the South. Its adoption as an official anthem was opposed because many believed it lacked dignity. —JES

Dockery, Thomas Pleasant. CSA b. N.C., 18 Dec. 1833, Dockery, whose family moved to Arkansas via Tennessee, commanded Arkansas troops in the Western theater and in the Trans-Mississippi throughout the war. He saw his first Confederate service as a colonel of state troops. At the Battle of WILSON'S CREEK, Dockery commanded the 19th Arkansas Infantry under Brig. Gen. BEN MCCULLOCH. When both were still colonels, THOMAS J. CHURCHILL credited Dockery with flanking the Federal position on his left and leading the charge that drove the Northern troops from their last position on the field.

CG

Dockery's regiment crossed to the east bank of the Mississippi with Maj. Gen. EARL VAN DORN for the defense of CORINTH May 1862, then Dockery briefly commanded the middle subdistrict of Arkansas. At VICKSBURG, he led a brigade in Maj. Gen. JOHN S. BOWEN's division and was captured when the city was surrendered. Brig. Gen. STEPHEN D. LEE commended the "cool and bravery" of Dockery and his men during their part in the defense.

Paroled, Dockery was promoted to brigadier general, 10 Aug. 1863. He led a brigade of Arkansans against Maj. Gen. FREDERICK STEELE during the 1864 CAMDEN EXPEDITION. His men again received commendations at the Battles of Marks' Mills and JENKINS' FERRY.

With his property destroyed during the war, Dockery turned to a career in civil engineering. d. New York City, N.Y., 27 Feb. 1898, after living in Houston for several years. —PLF

Dodge, Grenville Mellen. USA b. Danvers, Mass., 12 Apr. 1831. Prominent as a combat commander, railroad builder, land developer, congressman, and author during his 84 years, Dodge ranks with the most versatile of Civil War generals. He was educated at Durham Academy in New Hampshire and Norwich University in Vermont, earning a diploma as a military and civil engineer in 1851. Moving to Iowa in 1851, he worked as a railroad engineer and surveyor, and organized the Council Bluffs Guards. He was commissioned colonel of the 4th Iowa Infantry July 1861 and was soon given command of a brigade in the Army of Southwest Missouri.

Dodge had 3 horses shot under him at the Battle of PEA RIDGE, Ark., where he was wounded in the side. Promoted to brigadier general after that battle, he earned the favor of Maj. Gen. U. S. Grant and other commanders for his skill in organizing espionage networks and in rebuilding the Mobile & Ohio and other railroads during the Western campaigning of 1862–63.

NA

He was given command of the District of Mississippi in the Army of the Tennessee Sept. 1862, then commanded the 4th Division and the XVI Corps of that army, and was promoted to major general June 1864 at Grant's request.

Leading his corps under Maj. Gen. WILLIAM T. SHERMAN'S command in the ATLANTA CAMPAIGN, he was severely wounded in the head by a minié bullet near Atlanta, 19 Aug. 1864. Returning from sick leave Dec. 1864, he was appointed commander of the Department of Missouri, in which post he served until the end of the war.

Dodge's troops were kept busy subduing Indians and guerrillas during 1865; his camp in western Kansas was named Fort Dodge, later Dodge City. Resigning his commission in 1866, he became chief engineer of the Union Pacific Railroad and served in the U.S. House of Representatives from Iowa 1865–69.

Dodge was employed by financier JAY GOULD in 1873, directing the laying of 9,000 mi of railroad track; later he built a rail line in Cuba. In 1901 his private fortune was estimated at $25 million. Late in life he was prominent as a railroad lobbyist, a leader of patriotic organizations, and an author of books on his varied experiences. d. Council Bluffs, Iowa, 3 Jan. 1916. —DS

Doles, George Pierce. CSA b. Milledgeville, Ga., 14 May 1830. At the time of his death in combat, Doles was regarded as one of the best brigadiers in the Army of Northern Virginia. A businessman prior to the war, he served as captain of a militia company known as the Baldwin Blues. When Georgia seceded, the company formed part of the 4th Georgia.

The Georgians spent the war's first year stationed at Norfolk, Va., and elected Doles their colonel May 1862. Joining Gen. ROBERT E. LEE's Army of Northern Virginia, the 4th Georgia saw action at MALVERN HILL, where a shellburst temporarily disabled Doles. At SOUTH MOUNTAIN and at ANTIETAM,

LC

Doles and his regiment performed conspicuously. Without military training, the Georgia colonel possessed a natural talent for command and was promoted to brigadier general 1 Nov. 1862.

Assigned command of 4 Georgia regiments, Doles rendered gallant, capable service in the campaigns of 1863. At CHANCELLORSVILLE, 2 May, his brigade spearheaded the surprise attack of Maj. Gen. ROBERT E. RODES's division. The Georgians crashed into the Union right flank, with the entire division routing the Union XI Corps. The next day Doles's brigade participated in the successful assaults that doomed the Union army to defeat at Chancellorsville. On 1 July, at GETTYSBURG,

Rodes's brigades delivered another riveting attack, again crushing the Union XI Corps; Doles, once more, distinguished himself.

The brigadier earned increasing praise and renown in the battles during spring 1864, with his brigade fighting valiantly at the WILDERNESS. On 10 May at SPOTSYLVANIA, however, the brigade suffered a costly defeat. In a brilliantly planned and executed attack, Union Col. EMORY UPTON severed the Georgians' line along the "MULE SHOE." The surprised Confederates fought stubbornly but hundreds were captured. Doles rallied the remnants and, with additional units, finally recaptured the trenches.

Less than a month later, 2 June, while Doles supervised the building of his line near COLD HARBOR, a Federal sharpshooter killed him instantly. It was another loss Lee could ill afford in that spring of attrition. Doles's remains were returned to Milledgeville. —JDW

Donelson, Daniel Smith. CSA b. Sumner Cty., Tenn., 23 June 1801. On 9 July 1861 Donelson was made a brigadier general in the Confederate army at the age of 60. He had graduated 5th in the West Point

class of 1825, established himself as a prominent Tennessee planter and militia man, and was speaker of the Tennessee state legislature at the start of the Civil War. He had served only 5 months in the U.S. Army, as a 2d lieutenant of artillery after his graduation from the academy.

On Tennessee's secession Gov. ISHAM G. HARRIS appointed Donelson a brigadier general of state troops, asking that he select sites along the Tennessee River for the building of fortifi-

LC

cations. Donelson said there were no really good locations, but picked the 2 best he could find. Forts were built on them, the first named Donelson, for the brigadier; the second was named Fort Henry, for Tennessee Sen. Gustavus A. Henry. FORTS HENRY AND DONELSON would be the sites of important Union victories.

After being commissioned into the Confederate army, Donelson was sent to Brig. Gen. WILLIAM WING LORING's command in western Virginia; to duty in Charleston, S.C.; then to Gen. BRAXTON BRAGG for his campaign to Murfreesboro. With the Army of Tennessee 31 Dec. 1862, at the Battle of STONE'S RIVER, Donelson showed what a 61-year-old volunteer could do: after the repulse of Confederate Brig. Gen. JAMES R. CHALMERS' men in their attack on the "Round Forest," Donelson followed up with his brigade and, from a slightly different position, assaulted the same group of Federals. Though eventually driven back, he and his men captured 1,000 Union troops and 11 cannon.

On 17 Apr. 1863 Donelson died of natural causes while serving as head of the Confederate Department of East Tennessee. Uninformed of his death, the Confederate War Department promoted him to major general 22 Apr. —JES

Doubleday, Abner. USA b. Ballston Spa, N.Y., 26 June 1819. In Sept. 1838 Doubleday entered the U.S. Military

Academy, graduating 24th in the class of 1842. He was commissioned in the artillery, serving under Gen. Zachary Taylor in the Mexican War.

Between 1847, when he became a 1st lieutenant, and 1861 Doubleday fought Indians in Texas, saw service in Florida's Seminole Wars, and served at Atlantic Coast posts. In 1861 Doubleday, then a captain, was stationed at FORT SUMTER, where it was said he "was probably the most wholehearted in his belief that the fort should be held in spite of everything." Some authorities credit him with firing

USMHI

the Union's FIRST SHOT in defense of the post.

At the outbreak of war Doubleday was made a major of the 17th Infantry, and in Feb. 1862, a brigadier general, he took command of a brigade in Brig. Gen. IRVIN MCDOWELL's corps on the Rappahannock and at SECOND BULL RUN. He also commanded a division at the SOUTH MOUNTAIN battle, as well as at ANTIETAM and FREDERICKSBURG.

At GETTYSBURG the brigadier general came on the scene just as Maj. Gen. JOHN F. REYNOLDS was killed. Doubleday speedily sized up the situation, assumed command, and kept the corps in position, to the disadvantage of the enemy—belying his nickname "Forty-eight Hours" Doubleday.

Despite this, Maj. Gen. GEORGE G. MEADE doubted Doubleday's ability to move rapidly and put Maj. Gen. John Newton in command. Humiliated, Doubleday returned to his division and after the battle went to Washington, where he tried to vindicate himself by writing "the longest battle report of the Union army."

Doubleday saw no more active service through the rest of the war. However, he remained in the Regular Army until retiring in 1873, "more famous for the canard that he originated the game of baseball than for his military career." d. Mendham, N.J., 26 Jan. 1893. —AG

Douglas, Stephen Arnold. USP b. Brandon, Vt., 23 Apr. 1813, the "Little Giant" rose to prominence in Illinois. Like his longtime political opponent ABRAHAM LINCOLN, he was a lawyer, as well as the best-known, most influential Northern Democrat before the Civil War. From 1847 to 1861, as a senator, Douglas found himself at the center of the controversy over slavery and its territorial extension.

Douglas became a national figure during the debate over the COMPROMISE OF 1850, when Henry Clay relied on him to work the measure through Congress. According to "POPULAR SOVEREIGNTY," Douglas' answer to the crisis, people of a frontier

USMHI

region should themselves decide if slavery should exist in their territory. The KANSAS-NEBRASKA ACT, a direct result of this policy, failed miserably in practice, with "BLEEDING KANSAS" and further polarization between North and South the end results. To Douglas' credit, he took responsibility for the Kansas fiasco and continued working within a government framework to achieve slave- and free-state reconciliation.

Douglas is perhaps best remembered for his famous debates with Lincoln, who shrewdly posed a sovereignty question Douglas could not answer without alienating Southern voters and those of his own state; that alienation was the chief cause of Douglas' defeat at the 1860 Democratic convention. The resulting split in the party assured Lincoln's election and the chain of events that brought secession and civil war (see also ELECTIONS, UNITED STATES).

With war declared, Douglas worked fervently for the Union, defending Lincoln's war measures. Unfortunately, this work took its toll, and Douglas died 3 June 1861 at his home in Springfield, Ill. His support of the administration set a standard War Democrats would follow throughout the Civil War.

—MTC

Douglas Landing, Ark., eng. at. 22 Feb. 1865   On the morning of 21 Feb. Union Capt. Gurnsey W. Davis led a detachment of 50 men of the 13th Illinois Cavalry from Pine Bluff down the Arkansas River to Douglas Landing, camping that night in a torrential downpour. While there, Davis learned that Confederates had been seen down the river about 3 mi and were expected to move on the landing to burn cotton to prevent it from being captured by Federal troops.

With the rain too heavy to allow him to move out, Davis doubled his pickets and decided to wait out the storm. The Confederates, however, moved first and at about 1 a.m. attacked his outposts on both sides, then sent a volley directly into the main body of his small command, huddled for protection under a shed. The Federals returned fire, holding the enemy long enough to get their horses out into line. Davis mounted his command, cared for his casualties—4 wounded —and ordered his men to retire. They returned to Pine Bluff that night after encountering several other roaming parties of Confederate cavalry. Davis had been both scouting and foraging but returned without the cattle he sought—and with little information other than that small parties of Federals like his were in constant danger in the Arkansas outback. The identity of the Confederates who attacked him is uncertain, though he believed their leader to be a notorious Colonel Clark, one of scores of partisan and raider leaders who constantly tormented the Federals in Arkansas and throughout the Trans-Mississippi. These leaders were largely responsible for making it almost impossible for Lincoln to effectively take and hold the western Confederacy.   —WCD

Dowling, Richard William.   CSA   b. County Galway, Ireland, May or July 1838, Dowling immigrated with his family to America in the 1840s, settling in New Orleans. In the early 1850s, following the death of his parents, he moved with his brother and sister to Houston, Tex., opening a chain of billiard saloons there and a liquor importing company in Galveston.

In 1859 Dowling joined a volunteer artillery company in Houston. When this unit disbanded the next year, he became 1st lieutenant of the Davis Guards, originally an infantry outfit. His men were mostly Irish-American dockworkers and laborers, whom one contemporary described as "men of brawn and muscle; quiet in manner if you treated them right, but woe to

you if you offended one. . . ." Physically Dowling did not fit this model: a Union officer who met him in 1862 characterized him as "a modest, retiring, boyish-looking Irish lad." He tried to hide his youth behind a walrus mustache, which, combined with fiery red hair, gave him the look of a warrior.

Dowling's initial war service was in Col. John S. Ford's mid-1861 expedition down the lower Rio Grande against Fort Brown and other Union outposts. On 1 Jan. 1863 Dowling, second in command of Company F/3rd Texas Artillery (formed from the Davis Guards), helped recapture GALVESTON harbor from the Union navy and army. There he won praise for directing his cannon against a wharf where enemy infantry were barricaded, a key to the victory. But his most notable exploit—one that made him a legend in Texas history at 25— occurred the following September: in a 1-hour engagement at SABINE PASS, 8 Sept. 1863, his battery, ensconced in a harbor earthwork known as Fort Griffin, beat back 4 Union gunboats and several transports attempting to enter the Sabine River and invade the Texas interior. The feat won the admiration of local citizens and newspaper editors, the praise of Jefferson Davis, and the Thanks of the Confederate Congress (see also DAVIS GUARD MEDAL).

After Sabine Pass, Dowling saw no further battle action. Exploiting his overnight fame, Confederate officials assigned him to recruiting duties in Texas for the remainder of the conflict. After its close, he returned to Houston to manage his saloons, dabble in real estate, trade oil and gas leases, operate a steamboat concern, and direct a utility company. He died 23 Sept. 1867 during a yellow-fever epidemic in the city.

—EGL

draft riots.   Draft riots broke out in response to the Union's first national conscription act, passed 3 Mar. 1863. Prior to that law the North had obtained its troops from volunteers and state militia called into Federal service. The conscription act declared all able-bodied males between 20 and 45 liable for service and also itemized exemptions, permitted substitutes, and provided elaborate machinery for enforcement.

Opposition to the act was widespread, especially among Northerners already lukewarm to the war effort. Enforcement problems, coupled with defects in the law itself, increased hostility toward it. Secret societies for resisting the draft were formed, and in some areas draft officers were assaulted by mobs or run out of town. Protests, outbreaks of violence, and other forms of resistance occurred in virtually every state.

By far the worst explosion took place in New York City in July 1863. New York had strong Southern sympathies, and its Democratic political machine despised ABRAHAM LINCOLN, as did Gov. HORATIO SEYMOUR. The drawing of the first draftees' names 11 July touched off 3 days of rioting in which mobs roamed the streets and fought pitched battles with police. Despite a number of ugly incidents, such as lynchings of blacks and the burning of the Colored Orphan Asylum, lurid newspaper reports greatly exaggerated the extent of the riots and number of casualties. Only a small portion of the city was affected, and one scholar concluded that no more than 74 persons, rather than hundreds, "died anywhere but in the columns of partisan newspapers."

Army units rushed from Gettysburg joined police, militia, and naval forces in quelling the riots. The draft resumed in New York 19 Aug. without incident, but sporadic rioting continued to break out across the North. In the end the draft provided about 46,000 conscripts and 118,000 substitutes—only about 6% of the Union force. —MK

Dranesville, Va., eng. at. 20 Dec. 1861 By mid-December 1861, nearly 5 months of relative quiet had passed in northern Virginia since the Union defeat at FIRST BULL RUN in July. Except for the Federal disaster at BALL'S BLUFF in October, no significant engagement had occurred between the opposing armies. The Federals, under Maj. Gen. GEORGE B. MCCLELLAN, a superb organizer, drilled daily in their camps on the Virginia hills opposite Washington, D.C. 25 mi to the west, at Centreville, Gen. JOSEPH E. JOHNSTON's Confederates also trained.

With the approach of winter, both McClellan and Johnston wrestled with logistical problems. Food and rations for the men and forage for the thousands of horses and mules were a constant need. 5 days before Christmas, both armies sent foraging parties for hay. Both sides selected the same area— the lush farmland west of Dranesville, a town about midway between Alexandria and Leesburg on the Leesburg Turnpike.

At daylight, 20 Dec., the Confederate foraging party, composed of virtually every wagon in Johnston's army, rolled out of Centreville, 16 mi south of Dranesville. Brig. Gen. J.E.B. STUART, with 150 cavalrymen, 4 infantry regiments, and an artillery battery, accompanied the wagons as an escort. Almost simultaneously Brig. Gen. E.O.C. ORD left Camp Pierpont with 5 Pennsylvania infantry regiments, a battery of 4 cannon, and a squadron of cavalry. Ord had been ordered to capture Southern marauders and confiscate forage from loyal Confederates.

Having only 12 mi to cover, the Federals entered Dranesville first, about noon. Scattering a few Confederate horsemen, the Union troops occupied the town. An hour later the 1st Pennsylvania Reserve Rifles spotted Stuart's approaching force to the south. Lt. Col. Thomas L. Kane, commander of the Rifles, knew the terrain and quickly moved his regiment to a hill near the intersection of the Leesburg Pike and the Georgetown road. Kane deployed his soldiers while informing Ord of the oncoming Confederates. Stuart's approaching troopers soon exchanged fire with the Pennsylvanians.

Ord and Stuart, both uncertain about the situation, hurried their trailing regiments forward. The Union brigadier deployed 3 regiments on the right of Kane, south of the turnpike, keeping the 10th Pennsylvania and the cavalry squadron north of the road. The Federal battery unlimbered beside the 10th, soon sending its shells toward the deploying Southerners. Stuart, meanwhile, aligned his 4 regiments in the woodlands opposite the 4 Pennsylvania regiments. His artillery unit halted behind the infantry and replied to Ord's gunners.

The infantry action began when the 9th Pennsylvania accidentally stumbled into the 1st Kentucky, who had already mistakenly exchanged volleys with the 6th South Carolina. Stuart then attacked with the 11th Virginia and 10th Alabama. The Confederates cleared the woods and drove toward Kane's soldiers, many of whom occupied a 2-story brick house. A 30-minute fire fight ensued, with the Confederates suffering more. Stuart then shifted the 11th Virginia to the right, but the regiment passed across the front of a concealed company of the 10th Pennsylvania, whose slicing volley staggered the Virginians, sending them back into the woods.

Stuart, with his attack repulsed and certain the wagons were safe, ordered a withdrawal about 3 o'clock. Masked by the smoke and woods, the Confederates extricated themselves without additional loss. Stuart suffered 194 casualties; Ord lost

only 68. The next day both commands returned to their camps. —JDW

Drayton, Percival. USN b. S.C., 25 Aug. 1812, Drayton, a member of a distinguished Southern family, was appointed midshipman 1 Dec. 1827, rising to lieutenant in 1838 and commander in 1855. Despite his Southern birth and heritage, Drayton so identified himself with Philadelphia, where he had lived for 30 years, that when South Carolina seceded, he had his name entered in the U.S. Navy register as a native of that city. Drayton supported the Union to such an extent that he insisted its preservation would be worth sacrificing his family ties in the South.

USMHI

In Oct. 1861, Drayton, commanding the *Pocahontas,* participated in the PORT ROYAL Expedition; at the time, his brother, Confederate Brig. Gen. THOMAS F. DRAYTON, was in command of the military district there. Later, Mar. 1862, Drayton joined the SOUTH ATLANTIC BLOCKADING SQUADRON of Capt. SAMUEL F. DU PONT. Promoted to captain in July, Drayton engaged the enemy at Fort McAllister, Mar. 1863, and participated in the unsuccessful attack on Charleston Apr. 1863. His skill as an administrator and organizer brought him to the attention of Rear Adm. DAVID G. FARRAGUT, who made Drayton his fleet captain aboard the *Hartford.* Drayton again distinguished himself during the Battle of MOBILE BAY. In recognition of his accomplishments, he was appointed to the Bureau of Navigation in Washington. He died in that city 4 Aug. 1865, only 4 months after assuming the position. —NCD

Drayton, Thomas Fenwick. CSA b. Charleston, S.C., 24 Aug. 1808. Graduating 28th in the West Point class of 1828, Drayton was a classmate and a lifelong friend of Confederate Pres. JEFFERSON DAVIS. Resigning from the army in 1836, he ran his plantation and served as a railroad director and state legislator until the outbreak of the war.

With his military experience and connections, Drayton received his commission as brigadier general 25 Sept. 1861. Assigned commander of the military district at PORT ROYAL, S.C., he unsuccessfully defended his post in November against a Union naval force. His brother, Cmdr. PERCIVAL DRAYTON, commanded the leading Union warship.

USMHI

In June 1862 Drayton assumed command of a brigade in Maj. Gen. JAMES LONGSTREET's corps, leading his brigade at SECOND BULL RUN, SOUTH MOUNTAIN, and ANTIETAM. Drayton proved to be an incompetent field commander, and at South Mountain and Antietam his brigade, in the words of another friend, Gen. ROBERT E. LEE, "broke to pieces." For Lee it was an embarrassing and difficult decision, but the Confederate commander assigned Drayton's regiments to other brigades.

During the war's final 2 years, Drayton served in the Trans-Mississippi Department. He led a brigade in the District of Arkansas and then commanded the Subdistrict of Texas. Later he served as president of the court of inquiry investigating Maj. Gen. STERLING PRICE's raid into Missouri.

Drayton settled in Georgia as a farmer after the war, then moved to North Carolina, where he became a life-insurance agent. d. Florence, S.C., 18 Feb. 1891.   —JDW

Dred Scott Case. In Mar. 1857 Supreme Court Chief Justice ROGER B. TANEY delivered the majority opinion in a controversial case that challenged the MISSOURI COMPROMISE and pushed the nation closer to civil war. The case concerned a black slave, Dred Scott, who 11 years earlier had sued for his freedom on the grounds that he had lived intermittently for several years in free territory with his former owner, an army surgeon. A Missouri district court ruled in Scott's favor after a second trial, but the state supreme court reversed the decision on appeal from his current owner.

The legal battle continued in a series of petitions and appeals until it reached the Federal Supreme Court. National attention focused on the case, with Southerners demanding protection of their property rights in slaves and Northerners fearing that a court decision against Scott would nullify the Missouri Compromise, thus opening the Western lands to slavery.

The Supreme Court decision confirmed Northern apprehensions. The justices denied Scott the right to sue in Federal court because blacks did not have citizenship and dismissed his residence in the North as grounds for freedom. They further condemned the antislavery provision of the Missouri Compromise as unconstitutional because it contradicted the 5th Amendment, which guaranteed protection of private property.

Scott and his family were freed May 1857 after a transfer of ownership to one of his white friends, but in the North the court's landmark decision solidified antislavery support for Abraham Lincoln and the Republican party.   —PLF

Drewry's Bluff (Fort Darling), Va., First Battle of. 15 May 1862   When Confederates under Gen. JOSEPH E. JOHNSTON withdrew from YORKTOWN 3 May 1862, they exposed the port city of Norfolk to capture. If the Federals took Norfolk, the IRONCLAD CSS *VIRGINIA* would be helpless, without a port. To prevent the *Virginia*'s capture, its crew, led by Lt. JOHN TAYLOR WOOD, blew it up, destroying the only obstacle to the ascent of the James River by the Union navy. By mid-May the Federal ironclads *MONITOR* and *GALENA* were leading 3 wooden warships up the James.

The Confederates agreed that their best chance to stop the Union ships from advancing on Richmond lay at a place called Drewry's Bluff. The site, officially known as Fort Darling, was owned by a man named Drewry. Since the military had all but ignored the fort until Yorktown was abandoned, the place was called Drewry's Bluff. There, about 7 mi below Richmond, the river is fairly narrow and the south bank is a sheer cliff 80–100 ft high. After local farmers dug gun emplacements, Pres. JEFFERSON DAVIS and his military adviser, Gen. ROBERT E. LEE, took action to shore up the position. Lee's oldest son, Brig. Gen. G.W.C. LEE, supervised the installation of heavy guns and the sinking of weighted hulks in the river channel as obstructions.

USMHI

Exceeding his advisory authority, R. E. Lee detached a brigade of infantry to support the position, and, with Wood in command, the crew of the *Virginia* took charge of the guns on the bluff. These preparations were hastily executed and makeshift; there was no way to predict whether they would suffice when the Federal flotilla challenged Drewry's Bluff.

When the Federal fleet approached, 15 May, the channel obstructions blocked the heavy-draft ironclads, and neither the *Monitor* nor the *Galena* could elevate their guns enough to fire at the batteries on the bluff. Moreover, the *Galena* proved vulnerable to Southern shot and shell during the 4-hour battle. It sustained many casualties, and by the time the Federals broke off the engagement, the *Galena,* severely crippled, had been hit 18 times. The 3 wooden ships that accompanied the ironclads remained essentially out of the conflict. The valiant defense at Drewry's Bluff had saved Richmond.   —EMT

Drewry's Bluff (Fort Darling), Va., Second Battle of. 16 May 1864   The Union landing at BERMUDA HUNDRED 5 May 1864 seriously threatened both Richmond and Petersburg, Va. Confederate authorities, facing the numerically superior Union Army of the James, rushed reinforcements to the crucial railroad center of Petersburg. But the former Massachusetts politician, Maj. Gen. BENJAMIN F. BUTLER, commanding the Federals, lacked ability and initiative. For 5 days Butler cautiously lumbered across the peninsula between the James and Appomattox rivers. Repulsed at Swift's Creek on the 9th, Butler withdrew to a defensive position across Bermuda Neck.

Butler's retreat behind his newly constructed works enabled Confederate Gen. P.G.T. BEAUREGARD to assume the offensive. With nearly 20,000 troops Beauregard hoped to lure Butler's 39,000-man army from behind their strong line. The Southern commander thus sent 7 brigades under Maj. Gen. ROBERT F. HOKE to Drewry's Bluff, the Confederate works overlooking the James River, 5 mi below Richmond.

Butler complied 12 May, advancing northward toward Hoke. Leaving behind 2 infantry divisions and sending his cavalry on a raid against the railroads, the Union commander marched with 15,000 infantry of the XVIII and X corps. Butler had decided to threaten the Confederate capital.

By the morning of the 13th the Federals had pushed the Confederates from their outer works into the main line at Drewry's Bluff. The shallowness of the river, however, prevented an attack by Union monitors. The cautious Butler settled into a defensive posture on the 14th, with Maj. Gen. WILLIAM F. SMITH's XVIII Corps on the right and Maj. Gen. QUINCY A. GILLMORE's X on the left. Butler formulated an attack for the 15th but canceled it because he preferred to hold his troops for a strong defense.

Leaving only a garrison at Petersburg, Beauregard arrived at Drewry's Bluff on the 14th. Reinforced by troops from Richmond and North Carolina, he rapidly organized the 10 brigades at his disposal into 3 divisions and ordered an attack for 16 May. At 4:45 a.m. that morning, Confederate Maj. Gen. ROBERT RANSOM's 4 brigades charged into Smith's right flank. Slowed by a thick fog, the Southerners routed Brig. Gen. CHARLES A. HECKMAN's brigade, capturing 400 Federals, 5 flags, and the brigade commander. Ransom halted; his organization was gone and his ammunition low.

Hoke, delayed by the fog, soon attacked Gillmore's lines. The Federals stubbornly fell back, but again the fog disorganized the Confederate attackers. Gillmore counterattacked into a gap between the Southern brigades, halting the Confederate advance. By 10 o'clock Beauregard's brigades had been spent and Butler began withdrawing. Maj. Gen. W.H.C. WHITING, with 2 Southern brigades, had been ordered to attack Butler's rear. But Whiting halted before one of the Union divisions left behind at Walthall's Station. Whiting's lack of aggressiveness and a heavy rainstorm allowed Butler to reach his works across the neck of the peninsula.

On the morning of 17 May the Confederates arrived opposite the Federal works. Beauregard sealed the neck of Bermuda Hundred, effectively encasing Butler on the peninsula. This second battle at Drewry's Bluff cost the Confederates 2,506 men, while the Federals lost 4,160. The grave threat to Richmond and Petersburg had been temporarily eliminated.

—JDW

Droop Mountain, W. Va., Battle of. 6 Nov. 1863 On 1 Nov. 1863 Brig. Gen. WILLIAM W. AVERELL with a 5,000-man force of Union infantry and cavalry departed southward from Beverly, W. Va., into the Allegheny Mountains; 2 days later Brig. Gen. Alfred N. Duffié left Charleston, W. Va., with another 1,700 Federals. Ordered to wreck the East Tennessee and Virginia Railroad, these 2 raiding parties marched by separate routes toward an assigned junction at Lewisburg, W. Va.

Harassed by Confederate guerrillas and scouts, Averell's main body of 2 infantry, 4 cavalry regiments, and 2 artillery batteries followed the Staunton Pike to Greenbrier Bridge, then through Camp Bartow and Green Bank to Huntersville, arriving there about noon on the 4th. At Huntersville, Averell learned that approximately 600 troops of Confederate Col. WILLIAM L. JACKSON's command were stationed at Marling's Bottom and immediately dispatched 2 cavalry regiments to cut them off. Jackson's men eluded the Union troopers, deploying at Mill Point. The next day Averell carried out a similar movement, and Jackson retreated to the crest of Droop Mountain.

Jackson, a cousin of Lt. Gen. THOMAS J. "STONEWALL" JACKSON, who was derisively nicknamed "Mudwall," had requested reinforcements 4 Nov. The next day, as Jackson regrouped on Droop Mountain, Confed. Brig. Gen. JOHN ECHOLS

left Lewisburg with an infantry brigade and 6 cannon, reaching the mountain summit at 9 a.m., 6 Nov. Assuming command, Echols deployed his force, his artillery anchoring the center and his infantry on the right. Jackson's cavalrymen held the Confederate left.

Averell, meanwhile, deployed for an assault, sending his infantry to the right in a circuitous march beyond the Confederate western flank. While the infantrymen ascended the mountain, the Union cavalry and artillery demonstrated against the Confederate center. An artillery duel ensued, while the Federal flanking force, delayed by an inept guide, moved into position.

About 1:30 p.m. Averell's infantry charged into Jackson's dismounted horsemen. With the sound of musketry on the summit, the Northern dismounted cavalry advanced up the face of the mountain. Behind a crude breastworks of logs and stones, Echols' 1,700 soldiers clung to their position for over an hour. At 3 o'clock the Confederate line collapsed, its ranks retreating down the south side of the mountain. The Federals only captured 1 cannon and 1 battle flag. Content with the victory, Averell halted for the night.

The Federal march resumed early on the 7th, toward Lewisburg. Averell's advance entered the town at 2 p.m., finding Duffié already in possession. Duffié had had an uneventful march, reaching Lewisburg only hours before. The combined forces advanced the next day on Dublin, where Echols was reportedly re-forming. Delayed by felled trees across the road and the condition of the troops, Averell, with Duffié's concurrence, abandoned the raid.

The 2 Union commands separated for the return march, Duffié reaching Beverly on the 12th, Averell 5 days later. Little had been accomplished, for the Confederates reoccupied Lewisburg as the Federals departed. Averell had won a minor victory, captured some prisoners, stores, and livestock but failed to wreck the railroad, the raid's objective.   —JDW

"Drummer Boy of Chickamauga." *See* CLEM, JOHN L.

DuBose, Dudley McIver. CSA b. Shelby Cty., Tenn., 28 Oct. 1834, DuBose attended the University of Mississippi, graduated from Lebanon Law School in his native state, and practiced law in Tennessee and Georgia before the war.

When the conflict began DuBose, residing in Augusta, Ga., enlisted in the Confederate service as a lieutenant in the 15th Georgia. The regiment eventually was assigned to the brigade of Brig. Gen. ROBERT A. TOOMBS, the fiery Georgia politician and DuBose's father-in-law. The lieutenant fought in the SEVEN DAYS' CAMPAIGN, and at SECOND BULL RUN and ANTIETAM, rising in regimental rank. In Jan. 1863 he was promoted to colonel and assigned command of his regiment.

LC

DuBose and his Georgians, now under Brig. Gen. HENRY L. BENNING, were part of Maj. Gen. JOHN B. HOOD's division of the I Corps. At GETTYSBURG, 2 July 1863, the regiment participated in Hood's charge on the Union III Corps. Benning's brigade fought at DEVIL'S DEN and before LITTLE ROUND TOP. In

September DuBose led his regiment in another attack, at CHICK-AMAUGA, where he was wounded.

The I Corps returned to Virginia, where DuBose saw combat at the WILDERNESS, May 1864. On 16 Nov. he was promoted to brigadier general and command of a brigade in Maj. Gen. JOSEPH B. KERSHAW's division. He led his brigade in the PETERS-BURG and APPOMATTOX campaigns. On 6 Apr. 1865, at SAYLER'S CREEK, Va., DuBose and a number of Confederate generals were captured. Released from Fort Warren, Mass., in July, he returned to Georgia.

The attorney resumed his legal career in Washington, Ga., serving 1 term as a U.S. Congressman, 1871–73. DuBose died in Washington, Ga., 2 Mar. 1883.   —JDW

Duke, Basil Wilson. CSA b. Georgetown, Ky., 28 May 1838. Many in the Confederacy's high command became able historians of the conflict, but none more able than Duke. Duke studied law before the war and was practicing in St. Louis, Mo., when the crisis came. Associated briefly with partisan ranger M. JEFF THOMPSON, he soon returned to Kentucky, where he enlisted in the Lexington Rifles, commanded by his brother-in-law, Brig. Gen. JOHN HUNT MORGAN.

Duke rose rapidly, first to 2d lieutenant, then to lieutenant colonel of the 2d Kentucky Cavalry. He served with distinction throughout Morgan's campaigns, including the raid into

USMHI

Indiana and Ohio, in which both were captured. He did not take part in Morgan's celebrated escape from the Ohio State Penitentiary, 26 Nov. 1863, and was exchanged in 1864. Duke returned to the Kentucky cavalry that fall, serving in southwest Virginia, and on Morgan's death was promoted brigadier, taking over Morgan's cavalry.

Duke accompanied Pres. Jefferson Davis and the fleeing Confederate government Apr.–May 1865, his being the last organized command answering to the War Department.

Following the surrender, Duke returned to the law, moved to Louisville, and for the rest of his life took a prominent role in Kentucky affairs. A moderate, advocating reconciliation with the North, he devoted much of his time to preserving the history of the Confederacy. He edited *SOUTHERN BIVOUAC,* one of the best veterans' magazines of the 1880s, and wrote 2 first-rate books, *A History of Morgan's Cavalry* (1867) and *Reminiscences of General Basil W. Duke* (1911). d. New York City, 16 Sept. 1916.   —WCD

Dumfries, Va., Raid, Stuart's. 26–28 Dec. 1862 By Dec. 1862 Maj. Gen. J.E.B. STUART was an internationally famous cavalry raider. Now, on the day after Christmas, he led 1,800 horsemen out of Fredericksburg, Va., to harass Maj. Gen. AMBROSE E. BURNSIDE, Maj. Gen. GEORGE B. MCCLELLAN'S successor as leader of the Army of the Potomac. Crossing the Rappahannock River near Brandy Station, Stuart divided his column for simultaneous attacks on 2 supply bases along the Telegraph road. He hoped to deny Burnside provisions and force him to weaken his command by detaching pursuers.

At first it was Stuart who was discomfited. A 2-pronged assault by his main body against Dumfries, 22 mi above Fredericksburg, was thwarted on the 27th by an unexpectedly large garrison. While covering his retreat, a part of Stuart's 5th Virginia Cavalry was cut down before his eyes. Farther north at Occoquan, meanwhile, Brig. Gen. WADE HAMPTON, Stuart's ranking subordinate, nabbed only a few supplies while allowing his trapped enemy to escape. The raiders reunited at Cole's Store, 9 mi northwest of Occoquan, where their leader considered returning home empty-handed.

When he learned that Burnside had dispatched mounted pursuers, now massing to the north, Stuart felt renewed and pushed on during the 28th. Near Selectman's Fort on Occoquan Creek, his 1st Virginia spearheaded a charge that scattered the nearest Federal force. A swift pursuit by the rest of the Confederate column captured a hastily abandoned and well-stocked camp.

Avoiding other, larger forces, Stuart continued northwest, determined to crown his journey with a dramatic gesture. At Burke's Station, barely 12 mi from Washington, D.C., he seized dozens of depot guards, horses, mules, and supply wagons. There he also tapped telegraph lines to monitor the progress of the Federal pursuit. Shortly before starting on a frigid and weary but successful return march to the Rappahannock, Stuart wired Union Q.M. Gen. MONTGOMERY C. MEIGS to complain about the "bad quality of the mules lately furnished" to the raiders.   —EGL

Duncan, Johnson Kelly. CSA b. York, Pa., 19 Mar. 1827. After graduating from West Point 5th in the class of 1849, serving against the Seminoles in Florida, and exploring possible railroad routes in the Northwest, Duncan left the U.S. Army in 1855 to supervise government construction in New Orleans. By 1861 he was a Louisianian by adoption and sided with the South when civil war began.

His first assignment was as a colonel of artillery defending FORTS JACKSON AND ST. PHILIP below New Orleans. Commissioned a brigadier general 7 Jan. 1862, he had about 500 men and 80 guns at his disposal when Union Capt. DAVID G. FAR-RAGUT brought up his fleet and

CWTI

mortar boats to assail the forts. According to Duncan, on the first day of firing, 18 Apr. 1862, Farragut's mortars lobbed 2,997 rounds at Fort Jackson in a 10-hour bombardment. But Duncan held out, until 24 Apr. On that day Farragut successfully chanced a run with his fleet past Duncan's guns, landing infantry behind the Confederate fort.

Duncan surrendered and was taken prisoner; after being exchanged, he was assigned to Gen. BRAXTON BRAGG's staff in Tennessee. d. from a fever in Knoxville, Tenn., 18 Dec. 1862.   —JES

Dunkard Church, at Antietam, Md. 17 Sept. 1862 Some of the bloodiest, fiercest combat of the Battle of AN-TIETAM took place around a whitewashed brick church belonging to the German Baptist Brethren, also known as the Dunk-

ards (or Dunkers) because of their baptismal ceremonies. In the early morning hours of 17 Sept., Confederate Maj. Gen. THOMAS J. "STONEWALL" JACKSON massed his artillery in front of the church, which stood beside the Hagerstown road on a rise of ground before the West Woods. When the battle opened at dawn, Federal cannon across Antietam Creek unleashed an artillery barrage about the church and artillery shells pockmarked its white walls. The Union infantry attacked down the pike, and for 3 hours the 2 armies contested the nearby fields. 1 Union division passed by the church, penetrating the West Woods, only to be shattered by Confederate musketry. Of all the photographs of Antietam, none are more haunting than those of dead men and horses lying before the Dunkard Church. —JDW

Dunovant, John. CSA b. Chester, S.C., 5 Mar. 1825. During the war in Mexico, 1846–48, Dunovant was a sergeant in the Palmetto Regiment, a South Carolina volunteer unit. In 1855 he was appointed a captain in the 10th U.S. Infantry di-
rectly from civilian life. He resigned that commission shortly
after his state seceded, Dec.
1860, and served as a major in
the provisional army of South
Carolina during the bombardment of FORT SUMTER.

In 1862 Dunovant was
named colonel of the 1st South
Carolina Infantry and led the
regiment during the operations
outside Charleston as part of
the 2d Military District, Department of South Carolina and

Georgia. After holding a position on Sullivan's Island, east of Charleston, his command was transferred to James Island, below the city. In June 1862 Dunovant's penchant for hard drinking resulted in his dismissal from the Confederate service. Thereafter he seemed obsessed with cleansing his record, receiving an opportunity to do so later that year, when Gov. FRANCIS W. PICKENS appointed him colonel of the 5th South Carolina Cavalry.

Dunovant served more soberly and effectively in mounted service, especially after Mar. 1864, when the 5th South Caro-lina was sent to Virginia as part of Maj. Gen. J.E.B. STUART's division, Army of Northern Virginia. On 16 May his troopers fought dismounted at the Battle of DREWRY'S BLUFF, neutralizing a threat to the left flank of Gen. P.G.T. BEAUREGARD's infantry. Later he was conspicuous at COLD HARBOR and TREVILIAN STA-TION and in the early battles of the PETERSBURG CAMPAIGN, winning a brigadier generalship 22 Aug. 5 weeks later, how-ever, in opposing a Union thrust south of Petersburg, he made tactical errors both in reconnaissance and combat, which threatened to undo his previous good service. On 1 Oct., a day after his troopers had been driven back by a brigade of Union cavalry near the Vaughan road, Dunovant sought permission to make a dangerous assault against the enemy's left along the Duncan road. His division commander, Maj. Gen. M. CAL-BRAITH BUTLER, at first refused, then gave in to Dunovant's insistent urging. Launching the attack at the head of his troops, Dunovant encountered dismounted Union cavalrymen, who shot him dead. —EGL

Du Pont, Samuel Francis. USN b. Bergen Point, N.J., 27 Sept. 1803. Appointed midshipman 19 Dec. 1815, Du Pont rose to lieutenant, 1826; commander, 1843; and captain, 1855. In 1861 Sec. of the Navy
GIDEON WELLES recognized his
impressive record by naming
him head of the Blockade Strategy Board, which organized the
BLOCKADE against the Confederacy and planned amphibious
operations on the Southern
coast.

On 18 Sept. 1861 Du Pont
took command of the SOUTH
ATLANTIC BLOCKADING SQUAD-
RON and prepared to move
against strategically important
PORT ROYAL, S.C. There, on 7
Nov., the Union navy won an

impressive victory, which resulted in Du Pont's promotion to rear admiral 30 July 1862. Du Pont then moved against Beaufort and, with its capture, tightened the blockade of the Broad River. The squadron contributed to other victories dur-ing 1862 by capturing Cumberland Island, St. Mary's, and FORT PULASKI, Ga.; and Amelia Island, Fernandina, and Fort Clinch, Fla.

On 7 Apr. 1863 Du Pont moved against Charleston with a squadron of 7 monitors, an armored gunboat, and the NEW IRONSIDES, serving as flagship. After almost 2 hours of heavy action, unable to continue, he ordered a withdrawal. 5 vessels were damaged, 1 sinking the following day. Du Pont had been skeptical about the effectiveness of the monitors against the strong Charleston defenses and was convinced that his defeat was due to their unfitness. He wanted the facts made public, but Welles refused. Considering himself censured by Pres. Abraham Lincoln and Welles, Du Pont asked to be relieved of command. On 6 July 1863 he was replaced by Rear Adm. JOHN A. DAHLGREN.

Du Pont returned to his home near Wilmington, Del. In failing health, he served briefly on a naval board in Washing-ton. d. during a visit to Philadelphia, 23 June 1865.

—NCD

Duryée, Abram. USA b. New York City, N.Y., 29 Apr. 1815. In the years before the Civil War, Duryée was one of the most popular and dashing amateur soldiers in America. He made a fortune in importing ma-
hogany, but his heart was in storybook soldiering. He en-
tered the 142d New York Militia at 18, and by 1849 was colonel of the elite 7th Regiment, a nationally famous parade-ground force of young, wellborn New Yorkers.

USMHI

Duryée resigned from the 7th in 1859; the war of his dreams broke out 2 years later. He eas-
ily raised a regiment of ZOUAVES who saw action in the war's first real fight, at Big Bethel, 10 June 1861. But Duryée was a disap-
pointment as a leader in combat, and when he was promoted to brigadier general 31 Aug. 1862, he was assigned to drill recruits in Washington. When he begged a field assignment, he was sent to guard train depots with a brigade of New Yorkers and Pennsylvanians.

At his first big battle, SECOND BULL RUN, he was shot twice. Although he recovered quickly and led his men at SOUTH MOUNTAIN, 14 Sept. 1862, his brigade was left in the rear as the reserve and only entered the fight as it was ending. At ANTIETAM, 17 Sept. 1862, Duryée was a part of the doomed Union I Corps, which attacked the Confederates through a shot-torn patch of ground known as the Cornfield. Duryée's brigade fought gallantly, but his regiments were shot to pieces by the devastating Confederate fire, and Duryée himself was wounded 3 times.

The final humiliation awaited Duryée in November, when he returned to duty and found that his brigade had been split up, its command given to another, and that he had been passed over for promotion in favor of a junior officer. When no one in the military chain of command would listen to his complaints, he resigned 5 Jan. 1863.

Duryée's career was the story of many volunteer officers who found themselves slowly being squeezed out of the war by the Regular Army professionals. After the war he was made police commissioner of New York City in 1873 and dockmas-
ter in 1884. d. New York City, 27 Sept. 1890. See also DURYÉE'S ZOUAVES.   —ACG

Duryée's Zouaves. ABRAM DURYÉE was a wealthy New Yorker, active in the state's antebellum militia, who in Apr. 1861 organized a regiment in New York City. Made up of "some of the best material in the city and its suburbs," the regiment was accepted into state service 25 Apr. and into Federal service, for 2 years, 9 May 1861. Duryée was its first commander. Adopting the ZOUAVE uniform, the unit became the 5th New York and was assigned to the famed 2d Divi-
sion/V Corps, which contained many Regular Army units.

The regiment was especially distinguished at GAINES' MILL, where it lost 169 of its 450 men, and at SECOND BULL RUN, where it suffered 297 casualties. In both of these battles the regiment was used to delay an overwhelming Confederate assault.

GOUVERNEUR K. WARREN was colonel of the 5th New York

May 1861–May 1862, and H. JUDSON KILPATRICK, Joseph E. Hamblin, and HENRY E. DAVIES each served for a part of the war with the regiment before they, like Duryée and Warren, became generals and went on to higher commands.

The 5th New York was mustered out May 1863 on expira-
tion of its term of service. Maj. Gen. GEORGE SYKES, in whose division the regiment served 1862–63, reportedly called it the best volunteer regiment he ever saw. When the 5th New York was mustered out, 3-year volunteers in the unit who still had time to serve were assigned to the 146th New York. The 165th New York, organized late in 1862, was sometimes referred to as the 2d Duryée's Zouaves.   —RMcM

Dutch Gap Canal, Va. In May 1864, during a drive on Richmond, Union Maj. Gen. BENJAMIN F. BUTLER's Army of the James assaulted Petersburg from the south and was beaten back from the city's southern approaches and from Drewry's Bluff, overlooking the James River. The Confederates bottled up his army in an area below Petersburg called BERMUDA HUN-
DRED. Butler maintained that if his army was ever to move on Richmond again, U.S. Navy Flag Officer Melancton Smith's gunboats would first have to shell Confederates off their posi-
tion on Drewry's Bluff. Smith's gunboats, however, could not dislodge the enemy; obstructions placed in the James and fire from heavy Confederate artillery downriver at Trent's Reach kept Union vessels a safe distance from the bluff.

To break this impasse, Butler decided to build a canal at Dutch Gap, a 174-yd-wide neck of land created by a sharp bend in the James. A canal cut at the base of this neck would allow Union vessels traveling the river to circumnavigate obstructions and stay out of range of much of the artillery fire from Trent's Reach.

Simple in design, Butler's plan was brutal to execute. From August to 31 Dec. Union troops, most of them blacks, dug out a new channel under sniper fire. Occasionally, shells from Confederate guns or mortars fell among them; though casualties were often slight, their numbers mounted. As Butler's men labored, Lt. Gen. U. S. GRANT's assaults on the Confederates

USMHI

shifted the focal point of the fighting from the area around Drewry's Bluff. Whether the Siege of Petersburg, then under way, failed or succeeded, Grant did not anticipate a concentrated movement of either Union or Confederate troops back toward Butler's force. Intent on keeping Butler, an incompetent political appointee, out of the main Petersburg operations, Grant let him continue working on the canal.

Butler, equally determined to have an active part in the war, used his political clout to get command of an expedition against Fort Fisher, N.C., in December (see BUTLER'S NORTH CAROLINA EXPEDITION). Failing to capture the Confederate fortification he returned, and with renewed interest focused his attention on his canal. Dissatisfied with the time consumed digging the canal by hand, he decided to remove the remaining earth with explosives. On 1 Jan. 1865 a 12,000-lb powder charge Butler had ordered set was exploded at the work site. Instead of clearing the obstructions, the explosion showered dirt back into the excavation and collapsed some of the channel. This major setback kept the canal from being completed until Apr. 1865, the same month the Confederate armies in the East were surrendered. The Dutch Gap Canal had served no military purpose other than to preoccupy one of the war's poorest generals. —JES

Dwight, William. USA b. Springfield, Mass., 14 July 1831. Educated at a private military school, Dwight entered West Point in 1849. Dismissed 31 Jan. 1853 for deficient grades he went into the manufacturing business in Boston and Philadelphia until the outbreak of the war.

Dwight received a commission as lieutenant colonel of the 70th New York 29 June 1861 and was named its colonel 2 days later. At the Battle of WILLIAMSBURG, 5 May 1862, he bravely led the regiment, which suffered 50% casualties. Wounded 3 times, he was left for dead and captured by the Confederates. Exchanged a short time later, the recovered officer was promoted to brigadier general 29 Nov. 1862.

Assigned to the Western theater, Dwight commanded a brigade in Brig. Gen. CUVIER GROVER's division in Maj. Gen. NATHANIEL P. BANKS's Department of the Gulf. He then commanded a division of the XIX Corps in the successful capture of PORT HUDSON, La., July 1863. During the RED RIVER CAMPAIGN, Mar.–May 1864, Dwight served as Banks's chief of staff, allegedly assigned the duty of confiscating Southern cotton for mills in Massachusetts.

In July the XIX Corps, under Brig. Gen. WILLIAM H. EMORY, was transferred to Virginia, where it participated in the 1864 SHENANDOAH VALLEY CAMPAIGN under Maj. Gen. PHILIP H. SHERIDAN. At THIRD WINCHESTER, 19 Sept., Dwight's division was partially routed in a morning assault. Dwight subsequently blamed the poor conduct of Grover's division for his own command's misfortune. Grover countered by charging Dwight with neglect of duty, asserting that while Dwight's division charged, its commander was enjoying his lunch far in the rear. Though arrested, Dwight soon returned to duty with no official action taken. His division played a secondary role in the Union victory at FISHER'S HILL. At CEDAR CREEK, 19 Oct., the XIX Corps and another Union command were routed in the surprise morning attack by the Confederates. Mustered out 15 Jan. 1866, Dwight was not included in the mass of brevet promotions at the end of the war.

Settling in Cincinnati, Dwight entered the railroad business with his brothers. d. Boston, Mass., 21 Apr. 1888. —JDW

Dyer, Alexander Brydie. USA b. Richmond, Va., 10 Jan. 1815. One of the few native Southerners to reach the rank of general in the Union army, Dyer was a career U.S. Regular who graduated 6th in his 1837 West Point class. In 1838 he was attached to the ordnance department. While this did not involve much field duty, during the Mexican War Dyer participated in the occupation of what became New Mexico Territory and in fighting at Chihuahua and Santa Cruz de Rosales.

Dyer was promoted to captain 3 Mar. 1853, and in Aug. 1861, with 23 years of ordnance experience, he was put in charge of the Springfield Armory in Massachusetts. There he oversaw experiments and incredible advances in weaponry, and he soon increased production of rifles to 1,000 a day. In 1863, under the rule requiring advancement of 1 grade for 10 years of faithful service, Dyer was made a major in the Regulars. On 12 Sept. 1864, recognition of his work came with a leap to the full rank of brigadier general and appointment as the army's chief of ordnance. Dyer himself invented a lead-based heavy artillery shell for rifled ordnance, the 24-pounder Dyer Shell; more than 168,000 of them were made for the Union.

Inspired by events at the armory, many crank inventors descended on Dyer, begging his attention. What he called "charlatan inventors and knavish contractors" became the bane of his life, and Union Col. HIRAM BERDAN was among the most annoying. Berdan and others lodged complaints with congressional patrons, claiming Dyer did not give them his fair and full attention and had not awarded contracts to them. Dyer requested a court of inquiry, which reaffirmed his powers to make contract decisions, run the armory as he saw fit, and interview those inventors and contractors he pleased.

Following the war, Dyer was brevetted a major general in the Regulars for his war service. He ran the armory until 1869, when, in poor health, he resigned. d. Washington, D.C., 20 May 1874. —JES

Dyer's *Compendium*. One of the indispensable works on the war is the 1,796-page *Compendium of the War of the Rebellion,* first published in Des Moines, Iowa, in 1909. A labor of love, it was compiled over 40 years by Frederick H. Dyer, Connecticut veteran and reunion society official, who worked without assistance of secretary, stenographer, or typist. His work has been called "the most monumental war record ever undertaken and successfully completed by a single individual."

Though filled with general information on the conflict, the *Compendium* is primarily a guide to Union army units, their activities, and organization. Part I, in Dyer's words, is "devoted to vital and various statistics" on Federal forces, the "formation of the various Armies and Departments of the war, the troops assigned to and serving with each, and their various Commanders. . . ." Part II is a record of engagements, losses, and the Union units participating, arranged chronologically and by state. The major feature of Part III is a collection of service sketches for over 3,550 Federal units. A comprehensive 45-page index completes the work. Originally released in a single hefty volume, the *Compendium* was reissued in a 3-volume format in 1959 (Thomas Yoseloff: New York and London.) —EGL

E

Early, Jubal Anderson. CSA b. Franklin Cty., Va., 3 Nov. 1816. With his abrasive and sloppy image, Early emerged from the Civil War as one of its great characters. Hard-drinking and sharp-tongued, he projected anything but the clean, noble image of a military commander. But "Old Jubal" or "Jube" was one of the more popular Confederate generals.

USMHI

Early was born into a prominent line of Franklin County Virginians and attended schools in the area before being appointed to the U.S. Military Academy in 1833, 1 year after the devastating death of his mother. His West Point career ended in 1837, when he graduated 18th in his class with a commission as 2d lieutenant in the 3d Regiment Artillery for duty in Florida's Seminole War. Early's first taste of battle came near Jupiter Inlet in the Everglades. After the conflict ended, he resigned to pursue a law career in Rocky Mount, Va.

Although Early voted against secession in the 1861 state convention, he quickly stepped forward to defend his native soil, accepted a commission as colonel of state forces assigned to train volunteers at Lynchburg, and soon commanded the 24th Virginia Infantry. After Virginia officially seceded, he resigned his Lynchburg post, joined his regiment at Manassas Junction, commanded the 6th Brigade at BLACKBURN'S FORD, and performed well with Brig. Gen. P.G.T. Beauregard at FIRST BULL RUN. His superiors were so impressed with his performance that after the battle they appointed him brigadier general.

He fought with his brigade under Gen. JOSEPH E. JOHNSTON in the Army of Northern Virginia's defense of the peninsula against Maj. Gen. GEORGE B. MCCLELLAN's invading Federals, then took a minié bullet in the shoulder at WILLIAMSBURG. Early remained on the field, until he was removed to a hospital in Williamsburg.

He recuperated quickly, returning to Richmond in search of a command. Taking over for the wounded Brig. Gen. ARNOLD ELZEY, he filled a brigade command under Maj. Gen. THOMAS J. "STONEWALL" JACKSON just in time for the Battle of MALVERN HILL. There he and his men became lost in heavy woods and suffered 33 casualties without firing a shot. But Early fought valiantly at CEDAR MOUNTAIN and along the Rappahannock River prior to SECOND BULL RUN. On 22 Aug. 1862, near Warrenton Springs, his skillful maneuvering fooled Maj. Gen. JOHN POPE's Federals, and his brigade escaped without a casualty. In a similar situation at ANTIETAM, his cool head again saved his brigade.

Early fought brilliantly at FREDERICKSBURG, was promoted major general to rank from 17 Jan. 1863, and headed a division. But his major weakness again shone through. His failure to reconnoiter adequately brought him trouble at CHANCELLORSVILLE (in spite of the Confederate victory), at MINE RUN late in 1863, and again in the WILDERNESS in 1864. But Gen. Robert E. Lee still considered Early, who had performed well during the GETTYSBURG CAMPAIGN, an asset and appointed him lieutenant general as of 31 May 1864.

That year, after fighting at COLD HARBOR, he boldly crossed the Potomac River and won what was probably his most celebrated victory, at MONOCACY. But his actions there alerted Federal troops around Washington, and his plan to attack the capital had to be aborted. (*See* EARLY'S WASHINGTON RAID.) In retreat, Early took part in another action that would make him famous, the burning of CHAMBERSBURG, Pa., in restitution for Federal destruction in the Shenandoah Valley.

Early ended the war fighting against Maj. Gen. PHILIP H. SHERIDAN at FISHER'S HILL, WINCHESTER, CEDAR CREEK, and WAYNESBOROUGH. After Lee surrendered, Early, disguised, traveled west to Texas, then to Havana, Cuba, and Toronto, Ontario.

In Canada he wrote *A Memoir of the Last Year of the War* (1867), a lively, and colored, account of his activities during the closing battles. Early returned to Lynchburg in 1869 and reestablished his law practice. Unlike many of his old comrades, he never accepted the Confederate defeat graciously. During his later years he supervised the Louisiana State Lottery and served as the first president of the Southern Historical Society. His writings, including an *Autobiographical Sketch* (1912), a revision of his memoir, leave no doubt that Early chose to remain defiantly "unreconstructed." d. Lynchburg, Va., 2 Mar. 1894. —FLS

Early's Washington Raid. 23 June–12 July 1864 On 23 June 1864, 14,000 Confederates, half of them barefoot, filed into columns and began marching down the Shenandoah Valley. With Maj. Gen. DAVID HUNTER's Union army withdrawing beyond the Alleghenies, leaving Washington, D.C., exposed, Lt. Gen. JUBAL A. EARLY's veterans marched swiftly north, hoping to force Lt. Gen. U. S. Grant to detach part of his army to defend the capital. On 2 July the Confederates entered Winchester, where Early divided his army, sending one force against Harpers Ferry while the second command continued toward Martinsburg, W. Va. 4 days later the Confederate Army of the Valley encamped beyond the Potomac River.

Receiving new orders from Gen. Robert E. Lee, Early detached a cavalry brigade toward Baltimore to cut communications and assist in a scheme to free 18,000 Confederate prisoners at POINT LOOKOUT, Md. Shoes arrived, and 8 July Early crossed South Mountain. He exacted a ransom of $20,000 from Hagerstown, then entered Frederick, whose citizens added $200,000 to Confederate coffers 9 July.

East of Frederick behind the Monocacy River, Northern soldiers under Maj. Gen. LEW WALLACE were deployed, stubbornly resisting 5 Confederate assaults before withdrawing late in the day. Wallace's fierce defense delayed Early's advance for a crucial day. The Confederates, suffering from stifling heat and choking dust, reached the defenses of Washington, D.C., on the afternoon of the 11th. But Early was too late; veterans hurried northward by Grant from Petersburg manned the fortifications. The Confederates probed the defenses the next day before retreating that night.

The audacious raiders, burdened with booty and supplies, eluded and then repulsed an inept Federal pursuit. Though the scheme to free the prisoners failed, Early had fulfilled Lee's orders by relieving the pressure on the Southern troops defending Petersburg. As the crusty Confederate told an officer, "Major, we haven't taken Washington, but we've scared Abe Lincoln like hell!"   —JDW

East, Union Department of the.   Before the Civil War, the Department of the East was the U.S. Army's bureaucratic designation for all U.S. territory east of the Mississippi River. From 1857, Brig. Gen. JOHN E. WOOL served as department commander, with headquarters at Troy, N.Y.

Through early 1861, secessionist state governments seized military control of the department's southern districts. The approach of war and the loss of territory compelled the U.S. War Department to begin the dissolution of the department 19 Apr. 1861. This dissolution was completed 26 Oct., and the Department of the East temporarily went out of existence. Eastern areas remaining under Union military control were organized into smaller, regional departments; Wool took command of the Department of Virginia.

U.S. War Department General Order No. 2, issued 3 Jan. 1863, reestablished a Department of the East and named Wool its commander. It included all of New England and the state of New York, with headquarters established in New York City. Wool remained department commander until his retirement July 1863. Maj. Gen. JOHN A. DIX assumed command 18 July 1863 and held it until the end of hostilities. Under Wool and Dix, departmental military activity was confined to civil and police matters (see DRAFT RIOTS), guarding approaches to Canada, and pursuing Confederates who raided Portland harbor, Maine, 26 June 1863, and ST. ALBANS, Vt.   —JES

Eastport, USS.   In fall 1861 the Confederates bought the *Eastport,* a 700-ton steamer, one of the fastest on the Mississippi River. Properly fitted, the 280-ft-long vessel could carry a formidable battery, and it was taken up the Tennessee River to Cerro Gordo, a landing in Hardin Cty., Tenn., where work was begun to convert it into an ironclad gunboat.

The Federals learned as early as Dec. 1861 that the steamer was being outfitted. On 7 Feb. 1862, after the fall of Fort Henry, Lt. Samuel L. Phelps, with a fleet comprising the *CONESTOGA,* the *TYLER,* and the *LEXINGTON,* went up the Tennessee as far as navigable—to Florence, Ala.—and at Cerro Gordo captured the half-finished *Eastport* along with 250,000 ft of lumber and the ironwork, arms, and other items intended for it.

The *Eastport* was completed at the shipyard at Cairo, Ill. Fitted with 8 guns, it was commissioned Aug. 1862 and, commanded by Phelps, quickly became a formidable gunboat.

In Feb. 1863 the *Eastport* headed for Vicksburg to join the fleet of Cmdr. DAVID D. PORTER but en route struck a bar, breaking the timbers used to strengthen the bottom under the boiler. It was towed back to Cairo to be repaired.

In spring 1864 the gunboat took part in the RED RIVER CAMPAIGN, which was particularly hazardous because the water level had failed to rise as it usually did during that season. The *Eastport* and another vessel were hauled laboriously over the rocks before they continued upriver to Fort de Russy, which by that time had been taken by Union land forces.

Its work finished, the *Eastport* started back down the river, ran into a torpedo below Grand Ecore 15 Apr., and sank. Heroic efforts were made to rescue it. The *Eastport* was raised and moved downstream 52 mi, then ran into a bed of logs and could not be dislodged.

On 26 Apr., cleared of personnel and equipment, the vessel was blown to pieces by 3,055 lb of powder scattered around its interior.   —VCJ

East Tennessee, Confederate Army and Department of.   The Army of East Tennessee, never united, was the scattered Confederate military might within the geographic area composing the Department of East Tennessee. The department was established 25 Feb. 1862 in response to the consequences of the Confederate defeat at MILL SPRINGS, Ky., 19 Jan. In August troops within the department were temporarily named the Army of Kentucky when Maj. Gen. E. KIRBY SMITH transferred from the Army of Northern Virginia to assume command, with headquarters at Knoxville.

The department first comprised an area of roughly 17,000 sq mi, including Chattanooga. Its responsibility extended over the Cumberland Mts. on its northern and western borders, and took in a small portion of North Carolina extending to the Blue Ridge range on its southeastern limit. By the end of 1862 Chattanooga had been cut from the department, and by mid-1863 the western tip of Virginia along the Cumberlands had been added.

The number of troops fluctuated, ranging from 7,000 in Jan. 1863 to 14,000 by April of that year. Such a small force proved inadequate to the needs of the large, ill-constructed geographic entity, which stretched over some 200 mountainous miles from Virginia to Georgia. Effectiveness was further hampered since both the command and the boundaries of the department changed many times—9 men held the post in 1 year alone, Aug. 1862–July 1863—and because responsibilities overlapped with those of adjacent departments, resulting in redundancy of manpower. Also, most of the men were tied down to specific locations and were thus unavailable for reinforcing the principal armies at crucial points.

Technically the command ceased to exist 25 July 1863, when the department officially merged with the Department of Tennessee, under Gen. BRAXTON BRAGG. But the army continued under Lt. Gen. SIMON B. BUCKNER, whom Bragg ordered to report directly to Richmond. This blatant lack of unity in command adversely affected the South's responses to simultaneous Federal operations against KNOXVILLE and CHATTANOOGA. Lt. Gen. JAMES LONGSTREET later took command of the department when he moved his corps into it for the Knoxville Campaign, but Buckner returned thereafter and remained until Feb. 1865, when the area and the army at last merged into Lt. Gen. JUBAL A. EARLY's Department of Western and Southwestern Virginia.   —HH

Eaton, Amos Beebe. USA b. Catskill, N.Y., 12 May 1806. On 29 Sept. 1861, Eaton was made a lieutenant colonel in the U.S. Army and an assistant commissary general. For 23 years he had been in the commissary department and for 12 years before that, an officer in the U.S. Army. A graduate of West Point in 1826, Eaton was 36th in his class, and until the Florida campaigning of the late 1830s was an infantry lieutenant. Thereafter he was pressed into fighting service only once, during the Battle of Buena Vista in the Mexican War. For this action he was brevetted major.

At the start of the Civil War, Eaton was faced with difficult supply problems, since there was no system to accommodate the large numbers of men who suddenly entered Union service. Relying on experience gained as commissary chief of the Department of the Pacific in the 1850s, he applied himself to the job of provisioning and distributing and 29 June 1864 was rewarded with promotion to brigadier general's rank. At that time he replaced retiring Brig. Gen. JOSEPH P. TAYLOR as commissary general of the U.S. Army. Though his position was not glamorous, Eaton won a brevet to major general 13 Mar. 1865, which he held until retirement to New Haven, Conn., in 1874. There he died 21 Feb. 1877.   —JES

Ebenezer Church, Ala., eng. at. 1 Apr. 1865 In late March Union Brev. Maj. Gen. JAMES H. WILSON's cavalry and artillery force invaded northern Alabama, with Selma, the state's industrial center, its objective. The resulting fight at Ebenezer Church was a part of this operation, called WILSON'S RAID. Opposing Wilson, Lt. Gen. NATHAN B. FORREST had a force of 7,000–8,000 cavalry and state militia, but the Confederates were scattered to cover both Wilson's advance and a possible Union cavalry move from Pensacola, Fla.

On 1 Apr., Wilson's advance force, led by Brig. Gens. Eli Long and EMORY UPTON, moved out at dawn from positions in front of Maplesville Station, about 30 mi from Selma. Long's division was to travel south on the Randolph-Plantersville road. Upton's division was to move along Long's left flank down the Randolph-Mapleville road. Their orders were to "press the enemy vigorously and charge them whenever they attempted to make a stand." The divisions were to meet where the 2 roads joined, forming the Selma highway, Wilson's intended assault route to the city. Combined, the 2 divisions numbered about 9,000.

Forrest and the Federal vanguard skirmished heavily 30–31 Mar. On 1 Apr. he had about 2,000 men near Maplesville Station, expecting reinforcement from Brig. Gen. WILLIAM H. JACKSON's 3,000 troopers and from Brig. Gen. JAMES R. CHALMERS' division. None of the troops arrived. The Cahawba River kept Jackson from the enemy and Chalmers was farther away than Forrest believed. When Long and Upton began their morning moves, Forrest organized resistance and sent couriers looking for Chalmers. Early in the afternoon he received word that Chalmers was moving toward Dixie Station. Forrest decided to withdraw 4 mi to a little chapel called Ebenezer Church near the intersection of Long's and Upton's routes and 1 mi from Dixie Station. His men would make a stand there and wait for Chalmers' division.

The defenders were organized into 3 small brigades commanded by Brig. Gens. PHILIP D. RODDEY and DANIEL W. ADAMS, and Col. Edward Crossland. Their thin line stretched from the right of the Alabama & Tennessee River Railroad tracks and the head of the Selma highway across to a wooded hill near Ebenezer Church. Crossland commanded the Confederate left at the church, Roddey the center on the highway, and Adams the right. 4 cannon covered Long's approach on the Randolph-Plantersville road; 2 others supported Adams' troops. Forrest, with less than 200 men, held off the Federals until nearly 4 p.m., then fell back to the Ebenezer Church line.

After Confederate skirmishers were driven in by Long's cavalrymen, the Federal commander ordered elements of the 17th Indiana Mounted Infantry to charge Forrest's main line. They broke through a portion of Roddey's sector, assaulted the 4-gun battery, and began an extended hand-to-hand fight that involved Forrest himself. These Federals retreated; a second assault by 5 regiments of dismounted Illinois and Indiana troopers hit the center; elements of Upton's division attacked Adams on the Confederate right. Adams' men, mostly untried Alabama militia, were successful in helping throw back a brigade of Upton's force. But when Upton committed 2 more regiments, dismounted and linked with the men assaulting the Confederate center, he was able to break through Adams' sector. The Alabamians were routed, threw away their weapons, and ran for Selma. Pursuing Federals captured 250 of them and 225 stands of arms.

The disaster on the right compelled Forrest to call retreat. Roddey's and Crossland's men withdrew toward Selma and tried to fight off the Federal pursuit. The engagement lasted less than an hour, costing Forrest 3 cannon and 300–400 soldiers, most of whom were captured. Chalmers, who never arrived, was left to make his own way to Selma. Federal casualties were approximately 12 dead and 40 wounded.   —JES

Echols, John. CSA b. Lynchburg, Va., 20 Mar. 1823. A graduate of Washington College in Virginia, Echols studied law at Harvard, was admitted to the bar, and served as commonwealth attorney and Virginia state legislator.

With Virginia's secession, Echols recruited volunteers in the western part of the state before becoming lieutenant colonel of the 27th Virginia. He commanded the regiment at FIRST BULL RUN, where his unit and 4 other Virginia regiments won enduring fame as the STONEWALL BRIGADE under Brig. Gen. THOMAS J. JACKSON. Promoted to colonel, Echols participated in the early phases of Jackson's 1862 SHENANDOAH

USMHI

VALLEY CAMPAIGN, suffering a severe wound at KERNSTOWN Mar. 1862. During his recuperation he was commissioned brigadier general, 16 Apr.

An imposing man, standing 6 ft 4 in. and weighing 260 lb, the new brigadier assumed command of a brigade in the Army of Western Virginia. In September the brigade operated in the Kanawha Valley under Maj. Gen. WILLIAM WING LORING. On 16 Oct. Echols succeeded Loring as commander of the Army of Southwest Virginia, holding the position less than a month. During summer 1863 Echols served on the court of inquiry created to examine the surrender of Vicksburg, Miss., in July.

He returned to field command again in southwest Virginia, and 6 Nov. 1863 his forces suffered a defeat at DROOP MOUN-

TAIN. In spring 1864 he fought under Maj. Gen. JOHN C. BRECK-INRIDGE at the Battle of NEW MARKET. Sent east to reinforce the Army of Northern Virginia, Echols' brigade was engaged at COLD HARBOR. On 22 Aug. Echols assumed command of the District of Southwest Virginia, retaining the position until 30 Mar. 1865, when he replaced Lt. Gen. JUBAL A. EARLY as commander of the Department of Western Virginia. In this capacity Echols moved east to unite with Gen. ROBERT E. LEE's army but learned en route of the surrender at Appomattox. He then marched to North Carolina, joining Gen. JOSEPH E. JOHNSTON's army. He eventually surrendered in Augusta, Ga., in the party of the fleeing Pres. JEFFERSON DAVIS.

Echols resumed his law practice after the war, prospering as an attorney and businessman with interests in banking and railroads. d. Staunton, Va., 24 May 1896. —JDW

Ector, Matthew Duncan. CSA b. Putnam Cty., Ga., 28 Feb. 1822, Ector migrated to Texas in the late 1840s after attending Centre College, Ky., practicing law in Georgia, and serving a term in the Georgia state legislature. In Texas he maintained a law practice, and in 1855 was elected to its legislature.

LC

After joining the Confederate army as a private, he advanced himself to a brigade adjutant's post with Gen. P.G.T. BEAUREGARD's army at Corinth in spring 1862, then was elected colonel of the 14th Texas Cavalry in time for Gen. BRAXTON BRAGG's invasion of Kentucky. On 23 Aug. 1862, before the campaign got under way, he received his brigadier's appointment, and the 14th Texas, serving as infantry, was put into his command. He led it with distinction at RICHMOND, Ky., in August, and at the end of the year commanded it in a surprise dawn attack on Union Maj. Gen. Alexander M. McCook's men on the first day of fighting at STONE'S RIVER.

Ector was praised for his performance there, and in spring 1863 was selected with several others to rush to the relief of Vicksburg before it was surrounded. Among the first troops to arrive outside the city, Ector's and Brig. Gen. EVANDER MCNAIR's men were still 1 day late. Other troops followed shortly, but the city had been virtually cut off 19 May.

After brief service in Mississippi, he returned to Tennessee, taking part in some of the first fighting in the Battle of CHICKAMAUGA. He was again transferred to Mississippi, returning east to take part in the ATLANTA CAMPAIGN. Dispatched to the Georgia fighting, Ector was wounded badly, resulting in the amputation of a leg. It is believed he was invalided home. Then, in Lt. Gen. JOHN B. HOOD's campaign into Tennessee, Ector's brigade of Maj. Gen. SAMUEL G. FRENCH's division took part in the Battles of FRANKLIN and NASHVILLE. Though records are unclear, Ector probably did not accompany his men on this arduous march so soon after an amputation. However, after the Tennessee campaigning, Ector's brigade, along with several others, was dispatched to the defenses of Mobile, Ala., where Ector joined his men for one of the last battles of the war and to be surrendered with them.

Settling in Texas, in the postwar period Ector continued in

the legal profession, rose to the bench, and at the time of his death in Marshall, 29 Oct. 1879, was presiding justice on the Texas court of appeals. —JES

Edmonds (Edmundson), Sarah Emma. b. New Brunswick, Canada, 1842. Among the few documented cases of women serving as soldiers in the Federal army, one of the best known is that of Edmonds, who disguised herself as a man after running away from home to escape a marriage arranged by her father. Settling in Rhode Island, she used the alias "Franklin Thompson" to get a position selling Bibles.

Edmonds' employer transferred her to Michigan shortly before the war. When local military units started organizing early in 1861, she enlisted as a male nurse in the 2d Michigan Infantry. In July the regiment became part of the Army of the Potomac, arriving in the East in time to fight at FIRST BULL RUN. Though unsuspecting comrades joked about Edmonds' small stature, she diligently carried out her duties as a field nurse.

Until spring 1863, when the 2d Michigan was sent to Kentucky, Edmonds worked intermittently as a soldier, spy, and mail carrier. That April she fell ill with malaria. Certain that doctors would discover her masquerade, she deserted rather than submit to hospitalization. Edmonds then discarded her uniform and until the war ended worked for the U.S. CHRISTIAN COMMISSION.

Under the name Sarah E. Edmundson, she published her wartime adventure as *Nurse and Spy in the Union Army* (1865), a narrative of narrow escapes from "rebel vixens" that the author admitted she had embellished for an eager public. A later edition capitalized on the book's sensational aspect with a new title, *Unsexed: Or, the Female Soldier.* Edmonds married in Apr. 1867, preferring that her activities as a spy be forgotten. "So much mean deception," she wrote, "is not pleasant to think about in time of peace."

The memoirs did not bring much income, but they helped establish the validity of her wartime service. In 1884, the Federal government awarded her a monthly pension of $12, which she collected until her death, 5 Sept. 1898. During her last years, Edmonds lived in La Porte, Tex. She enjoys the distinction of being the only woman ever granted membership in the GRAND ARMY OF THE REPUBLIC. —PLF

Edwards, Oliver. USA b. Springfield, Mass., 30 Jan. 1835. At 21, Edwards moved to Warsaw, Ill., where he entered the foundry business, then returned to Massachusetts to enlist when the Civil War began.

Edwards mustered in as 1st lieutenant and adjutant of the 10th Massachusetts 21 June 1861. Subsequently appointed an aide on the staff of Maj. Gen. DARIUS N. COUCH, he served capably during the PENINSULA CAMPAIGN in spring 1862 and returned to field command 4 Sept. as colonel of the 37th Massachusetts. These Bay Staters were assigned to a brigade in Maj. Gen. JOHN NEWTON's division of the VI Corps, and Edwards led them with distinction in the battles of FREDERICKSBURG, CHANCELLORSVILLE, and GETTYSBURG.

NA

After the last engagement, Edwards temporarily commanded a special brigade that was rushed to New York City to quell the DRAFT RIOTS.

During the first 3 months of 1864 the Massachusetts colonel commanded a brigade. Returning to regimental command in the spring, Edwards led the 37th at the WILDERNESS, 5–6 May, resuming brigade command 2 days later at SPOTSYLVANIA. On 12 May his brigade charged the Confederate "MULE SHOE," and in the course of this vicious struggle, Edwards commanded 21 regiments for 13 hours.

In July the VI Corps transferred to the SHENANDOAH VALLEY, where it participated in the successful Union campaigning. During the Federal victory at THIRD WINCHESTER, on 19 Sept., Edwards gallantly led his brigade. For his distinguished conduct on this day and at Spotsylvania, he was brevetted brigadier general. When the Federals advanced up the valley after their victory, Edwards assumed command of Winchester, protecting hospitals and ensuring the flow of supplies. Offered the post of provost marshal general of the Middle Military District, he declined.

Edwards returned with the VI Corps late in 1864 to Petersburg, Va. When the Union army finally broke the Confederate lines, 2 Apr. 1865, he accepted the surrender of the city from its mayor. Some days later, at SAYLER'S CREEK, Edwards' brigade captured Confederate Gens. RICHARD S. EWELL and G.W.C. LEE, and an entire Confederate brigade. Brevetted major general for this exploit, he received the full rank of brigadier general 19 May 1865.

After the war Edwards returned to Warsaw, where he served as its mayor 3 times. He briefly entered the manufacturing business in Massachusetts but returned to his adopted community, dying there 28 Apr. 1904.   —JDW

Egan, Thomas Wilberforce. USA b. Watervliet, N.Y., 14 June 1834. The son of Irish immigrants, Egan lacked professional military experience but rose to command a brigade in the Army of the Potomac by the

NA

midpoint of the war. On 1 July 1861 he became the lieutenant colonel of the 40th New York Volunteers, leading his regiment so well at SEVEN PINES, during Maj. Gen. GEORGE B. MCCLELLAN'S 1862 PENINSULA CAMPAIGN, that he became its colonel in June.

Early that October, Egan's regiment was one of many that failed to intercept Lt. Gen. J.E.B. STUART'S raiders following their sacking of CHAMBERSBURG, PA. Egan was not present with his regiment at Fredericksburg 2 months later, but at CHANCELLORSVILLE the next May he was assigned a brigade in Maj. Gen. DANIEL E. SICKLES' III Corps. The command was so hotly engaged that it suffered 756 casualties, the second heaviest loss of any Union brigade involved in the campaign.

At GETTYSBURG Egan reverted to command of the 40th New York, which on 2 July 1863 held the far left flank of Sickles' displaced line, next to DEVIL'S DEN. The regiment was swept under by Lt. Gen. JAMES LONGSTREET'S attack late that afternoon, costing Egan "many of my bravest and most faithful men." Late

in the year he was given command of another, fresher brigade.

Upon his corps' demise early in 1864, Egan was transferred to a II Corps brigade, which he commanded at the WILDERNESS and SPOTSYLVANIA. At an early stage of the PETERSBURG CAMPAIGN, he received a wound that partially paralyzed him for 2 months. Returning to duty, he served so meritoriously that he won promotion to brigadier general of volunteers 3 Sept. 1864.

Soon after he took over the 2d Division/II Corps, which he directed at BURGESS' MILL, 27 Oct. He later received the brevet of major general, dating from this engagement. In November Egan was again wounded, but he was well enough by spring 1865 to lead a division in the Army of the Shenandoah.

Mustered out of the service Jan. 1866, he was appointed deputy collector in the New York Customs House, a position he retained for 15 years. He died in New York City, 24 Feb. 1887, and is buried in Brooklyn.   —EGL

elections, Confederate States. In May 1861 the Provisional Confederate Congress called for elections to be held in November. Until then, neither the legislators nor Pres. JEFFERSON DAVIS or Vice-President ALEXANDER H. STEPHENS would be confirmed by popular vote, but with fierce patriotism and spirit of unity prevailing, few incumbents doubted success at the polls.

The central government announced the election date in newspapers, leaving the states to conduct the voting under their old constitutions. As no official political parties existed in the Confederacy, voters generally chose candidates for the House of Representatives at public meetings. Senators were elected by the state legislatures. Candidates campaigned little, either because army duties preoccupied them or because they considered the times inappropriate for electioneering. With the war apparently going well and the Davis administration still in favor, local rather than national issues influenced the outcome at the polls. Voters tended to follow their prewar Whig or Democratic preferences, drawing few distinctions between secessionist and Unionist records as long as the contender professed devotion to the Confederacy now that the war had begun.

5 states—Virginia, North Carolina, Florida, Alabama, and Tennessee—provided absentee voting for soldiers, a practice adopted throughout the Confederacy by 1863. When officials tallied the ballots, Davis and Stephens won against no opposition and most provisional congressmen were elected to the first regular session.

By the second national elections in 1863, Davis' war policies were under severe attack, with popular support for his programs waning steadily as morale declined. Politicking regained its antebellum intensity, dominated now by heated debates between pro- and anti-administration men. Davis' opponents condemned him for violating states rights, particularly in the areas of CONSCRIPTION, exemption, martial law, IMPRESSMENT, *HABEAS CORPUS,* and taxation (*see* INCOME TAX, CONFEDERATE; TAX IN KIND)—measures widely despised as an unwarranted centralization of power. But critics offered no alternatives other than vague promises to do something different to ensure Southern independence and bring about the end of the war. Pro-administration candidates urged cooperation and self-sacrifice, gingerly avoiding mention of their voting records on unpopular issues. Peace men surfaced in both camps, and anti-administration candidates clamoring for a negotiated truce threatened to obstruct the Davis contingent, which endorsed the president's insistence on military victory as the only means to achieve independence.

The logistics of holding elections under wartime conditions confused the bitterly contested campaign. Congress approved voting by general ticket in Louisiana, Arkansas, Mississippi, Missouri, Kentucky, and Tennessee because Federal troops occupied large sections of those states. In others with substantial refugee populations, officials arranged absentee voting for their displaced citizens. Richmond set no date for the elections, which spanned June to November, prolonging the outcome for nearly 6 months. When the Second Regular Congress convened, May 1864, the number of anti-administration districts in the House had risen from 26 to 41 out of a total of 106. 12 of the 26 senators had been elected on opposition platforms. Even among the pro-Davis men there was a high turnover, clearly expressing the public's lack of confidence in the president.

Davis owed his continued congressional majority to the soldier vote, and to the returns that came in from occupied areas. Both constituencies showed pronounced support for his radical measures, helping the president hold his tenuous control in Congress until the Confederate collapse. But many of his staunchest allies had been defeated; discouraged, others had joined the army rather than seek reelection. Of the 236 Confederate legislators over the course of the war, only 27 served in all 3 congresses.   —PLF

elections, United States. As the nation prepared for the 1860 elections, divisions among the major political parties placed 4 presidential candidates before the public. 3 of the tickets represented desperate attempts to placate sectional antagonisms that Southerners insisted would lead to disunion if ABRAHAM LINCOLN won the election. On the Republican ticket with Lincoln was HANNIBAL HAMLIN of Maine, running on a platform that downplayed the slavery issue while endorsing government homesteads, free land and citizenship for German immigrants, and protection for American industries. The Constitutional Union party, a pro-compromise coalition of Whigs and Unionists, nominated Tennessee's John Bell for president and Edward Everett of Massachusetts as his running mate. The Democratic party split over the slavery issue, the Northern contingent nominating the POPULAR SOVEREIGNTY champion STEPHEN A. DOUGLAS of Illinois and Georgia's HERSCHEL V. JOHNSON; the Southerners, states-rights and proslavery men but not radical secessionists, put forward Kentucky's JOHN C. BRECKINRIDGE and Joseph Lane of Oregon. Each party made devotion to the Union the focal point of its campaign.

Voting split clearly along sectional lines. Lincoln carried the North with a sweeping majority of 180 electoral votes. Southerners divided, giving Breckinridge 72 electoral votes, Bell 39. Douglas, whom the Northern Democrats hoped would appeal to moderates in both sections, took only the 12 electoral votes from Missouri and New Jersey. The popular vote, however, was much closer. Lincoln polled 1,866,452 votes, but not one was cast for him in 10 of the Southern states. Douglas came in a surprisingly close second with 1,376,957. Breckinridge trailed with 849,781, Bell with 588,879.

Had the unsuccessful contenders consolidated their popular votes into a majority, the election's outcome would not have changed. With his victories in the densely populated North, and in California and Oregon, Lincoln's electoral votes outnumbered those of his 3 opponents combined. Unquestionably, the U.S. had elected in a valid contest a minority president who owed no part of his victory to the division of his political adversaries.   —PLF

Elk Creek, Indian Territory, eng. at. 17 July 1863 *See* HONEY SPRINGS, INDIAN TERRITORY, ENG. AT.

Elkhorn Tavern, Ark., Battle of. 7–8 Mar. 1862 *See* PEA RIDGE, ARK., BATTLE OF.

Ellerson's Mill, Va., Battle of. 26 June 1862 *See* MECHANICSVILLE, VA., BATTLE OF.

Ellet, Alfred Washington. USA b. Penn's Manor, Pa., 11 Oct. 1820, Ellet was one of 14 children. After being reared on the family farm, he studied engineering, as had his brother, CHARLES ELLET. As a civil engineer Alfred traveled around the country, and at the start of the Civil War lived in Bunker Hill, Ill. There, 20 Aug. 1861, he joined the 59th Illinois Infantry and was elected captain.

With the 59th he fought in the Battle of PEA RIDGE, Ark. While he was in the field, his brother Charles received permission from the War Department to build a ram fleet on the Mississippi River. As it neared completion, Charles was commissioned a colonel in the Union army and given command of the boats, asking that Alfred be made his second-in-command. On 29 Apr. 1862 Alfred learned of his new post and his promotion to lieutenant colonel, and set out for Charles' fleet at New Albany, Ind., with 3 officers and 50 men of the 59th Illinois. Under Charles, he and his men fought victoriously in the Battle of MEMPHIS on the Mississippi. But Charles received a wound in the fight and died of complications 21 June; Alfred was made colonel and ram-fleet commander in his stead.

Ellet spent the summer plying the Mississippi and Yazoo rivers, sparring with Confederate gunboats, discovering the construction of the Confederate ironclad *Arkansas,* and being assaulted by guerrillas firing at him from riverbanks. This last problem led to the creation of an amphibious army force called the MISSISSIPPI MARINE BRIGADE and Ellet's appointment as its commander and brigadier general 1 Nov. 1862. He retained nominal command of the ram fleet but reported to acting Rear Adm. David D. Porter. His subordination to the U.S. Navy, and the granting of commands and commissions to Ellet's son and nephews in the ram fleet, set off a series of unresolved squabbles between the army and the navy.

During the SECOND VICKSBURG CAMPAIGN, 2 of Ellet's rams ran the Confederate river batteries; the marine brigade operated against onshore guerrillas; and on 24 May 1863 Ellet ordered the burning of the town of Austin, Miss., in retaliation for its citizens' aid to Confederates in reporting his movements. His rams also performed transport duty during this period, and in 1864 both the rams and the marine brigade took part in Maj. Gen. ANDREW J. SMITH's operations in Arkansas and Louisiana, involving Ellet's men in significant but decreasing numbers of skirmishes and engagements. In August the marine brigade was disbanded. Having earlier lost command of the rams to Porter, Ellet was posted to New Orleans. He resigned his commission 31 Dec. 1864.

In the postwar years he returned to civil engineering, was involved in railroad development, and became a resident of Kansas. d. El Dorado 9 Jan. 1895.   —JES

Ellet, Charles. USA b. Bucks Cty., Pa., 1 Jan. 1810. Older brother of Brig. Gen. ALFRED W. ELLET, Charles became one of the country's outstanding engineers. Largely self-educated, with a natural aptitude for mathematics and languages, he became a designer and builder of suspension bridges. His bridge over the Wheeling and Ohio rivers, completed in 1849, was— at 1,010 ft—the longest of its type in the world. Ellet also devised methods of flood control and for improving navigation, but, lacking political support, his proposals were not acted on. Visiting the besieged city of Sebastopol during the Crimean War, Ellet became convinced that a naval siege could be bro-

LC

ken by the use of "ram-boats." But the Russians were not interested in the idea, nor was the Navy Department after Ellet returned to the U.S. (*see* RAMS).

During the first years of the Civil War, Ellet continued to be ignored—until the appearance of the Confederate ironclad *VIRGINIA (Merrimack).* In Mar. 1862 Sec. of War EDWIN M. STANTON commissioned Ellet a colonel subject only to his own authority. Working under deadlines imposed by Stanton, Ellet converted 9 old steamboats into a ram fleet. Though Ellet realized his unarmed rams seemed weak, he believed that audacity in striking the enemy would compensate for this. The test came during the Battle of MEMPHIS, which resulted in the destruction of the Confederate fleet and the surrender of the city to Flag Officer CHARLES H. DAVIS 6 June. The only casualty among the men aboard the rams was Ellet, who was wounded by an enemy shot. He died 21 June as his boat reached Cairo, Ill. Finally recognized for his services to his country, Ellet was given a state funeral at Independence Hall in Philadelphia.   —NCD

Elliot, Washington Lafayette. USA b. Carlisle, Pa., 31 Mar. 1825. The son of navy Capt. Jesse D. Elliot, Washington had the opportunity to travel extensively and receive a varied education. He attended Pennsylvania's Dickinson College, West Point (1841–44), and studied medicine before receiving an appointment into the Regular Army in 1846 as lieutenant in the mounted arm. Mexican War service and recruiting and frontier duty followed.

At the start of the Civil War Elliot was a captain, participated in the battles at Springfield and WILSON'S CREEK, Mo., then was commissioned colonel of the 2d Iowa Cavalry 14 Sept. 1861. Following the fortunes of Maj.

LC

Gen. JOHN POPE, he fought at NEW MADRID, Mo., and ISLAND NO. 10. He took part in the Siege of CORINTH, Miss., and a cavalry raid on the Mobile & Ohio Railroad, and was made a brigadier general 11 June 1862. Elliot was wounded at SECOND BULL RUN, where he was Pope's chief of cavalry for the Army of Virginia. On Pope's departure from the East, Elliot was given command of the Department of the Northwest, then led the

3d Division/III Corps/Army of the Potomac at CHANCELLORSVILLE and GETTYSBURG.

In the campaigning for KNOXVILLE late in 1863, he was transferred to command of the 1st Cavalry Division/Army of the Cumberland and served in Tennessee. Attached to Maj. Gen. GEORGE H. THOMAS's command for the campaigns to ATLANTA and in Tennessee, Elliot fought in the Battle of NASHVILLE in the latter campaign. Following this, he was transferred to command of the District of Kansas.

At the end of the war Elliot was brevetted major general for his extensive service and remained in the army until 1879, when he retired to take up banking in San Francisco, where he died 29 June 1888.   —JES

Elliott, Stephen, Jr. CSA b. Beaufort, S.C., 26 Oct. 1832 Bearing the same name as his grandfather, a distinguished naturalist, and his father, the first bishop of the Episcopal Church in Georgia, Elliott grew up in comfortable circumstances on the family plantation. There he was educated, and developed into an accomplished, popular sportsman elected to serve his district in the state legislature. On the outbreak of civil war he was commissioned captain of the Beaufort Artillery (later also called "Stuart's Battery"), a local organization begun in 1776, which he helped equip for Confederate service. Elliott led the company to Charleston, where it participated in the shelling of FORT SUMTER in April.

USMHI

He was then assigned to guard duty around Port Royal harbor in his native state. After Union forces captured the coastal islands, Elliott harassed the enemy in a series of daring night raids against Federal outposts, on 9 Apr. 1863 sinking the steamer *George Washington* near Chisholm's Island.

Advanced to major, then lieutenant colonel, in September he was appointed chief of artillery for the Third Military District and placed in charge of defense operations at Fort Sumter. The assignment provided Elliott opportunity to experiment further with torpedoes, weapons he had first tried using at Red Bluff on the Savannah River in spring 1862. 4 of the devices were placed among the Federal blockading fleet off Charleston the night of 10 Oct. 1863, with hopes of sinking the formidable monitor *NEW IRONSIDES.* Though they inflicted no apparent damage, Elliott's initiative induced departmental commander Gen. P.G.T. BEAUREGARD to endorse his qualities of leadership in a report to Sec. of War JAMES A. SEDDON.

Promoted to colonel with command of Holcombe's Legion, Elliott left South Carolina for the siege lines around PETERSBURG in spring 1864. With his advancement to brigadier general 24 May, 3 regiments were added to his command and deployed along the section of the Confederate line blown up in the mine explosion 30 July (*see* CRATER, BATTLE OF THE). Nearly 700 men in the brigade were killed or wounded. Elliott himself climbed out of the crater and was critically wounded while repositioning the remnants of his shattered command. The wounding disabled him for several months, but he returned to the field under Gen. JOSEPH E. JOHNSTON for the final battles in North Carolina, including BENTONVILLE, where he was again seriously wounded.

Following Johnston's surrender at Durham Station, Elliott returned to South Carolina. Though reelected to the legislature, he never fully recovered from his wounds, dying 21 Mar. 1866 in Aiken, S.C., before taking office. —PLF

Ellis, John Willis. war governor b. Rowan Cty., N.C., 23 Nov. 1820. A descendant of Welshmen who settled in New England in the 17th century, Ellis was privately tutored, attended Randolph-Macon College in Virginia, and graduated in 1841 from the University of North Carolina. He read law, was admitted to the state bar in 1842, and practiced in Salisbury. A Democrat, Ellis was a member of the state house of commons, 1844–48, and a legislative leader of his party's program of railway construction.

In 1848, the legislature elected Ellis to the state superior court, where for a decade he displayed an adeptness for judiciary service. With the support of aristocrats and slaveholders, he was nominated for the governorship in 1858, winning the election by more than 16,000 votes. As governor, he continued to champion internal improvements in the state, especially the construction of railroads and canals. 2 years later he won reelection, defeating a Whig candidate who campaigned in favor of a tax on slaves.

When Ellis first took office, he deprecated the notion that civil war and secession were imminent. Then, after Abraham Lincoln entered the White House, the governor promoted formation of a Confederacy to protect states rights, slavery, agricultural interests, and other aspects of Southern society. When war neared, he called for a convention of Southern states, a referendum on secession, and the expansion and reorganization of state troops. While the legislature appropriated $300,-000 to upgrade the militia, factions within the Whig and Democratic parties conspired to slow the progress of Ellis' other legislative programs, and Feb. 1861 his constituents voted down a secession convention.

Even Ellis resisted violent disunion, initially impeding those who wished to seize Federal property within the state. When Lincoln called for volunteers to suppress rebellion in the South, however, Ellis denounced the act as a "wicked violation of the laws of the country" and called on thousands of North Carolinians to arm and oppose invasion. On 20 May 1861, at his urging, a statewide convention was held, adopting a secession ordinance. On 7 July, having barely begun the task of placing North Carolina on a war footing, Ellis died in Red Sulphur Springs, (now W.) Va., reportedly of strain and overwork. —EGL

Ellsworth, Ephraim Elmer. USA b. Malta, N.Y., 11 Apr. 1837. As a boy Ellsworth longed for an appointment to West Point but had no opportunity to prepare for its entrance examination. Leaving home in early youth, he lived in New York City, then Chicago, working as a law clerk and a solicitor of patents.

Ellsworth's interest in soldiering led him to join a Chicago volunteer company about to disband for lack of interest. By his enthusiasm and organizational ability he revived the unit, attracting new members through his introduction of the ZOUAVE dress and drill, patterned after French colonial troops in Algeria. His National Guard Cadets, later renamed the U.S. Zouave Cadets of Chicago, became highly efficient and disciplined, thanks to a regimen that stressed not only tactics but the moral life. Their baggy pants, short jackets, fezzes, and gaiters, as well as their intricate drill evolutions, gained the

USMHI

zouaves attention throughout the Midwest. Soon Ellsworth was appointed a major on the staff of the commander of the Illinois National Guard, and his unit became the governor's guard. In 1860 his cadets made a triumphal tour of major cities in the North, including New York and Washington, D.C.

That August, temporarily abandoning the company, Ellsworth went to Springfield, Ill., to study law in the office of Abraham Lincoln. He remained to serve the future president in the fall campaign and accompanied him to Washington, D.C., early in 1861. Ellsworth's subsequent attempt to secure a War Department position was curtailed by the outbreak of the war, impelling him to go to New York City to raise a regiment of volunteers. He recruited heavily among the city's fire departments, clothing its members in zouave uniforms and training them according to the manual of his cadet company. The regiment was designated the 11th New York Fire Zouaves, with Ellsworth its colonel.

Returning to Washington, he led his zouaves aross the Potomac 24 May to occupy Alexandria, Va. Spying a Confederate flag atop the Marshall House hotel, Ellsworth climbed to the roof and tore it down. While descending the stairs, he was shot to death by the proprietor, James T. Jackson, who was killed a moment later by Pvt. FRANCIS BROWNELL, one of Ellsworth's men.

As the Union's first casualty, Ellsworth became its first martyr, stirring the North's will to fight. Lincoln openly mourned his loss, and his body lay in state at the White House before being returned to upstate New York for burial. —EGL

Ellsworth's Zouaves. USA When the war began, ELMER E. ELLSWORTH, well known in mid-19th-century military circles as the organizer, trainer, and popularizer of ZOUAVE units in several Northern states, raised a regiment from the firemen of New York City. In its early months the regiment adopted the zouave dress (scarlet trousers and blue jacket) and took the name 1st New York Fire Zouaves, or Ellsworth's Zouaves. Officially the unit was the 11th New York Infantry. Eventually it adopted a uniform similar to that worn by the Union army because the zouave uniform proved too conspicuous on the battlefield.

Ellsworth was elected its colonel, and 20 Apr. 1861 the regiment was accepted into state service. Mustered into U.S. service for 2 years on 7 May, the unit spent virtually its entire career in the area around the District of Columbia. The zouaves acquired a reputation for rowdy conduct, but they also helped extinguish a fire that threatened serious damage to the capital. Ellsworth became the first Union martyr when he was killed 24 May after removing a Southern flag from atop a hotel in Alexandria, Va.

The regiment fought at FIRST BULL RUN, 20 July, as part of Brig. Gen. SAMUEL P. HEINTZELMAN's division, and distinguished itself while supporting the Federal artillery. In that battle the zouaves lost 177 men.

Charles M. Leoser was colonel of the 11th New York Aug. 1861–Apr. 1862. That June the regiment was mustered out of service despite the fact that it still had almost a year of its original term of service left.   —RMcM

Elmira Prison. In May 1864 the U.S. War Department learned there were vacant barracks in Elmira, N.Y., that had been used as a rendezvous point earlier in the war. Men were sent to encircle the camp with a stockade fence and make it into Elmira Prison. By July about 700 Confederate prisoners were being transferred there from POINT LOOKOUT, Md., and other overcrowded Federal prisons, and before the end of August they numbered almost 10,000 enlisted men.

Living conditions were bad from the start, with insufficient shelter—the barracks held only half the prisoners; the others were crowded into tents, even in winter—and with a serious sanitary situation presented by a stagnant pond stretching the length of the enclosure, into which sinks drained. The 40-acre camp was below the level of the Chemung River, which bordered it, making drainage difficult.

The prisoners' diet lacked vegetables, and by August there were 793 cases of scurvy. Dr. Eugene F. Sanger, camp surgeon and commandant, feuded constantly about unfilled needs and 1 Nov. 1864 wrote U.S. Army Surgeon General JOSEPH K. BARNES: "Since August there have been 2,011 patients admitted to the hospital and 775 deaths. . . . Have averaged daily 451 in hospital and 601 in quarters, and aggregate of 1,052 per day sick. At this rate the entire command will be admitted to hospital in less than a year and thirty-six percent die."

Winter was severe and prisoners suffered greatly before additional barracks were completed. New prisoners brought the total number confined to 12,122 by 12 May 1865, the last day captives arrived. On 1 July the officer in charge made this accounting of those prisoners of war: released, 8,970; still in hospital, 218; died, 2,917; escaped, 17. 10 escapees had spent 2 months digging a tunnel 66 ft long under the stockade

perimeter, and at 4 a.m., 7 Oct. 1864, had crawled through to freedom.   —PR

Eltham's Landing (Barhamsville; West Point), Va., eng. at. 7 May 1862 The Confederate retreat up the Virginia peninsula from YORKTOWN began 3 May 1862. The Union Army of the Potomac pursued, and a vicious rearguard engagement occurred on the 5th at WILLIAMSBURG. Confederate Gen. JOSEPH E. JOHNSTON ordered a resumption of the withdrawal on the 6th, except for Maj. Gen. GUSTAVUS W. SMITH's wing covering the army's flank along the York River. Concerned about the army's wagon train, Johnston kept Smith's experienced soldiers at Barhamsville, a spot particularly vulnerable to a Federal attack from the river.

Smith waited throughout the morning of 6 May while the wagons rumbled past and the army's rear divisions closed. In the afternoon Smith learned that Federal transports, protected by gunboats, had arrived at the head of the river at Eltham's Landing. Union soldiers soon disembarked, forming a line on the south bank opposite Smith's flank. Johnston reacted swiftly to the news, redirecting the other units of the army toward Smith. By the morning of the 7th, the entire Confederate army was concentrated at Barhamsville.

Smith did not contest the Federal landing on the 6th, hoping to lure the Northerners inland beyond the range of the gunboats' heavy ordnance. But on the morning of the 7th, when the Federals remained behind their works, Smith decided to attack. The Confederate general ordered Brig. Gen. WILLIAM H. C. WHITING's division forward to clear the woods and to advance field artillery for a bombardment of the landing and the transports.

Whiting's brigades drove into the woods, pushing back the Union skirmishers a mile and a half. When Southern artillerists argued that the transports were beyond their range, and with

the Federal infantry sheltered by a bluff, Whiting abandoned the attack. Confederate losses amounted to 48; Federal casualties totaled 186, including 46 prisoners. This minor engagement lasted only 2 hours.

Whiting's advance secured the Confederate flank, permitting the uneventful passage of the wagon train. The other notable incident of the action was the insubordination of a soldier of the 4th Texas. Ordered to advance with unloaded rifles by Brig. Gen. JOHN B. HOOD, the Texans encountered Federal skirmishers. One Union corporal immediately aimed at Hood and a single rifle shot cracked. The Federal fell dead, killed by a Texan who refused to meet an enemy with an empty rifle. His disobedience of orders probably spared the life of one of the Confederacy's greatest generals.   —JDW

Elzey, Arnold. CSA b. "Elmwood," Somerset Cty., Md., 18 Dec. 1816, Arnold Elzey Jones was graduated from West Point in 1837, 33d in his class, at that time dropping his last name for his middle name, that

of his paternal grandmother. In the Seminole War he fought on the frontier against Indians, and in the Mexican War he was brevetted for gallantry.

At the beginning of the Civil War, Captain Elzey commanded the arsenal at Augusta, Ga., which he surrendered to Confederate troops Apr. 1861. Returning with his command to Washington, D.C., he resigned his commission in the U.S. Army on the 25th. Elzey then traveled to Richmond, receiving

LC

a commission as colonel of the 1st Maryland in the Confederate army. At FIRST BULL RUN, as senior colonel, Elzey resumed command of his own brigade when its temporary commander, Brig. Gen. E. KIRBY SMITH, fell severely wounded. As a reward for his performance, he was promoted to brigadier general, to date from 21 July 1861.

During the campaigns of 1862, Elzey commanded a brigade under Maj. Gen. THOMAS J. "STONEWALL" JACKSON, distinguishing himself in Jackson's brilliant 1862 SHENANDOAH VALLEY CAMPAIGN and having a horse shot under him at PORT REPUBLIC in June. At GAINES' MILL, during the SEVEN DAYS' CAMPAIGN, Elzey suffered a grievous wound in the head and face. Incapacitated for several months, he returned to duty with the rank of major general, dated 4 Dec. 1862.

In December the Marylander assumed command of the Department of Richmond, becoming responsible for the defenses of the Confederate capital. He was relieved in Apr. 1864, then in autumn organized the Local Defense Brigade of government clerks. He served briefly in Staunton organizing the Virginia reserves, and subsequently served as chief of artillery of the Army of Tennessee, but apparently was not present during its invasion of Tennessee late in 1864.

Paroled in Washington, Ga., 9 May 1865, Elzey returned to his native state, where he farmed until his death in Baltimore, 21 Feb. 1871.   —JDW

Emancipation Proclamation. Officially, the Civil War was a rebellion, and restoration of the Union was ABRAHAM LIN-

COLN's objective. Though Lincoln opposed slavery, he did not believe that he had authority to act against it. Throughout the war he favored voluntary compensated emancipation and colonization of the slaves once they were released. Concerned about keeping the loyal BORDER STATES within the Union, Lincoln was also influenced by the many Northerners who opposed any move to free the slaves.

Nevertheless, slavery was the cornerstone of the Confederacy, and the issue could not be avoided. Several military commanders tried to liberate slaves, but Lincoln countermanded their orders. Congress also passed several emancipation acts; in Apr. 1862 it abolished slavery in the District of Columbia with compensation, and later in the territories without it. Gradually Lincoln became convinced that he must take some antislavery action to win the war. On 22 Sept. 1862 he issued a preliminary emancipation proclamation, which stated that on 1 Jan. 1863 slaves in rebellious sections of the country should be free and that the government would not repress those attempting to gain their own freedom.

The Emancipation Proclamation of 1 Jan. 1863 followed through by declaring that all slaves in rebellious sections were free. The slaves did not rebel militarily but flocked to the Union lines. Thousands joined the Union armed forces, which now accepted their service. No longer did any European nation seriously consider intervention on the side of the Confederacy.

For the loyal slave states, however, Lincoln still favored compensated emancipation. Though none of them accepted his program, by early 1865 Maryland and Missouri had abolished slavery through state enactments. The 13TH AMENDMENT to the Constitution, Dec. 1865, outlawed slavery and forced its abolition in Delaware and Kentucky. *See also* DISTRICT EMANCIPATION ACT.   —LG

embalmed beef. The Civil War was the first American conflict that saw soldiers issued canned rations. "Embalmed beef" was Union soldier slang for canned beef.   —JES

Emmett, Daniel Decatur. composer b. Mount Vernon, Ohio, 29 Oct. 1815, Emmett was a performer and popular Northern composer, best remembered for having written "DIXIE," the unofficial Southern anthem. Prior to the Civil War he was a bandsman with the 6th U.S. Infantry, during which time he wrote *Emmett's Standard Drummer,* the army's first drum manual. After army service he worked as a performer in circuses and variety shows and by the 1840s had his own minstrel show in New York City.

After an unsuccessful tour in England, Emmett's troupe folded and he joined Bryant's Minstrels in New York City, working with them until 1865 and writing several compositions for them and for his own profit. As well as "Dixie," he composed other popular but now obscure Civil War favorites such as a song of praise to Union Maj. Gen. George B. McClellan, "Mac Will Win the Union Back." A "hit" songwriter, he was known as a popular entertainer by both the Northern and Southern public during the war. But Emmett, a War Democrat, was loyal to the Union cause and did not travel in the Confederacy. The South's adoption of "Dixie" during the war caused him frequent embarrassment.

In the postbellum era he continued in show business until retiring to rural Ohio in 1888. In 1895 he staged a final performing tour of the South. d. on his farm near Mount Vernon, 28 July 1904.   —JES

Emory, William Hemsley. USA b. "Poplar Grove," Anne's City, Md., 7 Sept. 1811. Emory's long and distinguished career with the U.S. Regular Army began with his graduation from the U.S. Military Academy, 14th in the class of 1831. Called "Bold Emory" by classmates, he received the rank of brevet 2d lieutenant in the 4th Artillery, resigning his commission after 4 years' service and reenlisting in 1838 as a 1st lieutenant in the Topographical Engineers. Over the next several years he developed exceptional skill as a surveyor, notably as second-in-command during the Northwest boundary dispute 1844–46. During the Mexican War he served as lieutenant colonel of

NA

volunteers, winning 2 brevets for gallant and meritorious service.

Until the Civil War Emory stayed in the Southwest as a surveyor, as commissioner by presidential appointment to establish the Gadsden Purchase boundaries, and as a writer and compiler of maps of the country west of the Mississippi. He was promoted to captain Apr. 1851, to major of the 2d Cavalry Mar. 1855, and at the outbreak of Civil War held rank as lieutenant colonel, 3d Cavalry.

In Mar. 1861 Emory was sent from Washington, D.C., to FORT SMITH, Ark., with orders to hold Indian Territory. Finding the Confederate position too strong, he withdrew the Federal troops to Fort Leavenworth, Kans., without losing a man in his command.

Emory was commissioned brigadier general of volunteers 17 Mar. 1862. He served under Maj. Gen. GEORGE B. McCLELLAN during the PENINSULA CAMPAIGN, receiving high praise, and 1 of his 4 wartime brevets, for his successful maneuvers to divide the wings of the Confederate army at Hanover Court House 27 May 1862. Ordered to Louisiana in 1863, he assumed division command under Maj. Gen. NATHANIEL P. BANKS and conspicuously led the XIX Corps during the RED RIVER CAMPAIGN in 1864. The expedition itself failed, but at the Battle of MANSFIELD, 8 Apr., Emory's determined stand inspired Brig. Gen. ROBERT A. CAMERON's disorganized division to rally long enough to permit an orderly retreat. Later that year Emory and the XIX Corps were transferred to Maj. Gen. PHILIP H. SHERIDAN's command in the Shenandoah Valley.

Though a dedicated and talented soldier repeatedly brevetted in both the volunteer and Regular armies, Emory did not receive rank as major general of volunteers until 25 Sept. 1865. He returned to the Regular Army and successively commanded the Department of West Virginia, the Department of Washington, and the Department of the Gulf before being retired with the rank of brigadier general 1 July 1876. In all, he devoted 45 years to the military. d. Washington, D.C., 1 Dec. 1887.

—PLF

Enchantress Affair. This early-war *cause célèbre* was created by the U.S. government's desire to eradicate Confederate privateering. On the morning of 6 July 1861, a licensed privateer, the *Jefferson Davis,* overtook a merchant schooner, the *Enchantress,* off the coast of southern Delaware. 5 seamen

from the Confederate raider, under Walter W. Smith, a former pilot from Savannah, boarded the schooner, made captives of her crew, and confiscated $13,000 worth of cargo. 16 days later, however, the *Enchantress* was captured off Hatteras Inlet, N.C., by the USS *Albatross,* a member of the Atlantic Blockading Squadron. The schooner was sent to North Carolina and the raiders were conveyed in irons to the Philadelphia Navy Yard.

On 22 Oct. Smith, the prize master, was tried in Philadelphia circuit court on piracy charges; 3 days later he was convicted and sentenced to death. Subsequently, the other raiders were tried, given the same sentence, and remanded to Philadelphia's Moyamensing Prison to await execution.

Believing that international maritime law, which legitimized privateering in wartime, had been violated, the prisoners' counsel, Nathaniel Harrison, petitioned Jefferson Davis on behalf of his clients. Late in November he asked the Confederate president to "submit some proposition to or to enter into some negotiation or arrangement with the Government of the United States" that would lead to an exchange of prisoners.

By then, however, the Davis government had already taken drastic steps to protect its privateer crews—and to win from its enemy a tacit admission of Confederate nationhood. On 9 Nov. acting Sec. of War JUDAH P. BENJAMIN had ordered Gen. JOHN H. WINDER, Richmond's provost marshal, to choose local prisoners to undergo the same fate as the crew of the *Enchantress* and other privateers convicted of piracy in the North. Winder arranged a lottery among captive Union officers in his department, resulting in the designation of Col. MICHAEL CORCORAN, 69th New York Volunteers, as hostage for Smith. The list of hostages also included 6 other colonels, 2 lieutenant colonels, 3 majors, and 3 captains.

This at last forced the U.S. War Department to alter its stance. Ultimately, none of the captured privateer crewmen were executed, all being declared prisoners of war. This gave the Confederacy a small but significant victory diplomatically and legally at a time when it needed every declaration of national legitimacy it could acquire. —EGL

Enfield rifle. English rifle muskets were extensively used in the Civil War by both sides. Enfield-made rifle muskets, generally referred to today as Enfields, after the British government's Royal Small Arms Factory in Enfield, England, were not used during the war. The British government, sensitive about maintaining neutrality, was not foolish enough to allow government-made weapons to end up in the hands of troops of either side. Instead, the rifle muskets used in this country were made by private contractors in England, in London and Birmingham.

WPC

The Enfield rifle muskets were of the pattern of 1853 with modifications, equipped with the angular bayonet. It was a well-made rifle musket in .577 caliber that fired a smooth-sided minié bullet, and was as accurate as the American Springfield rifle musket. A few other models, primarily 2-band rifles equipped with sword bayonets, were also imported. Unfortunately, parts were not interchangeable among any of these weapons. Only the Royal Small Arms Factory had machinery capable of producing weapons with interchangeable parts; the private contractors finished their weapons by hand. Commanders complained, and with good reason. For instance, if soldiers happened to be wearing bayonets in an emergency in which their arms were stacked, and if the arms were mixed up in the confusion, the consequences could have been serious.

Nonetheless, the Enfield was an extremely popular weapon, and each side imported roughly 400,000. It was considered second only to the Springfield as a primary arm for the infantry.
—LDJ

engagement. Today *engagement* refers to a combat of varying size: a full-scale battle or a limited fight in advance of a battle. A variant, *meeting engagement,* denotes an encounter that surprises either or both opponents. Apparently these definitions were also in use before and during the Civil War.

In the late 1870s, however, *engagement* took on a more specific meaning. During that period boards of army officers studied the varied terminology bestowed on combat through the ages and chose that most applicable to the American experience. The minutes of these boards are available today in the National Archives and reveal that panel members defined *battle* as a wide-scale encounter between major elements of independent commands directed by general officers. The records fail to specify the criteria developed to classify combats of lesser size but suggest that *engagement* denotes a combat of more limited scope, involving subordinate units or detachments of main armies. In size, an engagement ranks just below a battle and above such other loosely defined combats as skirmishes, actions, and affairs.
—EGL

engineers. When the war began, the Union had 2 engineer corps. The Corps of Topographical Engineers conducted explorations, surveys, and reconnaissances of uncharted areas and sites for defenses, first under the command of Col. John J. Abert, then, beginning Sept. 1861, under Col. Stephen H. Long. But for reasons of efficiency, the Corps of Engineers absorbed the topographical engineers in 1863.

The Corps of Engineers' duties included planning and erecting defenses, constructing and destroying roads and bridges, placing and removing obstructions, conducting topographical surveys during campaigns, reconnoitering enemy works, and preparing and distributing accurate maps. The wartime chiefs of engineers, Brig. Gens. JOSEPH G. TOTTEN and Richard Delafield (who succeeded to command in 1864), attempted to perform these duties with an assortment of Regular Army and volunteer officers and men, and with hired civilians.

The Confederacy established a Corps of Engineers com-

NA

manded by 4 chiefs during the war: Brig. Gens. JOSIAH GORGAS and DANVILLE LEADBETTER, Col. Alfred L. Rives, and Maj. Gen. JEREMY F. GILMER. Fortunately, the Confederate engineers obtained the services of trained officers who had resigned from the U.S. Army, but they lacked equipment and maps when the war began. Equipment was purchased from foreign countries, captured from the enemy, and manufactured in the South, but deficiencies continued throughout the war. Among other duties, engineer officers energetically prepared maps that were quickly distributed to the various army commands. The Confederacy also organized engineer troops and hired hundreds of civilians and slaves to work on fortifications, roads, and bridges.

Both Union and Confederate armies were unable or, at times, unwilling to furnish sufficient men and equipment to the corps to complete important tasks. In spite of deficiencies, the engineers performed valuable and diverse services, and many trained engineer officers—among them GEORGE G. MEADE, P.G.T. BEAUREGARD, JOSEPH E. JOHNSTON, and ROBERT E. LEE— became worthy commanders of troops.   —DEF

enlistments.   Neither ABRAHAM LINCOLN nor JEFFERSON DAVIS faced difficulty raising troops early in 1861. Large numbers of volunteers did not wait for the call to arms, but joined local companies being organized, reported to hastily established state camps of instruction, and drilled impatiently as they waited for their regiments to be accepted into national service. North and South, the recruits expected a quick, easy victory. The majority enlisted as short-term soldiers, certain a few months would give them more than enough time to defeat the enemy.

Short-term enlistments presented a dilemma for both chief executives from the start, with Lincoln and Gen. WINFIELD SCOTT in the North and Davis and Vice-President ALEXANDER H. STEPHENS in the South predicting a prolonged, bitter struggle. Nonetheless, state governors and private citizens busily recruited and tried to equip their volunteers. Lincoln's 15 Apr. call for 75,000 volunteers, and Davis' earlier call for 100,000 was answered within a matter of weeks, but there was no uniformity to the enlistments. Some of the state troops, particularly in the South, had signed up for 6-month or 1-year tours of duty. Many Northerners enlisted as 90-day men. New York authorized the enlistment of 30,000 2-year men, some to serve their full term in Federal service, others to serve 90 days at the national level then return home for 2 years' duty in the state.

On 3 May Lincoln issued a second call, asking for 42,034 volunteers to enlist for 3 years or the duration, for an additional 6,347 men to join the Regular Army, and for another 18,000 to join the navy. The same month the administration began trying to enforce extended enlistments. Sec. of War SIMON CAMERON informed each governor of his state's quota, advising him that the Federal government would accept only 3-year troops and a limited number of short-term regiments. Several compromises were made to calm the indignant protests. New York troops were mustered in for 2 years, and some companies mutinied when their enlistments were extended. Other short- or intermediate-term units also were accepted for politically prudent reasons. To an extent the War Department, unprepared to equip, feed, or discipline an untrained volunteer army, insisted on 3-year enlistments to limit the number of men sent to Washington. But the need for Federal control over length of service became more urgent as the nation prepared

for its first battle, in July, at the time the 90-day enlistments were about to expire.

On 6 Mar. the Provisional Confederate Congress called out the state militias and authorized the recruitment of 100,000 volunteers. Until the fall of FORT SUMTER, the Confederacy accepted only 6- and 12-month volunteers recruited at the state and local levels, but Davis had argued consistently for long-term enlistments. In late April the Provisional Congress permitted the president to accept volunteers directly into government service, and approved their enlistment for 3 years. Within a few weeks, the central government called for 400,000 enlistees. Predictably, the governors protested the legislation as a curtailment of STATES RIGHTS, also fearing that government-raised troops would not be counted into state levies. To appease them, Davis accepted the 6- and 12-month soldiers as state troops.

By the end of 1861 war fever had subsided and enlistments fell sharply. In December Confederate Sec. of War JUDAH P. BENJAMIN reported that the short- or intermediate-term enlistments of 148 regiments were due to expire. Though most of the men could be counted on to reenlist, the Confederate Congress began seriously considering the draft legislation that culminated in the Conscription Act of Apr. 1862. One part of it converted 6- and 12-month enlistments into 3-year tours of duty, to be counted from each soldier's original enlistment date. The provision caused bitter resentment among the men and a renewed burst of opposition from state officials, but most Confederates conceded to necessity.

Short-term enlistments led to disorganization and confusion for the rank and file, the commanders, and the bureaucrats of both nations. In its desperate struggle to keep men in the field, the Davis administration alienated large numbers of 6- and 12-month men by pitting voluntary reenlistment against the alternative of being subject to the draft. For the North, tightening Federal control over enlistments was one more step in the reorganization of the national army.   —PLF

***Enrica,* CSS.**   See ALABAMA, CSS.

envelopment.   The object of this offensive, directed against a flank of a fixed position, was to pour an efilading fire along the enemy's line. A double envelopment, usually a risky operation, involved an attack against both flanks simultaneously. A similar though longer-range operation was known as a TURNING MOVEMENT, or strategic envelopment, in which the offensive was directed not against the enemy position itself but toward a point in its rear, compelling the enemy to leave his works and defend that point, making him more vulnerable.

Most Civil War maneuvers were either envelopments or turning movements, since by 1861 the long-range accuracy of rifled small arms had rendered frontal assaults against fixed— especially entrenched—positions extremely costly. It should be noted, however, that Civil War–era tactics manuals did not apply specific definitions to either "envelopment" or "turning movement"; these were not rigidly defined until later in the century. Civil War tacticians used the terms only in their most general sense—in reference to any maneuver that was not a frontal attack.   —EGL

eprouvette.   A small mortar used in testing the strength of gunpowder was called an eprouvette. Its interior did not taper sharply near the base as in other mortars, where the round rested above the powder charge.   —JES

Ericsson, John. inventor b. Langbanshytten, Sweden, 31 July 1803, Ericsson was a mechanical and naval engineer who, while serving in the Swedish military, developed a "caloric" hot-air engine that brought him international attention in 1826. In the next 35 years he developed many ship engines and nautical designs and became a partner of American engineer Robert F. Stockton. Ericsson immigrated to the U.S. in 1839, having built what was then a high-speed English locomotive, the *Novelty,* and having developed a prototype screw-propeller ship design. He is remembered in American history as the inventor of the ironclad *MONITOR.*

LC

Ericsson and Commodore Stockton developed an experimental steam-powered warship, the USS *Princeton.* In 1844, as one of the ship's newly designed cannon was being demonstrated for Washington, D.C., dignitaries, it exploded, killing the U.S. secretaries of state and navy and several others; and, though Stockton had designed the flawed cannon, the tragedy clouded Ericsson's career for several years. From then until the Civil War he worked in New York City as an engineer.

The U.S. Navy was anxious to have a weapon to combat the Confederates' VIRGINIA, then under construction, and 7 Aug. 1861 announced interest in looking at IRONCLAD ship designs. At the urging of industrialist and contractor CORNELIUS S. BUSHNELL, Ericsson submitted a design for a ship he called an "ironclad battery." After initial rejection, the design was accepted 15 Sept., with the provision it be built within 100 days and cost no more than $275,000. Though construction fell slightly behind schedule, the ship slid down the ways at New York's Greenpoint Shipyard 30 Jan. 1862 and was christened *Monitor,* a name Ericsson had suggested.

Following the ship's success against the *Virginia* and in service on the James River, Ericsson worked on other "monitor" designs and successfully modified them to carry 2 revolving gun turrets and handle slightly better in deeper water. After the Civil War he remained a successful inventor until his death in New York City, 8 Mar. 1889.   —JES

Erlanger loan. On 28 Oct. 1862 the Confederate commissioner to France, JOHN SLIDELL, completed negotiations with Émile Erlanger and Co., a Parisian banking house, to manage the sale of a £5 million Confederate bond issue secured by cotton. Congress approved the contract 29 Jan. 1863, after reducing the face value of the issue to £3 million ($14,550,000).

To call the transaction a loan was to use polite businessmen's language for high-risk cotton speculation. The 20-year, 7% bonds were to be convertible into cotton at well below the world market price. The Confederacy hoped the promise of lucrative profits would attract European investors and restore its faltering credit rating abroad.

With the military situation then favoring the Confederacy, the scheme had appeal. Shortages in Europe caused by the Federal blockade had driven the price of cotton to 50 cents a pound in the overseas market, while a glut of cotton in Southern warehouses lowered domestic prices to 12 cents a pound.

The Treasury Department planned to stockpile the commodity at its depreciated value, then use it to redeem the Erlanger notes no later than 6 months after the anticipated peace. Prices were likely to remain high immediately after the war, so speculators could reasonably expect to reap enormous profits. For investors who wanted their cotton during the war, the government delivered it to within 10 mi of a railroad or navigable river; from there the bondholder assumed the risk of transportation.

As the clearinghouse, Erlanger and Co. anticipated large profits, paying £77 for every £100 bond the Confederacy offered. These were to be offered to the public at £90, with a guaranteed 5% commission to brokers. On 19 Mar. the bonds went on sale in Paris, London, Amsterdam, and Frankfurt and were oversubscribed by the end of the day. Success, however, was short-lived. Within a few weeks prices began to fall. Southern sympathizers suspected Union agents of tampering with the market, but prices declined irretrievably after the Confederate losses at VICKSBURG and GETTYSBURG in July.

Nonetheless, Confederate purchasing power had been restored for several months, allowing Southern agents to acquire desperately needed war materials. And though dramatically curtailed, trading did not stop entirely. By 11 Feb. 1865 five-sixths of the bonds had been sold, with the Confederacy realizing returns estimated at between $6 million and $8,535,000. Market manipulations and commissions accounted for the difference between these figures and the bond issue's face value.

—PLF

espionage. By the outbreak of the war, neither the Union nor the Confederacy had established a full-scale espionage system or a military intelligence network. The South, however, was already operating an embryonic spy ring out of Washington, D.C., set up late in 1860 or early in 1861 by THOMAS JORDAN. A former U.S. Army officer, now a Confederate colonel, Jordan foresaw the benefits of placing intelligence agents in the North's military and political nerve center.

By summer 1861, Jordan had turned the ring over to his most trusted operative, ROSE O'NEAL GREENHOW, a local widow of Southern birth. Mrs. Greenhow's high station in Washington society enabled her to secure intelligence of great value to the Confederacy. Much of it reportedly came from an infatuated suitor, HENRY WILSON of Massachusetts, chairman of the Senate Military Affairs Committee. Through a ring of couriers that included a woman named Bettie Duval, Greenhow smuggled information about the southward-marching army under Brig. Gen. IRVIN MCDOWELL to Confederate troops in the vicinity of Virginia's Manassas Junction. There it was received by Colonel Jordan, now chief of staff to the local commander, Gen. P.G.T. BEAUREGARD. The intelligence helped turn FIRST BULL RUN into a Confederate victory.

2 other intelligence networks in the Federal capital, both of later vintage, were supervised by cavalrymen turned spies, Capt. Thomas N. Conrad and Pvt. J. Franklin Stringfellow. These amazingly resourceful operatives were connected with the Confederacy's first organized secret-service bureau, formed in 1862 as a part of the CSA Signal Corps. The head of the bureau, Maj. William Norris, eventually coordinated the activities of dozens of espionage and counterespionage agents who operated along the "Secret Line," an underground link between Richmond and the Washington-Baltimore region. In time, Norris and his assistant, Capt. Charles Cawood, sought

to extend this network of intelligence outlets well above the Mason-Dixon line—as far north as that great base of Confederate espionage operations, Canada. Arguably the most effective military intelligence establishment of the war, Norris's bureau directed all espionage activity along the Potomac River, supervised the passage of agents to and from enemy lines, and forwarded dispatches from the Confederate War and State departments to contacts abroad.

A second Confederate secret-service unit was organized early in 1864. A prototype commando outfit, it was attached to the Torpedo Bureau of Brig. Gen. GABRIEL J. RAINS, but was neither as large nor as well administered as Norris's agency.

The Confederacy was also served by countless private operatives. Probably the most celebrated civilian spy was BELLE BOYD, who risked her life to bring intelligence to Maj. Gen. THOMAS J. "STONEWALL" JACKSON during his SHENANDOAH VALLEY CAMPAIGN of 1862. Less heralded was JAMES HARRISON, an itinerant Richmond actor who late in June 1863 rode to Gen. Robert E. Lee's Pennsylvania headquarters with word that the Army of the Potomac was about to enter the Keystone State in hot pursuit. The unexpected news permitted Lee to mass his scattered army prior to GETTYSBURG.

Confederate spies in uniform (known as "scouts" when wearing their own army's attire, and liable to summary execution if captured in enemy garb) included the cavalry raiders of the "Gray Ghost," JOHN S. MOSBY. Others served the equally daring TURNER ASHBY and the Marylander HARRY GILMOR. Among other soldier-spies were the young Kentuckian Jerome Clarke and SAM DAVIS, the Tennessee farmboy who died a hero's death after refusing to reveal to his Union captors the identity of his raiding leader.

Despite the triumphs of individual spies, most large-scale Confederate espionage efforts failed. Carefully planned but ultimately unsuccessful projects included the Oct. 1864 raid on ST. ALBANS, Vt.; the attempt the following month to burn large sections of New York City; and the NORTHWEST CONSPIRACY.

The Union waited till the shooting started to take steps toward creating an espionage establishment. Its first secret-service bureau was set up in mid-1861 by ALLAN PINKERTON, founder of the famous Chicago detective agency. While serving Maj. Gen. GEORGE B. MCCLELLAN in the Department of the Ohio during the war's first summer, Pinkerton, acting alone, penetrated the Confederacy as far as Jackson, Miss., before returning north with information on Southern war preparations. Following McClellan to Washington, Pinkerton almost singlehandedly broke up Greenhow's spy ring. As military intelligence experts, however, Pinkerton and his band of agents were out of their depth. In 1862, as secret-service chief for McClellan's Army of the Potomac, Pinkerton sent his employer outlandish estimates of enemy strength and dispositions, hindering rather than facilitating McClellan's operations.

The war's first double agent, Timothy Webster, regularly penetrated Southern lines, gathering intelligence in such diverse locales as Baltimore, Louisville, and Memphis, and infiltrating the militant Baltimore society of Confederate sympathizers known as the Knights of Liberty. Webster's services ended in Apr. 1862, however, when a combination of events led to his arrest and execution in Richmond.

One Union spy who made notable contributions throughout the war was ELIZABETH VAN LEW, a longtime resident of the Confederate capital. "Crazy Bett," as the eccentric Unionist was known to her neighbors, ran the largest and most successful spy ring concentrated in any city. Her team of operatives included a freed slave whom she placed as a servant in the Confederate White House to eavesdrop on Pres. Jefferson Davis and his visitors.

An equally infamous Union espionage leader was Brig. Gen. LAFAYETTE C. BAKER, chief of War Department detectives. As the bullyboy of Sec. of War EDWIN M. STANTON, he shadowed, apprehended, interrogated, and imprisoned a multitude of Washingtonians, many on the merest suspicion of disloyalty. Though personally brave, Baker was a ruthless, unsavory character whose high-handed methods and unassailable power made him feared even by associates.

Union espionage work was advanced by dozens of lesser-known Northerners, in and out of uniform. Civilian spies and counterspies included, as in the South, numerous women—whose sex usually spared them the harsher consequences of their actions, if apprehended. One of the most resourceful was SARAH EMMA EDMONDS, who gained entrance to Confederate camps near Yorktown, Va., disguised as a black slave. Much less enterprising and successful was the actress PAULINE CUSHMAN, whose double-agent activities won her undeserved fame as the "Spy of the Cumberland." Male civilians who spied for the North included William A. Lloyd and his business associate, Thomas Boyd, who, as Southern transportation agents of long standing, were able to roam, more or less freely, to Richmond, Savannah, Chattanooga, and New Orleans—Lloyd all the while carrying his espionage contract, signed by ABRAHAM LINCOLN.

Union spies in uniform were more numerous. Probably the most noted was Maj. Henry Young of Rhode Island, whose 58-man band of scouts served Maj. Gen. PHILIP H. SHERIDAN during the war's final year. In the APPOMATTOX CAMPAIGN, the scouts tapped enemy telegraph wires and misdirected supply trains critically needed by Lee's army. Another effective operative in uniform was Col. George H. Sharpe, who in 1864–65 ran the highly efficient military information bureau attached to ULYSSES S. GRANT's headquarters. One of the most publicized espionage operations was conducted by civilian agent JAMES J. ANDREWS in an ambitious but failed attempt to sabotage Confederate rail lines (see ANDREWS' RAID).   —EGL

Etheridge, Annie. vivandière b. Michigan, 3 May 1844. Though born in Michigan, "Gentle Annie" or "Michigan Annie," the best known of the women described as VIVANDIÈRES, spent most of her childhood in Wisconsin. Etheridge remained there when her father settled in Detroit after suffering business reverses sometime before the Civil War. Whether she was married and followed her husband to Detroit, or was visiting her father early in 1861 is uncertain, but she did enlist as a nurse in the 2d Michigan Infantry, transferring later to the 3d Michigan Infantry. At the end of her 3-year tour of duty she reenlisted with the veterans of the 5th Michigan, serving until the surrender.

Popular with the troops and with the public, Etheridge became a kind of folk heroine during and immediately after the hostilities. Many stories were told of her bravery under fire, and at Spotsylvania she is supposed to have rallied retreating troops. She was slightly wounded once, but claimed only services as a nurse in her postwar application for a pension. Following the Confederate surrender the government rewarded her with a civil-service clerkship in Detroit.   —PLF

Evans, Clement Anselm.

Evans, Clement Anselm. CSA b. Stewart Cty., Ga., 25 Feb. 1833, Evans was a young man in a hurry, becoming an attorney before he was 19, a judge at 22, a state senator 4 years later, and an 1860 presidential elector.

Enlisting in the 31st Georgia, Evans was commissioned a major 19 Nov. 1861 and promoted to colonel Apr. 1862, serving with his Georgians throughout the war in the Army of Northern Virginia. Evans commanded his regiment and later a brigade in the division successively belonging to Lt. Gens. THOMAS J. "STONEWALL" JACKSON and JUBAL A. EARLY, and Maj. Gen. JOHN B. GORDON.

LC

Participating in every major battle from the PENINSULA CAMPAIGN in spring 1862 to the surrender at APPOMATTOX 9 Apr. 1865, Evans temporarily succeeded to brigade command at FREDERICKSBURG Dec. 1862. Returning to regimental level, he performed gallantly at CHANCELLORSVILLE, GETTYSBURG, the WILDERNESS, and SPOTSYLVANIA. Promoted to brigadier general 19 May 1864, he assumed command of Gordon's excellent brigade of Georgians, leading it during Early's summer raid on Washington, D.C., during which he suffered a debilitating wound at MONOCACY, 9 July. Evans had been wounded 4 times previously, and this last maiming limited his duty for much of the year. In November he succeeded Gordon in command of the division, leading it at PETERSBURG and until APPOMATTOX, where the unit captured the army's final group of Federals.

The carnage of the war convinced Evans to enter the ministry of the Methodist Episcopal Church. He retired from the ministry in 1892, devoting his final years to veteran affairs and writing. Evans published the *Military History of Georgia* (1895) and edited the valuable 12-volume *Confederate Military History* (1899). Shortly before his death he served as commander in chief of the United Confederate Veterans. The highly esteemed officer died 2 July 1911 in Atlanta.   —JDW

Evans, Nathan George.

Evans, Nathan George. CSA b. Marion, S.C., 3 Feb. 1824. After attending Randolph-Macon College, Evans matriculated at the U.S. Military Academy, graduating 36th in the 38-man class of 1848. Posted to a regiment of dragoons, he served for the next dozen years on the Western frontier. In 1855, he was commissioned 1st lieutenant in the newly organized 2d U.S. Cavalry, in which he distinguished himself during numerous Indian skirmishes.

Evans resigned his captain's commission Feb. 1861 to enter the provisional army of his native state with the rank of major. During the firing on FORT SUMTER, he served as an adjutant general of South Carolina troops

USMHI

and by FIRST BULL RUN had risen to colonel in the Confederacy.

In that initial large-scale engagement of the war, "Shanks" (a nickname that his lean legs had won him) reached the peak of his career. Commanding a 2-regiment brigade on the Confederate left flank near Manassas Junction, he detected the Union advance that inaugurated the battle of 21 July 1861. Though heavily outnumbered, Evans moved swiftly and without specific orders to block the Union turning movement, allowing Gen. P.G.T. BEAUREGARD to meet the enemy on fairly even terms. Finally forced to retreat, Evans' small command was largely responsible for the Federal defeat that resulted.

After serving in the Oct. 1861 Battle of BALL'S BLUFF, winning the THANKS OF THE CONFEDERATE CONGRESS for his role in that morale-strengthening victory, he was promoted to brigadier general as of the date of the engagement. His new rank gained him a command so peripatetic that it became known as the "Tramp Brigade." Evans led it at SECOND BULL RUN and temporarily commanded a division during the ANTIETAM CAMPAIGN.

Early in 1863, the brigade became a part of Gen. JOSEPH E. JOHNSTON's army and fought near VICKSBURG. Later that year Evans' reputation waned, largely because of his intemperance, and he was tried for intoxication and disobedience of orders; though acquitted, he lost his command.

Evans returned to active duty in spring 1864, only to be incapacitated by a fall from his horse. With the collapse of the Confederacy, he fled Richmond with Jefferson Davis before surrendering. After the war, he became principal of a high school in Midway, Ala., where he died 23 Nov. 1868.

—EGL

Evarts, William Maxwell.

Evarts, William Maxwell. USP b. Boston, Mass., 6 Feb. 1818. An 1837 graduate of Yale and an alumnus of Harvard Law School, Evarts was an author of political articles, an assistant U.S. attorney, and the successful counsel in the *Lemmon Slave Case,* which gave freedom to a slave who had escaped in New York City while being taken from Virginia to Texas by ship. In 1860 he headed the New York delegation at the Republican national convention and led the fight for WILLIAM H. SEWARD's nomination.

Evarts was a strong Union man and the secretary of New York's Union Defense Committee in 1861. That year, during the *ENCHANTRESS* AFFAIR, he handled the prosecution involving the Confederate privateer crew and received national attention because of the life-or-death stakes and the delicacy the case required. With his reputation for sensitivity established, he was sent on 2 diplomatic missions to England, in 1863 and 1864, to negotiate for an end to the private construction of Confederate warships. During this period, until SALMON P. CHASE became available for the position, Evarts was under consideration as successor to U.S. Supreme Court Chief Justice ROGER B. TANEY.

Evarts' postwar career was long and distinguished. He served as Pres. ANDREW JOHNSON's attorney general, 1868–69, and chief defense counsel in the impeachment trials; successfully represented a British client in the *ALABAMA CLAIMS* cases; was Pres. Rutherford B. Hayes's secretary of state, 1877–81; and a 1-term U.S. senator 1885–91. d. New York City, 28 Feb. 1901.

—JES

Ewell, Richard Stoddert.

Ewell, Richard Stoddert. CSA b. District of Columbia, 8 Feb. 1817, Ewell moved with his family to Prince William Cty., Va., when he was 9. Like his brother Benjamin, he attended the U.S. Military Academy, graduating 13th in the class of 1840. Receiving a commission in the 1st U.S. Dragoons, he reported to Carlisle Barracks, Pa., for training, then went to Fort Wayne in present-day Oklahoma. Given a brevet captaincy for his conduct in the Mexican War, Ewell served in Baltimore, then returned to the Southwest. In Virginia on sick leave when the Civil War began, he resigned his commission as captain in the U.S. Army 7 May 1861.

USMHI

Initially a lieutenant colonel in the Virginia forces, Ewell became a colonel in the Confederate army, commanding a camp of cavalry instruction. He was promoted to brigadier general 17 June 1861, and major general 24 Jan. 1862. He served with distinction at FIRST BULL RUN and CEDAR MOUNTAIN and in the SHENANDOAH VALLEY and SEVEN DAYS' campaigns.

Losing a leg at GROVETON, Aug. 1862, Ewell was equipped with a wooden one and returned to duty 23 May 1863 as a lieutenant general to replace THOMAS J. "STONEWALL" JACKSON in command of the II Corps. Though riding was difficult, "Old Bald Head," an affectionate nickname given Ewell by his men, was an active campaigner from GETTYSBURG to SPOTSYLVANIA COURT HOUSE, even though he was wounded twice. At the "BLOODY ANGLE," a fall from his horse incapacitated him from further field command and thereafter he commanded the Department of Henrico and then the defenses of Richmond. Captured at SAYLER'S CREEK 6 Apr. 1865, he was imprisoned in Fort Warren, Mass., until 19 Aug.

Ewell retired to a farm near Spring Hill, Tenn., and died there 25 Jan. 1872. His final years were clouded because some blamed him for the Confederate defeat at Gettysburg. On the first day of the battle Ewell chose not to capture CEMETERY HILL, but control of that position could not by itself have ensured a victory.   —DEF

Ewing, Hugh Boyle. USA b. Lancaster, Ohio, 31 Oct. 1826. The scion of Ohio's privileged Ewing family, Hugh, brother of THOMAS and Charles, and foster brother of WILLIAM T. SHERMAN, started life as a worry to his kin. Privately tutored at home, he entered West Point with its 1848 class but, failing the engineering exams, was compelled to resign before graduation. Ewing joined the gold rush of 1849 but found no gold and came east in 1852, setting up a law practice in St. Louis, then trying to establish one in Leavenworth, Kans., with help from his brother Tom and William Sherman.

After returning to Ohio in 1858, Ewing received his first

NA

opportunity to exercise public responsibility May 1861, when Ohio Gov. WILLIAM DENNISON, a political associate of Hugh's family, appointed him brigade inspector of state volunteers. He soon served under Gens. GEORGE B. MCCLELLAN and WILLIAM S. ROSECRANS in the first western Virginia campaigning, and was

appointed colonel of the 30th Ohio Infantry 20 Aug. After the reorganization and reassignment of state troops, he was sent to the Army of the Potomac, in which he received favorable notice for his bravery at the Battle of SOUTH MOUNTAIN and industry at the Battle of ANTIETAM. In this theater he successively led a regiment, then a brigade of the IX Corps, and was appointed a brigadier general of volunteers 29 Nov. 1862.

During the SECOND VICKSBURG CAMPAIGN, Ewing served under Major General Sherman in the XV Corps. Capable performance won him command of Brig. Gen. WILLIAM SOOY SMITH's old XVI Corps division, which had been transferred to the XV Corps. He then took command of the XV Corps' 4th Division and led it through the Tennessee fighting. At the Battle of MISSIONARY RIDGE at Chattanooga his command headed the army's assault on Confederate Maj. Gen. PATRICK R. CLEBURNE's line. The Confederates were committed to desperate defense, hit Ewing's men with all their available ordnance, then pelted tnem with rocks and debris.

When the Confederates retreated to Georgia, Ewing was given charge of the occupation forces in Louisville, Ky. After a year of this duty he rejoined Sherman's army, then in North Carolina, and began plans for a thrust up the Roanoke River in the Confederate rear. But the war ended before this could happen, and Ewing was mustered out of volunteer service 15 Jan. 1866; on leaving he was brevetted a major general for more than 4 years of service.

Ewing's war record won him influence in peacetime. Appointed U.S. minister to Holland, he served there until 1870. After a brief period practicing law in Washington, D.C., in the early 1870s, he moved to a farm near Lancaster, Ohio, and pursued a career as a writer until his death there 30 June 1905.
                                                                —JES

Ewing, Thomas, Jr. USA b. Lancaster, Ohio, 7 Aug. 1829. Son of a prominent public official and brother of future Union Gen. HUGH B. EWING, Thomas also distinguished himself in the national spotlight. Ewing became a private secretary to Pres. Zachary Taylor in 1848, the year before his father, Thomas, Sr., began serving as U.S. secretary of the interior. He soon entered Brown University, graduating in 1854, and studied law in Cincinnati, where he was admitted to the bar.

He moved his practice to Leavenworth, Kans., in 1856 and joined the firm of Sherman & McCook until he became a member of the Kansas peace conference in 1861. Ewing

NA

fought to stop the admission of Kansas to the Union as a slave state and until the war served as Kansas' first supreme court chief justice.

Ewing joined the army in 1862 as a colonel in charge of recruiting for the 11th Kansas Cavalry. After commanding the regiment at Cane Hill and PRAIRIE GROVE, he accepted a promotion to brigadier general, 13 Mar. 1863, and command of the District of the Border. Here Ewing became known for issuing GENERAL ORDER NO. 11, dictating the evacuation of 4 Missouri counties thought to contain Southern sympathizers harboring

Col. WILLIAM C. QUANTRILL's guerrillas. In 15 days all inhabitants were to leave those counties; Ewing's command, backed by an order from Pres. Abraham Lincoln, was to execute all violators.

Ewing finished military service Feb. 1865 after notable performances against Maj. Gen. STERLING PRICE during his 1864 Missouri Raid and at the battle at Pilot Knob.

After the war he practiced law in Washington, D.C., for several years, turning down appointments of U.S. attorney general and secretary of war. He then served his home state in the U.S. House of Representatives for 2 terms, 1877–81, finally practicing law in New York City from 1881 until his death there 21 Jan. 1896.   —FLS

Excelsior Brigade. USA Civil War soldiers usually enlisted in regiments, which then formed brigades at the front. The Excelsior Brigade, however, was among the few outfits recruited as a brigade. The controversial Democratic politician DANIEL E. SICKLES raised the brigade of 5 regiments (1st–5th Excelsior, later designated 70th–74th New York) in New York City immediately after war erupted. Disputes between state and national officials threatened the brigade's survival, but Washington eventually accepted it. Immediately after FIRST BULL RUN, 3 of Sickles' regiments rushed to the capital, the other 2 joining them later in 1861.

His brigade became the 2d Brigade/Hooker's division/ Army of the Potomac (later 2d Brigade/2d Division/III Corps; 2d Brigade/4th Division/II Corps; and 4th Brigade/3d Division/II Corps). Sickles led it May 1861–Mar. 1862 and May–July 1862. Its subsequent generals were John J. Abercrombie, May 1862; Joseph W. Revere, Dec. 1862–May 1863; Charles K. Graham, Feb.–Mar. 1863; and Francis B. Spinola, July 1863. It also frequently served under Cols. Nelson Taylor, 1862, and William R. Brewster, 1863–64.

Though inseparably associated with its name, Sickles actually commanded it in battle only at SEVEN PINES and during the SEVEN DAYS' CAMPAIGN. It fared worse under its later generals —disastrously under Revere at CHANCELLORSVILLE, uselessly under Spinola at Manassas Gap. Its glory was won mostly under its colonels: Taylor at WILLIAMSBURG, FIRST BRISTOE STATION, and SECOND BULL RUN; and Brewster at GETTYSBURG, MINE RUN, the WILDERNESS, SPOTSYLVANIA, NORTH ANNA, COLD HARBOR, and PETERSBURG.

By early 1864 the brigade had received reinforcements: the 120th New York Regiment, Dec. 1862; and the 11th Massachusetts Regiment and 84th Pennsylvania Regiment, Mar. 1864, the latter 2 joining when the II Corps absorbed the III Corps. The Excelsior Brigade did not long survive its old corps. Four of its regiments did not reenlist. The 70th and much of the 72d and 74th went home in June 1864, the 71st departed in July, and the rest of the 74th left in August. By then the Excelsior Brigade was no more. On 5 July it was distributed among Brig. Gen. Gershom Mott's other 3 brigades. Only the 73d and 120th remained until Appomattox.   —RJS

exchange. *See* PAROLE.

Ezra Church, Ga., Battle of. 28 July 1864   Though Confederate Gen. JOHN BELL HOOD's savage sorties 20 and 22 July 1864 failed to wreck a portion of Maj. Gen. William T. Sherman's army and drive him away from Atlanta, they did, with the help of Atlanta's strong fortifications, block the Union drives on the city from the north and east. Consequently, Sherman looked to the west.

USMHI

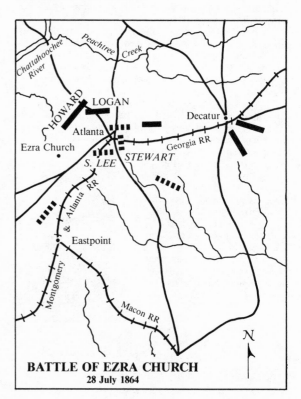

BATTLE OF EZRA CHURCH
28 July 1864

Between 25–27 July Sherman transferred the Army of the Tennessee, now commanded by Maj. Gen. OLIVER O. HOWARD, from his left to his right wing, ordering it 28 July to advance and cut the railroad between Atlanta and East Point, Hood's only remaining supply line.

Hood detected this maneuver, perceived its intent, and sought to turn it to Confederate advantage by sending portions of 2 corps, Lt. Gens. STEPHEN D. LEE's and A. P. STEWART's, to ambush Howard's column southwest of Atlanta. On the afternoon of 28 July Lee's Corps, followed by Stewart's, attacked Howard near Ezra Church. But instead of striking the Federals' open flank as planned, the Confederates ran against the front of Maj. Gen. JOHN A. LOGAN's XV Corps, which, in anticipation of the Confederate move, had formed a barricaded line at a right angle to the rest of Howard's force.

Although the Southern troops for the most part charged with their usual bravery, their attempt to overrun Logan was futile; 5,000 of them were killed, wounded, or captured, whereas Logan lost only 562 men. Further, only a misleading map prevented Sherman from falling on the left flank of the attacking force, thereby totally destroying it and opening the way for the quick capture of Atlanta.

Hood's foray at Ezra Church did stop Sherman from cutting Atlanta's supply line, but the heavy losses suffered by the Confederates in this and their previous sorties destroyed their offensive power and spirit. Henceforth Hood had no choice but to stand on the defensive.   —AC

F

Fagan, James Fleming. CSA b. Clark Cty., Ky., 1 Mar. 1828. After spending his first 10 years near Louisville, Fagan moved with his family to Arkansas, where his father worked as a state building contractor in Little Rock. His father died soon after, and his mother remarried. When his stepfather died, Fagan handled the affairs of the family farm near the Saline River and later served in the state general assembly as a Whig from Saline County.

In the Mexican War he fought under Col. Archibald Yell as a lieutenant and in 1861 was among the first military men to raise a company of recruits in defense of the state. After serving initially as captain of the company, he was appointed colonel of the 1st Arkansas Infantry and on 12 Sept. 1862 received a promotion to brigadier general in command of a brigade of Arkansas regiments. Fagan subsequently played vital roles in the battles at Helena, Hindman's Hill, Shreveport, Mansfield, and Pleasant Hill.

MC

His most important military accomplishment came in the 1864 Confederate repulse of Union Maj. Gen. FREDERICK STEELE's campaign against Camden, Ark. On 25 Apr. Fagan's division captured over 200 Federal wagons and inflicted 1,600 casualties at what has been called "the slaughter at Marks' Mills." This successful operation cut Steele off from sorely needed supplies and forced the Northerners to give up Camden (*see* CAMDEN EXPEDITION, ARK.).

For his service in Maj. Gen. STERLING PRICE's final raid through Missouri, Fagan, a major general since 25 Apr. 1864, was commended by Price as one who "bore himself throughout the whole expedition with unabated gallantry and ardor." Fagan fought to the end of the war in Apr. 1865.

After the war he turned to farming and public service, accepting appointments as U.S. marshal and land-office receiver. In 1890 he lost the election for Arkansas state railroad commissioner and died 1 Sept. 1893 in Little Rock.   —FLS

Fairbanks, Erastus. war governor b. Brimfield, Mass., 28 Oct. 1792. A 7th-generation descendant of Yorkshiremen, Fairbanks moved to St. Johnsbury, Vt., at 23. There he and his 2 younger brothers extended their family's saw and grist mill into a manufacturing concern that continued to expand for many years. The business doubled in value every 3 years between 1842 and 1857, turning out goods ranging from cast-iron plows to platform scales.

Fairbanks did not allow business success to dull his sense of public responsibility: in 1836 he was elected to the lower house of the Vermont legislature; in 1844 and 1848 he was a Whig presidential elector; and in 1852 he was elected governor, a position in which he promoted educational and social welfare.

Such advocacy hurt him politically. By signing a bill, passed by the legislature, that prohibited the sale of intoxicating liquors in the state, he made powerful enemies who helped deprive him of reelection. In 1856 he cast his lot with the fledgling REPUBLICAN PARTY, and 4 years later, though almost 70, he easily won another term as governor.

From the outset he promoted the war for the Union. On the day Abraham Lincoln issued his first call for troops, Fairbanks convened the legislature in special session to organize, arm, and equip the militia to answer that call. He went beyond duty by offering his firm's credit as backing for raising needed resources. These and other efforts gained him the thanks of the War Department, which praised his "patriotic ardor and energy." Later the governor won Lincoln's appreciation by persuading the legislature to empower Fairbanks to establish state recruiting stations and draft a sufficient number of Vermonters to make up for shortfalls in volunteering.

When Fairbanks left office in 1862, the administration in Washington lost one of its staunchest and most effective supporters. His health undermined by years of political battles, the former governor died in St. Johnsbury, 20 Nov. 1864.

—EGL

Fair Gardens (Kelly's Ford), Tenn., eng. at. 27 Jan. 1864 Ordered to push Lt. Gen. JAMES LONGSTREET's Confederates north from their East Tennessee winter quarters at Russellville and Morristown, Maj. Gen. JOHN G. FOSTER's Union cavalry began ineffective operations south of the French Broad River Jan. 1864. Foster's cavalry, led by Brig. Gen. SAMUEL D. STURGIS, saw only 3 days of significant fighting.

Operating from their temporary base at Sevierville, about 19 mi southeast of Knoxville, Sturgis' regiments fanned out north and east, probing fords on the French Broad and looking for forage in the depleted country around Newport. When Federal cavalry appeared at fords around Dandridge, a town roughly midway between Sturgis' base and Morristown, Longstreet dispatched Maj. Gen. WILLIAM T. MARTIN with Brig. Gen. JOHN T. MORGAN's cavalry division to cross the French Broad, travel south, and hit Sturgis in the rear. Brig. Gen. FRANK C. ARMSTRONG's Confederate cavalry division followed close behind.

Martin's horsemen, with artillery, advanced to the Fair Gardens area, 10 mi east of Sturgis' base, and 26 Jan. drove one of the Federal flank regiments west to the Dickey House, where the Sevierville road forked and became the Fair Gardens and Newport roads. Armstrong's division attacked a second Union regiment 6 mi northeast of Sevierville and pushed it to within 2.5 mi of the town. On the 27th, Sturgis advanced on the Confederate line that ran from a ridge near the Dickey House southeast to McNutt's Bridge, also called Kelley's Ford, on the Big East Fork of the Little Pigeon River. 2 mounted regiments, 1 dismounted regiment, and Capt. Eli Lilly's 18th Indiana Battery pressed Martin's line back a mile, then crossed the East Fork under cover of Lilly's guns. A brigade under Col. Oscar H. La Grange pressed Confederates from the Fair Gardens road toward McNutt's Bridge. Martin's troops put up stiff resistance at a wooded hill three-quarters of a mile behind the bridge, then fell back to Fair Gardens. A day of charges and countercharges climaxed with a rush down the Fair Gardens road by members of the 2d and 4th Indiana Cavalry, netting 112 Confederate prisoners and 2 cannon.

Confederates fell back to Swann's Island on the French Broad after skirmishing on the 28th. At the river, fighting broke off with the appearance of Armstrong's cavalry backed by Longstreet with elements of Brig. Gen. BUSHROD R. JOHNSON's infantry division. Sturgis' troops withdrew to Sevierville and Martin's force returned north of the French Broad. Skirmishes and maneuvers continued in the region through February.

In the 27 Jan. engagement Martin lost 200 men killed, wounded, and captured. Sturgis' force lost 60–70 troopers from all causes.   —JES

Fair Oaks, Va., Battle of. 31 May–1 June 1862 *See* SEVEN PINES, VA., BATTLE OF.

Falling Waters, Md., eng. at. 14 July 1863 The Confederate retreat from GETTYSBURG began 4 July 1863 as the defeated Army of Northern Virginia wearily filled the Pennsylvania and Maryland roads for 3 days, its wagon train of wounded alone stretching for 17 mi. Heavy downpours hampered the march, but Gen. ROBERT E. LEE's Confederates reached the Potomac River at Williamsport, Md., on the afternoon of the 6th and continued to arrive into the morning hours of the 7th.

Since the rains had swelled the river, making it unfordable, Lee ordered the construction of PONTOON BRIDGES while his infantry and artillery erected a defensive line from Williamsport to Falling Waters. Little occurred except cavalry clashes and skirmishes until 12 July, when Maj. Gen. GEORGE G. MEADE's pursuing Army of the Potomac arrived opposite the Confederate position. The Federals, battered at Gettysburg as badly as the Southerners, simply entrenched before the Confederate works.

By the next day the Potomac was passable at Williamsport, and the Southern engineers had completed the pontoon bridge at Falling Waters. Lee ordered the retreat. Under the cover of darkness, the Confederates crossed to Virginia in a skillfully executed move, and by 11 o'clock the next morning all units had reached the south bank, except for 2 divisions at Falling Waters.

Meade, meanwhile, had ordered a reconnaissance in force for 7 a.m. on the 14th. The advancing Federals found only abandoned works at Williamsport, while at Falling Waters the 2 Confederate divisions lay encamped over a mile from the river. Maj. Gen. JOHN BUFORD's and Brig. Gen. H. JUDSON KILPATRICK's cavalry divisions led the Federal advance at Falling Waters. Buford, approaching from the north, charged first.

Before his assault could develop, however, Kilpatrick permitted 2 small squadrons to attack the surprised Confederates of Maj. Gen. HENRY HETH's division. In the melee the Southerners, using rifles, fence rails, and axes, unhorsed most of these Federal horsemen. Alerted, the Confederates fought stubbornly when Kilpatrick attacked with strength and Buford struck from the east. Before the 2 Confederate divisions could cross, they lost 719 officers and men as prisoners and abandoned 2 cannon. Their most grievous loss was Brig. Gen. JAMES J. PETTIGREW, who was mortally wounded in the initial attack.

Because of the Federals' failure to destroy the Confederate army, Northern generals exaggerated considerably the South's losses at Falling Waters. The Union cavalry had only surprised Heth's soldiers, inflicting minimal casualties.   —JDW

Farnsworth, Elon John. USA b. Green Oak, Mich., 30 July 1837, Farnsworth entered the University of Michigan in 1855 but 2 years later was expelled for participating in a carousal that caused the death of a fellow student. As a civilian he accompanied Col. ALBERT SIDNEY JOHNSTON's Utah Expedition of 1858–59, serving as forage master. Soon after the outbreak of the Civil War, he joined the 8th Illinois Volunteer Cavalry, organized and originally commanded by his uncle, former congressman JOHN F. FARNSWORTH.

USMHI/MA

Young Farnsworth rose rapidly from adjutant to company commander and was reportedly present for each of the more than 40 battles and skirmishes in which his regiment participated until mid-1863. During this time he also won publicity for his patriotism and impetuousness, hauling an Episcopal rector from his Alexandria, Va., pulpit for omitting the customary prayer for the health of the president of the U.S.

In spring 1863 Farnsworth accepted a position on the staff of Brig. Gen. ALFRED PLEASONTON, commanding a cavalry division in the Army of the Potomac. Coveting promotion, Pleasonton induced Farnsworth to ask his uncle (once again a congressman) to intercede with his old friend, ABRAHAM LINCOLN, on Pleasonton's behalf. When, soon afterward, the cavalry leader received a second star and command of the army's cavalry corps, he advanced Farnsworth to brigadier general of volunteers.

Farnsworth saw his first service in brigade command at the outset of the GETTYSBURG CAMPAIGN. At Hanover, Pa., 30 June 1863, Farnsworth's men, part of Brig. Gen. H. JUDSON KILPATRICK's 3d Cavalry Division, were attacked and nearly routed by Maj. Gen. J.E.B. STUART's troopers. 3 days later, before PICKETT'S CHARGE, Kilpatrick went into position along the Union left flank below Gettysburg. After the charge he ordered Farnsworth to lead a regiment against Confederate infantry and artillery positioned behind stone walls atop high ground. By this action Kilpatrick hoped to divert attention from any counterattack Union troops might make in the wake of their repulse of Pickett's Charge. Farnsworth protested that the mission was suicidal, whereupon Kilpatrick questioned his courage and offered to lead the charge himself.

Stung by the affront, Farnsworth followed Kilpatrick's orders, losing a quarter of his command. Unharmed after a circuitous ride among the enemy, he was cut down when he inexplicably retraced his path past the Southerners' positions. Confederate observers claimed he died by his own hand after being wounded numerous times.   —EGL

Farragut, David Glasgow. USN b. Campbell's Station, Tenn., 5 July 1801. Through the influence of Cmdr. David D. Porter, who had adopted him, Farragut was commissioned a midshipman 17 Dec. 1810, serving under Porter during the War of 1812. A prize master at 12, Farragut was promoted to lieutenant in 1822, to commander in 1844, and to captain in 1855.

USMHI

Farragut was a resident of Norfolk, Va., when that state seceded Apr. 1861. Unwelcome because of his Union sympathy, he moved north, where his loyalty was initially suspected. But Dec. 1861 Sec. of the Navy GIDEON WELLES put Farragut in command of the West Gulf Blockading Squadron and ordered him to capture New Orleans. Farragut spent 2 months putting together a squadron at Ship Island, then moved against FORTS JACKSON AND ST. PHILIP, which guarded the river passage to New Orleans. His force consisted of 24 wooden vessels and 19 mortar boats under his adoptive brother, Cmdr. DAVID D. PORTER. On 24 Apr. 1862 the fleet succeeded in passing the forts and, 25 Apr., New Orleans surrendered. The impressive victory, in which the navy played a major part, brought Farragut's promotion to rear admiral 16 July 1862, along with a vote of thanks by a grateful Congress.

During summer 1862, Farragut operated on the Mississippi, but army and navy attempts to capture Vicksburg failed. He tightened the blockade of the Gulf Coast, but Mobile still held out, protected by Forts Gaines and Morgan. Early in 1864 Farragut was ordered to capture Mobile and, after months of meticulous planning, he began the Battle of MOBILE BAY, 5 Aug. The Federal fleet moved through the channel port and past the guns of FORT MORGAN. The waters were heavily mined, and when the *Tecumseh* struck a torpedo and sank, the rest of the squadron hesitated. Tied to the rigging of the *Hartford,* Farragut called out, "Damn the torpedoes! Full steam ahead!" Token Confederate naval resistance ended with the capture of the CSS *Tennessee* and her captain, Adm. FRANKLIN BUCHANAN. Fort Morgan surrendered 23 Aug. The Battle of Mobile Bay was Farragut's greatest victory and resulted in his promotion to vice-admiral.

Ill health prevented Farragut's participation in the FORT FISHER campaigning, but he recovered sufficiently to be on the James River early in 1865.

After the war, Farragut was made a full admiral, and in 1867–68 he commanded the European Squadron. d. Portsmouth, N.H., 14 Aug. 1870.   —NCD

fascine. A bundle of sticks or twigs used to reinforce earthworks, trench walls, or lunettes, a fascine was a field substitute for a sandbag or cotton bale, the most preferred reinforcing

materials. Usually buried in the earth interior of a wall, a fascine had a bristling top that would often protrude above hastily built field fortifications and give the impression of being a defensive feature like an ABATIS.   —JES

Fauntleroy, Charles Magill. CSN b. Winchester, Va., 1 Aug. 1822, Fauntleroy was appointed an acting midshipman from Virginia 3 Mar. 1838 and was promoted to lieutenant in 1852. On 7 Apr. 1861 he resigned from the service, but his resignation was not accepted and he was dismissed as of the 7th. After briefly serving in the Virginia navy, Fauntleroy was appointed lieutenant in the Confederate navy, 10 June. The next month he was temporarily assigned to duty in the army, as captain and aide-de-camp to Gen. JOSEPH E. JOHNSTON. An ordnance officer at FIRST BULL RUN, Fauntleroy later that year commanded the naval defenses at Harpers Ferry.

When the CSS *Nashville* ran the BLOCKADE out of Charleston in October, Fauntleroy was executive officer aboard. Then, after the *Nashville*'s return from England Feb. 1862, he was detached for army duty at Richmond. Because of his reputation as a gunnery expert, he was selected to command the batteries at DREWRY'S BLUFF, 15 May 1862. He also fought at SEVEN PINES, 31 May–1 June, being promoted to colonel in the Confederate army in September.

At sea again, Fauntleroy captained the blockade runner *Economist.* Then, while in France Mar. 1864, he received orders from Flag Officer SAMUEL BARRON in Paris to take command of the *RAPPAHANNOCK,* at Calais for repairs. A few weeks thereafter the ship's assistant paymaster, Douglas F. Forrest, described the new commander as "an exceedingly courteous gentleman, cheerful although not always gay, dignified . . . [who] gives the greatest promise of an efficient commander." But Forrest did not have the chance to serve under Fauntleroy at sea because the *Rappahannock* never sailed as a CONFEDERATE CRUISER. Convinced that the South was losing the war, Napoleon III detained the ship at Calais until war's end. Fauntleroy's last official duty was to pay off and discharge the *Rappahannock*'s officers and crew.

He returned to Virginia, where he married for a third time in July 1867 and settled on his wife's plantation near New Orleans, La. d. Leesburg, Va., 28 July 1889.   —NCD

Fayetteville, N.C., Union occupies. 11 Mar. 1865 By early Mar. 1865, the BUMMERS and incendiaries of Maj. Gen. WILLIAM T. SHERMAN's armies had laid waste to vast portions of South Carolina. Though milder, the Federals' treatment of North Carolina, into which they began crossing on the 3d, was harsh enough to linger in residents' minds for decades.

Early on the morning of the 11th, in advance of the main Union command, 67 horsemen under Capt. William R. Duncan clattered into Fayetteville, the first sizable Tarheel community on Sherman's route. At once they clashed with Lt. Gen. WADE HAMPTON and a small detachment of his cavalry that had spent the previous night there. The Federals might have nabbed the general but for the vigilance of one of his scouts, who rounded up a mounted force much smaller but more aggressive than Duncan's. Charging down from the other end of town, they stampeded the invaders, killing 11 and capturing 12, including the captain.

Fayetteville's deliverance was short-lived. Hampton and his men soon rode north, just before a 200-troop detachment of Brig. Gen. GILES A. SMITH's 4th Division/XVII Corps entered the city. Aided by Duncan's survivors, the newcomers took possession of Arsenal Hill, a commanding eminence; they chased Hampton's rear guard over the Cape Fear River Bridge but could not prevent the retreating cavalry from burning it. Soon Sherman's advance body trooped in, secured the town, and formally received its surrender from Mayor Archibald McLean.

During the 5 days the Northerners occupied Fayetteville, little personal violence was inflicted on the citizenry, but the destruction of property useful to the Confederacy was extensive. The Federals torched the city's U.S. arsenal, which had been furnishing weapons to the South since early in 1861, as well as all railroad property, factories, tanneries, gristmills, cotton mills, warehouses, and banks. The offices of 3 newspapers were also burned, while many private residences were ransacked before the establishment of a city-wide provost guard by Brig. Gen. ABSALOM BAIRD, whom Sherman appointed military governor of Fayetteville. Until the Federals marched north toward Goldsborough on the 15th, an area resident complained "there was no place, no chamber, trunk, drawer, desk, garret, closet, or cellar that was private to their unholy eyes. Their rude hands spared nothing but our lives...."   —EGL

Featherston, Winfield Scott. CSA b. Murfreesboro, Tenn., 8 Aug. 1820. In 1861 Featherston was elected colonel of the 17th Mississippi Infantry and sent to Virginia. By that time the colonel was already a combat veteran and a prominent member of the community of Holly Springs. He had fought in the Creek Indian Wars of the late 1830s when he was a teen-ager, then migrated to Mississippi. At the start of the Civil War he had been practicing law in the state for nearly 20 years and had been elected to the U.S. House of Representatives in 1847.

LC

Under senior Col. EPPA HUNTON, Featherston and the 17th went into combat at the Oct. 1861 Battle of Ball's Bluff. Near the end of the fight, on Hunton's order, Featherston led his men in a charge that pushed the men of Union Col. EDWARD D. BAKER off the edge of a towering cliff to the rocks below, putting a gruesome finish to the battle and causing a stir in the Federal capital.

Featherston spent that fall and all the next year in the Eastern theater. He was given a brigadier general's commission 4 Mar. 1862, at the beginning of the Siege of YORKTOWN; fought through the PENINSULA CAMPAIGN; was hotly engaged on the Confederate right at the Battle of GAINES' MILL; saw action at the SECOND BATTLE OF BULL RUN, badly beating Union Brig. Gen. GEORGE SYKES's force on the second day of combat; and fought at the BATTLE OF FREDERICKSBURG, under Maj. Gen. RICHARD H. ANDERSON, laying a punishing fire on assaulting Federal troops. Throughout this time his brigade was made up of the 12th, 16th, 19th, and 48th Mississippi regiments.

In 1863, at his request, Featherston was transferred to the Western theater, where he was assigned a brigade in Maj. Gen. WILLIAM WING LORING's division for service with the Vicksburg garrison. But along with other reinforcing units, Featherston's men did not arrive in time to prevent the Federals' envelop-

ment of the city. Though they were unable to help, they did escape capture when the city was surrendered. With the Army of Tennessee as part of Polk's Corps, he served through the ATLANTA CAMPAIGN and the FRANKLIN AND NASHVILLE CAMPAIGN, briefly led Loring's division, and soldiered through all the army's marches and fights to the surrender in North Carolina. Throughout the campaigning he commanded infantry, with one exception: at a little battle at Utoy Creek, outside Atlanta, Maj. Gen. JAMES P. ANDERSON gave him command of a section of Parrott guns, with which he held off the Federals' advance.

Following the war Featherston returned to Mississippi, became a militant Democrat, fought for the ouster of Reconstruction governor ADELBERT AMES, and served in the state legislature. On 28 May 1891, a year after completing work as a member of the state's 1890 constitutional convention, he died in Holly Springs.   —JES

feint. When a small, vigorous attack was launched by a detachment against a part of the enemy's line or in a sector other than the one targeted for the main attack, it was referred to as a feint. It was meant as a distraction, and ensured the commitment of enemy troops away from the point of the primary assault. *See also* DEMONSTRATION.   —JES

Fenton, Reuben Eaton. war governor b. Carroll, N.Y., 4 July 1819, Fenton ended his early education at 17, when his father's business failed, forcing the young man to go to work. After years of strenuous labor in lumber camps, he paid his father's debts and began a legal and political career. Admitted to the bar in 1841, Fenton became supervisor of his hometown 2 years later. In 1849 he was elected to the state assembly as a Democrat and was sent to Congress in 1852.

NA

Soon after taking his place in the House of Representatives, Fenton broke with his party over slavery, opposing its expansion into the territories. He became a founder of the Republican party in New York, in 1855 presiding over the first state convention there. The following year he was returned to Congress as a Republican, serving in the House from March 1857 until late in 1864, when he entered the gubernatorial race. Appreciating the importance of unseating Democrat HORATIO SEYMOUR, an intractable enemy of the Lincoln administration and particularly of the government's conscription policies, Fenton conducted a vigorous campaign. His efforts were rewarded when he won a larger proportion of the state vote than Abraham Lincoln himself.

In the executive mansion at Albany, Fenton was a strong supporter of the administration and placed his state's vast resources at the disposal of the war effort. He disagreed with Lincoln only in his belief that New York's 1865 draft quota was unrealistically high. Wishing to appease the governor, who had become a figure of national stature, Lincoln cut the quota by one-fourth. Fenton ran again for the governorship in 1866 and was reelected by a majority of more than 13,000 votes. During his tenure he was noted for his advocacy of prison and registry-law reform and for his firm support of public education. By the end of his second term, he was regarded as a master political organizer and strategist.

In 1869 Fenton won a Senate seat following a bitter struggle with former Gov. EDWIN D. MORGAN for the nomination. While in Washington, however, he was unable to maintain political power in his state. After leaving the Senate in 1875, Fenton busied himself with business interests, became a bank president, and gained a reputation as an expert on monetary affairs. d. Jamestown, N.Y., 25 Aug. 1885. —EGL

Ferguson, Samuel Wragg. CSA b. Charleston, S.C., 3 Nov. 1834, Ferguson was the son of a planter-politician who had fought in the War of 1812. After attending a local academy, he was graduated from West Point in 1857, ranking in the middle of his 38-man class, and went into dragoon service, participating in the 1857–58 expedition against the Mormons in Utah. He then served on garrison duty in Washington Territory, resigning his commission Mar. 1861 to enter the provisional army of his native state.

LC

Ferguson was on the staff of Gen. P.G.T. BEAUREGARD, with the rank of captain, at FORT SUMTER and FIRST BULL RUN, and was in the West from SHILOH to CORINTH. In Oct. 1862, shortly after marrying a daughter of one of Gen. Robert E. Lee's cousins, he became lieutenant colonel of the 28th Mississippi Cavalry. The following year, as a colonel, he campaigned against Union shipping on the Mississippi, opposed an enemy expedition in the Mississippi Delta, and was promoted to brigadier general to rank from 23 July 1863. In 1864 he served in many phases of the ATLANTA CAMPAIGN, leading a brigade in the Army of Mississippi, then in the Army of Tennessee. On 2 Sept. his command was the last body of troops to evacuate Atlanta before Maj. Gen. WILLIAM T. SHERMAN occupied the city.

A troublesome subordinate, Ferguson early in 1865 had a falling-out with Maj. Gen. JOSEPH WHEELER, who opposed his promotion to 2-star rank, calling him incompetent, insurbordinate, malcontented, and neglectful of his command—an example of "bad conduct and unsoldierly spirit." Later that year, nevertheless, Ferguson was ubiquitous in attacking the flanks, rear, and supply lines of Sherman's command during the CAROLINAS CAMPAIGN. At war's end, he joined JEFFERSON DAVIS and his fugitive party in an attempt to flee through Georgia.

Captured and paroled, Ferguson settled in Greenville, Miss., where he opened a law practice. He became the president of the Board of Mississippi Levee Commissioners and in 1885 a member of the U.S. Rivers Commission. Several years later he returned to Charleston, where he took up civil engineering. Retaining the martial spirit, he tried unsuccessfully to serve in the Spanish-American War of 1898. He lived long enough to see a larger, more deadly war break out, dying in Jackson, Miss., 3 Feb. 1917. —EGL

Ferrero, Edward. USA b. Granada, Spain, 18 Jan. 1831, Ferrero, like his Italian father, was a dance teacher. Both immigrated to America from Granada when Edward was an infant, and both taught ballroom technique in the New York City area during the antebellum period. At the outbreak of the Civil War, Edward was teaching dance to West Point cadets and was also a lieutenant colonel of the New York State Militia. With these qualifications, on 14 Oct. 1861 he was commissioned colonel of the 51st New York Infantry.

He and his men were first sent to Annapolis, Md., to be trained for Brig. Gen. AMBROSE E. BURNSIDE's amphibious expedition to NEW BERNE, North Carolina. From the expedition's start in Feb. 1862 until the end of the war, Ferrero, Burnside, and the army's IX Corps would be linked together. In summer 1862 Ferrero and others were quickly shuttled from the North Carolina coast to cooperate with Maj. Gen. JOHN POPE's Army of Virginia. Ferrero was given command of a IX Corps brigade there and served through SECOND BULL RUN. On 10 Sept. he was made a brigadier general and fought with the IX Corps through the Battle of ANTIETAM and Burnside's fiasco at FREDERICKSBURG in December.

With his corps Ferrero was sent to Kentucky for several weeks early in 1863 and in March his general's appointment lapsed for want of U.S. Senate confirmation. He was reappointed brigadier general 6 May and in June dispatched to siege duty at Vicksburg. There, because of the time that had elapsed since his unconfirmed first commission, he was subordinate to Brig. Gen. ROBERT B. POTTER, who had been his major in the 51st New York. In Apr. 1864 the IX Corps was sent back to Annapolis for reorganization and assigned a division of black troops with Ferrero its commander. In July this division was singled out to take the second assault line at the Battle of the CRATER in Virginia. The fight was an unqualified Union disaster.

At the Crater, Ferrero's troops were to follow those of Brig. Gen. JAMES H. LEDLIE out of their trenches. Ledlie and Ferrero sat in a bombproof during the battle, did not observe their men, and supposedly "passed a bottle of rum back and forth." Their ill-prepared and unguided troops were caught in the Crater and slaughtered. A court of inquiry and Ledlie's resignation from the army followed, but in an oversight, Ferrero was handed a major general's brevet for Petersburg service along with other brigadiers. He was given duty out of harm's way with the bottled-up Army of the James at BERMUDA HUNDRED until the Confederate surrender.

In the postwar years Ferrero returned to dance instruction, at different times running large ballrooms in New York City, where he died, 11 Dec. 1899. —JES

Ferry, Orris Sanford. USA b. Bethel, Conn., 15 Aug. 1823. The son of a prosperous businessman, Ferry graduated from Yale in 1844, became an attorney 2 years later, and subsequently served as a probate judge, state attorney, Connecticut senator, and in the U.S. House of Representatives, 1858–60.

The Connecticut Republican typified how leading politicians with the proper beliefs could rise to high military rank, regardless of merit or performance.

Ferry received a commission as colonel of the 5th Connecticut 23 July 1861. Seeing little action, he was nevertheless promoted to brigadier general 17 Mar. 1862. As a brigade commander, Ferry participated in the 1862 SHENANDOAH VALLEY CAMPAIGN, opposing Maj. Gen. Thomas J. "STONEWALL" JACKSON, and with the IV Corps in the PENINSULA CAMPAIGN.

In Jan. 1863 Ferry assumed command of a division in the

XVIII Corps in the Department of the South and in April transferred to the X Corps, commanding a division stationed at Seabrook Island, S.C. A year later the X Corps transferred to Virginia as part of Maj. Gen. BENJAMIN F. BUTLER's Army of the James, in which Ferry led a division at BERMUDA HUNDRED and in the early phases of the PETERSBURG CAMPAIGN. On 23 May 1865, for his services in the Army of the Potomac, Ferry was brevetted major general.

NA

After the war Ferry returned to Connecticut, where in 1866 the legislature elected him to the U.S. Senate. An outspoken, unswerving Radical Republican, Ferry nevertheless strongly advocated moderation toward the defeated South. Reelected in 1872, Ferry did not finish the term, dying in Norwalk, Conn., from a "progressive spinal disease" 21 Nov. 1875.   —JDW

Fessenden, Francis. USA b. Portland, Maine, 18 Mar. 1839. Though he was an able commander, all evidence shows that Fessenden's military appointments were purely political. He was the son of Pres. Abraham Lincoln's second treasury secretary, WILLIAM P. FESSENDEN, and younger brother of Brig. Gen. JAMES D. FESSENDEN. His first commission came directly from Sec. of War SIMON CAMERON 14 May 1861.

Fessenden attended school in Portland before entering Bowdoin College, graduating in 1858 and beginning law studies at Harvard; eventually he was admitted to the bar. When the war began Fessenden became a captain in the 19th U.S. Infantry and Apr. 1862 fought at the Battle of SHILOH. The battle was his first, and he received an incapacitating wound in the fighting. By Sept. 1862 he had returned to service as colonel of the 25th Maine in defense of Washington, D.C. On 10 July 1863 he was honorably mustered out of volunteer service.

NA

On 11 Jan. 1864 Fessenden rejoined the army as a colonel in the 30th Maine assigned to New Orleans. He served in Maj. Gen. Nathaniel P. Banks's RED RIVER CAMPAIGN and fought brilliantly at the Battle of PLEASANT HILL. On 23 Apr. 1864 Fessenden received orders to take a hill held by the Confederates near Monett's Ferry. Determining both flanks to be impregnable he successfully led his brigade in a bold charge up the steep slopes, directly into heavy Confederate fire. Of the brigade's 153 casualties Fessenden himself sustained a serious wound to his right leg and was forced to undergo amputation several days later.

Fessenden finished the war as a brigadier general as of 10 May 1864 and was appointed major general 9 Nov. 1865. 4 times during his career he was promoted for "gallant and meritorious service in the field." His last military service included desk duty in Washington as commissioner for the trial of Andersonville Prison commandant HENRY WIRZ. He then returned to Portland and became its mayor for a term before his death there 2 Jan. 1906.   —FLS

Fessenden, James Deering. USA b. Westbrook, Maine, 28 Sept. 1833. Graduating from Bowdoin College in 1852, Fessenden studied law, was admitted to the bar, and became a partner in his father's law office. He interrupted his career at the outbreak of the war, receiving a captaincy and recruiting a company of marksmen who became part of the 2d Regiment of U.S. Sharpshooters.

In Virginia during the first winter of the conflict his unit saw little action, and Mar. 1862 Fessenden accepted a position on the staff of Maj. Gen. DAVID HUNTER, commander of the Department of the South. That summer, at Hunter's headquarters in South Carolina, Fessenden organized and drilled the first body of black troops in uniform, the 1st South Carolina Volunteers. Because of Hunter's premature emancipation policies, the War Department disavowed his actions and ordered the regiment disbanded. Fessenden returned to staff duties, winning a colonelcy during the operations around Charleston that July.

After being injured in a riding accident, he quit active duty for a time, but on recovery, in Sept. 1863, he was transferred to the staff of Maj. Gen. JOSEPH HOOKER, then moving his XI and XII corps from Virginia to Tennessee. During the CHATTANOOGA CAMPAIGN, "Fighting Joe" complimented his staff officer's performance on several occasions. For his services at RESACA, May 1864, Fessenden was recommended for star rank, and again following PEACHTREE CREEK, in July. He received his brigadier's appointment 8 Aug. 1864, a promotion probably due as much to family prominence (his father being the new secretary of the treasury) as to Fessenden's military record.

At that grade, he was dispatched to the Shenandoah Valley to command a brigade in Maj. Gen. PHILIP H. SHERIDAN's XIX Corps, serving at THIRD WINCHESTER in September and the next month at CEDAR CREEK, where he was relegated to garrison duty in the valley. He led a provisional division there Mar.–Apr. 1865 but saw little active service.

Following the Confederacy's death, Fessenden was sent on special service to Georgia and South Carolina as a brevet major general of volunteers. Mustered out Jan. 1866, he returned to his law practice in Portland, Maine; served as state register of bankruptcy, 1868–78; and spent 3 terms in the state legislature. He was the son of WILLIAM P. FESSENDEN and brother of FRANCIS FESSENDEN. d. Portland, 18 Nov. 1882.   —EGL

Fessenden, William Pitt. USP b. Boscawan, N.H., 16 Oct. 1806. The illegitimate son of Ruth Greene and Samuel Fessenden, William was raised by Samuel's parents until he was 6 or 7. His father married, took him into his new household, and educated him at Bowdoin College. Because of "his general character and the bad influence of his example" he was denied his diploma for a year following his graduation in 1823.

Fessenden moved to Portland, Maine, after receiving a law degree in 1827, and was active in state affairs from 1830. 4 widely spaced terms in the state legislature, a distinguished law career, and election to 1 term in the U.S. House of Representatives in 1840 won him state-wide recognition as a Whig, then as a Republican backer of abolition. With antislavery sentiment in Maine and a factional coalition, Fessenden was elected to the U.S. Senate in 1854. Permanent disabilities resulting from ill health in 1857 and bitterness over his wife's death soured his personality, earning him a reputation for harshness and insensitivity. In 1857 he was also appointed to the Senate Finance Committee and with reelection to the Senate was made its chairman.

In 1861 Fessenden had 2 sons, JAMES and FRANCIS, serving in the Union army. With a reputation for austerity before war broke out, Fessenden urged economy during the conflict, voting down pork-barrel and patronage contracts and expenditures. At various times he allied himself with Sec. of the Treasury SALMON P. CHASE and Sen. JOHN SHERMAN on revenue legislation, but he opposed the portion of Sherman's Omnibus Revenue Act of Aug. 1861 that provided for issuing paper currency. In 1862 the Federal government printed legal-tender notes, which Fessenden railed against as dangerous and inflationary, supporting the ill-fated Collamer Amendment to have them eliminated. Until mid-1864 he urged heavier taxes and bond sales as the best positive public finance measures.

On 1 July 1864 Pres. ABRAHAM LINCOLN appointed the senator secretary of the treasury. Former secretary Chase, caught in a run to take the presidency for himself, had been eased from office and appointed to the U.S. Supreme Court, a post Ohio Gov. DAVID TOD had declined. Fessenden accepted the offer only on the condition that his service would be temporary. He stepped into a $1.7 billion national debt and financial management of a war costing $2 million a day. He quickly renewed bond sales, previously suspended for a few months. During this period New York financier Morris Ketchum, whom Fessenden had appointed to sell government bonds, was trying to manipulate prices for personal profit. Fessenden survived the embarrassment and, after being reelected to the Senate, resigned the secretaryship Mar. 1865 to return to the legislature. He left the cabinet with the treasury in better condition, and with bond sales and tax revenues meeting war costs.

After the war Fessenden, "a conservative Radical," opposed Pres. ANDREW JOHNSON's impeachment, which he claimed resulted from "general cussedness" on the part of RADICAL REPUBLICANS. His position erupted into an argument over party loyalty that was not resolved at the time of his death in Portland, 8 Sept. 1869.   —JES

Field, Charles William. CSA b. "Airy Mount," Woodford Cty., Ky., 6 Apr. 1828, Field was graduated from the U.S. Military Academy, 27th in the class of 1849, accepting a commission in the dragoons. He served on the frontier and instructed cavalry at West Point before resigning 30 May 1861 with the rank of captain.

The Kentuckian received a commission in the Confederacy as colonel of the 6th Virginia Cavalry. On 9 Mar. 1862 Field was promoted to brigadier general. Transferred to the infantry, he assumed command of a brigade in Maj. Gen. AMBROSE P. HILL's Light Division, fighting in the SEVEN DAYS' CAMPAIGN, at CEDAR MOUNTAIN, and SECOND

LC

BULL RUN. In the last battle, he suffered a crippling wound in the hips from which he never fully recovered. During his long convalescence, Field served temporarily as the superintendent

of the Bureau of Conscription.

Promoted to major general 12 Feb. 1864, Field was assigned command of fellow Kentuckian JOHN B. HOOD's division of the I Corps. Lt. Gen. JAMES LONGSTREET, corps commander, protested the appointment of the crippled Field to divisional command, a protest that resulted in a rebuke from Pres. Jefferson Davis.

Field's performance proved Longstreet's misgivings to be unfounded. An intelligent man with an indomitable will, Field led the division with skill and valor at the WILDERNESS, SPOTSYLVANIA, COLD HARBOR, and the battles of the PETERSBURG CAMPAIGN. His division fought particularly well at FORT HARRISON and DARBYTOWN ROAD, and when the army surrendered at Appomattox, he commanded its strongest division.

Field enjoyed a varied career after the war. A businessman in Georgia and Maryland, he also served in the Egyptian army for 3 years, acted as doorkeeper of the U.S. House of Representatives, worked as a government civil engineer, and acted as superintendent of the Indian reservation at Hot Springs, Ark. He died in the nation's capital 9 Apr. 1892, the 27th anniversary of Appomattox.   —JDW

field artillery. Civil War artillery provided ordnance chiefs with, at the least, mild headaches and, at worst, nightmares. The "long arm" was in a transitional stage; an army's artillery might have at least 6 different types of gun and as many as 18 varieties of projectile with 4 or 5 kinds of fuse. Early in the war the Confederates built up their artillery arm through capture; thus they often had 2 or even 3 types of gun in a single battery, necessitating a variety of ammunition.

Field artillery was of 2 classes: bronze smoothbores and rifles, mainly iron. The muzzle-loading smoothbores were 6- and 12-pounder; 12-, 24-, and 32-pounder howitzers; and the Model 1857 12-pounder NAPOLEON. The muzzle-loading rifles included 10- and 20-pounder Parrott, 3-in. ordnance (RODMAN), 12- and 24-pounder James, 6- and 10-pounder Wiard, and—for the South—ENGLISH BLAKELYS, WHITWORTHS, and ARMSTRONGS, some of which were also made as breechloaders.

The most popular gun was the efficient, trouble-free Napoleon, with its effective range of 1,619 yd at 5° elevation and its deadliness with canister at short range. Among the iron rifles the 3-in. ordnance, range 1,830 yd at 5° elevation, was a favorite with gunners. Its lighter tube (820 lb to the Napoleon's 1,227) made it ideal for the cavalry's horse artillery. Howitzers had shorter tubes than guns. Tubes were made shorter as bore and projectile weight were increased.

A regulation-size battery had 6 guns, each attached to a limber (ammunition chest) drawn by 6 horses hitched in pairs. Each was supplied by 1 or more caissons (4-wheel carts carrying 2 or more ammunition chests), also using 6-horse teams. In action, a gun team numbered 9 men under a "chief of piece." Except for canister at short range, standard firing rate was 1 shot in 2 minutes.   —JES

Fifteen-Negro Law. See TWENTY-NEGRO LAW.

"Fighting McCooks." Of the 14 "Fighting McCooks" of Ohio serving in the armed forces of the U.S. during the Civil War, 7 were sons of Maj. Daniel McCook, the other 7 cousins. In July 1863, at 57, Daniel led a unit of Ohio Home Guards into action against Brig. Gen. JOHN HUNT MORGAN's raiders near Buffington Island, Ohio, and was killed.

3 of Daniel's sons became generals during the war: Alexander McDowell, Robert Latimore, and Daniel, Jr. Another son, Roderick Sheldon (d. 1886), became a lieutenant in the navy; a cousin, Edward Moody McCook, reached the rank of major general of volunteers.

ALEXANDER M. MCCOOK was best known as the commander of the XX Corps of the Army of the Cumberland and for his actions in the Battles of PERRYVILLE, STONE'S RIVER, and CHICKAMAUGA.

Robert, an older brother, was a successful lawyer at the start of the war and in 1861 organized the 9th Ohio Infantry; as its colonel he was engaged in the western Virginia campaigning. In Jan. 1862 he was cited for distinguished service at the Battle of MILL SPRINGS, Ky., and was promoted to brigadier general. On 5 Aug. 1862 he was mortally wounded in an action with guerrillas near Huntsville, Ala., and died the next day.

Daniel, Jr., was a younger brother who had begun to practice law in Leavenworth, Kans., when the war began. In 1861 he was a captain in the 1st Kansas Infantry and the next year became Maj. Gen. George H. Thomas' chief of staff. As colonel he commanded brigades during the Battles of PERRYVILLE and CHICKAMAUGA and in Maj. Gen. William T. Sherman's ATLANTA CAMPAIGN. Daniel was mortally wounded at the Battle of KENNESAW MOUNTAIN, 27 June 1864, and died 17 July, the day after he was commissioned brigadier general.

Starting as a major in the 2d Indiana Cavalry in 1861, Edward Moody McCook rose to colonel and the command of a cavalry division in the Army of the Cumberland in 1863. Commissioned brigadier general in 1864, he commanded a cavalry division during the Atlanta Campaign and, according to one Confederate source, "made his name a horror." He also commanded a division during Brig. Gen. JAMES H. WILSON's 1865 campaign through Alabama and was commissioned major general. At the end of the war he was appointed military governor of Florida and 1866–69 was U.S. minister to Hawaii, then territorial governor of Colorado 1869–76. Involved in real estate, mining, and finance, McCook became the richest man in Colorado, dying in Chicago, 9 Sept. 1909.   —JWR

finance, Confederate. Confederate Sec. of the Treasury CHRISTOPHER G. MEMMINGER assumed his duties Feb. 1861 by floating government loans and creating an instant national debt. In 1861 the Confederacy sold bonds worth $150 million in the so-called Bankers Loan, which secured much-needed specie. The government also tapped agricultural staples through the Produce Loan, in which planters pledged their produce in exchange for government paper. Against the receipts of these loans, Memminger issued Treasury notes, circulating paper money with which the government paid its bills. In Aug. 1861 the Confederate Congress passed a war tax on various kinds of property to increase government resources. Unfortunately Memminger's department was inefficient in collecting the produce subscribed to the Produce Loan, and he allowed taxes to be paid in inflated state currency. Consequently government paper money fed inflation, which served as an inverse tax on Confederate citizens.

By 1863 Memminger realized that inflation was threatening the government's ability to support itself and the war. Accordingly he proposed and Congress passed a graduated INCOME TAX and a 10% TAX IN KIND on agricultural products. In Mar. 1863 the Confederacy accepted a $15 million loan from the French banking house of Emile Erlanger that yielded much less than its face value (about $8.5 million), but given the tenuous nature of Southern nationhood, the Confederates made the best deal possible. (*See also* ERLANGER LOAN.) Still, Memminger's printing presses moved faster than the government could collect revenue, and inflation accelerated. In desperation, in 1864 Memminger imposed a Compulsory Funding Measure, which devalued those Treasury notes not exchanged for noncirculating government bonds. This failed too, as Confederates continued to exchange government paper for goods and services.

In July 1864 JEFFERSON DAVIS replaced Memminger with another South Carolinian, GEORGE A. TRENHOLM, but there was little Trenholm could do. The Confederacy never had more than $27 million of specie. The national debt ran over $700 million and the overall inflation was about 6,000%. That the Confederacy persisted as long as it did amid this financial chaos was a wonder.   —EMT

Finegan, Joseph. CSA   b. Clones, Ireland, 17 Nov. 1814. Emigrating to America in his early twenties, Finegan settled in Florida, building a lumber mill at Jacksonville. Later he moved to Fernandina, practiced law, and constructed railroads. In 1861 he was a member of the state secession convention, following which Gov. JOHN MILTON chose him to handle all military affairs pertaining to Florida's role in the Confederacy.

From Apr. to Oct. 1862 Finegan commanded the Department of Middle and Eastern Florida with the rank of brigadier general; later his command was reduced to the District of East Florida. His troops were thinly scattered throughout the district,

LC

waging an arduous campaign to protect portions of the Atlantic coast from the U.S. Navy. In Feb. 1864 3 brigades under his direction made a stand near OLUSTEE against 5,500 Federals under Brig. Gen. TRUMAN SEYMOUR, sweeping inland after an amphibious landing at Jacksonville. On the 20th Finegan skillfully deployed his 6,500 troops against the front and flanks of the enemy, and after a four-and-a-half-hour battle put Seymour to flight. For chasing the Union troops to their base of operations on the Atlantic Coast, Finegan and his soldiers won the THANKS OF THE CONFEDERATE CONGRESS.

3 months later, Finegan was transferred to Virginia, where he led a consolidated brigade of Floridians in Brig. Gen. WILLIAM MAHONE's division of the III Corps/Army of Northern Virginia. On the morning of 3 June 1864 the command plugged a gap in the right flank of the Confederate army at COLD HARBOR, then assisted another force in repulsing troops of the II Corps/Army of the Potomac. That evening they repelled another assault, this against their skirmish line. Finegan's brigade performed with similar ability in many engagements in the PETERSBURG CAMPAIGN, but in winter 1864–65 it suffered heavily from desertion. 2 weeks before Gen. Robert E. Lee's surrender at Appomattox, Finegan was returned to Florida, where he finished out the conflict.

With the coming of peace, he returned to his law practice, was a member of the Florida senate, then relocated to Savannah, Ga., entering the cotton-brokerage business. He spent his last years in Rutledge, Fla., dying 29 Oct. 1885.   —EGL

Finley, Jesse Johnson. CSA b. Lebanon, Tenn., 18 Nov. 1812. The son of a wealthy planter, Finley attended a local academy, read law in Nashville, and opened a practice in his native village. Gaining a prominent place in the community, he was appointed captain of a company of mounted volun-
teers during the Seminole War of 1836. After the conflict he moved his residence several times, serving over a period of 10 years in the legislatures of Tennessee, Arkansas, and Florida, and briefly, 1845–46, as mayor of Memphis.

LC

In 1852 Finley was elevated to the Florida bench and 1853–61 served the western circuit of the state. At the out-
break of the Civil War he was a Confederate States judge, a post he resigned Mar. 1862 to become a private soldier in the 6th Florida Infantry. Soon he was commissioned colonel of the regiment, which he led during the Kentucky campaigning of Maj. Gen. E. KIRBY SMITH.

At CHICKAMAUGA, 20 Sept. 1863, Finley commanded not only his own unit but a Virginia infantry regiment, taking heavy losses but winning praise for his prompt reinforcement of Col. JOHN H. KELLY's brigade of Lt. Gen. SIMON B. BUCKNER's division. That November—the month in which he led the 6th Florida at MISSIONARY RIDGE—Finley was promoted to brigadier general. During the ATLANTA CAMPAIGN he was assigned the Florida brigade in the Army of Tennessee. Wounded at RESACA, he saw his brigade crushed and nearly routed by superior forces at Dallas, and was again wounded at JONESBOROUGH, while carrying 2 lines of Federal works.

Incapacitated by his latest injury, he served as president of courts-martial at Knoxville, Tenn., before surrendering under Maj. Gen. HOWELL COBB at Columbus, Ga., late in Apr. 1865.

Returning to Florida, Finley settled in Lake City, where he resumed his legal practice. In 1871 he moved to Jacksonville, served in Congress as a conservative Democrat, 1875–79, and was unseated in 1880 during a contested election. In Mar. 1887 he was designated to fill a vacancy in the U.S. Senate but his appointment was voided on a technicality. Later that year he returned to a Florida circuit-court judgeship, serving until 1903. He died in Lake City 6 Nov. 1904 and was buried in Gainesville.   —EGL

first shot. The first shot fired in the Civil War, the shot that began 4 years of military hostilities, is generally credited to Confederate Lt. Henry S. Farley. At precisely 4:30 a.m., 12 Apr. 1861, the lieutenant pulled the lanyard on his mortar and fired a shot that exploded 100 ft in the air above the walls of FORT SUMTER in Charleston harbor, S.C. Serving in the garrison and defenses of Confederate-held Fort Johnson at the harbor-
side, Farley fired on the direction of his captain, George S. James. James's fort had been directed by ROGER A. PRYOR to fire at that time; the shot let loose was the signal for each of the Confederate batteries positioned around the harbor to com-
mence firing, in turn, on Federal-held Fort Sumter.

Other men are given or take credit for the distinction of firing the first shot. At dawn, 9 Jan. 1861, the unarmed Federal supply ship *Star of the West* was fired at by Cadet George Haynesworth, a student at South Carolina's Citadel military academy on temporary assignment at the secessionist-held Morris Island battery on Charleston harbor. The *Star of the West* carried Union reinforcements and supplies for Maj. ROB-
ERT ANDERSON's Fort Sumter garrison. Haynesworth's shot set off general firing from other guns on Morris Island, then can-
non in the secessionists' Fort Moultrie joined in.

On the occasion of the Confederates' last demand for Sumter's surrender, 12 Apr., Pryor, unhappy with Anderson's response, handed the major a note, composed with Southern Capt. STEPHEN D. LEE, that informed him firing would begin at 4:30 a.m. Pryor then went to Fort Johnson by boat and instructed Captain James to fire the 4:30 signal gun. James of-
fered Pryor the opportunity of firing the first shot, but Pryor, reputedly unnerved or overcome with the import of this act, declined the privilege; some accounts have inaccurately credited him with the first shot.

Other accounts give credit to secessionist "fire-eater" ED-
MOND RUFFIN. An honorary member of South Carolina's Palmetto Guard manning the guns in the ironclad battery on Cum-
mings Point at Charleston harbor, Ruffin was offered and accepted the privilege of firing the guards' first shot of the war. However, this "first shot" was fired from Morris Island after firing on Sumter had commenced from other points.

Among the Union defenders of Fort Sumter, there was agreement that Capt. ABNER DOUBLEDAY fired the first shot in the fort's defense around 7 a.m.

Determination of a "first shot" is neither possible nor, per-
haps, a valid exercise. At least for a minority on both sides, a consensus had been reached as early as 1860 that the great national issues could only be settled by violence; many were anxious to be the first to provide it.   —JES

Fisher's Hill, Va., Battle of. 22 Sept. 1864 Maj. Gen. PHILIP H. SHERIDAN's Union Army of the Shenandoah achieved a signal victory 19 Sept. 1864 in the THIRD BATTLE OF WINCHES-
TER. The Federals sent Confederate Lt. Gen. JUBAL A. EARLY's Army of the Valley "whirling through Winchester." During the night of 19–20 Sept. the Confederates retreated southward to Fisher's Hill, 1 mi south of Strasburg and 21 mi from Winchester.

The veteran Southerners, members of Lt. Gen. THOMAS J. "STONEWALL" JACKSON's incomparable II Corps, filed into their old trenches on Fisher's Hill throughout the 20th. Early de-
cided to make another stand there, the only place he could defend without opening the upper Shenandoah Valley to the Federals. Fisher's Hill was a high, steep bluff, seemingly heaved up by mistake from the valley floor during the Creation. Flanked by Massanutten Mountain on the east and Little North Mountain on the west, the eminence dominated the Shenandoah at its narrowest point. It had long been, a Union officer remarked, "the bugbear of the valley," a position, if ade-
quately manned, that was nearly impregnable.

But with fewer than 9,000 effectives, the Confederate commander could not stretch his lines to make his works unassaila-
ble. He spread his troops even further by placing Brig. Gen. LUNSFORD L. LOMAX's undermanned, demoralized cavalry command on his vulnerable left, where the high bluff sloped down into a small valley before merging with Little North

Mountain. But Early's rugged fighters welcomed the stand—they wanted another chance at the Northerners.

The jubilant Federals arrived before Fisher's Hill late on the 20th. Sheridan had been halted in August by the high bluff, and he knew the difficulties of a frontal attack. That night he met with his 3 infantry corps commanders—Maj. Gens. HORATIO G. WRIGHT, WILLIAM H. EMORY, and GEORGE CROOK. Crook suggested using his command in a flanking maneuver similar to the one executed at Winchester. Though Wright and Emory demurred, Sheridan approved the plan. As a secondary phase, Sheridan ordered his cavalry commander, Maj. Gen. ALFRED T. A. TORBERT, to take 2 divisions, sweep up the Luray Valley, cross the Massanutten at New Market Gap, and cut Early's only avenue of retreat. Crook's attack was scheduled for 22 Sept.

Throughout the 21st and most of the 22d, Wright's and Emory's troops shifted into position to assault the bluff frontally. Skirmishing and artillery duels characterized the action. Concealed in woods on the 21st, Crook's 2 divisions on the 22d moved by a concealed route to Little North Mountain and beyond Early's flank and rear. The circuitous march consumed most of the day. By 4 p.m. the 2 divisions had scaled the mountain and wheeled to the east, facing perpendicularly to the Confederate line.

Down the boulder-strewn slope, Crook's cheering soldiers charged. The attack burst upon Lomax's startled troops, who ran away almost immediately. Maj. Gen. STEPHEN D. RAMSEUR, commanding the nearest Confederate infantry division, shifted his front. But Crook's attack was unrelenting, and, when Wright's and Emory's soldiers stormed up the hillside, the Southerners' line collapsed. Confederate units stood fast until enveloped on their front, flank, and rear. Darkness saved much of Early's army from capture or destruction.

At a cost of 456 casualties, Sheridan had completely routed the Confederate army, sending it toward the Blue Ridge Mts. and clearing the upper valley for his own troops. Though Torbert failed to seal off the Confederate retreat, Sheridan had again won a critical victory. His victories at Winchester and Fisher's Hill, within 4 days, provided Abraham Lincoln's reelection campaign with timely, sorely needed military successes. The twin Southern defeats also marked the beginning of the end for the Confederacy in Virginia.   —JDW

Fishing Creek, Ky., Battle of. 19 Jan. 1862 *See* MILL SPRINGS, KY., BATTLE OF.

Fisk, Clinton Bowen. USA b. York, N.Y., 8 Dec. 1828. Fisk moved to Michigan Territory in his infancy. His father died soon after the move and left his son on near "pinching poverty." Fisk enrolled at an academy in Albion and subsequently established himself as a businessman in Coldwater, a town on the Michigan Southern Railroad. After the Panic of 1857 ruined his milling business and small banking enterprise, he moved to St. Louis and sold insurance until the war broke out.

In 1861 Fisk entered military service with the home guards in time for the 10 May seizure of Camp Jackson, a reported "hot bed of Secessionists" near St. Louis. His official service in the U.S. Army started in late summer 1862, when he accepted an appointment as colonel of the 33d Missouri Volunteers. Fisk formed a brigade, was appointed brigadier general 24 Nov. 1862, and spent the rest of the war fighting against Confederate raiders in Missouri and Arkansas.

NA

As commander of the District of Northern Missouri, 1864–65, Fisk made his mark in Civil War history in 1864 during Confederate Maj. Gen. STERLING PRICE'S campaign through that state. When pro-Confederates enlisted in the state militia to sabotage Unionist activities, calling the infiltration the Paw Paw Rebellion, Fisk set out immediately to quell the uprising and replace the Southern sympathizers with new recruits. In 2 months he increased his troop strength enough to play a major part in forcing Price from the state.

Fisk's postwar career was extensive. In 1865 he served as assistant commissioner of the FREEDMEN'S BUREAU and opened a school for blacks in Nashville the next year; in 1867 it was chartered as Fisk University. Deeply religious, Fisk attended a number of national and international Methodist church conferences. In 1874 he served on the Board of Indian Commissioners; in 1886 he was the Prohibitionist party candidate for governor of New Jersey; and he ran for president on the same party's ticket in 1888. Fisk also operated a successful banking business in New York City, where he died 9 July 1890.   —FLS

Five Forks, Va., Battle of. 1 Apr. 1865 By nightfall of 31 Mar. 1865, the Confederate lines covering Petersburg, Va., were stretched precariously thin. Because of the Union flanking movement toward the Southern right, Confederate troops had to be shifted westward toward Five Forks, Va., a road junction. Gen. ROBERT E. LEE moved 19,000 soldiers there, nearly one-third of his entire army, to oppose almost 50,000 Federals. 2 days of heavy rain and Confederate counterattacks near DINWIDDIE COURT HOUSE delayed the Union offensive. Lee and Maj. Gen. GEORGE E. PICKETT, commanding that sector, knew that the Federal onslaught would resume 1 Apr.

Pickett crafted a line with his outnumbered defenders. Maj. Gen. W.H.F. "ROONEY" LEE's cavalry division covered the Confederate right, or western, flank. Pickett's 5 infantry brigades manned the center, digging in along White Oak road. Pickett refused the flank of his left brigade, forming a hook, a disposition necessitated by a dangerous 3-mi gap yawning from the Five Forks line to the main Confederate works to the east. Pickett screened this break in the front with Brig. Gen. WILLIAM P. ROBERTS' weak cavalry brigade and a dismounted regiment from another cavalry brigade. Lee told Pickett on 1 April that his line must be held "at all hazards."

For the last 3 days these Confederates had opposed Maj. Gen. PHILIP H. SHERIDAN's 3 Union cavalry divisions and 2 infantry corps, the II and V. Sheridan, pushed back to Dinwiddie Court House on 31 Mar., planned to assault the Confederate front while the V Corps, under Maj. Gen. GOUVERNEUR K. WARREN, stormed into the gap, rolling up Pickett's left.

2 Union cavalry divisions, commanded by Maj. Gen. GEORGE A. CUSTER and Brig. Gen. THOMAS C. DEVIN, initiated the action 1 Apr., pressing north into the wooded terrain. The horsemen fought dismounted except for 2 of Custer's brigades. Brig. Gen. RANALD S. MACKENZIE's cavalry brigade, meanwhile, reached the White Oak road 3 mi east of Five Forks and veered westward across the gap. The Confederate skirmishers

receded before the Federal cavalrymen, spilling into their main line. Sheridan, however, waited impatiently for Warren, whose advance had been delayed.

Finally, about 4 p.m., the Union infantry charged into the gap; unfortunately Warren had miscalculated the length of the Southern line and his 2 divisions attacked into a void. The left division under Brig. Gen. ROMEYN B. AYRES was suddenly caught in a crossfire by Pickett's refused infantry flank. Ayres wheeled to face the fire, and Sheridan, who was present, ordered the other 2 infantry divisions to adjust. Sheridan fumed over Warren's failure and, with permission from Lt. Gen. Ulysses S. Grant, removed the corps commander from command.

Ayres's veterans drove into the woods, crushing Pickett's left. Pickett, who had been at a shad bake in the rear when the Federal assault exploded, galloped through a gauntlet of fire to direct the defense. The Confederate general shifted his brigades to meet the threat but he had too few muskets. The 2 remaining divisions of the V Corps charged into the Confederate rear. At Five Forks, Devin's horsemen stormed over the Southerners' works, seizing cannon, flags, and over a thousand prisoners. Mackenzie sealed the direct route of a Confederate retreat. Their lines shattered, thousands of Southerners surrendered.

Sheridan had achieved a signal victory: 4 cannon, 11 flags, and about 5,200 Confederates were in Federal hands, secured with about 1,111 casualties. The remnant of Pickett's command was severed from the main army and Lee's right flank had been turned. Warren was eventually cleared by a court of inquiry, but his removal clouded the officer's record. The Battle of Five Forks permitted Grant to launch a massive assault the next day, which finally crushed Lee's Petersburg lines.
—JDW

fixed ammunition.   Most field cannon used fixed ammunition, any projectile attached to its cartridge or powder bag and loaded as one piece. All round fused shells, spherical case, canister, and the rare grape rounds were preferably loaded as fixed ammunition to ensure that the projectile's fuse faced outward at the gun's mouth. Otherwise the projectile might detonate in the barrel when the lanyard was pulled. However, the cartridge or powder bag and a round projectile could be loaded separately with care.

The second advantage of fixed ammunition was speed in loading and firing. A good gun crew could load, prime, and fire a projectile in 30 to 35 seconds with fixed ammunition. Separately loading the charge, then the projectile, added crucial time to the operation.

Spherical shells, solid shot, and spherical case shot had an additional piece fixed to them. These round projectiles were strapped on a wooden sabot, or shoe, with bands of tin or leather; this combination was, in turn, tied to its powder charge. When these loads were rammed into cannon, the sabot made for a tight fit between the shot or shell and the barrel wall, giving added push to the projectile when the powder was fired. With a sabot, less propelling gas escaped around the curvature of the projectile. In howitzers, these sabots were tapered to conform to the conical inner barrel wall at the breech.

In long, heavy cannon or mortars, fixed ammunition was not used. Loading hooks ensured the proper positioning of the projectile in these pieces.   —JES

flags, Confederate.   Sensitive to the importance of providing a symbol for the new Confederate nation, delegates to the Provisional Congress in Montgomery, Ala., appointed a Committee on Flag, Seal, Coat of Arms, and Motto within a week after they convened late in Jan. 1861. In their eagerness to have a flag flying over the provisional Capitol on the day of Lincoln's inauguration, less than a month away, the committeemen hastily chose the design submitted by Prof. Nicola Marschall. Marschall's design closely resembled the U.S. flag, a similarity the legislators endorsed since many Southerners harbored strong attachments to the old banner. The flag comprised a blue canton studded with 7 white stars, 1 for each state then part of the Confederacy, and 3 stripes, the top and bottom ones red, the middle one white. Congress adopted the flag 4 Mar., and that afternoon the granddaughter of former president John Tyler raised the Stars and Bars over the Capitol.

MC

MC

But the flag's lack of distinctiveness generated dissatisfaction instead of popular acceptance. Worse, its similarity to the U.S. flag led to confusion on the battlefield at FIRST BULL RUN. Southern generals urged Congress to authorize a more appropriate standard. When the politicians failed to respond, Gen. JOSEPH E. JOHNSTON asked for suggestions, selecting Gen. P.G.T. BEAUREGARD's design of a blue St. Andrew's cross edged in white on a red field, with a star representing each Confederate state set in the cross. Johnston modified the flag from a rectangle to a square, varying the size for each arm of the military: 4 ft by 4 ft, infantry; 3 ft by 3 ft, artillery; 2.5 ft by 2.5 ft, cavalry. The War Department approved the design 1 Oct. Congress never formally adopted the Battle Flag, but the public

MC

MC

accepted it wholeheartedly, and it remains the most powerful of Confederate icons.

Continued discontent with the Stars and Bars' similarity to the Federal flag prompted the legislators to authorize a National Flag 1 May 1863, adapting the Battle Flag as the union set into a white field. Called the Stainless Banner, this effort too fell short of success. Its width was half its length, creating an awkward effect, and, when it hung limp, its broad white expanse looked like a truce flag. Congress approved a second National Flag, a modified Stainless Banner, 4 Mar. 1865. The length was enlarged to two-thirds the width, and the white field ended in a broad red stripe. The Confederate collapse prevented widespread use of the improved design.

The Southern navy flew the Stars and Bars until Sec. of the Navy STEPHEN R. MALLORY authorized 3 new flags 26 May 1863. The New Ensign was the first National Flag reduced in size; the Naval Jack was the Battle Flag in rectangular form; and the Pennant was a 72-ft-long red, white, and blue star-studded banner 1 ft wide at its head and tapering to a point. The New Ensign holds the distinction of being the last flag flown in

Confederate service. Capt. JAMES I. WADDELL of the cruiser *SHENANDOAH* did not learn of the Confederate surrender until Aug. 1865. He immediately set sail for England and formally lowered his colors in Liverpool harbor 6 Nov.

In June 1887 Pres. Grover Cleveland approved the return of captured Confederate flags to the South, creating an outcry among indignant Northerners. He revoked the order, deferring to congressional authority. The flags were returned peacefully to the South in 1905.   —PLF

Flanagin, Harris. war governor b. Roadstown, N.J., 3 Nov. 1817. Moving to Arkansas from Illinois in 1837, the year he was admitted to the bar, Flanagin was elected to the state legislature on the Democratic ticket in 1842 but preferred the law to politics and 2 years later returned to his practice. As a delegate to the secession convention in spring 1861, he voted against taking Arkansas out of the Union. After the firing on FORT SUMTER, he reversed his position, entering Confederate service as a captain in the 2d Arkansas Mounted Rifles. Promoted to colonel and assigned to Knoxville, Tenn., he learned of his unsolicited election to the governorship of Arkansas a few days after HENRY M. RECTOR had been forced out of the office by a hostile legislature. Resigning from the army, he traveled to Little Rock to be inaugurated 15 Nov. 1862.

One of the poorer Southern states, Arkansas was ill equipped for war. The fighting taxed its already strained frontier economy, and divided loyalties among the citizens seriously undermined morale. Burdened with maintaining civil order, Flanagin worked diligently to relieve shortages of food, clothing, and medicine in the state. He tried to encourage manufacture both in the private and public sectors and to initiate welfare programs in the regions hardest hit by the war, but an empty treasury prevented success in either endeavor.

After Union troops captured Little Rock 10 Sept. 1863, the way was open for the appointment of a Union provisional governor, though Flanagin retained his office for several months. During this time he tried cooperating with the Unionists to establish a RECONSTRUCTION government acceptable to Washington. He finally left office 18 Apr. 1864, returning to his law practice. Shortly before hostilities ceased, he met at Marshall, Tex., with other Confederate leaders from the Trans-Mississippi states to discuss the possibility of seeking peace with the U.S. government independently of Richmond. Failing, he retired to Arkadelphia, where he died 23 Oct. 1874 while serving as a member of the state constitutional convention.   —PLF

flanking position. To arrange a defender's battle lines so that 1 or more lines thrust forward at an angle from the main lines, is to place them in a flanking position. These roughly perpendicular defensive lines bring their fire to bear on the enemy's flank. Units in flanking position need not connect with units on the main battle line, so long as provision is made that no gap can be exploited or defensive communications assaulted through any area between the end of the main battle line and troops in flanking position. Troops in this position should be placed to bring down a crossfire on the enemy or charge forward and hit undefended sides of his assault or communications lines. If troops in flanking position have sufficient strength and are anchored tightly near one end of the main defense line, they can be wheeled to squeeze the enemy between themselves and main-line defenders.   —JES

Fleetwood Hill, Va., Battle of. 9 June 1863 *See* BRANDY STATION, VA., BATTLE OF.

Fletcher, Thomas. war governor b. Randolph Cty., Ark., 18 Apr. 1819. For 11 days in Nov. 1862 Fletcher, a Democrat, was governor of Arkansas. The former teacher had achieved his highest elective political office earlier in the year when he became president of the Confederate state senate. When Gov. HENRY M. RECTOR left office late in 1862, Fletcher succeeded him, 4 Nov., as acting governor. He served only long enough to call a gubernatorial election and perform official duties until a new governor, HARRIS FLANAGIN, could be inaugurated 15 Nov. Fletcher then returned to the senate until the state government was taken over by the pro-Union faction Apr. 1864, 7 months after Federal troops occupied Little Rock.

In the postwar years he read law, ran unsuccessfully for governor in 1876 and 1878, and held various minor political offices. He left the Democratic party in the 1890s to become a Populist leader. d. Little Rock, 21 Feb. 1900. —PLF

Florida. On 10 Jan. 1861, Florida, with a population of about 140,000, almost half of whom were black slaves, became the third state to secede from the Union. The Florida convention meeting in Tallahassee adopted the secession ordinance 62 to 7, and the capital celebrated that night with a torchlight parade.

Warlike preparations had begun 2 months earlier with recruiting, equipping, and training militia, and warlike action took place even before secession. As the year began, Florida officials heard that the Federal government had authorized reinforcement of the forts at Pensacola and the destruction of the arsenal at Chattahoochee to prevent pro-Southern militia from seizing them. Moving quickly, and by order of Gov. MADISON S. PERRY, on 5 Jan. state troops took over the arsenal and on 7 Jan. seized Fort Marion at St. Augustine. Federal forces had to withdraw from McRee and Barrancas, the mainland forts at Pensacola, to Fort Pickens, on an island in Pensacola harbor.

The exchange of fire during this operation has been called "the first fighting of the war." On 12 Jan. a combined force of about 550 Florida and Alabama troops took over the Pensacola Navy Yard. The force was anxious to attack FORT PICKENS but several Southern leaders, hoping immediate war might be avoided, insisted on delay. At Abraham Lincoln's order, Union troops heavily reinforced Fort Pickens and it, along with Forts Jefferson and Taylor, remained under Federal control during the war, enabling the Union to keep Florida's coast and Confederate forts blockaded.

Florida was an important source of cattle and salt for the Confederacy. A Union officer boasted that the destruction of some saltworks near Pensacola during a Federal raid "hurt the South more than would have the loss of Charleston." And the demolition of saltworks on Florida's St. Joseph's Bay was hailed by the New York *Herald* as "a greater blow than capturing 20,000 troops."

Largely through the efforts of JOHN MILTON, Perry's successor as governor, Florida furnished 21 military organizations—14,000–15,000 men—to Confederate forces; over 1,300 men were killed in action or died of wounds and 1,100 or more died of disease. About 1,200 white Floridians and almost as many blacks served in Federal armies. —PR

Florida, CSS. Secretly built in England, the *Florida,* the first cruiser constructed abroad for the Confederacy, began as a hard-luck ship but developed into one of the South's most effective weapons against the North's sea commerce.

As the *Oreto,* a twin-bladed screw steamer, it was sneaked out of Liverpool, unarmed, by a British crew 22 Mar. 1862 and taken to Nassau, to be met by its first commander, JOHN N. MAFFITT. The ship at last got clearance from British authorities to depart Nassau and was spirited away 17 Aug., its guns put aboard, and its name changed to *Florida.*

Yellow fever had already struck her crew, killing several. Maffitt also became ill and narrowly escaped death. With only 1 fireman and 4 deck hands fit for duty, he ran the blockade 4 Sept. and reached Mobile. Refurbished, the ship ran back to sea 16 Jan. 1863, and 3 days later made its first capture. On 12 Feb. it bagged the *Jacob Bell,* the most valuable prize (estimated at $1.5 million) taken by a Confederate cruiser during the war.

In August, Maffitt went into Brest, France, for repairs. There, because of ill health, he was succeeded first by Cmdr. Joseph N. Barney, then, weeks later, by Lt. Charles M. Morris. The *Florida* left Brest 12 Feb. 1864 and continued its scourge of the sea. On 4 Oct. it put into Bahia, Brazil, leaving a trail of 37 captures. There the ship anchored close to the USS *WACHUSETT,* assuming safety under rules of international warfare. But at 3:15 a.m., 7 Oct., with part of its crew ashore, the Union vessel rammed and captured the ship, towing it to sea.

A gross outrage having been committed against the neutral government of Brazil, the U.S. agreed the vessel should be returned, with crew. But the Union had no intention of letting this ship get back to sea. The *Florida* was taken to the Chesapeake Bay and there, under highly questionable circumstances, sank after being rammed by an army transport. Brazil received only an apology. —VCJ

Florida, Union Department of. Created by order of Gen.-in-Chief WINFIELD SCOTT 13 Apr. 1861, one day after the bombardment of FORT SUMTER, and formed as part of the Department of the East, the Union Department of Florida consisted not only of Florida but also contiguous islands in the Gulf of Mexico. That same day Brev. Col. Harvey Brown of the 2d U.S. Artillery was placed in command. At that time Brown was in charge of a relief expedition bound for FORT PICKENS, at the entrance to Pensacola harbor. On 18 Apr. the expedition reached its destination, which thereafter served as departmental headquarters.

The department remained unchanged until 11 Jan. 1862, when it was designated to comprise Florida except for Key West, the Tortugas, and the mainland from Apalachicola to Cape Canaveral; the excluded territory was transferred to the Department of Key West. On 22 Feb. Brown was replaced by Brig. Gen. Lewis G. Arnold, who retained control when, 15 Mar. 1862, the department merged into the Department of the South. Later West Florida, Key West, and the Tortugas were transferred to the Department of the Gulf, then to the Division of West Mississippi.

The Department of the South was reorganized Apr. 1864, following the transfer of its field force, the X Corps, to Virginia. As part of the reorganization, a District of Florida emerged, dating from the 25th, and existed for 6 months, commanded by, successively, Brig. Gen. WILLIAM BIRNEY and George H. Gordon, Birney again, Col. William H. Noble, and Brig. Gen.

JOHN P. HATCH. In Oct. 1864 the forces composing it (most of them U.S. Colored Troops) were designated as the 4th Separate Brigade, Department of the South.

On 27 June 1865 the Department of Florida was reconstituted as part of the Reconstruction command known as the Division of the Gulf. Maj. Gen. JOHN G. FOSTER took command, with headquarters at Tallahassee, 1 Aug. of that year. On 6 Aug. 1866 the department again passed out of existence when merged into the Department of the Gulf.   —EGL

Floyd, John Buchanan.

CSA   b. Montgomery Cty., Va., 1 June 1806. A talented politician who might have been expected to accomplish great things for the Confederacy, Floyd lost both his military reputation and credibility.

Floyd attended South Carolina College, pursuing careers as a lawyer and planter until elected to the house of delegates in 1847 and then to the Virginia governorship in 1848. Appointed secretary of war by Pres. James Buchanan in 1857, Floyd resigned the post 29 Dec. 1860, when Buchanan maintained a policy at Charleston harbor that angered the South. Floyd was afterward accused in the North of transferring quantities of arms to Southern arsenals in preparation for war.

Floyd returned to western Virginia to raise a brigade of mountaineers and 23 May 1861 was appointed a Confederate brigadier, thereafter becoming involved in small battles at Cross Lanes, CARNIFIX FERRY, and Gauley Bridge in western Virginia.

Floyd's brigade was sent Dec. 1861 to serve in Gen. ALBERT SIDNEY JOHNSTON's army in Tennessee, where Feb. 1862 the brigade helped defend the vital Confederate defensive post of FORT DONELSON, threatened by an advancing Union force under Brig. Gen. U. S. Grant. Shortly after arriving, Floyd, the ranking commander, found his army surrounded on the land side of the Cumberland River. After an attack to break out was bungled, the vacillating Floyd agreed with Brig. Gen. SIMON B. BUCKNER that they would have to surrender. Saving himself and most of his brigade by steamboat, he allowed Buckner to surrender the main army. Floyd then retreated to Nashville, which he abandoned after an attempt to save supplies there. For his behavior in deserting his command, Floyd was relieved 11 Mar. 1862.

Floyd nevertheless continued to be active in the war effort in southwestern Virginia. Commissioned a major general in the militia, he used his influence to raise a band of PARTISANS who terrorized Unionists in the area and annoyed Confederate authorities trying to recruit troops for the Regular service in the same vicinity. But the constant campaigning ruined Floyd's health, and he died near Abingdon, Va., 26 Aug. 1863.
                                                                    —CMS

flying battery.

2 or more horse-drawn cannon whipping along the battlefield, unlimbering, firing, limbering up, and riding off to fire from another position were loosely referred to as a "flying battery." No Union or Confederate organization officially listed a gun section as a flying battery. The term refers to the light-artillery tactic of keeping guns moving and fighting. However, Confederate Maj. JOHN PELHAM, commander of Lt. Gen. J.E.B. STUART's HORSE ARTILLERY, and given great credit for refining this tactic, often heard his 4 guns referred to as a flying battery.

The technique was particularly effective when the flying battery's movements were concealed by forest or terrain, giving the illusion of several guns in different positions. A Confederate flying battery was even effective against the Union navy: near Wilmington, N.C., blockade runners pursued by naval vessels were often covered by a flying battery hauling a Whitworth rifled cannon, which would appear from behind sand dunes, race down the beach, unlimber, fire on the navy, move behind the dunes, and fire again—all of which kept the navy from taking its range and allowed the blockade runner time to make the shelter of the harbor.   —JES

Flying Telegraph Train.

The Union army's chief signal officer, Col. ABRAHAM J. MYER, first devised the idea of the Flying Telegraph Train to accommodate the short-distance capability, but high mobility, of the BEARDSLEE TELEGRAPH system. The appearance of the flying trains coincided with the experimental Beardslee system's brief use in spring 1862. The trains themselves were merely 2 wagons, with 2 Beardslees, 5 mi of wire (the short but effective range of the system), 150 15-ft lances or portable telegraph poles, 50 18-ft lances, 5 hand reels for the wire, and 2 hand-crank magnetos to power the sending sets. About 30 of these 2-wagon trains were set up and expected to keep pace with the army in the field, raising or removing wire as the campaign's needs dictated. The word flying was meant to summon images of these electronic messengers breezing along with the moving army. In a day when most telegraphy was tied to permanent stations and miles of heavy-duty poles, the system was effective.

On the elimination of the Beardslee system, the flying train stayed on in slightly different form. A battery wagon was added to compensate for the loss of the Beardslee magneto; this increased the telegraph's range. What was once the Flying Telegraph Train became the standard field telegraph train.
                                                                    —JES

foot cavalry.

Members of the II Corps/Army of Northern Virginia called themselves "foot cavalry," a proud appellation born during Maj. Gen. THOMAS J. "STONEWALL" JACKSON's 1862 SHENANDOAH VALLEY CAMPAIGN. In 6 weeks, Jackson's lean, rugged fighters marched 400 mi, fought 5 pitched battles, and baffled 3 Union commands. Throughout the harrowing campaign Jackson rode along the marching columns, saying, "Press on, men. Press on." "Close up. Close up."—words that forged a command and echo through history.

The foot cavalry became the Confederacy's hardest-marching, finest offensive body of troops. In the SECOND BULL RUN CAMPAIGN, they covered 50 mi in 2 days in a march beyond the Union army's flank. In June–July 1864, under Lt. Gen. JUBAL A. EARLY, the II Corps raided the North, marching over 500 mi in 5 weeks. An old Confederate could boast of no greater association than to say he belonged to "Old Jack's foot cavalry."
                                                                    —JDW

Foote, Andrew Hull.

USN   b. New Haven, Conn., 12 Sept. 1806. After attending West Point for several months in 1822, Foote left to accept an appointment as midshipman at Annapolis. While in the navy, Foote, deeply religious, became a crusader for temperance and against the African slave trade. He was also a fighter: while commanding the Portsmouth at Canton, China, 1856–58, he led 327 sailors and marines in action against several thousand Chinese after Chinese nationals fired on ships flying the American flag.

In Aug. 1861 Navy Sec. GIDEON WELLES, a friend of Foote's,

assigned him to command naval forces on the upper Mississippi. Working with Brig. Gen. ULYSSES S. GRANT, Foote was to move downriver and cut the South in two, thereby denying the Confederacy supplies from the West and Southwest. Foote's flotilla fought superbly at FORT HENRY, winning the victory 6 Feb. 1862, although the combined land/sea attack on FORT DONELSON, 14 Feb. 1862, was an army victory. During the action against Donelson, shell splinters struck Foote

USMHI

aboard the *St. Louis.* He refused to let his injuries slow him down, although he was on crutches during the attack on ISLAND NO. 10. Finally, because of ill health, Foote was unable to continue his command and was replaced by Capt. CHARLES H. DAVIS. Foote became an admiral and was put in charge of the Bureau of Equipment and Recruiting in Washington, D.C. Dissatisfied with being away from the action, Foote finally was given another command, the SOUTH ATLANTIC BLOCKADING SQUADRON. Completely dedicated to duty, he died while en route to his new command 26 June 1863.   —NCD

Foote, Henry Stuart. CSP b. Fauquier Cty., Va., 28 Feb. 1804. That Confederate Tennesseans elected pro-Union Foote to the Southern Congress is almost as puzzling as their representative's willingness to serve.

Throughout his tenure, Foote opposed almost every policy put forward by the administration, waging a battle against the war and against Pres. JEFFERSON DAVIS, and finally invoking the censure of his congressional colleagues.

NA

Foote practiced law in Richmond in 1823, relocated briefly in Alabama, then became a noted criminal attorney and politician in Mississippi. In 1847 the state legislature elected him to the U.S. Senate, where he began his personal and political feud with Davis, the state's other senator, partly over their divergent opinions on secession. Surprisingly, Foote won the governorship in 1853, but a year later, disgusted with Mississippi's powerful STATES-RIGHTS faction, he moved to California. He returned east in 1858 and settled in Nashville, Tenn. Despite his outspoken Unionism, he was elected to the CONFEDERATE CONGRESS in fall 1861 and reelected 2 years later.

Foote immediately established himself as an antagonist in Richmond, consistently voting against war measures. He vigorously opposed CONSCRIPTION, which he saw as a catalyst to civil war within the South; the suspension of *HABEAS CORPUS,* which, he argued, disregarded individual rights; and Davis' defensive military policy, which, ironically, he thought should embrace total offensive warfare. His fiery temper brought him to blows with colleagues on 2 occasions, and even his friends tired of his prolonged spontaneous outbursts on the House

floor. As a self-appointed one-man committee on the conduct of the war, he initiated no fewer than 30 inquiries into fraud in the commissary and quartermaster's departments, and repeatedly sought official sanction to open peace talks with the Federal government, to dismiss top officials, and to abolish the War Department.

Finally, on the failure of the HAMPTON ROADS CONFERENCE 3 Feb. 1865, he decided to open his own unofficial peace negotiations with Abraham Lincoln but was captured by the Confederacy before he could cross the Potomac River. A vote to expel him failed, though his colleagues as a body condemned his treasonous behavior. Again he attempted to reach Washington, this time succeeding, but Lincoln refused to see him. Rather than go back to the South, he went to Europe.

In the postwar years, after Foote returned to Washington and became a friend of Pres. ULYSSES S. GRANT's, the president appointed him superintendent of the New Orleans Mint. He finally returned home to Nashville, where he died 19 May 1880.   —PLF

foraging. 2 definitions of the word, "to live off the land" and "to plunder," apply to wartime conditions, and whether acting under orders or off on an independent foray, the Civil War soldier frequently resorted to foraging to vary his army rations. Much foraging was carried out by authorized details led by officers. Maj. Gen. WILLIAM T. SHERMAN followed the practice as part of his strategy on the MARCH TO THE SEA, and Maj. Gen. PHILIP H. SHERIDAN adopted it during his SHENANDOAH VALLEY CAMPAIGN of 1864. Generally, official foraging parties, Union or Confederate, issued receipts for stock or stores taken, these to be presented to the quartermaster for reimbursement. Commanding officers often took severe measures to protect civilian property from wanton pilferage, issuing restrictive orders, posting guards, and punishing offenders.

A vast amount of foraging, however, was "unauthorized," ignored if not encouraged by lower-grade officers lax in enforcing discipline, applauded by comrades sharing the spoils. Receipts might be issued to civilians professing loyalty, but they carried no guarantee of being honored. Some Southern soldiers felt entitled to civilian foodstuffs in exchange for fighting, and took what was not freely given. Occasionally observers reported the cavalry more prone to foraging than the infantry. No appreciable distinction was noted between Union and Confederate foragers. *See also* BUMMERS.   —PLF

Forbes, Edwin. artist b. New York, N.Y., 1839. In 1857 Forbes began studying art at the National Academy of Design in New York City, specializing in animal art. His instructor, Arthur F. Tait, achieved notice creating horse-racing and country scenes for the Currier & Ives firm. In later years features of Tait's instruction were apparent in Forbes's Civil War art.

Hired by *FRANK LESLIE'S ILLUSTRATED NEWSPAPER* as "special artist" in 1862 to cover the Civil War, Forbes in the next 2 and a half years sketched the SHENANDOAH VALLEY CAMPAIGN of 1862, the SECOND BATTLE OF BULL RUN, the Battle of ANTIETAM, the struggle on BURNSIDE'S MUD MARCH Jan. 1863, the CHANCELLORSVILLE CAMPAIGN, the Battle of GETTYSBURG, the WILDERNESS Campaign, the beginning of the Siege of PETERSBURG, and Confederate Lt. Gen. Jubal A. EARLY's WASHINGTON RAID in mid-July 1864.

Between his coverage of these great battles and events he sketched daily camp life in the Union army and incidents in the

LC

field. These became his favorite subjects, and he produced a large body of work that formed the basis of his famous postwar series of copper-plate etchings, *Life Studies of the Great Army* (1876). He also returned to animal studies and did many sketches of cavalry and artillery horses at work and in action. In these, like his teacher Tait and other artists, he drew a running mount with all 4 feet off the ground. Though not unique to Forbes's art, this "flying horse" is frequently used to identify his animal studies.

Forbes's coverage of Early's raid on Washington was his last field work for *Leslie's.* Thereafter he lived in Flatbush, Brooklyn, reworking his best Civil War themes. At the 1876 Centennial Exposition he was given a medal for *Life Studies,* then in 1890 a 2-volume work, *Thirty Years After: An Artist's Story of the Great War,* was published. This also contained memoirs of his life as a Civil War "special" for *Leslie's.* Though a paralytic stroke numbed his right side in the early 1890s, he continued to work, drawing with his left hand until his death in Brooklyn, 6 Mar. 1895.   —JES

Force, Manning Ferguson.   USA   b. District of Columbia, 17 Dec. 1824. When Force entered the 26th Ohio Infantry as a major in 1861, he had been a successful attorney in the state for several years, having graduated from Harvard in 1845 and
from its law school in 1848. He
had resided in Cincinnati since
1850.

USMHI

With Ohio troops, Force took
part in the Union army's first
Western successes at FORTS
HENRY AND DONELSON, and in the
Federal near-disaster at SHILOH,
Apr. 1862, where he fought on
the Union's far right, commanding a portion of Maj. Gen. LEW
WALLACE's troops on the second
day of fighting. Force was often
questioned about Wallace's
controversial performance in this battle and in 1881 wrote *From Fort Henry to Corinth* about this and other early war experiences. During the first years of the war Force was promoted twice: to lieutenant colonel 11 Sept. 1861 and to full colonel 23 May 1862, the latter for his performance at Shiloh.

In Brig. Gen. ULYSSES S. GRANT's army, he fought through the VICKSBURG Campaign, taking part in the engagement at RAYMOND and serving on the Vicksburg siege lines with the XVII

Corps. This last service won praise from corps commander Maj. Gen. JAMES B. MCPHERSON, the award of a XVII Corps Medal, and promotion to brigadier general 11 Aug. 1863. Force soldiered with this corps through the north Georgia fighting and the Battle of ATLANTA as a part of Brig. Gen. MORTIMER D. LEGGETT's division. As head of the division's 1st Brigade he saw hot combat 22 July 1864 on the Union left in front of the city and in the fighting distinguished himself for bravery, receiving the Medal of Honor in 1892. But the cost was high: Force was badly wounded in the face and permanently disfigured.

His wound kept him from the field until October, when he rejoined the Army of the Tennessee in Atlanta and with it set out on the MARCH TO THE SEA and the CAROLINAS CAMPAIGN. Through the latter campaign and until the Confederate surrender, he commanded the XVII Corps' 1st Division. In Jan. 1866 he was mustered out of service after being brevetted major general for his bravery in the Battle of Atlanta.

Force returned to Cincinnati a hero and was shortly elected to a judgeship, sitting on the state bench 1866–67 and finally serving as a superior court judge. He then accepted a post as head of the Ohio Soldiers' and Sailors' Home, which he held until his death in Cincinnati 8 May 1899.   —JES

Ford's Theater.   The theater at 10th St., Washington, D.C., where ABRAHAM LINCOLN was assassinated 14 Apr. 1865, was the second playhouse to occupy the site. The original building, erected 1833–34, housed the First Baptist Church of Washington. Services were held there until 1855, when the congregation merged with another and relocated. In 1861 the building

LC

was purchased by John Thomson Ford (1829–94), a Baltimore-born bookseller turned theater owner and manager.

The thought of a theater replacing a house of God disturbed many Washingtonians, and one, who had worshiped in the church, predicted a dire fate for its successor. The prophecy came true when, 9 months after its opening, Ford's Atheneum was gutted by a fire caused by a defective gas meter.

Undeterred by his misfortune, John Ford planned a larger and more modern structure, one equipped for the production of dramatic plays as well as musicals, the standard fare of the Atheneum. The cornerstone of the new edifice was laid 28 Feb. 1863, and 27 Aug. it opened as one of the finest theaters in the country. The auditorium sat almost 1,700, including 421 in the dress circle (first balcony). The orchestra pit, parquet, and dress circle, sloping downward toward the stage, were fitted with comfortable cane-bottomed chairs. On either side of the stage were 4 boxes, 2 upper and 2 lower.

From its first performance, of *The Naiad Queen*, until closed by the government following the assassination, Ford's Theater was one of the capital's most popular places of amusement. Some 495 performances were given there before Washington's political, military, and social elite. Lincoln attended 8 plays at the theater, his wife several more; on 9 Nov. 1863 the president saw a performance of *The Marble Heart*, starring one of the city's favorite actors, JOHN WILKES BOOTH.

On the night he was shot, Lincoln, his wife, and 2 guests occupied an enlarged box in the dress circle, to the right of the stage. The play was the sort that Lincoln favored, a farce about an English family's attempt to cheat a Yankee relation out of an inheritance they must share. *Our American Cousin* starred Laura Keene, a popular actress making her 1,000th appearance on the stage. As a benefit in her honor, the performance received a healthy advance booking; Lincoln's presence, and the rumored attendance of Gen. and Mrs. Ulysses S. Grant, made it a sellout. *See also* LINCOLN'S ASSASSINATION.   —EGL

foreign-born soldiers. Over half a million foreign-born soldiers fought in the American Civil War, the majority for the Union. Some enlisted hungry for advancement or adventure, others to collect substantial BOUNTIES. They were called hirelings and fodder for Confederate artillery, and suffered from an unfair draft. But most volunteered to defend a nation that gave them economic opportunities and freedoms denied them in their homelands. The subject of anti-immigrant hostility through the 1850s, they now embraced military service as a chance to show loyalty to their adopted country.

Recognizing their potential, Abraham Lincoln courted the foreign-born population in the 1860 presidential campaign, then, once elected, repaid its leaders with military appointments. He was not disappointed. They recruited energetically among their countrymen as war fever swept the North. Companies of German, Irish, Scandinavian, and French organized, elected officers from their ranks, and were mustered into the army.

Soldiers of almost every nation brought to the Union army experience their native-born comrades lacked. They were often veterans of military service in Europe, and some, especially those who had been officers, had served in the Crimean War or the revolutions of 1848. Their military discipline and bearing elicited favorable comment amid the confusion that marked the raw American recruits early in 1861. Language did present serious problems, particularly on the battlefield. Large numbers of recruits spoke only their native tongue or had

limited command of English, and at the beginning of the war needed officers of their own nationality to issue commands in a language they understood. A short time into the war recruiters made some efforts to teach basic English to newly arrived immigrant recruits before sending them to the front.

Foreign-born units were easily recognized by their colorful uniforms and regimental flags that often honored 2 countries. Several, such as the Garibaldi Guard and the IRISH BRIGADE, distinguished themselves with unrivaled bravery. Men and officers shared a fierce pride in their nation of birth. Favored was the German-American infantryman who could boast, "I fight mit [Franz] Sigel." Irish-born Brig. Gen. THOMAS F. MEAGHER submitted his resignation after the Battle of FREDERICKSBURG to protest the treatment of his Irish Brigade. In all, 6 men of foreign birth attained the rank of major general in the Union army: FRANZ SIGEL, CARL SCHURZ, and PETER J. OSTERHAUS, from the German states; ROBERT PATTERSON, Ireland; JACOB D. COX, Canada; and JULIUS H. STAHEL, Hungary.

Fewer talented foreign-born soldiers rose to high rank in the Confederacy, partly due to prejudice, partly because the South attracted fewer immigrants. Only 2 men, Irish-born PATRICK R. CLEBURNE and the affable Frenchman CAMILLE ARMAND JULES MARIE, PRINCE DE POLIGNAC, were promoted to major general. Perhaps the best known foreign-born Confederate was the dashing Prussian cavalryman HEROS VON BORCKE, chief of staff and close friend of Maj. Gen. J.E.B. STUART. Lower-grade officers and enlisted men tended to be distributed throughout the Southern armies rather than segregated, but 9 Confederate states did send more than 150 units (usually companies) of predominantly foreign-born soldiers into the field.

By 1863 few foreign units, South or North, could replenish their ranks with their own countrymen. As they accepted native-born replacements, their distinctiveness gave way to the regimentation of army life and to increased contact with native-born men. But by 1865, men who had been grudgingly tolerated before the war had earned full rights to the privileges and opportunities of citizenship, and many who fought as mercenaries stayed to enjoy the nation's bounty.   —PLF

Forney, John Horace. CSA b. Lincolnton, N.C., 12 Aug. 1829. In 1835 Forney's family migrated to Alabama, where he and his older brother, WILLIAM HENRY, also a future Confederate general, were educated by tutors. John entered West Point in 1848, graduating 22d in his class 4 years later. Through most of his U.S. Army career he was assigned to frontier garrisons or recruiting duty, achieving rank of 1st lieutenant 25 Aug. 1855. After participating in Col. ALBERT SIDNEY JOHNSTON's Utah Expedition, he taught tactics at West Point until resigning his commission 23 Jan. 1861.

Forney first joined Alabama troops as a colonel of artillery under Brig. Gen. BRAXTON BRAGG at Pensacola. In March he resigned from state service to accept a captaincy in the Confederate army, raised the 10th Alabama, and 4 June was commissioned colonel of the regiment. The career officer's insistence on strict discipline made him unpopular with some volunteer soldiers, though it earned him respect from his peers.

Through the early months of the war he fought in Virginia, being severely wounded in the right arm at DRANESVILLE 20 Dec. Advanced to brigadier general 10 Mar. 1862 and ordered to Mobile, he was given charge of the District of the Gulf 2 July. On 27 Oct. he was promoted to major general and at the end of the year he reported to Lt. Gen. JOHN C. PEMBERTON at

Vicksburg, where he held divisional command until the city was surrendered 4 July 1863, Forney along with it.

Following his exchange 13 July and a period of leave with his family, he oversaw the parole and exchange of troops in Mississippi Nov. 1863–July 1864 and commanded a division under Gen. E. KIRBY SMITH in Louisiana through 1864. By right of seniority he superseded Maj. Gen. JOHN G. WALKER as commander of the District of Texas Mar. 1865. He was paroled at Galveston 20 June, 18 days after Smith surrendered the Trans-Mississippi.

During the postwar years Forney operated a small military academy in Jacksonville, Ala., and worked as a surveyor and civil engineer. d. Jacksonville, 13 Sept. 1902.   —PLF

Forney, William Henry. CSA b. Lincolnton, N.C., 9 Nov. 1823. Accompanying his family to Alabama in 1835, Forney graduated from the state university 9 years later. He read law in

the Jacksonville, Ala., office of his brother Daniel, leaving to serve as a lieutenant in the 1st Alabama Volunteers in Mexico. Returning in 1848 to Jacksonville and the law, he was admitted to the bar and by 1859 was also a state legislator.

Forney entered Confederate service as a captain in the 10th Alabama Infantry, a regiment commanded by another brother, John, a West Pointer and future major general. At DRANESVILLE, VA., 20 Dec. 1861,

GG

Forney saw his first action and received the first of his 13 wartime wounds. Having risen to lieutenant colonel of his regiment by the start of the 1862 PENINSULA CAMPAIGN, he was again wounded at WILLIAMSBURG. Captured while hospitalized, he was exchanged in September. As a colonel, he led the 10th Alabama at FREDERICKSBURG and at CHANCELLORSVILLE, where he took another wound.

Forney's military service was temporarily halted 2 July 1863 while he was serving in the center of the Confederate line at GETTYSBURG. That afternoon, under Brig. Gen. CADMUS M. WIL-COX, the brigade to which the 10th Alabama belonged was struck by parts of 2 Union regiments making a reconnaissance in force. A sharp 20-minute engagement occurred astride a branch of Pitzer's Run, ending when Forney led his regiment in a counterattack that sent the enemy reeling. Though wounded in the arm and chest, he kept charging. Next, his right arm was shattered by a minié bullet, but he did not halt till a wound in the foot crippled him. Left behind during Gen. R.E. Lee's retreat, he was again captured, and was imprisoned for over a year.

After his exchange, he returned on crutches to his regiment and directed it through autumn 1864. Temporarily in command of Wilcox's brigade several times during the PETERSBURG CAMPAIGN, he received the unit permanently when promoted brigadier general 15 Feb. 1865. Still disabled, he accompanied the Army of Northern Virginia to Appomattox, where he surrendered the remnants of the brigade: 952 officers and men.

Though maimed for life, Forney enjoyed a successful postwar legal and political career, serving in the Alabama senate till ousted by the CARPETBAGGER regime. When local govern-

ment regained power, he was sent to the U.S. House of Representatives, where he served continuously 1875–93. d. Jacksonville, Ala., 16 Jan. 1894.   —EGL

Forrest, French. CSN b. St. Mary's Cty., Md., 4 Oct. 1796, Forrest was appointed midshipman in the U.S. Navy 9 June 1811, serving in both the War of 1812 and the Mexican War. In the latter he was a cap-tain, commanding the *Cumber-land* and the *Raritan* in action off Vera Cruz.

Resigning his commission, Forrest was appointed a captain in the Virginia navy after that state seceded. On 10 June 1861 he received the same rank in the Confederate navy, becoming third in seniority, which, Forrest believed, entitled him to an ac-tive command. Placed in charge of the Gosport Navy Yard at Norfolk, Forrest was ordered by Navy Sec. STEPHEN R. MALLORY to

USMHI

rebuild as an armored ship the hulk that was the USS *Mer-rimack*. This Forrest did, despite misgivings, resulting in the CSS *VIRGINIA*, the South's first IRONCLAD. Though Forrest expected to command the *Virginia,* the position was given to Capt. FRANK-LIN BUCHANAN. 3 months after the Battle of HAMPTON ROADS, 8–9 Mar. 1862, Mallory had Forrest replaced at Gosport for slowness in repairing the *Virginia* for service. Forrest became head of the Office of Orders and Details until Mar. 1863, when he finally received the command he coveted, becoming Flag Officer of the James River Squadron. The squadron, however, was not involved in any significant action during Forrest's ten-ure, and May 1864 he was replaced by Cmdr. John K. Mitchell. d. District of Columbia, 22 Nov. 1866.   —NCD

Forrest, Nathan Bedford. CSA b. Bedford Cty., Tenn., 13 July 1821. The son of a poverty-stricken, backwoods black-smith, no man had more to overcome during his rise to fame than Forrest. Forced to assume responsibility for a large family at 16, Forrest, who could make the most of meager resources, became a successful slave trader and planter by 1861.

Enlisting in the Confederate army as a private that year, he was promoted to brigadier gen-eral 21 July 1862, major general 4 Dec. 1863, and by war's end he was a lieutenant general. De-spite a lack of military educa-tion, he displayed extraordinary capability as a tactician and a firm grasp of strategic consider-ations. His underlying philosophy of warfare was "War means fightin' and fightin' means killin'." He applied this belief with such imagination and ferocity that he became the most feared of all Confederate cavalry leaders.

Forrest's escape with all his men from FORT DONELSON and his performance at SHILOH brought him to prominence early in the war, which allowed him to develop the raiding tactics that made his cavalry a superb strike force. Time after time, he led his men on raids behind enemy lines and invariably accomplished far more than could have been expected from the resources committed. Though such outstanding successes caused his other capabilities to be overlooked for much of the war, he was far more than a raider, which he clearly demonstrated at BRICE'S CROSS ROADS. There, in a head-on engagement, he inflicted one of the most humiliating defeats in the history of the U.S. Army.

Following the war Forrest devoted his life to farming and business interests. Maj. Gen. WILLIAM T. SHERMAN summed up the accomplishments of this charismatic leader and magnificent field commander when he said, "After all, I think Forrest was the most remarkable man our Civil War produced on either side." d. Memphis, 29 Oct. 1877. *See also* FORREST'S FIRST RAID; FORREST'S SECOND RAID.   —WRB/DKS

Forrest's First Raid, Tenn.   July 1862   Following reorganization of the Confederate army and his personal success at SHILOH, Col. NATHAN B. FORREST was recommended for promotion to brigadier general and given a command around Chattanooga June 1862. On 9 July he led this regimental-size cavalry force across the Cumberland Mts. to McMinnville, where it rendezvoused with 5 additional companies 11 July. Under Maj. Gen. E. KIRBY SMITH's orders, Forrest's 1,400 men were to raid, scout, and discourage the Union Army of the Cumberland's movements in Middle Tennessee.

At 1 p.m., 13 July, Forrest's brigade set out from McMinnville, riding northwest. They stopped at Woodbury at 11 p.m., received reports on the strength and supplies of the Federal garrison at Murfreesboro, and decided it was a good objective. The Confederates hit Murfreesboro at 4:30 a.m. and by early afternoon had captured Brig. Gen. THOMAS L. CRITTENDEN, his entire 1,040-man garrison, its artillery, small arms, and supplies. In 14 and a half hours Forrest's men had ridden 50 mi; within another 10 hours they were riding back toward McMinnville, their prisoners driving wagons loaded with $1 million in goods and arms.

Kirby Smith and Gen. BRAXTON BRAGG were readying Chattanooga troops for an invasion of Kentucky and ordered Forrest to make a feint at Nashville, distracting Brig. Gen. WILLIAM "Bull" NELSON and the new Federal garrison at Murfreesboro from campaign preparations. On 18 July Forrest's raiders left McMinnville at noon. Frightened by Forrest's success at Murfreesboro and alerted to his new moves, the Union commander at Nashville dispatched a force to Lebanon, northeast of the city, mistakenly believing that the troops in Forrest's command numbered 7,000.

After ranging through Middle Tennessee for 2 days, avoiding Murfreesboro, Forrest's brigade rode into Lebanon at dawn, 20 July, and found that Federals there had retreated the day before, concerned by the reported size of the Confederate force. At noon, 21 July, his men rode through the Hermitage, 12 mi from Nashville, and late that afternoon drove in Union pickets 5 mi from the city. The hours before dark were spent destroying rail lines to the Chattanooga area, telegraph lines, and railroad stockades. That same afternoon Confederate operations around the city compelled Federals in Nashville to wire Nelson to send infantry north to engage Forrest. The raiders returned south in the face of Nelson's column, avoiding them and the remaining Murfreesboro garrison by simple detours.

The last clash between Forrest and Federal troops in Middle Tennessee occurred at Manchester, southeast of McMinnville, 27 July. There Union Brig. Gen. WILLIAM S. SMITH's small force, guarding a branch rail line from Tullahoma to McMinnville, was bloodied by some of Forrest's troops operating against the railroad. There was additional maneuvering in Middle Tennessee between Forrest and the Federals into late August, when the Confederates' Kentucky campaigning was under way, but actual raiding stopped at the end of the month. *See also* FORREST'S SECOND RAID.   —JES

Forrest's Second Raid, Tenn.   11 Dec. 1862–3 Jan. 1863 While Gen. BRAXTON BRAGG campaigned against Federals in the Murfreesboro, Tenn., area, he granted a request for help from Confederate Lt. Gen. JOHN C. PEMBERTON, commanding at Vicksburg. Bragg ordered Brig. Gen. NATHAN B. FORREST to raid in West Tennessee, destroying the rail supply line to Maj. Gen. ULYSSES S. GRANT's troops campaigning to Vicksburg through north Mississippi. Forrest's new brigade, 2,100 men from Tennessee and Alabama, were to destroy the Mississippi Central Railroad track in the Jackson area and the Mobile & Ohio Railroad track running from Columbus, Ky., south through Jackson. Grant's army got all its supplies directly from Columbus by train, and if Forrest was successful, the army, cut off from its commissary goods and munitions, would be forced out of Mississippi; at the least, Confederate cavalry operating to the rear might slow the Federal advance.

On 15 Dec. Forrest's men arrived at Clifton from Middle Tennessee, crossed the Tennessee River on 2 flatboats, and entered hostile country. Because of a decision to cross the horses by boat, the ferrying was not completed until late on the night of 16 Dec. The movement was reported by Union intelligence, and by the time Forrest's men set out on the morning of the 17th, Grant had ordered troops to concentrate at Jackson, and a cavalry force under Col. Robert G. Ingersoll was moving to confront the Confederates.

Ingersoll's troopers clashed with Forrest's at Beech Creek on the 18th, fell back 5 mi to Lexington, and were routed by severe fighting. Ingersoll, 149 other Federals, 2 3-in. Rodman cannon, and 300 Sharps rifles and ammunition were captured. On the 19th Forrest demonstrated east of Jackson while Confederate detachments tore up Mobile & Ohio track 8 mi north of the town and wrecked Mississippi Central track south of it. District of Jackson commander Brig. Gen. JEREMIAH C. SULLIVAN organized for a desperate defense of the community, not realizing his force outnumbered Forrest's 4-to-1. The next day his men began a timid pursuit while Confederates split their force and took Humboldt and Trenton. Also on the 20th, Forrest paroled the 1,200 Union troops he had captured since entering West Tennessee.

On 23 Dec. Forrest captured Union City, near the Tennessee/Kentucky state line, where he made his headquarters through Christmas Eve. Since the 20th his men had torn up additional Mobile & Ohio track and burned trestles; on the 23d and 24th they ranged north across the state line and even destroyed railroad trestles at Moscow, Ky., 10 mi south of the Columbus railhead. No Union force came out of Columbus to meet them, presumably because of Federal Maj. Gen. HENRY W. HALLECK's orders to stay there protecting rail facilities.

On Christmas Day Forrest set out southeast, down the Northwestern Railroad's line, hoping to end the raid and cross the Tennessee River. But after passing into the country beyond the railroads, he found the small Obion River and other streams near flood level, Union gunboats active on the navigable waters, most bridges burned by Sullivan's men, and forces moving against him from all points.

After dodging Sullivan's 2d and 3d brigades 29–30 Dec. in the Huntingdon area north of Lexington, at 9 a.m., 31 Dec., Forrest was compelled to fight at PARKER'S CROSS ROADS. His troops escaped the battle and withdrew to Lexington 12 mi south.

In Lexington, Forrest paroled 300 Federals captured at Parker's Cross Roads and formed the march for Clifton. The next morning, as he neared the river, he clashed with a Union cavalry regiment from Maj. Gen. GRENVILLE M. DODGE's Corinth command, beat them, and reached the Clifton crossing by noon, 1 Jan. The concealed flatboats were brought out and in only 12 hours, the entire force crossed back into Middle Tennessee, with the horses made to swim.

On 2–3 Jan. leisurely Union pursuit and probing continued, but the raid was ended. *See also* FORREST'S FIRST RAID.   —JES

Forsyth, James William.

USA b. Maumee, Ohio, 8 Aug. 1835. An 1856 West Point graduate, 28th in his class, Forsyth served in Washington Territory until the outbreak of the Civil War. With the rank of 1st lieu-
tenant, he returned to his native state, where he acted as an assistant instructor of Ohio recruits at Mansfield. Promoted to captain 24 Oct. 1861, Forsyth commanded a brigade in the Army of the Ohio during the first 3 months of 1862. On 15 Mar. he accepted an appointment to the staff of Maj. Gen. GEORGE B. MCCLELLAN, acting as inspector general, then provost marshal general of the Army of the Potomac during the PENINSULA, SEVEN DAYS' and ANTIETAM campaigns.

NA

Forsyth eventually transferred to the Western theater, joining the staff of Maj. Gen. PHILIP H. SHERIDAN as acting assistant adjutant general and winning the brevet of major for his performance at CHICKAMAUGA. Forsyth remained with Sheridan as his chief of staff for the rest of the war and in spring 1864 went east with Sheridan, assuming command of the Cavalry Corps/Army of the Potomac. Forsyth participated in the Overland Campaign against Richmond and in Sheridan's victorious 1864 SHENANDOAH VALLEY CAMPAIGN. Forsyth was brevetted brigadier general of volunteers for gallantry in the valley, colonel in the Regular Army for FIVE FORKS, and brigadier general for his wartime service. On 19 May 1865 he received the full rank of brigadier general of volunteers.

Forsyth remained in the Regular Army after the war, for 2 years commanding a brigade of cavalry, then in 1867 rejoining Sheridan as an aide and military secretary. Promoted to lieutenant colonel in 1878, he served with the 1st Cavalry until 1886, when he became colonel of the 7th Cavalry. Between 1887 and 1890 Forsyth organized the School for Cavalry and Field Artillery at Fort Riley, Kans., which existed until World War II. To his discredit, Forsyth commanded the troops involved in the massacre of a band of Sioux Indians at Wounded Knee, S.D., 29 Dec. 1890. Promoted to brigadier general in

1894 and major general in 1897, Forsyth retired, dying in Columbus, Ohio, 24 Oct. 1906.   —JDW

Fort Bisland, La., eng. at.

13–14 Apr. 1863 *See* IRISH BEND AND FORT BISLAND, LA., ENGS. AT.

Fort Blakely, Ala., Siege of.

2–9 Apr. 1865 On 17–18 Mar. 1865, Union Maj. Gen. E.R.S. CANBY's troops of the XVI and XIII corps moved down the east and west shores of Mobile Bay driving Confederates into their defenses at Spanish Fort, opposite the bay from Mobile, and Fort Blakely, northeast of Mobile on the east bank of the Appalachee River. The movement of the XVI Corps down the western bay shore was a diversion; after 2 days they doubled back and joined XIII Corps troops pressing Blakely and Spanish Fort. Soon 13,000 Union troops arrived from Pensacola, Fla., and by 1 Apr. Federals had invested Spanish Fort and were within 700 yd of the walls.

Brig. Gen. RANDALL L. GIBSON's 2,000 Confederates tied up a portion of Canby's force at Spanish Fort, made a sortie against the Federals, and withstood periodic bombardment by Federal warships until the night of 8 Apr., when they evacuated to Mobile by boat. This allowed Canby to turn his force of 45,000 men on Blakely and besiege its garrison of about 4,000 men, commanded by Brig. Gen. ST. JOHN R. LIDDELL.

Liddell's men had been under siege 6 days when Union sappers' assault trench lines reached a point within 500 yd of the Confederate defenses. The remaining ground to Blakely's walls was covered with obstructions and torpedoes detonated by trip wires. Sniping had been relentless since the siege's beginning. On 9 Apr. Canby decided to try a general assault at 6 p.m. At the appointed hour 16,000 Union troops leaped from trenches and rushed the Confederates; 37 Union field pieces and 57 siege guns opened on the ground ahead of the charging troops. Liddell's men poured out a heavy small-arms fire but were crushed by artillery and force of numbers. Assaulting Federals easily avoided visible torpedo trip wires, negotiated obstructions, and routed Blakely's garrison within an hour. Some Confederates dispersed into nearby woods; others ran for the river landing, where they were trapped.

Federals captured nearly 3,200 of Liddell's men in their 9 Apr. assault. The few who escaped made their way to Mobile, and 11 Apr. were evacuated with Maj. Gen. DABNEY H. MAURY's 4,500-man city garrison. On 12 Apr. Mobile's mayor, R. H. Slough, surrendered the city to Canby's subordinate, Maj. Gen. GORDON GRANGER.

The fighting at Blakely was the last infantry combat of the war. Gen. Robert E. Lee's Confederates were surrendered the day the fort fell. This last engagement cost Federals 105 killed and 466 wounded.   —JES

Fort Brooke, Fla., engs. at.

16 Oct. and 25 Dec. 1863 Built in 1824 to protect peaceful Seminoles from more violent tribes, Fort Brooke commanded the head of Tampa Bay near the mouth of the Hillsborough River. Its proximity to that important Gulf Coast port made it a natural target for Union warships. Twice during fall and winter 1863, gunboats from the Federal blockading fleet in St. Mark's Bay moved against the fortress, hoping to gain control of the main channel adjacent to it. Both times they were turned back by a small Confederate garrison.

On 15 Oct. 1863, 2 gunboats steamed past Gadsden Point and on the next day moved up to the fort, which they pounded with 126 shells, including 200-pounder Parrott ammunition. That night 130 troops landed at Ballast Point, adjacent to the head of the bay, and marched overland to a point north of the fort, while the gunboats resumed their shelling of the garrison. Despite the barrage, the commander of Fort Brooke, Capt. John Wescott, 2d Florida Battalion, sent out a force that intercepted the Federals as they were about to raid local saltworks and other Confederate manufactories. Wescott took 5 prisoners and estimated that 50 others were killed or wounded.

On Christmas Eve the USS *Tahoma,* one of the gunboats that had attacked in October, returned to Fort Brooke, anchoring before the garrison. The next morning, it spent 2 hours blasting Wescott's garrison and the village along Tampa Bay with numerous 32- and 150-pounder shells. Meanwhile, a small schooner accompanying the *Tahoma* shelled the shore of the main channel. Wescott anticipated that his enemy would come ashore and was ready "to have received them properly." But the *Tahoma*'s skipper, Lt. Comdr. David B. Harmony, decided, once again, that the garrison was too energetic and its firepower too accurate. Harmony drew off about noon and proceeded down the bay, having inflicted no casualties.   —EGL

Fort Clark, N.C. *See* HATTERAS INLET, N.C., BATTLE OF.

Fort Darling, Va., First Battle of. 15 May 1862 *See* DREWRY'S BLUFF, VA., FIRST BATTLE OF.

Fort Darling, Va., Second Battle of. 16 May 1864 *See* DREWRY'S BLUFF, VA., SECOND BATTLE OF.

Fort Delaware. Built on Pea Patch Island in the Delaware River by Maj. Gen. GEORGE B. MCCLELLAN when he was a member of the Corps of Engineers, Fort Delaware housed political and naval prisoners from the beginning of the war. As the war progressed it became well known as a prison for Confederate soldiers, and it was this prison above all others that captives dreaded. Brig. Gen. Albin F. Schoepf, a Hungarian refugee who was commandant at the fort, was called "General Terror" by his prisoners.

With the arrival in 1861 of 2,000 Confederate soldiers,

AC

"shed barracks" were provided. These quarters were situated inside the wall surrounding the fort, on ground several feet below the high-water level of the river. Dikes kept water from washing over the ground, but winter was damp and cold.

After Fort Delaware was designated a permanent prison depot and thousands more began arriving, new barracks were built, with enough to house 5,000 completed by spring 1863. But as soon as they were occupied they began to sink in the mud, and some almost fell over. Col. William Hoffman, commissary general of Union prisons, denied accusations that prisoners at Fort Delaware were badly treated, despite the insistence of the Union surgeon general that the place was dangerously overcrowded with some 8,000 prisoners on a marshy site unsuited for the confinement of large numbers. In addition, the surgeon general charged, sick and well inmates were packed together without proper cooking facilities or adequate policing. Hoffman ignored recommendations for relieving the situation, removing only a few of the prisoners to another camp. Prisoners from Fort Delaware were described as "looking like the vanguard of the Resurrection. . . . Scores seemed to be ill; many were suffering from scurvy, while all bore marks of severe treatment in their thin faces and wasted forms."

In Sept. 1863, of the 7,000 prisoners at Fort Delaware, 331 died; in October smallpox broke out and the suffering and death increased. The last Confederates were not released from the prison until mid-July 1865.   —PR

Fort Donelson, Tenn., Battle of. 13–16 Feb. 1862 After the capture of FORT HENRY by Brig. Gen. ULYSSES S. GRANT, 6 Feb. 1862, only Fort Donelson on the Cumberland River stood in the way of Federal control of Kentucky and western Tennessee. Grant planned on taking Donelson by using his army to block the fort while Flag Officer ANDREW H. FOOTE's gunboats shelled it into submission.

Confederate Gen. ALBERT SIDNEY JOHNSTON had sent half of his force to Donelson and had placed Brig. Gen. JOHN B. FLOYD in command there. Floyd's second was Maj. Gen. GIDEON J. PILLOW, and third in command was Brig. Gen. SIMON B. BUCKNER. The fort itself consisted of shallow earthen entrenchments that extended in a semicircle.

At midafternoon, 14 Feb., Foote's small ironclad flotilla steamed upriver and began firing continuously until only 400 yd from the fort. With their guns on high ground above the river, the Confederates had the advantage as they shot into the flotilla with deadly effect. All of the boats took direct hits, one shot tearing through the pilothouse of the flagship *St. Louis,* wounding Foote. With their steering out of control, both the *St. Louis* and the *Louisville* drifted downstream. Recognizing his defeat, Foote ordered a withdrawal.

Despite this success, Floyd was convinced that Donelson was undefendable and decided to break out the next morning. Early on 15 Feb. the Confederates, including cavalry of Col. NATHAN B. FORREST, rushed the surprised Federals, driving them back. The escape route to Nashville was open. Then, inexplicably, Pillow ordered a withdrawal. After regrouping, Grant had his men countercharge, and the Federals soon regained most of what they had lost.

That night Floyd, with Pillow's approval, decided to surrender, but neither officer was willing to do the actual surrendering; that odious responsibility fell to Buckner. Floyd and Pillow, with about 2,500 men, escaped in boats, while Forrest and his cavalry left by the backwaters. On the morning of 16 Feb. Buckner requested terms of capitulation from Grant, who insisted on unconditional surrender. With the capture of Forts Henry and Donelson, Nashville surrendered 23 Feb., and both Kentucky and western Tennessee were lost to the Confederacy.   —NCD

Fort Fillmore, New Mexico Territory. See BAYLOR'S "BUFFALO HUNT."

Fort Fisher, N.C., Battle of. 23–27 Dec. 1864 See BUTLER'S NORTH CAROLINA EXPEDITION.

Fort Fisher, N.C., expedition to. 24 Dec. 1864–15 Jan. 1865 After removing Maj. Gen. BENJAMIN F. BUTLER for failing to attack or besiege Fort Fisher, Lt. Gen. Ulysses S. Grant vowed that there would be no repetition of this debacle (see BUTLER'S NORTH CAROLINA EXPEDITION). He wired Rear Adm. DAVID D. PORTER that he would "be back again with an increased force and without the former commander." The new expedition consisted of 8,000 men, several light cannon, and a siege train. Its commander was one of Butler's division leaders, Brig. Gen. ALFRED H. TERRY.

Terry teamed with the navy in a spirit of openness and cordiality that Butler and Porter never shared. Joining the latter off Beaufort 8 Jan. 1865, the general outlined a carefully considered plan of attack. After Porter suggested revisions and additions, the army and navy returned to Confederate Point on the 13th. By 3 p.m., under Porter's covering fire, 3 divisions of white soldiers and 1 of U.S. Colored Troops established a beachhead above the fort's land-face. The blacks then built a strong line of works across the upper neck of the peninsula, keeping at bay the Confederates near Sugar Loaf under Gen. BRAXTON BRAGG and Maj. Gen. ROBERT F. HOKE.

On the next day, Porter's 44 ships pounded Col. William Lamb's garrison at closer range. This time their fire was so heavy and so accurate that several of the fort's cannon were disabled, part of its land-face was destroyed, wires activating its land mines were severed, and its garrison was badly demoralized.

The land offensive began at 4 p.m., with an assault by 1,600 of Porter's sailors and 400 marines against the northeastern salient of the sea-face. The navy suffered heavily but diverted

USMHI

the garrison at a crucial time. Exploiting this opportunity, 3 brigades of infantry under Cols. N. Martin Curtis, GALUSHA PENNYPACKER, and Louis H. Bell, scrambled through the palisade and up the parapet of the land-face. All 3 brigade leaders were severely wounded in the assault, Bell mortally, and many of their men fell to Confederate marksmen and cannoneers. Survivors poured through the works and swarmed over the defenders, engaging in some of the fiercest close-quarters fighting of the war.

The outcome hung suspended until early evening, when Terry and his field leader, Brig. Gen. ADELBERT AMES, committed Col. Joseph C. Abbott's reserve brigade, which turned the tide. By 9 p.m. the garrison had fallen, several hundred defenders were casualties (including Lamb, severely wounded, and his local superior, Maj. Gen. W.H.C. WHITING, wounded mortally), and the Confederacy's only East Coast door to the outside world had been slammed shut.   —EGL

Fort Gaines, Ala. See FORT MORGAN, ALA.

Fort Gibson, Indian Territory, Siege of. Sept. 1864 Throughout summer 1864, Brig. Gen. STAND WATIE, chief of the pro-Confederate Cherokees, and his 7,000-man Indian brigade threatened Union troops in eastern Indian Territory. Their object was the eventual siege and reduction of the territory's strongest Union outpost, Fort Gibson. The Confederates' strategy was to threaten the larger Union force at nearby FORT SMITH, Ark., destroy civilian and military stores in the area, and interpose Confederate troops between Fort Gibson and potential reinforcement from Fort Smith. In theory, the Federals, threatened and unsupplied, would be forced to abandon Gibson.

On 15 June 1864 several hundred of Watie's troops used 3 artillery pieces to sink the Federal supply steamer *J. R. Williams* at Pleasant Bluffs on the Arkansas River. It was loaded with $120,000 worth of food and clothing for 5,000 Union troops and 5,000 pro-Union Indian refugees at Fort Gibson. Then, reinforced by Col. RICHARD M. GANO and a brigade of Texas cavalry, on 27, 28, 30 July and 2 Aug., Watie's force captured the garrison of a Fort Smith outpost; destroyed haying operations at Blackburn's Prairie; sacked a Fort Smith commissary post, destroying $130,000 in food and clothing; then shelled Fort Smith. Union Brig. Gen. JOHN M. THAYER, commanding the District of the Frontier, was inundated by hungry Unionist

USMHI

refugees and called the 2d Kansas Cavalry for reinforcement, detaching and dispatching a portion of the Kansas troops to duty at Fort Gibson and assigning the rest to Fort Smith.

At a combat at Gunter's Prairie, 24 Aug., Watie's force attacked 420 of the 2d Kansas, killing 20. Then 800 of Watie's men and Gano's 1,200 Texans circled northwest of Fort Gibson, attacked a 125-man Union force at Flat Rock Ford on the Grand River, and killed 40. This began the Siege of Fort Gibson; never actually confronted and invested by an enemy force, the fort was, just the same, cut off from supply and reinforcement.

Survivors of the Flat Rock Ford fight raced to Gibson; their exaggerated estimate of Confederate strength panicked Unionists there, who put their reserves on alert. Additional refugees arrived; running short of food, they requested supplies. Thayer dispatched 300 supply wagons and a 610-man escort under command of Maj. Henry Hopkins to relieve Gibson. On the night of 19 Sept., at the stockade at Cabin Creek, on the way to Gibson, Watie's and Gano's forces attacked Hopkins' camped wagons. Confederate artillery killed Union horse teams and destroyed the Federals' rickety stockade. Several charges, first by Watie's, then Gano's horsemen, broke and scattered the Union force. The Cabin Creek fight was Watie's last victory and later won him a commendation from the Confederate Congress.

Well over 10,000 soldiers and refugees at Fort Gibson found themselves with only a 2-week supply of food and, after hesitation, Thayer said no relief would come from Fort Smith. Meanwhile, without the Federals' knowledge, Watie's poorly disciplined force of Indian volunteers dispersed to winter in Texas. Gano could not continue the siege alone and also returned to the Lone Star State. For a time, unaware that the danger of Confederate attack had passed, Unionists at Gibson maintained their alert and rationed supplies. By the time they realized the siege had ended, the weather had begun turning and other supply problems arose. Unwilling to abandon Gibson, the westernmost Union outpost in hostile territory, the garrison and refugees lived at starvation level through the winter until the Confederate surrender in spring.   —JES

Fort Gregg, Va., Battle of. 2 Apr. 1865 The Confederate earthworks and defenders surrounding Petersburg, Va., had defied the Union Army of the Potomac for nearly 10 months. But the Federal victory at FIVE FORKS, 1 Apr. 1865, permitted the encirclement of the PETERSBURG defenses. Shielded by a heavy fog, the Federals launched a massive final assault at 4:40 a.m., 2 Apr.

The sparsely held Confederate lines collapsed under the onslaught. The Union IX Corps stormed over the lines along Jerusalem Plank Road. The VI Corps, in a relentless surge, crushed the works at Fort Fisher, wheeled to the left, and rolled up the Confederate defenders to Hatcher's Run. There the Southern lines vanished under an overwhelming attack by 2 divisions of the XXIV Corps, which then turned, charging down the Boydton Plank Road, across the front of the VI Corps, toward Forts Gregg and Baldwin.

Near noon the Union assault wave lapped against Fort Gregg. With the collapse of his western lines, Gen. ROBERT E. LEE notified authorities in Richmond that Petersburg would be evacuated that night, ordered a new temporary line rapidly built to guard the avenues of retreat, and shifted troops to danger spots. Lee needed time to extricate his army safely, and

that task fell to the defenders at Fort Gregg, the crucial hinge in the now beleaguered Confederate line.

Barely 500 Southerners and some artillery, belonging to Brig. Gen. NATHANIEL H. HARRIS' brigade and remnants of Maj. Gen. CADMUS M. WILCOX's division, manned the works when the Northerners attacked. The divisions of Brig. Gen. ROBERT S. FOSTER and Brig. Gen. JOHN W. TURNER assailed the fort. The proud Confederates repulsed the attack, then another, and still one more. The muzzles of the Southerners' rifles and cannon sizzled from the heat. Wounded Confederates loaded rifles, passing them with bloody hands to the unhurt defenders. The Federals finally found an uncompleted ditch that led into the fort. Surging over the parapet, the Northerners engulfed the garrison. But the Confederates fought them hand-to-hand for another 25 minutes, until overwhelmed.

The victorious Federals, suffering 714 casualties, counted 57 dead Confederates, 129 wounded prisoners, and 30 who were unhurt. The fighting spirit of Lee's veterans once more bought their commander precious time. When the fort fell, a new Confederate line to the rear was finished. The Confederate army abandoned Petersburg under the cover of night.

—JDW

Fort Harrison, Va., Battle of. 29–30 Sept. 1864 *See* CHAFFIN'S FARM, VA., BATTLE OF.

Fort Hatteras, N.C. *See* HATTERAS INLET, N.C., BATTLE OF.

Fort Henry, Tenn., Battle of. 6 Feb. 1862 Confederate Brig. Gen. LLOYD TILGHMAN had fewer than 3,400 poorly equipped troops to defend Fort Henry on the Tennessee River. By early Feb. 1862, several of the antiquated cannon were underwater due to flooding and the rest were in danger of being submerged. Neither Gen. ALBERT SIDNEY JOHNSTON nor Brig. Gen. LEONIDAS POLK could supply the help he needed.

Brig. Gen. ULYSSES S. GRANT landed his 1st Division north of Panther Creek, which flowed westward into the Tennessee River about 3 mi north of the fort. The division was to swing around the creek and approach the fort from the east, cutting off the garrison's escape. As soon as the transports could return with the 2d Division, it would seize the high ground, occupied by unfinished Fort Heiman, which commanded low-lying Fort Henry. Flag Officer ANDREW H. FOOTE would bombard the fort from his 7 gunboats, whose firepower was several times greater than that Tilghman commanded.

Tilghman made the sensible decision not to sacrifice his men. On 6 Feb., as the Federals approached, he started most of his troops to FORT DONELSON, 10 mi away. Then he returned to join the Tennessee artillerymen, whom he asked to delay the enemy for an hour. They did better than that and inflicted some damage on the gunboats before their 2 effective guns were disabled. Honor had been satisfied, and Tilghman surrendered. The Federal officers who accepted the surrender entered Fort Henry by rowing through the sallyport. To the delight of the navy, Grant arrived after the surrender. Federal losses were reported as 11 killed, 5 missing, and 31 wounded; the Confederates had 5 killed, 11 wounded, and about 94 captured.

3 gunboats then raided 150 mi upstream to Muscle Shoals, destroying bridges and boats in a spectacular demonstration of the importance of controlling the rivers. *See also* FORTS HENRY AND DONELSON CAMPAIGN, TENN.   —LHH

Fort Hindman, Ark., eng. at. 10–11 Jan. 1863 *See* AR-KANSAS POST, ARK., ENG. AT.

Fort Huger, Va. An open fortification named for Maj. Gen. BENJAMIN HUGER, the fort was constructed in 1861 by the Confederates to protect Suffolk, Va. The fort stood near the confluence of the western branch of the Nansemond River and the main stream. The Nansemond flows north into the James River, uniting with the latter west of Norfolk.

Fort Huger was an installation in the Confederate Department of Southern Virginia, an area extending from the James River to North Carolina. A fertile agricultural region, the department protected the southern flank of the vital railroad center of Petersburg. In spring 1862 the Federals seized Norfolk and also occupied Suffolk. Though the fort remained occupied it offered no resistance to the Union gunboats that patrolled the Nansemond.

Early in 1863 activity in the department increased. When Gen. ROBERT E. LEE learned in February that the Union IX Corps was moving toward the area, he sent Lt. Gen. JAMES LONGSTREET with 2 divisions to protect Petersburg and to garner badly needed supplies. After Federal orders were altered, only 1 Confederate division went to Suffolk. Longstreet assumed control of 3 divisions and ordered an operation against Union-held New Berne, N.C. Unsuccessful, Longstreet in April moved against Suffolk and its Union force, numbering 25,000.

As part of his siege of Suffolk, Longstreet ordered Maj. Gen. SAMUEL G. FRENCH, department commander, to place a heavy battery in Fort Huger. French complied, deploying 5 guns in "Old Fort," as the Confederates styled the works, and 2 32-pounders in the rear, supported by the 55th North Carolina and farther back Col. EVANDER M. LAW's brigade. By the evening of 18 Apr., the Confederates had completed the defenses.

French became ill the next day, and the fort remained ungarrisoned except for the battery. About 6 p.m., 270 Federals landed 400 yd above Fort Huger, rapidly bringing ashore 4 boat howitzers. Encountering no opposition, they rushed the fort. In a brief melee the Confederates surrendered. The Federals hurriedly took the 5 guns and 137 captured troops back across the river.

As a result of this embarrassing defeat, 2 of Law's aides accused the 55th North Carolina of cowardice. The regiment's commander, Col. John K. Connally, heatedly disputed the accusation. The result was a double duel, in which no one was hurt, though 3 shots were fired by 2 participants. —JDW

Fort Lafayette, N.Y. Since at the beginning of the Civil War neither North nor South had facilities for confining prisoners of war, captives frequently were sent to existing fortifications, thus turning them, at least in part, into military prisons. Such was the case of Fort Lafayette, N.Y. Some of its first inmates were citizens charged with disloyalty to the North and captured Confederate privateersmen. Most of the 670 prisoners taken at the fall of HATTERAS INLET late in Aug. 1861 were brought to Fort Lafayette, and in Feb. 1862 war-associated prisoners in the "Tombs," New York City's prison, were transferred there, among these the 13 men who had been taken when the privateer *Savannah* was captured off Charleston harbor 3 June 1861.

As the war progressed, Lafayette became important largely as a place of imprisonment for Confederate officers and persons accused of disloyalty. A number of them, including members of the Maryland legislature, had done nothing more than express sympathy for the South. James W. Wall, a New Jersey Democrat later sent to the U.S. Senate, was arrested and put in the fort for a time because of his criticism of the government in newspapers he was connected with. By order of Union Gen. WINFIELD SCOTT, officers who had resigned commissions in the U.S. Army to accept Confederate commands were, if captured, to be sent there.

Most of the prisoners were educated men who realized the importance of adjusting to confinement. They organized societies, published a handwritten newspaper, and quietly made the best of their situation.

An understanding of the fort's operation may be gained from Scott's statement about its commander, Col. Martin Burke: "Colonel Martin Burke is famous for his unquestioning obedience to orders. He was with me in Mexico, and if I had told him at any time to take one of my aides-de-camp and shoot him before breakfast, the aide's execution would have been duly reported." —PR

Fort Loudon, Tenn., Battle of. 29 Nov. 1863 *See* FORT SANDERS, TENN., BATTLE OF.

Fort McAllister, Ga. 13 Dec. 1864 Atop a bluff on the south bank of the Ogeechee River, Fort McAllister was a key to the defenses of Savannah, 15 mi to the north. During 1862 and 1863 Union warships repeatedly tried, in vain, to blast their way by the fort. Mounted by 22 large-caliber cannon, constructed of dirt and logs, and filled with bombproofs and traverses, it was as strong as it was important.

On 10 Dec. 1864, Maj. Gen. WILLIAM T. SHERMAN's troops, many of them hungry and subsisting entirely on poorly husked rice from local plantations, reached the outskirts of Savannah. On 12 Dec. Sherman ordered the commander of his right wing, Maj. Gen. OLIVER O. HOWARD, to capture Fort McAllister; once the fort was taken, the Union navy could land all the rations the men needed.

Howard assigned the mission to Brig. Gen. WILLIAM B. HAZEN's division of the XV Corps, a crack outfit Sherman himself had once commanded. On the afternoon of 13 Dec. Hazen deployed 1,500 troops for the assault. Awaiting them were 150 Confederates under Maj. George W. Anderson of Savannah. Determined "to defend the fort to the last extremity," they had spent several days strengthening the fort on its landward side.

With just 1 hour of daylight remaining, Hazen's veterans rushed forward. Without a pause they made their way over fallen trees, rows of ABATIS and CHEVAUX-DE-FRISE, a large ditch, and numerous 13-in. shells that had been converted into mines. Reaching the parapet, they scrambled to the top, then into the fort, where after ferocious hand-to-hand fighting they overwhelmed the garrison. 16 Confederates were killed, 55 wounded; the Union loss totaled 134, mainly from the mines. The defenders simply lacked the firepower to stop the attackers, who used sharpshooters to neutralize the fort's cannon.

Sherman called it "the handsomest thing I've seen in this war," and Hazen soon was promoted. More important, Sherman now had his "cracker line" to bring in supplies, and the fall of Savannah was merely a matter of time. —AC

Fort Macon, N.C., Siege of. 23 Mar.–25 Apr. 1862 In the middle of Mar. 1862, following his capture of ROANOKE

ISLAND and NEW BERNE, Maj. Gen. AMBROSE E. BURNSIDE was ready to accomplish the third objective of his North Carolina coastal campaign: the seizure of Fort Macon, on the eastern tip of Bogue Banks Island, just below Beaufort.

According to one of Burnside's colonels, Fort Macon was "an old-style, strong, stone, casemated work, mounting 67 guns, garrisoned by above 500 men, commanded by Colonel Moses J. White." Strong it might be, but it was vulnerable. Designed to protect Beaufort against a sea attack, it was easily isolated from the interior by a movement from the north; and isolation meant starvation for the garrison. Aware of the fact, Maj. Gen. JOHN G. PARKE, whom Burnside had selected to lead the movement against Fort Macon, sent a surrender demand to Colonel White 23 Mar. Showing more feistiness than prudence, the colonel—whose troops had been reduced to about 400 effectives, low on ammunition—politely but firmly refused. Accordingly, Parke made plans to blast him out.

On the 29th, the advance echelon of Parke's brigade landed on Bogue Banks, west of the fort, covered by warships from the fleet of Capt. LOUIS M. GOLDSBOROUGH. For the next 2 weeks, in Parke's words, "every available hour of night and day was spent in transporting men, siege train and supplies." With a beachhead firmly established, Union patrols moved gingerly toward the fort. Several days of small-unit clashes were followed 10 Apr. by a reconnaissance close to Macon's guns, which convinced Parke that a siege rather than an attack was his proper course.

It took only a few days to complete an investment. By the 15th, enough heavy cannon had been emplaced around the fort to doom its garrison, now reduced to 300 able troops. But Colonel White stubbornly rejected further demands for surrender, including one tendered by Burnside in person.

At dawn on the 25th, Parke's batteries opened a furious fire against the fort, accompanied for a brief time by salvos from the navy. The bombardment was amazingly accurate and effective, the fort's return fire sparse and poor. Late in the afternoon, with his works badly damaged and 25 of his men casualties, White ran up a flag of surrender. With his capitulation, the most strategic portion of the North Carolina coast fell into Union hands, enabling Burnside to plan a drive inland.

—EGL

Fort Monroe, Va. One of the bastions erected during the 1820s and 1830s for the coastal defense of the U.S., Fort Monroe was a stone and brick fortress squatting on Old Point Comfort at the tip of the Virginia peninsula. Its heavy guns swept the waters of Hampton Roads, where the James River spills into Chesapeake Bay.

With the outbreak of the Civil War and Virginia's secession, the fort became vitally important to the Union War Department. Garrisoned with a small body of Regulars Apr. 1861, it received reinforcements in May and became headquarters for the Union Department of Virginia, which subsequently merged into the Department of Virginia and North Carolina. The fortress also served as headquarters for the Army of the James, created Apr. 1864.

Several significant actions and events occurred near Fort Monroe during the war. On 10 June 1861 the Union force at Old Point Comfort advanced inland, resulting in the Battle of BIG BETHEL. The first clash of ironclad warships—the *Virginia* and the *Monitor*—occurred in the waters off the point 9 Mar. 1862 (*see* HAMPTON ROADS, BATTLE OF). The Union Army of the

Potomac converged on the fortress in spring 1862 for the PENINSULA CAMPAIGN. During the PETERSBURG CAMPAIGN, 1864–65, Union engineers laid a telegraph cable from army headquarters at City Point, Va., to Fort Monroe, where a line to Washington, D.C., connected. Finally, 3 Feb. 1865, aboard a steamer in Hampton Roads, Pres. ABRAHAM LINCOLN and Sec. of State WILLIAM H. SEWARD conferred with Confederate representatives at the abortive HAMPTON ROADS CONFERENCE. By war's end, Fort Monroe had nobly served the Union cause.

—JDW

Fort Morgan, Ala. Mobile Point is a long neck of land jutting out to cover the entrance of Mobile Bay on the east. French soldiers fortified its tip in 1699. A succession of colonial regimes and the U.S. government all thought it was an ideal site for a fort; in 1818 the U.S. Army commissioned masons to start building a brick fortress. By 1834 this fort was finished, named for Revolutionary War Gen. Daniel Morgan, and presented a military profile army engineers called "a classic." Landward fields behind it were cleared for a long distance, and smooth direct embankments sloped up to a series of outer brick walls covering the main ramparts—all surrounding a 10-sided brick building at its center called the "citadel." From the mouth of Mobile Bay, supported on the west by Fort Gaines on Dauphin Island and smaller Fort Powell in Grant's Pass, it looked imposing.

Alabama did not secede from the Union until 11 Jan. 1861, but on 5 Jan. eager state secessionists seized Fort Morgan for the defense of the port city of Mobile at the foot of the bay. State troops held it for 2 months, then it was garrisoned by Confederates. For 3 years its cannon covered the movements of blockade runners on the bay and kept the U.S. Navy at a respectful distance.

From 5 to 23 Aug. 1864, the garrisons at Forts Gaines, Morgan, and Powell fought the Battle of MOBILE BAY, were each invested, and in turn surrendered. Fort Morgan, commanded by Confederate Brig. Gen. RICHARD L. PAGE, was the last to capitulate, its walls and casemates breeched and crumbling. Federals garrisoned it for the next several months, then on 17 Mar. 1865, Maj. Gen. GORDON GRANGER's XIII Corps marched from it to besiege FORT BLAKELY on the outskirts of Mobile. As a Confederate fortress, Fort Morgan had the dubious distinction of being the site from which was launched the last large Federal land campaign of the Civil War.

In the postbellum years it was refurbished, continuing in military use as late as the 1890s, when concrete gun emplacements were built. It survives under the care of the National Park Service.

—JES

Fort Pickens, Fla. In Dec. 1860, Federal Lt. Adam J. Slemmer commanded a small force of U.S. soldiers at Pensacola, Fla. He also oversaw the care of mainland Forts Barrancas and McRee on the rim of Pensacola harbor, and was responsible for Fort Pickens, an unoccupied stone and masonry fortification on the west end of Santa Rosa Island a few thousand yards offshore. Built to repel foreign invaders, the 3 forts were erected for the protection of Pensacola harbor, the deepest along the Gulf of Mexico, and the Pensacola Navy Yard, the best shipyard in the Deep South. Slemmer's men, the forts, and naval personnel at the yard were supported by the commissary ship *Supply* and a few other small Federal supply and transport vessels in the harbor.

Throughout December, Florida secessionists planned to seize the military facilities at Pensacola. Late that month and early in Jan. 1861 secessionist militiamen gathered in the area, seized telegraph stations, and cut overland communications with the North. Thus Slemmer and the naval personnel could receive only delayed instructions from their superiors in Washington, D.C. On 10 Jan. Florida seceded, and that day, on their own initiative, Slemmer and 81 soldiers and sailors spiked the cannon at Fort Barrancas and withdrew to Pickens. Also on 10 Jan., Navy Lt. Henry Erben of the *Supply* landed at McRee, with the help of loyal seamen destroyed the fort's guns and powder, then withdrew to his ship. Secessionists seized the damaged mainland forts immediately after Slemmer and Erben departed, and 12 Jan. secured the surrender of the navy yard from U.S. Flag Officer James Armstrong.

3 times within the next several days Floridians demanded that Slemmer surrender Pickens. Each time he refused. Cut off from mainland supply and communication, the garrison at Pickens was effectively besieged, creating a crisis as volatile as the one then ongoing at FORT SUMTER in Charleston harbor, S.C. The outbreak of hostilities at either fort would bring on war.

News of the standoff at Pensacola reached Washington, D.C., by ship. Taking a cautious approach to the crisis, outgoing president James Buchanan dispatched to Pensacola harbor the warship *Brooklyn* with 200 reinforcements. The ship was ordered to anchor near Pickens but not to land the troops unless secessionists made a hostile move against the fort. The stalemate, called the Fort Pickens Truce, went into effect 29 Jan. when the *Brooklyn* came to rest within sight of Santa Rosa.

On 5 Mar., the day after his inauguration, Pres. ABRAHAM LINCOLN ordered the troops aboard the *Brooklyn* to reinforce Pickens; on 7 Mar. Confederates at Pensacola were organized into a unified command under Brig. Gen. BRAXTON BRAGG. The *Brooklyn*'s commander received the order to land reinforcements on the 31st, but he refused it, claiming that the order, which had been signed by Lt. Gen. WINFIELD SCOTT, was invalid because it had not been issued by the Navy Department. Meanwhile, at Bragg's direction, 5,000 Confederates prepared to invade Santa Rosa Island.

Orders issued quickly by the Navy Department reached the *Brooklyn* 12 Apr., as did news of the firing on Fort Sumter. The Fort Pickens truce ended, and that day the *Brooklyn* sailed behind Santa Rosa Island, landing Col. Harvey Brown and the 200 Union troops to the rear of Fort Pickens. Slemmer turned over command of the fort to Brown. The Confederates, who had been alerted to the arrival of the reinforcements, called off their invasion plans. 4 days later, a second seaborne Union relief expedition landed additional troops, increasing the garrison at Pickens to 1,000 men and bringing to 4 the number of Union warships anchored nearby.

The Federal troops never lost possession of the fort. The 6th New York Zouaves joined the Santa Rosa garrison June 1861 and Union warships blockaded Pensacola harbor for the next several months, denying Confederates use of the navy yard. Between 12 Apr. 1861 and the Confederate evacuation of Pensacola 9 May 1862, only 5 fights took place in the harbor: on 2 Sept. 1861 raiding Union seamen burned the navy-yard dock; on 14 Sept. Federal sailors burned the Confederate schooner *Judah;* on 8 Oct. Confederates invaded then retreated from Santa Rosa; and on 22–23 Nov. and again on New Year's Day 1862, artillerists at Fort Pickens dueled with

Confederate cannoneers on the mainland. Neither of these last 2 engagements, the largest staged, was conclusive, but the November artillery exchange nearly forced Confederates occupying Fort McRee to capitulate. Within about 28 hours, 5,000 shells were fired at ranges of 2,000–3,000 yd, but total casualties for both sides numbered only 8 killed. The 1 Jan. 1862 duel spent an equally impressive number of shells to no effect. Bragg's troops evacuated Pensacola 9 May, and Federals repossessed it 12 May.   —JES

Fort Pillow, Tenn., Battle of. 12 Apr. 1864   A Tennessee earthwork fortification, Fort Pillow, sat on east-bank bluffs overlooking the Mississippi River 40 land mi north of Memphis. Union Maj. Lionel F. Booth commanded its garrison of 295 white troops composing the 13th Tennessee Cavalry, and 262 blacks of the 11th U.S. Colored Troops and Battery F/4th U.S. Colored Light Artillery. Maj. William F. Bradford was second in command. On 12 Apr. 1864, Capt. James Marshall's tinclad *New Era* sat below Pillow covering its riverfront. Confederate cavalry Brig. Gen. JAMES R. CHALMERS, commanding 1,500 men of Maj. Gen. NATHAN BEDFORD FORREST's Cavalry Corps, assaulted the works at 5:30 a.m.

Pillow sat on sites of 2 older, larger forts. By 8 a.m. Chalmers' main force was holding the trenches of the older work, surrounding the Federals. Major Booth's 6 cannon could not be brought to bear on Chalmers' troops, the *New Era*'s support fire was ineffective, and the garrison was hemmed in tightly. Confederates took high knolls on the perimeter and covered the fort's interior with small-arms fire. Major Booth was killed at 9 and command passed to Major Bradford. Forrest arrived at 10, took command of the Confederates, and ordered a general assault at 11 that took the Federals' barracks on the fort's south side. Confederate fire from cover of the barracks swept Pillow's interior. At 1 p.m. the *New Era,* short of ammunition, dropped downriver to resupply. Forrest's adjutant, Capt. Charles W. Anderson, said that "it was perfectly apparent to any man endowed with the smallest amount of common sense that to all intents and purposes the fort was ours." At 3:30 Confederates received a fresh supply of ammunition and sent in a demand for surrender.

Bradford asked for an hour for consultation. Looking downriver Forrest saw a steamer heading north, loaded with reinforcements. Smoke from one or more boats could be seen in the opposite direction. Forrest told Bradford he could have 20 minutes. Truce flags went up. Forrest demanded surrender again and Bradford refused. Confederates charged the last line of works, driving the Federals to the bluff, down the riverbank, and into the face of Captain Anderson's Confederates, maneuvered there earlier. From that moment a controversy began that continues today.

Confederates lost 14 killed and 86 wounded in the day's fight, captured 226 Federals, killed 231, and wounded 100. Some Federals claimed that as Confederates scaled the earthworks they screamed racial epithets and killed black troops who had thrown down their arms in surrender. Others said Forrest's men killed wounded blacks and whites where they lay. Confederates claimed the high Union casualty rate came when garrison survivors ran, fighting their way to the river. Some Confederates said blacks picked up arms again after having surrendered and suffered the consequences. Other accounts attribute the high casualty rate among blacks to their tenacious defense at the earthworks, some Federals and

Confederates saying they were the last to break and run for the rear. Only 58 black troops of the 262 engaged were taken prisoner. The Union public called it a massacre.

The U.S. Congress' COMMITTEE ON THE CONDUCT OF THE WAR investigated, gathering blood-curdling testimony from some of the wounded left behind when Forrest's troops evacuated Pillow the night of 12 Apr. Response of the Confederate government was slow; Forrest's battle report, stalled in transit, was not brought to light until 4 months after the engagement. The general denied it was a massacre. Historical evidence remains divided between adherents of Union and Confederate views. There is general agreement that Confederates had extra animosity toward white members of the Union 13th Tennessee Cavalry, called "Tories," "renegades," or "homegrown Yankees." Racial antipathy toward black Union troops was well documented. It is probable, whether regarded as a massacre or not, Confederates hit the Fort Pillow defenders with more zeal than usually reserved for the enemy, and some excesses occurred.   —JES

Fort Powell, Ala. See FORT MORGAN, ALA.

Fort Pulaski, Ga., surrender of. 11 Apr. 1862 Savannah was guarded from ocean attack by Fort Pulaski at the Savannah River's mouth. Both Gen. Robert E. Lee, who helped build the fort, and the U.S. Army's chief engineer were certain that Pulaski's thick brick walls could not be breached by cannon, and its island location made assault by small boat suicidal. Yet in Feb. 1862 a U.S. Army expedition under Capt. QUINCY A. GILLMORE was on Tybee Island, a few miles from Pulaski. With mortars, smoothbores, and the accurate new Parrott rifles, Gillmore intended to shatter Pulaski's walls.

Col. Charles H. Olmstead commanded the fort. Though his garrison was small and his cannon few, he was confident. When a Federal officer demanded Pulaski's surrender at dawn, 10 Apr., Olmstead declined, and the Confederates prepared for battle.

Firing began at 8:15 a.m. In just 5 hours Gillmore's powerful rifles had begun to cut a breach. By nightfall a substantial hole was opened, and the next morning the Federals began to exploit it. Soon shells were flying through and striking against the magazine. Continued firing knocked a hole in the magazine's wall, and Fort Pulaski faced the threat of being blown up with its own powder.

At 2 p.m. on 11 Apr., Olmstead lowered his flag. Gillmore was rowed over to receive the surrender, and Savannah, as an effective blockade-running port, was sealed up by the loss of the fort built to defend it.   —MM

Fort Sanders (Fort Loudon), Tenn., Battle of. 29 Nov. 1863 Fort Sanders was a key to the defense of Knoxville, which stood on the right bank of the Holston River and on the East Tennessee & Georgia Railroad. To protect the town the Confederates built a number of fortifications, including Fort Loudon in the northwest quadrant. In summer 1863 a Union army invaded East Tennessee and occupied Knoxville, and in November Lt. Gen. JAMES LONGSTREET launched his KNOXVILLE CAMPAIGN to capture or drive it out. As the Confederates approached the town, cavalry under Brig. Gen. William P. Sanders intercepted them about a mile from the fort, delayed their advance, and gained for the Union precious time to strengthen Knoxville's defenses. In the fighting Sanders fell mortally

wounded, and Fort Loudon was renamed Fort Sanders in his honor.

Fort Sanders stood on an eminence that fell off sharply to the northwest, making impossible an unexposed advance to within about 200 yd. From there the approach was treacherous. A line of entrenched pickets skirted a field of stumps to which old telegraph wire was fastened. Beyond the field and surrounding the fort was a ditch about 12 ft wide and from 4 to 10 ft deep, the sides of which were almost vertical. The final obstacle was a sharply inclined parapet, difficult to mount because the berm at its foot had been cut away.

At dawn, 29 Nov., following a brief artillery barrage directed at the fort's interior, 3 Confederate brigades charged. They were covered by the fire of sharpshooters in trenches seized from the enemy pickets the night before. The WIRE ENTANGLEMENTS caused only momentary delay, but when the attackers reached the edge of the ditch, they stopped, unsure of what to do. Under murderous musketry and canister they began firing at the fort. Officers and color-bearers leaped into the ditch. Lacking ladders, they had to hoist men onto the parapet, but the only Confederates to enter the fort became prisoners of war.

In about 20 minutes the Confederates grudgingly withdrew. An attack by a fourth brigade was quickly repulsed. Shortly thereafter Longstreet received word of Gen. BRAXTON BRAGG's defeat at Chattanooga and retired northeastward.   —FDW

Fort Smith, Ark. Located on the Arkansas River near the present-day border of Oklahoma, Fort Smith was established in 1817 as the first U.S. military post on the Southwestern frontier. Initially it served as a peacekeeping garrison for Eastern Indians being relocated beyond white settlements.

By 1861 the fort had become the major supply depot for the army's frontier outposts. When Arkansas seceded in May, state troops advanced on the installation, which Col. WILLIAM H. EMORY had been ordered to evacuate with most of its stores and ordnance. The first Confederate offensive launched from the fort attempted unsuccessfully to intercept Emory's column before it reached Fort Leavenworth.

Strategically, Fort Smith operated as the Confederacy's strong point for troops guarding approaches to Texas, Louisiana, and Arkansas; as the major supply depot for the Trans-Mississippi; and as the command center for forces deployed within Indian Territory. No fighting occurred at the post, but it was the starting point for several expeditions, including those that culminated in the battles at WILSON'S CREEK, PEA RIDGE, and HONEY SPRINGS.

Maj. Gen. EARL VAN DORN commanded at Fort Smith briefly after Brig. Gen. BEN MCCULLOCH's death at Pea Ridge, Mar. 1862. His men plundered the stores and the countryside sufficiently to alienate townspeople, and he withdrew under pressure, sending Maj. Gen. THOMAS C. HINDMAN to restore order.

Hindman proclaimed martial law and began impressing supplies for the army since few were forthcoming from the East. But reports of a major Federal invasion in December prompted him to evacuate the fort. When Confederate Lt. Gen. THEOPHILUS H. HOLMES learned of the abandonment, he ordered Brig. Gen. WILLIAM STEELE to reoccupy the post. Steele held Fort Smith through summer, but during his expedition to trap Federal troops at Honey Springs, he received reports of a Union column marching toward the post and sent Brig. Gen. WILLIAM L. CABELL to defend it. Learning he was outnumbered and that Steele, pushed deep into Indian Territory, could not send reinforcements, Cabell withdrew from Fort Smith 30 Aug. 1863. Union troops easily captured the fort, holding it for the duration of the war. —PLF

Fort Stedman, Va., eng. at.

25 Mar. 1865 By early 1865 Gen. ROBERT E. LEE'S PETERSBURG defenses were perilously weak. When the Confederate leader learned of Maj. Gen. PHILIP H. SHERIDAN's 2 Mar. victory against Lt. Gen. JUBAL A. EARLY in the Shenandoah Valley, he realized that "Little Phil" was free to join the forces besieging him. Before Sheridan could reach Petersburg, Lee planned a final, desperate offensive, east of the city. If successful, a breakthrough might compel Lt. Gen. U. S. GRANT to shorten his lines, permitting at least some Confederates to escape into North Carolina, joining Gen. JOSEPH E. JOHNSTON.

USMHI/MA

Interior of Fort Stedman

The plan called for Maj. Gen. JOHN B. GORDON, with 3 divisions of Lee's II Corps, elements of the I and III corps, and a division of cavalry—almost half the besieged army—to capture Fort Stedman, a redoubt at the far right of Grant's line, only 150 yd from a strong Confederate salient. In a single rapid move Gordon was expected to overwhelm infantry from Brig. Gen. ORLANDO B. WILLCOX's IX Corps division and a regiment of heavy artillery. 3 columns of 100 men each would then seize 3 smaller forts believed to be in Stedman's rear, while the rest enfiladed the Union line from the rear and attached the route to CITY POINT, Grant's supply base.

At first the assault, begun at 4 a.m., 25 Mar., was successful. Gordon captured the nearest Union pickets, slipped through their works, and seized the redoubt and 3 supporting batteries. With both Grant and Maj. Gen. GEORGE G. MEADE, commander of the Army of the Potomac, absent from the front lines, a Federal response was slow to come. But when the Confederate columns discovered the satellite forts to be nonexistent and retreated to Stedman, the attack collapsed. Willcox's and Brig. Gen. JOHN F. HARTRANFT's divisions finally counterattacked, subjecting the enemy to a murderous hail of musketry and cannon fire. Hundreds surrendered rather than risk retreating. By 8 o'clock over 4,000 of Lee's men had become casualties against only 1,500 Federals, and his final offensive of the war had ended in a bloody fiasco. —EGL

Fort Stevens, District of Columbia.

Located on the 7th St. Pike running toward Silver Spring, Md., Fort Stevens was one of 60 enclosed forts composing the defenses of Washington, D.C. As the war progressed, the national capital became a fortress. 30 mi of unbroken lines rimmed the city, with an additional 20 mi of rifle trenches. The heavy ordnance included 762 guns and 74 mortars.

No Confederate force ever seriously threatened the capital and its works until July 1864. During the first week of the month, Lt. Gen. JUBAL A. EARLY's II Corps/Army of Northern Virginia, marching north down the Shenandoah Valley, entered western Maryland on an audacious raid. A patchwork Union force, though defeated, delayed the Confederate advance at the Battle of MONOCACY, 9 July. Hampered by heat and choking dust, the weary Confederates arrived in the suburbs of the capital opposite Fort Stevens on the 11th.

Skirmishing erupted between the Southerners and the Union defenders in Fort Stevens and the 2 fortifications on its flanks, Forts DeRussy and Slocum. Early pressed his skirmishers forward to ascertain the strength and composition of the Federal forces. Pres. and Mrs. Abraham Lincoln were visiting Fort Stevens and witnessed the action. Union soldiers had to order the chief executive from the parapets when his curiosity quickened with the fighting.

Early ordered an assault for 12 July, but Federal reinforcements, the leading elements of the veteran VI Corps, arrived during the night of the 11th and the morning of the 12th. The Confederate general abandoned his attack plan, electing to resume extensive skirmishing. Lincoln visited the fort again and once more came under fire. During a heated exchange, a young Union officer, Capt. Oliver Wendell Holmes, Jr., seeing the president watching intently, shouted, "Get down, you fool." Lincoln meekly complied.

During the night of the 12th–13th, the Confederates abandoned their raid, marching south toward Virginia. The formidable defensive works, properly manned, had dissuaded Early from making a costly frontal attack. The raid had caused little more than intense excitement and curiosity in the capital. —JDW

Fort Sumter, S.C.

12–14 Apr. 1861 On 12 Apr. 1861 Union Maj. ROBERT ANDERSON and 127 men held Fort Sumter in Charleston harbor, with Capt. ABNER DOUBLEDAY Anderson's second in command. The men had been neither supplied nor reinforced since occupying the fort the night of 26 Dec. 1860. Their presence caused a crisis between the U.S. government and the seceded state of South Carolina, offended at Federal troops sitting on sovereign territory. Secessionists commanded by Brig. Gen. P.G.T. BEAUREGARD had thrown up batteries on the harbor's shores north and south of Sumter and trained guns on it from Forts Moultrie and Johnson. Sumter mustered only 66 cannon, several unmounted. At 3:20 a.m. the crisis came to a head. Capt. STEPHEN D. LEE and Col. JAMES CHESNUT, secessionists, rowed out to Sumter and made a last demand for surrender. When Anderson declined, they informed him the fort would be shelled within the hour. The major had also declined previous surrender demands because ships loaded with troops and supplies were reported en route.

The first Confederate shell burst high over the fort at 4:30 a.m., and the firing continued. Anderson mustered his force on Sumter's parade ground, warned the men to take no unnecessary risks, and sent them to their guns. The major offered the honor of the Union's FIRST SHOT to Doubleday, who fired it around 7. A lopsided, 34-hour duel began. After firing a few rounds from different guns, the Federals restricted themselves to serving 6 cannon, since they were short of powder-bag cartridges; 43 loyal civilian workmen making up part of the garrison sewed more bags from linen, burlap scraps, and socks. The supply ships Anderson expected arrived in the afternoon of the 12th but were kept outside the harbor by Confederate artillery.

Federals in the fort concentrated fire on specific Confederate batteries but did little damage. No shells were sent into Charleston, but Doubleday put 2 rounds through the roof of the Moultrie House hotel near Fort Moultrie, northeast of Sumter. The Confederates' ironclad Point Cummings battery, south of Sumter, inflicted a heavy barrage on the fort. Through the night Federals ceased firing, and Confederates reduced their shelling to periodic shots. By dawn, 13 Apr., 3 separate fires had broken out in the fort's interior, threatening its powder magazine.

Confederate batteries resumed heavy shelling at daylight on the 13th. Suffering from smoke inhalation, Anderson's men lay low on the ground, rising only occasionally to reply with token shots. At 12:48 p.m. a Confederate shell blew away Sumter's flagstaff. Before it was replaced, secessionist Col. LOUIS T. WIGFALL, seeing the flag go down, set out by rowboat for the fort and demanded surrender again. Anderson conceded, firing stopped, and surrender ceremonies were planned for the next afternoon.

On 14 Apr., with Brig. Gen. P.G.T. Beauregard's permission, Anderson began firing a 100-gun salute to the American flag before hauling it down. The 50th gun exploded, wounding several of its crew and killing one. These were the only Federal casualties of the siege. The garrison was then transported to the waiting ships outside the harbor. —JES

Fort Sumter and Fort Pickens medals. In the opening weeks of the war, the North was enthralled by the gallant resistance of Maj. ROBERT ANDERSON's garrison at FORT SUMTER and of Lt. Adam J. Slemmer's troops at FORT PICKENS, Fla. On 6 June 1861 the New York State Chamber of Commerce voted to finance medals commemorating their heroics. A total of 168 were struck, one for each member of the garrisons; those present at the chamber of commerce's May 1862 meeting received the award in person.

Designed by Charles Miller of New York, the medals were struck in 8 styles and 4 sizes. The Sumter Medal had 4 classifications (for presentation to the garrison commander, his officers, noncommissioned officers, and privates), varying from 2 to 6 in. in diameter and each carrying Anderson's portrait on the obverse. The Pickens Medal, of the same classifications and in the same sizes, bore Slemmer's portrait. The reverse of the medals carried allegorical designs: "The Genius or Guardian Spirit of America Rising from Fort Sumter" and "Cerebus, or the Monster of War, Chained to Fort Pickens." —EGL

Fort Wagner, S.C., Siege and evacuation of. 10 July–6 Sept. 1863 *See* BATTERY (FORT) WAGNER, S.C., SIEGE AND EVACUATION OF.

Fort Warren, Mass. Built on George's Island, Boston harbor, Fort Warren has enormous granite pentagonal walls and gun emplacements originally meant for Massachusetts' seaward defense. The fort became a training camp for state volunteers and garrisoned the 14th Massachusetts Infantry. During the war it first held a few smugglers and political prisoners from Maryland and the border South. Then, Aug. 1861, following the capture of North Carolina's HATTERAS INLET forts, Confederate prisoners arrived from confinement on Governor's Island in New York City. The fort was prepared for 100 new arrivals, but many times that number came; food, furniture, and all facilities were insufficient. Appeals to the Boston public and gifts from families and friends of the Confederates kept prisoners supplied for the first weeks. Within 2 years Fort Warren became the elite Northern prison.

USN

Confederate officers, separated from enlisted men, wandered the island in the first months, on oath not to escape; exercise yards accommodated the others. Though prisoners were housed in gun casemates converted to cells, space was ample compared to other prisons. Some officers had private, lightly furnished cells. Food was sufficient.

Warren briefly reverted to a troop facility, but new prisoners arrived July 1863, mostly distinguished officers and Confederate personalities, all treated with some deference. Among them were Confederate privateer and naval officer Lt. Charles W. Read, cavalry raider Col. BASIL W. DUKE, and blinded cavalry Brig. Gen. ADAM R. "STOVEPIPE" JOHNSON. Rules were tightened, but those receiving money from home were free to spend limited sums on amenities, and exercise continued, though officers were now confined to the yards.

Greater crowding followed Confederate military losses, straining food supplies, but while rations were reduced, they remained adequate. On the Confederate surrender only 12 deaths marked Warren's record, all attributed to wounds or illness occurring before confinement. —JES

Forts Henry and Donelson Campaign, Tenn. 6–16 Feb. 1862 Located on the Tennessee and Cumberland rivers, Forts Henry and Donelson were in the middle of the South's defense line stretching from Columbus, Ky., to Bowling Green,

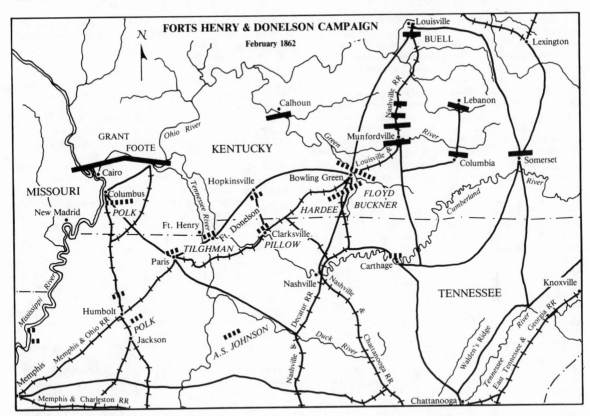

FORTS HENRY & DONELSON CAMPAIGN
February 1862

then southward to Cumberland Gap. Loss of the forts would allow the North invasion routes by land and by water. In Nov. 1861 the forts were placed under the command of Brig. Gen. LLOYD TILGHMAN, who was pessimistic about defending Fort Henry. The fort, located above a bend in the Tennessee River, commanded a stretch of river 3 mi long but had obvious weaknesses: on low ground and subject to flooding, it was also overshadowed by hills on both sides of the river. In response, Tilghman began work on another fort on a bluff across the river, but it was not completed in time for the battle at Fort Henry. Though he had 11 of Fort Henry's 17 guns placed on the riverfront, where they could command the main channel, Tilghman, still skeptical that the fort could withstand an attack, sent most of his men to Fort Donelson, only 10 mi away, leaving about 100 artillerymen behind.

Late in Jan. 1862, a reluctant Maj. Gen. HENRY W. HALLECK finally had given his approval to a joint military/naval attack on the forts. Brig. Gen. ULYSSES S. GRANT would command army forces, while Flag Officer ANDREW H. FOOTE would command the gunboat flotilla. The gunboats reached Fort Henry 4 Feb., and an attack plan was formulated by Grant and Foote. The action began 6 Feb. as the gunboats closed to a range of 600 yd. A devastating exchange resulted in heavy damage to the fort, putting all but 4 guns out of action. By the time Grant's men arrived, delayed by muddy roads, the battle had ended and Tilghman had surrendered.

After learning of the loss of Fort Henry, Gen. ALBERT SIDNEY JOHNSTON, at Bowling Green, decided to give up his position

and retire to Nashville. He sent half of his army to reinforce Fort Donelson and placed Brig. Gen. JOHN B. FLOYD in command there. 2 other officers—Brig. Gens. GIDEON J. PILLOW and SIMON B. BUCKNER—were sent to assist in the defense. Grant's force of 15,000 arrived at Fort Donelson 12 Feb., and he positioned his men while waiting for Foote's flotilla. The gunboats arrived on the 14th but were repulsed by the shore batteries in a sharp exchange. Unlike the Battle of FORT HENRY, the victory at FORT DONELSON was Grant's and the army's. Buckner surrendered the garrison 16 Feb. The victory brought Grant national prominence and provided the initiative in the river war that culminated in his impressive victory at VICKSBURG in 1863. The capture of Forts Henry and Donelson completely changed the war in the West, forcing the Confederates to evacuate Nashville and Columbus. They lost their grip on southern Kentucky and virtually all of Middle and western Tennessee.
                                                                                —NCD

Forts Jackson and St. Philip, La., Battle of.   18–28 Apr. 1862   Early in 1862 the Union undertook the campaign, championed by Gen. WINFIELD SCOTT, aimed at dividing the Confederacy and recovering the Mississippi River from its mouth to Cairo, Ill. Capt. DAVID G. FARRAGUT's oceangoing West Gulf Blockading Squadron was given the mission of ascending the Mississippi and capturing New Orleans, the South's largest city.

To guard the river approaches to New Orleans, the Confederates had occupied and strongly garrisoned 2 masonry forts

—Jackson on the right bank and St. Philip on the opposite shore—some 12 mi above Head of Passes. To hold Union warships under the fire of the forts' waterfront batteries, Southern engineers moored a line of hulks across the river. Auxiliary to the land defenses, the Confederates had a heterogeneous naval force consisting of 4 vessels of the Confederate navy, 2 belonging to the state of Louisiana, and 6 manned by the river defense fleet, 2 of which, *Louisiana* and *Manassas,* were ironclads. But the former's engines were not powerful enough to propel the ship, and in the ensuing battle it was moored to the bank above Fort St. Philip and employed as a floating battery.

From his advance base at Ship Island, Miss., Farragut prepared to ascend the Mississippi. Though the deep-draft screw sloops were lightened, considerable difficulty was experienced in dragging them over the Southwest Pass bar. It was 8 Apr. before Farragut assembled his 24 vessels and Cmdr. DAVID D. PORTER's 19 mortar schooners at Head of Passes. Each of Porter's ships mounted a 13-in. mortar.

To soften up defenses at Forts Jackson and St. Philip, the mortar schooners opened fire on the 18th, lofting their 200-lb shells into and around the works. The bombardment continued for the next 5 days, the Federals focusing on Fort Jackson. Meanwhile, on the night of the 20th, several gunboats opened a passage through the obstructions.

Satisfied that steam-powered warships could pass forts designed to cope with sailing vessels, Farragut put his squadron in motion at 2 a.m., 24 Apr. His ships, except 3 gunboats, fought their way upstream through the hulks and by the forts. Then, in a wild melee, they avoided fire rafts and the bull-like rushes of the ram *Manassas* and smashed the Confederate fleet. Continuing up the river 70 mi, Farragut went ashore to accept the surrender of New Orleans on the 25th. 3 days later the Forts Jackson and St. Philip garrisons, isolated by Farragut's bold dash, mutinied and surrendered. —ECB

Foster, John Gray.

USA b. Whitefield, N.H., 27 May 1823. At 10 Foster moved with his family to Nashua, N.H., where he completed his early education. In 1846 he graduated from the U.S. Military Academy, 4th in a class of 59. Commissioned a lieutenant in the construction engineers, Foster served throughout the Mexican War in a prestigious unit, the company of sappers, miners, and pontoniers; in Mexico he won 2 brevets and was severely wounded at Molino del Rey.

Returning north, Captain Foster handled routine engineering assignments and 1855–57 taught his specialty at West Point. When the Civil War began, he was at its center, as

LC

engineer in charge of fortifications in Charleston harbor. After surrendering with the garrison of FORT SUMTER, he went to Washington and 23 Oct. 1861 became a brigadier general of volunteers.

At that rank he commanded a New England infantry brigade during coastal operations in North Carolina, including the battles of ROANOKE ISLAND and NEW BERNE, winning in both engagements high praise from his superior, Maj. Gen. AMBROSE

E. BURNSIDE. On 15 Mar. 1862 he was named military governor of New Berne and vicinity and 6 July received command of a division and the DEPARTMENT OF NORTH CAROLINA, to which the DEPARTMENT OF VIRGINIA was later added, heading it till Nov. 1863.

Thereafter Foster held various administrative posts, each for several months, only occasionally engaging in active operations. Late in 1863 he was transferred to Tennessee as a member of the force that helped relieve the Siege of KNOXVILLE. In December, he replaced Burnside as commander of the Army of the Ohio, relinquishing that post 2 months later, having been injured in a fall from his horse.

Fully recovered in May 1864, Foster, a major general since 18 July 1862, was assigned to head the Department of the South, and cooperated with Maj. Gen. WILLIAM T. SHERMAN in the Sieges of SAVANNAH and CHARLESTON, the latter falling 18 Feb. 1865 to Foster's troops. The close of the war found him commanding in Florida as a brevet major general of Regulars.

From 1865 until his death in Nashua, 2 Sept. 1874, he was involved in surveys and construction along the New England coast, in assisting the chief of engineers, and in publishing works on various aspects of his profession. —EGL

Foster, Robert Sanford.

USA b. Vernon, Ind., 27 Jan. 1834. Educated in a local school, Foster at 16 went to Indianapolis, where he learned the trade of a tinner. Enlisting immediately after the war began, he was commissioned a captain in the 11th Indiana, a 90-day regiment, transferring in June to the 13th Indiana as its major. Foster saw action at Romney and Rich Mountain in western Virginia, rose in rank to colonel 30 Apr. 1862, and commanded the regiment in Brig. Gen. JAMES SHIELDS's division during the SHENANDOAH VALLEY CAMPAIGN of 1862. Transferred to Suffolk, Va., he commanded a brigade in the Union forces defending the town.

USMHI

Foster was promoted to brigadier general 12 June 1863 and participated in the Union siege operations against Charleston, S.C., in autumn 1863 and winter 1864. He commanded a brigade responsible for the protection of the harbor at Folly Island and in spring 1864 served briefly in Florida before returning to southeastern Virginia. The brigadier then accepted the position of chief of staff under Maj. Gen. QUINCY A. GILLMORE, commander of the X Corps/Army of the James.

Foster participated in the PETERSBURG Campaign as a brigade and then a division commander. On 2 Apr. 1865, the day the Confederates abandoned Petersburg, Foster's division and another Union division repeatedly charged FORT GREGG, the vital hinge of the broken Confederate lines. Brevetted major general, he served as a member of the military commission trying the conspirators in the assassination of Abraham Lincoln.

Foster resigned his commission 25 Sept. 1865, returning to Indianapolis, where he served as city treasurer, U.S. marshal, and president of the city board of trade. d. Indianapolis, 3 Mar. 1903. —JDW

fougasse. In Western military history, the use of this primitive land mine can be traced to the late Middle Ages. Most often a shallow hole in the ground filled with jagged stones and a charge of gunpowder, it was set off by a fuse that ran to a fortified position. Though its use was rarely reported in the Civil War, Capt. TRUMAN SEYMOUR of the Union garrison at FORT SUMTER altered its form to defend the works from an infantry assault in 1861. He filled barrels with stones and gunpowder, to be dropped from the fort walls in front of attackers and discharged with long lanyards. They were not used.   —JES

14th Amendment. Reconstruction politicians, determined to keep Southern legislators from discriminating against freedmen, Unionists, and Federal soldiers, framed the 14th Amendment in 1866; limiting state authority, it gave the Federal Supreme Court the power to protect basic civil rights of all citizens.

Agitation for the amendment grew out of severe dissatisfaction with Pres. ANDREW JOHNSON's moderate plans for restoring the Southern states to the Union. His lenient granting of amnesty (*see* AMNESTY PROCLAMATIONS, FEDERAL) had placed in power former Confederate leaders who in coalition with Northern Democrats would be able to threaten Republican political domination and possibly the party's future. Provisional Southern legislatures had resisted ratifying the 13TH AMENDMENT, infuriated Northern public opinion by refusing to accept defeat with sufficient humility, and undermined black freedom with a series of BLACK CODES. Military officials were also being harassed by the passage of state laws that left them liable to prosecution for carrying out orders issued by the Federal government. The amendment incorporated 2 critical pieces of legislation: it prevented states from depriving persons of life, liberty, and property without due process of law, and guaranteed equal protection under the law; it also imposed more rigid terms for restoring the South to the Union.

The restoration clause reapportioned representation by eliminating the three-fifths law, which determined the census value assigned to slaves in the prewar years, and adjusted population figures for those states refusing suffrage to blacks; disfranchised former Confederates who had broken any oath to the Federal government; repudiated the Confederate debt; and provided enforcement for the provisions enacted.

A compromise measure, the amendment did not include the universal suffrage Radicals wanted to tighten control over Southern governments, nor did it offer the unconditional amnesty favored by advocates of Presidential Reconstruction; but it did provide the cornerstone for future civil rights legislation by defining citizenship and strengthening the status of the individual.

On Johnson's recommendation, Southern legislators rejected the amendment, claiming it did not guarantee readmission to the Union, gave excessive power to Congress, deprived the South of its most talented leaders, and threatened to place blacks in control of state governments. When Congress responded by demanding universal suffrage and new elections under military supervision, all but 4 Southern states ratified the amendment. It became law 28 July 1868. The last few states soon fell into line, but Southerners resisted compliance by intimidating with violence those blacks trying to exercise their civil rights.

In 1883 the Supreme Court ruled that the word *person* applied to corporations as well, with the result that laws seeking to govern corporate practices could be interpreted as violations of "due process" and therefore unconstitutional. This allowed many desegregation laws to be struck down and led to passage in Southern states later in the 19th century of discriminatory Jim Crow laws, which were not overturned until the Civil Rights Acts of 1964 and 1965.   —PLF

Fox, Gustavus Vasa. USP   b. Saugus, Mass., 13 June 1821. Following 2 years of preparatory school at Phillip's Academy in Andover, Mass., Fox received an appointment as midshipman at the U.S. Naval Academy at Annapolis, graduating 12 Jan. 1838. He advanced to passed midshipman in 1845 during a tour of duty aboard the *Preble* and gained additional experience at sea and on troop transport duty during the Mexican War. In 1856 Fox resigned the lieutenant's commission he had earned 4 years earlier and became an agent for the Bay State Mills.

USMHI

Early in 1861 Fox's politically powerful brother-in-law, MONTGOMERY BLAIR, arranged to have him consult on the FORT SUMTER crisis. His proposal to send steam-powered supply ships past the Charleston harbor batteries at night was vetoed by Pres. James Buchanan. But ABRAHAM LINCOLN, the new president, admired his ideas and sent Fox to Charleston to seek some solution to the mounting tensions. But he did not arrive in the city until 12 Apr., too late to do anything except transport Maj. ROBERT ANDERSON and his men to New York after Anderson surrendered Sumter on the 13th. Though the peace-keeping attempt failed, Lincoln praised Fox's efforts and offered him command of a ship, which Fox turned down in favor of an appointment as chief clerk in the Navy Department. Recognizing his talent, Lincoln created the position of assistant navy secretary for Fox 1 Aug., under Navy Sec. GIDEON WELLES.

An experienced, diplomatic administrator, Fox made himself indispensable to Welles and earned respect in political circles for his competence and tact, particularly in matters of personnel management and initiating new procedures. He persuaded Welles to use IRONCLADS in battle, influenced favorable curriculum changes at the officers' school at Annapolis, and in his correspondence with ship contractors displayed exceptional skill as an engineer. He resigned the assistant secretaryship 22 May 1866 but was reappointed on the 31st to serve as courier to Russia.

On his return to the U.S. in December, Fox reentered the textile business in Massachusetts, dying in New York City 29 Oct. 1883. After her husband's death, Fox's widow gave his personal papers to Montgomery Blair and 2 of Blair's brothers. They later authorized publication of the papers by the Naval History Society. Volumes I (1918) and II (1919) of the 3 volumes projected in the preface to volume I were released in editions limited to 1,250 copies. They contain valuable detail concerning the administration of the Civil War navy.   —PLF

Fox's *Regimental Losses*. *Regimental Losses in the American Civil War 1861–65,* by William F. Fox (1889), is the most thorough and reliable of the 3 classic Civil War statistical registers, the other 2 being DYER'S *COMPENDIUM* and LIVER-MORE'S *NUMBERS AND LOSSES IN THE CIVIL WAR.* Fox analyzed regimental muster rolls and records from the various state adjutant generals' offices to assemble casualty figures, rank units by losses, draw statistical comparisons among them by battle, and enumerate death from disease and imprisonment. Of particular value are the brief Federal corps and regimental histories. The bulk of the work pertains to Union troops, with Confederate statistics covered to the extent permitted by fragmentary records. —PLF

Frank Leslie's Illustrated Newspaper.

Picture newspapers first became popular in England in the 1840s, with the *London Illustrated News* the preeminent pioneer. Frank Leslie, then known as Henry Carter, began work as an engraver for the *News* in 1842. After immigrating to the U.S. in 1848, legally changing his name to Frank Leslie, and working for a string of American illustrated papers, he launched *Frank Leslie's Ladies' Gazette of Paris, London, and New York Fashions* in 1854. Its success encouraged him to start *Frank Leslie's Illustrated Newspaper,* a weekly that first appeared 15 Dec. 1855.

In the competitive antebellum news market *Leslie's* stayed afloat but never really prospered until the Civil War. With a staff of field artists, or "specials," sketching the battle action, the war scenes were transferred to woodblock engravings and appeared before the public within 2 weeks of the event they depicted. This remarkably rapid, though rarely wholly accurate, presentation of the war's visual side made *Leslie's* eminent in its field, the only major rival being *HARPER'S WEEKLY. Leslie's* made its contribution to ART as well. Specials James E. Taylor, William Waud, and EDWIN FORBES all refined their talents during the Civil War working on its staff. In an age when photography was limited to still scenes, *Leslie's* staff made a contribution to history, recording action for future generations to see instead of imagine.

The paper appeared every Saturday, selling for 8 cents. Though its reportage never threatened to steal the literate audience of newspapers like the New York *Herald*, its simple format, broad display of war news, and ample sprinkling of humor kept it a best seller through the 1860s. Postbellum, Frank Leslie extended wartime profits by reproducing wood engravings from the war years in pictorial histories, and his magazine continued publication through the end of the century and the advent of news photography. —JES

Franklin, Tenn., Battle of.

30 Nov. 1864   Union Maj. Gen. JOHN M. SCHOFIELD's IV and XXIII corps troops threw up defenses around the town of Franklin on the morning of 30 Nov. 1864. After marching north 12 mi from SPRING HILL, pursued by Gen. JOHN B. HOOD's Army of Tennessee, Schofield's men had planned to cross the Harpeth River in back of the town, but found 1 of 2 bridges destroyed, the other badly damaged. Hood's army, 3 great columns come north from Florence, Ala., intended pushing on to take Nashville, 18 mi to the north, initiating the Army of Tennessee's FRANKLIN AND NASHVILLE CAMPAIGN.

Some restoration work on the damaged bridge allowed Federals to trickle across the Harpeth at midmorning, but Schofield's tired troops, in motion since early on the 29th, needed rest. Union cavalry Brig. Gen. JAMES H. WILSON, across the Harpeth, covered the Federal left rear, where Confederates

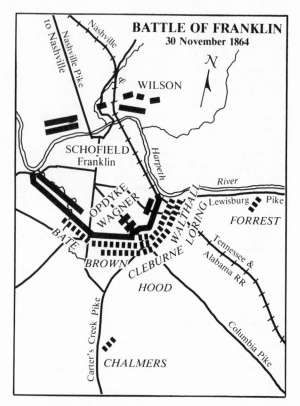

might ford upstream and attempt rear and flank attacks. Of the nearly 28,000 Union troops in Schofield's command, about 20,000 manned earthworks dug that morning from their left on the Tennessee & Alabama Railroad, in a curve around the Carter cotton gin on the Columbia Pike in front of town, across the Carter's Creek Pike, and bending to their right rear on the Harpeth. Schofield determined to halt his men a few hours in these positions, fighting Hood if necessary.

Hood's men appeared across the Federal front a little after noon. Against the advice of cavalry Maj. Gen. NATHAN B. FORREST and infantry column commander Maj. Gen. BENJAMIN F. CHEATHAM, Hood deployed battle lines for a frontal assault on the entrenched Federals across nearly 2 mi of open ground. 2 of his 3 columns, Lt. Gen. ALEXANDER P. STEWART's and Cheatham's, had arrived from Spring Hill, giving the Confederates a slight numerical advantage, since those of Schofield's troops already across the Harpeth could not be brought to bear in a sudden defense. It was said Hood disdained fighting from cover, believing "cold steel" and head-on attack built a fighting man's character. At 4 p.m. his men went forward on a broad front.

2 detached Federal brigades under Brig. Gen. GEORGE D. WAGNER sat astride the Columbia Pike about a half-mile in front of Franklin. Confused by an order to withdraw from an enemy advance, they held fast until, overwhelmed, they charged into 5 Union brigades on the Franklin front, leading the Confederates and forcing comrades in the trenches to hold their fire. Artillery in front of the Carter cotton gin also held off.

Hood, from his left to right, sent in Maj. Gens. WILLIAM B.

BATE, JOHN C. BROWN, PATRICK R. CLEBURNE, SAMUEL G. FRENCH, EDWARD C. WALTHALL, and WILLIAM WING LORING. Cleburne's and Brown's men, in the center, followed Wagner's troops hotly until the latter cleared their own defenses. The sudden fire Federals let loose once the retreating troops passed, leveled rows of Confederates and killed Cleburne. But momentum carried many over the works, driving the Federals from their cannon into the yard of the Carter house. Union Col. EMERSON OPDYCKE's brigade, 200 yd in the rear, rushed forward, driving Confederates to the entrenchments, pinning down the wounded Brown and a large part of his command. The railroad and rising ground hindered Confederates on the right. Crowded together, they were hit by point-blank artillery fire from a battery near the railroad. Bate's left-wing troops hit uneven resistance, took some outer works, and held until dark. Forrest's cavalry forded the Harpeth on the far right, hit Wilson's cavalry and infantry supports, fought until ammunition ran out, then retired. Confederate cavalry under Brig. Gen. JAMES R. CHALMERS, deployed on the left, only fought sporadically and with no clear objective.

Fighting continued fitfully until 9 p.m., Confederates withdrew to bivouac, and Schofield hurried a withdrawal at 11. Lead troops in his 7-mi train reached Nashville at dawn. All passed into Maj. Gen. GEORGE H. THOMAS' lines by noon. Hood opened fire on Franklin at daybreak 1 Dec., found it empty, and rushed on to invest Nashville. Those Confederates not in shock were bitter over his foolish frontal attack.

Franklin was Hood's great disaster, costing 6,200 Confederate casualties; Federals lost 2,326. PICKETT'S CHARGE at GETTYSBURG cost less than Hood's at Franklin. A total of 6 generals dead, 5 wounded, and 1, Brig. Gen. GEORGE W. GORDON, captured, vindicated critics of Hood's tactical skills but ruined the command of the Army of Tennessee.   —JES

Franklin, William Buel. USA b. York, Pa., 27 Feb. 1823. The top graduate of the West Point class of 1843 (ULYSSES S. GRANT ranked in the middle), Franklin won an appointment as an engineer, serving with distinction under Col. Philip Kearny in the South Pass Expedition and in the Mexican War. On the eve of the Civil War he was assigned to superintend the construction of a new dome for the Capitol. Appointed brigadier general 17 May 1861, Franklin rose from command of a brigade to a division, a corps, then 2 corps at the Battle of FREDERICKSBURG, 13 Dec. 1862. His military fortunes were closely tied to those of Maj. Gen. GEORGE B. MCCLELLAN, whom he greatly admired.

USMHI/MA

Fredericksburg was a disaster for the Army of the Potomac, and its commander, Maj. Gen. AMBROSE E. BURNSIDE, blamed Franklin. In fact, Franklin had executed Burnside's hazy orders literally, but attacked the Confederates with less vigor than he later exhibited in his public criticisms of Burnside. Sustained by the COMMITTEE ON THE CONDUCT OF THE WAR for political reasons, Burnside succeeded in shelving Franklin for more than 5 months.

In summer 1863 Franklin got a second chance through assignment to corps command in the Department of the Gulf. He participated in Maj. Gen. NATHANIEL P. BANKS's disastrous RED RIVER CAMPAIGN, from which Franklin emerged with a severe wound and further damage to his reputation. Disability and official disfavor kept him from active campaigning during the last year of the war despite Grant's request for his services.

After the war, as an executive of the Colt Fire Arms Manufacturing Co. for 22 years, Franklin again demonstrated his engineering and administrative ability. Only during the war did he fail to rise to the heights expected of him, and then he appears to have been a victim of misfortune rather than incompetence, a talented soldier in the wrong place at the wrong time. He died in Hartford, Conn., 8 Mar. 1903, after serving the state as an elector in the 1876 presidential election and the Federal government as commissioner general at the 1888 Paris Exposition.   —JYS

Franklin and Nashville Campaign, Tenn. (Hood's Tennessee Campaign). 29 Nov.–27 Dec. 1864 On 22 Nov. 1864 Gen. JOHN B. HOOD's 39,000 Confederates left Florence, Ala., in 3 columns commanded by Maj. Gen. BENJAMIN F. CHEATHAM and Lt. Gens. STEPHEN D. LEE and ALEXANDER P. STEWART. Following a plan originated by Hood and approved by Pres. JEFFERSON DAVIS, they invaded Tennessee to draw Union military attention from the Deep South, crush Maj. Gen. WILLIAM T. SHERMAN's Western support for his operations in Georgia, and perhaps take war through Kentucky to the North.

After the fall of ATLANTA, Hood had moved the Army of Tennessee northwest in September and October, drawing Sherman and a detached force from Atlanta, skirmishing and wrecking railroads, fighting at ALLATOONA, then withdrawing into northwest Alabama. Unwilling to pursue farther, Sherman had paused west of Rome, Ga., ordered the IV, XVI, and XXIII corps to Maj. Gen. GEORGE H. THOMAS, commanding at Nashville, and returned to Atlanta to begin his March to the Sea. Sherman knew Hood's intent and believed that, reinforced, Thomas would repel him.

Hood and Thomas spent more than 20 days preparing their parts in the campaign: Hood gathering supplies, reorganizing, and waiting for Maj. Gen. NATHAN B. FORREST's cavalry; Thomas creating a cavalry force under Brig. Gen. JAMES H. WILSON and moving the IV and XXIII corps from the Chattanooga area to positions west along the Tennessee & Alabama Railroad. The XVI Corps detachment Thomas looked for could not reach him until December. Forrest spent late October and early November raiding Nashville's Tennessee supply lines and wrecking the railhead at Johnsonville.

Forrest joined Hood at Florence, the expedition entered Tennessee, and its columns, traveling miles apart, moved for Columbia, midway to Nashville. The XXIII Corps' Maj. Gen. JOHN M. SCHOFIELD commanded his men and elements of the IV Corps at Pulaski along the railroad, west of invading columns. On Thomas' orders, he raced his force north to Columbia, arriving ahead of the Confederates 24 Nov., and covered bridges on the Duck River astride the invasion route. Federal cavalry sparred with Confederate horsemen from the Alabama line to Columbia. Schofield skirmished around Columbia from the 24th to the 26th, until Hood's columns converged on his front. Bridges over the Duck River were destroyed and Schofield's troops withdrew north, covering fords, until Forrest's cavalry crossed at Huey's Mill on Schofield's left

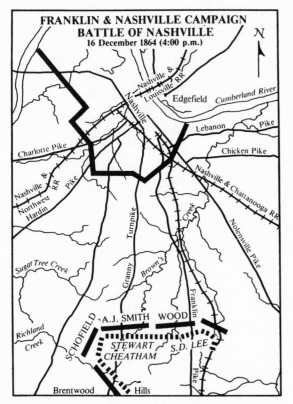

FRANKLIN & NASHVILLE CAMPAIGN
BATTLE OF NASHVILLE
16 December 1864 (4:00 p.m.)

on the 28th. Wilson sent word to Schofield: "Get back to Franklin without delay."

Union Maj. Gen. DAVID S. STANLEY, commanding IV Corps troops, hurried north to SPRING HILL 29 Nov. to hold the town until Schofield's troops passed through. Forrest, from his eastern crossing of the Duck, threatened the Federal right. Stanley's pickets held him off. Hood failed in his plan to hold Federals there, circumvent them, and press on to Nashville. He blamed Cheatham for bumbled enveloping maneuvers, and Schofield slipped through, marching his men from midnight to noon from Spring Hill to Franklin 30 Nov.

At the Battle of FRANKLIN late that afternoon, Federals faced Hood's 18 charging brigades; their center was pierced, resealed, and the enemy repulsed from the fortified town while Schofield tried repairing bridges across the Harpeth River at their backs. The Union retreat, stalled by destroyed crossings, began again at 11 p.m. and continued to Thomas' Nashville lines the next day. At Franklin, his last attempt to keep the IV and XXIII corps from reaching Thomas, Hood sacrificed over 6,000 men.

3 divisions of the XVI Corps, promised earlier, reached Nashville 30 Nov. from the Trans-Mississippi. Schofield's arrival brought Thomas' strength to nearly 70,000. Hood's men invested the city, and telegrams from Washington urged Thomas to finish the contest.

Thomas spent 2 weeks planning attack and pursuit. On 6 Dec. Lt. Gen. U. S. GRANT wired a direct order "to attack Hood at once," but Thomas ignored it. 9 days later Federals sallied out of the fortress city and in a day's fight wrecked and demor-

alized the Army of Tennessee in front of an enormous body of civilian spectators lining the hills around the battlefield. A 10-day pursuit followed, Wilson's cavalry in the advance, Forrest's cavalry providing the rear guard from Columbia south to the banks of the Tennessee. The last of Forrest's men crossed the river 27 Dec., and 2 days later Hood's men marched on to Tupelo, Miss., ending the Franklin and Nashville Campaign. The Army of Tennessee, fragmented, dispatched elements to Mississippi and Mobile, the remainder traveling east for the last campaign in the Carolinas. —JES

Franklin's Crossing (Deep Run), Va., eng. at. 5 June 1863 The leading elements of the Confederate Army of Northern Virginia abandoned their lines at Fredericksburg, Va., 3 June 1863. Gen. ROBERT E. LEE had decided to invade the North for a second time, and throughout the 3d and 4th the Confederates marched westward toward the Shenandoah Valley. Rumors of this Southern movement filtered into Union headquarters across the Rappahannock River, where Maj. Gen. JOSEPH HOOKER evaluated the information. To check the accuracy of the reports, Hooker ordered a reconnaissance in force for 5 June.

Maj. Gen. JOHN SEDGWICK's VI Corps veterans drew the assignment. Union infantry, supported by artillery, moved during the morning down to the river at Franklin's Crossing near Deep Run (the point used to cross the river during the Battle of FREDERICKSBURG). Confederates, shielded by rifle pits, fired upon the Federals, who, though replying with musketry and artillery charges, could not dislodge the Southerners. The 26th New Jersey and 5th Vermont, supported by 2 regiments, attempted a crossing but were repulsed.

Sedgwick personally oversaw the operations and ordered a crossing in pontoon boats. The 2 Union regiments pushed the pontoons to the river's edge, crawled in, and went across. Landing on the southern bank, the Federals charged into the Confederates, seizing the pits and 35 prisoners. Pushing into the adjoining woods, the Federals halted before more Confederates, supported by artillery. The Union troops withdrew, suffering 57 casualties. The presence of additional Southerners convinced Sedgwick that Lee still held his lines in strength.

Sedgwick's assessment was only partially correct. His veterans had encountered Lt. Gen. AMBROSE P. HILL's III Corps troops. Hill's, however, was the only corps left around Fredericksburg, under orders to follow if the Federals did not cross in force. Hill marched the next day. Hooker, still unconvinced, ordered reconnaissances by his cavalry, resulting 9 June in the Battle of BRANDY STATION. —JDW

Fraser, Trenholm & Co. A Charleston, S.C., shipping and banking firm, John Fraser & Co. had an English subsidiary during the Civil War: Fraser, Trenholm & Co. Established in antebellum years by the company's majority owner, GEORGE A. TRENHOLM, from Mar. 1862 it served the Confederate government as the Confederate Depository in Liverpool, England, keeping government banking accounts, converting currency, acting as receiver of funds, and taking part in all foreign aspects of Confederate finance.

E. L. Trenholm, George's brother, and James T. Welsman and Charles K. Prioleau ran its daily affairs. Capt. JAMES D. BULLOCH, Confederate navy purchasing agent, and Maj. CALEB HUSE, purchasing agent for the Southern army, both kept offices on its premises at 10 Rumford Place. Its services were invaluable to Confederate diplomats JAMES M. MASON and JOHN SLIDELL, and Southerners abroad came to know it as the Confederate government's unofficial European mission.

Among its patriotic chores, Fraser, Trenholm & Co. helped dispose of cotton certificates and advised Confederates in arranging the South's only sizable foreign debt, the ERLANGER LOAN. It disbursed funds to Huse and Bulloch for arms purchases and late in the war sold shiploads of Confederate cotton and credited the proceeds to Southern accounts for draw by European weapons and supply dealers.

Fraser, Trenholm & Co.'s Confederate connection remained only semiofficial. The company pursued profit for the parent firm by operating a 50-ship fleet of blockade runners and received .5% commission from the Confederate government for its banking and financial services. It sold 8 of its ships to the Confederacy for government shipping use while continuing to smuggle millions of dollars' worth of cotton out of the South yearly. At the end of the Civil War, as the last Confederate depository in Europe, it tried to satisfy all outstanding Southern accounts before closing its doors.

In postwar years, George Trenholm was caught up in Reconstruction tax problems and both Fraser, Trenholm & Co. and John Fraser & Co. shut down permanently. —JES

Frayser's Farm, Va., Battle of. 30 June 1862 *See* WHITE OAK SWAMP, VA., BATTLE OF.

Frazer, John Wesley. CSA b. Hardin Cty., Tenn., 6 Jan. 1827. After graduating 34th in the West Point class of 1849, Frazer went through routine assignments in the East and Far West, and by 1860 was an infantry captain serving in Washington Territory. He began his Confederate career when he resigned his U.S. Army commission Mar. 1861 and accepted the lieutenant colonelcy of the 8th Alabama Infantry, soon resigning again to become colonel of the 28th Alabama.

After leading the 28th Alabama through Gen. BRAXTON BRAGG's Kentucky campaigning, Sept. 1862, he served competently with the Army of Tennessee through spring 1863 and was nominated for brigadier general 19 May.

USMHI

In Sept. 1863 Union Maj. Gen. AMBROSE E. BURNSIDE commanded 25,000 men in East Tennessee and held Knoxville. The previous month Confederate Maj. Gen. SIMON B. BUCKNER had been compelled to withdraw from Burnside's superior numbers, leaving Frazer with 2,500 men to hold Cumberland Gap and prevent Federal reinforcement, while the main army prepared for the CHICKAMAUGA CAMPAIGN. A confident Frazer "boasted that he could hold the gap for at least a month under siege." While nothing in his combat experience indicated that he was an expert tactician, he believed the positioning of his 3 North Carolina and Georgia regiments and his lone battery made the gap a Confederate stronghold.

Either he felt abandoned by Buckner or overwhelmed by Burnside's numbers, but Frazer failed to hold the gap, surrendering 9 Sept. 6 days later Bragg learned that the garrison had

fallen. Frazer was lambasted by Confederate politicians, his commission was rejected by the Confederate Senate, and following his unconditional surrender he was imprisoned at FORT WARREN in Boston harbor, where he remained until the end of the war. Little was heard from him until 16 Apr. 1865, when he and 14 other imprisoned Confederate generals wrote to Lt. Gen. U. S. Grant to express condolences on the death of Abraham Lincoln.

Following his release in 1865, Frazer moved briefly to Arkansas, became a planter, then went to New York City, where he became a businessman. He died there 31 Mar. 1906.
—JES

Fredericksburg, Confederate Department of. Created soon after Virginia's secession, the Confederate Department of Fredericksburg, comprised the area between Powell's River and the mouth of the Potomac River, embracing the counties on both sides of the Rappahannock River from its mouth to Fredericksburg. Brig. Gen. THEOPHILUS H. HOLMES commanded the department until it was reorganized 22 Oct. 1861 into the District of Aquia. —JDW

Fredericksburg, Va., First Battle of. 13 Dec. 1862 On 19 Nov. 1862 Maj. Gen. AMBROSE E. BURNSIDE's Army of the Potomac, approximately 130,000 men, was encamped on Stafford Heights on the east bank of the Rappahannock River overlooking the city of Fredericksburg; there they waited for the arrival of PONTOON boats that would enable them to bridge the river and advance on Richmond. The pontoons finally arrived 25 Nov., but Burnside made no attempt to cross for almost another 3 weeks.

This unnecessary delay enabled Gen. ROBERT E. LEE to unite the 2 wings of his Army of Northern Virginia, recently reorganized into 2 corps under Lt. Gen. JAMES LONGSTREET and Lt. Gen. THOMAS J. "STONEWALL" JACKSON; Jackson had been in the vicinity of Winchester, Longstreet near Culpeper. Rather than contest the Federal crossing of the river, Lee chose to fortify the heights west of the city, varying from 1 to 2 mi distance from the river. Here, along a 7-mi front stretching from the Rappahannock on his left to Massaponax Creek on his right, he placed Longstreet on the left and Jackson on the right, with over 300 pieces of artillery in support. His force consisted of approximately 75,000 men. Longstreet's position, along a ridge known as Marye's Heights, was further fortified by a sunken road and a stone wall at the base of the heights. An open plain about 2 mi wide lay between Jackson's position and the river.

Despite the topographical advantage and strength of the Confederate position, Burnside finally decided to attack and 13 Dec. ordered a frontal assault by Maj. Gen. EDWIN V. SUMNER on the right and Brig. Gen. WILLIAM B. FRANKLIN on the left, with Maj. Gen. JOSEPH HOOKER in the center in reserve. All day the Federals charged the almost impregnable Confederate position only to be beaten back each time with heavy losses. Darkness put an end to the useless slaughter. 2 days later, under cover of a violent rainstorm, the Army of the Potomac retreated across the river. The Federals had suffered 12,653 casualties in killed, wounded, and missing; the Confederates 5,309. *See also* FREDERICKSBURG CAMPAIGN, VA. —JPC

Fredericksburg, Va., Second Battle of. 3–4 May 1863 This encounter was part of the Battle of CHANCELLORSVILLE. Maj.

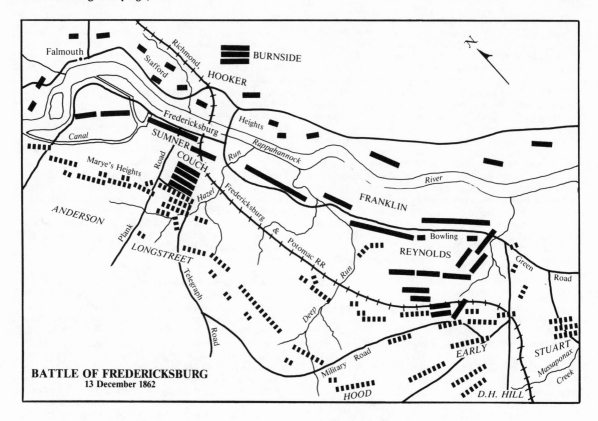

BATTLE OF FREDERICKSBURG
13 December 1862

Gen. JOSEPH HOOKER, commanding the Army of the Potomac, had taken the bulk of his forces up the Rappahannock River to a point northwest of Fredericksburg and had crossed both the Rappahannock and Rapidan rivers to get on the Confederate left flank and rear. He left Maj. Gen. JOHN SEDGWICK's VI Corps opposite Fredericksburg to attempt a diversionary attack to hold the Confederates there in their defensive positions.

Gen. ROBERT E. LEE, commanding the Army of Northern Virginia, was not deceived by the ruse. He moved his force west to meet Hooker's threat, leaving only Maj. Gen. JUBAL A. EARLY's division to hold the heights west of the city, including the stone wall and sunken road at the base of Marye's Heights.

When Hooker's advance was halted at Chancellorsville, Hooker ordered Sedgwick to seize Marye's Heights and then advance to attack Lee's right flank. Several times Sedgwick charged the heights and was driven back by Brig. Gen. WILLIAM BARKSDALE's brigade of Mississippians, who had seen heavy fighting on the same ground 5 months earlier. During a truce to remove the wounded, Sedgwick learned that the Mississippians had suffered severe losses and were barely able to cover their lines. Ordering his men to carry unloaded rifles so they would not stop to fire and reload, Sedgwick attacked again with a daring and gallant bayonet charge that drove the Confederates off the heights and back toward Richmond. Pausing only long enough to regroup, Early proceeded west toward Chancellorsville.

When Lee learned the heights had been lost and another Federal force was moving toward him, on 3 May he boldly split his army in Hooker's front and marched 2 divisions back toward Fredericksburg. Late that afternoon, Confederates under Maj. Gen. LAFAYETTE MCLAWS met Sedgwick's advance division near Salem Church on the Orange Turnpike and halted it. The next day Early also came up. Attacked furiously on 3 sides, Sedgwick wisely abandoned any idea of joining Hooker. Instead, he swung his corps around toward the Rappahannock to protect his flanks and that night crossed the river at Scott's Ford, just below Banks' Ford. Hooker made no move to help Sedgwick at any time. —JPC

Fredericksburg Campaign, Va. Nov.–Dec. 1862 On 7 Nov. 1862 Maj. Gen. AMBROSE E. BURNSIDE replaced Maj. Gen. GEORGE B. MCCLELLAN as commander of the Army of the Potomac. Burnside neither wanted the command nor felt certain that he was fit for the responsibilities. Within a week, however, he had reorganized the army into 3 Grand Divisions and secured Pres. ABRAHAM LINCOLN's approval of a new drive on Richmond.

When Burnside assumed command, the Union army covered the area of central Virginia north of the Rappahannock River near Warrenton. Across the river lay Confederate Lt. Gen. JAMES LONGSTREET's I Corps, while Lt. Gen. THOMAS J. "STONEWALL" JACKSON's II Corps remained in the Shenandoah Valley. Burnside abandoned McClellan's promising movement to strike Gen. ROBERT E. LEE's separate wings for an advance

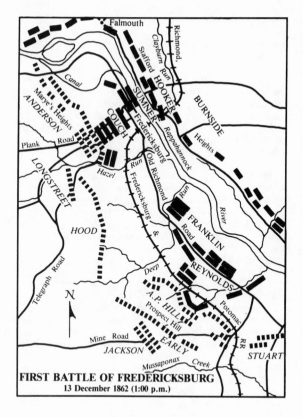

FIRST BATTLE OF FREDERICKSBURG
13 December 1862 (1:00 p.m.)

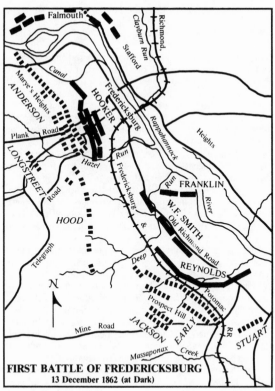

FIRST BATTLE OF FREDERICKSBURG
13 December 1862 (at Dark)

eastward toward Fredericksburg.

On 15 Nov. the Federals began moving down the Rappahannock, uncharacteristically marching rapidly, with the advanced corps covering the 40 mi to Falmouth, across the river from Fredericksburg, in 2 days. By the 19th the entire Union army blanketed the hills behind Falmouth. Burnside's swift, well-executed maneuver surprised Lee, who temporarily lost contact with the Federals. When Lee finally ascertained Burnside's objective, he ordered Jackson east and sent Longstreet toward Fredericksburg, which his leading units reached on the 18th.

Unfortunately for the Federals, their stolen march had been for nothing. Burnside had ordered PONTOONS for spanning the river, but they were sidetracked by bureaucratic bungling in the capital. Burnside compounded the error by refusing to permit a forced crossing recommended by Maj. Gen. EDWIN V. SUMNER, commanding the Right Grand Division. The pontoons finally arrived on the 25th, but too late, for many Confederates manned works on the hills west of Fredericksburg.

Burnside probed downriver for an unopposed crossing but, finding none, decided to cross at the town. On the morning of 11 Dec. Federal engineers, shielded by fog, began laying the bridges. When the fog lifted, Confederate sharpshooters hidden in buildings drove away the engineers. Union artillery responded with a massive barrage that reduced to rubble many buildings in Fredericksburg. The Confederate marksmen continued to pepper the bridge builders. Finally, Union volunteers, crossing in boats, dislodged the Southerners and secured the riverbank. On 12 Dec. the huge Union army crossed on 5 pontoon bridges. Burnside ordered a dawn assault against the 7-mi-long Confederate line.

Brig. Gen. WILLIAM B. FRANKLIN's Left Grand Division of 50,-000 men launched the Union attack on the southern part of the field against Jackson's veterans, who were behind a railroad embankment. 2 Union divisions penetrated a gap in the Southerners' lines, pressing back Jackson's ranks. Confederate counterattacks sealed the breach, repulsing Franklin's assault. To the north, directly behind the town, Sumner's and Maj. Gen. JOSEPH HOOKER's Grand Divisions hurled themselves in suicidal attacks against Lee's impregnable position on Marye's Heights. Waves of blue-coated soldiers stormed the stone wall, only to be engulfed in rifle and artillery fire. A Confederate gunner claimed that a chicken could not stay alive on the frozen ground before the Southerners. Piles of Federals covered the field at nightfall.

Burnside, nearly overcome with grief, ordered a renewal of the attacks for the next day. His Grand Division commanders, however, convinced him of the futility of such an assault and Burnside finally revoked the order. Jackson argued for a decisive Confederate counterattack, but Lee demurred, for Union artillery across the river dominated the open terrain. The battle on the 13th cost the Federals 12,653 in killed, wounded, and missing, while Southern casualties amounted to only 5,309.

During the night of 15 Dec. the Union army recrossed the river; Burnside had been decisively beaten. *See also* FREDER-ICKSBURG, VA., FIRST BATTLE OF.   —JDW

freedmen. When the U.S. Congress passed the CONFISCA-TION ACT OF 1862, thousands of Southern slaves became freed-men. Though they had eagerly awaited their liberators, free-dom was accompanied by frightening uncertainties.

Homeless, with few possessions, blacks fleeing to Union lines for protection found themselves as dependent on the Federal government for their existence as they had been on their masters. But Washington issued no concrete policy con-cerning their welfare, and field commanders saddled with car-ing for the refugees resorted to various means of providing them with food, shelter, and clothing.

Many freedmen, herded into CONTRABAND camps, were hired out to loyal Unionist plantation owners for low wages, and others in the Western theater were assigned parcels of confiscated lands for subsistence farming. Still others rendered service to the army.

Unaccustomed to administering refugee relief, the army gen-erally managed to maintain freedmen at a subsistence level. But many died of disease in overcrowded stockades, and some voluntarily returned to their homes because of deplorable con-ditions. Supplemental aid arrived from Northern relief societies that collected food and clothing for the freedmen and by 1862 began sending teachers to educate them. That year the New England Freedman's Aid Society was operating schools in South Carolina, and before war's end blacks in Mississippi and Georgia had founded schools for their own people.

Not all freedmen dared trust whites professing friendship. Abuses of slavery were fresh in their minds, and many suffered injustices at the hands of invading white soldiers. Knowing the war was not over, unsure of what or whom to believe, many preferred to stay with their masters, whose power over them would remain after Union forces moved on. Others joined the Federal army after 1863, or followed it aimlessly, not knowing what else to do. Some chanced reenslavement to search for relatives in areas still held by the Confederates. But in the minds of all blacks was a dread that freedom might not last.
                                                                            —PLF

Freedmen's Bank. Early in 1865 the U.S. Congress chart-ered the Freedmen's Savings and Trust Co. to encourage liber-ated slaves to save money to buy homes and land. With head-quarters in New York City, the bank opened 4 Apr. 1865. Only blacks were permitted to become depositors, and most of those who did invested their dreams as well as their hard-earned money in the institution. By 1872, 34 branch offices had been opened, all but 2 of them in Southern cities.

The Freedmen's Bank charter required at least two-thirds of all deposits to be invested in U.S. securities; this stipulation was later amended to include real estate. But poor management, an incompetent staff, and erratic bookkeeping undermined the bank's stability. Bad loans were made to speculators, often as a result of political influence. When the Panic of 1873 hit, many of them defaulted.

The trustees tried to restore confidence by convincing the prominent black leader Frederick Douglass that the bank was sound and would thrive with him as president, but within a few months he discovered the hopelessness of keeping the institu-tion solvent. Douglass petitioned the Senate Finance Commit-

tee for funds to save the bank and even invested $10,000 of his own money in the failing venture. Despite his efforts, the Freedmen's Bank closed 28 June 1874, with thousands of depositors losing their savings.   —PLF

Freedmen's Bureau. On 4 Mar. 1865 the U.S. Congress established the Bureau for the Relief of Freedmen and Ref-ugees, authorizing it to operate for 1 year. The bureau con-solidated several departments organized earlier to oversee the welfare of former slaves, and its responsibilities extended to thousands of Southern white refugees who were given food and clothing provided by the Federal government.

Within a few months, the bureau was operating in every Southern state under jurisdiction of the War Department. In May 1865 Maj. Gen. OLIVER O. HOWARD was appointed com-missioner of the bureau's far-reaching programs, and under his leadership government employees and volunteers from vari-ous relief societies helped freedmen find jobs, set wages and terms of labor contracts, settled blacks on public lands under the HOMESTEAD ACT OF 1862, and investigated the freedmen's claims of unfair treatment. More than a welfare agency, the bureau tried to help newly freed blacks adjust to living in a free society. Though promises of "40 acres and a mule" never materialized, Howard did establish an extensive system of schools, many of which continued to operate after the bureau was discontinued. For blacks, the agency represented a step toward independence, and the one guardian of civil rights among white Southerners who were moving quickly to enact a series of discriminatory BLACK CODES.

RADICAL REPUBLICANS drafted a revised, strengthened Freed-men's Bureau Act Dec. 1865 and included a provision to extend its operations indefinitely. But ANDREW JOHNSON, eager to carry out Lincoln's lenient Reconstruction policies, vetoed the legislation as an unwarranted extension of military jurisdic-tion in peacetime and an invitation to conflict between civil and military authority. Because congressmen were unable to marshal enough support to overrule the president, the bureau was gradually discontinued.

During its existence, the bureau was severely criticized for inefficiency and corruption. Howard, a deeply religious man noted for his integrity and his questionable judgment of people, was saddled with corrupt officials given to self-interest and misappropriation of funds. And he unfortunately became a pawn of the Radicals, whose use of the agency to consolidate Republican power in the occupied states engendered distrust among Southern whites.   —PLF

Free Soil party. The Free Soil party was an antebellum coalition of antislavery proponents from the Democratic, Whig, and Liberty parties as well as from smaller political groups. While many members favored abolition, the Free-Soil-ers' philosophy emphasized not the moral or religious implica-tions of slavery but its economic, social, and political conse-quences. Most Free-Soilers were less concerned with black men in chains than with free whites whose livelihood seemed threatened by the peculiar institution. The party's platform—founded on the values of economic development, social mo-bility, and political democracy—glorified the working class, while denouncing the degradation of the work ethic in South-ern society and accusing Southerners of trying to exclude white laborers from the territories.

Party spokesmen emphasized the pragmatic bent of Free-

Soil philosophy. Former Democrats in the party claimed to feel "no squeamish sensitiveness upon the subject of slavery, no morbid sympathy for the slave." Others professed no knowledge of the slave's plight and no desire to mix moral or religious issues with practical politics. They were primarily concerned with limiting the power of the South, which they viewed as a neofeudal society where workers, white and black alike, were held in thrall. One acerbic observer wrote that the typical Free-Soil speech was laden with "disjointed facts, and misapplied figures, and great swelling words of vanity, to prove that the South is, upon the whole, the very poorest, meanest, least productive, and most miserable part of creation. . . ."

The Free Soil party had a brief life, even by the standards of its politically volatile era; formed in 1848, it was dead by 1852, following 2 unsuccessful presidential campaigns.

At the outset the Free-Soilers' main issue was opposition to slavery's extension into the Western territories, which they held to be unconstitutional. They were particularly concerned with the 500,000 sq mi acquired as a result of the Mexican War. 2 years later, the COMPROMISE OF 1850—which many Americans saw as a corrupt device for spreading slavery throughout the West—and its offshoot, the FUGITIVE SLAVE ACT, broadened and deepened the party's ideological base and swelled its numbers.

Success at the polls, however, did not follow. In 1848 Free-Soilers were hopeful of returning their standard-bearer, Martin Van Buren, to the White House, but during the campaign Van Buren's opponents, sensing the national mood, appropriated the antislavery issue as their own. Even though he drew enough votes from the Democrats to cause the election of the Whig candidate, Zachary Taylor, Van Buren failed to carry a single state. 4 years later, the party fared even worse: its candidate for president, John P. Hale of New Hampshire, won less than 5% of the national vote.

These were bitter disappointments, especially for the radical antislavery men, who, though they composed a small portion of the party, gave it much of its vitality and vision. Combining their interest in socioeconomic issues with their moral repugnance to slavery, by 1856 they had joined with other politicians to create the REPUBLICAN PARTY.   —EGL

Frémont, John Charles.

Frémont, John Charles. USA b. Savannah, Ga., 21 Jan. 1813. Of the 4 major generals appointed by Pres. ABRAHAM LINCOLN at the outset of the war, John C. Frémont was easily the most celebrated. He had been a national hero since the 1840s, when he led trailblazing expeditions across the Rocky Mts. and took a leading part in the campaign to win California from Mexico. In 1856 the "Pathfinder" won the affection of many Northerners by carrying the standard of the REPUBLICAN PARTY in its first campaign for the presidency. Lincoln appointed him major general 14 May 1861. In July, at the urging of Frémont's many friends in Washington, New York, and Missouri, Lincoln gave him command of the important Western Department, headquartered in St. Louis. It was a decision the

USMHI

president would soon regret.

In St. Louis Frémont spent hundreds of thousands of dollars to fortify the city, while he let his field commanders, ill equipped and inadequately supported, blunder into Confederate traps. Stinging Union defeats at Springfield and Lexington turned many of Frémont's warmest friends into enemies, while the general's impetuous order freeing all slaves owned by Missouri secessionists cost him the president's confidence (see FRÉMONT'S EMANCIPATION PROCLAMATION). Frémont viewed his proclamation as a brilliant war measure; Lincoln saw it as a swipe at border-state loyalists—an ill-conceived attempt to turn the war to save the Union into a war to abolish slavery. 3 months after his arrival in St. Louis, Frémont was relieved of all duties as a Union commander.

He returned to service Mar. 1862 as commander of the newly created Mountain Department but again proved unequal to his task, coming off second best in a confrontation with Maj. Gen. THOMAS J. "STONEWALL" JACKSON. When Maj. Gen. JOHN POPE was named his superior, Frémont asked to be relieved of his duties. In the next presidential election, he made a half-hearted attempt to head a third party.

An explorer, a man of charm and unquestioned loyalty, Frémont in the Civil War proved to be one of the North's greatest military embarrassments.

From 1864 Frémont's personal fortunes also began to fail with the loss of his California properties. Between 1878 and 1883 he served as territorial governor of Arizona but depended on his wife's income from writing during most of his later years. d. New York City, 13 July 1890.   —BMcG

Frémont's Emancipation Proclamation.

Frémont's Emancipation Proclamation. In July 1861 ABRAHAM LINCOLN appointed JOHN C. FRÉMONT, explorer turned officer, commander of the Western Department in the hope that his popularity would strengthen Union support in the Trans-Mississippi territory. The assignment was difficult, since his command included volatile Missouri, held in terror by secessionist guerrillas.

By late August Frémont had placed Missouri under martial law. Reasoning that slavery aided guerrillas and that a direct strike at the institution would crush them, in a proclamation dated 30 Aug. he declared Missouri's slave population forever free. Injudiciously impinging on the executive powers, Frémont did not inform Lincoln of his act until a week later. The president asked him to modify the order to conform to official policy, which, under the Confiscation Act of 1861, freed only those slaves used by Confederates to aid the war effort but did not extend general abolition. Frémont refused.

Lincoln's position was politically complex: he could not risk alienating conservatives in the BORDER STATES with such a radical move; neither could he ignore Radical Republicans agitating for abolition. Within weeks Frémont was removed from command and his mandate revoked, but the controversy he stirred focused national attention on the war's objectives. The debate already smoldering between gradual emancipationists and Radicals escalated into demands that the war be waged to free slaves as well as preserve the Union. Radical newspapers took up the cause, forcing into the open dissension among government officials. Public opinion was divided. Elevating the war to a crusade for freedom justified it morally in a way no political goal could, but many soldiers were unwilling to fight to free blacks they considered economically and socially threatening.

Lincoln's cautious approach to emancipation with colonization abroad was undermined. Frémont's proclamation had altered the nature of the struggle. From fall 1861, the war for the Union became inseparably joined to the abolition of slavery.
—PLF

French, Samuel Gibbs. CSA b. Gloucester Cty., N.J., 22 Nov. 1818. In 1843 French graduated 14th in his West Point class, 7 places above classmate ULYSSES S. GRANT. After being wounded and brevetted captain for bravery with the artillery in the Mexican War, he left the army as an assistant quartermaster in 1856 to become a Mississippi planter. Marriage into a Southern family and his Mississippi interests compelled him to follow his adopted state out of the Union, and 23 Oct. 1861 he was appointed a brigadier general in Confederate service. Previously, he had been the state militia's ordnance chief.

LC

When state troops were sent east for service in Virginia, French followed, commanding in the Confederate rear guard on the peninsula during Gen. ROBERT E. LEE's 1862 SECOND BULL RUN CAMPAIGN. For this service he was made major general to rank from 31 Aug. 1862. After duty in the Petersburg and Suffolk districts, he was posted to a quiet sector of North Carolina. Because of Lee's need for reinforcement, French graciously gave up a large number of his men for service in the Army of Northern Virginia, reducing his command to 6,000.

Tiring of his duties in North Carolina, he requested transfer west and was assigned to Gen. JOSEPH E. JOHNSTON's troops at Jackson, Miss. Then, 18 May 1864, he was given duty with the Army of Tennessee. He saw the most combat of his Confederate career at this time, fighting for ATLANTA; in October he personally commanded the force that assaulted the Federal fort at ALLATOONA. In this battle he aroused controversy by breaking off the fight, anticipating reinforcement of the Federals; and by claiming his orders were not to attack, only to demonstrate against the railroad.

Holding division command under Johnston, French also briefly commanded a corps in Lt. Gen. JOHN B. HOOD's army. When Maj. Gen. BENJAMIN F. CHEATHAM was promoted over him to permanent corps command, French requested transfer to another district; Hood's FRANKLIN AND NASHVILLE CAMPAIGN intervened. French's division served in Cheatham's Corps for the Battle of FRANKLIN, but before the campaign proceeded further French was given medical leave for a severe eye infection. By the time he was prepared to return to duty, the old Army of Tennessee had been destroyed, and French was assigned to the beleaguered garrison at MOBILE.

French and Confederates at Mobile put up a stubborn defense throughout the siege of the city. On their surrender, 12 Apr., the war in the North had already ended. French returned to Mississippi, resumed planting, and wrote a memoir of his adventures, "Two Wars" (*Confederate Veteran*, 1901, Vol. XV). d. in retirement, Florala, Fla., 20 Apr. 1910. —JES

French, William Henry. USA b. Baltimore, Md., 13 Jan.

1815, French was appointed to the U.S. Military Academy from the District of Columbia and graduated 22d in the class of 1837. Like many junior officers of his era, he served in the Seminole War, and in the Mexican War acted as an aide to Gen. (later Pres.) Franklin Pierce.

USMHI

The secession crisis of 1861 found French in Texas, where he refused to surrender his garrison to state authorities, choosing instead to lead his men on a long journey to the Federal post at Key West, Fla. Appointed a brigadier general of volunteers 28 Sept. 1861, French commanded a brigade of the II Corps in Maj. Gen. George B. McClellan's PENINSULA CAMPAIGN and in the SEVEN DAYS' CAMPAIGN Mar.–July 1862. Directing a division at Antietam, French earned promotion to major general 29 Nov. 1862, fighting at FREDERICKSBURG and CHANCELLORSVILLE.

Given a detachment of the VIII Corps based at Harpers Ferry, in the GETTYSBURG CAMPAIGN French sent a force to destroy Gen. Robert E. Lee's PONTOON BRIDGES on the Potomac River. Replacing the wounded Maj. Gen. DANIEL E. SICKLES as III Corps commander 7 July 1863, French advised Maj. Gen. GEORGE G. MEADE against pursuing the defeated Lee too closely. A victim of his own caution, French allowed a Confederate rear guard to unduly delay him at Manassas Gap, thereby denying Meade a chance to strike at the retreating Confederates.

For the rest of 1863 French's corps participated in Meade's efforts to outmaneuver Lee. In the MINE RUN CAMPAIGN, French badly misdirected the march of his corps, and Meade considered him partly responsible for the failure of the operation. Obviously unfit for corps command, French was relieved early in 1864 as a result of the reorganization of the Army of the Potomac. He never again saw field service, spending the rest of the war in garrison and administrative posts. d. District of Columbia, 20 May 1881. —BNO

French's Field, Va., eng. at. 25 June 1862 *See* OAK GROVE, VA., ENG. AT.

frontal attack. Among the most common infantry assaults was the frontal attack, a holdover from 18th-century infantry tactics when troops with inaccurate smoothbore muskets charged the enemy directly and decided the battle with bayonets. In the face of an entrenched enemy wielding rifled firearms, frontal attacks had tragic consequences in the Civil War. In the most telling frontal attack, at COLD HARBOR, 3 June 1864, 7,000 Federal soldiers were killed in 8 minutes. —JES

Frontier, Union Army of the. Vacillation does not produce victory. Instead of overrunning Missouri in Sept. 1862, Confederate invaders from Arkansas halted before NEWTONIA, where they merely repulsed sorties. From Kansas and Missouri, Union regiments rushed to Newtonia's relief. Maj. Gen. JOHN M. SCHOFIELD, lately District of Missouri commander, took charge of these forces 26 Sept., and 12 Oct. they became the Army of the Frontier.

With 2 divisions he scared off (but did not trap) the secessionists 4 Oct. With an additional division, he spent the rest of October pursuing them through northwestern Arkansas. Exhausted by arduous marching over barren mountains, the Federals needed to rest and resupply. Brig. Gen. JAMES G. BLUNT's 1st Division bivouacked around Cane Hill, Ark.; Brig. Gen. (Missouri State Militia) James Totten's 2d Division and Brig. Gen. FRANCIS J. HERRON's 3d Division, however, withdrew to Camp Curtis, Mo. Schofield, ill, returned to St. Louis and Totten was detailed, leaving Herron in charge at Camp Curtis.

But the campaign was not over. Confederate Maj. Gen. THOMAS C. HINDMAN's bold counterthrust threatened to defeat Blunt and Herron. But again the Confederates halted instead of attacking, and a forced march by Herron's divisions, which moved 125 mi in 5 days to unite with Blunt on the battlefield, turned the tide. The resulting Battle of PRAIRIE GROVE, 7 Dec. 1862, was a tactical draw but a Northern strategic victory that forestalled the South's invasion of Missouri until Sept. 1864.

Schofield soon resumed command. Guarding Missouri against raiders and guerrillas was his duty. Arguing with Blunt, Herron, and Maj. Gen. SAMUEL R. CURTIS, his superior in St. Louis, was his preoccupation. By Mar. 1863 both Blunt and Schofield were gone, with Herron succeeding to command of the Army of the Frontier until it was discontinued 5 June 1863. Herron then took an enlarged division of that army to Vicksburg, the remaining regiments being distributed among garrisons in Missouri and Arkansas.   —RJS

Front Royal, Va., eng. at.   23 May 1862   After the Battle of MCDOWELL, Maj. Gen. THOMAS J. "STONEWALL" JACKSON moved back toward Harrisonburg, Va., where he had left Maj. Gen. RICHARD S. EWELL's division when he went west. Farther north, Union Brig. Gen. JAMES SHIELDS had left the Shenandoah Valley, stationing Maj. Gen. NATHANIEL P. BANKS at Strasburg with about 8,000 men to block Jackson if he came north again. To protect the area abandoned by Shields, Banks sent 1,000 men and 2 guns to Front Royal, east of Strasburg on the Manassas Gap Railroad.

Banks now had the only Union army in the valley. Jackson acted quickly, moving north on the Valley Pike, as though planning an attack at Strasburg, but sending Ewell's force north on the other side of Massanutten Mountain. At New Market, Jackson crossed the gap east and met Ewell at Luray, then moved north toward Front Royal with a force of about 17,000. As he neared Front Royal, 23 May, he was met by Confederate spy BELLE BOYD, who had information on the strength and location of the Union force. Brig. Gen. TURNER ASHBY's cavalry was sent west to hold the railroad line that ran to Strasburg, while the main force came into town, planning to capture and hold the 2 bridges over the forks of the Shenandoah River. Jackson sent the 1st Maryland Regiment, CSA, to attack the 1st Maryland Regiment, USA, commanded by Col. JOHN R. KENLY. The Federals fell back slowly and set fire to the North Fork Bridge, but the Confederates pursued and managed to save part of the structure. Col. Thomas S. Flournoy's 6th Virginia Cavalry forded the stream and in a wild cavalry charge captured almost the entire Union force near Cedarville. The Union lost 904 in casualties, while the Confederates lost about 50.

Jackson was now located between General Banks and Washington, D.C., while Winchester and Harpers Ferry were undefended. Both Jackson and Banks raced north, to meet again at WINCHESTER on the 25th. On the peninsula, Maj. Gen. IRVIN MCDOWELL's army was called back from Maj. Gen.

GEORGE B. MCCLELLAN's command near Richmond when Jackson became a new threat in the valley.   —FSK

Front Royal (Guard Hill), Va., eng. at.   16 Aug. 1864   On 7 Aug. 1864 Maj. Gen. PHILIP H. SHERIDAN assumed command of the Union forces in the Shenandoah Valley. 3 days later his army advanced southward up the valley against Lt. Gen. JUBAL A. EARLY. The outnumbered Confederates withdrew to the strong, natural defensive position at Fisher's Hill, where the 2 armies, constantly skirmishing, stalked each other for 4 days.

When Sheridan advanced, Early urgently requested reinforcements from Richmond. Gen. ROBERT E. LEE responded by sending an infantry and a cavalry division and an artillery battalion, all commanded by Lt. Gen. RICHARD H. ANDERSON. By the afternoon of 14 Aug. Anderson's command had reached Front Royal at the northern end of the Luray Valley, where the north and south forks of the Shenandoah River meet. The Confederate reinforcements threatened Sheridan's left, rear, and communications.

The Union commander ordered Brig. Gen. WESLEY MERRITT's cavalry division toward Front Royal. On the 15th, Merritt's pickets guarded the roads leading from Front Royal to the Union rear. Anderson responded to the presence of the Union cavalry by sending Brig. Gen. WILLIAM T. WOFFORD's infantry brigade and Brig. Gen. WILLIAMS C. WICKHAM's cavalry brigade across the Shenandoah River to Guard Hill to cover the fords.

About midafternoon on the 16th, Wickham charged the advance videttes of Brig. Gen. THOMAS C. DEVIN's brigade at Cedarville. Devin rapidly brought forward 2 regiments, which counterattacked down the road. A Confederate and a Federal regiment crashed together in a swirling fight with sabers. The Southerners broke, falling back on their reserves. Wickham personally led another charge that blunted the Federal drive until his troopers recrossed the river. Devin's horsemen had seized 2 flags and 139 prisoners and horses.

Wofford, meanwhile, held Guard Hill, coming under attack from Brig. Gen. GEORGE A. CUSTER's brigade. Custer's 5th Michigan, armed with Spencer repeaters, shoved the Confederate infantry off the hill. Wofford's troops quickly streamed toward the river, where many of them drowned or were helplessly shot by the pursuing horsemen. The Union victory had been sharp and decisive.

Merritt's confirmation of the presence of Confederate infantry, cavalry, and artillery at Front Royal forced Sheridan to order a withdrawal down the valley. That night the Federals began retreating back to their lines at Harpers Ferry.   —JDW

Frost, Daniel Marsh.   CSA   b. Schenectady Cty., N.Y., 9 Aug. 1823, Frost graduated 4th in his class of 1844 from the U.S. Military Academy, and was brevetted for gallantry in the Mexican War after serving nobly at the Battle of Cerro Gordo. Completing a year of duty in Europe, he resigned from the army in 1853. Moving to St. Louis, Frost entered the planing-mill business, served in the state legislature, and was a member of the Board of Visitors at West Point.

When the Civil War began, Frost, a brigadier general in the state militia, chose to follow the secessionist philosophy of Missouri's governor CLAIBORNE F. JACKSON. As the militia commander at St. Louis, Frost met secretly with Jackson and other secessionists to establish a militia camp named for the governor just outside the city, in Lindell Grove. Frost publicly denied his involvement in a secessionist plot to capture the U.S. arsenal at St. Louis as he trained his militiamen at Camp Jackson, claiming he was not one of the governor's men. Later in the war Federals captured a letter disclosing Frost's active involvement in the plot. Though he and all the occupants of Camp Jackson were forced to surrender to Capt. NATHANIEL LYON when Lyon threatened to attack the training facility, Frost was paroled and later exchanged.

DAM/LSU

He accepted an appointment to brigadier general in the Confederate army 3 March 1862 but declined a request to command a small brigade at PEA RIDGE. Frost subsequently served as inspector general for Gen. BRAXTON BRAGG and as a subordinate of Maj. Gen. THOMAS C. HINDMAN at the Battle of PRAIRIE GROVE.

In 1863 he fled with his family to Canada after his wife was forced from their home in St. Louis because of the family's Confederate sympathies. In 1865 he returned to Missouri and farmed his property near St. Louis, dying there 29 Oct. 1900.
—FLS

Fry, Birkett Davenport. CSA b. Kanawha Cty., Va., 24 June 1822. Educated at the Virginia Military Institute and Washington College, Fry entered West Point, from which he was dismissed for failure in mathematics. He then studied law, fought as a 1st lieutenant in the Mexican War, emigrated to California, filibustered in Nicaragua, and was in cotton manufacturing in Alabama.

With the beginning of the war, Fry was appointed colonel of the 13th Alabama. Transferred to Virginia, he led his regiment at SEVEN PINES, where he suffered his first wound. At ANTIETAM his arm was shattered, and at CHANCELLORSVILLE, after assuming command of Brig.

LC

Gen. JAMES J. ARCHER's brigade, Fry suffered a third wound. On 1 July 1863, at GETTYSBURG, Fry again succeeded Archer to command of the brigade after the latter's capture. 2 days later, he led the brigade in PICKETT'S CHARGE, falling into Federal hands with his fourth wound.

By a special exchange 9 months later, Fry returned to Confederate service. Appointed brigadier general 24 May 1864, he commanded 2 brigades at COLD HARBOR and saw action during the early stages of the PETERSBURG CAMPAIGN. Transferred south, he commanded a military district in South Carolina and Georgia, with headquarters at Augusta, until the end of the war.

Choosing not to stay in the reunited country, Fry emigrated to Cuba until 1868, when he returned to the U.S., engaging in a successful cotton-milling and manufacturing business in Alabama and Florida. A fellow Southern officer described him as a man with a "gunpowder reputation." d. Richmond, Va., 21 Jan. 1891.
—JDW

Fugitive Slave Act. Congress first passed a fugitive slave law in 1793 as a means to protect Southern "property" rights in chattel slavery. As the Northern states abolished the institution, they passed personal liberty laws to safeguard free blacks, and over time this legislation often made the Federal law useless.

With the spread of antislavery sentiment, a new fugitive slave law became a critical part of the COMPROMISE OF 1850. It was the one concession to the South written into the legislation, and a test of the North's willingness to guarantee personal property rights through strict enforcement of the provision. Under the law, Northern officials were responsible for returning a fugitive slave to his owner. Any person found guilty of assisting a fugitive was subject to 6 months' imprisonment, a $1,000 fine, and reimbursing the owner for the market value of the slave. The law denied fugitives a jury trial and protection under a writ of *habeas corpus.* Many Northerners regarded the law as a flagrant violation of fundamental American rights, and in response to their protests new personal liberty laws were enacted to weaken the 1850 legislation.

Though politicians had expected the fugitive slave law to relieve sectional tensions, they quickly realized that it had become a propaganda tool for abolitionists, who deliberately violated the legislation. In the decade before the Civil War fugitives were seldom returned to their masters, but the law's existence deepened the rift between North and South. More than anything, it grew into a symbol of determined resistance for both proslavery and antislavery factions, and one of the key issues leading to irreconcilable disunion in 1861.   —PLF

furlough. An enlisted man's leave from the Union or Confederate army, granted at his superior's discretion, was called furlough. Rules in both services specified that furloughs be granted by a commander actually quartered with the soldier's company or regiment. A furloughed soldier's arms and accoutrements remained behind, and he carried furlough papers giving a detailed description of his physical appearance, return and departure dates, unit designation, and pay and subsistence allowances furnished. Furlough papers warned the soldier to rejoin his unit by the date specified "or be considered a deserter."

Furloughs differed from leaves of absence. Officers were granted leaves, whose rules and stipulations were more extensive. Both leaves and furloughs were freely abused, and both armies had occasion to cancel all leaves and furloughs to account for deserters and malingerers. They were also used as inducements: on expiration of enlistment, entire Union army regiments were given "veterans' furloughs" if they reenlisted. These were for an extended time, allowing soldiers to return home, and accounted for a dramatic increase in the national birth rate 1863–64.   —JES

G

gabion. A cylindrical wicker basket several feet high, filled with dirt and stones, a gabion was used to reinforce fieldworks. Its use in earthworks preceded the Civil War by centuries. Crude English woodcuts from the 1640s show gabions shoring up the works of Oliver Cromwell and Charles I.   —JES

LC

Gaines' Landing, Ark., eng. at. 10–11 Aug. 1864 On 10 Aug. 1864 the steamer *Empress,* carrying passengers and cargo from New Orleans to St. Louis, came under heavy fire from Confederate artillery and infantry 2 mi below Gaines' Landing. Within minutes, 6 men on board the steamer, including its captain, were killed, several were wounded, and the *Empress* was disabled. Overcome by panic, the passengers demanded an immediate surrender, but the *Empress'* officers refused. Although capture seemed certain, the timely arrival of the *Romeo* enabled the *Empress* to be towed to a safe position on the river. After repairs were completed, the ship continued upriver to St. Louis the following day.

On 11 Aug. the *Prairie Bird* became the target of the same Confederate battery that had surprised the *Empress.* During the exchange of fire, the wooden steamer was struck repeatedly, with 1 crewman killed and another wounded. The enemy battery was finally silenced by the combined shelling of both the *Prairie Bird* and the *Romeo.*   —NCD

Gaines' Mill, Va., Battle of. 27 June 1862 The SEVEN DAYS' CAMPAIGN began 25 June 1862 with the secondary en-

gagement at Oak Grove, Va. The next day, to relieve Richmond, Gen. ROBERT E. LEE launched his offensive against Union Maj. Gen. FITZ JOHN PORTER's isolated V Corps north of the Chickahominy River. Lee's strike plan faltered when Maj. Gen. THOMAS J. "STONEWALL" JACKSON failed to reach the field, and Porter, entrenched east of Mechanicsville, bloodily repulsed the Confederate frontal attacks.

With Jackson on his right flank and rear, Porter abandoned his strong position behind Beaver Dam Creek during the night of 26–27 June. Leaving only a rear guard, the large Union corps, numbering nearly 30,000, retreated southward, closer to the bulk of Maj. Gen. GEORGE B. MCCLELLAN's Army of the Potomac, located south of the Chickahominy. McClellan reacted defensively to Lee's unexpected offensive by contracting his lines, ordering an evacuation of his supply base at White House, and directing Porter to withdraw to a strong position near bridges across the Chickahominy.

Porter's corps halted on a plateau south and east of New and Old Cold Harbor near Gaines' Mill. Porter formed a semicircular defensive line on the plateau behind Boatswain Swamp. Brig. Gen. GEORGE SYKES's tough division of Regulars manned the right; Brig. Gen. George W. Morell's division held the left; while Brig. Gen. George A. McCall's division acted as a reserve. Porter's ample artillery swept the approaches before the strong position.

The Federals waited throughout the morning for the approaching Confederates. When the latter found Porter's empty works at Mechanicsville early on the 27th, Lee pressed his advance, again ordering a convergence on the Union corps. By midafternoon Maj. Gen. AMBROSE P. HILL's leading division reached Gaines' Mill and formed. The impetuous Hill then charged the Union position. Across the boggy ground and ravines, the Confederates attacked; the Union infantry and artillery scorched the open ground, repulsing Hill's troops with heavy losses. Some of Hill's brigades made several attacks but failed against the firestorm.

Maj. Gen. JAMES LONGSTREET's command arrived on Hill's right, but Lee delayed the assault until Jackson arrived on the Confederate left. Jackson, however, as on the day before, was late. His strange behavior during this campaign has been ascribed to various causes, but his leadership clearly lacked the fire and skill of his recent SHENANDOAH VALLEY CAMPAIGN. Delayed by a countermarch, the lethargic general did not arrive until 3 p.m., with his command behind.

By the time he did arrive, Lee had resumed the attacks. Maj. Gen. DANIEL H. HILL's division stormed forward on the left only to be swept back by the fire of Sykes's veterans. On the right, Brig. Gen. GEORGE E. PICKETT's brigade suffered heavy casualties in a diversionary attack. Finally, about 7 o'clock, the Confederates launched a coordinated assault against Porter, who had been reinforced with 1 division. While Longstreet and D. H. Hill pressed the Union flanks, the brigades of Brig. Gen. JOHN B. HOOD and Col. EVANDER M. LAW pierced the Federal center in a riveting, gallant charge. Porter's line cracked, but the Northerners withdrew in an orderly fashion. A suicidal charge across the plateau by the 5th U.S. Cavalry and part of the 2d U.S. Cavalry ended the fighting.

The Confederates had wrenched the plateau from the Federals, but at a cost of 8,750 killed and wounded. Porter suffered 6,837 casualties in a defense that enabled McClellan to continue his retreat toward the James River. —JDW

Galena, **USS.** On 4 Oct. 1861 contracts were let for the construction of 3 new IRONCLADS, of which one was the *Galena*, a small corvette plated with iron 3 in. thick. It was launched at Mystic, Conn., 14 Feb. 1862. From the start there was doubt it would be able to withstand heavy gunfire. Of this opinion was the commander who led it into action, Cmdr. JOHN RODGERS, a veteran officer with a long career as a coast surveyor.

Stationed off Fort Monroe, the ship had its first test 15 May 1862. That day the *Galena* steamed up the James River along with 4 other ships, including the *MONITOR*. At DREWRY'S BLUFF, 7 mi below Richmond, the fleet encountered its first serious

USMHI

opposition. There, on a bluff overlooking a bend in the river, the Southerners, working in rain and mud for 2 days, had hastily erected a battery, Fort Darling, and, to block passage, had sunk the CSS *Jamestown* and some small sailing vessels in the channel.

The *Galena* came within 600 yd of the fort, swung about, and opened fire. The *Monitor*, of different design, and other ships remained behind the vessel. Although the attack lasted more than 3 hours, the ships were unable to silence the battery on the bluff, and the fleet fell back, the *Galena* badly damaged, having been struck 28 times and perforated 18; 13 crew had been killed and 11 wounded. The *Monitor* had not been damaged and no one on board had been injured, even though the ship once ran out in front of the *Galena* and bombarded the fort. *See also* DREWRY'S BLUFF, VA., FIRST BATTLE OF.

The *Galena* was not the effective weapon it was intended to be, so the vessel's armor plates were removed and it served out the war as a wooden gunboat, mostly on blockade duty. —VCJ

"Galvanized Yankees." Some 6,000 men organized into 6 regiments, "Galvanized Yankees" were Confederate soldiers, recruited in Federal prisoner-of-war camps, who served thereafter as U.S. Volunteers. (Conversely, there were a few hundred "Galvanized Rebels.") The nickname at first was used derisively, but it stuck and the men apparently came to like it. They had also been called "repentant Rebels," "transfugees," "Rebel prisoners," "deserters," and "white-washed Rebels." They soldiered for the Union Sept. 1864–Nov. 1866.

Many Federal officers mistrusted or had great contempt for Galvanized Yankees until, in episode after episode, they proved their valor, loyalty, and dependability. Some converts deserted, but the desertion rate only slightly exceeded that of Union state volunteer regiments. These Yankees reaped praise from their superiors, but that and the release from squalid prison camps was about all the thanks they ever received. After the war they scattered and sought new identities; some changed their names to escape the opprobrium heaped on them by other Southerners. Even other former Federal soldiers tended to reject them, and the GRAND ARMY OF THE REPUBLIC ignored them completely.

The North used these men exclusively in the Trans-Mississippi, where they provided frontier security and fought Indians. They restored stage and mail service, sometimes carried mail themselves, escorted supply trains, rebuilt telegraph lines, guarded telegraph stations and railroad surveying parties, manned outposts, scouted and secured trails, and searched for white women who had been captured by Indians. They fought numerous skirmishes and engaged in one bloody battle. Among all these military duties, some of them also found time to write poetry and publish a newspaper. —HH

Galveston, Tex., battle for. 1 Jan. 1863 Although the Federal blockade of Galveston began July 1861, another 15 months passed before a naval force succeeded in taking the port. Union Cmdr. William B. Renshaw, aboard the *Westfield*, commanded a squadron that included the *HARRIET LANE*, the *Owasco*, the *Clifton*, and the mortar schooner *Henry James*. On 4 Oct. 1862 Renshaw moved his ships into Galveston harbor and demanded unconditional surrender. Confederate Col. Joseph J. Cook, commanding the city's defenders, surrendered Galveston after Renshaw agreed to a 4-day truce, during which Cook withdrew his troops, guns, and equipment. To assist Renshaw in controlling the city and harbor, the *Sachem*, *Corypheus*, and 3 companies of the 42d Massachusetts Infantry were sent from New Orleans. The infantry took a position on one of the wharves to receive support from the squadron in the event of attack.

Galveston remained in Federal control for less than 3 months. After Confederate Brig. Gen. JOHN B. MAGRUDER assumed command of military forces in Texas 29 Nov. 1862, he made the recapture of the city a priority. Magruder planned a combined land/sea attack centered around 2 steamers, the *Bayou City* and the *Neptune*, which were converted into cotton-clad gunboats by the use of protective cotton bales.

Before dawn, 1 Jan. 1863, Southern forces launched their attack. Confederate Maj. Leon Smith commanded the cotton-clads and their tenders, the *John F. Carr* and the *Lucy Gwin.* Aboard the gunboats, acting as riflemen, were Col. THOMAS GREEN and his Texas cavalry. When the Massachusetts men came under attack by land, Renshaw moved the *Westfield* to assist them, but his ship became grounded and could not be floated, even with assistance from the *Clifton.*

While the *Westfield* lay helpless, the battle raged. Union Cmdr. Jonathan M. Wainwright rammed his *Harriet Lane* into the *Bayou City.* Both vessels suffered only minor damage, but when the *Neptune* rammed the *Harriet Lane,* the cotton-clad was severely damaged and sank. Then the *Bayou City* struck the *Harriet Lane,* and the 2 vessels locked together. The Texans on board the *Bayou City* boarded the *Harriet Lane* and engaged the Federal sailors in hand-to-hand combat. Both Wainwright and his executive officer were among those killed before the *Harriet Lane* was surrendered.

The Confederates arranged a truce with Renshaw, offering him a chance to leave with his men aboard one of the ships if he surrendered. But Renshaw was determined to destroy the *Westfield* rather than have it taken. After transferring most of his crew, he ordered Union Lt. Cmdr. Richard L. Law, commanding the *Clifton,* to withdraw all remaining vessels from the harbor while he attended to the destruction of the *Westfield.* Renshaw set the ship on fire and was leaving when the magazine exploded prematurely, killing him and the men with him. Law succeeded in moving the remaining 4 vessels to safety outside the harbor.

It was an impressive victory for the Confederates, who had also captured almost the entire Federal force ashore. The loss to the Confederates was 26 killed and 117 wounded, and the *Neptune.* The Federals lost 414 men killed or captured, along with the *Westfield* and the *Harriet Lane.*

Galveston remained the only major Southern port still in Confederate hands at the war's end. On 2 June 1865 the city was formally surrendered by Maj. Gen. E. KIRBY SMITH.

—NCD

Gamble, Hamilton Rowan. war governor b. Winchester, Va., 29 Nov. 1798, Gamble was admitted to the Virginia state bar in 1816, shortly after his graduation from Hampden-Sydney College. He soon moved to Missouri Territory, where he established a successful practice and became prominent in the territorial judiciary. Gamble interrupted his law career briefly to serve as Missouri's secretary of state, 1824–25, then left politics until elected to the legislature as a Whig in 1846. As a state supreme court justice, 1851–54, Gamble delivered a dissenting opinion in Dred Scott's first unsuccessful bid for freedom, basing his argument on a slave's rightful claim to emancipation if taken to free territory by his master (*see* DRED SCOTT CASE).

Ill health prompted Gamble to resign in 1854, and he retired to Norristown, Pa., until the secession crisis threatened to take Missouri out of the Union. Believing secession would ruin the state, he returned home and was elected to a convention called by local leaders to consider Missouri's standing in the Union. As a conservative, antisecessionist politician in favor of compromise, Gamble helped organize the Conditional Unionist party. When secessionist leaders fled the state in June to establish a Confederate government in exile, the convention declared the governorship vacant and appointed Gamble provisional governor.

Gamble supported the Lincoln administration to keep the

Confederacy from gaining a stronghold in the state but frequently came under criticism for refusing to reinforce Federal troops with state militia. Military commanders also complained that he allowed Southern sympathizers into the ranks, and these often deserted to the Confederate army or to guerrilla bands as soon as they were issued arms. Politically, Gamble tried to quell a bitter struggle between pro- and antislavery factions by offering a program of gradual emancipation. When the legislature approved the plan early in 1863, Radicals called for Gamble's resignation. Refusing to be forced out of office, he commanded sufficient support from moderates to retain the governorship until his death in Jefferson City, 31 Jan. 1864. He had achieved his goals of keeping Missouri in the Union and effecting emancipation. *See also* MISSOURI.   —PLF

Gano, Richard Montgomery. CSA b. Bourbon Cty., Ky., 17 June 1830, Gano entered Confederate service in 1861 with no military experience other than a few skirmishes with Indians in his adopted state of Texas. He had attended Bacon College in Harrodsburg, Ky., and Bethany College in Virginia before beginning his studies at Louisville University Medical School.

LC

For 8 years he practiced medicine in Bourbon County, then moved to Texas in 1859. Gano served 1 term in the state legislature in the prewar years, joining the army as a cavalry officer in Capt. JOHN HUNT MORGAN'S command shortly after the fighting began. He accompanied Morgan on the 1862 invasion of his native state and by 1863 had advanced to colonel of the 7th Kentucky Cavalry.

Reassigned to command a brigade of cavalry and artillery in Indian Territory, he finished his Confederate career in the Trans-Mississippi. In recognition of Gano's performance in the CAMDEN EXPEDITION, during which he was wounded, Lt. Gen. E. KIRBY SMITH promoted him to brigadier general; Pres. JEFFERSON DAVIS later confirmed the appointment to rank from 17 Mar. 1865. After the Camden operations, he raided around Forts Gibson and Scott, disrupting communications between the 2 Federal garrisons and capturing a 300-wagon supply train at Cabin Creek 19 Sept. 1864 in a combined attack with Brig. Gen. STAND WATIE's Indian troops.

When the war ended, Gano returned to Texas and served for 45 years as a Protestant clergyman. He was active in the United Confederate Veterans until his death in Dallas 27 Mar. 1913.   —PLF

Gardner, Alexander. photographer b. Paisley, Scotland, 27 Oct. 1821, Gardner, reared in genteel poverty, left school at 14 to work as a jeweler's apprentice. At 21 he joined the Glasgow *Sentinel* as a reporter and pursued interests in science, philosophy, and photography; the extent of his photographic work in Scotland is unknown. He became editor of the *Sentinel,* then emigrated to New York City in 1856 and took a position at popular photographer MATHEW BRADY's New York gallery. After training, he assumed management of Brady's Washington, D.C., studios in 1858, looking after its business affairs and working mostly in portraiture.

Joined in Brady's employ by his brother, James, Alexander received no credit for his antebellum and early Civil War photography. His famous images of Pres. ABRAHAM LINCOLN's first inaugural and, later, his shocking views of the dead at Antietam, all bore the back mark "Brady's Album Gallery" or "Brady & Co." Photographic historian William A. Frassanito states that it was on Gardner's initiative that Brady's corps of photographers and assistants was organized to follow Union troops in the field. Gardner served as Brady's chief field operative. As well as making battlefield images, he also took photographs of troops and notables in the field. Frequently Brady sold Gardner's images, and those of other operatives, to illustrated news weeklies. Woodcuts were modeled from them and, in print, credited to Brady.

Gardner quit the Brady organization early in 1863, opened a studio at 7th and D streets in Washington, D.C., organized his own corps of photographers, personally led them to Gettysburg to photograph the aftermath of that battle, and was briefly detained by Confederate forces 5 July 1863 when he crossed their path at Emmitsburg, Maryland.

All of Gardner's photographers received full credit for their work. Talented and vigorous cameraman TIMOTHY O'SULLIVAN became head of Gardner's photographic corps, while Gardner himself remained in Washington through most of the last months of the war. His photographers covered the Virginia theater and the Carolinas along the coast.

Gardner continued his photographic work after the Civil War, shooting the grand reviews of the Army of the Potomac and the Army of Tennessee, the portraits and executions of the Lincoln murder conspirators, and the execution of Andersonville's Confederate commander Maj. HEINRICH H. WIRZ. He then published a *Photographic Sketch Book of the Civil War* (1865), featuring the best of his and his operatives' wartime images. In 1867 he closed his studio and went west, photographing the developing frontier. Visiting Arizona, then working out of Abilene and Hays City, Kans., he produced 150 images of construction on the Union Pacific Railroad for the line's use in engineering and promotion work. Returning east, he was struck by a long, debilitating illness, and died December 1882.   —JES

Gardner, Franklin. CSA b. New York, N.Y., 29 Jan. 1823, Gardner is remembered as commander of the Confederate garrison during the Siege of PORT HUDSON. Ranked 17th in the West Point class of 1843, he

served the U.S. Army in Florida and Texas, fought in 6 Mexican War battles, did frontier garrison duty, and was captain at Fort Bridger, Utah Territory, through early 1861. Though a scion of a Unionist family, son of former Adjutant General of the U.S. Army Charles K. Gardner, he married into the clan of Louisiana secessionist ALFRED MOUTON, identified with Southern interests, and accepted a commission as lieutenant colonel in the Confederate army 16 Mar.

USMHI

1861. Charged with abandoning his post at Fort Bridger, he was dropped from U.S. Army rolls 7 May.

Gardner exercised brigade command without commensurate rank, performing duty in Mississippi, Tennessee, and at SHILOH until promotion to brigadier general 11 Apr. 1862. He led a brigade through Gen. BRAXTON BRAGG's 1862 Kentucky campaigning and, given an unconfirmed appointment as major general 13 Dec., was transferred to the VICKSBURG theater by the Confederate War Department over Bragg's protests.

Posted to Port Hudson, La., in support of the Vicksburg garrison to the north, Gardner sustained his men through a protracted siege, 3 heavy Union assaults, and life on the edge of starvation until compelled to ask Union Maj. Gen. NATHANIEL P. BANKS for surrender terms 8 July 1863. Gardner surrendered unconditionally the next day and was taken prisoner with his force of approximately 7,000 Confederates. Exchanged in August the following year, he ended the war in Lt. Gen. RICHARD TAYLOR's service in the Department of East Louisiana, Mississippi, and Alabama. His commission as major general was confirmed 10 June 1864, during his confinement.

Gardner worked as a farmer in Louisiana until his death at Vermillionville, 29 Apr. 1873.   —JES

Gardner, William Montgomery. CSA b. Augusta, Ga., 8 June 1824. On graduation from West Point in 1846, ranking 55th of 59 cadets, Gardner joined the army in Mexico. As a brevet 2d lieutenant in the 1st

U.S. Infantry, he was at the Siege of Vera Cruz and in the Battles of Contreras and Churubusco, in the latter receiving a severe wound and a brevet for gallantry. From 1848 to 1861 he was on garrison and scouting duty, slowly rising to the rank of captain.

Gardner resigned this commission 19 Jan. 1861, the day his state seceded, to become lieutenant colonel of the 8th Georgia Infantry. As executive officer to former Confederate

LC

congressman FRANCIS S. BARTOW, he drilled and disciplined the 8th, one of the first Deep South regiments to be sent to Virginia to oppose a Union invasion. At FIRST BULL RUN, 21 July 1861, Bartow was killed and Gardner's leg was shattered by a rifle ball. As one of Gardner's men recorded, at a crucial moment the regiment was ordered to support the right flank of Brig. Gen. BARNARD E. BEE's brigade: "When we arrived at Genl. Bee's position he told us to charge down a hill and up another one to a thicket which was on the left and front of the enemy. We did this through a perfect hail storm of bullets. . . . [H]ere Col. Gardner fell with his leg broken. . . ."

The wound nearly took Gardner's life, requiring repeated surgery and incapacitating him for further field service. Nevertheless he recovered sufficiently to hold administrative posts during the rest of the war, with the rank of brigadier general. In mid-Nov. 1861 he took over the District of Middle Florida and almost returned to the field for the Feb. 1864 Battle of OLUSTEE. Gen. P.G.T. BEAUREGARD, his immediate superior, remarked that he would have given Gardner a battlefield command "had I been confident of Brigadier-General Gardner's physical ability for the field. . . . I have great confidence in his soldierly qualities."

Late in 1864 Gardner became commandant of military prisons east of the Mississippi. By war's end he headed the post at Richmond, Va. Despite his wound, he lived in Georgia and Tennessee for 35 years after the war, dying in Memphis 16 June 1901.   —EGL

Garfield, James Abram. USA/USP b. Cuyahoga Cty., Ohio, 19 Nov. 1831. News of FORT SUMTER reached Garfield as he sat in the Ohio senate, a freshman member and ardent antislavery Republican. Realiz-

ing the path to political advancement led through the battlefield, he angled for command until appointed lieutenant colonel, later colonel, of the 42d Ohio Volunteers. His first task was recruiting men, and he drew on the students of Western Reserve Eclectic Institute, which he had attended and then returned to as a teacher after graduating from Williams College. Once in camp, Garfield studied military manuals at night, practicing by moving

USMHI

blocks across a table, to stay one step ahead of his recruits.

Sent to Kentucky, the scholarly colonel so impressed Maj. Gen. DON CARLOS BUELL that he was entrusted with a brigade and sent to Sandy River to stop an invasion of eastern Kentucky. There Garfield fought Brig. Gen. HUMPHREY MARSHALL at Middle Creek 10 Jan. 1862 and routed the remnants of the general's army at Pound Gap 16 Mar. These minor battles came early enough in the war to bring popularity to the "Hero of the Sandy Valley" and a commission as brigadier general to rank from 11 Jan.

His presence at SHILOH and the advance on CORINTH had no military effect, but his accomplishments in the field led to election to the U.S. House of Representatives in fall 1862. Since Congress did not meet until Dec. 1863, he remained in service. Late in 1862, when illness drove him from camp, Garfield sat on the court-martial of Maj. Gen. FITZ JOHN PORTER. When he returned to the army, Maj. Gen. WILLIAM S. ROSECRANS offered to give him brigade command or the appointment as chief of staff, Army of the Cumberland. Wisely choosing the latter, Garfield found scope for his organizational abilities.

When Rosecrans was defeated at the Battle of CHICK-AMAUGA, 19–20 Sept., Garfield distanced himself from his discredited leader and emerged a major general. He was on his way to Congress anyway, where his military career gave him more recognition than other new congressmen received, and his alliance with powerful Ohio Radical Republicans, especially Sec. of the Treasury SALMON P. CHASE, started him on the road to the White House.   —JYS

Garland, Samuel, Jr. CSA b. Lynchburg, Va., 16 Dec. 1830. A collateral descendant of Pres. James Madison, Garland was a graduate of the VIRGINIA MILITARY INSTITUTE and the University of Virginia Law School. A practicing attorney in Lynchburg, he organized the Lynchburg Home Guard, a militia company, after JOHN BROWN's Raid Oct. 1859 (see HARPERS FERRY, WESTERN VA., JOHN BROWN'S RAID ON). When Virginia seceded, Garland mustered into Confederate service as captain of

Company C/11th Virginia.

A few days later the members of the infantry regiment elected him colonel, and for a year he commanded with distinction. In 1861, at FIRST BULL RUN and at DRANESVILLE, he led the regiment with skill, winning praise in his superiors' reports for his performance. At WILLIAMS-BURG, May 1862, Garland was wounded, but his combat prowess earned him promotion to brigadier general on the 23d of that month.

USMHI

Assigned to a brigade in Maj. Gen. DANIEL H. HILL's division, the Virginian earned increasing renown during the Peninsula and Seven Days' campaigns. At SEVEN PINES, 31 May, his brigade charged with the division, suffering grievous casualties. With reckless daring Garland exposed himself constantly, having 2 horses shot under him, and was among the officers most distinguished for their conduct during the battle.

Garland fought at SECOND BULL RUN and joined in the Confederate invasion of Maryland in the ANTIETAM CAMPAIGN. On the morning of 14 Sept. 1862, Garland's brigade of North Carolinians held Fox's Gap, the right-flank position of Hill's line on SOUTH MOUNTAIN. By 9 a.m. the leading division of the Union IX Corps had charged Garland's line, which clung tenuously to its position. While Garland was examining his right, he fell mortally wounded, dying later that day.

Hill said that Garland was "the most fearless man I ever knew." Gen. ROBERT E. LEE characterized the capable Virginian as "that brave and accomplished young officer." Garland was buried in Lynchburg beside his wife and son.   —JDW

Garnett, Richard Brooke. CSA b. "Rose Hill," Essex Cty., Va., 21 Nov. 1817. Attending West Point with his cousin, later Brig. Gen. ROBERT S. GARNETT, Richard graduated 29th in

the class of 1841, served in the Seminole War in Florida, and was with the U.S. Army until the Civil War, although he did not serve in the Mexican War. He was commissioned a major in the Confederate States Army early in the war and was promoted to brigadier 14 Nov. 1861.

During the SHENANDOAH VALLEY CAMPAIGN of 1862 Garnett commanded the famous Stonewall Brigade, succeeding Maj. Gen. THOMAS J. "STONEWALL" JACKSON. At KERNSTOWN, he an-

USMHI

gered Jackson when he retreated in the face of an overwhelming Federal assault; charges were preferred for a court-martial but a trial was never held. Garnett never quite forgave Jackson for the unjust charges, though he later grieved at his commander's death and served as a pallbearer at his funeral. Garnett was transferred from Jackson's command to Lt. Gen. JAMES LONGSTREET's I Corps and took command of a Virginia brigade in Maj. Gen. GEORGE E. PICKETT's division, leading it at SOUTH

MOUNTAIN, ANTIETAM, and FREDERICKSBURG, winning the love and respect of his men.

On the third day at GETTYSBURG, during PICKETT'S CHARGE, Garnett cleared his tarnished reputation. Too sick to walk, he refused to watch from the rear while his men advanced; instead, he rode in the front rank of the charge, galloping up and down the line and encouraging his Virginians. Near the stone wall on Cemetery Ridge, Garnett was killed; his body was never recovered. —JTP

Garnett, Robert Selden. CSA b. Essex Cty., Va., 16 Dec. 1819, Garnett gained the unenviable distinction of being the first general officer, Union or Confederate, killed in action in the Civil War. Commander of a small army in northwestern Virginia, he was regarded by his superiors as a promising soldier.

Garnett graduated 2 places ahead of his cousin, RICHARD B. GARNETT, 27th in the class of 1841 at West Point. He fought in the Seminole War and distinguished himself in the Mexican War, winning brevets as captain and major at Monterrey and Buena Vista, respectively. Serving as commandant of cadets at West Point, Garnett taught infantry tactics there for 3 years.

LC

At the outbreak of the war he was on leave in Europe, but he returned home, resigned his commission, and was commissioned brigadier general in the Confederate army 6 June 1861.

Assigned to command the Confederate troops in the mountains of northwestern Virginia, he was hampered by a lack of supplies, food, ammunition, and soldiers. In June–July 1861 Garnett's small force was steadily pushed back from Rich Mountain and then from Laurel Hill by superior Federal forces under Maj. Gen. GEORGE B. MCCLELLAN and Brig. Gen. WILLIAM S. ROSECRANS.

In the first 2 weeks of July Garnett's men were forced to retreat across the mountains, and on the 13th they crossed the Cheat River at CORRICK'S FORD. Garnett was supervising the fording of the river and arranging the positions of his rear guard when he was mortally wounded by Union troops crossing the river. His body fell into enemy hands but was returned to his family by McClellan. Originally buried in Baltimore, his body was reinterred near his wife's grave in Greenwood Cemetery, Brooklyn, N.Y. —JTP

Garrard, Kenner. USA b. Bourbon Cty., Ky., 30 Sept. 1827. After attending Harvard and transferring to West Point, where he graduated 8th in the class of 1851, Garrard began a 10-year cavalry career in the Southwest. In Apr. 1861, while evacuating from Texas with other U.S. Regulars, he was imprisoned by zealous state patriots and paroled. Parole terms kept him at commissary-general and West Point posts until his official exchange 27 Aug. 1862 and appointment as volunteer colonel of the 146th New York Infantry.

Garrard served with the 146th and the Army of the Potomac through the Battle of GETTYSBURG, where, 2 July 1863, he assumed command of slain Brig. Gen. STEPHEN H. WEED's infan-

try brigade. Appointment to brigadier general 23 July and service in the inconclusive autumn campaigning at Mine Run and along the Rappahannock River followed. In November he was commissioned a major in the Regulars. Then a brief midwinter appointment as chief of the Cavalry Bureau in Washington, D.C., ended Feb. 1864 with assignment to the Army of the Cumberland.

LC

Through Maj. Gen. WILLIAM T. SHERMAN's Georgia campaign, Garrard led the 2d Cavalry Division. During the Battle of ATLANTA in July he raided Covington, Ga., and the South River area. Commendation for his efforts won him assignment as leader of the 2d Division in Maj. Gen. ANDREW J. SMITH's XVI Corps for Tennessee campaigning. Garrard's contingent was among the last of the major reinforcements to reach Maj. Gen. GEORGE H. THOMAS' force at Nashville; for his part in the Battle of Nashville he was brevetted major general of volunteers.

At the end of the war Garrard served as military commander of Mobile, Ala. With other old elements from the FRANKLIN AND NASHVILLE CAMPAIGN, he had participated in the siege and surrender of the city. On 13 Mar. 1865 he was brevetted brigadier general and major general in the Regulars for war service; his resignation followed 9 Nov. 1866. Dabbling in real estate, Garrard took up residence in Cincinnati, Ohio, where he died 15 May 1879. —JES

Garrott, Isham Warren. CSA b. Anson Cty., N.C., 1816. A graduate of North Carolina State University, Garrott, a young attorney, moved to Marion, Ala., in 1840 and made a home there, with a career in law and holding minor public offices. After election to terms in the state legislature, 1845 and 1847, he became an active Southern separatist, a member of the 1860 electoral college, and Alabama commissioner to North Carolina during the early days of the secession crisis.

With the advent of civil war, he helped organize the 20th Alabama and was appointed its colonel 8 Oct. 1861. Garrison duty in Mobile followed until spring 1863, when Garrott and

LC

the 20th were sent to the VICKSBURG, Miss., theater and placed under command of Garrott's old state political ally, Brig. Gen. EDWARD D. TRACEY. In action at PORT GIBSON, Miss., 1 May, Tracey died and Garrott assumed brigade command. In the next 6 weeks his brigade fought at Baker's Creek and in other minor actions around Vicksburg. On 17 June 1863, reputedly bored with duty in the newly besieged city, Garrott borrowed a soldier's rifle, took a place on the Confederate skirmish line, and was killed. A commission as brigadier general dated 28 May arrived for Garrott several days later. —JES

Gartrell, Lucius Jeremiah. CSA/CSP b. Wilkes Cty., Ga., 7 Jan. 1821. The son of a prosperous planter, Gartrell was educated at Randolph-Macon College and the University of Georgia, graduating from nei-
ther. Taking up law, he was elected solicitor general, then judge, of the northern judicial circuit of his state. In 1847 he entered the Georgia General As-sembly as a Whig; by 1849 he was a Democrat and one of the radical pro-slavery leaders of the legislature. He bitterly op-posed colleagues who pro-moted compromise measures such as those of Henry Clay, and when he entered the U.S. House of Representatives in 1857 he was an outspoken ad-vocate of secession.

LC

When his state left the Union, Gartrell eagerly took up arms in the cause of Confederate liberty. He organized the 7th Georgia Infantry, was elected its colonel, and led the regiment at FIRST BULL RUN as a part of the understrength brigade under Col. FRANCIS S. BARTOW. Winning a seat in the CONFEDERATE CONGRESS Nov. 1861, he resigned his commission and re-turned to political life. He became chairman of the House Committee on the Judiciary and strongly supported the ad-ministration of JEFFERSON DAVIS. He voted to make Confederate Treasury notes legal tender, to end all military exemptions—even those held by state government officials—to strengthen the field army, and to curb speculation by placing price limits on certain staple commodities. Most controversial was his sponsorship of a bill to suspend *HABEAS CORPUS* whenever the Davis administration thought necessary.

Preferring the military, Gartrell refused to seek reelection, then returning to uniform, and 22 Aug. 1864 he was named briga-dier general. Organizing 4 regiments of Georgia Reserves, he led them in a spirited but futile attempt to halt Maj. Gen. WILLIAM T. SHERMAN's march up the Georgia coast into South Carolina. His brigade's tenacious fighting at Coosawhatchie, S.C., late that year, enabled Lt. Gen. WILLIAM J. HARDEE's garri-son to withdraw successfully from Savannah, though nearly hemmed in by Sherman.

Wounded shortly before war's close, Gartrell was sent home to Augusta. In peacetime, he moved to Atlanta and resumed his legal practice, establishing a reputation as the state's most able criminal lawyer. A member of the Georgia constitutional convention of 1877, he lost the 1882 gubernatorial race to former Confederate vice-president ALEXANDER H. STEPHENS. d. Atlanta, 7 Apr. 1891.   —EGL

Gary, Martin Witherspoon. CSA b. Cokesbury, S.C., 25 Mar. 1831, Gary entered Harvard, where he studied law, grad-uating in 1854. He succeeded as a criminal lawyer and a secessionist member of the state legislature.

When South Carolina seceded, Gary was captain of the Watson Guards, a militia company that joined Confederate service as part of the HAMPTON LEGION, a command of infantry, cavalry, and artillery formed by Col. WADE HAMPTON. Gary led the legion at FIRST BULL RUN when Hampton and its lieutenant colonel fell wounded. Promoted to lieutenant colonel, then

colonel, Gary commanded the legion throughout most of the conflict. As dismounted cavalry, 1862–63, the legion fought in the PENINSULA CAMPAIGN, at SEC-OND BULL RUN, ANTIETAM, FRED-ERICKSBURG, Suffolk, CHICK-AMAUGA, and KNOXVILLE.

During the campaigns of 1864–65 the legion was mounted as cavalry. On 19 May 1864 Gary was promoted to brigadier general and com-manded a cavalry brigade. Dur-ing the PETERSBURG CAMPAIGN he

USMHI

participated in the engagements on the north side of the James River. When the Confederate troops abandoned Richmond Apr. 1865, his command was the last to leave the capital. After the surrender at APPOMATTOX, Gary led his unit through the Federal lines and joined Pres. Jefferson Davis' fleeing entour-age.

A thin, balding, erect man, Gary, nicknamed the "Bald Eagle," resumed his legal and political career after the war. Allying himself with his old commander, Hampton, he es-poused white supremacy and was elected to the South Caro-lina state senate. Twice Gary ran for the U.S. Senate, but was defeated by former political associates. d. Edgefield County 9 Apr. 1881.   —JDW

Gatlin, Richard Caswell. CSA b. Lenoir Cty., N.C., 18 Jan. 1809. After attending the University of North Carolina and graduating from West Point 35th in the class of 1832, Gatlin was an infantry officer in many parts of the West and South-west. During the Mexican War, he defended Fort Brown, Tex., then crossed the Rio Grande, being wounded while storming enemy works at Monterrey. Fol-lowing the conflict, he fought Seminoles in Florida, served on the Kansas and Dakota frontier, and joined Col. ALBERT SIDNEY JOHNSTON's Utah Expedition in 1858.

In Apr. 1861, as a major in the 5th U.S. Infantry, Gatlin was apprehended by Arkansas state

LC

forces at FORT SMITH. Released on parole, he decided to join his captors' cause and was appointed adjutant general of his native state. In this capacity he received the rank of major general of North Carolina Militia as well as the stars of a Confederate colonel. Later that year he was named to com-mand the North Carolina coastal defenses and the military department that encompassed the state. As a brigadier general, his appointment dating from 8 July 1861, he administered the post from his headquarters in Wilmington.

In August, Union army and navy forces captured Fort Hat-teras (*see* HATTERAS INLET, N.C.), gaining a foothold on the Carolina coast, an act that brought Gatlin much criticism, even abuse. Moving his headquarters to Goldsborough in Septem-ber, he made efforts to defend other parts of the state, including New Berne. His superiors, however, denied his requests for reinforcements, which helped account for NEW BERNE's seizure by Brig. Gen. AMBROSE E. BURNSIDE Mar. 1862. Soon afterward, Gatlin lost his command. Illness was cited as the official reason for his relief. In published reports Gatlin defended himself, maintaining that insufficient defense forces and his inability to control offshore waters were to blame for the enemy's success: "these failures do not by right rest with me."

Nevertheless, he was provided no new command, prompting him to resign his commission Sept. 1862 and return to his adjutant general's post in North Carolina. After the war he moved to Sebastian Cty., Ark., where he farmed until his death in Mount Nebo 8 Sept. 1896. —EGL

Gatling gun. The Gatling gun saw only limited use in the Civil War, but the conflict tested this weapon, perhaps the first successful true machine gun used in warfare. Invented by Dr. Richard Jordan Gatling, the Civil War model served as the precursor of more successful models.

The Gatling gun was a hand-crank-operated weapon with 6 barrels revolving around a central shaft. The cartridges were fed to the gun by gravity through a hopper mounted on the top of the gun. 6 cam-operated bolts alternately wedged, fired, and dropped the bullets, which were contained in steel chambers. Gatling used the 6 barrels to partially cool the gun during firing. Since the gun was capable of firing 600 rounds a minute, each barrel fired 100 rounds per minute.

The gun had a number of problems, however. The bores were tapered, and often the barrels and chambers did not exactly align, affecting accuracy and velocity. The chamber system itself, in which a paper cartridge was contained inside a capped steel chamber, was both expensive and fragile. While the gun showed much promise and fired the standard .58-caliber ammunition, it had so many drawbacks and was so radical in both design and purpose that Gatling was unable to interest the U.S. government. The army purchased none of his guns, but Maj. Gen. BENJAMIN F. BUTLER, after a field test, purchased 12 for $1,000 each. They were used on the Petersburg front in 1864 and apparently were considered successful. That, however, was the only service the guns saw.

In Jan. 1865 Gatling's improved Model 1865 gun was tested by the Ordnance Department. Among other things, this weapon used rimfire copper-cased cartridges instead of the steel-chambered paper variety. Though this model did not see service, it was adopted officially in 1866. Having at last received government approval, Gatling began to sell his guns throughout the world; they achieved lasting fame in the postwar years. —LDJ

Geary, John White. USA b. Mount Pleasant, Pa., 30 Dec. 1819, Geary was a man equally at home in politics and the military. He was a student at Jefferson College in Canonsburg, Pa., when the death of his father forced him to begin adult life early. Geary tested a number of professions before settling on law. Enlisting in the volunteer army for the Mexican War, he won praise as colonel of the 2d Pennsylvania Infantry, then organized postal service in California, served for a time as mayor of San Francisco, and was territorial governor of Kansas until his strong antislavery views forced his resignation.

When the Civil War began, Geary immediately issued a call in his home state for troops; so well respected was he that 68 companies responded to his proclamation. Geary selected 15

USMHI

and organized the oversized 28th Pennsylvania Infantry. Service with Brig. Gen. NATHANIEL P. BANKS along the upper Potomac River brought him a brigadier's commission 25 Apr. 1862. At the Battle of CEDAR MOUNTAIN in August of that year, Geary was wounded in the foot and shoulder. Yet this tall, full-bearded officer with sharp eyes and an equally sharp tongue soon returned to duty and assumed command of a division in the XII Corps. He displayed resoluteness at CHANCELLORSVILLE, steadfastness at GETTYSBURG, extraordinary valor at LOOKOUT MOUNTAIN, and administrative skills in Maj. Gen. WILLIAM T. SHERMAN'S ATLANTA CAMPAIGN. Geary received brevet promotion to major general while military governor of Savannah.

In 1866 he was elected to the first of 2 consecutive terms as Republican governor of Pennsylvania. On 8 Feb. 1873, less than 3 weeks after leaving the governor's post, Geary was fatally stricken while preparing breakfast for his infant son. He was buried with state honors in Mount Kalma Cemetery, Harrisburg, Pa. —JIR

General Orders No. 9, Appomattox, Va. 10 Apr. 1865 *See* LEE'S FAREWELL TO THE ARMY OF NORTHERN VIRGINIA.

General Orders No. 11, Holly Springs, Miss. 17 Dec. 1862 *See* GRANT'S ANTI-JEW ORDER.

General Orders No. 11, Missouri. 25 Aug. 1863 With only 2,500 men spread over the vast Border District, which included Colorado Territory, Brig. Gen. THOMAS EWING was frustrated in his campaign to suppress Confederate guerrillas in Missouri. After he had ordered the arrest in summer 1863 of disloyal men and women who willingly aided Confederate guerrillas in the state, several of the women, among them kin to some of Confederate Col. WILLIAM C. QUANTRILL's men, were imprisoned at an old brick warehouse in Kansas City. On 18 Aug. the building collapsed, killing 5 of them. In retaliation, Quantrill decided to raid the abolitionist stronghold of LAWRENCE, KANS., kill Brig. Gen. JAMES LANE, the hated soldier-politician responsible for previous depradations against Confederate families, and as many men as they found in the town. His 450 guerrillas rode into Lawrence early on the morning of the 21st. When they left the next day, about 150 men and boys lay dead and the town was in ruins.

Infuriated, Lane, who had left Lawrence before Quantrill's men arrived, insisted that Ewing deal harshly with Confederate sympathizers, helped write the vindictive retaliatory General Orders No. 11, then threatened to ruin Ewing's military career if he failed to enforce them stringently. Issued 25 Aug., the orders dictated the depopulation by 9 Sept. of all civilians living more than 1 mi from any military post in Jackson, Cass, Bates, and (half of) Vernon counties. Assigned to carry out the mandate was the 15th Kansas Cavalry, led by jayhawker Col. Charles R. Jennison.

Many Kansans suffered grievously from the violence that marked their forced evacuation. Refugees, most of them old men, women, and children, fleeing in terror to Arkansas with wagonloads of household goods, reported indiscriminate robbery and murder by U.S. troops. So devastated was the region by arson that for years after the war the area was called the "Burnt District."

Of the 10,000 people who lived in Cass County before the war, only 600 able to prove their loyalty to the Union remained after Ewing's orders took effect. General Orders No. 11 ruined the western part of the state's economy. Amid public outrage, Missouri genre artist George Caleb Bingham made Ewing immortal by recording the tragic effect of his decree in the painting *Orders Number Eleven* (1869–70). Orders No. 11 was the most severe military act of the war aimed at civilians.   —PLF

General Orders No. 28, New Orleans, La.   15 May 1862
See "WOMAN'S ORDER."

General Sterling Price, CSS.   Constructed as the *Laurent Millaudon* at Cincinnati, Ohio, the *General Sterling Price* was a stern-wheeler, 182 ft long, 30 ft in beam, and slightly over 9 ft in draft. In 1861 it was commandeered by the Confederacy and fitted out at New Orleans for the CONFEDERATE RIVER DEFENSE FLEET. In Jan. 1862 Capt. James E. Montgomery, in command of the river defense fleet, began fitting out the vessel as a ram. Its bow was covered with 4 in. of heavy timber and iron an inch thick, and was strengthened by wooden bulkheads filled with compressed cotton bales. Though its battery apparently varied, the ram generally carried 1 32-pounder forward and 1 24-pounder aft.

USMHI

On 25 Mar. 1862 the converted steamboat left New Orleans for Memphis, where it was prepared for combat. In April it was ordered to Fort Pillow, Tenn., to help guard the river approaches to Memphis. On 10 May, near Fort Pillow, the *General Sterling Price*, along with 7 other vessels of the river defense fleet under Montgomery, attacked the ironclad gunboats of the Union "Western Flotilla." In the Battle of PLUM RUM BEND that followed, the *General Price* rammed the ironclad *Cincinnati*, which, rammed by 2 other river defense fleet vessels, sank in shallow water. The *General Price* also disabled *Federal Mortar Boat No. 16* and was itself only slightly damaged during the engagement.

After cooperating with other Confederate vessels in holding the river, early in June it returned to Memphis to take on coal. When the Union river flotilla arrived above Memphis, Montgomery's vessels, including the *General Price,* attacked the Union warships. The *General Price* concentrated on the *Monarch,* one of Col. CHARLES ELLET's wooden rams, but in the battle the Confederate vessel collided with the *General Beauregard* and was disabled. The *Queen of the West* then rammed the *General Price,* which sank in shoal waters. The ram was later raised by Union forces and taken into Federal service. It was scrapped after the war.   —WNS

"Gentle Annie."   *See* ETHERIDGE, ANNIE.

Georgia.   With the largest acreage and, in 1861, the largest population of the states in the Deep South, Georgia was the strategic connecting area between the mid-Gulf South and the seaboard. Thus it was vital to the secessionist movement. After South Carolina seceded 20 Dec. 1860 and Mississippi, Florida, and Alabama followed 9, 10, and 11 Jan., respectively, only Georgia was needed for seceded territory to stretch from North Carolina's southern border to the Mississippi River.

In Nov. 1860 Georgia's governor, JOSEPH E. BROWN, a strong secessionist, asked his legislature to call for a convention to vote for secession; after 2 weeks of debate a convention was called for 16 Jan. On 19 Jan., after speeches made by visitors from South Carolina, Alabama, and Mississippi stirred enthusiasm for leaving the Union, Georgia seceded.

In an extended disagreement between the state of Georgia and the Confederate government, Brown, as ardent in his defense of STATES RIGHTS as of secession, objected to military conscription being withdrawn from state control. Nevertheless, Brown armed Georgia efficiently, and more completely than any other Southern state. According to the governor, over 100,000 Georgians, in addition to the GEORGIA MILITIA, fought for the Confederacy.

Relatively little fighting took place on Georgia soil—largely unsuccessful Federal raids—until spring 1864, when Maj. Gen. WILLIAM T. SHERMAN began his march south from Tennessee through Georgia to the sea (*see* MARCH TO THE SEA). En route, Sherman offered to spare the state further destruction if Georgia's forces were withdrawn from Confederate armies. While Brown still believed in the right of each state to act independently, he refused to violate Georgia's pledge to the South and made a public statement rejecting the offer. Sherman returned to the devastation of Georgia, later estimating the damage to the state at $100 million.   —PR

Georgia, Confederate Department of.   Defended by state forces and a Georgia navy that existed only on paper, the coastline of Georgia was rendered vulnerable in the extreme with the fall of PORT ROYAL, S.C., late in 1861. On 26 Oct., after Confederate troops were sent to the coast, Special Order No. 190 from the Adjutant and Inspector General's Office in Richmond designated Georgia a separate military department. Named to command, with headquarters at Savannah, was Brig. Gen. ALEXANDER R. LAWTON, formerly colonel of the 1st Georgia Infantry.

By the end of the month, the department was defended by 5,982 officers and men (of whom 5,497 were listed as present for duty), plus 33 siege and 17 field cannon. The soldiers were scattered over 21 posts such as Savannah, Fort Pulaski, Brunswick, Waynesville, and several islands off the coast, including Tybee, which had the largest contingent—1,086 troops.

Lawton's department existed for barely 10 days. On 5 Nov. it was merged into the DEPARTMENT OF SOUTH CAROLINA AND GEORGIA, a military district assigned to Gen. ROBERT E. LEE. 19 days later, despite Lee's and Lawton's efforts, Federals captured both Tybee and Wassaw islands. These lodgments enabled the invaders the following April to seize FORT PULASKI and threaten Savannah. This was the extent of Union gains in Georgia until Maj. Gen. WILLIAM T. SHERMAN's invasion May 1864.   —EGL

***Georgia,* CSS.** In Mar. 1863 Cmdr. MATTHEW F. MAURY, Confederate naval agent in Great Britain, purchased the iron steamer *Japan* at Dumbarton, Scotland. Maury had been unable to secure a wooden vessel, which would have been better suited for use as a cruiser. The *Japan,* built in 1862 as a merchant ship, weighed 600 tons, was 212 ft long, and had a draft of 13 ft. The ship departed Greenock, Scotland, reputedly

OR

bound for the East Indies, 1 Apr. 1863. 8 days later, off Ushant, France, it was commissioned the CSS *Georgia,* under command of Lt. William L. Maury, and supplies and equipment were transferred from the steamer *Alar.* The battery consisted of 2 100-pounders, 2 24-pounders, and 1 32-pounder.

The *Georgia* was not in the same class as the *FLORIDA* and the *ALABAMA,* both specially designed for use as cruisers. One Confederate officer referred to the ship as "a poor miserable little tin kettle." Among its other deficiencies, the rapid accumulation of sea growth on the vessel's iron hull reduced its speed considerably. Nevertheless, during 6 months spent cruising from the Cape Verde Islands and off Brazil and Africa, the *Georgia* took 9 prizes. Finally, in "almost broken down condition," it arrived at Cherbourg, France, for repairs.

Early in 1864, while Maury was on detached duty, Lt. William E. Evans brought the *Georgia* to the coast of Morocco for a secret rendezvous with the *RAPPAHANNOCK,* which had been designated its replacement. The guns of the *Georgia* were to be transferred to the vessel, but the *Rappahannock,* detained at Calais by Napoleon III, never appeared.

On 2 May 1864 the *Georgia* was taken to Liverpool and sold to an English merchant. Despite this, the ship was seized

by the *Niagara* at sea and taken to Boston. A Federal court ruled that it was a lawful prize of the U.S.   —NCD

Georgia, Union Army of. To "march to the sea," Maj. Gen. WILLIAM T. SHERMAN divided his "army group" into two wings. The Army of the Tennessee constituted the right wing; 2 corps of the Army of the Cumberland composed the left wing. But because the commander of the latter army was in Nashville, the left wing could not use the name Army of the Cumberland. It was called instead—first informally; after 28 Mar. 1865, formally—the Army of Georgia.

Senior corps commander Maj. Gen. HENRY W. SLOCUM led this new army. In his absence, his XX Corps was directed first by Brig. Gen. Alpheus S. Williams, then by Brig. Gen. JOSEPH A. MOWER. Throughout Sherman's advance, Maj. Gen. JEFFERSON C. DAVIS commanded the XIV Corps. Sometimes, Brig. Gen. H. JUDSON KILPATRICK's cavalry division also served under Slocum.

Leaving Atlanta 15 Nov. 1864, the left wing feinted toward Augusta, then shifted southward, occupied Milledgeville, and closed on Savannah. During the mild siege there, 9–21 Dec., it anchored Sherman's left on the Savannah River and crossed 1 brigade to South Carolina, causing Lt. Gen. WILLIAM J. HARDEE to abandon the city. From Savannah the army moved northward around Columbia to Cheraw and Sneedsboro, S.C.

The Army of the Tennessee was the wing most often involved in the few battles in Georgia and South Carolina after 15 Nov. but in North Carolina, Slocum bore the brunt. On 15–16 Mar. he finally drove Hardee from AVERASBOROUGH, then 19 Mar. the great Confederate counterattack at BENTONVILLE slammed into his incautious XIV Corps; 2, then 4 of his divisions became embroiled before he stabilized the defense. The South's lack of cohesion and the North's skill and bravery saved his wing from disaster. The other wing eventually joined him; the Secessionists' opportunity passed, and they withdrew.

Slocum's command briefly rested around Goldsborough, then advanced to Raleigh, helping to force Gen. JOSEPH E. JOHNSTON's surrender. It next marched north, participated in the GRAND REVIEW 24 May, and was disbanded 1 June 1865.

Like its "parent" Army of the Cumberland, the Army of Georgia showed a propensity for the bold strategic sweep, a powerful attack, and a steadfast defense.   —RJS

Georgia, Union Department of. Georgia formally came under Union military rule 10 Feb. 1865, when Maj. Gen. GEORGE H. THOMAS, from his headquarters in Nashville, assumed command of the Department of Kentucky and the DEPARTMENT OF THE CUMBERLAND. The latter comprised that portion of northern Georgia occupied by his troops as well as Tennessee and parts of Alabama and Mississippi. This arrangement was effective until Military Reconstruction began in the South. On 7 June 1865 Pres. ANDREW JOHNSON assigned Thomas the MILITARY DIVISION OF THE TENNESSEE, including the Department of Georgia. In immediate command of the latter, which embraced the entire state of Georgia, was Maj. Gen. JAMES B. STEEDMAN, with headquarters at Augusta. Steedman retained control under General Order No. 118, 27 June 1865, which formalized the organization of RECONSTRUCTION divisions and departments.

The Department of Georgia was in existence for less than a year. On 10 Dec. 1865 Steedman was succeeded by his senior subordinate, Maj. Gen. JAMES H. WILSON, who was in turn replaced 9 days later by Brev. Maj. Gen. JOHN M. BRANNAN, who held the post until 19 May 1866, when the department was merged into the Department of the South.   —EGL

Georgia Militia. The extreme STATES-RIGHTS views of Georgia Gov. JOSEPH E. BROWN placed him at odds with Confederate officials throughout the war. One of their most bitter clashes involved the government's authority to press state troops into Confederate service, which Brown considered a flagrant violation of state sovereignty. He was incensed by the Confederate CONSCRIPTION Act of Apr. 1862, which swallowed whole the state army he had organized. Eventually, however, the governor built a new force by exempting local civil and military officers from later draft calls and by recruiting men above and below draft age. By mid-1864, he had gathered several thousand militiamen. The lengths to which he went to keep these citizen soldiers from government service earned them the nickname "Joe Brown's Pets."

Although Brown's original militia served in the field from the war's early days, his "pets" did not see active service till spring 1864, when he consented to make them available to the Confederacy under certain conditions. Alarmed by Maj. Gen. WILLIAM T. SHERMAN's advance through his state, Brown on 18 and 21 May and 24 June ordered his officers to turn out for local defense. On 9 July he called out every able-bodied man between 16 and 55, including those previously exempt. Soon 3,000 military and civil officers massed near Atlanta, the point most in need of protection. Organized into 2 brigades, they were initially led by the state adjutant general, Maj. Gen. HENRY C. WAYNE, then by Maj. Gen. GUSTAVUS W. SMITH. The old men and boys joined them in mid-July. Clad in motley attire and armed with antique weapons, they raised Smith's force to 10,000.

Derided by the veterans of the Army of Tennessee, whom they augmented during the ATLANTA CAMPAIGN, the militia nevertheless proved their courage and ability 2–3 July along the CHATTAHOOCHEE RIVER and 3 weeks later in the Battle of ATLANTA, winning praise from Gen. JOHN BELL HOOD. After the city's fall, Smith's men constituted the only organized infantry opposition to Sherman's MARCH TO THE SEA. Though battered by Sherman at Griswoldville, 22 Nov., they defeated a large force of Federals at HONEY HILL, S.C., 8 days later. Despite their good service, government resentment against the militiamen revived with Brown's decision to furlough them in September and December, while Sherman's invasion continued.   —EGL

Getty, George Washington. USA b. District of Columbia, 2 Oct. 1819, Getty entered West Point at 16, graduating 15th in the class of 1840. An artillerist, he was brevetted for gallantry in the Mexican War, fought in the Seminole Wars, and served on the frontier. At the outbreak of the Civil War, he held the rank of captain of the 4th Artillery.

Getty transferred to the 5th Artillery until appointed lieutenant colonel and additional aide-de-camp of volunteers 28 Sept. 1861. Commanding 4 batteries, he distinguished himself during the PENINSULA and SEVEN DAYS' campaigns and at SOUTH MOUNTAIN. At ANTIETAM he served as chief of artillery of the IX Corps. Promoted to brigadier general to date from 25 Sept. 1862, the artillerist assumed command of the 3d Division/IX Corps, leading it in the Battle of FREDERICKSBURG.

In Mar. 1863 Getty's division transferred to southeastern

Virginia, where it participated in the successful Union defense of Suffolk. Getty served on engineering duty before commanding a diversionary movement to the South Anna River in Virginia during the GETTYSBURG CAMPAIGN.

LC

Early in 1864 he temporarily acted as inspector general of the Army of the Potomac. When the year's campaigning began in spring, Getty assumed command of a division of the VI Corps, leading it at the WILDERNESS, where he was severely wounded. Returning to command, he participated in the PETERSBURG and SHENANDOAH VALLEY campaigns. During the Battle of CEDAR CREEK, 19 Oct., Getty commanded the VI Corps. For his gallant services during the year, he was brevetted brigadier general in the Regular Army and major general of volunteers. On 2 Apr. 1865 his division made the initial penetration of the Confederate lines at Petersburg, which resulted in the abandonment of the city and the Confederate retreat ending at Appomattox.

Getty remained in the Regular Army following the war and was appointed colonel of the 38th Infantry in 1866. He subsequently transferred to the 3d Artillery, commanded the army school at Fort Monroe, Va., and served as a member of the board that reversed the court-martial of FITZ JOHN PORTER for that officer's role in SECOND BULL RUN. Retiring in 1879, the career soldier lived on a Maryland farm, "Forest Glen," where he died 1 Oct. 1901.   —JDW

Gettysburg, Pa., Battle of.   1–3 July 1863

Day 1, 1 July 1863

Neither Gen. ROBERT E. LEE nor Maj. Gen. GEORGE G. MEADE had planned to fight at the southern Pennsylvania crossroads village of Gettysburg. But when a Confederate infantry brigade, marching eastward on the Chambersburg Pike in search of shoes, clashed with 2 Union cavalry brigades west of the town, the 2 armies were drawn into battle.

Maj. Gen. HENRY HETH's Confederate division encountered the Union cavalry, under Brig. Gen. JOHN BUFORD, about 4 mi west of Gettysburg. Buford had recognized the strategic importance of the village, where 9 roads converged, and had deployed his troopers to confront the approaching Confederates. At 8 o'clock Heth's veterans charged the dismounted cavalrymen, who were armed with the new Spencer carbines. The Federals fought stubbornly, repulsing several Confederate attacks.

About 10:30 a.m. Maj. Gen. JOHN F. REYNOLDS' Union I Corps relieved Buford's veterans. The unwanted and unplanned battle soon escalated. After Lt. Gen. AMBROSE P. HILL, Heth's commander, ordered an assault, Heth's and then Maj. Gen. WILLIAM D. PENDER's division stormed into Reynolds' lines on McPherson's Ridge. The battle raged; Reynolds died from a sharpshooter's bullet and the famous Union IRON BRIGADE was devastated. The Confederates seized the ridge, pushing the Federals back to Seminary Ridge, where they regrouped.

Shortly after noon Maj. Gen. OLIVER O. HOWARD's Union XI Corps reached the field, deploying north of Gettysburg. 2 of

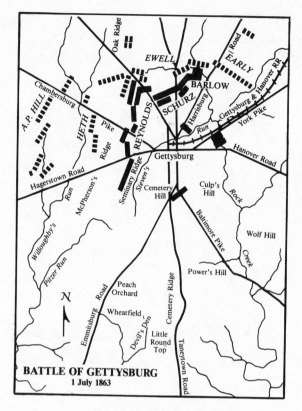

BATTLE OF GETTYSBURG
1 July 1863

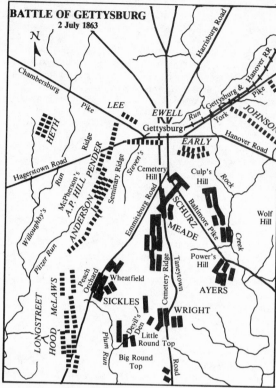

BATTLE OF GETTYSBURG
2 July 1863

Lt. Gen. RICHARD S. EWELL's Confederate divisions soon arrived opposite Howard's lines. Ewell charged, rolling up the luckless XI Corps ranks with heavy losses. Howard's men fled into and through the town. Hill then renewed his attacks, and the Union I Corps, assailed front and flank, crumbled.

South of the village, on Cemetery Hill, Maj. Gen. WINFIELD S. HANCOCK rallied the fleeing Union troops. Lee, who arrived mid-afternoon, ordered Ewell, "if possible," to attack Hancock's position, but Ewell hesitated and never did attack. Though his orders not to bring on a general engagement had been disregarded, Lee ordered a concentration after the day's decisive victory. Meade, likewise, redirected his scattered corps toward Gettysburg during the night.

Day 2, 2 July 1863

At dawn Union forces manned a naturally strong defensive position south and east of Gettysburg. Resembling a giant fishhook, the line stretched from CULP'S HILL to CEMETERY HILL, along CEMETERY RIDGE to the base of LITTLE ROUND TOP. The southern anchor, Little and Big Round Tops, were unoccupied.

The Confederates reconnoitered the Union position during the morning. Lt. Gen. JAMES LONGSTREET argued for a flanking movement beyond the Union left. Lee, thinking he had to fight or retreat, rejected Longstreet's plan and resolved to renew the offensive. When Ewell stated that the Union right at Culp's and Cemetery hills was too strong to attack, Lee ordered Longstreet to assault Meade's left in front of the Round Tops.

Longstreet's march beyond Meade's left and the Federal observation posts consumed most of the afternoon. About 4 o'clock Longstreet launched his attack with 2 divisions. Maj. Gens. LAFAYETTE MCLAWS' and JOHN B. HOOD's Confederates struck Maj. Gen. DANIEL E. SICKLES' III Corps. Sickles, who without orders had advanced to higher ground along the Emmitsburg road, manned a salient when the Southerners charged. The severe fighting raged along places that became famous because of the carnage there—the PEACH ORCHARD, the WHEATFIELD, DEVIL'S DEN, and Little Round Top. Meade shifted troops from the right to the left, and Confederate charges were met with riveting Federal counterattacks. Regiments, brigades, and divisions were mowed down in the mounting fury. A valiant Union defense saved Little Round Top and secured Meade's position.

The fighting then shifted toward the Union center as Lee's plan of en echelon attacks unfolded. Though Hill assaulted with inadequate numbers, 1 Confederate brigade made a temporary lodgment on Cemetery Ridge. At twilight 2 Confederate brigades gallantly stormed up Cemetery Hill, momentarily succeeding until overwhelmed by Union reinforcements. The day's bloody action ended with another abortive Confederate attack on Culp's Hill.

Day 3, 3 July 1863

2 days of savage combat had battered each army. The Federals, assailed on both flanks, still clung to their strong position. In the early minutes of 3 July Meade held a council of war, during which he and his corps commanders resolved to stay

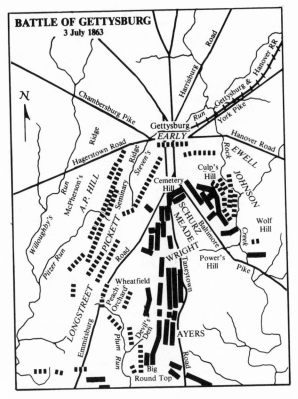

BATTLE OF GETTYSBURG
3 July 1863

in a lethal hail of musketry and canister. A handful of brave Confederates pierced the line but most never had a chance. Streaming back to Seminary Ridge, Lee met them, saying, ''It's all my fault. My fault.''

Stuart, likewise, was repulsed in a swirling cavalry fight lasting 3 hours. The most crucial battle of the war was over, but at a fearful cost. The 3 days' casualties were staggering: 3,155 Federals killed, 14,529 wounded, and 5,365 missing; 3,903 Confederates killed, 18,735 wounded, and 5,425 missing. The country had never seen such carnage. *See also* GETTYSBURG CAMPAIGN.
—JDW

Gettysburg Address. Shortly after the Battle of GETTYSBURG, Pennsylvania Gov. ANDREW G. CURTIN commissioned David Wills, a local attorney, to purchase land for a cemetery for the Union dead. Wills bought 17 acres adjoining the private Evergreen Cemetery on Cemetery Hill and employed a noted landscape artist, William Saunders, to lay out what was to become a national shrine. To give the dead equal honor Saunders devised a plan with a section for each state radiating from a central point, like segments of a pie.

In early autumn 1863, though the task of transferring more than 3,500 dead from their battlefield graves was far from completed, a committee began planning a dedication service. Edward Everett, an outstanding orator of the day, was to make the principal speech. At his request the date was set for Thursday, 19 Nov. Almost as an afterthought, as a gesture of courtesy, Pres. ABRAHAM LINCOLN was invited to ''make a few remarks.'' To the committee's surprise Lincoln accepted. Seeing an opportunity to state what he felt underlay the Union's purpose in the war, the president spent much time and thought in preparing his speech.

Lincoln arrived in Gettysburg 18 Nov. The next day, after an elaborate procession to the cemetery, Everett delivered his eloquent, 2-hour speech from a platform erected at the northwest edge of the burial ground. When the applause died, Lincoln, a tall, shambling figure in black broadcloth, rose and adjusted his spectacles, took out 2 sheets of paper, and began reading with his deliberate, high-pitched Western twang. Some in the audience, restive after 2 hours of standing, failed to appreciate his words, and rumors persist that Lincoln sat down after perfunctory applause, deeply disappointed at what he felt was a failure. But contrary to legend, the speech was received enthusiastically and some perceptive reporters immediately recognized its significance.
—RDH

Gettysburg Campaign, Pa. June–July 1863 The spectacular Confederate victory at CHANCELLORSVILLE during the first week of May 1863 did not relieve the enormous problems confronting the Confederacy. On all fronts, superior Northern resources in manpower and matériel were beginning to overwhelm the South. With the Confederacy strangled by the Union blockade, wracked by worsening inflation, and outnumbered from Virginia to Mississippi, authorities wrestled with the strategic options.

Pres. JEFFERSON DAVIS, cabinet members, and generals conferred during May. Gen. ROBERT E. LEE, commander of the Army of Northern Virginia, opposed plans to send detachments from his army to relieve Tennessee and a besieged VICKSBURG, arguing for a second invasion of the North. Such an offensive, Lee stated, would relieve Richmond, allow the Confederates to garner supplies from the lush Pennsylvania

and fight rather than retreat. Meade believed that if the Confederates renewed their offensive, they would attack his center.

Lee was also determined to fight. Having unsuccessfully attacked both Federal flanks, he planned a massive assault against Cemetery Ridge, as Meade had predicted. Again over the sound objections of Longstreet, the Confederate commander fashioned a plan. Even as he prepared, Confederates, attacking Meade's right at Culp's Hill, were making no progress. Convinced that Union morale was low and that his veterans were invincible, Lee committed to the assault 11 brigades, spearheaded by Maj. Gen. GEORGE E. PICKETT's fresh division. As a secondary phase, Lee ordered Maj. Gen. J.E.B. STUART, who had finally rejoined the army, to attack the Union rear from the east with his cavalry.

The 7-hour struggle for Culp's Hill ended about noon, and a silence pervaded the field. An hour later some 140 Confederate cannon unleashed a furious barrage. For 2 hours Southern gunners hurled a firestorm of shot and shell against the Union center, but most of the shells overshot the target.

Just before 3 o'clock the cannon fell silent. Another ominous stillness followed. Then, with admirable precision, 13,000 Confederates emerged from the woods on Seminary Ridge. Stepping out, they marched steadily across the open ground toward a clump of trees in the Union line. Union artillerists opened fire, and Confederates fell in clumps. But they came on, across the Emmitsburg road and up the slope toward the trees. Federal infantry fired, and PICKETT'S CHARGE was halted

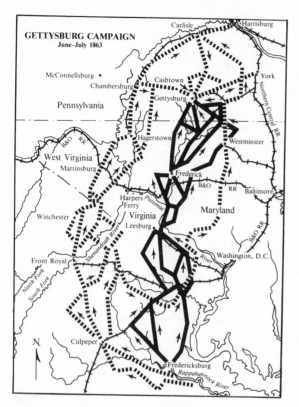

GETTYSBURG CAMPAIGN
June–July 1863

countryside, encourage the Northern peace movement, re-open the possibility of European recognition, and perhaps result in the capture of the Union capital and other Northern cities. The civilian authorities approved Lee's scheme.

On 3 June the advance elements of the reorganized Confederate army abandoned their lines at Fredericksburg, with only Lt. Gen. AMBROSE P. HILL's III Corps remaining to deceive Union Maj. Gen. JOSEPH HOOKER. By the 8th Lee had concentrated 2 infantry corps and his cavalry at Culpeper, east of the Blue Ridge Mts. Confronted with rumors of a major Southern offensive, Hooker ordered cavalry reconnaissances that resulted in battles at FRANKLIN'S CROSSING on the 5th and at BRANDY STATION on the 9th.

Lee's march accelerated on the 10th when Lt. Gen. RICHARD S. EWELL's II Corps, Lt. Gen. THOMAS J. "STONEWALL" JACKSON's former command, moved toward the Shenandoah Valley. Marching swiftly, on 13 June Ewell's foot cavalry reached Winchester, where Maj. Gen. ROBERT H. MILROY's Union force was stationed. Ewell attacked the next day and on the 15th, virtually destroying the Federal command. With the lower valley cleared of Union troops, Lee's army drove across the Potomac River into Maryland. By 25 June the III Corps of Confederate infantry had entered Northern territory.

Hooker, meanwhile, reacted swiftly to the invasion. Marching northward, his army remained between the Southerners and Washington, D.C. Hooker, however, complained about superior Confederate numbers and the lack of support from the Lincoln administration. When he quarreled with Maj. Gen. HENRY W. HALLECK, Union general-in-chief, over the garrison at

Harpers Ferry, the army commander submitted his resignation. Lincoln accepted it, appointing Maj. Gen. GEORGE G. MEADE to command 28 June.

On the day Meade replaced Hooker, Lee learned through a spy that the entire Union army lay north of the Potomac. The Confederate army had been stumbling blindly into Pennsylvania since 24 June, when Maj. Gen. J.E.B. STUART abandoned Lee's flank for a raid around the Union army. Censured for his near-defeat at Brandy Station, Stuart, using Lee's discretionary orders, had cantered off in another dramatic ride. His absence crippled the Confederate invasion, denying Lee vital intelligence.

When Lee learned of Meade's position, he rapidly regrouped his infantry units scattered across southern Pennsylvania. Opposed only by weak Union militia, the Confederates had seized all the livestock, food, clothing, and shoes they could find, while levying tribute on towns. Advance elements were threatening Harrisburg when Lee ordered a concentration at Cashtown, 8 mi west of Gettysburg. On 1 July, a Confederate brigade, seeking shoes, engaged Union cavalry west of Gettysburg, a village where 9 roads converged.

For 3 days the armies grappled in battle. The Union defenders, assailed on both flanks and in front, clung to their strong natural position. The 2 armies suffered more than 50,000 casualties. (*See* GETTYSBURG, PA., BATTLE OF.) On 4 July Lee began his retreat, crossing back into Virginia 14 July.

The Gettysburg Campaign has been the focus of more study than any other Civil War engagement. Controversies surround the battle. Stuart's ride, the earlier death of Jackson, the inefficiency of Confederate staff work, Lt. Gen. JAMES LONGSTREET's reluctance to fight offensively, Ewell's indecisiveness 1 July, and Lee's belief in the invincibility of his army have all been argued as the causes of the Confederate defeat. Meade's battlefield generalship and the defiant valor of his veterans had much to do with the outcome. The Union victories at Gettysburg and Vicksburg were the military turning points of the war. The Confederacy had begun an inexorable descent toward defeat.
—JDW

Gettysburg, Pa., Raid, Stuart's. 24 June–3 July 1863
The 3-day battle at Gettysburg has generated more literature than any other battle of the Civil War. The historical controversy, begun soon after the conflict ended, has posited a series of "ifs," especially regarding Confederate operations. Of these "might-have-beens," few have been debated more intensely than Maj. Gen. J.E.B. STUART's cavalry raid behind the Union Army of the Potomac.

The second Confederate invasion of Northern soil began 3 June when part of Gen. Robert E. Lee's Confederate army abandoned their lines near Fredericksburg, Va. 6 days later Federal cavalry, seeking intelligence, attacked and nearly defeated Stuart at BRANDY STATION. As both armies marched northward, the cavalry opponents dueled in classic engagements at Aldie, Middleburg, and Upperville, Va., 18–21 June. On the 22d Lee gave Stuart vague, discretionary orders, permitting the cavalry officer to harass the Union infantry and directing him to guard the army's right flank, remain in communication, and gather supplies. On the 24th, Stuart prepared to ride around the Federals in an undertaking similar to the one he had accomplished brilliantly a year before on the Peninsula (*see* STUART'S RIDE AROUND MCCLELLAN).

At 1 a.m., 25 June, Stuart, with 3 brigades, rode eastward

in the darkness toward the Bull Run Mts. Encountering Union infantry marching east of the mountains, the Southerners halted for the night. On the 26th, Stuart detoured widely around the passing Federals, covering 23 mi. The next day, in the saddle early again, the Confederates reached Fairfax Court House, routed a few Northern horsemen, then rested for several hours. Resuming the weary march on the 27th, Stuart shoved his brigades across the Potomac River late that day, hours behind schedule. 28 June brought no rest as the Confederates moved across Maryland. At Rockville, Stuart attacked and captured 125 wagons, an encumbrance that only slowed the march.

The Southerners rode all night toward Pennsylvania, burdened with prisoners and wagons. Halting near Hood's Mill, Md., they wrecked rails of the Baltimore & Ohio and waited for approaching trains. About noon Stuart moved toward Westminster, where his men were suddenly attacked by Union cavalry. The Confederates repulsed the Federals, fed their mounts, and gathered a little sleep. Before 10 a.m. on the 30th, they entered Hanover, Pa., and within minutes a Union brigade charged them. A savage battle ensued with the Southerners repulsing the Federals. Stuart pushed his men all night again before halting at Dover.

On the morning of 1 July, he rested the command for several hours. To the southwest Lee's army, having received no information from Stuart about the location of the Union army, stumbled into battle at Gettysburg. Later on the 1st an army messenger found Stuart. On the afternoon of 2 July, the cavalry commander, riding ahead of his brigades, reported to Lee at Gettysburg. Lee, according to tradition, said, "Well, General Stuart, you are here at last." —JDW

Gholson, Samuel Jameson. CSA b. Madison Cty., Ky., 19 May 1808, Gholson migrated to Mississippi in 1830 from his family's Alabama home, where he had studied law privately. Appointed in 1839 by the Van Buren administration to the Federal bench in Mississippi, Gholson was a U.S. judge for 22 years before the Civil War. His early public career also included terms in the state legislature and a brief, stormy period in the U.S. House of Representatives marked by an argument, nearly ending in a duel, with HENRY A. WISE, a future Confederate governor of Virginia.

LC

A STATES-RIGHTS advocate, Gholson was a delegate to the 1860 Democratic convention and a member of the 1861 Mississippi secession convention. When civil war began he joined state troops as a private, rose to major, then colonel of the 14th Mississippi. At the Battle of FORT DONELSON, he served with the rank of brigadier general of state troops. He was shot through the right lung and surrendered with the garrison. After exchange, he served under Maj. Gen. STERLING PRICE in the Battles of IUKA and CORINTH, was made major general of state troops in 1863, then was commissioned brigadier general in the Confederate army to rank from 6 May 1864. His last assignment, under cavalry commander Brig. Gen. JAMES R.

CHALMERS in the Department of Mississippi and East Louisiana, ended 27 Dec. 1864, when he was wounded in a skirmish at Egypt, Miss., and his left arm was amputated. After the war Gholson returned to the state legislature and fought Reconstruction policies. d. Aberdeen, Miss., 16 Oct. 1883.

—JES

Gibbon, John. USA b. Philadelphia, Pa., 20 Apr. 1827, Gibbon moved when a small boy to Charlotte, N.C.; he entered West Point from that state, graduating 20th in the class of 1847 with AMBROSE E. BURNSIDE and AMBROSE P. HILL. After service in the Mexican and Seminole wars and 5 years at West Point as artillery instructor, he was sent to Fort Leavenworth as captain of the 4th U.S. Artillery. Though 3 of his brothers went south when war began, he remained with the North.

LC

Gibbon had written the basic *Artillerist's Manual,* published by the War Department in 1860. Because of his qualifications, Brig. Gen. IRVIN MCDOWELL made him chief of artillery Oct. 1861. However, when he became a brigadier, 2 May 1862, he was given a brigade of 1 Indiana and 3 Wisconsin regiments; to bolster their morale he had them distinctively outfitted with tall black felt hats and white gaiters, and they became known as the Black Hat Brigade. A few months later, at SOUTH MOUNTAIN, thanks to a compliment from Maj. Gen. JOSEPH HOOKER, it became known as the IRON BRIGADE. Gibbon went on to divisional command in Maj. Gen. JOHN F. REYNOLDS' I Corps, was wounded at FIRST FREDERICKSBURG, and returned to lead the 2d Division of Maj. Gen. WINFIELD S. HANCOCK's II Corps. He was wounded again at GETTYSBURG, commanded briefly the draft depots at Philadelphia and Cleveland, returned to his division in time to fight through all the battles of Lt. Gen. ULYSSES S. GRANT's campaign against PETERSBURG, and became major general as of 7 June 1864. By January 1865 he was commanding the XXIV Corps and at Appomattox was one of the commissioners who received the surrender of Gen. Robert E. Lee's army.

After the war Gibbon fought Indians in the West, became Regular Army brigadier 10 July 1885, wrote his *Personal Recollections of the Civil War* (1928), and was commander in chief of the MILITARY ORDER OF THE LOYAL LEGION when he died in Baltimore 6 Feb. 1896.

Theodore Lyman, a Union soldier and prominent zoologist, called him "steel-cold General Gibbon . . . the most American of Americans." —RDH

Gibson, Randall Lee. CSA b. Woodford Cty., near Versailles, Ky., 10 Sept. 1832. After a public and private education at his parents' Louisiana plantation, Gibson received a degree from Yale University in 1853, studied law in New Orleans, spent years traveling in Europe, and briefly served as U.S. embassy attaché in Madrid.

Returning home shortly before the Civil War, when Louisiana seceded from the Union he became an aide to Gov. THOMAS O. MOORE, in Mar. 1861 joining the 1st Louisiana

Artillery as captain. Later commissioned colonel of the 13th Louisiana Infantry, he led the regiment to SHILOH and there commanded the 1st Brigade of Brig. Gen. DANIEL RUGGLES' division in early assaults on the Federal "HORNETS' NEST" position. Commended for his efforts, he went on to fight through the Army of Tennessee's 1862 KENTUCKY CAMPAIGN and at the Battle of CHICKAMAUGA. He was promoted to brigadier general 11 Jan. 1864 and fought at AT-

GG

LANTA and in the FRANKLIN AND NASHVILLE CAMPAIGN. On the dispersal of Gen. JOHN B. HOOD's army, he was assigned to the defense at MOBILE, Ala.

A suave, polished officer, Gibson, commanding besieged Spanish Fort, inspired his men to hold to the last extremity, then led them in a daring night escape 8 Mar. 1865. This ended his Civil War service.

His postbellum career included the practice of law and election to 4 terms in the U.S. House of Representatives, 1872–82, and 2 in the Senate, beginning in 1883. He died in Hot Springs, Ark., 15 Dec. 1892 during his second senatorial term.   —JES

Gilbert, Charles Champion.

USA   b. Zanesville, Ohio, 1 Mar. 1822, Gilbert was appointed to West Point from Ohio, graduated 21st in the class of 1846, and served with distinction in the Mexican War and on frontier duty.

Wounded as a captain commanding Regulars at the 1861 Battle of WILSON'S CREEK, Mo., in 1862 he saw duty as inspector general for the Department of the Cumberland, then the Army of the Ohio; service in the Battles of SHILOH, Tenn., and RICHMOND, Ky.; and temporary duty as "acting major general" of the small Army of Kentucky. Brevetted a major in the Regulars 7 Apr. 1862, then brigadier general of volunteers 4 Sept. 1862,

LC

he met his military downfall the next month at the Battle of PERRYVILLE. In a series of articles written after the war for the *Southern Bivouac* and condensed in *Battles and Leaders of the Civil War* (1885–87), Gilbert claimed that his Provisional III Corps, making up the Union center at Perryville, had saved Maj. Gen. ALEXANDER M. MCCOOK's corps from destruction. At the time, Gilbert's superiors had charged him with mishandling his men and had him relieved from field command.

Though Gilbert was routinely brevetted lieutenant colonel in the Regulars for his Perryville service, his commission as brigadier general was not reconfirmed by the Senate and lapsed 4 Mar. 1863. For the rest of the war he assumed a desk position as major of the 19th Infantry.

Postbellum, Gilbert continued in the army on frontier duty as colonel of the 17th Infantry until compulsory retirement 1 Mar. 1886. d. Baltimore, 17 Jan. 1903.   —JES

Gillem, Alvan Cullen.

USA   b. Gainesboro, Tenn., 29 July 1830. Reared and educated in rustic central Tennessee, Gillem studied in Nashville, then attended West Point, graduating 11th in the class of 1851.

After duty in Florida and on the frontier, he began his Union Civil War service as a captain and assistant quartermaster in the Tennessee theater.

After duty at the Battles of MILL SPRINGS and SHILOH, and a period as chief quartermaster for the Army of the Ohio, Gillem was made colonel of the Union 10th Tennessee Infantry 13 May 1862. He took part in Maj. Gen. HENRY W. HALLECK's march on CORINTH, Miss., then became provost marshal of

LC

Nashville. Influential friend and fellow Tennessean ANDREW JOHNSON saw that Gillem was made adjutant general of that state June 1863 and appointed brigadier general to rank from 17 Aug. Until 1868 he retained positions with the state Reconstruction regime; in Jan. 1865 he was appointed vice-president of the Tennessee constitutional convention; in Apr. 1865 he became a state legislator; and through 1866 he was commander of the military District of East Tennessee.

Concurrent with his civil service, Gillem saw cavalry duty in East Tennessee in 1864, fighting engagements at Greenville and Morristown, raiding in southwest Virginia, riding with Maj. Gen. GEORGE STONEMAN in western North Carolina raids, and fighting at Salisbury, N.C.

Gillem was brevetted brigadier general in the Regulars 13 Mar. 1865 for his war service, major general in the Regulars 12 Apr., and was appointed major general of volunteers 3 Nov. 1865. After reassignment to Mississippi and Arkansas in 1868, service in Texas, and commanding troops in the 1873 Modoc Indian War, he went on sick leave. d. Soldier's Rest, Tenn., 2 Dec. 1875.   —JES

Gillmore, Quincy Adams.

USA   b. Lorain Cty., Ohio, 28 Feb. 1825. Graduation at the top of the U.S. Military Academy class of 1849 gave Gillmore a commission in the Corps of Engineers. Before the Civil War he helped build forts, 1849–52; taught at West Point, 1852–56; headed the Engineer Agency in New York City, 1856–61; and attained the rank of 1st lieutenant.

Assigned chief engineer of the PORT ROYAL Expedition, he first won recognition for the bombardment and capture of FORT PULASKI, Ga., outside Savannah, where he used rifled guns to destroy masonry fortifications designed to withstand artillery. Consequently, he was

USMHI

appointed brigadier general as of 28 Apr. 1862 and sent to Kentucky, where he served competently but had no opportunity to display his strongest talents.

On 10 July 1863 he was promoted to major general and assigned to command the Department of the South and the X Corps. Conducting operations against Charleston, S.C., he achieved the captures of Morris Island and BATTERY (FORT) WAGNER and the destruction of Fort Sumter.

In May 1864 Gillmore's X Corps was assigned to serve in the Army of the James under Maj. Gen. BENJAMIN F. BUTLER, a man of dazzling ineptitude in battle and of equally dazzling brilliance in political warfare. When the Army of the Potomac struck Gen. ROBERT E. LEE in the spring campaign, the way to Richmond lay open to the Army of the James, but Butler bungled. To recover, he managed to blame a series of fiascoes on Gillmore, who deserved only a proportionate share, and sent his subordinate to Washington in disgrace. In July, Gillmore participated in the defense of Washington against Lt. Gen. JUBAL A. EARLY, during which his horse fell, injuring him so severely that he could undertake only nominal duty for the rest of the war.

Gillmore remained in the Corps of Engineers until his death in Brooklyn, N.Y., 7 Apr. 1888. For many years he worked to improve the fortifications off the south Atlantic coast, including some he had helped destroy during the Civil War, and to improve some of the harbors he had helped close. *See also* GILLMORE MEDAL. —JYS

Gillmore Medal. Union Maj. Gen. QUINCY A. GILLMORE had 400 bronze medals struck by Ball, Black, & Company of New York to reward enlisted personnel who had distinguished themselves in operations against Charleston, S.C., and Fort Sumter in summer 1863. On the obverse, Fort Sumter was shown in ruins; Gillmore's engraved autograph sat on the reverse. Called "medals of honor," they featured clasps engraved with the recipient's name, rank, and regiment. A certificate was supplied explaining why the medal had been awarded. Gillmore requested that regimental commanders submit the names of soldiers deserving the honor. —JES

Gilmer, Jeremy Francis. CSA b. Guilford Cty., N.C., 23 Feb. 1818. Son of a U.S. Army officer and brother of a Confederate congressman, Gilmer graduated 4th in the 31-man West Point class of 1839. His class standing brought him a lieutenancy in the Corps of Engineers and an instructorship at his alma mater. Later he assisted in the construction of Fort Schuyler, N.Y., and served as assistant chief of engineers in the Federal capital, 1844–46. During the Mexican War he was chief engineer of the army in New Mexico, building Fort Marcy at Santa Fe. Harbor and river improvement projects lasted many months after the war, as did the construction of Forts Jackson

LC

and Pulaski. Shortly before the outbreak of the Civil War, he was in charge of erecting defenses at the entrance to San Francisco Bay.

In June 1861 Gilmer resigned his captain's commission to enter the Confederate army as a lieutenant colonel of engineers. He headed the engineer staff of Gen. ALBERT SIDNEY JOHNSTON, commander of Confederate Department No. 2. Gilmer was present for the campaign of FORTS HENRY AND DONELSON and during the second day at SHILOH was severely wounded. On 4 Aug. 1862, having recovered from his wound, he was named chief engineer of the Department of Northern Virginia; 2 months later he became head of the Bureau of Engineers in the Confederate War Department. Richmond remained his home for almost a year.

On 25 Aug. 1863 Gilmer was jumped to major general and was sent to South Carolina to improve the defenses of Charleston. As second-in-command of the DEPARTMENT OF SOUTH CAROLINA, GEORGIA, AND FLORIDA, he served through the formative period of the Siege of CHARLESTON before his transfer to defense duty at Atlanta and Savannah. He relinquished the post at Savannah 2 Apr. 1864, when he returned to Richmond to resume his duties in the Bureau of Engineers. He remained behind a desk for the rest of the war; by its close he was generally regarded as the ablest military engineer in Confederate service.

Postbellum, Gilmer was a civil engineer in Savannah and was briefly involved in railroad enterprise. He also served as president of the Savannah Gas Light Co. from 1867 until his death in that city 1 Dec. 1883. —EGL

Gilmor, Harry. CSA b. Baltimore Cty., Md., 24 Jan. 1838. Given a private education and farm experience on the family estate, "Glen Ellen," Gilmor left Maryland, tried homesteading in Wisconsin and Nebraska territories, then returned to join the Maryland Militia and take part in local secessionist politics. When his state came under Federal occupation he was arrested and jailed for 2 weeks on suspicion of subversive activity. On 31 Aug. 1861, after riding into Virginia, he enlisted in Confederate Col. TURNER ASHBY'S cavalry near Charlestown and served 6 months on scouting and regular duties in early Shenandoah Valley operations.

USMHI

Though inspired by Ashby's example of independence in the field, he was unable to secure command of a Virginia Partisan Ranger unit. On 12 Mar. 1862 he accepted a commission as captain of Company F/12th Virginia Cavalry.

Until early 1865 Gilmor participated in most of the major battles fought by the Army of Northern Virginia. His most distinguished service consisted of raiding, scouting, and supporting Confederate partisans Col. JOHN S. MOSBY and Capt. JOHN H. MCNEILL. During the Sept. 1862 Confederate advance into Maryland, Gilmor unwisely left the main force to visit a friend 7 mi outside Baltimore. Captured there by Federals, and first charged with espionage and locked in the Baltimore city jail, he was later transferred to Fort McHenry, then exchanged as a prisoner of war Feb. 1863. Promoted to major late in spring and given command of the 1st Maryland Battalion (later reorganized as the 2d Maryland) for independent service, he fought through the GETTYSBURG CAMPAIGN attached to Lt. Gen. RICHARD S. EWELL'S II Corps, then accelerated partisan raiding in the Shenandoah, he and his men often disguised as Union cavalry or civilians. In Feb. 1864, at the direction of Mosby, Gilmor and 28 men tried to cut Baltimore & Ohio Railroad lines as a distraction from Confederate operations to the west. A train was stopped; some of Gilmor's men reportedly robbed passengers and bothered women. Shocked Southern authorities brought charges against the major. Acquitted by court-martial, he participated in raids around Baltimore, took part in the 30 June 1864 burning of CHAMBERSBURG, Pa., and was wounded and briefly disabled in a skirmish before the Battles of WINCHESTER and FISHER'S HILL. His activities earned him Maj. Gen. PHILIP H. SHERIDAN's personal enmity. On 5 Feb. 1865, Union Maj. Harry Young and a small party disguised as Confederate cavalry rode into Moorefield, Va., and abducted Gilmor from a bed in a private home. Hurried back to Federal lines, he was sent to FORT WARREN, Boston harbor, for the duration of the war.

After parole Gilmor authored a partly ghost-written memoir of his unusual service, *Four Years in the Saddle* (1866), then became a Baltimore businessman and police commissioner, 1874–79. He died in that city, 4 Mar. 1883. —JES

Gilmore, Joseph Albree. war governor b. Weston, Vt., 10 June 1811. His education cut short by his father's death, Gilmore went to Boston to join an older brother in business. At 21, after clerking in a store, he went to work for himself. In 1842 he moved to Concord, N.H., where he established a store at the northern terminus of the New England railway system; its location made him prosperous. 6 years later he became construction agent of the Concord & Claremont Railroad and in 1856 superintendent of the road.

An old-line Whig, Gilmore joined the Republican party in the late 1850s and was elected to the New Hampshire legislature under its standard; in 1859 he became president of the state senate and in 1863 was his party's regular nominee for governor. "Lacking fire and enthusiasm," he ran a lackluster race; neither he nor his opponents, who included an independent Republican, received a majority of the vote. The race was thrown into the legislature, which elected Gilmore despite his having won 2,500 fewer votes than his Democratic rival.

Gilmore entered the gubernatorial mansion at a time of bleak Union military and political prospects. ABRAHAM LINCOLN's government viewed him warily, especially when he remonstrated against CONSCRIPTION and demanded the removal of provost marshals from his state. Later, however, he made strenuous efforts to spur statewide enlistments. He proclaimed that New Hampshire would need no further draft, because "her sons will rise in their might, and, like an avalanche from their icy hills, sweep the last traces of armed treason into the Gulf of Mexico." Backing rhetoric with action, he raised enough recruits to ease Lincoln's mind.

Renominated by his party, Gilmore won a second term Mar. 1864 with a majority of nearly 6,000 votes. Grateful for the improved military situation, he wired Sec. of War EDWIN M. STANTON that "the soldiers of New Hampshire have aided civilians and citizens to achieve a great constitutional victory." Thereafter he strove to cut red tape hindering his continued support of the war, an effort that involved him in feuds with the legislature but also, as one biographer writes, "earned him an honorable place among the war governors." In failing health by the end of his second term, he retired from public life in 1865. After a lengthy illness, he died in Concord 17 Apr. 1867. —EGL

Girardey, Victor Jean Baptiste. CSA b. Lauw, France, 26 June 1837, Girardey, at 5, emigrated with his family to the U.S., settling in Augusta, Ga. Orphaned at 16, he moved to New Orleans, completed his education, and married. When the Civil War began, he enlisted as a 1st lieutenant and aide-de-camp of the 3d Georgia.

LC

Transferring to Virginia in 1862, with the rank of captain Girardey joined the staff of Brig. Gen. AMBROSE R. WRIGHT as assistant adjutant general. He served on Wright's staff until May 1864, when he was transferred to the divisional staff of Brig. Gen. WILLIAM MAHONE. His performance during the campaigning of 1862 and 1863 was repeatedly commended by Wright and his superiors.

On 30 July 1864, when the Union army exploded its mine at Petersburg and assaulted the ruptured Confederate lines, Girardey organized and timed Mahone's counterattack in the Battle of the CRATER. For his brilliant performance, he was promoted from captain to brigadier general, the only instance of this in the army during the war. 17 days later, 16 Aug., while commanding Wright's brigade, the new brigadier was killed near Fussell's Mill on the Darbytown road. Girardey was buried in Augusta. —JDW

Gist, States Rights. CSA b. Union, S.C., 3 Sept. 1831, Gist was a graduate of South Carolina College and the Harvard University Law School. An attorney in his home state, he became active in the militia, rose to state brigadier general in 1859, and prepared South Carolinians for war. After South Carolina seceded, as state adjutant and inspector general he acquired arms for and oversaw the bombardment of FORT SUMTER. As a volunteer aide to South Carolina Brig. Gen. BARNARD E. BEE, he witnessed the FIRST BATTLE OF BULL RUN, and on Bee's death the day after the battle assumed temporary command of his brigade.

LC

After returning to South Carolina and duties as adjutant general, Gist received appointment as a Confederate brigadier general 20 Mar. 1862 and was sent to state coastal defenses commanded by Maj. Gen. JOHN C. PEMBERTON. On Pemberton's encirclement at VICKSBURG, Miss., Gist joined Gen. JOSEPH E. JOHNSTON's failed relief expedition to the city. His reassignment to the Army of Tennessee and combat duty at CHICKAMAUGA, CHATTANOOGA, and the battle for ATLANTA followed.

Gist commanded a brigade in Maj. Gen. JOHN C. BROWN's division during Gen. JOHN B. HOOD's FRANKLIN AND NASHVILLE CAMPAIGN. In the assault on the Federal center at the Battle of FRANKLIN, while leading his troops on foot, he was killed 30 Nov. 1864, 1 of 6 Confederate generals to die as a result of the fight. —JES

Gladden, Adley Hogan. CSA b. Fairfield, S.C., 28 Oct. 1810. A Columbia, S.C., cotton broker and postmaster, and a veteran volunteer of the Seminole and Mexican wars, Gladden was a resident of New Orleans at the start of the Civil War. He briefly held the lieutenant colonelcy of a South Carolina regiment, resigned it to join the Louisiana secession convention, then accepted appointment as colonel of the 1st Louisiana.

_LC_

Throughout the Civil War, Gladden served under Gen. BRAXTON BRAGG, first at Pensacola and the Siege of FORT PICKENS, later in the occupation of CORINTH, Miss., in 1862, then in the Battle of SHILOH. He was appointed brigadier general 30 Sept. 1861 and, on organization of the campaign to Shiloh, took command of a brigade made up of his 1st Louisiana, Maj. FELIX H. ROBERTSON's battery, and the 21st, 22d, 25th, and 26th Alabama regiments. As the 1st brigade of Brig. Gen. JONES M. WITHERS' division in Bragg's Corps, at Shiloh Gladden's men were so heavily engaged that in a short time Gladden and his second- and third-in-command were all severely wounded.

Gladden had an arm amputated on the field and died 12 Apr. 1862.   —JES

Glendale, Va., Battle of. 30 June 1862 _See_ WHITE OAK SWAMP, VA., BATTLE OF.

Globe Tavern, Va., Battle of. 18–21 Aug. 1864 _See_ WELDON RAILROAD OPERATIONS 22 June–21 Aug. 1864.

Glorieta Pass, New Mexico Territory, Battle of. 26–28 Mar. 1862 _See_ LA GLORIETA PASS, NEW MEXICO TERRITORY, BATTLE OF.

Godwin, Archibald Campbell. CSA b. Nansemond Cty., Va., date unknown, 1831. Moving to North Carolina early in life, Godwin went into business there before seeking a new life on the Pacific Coast. In his early twenties he was a successful miner and rancher in California. Some years later he entered politics and barely lost the Democratic nomination for governor in 1860.

When war came, Godwin hastened east. In Virginia he received a Confederate staff appointment and was detailed provost marshal in charge of Richmond's LIBBY PRISON, with the rank of major. He returned to North Carolina to supervise construction of SALISBURY PRISON, an assignment he relinquished to raise and command the 57th North Carolina Infantry.

In his first 4 battles, Godwin performed with skill and tenacity. At FREDERICKSBURG, 13 Dec. 1862, his regiment held the extreme Confederate right, a position assailed by a large enemy force at the height of the battle. The 57th North Carolina counterattacked and shoved their antagonists far to the rear, saving a beleaguered artillery unit. The following May, at CHANCELLORSVILLE, Godwin's outfit was one of those in Maj. Gen. JUBAL A. EARLY's division that repulsed a series of Union efforts to seize much of the same ground contested at Fred-

icksburg. At GETTYSBURG, 2 July 1863, Godwin took command of Brig. Gen. ROBERT F. HOKE's brigade on the mortal wounding of its senior colonel and led a gallant though unsuccessful attack on a bank of Union cannon west of CULP'S HILL. And during the disastrous defeat at RAPPAHANNOCK STATION, 4 months after Gettysburg, he was captured after refusing to surrender, even though surrounded, heavily outnumbered, cut off from his supports, and with his brigade reduced to about 70 effectives. Until his capture, he threatened to shoot any man who surrendered before being physically overpowered.

For his gallantry, the Army of Northern Virginia made exceptional efforts to secure Godwin's parole and exchange. Returning to the field in mid-1864, he was raised to brigadier general 5 Aug. 5 weeks later, 19 Sept., he was killed by a shell fragment at THIRD WINCHESTER, "nobly doing his duty" to the end.
                                                                              —EGL

Goggin, James Monroe. CSA b. Bedford Cty., Va., 23 Oct. 1820, Goggin enjoyed a varied antebellum career. He attended West Point but did not graduate; emigrated to the Republic of Texas, serving in its army as a lieutenant; traveled in 1848 to California, where he established mail routes; and eventually settled in Memphis, Tenn., in the cotton-brokerage business.

_GG_

With the advent of war, Goggin enlisted as major of the 32d Virginia, serving under Maj. Gen. JOHN B. MAGRUDER until spring 1862, when he transferred to staff. Assigned to Maj. Gen. LAFAYETTE MCLAWS' division as assistant adjutant general, Goggin served on the division's staff for the rest of the war. Under McLaws and later under Maj. Gen. JOSEPH B. KERSHAW, he participated in all the major campaigns in the East and at CHICKAMAUGA. Goggin was cited often for bravery and fidelity.

During the Battle of CEDAR CREEK, 19 Oct. 1864, Goggin commanded the brigade of Brig. Gen. JAMES CONNER, who was temporarily absent. For his service as a staff officer and his performance in the latter battle, he was promoted to brigadier general 4 Dec. 1864. The commission, however, was revoked, and he returned to Kershaw's staff. On 6 Apr. 1865, at SAYLER'S CREEK, Va., Goggin and Kershaw fell into Federal hands.

After the war Goggin returned to Texas, subsequently living in Austin, where he died 10 Oct. 1889.   —JDW

Gold Hoax of 1864. On the morning of 18 May 1864, 2 New York newspapers, the _World_ and the _Journal of Commerce,_ hit the streets containing another proclamation from the president of the U.S. In doleful words, Abraham Lincoln recounted recent military disasters, asked for a day of humiliation, prayer, and fasting, and the conscription of another 400,-000 men.

The public document created an immediate furor—the stock exchange shuddered in feverish activity; the price of gold shot up 10%. The other 5 dailies had not printed the proclamation and word rapidly spread along Wall Street that it was spurious, perpetrated by the 2 papers or some cunning villain. Businessmen stormed the *Journal*'s office. Before the uproar subsided, this skillfully fabricated and executed scheme had far-reaching ramifications.

The perpetrator of the hoax was the city editor of the Brooklyn *Eagle,* JOSEPH HOWARD, JR. A man of notorious reputation, Howard surmised that more dire news would send the price of gold upward. By speculating in the market a few days earlier, Howard hoped to realize a quick profit. Enlisting the aid of Francis A. Mallison, a young reporter for the *Eagle,* Howard duplicated an Associated Press dispatch and foisted it on the 2 newspapers. An alert night editor prevented the other 5 papers from publishing the feature.

When Lincoln and 2 of his cabinet officers, EDWIN M. STANTON and WILLIAM H. SEWARD, learned of the bogus proclamation, they overreacted. Believing the newspapers were to blame, they ordered Maj. Gen. JOHN A. DIX, commandant of the Department of the East, to seize the 2 publications and the Independent Telegraph line, which had been accused of sending the dispatch. Dix obeyed reluctantly, convinced that the businesses were innocent victims.

Howard was arrested 20 May, having boasted that there would be changes in the stock market. He immediately implicated Mallison and exonerated the papers and the telegraph company. Lincoln released Howard after 3 months of incarceration.

The president had been publicly embarrassed by his rash suppression of the newspapers; seeking reelection, he could ill afford additional attacks on his record. Though New York Democratic Gov. HORATIO SEYMOUR vainly tried to have Dix indicted, he was cleared. Ironically Lincoln had indeed planned a call for the draft of more men, but the public outcry delayed it 2 months. Nothing, said a witness, angered Lincoln more during the war than the Gold Hoax.   —JDW

Goldsborough, John Rodgers. USN b. District of Columbia, 2 July 1809. Though designated passed midshipman by Capt. David Porter 1 Dec. 1823, Goldsborough did not receive his official appointment from the Navy Department until 16 Nov. 1824. Before that date he served under Porter aboard the *North Carolina* in an expedition against pirates. Goldsborough became a lieutenant in 1837, commander in 1855, and captain in 1862.

From May 1861 until Sept. 1863, Goldsborough performed effective service in blockading the South as commander of the *Union,* the *Florida,* and the *Colorado.* Aboard the *Union* May 1861, he initiated the

USMHI

blockade of Savannah. The following year, as commander of the *Florida,* he was senior officer of the blockading squadron off Charleston. From Mar. to Sept. 1863 he was in command of the blockaders off Mobile.

In Nov. 1863 Goldsborough became inspector in charge of ordnance at the Portsmouth, N.H., Navy Yard. From 1865 to 1868 he commanded the *Shenandoah* on a cruise to Japan and Korea. His promotion to commodore came in 1867. Goldsborough's last years of naval service were spent as head of the

Mare Island Navy Yard and the naval station at Mound City, Ill.

He retired in 1872 and died in Philadelphia 22 June 1877. His older brother was career naval officer LOUIS M. GOLDSBOROUGH.   —NCD

Goldsborough, Louis Malesherbes. USN b. District of Columbia, 18 Feb. 1805. Goldsborough received his lieutenant's commission in 1825. During the decades prior to the Civil War, he served on various foreign stations, commanded a steamboat expedition in the Seminole War and the ship of the line *Ohio* during the Mexican War, and served as superintendent of the Naval Academy. He held the rank of captain in 1861.

On the outbreak of war he was appointed to command the Atlantic Blockading Squadron and, when it was divided, the NORTH ATLANTIC BLOCKADING SQUADRON. Commanding the fleet that in Feb. 1862 attacked ROANOKE ISLAND, N.C., Goldsborough earned the THANKS OF CONGRESS for the capture of the island and the closing of the North Carolina sounds. He was subsequently criticized for not being present at the Battle of HAMPTON ROADS when the Confederate ironclad *VIRGINIA* attacked units of his squadron, as well as for his policy during Maj. Gen. GEORGE B. MCCLELLAN'S PENINSULA CAMPAIGN. When in July 1862 the James River Flotilla, an independent command, was created from his squadron, Goldsborough asked to be relieved from command of the North Atlantic Blockading Squadron. The day after he requested this relief, he was promoted to rear admiral.

From Sept. 1862 until Apr. 1865 Goldsborough performed administrative duties for the Navy Department in Washington, D.C. In Feb. 1865 the department decided to reestablish a squadron in European waters and appointed Goldsborough to the command. His major responsibility was to destroy the Confederate commerce cruisers *RAPPAHANNOCK, SHENANDOAH* and *TALLAHASSEE* and the ironclad ram *STONEWALL,* believed to be somewhere in European waters (*see* CRUISERS, CONFEDERATE). Though the Civil War was over by July, when Goldsborough reached Europe, he was ordered to seize any former "rebel vessels." None was captured, however, and after 2 years he relinquished command of the squadron and returned to the U.S. He retired in 1871 and died in the District of Columbia, 20 Feb. 1873. Cmdr. JOHN R. GOLDSBOROUGH was his younger brother.   —WNS

Goodwin, Ichabod. war ˙governor b. North Berwick, Maine, 8 Oct. 1794, Goodwin, descended from colonial stock, attended a local academy, then became a clerk in a mercantile firm in Portsmouth, N.H. At 20 he served the firm as supercargo on a merchant vessel and, after 2 sea voyages, spent a dozen years as ship's master and owner. He then founded a trading house in Portsmouth, amassed considerable wealth, and entered politics. As a Whig he spent 6 terms in the New Hampshire legislature and was a delegate to 3 national conventions. He pursued several unsuccessful bids for a congressional seat, as well as one for the governor's chair. After joining the Republican fold, he was elected governor of New Hampshire in 1859 and reelected the following year.

From the first, Goodwin enjoyed the support of ABRAHAM LINCOLN's administration; Lincoln himself made several speeches promoting his reelection. In 1860, the governor at first downplayed Southern threats to secede, considering sectional unrest "not unusual upon the recurrence of each presidential canvass." But when war beckoned, he made good his pledge that the Granite State would defend the Union with all its might. When Lincoln called for volunteers, New Hampshire's legislature was not sitting. Unwilling to delay the state's response by calling a special session, Goodwin gained the cooperation of local bankers and borrowed $680,000 to supply and arm 2 regiments. Though frugal in spending the outlay, he produced impressive results. One historian has commented that the 1st New Hampshire Volunteers went to war "so fully equipped that it could have lived entirely to itself and conducted an independent campaign for weeks." Though many of his actions in behalf of the war effort were extra-legal, Goodwin had the satisfaction of seeing them sanctioned by the passage of enabling laws during the legislature's next session.

Despite being a candidate for reelection Mar. 1861, the moderate governor was passed over by the RADICAL REPUBLICANS, who had gained control of the state party. His successor, Nathaniel S. Berry, benefited from the smooth-running governmental machinery Goodwin had constructed. In private life, Goodwin pursued various business ventures, including the presidencies of several railroads, until his death in Portsmouth 4 July 1882. —EGL

Gordon, George Washington. CSA b. Giles Cty., Tenn., 5 Oct. 1836. Reared and educated in rural Mississippi and Texas, Gordon went to the Nashville, Tenn., Western Military Institute, where he studied engineering under future Confederate Gen. BUSHROD R. JOHNSON. Graduating in 1859, he took up surveying and entered Confederate service in 1861 as drillmaster of the 11th Tennessee Infantry.

Under Brig. Gen. FELIX K. ZOLLICOFFER, then Maj. Gen. E. KIRBY SMITH, he served in East Tennessee; was successively promoted captain, lieutenant colonel, then colonel in Dec. 1862; and fought in the Battle of STONE'S RIVER as part of the 2d

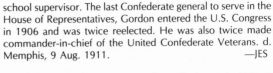

LC

Brigade in Maj. Gen. JOHN P. MCCOWN's division. Gordon soldiered through the Battles of CHICKAMAUGA, CHATTANOOGA, and the ATLANTA fighting, and was made brigadier general to rank from 15 Aug. 1864. He led a brigade in Maj. Gen. JOHN C. BROWN's division in Gen. JOHN B. HOOD'S FRANKLIN AND NASHVILLE CAMPAIGN, and at the Battle of FRANKLIN 30 Nov. 1864 led the group of Brown's men that made the deepest penetration of the Federal center. Wounded and captured there, he was shipped east and finished the war a prisoner in FORT WARREN, Boston harbor.

Released from prison July 1865, Gordon settled in Memphis and studied law. He then became an attorney, a state railroad commissioner, a U.S. Indian agent in the West, and a Memphis

school supervisor. The last Confederate general to serve in the House of Representatives, Gordon entered the U.S. Congress in 1906 and was twice reelected. He was also twice made commander-in-chief of the United Confederate Veterans. d. Memphis, 9 Aug. 1911. —JES

Gordon, James Byron. CSA b. Wilkesborough, N.C., 2 Nov. 1822, Gordon, distant kin of the more famous Confederate Gen. JOHN B. GORDON, was a graduate of Emory and Henry College in Virginia. He then engaged in the mercantile business and served a term in the North Carolina legislature.

Gordon enlisted in 1861 as a private in the Wilkes Valley Guards and was elected its 1st lieutenant, then captain. In May he received an appointment as major of the 1st North Carolina Cavalry. Transferring to Virginia, the regiment joined the brigade of the distinguished South Carolinian Brig. Gen. WADE HAMPTON. Under Hampton, Gordon and the regiment participated in the major campaigns of the Cavalry Corps. Promoted to lieutenant colonel in 1862, colonel in spring 1863, and to brigadier general 28 Sept. 1863, Gordon performed with distinction.

As commander of the North Carolina brigade in these corps, he fought with particular gallantry during the BRISTOE CAMPAIGN in October. In the campaigning of May 1864, Gordon participated in the cavalry operations against Union Maj. Gen. PHILIP H. SHERIDAN's raid on Richmond. Near Meadow Bridge, 12 May, while engaging Federal horsemen, Gordon fell mortally wounded. d. Richmond, 18 May 1864. —JDW

Gordon, John Brown. CSA b. Upson Cty., Ga., 6 Feb. 1832, Gordon attended the University of Georgia but dropped out to study law and become a member of the Atlanta bar. When the Civil War started, he was engaged in a mining operation in the northwest part of the state. Raising a company of mountain men known as the Raccoon Roughs, he was elected its captain. A capable organizer and a hard fighter, Gordon rose swiftly in the Confederate army. On 1 Nov. 1862, after the Battle of ANTIETAM, where he was seriously wounded, he was promoted to brigadier general. He went on to become one of Gen. ROBERT E. LEE's most capable and trusted

LC

officers and was made a major general 14 May 1864. During the last days of the war, he commanded the II Corps/Army of Northern Virginia. He surrendered with the remnants of his corps at APPOMATTOX 9 Apr. 1865.

Gordon returned to Atlanta after the war, resumed the practice of law, became active in Democratic party affairs, and was a leader in the struggle to return Georgia to home rule. The legislature elected him to the U.S. Senate in 1873 and again in 1879. He resigned 26 May 1880 and went to work promoting a railroad venture. Returning to politics in 1886, he was elected governor. At the close of his term, the legislature elected him to the U.S. Senate, where he served a third term, 1891–97.

When the United Confederate Veterans was organized in

1890, Gordon was made commander in chief, a post he held until his death. In 1903 he published an excellent account of his wartime service, *Reminiscences of the Civil War.* He died in Miami, Fla., 9 Jan. 1904 and was buried in Oakland Cemetery, Atlanta. —JOH

Gorgas, Josiah. CSA b. Running Pumps, Pa., 1 July 1818, Gorgas became one of the South's greatest assets during the Civil War. A poor boy who sought to improve himself by securing an appointment to West Point, Gorgas graduated 6th in the class of 1841 and spent most of his years as a junior officer studying and working in ordnance depots and arsenals. His marriage to an Alabama woman, together with his Southern friendships and resentment against abolitionist extremism, induced him to go south in Apr. 1861 and offer his services to the Confederacy.

LC

Gorgas accepted a position as chief of the Ordnance Bureau and the enormous task of arming Confederate armies, directing the collection and distribution of weapons and ammunition available in the South. At the same time he dispatched agents to Europe to purchase arms and began establishing mills and factories throughout the South to manufacture the tools of war at home. His success was extraordinary. Gorgas displayed sound judgment and organizational genius in selecting his subordinates and managing what became a huge war industry.

Early in 1864 he reflected in his diary: "I have succeeded beyond my utmost expectations. . . . Where three years ago we were not making a gun, pistol nor a sabre, no shot nor shell —a pound of powder—we now make all these in quantities to meet the demands of our large armies." Very soon, however, the Confederacy began losing control of its manufacturing establishment because of military capture, and Gorgas spent his final year of the war attempting to patch up his organization and maintain as much efficiency as possible.

At war's end Gorgas was a brigadier general (as of 10 Nov. 1864), but he and his adopted nation had lost all. After a brief attempt at business, he became an educator, first at the University of the South at Sewanee, Tenn., then as president of the University of Alabama. Gorgas died at his home in Tuscaloosa, 15 May 1883. His *Civil War Diary* (1947) and Frank E. Vandiver's *Ploughshares into Swords* (1952) provide an excellent comprehensive history of Confederate ordnance.   —EMT

Govan, Daniel Chevilette. CSA b. Northampton Cty., N.C., 4 July 1829. Born into a family whose ancestors had fled Scotland after the Jacobite uprising of 1747, Govan was the son of a South Carolina congressman. He experienced a peripatetic youth: raised in Mississippi, he spent some years at the University of South Carolina, then moved to California to seek his fortune in company with another future Confederate general, BEN MCCULLOCH. In 1850 the latter was elected sheriff of Sacramento, and Govan left the gold fields to serve as his deputy. 2 years later he returned to Mississippi, farmed, and married. He accompanied his bride to Phillips Cty., Ark., where he lived the

life of a planter till the Civil War erupted.

USMHI

When the Confederacy mobilized, Govan raised a company that became part of the 2d Arkansas Infantry. Elected lieutenant colonel of the regiment, he led it during the Army of Tennessee's operations in Tennessee, including SHILOH; Kentucky, including PERRYVILLE; Mississippi; and Georgia. By late 1862 his conspicuous gallantry under fire had gained him command of a brigade in the division of Maj. Gen. PATRICK R. CLEBURNE, which he directed at STONE'S RIVER, CHICKAMAUGA, MISSIONARY RIDGE, and Ringgold. He was elevated to brigadier general as of 29 Feb. 1863. During the ATLANTA CAMPAIGN he led his 4 Arkansas regiments with skill and courage, receiving accolades from several superiors, including Gen. JOSEPH E. JOHNSTON, who especially praised his conduct at the battle of Pickett's Mills 27 May 1864.

On 1 Sept., at JONESBOROUGH, the battle that doomed Atlanta to Union capture, Govan's brigade and supporting troops were overwhelmed by attacking Federals. Most of the Arkansas troops fought stubbornly, refusing to surrender until overrun. Before part of his brigade broke free and established a new line, Govan and many others were captured. He was parted from the Army of Tennessee for only a short time; paroled and exchanged, he fought under Gen. JOHN BELL HOOD at FRANKLIN and NASHVILLE, as well as in the CAROLINAS CAMPAIGN.

The war over, Govan returned to his Arkansas plantation and resumed farming. In 1894 he moved to Washington State as an Indian agent, a position tendered him by Pres. Grover Cleveland. He returned east 2 years later, following the death of his wife, and lived in Mississippi and Tennessee until his death in Memphis 12 Mar. 1911.   —EGL

Gracie, Archibald, Jr. CSA b. New York, N.Y., 1 Dec. 1832. The son and grandson of prominent New Yorkers, Gracie studied in Heidelberg, Germany, and at the military academy at West Point, graduating 14th in the class of 1854. Following service on the Northwestern frontier, he resigned from the army in 1856, entered a Mobile, Ala., cotton-brokerage business with his father, and became active in the state militia.

USMHI

At the outbreak of the secession crisis, his Unionist father returned to New York City, while Gracie, militia captain of the Washington Light Infantry, allied himself with Alabama Gov. ANDREW B. MOORE. Before the state left the Union, on Moore's order Gracie seized the Federal arsenal at Mount Vernon, Ala. Later, with his men, he joined the 3d Alabama Infantry and went on duty in Virginia. On 12 July 1861 he was made major of the 11th Alabama; early in 1862 he returned home, organized the 43d Alabama, and was elected its colonel. After service in East Tennessee, the Kentucky campaigning, and promotion to brigadier general to rank from 4 Nov. 1862, he fought through the Battle of CHICK-AMAUGA, the Siege of KNOXVILLE, and took a severe wound at BEAN'S STATION, Tenn., 14 Dec. 1863.

Following recuperation and reassignment to Gen. P.G.T. BEAUREGARD's Virginia command May 1864, Gracie saw duty on the PETERSBURG siege lines. He was killed by Union artillery 2 Dec. 1864 while observing enemy movements. The elder Gracie removed his son's body to New York City after the war. Gracie, overweight and with a less than martial appearance, still inspired his men and superiors, and was eulogized in a poem "Gracie, of Alabama" by Francis O. Ticknor.   —JES

Graham, William Alexander. CSP b. Lincoln Cty., N.C., 5 Sept. 1804. Through the antebellum years, Graham condemned secession as disastrous for the South. When the move toward Southern independence peaked in 1861, he participated in the WASHINGTON PEACE CONFERENCE, hoping to find some last-minute compromise to avert disunion. Yet 5 of his sons became officers in the Confederate army and Graham accepted election to the Second CONFEDERATE CONGRESS, where he took a leading role in opposing the Davis administration.

Graham had graduated from the University of North Carolina in 1824, read law under jurist Thomas Ruffin, and settled in Hillsborough, establishing himself as a respected attorney over the next decade. As a moderate Unionist Whig he served as state legislator, 1833–40; U.S. senator, 1840–43; and governor of North Carolina, 1845–49. Pres. Millard Fillmore appointed Graham secretary of the navy in 1850, a position he resigned 2 years later to accept the Whig vice-presidential nomination. Reelected to the Senate in 1854, he supported internal improvements and the expansion of public education much as he had at the state level.

Graham helped organize the Constitutional Union party in hopes of preventing ABRAHAM LINCOLN's election in 1860. When the effort failed, as a delegate to the secession convention, he tried to prevent North Carolina from seceding, standing firm for the Union until Lincoln's call for volunteers. He served in the state senate until defeating GEORGE DAVIS for a seat in the Second Confederate Congress. A consistent peace advocate, he opposed all of JEFFERSON DAVIS' war programs. Though he favored peace with independence, in Feb. 1865 he joined several colleagues in a direct bid to Davis to negotiate a reconstructionist truce that would have restored the South to the Union on an equal footing with the Northern states. A few weeks before Gen. ROBERT E. LEE surrendered, Graham was urging the individual Confederate states to seek peace independently for whatever terms they could secure.

Graham was elected state senator in 1865 but was denied his seat under FEDERAL AMNESTY conditions barring former Confederate politicians from holding office. Though he never again held elected office, Graham remained influential in the conservative faction of North Carolina politics. He returned to his law practice and served as a trustee of the Peabody Fund. Graham died 11 Aug. 1875, at Saratoga Springs, N.Y., while arbitrating a Virginia-Maryland boundary dispute.   —PLF

Granbury, Hiram Bronson. CSA b. Copiah Cty., Miss., 1 Mar. 1831. After an education at Oakland College in Rodney, Miss., Granbury moved to Waco, Tex., in the 1850s, becoming an attorney and an official in McLennan County

government. On the secession of Texas from the Union, he organized the Waco Guards, was sent to duty in Kentucky and Tennessee, and Oct. 1861 was made major of the 7th Texas.

LC

Granbury was captured in the fall of FORT DONELSON Feb. 1862, was exchanged, then received promotion to colonel of the 7th on 29 Aug. 1862. He served in north Mississippi through the VICKSBURG CAMPAIGN; fought at CHICKAMAUGA, the Siege of CHATTANOOGA, the Battle of MISSIONARY RIDGE; and on the Army of Tennessee's Nov. 1863 retreat to north Georgia took over a brigade, receiving praise from division commander Maj. Gen. PATRICK R. CLEBURNE. Granbury became a brigadier general 29 Feb. 1864, leading the 6th, 7th, 10th, 15th, 17th, 19th, 24th, and 25th Texas regiments through the fighting to Atlanta and north again on Gen. JOHN B. HOOD's FRANKLIN AND NASHVILLE CAMPAIGN. At the Battle of FRANKLIN, 30 Nov. 1864, he charged the Union center with Cleburne, was killed before reaching the enemy breastworks, and became one of 6 Confederate generals to die as a result of the battle.   —JES

Grand Army of the Republic. When Federal soldiers returned from the war, they expected to be accorded the honors and privileges due saviors of the Union. Instead they found hard times, few jobs, and little compensation for service-related disabilities. Many disgruntled veterans banded together in political-action groups. By the end of 1865, organizations such as the Soldiers' and Sailors' National Union League and the United Service Society had begun to infiltrate established political parties.

A much larger soldiers' organization began when 2 former generals from Illinois, Richard J. Oglesby and JOHN A. LOGAN, sought to exploit the grievances of veterans to further their political ambitions. Early in 1866, along with a political errand boy, Dr. Benjamin F. Stephenson, the pair laid the basis for the Grand Army of the Republic. A former army surgeon, Stephenson devised an elaborate system of oaths and rituals that played on anti-Confederate sentiment, and on 1 Apr., at Springfield, organized the GAR's first post. The stated goals of the new organization included the promotion of fraternal feelings among veterans, the aiding of needy or disabled comrades, the support of veterans' widows and children, the facilitation of service benefits, and the encouragement of public allegiance to the government. The society also had definite political ends, seeking a mutually advantageous association with the party that had administered the war effort. Wags soon claimed that GAR stood for "Generally All Republicans."

The organization's importance to the Republican party grew with its membership. Within 6 months of the army's formation, Illinois alone boasted 157 posts. Soon neighboring states added chapters, and the society expanded eastward and southward. By mid-1867 virtually every Northern state had GAR posts, as did those former Confederate states where large numbers of Federal veterans had settled. (The latter accepted black members reluctantly or not at all, despite an official policy that accorded them full membership status.)

Late in 1866 the GAR held its first encampment, electing former Maj. Gen. Stephen A. Hurlbut national commander. It was under his successor, General Logan, however, that the society experienced its most significant growth and muscle-flexing. Taking Logan's lead, the GAR vigorously pursued the equalization of wartime bounties, the passage of a national pension law, and the establishment of homes for veterans' orphans. By 1867, thanks to such agitation, the society had become the principal organ through which servicemen expressed their demands. Its clout was demonstrated by the crucial support it gave to ULYSSES S. GRANT's presidential bid the following year.

Over the next 6 decades, the power of the organization waxed and waned according to how badly the Republican party needed its help. The GAR did succeed in enacting many of its pet programs, such as the establishment of Decoration Day (forerunner of Memorial Day) as a national holiday and the passage of a liberal pension bill that, by the first decade of the 20th century, had cost the Treasury over $1 billion. Other programs for which it lobbied achieved partial success, including the addition of patriotic exercises, military instruction, and "loyal" history to the public-school curricula.

The apogee of the GAR's power occurred in 1890, when its membership peaked at 427,981, exclusive of its women's and Sons of Union Veterans auxiliaries. From that time, its strength and influence diminished rapidly and its orientation became increasingly nonpartisan. In 1949 the GAR's 83d and final encampment was attended by 6 of its 16 surviving members. The last comrade, Albert Woolson of Minnesota, a former drummer boy, died in 1956.   —EGL

USMHI

Sherman's Grand Review

Grand Review of the Armies. To celebrate Union victory and power, on 18 May 1865 the War Department ordered a grand review in Washington of the main Northern armies—Maj. Gen. GEORGE G. MEADE's Army of the Potomac and Maj. Gen. WILLIAM T. SHERMAN's Army of Georgia and Army of the Tennessee. The Army of the Potomac passed in review 23 May, with Meade leading more than 80,000 veterans in a proud march down Pennsylvania Avenue.

The next day was the turn of Sherman's forces, and Sherman was apprehensive about the showing his troops would make. They had just completed a 2,000-mi march through Georgia, the Carolinas, and Virginia; they had had little time or use for formal drill; and their uniforms were threadbare and ragged. As Sherman watched the natty-looking Army of the Potomac, he said to Meade, "I'm afraid my poor taddermalion corps will make a poor appearance tomorrow when contrasted with yours."

At 9 a.m., 24 May, beneath a sunny sky, Sherman's 65,000 veterans marched down a Pennsylvania Ave. lined with cheering spectators. Sherman, with his staff and Maj. Gen. OLIVER O. HOWARD, rode at the head. As he looked back, "the sight was simply magnificent. The column was compact, and the glittering muskets looked like a solid mass of steel, moving with the regularity of a pendulum." It was, he later declared, "the happiest and most satisfactory moment of my life."

To observers it seemed as if Sherman's men, most of whom were from the West, were rangier and leaner than the predominantly Eastern soldiers of the Army of the Potomac; they marched with a longer, more swinging stride; and their faces bore a "glory look." Their bands played "The Battle Hymn of the Republic," which they had sung when setting out from Atlanta on the MARCH TO THE SEA. Among their divisions were bodies of stalwart black laborers carrying shovels and picks; squads of the famous BUMMERS brandishing hams and chickens; herds of goats, cattle, and mules; and families of freed slaves.

At 4:30 p.m. the last regiment passed the platform occupied by Pres. ANDREW JOHNSON. The grand review had been, stated Sherman proudly, "a fitting conclusion to the campaign and the war." —AC

Granger, Gordon. USA b. Joy, N.Y., 6 Nov. 1822, Granger was one of many Union generals who served exclusively in the West. Graduating from West Point 35th in the class of 1845, he earned 2 brevets, first lieutenant and captain, for meritorious conduct in the Mexican War, then served in the Mounted Rifles on the frontier until the outbreak of the war.

Granger fought under Brig. Gen. SAMUEL D. STURGIS in Missouri at Dug Spring and WILSON'S CREEK, winning colonelcy of the 2d Michigan Cavalry. Made brigadier 26 Mar. 1862, he commanded a brigade during the succeeding NEW MADRID, ISLAND NO. 10, and CORINTH campaigns. For about a month,

USMHI

during Sept. 1862, Granger led several brigades in the Army of the Ohio. His major generalcy dated from 17 Sept. 1862.

Granger's most significant service came 20 Sept. 1863, at the Battle of CHICKAMAUGA. When the Union line broke and began a confused withdrawal to CHATTANOOGA, Maj. Gen. GEORGE H. THOMAS's corps made a desperate stand on HORSESHOE RIDGE to cover that retreat. Without orders, Granger sent 2 of the 3 brigades of his Reserve Corps to Thomas' aid; they arrived just in time to beat back a Confederate charge and, with Thomas' men, held back the Southerners' assaults until dark, ensuring the safety of Maj. Gen. WILLIAM S. ROSECRANS' army. Granger commanded the IV Corps at Chattanooga, aided in raising the Siege of KNOXVILLE, and served against Forts Gaines and Morgan and in the capture of MOBILE. On sick leave much of the time after the war, he died in Santa Fe, New Mexico Territory, 10 Jan. 1876.

A short, peppery, profane disciplinarian, Granger was not especially well liked by his troops. But he had what was needed to be a good soldier. A note he wrote to Rosecrans might well have been written for himself and Thomas at Chickamauga: "The battle is neither to the swift nor to the strong but to him that holds on to the end." —RDH

Grant, Lewis Addison. USA b. Winhall, Vt., 17 Jan. 1828. Educated in the common schools of Vermont, Grant taught school in New Jersey and Massachusetts, then studied law and successfully practiced his profession in his native state.

On 15 Aug. 1861 Grant was commissioned major of the 5th Vermont. Promoted to lieutenant colonel, he participated in the 1862 campaigns in the East. At SAVAGE'S STATION in June the 5th Vermont suffered grievous casualties. Grant was promoted to colonel 15 Sept., assumed command of the famed Old Vermont Brigade, and led it at FREDERICKSBURG, where he fell wounded.

USMHI

Given permanent command of the brigade, Grant gallantly performed during the battles of 1863–64. In the CHANCELLORSVILLE CAMPAIGN in May 1863, the Vermonters captured 3 Confederate flags in the action at SALEM CHURCH, for which Grant was awarded the MEDAL OF HONOR 11 May 1893. He participated in the GETTYSBURG CAMPAIGN and, with the rank of brigadier general, dated 27 Apr. 1864, fought at the WILDERNESS, SPOTSYLVANIA, and COLD HARBOR. At the Wilderness his brigade lost nearly half its members. During the SHENANDOAH VALLEY CAMPAIGN of 1864, Grant commanded his division at CEDAR CREEK, 19 Oct. In this battle the Confederates launched a surprise attack at dawn, crushing the Union lines. The routed Federals re-formed on Grant's line, from which they counterattacked in the afternoon, defeating the Southern troops. For his distinguished conduct, Grant received the rank of brevet major general. Wounded during the war's final week, he mustered out Aug. 1865.

Declining a commission in the Regular Army, Grant journeyed westward after the war. He lived in Illinois and Iowa before settling permanently in Minneapolis, Minn. From 1890 to 1893 the veteran officer served as assistant secretary of war. Living to the age of 90, Grant died in his adopted city 20 Mar. 1918. —JDW

Grant, Ulysses Simpson. USA b. Point Pleasant, Ohio, 27 Apr. 1822. Christened Hiram Ulysses (his name change began with an error by the congressman who appointed him to West Point), Grant was de-scended from Puritans who emigrated to New England in the early 17th century. The son of a hardworking, acquisitive tanner, he nevertheless grew up quiet, introspective, and seemingly lazy. Despairing for his son's future in business, Jesse Root Grant secured a U.S. Military Academy appointment for the young man in 1839. At West Point, despite a later reputation as an abysmal student, Grant consistently ranked near the class median. He had poor

USMHI

study habits and preferred romance novels to tactics, but was strong in mathematics and equestrianism. Graduating in 1843, he ranked 21st of 39 cadets.

Despite his preference for cavalry service, Grant became a lieutenant in the 4th U.S. Infantry. 4 years after graduating, he fought in Mexico. Though convinced American politicians had provoked the war for territorial gain, he admired its military leaders, especially Zachary Taylor and WINFIELD SCOTT. Laying misgivings aside, he fought well enough to win brevets for gallantry at Molino del Rey and Chapultepec.

After the conflict he served in several remote garrisons, including Fort Humboldt, Calif., early in 1854. There, without Julia, his wife of 6 years, and their 2 children (2 others would follow), he fought boredom and loneliness by drinking—a habit he indulged at various stages of his later career. Though he drank much less frequently than legend has it, he seemed unable to stop until family, friends, or events intervened. In July 1854, smarting under the condemnation of his regimental commander, he resigned his recently received captaincy and returned to his family in Missouri.

There Grant led a hardscrabble existence and was eventually reduced to peddling firewood on St. Louis streets. Forced to rely on the grudging charity of his father, he moved to his parents' home in Galena, Ill., and worked at a variety of jobs—none successfully—till rescued by the Civil War. At first his efforts to join the volunteer army were rebuffed. Finally, thanks to a patronage-minded congressman, ELIHU B. WASHBURNE, and to Gov. RICHARD YATES, Grant became colonel of the 21st Illinois Infantry June 1861. 2 months later, after whipping a rebellious mob into military trim, "Captain Sam" Grant, the Galena ne'er-do-well, found himself a brigadier general of volunteers.

His first effort in command began well but ended in near-disaster during a November offensive against Confederate camps near BELMONT, Mo. Afterward Grant returned to an administrative post until able to recoup lost honor. In Feb. 1862, under the remote supervision of Maj. Gen. HENRY W. HALLECK, ranking commander in the West, he broke the center of the Confederate defense line in that theater by capturing FORTS HENRY AND DONELSON on the Tennessee and Cumberland rivers. His brilliant turning movement against Donelson and his refusal to accept less than its UNCONDITIONAL SURRENDER brought him instant, nationwide fame.

The glory seemed transitory. On 6 Apr. his scattered army

was surprised and almost routed near Pittsburg Landing and SHILOH Church, Tenn., by Confederates under Gen. ALBERT SIDNEY JOHNSTON. On the next day, Grant made amends by repulsing the enemy, but for months public criticism of his military and personal habits blighted his career. His reputation further suffered when his initial attempt to seize the Mississippi River stronghold VICKSBURG was frustrated that December by Confederate supply-line raiders.

Mid-1863 marked the turning point of Grant's career. Aggressive, inspired strategy—characterized by an amphibious movement to a point below Vicksburg and a swift drive inland, without supply lines—melded with hard-hitting TACTICS to cause the city's fall and the Confederacy's division 4 July 1863. His success was rewarded with a promotion to major general in the Regular Army. When, 4 months later, his mission to East Tennessee resulted in raising the Siege of CHATTANOOGA and in the dramatic victories of LOOKOUT MOUNTAIN and MISSIONARY RIDGE, Grant became the Union's preeminent warrior. Formalizing this distinction, Abraham Lincoln made him general-in-chief, at a revived 3-star rank, the following March.

Provided with mammoth resources for the 1864 Virginia campaigning, Grant would go into textbooks as a butcher who slashed and pounded his way to triumph, heedless of cost. This image is false. The multitheater strategy Grant mapped and coordinated in the war's final year (including Maj. Gen. WILLIAM T. SHERMAN's operations in Georgia, Maj. Gen. BENJAMIN F. BUTLER's foray up the James River, and the Shenandoah Valley campaigns of Maj. Gen. PHILIP H. SHERIDAN and his predecessors) was aimed at flanking the enemy and reaching his rear, there to destroy his communications and subsistence. From the WILDERNESS to APPOMATTOX—with a single, costly lapse at COLD HARBOR—Grant sought to outmaneuver rather than outfight Gen. ROBERT E. LEE. Failing to make headway above Richmond, he bypassed Lee in mid-June by an artful turning movement toward PETERSBURG. Frustrated there, Grant employed various indirect offensives that eventually lengthened Lee's lines beyond the breaking point, making inevitable Lee's surrender 9 Apr. 1865. In his most decisive campaign, Grant succeeded not by brute force but by agility, speed, and craft.

In peace, Grant proved unable to utilize effectively the talents that had made him a warrior equal to George Washington and Winfield Scott. As president of the U.S., 1869–77, he lived by the same simple code of ethics that had sustained him since youth. His political naïveté, elementary view of complex situations, and inability to judge the character of his governmental subordinates infused his administration with controversy, corruption, and scandal. Returning glumly to private life, he traveled the world, briefly and disastrously entered business, and finally, to provide for a near-destitute family, began to write. By taking up the pen he regained the stature he had forfeited in laying down the sword. His *Personal Memoirs* (1885), which he completed during a pain-wracked race with throat cancer—to which he succumbed at Mount McGregor, N.Y., 23 July 1885—constitute his greatest monument. His words, like his battlefield tactics, display vigor, precision, economy, and an ironic brilliance.   —EGL

Grant's "Anti-Jew Order" (General Orders No. 11, Holly Springs, Miss.). 17 Dec. 1862 In Nov. 1862 Maj. Gen. ULYSSES S. GRANT, commanding the Department of the Tennessee, sat idle and dejected at La Grange, Tenn. His advance toward Vicksburg had bogged down, and he was not certain that the War Department would support him fully in his present command. Gen.-in-Chief HENRY W. HALLECK was criticizing him for failing to press the Confederate retreat from Corinth, Miss., and a subordinate, Maj. Gen. JOHN A. MCCLERNAND, was trying to usurp Grant's effort to seize control of the Mississippi.

Grant vented his frustration by lashing out at civilian speculators, who had descended *en masse* on his department, buying up confiscated enemy supplies, primarily cotton. These they sold for obscene profits in the North, often with the connivance of army officers and U.S. Treasury agents. Many of these businessmen, including some Jews, had secured favors from Grant through the mediation of his avaricious father. Grant, on 9 and 10 Nov., ordered 2 of his commanders to refuse permits to businessmen wishing to travel south of Jackson, Tenn., adding that "the Israelites especially should be kept out." On 17 Dec. at Holly Springs, Miss., the departmental commander went even further, issuing what one historian has called "the most sweeping anti-Jewish regulation in all American history." His General Orders No. 11 proclaimed that "the Jews, as a class violating every regulation of trade established by the Treasury Department and also department orders, are hereby expelled from the department within twenty-four hours." Evidence indicates that this ban was prompted by the urging of Halleck. Nevertheless, it reflected Grant's unconscious acceptance of the widespread antisemitism of his day.

Several prominent Jewish residents within Grant's department, evicted by the decree, hastened to Washington. To Abraham Lincoln himself they expressed their outrage over this libel against an entire social and religious class. The president, who appeared unaware of the order, had it revoked by Halleck 4 Jan. 1863, but not before it created a controversy in the press, in Congress, and in Jewish and gentile communities throughout the North.　　—EGL

grape shot; canister. Grape shot and canister were scatter-shot projectiles used extensively in the Civil War. Though the army and the navy used both types, the army had officially deleted grape shot from its ammunition tables in favor of canister. Either type of projectile was effective at ranges from about 300–600 yd; extension to 800 yd was possible when the ground was hard enough to allow the balls to ricochet. If grape or canister was fired at too short a range, it would fail to disperse, and while murderous in a small area, it would not be as effective as at longer ranges. On the other hand, at too long a range the balls were overly dispersed. One method used by field batteries to counter close-range problems with canister was to load 2 or 3 and fire them at once. This double or triple canister could be gruesomely effective.

Grape shot consisted of a bottom and top iron plate, the 2 connected by a long bolt. Between were stacked iron balls, usually 9 of them, which were held in place by iron rings. Some Confederate grape shot had more than 9 balls, including some models with as many as 21 balls usually smaller than standard grape, arranged in 7 tiers of 3 each. Another form of grape shot that could accommodate almost any number of balls was "quilted grape." This type consisted of an iron bottom plate with an upright pin around which the balls were piled. The entire round was then encased in a canvas bag and the balls held in place with rope or heavy twine, giving the round a quilted appearance.

Canister was made of iron top and bottom plates over which

ends of a sheet-iron cylinder were bent. Iron balls were placed inside in 4 tiers, the spaces between tightly packed with sawdust. Generally there were 48 iron balls in a round. Sometimes lead musket balls were used, and the navy may have occasionally used brass canister balls.

Both rounds worked essentially the same way. When fired, the fixed round broke apart, producing a massive shotgun effect. Charging enemy troops were usually badly hurt and in some cases virtually annihilated.　　—LDJ

Gray, Henry. CSA　b. Laurens District, S.C., 19 Jan. 1816. After graduating from South Carolina College in 1834, Gray moved to Mississippi, where he served as Winston County district attorney and as a state congressman. He also ran for a U.S. congressional seat as a Whig but lost the election and moved to Louisiana, a state he would adopt as his home. In 1856 he was an elector for James Buchanan and in 1860 lost the U.S. Senate election to JUDAH P. BENJAMIN by 1 vote.

LC

As the war broke out Gray enlisted in a Mississippi state regiment before he took the reins of the 28th Louisiana Infantry as its colonel. His most noteworthy service took place almost entirely within the boundaries of Louisiana, leading his regiment along the Teche, where he was wounded; at Fort Bisland (see IRISH BEND AND FORT BISLAND), "one of those desperate affairs"; and at MANSFIELD and PLEASANT HILL, and in the RED RIVER CAMPAIGN, where he led a brigade in Brig. Gen. ALFRED MOUTON's division.

Had it been up to Gen. E. KIRBY SMITH, commander of the Trans-Mississippi, Gray would not have received his promotion to brigadier general. The officers had become bitter enemies, and Smith refused the promotion because he considered Gray's habits "not good." But Gray had a powerful friend in Confederate Pres. JEFFERSON DAVIS, and 17 Mar. 1865 received his brigadier's star to date from the Battle of MANSFIELD, 8 May 1864.

Despite the disparaging remarks made by Smith, Lt. Gen. RICHARD TAYLOR reported: "Colonel Gray and his regiment, officers and men, deserve most favorable mention. Their gallantry in action is enhanced by the excellent discipline which they have presented. . . ."

In Oct. 1864 Gray was elected to the Confederate Congress while still in the army. After the war he served a term in the Louisiana state senate and retired "in virtual seclusion" until his death 11 Dec. 1892 in Coushatta, La.　　—FLS

Graybeard Regiment. USA　The 37th Iowa Volunteer Infantry, authorized by the Union War Department and Iowa Gov. SAMUEL J. KIRKWOOD, and raised by George W. Kincaid, was a 3-year regiment made up of men 45 years old and older. Organized to relieve able-bodied veteran troops from garrison, prisoner, and guard duties, it boasted some of the oldest soldiers in active service, one being 80. Called the Graybeard Regiment, it mustered into service 914 officers and men Dec. 1862, and on discharge, 24 May 1865, carried 460 names on its roll. Since the regiment served at ALTON PRISON in Illinois; ROCK ISLAND PRISON in the Mississippi; CAMP MORTON, Ohio; and rode guard on the Memphis & Charleston Railroad, most of its casualties came from disease and some rail accidents. Several other men were lost to discharge based on the infirmities of age. —JES

"Gray Ghost of the Confederacy." *See* MOSBY, JOHN S.

Grayson, John Breckinridge. CSA b. Fayette Cty., Ky., 18 Oct. 1806. Entering the U.S. Military Academy in 1822, Grayson graduated 4 years later, 22d in his 41-man class. As an artillery subaltern he served at Fort Monroe, Va.; Augusta, Ga.; and other garrisons in the South. In 1835–36 he was in Florida fighting the Seminoles, thereafter joining the Commissary of Subsistence. He was on staff duty in New Orleans 1836–47, then became chief of commissary to Gen. WINFIELD SCOTT in Mexico. Service at Vera Cruz, Cerro Gordo, Churubusco, Molino del Rey, Chapultepec, and Mexico City brought him the brevets of major and lieutenant colonel for "gallant and meritorious conduct."

GG

Grayson was chief commissary of the post at Detroit 1848–55, then served in New Mexico Territory from 1855 till 1 July 1861, when he resigned his full rank of major. His long experience in the military immediately brought him the rank of brigadier in the PROVISIONAL ARMY OF THE CONFEDERATE STATES, to date from 15 Aug. 1861. 6 days later he took command of the DEPARTMENT OF MIDDLE AND EASTERN FLORIDA, a position tendered him despite his rapidly deteriorating health.

Dutifully shouldering this burden, he sought to prepare the state's coastal defenses for an attack by Union soldiers and sailors. But he found his situation gloomy, wiring the Confederate War Department that "unless cannon powder, etc., be sent to Florida in the next thirty days, she will fall into the hands of the North. Nothing human can prevent it. There are not 4,000 pounds of powder at every post combined. The batteries are incorrectly put up and not finished. The enemy can land where they please."

The chaos throughout his department, and his anxiety over the strength and intentions of the enemy, further weakened Grayson's health, and he fell victim to power plays among his subordinates and local politicians. His inability to command effectively became a statewide issue that led to his relief 10 Oct. 11 days later he died in Tallahassee of tuberculosis. His remains were moved to New Orleans for burial. —EGL

Great Bethel, Va., Battle of. 10 June 1861 *See* BIG BETHEL, VA., BATTLE OF.

"Great Locomotive Chase." 12 Apr. 1862 *See* ANDREWS' RAID.

Greek fire. An incendiary substance used to charge shells, Greek fire saw little service during the Civil War because of its

tendency to explode in a loaded gun before it was fired. In the 7th century the general of Constantine IV's fleet used it to destroy the Saracens' ships; 19th-century military encyclopedias speculated that the combustible was principally naphtha. Inventor Levi Short of Philadelphia developed the Greek fire of Civil War vintage, probably a combustible achieved by making a solution of phosphorus in bisulfide of carbon.

Maj. Gen. QUINCY A. GILLMORE used Greek fire in the bombardment of Charleston, S.C., 21–22 Aug. 1863, until the last shell blew out the breech of the "SWAMP ANGEL," the 8-in., 200-pounder Parrott in use on Morris Island. Gen. P.G.T. BEAUREGARD, the Confederate commander at Charleston, criticized it as a barbaric tool of war being used against women and children. Confederates are credited with using Greek fire to burn the Barnum Museum during the plot to burn NEW YORK CITY, 25 Nov. 1864. —PLF

Greeley, Horace. editor b. Amherst, N.H., 3 Feb. 1811, of poor parents, Greeley learned the printer's trade before coming to New York City in 1831. After a succession of ventures he founded the NEW YORK *TRIBUNE* in 1841 and made it the largest, most powerful newspaper in the country. By 1860 its circulation had reached 287,-750, and Greeley enjoyed a national reputation as political savant, social crusader, moralist, and eccentric who espoused every new cause or fad. With Greeley its shrewd, perceptive editor, his paper set new standards in taste and intellectual appeal.

LC

During the Civil War Greeley opposed the CRITTENDEN COMPROMISE and any concessions to slavery, arguing that disunion was preferable. Once the fighting began, he supported the war effort vigorously. Allying himself with Radicals such as CHARLES SUMNER, THADDEUS STEVENS, and SALMON P. CHASE, he opposed conciliation and demanded immediate emancipation of slaves.

As the war progressed, Greeley pursued what others regarded as an erratic course. Convinced that Abraham Lincoln could not win the presidency in 1864, he hesitated to support him. As early as 1863 he flirted with the idea of foreign mediation. His growing urge to promote peace led him in 1864 to attempt direct negotiations with the Confederacy, a move that brought him ridicule. Nor did his plea for amnesty and pledging of bail for JEFFERSON DAVIS in 1867 win him friends.

In 1872 liberal Republicans joined with Democrats to nominate Greeley for the presidency, but his campaign turned into a fiasco. Pilloried and abused unmercifully by his enemies, he asked plaintively whether he was running for the presidency or the penitentiary. His crushing defeat, coupled with the death of his wife and other personal reverses, broke his mind and health. He died in New York City, 29 Nov. 1872, less than a month after the election. For decades Americans had tolerated or admired Greeley as a national eccentric; at the end their affection for his oddities soured into scurrilous derision. —MK

Green, Martin Edwin. CSA b. Fauquier Cty., Va., 3 June 1815. As a young man Green immigrated to Lewis Cty., Mo., and opened a lumber-milling business with his brothers, extending his interests in the state during the decades before the Civil War. In 1861 he recruited cavalry in northeast Missouri for the commander of the secessionist Missouri militia, Maj. Gen. STERLING PRICE; Green's Missouri Cavalry Regiment elected him colonel.

LC

Green served with Price during his entire Civil War career, taking part in the Siege of Lexington and the Battles of PEA RIDGE, IUKA, and CORINTH. In the interim he was promoted brigadier general, 21 July 1862. At Corinth he showed he had risen above his abilities. There, on the second day of battle, 4 Oct. 1862, Brig. Gen. LOUIS HÉBERT, despondent of success, reported himself sick, and Green was thrust into command. A subordinate said Green seemed "hopelessly bewildered, as well as ignorant of what ought to be done."

During north Mississippi and early VICKSBURG campaigning, he fought in Maj. Gen. JOHN S. BOWEN's divisions, taking a slight wound 25 June 1863. 2 days later, observing Union troops in front of the Vicksburg defenses, he was killed by an enemy sharpshooter.   —JES

Green, Thomas. CSA b. Amelia Cty., Va., 8 Jan. 1814. When Green was killed by gunboat fire in a reckless but daring charge at BLAIR'S LANDING, another Confederate officer lamented the loss as one the Trans-Mississippi command could least afford. Educated as a lawyer at the University of Nashville, but better suited to soldiering, Green spent most of his career engaged in military activity. He moved to Texas in 1835, fought for Texas independence at San Jacinto the next year, skirmished with Indians on the frontier, and served as captain of the 1st Texas Rifles during the Mexican War.

LC

A "hero of heroes" in his adopted state, Green entered Confederate service as a colonel of the 5th Texas Cavalry, which he commanded commendably at VALVERDE, New Mexico Territory. He joined Maj. Gen. RICHARD TAYLOR's command in Louisiana after distinguishing himself at GALVESTON Jan. 1863. Both Taylor and Lt. Gen. E. KIRBY SMITH praised Green repeatedly for his valiant assaults against heavy odds. He was advanced to brigadier general 20 May 1863. While Taylor favored promoting the cavalryman to major general, apparently JEFFERSON DAVIS never acted on the recommendation.

Green covered the Confederate retreat from Fort Bisland (*See* IRISH BEND AND FORT BISLAND) during operations on Bayou Teche in spring 1863. That November he routed Federal troops under Maj. Gen. STEPHEN G. BURBRIDGE in a brief but bloody engagement at BAYOU BOURBEAU, which was lauded by a fellow officer as a "brilliant victory." Green fought aggressively at MANSFIELD Apr. 1864 during Maj. Gen. NATHANIEL P. BANKS'S RED RIVER CAMPAIGN. In the battle at BLAIR'S LANDING on the 12th, Green, well fortified with rum, led an impetuous charge on Adm. DAVID D. PORTER's gunboats. Green fell in the advance; about 300 of his Texans were mowed down by grape and canister from the river. Taylor had lost one of his best commanders. Banks, acknowledging the cavalryman's bravery in his report to Maj. Gen. WILLIAM T. SHERMAN, praised Green as "the ablest officer in their [the Confederates'] service."

—PLF

"Greenback Raid." 13 Oct. 1864 *See* HARPERS FERRY, W. VA., MOSBY'S RAID ON.

greenbacks. Authorized by the Legal Tender Act of 25 Feb. 1862, non-interest-bearing government notes, printed on one side in green ink, were issued to serve as currency in place of gold; soon these were popularly called "greenbacks." Opponents challenged the constitutionality of greenbacks and condemned them as a source of runaway inflation, but during the congressional debates leading to passage of the legislation, Sec. of the Treasury SALMON P. CHASE declared them "indispensably necessary" to finance the war. The second Legal Tender Act passed 11 July 1862, and by the end of the month greenbacks were worth only 91 cents in gold. But the public liked them, especially Westerners, who had long opposed an economy based on hard money. Confederates living in occupied territory accepted Federal greenbacks willingly and used them instead of their worthless Confederate currency after Union troops moved on.

In all, the greenback issues amounted to $450 million. On 18 Dec. 1865 Congress passed a resolution to retire the notes, but it was never put into effect because the public favored paper money. *See also* LEGAL TENDER ACTS.   —PLF

Greenbrier River, western Va., eng. at. 3 Oct. 1861 A fortnight of inactivity followed the Union victory at CHEAT MOUNTAIN 11–13 Sept. 1861. The torrential rains that hampered Confederate movements during the operation continued incessantly for 2 weeks, churning the mountain roads into impassable troughs. Both armies remained in camp along this Staunton, Va.–Beverly, western Virginia, line. Union Brig. Gen. JOSEPH J. REYNOLDS retained possession of Cheat Mountain, which his soldiers had successfully defended. 12 mi to the east of the Federals, Brig. Gen. HENRY R. JACKSON's Confederates occupied Camp Bartow, on the south fork of the Greenbrier River.

Near the end of September the rains finally ceased, and Reynolds decided to make "an armed reconnaissance of the enemy's position." At midnight, 2 Oct., the Union command, numbering 5,000, abandoned their base at Cheat Mountain, marching on the Staunton-Parkersburg Turnpike. About daylight on the 3d, Reynolds' vanguard encountered Jackson's advanced pickets, who withdrew immediately, sounding the alarm. The Federals arrived at 7 a.m. opposite Camp Bartow. Opposing skirmishers soon exchanged musketry as Reynolds deployed for an attack.

Union batteries initiated the Federal advance, concentrating their fire on Jackson's center brigade. Confederate artillery crews replied as the fighting escalated. About 9:30 a.m. a Union brigade forded the river and charged toward the Southern left. The Confederates, who numbered only 1,800, repulsed this attack, driving the Northerners back across the stream. Reynolds then shifted the bulk of his forces to his left, where they renewed the offensive. Jackson countered by reinforcing his endangered flank. This second Federal attack was also quickly stopped by the Confederates.

Reynolds, unable to envelop either flank, soon disengaged. His casualties amounted to only 8 killed and 36 wounded, while Jackson lost 6 killed, 33 wounded, and 13 missing. The Federals retraced their march to Cheat Mountain, arriving at sundown. Another period of quiet, stretching into the winter, followed this minor engagement. —JDW

Greene, Samuel Dana. USN b. Cumberland, Md., 11 Feb. 1840. Appointed to the U.S. Naval Academy 21 Sept. 1855, Greene graduated with the class of 1859. He served as midshipman aboard the *Hartford* and was promoted to lieutenant 31 Aug. 1861. Early in 1862 Greene became executive officer of the new *MONITOR,* serving under 5 different commanders of that vessel. During the 9 Mar. 1862 engagement with the *VIRGINIA (Merrimack)* at HAMPTON ROADS, Greene directed the *Monitor*'s turret and guns. Lt. JOHN L. WORDEN, commanding the ship, credited Greene with "great courage, coolness, and skill." When Worden was wounded during

USMHI

the action, Greene took command and followed Worden's orders to protect the *Minnesota.* The action ended as the ironclads withdrew, both sides claiming victory.

Greene was on board the *Monitor* when it foundered off Cape Hatteras on the night of 30–31 Dec. 1862. Following the loss of the ship, he served as executive officer of the *Florida* and the *Iroquois.* He was promoted to lieutenant commander in 1865 and commander in 1872.

After 1866 Greene served as an instructor at the Naval Academy, with occasional sea duty. He was executive officer at the Portsmouth, N.H., Navy Yard at the time of his death, by suicide, 11 Dec. 1884. —NCD

Greenhow, Rose O'Neal. spy b. District of Columbia, about 1815–17. As a teen-ager O'Neal moved from her family's Maryland farm to her aunt's fashionable boardinghouse in Washington, D.C. Personable, intelligent, and outgoing, she adapted easily to the social scene of the capital, and people in Washington's highest circles opened their doors to her. Regarded as a beautiful, ambitious, seductive woman, she disappointed an army of suitors by marrying Dr. Robert Greenhow, an influential, learned man under whose tutelage she flourished and to whom she bore 4 daughters.

Among her friends were presidents, senators, high-ranking military officers, and less important people from all walks of life, many of whom played knowing or unknowing roles in the espionage ring she organized in 1861. One of her closest

LC

companions had been JOHN C. CALHOUN, whose political instruction sealed Rose's identification with and loyalty to Southern interests.

A widow when war broke out, Greenhow immediately used her contacts and talents to provide Gen. P.G.T. BEAUREGARD with information resulting in the Union rout at FIRST BULL RUN. Suspected of espionage and imprisoned Aug. 1861, she continued gathering and forwarding information vital to Confederate operations. News of her activities brought publicity and tremendous popularity among Southern sympathizers. After being brought to trial in spring 1862, Greenhow was deported to Richmond, where cheering crowds greeted her.

That summer JEFFERSON DAVIS sent her to Europe as a courier. She stayed there collecting diplomatic intelligence and writing her memoirs until recalled in 1864, apparently bearing dispatches urgent to the Confederacy. Sailing on the blockade runner *Condor,* she reached the mouth of the Cape Fear River just outside Wilmington, N.C., when a Union ship gave chase, forcing the *Condor* aground on a sandbar early on the morning of 1 Oct. Greenhow, fearing capture and reimprisonment, persuaded the captain to send her and 2 companions ashore in a lifeboat, but in stormy seas the small vessel overturned. Rose drowned, dragged down by the $2,000 in gold she carried. Her body was found and identified a few days later and buried with honors in Wilmington. —PLF

Greer, Elkanah Brackin. CSA b. Paris, Tenn., 11 Oct 1825, Greer moved to Mississippi while still a young man. Under Col. JEFFERSON DAVIS, future Confederate States president, he fought with the 1st Mississippi Rifles in the Mexican War, then established himself as a planter and merchant in Marshall, Tex. In 1859 he was elected grand commander of the secret, pro-slavery order KNIGHTS OF THE GOLDEN CIRCLE.

Greer entered the Civil War as a colonel 1 July 1861. In the battle at WILSON'S CREEK, Mo., 10 Aug., Greer and his 3d Texas Cavalry charged Federal Brig. Gen. NATHANIEL LYON's right flank. Greer reported after the fighting: "The

LC

enemy was thrown into considerable confusion." Though Federal reports disagreed with that account of the charge, the Confederates had won, and Greer had proven his ability to command.

In 1862 Greer suffered a painful wound at the Battle of PEA RIDGE, Ark., and received his commission as brigadier general 8 Oct. In a short time he accepted the post of Conscription Bureau chief for the Trans-Mississippi Department. There he worked with Maj. Gen. JOHN B. MAGRUDER to settle differences between Confederate conscription laws and those of Texas. In

1864 he also commanded the reserve forces in the Trans-Mississippi.

Greer lived in Marshall until 25 Mar. 1877, when he died at the home of his sister, in DeVall's Bluff, Ark. He was buried in his home state of Tennessee, in Elmwood Cemetery, Memphis. —FLS

Gregg, David McMurtrie. USA b. Huntington, Pa., 10 Apr. 1833, Gregg was first cousin to ANDREW GREGG CURTIN, wartime governor of Pennsylvania. He graduated from West Point 8th in the class of 1855 and saw duty on the Indian frontier until the Civil War began. After being named colonel of the 8th Pennsylvania Cavalry Jan. 1862, Gregg carved out a distinguished fighting record. His performance during the PENINSULA CAMPAIGN earned him promotion to brigadier general of volunteers, to rank from 29 Nov. 1862. He led a division during Maj. Gen. GEORGE STONEMAN's ill-advised raid on Richmond in the CHANCELLORSVILLE CAMPAIGN and protected the

USMHI

Federal right at GETTYSBURG, where his 2d Cavalry fought a sharp engagement with Maj. Gen. J.E.B. STUART.

As commanding officer of the 2d Cavalry, Gregg performed in exemplary fashion during the campaigning against Richmond in 1864. In August he earned promotion to major general of volunteers. Yet on 3 Feb. 1865 he abruptly resigned both his Regular and volunteer commissions for reasons that have never come to light; years later Gen. PHILIP H. SHERIDAN said of Gregg in his autobiography: "it is to be regretted he felt obliged . . . to quit the service."

After leaving the army Gregg lived in Reading, Pa., until named U.S. consul at Prague in 1874. Later he wrote *The Second Cavalry Division of the Army of the Potomac in the Gettysburg Campaign* (1907). He died in Reading 7 Aug. 1916. Active in municipal and charitable affairs, Gregg was described as "a rare combination of modesty, geniality and ability" who was "universally liked and respected." —MK

Gregg, John. CSA b. Lawrence Cty., Ala., 28 Sept. 1828, Gregg was a graduate of La Grange College and studied law in Tuscumbia. In 1852 he moved to Fairfield, Tex., where he was elected a district judge 4 years later. A member of the state secession convention, Gregg then served in the Provisional Confederate Congress until after FIRST BULL RUN in July 1861.

Returning to Texas, he recruited the 7th Texas and was elected its colonel. The regiment reported for duty in Tennessee, where it and its commander surrendered to Union forces at FORT DONELSON Feb. 1862. Following his ex-

USMHI

change, Gregg received promotion to brigadier general 29 Aug. 1862 and command of a brigade of Texas and Tennessee troops, which participated in Gen. JOSEPH E. JOHNSTON's operations during the VICKSBURG CAMPAIGN, May–July 1863. Transferred to Lt. Gen. JAMES LONGSTREET's I Corps/Army of Northern Virginia, he and his brigade stormed the Federal lines 20 Sept. 1863 in the Confederate victory at CHICKAMAUGA.

Gregg fell severely wounded in the attack, but after his recovery he assumed command of the famed Texas Brigade of Lt. Gen. JOHN B. HOOD (*see* HOOD'S TEXAS BRIGADE). He led these tough veterans in the Battles of the WILDERNESS, SPOTSYLVANIA, COLD HARBOR, and PETERSBURG. At the Wilderness, 6 May 1864, Gregg's Texans refused to counterattack until Gen. ROBERT E. LEE, who was along the searing battlefront, moved to the rear and safety. It was the first of 2 famous "Lee to the rear" incidents of the Overland Campaign.

During the engagements of the PETERSBURG Campaign, Gregg's brigade saw nearly constant action. On 7 Oct. 1864, while leading a counterattack along the DARBYTOWN ROAD, Gregg was killed. This excellent combat officer was buried in Aberdeen, Miss. —JDW

Gregg, Maxcy. CSA b. Columbia, S.C., 1 Aug. 1814. Few Southerners greeted the dissolution of the Union with greater pleasure than did Gregg. A man of keen intellect, with eclectic intellectual tastes, he attended South Carolina College, studied law with his father, and was admitted to the bar. For 2 decades, interrupted only by duty in the Mexican War, Gregg was extensively involved in state and regional politics.

A member of the state secession convention, Gregg jubilantly voted to leave the Union Dec. 1860. The convention authorized a 6-month regiment, giving the command to Gregg, with the rank of colonel. After Gregg and his volunteers participated in the bombardment of FORT SUMTER, Apr. 1861, they moved north to Virginia, where they spent the spring months drilling and picketing. When their term expired, many in the regiment returned to their homes, missing the FIRST BULL RUN CAMPAIGN.

With the newly formed 1st South Carolina, Gregg was ordered to the Suffolk, Va., area in autumn 1861. On 14 Dec. he received his commission of brigadier general and command of a brigade of 3 South Carolina regiments. His old regiment and another one joined the brigade in spring 1862, and Gregg led this unit in the rest of the battles of that year.

In the SEVEN DAYS' CAMPAIGN Gregg's South Carolinians suffered more casualties than any other brigade in Maj. Gen. AMBROSE P. HILL's Light Division. Assigned a reserve role at CEDAR MOUNTAIN, 9 Aug., the brigade fought tenaciously 3 weeks later at SECOND BULL RUN. During this searing battle, Gregg walked along the brigade's line, fearlessly exposing himself and encouraging his men. His conduct moved Hill to say that "he is the man for me." At ANTIETAM 17 Sept. Gregg was slightly wounded by the Federal volley that killed Brig. Gen. LAWRENCE O. BRANCH.

3 months later, at FREDERICKSBURG, Gregg's brigade held a reserve position behind a dangerous gap in the Confederate lines on the right. When the Federals stormed into the hole 13 Dec. 1862, Gregg hurriedly rallied his unprepared command. Riding toward the front, the brave South Carolinian fell from a rifle ball that entered his side and passed through his spine. He lingered in agony for 2 days, dying 15 Dec. 1862. —JDW

Grierson, Benjamin Henry. USA b. Pittsburgh, Pa., 8 July 1826, Grierson was educated in Ohio and moved to Illinois, where he taught music before entering business. At the start of the Civil War he enlisted as a private. Appointed major of the 6th Illinois Cavalry as of 24 Oct. 1861 and promoted to colonel as of 12 Apr. 1862, he participated in numerous raids and skirmishes in West Tennessee and northern Mississippi. In December his aggressive pursuit of Confederate forces, after their successful raid against the Union supply depot at HOLLY SPRINGS, Miss., earned him the command of a cavalry brigade.

USMHI

Grierson gained national renown when, under orders from Maj. Gen. ULYSSES S. GRANT, he cast off from La Grange, Tenn., and led a 16-day cavalry raid, 17 Apr.–2 May 1863, through Confederate Mississippi, fighting small battles, disrupting communications, and destroying military matériel before emerging at Baton Rouge, La. (see GRIERSON'S RAID). Grierson demonstrated that Union forces could operate successfully in Confederate territory without a supply line. This daring raid drew the attention of Confederate troops away from critical movements being made in the campaign against VICKSBURG, and Grant noted that Grierson had "taken the heart out of Mississippi." For this exploit, he was promoted to brigadier general of volunteers as of 3 June 1863.

Grierson was an outstanding Union cavalry leader and, despite his lack of military education, demonstrated an aptitude for war. After the conflict he was appointed colonel, 10th U.S. Cavalry, and participated in numerous actions against hostile Indians. He died in Omena, Mich., 1 Sept. 1911, one of only a few civilians to attain the rank of brigadier general in the Regular Army. —DLW

Grierson's Raid. 17 Apr.–2 May 1863 To divert the Confederates' attention from his march south from Milliken's Bend, La., Maj. Gen. U. S. Grant called for help from the cavalry. Late in Mar. 1863, Maj. Gen. Stephen A. Hurlbut, Grant's subordinate in Memphis, framed a proposal for a raid on the Southern Railroad. Coincidentally, Union Maj. Gen. WILLIAM S. ROSECRANS was readying a mounted column to strike the Western & Atlantic Railroad in northwest Georgia. Learning of each other's plans, Hurlbut and Rosecrans hammered out a scheme to keep the northern Mississippi and Alabama Confederates busy, thus freeing their mounted columns to penetrate deep into the Southern heartland.

On 15 Apr. the joint operations began when a Union column struck eastward from Corinth and drove the Confederates back into the Tennessee Valley. Tuscumbia was captured on the 24th. Meanwhile, infantry columns had marched from Memphis and La Grange, and between them engrossed the attention of the Confederate cavalry posted in northwest Mississippi.

Covered by these thrusts, 2 great cavalry raids started. Col. ABEL D. STREIGHT's mule-mounted soldiers left Tuscumbia 26 Apr., heading for the Western & Atlantic. This sweep failed when Brig. Gen. NATHAN B. FORREST compelled Streight's men to lay down their arms 3 May near Cedar Bluff, Ala.

The second column, 1,700 strong, led by Col. BENJAMIN H. GRIERSON, had ridden out of La Grange 17 Apr. Near West Point on the 21st, when hard-pressed by pursuing Confederate cavalry, Grierson detached Col. EDWARD HATCH with a third of the command. Hatch, after threatening the Mobile & Ohio Railroad, returned to La Grange. The Confederate forces in northeast Mississippi trailed Hatch, allowing Grierson to proceed south unopposed.

On the 24th Grierson's men struck the vital Southern Railroad at Newton Station. After breaking up the railroad and cutting the telegraph, his primary mission, Grierson determined to take advantage of his discretionary orders and strike for the Mississippi River.

Apprised of the raid on Newton Station, Confederate Lt. Gen. JOHN C. PEMBERTON focused his efforts on hunting down and destroying Grierson's horse soldiers. Grierson's column, however, slipped through the net Pemberton spread. After cutting the New Orleans, Jackson, & Great Northern Railroad, Grierson's troopers entered the Union lines at Baton Rouge 2 May. Since leaving La Grange, Grierson had ridden through the heart of Mississippi, wreaking havoc on communications. More important, he had diverted Pemberton's attention from Grant's march south. In futile efforts to destroy Grierson's command, Pemberton had worn down and scattered his strategic reserve. —ECB

Griffin, Charles. USA b. Granville, Ohio, 18 Dec. 1825. One of several excellent generals the artillery service contributed to the Union army, Griffin commanded infantry for most of the Civil War but never lost his love for cannon. Graduating 23d in the West Point class of 1847, Griffin practiced artillery skills as a field officer in the Southwest until his assignment in 1860 as an instructor at the Military Academy.

USMHI

While at West Point he organized a field battery; conspicuous conduct while commanding those guns at FIRST BULL RUN brought him a major's commission. After a solid performance in the 1862 PENINSULA CAMPAIGN Griffin was promoted to brigadier general, 9 June, and commanded infantry brigades at FREDERICKSBURG and CHANCELLORSVILLE. Sickness delayed his arrival at GETTYSBURG, but when he reached the field, his men were so glad to see him that they pulled him from his horse and carried him to his tent on their shoulders.

Though Griffin had an aura of parade-ground smartness, he slipped into profanity easily and was noted for a choleric temper and a readiness to take offense. But he was a splendid combat officer. During fighting from the Wilderness to Appomattox, he led a division ably and enjoyed the confidence of both Lt. Gen. U.S. GRANT and Maj. Gen. PHILIP H. SHERIDAN. However, he could not escape controversy, and his outspokenness got him into trouble with Maj. Gen. GEORGE G. MEADE on at least one occasion.

After the war Griffin became colonel of the 35th U.S. Infantry and took charge of the District of Texas. He refused to leave Galveston when a yellow-fever epidemic swept through the city, and 15 Sept. 1867 he died of the disease. Griffin was buried in Oak Hill Cemetery, District of Columbia.   —JIR

Griffin, Simon Goodell. USA b. Nelson, N.H., 9 Aug. 1824. The grandson of 2 Revolutionary War soldiers, Griffin grew up on his uncle's farm near Roxbury. Despite a sketchy education, he secured a teaching job and studied law, gaining admission to the bar in 1860. By then he had served 2 years in the state legislature.

In mid-1861 Griffin helped organize a company of the 2d New Hampshire Volunteers, being named its captain 6 weeks before FIRST BULL RUN. In that engagement his regiment, part of Col. AMBROSE E. BURNSIDE'S brigade, held an important position on the Union right, participating in the initial assault of Brig. Gen. IRVIN MCDOWELL'S

NA

army. After the Federal retreat to the defenses of Washington, Griffin visited his native state on an errand relating to equipping new regiments with SHARPS RIFLES, a weapon the 2d Volunteers had used to good effect at Bull Run. On this trip, he was offered executive command of the 6th New Hampshire Infantry, an appointment he accepted 28 Nov. 1861.

As a lieutenant colonel, he sailed on the expedition that captured ROANOKE ISLAND and pushed into the North Carolina interior. On 22 Apr. 1862 he became colonel of his regiment and led it, as part of the IX Corps, at SECOND BULL RUN and ANTIETAM. In the latter battle, his men were heavily engaged at Burnside Bridge, suffering severely.

Early in 1863 Griffin and his outfit joined Burnside's Department of the Ohio and that spring went to Mississippi to counter Gen. JOSEPH E. JOHNSTON's efforts to reinforce VICKSBURG. Following this successful campaign, the colonel was transferred from his new position of brigade leader to command Camp Nelson, Ky. When the IX Corps returned east Apr. 1864, he won recognition at SPOTSYLVANIA, receiving a brigadier generalship, 12 May, as well as Burnside's praise for being "conspicuous for his bravery and gallantry." Among other actions that year, he had the misfortune to participate in the disastrous Battle of the CRATER.

In Mar. 1865 Griffin moved up to division command, which he held throughout the APPOMATTOX CAMPAIGN. Mustered out 24 Aug., he spent the postwar years as a manufacturer in his native state, a railroad and land speculator in Texas, and a 3-time member of the New Hampshire legislature. d. Keene, N.H., 14 Jan. 1902.   —EGL

Griffith, Richard. CSA b. near Philadelphia, Pa., 11 Jan. 1814. After graduating in 1837 from Ohio University, Griffith settled in Vicksburg, Miss., as a schoolteacher. During the Mexican War he served as regimental adjutant of the 1st Mississippi Rifles, commanded by Jefferson Davis. Returning to Mississippi after the war, he lived in Jackson, where he was a

banker, U.S. marshal, and state treasurer for 2 terms.

When Mississippi seceded, Northern-born Griffith was elected colonel of the 12th Mississippi. On 12 Nov. 1861 this close friend of the Confederate president secured a commission as brigadier general and the command of a brigade. Griffith served under Maj. Gen. JOHN B. MAGRUDER during the PENINSULA and SEVEN DAYS' campaigns. On 29 June 1862, in the action at SAVAGE'S STATION, he fell mortally wounded, dying later in the day.   —JDW

LC

Grimes, Bryan. CSA b. Pitt Cty., N.C., 2 Nov. 1828. After graduating from the state university, traveling, and farming, Grimes became a member of the North Carolina secession convention. Despite his Whig origins, he was a passionate advocate of the Confederate cause, rushing to enlist in the wake of the FORT SUMTER crisis. He entered service as major of the 4th North Carolina Infantry, under Col. (later Brig. Gen.) GEORGE B. ANDERSON.

Sent with his regiment to Virginia shortly after FIRST BULL RUN, Grimes advanced to lieutenant colonel May 1862 and to colonel the following month. At SEVEN PINES, the first of many battles in which he barely eluded

LC

death, he was the only officer in the 4th to emerge unwounded, 462 of the regiment's 520 men becoming casualties. The survivors served gallantly at MECHANICSVILLE and on the fringes of other battles during the PENINSULA CAMPAIGN. Before that campaign ended, his immediate superior declared that "Colonel Grimes and his regiment are the keystone of my brigade."

Disabled by typhoid fever and a riding accident, Grimes nevertheless served at ANTIETAM, where a horse was shot beneath him; by war's end, 7 of his mounts would be killed in battle. He led Anderson's brigade at FREDERICKSBURG, and May 1863 he was conspicuous during all 3 days at CHANCELLORSVILLE, again as regimental commander. At GETTYSBURG, his men helped drive the Union XI Corps through the town 1 July, and during the retreat from Pennsylvania they efficiently guarded the army's rear.

Grimes was no less conspicuous in the campaigns of 1864. At SPOTSYLVANIA, he took over the brigade of Brig. Gen. STEPHEN D. RAMSEUR following the latter's wounding, and led it in a successful counterattack 12 May, recovering much of the ground lost at the "BLOODY ANGLE." This won him high praise from Gen. Robert E. Lee, a brigadier's commission, 19 May, and permanent command of Brig. Gen. JUNIUS DANIEL's old brigade. That summer he served under Lt. Gen. JUBAL A. EARLY in the SHENANDOAH VALLEY CAMPAIGN, being conspicuous in division command at CEDAR CREEK.

On 15 Feb. 1865 he was elevated to major general, at which grade he fought at FORT STEDMAN and through the APPOMATTOX CAMPAIGN, leading one of the final assaults on the day that Lee surrendered. After the war, he returned to farming on his North Carolina plantation. He was assassinated 14 Aug. 1880 by a killer hired by local residents whom Grimes had sought to expel from the community as undesirables. —EGL

Griswold and Gunnison. Samuel Griswold and A. W. Gunnison manufactured for the Confederacy brass-framed copies of the Colt 1851 Navy revolver. Their firm was one of the most successful of Confederate handgun manufacturers.

Practically nothing is known of Gunnison, but Griswold had operated a cotton-gin manufactory before the war at Griswoldville, Ga., a hamlet located on the Georgia Central Railroad

HTIC

about 10 mi south of Macon. His factory dominated the settlement, and he built a 3-story residence for himself and 50 or more cottages for his workers. In May 1862, Capt. Richard E. Cuyler was authorized by the Confederate Ordnance Department to accept from Griswold and Gunnison, at $40 each, all the revolvers they could make in 8 months. Within 2 months the firm was turning out 50–60 revolvers per week, using 22 machines operated by 24 hands, 22 of whom were slaves. Yet while the revolvers were being produced, a number of production problems came to light, particularly the iron used in the barrels and cylinders, some of which would not stand the proofing tests. As a result, the first 22 revolvers were not delivered until October, and only 5 of them passed the tests administered by the Macon Arsenal. Though the firm continued to be plagued by iron of insufficient quality, they were eventually able to turn out an average of 100 revolvers a month.

The revolvers themselves were almost exact copies of the Colt 1851 Navy, but with a round barrel and a brass frame. Most of the revolvers had the serial number stamped in the frame, and a few also had *CS* or *CSA* stamped into the frame. Approximately 3,600 revolvers were turned out during the 3-year period the factory existed.

On 20 Nov. 1864 Maj. Gen. WILLIAM T. SHERMAN's columns, on their MARCH TO THE SEA, engaged Georgia militia at Griswoldville. Their victory was in little doubt, and probably the same day they destroyed the entire pistol-making factory. Only a few buildings, including Griswold's house, escaped the destruction, and the factory was never reestablished. —LDJ

Grover, Cuvier. USA b. Bethel, Maine, 29 July 1828, Grover was an 1850 graduate of West Point, standing 4th in a class of 44. He served on the frontier during the decade before the Civil War, participating in the Northern Pacific Rail-

road exploration 1853–54 and the Utah Expedition against the Mormons 1858–59. With the rank of captain of the 10th Infantry, he was commanding at Fort Union, New Mexico Territory, when the war began.

KA

Returning east, Grover went on a leave of absence Nov. 1861–Apr. 1862, when he was promoted to brigadier general, to rank from 14 Apr. Assigned a brigade in Maj. Gen. JOSEPH HOOKER's division, he fought at YORKTOWN, WILLIAMSBURG, SEVEN PINES, SAVAGE'S STATION, and MALVERN HILL. His conduct earned him 2 brevets. In July his brigade was transferred to Maj. Gen. JOHN POPE's Army of Virginia. Under Pope, Grover fought in the SECOND BULL RUN CAMPAIGN.

In Jan. 1863 Grover was assigned command of a division of the XIX Corps/Department of the Gulf. For 18 months he participated in the operations of Maj. Gen. NATHANIEL P. BANKS in Louisiana and Mississippi, commanding the army's right wing at the Siege of PORT HUDSON. The XIX Corps, under Brig. Gen. WILLIAM H. EMORY, was then transferred to Virginia July 1864.

Assigned to the Middle Military District, Emory's corps participated in Maj. Gen. PHILIP H. SHERIDAN's victorious 1864 SHENANDOAH VALLEY CAMPAIGN. On the morning of 19 Sept. 1864, Grover's division charged the Confederate left in the THIRD BATTLE OF WINCHESTER. Wrecking a Confederate brigade, Grover's veterans became disorganized in this charge and were routed in a lashing Southern counterattack. The collapse of his division resulted in charges and countercharges between Grover and Brig. Gen. WILLIAM DWIGHT, commander of Emory's other division. No official action was taken, and Grover commanded capably at FISHER'S HILL and CEDAR CREEK, where he suffered a wound. For his services during this campaign Grover was brevetted brigadier general, U.S. Army, and major general of volunteers. He subsequently earned the brevet of major general in the Regular Army and commanded the District of Savannah, Georgia, at the war's end.

The career officer remained in the postwar army. As a lieutenant colonel he commanded the 38th Infantry, a black regiment, and later, as colonel, the 1st Cavalry. In 1885 Grover, plagued by poor health, visited Atlantic City, N.J., where he died 6 June. The 39-year veteran was buried at West Point. —JDW

Groveton, Va., Battle of. 28 Aug. 1862 On the evening of 26 Aug. 1862, Maj. Gen. THOMAS J. "STONEWALL" JACKSON's II Corps/Army of Northern Virginia descended on the huge Union supply depot at Manassas Junction. To the hungry Confederates the bulging warehouses were a prize of nearly incomprehensible size, and they reveled in the plunder. Throughout the night and into the 27th they dined on fruits, pickled oysters, canned lobster salad, wines, and whiskey while stuffing their haversacks with cakes, canned goods, meats, candy, and the abundant liquor. What Jackson's troops could not carry, they burned. By the afternoon of the 27th Manassas Junction lay smoldering and black.

Jackson's 50-mi, 2-day march to the supply depot had

turned Union Maj. Gen. JOHN POPE's right and destroyed his supply base. Pope initially had considered Jackson's march a raid into the Shenandoah Valley. When reports confirmed the Confederate seizure of the supply base, Pope ordered a withdrawal from his outflanked positions along the Rappahannock River. Throughout 27 Aug., while Jackson's men feasted, the Army of Virginia shuttled northward toward Manassas. Confusing intelligence and contradictory orders from Pope hampered the Union march.

Hoping to capture the isolated Jackson, Pope finally reached Manassas Junction about noon on the 28th. The Union commander found only the charred ruins of his base. During the night "Old Jack" had withdrawn by 3 separate routes to a long, steep, abandoned railroad embankment running from Groveton to Sudley Springs, north of the old Bull Run battlefield. Receiving conflicting reports of the elusive Confederates' whereabouts, Pope ordered a concentration at Centreville. Throughout the afternoon of the 28th the Federals groped toward Centreville while Jackson's men rested in the shade and enjoyed their full haversacks.

Shortly before 5:30 p.m. Brig. Gen. JOHN GIBBON's leading brigade of Brig. Gen. RUFUS KING's Union division approached Jackson's concealed lines along the Warrenton Turnpike. Jackson, who was waiting for the arrival of Gen. ROBERT E. LEE and Maj. Gen. JAMES LONGSTREET's I Corps, could not resist the temptation to lash into the marching Federals. A Confederate battery rumbled into position and hurled 6 shells into woods near the pike. Gibbon rapidly deployed his 4 regiments and brought up Battery B/4th U.S. Artillery.

Brig. Gen. WILLIAM B. TALIAFERRO's Confederate division, supported by 2 brigades of Maj. Gen. RICHARD S. EWELL's division, charged with a cheer. The attacking Confederates surged down the slope as Gibbon's regiments replied with searing volleys. The Southerners abruptly halted and responded. For the next 2 hours, at a distance of about 100 yd, the opponents lashed at each other in a stand-up fight. Gibbon's 1 Indiana and 3 Wisconsin regiments, nicknamed the Black Hat Brigade because of their black slouch hats, had never been in battle before.

Volleys of musketry rolled up and down the hillside as regiments on both sides suffered grievous casualties, their lines marked by neat rows of maimed and dead bodies. The Stonewall Brigade lost a third of its men, including 3 regimental commanders. Confederate Brig. Gen. ISAAC R. TRIMBLE fell with 3 wounds, while Ewell, a brilliant division commander, had his knee shattered, which resulted in an amputation that night. He was gone for months. Gibbon's Black Hats also lost a third of their numbers.

Darkness finally ended the battle, with the Confederates having halted the Federal assault. Pope had found Jackson, and Gibbon's men—soon to be named the IRON BRIGADE—had been baptized into combat. One of them wrote after the war that the brigade was always ready for combat, but after Groveton, "we were never again eager."   —JDW

Grow, Galusha Aaron. USP b. Ashford, Conn., 31 Aug. 1823. The fifth of 6 children, Grow moved with his widowed mother to Susquehanna Cty., Pa., while in his teens. The family worked a 400-acre farm, then established a lumber business. Profits were sufficient to send Grow to an academy near Philadelphia and later to Amherst College, from which he was graduated in 1844. 3 years later he was admitted to the bar and

joined the Towanda, Pa., law office of DAVID WILMOT, stalwart of the FREE SOIL PARTY.

In 1850 a split in Pennsylvania Democratic ranks prevented Wilmot from being reelected to the House of Representatives but permitted him to nominate Grow in his place. The latter was elected, taking his seat in Washington, D.C., as the youngest member of the 32d Congress. He remained in the House of Representatives for the next 12 years.

LC

Grow was primarily a spokesman for the hopes and needs of frontier settlers, whose interests he identified with. From his earliest days in Congress he pressed for government liberality in opening public lands to settlement. In his second term he promoted a measure to give every applicant a free plot of 160 acres, but not until 20 May 1862 did the principal achievement of his legislative career, the HOMESTEAD ACT, become law.

In the years leading up to the Civil War, Grow was a leader among Northern and Western congressmen allied to combat the influence of Southern Democrats. Restive in conservative surroundings, he bolted to the Republican fold in 1856. Thanks to support from powerful colleagues, including THADDEUS STEVENS, he was named Speaker of the House during the special congressional session of summer 1861.

Grow also had mighty enemies, including SIMON CAMERON, Abraham Lincoln's first secretary of war and boss of Pennsylvania Republicans. Further, as one historian notes, "although a fighter, Grow lacked ability to sense popular opinion, to appraise properly political situations, and to perceive practical implications." These factors combined to deny him reelection in 1863 and for 30 years thereafter. During that period he held several commercial positions, including the presidency of a Texas railroad. Finally returned to Congress in 1894, through the errors of power brokers opposed to him, he served 3 more terms. In 1896 he won reelection by almost 300,000 votes, at that time the largest margin of any American office holder. d. Glenwood, Pa., 31 Mar. 1907.   —EGL

Guard Hill, Va., eng. at. 16 Aug. 1864 *See* FRONT ROYAL, VA., ENG. AT.

Gulf, Confederate Department of the. *See* GULF, CONFEDERATE DISTRICT OF THE.

Gulf, Confederate District of the. Regular troop-strength reports from Confederate Brig. Gen. JOHN H. FORNEY, 30 June 1862, showed him in command of an area around Mobile, Ala., informally called the District of the Gulf. General Orders No. 89, from Confederate Department No. 2, 2 July 1862, formally created the District of the Gulf, assigned Forney its command, and defined its boundaries as "the country east of the Pearl River [Miss.] to the Apalachicola [River, Fla.] and as far north as the 32d parallel of latitude," a latitude 40 mi south of Montgomery, Ala. On 3 Nov. the northern boundary was extended to the 33d parallel to include Montgomery. Brig. Gen. WILLIAM W. MACKALL assumed district command 14 Dec.;

Maj. Gen. SIMON B. BUCKNER relieved him 23 Dec. and, 27 Apr. 1863, was ordered to leave for Tennessee at the first opportunity. Maj. Gen. DABNEY H. MAURY replaced Buckner in mid-May.

Sometime between 28 Feb. 1863 and 1 Apr., the district briefly achieved departmental status. While no extant records give a date for the inception of the Confederate Department of the Gulf, Buckner's last troop-strength reports for April through 1 May and Maury's first correspondence on taking command are both headed "Department of the Gulf." Lt. Gen. LEONIDAS POLK's 7 Feb. 1864 Special Orders No. 38 defined the department as existing approximately within the original boundaries of the District of the Gulf, with its northern border at the 32d parallel. On 9 May 1864, the DEPARTMENT OF ALABAMA, MISSISSIPPI, AND EAST LOUISIANA came into being, encompassing and eliminating the former Gulf department, and Maury reverted to command of the District of the Gulf, an area existing within the boundaries of the old department.

Maury retained command through the fall of MOBILE until his troops were surrendered by Lt. Gen. RICHARD TAYLOR, 4 May 1865. —JES

Gulf, Union Army of the. Initiated 23 Feb. 1862, the Union's Department of the Gulf and Army of the Gulf coincided, with those troops, most of them New Englanders, assigned to the Department of the Gulf composing the Army of the Gulf. With headquarters at New Orleans, the department included all the coast along the Gulf of Mexico west of Pensacola, Fla.

Army commanders were Maj. Gens. BENJAMIN F. BUTLER, 20 Mar.–17 Dec. 1862; NATHANIEL P. BANKS, 17 Dec. 1862–23 Sept. 1864; Stephen A. Hurlbut, 23 Sept. 1864–22 Apr. 1865; Banks again, 22 Apr.–3 June 1865; and E.R.S. CANBY, 3–27 June 1865.

The primary operations involving the army were the siege and capture of PORT HUDSON, La., and smaller operations along the Texas coast 26 Oct. 1863–4 Jan. 1864. The major force associated with the army was the XIX Corps; the XII, XVI, and XVII corps, or units thereof, were also assigned to the department at various times. The department and its army continued to function virtually as a separate entity until both were abolished 27 June 1865, though technically they were merged into the Military Division of West Mississippi (Trans-Mississippi Division) 7 May 1864. —RAP

Gulf, Union Department of the. *See* GULF, UNION ARMY OF THE.

Gulf, Union Military Division of the. *See* WEST MISSISSIPPI, UNION MILITARY DIVISION OF.

Gulf Blockading Squadron. On 7 May 1861 Capt. William Mervine was ordered to command a squadron of warships "to establish and enforce a blockade . . . [of] all the ports . . . south of Key West to the Rio Grande." 17 vessels were to comprise his command, designated the Gulf Blockading Squadron. During the 4 months Mervine commanded the squadron, efforts were made to blockade ports in the Gulf, but his few vessels proved ineffective. At the end of July, 13 of his warships were dispersed among 9 ports, the 4 remaining vessels guarding the various passes to the Mississippi River. Sec. of the Navy GIDEON WELLES's dissatisfaction with the BLOCKADE resulted in Mervine's being relieved by Capt. William W. McKean in September.

McKean had more success. Late in September, 4 of his warships moved up the passes in the Mississippi River and sealed off the river to BLOCKADE RUNNERS. As he received additional vessels, McKean strengthened forces guarding the larger ports, particularly Mobile and Galveston. In November he had 20 warships on blockade duty.

The squadron also cooperated with the army in military operations along the coast. In Nov. 1861 2 vessels joined in an attack on Fort McRee, Fla. On 3 Dec., Ship Island, off the Mississippi coast, was occupied and became the base of operations for the successful campaign for New Orleans.

In Dec. 1861 the Navy Department decided to divide the Gulf Blockading Squadron into 2 squadrons, east and west. The Eastern squadron was responsible for all of Florida east of Pensacola, including its Atlantic coast, as well as the Bahamas and Cuba. McKean retained command of this squadron. The Western squadron was placed under Capt. DAVID G. FARRAGUT, who, in addition to blockading the Gulf ports west of Pensacola, had the responsibility of taking New Orleans. The Gulf Blockading Squadron ceased to exist when Farragut arrived at Ship Island 25 Feb. 1862 and relieved McKean of those vessels that were to be under his command. —WNS

Guntown, Miss., Battle of. 10 June 1864 *See* BRICE'S CROSS ROADS, MISS., BATTLE OF.

H

habeas corpus, suspension of the writ of. Following the hostilities at FORT SUMTER, Apr. 1861, Pres. ABRAHAM LINCOLN suspended the writ of *habeas corpus* by presidential proclamation in the North and imposed martial law in several of the critical BORDER STATES, an action that saved them for the Union. In the wake of suspension, some 18,000 civilians were arrested throughout the North. The president regarded these arrests as a warning against disloyalty, and was initially supported by a public who had criticized civilian police for not arresting secessionist sympathizers. A few people taken into custody were held for trial, but military authorities released most of them quickly.

When martial law remained in force in those loyal border states susceptible to invasion, and arrests, many of them arbitrary, continued, public opinion turned sharply against the administration. Critics accused Lincoln of going too far in interpreting the constitutional clause permitting *habeas corpus* to be suspended in the event of invasion or to protect public safety, and charged him with permitting the military to dominate civil law in states not in rebellion. Lincoln saw suspension of the writ as a deterrent to peace agitators and subversive activities, reminding his opponents that arrests were made publicly and received wide coverage by the press. On 5 July 1861 Atty. Gen. EDWARD BATES gave an opinion supporting the presidential power to suspend the writ, but in an effort to find a fair solution to popular disapproval, on 14 Feb. 1862 Lincoln ordered the release on PAROLE of all military prisoners, granting them AMNESTY for past offenses.

Despite the public's indignation, national legislators recognized suspension of *habeas corpus* as a wartime necessity, passing the *Habeas Corpus* Act of Mar. 1863 to legally sanction Lincoln's earlier proclamation and authorize suspension in the future. The controversial legislation also gave the Federal government greater control over state courts by protecting military officers from being prosecuted at the local level for carrying out their orders, especially in their enforcement of CONSCRIPTION laws. In exchange the act placed certain restrictions on the military, requiring commanding officers to report all civilian arrests to Federal district and circuit judges. Widespread arrests for suspected disloyalty resumed after the act was passed, continuing until the war ended.

Habeas corpus was also suspended by JEFFERSON DAVIS in the Confederate States, but the Confederate Congress, conscious of protecting STATES RIGHTS, imposed harsh restrictions on suspension. Legislators first approved revocation of *habeas corpus* 27 Feb. 1862 as a means to quell civil disorder in invaded territory and to enforce the Draft Act of 1862, which extended 12-month ENLISTMENTS to the duration of the war. The law was amended 19 Apr., authorizing the military to arrest civilians for offenses against the government, but re-

mained in force for only 30 days after the congressional session dissolved. Congress suspended *habeas corpus* a second time 20 Sept., but in a weakened form that proved insufficient. On 13 Oct. the legislators reinstated the February law but allowed it to expire because of strenuous public opposition.

Most Southerners considered suspension of the writ a step toward despotism by the central government, even though Davis used it sparingly. At the president's request, a third law revoking *habeas corpus* passed 5 Feb. 1864, defining treasonable offenses rather than allowing blanket suspension. Again extreme public disapproval induced legislators to let the act expire. Despite Davis' pleas to have the act renewed that November, the Confederate Congress passed no further legislation suspending *habeas corpus*.   —PLF

Hagood, Johnson. CSA b. Barnwell Cty., S.C., 21 Feb. 1829, Hagood attended Richmond Academy in Augusta, Ga., then South Carolina Military Academy in Charleston, graduating from the latter school in 1847. Before the war interrupted his career, he practiced law, operated a successful plantation, and in 1851 was elected commissioner-in-equity of the county. His tenure as deputy adjutant general of militia, which also began in 1851, provided him with experience valuable in raising the 1st South Carolina Infantry, which was stationed in Charleston for the reduction of FORT SUMTER Apr. 1861.

Elected colonel of the regiment, Hagood fought at FIRST BULL RUN, then returned with his command to his native state, where he remained until mid-1864. In May of that year he was ordered to Virginia for the defense of PETERSBURG. Arriving at Walthall Junction, he helped turn back the Union advance ordered by Maj. Gen. BENJAMIN F. BUTLER, on the 16th fought at DREWRY'S BLUFF, and in June at COLD HARBOR. Sent south again in December, Hagood battled under Gen. JOSEPH E. JOHNSTON during the Confederate retreat through the Carolinas.

When the war ended, he returned to his plantation, becoming an influential promoter of diversified farming and in 1869 the first president of the South Carolina Agricultural Mechanical Society. His interest in educational reforms led to his appointment to several school boards over the years, and his keen business sense, to membership on a commission empowered to investigate banking practices in the state. A staunch Democrat allied with WADE HAMPTON in his efforts to free South Carolina from Reconstruction politics, Hagood was elected comptroller general when Hampton won the governorship in 1876. Reelected 2 years later, he went on to become his state's 51st governor in 1880.

Before his death in Barnwell, 4 Jan. 1898, Hagood wrote his autobiography, *Memoirs of the War of Secession* (1910), a tome filled with more words than necessary to describe the author's contribution to the war effort. —PLF

Hahn, Michael. war governor b. Bavaria, Germany, 24 Nov. 1830. Brought to the U.S. as an infant by his widowed mother, Hahn was reared in New Orleans, La. Through the 1850s, Hahn, an 1851 graduate of University of Louisiana Law School, gained a reputation as an avid antisecession, antislavery Democrat, actively supporting STEPHEN A. DOUGLAS for the presidency in 1860. When Douglas lost to ABRAHAM LINCOLN, Hahn toured Louisiana as a member of a committee agitating against secession. Almost immediately after Federal occupation troops arrived in New Orleans in 1862, he took the oath of allegiance to the U.S. government. Respected for his integrity, in December he was elected as a Unionist to the U.S. House of Representatives. Though prohibited from taking his seat until Feb. 1863, he began working toward reconstructing the state. Once in Washington, he threw his full support behind Lincoln's war measures, including emancipation short of immediate equal rights for blacks.

With Maj. Gen. NATHANIEL P. BANKS's backing, in Feb. 1864 Hahn easily won election to the Louisiana governorship as a moderate on the Free State ticket. Lincoln appointed him military governor as well 2 weeks after the president's inauguration in March, but Hahn assumed little power in his dual role and was in constant conflict with occupation army commanders who overrode his authority in civil matters. The legislature elected Hahn to the U.S. Senate Jan. 1865, but because of the questionable success of wartime Presidential Reconstruction, he was refused his seat.

In 1867 Hahn, who had purchased and edited the *Daily True Delta* in 1864, launched the second of his 3 newspaper ventures, the New Orleans *Republican,* which he published until 1871. After spending 4 years in retirement at his sugar plantation, he returned to public service as state registrar of voters, superintendent of the U.S. mint, and district judge until being elected as a Republican to the House in 1884. He died suddenly in the District of Columbia, 15 Mar. 1886, before the first session was adjourned. —PLF

Hall, Maria. nurse b. date unknown, District of Columbia. After DOROTHEA DIX refused Hall service as a nurse because she was too young, she was accepted at Indiana Hospital in Washington, D.C. Hall worked in the capital July 1861–July 1862, then joined the hospital transport service, working aboard the *Daniel Webster,* a U.S. SANITARY COMMISSION vessel readied to carry sick and wounded soldiers to stationary hospitals. Later that summer she worked with ELIZA HARRIS at Harrison's Landing, attending the wounded from the PENINSULA CAMPAIGN, and in September was sent to the battlefield at ANTIETAM.

When the wounded from Antietam were moved to permanent hospitals, Hall was assigned to Smoketown General Hospital in Maryland, where she stayed for 9 months. An able organizer, she transferred to the Naval Academy Hospital at Annapolis, with responsibility for 1 section of the tent hospital on the academy's campus. In spring 1864 she was named superintendent of the naval hospital, a position she held until the facility closed in summer 1865.

During her final months of service, Hall administered to many of the prisoners released from ANDERSONVILLE PRISON. Of the hundreds she had cared for, she felt few had suffered as tragically as these. They seemed, she wrote in the soldiers'

weekly newspaper *The Crutch,* creatures of "some strange outer world, some horrible land of dimness and groans." d. place and date unknown. —PLF

Halleck, Henry Wager. USA b. Westernville, N.Y., 16 Jan. 1815, Halleck was one of the Union army's most brilliant officers and one of its most unsuccessful generals. A spit-and-polish West Pointer, graduating 3d in the class of 1839, Halleck was adept at military theory. Hobbled in the field by his excessive caution, he was also isolated at headquarters by an aloof, forbidding manner. ULYSSES S. GRANT acknowledged his "gigantic intellect." WILLIAM T. SHERMAN praised his "great capacity" and "large acquirements." Others reviled him as a "cold, calculating owl" who "plans nothing, suggests nothing, is good for nothing."

USMHI

Before the war, Halleck had a brilliant career as a soldier, teacher, writer, and lawyer. He taught at West Point, became an expert on fortifications, published books on legal and military subjects, fought in Mexico, served as secretary of state of California, and established himself as the leading lawyer in gold-rush San Francisco. But when war broke out in 1861 the army was still in Halleck's blood. That August he returned from California to accept a commission as major general, to rank from 19 Aug., in the Union army. In November he succeeded Maj. Gen. JOHN C. FRÉMONT, at St. Louis, as commander of the newly formed Department of the Missouri, where he restored discipline and efficiency to a lax command, earned the nickname "Old Brains," and received overall credit for the battlefield glories of Grant and Maj. Gens. SAMUEL R. CURTIS and DON CARLOS BUELL. But his one excursion into the field—at CORINTH, Miss., May 1862—revealed him to be a plodding tactician and an excessively cautious commander.

Named ABRAHAM LINCOLN's general-in-chief July 1862, Halleck displayed great administrative ability, but his grasp of field affairs was poor, and his personality made him many more enemies than friends. In Mar. 1864 Grant was named supreme commander of all Union armies and Halleck was "kicked upstairs" to the new post of chief of staff, where he remained until the end of the war.

Halleck commanded the Military Division of the James after Gen. ROBERT E. LEE's surrender. In Aug. 1865 he was assigned to the Division of the Pacific, and 4 years later was transferred to the Division of the South. d. Louisville, Ky., 9 Jan. 1872. —BMcG

Hamilton, Andrew Jackson. USA/USP b. Huntsville, Ala., 28 Jan. 1815, Hamilton clerked, studied, and practiced law in Alabama until 1847. Moving to Texas, he became state attorney general, a state legislator, and in 1859 a U.S. congressman backed by Austin's Travis County Unionists. He clung to an antisecessionist position throughout the political crisis of early 1861 and by spring was the lone Texas representative in Congress. He returned to his district in March and successfully stood for reelection, his stubborn constituents refusing to recognize that Texas had been admitted to the Confederacy 2 Mar. In the South, the election and Hamlin were called treasonous. U.S. diplomatic personnel in Mexico reported rumors that Hamilton was expected to lead Austin citizens in antisecessionist rebellion. Impending arrest compelled his flight to Mexico in 1862.

LC

From Mexico he traveled to Washington and 14 Nov. 1862 was commissioned brigadier general of volunteers and appointed military governor of Texas. Reporting for duty in New Orleans, he wanted his governorship to be a working appointment and urged Rear Adm. DAVID G. FARRAGUT and Maj. Gens. BENJAMIN F. BUTLER and NATHANIEL P. BANKS to move ahead their planned operations at GALVESTON, Tex. Among the battles for Galveston, the 1 Jan. 1863 Union naval and land operation was a disaster, one Banks attributed to Hamilton's impatience. Hamilton also included several of his creditors aboard the expedition's ships, intending to pay off obligations after Union success there by allowing them first opportunity at cotton speculations. In 1864 he secured permission to export Texas cotton.

Banks's appraisal of Hamilton as without "force of character," and doubts about him expressed by Union Sec. of the Navy GIDEON WELLES and others, relegated Hamilton to a secondary role for the rest of the war. His first appointment as general had gone unconfirmed by the Senate and expired 4 Mar. 1863. Reappointed by Lincoln 18 Sept. 1863, he resigned the commission June 1865 when Pres. ANDREW JOHNSON reaffirmed his appointment as military governor of Texas.

Postwar, with the return to civil government, Hamilton sat on the Texas supreme court, ran unsuccessfully for governor in 1869, and litigated against state anti-Reconstruction Democrats. d. Austin, 11 Apr. 1875.   —JES

Hamilton, Charles Smith. USA b. Westernville, N.Y., 16 Nov. 1822. After private schooling in Erie Cty., N.Y., and appointment to West Point, Charles Hamilton, classmate of U. S. GRANT, graduated 26th in the class of 1843. Garrison duty in the East and Midwest, Mexican War service in 5 battles, and brevet promotion to captain were followed by routine assignments and Hamilton's resignation in 1853. He ran a flour-milling business in Fond du Lac, Wisc., until the Civil War.

LC

Hamilton organized the 3d Wisconsin Infantry, was commissioned colonel 11 May 1861, and was made brigadier general 17 May. His service, distinguished by the number of celebrated generals he displeased, took him to the Potomac River, the Shenandoah Valley, and divisional command at the Siege of YORKTOWN. Removed from the Army of the Potomac by Maj. Gen. GEORGE B. MCCLELLAN as "unfit to command a division," he exercised Western divisional command for Maj. Gen. WILLIAM S. ROSECRANS at the Mississippi battles at IUKA and CORINTH, and reputedly on Maj. Gen. U. S. Grant's intercession was made major general to rank from 19 Sept. 1862 for his part in the Union forefront at Iuka. Duplicitous, Hamilton criticized Grant to Washingtonians while politicking for a better command under him. His machinations provoked protests from Grant and threats of resignation from Hamilton if advancement was not forthcoming.

Maj. Gen. HENRY W. HALLECK referred to Hamilton's offers to resign as a "game." On 13 Apr. 1863 Hamilton's resignation was accepted. He returned to Wisconsin, manufactured Colzac Oil for lighthouses, later became president of the Hamilton Paper Co., a regent of Wisconsin State University, and a leader of the GRAND ARMY OF THE REPUBLIC and the MILITARY ORDER OF THE LOYAL LEGION OF THE UNITED STATES. Ironically, he received a Republican patronage appointment as a U.S. marshal during Grant's first presidential term. d. Milwaukee, 17 Apr. 1891.
                                                                                       —JES

Hamlin, Charles. USA b. Hampden, Maine, 13 Sept. 1837, Hamlin, the son of vice-president HANNIBAL HAMLIN, attended Hampden, Bridgton, and Bethel academies before studying at Bowdoin College. Graduating in 1857, he read law under his father's supervision, then established his own practice in Orland.

Hamlin spent the early part of the Civil War in Washington as a recruiter. On 21 Aug. 1862 he enlisted in the 18th Maine Infantry, which became the 1ST MAINE HEAVY ARTILLERY. First assigned as a commissary major, then to construction duty on the Washington defenses, Hamlin did not enter field service until May 1863, when he became adjutant general of the 2d Division/III Corps/Army of the Potomac. Though Hamlin held administrative positions through most of the war, he participated in the fighting for the Round Tops at GETTYSBURG, 2 July 1863, at Kelly's Ford, Locust Grove, and Mine Run. He finished the war as an inspector of artillery. Immediately after ABRAHAM LINCOLN's assassination, Hamlin commanded the troops detailed to keep order in Washington in the face of rumored uprisings.

He resigned from the army 14 Sept. 1865, settling in Bangor to resume his law practice. Before his death 15 May 1911, he became a powerful influence on banking in Maine, lectured on banking at the University of Maine, and held several minor political appointments in the state. The founder and early president of the Maine chapter of the MILITARY ORDER OF THE LOYAL LEGION OF THE UNITED STATES, he wrote several magazine articles about the war and contributed to the book *Maine at Gettysburg* (1898). His detailed notes on wartime politics in Washington formed the basis of the biography *The Life and Times of Hannibal Hamlin* (1899).   —PLF

Hamlin, Hannibal. USP b. Paris, Maine, 27 Aug. 1809. Only the fact that Hamlin was ABRAHAM LINCOLN's first vice-president saved him from the near oblivion of a footnote in U.S. history. Yet he was a successful lawyer who had been admitted to the bar in 1833; served 6 terms in the Maine legislature, 1836–40 and 1847; represented his state as a Democrat in the House of Representatives for 2 terms, 1843–47; and interrupted the last 2 of his 3 terms in the Senate, 1848–61, to serve as governor of Maine in 1857. From 1856, when Hamlin broke with the Democratic party over the KANSAS-NEBRASKA ACT, he served the people of Maine as a Republican.

Hamlin won his party's nomination as Lincoln's running mate 18 May 1860 in the national convention in Chicago. On the first ballot, fire-eating abolitionist CASSIUS M. CLAY of Kentucky received more than 100 votes, and the galleries were chanting, "Clay! Clay!," but Clay was a radical from west of the Allegheny Mts. and a former Whig; Hamlin was thought to give a better balance to the

USMHI

ticket as a moderate, an Easterner, a friend of WILLIAM H. SEWARD's (Seward had just lost the presidential nomination), and a former Democrat. He won on the second ballot.

Hamlin had not wanted the vice-presidency, but he realized the necessity of balancing the ticket. Having traded an influential Senate seat for a traditionally powerless office, he hoped Lincoln would assign him an important role in the war effort, but he was disappointed. While he urged the president to issue an emancipation proclamation and enlist free blacks in the army, he resented being relegated to the background. In frustration he enlisted as a private in the Maine Coast Guard and invoked public criticism by taking his place among the ranks during the 1864 summer encampment at Kittery.

Despite his unhappy position, Hamlin preferred another term as vice-president to leaving political life, and he expected to be renominated. Lincoln, however, wanted ANDREW JOHNSON, the military governor of Tennessee, on the ticket, so Hamlin lost to political expediency.

After his vice-presidency Hamlin again served in the Senate, 1869–81, and ended his public career by representing the U.S. as minister to Spain, 1881–82, during Chester A. Arthur's administration. He then retired to a quiet life in Maine, dying suddenly 4 July 1891 at his club in Bangor.

In later years, Hamlin, a political moderate recalling his wartime eagerness for emancipation, paid the martyred war president this tribute: "I was more radical than Lincoln. I was urging him; he was holding back . . . and he was the wiser." —RDH

Hammond, William Alexander. USA b. Annapolis, Md., 28 Aug. 1828, Hammond received his medical degree from the University of the City of New York in 1848. He entered the U.S. Army in 1849 as an assistant surgeon, serving in the West and at West Point Military Academy. In 1857 the American Medical Association commended his work on nutrition. He resigned from the army in 1859 to accept a professorship of anatomy and physiology at the University of Maryland.

At the outbreak of civil war he rejoined the army at the bottom of the list of assistant surgeons, having lost his seniority. As inspector of camps and hospitals, he gained the attention of the

USMHI

U.S. SANITARY COMMISSION for his excellent work at a time when the army medical service was in a disastrous condition. With the assistance of the sanitary commission he was appointed surgeon general with the rank of brigadier general as of 25 Apr. 1862.

Hammond brought efficiency, order, and reform to the chaotic army medical service, which had been overwhelmed by battle casualties and sick soldiers because of outmoded procedures. Wounded soldiers were often left lying on the field for days only to find themselves finally placed in makeshift hospitals with little or no care provided by the army medical service. Hammond created a general hospital service and was instrumental in the introduction of an efficient AMBULANCE CORPS. He also established the Army Medical Museum and started the systematic collection of data about all soldiers in the army that became the basis for the *Medical and Surgical History of the War of the Rebellion* (1870–88).

In 1864, however, Hammond clashed with Sec. of War EDWIN M. STANTON over the direction of the army medical service. As a result, he was court-martialed on a petty charge and dismissed from the army as of 18 Aug. 1864. Hammond's administration of the medical service had been efficient, and his innovations reduced some of the horrors of the war for Union soldiers. Vindicated after the war, he was restored to brigadier general on the retired list as of 27 Aug. 1879 and died 5 Jan. 1900 in the District of Columbia. —DLW

Hampton, Wade. CSA b. Charleston, S.C., 28 Mar. 1818, Hampton graduated from South Carolina College in 1826 and studied law, but rarely practiced. He was a man of great physical strength and great moral and political courage. Under his management the family plantations in South Carolina and Mississippi prospered greatly. Though he believed in the right of secession, he disputed its economic value and doubted the soundness of slave labor. When South Carolina seceded, he raised a command of cavalry known as the HAMPTON LEGION, which served most of the war with the Army of Northern Virginia in Maj. Gen. J.E.B. STUART's Cavalry Corps.

USMHI

Hampton was slightly wounded at FIRST BULL RUN, fought during most of the PENINSULA CAMPAIGN, and was commissioned brigadier general 23 May 1862. He was wounded again at SEVEN PINES but recovered to fight at ANTIETAM, in the CHAMBERSBURG raid, and at GETTYSBURG, where he was wounded a third time. Hampton was promoted to major general as of 3 Aug. 1863. After the Battle of the WILDERNESS, he succeeded Stuart on the latter's death as commander of the cavalry corps and participated in the PETERSBURG CAMPAIGN. As horses became scarce, he trained his men to fight on foot.

On 15 Feb. 1865 Hampton was promoted to lieutenant general and ordered to support Gen. JOSEPH E. JOHNSTON's retreat through South Carolina. Technically he was not under Johnston's command, so was exempt from the surrender.

Hampton returned to his ruined estates, restoring their original productivity. Vigorously opposing the Radicals, he was elected governor of South Carolina in 1876 and 1878, then was sent to the U.S. Senate, where he served until 1891. His political career ended when Populists defeated his conservative "Old South" party. He died in Columbia 11 Apr. 1902, 1 of only 3 Confederate lieutenant generals who attained that rank without formal military education.   —DBS

Hampton Legion. CSA In spring 1861 the wealthy South Carolina planter WADE HAMPTON organized a "legion"—a mixed command of infantry, cavalry, and artillery. The unit, which took the name of its founder, attracted to its ranks members of some of the wealthiest families of the state. With his private funds Hampton purchased much of the legion's equipment, including some of its artillery pieces.

In July 1861 he took the legion's infantry, some 600 men, to participate in the FIRST BATTLE OF BULL RUN. The unit lost 121 of its men in that engagement but won great praise. Hampton himself was wounded.

It soon became evident that the legion's organization was impractical. Hampton's artillery, organized as (Maj. James F.) Hart's South Carolina Battery, was assigned to the artillery units; the cavalry companies were transferred to the mounted arm; the infantry companies became, in effect, a battalion, though they retained the name "Hampton Legion" until the end of the war.

In early summer 1862 the infantry of the legion, under command of Lt. Col. MARTIN W. GARY, was assigned to Brig. Gen. JOHN B. HOOD'S Texas Brigade. The legion fought through the SEVEN DAYS', SECOND BULL RUN, and ANTIETAM campaigns as part of that brigade.

In the reorganization of the Army of Northern Virginia, fall 1862, the infantry of the legion became part of Brig. Gen. MICAH JENKINS' brigade of Maj. Gen. GEORGE E. PICKETT'S division. The brigade was left in Virginia during the GETTYSBURG CAMPAIGN but was at CHICKAMAUGA and KNOXVILLE.

In spring 1864 the legion was designated mounted infantry and assigned to a cavalry brigade. Gary, promoted to brigadier 19 May, had his command expanded to a brigade by the addition of 3 regiments. The legion fought with his brigade on the north side of the James during the Sieges of Richmond and Petersburg and was among the last units to leave Richmond Apr. 1865. Under the command of Lt. Col. Robert B. Arnold, the legion was surrendered and paroled at Appomattox Court House.

A soldier of the Texas Brigade who fought beside the Hampton Legion in several battles of 1862 expressed admiration for the unit's "grit . . . staying quality and . . . dash."   —RMcM

Hampton Roads, Va. Hampton Roads is the channel, about 8 mi long, formed by the James, Nansemond, and Elizabeth rivers as they come together and flow into Chesapeake Bay. During the Civil War, it was of major strategic importance to the Federals in their operations against Richmond. On the north it was bordered by the peninsula, between the York and James rivers, while at its eastern corner—Old Point Comfort—was Fort Monroe, which remained in Union control. The main channel in and out of Hampton Roads lay between the Rip Raps, a small artificial stone island built by the Federals, and FORT MONROE; both were heavily fortified. Confederate batteries at Sewell's Point protected the entrance to the Elizabeth, while Union positions at Pig Point guarded the entrance to the Nansemond. Vessels of the Federal blockading squadron were concentrated at Hampton Roads after the Confederates seized

Norfolk and its important Gosport Navy Yard. Then, after the South began building a powerful IRONCLAD at Gosport—the *VIRGINIA (Merrimack)*—it became even more important for the Federals to keep the 3 rivers closed.

Hampton Roads was the scene of 3 important events during the war: On 3 Aug. 1861 the war's first aerial reconnaissance took place as a balloon ascended from the USS *Fanny* to observe the Confederate batteries at Sewell's Point. (*See also* BALLOONS.) Then, 8–9 Mar. 1862, at the Battle of HAMPTON ROADS, the *Virginia* challenged the blockaders off the Roads and engaged the *Monitor* in the first battle between ironclads. And at the HAMPTON ROADS CONFERENCE, 3 Feb. 1865, Pres. ABRAHAM LINCOLN met with Confederate negotiators at a secret meeting to discuss terms for ending the war.   —NCD

Hampton Roads, Va., Battle of. 8–9 Mar. 1862 When Capt. FRANKLIN BUCHANAN accepted command of Confederate defenses of the lower James River Feb. 1862, his most significant defense was a novel and untested warship. For months the Confederate navy had worked to raise and refit the hull of the USS *Merrimack,* rechristening it the CSS *VIRGINIA.* The superstructure and deck of the ship were covered with iron plates to render the exposed area impervious to shot and shell.

On 8 Mar. Buchanan first took his cumbersome vessel from its mooring near Norfolk, not for a trial cruise, but into combat. At a maximum speed of 6 knots the *Virginia* sailed into HAMPTON ROADS and engaged Federal warships off Newport News. The Southern IRONCLAD first rammed the USS *Cumberland* and punched a huge hole below its waterline. Leaving the broken point of its ram in the victim's side, the *Virginia* then turned on the *Congress.* The Federal crew ran their vessel ashore to prevent the heavy-draft (22-ft) ironclad from ramming it. Buchanan, however, blasted the *Congress* into a burning hulk. The Confederates broke off the engagement in the late afternoon. Buchanan suffered a wound in the aftermath of the fight, and Lt. CATESBY AP R. JONES assumed command.

On 9 Mar. Jones set out to continue the work of destruction against wooden ships. As he stalked the USS *Minnesota,* however, the ironclad USS *MONITOR* intervened. The *Monitor,* product of inventor JOHN ERICSSON, was smaller than the *Virginia,* but more maneuverable; it had better engines and drew only 10.5 ft of water. Dubbed the "Yankee cheese box on a raft," the *Monitor* had a revolving turret in which there were 2 guns.

The duel between the ironclads began about 9 a.m. The ships pounded each other to no significant effect until 11. Then Lt. JOHN L. WORDEN, who commanded the *Monitor,* withdrew to replenish his ammunition and returned to fight again. Around noon the Confederates hit one of the *Monitor's* viewing slits and temporarily blinded Worden. At this point the Federal ship broke off the conflict.

For the next 2 months the 2 ironclads shadowed each other without renewing combat. The Federals attempted to lure the Confederate ship into shallow water; the Southerners tried to draw the *Monitor* into open water. When the Union took Norfolk 9 May, the *Virginia* became a ship without a port, and the Confederates had to scuttle her, at Craney Island.

The 2 combatants in the indecisive Battle of Hampton Roads had made wooden warships obsolete.   —EMT

Hampton Roads Conference. 3 Feb. 1865 The conference initially began with a wild scheme concocted in the fertile

Battle of Hampton Roads NA

imagination of politician FRANCIS P. BLAIR, SR. Blair believed that if the Union and Confederate governments could band together long enough to drive the French out of Mexico, then, in a spirit of harmony, a reconciliation could be negotiated.

ABRAHAM LINCOLN, hopeful peace could be won without conceding to the demands by Radical Republicans for a harsh RECONSTRUCTION, agreed to Blair's unofficial visit to Richmond at the end of 1864 to confer with JEFFERSON DAVIS. While the Confederate president failed to appreciate Blair's scheme, he saw it as an excellent opportunity to silence defeatist sentiment and steel his nation for another year of hard war. Late in January, JOHN A. CAMPBELL, ROBERT M. T. HUNTER, and Confederate Vice-Pres. ALEXANDER H. STEPHENS, all vociferous critics of Davis, crossed through the Petersburg lines to request a peace conference, which eventually took place at HAMPTON ROADS.

Stephens was pessimistic from the start. Davis had locked his delegates into negotiations "between the two countries," while Lincoln would discuss only reunion. The commissioners were shocked and outraged when they heard the Union president's demands. He told them the South was in no position to bargain at this stage of the war. Moreover, no armistice would be considered until the Confederates gave up their arms and recognized reunion and emancipation as fact. Tragically, the commissioners failed to investigate the generous terms Lincoln was prepared to offer toward Reconstruction. If accepted they might have eliminated much sectional bitterness after the war.

The conference ended with nothing accomplished. Davis made sure the Union demands were widely circulated, thus provoking a resurgence of Southern patriotism and stifling de-

featist talk for the time being. Lincoln's plan for Reconstruction caused an uproar within Republican ranks. Radicals retrenched and laid plans to mete out a just retribution on the South.

—MTC

Hampton-Rosser cattle raid, Va. 16 Sept. 1864 The Union army's grip on PETERSBURG, marked by lengthening trenches, tightened throughout summer 1864. By September the food supply of the Army of Northern Virginia had become critical. On the 5th a resourceful Confederate cavalry scout, Sgt. George D. Shadburne, reported that 2,500–3,000 weakly guarded Federal cattle were corraled at Coggins' Point on the south bank of the James River, 6 mi below Union headquarters at CITY POINT. Maj. Gen. WADE HAMPTON, commander of the Confederate cavalry corps, immediately submitted and obtained approval of an audacious plan to capture the herd.

At 1 a.m., 14 Sept., with Shadburne and Hampton in the lead, nearly 4,000 Southern horsemen cantered into the darkness. While Confederate infantry and other cavalry diverted the Federals, Hampton's raiders rode southwestward, away from Union lines. At Dinwiddie Court House, the gray-clad horsemen turned to the southeast, rode another 11 mi, and veered northeastward. By nightfall the Confederates had reached Wilkinson's Bridge on the Rowanty Creek.

Again, on the 15th, the raiders rode before dawn. 18 circuitous mi led them to Blackwater Creek, where Hampton had a bridge repaired. After midnight the Confederates crossed, deploying for a dawn attack against the Federal pickets at Sycamore Church, 4 mi from Coggins' Point.

At 5 a.m., 16 Sept., Brig. Gen. THOMAS L. ROSSER's Laurel Brigade charged into the camp of the 1st D.C. Cavalry. In 30 minutes Confederates killed, wounded, or captured 219 startled Federals. Rosser hurriedly regrouped and within an hour attacked 150 members of the 13th Pennsylvania Cavalry, who were guarding the herd. Rosser's charge destroyed the Union detail. The Confederates soon calmed the frightened cattle, seized many supplies, cut telegraph wires, and started southward with their prize.

The Union command initially reacted incredulously to the news of the Confederate attack and capture. Not until after Hampton had abandoned Coggins' Point did Union gunboats arrive to shell the area. The Confederate cowboys herded their 2,486 head of cattle back along their route of advance. The column stretched for nearly 7 mi through choking clouds of dust. At Ebenezer Church, about 4 p.m., Rosser began a 4-hour duel with Federal cavalry while Hampton pushed the herd. The Confederates rode throughout the night, reaching their lines about 9 a.m. on the 17th. At a cost of 61 casualties, Hampton and Rosser had completed one of the largest cattle-rustling operations in American history.   —JDW

Hancock, Cornelia. nurse b. Hancock's Bridge, near Salem, N.J., 1839. Of the women arriving in Philadelphia 5 July 1863 as volunteer nurses for GETTYSBURG, DOROTHEA DIX rejected only one, 23-year-old Cornelia Hancock. Undaunted, the young Quakeress sat down on the train scheduled to carry the women west and remained in her seat until disembarking at the battle-torn town the next day. Immediately she went to work with a dedication and efficiency that won respect from the doctors and affection and a silver medal of appreciation from admiring patients.

A compassionate woman of boundless initiative, Hancock stayed with the army, usually as a paid nurse, until 13 May 1865. Her brief term in the Contraband Hospital in Washington, D.C., discouraged her because blacks received such degrading treatment. "Where are all those good abolitionists north," she wrote home after witnessing the freedmen's destitution, "that do so much *talking* and so *little* acting?" (*See also* CONTRABANDS.)

Hancock preferred working in field hospitals and there her reputation thrived as an organizer and as a source of desperately needed supplies that she was able to get from civilians. With severe fighting to the south in mid-1864, her services were requested at the II Corps Hospital at Brandy Station, Va. She was the first woman to arrive at Belle Point, where she tended wounded from the WILDERNESS, then served at Fredericksburg, Port Royal, White House Landing, CITY POINT, and Petersburg.

Letters to her family richly describe hospital life and the suffering among her patients. She subjected colleagues to blunt criticism or approval as she judged their usefulness, but her soldiers received only praise for their endurance under extreme suffering. To her, the most difficult of tasks was writing to the family of a dying man. Even laboring under fire distressed her less, though the carnage she condemned "as a hellish way to settle a dispute." Gen.-in-chief U. S. GRANT she regarded a mere instrument of war after the Wilderness. "The idea of making a *business* of *maiming men* is not worthy of a civilization," she wrote in disgust over the number of casualties during the Overland Campaign.

On 9 Apr. 1865 Hancock visited Richmond, and a few days later she joined in the surrender celebrations at Grant's head-

quarters. Before going home, she stopped in Washington to see the GRAND REVIEW OF THE ARMIES.

Hancock's stint in the Contraband Hospital convinced her of the need to labor among freed slaves. Sponsored by the Society of Friends, she opened the Laing School for Negroes in Pleasantville, S.C. After teaching for a decade, she settled in Philadelphia. She helped found the Society for Organizing Charity in 1878 and the Children's Aid Society and Bureau of Information 4 years later. She never married, remaining active in social work and in urban development almost until her death, in Philadelphia in 1926.

Hancock's letters, written 7 July 1863–13 May 1865, were first published in 1937 under the title *South After Gettysburg*. Demand for the superb collection led to a second printing the same year. They provide a valuable description of the tragic aftermath of battle and a front-line nurse's attempt to cope with suffering. A third edition, with a foreword by historian Bruce Catton, was published in 1956.   —PLF

Hancock, Winfield Scott. USA b. Montgomery Square, Pa., 14 Feb. 1824. Graduating 18th in the West Point class of 1844, Hancock impressed his fellow soldiers with his military bearing and his thoroughly professional attitude. After his appointment as brigadier general as of 23 Sept. 1861, Hancock fought creditably in the campaigns of the Army of the Potomac as brigade and division commander, but it was at GETTYSBURG that he won great acclaim. Commanding the II Corps, he played a vital role in selecting the Union position on the first day of battle, thwarted Gen. ROBERT E. LEE's attempt to turn the left flank on the second day, and repelled the desperate

USMHI

attempt to break the center on the third day. He never fully recovered from the serious wounds he received there.

After a recuperation of nearly 6 months, Hancock returned to his corps and fought through the Virginia campaigns of 1864 until November, when his health drove him back to Washington. There he recruited for a corps of veterans (*see* VETERAN RESERVE CORPS). During the summer, rumors of the removal of Maj. Gen. GEORGE G. MEADE from the command of the Army of the Potomac carried the corollary that Hancock would replace him.

Through the vicissitudes of that army's campaigns, he refrained from intrigue and criticism, concentrating instead on the discipline of his men and their obedience to orders. Assessing his career, Lt. Gen. ULYSSES S. GRANT called him the "most conspicuous" of all Union commanders who had never exercised independent command. During RECONSTRUCTION, Hancock, while commander of the Fifth Military District, offended Republicans by his reluctance to use military power to replace civil courts. A major general in the Regular Army by 1866, he eventually assumed command of the Department of the East.

Needing a war hero to counter Republicans, who were stressing their patriotic war record, Democrats nominated Hancock for the presidency in 1880. Ridiculed during the campaign for apparently betraying ignorance of the meaning of a tariff, he lost to JAMES A. GARFIELD by a small margin of the popular vote and 59 electoral votes.

d. Governors Island, N.Y., 9 Feb. 1886.　　　—JYS

Hanson, Roger Weightman. CSA b. Winchester, Ky., 27 Aug. 1827. As a young 1st lieutenant of Kentucky Volunteers, Hanson served under Capt. JOHN S. WILLIAMS, a future Confederate general, during the Mexican War, making numerous military and political contacts. Following prospecting in the 1849 gold rush, he practiced law in Kentucky, lost a seat in the state legislature to Williams in 1851, was elected to the state legislature in 1853 and 1855, lost a bid for the U.S. Congress in 1857, and was a presidential elector in 1856 and 1860.

LC

In 1861, as a colonel of the Kentucky State Guard and a former Unionist in the secession controversy, Hanson traveled to Tennessee, accepted Confederate commission as colonel of the 2d Kentucky Infantry, and, under Brig. Gen. SIMON B. BUCKNER, the next year fought conspicuously at FORT DONELSON. Captured there, then exchanged, in Oct. 1862 he assumed brigade command without commensurate rank. During Gen. BRAXTON BRAGG's autumn campaigns, Hanson's brigade took part in diversionary action, threatening Nashville in November and took part in Col. JOHN HUNT MORGAN's capture of Hartsville, Tenn., 7 Dec. Hanson was made brigadier general 13 Dec. 1862, to serve under Maj. Gen. JOHN C. BRECKINRIDGE for the upcoming STONE'S RIVER campaign.

On the final day of fighting at the Battle of Stone's River, in a charge that cost his brigade 400 casualties, Hanson was mortally wounded. He died near the battlefield 4 Jan. 1863.　　—JES

Hardee, William Joseph. CSA b. Camden Cty., Ga., 12 Oct. 1815. In Jan. 1861, 45-year-old Lt. Col. William J. Hardee resigned from his U.S. Army career and 17 June accepted a commission as Confederate brigadier general. On 7 Oct. the West Point graduate, 26th in the class of 1838, was advanced to major general. Early in the war Hardee organized an Arkansas brigade and operated in that state and central Kentucky until the Army of Mississippi's concentration at Corinth, Mar. 1862, when he was assigned command of its III Corps. He performed creditably at SHILOH in April and perfected his corps, redesignated the I Corps or, while he commanded it, Hardee's Corps of the Army of Tennessee. In the KENTUCKY CAMPAIGN, particularly in maneuvers around Murfreesboro, Tenn., Hardee's troops, heavily engaged, continued to show skill taught them by their commander, author of the 1850s classic *Rifle and Light Infantry Tactics* (see HARDEE'S *TACTICS*). He was

LC

admired by his men, who affectionately called him "Old Reliable." On 10 Oct. 1862 Hardee was promoted to lieutenant general.

Along with much of the Army of Tennessee, Hardee was unimpressed with Gen. BRAXTON BRAGG's leadership. However, he continued under Bragg through CHICKAMAUGA and disastrous LOOKOUT MOUNTAIN and MISSIONARY RIDGE, where one of his divisions served as rear guard. After Bragg's resignation and Gen. JOSEPH E. JOHNSTON's assignment to army command, Hardee continued command of his corps through the ATLANTA CAMPAIGN. When Gen. JOHN BELL HOOD was assigned to replace Johnston July 1864, Hardee's lack of confidence in Hood caused him to request transfer. In Sept. 1864 he was assigned command of the Department of South Carolina, Georgia, and Florida and by year's end found himself attempting to defend SAVANNAH with few troops against Maj. Gen. WILLIAM T. SHERMAN's hordes. Forced out of that city, he had to yield Charleston and Columbia as his small army was driven north through the Carolinas (see CAROLINAS CAMPAIGN). Eventually, home guards and survivors of the FRANKLIN AND NASHVILLE CAMPAIGN joined Hardee's command, then were put under Johnston and designated the Army of Tennessee. Hardee fought his last battle at BENTONVILLE, N.C., and surrendered 26 Apr. 1865 at Greensborough.

Hardee settled in Selma, Ala., after the war and became a planter. d. 6 Nov. 1873 while traveling in Virginia.　—LDJ

Hardee Hat. The black-pattern 1858 army hat, known familiarly as the "Hardee Hat," had a tall, round crown and wide brim, generally rolled up on the right side and fastened with a brass eagle. A black plume decorated the left side. It was regulation U.S. Army headgear until the advent of the Civil War, and several volunteer and regular units wore it through the first months of war. Maj. WILLIAM J. HARDEE, later a Confederate lieutenant general, was on the first army board to review the hat pattern in 1855. His involvement with its adoption was minimal, but his name remained associated with it. It is also sometimes known as the Jeff Davis Hat, referring to Davis' tenure as secretary of war at the time it was first considered.　—JES

Hardee's *Tactics*. The introduction in the 1850s of the RIFLE, which doubled the foot soldier's range of accuracy, rendered Napoleonic TACTICS obsolete. Consequently, infantry manuals prepared in Europe began to reject the precise, slow formations of earlier wars, stressing instead speed and flexibility of maneuver. Noting these developments, American military observers realized that their own tactics, which paid homage to Napoleon's brand of warfare, required revision.

At the behest of Sec. of War JEFFERSON DAVIS, Maj. (and future Confederate Lt. Gen.) WILLIAM J. HARDEE, a Georgia-born West Pointer with 15 years' dragoon and infantry experience, began work on a new manual Nov. 1853. 8 months later he submitted his product to the War Department, which quickly approved it. Hardee's *Rifle and Light Infantry Tactics* (soon universally known as Hardee's *Tactics*) was published in 1855 under government subsidy. Immediately popular with West Point cadets and militiamen, the *Tactics* also served as a pocket-size bible for the thousands of men, North and South, who became infantry officers during the Civil War. New editions appeared in 1860 and 1861, and several Confederate versions were printed. None, however, made major changes in the original text.

Based to a large extent on the 1848 French manual *Ordonnance du roi sur l'exercice et les manoeuvres des bataillons de chasseurs à pied,* Hardee's work adapted European concepts to American usage, emphasizing speed over mass in battle. 2 ingredients of the French model received particular emphasis: an increase in the accepted rate of advance of an attack column and a "comrades in battle" theory that sought to enhance the effectiveness of small unit formations. Hardee doubled the rate of advance approved by older manuals to 180 steps per minute at a stride of 33 in. Associated concepts increased the speed with which units deployed from column into line. Meanwhile, the "comrades in battle" theory stressed a formation wherein blocks of 4 soldiers trained and fought together. This facilitated mutual support and supposedly enabled foot troops to repulse larger forces of infantry and even of horsemen.

Such innovations failed to overcome fully the deadly effectiveness of the rifle; moreover, their application was limited to battalion-size formations. Nevertheless, they represented a great advance over older, less flexible concepts such as those embodied in WINFIELD SCOTT's *Infantry-Tactics,* published in 1846 and considered the standard manual prior to Hardee's.

—EGL

Hardeman, William Polk. CSA b. Williamson Cty., Tenn., 4 Nov. 1816. At 19 Hardeman moved to Texas, becoming one of the state's most vigorous defenders. After fighting in the War for Texas Independence and the Mexican War, he accepted a commission as captain in the 4th Texas Mounted Volunteers in time for Confederate service in Brig. Gen. HENRY HOPKINS SIBLEY's campaign to acquire New Mexico Territory for the Confederacy early in 1862.

At VALVERDE, 21 Feb., Lt. Col. William R. Scurry cited Hardeman for conspicuous gallantry as a leader in one of 6 companies in the 4th Texas that spearheaded "the last brilliant and successful charge which decided the fortunes of the day." The Confederates had driven Col. E.R.S. CANBY's Federals back to their outpost at Fort Craig, and for his part in the victory Hardeman received a commendation from Sibley and a promotion to lieutenant colonel.

By the end of 1862 he had been promoted to colonel and commanded Col. THOMAS GREEN's brigade for a short time. Early in 1864 Hardeman's command participated in the RED RIVER CAMPAIGN against Maj. Gen. NATHANIEL P. BANKS and his Union troopers. His regiment performed conspicuously in the battles at MANSFIELD and PLEASANT HILL, 8–9 Apr., and pursued Banks after the campaign. On 28 Oct. Gen. E. KIRBY SMITH recommended Hardeman for a promotion to brigadier general, citing him as among "the best brigade commanders in the Trans-Mississippi department." The promotion was conferred 17 Mar. 1865.

After the war Hardeman was a planter in Texas, assistant sergeant-at-arms in the state house of representatives, inspector of railroads, and supervisor of the Texas Confederate Soldiers' Home. On 8 Apr. 1898 Hardeman died at his home in Austin.

—FLS

Hardie, James Allen. USA b. New York City, N.Y., 5 May 1823, Hardie served 37 years in the U.S. Army, earning promotion and respect not as a combat officer but in staff command. An 1843 West Point graduate, 11th in his class, Hardie taught at his alma mater, served in California during the Mexican War, participated in the Indian campaigns, and acted as an aide to Brig. Gen. JOHN E. WOOL. Captain Hardie was adjutant general of the Department of Oregon when the Civil War commenced.

LC

Promoted to lieutenant colonel 28 Sept. 1861, he joined the staff of Maj. Gen. GEORGE B. MCCLELLAN, serving the general during the PENINSULA, SEVEN DAYS' and ANTIETAM campaigns. When Maj. Gen. AMBROSE E. BURNSIDE replaced McClellan, Hardie remained at army headquarters. During the Battle of FREDERICKSBURG, 13 Dec. 1862, he kept Burnside informed of the operations on the Union left. So accurate were his field dispatches that Burnside and Maj. Gen. WILLIAM B. FRANKLIN, commander of the Left Grand Division, accepted them as correct assessments of the disastrous Union defeat.

Hardie was promoted to brigadier general to rank from 29 Nov. 1862. His name, however, was never submitted for Senate confirmation, and his commission was revoked 22 Jan. 1863. On 19 Feb. the War Department promoted him to major and appointed him assistant adjutant general in the Regular Army. For the remainder of the war Hardie executed special assignments for the department. In June 1863 he carried the secret orders replacing Maj. Gen. JOSEPH HOOKER with Maj. Gen. GEORGE G. MEADE as commander of the Army of the Potomac during the GETTYSBURG CAMPAIGN. In Mar. 1864 he was promoted to colonel and inspector general and a year later received the brevets of brigadier and major general, U.S. Army.

During the postwar years Colonel Hardie served as one of the army's 4 inspector generals. d. 14 Dec. 1876 while on active duty.

—JDW

Hardin, Martin Davis. USA b. Jacksonville, Ill., 26 June 1837. The grandson of a U.S. senator and the son of a militia general killed in the Mexican War, Hardin entered West Point, graduating 11th in the class of 1859. Until the outbreak of the Civil War, he served as an artillery lieutenant in Oregon.

Hardin was promoted to 1st lieutenant 14 May 1861 and assigned to the staff of Col. HENRY J. HUNT. He saw little action until spring 1862, when he served Hunt, who was Maj. Gen. GEORGE B. MCCLELLAN's chief of reserve artillery, during the PENINSULA and SEVEN DAYS' campaigns. On 8 July 1862 the young staff officer was promoted to lieutenant colonel and command of the 12th Pennsylvania Reserves. He gallantly led his regiment at GROVETON and SECOND BULL RUN, where he was wounded twice. Promoted to colonel 1 Sept., Hardin temporarily commanded 2 brigades in succession, then returned to his regiment during the Battle of GETTYSBURG.

His conduct there earned him permanent command of a brigade in the V Corps, which he led during the BRISTOE and MINE RUN campaigns in autumn 1863. In December, while inspecting pickets near Catlett's Station, Hardin was ambushed by Confederate guerrillas. Surgeons amputated his left arm, and he did not return to duty until spring 1864.

LC

Hardin sustained another wound in May in the operations along the NORTH ANNA RIVER. While recuperating, he received his promotion to brigadier general 2 July and command of the defenses north of the Potomac, XXII Corps, Washington, D.C. In this capacity he defended the capital against Lt. Gen. JUBAL A. EARLY's Confederate raiders in mid-July (*see* EARLY'S WASHINGTON RAID). He was brevetted brigadier general, U.S. Army, for his combat record.

When the war ended, the one-armed Hardin remained in the Regular Army. Named major of the 43d Infantry in 1866, he retired 4 years later because of his wounds. Hardin studied law and prospered in Chicago, devoting much time to veteran affairs and to writing. He died in obscurity in St. Augustine, Fla., 12 Dec. 1923, the last survivor of his class at West Point. —JDW

hardtack. Called "Army Bread" by manufacturers, hardtack was a quarter-inch-thick cracker made of unleavened flour. A staple of Union and Confederate soldiers' diets, it was unpopular and unpalatable, and its impervious character made it legendary. In 1861, Union recruits joked that they had been issued unopened barrels of hardtack from the Mexican War, not much less edible than recent issues. —JES

Harker, Charles Garrison. USA b. Swedesboro, N.J., 2 Dec. 1835. A retail clerk appointed to West Point by his employer, Congressman Nathan T. Stratton, Harker graduated 16th in the class of 1858, went on to serve at Governors Island, N.Y., and in Oregon and Washington territories. As 1st lieutenant of the 15th U.S. Infantry, he trained Ohio volunteers for civil war early in 1861. Promoted captain in the Regulars 24 Oct. 1861, he was made colonel of the 6th Ohio Volunteers 11 Nov., attached to Brig. Gen. DON CARLOS BUELL's command, and through the next year fought at SHILOH, the Siege of CORINTH, and the Battles of PERRYVILLE and STONE'S RIVER. At Stone's River, in the first day of fighting he distinguished himself under Brig. Gen. PHILIP H. SHERIDAN in supporting Brig. Gen. Horatio P. Van Cleve's tenuous position and in saving the army from rout. At the Battle of CHICKAMAUGA, 20 Sept. 1863, Harker made a last-ditch stand with Maj. Gen. GEORGE H. THOMAS at Snodgrass Hill. For consistent daring in desperate straits, he was made

brigadier general to date from 20 Sept. After fighting at CHATTANOOGA and MISSIONARY RIDGE, and service in the relief expedition to besieged Maj. Gen. AMBROSE E. BURNSIDE at KNOXVILLE, he commanded a brigade in the IV Corps early in the ATLANTA CAMPAIGN. At the Battle of KENNESAW MOUNTAIN, 27 June 1864, he was shot from his horse and killed in the assault on entrenched Confederates. —JES

Harlan, James. USP b. Clark Cty., Ill., 26 Aug. 1820. Descended from English Quaker stock, at 4 Harlan moved with his family to Indiana, where he gained a local education and in 1841 entered Asbury University. Graduating with highest honors, he became principal of an academy in Iowa City, Iowa, meanwhile joining the Whig party. Later he studied law, was called to the bar, and in 1850 declined an opportunity to run for the governorship of Iowa. In 1853 he was chosen to serve as head of what became Iowa Wesleyan University, one of the earliest trans-Mississippi institutions of higher learning. After 2 years, however, politics—specifically agitation over the free-soil movement, which he ardently supported—drew him into public life.

In 1855 Harlan was elected to the U.S. Senate on the Whig ticket. His energy and forthrightness, displayed throughout his campaign, helped him win the position. He publicly vowed that on constitutional questions he would be guided by Supreme Court decisions, in legislative matters by the views of the people and the lawmakers of Iowa, and "in all questions of *Conscience* by the Bible." Through irregularities in the Iowa legislature, his seat was declared vacant in 1857, but he regained it as a Republican candidate later that year and was reelected in 1861. In Congress, Harlan was at first considered a moderate on sectional matters, but during the Civil War he allied himself with the more RADICAL REPUBLICANS on numerous issues. He became a loyal supporter of ABRAHAM LINCOLN as war administrator, and also a family intimate; in later years his daughter married Lincoln's eldest son. In nonmilitary matters, he favored westward expansion, homestead and land-grant-college legislation, and the Pacific Railroad Acts, which he sponsored. (*See also* HOMESTEAD ACT OF 1862 and MORRILL ACT.)

Shortly before his assassination, the president appointed Harlan secretary of the interior. Though he held the post for 14 months under Pres. ANDREW JOHNSON, political differences between the two finally prompted Harlan's resignation. As secretary, he was a conscientious but controversial administrator, engaging in numerous disputes with other government authorities—some of whom charged him, apparently without basis, of corrupt land transactions and personnel appointments.

Harlan won a third Senate term in 1867, but political rivals banded to prevent his further service in elective office. Though he retired to private life in 1873, he presided over the ALABAMA CLAIMS 1882–86. d. Mount Pleasant, Iowa, 5 Oct. 1899. —EGL

Harpers Ferry, western Va., capture of. 15 Sept. 1862 A key element in Gen. R. E. LEE's plans for his ANTIETAM CAMPAIGN called for the capture of a 12,000-man Federal force threatening the Confederate rear from a position at Harpers Ferry. On 9 Sept. Lee issued orders that dispatched columns toward Harpers Ferry along 3 different routes. By the evening of the 13th, Maj. Gen. LAFAYETTE MCLAWS' Confederates were on Maryland Heights opposite Harpers Ferry and Brig. Gen.

USMHI

JOHN G. WALKER's column was in position on Loudoun Heights east of the town. Maj. Gen. THOMAS J. "STONEWALL" JACKSON, in overall command, sealed the trap with his third column, which had come in from the west via Martinsburg.

The Federals were in an untenable position on low ground, surrounded by strong Confederate forces on the hills overlooking the town. Brig. Gen. JULIUS WHITE had retreated into Harpers Ferry from Martinsburg in the face of Jackson's advance. White left Col. Dixon S. Miles in command at Harpers Ferry, because Miles was more familiar with the situation there. On the night of 14 Sept. Col. Benjamin F. Davis led 1,300 Union cavalry out of the doomed town, across the Potomac, and on to freedom by a route the Confederates had carelessly left unguarded. This dramatic exploit was made even more amazing when the cavalry column captured a number of Confederate wagons and men en route to safety.

On the morning of the 15th Jackson made ready to assault the Federal lines around Harpers Ferry. Before the preliminary artillery barrage had concluded, the defenders raised a white flag and White surrendered the town. Colonel Miles was killed during the shelling. Jackson's success came not a moment too soon, since Federal pressure was building following their attacks on the South Mountain gaps, and Jackson was obliged to hurry his victorious troops to join Lee at Antietam Creek. About 12,000 Federals were captured, together with 13,000 badly needed arms, 73 cannon, and innumerable smaller supplies and equipment.   —RKK

Harpers Ferry, western Va., John Brown's Raid on.
16–18 Oct. 1859   JOHN BROWN, an unyielding abolitionist and religious fanatic and a product of the bitter sectional controversy of the 1850s, quoted from the Bible while wielding a sword. He believed that he was God's appointed instrument to rid the country of the sin of slavery. After murdering 5 proslavery settlers near Pottawatomie, Kans., Brown planned to strike out against slavery in the South itself.

For 3 years Brown worked on the details of his assault. He proposed to lead a band of raiders into the mountains of Virginia, gather slaves from plantations and farms, arm them, establish a freedmen's republic, and incite slave insurrections throughout the region. Brown convinced several leading abolitionists, called the "Secret Six," to finance the undertaking and recruit volunteers. In summer 1859 he rented a farm in Maryland across the Potomac River from Harpers Ferry, where a Federal arsenal was located. On the night of 16 Oct. Brown and 21 recruits stole into the ferry, seizing the undefended armory, arsenal, and rifle works.

Unrealistic from the outset, the scheme faltered almost immediately. Brown had neither informed nearby slaves of his plot nor developed an escape route. He simply gathered a handful of white hostages and black slaves and waited. Virginians reacted swiftly to the raid, and by the 17th militia and armed citizens had surrounded the band. The aroused Southerners attacked, driving Brown's men out of the buildings and into the fire-engine house. In the melee 3 local men and several raiders, including 2 of Brown's sons, were killed or mortally wounded. During the night Bvt. Col. ROBERT E. LEE arrived with a detachment of marines from Washington, D.C. When Brown refused to surrender on the 18th, the marines, led by Lt. J.E.B. STUART, stormed the fire-engine house. Brown was wounded and 2 raiders were killed.

With 6 confederates, the abolitionist was tried for treason and sentenced to execution. On 2 Dec. 1859, in Charlestown, western Virginia, John Brown calmly walked to the gallows.

Enraged Southerners blamed Republicans for this attempt at slave insurrection and warned that if a Republican was elected president in 1860 they would secede. A martyr in the eyes of many Northerners, Brown predicted that the sin of slavery "will never be purged away; but with Blood." He had done much to make this come true.   —JDW

Harpers Ferry, W.Va., Mosby's ("Greenback") Raid on.

13 Oct. 1864   Maj. Gen. PHILIP H. SHERIDAN's campaign in the Shenandoah Valley against Lt. Gen. JUBAL A. EARLY's Confederates had achieved decisive results by Oct. 1864. Twice, at WINCHESTER 19 Sept. and at FISHER'S HILL 3 days later, the Union army had defeated the Confederates. By early October the Federals had occupied the upper valley near Harrisonburg, destroying crops, farms, and mills. Sheridan's successful campaign was hampered only by the operations in his rear waged by the Confederacy's incomparable guerrilla officer Lt. Col. JOHN S. MOSBY.

Mosby had forged the 43d Virginia Battalion, since its formation Jan. 1863, into an indestructible body of partisan rangers. Operating from the region east of the Blue Ridge Mts. known as "Mosby's Confederacy," the rangers descended on Union wagon trains, outposts, and railroad trains and crews. Superb horsemen, they defied all attempts at eradication. Sheridan wrestled with solutions, even creating an elite body of scouts with the sole mission of destroying the ubiquitous rangers. But time and again Mosby struck, inflicting casualties, destroying or capturing supplies, and frustrating Union commanders.

On the night of 12 Oct. 1864 Mosby, with 84 rangers, reentered the valley on another raid. All day on the 13th the raiders hid north of Winchester. With nightfall, they remounted and rode northward, halting about 10 o'clock at a deep cut near Brown's Crossing on the Baltimore & Ohio Railroad, several miles west of Harpers Ferry. A detachment hurriedly displaced a few rails in the cut, then patiently waited.

Between 2 and 3 in the morning the westbound passenger express came rattling out of the darkness. When the engine hit the gap in the rails, it lurched suddenly into the bank in a loud crash. Inside the cars passengers tumbled from their seats. Within minutes the rangers swarmed through the damaged cars. A Federal soldier resisted and was shot instantly. The rangers herded the passengers outside, and Mosby ordered the cars and engine burned. 2 rangers held a satchel and a tin box they had taken from 2 army paymasters. Inside was $173,000 in GREENBACKS, which would be divided in 84 shares. While the train burned, the rangers rode away into the West Virginia blackness. Mosby's "Greenback Raid" brought operations on the vital railroad to a temporary standstill.   —JDW

Harpers Ferry rifle.

The U.S. rifle Model 1841, Mississippi rifle, or Harpers Ferry rifle, saw its first service in the Mexican War, where future Confederate Pres. JEFFERSON DAVIS' 1st Mississippi Rifle Regiment made its accuracy famous in the 1840s. The first U.S. Army standard-issue rifled small arm using percussion caps, it fired a .54-caliber conical projectile, had a 33-in. barrel, weighed 9.75 lb, and, with skillful handling under ideal conditions, found its target at 1,000 yd. The U.S. Harpers Ferry, Va., Arsenal first produced it, manufacturing 25,296 1846–55. The arsenal's name stuck to the weapon, carried by Federals and Confederates at the outset of the Civil War. U.S. manufacture was discontinued in favor of the U.S. Model 1861 rifle musket. Confederate manufacturers continued producing limited numbers of the 1841 model throughout the war.

—JES

Harper's Weekly.

In 1857 Fletcher Harper, of Harper and Brothers publishers, launched *Harper's Weekly.* An illustrated newspaper selling for 5 cents a copy, it capitalized on the popularity of illustrated newspapers originating in Britain, bringing the public woodcut engravings of news events in the age before printing technology could reproduce photographs. The newspaper was distributed each Saturday, had a national circulation, and, borrowing from the successful format of the established *Harper's Monthly Magazine,* featured serializations of novels by such popular contemporary authors as Charles Dickens and Wilkie Collins.

At Fletcher Harper's direction, the newspaper, selling at an inflated wartime price of 6 cents an issue, kept an unflagging pro-Union, pro-war policy throughout the Civil War. Through its graphics most Federal servicemen were depicted as noble martyrs and heroes, and most Confederates as flea-bitten villains. It served as a propaganda organ for the Union cause, though it featured cartoons and jokes that, by 20th-century standards, are racist and ethnocentric. Beginning in 1862 George William Curtis, essayist and speaker, assumed its editorship.

Harper's Weekly's contribution to the history of the Civil War lay chiefly in its art. News artists ALFRED R. WAUD, Henry Mosler, and Theodore Davis contributed to *Harper's* reputation for graphics. *Harper's* news artist, WINSLOW HOMER, later won personal recognition for his fine art, and Thomas Nast, who joined *Harper's* in the middle of the war, later brought the paper national note for his caricatures of corrupt New York City mayor William Marcy "Boss" Tweed. The paper's artwork received censure as well as praise. A 2-page spread published in 1862 depicting Confederate defenses at YORKTOWN, Va., and the position, strength, and location of besieging Federal units caused Union Sec. of War EDWIN M. STANTON, an advocate of CENSORSHIP, to order publication of the newspaper suspended. Fletcher Harper's diplomatic skills got the order reversed.

The paper's popularity during the war eclipsed its nearest national rival, *FRANK LESLIE'S ILLUSTRATED NEWSPAPER.* Its growth continued through the 1870s, but with the advent of news photography and changing public tastes, its appeal waned in the late 19th century. In 1916 it was absorbed by a publication called the *Independent.*   —JES

Harriet Lane, USS.

Named for the niece who had served as Pres. James Buchanan's hostess in the White House, the *Harriet Lane,* a sidewheel steamer, was built in New York and launched Nov. 1857, the first engine-driven REVENUE CUTTER. It was a fast ship but could store only enough coal to last 6 days.

THE REISSUE OF

HARPER'S WEEKLY.

A JOURNAL OF CIVILIZATION

VOL. VI.—No. 304.]   NEW YORK, SATURDAY, OCTOBER 25, 1862.   [SINGLE COPIES SIX CENTS.
$2 50 PER YEAR IN ADVANCE.

Entered according to Act of Congress, in the Year 1862, by Harper & Brothers, in the Clerk's Office of the District Court for the Southern District of New York.

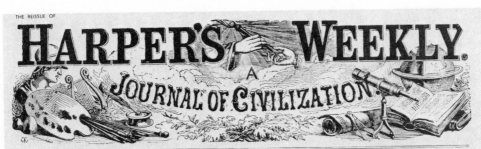

GARIBALDI, WOUNDED AND A PRISONER.—[See next page.]

Early in Apr. 1861, the *Harriet Lane* was sent to Charleston, S.C., to reprovision FORT SUMTER, and there, on the 12th, its crew witnessed the first bombardment of the war. For most of the summer, it served as a blockade ship off Fort Monroe. On 26 Aug. it became part of a fleet sent to North Carolina to capture HATTERAS INLET, the first expedition of the Union navy in the Civil War. Forts Clark and Hatteras were taken quickly, but on the afternoon of 29 Aug. the *Harriet Lane* was grounded on a shoal, where it remained for 2 days.

The ship participated in the attack on FORTS JACKSON AND ST. PHILIP 18–28 Apr. 1862, then served as the flagship of the Potomac Blockading Fleet. In Oct. 1862 it was part of a fleet sent to capture GALVESTON, TEX. There the attack was delayed until New Year's Day, by which time the Confederates were prepared. Loaded with bales of cotton to protect their crews, vessels came out into the harbor, captured the *Harriet Lane*, forced the USS *Westfield* to be blown up, drove off the invading fleet, and temporarily lifted the blockade.

For months, the Union navy made plans to recapture the *Harriet Lane* but could never locate the ship. Various reports indicated that it had been dismantled at Galveston, had escaped to sea, or had been moved to Harrisburg, Miss., to undergo alterations.

After the war, the ship was recovered at Havana, Cuba, and sold to developers in Boston, Mass., who transformed it into a bark. It sailed the seas until it foundered in the Caribbean Sea 13 May 1884.

—VCJ

Harris, Eliza. nurse b. place and date unknown. Though characterized by acquaintances as despondent and pessimistic, Harris worked strenuously to better conditions among the wounded in Northern hospitals during the war. An organizer of the Ladies' Aid Society of Philadelphia, she was chosen by her colleagues as their field correspondent, with responsibility for distributing supplies collected by the society. She ultimately served in the same capacity for soldiers' aid societies across Pennsylvania and as an agent for both the U.S. SANITARY COMMISSION and the U.S. CHRISTIAN COMMISSION.

During the war Harris visited more than 100 hospitals, served aboard a hospital transport after the battle at SEVEN PINES, nursed in field hospitals during the PENINSULA CAMPAIGN and at SECOND BULL RUN, and worked with MARIA HALL at Antietam Nov. 1862. Over the War Department's protests, Harris traveled to GETTYSBURG July 1863 immediately following the battle. From there she followed the army south to Tennessee, serving in the Western theater from the battle at CHICKAMAUGA in September through May 1864. During the latter months of war she worked with CONTRABANDS and white refugees in Tennessee, Virginia, and North Carolina.

After the surrender Harris returned to Philadelphia, where she and her husband, prominent physician John Harris, were active in community affairs. d. place and date unknown.

—PLF

Harris, Isham Green. war governor b. Franklin Cty., Tenn., 10 Feb. 1818, Harris was educated in local common schools and at Winchester Academy. He moved to Paris, Tenn., in 1832, taking a position as clerk in a mercantile house. At the same time he studied law with a local attorney and in 1841 passed his bar examinations. Elected to the state legislature as a Democrat in 1847, he served the next year as elector for unsuccessful presidential candidate Lewis Cass, senator

LC

from Michigan. Harris won seats in the U.S. House of Representatives in 1849 and 1851, but declined a third nomination to return to his law practice in Memphis.

His retirement from politics lasted until 1856, when he became a presidential elector for James Buchanan. The STATES-RIGHTS secessionist Democrat received the gubernatorial nomination in 1857, defeating Whig opponents that year and again in 1859. After ABRAHAM LINCOLN'S election to the presidency, Harris urged Tennesseans to pass a secession ordinance, refusing Lincoln's call for troops and pledging men and loyalty to the Southern government. By July 1861 he had equipped for state service or made available to the Confederacy 100,000 Tennessee troops, earning his reputation as the "War Governor of Tennessee."

Reelected in August, Harris called for the legislature to convene in Memphis Feb. 1862. Less than a month later, Federal troops occupied large sections of the state and Lincoln appointed ANDREW JOHNSON military governor; thereafter Harris held office nominally. Determined to play an active role in achieving Southern independence, he volunteered as an aide-de-camp on the staffs of, successively, Gens. ALBERT SIDNEY JOHNSTON, BRAXTON BRAGG, and JOSEPH E. JOHNSTON, serving in most of the major battles in the Western theater. Toward the end of the war the Confederate Congress repaid his devotion by voting him a courtesy seat in the legislature.

After the Confederate surrender, Harris faced Federal charges of treason, and, with a $5,000 reward offered for his capture, fled to England. He returned to Memphis in 1867, reestablished his law practice, and reentered politics as a U.S. Senator in the post-Reconstruction years. Elected to 3 consecutive terms beginning in 1883, Harris died in office in Washington, D.C., 8 July 1897. During his latter years he was an active and popular officer in the Southern Historical Society.   —PLF

Harris, Nathaniel Harrison. CSA b. Natchez, Miss., 22 Aug. 1834. A law graduate of the University of Louisiana, Harris practiced his profession in Vicksburg. Early in 1861 the attorney organized the Warren Rifles, a militia company that was mustered into state service 8 May. Less than a month later the unit entered Confederate service as Company C/19th Mississippi, with Harris its captain.

The 19th Mississippi soon transferred to Virginia but saw little action until spring 1862. Promoted to major 5 Mar. 1862, Harris fought bravely at WILLIAMSBURG 5 May, earning commendation for his performance. He participated in the campaigns of SEVEN DAYS', SECOND

USMHI

BULL RUN, and ANTIETAM, earning promotion to lieutenant colonel after the Antietam Campaign.

Harris assumed command of his regiment 2 Apr. 1863, with the rank of colonel, and led the Mississippians at CHANCELLORS-VILLE and GETTYSBURG. He was commissioned brigadier general 20 Jan. 1864 and given a brigade in Maj. Gen. WILLIAM MA-HONE's veteran division. In the scorching struggle for the "MULE SHOE" at SPOTSYLVANIA, 12 May, Harris distinguished himself when his brigade delivered a riveting counterattack. A steady and hard-hitting combat officer, he earned increasing distinction during the PETERSBURG CAMPAIGN. On 21 Aug., at Globe Tavern, his brigade suffered casualties totaling over half its number. In Mar. 1865 Harris commanded the inner defenses of Richmond. He surrendered with the army at Appomattox.

Returning to Vicksburg, Harris resumed his law practice. He eventually served as a railroad president and as registrar of a land office in South Dakota. Moving to California in 1890, he prospered as a businessman. He died, while on a business trip, in Malvern, England, 23 Aug. 1900. His cremated remains were returned to Brooklyn, N.Y., for burial.   —JDW

Harris, Thomas Maley. USA b. Wood Cty., Va., 17 June 1817, Harris studied then practiced medicine in the section of his native state that in 1863 became part of West Virginia.

Prominent in his community, he played a major role in recruiting a local regiment, the 10th West Virginia Infantry, late in 1861. On the outfit's muster-in, he became its lieutenant colonel, rising to colonel 20 May 1862.

Harris' regiment participated in the unsuccessful pursuit of Maj. Gen. THOMAS J. "STONE-WALL" JACKSON during the latter's spring 1862 SHENANDOAH VALLEY CAMPAIGN. Early in 1863, the 10th West Virginia was returned to its home region, to become part of Brig. Gen. WILLIAM

LC

W. AVERELL's brigade of the VIII Corps. Through that year and well into 1864 the 10th saw frequent action in the West Virginia mountains, sometimes against Confederate Regulars, often against Southern partisans and bushwhackers. It fought skillfully enough to win its colonel temporary command of a brigade Mar. 1864. That August, following participation in a railroad-wrecking expedition under Averell, Harris led a division in the VIII Corps. Later he distinguished himself during Maj. Gen. PHILIP H. SHERIDAN's operations in the Shenandoah, especially at THIRD WINCHESTER and CEDAR CREEK.

In December Harris' command was transferred to the Petersburg front and became the Independent Division of the XXIV Corps/Army of the James. When Brev. Maj. Gen. JOHN W. TURNER was assigned to lead the division, Harris attempted to resign his commission in protest but was persuaded to remain on duty as a brigadier of volunteers. He led the 1st Brigade of Turner's "Wild Cat Division" in the final operations in Virginia, including the seizure of FORT GREGG, 2 Apr. 1865. A week later his troops helped curtail Gen. ROBERT E. LEE's retreat toward Appomattox Court House.

As a brevet major general, Harris served on the postwar commission that tried those charged in LINCOLN's ASSASSINA-TION. Mustered out of the army in 1866, he spent 1 term in the West Virginia legislature, was adjutant general of the state,

1869–70, then a pension agent. He also wrote on medicine, the Lincoln murder conspiracy, and religion, praising Calvinism and condemning Roman Catholicism. d. Harrisville, W. Va., just shy of 90, 30 Sept. 1906.   —EGL

Harrisburg, Miss., Battle of. 14–15 July 1864 See TUPELO, MISS., BATTLE OF.

Harrison, James. spy b. Baltimore, Md. (?), 1 Nov. 1834. More is known of Harrison's activities before and after the war than during the conflict. He made his acting debut in Baltimore 8 Sept. 1852, toured with various acting companies including Edwin Booth's, and shortly before the war managed a theater in Petersburg. He enlisted in the Confederate army at Richmond, but his specific duties and rank remain unknown. Both the Confederate War Department and several commanders, Lt. Gen. JAMES LONGSTREET in particular, regarded him as a reliable, effective spy. Gen. ROBERT E. LEE trusted him enough to alter his plans just before the Battle of GETTYSBURG when Harrison informed him that Maj. Gen. JOSEPH HOOKER had started to cross the Potomac and that Maj. Gen. GEORGE G. MEADE had been given command of the Army of the Potomac. As badly mauled as Lee's troops were, the information prevented his Army of Northern Virginia from being defeated in detail.

Harrison continued to appear on the stage while he engaged in espionage. The agent hinted as much to Brig. Gen. G. MOX-LEY SORREL in Longstreet's camp early in Sept. 1863. The next week Sorrel recognized him in a performance of *Othello* at the New Richmond Theater. At the same time, the officer learned of Harrison's fondness for liquor and gambling, and cautioned Longstreet against employing him again. When the general sought his services during the Tennessee campaigning, Harrison was nowhere to be found, though he appears to have been well known among the high command.

The actor kept silent about his activities after the war, even though he occasionally found himself in reduced circumstances that might have been relieved by capitalizing on his exploits. In 1906, after becoming ill on the way to a performance, he retired. Harrison lived his last years in Louisville, supported in part by money from the Actors' Fund. After his death 21 Feb. 1913, the organization destroyed whatever papers they possessed concerning him.   —PLF

Harrison, James Edward. CSA b. Greenville District, S.C., 24 Apr. 1815. The elder brother of THOMAS HARRISON, who would also become a Confederate general, James moved with his family first to Alabama, then to Mississippi. He served 2 terms in the Mississippi legislature before settling near Waco, Tex., in 1854. EDWARD CLARK chose him as part of the Texas delegation to the Five Civilized Tribes, Feb. 1861, which sought to persuade them to ally with the Confederacy in the likely event of war. The optimistic report the emissaries submitted formed the basis of Clark's advice to JEFFERSON DAVIS regarding the urgency of Confederate alliances with the various tribes, a matter of utmost importance to borderland Texans fearful of depredations should the tribes pledge loyalty to the Northern government. On his return, Harrison participated in the state secession convention.

When the fighting started, he accepted a commission as lieutenant colonel in the 15th Texas Infantry, a unit usually detached for scouting and skirmishing details into 1863. He served under Brig. Gen. THOMAS GREEN during the Louisiana campaigning that year and until Green's death at BLAIR'S LANDING Apr. 1864. The 15th Texas was heavily engaged in a successful charge on the enemy rear in the Sept. 1863 operations along the Atchafalaya.

LC

Harrison proved himself an adequate commander, receiving commendations from Green, but did not achieve military greatness. He was nonetheless promoted to brigadier general to rank from 22 Dec. 1864, with command of the 15th, 17th, and 31st Texas regiments and (Col. James G.) Stevens' Texas Regiment (22d Texas Cavalry, dismounted)/Maj. Gen. CAMILLE DE POLIGNAC's division. His brigade resisted surrender, voting at a camp meeting early in May 1865 its "unalterable determination never to yield."

After Gen. E. KIRBY SMITH surrendered the Trans-Mississippi troops later that month, Harrison returned to Waco, where he died 23 Feb. 1875. —PLF

Harrison, Thomas. CSA b. Jefferson Cty., Ala., 1 May 1823. Brother of Confederate Brig. Gen. JAMES E. HARRISON, Thomas was reared in Monroe Cty., Miss. After moving to Texas and establishing a law practice in 1843, he briefly returned to Mississippi, fought in the Mexican War as a member of Col. JEFFERSON DAVIS' 1st Mississippi Rifles, then took up permanent residence in Texas, first near Houston, then Waco, serving a term in the state legislature. At the outbreak of civil war he was prominent in Waco's affairs.

From 1861, as captain of state militia, Harrison was assigned to the West Texas frontier. Early in 1862, following an epidemic of measles that seriously reduced the ranks of the 8th Texas Cavalry in Tennessee, he and his company were enlisted in the regiment as replacements. On 8 Nov. 1862 Harrison was commissioned colonel of the 8th Texas, called TERRY'S TEXAS RANGERS, and served with it until the war ended. Throughout the war, the unit was attached as scouts to the Army of Tennessee, as a part of Maj. Gen. JOSEPH WHEELER's Cavalry Corps. Often in brigade command without commensurate rank, he saw action in the STONE'S RIVER, CHICKAMAUGA, CHATTANOOGA, KNOXVILLE, and ATLANTA campaigns, and in resistance fighting during Union Maj. Gen. WILLIAM T. SHERMAN's MARCH TO THE SEA. Following the fall of SAVANNAH, Harrison was made brigadier general to rank from 14 Jan. 1865 and given command of the 8th and 11th Texas, 4th Tennessee, 3d Arkansas, and 1st Kentucky. His command was absorbed into Lt. Gen. WADE HAMPTON's cavalry for the final campaign in the Carolinas (see CAROLINAS CAMPAIGN).

In postwar years, Harrison was an anti-Reconstruction Democrat and district judge, dying in Waco 14 July 1891.

—JES

Harrison's Island, Va., Battle of. 21 Oct. 1861 See BALL'S BLUFF, VA., BATTLE OF.

Harrison's Landing, Va., action at. 2 July 1862 On that date, in a heavy rainstorm, the Army of the Potomac aban-

doned its battlefield position on Malvern Hill, continuing its retreat across the Virginia peninsula. For a week the Federals, constantly withdrawing, had battled the Army of Northern Virginia. The SEVEN DAYS' CAMPAIGN had been a series of running battles as Maj. Gen. GEORGE B. MCCLELLAN shifted his supply base from White House on the Pamunkey River to Harrison's Landing on the James River. McClellan termed it a strategic withdrawal, though some critics labeled it a "great skedaddle."

Harrison's Landing was a wharf on the 3-mi riverfront of the Berkeley plantation, the former manor home of the Harrison family and the birthplace of William Henry Harrison, the nation's ninth president. McClellan had selected the site because there was no place closer to Richmond where the Federal army could be supplied by water and protected by naval gunboats.

The Federals' arrival at the landing 2 July signaled the end of the 2-month Peninsula Campaign. After the past week's vicious battles, neither the Union troops nor the Southerners were capable of renewing combat. Gen. ROBERT E. LEE's Confederates pursued to Harrison's Landing, but McClellan's lines, anchored between 2 creeks and supported by the gunboats' heavy ordnance, were too strong. Both armies needed a respite and only sporadic skirmishing characterized the action at the landing.

ABRAHAM LINCOLN visited McClellan 8 July. Unwilling to admit his faults or accept blame, the army commander gave Lincoln his HARRISON'S LANDING LETTER. In it McClellan boldly advised Lincoln on political and military policy.

The Union army remained at Harrison's Landing until ordered north 3 Aug. As usual, McClellan moved tardily, with the final contingent not leaving until after the 20th. —JDW

Harrison's Landing letter. Late in June 1862 Maj. Gen. GEORGE B. MCCLELLAN asked for and received from Pres. ABRAHAM LINCOLN permission to present his views on the conduct of the war. When Lincoln arrived at Harrison's Landing 8 July, after the failed PENINSULA CAMPAIGN, McClellan had the confidential and subsequently controversial letter ready. In it he advised the president to follow a conservative policy, to wage war against military and political organizations but not against the civilian population of the South. Confiscations, political executions, and territorial reorganization should not be carried out, nor should oaths be required or military government enacted outside hostile areas. Protection of private property should extend to slavery, including compensation to masters for blacks given refuge as CONTRABANDS behind Union lines. Abolition, McClellan urged, must not be pursued because such radicalism would alienate the troops. Lincoln should concentrate the armies into large bodies rather than keep them divided into smaller, independent commands and appoint a general-in-chief to direct them. He did not ask for the job but expressed his willingness to accept the position.

McClellan personally handed the letter to Lincoln. The president read it and thanked him but did not respond to the contents. A few days later, in Washington, Lincoln recommended the appointment of a general-in-chief, a decision he had made before inspecting the troops at Harrison's Landing, and chose Maj. Gen. HENRY W. HALLECK to fill the position.

The pompous "Little Mac" drew sharp criticism when rumors of the letter circulated, and his languishing military career was destroyed. Radical Republicans anxious to dispose of him labeled his political advice a tool to win Democratic support for the presidency. McClellan, however, had acted out of genuine concern for the safety of the country. His audacity lay in trying to deliver the nation when he could not deliver victories on the battlefield.   —PLF

Hart, John Elliott. USN b. Schenectady, N.Y., date unknown. Appointed midshipman 23 Feb. 1841, Hart became a lieutenant in 1855. During the first 18 months of the Civil War, he served aboard the *Vincennes* and the *Santee*. On 5 Aug. 1862 he was promoted to lieutenant commander and in October was assigned command of the *Albatross* of the West Gulf Squadron. Needing extra protection for his wooden steamer, Hart had its decks piled with cotton bales and both bales and lumber attached to its sides. At St. Andrew's Bay, Fla., in an expedition 24 Nov.–8 Dec. 1862, the men of the *Albatross* destroyed a major saltworks. They participated in Rear Adm. DAVID G. FARRAGUT's attack on PORT HUDSON Mar. 1863, losing 1 *Albatross* sailor.

On 4 May 1863, while reconnoitering Confederate Fort De Russy on the Red River, the *Albatross* engaged the iron steamers *Grand Duke* and *Mary T* and Confederate cavalry on shore. After receiving extensive damage and suffering 4 casualties, the *Albatross* withdrew. Hart complained to Farragut that he could have captured both steamers, which he claimed were preparing to surrender, had his signals for assistance been heeded by the other vessels of the expedition.

On 11 June 1863, irrational from fever, Hart shot himself while aboard the *Albatross*. His body was interred in the Grace Episcopal Cemetery in St. Francisville, La.   —NCD

Hartford, USS. Built at the Boston Navy Yard, the *Hartford* was launched 22 Nov. 1858. A screw sloop, it was 225 ft in length, 44 ft in beam, drawing slightly over 17 ft and displacing 2,900 tons. Its battery consisted of 20 9-in. Dahlgren smoothbores, 2 20-pounder Parrotts, and 2 12-pounders. The *Hartford* spent its entire pre–Civil War career as flagship of the East India Squadron. On the outbreak of hostilities the vessel departed for the U.S., arriving at Philadelphia 2 Dec. 1861. On 28 Jan. 1862 it departed for the Gulf of Mexico, carrying the flag of Capt. DAVID G. FARRAGUT, commander of the newly created West Gulf Blockading Squadron. Until Dec. 1864 the *Hartford* served as the squadron's flagship.

Flag Officer Farragut, with orders to capture New Orleans, assembled his squadron off Ship Island on the Mississippi coast. By early April his vessels, including the *Hartford,* were over the bar and in the Mississippi River. On 24 Apr. the squadron sortied up the river, engaging Confederate forts and warships. In the wild night action that followed, the *Hartford* successfully avoided the Confederate IRONCLAD *Manassas* attempting to ram, but ran aground trying futilely to escape from a fire raft. Slightly damaged, the flagship backed free from the bank and continued upriver to New Orleans. After the Crescent City surrendered on the 29th, the *Hartford* spent months in action against Vicksburg and patrolling. (*See also* FORTS JACKSON AND ST. PHILIP, LA., BATTLE OF.)

Farragut then turned his attention to Mobile, Ala. On 5 Aug. 1864, the admiral, with the *Hartford* as his flagship, led into Mobile Bay a fleet consisting of 4 monitors and 14 wooden vessels. The bay was defended by Forts Morgan and Gaines and a small Confederate naval force including the ironclad *TENNESSEE*. The 3-hour engagement ended when the *Tennessee* surrendered and the other Confederate vessels were captured or fled. The *Hartford* suffered minor damage. (*See also* MOBILE BAY, ALA., BATTLE OF.)

The *Hartford* remained in Mobile Bay for 4 months, until Farragut received orders to return to New York. The ship entered the New York Navy Yard for repairs 13 Dec. 1864 and remained there until spring 1865.   —WNS

Hartranft, John Frederick. USA b. near Fagleysville, Pa., 16 Dec. 1830. After a youth spent in the suburbs of Philadelphia Hartranft attended Virginia's Marshall College and in 1853 was graduated from Union College in New York. Trained as a civil engineer, he switched to politics and law; in 1854 he became deputy sheriff of Montgomery Cty., Pa., and in 1860 was called to the bar. Shortly before the Civil War he was named colonel of the 1st Regiment/Montgomery County Militia.

In spring 1861 Hartranft's outfit became a 90-day volunteer regiment. Sent to Washington, D.C., it accompanied Brig. Gen. IRVIN MCDOWELL's advance to Manassas Junction, Va., in

LC

mid-July. On the eve of FIRST BULL RUN, however, the regiment turned its back on the enemy and marched home, its enlistment period over, despite McDowell's plea that it remain for the battle. Humiliated by his men's decision, Hartranft stayed with the army, an act that won him a MEDAL OF HONOR in 1886.

After Bull Run, he raised the 51st Pennsylvania Infantry, of which he became colonel Nov. 1861. The 51st served for a time in North Carolina, mainly on occupation duty. At ANTIETAM, 17 Sept. 1862, it braved a storm of rifle and cannon fire to cross Burnside Bridge and threaten the Confederate right flank. By Feb. 1863 Hartranft was commanding a brigade in the IX Corps/Army of the Potomac; later he led a comparable unit in the Army of the Ohio. After exercising divisional command several times temporarily, he took permanent charge of the 3d Division/IX Corps, leading it competently during many of the Army of the Potomac's final battles. He was particularly conspicuous at SPOTSYLVANIA while still in brigade command, winning the star of a brigadier to date from 12 May 1864, and as a division leader at FORT STEDMAN, where his role in helping repulse Gen. ROBERT E. LEE's last offensive made him a brevet major general of volunteers.

After the war Hartranft was appointed a special provost marshal during the trial of those accused in LINCOLN'S ASSASSINATION. Returning to civil life, he was auditor general, then a 2-term governor, 1873–79, of Pennsylvania. In 1879 he became postmaster of Philadelphia and 1881–85 was collector of the city port. d. Norristown, Pa., 17 Oct. 1889.   —EGL

Hartsuff, George Lucas. USA b. Tyre, N.Y., 28 May 1830, Hartsuff, at 12, moved with his parents to Michigan, where he lived until entering West Point in 1848. Graduating 19th in his class 4 years later, he served briefly in Texas before fighting against the Seminoles in Florida, where, in a skirmish, he suffered 2 severe wounds. He then returned to West Point as an instructor until the outbreak of the Civil War.

With the brevet rank of captain in the adjutant generals department, Hartsuff participated in the secret expedition that reinforced FORT PICKENS, Fla. In July 1861 he was appointed chief of staff to Brig. Gen. WILLIAM S. ROSECRANS, who com-

USMHI

manded the Department of West Virginia. He served with Rosecrans until he received his appointment to brigadier general 15 Apr. 1862. Assigned a brigade in Maj. Gen. Irvin McDowell's corps, he led his command at CEDAR MOUNTAIN, SECOND BULL RUN, SOUTH MOUNTAIN, and ANTIETAM, where he suffered another grievous wound.

Promoted to major general 19 Nov. 1862, Hartsuff, for the remainder of the war, shuttled between field command and court-martial duty, his wounds periodically incapacitating him during these years. He served on boards and commissions Dec. 1862–28 May 1863, when he was appointed commander of the XXIII Corps. In September he again relinquished field duty because of his health. The disabled general finally returned to field command Mar. 1865 as commander of the defenses of BERMUDA HUNDRED in the Department of Virginia and North Carolina.

Brevetted brigadier and major general in the Regular Army for his war record, Hartsuff remained in the army after the war. With the rank of lieutenant colonel of staff, he resumed his duties in the adjutant general's department. In 1866 he transferred to the Department of the Gulf, eventually serving in the Fifth Military District and the Division of the Missouri. Because of his wounds, Hartsuff retired June 1871. He died in New York City, on 16 May 1874, from pneumonia caused by a scar left on his lung from a wound received in the Seminole War.   —JDW

Harvey, Louis Powell. war governor b. East Haddam, Conn., 22 July 1820, Harvey moved with his parents to Ohio during his childhood. Because he worked to help support the family, he was largely self-educated. He attended Western Reserve College for 2 years, 1835–37, but because of ill health

left without graduating. Hoping a change of climate would benefit him, he taught school in Nicholasville, Ky., tutored at Woodward College in Cincinnati, then moved to Wisconsin to work successively as teacher, mill owner, and shopkeeper. Briefly, 1843–44, he edited the Southport *American,* a Whig newspaper that brought him to the attention of local politicians.

With a reputation for scrupulous honesty and with few enemies, Harvey won a series of elected offices as delegate to the second state constitutional convention in 1847, state senator on the Whig ticket in 1853 and as a Republican in 1855, and secretary of state in 1859. Nominated governor in 1861 by both the Union and Republican parties, he defeated the Democratic candidate by a comfortable margin, taking office Jan. 1862. During the early months of Harvey's administration, the legislature resisted voting war funds, particularly for soldier and dependent relief. Following the lead of other Northern governors, he did secure permission for Wisconsin to apply the direct tax levied against the state toward Wisconsin's war claims against the Federal government.

Interested in soldiers' needs, Harvey assigned agents to look after them in camp and frequently traveled to camps and hospitals himself. Learning that many Wisconsin soldiers had been wounded at SHILOH, the governor organized a relief expedition to care for state troops. As his party moved down the Mississippi River, he visited the hospital transports en route. Late on the night of 19 Apr., he slipped stepping from one boat to another. His body was recovered 65 mi downstream a few weeks later and returned to Madison for burial. Harvey had been in office just over 100 days.   —PLF

Hascall, Milo Smith. USA b. LeRoy, N.Y., 5 Aug. 1829. As a teen-ager Hascall moved to Goshen, Ind., worked as a clerk and schoolteacher, then entered West Point, graduating 14th in the class of 1852. After a year of artillery service at Fort Adams, R.I., Hascall resigned, returned to Indiana, became a contractor for the Michigan Southern & Northern Indiana Railroad, then was an attorney, district attorney, and clerk of courts.

With the start of the Civil War, Hascall joined a 3-month regiment as a private. After an appointment as an aide-de-camp with state troops, he saw action at Phillipi, in western Virginia. On 12 June 1861, 9 days after

LC

the skirmish at PHILLIPI, he was commissioned colonel of the 17th Indiana. That December, assignment to Louisville, Ky., brought him brigade command in the Army of the Cumberland.

Hascall went to Tennessee, missed the Battle of SHILOH, was promoted brigadier general 25 Apr. 1862, then took part in the march to Corinth, Miss., and the Battle of STONE'S RIVER that winter. Commanding the 1st Brigade/1st Division in Maj. Gen. THOMAS L. CRITTENDEN's left wing, and fighting around the "Round Forest" at Stone's River, Hascall was thrust into division command when Brig. Gen. THOMAS J. WOOD was wounded. He later transferred to Maj. Gen. AMBROSE E. BURNSIDE's Army of the Ohio, briefly commanded the District of Indiana, then fought in the Siege of KNOXVILLE late in 1863.

Commanding the 2d Division/XXIII Corps in Maj. Gen. WILLIAM T. SHERMAN's spring 1864 ATLANTA CAMPAIGN, Hascall won praise from Maj. Gen. JOHN M. SCHOFIELD and recommendation for promotion. Advancement was denied and Hascall resigned 27 Oct., returned to Goshen, and took up banking. He moved to Galena, Ill., and in 1890 to Chicago, to enter the real-estate business. d. Oak Park, Ill., 30 Aug. 1904.   —JES

Haskin, Joseph Abel. USA b. Troy, N.Y., 21 June 1818. The 10th-ranked graduate of the West Point class of 1839, Lieutenant Haskin spent several years in Maine during Canadian border controversies, then fought in the Mexican War. He lost his left arm in the storming of Chapultepec Castle and received brevets to captain and major, then drew recruiting, quartermaster, and garrison duty until 1861.

LC

Haskin's Civil War career began badly. As captain, 1st U.S. Artillery, commanding at the Baton Rouge, La., Federal arsenal and barracks, he telegraphed War Department superiors 10 Jan. 1861 that he had been compelled to surrender the facilities to state secessionists. Through 1864 his service comprised more garrison duty, routine promotion to major of Regulars 20 Feb. 1862, responsibility for the northern defenses of the District of Columbia, and assignment as chief of artillery at Washington, D.C. Confederate Lt. Gen. JUBAL A. EARLY's July 1864 Washington Raid thrust Haskin out of the background.

On 10, 11, and 12 July, Haskin, in charge of Forts Stevens and Slocum, sent out cavalry to delay Early's advance on the city and prepared his garrisons for action. His quick response and cool deportment in the fighting won him promotion to brigadier general of volunteers to rank from 5 Aug. After more duty in Washington, he was brevetted brigadier general in the Regulars 13 Mar. 1865 for his war service. (See also EARLY'S WASHINGTON RAID.)

After the war, Haskin commanded posts at Boston and New York harbors, then was retired for disabilities 15 Dec. 1870. d. of tuberculosis, Oswego, N.Y., 3 Aug. 1874.   —JES

Hatch, Edward. USA b. Bangor, Maine, 22 Dec. 1832. An Iowa lumber dealer, a one-time student at Vermont's NORWICH UNIVERSITY, and a former merchant seaman, Hatch joined the 2d Iowa Cavalry as captain 12 Aug. 1861, remaining in the military until his death.

Service with the 2d Iowa at Island No. 10 and in the spring 1862 campaign to Corinth, Miss., was followed by promotion to colonel 13 June 1862 and command of a brigade for the autumn Battle of CORINTH. The next spring, he led a regiment in GRIERSON'S RAID, destroying rail lines between La Grange, Tenn., and Columbus, Miss. After raiding in north Alabama late in 1863, Hatch was badly wounded in a December skirmish south of Moscow, Tenn. During his recuperation he commanded the St. Louis, Mo., cavalry depot.

For past performance and on Brig. Gen. BENJAMIN H. GRIERSON's endorsement, Hatch was made brigadier general to rank from 27 Apr. 1864. Sent to Memphis, Tenn., in June, he operated into north Mississippi against elements of Maj. Gen. NATHAN B. FORREST's cavalry until recalled to Middle Tennessee and assignment to command a division in Maj. Gen. JAMES H. WILSON's cavalry during the FRANKLIN AND NASHVILLE CAMPAIGN. His highly commended performance at the Battles of Franklin and Nashville ended his combat service.

LC

Mustered out of volunteer service Jan. 1866, Hatch continued in the army and was commissioned colonel of the 9th U.S. Cavalry 28 July. He briefly commanded the Department of the Southwest, disputed a reservation treaty with the Ute tribe, and unsuccessfully pursued Mescalero Apache Chief Victorio on his escape from government lands. His parts in the Battles of Franklin and Nashville were recognized 2 Mar. 1867, when brevets to brigadier and major general in the Regulars were awarded him for those actions. d. Fort Robinson, Nebr., 11 Apr. 1889.

—JES

Hatch, John Porter. USA b. Oswego, N.Y., 9 Jan. 1822. Graduating 17th in the West Point class of 1845, Hatch was assigned to the Mounted Rifles. He served meritoriously as a 2d lieutenant in the Mexican War, thereafter drawing garrison duty in Oregon, Texas, and New Mexico Territory until the Civil War began. In Apr. 1861 Hatch was ordered east from his post as commissary chief in the Department of New Mexico and given command of a cavalry brigade under Maj. Gen. GEORGE B. MCCLELLAN. Promoted to brigadier general of volunteers as of 28 Sept. and named chief of cavalry for Maj. Gen. NATHANIEL P. BANKS, Hatch fought in the Shenandoah Valley through spring and summer 1862 (see SHENANDOAH VALLEY CAMPAIGN, JACKSON'S).

Noted for determination and bravery in battle—Confederate cavalryman Col. THOMAS T. MUNFORD singled him out for his boldness around Strasburg in May—he lacked the ability to carry out successfully a cavalry raid that depended on swiftness and surprise. Twice he was ordered to destroy a stretch of the Virginia Central Railroad between Gordonsville and Lynchburg in preparation for Maj. Gen. JOHN POPE'S SECOND BULL RUN CAMPAIGN, and twice he failed, encumbered in the first attempt by taking along an infantry force and a supply train, in the second by roads he claimed were impassable because of heavy rains. In anger Pope demoted Hatch to an infantry brigade, which he led at Second Bull Run and CHANTILLY.

Following Pope's defeat, Hatch was assigned to Maj. Gen. JOSEPH HOOKER's I Corps and given command of the 1st Division, which he was leading when severely wounded at Turner's Gap during the Battle of SOUTH MOUNTAIN, 14 Sept. 1862. Thereafter Hatch held a series of administrative posts in the Southeast, directed a supply depot, and sat on courtsmartial. He commanded the District of Florida, 24 Mar.–25 Apr. 1864; the Department of Florida, 1–26 May; the District of Hilton Head, 2 June–1 Aug.; the District of Florida again, 4 Aug.–26 Oct.; and Morris Island, 14–30 Nov. and 23 Jan.–26 Feb. 1865. On occasion he held temporary command of the

Department of the South. From Nov. 1864 to Mar. 1865 he commanded the Coast Division, and at the end of the war in April he headed the District of Charleston.

Mustered out of the volunteers, Hatch rejoined the Regular Army as major of the 4th Cavalry, on duty against Indians in the West. He was promoted to lieutenant colonel in 1873 and to colonel, his highest rank, in 1881; at that time he transferred to the 2d Cavalry. In 1893, a decade after his retirement from active service, he received the MEDAL OF HONOR for bravery at South Mountain. Hatch lived in New York City from 1883 until his death there 12 Apr. 1901.   —PLF

Hatcher's Run (Armstrong's Mill; Boydton Plank Road; Dabney's Mill; Vaughan Road), Va., Battle of.

5–7 Feb. 1865   After the failure of the Union's fifth offensive at Petersburg in late Sept. and early Oct. 1864, the deadly tedium of trench warfare characterized the campaign's operations for several months. Early in Feb. 1865, however, Lt. Gen. ULYSSES S. GRANT ordered another extension of Federal lines south and west of Gen. ROBERT E. LEE's beleaguered Confederate lines guarding the vital Southside Railroad. The Union commander committed over 35,000 troops to the operation against the Boydton Plank Road, a route supposedly used by Confederate wagon trains to supply the defenders.

On the morning of 5 Feb. the Union force advanced. The 2d Cavalry Division, commanded by Brig. Gen. HENRY E. DAVIES, spearheaded the march, supported by Maj. Gen. GOUVERNEUR K. WARREN's V Corps and Maj. Gen. ANDREW A. HUMPHREYS' II Corps. Despite inclement weather, the cavalry, moving via Reams' Station, occupied Dinwiddie Court House on the Boydton road. The Federal troopers gathered a few Confederate prisoners before being ordered back on the infantry.

Humphreys' corps, meanwhile, reached Hatcher's Run near the Vaughan road crossing. Humphreys halted, deploying in line about 1,000 yd from new Confederate entrenchments. 2 mi to the south of the II Corps, Warren deployed his veterans in support near Monks Neck. The Confederates, members of Lt. Gen. AMBROSE P. HILL's and Maj. Gen. JOHN B. GORDON's corps, responded tentatively to these Federal dispositions until late in the afternoon of the 5th. About 5 p.m. Maj. Gen. WILLIAM MAHONE's division launched a counterattack against Humphreys, but was repulsed by Brig. Gen. THOMAS A. SMYTH's division.

Davies' troopers rejoined the infantry during the morning of the 6th. About 1 p.m. Warren reconnoitered toward Gravelly Run and Dabney's Mill. To counter Warren's advance, Gordon sent forward Brig. Gen. JOHN PEGRAM's veteran division, which lashed into the Federals but was repulsed by Union strength. Pegram was killed in the attack.

The next day the Federals abandoned their tentative hold on the Boydton Plank Road. Humphreys and Warren remained, however, fortifying their new lines to the Vaughan road crossing of Hatcher's Run. Grant's operation cost him 1,512 men: 170 killed, 1,160 wounded, and 182 missing. This successful action forced Lee to further extend his precariously thin lines and was the last principal Union shift to the left before the final push in late March and early April that resulted in the Battle of FIVE FORKS.   —JDW

Hatcher's Run, Va., eng. at.

27 Oct. 1864   *See* BURGESS' MILL, VA., ENG. AT.

Hatteras, USS.

Built to be a passenger ship on the Delaware River, the *Hatteras* was purchased by the U.S. Navy 25 Sept. 1861. The sidewheel steamer—210 ft long, weighing 1,126 tons, with an 18-ft draft—could manage speeds up to 13 knots. After conversion to a warship, the *Hatteras* was provided with a battery of 4 32-pounders, 2 30-pounders, 1 20-pounder, and 1 12-pounder howitzer. The ship was converted in haste, and serious problems remained: its engines were unprotected; its boilers were only partially shielded by coal bunkers; and its sails were useless except to help keep the ship steady.

George F. Emmons, the first commander of the *Hatteras,* was assigned to the blockade of the Gulf Coast, first off Cedar Keys, Fla., then off Mobile. The ship was credited with the capture of 14 BLOCKADE RUNNERS in approximately 1 year. In Nov. 1862 Emmons was replaced by Cmdr. Homer C. Blake. Under his command, the *Hatteras* was at New Orleans for repairs when news arrived of the Confederates' capture of GALVESTON. Despite uncompleted work on its hull, the *Hatteras* joined the Federal squadron off Galveston, where 4 vessels were already on duty.

On the afternoon of 11 Jan. 1863, an unidentified vessel was seen approaching the Texas coast, and Blake was ordered to investigate. He suspected, correctly, that the vessel was the CSS *ALABAMA,* commanded by Capt. RAPHAEL SEMMES. After luring the *Hatteras* 20 mi from the squadron while awaiting darkness, Semmes opened fire. The battle lasted only 13 minutes, killing 2 men and wounding 5 others aboard the *Hatteras.* All 121 survivors were brought aboard the *Alabama* before their ship sank. They were later released in Jamaica. A naval court of inquiry concluded that Blake's conduct had been "commendable and proper" and that he was not to blame for the loss of his ship. The battle with the *Hatteras* contributed greatly to the reputation of Semmes and the *Alabama.* Their engagement was the first in which a steam warship sank another steam warship in open sea. On 17 Jan. 1976 the *Hatteras* was discovered by civilian divers who had been searching for it.   —NCD

Hatteras Inlet (Forts Hatteras and Clark), N.C., Battle of.

27–29 Aug. 1861   At the war's outset, North Carolina troops fortified the sea approach to Hatteras Inlet, one of the state's busiest ports, a haven for BLOCKADE RUNNERS, and a major supply conduit for Confederate forces in Virginia. 2 defensive positions were constructed: Fort Hatteras, one-eighth of a mile west of the inlet, on ground that commanded the sea channel, and Fort Clark, a smaller installation east of Hatteras. The larger fort mounted a dozen 32-pounder smoothbore cannon, Fort Clark 7 smoothbores. This arrangement permitted a crossfire to be leveled at any invaders. Soon almost 600 North Carolinians manned the works.

The guns were not needed until Aug. 1861, when blockade runners began to hurt Union shipping. On the 9th, the commander of the Atlantic Blockading Squadron, Flag Officer SILAS H. STRINGHAM, was sent to neutralize the defenses. Accompanying his fleet of 7 warships were 2 transports carrying 880 soldiers under Maj. Gen. BENJAMIN F. BUTLER, who had suggested such an expedition to the War Department. Smarting over his recent removal from command at FORT MONROE, Va., the former Massachusetts legislator regarded the expedition as a means of recouping lost prestige.

On the afternoon of 27 Aug. Stringham's fleet reached Hatteras Inlet from Fort Monroe, and Butler readied a landing. The plan called for the army to attack the land-face of Fort Hatteras, while the navy, with 143 rifled cannon, shelled both works. At 10 the next morning, Stringham began to pound the forts with accurate firepower. Attempting to reply, the Confederates' shells fell short of their mark.

Just before noon, Butler's troops took to surfboats, but heavy breakers dashed many of the vessels against the shore, drowning dozens of men. Even so, by day's end the Confederates had abandoned Fort Clark and resistance from Fort Hatteras had weakened considerably. That night, the latter's garrison was augmented by support from Portsmouth, Va., under Flag Officer SAMUEL BARRON, chief of coastal defenses in Virginia and North Carolina. The additional troops failed to help; under the ceaseless pounding of Federal guns, Barron surrendered Hatteras and its environs early on the afternoon of the 29th. The capitulation buoyed Union morale, sinking since FIRST BULL RUN, advanced Butler's standing (despite his troops' lack of participation), and shook Southern confidence.   —EGL

Hatton, Robert Hopkins. CSA b. Steubenville, Ohio, 2 Nov. 1826. An 1847 graduate of Tennessee's Cumberland University, Hatton continued there as a teacher while studying law under Judge ROBERT L. CARUTHERS. He practiced law in the 1850s, served 2 terms in the Tennessee legislature; lost the 1859 gubernatorial election to incumbent ISHAM G. HARRIS, and was sent to the U.S. House of Representatives in 1860 on the National American ticket.

LC

Hatton was an early casualty of the war. Commissioned colonel of the Confederate 7th Tennessee Infantry 26 May 1861, he fought in the Battle of CHEAT MOUNTAIN, Va., and served in winter quarters in western Virginia early in 1862. Shuttled to the Virginia peninsula, at the head of a brigade he clashed with Brig. Gen. ERASMUS D. KEYES's Union corps near Savage's Station 23 May 1862, received promotion to brigadier general to rank from that date, and 8 days later, riding to the front of his troops with Maj. Gen. GUSTAVUS W. SMITH, was killed 31 May in the Battle of SEVEN PINES. His death was immediate. His troops passed to Col. JAMES J. ARCHER's command.   —JES

Haupt, Herman. USA b. Philadelphia, Pa., 26 Mar. 1817. As U.S. railroad superintendent from spring 1862 until fall 1863, engineer Haupt had the power to seize, maintain, and operate all railroads and utilize all equipment needed to facilitate military transportation. His efficient operation made the Union's transportation problems far less serious than those of the Confederacy.

Haupt graduated 31st in the U.S. Military Academy's class of 1835 but resigned his commission 3 months later to enter railroad engineering and teach civil engineering, architecture, and mathematics at Pennsylvania College in Gettysburg. Haupt's *General Theory of Bridge Construction* (1851) established him as an authority on the subject.

During 1851–52 Haupt was general superintendent of the Pennsylvania Railroad and later served on the company's

board of directors. In the late 1850s, despite construction difficulties and criticism, he engineered and helped finance the 5-mile Hoosac Tunnel in the Massachusetts Berkshires.

A telegram from Sec. of War EDWIN M. STANTON called Haupt to Washington Apr. 1862 to take charge of U.S. military railroading. He was soon appointed aide-de-camp to Maj. Gen. IRVIN MCDOWELL with the rank of colonel. He first sought to safeguard lines in the Wash-

LC

ington area from Confederate raiders by building blockhouses at vulnerable points and by constructing stockades around machine shops. Haupt armed and drilled railroad personnel to make them self-protective and greatly improved telegraphic communications along the lines. The secret of his spectacular success in repairing damaged rail lines and bridges was his personal supervision and detailed inspection.

On 5 Sept. 1862, for "exceptional and meritorious service," he was promoted to brigadier general of volunteers, but he later refused the appointment, saying he would gladly serve without official rank and without pay, but he would not consent to a limitation on his freedom to continue private business. Faced with the demand that he accept the commission, with its restrictions, he resigned from military service 14 Sept. 1863.

Until his death, more than 40 years later, Haupt worked for a variety of railroads as an engineer and general manager. He died of a heart attack 14 Dec. 1905, aboard a train in New Jersey. *See also* RAILROADS, U.S. MILITARY.   —PR

havelock. A white KEPI cover with a long tail draping over the wearer's neck and shoulders, the havelock was named for Sir Henry Havelock, the British military man who made it popular in India in the 1850s. Considered smart martial apparel in hot climates, it was worn early in the Civil War by Northerners and Southerners to ward off sunstroke. The havelock was eliminated from uniform requisitions when Americans found that it cut off air circulation around the head and face.
          —JES

haversack. A white canvas bag about a foot square, the haversack held the Civil War soldier's daily rations. Slung on a strap over the right shoulder, it had a waterproof lining and a flap that buckled over its top, and hung on the left hip. Some, custom-made officers' and militia models, were made of patent leather. Most had a number or other company identification painted or stenciled on them.   —JES

Hawes, James Morrison. CSA b. Lexington, Ky., 7 Jan. 1824, Hawes graduated 29th in the 41-man West Point class of 1845. In the Mexican War he was brevetted 1st lieutenant but declined a second brevet awarded to him for meritorious service. After the war with Mexico, Hawes returned to the Military Academy as an instructor of infantry and cavalry tactics and of mathematics. For 2 years he attended the cavalry school in Saumur, France, returning in time for service in Kansas, where he took part in the border conflicts before the war.

After resigning from the U.S. Army 9 May 1861, he accepted a commission as captain in the Confederate Regular Army and was promoted to major the following month. On 26 June he was elected colonel of the 2d Kentucky Cavalry but declined the appointment in favor of remaining with the Regular Army (see REGULAR ARMY, CONFEDERATE).

LC

In 1862 Gen. ALBERT SIDNEY JOHNSTON recommended Hawes for a promotion to brigadier general in the Provisional Army. Hawes officially received the commission 14 Mar. and took command of all cavalry in the Western Department under Johnston until the day after the Battle of SHILOH, 8 Apr. Hawes requested relief of command to attach himself to Maj. Gen. JOHN C. BRECKINRIDGE's division. He later served commendably in Arkansas as a brigade commander near Little Rock. Hawes saw service at Milliken's Bend during the VICKSBURG siege in 1863 and transferred to Galveston Island just before the war ended.

After the war he returned to Kentucky and operated a hardware store in Covington, where he died 22 Nov. 1889. —FLS

Hawes, Richard. war governor b. Caroline Cty., Va., 6 Feb. 1797. Moving from Virginia to Kentucky in 1810, Hawes's family lived first in Fayette County, then in Jefferson County. He graduated from Transylvania College in Kentucky, was admitted to the bar in 1818, and the next year opened a law office in Winchester. After serving 3 terms in the state legislature in 1828, 1829, and 1836, he was elected on the Whig ticket to 2 terms in the U.S. House of Representatives, 1837–41. When the Whig party broke apart, Hawes joined those moderate secessionists who allied with the Democrats. In 1861 the Kentucky legislature appointed him to a committee of 6 charged with furthering the state's policy of armed neutrality.

Regardless of his role as a promoter of peace, Hawes's sympathies lay with the Confederacy, and he preferred to take Kentucky out of the Union. Though the state never seceded, an extralegal Confederate government was established. When the "provisional" Confederate governor of Kentucky was killed at SHILOH, Hawes succeeded him in office. He traveled with Gen. BRAXTON BRAGG to Frankfort, where the commander inaugurated him 4 Oct. 1862. Within hours of the ceremony Bragg, with Hawes in tow, retreated before Brig. Gen. DON CARLOS BUELL's advancing Federal troops. The exiled governor never performed any official duties. He later criticized Bragg vociferously, blaming Confederate failures on the general's incompetence.

In postwar years Hawes lived in Paris, Ky. From 1866 until his death 25 May 1877, he held an appointment as county judge.   —PLF

Hawkins, John Parker. USA b. Indianapolis, Ind., 29 Sept. 1830. For 42 years Hawkins held thankless positions in the Quartermaster and Commissary departments but managed to gain some measure of recognition for his service in the Civil War.

After graduating 40th in the 43-man West Point class of 1852, he waited almost 2 years to be promoted from brevet

2d lieutenant in the 6th Infantry to full 2d lieutenant in the 2d Infantry. From 1858 to 1861 he served as regimental quartermaster in the Northwest as a 1st lieutenant.

At the beginning of the war, Hawkins joined the army Commissary Department as a captain and served in several posts throughout Missouri as assistant inspecting, then chief commissary.

As chief commissary of the Army of the Tennessee in 1863,

LC

Hawkins became ill and missed 3 months' service. On his return to duty he was transferred to Louisiana, placed in command of the District of Northeastern Louisiana and a black brigade, and promoted to brigadier general of volunteers 13 Apr. 1863. In Feb. 1864 Hawkins joined the Federal garrison near Vicksburg, Miss., as the commander of an all-black division, one he led in the siege and capture of Mobile in Mar. 1865. He attained the brevet of major for "gallant and meritorious service" during the siege, and the ranks of brigadier general and major general in the Regular Army and major general of volunteers.

After the war Hawkins joined the Subsistence Department as a captain in the Regular Army and served for 28 years until he retired in 1894 as commissary general of subsistence. He retired to Indianapolis, where he died 7 Feb. 1914. —FLS

Hawthorne, Alexander Travis. CSA b. Conecuh Cty., Ala., 10 Jan. 1825. After completing his education at Georgia's Mercer University and at Yale, in 1847 Hawthorne settled in Camden, Ark., to practice law. He joined the 6th Arkansas Infantry when it organized at Little Rock June 1861 and was elected lieutenant colonel of the regiment. By spring 1862, before his unit engaged in its first major battle, at SHILOH, he had been promoted to colonel. Hawthorne participated in Gen. BRAXTON BRAGG'S KENTUCKY CAMPAIGN, commanded the 6th at STONE'S RIVER, and was cited for gallantry in an attack on Fort Hindman in 1863 during the Federal assault on Helena, Ark. (see ARKANSAS POST, ARK.).

LC

With his promotion to brigadier general to rank from 18 Feb. 1864, Hawthorne assumed command of the 5th Brigade (17th, 21st, and 23d Tennessee; 33d Alabama; and Austin's Light Battery)/Brig. Gen. THOMAS J. CHURCHILL's division/III Corps/Army of Mississippi. For the rest of the war he served under Churchill, leading his brigade in operations to halt Maj. Gen. NATHANIEL P. BANKS'S RED RIVER CAMPAIGN of 1864 and fighting conspicuously at JENKINS' FERRY.

Hawthorne was among the contingent of Trans-Mississippi officers who refused to accept defeat. He traveled to Mexico with Gen. E. KIRBY SMITH's party of exiles but apparently went immediately to Brazil to establish a Confederate community and a home for himself on a small island in the bay near Rio de Janeiro. Until summer 1868, when his wife became ill, the devout Baptist involved himself in missionary work. At that time, the family returned to the U.S., settling in Atlanta. Hawthorne engaged in business until his ordination as a Baptist minister in 1880, then moved to Marshall, Tex. During his later years he worked as an agent to solicit material for publication in the *Southern Historical Society Papers.* d. 31 May 1899 in Marshall.   —PLF

Hay, John Milton. USP b. Salem, Ind., 8 Oct. 1838, Hay served as Pres. ABRAHAM LINCOLN's personal secretary and biographer. Following local elementary schooling and a private

secondary education, he entered Brown University in Rhode Island, graduated in 1858, and in 1859 took a job in his uncle's Springfield, Ill., law office. Attorney Abraham Lincoln's offices were next door. When Lincoln received the 1860 Republican presidential nomination, his secretary, JOHN G. NICOLAY, persuaded him to hire Hay as an assistant secretary.

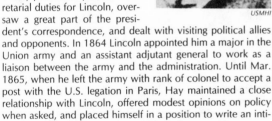
USMHI

Hay performed personal secretarial duties for Lincoln, oversaw a great part of the president's correspondence, and dealt with visiting political allies and opponents. In 1864 Lincoln appointed him a major in the Union army and an assistant adjutant general to work as a liaison between the army and the administration. Until Mar. 1865, when he left the army with rank of colonel to accept a post with the U.S. legation in Paris, Hay maintained a close relationship with Lincoln, offered modest opinions on policy when asked, and placed himself in a position to write an intimate history of the president and his administration.

A young man when he left Lincoln's employ, Hay built a distinguished career as a diplomat, novelist, poet, historian, and political adviser. After working in the U.S. legations in Paris, Vienna, and Madrid, he left Europe in 1870; became an editorial writer for the New York *Tribune,* 1870–75; married into a wealthy family; served as assistant secretary of state, 1879–81, under Pres. RUTHERFORD B. HAYES; then became Pres. WILLIAM MCKINLEY's ambassador to Great Britain, 1897–98, and secretary of state, 1898, maintaining that cabinet post under Pres. Theodore Roosevelt until his death in Lake Sunapee, N.H., 1 July 1905. Hay's literary output includes 2 books of poetry, *Pike County Ballads* (1871) and *Collected Poems* (1890), the novel *Bread-Winners* (1884), and the travel book *Castilian Days* (1871). With John Nicolay he wrote the 10-volume *Abraham Lincoln: A History* (1890), to which they devoted 15 years. The book, still considered one of the best biographies of the president, not only used Hay's and Nicolay's personal papers but, with the cooperation of Robert Lincoln, the president's surviving son, incorporated Lincoln family papers.   —JES

Hayes, Rutherford Birchard. USA b. Delaware, Ohio, 4 Oct. 1822. Hayes's father died before his son's birth, but a

wealthy uncle provided the boy's education at Kenyon College and Harvard Law School. For 5 years Hayes practiced law in Lower Sandusky, Ohio, before seeking greater opportunity in Cincinnati, where he became active, but not prominent, in Whig-Republican politics.

Recruiting troops in Cincinnati, he was commissioned major of the 23d Ohio. The 3d-ranking officer of the regiment, Hayes had a chance to learn military procedures before advancing to higher rank. He commanded the regiment late in 1861, though he was not for-

USMHI

mally commissioned colonel until 24 Oct. 1862. He later commanded a brigade and, temporarily, a division during the SHENANDOAH VALLEY CAMPAIGN of 1864. Promoted to brigadier general as of 19 Oct. 1864, he held that rank when the war ended and later received appointment as brevet major general. Nonetheless, he never commanded troops in battle holding rank higher than colonel.

The 23d Ohio first campaigned inconspicuously in what is now West Virginia. Sent east to join Maj. Gen. JOHN POPE, the 23d fought at SOUTH MOUNTAIN, where Hayes received the first of 4 wounds. In summer and fall 1864, he commanded a brigade under Brig. Gen. GEORGE CROOK. His men fought in the Shenandoah Valley in the army first led by Maj. Gen. DAVID HUNTER, then more successfully by Maj. Gen. PHILIP H. SHERIDAN. Hayes participated with minor distinction in Sheridan's triumphs over Confederate Lt. Gen. JUBAL A. EARLY and was given a relatively inactive command for the rest of the war. *See also* SHENANDOAH VALLEY CAMPAIGN, SHERIDAN'S.

In 1864 Hayes was nominated to run for the U.S. House, despite having written: "An officer fit for duty who at this crisis would abandon his post to electioneer for a seat in Congress ought to be scalped." No other statement could have pleased his superiors more or served better to guarantee his election. Hayes was elected twice to Congress, in 1865 and 1867, but resigned to run for governor of Ohio before serving his second term. Governor 1868–72, he was reelected in 1875 and entered the White House in 1877. By no means a failure as president, Hayes was nevertheless disappointed with his administration. He told a group of veterans that the war years were "the best years of our lives." d. Fremont, Ohio, 17 Jan. 1893.

—JYS

Hays, Alexander. USA b. Franklin, Pa., 8 July 1819, Hays attended 2 academies and Allegheny College before leaving during his senior year to enter the U.S. Military Academy. By the time he graduated, 20th in the class of 1844, he had formed a lasting friendship with Ulysses S. Grant, who graduated a year ahead of him. Hays fought in the Mexican War, earning a brevet for gallantry. He resigned from the army in 1848, went to California for gold, then returned to Pennsylvania, where he became a construction engineer specializing in bridge building.

When the Civil War began, Hays reenlisted 14 May 1861 in the Regular Army as captain of the new 16th Infantry. On 9 Oct. he received a commission as colonel of the 63d Pennsylvania. For nearly a year he commanded the regiment in Maj. Gen. PHILIP KEARNY's division of the III Corps. He distinguished himself at YORKTOWN, WILLIAMSBURG, SEVEN PINES, SAVAGE'S STATION, and MALVERN HILL. At SECOND BULL RUN he fell severely wounded during the numerous Union attacks. Promoted to brigadier general 29 Sept. 1862, Hays was stationed after his recovery in the defenses of Washington, D.C.

USMHI

On 28 June 1863 he secured command of the 3d Division of the II Corps. 5 days later, 3 July, his new command and another division manned the low stone wall toward which PICKETT'S CHARGE was directed. He performed conspicuously during this climax at GETTYSBURG. In spring 1864 Hays was relegated to brigade command when the ravaged III Corps was merged into the II. On the morning of 5 May 1864 he was killed at the WILDERNESS. Brevetted throughout the war for his combat prowess, he received his final brevet of major general posthumously, to date from his death. —JDW

Hays, Harry Thompson. CSA b. Wilson Cty., Tenn., 14 Apr. 1820. Orphaned at an early age, Hays lived with an uncle in Mississippi. A graduate of St. Mary's College in Baltimore, he studied law in the Maryland city and established a practice in New Orleans. He fought with distinction in the Mexican War and during the 1850s was active in the Whig party.

Hays entered Confederate service as colonel of the 7th Louisiana. The regiment reached Virginia in time for the FIRST BATTLE OF BULL RUN, where Hays led his recruits with the skill of a veteran, and eventually it joined the famed Louisiana Brigade of Brig. Gen. RICHARD TAYLOR. The Louisianans participated in Maj.

LC

Gen. THOMAS J. "STONEWALL" JACKSON's brilliant SHENANDOAH VALLEY CAMPAIGN of 1862. On 9 June, at PORT REPUBLIC, they were badly repulsed when they charged a strong Union line. Hays fell severely wounded in the attack. On 25 July, while recuperating, he was promoted to brigadier general.

The new brigadier returned to active duty as commander of the restructured Louisiana Brigade. In his initial battle as brigade commander, Hays led his tough veterans in a charge into Miller's Cornfield at ANTIETAM, where nearly half of them were slaughtered by Union gunfire. As a part of Maj. Gen. JUBAL A. EARLY's division, Hays's brigade delivered a counterattack at FREDERICKSBURG in December and, at CHANCELLORSVILLE, May 1863, assisted in the defense of Marye's Heights. During the Battle of GETTYSBURG, in the twilight of 2 July, the Louisianans and another Confederate brigade, both under Hays, stormed up CEMETERY HILL, momentarily wrenching this vital position from the Union forces in a futile but brilliant assault.

On 7 Nov. 1863, at RAPPAHANNOCK STATION, a superior Fed-

eral force in a skillful attack overran and routed Hays's brigade. Though briefly captured, Hays galloped to safety through a gauntlet of musketry. His depleted command again fought well at the WILDERNESS, May 1864, and at SPOTSYLVANIA, where Hays was wounded 10 May. When he recovered, he was transferred to the Trans-Mississippi, remaining there until war's end.

Hays returned after the conflict to New Orleans, where he served as sheriff of Orleans Parish until removed by Federal authorities. He then practiced law until his death in New Orleans, from Bright's disease, 21 Aug. 1876. —JDW

Hays, William. USA b. Richmond, Va., 9 May 1819. Appointed to West Point in 1836 from his new home in Nashville, Tenn., Hays graduated 4 years later, ranking 18th in a class of 42. Posted to the artillery as a 2d lieutenant, he gained a position in one of the most prestigious horse batteries of the pre–Civil War army, Capt. James Duncan's A/2d U.S. Artillery. In this unit, fighting beside Lt. HENRY J. HUNT, later the artillery commander of the ARMY OF THE POTOMAC, he saw action in the Mexican War battles at Molino del Rey and at the San Cosme Garita outside the enemy capital. In these engagements he won the brevets of captain and major.

LC

In the years immediately preceding the Civil War, Hays served in numerous garrisons, for a time fighting the Seminoles in Florida. By mid-1861 he was a full-rank captain in the defenses of Washington; thereafter he led a 4-battery brigade in the Artillery Reserve of the Army of the Potomac, under Hunt. He served so ably during the Peninsula Campaign, especially at WILLIAMSBURG and GAINES' MILL, that he succeeded his old colleague as Artillery Reserve leader. He was promoted to brigadier general of volunteers as of 29 Nov. 1862.

Leaving the artillery early in 1863, Hays assumed command of a brigade in the 1st Division/II Corps just before CHANCELLORSVILLE, where he was captured 3 May. Exchanged promptly, he rejoined the army at the outset of the GETTYSBURG CAMPAIGN. At first there was no field position for him, but on 3 July, wounds to Maj. Gen. WINFIELD S. HANCOCK and Brig. Gen. JOHN GIBBON led to Hays's assignment to command the II Corps. Unable to obtain the major generalship required to retain the position, he relinquished it that September. Until Feb. 1865, he served on provost duty in New York City, retaking the field as commander of the 2d Division/II Corps at the outset of the APPOMATTOX CAMPAIGN.

Hays's career crumbled on the morning of 6 Apr. 1865, when his corps leader, Maj. Gen. ANDREW A. HUMPHREYS, relieved him for sleeping on duty after having been cautioned to be vigilant. Though awarded the brevet of brigadier general of volunteers for his war service, he never rose above major in the Regular service. He died while in command of Fort Independence, Mass., 7 Feb. 1875. —EGL

Hazen, William Babcock. USA b. West Hartford, Vt., 27 Sept. 1830. Moving with his parents to Ohio at 3, Hazen grew up in the village of Hiram. In 1855 he graduated from West Point, 28th in his class, in fulfillment of a long-standing

355 Hébert, Paul Octave

ambition. Thereafter he served in Oregon Territory against Klamath and Rogue River Indians and in 1859 was wounded by Comanches in Texas. When the Civil War began, he was a brevet 1st lieutenant and an assistant instructor of infantry tactics at his alma mater.

LC

Through the aid of a boyhood friend, Lt. Col. JAMES A. GARFIELD, Hazen secured the colonelcy of an Ohio infantry regiment. In Nov. 1861 he was raised to brigade leadership in Brig. Gen. DON CARLOS BUELL's Army of the Ohio. On the second day at SHILOH, he led his command in a charge that protected the right wing of Brig. Gen. WILLIAM NELSON's division. 9 months later, at STONE'S RIVER, he added to his reputation with a sterling performance near the Round Forest, where he repulsed a series of assaults on the far left of Maj. Gen. WILLIAM S. ROSECRANS' Army of the Cumberland. This success cost his brigade one-third of its strength in casualties. Late in 1863 Hazen erected on that ground, in their memory, the first Civil War battlefield monument.

At CHICKAMAUGA, he again held Rosecrans' left; afterward, he played a major role in the CRACKER LINE OPERATION that raised the Siege of CHATTANOOGA. At MISSIONARY RIDGE, Hazen's troops were among the first to reach the summit, sending the enemy into headlong flight.

In Aug. 1864, after fighting skillfully on the road to Atlanta, Hazen took command of the 2d Division/XV Corps/Army of the Tennessee, which he led during Maj. Gen. WILLIAM T. SHERMAN's MARCH TO THE SEA. He capped that campaign by a fierce attack on FORT MCALLISTER 13 Dec., the climax of the Siege of SAVANNAH. By war's close he was a major general by full rank in the volunteers and by brevet in the Regulars.

Following the hostilities, he became colonel of the 38th, and later the 6th, U.S. Infantry. He fought in numerous Indian campaigns, observed the Franco-Prussian War, and engaged in controversies with Gens. PHILIP H. SHERIDAN and GEORGE A. CUSTER and war secretaries WILLIAM W. BELKNAP and Robert Todd Lincoln. A brigadier general and chief signal officer of the army, he died in the District of Columbia, 16 Jan. 1887.

—EGL

Hébert, Louis. CSA b. Iberville Parish, La., 13 Mar. 1820. Hébert's family, descendants of 17th-century French settlers who came to Canada, belonged to the wealthy class of Louisiana sugar planters. First cousin of future Confederate brigadier PAUL O. HÉBERT, Louis was educated at home by private tutors, attended Jefferson College in Louisiana, and graduated 3d in the West Point class of 1845. Brevetted 2d lieutenant of engineers, he completed his assignment as assistant engineer in the construction of Fort Livingston, then resigned in 1846 to manage the family sugar interests. During the antebellum years he served as a militia officer, state senator, and chief engineer of Louisiana.

Hébert entered Confederate service as colonel of the 3d Louisiana Infantry, which was placed under Brig. Gen. BEN MCCULLOCH's command. McCulloch singled out Hébert and the 3d for gallantry at WILSON'S CREEK, the unit's first major battle. A large part of the Louisianans and their colonel were

captured at PEA RIDGE, Mar. 1862, which misled Maj. Gen. EARL VAN DORN to report Hébert killed along with McCulloch and Col. JAMES M. MCINTOSH.

LC

After his exchange 26 May, Hébert was promoted to brigadier general with command of the 2d Brigade of Brig. Gen. LEWIS H. LITTLE's division in Maj. Gen. STERLING PRICE's Army of the West. At IUKA, Hébert's men bore the brunt of the Federal attack and again received praise for their stalwart defense. Hébert fought again at CORINTH and was surrendered at VICKSBURG when the city fell. Following his second exchange, he was transferred to the Army of Tennessee and sent to North Carolina. Until the end of the war he had charge of heavy artillery around Fort Fisher, also serving in the state as chief engineer for the Confederate War Department.

Hébert did not return to public life in the postwar years. He edited a newspaper in Louisiana and taught at private schools until his death in St. Martin Parish, 7 Jan. 1901.   —PLF

Hébert, Paul Octave. CSA b. Iberville Parish, La., 12 Dec. 1818. First cousin of LOUIS HÉBERT, who became a Confederate general, Paul graduated 1st in his class both at Jefferson College, La., in 1836 and 4 years later at West Point. The classmate of WILLIAM T. SHERMAN and GEORGE H. THOMAS received a commission as 2d lieutenant in the Corps of Engineers, with assignment as assistant professor of engineering at the Military Academy. From July 1842 until he resigned from the army in 1845 Hébert was stationed at Barataria, La., to superintend the construction of Mississippi River defenses.

LC

He reenlisted with the rank of lieutenant colonel of the 14th Infantry Volunteers, serving under Gen. Franklin Pierce during the Mexican War. By the end of the war he had been brevetted colonel for gallantry at Molino del Rey. Between wars, Hébert managed his plantation, participated in the state constitutional convention of 1852, and that year was elected to the governorship on the Democratic ticket.

Early in 1861 Hébert was elected colonel of the 1st Louisiana Artillery, immediately received an appointment as brigadier general of state troops, and 17 Aug. 1861 was commissioned brigadier general in the Confederate army. Over the course of the war Hébert commanded the Department of Texas, the District of West Louisiana and Texas, and the District of Texas and Territory of Arizona. He engaged in significant fighting only once, at Milliken's Bend. Aside from some skirmishing, he was caught up principally in administrative duties, and established the system of licensing cotton speculators that formed the basis of Maj. Gen. JOHN B. MAGRUDER's hated "Cotton Order."

Hébert took the oath of allegiance and applied for a pardon

immediately after hostilities ceased. Pres. ANDREW JOHNSON granted it in 1865, freeing Hébert of the political restrictions placed on former Confederate officers. While Hébert did not seek elective office, he led a faction of Louisiana Democrats in support of HORACE GREELEY for president in 1872. Over the next several years he held engineering appointments from both the state and Federal governments.

Hébert suffered from cancer during the last year of his life. d. New Orleans, 29 Aug. 1880. —PLF

Heckman, Charles Adam.

Heckman, Charles Adam. USA b. Easton, Pa., 3 Dec. 1822. After being educated at Minerva Seminary, working as a hardware clerk, and serving in the Mexican War as a sergeant in the VOLTIGEURS, Heckman moved to Phillipsburg, N.J., and became a conductor on the New Jersey Central Railroad. He left the railroad to accept a commission as lieutenant colonel in the 9th New Jersey Infantry 8 Oct. 1861.

Heckman took part in Brig. Gen. AMBROSE E. BURNSIDE's amphibious operations on the North Carolina coast, and was made colonel to rank from 10 Feb. 1862 and brigadier general to rank from 29 Nov. 1862, all the while on occupation duty in

LC

the Carolinas. Next assigned to the Army of the James, he commanded garrisons at Norfolk and Portsmouth, Va., through 1863 and early 1864. He saw his first real action near DREWRY'S BLUFF 16 May 1864, and because of heavy fog and his own blunders his brigade was swept away and he was captured. As a prisoner Heckman, with 50 others, was taken to Charleston, S.C., and placed in range of Union artillery, to prevent batteries from firing on the city.

After his exchange, Sept. 1864, Heckman, with little combat experience, assumed command of the 2d Division/XVIII Corps for Maj. Gen. E.O.C. ORD's assault on Fort Harrison at Petersburg, Va. The disastrous 29 Sept. attack ended with Heckman leading Ord's men to defeat after Ord, wounded, passed command to him. Though he claimed unfamiliarity with the battle plans, superiors' claims that his actions showed little common sense were upheld.

He briefly commanded the XXV Corps in Maj. Gen. GODFREY WEITZEL's absence Jan.–Feb. 1865, but opinion prevailed that he was not suited to command. Lt. Gen. U. S. GRANT sent him home 23 Mar.; Heckman resigned 25 May 1865.

Postwar, he returned to the New Jersey Central and worked as a train dispatcher. d. Germantown, Pa., 14 Jan. 1896.

—JES

Heintzelman, Samuel Peter.

Heintzelman, Samuel Peter. USA b. Manheim, Pa., 30 Sept. 1805, Heintzelman devoted over 4 decades to the service of his country, rising from 2d lieutenant to major general and corps commander in the Civil War. While his experience, devotion to duty, and bravery were undeniable, he lacked initiative, imagination, and administrative ability. Leading a squad or regiment in combat, Heintzelman possessed the requisite skill and enough courage for a dozen men; but when asked to command a Union corps, he floundered.

USMHI

An 1826 graduate of West Point, 17th in his class, Heintzelman spent 2 decades on garrison duty and in recruiting and quartermaster service. During the Mexican War he earned the brevet of major for gallantry; in 1851 he was brevetted lieutenant colonel for his services in the Southwest. With the advent of the Civil War, he received a commission of colonel, 14 May 1861, and command of the newly formed 17th U.S. Infantry; 3 days later he was promoted to brigadier general.

Heintzelman's troops seized ALEXANDRIA 24 May, and 4 days later Heintzelman received command of a division in Brig. Gen. IRVIN MCDOWELL's army. At FIRST BULL RUN he fought with his usual valor, suffering a wound while vainly trying to rally his broken division in the Union rout. He remained in divisional command throughout fall 1861 and winter 1862. On 13 Mar. he assumed command of the III Corps/Army of the Potomac and was promoted to major general 5 May.

Maj. Gen. GEORGE B. MCCLELLAN's PENINSULA CAMPAIGN revealed Heintzelman's shortcomings as a commander of a large body of troops. His natural caution and penchant for magnifying the difficulties before him increased during the campaign. Leading the Union advance at YORKTOWN, he vastly overestimated the strength of the Confederate defenders, convincing a naturally cautious McClellan to lay siege to the village. He commanded 2 of the army's best combat divisions under Brig. Gens. JOSEPH HOOKER and PHILIP KEARNY, who led the units with skill and courage. At WILLIAMSBURG Hooker's and Kearny's men fought valiantly while Heintzelman exercised little control. At SEVEN PINES the corps commander rallied broken Federal units but with minimal effect. During the SEVEN DAYS' CAMPAIGN the corps performed well, again under Hooker and Kearny.

The SECOND BULL RUN CAMPAIGN was Heintzelman's last as a corps commander. Once more he failed to exhibit the attributes of an officer destined for further responsibilities. During the ANTIETAM CAMPAIGN the III Corps remained in the Washington, D.C., defenses. On 12 Oct. Heintzelman was relieved of corps command and assigned to the Military District of Washington. For nearly 2 years he remained at the capital and later was in charge of the Northern Department, with headquarters in Columbus, Ohio. He served on court-martial duty during the war's final months.

A stern man of blunt speech and abundant energy, Heintzelman retired in 1869, dying in the District of Columbia, 1 May 1880. —JDW

Helm, Benjamin Hardin.

Helm, Benjamin Hardin. CSA b. Bardstown, Ky., 2 June 1831, Helm, called Ben Hardin Helm, ranked 9th in the West Point class of 1851. He resigned his lieutenant's commission in 1852 after duty at the Carlisle, Pa., cavalry school and at Fort Lincoln, Tex., and became a law student, a 1-term Kentucky state legislator, a state attorney for Kentucky's 3d District, and a prosperous lawyer.

At the start of civil war Helm recruited the 1st Kentucky Cavalry for the Confederacy, then received a colonel's commission 19 Oct. 1861, occupied Bowling Green, Ky., with

Brig. Gen. SIMON B. BUCKNER, was sent south, and received promotion to brigadier general 14 Mar. 1862. On 6 April, at the end of the first day of fighting in the Battle of SHILOH, Helm incorrectly sent word from his post in north Alabama that Union Maj. Gen. Don Carlos Buell's force was pressing for Decatur, Ala., instead of moving to Brig. Gen. U. S. GRANT's aid. Gen. P. G. T. BEAUREGARD, who assumed command after Gen. Albert Sidney Johnston's death

USMHI

at Shiloh, later claimed that he disregarded Helm's message, yet he did not press his advantage on the 6th. By morning, the reinforcements had arrived, strengthening the Federal position and denying victory to the Confederate troops.

Shiloh did not affect Helm's career. Posted to Vicksburg in summer 1862, he took part in Maj. Gen. JOHN C. BRECKINRIDGE's expedition to BATON ROUGE but missed the battle because of injuries in a fall from his horse. In Jan. 1863 he joined the Army of Tennessee and served in the TULLAHOMA and CHICKAMAUGA campaigns under Breckinridge. On 20 Sept., he was mortally wounded at Chickamauga and died that night.

Helm is remembered less for his Confederate service than for marrying Emily Todd in 1856. Before the war, Mrs. Helm, MARY TODD LINCOLN's half sister, brought her husband into Pres. ABRAHAM LINCOLN's family circle. The president offered Helm a Union major's commission in 1861, which he declined to raise the 1st Kentucky. After Helm's death, his widow passed through Union lines to visit her sister at the White House in December, causing a furor in the Northern press. On 14 Dec. Emily Helm took a Union loyalty oath in Washington and was granted amnesty.   —JES

Helper, Hinton Rowen. author b. Rowan (Davie) Cty., N.C., 27 Dec. 1829. Appointed by Abraham Lincoln to Buenos Aires as U.S. consul early in 1861, Helper had no direct involvement in the war, but a book written 4 years earlier by the enigmatic young Southerner ranked with John Brown's Raid in inflaming the passions of a nation on the brink of civil war (see HARPERS FERRY, WESTERN VA., JOHN BROWN'S RAID ON).

Helper's controversial work, *The Impending Crisis of the South: How to Meet It* (1857), contrasted the economic status of the free-labor North with the slave-labor South. Helper emphasized the sectional discrepancies with a series of statistics unfavorable to the South and attributed Southern backwardness to slavery. Without condemning slaveowners, he directed his arguments to nonslaveholding whites, whom he believed suffered the greatest disadvantages from the regional dependence on slave labor.

The book sold 14,000 copies, an extraordinary achievement in a time marked by economic crisis. Few copies circulated outside the North, where ABOLITIONIST and antislavery advocates embraced his work as documented confirmation of the evil effects of slavery. Southern critics never developed a cohesive refutation of Helper's theses, largely because they refused to read them. Rather, they based their outrage on summaries written by Northern reviewers. Almost without exception, the author, not the book, was attacked, accused of trying to incite a slave uprising and charged with treason against the South.

Labeling the material seditious, Southern politicians managed legally to block the book from being distributed in the slave states, and people possessing copies were persecuted by local officials with arrest, imprisonment, fines, and, on at least one occasion, hanging. Often copies of *The Impending Crisis* were destroyed in book-burnings. Helper recognized that his fellow Southerners' ire stemmed from his attempt to present facts instead of an emotional appeal. Without a fictionalized format to discredit it, the book provoked a far greater outcry than had *Uncle Tom's Cabin* a few years earlier.

Understanding that Helper's reasoned arguments and statistics could benefit the 1860 elections, Republicans raised a special fund to print 100,000 copies for distribution as campaign literature, capitalizing as well on the author's Southern origins. Once Lincoln won the presidency, *The Impending Crisis* lost its significance, overshadowed by a military confrontation that Helper had hoped would be averted at the ballot box by nonslaveholders within the South.

Ironically, Helper hated blacks more than he hated slavery. His second book, *Nojoque* (1867), denounced them as a threat to free white labor, with the author professing in the preface his intent "to write the Negro out of America . . . and out of existence." He approached the majority of his endeavors with an intensity similar to that of his Negrophobia, sacrificing family, friends, and fortune to his fanaticisms. Alone, embittered, and impoverished, he committed suicide in the District of Columbia, 8 Mar. 1909.   —PLF

Henrico, Confederate Department of. Encompassing Henrico Cty., Va., in which Richmond, the Confederate capital, was located, the Confederate Department of Henrico was probably created officially Dec. 1861 and was expanded to include Petersburg and vicinity Mar. 1862. Brig. Gen. JOHN H. WINDER was appointed department commander on its authorization.

Winder, who also was provost marshal general of the Confederacy and provost marshal of Richmond, had primary responsibility for the prisons of LIBBY and BELLE ISLE. During spring 1862, when Maj. Gen. GEORGE B. MCCLELLAN's Union army lumbered up the peninsula toward Richmond (see PENINSULA CAMPAIGN), Confederate authorities proclaimed martial law in the capital. The enforcement fell on Winder, who soon became quite unpopular.

The Confederate brigadier initially forbade liquor sales and required all citizens to surrender their firearms. To enforce the rules, he created a body of civilian detectives, who soon earned the derisive nickname "Plug Uglies." His soldiers and authorized civilians arrested citizens suspected of disloyalty, issued passports, and vainly tried to limit the unquenchable thirst of the citizens for liquor.

Winder continued in his post until May 1864, when the department was disbanded. He had wrestled with price fixing, witnessed the BREAD RIOT in spring 1863, closed the "Hells" (the city's notorious gambling houses), and even dismissed all but one of his "Plug Uglies" for malfeasance, corruption, or bribery. The Department of Henrico and its commander were burdened with the problems of a small state capital transformed into a bustling wartime capital of a new nation.   —JDW

Henry rifle. One of the most advanced small arms in use during the Civil War, the Henry rifle saw limited but effective service as the war drew to a close. The invention of B. Tyler Henry, plant superintendent of the New Haven Arms Co., the Henry rifle was patented 16 Oct. 1860. Henry's concept was not entirely new, and to a degree represented improvements on Smith and Wesson's "Volcanic" rifle. Still, Henry was able to add several distinctive features: fixed, metallic ammunition; a split firing pin that struck the cartridge at 2 points, reducing the chances of misfire; and a successful system of cartridge extraction. As produced, the Henry carried 15 rounds of .44-caliber rimfire cartridges in its magazine, located directly under the barrel. The cartridge closest to the breech was fed by dropping the loading lever, which forced the block backward and cocked the hammer, and by closing the lever, which forced the cartridge into the chamber.

The U.S. government purchased 1,730 Henrys 23 July 1863–7 Nov. 1865. However, as many as 10,000 of them may have seen Civil War service through purchases by states or individual regiments. The Henry was particularly popular in the West among Maj. Gen. WILLIAM T. SHERMAN's troops, but saw only limited use in the Eastern theater; the only regiment in the Army of the Potomac known to have used Henrys was the 1st Main Cavalry. Henrys were used at DINWIDDIE COURT HOUSE, FIVE FORKS, and SAYLER'S CREEK.

Confederates picked up an occasional Henry, but its use in the South was limited. Still, Confederate Col. George Martin was presented with a Henry at Greensborough, N.C., just before the end of the war "for the President's defense." It is doubtful, however, whether this weapon, now in the Museum of the Confederacy in Richmond, was ever used. Confederates in the West applied the same phrase to the Henry that Eastern Confederates applied to the Spencer: "that damn Yankee rifle they load up on Sunday and fire all week."   —LDJ

Heroes of America, Order of the. *See* PEACE SOCIETIES.

Herron, Francis Jay. USA b. Pittsburgh, Pa., 17 Feb. 1837. Known for his gallantry and leadership at the Battle of PEA RIDGE, Ark., 7–8 Mar. 1862, Herron was one of the most admired officers of the war, at least by his commanders. While he received the MEDAL OF HONOR for Pea Ridge (30 years after the war), he also led his troops in the battles at WILSON'S CREEK, Mo., PRAIRIE GROVE, Ark., and the Siege of VICKSBURG, Miss.

In 1855 Herron moved from Pennsylvania to Iowa after attending the University of Pittsburgh. Using experience he had gained from working in a Pittsburgh bank, he and 2 brothers established one of their own in

LC

Dubuque. There he also established a militia company and remained in the banking business until 14 May 1861, when he joined the 1st Iowa Infantry as a captain. 10 days after the disastrous Federal defeat at Wilson's Creek, 10 Aug., he was honorably mustered out to take over as a lieutenant colonel in the 9th Iowa. For his personal bravery at Pea Ridge, he was commissioned a brigadier general of volunteers to rank from

16 July 1862. He was captured in the battle and saw little action until he returned to his command later that year.

In Dec. 1862 Herron's 2-division command, encamped on Wilson's Creek, marched 150 mi in 4 days to do battle at Prairie Grove, answering a request from Brig. Gen. JAMES G. BLUNT. Blunt's 7,000 Federals were being chased by 11,500 Confederates under Maj. Gen. THOMAS C. HINDMAN. Collecting his 6,000 men and 30 guns, Herron marched them incessantly; by 7 Dec. he had arrived on the field in Blunt's support. Said Herron after the battle, "I think this section is rid of Hindman." For his actions at Prairie Grove, Herron became a major general of volunteers to rank from 29 Nov. 1862 and finished the war as a corps commander at Brownsville, Tex., and as an Indian treaty commissioner.

From 1865 to 1877 Herron lived in Louisiana, serving as an attorney, a U.S. marshal, and acting state secretary of state. In 1877 he moved to New York City, where he died a pauper, according to his death certificate, 8 Jan. 1902.   —FLS

Heth, Henry. CSA b. Chesterfield Cty., Va., 16 Dec. 1825, Heth has received mixed reviews as a military leader. He graduated from West Point in 1847, last in a class of 38 cadets. Following graduation he served briefly in Mexico (he missed the war), then on the Western frontier, where he rose to the rank of captain and attracted some attention in minor actions against the Brulé Sioux.

NA

When the Civil War came, he resigned his Regular commission to join the Confederacy. A favorite of JEFFERSON DAVIS', he won an appointment to the rank of brigadier general as of 6 Jan. 1862. After sometimes frustrating but usually praiseworthy service in western Virginia and Kentucky, he was given a brigade in Maj. Gen. AMBROSE P. HILL's division/Lt. Gen. THOMAS J. "STONEWALL" JACKSON's Corps, just in time for CHANCELLORSVILLE. Heth received recognition for his field leadership in that battle and in the reorganization that followed gained command of a division.

On 1 July 1863, Heth's division made the first major contact with the Union forces at GETTYSBURG, while presumably looking for shoes for Confederate troops. Heth pressed forward without regard for the formality of reconnaissance and in the subsequent fighting his division was severely bloodied. He was taken out of action for several days by wounds but recovered in time to command the rear guard during Gen. ROBERT E. LEE's retreat from Pennsylvania. He remained embarrassed by his precipitate action, though both he and Hill, commanding the III Corps, had underestimated the numbers and the fighting ability of the Union forces.

Heth served out the war in the Army of Northern Virginia, in the thick of the fighting at BRISTOE STATION, the WILDERNESS, and around PETERSBURG. He left the army with a reputation for personal bravery and tenacity, but with an unfortunate tendency toward rashness when deliberation was called for. He seemed to recognize his limitations, admitted his mistakes on occasion, and impressed everyone with his charm and spirit.

After the war, he followed a business career with indifferent success and served briefly as an agent of the Office of Indian Affairs. In spite of ill health, before his death he managed to finish his memoirs, finally published in 1974 as *The Memoirs of Henry Heth.* d. District of Columbia, 27 Sept. 1899 and was buried in Richmond.   —JTH

Hickenlooper, Andrew.

USA   b. Hudson, Ohio, 10 Aug. 1837. Reared in Circleville and Cincinnati, Hickenlooper attended St. Xavier and Woodward colleges in Cincinnati, became Cincinnati city engineer in 1856 and city surveyor in 1859. The 5th Ohio Independent Battery Light Artillery, raised by Hickenlooper for Civil War service, was mustered in Sept. 1861 and Hickenlooper was commissioned its captain. Known as HICKENLOOPER'S BATTERY, it built his reputation as a tough, intelligent, though very young subordinate officer.

NA

After quiet service with Maj. Gen. JOHN C. FRÉMONT's troops in Missouri, the battery joined Maj. Gen. ULYSSES S. GRANT's forces in Tennessee. Hickenlooper distinguished himself at the Battle of SHILOH and in the pursuit of the Confederate forces to CORINTH, Miss., then assumed division command of artillery for the Oct. 1862 Battle of Corinth. Maj. Gen. JAMES B. MCPHERSON assigned him to his staff the same month. With the Army of the Tennessee for the remainder of the war, Hickenlooper performed his greatest service during the Siege of VICKSBURG, when as chief engineer he orchestrated artillery operations and work on the Vicksburg mine, an attempt to blow up Fort Hill on the Confederate lines by tunneling beneath it. For his performance he won the XVII CORPS MEDAL. Under McPherson he held the positions of judge advocate and chief of artillery in the ATLANTA CAMPAIGN; under Maj. Gen. OLIVER O. HOWARD he was promoted to lieutenant colonel 14 Sept. 1864 and joined in the MARCH TO THE SEA and the CAROLINAS CAMPAIGN. Before being mustered out of service, Hickenlooper was brevetted brigadier general of volunteers for war service, on the recommendations of Lieutenant General Grant and Maj. Gens. WILLIAM T. SHERMAN and Howard.

In his postwar career Hickenlooper served as a U.S. marshal in Ohio, Cincinnati city engineer, vice-president and president of the Cincinnati Gas Light & Coke Co., and lieutenant governor of Ohio. Intensely interested in lighting technology, he wrote 3 books on the subject, as well as the history *The Battle of Shiloh* (1903). d. Cincinnati, 12 May 1904.   —JES

Hickenlooper's Battery.

USA   The 5th Ohio Independent Battery Light Artillery, raised by 24-year-old Cincinnati engineer ANDREW HICKENLOOPER, is better remembered as Hickenlooper's Battery. Mustered into Union service 22 Sept. 1861, at St. Louis, Mo., for duty with Maj. Gen. JOHN C. FRÉMONT's Department of Missouri, it saw no action until transferred to the 6th Division/Army of the Tennessee Mar. 1862. It fought in the Battle of SHILOH the next month. Under Hickenlooper, the battery pursued the Confederates to Corinth, Miss., occupied a position in the town's defenses, then, on Hickenlooper's assumption of divisional artillery command, fought in the Oct. 1862 Battle of CORINTH under Lt. Bellamy S. Matson.

At both Shiloh and Corinth it won distinction for fighting on desperately contested ground.

As a part of the XIII Corps the battery took part in Maj. Gen. ULYSSES S. GRANT's first Mississippi campaign late in 1862, transferred to the XVII Corps for operations in Tennessee, then joined the XVI Corps in 1863 for the Siege of VICKSBURG. Following the surrender of Vicksburg and the campaign to JACKSON, Miss., the cannoneers' relationship with Hickenlooper dissolved when their old commander remained with the Army of the Tennessee and the battery was assigned to Maj. Gen. FREDERICK STEELE's CAMDEN EXPEDITION. The battery participated in the seizure of Little Rock, Ark., then, as part of the Army of Arkansas and Department of Arkansas, ended the war on garrison duty in the town. The last of its men were mustered out of service 31 July 1865, members of an artillery unit distinguished by a heavy combat record and comparatively light casualty figures. Only 5 men of the 5th Ohio died in combat.   —JES

Hicks, Thomas Holliday.

war governor b. Dorchester Cty., Md., 2 Sept. 1798. A farmer's son with a rudimentary education, Hicks held elective or appointive office in Maryland for over 4 decades. A local constable, he eventually became the state's chief executive, serving during the secession crisis in 1861. His actions and inactions, berated or supported by factions in the badly divided state, contributed to Maryland remaining in the Union.

Hicks was a constable at 21, a sheriff at 26, and a state legislator at 32. Initially a member of the Democratic party, he switched in the 1830s to the newly formed Whigs, serving as an 1836 presidential elector.

USMHI

That year the experienced young politician returned to the house of delegates and was elected by the legislature to the governor's council. When this latter body was abolished in 1838, Hicks received an appointment as registrar of wills in Dorchester County, a post he held almost continuously for 17 years. In 1850–51 he served as a member of the Maryland constitutional convention.

With the dissolution of the Whigs after the 1854 presidential election, Hicks joined the American, or Know Nothing, party, an organization espousing nativism. The party expanded rapidly in the mid-fifties, and in fall 1857 Hicks was elected governor of the state. Never a gifted orator, he nonetheless possessed a steady sense of justice and a natural common wisdom. Slow to make decisions, he usually adhered to them tenaciously once he decided on a course of action.

Hicks's term of office coincided with the climax of mounting sectional controversies. After the election of ABRAHAM LINCOLN, Maryland secessionists and Unionists clamored for a special session of the legislature to define Maryland's position on the crisis. Resisting the mounting pressure, Hicks did nothing, and mass meetings either denounced or praised his inaction. But the firing on FORT SUMTER and Lincoln's subsequent call for volunteers forced the issue.

Hicks remained steadfast, but the state, especially Baltimore, was volatile. On 19 Apr. a mob of Baltimoreans attacked the

6th Massachusetts, which was switching trains en route to Washington, D.C. (*see* BALTIMORE RIOTS). At least 13 soldiers and civilians were killed. Seizing the city for several days, pro-secessionists arrested some Unionists, terrorized others, and several times threatened Hicks's life. But the governor still did not act.

Finally, on 26 Apr. he called a special session of the legislature to meet in Frederick, an area of strong Unionist sentiment. Hicks urged neutrality and the legislature agreed, stating that it lacked the constitutional authority to adopt an ordinance of secession. Hicks rendered the North an invaluable service by keeping Maryland from seceding until the legislature declared for the Union and Federal troops were stationed in Baltimore.

When his term expired in 1862, he rejected a brigadiership in the Union army, then accepted a vacancy in the U.S. Senate created by the death of a Maryland senator. Failing health, however, limited his participation. In 1863 he injured his ankle, which did not heal, resulting in the amputation of his foot. Reelected in 1864, Hicks died 13 Feb. 1865 due to complications from the amputation. —JDW

Higgins, Edward. CSA b. Norfolk, Va., 1821. As a boy Higgins lived with an uncle in Louisiana, accepted an appointment as midshipman in the U.S. Navy in 1836, and served until resigning as a lieutenant in 1854. Until the Civil War he was a civilian executive officer on mail steamers plying East Coast waters.

In spring 1861 Higgins joined the 1st Louisiana Artillery as captain, became aide-de-camp to Confederate department commander Maj. Gen. DAVID E. TWIGGS, supervised construction of the Ship Island defenses, and during the early blockade of Galveston, Tex., was recommended by Twiggs to head a relief expedition to drive off the

LC

U.S. Navy from the city. The expedition proved to be unnecessary, and Higgins was promoted lieutenant colonel of the 21st Louisiana Infantry. As Col. JOHNSON K. DUNCAN's second-in-command, he oversaw the garrisons at FORTS JACKSON AND ST. PHILIP and the defense of New Orleans. After brief imprisonment when Federal troops captured the forts in 1862, he was exchanged and sent to duty in the Vicksburg river batteries. As a part of Brig. Gen. STEPHEN D. LEE's brigade, Higgins commanded the 22d Louisiana Artillery at the Snyder's Mill defenses. On Confederate surrender of Vicksburg, July 1863, he again became a prisoner. Exchanged a second time, he was promoted brigadier general to rank from 29 Oct. on the request of Maj. Gen. DABNEY H. MAURY, with whom he had served at Vicksburg. Higgins reported to the defenses at Mobile, Ala., serving there through much of 1864. Then, for reasons unknown, he was relieved of duty and left to await orders until the end of the war.

Postbellum Higgins returned to Norfolk and worked as an importer and insurance agent until 1872. He moved to San Francisco, Calif., to become a steamship agent and died there 31 Jan. 1875. —JES

High Shoal, Indian Territory, eng. at. 9 Dec. 1861 *See* BIRD CREEK, INDIAN TERRITORY, ENG. AT.

Hill, Adams Sherman. journalist b. Boston, Mass., 30 Jan. 1833. Raised in Worcester, Mass., Hill, a minister's son, entered Harvard, graduated from its law school in 1855, worked briefly as a law reporter, then joined the NEW YORK TRIBUNE as a night editor in 1858. He went to the *Tribune's* Washington, D.C., bureau as assistant to veteran correspondent Edward E. House in spring 1861, and with House witnessed an infantry engagement at BLACKBURN'S FORD, Va., 18 July. Described as extremely nearsighted and highly nervous, Hill panicked under fire, fled the field, and submitted an exaggerated, inaccurate story to the *Tribune,* claiming Union defeat and the loss of 500 dead. He received no more combat assignments, instead excelling in administering the *Tribune's* reportage of the war and events in Washington.

First as assistant bureau chief, from Aug. 1861 under the frequently absent Samuel Wilkeson, then as bureau chief, from Jan. 1863, Hill established news contacts for the *Tribune,* counting among his confidential sources Pres. ABRAHAM LINCOLN's personal staff, Sen. CHARLES SUMNER, Assistant Sec. of the Navy GUSTAVUS V. FOX, Speaker of the House SCHUYLER COLFAX, and Sec. of the Treasury SALMON P. CHASE. Hill assigned and supplied reporters on combat duty in the Eastern theater and hired several noteworthy journalists, among them CHARLES A. PAGE. An advocate of impartial journalism, Hill forwarded to New York *Tribune* offices stories that lacked the partisanship typical of 19th-century journalism. *Tribune* publisher HORACE GREELEY, an advocate of the old style, disliked Hill, which led to Hill's resignation from the newspaper Dec. 1863 and the formation, with fellow journalists HENRY VILLARD and Horace White, of the capital news service the Independent News Room. Disseminating information to newspapers in Boston, Chicago, St. Louis, and New York, the service was the first to compete with the ASSOCIATED PRESS. But because of its competitor's exclusive contract with the American Telegraph Co., it was forced to use the small Independent Telegraph Co. This association, and the Independent News Room's competitiveness, caused Hill's detention by Federal authorities 19–20 May 1864 as a suspect in the GOLD HOAX. War Department officials briefly believed Hill's service might have perpetrated the hoax to discredit the Associated Press. But the Independent Telegraph Co. had been manipulated in the scheme.

In the latter months of the war the Independent News Room prospered. Hill remained active in journalism in immediate postwar years, then in 1872 left reporting to join the faculty at Harvard as an assistant professor of rhetoric. A full professor in 1876, he later became chairman of the university's English department and wrote *Our English* (1889) and *Foundations of Rhetoric* (1892). d. Boston, 25 Dec. 1910. —JES

Hill, Ambrose Powell. CSA b. Culpeper, Va., 9 Nov. 1825, Hill graduated from West Point 15th in his class in 1847 and was commissioned a 2d lieutenant. He saw service in the Mexican War, duty in the office of the superintendent of the Coast Survey, participated in the Third Seminole War, and served at a number of posts.

On 1 Mar. 1861 Hill resigned from the U.S. Army, entering Confederate service as colonel of the 13th Virginia Infantry. He was named a brigadier general 26 Feb. 1862 and at WILLIAMSBURG, 5 May, assailed the Federals as they advanced up the peninsula. His conduct earned him command of a division and promotion to major general 26 May. A month later, at MECHANICSVILLE, Hill opened the SEVEN DAYS' CAMPAIGN. He and his unit, known as Hill's LIGHT DIVISION, also spearheaded Confederate attacks at GAINES' MILL and Frayser's Farm.

NA

He joined Maj. Gen. THOMAS J. "STONEWALL" JACKSON on the Rapidan River in late July and, while teamed with him, Hill and his division earned a deserved reputation as one of America's great fighting units. They distinguished themselves at CEDAR MOUNTAIN, SECOND BULL RUN, ANTIETAM, FREDERICKSBURG, and at CHANCELLORSVILLE were in the forefront on Jackson's last and greatest march.

When Gen. ROBERT E. LEE reorganized his army following Jackson's death, Hill was promoted to lieutenant general 24 May 1863 and was placed in command of the newly constituted III Corps. Whether he displayed behavior that today would be attributed to psychosomatic problems or whether his capabilities were unequal to the challenge, his performance as corps commander was undistinguished. At GETTYSBURG, despite his corps' role in bringing on the fight, he was passive; at BRISTOE STATION his impetuous assault cost more than 1,300 casualties; at the WILDERNESS, his corps was saved from disaster by Lt. Gen. JAMES LONGSTREET's arrival; he became sick and missed the SPOTSYLVANIA fighting; and in the contest for PETERSBURG, whenever a crisis threatened, he generally reported himself sick and yielded his responsibility.

On 2 Apr. 1865 Hill returned from sick leave, rode to rally his men, whose lines had been shattered, and was shot and killed by 2 Union VI Corps soldiers. He was buried in Richmond.   —ECB

Hill, Benjamin Harvey. CSP b. Jasper Cty., Ga., 14 Sept. 1823. With considerable sacrifice on the part of his family, Hill attended the University of Georgia, graduated with honors in 1843, and the next year was admitted to the bar. He enjoyed professional success in criminal and civil law, earning praise from his colleagues and sufficient wealth from his clients to become a slaveholding landowner. In 1851 he won a seat in the state house of representatives, his only elected office before the war.

Hill spent his political career altering his party affiliations whenever practicality demanded. After the Whigs dissolved, he joined the American (Know Nothing) party, then the Constitutional Unionists, and finally the Democrats in support of John Bell for the presidency in 1860. A consistent proponent of compromise, he attended the Milledgeville convention Jan. 1861 opposed to disunion, but changed his position and signed the ordinance of secession later that month. In the Provisional Congress he quickly established himself as a supporter of JEFFERSON DAVIS' insistence on strong central government. The Georgia legislature elected him to the Senate of the 2 Regular Congresses, where he served as chairman of the Committee on the Judiciary. Though he professed to disagree with the president on such issues as CONSCRIPTION, excessive IMPRESSMENT, and suspension of the writ of *HABEAS CORPUS*, he

consistently defended these unpopular measures as necessary to the war effort. As the Confederate military situation deteriorated, Hill joined the peace faction urging Davis to seek a negotiated end to the war.

Federal authorities arrested Hill following Gen. ROBERT E. LEE's surrender and imprisoned him for 3 months at FORT LAFAYETTE in New York. When Pres. ANDREW JOHNSON paroled him in July, he retired to his home in La Grange, Ga., avoiding public life until lashing out against Radical Reconstruction in 1867. Characteristically, he reversed his position 3 years later, promoting acceptance of the measures already imposed on the state. Georgia Democrats responded by politically ostracizing him for the next 5 years. Finally elected to the House of Representatives as a Republican in 1875, he astounded his new colleagues by vigorously defending Southern rights, the Confederacy, and Jefferson Davis. He returned to the Democratic fold and was elected to the Senate Jan. 1877. Hill died in Atlanta, 16 Aug. 1882, before his term expired.   —PLF

Hill, Benjamin Jefferson. CSA b. McMinnville, Tenn., 13 June 1825, Hill acquired his education in local common schools and by the 1850s had established a successful mercantile business. From 1855 until the Civil War, he served in the state senate. He entered the Provisional Army of Tennessee with the colonelcy of the 5th Tennessee Volunteers (later the 35th Tennessee), resigning Sept. 1861 to enter Confederate service at the same rank.

At SHILOH, 6 Apr. 1862, he fought under Brig. Gen. PATRICK R. CLEBURNE, with whom he served until Cleburne's death at FRANKLIN Nov. 1864. In the 18 months following Shiloh, his regiment initiated the Confederate attack at RICHMOND, Ky., fought at STONE'S RIVER, and participated in the failed defense of MISSIONARY RIDGE during the battles for CHATTANOOGA. Through the remainder of 1863 and until 24 Aug. 1864, Hill was provost marshal for the Army of Tennessee. He returned to field service in the last weeks of the ATLANTA CAMPAIGN.

LC

Though an experienced infantry commander, he was transferred to cavalry, leading a brigade through the FRANKLIN AND NASHVILLE CAMPAIGN. His promotion to brigadier general dates from 30 Nov. He ended the war fighting around Selma, Ala., in Lt. Gen. NATHAN B. FORREST's command.

Hill spent the postwar years practicing law and rebuilding his business in McMinnville, where he died 5 Jan. 1880.

—PLF

Hill, Daniel Harvey. CSA b. York District, S.C., 12 July 1821. The youngest of 11 children, Hill decided early on a military career. Entering West Point in 1838, he graduated in 1842, 28th in a class of 56 and 1 of 15 who would become Civil War generals. After gallant service at Vera Cruz, Cerro Gordo, Contreras, and Chapultepec during the Mexican War, he left the army to teach at Washington College in Virginia and Davidson College in North Carolina. He was superintendent of North Carolina Military Institute when war began.

Hill won the first engagement of the war, at BIG BETHEL, 10 June, receiving rank as brigadier general that day. Promoted to major general 26 Mar. 1862, he fought under Gen. JOSEPH E. JOHNSTON at YORKTOWN, WILLIAMSBURG, and SEVEN PINES, and under Gen. ROBERT E. LEE during the SEVEN DAYS' CAMPAIGN and at SECOND BULL RUN, SOUTH MOUNTAIN, and ANTIETAM. Between the PENINSULA CAMPAIGN and South Mountain, Hill briefly commanded the Department of North Carolina.

LC

Historian Hal Bridges has called Hill "Lee's maverick general." Possessed of a bravery that approached recklessness, he earned respect and affection from his men. He was also abrasive and outspoken toward his fellow officers, and his relations with them suffered. An individualist among an army of individualists, he had the temerity to criticize two full generals, first Lee, then BRAXTON BRAGG—JEFFERSON DAVIS' favorites. This Davis could not forgive. Hill's caustic criticism of Lee for the Confederate defeat at MALVERN HILL and for his poor showing at South Mountain, and Hill's refusal to admit any responsibility for the loss of Special Order No. 191 (*see* LEE'S LOST ORDER) containing Lee's Antietam battle plan, led to a rift between the two men that ended only with Lee's death.

Appointed lieutenant general 11 July 1863, Hill was transferred to the Army of Tennessee, under Bragg's command. He fought brilliantly at CHICKAMAUGA, 19–20 Sept., and deserves much of the credit for delivering a crushing defeat to the Union troops under Maj. Gen. WILLIAM S. ROSECRANS. In a bitter controversy after the battle, Hill publicly condemned Bragg's failure to pursue the defeated Union army, and the ambiguous, confusing orders issued by the commander invited Hill and several other officers to accuse him of incompetency and recommend his removal. Believing Hill responsible for the affront, Bragg retaliated by unfairly accusing him of delaying an attack that had been ordered for but not begun at dawn on the 20th. Though the charge was unwarranted, Hill was removed from command and his lieutenant generalcy not confirmed. Except briefly at PETERSBURG in 1864 and at BENTONVILLE in 1865, he saw no further service.

After the war Hill edited 2 publications, *The Land We Love* (1865–69), a magazine of Southern literature and articles concerning the Confederate military, and *The Southern Home* (1870–77). He then resumed his career as an educator, accepting the presidency first of the Arkansas Industrial University (later the University of Arkansas), then of the Georgia Military Academy. Most of Hill's extensive postwar writings were defenses of his military reputation. d. Charlotte, N.C., 24 Sept. 1889.   —RDH

Hill's Point, N.C., eng. at. 2 Apr. 1863 His Mar. 1863 offensive against New Berne having failed, Maj. Gen. DANIEL H. HILL ranged eastward toward the North Carolina coast. He hoped to reverse his ill luck by assailing a second objective recently given him by Lt. Gen. JAMES LONGSTREET: the Union garrison at Washington. Hill planned this operation carefully. By 30 Mar. he had erected batteries along the Pamlico River east of the town, to prevent a 3-gunboat flotilla anchored in the

stream from reinforcing the garrison. He also mounted guns along the south bank of the Pamlico at Hill's Point, as well as farther up the north bank, at Swan's Point. Yet another battery swept the south bank a short distance below Washington. Hulks and pilings sunk in the river further precluded amphibious relief of the garrison. To prevent the Federals at New Berne from interfering, Hill placed 2 brigades of infantry across the roads running south from Washington. Meanwhile, a brigade under Brig. Gen. RICHARD B. GARNETT held at bay the 1,200 troops at Washington, led by Brig. Gen. JOHN G. FOSTER, commander of the Union Department of North Carolina.

Enjoined to refrain from storming the village, Hill kept Garnett's brigade well in hand and contented himself with exchanging artillery fire with his enemy. Within 2 days, supplies and rations began to run low in Washington. When 2 efforts to bring reinforcements from New Berne failed, the Federals seemed doomed to surrender.

On 2 Apr., however, the gunboats below the obstructed stretch of river suddenly turned their firepower on the Hill's Point battery, silencing its guns. The following morning, a Confederate emplacement just outside Washington opened on the ships. The latter in turn concentrated on the new obstacle and quickly overwhelmed it. This success showed General Foster that the Confederate positions were not invincible.

When the next 12 days failed to bring relief from New Berne, Foster ran the batteries in a steamer protected by hay bales stacked on its deck. Though struck 40 times by the guns at and near Hill's Point, the ship passed the obstructions early on the 15th and reached New Berne. Aware that Foster could now bring reinforcements against him, Hill called off the siege and again withdrew in dejection and disgust from a strategic objective.   —EGL

Hincks, Edward Winslow. USA b. Bucksport, Maine, 30 May 1830. Dropping the *c* from his family name early in life (he reinstated it in 1871), Hincks received a common-school education, then traveled to Bangor to become a printer. In 1849 he moved to Boston, attained prominence, and by 1855 was a member of the Massachusetts legislature. By all accounts he was modest and unassuming but "very sociable"—"a most agreeable man."

When the Civil War erupted, Hincks became both a lieutenant in the 2d U.S. Cavalry and the lieutenant colonel of the 8th Massachusetts Volunteers. By mid-May 1861 he was colonel of the 8th and soon afterward resigned his Regular commission. He then gave up his position with the 8th, taking command of the 19th Massachusetts 3 Aug.

His active service began near Annapolis, Md., where his men repaired and guarded railroads and bridges. Late in 1861 he participated in the debacle at BALL'S BLUFF and the following spring served under Maj. Gen. GEORGE B. MCCLELLAN in the PENINSULA CAMPAIGN. Wounded at WHITE OAK SWAMP, he became a casualty again at ANTIETAM. The wound disabled him for 6 months and caused him pain and debility for the rest of his life.

While on convalescent leave, he was promoted brigadier

general of volunteers to rank from 29 Nov. 1862. After partially recovering, he went on recruiting duty until given command of a Maryland prison camp Mar. 1864. A month later, he took over a XVIII Corps division composed of BLACK SOLDIERS. As a member of Maj. Gen. BENJAMIN F. BUTLER's Army of the James, he served creditably during the first part of the campaigning for Richmond and Petersburg, though often ill or prostrated by his wounds. His afflictions helped persuade Butler to suspend a promising assault by Hincks's division against Petersburg 9 May.

By July 1864 he was forced to quit active service. Till war's close, by which time he was a brevet major general of volunteers, he was again on recruiting service. Resigning his volunteer commission June 1865, he later became lieutenant colonel of a regiment of Regulars. He retired Dec. 1870 as colonel of the 25th Infantry, to serve as governor of the National Home for Disabled Volunteers in Virginia and later of another soldiers' home in Wisconsin. d. Cambridge, Mass., 14 Feb. 1894.
—EGL

Hindman, Thomas Carmichael. CSA b. Knoxville, Tenn., 28 Jan. 1828. When Hindman was 4, his parents moved to Jacksonville, Ala., where his father served as an Indian agent. In 1841 the family headed west, settling on and operating a large plantation in Tippah Cty., Miss. Hindman was educated in local common schools and matriculated at the Classical and Commercial High School in Lawrenceville, N.J.

7 months after the outbreak of the Mexican War, Hindman was mustered into service at Vicksburg as a 2d lieutenant in the 2d Mississippi Infantry. The regiment served in northern Mexico but saw little action, though its ranks were severely reduced by disease. On Hindman's return from the war, he was admitted to the state bar, and, 1854–55, represented Tippah County in the state legislature. In 1856, he immigrated to Arkansas, locating in Helena, where he continued to practice law. He was elected and reelected to Congress as a Democratic representative in 1858 and 1860, though he did not take his seat in the 37th Congress.

Hindman played a leading role in agitating for the secession of Arkansas. At the conclusion of this campaign, he resigned from Congress, raised the 2d Arkansas Infantry, and entered Confederate service as its colonel. He was promoted brigadier general to rank from 28 Sept. 1861. At SHILOH, he led a division in Maj. Gen. WILLIAM J. HARDEE's Corps, until disabled as he hurled his troops against the "HORNETS' NEST."

Named a major general to rank from 14 Apr. 1862, in late May Hindman returned to Arkansas as commander of the Trans-Mississippi Department. His vigorous enforcement of conscription and imposition of martial law caused an uproar. To appease local politicians, the War Department replaced him with Lt. Gen. THEOPHILUS H. HOLMES. Then, as commander of the Confederate forces in northwest Arkansas, Hindman seized the initiative but was defeated at PRAIRIE GROVE.

Soon, at his own request, Hindman was reassigned, to the Army of Tennessee. He led a division at CHICKAMAUGA, where

he was wounded, and in the ATLANTA CAMPAIGN from Rocky Face to KENNESAW MOUNTAIN, where he was wounded in the eye, incapacitating him for active duty.

On the collapse of the Confederacy, Hindman fled to Mexico to become a coffee planter, but returned to Arkansas in 1867. On 28 Sept. 1868 he was killed by an assassin in his Helena home and was buried in a local cemetery.   —ECB

Hinks, Edward Winslow. *See* HINCKS, EDWARD WINSLOW.

Hitchcock, Ethan Allen. USA b. Vergennes, Vt., 18 May 1798, Hitchcock resigned from the U.S. Army in 1855 and retired to St. Louis to repair his broken health and continue his study of philosophy. An 1817 West Point graduate, he had acquired a reputation as an administrator that twice brought him offers of appointment as governor of Liberia. His work in hermetic philosophy, which led to books on Swedenborg, Spinoza, alchemy, and fairy tales, mystified readers then and now.

Hitchcock's efforts early in the Civil War to assist the Union cause in St. Louis brought him an appointment as major general Feb. 1862. He at first declined for reasons of health, while rumors spread that Sec. of War EDWIN M. STANTON intended to send him to replace Brig. Gen. ULYSSES S. GRANT, then in front of FORT DONELSON. Eventually persuaded to accept the commission, he was called to Washington. There he was shocked when Stanton urged him to take command of the Army of the Potomac in place of Maj. Gen. GEORGE B. MCCLELLAN. Convincing Stanton that because of his health, age, and inclinations he was unsuited for field command, he remained in Washington as military adviser, serving frequently on major courts-martial.

Appointed commissioner for the exchange of prisoners Nov. 1862, Hitchcock found his niche. Comfortable behind a desk, he drew on his long acquaintance with military procedure and administration to direct the complex negotiations and bookkeeping involved in prisoner exchange, finding enough spare time to explore hidden meanings in the poetry of Shakespeare and Edmund Spenser. A fervent patriot, the soldier-scholar served his country to the best of his ability. Aware of his own limitations, perhaps he rendered his greatest service by rejecting Stanton's impetuous and flattering offers of field command. He was mustered out of the service 1 Oct. 1867, retiring to the South because of ill health. d. Sparta, Ga., 5 Aug. 1870.
—JYS

***H. L. Hunley,* CSS.** Conceived in New Orleans and constructed in Mobile, the submarine *Hunley* recorded its only victory, the first submarine sinking of an enemy vessel, off Charleston harbor 17 Feb. 1864.

The *Hunley* was the creation of Horace L. Hunley of New Orleans, originally an investor in a submarine privateer scheme, eventually a victim of the vessel that bore his name. The vessel was built from a boiler—cut, tapered, rigged with conning towers, diving planes, ballast tanks, a keel, and a 90-lb TORPEDO mounted on a pole attached to its bow. Propulsion was crude: a propeller shaft ran the length of its interior, and 8 crewmen cranked it by hand.

In its early days the ship more than once sank with all hands: 3 crews were lost testing the vessel, 1 an experienced group from Mobile who perished with Hunley in command. Operated by army Lt. George E. Dixon, who had helped build it, the submarine eventually began to function smoothly.

Training cruises turned into nighttime forays against Federal blockaders outside Charleston harbor's bar. But the intended victims were 12 mi away, and favorable winds and tides as well as muscle were necessary to reach them. All the variables came together on the night of 17 Feb., when, with seas calm and the tides right, the *Hunley* began a run that took it to the U.S. sloop *HOUSATONIC.* A light mist hung on the water, masking the submarine as it cruised just beneath the surface.

At 8:45 p.m. it was spotted, closing on the sloop from abeam. The alarm was given, the cable slipped, and the *Housatonic* began backing out of danger. But the *Hunley* changed directions, swinging around to the stern quarter, and the sloop backed into her. The *Hunley's* torpedo exploded between the *Housatonic's* main and mizzen masts, and the blockader went down within minutes.

Nothing was seen of the *Hunley.* It was not captured, nor did it return to Charleston. Years later, the ship was found lying on the bottom, sunk along with its victim.   —MM

Hodge, George Baird.

CSA   b. Fleming Cty., Ky., 8 Apr. 1828, Hodge, an 1845 graduate of the U.S. Naval Academy, resigned his passed midshipman's commission in 1850, studied law, and in 1852 failed in a bid for a U.S. congressional seat. After being elected to Kentucky's state legislature in 1859, voting for JOHN C. BRECKINRIDGE in the 1860 electoral college, and enlisting in the Confederate army as a private in 1861, Hodge was appointed to the Provisional Confederate Congress by Kentucky's secessionist governor, GEORGE W. JOHNSON, then elected to the First Regular Congress Jan. 1862.

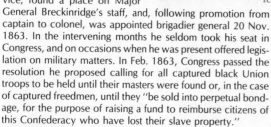

LC

Hodge preferred army service, found a place on Major General Breckinridge's staff, and, following promotion from captain to colonel, was appointed brigadier general 20 Nov. 1863. In the intervening months he seldom took his seat in Congress, and on occasions when he was present offered legislation on military matters. In Feb. 1863, Congress passed the resolution he proposed calling for all captured black Union troops to be held until their masters were found or, in the case of captured freedmen, until they "be sold into perpetual bondage, for the purpose of raising a fund to reimburse citizens of this Confederacy who have lost their slave property."

The Confederate Senate did not endorse Hodge's commission as brigadier general. As a colonel commanding a cavalry brigade, he fought under Maj. Gen. JOSEPH WHEELER and Brig. Gen. NATHAN BEDFORD FORREST in the CHATTANOOGA operations and rode in WHEELER'S RAID, 1–9 Oct. 1863. On 2 Aug. 1864 his name was resubmitted for promotion to brigadier general and again went unconfirmed. Hodge was then assigned to head the District of Southwest Mississippi and East

Louisiana; under him the command deteriorated. In Jan. 1865 he was brought up on charges of incompetency and cowardice and, though absolved, at Forrest's request Hodge was asked to relinquish his district command. Forrest relieved him in March, dispatching him to Richmond for assignment. Hodge did not go, and instead was paroled as a brigadier general 10 May 1865 at Meridian, Miss.

Postwar, Hodge practiced law in Newport, Ky., was a Democratic elector in 1872, and a Kentucky state legislator 1873–77, after which he retired to Florida, dying in Longwood, 1 Aug. 1892.   —JES

Hodgers, Jennie.   *See* CASHIER, ALBERT D. J.

Hoge, Jane Currie Blaikie.

U.S. Sanitary Commission   b. Phila., Pa., 31 July 1811. Following her graduation from Young Ladies' College in Philadelphia, Jane Blaikie married A. H. Hoge, a merchant from Pittsburgh. The couple lived in Pittsburgh for 14 years, moving in 1848 to Chicago, where they resided at the outbreak of civil war. With 2 sons serving in the Union army, Jane began corresponding with prominent women in soldiers' aid societies throughout the Midwest, urging them to coordinate and systematize their efforts. She and her close friend MARY A. LIVERMORE were the principal organizers in their region of the U.S. SANITARY COMMISSION. In Jan. 1862 the

LC

commission appointed Hoge its agent in Chicago. That November she and Livermore represented the Chicago branch at the Women's Council in Washington, D.C.

Hoge lectured extensively throughout the North, relying on emotional appeals to raise funds and supplies, whose distribution to hospitals she oversaw. She visited troops during her inspection tours but was more than an administrator than a nurse. She was characterized as humorless by colleagues, and her efficiency and keen understanding of logistics frequently resulted in an impersonal approach to her work and an inability to see sick and wounded soldiers as individuals. A high point in Hoge's wartime career was the phenomenally successful Chicago Sanitary Fair, the first of its kind, opened Oct. 1863 (*see* SANITARY FAIRS).

In 1867 Hoge published *The Boys in Blue: Or, Heroes of the "Rank and File,"* one of the first wartime memoirs written by a woman. Like her fundraising speeches, the book is charged with emotionalism, so must be read with caution. During the postwar years Hoge served as president of the Women's Board of Foreign Missions and was employed as a social-service worker in Chicago, where she died 26 Aug. 1890.   —PLF

Hogg, Joseph Lewis.

CSA   b. Morgan Cty., Ga., 13 Sept. 1806, Hogg became a plantation owner near Tuscaloosa, Ala., and at 33 migrated to the Republic of Texas, taking part in its congress and, with annexation, fighting in the Mexican War as a volunteer private. In the 1850s he served as a state legislator, railroad promoter, and worked as an attorney before becoming a delegate to the Texas secession convention.

After voting for secession, with a state commission Hogg raised troops through 1861. On 14 Feb. 1862 he was commissioned brigadier general and given command of the 1st Texas Battalion Dismounted Cavalry, (Maj. Thomas H.) McCray's Arkansas Battalion, the 10th and 11th Texas Infantry, and Goode's Battery of light artillery, all brigaded for service with the Confederate Army of the West. Hogg and his troops were sent to Corinth, Miss., to

LC

prepare for the SHILOH campaign. In crowded camps there the brigadier contracted dysentery and died 16 May. Ezra Warner's *Generals in Gray* notes that many said he was taken so quickly he never put on a Confederate uniform. The photograph above may be a painted composite.   —JES

Hoke, Robert Frederick. CSA b. Lincolnton, N.C., 27 May 1837. Of Alsatian, Swiss, and English descent, Hoke was the son of a Democratic politician who was nominated governor of North Carolina in 1844.

Educated in his hometown and later at the Kentucky Military Institute, by 17 he was managing his family's cotton mill, iron works, and other commercial enterprises.

Early in 1861 Hoke entered Confederate service as 2d lieutenant in Col. DANIEL H. HILL'S 1st North Carolina Infantry, a 6-month regiment. Fighting that June at BIG BETHEL, he won Hill's praise for his "coolness, judgment and efficiency." In September he moved up to major of

NA

the 1st, soon afterward becoming lieutenant colonel of the 33d North Carolina. After leading 5 companies of the latter regiment at NEW BERNE, 14 Mar. 1862, and the entire outfit during the PENINSULA CAMPAIGN, he transferred to the 21st North Carolina, of which he was appointed colonel. By this time he had acquired a reputation as one of the most talented young officers in Gen. ROBERT E. LEE'S Army of Northern Virginia.

Hoke led the 21st with quiet ability during the SECOND BULL RUN and ANTIETAM campaigns. Commanding the brigade of Brig. Gen. ISAAC R. TRIMBLE at FREDERICKSBURG, he drove back an enemy division that had pierced the Confederate right, pursuing it so hotly that he captured 300 prisoners. On 17 Jan. 1863 he was elevated to brigadier general and given a command composed of 5 North Carolina infantry units. At the head of this force he was seriously wounded at CHANCELLORS-VILLE, 4 May, while holding the Confederate line atop Marye's Heights. The injury kept him out of the Gettysburg Campaign.

Sent to his native state after recuperating, on 17 Apr. 1864 Hoke attacked Union fortifications outside the coastal city of Plymouth. Through his aggressive tactics the 3,000-man garrison surrendered 3 days later. The feat brought him the THANKS OF THE CONFEDERATE CONGRESS and a major generalship as of

20 Apr. Later that year he served under Gen. P.G.T. BEAURE-GARD in the Petersburg and Richmond campaigning, then led the field forces of Gen. BRAXTON BRAGG during the Union attacks on FORT FISHER. He finished the war by fighting at KINSTON and BENTONVILLE, relinquishing his sword 1 May 1865.

After the war, Hoke returned "to inconspicuous private pursuits," his only public service being a state-sponsored directorship of the North Carolina Railroad Co. d. Raleigh, 3 July 1912.
—EGL

Hollins, George Nichols. CSN b. Baltimore, Md., 20 Sept. 1799. The son of a prominent merchant, Hollins went to sea with a midshipman's warrant in the navy when he was 14 and served actively in the War of 1812. After the war he remained in the navy, rising to the rank of captain by 1855. He was in command of the USS *Susquehanna* at Naples when the Civil War began.

Ordered to return to the U.S., Hollins did so, then resigned his commission to go South. He accepted an appointment as commander in the Confederate navy 20 June 1861 and 9 days later captured a Union ship to command, the steamer *St. Nicholas.* Aboard the *St. Nicholas* Hollins

LC

took 3 prizes in Chesapeake Bay waters. In July 1861 he received command of the New Orleans Naval Station. He rapidly outfitted a small fleet and with it drove off the Union ships attempting to blockade the Mississippi River. In Oct. 1861 Hollins assumed command of Confederate naval forces on the upper Mississippi. He saw action off Columbia, Ky., NEW MADRID, ISLAND NO. 10, Fort Pillow, and Memphis. In Apr. 1862 he returned to New Orleans to assist in the defense of the city against the threat posed by Capt. DAVID G. FARRAGUT'S Union fleet (*see* FORTS JACKSON AND ST. PHILIP, LA., BATTLE OF).

With strong opinions about how to defend New Orleans, Hollins wanted to station his fleet below the city. But he never received the opportunity to translate his ideas into action. Instead he received orders to report to Richmond, and there he spent the remainder of the war serving on naval boards and courts. It is likely that the vigor with which he pressed his plans for New Orleans on Sec. of the Navy STEPHEN R. MALLORY contributed to the brevity of his active service.

After the war Hollins returned to Baltimore and civilian life. d. Baltimore, 18 Jan. 1878.   —EMT

Holly Springs, Miss., Raid on. 20 Dec. 1862 Late in 1862, Col. John S. Griffith of the Texas Cavalry Brigade suggested to Lt. Gen. JOHN C. PEMBERTON that Pemberton organize into a division 3 mounted brigades then in north Mississippi, that he place Maj. Gen. EARL VAN DORN in charge, and that he send this formidable force against Maj. Gen. ULYSSES S. GRANT'S supply depot at Holly Springs. At Pemberton's request, Gen. BRAXTON BRAGG ordered Brig. Gen. NATHAN B. FORREST to distract Grant by striking the Mobile & Ohio Railroad, the Federal supply line running from Columbus, Ky., south through Jackson, Tenn. When Grant learned that Forrest's cavalrymen were tearing up track in West Tennessee, he suspended his march beyond the Yocona River 19 Dec. 1862 (see FORREST'S SECOND RAID, TENN.).

Though Grant did not know it, Van Dorn had left Grenada, Miss., on the evening of the 17th at the head of 3,500 men. Swinging well to the east of the Federals, he rode northeast through Pontotoc and New Albany toward Ripley, then cut west to Holly Springs. Though he was sighted at Pontotoc on the 18th by Federal cavalry returning from a raid on the Mobile & Ohio Railroad, more than 24 hours passed before Grant was alerted to the danger. Late on the 19th Grant warned Col. Robert C. Murphy at Holly Springs and the commanders of other posts on the Mississippi Central Railroad.

That night, a few miles east of Holly Springs, Van Dorn divided his force, sending half to the town by way of a side road, the rest by the Ripley road. At daybreak on the 20th his brigades swept into Holly Springs, the horse soldiers attacking from the east, northeast, and north. On the road leading south out of the supply depot, Van Dorn posted a patrol to prevent Federal reinforcements from reaching Holly Springs. Most of the Northern troops were surprised out of their sleep, trying in their confusion to form a defense. But Van Dorn's men routed them, and the vital supply depot with its tons of medical, quartermaster, ordnance, and commissary stores quickly fell into Confederate hands. While about 1,500 prisoners were being paroled, the Confederate raiders plundered warehouses, cut telegraph lines, and tore up track. After putting the torch to those supplies they could not carry with them, the Confederates remounted and withdrew. In 10 hours they had destroyed $1.5 million worth of supplies and burned several buildings, including a new 2,000-bed hospital.

Van Dorn headed north, away from Grant's headquarters at Oxford, Miss., hoping to delay pursuit. Sweeping to the west of La Grange, Tenn., his column lunged toward Bolivar, then returned to Grenada, Miss., on the 28th by way of Saulsbury, Tenn. Though Grant pushed his cavalry hard, it failed to overtake the daring Confederates.

The Holly Springs raid had immediate and far-reaching repercussions for Grant's campaign against VICKSBURG. Van Dorn had destroyed the general's most important supply depot, and the countryside had been exhausted by the belligerents. Grant now yielded the initiative and 21 Dec. began to pull back to Memphis.   —ECB

Holmes, Theophilus Hunter. CSA b. Sampson Cty., N.C., 13 Nov. 1804, Holmes, a classmate of Robert E. Lee's, graduated from West Point in 1829, ranked 44th in his class. Commissioned a 2d lieutenant in the 7th U.S. Infantry, he served on the Southwestern frontier, fought in the Second Seminole War, marched with Gen. Zachary Taylor from Corpus Christi to the Rio Grande, and was brevetted major for gallantry in the Mexican War.

Holmes spent most of the 1850s on garrison duty at Jefferson Barracks, Forts Washita, Arbuckle, and Bliss, and other frontier posts. From 1859 to 1861 he was on recruiting duty. On 22 Apr. 1861 Major

LC

Holmes, 1 of 15 field-grade army officers to cast their lot with the South, resigned his commission and returned to North Carolina, where he assisted in organizing state troops.

On 5 June 1861 he was made brigadier general in the Provisional Confederate Army and was called to Virginia. The brigade he commanded at FIRST BULL RUN saw little action. Promoted to major general 7 Oct. 1861, he was ordered in mid-March to the Department of North Carolina, where he reorganized defenses to guard against Union amphibious attacks. Late in June 1862 he reinforced Gen. ROBERT E. LEE before Richmond, but at MALVERN HILL he "allowed the day to pass and the battle to be decided in his hearing without doing more than forming his men in line of battle."

In July 1862 Holmes was sent to command the vast Trans-Mississippi Department. Though promoted to lieutenant general to rank from 10 Oct. 1862, he proved a poor choice for this difficult assignment, clashing with strong-willed subordinates who bombarded Richmond with stories of his administrative shortcomings.

Superseded by Lt. Gen. E. KIRBY SMITH as department commander, Holmes took charge of the District of Arkansas, where he helped botch the 4 July 1863 assault on Helena. In Mar. 1864, he returned to North Carolina, where he commanded the state reserves.

After the return of peace, Holmes lived near Fayetteville, N.C. d. on his farm 21 June 1880.   —ECB

Holt, Joseph. USA b. Breckinridge Cty., Ky., 6 Jan. 1807, Holt, educated at St. Joseph's and Centre colleges, began practicing law in Elizabethtown when he was 21. Following 3 years in Louisville, he moved to Port Gibson, Miss., acquiring considerable wealth and attaining prominence in his profession. After the death of his first wife, he returned to Louisville and took only cases that interested him.

A newspaper editor and a fine speaker, Holt was active in Kentucky Democratic politics, becoming a strong influence in the state. In 1856 he supported James Buchanan and was subsequently appointed commissioner of patents; postmaster general, 1859–60; and secretary of war during the last few weeks of Buchanan's presidency.

LC

With the Civil War, Holt, formerly a strong believer in Southern rights, became an ardent Union man. Pres. ABRAHAM LINCOLN appointed him judge advocate general of the army 3 Sept. 1862, with the rank of colonel. In 1864 Holt became the first head of the Bureau of Military Justice, ranking as brigadier general from 22 June. With the support of Lincoln and Sec. of War EDWIN M. STANTON, Holt expanded the jurisdiction of his office to include trials of civilians before military commissions, such as the subversion cases against CLEMENT L. VALLANDIGHAM and Lambdin P. Milligan.

The assassination of Lincoln made Holt a national figure when Pres. ANDREW JOHNSON appointed a military commission to try those charged in JOHN WILKES BOOTH's conspiracy and Holt conducted the government's case. All on trial were convicted 30 June 1865. A majority of the military recommended in writing that the president commute to life imprisonment the death sentence of MARY ELIZABETH SURRATT, convicted as an accomplice in the assassination. What happened when Holt took the verdicts to the president is disputed. Johnson later maintained that Holt did not show him the recommendation for mercy. For the rest of his life, Holt insisted that Johnson had seen the clemency recommendation. Regardless of where the truth lies, the president approved the sentences.

Holt retired as judge advocate general 1 Dec. 1875 and spent his remaining years in Washington, where he died 1 Aug. 1894, alone, blind, and bitter. He was buried near Stephensport, Ky.   —JOH

Holtzclaw, James Thadeus.   CSA   b. Henry Cty., Ga., 17 Dec. 1833. After a local secondary education in Chambers Cty., Ala., Holtzclaw moved to Montgomery and from 1855 practiced law.

First a militia lieutenant, Holtzclaw was commissioned major of the 18th Alabama Infantry Aug. 1861, and the next spring, as a member of the 3d Brigade in Brig. Gen. JONES M. WITHERS' division, fought and took a near-fatal lung wound at the Battle of SHILOH. A surprisingly speedy recovery was followed by his promotion to lieutenant colonel 1 July 1862, then to colonel 10 May 1863, while serving in garrison at Mobile, Ala., with the 18th. He went

LC

with Gen. BRAXTON BRAGG's Army of Tennessee to the Battles of CHICKAMAUGA and CHATTANOOGA, serving in Brig. Gen. HENRY D. CLAYTON's brigade, which he briefly led during the Chattanooga fighting. Made brigadier general 7 July 1864, Holtzclaw fought in the ATLANTA CAMPAIGN and the FRANKLIN AND NASHVILLE CAMPAIGN, during the latter as a part of Lt. Gen. STEPHEN D. LEE's Corps. Holtzclaw's troops, taking only slightly less damaging losses than other brigades in the Tennessee campaigning, fought as Gen. JOHN B. HOOD's rear guard on the retreat, then took up duty in the Mobile, Ala., forts until their surrender.

Postwar, Holtzclaw resumed his Montgomery law practice, and shortly before his death there, 19 July 1893, was a state railroad commissioner.   —JES

Homer, Winslow.   artist   b. Boston, Mass., 24 Feb. 1836. At 19, Homer was apprenticed to a local lithographer, and his drawings were soon appearing in the illustrated periodicals of the day.

In 1859 he moved to New York City to study at the National Academy of Design, supporting himself by contributing drawings to HARPER's WEEKLY. In 1861 Harper's sent him to Washington to sketch ABRAHAM LINCOLN's first inauguration. Homer's initial war drawings for Harper's depicted Maj. Gen. GEORGE B. MCCLELLAN's army on the banks of the Potomac in Oct. 1861. The following year he was dispatched as a "special artist" to cover the PENINSULA CAMPAIGN. Though he did not serve again as a special, he made frequent excursions to the battlefronts and filled his sketchbook with drawings, from which he worked in his studio in New York.

Double-page woodcuts of his illustrations depicting battles and camp scenes appeared in *Harper's* throughout the war years. Homer was not specifically a combat artist; his work was concerned with the intimate moments of camp life and human interest rather than with the panorama of clashing armies. Supplied with his firsthand observations made at the front, he translated these drawings into canvases such as *Yankee Sharpshooter* (1862). In 1865 his painting *Prisoners at the Front,* depicting Brig. Gen. FRANCIS C. BARLOW questioning Confederate captives, was acclaimed by critics and immediately established his reputation as a painter of note.

After the war Homer contributed to *Harper's* illustrations dealing with a variety of subjects. He then devoted his talents exclusively to genre painting, becoming one of the foremost artists in America. He is famous for his Maine seascapes, woodland scenes in the Adirondacks and, in later years, watercolors of the Bahamas. d. Prout's Neck, Maine, 29 Sept. 1910.
                                                              —FR

Homestead Act of 1862.   For a decade preceding civil war, Southern congressmen blocked homesteading legislation providing free distribution of public lands, most located in the trans-Mississippi states and territories. Realizing the abundance of rich farmland in the Midwest, they argued against the free farm program as a drain of men and money from the South, fearing also that the movement of Northern antislavery men and foreigners into the region would destroy the precarious balance of sectional power in Congress as new states formed.

But the idea of colonizing the Western expanses through the distribution of free land appealed to the Northern public. Looking toward the elections later in the year, Republicans and Democrats passed a weak compromise homestead measure Mar. 1860, each party hoping to strengthen its power in the pro-homesteading Northern and border states. As anticipated, Pres. James Buchanan vetoed the bill, questioning the Federal government's right to give public lands to individuals.

During the fall campaigning, Republican presidential candidate ABRAHAM LINCOLN ardently supported the homesteading issue. Once the Southern states seceded after his election, he was confident the legislation would face little opposition in Congress, which passed the Homestead Act, 20 May 1862. Its liberal terms went into effect 1 Jan. 1863, permitting any citizen or future citizen, man or woman, who was over 21; citizens under 21 who were heads of households; and anyone who had fulfilled 2 weeks' military service to file for title to a quarter-section (160 acres) of public land. Of the nearly 2 billion acres of government land, most stretching from Michigan to Dakota and from Missouri to Minnesota, settlers had claimed 1,261,000 acres by June 1864. To secure title, the law required a pioneer to live on his land for 5 years, make improvements, and pay $10 in miscellaneous legal fees. The real price exacted was his considerable investment in labor.

The legislation editor HORACE GREELEY praised as the chance to "give every poor man a home" did not operate entirely as intended. Speculators managed to acquire large tracts, as they had when the Federal government previously sold land, and many urban working men and immigrants lacked the money, equipment, and experience necessary to succeed as farmers. Some soldiers protested that the best land would be taken before their enlistments expired. On the whole, however, the legislation enhanced popular support for Lincoln and hastened the agricultural and industrial development of the Midwest.

—PLF

Honey Hill, S.C., eng. at. 30 Nov. 1864 By the last week in Nov. 1864 Maj. Gen. WILLIAM T. SHERMAN's march on SAVANNAH was well advanced. To prevent reinforcements from reaching that city from the Carolinas, cooperating Federals sought to sever the railroad between Charleston and Savannah. On the evening of the 28th, Maj. Gen. JOHN G. FOSTER, head of the Department of the South, left Hilton Head, S.C., with 5,500 men ("all the disposable troops in this department") and sailed down the Broad River toward Boyd's Neck, S.C., 35 mi northeast of Savannah. From there he planned to move 10 mi eastward to cut the rail line near Grahamville.

When the first contingent of his transport fleet landed at Boyd's Neck the following afternoon, Foster passed command of his expedition to the leader of his Coast Division, Brig. Gen. JOHN P. HATCH. Before all the units could disembark, Hatch moved inland with 1 infantry brigade, a contingent of sailors, and an 8-gun battery worked by the seamen. Delays caused by errors in marching prevented his advance from reaching the Grahamville depot until after 9 a.m. 30 Nov.

There Hatch found that his errant trek had given Confederates time to mass in his front. His opponents, however, seemed unprepossessing: fewer than 2,000 GEORGIA MILITIA and state troops under Maj. Gen. GUSTAVUS W. SMITH, plus a few Confederate cavalry and artillery units. The force had started from Macon 8 days before and, though not bound to serve outside Georgia, had marched to Grahamville in response to a plea from the area commander, Lt. Gen. WILLIAM J. HARDEE. Having learned of Foster's advance, Hardee wanted Smith to protect the station for a few hours, until supports came from the north.

Fighting began when Hatch advanced 4 of his regiments, supported by a second brigade that had just reached him. After driving some Confederates, he found others ensconced behind earthworks 3 mi below the depot, on a stream-bordered crest known as Honey Hill. Erected 2 years before to obstruct just such an attack, these defenses, as well as the difficult terrain, prevented a flank movement. Hatch therefore launched 3 direct attacks, each of which failed emphatically. Confederate artillery fire proved deadly, and soon the attackers' ammunition ran low. When he learned of Smith's imminent reinforcement, Hatch pulled back, then retreated, having suffered 746 casualties to the militia's 50. —EGL

Honey Springs (Elk Creek), Indian Territory, eng. at. 17 July 1863 On 15 July Confederate Brig. Gen. DOUGLAS H. COOPER, commanding the 1st Brigade/Indian Troops, learned that the Arkansas River had become fordable and feared a threat to his security should Federal Brig. Gen. JAMES G. BLUNT decide to cross and attack him in his position along Elk Creek, 25 mi south. That is exactly what Blunt intended to do. On the night of the 15th he began his crossing and the next evening had some 3,000 men—mostly Indian and black troops, along with 2 batteries—on the march toward Cooper.

Skirmishing began early 17 July as Blunt approached Cooper. The Confederate troops, themselves composed largely of Cherokee and Choctaws, somewhat outnumbered their attackers, but almost from the first they began to suffer from inferior powder and ammunition. Blunt advanced toward the enemy in a single line of battle, his small detachment of cavalry dismounted and fighting on foot.

Starting about 10:30 a.m., the fighting continued for 2 hours. Cooper believed that he had repulsed at least 1 Federal attack before it started to rain on the battlefield. The downpour rendered useless many of the weapons already suffering from damp powder, and Cooper had to retire to find fresh ammunition. Reconnoitering from high ground near the creek, he soon saw the full extent of Blunt's command and that it threatened to turn his left flank. His situation then began to disintegrate. Col. Tandy Walker, with 2 Indian regiments, misunderstood Cooper's orders and marched away from the battle. Then Cooper found that his men holding a vital crossing on Elk Creek were giving way, threatening to allow Blunt to cross and flank him once again. From then, the retreat spread through the Southern command without orders. Cooper managed a fair rearguard action; his war-whooping Choctaws charged into Blunt until they too were demoralized and retreated.

In this engagement, the largest of the war in Indian Territory, perhaps 8,000 men took part. Blunt's losses were 13 killed and wounded, and another 47 taken prisoner. Honey Springs was another in a long series of small victories for Blunt that kept the Confederate attempt to hold the territory constantly discomfited. —WCD

Hood, John Bell. CSA b. Owingsville, Ky., 1 June 1831. Influenced by his grandfather's stories of Indian fighting and by popular accounts of the Mexican War, Hood sought a military career at 18. With the assistance of his uncle, Congressman Richard French, Hood received an appointment to the U.S. Military Academy 20 Feb. 1849, on condition of being able to pass the entrance examinations. Though a poor student and a persistent discipline problem, Hood graduated 44th in a class of 52 in 1853.

On graduation Hood was brevetted 2d lieutenant, assigned briefly to Fort Columbus, N.Y., then transferred to Fort Jones in northern California.

LC

When Congress approved the formation of 2 new regiments of infantry and 2 regiments of cavalry to protect the frontier, 3 Mar. 1855, Hood received his commission as 2d lieutenant, 2d U.S. Cavalry, a unit to become well known for the officers who served in it. Several, including Col. ALBERT SIDNEY JOHNSTON, Lt. Col. ROBERT E. LEE, Maj. WILLIAM J. HARDEE, and Maj. GEORGE H. THOMAS, became high-ranking Union or Confederate officers.

Hood developed a preference for aggressive military tactics early in his career on garrison duty and on the Texas frontier. His often reckless daring later proved to be a key to his military successes and also one of the reasons for his failures.

After resigning his Regular Army commission 17 Apr. 1861, Hood joined the Confederate army with appointment as 1st lieutenant of cavalry. He served on recruitment duty in Kentucky until May, when he was ordered to report to Col. JOHN B. MAGRUDER at YORKTOWN, Va. Hood acquitted himself well during the early months of war, rising rapidly in rank. On 6 Mar. 1862 he was promoted to brigadier general and assigned command of the hard-fighting Texas Brigade, soon known as HOOD'S TEXAS BRIGADE. His aggressive leadership brought him to the favorable attention of the Confederate high command. Admired for his courage and well respected by his men, Hood led his troops through the PENINSULA CAMPAIGN, fighting conspicuously at GAINES' MILL, MALVERN HILL, and SECOND BULL RUN. Promoted to major general 10 Oct. 1862, he was given command of a division under Maj. Gen. JAMES LONGSTREET, leading it during the ANTIETAM CAMPAIGN, at FREDERICKSBURG, and at GETTYSBURG, where he was severely wounded in the left arm. At CHICKAMAUGA Hood commanded several divisions in Longstreet's left wing. When he was again wounded, doctors were forced to amputate his right leg, and he recuperated in Richmond before returning to the field.

Hood was promoted to lieutenant general 1 Feb. 1864, to rank from Chickamauga, and given command of a corps during the ATLANTA CAMPAIGN. When Gen. JOSEPH E. JOHNSTON was removed from command of the Army of Tennessee 17 July, Hood was appointed to temporary rank of general to succeed him. Reluctant to take command in the middle of the campaigning, Hood protested to Pres. JEFFERSON DAVIS, but Davis refused to change the orders. Hood took the offensive unsuccessfully at PEACHTREE CREEK, 20 July, and again 2 days later in the Battle of ATLANTA. At JONESBOROUGH, 1 Sept., it became clear that the Confederates could not hold off Maj. Gen. WILLIAM T. SHERMAN's forces. Hood retreated, hoping to draw Sherman away from Atlanta by attacking his supply lines northwest of the city. Bad weather, greater enemy troop strength, and the slow arrival of supplies due to Hood's poor planning prevented him from attacking. He withdrew instead to Tennessee, intending to retake the state, move into Kentucky and secure it north to the Ohio River, then reinforce Gen. ROBERT E. LEE in Virginia.

The campaign failed disastrously. At FRANKLIN, 30 Nov., Hood sustained heavy losses and defeat in a futile frontal assault protested by his corps commanders. 2 weeks later, at NASHVILLE Maj. Gen. GEORGE H. THOMAS attacked his weakened, demoralized army, inflicting the only decisive defeat of the war and effectively destroying the once-formidable Army of Tennessee (see FRANKLIN AND NASHVILLE CAMPAIGN). On 23 Jan. 1865 Hood, a capable subordinate whose abilities were not sufficient for leading an army, was relieved at his own request and held no further field command. His military career ended with his surrender at Natchez, Miss., 31 May 1865, while on orders to join the Trans-Mississippi Department.

After the war Hood settled in New Orleans, working as a factor and commission merchant, and later in the insurance business. Though he was at first moderately prosperous, business reverses deprived him of an adequate livelihood. Impoverished, he died of yellow fever 30 Aug. 1879, a few days after the death of his wife of 11 years and their eldest child; 10 other children, including 3 sets of twins, survived him. To provide for the orphans, friends arranged to have his wartime memoirs published. The book, *Advance and Retreat* (1880), is a classic among Civil War literature, though it is largely a work of self-defense. —JDK

Hood's First Sortie. 20 July 1864 *See* PEACHTREE CREEK, GA., BATTLE OF.

Hood's Second Sortie. 21–22 July 1864 *See* ATLANTA, GA., BATTLE OF.

Hood's Tennessee Campaign. *See* FRANKLIN AND NASHVILLE CAMPAIGN, TENN.

Hood's Texas Brigade. CSA Federals learned to dread facing the hard-fighting Texas Brigade early in the war. Their first clash with Hood's Texans came 7 May 1862, near ELTHAM'S LANDING, Va., when the Texans pushed Union troops back to the safety of their gunboats. They continued to overwhelm Federal lines in almost every major Civil War battle.

JEFFERSON DAVIS authorized the Texas Brigade Sept. 1861 when the rowdy volunteers arriving from the Lone Star State showed indifference toward military regulations. But they were crack marksmen, aggressive soldiers of unquestioned loyalty whose supremacy on the battlefield commanded their superiors' praise.

JOHN B. HOOD, the general with whom they were always identified, understood that the Texans needed a loose rein and gave it to them. To Gen. ROBERT E. LEE, the Texans were his most dependable troops, always first on the field and last to leave it. As devoted to him as they were to Hood, the brigade refused to disappoint either.

Their daring, almost reckless charge that routed the 10th New York from a seemingly impregnable position at GAINES' MILL has been called the most brilliant achievement in the SEVEN DAYS' CAMPAIGN. At SECOND BULL RUN they faced the same New York troops, capturing the guns that had destroyed their ranks at Gaines' Mill. Nearly two-thirds of the brigade fell at ANTIETAM. And because it repeatedly saw frontline action, its total losses were staggering.

Hood's Texans prided themselves on effectiveness as a fighting unit. When depleted ranks forced Davis to reorganize the army in 1864, the brigade balked at being disbanded. Afraid to destroy its morale, Davis kept them intact.

Hood's Texas Brigade surrendered with Lee at Appomattox. Of the estimated 5,300 men who had enlisted since 1861, only 617 veterans remained to lay down arms Apr. 1865. Welcomed as heroes in Houston that summer, the survivors parted company for homes many had not seen in 4 years.   —PLF

Hooker, Joseph. USA b. Hadley, Mass., 13 Nov. 1814. The grandson of Joseph Hooker, a captain during the American Revolution, this Hooker attended Hopkins Academy in Hadley, and in 1833 entered the U.S. Military Academy, graduating 29th in a class of 50 in 1837. His early service included the Second Seminole War and duty along the Canadian border. He was then appointed adjutant at West Point.

In the Mexican War, Hooker served in the campaigns of both Gen. Zachary Taylor and Gen. WINFIELD SCOTT, winning brevets as captain for gallantry at Monterrey, major at National Bridge, and lieutenant colonel at Chapultepec. During this period

USMHI

Hooker testified in defense of GIDEON PILLOW, an officer accused of disloyalty to Scott. The testimony did not endear Hooker to Scott.

On 21 Feb. 1853 Hooker resigned from the army, settled in

Sonoma, Calif., as a farmer, and joined the state militia. When the Civil War broke out, he volunteered but was at first rejected, possibly due to Scott's influence. But 17 May 1861 he was appointed brigadier general of volunteers and assigned the Washington defenses.

On 5 May 1862, at WILLIAMSBURG, Hooker's division sustained a heavy assault by Confederates and Hooker obtained the nickname "Fighting Joe" for the bravery he displayed even after falling in the mud with his dying horse. He showed similar courage and professionalism at SEVEN PINES, WHITE OAK SWAMP, MALVERN HILL, SECOND BULL RUN, BRISTOE STATION, and Williamsburg road. As commander of the I Corps, he engaged in the ANTIETAM CAMPAIGN and was successful at SOUTH MOUNTAIN. At Antietam he was wounded in the foot and took sick leave. Major General of Volunteers as of 5 May, he was advanced to the rank of brigadier general in the Regular Army, 20 Sept. 1862.

After recuperating from his injury, Hooker suffered defeat at FREDERICKSBURG. He was one of several officers to criticize the conduct of his superior, Maj. Gen. AMBROSE E. BURNSIDE, during the campaign. After Burnside requested that either he or some of these dissident officers be relieved, Lincoln relieved him and appointed Hooker to replace him in the command of the Army of the Potomac. The transfer of responsibility was effected in a letter from President Lincoln to General Joseph Hooker, 26 Jan. 1863. In this letter Lincoln expressed great confidence in Hooker's bravery and skill but criticized him for having thwarted Burnside. Lincoln also wrote, "I have heard, in such a way as to believe it, of your recently saying that both the Army and the Government needed a dictator. Of course, it was not for this, but in spite of it, that I have given you the command. Only those generals who gain successes can set up dictators. What I now ask of you is military success, and I will risk the dictatorship."

Hooker accepted his assignment with vigor and initiated a badly needed reorganization of the army by eliminating grand divisions and forming the cavalry into a corps, thus preparing the army to be tested at CHANCELLORSVILLE 1–4 May 1863. At first Hooker advanced but decided to retreat as Gen. ROBERT E. LEE approached. On 2 May Lee sent Lt. Gen. THOMAS J. "STONEWALL" JACKSON and Jackson's 32,000 men on a march around Hooker's flank, leaving Lee vulnerable, with only 14,-000 men. Hooker, however, declined to act, sacrificing a situation in which he had an overwhelming advantage.

Anticipating the movement of Confederate forces into Pennsylvania early in summer 1863, Hooker requested as reinforcements the 10,000 troops stationed at Harpers Ferry. He interpreted Maj. Gen. HENRY W. HALLECK's refusal as a breach of faith by the government and asked to be relieved of his command. On 28 June 1863, 3 days before the decisive battle at GETTYSBURG, Maj. Gen. GEORGE G. MEADE replaced him.

Hooker then became commander of the XI and XII corps and was ordered to the Western theater. Under Maj. Gens. GEORGE H. THOMAS and WILLIAM T. SHERMAN during the battles for CHATTANOOGA, he demonstrated his abilities at LOOKOUT MOUNTAIN, 24 Nov. 1863, and was brevetted major general in the Regular Army for his aggressive leadership.

Hooker showed great strength as a corps commander at Mill Creek Gap, RESACA, Cassville, NEW HOPE CHURCH, Pine Mountain, and during the Siege of ATLANTA. When Maj. Gen. JAMES B. MCPHERSON was killed, Hooker seemed appropriate choice to succeed. Sherman gave command to Maj. Gen. OLIVER O.

HOWARD, Hooker's subordinate. Feeling he had been treated unfairly, Hooker asked to be relieved of his position. His request was accepted, bringing to an end his field service.

Hooker was transferred to various commands, including the Department of the East and the Department of the Lakes. He was retired from the army 15 Oct. 1868 after a stroke left him partially paralyzed. d. Garden City, N.Y., 31 Oct. 1879.

—JDK

"Hornets' Nest," at Shiloh, Tenn. 6 Apr. 1862 In the Battle of SHILOH, following the rout of Union Brig. Gen. BENJAMIN M. PRENTISS' troops from their camps early 6 Apr. 1862, an arched battle line, supported by 3 batteries, was thrown up opposite the Peach Orchard. Made up of Brig. Gens. Stephen A. Hurlbut's, W.H.L. WALLACE's, and Prentiss' men, it held nearly 6 hours until, between 5 and 5:30, it was surrounded and crushed by Confederates. There bullets flew like angry hornets, prompting Confederate troops to call it the "Hornets' Nest."

—JES

hors de combat. Civil War–era Americans thought French the language of war, not love. In contemporary literature, a wounded soldier was said to have been rendered *hors de combat*—out of combat.

—JES

horse artillery. Horse-drawn field artillery was commonly called horse artillery. Based on 18th-century French innovations in artillery systems, a cannon on its 2-wheeled carriage, coupled to its 2-wheeled limber carrying an ammunition chest, was pulled by a 6-horse team. 3 drivers rode the 3 team horses on the left, perhaps 2 cannoneers rode atop the ammunition chest, the others in the platoon following on a second team and limber hauling a 2-wheeled caisson. The horse artillery was a highly maneuverable system generally used with field guns in the 6-to-24-pounder classes. A FLYING BATTERY, where each cannoneer rode a team horse, was sometimes incorrectly identified as a horse artillery.

—JES

Horseshoe Ridge, Snodgrass Hill, at Chickamauga, Ga. 20 Sept. 1863 On that date, following the breakthrough of Confederate Lt. Gen. JAMES LONGSTREET's troops at the Battle of CHICKAMAUGA, Union Maj. Gen. GEORGE H. THOMAS pulled back his forces for a desperate defense of Snodgrass Hill in the northwest quadrant of the battlefield. The west end of the hill, an extension of the Lookout Mountain range, became known in postwar literature as Horseshoe Ridge. Though the afternoon attacks on the hill have been called vicious, at Horseshoe Ridge they were the most desperate. There, Brig. Gen. JAMES B. STEEDMAN, arriving with Maj. Gen. GORDON GRANGER's Union Reserve Corps, held off repeated Southern assaults and led his troops, carrying the flag of the 115th Illinois. At dusk, as Thomas pulled his men off for retreat through McFarland's Gap, on the ridge the 21st and 89th Ohio and the 22d Michigan, their ammunition exhausted, were ordered by Granger to hold it with the bayonet. They obliged until the Union army escaped, then the 3 regiments surrendered.

—JES

Hotchkiss, Jedediah. CSA b. near Windsor, N.Y., 30 Nov. 1828, Hotchkiss sketched himself into the annals of the Civil War. A self-taught map maker, he was the best topographical engineer of the Army of Northern Virginia. More than any other man, he was responsible for Lt. Gen. THOMAS

J. "STONEWALL" JACKSON's ability to march with celerity, guided by a firm knowledge of the terrain.

Emigrating to Virginia as a teacher, Hotchkiss was successful in his profession, and he and his brother Nelson founded the Loch Willow Academy. When the war began, Hotchkiss, deeply attached to his adopted state, closed his school and entered the army, performing engineering duties in western Virginia before securing an appointment to Jackson's staff early in 1862.

LC

Possessing a quick perception of terrain, Hotchkiss immediately rendered invaluable service to Jackson, reconnoitering, drawing accurate maps, and offering advice on land features. Jackson relied heavily on his map maker for this knowledge, for the general lacked such skills. After Jackson's death, Hotchkiss, though deeply grieved and disgusted with war, continued as topographical engineer for the general's successors. At CEDAR CREEK, for instance, his knowledge of the terrain allowed Lt. Gen. JUBAL A. EARLY to surprise the Federal army.

Hotchkiss resumed his teaching career after the war, but in a few years he left the profession to promote the restoration and development of Virginia's natural resources. For the rest of his life this mission and the Presbyterian church dominated his activities. With William Allen, Hotchkiss published *The Battlefields of Virginia* (1867), then wrote a volume for *Confederate Military History* (1899) on Virginia's role in the war and contributed nearly half the Confederate maps found in the *Atlas of the Official Records* (1891–95). d. Staunton, Va., 17 Jan. 1899. *Make Me A Map of the Valley: The Civil War Journal of Jackson's Topographer* was published in 1973.

—JDW

Hotchkiss projectile. A shell for rifled artillery in calibers 2.5–7 in., the Hotchkiss projectile was cast in 2 sections: a knob-shaped base and shell with a tapered bottom, held together by a tight-fitting lead band. When fired, the base shoved the lead band over the end of the shell and into the rifling, sending the shell spiraling out of the cannon on a straight course. It was a popular round for the 3-IN. ORDNANCE GUN. Some sources claim that the ragged end of the lead band flying along with the shell made a screaming sound that demoralized the enemy.   —JES

hot shot. Intended for maritime use, hot shots were solid iron shot heated in a furnace and fired at wooden vessels. Shot furnaces were found in seacoast fortifications as well as aboard ships. Armored shipping reduced hot shot's effectiveness. It was used to set afire the wooden interior at FORT SUMTER Apr. 1861, and Confederates at FORT FISHER, N.C., used it against the bombarding Union fleet Jan. 1865. At its most efficient, it was fired to just pierce the hull of a vessel, then sit smoldering inside a bulkhead, eventually setting the ship afire.   —JES

Hotze, Henry. propagandist b. Zurich, Switzerland, 1834. Immigrating to the U.S. while a child, Hotze settled in

Mobile, Ala., becoming a naturalized citizen in 1856. He adapted thoroughly to Southern customs and attitudes toward slavery and the inferiority of blacks. Hotze was admired for his exceptional intellect and affability, and in 1858 Sec. of State Lewis Cass secured for him a provisional appointment as secretary and chargé d'affaires at the U.S. legation in Brussels, a position that ended the next year. Hotze returned to Mobile to work as a journalist for the Mobile *Register,* at which time he probably became acquainted with LEROY P. WALKER, a future Confederate secretary of war.

Early in 1861 Hotze belonged to the Mobile Cadets, an elite military company mustered into the 3d Alabama and ordered to Virginia that spring. At the end of May he was placed on detached duty as a clerk in the assistant adjutant general's office and sent by Walker on a special mission to London. On his return, Hotze left the army to accept an appointment from Sec. of State ROBERT M. T. HUNTER as commercial agent in London, with discretionary orders to use his journalistic talents to create a favorable image of the Confederacy in the British press.

Hotze arrived in London 29 Jan. 1862 and within weeks began placing editorials in newspapers by supplying professional agents with copy they sold to editors for publication. By doing so he gained favor with the agents, who received the payment for his work, and he was able to avoid tying the articles directly to his activities. With backing from 2 expatriated Southerners and James Spence, an Englishman sympathetic to the Confederacy, he began publishing a pro-Confederate general-interest newspaper, *The Index: A Weekly Journal of Politics, Literature, and News.* Never widely circulated, it nonetheless became a powerful propaganda organ directed toward Englishmen capable of shaping public opinion. To fill his paper he hired freelance part-time writers who had valuable connections with other European newspapers, where they frequently placed stories favorable to the South. His contacts extended beyond England to France, Scotland, Germany, and Ireland, and from correspondents in the North came some of the information appearing in his columns.

Hotze's superior, Confederate propagandist EDWIN DE LEON, praised the young journalist's work lavishly. Sec. of State JUDAH P. BENJAMIN offered restrained but marked admiration for his achievements, arranging appropriations for Hotze to continue his work but refusing his request to extend his propagandizing to Germany.

Hotze once referred to *The Index* as his "little kingdom," explaining his ambition to make it the showcase of Southern journalistic accomplishment. He hoped to continue publishing *The Index* after the war as a Southern commercial newspaper, but the devastated Southern economy could not financially support the endeavor. The paper continued to appear until Aug. 1865, but its usefulness ended with the Confederate surrender.

Embittered when the newspaper folded, Hotze remained in Europe after the war, working as a journalist in England and France. He died in spring 1887 and was buried in Zug, Switzerland. Among the more accessible of his writings is *Three Months in the Confederate Army,* a book originally serialized in *The Index.* It presents an idealized account of the early months of Confederate camp life and patriotic enthusiasm, and was part of Hotze's attempt to convince Europeans that high morale and well-being characterized the Confederacy.

—PLF

Housatonic, USS. Built at the Boston Navy Yard and launched 29 Nov. 1861, the *Housatonic* was a screw sloop of war, 207 ft long, 38 ft in beam, with an 8-ft, 7-in. draft, and displacing 1,240 tons. It was armed with a 100-pound Parrott rifle, 3 30-pound Parrott rifles, 1 11-in. Dahlgren smoothbore, 2 32-pounder smoothbores, and 3 howitzers. The vessel remained in Northern waters through the summer of 1862 and joined the SOUTH ATLANTIC BLOCKADING SQUADRON off Charleston, S.C., in September.

For the next 17 months the *Housatonic* was a unit of the squadron, usually on blockade duty off the Charleston harbor bar, occasionally shelling targets along the shore. Its small boats patrolled close inshore, and raiding parties from the warship were landed to attack the outer defenses of Charleston. The ship also helped capture a number of blockade runners including the *Neptune,* the *Secesh,* and the *Princess Royal.* Early in 1863 the *Housatonic* was involved in a night engagement with the Confederate ironclads *CHICORA* and *PALMETTO STATE* but suffered no damage. It was not so fortunate 17 Feb. 1864 when the *H.L. HUNLEY* rammed a spar torpedo into the Union warship's starboard side, and it sank within a few minutes. The ship went down in water so shallow that its rigging remained above the waterline, providing a refuge for many of the crew. Only 2 officers and 3 men were lost. In this way the *Housatonic* had the unwanted honor of being the victim of one of the first successful submarine attacks in history.

The ship remained on the bottom for the rest of the war and was partially salvaged in the postwar years. —WNS

Houston, Samuel. governor b. Rockbridge Cty., Va., 2 Mar. 1793. Removed to Maryville, Tenn., young Sam Houston grew up with little formal education, instead studying the Cherokee Indian life and language. After accepting a commission as ensign in Gen. Andrew Jackson's army, serving 1813–18 and fighting in the Creek Indian Wars, he studied law, and over the next 40 years, became district attorney of Nashville; a 2-term U.S. congressman, 1823–27; governor of Tennessee, 1827–29; a trader in Indian Territory; a Texas pioneer and revolutionist; commander of the Texas revolutionary army; a 2-term president of the Republic of Texas; a Texas legislator; and, 1846–59, a U.S. senator. Though he was one of the most amazing men of his age, the Civil War cast a pall over his last years.

In 1861 Houston was governor of Texas, having been elected in 1859. He opposed secession, declaring, "I am for the Union without any 'if' in the case"; further, he opposed alliance and confederation with other seceding Southern states, believing Texas' best interest lay in independence, if not union. While this latter view gained credence with a large minority of Texas secessionists, it was defeated in debate in the secession convention. Before the WASHINGTON PEACE CONFERENCE was called, Houston proposed a convention of Southern states to discuss conciliation but was ignored.

Adhering to state law, on petition of the legislature Houston called a state secession convention. On 2 Feb. 1861 it voted to secede, and 4 Mar. he was compelled to issue the Proclamation of Secession. Shortly thereafter, an oath of loyalty to the Confederacy was required of all Texas authorities. In a drama in the statehouse, Houston was called 3 times to stand and take the oath. Reportedly, he sat, whittling through the proceedings, not answering to his name. His resignation was accepted 18 Mar., and he removed to his home in Huntsville, Tex.,

declining Pres. ABRAHAM LINCOLN's offer of troops to maintain his seat in office. d. San Antonio, 26 July 1863. —JES

Hovey, Alvin Peterson. USA b. near Mount Vernon, Ind., 26 Sept. 1821. The youngest of 8 children and an orphan by 15, Hovey became an apprentice bricklayer. In his late teens he taught school, read law, and was admitted to the bar. At the outbreak of the Mexican War he received a lieutenancy in a local volunteer company but saw no service. Later he was a member of Indiana's constitutional convention, a circuit judge, and by 1854 the youngest Indiana supreme court justice to that time. After serving 2 years on the bench, he became a U.S. district attorney, and in 1858, having switched his political affiliation from Democrat to Republican, he was an unsuccessful candidate for Congress.

LC

When the Civil War began, Hovey's political standing helped him gain a colonel's eagles as commander of the 24th Indiana Infantry. He led his regiment in Missouri and Apr. 1862 comported himself gallantly at SHILOH, a performance that earned him a brigadier generalship as of the 28th of that month. That autumn he commanded a brigade as head of the 2d District/Department of Eastern Arkansas, and by Feb. 1863 he was leading the 12th Division of the XIII Corps in Maj. Gen. ULYSSES S. GRANT'S ARMY OF THE TENNESSEE. This command served conspicuously in the VICKSBURG CAMPAIGN, especially at CHAMPION'S HILL, where it lost a third of its strength in casualties while winning Grant's praise for its key role in the Union victory.

In Dec. 1863 Hovey returned to Indiana, where he organized and forwarded to the front newly organized troops. He left his native state to take part in the opening stages of the ATLANTA CAMPAIGN but returned on leave June 1864, a move Maj. Gen. WILLIAM T. SHERMAN thought so poorly timed that he disbanded Hovey's division. Hovey finished the war as commander of the District of Indiana. There, as a brevet major general of volunteers, he handled administrative chores, battled militant Copperheads (*see* PEACE DEMOCRATS), and recruited 10,000 troops, who, answering his call for young, unmarried men, became known as "Hovey's Babies."

After the conflict, he practiced law, spent 5 years as U.S. minister to Peru, sat in the House of Representatives 1888–89, and Jan. 1889 was sworn in as governor of Indiana. He died in office at Indianapolis, 23 Nov. 1891. —EGL

Howard, Joseph, Jr. journalist b. Brooklyn, N.Y., about 1833. A professional newspaperman, Howard was described by a contemporary as "a dashing and somewhat reckless fellow in his way, ready to supply on short notice any sort of sensation that might be desired."

Howard was a shadowy figure, and little is known of his antebellum career. But he burst upon the journalistic world in 1861 with a fraudulent story of president-elect ABRAHAM LINCOLN's furtive passage through Baltimore "in a Scotch cap and military cloak." By summer of that year, Howard was working for the New York *Times,* filing a story on the FIRST BATTLE OF BULL RUN.

Without scruples, Howard used any means to cover and report a story: once he kept a telegraph line open for his paper by wiring the genealogy of Jesus. In Sept. 1862, wearing a surplice and holding a prayerbook, Howard infiltrated the funeral procession of Maj. Gen. PHILIP KEARNY, from which newspapermen had been banned. His skillful reporting earned him one of the first regular bylines in the *Times*.

By spring 1864 Howard was the city editor of the Brooklyn *Eagle*. With the assistance of one of his reporters, Francis A. Mallison, he perpetrated the infamous GOLD HOAX. Howard and Mallison wrote a bogus presidential proclamation, which recounted military defeats, asked for a day of humiliation and prayer, and called for the draft of 400,000 men. 2 of New York City's 7 dailies accepted the skillfully forged ASSOCIATED PRESS dispatch and published the proclamation. It immediately created a furor, causing the price of gold to shoot up, infuriating Lincoln, and eventually leading to the suppression of the newspapers and a court case.

Howard was arrested 2 days later, having boasted that he would make money in the gold market. He and Mallison spent less than 3 months in prison. Rev. HENRY WARD BEECHER, arguing that Howard was "the only spotted child of a large family," interceded with Lincoln, who released the pair.

Howard worked for several city papers after the war. A president of the New York Press Club, his "Howard's Column" was by 1886 very popular and widely syndicated. d. New York City, 31 Mar. 1908.   —JDW

Howard, Oliver Otis. USA b. Leeds, Maine, 8 Nov. 1830, Howard graduated from Bowdoin College in 1850, and in 1854 4th in his class at West Point, where he was teaching mathematics when war erupted. Placed in command of the 3d Maine Regiment, he led a brigade at FIRST BULL RUN and performed well enough to earn a brigadier general's star 3 Sept. 1861, despite the fact that his troops left the field in disorder.

Howard was awarded the MEDAL OF HONOR in 1893 for his heroic leadership in the Battle of SEVEN PINES, 31 May 1862, where he suffered 2 wounds that forced amputation of his right arm. After a brief recuperation he commanded a division

USMHI

at ANTIETAM and FREDERICKSBURG and earned promotion to major general 29 Nov. 1862.

At CHANCELLORSVILLE, commanding the XI Corps, he suffered a humiliating rout at the hands of Lt. Gen. THOMAS J. "STONE-WALL" JACKSON. His failure to protect Maj. Gen. JOSEPH HOOKER's flank was cited as a major reason for the Union defeat.

Not long thereafter, at GETTYSBURG, he became the senior commander for a brief period after Maj. Gen. JOHN F. REYNOLDS was killed. Howard's selection of CEMETERY HILL and CEMETERY RIDGE as sites on which to anchor the Union position earned him a THANKS OF CONGRESS citation.

In the ATLANTA CAMPAIGN he commanded the IV Corps under Maj. Gen. WILLIAM T. SHERMAN, who placed him in command of the Army of the Tennessee during the MARCH TO THE SEA and the CAROLINAS CAMPAIGN.

A devout churchgoer who opposed drinking and gambling among his men (Sherman declared he "ought to have been born in petticoats and ought to wear them"), Howard was the choice of ABRAHAM LINCOLN and Sec. of War EDWIN M. STANTON to head the FREEDMEN'S BUREAU at war's end. Though his own behavior was beyond reproach, his refusal to acknowledge activities of his subordinates resulted in an agency marked by corruption. He was called before a court of inquiry in 1874 but cleared of the charges against him. Howard's devotion to blacks subsequently led him to take a leading role in establishing Howard University in Washington, D.C.

During the late 1870s and 1880s Howard fought in the West against Indians and served as superintendent of the U.S. Military Academy. He was commissioned major general in the Regular Army in 1886 and assumed command of the Division of the East. Retiring in 1894, he devoted his last years to religious and educational endeavors, helping found Lincoln Memorial University at Harrogate, Tenn. During this time he lived in Burlington, Vt., where he died 26 Oct. 1909.

—DS

Howe, Julia Ward. author, reformer b. New York, N.Y., 27 May 1819. The daughter of wealthy banker Samuel Ward and wife of abolitionist Samuel Gridley Howe, Julia is remembered as the author of the poem "Battle Hymn of the Republic." Written after a tour of army camps in the Washington, D.C., area with her friend Massachusetts Gov. JOHN A. ANDREW, it was published Feb. 1862 in the *Atlantic Monthly,* which paid her $4 for the rights. Set to the tune "John Brown's Body," the poem became the best remembered of Civil War songs. Howe died in Hartford, Conn., 17 Oct. 1910, known in her own day as an abolitionist, suffragette, and peace activist.   —JES

howitzer. The howitzer is an artillery piece developed in the Netherlands around the turn of the 18th century. Most

LC

often made of bronze, in the Civil War howitzers were manufactured in standard projectile weight classes: 12-, 24-, and 32-pounders; their respective shell weights were 8.9, 18.4, and 25.6 lb. Generally smoothbores, they had short tubes with chambered interiors that allowed a light powder charge to lob a shell on a high trajectory and made them adaptable to multiple field uses. They were effective antipersonnel weapons capable of firing CANISTER or CASE SHOT and vied with the MORTAR in their ability to arch a projectile over walls and fortifications. The Model 1841 mountain howitzer was a 12-pounder of lighter design that could be broken down and transported on muleback, unlike its standard 12-pounder howitzer counterpart. A howitzer with an 8-in. bore diameter was also a good siege and garrison weapon, throwing a 50.5-lb shell over 1,200 yd on a 4-lb powder charge. Unlike the field howitzer, the 8-in. seacoast howitzer Model 1841 had a swell at its muzzle. Confederate gunmakers turned out some iron models and an experimental 8-in. rifled piece.   —JES

Huger, Benjamin. CSA b. Charleston, S.C., 22 Nov. 1805. Scion of an old military family (his father was adjutant general during the War of 1812, and his mother was the daughter of a Revolutionary War commander), Huger graduated 8th in the West Point class of 1825. Though assigned to the artillery, he spent 3 years on topographical duty before becoming an ordnance officer. For a dozen years he commanded the armory at FORT MONROE, Va. He also sat on a War Department ordnance board and spent a year in Europe studying modes of Continental warfare.

During the Mexican War, Huger (pronounced *Eú*-zhay)

LC

was chief of ordnance to WINFIELD SCOTT. For gallantry in 3 campaigns he won as many brevets, including that of colonel. Returning to the U.S. in 1848, he served on a board that developed new artillery tactics, then superintended armories in Virginia, Maryland, and elsewhere in the South. In 1852 South Carolina officials presented him with a dress sword "in recognition of the honor his career had cast upon his native State."

Joining the Confederate army, he was named brigadier general 17 June 1861 and major general less than 4 months later. Placed in charge of the Department of Norfolk, he promptly declared his district too weakly held to prevent a Union invasion. When Federals approached in May 1862, Huger dismantled his works, torched the city's naval yard, destroyed the CSS *VIRGINIA*, and evacuated Norfolk as well as neighboring Portsmouth.

His actions while in command of ROANOKE ISLAND, N.C., had also been controversial. When troops there surrendered to a Union expeditionary force Feb. 1862, Huger's failure to reinforce them was investigated by the Confederate Congress. Nevertheless, JEFFERSON DAVIS subsequently gave him a division under Gen. JOSEPH E. JOHNSTON, which he led at SEVEN PINES and in many of the SEVEN DAYS' battles. In several of these engagements, notably WHITE OAK SWAMP and MALVERN HILL, his

leadership left much to be desired, resulting in his relief from active command 12 July 1862 and his relegation to artillery and ordnance-inspection duties.

In this capacity he did an efficient job both in the Western theater and, after mid-1863, in the TRANS-MISSISSIPPI DEPARTMENT. In poor health by the close of hostilities, he retired to a life of farming in North Carolina, then in Virginia. Late in life he returned to Charleston, dying there 7 Dec. 1877.

—EGL

Humes, William Young Conn. CSA b. Abingdon, Va., 1 May 1830. Despite his family's financial misfortunes, Humes secured a good education, graduating with honors in 1851 from the Virginia Military Institute. After teaching in order to obtain funds to repay educational debts, he moved to Knoxville, Tenn., studied law, and practiced the profession there and later in Memphis.

Humes traded his prosperous practice for a Confederate artillery lieutenant's commission shortly after the Civil War began. His military training soon brought him captain's bars and command of batteries on ISLAND NO. 10 in the Mississippi River above NEW MADRID, Mo. Union

LC

Maj. Gen. JOHN POPE attacked that position Apr. 1862, capturing some 7,000 Confederates, including Humes, who was quickly exchanged and paroled. Backed by commendations from his superiors for his performance on Island No. 10, he received command of all horse artillery units in Maj. Gen. JOSEPH WHEELER's cavalry corps/Army of Tennessee early in 1863. That November he was named a brigadier general in charge of one of Wheeler's mounted brigades.

In cavalry service, Humes forged a notable career, especially during and after the ATLANTA CAMPAIGN. At Varnell's Station, 4–5 May 1864, in command of a 3-brigade division, he helped repulse an attack by Union cavalry who outnumbered his men 5-to-1. On 27 May, with supporting units, he defeated "with immense slaughter" another Union cavalry force of superior size, which had aimed at the Confederate rear at Pickett's Mills. In an August raid against the communication lines of Maj. Gen. WILLIAM T. SHERMAN, the young brigadier drove enemy forces out of Dalton, Ga., capturing and sacking its supply depot. At BUCK HEAD CREEK, 28 Nov., Humes's division and another force under Wheeler scattered troops in bivouac under Brig. Gen. H. JUDSON KILPATRICK, almost nabbing "Kill-Cavalry" himself. Humes performed this same feat 9–10 Mar. 1865 at MONROE'S CROSS ROADS, N.C., where he fell wounded. On that same date he was elevated to major general.

Returning to Memphis after surrendering with Gen. Joseph E. Johnston, Humes resumed his law practice. Later he transferred his office to Huntsville, Ala., where he died 11 Sept. 1882.

—EGL

Humphreys, Andrew Atkinson. USA b. Philadelphia, Pa., 2 Nov. 1810, Humphreys, the son and grandson of men who designed and built ships for the U.S. Navy, graduated from the U.S. Military Academy 13th in his class in 1831. He left the U.S. Army for 2 years in the 1830s to pursue a career as an engineer, then was appointed an engineer officer. At the outbreak of the Civil War Humphreys was considered one of the finest engineers in the army but had not been in combat for a quarter-century, and then as a junior officer in the Seminole War.

USMHI

Humphreys served first in the Army of the Potomac as a staff officer for Maj. Gen. GEORGE B. MCCLELLAN, gaining command of a division only shortly before the Battle of ANTIETAM. As division commander he won particular distinction at FREDERICKSBURG and GETTYSBURG, but soon after the latter battle was assigned chief of staff to Maj. Gen. GEORGE G. MEADE with the rank of major general to rank from 8 July 1863. Only through accepting this post could he gain the promotion he thought he deserved, but it deprived him of the chance to lead troops, the only military duty he wanted. In Nov. 1864 Humphreys replaced the wounded Maj. Gen. WINFIELD S. HANCOCK in command of the II Corps, which Humphreys led through the surrender at Appomattox.

After the war Humphreys commanded the Corps of Engineers for 13 years, then wrote 2 studies covering the campaigns of the Army of the Potomac, *From Gettysburg to the Rapidan* (1883) and *The Virginia Campaigns of 1864–1865* (1883). Both are meticulously accurate and deadly dull, neither revealing much of Humphreys himself. A man of quiet competence, a superb engineer and talented scientist, a loyal and accomplished soldier, Humphreys perhaps contributed much to the winning of the Civil War for which he never received adequate credit. He retired from his military career in 1879, dying in the District of Columbia 27 Dec. 1883.   —JYS

Humphreys, Benjamin Grubb. CSA b. Claiborne Cty., Miss., 24 or 26 Aug. 1808. One of 16 children, Humphreys attended schools in Kentucky and New Jersey before entering West Point in 1825. After being dismissed with many others following a Christmas Eve riot in 1826, he returned to his native state, studied law, farmed, and served in both houses of the state legislature.

Though an opponent of secession, Humphreys raised an infantry company for the Confederacy and was commissioned captain in the 21st Mississippi 18 May 1861. 4 months later he was elected colonel of the regiment, commanding it until summer 1863. He performed capably as a regimental commander, and as part of Brig. Gen. WILLIAM BARKSDALE's brigade, Humphreys and the 21st Mississippi participated in the SEVEN DAYS', ANTIETAM, FREDERICKSBURG, and CHANCELLORSVILLE campaigns. In the last campaign Barksdale's Mississippians stubbornly defended

LC

Marye's Heights at Fredericksburg until overwhelmed by Federal numbers.

When Barksdale fell mortally wounded at GETTYSBURG 2 July 1863, Humphreys, as senior colonel, assumed command of the brigade. His well-earned promotion to brigadier general came 14 Aug., to date from 12 Aug. Humphreys and his brigade of Mississippians went west with Lt. Gen. JAMES LONGSTREET's I Corps in September, fighting at CHICKAMAUGA and KNOXVILLE. In spring 1864 Humphreys saw action at the WILDERNESS, SPOTSYLVANIA, and COLD HARBOR. In August his division, commanded by Maj. Gen. JOSEPH B. KERSHAW, was sent to the Shenandoah Valley to reinforce Lt. Gen. JUBAL A. EARLY's II Corps. On 3 Sept., near Berryville, Humphreys suffered a wound that eventually incapacitated him from field service. At the close of hostilities, he commanded a military district in his home state.

Pardoned by Pres. ANDREW JOHNSON, the esteemed brigadier was elected his state's first postwar governor. Inaugurated 16 Oct. 1865, Humphreys served until 15 June 1868, when he was ejected by Federal military authorities. Until his death, on his plantation in Leflore Cty., Miss., 20 Dec. 1882, Humphreys was an insurance agent and planter.   —JDW

Hunt, Henry Jackson. USA b. Detroit Barracks, Mich., 4 Sept. 1819, Hunt carried on the family military tradition by attending West Point, where he became interested in service with the new light artillery, graduating 19th in his class in 1839. On the eve of civil war, Hunt, a major who had served on a board to revise light artillery tactics, was considered one of the foremost authorities on artillery.

USMHI

Under fire at FIRST BULL RUN, he acted coolly and competently, using his artillery to turn back a Confederate assault on the left flank that might have finished the beaten Federals. When Maj. Gen. GEORGE B. MCCLELLAN took command of the Army of the Potomac, he demonstrated his faith in Hunt by promoting him to colonel and putting him in charge of the Artillery Reserve, an idea Hunt had masterminded. Hunt returned the favor by continued loyalty to "Little Mac" long after it became politically inexpedient.

Hunt served notably on the peninsula, where his Artillery Reserve smashed Gen. ROBERT E. LEE's assault on MALVERN HILL. Promoted to brigadier general and chief of artillery 15 Sept. 1862, he led his guns into battle at ANTIETAM harassed by uncooperative infantry commanders.

At FREDERICKSBURG Hunt's 147 guns were used to destroy the town but were unable to push the Confederates off Marye's Heights. In 1863 Maj. Gen. JOSEPH HOOKER chose to lessen Hunt's authority, then suffered a defeat caused in part by the ineffective artillery support of an arm reduced to chaos. Restored to his command by Maj. Gen. GEORGE G. MEADE at GETTYSBURG, Hunt mustered the 70 CEMETERY HILL guns that threw back PICKETT's CHARGE. This action proved to be the height of Hunt's career. Under Lt. Gen. U. S. Grant he remained chief of artillery until 1864, when he was put in command of siege operations at PETERSBURG.

Throughout the war Hunt's attempts to make the artillery an independent branch were hampered by infantry commanders who bitterly attacked him, feeling they should have complete control of the artillery.

Though brevetted a major general, Hunt reverted to the rank of colonel at war's end. He served with the Regular Army and after retirement became governor of the Soldiers' Home in Washington, D.C., where he died 11 Feb. 1889. —CMS

Hunter, David. USA b. District of Columbia, 21 July 1802, Hunter graduated from West Point ranked 24th in the class of 1822, serving in minor positions on the Northwest frontier before the war. On 14 May 1861 he was made colonel of the 3d U.S. Cavalry, 3 days later was appointed brigadier general in charge of the 2d Division of Brig. Gen. IRVIN MCDOWELL's army, and 13 Aug. was promoted to major general. When the war commenced, he was severely wounded at the onset of FIRST BULL RUN.

USMHI

Hunter was later called to Missouri to command a division under Maj. Gen. JOHN C. FRÉMONT, whom he relieved as commander of the Western Department. In 1862 he took over the Department of the South and subsequently captured and demanded the surrender of FORT PULASKI, Ga. On 9 May he abolished slavery in his department of the army, an action repudiated by Pres. ABRAHAM LINCOLN on the grounds that Hunter had surpassed his authority. Hunter then raised a black regiment, the 1st South Carolina, which was approved by Congress.

In an effort to capture Charleston, he was defeated at SECESSIONVILLE, 16 June 1862, after which he temporarily suspended his military duty. When Maj. Gen. FRANZ SIGEL was deterred in the Shenandoah Valley, May 1864, Hunter was called to take over the Department of West Virginia in the valley region. He cut Southern supply lines, communication lines, and railroad lines as he moved throughout the valley and was victorious at the Battle of PIEDMONT. At Lynchburg he encountered Lt. Gen. JUBAL A. EARLY, who threatened his forces and caused him to withdraw into West Virginia. The move left the valley open for EARLY'S WASHINGTON RAID, and Hunter received much criticism for his retreat. After meeting with Lt. Gen. U. S. GRANT and Maj. Gen. PHILIP H. SHERIDAN, he decided to resign his command 8 Aug. 1864, so that Sheridan could effectively rid the Shenandoah Valley of Confederate forces (see SHENANDOAH VALLEY CAMPAIGN, SHERIDAN'S). Known for the numerous defeats he suffered, Hunter is not considered among the more adept Union military officers.

After Lincoln's assassination, Hunter served as president of the committee that tried the conspirators. Following the war, he was brevetted to brigadier and major general in the Regular Army. He lived in Washington, D.C., until his death there 2 Feb. 1866. —KAK

Hunter, Robert Mercer Taliaferro. CSP b. Essex Cty., Va., 21 Apr. 1809, Hunter was educated by private tutors and at the University of Virginia. He practiced law and sat in the

Virginia legislature 1834–37.

LC

Serving in the U.S. Congress as a STATES-RIGHTS Whig 1837–43, Hunter was Speaker of the House of Representatives 1839–41. Coming increasingly under the influence of JOHN C. CALHOUN, he followed the South Carolinian into the "Southern Rights" wing of the Democratic party and was active in the unsuccessful movement in 1844 to elect Calhoun president. He was sent back to the House of Representatives in 1845 and was elected to the U.S. Senate in 1847.

In the Senate, 1847–61, Hunter emerged as a leading Southern spokesman, though his natural conservatism and conciliatory manner won admirers in all sections. He tried to work out a compromise between North and South 1860–61 but, realizing that such an undertaking could not succeed, he withdrew from Congress.

Hunter served in the Confederate Congress until July 1861, when he became secretary of state. In Feb. 1862 he became one of Virginia's Confederate senators, a post in which he served with no special distinction for the rest of the war. Early in 1865 he was one of the Confederate commissioners to the HAMPTON ROADS CONFERENCE, where peace negotiations failed when Southerners insisted on independence. In the last months of the war he struggled with no success to help Pres. JEFFERSON DAVIS rally public support for a last-ditch effort.

Much of Hunter's property was destroyed during or immediately after the war, and Hunter himself was briefly imprisoned. In 1867 he again became active in politics and helped organize Virginia conservatives in opposition to RECONSTRUCTION. From 1874 to 1880 he was state treasurer. At his death at "Fonthill," near Lloyds, Va., 18 July 1887, he was collector of the port of Rappahannock, Va. —RMcM

Hunter's Raid. 26 May–18 June 1864 4 days after Union Maj. Gen. FRANZ SIGEL's defeat at NEW MARKET, 15 May 1864, Maj. Gen. DAVID HUNTER replaced him as commander of the Department of West Virginia. Hunter's instructions outlined a campaign toward Lynchburg and Charlottesville, its primary objective the destruction of the Virginia Central Railroad, the James River Canal, and major industrial facilities and resources in the Shenandoah Valley. Lt. Gen. U. S. Grant ordered Hunter to march eastward and join the Army of the Potomac after the mission was completed.

On 26 May Hunter's 8,500-man command initiated the movement. Confederate Brig. Gen. WILLIAM E. "GRUMBLE" JONES surprised Hunter on 5 June at PIEDMONT, but the Federal general counterattacked, turning the Confederate right flank and killing Jones. 3 days later Brig. Gen. GEORGE CROOK's command, numbering 10,000, joined Hunter. Personally committed to a campaign of destruction, Hunter entered Staunton, where his soldiers wrecked miles of railroad tracks and the depot, factories, and mills. On 11 June the Union army entered Lexington, soon engulfing that town in flames. Soldiers looted Washington College and ransacked the Virginia Military Institute before burning the military school and the home of Virginia governor JOHN LETCHER. For 3 days the town and neighboring villages were plundered and burned.

Hunter crossed the Blue Ridge Mts. and reached his major objective, Lynchburg, on the 17th. Manning the Confederate lines was Lt. Gen. JUBAL A. EARLY's II Corps, dispatched by Gen. ROBERT E. LEE to stop Hunter. Though his troops were numerically superior, Hunter panicked before these seasoned Confederates and retreated the next night. Early pursued and overtook the fleeing Federals at Liberty, inflicting casualties and capturing wagons. The Union general abandoned the valley and retreated into West Virginia. On 6 Aug. Grant replaced Hunter with Maj. Gen. PHILIP H. SHERIDAN.   —JDW

Hunton, Eppa. CSA b. Fauquier Cty., Va., 22 Sept. 1822, Hunton was a schoolteacher, then a prosperous lawyer during the antebellum period. Elected as commonwealth attorney in his county, he engaged in Democratic politics and served in the state militia, becoming a colonel, then a brigadier general. A member of the Virginia secession convention, Hunton was elected colonel of the 8th Virginia, which he recruited and equipped, after the Old Dominion withdrew from the Union.

At FIRST BULL RUN Hunton and his novice regiment performed gallantly, participating in the defense of Henry Hill and charging gamely in the final Confederate assault that routed the Union

LC

army. Hunton's conduct earned him commendation in the battle reports. Assigned to the brigade of Brig. Gen. GEORGE E. PICKETT, the 8th Virginia's next major action was in the SEVEN DAYS' CAMPAIGN, June–July 1862. When Pickett fell wounded at GAINES' MILL, Hunton assumed command of the brigade, leading it for 3 days until he collapsed from exhaustion.

Hunton commanded the regiment for another year, leading it at ANTIETAM Sept. 1862 and at GETTYSBURG July 1863. During Pickett's famed charge, 3 July, Hunton suffered a severe wound. His deserved promotion to brigadier general, delayed because of his health, finally came 9 Aug. 1863. As a brigade commander, he fought at the WILDERNESS, SPOTSYLVANIA, COLD HARBOR, and PETERSBURG. At FIVE FORKS, 1 Apr. 1865, he and his brigade fought bravely against overwhelming Federal forces. 5 days later he was captured, along with other Confederate generals, at SAYLER'S CREEK and imprisoned in FORT WARREN.

Hunton's postwar career was even more distinguished than

his prewar endeavors. He resumed his legal practice, in Warrenton, served 4 terms as a U.S. congressman, 1873–81, and 3 years as a senator, 1892–95. Hunton was the only Southern member of the electoral commission that decided the disputed presidential election of 1876 between Samuel Tilden and RUTHERFORD B. HAYES. Retiring from the Senate in 1895, he lived in Warrenton until his death in Richmond 11 Oct. 1908.
          —JDW

Huse, Caleb. CSA b. Newburyport, Mass., 11 Feb. 1831, Huse graduated 7th in the West Point class of 1851, briefly went on artillery duty at Key West, Fla., and 1852–59 was professor of chemistry, mineralogy, and geology at the Military Academy. After taking an indefinite leave of absence to travel in Europe 1859–60, he accepted a post at the University of Alabama. Ordered to return to the army Feb. 1861, he resigned, accepting a commission as captain in Confederate service.

CMH

In April, Huse's background in science, administration, and ordnance won him special assignment as the Confederate army's European purchasing agent. Through Trenholm Brothers, the New York office of FRASER, TRENHOLM, & CO., he financed passage to England from Canada, arriving in Liverpool 10 May 1861. He spent his years of Confederate service working out of the Fraser, Trenholm & Co. offices in Liverpool, traveling in France and Austria, and buying guns and equipment from any nation that would accept Confederate business. Though he was successful, interdepartmental rivalries brought bribery and kickback charges against him in 1863 for his association with a disreputable English firm. Confederate financial agent Colin J. McRae conducted an audit and investigation that absolved Huse of wrongdoing. Though exact figures and inventory of Huse's purchases are unavailable, they ran into millions in pounds sterling and encompassed everything from rifles to drugs. Both he and Confederate naval Cmdr. JAMES D. BULLOCH are credited with prolonging the war through their ability to procure supplies and equipment.

Destitute at the end of the war, Huse returned to the U.S. late in 1867 or 1868. For several years he floundered as a businessman, until in 1876 he opened a military preparatory school in Sing Sing, N.Y. 3 years later he relocated the school in Highland Falls, operating it there successfully for 20 years. d. Highland Falls, 11 Mar. 1905.   —JES

I

Île à Vache. In Apr. 1863, 468 freedmen boarded the *Ocean Ranger* in Fort Monroe, Va., and sailed for the Haitian Île à Vache in an experiment ABRAHAM LINCOLN hoped would lead to extensive colonization of blacks outside the U.S. In 1862, with emancipation imminent, many Northerners, particularly those in the border states, had feared a heavy northward migration by former slaves. Thus the president wanted to present to the public a workable plan of voluntary colonization before issuing his EMANCIPATION PROCLAMATION Jan. 1863. Lincoln himself did not believe blacks and whites could live together in peace as social and political equals, but neither would he sanction the forced removal of blacks. The Île à Vache scheme, like others he investigated, made colonization conditional on the willingness of blacks to leave the country and on the promises of the host country to protect the emigrants' freedom.

The Île à Vache venture was presented early in Oct. 1862 when promoter Bernard Kock approached Lincoln offering to provide homes for 1,000 blacks on an island he had leased in the West Indies and to put them to work growing cotton. The U.S. government would assume responsibility for transporting the colonists, providing supplies for the enterprise, and pay Kock $50 for each person settled. Facing disapproval from Radical Republicans, Lincoln had Kock investigated carefully and canceled the arrangement on learning of Kock's reputation as a speculator. A few weeks later 2 New York financiers, Charles K. Tuckerman and Paul S. Forbes, presented the same proposal to the president and had their contract approved after Lincoln limited to 500 the number of colonists to be settled.

The colonists' initial enthusiasm for Île à Vache faded when they arrived to find neither the homes nor the school or hospital they had been promised, but an island covered with thick jungle. Kock, hired by Tuckerman and Forbes to lead the expedition without Lincoln's knowledge, was replaced at the president's insistence in July. Within months the backers abandoned the project as a bad investment, leaving the colonists with no assistance in their struggle to survive. In November the rumors of death and starvation that reached Washington moved Lincoln to send an agent to the island, but nothing could be done to salvage the colony. On 20 Mar. 1864, less than a year after their hopeful departure, 368 embittered survivors were returned to the U.S. aboard the *Marcia C. Day*.

The failure of the colony on Île à Vache and the Jan. 1863 legislation allowing blacks to enlist in the army ended Lincoln's plans to colonize freedmen abroad. Outraged by the tragedy, Congress permanently withdrew all colonization appropriations 2 July 1864. —PLF

Illinois. Organized as a territory in 1809, Illinois became the 21st state in 1818, with the motto "State Sovereignty, National Union." It was in Alton that the murder of abolitionist Elijah P. Lovejoy in 1837 helped arouse antislavery sentiment that eventually led to the formation in 1854 of the REPUBLICAN PARTY. In Illinois the Lincoln-Douglas senatorial debates were heard in 1858, and in 1860, in the Wigwam in Chicago, ABRAHAM LINCOLN received the Republican party's nomination for the presidency.

When war came, Illinois lived up to its motto. Vigorously led by Gov. RICHARD YATES, the state responded overwhelmingly to the call for volunteers. By the end of the war 259,092 men had served the Union, mostly in the Western armies. Of these, 255,057 composed 150 white infantry regiments, 17 cavalry units, 2 light artillery units, and 8 independent batteries; 2,224 more were sailors and marines; the remaining 1,811 were in the 29th U.S. Colored Infantry and other black regiments. Only 3,538 Illinoisans were conscripts; only 55 men paid the $300 COMMUTATION fee to avoid service. At the end of the war their dead numbered 34,834.

Illinois furnished the Union with 53 brigadier generals; 9 became major generals, and 1, ULYSSES S. GRANT, led the Union armies in the war's final year as lieutenant general. Of the major generals, JOHN A. "BLACK JACK" LOGAN and JOHN M. PALMER distinguished themselves in the ATLANTA CAMPAIGN, JAMES H. WILSON led the Western Cavalry Corps in the war's last months, and BENJAMIN H. GRIERSON is remembered for his famous cavalry raid. Notable too, though less accomplished, were BENJAMIN M. PRENTISS of "HORNETS' NEST" fame at SHILOH and political general JOHN A. MCCLERNAND. Island No. 10 had its JOHN POPE and Gettysburg its JOHN BUFORD and WESLEY MERRITT.

And over them all was the greatest Illinoisan, their commander-in-chief, ABRAHAM LINCOLN. —RDH

Imboden, John Daniel. CSA b. near Staunton, Va., 16 Feb. 1823. A man of varied interests, and 5 wives, Imboden attended Washington College for 2 years, then taught school and practiced law in Staunton. He served 2 terms in the state legislature but failed to be elected a delegate to the Virginia secession convention, perhaps because of his strong secessionist views.

Immediately after Virginia seceded, Imboden led the military unit he had organized, the Staunton Artillery, to Harpers Ferry and captured the U.S. arsenal there. He fought at FIRST BULL RUN and in 1862 organized a cavalry command, the 1st Partisan Rangers, to fight with Maj. Gen. THOMAS J. "STONEWALL" JACKSON in his Shenandoah Valley Campaign of 1862.

Promoted to brigadier general to rank from 28 Jan. 1863, Imboden displayed resourcefulness and skill in semi-independent command. He led the "Imboden Raid" in spring 1863, during which he cut Baltimore & Ohio Railroad lines and captured large numbers of livestock from western Virginia. During the GETTYSBURG CAMPAIGN he guarded the Confederate left flank in the advance and performed with distinction in covering the South's retreat.

In 1864 Imboden commanded the cavalry accompanying Lt. Gen. JUBAL A. EARLY during his threatening raid on Washington (*see* EARLY'S WASHINGTON RAID) and during his subsequent operations against Maj. Gen. PHILIP H. SHERIDAN in

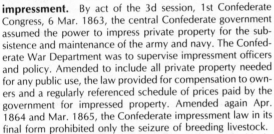

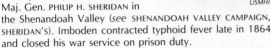

USMHI

the Shenandoah Valley (*see* SHENANDOAH VALLEY CAMPAIGN, SHERIDAN'S). Imboden contracted typhoid fever late in 1864 and closed his war service on prison duty.

Following the war, he promoted the development of the mineral and mining resources of Virginia. d. Damascus, Va., 15 Aug. 1895.   —EMT

impressment. By act of the 3d session, 1st Confederate Congress, 6 Mar. 1863, the central Confederate government assumed the power to impress private property for the subsistence and maintenance of the army and navy. The Confederate War Department was to supervise impressment officers and policy. Amended to include all private property needed for any public use, the law provided for compensation to owners and a regularly referenced schedule of prices paid by the government for impressed property. Amended again Apr. 1864 and Mar. 1865, the Confederate impressment law in its final form prohibited only the seizure of breeding livestock.

Food, clothing, horses, cattle, coal, iron, railroads, blacks (slaves and freedmen), domestic and industrial property were seized by officers appointed by state governors; compensation was determined by the price schedule and 2 disinterested parties, 1 selected by the impressment officer and 1 by the property owner. Impressment of freedmen, specifically for work with the NITER AND MINING BUREAU, functioned like a draft, the laborers being compensated at an established minimum wage.

Previously all Confederate armies and state governments had resorted to impressment in specific emergencies, later paying damage or compensation claims brought by individual property owners. In Nov. 1862 the Georgia and Alabama state legislatures vested their governors with impressment powers. But passage of the Mar. 1863 law brought official protests from the legislatures of Alabama, Mississippi, Georgia, Texas, Virginia, Arkansas, Florida, and North Carolina, these bodies claiming that impressment power in the hands of the Richmond administration constituted a violation of STATES RIGHTS. Protests from the public and from state governments grew more heated in the late months of the war when the amended law eliminated the price schedule and substituted the phrase "just price" when instructing impressment officers in the amount of compensation required. Inflation of Confederate currency was not considered in establishing the "just price," and several impressment officers stood accused of using this provision to indulge in personal financial speculation.

Confederates relied on impressment as a regular means of augmenting supplies to the armed services. By contrast, standing Federal legislation permitted Union forces to impress private property in emergencies. But because of an adequate supply system, Federal use of impressment powers was not extensive.   —JES

imprints, Confederate. During the Civil War Confederate printers produced approximately 4,000 known different kinds of printed materials ranging from reports of military operations and government proceedings to newspapers, speeches, literature, and ephemera. The material is of particular importance to Civil War historians because of the insights it offers into the thoughts, values, and beliefs of the Confederate people.

South Carolina issued the first Confederate imprint in the form of the 20 Dec. 1860 "extra" edition of the Charleston *MERCURY*. Within 15 minutes after the state had withdrawn from the Union, overjoyed South Carolinians were buying the newspaper to read the text of the anticipated Ordinance of Secession. The last Confederate imprint was the surrender terms (General Order No. 54) issued by Lt. Gen. RICHARD TAYLOR at Meridian, Miss., dated 6 May 1865.

Any material published within the Confederacy is eagerly sought by collectors, with the limited amount available resulting in high prices.

The most extensive public collections of Confederate imprints accessible to researchers are located at the Library of Congress; the Boston Athenaeum; Princeton University; Huntington Library, San Marino, Calif.; the Confederate Museum in Richmond, Va.; and the Western Reserve Historical Society, Cleveland, Ohio. Large collections are also found in the libraries at Duke University, Durham, N.C.; Emory University, Atlanta, Ga.; the University of Virginia, Richmond; and the University of North Carolina, Chapel Hill.   —PLF

income tax, Confederate. During the Civil War, 8 Confederate states enacted income taxes ranging from .025% in Louisiana to 10% in Virginia; yet, because Southerners strenuously opposed direct taxation, national legislators waited until Apr. 1863 before passing a desperately needed income tax to finance the war.

Sec. of the Treasury CHRISTOPHER G. MEMMINGER first proposed a direct tax on income, a 10% levy on salaries, 10 Jan. 1863, projecting that revenue from this tax and a 1% property tax would add $60 million to the Confederate treasury at the end of the first year of enforcement. Nearly 7 weeks later the House Ways and Means Committee put forward a more stringent schedule, calling for a 14% tax on incomes up to $10,000 and 24% on sums exceeding that amount. Both plans failed to meet the approval of the more conservative Senate Finance Committee, which offered its own moderate version of income-tax legislation 2 Apr. The Senate bill proposed 5% on salaries ranging from $500 to $1,500; 10% on those from $1,500 to $10,000; 12.5% from $10,000 to $15,000; and 15% on earned income in excess of $15,000. The bill that was finally passed 24 Apr. called for a milder graduated income tax exempting wages to $1,000, and levying a 1% tax on the first $1,500 over the exemption and 2% on all additional income. Initially the public accepted the tax willingly, believing it would bring in high receipts and reduce inflation; but the cumbersome mechanisms for collection were ineffective and the amount of the tax too low to relieve the Confederacy's financial dilemma.

The Confederate Congress did not alter the income-tax rates

in their subsequent tax legislation, though levies on earned income were ruled deductible from other taxes passed in the comprehensive tax act of 17 Feb. 1864. The legislators refused Memminger's desperate plea later that year for a 20% tax on incomes over $5,000 and 50% on sums of more than $10,-000. —PLF

income tax, Federal. In his report to the special session of Congress 4 July 1861, Sec. of the Treasury SALMON P. CHASE estimated that in the coming fiscal year the Federal government would have to spend $320 million to finance the war. He recommended that $240 million be borrowed and the rest be obtained from revenues. Of the latter amount, Chase suggested that existing duties, new or increased duties, sales of public lands, and miscellaneous sources would provide about $60 million to the Treasury. The remaining $20 million he thought obtainable from direct taxes, internal duties, or both —whichever "the superior wisdom of Congress" decreed.

The House Ways and Means Committee met his challenge by preparing 2 revenue measures. The first, termed a tariff bill, was directed at import duties. Then, 24 July, the House considered a domestic tax bill. As drawn up by Treasury officials, it authorized 2 types of levies: direct taxes on real estate, apportioned among the states on the basis of population, and excise taxes on items ranging from liquor to bank notes.

This "additional revenue" bill encountered much opposition, for a property tax would hit Midwestern farmers hard, while barely touching Eastern bankers and merchants. Various proposals for a substitute tax were considered and rejected, until the House committee agreed on a bill to tax personal and corporate incomes. Like the LEGAL TENDER ACTS, this legislation was a radical assertion of Federal power. After its merger with the tariff bill, however, it quickly passed both houses and was approved by ABRAHAM LINCOLN. Still, it never went into operation.

Early in 1862 a new bill was introduced in Congress that, in its final form, imposed a 3% tax on yearly incomes between $600 and $10,000 and 5% on higher incomes. Passed that spring by a wide majority in both houses, it was signed into law by Lincoln 1 July. On 30 June 1864 it was amended to increase the tax rate to 5% on incomes of $600 to $5,000, 7.5% on incomes from $5,000 to $10,000, and 10% thereafter.

This first income tax to be enacted by Congress set a minimum taxable salary figure too high to ensure maximum effectiveness. Even so, it brought the Treasury $2 million in revenues in 1863 and 10 times as much the following year. Repealed in 1872 and later ruled unconstitutional, it nevertheless formed the basis of the present-day income tax.

—EGL

Indiana. When war came in 1861, Indiana was unprepared, largely because the militia had been neglected by the state government and there were no trained soldiers. But within a year, many civilians who had had military service, including veterans of the Mexican War, were back in uniform, and 61,-341 Hoosiers enlisted, nearly twice the quota set for the state. OLIVER P. MORTON, who became governor in 1861, led a large faction that believed the Union had no choice but to crush the rebellion. A man of extraordinary organizing ability, Governor Morton saw that training camps were organized, bought war equipment, started a state arsenal, and provided for soldiers' welfare, hospital care, and dependents' welfare—all of which

was done largely on money he induced a New York bank to loan the state, which at the time had bad credit.

There were no battles in Indiana until July 1863, when Brig. Gen. JOHN HUNT MORGAN and about 3,000 Confederate cavalrymen crossed the Ohio River and invaded the state. For 5 days they plundered, looted, and burned between fights, until, their numbers considerably reduced, they were chased into Ohio by Union troops.

Prior to Morgan's raid there were thought to be large numbers of Copperheads (see PEACE DEMOCRATS), Northerners sympathetic to the South, in southern Indiana, and it was believed that they would actively support and join a Confederate invasion. Certainly the raid was through the part of the state friendliest to the South, which was, possibly, a Confederate error. Either the Copperheads were not so numerous as thought or they resented the Confederates taking their money, horses, hams—even bolts of calico and a bird cage with canaries in it—because Morgan's invasion failed to rally Southern sympathizers.

The fifth largest of the Union states, Indiana was particularly important as a principal source of food for the Federal armies. The state's military contribution included 129 infantry regiments, 13 regiments and 3 companies of cavalry, 1 regiment of heavy artillery, and 26 batteries of light artillery, totaling 196,363 men; 7,243 were killed and 17,785 died of disease. Hoosier soldiers fought in more than 300 engagements in all theaters of the war. —PR

19th Indiana. Recruited in the central part of the state, including Indianapolis and Muncie, the 1,046 volunteers of this outfit were mustered into Federal service 29 July 1861. Under their towering colonel, SOLOMON MEREDITH, they reached Washington, D.C., by train early in August. The next month, with 40% of the regiment suffering from illness, able-bodied members absorbed heavy casualties in a clash with Col. J.E.B. STUART's cavalry at Lewinsville, Va., the 19th's first fight.

In October the outfit was attached to the 1st Brigade/3d Division/I Corps/Army of the Potomac. Along with the 2d, 6th, and 7th Wisconsin (and later the 24th Michigan) it formed one of the most famous units in American military history, the IRON BRIGADE OF THE WEST. It first saw battle 28 Aug. 1862, at GROVETON, during the SECOND BULL RUN CAMPAIGN, where it engaged in a stand-up, 2-hour fight at close range with the Confederates of Maj. Gen. THOMAS J. "STONEWALL" JACKSON. The Hoosiers lost 259 of 432 engaged but held their ground till darkness fell. At ANTIETAM, 3 weeks later, the regiment was again heavily engaged, as was the whole of the brigade under Brig. Gen. JOHN GIBBON. Holding Gibbon's left, the regiment fought in the West Woods, then enfiladed a Confederate line near Miller's Cornfield. Later the 19th was itself enfiladed by the division of Brig. Gen. JUBAL A. EARLY, sustaining numerous casualties, including the mortal wounding of Lt. Col. Alois O. Bachman. Still, it held its position so stubbornly that after the battle Maj. Gen. GEORGE B. MCCLELLAN remarked to Indiana Gov. OLIVER P. MORTON that his army possessed "no better regiment" than the 19th.

The outfit was lightly engaged at FREDERICKSBURG, not at all at CHANCELLORSVILLE. On the first day at GETTYSBURG, however, it lost 72% of its strength. Early in the day it shattered Brig. Gen. JAMES J. ARCHER's brigade along McPherson's Ridge, northwest of town, but late that afternoon parts of 3 Confederate brigades overwhelmed it, compelling it to retreat with the rest of the brigade, now led by Brigadier General Meredith. In the weeks that followed, the 19th was partially recruited and fought in the II Corps from BRISTOE STATION to PETERSBURG; another commander, Col. Samuel J. Williams, was killed at the WILDERNESS. Additional battle losses sapped its strength and forced it to merge with the 20th Indiana Oct. 1864, whereupon it lost its regimental identity.   —EGL

27th Indiana.   Organized in Indianapolis in summer 1861, the regiment entered Federal service 12 Sept., entraining for Washington, D.C., 3 days later. In the capital the regiment became part of the division of Maj. Gen. NATHANIEL P. BANKS. Under Col. Silas Colgrove it served on guard duty at Frederick, Md., until Mar. 1862, when assigned to the 3d Brigade/1st Division/Banks's corps. That May it saw its first battle action against the FOOT CAVALRY of Maj. Gen. THOMAS J. "STONEWALL" JACKSON in the lower Shenandoah Valley. Subsequently, the 27th was heavily engaged at CEDAR MOUNTAIN, 9 Aug. 1862, a prelude to SECOND BULL RUN.

On 13 Sept. 1862, during the ANTIETAM CAMPAIGN, members of the regiment discovered LEE'S LOST ORDER near their old bivouac outside Frederick. 4 days later, more than 200 of their comrades fell during the war's bloodiest day; afterward, survivors garrisoned Harpers Ferry for 3 months. As a part of the XII Corps, the outfit then joined the Army of the Potomac at Falmouth, Va. It missed the debacle at FREDERICKSBURG but did not escape BURNSIDE'S MUD MARCH.

Colonel Colgrove and his men again saw action at CHANCELLORSVILLE. On 3 May 1863 they held high ground between Fairview and Hazel Grove, stubbornly resisting the Confederate flanking offensive that had routed the XI Corps. Finally forced to withdraw, the regiment left dozens of casualties behind and later re-formed in good order. Exactly 2 months later, at GETTYSBURG, the 27th, in concert with the 2d Massachusetts Infantry, made a suicidal charge on a Confederate brigade along CULP'S HILL. After losing one-third of its men in a fruitless effort to clear the hill, it was forced into rapid retreat. Much of its loss was attributable to the unrealistic strategy of the army's right wing commander, Maj. Gen. HENRY W. SLOCUM, and to the faulty attack dispositions of Colonel Colgrove, now commanding the 27th's brigade.

The following September, the regiment headed west with the rest of the XII Corps. Joining the Army of the Tennessee, it was conspicuous at RESACA, where it inflicted 5 times as many casualties as it absorbed, and in several other battles during the ATLANTA CAMPAIGN. When mustered out Nov. 1864, the regiment was on occupation duty in the recently fallen Confederate citadel.   —EGL

Indians, Confederate.   The Confederacy had several reasons for seeking alliances with the tribes in Indian Territory, but uppermost was the potentially valuable manpower that might be recruited to form a buffer between Kansas and the thin line of Confederate soldiers strung along the Arkansas, Louisiana, and Texas borders.

Early in 1861 Gov. EDWARD CLARK of Texas optimistically assured JEFFERSON DAVIS that 20,000 warriors might be enlisted in the Southern army to protect the vulnerable Western approach to the Confederacy from invasion by Federal troops. He was wrong. Brig. Gen. ALBERT PIKE, whose extensive dealings with Indians convinced Davis in March to appoint him

special commissioner in charge of treaty making, more realistically predicted he could raise 3,500, certainly no more than 5,000, Indians to defend themselves from Federal invasion. After an exhausting swing through the territory that summer and early fall, Pike negotiated the last treaty with Chief John Ross of the Cherokee Nation 7 Oct. 1861. For the Five Civilized Tribes—Cherokee, Creek, Choctaw, Chickasaw, and Seminole—the terms were generous, granting them several rights denied for years by the Federal government, and at least on paper establishing these Indians as near-equals to white men. This far exceeded anything offered by Washington, which was not even living up to existing treaties.

If Southern politicians genuinely expected to profit militarily from Indian alliances, they were mistaken. Indian commanders Daniel McIntosh and his brother Chilly, John Drew, and John Jumper never managed to keep more than a few thousand cavalrymen in the field at any one time. Confederate Col. DOUGLAS H. COOPER fared little better with his regiment of Choctaws and Chickasaws. Ill-adapted to the strict discipline demanded in an organized army, disgusted when promised arms and supplies failed to arrive, they deserted in large numbers. Many defected when in Nov. 1861 their white commanders ordered the relentless pursuit of some 4,000 Creeks under Chief Opothleyahola as the refugees fled for protection to the Union lines in Kansas. The Indians who wore gray would fight Federals, but they could not slaughter their own people.

The only major battle in which Indian troops fought was PEA RIDGE, on the first day, 7 Mar. 1862. Rarely would they stand up under artillery fire, but here they performed well, holding their charge against Col. PETER J. OSTERHAUS' cannoneers to break the Union line. Thereafter their service was confined to Indian Territory.

Indian troops did render valuable service as scouts and on raiding forays, warfare to which they were particularly well suited. But consistently, only STAND WATIE, the one Indian to attain general rank in the Confederate army, provided the South with significant military assistance, by harassing Federal troops after they reoccupied the territory early in 1863.

Most damaging to the Confederate use of Indian troopers was the ammunition their warfare provided for the Northern press. Newspaper headlines railed against atrocities committed by Indians on the Union dead and wounded left on the battlefield. Some did take scalps or mutilate corpses, and neither protests from the Confederate government nor assurances of "civilized warfare" from tribal leaders could stop them.

The war kept these Indians from realizing the social, legal, and political gains won in the treaties, and traditional rivalries flared violently as tribal factions chose between North and South. Homes were burned, livestock confiscated, land laid waste, and families left to starve because Richmond was unable to send desperately needed provisions or provide protection against invading Federal soldiers.

The Confederacy reaped little military benefit from its Indian allies, and pro-Southern Indians paid dearly for their sympathies during and after the war. Because they had fought for the Confederate government, all existing Federal treaties with them became void. An impoverished, embittered people traded their Southern loyalty for the indignities of a harsh RECONSTRUCTION.   —PLF

industry.   The Civil War's effect on Northern industry was uneven, ambiguous, even contradictory. A wealth of economic data offers evidence that the industrial capacity of the North was greatly expanded by the conflict. Other statistical information, equally abundant, suggests that the war exercised no major influence on Northern industry or actually retarded its growth.

One major economic result of the war was that it helped change the U.S. from a country with an essentially agrarian society to one dependent on mechanization and a national market system. Only the North possessed an industrial base, small as it was, before the shooting started. During the fiscal year ending 1 June 1860, the country possessed some 128,300 industrial establishments. Of these, 110,274 were located in states that remained in the Union. The most heavily industrialized states, New York and Pennsylvania, each had more industry than all the seceding states combined. In 1860, too, America had a total of $1,050,000,000 invested in real and personal property devoted to business, with $949,335,000 concentrated in the North; Pennsylvania, New York, and Massachusetts each had a larger investment than the South as a whole. Finally, the North contributed 92.5% of the $1.9 billion that comprised the total value of annual product in the country in 1860.

One body of evidence indicates that the war widened this sectional disparity by destroying the South's minute industrial base and expanding that of the North to prodigious dimensions. Statistics on specific industries provide what appears to be convincing proof. While the loss of the Southern crop produced a steep war-long decline in production in the North's largest industry, cotton textiles, its woolen industry enjoyed a 100% production rise during the conflict. The second largest consumer industry in the Union, shoes and leather, also enjoyed tremendous growth, thanks to army contracts that more than offset the loss of the Southern market. Other war-related industries, especially firearms, gunpowder, and wagon manufacturing, grew rapidly on the strength of military contracts. Meanwhile, iron production in the North experienced a slump early in the war but boomed 1863–64, in the latter year reaching a production level 29% higher than that of the entire country in the busiest prewar year, 1856. The coal industry experienced similar growth, in 1861–65 enjoying an expansion rate 21% higher than that for the nation as a whole during the 4 years immediately preceding civil strife.

The war years stimulated production of new inventions and accelerated the growth of established technology. Due to a deluge of government contracts, sewing machines became an integral part of the clothing industry, and the 50-year-old system of machine-made interchangeable parts became firmly entrenched in the production system. Agriculture-related industrial goods also witnessed production spurts attributable to the war: Gail Borden's condensed-milk process, patented in 1856, became essential to the diets of many Union soldiers, while implements including the thresher and the rotary plow experienced sales booms as machinery took over work abandoned by farm hands gone to war. In other ways, such as by easing unemployment and by promoting the enactment of protective tariffs, the war encouraged wide-scale industrial expansion. No wonder that by 1864 the Union's manufacturing index had risen to a level 13% greater than that of the country as a whole in 1860.

But the war gave rise to no important new industries and, despite the statistics quoted above, generated no unusual increase in basic industrial production. It did not, as some econo-

mists later asserted, spawn an American industrial revolution; most of the innovations that did revolutionize American industry later in the century originated in the period 1820–60. Sharp declines marked the production expansion of many Northern industries during wartime. The nation's railroads, for example, increased their trackage by 70% during the 1860s, as against over 200% in a brief period prior to the 1860s. The war saw only a 1% rise in the production of pig iron, though that industry had experienced a 17% increase 1855–60 and in the 5 years following Appomattox grew by 100%. Though the coal industry as a whole expanded, bituminous coal production failed to increase during the conflict, while the copper industry's rate of growth was dramatically low, especially given its importance to war matériel production. Perhaps a more revealing ratio is the 22% increase in total American commodity output in the 1860s, compared to a 62% growth rate in both the 1850s and 1870s. Another striking comparison is the 3% decline in American output per capita in the 1860s, as against an average decennial increase of 20% for the balance of the period 1840–1900.

The war may also have exerted a negative influence on Northern industry in more generalized ways. The state of the wartime economy, which inspired the issuance of paper currency throughout the Union, produced a steady inflation, a general rise in commodity prices, and a decrease in purchasing power. It also gave rise to trade unions, work strikes, and other conditions considered injurious to industrial growth. By discouraging immigration, the war reduced a source of cheap labor. The conflict also helped unsettle business conditions by drawing off capital and labor from North and South alike, a trend whose impact on the economy lasted well into the 1870s. Predictions early in the war of a quick Union victory hindered industrial growth by making entrepreneurs wary of overexpanding. As late as Aug. 1862, the New York *Tribune* complained about "our paralyzed industry."

But wartime statistics, positive or negative, fail to tell the full story of the Civil War's impact on Northern industrialism. Perhaps the primary economic effect of this period of upheaval was to prepare the U.S. for an intense industrialization in the decades following 1865. The conflict helped do away with industry-stifling government regulation; nationalized the regional market system of antebellum years; created a generation of war-weary young men motivated by the acquisitive ethic; reduced the energy-sapping political strife that had adversely affected industrialism prior to 1861; and brought to long-term power a political party that favored business growth. Thus, regardless of the immediacy of its effects, the war contributed much to the long-term economic climate that made a reunited America the industrial giant of the 20th century. —EGL

"infernal machines." Any number of hidden explosive devices were called "infernal machines." In an age when gentlemen's rules were applied to war, land or sea mines, torpedoes, concealed bombs, or incendiary devices were thought cowardly. They first saw limited naval use by the Russians in the Crimean War. Land mines, live artillery shells with contact fuses buried just below the earth's surface, caused controversy when first used by Confederates at YORKTOWN, Va., in 1862. Confederate Brig. Gen. GABRIEL J. RAINS was lambasted by his own superiors for ordering their deployment. Federals were frightened and outraged by a "horological torpedo," or time-bomb, that destroyed Union docks at CITY POINT, Va., 9 Aug.

1864. Though Confederates later set up a "torpedo bureau" and Union naval personnel later adopted some torpedoes, the rank-and-file on both sides continued to think these devices diabolical. —JES

Ingalls, Rufus. USA b. Denmark, Maine, 23 Aug. 1818, Ingalls graduated 32d in the West Point class of 1843, joined the mounted rifles and dragoons, fought as a lieutenant in Mexican War engagements in New Mexico Territory, and, 12 Jan. 1848, as a captain, became an assistant quartermaster. He stayed in quartermaster service for the rest of his army career.

LC

After duty in the Far West Ingalls was stationed at FORT PICKENS, Fla., for the crisis of early 1861, sent north to the Army of the Potomac after the FIRST BATTLE OF BULL RUN, and made chief quartermaster in September. He remained the chief of Eastern supply throughout the war and, after promotion to major in the Regulars 12 Jan. 1862, became brigadier general of volunteers 23 May 1863 and brevet brigadier general of Regulars 6 July 1864. Lt. Gen. ULYSSES S. GRANT placed him in charge of supply June 1864, with responsibility for all armies operating against Richmond. In this capacity he built up the huge supply depot at CITY POINT, Va.

Ingalls was relieved of duty at City Point 9 May 1865, after being brevetted major general in the volunteers and Regulars 13 Mar. 1865. He retired from the army 1 July 1883 as quartermaster general and brigadier general, and died 15 Jan. 1893 in New York City. —JES

Invalid Corps. A great number of Civil War soldiers were disabled by weapons, disease, and accidents. Initially, the permanently disabled received medical discharges from the army, but later they remained in the service and performed noncombat duties, relieving other soldiers to fight.

In 1862 the Union army allowed chief medical officers to employ "convalescent wounded and feeble men" as nurses, cooks, and hospital attendants and subsequently to organize them into detachments. Unfortunately, these methods were inefficient, and many convalescents did not return to their combat units when well.

Therefore, in Apr. 1863 the U.S. War Department created an Invalid Corps of worthy disabled officers and men who were or had been in the army. Ridicule influenced the corps to exchange its sky blue uniform for one similar to those worn by the other soldiers. The corps formed 2 "battalions," the first for those who could bear arms and perform garrison duty and the second for the severely handicapped fit only for hospital service. Late in the war the surgeon general took command of the second battalion. Like the combat units, the Invalid Corps organized officers and men into companies and regiments.

Renamed the VETERAN RESERVE CORPS 18 Mar. 1864, it was abolished during summer 1866. Between 1863 and 1866 more than 60,000 individuals served in the organization and performed valuable services, including garrisoning fortifications and quelling an 1863 DRAFT RIOT in New York City.

The Confederacy established an Invalid Corps in 1864, in which officers and men disabled in the line of duty had to serve if they wished to receive pay. Also, if their physical condition improved sufficiently, they had to return to their combat unit. Unlike its Union counterpart, the Confederate Invalid Corps never organized companies and regiments, but a high percentage of its officers and men did perform worthwhile duties based on their disabilities and army requirements. —DEF

Iowa. In the years before the Civil War, Iowa played an important role in agitating for the emancipation of slaves, and many slaves found freedom through the Underground Railroad in the state, which had "stations" in Quaker towns. Abolitionist JOHN BROWN maintained headquarters at the Quaker village of Springdale, Iowa, for some years, and trained followers there.

When Pres. ABRAHAM LINCOLN called for troops in 1861, and Gov. SAMUEL J. KIRKWOOD announced that a regiment must be formed, 10 times the required number of Iowans offered themselves for enlistment. After that, until Sept. 1864, every call for military, political, and financial support for the Union was met with enthusiasm. By fall 1864, with the end of the war in sight, that enthusiasm had waned and the governor was forced to resort to the draft to supply the state quota of soldiers.

During the 4 years of war Iowans served with distinction in Union campaigns throughout the country. About one-half of all the men of military age in the state—more than 76,000—served in the army. There were 46 Iowa infantry regiments, with from 800 to 1,000 men in each regiment; 440 blacks in another regiment; 4 batteries of light artillery; 9 regiments of cavalry; and thousands of troops in replacement units. Iowa, in proportion to its population, supplied more men to the Union forces than any other state; few states suffered a higher percentage of lives lost. Of the 13,001 who died, 3,540 were killed or mortally wounded in battle, 515 died while prisoners of war, 8,498 died of disease (most of them while serving in the lower Mississippi Valley or in Georgia), and 448 died of accidents and other causes. More than 8,500 were seriously wounded. —PR

Irish Bend and Fort Bisland, La., engs. at. 13–14 Apr. 1863 These engagements took place during Maj. Gen. NATHANIEL P. BANKS's Teche River Campaign while he opposed forces of Confederate Maj. Gen. RICHARD TAYLOR. Banks had Brig. Gen. CUVIER GROVER move a force by transports across Grand Lake to Indian Bend, near Franklin, to attack enemy troops there. Meanwhile, the main Federal force moved against Bisland, below Franklin, to attack the Confederates.

On 10 Apr. Confederate Brig. Gen. ALFRED MOUTON arrived at Bisland. Finding entrenchments on the west side of the Teche but none on the east side, he impressed local blacks and sent them to work building fortifications until the early morning of the 13th. It was from the west bank of the Teche that the battle commenced, at daybreak, 13 Apr.

Taylor ordered his Texas Brigade to attack, then moved to the rear to direct his men there against the threat from Grover. Banks ordered his entire line to advance. During the action the Confederates used the gunboat *Diana,* which they had captured earlier, but the vessel was soon put out of action by engine damage from a shell. As infantry advanced on both sides of the Teche, heavy artillery fire forced the men to take cover. By evening the Federals were in position to charge the west bank, but Banks postponed the assault until the next morning. That night the Confederates evacuated Bisland, and the Federals found the works empty on the 14th.

Banks caught up with Taylor's force at Irish Bend (Nerson's Woods), where the Confederates were prepared and expecting an attack. Though outnumbered 5-to-1, the Confederates had the advantage of concealment, while the Federals were hindered by rough and swampy terrain. As at Bisland, a heavy exchange of artillery fire began the action. The Confederates charged, causing the Federals to fall back temporarily. The *Diana* arrived from Franklin, though still crippled from the earlier action. Taking advantage of delays and of Grover's indecision, Taylor withdrew his men to safety, then burned the only bridge that could be used to pursue them. The *Diana* and all the Confederate transports on the lower Teche were destroyed to prevent their capture. Though Banks lost an opportunity to destroy Taylor's army, the navy did better that day. On Grand Lake 3 Federal gunboats engaged and destroyed the ram *QUEEN OF THE WEST.* —NCD

Irish Brigade. USA The Civil War was America's first conflict in which the Catholic Irish were significant participants. In both the North and the South, they enthusiastically formed units and bravely battled for their respective sides.

Their most famous unit was "Meagher's Irish Brigade." Spawned by the Irish 69th New York State Militia Regiment right after FIRST BULL RUN, it originally contained the 63d, 69th, and 88th New York Volunteer regiments. The non-Irish 29th Massachusetts Regiment reinforced it during the PENINSULA CAMPAIGN, only to be traded to the IX Corps for the Irish 28th Massachusetts Regiment Nov. 1862. The Irish 116th Pennsylvania Regiment joined Oct. 1862. Despite these additions, the undersized brigade, its ranks depleted by many casualties, had difficulty remaining intact. Still, it survived as the 2d Brigade/ (Maj. Gen. Edwin V.) Sumner's Division/Army of the Potomac, later the 2d Brigade/1st Division/II Corps, until June 1864, when its New York regiments joined the 3d Brigade as the Consolidated Brigade/1st Division/II Corps. That Novem-

Officers of the Irish Brigade

USMHI

ber the Irish 2d Brigade was reconstituted, containing the 7th New York Heavy Artillery Regiment and the 28th, 63d, 69th, and 88th. The 4th New York Heavy Artillery Regiment replaced the 7th early in 1865.

The brigade's only commanding general was the Irish revolutionary THOMAS F. MEAGHER. Acting brigadiers included Robert Nugent, Patrick Kelly, Richard Byrnes, and Richard C. Duryea. Both Kelly and Byrnes were killed in action leading the brigade.

Such combat losses were understandable, for the Irish Brigade made some of the most gallant charges of the war: to the "BLOODY LANE" at ANTIETAM, toward Marye's Heights at FREDERICKSBURG, across the WHEATFIELD at GETTYSBURG. It was involved in virtually all the Army of the Potomac's major battles from SEVEN PINES to First Weldon Railroad. After being reconstituted, it engaged from Watkins' Farm to Cumberland Church. Following the GRAND REVIEW, its infantry mustered out June 1865, and the 4th left service that September.   —RJS

Iron Brigade, Confederate. *See* SHELBY'S IRON BRIGADE.

Iron Brigade of the West (Black Hat Brigade). USA In autumn 1861, in Washington, D.C., the 2d, 6th, and 7th Wisconsin and the 19th Indiana regiments were organized as a brigade, the only all-Western brigade in the Army of the Potomac; its first commander was Brig. Gen. RUFUS KING. When corps were created in 1862, it was assigned to the I Corps.

Brig. Gen. JOHN GIBBON became commander of the brigade May 1862, improving its training and discipline and giving it the black felt hats that came to symbolize the unit. The brigade's first major action was at GROVETON, 28 Aug. 1862, where it lost 751 men (33% of its strength). At SOUTH MOUNTAIN, 14 Sept. 1862, it lost 318 men (25%). Its heroic conduct on that day led the I Corps commander, Maj. Gen. JOSEPH HOOKER, to refer to it as his "iron brigade." At ANTIETAM 3 days later, the Iron Brigade lost another 348 men (42%).

In fall 1862 the 24th Michigan was added to the brigade, bringing much-needed reinforcements and preserving its all-Western character. The unit was only slightly engaged at FREDERICKSBURG and CHANCELLORSVILLE.

On 1 July 1863, the brigade was with the I Corps as it deployed to defend McPherson's Ridge and Seminary Ridge west and northwest of GETTYSBURG. In the heavy fighting that followed, it slowed the Confederate advance and thereby gained time for the deployment of other units. It paid a heavy price, losing 1,212 of its 1,883 men (65%); the 24th Michigan lost 80%, the 2d Wisconsin 77%, and the 19th Indiana 72%.

The battle of 1 July destroyed the Iron Brigade, but the name continued in use. Eastern regiments were added to the brigade, draftees and substitutes came into the ranks, and old regiments left the service as their time expired or they were consolidated with other units. Only the memory of the old brigade lingered.   —RMcM

Ironclad Oath. The Ironclad Oath originated in a stringent loyalty oath passed by the Federal Congress 2 July 1862. Largely because of Pres. ABRAHAM LINCOLN's conciliatory approach toward reconstructing the Confederate states and citizens, the oath had little effect during the war despite the heated debate it prompted in Congress. The oath as written into the Reconstruction Act of 23 Mar. 1867 called for allegiance to the U.S. government. While earlier loyalty oaths included only a pledge of future loyalty, Radical congressmen insisted on a pledge of past as well as future allegiance.

Subsequent Reconstruction enforcement acts complicated already onerous conditions by giving administering officers discretionary power to decide whether a resident of a former Confederate state, based on his past activities, was eligible to swear loyalty. Few Southerners could or would swear to "past allegiance," thus the majority of white Southern males were barred from the franchise and from holding political office. After 2 years of relatively mild RECONSTRUCTION, the Ironclad Oath embittered Southerners because it so effectively wrenched state governments from their control. The net of exclusion even entrapped Unionists who could not prove they had been faithful to the Federal government during the war. The oath could be waived on an individual basis by a two-thirds vote of Congress.   —PLF

ironclads. Though ironclad warships were already being built in France and Great Britain, the Civil War demonstrated conclusively their superiority over wooden warships, revolutionizing naval warfare. Because the South lacked the means of producing a navy equal to the North's wooden fleet, much of its limited resources were spent in building ironclads. In May 1861 Confederate Sec. of the Navy STEPHEN R. MALLORY requested Congress to support the building of an ironclad warship that could challenge the Federal BLOCKADE. A month later, Confederate Lt. JOHN M. BROOKE began working on a design for such a vessel. Though some naval traditionalists looked with disfavor on ironclads, the U.S. Congress made an important first step in their development by establishing a 3-member Ironclad Board, which examined proposals for an experimental ironclad, then made recommendations.

The South's first ironclads were designed to operate both on open sea and inland waters, reflecting the offensive strategy advocated by Mallory. The South's and North's first efforts at building ironclads resulted in the CSS *VIRGINIA* and the USS *MONITOR*. The superiority of an ironclad over wooden adversaries was dramatically illustrated when the *Virginia* went into action at HAMPTON ROADS, Va., 8 Mar. 1862. Then, on 9 Mar., the *Virginia* and the *Monitor* fought to a stand-off in one of the most important naval battles in American history. The lessons of Hampton Roads were obvious, and for the rest of the war both North and South concentrated on building ironclads. By mid-1862 Mallory had changed to a more realistic defensive strategy, resulting in smaller, shallow-draft ironclads built for river and harbor defense.

In all, about 50 ironclads were either laid down or contracted for within the Confederacy, but only 22 of these were actually commissioned and put into operation. The shortage of iron and lack of suitable engines greatly handicapped their completion, and continuous loss of waterways and ports to Northern forces led the Confederates themselves to destroy many of these ships, both finished and unfinished.

Though the ironclads used were unseaworthy, slow, and plagued by mechanical problems, they nevertheless contributed much to the South's war effort. The threat they posed led to "ram fever" in the North, an exaggerated fear that invincible Southern ironclads would soon break the BLOCKADE and move against Northern coastal cities. This fear was shared by the public and official Washington circles alike and resulted in the diversion of Federal vessels and troops to counter the menace.

It also led to "MONITOR FEVER" following the success of the *Monitor* at Hampton Roads. Some 60 monitor-type vessels were built by the North after *Monitor* I, varying greatly in size and design. 1 of these, the *NEW IRONSIDES*, was the most powerful ironclad built by the Federals and the only ocean-going armored cruiser to be completed during the war. Though the other ironclads were unsuited for blockade duty, they proved invaluable in operations on Western waters and against the South's harbor defenses.

Even before the *Virginia-Monitor* encounter, Federal ironclad gunboats (referred to as "POOK TURTLES" after their designer, Samuel M. Pook) had been hurriedly built and were contributing to Federal army and navy successes on the Mississippi and its tributaries. River steamers were also converted into ironclads and participated in the RIVER WAR.   —NCD

Isherwood, Benjamin Franklin.

Isherwood, Benjamin Franklin. USN b. New York, N.Y., 6 Oct. 1822. In 1844 Isherwood was appointed first assistant engineer in the newly established Corps of Engineers of the U.S. Navy. In 1848 he was promoted to chief engineer. In 1861, anticipating hostilities against FORT SUMTER, Navy Sec. GIDEON WELLES sent Isherwood to the Norfolk Navy Yard 11 Apr. to repair the engines of the USS *Merrimack* so that the ship could be brought to sea if the yard was threatened. Isherwood had it repaired and ready by 18 Apr., but 2 days later the yard was partially destroyed by withdrawing Federal forces. The *Merrimack* was among the vessels burned and sunk.

LC

In 1862 Isherwood became the first head of the new Bureau of Steam Engineering. His work involved directing the design and construction of all machinery connected with the new steam navy. Isherwood designed the *Wampanoag* class of ships especially for use on the Southern BLOCKADE. For a time these were the fastest ships afloat, capable of speeds up to 17.75 knots. By war's end the navy had expanded its fleet to include 600 new steam warships.

After serving 8 years as head of the Bureau of Steam Engineering, Isherwood turned his attention to the study of foreign navies and naval bases. He retired with the rank of commodore 6 June 1884 and was later promoted to rear admiral on the retired list. d. New York City, 19 June 1915.   —NCD

Island No. 10, Mo., Battle of.

Island No. 10, Mo., Battle of.   7 Apr. 1862   About 60 mi below Columbus, Ky., Confederates fortified bluffs overlooking the Mississippi River and constructed batteries on the eastern side of an island there, Island No. 10. At NEW MADRID, Mo., about 10 mi downriver, a few Confederate guns and boats protected the western approaches to the elongated peninsula area called New Madrid Bend. Created by the river, this neck of land provided ready communications with Confederate defenses along the crescent-shaped bend in the river where the island lay. Together, these defenses, manned by 7,000 Confederates, barred passage to Union troops and boats.

Opposing this formidable array was Maj. Gen. JOHN POPE's Army of the Mississippi and Flag Officer ANDREW H. FOOTE's

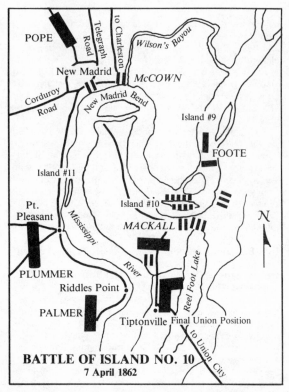

BATTLE OF ISLAND NO. 10
7 April 1862

flotilla of 6 gunboats and 11 mortar boats. At daylight 13 Mar. 1862 Pope's troops appeared before New Madrid, and that night Confederate Brig. Gen. JOHN P. MCCOWN evacuated the town and its defenses to the peninsula area across the river. River communications and means of supply were now cut off from above and below Island No. 10, and the generally impassable swamps east of New Madrid Bend essentially trapped the consolidated Confederate units.

With the arrival of the Federal gunboat flotilla above Island No. 10 on 17 Mar., a naval assault was attempted but defeated. Pope determined to attack the Confederates by crossing the river below New Madrid. A gunboat, the *CARONDELET*, ran past the Confederate batteries during a storm the night of 4 Apr.; another boat, the *Pittsburg,* ran past at 2 a.m. on the 7th; and Pope readied 4 steamers loaded with troops, which landed on the eastern shore about noon.

Confederate Brig. Gen. WILLIAM W. MACKALL, who had replaced McCown, found himself trapped and surrendered about 3,500 men with all their equipment and ordnance 8 Apr. The Mississippi was now opened as far south as Fort Pillow, Tenn.   —WS

Iuka, Miss., Battle of.

Iuka, Miss., Battle of.   19 Sept. 1862   Maj. Gen. STERLING PRICE's small Confederate Army of the West occupied Iuka, Miss., near the Tennessee border, early on 14 Sept. 1862. On Gen. BRAXTON BRAGG's instructions, Price had run from the town elements of Maj. Gen. WILLIAM S. ROSECRANS' force, believing they were bound for Middle Tennessee to reinforce Maj. Gen. DON CARLOS BUELL's Union army. His orders were to prevent Union troops in north Mississippi led by Maj. Gens.

U. S. GRANT, E.O.C. ORD, and Rosecrans from moving to Tennessee while Bragg campaigned there. With only 14,000 men, he was to call on Maj. Gen. EARL VAN DORN's Vicksburg garrison if needed.

Conversely, in his Corinth, Miss., headquarters northwest of Iuka, Grant feared Price's men would move north to reinforce Bragg's assaults on Buell. He planned to have Ord's 8,000-man force move on Price from Burnsville, 7 mi northwest of Iuka, and Rosecrans' 9,000 men march about 14 mi east from Jacinto to the city's southern outskirts for a coordinated attack. All elements were to arrive around Iuka the night of 18 Sept. and Ord's men to begin the battle early the next morning. Rosecrans' troops, smashing the Confederate left, would cut off Price's southern retreat route.

Early on the evening of the 18th, Price learned that Ord's men were marching on him from Burnsville. In a few hours he received orders from Van Dorn to remove his force southwest of Jacinto to Rienzi and form a joint command with Van Dorn at its head. Together they would campaign to West Tennessee. Price, not fully apprised of Rosecrans' march, decided to avoid battle with Ord and retreat west-southwest to Rienzi.

A portion of Rosecrans' force became lost on the march from Jacinto. While Ord was prepared for battle, Rosecrans could not take up his post until early afternoon on the 19th. From the Burnsville headquarters Grant changed plans, sending word to Rosecrans that Ord would attack only after Rosecrans began the action, thus preserving coordination. Meanwhile, Ord sent a message to Price calling on him to surrender. In the message Ord lied, saying Gen. ROBERT E. LEE's Eastern army had been smashed in Maryland and the war was effectively over. Discounting Ord's message, Price speeded evacuation plans. By early afternoon, as his first elements moved southwest of the city, they collided with Rosecrans' men. He decided Grant's and Ord's presence to the northwest was a ruse, pulled troops from that front to face Rosecrans, and started a pitched battle south of the city.

As more reinforcements were needed, elements of Confederate Brig. Gen. LEWIS H. LITTLE's division were called down from Ord's front. After Little was killed in the move, Brig. Gen. LOUIS HÉBERT assumed his command, assaulting Union Brig. Gen. CHARLES S. HAMILTON's division at the head of Rosecrans' force deployed across the Jacinto road 1.5 mi south of the city. Federals there were also to cover the southerly Fulton road, but Rosecrans, hesitant to split his force, left it unguarded.

All through the fighting on the 19th Ord sat northwest of Price, claimed he heard no fighting, and wondered at Rosecrans' whereabouts. This rare instance of ACOUSTIC SHADOW left Rosecrans to fight alone the entire afternoon. By evening only a light Confederate cavalry screen covered Ord's front. Price planned more fighting south of Iuka on the 20th.

Before daylight Hébert and Confederate Brig. Gen. DABNEY H. MAURY convinced their general that the force to the north was more substantial than assumed and provoked his order to disengage and retreat. Price's men marched south off the battlefield on the uncovered Fulton road, keeping their wagons far in front and maintaining a heavy rear guard. Pursuit by Rosecrans was pointless. Tangled terrain and poor roads reduced the chase to a shambles. Price joined Van Dorn and planned the Battle of CORINTH for the next month.

Confederate losses at Iuka totaled 1,516 in killed, wounded, captured, and missing; the Federals lost 790. There were mutual recriminations among the Federal commanders over Price's army eluding capture. Later Grant conceded that Rosecrans had been correct to keep his force together and leave the Fulton road uncovered, but Rosecrans always doubted Ord's claim that he had not heard the fight.   —JES

Iverson, Alfred, Jr. CSA b. Clinton, Ga., 14 Feb. 1829. The son of a U.S. senator, Iverson was reared in Columbus, Ga., and Washington, D.C. He dropped out of military school in Alabama Aug. 1847 to serve in the Mexican War as 2d lieutenant in a regiment of Georgia volunteers his father had helped equip. After the conflict he returned home and began a law career, then quit to become a professional soldier. In 1855 he was commissioned directly into the new 1st U.S. Cavalry, with which he served at posts including Fort Leavenworth, Kans., and Carlisle Barracks, Pa.

In Mar. 1861, Iverson resigned his commission to accept a captaincy in the PROVISIONAL ARMY OF THE CONFEDERATE STATES. Soon he went to Wilmington, N.C., to command troops guarding the Cape Fear River. That August he became colonel of the 20th North Carolina Infantry, having recruited the regiment almost singlehandedly. He and his men were sent to Virginia shortly before the SEVEN DAYS' CAMPAIGN, during which Iverson comported himself meritoriously at GAINES' MILL, where the 20th captured a Federal battery whose fire had enfiladed comrades' positions.

Wounded later in the campaign, Iverson recovered to fight at SOUTH MOUNTAIN and ANTIETAM, in the latter battle leading the brigade formerly under Brig. Gen. SAMUEL GARLAND, Jr. Named a brigadier general 1 Nov. 1862, he served competently 6 months later at CHANCELLORSVILLE. On 1 July 1863, however, his brigade was savaged by the Union I Corps northwest of GETTYSBURG, partly through errors made by its leader. Seeing most of his men killed, wounded, or captured, Iverson, in the words of one historian, "went to pieces and became unfit for further command." Though he recovered to perform well during the Confederate retreat from Pennsylvania—especially at Hagerstown, Md., 6 July—his record remained tarnished. Eventually he was exiled to Georgia, where he led state forces.

He recouped his reputation during the 1864 campaigning in the West, after being given a brigade in the cavalry corps of Maj. Gen. JOSEPH WHEELER. His most notable performance was his capture of Maj. Gen. GEORGE STONEMAN and large numbers of the latter's troopers during STONEMAN'S AND MCCOOK'S RAID that July.

When the conflict closed, Iverson went into business in Macon, Ga., moving to Florida in 1877 to manage orange groves near Kissimmee. Returning to his native state, he died in Atlanta 31 Mar. 1911.   —EGL

Ivy Mountain, Ky., eng. at. 8 Nov. 1861 Confederate Col. JOHN S. WILLIAMS, recruiting in southeast Kentucky, had 1,010 raw volunteers gathered around Piketon (or Pikesville), 28 mi southeast of Prestonburg. To entrap Williams, Union Brig. Gen. WILLIAM NELSON sent Col. Joshua W. Sill from the Louisa area, north-northeast of Prestonburg, south about 38 mi to the east of Piketon to cut off Williams' retreat across the nearby Virginia state line. Sill left Louisa late on the morning of 7 Nov. with a regiment, a small battalion, and some artillery. Nelson left Prestonburg at 5 a.m. 8 Nov. with 3 regiments, a volunteer battalion, and 2 artillery sections, marching straight for Piketon down the open state road.

Williams' men, armed with shotguns and flintlocks, were no

test for Nelson's force, and Williams only hoped for time to retreat to Virginia. Nelson's troops ran into enemy cavalry 8 mi into their march. Williams' horsemen skirmished and withdrew. Undeterred, the Federals marched toward Piketon with great speed. His evacuation incomplete, Williams decided to fight Nelson for time at a narrow gorge northeast of Piketon where the state road ran between Ivy Creek and the side of Ivy Mountain. As Nelson's Federals rounded a sharp, blind bend in the road, half of Williams' force opened fire on them, beginning a 1-hour-and-20-minute engagement fought mostly with small arms. Nelson's men outnumbered the Confederates, but since the road narrowed at the bend to a width of 7 ft, rein-

forcements could not be brought up and the artillery could not be effectively deployed.

When the fight broke off, Williams' Confederates felled trees across the road and burned bridges behind them, slowing Nelson's pursuit. The Federals marched 4 mi, then bivouacked in a heavy rain. Night, rain, and obstructions gave Williams time to pull out of Piketon and retreat to Abingdon, Va., 9 Nov. Sill's force from Louisa, too late to cut the retreat, skirmished with the last departing Confederates at Piketon on the 9th, then occupied the village. Nelson claimed he lost 6 killed and 24 wounded in the engagement; Confederate losses are undetermined. —JES

J

Jackson, Alfred Eugene. CSA b. Davidson Cty., Tenn., 11 Jan. 1807. After attending Washington College in Virginia and Greenville College in Illinois, Jackson farmed in East Tennessee, building a wholesale produce, mercantile, and shipping business.

LC

Enlisting in Confederate service in 1861 and made a staff major, Jackson was quartermaster under Brig. Gen. FELIX K. ZOLLICOFFER and later paymaster in Knoxville during its Confederate occupation. Jackson's service record is not as well documented as some Confederate officers. Fighting in contested East Tennessee through most of the war, often in guerrilla actions with local Union loyalists, he was kept in a political and military backwater. He was commissioned brigadier general 9 Feb. 1863 and given a composite brigade of infantry and cavalry that changed regularly throughout the next 18 months and at one time included a company of Cherokee Indians. Through early 1863 his force fought Union bushwhackers, pursued deserters, and raided in Kentucky and southwest Virginia. In Sept. 1863 it captured the entire 100th Ohio Infantry in a fight at Telford's Station, Tenn., supported Brig. Gen. JOHN S. WILLIAMS in the October retreat from BLUE SPRINGS, skirmished with Union Maj. Gen. AMBROSE E. BURNSIDE's troops along the East Tennessee & Virginia Railroad, and helped protect Lt. Gen. JAMES LONGSTREET's troops while they were in winter quarters.

Gen. BRAXTON BRAGG reported in May 1864 that an inspection of Jackson's command showed the men to be "in miserable order." He recommended their transfer to another command in western North Carolina and Jackson's relief, pending his assignment to a better-disciplined organization. Jackson's last assignment mentioned in the *OFFICIAL RECORDS* was to light staff duty under Maj. Gen. JOHN C. BRECKINRIDGE 23 Nov. 1864, which implies that he was in poor health.

Jackson lost his Tennessee property and assets during the war. In postbellum years he was a tenant farmer in Virginia until a special pardon by Pres. ANDREW JOHNSON partially restored some of his antebellum holdings. d. Jonesborough, Tenn., 30 Oct. 1889. In reports of the Southern Historical Society he is sometimes confused with WILLIAM "MUDWALL" JACKSON. —JES

Jackson, Claiborne Fox. war governor b. Fleming Cty., Ky., 4 Apr. 1806. During his brief Civil War career, the fiery governor of Missouri led a contingent of untrained, poorly equipped secessionists in a futile attempt to take the state out of the Union and into the Confederacy. Jackson had arrived in Missouri more than 40 years earlier and quickly established himself as a successful businessman. He compensated for a scanty formal education with practical experience acquired under his father-in-law's tutelage and with eloquent forcefulness as a public speaker. His political career spanned 26 years, beginning with election to the state legislature in 1836, and survived opposition from powerful Missouri Sen. Thomas Hart Benton to win the governorship in 1860 as an ardent proslavery Democrat.

At his inauguration in December, Jackson publicly avowed compromise but privately worked to encourage secession. The convention he called in February voted against leaving the Union and turned down his bill to authorize the formation of the Missouri State Guard. 2 months later, Jackson refused ABRAHAM LINCOLN's call for troops, declaring that the state would not supply men for the president's "unholy crusade" to hold the Southern states by force. Though formally issuing a statement of neutrality, the governor sanctioned the training of state militia at Camp Jackson, an encampment near the St. Louis arsenal, which Jackson wanted to place under state control. Federal authorities labeled the militia pro-secessionist, an assumption proven correct when Unionist militia and Regulars stormed the camp 10 May and found a large cache of ordnance supplied by the Confederacy.

That day, the legislature passed a bill to establish the State Guard, Jackson fled with his supporters from the capital at Jefferson City to Neosho, and a rump legislature voted to secede and join the Confederacy. For more than a year, the deposed governor claimed legitimacy for his "government in exile," but the claims carried no substance as Missouri remained largely under Union control. His troops eventually disbanded or were absorbed into the Confederate army. Jackson finally settled in Little Rock, Ark., where he died of illness 2 Dec. 1862. —PLF

Jackson, Henry Rootes. CSA b. Athens, Ga., 24 June 1820. The son of a college professor, Jackson grew up an esthete, with particular talent as a poet. Graduating near the top of the Yale class of 1839, he studied law, soon opened a practice in Savannah, and was appointed a U.S. district attorney. During the war in Mexico, he served as colonel of the 1st Georgia Infantry, then became a judge of his state's superior court. Attaining national prominence in politics, he was U.S. ambassador to Austria 1853–58 and in 1859 declined the chancellorship of the University of Georgia. He was a delegate to 2 Democratic conventions in 1860, became a presidential elector for JOHN C. BRECKINRIDGE, and early in 1861 served on the

Georgia secession commission.

When the Southern nation took shape, Jackson was tendered a judgeship in the Confederate courts in Georgia but soon resigned to accept a brigadier géneralship, an appointment dated 4 June 1861. He led a brigade under Gen. ROBERT E. LEE in the western Virginia campaigns that summer and fall, being conspicuous in action near CHEAT MOUNTAIN, where his well-drilled and well-disciplined command repulsed a Union attack 3 Oct.

LC

That December Gov. JOSEPH E. BROWN offered him a division of Georgia state troops, with the rank of major general. Against the wishes of Lee and JEFFERSON DAVIS, he accepted the appointment but returned to Confederate service after a CONSCRIPTION act of 1862 gave the Confederacy jurisdiction over his command. After serving as a volunteer aide on the staff of Brig. Gen. W.H.T. WALKER, Jackson was recommissioned a Confederate brigadier 23 Sept. 1863.

During the ATLANTA CAMPAIGN, he again served Governor Brown, this time by helping organize state troops to oppose Maj. Gen. WILLIAM T. SHERMAN. In mid-1864 he commanded the District of Georgia. After the city's fall, he joined Gen. JOHN BELL HOOD for the invasion of Tennessee and fought at FRANKLIN and NASHVILLE, commanding a brigade in the corps of Maj. Gen. BENJAMIN F. CHEATHAM. Captured in the latter battle, he was imprisoned in Massachusetts until July 1865. He then resumed his law practice in Georgia, was minister to Mexico 1885–86, directed railroad and banking companies, and from 1887 until his death in Savannah, 23 May 1898, was president of the state historical society. —EGL

Jackson, John King. CSA b. Augusta, Ga., 8 Feb. 1828. An honors graduate of South Carolina College, Jackson studied law and at 20 was admitted to the Augusta bar. In pre–Civil War years he commanded a local militia company, rising to lieutenant colonel of all militia units in his native city.

One of the first in his state to rally to the Confederate colors, Jackson became colonel of the 5th Georgia Infantry May 1861, commanding the regiment in camp at Pensacola, Fla. Early in October he led one of the 3 Confederate forces that attacked Union encampments on Santa Rosa Island. He left Pensacola as a brigadier general Feb. 1862 to head the post at

LC

Grand Junction, Tenn., where he helped organize the ARMY OF TENNESSEE and prepared it for its first large-scale action at SHILOH. On that field, Jackson led a brigade of Alabama and Texas infantry, plus a Georgia battery. He participated in the second wave of attack 6 Apr., then pressured the Union left flank near Wicker Field till virtually out of ammunition.

After Shiloh, Jackson was sent to Bridgeport, Ala., where he guarded railroad lines. He then served under Gen. BRAXTON BRAGG at STONE'S RIVER, where his command was destroyed 31 Dec. 1862 as the result of a disastrous attack against the far Union left. When Bragg retreated, the remnant of Jackson's brigade returned to Bridgeport. Soon afterward its leader was charged with protecting communication lines between Atlanta and Tullahoma, Tenn.

In Sept. 1863 Jackson's refurbished command served with distinction at CHICKAMAUGA in the division of Maj. Gen. BENJAMIN F. CHEATHAM. Here too it was savaged, losing 61% of its strength, the second greatest casualty rate of any Confederate brigade engaged. Nevertheless, its survivors fought ably 2 months later, helping check the assault that had broken the South's line on MISSIONARY RIDGE.

In 1864 Jackson performed skillfully in the first part of the ATLANTA CAMPAIGN. That July he and 2 of his regiments were sent to Charleston. Afterward he commanded the District of Florida, participated in the Siege of SAVANNAH, and near war's end guarded ordnance depots at Branchville, S.C. When peace came, he practiced law in Augusta, then served as a bank employee until his death from pneumonia in Milledgeville, Ga., 27 Feb. 1866. —EGL

Jackson, Richard Henry. USA b. Cty. Westmeath, Ireland, 14 July 1830. Coming to America with his family as a youth, Jackson enlisted at 21 in Company L/4th U.S. Artillery. He served in Florida against the Seminoles and fought various tribes on the Western plains, rising to first sergeant of his company Apr. 1860, then entering the commissioned ranks. By the start of the Civil War he was a 1st lieutenant in the 1st Artillery.

Jackson spent the early months of the conflict in Florida, as part of the relief expedition sent to FORT PICKENS. On 20 Feb. 1862, while in Pensacola harbor, he was promoted to captain of his company. Late that year and through most of

LC

1863 he was engaged in the Siege of CHARLESTON, where his Regular Army experience proved invaluable to his commander, Maj. Gen. David Hunter. In mid-Apr. 1863 Hunter named him an assistant inspector general and a lieutenant colonel of volunteers. Jackson spent several months as chief of artillery, X Corps, under Hunter's successor, Maj. Gen. QUINCY A. GILLMORE. He held that position when the corps was transferred from South Carolina to Virginia early in 1864 to operate against Richmond as part of the Army of the James.

In Virginia as well as in the Deep South, his Regular Army notions of discipline and deportment antagonized many volunteers. On one occasion, an observer reported that Jackson struck with his saber limber-riding members of the 1st Connecticut Battery "because he thought they were not sitting up straight enough." The man added: "Colonel Jackson . . . had but few friends among officers and men of the volunteer regiments."

Jackson's abrasive personality may have impeded his advancement. Though he rendered valuable service during the PETERSBURG CAMPAIGN and was given a division in the XXV

Corps early in 1865, he was not appointed a brigadier general until 6 weeks after Appomattox. Promotion came even more slowly after Jackson's return to the Regular Artillery Feb. 1866: not till 1880 did he rise to captain, and he made lieutenant colonel only 4 years before his death at Fort McPherson, Ga., 28 Nov. 1892. —EGL

Jackson, Thomas Jonathan "Stonewall." CSA b. Clarksburg, Va., 21 Jan. 1824. Known best by his nickname "Stonewall," Jackson was of Scotch-Irish descent. After his parents died in poverty when he was young, Jackson was raised by his uncle. Though ill-prepared for higher education, nonetheless he entered the U.S. Military Academy at West Point July 1842 and applied himself to his studies. His grades improved steadily each year, and in 1846 he graduated 17th in a class of 59.

USMHI

Assigned to Mexico, Jackson performed well at Vera Cruz, Cerro Gordo, and Chapultepec. Within 18 months of his assignment, he was brevetted major and received praise from Gen. WINFIELD SCOTT. During the late 1840s Jackson was assigned to forts in New York and Florida. In 1851 he became a professor of artillery and natural philosophy at VIRGINIA MILITARY INSTITUTE in Lexington, resigning from the army shortly thereafter. At the hanging of JOHN BROWN, 2 Dec. 1859, Jackson commanded the VMI Cadet Corps.

On 21 Apr. 1861, Jackson, a relatively unknown major in the Virginia Militia, was ordered to Richmond. Made a colonel of Confederate infantry and sent to Harpers Ferry, within a matter of weeks, 17 June 1861, he was elevated to brigadier general as part of Gen. JOSEPH E. JOHNSTON's army. At FIRST BULL RUN Jackson acquired his nickname when Brig. Gen. BARNARD E. BEE said, "There is Jackson standing like a stone wall." Due to his reputation in battle, he was elevated to major general 7 Oct. 1861.

On 5 Nov. 1861, Jackson assumed command in the SHENANDOAH VALLEY, a district of the Department of Northern Virginia. A winter raid against Romney Jan. 1862 proved futile, and controversy followed when Brig. Gen. WILLIAM WING LORING complained that Jackson had assigned Loring's men to outpost duty in bitter-cold weather. Still, his aggressive fighting and ability to move his FOOT CAVALRY quickly made him a hero in the Confederacy.

Jackson left his winter headquarters at Winchester several days after Johnston evacuated Manassas, 8–9 Mar., marking the beginning of the SHENANDOAH VALLEY CAMPAIGN of 1862. Taking the offensive, Jackson suffered heavy losses when he moved against Maj. Gen. JAMES SHIELDS at KERNSTOWN, but he managed to divert 3 Federal armies. At first criticized, he later received praise for keeping in western Virginia significant numbers of troops that might otherwise have been sent to aid Maj. Gen. GEORGE B. MCCLELLAN's unsuccessful advance on Richmond during the PENINSULA CAMPAIGN.

From 17 Apr. to 12 May, Jackson worked closely with Gen. ROBERT E. LEE, devising a plan to attack Brig. Gen. NATHANIEL P. BANKS's troops and prevent them from joining Maj. Gen. IRVIN

MCDOWELL in his movement toward Fredericksburg to reinforce McClellan. On 8 May, as McClellan's army advanced toward Richmond, Jackson made an initial attack against Maj. Gen. JOHN C. FRÉMONT's army west of Staunton. Gen. Joseph E. Johnston, Jackson's commander, thought Banks was too strong to be attacked and thus ordered Jackson not to strike as planned. Certain of success, Jackson appealed directly to Richmond for permission to make his assault. With Lee's approval, on 23 May 1862 Jackson ordered a pivotal attack against Banks at FRONT ROYAL, driving Banks's forces back across the Potomac. Early in June he defeated Frémont at CROSS KEYS and Shields at PORT REPUBLIC. Historians cite the maneuvers in Jackson's Valley Campaign as some of the finest examples of military strategy and deployment.

In May 1862, after Johnston was wounded at SEVEN PINES, Lee assumed command of the forces around Richmond, reorganizing them into the Army of Northern Virginia. Jackson and his command were transferred to the Richmond area, arriving by train 23 June to fight in the SEVEN DAYS' CAMPAIGN. Fatigue and unfamiliarity with the terrain prevented him from attacking Federal troops at MECHANICSVILLE as Lee had planned, but on 27 June his men fought well at GAINES' MILL and on the 29th they pursued McClellan to WHITE OAK SWAMP. There Jackson's physical exhaustion affected his ability to direct troops. His failure to cross the swamp as Lee had ordered impaired Lee's plan to corner McClellan at Glendale 30 June.

After several inconsequential engagements, Lee and Jackson conferred 24 Aug. 1862 to plan an offensive against Maj. Gen. JOHN POPE at Manassas Junction. With 20,000 of his men, Jackson traveled 51 mi in 2 days, destroying Pope's base 27 Aug. 1862. Regrouping at GROVETON, some 6 mi northwest of Manassas, Jackson held off Federal forces in fierce fighting 28–29 Aug. By holding and then slowly deploying his reserve, he skillfully resisted Federal attacks and ultimately aided in driving Pope back to Washington after the Union commander's defeat at SECOND BULL RUN.

On 15 Sept. 1862, Jackson led the advance effort in capturing HARPERS FERRY, taking 12,520 prisoners. He and his men then marched rapidly to ANTIETAM, where their hard fighting saved Lee from being overwhelmed by an unexpectedly large Union force. On 10 Oct. 1862, Jackson was promoted to lieutenant general and was given command of the II Corps in the Army of Northern Virginia. At the Battle of FREDERICKSBURG, 13 Dec., he led the right wing of the army to victory.

Jackson's forces wintered at Moss Neck on the Rappahannock River, near Fredericksburg. Devoted to his family, Jackson took leave to visit his wife and see his infant daughter for the first time. News that 134,000 Federal troops were crossing the Rappahannock on both sides of Fredericksburg cut short his leave 29 Apr. 1863.

Dividing his forces, Jackson sent a contingent to defend against Maj. Gen. JOHN SEDGWICK's left wing while taking the majority of his men into the Wilderness near Spotsylvania 30 Apr. Joining Lee, he aided in stopping Maj. Gen. JOSEPH HOOKER's advance down the Rappahannock toward Fredericksburg 1 May. The Federals were driven back to CHANCELLORSVILLE. That night Lee and Jackson decided to split the army again, Lee staying at Chancellorsville to face Hooker's front and Jackson making a sweeping flank movement around Hooker's right to attack from the rear. The morning of 2 May Jackson completed his famous flank march around the Federal right and routed the Federal XI Corps.

This, one of the most dramatic victories in the war, was marred by tragedy when in the faint light of dusk some of Jackson's own men mistakenly fired at him. Badly wounded, he was carried to a nearby home, where late that night doctors amputated his left arm. Though he rallied briefly, his condition deteriorated, complicated by pneumonia. He died 10 May, depriving Lee of a brilliant military leader just 25 months into the war. —JDK

Jackson, William Hicks. CSA b. Paris, Tenn., 1 Oct. 1835, Jackson attended West Tennessee College, received appointment to West Point, and graduated 38th in the class of 1856. He fought in Texas and New Mexico Indian campaigns before resigning his lieutenant's commission 16 May 1861 to become a Confederate artillery captain.

LC

Jackson served briefly in Kentucky, then, as a volunteer on Brig. Gen. GIDEON J. PILLOW's staff, fought with the 11th Louisiana Infantry in the Nov. 1861 Battle of BELMONT, where his horse was riddled and he was badly wounded in the fight. After a lengthy recovery, he accepted a commission as colonel of the 1st Tennessee Cavalry and assignment to a string of excellent commands. From 1862 he served under Maj. Gen. EARL VAN DORN, Gen. JOSEPH E. JOHNSTON, Lt. Gen. STEPHEN D. LEE, Maj. Gen. JOSEPH WHEELER, Lt. Gen. JOHN B. HOOD, and Lt. Gen. NATHAN BEDFORD FORREST.

Known to his troops as "Red," Jackson distinguished himself in the HOLLY SPRINGS RAID, won promotion to brigadier general 29 Dec. 1862, campaigned in Middle Tennessee, and, following Van Dorn's murder, was sent to the VICKSBURG theater. After taking part in Johnston's efforts to relieve Vicksburg in 1863, he commanded a cavalry division under S. D. Lee in the Department of Mississippi, Alabama, and East Louisiana and fought Federal infantry during the Feb. 1864 MERIDIAN CAMPAIGN. Assigned to Wheeler's command during the ATLANTA CAMPAIGN, Jackson participated in the battle of KENNESAW MOUNTAIN and suffered an embarrassing personal defeat at LOVEJOY'S STATION, Ga., in Aug. 1864. He took 2,000 cavalry to Tuscumbia, Ala., in October to join Hood's command for the FRANKLIN AND NASHVILLE CAMPAIGN. Made commander of Hood's cavalry for that campaign, Forrest assigned Jackson some peripheral service, sent him to demonstrate around Murfreesboro, Tenn., during the Battle of Nashville, and placed him in the Confederate rear guard for the retreat to Alabama. Thereafter, Jackson held divisional command under Forrest in the final campaigns and took part in a series of hot engagements during Union Maj. Gen. JAMES H. WILSON'S RAID TO SELMA.

In peacetime, Jackson's years on horseback served him well. He became a nationally known breeder of thoroughbred horses and from his Belle Meade stables produced champions Bonnie Scotland, Iroquois, Inspector, and Great Tom. d. at his farm near Nashville, Tenn., 30 Mar. 1903. —JES

Jackson, William Lowther. CSA b. Clarksburg, western Va., 3 Feb. 1825. A lawyer, commonwealth attorney, judge,

state legislator, and lieutenant governor of Virginia, Jackson had a distinguished antebellum career. When civil war began, he resigned as judge of the 19th judicial circuit, enlisting as a private in the Confederate army.

LC

He soon received a commission as colonel of the 31st Virginia and led the regiment in the summer and fall 1861 campaigning of Brig. Gen. ROBERT S. GARNETT in western Virginia. Following this disastrous Confederate operation, he joined the staff of his second cousin, Maj. Gen. THOMAS J. "STONEWALL" JACKSON, serving his famous kinsman in the SHENANDOAH VALLEY, SEVEN DAYS', CEDAR MOUNTAIN, SECOND BULL RUN, ANTIETAM, and FREDERICKSBURG campaigns. On 17 Feb. 1863, Jackson received authorization to recruit a regiment for operations within the Union lines in western Virginia. In April he was elected colonel of a new command, the 19th Virginia Cavalry. He and his unit then joined the brigade of Brig. Gen. ALBERT G. JENKINS, who operated in western Virginia, the Shenandoah Valley, and southwestern Virginia. During 1863 Jenkins' brigade rode on several raids, with Jackson commanding his regiment and acting as the brigade's adjutant general.

Jackson saw considerable duty in the various campaigns of 1864. He fought at CLOYD'S MOUNTAIN 9 May, assisted in the defense of Lynchburg in June, and commanded a brigade during Lt. Gen. JUBAL A. EARLY's July raid on Washington (*see* EARLY'S WASHINGTON RAID). Jackson's performance as a cavalry officer had earned him, justifiably or not, the derisive nickname of "Mudwall" in reference to his cousin. During the late summer and fall his brigade fought at Winchester, Fisher's Hill, Tom's Brook, and Cedar Creek. On 19 Dec. 1864 he received his promotion to brigadier general.

When the war ended in Virginia, Jackson refused to surrender. He journeyed west, finally receiving a parole in Brownsville, Tex., 26 July. The unreconstructed Confederate temporarily emigrated to Mexico, returning to West Virginia, where he learned that ex-Confederates were prohibited from practicing law. He moved to Kentucky and gained appointment as a jurist, remaining on the bench until his death in Louisville 24 Mar. 1890. —JDW

Jackson, Miss., eng. at. 14 May 1863 On 9 May 1863, at Tullahoma, Tenn., Confederate Gen. JOSEPH E. JOHNSTON received orders from the War Department to take command of military affairs in Mississippi. He left immediately to relieve Lt. Gen. JOHN C. PEMBERTON. On 13 May, 50 mi east of Jackson, Miss., Johnston received word that elements of the Union XV and XVII corps under Maj. Gens. WILLIAM T. SHERMAN and JAMES B. MCPHERSON were moving toward Jackson to cut the railroad leading west to VICKSBURG. When Johnston arrived in Jackson later that day, commander Brig. Gen. JOHN GREGG told him that just 6,000 Confederates held the town. Johnston wired Sec. of War JAMES A. SEDDON, "I am too late," and shortly before 3 a.m., 14 May, ordered the evacuation of Jackson. Gregg was to hold the town until evacuation was complete.

McPherson's XVII Corps column marched southeast from

Clinton; Sherman's XV Corps column traveled northwest from Mississippi Springs. Near 9 a.m., 3 mi northwest of Jackson on the Clinton road, McPherson's force, hiking in heavy rain, collided with a brigade and artillery battery commanded by Col. Peyton H. Colquitt. At 10 Sherman's troops hit resistance on the road southwest of town at a bridge crossing a tributary of the Pearl River. Stiff Confederate opposition, the rain, and a poor line of Southern trenches in front of Sherman delayed heavy fighting, but only until 11. The rain stopped and Brig. Gen. MARCELLUS M. CROCKER's XVII Corps troops attacked Colquitt's force on the Clinton road, driving it southeast to the intersection of the Clinton and Robinson roads. Gregg dispatched Col. Robert Farquharson from Jackson to feint at McPherson's left, a move the Federals fended off. Sherman's batteries drove back Col. Albert P. Thompson's Southerners from the bridge to trenches in their rear. Troops of the 95th Ohio probed Thompson's left and struck his rear as Confederates in the northwest and southwest pulled in closer to the town.

Between 2 and 3 p.m., word from Johnston reached Gregg that the bulk of the men and matériel from Jackson were on the road to Canton, north of town on the Mississippi Central Railroad line. Gregg ordered his men to disengage and followed Johnston north. Federals entered Jackson, found it empty, and at 4 p.m. Maj. Gen. U.S. GRANT, traveling as an observer with Sherman's troops, held a victory celebration in the Bowman House hotel a block north of the abandoned state capitol building.

Johnston's evacuation of Jackson, then and now, was called a strategic blunder. Reinforcements were available; had Johnston chosen to delay, by dawn, 15 May, he could have had 12,000 men to resist a Federal force estimated at 20,000. Lieutenant General Pemberton's troops, at the Federals' backs, could have attacked, placing Sherman and McPherson in a vise. Instead, the Federals were able to burn much of the town and destroy rail connections on the Southern Railroad of Mississippi, the Mississippi Central, and the New Orleans, Jackson, & Great Northern lines. This further isolated Vicksburg and made siege likely.

Confederate losses at this engagement were light, estimated by Gregg at 200 from all causes. Sherman claimed 250 Confederate prisoners were taken, while total Federal losses were 42 killed, 251 wounded, and 7 missing.   —JES

Jackson, Miss., Siege of. 10–16 July 1863 On 1 July 1863, after time had run out for the defenders of VICKSBURG, Gen. JOSEPH E. JOHNSTON put his 32,000-man army in motion to go to their relief. He spent several days searching for lightly guarded crossings of the Big Black River, but Maj. Gen. WILLIAM T. SHERMAN, sent by Maj. Gen. U. S. GRANT to guard the approaches to the army's rear, frustrated his effort.

The surrender of Vicksburg enabled Grant to reinforce Sherman, and 5 July Sherman advanced to attack Johnston. Covered by cavalry, Johnston abandoned the line of the Big Black, retreating into earthworks covering the approaches to Jackson. The Union army crossed the river on a broad front. Columns tramped east; advance guards clashed with Confederate cavalry. Clinton was occupied on the 9th, and the next day Sherman's 3 corps closed in on Jackson.

On 12 July, Union Brig. Gen. JACOB G. LAUMAN's division of the XIII Corps was directed to make a forced reconnaissance of the defenses between the New Orleans railroad and the Pearl River. Charging into an ABATIS, one of his brigades was

cut to pieces, losing more than one-half of its 1,000 men.

While awaiting arrival of a wagon train with artillery ammunition, en route from Vicksburg, Sherman's troops inched their way closer to the perimeter of Jackson. Johnston sent his cavalry sweeping to the west to intercept the train, but the Confederate horse soldiers failed, and the wagons arrived at Sherman's headquarters. Apprised of this, Johnston ordered his army to prepare to abandon the siege lines.

Under cover of darkness on 16 July, the Confederates evacuated Jackson, crossed the Pearl River, and retired to Morton. Sherman's army occupied the city on the 17th, and 1 division followed Johnston's rear guard as far as Brandon. After wreaking additional havoc on the railroads and city, Sherman's columns were recalled and returned to the Vicksburg area 25 July.
                                                              —ECB

James, Union Army of the. The Union's X Corps joined the XVIII Corps to form Maj. Gen. BENJAMIN F. BUTLER's Army of the James/Department of Virginia and North Carolina in Apr. 1864. It boldly sailed to BERMUDA HUNDRED in May but captured neither Richmond nor Petersburg. Trounced at the SECOND BATTLE OF DREWRY'S BLUFF, it was "corked in the bottle" at Bermuda Hundred, where it was joined by Brig. Gen. AUGUST V. KAUTZ's raiding cavalry division.

Butler's army secured Bermuda Hundred but failed to take PETERSBURG 9 June. The XVIII Corps, returning from detached service at COLD HARBOR, captured Petersburg's outer defenses but not the city 15 June. Nor could the X Corps long hold the Howlett line, the Confederate defense line across Bermuda Hundred Neck. In the ensuing Siege of Petersburg, Butler administered all Department of Virginia and North Carolina units but initially directed only the one corps at Bermuda Hundred, Dutch Gap, Deep Bottom, and downriver garrisons. Maj. Gen. GEORGE G. MEADE, commanding the Army of the Potomac, controlled the other corps and Kautz while they were detached south of the Appomattox and during the July-Aug. strikes.

Not until 29 Sept. was the army reunited under Butler's command. Its great CHAFFIN'S FARM breakthrough imperiled Richmond, but the secessionists' bravery and Union blunders saved the city. Butler's army thereafter had its own Virginia peninsula–Bermuda Hundred sector. Butler repulsed Southern counterattacks 30 Sept. and 7 Oct. but was checked 13 and 27 Oct.

The Army of the James reshuffled into the white XXIV Corps and largely black XXV Corps 3 Dec. Greater change occurred 8 Jan. 1865, when Butler was relieved after his Fort Fisher fiasco (see BUTLER'S NORTH CAROLINA EXPEDITION). Maj. Gen. ALFRED H. TERRY's 2 Army of the James divisions stormed that stronghold 15 Jan. (see FORT FISHER, N.C., EXPEDITION TO). The army lost those troops and North Carolina too, becoming the Army of the James/Department of Virginia 31 Jan.

New commander Maj. Gen. E.O.C. ORD led 4 of his 7 divisions back to Petersburg for the final fighting there. Then his forced march with the XXIV and attached V corps provided the weight needed to trap Gen. ROBERT E. LEE at APPOMATTOX Court House. The army occupied Virginia until effectively discontinued when Terry succeeded to command at the Department of Virginia 14 June 1865.   —RJS

James, Union Military Division of the. Union authorities created the Military Division of the James 19 Apr. 1865, 10

days after the war ended in Virginia. The military division encompassed the Union Department of Virginia and the parts of North Carolina not occupied by the command of Maj. Gen. WILLIAM T. SHERMAN. Maj. Gen. HENRY W. HALLECK, former Union chief of staff, commanded the division from its headquarters at Fort Monroe until 7 June 1865, when the division was discontinued. —JDW

James River bridge. By dawn, 13 June 1864, the trenches of the Army of the Potomac before COLD HARBOR lay empty. Under the Virginia night, the Federals abandoned their works, swinging south and east toward the James River. 40 days of continuous harrowing combat between the Federals and the Army of Northern Virginia had resolved little, and produced mounting casualties. Lt. Gen. ULYSSES S. GRANT had decided to shift the area of operations to the south side of the James, against the vital Southern railroad center of Petersburg.

It was a bold, dangerous movement in the face of the formidable Confederates of Gen. ROBERT E. LEE. If the Federals were to capture the weakly defended railroad junction, the march demanded celerity and the construction of a PONTOON BRIDGE across the river. Planning for such a bridge had been under way for 2 months, but it was a prodigious undertaking, an engineering feat the army had never attempted before.

Early 14 June a team of 450 engineers, directed by Capt. George H. Mendell, began the work. At the site selected, between Windmill Point and Fort Powhatan, the James sprawled to a width of 2,100 ft and was 15 fathoms deep in midstream, with a strong tidal current. Working from both banks, the engineers linked together 101 pontoons in 8 hours. 3 schooners, anchored in the deep water, supported the central section. When completed, the James River bridge was the longest continuous pontoon bridge in military history.

Late on the 14th Grant's legions began crossing the bridge. The steady tread of marching men continued through the night and on into the 15th. By morning, all the infantry and 4 batteries had filed over to the south bank. The final elements of the army crossed late on 18 June. The engineers then dismantled the bridge into 3 giant rafts and floated them downstream to CITY POINT, where Grant had established headquarters. Though Grant's brilliant maneuver failed to capture Petersburg because of faulty generalship and staff work, the James River bridge was a marvelous accomplishment. —JDW

Jenkins, Albert Gallatin. CSA b. Cabell Cty., Va., 10 Nov. 1830, Jenkins was a distinguished attorney and U.S. congressman before the war. An 1848 graduate of Jefferson College in Pennsylvania and an 1850 graduate of Harvard Law School, he practiced law in Charlestown, Va., until his election to the House of Representatives in 1856. Reelected twice, he resigned his seat Apr. 1861 to recruit for the Confederacy a cavalry company in western Virginia.

Appointed lieutenant colonel of the 8th Virginia Cavalry, Jenkins soon assumed the colonelcy of the regiment, participating in numerous raids in the Allegheny Mountain region of western Virginia throughout 1861. In Feb. 1862 he was elected to the Confederate Congress, holding his seat until 5 Aug., when he secured promotion to brigadier general. Later that month Jenkins led his new brigade of home guards, guerrillas, and regular cavalrymen on a 500-mi raid through western Virginia and into Ohio.

In summer 1863 Jenkins' brigade transferred to the Army of

Northern Virginia to participate in the GETTYSBURG CAMPAIGN. His brigade led the army's advance, capturing Chambersburg, Pa., and threatening Harrisburg, the state capital. In the 3-day battle at GETTYSBURG, Jenkins suffered a wound that incapacitated him briefly and in autumn he returned to his command in West Virginia. On 9 May 1864, at CLOYD'S MOUNTAIN, he commanded a patchwork defense that contested the advance of Brig. Gen. GEORGE

USMHI

CROOK's Union force. In this vicious engagement, Jenkins, while rallying his broken lines, again fell wounded. A Union surgeon amputated his arm, but he never rallied, dying 21 May 1864. —JDW

Jenkins, Micah. CSA b. Edisto Island, S.C., 1 Dec. 1835. Of Welsh stock, Jenkins was the son of a wealthy planter. In 1855 he graduated at the head of his class from the South Carolina Military Academy, then helped establish a military school of his own at Yorkville.

Jenkins left his academy in mid-1861 to join the Confederate army and fight for a cause in which he passionately believed. His military training helped him in raising and drilling the 5th South Carolina Infantry, of which he was elected colonel. Sent to Virginia and assigned to the brigade of Brig. Gen. DAVID R. JONES, the 5th held the far Confederate right at FIRST BULL

GG

RUN and participated in an ill-timed attack on enemy artillery late in the fight. By the latter part of the year, Jenkins had replaced Jones in command of the brigade.

By early 1862 Jenkins was highly regarded as a troop commander, especially by his division leader, Maj. Gen. JAMES LONGSTREET. He was also popular with his troops. One of his officers remarked that "whatever could be done by untiring energy in camp and on the field, Jenkins was sure to accomplish. He was noted for his cheerfulness, and usually wore a bright smile, which attended him even on the battle field." He solidified his standing in the Army of Northern Virginia by fine performances in the PENINSULA CAMPAIGN, especially at WILLIAMSBURG, SEVEN PINES, GAINES' MILL, and WHITE OAK SWAMP, where his troops captured a full battery by an attack notable for its boldness, energy, and tactical skill.

On 22 July 1862 Jenkins was raised to brigadier general. His outstanding career continued at CEDAR MOUNTAIN, SECOND BULL RUN, FREDERICKSBURG, Suffolk, and, after he was sent west late in 1863, CHATTANOOGA and KNOXVILLE. Returning to Virginia for the spring operations, he was at Longstreet's side when the army entered the second day's battle in the WILDERNESS. Early on 6 May 1864, riding ahead of their corps on a reconnaissance, both generals were mistaken for Federals and fired on by their troops. Longstreet fell wounded and Jenkins took a bullet through the brain, dying a few hours later. Mourned by the entire Army of Northern Virginia, he was buried in Charleston. —EGL

Jenkins' Ferry, Ark., eng. at. 30 Apr. 1864 Jenkins' Ferry was the final blow against the Union army's CAMDEN EXPEDITION through Arkansas, one that would clear the way for a Confederate invasion of Missouri.

Though Maj. Gen. FREDERICK STEELE had reached his initial goal, the town of Camden, he learned 26 Apr. that Lt. Gen. E. KIRBY SMITH and Maj. Gen. STERLING PRICE had joined their forces, and Brig. Gen. JAMES F. FAGAN's troops had captured and destroyed a wagon train on its way from Camden to Pine Bluff. At dawn the next morning, the Federals began a retreat toward Little Rock, and the Confederates retook Camden.

As soon as his men had constructed a PONTOON BRIDGE, Kirby Smith crossed the river in pursuit of Steele, covering 52 mi in 46 hours through steady rain. It would be a mudbath for both sides. From dusk until midnight the Confederates rested, hoping that Fagan would catch up with the Federal front. But he learned of Steele's retreat too late, and the Southerners had to settle for a rear assault. Throughout the morning hours they marched, until before dawn Brig. Gen. JOHN S. MARMADUKE's advance column encountered Federal pickets 2 mi from Jenkins' Ferry. They had stumbled onto the main body of Steele's army, waiting to cross the Saline River. Steele had cleverly posted 4,000 men in a defensive position with both flanks protected. For most of the morning and into the afternoon the shooting continued as the Federals slowly moved across the river on a pontoon bridge. Finally, Steele withdrew his rear guard and crossed the river uncontested, the weary Confederates content to allow the retreat.

Federal troops suffered 528 casualties at Jenkins' Ferry, Confederate losses amounted to 443. By putting an end to the Federal Camden Expedition, Southerners inflicted a severe setback on the Union's Western armies. —FLS

Jericho Mills, Va., eng. at. 23 May 1864 *See* NORTH ANNA RIVER, VA., BATTLE OF.

Joe Brown's Pikes. Hard-pressed to furnish enough weapons to arm his militia and volunteers, Gov. JOSEPH E. BROWN of Georgia promoted a simple, efficient, and relatively inexpensive form of weaponry. On 20 Feb. 1862 he appealed to state mechanics to produce 10,000 pikes, each to carry an 18-in. knife atop a staff 6 ft long. Brown saw this as an improvement over conventional small arms, noting that while the latter might misfire or prove inaccurate, the "short range pike . . . wielded by a stalwart patriot's arm, never fails to fire, and never wastes a single load." The governor expected pikes to be particularly useful in following up a victory: "let the pursuit be rapid, and if the enemy throw down their guns and are likely to outrun us . . . keep close at their heels, till each man has hewed down at least one of his adversaries."

By the close of 1862 Brown had purchased some 7,100 pikes, with staffs made of ash or hickory and blades of polished steel. However, partially owing to the ridicule of critics who considered such weapons impractical as well as anachronistic, fewer than 1,300 were issued to Georgians. Rarely used in the field, they were chiefly notable as a symbol of Brown's fondness for the warfare of antiquity. —EGL

"Johnny Shiloh." *See* CLEM, JOHN LINCOLN "JOHNNY."

Johnson, Adam Rankin. CSA b. Henderson, Ky., 8 Feb. 1834. In 1854 Johnson migrated to Texas and settled near Austin, working as a surveyor, Indian scout, guide, and contractor for the Overland Mail stagecoach company until the Civil War. From a Unionist family, Johnson returned to Kentucky to enlist in Confederate service. En route, at Hopkinsville, he met Col. NATHAN BEDFORD FORREST, who enlisted Johnson as a scout, taking him to an engagement at Sacramento, Ky., and action at FORT DONELSON, Tenn., Feb. 1862.

Johnson escaped capture in the fall of Donelson, continued scouting, and in early summer 1862 was recruiting troops

USMHI

around his hometown. Following a 30 June affair at Henderson, where he and 2 companions frightened off local militia, Johnson was accused of outlawry, the citizens believing he carried no Confederate commission; it is now supposed that he was a captain. In another ruse he routed a Federal cavalry regiment near Madisonville, Ky., 5 July. On 18 July, with a small force, he crossed the Green River north into Indiana, burning and pillaging the Federal arsenal at NEWBURGH and quelling resistance by displaying 2 cannon, with which he threatened to shell the town. Johnson's force escaped to Kentucky, later revealing that the illusory cannon were lengths of stovepipe laid across wagon wheels and axles; thus Johnson was nicknamed "Stovepipe." He was promoted to colonel Dec. 1862 to rank from 13 Aug., then joined Brig. Gen. JOHN HUNT MORGAN's command, participating in all his operations through his July 1863 Ohio raid (*see* MORGAN'S OHIO RAID). Near the end of this raid, Johnson eluded capture, swimming to freedom across the Ohio River 19 July.

Assuming his own command, and commissioned brigadier general as from 1 June 1864, he was accidentally shot and permanently blinded by his own troops in action at Grubb's Cross Roads, Ky., 21 Aug. 1864. Captured and briefly held prisoner at FORT WARREN, Boston harbor, he was exchanged. Despite his disability, he refused to resign from Confederate service, instead surrendering himself with others near Macon, Miss., Apr. 1865.

Postwar, Johnson returned to Texas, becoming prominent in local affairs, founding the town of Marble Falls, and dictating a history, *The Partisan Rangers of the Confederate States Army* (1904). d. Burnet, Tex., 20 Oct. 1922. —JES

Johnson, Andrew. war governor b. Raleigh, N.C., 29 Dec. 1808. Johnson moved with his family to eastern Tennessee in 1826. Without formal schooling, he nevertheless opened and successfully managed a tailor shop in Greeneville that provided him the means to accumulate a small estate.

Before Johnson was 21, he organized a workingman's party that twice elected him alderman, then mayor of Greeneville. He was elected to the state legislature in 1835 to represent the district comprising Greene and Washington counties. Defeated for reelection in 1837, he ran again and won in 1839; in 1841 he was elected state senator. Self-educated, Johnson retained a roughness of demeanor that helped him win the loyalty of Tennessee mountaineers and small farmers whose causes he outspokenly championed in Congress as their representative 1843–53. Johnson became governor of Tennessee in 1853 and served until he was again elected to national office in 1856, this time as a U.S. senator.

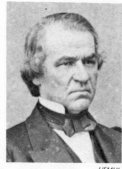

USMHI

After Fort Sumter, June 1861, Tennesseans, led by those in the central and western parts of the state, approved secession and embraced the Confederacy. When counties in the eastern section, adhering to the Union, tried to secede from the state, they were stopped by Confederate forces. By early 1862 Tennessee was the major battleground in the Western theater. Union armies in mid-February captured Forts Henry and Donelson (*see* FORTS HENRY AND DONELSON CAMPAIGN) and, within days, the Federals occupied Nashville.

A firm Unionist, Johnson refused to abide by the state's decision to secede and retained his Senate seat, supporting measures suppressing the rebellion. When Union Pres. ABRAHAM LINCOLN in Mar. 1862 sought to appoint a military governor of Tennessee, Johnson seemed the ideal choice.

With instructions to reestablish Federal authority in the state, Johnson remained in office for nearly 3 years. His authority extended, at first, only over central and western Tennessee, areas in which Confederate forces had been subdued by the Federals but where Confederate sentiments were still the most pronounced. Despised there, the governor consequently exercised arbitrary power, supported by Union soldiers. With Tennessee remaining a battleground, frequent disputes arose between Johnson and army commanders with military priorities. The governor, however, acted steadfastly to fulfill the political purpose of his appointment, even during the many alarms sounded about the advances of Confederate forces on Nashville. In the summer of 1863 Federals seized Knoxville and, that fall, were victorious at CHATTANOOGA, largely clearing the state of Southern troops. With the assistance of loyal East Tennesseans, Johnson then restored civil government in the state.

By Jan. 1865 the governor had reported to Lincoln that a constitutional convention had abolished slavery. Johnson's tenure was ending, for he had been elected Lincoln's vice-president. The Republican party had selected the Southerner as a running mate because of his steadfast adherence to the Union and because of his performance, under difficult circumstances, as military governor.

With LINCOLN'S ASSASSINATION, Apr. 1865, Johnson assumed the presidency and soon enacted an executive RECONSTRUCTION program that his congressional opponents, many of whom were RADICAL REPUBLICANS, found too lenient. During speaking tours Aug.–Sept. 1866, Johnson tried to explain and defend his policies; the 1866 elections, in which Radicals won a majority, made clear his failure to garner support.

On 2 Mar. 1867, Congress passed, over Johnson's veto, its original Reconstruction bill, which was based on military administration of Southern states and black suffrage. The legisla-

ture continued, bill after bill, to override presidential vetoes, including Johnson's rejection of the Tenure of Office Act. Forbidding the president to remove, without the approval of the Senate, certain appointed Federal officials, the new law stripped Johnson of even more power: by its terms, he could not dismiss from his own cabinet Sec. of War EDWIN M. STANTON, an ally of the Radicals.

In a defiant action intended to test the constitutionality of the Tenure of Office Act, Johnson removed Stanton from his post Aug. 1867. The Senate did not concur with the president's dismissal, nor would it confirm Johnson's nomination of a new secretary of war; Stanton retained his office. Johnson's enemies in Congress used his technical violation of the act as a reason to vote articles of impeachment. Though the charges were weak, in trial Johnson was nearly convicted. Finally, 7 Republican senators sided with the Democrats and the vote 26 May 1868 fell one short of the two-thirds required for conviction.

At the end of his presidential term, Johnson returned to Tennessee. He became active again in state politics and finally won a U.S. Senate seat in 1874, months before his death 31 July 1875 near Carter Station, Tenn.   —JDW

Johnson, Bradley Tyler. CSA b. Frederick, Md., 29 Sept. 1829, Johnson was one of the most prominent Marylanders to cast his lot with the Confederacy. An 1849 graduate of The College of New Jersey, he was admitted to the Maryland bar 2 years later. The able lawyer soon became a state's attorney and chairman of the state Democratic committee. A delegate to the 1860 Democratic presidential nominating conventions at Charleston and Baltimore, he staunchly supported Vice-Pres. JOHN C. BRECKINRIDGE.

When war came, Johnson assisted in recruiting the 1st Maryland, CSA, receiving a commission as its major. The regiment fought at FIRST BULL RUN, subsequently being placed under the command of Maj. Gen. THOMAS J. "STONEWALL" JACKSON. During Jackson's 1862 SHENANDOAH VALLEY CAMPAIGN, Johnson, who now commanded the 1st Maryland as colonel, fought the 1st Maryland, USA, in the streets of FRONT ROYAL, 23 May. Johnson led the regiment in the SEVEN DAYS' CAMPAIGN and at the Battle of CEDAR MOUNTAIN. During the SECOND BULL RUN CAMPAIGN, he temporarily commanded a brigade with such ability that one veteran Southerner claimed no one had ever done it better.

Johnson's excellent combat record should have secured his promotion to brigadier general. Jackson on several occasions urged a promotion, but it was not granted until 28 June 1864, when Johnson assumed command of the cavalry brigade of Brig. Gen. WILLIAM E. JONES, who had been killed earlier in the month. The unjustified delay probably resulted from lack of a brigade of Maryland units for him to command.

Johnson led his brigade in Lt. Gen. JUBAL A. EARLY's July 1864 raid on Washington (*see* EARLY'S WASHINGTON RAID). During this bold operation he attempted to free Confederate prisoners at POINT LOOKOUT, Md., but the task was too great. On 30 July he and Brig. Gen. JOHN MCCAUSLAND executed Early's orders to burn CHAMBERSBURG, Pa., in retaliation against the Union Army's destruction of Lexington, Va. Returning from Pennsylvania, his and McCausland's brigades were surprised and routed at MOOREFIELD, W. Va., 7 Aug. Narrowly escaping in the stampede, Johnson participated in the battles of the SHENANDOAH VALLEY CAMPAIGN of 1864, which destroyed Early's cavalry. When the ravaged mounted units were consolidated, Johnson lost his brigade. He spent the war's final months as commandant of the prison at Salisbury, N.C.

Johnson settled in Richmond when the war ended, resuming his legal practice and eventually serving in the Virginia state senate. In 1879 he returned to Baltimore, where he wrote 2 biographies and several articles for Confederate historical publications. d. Amelia, Va., 5 Oct. 1903.　　　　—JDW

Johnson, Bushrod Rust. CSA　b. Belmont Cty., Ohio, 7 Oct. 1817, Johnson was one of the many excellent but unsung commanders whose skill kept the Confederacy alive for 2 years after VICKSBURG and GET-
TYSBURG. With WILLIAM T. SHER-
MAN and GEORGE H. THOMAS, he graduated from West Point in 1840, 23d in his class. During the next 7 years he served creditably in the Seminole and Mexican wars.

In 1847 he resigned from the army to teach, first at the Western Military Institute in George-town, Ky., then at the University of Nashville. When war came, he joined the Confederacy as a colonel of engineers. On 24 Jan.

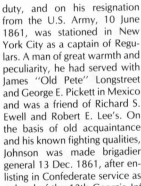

USMHI

1862 he was appointed brigadier general. He escaped after being captured at FORT DONELSON but was badly wounded at SHILOH, recovering in time to lead his brigade in Gen. BRAXTON BRAGG'S KENTUCKY CAMPAIGN in autumn and in the bloody Battle of STONE'S RIVER at the end of the year.

The high point of his career came at CHICKAMAUGA, when his division of Maj. Gen. JOHN B. HOOD's Corps spearheaded the breakthrough of the Union line at the gap left by the mistaken withdrawal of Brig. Gen. THOMAS J. WOOD's division. It was the turning point of the battle. Following this victory, Bragg sent Johnson with Lt. Gen. JAMES LONGSTREET to besiege Maj. Gen. AMBROSE E. BURNSIDE at KNOXVILLE; with the lifting of the siege at Maj. Gen. WILLIAM T. SHERMAN's approach, Longstreet returned to the East, and Johnson's division joined Gen. ROBERT E. LEE's army to serve at BERMUDA HUNDRED and the CRATER at Petersburg. His major general's commission dates from 21 May 1864.

After being paroled at Appomattox, Johnson became chancellor of the University of Nashville but, lacking funds, the school closed and he moved to Macoupin Cty., Ill., to become a farmer. With his health undermined by wartime hardships, he soon became a semi-invalid. d. on his farm near Brighton, 12 Sept. 1880.　　　　—RDH

Johnson, Edward. CSA　b. Salisbury, Va., 16 Apr. 1816, Johnson, ranked 32d in the West Point class of 1838, fought in the Seminole and Mexican wars, served on Western outpost

duty, and on his resignation from the U.S. Army, 10 June 1861, was stationed in New York City as a captain of Regulars. A man of great warmth and peculiarity, he had served with James "Old Pete" Longstreet and George E. Pickett in Mexico and was a friend of Richard S. Ewell and Robert E. Lee's. On the basis of old acquaintance and his known fighting qualities, Johnson was made brigadier general 13 Dec. 1861, after enlisting in Confederate service as colonel of the 12th Georgia Infantry.

LC

Called "Old Allegheny" and "Allegheny Ed," Johnson first went on Confederate duty in western Virginia, fought in Maj. Gen. THOMAS J. "STONEWALL" JACKSON's SHENANDOAH VALLEY CAMPAIGN of 1862, and was shot through the foot at the Battle of MCDOWELL. His wound healed poorly, forcing him to spend nearly a year on convalescent leave. Nonetheless he advanced to major general 28 Feb. 1863. Following Jackson's death at CHANCELLORSVILLE, Johnson took command of that general's old division, leading it at GETTYSBURG in the fighting at CULP'S HILL, and in the WILDERNESS and SPOTSYLVANIA campaigns. With his artillery withdrawn preparatory to a move to new entrenchments, Johnson and his men were overrun and captured at the "BLOODY ANGLE" at Spotsylvania, 12 May 1864. As a result of his old foot wound, Johnson carried an outsized club into battle, using it as a cane in daily life. He used it to club several of his captors before an old army friend, Union Maj. Gen. MARSENA R. PATRICK, recognized Johnson, realized his embarrassment at being captured, and saw to his kind treatment.

Exchanged shortly thereafter, Johnson was sent to the Army of Tennessee, fought in Lt. Gen. JOHN B. HOOD's FRANKLIN AND NASHVILLE CAMPAIGN in Lt. Gen. STEPHEN D. LEE's Corps, and was taken prisoner in the Battle of Nashville, Dec. 1864. Following his release from OLD CAPITOL PRISON July 1865, he took up farming in Virginia, dying in Richmond 2 Mar. 1873. He was remembered as a gruff, badly dressed, voluble swearer, and as one of the Confederacy's best division commanders.　—JES

Johnson, George W. war governor　b. Georgetown, Ky., 27 May 1811. Johnson's grandfather, Revolutionary War Col. Robert Johnson, was among the early settlers of Kentucky. On graduating from Transylvania University, George read law and established a practice in Georgetown, but he abandoned his legal career to farm in Kentucky and Arkansas. From 1838 to 1840 he represented Scott County, Ky., in the state legislature; twice, in 1852 and 1860, he was a defeated candidate for Democratic presidential elector.

Johnson advocated secession through 1861, though he assisted Gov. BERIAH MAGOFFIN in his efforts to keep Kentucky out of the war. It was Johnson who carried Magoffin's letter of Aug. 1861 to JEFFERSON DAVIS asking the Confederacy to respect his state's neutrality. When Brig. Gen. ULYSSES S. GRANT invaded Kentucky in September, Johnson aligned himself with the South. He organized a secession convention at Russellville, where, 18–20 Nov., delegates from those counties under Confederate control met with refugee politicians from regions occupied by Federal troops. They passed an ordinance of secession, established a provisional government, elected Johnson governor, and had Kentucky admitted to the Confederacy 10 Dec., though the presence of the Union army in the state prevented the rump government from being put into effect.

Johnson fled Russellville and attached himself to Brig. Gen. JOHN C. BRECKINRIDGE's command as a civilian aide, holding a staff position on the first day of fighting at SHILOH, 6 Apr. 1862. That night he enlisted in Confederate service. On the 7th, he was mortally wounded, lying on the battlefield through the next day until taken to a Union hospital. He died behind enemy lines on the 9th, his body being sent to Georgetown for burial.
—PLF

Johnson, Herschel Vespasian.

CSP b. Burke Cty., Ga., 18 Sept. 1812. A lawyer, jurist, legislator, and governor of Georgia from 1853 to 1857, Johnson gradually changed his position from pro-Southern extremism to one of moderation during the antebellum sectional conflict. He briefly incurred disfavor among Southerners by accepting the Democratic vice-presidential nomination at the Baltimore convention in 1860, running on a POPULAR SOVEREIGNTY ticket with STEPHEN A. DOUGLAS. On ABRAHAM LINCOLN's victory at the polls, he urged secessionists to give the president a chance to effect compromise. He did not believe a confederacy of Southern

LC

states could succeed, yet when Georgia passed the ordinance of secession, Johnson cast his lot with the government soon to form in Montgomery, Ala.

He then returned to his plantation until the state legislature elected him to replace ROBERT A. TOOMBS in the Regular Confederate Congress Nov. 1862. Once in office, he generally opposed JEFFERSON DAVIS' war measures, writing in his postwar autobiography of those times when he "acquiesced in what [he] could not approve." He never abandoned his advocacy of STATES RIGHTS, opposing IMPRESSMENT, arming slaves (see BLACK TROOPS, CONFEDERACY APPROVES USE OF), suspension of HABEAS CORPUS, and all taxes except those on incomes (see INCOME TAX, CONFEDERATE). Shortly after taking his seat, he proposed a constitutional amendment that would have permitted peaceful secession from the Confederacy, and by spring 1864 he was actively involved with the faction seeking a negotiated peace with independence.

The war resulted in severe financial losses for Johnson, from which he never recovered. He applied for a pardon from Pres. ANDREW JOHNSON within a few months after the Confederacy's defeat. It was granted, and in fall 1865 the Georgian served as president of the state constitutional convention. He also devoted considerable energy to securing a pardon for his old friend ALEXANDER H. STEPHENS.

Johnson's postwar political career ended when, after winning a bitter contest in the state legislature, he was denied his seat in the U.S. Senate. From 1873 until his death near Louisville, 16 Aug. 1880, Johnson held an appointment as circuit judge.
—PLF

Johnson, Reverdy.

USP b. Annapolis, Md., 21 May 1796. A graduate of St. John's College, Johnson became a lawyer with an active practice in Baltimore for almost 60 years, winning recognition as one of the great attorneys of his day. He was known particularly for his extraordinary memory, which served him well especially in his latter years as his eyesight failed. Noted as a constitutional lawyer, he won the case upholding the validity of Cyrus McCormick's reaper patent and as defense attorney in the DRED SCOTT CASE contributed much to the controversial majority opinion of the Supreme Court.

In politics he was at first an

LC

ardent Whig in the Maryland legislature that sent him to the U.S. Senate in 1845. While supporting the war with Mexico, he opposed annexing any territory. Though he thought slavery wrong, he sought to dodge the question of extending it and favored compromise to avert disunion. He continued to be sympathetic to the South during the 1850s but opposed secession as unconstitutional. As a member of the WASHINGTON PEACE CONFERENCE, in Feb. 1861 he tried in vain to devise a formula to preserve the Union, and in the Maryland legislature he worked to keep his state in the Union. Reelected to the Senate in 1862, he served as a voice of moderation. At first he opposed ABRAHAM LINCOLN's EMANCIPATION PROCLAMATION as too sudden, but he did vote for the 13TH AMENDMENT.

During Reconstruction, Johnson urged continuing Lincoln's moderate policy toward the South, generally supported Pres. ANDREW JOHNSON, was legal counsel for MARY SURRATT in the Lincoln assassination trial, and served on the Congressional Joint Committee on Reconstruction. At first opposing the FREEDMEN'S BUREAU and black suffrage, he did vote for the 14TH AMENDMENT, hoping it would end military occupation of the South. In Johnson's impeachment trial he voted for acquittal. In 1868, as minister to England, he worked out a reasonable agreement on the ALABAMA CLAIMS, only to see it rejected by Congress. Back in America in 1869, he spent much time defending Southerners in court cases till his death in Annapolis 10 Feb. 1876.
—DL

Johnson's Island Prison.

As the Civil War progressed and prisoners in large numbers were held, some confinement areas were established by enclosing existing camps, others by constructing new facilities. Of the latter type in the North, Johnson's Island Prison, Ohio, in Sandusky Bay on Lake Erie, was one of the most important. The prison site, a mile from the mainland and 2.5 mi from Sandusky, encompassed 300 acres rented for $500 annually; half of it was wooded, sparing the camp a fuel problem. In a 40-acre waterfront clearing, quarters were built for 100 guards and an estimated 1,000 prisoners. The prisoners' quarters were army-type barracks, each 125 ft by 24 ft with 9-ft walls; each was divided into 3 rooms and designed for 180 men. A washhouse, a hospital, and 2 mess halls were added. Johnson's Island was one of few military prisons in which captives did not do their own cooking. A fence, topped by a walkway and guard posts for sentinels, encircled the buildings. A blockhouse with howitzer and guard boat completed the installation. The total cost of construction was $30,000.

In Jan. 1862 Maj. William S. Pierson of Sandusky was given command of the prison, and in February the first 500 to 600 prisoners arrived. Soon there were more prisoners than the expected 1,000, almost all officers. Shelter was adequate, but there was a shortage of clothing and food. The Confederate officers, who included 7 generals, struggled to keep up their courage, organizing their own government, holding debates, and giving French, music, and dancing lessons.

In 1863 Confederate Capt. Charles H. Cole (of Brig. Gen. Nathan B. Forrest's Cavalry Corps) escaped from Johnson's Island to Canada. With information supplied by Cole, a plot to free island prisoners developed, and Confederate Navy Capt. John Y. Beall was chosen in 1864 to lead the rescue. Captured, Beall was tried by a military court and hanged in New York Feb. 1865. There were about 3,000 Confederates confined in Johnson's Island at the end of the war.   —PR

Johnsonville Raid, Forrest's. 19 Oct.–9 Nov. 1864 "That devil Forrest was down about Johnsonville making havoc among the gunboats and transports." This vitriolic comment by Union Maj. Gen. WILLIAM T. SHERMAN captured the essence of Maj. Gen. NATHAN B. FORREST'S raid against Johnsonville, Tenn., late in 1864. Unremitting pressure was being applied to the Confederate army and Forrest's purpose was to make every effort to relieve it.

Forrest's cavalry left Corinth, Miss., 19 Oct. 1864 to begin what would be a 23-day foray. Traveling northwest through Jackson, Tenn., the Confederates swung on a northeasterly path to Paris. Turning abruptly eastward, they crossed the Big Sandy River and arrived at Paris Landing on the Tennessee River 28 Oct. The following day, the raiders effectively blocked that waterway in the vicinity of Fort Heiman and Paris Landing. After off-and-on engagements between Confederate shore batteries and several Union gunboats, Forrest and his men commandeered 2 Federal steamers on the Tennessee River.

On 1 Nov. Forrest's "cavalry afloat" moved downriver to Johnsonville while a portion of his force struggled with the artillery pieces along the muddy riverbanks. Following a day of desultory action, the Confederates made their final move against Johnsonville 3 Nov. A combination of bluff and clever artillery emplacement brought about a significant Confederate victory. Federal gunboats and great mounds of supplies went up in a wild, wind-whipped inferno as Forrest's massed cannon belched successive salvos of unerring iron on them. The Johnsonville Raid resulted in Union losses of 4 gunboats, 14 steamboats, 17 barges, 33 guns, 150 prisoners, and over 75,000 tons of supplies. Total damages were estimated at $6.7 million. The episode once again showed Forrest's fierce but ingenious capabilities and strengthened his reputation as one of the war's premier field commanders   —WRB/DKS

Johnston, Albert Sidney. CSA b. Washington, Ky., 2 Feb. 1803, Johnston, one of the most promising Confederate generals, was a distinguished leader of great reputation in 1861. A close friend of Pres. JEFFERSON DAVIS, Johnston considered himself a Texan, though born in Kentucky. Following his graduation from West Point, 8th in the class of 1826, he served with distinction as an officer in both the Black Hawk and Mexican wars. Drawn to Texas in 1836, he fought for that

republic as senior brigadier general and became its secretary of war. Appointed colonel of the 2d U.S. Cavalry in 1855, he led the Utah Expedition against the Mormons in 1857 and when civil war began was a brevet brigadier general commanding the Department of the Pacific. His resignation was submitted after Texas seceded, and Johnston was soon placed in command of the huge Confederate Department No. 2 by Davis, with the rank of full general.

LC

Johnston was expected to defend an enormous region of the South, stretching from the Appalachian Mountains in the East to Indian Territory in the West. Failures of his subordinates at Forts HENRY and DONELSON and at MILL SPRINGS resulted in the loss of virtually all of Kentucky and most of Tennessee early in 1862. Withdrawing to a line along the northern Mississippi border, Johnston concentrated his forces for a bold attempt to recoup the earlier disasters. Aided by Gen. P.G.T. BEAUREGARD, Johnston marched from Corinth, Miss., against the Federal concentration at Pittsburg Landing, on the Tennessee River. 2 days of delays and a heavy rain thwarted the anticipated quick Confederate thrust, but Johnston decided to attack anyway. His assault *en masse* on the morning of 6 Apr. 1862 caught the Federal army by surprise and began the 2-day Battle of SHILOH.

Entangled in thick woodlands and strung out by faulty troop dispositions, Johnston's men struggled to apply pressure to the critical Federal left flank along the river. Leading an attack in the vicinity of the Peach Orchard about 2 p.m., Johnston was struck in the right leg by a stray minié bullet and bled to death before the flow was staunched.

Though his career terminated before the merits of his generalship were fully tested, if for no other reason than that his successors proved woefully lacking, Johnston's death was a staggering blow to the Confederacy.   —WS

Johnston, George Doherty. CSA b. Hillsborough, N.C., 30 May 1832. Reared and schooled in Alabama, Johnston was a graduate of Alabama's Howard College and Cumberland University Law School in Tennessee. He became an attorney in Marion, Ala., the mayor of Marion in 1856, and a state legislator in 1857 and 1858. At the start of the Civil War he joined the 4th Alabama as 2d lieutenant and went to the thick of the fighting at FIRST BULL RUN, where he served under Brig. Gen. BARNARD E. BEE.

Following a brief return home and a new commission as major of the 25th Alabama, Jan. 1862, he fought at the Battle of SHILOH in Brig. Gen. JONES M. WITHERS' division. There, Gen. ALBERT SIDNEY JOHNSTON so impressed him that he said, "had [Johnston] been spared a longer career

LC

I believe he would have proved himself to be the equal of any military chieftain of modern times.'' Johnston was appointed colonel of the 25th Alabama Sept. 1862, and, after fighting the Battle of STONE'S RIVER under Brig. Gen. ZACHARIAH C. DEAS, went on to the CHICKAMAUGA, CHATTANOOGA, and ATLANTA campaigns. Johnston was promoted to brigadier general 26 July 1864.

Wounded in the leg at the Battle of EZRA CHURCH, 28 July, he followed Gen. JOHN B. HOOD's army on crutches for its invasion of Tennessee. It is presumed that Johnston stayed with the Army of Tennessee to its end in North Carolina, but he was not surrendered with it. Historian Ezra Warner's *Generals in Gray* places him in the field attempting to join those Confederates still fighting in the West.

After the war he held positions as commandant of cadets at the University of Alabama, superintendent of the South Carolina Military Academy, U.S. civil service commissioner, and an Alabama state senator. d. Tuscaloosa, Ala., 8 Dec. 1910.

—JES

Johnston, Joseph Eggleston. CSA b. Farmville, Va., 3 Feb. 1807, Johnston attended Abingdon Academy in Virginia and entered West Point in 1825. Graduating 13th in a class of 46 in 1829, he was appointed 2d lieutenant in the 4th Artillery. After 8 years of service against Indians and on frontier duty, he resigned to become a civil engineer.

As an engineer, Johnston joined geologist John Wesley Powell's expedition to Florida. On 15 Jan. 1838 the group was attacked by Indians, and Johnston, in spite of wounds, led the rear guard in a skillful retreat. As a result he was recommissioned a 1st lieutenant in the Topographical Engineers. In 1846 he

USMHI

was promoted to captain and served with distinction in Mexico under Gen. WINFIELD SCOTT. After the war Johnston returned to the Topographical Engineers, progressing to lieutenant colonel in the 1st Cavalry in 1855, and, 28 June 1860, to quartermaster general and brigadier general.

He resigned from the U.S. Army 22 Apr. 1861, shortly after Virginia seceded from the Union, and offered his service to his state. Initially appointed major general of Virginia troops, on 14 May he was commissioned brigadier general in the Confederate army. His first assignment was at Harpers Ferry. There he withdrew his troops quietly before the superior Federal force led by Brig. Gen. ROBERT PATTERSON, eluded pursuit, and by rail and on foot took his men to reinforce Brig. Gen. P.G.T. BEAUREGARD at FIRST BULL RUN. Assigned to the right flank, with orders to advance, Johnston quickly shifted to the sagging Confederate left. His timing enabled him to drive back the enemy, turning a losing situation into victory. On 31 Aug. he became a full general, to rank from 4 July.

The appointment created a lasting animosity between Johnston and Pres. JEFFERSON DAVIS when Johnston complained that the appointment placed him fourth (after SAMUEL COOPER, ALBERT SIDNEY JOHNSTON, and ROBERT E. LEE) instead of first in seniority among full-rank generals. Having been senior brigadier in the U.S. Army, he had expected to retain that position in the Confederacy.

A consummate professional in his ability to plan, gather intelligence, and take defensive action, Johnston defended the Virginia peninsula against Maj. Gen. GEORGE B. MCCLELLAN in spring 1862 (see PENINSULA CAMPAIGN). Having observed the Federal build-up around YORKTOWN, he recommended retrenching the army closer to Richmond, but Davis ordered Johnston to hold. Finally forced to retreat 4 May, he conducted a rearguard fight at WILLIAMSBURG on the 5th, successfully covering his troops' withdrawal.

Johnston struck McClellan at SEVEN PINES 31 May. Though he had planned the offensive carefully, the battle was poorly executed, owing in large part to his subordinates' failure to convey orders efficiently or oversee their outcome. Twice wounded in the battle, he left the army for several months to recuperate.

On returning to duty in November, he was placed in charge of the Department of the West, with orders to halt Brig. Gen. ULYSSES S. GRANT's advance in Mississippi. The ill-defined command and the contradictory orders issued by Davis from Richmond left Johnston unsure of his authority. Though he advised Lt. Gen. JOHN C. PEMBERTON to evacuate VICKSBURG rather than risk losing his entire army, Pemberton refused to withdraw when Davis ordered him to hold the city. Lacking sufficient manpower, Johnston was unable to relieve Pemberton once Grant blocked access to Vicksburg, and the garrison was surrendered 4 July.

In Dec. 1863, after Bragg's failure at CHATTANOOGA, Johnston was assigned to the Army of Tennessee with instructions to reorganize it and take the offensive. The reorganization went well, but Johnston hesitated in taking the offensive, claiming he had insufficient troops to oppose the powerful Federal army. He preferred waiting for the enemy to attack and expend its strength, allowing him to counterattack a weakened foe. In May 1864, pitted against Maj. Gen. WILLIAM T. SHERMAN during the ATLANTA CAMPAIGN, he was dependent on this strategy, which Davis refused to approve. Johnston fell back skillfully through northern Georgia before a numerically superior enemy. Davis, increasingly frustrated by Johnston's failure to stop the Federal advance, relieved him of command 17 July in front of Atlanta, replacing him with Lt. Gen. JOHN B. HOOD. A cautious soldier, Johnston had recorded neither great victories nor defeats, but he had kept his forces intact and safe from destruction.

After Hood's failure to hold Atlanta and his disastrous FRANKLIN AND NASHVILLE CAMPAIGN, Gen. ROBERT E. LEE restored Johnston to command 23 Feb. 1865. Through spring he led the remnants of the once-formidable Army of Tennessee in the CAROLINAS CAMPAIGN. After Lee capitulated in Virginia, he negotiated an armistice with Sherman, 18 Apr. Davis ordered him South to continue the war, but, realizing the hopelessness of further resistance, Johnston signed final surrender terms 26 Apr., bringing his military career to a close (see SURRENDERS: Johnston).

After the war, Johnston lived in various southern cities and engaged in the insurance business. His memoirs, *Narrative of Military Operations Directed During the Late War Between the States* (1874), are justification of his military record. In 1878 he was elected from Virginia to a term in the U.S. House of Representatives, 1879–81; and 1885–91, during Grover Cleveland's administration, he held an appointment as commissioner of railroads. d. District of Columbia, 21 Mar. 1891. —JDK

Johnston, Robert Daniel. CSA b. Lincoln Cty., N.C., 19 Mar. 1837. After attending a preparatory school in Rutherfordton, Johnston graduated in 1857 from the state university and studied law at the University of Virginia 1860–61. By the time North Carolina seceded, he was a practicing attorney, an elder of the Presbyterian church, and a 2d lieutenant of militia.

LC

On 15 July 1861 Johnston became captain of Company K/23d North Carolina Infantry. His regiment was sent to the Virginia peninsula, where it opposed Maj. Gen. GEORGE B. MCCLELLAN's spring 1862 offensive. Johnston fought well at WILLIAMSBURG and, 21 May 1862, became lieutenant colonel of his outfit. At SEVEN PINES, 10 days later, he went down with a wound but recovered in time to fight in the ANTIETAM CAMPAIGN as a member of Brig. Gen. SAMUEL GARLAND's brigade of Maj. Gen. DANIEL H. HILL's division. At ANTIETAM, 17 Sept. 1862, the 23d North Carolina held the center of Gen. ROBERT E. LEE's line near the sunken road later known as "BLOODY LANE." Johnston's conduct in that sector prompted Hill to refer to him in his battle report as "the gallant Lieutenant-Colonel."

At CHANCELLORSVILLE, Johnston was chosen by Brig. Gen. ROBERT E. RODES to command the 12th North Carolina, following the death of that regiment's senior officer. The 12th took part in Lt. Gen. THOMAS J. "STONEWALL" JACKSON's flank march of 2 May 1863, which turned the tide of battle; during the maneuver, the regiment fought stubbornly, capturing a stand of Union colors.

Johnston soon returned to his old regiment and accompanied it to Pennsylvania. Early on 1 July, representing Brig. Gen. ALFRED IVERSON's brigade of Lt. Gen. RICHARD S. EWELL's II Corps, the 23d North Carolina rammed into Union troops above GETTYSBURG. In the melee Johnston fell with a wound that kept him out of the rest of the battle.

After his recovery he received a brigadier's star, dating from 1 Sept. 1863, plus command of 4 regiments and 1 battalion of North Carolina infantry. He participated ably in the 1864 campaigns from the WILDERNESS to PETERSBURG and afterward in the Shenandoah Valley, where he was CONSPICUOUS at THIRD WINCHESTER. Johnston closed out the war in his home state, guarding the line of the Roanoke River.

After the war, he moved to Charlotte, where for 20 years he practiced law. He later worked as a banker in Birmingham, Ala., and Winchester, Va., dying in the latter town 1 Feb. 1919. —EGL

Jomini's _Treatise on Grand Military Operations._ The military theorist generally considered to have exercised the greatest influence on Civil War commanders was Baron Antoine Henri Jomini (1779–1869). Born in Switzerland, he quit the life of a bank clerk at 17 to enter Napoleon's army, within 10 years becoming a colonel on the staff of Marshal Ney. Later

he was a brigadier general and staff officer to Napoleon himself, before joining the czarist army and attaining a full generalcy.

The event that brought Jomini to Napoleon's attention was the publication of his _Traité des grandes opérations militaires (Treatise on Grand Military Operations),_ released in 8 volumes in Paris, 1804–06. This was the first of many works on the theory and practice of war that Jomini was to produce, his _magnum opus_ being _Précis de l'art de la guerre_ (2 vols; Paris: 1838). In most of these works Jomini canonized the strategist from Corsica. As the foremost 19th-century interpreter of Napoleon's campaigns, the baron himself acquired a name synonymous with military wisdom.

His influence on Civil War generals, notably HENRY W. HALLECK, GEORGE B. MCCLELLAN, and ROBERT E. LEE, was considerable. Until 1832, selections from Jomini's _Traité_ constituted the only text on strategy available to West Point cadets. Inevitably, the maxims articulated in the work, framed around a study of the campaigns of Frederick the Great during the Seven Years' War, paralleled by observations on Napoleon's operations, found application in numerous engagements 1861–65.

The _Traité_ is permeated by Jomini's patterned, almost geometrical approach to tactics and strategy, an emphasis reflecting his belief that war could be limited and its violence controlled. Such a conviction may have deluded such disciples as McClellan into thinking they could triumph by maneuver rather than by battle. Among Jomini's cherished "fundamental principles" is the necessity for an army to concentrate superior numbers, through interior lines of operations, against an opponent confined to exterior lines. Stressed too is the danger of surrendering the offensive and awaiting attack. The _Traité_ also emphasizes the superiority of the TURNING MOVEMENT over the direct attack, the threatening of enemy communications, the selection of lines of operations based on logistical criteria, the vigorous pursuit of a beaten foe, and the exploitation of surprise to defeat the enemy psychologically as well as physically. —EGL

Jones, Catesby ap Roger. CSN b. Fairfield, Va., 15 Apr. 1821. This capable and energetic officer entered the service as midshipman 18 June 1836, was promoted to passed midshipman in 1842, and to lieutenant in 1849. During 1853, while assigned to the Washington Navy Yard, he worked with Lt. JOHN A. DAHLGREN in experiments that led to the improved DAHLGREN GUN. After the secession of Virginia, Jones resigned his commission and became a captain in the Virginia navy. On 10 June 1861, he was appointed a lieutenant in the Confederate navy and commanded the batteries on Jamestown Island at a time when Navy Sec. STEPHEN R. MALLORY placed top priority on the building of an ironclad warship. Jones and Lt. JOHN M. BROOKE worked together in testing iron plating for this vessel, the _VIRGINIA (Merrimack)._

In Nov. 1861 Jones was at Norfolk preparing the battery of the new IRONCLAD. His knowledge of ordnance was an important factor in his selection as the ship's executive officer. He served well during the engagement off HAMPTON ROADS, 8–9 Mar. 1862, and he took command following the wounding of Capt. FRANKLIN BUCHANAN during action with the USS MONITOR. He continued as executive officer under Franklin's successor, Capt. JOSIAH TATTNALL, until the ironclad was destroyed to prevent its capture.

In May 1862, Jones established a land battery on the James

River below DREWRY'S BLUFF. Manned by his sailors, it was meant to protect Richmond from Federal gunboats. On 15 May the battery contributed to the defeat of an enemy flotilla commanded by Capt. JOHN RODGERS.

Jones commanded the *Chattahoochee* off Columbus, Ga., and headed the naval works at Charlotte, N.C., before assuming command of the Selma (Ala.) Iron Works 9 May 1863. This foundry became the Confederate Naval Foundry and Ordnance, which produced cannon for vessels at Mobile and for Forts Morgan and Gaines. Jones made a point of personally supervising each large casting and on one occasion narrowly escaped death or injury from an explosion and fire.

After the war Jones formed a business partnership with former navy associates Brooke and Robert D. Minor, in which they purchased military supplies in the U.S. and sold them to foreign governments. Jones died 20 June 1877, after being shot by a Selma neighbor over a quarrel between two of their children.

—NCD

Jones, David Rumph. CSA b. Orangeburg District, S.C., 5 Apr. 1825. Having received his basic education at local common schools, Jones entered West Point in 1842 and graduated 41st in the class of 1846. The new 2d lieutenant fought in the Mexican War, winning brevets for gallantry at Contreras and Churubusco. He spent several years in garrison duty and as an assistant instructor of tactics at the Military Academy before transferring to the adjutant general's department in 1853. On 15 Feb. 1861, when he resigned from the army to join Confederate service, he was on duty in the Department of the West.

Sometimes addressed by the nickname "Neighbor," Jones entered the secessionist army designated major and chief of staff to Brig. Gen. P.G.T. BEAUREGARD at Charleston, S.C. He carried the surrender terms to FORT SUMTER after the bombardment of the installation Apr. 1861 and has been credited with lowering the American flag at the garrison. Given his brigadier's star 17 June and transferred to Virginia, he and his brigade demonstrated effectively against the Union flank at FIRST BULL RUN. During 1862 Jones fought on the peninsula from YORKTOWN to MALVERN HILL and on the Bull Run battlefield, where Southern troops defeated the Union army for the second time.

Though he lacked the flair displayed by several other Confederate officers, Jones possessed the good judgment and steadiness desirable in a reliable military officer. The tenacious defense he staged at Thoroughfare Gap 27 Aug. 1862 allowed Maj. Gen. JAMES LONGSTREET to reach Maj. Gen. THOMAS J. "STONEWALL" JACKSON at Manassas Junction on the 30th, in time for Second Bull Run, and he performed with equal skill at SOUTH MOUNTAIN that September. His grandest performance in battle occurred at ANTIETAM. Deployed on the right flank of the Confederate line south of Sharpsburg with only part of his command—fewer than 2,800 men—he defended the vital Boteler's Ford road, the Confederate army's escape route to the Potomac River. He emerged from the Antietam Campaign with divisional command and a major generalcy as of 10 Mar. 1862.

Jones did not long survive his promotion, dying in Richmond, Va., 15 Jan. 1863, the result of heart disease he had suffered for several years.

—PLF

Jones, John Beauchamp. diarist b. Baltimore, Md., 6 Mar. 1810. As a prewar journalist and author of minor impor-

tance, Jones wrote several marginally successful novels and edited various newspapers, the most prominent being the *Madisonian,* political organ of John Tyler's administration. He lived briefly in Kentucky and Missouri, spent a few months in Europe, then settled in Burlington, N.J. Out of Philadelphia he published the *Southern Monitor* from 1857 until the abortive attempt to resupply FORT SUMTER in spring 1861. Though sympathetic to Southern sectional interests, Jones's weekly was a platform from which he cautioned against the dangers of disunion. His last prewar book, *Wild Southern Scenes* (1859, reissued in 1861 under the title *Secession, Coercion, and Civil War*), adopted the same theme. While it showed signs of matching in popularity his one earlier success, *Wild Western Scenes* (1841), it failed with the advent of war.

Jones traveled to Montgomery, Ala., to obtain a clerkship with the Confederate War Department while the Provisional Congress was in session, intending from the outset to apply his journalistic skills to record the details of the Southern government. From his vantage point, he ultimately produced a piece of literature invaluable to the study of the Confederacy. First published in 1866 as the 2-volume *A Rebel War Clerk's Diary,* it gives an extensive account of War Department proceedings through the eyes of an insider who did not hesitate to comment on the personalities he observed. Little escaped his attention. His is a microscopic view of the Confederacy: of alternating waves of hope and despair; of privation and suffering among civilians; of bickering between JEFFERSON DAVIS and the military figures; of discord between Davis and Congress; of the destructive conflict between state and central governments.

Jones wrote for accuracy rather than from inspiration, and his prose tends to be tedious and overwritten, in places needlessly bogged down in tirades against Confederate bureaucracy. There are occasional inaccuracies, the result of lapses in communication with the front and a tendency toward conjecture, the latter largely flaws of his postwar editing. As a whole, however, no other work so thoroughly portrays the social, economic, and political trials of a nation struggling for survival.

Jones did not live to see his diary in print. He returned to Burlington after the war, completing work on his manuscript before dying 4 Feb. 1866 from an illness aggravated by wartime deprivations. The work, in press at the time of his death, enjoyed only moderate popularity until postwar generations of historians recognized its worth. 2 subsequent editions have been published: The first, edited by Howard Swiggett and issued as *A Rebel War Clerk's Diary at the Confederate States Capital* (1935), contains a helpful introduction and editorial notes of value; like the highly prized original edition, it is complete and was released in 2 volumes. A 1-volume edition, edited by Earl Schenck Meirs (1958), suffers from extensive abridgment but retains the essential commentary of interest to the general reader.

—PLF

Jones, John Marshall. CSA b. Charlottesville, Va., 26 July 1820, Jones graduated from the U.S. Military Academy in the class of 1841, ranking 39th of 52 cadets. As an infantry subaltern, he served in garrisons in Michigan, Florida, and Texas before returning to West Point to teach infantry tactics. From the end of his instructorship in 1852 until the Civil War, he served mainly on the frontier, participating in the Utah Expedition of 1857–58, and also helped revise army tactics.

On 27 May 1861 Jones resigned his captaincy in the 7th U.S. Infantry to enter Confederate service at an equal rank.

Though assigned to the artillery, where he was soon appointed a lieutenant colonel, he spent most of his early war service as adjutant to Brig. Gens. JOHN B. MAGRUDER and RICHARD S. EWELL. Under the latter, he participated in Lt. Gen. Thomas J. "Stonewall" Jackson's SHENANDOAH VALLEY CAMPAIGN of 1862, seeing action at FRONT ROYAL, FIRST WINCHESTER, CROSS KEYS, and PORT REPUBLIC. He continued on Ewell's staff when Jackson's Corps was transferred

LC

to Virginia, serving ably through the SEVEN DAYS' CAMPAIGN. In the SECOND BULL RUN CAMPAIGN, he was with Ewell at CEDAR MOUNTAIN and GROVETON, where the division leader was wounded. Later Jones became inspector general to Brig. Gen. JUBAL A. EARLY, who praised his service that December at Fredericksburg.

Jones's final battle in a staff position was CHANCELLORSVILLE. Promoted brigadier general to rank from 15 May 1863, he received command of a brigade under the recuperated Ewell, now a lieutenant general commanding the II Corps/Army of Northern Virginia. Despite an apparent earlier tendency to frequent drink, Jones led his 6 Virginia regiments with energy and skill at GETTYSBURG, where, near sundown, 2 July, he fell wounded on the slope of CULP'S HILL.

Jones received a second wound that November after rejoining the army for the MINE RUN CAMPAIGN. Despite the seriousness of the injury, he reported for duty a few days later. He was mostly inactive through that winter, but 5 May 1864 his brigade opened the Battle of the WILDERNESS, driving in the advance of the Union V Corps near Wilderness Run. That afternoon, however, the enemy returned in force, crumpled Jones's right flank, and shoved his men back a quarter of a mile. In the melee, reportedly while attempting to rally his men, Jones was shot dead. In his campaign report, Ewell termed his loss "irreparable." —EGL

Jones, John Robert.

CSA b. Harrisonburg, Va., 12 Mar. 1827. Graduating from the Virginia Military Institute in 1848, Jones taught school in Florida, then became principal of a military academy in Maryland. He returned to his native town when civil war erupted, recruiting and commanding a company that entered Confederate service as part of the 33d Virginia Infantry.

With his regiment Jones saw action at FIRST BULL RUN, taking part in an attack that captured 2 Union batteries. Early in 1862, under Maj. Gen. THOMAS J. "STONEWALL" JACKSON, the 33d participated heavily in the SHENANDOAH VALLEY CAMPAIGN and Jones performed adroitly

USMHI

enough to advance to lieutenant colonel. That June, on the recommendation of Jackson himself, he was appointed a briga-

dier general (though never confirmed by the Confederate Senate). By then Jackson's victorious troops had rejoined Gen. ROBERT E. LEE for the SEVEN DAYS' CAMPAIGN before Richmond. In charge of a brigade in Jackson's division, Jones was conspicuous at GAINES' MILL and MALVERN HILL, being wounded on the night of the latter battle. While the wound prevented his participation at SECOND BULL RUN, he soon returned to his command.

Jones resumed his rise to prominence by a solid performance in command of Jackson's old division during the Battle of HARPERS FERRY, 15 Sept. 1862. He then hastened to the ANTIETAM battlefield, where on the 17th his men held Lee's far left against an artillery barrage, then repulsed an enemy advance. Jones himself, however, missed much of the fight after being disabled by a shellburst.

Another disability, an ulcerated leg, removed him from the fighting at CHANCELLORSVILLE 2 May 1863. His absence left his command, in the words of one historian, "confused and irresolute." It also led to his relief from duty in disgrace. Considering his excuse to go to the rear unconscionably weak, his superiors soon cashiered him for cowardice.

Jones drifted westward and as a civilian was captured at Smithtown, Tenn., 2 months after Chancellorsville. He spent the rest of the war in prison, not being released from FORT WARREN, Mass., until 24 July 1865. He returned to Harrisonburg, where he was employed in the farm-implement business, filled a circuit court position, and died 1 Apr. 1901.   —EGL

Jones, Patrick Henry.

USA b. Cty. Westmeath, Ireland, 20 Nov. 1830, Jones emigrated at the age of 10, settling with his family on a farm in Cattaraugus Cty., N.Y. He read law in Ellicottville, was admitted to the bar, and practiced his profession until the onset of the war.

Jones enlisted in the 37th New York, known as the Irish Rifles, receiving a commission of 2d lieutenant 7 July 1861. 2 weeks later, at FIRST BULL RUN, the regiment held a reserve position. Jones was promoted to 1st lieutenant 4 Nov., then major 21 Jan. 1862. He participated in the PENINSULA CAMPAIGN, fighting at WILLIAMSBURG and SEVEN PINES. He also saw action at SECOND BULL RUN. On 8

LC

Oct. he became colonel of the 154th New York in Brig. Gen. ADOLPH VON STEINWEHR'S division of the XI Corps. On 2 May 1863, at CHANCELLORSVILLE, when the XI Corps was surprised and routed by a Confederate attack, Jones fell wounded and was captured.

Exchanged in October, he went west with the XI and XII corps to Tennessee. In the Union assault on MISSIONARY RIDGE in November, Jones and the 154th New York had only a nominal role. In spring 1864 the 2 Union corps were consolidated into the XX Corps in Maj. Gen. WILLIAM T. SHERMAN'S command. On 7 June Jones secured the command of a brigade, which he led in the ATLANTA CAMPAIGN, in Sherman's MARCH TO THE SEA, and in the CAROLINAS CAMPAIGN. On 18 Apr. 1865 he received his promotion to brigadier general, to date from 6 Dec. 1864.

Resigning his commission 17 June, Jones returned to Ellicottville. Later that year he secured the position of clerk of the New York Court of Appeals. In 1869 Pres. Ulysses S. Grant appointed him postmaster of New York City. He resigned in 1873 and was elected register of New York the next year. In 1877 he returned to the legal profession, dying on Staten Island, N.Y., 23 July 1900.   —JDW

Jones, Samuel. CSA b. Powhatan Cty., Va., 17 Dec. 1819. Graduating 19th in the 52-man West Point class of 1841, Jones became a subaltern in the 1st U.S. Artillery. For the next 5 years he performed garrison duty in Maine and Florida, returning to the Military Academy as an instructor of infantry and artillery tactics. From 1851 to 1858 he served in Louisiana and Texas before being named assistant to the judge advocate of the army. He was still a member of the War Department staff, with the rank of captain, when the Civil War broke out. Immediately he resigned his commission and returned to his native state.

USMHI

Jones entered the Confederate ranks as a major of artillery. By July 1861 he was a colonel, serving at that rank as chief of artillery to Brig. Gen. P.G.T. BEAUREGARD. His success in that role during FIRST BULL RUN brought him acclaim in commanders' reports and the rank of brigadier general. From that time until Jan. 1862 he led a brigade of Georgia regiments along the Potomac River. Subsequently he relieved Gen. BRAXTON BRAGG at Pensacola, Fla., then commanded the Department of Alabama and West Florida, headquartered at Mobile.

He was in departmental command only until April, when sent west to lead a division in Maj. Gen. EARL VAN DORN's Army of Mississippi. After fighting at CORINTH, he returned to a desk job as a major general in command of the Department of East Tennessee. In December Bragg asked for troops to reinforce his army in Kentucky; when Jones failed to detach them, he lost that command and was sent to take over the Department of Western Virginia, at Dublin. There he served until Mar. 1864, by which time he had lost favor with his superiors, including Gen. ROBERT E. LEE, whose summer 1863 invasion of Pennsylvania had received little aid from Jones. This may have been a factor in his eventual relief, though he argued that a lack of troops and supplies handicapped any cooperative effort.

In Apr. 1864 Jones succeeded Beauregard to head the Department of South Carolina, Georgia, and Florida, in which command he defended Charleston against various Union threats. 6 months later he was named commander of the District of South Carolina, and 11 Jan. 1865 was assigned to head the Military District of Florida. At the close of the war he surrendered at Tallahassee, was paroled, and returned to Virginia to farm. In later life he held positions in the offices of the U.S. adjutant general and judge advocate general. d. Bedford Springs, Va., 31 July 1887.   —EGL

Jones, William Edmondson "Grumble." CSA b. Washington Cty., Va., 9 May 1824, Jones was one of the most controversial figures of the Civil War. Described as "the best

outpost officer" in the Army of Northern Virginia, he was one of the few general officers court-martialed from its ranks. Eccentric, cantankerous, with a razor-sharp tongue, Jones cared little for pretense or appearance. As a cavalry officer, he possessed a combat record rivaled by few. His men idolized him, ROBERT E. LEE regarded him highly, and THOMAS J. "STONEWALL" JACKSON seemingly placed unwavering trust in the dour mountaineer. J.E.B. STUART, however, could barely abide him.

LC

Jones attended Emory and Henry College before entering West Point, where he graduated in 1848 ranked 10th in his class. He served on the frontier until 1857, when he resigned from the army, returning to his Virginia farm. During a furlough in 1852, he married, but, while en route to his command, his bride died in a shipwreck off the Texas coast. He was never the same.

When Virginia seceded, Jones was elected captain of the Washington Mounted Rifles, which he organized. He fought at FIRST BULL RUN under Stuart, and the feud between the two began. He briefly served as colonel of the 1st Virginia before assuming command of the 7th Virginia Mar. 1862. His solid performances at CEDAR MOUNTAIN, SECOND BULL RUN, and ANTIETAM earned him promotion to brigadier general 19 Sept. With Jackson's recommendation, but without Stuart's, Jones received the Laurel Brigade, a tough, veteran unit. In December he was given command of the Valley District.

In Apr.–May 1863 Jones undertook a spectacular raid into western Virginia. Penetrating nearly to the Ohio River, he inflicted heavy Union casualties while losing only a dozen men in a raid nearly unparalleled in Confederate history. Over his objections and Stuart's, Jones served under his old antagonist in the GETTYSBURG CAMPAIGN. At BRANDY STATION, his brigade bore the brunt of the fighting, suffering the most casualties. The animosity between the two men festered until September, when Jones, either verbally or in writing, abused Stuart. The corps commander ordered court-martial proceedings, and 9 Oct. Jones was found guilty and transferred to the Department of Western Virginia.

In his new assignment Jones once again performed brilliantly, constantly raiding into East Tennessee and blocking a Union thrust at Saltville. On 5 June 1864, at an engagement at PIEDMONT, while rallying his men, Jones died instantly with a bullet through his forehead. He was buried on the field by Federals, and his remains were reinterred near his home after the war.   —JDW

Jonesborough, Ga., Battle of. 31 Aug.–1 Sept. 1864 Maj. Gen. WILLIAM T. SHERMAN realized Atlanta was too strongly fortified to be taken by direct assault. Only the indirect approach—cutting its last open supply line from the south, the Macon & Western Railroad—could force Gen. JOHN B. HOOD's Confederates to evacuate the city. Attempts by cavalry raids and infantry detachments had failed, so Sherman decided to throw his entire army against the Macon & Western.

During the night of 25 Aug. he pulled his troops out of

trenches north and west of Atlanta. One corps, the XX, fell back to the railroad bridge spanning the Chattahoochee River. With his other 6 corps—the IV, XIV, XV, XVI, XVII, and XXIII—Sherman advanced from the northwest to strike the Macon & Western between Rough and Ready and Jonesborough.

Having sent his elite cavalry under Maj. Gen. JOSEPH WHEELER to raid Sherman's communications, Hood at first questioned Sherman's intent, hoping Wheeler had succeeded and the Federals were retreating north. But by 27 Aug. he perceived that large enemy forces were moving south of Atlanta. Accordingly he sent Lt. Gen. WILLIAM J. HARDEE with 2 corps, his own and Lt. Gen. STEPHEN D. LEE'S, to drive back the Union columns. Hood remained in Atlanta with the rest of his army—Lt. Gen. A. P. STEWART's Corps and the GEORGIA MILITIA.

On 31 Aug. Federals repulsed a poorly coordinated and generally feeble attack by Hardee on the Union XV and XVI corps west of Jonesborough. Meanwhile, Hood had learned that a strong Federal force was approaching Rough and Ready. Fearing that Sherman planned to attack Atlanta from the southwest, Hood recalled S. D. Lee's Corps the night of 31 Aug. Hardee was left with hopelessly inadequate strength.

On 1 Sept. the Union XIV Corps broke the thin Confederate defense at Jonesborough and forced Hardee to retreat to Lovejoy's Station. Only Sherman's failure to use his full available strength enabled Hardee to escape total destruction. However, Sherman cut the Macon & Western, making it impossible for Hood to hold Atlanta any longer. —AC

Jordan, Thomas. CSA b. Luray, Va., 30 Sept. 1819, Jordan graduated 41st in the West Point class of 1840, served as a lieutenant in the Seminole War, became a captain and assistant quartermaster in 1847, and served with the 3rd U.S. Infantry in the Mexican War. He resigned from U.S. service 21 May 1861, having performed the same duty at the same rank for more than 13 years, and went to Virginia to accept a commission as lieutenant colonel in the Confederate army.

Ambitious, Jordan attached himself to Gen. P.G.T. BEAUREGARD as adjutant general at FIRST BULL RUN, personally maneuvered troops on the field, and won his general's attention. His fortunes were linked to Beauregard's for the duration of the war. On staff duty in Corinth, Miss., in 1862, he drew up Gen. ALBERT SIDNEY JOHNSTON'S battle orders for the SHILOH campaigning, inserted his and Beauregard's changes, and on the field prior to Johnston's death, according to historian James Lee McDonough's *Shiloh: In Hell Before Night,* handled the disposition of troops. When Brig. Gen. BEN HARDIN HELM erroneously reported that Maj. Gen. DON CARLOS BUELL was moving toward Decatur, Ga., rather than to Maj. Gen. ULYSSES S. GRANT's assistance at Pittsburg Landing, Jordan insisted to Beauregard that the report was accurate. Jordan is also credited with recommending that Beauregard begin to withdraw from Shiloh 7 Apr., when Confederate resistance collapsed after Buell arrived to reinforce Grant.

Jordan was promoted brigadier general 14 Apr. 1862 for his performance at Shiloh. Thereafter, his fortunes diminished along with Beauregard's. He lobbied to have Beauregard given greater responsibilities in the Army of Tennessee. When the effort failed, he accepted a position as chief of staff to Gen. BRAXTON BRAGG, Johnston's replacement as commander in chief of the Western army, July 1862. In 1863 he returned to Beauregard's staff, administering the defense of Charleston, S.C. He remained in that theater through the surrender in

1865, at war's end commanding the 3d District of South Carolina.

After the war Jordan became an editor of the Memphis *Appeal* under editor-in-chief (former Confederate Brig. Gen.) ALBERT PIKE. Late in the 1860s he joined Cuban revolutionaries and when their insurrection failed, he founded and edited the *Financial and Mining Record* in New York City, where he died 27 Nov. 1895. —JES

Judah, Henry Moses. USA b. Snow Hill, Md., 12 June 1821, Judah graduated 35th in the West Point class of 1843, won brevets to 1st lieutenant and captain for action at Molino del Rey and Chapultepec in the Mexican War, and at the outset of the Civil War led the 4th California, being made colonel of volunteers 6 Sept. 1861.

Briefly resigning his volunteer commission 8 Nov., Judah traveled to Washington, D.C., served in the city defenses, was made brigadier general of volunteers 21 Mar. 1862, and the next month became inspector general of the Army of the Tennessee. Following the Battle of SHILOH, Judah led a division in the march on CORINTH while still

LC

serving as inspector general. He resigned that post July 1862, transferred to Kentucky, and was appointed acting inspector general of the Army of the Ohio in October.

Events thrust Judah into the forefront following his assignment to command the 3d Division/XXIII Corps early in June 1863. Stationed at Cincinnati, he was sent in pursuit of Confederate raider JOHN HUNT MORGAN and was outmaneuvered during MORGAN'S OHIO RAID. Judah's part in the Confederates' capture reflected poorly on his skill in the field. After a period in command of the 2d Division/XXIII Corps, he was relegated to desk duties in the Department of the Cumberland until the end of the war.

Brevetted lieutenant colonel and colonel in the Regulars 13 Mar. 1865 for his war service, Judah went on garrison duty in Plattsburg, N.Y., as a major and died there 14 Jan. 1866. —JES

Jug Tavern, Ga., eng. at. 3 Aug. 1864 Begun in the hope of wrecking railroads south of Atlanta and freeing prisoners at ANDERSONVILLE, STONEMAN'S AND MCCOOK'S RAID ended ignominiously. Surrounded by Confederate horsemen at Sunshine Church, Ga., 31 July 1864, Maj. Gen. GEORGE STONEMAN was forced to surrender with 1 of the 3 brigades of his cavalry division, Army of the Ohio. The rest of his command, the brigades of Cols. Horace Capron and Silas Adams, managed to work their way free of encirclement late that afternoon and to race to safety. Soon, however, a brigade of Confederate cavalry from the Army of Tennessee, several Kentucky regiments under Col. William C. P. Breckinridge, took up a spirited pursuit.

Colonel Capron, commanding the 14th Illinois, the 8th Michigan, and a squadron of the 1st Ohio, fled in company with only a few hundred men, though numerous escapees later joined him. At first separated from Adams' brigade, by pressing northeastward he linked with it near Rutledge Station late on 1 August. On the next day, the combined force moved against Athens, planning a 2-pronged strike on that well-garrisoned river town. While Adams demonstrated above the town, Capron took up a detached position, then sought to rejoin him to force a crossing of the Oconee River 2.5 mi above Athens. But a local guide misled Capron's column, and the Union forces remained apart. With Breckinridge still baying at his heels, a disgruntled Capron moved on northeastward, stopping after dark on the 2d at Jug Tavern (present-day Winder), almost within reach of Maj. Gen. WILLIAM T. SHERMAN's infantry. Having ridden 56 mi in 24 hours, Capron's men were exhausted, and he permitted them a 2-hour rest.

Just before dawn on the 3d, Breckinridge's cavalry struck the Union position. Having slipped around Capron's pickets in the darkness, the Kentuckians plowed into a mob of runaway slaves who had camped in the rear of the Federal column. The blacks fled in fear as the attackers rode over them, shouting and shooting. Soon, Capron later wrote, the Confederates burst through his bivouac, "driving and scattering everything before them. Every effort was made by the officers to rally the men and check the enemy's charge, but . . . a stampede now took place." As panicky Federal troopers remounted and galloped across a bridge over Mulberry Creek, the span collapsed under the weight and numerous men and animals drowned. Others, including Capron, fled to safety through dark forests. By then perhaps as many as 250 Federals had been killed or captured. —EGL

Julian, George Washington. USP b. Centreville, Ind., 5 May 1817, Julian was reared in a Quaker household headed by his widowed mother. The family's financial circumstances prevented him from attending school, though through reading he acquired a substantial education on his own. At 18 he found employment as a teacher, but friends encouraged him to read law and in 1840 he was admitted to the bar. After practicing briefly in Henry County, he returned to Centreville to be near his family.

His election in 1845 to the state legislature as a Whig marked the beginning of a long political career. A persistent idealist whose sincerity few doubted, Julian belonged to 5 different political parties during the years he held public office. At odds with the Whigs over the slavery issue, he allied with the FREE SOIL PARTY in 1849, winning a seat the next year in the U.S. House of Representatives. His abolitionist stance placed him

LC

in opposition to the COMPROMISE OF 1850 and out of political favor. Defeated for reelection in 1851, he did not hold office again until 1861. In the interim, he joined the People's party, which in 1856 became the REPUBLICAN PARTY.

With Republican backing in 1861 Julian won the first of 5 consecutive terms in the House. With Senators BENJAMIN F. WADE and ZACHARIAH CHANDLER, he became one of the most powerful Radical Republicans in Congress, an outspoken critic of Pres. ABRAHAM LINCOLN's refusal to issue an EMANCIPATION PROCLAMATION at the beginning of the Civil War, and an opponent of the president's colonization efforts (see ÎLE À VACHE). His insistence on the confiscation of Confederate property, the enlistment of blacks into the army, and the guarantee of civil and political equality for blacks won the favor of Radical colleagues and an appointment to the joint COMMITTEE ON THE CONDUCT OF THE WAR.

After the 13th and 14th amendments were passed during Reconstruction, Julian tried unsuccessfully to introduce a bill to give women the suffrage, then focused his attention on attacking land monopoly, corruption in government, and declining morality among Americans. He disapproved when the Republican party chose ULYSSES S. GRANT for the presidency in 1868 and made the corruption-riddled administration a target for his criticism. A failed attempt to organize a Liberal Republican party in 1870 resulted in his defeat for reelection in 1871 and his expulsion from the Republican party the next year.

Shortly thereafter Julian took the only choice open to him and joined the Democrats, but he never again held elected office. In Nov. 1873 he moved to Irvington, near Indianapolis. His zeal as a reformer waned, but an appointment as surveyor general of New Mexico during Pres. Grover Cleveland's administration allowed him to continue his crusade against land monopoly. Never a wealthy man, he supported himself largely by writing for magazines after he withdrew from politics. In 1884 he published his *Political Recollections: 1840–1872,* for the most part a discussion of antislavery politics during his career. d. Irvington, 7 July 1899. —PLF

K

Kanawha, Confederate Army of the. In 1861 Confederate operations in what is now West Virginia were notable for their abysmal failures in all respects. The Confederate Army of the Kanawha, formed 6 June 1861, was one of several commands operating in the area and was initially commanded by Brig. Gen. HENRY A. WISE. The zone of operation was then western Virginia, a wild, remote area in which both Union and Confederate sentiments existed. This army is not to be confused with Confederate troops under Brig. Gens. ROBERT S. GARNETT and WILLIAM WING LORING operating in southwestern Virginia during the same period.

After much marching, countermarching, and inconclusive skirmishing, Wise was superseded by Brig. Gen. JOHN B. FLOYD, previously secretary of war under Pres. James Buchanan and now under direct orders from Pres. JEFFERSON DAVIS. Wise and Floyd, both politicians and past governors of Virginia, were incapable of cooperation. Wise refused to acknowledge his subordinate position and continued to act independently. Gen. ROBERT E. LEE was sent from Richmond to assume overall command of the area Aug. 1861 but could do nothing with the constantly quarreling men.

Floyd failed to form any cohesive force and was unable to contain even a halfhearted Union assault at Cross Lanes and CARNIFIX FERRY, 10 Sept. On 25 Sept. Sec. of War JUDAH P. BENJAMIN flatly ordered Wise to turn over command of all forces to Floyd and report to Richmond for reassignment. Still, failure continued to follow failure.

In November, after a campaign remembered for dismal disasters and lackluster performances by all participants, the Army of the Kanawha was officially disbanded. Floyd was sent south to Bowling Green, Ky., with his brigades and those of Col. JOHN MCCAUSLAND to form the 3d Division/Central Army of Kentucky. Wise, his brigade restored to him, went to Norfolk, and Lee repaired to Charleston, S.C., to command defenses of that state, leaving behind a portion of his military career best forgotten. —RAP

Kansas. Kansas entered the Union 29 Jan. 1861, just as the Southern states were leaving it. Still a frontier society during the Civil War, the state had fewer than 100,000 citizens, concentrated in the eastern part of the state, and only 10 towns with over 500 inhabitants. Most of its people farmed or raised livestock, living in log cabins or dugouts.

Kansans overwhelmingly and enthusiastically supported the Union cause. Hailing mainly from the Great Lakes region, they were strongly Republican and antislavery, though few were abolitionists. Moreover, many felt they had a score to settle with Missouri dating back to the "BLEEDING KANSAS" turmoil of the 1850s. Throughout the war Kansas jayhawkers and "Red Legs" raided western Missouri as pro-Confederate Missouri

bushwhackers retaliated. The awful climax came 21 Aug. 1863, when 450 bushwhackers under Col. WILLIAM C. QUANTRILL destroyed LAWRENCE, Kans., and murdered about 15 of its male residents—the bloodiest affair of its kind to occur anywhere during the war. On 6 Oct. Quantrill also massacred nearly 100 Federal soldiers at BAXTER SPRINGS, Kans.

In October 1864 a 12,000-man Confederate army under Maj. Gen. STERLING PRICE marched from Arkansas into Missouri and approached Kansas City. Kansas militia joined Regular Union forces in defeating Price at an engagement at WESTPORT, Mo., 23 Oct. 2 days later, pursuing Federal cavalry routed Price at Mine Creek, the only full-scale battle fought in Kansas during the war.

Throughout the war Kansas raised 20,097 troops, most of whom served in or near the state, suffering 8,498 casualties. Both figures were the highest for all Northern states in proportion to population. Yet, despite the war and in some ways because of it, Kansas prospered between 1861 and 1865 and its population grew. —AC

1st Kansas Colored Volunteers. *See* 79TH U.S. COLORED TROOPS.

Kansas, Union Department of. Originally part of the Western Department, the Department of Kansas was established by General Order No. 97, 9 Nov. 1861. It consisted of a vast area that included the state of Kansas, all of Indian Territory, and the territories of Colorado, Nebraska, and Dakota. Maj. Gen. DAVID HUNTER was assigned command and established his headquarters at Fort Leavenworth. The boundaries were readjusted slightly 14 Feb. 1862 when Fort Garland in Colorado Territory was transferred to the Department of New Mexico.

A month later, 11 Mar., the command was absorbed into the Department of the Mississippi. The temporary merger lasted only until the Department of Kansas was reestablished by General Order No. 50, 2 May, with its previous boundaries intact, under the administration of Brig. Gen. JAMES G. BLUNT. Blunt's territory was reduced 6 Sept. when Nebraska and Dakota territories were transferred to the Department of the Northwest. On 19 Sept. the Department of Kansas was merged into the Department of the Missouri.

The department came into existence for the third time by General Order No. 1, 1 Jan. 1864, at which time its boundaries were expanded to again include Nebraska, and Fort Smith, Ark., was added. Maj. Gen. SAMUEL R. CURTIS was assigned command of the department from 16 Jan. The Indian Territory and the military post at Fort Smith were transferred to the Department of Arkansas 17 Apr. On 30 Jan. 1865 the Department of Kansas was merged permanently into the Department of the Missouri.   —PLF

Kansas-Nebraska Act. Of the legislation passed by Congress in the decade preceding civil war, none so completely undermined the chances for compromise between North and South on the issue of slavery as the Kansas-Nebraska Act of 1854. Written by Sen. STEPHEN A. DOUGLAS after the acquisition of Oregon and California called into question the status of the Great Plains, the act divided into 2 territories, along the 40th parallel, the unorganized land of the Louisiana Purchase.

As initially drafted, the legislation conformed to the precedent set by the COMPROMISE OF 1850 for the organization of Utah and New Mexico, giving the inhabitants territorial discretion over slavery without repealing the MISSOURI COMPROMISE (1820) (*see* POPULAR SOVEREIGNTY). Southern congressmen protested vehemently, arguing that unless the 36° 30' line was nullified, slaveholders would be excluded from settling in a large block of land open to free-soilers, who would then vote against slavery. At first, Douglas objected to amending the act to rescind the Missouri Compromise, but finally he revised his proposals to comply with the Southerners' demands, and the 36° 30' line was repealed. Though the apparent victory legitimized Southern insistence on Federal nonintervention into territorial government, the South had won an empty concession guaranteeing only against a state being refused admittance to the Union because its constitution provided for slavery. Congress passed the act 30 May 1854, after 5 months of bitter debate over its provisions.

Douglas' motives for conceding to the Southerners were challenged at the time and have been disputed ever since. His desire to speed the development of railroads in the West, his presidential aspirations, even his marriage to the daughter of a slaveowner are offered as possible explanations for his actions, but most often cited is his sincere belief that the Great Plains presented a natural barrier to the expansion of slavery.

The Kansas-Nebraska Act angered the free-soil North and cost Douglas much of his popularity in the South, especially after ABRAHAM LINCOLN skillfully attacked popular sovereignty during the widely publicized series of debates between the 2 men in 1858. By limiting the political avenues open to resolving subsequent disputes over slavery, the legislation destroyed the balance of power provided for in the Missouri Compromise and upheld by the Compromise of 1850. Free-soil advocates polarized against the pro-slavery faction, leading to the formation and rapid growth of the Republican party, while the struggle for control of Kansas Territory erupted into tragic internecine conflict known thereafter as "BLEEDING KANSAS."   —PLF

Kautz, August Valentine. USA b. Baden, Germany, 5 Jan. 1828, Kautz was brought to the U.S. as an infant, and his family eventually settled in Georgetown, Ohio, the same small town in which ULYSSES S. GRANT spent his boyhood. The 2 future generals, however, 6 years apart in age, were not friends. Kautz enlisted as a private in a volunteer regiment that fought in the Mexican War and returned determined on a military career. Graduating 35th in his class from West Point in 1852, he served on the Pacific Coast in the 4th Infantry, Grant's regiment, but the 2 did not serve together.

Kautz fought in the PENINSULA CAMPAIGN of 1862 as a captain, 6th Cavalry, and in September was appointed colonel, 2d Ohio Cavalry. Spending the winter in command of CAMP CHASE in Columbus, Ohio, he used the undemanding assignment

profitably by writing *The Company Clerk* (1863), a book reprinted 12 times during the war. Though he served as chief of cavalry, XXIII Corps, late in 1863, he made little mark before his appointment as brigadier general as of 7 May 1864.

USMHI

Assigned to command the cavalry division of the Army of the James, Apr. 1864, Kautz served in an army largely immobilized, first by the ineptitude of its commander, Maj. Gen. BENJAMIN F. BUTLER, then by its role in the Siege of PETERSBURG. Only the cavalry could move, and Kautz took a prominent but undistinguished role in expeditions to cut Confederate railroads. Overly cautious, the cavalryman succeeded largely because of the improvement in the strength and ability of the U.S. Cavalry and the corresponding decline of its opponents. In fact, Kautz performed best as a subordinate and shortly before the close of the war was assigned to command an infantry division.

He remained in the Regular Army after the war, serving predominantly on frontier duty. Kautz died in Seattle, Wash., 4 Sept. 1895 and was buried in Arlington National Cemetery.

—JYS

Kearny, Philip. USA b. New York, N.Y., 2 June 1815. After Kearny's mother died when he was 9, he spent his childhood and youth with his maternal grandfather, a man of wealth and high social position. Kearny's uncle, Gen. Stephen Watts Kearny, was a U.S. dragoon and Philip favored a military life, but his grandfather, who had lost all his sons, persuaded him to go to Columbia University.

USMHI

After graduating in 1833, Kearny traveled widely. When his grandfather died, leaving him a million dollars, he returned home and in 1837 obtained a commission as 2d lieutenant in the 1st U.S. Dragoons. After 2 years' service with them, the secretary of war sent him to the French Cavalry School at Saumur to study cavalry tactics. While there, Kearny saw action in Algiers, serving with the Chasseurs d'Afrique. On his return to the U.S., he served as aide-de-camp to, successively, Alexander Macomb and WINFIELD SCOTT, generals-in-chief of the army. In the Mexican War, Kearny accompanied Scott to Mexico City and at Churubusco was wounded so severely that his left arm had to be amputated. He was brevetted major for gallantry and, after service in California, resigned from the army, married, and made his home in New Jersey.

The military attracted him again in 1859, when he served in Napoleon III's Imperial Guard in the Italian War, winning the French Legion of Honor for bravery at Solferino. When the Civil War started, Kearny was appointed brigadier general of volunteers, commanding a brigade of New Jersey regiments in

Brig. Gen. WILLIAM B. FRANKLIN's division. One of the best known and respected soldiers in the army, he distinguished himself during the PENINSULA CAMPAIGN, rising to major general in command of the 1st Division of Maj. Gen. SAMUEL P. HEINTZELMAN's III Corps. After SECOND BULL RUN, he accidentally rode into the enemy lines during the indecisive Battle of CHANTILLY, 1 Sept. 1862, and was killed instantly. He was buried in Trinity Churchyard in New York City but was later moved to the National Cemetery at Arlington, Va. The New Jersey town in which he had resided was renamed Kearny in his honor. *See also* KEARNY MEDAL AND KEARNY CROSS.   —DBS

Kearny Medal and Kearny Cross.   These decorations, issued to men of the 1st Division/III Corps/Army of the Potomac, were named for Maj. Gen. PHILIP KEARNY, who commanded the division until his death at the Battle of CHANTILLY, Va., 1 Sept. 1862. Authorized in his honor after his death, the decorations were official only insofar as Kearny's old division was concerned; they were not recognized officially at any other level of the army.

The Kearny Medal was made of gold and was in the form of a Maltese cross under a circle bearing the words *Dulce et decorum est pro patria mori*. In the center was a circular gold device with the word *Kearny*. The medal was suspended by a ribbon and the back of the cross was engraved with the name of the recipient. These medals were issued by officers of Kearny's division to officers who had served honorably in battle while Kearny was still in command. The medal was adopted 29 Nov. 1862, and about 317 were distributed. They were manufactured by the New York firm of Ball, Black, & Co.

The Kearny Cross was authorized 13 Mar. 1863 while Brig. Gen. DAVID B. BIRNEY was in command. It was designated "the division decoration" and was designed as a "cross of valor" for enlisted men of the division. A bronze "cross pattee" with the words *Kearny Cross* on one side and *Birney's Division* on the other, it too was suspended from a ribbon. Far more of these were awarded than the Kearny Medal but the exact number is unknown.   —LDJ

***Kearsarge*, USS.**   A 1,031-ton vessel launched Sept. 1862 and commissioned 4 months later, the U.S. steamer *Kearsarge* was first commanded by Charles W. Pickering. Beginning a 3-year cruise, it joined 2 other Federal warships blockading the steamer CSS *SUMTER* at Gibraltar. On 8 Apr. 1863, Capt. JOHN A. WINSLOW replaced Pickering, and for the next 14 months the *Kearsarge* cruised off Europe, the Canaries, Madeira, and the Western Islands.

In June 1864 Winslow learned that the CSS *ALABAMA*, commanded by Capt. RAPHAEL SEMMES, was at Cherbourg harbor, and he steamed to that port. On 19 June Semmes brought the *Alabama* to sea in order to fight the *Kearsarge*, since he had concluded that the 2 ships were evenly matched and that he had a good chance of winning. The contest, which lasted just over an hour before the *Alabama* was sunk, demonstrated the superiority of the *Kearsarge*'s battery, especially its 2 11-in. pivot guns, as well as the crew's superb handling of these guns. 15 sailors on the *Kearsarge* received Medals of Honor for gallantry during the fight.

Several months before his encounter with the *Alabama*, Winslow, following the suggestion of one of his officers, had had chains slung over the *Kearsarge*'s midsection to protect its engines, and these were covered with boards. After his defeat Semmes accused Winslow of "cheating" by having secretly converted the *Kearsarge* into an "ironclad."

Following its victory over the *Alabama*, the *Kearsarge* finished its cruise and returned to Boston 7 Nov. 1864, to be decommissioned 3 weeks later. The ship continued in active naval service until wrecked off Central America in 1894.

The sternpost of the *Kearsarge*, containing an unexploded shell from the *Alabama*, can be seen today at the Naval Historical Display Center, Washington, D.C., and the powerful pivot guns are on permanent display at Mare Island Navy Base, Calif.   —NCD

Kell, John McIntosh.   CSN   b. Darien, Ga., 23 Jan. 1823. Appointed midshipman in the U.S. Navy in 1841, Kell graduated from the Naval Academy in 1848 and was assigned as

USMHI

passed midshipman to the *Albany.* His refusal to obey an order he considered illegal and beneath his rank resulted in court-martial and dismissal in 1849. During the proceedings he won the admiration of Lt. RAPHAEL SEMMES, the officer who defended him and who would later request him as his second-in-command in the Confederate navy. Dissatisfied with civilian life, Kell sought to reenter naval service and through the intervention of his family's political

PHCW

acquaintances was reinstated in 1850. Promoted to lieutenant 15 Sept. 1855, he spent most of his remaining years in U.S. service at sea, participating in Perry's Expedition to Japan and in the Paraguay Expedition of 1858.

Kell resigned his commission 23 Jan. 1861 and was appointed a commander in the Georgia navy. His assignment to the *Savannah* ended in April on receipt of orders from the Provisional Confederate Congress to report to New Orleans as 1st lieutenant and executive officer to Commander Semmes aboard the *SUMTER,* the first of the Confederate commerce raiders (*see* CRUISERS, CONFEDERATE). A small vessel ill-suited as a raider, the *Sumter* nonetheless performed admirably until decommissioned at Gibraltar in 1862.

Shortly thereafter, Semmes was given command of the raider *ALABAMA,* retaining Kell as executive officer. Semmes depended on Kell, who carried out his administrative duties with thoroughness and efficiency. As the man responsible for managing a crew of rough seamen, he earned a reputation as a strict but fair disciplinarian. He left the ship for only a few days during its more than 2 years afloat, giving little opportunity for critics to challenge his devotion to duty.

Kell became one of the few men with whom Semmes shared a close friendship. After their rescue by the *Deerhound* when the *Alabama* was sunk off Cherbourg, France, 19 June 1864, the two men spent much time together in England until receiving new assignments. Kell reported to the Confederate capital to take command of the ironclad *Richmond,* one of the ships in the James River Squadron, and participated in the unsuccessful attack on the Union fleet 23–24 Jan. 1865. At the time of the Confederate surrender, he was in Georgia on sick leave.

After the war Kell bought a small tract of land in Sunnyside, Ga., supporting his family meagerly by farming. During these years he refrained from defending the *Alabama* against charges of piracy, believing it was Semmes's place to defend himself and his crew. After Semmes's death in 1877, he became the chief vindicator of both the ship and its captain. Gov. JOHN B. GORDON, former Confederate general and a prominent postwar politician, appointed Kell state adjutant general in 1886 to help relieve the financial burden of a growing family. An office of prestige rather than purpose when he inherited it, Kell worked energetically to reorganize the position into a useful branch of state government. He held the appointment despite failing health until shortly before his death at Sunnyside, 5 Oct. 1900. —PLF

Kelley, Benjamin Franklin. USA b. New Hampton, N.H., 10 Apr. 1807, Kelley moved to Wheeling, in western

Virginia, at the age of 19. For over 2 decades he was a merchant, then in 1851 became a freight agent of the Baltimore & Ohio Railroad.

When the war began, Kelley raised the 1st (West) Virginia and was named its colonel 22 May 1861. On 3 June at PHILIPPI, the 90-day regiment fought Confederate volunteers and Kelley suffered a severe wound. When he returned to duty, he received promotion to brigadier general, to date from 17 May. His rapid rise had little basis in military experience and prowess but probably occurred

USMHI

because of his staunch pro-Union efforts in western Virginia.

Kelley's principal duty and service throughout the war was to guard the vital BALTIMORE & OHIO RAILROAD in Maryland and West Virginia. His command constantly operated against Confederate raiding parties that tried to sever the railroad line and destroy the depots. He participated in the Union pursuit after GETTYSBURG and the Nov. 1863 attack on Brig. Gen. JOHN D. IMBODEN's camp at Moorefield. In 1864 his command fought at Cumberland, Md., and again at MOOREFIELD, W.VA. In November a Confederate raiding party surprised and captured the Union depot at New Creek, W.Va. Kelley's performance in this disaster and his bungled pursuit drew severe criticism from his superior, Maj. Gen. PHILIP H. SHERIDAN.

On 21 Feb. 1865 Confederate guerrillas, under the cover of darkness, entered Cumberland, Md., capturing Kelley and his department commander, Maj. Gen. GEORGE CROOK. The affair created an uproar and both officers soon secured a special exchange. With the brevet rank of major general, Kelley resigned 1 June 1865.

After the war Kelley held a number of government posts. He was, successively, collector of internal revenue for West Virginia, superintendent of the Hot Springs, Ark., reservation, and examiner of pensions in Washington, D.C. d. Oakland, Md., 16 July 1891. —JDW

Kelly, John Herbert. CSA b. Pickens Cty., Ala., 31 Mar. 1840. After appointment to West Point in 1857, Kelly resigned 29 Dec. 1860 to fight for the South. At first opportunity he enlisted as a Confederate 2d lieutenant, was promoted to captain, placed on Brig. Gen. WILLIAM J. HARDEE's staff, and 23 Sept. 1861 became major of the 14th Arkansas.

He commanded the 9th Arkansas Battalion at the Battle of SHILOH and, late on the morning of 7 Apr. 1862, led it in a counterattack on Federals northeast of Shiloh Church. Commended and promoted to colonel of the 8th Arkansas in May, he led his regiment at the Battles of PERRYVILLE and STONE'S

PHCW

RIVER. On 20 Sept. 1863, at CHICKAMAUGA, Kelly took one of

Maj. Gen. SIMON B. BUCKNER's brigades into the final assault on Union Maj. Gen. GEORGE H. THOMAS' Snodgrass Hill position. For this he was made brigadier general 16 Nov. 1863, given a cavalry command under Maj. Gen. JOSEPH WHEELER, and in December exercised independence by signing Maj. Gen. PATRICK R. CLEBURNE's memorandum recommending emancipation for slaves willing to join the Confederate army. Through the fall of ATLANTA, Kelly headed a division in Wheeler's Cavalry Corps.

On 2 Sept. 1864, during a raid on Union Maj. Gen. WILLIAM T. SHERMAN's communication lines, Kelly was mortally wounded in a fight with Maj. Gen. LOVELL H. ROUSSEAU's Federal cavalry at Franklin, Tenn. Left at the nearby home of William H. Harrison, he died 4 Sept. and was buried on the property. His remains were moved to Mobile in 1866.

—JES

Kelly's Ford, Tenn., eng. at.   27 Jan. 1864   *See* FAIR GARDENS, TENN., ENG. AT.

Kelly's Ford, Va., action at.   7 Nov. 1863   Following the engagement at BRISTOE STATION, 14 Oct. 1863, Gen. ROBERT E. LEE removed his army south of the Rappahannock River, on the assumption that Maj. Gen. GEORGE G. MEADE might renew the offensive, even in a limited fashion. Meade proposed to retake the area between the Rappahannock and the Rapidan, the Lincoln administration having vetoed a general movement toward Fredericksburg. Lee fortified the major crossings of the Rappahannock, especially at Rappahannock Station and at Kelly's Ford a few miles below. At the latter crossing, he would allow Meade to cross, then attack the Union troops in force while holding the main crossing upstream. On 7 Nov. the Federal left wing, commanded by Maj. Gen. WILLIAM H. FRENCH, crossed at Kelly's Ford, seized some 300 prisoners, and established a strong lodgment on the south bank. Lee was not at first concerned since he expected to hit hard in a counterattack. However, his plans were thwarted by the success of the Federal right, a contingency he had not anticipated.

—JTH

Kelly's Ford, Va., Battle of.   17 Mar. 1863   Early on the afternoon of 25 Feb. 1863, about 400 of Brig. Gen. FITZHUGH LEE's Confederate cavalrymen surprised and routed Union cavalry outposts near Hartwood Church, capturing 150 Federals belonging to Brig. Gen. WILLIAM W. AVERELL's division. Lee and Averell were close friends, and Lee jestingly left a note behind, asking his old West Point classmate to return the visit and bring some coffee.

While this Confederate attack embarrassed Averell, it infuriated Maj. Gen. JOSEPH HOOKER, commander of the Union army. Hooker, who had reorganized the Union cavalry into a corps, wanted these Confederate forays stopped and ordered his cavalry commander, Maj. Gen. GEORGE STONEMAN, to end them or face relief from command. Within 3 weeks, Averell's scouts reported the presence of Lee's horsemen near Culpeper Court House, and the Union officer secured Stoneman's permission to return the visit.

Averell's division departed their lines 16 Mar. and long before sunrise on the 17th the 2,100 Federals arrived opposite Kelly's Ford on the Rappahannock River. Forewarned, Lee's pickets, behind felled trees, stubbornly prevented a crossing for 2 hours. Once on the south side, Averell advanced cautiously, halting a mile from the ford, near 2 farms. Lee, mean-

while, with only 800 troopers, moved toward the Union force. The Confederates met them at noon and soon charged.

For the next 5 hours the commands fought each other in a series of attacks and counterattacks. Mounted and dismounted, they battled across the farmlands and along stone walls. Averell, using his numerical advantage and an artillery battery, repulsed Lee's galloping thrusts, and the 2d Virginia Cavalry, for the first time in the war, fled before a Union cavalry charge. Union artillery blasts erased entire squadrons of Virginians. In one Confederate assault near the Wheatley farmhouse, Maj. JOHN PELHAM, the 25-year-old commander of the cavalry's horse artillery, having come along as a spectator, died instantly from a piece of shell in his skull.

Averell finally pushed the Confederates back a mile, but Lee again counterattacked. The gray-clad horsemen crashed into the Federals in a classic cavalry attack. Sabers and pistols emptied saddles, but the Northerners held. About 5:30 p.m. Averell withdrew; Union casualties amounted to 78, Confederate 170. For the first time in battle Union horsemen had matched the superb Confederate cavalry blow for blow. Before Averell recrossed the river, he left Lee a sack of coffee and a note asking how his old comrade had enjoyed the visit.

—JDW

Kemper, James Lawson.   CSA   b. Madison Cty., Va., 11 June 1823, Kemper was a student at Virginia Military Institute and graduated in 1842 from Washington College, after which he read for the law. He was a captain in the Virginia Volunteers during the war with Mexico and later was a prominent member of the Virginia house of delegates, where he gave special attention to militia affairs. Largely due to his efforts, Virginia troops were generally prepared in 1861.

USMHI

When the Civil War began, Kemper became colonel of the 7th Virginia and advanced in rank as he distinguished himself in major battles from FIRST BULL RUN to GETTYSBURG. He was promoted to brigadier general 3 June 1862, fought in the Battles of SEVEN PINES and the SEVEN DAYS', and in August was a division commander at SECOND BULL RUN. He figured prominently at SOUTH MOUNTAIN, ANTIETAM, and FREDERICKSBURG, and at GETTYSBURG he commanded a brigade in Maj. Gen. GEORGE E. PICKETT's division of Lt. Gen. JAMES LONGSTREET's Corps. Kemper's brigade, Longstreet's old command, stepped off in the right of Pickett's division, reached the Emmitsburg road, and guided to the left. Encountering severe flanking fire, it was eventually repelled, and withdrew with the battered remnants of that fateful charge. Its commander remained on the field, desperately wounded and a captive of the Union forces.

In 1864 Kemper was exchanged and returned to Richmond, where he served in a staff position. He was promoted to major general 19 Sept. 1864 and commanded the defense of Richmond after its evacuation near the end of the war. With the final surrender, Kemper, respected as a courageous and effective field commander, advised his fellow Virginians to accept the verdict of the war and look to rebuilding the state. He continued his law practice and served as governor of Virginia 1874–77. His years in office were stressful as a result of the Readjuster movement, but he sought to bring his state into the new order. Retiring at the end of his term, he died in Orange Cty., Va., 7 Apr. 1895. —JTH

Kenly, John Reese. USA b. Baltimore, Md., 11 Jan. 1818. Educated in the public schools of Baltimore, Kenly studied law and was admitted to the bar in 1845. During the Mexican War he served as a captain and major of volunteers, subsequently earning the thanks of the Maryland legislature for his gallantry in the Battle of Monterrey. After the conflict he returned to the legal profession.

On 11 June 1861 Kenly was commissioned colonel of the 1st Maryland, USA. During the war's first year the regiment served along the upper Potomac River in garrison duty. On 23 May 1862 Kenly's regiment fought the 1st Maryland, CSA, in the streets of FRONT ROYAL,

LC

Va. The Union regiment suffered some 900 casualties in the action, including a severely wounded Kenly, who was captured along with hundreds of his men. Exchanged 15 Aug. he was promoted 7 days later to brigadier general.

Kenly assumed command of the Maryland Brigade—1st, 4th, 6th, 7th, and 8th Maryland regiments—and was assigned to western Maryland. Throughout fall 1862 and for most of 1863 the brigade guarded the BALTIMORE & OHIO RAILROAD against Confederate raids. Kenly temporarily commanded a division of the I Corps during the BRISTOE CAMPAIGN in October. In spring 1864 the Maryland brigadier was relieved from command in the Army of the Potomac and assigned command of the District of Delaware, headquartered at Wilmington.

In July 1864 Kenly participated in the Union pursuit of Lt. Gen. JUBAL A. EARLY's Confederates, who had raided toward Washington (see EARLY'S WASHINGTON RAID). Commanding a brigade of militia and home guards, Kenly and his command guarded a wagon train. Near Winchester, Va., Southerners attacked the wagons, destroying numbers of them. After an official inquiry, Kenly transferred to the command of the District of Eastern Shore, Maryland, where he remained until the war's end, mustering out 25 Aug. 1865 with the rank of brevet major general.

Kenly returned to Baltimore, where he resided for the rest of his life. The city presented him with a sword, and the state legislature voted him a second thanks for his war service. The esteemed Marylander died in his home 20 Dec. 1891.

—JDW

Kennedy, John Doby. CSA b. Camden, S.C., 5 Jan. 1840. After attending South Carolina College, Kennedy studied law and was admitted to the bar Jan. 1861, 1 month after his state seceded. Deferring his law practice, in April he became a captain in the 2d South Carolina Infantry. 3 months later his regiment, under Col. JOSEPH B. KERSHAW, was engaged along the Confederate left at FIRST BULL RUN. During the battle, the

captain was wounded by a minié bullet.

LC

Thereafter Kennedy rose steadily, becoming colonel of the 2d on Kershaw's promotion to brigadier general early in 1862. On the Virginia peninsula he led his regiment through most of the SEVEN DAYS' CAMPAIGN, before being incapacitated by illness after SAVAGE'S STATION. He recovered in time to participate in the ANTIETAM CAMPAIGN, including Lt. Gen. THOMAS J. "STONEWALL" JACKSON's capture of HARPERS FERRY. In December, at FREDERICKSBURG, he led his own and a second regiment in supporting the brigade of Brig. Gen. THOMAS R. R. COBB by the stone wall at the base of Marye's Heights. Almost 7 months later, he served gallantly during the second day at GETTYSBURG, falling severely wounded while leading a charge against a Federal battery near the PEACH ORCHARD.

In 1864 Kennedy fought from the WILDERNESS to PETERSBURG, then in the Shenandoah Valley during Lt. Gen. JUBAL A. EARLY's operations, for part of that period commanding Kershaw's brigade. His final battle in Virginia was CEDAR CREEK, 19 Oct. On 22 Dec. he was raised to brigadier general and dispatched to South Carolina at the request of Gov. ANDREW G. MAGRATH, who foresaw Maj. Gen. WILLIAM T. SHERMAN's invasion of the state.

In the CAROLINAS CAMPAIGN, the new brigadier fought at AVERASBOROUGH and BENTONVILLE under Gen. JOSEPH E. JOHNSTON, reportedly being wounded 6 times as well as "hit fifteen times by spent balls." Following Johnston's surrender, Kennedy returned to Camden and took up his law career. Elected to Congress Dec. 1865, he was denied his seat after refusing to take the IRONCLAD OATH of allegiance to the Federal government. Later he was prominent in the campaign to return his state to white majority rule. Following military Reconstruction, he served as a state legislator, then as lieutenant governor. He died of a stroke in his native city 14 Apr. 1896.

—EGL

Kenner, Duncan Farrar. CSP b. New Orleans, La., 11 Feb. 1813 into a wealthy Louisiana family, Kenner received his early education from private tutors and in the public schools of New Orleans. He graduated from Miami University, Ohio, in 1831, and toured Europe for 4 years. On his return he read law with JOHN SLIDELL, but rather than practice settled on "Ashland," a plantation in Ascension Parish, as a sugar planter and horse breeder of repute.

Kenner served several terms in the state legislature beginning in 1836, as a delegate to the state constitutional convention in 1844, and as the convention president in 1852. The state sent him to the Provisional CONFEDERATE CONGRESS Feb. 1861. He was elected without opposition to the House of Representatives of both Regular Congresses. As chairman of the Ways and Means Committee, he supported an aggressive economic plan to finance the Confederacy, calling for a protective tariff, higher taxes, and government aid for railroad construction. Unlike the majority of his colleagues, Kenner embraced a nationalistic vision for the Confederacy, believing popular opinion should not obstruct the goal of establishing a nation.

As the war progressed Kenner, with increasing conviction, believed the South could win only with European recognition. Believing also that recognition would be forthcoming only if the Confederacy abolished slavery, he urged Sec. of State JUDAH P. BENJAMIN to consider emancipation. Finally, late in 1864, Pres. JEFFERSON DAVIS in desperation appointed Kenner minister plenipotentiary to attempt a secret mission to Europe to propose emancipation in exchange for recognition of the Confederate nation. Hoping to sail from Wilmington, N.C., Kenner arrived in time to see FORT FISHER fall Jan. 1865, and with it the last Southern port on the East Coast. In disguise, he traveled overland to New York City, departing 11 Feb. aboard the *America.* In Europe, he met a cool reception: Napoleon III agreed to follow England's lead, but British Prime Minister Lord Palmerston rebuffed Kenner's offer, and the last-ditch mission ended in failure.

Kenner returned home to find his house standing but the plantation in ruins. Within a few years, with hard work and his astute business sense, he had rebuilt the estate to exceed its prewar value. He encouraged the introduction into the state of advanced agricultural methods and machinery and helped organize the Sugar Planters' Association, 1877, and the Sugar Experiment Station, 1885, serving as the first president of each organization.

Politically Kenner remained active on the local level in opposing the Republican Reconstruction regime, losing a bid for a Senate seat in 1879. 3 years later Pres. Chester A. Arthur appointed him to the U.S. Tariff Commission. Kenner served for several years on the Louisiana Levee Board and chaired the building committee for the New Orleans Cotton Exposition, 1884–85. He held the presidency of the Louisiana Jockey Club from its founding until his death in New Orleans 3 July 1887.
—PLF

Kennesaw Mountain, Ga., Battle of. 27 June 1864

"An army to be efficient," wrote Maj. Gen. WILLIAM T. SHERMAN, "must not settle down to a single mode of offense, but must be prepared to execute any plan which promises success." By late June 1864, his 3 armies had spent the first 7 weeks of the ATLANTA CAMPAIGN employing essentially one mode of offense, a continual movement toward the flanks of Gen. JOSEPH E. JOHNSTON's Army of Tennessee. But the wily Johnston had slipped away every time, digging in behind new and formidable earthworks. Now, at last, the frustrated Sherman adopted new tactics based on the "moral effect" of a direct attack.

Currently Sherman's opponent held a position on high ground about 2 mi northwest of Marietta, Ga. His 7-mile-long line stretched north from Olley's Creek along a ridgeline that held his center and right flank. The high ground—Cheatham's Hill and, farther north, Kennesaw Mountain (comprising Big and Little Kennesaw, plus Pigeon Hill)—featured steep slopes covered by trees and boulders. Sherman, however, believed Johnston had stretched his army so thinly along that ground that his center and right lay vulnerable to assault. Further, rain-induced quagmires at least temporarily prevented any further resort to movements around the enemy's flanks.

Sherman scheduled his offensive for the 27th. The day before, in an effort to immobilize Johnston's lower flank, he sent part of Maj. Gen. JOHN M. SCHOFIELD's Army of the Ohio to demonstrate near Olley's Creek. To Sherman's surprise, 3 of Schofield's brigades gained a foothold on the south bank of the stream, though opposed by Confederate horsemen.

Despite Schofield's gains, Sherman proceeded with his assault against the Confederate center and right. By 6 a.m. on the 27th, with the temperature beginning its climb toward 100°, 3 brigades from Maj. Gen. JOHN A. LOGAN's XV Corps/Army of the Tennessee had moved toward the hills along the southern end of Kennesaw Mountain. After 2 hours of skirmishing, the Federals, two-thirds of them from Brig. Gen. Morgan L. Smith's division, rushed uphill and closed in hand-to-hand combat with the nearest Confederates, the advance guard of Maj. Gen. WILLIAM WING LORING's corps. In a desperate struggle with bayonets and clubbed rifles, Smith's men captured the first line of works. But when they pressed upward to Loring's main position, a solid wall of rifle and artillery fire collapsed on them. Hundreds fell dead or wounded; survivors huddled behind trees and rocks, unable to advance or retreat without exposing themselves to quick death.

Shortly after the Army of the Tennessee started forward, 2 divisions of the Army of the Cumberland assaulted the Confederate center on and north of Cheatham's Hill, ground held by the corps of Lt. Gen. WILLIAM J. HARDEE. 2 brigades from the XIV Corps division of Brig. Gen. JEFFERSON C. DAVIS and 3 brigades of Brig. Gen. JOHN NEWTON's division of the IV Corps made their way up the treacherous slope in the wake of an artillery barrage. The covering fire provided little help. One of Davis' brigades captured a line of trenches but was blown short of the main enemy works. Farther north, Newton's men scrambled up the steep, rocky incline in 2 columns, only to be cut down or forced to flee under a blizzard of shot and shell. A second attack also fell short of the Confederate trench line.

By noon, the Union offensive lay in a crumpled heap. It had cost about 3,000 casualties; among the dead were 2 brigade leaders, Brig. Gen. CHARLES G. HARKER and Col. Daniel McCook. Confederate losses amounted to perhaps 750. Sherman had paid a terrible price for his impatience with flank movements.
—EGL

Kentucky.

The border state of Kentucky, native state of both ABRAHAM LINCOLN and JEFFERSON DAVIS, was strongly nationalistic but economically pro-South. For a generation prior to the Civil War, the state had straddled the borderline of conflict, with its statesmen working for compromise. With the coming of war, its governor refused to honor Lincoln's call for troops after FORT SUMTER, and the state legislature, 20 May 1861, resolved to remain neutral. President Lincoln assured Kentuckians that no Federal troops would be sent into their state as long as it remained peaceful. The important position of the state geographically, and the even balance of its pro-North and pro-South inhabitants, made both sides honor its neutrality.

During the early months of war many Kentuckians volunteered for army service, with Union volunteers accepted at camps north of the Ohio and Confederates at a camp in northern Tennessee established especially for their recruitment. Within Kentucky the state militia, on home-guard duty, divided into 2 organizations, one friendly to the North and one to the South. Probably to a greater extent than in any other state, the war became literally, tragically, a struggle of brother against brother.

Kentucky's precarious neutrality could not last. On 3 Sept. 1861 Confederate Maj. Gen. LEONIDAS POLK led his forces from Tennessee into Kentucky, seizing Hickman and Columbus on the Mississippi River. Brig. Gen. U. S. GRANT speedily countered by occupying Paducah. Pro-South and pro-North militia forgot they were home guards and rushed to assist their corresponding armies. Kentucky soldiers in the Confederate army held a convention at Russellville Nov. 1861 and adopted an ordinance of secession. With a pro-South governor and a largely pro-North legislature, the state reeled in confusion.

Confederate forces enjoyed some victories in Kentucky, but after the fall of FORTS HENRY AND DONELSON in Tennessee, Feb. 1862, Confederate defenses gave way and the border state fell under Union control to the extent that future campaigns into the state by Confederates achieved only minor success.

Nearly 76,000 Kentuckians served with Union forces and about 25,000 with the Confederacy. Of all Kentuckians serving, approximately 30,000 died, 10,000 of battle wounds and 20,000 of disease and exposure. —PR

5th Kentucky. USA Commanded by Col. LOVELL H. ROUSSEAU, the Union's 5th Kentucky, known as the "Louisville Legion," numbered 1,020 men and officers when mustered into service 9 Sept. 1861 at Camp Joe Holt, Ind. Moving into camp at Muldraugh's Hill, Ky., Col. Harvey M. Buckley became its new commander in October on Rousseau's promotion to brigadier general. First in a brigade under Rousseau, it joined the Army of the Ohio Dec. 1861, serving in the 4th Brigade/2d Division until Nov. 1862, then entered the Army of the Cumberland, soldiering in the XIV, XX, and IV corps until the expiration of its original enlistment 14 Sept. 1864.

Survivors of the 5th Kentucky saw action at SHILOH, STONE'S RIVER, CHICKAMAUGA, the Siege of CHATTANOOGA and the Battles of ORCHARD KNOB and MISSIONARY RIDGE, Dalton, RESACA, KENNESAW MOUNTAIN, the Battle of ATLANTA, and more than 15 other engagements and battles. At its Sept. 1864 mustering-out, 157 members were counted as killed in combat, 15.3% of its original strength. At Chickamauga it had lost 125 killed, wounded, and missing, and in the battles for Chattanooga, as a part of Brig. Gen. WILLIAM B. HAZEN's brigade, lost 22 more from all causes.

A large number of 5th Kentucky veterans reenlisted Sept. 1864, garrisoned Nashville, and fought the Battle of NASHVILLE; they were transferred to North Carolina Apr. 1865, where they were present at the surrender of Confederate Gen. JOSEPH E. JOHNSTON's forces. Following the GRAND REVIEW of the Western armies, its veterans returned to Louisville and mustered out 25 July 1865. When casualties from original and veteran service were added to the number of officers and men killed by disease, the 5th Kentucky tallied 302 deaths from all causes during the war. —JES

Kentucky, Confederate Army of. When in late summer 1862 Confederate Maj. Gen. E. KIRBY SMITH invaded Kentucky as part of Gen. BRAXTON BRAGG's major Western offensive, the Southern forces previously in the Department of East Tennessee were renamed the Confederate Army of Kentucky. On 30 Aug. 1862, just 5 days after the government made the official designation, Kirby Smith's men won a decisive victory at the Battle of RICHMOND.

The closest thing to a battle of annihilation in the entire war, Richmond helped secure Kirby Smith's promotion, some 7 weeks later, to lieutenant general. The Federals had 6,000 hastily assembled raw recruits, Kirby Smith 6,000 veteran infantry and 850 cavalry. The hotly contested fight lasted all day,

the Federals making stand after stand while being successively pushed back.

Kirby Smith then quickly secured the area between Richmond and Lexington, Ky. Remaining in Lexington through September, he established virtually complete control over central Kentucky. Augmented by Col. JOHN HUNT MORGAN's horsemen, the Confederate cavalry periodically raided to the outskirts of Louisville and even to Covington, just across the Ohio River from Cincinnati. Unfortunately Bragg's larger scheme did not go as well as his subordinate's, and the Western offensive culminated 8 Oct. in Confederate frustration at the Battle of Perryville. That forced the end of the Kentucky invasion, and in subsequent reorganizations the army lost its identity. Kirby Smith briefly gained a corps command in Bragg's Army of Tennessee, but 20 Nov. his command reverted to that of the Department of East Tennessee. Those troops remained, becoming again the Army of East Tennessee, though widely scattered and not numerous. In December Kirby Smith departed to take command of the Army of the Southwest.

—HH

Kentucky Campaign. Aug.–Oct. 1862 Late in the summer of 1862, all the principal Confederate armies undertook offensive operations. While the army of Gen. ROBERT E. LEE invaded Maryland, resulting in the ANTIETAM CAMPAIGN, the commands of Maj. Gens. E. KIRBY SMITH and BRAXTON BRAGG launched a 2-pronged thrust into Kentucky. Confederate authorities hoped that these movements into Union territory would result in the recognition of their nation by European countries and would secure supplies and thousands of recruits from the 2 border states.

The Southern advance into Kentucky began 14 Aug. when Smith's 10,000 troops departed from Knoxville, Tenn. Bypassing the Union-held Cumberland Gap, Smith moved swiftly into the state. On the 30th, the Confederates defeated and captured most of an inexperienced 6,500-man Union garrison at RICHMOND, in the central part of the state. 2 days later Smith entered Lexington, then scattered his troops throughout the Lexington-Frankfort-Harrodsburg region with an apparent disregard for Bragg's movements.

Positioned at Chattanooga, Tenn., Bragg started northward 28 Aug., 2 weeks after Smith. His 30,000-man Army of Mississippi moved on a parallel route 100 mi west of Smith, entering Kentucky by way of Tompkinsville and Glasgow. On 17 Sept. a Federal garrison at MUNFORDVILLE surrendered to Bragg. A week later the Confederates were located at Bardstown, where they remained until 3 Oct. During this lull, Bragg conferred with Smith at Lexington and installed RICHARD HAWES as provisional Confederate governor of Kentucky, at Frankfort.

The presence of the Confederates in Kentucky, threatening the Ohio River, caused alarm in Louisville and Cincinnati and drew Union Maj. Gen. DON CARLOS BUELL's Army of the Ohio out of Tennessee. Moving on Chattanooga, Buell reacted slowly at first to Smith's and Bragg's movements, but once their intention became evident, he raced northward to save Louisville. Having received 3 divisions from Maj. Gen. ULYSSES S. GRANT, Buell's army numbered 50,000. On 29 Sept. they reached Louisville, their advance uncontested by Bragg.

The Federals moved against the Confederates 1 Oct., in 4 parallel columns. The main Union thrust was directed toward Bardstown. But Bragg, expecting Buell to move on Frankfort, sent a division to reinforce Smith and concentrated his remaining divisions at Perryville. On 7 Oct. the vanguard of the Union army struck Bragg's force, now reduced to 16,000. At dawn the next day, a brigade of Brig. Gen. PHILIP H. SHERIDAN's division attacked, opening the Battle of PERRYVILLE, the only major engagement of the campaign. A battle of attacks and counterattacks by both sides, Perryville resulted in 4,200 Union and 3,400 Confederate casualties. The Federals eventually held firm and Buell planned an all-out attack for the 9th, but Bragg withdrew during the night.

Smith's and Bragg's commands finally united at London, Ky. With his men outnumbered, short of supplies, and burdened with sick and wounded, Bragg decided to abandon the campaign. The Southerners, with their hopes of victory and of thousands of volunteers unfulfilled, retreated through Cumberland Gap. Buell pursued timidly, and the final Southern units reentered Tennessee 26 Oct. Kentucky was secured for the remainder of the war. Neither Bragg nor Smith had performed particularly well. Because of his lame pursuit, Buell was relieved of command.   —JDW

kepi. Adaptations and variations of the 1858 U.S. Army forage cap were colloquially and generally referred to as kepis. A French word derived from the Swiss-German diminutive for "cap," kepi usually denoted the French-style military cap with a short, round, flat crown and leather visor. In American Civil War use, it most often implied the ZOUAVE-, chasseur-, or McClellan-pattern cap. The original 1858 forage cap had a taller crown flopping forward, in some cases its top standing almost vertical to the visor, and was used throughout the war in both armies. The chasseur model, close to the French cavalry fatigue hat, was a nattier number, its shorter crown pinched forward at about a 35° angle and its officer models decorated with a crown and band of contrasting colors and perhaps some gold braid around the top of the crown. Kepis are the hats most closely associated with Civil War service.
                                                                        —JES

Kernstown, Va., First Battle of. 23 Mar. 1862 Maj. Gen. THOMAS J. "STONEWALL" JACKSON's tiny Valley Army of about 4,500 volunteers and militia had moved some 40 mi south of Winchester in Mar. 1862 when the general received information that a large Union force under Maj. Gen. NATHANIEL P. BANKS was leaving Winchester to go to Manassas. On 21 Mar. cavalry scouts under Col. TURNER ASHBY reported that Winchester was almost abandoned. Jackson immediately decided to demonstrate that Confederates still occupied the valley. After a hasty march, he arrived on Sunday afternoon, 23 Mar., at the village of Kernstown, just south of Winchester on the Valley Pike.

Assuming that he would find only a small enemy force, Jackson quickly planned a feint attack along the level ground near the pike, sending his main force toward Sandy Ridge on the west to strike the flank and rear of the Federals. Ashby had been skirmishing along the pike since morning and was now reinforced by Col. Jesse S. Burks's brigade to hold the valley road, while Col. Samuel V. Fulkerson's brigade, supported by Brig. Gen. RICHARD B. GARNETT with the STONEWALL BRIGADE, moved to the ridge. But Pritchard's Hill, northwest of the pike, was occupied by Union artillery in a commanding position to shell both Confederate groups, and 2 large Union brigades under Col. Erastus B. Tyler and Col. NATHAN KIMBALL moved onto the ridge to block the flank attack.

Opposing regiments fought back and forth in a bitter struggle for possession of a stone fence on the ridge. The unexpected strength of the Union resistance caused confusion among the Confederates. Jackson was not at the ridge and had kept his plans to himself. His regiments found themselves being pushed back and called for support. Garnett's brigade ran out of ammunition, and since he had no orders and no support, he moved to the rear, and the rest of the line followed. Jackson was trying to send up reserves and was furious to find his Stonewall Brigade falling back without orders. The army retreated, saving some artillery and wagons but having lost 455 killed or wounded and several hundred prisoners. Brig. Gen. JAMES SHIELDS ordered more Union troops to return to the valley.

The vigorous attack at Kernstown alarmed Washington and kept it in constant fear of an enemy force in the valley and of the unpredictable activities of "Stonewall" Jackson.   —FSK

Kernstown, Va., Second Battle of. 24 July 1864 The July 1864 raid on Washington, D.C., by Lt. Gen. JUBAL A. EARLY's II Corps/Army of Northern Virginia, embarrassed the Union authorities. When the Confederates departed from in front of the capital during the night of 12–13 July, a Federal pursuit was ordered. Early's raiders, however, eluded capture and destruction, bloodily repulsing a Union attack at Cool Spring on the Shenandoah River on the 18th. Brig. Gen. WILLIAM W. AVERELL's Federals routed one of Early's divisions 2 days later at Stephenson's Depot, north of Winchester, Va. The Confederates escaped basically unscathed, marching south up the Shenandoah Valley.

The main part of the Federal pursuit force, the VI Corps under Maj. Gen. HORATIO G. WRIGHT, retraced its march 21 July. To watch Early's command and protect the lower valley, Brig. Gen. GEORGE CROOK's Army of West Virginia occupied Winchester on the Valley Pike. With 7,000 infantry and 1,500 cavalry, Crook encamped a mile south of the town. Uncertain of Early's intentions and location, Crook sent Averell's cavalry division south on the 23d. At Kernstown, only a short distance south of Winchester, Averell's troopers encountered Early's advanced cavalry videttes, and the horsemen skirmished throughout the day. Both commands disengaged late that afternoon, with the Federals maintaining pickets at Kernstown.

Early, who had retreated to Strasburg, 20 mi south of Winchester, decided to advance against Crook on the 24th. At dawn the Confederates filled the pike, marching north. Southern cavalry renewed their clash with the Federals near 7:30 a.m. The blue-clad cavalrymen soon informed Crook of the Confederate activity, and by noon the Union commander had most of his 3 infantry divisions deployed on the north side of a small stream called Hogg Run. When Early arrived, he probed the Union position with Maj. Gen. JOHN B. GORDON's leading division.

Gordon's strong demonstration opened the battle's heavy fighting. While the Confederates occupied the Federals' front, Maj. Gen. JOHN C. BRECKINRIDGE's division swung wide to the right, coming in on Crook's exposed left flank. Breckinridge and Gordon soon charged together in 2 magnificent lines. The Federals fought stubbornly until Breckinridge's soldiers crumbled the flank, forcing a retreat that turned into a rout as Southern cavalry charged Crook's wagon train. During the stampede Crook's men abandoned or burned 72 wagons and 12 caissons.

The Confederates inflicted 1,185 casualties, including the capture of 479 prisoners. Early's losses are unknown, but he enjoyed another victory. This defeat and rout at Kernstown opened the lower Shenandoah to the Confederates and convinced Union authorities that a change was needed in the vital area. 2 weeks later Maj. Gen. PHILIP H. SHERIDAN assumed command of the new MIDDLE MILITARY DIVISION and army formed to oppose Early. —JDW

Kershaw, Joseph Brevard. CSA b. Camden, S.C., 5 Jan. 1822. Born into the antebellum Southern planter aristocracy, Kershaw lived up to his birthright. During his youth he practiced law, served creditably in the Mexican War, and won election to the South Carolina legislature in 1852 and 1854.

A member of his state's secession convention, Kershaw acted out his vote to dissolve the Union by raising a regiment and joining the Confederate army as a colonel. After commanding the Morris Island fortifications during the bombardment of FORT SUMTER, he went to Virginia with his regiment and saw action at FIRST BULL RUN. Promoted to brigadier general 13 Feb. 1862, he commanded a brigade of Brig. Gen. LAFAYETTE MCLAWS' division in Maj. Gen. JAMES LONGSTREET'S Corps of the Army of Northern Virginia.

USMHI

Kershaw and his brigade saw active service in the campaigns of the Eastern theater during 1862 and 1863. At FREDERICKSBURG he held the crucial sunken road in front of Marye's Heights against repeated assaults of massed Federals. At CHANCELLORSVILLE his command also distinguished itself. And at GETTYSBURG he was involved in the desperate fighting for the PEACH ORCHARD and WHEATFIELD on the second day, losing half his brigade.

In fall 1863 Kershaw and his command went west with Longstreet and fought at CHICKAMAUGA. Returning to Virginia for the campaigns of 1864, Kershaw was promoted to major general 18 May and given command of a division in Longstreet's Corps. He fought in the WILDERNESS, at SPOTSYLVANIA, COLD HARBOR, and PETERSBURG. After the Battle of SAYLER'S CREEK, he surrendered with Lt. Gen. RICHARD S. EWELL'S corps 6 Apr. 1865.

After the war Kershaw returned to South Carolina and the law. He served as a circuit court judge for 16 years and died in Camden 13 Apr. 1894. —EMT

Keyes, Erasmus Darwin. USA b. Brimfield, Mass., 29 May 1810. The son of a doctor, Keyes had a distinguished antebellum career in the Regular Army. An 1832 graduate of West Point, ranked 10th in his class, he fought Indians on the frontier, performed garrison duty, acted as Gen. WINFIELD SCOTT's aide and military secretary on 3 occasions, instructed cadets at the academy in artillery and cavalry, while rising to colonel of the 11th Infantry by the outbreak of the Civil War.

A favorite of Scott, Keyes was given a brigade in Brig. Gen. Daniel Tyler's division. The brigade fought at FIRST BULL RUN with no particular merit. In August Keyes received his promotion to brigadier general, to date from 17 May and remained

USMHI

in brigade command until November, when he assumed command of a division. In Mar. 1862 Pres. ABRAHAM LINCOLN named him commander of the newly created IV Corps.

Promoted to major general 5 May, Keyes led the corps throughout Maj. Gen. GEORGE B. MCCLELLAN'S PENINSULA CAMPAIGN. His performance was solid, though unexceptional. When McClellan abandoned the peninsula in July and August, Keyes' corps remained, transferring to Maj. Gen. JOHN A. DIX's Department of Virginia. Keyes served under Dix for a year. During the GETTYSBURG CAMPAIGN, Dix advanced against Richmond in a demonstration to prevent Confederate reinforcements from moving north to augment Gen. ROBERT E. LEE's army. Keyes, in the operation, retired before a Confederate force that Dix considered to be inferior. On 1 Aug. 1863 the War Department disbanded the IV Corps and removed Keyes from command. Keyes asked for an official investigation of Dix's charges, but his request was never granted. After a year of serving on boards and commissions, he resigned from the army 6 May 1864.

The Union general then moved to San Francisco, where he prospered as a gold miner, banker, and winemaker. While on a vacation in Europe, he died in Nice, France, 14 Oct. 1895. —JDW

Key West, Fla., Union Department of. By the outset of the Civil War, Key West, Fla., was a Confederate stronghold; at least 80% of its population was secessionist. The island's military and political structure, however, remained in Union hands. The U.S. Navy maintained gunboats and an artillery force at the Key West Naval Base, while army troops garrisoned Key West Barracks and nearby Fort Taylor. Meanwhile, the island's district court and customs house were headed by Unionist officials who refused to resign following the state's secession Jan. 1861.

The War Department sought to preserve this small enclave by imposing a departmental structure on the island. General Orders No. 3, dated 11 Jan., assigned Brig. Gen. JOHN M. BRANNAN, former commander of Key West Barracks, to head the department, a part of the Department of Florida. His territory encompassed the island itself, the Tortugas (including Fort Jefferson), and the Florida mainland as far as Apalachicola on its west coast and Cape Canaveral on the east coast.

Brannan did not assume control until 21 Feb., and he remained an independent commander for barely 3 weeks. On 15 Mar. his domain, as well as the rest of Florida, became part of the Department of the South, under Maj. Gen. DAVID HUNTER. Because of its inaccessible location and strong defense force, Key West remained in Federal hands throughout the war.

—EGL

Kiernan, James Lawlor. USA b. Mt. Bellew, Cty. Galway, Ireland, 26 Oct. 1837. The son of a retired surgeon in the Royal Navy, Kiernan served as assistant surgeon and chief surgeon during the Civil War. The records of his life, both private and military, are sketchy. He attended Dublin's Trinity

College and sometime before 1854 made the voyage to the U.S. He resided in New York City, where he attended the New York University Academy of Medicine and eventually copublished the weekly journal *Medical Press* with his brother-in-law.

USMHI

In 1861 he joined the 69th New York Militia as an assistant surgeon, serving at FIRST BULL RUN. On 1 Mar. 1862 he left the 69th in favor of Western service with the 6th Missouri Cavalry. There, after the Battle of PEA RIDGE, he left the Medical Corps, though he officially resigned as a surgeon May 1863. Apparently he became a major in the 6th Missouri. He was subsequently appointed brigadier general 1 Aug.

At PORT GIBSON, Miss., he is reported to have taken a wound in the left lung, one that debilitated him for the remainder of his life. Kiernan then took command of the Federal outpost at Milliken's Bend, but resigned 3 Feb. 1864 because of his lung ailment.

After the war he served as a consul to China, a doctor in New York City, and a pension-bureau physician until his death 29 Nov. 1869 in New York, of "congestion of the lungs."

—FLS

Kilpatrick, Hugh Judson. USA b. Deckertown, N.J., 14 Jan. 1836. Characterized as "Kilcavalry" by subordinates because of recklessness in combat, Kilpatrick was an extremely ambitious Union officer. Born into modest circumstances, he acquired early his lifelong habit of cultivating influential friends. One such connection secured him an appointment to West Point. Graduating 19th in his class in 1861, he accepted his commission as a 2d lieutenant and, 3 days later, a captain's commission in the 5th New York. In just over a month, 10 June, he became the first Regular Army officer wounded in action, in the skirmish at BIG BETHEL. By September he had recovered from his wound and accepted promotion to lieutenant colonel in the 2d New York Cavalry. He served primarily on the Virginia front 1862–63. His aggressiveness and attention to influential friends assisted his rise to colonel Dec. 1862, then to brigadier general 14 June 1863.

USMHI

Kilpatrick's cavalry commands usually looked good on parade and in battle. Nevertheless, their camps reflected the young general's lack of discipline and good order. While he never drank, no one could accuse him of excess morality, and women of questionable virtue frequented his camps.

During the GETTYSBURG CAMPAIGN, Kilpatrick commanded a division of cavalry and was accused of poor judgment for ordering a disastrous charge on the third day of battle. Attempting to recoup his reputation and enhance his postwar political

ambitions, he planned an extensive raid on Richmond early in 1864. Hoping to swoop down on the Confederate capital, free Union prisoners there, and wreak as much havoc as possible on the city, he seemingly lost his nerve at the very gates of Richmond 1 Mar. 1864 (see KILPATRICK–DAHLGREN RAID).

In the aftermath of the raid, Kilpatrick commanded a cavalry division in Maj. Gen. WILLIAM T. SHERMAN's drive to Atlanta. Wounded at Dalton, Ga., he returned to participate in Sherman's MARCH TO THE SEA and the Union drive through the Carolinas (see CAROLINAS CAMPAIGN). At war's end he resigned a major general's commission, accepting instead an appointment as minister to the Republic of Chile. He ran unsuccessfully for Congress in 1880, then returned to his diplomatic post. Kilpatrick died in Santiago 4 Dec. 1881. His remains were eventually reburied at West Point.   —EMT

Kilpatrick–Dahlgren Raid. 28 Feb.–3 Mar. 1864 During the early weeks of 1864 Union cavalry general H. JUDSON KILPATRICK plotted a daring raid on Richmond to release the large number of Federal prisoners held there. The scheme impressed his influential friends in Washington; ABRAHAM LINCOLN added his blessing; and on the evening of 28 Feb. 1864 about 4,000 troopers set out toward Ely's Ford on the Rapidan River.

The Federals rode all night and before dawn reached Spotsylvania Court House, where a detached force of 500 turned due south on a route to Goochland Court House. Commanding this detachment was Col. ULRIC DAHLGREN, whose mission it was to cross the James River and dash into Richmond from the south while Kilpatrick entered from the north. Both parties advanced relatively on schedule during 29 Feb., despite heavy rains that turned to sleet toward nightfall. A small force of 300 Confederate cavalry was in pursuit of Kilpatrick but well behind the raiders.

On 1 Mar. Kilpatrick reached Richmond's intermediate defense line. Though there were only about 500 defenders, Kilpatrick hesitated, then retreated some distance. He contemplated a night attack, but the pursuing Confederate cavalry caught up and launched an attack on his camps. After the Federals fought them off, Kilpatrick decided to withdraw down the peninsula to friendly lines.

Meanwhile, Dahlgren was having difficulties. High water prevented him from crossing the James; thus he approached Richmond from the west instead of the south. Late on the afternoon of 1 Mar., his troopers were repulsed on the outskirts of the city by the home guards. During the confusion Dahlgren and about 100 men were separated from the rest of the force. Most of the troops circled north of Richmond and finally found Kilpatrick. Dahlgren's smaller body took a wider arc around the city and on the night of 2 Mar. rode into an ambush in King and Queen County. Dahlgren was killed and most of the raiders were taken captive. Papers found on Dahlgren's body contained instructions to burn Richmond and kill Confederate leaders, inflaming public opinion in the South (see DAHLGREN PAPERS).   —EMT

Kimball, Nathan. USA b. Fredericksburg, Ind., 22 Nov. 1822. After attending what is now DePauw University, Kimball taught school at Independence, Mo., farmed for a time, then studied medicine under the supervision of his brother-in-law, a local physician. During the Mexican War he was a captain in the 2d Indiana Volunteers, serving ably in the Battle of Buena

Vista, where he held his position despite the disorderly retreat of much of his regiment. On his return to Indiana he practiced medicine in the village of Loogootee until the outbreak of the Civil War.

LC

Early in 1861 Kimball regained a captaincy in the volunteers and soon became colonel of a regiment he had helped raise, the 14th Indiana Infantry. Later that year, serving in western Virginia, his outfit fought at CHEAT MOUNTAIN and GREEN-BRIER RIVER. Sent to the Shenandoah Valley, he distinguished himself in the fighting at KERNSTOWN 23 Mar. 1862. In that battle, during Maj. Gen. THOMAS J. "STONEWALL" JACKSON'S SHENANDOAH VALLEY CAMPAIGN, he succeeded to the command of the division formerly led by the wounded Brig. Gen. JAMES SHIELDS. Kimball directed the command so well that he inflicted on Jackson one of the few tactical defeats of his career, and the victory enabled the Indiana officer to gain the star of a brigadier general 16 Apr.

In Sept. 1862 Kimball's new command, the 1st Brigade/3d Division/II Corps, lost heavily at ANTIETAM. 3 months later it made one of the energetic but ill-fated attacks against Marye's Heights at FREDERICKSBURG, in which Kimball was severely wounded. After recovering, he was sent west in spring 1863 and led a XVI Corps division in the VICKSBURG CAMPAIGN. Following the fall of the city, he served for some time in Arkansas, opposing the forces of Maj. Gen. STERLING PRICE and helping organize the state's Unionist government.

At the outset of the 1864 ATLANTA CAMPAIGN, Kimball was reduced to command of a brigade in the IV Corps but returned to divisional leadership in late July, after gallant participation at PEACHTREE CREEK. That summer his services were required in his home state, where he helped combat the subversive KNIGHTS OF THE GOLDEN CIRCLE. Returning to field command, he fought at FRANKLIN and NASHVILLE, and was brevetted a major general of volunteers 1 Feb. 1865.

After the war, Kimball was Indiana commander of the GRAND ARMY OF THE REPUBLIC, then state treasurer and legislator. Moving west in 1873, he became surveyor general of Utah and postmaster of the city of Ogden, where he died 21 Jan. 1898.   —EGL

King, Rufus. USA b. New York, N.Y., 26 Jan. 1814. After attending Columbia College in New York City, King was appointed to West Point, graduated 4th in the class of 1833, and, after service in the engineers, resigned his commission 30 Sept. 1836 to become a civil engineer for the New York & Erie Railroad. From 1839 to 1845 he edited the Albany *Daily Advertiser* and Albany *Evening Journal* and served as adjutant general of New York militia until moving to Milwaukee, Wis. In 1845 he became an owner/editor of the Milwaukee *Sentinel and Gazette* and until the Civil War was prominent in Midwestern public life and politics. In 1861 Sec. of State WILLIAM H. SEWARD secured King's patronage appointment as U.S. minister to the Papal States. The FORT SUMTER crisis compelled him instead to offer his military service, and he was appointed brigadier general of volunteers 17 May 1861.

King's wealthy and distinguished New York family and his own experience in the Midwest helped him organize the IRON BRIGADE OF THE WEST in Washington. After a year in Washington, D.C., and along the Rappahannock River, his troops went into combat in the SECOND BULL RUN CAMPAIGN, fighting well without him. Brig. Gen. JOHN GIBBON led them in his stead. King, assigned a division in Maj. Gen. IRVIN MCDOWELL'S corps, mishandled his part in

LC

maneuvers around Gainesville, Va., and Thoroughfare Gap days before the Battles of GROVETON and SECOND BULL RUN. Confederates filtered through Thoroughfare Gap to attack Maj. Gen. JOHN POPE'S army. Since King was an epileptic with a reputation as a drinker, his actions are difficult to account for between 27 and 30 Aug. He missed the Battle of Groveton, remaining in Gainesville; reporting on the fight, which he had not witnessed, he greatly overestimated the numbers in Maj. Gen. THOMAS J. "STONEWALL" JACKSON'S force. King missed both days at Second Bull Run, claiming illness. Pope believed him drunk at least 2 of those 4 days and had him court-martialed. Found guilty of disobedience and errors in judgment, he was given minor duties until his resignation 20 Oct. 1863. Paradoxically, during this period he sat on the court-martial of Brig. Gen. FITZ JOHN PORTER, accused of dereliction in the same campaign.

Concurrent with his resignation, King accepted reappointment to the Papal States ministry 7 Oct. 1863, serving there until 1 Jan. 1868. In that post he helped secure the arrest and extradition of JOHN H. SURRATT, a conspirator in Lincoln's assassination. Briefly serving as deputy customs collector in New York City, he retired in 1869 in poor health, and died in that city 13 Oct. 1876. Whether King was ill or drunk during the Second Bull Run Campaign is a perennial issue in discussing its history. The blame for the mishandling of his division at Thoroughfare Gap must be shared by McDowell.   —JES

King's School House, Va., eng. at. 25 June 1862 *See* OAK GROVE, VA., ENG. AT.

Kinston, N.C., Battle of. 8–10 Mar. 1865 The fall of Wilmington, 22 Feb. 1865, enabled Maj. Gen. JOHN M. SCHOFIELD, the recently installed commander of the Union Department of North Carolina, to plan an inland campaign. His first task was to prepare a line of communications from the Atlantic Coast to Goldsborough, which Maj. Gen. WILLIAM T. SHERMAN, about to begin his invasion of the state, could use on his trek north. Since supply vehicles and rolling stock were scarce at Wilmington, Schofield found it expedient to operate instead from New Berne. On the 25th he ordered the latter's garrison commander, Brig. Gen. INNIS N. PALMER, to move westward with his mobile forces, shielding laborers who had begun to repair the railroad to Goldsborough.

Dissatisfied with Palmer's progress, Schofield placed over him Maj. Gen. JACOB D. COX, who had come east with Schofield's XXIII Corps following the Battle of NASHVILLE. Soon Cox commanded a provisional corps embracing not only Palmer's division but that of Brig. Gen. SAMUEL P. CARTER from the District of Beaufort. A third division, under another XXIII Corps commander, Brig. Gen. THOMAS H. RUGER, would join Palmer and Carter on the road to Goldsborough. The Union force numbered over 13,000 infantry, a small cavalry contingent, and several artillery units.

The advance brigades of the command marched out of New Berne early in March. On the 7th, they found their progress stopped at Southwest Creek, just below Kinston. On the west bank of the stream the local Confederate commander, Gen. BRAXTON BRAGG, had entrenched about 6,500 effectives from the division of Maj. Gen. ROBERT F. HOKE. With these troops and those to come, under Lt. Gen. DANIEL H. HILL (including remnants of the Army of Tennessee), Bragg hoped to slow the Federals' march, if not stop it altogether.

Bragg held his enemy stationary throughout the 7th with an effective artillery barrage. The following day, Hill joined him with 2,000 troops, enough to take the offensive against the Federals now dug in near Wise's Forks. Bragg sent Hoke against the enemy left, while Hill made ready to advance on the other flank. Hoke crossed the stream and swooped down on 2 regiments under Col. Charles Upham, posted 1 mi in advance of Cox's main line. Upham's little brigade disintegrated under the pressure, but Hoke accomplished nothing further. Meanwhile, Hill was sent on a fruitless effort to stanch Upham's retreat from the rear instead of being allowed to link with Hoke for a push farther eastward. Bragg's faulty tactics thus prevented Hill from exploiting Hoke's gains.

On the 9th, Ruger's division having arrived to guard the Federal center, Cox fought off a feeble attempt by Hoke to break his line. Still confident he could turn the enemy out of its position, Bragg attempted another flank envelopment just before noon 10 Mar. On this day Hoke initially gained ground, gouging some of Carter's men from their works; meanwhile, Hill, on the Confederate left, captured one of Palmer's trench lines. Ruger shored up weak points in the line, and Union strength forced Hoke backward. Caught ahead of his supports, Hill had to fall back too.

Finally, Bragg pulled the entire force across the Neuse River to Kinston, part of Ruger's division in hot pursuit. The latter was soon recalled, permitting the Confederates, who had suffered heavy casualties, to escape. They had grown too weak to prevent Schofield from capturing Kinston on the 14th. A week later, without strong opposition from Bragg, the Federals rode their momentum into Goldsborough, securing Sherman's much-needed base of supply.   —EGL

Kirby, Edmund. USA b. Brownsville, N.Y., 11 Mar. 1840, Kirby was a grandson of Maj. Gen. Jacob Brown, commander in chief of the Regular Army 1815–28, and son of Brev. Col. Edmund Kirby, an army paymaster who died when his son was 9. The younger Edmund entered West Point in 1856, graduating 10th in the class of 1861. The Civil War split the allegiance of his family, including more than a dozen cousins, among them a second cousin, Confederate Gen. EDMUND KIRBY SMITH.

Commissioned a 2d lieutenant 6 May, Kirby was promoted to 1st lieutenant 8 days later. He immediately received an assignment to the 1st U.S. Artillery, initially commanding a section and later the battery. Kirby fought in nearly all the major campaigns in the East: FIRST BULL RUN, BALL'S BLUFF, PENINSULA, SEVEN DAYS', ANTIETAM, FREDERICKSBURG, and CHANCELLORSVILLE.

_LC_

In this last campaign, 3 May 1863, Kirby's battery was engaged near the Chancellor House. As the opposing artillerists exchanged charges, a piece of Confederate case shot fractured Kirby's thigh. He reluctantly abandoned his post and was eventually sent to a hospital in Washington. Infection set in and surgeons amputated the leg. Told that he could not recover, the 23-year-old lieutenant serenely accepted his fate, except for voicing concern over his widowed mother and sisters. Pres. ABRAHAM LINCOLN, during a visit to the hospital, learned of Kirby, and commissioned him a brigadier general of volunteers 28 May 1863, the day he died. Lincoln's magnanimity ensured that Kirby's family would receive a generous pension.   —JDW

Kirby Smith, Edmund. See SMITH, EDMUND KIRBY.

Kirby Smithdom. See TRANS-MISSISSIPPI, CONFEDERATE DEPARTMENT AND ARMY OF THE.

Kirkland, Richard Rowland. See "ANGEL OF MARYE'S HEIGHTS."

Kirkland, William Whedbee. CSA b. "Ayrmont," Hillsborough, N.C., 13 Jan. 1833, Kirkland entered the U.S. Military Academy in 1852 but never graduated. Commissioned a 2d lieutenant in the U.S. Marine Corps in 1855, he served until Aug. 1860. Joining the Confederate Regular Army before the firing on FORT SUMTER, he was commissioned a captain of infantry 16 Mar. 1861.

Elected colonel of the 21st North Carolina in June, Kirkland led his regiment at FIRST BULL RUN and in the SHENANDOAH VALLEY CAMPAIGN of 1862. During the latter operation, he was severely wounded at FIRST WINCHESTER in May. Incapacitated for months, the North Carolinian spent more than a year recovering. He was able, however, to act as Maj. Gen. PATRICK R. CLEBURNE's chief of staff in the Battle of Stone's River in late Dec. 1862 and early Jan. 1863.

Kirkland returned to his regiment in time for the Battle of GETTYSBURG. Promoted to brigadier general 29 Aug. 1863, he commanded a brigade in Maj. Gen. HENRY HETH's division during the BRISTOE CAMPAIGN in October. At BRISTOE STATION on the 14th, his brigade was slaughtered and he was again wounded, disabling him until spring 1864. He led his brigade at the WILDERNESS and SPOTSYLVANIA before suffering a third wound 2 June near Gaines' Mill. Returned to active duty in August, Kirkland was assigned to a brigade in the division of Maj. Gen. ROBERT F. HOKE. He participated in the engagements north of the James River until transferred to North Carolina in December. Kirkland fought at FORT FISHER and at BENTONVILLE, where he was surrendered with the rest of Gen. JOSEPH E. JOHNSTON's army.

Settling in Savannah, Ga., Kirkland engaged in the commission business. He subsequently moved to New York City, where his daughter, Bess, had become a famous actress, under the stage name of Odette Tyler. Invalided about 1900, Kirkland lived in a soldiers' home in Washington, D.C., until his death there 12 May 1915. —JDW

Kirkwood, Samuel Jordan. war governor b. Harford Cty., Md., 20 Dec. 1813. Educated in Washington, D.C., Kirkwood worked there as a druggist until moving to Richland Cty., Ohio, in 1835. There he read law and was admitted to the bar in 1843. During his 12 years in the state, he held an appointment as county prosecuting attorney, 1845–49, and was a member of the 1850–51 Ohio constitutional convention. On relocating to Iowa in 1855 he abandoned his legal practice to become a farmer and miller near Iowa City.

A rough-hewn man highly regarded for integrity and financial good sense, Kirkwood appealed to the frontier electorate, winning a seat in the state senate in 1856 and the governorship in 1859. As a conservative, but fiercely pro-Union, antislavery member of the Republican party, he opposed compromise beyond reinstating the MISSOURI COMPROMISE to appease Southern radicals during the secession crisis of winter 1860–61. Responding to ABRAHAM LINCOLN's appeal for troops, he had a regiment of Iowans ready for duty within 2 weeks of the call to arms.

Kirkwood labored vigorously to prepare the state for war. Satisfied with his support of Lincoln's policies, the governor's constituents reelected him in 1861. He urged the president toward emancipation and the use of 'black soldiers, offering to recruit blacks in Iowa to take the place of white men in the ranks. Though he favored CONSCRIPTION, under his direction Iowa was one of the few states able to fulfill its troop quota without resorting to the draft.

Except for traveling east to attend the convention of governors held in Altoona, Pa., 24 Sept. 1862, Kirkwood remained in Iowa to apply his administrative abilities to problems within the state. Much of his time was spent selling bonds to finance Iowa's war effort, seeking Federal assistance to equip the 50 3-year regiments he raised for the Union army, providing soldiers' aid and relief to widows and orphans, and countering Copperhead activities in the region (see PEACE DEMOCRATS).

Unable to succeed himself for a third term as governor, he campaigned in 1863 for the election of Republican William M. Stone. From Kirkwood, Stone inherited a well-organized, efficient state government.

Kirkwood's retirement from elected office was interrupted briefly by an appointment to fill a vacant Senate seat in 1866. When the term expired in 1867, he accepted the presidency of the Iowa & Southwestern Railroad. He served 1 additional term in the U.S. Senate, 1877–81, and was as secretary of the interior, Mar. 1881–Apr. 1882, in the James A. Garfield administration. d. Iowa City, 1 Sept. 1894. —PLF

knapsack. Both Union and Confederate volunteers first went to the Civil War carrying a standard backpack, or knapsack. Most often riding on a light wooden frame, it was made of heavily painted canvas, had the number of the soldier's unit stenciled on the back, and strapped over his shoulders and around his chest. Some were made of rubber; all fit poorly, sagged onto the small of the soldier's back, and were too hot to carry in summer. Both armies discarded them during the war. Soldiers preferred a blanket roll filled with bare necessities slung over the left shoulder and tied with string at the right hip. —JES

Knights of the Golden Circle. Originally a Southern organization, the Knights of the Golden Circle was founded in 1854 by GEORGE W. L. BICKLEY, its goal to bring about the annexation of Mexico in order to extend the area of slavery. The movement languished until 1859, when the sectional struggle was approaching its climax. Then, under Bickley's tireless leadership, chapters ("castles") sprang up throughout the South. Though still concerned with creating a Mexican slave empire, the Knights focused their attention on secession, which they favored. During this period castles also were formed in the border states by individuals who favored the Southern cause. After civil war broke out, the Knights and other groups gained notoriety for their subversive activities behind the Federal lines. Through the war they engaged in practices ranging from providing the Confederacy with intelligence to acts of sabotage such as blowing up warehouses and ammunition dumps.

It is impossible to determine even approximately how many Knights there were or how effectively they performed. They were sworn to secrecy under threat of death by torture and of course sought to avoid detection and arrest for their activities. Estimates of the membership in Missouri alone range from 10,000 to 60,000, and the Chicago *Tribune* reported that there were at least 20,000 Knights in Illinois. Most likely the actual numbers were fewer. What they accomplished will never be known, for it was commonplace during the war to attribute every accident or misfortune to the work of the Knights or some other group collectively known as Copperheads (see PEACE DEMOCRATS). —RJM

Knoxville Campaign. Nov.–Dec. 1863   During the stalemated investment of Chattanooga, Tenn., Confederate Gen. BRAXTON BRAGG and Lt. Gen. JAMES LONGSTREET quarreled. On Pres. JEFFERSON DAVIS' approval, to ease command tensions and divert Federal attention from Chattanooga operations, Longstreet, 2 divisions led by Maj. Gen. LAFAYETTE MCLAWS and Brig. Gen. MICAH JENKINS, and 2 artillery battalions under Col. E. PORTER ALEXANDER and Maj. Austin Leyden were sent to attack Maj. Gen. AMBROSE E. BURNSIDE's East Tennessee troops at Knoxville. Maj. Gen. JOSEPH WHEELER's 5,000 cavalry, directed to lend support, brought Longstreet's strength to 17,000 men.

Departing 4 Nov., Longstreet's force struggled northeast up the East Tennessee & Georgia Railroad, arriving in front of the Little Tennessee River near Loudon on the 14th. Wheeler traveled east of Longstreet's force to Maryville, which is south of Knoxville. From the 13th, he moved north probing Knoxville's southern approaches; through the 17th, he scouted the south banks of the Holston River west of the city. Longstreet's infantry and artillery crossed the Little Tennessee the night of 14 Nov., west of Loudon, alerting a Union outpost. Burnside rushed from Knoxville to organize the withdrawal of advanced IX and XXIII corps troops in the Loudon area.

Traveling parallel northeast routes from the Little Tennessee, Union and Confederate forces shadowed one another through the 15th, Longstreet hoping to attack the Federals near Lenoir. Burnside's troops slipped away and a race began between Confederate and Union forces to reach CAMPBELL'S STATION, a strategic intersection on the Kingston road to Knoxville; the first to reach it might fend off or capture the other. On the 16th, Burnside's men arrived at the intersection 15 minutes ahead of Longstreet's troops, fought a delaying action until nightfall, and, behind a cavalry screen, retreated into the safety of Knoxville's fortified lines on the 17th. Confederates advanced, probing Knoxville's lines, and drove in an advanced brigade of Federal cavalry, killing its commander, Brig. Gen. William P. Sanders. This began the Siege of Knoxville.

The city's lines were strengthened by several lunettes; Fort Sanders on the northwest was the most prominent and easily approached. Longstreet targeted it for assault 20 Nov. but postponed the attack several times: 2 night attacks were planned and canceled; an attack was postponed to await the arrival of 2 reinforcing brigades under Brig. Gen. BUSHROD R. JOHNSON; and Sanders was briefly dropped as an objective on advice of consulting engineer Brig. Gen. DANVILLE LEADBETTER. Longstreet at last settled again on Sanders, assaulting it at dawn 29 Nov. A deep ice-and-rain-slicked ditch around the fort helped defeat the attack. Troops caught there could not mount the parapets and were shot up badly. After withdrawal, a second attack was called off; Longstreet, observing the assault, had been handed a telegram announcing Bragg's retreat from Chattanooga into north Georgia and ordering Longstreet to his support.

Confederate intelligence reported Federal troops in the field, either to pursue Bragg or intercept Longstreet. Longstreet decided to remain at Knoxville, draw Federals away from Bragg, then escape. Knoxville stayed besieged until Confederate withdrawal northwest on the night of 4 Dec. Union Maj. Gen. JOHN G. PARKE headed a feeble pursuit. Confederates hiked 5 days to Rogersville, resting and gathering supplies there until the night of the 13th, when they backtracked southeast for a dawn attack on Parke's advance at BEAN'S STATION. The engagement there, where Federals under Brig. Gen. JAMES M. SHACKELFORD escaped capture, effectively ended the Knoxville Campaign.

Skirmishes occurred in the surrounding Clinch Mountains district through December. Longstreet marched his troops south of the Holston to winter quarters at Russellville on the East Tennessee & Virginia Railroad, remaining there until Mar. 1864, when ordered to the Army of Northern Virginia. Confederate losses in the Knoxville Campaign totaled 1,296 in killed, wounded, and missing. The Federals lost 681. The campaign is widely held to be the Confederates' poorest, its major failing most often cited as the splitting of Bragg's forces around Chattanooga, leaving insufficient numbers and supplies for success either there or at Knoxville. *See also* CHATTANOOGA, TENN., BATTLES FOR.   —JES

Krzyzanowski, Wladimir. USA b. Raznova, Poland, 8 July 1824, Krzyzanowski fled Prussian-held Poland after fighting in the failed nationalist uprising of 1846. He settled in New York City, became a naturalized U.S. citizen, practiced civil engineering, and worked for the Republican party. Well-educated, multilingual, prominent in America's small Polish emigré community, and friendly with other European refugee groups, he declared publicly that first-generation Yankees were as willing to die for the flag as native-born Northerners. In Aug. 1861 he began raising a Polish regiment and, after gathering 4 companies, combined them with 6 German-speaking companies to form the 58th New York Volunteer Infantry. He was commissioned its colonel Oct. 1861 and in November was assigned to duty in Brig. Gen. LOUIS BLENKER's division.

Krzyzanowski performed competently in the undistinguished commands of Maj. Gen. JOHN C. FRÉMONT and his close friend Maj. Gen. CARL SCHURZ, fighting in the SHENANDOAH VALLEY, SECOND BULL RUN, CHANCELLORSVILLE, and

LC

GETTYSBURG campaigns. When Schurz's XI Corps was reduced to 2 divisions in autumn 1862, Krzyzanowski received appointment to brigadier general 29 Nov. His appointment, unconfirmed by the U.S. Senate, expired 4 Mar. 1863 and went unrenewed. Later Schurz bitterly said that Krzyzanowski's commission had lapsed because no U.S. Senator could pronounce his name.

After Gettysburg, Krzyzanowski joined Maj. Gen. JOSEPH HOOKER's relief expedition to CHATTANOOGA, fought through the siege there, then was transferred to successive commands at the supply posts of Bridgeport and Stevenson, Ala. For war service he received a brevet to brigadier general 2 Mar. 1865 and mustered out 1 Oct.

As a veteran, a prominent immigrant Republican, and postwar political partisan of Schurz, he received a civil service appointment with the Treasury Department, working for the Internal Revenue Service in the West and Deep South. In 1871 he was arrested for malfeasance and charged with theft of public monies. Schurz's conservative Republican enemies used this to embarrass him, since he had secured Krzyzanowski's appointment. The controversy faded, charges were dropped, and Krzyzanowski took assignment as a customs inspector in Central America. He then served as a customs agent in New York City until his death there, 31 Jan. 1887.
                                                                             —JES

Kueffner, William C. USA b. Mecklenburg, Germany, date unknown. Emigrating as a youth to the U.S., Kueffner settled in Texas but soon found slavery and STATES RIGHTS offensive to his taste. Before the outbreak of the Civil War he moved to Illinois and 25 Apr. 1861 became a sergeant in Company D/9th Illinois Volunteer Infantry. A month later, his military abilities brought him advancement to 1st lieutenant, and by late July he wore a captain's bars.

Kueffner served with remarkable fidelity and durability, seeing action in 110 engagements, one of the longest continuous combat records of any Union veteran. He received wounds in 4 of these actions, including SHILOH and CORINTH. By Oct. 1863 he had been forced to accept a captaincy in the VETERAN RESERVES, composed of soldiers with disabilities or wounds that left them unfit for front-line duty. Early in 1865, however, he recovered sufficiently to return to active service. His war record and his statewide prominence resulted that February in his receiving the colonelcy of the 149th Illinois Volunteers. He led his regiment in the West, as part of the brigade commanded by the Prussian-born Prince FELIX SALM-SALM. Remaining in the army at war's close, he was mustered out as a brevet brigadier general of volunteers 27 Jan. 1866. He survived his military service by 27 years. d. place unknown, 18 Mar. 1893.
                                                                             —EGL

L

Ladies' Gunboat Societies. Established by patriotic women of the South, these societies helped raise funds for building Confederate IRONCLADS. The first gunboat society was organized in New Orleans late in 1861, and others sprang up rapidly throughout the South. Competition among societies brought auctions, raffles, concerts, even "gunboat fairs," as methods of raising funds. 3 ironclads—the *Charleston, Fredericksburg,* and *Georgia*—were referred to as "ladies' gunboats" because they were built almost exclusively with funds raised by the societies. Enthusiasm peaked during spring 1862, then fell off rapidly after the loss of New Orleans, Memphis, and Norfolk and the destruction of all but 5 of the original ironclad gunboats. By 1863 donations had all but ceased.

—NCD

La Glorieta Pass, New Mexico Territory, Battle of.
26–28 Mar. 1862   At the southern tip of the Sangre de Cristo Mts., 20 mi southeast of Santa Fe in northern New Mexico, is La Glorieta Pass, through which runs the old Santa Fe Trail. Sometimes called Apache Canyon, the pass is several miles long, about a quarter-mile wide at the middle, and tapers to narrow defiles at both ends. Ordered on 25 Mar. 1862 to move against the Confederate force at Santa Fe, Maj. JOHN M. CHIVINGTON and a raiding party of 418 Union soldiers arrived at Kozlowski's ranch, about 5 mi southeast of La Glorieta. From Confederate pickets captured that night Chivington learned of the presence of 250–300 Texas under Maj. Charles L. Pyron bivouacked at Johnson's ranch at the far end of the pass.

Early on the morning of 26 Mar., Chivington moved toward the enemy. About 2 p.m. his men captured a 30-man Confederate advance, then fell on Pyron's main force 1.5 mi west of Pigeon's ranch, which lay 6 mi northeast of Johnson's ranch. With his advance guard taken by the enemy, Pyron was caught by surprise, but the Confederate commander quickly threw out a skirmish line, and his 2 6-lb howitzers began firing grape and shell at the Federals. The artillery fire sent the Federals into confusion until Chivington divided his troops, sending 3 companies to find cover in the rocks and deploying 2 companies in the cottonwood and pines along the mountain slopes on each side of the canyon; this placed the Confederates in a crossfire. The Texans held their ground briefly before Pyron withdrew about 1.5 mi to where the pass narrows; there he was able to establish a stronger defense. As they pulled back, the Texas destroyed the bridge they had used to cross a 15-ft arroyo.

Again Chivington sent men to the slopes, but in increased numbers, to counter the Confederate skirmishers Pyron had ordered to the brush. The Federals flanked the Texans and poured another severe enfilading fire on them for an hour before Pyron's men broke. As the Confederates retreated with their guns, the Federal cavalry charged, jumping their hoses across the arroyo and landing in the midst of the Confederate rear guard. Gathering 60 or 70 prisoners, Chivington withdrew to Kozlowski's ranch, having lost 19 killed, 5 wounded, and 3 missing. The Confederates claimed casualties of 16 dead and 30–40 wounded in the day's fighting.

As his men reorganized at Johnson's ranch, Pyron sent for reinforcements from Lt. Col. WILLIAM R. SCURRY at Galisteo, 15 mi south of La Glorieta. Scurry arrived with the 4th Texas on the morning of the 27th, bringing the Confederate force to 1,100. They waited 24 hours at Johnson's ranch, expecting Chivington to renew the attack. When the Federals failed to act, Scurry decided to take the offensive. On the morning of the 28th he moved down the canyon toward Pigeon's ranch, leaving behind his 73-wagon supply train and, to guard the camp, a detachment of 200 men, most of them wounded, drivers, or cooks.

About 2 a.m. the same morning, Union Col. JOHN P. SLOUGH had reached Kozlowski's ranch with reinforcements. Chivington briefed him on the Confederate position and Slough decided to launch an attack against Johnson's ranch, moving toward Pigeon's ranch about 8:30. He ordered Chivington to take his men and circle around La Glorieta Pass to attack the Texans from the west, intending to catch the Confederates between the 2 Federal forces. Slough moved toward La Glorieta with about 900 men, arriving a mile west of Pigeon's ranch about 10:30.

By that time Scurry had advanced down the canyon, and his scouts saw the Federal column approaching. Immediately he ordered his cavalry to the rear, where they dismounted and formed a battle line. Slough discovered the Confederate front at 800 yd, and the battle began 10:30–11 a.m. Slough's 8 field guns battered the Texans' artillery into uselessness, but the Southerners were able to keep a company of the 1st Colorado from moving around their flank. Slough yielded ground. 5 times the Confederates charged, losing all their field officers killed or wounded. They finally broke under 6 volleys from Slough's artillery, followed by a bayonet charge, but retook their lines when the Federal troopers were repelled by a deadly barrage of gunfire from the Texas sharpshooters. The fighting ended about 5 p.m., when Slough retreated to Pigeon's ranch. Scurry also withdrew, leaving his wounded on the field where they had fallen.

Initially Scurry believed he had repeated the Confederate victory at VALVERDE, where a month earlier, Brig. Gen. HENRY HOPKINS SIBLEY's troops had defeated a Union force under Col. E.R.S. CANBY. Later he learned that Chivington had reached Johnson's ranch, burned the Confederate supply wagons, bayoneted 500–600 mules and horses, and captured 17 prisoners. Chivington had destroyed nearly all of the Confederates' supplies, forcing the Southerners to withdraw to Texas, thus giving the victory to the Union.

Chivington had delivered a severe blow to the Confederate incursion into the Southwest, one from which the Southerners never recovered. The Confederate defeat at La Glorieta Pass marked the military turning point of the war in New Mexico Territory. Of the 1,100 Confederates engaged in the fighting at Pigeon's ranch, Scurry lost 36 killed, 60 wounded, and 25 missing. Slough, with 1,345 men including Chivington's, listed 31 killed, at least 50 wounded, and 30 missing.   —PLF

Laird Rams.   During summer 1862, JAMES D. BULLOCH, Confederate naval agent in England, contracted with John Laird & Son at Birkenhead for the building of 2 powerful ram-type vessels. The twin-turreted rams would have iron rammers protruding 7 ft beyond their prows. When the vessels were in motion, these rammers would be below the waterline, thereby striking enemy ships below their protective plate. Each of the Laird Rams was 230 ft long, weighed 1,180 tons, and had a draft of 18 ft. Their 350-horsepower engines enabled them to reach speeds up to 10 knots.

Laird Hulls Nos. 294 and 295 were to become the *North Carolina* and the *Mississippi*. Though Flag Officer SAMUEL BARRON was sent to Europe with orders to assume command of the rams when they were completed, no Confederate would see service aboard either vessel. Despite Bulloch's efforts to have their ownership transferred to a French firm, the ships' true purpose became known, and they were seized by the British government for violating that nation's neutrality laws. Taken over by the British navy, the rams became the HMS *Scorpion* and the HMS *Wivern*. Their loss dashed Confederate Navy Sec. STEPHEN R. MALLORY's plan to change the course of the war by breaking the blockade.   —NCD

Lake Chicot (Ditch Bayou), Ark., eng. at.   6 June 1864 Determined to end Confederate Brig. Gen. JOHN S. MARMADUKE's guerrilla operations around Lake Village, Ark., Maj. Gen. ANDREW J. SMITH, 10,000 men, and 26 gunboats and transports left Vicksburg, Miss., 4 June 1864. Traveling north 90 mi on the Mississippi River, the Federals debarked at 5 p.m., 5 June, at Sunnyside Landing, Ark., 8 mi east of Lake Village. Marmaduke's subordinate, Col. Colton Greene, 3d Missouri Cavalry, and elements of his 600-man command skirmished to the west with Union Lt. Col. George E. Currie, members of his MISSISSIPPI MARINE BRIGADE, and the 2d Wisconsin Cavalry, until they neared the edge of Ditch Bayou, a swamp bordering Lake Chicot. Dusk and light rain ended the fighting.

At 6 a.m., 6 June, Smith's force, troops of the XVI and XVII corps under Brig. Gen. JOSEPH A. MOWER, the 3d Indiana Battery, the 2d Wisconsin, and Currie's marines, set out from Sunnyside Landing, moving toward Ditch Bayou on the narrow Old Lake road, a rude byway paralleling the west shore of the lake. On reaching Ditch Bayou, the Federal troops had to cross the one bridge spanning the swamp in order to reach the lake.

Greene's Confederates first attacked 2 mi inland on the Union route of march. Throughout the day, in a heavy rain that turned the road to mire, Confederates launched piecemeal attacks and skirmished slowly backward toward the bayou, about 5 mi distant. Forest and thick undergrowth prevented the Federals from bringing up the bulk of their force and deploying a broad battle line. Against the advice of Marine Bri-

gade guerrilla fighters, Smith pressed on until reaching a small clearing and a sparse Confederate line stretching three-fourths of a mile near the plantation "Red Leaf." There, supported by 1 cannon, Confederates briefly held up the Federals, then retired 2 mi to the edge of Ditch Bayou, heavy cover, and the support of 4 cannon.

Greene's cannon fire threw Smith's men into confusion; an attempt to deploy the 3d Indiana for counterbattery fire ended with Union cannon, caissons, and equipage stuck in mire and underbrush with no clear shot at the Confederates. Fighting from cover of the bayou, the Confederates held off a force outnumbering them 7-to-1. At 2:30 p.m., ammunition exhausted, they withdrew beyond Lake Chicot to Bayou Mason, 3 mi west of Lake Village.

The fighting ended indecisively, with Confederate casualties totaling 37 and Federal casualties 250. Outraged at their military embarrassment, that night Smith's troops marched on and sacked Lake Village.   —JES

Lamar, Lucius Quintus Cincinnatus.   CSP   b. Putnam Cty., Ga., 17 Sept. 1825, Lamar graduated from Emory College in Oxford, Ga., in 1845, studied law under a kinsman in Macon, and was admitted to the bar in 1847. Hoping for greater opportunities in a less settled state, he moved with his wife to Oxford, Miss., 2 years later to establish his practice and teach mathematics at the University of Mississippi. He returned to Georgia in 1852 and served in the state legislature, but moved permanently to Mississippi Oct. 1855.

LC

Lamar stood firmly for the Union as the sectional crisis festered, but his commitment to slavery and STATES RIGHTS identified him with the Southern Democrats, and as a Southern Democrat his constituents elected him to the House of Representatives in 1857 and in 1859. He backed the JOHN C. BRECKINRIDGE–Joseph Lane ticket at the 1860 Democratic national convention in Charleston, urging his colleagues not to support the rump session later held in Baltimore to nominate STEPHEN A. DOUGLAS.

Regardless of his Unionist sympathies, Lamar never questioned the right of secession and saw dissolving the Union to preserve Southern rights as the only response to ABRAHAM LINCOLN's election. Early in 1861 he resigned his congressional seat and returned home to draft the Mississippi ordinance of secession.

Though a military career seemed out of character, Lamar helped recruit the 18th Mississippi. He served as the regiment's lieutenant colonel until May 1862, resigning officially a few months later, after suffering an "apoplectic stroke" that would recur throughout his life.

Still eager to serve the Confederacy, he accepted from Pres. JEFFERSON DAVIS an appointment as special commissioner to Russia. Arriving in London Mar. 1863, he was recalled after the Russian fleet sailed into New York harbor that fall in a diplomatic show of friendship toward the Lincoln administration. In Richmond he lobbied faithfully against Davis' critics. The president rewarded him with the judge advocacy of the III Corps/

Army of Northern Virginia, a post he held from Dec. 1864 until the Confederate collapse.

Immediately following the war Lamar returned to law and teaching, reentering politics in 1872 as Mississippi's first Democratic congressman since the imposition of Radical RECONSTRUCTION. The elegy he delivered in Congress when CHARLES SUMNER died attracted national attention, in a limited way easing some of the bitterness Northerners felt toward the South. Lamar emerged as Mississippi's foremost politician, becoming popular nationally for his sincere and thoroughly pragmatic pleas for reconciliation.

Mississippians elected him to the Senate Jan. 1876, though he did not take his seat until Mar. 1877. In Washington he championed the "New South" and enhanced his growing reputation by opposing the free silver movement, against instructions from his state. Pres. Grover Cleveland named him secretary of the interior in 1885 and nominated him to the Supreme Court 2 years later. The Senate confirmed the appointment reluctantly because of his status as a former Confederate, but he served competently on the court until his death in the District of Columbia 23 Jan. 1893. —PLF

Land-Grant College Act. *See* MORRILL ACT.

Lane, James Henry. CSA b. Mathews Court House, Va., 28 July 1833. Lane's troops affectionately called their intellectual commander the "Little General." What he lacked in stature he possessed in vigorous fighting spirit. The popular, aggressive professor supported Gen. ROBERT E. LEE dependably through all the major campaigns waged by the Army of Northern Virginia.

USMHI

Lane graduated from Virginia Military Institute in 1854, from the University of Virginia 3 years later, and taught mathematics and military tactics at VMI and North Carolina Military Institute. He resigned his position at the latter school in 1861 when elected major of the 1st North Carolina Volunteers. His scouting detail encountered the enemy in the skirmishing that initiated the engagement at BIG BETHEL 10 June. That September, Lane transferred to the 28th North Carolina with the rank of colonel in Brig. Gen. LAWRENCE O. BRANCH's command. A Virginian leading North Carolina troops might have proven difficult given the competitiveness between the 2 states, but Lane's men respected his abilities to the point of petitioning for his promotion to brigadier general after Branch died at ANTIETAM. Based on Lane's skillful rearguard actions covering Lee's retreat from Maryland, the War Department approved the promotion 1 Nov. 1862.

Lane's command comprised the 7th, 18th, 28th, 33d, and 37th North Carolina regiments. The 18th bore heavy guilt as the unit responsible for Lt. Gen. THOMAS J. "STONEWALL" JACKSON's wounding at CHANCELLORSVILLE. As if to atone, the command fought relentlessly at GETTYSBURG 2 months later. After Maj. Gen. WILLIAM D. PENDER's wounding on the second day, Lane assumed divisional command. Lacking confidence in Lane's ability as a divisional commander, Lee placed Maj. Gen.

ISAAC R. TRIMBLE over him. When Trimble fell wounded at the outset of PICKETT'S CHARGE, Lane valiantly led the left-flank assault on CEMETERY RIDGE. He stopped before the wall, urging his men forward. His horse was shot under him, but he rose unhurt, continuing to rally the North Carolinians until forced to order a retreat. Watching the persistent charge from afar, Trimble insisted that if Lane's men could not take the ridge, no assault could. Lane boasted later that his men were the last to leave the field, a claim Trimble confirmed. Nearly 50% of the brigade lay dead or wounded on the field.

Lane himself suffered 3 wounds in battle: at WHITE OAK SWAMP, at MALVERN HILL, and at COLD HARBOR. He was surrendered with his men at APPOMATTOX Apr. 1865. After the war he taught at schools in North Carolina, Virginia, and Alabama, ending his career as a professor of civil engineering at the Alabama Polytechnic Institute shortly before his death in Auburn 21 Sept. 1907. —PLF

Lane, James Henry. USA/USP b. Lawrenceburg, Ind., 22 June 1814. A shrewd, personable opportunist trained as a lawyer but obsessed with his own political advancement, Lane maneuvered himself into position as a favorite of ABRAHAM LINCOLN early in the Civil War years. He had entered politics on the strength of his military achievements during the Mexican War, winning the lieutenant governorship of Indiana in 1849 and a Democratic seat in the U.S. House of Representatives in 1853. There he made the mistake of voting for the KANSAS-NEBRASKA ACT, which alienated his constituents so thoroughly that he did not run for reelection. When his term expired, he

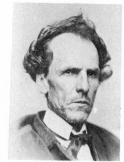

USMHI

migrated to Kansas Territory, where he tried unsuccessfully to organize the Democratic party. He then joined the Free State movement, becoming embroiled in the "BLEEDING KANSAS" controversy, leading antislavery factions in the territory.

Lane's political plans were interrupted again when he killed a neighbor in a duel June 1858, but he was elected to the Senate as a Republican in 1861 after a 2-year campaign to regain support. On his arrival in Washington in April, he recruited the "Frontier Guards," about 50 men, most of them politicians, who volunteered to guard the capital and were bivouacked in the White House. A grateful Lincoln permitted Lane to become the leader of Kansas interests, and the senator used his position to obtain patronage appointments for his friends.

The soldier-politician returned to Kansas to raise several regiments in anticipation of an invasion by Confederates from Missouri. His 1,500-man Kansas Brigade halted Brig. Gen. STERLING PRICE's advance, and when the Confederate troops retreated, Lane's men moved into Missouri on a spree of plundering and destruction that intensified the border war. Among the troops raised by Lane was a regiment of blacks, one of the first mustered into the Federal army, 13 Jan. 1863. That year Lane's enemies mounted a campaign to oust him from power, and he began stumping the state to ensure the election of a legislature that would return him to the Senate. He reversed several political setbacks just before his term expired when he turned Price's Oct. 1864 raid into Kansas to his advantage by accusing his adversary, Gov. Thomas Carney, of not providing the state with adequate defense (*see* PRICE'S MISSOURI RAID OF 1864).

Retaining his Senate seat, Lane supported the HOMESTEAD and Pacific Railroad acts, both favored by Kansans, but destroyed his career by going against popular opinion to support Pres. ANDREW JOHNSON's veto of the Civil Rights bill of 1866. Accused of graft in connection with Indian contracts and depressed by Kansans' aloofness toward him on his return to the state, he committed suicide near Leavenworth, 1 July 1866, dying 10 days later.   —PLF

Lane, Walter Paye. CSA b. Cty. Cork, Ireland, 18 Feb. 1817. Lane's family immigrated to Baltimore in 1821 but soon relocated to Fairview, Ohio. Lane moved on to Texas in 1836 and fought at San Jacinto in the Texas War for Independence. Thereafter his varied career included privateering in Gulf waters, an attempt at establishing a farm on the frontier, fighting Indians, and teaching school. During the Mexican War he enlisted in the 1st Texas Cavalry, a unit heavily engaged in scouting. From 1849 to 1858, when he settled in Marshall, Tex., Lane traveled between Texas, Peru, and the Western gold fields, amassing and losing several small fortunes. He entered Confederate service in 1861 as a lieutenant colonel in the 3d Texas (South Kansas–Texas) Cavalry, later becoming colonel of the 1st Texas Partisan Rangers.

The 3d Texas first saw action at WILSON'S CREEK, Mo., where Lane had a horse shot under him and fought part of the battle dismounted. Later that year he led 5 companies of his Texans in a successful strike against pro-Union Indians at Chustenahlah in Indian Territory. At PEA RIDGE, Ark., 7–8 Mar. 1862, Lane commanded a brigade in Brig. Gen. JAMES M. MCINTOSH's division. Amid the confusion of that disorganized battle he proved himself capable of handling a larger body of troops, but no promotion was forthcoming. That May the impressive charge he led against a superior force near Corinth, Miss., induced Gen. P.G.T. BEAUREGARD to single him out for special praise in the records.

Except for limited duty in Indian Territory—which he avoided whenever possible—Lane completed his Civil War service in Louisiana, notably at BAYOU LA FORCHE July 1863 and at BAYOU BOURBEAU that November. Assigned for a time to Maj. Gen. JOHN B. MAGRUDER's command along the Texas coast, he traveled to northern Louisiana for Lt. Gen. RICHARD TAYLOR's defense against Maj. Gen. NATHANIEL P. BANKS's RED RIVER CAMPAIGN of spring 1864. He was severely wounded at MANSFIELD but was back in the field by October, when Gen. E. KIRBY SMITH, who considered him a superior cavalry officer and one of the 3 best brigade commanders in the Trans-Mississippi, recommended him for promotion. His advancement to brigadier general, to rank from 10 Mar. 1865, was confirmed in the last session of the Confederate Congress.

After Smith surrendered the Trans-Mississippi and the army disbanded, Lane returned to Marshall. The amiable bachelor became a successful merchant and colorful celebrity in the state, particularly beloved among the Daughters of the Confederacy and the Daughters of the Republic of Texas. In 1887 he published his memoirs, *The Adventures and Recollections of Gen. Walter P. Lane* (reprinted in 1928 with an addendum by Mary Jane Lane), of which about one-third covers his Civil War

career. d. Marshall, Tex., 28 Jan. 1892.   —PLF

Lanier, Sidney. poet b. Macon, Ga., 3 Feb. 1842. A Southern esthete reared in Macon, Lanier became known through his allegorical poetry as a spokesman for the defeated Confederacy.

The 1860 graduate of Oglethorpe University tutored at his alma mater until the Civil War. In June 1861 he joined the Macon Guards and was assigned to the Virginia theater through most of the war. He transferred to mounted signal duty in late summer 1862, serving variously as a scout, courier, and signalman. Transferred to Wilmington, N.C., in spring 1864, he was a signalman aboard BLOCKADE RUNNERS until being captured at sea 2 Nov. 1864 and sent to POINT LOOKOUT Prison, Md., where he sat out the end of the war.

Lanier's antebellum view of the South as a bastion of chivalric and social refinement, his wartime hope that the Confederacy would survive to become a cradle of art and grace, and his bitterness at loss and Reconstruction were shared by others. But his 1867 novel of the war period, *Tiger-Lilies,* and his poems brought these sentiments before the Northern and Southern public. "The Raven Days," "Civil Rights," "Betrayal," "Laughter in the Senate," "Corn," "The Revenge of Hamish," and other poems struck readers with Lanier's sense of frustration and alienation over the social and political realities that had come to pass.

Before pursuing writing full-time, Lanier practiced law, and was a lecturer at Johns Hopkins University in 1879. He died of consumption 7 Sept. 1881, in Lynn, N.C., as unhappy over the hack work he wrote to support his family as he was over the late war. Critics find his work disciplined but inconsistent.   —JES

Lauman, Jacob Gartner. USA b. Taneytown, Md., 20 Jan. 1813, Lauman, raised and educated in York Cty., Pa., migrated to Burlington, Iowa, in 1844 and pursued a business career. Appointed colonel of volunteers 11 July 1861, he helped raise the 7th Iowa Infantry and went on duty at Pilot Knob, Mo.

After skirmish action in September, Lauman took a severe wound in the Battle of BELMONT, 7 Nov. At the head of the 7th Iowa, he took part in the capture of Fort Henry, Tenn., Jan. 1862, and at the head of a brigade breached the works of Fort Donelson in February (*see* FORTS HENRY AND DONELSON CAMPAIGN). For his Fort Donelson service he received promotion to brigadier general to rank from 21 Mar. and was given command of a brigade of Indiana and Kentucky troops for the Battle of SHILOH. There elements of his command were heavily engaged in fighting at the "HORNETS' NEST."

Lauman went on garrison service in Memphis, assumed command of the 4th Division/XVI Corps, skirmished with Confederate partisans near Greenville, Miss., May 1863, then oversaw sappers and trench-fighting at VICKSBURG until the end of the siege. Under Maj. Gen. E.O.C. ORD, he led his division in the XIII Corps march on JACKSON, Miss., and on the morning of 12 July, independent of his instructions and the cooperation of other divisional commanders, pressed more than 1,000 men into a suicidal blind assault on a screened Confederate fortification. After Ord inspected the scene, he ordered Lauman to get his men to cover, call the roll, and assemble stragglers. The major general reported, "I found he did not know how to do it." Relieved on the spot by Ord, Lauman was replaced by Brig. Gen. ALVIN P. HOVEY.

Maj. Gen. U. S. GRANT called Lauman to account, then sent him to Iowa to await orders. His services were not called on again, and following a *pro forma* brevet to major general 13 Mar. 1865, he was mustered from service 24 Aug. Briefly resuming his business career, Lauman died in Burlington, Iowa, 9 Feb. 1867. —JES

Laurel Hill, western Va., skirmish at. 7 July 1861 Laurel Hill, or Mountain, was the northeastern extension of Rich Mountain. Divided by the Tygart River, the 2 peaks formed a part of the most westerly range of the Allegheny Mountains. The 2 mountains towered above the Tygart River Valley, where the Parkersburg-Staunton Turnpike passed through Beverly on its circuitous path to the Shenandoah Valley. The army that occupied the eminences held the gateway to northwestern Virginia.

Confederate forces under Brig. Gen. ROBERT S. GARNETT seized Laurel Hill 16 June 1861. Garnett entrenched immediately, while blocking all the country roads from the northwest with fallen trees. The Confederates also built fortifications on Rich Mountain, with Garnett dividing his command between both camps. 5 days after Garnett manned the mountain gateway, Union Maj. Gen. GEORGE B. McCLELLAN entered western Virginia, his command consisting of 27 infantry regiments, 4 batteries, and 2 troops of cavalry. On 2 July the Union force occupied Buckhannon, 8 mi west of Laurel Hill.

On 6 July McClellan began a full-scale advance on Garnett's position. Col. Robert L. McCook, with 2 regiments, led the Union march, arriving before Garnett's 2 regiments on Laurel Hill. The next day McCook's Ohio volunteers probed the Confederate works on the hill; skirmishing flared and continued for 4 days. While the opponents dueled on the mountainside, McClellan attacked the RICH MOUNTAIN works 11 July, resulting in a Confederate defeat. With Federals in his rear, Garnett abandoned Laurel Hill that night. —JDW

Law, Evander McIvor. CSA b. Darlington, S.C., 7 Aug. 1836. Law's division commander described him as "one of the best men in battle I ever saw." A brigadier by autumn 1862, this brilliant fighter never rose to higher rank, for a year later he engaged in a bitter feud with his commander, Lt. Gen. JAMES LONGSTREET.

An 1856 graduate of the South Carolina Military Academy, Law was an instructor during his senior year. On graduation he moved to Tuskegee, Ala., where he helped establish the Military High School. With Alabama's secession, he enlisted as a captain in the 4th Alabama, which participated in the early operations at Pensacola before transferring to Virginia. Elected lieutenant colonel, Law fought at FIRST BULL RUN, where he suffered a serious wound. He was elected colonel of the 4th that autumn.

Law led his Alabamians during the PENINSULA CAMPAIGN, then assumed command of 1 of the 2 brigades in Brig. Gen. WILLIAM H. C. WHITING's division in the SEVEN DAYS' battles.

USMHI

Law's brigade and Brig. Gen. JOHN B. HOOD's brigade penetrated the Union lines at GAINES' MILL in a riveting attack in the twilight of 27 June 1862. Their assault doomed the Federals to defeat. In August the 2 commands again distinguished themselves at SECOND BULL RUN, in the massive Confederate counterattack that wrecked the Union Army of Virginia. 3 weeks later the small division, now commanded by Hood, was hurled into the Cornfield at ANTIETAM, where they fought unsupported, buying time for Maj. Gen. THOMAS J. "STONEWALL" JACKSON. When asked later where his division was, Hood replied, "Dead on the field."

On 2 Oct. 1862 Law received his well-deserved promotion to brigadier general. His new brigade saw little action at FREDERICKSBURG and missed CHANCELLORSVILLE, being on detached duty with the I Corps. Law then assumed command of a brigade composed of Alabama regiments, which he led at GETTYSBURG. In this battle, 2 July 1863, part of Law's brigade initiated the Confederate attacks on LITTLE ROUND TOP. In one of the war's most vicious struggles, the Alabamians were repulsed. Law, meanwhile, had assumed command of the division when Hood fell severely wounded.

With Hood's fall, Law's difficulties with Longstreet began. The corps commander requested that Brig. Gen. MICAH JENKINS, like Longstreet and Law a Carolinian, and a rival of Law, replace Hood in command of the division. Jenkins was Law's senior in rank by 2 months, but Law had been with the division longer. Pres. JEFFERSON DAVIS wanted Law for the post but Longstreet demurred. Hood, however, returned to the command. When Longstreet and 2 divisions were sent west to Georgia to reinforce Gen. BRAXTON BRAGG's army, Hood was again wounded, at CHICKAMAUGA. In the subsequent operations around CHATTANOOGA, Law commanded a detached brigade and Jenkins the division. Twice Jenkins accused Law of failing to support him in actions. The animosities between the 2 festered until 19 Dec., when Law resigned, alleging that he wanted a transfer to the cavalry. In a complicated case, Longstreet eventually preferred charges, even threatening his own resignation if Law was not court-martialed. But the War Department never preferred charges, and Law returned to corps.

He led his brigade at the WILDERNESS, SPOTSYLVANIA, and COLD HARBOR, where he was wounded. On recovering, Law requested a transfer to the Carolinas. At war's end he commanded a cavalry unit in Gen. JOSEPH E. JOHNSTON's army.

Postbellum, Law moved to Florida, where he helped establish the state's educational system and was a newspaperman. Active in veteran affairs, he died in Bartow 31 Oct. 1920. —JDW

Lawler, Michael Kelly. USA b. Cty. Kildare, Ireland, 16 Nov. 1814, Lawler immigrated to the U.S. with his family in 1816, eventually settling in Illinois. Active in the state militia, he fought in the Mexican War, commanding the 3d Illinois; in the 1850s farmed and ran a mercantile business near Shawneetown, Ill.; and in 1861 entered volunteer service as colonel of the 18th Illinois.

After Lawler served in Missouri operations under Brig. Gen. U. S. GRANT, he was court-martialed and acquitted of charges that he had used brutality in the discipline of his troops. In Feb. 1862 he fought in Brig. Gen. JOHN A. MCCLERNAND'S command at FORT DONELSON, where he was wounded, and under Brig. Gen. JOHN A. LOGAN policed the Tennessee and Kentucky countrysides until 1863. He was promoted to brigadier general to rank from 29 Nov. 1862.

LC

In the VICKSBURG CAMPAIGN, Lawler, in brigade command, fought at PORT GIBSON, CHAMPION'S HILL, and BIG BLACK RIVER BRIDGE. On 22 May he took part in the assault on Confederate Maj. Gen. STEPHEN D. LEE's troops along the Vicksburg lines and participated in the siege until its conclusion. Transferred to the Department of the Gulf, he commanded the 4th and 1st divisions/XIII Corps, then on dissolution of the corps was given divisional command in the Gulf Coast reserve corps until the Confederate surrender. Brevetted major general 13 Mar. 1865, he was mustered out 15 Jan. 1866.

Postwar, Lawler returned to his farm near Equality, Ill., until his death there 26 July 1882.   —JES

Lawrence, Kans., Raid on. 21 Aug. 1863   1 of 4 principal towns that the original settlers established in the territory, Lawrence, Kans., was also 1 of 2 towns peopled by pro-Unionists with antislavery sentiments. On 21 Aug. 1863, beginning at dawn, some 450 Confederate and Missouri guerrillas, under Col. WILLIAM C. QUANTRILL, entered Lawrence, wantonly burning, pillaging, and massacring its citizens.

The "Kansas War," one within the larger struggle, was characterized by personal enmity and bitterness. The Unionists had raided Osceola, Mo., and the Lawrence raid ostensibly was in retaliation. But Quantrill, who had previously conducted several irregular operations, also had a personal grudge against the abolitionist town and its people.

About 150 men and boys died (some sources put the figure at 180); only women and smaller children were spared by the raiders, though a few men did manage to escape. The attackers also destroyed $1.5 million worth of property. An eyewitness asserted, "The town is a complete ruin. The whole of the business part, and all good private residences are burned down. Everything of value was taken along by the fiends. . . . I cannot describe the horrors."

Quantrill's men withdrew the next day, leaving little but a smoldering ruin. They struck again about 6 weeks later at BAXTER SPRINGS, Kans., then went into Texas.   —HH

Lawton, Alexander Robert. CSA b. Beaufort District, S.C., 4 Nov. 1818. To his good breeding and natural refinement, Lawton added degrees in 1839 from the U.S. Military Academy, graduating 13th in his class, and in 1842 from Harvard Law School. In 1843 he settled in Savannah, Ga., and was associated with that state until his death. He occupied himself with the law, railroad administration, and state politics until the secession of Georgia, a step he encouraged.

Lawton commanded the state troops that seized FORT PULASKI, the first act of war in Georgia. Soon after, 13 Apr. 1861, he received a commission as Confederate brigadier and was ordered to Virginia, where he compiled an admirable record as brigade and division commander in the battles of the SHENANDOAH VALLEY CAMPAIGN of 1862, the SEVEN DAYS', SECOND BULL RUN, and ANTIETAM, where he was severely wounded.

LC

In Aug. 1863 Jefferson Davis named Lawton the second quartermaster general of the Confederacy, replacing Col. ABRAHAM C. MYERS. In this office Lawton proved energetic and resourceful, but he could not solve the basic problem of material shortages and failed to provide the sweeping regulation of railroads needed in the struggle.

After the war Lawton's stature as a political figure in Georgia grew. In 1880 he lost a contest to JOSEPH E. BROWN for a Senate seat, which was viewed as a victory for the "New South" over the Old. He was chosen president of the American Bar Association in 1882 and appointed minister to Austria in 1887. d. Clifton Springs, N.Y., 2 July 1896.   —PMM

Leadbetter, Danville. CSA b. Leeds, Maine, 26 Aug. 1811, Leadbetter graduated 3d in the West Point class of 1836, and held positions in the artillery and engineers until being assigned permanently to the engineers July 1837. His engineering service ended with his resignation as captain 16 Oct. 1852 to accept appointment as chief engineer for the state of Alabama. He lived and worked in Mobile until secession, advising state Confederates early in 1861 on the defense of Mobile Bay.

Leadbetter's reputation in engineering won him a commission as colonel in the Confederate army and an appointment as acting chief of the Bureau of Engineers. From his Richmond office he corresponded with officers on the defense of Mobile and other coastal fortifications, traveled to Virginia's peninsula advising on the defense of YORKTOWN, and 10 Nov. 1861 was sent west to oversee railroad, bridge, and communications construction and repair in East Tennessee. He briefly commanded troops in the field, guarded against Unionist sabotage in the area, and 27 Feb. 1862 was dispatched to Cumberland Gap.

LC

Next attached to Gen. BRAXTON BRAGG's Army of Tennessee, Leadbetter arranged the Confederate lines overlooking CHATTANOOGA. He was then sent to assist Lt. Gen. JAMES LONGSTREET, who was besieging KNOXVILLE; there his work was criticized and rejected by Longstreet's subordinates. He stayed with the Army of Tennessee until it was expelled from the state, then spent the remainder of the war supervising the defenses of Mobile.

After the war, Leadbetter went to Mexico, then Canada, dying near Niagara Falls, Ontario, 26 Sept. 1866. —JES

Ledlie, James Hewett. USA b. Utica, N.Y., 14 Apr. 1832, Ledlie has been described as the Union's worst general. Contemporaries considered him a drunkard, a poltroon, and a gloryseeker. Though he combined incompetence with cowardice, he rose to the rank of brigadier general, proving that lack of qualifications did not necessarily hamper a Civil War officer with the proper connections and influential friends.

Educated at Union College in his native state, Ledlie was a civil engineer before the war. With the outbreak of the conflict, he helped raise the 19th New York and was unanimously chosen its major 22 May 1861. Ledlie eventually was promoted

LC

to lieutenant colonel in September and colonel 3 months later. His regiment, redesignated the 3d New York Artillery, was transferred to the Department of North Carolina early in 1862.

For nearly a year the New Yorkers remained in North Carolina. In December Ledlie, commanding a Union artillery brigade, saw his first significant action in the expedition against Goldsborough, N.C. Though he blundered in the operation, Maj. Gen. JOHN G. FOSTER praised him, recommending him for promotion to brigadier general.

On 24 Dec. 1862 Ledlie secured his promotion, but the Senate did not confirm it before adjourning Mar. 1863. Maneuvering to secure his appointment, he wrote to ABRAHAM LINCOLN and Sec. of State WILLIAM H. SEWARD, a New York neighbor and friend. His efforts succeeded with his reappointment 27 Oct. 1863.

In spring 1864 Ledlie secured command of a brigade in the IX Corps. His incompetence, cowardice, and drunkenness were soon starkly revealed. On 24 May, along the North Anna River, his brigade attacked a Confederate position. Ledlie charged rashly, against orders, and his brigade was easily repulsed. He was, however, assigned a division, which, 17 June, charged at PETERSBURG. While his men suffered 841 casualties, Ledlie lay on the ground in a drunken stupor. His greatest blunder came 30 July, when his division spearheaded the Union assault after the explosion of the Petersburg mine (*see* CRATER, BATTLE OF THE). While his division stumbled into the crater and was slaughtered, Ledlie stayed behind in a bombproof, drinking rum with another division commander. A court of inquiry criticized him in September, and in December Maj. Gen. GEORGE G. MEADE read him out of the army. Ledlie resigned 23 Jan. 1865.

The New Yorker prospered as a civil engineer after the war, working on the Union Pacific Railroad and Chicago's harbor. d. Staten Island, N.Y., 15 Aug. 1882. —JDW

Lee, Albert Lindley. USA b. Fulton, N.Y., 16 Jan. 1834. In 1853 Lee graduated from Union College in Schenectady preparatory to his law studies. Moving to Kansas Territory, he opened a practice during the volatile years of hostility between pro- and antislavery factions in the region. Lee became a state

supreme court justice in 1861 but resigned the position to enter the Federal volunteer service in October as major of the 7th Kansas Cavalry.

USMHI

Most of his early duty was confined to skirmishing in Kansas and western Missouri, where he displayed talent as a cavalry commander despite his lack of military training and experience. He advanced in rank rapidly, receiving a brigadier generalship Apr. 1863, to rank from 29 Nov. 1862, without having fought in any large battles. When Maj. Gen. U. S. GRANT began moving against VICKSBURG, Lee was transferred east of the Mississippi River to take part in support operations. At CHAMPION'S HILL and again during the engagement at the BIG BLACK RIVER BRIDGE, he served as chief of staff to Maj. Gen. JOHN A. MCCLERNAND.

Lee was wounded during the Siege of VICKSBURG but recovered quickly and transferred to Maj. Gen. NATHANIEL P. BANKS'S command in New Orleans. As chief of cavalry in the Department of the Gulf, he commanded mounted forces during the RED RIVER CAMPAIGN in 1864. His men engaged heavily in skirmishing, particularly at MANSFIELD and PLEASANT HILL, but Lee, while capable enough, did not distinguish himself as an outstanding commander. The amicable relationship he enjoyed with departmental headquarters deteriorated after Maj. Gen. E.R.S. CANBY, a Regular Army officer, replaced Banks. Hoping to have Lee transferred, Canby ordered him to Washington for assignment, but the adjutant general returned him to the Gulf. In Apr. 1865 Canby sent Lee to New Orleans to await orders. With no command and the war nearly over, he resigned his commission 4 May.

Lee traveled extensively in Europe and in the U.S. after the war, discarding his legal practice to pursue business interests. d. 31 Dec. 1907 at his home in New York City. —PLF

Lee, Edwin Gray. CSA b. "Leeland," Loudoun Cty., Va., 27 May 1836. A graduate of William and Mary College, Lee was a lawyer before the war, marrying a daughter of future Confederate Gen. WILLIAM N. PENDLETON.

Lee entered Confederate service Apr. 1861 as a 2d lieutenant in the 33d Virginia. Soon elected 1st lieutenant, he served as an aide-de-camp to Brig. Gen. THOMAS J. "STONEWALL" JACKSON at FIRST BULL RUN. Rejoining the 33d, which was now a part of the STONEWALL BRIGADE, Lee rose in rank to major, then lieutenant colonel. He fought in the SHENANDOAH VALLEY CAMPAIGN of 1862 and in the SEVEN DAYS' battles. Promoted

GG

to colonel, he led his regiment at SECOND BULL RUN, ANTIETAM, and FREDERICKSBURG.

Shortly after the last engagement, Dec. 1862, Lee resigned because of ill health. But he soon returned to duty, and was commissioned and assigned to Richmond. On 17 May 1864 he was transferred to Staunton, where he recruited local troops for the defenses in the Shenandoah Valley. Promoted to brigadier general 23 Sept., to rank from 20 Sept. in November he again left the army for reasons of health. On 24 Feb. 1865 the Confederate Senate rejected his appointment to brigadier. Shortly before the war ended, he and his wife ran the blockade and settled in Montreal.

In spring 1866, the couple returned to Virginia. d. Yellow Sulphur Springs, 24 Aug. 1870, from a "disease of the lungs."
—JDW

Lee, Fitzhugh. CSA b. Fairfax Cty., Va., 19 Nov. 1835. Even if he had not been a nephew of ROBERT E. LEE, Fitzhugh Lee would be remembered as one of the youngest and ablest cavalry commanders in the Civil War. "Fitz" graduated 45th in the West Point class of 1856, though he had almost been expelled for misbehavior by his famous uncle, who was superintendent of the academy. Badly wounded in the Indian wars, he was an assistant instructor at West Point in 1861, resigning his first lieutenancy in May to join Confederate service at the same rank. During the PENINSULA CAMPAIGN he served as a Confederate staff officer.

USMHI

His cavalry career began shortly thereafter with Maj. Gen. J.E.B. STUART. Lee became a brigadier general 24 July 1862, at 27, and a major general the following year, to rank from 3 Aug. He led a brigade in the ANTIETAM CAMPAIGN, at CHANCELLORSVILLE, and at GETTYSBURG. The following year he was severely wounded at the third Battle of WINCHESTER and remained out of action until near the end of the war, when he became R. E. Lee's chief of cavalry corps. He surrendered just after Appomattox.

Lee served as governor of Virginia 1885–89; farmed; served as consul general in Havana, Cuba, 1896–98, on the eve of the Spanish-American War; then became a major general in the U.S. Volunteer Army at the head of the VII Corps in Cuba, retiring in 1901.

Besides farming and politicking, Lee wrote a biography of his uncle and other works about the war in which he played such a vital part. d. District of Columbia, 28 Apr. 1905. —RHF

Lee, George Washington Custis. CSA b. Fort Monroe, Va., 16 Sept. 1832. ROBERT E. LEE had Custis, the eldest of his 3 sons, educated at private schools in Virginia. Young Lee then received an at-large appointment to the U.S. Military Academy in 1850, graduating 1st in his class 4 years later. Assigned to the Corps of Engineers with rank as 2d lieutenant, he worked at improving river and harbor facilities until being assigned to the office of the chief engineer in Washington, D.C., a post he held when he resigned a 1st lieutenant's commission, 2 May 1861. 2 months later, 1 July, he entered Confederate service as a captain of engineers and was assigned to building fortifications around Richmond.

Though Custis Lee was anxious to receive a field command, he spent most of the war away from the fighting, serving on

LC

Pres. JEFFERSON DAVIS' staff as a military aide. Davis valued his services and advice, often sending him to the front lines to evaluate defenses, deliver confidential dispatches, and consult on the reorganization of the army. Lee was promoted to brigadier general 25 June 1863 and to major general 20 Oct. 1864.

More than the president's reluctance to release Custis Lee kept him from the field. Unsure of his own abilities, Lee believed himself too inexperienced to lead troops in battle. Davis offered him command of the Department of Western Virginia Aug. 1864, but illness and uncertainty prevented him from accepting. Finally, during the last retreat from PETERSBURG, he joined the fighting at the head of a regiment of mechanics he had recruited in Richmond. Attached to Lt. Gen. RICHARD S. EWELL's command, Custis Lee's men were heavily engaged at SAYLER'S CREEK, where the overwhelming Federal troops surrounded Lee. Rather than endanger his Confederates further, he surrendered. He was paroled soon after capture to visit his ailing mother.

With his inheritance, the Custis family estate "Arlington," in Federal hands, in Oct. 1865 Custis Lee accepted a position teaching engineering at the Virginia Military Institute. He succeeded his father as president of Washington and Lee College 1 Feb. 1871, holding the post until illness necessitated his resignation 1 July 1897. Less successful than his outgoing brother, W.H.F. LEE, Custis Lee seemed to friends unable to escape the shadow of his famous father, who had impressed on his eldest son a need to excel. He lived out his retirement years at "Ravensworth," the family estate W.H.F. Lee had inherited in Fairfax Cty., Va., dying there 18 Feb. 1913.
—PLF

Lee, Robert Edward. CSA b. Westmoreland Cty., Va., 19 Jan. 1807. Winfield Scott called him "the best soldier I ever saw in the field." Viscount Garnet Wolseley said, "He is stamped upon my memory as a being apart and superior to all others in every way." ABRAHAM LINCOLN, through an emissary, offered him field command of the armies of the U.S. after FORT SUMTER, but Robert E. Lee, who considered duty "the most sublime word in the English language," chose loyalty to his beloved Virginia, though personally opposed to slavery and secession.

USA

Had he accepted Lincoln's offer, the Civil War might well have been ended earlier, with far less bloodshed, for Lee and his Army of Northern Virginia held off the ultimate Confederate defeat for months, if not years.

Lee was the fourth child of "Light Horse Harry" Lee, the Revolutionary War cavalry hero. Disaster befell the family when Lee's father was imprisoned for debt and later died of wounds suffered in suppressing a riot in Baltimore. The young Robert was reared by his widowed mother in Alexandria, where he attended private schools. Noted for his intellect and character, as well as his handsome appearance, he seemed born to command.

Appointed to West Point in 1825, he became corps adjutant, the chief post of honor for a cadet, and graduated 2d in his class, without a demerit on his record. He was commissioned a 2d lieutenant in the elite Corps of Engineers and, 2 years later, married Mary Custis, the great granddaughter of Martha Washington and heiress of several estates. A devoted family man, Lee fathered 7 children.

Promoted to 1st lieutenant in 1836 and to captain 2 years later, Lee undertook various civil and military engineering projects for the Corps of Engineers before the Mexican War, in which he was assigned to Gen. WINFIELD SCOTT's staff. He was instrumental in the U.S. victory at Cerro Gordo and distinguished himself in the assault at Chapultepec, where, 13 Sept. 1847, he was wounded. On his return to the U.S., he was promoted to brevet colonel for his heroism.

During a 3-year term as superintendent of West Point, 1852–55, Lee not only revitalized the curriculum but formed lasting relationships with the students. His career for the next few years was overshadowed by concerns for the health of his wife and management of her estate. He served with the cavalry in Texas 1856–57, and was on leave at Mrs. Lee's family seat, "Arlington," when put in command of a contingent of marines to recapture HARPERS FERRY from JOHN BROWN and his followers.

On cavalry duty in Texas, Feb. 1861, when that state seceded, Lee returned to "Arlington" to await events. It was there that he received and declined Lincoln's offer. He resigned his commission and, 23 Apr., accepted command of Virginia's defenses. On 31 Aug. he was promoted to full general as special military adviser to Confederate Pres. JEFFERSON DAVIS. Though unable to prevent Federal seizure of the mountainous sections of western Virginia, he did carry out an important mission to oversee coastal defenses in South Carolina and Georgia. In Mar. 1862 he returned to his position as adviser to Davis, whose confidence in him never slackened. Then, 31 May, with the 100,000-man Union army of Maj. Gen. GEORGE B. MCCLELLAN on the outskirts of Richmond, Lee replaced the wounded Gen. JOSEPH E. JOHNSTON as commander of what he, Lee, named "The Army of Northern Virginia," and proceeded to create an unparalleled military record.

Lee quickly reorganized his new army, called Maj. Gen. THOMAS J. "STONEWALL" JACKSON from the Shenandoah Valley, and 26 June, launched an offensive that came to be known as the SEVEN DAYS' CAMPAIGN. Though casualties were high, Lee drove McClellan back down the peninsula to the protection of his gunboats, then turned north and delivered a smashing defeat to a second Union army, commanded by Maj. Gen. JOHN POPE, in the SECOND BATTLE OF BULL RUN. Thereupon he launched an invasion aimed at penetrating deep into Pennsylvania. Though Jackson captured Harpers Ferry and 12,000 Federals, the discovery of a copy of Lee's marching orders led him to take up defensive positions along Antietam Creek, just north of the Potomac (see LEE'S LOST ORDER). There, in the bloodiest day of the war, 17 Sept. 1862, he won a tactical victory but a strategic defeat when he retired to Virginia.

At FREDERICKSBURG, 13 Dec., he soundly defeated the Army

of the Potomac under Maj. Gen. AMBROSE E. BURNSIDE and won an even more decisive victory the following May, at CHANCELLORSVILLE, when the Federals, now under Maj. Gen. JOSEPH HOOKER, tried to trap him along the Rappahannock River. But there Lee suffered an irreparable loss in the accidental wounding and death of Jackson, his chief lieutenant.

Again Lee demonstrated his administrative genius when, in a few weeks, he reorganized his army and devised a strategy for a new invasion of the North. Launching this movement early in June, by the end of the month he had occupied the entire Cumberland Valley and other parts of Pennsylvania, and was approaching the state capital at Harrisburg. Discovering that Hooker had been replaced as Federal commander by Maj. Gen. GEORGE G. MEADE, who was threatening his lines of communications, Lee concentrated his army near GETTYSBURG. There, 1–3 July 1863, in the largest battle of the war, Lee, without Jackson, suffered his first outright defeat and retreated to Virginia, his numbers much depleted.

Lee's greatest test came the following spring when, with only 60,000 men, he opposed the overland drive of Lt. Gen. U. S. GRANT's 120,000-man army against Richmond. Though Lee balked Grant's progress in the Battles of the WILDERNESS, SPOTSYLVANIA COURT HOUSE, the NORTH ANNA, and COLD HARBOR, inflicting over 50,000 casualties on the Federals, he found himself that summer backed into defensive works protecting Richmond and Petersburg. With Maj. Gen. WILLIAM T. SHERMAN marching through Georgia and South Carolina and morale on the homefront diminishing, it was only a matter of time before Federal superiority in numbers and matériel prevailed.

Too late to save the Southern cause, Davis appointed Lee commander of all Confederate armies, and the Congress adopted his advice to authorize recruitment of black slaves (see BLACK TROOPS, CONFEDERACY APPROVES USE OF).

By now Lee's health had been impaired as well. In Mar. 1865 he abandoned the defenses of the Confederate capital in a desperate effort to unite with Johnston against Sherman in North Carolina. But Grant brought him to bay at APPOMATTOX Court House, where, 9 Apr. 1865, the proud Lee reluctantly surrendered his starving, ragged army of only 28,000.

Lee ranks among the ablest field commanders in American history. In battle he was imperturbable. He enjoyed a rare ability to command respect and affection from his troops, was a master in the art of field fortifications, and possessed an uncanny understanding of his opponents. He was also quick to seize the initiative. Among his faults were his sometimes cavalier attitude toward supply and his habit of devising and explaining his general plans for a campaign or battle, then leaving the execution to his subordinate generals—a practice that contributed to his defeat at Gettysburg.

His victories in the Seven Days', Second Bull Run, Fredericksburg, Chancellorsville, and Cold Harbor were won against superior numbers. Not until the last days of the war, at FIVE FORKS, was Lee's army driven from a battlefield in disorder. At both Antietam and Gettysburg he continued to occupy his positions until he chose to retreat.

But Lee demonstrated his greatest strength of character after the war, when he spurned prestigious job offers for the post of president of Washington College in Lexington, Va., at a salary of $1,500 per year. As he had done at West Point, he transformed the curriculum, creating the nation's first departments of journalism and commerce. Deprived of his citizenship, he nonetheless urged his fellow Southerners to put the bitterness of war and defeat behind them and become loyal Americans once more.

By the time of his death, 12 Oct. 1870, at 63, he had become a genuine American hero, admired in the North, revered in the South. —RHF

Lee, Stephen Dill. CSA b. Charleston, S.C., 22 Sept. 1833, Lee was born into a family distantly related to the Virginia Lees. He graduated from West Point in 1854, standing 17th in a class of 46.

For 7 years he served in the U.S. Army (artillery and staff), resigning Feb. 1861 to enter Confederate service. On Brig. Gen. P.G.T. BEAUREGARD's staff at FORT SUMTER, he was then assigned to the army in Virginia. Lee won great praise as an artillerist at SECOND BULL RUN and at ANTIETAM.

Selected to fill a vacancy for an artillery brigadier general in Mississippi, he fought at Chickasaw Bayou, CHAMPION'S HILL, and the Siege of VICKSBURG,

LC

commanding an infantry brigade part of this time. Captured at Vicksburg and exchanged Aug. 1863, Lee was promoted to major general. He commanded cavalry in Mississippi and Alabama until May 1864, when he was named commander of the Department of Alabama, Mississippi, and East Louisiana.

The following July, Lee was made lieutenant general, to rank from 23 June, and assigned to corps command in the Army of Tennessee, then defending Atlanta. He fought in the remainder of the ATLANTA CAMPAIGN, playing a prominent role at EZRA CHURCH, and led his corps in the FRANKLIN AND NASHVILLE CAMPAIGN. Wounded on the retreat from Nashville, he did not return to duty until the final CAROLINAS CAMPAIGN, and was surrendered Apr. 1865.

After the war, Lee lived in Mississippi, where he worked as a farmer, state legislator, and first president of the Mississippi Agricultural and Mechanical College, 1878–97. He also helped found and was active in the UNITED CONFEDERATE VETERANS as its president 1904–08, promoted women's rights, worked for the preservation of the Vicksburg battlefield sites, and wrote history. d. Vicksburg, 28 May 1908. —RMcM

Lee, William Henry Fitzhugh. CSA b. "Arlington," Va., 31 May 1837. The second son of ROBERT E. LEE, "Rooney" Lee was a graduate of Harvard. In 1857 he entered the Regular Army as a 2d lieutenant, 6th Infantry, participating in the Utah Expedition before resigning in 1859 to farm at "White House," the plantation on the Pamunkey River he inherited from his maternal grandfather.

When Virginia seceded, Lee immediately volunteered and was commissioned a captain, then a major in the Confederate cavalry. He served as Brig. Gen. WILLIAM WING LORING's cavalry commander in western Virginia during summer 1861 and spent the rest of the year and part of 1862 near Fredericksburg. He was then appointed lieutenant colonel and, shortly afterward, colonel of the 9th Virginia Cavalry, leading it in Maj. Gen. J.E.B. STUART's operations throughout the summer of 1862. At SOUTH MOUNTAIN in September, Lee was unhorsed

and knocked unconscious. His capable performance earned him promotion to brigadier general, to date from 15 Sept.

Lee proved to be an exceptional brigade commander, leading the 3d Brigade at FREDERICKSBURG and at CHANCELLORSVILLE. On 9 June 1863, at BRANDY STATION, he suffered a severe leg wound, and on the 26th, while recuperating, he was captured by Federal raiders. He languished in a Union prison for 9 months, not exchanged until Mar. 1864.

USMHI

Promoted to major general 23 Apr. 1864, Lee became the youngest officer of that rank in the Confederacy. During the war's final year, he assumed greater responsibility as attrition thinned the officers' ranks. At Globe Tavern, near Petersburg, Aug. 1864, he commanded the cavalry. In the war's final week in Apr. 1865 he was second-in-command, responsible for the army's right flank in its retreat from Petersburg to Appomattox.

After the war Lee returned to White House, which had been destroyed by Union troops in 1862. He rebuilt his home, farmed, and served as president of the Virginia Agricultural Society and as a state senator. Elected to the House of Representatives in 1887, he was in his second term when he died 15 Oct. 1891 at "Ravensworth," his wife's Alexandria, Va., estate. He is buried in the Lee mausoleum on the campus of Washington and Lee University in Lexington. —JDW

Leech & Rigdon. Thomas Leech of Memphis, Tenn., was employed before the war as a gun dealer and cotton broker. Following the outbreak of hostilities, he founded the Memphis Novelty Works for the manufacture of all types of military cutlery and arms repair. Charles H. Rigdon of Saint Louis, Mo., was a scale maker prior to the war. He gained experience with revolvers by working with William Able Shawk, who produced a small quantity of brass-framed imitation Colts using Rigdon's equipment.

HTIC

A Southern sympathizer, Rigdon floated his machinery downriver from Saint Louis to Memphis, where he joined in partnership with Leech in late 1861 or early 1862. Operating as Leech & Rigdon, this firm continued to produce a complete line of edged weapons as the Memphis Novelty Works.

Before Rigdon's revolver-making equipment could be put to good use, however, Memphis was evacuated. In May 1862 Leech & Rigdon reestablished their plant at the Confederate States armory, known as Briarfield, in Columbus, Miss. Here they deleted "Memphis" from their trade name and continued as the Novelty Works. When Columbus was threatened in fall 1862, they moved again, to Greensboro, Ga., where they operated until their partnership was dissolved Dec. 1863.

Leech & Rigdon manufactured 1,500 serviceable revolvers under a Confederate States contract. As the South's second largest producer of handguns, after GRISWOLD & GUNNISON, they produced a finely engineered copy of Colt's Model 1851 revolver. Manufacture of these 6-shot, .36-caliber weapons began at the Briarfield armory in 1862. After the firm broke up, Rigdon moved to Augusta, Ga., taking his machinery with him. He went into business with Jesse Ansley Jan. 1864. Under the terms of his dissolved partnership with Leech, his new company completed the Confederate contract for 1,500 revolvers, while continuing to stamp them "Leech & Rigdon, C.S.A."

—MJO'D

Leesburg, Va., Battle of.   21 Oct. 1861   *See* BALL'S BLUFF, VA., BATTLE OF.

Lee's Farewell to the Army of Northern Virginia.   On 10 Apr. 1865, the day after Gen. ROBERT E. LEE surrendered the Army of Northern Virginia to Lt. Gen. ULYSSES S. GRANT, the Confederate commander-in-chief issued General Orders No. 9, his eloquent "farewell" to his army:

> After four years of arduous service marked by unsurpassed courage and fortitude, the Army of Northern Virginia has been compelled to yield to overwhelming numbers and resources.
>
> I need not tell the brave survivors of so many hard fought battles, who have remained steadfast to the last, that I have consented to this result from no distrust of them; but feeling that valor and devotion could accomplish nothing that could compensate for the loss that must have attended the continuance of the contest, I determined to avoid the useless sacrifice of those whose past services have endeared them to their countrymen.
>
> By the terms of the agreement, officers and men can return to their homes and remain until exchanged. You will take with you the satisfaction that proceeds from the consciousness of duty faithfully performed; and I earnestly pray that a Merciful God will extend to you His blessing and protection.
>
> With an unceasing admiration of your constancy and devotion to your Country, and a grateful remembrance of your kind and generous consideration for myself, I bid you all an affectionate farewell.

On the morning of 11 Apr., following a spartan breakfast and tearful good-byes from his staff, the general mounted his horse, Traveller, and with a Union honor guard left Appomattox for home to take his place in history.   —EMT

Lee's Lost Order.   On the morning of 13 Sept. 1862, Maj. Gen. GEORGE B. MCCLELLAN's Army of the Potomac, in pursuit of the Confederates who had invaded Maryland, closed up on Frederick City. Shortly before noon, the infantry of the XII Corps bivouacked on ground recently occupied by the Confederate division of Maj. Gen. DANIEL H. HILL. Lolling in a field south of the city, Pvt. Barton W. Mitchell of the 27TH INDIANA spied in the grass a package wrapped in paper. The package held 3 cigars, which Mitchell shared with comrades while he inspected their covering. He sat bolt upright when he realized he was holding a copy of Special Order No. 191, dated 9 Sept. 1862 and signed by the adjutant general of the Army of North-

ern Virginia, Col. ROBERT H. CHILTON. At once he showed the order to Sgt. John M. Bloss, who hastened it to their commander, Col. Silas Colgrove. The colonel saw that it was presented to McClellan himself.

The document handed to "Little Mac" was one of 7 copies of an order Gen. ROBERT E. LEE had sent to his ranking subordinates. This particular copy had been intended for General Hill; apparently a careless staff officer had lost it, though the information had reached its intended recipient through another source. It told McClellan that Lee had divided his army, sending 3 of its 4 parts southwestward from Frederick to capture the Union garrison at HARPERS FERRY. With such information the Union commander could interpose among the detachments, defeating each in detail. No wonder he could not repress his glee, despite the presence of a group of local citizens whose audience with him the letter's arrival had interrupted. Later he exclaimed to a subordinate: "Here is a paper with which if I cannot whip Bobbie Lee I will be willing to go home!"

Yet McClellan failed to exploit fully this remarkable stroke of luck. His army did not start for Harpers Ferry till the next morning. In the interim, he painstakingly confirmed the authenticity of the order and scrutinized reports of large enemy forces in his front. Meanwhile, one of the citizens who had been at McClellan's side when the order arrived hastened to Lee's army with the news, enabling Lee to block McClellan's path on the 14th long enough to capture Harpers Ferry and reunite his army.   —EGL

Legal Tender Acts.   By the end of 1861 the Northern banking community was facing a crisis, the result of a gold shortage. A series of events casting doubt on the Union's ability to win the war—including Southern victories at FIRST BULL RUN and BALL'S BLUFF, and the possibility of British intervention on behalf of the Confederacy as result of the *TRENT* AFFAIR—had prompted panic buying of precious metals. Increased speculation and hoarding had depleted the gold reserves not only of the banks but also of the Federal Treasury. This situation complicated government efforts to obtain loans needed to pay the continuing cost of the war and to cover debts already incurred in the course of recruiting 600,000 volunteers to increase its armed force of 16,000 Regulars.

The signal that drastic action was needed came late in December, when New York banks, whose gold reserves had shrunk by almost a third during the previous 3 weeks, suspended payment of specie as backing for their notes. Banks in Boston and Philadelphia quickly followed suit; soon, throughout the North, debtors could make payments only by check or by Treasury or bank notes. Clearly the government needed to devise a new medium of exchange.

At the height of the crisis, Republican Congressman Elbridge G. Spaulding of New York, a member of the House Ways and Means Committee, proposed a solution. He drafted a bill making paper currency, payable on demand by the U.S. Treasury but unbacked by gold or silver, legal tender for all debts, public and private, except duties on imports and interest on the public debt. The constitutionality of fiat money was questionable, but Atty. Gen. EDWARD BATES upheld its legality, touching off intense congressional debate.

Wartime exigencies finally prompted the passage of a Legal Tender Act much like Spaulding's. ABRAHAM LINCOLN signed it into law Feb. 1862, and "GREENBACKS" began to circulate early in April. The first act authorized an issuance of $150 million in Treasury notes; acts of July 1862 and Mar. 1863 provided for additional issues totaling $300 million. In later months, especially when Union military fortunes sagged, the value of the greenback depreciated sharply but not enough to vitiate its value to the wartime economy of the North.   —EGL

Leggett, Mortimer Dormer. USA b. near Ithaca, N.Y., 19 Apr. 1821. Raised on a farm, as a teenager Leggett moved with his family to Geauga Cty., Ohio. In 1839, after months of preparatory study by night, he entered a teacher's academy in Kirtland, Ohio, graduating 1st in his class. Seeking to combine careers in law and medicine, he attended Western Reserve College and took supplementary courses at Willoughby Medical School. After admittance to the bar, he settled in Akron, where he promoted primary education and served as school superintendent, a post he later held in 2 other Ohio cities. In 1850 he began to practice law and 6 years later became a member of the faculty of the Ohio Law College.

LC

When the Civil War commenced, Leggett joined the staff of his friend Maj. Gen. GEORGE B. MCCLELLAN, serving under him during the western Virginia campaigning of 1861. Later Gov. WILLIAM DENNISON authorized Leggett to raise a regiment of infantry, the 78th Ohio Volunteers. He led the outfit in Brig. Gen. ULYSSES S. GRANT's Army of the Tennessee at FORT DONELSON, CORINTH, and SHILOH. Though his troops were only marginally engaged in these battles, the former lawyer-physician-educator showed himself adept at military command; as a result, he was awarded a brigadier's star to rank from 29 Nov. 1862.

At the head of an Ohio brigade, Leggett distinguished himself in several phases of the VICKSBURG CAMPAIGN. During siege operations against the enemy citadel, May–July 1863, his troops handled a variety of engineering chores. Late that year he was leading a division in the XVII Corps of Grant's army. He won even greater notice in the ATLANTA CAMPAIGN of 1864, on 21 July leading a successful assault on Bald Hill, a commanding eminence northeast of the Gate City; thereafter the site was known as LEGGETT'S HILL.

As a brevet major general of volunteers, Leggett finished the conflict by playing a leading role in Maj. Gen. WILLIAM T. SHERMAN's MARCH TO THE SEA and CAROLINAS CAMPAIGN, for a time leading the XVII Corps. He attained a full major generalship Aug. 1865 but resigned his commission a month later to return to civilian pursuits. He practiced law in Zanesville, Ohio, then went into manufacturing, before being appointed commissioner of patents Jan. 1871 by President Grant. Later he founded a firm that became a part of the General Electric Co. d. Cleveland, 6 Jan. 1896.   —EGL

Leggett's Hill, Ga., eng. at. 21 July 1864 On 20 July 1864, as Gen. JOHN BELL HOOD's Confederates battled Maj. Gen. GEORGE H. THOMAS's Federals along PEACHTREE CREEK, northeast of Atlanta, the balance of Maj. Gen. WILLIAM T. SHERMAN's forces advanced on the city from the east. That after-

noon Sherman's Army of the Tennessee, under the direct command of Maj. Gen. JAMES B. MCPHERSON, pressed Confederate skirmishers into the city works. At length McPherson drew up about 2.5 mi from Atlanta, his XV Corps forming his right flank, Maj. Gen. FRANCIS P. BLAIR's XVII Corps going into position farther south. A long burst of rifle fire flamed out of the Confederate works, persuading Sherman to delay an assault along McPherson's front.

One point on the Southern line, an eminence just southwest of Blair's position known as Bald Hill, offered particular resistance. On its tree-cleared summit, well-entrenched Confederates raked Blair's left with a galling fire; those wounded by it included Brig. Gen. Walter Q. Gresham, leader of Blair's 4th Division. To remove this deadly annoyance, McPherson ordered Blair to attack the hill. Blair relayed the order to Brig. Gen. MORTIMER D. LEGGETT, leader of his 3d Division. Since Leggett apparently did not receive the order before darkness fell, he prepared an assault for the next morning.

At sunrise on the 21st, Leggett went forward, Brig. Gen. MANNING F. FORCE's Illinois and Wisconsin brigade in the lead, the rest of the division behind. On the right, Gresham's division, now led by Brig. Gen. GILES A. SMITH, advanced to neutralize opponents in its front.

Before Force reached the hill, its summit was swept by a torrent of artillery fire from batteries in his rear. Confederate Brig. Gen. JAMES A. SMITH described the barrage as "committing dreadful havoc in the ranks. I have never before witnessed such accurate and destructive cannonading." Without this covering fire, an attack on a hill so steep, crowned by works so strong, would have been suicidal. With such assistance, Force's men scrambled up its slope and drove out the defenders at bayonet point. In routing part of Maj. Gen. PATRICK R. CLEBURNE's veteran division, Leggett's men absorbed perhaps 350 casualties; supporting troops, including Giles Smith's, lost about as many. Their prize was worth the cost: atop what soon became known as Leggett's Hill, the Federals built, an Ohio officer said, "almost a Gibraltar." From there guns could fire into Atlanta and enfilade a large section of its works.   —EGL

LeMat revolver. Dr. Jean LeMat of New Orleans acquired a U.S. patent on his formidable .40-caliber, 9-shot revolver in 1856. The first of several patented designs carried an 18-gauge shotgun load under its .40-caliber barrel; by flicking the thumb over a stud on the hammer one could switch from firing pistol rounds to letting off a "grapeshot" load. LeMat built the revolver for cavalry and navy use in close personal combat. Manufactured in France, under license by C. Girard & Co. for Southern buyers, they were given to prestigious Confederates as promotional gifts. Cavalry Maj. Gen. J.E.B. STUART and Gen. P.G.T. BEAUREGARD, the latter rumored to be a partner in their manufacture, both carried LeMats. The pistol came in 2 models of 2 types each, the first model having a half-octagon barrel, the second having a full-octagon barrel. One type could be adapted to take a full-length extension on the shotgun barrel. Most manufactured models were inferior to custom-made prototypes, and Confederate arms buyers in Europe condemned entire lots before delivery. The LeMat was more often spoken of than seen.   —JES

Letcher, John. war governor b. Lexington, Va., 29 Mar. 1813. After attending Randolph-Macon and Washington colleges in Virginia, Letcher graduated from the latter in 1833 and

6 years later was admitted to the bar. The editor of the Democratic *Valley Star* 1839–50, he supported STATES RIGHTS and a strict interpretation of the Constitution, calling at the same time for democratic reform of the state government. In his efforts to get an equitable distribution of power between eastern and western interests in Virginia, he fleetingly gave his endorsement to the separatist movement and gradual emancipation in the western counties

NA

of the state. At the constitutional convention of 1850–51 Letcher played a major role in creating a new constitution granting universal white manhood suffrage, which gave his constituents a greater share of the power they sought. His popularity among the westerners resulted in his election to the U.S. House of Representatives, 1851–59, where Letcher, himself a slaveowner, became a proslavery spokesman cautioning moderation and conciliation. He nearly lost the gubernatorial election of 1859 to Whigs, who labeled him an abolitionist, but won by a narrow margin and was inaugurated 1 Jan. 1860.

Letcher tried to dissuade secessionists in his state, supporting for the presidency the compromise politician STEPHEN A. DOUGLAS. At the same time, as a precautionary measure, he encouraged legislation to strengthen the militia. When the Deep South began seceding he helped organize the WASHINGTON PEACE CONFERENCE in hopes of finding some resolution to Southern grievances.

With the firing on FORT SUMTER and the passage a few days later of an ordinance of secession, 17 Apr., Letcher became governor of the most powerful of the Confederate states. As such, he cooperated fully with the Confederate central government, even on IMPRESSMENT and CONSCRIPTION, issues he believed infringed on powers reserved to the states. He tried to keep the western counties from seceding, encouraged guerrilla warfare, pleaded with other governors to put aside their insistence on states rights in favor of unity until independence was won, and withheld his public criticism of the JEFFERSON DAVIS administration for the sake of harmony. Letcher appointed ROBERT E. LEE commander of all state troops; commissioned THOMAS J. "STONEWALL" JACKSON colonel, then defended him against criticism from Sec. of War JUDAH P. BENJAMIN; and relinquished the state forces to Confederate authority before any other states did so.

As an administrator Letcher spent an excessive amount of time planning and carrying out details that could have been delegated to staff. He failed to control speculation or check inflation, and his program to alleviate shortages of salt ended in bureaucratic disaster. His relationship with the legislature deteriorated sharply as a result of his pragmatic cooperation with the central government, and Virginians in general disapproved of his subordination of state power to Confederate authority. When his term expired at the end of 1864, he left office and retired to Lexington, having been defeated for a seat in the Confederate House earlier that year.

Letcher was financially ruined by the war, his home in Lexington burned by Maj. Gen. DAVID HUNTER's troops in 1864. The former governor was imprisoned for 6 weeks after the surrender but was released without being tried for treason. He then practiced law, playing only a minor role in postwar Virginia politics as a member of the state house, 1875–77. d. Lexington, 26 Jan. 1884.   —PLF

Leventhorpe, Collett. CSA b. Exmouth, England, 15 May 1815. Descended from "an ancient and knightly family" of Yorkshire, Leventhorpe was educated at Winchester College and at 17 was commissioned by William IV an ensign in His Majesty's 14th Regiment of Foot. After serving 3 years in Ireland and several more in the West Indies and Canada, he relinquished his captaincy in 1842 and emigrated to the U.S. Settling in North Carolina, he married into a prominent local family.

LC

At the outbreak of the Civil War, Leventhorpe hastened into the Confederate ranks. His community standing and military background won him the colonelcy of the 34th North Carolina Infantry. As one biographer has it, he "brought his regiment to such a remarkable state of discipline and training" that by December he was given temporary command of a brigade. In Apr. 1862 he was transferred to the 11th North Carolina and soon was sent to the Atlantic coast to head the District of Wilmington. Later that year he manned the defenses along Virginia's Blackwater River, where his regiment guarded a line some 26 mi long. Returning to North Carolina in December, he was conspicuous in midmonth in skirmishing at White Hall, which slowed Federals under Brig. Gen. JOHN G. FOSTER in their advance toward Goldsborough.

After helping repulse a sortie during the Siege of Washington, Apr. 1863, the 11th North Carolina joined Gen. ROBERT E. LEE's Army of Northern Virginia. During the GETTYSBURG CAMPAIGN, the outfit formed part of Brig. Gen. JAMES J. PETTIGREW's brigade of Maj. Gen. HENRY HETH's division, Lt. Gen. AMBROSE P. HILL's Corps. With the rest of Heth's command, it participated in the first day's fighting at Gettysburg, where Leventhorpe was seriously wounded. Captured during the Confederate retreat to Virginia, he was forced to submit to a painful operation without benefit of anesthesia. He survived but was not released from imprisonment for 9 months.

Thereafter, as a brigadier general of North Carolina troops, he operated along the Roanoke River and the Petersburg & Weldon Railroad. On 18 Feb. 1865 he also became a brigadier in the Confederate ranks, but 3 weeks later he refused the appointment. After the war, he was involved in several business enterprises, traveled frequently to his native land, lived for a time in New York City, and ultimately settled in Wilkes Cty., N.C., where he died 1 Dec. 1889.   —EGL

Lewis, Joseph Horace. CSA b. near Glasgow, Ky., 29 Oct. 1824. Scion of a prosperous family, Lewis was educated at Centre College, graduating in 1843, 2 years before being admitted to the bar. He entered politics and was 3 times elected to the lower house of the Kentucky legislature. Twice, however, his bid for a U.S. congressional seat was thwarted. Initially a Whig, by the late 1850s he had become a secessionist Democrat and in the presidential campaign of 1860 was an elector for JOHN C. BRECKINRIDGE.

LC

Lewis entered Confederate service as colonel of the 6th Kentucky Infantry, which he had organized in Barren County. He quickly won a reputation as a stern disciplinarian, a martinet whom his troops nevertheless respected and admired. As part of the ORPHAN BRIGADE, he was conspicuous at SHILOH, his horse being shot under him during an attack on Union troops just northeast of the church that lent the battlefield its name. That winter he served capably at STONE'S RIVER, on 2 Jan. holding the left of the brigade of Brig. Gen. ROGER W. HANSON, though pounded by enemy artillery.

Under Breckinridge, now a major general, Lewis again distinguished himself at CHICKAMAUGA, where he gained command of the Orphan Brigade on the death of Brig. Gen. BEN HARDIN HELM. Because of his spirited service along the Confederate right during that great victory, "Old Joe" received promotion to brigadier general as of 30 Sept. 1863. He was less fortunate at MISSIONARY RIDGE, where his line was broken by Federals who made a spectacular charge up the mountainside.

During the ATLANTA CAMPAIGN, he turned in a series of solid performances in battles including RESACA, NEW HOPE CHURCH, Dallas, Pine Mountain, KENNESAW MOUNTAIN, PEACHTREE CREEK, and Utoy Creek. Following Atlanta's fall, Lewis' brigade was mounted and fought in the saddle for the rest of the war, which for Lewis concluded with participation in the CAROLINAS CAMPAIGN. He then took his Kentuckians to Washington, Ga., where they lay down their arms 6 May 1865.

Returning home, Lewis resumed his legal career. He served in the state legislature; spent 3 terms in the U.S. House of Representatives, 1871–77; then held a judicial position for 17 years, the last 4 of which he spent as chief justice of the Kentucky Court of Appeals. d. on his farm in Scott County 6 July 1904.
—EGL

Lewis, William Gaston. CSA b. Rocky Mount, N.C., 3 Sept. 1835. The descendant of Revolutionary War veterans, Lewis was educated at a military academy in Raleigh before graduating at 19 from the University of North Carolina. After teaching school in Florida as well as in his native state, he spent a year in the Northwest as a government surveyor. From that time until the Civil War, he was assistant engineer on a branch of the Wilmington & Weldon Railroad.

GG

Early in the conflict Lewis served as a junior lieutenant in the 1st North Carolina Infantry, taking part in BIG BETHEL, the first sizable clash of arms in Virginia. Promoted to major of the 33d North Carolina, he soon went to New Berne, N.C., to defend

his state's coast against Federal incursion. Though the campaign failed, his participation was meritorious, elevating him to lieutenant colonel of his third regiment, the 43d North Carolina, which became a part of Lt. Gen. Thomas J. "Stonewall" Jackson's corps.

The 43d accompanied Jackson's successor, Lt. Gen. RICHARD S. EWELL, into the SECOND BATTLE OF WINCHESTER, early in the Gettysburg Campaign. Following the seizure of that Virginia town, Lewis's regiment proceeded into Pennsylvania, fighting all 3 days at Gettysburg, including the combat on CULP'S HILL, 3 July 1863. That day, Lewis succeeded to regimental command and performed so ably that his brigade leader lauded his "bravery and coolness" under fire. He then served at BRISTOE STATION and MINE RUN before returning to North Carolina in spring 1864 to fight under Maj. Gen. ROBERT F. HOKE. In April, during Hoke's capture of Plymouth, Lewis served gallantly enough to win a colonelcy.

From Plymouth he was sent to lower Virginia. Early in May he was given command of Hoke's old brigade, which he led under Gen. P.G.T. BEAUREGARD at the SECOND BATTLE OF DREWRY'S BLUFF, on the 16th. In that fight he conducted a slashing attack against the right flank of Maj. Gen. BENJAMIN F. BUTLER's Army of the James, helping repulse its thrust at lightly guarded Richmond. 15 days later, Lewis was a brigadier general and as such participated in EARLY'S WASHINGTON RAID, in the subsequent SHENANDOAH VALLEY CAMPAIGN, and in the APPOMATTOX CAMPAIGN under Gen. ROBERT E. LEE. Severely wounded 7 Apr. 1865 at Farmville, Lewis was captured but quickly paroled. Thereafter he resumed his civil-engineering career in North Carolina, for 13 years serving as state engineer. d. Goldsborough, N.C., 7 Jan. 1901.
—EGL

Lexington, Mo., Siege of. 12–20 Sept. 1861 Instilled with confidence from the Confederate victory at WILSON'S CREEK, near Springfield, Mo., 10 Aug., Maj. Gen. STERLING PRICE determined to rid the state of Kansas jayhawkers and Northern sympathizers. By 13 Sept. former governor Price had led his 7,000 men of the Missouri State Guard to the outskirts of Lexington, a town of 1,000 overlooking the Missouri River. 2 encounters with Union pickets that day marked the beginning of the siege.

Just north of town, on the Masonic College campus, was a garrison of 2,800 troopers under the command of Col. James A. Mulligan, guarding several items they had confiscated from the town. Included in the cache were the great seal of the state and nearly a million dollars from the bank in town, the latter buried under Mulligan's tent. His orders were to hold Lexington "at all hazards."

The second exchange on the 13th drove the Federal garrison back into its fortifications of 12-by-12-foot earthen ramparts, which housed 7 cannon. For 5 days the 2 commanders waited. Mulligan hoped for support from Maj. Gen. JOHN C. FRÉMONT; the help would never come. Price waited for his ammunition train to arrive as volunteers poured in from all over the state. The Federals were doomed.

On 18 Sept. Price's overwhelming force surrounded the garrison and forced it to abandon the only supply of water near the fortification. Still the Federals resisted with artillery and fought fiercely at the Anderson house, 125 yd from the Union ramparts. Because of its position on a hill, the brick building was militarily strategic; but the Northerners used it only as a hospital, and eventually they lost it.

On the 19th, Price's artillery fired into the thirsty garrison and the surrounding town, which had been evacuated. The relief column Mulligan had hoped for was on its way under Brig. Gen. SAMUEL D. STURGIS, but it was scared away by the threat of an encounter with a 3,000-man detachment sent out by Price. Mulligan was on his own, and his command was crumbling.

By the morning of the 20th the Missouri troopers were closing in on the Federal garrison, moving behind huge hemp bales for protection. In a few hours several of Mulligan's subordinates raised the surrender flag on their own initiative, the firing stopped, and Price sent a courier with a note to Mulligan to arrange a truce. At first the colonel refused to surrender, and rifles and hemp bales burst into motion once again. Finally Mulligan conferred with his officers, who voted to capitulate, and at 2 p.m. the garrison was surrendered with 159 casualties, 3,000 rifles, 750 horses, and the 7 cannon.

Despite the sensational victory, Price was unable to equip his entire force of volunteers, and enthusiasm dropped so much that his command dwindled to its original complement of 7,000. Frémont's strong, newly formed army of 38,000 eventually forced him from the state.　　—FLS

Lexington, Tenn., eng. at. 18 Dec. 1862 Union informants reported 16 Dec. that Confederate Brig. Gen. NATHAN B. FORREST had crossed the Tennessee River west from Clifton, a community north of Savannah, Tenn. According to the report, Forest, with 2,100 men, would raid in West Tennessee and assault the Mobile & Ohio and Mississippi Central railroads supplying Maj. Gen. ULYSSES S. GRANT's Union campaign in Mississippi. Union Brig. Gen. JEREMIAH C. SULLIVAN, commanding at Jackson, Tenn., acted on other intelligence reports and 16 Dec. dispatched Col. Robert G. Ingersoll 28 mi east to command Federal cavalry at Lexington, the probable first objective of FORREST'S SECOND RAID. Gathering Illinois, Ohio, and Unionist West Tennessee troops and a 2-gun section of an Indiana battery, Ingersoll defended the town with about 706 men.

Forrest's cavalrymen marched 8 mi west of the Tennessee 17 Dec., camped, and prepared to move north, then west on Lexington. Anticipating this approach, Ingersoll deployed pickets 5 mi east of town along Beech Creek and ordered bridges burned on the 2 northwest-southwest roads crossing the creek to the southeast. Late on the 17th, Forrest's advance troops were sighted. Ingersoll pulled back to a position half a mile from Lexington and prepared to fight along the 2 roads, the more northerly one being called the State road, the more southerly called the Lower road. He positioned his 2 cannon north of the creek crossings. Unknown to Ingersoll a Lieutenant Fox, with the force on the Lower road, for unknown reasons failed to burn the bridge crossing his front.

Union Maj. Otto Funke led troops 4 mi down the State road at dawn, 18 Dec., hit a large body of Confederates, and began a fight lasting several hours. Forrest's troops, able to overrun Funke's men at any time, gave the impression of forming for a major assault. Intent on assaulting the Federal left, Confederates instead sent the bulk of their forces up the Lower road, crossed the undestroyed bridge, and routed troops commanded by Col. Isaac R. Hawkins. Ingersoll tried too late to mass his troops along the Lower road, was enfiladed on all sides, driven back to his cannon, and after repelling 3 charges was overrun. His West Tennessee troops fled the field.

Ingersoll became a prisoner along with 149 of his men. Both his cannon were captured. Records of the numbers of Union and Confederate troops killed and wounded in the engagement are neither complete nor reliable.

Though overwhelmed, most Federals gave a good account of themselves, according to Forrest's men. The prisoners were held 2–3 days, then paroled at Trenton, Tenn. Those Federals who escaped alarmed Sullivan at Jackson, stating that Forrest commanded a force as large as 10,000 men. This ensured Federal timidity for the duration of Forrest's raid.　　—JES

Lexington, USS. Originally a wooden sidewheel steamer built in Pittsburgh in 1860, the *Lexington* was designed to carry freight and passengers, and completed 2 trips between Pittsburgh and New Orleans before being purchased by the U.S. government May 1861. By August the ship had been converted to a gunboat and was ready for service. Weighing 448 tons, the *Lexington* was 177 ft long and had a draft of 7 ft. It was powered by 3 boilers and 2 high-pressure engines, and its original battery consisted of 2 32-pounders and 4 8-in. Dahlgrens.

The *Lexington* contributed significantly to Federal successes in the RIVER WAR. It saw action at Paducah and Smithfield, Ky., and at BELMONT, Mo., during 1861. The next year it contributed to Federal successes at FORT HENRY, ISLAND NO. 10, SHILOH, and St. Charles, Ark. The gunboat participated in the action against Fort Hindman at ARKANSAS POST, Jan. 1863, and against Fort Donelson in February. In retaliation for guerrilla activities, the *Lexington* shelled the town of Palmyra, Tenn., Apr. 1863, and during 1864 participated in the RED RIVER CAMPAIGN. Its commanders, through the end of the war, were Commander Roger N. Stembel, Commander James W. Shirk, Lt. Commander Samuel L. Phelps, Lt. Commander LeRoy Fitch, and Acting Lt. William Flye.

On 17 Aug. 1865, the *Lexington* was sold at auction at Mount City, Ill.　　—NCD

Libby Prison. After Andersonville, Libby, in Richmond, Va., is the most famous of the Confederate military prisons. Andersonville held enlisted men; Libby was for Federal officers.

Formerly the Libby & Son Ship Chandlers & Grocers (confused in some accounts with the Pemberton Factory Prison, originally a tobacco manufactory), Libby Prison faced north on Carey St., west on 20th St., east on a large vacant lot, and south on Canal St. Thus the 3-story 150-by-100-foot building stood isolated, making it easier to guard.

The 3 floors were divided into 8 large rooms that the prisoners identified as Streight's room, Milroy's room, Chickamauga room, Gettysburg room, and the like, depending on who their commander was or the battle in which they were captured. By 1863 the rooms were crowded; at night the men slept in squads, lined up on their sides for warmth and to save space. When the hard floor became unendurable, the entire squad would turn over on order of an elected leader. The quality of the food was poor and the quantity inadequate, and officers who had contrived to save any money or valuables on the way to Libby bartered these or even clothing for additional food. Prisoners dared not show themselves at windows for fear of being fired on by guards.

Naturally, the men's thoughts turned toward escape, the most famous of which was engineered by Col. Thomas E. Rose of the 77th Pennsylvania, captured at CHICKAMAUGA 20 Sept. 1863. The cellar at Libby was partitioned into 3 sections. By

USMHI

USMHI

making a hole in the fireplace of an unused kitchen on the first floor, Rose was able to descend the chimney and break out into the east section, or vermin-filled "Rat Hell," as the tunnelers came to call it. Rose and his companions dug a tunnel 50 ft long from the cellar to a warehouse shed on the far side of the vacant lot. On the night of 9 Feb. 1864, 109 officers crawled through to freedom. 48 were recaptured, including Rose. Libby Prison was dismantled in 1889 and rebuilt as a museum in Chicago. —RDH

Liddell, St. John Richardson. CSA b. near Woodville, Miss., 6 Sept. 1815. Liddell's early military career ended abruptly in 1833 when lackluster grades encouraged his resignation from West Point after a year at the academy. Thereafter he operated the plantation his father purchased for him in Catahoula Parish, La. Apparently he retained some visions of martial glory, for at 46 he entered Confederate service with rank of colonel as a volunteer aide to Maj. Gen. WILLIAM J. HARDEE, occasionally serving as confidential courier for Gen. AL-BERT SIDNEY JOHNSTON. Hardee admired Liddell's qualities of leadership enough to give him brigade command under Brig.

LC

Gen. PATRICK R. CLEBURNE, who concurred in Hardee's opinion after Liddell's distinguished performance at CORINTH. He was promoted to brigadier general from 17 July 1862.

At PERRYVILLE and at STONE'S RIVER Liddell matched his growing reputation as a reliable, hard-hitting infantry commander, thoroughly dedicated to Confederate victory. Assigned by Cleburne to hold Liberty Gap, Tenn., 24 June 1863, Liddell's Arkansas brigade fought off 3 attacking Federal brigades. Though absent on leave at the time of Cleburne's operations around CHICKAMAUGA, Liddell reported for duty at word of the fighting. He was one of the committee members appointed to draft the constitution of the COMRADES OF THE SOUTHERN CROSS, an officers' fraternal organization begun by Cleburne during the war.

Late in 1863 Liddell requested transfer to the Trans-Mississippi. From then until the war ended he held various district commands, fought under Lt. Gen. RICHARD TAYLOR to oppose Maj. Gen. NATHANIEL P. BANKS'S incursions during the RED RIVER CAMPAIGN, helped track down draft evaders and parolees, and operated against jayhawkers in northeastern Louisiana. He reported to Maj. Gen. DABNEY H. MAURY Aug. 1864, first being assigned to southern Mississippi and the next spring to the defenses of MOBILE, Ala. He was captured when Union forces overcame FORT BLAKELY 9 Apr. 1865.

Liddell returned to his plantation after his release. On 14 Feb. 1870 the 2 sons of a neighbor with whom he had been quarreling helped their father murder Liddell on board a steamboat on the Black River. His body was returned to his plantation for burial. —PLF

Light Division. USA The Light Division of the Army of Northern Virginia was created late in the spring of 1862 as Confederates concentrated to defend Richmond during the

PENINSULA CAMPAIGN. The division's first commander was Maj. Gen. AMBROSE P. HILL.

At its creation it contained the brigades of Maj. Gen. CHARLES W. FIELD (Virginia troops) and Brig. Gens. MAXCY GREGG (South Carolina), JOSEPH R. ANDERSON (Georgia), and JAMES J. ARCHER (Tennessee and Alabama), and the North Carolina brigades of Brig. Gens. LAWRENCE O. BRANCH and WILLIAM D. PENDER. Archer's and Field's brigades were reassigned May 1863, and casualties brought new commanders to the other brigades as the war went on.

Some writers speculate that the division's name referred to its ability to march rapidly. Many of its soldiers believed that the name referred to the fact that they traveled light—without coats, shoes, food, and other necessities.

The division was prominent in the SEVEN DAYS' battles and at SECOND BULL RUN. Its best-known service was its march from Harpers Ferry, Va., to Sharpsburg, Md., to save the Confederate flank at ANTIETAM, 17 Sept. 1862.

When the army was reorganized in fall 1862 the division was assigned to the II Corps. In May 1863 it was put under Pender and assigned to the III Corps commanded by Hill.

The division was prominent in the first day's fighting at Gettysburg, where Pender was mortally wounded. Maj. Gen. ISAAC R. TRIMBLE took command, only to be wounded and captured 2 days later. In Aug. 1863 Maj. Gen. CADMUS M. WILCOX became the division's last commander.

The unit fought at the WILDERNESS and at PETERSBURG held part of the III Corps position on the Confederate right. Its line was shattered by a Federal attack 2 Apr. 1865, and Hill was killed in the assault. The remnant of his corps was consolidated with the I Corps and fought as part of that command in the APPOMATTOX CAMPAIGN. —RMcM

Lilley, Robert Doak. CSA b. Greenville, Va., 28 Jan. 1836. After graduating from Washington College in Lexington, Lilley sold surveying instruments invented by his father. He was in Charleston when the Civil War erupted 12 Apr. 1861 with the bombardment of FORT SUMTER in the city's harbor.

Returning to Virginia, Lilley recruited the Augusta Lee Guards and was appointed its captain. The volunteer company soon became a part of the 25th Virginia. During summer and fall 1861 the regiment fought in western Virginia at RICH MOUNTAIN and GREENBRIER RIVER and subsequently joined the brigade of Brig. Gen. JUBAL A. EARLY in Maj. Gen. RICHARD S.

USMHI

EWELL's division. Under Early, Lilley fought at MCDOWELL, Va., and in the SHENANDOAH VALLEY CAMPAIGN May–June 1862, at CEDAR MOUNTAIN and SECOND BULL RUN in August, and at ANTIETAM a month later.

Promoted to major Jan. 1863, Lilley served under Brig. Gen. JOHN D. IMBODEN in western Virginia in spring 1863. He and the 25th served in the STONEWALL BRIGADE for the GETTYSBURG CAMPAIGN. His performance in Pennsylvania earned him promotion to lieutenant colonel. Lilley also fought at MINE RUN in autumn 1863 and at the WILDERNESS and SPOTSYLVANIA May

1864. On 31 May 1864 he was promoted to brigadier general and assumed command of Early's old brigade.

As a brigade commander under Early, who now commanded the II Corps, Lilley participated in EARLY'S WASHINGTON RAID, July 1864. On 20 July, at Stephenson's Depot, Lilley suffered 3 wounds and fell into Federal hands. Placed in a Union hospital in Winchester, he was freed 4 days later when the Federals abandoned the town after their decisive defeat at Kernstown, 5 mi to the south. In November, he returned to duty, commanding the reserve forces in the Shenandoah Valley until the war's end.

Lilley spent most of the postwar years as a financial agent for his alma mater, raising substantial sums for the college, whose president was Robert E. Lee until his death in 1870. Lilley died in Richmond 12 Nov. 1886 while attending a meeting of the Presbyterian Synod of Virginia.   —JDW

Lincoln, Abraham. USP b. near Hodgenville, Ky., 12 Feb. 1809. The central figure of the Civil War, Lincoln is regarded by many historians and laymen as not only the foremost of our presidents but also the greatest American of all time. With scant formal education, from a poor family, this frontier lawyer held the nation together through the worst crisis in its history. A leader of weaker will or fainter vision might well have failed either to win the Civil War or end the institution of slavery. With good reason, he is viewed as the savior of the American union and the "Great Emancipator."

KA

Lincoln was born into an obscure backwoods family who moved to Indiana when he was 7. His mother died 2 years later and his father married a widow, Sarah Bush Johnston, who exerted a good influence on the boy. Though his education was limited to a few months in a 1-teacher school, Lincoln avidly read books such as the Bible, *Pilgrim's Progress* and Weems's *Life of Washington.*

Growing to a muscular 6'4", he supported himself by manual labor until he was 21, when he settled in New Salem, Ill. There he continued his self-education while serving as storekeeper, militia captain in the Black Hawk War, and postmaster. In 1832, he lost a race for the state legislature but won a seat as a Whig 2 years later, serving 4 terms and gaining statewide popularity for his homespun wit and integrity.

During this period, Lincoln also began his private study of law, borrowing books from a local attorney, and was licensed to practice in 1836. Increasingly successful as a circuit rider, he settled in Springfield, the new capital. In 1844, 2 years after his marriage to Mary Todd of Lexington, Ky., a young woman of aristocratic pretensions, he formed a partnership with William H. Herndon and went on to become one of Illinois' ablest lawyers.

In 1847, he was elected to the U.S. House of Representatives and during his single term became known for both his opposition to the Mexican War and the institution of slavery. After switching allegiance to the new REPUBLICAN PARTY in 1856, Lincoln ran for the U.S. Senate against the "Little Giant,"

STEPHEN A. DOUGLAS. Though Lincoln lost, the race attracted national attention because of the candidates' widely reported debates over the issue of slavery in the territories. Lincoln's standing was further enhanced 27 Feb. 1860, when, in New York City, before an influential audience, he delivered his brilliant Cooper Union speech, in which he argued the Federal government's power to limit slavery in the territories.

In July the Republicans nominated Lincoln for the presidency on the third ballot at the convention in Chicago. The DEMOCRATIC PARTY split into Northern and Southern factions, each with its own presidential candidate. Lincoln's election the following November, over 3 other candidates, with only 40% of the popular vote, was unacceptable to Southern politicians and became the pretext for first South Carolina and in quick order 10 other states to secede from the Union.

By the time Lincoln arrived in Washington to be sworn in as the nation's 16th president, 4 Mar. 1861, the Confederate States of America had been formed. In his first inaugural address, Lincoln tried to woo the South back into the Union, but after the bombardment of FORT SUMTER, 12 Apr., he called for 75,000 volunteers to suppress "the insurrection," declared a BLOCKADE of Southern ports, and authorized the suspension of *HABEAS CORPUS* in areas threatened by pro-secessionist elements. Only after the war was under way and the reins of the presidency were firmly in his hands did Lincoln call Congress to meet 4 July 1861, in a special session that he had already enacted by executive decree (*see* CONGRESS, U.S.). Thereafter the history of Lincoln's administration followed the course of the Civil War.

A man of gentle spirit, Lincoln accepted the fact that only a vigorous prosecution of the war would restore the Union. His will to win never flagged despite enormous battle casualties and much political opposition, a substantial amount of it coming from members of his cabinet (*see* CABINET, UNITED STATES) and from among the RADICAL REPUBLICANS.

As commander in chief, Lincoln not only took care to win and keep the affection of the ordinary Union soldier but also displayed a surprising aptitude for military strategy. While he fumbled in his selection of generals, he learned from his mistakes. At considerable political risk, he dismissed the popular Maj. Gen. GEORGE B. MCCLELLAN because of his failure to lead the Army of the Potomac to victories. And despite pressure from ardent abolitionists, he countermanded premature efforts by army commanders to ban slavery in their jurisdiction.

Ever the masterful politician, he always took care not to alienate his basic constituency, the ordinary citizenry of Northern and Western states, while advancing the progress of the war. His EMANCIPATION PROCLAMATION was carefully framed to avoid offense to loyal but slaveowning states; only those slaves in Confederate-controlled areas were declared free at that early stage of the war.

Though charges of disloyalty were made against his wife because 4 of her brothers and 2 of her brothers-in-law served in the Confederate army, Lincoln ignored them, as he did much brutal criticism of his administration and his personal character. Added to the crushing burdens of his office were private griefs over the death of his 12-year-old son, Willie, in 1862, and the often shrewish behavior of his emotionally unstable wife (*see* LINCOLN, MARY TODD). To conceal his melancholy, he often told earthy stories, to the disgust of some of his more polished cabinet members.

In general, Lincoln was an inefficient administrator, running his office like a large law firm, with a staff of 2 male secretaries, JOHN HAY and JOHN NICOLAY. He also made himself needlessly accessible to office seekers and special pleaders. But he was a superb leader, unswerving in his goal of restoring and preserving the Union. He also used his skills as a speaker to great advantage. His inaugural speeches and his GETTYSBURG ADDRESS are masterpieces of American oratory.

Lincoln showed a surprisingly sure grasp of foreign affairs, skillfully avoiding a war with Great Britain in the *TRENT* AFFAIR and winning European goodwill with his Emancipation Proclamation. In domestic affairs, the HOMESTEAD ACT of 1862 is the most notable achievement of his administration.

But the war overshadowed nonmilitary congressional concerns. Though by 1864 Federal forces had reopened the Mississippi River and brought large sections of the South under Federal control, many in the North despaired of victory as casualties mounted in Lt. Gen. ULYSSES S. GRANT's offensive against Gen. ROBERT E. LEE's Confederate Army of Northern Virginia. Lincoln himself doubted first his chances of renomination, then his ability to defeat the Democratic candidate, the still-popular former general McClellan, who ran on a "Peace Platform" and who blamed Lincoln for prolonging the war.

Adm. DAVID G. FARRAGUT's naval success at MOBILE BAY 5 Aug., the fall of ATLANTA to Maj. Gen. WILLIAM T. SHERMAN 2 Sept., and Maj. Gen. PHILIP H. SHERIDAN's successful SHENANDOAH VALLEY CAMPAIGN later that fall vindicated Lincoln's firm war policy. McClellan carried only 3 states, with 12 electoral college votes to Lincoln's 212. By Christmas, Sherman had marched to the sea and the Confederacy was rapidly falling apart. With the surrender of Lee's army at APPOMATTOX 9 Apr. 1865, the war ended.

The humane character of Lincoln was best demonstrated by his policy of reconciliation with the South, as expressed in his second inaugural address, 4 Mar. 1865, in which he spoke of "malice toward none" and "charity for all." His death from an assassin's bullet a few weeks later, 15 Apr., not only cut short a great man's life but also delayed the restoration of the American union. The fate of the nation passed into the hands of lesser men. *See also* LINCOLN'S ASSASSINATION.   —RHF

Lincoln, Mary Todd. b. Lexington, Ky., 13 Dec. 1818. The temperamental wife of ABRAHAM LINCOLN was born into a wealthy, influential Kentucky family that provided her with a quality education at private local academies. In 1839, 2 years after visiting her sister in Springfield, Ill., she became a permanent member of the household and a popular belle in the political circles to which her sister's father-in-law, Gov. Ninian Edwards, belonged. Here she met Lincoln, and the two became engaged. Their relationship was interrupted abruptly when he failed to arrive at the wedding, attributing his nonappearance to nervousness. Over the protests of Todd's family, the courtship resumed, and the couple married hastily 4 Nov. 1842. Lincoln's law partner and biographer, William H. Herndon, intensely disliked Mary, and later wrote scathingly of her as a "shrill" who made Lincoln's life miserable. But while stubborn, willful, and given to biting sarcasm, she adored her husband and in their years together worked to make a comfortable home for him and their sons.

Mary's years as First Lady after Lincoln's inauguration in 1861 were not happy. Many in Washington distrusted her because of her Southern roots (her brother-in-law BENJAMIN H. HELM was a Confederate general), her erratic temperament,

LC

and her obsession for expensive clothes and lavish entertainment. The death of her 12-year-old son, Willie, in 1862 left her severely depressed, and Lincoln's assassination devastated her.

Despite a substantial inheritance from her husband's estate, Mary's extravagance resulted in reduced circumstances. In 1870 Congress awarded her a yearly pension of $3,000 in response to her indignant petitions for assistance as the widow of the martyred president. Her instability became more pronounced after the death of her youngest son, Tad, in 1871. 4 years later she was declared insane and committed to a private sanitarium at Batavia, Ill., where she remained for several months until judged competent to manage her affairs.

For the next few years Mary traveled abroad, returning to her sister's home in Springfield toward the end of her life. Shortly before her death Congress increased her pension to $5,000 and voted to give her a lump-sum gift of $15,000. d. Springfield, 16 July 1882.   —PLF

Lincoln's assassination. 14 Apr. 1865 Late in 1864 popular actor JOHN WILKES BOOTH, working out of Mrs. MARY SURRATT's Washington, D.C., boardinghouse, recruited conspirators JOHN H. SURRATT (Mrs. Surratt's son), Lewis T. Paine (born Powell), Samuel Arnold, Michael O'Laughlin, David Herold, and George Atzerodt for a plot to kidnap Pres. ABRAHAM LINCOLN and exchange him for Confederate prisoners of war. The scheme failed Mar. 1865. About the time of the surrender of the Confederate Army of Northern Virginia, Booth committed himself to the assassination of top Union officials and secured help from his associates in the kidnapping plot.

Between 8:30 and 9 p.m. 14 Apr. 1865, Abraham and Mary Lincoln and their guests, Maj. Henry Rathbone and Miss Clara Harris, entered the FORD'S THEATER presidential box to see a performance of *Our American Cousin*. Booth, a familiar face at that Washington theater, entered with little notice, and between 10:15 and 10:30 approached Lincoln's box. The box guard was unaccountably absent. Booth stepped in behind Lincoln, shot him in the head with a single-shot 44.-caliber derringer, slashed Rathbone with a hunting knife, and leaped 10 ft down to the stage. In his leap his spur caught in a flag draped in front of the box. The fall broke Booth's left leg. Standing painfully, he shouted to the audience, *"Sic semper tyrannus,"* limped backstage, mounted his horse waiting in the alley back of the theater, and rode out of Washington.

Concurrent with Booth's act, Lewis Paine, once a Confederate guerrilla, forced his way into Sec. of State WILLIAM H. SEWARD's Washington home, assaulted Seward's family, and tried to kill the secretary with a knife. Unsuccessful, Paine also escaped.

The unconscious Lincoln was carried across the street from Ford's to the William Peterson home, where he died at 7:22 a.m., 15 Apr. Meanwhile, Booth began a tortured odyssey through the Maryland and Virginia countryside, accompanied by David Herold. Around 4 a.m., near Bryantown, Md., the two men arrived at the home of Dr. SAMUEL A. MUDD, who set Booth's leg and gave him a place to rest and material assistance. Herold and Booth left Mudd at about 4 p.m., and until 25 Apr. alternately hid and ran south to Virginia, where they were surrounded by Union troops south of the Rappahannock River on Richard Garrett's farm. Herold surrendered, Booth was shot and killed, and the body and prisoner were taken to Washington.

Except for John Surratt, all Booth's associates from the original kidnap plot, Dr. Mudd, a Ford's theater stagehand, and Mrs. Surratt were arrested. They were tried by a controversial military tribunal who believed they had also intended to murder Vice-Pres. ANDREW JOHNSON and Lt. Gen. U. S. GRANT. All were found guilty of various charges. Paine, Herold, Atzerodt, and Mrs. Surratt (later widely believed to be innocent of any involvement in Booth's scheming) were hanged. Arnold, O'Laughlin, and Mudd were given terms of life imprisonment. Edward Spangler, the stagehand, was sentenced to 6 years. John Surratt was extradited from Alexandria, Egypt, in 1866; a U.S. jury voted 8 to 4 to acquit him. O'Laughlin died in prison. President Johnson pardoned the survivors in 1869.

—JES

Lincoln's first inauguration. Amid fears of violence and possible assassination, large crowds gathered in Washington, D.C., 4 Mar. 1861, to see ABRAHAM LINCOLN inaugurated as president of the U.S. Cavalrymen guarded the intersections, riflemen watched from rooftops, artillerymen stood with howitzers ready. Plainclothes detectives milled through the throng.

Lincoln arose at 5 a.m., had breakfast, and spent time with his family. Then the president-elect asked to be alone. He meditated, listened to the soldiers marching in the streets, and offered a prayer. He saw only Sec. of State WILLIAM H. SEWARD, who helped make a few last-minute changes to Lincoln's inaugural speech.

The noontime procession included 34 girls in costumes representing the states and Lincoln in a simple open carriage. The Capitol's marble front was stained with spattered tobacco juice, and the arm of a crane protruded from the still-uncompleted dome. Sen. STEPHEN A. DOUGLAS held Lincoln's hat and cane while the new president spoke. Lincoln's words reflected firm resolution: the states that had proclaimed themselves out of the Union must come back. No concession would be made. No terms. But, he said, "in *your* hands, my dissatisfied fellow countrymen, and not in *mine,* is the momentous issue of civil war." He then went to the White House. "Thank God," said the aged general-in-chief, WINFIELD SCOTT, "we now have a government."   —HH

Lincoln's second inauguration. Great differences distinguished Lincoln's second inauguration, 4 Mar. 1865, from the first: the Capitol building was now complete, the end of the bitter war was in sight, and the threat to the Union had ended. Lincoln rode from the White House to the Capitol escorted by bands, cavalry, and a crowd of spectators. At the Senate Chamber ANDREW JOHNSON was sworn in as vice-president. Everyone then moved to the platform along the east front to hear Lincoln speak.

His address was the briefest ever made by a president. In it he reminded his audience that "impending civil war" had faced the nation when he took office four years before. "All

dreaded it—all sought to avert it. . . . And the war came." Of the contending governments, he noted that "both read the same Bible, and pray to the same God; and each invokes His aid against the other." Lincoln expressed everyone's sentiments when he said, "Fondly do we hope—fervently do we pray—that this mighty scourge of war may speedily pass away." Lincoln closed with his speech with his now-famous injunction, "With malice toward none; with charity for all," urging a torn nation to unite and "do all which may achieve and cherish a just and lasting peace, among ourselves, and with all nations."

The oath of office was administered by Chief Justice SALMON P. CHASE, and Lincoln kissed the Bible. After an artillery salute a procession followed his carriage to the White House. At the reception that evening he shook hands with 6,000 people and found time to meet with army officers present to discuss ever-pressing military matters. A month later Gen. ROBERT E. LEE surrendered at Appomattox and Lincoln was assassinated. His death ended the South's chances for a moderate Reconstruction.   —AG

Little, Lewis Henry. CSA b. Baltimore, Md., 19 Mar. 1817. The son of a longtime member of Congress, Little was commissioned into the army as 2d lieutenant in 1839. He served with the 7th Infantry during the Mexican War, advancing in Aug. 1847 to captain, the rank he held by brevet for gallantry at Monterey the previous year. Little stayed in the army until 7 May 1861, when he resigned to join the Confederate States Army with the rank of major.

Following a brief assignment with the artillery, Little was attached to Maj. Gen. STERLING PRICE'S staff as colonel and adjutant general. Price admired his leadership ability and 23 Jan. 1862 placed him in command of the 1st Missouri Brigade. These men Little led with distinction in March at PEA RIDGE, which contributed to his promotion to brigadier general 16 Apr. His well-disciplined brigade attracted the attention of Gen. BRAXTON BRAGG, who assigned him to command the 1st Division/Army of the West. On 19 Sept. at IUKA, Miss., 2 of Little's brigades withstood an assault by Federal troops under Maj. Gen. WILLIAM S. ROSECRANS before giving ground to superior numbers. That evening, while the fighting continued, Little was shot through the head and fell dead from his horse as he conferred with Price on the field.

Badly shaken by the sudden loss of one of his most dependable officers, Price decided against launching a counterattack on the 20th. Before the Confederates withdrew, they buried Little by torchlight in the garden behind his headquarters. His successor, Brig. Gen. LOUIS HÉBERT, led the division to Baldwyn, Miss., to reorganize and named the camp there Camp Lewis Henry in honor of the fallen general. Little's remains were later removed to Greenmount Cemetery in Baltimore.

—PLF

Little Round Top at Gettysburg, Pa. 2 July 1863 The struggle for Little Round Top on the afternoon of 2 July 1863 was fought on a rock-strewn, partly wooded hill rising to a height of 650 feet. The peak had been virtually unmanned, except for a signal station, throughout the night of the 1st and the morning and afternoon of the 2d. When the Confederate attack exploded against Maj. Gen. DANIEL E. SICKLES' III Corps at the Peach Orchard at 4 p.m., occupation of the hill suddenly became critical for the army of Maj. Gen. GEORGE G. MEADE.

What followed for nearly 3 hours was a deadly fight for its possession.

Sickles's unauthorized advance to the PEACH ORCHARD had unhinged the Union's left flank. When Meade learned of this movement, he ordered Maj. Gen. GEORGE SYKES's V Corps forward and dispatched his chief of engineers, Maj. Gen. GOUVERNEUR K. WARREN, to reconnoiter on the left. Warren scaled Little Round Top, recognized the peak's importance, found the woods below full of Confederates, and immediately sent a messenger to bring up troops to occupy the hill. Warren's aides located Union Col. STRONG VINCENT, who commanded a V Corps brigade, and, assuming full responsibility for advancing up the slopes, the colonel double-quicked his 4 regiments. Confederate artillery crews spied the Federals on the hill and opened fire as the regiments lined Little Round Top's southern and western sides.

Vincent's men had barely settled in when out of the woods to the southwest came 3 Confederate regiments, the 4th Alabama and the 4th and 5th Texas. The Union line suddenly blazed with musketry as the Southerners climbed the slope. Then, on the Union left, where the 20TH MAINE, under Col. JOSHUA L. CHAMBERLAIN, was positioned, 2 more Confederate regiments stormed across the saddle between the two Round Tops. Tired and thirsty, these Southerners, the 15th and 47th Alabama, under Col. William C. Oates, were looking for a fight; in minutes they would have more than they bargained for.

For the next hour Chamberlain's 20th Maine and Oates's Alabamians slaughtered each other. Volleys of minié bullets tore into bone and flesh. The Confederates flailed at the flanks of the Federals, charging repeatedly up the slope, but the Maine soldiers clung to their ragged line. Around the hill's western slope, the rest of Vincent's regiments repulsed the Confederate charges. Brig. Gen. STEPHEN H. WEED's brigade soon arrived to lengthen Vincent's right. In the furious combat Weed was killed, but the Union line held. Chamberlain's stalwart conduct earned him the MEDAL OF HONOR. Little Round Top was secured with valor and appalling casualties.

—JDW

Livermore, Mary Ashton Rice. U.S. Sanitary Commission b. Boston, Mass., 19 Dec. 1820. As it did for many Americans, the Civil War opened new worlds to Mary Livermore. For the author and temperance leader the conflict led to a career as a suffragist and earned her praise for "executive ability far beyond the average."

Livermore began a vigorous 70-year career by teaching at the New England female seminary where she was educated. A dedicated, tireless reformer, she married in 1854. For the next 3 years she and her husband, a minister, organized study groups among Massachusetts factory workers; education and alleviating poverty remained lifelong concerns.

LC

The Livermores moved in 1857 to Chicago, where Mary worked as associate editor of her husband's religious publica-

tion, the *New Covenant.* The paper offered an outlet for her writings about charity work. The staunch Unionist was also the only woman to report on the convention that nominated Abraham Lincoln.

When war broke out, Livermore used her pen to stir women into devoting time and talents to soldiers' relief work. Largely through her appeals the Northwestern branch of the U.S. SANITARY COMMISSION was established to serve soldiers in the Western theater. Appointed an agent in charge of securing money and supplies, she welded the organization into one of influence and effectiveness. Severely critical of civilian and military negligence, she wrote exposés on the hardships wounded soldiers suffered from insufficient supplies and sanitary conditions, prompting a series of charity fairs that united Northern efforts to provide soldiers' relief.

Convinced by her wartime experiences that women's power over social issues depended on their right to vote, she redirected her energies toward enfranchisement and championed higher education and professional training for women. The first of Livermore's memoirs, *My Story of the War* (1888), is a valuable source of information on Civil War hospitals and nursing. She died 23 May 1905 in Melrose, Mass., her home for several years.

—PLF

Livermore's *Numbers and Losses in the Civil War.* Compiled by former Federal Col. Thomas L. Livermore and published in 1900, *Numbers and Losses in the Civil War in America 1861–65* is the standard statistical reference for Union and Confederate armies. Livermore's analysis takes into account figures published in the 1860 census, the OFFICIAL RECORDS of the Union and Confederate Armies, FOX'S REGIMENTAL LOSSES, state muster rolls, pension records, postwar estimates by contemporaries, and local defense forces. Strength of armies, number of forces engaged, and casualty figures are broken down by battle. All statistics are carefully documented. When *Numbers and Losses* was first published, it challenged late-19th-century assumptions about the disparity between the sizes of the Union and Confederate armies, revising the number in Confederate service from an estimated 600,000 to possibly as many as 1.5 million, the true figure probably falling midway between the 2 totals. Livermore calculated the number of enlistments in the Union army at 2,898,304, including state militia and short-term emergency troops. The book was reissued in 1957, with a biographical sketch about Livermore.

—PLF

Lockwood, Henry Hayes. USA b. Kent Cty., Del., 17 Aug. 1814. A graduate of the West Point class of 1836, ranking 22d among 49 cadets, Lockwood was assigned to the 2d U.S. Artillery and was sent to Florida to oppose the Seminole uprising. On 12 Sept. 1837 he resigned his commission and spent 4 years on his Delaware farm until he was appointed professor of mathematics in the U.S. Navy. He taught aboard ships, then at a naval facility in Philadelphia, and finally at the NAVAL ACADEMY, Annapolis, Md. In 1851 he transferred to the chair of field artillery and infantry tactics, with the additional duty of professor of astronomy.

With the outbreak of the Civil War, Lockwood returned to army service as colonel of the 1st Delaware Infantry. On 8 Aug. 1861 he was appointed a brigadier general of volunteers. Soon afterward he led an expedition to the eastern shore of Virginia, then took command of the prison at POINT LOOKOUT and the defenses of the lower Potomac. He did not see field service till GETTYSBURG, where he led a XII Corps brigade, composed primarily of Maryland regiments, in the Army of the Potomac.

USMHI

At the close of the campaign in Pennsylvania, Lockwood's command was detached for garrison duty outside Harpers Ferry. He spent 5 months at this post before going to Baltimore, Dec. 1863, to succeed Maj. Gen. ROBERT C. SCHENCK in charge of the Middle Department. Rejoining the Army of the Potomac the following spring, Lockwood directed a V Corps division at COLD HARBOR. Afterward he was again detached to head a portion of the Middle Department, encompassing Baltimore and the eastern shore of Maryland. In July he led a conglomeration of provisional units against Lt. Gen. JUBAL A. EARLY's Confederate raiders; after the latter's retreat to Virginia, Lockwood returned to departmental duties.

On his muster-out, Aug. 1865, he returned to Annapolis, where he taught gunnery and other subjects of a mathematical, scientific, and tactical nature. In 1870 he was assigned to the Naval Observatory in Washington, serving there until his retirement 6 years later. His remaining years were spent in Washington, D.C., where he died 7 Dec. 1899. Because of his long service at the Naval Academy, he was accorded the distinction of burial in its cemetery at Annapolis.   —EGL

Logan, John Alexander. USA b. Jackson Cty., Ill., 9 Feb. 1826. The best known of ABRAHAM LINCOLN's political generals, the fiery Logan was educated by tutors and in the common schools near his home. He attended Louisville University in Kentucky and served in the Mexican War as a 2d lieutenant of Illinois volunteers. A lawyer in civilian life, Logan was elected on the Democratic ticket to the state legislature in 1852, 1853, 1856, and 1857. In 1856 he served as a presidential elector for James Buchanan, was elected to the U.S. House of Representatives 2 years later, and was reelected in 1860.

USMHI

Logan's loyalty to the Union raised speculation through the secession winter of 1860–61. His family had migrated to Illinois from the South, and he was best known for sponsorship of harsh laws barring free blacks from the state and vehement defense of the FUGITIVE SLAVE ACT. His name had been used to promote Confederate recruiting in his district in the southern tip of Illinois, and his brother-in-law had enlisted in the Confederate army. In Springfield, June 1861, when he addressed a regiment of Union volunteers soon to be mustered, Col. ULYSSES S. GRANT feared the worst until Logan delivered a patriotic speech that removed all doubt about his loyalty.

Logan resigned his congressional seat in spring 1861, raised

a regiment that joined Grant's army at Cairo, and fought with distinction at BELMONT and FORT DONELSON. Owing in part to Lincoln's policy of placing prominent Democrats in command, Logan was appointed brigadier general as of 21 Mar. 1862 and promoted to major general to rank from 29 Nov. of that year. Loyal and aggressive service with the Army of the Tennessee won Grant's favor as well as that of Maj. Gen. WILLIAM T. SHERMAN.

In 1864 Logan commanded the XV Corps in the ATLANTA CAMPAIGN and succeeded to command of the Army of the Tennessee when Maj. Gen. JAMES B. MCPHERSON was killed. When Sherman replaced him with a West Pointer, Logan developed a resentment against professional soldiers that he cherished the rest of his life. Sherman understood that Logan was a competent officer but foremost a politician, sometimes an inspired fighter but never a trustworthy administrator. Logan went to Illinois to campaign for the Republican party, then returned to the field to lead his corps through the CAROLINAS CAMPAIGN.

After the war he resumed his political career, as a Radical Republican, serving as U.S. congressman 1867–71, and U.S. senator 1871–77 and 1879–86, and running unsuccessfully for the vice-presidency in 1884. He served Grant as loyally in politics as he had in war, meanwhile advancing his own career through corrupt and ruthless methods. Credited with the idea of establishing Memorial Day, Logan characteristically promoted the holiday to use the war dead for political advantage, eager to "wave the bloody shirt" whenever the opportunity presented itself. He kept active in veterans' organizations and wrote extensively about the war, usually in spirited prose with strong political overtones. His 2 books, *The Great Conspiracy* (1886) and *The Volunteer Soldier in America* (1887), are largely embellished memoirs. d. District of Columbia, 26 Dec. 1886.   —JYS

Logan, Thomas Muldrup. CSA b. Charleston, S.C., 3 Nov. 1840. A year after graduating 1st in his class at South Carolina College, Logan served as a volunteer during the bombardment of FORT SUMTER. Helping to organize part of the HAMPTON LEGION, he became a 1st lieutenant in one of its companies. He served capably at FIRST BULL RUN, where the legion shored up the Confederate line on Henry Hill during a crucial phase of the fighting. Promotion to captain followed the battle.

LC

At the head of his company, Logan was wounded 27 June 1862 at GAINES' MILL. Kept out of action during the rest of the PENINSULA CAMPAIGN, he returned to the legion in time to serve at SECOND BULL RUN, where the unit was not prominently engaged. He won plaudits, however, at ANTIETAM, where his outfit held a strategic position along Gen. ROBERT E. LEE's left flank and helped parry the initial Federal thrust 17 Sept. For his part in this feat, Logan won a commission as major. Joining the brigade of Brig. Gen. MICAH JENKINS soon afterward, he was promoted to lieutenant colonel in time for service near Suffolk, Va., in spring 1863. In that campaign, he conducted a successful reconnaissance mission "fifteen miles in advance of the Confederate lines."

Sent to Tennessee late in 1863, Logan's outfit fought conspicuously at CHICKAMAUGA and at KNOXVILLE, where he led a unit of sharpshooters that spearheaded Lt. Gen. JAMES LONGSTREET's effort to press Maj. Gen. AMBROSE E. BURNSIDE's army into the city. Returning east in spring 1864, Logan became colonel of the Hampton Legion 19 May, following detached service on Gen. P.G.T. BEAUREGARD's staff during an unsuccessful Union offensive against Richmond. Wounded at Riddle's Shop, 13 June, he recuperated during the PETERSBURG CAMPAIGN, then went to North Carolina to lead the cavalry brigade formerly under Brig. Gen. MATTHEW C. BUTLER. United there with his old superior, Lt. Gen. WADE HAMPTON, he was appointed a brigadier general Feb. 1865. A month later he led a determined though unavailing charge at BENTONVILLE.

After accompanying Gen. JOSEPH E. JOHNSTON to the surrender ceremonies at Durham Station, Logan settled in Virginia, where he married and went into railroad development. Within a few years he had parlayed a modest investment into control of what became the Southern Railway. Following a varied career that included sponsoring inventions and speculating on Wall Street, he died in New York City, 11 Aug. 1914.   —EGL

Logan's Cross Roads, Ky., Battle of. 19 Jan. 1862 *See* MILL SPRINGS, KY., BATTLE OF.

Lomax, Lunsford Lindsay. CSA   b. Newport, R.I., 4 Nov. 1835. The son of an artillery captain from Virginia, Lomax grew up with an abiding affection for his Southern heritage. He was educated in schools at Richmond and Norfolk before entering West Point. Graduating in 1856, he ranked 21st in his 49-man class. In prewar years he served in the cavalry, mostly on the frontier, rising to 1st lieutenant, a commission he resigned 25 Apr. 1861 to become a captain of Virginia state troops.

Until early 1863 Lomax served in the West as a staff officer to Brig. Gen. BEN MCCULLOCH, Gen. JOSEPH E. JOHNSTON, and Maj. Gen. EARL VAN DORN. Probably at the urging of his

USMHI

West Point classmate and longtime friend, Brig. Gen. FITZHUGH LEE, he left his post in East Tennessee to accept the colonelcy of an Eastern unit, the 11th Virginia Cavalry. Though at first mistrusted by the officers of the regiment, former subordinates of the lamented Brig. Gen. TURNER ASHBY, he soon gained their confidence and respect. He proved his fitness for higher command during Brig. Gens. WILLIAM E. JONES's and JOHN D. IMBODEN's raid of Apr. 1863 and in the epic cavalry battle at BRANDY STATION 2 months later. During the balance of the GETTYSBURG CAMPAIGN, he scouted, guarded the main army of Gen. ROBERT E. LEE, and fought in the 21 June battle at Upperville as well as in several engagements during the Confederate retreat from Pennsylvania.

In Oct. 1863, by now a brigadier general, Lomax lost some prestige by failing to protect the rear of Maj. Gen. J.E.B. STUART's cavalry at Auburn Mills. He redeemed himself by so many fine performances that by 10 Aug. 1864 he was a major general commanding a division. That year he was conspicuous at YELLOW TAVERN, then in the Shenandoah Valley at FISHER'S HILL, Tom's Brook, and during the repulse of a Union cavalry raid on Gordonsville. His detaching at CEDAR CREEK and WAYNESBOROUGH was a major factor in both Confederate defeats.

Late in Mar. 1865 Lomax received command of the VALLEY DISTRICT. Refusing to surrender in Virginia, he made his way into North Carolina that May, laying down his arms with Johnston at Greensborough.

After the conflict, he farmed near Warrenton, Va., served as president of what became the Virginia State University at Blacksburg, and helped compile the *OFFICIAL RECORDS of the Union and Confederate Armies.* d. District of Columbia, 28 May 1913, the next-to-last surviving Confederate major general.   —EGL

Long, Armistead Lindsay. CSA   b. Campbell Cty., Va., 3 Sept. 1825, Long was among a handful of men who formed a close association with Gen. ROBERT E. LEE while serving on his personal staff. For nearly 2 years he acted as Lee's military secretary, proving to be an indispensable staff officer.

Graduating 17th in the West Point class of 1850, Long served for 11 years in the artillery in Florida, on the frontier against Indians, and in garrison duty. On 20 May 1861, he was appointed aide-de-camp to his father-in-law, Union Brig. Gen. EDWIN V. SUMNER. The Virginian, however, resigned his commission and entered Confederate service as a major of artillery,

LC

initially serving on the staff of Brig. Gen. WILLIAM WING LORING in Western Virginia. In autumn 1861 he was ordered to Charleston, where he joined Lee's staff.

On 1 June 1862 Lee assumed command of the Army of Northern Virginia, and Long became his military secretary with the rank of colonel. Though Lee never created an adequate personal staff, the men who served him, like Long, were quite capable. The Confederate commander detested paperwork, and Long or Maj. Charles Marshall did much of this onerous task. To his close aides, Lee was known as the "Tycoon."

During much of Long's service on the staff, he assisted in the deployment and use of the army's batteries. His exceptional judgment in artillery operations ultimately caused Lee to appoint him commander of the artillery of the II Corps. He was promoted to brigadier general of artillery 21 Sept. 1863 and until the war's end served with the II Corps.

In the postwar era, the former artillerist became chief engineer of a Virginia canal company, but in 1870 he suffered total blindness and could no longer work. Pres. ULYSSES S. GRANT then appointed his wife postmistress of Charlottesville, Va. In 1886, using a special slate, Long wrote the valuable *Memoirs of Robert E. Lee, His Military and Personal History.* d. Charlottesville 29 Apr. 1891.   —JDW

Longstreet, James. CSA   b. Edgefield District, S.C., 8 Jan. 1821. The son of a farmer, Longstreet spent his early years in

Augusta, Ga. On the death of his father in 1833 he moved with his mother to Somerville, Ala.

Admitted to West Point in 1838, he attended with U.S. GRANT, HENRY W. HALLECK, IRVIN MC-DOWELL, GEORGE H. THOMAS, and WILLIAM T. SHERMAN, graduating 54th in a class of 62 in 1842. Brevetted 2d lieutenant of the 4th Infantry for tours in Missouri and Louisiana, he served with the 8th Infantry in Florida.

Longstreet participated in the Mexican War under Gen. Zachary Taylor up to and including the Battle of Monterey, and

USMHI

joined the forces under Gen. WINFIELD SCOTT for the expedition to Mexico City. Wounded at Chapultepec, he was brevetted major, a rank he maintained until 1 June 1861, when he resigned to join the Confederate army. He was commissioned brigadier general 17 June 1861, in spite of his desire to assume an administrative rather than a military role.

Longstreet was in command of troops at FIRST BULL RUN, where he did an excellent job of deployment. As a result of his skillful leadership, he was promoted to major general 7 Oct. 1861 and given command of a division under Gen. JOSEPH E. JOHNSTON. Longstreet distinguished himself in the rearguard action at WILLIAMSBURG, 5 May 1862, as Johnston's forces pulled back toward Richmond from YORKTOWN. But his lateness to the field and misunderstanding of orders contributed to the failure at SEVEN PINES, 31 May 1862.

Longstreet recouped his reputation somewhat during the SEVEN DAYS' battles, 25 June–1 July 1862. In fighting around Richmond after Gen. ROBERT E. LEE had assumed command, Longstreet showed courage and willingness to fight. Favorably impressed, Lee entrusted him with greater than half of his infantry forces. On 13 Aug. he was sent to aid Maj. Gen. THOMAS J. "STONEWALL" JACKSON, who was engaged against the Federals under Maj. Gen. JOHN POPE near Orange Court House. The maneuver marked the beginnings of the SECOND BULL RUN CAMPAIGN. Longstreet crossed the Rapidan River slowly but moved skillfully up the Rappahannock. On the morning of 29 Aug. 1863, he joined Jackson, who had just completed his march to Manassas Junction. Though Lee wanted Longstreet to take the offensive, Longstreet deliberated until 30 Aug. 1862 before entering the contest. Here emerged one of Longstreet's greatest flaws as a military leader: he was slow to act on orders if he did not fully agree with his superior's plans.

Longstreet participated in the ANTIETAM CAMPAIGN Sept. 1862, and, though not wholeheartedly behind the invasion, he fought skillfully. On 11 Oct. Lee recommended Longstreet for a lieutenant generalship, with his division grouped as the I Corps. This unit sustained heavy fighting at FREDERICKSBURG 13 Dec.

On 17 Feb. 1863 Longstreet moved southeast with Maj. Gens. GEORGE E. PICKETT and JOHN B. HOOD to guard Richmond. Known as the Suffolk Campaign, it was Longstreet's first experience with a relatively independent command. When he initiated no significant action, Lee suggested he either fight or return to join the Army of Northern Virginia. He finally advanced on Suffolk 11 April.

Longstreet's relationship with Lee became closer after Jackson died 10 May 1863. In planning the GETTYSBURG CAMPAIGN, Longstreet advocated defensive tactics as part of an overall, offensive strategy, while Lee chose to attack Maj. Gen. GEORGE G. MEADE in Gettysburg 1 July 1863. Ordered to assault CEMETERY RIDGE at dawn on the 2d, Longstreet delayed, reluctant to advance until Brig. Gen. EVANDER M. LAW's reinforcements arrived. Marching and countermarching his men west of SEMINARY RIDGE, he finally hit the Federal lines at 4:30 p.m. His men fought courageously for 4 hours, holding their ground until the battle was halted for the day. His initial delay, however, had allowed Union commanders to bring up reinforcements, and when the attack resumed on the 2d, it resulted in tremendous loss of life. For years after the war Longstreet would be blamed, not altogether fairly, for costing Lee the battle.

Reassigned to Georgia Sept. 1863, Longstreet served well at CHICKAMAUGA but ran into difficulty against opposing forces at KNOXVILLE in November, marking a low ebb in his career; despondent, he considered resigning. He proposed plans to Pres. JEFFERSON DAVIS for offensive action in Tennessee and Kentucky, but these were not adopted. Summoned back to Virginia Apr. 1864, Longstreet and his troops arrived to effectively assist Lt. Gen. AMBROSE P. HILL's Corps in the second day of battle at the WILDERNESS, where he was wounded. In November he resumed service, this time in defense of Richmond. He and the remainder of his corps continued to fight until the surrender at Appomattox, 9 Apr. 1865.

Longstreet was a superior corps leader but did not have prowess in strategy or independent command. Often slow or reluctant to take the offensive, he was, nonetheless, a fearless soldier when engaged in battle. Lee referred to him affectionately as "My Old War Horse," and his men called him "Old Pete."

In the postwar years he entered business as an insurance agent, supervised the Louisiana State Lottery, and held various Federal appointments, finally settling in Gainesville, Ga. He alienated Southerners by becoming a Republican, yet was instrumental in easing tensions between "Old" and "New South" Democrats. Longstreet wrote extensively after the war, usually in defense of his performance at Gettysburg. d. Gainesville 2 Jan. 1904. His autobiography, *From Manassas to Appomattox* (1896), is one of the finest memoirs written by a member of the Confederate high command. It was republished in 1960, with a valuable introduction and annotations by James I. Robertson.   —JDK

Lookout Mountain, Tenn., Battle of. 24 Nov. 1863 Early in November, Union Maj. Gen. U. S. GRANT devised a broad plan for the battles for CHATTANOOGA, Tenn. Troops under Union Maj. Gen. WILLIAM T. SHERMAN would assault the right of Confederate Gen. BRAXTON BRAGG's Missionary Ridge lines east of Chattanooga. Union Maj. Gen. George H. Thomas' troops would hold the Federal center, facing Missionary Ridge. With 2 divisions, Union Maj. Gen. JOSEPH HOOKER would move on Rossville Gap, to the southwest. After securing the gap, a frequently used avenue of invasion and retreat in the Missionary Ridge range at the Tennessee and Georgia border, Hooker would maneuver on Bragg's left and rear.

Hooker's part in Grant's strategy brought on the 24 Nov. 1863 Battle of Lookout Mountain. An 1,100-ft craggy tower southwest of Chattanooga, Lookout Mountain rose south of a bend in the Tennessee River opposite a finger of land called

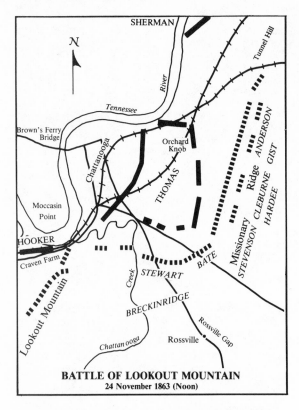

BATTLE OF LOOKOUT MOUNTAIN
24 November 1863 (Noon)

Moccasin Point. To reach Rossville Gap, Hooker would have to fight his way around or through Confederates occupying Lookout Mountain.

On 23 Nov. 1863, circumstances changed the particulars of Grant's plan for an assault on the Confederate left. Earlier he had decided that 4 Federal divisions would cross the Tennessee River, west of Chattanooga, on a makeshift bridge at Brown's Ferry. (The bridge, connecting Moccasin Point with Lookout Creek and the entrance of Lookout Valley, had been thrown up during Oct. 1863 Cracker Line Operation.) These divisions, after crossing the Brown's Ferry bridge, would march up Moccasin Point, maneuver across the Union rear, and join Sherman's force for the attack on Bragg's right. On 23 Nov. the divisions began their movement. But the crude Brown's Ferry bridge, under much stress and use, virtually collapsed after 3 divisions had crossed. Brig. Gen. PETER J. OSTERHAUS' division was stranded on the Tennessee's west bank, opposite Moccasin Point.

On that same day, as thé 3 divisions maneuvered in Chattanooga's rear, an elaborate reconnaissance in force of the Confederate center by Thomas' troops resulted in the unexpected Battle of ORCHARD KNOB. Union victory in this small battle allowed Chattanooga's entire Federal garrison to move their front to Orchard Knob and the very foot of Missionary Ridge.

Assessing the day's events, Grant decided to alter his strategy. He ordered Osterhaus' division to join Hooker for the latter's movement against Bragg's left, then he urged Hooker to show initiative: the general was to capture Lookout Moun-

tain, if possible. By capturing the mountain, instead of merely fighting his way over or around it, Hooker would secure his rear when he entered Rossville Gap and, at the same time, shorten Bragg's defense line.

With his force now bolstered to 3 divisions, Hooker approached Lookout Mountain long after dawn, 24 Nov., and immediately met resistance. For 24 hours the progress of the Battle of Lookout Mountain was a mystery to Federals around Chattanooga. Rain, mist, fog, and chill winds played on the mountain throughout the day. Because of the inclement weather, the fight, though heard, could not be seen from Grant's Orchard Knob headquarters at the Union center. Late in the day, when fog lifted briefly to reveal Union troops firing and scaling the mountainside, Brig. Gen. MONTGOMERY C. MEIGS, watching from Orchard Knob, dubbed Hooker's fight the "Battle Above the Clouds." This phrase became popular in press reports of the action.

Lookout Mountain was defended by Confederate Maj. Gen. CARTER L. STEVENSON, whose small division, with a few cavalry and cannon, held the mountaintop plateau. A force of 2,694 men under Brig. Gens. EDWARD C. WALTHALL and JOHN C. MOORE held the mountain's slopes. Brig. Gen. ALFRED CUMMING's brigade, of Stevenson's division, and Brig. Gen. JOHN K. JACKSON's brigade, for that 1 day commanded in the field by Col. John C. Wilkinson, served as Moore's and Walthall's supports. Walthall and elements of his command were to fight as skirmishers along Lookout Creek at the mountain's base. Jackson would be in overall command of a line established midway up the mountain's slopes.

Prior to 23 Nov. Stevenson's superior, Lt. Gen. WILLIAM J. HARDEE, had been charged with Lookout Mountain's defense. His force had included Maj. Gen. STATES RIGHTS GIST's division, manning a line along Lookout Creek. But on the night of 23 Nov. Hardee informed Stevenson that he and Gist's division had been ordered to the right of Bragg's Missionary Ridge line. Stevenson would command the defense of the mountain.

Stevenson complained that, as a division commander, he did not have sufficient knowledge of all the terrain in his front. Previously he had only been concerned with that part of the Confederate line held by his division. He told superiors he had too few men to make an adequate stand against a Federal assault. Bragg, tacitly acknowledging these complaints, sent word that he would supply Stevenson with reinforcements if they were requested. But Bragg, concerned with Sherman's movements, did not believe an attack would be made against his left.

At about 8 a.m., 24 Nov., the first elements of Hooker's force, Union Brig. Gen. JOHN W. GEARY's division, having marched northeast up Lookout Valley from its Wauhatchie post, felled trees for use as crude bridges and forced a crossing of Lookout Creek to assault the northwest face of Lookout Mountain. Union Brig. Gen. Charles Cruft's division crossed the creek and hit the mountain on Geary's left. A short time later, Osterhaus' division crossed the creek and attacked on Cruft's left. Federals drove back Walthall's skirmishers, men sent forward from an established line at the Craven farm on the northeast face. Hit in flank and rear, this portion of Walthall's force lost several men taken prisoner, then fell back to the Craven farm line. There Walthall's and Moore's men fought around the Craven farmhouse (called the "white house" in initial Union reports), commanded by Jackson.

Fog hindered both Union and Confederate infantry. At Moccasin Point, Union batteries supporting Hooker's 3 divisions had difficulty finding their range in the haze, as did Stevenson's few cannon atop Lookout Mountain. Confederate Brig. Gen. EDMUND W. PETTUS' brigade, detached from Stevenson's division, descended the mountain to the Craven farm line at about 1 p.m. After the arrival of Federal reinforcements, commanded by Brig. Gen. WILLIAM P. CARLIN, and repeated Union assaults, the Confederate line was reestablished about 400 yd in the rear of the Craven house.

Meanwhile, atop the mountain, Stevenson repeatedly requested reinforcements from Bragg. The requests were not acknowledged. Then, at 2:30 p.m., word came from Bragg that Stevenson was to withdraw all his troops to the extreme right of the Missionary Ridge line. Stevenson's division was to take a place beside Gist's, and both were to support Maj. Gen. PATRICK R. CLEBURNE's troops then engaged with Sherman's advance at TUNNEL HILL.

Distressed at having to remove his entire force to a new front while engaged with Hooker's troops, Stevenson received help from Maj. Gen. BENJAMIN F. CHEATHAM in supervising the withdrawal. Confederates on the plateau were removed first, while men fighting behind the Craven farm continued to hold their line. At 8 p.m. this last line of defense was withdrawn under cover of fire from Confederate Col. JAMES T. HOLTZCLAW's brigade. This ended the day's fighting on Lookout Mountain.

On the morning of 25 Nov. members of the Federal 8th Kentucky Infantry raced for the unoccupied mountain summit and raised the U.S. flag, signaling victory to Union troops in the valley below. Hooker then moved on Rossville Gap.

Union and Confederate casualty figures at Lookout Mountain are difficult to ascertain. Both sides gave aggregate numbers for the battles for Chattanooga. On many maps and in many battle accounts, Moore's and Walthall's troops are listed as Cheatham's division. While they were members of that division, Cheatham was not present for most of the fighting at Lookout Mountain. Except for the period in which he helped Stevenson supervise the Confederate withdrawal, Cheatham executed duties on Bragg's right 24 Nov. See also CHATTANOOGA CAMPAIGN.   —JES

Loring, William Wing.

CSA b. Wilmington, N.C., 4 Dec. 1818. By the end of the Civil War, William Wing "Old Blizzards" Loring had become the senior major general on active Confederate field duty. Though he was a planter, builder of a sugar mill, a lawyer, and a minor politician, his real flair was for the military. He first tasted combat at the age of 14 against Indians in the Florida Everglades. In the Seminole War he rose to the rank of major. During the Mexican War he attained the brevet rank of colonel and in fighting before Mexico City lost his left arm. He remained in the U.S. Army, held a variety of jobs, and studied military science in Europe. On resigning his commission 13 May 1861, he held full colonel's rank.

LC

Appointed a brigadier general in the Confederate army 20 May he took charge of Southern forces in western Virginia. He was in the CHEAT MOUNTAIN fighting, later feuding with Maj.

Gen. THOMAS J. "STONEWALL" JACKSON (see LORING–JACKSON CONTROVERSY). On 15 Feb. 1862 he was promoted to major general and given command of the Army of Southwestern Virginia. In December he transferred to command of the I Corps/Army of Mississippi.

Loring got his nickname during his successful fending off of Maj. Gen. U.S. GRANT's effort to reach VICKSBURG through the complex system of waterways above the city. Under his personal direction at Fort Pemberton on the Tallahatchie River, aided by the channel block provided by a sunken steamer, Loring's men rained effective fire. Pacing the parapet of cotton bales, he called excitedly: "Give them blizzards, boys! Give them blizzards!"

Cut off from the main Confederate body at Baker's Creek, in May 1863 he and his force escaped capture at Vicksburg. Loring served under Lt. Gen. LEONIDAS POLK in northern Mississippi and after the general's death took command of Polk's Corps in the Army of Tennessee. After participating in the ATLANTA CAMPAIGN, he ended his service in the Carolinas (see CAROLINAS CAMPAIGN).

Loring fled the country after the war and in 1869 entered the service of the khedive of Egypt. 10 years later he returned to the U.S., publishing A Confederate Soldier in Egypt in 1884. d. New York City, 30 Dec. 1886.   —HH

Loring–Jackson controversy.

Jan.–Feb. 1862 Confederate Brig. Gen. WILLIAM WING LORING and his brigade were assigned to duty with Maj. Gen. THOMAS J. "STONEWALL" JACKSON Dec. 1861. Though retaining a separate brigade command, Loring was to act on Jackson's orders.

After their lackluster performance in Jackson's midwinter operations in the mountains west of Winchester, Va., 10 Jan., the major general ordered Loring to put his men into winter quarters at Romney. Loring believed the assignment of his brigade to outpost duty was meant as a slight to his men and showed preference toward the major general's regular command. Jackson's Confederates withdrew about 30 mi east-southeast to Winchester. Unhappy under Jackson, subscribing to common army prejudice that the general suffered deficient mental capacity, and claiming his brigade was dangerously exposed and unsupported at Romney, Loring wrote the Confederate War Department requesting his troops be recalled to Winchester.

Jackson considered his brief mountain campaign successful. Union troops had abandoned Romney and the surrounding area. Loring's occupation of the town would guard his western perimeter and secure it as a starting point for fair-weather campaigning. An expert at quick marches, Jackson believed his Winchester troops were within easy supporting distance of Loring. But on 30 Jan. he received a directive from Sec. of War JUDAH P. BENJAMIN, who claimed that he had heard Loring was in danger at Romney and ordered Jackson to recall him to Winchester.

Outraged, on 31 Jan. Jackson wrote the secretary, stating that Loring had been ordered back at Benjamin's direction, adding "with such interference in my command I cannot expect to be of much service in the field." Jackson also requested transfer to the Virginia Military Institute faculty. Failing that, he asked that his resignation be accepted. He wrote Virginia Gov. JOHN LETCHER, informing him of his decision and requesting his intercession to ensure the faculty appointment.

Letcher and Gen. JOSEPH E. JOHNSTON, on duty at the War

Department offices, jumped in to ease the issue. Johnston wrote Jackson begging him to reconsider his decision and asking his patience in dealing with politicians. Letcher, in a public scene in Benjamin's office, tongue-lashed the secretary and his staff, then traveled to Winchester to ask Jackson to stay with the army. On 6 Feb. Jackson agreed to remain on duty. Benjamin partially recanted and, appeasing Loring in the bargain, secured his promotion to major general and transfer to southwest Virginia. This ended the feud that nearly cost the Confederacy its best strategist.   —JES

losses.   Losses in a time of war are usually taken to mean the men who were killed in action or died of mortal wounds. Estimates of losses in the Civil War depend on whose figures one reads and how closely the records are examined. According to Thomas L. LIVERMORE's *NUMBERS AND LOSSES IN THE CIVIL WAR,* the "records show that 385,245 men were killed and wounded in the Union army, and that the Confederate army lost 94,000." Other authorities claim that the Union lost 360,-000 men and the Confederacy a total of 258,000, pointing out that Union and Confederate casualties of 249,458 and 59,297, respectively, were due to disease and accidents. More than 12,912 Union soldiers died at Andersonville prison alone, and Confederate prisoners who also died in detention camps must be numbered among the casualties of the war.

Gen. SAMUEL COOPER, adjutant general of the Confederate army, claimed that his side lost 53,973 killed in battle, 194,026 wounded, and 202,283 captures. Confederate muster-roll figures show the Confederate army losing 52,954 killed in action, 21,570 dead of wounds, and 59,297 dead of disease. In another estimate Union losses came to 110,070 killed or

dead of wounds and 249,458 dead of disease or accidents.

Somewhere in this range of estimates are the correct figures. Perhaps some reliance should be placed on the Confederate muster-roll figures, since they are based on documents that were prepared during the war years. If one reads the summary lines at the bottom of the many regimental histories in DYER'S *COMPENDIUM,* one grim fact stands out in endless repetition: the loss of men by disease and accidents consistently exceeds the loss in battle. Of the total losses for both Union and Confederate armies it is estimated that 204,070 were killed or mortally wounded, whereas 308,755 died of disease or by accident.   —AG

Lost Cause.   Journalist EDWARD A. POLLARD's book *The Lost Cause* (1866) first defined "lost cause" as the South's failed attempt to dissolve peacefully a Federal Union it believed had been formed as a voluntary association. To the men and women of the defeated Confederacy, the War for Southern Independence assumed a sacredness akin to religion. Proud and determined, the people of the South, subjected to military occupation and hated political legislation during 10 years of harsh Congressional Reconstruction, refused to be conquered in spirit. Before Pres. Rutherford B. Hayes withdrew the last Federal troops in 1877, the South labored vigorously to keep its sacrifices fresh in the hearts of its youth. Those of the war generation saw the conflict as one to preserve their civilization. They were neither willing nor able to see their defeat as anything but subjugation by Northern industrial might and superior manpower reserves.

From the pulpit, in the classroom, in literature, and at home grew the myth of an idealized past, of an "Old South" blessed

with pastoral simplicity trampled by Northern aggressors guilty of betraying the democratic principles on which the Founding Fathers had based the Constitution. Politicians "reminded" voters unceasingly of their subjugation at the hands of invaders. Veterans became venerated as heros, patriotic organizations were formed, magazines flourished to retell the battle stories, holidays were established to honor great leaders, and relics of the Confederacy were preserved as monuments to a just cause that fell before avarice and materialism.

At first Northerners angrily interpreted the South's refusal to submit meekly as an arrogant lack of repentance to which the conquerers felt entitled. In time, the victors mellowed, developing a respect for the tremendous price paid by the South in its doomed bid for independence. Tragically, the sympathy came at the expense of blacks, as the civil rights they had gained during Reconstruction were suppressed by discriminatory Jim Crow laws.

For Southerners, belief in the Lost Cause gave meaning to their sacrifices, infusing them with the self-righteousness of a superior race struggling to survive under the yoke of an oppressor, albeit a generous one. The Lost Cause mentality proved to be the psychological salvation for a South dominated by former Confederates and "unreconstructed" Rebels. It endured well into the 20th century. —PLF

Loudoun Rangers. USA An independent Union command of disaffected Virginians, the Loudoun Rangers were authorized under a special order of Sec. of War EDWIN M. STANTON and mustered into Federal service at Lovettsville, 20 June 1862. Most of its recruits came from the German settlement northwest of Leesburg, in the Piedmont region of Virginia east of the Blue Ridge Mts. Samuel C. Means of Waterford and Capt. Daniel M. Keyes of Lovettsville commanded the unit.

Created to operate against Confederate guerrillas in northern Virginia, the Loudoun Rangers enjoyed some initial successes until the arrival in the area of Lt. Col. JOHN S. MOSBY's 43d Battalion of Virginia Partisan Rangers. Mosby's lethal daredevils, many recruited from the same area as the Loudoun Rangers and operating out of the region, eventually became the target of the Federals. The Loudoun Rangers, however, never matched the superb Southern partisans, though they remained a major annoyance to the Confederates.

The antagonists battled for nearly 2 years in the Piedmont area known as "Mosby's Confederacy," among the Blue Ridge Mts., and into Maryland. Mosby's men, who seemed to suddenly appear from the mists, enjoyed most of the successes. On 4 July 1864 the Confederate guerrilla chieftain, with 150 men, attacked a body of Federals, including 2 companies of Loudoun Rangers, near Point of Rocks, Md. In a fierce attack, the Southerners routed the entire Union command, burning storehouses and a canal boat. Capt. William H. Chapman of Mosby's band duplicated the feat 14 Oct., again scattering the blue-clad rangers in Maryland and destroying stores and boats. The rangers achieved minor revenge a month later when one of them killed Capt. R. P. Montjoy, one of Mosby's best and most fearless officers.

The final showdown between the foes occurred a few days before the war ended. Mosby's raiders suddenly galloped into the camp of the Loudoun Rangers near Halltown, Va., 5 Apr. 1865, and in a brief melee captured nearly the entire Federal command. When a Union general learned of the defeat, he tersely and aptly remarked, "Well, that's the last of the Loudoun Rangers." —JDW

Louisiana. Seceding 26 Jan. 1861, Louisiana had no warfare within its borders until Apr. 1862, when Capt. DAVID G. FARRAGUT, a former resident of the state, entered the Mississippi with an expedition of 43 Federal ships. For 5 days he bombarded FORTS JACKSON AND ST. PHILIP near the mouth of the river, then took 17 ships past the forts and occupied New Orleans without opposition. On 1 May, Maj. Gen. BENJAMIN F. BUTLER brought 15,000 Federal troops into the city and began his controversial and unpopular military rule. Farragut took his fleet up the river and seized BATON ROUGE and Bayou Sara. Federal-controlled Louisiana had its capital at New Orleans.

Almost all of the state west of the Mississippi River remained under Confederate control until early 1863 and was governed first from Opelousas, then from Shreveport. Maj. Gen. RICHARD TAYLOR and his Confederates kept Butler pinned in the New Orleans area but were not able to prevent his successor, Maj.

Gen. NATHANIEL P. BANKS, from taking over a large part of southern Louisiana. However, in Apr. 1864, far up the Red River at MANSFIELD and PLEASANT HILL, La., Taylor, with fewer than 9,000 men, so thoroughly defeated Banks, with a force of at least 20,000, that the Union soldiers fled in disorderly retreat. That largely ended the fighting in the state.

Louisiana at the beginning of the Civil War had a total white population of 350,000, from whom about 1,000 military companies numbering some 56,000 troops were raised and served in the Confederate armies. In addition, some 10,000 boys too young for the army and men too old for it served in homeguard units. Between 6,500 and 7,000 Louisianians serving in Confederate armies died from all causes. Between 500 and 600 battles, skirmishes, and raids, the majority of them relatively minor, took place within the state. In general, the war in Louisiana was different from the campaigns in other parts of the nation because the field of action usually included bayous, swamps, and marshes where established military procedures could seldom be successfully applied.   —PR

Louisiana, CSS. In its early plans to offset the Union BLOCKADE, the South designed 2 powerful ironclads, the *Louisiana* and *Mississippi,* which were to be built at New Orleans with all possible speed. The more formidable *Louisiana* was begun 15 Oct. 1861 but ran into trouble at the start. Laborers struck for higher pay, and the blockade made it difficult to assemble necessary lumber and railroad iron.

When the Union fleet started up the Mississippi Apr. 1862, the Southerners were desperate. The *Louisiana* was only partially complete, and the *Mississippi* was far less advanced. Only FORTS JACKSON AND ST. PHILIP and 4 or 5 ships stood in the way of the capture of New Orleans.

On 20 Apr. the *Louisiana* was sent downriver with orders to tie up to the left bank a half-mile above St. Philip. In its unfinished state it could serve only as a stationary floating battery. The ship was badly designed, its engines would not work, its propellers were incomplete, and labor crews were still on board.

The Union ships neared the forts 24 Apr. In early combat the *Louisiana*'s commander, Charles F. McIntosh, was mortally wounded. His place was taken by Fleet Cmdr. John K. Mitchell. At noon, 27 Apr., a Union ship came up under a flag of truce and demanded surrender of the forts, which was refused. Later that night, however, their commander decided to capitulate. At 3 p.m. on the 28th the U.S. flag was raised above the fortifications, but Mitchell decided not to give up the *Louisiana.* Instead, he set it on fire, blowing it up in a mighty explosion that shook Union officers in their seats. Adm. DAVID D. PORTER, to whom Mitchell and his fellow officers surrendered, was furious that this was done while flags of truce were still flying and charged that the Confederate officers had "forfeited all claim to any consideration." They were held in close confinement until being sent north as regular prisoners.
—VCJ

Lovejoy's Station, Ga., Kilpatrick's Raid to. 18–23 Aug. 1864 In mid-Aug. 1864, following his rout of STONEMAN'S AND MCCOOK'S RAID, Confederate Maj. Gen. JOSEPH WHEELER began an expedition of his own, aimed at Maj. Gen. WILLIAM T. SHERMAN's supply lines. Having secured his communications, Sherman was not concerned. Instead, exploiting Wheeler's absence, he mounted another raid on the Confeder-

ate supply lines south of Atlanta. This he entrusted to the leader of the 3d Cavalry Division/Army of the Cumberland, Brig. Gen. H. JUDSON KILPATRICK.

On the 18th the impulsive young Irishman set out from Sandtown, Ga., with 4,000 troopers and 2 horse artillery units. His force comprised the brigades of Lt. Cols. Robert Klein, Fielder A. Jones, and Robert H. King, grouped under the immediate supervision of Col. Eli H. Murray, plus 2 brigades from the 2d Cavalry Division, led by Cols. Robert H. G. Minty and Eli Long. That evening the column struck 1 of its 2 objectives, the Atlanta & West Point Railroad. After ripping up a small section of track near Fairburn, the men remounted and headed southeastward toward their primary target, Lovejoy's Station, some 20 mi southeast of Atlanta, on the Macon & Western Railroad. Kilpatrick led the main body, Colonel Klein a 305-man advanced detachment that was to reunite with Kilpatrick at Griffin, along the railroad to Macon.

On the evening of the 19th the main body reached the Macon Railroad and the supply depot at Jonesborough, a major support base for Atlanta. The troopers held off the local guard long enough to burn large quantities of stores. The next afternoon, Kilpatrick's men reined in at Lovejoy's but had barely begun their work of destruction when Confederate infantry appeared in force. Compelled to fight into the night, the raiders had little time for wrecking trackage, especially when horsemen Wheeler had left at Atlanta, the division of Brig. Gen. WILLIAM H. JACKSON, came up to thrash their rear. Almost encircled, the Federals finally broke free, returning to Sherman's army on the 23d by a long circuit east of Atlanta.

Kilpatrick told his superior that he had done enough damage to keep the railroad out of operation for 10 days, thanks largely to Klein's detachment, which on the 19th had ripped up 3 mi of track and telegraph wire near Lovejoy's. Sherman discovered, however, that the Macon line was back in operation 2 days after his troopers' return, confirming his low opinion of cavalry and forcing him to move his entire army below Atlanta to accomplish the job the raiders had failed to do.   —EGL

Lovell, Mansfield. CSA b. District of Columbia, 20 Oct. 1822. The 9th-ranked graduate in the West Point class of 1842, Lovell took a commission in the U.S. artillery, received a wound and brevet promotion to captain in the Mexican War, and 18 Dec. 1854, with his friend and West Point classmate GUSTAVUS W. SMITH, resigned from the army. After dabbling in business in New York City, he found work with Smith on the city street commission, and 19 Sept. 1861, with Smith, resigned as deputy street commissioner to accept an appointment as a Confederate officer.

Made major general 7 Oct. 1861, following lobbying efforts by Smith, Lovell assumed command of the defenses of New Orleans, supervising the arming of its forts and batteries and instigating creation of the CONFEDERATE RIVER DEFENSE FLEET. Noted for enjoying liquor, bonhomie, and hotel life, Lovell unfortunately bragged about the New Orleans defenses. In Apr. 1862, driven from the city with

NA

little effort by Union Navy Capt. DAVID G. FARRAGUT, he was vilified by his troops and superiors.

Lovell was next assigned an infantry division in the Vicksburg command of another West Point classmate, Maj. Gen. EARL VAN DORN, under whom he performed miserably on the second day of the Oct. 1862 Battle of CORINTH. Lovell's division, acting in concert with the Confederate center and left, was to hit the north end of the Union lines. His men did little more than skirmish heavily on the Union left, and Lovell seemed not to urge them on. On 5 Dec. 1862 he successfully fought the engagement of COFFEEVILLE in north Mississippi with Van Dorn's troops, then was relieved of command later in the month for his loss of New Orleans Apr. 1862. At Lovell's request, a Confederate court of inquiry met Apr. 1863 and absolved him of charges of incompetence. However, he received no other assignment for the duration of the war.

After the Confederate surrender Lovell returned to New York City, helped in the removal of naval obstructions from the East River, and worked as a civil engineer. He died there 1 June 1884.

In defense of Lovell's martial talents it should be noted that Gens. JOSEPH E. JOHNSTON and JOHN B. HOOD, and board of inquiry members Brig. Gens. THOMAS C. HINDMAN and WILLIAM M. GARDNER all believed his defense of New Orleans adequate. Most of the blame for the defeat fell to Confederate naval inferiority. Historian Albert Castel attributes Lovell's conduct on the second day at Corinth to common sense: seeing the superiority of the Union position, he declined wasting his men in an all-out assault. Confederate enlisted men were not so kind and fondly sang the satirical "New Ballad of Lord Lovell," memorializing his loss of New Orleans and his veteran drinker's red nose.   —JES

Low, John. CSN b. Aberdeen, Scotland, 24 Jan. 1836. Relatives in England raised Low when his parents died soon after his birth. At 16 he joined the British Merchant Marine and for most of his life was involved in some aspect of seafaring. He settled in Savannah, Ga., in 1856 and was operating his own merchant-supply business there when the Civil War began.

Low enlisted as a private in the Georgia Hussars 19 Jan. 1861 but resigned from the cavalry unit to accept an appointment in the Confederate States Navy as acting master with rank of lieutenant. That autumn, JAMES D. BULLOCH, an antebellum acquaintance of Low and the man named by Pres. JEFFERSON DAVIS to secure ships for the Confederacy in Europe, arranged to have the young naval officer ordered to Liverpool to assist him in acquiring ships and transporting them to Southern ports. Leaving Liverpool, Low sailed as 2d officer to Bulloch aboard the first vessel purchased for Confederate service, the *Fingal*, a former British merchant ship later renamed the *ATLANTA*. The vessel was converted to a warship at sea. Carrying a cargo of 15,000 Enfield rifles and 4 cannon, the largest single shipment of military supplies to reach the South, it arrived in Savannah 12 Nov.

On his return to Liverpool Mar. 1862, Low was assigned by Bulloch to deliver the recently completed Confederate cruiser *Oreto* (renamed the *FLORIDA*) to Lt. JOHN N. MAFFITT at NASSAU; that July he also assisted Bulloch in getting the *Enrica* (renamed the *ALABAMA*) to sea, but this time his superior ordered him to stay with the ship, which had been placed under the command of Capt. RAPHAEL SEMMES. Semmes gave the 1st lieutenant's billet to JOHN MCINTOSH KELL, who had served under him aboard the *SUMTER*, demoting Low to 4th lieutenant and ap-

pointing him boarding officer. But Semmes realized Low was eager for his own command, and when the *Alabama* overtook and captured the *Conrad,* 21 June 1863, he renamed it *Tuscaloosa* and commissioned Low its captain.

For nearly 6 weeks the *Tuscaloosa* had few encounters and made no captures, largely because fear of the cruisers had cleared the seas of Northern merchant vessels. Finally, off the coast of Cape Town, 31 July, the crew boarded the American-owned *Santee*. Because it carried neutral cargo, the property of British subjects, Low ransomed the ship for $150,000 rather than destroy it. He took few additional prizes before British authorities seized the *Tuscaloosa* 26 Dec., when Low anchored at Simon's Bay off the coast of South Africa to take on supplies.

In February Low returned to Liverpool and learned that Bulloch had recommended him for permanent promotion to 1st lieutenant, to rank from 6 Jan. 1864. During the last year of the war he was assigned to oversee the construction of 4 additional ships for the Confederacy. Only 1 of these, the *Ajax,* a light-draft gunboat, put to sea. It cleared Nassau Jan. 1865 and reached St. George, Bermuda, 4 May, where local authorities prevented its departure until they learned the Confederacy had fallen. Low sailed the *Ajax* back to Liverpool, surrendering it there 9 June.

Rather than return to Georgia, Low, whose wife had died during the war, sent for his son and stayed in England. He prospered in business, first managing cotton mills, then working as a commission agent for naval stores and a representative for marine insurance companies. d. Liverpool, 6 Sept. 1906, after a 2-month illness.   —PLF

Lowe, Thaddeus Sobieski Constantine. aeronaut b. Jefferson Mills, N.H., 20 Aug. 1832. Despite a limited education, Lowe demonstrated an early aptitude for applied science. In his twenties, he had already adopted aeronautics as his profession, an outgrowth of his interest in upper air currents. In 1858 he built the first of many BALLOONS and made an ascent at Ottawa, Canada, in celebration of the laying of the Atlantic cable. A year later, thanks to donations from patrons and profits from traveling exhibitions, he built a huge balloon, the *City of New York.* Attempts at a transatlantic voyage late in 1859 and the following summer failed when the airship's gas envelope was damaged during inflation.

Deferring a third effort at reaching Europe by air, "Professor" Lowe used a smaller balloon to make a 9-hour, 900-mile flight from Cincinnati, Ohio, to Unionville, S.C. 19–20 Apr. 1861. Coming a week after the firing on FORT SUMTER, the voyage ended with his imprisonment as a suspected Union spy. On his release, he hastened to Washington and offered his services to the Union army. Impressed by Lowe's exploits, which had gained him recognition both within and outside the scientific community, ABRAHAM LINCOLN made him chief of army aeronautics in August, with the pay of a colonel. The War Department also provided him a small appropriation, labor details, and technological resources.

Lowe proved his value by conducting numerous aerial experiments with military applications. From the defenses of Washington, 18 June 1861, he sent the first telegraphic message from a balloon. 3 days after FIRST BULL RUN, he went aloft to gather information on Confederate dispositions south of the Potomac. During an ascent 24 Sept. he became the first aerial observer to provide fire direction for artillery.

At first confined to a base that offered the facilities of a gas works, Lowe took the field with the Army of the Potomac in spring 1862, accompanied by portable coal-gas generators he had devised. He served Maj. Gen. GEORGE B. MCCLELLAN throughout the PENINSULA CAMPAIGN, conducting daily aerial observation and even photographic reconnaissance. The army leader so appreciated his services that he provided Lowe with an additional appropriation of $8,600, enabling him to enlarge his fleet of balloons. Soon he possessed 7 airships, ranging in capacity from 15,000 to 32,000 cu ft; the latter included his most famous balloon, *Intrepid.*

Malaria contracted on the peninsula sidelined Lowe during the ANTIETAM CAMPAIGN, but he went aloft and supervised the ascents of others during and after FREDERICKSBURG, providing valuable intelligence to McClellan's successors. Shortly before CHANCELLORSVILLE, however, Maj. Gen. JOSEPH HOOKER subordinated him to the chief engineer of the army, reducing the aeronaut's pay, pruning his staff, and obstructing his work. As a result, Lowe resigned his position 8 May 1863. By then his balloon corps had made more than 3,000 ascensions.

Soon Lowe turned to new inventions and enterprises, devising a process for manufacturing artificial ice and improving the method of producing water-gas for use as fuel. In later years he moved to California, where he built an electric railway up a steep mountain that later bore his name. At its summit was erected another monument to his scientific work, the Lowe Observatory. d. Pasadena, Calif., 16 Jan. 1913.   —EGL

Lowell, Charles Russell. USA b. Boston, Mass., 2 Jan. 1835, Lowell was graduated 1st in his class from Harvard in 1854. A nephew of the poet James Russell Lowell, he toured Europe for several years before returning to the U.S., where he engaged in the railroading and the ironworks business.

With the commencement of war, Lowell accepted a captaincy in the 3d (later 6th) U.S. Cavalry 14 May 1861. In spring 1862 he participated in the PENINSULA CAMPAIGN, where his younger brother, James Jackson Lowell, was killed. At the conclusion of the campaign, Lowell joined the staff of Maj. Gen. GEORGE B. MCCLELLAN. During the Battle of ANTIETAM the staff

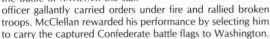
USMHI

officer gallantly carried orders under fire and rallied broken troops. McClellan rewarded his performance by selecting him to carry the captured Confederate battle flags to Washington.

After the battle Lowell returned to Massachusetts, where he recruited and organized the 2d Massachusetts Cavalry. Commissioned its colonel 10 May 1863, Lowell served with his men in the defenses of the capital for over a year, during which time he commanded the Independent Cavalry Brigade XXII Corps. In July 1864 his command assisted in the defense against Lt. Gen. JUBAL A. EARLY's Confederate corps.

During the 1864 SHENANDOAH VALLEY CAMPAIGN between Early and Maj. Gen. PHILIP H. SHERIDAN, Lowell commanded the tough Reserve Brigade, a unit of 3 regiments of Regulars and 2 of the veteran volunteers. Intelligent, experienced, and fearless, Lowell was a superb combat officer. At THIRD WIN-

CHESTER, 19 Sept., and at Tom's Brook, 9 Oct., he distinguished himself, handling his brigade with skill in its charges. On 19 Oct., at CEDAR CREEK, Early's Confederates charged the Federals at dawn, routing 2 Union corps. During the morning's action Lowell suffered a wound but refused to leave the field. When the Federals counterattacked in the afternoon, he suffered a second and mortal wound. The well-liked and highly regarded officer died 20 Oct. 1864. On Sheridan's intercession, Lowell was posthumously commissioned a brigadier general to rank from 19 Oct.   —JDW

Lowrey, Mark Perrin. CSA b. McNairy Cty., Tenn., 30 Dec. 1828. In youth Lowrey moved to Tishomingo, Miss. A desperately poor, illiterate bricklayer, he enlisted as a private in the 2d Mississippi Infantry for the Mexican War, saw no action, and on his discharge arranged to be privately tutored. At 24, while still pursuing his education, he entered the Baptist ministry. In 1861, with several congregations and influence in the community, he was urged by neighbors to accept the colonelcy of the 4th Regiment of state volunteers for temporary Civil War duty.

GG

A 60-day unit, the 4th was disbanded after brief garrison service in Kentucky. Lowrey raised the 32d Mississippi Infantry Apr. 1862, became its colonel, and at PERRYVILLE, when Brig. Gen. S. A. M. WOOD was wounded, assumed brigade command in his first battle. Without previous combat experience, he performed well, winning notice in the KENTUCKY CAMPAIGN and praise from Maj. Gen. PATRICK R. CLEBURNE in the Battle of CHICKAMAUGA. He was promoted brigadier general 4 Oct. 1863, fought at MISSIONARY RIDGE, through the ATLANTA CAMPAIGN, and, on Cleburne's assumption of corps command, led a division in the Battle of JONESBOROUGH. Lowrey resumed brigade command for Gen. JOHN B. HOOD's FRANKLIN AND NASHVILLE CAMPAIGN, fought in the second line at the Battle of Franklin, briefly led his division in the days before the Battle of Nashville, and on the second day of that fight assumed command of Maj. Gen. BENJAMIN F. CHEATHAM's division. He remained in division command 4 months while on duty in South Carolina, then resigned his commission 14 Mar. 1865.

Lowrey returned to the ministry, established Mississippi's Blue Mountain Female Institute in 1873, and wrote for a religious newspaper, *The Christian Index.* He was proudest of having taken part in a religious revival in the army, baptizing 50 men within 2 weeks in spring 1864. His explanation of his army resignation read eloquently: "I had been separated from the men and officers with whom I had borne the 'burden and heat of the day,' and to whom I was endeared by a thousand sacred ties, and although I was willing to stand with our broken forces until the end of the struggle, I was unwilling to mourn with strangers at the funeral of 'The Lost Cause.'" Lowrey died traveling in Tennessee, 27 Feb. 1885.   —JES

Lowry, Robert. CSA b. Chesterfield District, S.C., 10 Mar. 1830. Before 1840, Lowry moved with his Scotch-Irish family

to Mississippi, where he was raised by his uncle, a judge. In partnership with him, Lowry engaged in various mercantile pursuits before marrying and moving to Arkansas, where he read law. Returning to Mississippi 5 years later, he was elected to the state legislature, first the lower, then the upper, house.

LC

An avid secessionist, Lowry enlisted in 1861 as a private in Company B/6th Mississippi Infantry, moving up to major when the regiment was formally organized. At that grade he fought at SHILOH, 6–7 Apr. 1862, where he was twice wounded and his regiment, in the words of one historian, "was reduced to a burial squad." The 6th's colonel, also wounded in the battle, soon resigned and Lowry succeeded him 23 May. Joining the army of Gen. JOSEPH E. JOHNSTON in Mississippi, he led his regiment in several battles of the VICKSBURG CAMPAIGN. At PORT GIBSON his "coolness and promptness in executing every order" won the praise of his superiors.

During the ATLANTA CAMPAIGN of 1864, Lowry received new accolades, especially at KENNESAW MOUNTAIN, 27 June. In charge of his brigade's skirmish line, he was instrumental in repulsing 2 of the many ill-fated Union attacks on that field. For part of the campaign he commanded the brigade of Brig. Gen. WINFIELD S. FEATHERSTON, proving himself qualified for higher command.

Permanent brigade leadership came to him at FRANKLIN, 30 Nov. 1864. In that battle, so deadly to Confederate generals, his direct superior was killed, and Lowry stepped into his place at the head of 6 Mississippi infantry regiments. He skillfully maneuvered these outfits 3 weeks later at Nashville and during the subsequent retreat of Gen. JOHN BELL HOOD's Army of Tennessee from its namesake state.

Receiving a brigadier generalship 4 Feb. 1865, Lowry returned to a position under Johnston in the war's closing weeks, fighting at BENTONVILLE and in other actions during the CAROLINAS CAMPAIGN. After Johnston's surrender, Lowry became a Mississippi senator, 1865–66; a 2-term governor, 1881–89; the co-author of a history of his state; and, from 1903 until his death in Jackson 19 Jan. 1910, state commander of the United Confederate Veterans.   —EGL

loyalty leagues. *See* UNION LEAGUE OF AMERICA.

loyalty oaths. Whenever Union commanders occupied Southern territory, they immediately tried to subdue the local population by requiring them to pledge loyalty to the Federal government. The severity of the oaths depended on the attitude of the commanding officer, who might require oath-takers to swear past as well as future allegiance to the U.S. By late 1862, hoping to accomplish mild reconstruction and cultivate goodwill, Pres. ABRAHAM LINCOLN, had directed the army high command to require only a simple oath of future loyalty.

The oaths, usually administered by a provost marshall, became a means of controlling Confederate sympathizers. A printed document was issued as proof of having taken the oath, and possessing the properly signed piece of paper could deter-

mine freedom of mobility, protection for private property (including slaves), and frequently the right to food and other supplies from Union stores or to sell crops. The Northern public clamored for strict loyalty oaths because Confederates flagrantly disregarded them at every opportunity. Papers "proving" a man or woman had taken the oath could be purchased from corrupt military authorities without any utterance of allegiance. Sometimes neighbors banded together, one of them taking the oath, then conducting business for the others. Men sometimes sent their wives to take the oath rather than do so themselves, and frequently a woman alone would charm a Union officer into providing her with the necessary papers, later making no pretense at where her loyalty lay. Prisoners sometimes took the oath to get paroled and immediately violated it by rejoining their old commands.

The traffic in oaths and Southerners' blatant attitude toward them created one more sore point between congressional Radicals and the president. Eventually the Radicals pushed through the despised IRONCLAD OATH as part of the Reconstruction Act of 1867.   —PLF

Lubbock, Francis Richard. war governor b. Beaufort, S.C., 16 Oct. 1815, Lubbock worked in several different businesses from 1829 until he moved to Texas in 1836. He opened stores of his own in Valesco and later in Houston, where he settled. As a Texas militiaman he skirmished with Indians and Mexicans on the frontier, then entered public life as clerk of the Texas house of representatives, comptroller of the state treasury, and district clerk of Harris County, the last an elected position he held for 16 years. More popular than talented, he won the lieutenant governorship in 1857 and attended the 1860 Democratic national convention in Charleston as a solid pro-secessionist. When Texans elected him governor Nov. 1861, he devoted his energies to strengthening state defenses and replenishing the empty state treasury.

Lubbock achieved considerable success during his 2 years in office. On his recommendation the legislature raised a Frontier Regiment to quell Indian hostilities in the western counties and created the Texas State Military Board to procure arms and equipment for troops stationed in the state. To raise money, he encouraged cotton trade with Mexico and sold U.S. indemnity bonds the state had received in 1850 for selling the area around Santa Fe to the Federal government. He established a state foundry and a percussion-cap factory to alleviate the shortage of arms and ammunition. Neither satisfied demand, but the cloth manufactory he operated at the state penitentiary in Huntsville turned out more fabric than any other facility of the kind in the Southwest. Ultimately it provided 38% of the revenue coming into the state treasury.

Lubbock's commitment to Confederate independence extended to courting good relations with the army. He cooperated extensively with district commander Maj. Gen. JOHN B. MAGRUDER by impressing several thousand slaves to build coastal defenses, assigned the militia to help return deserters to Louisiana, and turned over the Frontier Regiment to the army for duty outside of the state despite the disaffection its removal caused among West Texans. After the massacre of German Unionists at Neuces, Oct. 1862, he tried to pacify the German communities in northern Texas by exempting them from draft laws.

Rather than run for reelection late in 1863, Lubbock accepted an appointment as colonel on the staffs of Magruder, then Maj. Gen. JOHN A. WHARTON. Impressed by his dedication to Confederate goals, JEFFERSON DAVIS invited him to Richmond in 1864 to advise him on affairs in the Trans-Mississippi. He was captured with Davis May 1865 and imprisoned for several months at FORT DELAWARE.

On being released in December, Lubbock returned to Texas. After failing at the meat-packing business, he returned to public office as tax collector in Galveston, state treasurer, and member of the Board of Pardons. d. Austin, Tex., 22 June 1905.
—PLF

lunette. A 2- or 3-sided field fort, its rear open to interior lines, was called a lunette. Lunettes were often named in honor of battery commanders or commanding brigadier generals.
—JES

Lynchburg, Va., eng. at. 16–18 June 1864 Maj. Gen. DAVID HUNTER's raid into the upper SHENANDOAH VALLEY, with its valuable railroad facilities, forced Gen. R. E. LEE to detach part of his army to meet the threat. Assigning the task to Lt. Gen. JUBAL A. EARLY and the II Corps, Lee instructed that officer to punish Hunter and then, by swift marches northward down the valley, cross the Potomac and menace Washington, D.C.

Early evacuated his lines at Cold Harbor before dawn 13 June. While Hunter ravaged the Lexington area, Early's veterans marched westward to Charlottesville, where on the 16th Early communicated with Maj. Gen. JOHN C. BRECKINRIDGE, whose 2 small brigades held Lynchburg. The II Corps began boarding the trains at Charlottesville, but it was not until 1 p.m. on the 17th that Early and his vanguard arrived at Lynchburg.

Late that day Hunter, after a deliberate march, reached the northern outskirts of the Virginia town, where 3 railroads intersected. Federal artillerists shelled the weakly held lines sporadically throughout the afternoon. While Hunter prepared plans that night for a morning attack, the rest of Early's veterans arrived on snail-slow trains. The newly extended Confederate works bristled with 8,000 additional muskets when the Federals cautiously probed forward. Hunter delivered a few small-scale attacks that were easily repulsed.

On the night of 18–19 June Hunter abandoned the enterprise, retreating northward. Early pursued at dawn, harassing the Union rear guard, turning the withdrawal into a precipitate flight beyond the Alleghenies into West Virginia. Early had saved Lynchburg and the railroad network. The Shenandoah Valley, the Confederate avenue of invasion, once more lay open.
—JDW

Lyon, Hylan Benton. CSA b. Caldwell Cty., Ky., 22 Feb. 1836, Lyon was orphaned as a child and educated in local Kentucky schools. He received appointment to West Point, graduated 19th in the class of 1856, then spent his army service in Florida and in Indian campaigns around Spokane in Washington Territory. On leave of absence at the time of his resignation from the Federal military, 30 Apr. 1861, he entered the Confederate army as an artillery captain.

After 9 months of service, troops elected Lyon lieutenant colonel of the 8th Kentucky Infantry. He fought at FORT DONELSON, was taken prisoner 16 Feb., then was confined to JOHNSON'S ISLAND. Released early in autumn and promoted to colonel, Lyon held brigade command in the Army of Tennessee during campaigning in north Mississippi, at VICKSBURG, and CHATTANOOGA. He led his brigade safely out of Confederate lines in the Siege of Vicksburg and had charge of removing

Gen. BRAXTON BRAGG's artillery after the defeat at MISSIONARY RIDGE. He then joined Maj. Gen. NATHAN B. FORREST's cavalry, commanding a Kentucky brigade in Brig. Gen. ABRAHAM BUFORD's division.

Lyon won distinction for his part in the Battle of BRICE'S CROSS ROADS, 10 June 1864. At the head of his 800-man brigade he began the battle for General Forrest and fought almost unsupported for the first hour of the combat. He won promotion to brigadier general, to date from 14 June, went on an unsuccessful recruiting mission behind enemy lines, then rode in Forrest's Johnsonville raid. He served in FRANKLIN AND NASHVILLE CAMPAIGN operations before being assigned to district command of enemy-occupied western Kentucky. This posting, presumably one of many meant to eliminate surplus officers from Forrest's rapidly dwindling command, effectively ended Lyon's war career.

After a brief period of self-imposed exile in Mexico, Lyon spent the postwar years as a Kentucky farmer active in veterans' affairs. Kentucky property holdings made him a lessee of the state penitentiary and earned him an appointment as state prison commissioner. d. Eddyville, Ky., 25 Apr. 1907.   —JES

Lyon, Nathaniel. USA b. Ashford, Conn., 14 July 1818, Lyon began his brief Civil War career with the advantage of long military service and the disadvantage of a hot temper. Graduating 11th in his class of 52 from West Point in 1841, he served in the Seminole and Mexican wars. A captain in the 1850s at Fort Riley, Kans., Lyon found himself in the middle of the murderous political climate of "BLEEDING KANSAS." He had been a Democrat with few convictions about slavery, but after witnessing the slavery controversy in Kansas, he hardened into a furious Republican who detested that institution.

USMHI

In 1861, when Lyon was transferred to St. Louis, Missouri was sharply divided between a pro-Confederate governor, CLAIBORNE F. JACKSON, and a pro-Union legislature, with a valuable arsenal in St. Louis as the prize for the victor. Lyon was only too willing to overstep any boundaries to keep Jackson from taking control of the arsenal and using the guns against the Union. When the governor called out the state militia, allegedly to train for home defense, Lyon grew suspicious and disguised himself as a farm woman to spy out the militia's camp. Concluding that Jackson intended to use the militia to seize the arsenal for the Confederacy, he surrounded the camp with his own soldiers and captured it. It was an ill-timed, hotheaded gesture, and a riot broke out in St. Louis when Lyon paraded his prisoners through the town. Nevertheless, he had saved the arsenal, and probably Missouri, for the Union.

His action provoked Jackson to openly declare for the Confederacy and call for outright insurrection, and Lyon, who had been promoted to brigadier general 17 May, mounted a campaign to drive him from the state. The Confederates were waiting for Lyon 10 Aug. 1861 at WILSON'S CREEK. In a bloody, inconclusive battle considered a Confederate victory, he was killed, impetuously trying to lead a last charge.   —ACG

M

McArthur, John. USA b. Erskine, Scotland, 17 Nov. 1826. Interested in smithing and ironwork, McArthur studied the trade, immigrated to the U.S. in 1849, worked as a boilermaker in Chicago, and with a brother-in-law began the successful Excelsior Iron Works in 1854. Sole owner of the iron business in 1861, McArthur, active in the state militia's Highland Guards, was made colonel of the 12th Illinois Infantry for Civil War service 3 May.

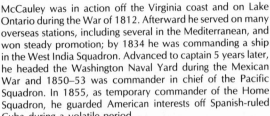
LC

With the 12th Illinois, McArthur served at Cairo, Ill., through Sept. 1861, participated in Missouri and Kentucky operations, and garrisoned Paducah, Ky., until Jan. 1862. He went on maneuvers against FORT HENRY and led a brigade made up of the 9th, 12th, and 41st Illinois for the Feb. 1862 assault on FORT DONELSON. For efficient service he received promotion to brigadier general 21 Mar. and went to the Battle of SHILOH, fighting on the left of the "HORNETS' NEST" until forced to retreat about 1:30 p.m., 6 Apr. He was wounded there, and 1 of his regiments sustained 59% casualties, the highest of any Union unit in the fight. McArthur succeeded to Brig. Gen. W.H.L. WALLACE's divisional command after the battle.

First under Maj. Gen. E.O.C. ORD, then Maj. Gen. JAMES B. MCPHERSON, he led divisions at IUKA, CORINTH, and in the VICKSBURG CAMPAIGN and siege, then was military governor of Vicksburg until 5 Aug. 1864. McArthur protected supply lines from Atlanta to Tennessee, briefly served under Maj. Gen. ANDREW J. SMITH in Missouri, and in December fought in the Battle of NASHVILLE. On the first day of fighting there, at the head of Smith's 1st Division/XVI Corps, he distinguished himself in a smashing assault on the Confederate left that won him a brevet as major general dated 15 Dec. 1864. Though recommended for promotion, McArthur lacked the political associations necessary for appointment to major general of volunteers. He was assigned to the Army of the Gulf for the remainder of the war and mustered out 24 Aug. 1865.

Postbellum, McArthur's iron business foundered, a position as Chicago's public works commissioner ended abruptly after the Chicago fire, and courts found against him as postmaster of Chicago for a $73,000 loss of postal funds in a bank failure. He died in retirement in Chicago 15 May 1906.   —JES

McCauley, Charles Stewart. USN b. Philadelphia, Pa., 3 Feb. 1793. Appointed a U.S. Navy midshipman at 15, McCauley was in action off the Virginia coast and on Lake Ontario during the War of 1812. Afterward he served on many overseas stations, including several in the Mediterranean, and won steady promotion; by 1834 he was commanding a ship in the West India Squadron. Advanced to captain 5 years later, he headed the Washington Naval Yard during the Mexican War and 1850–53 was commander in chief of the Pacific Squadron. In 1855, as temporary commander of the Home Squadron, he guarded American interests off Spanish-ruled Cuba during a volatile period.

By the start of the Civil War McCauley was overage and unwell, quite possibly unfit for duty. The Navy Department nevertheless sent him to command the vital and vulnerable Gosport Navy Yard at Norfolk, shortly before Virginia seceded. Warned by his superiors to do nothing to disturb the local *status quo,* he failed to take timely measures to safeguard the ships, ordnance, and other property of the yard. In mid-Apr. 1861 several emissaries from Washington relayed orders to evacuate the most valuable ships in the yard's fleet, especially the mighty steam frigate *Merrimack,* and to take steps to prevent Virginians from seizing whatever resources he could not remove. Stubbornly adhering to his earlier orders to refrain from provocative actions, he refused to act until the Fall of Norfolk, 20 Apr. By then Virginia had seceded, and local troops, whose numbers McCauley overestimated, prepared to storm the yard. At his direction, 8 of the 11 ships at Gosport, including the *Merrimack,* were burned or scuttled, while government buildings, docks, and supplies were torched. Still, as soon as his garrison fled to sea, state troops swarmed in, salvaging $3 million worth of property, including over 1,000 cannon and 2,000 barrels of gunpowder. The Confederate navy later raised and refit 4 vessels, including the *Merrimack,* which it transformed into the war's first ironclad, CSS *VIRGINIA.*

The destruction of a ten-million-dollar facility brought McCauley a torrent of censure from the government and the Northern public. A Senate investigating committee concluded that he had acted hastily and irresponsibly. Smarting from such criticism, including charges that he had been drunk 20 Apr., he soon retired. He went into exile at his home in Washington, D.C., where he died 21 May 1869.   —EGL

McCausland, John. CSA b. St. Louis, Mo., 13 Sept. 1836. The son of Irish immigrants, McCausland was only 7 when both parents died. Growing up on an uncle's farm in what is now West Virginia, in 1857 he graduated from Virginia Military Institute at the top of his class. After studying a year at the University of Virginia, he returned to the institute as an assistant professor of mathematics.

In spring 1861 he organized and became colonel of the 36th Virginia Infantry, which saw service in its home area of western

Virginia as well as at FORT DON-
ELSON, where it was one of the
few Confederate units to escape
capture. McCausland per-
formed dependably thereafter
in southwestern Virginia. On 9
May 1864, at the engagement at
CLOYD'S MOUNTAIN, he suc-
ceeded to command after the
death of Brig. Gen. ALBERT G.
JENKINS; a brigadier's commission came 9 days later.

McCausland led cavalry for
the remainder of the war, campaigning actively in the Shenan-
doah Valley while serving under Lt. Gen. JUBAL A. EARLY. He is
best remembered for a July 1864 raid into Pennsylvania: Acting
under orders, he demanded $100,000 in gold from the inhabi-
tants of Chambersburg in retribution for destruction of private
homes in the valley by Federal Maj. Gen. DAVID HUNTER. When
merchants refused to pay, McCausland evacuated Chambersburg's 300 residents and set fire to the business district.

With Gen. R. E. LEE in the final fighting, McCausland cut his
way through the Federal lines at Appomattox rather than surrender. After journeying to Europe to avoid arraignment for the
Chambersburg "atrocity," he returned to the U.S. in 1867,
ultimately acquiring a 6,000-acre tract in Mason Cty., W. Va.
There, in self-imposed isolation, he spent the rest of his life.
McCausland was the next-to-the-last Confederate general to
die. Succumbing to a heart attack 22 Jan. 1927, he was buried
at Henderson, W. Va.   —JIR

McClellan, George Brinton. USA b. Philadelphia,
Penna., 3 Dec. 1826. A member of an old and distinguished
family, McClellan left the University of Pennsylvania in 1842 for
a brilliant career at West Point.

He ranked 2d in the class of
1846, became an engineer
officer, and won 2 brevets for
distinguished service in the Mexican War. Later he built forts, improved harbors, taught at his
alma mater, mapped railroad
routes, observed European tactics during the Crimean War,
and designed a comfortable saddle that bore his name. Resigning his captain's commission in
1857, he became chief engineer, then vice-president, of the
Illinois Central Railroad and in

1860 president of the Ohio & Mississippi.

Residing in Cincinnati when war broke out, McClellan was
appointed a major general of Ohio volunteers by Gov. WILLIAM
DENNISON. His administrative expertise and the credit he accepted for victories at RICH MOUNTAIN and CORRICK'S FORD in
western Virginia brought him national attention. On 27 July
1861 ABRAHAM LINCOLN placed him at the head of the army
defeated at FIRST BULL RUN. In a few months, "Little Mac"
turned the ARMY OF THE POTOMAC into a command capable of
standing with the Confederacy's best, thereby winning his
troops' undying devotion. But because of his anti-Republican

bias, he feuded with government officials, showing particular
animosity toward Sec. of War EDWIN M. STANTON and Treasury
Sec. SALMON P. CHASE; both cordially reciprocated. He also
clashed with Gen. WINFIELD SCOTT, whom he replaced as general-in-chief 1 Nov., as well as with Maj. Gen. HENRY W. HAL-
LECK, who in turn supplanted McClellan July 1862.

Given to unconscionable dawdling, McClellan refused to
begin field campaigning until Lincoln commanded him to do
so in his PRESIDENT'S GENERAL WAR ORDERS NO. 1. Finally, late
in Mar. 1862 he made an amphibious movement to FORT
MONROE, then led his 118,000 troops up the Virginia peninsula
toward Richmond. In subsequent weeks, he allowed much
smaller Confederate forces, whose strength he habitually magnified, to slow or stymie him. He was reluctant to seize the
offensive, insistent about reinforcements, and so poor a strategist that he had to change his base of operations in midcam-
paign. These and other factors compelled him to abandon his
offensive and retreat to the James River early in July, despite
having emerged victorious from almost every battle between
WILLIAMSBURG, 5 May, and MALVERN HILL, 1 July.

Distressed by McClellan's slowness, his proclivity for maneuvering instead of fighting, and his political posturing, early
in August Lincoln removed his army to another theater and
placed it under Maj. Gen. JOHN POPE's command. However,
when it was defeated and demoralized at SECOND BULL RUN
under Pope, the president had no alternative but to return the
army to McClellan. As he had the year before, McClellan
brought order from chaos and restored his troops' spirit, but
in the ensuing ANTIETAM CAMPAIGN he displayed many of the
same flaws exhibited on the peninsula. His tactical draw
against Gen. ROBERT E. LEE 17 Sept. ended Lee's invasion of
Maryland but highlighted McClellan's enigmatic ineptitude in
combat. When McClellan plodded after the retreating enemy,
Lincoln relieved him again, this time for good.

While on inactive duty, McClellan fully embraced politics,
for some time his consuming love. In 1864, as the Democratic
presidential candidate, he opposed Lincoln's reelection.
Though he repudiated his party's antiwar platform, his aura of
defeatism led to his failure at the polls in November. Thereafter, as a civilian, McClellan traveled extensively; worked at
civil-engineering and other business ventures; wrote a self-
serving memoir, *McClellan's Own Story* (1887), and served 1
term, 1878–81, as governor of New Jersey. d. Orange, N.J., 29
Oct. 1885.   —EGL

McClernand, John Alexander. USA b. near Hardins-
burg, Ky., 30 May 1812. After his father's death, McClernand
moved with his mother to Shawneetown, Ill., where he attended school and read law. He settled in Springfield, establishing a practice and entering politics. The Democratic U.S.
representative from Abraham Lincoln's home district, McClernand was appointed a brigadier general to rank from 17 May
1861. His only military experience dated back nearly 30 years
to service as a private in the Black Hawk War; 5 terms in
Congress, 1843–51 and 1859–61, and popularity among Illinois Democrats constituted his qualifications for command.

Ambitious, selfish, and pompous, McClernand irritated professional soldiers but was intelligent and bold enough to compile a decent war record. Almost immediately he was placed
under Brig. Gen. ULYSSES S. GRANT, a position that enabled him
to share the credit for battles at BELMONT and FORTS HENRY AND
DONELSON but led him to believe that he could do better on his

own. Promoted to major general as of 21 Mar. 1862, he outranked every officer in Grant's army except Grant himself and resented the West Pointers Grant trusted.

USMHI

In Oct. 1862 McClernand received permission from Lincoln to raise troops for an expedition against VICKSBURG. Once the new troops reached Memphis, Grant appropriated them for an expedition to Vicksburg led by Maj. Gen. WILLIAM T. SHERMAN. After the assault failed miserably in December, McClernand reclaimed his army and led it to a splendid victory at ARKANSAS POST, which Grant labeled a "wild goose chase" before he learned that Sherman had planned it. When the army returned to a position near Vicksburg, Grant assumed personal command, placing the outraged McClernand in command of only 1 of the 3 army corps, the XIII.

While Grant detested McClernand, he had no justification for shelving him. On 22 May 1863 Grant assaulted the Vicksburg entrenchments for a second time, and reports from McClernand exaggerating his troops' success led Grant to commit more men to a hopeless and bloody effort. Though the assault was Grant's mistake, McClernand had compounded it. In June Grant removed him from command for issuing a bombastic congratulatory order to his men without sending it through headquarters. McClernand protested, but when Vicksburg fell 3 weeks later, so did McClernand.

Briefly restored to command of the XIII Corps Feb. 1864, McClernand served in the RED RIVER CAMPAIGN long enough to damage his reputation and become so ill that he resigned his commission. McClernand returned to Springfield and to his career as a Democratic politician. d. 20 Sept. 1890.   —JYS

McComb, William. CSA b. Mercer Cty., Pa., 21 Nov. 1828, McComb went with the Confederacy though he had lived in the South for only 7 years, moving in 1854 to Clarksville, Tenn., where he was a manufacturer.

With the outbreak of the war, he enlisted as a private in the 14th Tennessee, soon being elected 2d lieutenant and adjutant of the regiment, which, transferred east, fought at CHEAT MOUNTAIN in September. Early in 1862 McComb was promoted to major. He participated in the SHENANDOAH VALLEY, SEVEN PINES, SEVEN DAYS', CEDAR MOUNTAIN, and SECOND BULL RUN battles and campaigns. His gallant, capable performance

LC

earned him promotion to lieutenant colonel in June and colonel 2 Sept.

McComb led his regiment, which belonged to Brig. Gen. JAMES J. ARCHER's brigade, at ANTIETAM, where he was seriously wounded. He returned to his command in time for the Battle of CHANCELLORSVILLE, again suffering a grievous wound. After

another extended period of convalescence, McComb led his Tennesseans at the WILDERNESS, SPOTSYLVANIA, COLD HARBOR, and PETERSBURG during spring and summer 1864. In October he assumed command of the brigade, with subsequent promotion to brigadier general from 20 Jan. 1865. He surrendered with the army at Appomattox.

McComb lived briefly in Alabama and Mississippi before settling in Virginia in 1869. There he farmed in Louisa County for nearly half a century, dying on his plantation 21 July 1918.   —JDW

McCook, Alexander McDowell. USA b. Columbiana Cty., Ohio, 22 Apr. 1831, McCook is best known as the commander of the XX Corps of the Army of the Cumberland and for his participation in the Battles of PERRYVILLE, STONE'S RIVER, and CHICKAMAUGA.

One of the famous "FIGHTING MCCOOKS" of Ohio, Alexander graduated 30th in the West Point class of 1852. He served in Western posts until 1858, then was an instructor at West Point until 1861. His first Civil War service was in the defenses of Washington and in the FIRST BATTLE OF BULL RUN.

LC

McCook was appointed colonel of the 1st Ohio Infantry in August and brigadier general of volunteers 3 Sept. 1861. He commanded a brigade of the Army of the Ohio during the second day of the Battle of SHILOH and was promoted to major general 17 July 1862. He commanded a corps of the Army of the Ohio at Perryville in October and the right wing of the Army of the Cumberland, later the XX Corps, at Stone's River, Dec. 1862–Jan. 1863.

With others, McCook was blamed for the disaster at Chickamauga, Sept. 1863, where the XX Corps was routed and driven from the field. Though he was exonerated by a court of inquiry, he was not given another field command. From Feb. to May 1865 he commanded the District of Eastern Arkansas.

McCook remained in the Regular Army after the war, serving mostly in the West. During the 1880s he commanded the cavalry and infantry schools at Fort Leavenworth. He was commissioned brigadier general, Regular Army, in 1890 and major general in 1894. He retired in 1895 and died in Dayton, Ohio, 12 June 1903.   —JWR

McCown, John Porter. CSA b. Sevierville, Tenn., 19 Aug. 1815. McCown, who graduated 10th in the West Point class of 1840, spent the antebellum years with the 4th U.S. Artillery, rising to captain after receiving commendation for Mexican War service at the Battle of Cerro Gordo. He formally resigned from the U.S. Army 17 May 1861, having accepted a commission as lieutenant colonel in the Confederate army 16 Mar. He was then commissioned colonel in command of the artillery corps/Provisional Army of Tennessee, and promoted to brigadier general 12 Oct. 1861.

McCown served at the Battle of BELMONT, Mo., prematurely evacuated the garrison at NEW MADRID, Mo., and escaped in the collapse of FORT PILLOW, Tenn. Promoted to major general 10 Mar. 1862, he led the Army of the West (his division and those of Brig. Gens. DABNEY H. MAURY and LEWIS H. LITTLE) 20 June–3 July; in September took command of the Department of East Tennessee; then assumed divisional command under Lt. Gen. E. KIRBY SMITH. While serving in the Army of Tennessee, McCown came under Gen. BRAXTON BRAGG'S scrutiny. Bragg thought him his worst divisional commander but inexplicably chose him to begin the Battle of STONE'S RIVER 31 Dec. 1862, then complained when all

USMHI

went poorly. He charged McCown with disobedience of orders. McCown wanted Bragg relieved, and claimed he would leave the service to raise potatoes on his 4-acre Tennessee farm unless he was. A court-martial 16 Mar. 1863 found against the major general, relieving him of rank and pay for 6 months. An embittered McCown thought the Confederacy "a *damned* stinking cotton oligarchy . . . gotten up for the benefit of [Tennessee governor] Isham G. Harris and Jeff Davis and their damned corrupt cliques." Given his frankness, McCown saw little more Confederate service.

His last reported Confederate combat was in a skirmish at Morgantown, N.C., 17 Apr. 1865. Postwar, he taught school in Tennessee and farmed in Arkansas, dying in Little Rock 22 Jan. 1879.   —JES

McCullagh, Joseph Burbridge. journalist b. Dublin, Ireland, Nov. 1842. McCullagh, one of a poor family of 16 children, at 11 worked his way to the U.S. alone. In New York City he learned the printing trade, worked for the New York *Freeman's Journal,* migrated to Missouri to join the St. Louis *Advocate* in 1858, learned stenography, served on the St. Louis *Democrat's* staff in 1859 and as stenographer for the Missouri General Assembly 1859–60, then moved to Ohio in 1860 as a reporter for the Cincinnati *Daily Gazette,* becoming one of its first and best Civil War correspondents.

Assigned by the *Gazette* to cover Maj. Gen. JOHN C. FRÉMONT's activities in the Department of the West, McCullagh found that he disliked Frémont, his plans, and his conduct of the war in Missouri. He next moved to Tennessee, from a unique vantage point aboard the Federal gunboat *St. Louis* reported Brig. Gen. ULYSSES S. GRANT's victory at FORT DONELSON, and won distinction for working under Confederate artillery fire. In Apr. 1862 he covered the Union force's disastrous first day at SHILOH. The *Gazette*'s editor thought his story defamed the army's character and refused to publish it. Consequently, McCullagh quit to join the staff of the competitive Cincinnati *Commercial,* for which he covered operations in Mississippi and the 1863 fall of Vicksburg, and reported the Ohio gubernatorial election of 1863. He then became the *Commercial's* Washington, D.C., correspondent and briefly followed Maj. Gen. WILLIAM T. SHERMAN's army marching through Georgia. In the history of American journalism he is remembered for perfecting the technique of the personal interview and during his war years in Washington conducted many, all published under his byline, "Mack." He continued as the *Commercial's* correspondent in the capital and also worked as U.S. Senate reporter for the ASSOCIATED PRESS until 1868.

From 1868 to 1870 McCullagh was managing editor of the Cincinnati *Enquirer,* in 1870 bought a partial interest in the Chicago *Republican,* in 1871 lost most of his personal property and financial interests in the Chicago fire, then rejoined the St. Louis *Democrat* as editor. In a policy dispute, he left the *Democrat* for the new St. Louis *Globe* in 1873 and, following a merger in 1875, edited the consolidated St. Louis *Globe-Democrat* until his death in a household accident on 31 Dec. 1896.   —JES

McCulloch, Ben. CSA b. Rutherford Cty., Tenn., 11 Nov. 1811. Older brother of Confederate Brig. Gen. HENRY E. MCCULLOCH, Ben was one of the most colorful and popular figures of early Texas history. Following his neighbor Davy Crockett to Texas, he fought at the Battle of San Jacinto, became a surveyor in the new republic, and was a leader in the Texas Rangers.

Commissioned a brigadier general in the Confederate States Army 11 May 1861, McCulloch was placed in command of Indian Territory. He obtained the Cherokees' promise to fight for the Confederacy and authorized STAND WATIE to organize a Cherokee force.

USMHI

As commander of Arkansas, Louisiana, and Texas troops operating in northern Arkansas and southern Missouri, he led Confederate forces against Brig. Gen. NATHANIEL LYON's Union troops at the Battle of WILSON'S CREEK, 10 mi south of Springfield, Mo., 10 Aug. 1861. McCulloch personally led 2 companies of Louisiana infantry in a charge that captured 5 guns of Col. FRANZ SIGEL's command and routed the Union force. Because of casualties and lack of ammunition, the Confederates did not follow up their advantage.

McCulloch was a frontier fighter with little regard for formal military protocol or theory and usually wore a black velvet suit in the field. He had a stormy relationship with Maj. Gen. STERLING PRICE, with whom he was teamed at Wilson's Creek and other actions. Friction between the two was eased by the appointment of Maj. Gen. EARL VAN DORN as commander of the Trans-Mississippi District early in 1862.

McCulloch, Price, and Brig. Gen. ALBERT PIKE were Van Dorn's top commanders at the Battle of PEA RIDGE near Fayetteville, Ark., 7–8 Mar. 1862. About 10:30 a.m. on 7 Mar., McCulloch rode forward to reconnoiter enemy positions and was killed by enemy sharpshooter fire. His death was a contributing factor in the Confederate defeat at Pea Ridge, which gave the Union control of northern Arkansas and southern Missouri. At his death he was the second-ranking Confederate brigadier general.   —DS

McCulloch, Henry Eustace. CSA b. Rutherford Cty., Tenn., 6 Dec. 1816, the reserved younger brother of Brig. Gen. BEN MCCULLOCH settled in Guadalupe Cty., Tex., in 1837. 6 years later his neighbors elected him sheriff, an office he filled in addition to his farming. During the Mexican War he served as captain of a company of Texas Rangers, usually skirmishing against Indians along the frontier. He was elected to the state legislature in 1853, to the senate in 1855, and accepted an appointment as U.S. marshal in eastern Texas during James Buchanan's presidency.

McCulloch attended the state convention in 1861 as a secessionist, entering Confederate service as colonel of the 1st Texas Mounted Rifles in April. During the early months of fighting he helped clear the state of U.S. troops, posting Confederate garrisons at the frontier forts along the eastern edge of

LC

the Panhandle. McCulloch spent nearly all of his military career within the state's borders, and much of it assigned to frontier duty. He was promoted to brigadier general to rank from 14 Mar. 1862, refusing the gubernatorial nomination the next year in favor of army service.

He fought outside Texas once, commanding a brigade in Maj. Gen. JOHN G. WALKER's division during the campaign to relieve Vicksburg. On 7 June Walker sent McCulloch to lead the division's assault on Milliken's Bend. Though the attack ended in victory, his hesitance in battle prompted Maj. Gen. RICHARD TAYLOR to praise his bravery but criticize his inability to handle a large command.

McCulloch returned to Texas for the duration of the war, commanding districts and subdistricts within the state. After Gen. E. KIRBY SMITH surrendered the Trans-Mississippi, McCulloch retired to Guadalupe County to live his last 30 years as a farmer. d. Rockport, Tex., 12 Mar. 1895.   —PLF

McCulloch, Hugh. USP b. Kennebunk, Maine, 7 Dec. 1808. Descended from Scotsmen who had emigrated in the 1760s, McCulloch was the son of a shipbuilder and merchant.

He spent a year at Bowdoin College, taught school, studied law, and in 1832 was admitted to the bar. A year later he moved to Fort Wayne, Ind., where he became cashier and manager of the local branch of the state bank. In 1856 he was named to manage the parent institution, of which he also became president. Though initially reluctant to enter banking, he demonstrated a natural aptitude for it. Through his guidance, the State Bank of Indiana prospered, even during depressions: in 1857 it

LC

was one of a handful of banks nationwide that avoided suspension of specie payments.

In 1862 McCulloch went to Washington to lobby against a national bank bill, which he considered ruinous to the state banking system. Despite his efforts, the measure was enacted a year later and in a dramatic turnabout he accepted Treasury Sec. SALMON P. CHASE's offer to enforce the new law as comptroller of the currency. Largely because of his influence with state banks, he succeeded at this formidable task. Despite being a militant contractionist—he once remarked that God

had placed gold and silver on earth expressly to provide man a standard of value and medium of exchange—he ably administered the circulation of $450,000 in GREENBACKS as provided for in the LEGAL TENDER ACTS.

In 1865 McCulloch replaced Chase's successor, WILLIAM P. FESSENDEN, as secretary of the treasury. His major effort in this office was his attempt to retire, as quickly as possible, all greenbacks in circulation, which had depreciated considerably since their issuance. Despite support in Congress, a law to this end was not passed for more than a decade—the result, in one historian's words, of the public view that "an abundant currency based simply on federal credit and the country's worth was required for the general good."

In postwar years McCulloch labored to reduce the national debt, readjust public revenues, and reinstate Federal taxation in the South. Retiring from office in 1869, he spent several years in London as a representative of a U.S. banking house before returning briefly, 1884–85, as treasury secretary under Chester A. Arthur. In his final years he resided near Washington, D. C., dying in Prince George's Cty., Md., 24 May 1895.   —EGL

McDowell, Irvin. USA b. Columbus, Ohio, 15 Oct. 1818. McDowell graduated from West Point in 1838, 23d in a class of 45. From 1841 to 1845 he was an instructor of tactics at

his alma mater. During the Mexican War he served on the staff of Brig. Gen. JOHN E. WOOL and was brevetted captain. Until the outbreak of the Civil War he was a staff officer in the adjutant general's office in Washington.

Elevated to brigadier general of volunteers 14 May 1861, McDowell had the misfortune to lead the ill-prepared Union army against the Confederates under Brig. Gen. P.G.T. BEAUREGARD at Manassas Junction July 1861. The pressures of the moment, the "on to Richmond" mental-

USMHI

ity, and Pres. ABRAHAM LINCOLN's perception of a need for action forced McDowell's hand. His plan of attack has been described as "good on paper," but it demanded staff work and field leadership beyond Union resources. On the other hand, the equally ill-prepared Confederates were able to maintain a defense, inexperienced as they were. In the ensuing "battle of amateurs" the Union forces were scattered and forced into a humiliating retreat back to Washington.

McDowell was superseded by Maj. Gen. GEORGE B. MCCLELLAN and relegated to a corps command, but he was promoted to major general Mar. 1862. To McClellan's dissatisfaction, McDowell's corps was detached to protect the capital while McClellan embarked on his ill-fated PENINSULA CAMPAIGN of 1862. Had McDowell advanced on Richmond from the north and joined McClellan, he might have effected a decisive move against the Confederates. As it was, he was drawn away by Maj. Gen. THOMAS J. "STONEWALL" JACKSON's masterful foray into the Shenandoah Valley, which to a nervous Lincoln administration appeared as a threat to Washington.

This missed opportunity, not McDowell's fault, was compounded by the Union defeat under Maj. Gen. John Pope at SECOND BULL RUN. McDowell shared the blame with Pope for this debacle and filled no field command for the remainder of the war. He was posted to the Department of the Pacific in 1864 and thereafter commanded departments in the South and West. He retired in 1882, dying in San Francisco 4 May 1885. —JTH

McDowell, Va., Battle of. 8 May 1862 After his defeat at the Battle of KERNSTOWN, 23 Mar. 1862, Maj. Gen. THOMAS J. "STONEWALL" JACKSON withdrew his 6,000 troops southward up the Shenandoah Valley. The Confederate general halted at Swift Run Gap in the Blue Ridge Mts., where he regrouped and recruited new volunteers. Maj. Gen. NATHANIEL P. BANKS, who had defeated Jackson at Kernstown, cautiously trailed the Southerners with 15,000 men. Confederate guerrillas and cavalrymen harassed the Union march.

By late April, however, Jackson's command numbered 17,-000. Maj. Gen. RICHARD S. EWELL had arrived with 8,000 men, and Jackson assumed control of Brig. Gen. EDWARD JOHNSON's brigade of 3,000, stationed at West View, 7 mi west of Staunton. Additionally, from Richmond, came orders from Gen. ROBERT E. LEE, military adviser to JEFFERSON DAVIS, suggesting that Jackson undertake a diversionary attack in the valley to prevent further Union reinforcements from being sent against Richmond.

Jackson formulated a difficult, secret plan. Leaving Ewell at Swift Run Gap on Banks' flank, he decided to advance against Maj. Gen. JOHN C. FRÉMONT, whose 20,000-man Federal command was advancing on Staunton from the west. With Brig. Gen. TURNER ASHBY's cavalry preoccupying Banks, Jackson, with his brigades, started on the afternoon of 30 Apr. Heading eastward to deceive Banks, Jackson's men marched in a driving rainstorm. The roads soon turned into troughs of sodden clay, with the Confederates barely crawling along. Past Port Republic, through Brown's Gap to Mechum's Station on the Virginia Central Railroad, the weary Confederates advanced in one of the war's most harrowing marches.

Spilling onto railroad cars, the Southerners steamed toward Staunton, arriving 6 May. In what would become a hallmark of his command, Jackson's FOOT CAVALRY had covered, in terrible conditions, 92 mi in 4 marching days, with another 25 mi by rail. Meeting Johnson at West View, Jackson pushed the combined forces, numbering roughly 10,000, westward toward Frémont's leading units. Late on the afternoon of 7 May, Johnson's skirmishers encountered the pickets of Brig. Gen. ROBERT H. MILROY's Union brigade.

Milroy's troops withdrew across Bull Pasture River, the brigadier informing Brig. Gen. ROBERT C. SCHENCK of the Confederates' advance. Schenck rapidly started his brigade toward Milroy, marching his troops all night. Senior to Milroy, he assumed command when he arrived, deploying their 6,000 men in a defensive position at McDowell. Setlinger's Hill to the east dominated the town and the Union line and, when Jackson's troops started filing onto the hill, Schenck decided to withdraw his outnumbered brigades before they were trapped.

As Jackson was surveying the Federal lines for a way to turn them, Schenck launched an early afternoon attack. The Union commander only hoped to delay the Confederates long enough to ensure his troops' safe escape. The battle flared for nearly 4 hours as the Union thrusts were repulsed by the Southerners. Schenck finally ceased the attacks and withdrew toward the Allegheny Mts., with Ashby's cavalry in pursuit. The Confederates held the field and claimed a victory. Jackson lost 45 killed and 423 wounded, while Schenck counted 26

killed, 227 wounded, and 3 missing. The Confederacy suffered a grievous loss when Johnson, an excellent officer, was so severely wounded that he stayed out of the war for a year.

Jackson followed with his infantry the next day, but his pursuit floundered because of poor roads and effective Federal rearguard actions. He abandoned the pursuit at Franklin, in western Virginia, on the 12th, when he turned eastward toward the valley. With Ashby's horsemen screening his rear, Jackson headed toward Banks. The Battle of McDowell marked the initial engagement of Jackson's 1862 SHENANDOAH VALLEY CAMPAIGN. —JDW

McGowan, John, Jr. USN b. Port Penn, Del., 4 Aug. 1843. The son of JOHN MCGOWAN, SR., John, Jr., was appointed acting master's mate 8 Mar. 1862 and acting master 8 May. He commanded the *Wyandank* in operations of the Potomac flotilla and the NORTH ATLANTIC BLOCKADING SQUADRON, 1862–65. A senior officer credited him with "zealous and efficient conduct" in helping to run aground and destroy 2 BLOCKADE RUNNERS Feb. 1864. McGowan also participated in the naval attacks on FORT FISHER Dec. 1864 and Jan. 1865.

In 1866 he was appointed master. At the end of a distinguished career, he became a rear admiral 13 Apr. 1901, the day he retired. d. Twilight Park, N.Y., 13 Aug. 1915. —NCD

McGowan, John, Sr. U.S. Revenue Cutter Service b. Philadelphia, Pa., 3 Dec. 1805. In 1832 McGowan was appointed a lieutenant in the U.S. Revenue Cutter Service, a division of the Treasury Department, becoming a captain in 1852. Early in Jan. 1861 he was chosen by the government to captain the chartered steamer STAR OF THE WEST, carrying supplies and reinforcements to the beleaguered Federal garrison at FORT SUMTER in Charleston harbor, S.C. While attempting to enter that harbor 9 Jan., the *Star of the West* was fired on and hit by Confederate artillery on Morris Island. Unwilling to risk his ship and those aboard, he returned to New York.

During 1862 McGowan helped organize and direct the operation of the Federal Mosquito Fleet in Chesapeake Bay. While commanding the USRC *Cuyahoga* at New York, June 1863, he joined in the search for the Confederate bark *Tacony* off the northeast coast. McGowan continued in the employ of the Treasury Department until his retirement in 1871. His son, JOHN MCGOWAN, JR., rose to rear admiral. d. Elizabeth, N.J., 18 Jan. 1891. —NCD

McGowan, Samuel. CSA b. Laurens District, S.C., 9 Oct. 1819. An 1841 graduate of South Carolina College, McGowan studied law; volunteered for the Mexican War, rising to the rank of staff captain with a commendation for gallantry; and entered politics, serving for 13 years as a state legislator. By 1861 McGowan also had risen to the rank of major general in the militia, commanding a brigade during the bombardment of FORT SUMTER in 1861.

The South Carolinian then volunteered for Confederate service, acting as an aide-de-camp to Brig. Gen. MILLEDGE L. BONHAM at FIRST BULL RUN. That autumn he was appointed lieu-

USMHI

tenant colonel of the 14th South Carolina. Promoted to colonel early in 1862, he was assigned to Brig. Gen. MAXCY GREGG'S South Carolina brigade, and with the 14th saw bloody action in the SEVEN DAYS' CAMPAIGN, at CEDAR MOUNTAIN, SECOND BULL RUN, and FREDERICKSBURG. He was wounded twice, initially during the Seven Days', then severely at Second Bull Run. Throughout the campaigns McGowan displayed exceptional battlefield prowess and perception, reacting energetically and capably to the demanding combat.

When Gregg fell mortally wounded at Fredericksburg, McGowan assumed command of the brigade. Promoted to brigadier general to date from 17 Jan. 1863, he led it in battle at CHANCELLORSVILLE, where 3 May it suffered grievous losses in attacking the strong Union works. McGowan was wounded for a third time, resulting in an extended period of convalescence.

He returned to duty in time for the spring campaigns of 1864, leading the brigade at the WILDERNESS and SPOTSYLVANIA. In the latter battle he suffered his fourth wound in the searing combat at the "BLOODY ANGLE," 12 May. McGowan subsequently participated in the PETERSBURG CAMPAIGN and surrendered with the army at Appomattox, his combat record unexcelled by any other brigade commander.

Returning to his home in Abbeville, S.C., the distinguished general was elected to Congress but was denied his seat. In 1878 he gained a seat in the state legislature, and the following year was elected an associate justice of the state supreme court. McGowan served on the bench until defeated for reelection in 1893. He died at his home 9 Aug. 1897.

—JDW

McGuire, Hunter Holmes. CSA b. Winchester, Va., 11 Oct. 1835, McGuire, a doctor's son, attended local secondary schools and graduated from Winchester Medical College in

1855. He briefly studied at Jefferson Medical College in Philadelphia, returned home with a slight rheumatic ailment, briefly taught at Winchester, then returned to Jefferson, studying there until Dec. 1859. Following John Brown's HARPERS FERRY RAID and the rise of strong anti-Southern prejudice at his school, McGuire left Jefferson, entered the Medical College of Virginia at Richmond, took a second medical degree, then taught a class at the University of Louisiana until he entered

LC

Company F/2d Virginia Infantry as a private in 1861. He is remembered as THOMAS J. "STONEWALL" JACKSON'S personal friend and physician.

With his regiment, McGuire went to Harpers Ferry to serve under Colonel Jackson and was commissioned a surgeon in the medical department 4 May 1861. Jackson became a brigadier general in June and, on organizing the 1st Virginia Brigade, asked that McGuire be made brigade surgeon. As brigade surgeon and chief medical officer of the short-lived Confederate Army of the Shenandoah, McGuire went to the FIRST BATTLE OF BULL RUN with Jackson and on all his subsequent operations until Chancellorsville. With Henry Kyd Douglas and ALEXANDER S. "SANDY" PENDLETON, he became part of Jackson's colorful

staff, attended the medical needs of many Confederate notables, and benevolently dealt with his general's exotic physical complaints and theories. When Jackson was wounded at Chancellorsville, McGuire decided to amputate his left arm. The complications that set in and Jackson's death after a 10-day struggle deeply affected McGuire. For the rest of his life he remained a staunch supporter of the general's image and accomplishments and wrote several biographical sketches of Jackson.

For the rest of the war, McGuire, attached to the II Corps/Army of Northern Virginia, served as chief corps surgeon, organized its ambulance service, became medical director of the Army of Northern Virginia, then medical director of Lt. Gen. JUBAL A. EARLY's Valley Army. He was captured by Federal forces Mar. 1865 and shortly released in reciprocity for his policy of never holding Union surgeons.

Following the Confederates' surrender, he joined the Virginia Medical College faculty as professor of surgery, helped organize the Richmond University College of Medicine, became its president, and wrote extensively on gynecology and obstetrics. An account of his service and impressions of Jackson appeared in the Richmond *Dispatch* in 1891 and was reprinted in the *SOUTHERN HISTORICAL SOCIETY PAPERS* (vol. XIX). He died of a stroke 19 Sept. 1900 and was memorialized by a statute in Richmond's Capitol Square.

—JES

McIntosh, James McQueen. CSA b. Ft. Brooke, Fla., 1828, McIntosh was the son of a career soldier killed in the Mexican War and brother of JOHN B. MCINTOSH, who became

a brigadier general in the Federal army during the Civil War. Entering West Point in 1845, James graduated last in his class, leaving the academy as brevet 2d lieutenant in the 1st Infantry. He received his commission May 1851, transferred to the 1st Cavalry in 1855 as 1st lieutenant, and had advanced to captain by the time he resigned to join the Confederate Regular Army at the same rank May 1861. He carried south a solid reputation as an aggressive cavalry leader. In the Battle of WIL-

LC

SON'S CREEK in August, he led the 2d Arkansas Mounted Rifles and was a favorite of his commander, Brig. Gen. BEN MCCULLOCH. The next January, McIntosh received a commission as brigadier general in the Confederate Provisional Army. At PEA RIDGE, 7 Mar., he held command of McCulloch's cavalry. McCulloch fell dead early in the fighting and McIntosh took charge of the battle. Within minutes of his friend's death, the cavalryman was shot through the heart leading a daring and foolhardy charge on Union troops under Col. PETER J. OSTERHAUS and Brig. Gen. JEFFERSON C. DAVIS.

In his official battle report, Maj. Gen. EARL VAN DORN described McIntosh as alert, daring, and devoted to duty, his death a loss to any commander partly because of his great popularity with his men. He was one of the few to die in his "brilliant cavalry charge." DABNEY H. MAURY, also praised and promoted to brigadier for his performance at Pea Ridge, wrote after the war that McIntosh died from being in a place where he did not belong. Regardless, the simultaneous deaths of

McCulloch and McIntosh made the two the foremost heroes of Pea Ridge.

McIntosh's body, first buried at the Fort Smith National Cemetery in Arkansas, was later moved to Austin, Texas.

—PLF

McIntosh, John Baillie. USA b. Fort Brooke, Fla., 6 June 1829, McIntosh was the descendant of a Revolutionary War commander and the son of a Regular Army colonel. During the Mexican War, he served as a naval midshipman. Resigning in 1850, he settled in New Jersey, where he married and went into business with his father-in-law.

USMHI

Despite his family's social ties to the South, McIntosh cast his lot with the Union June 1861, even as his brother, West-Point-educated JAMES M. MCINTOSH, joined the Confederacy. Having applied for a Regular Army commission, he became a lieutenant in the 2d (later the 5th) U.S. Cavalry. Late in 1861 and early in 1862 he acquired a reputation for bravery and tactical expertise while serving in the Shenandoah Valley and on the Virginia peninsula. That June McIntosh commanded a volunteer infantry regiment at WHITE OAK SWAMP. Returning to the 5th Cavalry, he fought ably at SOUTH MOUNTAIN and ANTIETAM.

His service in the PENINSULA CAMPAIGN recommended him for a permanent position with the volunteers. In Nov. 1862 he was named colonel of the 3d Pennsylvania Cavalry, which he molded into one of the most effective mounted regiments in the Union. Noting this, Brig. Gen. ALFRED PLEASONTON gave him a brigade in spring 1863. In his new position McIntosh served at the Battle of KELLY'S FORD, 17 Mar., the first successful combat showing of the Federal cavalry in the East, and on Maj. Gen. GEORGE STONEMAN's raid during the Chancellorsville Campaign. Early that June he nearly resigned his commission in outrage at the demotion of a superior and friend, Brig. Gen. WILLIAM W. AVERELL. Persuaded to remain with the volunteers, he played a key role in keeping Maj. Gen. J.E.B. STUART from striking the Union right and rear at GETTYSBURG. In 1864 he fought in numerous engagements under Maj. Gen. PHILIP H. SHERIDAN, ultimately as a brigadier general.

McIntosh's active service ended at THIRD WINCHESTER, where a leg wound led to amputation. After the conflict, however, he rose to command the 42d U.S. Infantry. Before retiring in 1870, he also became governor of the Soldiers' Home in Washington, D.C., and superintendent of Indian affairs in California. d. New Brunswick, N.J., 29 June 1888.   —EGL

Mackall, William Whann. CSA b. Cecil Cty., Md., 18 Jan. 1817, Mackall graduated 8th in the 1837 class at West Point, served in the Seminole War, was a twice-brevetted officer of the Mexican War, and commanded artillery. After assignment as an assistant adjutant general in 1846, he spent much of the rest of his military life as a staff officer.

Offered a Union staff position as lieutenant colonel 11 May 1861, Mackall declined, resigned from Federal service 3 July, accepted a corresponding Confederate offer, and took assignment as Gen. ALBERT SIDNEY JOHNSTON's adjutant general.

LC

Mackall thought Johnston overrated and inefficient, became a partisan of Gen. P.G.T. BEAUREGARD in army politics, and through him was promoted to brigadier general as of 27 Feb. 1862. Replacing Brig. Gen. John P. McCown as commander of the men and batteries at ISLAND NO. 10 in Missouri, he lost the island in April. Captured and later exchanged, Mackall led a brigade briefly in Tennessee. For several days in Dec. 1862 he commanded the District of the Gulf, then, until spring, he headed a subdistrict.

West Point classmate Gen. BRAXTON BRAGG requested Mackall's assignment as chief of staff in the Army of Tennessee early in 1863. After the transfer came through in April, Mackall, dissatisfied, served through late September, requested relief, then received a brigade command in Mississippi. He became Gen. JOSEPH E. JOHNSTON's chief of staff Jan. 1864, but served only until July, when, unhappy about Gen. JOHN B. HOOD's assignment as head of the Army of Tennessee, he was relieved at his own request. Mackall received no more assignments and surrendered himself to Union authorities in Macon, Ga., 20 Apr. 1865.

Postwar, he farmed and speculated in Virginia real estate. d. on one of his farms in Fairfax Cty., 12 Aug. 1891.   —JES

McKean, William Wister. USN b. Philadelphia, Pa., 19 Sept. 1800, McKean was appointed acting midshipman 30 Nov. 1814, being promoted to lieutenant in 1825, commander in 1841, captain in 1855, and commodore in 1862. In Apr. 1861, commanding the *Niagara,* McKean returned to the U.S. from the Far East. While his ship was being refitted at the Boston Navy Yard, he "purged" disloyal Southerners among his officers by requiring all to take an oath of allegiance to the U.S. In Sept. 1861 McKean became flag officer commanding the GULF BLOCKADING SQUADRON. Still commanding the *Niagara,* he participated in the shelling of Fort McRee, Pensacola Navy Yard, and the town of Warrington, off the coast of western Florida, 22–23 Nov. 1861.

From January to June 1862 McKean commanded the Eastern Gulf Blockading Squadron, which covered the Florida gulf and east coast plus Cuba and the Bahamas, with Capt. DAVID G. FARRAGUT in control of the Western Gulf Blockading Squadron. In June 1862, ill health forced McKean to retire. He died at his home near Binghamton, N.Y., 22 Apr. 1865.   —NCD

Mackenzie, Ranald Slidell. USA b. Westchester Cty., N.Y., 27 July 1840. After attending Williams College, Mackenzie received appointment to West Point, graduating 1st in the class of 1862, and was commissioned a lieutenant of engineers 17 June.

Mackenzie's Civil War service was relentless. Until the Battle of the WILDERNESS, Mackenzie engaged in defensive and bridge-building projects, fought at SECOND BULL RUN, served on engineer duty in the ANTIETAM CAMPAIGN, and saw combat at FREDERICKSBURG, CHANCELLORSVILLE, and GETTYSBURG. Wounded at Second Bull Run, by June 1864 he had been brevetted to lieutenant colonel of Regulars for bravery. The next month he became colonel of volunteers to the 2d Connecticut Heavy Artillery, having already served in regimental command in the battles at the Wilderness and SPOTSYLVANIA.

NA

He took part in the early investment of PETERSBURG and received another wound. During Confederate Lt. Gen. JUBAL A. EARLY'S Raid on Washington, D.C., Mackenzie and the 2d Connecticut, serving as infantry, were hustled to the city's defenses. A brigade command and campaigning in the Shenandoah Valley with Maj. Gen. PHILIP H. SHERIDAN followed. After fighting at Opequon Creek, FISHER'S HILL, and Middletown, and taking another wound at CEDAR CREEK, he was made brigadier general of volunteers to rank from 19 Oct. 1864, given a divisional cavalry command at Petersburg, and fought at the Battle of FIVE FORKS and in the APPOMATTOX CAMPAIGN. He ended the war brevetted major general of volunteers and brigadier general of Regulars, as of 13 Mar. 1865.

After the war Mackenzie continued his military career in the Regular Army. Made colonel of the 41st Infantry 6 Mar. 1867 and transferred to the 4th Cavalry late in 1870, he forged an impressive army reputation in the West, chasing renegade Indians into Mexico and fighting hostile tribes and bandits through 1876. Promoted brigadier general of Regulars 26 Oct. 1882, he took disability retirement 10 July 1885 because of the wounds he had received in both the Civil and Indian wars. Suffering from chronic pain and severe psychological problems, Mackenzie died on Staten Island, N.Y., 19 Jan. 1889. He was a nephew of Confederate diplomat JOHN SLIDELL and nephew by marriage to Confederate Gen. P.G.T. BEAUREGARD.

—JES

McKinley, William. USA b. Niles, Ohio, 29 Jan. 1843. When he was 9, the future 25th president of the U.S. moved with his parents to Poland, Ohio, where he attended public

school and Union Seminary. In 1860 he entered Allegheny College in Meadville, Pa., but left because of poor health resulting from overstudy. He taught school briefly, then enlisted as a private in Company E of the 23d Ohio Volunteer Infantry Regiment, which was organized at Columbus and mustered in at Camp Chase 11 June 1862 with 950 men.

LC

In the 23d Ohio, more commanding and ranking officers would become famous than in any other regiment in the Union armies. Its first colonel was Maj. Gen. WILLIAM S. ROSECRANS; Eliakim P. Scammon, succeeding him, became a brigadier general; RUTHERFORD B. HAYES, following Scammon, was a brevet major general and the 19th president; James M. Comly, Hayes's successor, served as American minister to Hawaii; and Brev. Maj. WILLIAM MCKINLEY became the second president to have served in the regiment.

As part of the Kanawha Division, the regiment served in the ANTIETAM CAMPAIGN, and with Maj. Gen. PHILIP H. SHERIDAN in the Shenandoah Valley in 1864, but spent most of the war in minor but unpleasant duty in West Virginia, fighting miniature battles, cleaning out guerrillas, patrolling roads, and protecting Union sympathizers. Out of 2,230 who served in the regiment, 290 died of wounds and disease, placing it among the 300 fighting regiments suffering the highest losses during the war.

From private, McKinley advanced to captain as the regiment saw action at CARNIFIX FERRY, Princeton, SOUTH MOUNTAIN, ANTIETAM, Lynchburg, Berryville, THIRD WINCHESTER, FISHER'S HILL, and CEDAR CREEK. He was brevetted major 13 Mar. 1865 for "gallant and meritorious service during the campaign in West Virginia and in the Shenandoah Valley."

McKinley escaped Confederate bullets for 4 years; he died of an assassin's bullet in Buffalo, N.Y., 14 Sept. 1901.

—RDH

McKinstry, Justus. USA b. Columbia Cty., N.Y., 6 July 1814. Moving with his parents to Michigan as a youth, McKinstry entered West Point in 1834, graduating 40th in his

class. In the Mexican War, though a quartermaster captain, he led a company of volunteers at Contreras and Churubusco, winning the brevet of major. He remained in the supply service through the opening months of the Civil War, which he spent in St. Louis as chief quartermaster of Maj. Gen. JOHN C. FRÉMONT'S Department of the West.

LC

In mid-1861, under the exigencies of war, McKinstry was authorized to purchase for Frémont all manner of goods—supplies, weapons, rations, ammunition—at any price and on any terms he found acceptable. This opened irresistible opportunities for personal gain. Soon he was deep in graft and fraud, primarily through his collusion with a St. Louis hardware concern, Child, Pratt, & Fox. In exchange for a portion of the proceeds, McKinstry permitted the firm to make as much as a 300% profit on SHODDY, exorbitantly priced goods it sold to the government. Eventually, he forced all other contractors to sell first to Child, Pratt, & Fox, at prices the firm doubled when reselling the goods to McKinstry.

The quartermaster chief also purchased cavalry, artillery, and dray horses at outlandish prices. In one 400-head lot he bought, 5 horses soon died and 330 others proved too young, old, or sickly to meet government standards. At other times, McKinstry padded civilian-employee payrolls and skimmed the excess. He sometimes forged vouchers to show that contractors had received payments greater than they had asked, enabling him to pocket the difference. He also demanded kickbacks for construction contracts awarded in the department.

Though he escaped detection for many months and was even promoted to brigadier general of volunteers Sept. 1861, McKinstry was finally betrayed by disgruntled associates. Condemned by a congressional investigating committee for perpetrating "stupendous frauds," he was jailed, court-martialed, and Jan. 1863 became the only Civil War commander to be cashiered "for neglect and violation of duty, to the prejudice of good order and military discipline."

Though disgraced, he flourished in postwar life as a New York City stockbroker and a Missouri land agent, dying in St. Louis, Mo., 11 Dec. 1897. —EGL

McLaws, Lafayette. CSA b. Augusta, Ga., 15 Jan. 1821, McLaws was a division commander in the Army of Northern Virginia, an army that boasted such major generals as JUBAL A. EARLY, JOHN B. GORDON, AMBROSE P. HILL, JOHN B. HOOD, WILLIAM DORSEY PENDER, WILLIAM MAHONE, and ROBERT E. RODES. McLaws' commission as major general preceded that of all these men, yet they are much better known than he. His service in the I Corps under JAMES LONGSTREET from WILLIAMSBURG to the WILDERNESS was that of a good leader and a dependable soldier but not that of a spectacular fighter.

LC

McLaws graduated 48th in the West Point class of 1842, which was also Longstreet's graduating class, and served with the U.S. Army in the Mexican War. He resigned from the army Mar. 1861 and helped organize the 10th Georgia Infantry. He was soon promoted to brigadier, 25 Sept. 1861, and to major general, 23 May 1862, after serving in the PENINSULA CAMPAIGN under Maj. Gen. JOHN B. MAGRUDER. From the SEVEN DAYS' to the opening of the Wilderness and Spotsylvania campaigns, McLaws commanded a division of Georgians, South Carolinians, and Mississippians.

The Georgian served well in the ANTIETAM CAMPAIGN and at FREDERICKSBURG, but at CHANCELLORSVILLE and GETTYSBURG did not distinguish himself. After the failure of Longstreet's KNOXVILLE CAMPAIGN in fall 1863, McLaws was blamed for the disaster at FORT SANDERS and relieved of his command by Longstreet. Transferred to Georgia in the midst of controversy, he was cleared of all charges against him. McLaws was commanding troops under Gen. JOSEPH E. JOHNSTON when the latter surrendered near Durham Station, N.C., 26 Apr. 1865.

McLaws settled in Savannah, Ga., after the war and served with the U.S. Internal Revenue Service and as postmaster of Savannah after Reconstruction. He was active in Confederate veterans' organizations for many years after the war and wrote several articles on his division's part in battle. He died in Savannah, 24 July 1897, and is buried there. —JTP

McLean, Wilmer. McLean was a farmer whose home was located near Manassas Junction along the banks of Bull Run in Virginia. According to one story, a shell smashed through his window during the FIRST BATTLE OF BULL RUN. Whether or not this is true, he decided to find a new place for his family "where the sound of battle would never reach them." He bought a 2-story brick house with a veranda running across its front in a small village of no strategic value southwest of Richmond. The name of the village was Appomattox Court House, or Appomattox Station, as it was sometimes called.

When early in Apr. 1865 Gen. ROBERT E. LEE decided to surrender his forces, the ceremony was to be held in Appomattox. Lee sent an aide, Col. Charles Marshall, to the town to find a suitable place. There Marshall encountered McLean, who

suggested an abandoned home nearby. When Marshall said it would be unsatisfactory, McLean took the colonel to his own house. Soon after arrangements were made, Lee arrived to wait for Lt. Gen. ULYSSES S. GRANT. And so the man who had sought to escape the conflict found it ended in his front parlor.

After about 3 hours, when terms were agreed on, Grant and Lee departed. Almost immediately, according to an officer who was there, "Relic-hunters charged down upon the manor house and began to bargain for the numerous pieces of furniture." Some tried to pay McLean, who angrily refused their money; others simply carted off whatever they could carry or tore heavy items to shreds and splinters for souvenirs. It was a costly peace for Wilmer McLean. —RJM

McMillan, James Winning. USA b. Clark Cty., Ky., 28 Apr. 1825, McMillan fought in the Mexican War, then engaged in business in Indiana for 10 years before he became colonel of the 21st Indiana July 1861. In 1862 he served in Louisiana under Maj. Gen. BENJAMIN F. BUTLER, fought in an engagement at BATON ROUGE, and engaged in the disreputable cotton trade in the La Fourche District. After the 4 Sept. Confederate ambush near Boutte Station and Bayou des Allemands, McMillan's regiment trapped a Texas cavalry battalion and sent it to the swamps in retreat. His men captured 300 horses, 50 Confederates, and various pieces of equipment.

LC

McMillan was appointed brigadier general as of 29 Nov. 1862. He commanded a brigade and frequently a division during the RED RIVER CAMPAIGN of 1864, fighting at MANSFIELD, PLEASANT HILL, and CANE RIVER CROSSING, all in Louisiana, until the XIX Corps, to which his troops belonged, was sent to support Maj. Gen. PHILIP H. SHERIDAN in the Shenandoah. His men fought ably at THIRD WINCHESTER as well as at CEDAR CREEK, 19 Oct. 1864, where his division helped repulse Lt. Gen. JUBAL A. EARLY's attacking Confederates. Having been driven from his camp, McMillan turned his troops around, facing the threatening Confederates and allowing the troops to build a defense. Early wrote after the war: "The delay . . . [gave the enemy] a glorious victory given up by my own troops after they had won it."

Until the war ended McMillan served as a division commander in the Department of West Virginia. On 15 May 1865 he resigned from the army, moved to Kansas, and in 1871 received an appointment to the pension-office board of review in Washington, D.C., a post he held until he died in Washington 9 Mar. 1903. —FLS

McNair, Evander. CSA b. Richmond Cty., N.C., 15 Apr. 1820. As a child, McNair moved with his family to Mississippi, finally settling in Simpson County. He interrupted his business career during the Mexican War to enlist in the 1st Mississippi Rifles, the regiment commanded by future Confederate president JEFFERSON DAVIS. After the war McNair relocated in Washington, Ark., where he was living in 1861. When the state seceded, he raised an infantry battalion. By August the unit had been recruited to regimental strength and McNair elected its colonel.

Initially assigned to the Trans-Mississippi under Brig. Gen. BEN MCCULLOCH, McNair led his Arkansans into their first battle at WILSON'S CREEK, 10 Aug. 1861. The following March he assumed command at PEA RIDGE after McCulloch was killed and Col. LOUIS HÉBERT captured. From that time he held brigade command. His first chance to prove himself in combat came that September in the fighting at RICHMOND, Ky. Assigned to Brig. Gen. THOMAS J. CHURCHILL's division/Maj. Gen. E. KIRBY SMITH's corps, McNair distinguished himself in the flank attack to push back the Federal advance. Superiors praised his bravery, recommending promotion to brigadier general. Congress confirmed the appointment as of 4 Nov.

At his new rank, McNair led his men in some of the heaviest fighting at STONE'S RIVER during the determined but unsuccessful assault on the right flank of Union Brig. Gen. JEFFERSON C. DAVIS' division. He was subsequently attached to Gen. JOSEPH E. JOHNSTON's command in the effort to relieve VICKSBURG, and remained in the Western theater through the battle at CHICKAMAUGA, 19–20 Sept. 1863. Leading a force of 1,207 effectives, McNair played a key role in beating back the Federal brigade under Col. Hans C. Heg at Viniard's farm on the 19th. The next day, McNair fell severely wounded as his brigade was bloodied in the attack on the Union center. His men went on to capture 2 Federal batteries and win renown as the "Star Brigade of Chickamauga."

Recovered, McNair accepted permanent transfer to the Trans-Mississippi, with a brigade composed entirely of Arkansas troops. He participated in the last major Confederate offensive under Maj. Gen. STERLING PRICE during PRICE'S MISSOURI RAID OF 1864. When the war ended, McNair reentered business, first in New Orleans, later in Mississippi. d. Hattiesburg, Miss., 13 Nov. 1902.   —PLF

McNeill, John Hanson. CSA b. Moorefield, Va., 12 June 1815. Confederate partisan John Hanson "Hanse" McNeill, reared in Hardy County, migrated to Kentucky in 1838 and farmed there until 1843 or 1844. Returning to Virginia, he farmed near Moorefield, then moved to Missouri in 1848, settling 3 mi south of Columbia, where he became a nationally known breeder of Shorthorn cattle. During the secession crisis McNeill sided with Missouri Confederates, captained a company of secessionist militia serving under militia commander STERLING PRICE, fought in early Missouri engagements, and was wounded, captured, and imprisoned in Columbia. After brief

USMHI

parole and reconfinement in a St. Louis prison late in 1861, he escaped, making his way back to Virginia with his sons Jesse, William, and George.

McNeill solicited for a command in South Branch Valley, surrounding Moorefield. Through Aug. 1862 he raised volunteers and 5 Sept. became captain of Company E/18th Virginia Cavalry, authorized by Col. JOHN D. IMBODEN to operate in concert with his 1st Virginia Partisan Rangers. Son Jesse, com-

missioned a 1st lieutenant, served as McNeill's second-in-command. Known as MCNEILL'S RANGERS, the force operated successfully against troops of Union Maj. Gens. BENJAMIN F. KELLEY, GEORGE CROOK, and PHILIP H. SHERIDAN for the duration of the war, McNeill often serving with fellow partisans HARRY GILMOR and JOHN S. MOSBY in guerrilla operations in the SHENANDOAH VALLEY and against the BALTIMORE & OHIO RAILROAD.

Though most often operating independently, McNeill helped plan and execute an Apr. 1863 raid in western Virginia, screened movements of Confederates in West Virginia during the GETTYSBURG CAMPAIGN, served under Col. THOMAS L. ROSSER in operations against Federals in the Moorefield area, and fought in peripheral operations against Maj. Gen. FRANZ SIGEL's troops during the BATTLE OF NEW MARKET.

Raiding Union supply trains, camps, and railroads made him notorious. To frighten him, in summer 1863 his wife, daughter, and 4-year-old son, living as refugees in Ohio, were arrested while trying to reach family members in West Virginia, then imprisoned briefly in CAMP CHASE, Columbus, Ohio.

McNeill's tactics alienated his superiors. Rosser denigrated his field performance, and in spring 1864 Imboden had him court-martialed for accepting into his command deserters from Confederate national service and refusing to return them when ordered. He was acquitted of the charge.

McNeill fought with unremitting success until 3 Oct. 1864, when, leading 60 Rangers, he attacked 100 Union troops at Mount Jackson, Va., in the Shenandoah Valley. Badly wounded in the fight, he ordered his men to leave him at a nearby home, then withdraw. Days later he was captured by Federals and interrogated by Sheridan. On 7 or 8 Oct., he was rescued by a stealthy party of Confederates sent by Lt. Gen. JUBAL A. EARLY. Taken to Harrisonburg, he died of his wound 9 Nov. 1864.   —JES

McNeill's Rangers. CSA Raised in Hardy Cty., Va., by prominent native son Capt. JOHN H. MCNEILL, McNeill's Rangers entered Confederate service as Company E/18th Virginia Cavalry 5 Sept. 1862 to fight as PARTISAN RANGERS under the nominal command of Col. JOHN D. IMBODEN. As a guerrilla unit, its complete roster has never been fully documented. Though the Southern Historical Society published a partial listing in postwar years, it is believed the rangers rarely mustered 100 members. Late in 1862 Adj. Gen. SAMUEL COOPER ordered Imboden, with the individual rangers' consent, to muster the unit into Confederate national service. All but 17 men left McNeill at that time, and the captain was permitted to recruit replacements for partisan service.

Under Captain McNeill, the rangers rode on the Apr. 1863 cavalry raid in western Virginia led by Brig. Gen. WILLIAM E. "GRUMBLE" JONES and Colonel Imboden, fought in diversionary actions during the GETTYSBURG CAMPAIGN, raided in southern Pennsylvania and around New Creek, W.Va., served in Maj. Gen. John C. Breckinridge's 1864 campaign against Maj. Gen. Franz Sigel's Federals in the SHENANDOAH VALLEY, and raided Union lines of supply and communication, several times cutting the BALTIMORE & OHIO RAILROAD. Using the town and country around Moorefield, W.Va., as a base, the rangers captured tons of Federal supplies during the war, on 10 Sept. 1863 captured almost the entire Federal 1st West Virginia Infantry camped outside Moorefield, and during Union Maj. Gen. DAVID HUNTER's summer 1864 campaign in the Shenandoah Valley, won their first major propaganda victory when they seized 60 members of the Federal 6th West Virginia Cavalry, caught bathing nude in the South Branch River.

This humorous success was eclipsed on 3 Oct. 1864, when Captain McNeill received a mortal wound in a raid on Mount Jackson, Va. His son, 1st Lt. Jesse McNeill, assumed command of the unit, led it during Brig. Gen. THOMAS L. ROSSER'S raid on the Federal supply depot at New Creek (see ROSSER'S NEW CREEK, W.VA., RAID), then engineered its second major coup, the 21 Feb. 1865 kidnapping of Union Maj. Gens. GEORGE CROOK and BENJAMIN F. KELLEY from the Revere House hotel in Cumberland, Md. The rangers' guerrilla activity continued until Jesse McNeill, 24 Apr. 1865, conceded that he was operating without orders and surrendered himself and 30 men to Brig. Gen. Rutherford B. Hayes at New Creek.

Some histories of campaigns and actions involving McNeill's Rangers indicate that the unit was commanded by John H. McNeill during late 1864. This error is attributable to Federal records and recordkeepers, unaware of the captain's death behind Confederate lines in November of that year. —JES

McPherson, James Birdseye. USA b. near Clyde, Ohio, 14 Nov. 1828, McPherson grew up in extreme poverty. Thanks to a merchant who befriended him, he secured an appointment to West Point, from which he graduated in 1853, 1st in his class. Posted to the Corps of Engineers, he gained a reputation as one of the most promising young officers in the army. Following the outbreak of the Civil War he served as an aide to Maj. Gen. HENRY W. HALLECK, then as chief engineer to Maj. Gen. U. S. GRANT during the FORTS HENRY AND DONELSON CAMPAIGN, the Battle of SHILOH, and the Federal occupation of West Tennessee. On the recommendations of

USMHI

Halleck and Grant he was promoted to brigadier general 19 Aug. 1862 and to major general 2 months later. In Jan. 1863 he became commander of the XVII Corps in Grant's army. In that capacity he performed excellently during the VICKSBURG CAMPAIGN, his corps taking the leading part in winning the decisive Battle of CHAMPION'S HILL, 16 May 1863.

In Feb. 1864 he led his corps in Maj. Gen. WILLIAM T. SHERMAN'S MERIDIAN CAMPAIGN, Miss. The following month he took command of the Army of the Tennessee after Sherman succeeded Grant as head of Union forces in the West. Early in May 1864, at the outset of the ATLANTA CAMPAIGN, Sherman sent him on an unsuccessful maneuver through SNAKE CREEK GAP to strike at the rear of Gen. JOSEPH E. JOHNSTON'S retreat. During subsequent operations in north Georgia, Sherman repeatedly used McPherson's army to outflank strong Confederate defense lines. On 22 July, as McPherson again sought to do this, the Confederates, now under Gen. JOHN B. HOOD, delivered a surprise counterattack southeast of Atlanta. Riding forward to investigate, McPherson encountered a force of Confederates, who shot and killed him when he tried to escape.

By all accounts McPherson's personality was charming, his character noble, and his mind brilliant. Sherman once predicted that if the war lasted long enough, McPherson would eclipse in military reputation not only himself but also Grant. Since McPherson never held independent command, the most that definitely can be said is that he was a highly competent corps commander. —AC

McRae, CSS. The *Marquis de la Habana,* an 830-ton seagoing steamer of Mexican origin seized by the U.S. as a pirate vessel, was renamed the *McRae,* becoming one of the first 2 ships acquired by the Confederacy in its efforts to build a navy. The vessel became a part of the small fleet, commanded by Capt. GEORGE N. HOLLINS, assembled around New Orleans to protect the Mississippi River from the advance of Federal ships.

Early on the morning of 12 Oct. Federal vessels were detected in the darkness coming up the river. Hollins rushed down with his fleet, driving the enemy back to Southwest Pass. He reported to the Navy Department in Richmond: "It was a complete success." The *McRae,* most heavily armed of the Confederate craft with 8 guns, aided in the shelling.

Early in 1862 the *McRae,* which had been moved during the winter to near New Madrid, Mo., served as Hollins' flagship until he was transferred to other duty 18 Apr. Meanwhile, it was called back to the defense of New Orleans, anchoring just below the city at FORTS JACKSON AND ST. PHILIP.

At 3 a.m., 24 Apr., Federal ships again came up the river. The *McRae,* commanded by 1st Lt. Thomas B. Huger, formerly a lieutenant in the U.S. Navy, led the Confederate attack. Early in the firing one of its guns exploded, setting fire to the ship. The flames were extinguished, but shortly afterward Huger was mortally wounded by a shot from the USS *Iroquois,* the vessel on which he had served before resigning to fight for the Confederacy. He was succeeded by 23-year-old Lt. Charles W. Read of Mississippi.

The *McRae* was so badly damaged by the more powerful Union ships that it had to be run ashore near Fort St. Philip. 2 days later, after the forts had surrendered, it was delegated to take the wounded to New Orleans under a flag of truce, then to return.

After unloading the wounded, the *McRae* headed back to the forts. But once out in the river, it struck something under the water and began to leak badly. Though aided by a police force from the city, Read had to abandon the ship. It sank the morning of 29 Apr. —VCJ

McRae, Dandridge. CSA b. Baldwin Cty., Ala., 10 Oct. 1829, McRae settled in Searcy, Ark., after graduating from South Carolina College in 1849. He practiced law and for 6 years held an appointment as clerk of the county and circuit courts.

In 1861 McRae resigned his post as state inspector general to enter Confederate service as major of the 3d Battalion of Arkansas Infantry. The 3d Battalion became the 21st Arkansas, with McRae commanding as colonel during the unit's first fight at WILSON'S CREEK. Brig. Gen. BEN MCCULLOCH, McRae's immediate superior, praised the civilian commander's coolness

USMHI

under fire as he led his men in their advance. He fought again at PEA RIDGE, 7–8 Mar. 1862. Later that spring Brig. Gen. THOMAS C. HINDMAN lauded McRae as "indomitable" for force-marching his men 25 mi in a day to reinforce Brig. Gen. ALBERT RUST for operations around Des Arc.

If McRae shaped his men into good soldiers, he did so indifferent to military protocol. In Oct. 1862, Maj. Gen. THEOPHILUS H. HOLMES reported that McRae's Arkansans were a "crude mass of undisciplined material," almost as poorly armed as drilled. The antipathy between the 2 men resurfaced after the July 1863 attack on Helena, Ark., during the campaign to relieve VICKSBURG, when Holmes accused McRae of "misbehavior before the enemy" for having failed to reinforce Brig. Gen. Thomas Fagan in the lines in front of Hindman's Hill. Fagan and Maj. Gen. STERLING PRICE came to his defense and Gen. E. KIRBY SMITH cleared him of the charges Dec. 1864. The aggrieved commander later served under Price during the RED RIVER CAMPAIGN, fighting at Marks' Mills and JENKINS' FERRY.

McRae resigned his commission later in 1864, returned to his law practice in Searcy, and in 1881 was elected deputy secretary of state. d. Searcy, 23 Apr. 1899. —PLF

MacRae, William. CSA b. Wilmington, N.C., 9 Sept. 1834, MacRae was a civil engineer during the antebellum years. When North Carolina seceded, he enlisted as a private in the Monroe Light Infantry but was soon elected its captain when it became a part of the 15th North Carolina.

LC

The regiment saw little action during the war's first year. In spring 1862 the 15th, now a part of Brig. Gen. HOWELL COBB's brigade, fought in the Virginia campaigns. MacRae, promoted to lieutenant colonel in April, gained battle experience in the PENINSULA, SEVEN DAYS', and SECOND BULL RUN campaigns. At Antietam he temporarily commanded the brigade's 250 men, repelling 3 Federal assaults before withdrawing with only 50 men still in the ranks. Returning to the regiment, he fought at Marye's Heights in the Battle of FREDERICKSBURG.

Early in 1863 the 15th transferred to North Carolina, where it served under Brig. Gen. JOHN R. COOKE. MacRae was promoted to colonel in February. The regiment returned to the Army of Northern Virginia after the invasion of Pennsylvania. During the BRISTOE CAMPAIGN in October, MacRae assumed temporary command of Brig. Gen. WILLIAM W. KIRKLAND's brigade when Kirkland fell wounded at Bristoe Station.

Noted for his discipline, MacRae particularly distinguished himself in the campaigns of 1864. When Kirkland was again wounded, near Gaines' Mill early in June, MacRae, with the temporary rank of brigadier general, once more led the brigade. His promotion was later made permanent, to date from 4 Nov. As a brigadier, MacRae excelled on 2 occasions during the battles around Petersburg. On 25 Aug., at REAMS' STATION, his brigade and 2 others, without firing a shot, charged the Union works, dislodging Federal infantry and capturing a battery. At BURGESS' MILL, 27 Oct. he displayed remarkable bravery and coolness. After his brigade had broken a Federal line and seized a battery, it fought, unsupported, against mounting Union numbers until darkness allowed the men to withdraw safely. He surrendered with his veterans at Appomattox.

Penniless, MacRae returned to North Carolina but eventually prospered as superintendent of a number of railroads. His devotion to work, however, wrecked his health, and he died in Augusta, Ga., 11 Feb. 1882. —JDW

Maffitt, John Newland. CSN b. at sea, 22 Feb. 1819. After Maffitt's father became a Methodist minister, the family was in such reduced circumstances that the boy was adopted by his uncle, Dr. William Maffitt, who lived near Fayetteville, N.C. Later John attended school in Westchester Cty., N.Y., and at 13 was appointed midshipman in the U.S. Navy.

LC

On 28 June 1838 Maffitt was promoted to passed midshipman, remaining on sea duty until spring 1842, when he was ordered to the Coast Survey. There, for more than 15 years, he was engaged in charting Atlantic coastal waters. Placed on the reserve list in 1857, he appealed and was restored to service with sea commands.

When the Civil War began, Maffitt resigned and 8 May 1861 was commissioned lieutenant in the Confederate States Navy. He served 3 tours of duty on Confederate combat vessels: on the gunboat *Savannah,* the cruiser *FLORIDA,* and the ironclad *ALBEMARLE.* Officially credited with the capture of 22 enemy merchantmen, he was promoted to commander 29 Apr. 1863. Maffitt is primarily remembered for his extraordinary skill in running the blockade in merchant ships. At various times during the war he commanded the *Cecile,* the *Theodora,* the *Florie,* the *Lillian,* and the *Owl.* His service on the *Owl* was a classic in the art of running the blockade.

After the war Maffitt commanded a British ship chartered to Brazil and, for a short time in 1870, a Cuban revolutionary ship. That ended his life at sea. On 23 Nov. 1870, he married for the third time and settled at "The Moorings" near Wilmington, N.C. There he wrote a novel, *Nautilus* (1871), and a number of excellent magazine articles about his Confederate naval career. When he died, 16 May 1886, in Wilmington, N.C., he left an unfinished memoir about piracy in the West Indies. Maffitt was buried in Oakdale Cemetery, Wilmington. —JOH

Magoffin, Beriah. war governor b. Harrodsburg, Ky., 18 Apr. 1815. Having graduated from Centre College in 1835, Magoffin studied law at Transylvania College and opened a practice in 1839. A Democrat, he served as a presidential elector 1844–56; in the state senate, 1850; and in the governor's chair, 1859–62. When fighting supplanted the threat of civil war in 1861, Magoffin tried to keep Kentucky neutral, refusing both Confederate and Federal calls for troops. Contemporaries accused him of being a secessionist working secretly to take Kentucky out of the Union. While he did allow Confederate recruiters to operate in the state, his private and public correspondence support the sincerity of his insistence on neutrality. Idealistic almost to the point of foolishness, he hoped to spare the state from war and serve as a mediator between the warring sections.

LC

Pressed to choose sides as Confederate and Federal troops invaded the state, Magoffin wanted to submit the issue of loyalty to the voters, whom he believed should make the decision. The pro-Union legislature refused to cooperate, and 18 Aug. 1862, facing threats of assassination, Magoffin resigned. He returned to his legal practice in Harrodsburg, interrupting his retirement from politics to serve again in the state legislature 1867–69. d. Harrodsburg, 28 Feb. 1885.   —PLF

Magrath, Andrew Gordon. war governor b. Charleston, S.C., 8 Feb. 1813, Magrath was the son of an immigrant who had fought in the Irish rebellion of 1798. He attended a local academy, was graduated at the head of his class at South Carolina College in 1831, spent some months at Harvard Law School, and, except for 2 years in the state legislature, practiced law in Charleston 1835–56. From 1856 until shortly before the Civil War, he was a judge of the U.S. District Court.

A pro-slavery Democrat, Magrath counseled against disunion when his state considered it in the early 1850s. Less than a decade later, however, he so ardently supported STATES RIGHTS that he urged secession. On 7 Nov. 1860 he resigned his judgeship; in a letter to Pres. James Buchanan he decreed that if South Carolina left the Union he "would not hesitate" to go with her. His words circulated widely and he became a local hero.

Thereafter Magrath increased his efforts to make secession a reality, achieving success 20 Dec. 1860. When South Carolina reorganized as an independent republic, he became secretary of state in the executive council of Gov. FRANCIS W. PICKENS. Before the firing on FORT SUMTER, he held extensive negotiations with the Buchanan and Abraham Lincoln administrations over the garrison's disposition. When war commenced, he became a Confederate judge. Soon his court decisions in favor of state sovereignty, especially that striking down the Confederate war tax on state securities, made him *persona non grata* in Richmond.

On 14 Dec. 1864 Magrath succeeded MILLEDGE L. BONHAM as governor of South Carolina. In office he supported some measures instituted by JEFFERSON DAVIS' government, including conscription, but more often joined Govs. JOSEPH E. BROWN of Georgia and ZEBULON B. VANCE of North Carolina in opposing Davis' concept of centralized rule. He resisted Confederate confiscation, blamed Davis for widespread abuse of civil rights, and criticized the military strategy that emanated from Richmond. In the last weeks of the conflict he plotted with Brown and Vance to pool state troops and force reforms in Confederate military and political philosophy.

Magrath fled his office mid-Feb. 1865 on Maj. Gen. WILLIAM T. SHERMAN's approach; in April, after returning, he was captured at Columbia and imprisoned. He eventually resumed his law practice, dying in Charleston, 9 Apr. 1893.   —EGL

Magruder, John Bankhead. CSA b. Port Royal, Va., 1 May 1807. "He's the hero for the times," boasted one Civil

War ballad, "the furious fighting Johnny B. MaGruder."

LC

An artillerist, the West Point graduate ranked 15th in the class of 1830, proved himself a good soldier in the Seminole War and again during the Mexican War, when cited for meritorious conduct. Commanding an artillery battery in Washington, Magruder resigned from the U.S. Army when civil war came. Commissioned a colonel in the Confederate infantry June 1861, he was assigned to the Virginia peninsula and commanded at BIG BETHEL, where Confederates were victorious in the first land battle of the war.

Though a relatively small engagement involving scarcely more than 300 Confederates at any time, Big Bethel made Magruder a celebrity. Pompous, egotistical, and given to theatrical behavior, he thrived on the recognition. His comrades nicknamed him "Prince John" because of his fondness for lavish entertainment, courtliness toward the ladies, and fashionable military dress. He ordered dress parades and reviews followed by elaborate dinner parties for even marginal dignitaries visiting his commands. At the height of his popularity the Richmond *Dispatch* called him "The picture of the Virginia gentleman, the frank and manly representative of the chivalry of the dear Old Dominion."

Magruder advanced to brigadier general 17 June 1861 and to major general 7 Oct., but his failures at MALVERN HILL, attributed to drunkenness and recklessness, led to public disfavor and loss of his command. His requested transfer to the Trans-Mississippi theater was delayed when Richmond recalled him to defend his conduct during the SEVEN DAYS' CAMPAIGN. Finally assigned to the District of Texas, he remained there until the war's end. He redeemed himself somewhat by capturing the Federal ship *Harriet Lane* to break the Texas blockade, then defeated Union troops to recapture GALVESTON Jan. 1863.

Proud, defiant, and unwilling to apply for parole, after the war he migrated to Mexico and fought under Maximilian. On the emperor's defeat he settled in Houston, Tex., where he died 18 Feb. 1871.   —PLF

Mahan, Dennis Hart. USA b. New York City, 2 Apr. 1802, Mahan abandoned medical school to attend the U.S. Military Academy, where he studied drawing. In 1824 he graduated at the head of his class with an outstanding academic record that earned him a commission as 2d lieutenant in the Corps of Engineers and a 2-year appointment as assistant professor of mathematics and engineering at the academy. Impressed by his hard work and exceptional ability as a military theorist, the War Department sent him to Europe to observe military institutions and public works projects. He stayed abroad 4 years, studying under Napoleon's officers at the School of Application for Engineers and Artillery at Metz, France.

2 years after his return to West Point in 1830, he was promoted to professor of civil and military engineering. Through his classroom passed most of the men destined to become important commanders in the U.S. and Confederate armies. A strict disciplinarian who demanded respect and excellence from his students, Mahan taught the leading European theories

of military science adapted to his perceptions of the changing nature of warfare. Stressing the importance of defensive tactics, he instructed cadets in the art of entrenchment and fortification, principles critical to the siege warfare and the technical advances in weaponry that evolved during the Civil War. Fixed trench warfare, he taught, should be combined with the skillful maneuvering of troops and the use of the flank attack to achieve victory.

His 2 most important works, *Complete Treatise of Field Fortification* (1836) and *Elementary Treatise of Advance-Guard, Out-Post, and Detachment Service of Troops* (1847), were widely read by Regular Army officers through the antebellum years, and both were reprinted in Richmond for Confederate officers' use during the Civil War.

Rather than discard the Jominian preference for the direct frontal assault, Mahan advocated its use to counterattack after the enemy had been repulsed from one's own trenches (*see also* JOMINI'S *TREATISE ON GRAND MILITARY OPERATIONS*). That Revolutionary-era military thought continued to influence Civil War generals is evident by the number of frontal attacks they ordered, but the early proponents of entrenching during the Civil War had been Mahan's students at West Point.

The nation's preeminent military educator continued to teach at West Point while his theories were being tested on Civil War battlefields. Later they would exert a profound effect on 20th-century trench warfare. Mahan's 47-year army career ended 16 Sept. 1871, when he accidentally walked off the side of a ship in New York City and drowned. His son, Alfred Thayer Mahan, became the nation's leading theorist on naval warfare. *See also* STRATEGY and TACTICS.   —PLF

Mahone, William. CSA b. Southampton Cty., Va., 1 Dec. 1826, Mahone was one of the officers of the Army of Northern Virginia who emerged as leaders of high rank and reputation in the campaigns after CHANCELLORSVILLE. From the WILDERNESS to APPOMATTOX, Mahone's troops were considered some of the best fighters in the army, making their commander one of Gen. ROBERT E. LEE's most trusted generals.

NA

Mahone was a graduate of the Virginia Military Institute at Lexington. Before the war he was a civil engineer, working for numerous railroads in the state. When Virginia seceded, Mahone was president and superintendent of the Norfolk & Petersburg Railroad. He was almost immediately appointed colonel of the 6th Virginia Infantry, which he commanded at the capture of Norfolk.

Commissioned brigadier general 16 Nov. 1861, Mahone served with his Virginia brigade in the Army of Northern Virginia from SEVEN PINES to the CRATER. He fought in all the army's major battles except ANTIETAM, when he was recovering from a serious wound suffered at SECOND BULL RUN. For his part in repulsing the Federal assault at the Crater, near Petersburg, 30 July 1864, the Virginian was promoted to major general and given command of a division, which he led until the surrender at Appomattox.

After the war Mahone returned to his work with the Norfolk & Petersburg Railroad and quickly became involved in Virginia politics. He was elected for a term to the U.S. Senate in 1880 on the Readjuster ticket, a Virginia version of the Republican party. The control of state politics was virtually in Mahone's hands for a time, and he remained active in the affairs of Virginia until his death in Washington, D.C., 8 Oct. 1895.
—JTP

Maine. In the 1860 election Maine voters fully endorsed ABRAHAM LINCOLN and native son HANNIBAL HAMLIN, who would serve as vice-president until the closing months of civil war in 1865. An abolition stronghold, Maine saw the war as a crusade to end slavery and gave vigorous support. All together, some 67,000 Maine men saw duty in 35 state military regiments, special units, or in marine or navy outfits. Of these almost 9,000 lost their lives, while 11,000 were incapacitated by illness or wounds. Maine troops played a sizable part in the Gettysburg victory in 1863.

Several Maine officers achieved distinction during the war and afterward. Among them, Maj. Gen. OLIVER O. HOWARD commanded Maj. Gen. WILLIAM T. SHERMAN's right wing on the march through Georgia, later headed the FREEDMEN'S BUREAU, and helped set up Howard University in Washington (serving as its president for 5 years) and Lincoln Memorial University in Tennessee. Brig. Gen. JOSHUA L. CHAMBERLAIN, a college professor before the war, fought from ANTIETAM to APPOMATTOX (where he headed troops accepting the Confederate surrender), later served as 4-term governor of Maine, then became president of Bowdoin College. After a fine wartime record, Brig. Gen. ADELBERT AMES served as Reconstruction senator, then governor, of Mississippi.

The maritime segment of the Maine population—shipbuilders, merchants, agents who served the disrupted transatlantic cotton trade—were less then enthusiastic about a war that wreaked havoc with trade and destroyed scores of Maine-based vessels. But a majority of Maine residents, imbued with reforming zeal, cheered that the war had eliminated slavery in America.
—DL

1st Maine Heavy Artillery. Organized at Bangor in summer 1862, this regiment was mustered in as the 18th Maine Volunteer Infantry. Under Col. Daniel Chaplin, it was sent to Washington late in August as part of the capital's defense force. It drilled alternately as infantry and artillery until Dec. 1863, when it was reorganized, reinforced, and redesignated the 1st Maine Heavy Artillery.

5 months later it joined a 10,000-man force that Lt. Gen. ULYSSES S. GRANT withdrew from the capital defenses to replenish losses suffered by the Army of the Potomac in the BATTLE OF THE WILDERNESS. On 15 May 1864 Chaplin's "heavies" joined the II Corps near Spotsylvania Court House and were immediately employed as infantry. The regiment was showered by taunts from veteran troops until it proved itself as a fighting force in its first engagement. On 19 May, when part of Lt. Gen. RICHARD S. EWELL's corps attacked II Corps supply trains, it repulsed the assault, fighting with a spirit and energy that only rookie troops could have mustered. For their success the Maine men suffered 155 killed or mortally wounded and 369 wounded.

Throughout the next 4 weeks, during which the army crossed the James River to Petersburg, the regiment saw limited action, but on 18 June, during a series of attacks east of the city, the heavies were chosen to spearhead an offensive against Confederate works near the Hare house. When the enemy unleashed its rifle and cannon fire, the regiment's supports halted, leaving the newcomers to attack alone across open ground. This they did, much to the surprise of their more experienced comrades, though they found the field "a burning, seething, crashing, hissing hell." Only a few survivors reached the works; 635 were killed or wounded, the greatest loss of any Union regiment in any battle.

The remnant of the 1st Maine served under Colonel Chaplin, and, following his death by a sharpshooter's ball 17 Aug., under Lt. Col. Thomas H. Talbot, until Appomattox. By war's end it had lost 23 officers and 418 men killed or dead of wounds, 215 dead of disease, and 922 wounded. Truly the regiment lived up to its nickname, the "Bloody First Maine." —EGL

17th Maine. Recruited in the state's southern counties, this outfit was organized at Cape Elizabeth, where it mustered in 18 Aug. 1862. 3 days later it moved to Washington, D.C., and remained there on garrison duty under Col. Thomas A. Roberts for 2 months. It was then attached to the 3d Brigade/1st Division/III Corps/Army of the Potomac. After its first action, at FREDERICKSBURG, where the regiment was lightly engaged along the Union left center, it took part in BURNSIDE's "MUD MARCH."

At CHANCELLORSVILLE, 3 May 1863, the 17th Maine experienced its first extensive battle service as part of Brig. Gen. DAVID B. BIRNEY's division. Positioned along the Orange Turnpike west of the Chancellor house, it was devastated by Confederate cannon and sharpshooters on high ground nearby. Forced to retreat after taking heavy losses, the regiment regrouped at Falmouth, Va., till ordered north to Pennsylvania in mid-June. At GETTYSBURG, 2 July, the 17th was again savaged, this time when the enemy assailed the III Corps' salient in the valley of Plum Run. General Birney noted that the regiment was "driven back from its position by overwhelming force, but, responding to my personal appeal, again charged the enemy across the small wheat-field, and retook their position. This regiment behaved most gallantly, and evinced a high state of discipline," but at a cost of 133 casualties, including 8 officers.

Active at BRISTOE STATION and MINE RUN and in operations along the Rapidan River, the 17th was transferred to the II Corps for the 1864 campaign. That May Col. George W. West led it into WILDERNESS, where in savage fighting it lost 192 of 500 men engaged. 6 weeks later, following service in all II Corps engagements from SPOTSYLVANIA to the initial assaults on Petersburg, the 17th was reduced to 200 effectives. It struggled through the Siege of PETERSBURG and shouldered its share of the fighting on the road to APPOMATTOX under Col. (later Bvt. Brig. Gen.) Charles P. Mattocks. By its muster-out, 4 June 1865, the outfit had lost 12 officers and 195 men killed or mortally wounded. It ranked 22d in this statistic among all Union regiments. —EGL

20th Maine. The 20th Maine Infantry Regiment was organized at Portland in late summer 1862 and mustered into Federal service on 29 Aug. of that year. Its first commander was Col. ADELBERT AMES. Later commanders were Brig. Gen. JOSHUA L. CHAMBERLAIN and Cols. Charles L. Gilmore and Ellis Spear. When the regiment reported to the Army of the Poto-

mac Sept. 1862, it was assigned to the 1st Division/V Corps, the unit with which it served throughout the war.

The regiment was in reserve at ANTIETAM, only slightly engaged at FREDERICKSBURG, and quarantined with smallpox at CHANCELLORSVILLE, where it was used to guard a telegraph wire.

On 2 July 1863, the 20th Maine approached the left of the Federal line at GETTYSBURG at the head of the 3d Brigade/1st Division/V Corps. When word came that LITTLE ROUND TOP, the hill that was the key to the area, was undefended and threatened by Confederates, the brigade commander, Col. Strong Vincent, sent his men forward at the double quick.

Chamberlain led the 360 men of the 20th into position on the extreme left of the Federal line. His orders from Vincent were to hold at all hazards. The regiment arrived just in time to meet an attack from Brig. Gen. EVANDER M. LAW's Alabama brigade. The fighting that followed was among the most bitter of the war. Chamberlain's leadership was beyond praise, and his men fought well. When the long day's struggle ended, the 20th Maine had lost 125 men, but the Federal left was secure.

The regiment fought in the Virginia campaigns of 1864 and 1865. At APPOMATTOX it was one of the regiments chosen to receive the Confederate surrender. The unit was mustered out of service in summer 1865. Almost 300 of the men from the 20th died in military service during the war. —RMcM

Major, James Patrick. CSA b. Fayette, Mo., 14 May 1836. Having graduated 23d in the West Point class of 1852, Brevet 2nd Lieutenant Major was given a 1-year assignment at the Carlisle Barracks in Pennsylvania. He received his commission and transfer to the prestigious 2d Cavalry 1 Dec. 1856 and was sent to the Texas frontier.

Since Major's loyalty lay with the South, he resigned his commission 21 Mar. 1861 to enter Confederate service on the staffs of Brig. Gens. EARL VAN DORN and DAVID E. TWIGGS. At WILSON'S CREEK in August he fought as a lieutenant colonel in the Missouri State Guard, serving afterward as chief of artillery to Van Dorn at Vicksburg in 1862,

LC

where he helped check the Union fleet from advancing on the city. The next year he fought conspicuously as colonel of 3 Texas cavalry regiments during operations along the Teche River. Promoted to brigadier general from 21 July 1863, he rendered his most important service thereafter during the RED RIVER CAMPAIGN of 1864 leading his dismounted troops aggressively at the battles of MANSFIELD and PLEASANT HILL. Toward the end of the war he had charge of a cavalry brigade in Maj. Gen. JOHN A. WHARTON's command. Major was paroled at New Iberia, La., 11 June 1865.

Unwilling to accept defeat, he lived briefly in France before establishing himself as a planter in Louisiana and Texas. d. Austin, Tex., 7 May 1877. —PLF

Mallory, Stephen Russell. CSP b. British Trinidad, c. 1813, Mallory served as Confederate secretary of the navy, the only cabinet officer to keep his position throughout the war. Many Southerners blamed him for the South's numerous naval failures, but history has been kinder to his reputation, crediting him with remarkable initiative and resourcefulness.

Mallory lived in Key West, Fla., and at a young age assisted his widowed mother in operating a boardinghouse. He read law and in 1840 was admitted to the bar, later became a customs inspector and judge in Key West, and saw service in the Seminole War. In 1851 Mallory was elected U.S. senator from Florida, a position he held at the time of the state's secession. Throughout his Senate career he served on the Committee on Naval Affairs and became its powerful chairman in 1855, pushing for a larger and stronger navy and for expansion.

When JEFFERSON DAVIS appointed him secretary of the Confederate States Navy, Mallory sent Southern naval officers and civilians to the North, to Canada, and later to Europe to purchase vessels for the embryonic navy. He directed efforts in England for the purchase and construction of CRUISERS intended to harass and destroy Northern shipping, thus hurting the North's economy and diverting Union warships from the BLOCKADE. The LAIRD RAMS, built in England but never delivered to the South, were also the result of Mallory's determination to break the blockade. To finance these operations, cotton was shipped through the blockade for sale abroad. Confederate purchasing agents, including JAMES D. BULLOCH in England, were given broad discretionary control of these funds.

In addition to his efforts abroad, Mallory supported the building of IRONCLAD vessels within the Confederacy and organized the Confederate Torpedo Bureau, which built torpedoes, floating mines, and the torpedo boat *H.L. HUNLEY.*

Mallory received increasing criticism after the loss of New Orleans, Memphis, and Norfolk, and the destruction—to avoid capture—of the ironclads *VIRGINIA (Merrimack)* and *Mississippi.* His conduct of the Navy Department was investigated by a joint committee of the Confederate Congress, but he was cleared of all charges.

Arrested by Federal forces after the war, Mallory was imprisoned for 10 months before being released. He returned to his law practice in Florida and died in Pensacola 9 Nov. 1873.
—NCD

Malvern Hill (Crew's Farm; Poindexter's Farm), Va., Battle of.

1 July 1862   6 days of running battles along the Virginia peninsula, characterized by a Union withdrawal pounded by uncoordinated Confederate assaults, had convinced Gen. ROBERT E. LEE that Maj. Gen. GEORGE B. MCCLELLAN's Union army was demoralized. One more offensive thrust, Lee believed, might destroy the Federals before they reached the James River. In one of his worst decisions, the Confederate commander hurled his legions against a nearly impregnable Union position on Malvern Hill in the final engagement of the SEVEN DAYS' CAMPAIGN. Confederate Maj. Gen. DANIEL H. HILL, describing the battle, said that it "was not war—it was murder."

On 30 June, the day before the battle, Lee's divisions had intercepted the Union retreat. But as they had throughout the week, faulty staff work and uncoordinated Southern attacks failed to destroy or cripple seriously the Union army. Even while this Battle of WHITE OAK SWAMP raged, Union Maj. Gen. FITZ JOHN PORTER, commander of the V Corps, was preparing a new defensive position at MALVERN HILL, 5 mi from Harrison's Landing, McClellan's objective.

Throughout the 30th and into 1 July the Federals filtered into Porter's position. Malvern Hill towered above the surrounding terrain, a 150-ft-high slope protected on its flanks by deep ravines and swamps with an open field of fire in its front. While the blue-clad infantry shuffled into line, Brig. Gen. HENRY J. HUNT, commanding the Union artillery, rimmed the slope with 100 guns in front and another 150 in reserve and on the flanks. Hunt's gunners swept the approaches, dominating the terrain.

Lee's men approached the formidable Union position disjointedly throughout the morning of the 1st. Warned of the natural strength of the high slope, Lee nevertheless ordered an attack. Against McClellan's right, or northern flank, Lee assigned the assault to the 3 divisions of Maj. Gen. THOMAS J. "STONEWALL" JACKSON, whose lethargic performance in the campaign had seriously hampered Confederate operations. Maj. Gen. JOHN B. MAGRUDER's division, trailing Jackson, was directed to form on Jackson's right. Farther to the right, opposite the Union left center, Maj. Gen. BENJAMIN HUGER's division was deployed. The divisions of Maj. Gens. JAMES LONGSTREET and AMBROSE P. HILL, which had fought heavily on the 30th, formed the reserve.

As though it were fated, however, Lee's plan went askew. Jackson, encountering a formidable swamp, halted to reconnoiter; Magruder, misinformed by local guides, veered from the field before correcting his march. When Huger arrived, Lee assigned him to the missing Magruder's sector. Shortly after noon, with everyone at hand except Magruder, Lee made the final plans for the attack. Massing his artillery behind Huger and Brig. Gen. WILLIAM H. C. WHITING's division of Jackson's command, the Southern chieftain ordered a bombardment followed by an infantry assault. Lee designated the advance of Brig. Gen. LEWIS A. ARMISTEAD's brigade of Huger's division as the signal for the attack.

About 1 p.m. Hunt's Federal gunners opened the battle, directing their fire against the Confederate batteries. For more than 2 hours the Union artillery systematically silenced Lee's cannon. About 3:30 p.m. Armistead, without artillery support, advanced. Hunt's gunners replied, stopping the Southern brigade cold, pinning the unit down until after dark. Lee then sent in Magruder, who had finally arrived. But once again the Confederate command structure failed; Magruder charged with only a third of his 15,000 men. Ramming home charges of canister and shells, the Union gunners raked Magruder's lines, causing heavy casualties. D. H. Hill, hearing Magruder's advance, came in on the left. Sheets of artillery projectiles ripped into Hill's ranks; Southerners fell in clusters, their bodies mangled by the burning artillery charges. 8 additional Southern brigades entered the fighting, only to be blown away. Darkness finally ended the murderous attacks.

The superiority of the Union artillery counted for more in this battle than in any other in the Civil War, inflicting half of the Southern casualties. Lee lost 5,355, while McClellan suffered 3,214 casualties. Though some Union generals wanted to counterattack, McClellan ordered another withdrawal to the James. The Seven Days' Campaign ended along the bloody slope of Malvern Hill.
—JDW

Manassas, Va., First Battle of. 21 July 1861 *See* BULL RUN, VA., FIRST BATTLE OF.

Manassas, Va., Second Battle of. 29–30 Aug. 1862 *See* BULL RUN, VA., SECOND BATTLE OF.

Manassas Campaign, Va., First. 16–22 July 1861 *See* BULL RUN, VA., FIRST CAMPAIGN.

Manassas Campaign, Va., Second. 26 Aug.–1 Sept. 1862 *See* BULL RUN, VA., SECOND CAMPAIGN.

Manassas Gap, Va., Battle of. 22 July 1863 Maj. Gen. GEORGE G. MEADE was sensitive to the charge that he had not pressed Confederates as vigorously as he might have when Gen. R. E. LEE led his beaten army away from GETTYSBURG and safely crossed the Potomac. Thus, when on 22 July Meade saw a chance to strike Lee's flank at Manassas Gap and destroy a good portion of his army, he seized upon it. Unfortunately, the Union advance corps under Maj. Gen. WILLIAM H. FRENCH was slow to move and was delayed for a day by Lee's rear guard. By then the Army of Northern Virginia had passed by to safety. Meade has been criticized for entrusting the advance to an inexperienced and unimaginative corps commander.

—JTH

Manassas Gap Railroad. At midnight on 17 July 1861, Confederate Gen. JOSEPH E. JOHNSTON, stationed near Winchester, Va., in the Shenandoah Valley, received orders to move immediately to Manassas Junction and reinforce Gen. P.G.T. BEAUREGARD's army behind Bull Run Creek. Johnston's columns rapidly filled the roads, marching through the Blue Ridge Mts. toward Piedmont. At this hamlet engines and cars of the Manassas Gap Railroad were waiting for the dusty marchers. The Confederates spilled into the cars and, hissing steam, the engines carried them to Bull Run, where on the 21st Johnston's army was the decisive factor in the Confederate victory. This movement on the Manassas Gap Railroad was the first time in military history that a railroad was used to achieve strategic mobility.

Completed in the mid-1850s, the railroad linked Manassas Junction with Strasburg in the valley. Stretching for 60 mi, it passed through the Blue Ridge Mts. at Manassas Gap, giving the track its name. Built during the railroad boom of the antebellum era, it served as a direct line from the fertile farms of the valley to Manassas Junction, where it connected with the ORANGE & ALEXANDRIA RAILROAD.

For the Confederacy, the railroad's usefulness was limited after FIRST BULL RUN. It continued to haul foodstuffs and equipment throughout the year and into winter 1862. But when Johnston abandoned his lines in northern Virginia Mar. 1862, the line became vulnerable to Union forces. The railroad moved its valuable rolling stock and shop machinery to Greensborough, N.C., where it was leased to other companies. The Confederates then destroyed the track to deny its use to the Federals.

The railroad figured again in the war in autumn 1864. The final struggle for the Shenandoah Valley was under way and by October Maj. Gen. PHILIP H. SHERIDAN's Union army had won 2 signal victories and controlled the upper valley south of Strasburg. For more than a year Union authorities had considered rebuilding the line but had been hampered by Lt. Col.

JOHN S. MOSBY's matchless partisan rangers. The possibility of linking Sheridan by rail to Washington or to Charlottesville, Va., convinced the Union government to undertake the reconstruction. For 2 weeks in September and October repair crews, guarded by soldiers, labored on the line. But Mosby's guerrillas conducted a quick succession of raids against the railroad. Desperately the Federals tried to catch the raiders, but the elusive Confederates defied capture. Sheridan finally halted the operation, and the Manassas Gap Railroad remained abandoned.

—JDW

Maney, George Earl. CSA b. Franklin, Tenn., 24 Aug. 1826, Maney graduated from the University of Nashville in 1845, went to the Mexican War as a volunteer, transferred as a 1st lieutenant to the U.S. Army regular infantry and dragoons, left service in 1848, and started a law practice in Nashville in 1850. Early in 1861 he became captain of the 11th Tennessee and 8 May was elected colonel of the 1st Tennessee.

USMHI

After briefly campaigning in Virginia at CHEAT MOUNTAIN and serving under Brig. Gen. THOMAS J. "STONEWALL" JACKSON, Maney was commissioned brigadier general 16 Apr. 1862, sent west to Maj. Gen. LEONIDAS POLK's I Corps/Army of Mississippi, and given command of the 2d Brigade/2d Division. When the corps was absorbed into the Army of Tennessee soon thereafter, Maney fought at the Battles of PERRYVILLE, STONE'S RIVER, CHICKAMAUGA, and CHATTANOOGA in Maj. Gen. BENJAMIN F. CHEATHAM's division.

Though few accounts report his personal actions in these fights, Maney's brigade is prominent in battle reports. It served well in the ATLANTA CAMPAIGN, and fought in the vanguard in the 22 July 1864 contest for the city. In temporary command of Cheatham's division, during the Battle of JONESBOROUGH, Maney was relieved of combat duty for unrecorded reasons and appears in no reports until his parole 1 May 1865 in North Carolina. Limited evidence suggests he served on staff duty in Georgia while his former brigade fought in Gen. JOHN B. HOOD's FRANKLIN AND NASHVILLE CAMPAIGN. Postwar, Maney supported Reconstruction, became president of the Tennessee & Pacific Railroad in 1868, failed to win the Republican gubernatorial candidacy in Tennessee in 1876, and served in the State Department with appointments to Columbia, Bolivia, Paraguay, and Uruguay. d. District of Columbia, 9 Feb. 1901.

—JES

Manigault, Arthur Middleton. CSA b. Charleston, S.C., 26 Oct. 1824. The son of a well-to-do rice planter, Manigault received a solid education but left the College of Charleston in 1841 to enter the export business. In 1846 he fought in Mexico as a lieutenant in the Palmetto Rifles, a commission he won through his experience as a sergeant major of militia. After serving under WINFIELD SCOTT, which he considered "perhaps the happiest and most romantic period" of his life, he returned to Charleston and worked as a commission merchant till the outbreak of civil war.

When his state seceded Dec. 1860, Manigault was elected

captain of a local company of mounted riflemen. He went on staff duty, serving as inspector general to Brig. Gen. P.G.T. BEAUREGARD, with the rank of lieutenant colonel. He was at Beauregard's side during the bombardment of FORT SUMTER. 6 weeks later he became colonel of the 10th South Carolina Infantry and shortly afterward commander of the state's First Military District, headquartered at Georgetown. There he erected batteries and built

LC

works to protect the local coastline, but at the end of Mar. 1862 he was ordered by his departmental commander, Maj. Gen. JOHN C. PEMBERTON, to dismantle the works and abandon the position. Reporting at Charleston, he served briefly under Brig. Gen. ROSWELL S. RIPLEY. Later that spring he and his regiment were sent to Mississippi to join the Army of Tennessee.

For the remainder of the war, he served in the West, from the outset as a brigade commander. He fought conspicuously at CORINTH, STONE'S RIVER (where his command ably supported the center of the Confederate line), and CHICKAMAUGA (where his troops menaced the Union left under Maj. Gen. GEORGE H. THOMAS). On 26 Apr. 1863 he was elevated to brigadier general, a promotion whose long delay he attributed to the influence of his family's enemies in the Confederate War Department.

During the 1864 ATLANTA CAMPAIGN, Manigault was wounded at RESACA but fought through to EZRA CHURCH. Later that year he served under Gen. JOHN BELL HOOD until again wounded, this time severely, at FRANKLIN. The prolonged effects of this wound eventually caused his death 17 Aug. 1886 at South Island, S.C., after he had spent several years as a planter and 6 more as adjutant and inspector general of his state.   —EGL

Mann, Ambrose Dudley.

diplomat b. Hanover Court House, Va., 26 Apr. 1801, Mann received his early education in Virginia and attended the Military Academy at West Point but resigned shortly before graduation to avoid military service. He studied law, abandoning his practice in 1842 to accept a series of minor diplomatic posts abroad. In 1853 he returned to the U.S. for a 3-year term as assistant secretary of state.

An outspoken proponent of STATES RIGHTS, Mann published several articles in *DEBOW'S REVIEW* encouraging Southern economic independence and the establishment of a Southern merchant marine. His advocacy of a direct trade route to Europe attracted the attention of radical secessionists and of Confederate Pres. JEFFERSON DAVIS, who appointed Mann a member of the first Confederate diplomatic mission to Europe Apr. 1861.

Unfortunately for the South, Mann was a thoroughly inept diplomat, lacking tact, common sense, and good judgment. Over the course of 1 year in London and 3 in Belgium, his lengthy, bombastic reports to Sec. of State JUDAH P. BENJAMIN proved consistently unreliable and exaggerated, and would have been dangerous to Confederate foreign affairs had Benjamin not disregarded them. Mann did exert some favorable influence on the press in London and Paris early in 1861 before

the Confederacy had propagandists working regularly in Europe. Beyond that, his great achievement—a trip to the Vatican in winter 1863–64 to get the pope to interfere with Federal recruitment of Irish and German Catholics—ended in humiliating failure when Davis and Benjamin correctly read nothing more than courtesy into a letter from the pope addressing Davis as president of the Confederacy. Davis' refusal to replace Mann defies explanation.

When Mann had departed from Richmond in 1861 he vowed not to return until the South achieved independence. True to his word, he lived alone and forgotten in and around Paris until his death Nov. 1889.   —PLF

Mansfield, Joseph King Fenno.

USA b. New Haven, Conn., 22 Dec. 1803, Mansfield entered the Military Academy at 13, graduating 5 years later in the class of 1822. For more than 2 decades he was involved, as an engineer officer, in the construction of defenses along the Southern coast. During the Mexican War he served with conspicuous gallantry as Gen. Zachary Taylor's chief engineer. His performance earned him the brevets of major, lieutenant colonel, and colonel. In 1853 Sec. of War JEFFERSON DAVIS, who had also been an officer in Taylor's army, recommended Mansfield's promotion to staff colonel in the inspector general's department. He held this post until the beginning of the Civil War.

LC

On 28 Apr. 1861, Mansfield assumed command of the Department of Washington, D.C. Within a month, on 18 May, he was promoted to brigadier general. His troops then seized and fortified positions on the Virginia side of the Potomac River. Mansfield commanded the department until Mar. 1862, when he served under Maj. Gen. JOHN E. WOOL at Fort Monroe. He briefly led a division of the VII Corps in operations around Suffolk. On 12 Sept. he assumed command of the XII Corps Army of the Potomac, which he joined at Frederick, Md., in pursuit of Gen. ROBERT E. LEE's invading Confederates.

5 days later, at ANTIETAM, the white-haired general led his new command into battle. The battle had been raging for 2 hours across a 40-acre cornfield when Mansfield, in the very forefront, led his corps through the East Woods. When his leading brigade reached the edge of the trees, Confederates, concealed in the cornfield, opened fire. The Federals hesitated and Mansfield rode forward. Thinking the Confederates were Federals, he ordered his men to cease firing. Suddenly another volley crashed from the stalks, and Mansfield was hit in the stomach. He was carried to a field hospital, where he died 18 Sept. 1862. He was promoted posthumously to major general 12 Mar. 1863, to date from 18 July 1862.   —JDW

Mansfield (Pleasant Grove; Sabine Cross Roads), La., Battle of.

8 Apr. 1864 In mid-Mar. 1864 an army of 25,000 Federals under Maj. Gen. NATHANIEL P. BANKS began moving up the west bank of the Red River in central Louisiana. Accompanying it on the river was a large flotilla of gunboats and transports commanded by Rear Adm. DAVID D. PORTER.

Late in March another Union army, 13,000 strong under Maj. Gen. FREDERICK STEELE, headed south from Little Rock, Ark. The objective of both expeditions was Shreveport, the military, political, and economic center of the Confederate Trans-Mississippi Department.

To meet this 2-pronged invasion, Gen. E. KIRBY SMITH, commander of the department, had barely 25,000 men divided between Lt. Gen. RICHARD TAYLOR in western Louisiana and Maj. Gen. STERLING PRICE in Arkansas. Correctly perceiving the Banks-Porter expedition as the more dangerous, he sent Brig. Gen. THOMAS J. CHURCHILL with 5,000 of Price's infantry to reinforce Taylor, who meanwhile fell back to Sabine Cross Roads south of Mansfield.

On 8 Apr. Taylor decided to give battle to Banks even though he had only 9,000 men and Churchill had not yet arrived. Late that afternoon one of his divisions attacked the head of the Union column, which had been reduced to 20,000 men by detachments. Charging forward like "infuriated demons," the Confederates smashed one, then another of Banks's division, causing them to flee in a panic-stricken rout. Taylor pursued vigorously, capturing 20 cannon, scores of wagons, and hundreds of prisoners. Finally, with darkness descending, a third Union division checked the Confederate pursuit. The Federals resumed their retreat, which continued through the night to Pleasant Hill.

Of the 12,000 Union troops actually engaged, 2,235 were killed, wounded, or captured; Taylor lost less than half that number. Banks's expedition had been defeated and his army was threatened with destruction. —AC

Marais des Cygnes River, Mo., eng. at. 25 Oct. 1864 The last major fighting of Confederate Maj. Gen. STERLING PRICE's raid into Missouri came at the Marais des Cygnes River. For almost a full month Federal Maj. Gen. ALFRED PLEASONTON had been chasing Price's raiders throughout Missouri. At Jefferson City, his defenses were extensive and threatening enough to send Price into a westward retreat. On hearing of Price's movements, Pleasonton immediately ordered a cavalry division to follow in pursuit. He struck 22 Oct. near Westport, then withdrew. Maj. Gen. SAMUEL R. CURTIS' Federal Army of the Border struck Price again the next day just south of Westport, as Pleasonton attacked one of Price's 3 divisions along the Big Blue River. Since the fighting had greatly reduced his forces, Price hastily retreated southward. Pleasonton immediately resumed his pursuit, chasing Price's demoralized troops for 60 mi to the Marais des Cygnes on the Kansas border.

By the 25th Pleasonton had reached the Confederate lines at the river and planned an attack for daybreak. Beginning with an artillery bombardment, Pleasonton's command, heavily outnumbered, made a gallant charge against the weakened Confederates. According to Pleasonton, the enemy "left in great haste, dropping trees in the road to bar our progress, and fighting a running contest to the Osage River, . . . after a brilliant charge the enemy was routed." Price's troops were "effectively crippled," and except for a few skirmishes, PRICE'S MISSOURI RAID was over. —FLS

March to the Sea. Nov.–Dec. 1864 After its fall 2 Sept. 1864, Maj. Gen. WILLIAM T. SHERMAN occupied Atlanta for 10 weeks, resting his army, damaging local communications, plotting new strategy. Meanwhile, Gen. JOHN BELL HOOD's Army of Tennessee began to range north and west on a march that

would carry it into Tennessee. Sherman briefly pursued but soon adopted a more productive course. He resolved to send his trusted subordinate Maj. Gen. GEORGE H. THOMAS, with 2 infantry corps and the majority of the cavalry, to Nashville for a showdown with Hood. The remainder of Sherman's command, some 62,000 troops of all arms and 64 cannon, he would lead through Georgia to the Atlantic Ocean.

Sherman had several reasons for waging such a campaign. He wanted to split the interior of the Deep South, "smashing things generally," especially supply lines that supported the Confederates in Virginia. He also wished to "demonstrate the vulnerability of the South" by laying a heavy hand on a region thus far spared war's suffering. In brief, Sherman wished to "make Georgia howl."

His troops departed Atlanta 15 Nov., simultaneously moving east toward Augusta and southeast in the direction of Macon, thereby deceiving the enemy as to his ultimate objective, Savannah. He accompanied the column taking the upper route, the XIV and XX corps of the Army of Georgia, under Maj. Gen. HENRY W. SLOCUM. The lower column, led by Maj. Gen. OLIVER O. HOWARD, commander of the Army of the Tennessee, consisted of the infantry of the XV and XVII corps, plus the cavalry division of Brig. Gen. H. JUDSON KILPATRICK. Pontoon trains and engineer units accompanied each wing, but provisions wagons were left behind; the troops would forage off the land.

The first leg of the march, which ended with the columns converging on the state capital, Milledgeville, was an easy one, principally due to Sherman's lack of opposition, and set the

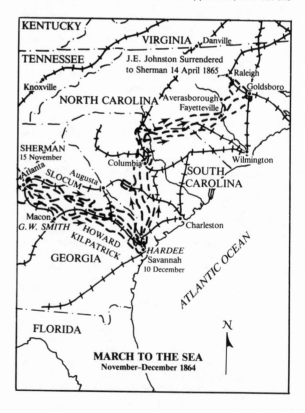

MARCH TO THE SEA
November–December 1864

tone for the entire journey. With Hood gone, the nearest sizable enemy force was the 18,000-man garrison under Lt. Gen. WILLIAM J. HARDEE at Savannah. The only others who remained to challenge him were 3,000 Georgia militia and state troops under Maj. Gen. GUSTAVUS W. SMITH, Maj. Gen. JOSEPH WHEELER's understrength cavalry corps, and miscellaneous local forces. Smith, who had concentrated at Macon, was caught by surprise when Howard's column veered sharply east above the city. And Wheeler's troopers had to be content with harassing the main Federal body and battling Kilpatrick's cavalry at WAYNESBOROUGH, Millen Grove, Rocky Creek Church, Thomas' Station, Brier Creek, and Ebenezer Creek.

After wrecking supply depots and several railroads, the convergent columns destroyed the military utility of Milledgeville 22–24 Nov. and sacked state government buildings. The columns again spread apart when leaving the capital, continuing to rip up railroad track (over 200 mi of it, eventually), which they burned and twisted into SHERMAN'S HAIRPINS. Meanwhile, marauding BUMMERS looted and torched along a path up to 60 mi wide, conduct tolerated if not condoned by Sherman's philosophy.

The only general engagement fought by the infantry was at Griswoldville, 22 Nov., where 523 overconfident militiamen fell dead or wounded while attacking a well-fortified XV Corps brigade. Otherwise, the foot soldiers brushed aside Wheeler's troopers, easily occupying Sandersville 26 Nov., Louisville 29 Nov., Millen 3 Dec., and numerous other towns. By 10 Dec., when they pulled up outside Savannah, having come 250 mi in 26 days, Sherman's soldiers had done $100 million in damage, reducing Georgia's midsection to debris and desolation.

—EGL

Marine Corps, Confederate States. The Confederate States Marine Corps (CSMC) was established by an act of the Confederate Congress 16 Mar. 1861. Corps strength was authorized at 46 officers and 944 enlisted men but actual enrollment never came close to that number. (A figure for 30 Oct. 1864 lists only 539 officers and men.) Though the officers were mostly former U.S. Marine officers, the head of the corps, Commandant-Col. LLOYD J. BEALL, was a former U.S. Army paymaster with no marine experience.

The CSMC was modeled after the U.S. Marine Corps, but there were some differences: the Confederates organized themselves into permanent companies, replaced the fife with the light infantry bugle, and wore uniforms similar to those of British marines. Ashore they provided guard detachments for Confederate naval stations at Mobile, Savannah, Charleston, Charlotte, Richmond, and Wilmington and manned naval shore batteries at Pensacola, Hilton Head, Fort Fisher, and Drewry's Bluff. Seagoing detachments served aboard the various warships and even on commerce destroyers.

Confederate marines saw their first naval action aboard the CSS VIRGINIA (Merrimack) off Hampton Roads, Va., 8–9 Mar. 1862, and near war's end were part of the naval brigade that fought at SAYLER'S CREEK, Va.

Despite desertions and even near-mutinies, most marines served well and deserved Navy Sec. STEPHEN R. MALLORY'S praise for their "promptness and efficiency." The corps' weakness was due largely to internal squabbles over rank, shore duty, and administrative assignments. And, with no funds for bounties, the corps could not easily enlist recruits. Until 1864 the monthly pay of enlisted men was $3 less than that of

equivalent army grades. Only late in the war were the marines allowed to draw from army conscripts to augment their ranks.

—NCD

Marine Corps, United States. The United States Marine Corps (USMC) was not utilized to full advantage during the Civil War. Already weakened by the resignations of many of its best officers, the USMC's morale suffered further as a result of feuding between staff and line officers and senior officers who regarded themselves administrators rather than field commanders. Another blow to morale was the practice of appointing new junior officers by patronage.

In 1861 Congress authorized the United States Marine Corps to be enlarged to 93 officers and 3,074 enlisted men, and ABRAHAM LINCOLN increased that number by another thousand. However, recruiting was hindered by a lack of funds for bounties and longer terms of enlistment than for men in the volunteer army. By 1863 negative feelings toward the USMC resulted in a congressional resolution that would have transferred the corps to army control. The resolution was defeated, however, and when Marine Commandant-Col. John C. Harris died in 1864, Sec. of the Navy GIDEON WELLES retired several senior officers to appoint Maj. Jacob Zeilin his successor. Zeilin, at 59, was a combat veteran of the Mexican War and an officer of proven ability.

Harris had governed the corps by carefully following all naval regulations and by staying clear of army operations, and Zeilin continued this policy. As a consequence, marines did not play a major role in expeditions and amphibious operations during the war. Both Harris and Zeilin failed to recognize the possibilities of amphibious assault, regarding such operations as a responsibility of the army. Some 400 marines did participate in the navy's unsuccessful landing operation against FORT FISHER, 13–14 Jan. 1865; the army landing finally won the battle there.

During the war marines continued their traditional role as ship guards, also manning batteries and participating in limited operations ashore. They did not always perform well, as at FIRST BULL RUN, where a marine battalion of mostly raw recruits was routed. But other marines distinguished themselves during landing and gunboat attacks and especially as members of gun crews. 17 marines received the MEDAL OF HONOR for conspicuous bravery; 13 of these were sergeants and corporals serving as gun captains and gun-division commanders.

Marine recruiting improved by 1864 with changes in the conscription laws and with bounty money finally available. When the war ended, the corps was at full strength. A total of 148 marines were killed in action, while 312 more died from other causes.

—NCD

Marmaduke, John Sappington. CSA b. near Arrow Rock, Mo., 14 Mar. 1833, Marmaduke served with distinction in the Confederate Trans-Mississippi Department. He studied at both Harvard and Yale before his appointment at West Point, graduated 30th in a class of 38 in 1857, and saw service on the Utah Expedition. Promoted to 2d lieutenant in the 7th Infantry during the Mormon Campaign, 1859–60, he resigned from the army in 1861 and was appointed a colonel in the Missouri Militia. Soon after, he became lieutenant colonel of the 1st Arkansas Battalion and finally colonel of the 3d Confederate Infantry.

Praised for his conduct at SHILOH, where he was wounded,

Marmaduke was promoted to brigadier general as of 15 Nov. 1862 and soon was conspicuous at the Battle of PRAIRIE GROVE. He was assigned to the command of a cavalry division in the Trans-Mississippi Department under Maj. Gen. THOMAS C. HINDMAN, and in 1863 his command twice accompanied Maj. Gen. STERLING PRICE on raids into Missouri.

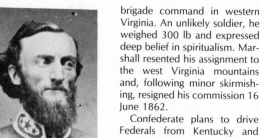
LC

In July 1863 Marmaduke was in fighting at Fayetteville and Helena, Ark., and in September commanded Price's cavalry during the defense of Little Rock. At this time, he fought a duel with and killed Brig. Gen. LUCIUS M. WALKER, for which he was arrested but soon released. He attacked Pine Bluff Oct. 1863 and was brilliant at the engagement at POISON SPRINGS during the 1864 RED RIVER CAMPAIGN. During PRICE'S MISSOURI RAID in October, Marmaduke was captured at Mine Creek, Kans., and spent the rest of the war in FORT WARREN prison in Boston harbor. While there, he was the last Confederate to be appointed major general, 18 Mar. 1865.

After the war Marmaduke turned to insurance and politics. He died in Jefferson City, 28 Dec. 1887, as governor of Missouri.   —LDJ

Marr, John Quincy. CSA b. Warrenton, Va., 27 May 1825, Marr was the first Confederate to die in combat. Ranked 2d in the class of 1846 at the VIRGINIA MILITARY INSTITUTE, he briefly taught there, then took over management of family land holdings. In the years before the Civil War he was county treasurer, high sheriff, and presiding justice of county courts. Following John Brown's raid on HARPERS FERRY in 1859, Marr organized the Warrenton Rifles militia for home defense and in 1861 sat as a delegate in the Virginia secession convention.

Commissioned lieutenant colonel 5 May 1861, he served on garrison duty with the Warrenton Rifles at Dumfries, Bristoe Station, and Fairfax Court House. In the predawn hours of 1 June, 50 men of the 2d U.S. Cavalry under Lt. Charles H. Tompkins rode through Fairfax Court House firing their weapons. One random bullet killed Marr, who was standing in a clover field at the roadside. His body was undiscovered for a few hours, while others skirmished with the 2d Cavalry. There were a few more casualties in the fighting, but as the first of the war, Marr is memorialized with a stone monument at Fairfax Court House.   —JES

Marshall, Humphrey. CSA/CSP b. Frankfort, Ky., 13 Jan. 1812, Marshall graduated 42d in the West Point class of 1832, resigned from the U.S. Army in 1833, studied and practiced law in Kentucky, and was a colonel of the 1st Kentucky Cavalry during the Mexican War. He was a U.S. congressman for 8 terms, 1848–59, during which time he served for a year as U.S. minister to China.

Marshall initially backed his state's neutrality in the secession crisis, then came to believe that it remained in the Union only through coercion by the Federal government. He accepted a Confederate commission as brigadier general 30 Oct. 1861, fled Kentucky under indictment for treason, and took

brigade command in western Virginia. An unlikely soldier, he weighed 300 lb and expressed deep belief in spiritualism. Marshall resented his assignment to the west Virginia mountains and, following minor skirmishing, resigned his commission 16 June 1862.

NA

Confederate plans to drive Federals from Kentucky and arouse Confederate loyalties required the presence of Kentuckians in responsible command. Marshall was cajoled into accepting reappointment as brigadier general 19 June and was ordered in September to pass through Pound Gap into Kentucky to take part in Gen. BRAXTON BRAGG'S KENTUCKY CAMPAIGN. He was unaccountably slow in arriving in the state, politicked with Maj. Gen. E. KIRBY SMITH against Bragg, and rarely took his position on time for any maneuver. When Bragg retreated from Kentucky, Marshall requested and was granted permission to follow his own route back to western Virginia. No significant assignments were given him thereafter. He resigned his commission again 17 June 1863 and entered the Second Confederate Congress, remaining with that body until its final adjournment.

In peacetime Marshall practiced law in Louisville, where he died 28 Mar. 1872. Bragg recalled that during the Mexican War Marshall and his men did "some fine running & no fighting" and rated Marshall in the U.S. Congress as a "humbug and a superficial, tho' fluent fool."   —JES

Marston, Gilman. USA b. Orford, N.H., 20 Aug. 1811. A farmer's son, Marston taught school, entered Dartmouth, and was graduated in 1837. After serving as the head of an Indianapolis preparatory school, he attended Harvard Law School, graduating in 1840. He began his legal practice in Exeter, N.H., in 1841 and 4 years later was elected to his first of 13 terms in the state legislature. In 1859 his constituents elected him to the House of Representatives, reelecting him 2 years later.

With his second term interrupted by the advent of the Civil War, Marston returned to his state and recruited the 2d New Hampshire. Appointed its colonel 10 June 1861, he led the unit at FIRST BULL RUN. A year later, in the PENINSULA CAMPAIGN, his regiment served in the division of Brig. Gen. JOSEPH HOOKER. Marston then took a temporary leave of absence. In fall 1862 he commanded the Union garrison at Centreville, Va., which protected the ORANGE & ALEXANDRIA RAILROAD. On 29 Nov. the New Hampshire officer received his promotion to brigadier general. He returned to his regiment in time to participate in the Battle of FREDERICKSBURG 13 Dec.

Marston was relieved of duty with the Army of the Potomac

in spring 1863. He then reported for duty under Maj. Gen. SAMUEL P. HEINTZELMAN in the Department of Washington. In July the War Department directed him to establish a prison camp in Maryland, which became the POINT LOOKOUT facility. Marston returned to field duty in spring 1864, commanding a brigade in the XVIII Corps. His brigade participated in the disastrous Federal assault at COLD HARBOR 3 June. Transferred once more, he served in the XVII Corps in eastern Virginia until resigning 20 Apr. 1865.

The Union general returned to New Hampshire, where the citizens of his district reelected him to another term in Congress. In 1867 he resumed his legal practice and subsequently served again in the state legislature and as a member of the state constitutional convention. Marston was appointed to the U.S. Senate for 4 months in 1889. The esteemed legislator and veteran died at Exeter, N.H., a year later 3 July 1890.

—JDW

Marston, John. USN b. Boston, Mass., 12 June 1795. Appointed midshipman in 1813, Marston was captain of the USS *Cumberland* at the Norfolk Navy Yard when the Civil War began. Still commanding the *Cumberland,* he participated in the joint army/navy expedition against HATTERAS INLET, N.C. Following the surrender of Forts Hatteras and Clark, Aug. 1861, Marston, now commanding the *Roanoke,* was assigned to the Charleston BLOCKADE.

In Dec. 1861 the *Roanoke,* badly in need of engine repairs, arrived at HAMPTON ROADS, Va. As senior naval officer at that station, Marston assumed responsibilities of that position in addition to being a ship's captain. When the CSS *VIRGINIA* *(Merrimack)* approached Hampton Roads 8 Mar. 1862, the *Roanoke* was still in disrepair. Nevertheless, since its battery was formidable, Marston had her taken in tow by 2 tugboats. The *Roanoke* arrived too late to take on the *Virginia,* which may well have saved it from suffering the fate of the doomed *Cumberland,* now commanded by William Radford, and the *Congress.*

The next day the Confederate advantage changed dramatically with the arrival of the USS *MONITOR.* After conferring with Lt. JOHN L. WORDEN, Marston decided to ignore Navy Sec. GIDEON WELLES's order to have the ironclad sent immediately to Washington. As he felt it should, the *Monitor* remained at Hampton Roads as defense against the *Virginia.*

In Mar. 1862 Marston finished his long naval career by bringing the *Roanoke* to the New York Navy Yard. He is listed as a rear admiral on the retired list in 1881. d. in Philadelphia, Pa., 8 Apr. 1885.

—NCD

Martin, James Green. CSA b. Elizabeth City, N.C., 14 Feb. 1819. The son of a physician, shipbuilder, and state legislator, Martin graduated 14th in the West Point class of 1840. As a lieutenant of artillery, he served in forts along the Atlantic Coast and on the Canadian border. During the Mexican War he distinguished himself on several fields, especially at Monterrey under Gen. Zachary Taylor and, under Gen. WINFIELD SCOTT, at Churubusco, where his right arm was amputated after being maimed by grapeshot. He remained in the army after recuperating, serving in Virginia, Pennsylvania, and on the frontier until the outbreak of the Civil War.

Martin entered the state armed forces June 1861, shortly after North Carolina seceded, and served as adjutant general for the first 10 regiments the state mustered in. That September

LC

he became a major general of militia and took charge of the defense of North Carolina. Through his administrative expertise, North Carolina troops entered the war as the best-equipped and best-organized in the South. They were also the most numerous, for he raised 12,000 more than the state's original quota.

When his organizational work was done, Martin requested field duty. He was named a brigadier general 15 May 1862 but was given another desk job as commander of the District of North Carolina, headquartered at Kinston. Perhaps disgruntled over this assignment, he resigned his commission late in July but was reappointed 11 Aug., retroactive to May. Finally, in fall 1863, he took charge of a brigade of 4 North Carolina infantry regiments. In camp at Wilmington he subjected his troops to rigorous training; nevertheless, they gave him the affectionate sobriquet "Old One Wing."

On 2 Feb. 1864, in conjunction with Maj. Gen. GEORGE E. PICKETT's operations against NEW BERNE, Martin routed the Union garrison at Newport Barracks. Transferred to Virginia, he fought just as ably at SECOND DREWRY'S BLUFF, in attacking Federal works at BERMUDA HUNDRED (a section of which he captured 20 May 1864), and during the SIEGE OF PETERSBURG.

While serving in the last campaign his health broke, and he returned to an administrative post in his native state. His loss pained Gen. ROBERT E. LEE, who remarked that Martin was "one to whom North Carolina owes a debt she can never repay." After the war Martin practiced law in Asheville, where he died 4 Oct. 1878.

—EGL

Martin, William Thompson. CSA b. Glasgow, Ky., 25 Mar. 1823. At 17 Martin graduated from Centre College in Kentucky, then moved to Natchez, Miss., and was admitted to the bar. He had a shrewd mind and a forceful voice, traits that promoted his subsequent career as a district attorney. One biographer notes that "he was a man of moral as well as physical courage, and he did not hesitate to take unpopular stands in following his own best judgment." His most unpopular stand was his opposition to secession, which faded only after the Civil War began. In 1861 he organized a local cavalry troop, which he led to Richmond. There it became part of the 2d

LC

Mississippi Cavalry with Martin as major of the regiment.

Early in 1862 Martin, now colonel of the Jeff Davis Legion, participated in several expeditions in Virginia, including Maj. Gen. J.E.B. STUART'S RIDE AROUND MCCLELLAN during the PENINSULA CAMPAIGN. He then served as an aide to Gen. ROBERT E. LEE until sent west Mar. 1863 as a brigadier general, to which he had been promoted the previous 2 Dec.

In the Western theater he led a division in Maj. Gen. JOSEPH WHEELER's cavalry corps. He saw action in the TULLAHOMA and CHICKAMAUGA campaigns and performed ably enough during WHEELER's RAID of 1–9 Oct. 1863 in the Sequatchie Valley to receive a major generalship as of 10 Nov. At that rank Martin served as one of Lt. Gen. JAMES LONGSTREET's cavalry leaders in the KNOXVILLE CAMPAIGN, during part of that period leading Wheeler's command.

The relationship between Wheeler and Martin became strained late in the Atlanta Campaign. According to one historian, "Gen. Martin seems to have adopted [Maj. Gen. Nathan Bedford] Forrest's attitude of distrust of Wheeler." Additionally, there may have been repercussions from Martin's heated criticism of his corps leader's failure to keep him supplied with able men and horses. A confrontation developed 14 Aug. 1864, after Wheeler attacked the Union garrison at Dalton, Ga. The assault proved unsuccessful, partly because Martin had placed his division in camp 7 mi from the town rather than participating as ordered. Wheeler relieved him at once and ensured that he never again served in the Army of Tennessee. Martin closed out the war in command of the District of Northwest Mississippi.

Once peace returned, he became active in Mississippi and national politics as a Democrat. He also served as president of a railroad and as a trustee of both the University of Mississippi and Jefferson College. d. near Natchez, Miss., 16 Mar. 1910.   —EGL

Martindale, John Henry. USA b. Sandy Hill, N.Y., 20 Mar. 1815. The son of a Whig congressman, Martindale entered the U.S. Military Academy in 1831, graduating 3d in his class 4 years later. He resigned from the army within a year, after failing to secure a post in the Corps of Engineers. He then studied law, was admitted to the bar in 1838, and practiced until 1861.

LC

With the outbreak of war, Martindale was among those who advocated using Regular Army officers as drill instructors and graduating immediately the top 2 classes at West Point. The War Department adopted both proposals. Martindale secured a commission as brigadier general of volunteers 9 Aug. He initially served in the defenses of Washington before being assigned to the command of a brigade in Brig. Gen. FITZ JOHN PORTER's division of the III Corps.

Martindale led his brigade in the PENINSULA and SEVEN DAYS' campaigns, seeing rugged combat at MECHANICSVILLE, GAINES' MILL, and MALVERN HILL. Stricken with typhoid fever, he relinquished his command. Porter, however, preferred charges against him, declaring that the brigade commander had openly asserted that he would surrender rather than desert his wounded at Malvern Hill. A court of inquiry investigated Porter's allegations and exonerated Martindale.

Restored to duty, he assumed command as military governor of the District of Columbia 2 Feb. 1863; serving in this capacity until 2 May 1864, when he led a division in Maj. Gen. WILLIAM F. SMITH's XVIII Corps. He directed his division at BERMUDA HUNDRED and at COLD HARBOR and in July commanded the corps for 2 weeks in the operations against PETERSBURG. On 13 Sept. Martindale resigned because of ill health. He was brevetted major general 13 Mar. 1865—ironically, for his services at Malvern Hill.

Martindale resumed his legal practice during the postwar years, often handling cases for the New York Central Railroad. From 1867 to 1869 he served as attorney general of the state and for 11 years was vice-president of the National Asylum for Disabled Volunteer Soldiers. While on a trip to Europe for his health, he died in Nice, France, 13 Dec. 1881.   —JDW

Maryland. Preferring compromise and neutrality, Maryland remained indecisive during the sectional crisis. The eastern portion of the state had strong social and economic ties with the South; the west was bound to the North. Maryland would eventually remain loyal to the Union, but Marylanders experienced serious trauma in their decision.

The war's first bloodshed occurred 19 Apr. on President St. in Baltimore. The 6th Massachusetts Militia, marching crosstown en route to Washington, was pelted with paving stones hurled by an angry mob of pro-secessionist civilians. Shots were exchanged, and 4 soldiers and 12 Baltimoreans were killed. The incident angered the South and caused poet James Ryder Randall to write the song "Maryland, My Maryland."

To ABRAHAM LINCOLN, Maryland was a vital border state that had to be kept from defecting to the Confederacy. For a month Gov. THOMAS H. HICKS, of the American (Know Nothing) Party, delayed calling the legislature into session. His "masterly inactivity" forestalled disunionists from pressuring the legislature into calling a secession convention. After Brig. Gen. BENJAMIN F. BUTLER occupied Federal Hill, overlooking downtown Baltimore, the Federal government supervised state affairs. Elections were manipulated, Unionists installed in key political posts, the writ of HABEAS CORPUS was suspended, and persons deemed subversive were arrested, including Baltimore's mayor and 19 members of the legislature. In 1864, anticipating the 13TH AMENDMENT, the general assembly abolished slavery in the state.

Because the nearby Shenandoah Valley offered an inviting avenue of invasion, a host of battles and skirmishes took place in central Maryland. Gen. ROBERT E. LEE, anticipating recruits, invaded the state in 1862 but was met with coldness by Unionist-minded western Marylanders. Hard fighting took place in the South Mountain passes before the Confederates concentrated along Antietam Creek near Sharpsburg. Maj. Gen. GEORGE B. MCCLELLAN attacked 17 Sept., the deadliest single day in American history. Lee maintained his position, but heavy odds forced his retreat to Virginia (see ANTIETAM CAMPAIGN).

The Confederates returned in 1864 during Lt. Gen. JUBAL A. EARLY's Raid on Washington. Early levied a requisition of $200,000 from Frederick, while Brig. Gen. JOHN MCCAUSLAND levied $20,000 from Hagerstown. The Battle of MONOCACY, near Frederick, 9 July, forced Maj. Gen. LEW WALLACE to fall back toward Baltimore and Early advanced to Silver Spring, but after skirmishing around Ft. Stevens, he decided against assaulting the Washington defenses and retired.   —DPK

Maryland, Union Department of. Constituted 19 July 1861, the Union Department of Maryland existed for 6 days. It coincided with the former Department of Annapolis, which encompassed Maryland counties for 20 mi on each side of the railroad linking Annapolis to Washington, D.C. Maj. Gen. JOHN A. DIX commanded the department. On 25 July it was merged into the Department of Pennsylvania. —JDW

Maryland Campaign. 4–22 Sept. 1862 *See* ANTIETAM CAMPAIGN.

Mason, James Murray. diplomat b. District of Columbia, 3 Nov. 1798, Mason, a Virginia aristocrat, was arrogant, domineering, and unconventional. Graduating from the College of William and Mary, he practiced law in Winchester, then entered politics in 1826, actively supporting backcountry interests on state and Federal levels.

As a senator, 1847–61, Mason was a staunch Calhoun STATES-RIGHTS Democrat. Though he favored counting only whites to allocate representation, he drafted the FUGITIVE SLAVE ACT, part of the COMPROMISE OF 1850, firmly believing slavery to be a cornerstone of Southern society. By the time of ABRAHAM LINCOLN'S

LC

election he was convined that compromise was impossible and that the South could preserve its identity only by establishing its sovereignty. With the outbreak of war, he offered his services to the Confederacy.

An old friend of JEFFERSON DAVIS and a 10-year veteran of the Senate Foreign Relations Committee, Mason was the ideal choice for the Confederacy's diplomatic envoy to Britain. The mission was eased by English indignation over the *TRENT* AFFAIR. Enthusiastic reception by the business community aided Mason in coordinating purchases for Confederate agents. While he was able to raise money from Confederate sympathizers and sell bonds in the private sector, the British government never received him officially.

Mason intended to convince Britain that its best interests lay in sanctioning an independent Southern nation which, rather than compete with Britain's industrial supremacy, would function as an agricultural satellite, albeit a sovereign one. The Confederacy would buy manufactured goods from England and supply cotton for its mills. But England's 2-year inventory of the staple undercut "COTTON DIPLOMACY." A divided Union that cut off the flow of cotton threatened Britain less than the possibility of war with the North and the loss of the lucrative Northern wartime market.

A year after the war Mason retired to Canada, where he remained until Andrew Johnson's second amnesty proclamation in 1868. Secure from arrest, he lived out his life in Alexandria, Va., dying 28 Apr. 1871. —PLF

Massachusetts. The center of the antislavery movement in America, Massachusetts viewed the coming of civil war as a moral crusade, since radical leaders like William Lloyd Garrison, CHARLES SUMNER, and Wendell Phillips had been denouncing the evils of slavery for many years. Secession brought early preparations for possible war, encouraged by controversial militia general BENJAMIN F. BUTLER and impatient Gov. JOHN A.

ANDREW. Massachusetts troops were the first armed soldiers to respond to ABRAHAM LINCOLN'S call for volunteers 15 Apr. 1861. A well-equipped militia was mustered in the next day, to proceed to Washington. En route, a mob attack in Baltimore brought the first casualties of the war to the 6th Massachusetts Infantry. The state was outraged by this unprovoked attack, and volunteers soon provided twice the quota assigned.

Massachusetts citizens were prominent in many ways. The diplomacy of CHARLES FRANCIS ADAMS as minister to England may have kept England out of the war. The inspiring "Battle Hymn of the Republic" was written by JULIA WARD HOWE, to the tune of "John Brown's Body." The dedication of Col. ROBERT GOULD SHAW to the training and fighting of the famous 54TH MASSACHUSETTS Colored Regiment is honored by a memorial on Boston Common. The valiant stand of Capt. John Bigelow's 9th Massachusetts Battery at GETTYSBURG is legendary. Maj. Gen. JOSEPH HOOKER commanded the Army of the Potomac, and NATHANIEL P. BANKS and DARIUS COUCH were corps commanders.

The Bay State contributed 77 infantry regiments and a total of 152,048 men to the Union cause. The seafaring traditions of the state led to the enlistment of the second largest number of navy recruits from any state, while GUSTAVUS V. FOX of Massachusetts was assistant secretary of the navy. In addition to the industrial output of shoes and uniforms from factories, the basic new weapon of the war, the .58-caliber rifled musket, was the product of the armory at Springfield, which made almost 800,000 during the war years. —FSK

22d Massachusetts. Known as "HENRY WILSON'S Regiment," after the senator who helped organize it and served briefly as its first colonel, the 22d Massachusetts was formed at Lynnfield, Mass., Sept. 1861, and reached Washington, D.C., 11 Oct. There it spent 5 months on picket and outpost duty as part of Brig. Gen. JOHN H. MARTINDALE's brigade/ARMY OF THE POTOMAC. In mid-Mar. 1862, under Col. Jesse A. Gove, a Regular Army officer and Mexican War veteran, the regiment embarked for the Virginia peninsula.

During the ensuing offensive against Richmond, the 22d was heavily engaged 27 June at GAINES' MILL, where it suffered its greatest combat loss of the war. Among the 84 men killed or mortally wounded was Colonel Gove, whose body fell into enemy hands and was never recovered. By the end of the campaign, the regiment had seen almost 100 of its members killed in battle, dozens of others having been wounded. It was lightly engaged at SECOND BULL RUN and at ANTIETAM was held in reserve throughout the fighting.

At FREDERICKSBURG, 13 Dec. 1862, the 22d was in the thick of the struggle; posted on the edge of the city, it supported the repeated attacks on Marye's Heights. After wintering at Potomac Creek, Va., it marched under Col. William S. Tilton to CHANCELLORSVILLE, where it was not engaged, and then to GETTYSBURG, during which campaign Tilton led the 1st Brigade/1st Division/V Corps, comprising his own regiment and 3 others. On 2 July 1863, the 22d was among those units hastened into action west of CEMETERY RIDGE to shore up the crumbling line of the III Corps. Twice attacked near the WHEATFIELD by strong Confederate forces, Tilton's brigade repulsed both efforts, holding on till the line along Cemetery Ridge was restored. Afterward, the 22d fell back in proper order, demonstrating, according to Tilton, "the greatest coolness and courage."

Following Gettysburg, the regiment was engaged at RAP-

PAHANNOCK STATION and MINE RUN. It fought stubbornly through the first part of the 1864 campaign, though reduced to fewer than 300 effectives. It lost many of these at the WILDERNESS, SPOTSYLVANIA (especially at Laurel Hill, 8 May), and COLD HARBOR. After participating in the 18 June assault on PETERSBURG, the outfit was placed on guard duty at CITY POINT until early October when it returned to Washington for muster-out. —EGL

54th Massachusetts Colored Regiment. In 1863 JOHN A. ANDREW, the antislavery governor of Massachusetts, won approval of a proposal to form a regiment from blacks living in his state. Andrew believed that such a regiment would offer "an opportunity for a whole race of men" and would "go far to elevate or depress the estimation in which the character of colored Americans will be held throughout the world." The result was the organization of the 54th Massachusetts Infantry, the most famous of the Union's black regiments.

Since it proved impossible to get enough black troops from Massachusetts, the 54th was filled by blacks from all over the North. As with all black units, almost all the officers were white. The regiment's first commander was Col. ROBERT GOULD SHAW, who had been a captain in the 2d Massachusetts.

In May 1863 the 54th was mustered into Federal service and assigned to the Department of the South. The regiment spent most of the war on the South Carolina coast, but it was often used in expeditions into Georgia and Florida, most notably in the campaign that led to the Battle of OLUSTEE, Fla., early in 1864.

The regiment's most renowned service was in the assault on BATTERY WAGNER, Morris Island, S.C., 18 July 1863. The 54th made a gallant attack that reached the top of the fort's wall before it was beaten back. Shaw was killed on the wall, and the regiment lost 272 of its 650 men. After Shaw's death, the unit was led by Col. Edward N. Hallowell.

The regiment set an example by refusing to accept pay until the law was changed to provide black troops with the same compensation white soldiers received. The 54th Massachusetts fulfilled Andrew's hope and returned to a great welcome in Boston in 1864. —RMcM

57th Massachusetts. Staffed largely by veterans of other outfits, this regiment was organized during winter 1863–64. It was mustered in at Worcester Jan.–Apr. 1864 under Col. (later Bvt. Maj. Gen.) WILLIAM F. BARTLETT. Toward the close of that month it traveled to Annapolis, Md., joining the 1st Brigade/1st Division/IX Corps/Army of the Potomac.

In its first battle, the 6 May fighting in the Virginia WILDERNESS, the 57th as well as its entire division supported the II Corps along the Orange Plank road. Hotly involved in that sector, the regiment lost 47 killed, 161 wounded, and 43 missing. Among the wounded was Colonel Bartlett, who never returned to regimental command. Under his successor, Lt. Col. Charles L. Chandler, the Bay Staters accompanied the army to SPOTSYLVANIA, where 12 and 18 May the unit lost 16 killed, 69 wounded, and 4 missing.

On the 24th, the regiment crossed the NORTH ANNA RIVER, heading south. Attempting to clear Ox Ford for the rest of its corps, it was outflanked and driven back with heavy loss, Lieutenant Colonel Chandler being killed. Under Capt. Julius M. Tucker, the survivors served on the far Union right at COLD HARBOR, where they were marginally engaged. On 13 June

they left their trenches and 2 days later, along with the rest of the army, crossed the James River to Petersburg.

On the evening of the 17th, Tucker, now a major, led his men in an attack east of the city, which cost the 57th 44 casualties, Tucker himself falling wounded. For several weeks the regiment served in the rifle pits outside Petersburg, then joined in the ill-fated assault at the Battle of the CRATER, 30 July. Leading the second wave of attack, Brig. Gen. Bartlett, commanding the 57th's brigade, was disabled and captured and his old regiment shredded. When the smoke cleared, only 47 effectives remained.

Rebuilt by recruits and returned convalescents, the 57th fought through the remainder of the PETERSBURG CAMPAIGN. On 25 Mar. 1865, it helped repulse Gen. ROBERT E. LEE's last offensive, at FORT STEDMAN. One of the first units to occupy evacuated Petersburg, it was soon transferred to Tenleytown, Md., doing guard duty there until mustered out 30 July 1865. Though in service less than 16 months, the regiment had lost almost 20% of its total enrollment. —EGL

massacres. *See* BAXTER SPRINGS, KANS., MASSACRE AT; CENTRALIA, MO., MASSACRE AT; FORT PILLOW, TENN., BATTLE OF; POISON SPRINGS, ARK., ENG. AT; SALTVILLE, VA., MASSACRE AT; SAND CREEK MASSACRE, COLORADO TERRITORY; SHELTON LAUREL, N.C., MASSACRE AT.

Matamoros, Mexico. Situated 25 mi from the mouth of the Rio Grande, Matamoros sits opposite Brownsville, Tex., in the Mexican state of Tamaulipas. During the Civil War its crude port facilities, adjacent to Confederate Texas, made it a major point of entry for Southern BLOCKADE RUNNERS bound from Havana, Cuba. A bar at the mouth of the Rio Grande limited entry to shallow draft schooners, but Mexico's nonbelligerent status prevented Union warships from interfering with these craft once they entered Mexico's territorial waters.

With a population of 9,000, Matamoros was virtually an open city to Confederates. Mexico's own political difficulties kept its civil administration in doubt. Mexican Gen. Santiago Vidaurri, governor of the neighboring state of Nuevo León and a friend of the Confederacy, exercised political control in the town through much of the war by remaining loyal to the French-supported government of Mexican Emperor Maximilian. Mexican rebels under Benito Juárez drove Vidaurri into exile in Texas Mar. 1864 and took control of the town until driven out by the French army in August. Vidaurri returned to control in September, but the French eased him from office and administered his affairs thereafter. Under all administrations Confederate imports and exports were heavily taxed, and frequent bribes were required to keep commercial traffic moving smoothly into Brownsville or, after that city fell to Federal troops, farther west for entry into Texas. The least efficient of all blockade-running ports, technically it remained the only one never closed by the Union navy.

Matamoros on the Rio Grande is sometimes confused in records with a smaller town of the same name in Coahuila. —JES

Maury, Dabney Herndon. CSA b. Frederick, Va., 21 May 1822. In his report of the Battle of PEA RIDGE, Maj. Gen. EARL VAN DORN praised Maury for his courage and patriotism. His subsequent military career confirmed his bravery; his men respected him as an honorable man who did not shirk his duty.

Maury graduated from the University of Virginia in 1842, studied law, but entered West Point rather than establish a legal practice. He graduated 37th in the class of 1846, with rank as 2d lieutenant of Mounted Rifles. Twice during the Mexican War the young cavalryman received brevets for gallantry and bravery. He taught geography, history, ethics, and infantry tactics at the U.S. Military Academy 1847–52, then spent 4 years stationed along

USMHI

the Texas frontier. From 1856 to 1860 he was superintendent of the cavalry school at Carlisle, Pa., in 1859 publishing the classic *Skirmish Drill for Mounted Troops.*

In May 1861 he resigned his commission as captain and the assistant adjutant generalcy of the Department of New Mexico, though the resignation was not accepted and 25 June he was dismissed from the army. Traveling to Richmond, Maury entered Confederate service as a captain of cavalry, and early in 1862 was promoted to colonel and assigned as chief of staff to Van Dorn in the Trans-Mississippi. The brilliant performance Van Dorn praised after Pea Ridge won for Maury promotion to brigadier general 18 Mar. 1862. At IUKA and CORINTH, Miss., and Hatchie Bridge, Tenn., he again fought skillfully. On 4 Nov. he was promoted to major general and assigned briefly to East Tennessee.

In July 1863 Maury took command of the District of the Gulf, a position he retained until the war ended. Through skillful defense he held MOBILE BAY until Aug. 1864, when Rear Adm. DAVID G. FARRAGUT overpowered the Confederate naval defense. Maury held Mobile until 12 Apr. 1865, when he retreated to Meridian, Miss., his 9,200 men withstanding for 3 weeks a combined assault by Farragut's fleet and Maj. Gen. E.R.S. CANBY's 45,000 infantrymen.

Maury returned to civilian life in poverty. He held teaching positions in Virginia and Louisiana, volunteered as a nurse in New Orleans during the yellow-fever epidemic of 1868, and settled for a time in Richmond. In 1868 he was among the founders of the Southern Historical Society, serving as chairman of its executive committee until 1886. Between 1885 and 1889, he held an appointment as U.S. minister to Colombia, and was a National Guard executive committee member until 1890.

Maury spent his latter years at his son's home in Peoria, Ill., dying there 11 Jan. 1900. He wrote several articles for the *SOUTHERN HISTORICAL SOCIETY PAPERS* and an interesting memoir, *Recollections of a Virginian* (1894), part of which covers the Civil War years. —PLF

Maury, Matthew Fontaine. CSN b. Spotsylvania Cty., Va., 14 Jan. 1806, Maury made his place in history well before the Civil War. He attended Harpeth Academy in Tennessee and in 1825 entered the U.S. Navy as a midshipman, performing so well that he was promoted to lieutenant in 1836. 3 years later he injured his leg in an accident and was crippled for life.

Unable to go to sea, he was assigned to the Navy Department's Depot of Charts and Instruments in Washington. During the next 19 years he devoted himself to various meteorologic

and oceanographic studies, contributing greatly to the science of marine navigation and writing several books on the subject. So widely recognized was his work that it led to an international conference in Brussels in 1853 that benefited navies all over the world. That year he was made a commander.

LC

Suddenly, in 1855, he was placed on the reserve list by the Naval Retiring Board. He and his friends voiced an immediate protest. The man Maury held most responsible was the committee chairman, Sen. STEPHEN R. MALLORY of Florida, later Confederate Navy secretary.

At the outbreak of war Maury joined the Confederate navy and was attached to the Office of Orders and Detail at Richmond. He came in frequent contact with Mallory, with whom he disagreed over the type of ships the South should build. Mallory favored IRONCLADS, Maury small gunboats with from 2 to 4 guns each.

Maury was put in charge of devising and placing submarine batteries in the James River. He did his job well, but late in 1862, because of his international reputation, he was sent to England as a Confederate naval agent, there to buy ships and supplies. He served out the war in London.

After the surrender he settled first in Mexico, then in England. In 1868 he returned to the U.S. and became professor of meteorology at the Virginia Military Institute in Lexington, where he died 4 Feb. 1873. —VCJ

Maxey, Samuel Bell. CSA b. Tompkinsville, Ky., 30 Mar. 1825, Maxey received his early education locally, then graduated 58th in the West Point class of 1846. He held a commission as 2d lieutenant with the 8th Infantry during the Mexican War, winning brevet rank as 1st lieutenant for gallantry at Contreras and Churubusco. Bored with his postwar assignment to Jefferson Barracks, Mo., he resigned from the army 17 Sept. 1849 to study law. With his father, also an attorney, he moved to Paris, Tex., in 1857 and set up a partnership.

A secessionist, Maxey resigned his seat in the Texas senate early in 1861 to organize the 9th Texas Infantry. Elected colonel in September, he took his

NA

regiment to join Gen. ALBERT SIDNEY JOHNSTON's command in Kentucky. Military experience and leadership ability resulted in his promotion to brigadier general as of 4 Mar. 1862. After fighting in East Tennessee, at PORT HUDSON, and in the campaign to relieve VICKSBURG, on 11 Dec. 1863 Gen. E. KIRBY SMITH gave him command of Indian Territory.

Of the generals who held this difficult assignment, none succeeded more effectively than Maxey. He waged a broad-based propaganda campaign to revitalize the demoralized Indian alliances with the Confederacy, operated a press at Fort

Towson to print pro-Southern literature, and used his skills as a fiery orator to cultivate goodwill among the loyal tribes. Orders to join Maj. Gen. STERLING PRICE to halt the Federal RED RIVER CAMPAIGN interrupted his reorganization of troops in the territory, but he was able to keep relatively reliable Indian brigades in the field by allowing them to fight as irregulars. Choctaws under Col. Tandy Walker fought well for him at POISON SPRINGS, Ark., 18 Apr. 1864, and Brig. Gen. STAND WATIE's raiding forays harassed Federal soldiers reoccupying large blocks of Indian Territory. Kirby Smith named him major general 18 Apr. 1864, but Jefferson Davis never formally confirmed the rank. Maxey finally lost command of the territory Mar. 1865 to the unscrupulous political maneuverings of Brig. Gen. DOUGLAS H. COOPER.

After the war Maxey returned to his law practice in Paris and in 1873 turned down an appointment to the state bench. 2 years later he won a seat in the U.S. Senate and was reelected in 1881. During his 12 years in office he supported Federal funding for the improvement of Texas roads, waterways, and railroads, and delivered eloquent speeches on behalf of dealing fairly with Indians. Defeated for a third congressional term, he retired to his law practice in Paris. Maxey died in Eureka Springs, Ark., 16 Aug. 1895. His body was returned to Paris, Tex., for burial.   —PLF

Meade, George Gordon. USA   b. Cádiz, Spain, 31 Dec. 1815, Meade was born on foreign soil while his father, Richard Worsam Meade, was a naval agent for the U.S. The family lived well abroad, but economic cir-
cumstances changed when Meade's father died in Washington, D.C., unable to collect on a debt legitimately owed to him by the government. Because of these financial reverses, Meade was forced first to withdraw from school in Philadelphia and attend one in Washington conducted by SALMON P. CHASE, then to enter the U.S. Military Academy 1 Sept. 1831. Despite his lack of enthusiasm for the academy, he did well, graduating 19th in a class of 56 in 1835. On

USMHI

a brief leave Meade aided in the survey for the Long Island Railroad. Then, during the Seminole War, he was sent to Florida as a brevet 2d lieutenant of the 3rd Artillery. After contracting a fever he was returned to duty at Watertown Arsenal in Massachusetts, where he was engaged in ordnance. On 26 Oct. 1836 he resigned from the army to do engineering work for the Alabama, Florida, & Georgia Railroad as well as to work on the survey of the Mississippi and the Texas border.

Having married, Meade rejoined the army 19 May 1842. He was appointed a 2d lieutenant in the Corps of Topographical Engineers and was assigned to the northeastern border survey. In 1843 he was transferred to Philadelphia to work on lighthouse construction in Delaware Bay until transfer to Texas and service in the Mexican War, where he saw action at Palo Alto and Resaca de la Palma. At Monterrey, 23 Sept. 1846, he was brevetted a 1st lieutenant for bravery and went on to action with Gen. WINFIELD SCOTT at Vera Cruz. From the close of the Mexican War to the Civil War, he did considerable engineering

work on coastal lighthouses and was in charge of the surveys of the Great Lakes.

Meade was made a brigadier general of volunteers 31 Aug. 1861, leading 1 of 3 Pennsylvania brigades along with Brig. Gens. JOHN F. REYNOLDS and E.O.C. ORD. His first duty in command was in the defense of Washington, D.C., where he aided in the construction of Fort Pennsylvania. His command was transferred Mar. 1862 to Maj. Gen. IRVIN MCDOWELL's army and after the evacuation of Manassas was absorbed into the Department of the Shenandoah.

In June 1862 Meade was assigned to the Virginia peninsula under Maj. Gen. GEORGE B. MCCLELLAN, then was promoted to major in the Corps of Topographical Engineers in the Regular Army. His brigade participated in the Battles of MECHANICSVILLE, GAINES' MILL, and WHITE OAK SWAMP, where, wounded in the hip and arm, he directed the battle until he physically could not continue.

After a less than adequate period of recovery, Meade was back in the fighting at SECOND BULL RUN, 29–30 Aug. 1862. At South Mountain he received written commendation from his superiors while in temporary command of Reynolds' division. On 16–17 Sept. at ANTIETAM, he showed courage by pushing forward until lack of ammunition prevented further pursuit. When Maj. Gen. JOSEPH HOOKER was carried from the field after being wounded, Meade assumed temporary command of the I Corps for the duration of the battle.

In Oct.–Nov. 1862, he was given Reynolds' old division under the leadership of McClellan in pursuit of Gen. ROBERT E. LEE to Falmouth, Va. On 29 Nov. he was made major general of volunteers and 25 Dec. was given command of the V Corps, after considerable losses at FREDERICKSBURG. On 26 Jan. 1863, he received command of the Center Grand Division, which included the former III and VI corps. After Hooker abolished the grand divisions, Meade returned to command of the V Corps. As its leader he participated in the Battle of CHANCELLORSVILLE, 4 May 1863. Though his unit performed well there when called upon, Hooker did not use it aggressively.

Meade's own thoughts on aggressive strategy during that battle brought his name forward as a candidate for commander of the Army of the Potomac. The appointment was received 28 June while he was tracking Lee's troops as they made their way north toward Pennsylvania. Meade was surprised and not entirely pleased with the appointment but accepted it as his duty. Though he concentrated his forces, he did not strike Lee's lines. By chance the armies met at Gettysburg just 3 days after his appointment. There Meade did a respectable job of managing his troops but some critics felt he might have done better by reinforcing his flanks, holding reserves, and being more aggressive. Meade did not press his advantage when he might have done so on 2–3 July but received the THANKS OF CONGRESS for his leadership in repelling the Army of Northern Virginia and was promoted to brigadier general in the Regular Army from 3 July 1863. He continued in command for campaigning along the Rapidan Ring that fall.

Following the MINE RUN operation, Maj. Gen. U. S. GRANT, who had been promoted to lieutenant general in command of all Union forces, decided to accompany the Army of the Potomac. Though Meade remained in command of that army until Appomattox, the presence of Grant somewhat preempted his leadership. With a few exceptions, Meade was patient and skillful in carrying out orders and 18 Aug. 1864 was promoted to major general in the Regular Army.

After the war Meade was placed in command of the Military Division of the Atlantic and the Department of the East in Philadelphia. On 2 Jan. 1868 he reported to Atlanta to administer Reconstruction policy, performing his duties thoughtfully and with a sensitivity to fairness in the light of often unjust regulations.

In 1866, he became commissioner of Fairmount Park in Philadelphia, a post he held until his death. He died in Philadelphia 6 Nov. 1872 as a result of old war wounds complicated by pneumonia.   —JDK

Meagher, Thomas Francis. USA b. Waterford, Ireland, 3 Aug. 1823. The son of a wealthy merchant, Meagher studied at an Irish Jesuit school and an English college, and belonged to several Irish independence organizations. Following a trip to the Continent to gauge revolutionist sympathies, Meagher was arrested by British authorities for a seditious speech and exiled to Tasmania in 1849. He fled to California in 1852, migrated to New York City, acquired U.S. citizenship, then became an attorney, lecturer, and a political power among Irish immigrants and partisans of an independent Ireland.

USMHI

Convinced that British sympathy lay with the Confederacy, Meagher mustered into Union service Apr. 1861 with a ZOUAVE company he raised for the 69th New York Militia. As a major he fought at FIRST BULL RUN under his friend Col. MICHAEL CORCORAN. On Corcoran's capture and the militia's dissolution, he returned to New York City and spent the fall and winter raising an IRISH BRIGADE.

The first of his regiments, the 69th New York Infantry, was mustered in Nov. 1861, and Meagher received commission as brigadier general 6 Feb. 1862. He led his brigade at the Siege of YORKTOWN, the Battle of SEVEN PINES, in the SEVEN DAYS' battles and the SECOND BULL RUN CAMPAIGN, and at the Battles of ANTIETAM, FREDERICKSBURG, and CHANCELLORSVILLE, in the last 2 fights pressing his men with bravery and abandon. At Marye's Heights in the Fredericksburg fighting the unit was shattered, and after Chancellorsville its survivors were slated for transfer and consolidation with other units. Protesting the reorganization and the end of the brigade's Irish character, on 14 May 1863 Meagher submitted his resignation, which was shelved.

On a ride with Corcoran, 22 Dec. 1863, his friend's horse fell, killing him. With Corcoran's death the mantle of Irish-American military leadership passed to Meagher. His resignation was canceled 23 Dec., and he was sent to Maj. Gen. WILLIAM T. SHERMAN. Though the transfer kept Meagher in service, Sherman had to find a position for him. In Nov. 1864 he took assignment with Maj. Gen. GEORGE H. THOMAS in the Department of the Cumberland, briefly commanded the Georgia District of Etowah, and in Savannah assumed command of MEAGHER'S PROVISIONAL DIVISION, leading its disparate elements to New Berne in the CAROLINAS CAMPAIGN. Unsatisfied with his duties, he resigned 15 May 1865.

Later that year Meagher's service was rewarded with appointment as territorial secretary to Montana. In the governor's absence he performed gubernatorial duties from Oct. 1865 through the next autumn. On 1 July 1867, during a drinking bout aboard a steamboat at Fort Benton, he fell overboard and drowned.   —JES

Meagher's Provisional Division. USA Union Brig. Gen. THOMAS F. MEAGHER, posted in Georgia early in 1865, took command of a temporarily organized division made up of stragglers and late arrivals to Maj. Gen. WILLIAM T. SHERMAN's Army of the Tennessee, already departed for the CAROLINAS CAMPAIGN. The exact date of its organization is unknown but is presumed to have fallen between 14 Jan. and 1 Feb. 1865. The journal of Maj. Gen. JACOB D. COX notes that on 25 Feb. Meagher's Provisional Division was shipped to New Berne, N.C., and awaited orders there. Though Confederate sources refer to Meagher's force in transit, the unit saw no action under the brigadier general. Meagher relinquished command 1 Mar. 1865, and the troops were joined to Brig. Gen. INNIS N. PALMER's division. This force split in two, with Palmer and Brig. Gen. SAMUEL P. CARTER each commanding half.   —JES

Mechanicsville (Beaver Dam Creek; Ellerson's Mill), Va., Battle of. 26 June 1862 On this date, Gen. ROBERT E. LEE's Confederates, 47,000 of them, were supposed to fall upon Maj. Gen. FITZ JOHN PORTER's corps, which composed the right flank of Maj. Gen. GEORGE B. MCCLELLAN's Union army. In addition, Lt. Gen. THOMAS J. "STONEWALL" JACKSON's Valley Army was to hit Porter from the rear. Across the Chick-

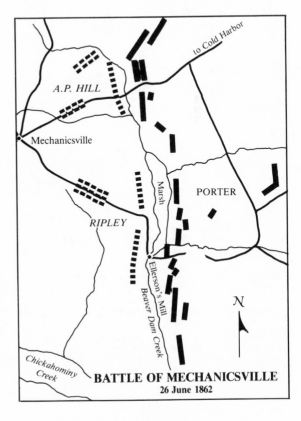

BATTLE OF MECHANICSVILLE
26 June 1862

ahominy from Mechanicsville, Maj. Gen. AMBROSE P. HILL waited to launch the attack, hoping for some sign of Jackson's approach. At 3 p.m. he could restrain himself no longer and, on the assumption that Jackson must be nearby, gave the order to advance.

5 infantry brigades with attendant artillery swept through the small hamlet of Mechanicsville. Then, as they advanced in line, they encountered Porter's well-prepared position behind Beaver Dam Creek, about a mile from Mechanicsville. Federal artillery raked the Southern ranks, followed by rifle fire. Southern commanders attempted to turn the Federal flank to no avail.

As darkness came, Lee determined to make one final charge and attempt to turn Porter's left flank. Brig. Gen. ROSWELL S. RIPLEY's brigade from Maj. Gen. DANIEL H. HILL's division had finally struggled across the Chickahominy, and Lee ordered it into action. Ripley's 2 regiments surged forward into the open twilight before the darkening undergrowth that fringed Beaver Dam Creek. As they came, the Federals opened fire with artillery and small arms. A few Confederates reached the opposite bank of the creek—too few to carry the Union works. In the end they all fell back—all but 477 casualties left behind in the growing darkness.

Lee's masterful plan had miscarried. Instead of forcing Porter's troops out of their entrenchments, the Confederates had assaulted them frontally. The day's action cost the Union 361 casualties and the Confederacy 1,484. The main blame was Jackson's. He never reached the action; indeed, he marched to within a few miles of Mechanicsville and made camp.   —EMT

Medal of Honor.   On 21 Dec. 1861, 8 months after the start of the Civil War, a bill was passed by the U.S. Congress and approved by Pres. ABRAHAM LINCOLN establishing a Medal of Honor to be awarded by the secretary of navy to enlisted men of the navy and the Marine Corps. On 12 July 1862 the army Medal of Honor was authorized for enlisted men and amended 3 Mar. 1863 to include army officers.

The first army Medals of Honor were presented by Sec. of War EDWIN M. STANTON 25 Mar. 1863 to 6 participants of the ill-fated ANDREWS' RAID. A few days later, 3 Apr., the first medals were awarded to sailors and marines. The medal was not authorized for navy officers until the eve of World War I.

LC

Creation of the medal gave the U.S. a military equivalent to the Victoria Cross of England and the Iron Cross of Germany. It was, and still is, the nation's highest award for valor.

Today the medal is awarded by the president in the name of Congress to such a person who, while an officer or enlisted man of the U.S. military or naval forces, has in action involving actual contact with an enemy distinguished himself conspicuously by gallantry and intrepidity at the risk of his life above and beyond the call of duty.

At the time of its authorization, however, it was not only the country's highest tribute for valor, it was the only medal given by the U.S. to its armed forces. Coupled with that, the wording of the congressional acts establishing the medals were vague

and allowed for liberal interpretation. As a result, many were dispensed to those who, by current standards, would not qualify for the medal.

In 1916 a board of 5 retired general officers was appointed to investigate all Medals of Honor previously issued to army personnel. 911 names were stricken from the list, most of them recipients of the medal for service during the Civil War.

—SWS

medicine.   A Civil War soldier quickly came face-to-face with his deadliest foe: disease. Poor diet, unsanitary camp conditions, pesky insects, and bad weather contributed to the soldier's general breakdown in health. Diarrhea in its various forms, including dysentery, claimed more lives than battlefield wounds. Sporadic outbreaks of measles, smallpox, and malaria added to the chronic woes of pneumonia, bronchitis, scurvy, and "camp itch."

Each day at sick call in the field or in hospitals, doctors examined their patients and prescribed medication to combat soldiers' ills. Since a majority of these cases were bowel complaints, dosage generally fell into one of two categories: astringents or purgatives. Open bowels placed the patient into the first category and either a plug of opium or a tree-bark substitute concocted from willows or sweet gums was administered. Closed bowels were treated with a dose of blue mass (mercury and chalk) or a vegetable cathartic. Pneumonia and bronchitis were dealt with by alternate bleeding, dosing with opium or quinine, and the application of mustard plasters. Scurvy was treated through a diet consisting of green vegetables and fruit. Onions and lemons were particularly effective; wine vinegar was a readily available substitute.

Camping in damp areas brought many cases of malaria, which were dosed with quinine or tree-bark derivatives from dogwoods or poplars; turpentine served in the absence of these potions. "Camp itch" caused by either insects or skin disease was a persistent problem. Delousing usually cured the first problem and poke-root solution taken internally took care of the second.

To halt communicable diseases such as measles and smallpox, quarantine and vaccination were employed. Measles, particularly in the early years of the war, incapacitated so many men that some army operations were delayed or even canceled.

The most commonly used wartime "cure-all" was alcohol, usually given in the forms of whiskey and brandy. While its true medicinal value was questionable, it did help ease pain and met few complaints from patients.

Chief medical officer for the Army of the Potomac Jonathan Letterman restructured the U.S. Army Medical Department into the form that existed through World War II. This reorganization authorized the inclusion of a medicine wagon for each brigade. Among its drug contents were chloroform, ether, morphine, opium (anesthetics), alcohol, asafedita, calomel, castor oil, digitalis, spirits, turpentine, and various acids.

Local manufacture of drugs was minimal and most were imported by the Federal government throughout the war. The Confederacy relied on BLOCKADE RUNNERS for its imports, and as the blockade tightened the need for local production increased. Pioneer Southern pharmacists such as Joseph Le Compte produced alcohol, silver chloride, sulfuric ether, nitric ether, and blue mass from native plants. Francis P. Porcher compiled a field guide of wild herbs and trees for medicinal substitutes: for example, juice from a green persimmon served as a styptic, wood turpentine as an antiseptic, and red garden poppy opium as an anesthetic. Despite these domestic alternatives, in the later years of war medicines were still in short supply, and Confederate soldiers increasingly endured illnesses, woundings, and amputations without medication.

In an era before antitoxins and the science of bacteriology existed, when crude sanitation and ignorance of water- and insect-related disease were prevalent, Civil War doctors became medicinal explorers. By recording successes and failures in their battle against disease, they contributed significantly to postbellum development of pharmacology.   —LJB

Meigs, John Rodgers. USA b. District of Columbia, 9 Feb. 1842, Meigs is remembered for the controversy surrounding his death. The bright eldest son of U.S. Army Quartermaster Gen. MONTGOMERY C. MEIGS and grandson of U.S. Navy hero Commodore John Rodgers, he received appointment to West Point in 1859, took a leave of absence to serve as an aide during the FIRST BULL RUN CAMPAIGN, then graduated 1st in the class of 1863, becoming a 2d lieutenant of engineers.

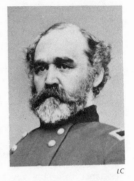

LC

After participating in the pursuit of the Confederate army following the Battle of GETTYSBURG, young Meigs served on Brig. Gen. BENJAMIN F. KELLEY's staff in West Virginia, fought at the Battle of NEW MARKET, Va., and campaigned in Maj. Gens. DAVID HUNTER's and PHILIP H. SHERIDAN's operations in the Shenandoah Valley. Sheridan appointed Meigs his chief engineer Aug. 1864 and had him brevetted to captain and major for gallantry at battles at Winchester and Fisher's Hill.

On 3 Oct. 1864, returning from a surveying assignment with 2 enlisted men, he overtook 3 Confederate cavalrymen on the Swift Run Gap road in the Shenandoah Valley and was shot and killed. One enlisted man was taken prisoner, the other escaped and told Sheridan that Meigs, without an opportunity to defend himself, had been killed in cold blood. Believing Meigs had been murdered by Confederate partisans, Sheridan ordered burned the town of Dayton, Va., and all homes and farms within 5 mi of Meigs's death. Dayton was spared—possibly, as writer George F. Skoch points out, because of the immediate parole of Meigs's other companion by Confederates. However, some homes were burned in retaliation.

Montgomery Meigs, unconvinced that his son's death constituted a legitimate casualty of war, placed $1,000 on the killer's head. The 3 Confederates, 1 of whom had been wounded by young Meigs in the encounter, claimed in postwar years that the fight had been fair. *Confederate Veteran* magazine gave a more balanced account of the incident Mar. 1914, one exonerating the cavalrymen. Many similar incidents may have occurred during the war, but young Meigs's social prominence made his case famous.   —JES

Meigs, Montgomery Cunningham. USA b. Augusta, Ga., 3 May 1816. A man of irascible personality who made his nation his career, Meigs graduated from West Point 5th in the class of 1836 and embarked on army engineering work distinguished by the building of the Washington, D.C., aqueduct and near-completion of the Capitol dome. With the outbreak of war in 1861, Unionist Meigs found that his lifelong interest in mechanics and science and his experience with the tricky mixture of public works and private contracts qualified him for the post of quartermaster general of the U.S. Army. Made an infantry colonel 14 May 1861, he protested that his talents lay elsewhere. The next day he was promoted to quartermaster general with the rank of brigadier, replacing JOSEPH E. JOHNSTON, who had joined the Confederacy.

Through 4 years of desperate management problems, Meigs's task was to change a small peacetime army-supply system to one accommodating a force of more than a million men. Beset with problems of corruption, kickbacks, and poor supply contracts, he weathered scandals in his administration (particularly in the West), geared up the supply system for the nation's largest army, advocated the iron-armoring of Union river fleets, dispensed $1.5 billion (the largest amount the army had spent until that time), and accounted, for good or ill, for every penny spent.

His Civil War career was not without tragedy. His eldest son, JOHN RODGERS MEIGS, was killed in the Shenandoah Valley while serving on Maj. Gen. PHILIP H. SHERIDAN's staff. Rumored to be a guerrilla murder, not a combat death, the loss provoked Sheridan to exact harsh revenge on valley residents. But to Georgian Meigs the only real consolation was that his son died serving the Union.

After the peace Meigs served on in the army as a major general until 1882. d. District of Columbia, 2 Jan. 1892.
          —JES

Memminger, Christopher Gustavus. CSA b. Wurtemberg, Germany, 9 Jan. 1803. Jefferson Davis appointed this German-born South Carolinian to the CONFEDERATE CABINET as secretary of the treasury Feb. 1861. A conscientious, industrious man, he struggled to finance the Confederate budget for 3 years in the face of severe criticism and insurmountable odds.

Orphaned shortly after his family immigrated to Charleston, Memminger was accepted into a wealthy family and educated as a lawyer. As his practice grew, so did his political aspirations. Elected to the state house of representatives in 1836, he chaired the Committee on Finance. His persistent

VM

efforts to establish controls over the banking industry earned him recognition as a sound financier.

A conservative Democrat, he opposed independent action

by South Carolina in response to the issue of slavery but defended slavery as an institution. By the time of John Brown's Raid (*see* HARPERS FERRY, WESTERN VA., JOHN BROWN'S RAID ON) he firmly believed both secession and unified action by the Southern states a necessary defense against Northern domination. In his frustrating position as Treasury secretary, Memminger tried to stabilize the Confederate economy, establish its credit, and draw money from the states into the Richmond government coffers. Though he agitated to increase bond sales, restrict currency issues to control inflation, and prod Congress into passing a comprehensive tax bill, the STATES-RIGHTS faction thwarted his attempts to control the flow of cash and credit at a national level. Considering Congress' sluggishness, cotton's uselessness as a cash crop, and widespread resistance to central government, it is unlikely that anyone could have done better. Memminger resigned July 1864 in the face of harsh criticism from Congress and the press.

Back in South Carolina after the war, he reopened his law practice and entered business. Already distinguished as the founder of Charleston's public-school system, Memminger devoted his later years to promoting free education for blacks and whites in the state. d. Charleston, 7 Mar. 1888.   —PLF

Memphis, Tenn., Battle of. 6 June 1862 Sharing command of the rams and fighting men of the CONFEDERATE RIVER DEFENSE FLEET, Capt. James E. Montgomery and Brig. Gen. M. JEFF THOMPSON (Missouri Militia) retreated to Memphis after being defeated by Union ironclad gunboats in the Battle of PLUM RUN BEND, Tenn., 10 May 1862. Following Union Maj. Gen. HENRY W. HALLECK's occupation of CORINTH, Miss., Confederate Gen. P.G.T. BEAUREGARD ordered troops evacuated from Fort Pillow and Memphis 4 June. The city could not be defended on land, and Beauregard withdrew his men from Halleck's front and Federal naval advances south on the Mississippi. Thompson's token force camped outside Memphis and Montgomery's rams were to contest any Union naval attack on the city.

Union naval Capt. CHARLES H. DAVIS, commanding ailing Flag Officer ANDREW H. FOOTE's fleet of IRONCLADS, moved on Memphis at 4:20 a.m., 6 June, from Island No. 45, 2 mi north of the city. His approach with the *Benton, Louisville, Carondolet, Cairo,* and *St. Louis* was joined by the armored rams *Queen of the West* and *Monarch* commanded by army Col. CHARLES ELLET. Several of Ellet's other rams followed within supporting distance. Warned of Davis' approach by a picket boat, Montgomery's rams moved slightly south of Memphis to organize for battle. Davis' fleet overtook and captured the fleeing Confederate transport *Sovereign* north of the city. Many of Thompson's force manned guns and took up small arms on Montgomery's rams *General Beauregard, General Bragg, General Price, General Van Dorn, General Thompson, Colonel Lovell, Sumter,* and *Little Rebel.* Thompson himself joined a large crowd of Memphis civilians to watch the fight from bluffs overlooking the river. The combat began in front of the city at 5:40 a.m. Thompson called it "one of the grandest, yet saddest scenes of my life."

After some desultory cannon fire from both sides, the Union *Queen of the West,* with Colonel Ellet in the pilot house, rushed in front of Davis' ironclads and rammed and sank the *Lovell.* A Confederate ram retaliated, disabling the *Queen.* The Union ram *Monarch* plowed into the *Beauregard.* As the *Beauregard* prepared to ram the *Monarch* in return, the *Price*

moved to ram the Union vessel on its opposite side. The *Monarch* moved out of the way, and the *Price* and *Beauregard* rammed each other. The *Sumter* and *Bragg,* both badly shelled by Davis' gunboats, were run aground. Montgomery, aboard the *Little Rebel,* fled into woods on the Arkansas banks opposite Memphis after his boat's machinery was blasted by Federal cannon fire and the vessel run aground by a ramming from the *Monarch.* Set afire by cannon shots from the *Benton,* the *Thompson* burned almost to the waterline, then exploded.

Smoke from cannon fire blanketed the river, making observation difficult for the combatants and the civilians ashore. Late in the fight the *Beauregard* drifted near shore and sank. Small-arms fire from the vessels was occasionally heavy. Colonel Ellet, badly wounded above one knee by a pistol bullet, died several days later from complications, the only Union fatality. Confederate deaths, though poorly counted, may have neared 100; between 70 and 100 were captured. Only the *Van Dorn* escaped the battle. Damaged, it traveled up the Yazoo River and was later scuttled. Federals captured, repaired, and later refitted the *Price, Bragg, Sumter,* and *Little Rebel* as Union rams.

Lt. Charles R. Ellet, son of Colonel Ellet, went ashore with 2 enlisted men, demanded Memphis' surrender from its mayor, and hauled down the Confederate flag over city hall. Captain Davis officially accepted the mayor's surrender between 10 and 11 a.m., and troops began occupying the city before noon. The capture of Memphis began a program of consolidation of Union gains on the Mississippi that would be completed the next summer with the seizure of PORT HUDSON.
                                                            —JES

Memphis & Charleston Railroad. Begun by farsighted Southerners in 1850, the Memphis & Charleston Railroad was intended to link the middle South with the seacoast. By 1859 company president Samuel Tate reported a profit of over $100,000 and an inventory that included 36 engines and 2 sleeper cars. Interested in seeing the line completed, the city of Charleston invested nearly $1 million with the railroad's developers in its first 6 years. But at the start of the Civil War it had only 271 mi of track and 20 mi of siding. Though it ran from Memphis, Tenn., through north Mississippi and Alabama, from Stevenson, Ala., it had to pay the Chattanooga & Nashville Railroad $20,000 annually to use its track to enter Chattanooga. Future Confederate general NATHAN B. FORREST, with 2,000 shares of stock, was one of its 10 heaviest private investors.

Despite its brief length, according to railroad historian Robert C. Black III, the line remained the only "trans-Confederate railroad," crossing 3 states west to east and intersecting the north-to-south line of the Mobile & Ohio Railroad at Corinth, Miss. Confederate cabinet member JUDAH P. BENJAMIN told officers that the line "must be defended against all hazards." As well as hauling equipment, its first major Confederate service consisted of shuttling Gen. ALBERT SIDNEY JOHNSTON's troops to Corinth in 1862 to begin the march to SHILOH. Following the battle, on 11 Apr. Brig. Gen. ORMSBY M. MITCHEL's Union troops severed the line at Huntsville, Ala., destroyed Memphis & Charleston repair shops there, and captured 106 cars and 18 engines.

Federals skirmished along the line 3–15 May 1862, the Corinth juncture with the Mobile & Ohio was captured 3 June, and the Memphis railhead fell 6 June. Maj. Gen. EARL VAN DORN attacked CORINTH 3 and 4 Oct., in part to gain access to the line. Federals used the track, the Stevenson terminus was in Union possession by autumn 1863, and in November stockholder Forrest attacked the M&C to prevent its use in supplying enemy forces in CHATTANOOGA. A destroyed section from Decatur, Ala., to Florence, Ala., underwent Confederate repairs at Gen. JOHN B. HOOD's order in autumn 1864 to afford him logistical support for the FRANKLIN AND NASHVILLE CAMPAIGN. A small spur line at Florence was the last to fall to Union troops, Mar. 1865.

Tate retained the presidency of the line through the war, reviving the railroad in postwar years. It became profitable again in the 1870s.   —JES

Memphis *Appeal*.   Col. Henry Van Pelt bought *The Western World and Memphis Banner of the Constitution* in 1840 to appeal the election results of the Harrison–Van Buren presidential contest. Accordingly, the newspaper's name changed to the Memphis *Appeal*. Like Van Pelt, the paper was always Democratic, and in 1860 its owners were Leonidas Trousdale, Robert McClanahan, and BENJAMIN F. DILL. They and their paper were conciliatory on the secession question. Douglas Democrats McClanahan and Dill bought out Breckinridge supporter Trousdale during the 1860 presidential election and later threw all editorial support behind the Confederacy when secession became an accomplished fact. When war threatened, the owners recruited, funded, and fielded an artillery unit, the "Appeal Battery."

The most Confederate and widely read of Tennessee's newspapers, the *Appeal* stated editorially its owners' preference to throw their equipment and business into the Mississippi River rather "than continue publication under Union occupation." On the morning of 6 June 1862, as Union gunboats defeated Confederate vessels on the river before Memphis, *Appeal* staffers sent equipment and materials by rail to Grenada, Miss., and resumed publication there. On 29 Nov. 1862, as Union troops approached, the *Appeal* moved to Jackson, Miss., producing its first issue there 13 Dec. 1862. Avoiding Federal capture, it moved again 14 May 1863 to Atlanta, Ga., stopping en route to put out a 1-page edition in Meridian, Miss. Remaining in Atlanta more than a year, it daily put out an 8,000-copy morning edition and a 6,000-copy evening edition. Contrary to belief, its name was not changed to the Memphis-Grenada-Jackson-Meridian-Atlanta *Appeal*. Federal occupation authorities established a counter-propaganda organ in Memphis titled the *Union Appeal*.

Supporting itself with advertising sales and job printing, the *Appeal* survived the Siege of Atlanta, then escaped to Montgomery, Ala., in summer 1864. In Apr. 1865, as WILSON'S RAID threatened Montgomery, the *Appeal*'s press was sent ahead to Macon, and McClanahan and some staff escaped across the Chattahoochee River. Dill and some equipment were captured by Union cavalrymen. Forced to sign a "seriocomic bond" for $100,000 renouncing the *Appeal*'s Confederate sympathies and pledging Union loyalty, Dill was released, returned to Memphis, and reestablished the *Appeal*.

Both Dill and McClanahan died shortly thereafter. Postwar the *Appeal* was badly run by Dill's widow, Americus, then taken over by a trio of owners headed by former Confederate general Albert Pike. Former part-owner Trousdale joined the editorial staff. Today, the newspaper continues as the Memphis *Commercial-Appeal*.   —JES

Mercer, Hugh Weedon.   CSA   b. Fredericksburg, Va., 27 Nov. 1808. Grandson and namesake of a Revolutionary War general, Mercer graduated from West Point in 1828, 3d in his class. As a lieutenant in the 2d U.S. Artillery, he spent a long tour of garrison duty in Georgia, manning the post of Savannah and the Augusta arsenal. For 2 years he was an aide to Bvt. Lt. Gen. WINFIELD SCOTT, then quit the army to marry a Savannah girl and settle in her hometown. Prior to the Civil War he was a bank cashier and an artillery officer in the local militia.

LC

Early in 1861 Mercer enlisted in the Confederate army as colonel of the 1st Georgia Infantry. By late October he was a brigadier general commanding the 1st, 54th, 57th, and 63d Georgia. Intimately acquainted with the defenses of Savannah, he was given command of them and spent most of the war in the city. In Aug. 1862 he was instrumental in impressing the first contingent of slaves and free blacks into Confederate service, to labor on the local works. Initially he petitioned slaveholders to lease 20% of their able-bodied chattels, whose transportation and rations were to be provided by the government. At first the appeal seemed effective, but soon it met with "a howl of indignant condemnation" from slavemasters throughout Georgia. By November the government had stripped Mercer of power to impress workers, and thereafter he relied on Gov. JOSEPH E. BROWN and local sheriffs to supply him with slaves.

Mercer left Savannah at the outset of the ATLANTA CAMPAIGN to accept field command in the Army of Tennessee. He fought ably at Dalton, Marietta, and KENNESAW MOUNTAIN, his brigade winning high praise in the last battle. After the BATTLE OF ATLANTA, he rose to command the division of the mortally wounded Maj. Gen. W.H.T. WALKER. He was ill during most of the subsequent campaign in Tennessee, eventually being relieved and sent back to Savannah to serve under Lt. Gen. WILLIAM J. HARDEE.

Departing the city on Hardee's retreat Dec. 1864, Mercer returned after hostilities ended to resume his banking career. In 1869 he moved to Baltimore, taking a position as a commission merchant. He died in Baden-Baden, Germany, where he had gone to seek a cure for ill health, 9 June 1877.   —EGL

Mercer, Samuel.   USN   b. Maryland, date unknown. Appointed midshipman 4 Mar. 1815, Mercer was promoted lieutenant in 1825, commander in 1841, and captain in 1855. At the outbreak of civil war he was captain of the *Powhatan*, which had finished a cruise and was at New York Mar. 1861. On 5 Apr. 1861 he was senior officer of the naval force (comprising the *Powhatan*, the *Pawnee*, the *Pocahontas*, and the revenue cutter *HARRIET LANE*) sent to Charleston harbor to provision the Federal garrison at Fort Sumter. A month later, Mercer was off the coast of Charleston again, this time commanding the *Wabash* of the Atlantic Blockading Squadron. He performed well, despite the ineffectiveness of the BLOCKADE at this time. In Aug. 1861, he participated in the combined navy/army expedition against the Confederate forts at HATTERAS INLET, N.C. During the engagement, the *Wabash* was struck twice by enemy shot. After bringing his ship to New York 8 Oct. 1861, Mercer was relieved of active command and appointed to the Navy Retiring Board. d. Brooklyn, N.Y., 6 Mar. 1862. —NCD

Meredith, Solomon. USA b. Guilford, Cty., N.C., 29 May 1810. In 1829 Meredith migrated to Indiana, worked as a laborer to pay for a private education, won election to 2 terms as sheriff of Wayne County and 4 terms in the state legislature, and in 1849 was made U.S. marshal for Indiana. Gov. OLIVER P. MORTON appointed him colonel of the 19th Indiana Infantry in summer 1861.

Brigaded with the 2d, 6th, and 7th Wisconsin regiments, Meredith's 19th served around Washington, D.C., and along the Rappahannock River until the Battle of GROVETON Aug. 1862. Fighting under Brig. Gen. JOHN GIBBON, the brigade, later known as the IRON BRIGADE OF THE WEST,

USMHI

distinguished itself. One of the 19th's casualties, Meredith convalesced through autumn, received a commission as brigadier general 6 Oct. 1862, and at the Battle of FREDERICKSBURG in December commanded the Iron Brigade in Brig. Gen. ABNER DOUBLEDAY's division in the I Corps. Meredith fought at CHANCELLORSVILLE and took a disabling wound on the first day of the battle at GETTYSBURG. In Apr. 1864 he was given garrison duty at Cairo, Ill., then was made post commander at Paducah, Ky., in September, serving there until the Confederate surrender.

Meredith was a political appointee and an older soldier; with his former brigade decimated by the Gettysburg fighting, no combat unit or position was sought for him. During his tour of duty at Paducah, Confederate cavalry raider Maj. Gen. NATHAN B. FORREST injected some excitement, but, in general, it was a quiet posting. After being brevetted major general of volunteers 14 Aug. 1865, he was mustered out 24 Aug.

In peacetime, Meredith accepted an appointment as government surveyor in Montana 1867–69, then retired to his farm near Cambridge City, Ind., dying there 2 Oct. 1875. —JES

Meridian Campaign. 3 Feb.–4 Mar. 1864 Union Maj. Gen. WILLIAM T. SHERMAN planned to march 120 mi east from Vicksburg, Miss., take Meridian, the state's largest remaining Confederate railroad center, and secure a broad corridor along the Mississippi River. If successful, he would cripple Western Confederate rail transport, eliminate an area supplying Southern troops with staples, restrict enemy operations south of Memphis, Tenn., and reduce the number of Union troops needed to secure Federal navigation of the Mississippi River.

He ordered Brig. Gen. WILLIAM SOOY SMITH to take 7,000 cavalry from the Memphis area 1 Feb., raid south through Okolona, down the Mobile & Ohio Railroad, and meet the main force at Meridian 10 Feb. Sherman left Vicksburg 3 Feb. with 20,000 men traveling in 2 columns: XVI Corps troops under Maj. Gen. Stephen A. Hurlbut departing north of the city, XVII Corps troops under Maj. Gen. JAMES B. MCPHERSON taking the direct easterly route on the Jackson road. To disperse Confederates from Sherman's front, diversions and feints

were ordered on Mobile, Ala., and Rome, Ga., along the Yazoo River; and on Pascagoula, Miss.

Confederate Lt. Gen. LEONIDAS POLK, commanding the Department of Alabama, Mississippi, and East Louisiana, had Meridian defended by 3,000 men under Maj. Gen. SAMUEL G. FRENCH, 2,500 cavalry under Maj. Gen. NATHAN B. FORREST along the Mobile & Ohio, 6,000 infantry under Maj. Gen. WILLIAM WING LORING northeast of Vicksburg at Canton, and 2,000 cavalry under Maj. Gen. STEPHEN D. LEE in Sherman's path west of Jackson. Forrest's and Lee's cavalry were the only Confederates seriously engaged in the campaign.

Lee's cavalry skirmished with Sherman's infantry 3–5 Feb. French, marching his men west to Jackson, arrived on the 4th, linked with Lee, abandoned plans for a battle northwest of Jackson at Clinton, and retreated east 5 Feb. Federal elements occupied Jackson late that day. On 8 Feb. Loring and French met at Morton, west of Meridian, skirmished with Federals 9 Feb., then retreated to Meridian. Other Southern departments, worried by Sherman's ordered diversions, sent Polk no reinforcements. Polk ordered Meridian abandoned 14 Feb. and removed his infantry and railroad rolling stock to Demopolis, Ala. Sherman's men entered Meridian the same day and through 19 Feb. destroyed 115 mi of railroad track surrounding the town.

Brigadier General Smith's Union cavalry never arrived at Meridian. Concerned, Sherman headed west 20 Feb., marching in a northerly arc through small towns and sending mounted scouts farther north to look for the lost force. The Federals assembled in Canton on the 26th, waited 5 days for word of Smith, then hiked back to Vicksburg, arriving there 4 Mar. Sherman's official report of 7 Mar. recorded Union losses in the brief campaign as just 170 killed, wounded, and missing, and claimed that the army lived chiefly off enemy civilians, took 400 prisoners, seized 3,000 draft animals, destroyed untotaled amounts of Confederate cotton, and escorted 5,000 slaves and 1,000 white refugees into Federal lines. The general praised McPherson and Hurlbut, saying that their handling of the campaign "left me an easy task, partaking more of the character of a pleasant excursion than of hard military service."

In Vicksburg Sherman received word that Smith had not launched his cavalry strike until 11 Feb., a day after he was expected at Meridian. He skirmished with Confederate militia, burned property, and tore up approximately 55 mi of railroad track until hitting Forrest's cavalry near West Point 20 Feb. Halting there because he was concerned about the topography, an extensive baggage train, and the safety of 1,000 slaves following his command, Smith turned back, skirmished north, fought and lost the engagement at Okolona, 22 Feb., then retired to Memphis with a loss of about 700 men killed, wounded, and captured. Sherman called his late start "unpardonable," his performance "unsatisfactory." —JES

***Merrimack,* USS.** See *Virginia,* CSS.

Merritt, Wesley. USA b. New York City, N.Y., 16 June 1834. One of the lesser-known but most successful "boy generals" of the war, Merritt was graduated from West Point 22d in the class of 1860. A dragoon before the war, he was a lieutenant in the 2d U.S. Cavalry when hostilities began. Until mid-1863 he served mostly on staff duty in Washington, including 2 stints as aide to Maj. Gen. GEORGE STONEMAN, commander of cavalry in the Army of the Potomac. Returning to field duty as a captain, he won notice for daring and gallantry at BRANDY STATION 9 June 1863, the largest mounted battle waged in North America. This, plus his capable performance near Middleburg 11 days later, enabled him to make an unprecedented leap to brigadier general of volunteers.

During the remainder of the GETTYSBURG CAMPAIGN, Merritt commanded the Reserve Cav-

USMHI

alry Brigade, Army of the Potomac, comprising 4 regiments of Regulars and 1 of volunteers. That autumn, in a host of battles and skirmishes, he demonstrated his fitness for higher command. Temporarily given a division May 1864, he served capably at Todd's Tavern, the war's largest dismounted cavalry fight, and during Maj. Gen. PHILIP H. SHERIDAN's raid on Richmond, especially at YELLOW TAVERN. That August he received permanent command of the 1st Cavalry Division in Sheridan's Army of the Shenandoah, which he led at THIRD WINCHESTER, Luray, CEDAR CREEK, and Tom's Brook. In the last engagement he helped inflict on Maj. Gen. THOMAS L. ROSSER's division one of the worst defeats suffered by Confederate cavalry during the war. In 1865 at WAYNESBOROUGH and during the APPOMATTOX CAMPAIGN he commanded Sheridan's cavalry corps as a brevet major general of volunteers.

Remaining in the army after the war, Merritt became a major general, fought Indians, served as superintendent of West Point, and commanded the first Philippine Expedition of 1898. Till the close of his career in 1900 he remained a highly capable officer, his lack of fame largely owing to his quiet and modest nature. d. at his home in Natural Bridge, Va., 3 Dec. 1910.   —EGL

Mervine, William. USN b. Philadelphia, Pa., 14 Mar. 1791. Mervine's long record of naval service gained him renown in both the War of 1812 and the Mexican War. He entered the navy as midshipman 16 Jan. 1809 and was promoted to lieutenant in 1815 and captain in 1841. In 1861 he was on waiting orders when war began. Flag Officer Mervine left Boston aboard the *Mississippi* to organize a Gulf blockading squadron, but sabotage to his ship's condensers caused temporary delays before he reached the Florida coast. There, Mervine established a BLOCKADE from Key West to Galveston. After Confederate forces occupied Ship Island July 1861, Navy Sec. GIDEON WELLES became displeased with Mervine for what he believed to be a lack of energy and initiative. In Sept. 1861 he replaced him with Flag Officer WILLIAM W. MCKEAN.

Though officially retired, Mervine was assigned desk duty in Washington and Philadelphia. He became president of the Navy Retiring Board in New York. While on the retired list, he was promoted to commodore in 1862 and rear admiral in 1866. d. Utica, N.Y., 15 Sept. 1868.   —NCD

Michigan. In 1861 Michigan had a population of 749,113, of which 394,694 were males. Over the next 4 years the state sent 87,000 men into Federal service; 14,700 of them lost their lives.

Immediately after FORT SUMTER was fired on, the 1st Michigan Volunteers was organized, arriving in Washington, D.C., as the first fully equipped regiment from the West. Some 75 other military units were organized, equipped, and followed the 1st to the battlefields. One of the most celebrated was the IRON BRIGADE OF THE WEST's 24th Michigan, which, with other Michigan units, was in such battles as ANTIETAM, STONE'S RIVER, CHICKAMAUGA, CHATTANOOGA, CHANCELLORSVILLE, GETTYSBURG, the WILDERNESS, SPOTSYLVANIA, and PETERSBURG. At Gettysburg the division that included the 24th came under fire for the first time, the Iron Brigade lost two-thirds of its troops, and the 24th's commander, Virginia-born Col. Henry A. Morrow, was wounded.

Michigan had its share of valor, including the 1st Regiment Colored Infantry and the 17th (Stonewall) Regiment, the latter losing 7 officers and 128 enlisted men killed in battle and 154 enlisted men by disease. Brig. Gen. GEORGE A. CUSTER commanded the Michigan Cavalry Brigade. Killed in battle with the 4th Michigan were Cols. Dwight A. Woodbury, Harrison H. Jeffords, and George W. Lombard. The state produced 4 generals: HENRY J. HUNT, HENRY HASTINGS SIBLEY, Orlando B. Willcox, and ELON J. FARNSWORTH.

Michigan also had its share of courageous women. ANNIE ETHERIDGE joined the 2d Michigan as a nurse and served from FIRST BULL RUN to R. E. Lee's surrender. As "Michigan Annie" or "Gentle Anna," she also served with the 3d and 5th Michigan. Other Michigan nurses were SARAH EMMA EDMONDS, Julia S. Wheelock, and BRIDGET DIVERS ("Michigan Bridget").

At the end of the war, the 4th Michigan Cavalry figured in the capture of Jefferson Davis (*see* DAVIS, JEFFERSON FINIS, CAPTURE OF), and the regiment, which included the 24th, was selected as an escort at the funeral of Pres. ABRAHAM LINCOLN.   —AG

"Michigan Annie." *See* ETHERIDGE, ANNIE.

7th Michigan Infantry. Of the 1,315 men who enlisted or reenlisted in the 7th Michigan Infantry, 729 fell killed or wounded to enemy guns. Fully 15.8% of the regiment—208 men—died in action or as a result of mortal wounds; 147 died of disease and another 42 died in Confederate prisons, placing the regiment among those that suffered the highest percentage of losses during their Civil War service.

Organized at Monroe, Mich., and mustered into Federal service 22 Aug. 1861, the 7th embarked for Washington, D.C., 5 Sept. under the command of Col. Ira R. Grosvenor. Attached to Brig. Gen. Frederick W. Lander's brigade/Brig. Gen. Charles P. Stone's division/Army of the Potomac, the regiment first fought in the disastrous battle of BALL'S BLUFF, 21 Oct. Transferred to the 3d Brigade/2d Division/II Corps Mar. 1862, it was heavily engaged during the PENINSULA CAMPAIGN, losing 22 men at SEVEN PINES and 23 at the Battles of SAVAGE'S STATION and WHITE OAK SWAMP.

Though withheld from the SECOND BATTLE OF BULL RUN, the 7th formed part of the rear guard as Maj. Gen. JOHN POPE retreated after his defeat. Grosvenor resigned at the end of the campaigning and was replaced by Col. Norman J. Hall, a Regular Army officer who led the regiment at ANTIETAM. In the slaughter on that field it suffered a staggering loss of 59 men killed and mortally wounded, 158 wounded, and 4 missing, slightly more than one-half of the number engaged. Shortly thereafter Col. Henry Baxter took over the 7th when Hall rose to brigade command. At FREDERICKSBURG, 13 Dec. 1862, Baxter, against great odds, led his men across the Rappahannock River to dislodge Confederate sharpshooters whose deadly fire had frustrated the Federal attempt to construct a PONTOON BRIDGE across the river. The 7th rushed into the open, jumped into empty pontoon boats, rowed rapidly to the enemy bank, sustaining few casualties, and drove the Southerners out of their rifle pits.

From 25 Jan. to 3 May 1863 the 7th served on provost guard. Only lightly engaged at CHANCELLORSVILLE, the regiment was heavily committed at GETTYSBURG on CEMETERY HILL 1–2 July, losing 65 killed and wounded of the 165 men engaged. Among the dead was Lt. Col. Amos E. Steele, who had been in command during the battle. A few weeks later the 7th reported to New York City to help quell the draft riots but returned to the field for the BRISTOE and MINE RUN campaigns.

Reassigned Dec. 1863 to the 1st Brigade/2d Division/II Corps, the 7th was furloughed for 30 days. It returned to hard campaigning at the WILDERNESS, SPOTSYLVANIA (where it fought at the "BLOODY ANGLE" 12 May), the NORTH ANNA RIVER, COLD HARBOR, PETERSBURG, WELDON RAILROAD, DARBYTOWN, REAMS' STATION, BURGESS' MILL, and at HATCHER'S RUN in 1865. When Petersburg fell, the 7th pursued the Confederates to Appomattox and was present when Gen. ROBERT E. LEE surrendered his army.

Led to Washington, D.C., by Lt. Col. George W. La Pointe, regimental commander since Nov. 1864, the veterans marched down Pennsylvania Ave. 23 May, proud participants in the Grand Review of Meade's Army of the Potomac. With peace again assured, they were ordered to Jeffersonville, Ind., and were mustered out of service 5 July. 2 days later La Pointe disbanded the men at Jackson, Mich. —PLF

24th Michigan Infantry. A latecomer to Brig. Gen. JOHN GIBBON's famed IRON BRIGADE OF THE WEST, the 24th Michigan was organized by Col. Henry A. Morrow in Detroit and mustered into the army 15 Aug. 1862. After a scant 2 weeks in training, it departed for Washington, D.C. There it was assigned to the capital's defenses until October, when the threat posed by Gen. ROBERT E. LEE'S ANTIETAM CAMPAIGN had ended. This inexperienced regiment then reported to Gibbon to augment his depleted 5 regiments of battle-seasoned veterans, which among them could muster fewer than the 900 recruits now added to their ranks. Not until the 24th had proven its mettle in several battles would the veterans of the original Iron Brigade discard their hostility toward the newcomers.

The 24th first battled at FREDERICKSBURG in December, the next month participated in Maj. Gen. AMBROSE E. BURNSIDE'S calamitous "Mud March," and Apr. 1863 fought stubbornly at Fitzhugh's Crossing below Fredericksburg early in the CHANCELLORSVILLE CAMPAIGN. At GETTYSBURG it was assigned to the 1st Division, the first infantry force to come under fire, and struggled to hold the contested ground at McPherson's Woods near Willoughby Run. During the fierce 3-day struggle, the 24th suffered more casualties than any other regiment on the field. Of the 496 men engaged, 69 were killed, 247 wounded, and 47 missing (one-half the missing having been wounded or killed). In the final tally the regiment lost 363 men and its colonel, Morrow, who was wounded and captured. Remembering the terrible carnage years later, one survivor stated with grim satisfaction that "no Rebel crossed that stream [Willoughby Run] and lived."

The remnants of the 24th pursued Lee as he retreated to Virginia. Lt. Col. Albert M. Edwards temporarily commanded the men in Morrow's absence, as he would on several occasions before assuming command 25 Jan. 1865, when Morrow was promoted to brigade command. Through 1864 the regiment fought at the WILDERNESS, SPOTSYLVANIA, the NORTH ANNA RIVER, MINE RUN, COLD HARBOR, WELDON RAILROAD, and PETERSBURG. Its losses had been so devastating that on 18 June 1864 it could muster only 120 men for the assault on the Petersburg defenses.

The 24th was withdrawn from the field after the BATTLE OF HATCHER'S RUN, 5–7 Feb. 1865, and sent to Camp Butler, near Springfield, Ill., to do guard duty at the draft rendezvous. In May the 24th was chosen to be the military escort for ABRAHAM LINCOLN's funeral procession as it passed through Springfield.

The regiment was mustered out of service 30 June in Detroit, where it had been met 10 days earlier with a hero's welcome. Ranked 19th of the "Three Hundred Fighting Regiments" listed in FOX'S *REGIMENTAL LOSSES,* the 24th saw 189 of its men killed or mortally wounded. In its 3 years' service, the regiment lost 589 killed and wounded, 153 missing and captured, and 139 dead of disease (30 of these in Confederate prisons). Of the 1,030 original enlistees, only 180 were present to be mustered out. —PLF

Middle and Eastern Florida, Confederate Department of. With headquarters at Fernandina, the department was established 21 Aug. 1861 under Brig. Gen. JOHN B. GRAYSON. Its principal area of defense was the Atlantic coast, a point continually threatened by Union land and naval forces. By late October the western limit of the department had been extended to the Choctawhatchee River.

Grayson made little headway in organizing the department's forces and building up its defensive works. Ill health forced him to pass command to Brig. Gen. JAMES H. TRAPIER 22 Oct. 2 weeks later, however, Trapier lost jurisdiction over the coastal region, which, along with the coasts of South Carolina and Georgia, was designated a separate department under Gen. ROBERT E. LEE. By the close of the year, Trapier's domain was defended by 3 regiments and 1 battalion of infantry, 1 battalion and 4 troops of cavalry, 2 artillery units, and a ship-bound contingent of coast guards, a total of almost 4,000 officers and men present for duty.

At his own request, Trapier relinquished command 19 Mar. 1862 to report to Gen. JOSEPH E. JOHNSTON in the Western theater. That day he was succeeded by Col. William S. Dilworth of the 3d Florida Infantry, who had been stationed at Fernandina since Grayson's regime. Dilworth held the post until 7 Apr., when Maj. Gen. JOHN C. PEMBERTON's Department of South Carolina and Georgia expanded to include middle and east Florida. Those areas remained a part of the larger district for only 2 days; as of the 9th they again formed a separate department, under Brig. Gen. JOSEPH FINEGAN.

Finegan, who assumed command at Tallahasse, immediately set out to enlarge his forces and stamp out "the vice of intemperance" prevalent among them. Whatever the success of this latter endeavor, he failed to prevent a continuing drain on manpower; by the end of June he commanded 2,686 officers and men present for duty, down from 3,790 in May. Many of the losses represented troops sent to shore up crumbling Confederate defense lines in the West. By July 1862 only 1,158 officers and men remained in Finegan's department. On

7 Oct. the command was reorganized into the Districts of East and Middle Florida, which became components of Gen. P.G.T. BEAUREGARD's Department of South Carolina, Georgia, and Florida. The District of East Florida was assigned to Finegan, while Brig. Gen. HOWELL COBB received the District of West Florida; the latter subsequently passed to Brig. Gen. WILLIAM M. GARDNER. Both districts were again consolidated 23 Feb. 1864, this time as the Military District of Florida, under Maj. Gen. J. PATTON ANDERSON. Brig. Gen. JOHN K. JACKSON succeeded Anderson 28 July of that year and in turn gave way to Brig. Gen. WILLIAM MILLER 29 Sept. The district's final commander was Maj. Gen. SAMUEL JONES, who assumed the position 11 Jan. 1865.   —EGL

Middle Creek, Ky., eng. at.   10 Jan. 1862   Over a month after the engagement at IVY MOUNTAIN, Confederates returned to recruit in southeast Kentucky. With headquarters outside Paintsville, about 12 mi north-northwest of Prestonburg along the west fork of the Big Sandy River, Brig. Gen. HUMPHREY MARSHALL gathered volunteers through late December and by 3 Jan. 1862 had 2,240 men; only 1,967 of them were reported fit for duty. Suffering from camp disease and food shortages, the men (a portion of them brought from Virginia) had an insufficient number of small arms and 4 cannon.

Union Col. JAMES A. GARFIELD, instructed to drive Marshall back to Virginia, moved troops south from Louisa 23 Dec. The next day they arrived at George's Creek, 18 river mi northeast of Paintsville, and by 5 Jan. 1862 had begun pressing Confederates from the town. Federals occupied Paintsville 6 Jan., while Marshall retreated overland south to Middle Creek at a point about 2.5 mi west of Prestonburg. Marshall claimed that it was his strategy to keep Garfield away from the west fork of the Big Sandy, where he could be reinforced and resupplied by boat. The strategy was partially successful. Boggy roads and country cut up by numerous creeks slowed Garfield's 1,100 infantry and 450 cavalry as it hiked south. Bivouacking 9 Jan. at the mouth of Abbot's Creek, a stream parallel to Middle Creek a mile north of Prestonburg, Garfield ordered reinforcements to move from Paintsville by boat. He planned to march a mile south the next day to the mouth of Middle Creek, then drive west after Marshall.

Setting out at 4 a.m., 10 Jan., Federals hit Confederate cavalry at 8 a.m. at the mouth of Middle Creek and skirmished west. By noon they had confronted Marshall's force, which was drawn up for battle at a hillside west of the creek, just north of its juncture with Lost Fork, and with regiments under Cols. JOHN S. WILLIAMS and Alfred C. Moore deployed on a hillside east of the stream. The 4 Confederate cannon were positioned on the hill on Marshall's left. Dispatching a portion of his force to cross Middle Creek and hit the Confederate right, Garfield tried pressing the Southerners from both hills. Poor ammunition made Marshall's cannon fire ineffective. A lack of food, equipment, and experience on both sides allowed the fighting to continue indecisively until 4 p.m., when Garfield received 700 reinforcements. Troops on the Confederate left had moved across Middle Creek through the afternoon and consolidated their force against Garfield's left. But facing additional Northern forces, they broke off the fight and withdrew south rather than trying to turn the Union flank.

Both sides claimed victory and wildly overestimated enemy losses. Garfield received congratulations from Maj. Gen. DON CARLOS BUELL. Marshall's troops occupied the area around

Martindale, moved farther south, then were ordered through Pound Gap to Virginia 24 Jan. Garfield's troops occupied Prestonburg after the engagement, then withdrew to Paintsville. Marshall actually lost 10 killed, 15 wounded, and 25 captured. Garfield claimed only 1 dead and 20 wounded.   —JES

Middle Department, Union.   The Middle Department was created 22 Mar. 1862 to consist of New Jersey, Pennsylvania, Delaware, the eastern shores of Maryland and Virginia, and Cecil, Harford, Baltimore, and Anne Arundel counties in Maryland; in Mar. 1863, western Virginia was added to its territory. The command, which formed part of the Department of the Potomac, was originally placed under Maj. Gen. JOHN A. DIX, who established headquarters at Baltimore.

Throughout its existence, the department was primarily a garrison and administrative command. Its tactical units were so widely dispersed that they could neither facilitate mutual support nor oppose the enemy at a critical point. Its busiest and most vulnerable posts were 2 garrisons in the lower Shenandoah Valley, Harpers Ferry and Winchester. They were situated mainly to guard the crossings of the Potomac River and to block enemy raids on communications lines including the BALTIMORE & OHIO RAILROAD and the Chesapeake & Ohio Canal.

At the height of its strength, summer 1863, the Middle Department comprised 49,961 troops present and absent and 108 cannon, scattered from Philadelphia to Wheeling, W. Va. By then Maj. Gen. ROBERT C. SCHENCK was in command, having replaced Maj. Gen. JOHN E. WOOL, Dix's successor, Dec. 1862. Schenck headed the department in its most active period, serving until he took a congressional seat at the close of 1863. As a desk officer he was capable, as a strategist inept. In June 1863, during the Confederate invasion of Pennsylvania via the Shenandoah Valley, his shortsightedness, vacillation, and failure to heed War Department warnings made possible the capture of Winchester, with a loss of 3,358 troops and 23 guns.

On Schenck's departure, Brig. Gen. HENRY H. LOCKWOOD commanded the department (now reduced by the transfer to other departments of New Jersey, Pennsylvania, and most of West Virginia) until 22 Mar. 1864, when relieved by Maj. Gen. LEW WALLACE. That July the latter was temporarily superseded by Maj. Gen. E.O.C. ORD, who directed a campaign against Confederates involved in EARLY'S WASHINGTON RAID. Wallace regained the command shortly before it became a part of Maj. Gen. PHILIP H. SHERIDAN's Middle Military Division 7 Aug. In June 1865 the department again expanded and was attached to the Reconstruction command known as the Division of the Atlantic. Until its merger into other departments 6 Aug. 1866, it was headed by Maj. Gen. WINFIELD S. HANCOCK.   —EGL

Middle Military Division, Union.   Confederate Lt. Gen. JUBAL A. EARLY's WASHINGTON RAID, July 1864, and his subsequent escape to Virginia embarrassed the administration of Pres. ABRAHAM LINCOLN and revealed serious bureaucratic flaws in the departments committed to the defense of the capital, Maryland, and Pennsylvania. The authority of 4 Union departments—the Middle, West Virginia, Susquehanna, and Washington—overlapped in the region penetrated by the Confederates. Maj. Gen. HENRY W. HALLECK, Union chief of staff, had the responsibility of coordinating the department but avoided active direction. When Early routed a Union force at KERNSTOWN, Va., 24 July, and Confederate cavalry burned

CHAMBERSBURG, Pa., on the 30th, Northern authorities had to act.

The officer ultimately responsible for the protection of the capital and the vital BALTIMORE & OHIO RAILROAD, which traversed the region, was Union Gen.-in-Chief ULYSSES S. GRANT. Early in August Grant recommended to Lincoln the appointment of Maj. Gen. PHILIP H. SHERIDAN to the command. Lincoln, Sec. of War EDWIN M. STANTON, and Halleck reluctantly agreed to the appointment of Sheridan, who was only 34. On 7 Aug. the 4 departments were merged into the Middle Military Division and Sheridan assumed command.

Within 2 months the aggressive "Little Phil" had vindicated Grant's faith in him. His Army of the Shenandoah—composed of the VI Corps, 2 divisions of the XIX Corps/the Army of West Virginia, and 2 cavalry divisions—defeated Early's rugged fighters at THIRD WINCHESTER, 19 Sept., and FISHER'S HILL on the 22d. The Federals then devastated the Shenandoah Valley, burning the lush harvest, farms, and mills of the Confederacy's granary. On 9 Oct. Sheridan's cavalry routed the Southern horsemen at Tom's Brook, and on the 19th at CEDAR CREEK the Union army inflicted its third defeat on Early's outnumbered veterans.

During winter 1865 most of the infantry departed the valley. On 28 Feb. 1865 Sheridan relinquished command to Maj. Gen. ALFRED T. A. TORBERT. 2 days later the Federal cavalry destroyed the final remnant of Early's army at Waynesborough. Maj. Gen. WINFIELD S. HANCOCK succeeded Torbert and remained in command until 27 June, when the Middle Military Division was abolished.   —JDW

Middle Tennessee, Confederate Army of.

On 27 Sept. 1862 Confederate Maj. Gen. SAMUEL JONES assumed command of the District of Middle Tennessee, delineated generally by the 2 paths of the Tennessee River through the state. At first the only Confederate forces were some 2,000 cavalry under Brig. Gen. NATHAN B. FORREST, in the Murfreesboro vicinity, threatening Nashville in support of Gen. BRAXTON BRAGG's invasion of Kentucky. On 28 Oct. Maj. Gen. JOHN C. BRECKINRIDGE with a division of 6,000 men arrived in the district. The combination of Breckinridge's and Forrest's forces then constituted the Army of Middle Tennessee. Breckinridge held the field command while Jones retained charge of the administrative district.

But the army was to be a short-lived one, because even before its formation Bragg had been defeated in Kentucky, 8 Oct., at PERRYVILLE. The victorious Federal army, under Maj. Gen. WILLIAM S. ROSECRANS, had quickly massed at Nashville and threatened to move against Breckinridge before Bragg could regroup. Breckinridge took the initiative and sent cavalry on raids against the Federal supply line. Only partly successful, the raids nevertheless induced Rosecrans to be overly cautious and bought sufficient time for Bragg to reach Murfreesboro.

During November Breckinridge's army conducted intelligence-gathering operations and communicated information to Bragg. Meanwhile, Bragg spent the month marshaling forces and reorganizing his command. The Army of Middle Tennessee was dissolved. Forrest's cavalry united with that of Maj. Gen. JOSEPH WHEELER and detached for a campaign in western Tennessee with hopes of diverting Maj. Gen. ULYSSES S. GRANT from VICKSBURG; Breckinridge's remaining force became a division in Lt. Gen. WILLIAM J. HARDEE's corps.   —HH

Miles, Nelson Appleton.

USA b. Westminster, Mass., 8

Aug. 1839. Miles's desire for an education beyond the academy level led him at age 17 to Boston, where he worked in a crockery store by day and went to school by night. A Colonel M. Salignac, a former French officer, also gave him some military instruction.

When the Civil War broke out, Miles recruited 100 volunteers for Col. Henry Wilson's 22d Massachusetts regiment. He was commissioned captain of infantry, but because his superior officers considered him too young to command in battle, he served on Brig. Gen. OLIVER O. HOWARD's staff throughout the PENINSULA CAMPAIGN. He

LC

was wounded, won an official commendation for gallantry, and was promoted to lieutenant colonel. He was wounded again at FREDERICKSBURG and again at CHANCELLORSVILLE, where he was brevetted brigadier general and won the MEDAL OF HONOR. Miles fought bravely at the Battles of the WILDERNESS and SPOTSYLVANIA, commanding a brigade of Brig. Gen. FRANCIS C. BARLOW's division of Maj. Gen. WINFIELD S. HANCOCK's II Corps. He sustained his fourth wound at PETERSBURG and was promoted to brigadier general of volunteers as of 12 May 1864 and major general 21 Oct. 1865.

When the Regular Army was reorganized in 1866 Miles determined to make the army his lifetime career. He was appointed colonel of the 40th U.S. Infantry (Colored Troops) and later of the 5th U.S. Infantry. Between these assignments he was commandant of Fort Monroe and, as such, was JEFFERSON DAVIS' custodian. Later his remarkable successes in pacifying Indians in the West included the capture of Geronimo. He was promoted to brigadier general in the U.S. Army in 1880, then to major general in 1890 and lieutenant general in 1900. In 1895 he was named commander in chief of the army, a position he filled through the Spanish-American War and until he retired in 1903.

During his retirement he lived in Washington and wrote a 2-volume autobiography and a second book, *Serving the Republic*. When he died in the District of Columbia, 15 May 1925, he was the last of the full-rank major generals of the Civil War.   —DBS

Miles, William Porcher.

CSP b. Walterboro, S.C., 4 July 1822, Miles studied 1 year at the Willington Academy, transferring to the College of Charleston, from which he graduated in 1842 with highest honors. The following year he abandoned his law studies to accept a position as assistant professor of mathematics at the college. During his 12-year tenure there he became well known and well liked in Charleston political circles. His popularity grew when in 1855 he volunteered as a nurse during a yellow-fever epidemic in Norfolk, Va., and on his return his friends nominated him for mayor in a successful effort to defeat the Know Nothing party in the city.

A solid pro-slavery secessionist, Miles was elected to the U.S. House of Representatives in 1857, but he resigned his seat 13 Dec. 1860, convinced the South had no choice but to seek independence. He chaired the South Carolina secession convention Committee on Foreign Affairs, signed the ordinance of secession, and traveled to Washington to negotiate the state takeover of Charleston's forts. Brig. Gen. P.G.T. BEAUREGARD appointed him 1 of a 3-man committee to arrange with Maj. ROBERT ANDERSON the surrender terms of FORT SUMTER.

Miles represented the Charleston district in the House of all 3 Confederate Congresses and as chairman of the Committee on Military Affairs was among the most powerful men in government. His vigorous support of administration policy on all matters concerning the army labeled him a close friend of JEFFERSON DAVIS. Though he opposed the president on railroad grants and the establishment of a powerful Supreme Court (see SUPREME COURT, CONFEDERATE STATES), he favored CONSCRIPTION, ending all exemptions, and voted to give complete powers of detail to Davis and the secretary of war.

In 1863 Miles married the daughter of a wealthy man who had been able to keep his property through the war. For 15 years he lived in leisurely retirement at Oakridge, Va., where he entertained lavishly and assembled an extensive collection of rare books. He accepted the presidency of the University of South Carolina in 1880, resigning the post 2 years later to manage his father-in-law's plantations in Louisiana.

Miles kept out of politics but was an outspoken opponent of the Republican party and much in demand as a public speaker. By the time of his death near Burnside, La., 11 May 1899, he had become prominent among the state's sugar planters.

—PLF

Miles Court of Inquiry.

Miles Court of Inquiry. Union Col. Dixon S. Miles, 57 years old, a U.S. Army Regular, commanded Brig. Gen. IRVIN MCDOWELL's 5th Division in operations during the FIRST BULL RUN CAMPAIGN. Known to be a heavy drinker, he had been ill for several days before the battle of 21 July 1861. His doctor unfortunately prescribed small drams of brandy for his condition on the day of the fight.

Miles's troops, relegated to reserve status for much of the battle, covered Blackburn's Ford during the late morning and afternoon. From his headquarters at Centreville, Miles rode back and forth during the day, quibbling with his junior officers' troop dispositions and drinking steadily. During one afternoon stop in Centreville, a staff officer tried to tell him of the Union rout on the distant Federal right. Heavily intoxicated, Miles dismissed him, saying, "I have something else to attend to." Eventually, his troops fell back on Centreville and subordinates complained of his condition to Col. ISRAEL B. RICHARDSON; McDowell ordered Miles relieved and placed Richardson in command. Miles either did not comprehend or care to comprehend the order, argued with Richardson over command, then threatened him with arrest.

Days later, Richardson preferred charges of drunkenness against Miles. A court of inquiry convened 21 Aug. 1861, its attending officers finding that Miles had been drunk and had been ill. A court-martial was not called for. Court-of-inquiry members found his illness to be an extenuating circumstance and believed a court-martial to be an inconvenient, inappropriate, time-consuming exercise. Court members may have also believed the embarrassment of the Union defeat at Bull Run would have been unpleasantly compounded by the publicity attending Miles's trial.

Miles's drinking habits were mentioned again following his death at Harpers Ferry, Sept. 1862, when his command was surrendered to Confederate Maj. Gen. THOMAS J. "STONEWALL" JACKSON during the ANTIETAM CAMPAIGN. Killed just as his

troops were being given up, Miles was suspected by some of being drunk at the time he ordered the surrender.   —JES

Military Academy, United States.

Military Academy, United States. Established as an army engineering school 16 Mar. 1802 and organized into an academy for training a young officer corps 29 Apr. 1812, the U.S. Military Academy at West Point, N.Y., contributed 1,008 general officers to the contending Civil War armies. The school, known colloquially as West Point, offered a 4-year baccalaureate college program in its antebellum years and, under an experimental program instituted by Sec. of War JEFFERSON DAVIS during Pres. Franklin Pierce's administration, briefly expanded to a 5-year course of study. The 5-year program ceased at the outbreak of the Civil War.

The alumnus with the greatest influence on the tactics and strategy of the Civil War was Prof. DENNIS HART MAHAN, member of the class of 1824, full-time faculty member from 1830, and dean of the faculty from 1838. Mahan molded the curriculum to emphasize more than military engineering, requiring students to study history, classical literature, and French, as well as STRATEGY and TACTICS. Almost all predominant Civil War generals were his former pupils.

Students were appointed to the academy by members of the U.S. Congress and, on graduation, ranked according to their standing in their class. Those at the top of the class were assigned to the Corps of Engineers; those at the bottom were assigned infantry duty. Confederate Gen. ROBERT E. LEE, graduating 2d in the 46-man class of 1829, became an engineer working on East Coast fortifications. Union Lt. Gen. ULYSSES S. GRANT, graduating 21st in the 39-man class of 1843, went to serve with the 4th Infantry in Missouri. (Grant, a good horseman, found no openings in the cavalry.) All graduates were appointed to the rank of 2d lieutenant. If no openings at that rank were available, the graduate received a brevet 2d lieutenant appointment.

During the secession crisis, many academy cadets from Southern states resigned from the institution as their states seceded. They did so without hindrance: in antebellum and war years, graduates were under no obligation to serve a mandatory term in the U.S. Army. In this way the Confederacy was supplied with a talented young officer corps. Of the Confederacy's 425 general officers, 146 were West Point graduates and 10 others had attended the institution. Of the Union's 583 generals, 217 were academy graduates and 11 others were once students there. The academy class of 1854 perhaps provided more distinguished Civil War officers than any other, including OLIVER O. HOWARD, J.E.B. STUART, JOHN PEGRAM, STEPHEN D. LEE, WILLIAM D. PENDER, ARCHIBALD GRACIE, JAMES DESHLER, and STEPHEN H. WEED.

The academy also provided a ready-made "old-boy" network or influential fraternity of alumni. Confederate Pres. Jefferson Davis, a graduate of the 1828 class, gave consideration to fellow alumni and classmates when making officer appointments. Confederate Maj. Gen. GUSTAVUS W. SMITH secured classmate MANSFIELD LOVELL's major generalcy for him. Union Maj. Gen. PHILIP H. SHERIDAN provided a prominent command for his classmate Brig. Gen. GEORGE CROOK. Academy connections also occasionally ensured wartime dramas. Confederate Brig. Gen. FELIX H. ROBERTSON was compelled to surrender Montgomery, Ala., to classmate Union Brig. Gen. JAMES H. WILSON. Prevailing on friendship won Robertson nothing. Wilson threatened to have him run down if he did not get himself and his white flag out of the road.   —JES

military bands. Confederate and U.S. Army regulations stated that each regiment would be provided with a military band at its commander's request. This regulation, retained from antebellum army organization, did not anticipate forces made up of thousands of volunteer regiments and, subsequently, thousands of bands. In December 1861 the Union War Department suggested eliminating military bands to realize a savings of $5 million. Instead, Federal musicians were reorganized July 1862. Volunteer members of regimental bands were ordered back to the fighting ranks or offered the opportunity of joining consolidated brigade-band organizations.

Confederate army bands, less numerous at the outset of the war, were never reduced by order. Southern manpower shortages dictated that more men serve in the ranks than in bands. Regulations for both armies stated that musicians should be trained as infantry, organized as a squad, and led by its chief musician, usually a noncommissioned officer. In crisis they could be pressed into combat service. During most battles, large numbers of band members were detailed to duty as stretcher-bearers, messengers, or hospital orderlies.

In Federal service, each month members of 16-man mounted bands or 24-man infantry bands earned from $45, for the leader, to $17, for junior members. Individual musicians, and drummers and buglers who were not band members, earned $12 each month. Confederate principal musicians earned $21 a month, cavalry musicians $13 a month, and infantry and artillery musicians each received $12 monthly.

In both armies these bandsmen were often recruited from existing civilian organizations. Sometimes entire civilian bands enlisted as a group. The Mountain Saxhorn Band from Staunton, Va., organized in 1855, became the 5th Virginia Regiment Band, known later as the Stonewall Brigade Band. Civilian band leaders with outstanding reputations were often recruited for specific volunteer bands seeking to enhance their reputations.

In addition to the traditional brass, woodwind, and percussion instruments found in each Civil War military band, several members played a rotary-valve horn called a saxhorn, a brass instrument with a bell extending over the player's shoulder. Rarely seen in the 20th century, they gave military bands a unique sound.

The Civil War, the last major conflict in which bands played on the field of combat, produced several notable organizations. Musicians from the 7th New York Regiment, organized as militia before the war, had outstanding reputations, as did the members of the U.S. Marine Band, then as now composed solely of U.S. Marine Corps Regulars. Among Confederate bands, from Salem, N.C., the 26th North Carolina Regimental Band was made up of members of a Moravian musical group. Its history and sheet music were preserved by its descendant organization, the Salem Band, and provide one of the best records of band music and service.   —JES

Military Order of the Loyal Legion of the United States.
A group of Union veterans agreed 9 Apr. 1865 to the perceived necessity of forming cadres of former officers pledged to the preservation of the Union. Unsure that the approaching peace would be permanent, they met in Philadelphia, Pa., and 15 Apr. instituted a constitution and bylaws. Membership was open to army, navy, and Marine Corps officers who had served the Union honorably, their descendants, and collateral descendants. Naming the organization the Military Order of the Loyal Legion of the United States, its members pledged fidelity to the Federal government and willingness to come to its aid in the face of insurrection. Its constitution provided for the establishment of local, state, and national headquarters called "comanderies." Rebellion did not reoccur and the organization quickly assumed the character of a fraternal veterans' association, pursuing the relief of war widows and orphans and compiling histories of campaigns its members served in.
                    —JES

Miller, Stephen. USA/war governor b. Carroll, Pa., 7 Jan. 1816. Locally educated, Miller drifted into politics as court clerk for Dauphin County and later was retained as flour inspector for the city of Philadelphia. For 2 years, 1853–55, he edited a Whig newspaper in Harrisburg, moving to St. Cloud, Minn., in 1858 to establish himself as a businessman. A devout Unionist, he was a delegate to the Republican convention in Chicago and an elector for ABRAHAM LINCOLN in 1860.

LC

In Apr. 1861 the 1st Minnesota Infantry elected Miller lieutenant colonel; as such he led the regiment at FIRST BULL RUN and at the disastrous Battle of Ball's Bluff, where his men provided the rear guard as the Federal army retreated across the Potomac. His career in the Eastern theater included a brief tour in the Shenandoah Valley and combat at SEVEN PINES and in the SEVEN DAYS' CAMPAIGN.

On 24 Apr. 1862 Miller was promoted to colonel of the 7th Minnesota and sent to help put down the SIOUX UPRISING around New Ulm. He had no more direct involvement with the Civil War but was advanced to brigadier general 26 Oct. 1863, resigning from the army 18 Jan. 1864 to accept the Minnesota governorship, 1864–65.

After 1871 Miller made a career in the employ of the St. Paul & Sioux City Railroad. In neither his civilian nor military career did he achieve widespread recognition, but he performed competently the jobs he undertook. d. Worthington, Minn., 18 Aug. 1881.   —PLF

Miller, William. CSA b. Ithaca, N.Y., 3 Aug. 1820. Relocating with his family to Louisiana in his infancy, Miller attended college there before joining a volunteer outfit during the Mexican War. After serving under Gen. Zachary Taylor in northern Mexico, he settled in Pensacola, Fla., to practice law and manage a sawmill.

Miller did not hesitate to join the Confederate army once secession became war. In mid-1861 he assumed command of a 6-company battalion, which early the next year became part of the 1st Florida Infantry. His troops saw heavy service during Gen. BRAXTON BRAGG's 1862 invasion of Kentucky, culminating 8 Oct. in the Battle of PERRYVILLE. During that struggle Miller's brigade leader, Brig. Gen. JOHN C. BROWN, was wounded; replacing him for the balance of the fight, Miller displayed fitness for higher command.

He reached the apogee of his field career 2 Jan. 1863, at STONE'S RIVER when leading the 1st and 3d Florida regiments. This force, part of the brigade of Brig. Gen. WILLIAM PRESTON, conducted a "magnificent but disastrous charge" aimed at driving several Federal brigades from high ground north of the battle's namesake stream. Miller was in the thick of the action as the attackers bounded up the heights, drove out the enemy,

USMHI

pursued them down the back slope—and were devastated by the fire of 60 Union cannon across the river. In the carnage preceding his men's repulse Miller was wounded; superiors' reports praised him for refusing to quit the field until the battle's conclusion.

Miller returned to Florida to recuperate and while there took charge of a Confederate conscription bureau encompassing manpower in the southern part of the state as well as in Alabama. Named a brigadier general 2 Aug. 1864, he received command of Florida reserve forces 5 weeks later. In addition to training and organizing these units, he carried administrative burdens as the head of the District of Florida. He left his desk job intermittently, such as in Mar. 1865, when he helped block a Union amphibious expedition against St. Mark's and Tallahassee.

After the war Miller resumed his lumber business and managed large farming interests. He spent 3 terms in the Florida legislature and lived in retirement in Washington County, dying in Point Washington, 8 Aug. 1909. —EGL

Miller's *The Photographic History of the Civil War.*

Francis Trevelyan Miller's history was first published 1911–12 on the 50th anniversary of the war's beginning. Editor-in-Chief Miller and his staff spent years collecting thousands of Civil War–era photographs, which were assembled into this 10-volume work. The Mathew Brady photographs from the National Archives form the basis of the collection, but Miller's researchers also scoured the country in search of images in private hands and in public repositories. Miller corresponded extensively with survivors, sometimes with the photographers themselves. Many of the accompanying narratives were written by veterans. For years, "Miller's" has remained the standard photographic reference on the war years.

Neither Miller nor his staff members were trained historians, and they relied heavily for identification on the individuals who supplied pictures, on veterans' memories, and on descriptions appended to the original prints. Consequently, some captions contain inaccuracies, but the *Photographic History* is nonetheless a valuable visual resource of the era. Because photographic technology did not permit cameramen to record action, they devoted most of their efforts to documenting soldier life. 3 volumes are given to images taken before or after battles; the remaining 7 chronicle navies, commanders, camp scenes, fortifications, ordnance, artillery, cavalry, infantry, and civilian scenes.

The complete set was reprinted in 5 volumes in 1957, with a new introduction by Henry Steele Commager. —PLF

Mill Springs (Beech Grove; Fishing Creek; Logan's Cross Roads; Somerset), Ky., Battle of. 19 Jan. 1862

One of the early disasters for the Confederacy, this battle reflected the crisis in leadership that was ultimately to plague the South in the vital Western theater. Although committed to the defense of the Cumberland Gap, Confederate Brig. Gen. FELIX K. ZOLLICOFFER advanced about 70 mi into Kentucky to Mill Springs during late Nov. 1861. Instructions from department commander Gen. ALBERT SIDNEY JOHNSTON to Zollicoffer's superior, Maj. Gen. GEORGE B. CRITTENDEN, not to cross the Cumberland River were received a day too late.

When confronted by an advance of the Federal army, under Brig. Gen. GEORGE H. THOMAS, from Lebanon, Ky., mid-Jan. 1862, Crittenden considered his plight. With approximately 4,000 effective troops, he was too weak to defend his meager entrenchments on the north bank and was unable to effectively withdraw to the south bank due to the rain-swollen river and inadequate transportation. Crittenden decided to attack. Thomas, meanwhile, was awaiting additional reinforcements at Logan's Cross Roads, about 10 mi from the Confederates.

Advancing in column in a heavy rain during the night, Zollicoffer's leading troops struck Thomas' pickets about daylight on 19 Jan. The 10th Indiana, attacked initially, was largely driven in disorder back to their encampments. Yet the 4th Kentucky, sent to reinforce the thin Federal line, held along the edge of a ravine, aided by the intense rain and fog. Zollicoffer, by mistake, rode up to Federal Col. Speed S. Fry and was fatally shot. When Crittenden rallied Zollicoffer's disorganized troops, he sent them forward with another brigade in a mass frontal attack. The charge failed spectacularly and a counterattack launched by Col. SAMUEL P. CARTER's brigade pushed back the Confederate right.

On the Confederate left a flank attack by the 9th Ohio Infantry enveloped the entire line. Many of the Southern troops' obsolete flintlock muskets failed to fire in the rain, and the entire force broke up in a disorderly retreat. Crittenden was compelled to abandon 12 cannon and large quantities of stores at his Beech Grove encampment. Hastily recrossing the Cumberland River that night, his dispirited troops withdrew toward Knoxville, abandoning Kentucky to Federal control. The operation had cost Crittenden 533 in killed, wounded, and missing; Thomas' losses totaled 261. —WS

Milroy, Robert Huston. USA b. near Salem, Ind., 11 June 1816.

At the age of 24 Milroy entered Captain Partridge's Academy in Norwich, Vt., graduating in 1843 with Bachelor of Arts and Master of Military Science degrees. During the Mexican War, he served as a captain in the 1st Indiana Volunteers. He studied law at Indiana University, then entered the legal profession and served briefly as a judge before resuming his practice in 1854.

When the Civil War erupted, Milroy had already recruited a militia company and was mustered in as colonel of the 9th Indiana 27 Apr. A 3-month regiment, the 9th reenlisted in July and participated in Union operations in western Virginia. On 3

USMHI

Sept. Milroy was promoted to brigadier general and assigned to command of the Cheat Mountain district in western Virginia. During 1862 the Hoosier general fought in the SHENANDOAH VALLEY CAMPAIGN and led a brigade of the I Corps/Army of Virginia at SECOND BULL RUN. He received his commission as major general 29 Nov. 1862.

He then commanded Milroy's Upper Potomac Division/VIII Corps/Middle Department. By June 1863 his command guarded the northern end of the Shenandoah Valley, with headquarters at Winchester. On 13 June the vanguard of Lt. Gen. RICHARD S. EWELL's II Corps, leading the Confederate army on its planned invasion of Pennsylvania, drove in Milroy's outpost. Ewell deployed his forces the next day to envelop the Union command. At 6 p.m. the Confederates attacked at Winchester, driving back the Federals; Milroy held a council of war and ordered a retreat. But Ewell, anticipating a withdrawal, severed Milroy's columns in the morning darkness of 15 June. It was a disaster for the Union, with 3,400 men captured, all 23 cannon lost, and more than 1,000 killed and wounded.

A court of inquiry eventually exonerated Milroy of responsibility for the disaster, but he never held field command again. During the war's final year, he organized and assigned militia regiments in Tennessee and guarded the Chattanooga Railroad. His vigorous suppression of guerrillas in West Virginia moved the Confederate government to place a price on his head.

Milroy resigned from the army 26 July 1865 and returned to Indiana, where he served as a trustee of the Wabash & Erie Canal Co. In 1872 the veteran officer became the Indian agent in Olympia, Wash., where he died 29 Mar. 1890. —JDW

Milton, John. war governor b. Jefferson Cty., Ga., 20 Apr. 1807. Educated at Louisville Academy in Georgia, Milton read law and was admitted to the state bar. He migrated in the early 1830s to Mobile, Ala., where he established a thriving practice. During the Seminole War of 1835–37 he served as a captain of volunteers, then lived in Marion, Ark., and New Orleans, moving to Jackson Cty., Fla., in 1846 as a farmer.

2 years later he was elected to the state senate on the Democratic ticket. An unbending advocate of STATES RIGHTS and slavery and an effective orator, he spoke throughout the state in favor of secession. At the national Democratic presidential convention at Charleston in 1860, Milton was a member of the Florida delegation, which joined representatives from other Southern states in withdrawing after the party split on the slavery issue.

Elected governor in 1860, he eagerly supported the convention that took Florida out of the Union 10 Jan. 1861, and signed the ordinance of secession on the 11th. 4 days before the delegates voted to secede, incumbent governor Madison S. Perry had ordered state troops to seize the Federal arsenal at Apalachicola; 12–18 Jan. the militia took over Forts Barrancas, Marion, Augustine, McRee, and the Pensacola Navy Yard, and Perry demanded the surrender of FORT PICKENS. Milton, who believed secession was "the most glorious event in the history of Florida," endorsed the action notwithstanding his personal dislike for Perry.

After his inauguration 7 Oct. 1861, Milton worked tirelessly toward the success of Confederate independence, trying to enforce acts passed by the state legislature that would limit the production of cotton and tobacco in favor of staple crops and curtail unlawful speculation and monopoly. He also opposed

IMPRESSMENT that he believed unfair to citizens of the state. Disgusted with BLOCKADE RUNNERS who wasted cargo space on luxury goods, he urged the JEFFERSON DAVIS administration to permit blockade running only by government-authorized agents in hopes of reducing speculation inconsistent with the public good and retaliation by the Federal fleet.

Faced with the difficulty of keeping militia under arms, Milton turned over to the Confederate army most of those troops raised in the state. Motivated by his inability to equip large numbers of recruits and by his belief that the government in Richmond should have the troops to use where they were most needed, he retained an insufficient number of men to guard the state. Fearful of internal insurrection by inadequately supervised slaves within the state and of the vulnerability of the 1,500-mi Florida coastline to invasion by Federal forces, he repeatedly asked Davis to send guns and reinforcements, often receiving no reply to his pleas.

Though Federal troops reoccupied Pensacola 10 May 1862 after Gen. BRAXTON BRAGG was transferred to Kentucky to meet Brig. Gen. ULYSSES S. GRANT's invasion, and although there was skirmishing within the state throughout the war, Milton contended with only one serious military threat, at OLUSTEE, 20 Feb. 1864, in a battle won by Confederate forces.

Milton, governor at Marianna, the one Confederate state capital uncaptured during the war, became increasingly depressed as the war progressed and he realized the South was being defeated. Rather than await surrender, he committed suicide in Marianna, 1 Apr. 1865. —PLF

Milwaukee, USS. A double-turreted river monitor, the USS Milwaukee was built by James B. Eads at Carondelet, Mo. It displaced 1,300 tons and was 299 ft in length and 56 ft in beam, with a 6-ft draft. The vessel carried 4 11-in. Dahlgren smoothbores, 2 per turret. One of its turrets was designed by Eads and the other by JOHN ERICSSON. The Milwaukee and the other vessels of the screw and steamer class were the only MONITORS ever built with triple screws and rudders. Commissioned 21 Aug. 1864, the ship soon received orders to join the West Gulf Blockading Squadron.

On 1 Jan. 1865, the Milwaukee arrived in Mobile Bay and joined the naval forces of Commodore Henry K. Thatcher. Although Rear Adm. DAVID G. FARRAGUT, while in command of the squadron, had captured Mobile Bay and the forts guarding it, the city of Mobile was still in Confederate hands. The Milwaukee's brief career was spent in the operations designed to take the port.

Union Maj. Gen. E.R.S. CANBY, with approximately 45,000 men, advanced towards Mobile along the rivers east of the city. The key to the city's defense was 2 forts, Blakely at the junction of the Apalachee and Tensas rivers, and Spanish Fort, directly across the bay from Mobile. With the support of the Milwaukee and other warships, in late March Canby's forces attacked the forts. In addition to providing fire support when needed, the Milwaukee was used to sweep the bay and rivers for torpedoes and transport army troops. On 28 Mar. the ship struck a torpedo in the Blakely River as it was chasing a Confederate transport carrying supplies to one of the forts. Its stern went under in 3 minutes, but its forward compartments remained afloat for nearly an hour, enabling the entire crew to abandon ship with most of their possessions.

The hulk of the Milwaukee was raised in 1868 and towed to St. Louis, where some of its materials were used in the construction of the James B. Eads Bridge across the Mississippi River.   —WNS

Mine Run Campaign.   26 Nov.–2 Dec. 1863   Following the effective Federal action at RAPPAHANNOCK STATION 7 Nov., Maj. Gen. GEORGE G. MEADE was inactive except for cavalry actions. On 26 Nov. he began a maneuver calculated to turn Gen. ROBERT E. LEE's right, which was the nearest and most exposed Confederate flank. The advance was slow, largely due to the tentativeness, even ineptness, of Maj. Gen. WILLIAM H. FRENCH, who commanded the lead corps. The delay allowed Lee to effect countermoves. When he ascertained that Meade meant to attack his army rather than attempt to cut the Fredericksburg & Richmond Railroad, he could scarcely believe his good fortune. His numerically inferior army would be in a position to fight a defensive action. Thus, on 28–29 Nov. he established strong field fortifications along the west bank of Mine Run.

In the meantime Maj. Gen. GOUVERNEUR K. WARREN had arrived below Lee's position and notified Meade that he believed he could turn that portion of the Confederate line. But during the bitter-cold night of 29–30 Nov. Lee had extended and fortified his line, and Warren realized that a general assault would be futile. Meade had the moral courage to countermand the orders for an attack that no doubt would have entailed severe losses for him with little effect on Lee. On 2 Dec., when the Federal attack had not materialized, Lee determined to take the offensive himself. When he learned that Meade had retreated, he exclaimed, "I am too old to command this army. We should never have permitted those people to get away." Meade expected to pay for what some termed a "fiasco" at Mine Run, but sensible observers realized that he had saved his army from useless casualties.   —JTH

minié bullet.   The standard infantry projectile of the Civil War, the minié bullet is often referred to as a minié ball. Actually a hollow-base lead bullet of cylindro-conoidal shape, it was developed in the 1840s by Capts. Henri-Gustave Delvigne and Claude-Étienne Minié of the French army. Both officers were looking for a way to improve the loading speed of the rifle, an expensive and specialized weapon issued in those days only to elite corps of riflemen. The rifle was accurate but slow to load because of the need to seat the ball in such a way that it would take the grooves of the rifling in the barrel. That was accomplished by using a tight-fitting ball and wrapping it in a patch, which then had to be forced down the barrel.

U.S.S. Milwaukee

USMHI

Standard infantry smoothbore muskets, on the other hand, were quick to load because they used undersized balls with no patch. The volume of fire that could be achieved tended to make up for the accuracy that was sacrificed.

Together, Delvigne and Minié developed a slightly undersized hollow-base projectile. It could be loaded like a musket ball, but when the rifle was fired, the gas of the explosion expanded the bullet at the base and forced it into the rifling grooves. Minié's contribution to the design was the insertion of an iron cup in the base, so that the cup was wedged into the bullet, thus expanding it. The British substituted boxwood or clay plugs, but the American army used no expansion agent.

The minié bullet was adopted for U.S. troops in 1855, and it brought a revolutionary change in warfare. Now all troops, not just the elite riflemen, carried the rifle. The greater accuracy of the weapon, combined with a lag in changing battle tactics to suit the new projectile, was responsible for the appalling battle casualties of the Civil War.   —LDJ

Minnesota. "We are a young state, not very numerous or powerful," declared Minnesota Gov. ALEXANDER RAMSEY 9 Jan. 1861, "but we are for the Union as it is, and the Constitution as it is." Minnesota, admitted to the Union less than 3 years earlier, took its stand. On 22 Jan. the state legislature passed a resolution offering both men and money to preserve the Union.

Ramsey chanced to be in Washington 13 Apr. When he learned of the attack on FORT SUMTER, he rushed to Sec. of War SIMON CAMERON and offered 1,000 Minnesota men for Federal service. Cameron asked him to submit his proposal in writing, and he did so. Thus Minnesota became the first state to make a formal offer of troops for the Northern armies of the Civil War, 2 days before Pres. ABRAHAM LINCOLN issued his call for 75,000 men.

The 1ST MINNESOTA INFANTRY, commanded by Col. Willis A. Gorman, left Fort Snelling, Minn., 22 June, arrived in Washington on the 26th and fought at FIRST BULL RUN. On that bloody field on 21 July the Minnesotans suffered 180 casualties, more than any other Union regiment engaged.

During the war Minnesota furnished some 24,000 men for Union service and Indian fighting. Maj. Gen. WILLIAM S. ROSECRANS said that the 5th Minnesota "saved the day" at CORINTH, 4 Oct. 1862. The 4th Minnesota suffered heavy casualties in Maj. Gen. U. S. GRANT's frontal attack on VICKSBURG 22 May 1863. The 2d Minnesota stood with Maj. Gen. GEORGE H. THOMAS at CHICKAMAUGA and, led by Lt. Col. Judson W. Bishop, scaled MISSIONARY RIDGE to help rout the Confederate defenders at CHATTANOOGA.

Perhaps the most storied feat of Minnesota arms came late on the second day at the Battle of GETTYSBURG, when the 1st Minnesota, under Col. William Colvill, charged against a Confederate advance, losing 215 of its 262 men.

Despite the drain of manpower necessary to put down the Sioux uprising at home late in 1862, Minnesota continued to send thousands to Civil War battlefields. The Minnesota 5th, 7th, 9th, and 10th regiments took part in the Battle of Nashville 15–16 Dec. 1864; the 2d and 4th marched with Maj. Gen. WILLIAM T. SHERMAN to the sea; and Minnesotans were on hand when Gen. R. E. Lee surrendered at Appomattox.   —DS

1st Minnesota Infantry. The first regiment of Union volunteers, the 1st Minnesota was tendered to the government in

1861. On the day after FORT SUMTER's surrender, Gov. ALEXANDER RAMSEY offered the unit to Sec. of War SIMON CAMERON, who immediately accepted it for Federal service. By 29 Apr. 10 companies had been mustered in under Col. Willis A. Gorman, the first of 3 regimental commanders who would become brigadier generals (the others being Napoleon J. T. Dana and Alfred Sully). Its first lieutenant colonel, STEPHEN MILLER, would succeed Ramsey as governor Jan. 1864.

Following state garrison duty, the regiment, clad in black pants and hats and red flannel shirts (an outfit that later gave way to Union blue), was sent to Washington. It reached the capital 26 June 1861 following the longest journey to war of any regiment serving in the East. 3 weeks later it participated in Brig. Gen. IRVIN MCDOWELL's attack on the Confederate left at FIRST BULL RUN. Heavily engaged, the 1st suffered the most casualties of any Union outfit in that action but refused to retreat with the rest of the army until commanded to do so 3 times.

That October, under Colonel Dana, the 1st guarded the rear of Col. EDWARD D. BAKER's force at BALL'S BLUFF. Early in 1862 it served briefly in the Shenandoah Valley, then went to the Virginia peninsula, where Colonel Sully led it ably at YORKTOWN, SEVEN PINES, SAVAGE'S STATION, WHITE OAK SWAMP, and MALVERN HILL. At ANTIETAM, as part of Maj. Gen. JOHN SEDGWICK's II Corps, it attacked the Confederate center. Exposed to heavy fire when its supports melted away, the regiment again refused to retreat until nearly overwhelmed.

Lightly engaged at FREDERICKSBURG and CHANCELLORSVILLE, the Minnesotans were called on to make a forlorn-hope attack at GETTYSBURG, 2 July 1863, following the rout of the III Corps. Reportedly, Maj. Gen. WINFIELD S. HANCOCK said of the effort: "There is no more gallant deed recorded in history." It cost the outfit 215 of 262 men engaged, the highest casualty rate of any Union regiment in any battle. 7 months later, following BRISTOE STATION and MINE RUN, many of the surviving veterans were discharged. Though recruited back to strength, fighting all the way from the WILDERNESS to APPOMATTOX, the regiment never matched its earlier combat performances.   —EGL

Missionary Ridge, Tenn., Battle of. 25 Nov. 1863 After consulting with Maj. Gen. U. S. GRANT during the campaign for CHATTANOOGA, Maj. Gen. WILLIAM T. SHERMAN rejoined his troops at Bridgeport, Ala., then marched them up Lookout Valley. 3 divisions led by Brig. Gens. PETER J. OSTERHAUS, JOHN E. SMITH, and Morgan L. Smith hiked for Brown's Ferry, opposite Moccasin Point. A fourth division under Brig. Gen. HUGH B. EWING made an ineffective feint toward Trenton at the rear of Lookout Mountain, then rejoined Sherman's column.

On 23 Nov. Morgan Smith's, John Smith's, and Ewing's divisions crossed the Brown's Ferry pontoon bridge to Moccasin Point and marched east behind Chattanooga to a point on the Tennessee River opposite its juncture with Chickamauga Creek and the north end of Missionary Ridge. Osterhaus' division could not cross the Brown's Ferry bridge, which had been weakened by recent high water and was near collapse. Grant ordered Osterhaus to join Maj. Gen. JOSEPH HOOKER for the Battle of LOOKOUT MOUNTAIN and had Brig. Gen. JEFFERSON C. DAVIS' division of the XIV Corps meet Sherman's 3 remaining divisions at the Tennessee opposite their point of attack.

On 24 Nov. Hooker's force assaulted Lookout Mountain; Maj. Gen. GEORGE H. THOMAS' Army of the Cumberland sat at

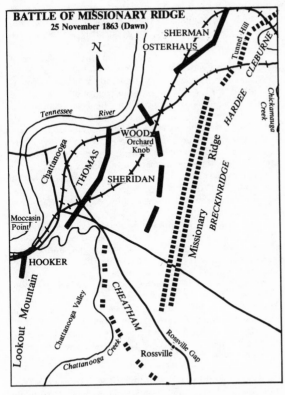

BATTLE OF MISSIONARY RIDGE
25 November 1863 (Dawn)

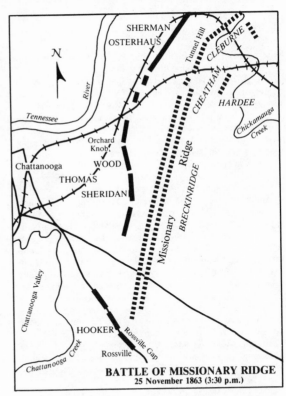

BATTLE OF MISSIONARY RIDGE
25 November 1863 (3:30 p.m.)

the Union center around ORCHARD KNOB facing the center and left center of the Confederates' lines on Missionary Ridge; and Sherman forced a pontoon-bridge crossing of the Tennessee, just south of Chickamauga Creek, at about 1 p.m. His divisions threw back 1 brigade opposing their crossing, then skirmished into the foothills along the north face of Missionary Ridge. Davis' division remained behind covering the bridge.

At the center Confederate Gen. BRAXTON BRAGG had trench lines at the foot, on the slope, and at the crest of Missionary Ridge. Though the lines were manned by the understrength divisions of Maj. Gen. ALEXANDER P. STEWART and Brig. Gens. WILLIAM B. BATE and J. PATTON ANDERSON, Bragg claimed that their superior physical positioning allowed them to be held successfully by only a skirmish line. Maj. Gen. JOHN C. BRECKINRIDGE commanded the center divisions. Lt. Gen. WILLIAM J. HARDEE commanded Maj. Gen. BENJAMIN F. CHEATHAM's, Brig. Gen. STATES RIGHTS GIST's, and Maj. Gens. CARTER L. STEVENSON's and PATRICK R. CLEBURNE's divisions on the right. Before the Union capture of Orchard Knob, Bragg had dispatched Cleburne's and Brig. Gen. BUSHROD R. JOHNSON's divisions east to reinforce Lt. Gen. JAMES LONGSTREET in the KNOXVILLE CAMPAIGN. Johnson's troops were beyond recall. Cleburne's were rushed back 23 Nov. and placed on the extreme Confederate right near Tunnel Hill.

After victory on 24 Nov., Hooker's divisions left Lookout Mountain to cross Chattanooga Valley and Chattanooga Creek, occupy Rossville Gap, and move on the Confederate left. Retreating Confederates burned the Chattanooga Creek bridge. Delayed midway to Rossville Gap, Hooker fell behind

schedule and took little part in winning Missionary Ridge.

Sherman's divisions fought up to Tunnel Hill at the base of Missionary Ridge on the 24th. That night Cleburne strengthened his positions. Having acquired most of the Chattanooga garrison's cannon, Sherman started shelling his front at midmorning 25 Nov. and at 11 began a general assault on Tunnel Hill. This Confederate position, truly superior, withstood the best Union efforts all day. Unable to progress, Sherman signaled Grant's headquarters several times, asking for Thomas' troops to assault the center and weaken the Southern defense. By 3 p.m. Hooker had not appeared on the Confederate left, and several reinforcements had been sent from Thomas' force to Sherman's front. Grant advised Thomas to attack the first Confederate trench line with his remaining troops. The divisions of Brig. Gen. THOMAS J. WOOD and Maj. Gen. PHILIP H. SHERIDAN drove out Confederate defenders from the first trench, then found themselves without cover under heavy fire from second-line trenches. Against orders, rather than stand under severe fire, Wood's and Sheridan's men drove on up hill, pushing the Southerners down the opposite slope in badly organized retreat. Cleburne's division was pulled from its successful right-wing defense and made the rearguard for Bragg's defeated army. Sheridan's troops pursued, and Hooker's divisions, at last on the ridge, followed, unsuccessfully trying to bring on an engagement the next day at Rossville. Bragg's force retreated south to Dalton, Ga. Both sides gave aggregate casualty figures for the battles of Chattanooga; Missionary Ridge losses are among them.

Union victory at Missionary Ridge won Grant promotion to lieutenant general and prompted Bragg, after lambasting in his report Breckinridge and commanders of the center-line division, to request relief from command. Pres. JEFFERSON DAVIS recalled him to Richmond, Va.
—JES

Mississippi. Mississippi became the second state to leave the Union by its ordinance of secession enacted in Jackson 9 Jan. 1861. The move surprised no one since Mississippians had chosen an overwhelming majority of disunionist delegates to a secession convention 7 Jan. There was rejoicing in Jackson, reported a New York *Herald* correspondent, who noted: "The churches are decorated with evergreens and the lone star is prominent." Jackson ladies had presented to the convention a special flag bearing a single star to denote the state's "independent nation status." The flag, called the "Bonnie Blue Flag," was to become a wartime symbol.

The "Republic of Mississippi" became one of the Confederate States of America with the organization of that government in MONTGOMERY, Ala., early in February. The fact that a Mississippi resident, JEFFERSON DAVIS, was president of the Confederacy gave the state a particular closeness to the new government. So many Mississippians rushed to join the Confederate army that authorities could not place them or furnish them equipment and supplies. Gov. JOHN J. PETTUS wrote frantically to President Davis for instruction as to procedure, adding that "all Mississippi is in a fever to get to the field."

Beginning in spring 1862, Mississippi became a battleground. There were few sections of it that did not experience the war's destruction, and, when the fighting ended, the state lay in ruins. After VICKSBURG fell, 4 July 1863, the majority of the Confederate forces were transferred to other states, leaving only cavalry units to protect the population and hamper the march of the Union soldiers across the state.

During the 4 war years, Mississippi contributed to the Confederate army some 80,000 men, a number greater than the state's total number of white males between the ages of 18 and 45 as counted in the 1860 census. Less than 20,000 of them were "present or accounted for" in Apr. 1865. —PR

Mississippi, Confederate Army of. The first of the 3 Confederate armies of this name was formed 5 Mar. 1862 by the proclamation of Gen. P.G.T. BEAUREGARD. His troops soon melded with others under Gen. ALBERT SIDNEY JOHNSTON, but the name stuck temporarily. 42,000 strong, the army fought the Battle of SHILOH, in which Johnston was killed, and under Beauregard it withstood the Siege of CORINTH. Successfully evacuated to Tupelo, its command went to Gen. BRAXTON BRAGG, and Nov. 1862 it merged with the Army of Kentucky to become the ARMY OF TENNESSEE.

On 7 Dec. 1862 the troops that had been Maj. Gen. EARL VAN DORN's Army of West Tennessee formed the second Army of Mississippi, under Lt. Gen. JOHN C. PEMBERTON. In Jan. 1863 Pemberton reorganized his forces and dropped the name Army of Mississippi; a series of hapless struggles against Maj. Gen. ULYSSES S. GRANT followed, and 4 July 1863 what was left of the army, 31,600 men, surrendered at VICKSBURG.

On 12 May 1864 Lt. Gen. LEONIDAS POLK joined his corps, about 20,000 cavalrymen in 2 divisions, to Gen. JOSEPH E. JOHNSTON's Army of Tennessee and at the same time proclaimed the corps to be the third Army of Mississippi. After Polk's death 14 June at Pine Mountain, in battle against Maj. Gen. WILLIAM T. SHERMAN, the corps lost its designation as an army and took the name Stewart's Corps after its new commander, Maj. Gen. ALEXANDER P. STEWART. —HH

Mississippi, Union Army of the. Not to be confused with Maj. Gen. JOHN A. MCCLERNAND's later Army of the Mississippi

(which captured Fort Hindman at ARKANSAS POST, Ark., 10–11 Jan. 1863), this army was a Western theater force created to achieve a specific objective, the eventual Federal control of the entire Mississippi River.

Brig. Gen. JOHN POPE organized the force, consisting of about 19,000 effectives plus a river fleet for the NEW MADRID–ISLAND NO. 10 Campaign, the northernmost phase of operations in the North's attempt to regain control of the river. The army was composed of 5 divisions of 2 brigades each, several cavalry brigades, and a flotilla brigade, and existed 23 Feb.–26 Oct. 1862, when the organization was discontinued.

Much to the credit of Pope and his Army of the Mississippi, New Madrid and Island No. 10 were captured by early April after thorough siege operations, construction of a canal, and a difficult crossriver flanking movement. As a direct result of this successful operation, Pope was selected to command in the Eastern theater and was succeeded by Maj. Gen. WILLIAM S. ROSECRANS 26 June 1862.

Rosecrans led the army at the Battle of IUKA, Miss., 19 Sept. 1862, against Confederate Maj. Gen. STERLING PRICE and some 17,000 Southern troops. The Federals, divided and lacking coordination, did not achieve a decisive victory, although the Confederate forces withdrew from the field.

That battle began the Corinth Campaign, in which the army performed adequately. It participated as a unit in the initial phases of the STONE'S RIVER and VICKSBURG campaigning, but subsequently, during a periodic army reorganization, most of its troops were absorbed into the original XIII Corps commanded by Maj. Gen. WILLIAM T. SHERMAN, and performed excellent service throughout those campaigns. —RAP

Mississippi, Union Department of the. President's War Order No. 3, 11 Mar. 1862, established the Union Department of the Mississippi in an area defined as all Civil War theater commands west of Knoxville, Tenn. Incorporating the troops of Maj. Gens. HENRY W. HALLECK, DAVID HUNTER, and DON CARLOS BUELL, the creation of the department resulted in Hunter's transfer east and Halleck's assumption of full command over Missouri, Kansas, Mississippi, and West Tennessee. With 128,810 men scattered through 4 states, Halleck directed department policy and campaigns from his St. Louis, Mo., headquarters. The arrangement proved ineffective during a period when the Battles of SHILOH, NEW MADRID, and ISLAND NO. 10 were fought within the department. In August the DEPARTMENT OF THE OHIO was assigned the West Tennessee and Mississippi districts of the department, and 19 Sept. the newly created DEPARTMENT OF THE MISSOURI absorbed and eliminated what remained of Halleck's original command.

2 Departments of Mississippi followed. The first, organized 28 Nov. 1864 under Maj. Gen. Napoleon J. T. Dana, with headquarters at Memphis, Tenn., comprised all of West Tennessee and the state of Mississippi. Department troops were expected to secure Maj. Gen. WILLIAM T. SHERMAN's rear during his campaign through Georgia. Maj. Gen. GOUVERNEUR K. WARREN relieved Dana 14 May 1865, serving until Maj. Gen. HENRY W. SLOCUM took charge of a new Department of Mississippi, instituted 27 June 1865 to oversee Reconstruction in the state of Mississippi. —JES

Mississippi, Union Military Division of the. Prior to the relief of Maj. Gen. WILLIAM S. ROSECRANS, Union success at Chattanooga, and Maj. Gen. ULYSSES S. GRANT's elevation to lieutenant general, ABRAHAM LINCOLN ordered the consolidation of the Departments of the Ohio, the Cumberland, and the Tennessee under Grant's command 16 Oct. 1863 and named the organization the Military Division of the Mississippi. With Maj. Gens. WILLIAM T. SHERMAN, GEORGE H. THOMAS, and AMBROSE E. BURNSIDE now under Grant's direct control, this organization allowed coordinated action in the Western theater and was the first significant step toward Union victory.

Forces in the division fought in Tennessee, Mississippi, Alabama, Georgia, and South and North Carolina. On Grant's promotion to general-in-chief, Sherman assumed command of the division, 18 Mar. 1864, until the organization's dissolution 27 June 1865. The departments within the division assumed largely bureaucratic status under Sherman's tenure, while their namesake armies, along with the Union Army of Georgia, were assigned roles in front or rear for the march to Atlanta and sea. —JES

Mississippi and East Louisiana, Confederate Department of.

Confederate Adj. Gen. SAMUEL COOPER's Special Orders No. 73, of 1 Oct. 1862, stated, "The State of Mississippi and that part of Louisiana east of the Mississippi River is constituted a separate military department." Formerly the District of Mississippi commanded by Maj. Gen. EARL VAN DORN, the new department encompassed that portion of Louisiana containing Union-occupied New Orleans and contested ground around Baton Rouge, as well as Corinth and other Federal-held parts of Mississippi. Special Orders No. 73 designated Lt. Gen. JOHN C. PEMBERTON department commander.

Pemberton's 21 Oct. order subdivided the department into Districts 1, 2, and 3, commanded, respectively, by Brig. Gens. DANIEL RUGGLES, MARTIN L. SMITH, and WILLIAM N. R. BEALL. Ruggles maintained headquarters at Jackson, Smith established his at Vicksburg, and Beall was headquartered at Port Hudson, La.

The Confederate Department of Mississippi and East Louisiana (subsequently commanded by Lt. Gen. LEONIDAS POLK after Pemberton's surrender of VICKSBURG) was renamed the Department of the Southwest 23 Dec. 1863, and 9 May 1864, under Maj. Gen. STEPHEN D. LEE, was restructured and designated the Department of Alabama, Mississippi, and East Louisiana, an area including beleaguered Mobile. Maj. Gen. DABNEY H. MAURY, commander of Mobile's defense and the Confederate District of the Gulf, briefly assumed responsibility for the department 26 July–15 Aug. 1864, at which time Lt. Gen. RICHARD TAYLOR, hero of the Battle of MANSFIELD, took command. Taylor surrendered his department to Union Maj. Gen. E.R.S. CANBY 2 May 1865. —JES

Mississippi Marine Brigade.

Late in summer 1862 Acting Rear Adm. DAVID D. PORTER and Lt. Col. ALFRED W. ELLET, commanding the Union army's River Ram Fleet, proposed forming a unit to operate against Confederate partisans along the Western rivers. The War Department approved. Commissioned brigadier general and ordered to Washington, D.C., to organize the force, Ellet assembled the 1st Battalion Mississippi Marine Brigade Infantry and the 1st Battalion Mississippi Marine Brigade Cavalry (recruited in Missouri), and Walling's Light Artillery Battery (raised in Philadelphia, Pa., for service in Missouri).

Named the Mississippi Marine Brigade by the War Department, the troops were army volunteers operating from specially outfitted transport boats that allowed them to land quickly and pursue guerrillas inland. Ellet named his nephew, Col. Charles Ellet, second-in-command and arrived with the brigade ready for duty at Milliken's Bend, La., 22 Mar. 1863.

Within a week of its arrival, the brigade was dispatched to Tennessee to support Maj. Gen. WILLIAM S. ROSECRANS. In its 17-month lifespan it fought in Tennessee, Mississippi, Arkansas, and Louisiana; among its notable actions were the burning of Austin, Miss., 24 May 1863; service at PORT GIBSON, Miss., and in the RED RIVER CAMPAIGN; and guerrilla fighting in Arkansas highlighted by the engagement at LAKE CHICOT, 6 June 1864. From the Red River Campaign until its dissolution, the brigade served in Maj. Gen. ANDREW J. SMITH's command.

From its beginning, the marine brigade, an innovative and potentially effective amphibious force, was hamstrung by interservice rivalries. Naval officers and Maj. Gen. U. S. GRANT quarreled with the contentious Ellet family, seeking control of the army ram fleet and removal of the Ellets from the scene of active operations.

Modestly effective, the brigade also experienced internal controversy. In summer 1863, in a family quarrel, Brigadier General Ellet arrested Colonel Ellet, who resigned from the army 8 Sept. for reasons of health. His cousin John R. Ellet became colonel. In all, 4 Ellets served in the brigade.

During its last weeks the brigade was commanded by Lt. Col. George E. Currie, while Alfred Ellet pursued personal feuds and opportunities in Louisiana. Ellet was assigned administrative duties in New Orleans and the brigade was disbanded Aug. 1864. —JES

Missouri.

In Missouri, prior to the Civil War, there were 4 distinct parties of conflicting sentiment: militant secessionists; equally militant Unionists; moderates of Southern sympathy; and Union moderates. The moderates struggled to keep peace in the state and, even after the fall of FORT SUMTER, 14 Apr. 1861, it appeared that they might do so, despite the fact that newly elected Gov. CLAIBORNE F. JACKSON was strongly pro-South. Then, on 10 May, Federal troops under Capt. NATHANIEL LYON seized Camp Jackson, a training camp on the outskirts of St. Louis that a week earlier had been garrisoned with pro-Southern state militia. Lyon had little difficulty in forcing the camp to surrender and holding the arsenal supplies, but the Federals were set upon in the city streets by Southern sympathizers, causing a riot leaving 28 people dead. With that, hope of maintaining peace in the state was lost.

Governor Jackson called out 50,000 state troops "to repel the invasion" of Missouri and moved the state government from Jefferson City just before the capital was taken over by Lyon. In Oct. 1861, pro-Southern legislators met in Neosho, in southwest Missouri, and passed an act of secession "declaring the ties heretofore existing between the United States and the State of Missouri dissolved." On that basis, the state was declared by some Southerners to be a member of the Confederacy. But a pro-Union state convention had already convened at Jefferson City; with the support of the Federal government, it had deposed Jackson and his refugee legislators and had set up a new state government. It was thus that Missouri was saved for the Union, "remained politically neutral throughout the war," and escaped major problems of Reconstruction after the war.

Missouri provided 447 separate military organizations, involving more than 109,000 men, to the Federal armies, and more than 100 military units, about 40,000 men, to the Confederacy. 1,162 battles and skirmishes were fought within the state, a total exceeded only in Virginia and Tennessee.

—PR

Missouri, Confederate Army of. Gen. E. KIRBY SMITH, commander of the Trans-Mississippi Department, directed the former Missouri governor, congressman, and militia leader, Maj. Gen. STERLING PRICE, to plan a raid in autumn 1864. It was to be the last gasp of the Confederacy in the West. Price hoped his raid would regain Missouri for the Confederacy or at least cause enough havoc to defeat Lincoln in the 1864 election and gain a better peace settlement for the South.

On paper, Price assembled a formidable army of 12,000 men. 3 divisions were formed, commanded by able Brig. Gens. JOSEPH O. SHELBY and JOHN S. MARMADUKE and Maj. Gen. JAMES F. FAGAN, each with a nucleus of battle-wise Missourians and other Westerners. There were only 14 cannon, all small and some homemade. To Price's deep irritation, THOMAS C. REYNOLDS, Missouri's governor in exile, went along to protect his political interests and later delivered a scathing criticism of Price's leadership.

The Army of Missouri crossed into Missouri from northeast Arkansas 19 Sept., heading for St. Louis. Blocked from that objective by Federal Maj. Gen. ANDREW J. SMITH, Price turned west and fought a series of engagements in a drive across the state to the outskirts of Kansas City.

Bravely taking on superior Federal forces under A. J. Smith and Maj. Gens. JAMES G. BLUNT, ALFRED PLEASONTON, and SAMUEL R. CURTIS, Price was at last defeated at Westport, Mo., and headed southwest. Both Marmaduke and Brig. Gen. WILLIAM L. CABELL were captured at the MARAIS DES CYGNES RIVER in Missouri, 25 Oct., and Price barely escaped to the Confederate lines with 6,000 survivors. —DS

Missouri, Union Department of the. Established by General Orders No. 97, 9 Nov. 1861, the Department of the Missouri initially consisted of Missouri, Iowa, Minnesota, Illinois, Arkansas, and Kentucky west of the Cumberland River, Maj. Gen. HENRY W. HALLECK commanding from headquarters at St. Louis.

On 11 May 1862 the department was merged into the Department of the Mississippi but was reestablished 19 Sept. to consist of Missouri, Kansas, Arkansas, the borderlands of Indian Territory, and Alton, Ill. 4 days later Maj. Gen. SAMUEL R. CURTIS was placed in command of the department at its former headquarters in St. Louis. On 11 Oct. Curtis' jurisdiction was expanded to include Colorado (excluding Fort Garland) and Nebraska territories. He retained command of the enlarged department until Maj. Gen. JOHN M. SCHOFIELD replaced him 24 May 1863.

3 times in Jan. 1864 the department was reduced: all territory except Missouri, Arkansas (excluding Fort Smith), and Alton, Ill., were transferred from the department on the 1st; Arkansas was withdrawn and assigned to the Department of Kansas on the 6th; and Alton, Ill., was attached to the Northern Department on the 12th. Maj. Gen. WILLIAM S. ROSECRANS received orders to assume command 20 Jan. 2 weeks later Alton was restored to his jurisdiction. On 27 May the department was attached to the Division of West Mississippi.

Maj. Gen. GRENVILLE M. DODGE replaced Rosecrans 9 Dec. The state of Missouri and Nebraska and Colorado (except Fort

Garland) territories were restored 30 Jan. 1865. The same day the department was attached to the Division of the Missouri. Utah Territory and Dakota west of 27° longitude were added 17 Feb.

In the major postwar reorganization of military territory, 27 June 1865, Alton was transferred to the Department of the Ohio, and Wisconsin, Minnesota, Iowa, all of Dakota, Montana, and Fort Garland were added to the Department of the Missouri, which was attached to the Division of the Mississippi. Reorganized several times during the postbellum years, the department continued to exist until 18 Dec. 1880.

—PLF

Missouri, Union Military Division of the. The Division of the Missouri was established by Gen. Orders No. 11, 30 Jan. 1865, to combine the Departments of the Missouri and the Northwest. Within its jurisdiction fell the states of Missouri, Kansas, Wisconsin, Iowa, and Minnesota, and the Nebraska, Dakota, and Colorado territories (except Fort Garland in Colorado). Maj. Gen. JOHN POPE assumed command of the division 3 Feb., establishing his headquarters in St. Louis. On 17 Feb. Utah Territory was transferred to the division from the Department of the Pacific and assigned to the Department of the Missouri, a part of the Division of the Missouri. Gen. Orders No. 44, issued 21 Mar., added the Department of Arkansas, which included Indian Territory, to the division. On 17 May the territory south of the Arkansas River was transferred to the Division of the Southwest.

By the time the division was organized, the fighting had ended in the area under Pope's command, except for skirmishing and guerrilla warfare. On 11 May 1865 Confederate Lt. Col. M. JEFF THOMPSON surrendered his brigade at Chalk Bluff, Ark. The last of the active Confederate field commands was surrendered by Brig. Gen. STAND WATIE, 23 June, at Doaksville, near Fort Towson, in Indian Territory. 4 days later the Division of the Missouri was discontinued. —PLF

Missouri Compromise, 1820. When the Missouri territorial assembly petitioned Congress for admission to the Union in 1818, the U.S. comprised 22 states: 11 slave, 11 free. Until that time, the legislators had consciously alternated between admitting slave and free states to preserve the balance of power among sectional interests. But some 2,000 to 3,000 slaves were then living in Missouri Territory. To receive Missouri with a constitution permitting slavery would have upset the balance in favor of the South in the Senate, though not in the House, where the difference in population gave Northerners 105 votes to the Southerners' 81.

In a move to limit slavery in Missouri and in the West, on 13 Feb. 1819 New York Rep. James Tallmadge proposed an amendment to exclude slavery from the territory, which passed in the House but was blocked by Southern legislators in the Senate. Through fall the Missouri issue dominated national politics, but the apparent stalemate broke when Maine separated from Massachusetts in 1819 and petitioned for admission to the Union as a free state. Legislators seized the opportunity to settle the immediate dilemma by passing enabling acts authorizing the people of Maine and Missouri to draft constitutions and form state governments.

The Maine constitution passed unchallenged, but rising antislavery sentiment in the nation forced legislators to address the extension of involuntary servitude into the Louisiana Purchase, where slaveholders had already begun to settle. Hoping to avoid political imbalance as states were organized in the Purchase territory, Illinois Sen. Jesse B. Thomas proposed admitting Missouri as a slave state but restricting slavery thereafter in the Louisiana Purchase to land below latitude 36° 30'. The Senate passed this Missouri Compromise quickly, the House accepting the amendment after some debate. Missouri was admitted to the Union the next year, 2 Mar. 1821.

When slavery again threatened to split the nation 30 years later, another generation of legislators honored the 36° 30' line in the COMPROMISE OF 1850, but 4 years later the KANSAS-NEBRASKA ACT voided the Missouri Compromise, pushing the nation toward war. —PLF

Mitchel, Ormsby MacKnight. USA b. Morganfield, Ky., 28 July 1809. Moving to Lebanon, Ohio, with his widowed mother, Mitchel completed his basic education, then clerked in a store in Xenia until being appointed to West Point. He graduated 15th in his class in 1829, staying at the academy for 7 years as an instructor of mathematics.

Resigning from the army in 1836, he returned to Ohio to teach mathematics, philosophy, and astronomy at Cincinnati College. The country's most respected authority on astronomy and a charismatic speaker on the subject, Mitchel was acclaimed by the scientific community for his influence in establishing the Naval Observatory and the Harvard Observatory. He served as the director of both the Cincinnati and Dudley observatories, the latter in Albany, N.Y. During the antebellum years he wrote 2 books based on his scientific studies and 1846–48 published the *Sidereal Messenger,* a magazine of popular astronomy.

In his search for competent military officers in spring 1861, ABRAHAM LINCOLN appointed Mitchel brigadier general 9 Aug., placing him in command of the Department of the Ohio. No major battles took place while Mitchel held the assignment, but raiding parties sent by him into Alabama seized the Memphis & Charleston Railroad at Huntsville, cut Confederate lines of communication, and harassed secessionists in the northern part of the state. Despite the success of his men in the field, Mitchel quarreled with his superior, Maj. Gen. DON CARLOS BUELL, over the lax discipline among Mitchel's troops.

Promoted to major general 11 Apr. 1862, he decided to leave the army rather than continue to serve under Buell. Buell, however, considered him a good soldier and recommended his transfer instead. Refusing his resignation, the War Department ordered Mitchel to Hilton Head, S.C., as commander of the Department of the South and the X Corps. Within a few weeks of his arrival he contracted yellow fever, dying in Beaufort, 30 Oct. His body was shipped to Brooklyn for burial. —PLF

Mitchell, John Grant. USA b. Piqua, Ohio, 6 Nov. 1838. An 1859 graduate of Kenyon College, Mitchell studied law privately until the Civil War. He enlisted in the Ohio Reserves June 1861 and received a commission as 1st lieutenant of the 3d Ohio infantry 30 July. With other Western units he took part in early mountain campaigns in western Virginia.

An able combat officer, Mitchell is distinguished for his progress through the ranks to a generalship at age 26, making him one of the youngest major generals in the Union army. Following the spring 1862 campaign against the Memphis & Charleston Railroad in Alabama and Tennessee, Mitchell was

promoted captain, recruited in Ohio, received commission as lieutenant colonel of the 113th Ohio 2 Sept. 1862, then became colonel of the 113th 6 May 1863.

LC

As a member of the Army of the Cumberland, he served in the TULLAHOMA CAMPAIGN, fought in Maj. Gen. GORDON GRANGER's Reserve Corps at HORSESHOE RIDGE at Chickamauga, and held brigade command in the XIV Corps for the battles at Dalton, RESACA, and KENNESAW MOUNTAIN. In the 27 June 1864 fighting at Kennesaw, Mitchell led his brigade in support of Col. Daniel McCook's spearhead brigade in Maj. Gen. GEORGE H. THOMAS' assault on the Confederate center. Under withering fire, he could not help McCook. McCook was killed, and Mitchell was driven back with heavy losses.

With Thomas, he left Georgia to go to the defense of Nashville, fought in the December battle there in command of a brigade in a provisional division, then was transferred east for the CAROLINAS CAMPAIGN, having been commissioned brigadier general 12 Jan. 1865. After brevet promotion to major general of volunteers 13 Mar., he fought at AVERASBOROUGH and BENTONVILLE and, following the Confederate surrender, resigned from service 3 July 1865.

In peacetime, Mitchell became an attorney and city councilman in Columbus, Ohio, and was a Federal pension agent for the state. d. Columbus, 7 Nov. 1894. —JES

Mobile, Siege of. 25 Mar.–12 Apr. 1865 Overlooking Mobile Bay, one of the major channels through which the Confederacy received its supplies from abroad, Mobile, Ala., is situated 30 mi from the Gulf of Mexico. It was defended by nearly 400 guns in 3 major forts (the most important of which was Fort Morgan) and several batteries, as well as by lines of piles, torpedoes, and numerous floating mines. Mobile was also defended by an inner line of works, principal of which was Spanish Fort, looked upon as the key to the city.

Rear Adm. DAVID G. FARRAGUT wanted to capture Mobile in 1862, after he had taken New Orleans, but it was not until 5 Aug. 1864 that he stormed into the bay with his fleet. In this effort Farragut managed to capture Fort Morgan and gain absolute control of the bay, but no attempt was made to move against Mobile.

By Mar. 1865 a new movement had begun against the city, both by land and water. Farragut had retired and in his place was Rear Adm. Henry K. Thatcher; army troops were led by Maj. Gen. E.R.S. CANBY. The navy had about 20 ships with which to battle Confederate Adm. FRANKLIN BUCHANAN's 4.

In a cooperative land/sea operation, 1 column moved up the coast 17 Mar., while another column moved by water to a point on the other side of the bay. There were to be simultaneous attacks, each drawing attention from the other. In 10 days the army was near Spanish Fort, while the gunboats were continually bombarding the forts.

On 4 Apr. the bombardment was stepped up and continued throughout the night at the rate of a shell every 3 or 4 minutes. On 8 Apr. Spanish Fort was evacuated by the Confederates.

Other forts began to fall, and on the 12th it was discovered that the Southerners had abandoned all their defenses. A formal demand was made for the surrender of Mobile and, at 12:30 p.m. that day, the U.S. flag was raised over city hall.

But the North had paid a high price for its victory. 9 vessels, large and small, had been sunk by torpedoes and mines, taking the lives of 114 men. —VCJ

Mobile Bay, Ala., Battle of. 5 Aug. 1864 In Jan. 1864 Rear Adm. DAVID G. FARRAGUT began planning the capture of Mobile Bay. By August his fleet (14 wooden ships, 4 monitors) was ready for battle with Fort Morgan and Adm. FRANKLIN BUCHANAN's flotilla—3 gunboats and the ironclad TENNESSEE.

Farragut's fleet entered the main channel at dawn on 5 Aug., the monitors ahead, the wooden ships lashed in pairs behind. Firing began as they approached Fort Morgan. Under the guns of the fort, the monitor TECUMSEH struck a mine and went down. The ships behind halted in confusion, and Morgan raked their decks with fire until Farragut forced his flagship, the HARTFORD, through the minefield, the fleet following. Buchanan's Tennessee attacked as they entered the bay, but superior speed and handling allowed the Federals to pass.

With the fleet in the bay, the Tennessee took brief refuge at Fort Morgan. But soon it steamed back out, ready to fight on alone. Farragut's fleet moved to meet the vessel and, outnumbered 17-to-1, the Tennessee plunged into the fray. Again and again it was rammed, and broadsides swept away its smokestack, destroying its steam power. Then its steering chains were shot away, and the Tennessee was adrift with the tide. His ship helpless and its armor beginning to give way, Buchanan surrendered. Fort Morgan fell soon after, and the U.S. Navy controlled Mobile Bay. —MM

Monett's Ferry, La., eng. at. 23 Apr. 1864 *See* CANE RIVER CROSSING, LA., ENG. AT.

Monitor, USS. The USS Monitor was designed and built by JOHN ERICSSON, a Swedish inventor. He laid its keel 25 Oct. 1861, and by the end of Jan. 1862 the vessel was ready for launching.

The Monitor was a unique warship. Instead of a standard ship hull, it had a large armored "raft," 172 ft by 41 ft 6 in., supported by a lower section of wood 122 ft long and 34 ft wide. The revolving turret carrying 2 11-in. Dahlgren smoothbores was considered its most novel feature.

On 25 Feb. 1862, the vessel was commissioned with Lt. JOHN L. WORDEN commanding officer. On 4 Mar. it left New York City under tow for blockade duty in North Carolina waters. On 8 Mar., while the ship was under way, the Confederate ironclad VIRGINIA (Merrimack) attacked Union blockaders in Hampton Roads, Va. That night the Monitor arrived and prepared to challenge the Confederate warship. The following day, 9 Mar., for 4 hours the 2 ironclads fought each other, "mercilessly, but ineffectively." Early in the afternoon the Virginia returned toward Norfolk, leaving the Roads in possession of the Monitor. The Monitor had won a tactical victory in preventing the destruction of Union vessels in Hampton Roads, but the Virginia controlled the river approach to Richmond. (*See* HAMPTON ROADS, VA., BATTLE OF.)

Early in May the Confederate ironclad was destroyed by its own crew to prevent its capture after Confederates evacuated Norfolk. As a result, the James River was opened to Union warships. The Monitor, reinforced by the ironclads Galena and Naugatuck, ascended the James but withdrew after an engagement with Confederate batteries at DREWRY'S BLUFF, 15 May. The Monitor spent the remainder of the summer in Hampton Roads and September–November was in the Washington Navy Yard undergoing repairs and alterations. Late in November it returned to Hampton Roads.

On 29 Dec. 1862, under the tow of the USS Rhode Island, the ship left the Roads for North Carolina waters. Shortly after midnight, 30 Dec., the vessel foundered in a storm off Cape Hatteras with the loss of 4 officers and 12 men. In 1973 it was found, bottom up, lying in some 220 feet of water. —WNS

"monitor fever." This expression refers to the enthusiasm and relief that swept the North after the USS MONITOR had proven a match for the Confederate ironclad VIRGINIA (Merrimack) during their engagement off HAMPTON ROADS, VA., 9 Mar. 1862. The Monitor restored Northerners' faith in their navy, a faith badly shaken by the initial successes of the Virginia. Enthusiasm for monitors continued as the navy concentrated on building this type of vessel for the rest of the war. —NCD

Monocacy, Md., Battle of. 9 July 1864 On 5 July the vanguard of Lt. Gen. JUBAL A. EARLY's command forded the Potomac River into Maryland. Union authorities in Washington, D.C., plagued by conflicting reports, responded slowly to this Confederate invasion. Only Maj. Gen. LEW WALLACE, commander of the Middle Department in Baltimore, reacted decisively. Sifting through the vague intelligence, Wallace readied his small command and selected a defensive position behind the Monocacy River east of Frederick, Md., where the road forked into the Baltimore and Washington pikes. Lt. Gen. U. S. GRANT, belatedly realizing that Early's corps had departed Petersburg, finally dispatched Brig. Gen. JAMES B. RICKETTS' division of the VI Corps northward. Ricketts joined Wallace on the 8th, thereby bringing the Union forces to more than 5,000 men.

The Confederate army, slowed by diversions and a leisurely pace, arrived at Frederick at sunrise the next morning. One division cleared the town, and skirmishing continued until Early decided to assault Wallace's left flank, where Ricketts' seasoned veterans were deployed. The Federals, in fierce fighting in a wheatfield and cornfield, repulsed 3 Confederate charges. About 4 p.m. Maj. Gen. JOHN B. GORDON launched a riveting, massive attack that broke 2 Federal lines before a third hurled him back. Gordon regrouped and in another vigorous charge cracked Ricketts' front. Wallace ordered a withdrawal, and the Federals retreated toward Baltimore.

Wallace's valiant, stubborn defense, costing him 1,880 men, delayed Early's advance on Washington for one vital day. When Early reached the capital's outskirts 2 days later the remainder of the VI Corps manned the works. The Battle of Monocacy perhaps saved the Northern capital. —JDW

Monongahela, Union Department of the. Late in Apr. 1863 Confederate cavalry under Brig. Gens. JOHN IMBODEN and WILLIAM E. JONES raided so near southwestern Pennsylvania that Gov. ANDREW G. CURTIN feared for the safety of his state. A month later not only Curtin but Sec. of War EDWIN M. STANTON placed credence in a rumor that a larger Confederate force, under Maj. Gen. J.E.B. STUART, was about to raid the

Aboard the U.S.S. **Monitor**

Pittsburgh vicinity. This time state and national governments cooperated in a defense effort.

On 9 June the War Department established the Department of the Monongahela, headquartered at Pittsburgh under Maj. Gen. WILLIAM T. H. BROOKS. His domain comprised Pennsylvania west of Johnstown and the Laurel Hill Mts., plus 6 counties in Ohio and western Virginia, including the Wheeling region, that were later transferred to other departments. Brooks's territory had been carved out of the Middle Department and the Department of the Ohio for the purpose of safeguarding possible objectives of a Confederate invasion during that summer of crisis.

On the 11th Brooks assumed command and set about to raise a force of local militia to augment the few volunteer units assigned to him. Because of War Department restrictions on militia recruiting (the government favored volunteer enlistments), Brooks enjoyed little success, raising 1 partially armed infantry regiment and 1 artillery unit without cannon. His mili-

tary prospects appeared ominous, for on 14 June Gen.-in-Chief HENRY W. HALLECK warned him of an imminent invasion by Gen. ROBERT E. LEE's Army of Northern Virginia, not merely Stuart's cavalry (*see* GETTYSBURG CAMPAIGN).

Though no coherent enemy force would violate Brooks's territory, he mustered enough military and civilian laborers to erect strong works at Pittsburgh and Wheeling as well as at several less strategic points. To garrison them, he somehow gathered more than 1,000 troops by late June, including a small regiment of volunteer infantry. Soon, however, the volunteers were ordered elsewhere, for a time leaving him with fewer than 800 troops, mostly short-term "emergency" men.

The Confederate invasion of Pennsylvania eventually worked in Brooks's favor. By 5 July the crisis had prompted more than 3,600 troops to report to him, including mounted and artillery units. By then defeated at Gettysburg, the Confederates had already left the state for Maryland, but most of

Brooks's men remained with him until his department was discontinued 6 Apr. 1864. On that date it was merged into a larger Pennsylvania military district, the DEPARTMENT OF THE SUSQUEHANNA. —EGL

Monroe's Cross Roads, N.C., eng. at.   10 Mar. 1865

In advance of Maj. Gen. WILLIAM T. SHERMAN's infantry, the cavalry division of Brig. Gen. H. JUDSON KILPATRICK crossed from South to North Carolina 6 Mar. 1865. 2 nights later, some 10 mi above the Lumber River, the Union leader captured members of Lt. Gen. WILLIAM J. HARDEE's rearguard. They told him that Lt. Gen. WADE HAMPTON's Confederate cavalry was in his rear, heading north toward Fayetteville.

Kilpatrick set a trap for them. He spread 3 brigades of troopers across every road Hampton could take, then bivouacked with the brigade of Col. George E. Spencer on forest- and swamp-bordered land near Monroe's Cross Roads and Solemn Grove. He set up headquarters in an abandoned house, where he also lodged his comely traveling campanion, Mary Boozer.

Unknown to Kilpatrick, one of his officers blundered into Hampton's troops late on the 9th and was forced to reveal the Union dispositions. At once, the Confederate leader plotted to turn the tables on his opponents. Learning that Spencer's bivouac lacked pickets, he planned to attack the next morning from the west with the division of Maj. Gen. MATTHEW C. BUTLER, while Maj. Gen. JOSEPH "Fightin' Joe" WHEELER led his division across the swamp in Kilpatrick's rear.

At dawn on 10 Mar., the Union bivouac became pandemonium. Reported the commander of Spencer's 5th Kentucky: "We were awakened from our slumbers by the deadly missiles and fiendish shouts of the rebel cavalry." Butler's men, then Wheeler's, raced through the camp, trampling still-sleeping troopers. Some Federals surrendered on the spot; others ran for the trees.

Hearing the commotion, Kilpatrick bolted from his headquarters, clad in nightshirt and boots. A Confederate horseman swooped down on him and, taking him for a private soldier, demanded to know General Kilpatrick's whereabouts. Thinking quickly, the disheveled commander pointed to a passing rider, and his would-be captor sped off. In an instant Kilpatrick fled to safety in the woods. Meanwhile, his paramour took refuge in a ditch until the shooting stopped.

When neither Butler nor Wheeler followed up his initial success, the Federals rallied. Joined by members of Kilpatrick's outlying brigades, under Cols. Thomas J. Jordan and Smith D. Atkins and Lt. Col. William B. Way, they counterattacked. With their horse artillery and repeating carbines, they put the attackers to flight and retook the bivouac. The Confederates captured the now-open road toward Fayetteville, having inflicted a reported 500 losses. Kilpatrick claimed to have lost (in addition to his dignity) 190 casualties, while killing 80 Confederates and capturing 30 others. —EGL

Montgomery, Ala.

When delegates to the Provisional Confederate Congress met in Montgomery 4 Feb. 1861, residents of Alabama's second largest city extended an eager welcome to the representatives of the new government. Capital of the state since 1846, Montgomery bustled as a center of commerce and trade, yet it was a small, provincial town ill-equipped to function as the seat of a federal government. Only 2 hotels operated in Montgomery, the better of these the Exchange Hotel. It filled quickly as politicians arrived with their families, soon becoming as notorious for its filth and exorbitant prices as for being a political meeting place. Some legislators sought accommodations in private homes, but these too were scarce and inadequate.

The newcomers nonetheless re-created in Montgomery a society of parties and receptions similar to the one they were accustomed to in Washington. The Provisional Congress met in the old state Capitol in the chamber of the house of representatives. President-elect JEFFERSON DAVIS was inaugurated in Montgomery 18 Feb., and the first Confederate flag, the "Stainless Banner," was raised over the provisional capital 4 Mar.

But the facilities in Montgomery could not satisfy the needs of the bureaucracy being established, and in March the legislators began to discuss relocating the national capital. Though their reasons for wanting to move stemmed in part from lack of housing and the discomforts inflicted by Alabama's prodigious mosquito and fly population, their choice of another city rested on more practical grounds. Congress rejected offers from several Southern cities and from Alabama legislators who offered to designate a capital district patterned after the District of Columbia. On 27 Apr. officials in RICHMOND, Va., the wealthiest and most influential of Southern cities, invited the legislators to relocate in the Old Dominion.

Essential to the Confederacy's future, Virginia was the leading producer of diversified staple crops in the South, and Richmond possessed the TREDEGAR IRON WORKS, the only foundry in the Confederacy capable of manufacturing the cannon and heavy industrial machinery critical to Confederate success. Equally important, the legislators expected the war to center on Virginia because of its proximity to Washington, and Davis, commander in chief of the Confederate army, believed he could better control military operations from Richmond. On 1 May legislator Walter Brooke introduced a bill to move the capital from Montgomery to Richmond. It passed overwhelmingly, and later that month the government was transported to its permanent site.

Spared from becoming a target for Union forces, Montgomery weathered raids against its rail lines but never suffered a major assault. Union cavalry under Brig. Gen. JAMES H. WILSON occupied the city 12 Apr. 1865. —PLF

Montgomery Convention (Convention of Rebel States).

On 4 Feb. 1861, the day the WASHINGTON PEACE CONFERENCE assembled, delegates of the states of the Lower South, noticeably missing at that gathering, met at Montgomery, Ala., to establish a Southern Confederacy. With considerable purpose, they hastened to create a new government before ABRAHAM LINCOLN took office. The Montgomery Confederate Congress managed to accomplish much before 16 Mar. It adopted a provisional constitution, chose a provisional president, declared all U.S. laws in force with exceptions to protect slavery, picked JEFFERSON DAVIS as president, authorized contracts, loans, and treasury notes, declared Mississippi River navigation open, admitted Texas to the Confederacy, adopted the "Stars and Bars" flag (see FLAGS, CONFEDERATE), confirmed STEPHEN R. MALLORY as secretary of the navy and JOHN REAGAN as postmaster general, authorized an army, adopted the CONFEDERATE CONSTITUTION, organized a government, and prepared for war.

The haste with which this was done also planted the seeds for future discontent and friction within the Confederacy. One of the most worrisome issues, STATES RIGHTS, was written into the constitution's preamble. Another was the failure to establish a CONFEDERATE STATES SUPREME COURT. Though delegates chose Davis as the Confederacy's first president, they were not unanimous in reaching that decision. Other contenders were WILLIAM L. YANCEY, HOWELL COBB, ROBERT A. TOOMBS, and ALEXANDER H. STEPHENS.

Personality clashes were to leave permanent wounds, and the election of Georgia's Stephens as vice-president displeased some delegates because of his pronounced Unionism during the antebellum decades. This discord was not dissipated in the euphoria following the raising of the new Confederate flag by former president John Tyler's granddaughter on the day Lincoln was inaugurated. Rather, the controversial elements that came out of Montgomery proved to be the imperceptible cancer that helped destroy the Confederate states. —AG

Moody, Young Marshall. CSA b. Chesterfield Cty., Va., 23 June 1822, Moody migrated to Alabama in the early 1840s and until the Civil War worked as a schoolteacher, shopkeeper, and clerk of the circuit court in Marengo County.

Joining the 11th Alabama Infantry as captain, he made the acquaintance of Maj. ARCHIBALD GRACIE; his career was tied to Gracie's for the duration of the war. With the major he helped raise the 43d Alabama, and on Gracie's promotion to brigadier general, Moody became colonel 4 Nov. 1862. With the 43d, he fought in East Tennessee, Gen. BRAXTON BRAGG's KENTUCKY CAMPAIGN, CHICKAMAUGA, the Siege of CHAT-

LC

TANOOGA, the Siege of KNOXVILLE, the engagement at BEAN'S STATION, and on Gracie's wounding took temporary brigade command, overseeing the unit's transfer to Gen. P.G.T. BEAUREGARD in Virginia, along the James River near Petersburg. He was wounded in action at DREWRY'S BLUFF 12 May 1864.

Returning to duty, he and Gracie served in the Petersburg trenches, and on his friend's death he took brigade command again, serving without commission until promoted to brigadier general 4 Mar. 1865. He was surrendered with the Army of Northern Virginia in April.

Moody tried to establish a business career in Alabama for a few months after the war, then died of yellow fever 18 Sept. 1866. —JES

Moore, Andrew Barry. war governor b. Spartanburg, S.C., 7 Mar. 1807, Moore moved from South Carolina to Perry Cty., Ala., in 1826. 6 years later the well-educated son of a planter was admitted to the state bar but taught school rather than devote himself to a law practice. He served as justice of the peace for 8 years, entering politics as a member of the Alabama house of representatives in 1839. His constituency reelected him to the house consistently 1842–45; during the last 2 years he held the speakership.

Moore continued in public service as a Whig presidential elector in 1848 and sat on the bench as circuit-court judge from 1851 until 1857, when he was elected governor on the Democratic ticket. 2 years later he retained the office by

soundly defeating a Southern rights Democrat.

Though a moderate secessionist, Moore called for a secession convention to be held 7 Jan. 1861, but 3 days before the delegates assembled, he ordered state troops to seize all Federal forts and military facilities. The convention endorsed his actions by passing an ordinance of secession 11 Jan. At Moore's request, the legislature appropriated half a million dollars for defense and authorized

LC

a 3 million-dollar indebtedness to prepare the state for war. Over the next several months he encouraged enlistments and generally supported the Jefferson Davis administration. The Alabama constitution prohibited a governor from serving more than 4 consecutive years, and in December Moore relinquished the office to the duly elected JOHN G. SHORTER, whom he served through the war as aide-de-camp.

Federal officials imprisoned Moore in 1865 but released him quickly because of his poor health. He practiced law in Marion, Ala., until his death there 5 Apr. 1873. —PLF

Moore, John Creed. CSA b. Hawkins Cty., Tenn., 28 Feb. 1824. After attending Emory and Henry College in Virginia, Moore was appointed to West Point, graduating 17th in the class of 1849. He resigned from the U.S. Army 28 Feb. 1855 to teach at Shelby College, Ky., after having served in Florida, the Southwest, and on garrison duty at Baton Rouge, La. In 1861 he left Kentucky and raised the Confederate 2d Texas Infantry in Galveston.

Elected colonel of the 2d Texas, Moore spent most of his Civil War career with the short-lived Confederate Army of the West and under Maj. Gen. DAB-NEY H. MAURY. At SHILOH, his first battle, he won praise fighting in

LC

Brig. Gen. JONES M. WITHERS' division of the Army of the West, then assumed command of the 3d Brigade/3d Division under Maury for campaigning in north Mississippi and in the battles at IUKA and CORINTH. He was promoted brigadier general 26 May 1862.

Moore's brigade (the 37th, 40th, and 42d Alabama regiments; the 2d Texas; and the 35th Mississippi) was taken prisoner in the surrender of Vicksburg along with Maj. Gen. CARTER L. STEVENSON's division. Exchanged 12 Sept. 1863, they fought together at Chattanooga in the Battle of LOOKOUT MOUNTAIN. Union Lt. Gen. U. S. GRANT later stated that these men had not been officially exchanged and fought in Tennessee in violation of agreements. This precipitated an argument that lasted until Jan. 1876, when the prisoner-exchange records were found and the minor matter of honor was laid to rest in favor of the Southerners.

While Moore served at Lookout Mountain, Maury, claiming

that the brigadier was not adequately employed there, arranged for his transfer to the defenses at Mobile, Ala. This was Moore's last assignment. He resigned 3 Feb. 1864 for reasons unclear.

In postwar years, Moore lived and worked in Texas as a teacher and free-lance writer. d. Osage, Tex., 31 Dec. 1910. Due to an indexing error in the postwar compilation of the *OFFICIAL RECORDS*, he is confused in some histories with Lt. Col. John C. Moore of the arsenal at Selma, Ala.   —JES

Moore, Patrick Theodore. CSA b. Galway, Ireland, 22 Sept. 1821. The son of a British government official, Moore moved with his family to Canada in 1835. His father, appointed a British consul, soon relocated in Boston. The younger Moore eventually settled in Richmond, Va., where he became a merchant and joined a militia company, with the rank of captain.

LC

When Virginia seceded, Moore entered Confederate service, commissioned colonel of the 1st Virginia. Leading his regiment at FIRST BULL RUN in Col. JAMES LONGSTREET's brigade, he suffered a severe wound in the head, incapacitating him for further regimental command. During the PENINSULA CAMPAIGN in spring 1862 he served as a volunteer aide on the staff of Gen. JOSEPH E. JOHNSTON. After Johnston fell wounded at SEVEN PINES, he joined Longstreet's staff for the SEVEN DAYS' CAMPAIGN.

For the next 2 years Moore served on court-martial duty. In May 1864, under Brig. Gen. JAMES L. KEMPER, he assisted in the organization of the reserve forces of Virginia. Promoted to brigadier general 20 Sept. 1864, Moore commanded a brigade of Richmond local defense troops until the war's conclusion. He was paroled 30 Apr. 1865.

With his antebellum business ruined by the war, Moore opened an insurance agency in Richmond. He lived and worked in his adopted city until his death there, 19 Feb. 1883.
—JDW

Moore, Thomas Overton. war governor b. Sampson Cty., N.C., 10 Apr. 1804, Moore stayed in North Carolina to receive his education, moving in 1829 to Rapides Parish, La., where he managed an uncle's sugar plantation. A shrewd businessman, Moore later purchased his own estate, becoming an important planter himself.

Criticized for possessing a volatile, uncompromising temperament, Moore was nonetheless an effective, well-liked politician at the local level. He was elected to the state house of representatives in 1848 and to the senate in 1856. Nominated for governor by the Democratic party in the 1859 elections, Moore won, taking office in Jan. 1860 as the nation approached the secession crisis. He attended the Democratic national convention in Charleston and campaigned actively for the John C. Breckinridge–Joseph Lane ticket.

On Lincoln's election Moore called a secession convention for 23 Jan. 1861. Confident that the delegates would vote Louisiana out of the Union, the governor ordered state troops

to take over and occupy Forts Jackson, St. Philip, and Pike. On the 10th the Federal arsenal at Baton Rouge surrendered to Moore's forces, who captured 50,000 stands of small arms and about 40 pieces of ordnance. Some of the guns he gave to Mississippi Gov. JOHN J. PETTUS, who feared his state would be defenseless against a Federal invasion. Moore also seized $500,000 in gold and silver at the U.S. mint and turned over $147,519.66 in custom-house receipts to the Confederate treasury.

As anticipated, the secession ordinance passed overwhelmingly. Moore stepped up recruiting, established a supply network under the jurisdiction of a military board, and urged banks to suspend specie payment in favor of conducting business in Confederate Treasury notes.

His government was forced to move north, first to Opelousas then to Shreveport, after Union Gen. BENJAMIN F. BUTLER occupied New Orleans June 1862. Loss of the city limited the assistance he could give to Pres. JEFFERSON DAVIS in Richmond, but to keep cotton from Union brokers, he forbade trade with the enemy and ordered burned any cotton accessible to the enemy. After the surrender of VICKSBURG cut the Trans-Mississippi Department from the Eastern Confederacy, Moore attended the August convention of Far Western governors in Marshall, Tex., and agreed to recognize departmental commander Lt. Gen. E. KIRBY SMITH as the Confederate authority in the region.

Moore's plantation in Rapides Parish was confiscated and his house destroyed during Maj. Gen. NATHANIEL P. BANKS'S RED RIVER CAMPAIGN in spring 1864. With his property gone and a warrant for his arrest outstanding, Moore fled to Cuba. Friends secured a pardon on his behalf, however, and he returned to the country to rebuild his plantation. He died there 25 June 1876, without having reentered politics or recouping his once considerable fortune.   —PLF

Moorefield, W.Va., Battle of. 7 Aug. 1864 The Confederate cavalry brigades of Brig. Gen. JOHN MCCAUSLAND and BRADLEY T. JOHNSON entered CHAMBERSBURG, Pa., about 5:30 a.m., 30 July 1864, demanding from the townspeople a levy of $100,000 in gold or $500,000 in greenbacks. When the citizens refused to comply, McCausland, under orders from Lt. Gen. JUBAL A. EARLY, had the town burned, in retaliation against Union depredations in the Shenandoah Valley. While the flames engulfed houses and businesses, consuming nearly two-thirds of the village, the Southern horsemen departed, encamping that night at McConnellsburg.

At sunrise on the 31st, the raiders, a mounted column of nearly 2,000 troops, began passing out of Pennsylvania into Maryland, halting at Bevansville. In intense heat and choking dust, the Confederates moved out early on 1 Aug. Late in the afternoon, near Cumberland, they skirmished with Federal cavalry, then withdrew to the Potomac River in an all-night march. Arriving in Old Town at daylight they encountered a small Union force, whom they captured after a brief melee. They rested that day and the next. Commanding the force, McCausland decided on a bold raid against New Creek, W. Va., a depot and repair shop on the Baltimore & Ohio Railroad. The Confederates moved against it on the 4th, but the strong position defied attack. On 5 Aug. the 2 brigades were encamped near Moorefield, resting and grazing their worn mounts.

The raiders had eluded Federal pursuers for nearly a week. Union troops had arrived too late at Chambersburg and had been too few at Cumberland. On 3 Aug. as the Confederates rested near Old Town, Union Maj. Gen. DAVID HUNTER, commander of the Department of West Virginia, ordered Brig. Gen. WILLIAM W. AVERELL to find them "by the most expeditious route" and attack them. Averell's 2 brigades of about 1,500 horsemen crossed the Potomac the next day. Conflicting reports of the Confederates' whereabouts slowed the march, so Averell pushed the columns all night. Late in the afternoon of the 5th, the Federals reached Springfield, where they learned of McCausland's abortive raid on New Creek and his withdrawal toward Moorefield.

Averell renewed his pursuit early 6 Aug. Arriving at Romney before noon, he received intelligence that the Southerners had passed through the village the day before, marching toward Moorefield. To cut off the Confederate retreat, the Union general dispatched a battalion of the 22d Pennsylvania Cavalry to Lost River Gap in the Allegheny Mts. After Averell resumed his march at 1 p.m., his vanguard captured a Southern courier carrying a letter from McCausland dated the 6th at Moorefield. Having located the Confederates, Averell halted early, resting the men and mounts, and ordered a move at 1 a.m., 7 Aug., to reach the Confederates at daylight.

The Federals trotted into the darkness of the 7th, snatched some Southern pickets en route, passed through Reynolds' Gap at 5 a.m., then deployed into line. Before them lay Johnson's camp north of the south branch of the Potomac River and 3 mi from McCausland's sleeping troopers. Within 30 minutes Averell's leading brigade, commanded by Maj. Thomas Gibson, charged. The galloping Federals burst into the startled Confederates. Pockets of Southerners offered some resistance but most wildly fled across the river. Johnson barely eluded capture in the rout.

With most of Johnson's brigade scattered or pushed back, Averell's second brigade, under Col. William H. Powell, splashed through the waters toward McCausland. The 21st Virginia Cavalry momentarily checked the assault, but the Union troops routed the horsemen and pursued the fleeing Southerners, capturing more prisoners, cannon, flags, and horses. Averell had scored a stunning victory. He reported that his men had captured 3 flags, 4 artillery pieces, 420 prisoners, and 400 horses, while losing only 9 killed and 32 wounded. Johnson reported his total casualties at 150 but McCausland filed none.

The Union victory at Moorefield partially compensated for the burning of Chambersburg and other recent Confederate successes in Maryland and the lower Shenandoah Valley. Averell deserved credit for his pursuit, the battle scheme, and its execution. Johnson accused McCausland of neglect of duty and asked for a court of inquiry, which was never convened. This defeat soured the relations between the two brigadiers. —JDW

Morgan, Charles Hale. USA b. Manlius, N.Y., 6 Nov. 1834. An 1857 graduate of West Point, finishing 12th in his class, Morgan served on garrison and frontier duty in the antebellum Regular Army. Stationed on the frontier when the war exploded, he did not return to the East until Dec. 1861. As 1st lieutenant, 4th U.S. Artillery, he participated in the PENINSULA and SEVEN DAYS' campaigns. Promoted to captain 5 Aug. 1862, he was on sick leave until 1 Oct., when he assumed command of the artillery of the II Corps. After directing the corps batteries at FREDERICKSBURG, on 1 Jan. 1863 the New Yorker became

Maj. Gen. WINFIELD S. HANCOCK's chief of staff, with the rank of lieutenant colonel.

Morgan served under Hancock until the conclusion of the war. Throughout the campaigns of 1863 and 1864—CHANCELLORSVILLE, GETTYSBURG, BRISTOE, MINE RUN, the WILDERNESS, SPOTSYLVANIA, COLD HARBOR, and PETERSBURG—Morgan directed the staff and assisted in the deployment of artillery. He earned 5 brevets for his performance.

NA

When an old wound of Hancock's forced him to relinquish field command, Morgan went with his commander to Washington, D.C., where they recruited for the VETERAN RESERVE CORPS. When the war ended, Morgan was serving Hancock as chief of staff of the Middle Military Division. On 21 May 1865 he received his commission of brigadier general of volunteers.

After the war Morgan remained in the Regular Army, reverting to his rank of captain. He served in a number of artillery garrisons, earning promotion to major 5 Feb. 1867. He died while on duty at Alcatraz Island, Calif., 20 Dec. 1875. —JDW

Morgan, Edwin Denison. USA/war governor b. Washington, Mass., 8 Feb. 1811. With his family Morgan moved to Windsor, Conn., in 1822, attending the local school there. For 2 years he studied at Bacon Academy in Colchester, leaving in 1828 to clerk in his uncle's grocery store in Hartford. He was elected to the city council at age 22 and at 26 moved to New York City. After a brief partnership in the wholesale grocery business, he amassed a fortune independently in merchandising and finance. His success extended to politics with his election as a city alderman in 1849 and to 2 terms in the state senate, 1851–55. Declining a third term, Morgan accepted one of the prestigious positions of commissioner of emigration, 1855–58.

An antislavery Whig during his early political career, Morgan left the party in 1855 to help organize the Republicans in New York. The next year he became chairman of the Republican National Committee, a position he held until 1862, and he was elected governor. During his first term he worked diligently to improve the state's finances and the canal system. His popularity among voters, and his reputation for honesty, gave him a wide margin of victory in his bid for a second term in 1860.

Morgan devoted himself to supporting ABRAHAM LINCOLN's war programs, raising and equipping 223,000 men for the Federal army. To give his valuable ally both civil and military authority in the state, an industrial and financial center critical to the war effort, on 28 Sept. 1861 the president appointed Morgan major general with command of the Department of New York. For more than a year Morgan labored to counter the strong antiadministration Democratic influences in New York but declined to run for a third term when his moderate stance toward slavery alienated Radicals within his party as they agitated for abolition. During the remaining months of his term he applied his energies to developing a system of defenses for New York harbor.

Morgan resigned his army commission 1 Jan. 1863 and shortly before his gubernatorial term expired was elected to the U.S. Senate. There he distinguished himself for his indefatigable work in committee. Though ANDREW JOHNSON admired Morgan's abilities and nominated him secretary of the treasury in 1865, Morgan opposed many of Johnson's policies, voting to convict the president after his impeachment trial.

Morgan's political career waned after 1869, when he was defeated in his second Senate race. Again between 1872 and 1876 Republicans chose him to head their national committee, but he retired from politics after losing the New York gubernatorial contest in 1876. The highly respected politician declined a second appointment to the treasury secretaryship in 1881. During his retirement he pursued his philanthropic interests, giving generously to several medical and educational institutions. d. New York City, 14 Feb. 1883.   —PLF

Morgan, George Washington. USA b. Washington Cty., Pa., 20 Sept. 1820, Morgan showed himself to be a leader when he fought in the War for Texas Independence and at 16 was commissioned an officer by Texas president SAM HOUSTON. He returned home in 1839, entered West Point in 1841, and resigned in his third year because of poor grades. He then studied law intermittently until moving to Mt. Vernon, Ohio, where he passed the bar and became prosecuting attorney for Knox County.

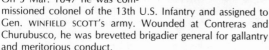

Morgan fought conspicuously as colonel of the 2d Ohio Volunteers under Gen. Zachary Taylor during the Mexican War. On 3 Mar. 1847 he was com-   *NA*
missioned colonel of the 13th U.S. Infantry and assigned to Gen. WINFIELD SCOTT's army. Wounded at Contreras and Churubusco, he was brevetted brigadier general for gallantry and meritorious conduct.

For the next 13 years, Morgan practiced law and farmed in Mt. Vernon, in 1856 accepting an appointment as U.S. consul at Marseilles and later the ministry at Lisbon, a post he resigned at the onset of the Civil War. ABRAHAM LINCOLN commissioned Morgan brigadier general of volunteers 12 Nov. 1861, giving him command of a division in Maj. Gen. DON CARLOS BUELL's Army of the Ohio. His great Civil War triumph was expelling the Confederates from Cumberland Gap in 1862. Transferred to Maj. Gen. WILLIAM T. SHERMAN's army the next year, Morgan led a division during the VICKSBURG CAMPAIGN and the XIII Corps in the capture of ARKANSAS POST.

Though Morgan was a competent soldier, Sherman blamed him for the failure of the Federal advance on CHICKASAW BLUFFS, 27–29 Dec. 1862. Because he disapproved of using blacks as soldiers, he resigned 8 June 1863, following several months of illness.

At the national Democratic convention in 1864, Morgan supported Maj. Gen. GEORGE B. MCCLELLAN for the presidential nomination. The next year he was defeated in the Ohio gubernatorial election, but in 1866 his constituents voted him into the U.S. House of Representatives. Unseated by a Republican opponent June 1868, he was reelected in 1869 and 1871, opposing harsh Reconstruction measures during his tenure. When his last term expired, Morgan reestablished his law practice in Mt. Vernon. He died during a visit to Ft. Monroe, Va.,

26 July 1893, and his body was returned to Mt. Vernon for burial.   —PLF

Morgan, John Hunt. CSA b. Huntsville, Ala., 1 June 1825. A member of a prominent Kentucky family, Morgan attended Transylvania College in Lexington for 2 years. He left school in 1842 under suspension for trouble he had gotten into with another student. From 1846 to 1847 he served in the Mexican War as a lieutenant of volunteers, purchasing a hemp factory and a woolen mill on his return home. In 1857 he organized the Lexington Rifles, a local militia unit that in Sept. 1861 followed him into the Confederate army. Serving first under Maj. Gen. SIMON B. BUCKNER, Morgan was promoted to colonel of the 2d Kentucky Cavalry 4 Apr. 1862 and

USMHI
to brigadier general 11 Dec. the same year.

Morgan, Kentucky's contribution to the ranks of legendary Southern cavalry commanders, was noted for his daring, headline-producing raids. Like his counterpart in the East, Maj. Gen. J.E.B. STUART, Morgan was the epitome of a cavalry leader. He stood arrow-straight, over 6 ft tall, and was always impeccably dressed and finely mounted, with the manner of a polished gentleman. While his military background was limited, innate talent offset any lack of formal training. Shrewd and fearless, he firmly established a reputation as a winner and earned the devotion and dedication of his men.

Morgan's cavalry operated in the Western theater under the command of Maj. Gen. JOSEPH WHEELER. Morgan's primary contribution to the war lay not so much in what his own raids accomplished but in what that added to the total impact of cavalry operations in the West. He conducted a series of raids into Tennessee and Kentucky, the raid of July 1862 lasting 3 weeks as his cavalry rampaged through the latter state seemingly invincible to Union cavalry sent against them. In alarm, Federal military leaders in Kentucky asked the War Department for help and warned of imminent Confederate uprisings in the state. In exasperation, ABRAHAM LINCOLN wired Maj. Gen. HENRY W. HALLECK, the ranking Federal commander in the department: "They are having a stampede in Kentucky. Please look to it."

Morgan's final cavalry exploit, July 1863, was a wild, 24-day ride through southern Indiana and across Ohio, ending with Morgan's capture and confinement in the OHIO PENITENTIARY. Although he escaped, the incurable adventurer was killed in a surprise cavalry encounter at Greeneville, Tenn., 3 Sept. 1864. *See* MORGAN'S OHIO RAID, MORGAN'S SECOND KENTUCKY RAID, and MORGAN'S THIRD ("CHRISTMAS") KENTUCKY RAID.

—WRB/DKS

Morgan, John Tyler. CSA b. Athens, Tenn., 20 June 1824, Morgan moved with his family to Calhoun, Ala., when he was 9. Educated at home and in local schools, he went to Tuskegee, Ala., studied law privately, became an attorney in 1845, and established a practice in Selma 10 years later. Morgan ardently advocated states rights and white supremacy,

served as an elector for JOHN C.
BRECKINRIDGE in the 1860 presidential election, and was a delegate to the state secession convention.

In 1861 he enlisted as a private in the Cahaba Rifles, became a member of the 5th Alabama, rose to major and
lieutenant colonel, and fought at
FIRST BULL RUN in July. Returning
to Alabama, he resigned his
commission, raised the 51st Alabama Cavalry (Alabama Partisan
Rangers), became its colonel,

LC

and participated in the fighting at STONE'S RIVER. With the Army
of Tennessee he also fought at CHICKAMAUGA Sept. 1863, rode
on Maj. Gen. JOSEPH WHEELER's raid on the supply lines at
Chattanooga, and, under Wheeler, supported the KNOXVILLE
CAMPAIGN.

Having declined promotion and service in Virginia, Morgan
accepted commission as brigadier general 16 Nov. 1863. He
fought in the ATLANTA CAMPAIGN and harassed Federals on their
MARCH TO THE SEA Nov.–Dec. 1864. Assigned to service at
Demopolis, Ala., he ended the war organizing home defense.
Given his racial views, biographers make a point of noting that
his final assignment involved raising black troops for Confederate military service.

Postwar, Morgan resumed his law practice, then won a seat
in the U.S. Senate in 1876. He remained in office until his
death in the District of Columbia, 11 June 1907. He had made
a national reputation as a rockbound conservative, a supporter
of Jim Crow laws, and an advocate of a Central American
canal.   —JES

Morgan's Ohio Raid. 2–26 July 1863 Brig. Gen. JOHN
HUNT MORGAN conducted his famous Ohio Raid in defiance of
orders from Gen. BRAXTON BRAGG to operate only south of the
Ohio River. Morgan believed that the pressure being applied
to the South could be relieved only by bringing war to the
citizens of the North and persuading Copperheads (see PEACE
DEMOCRATS) to rise in support of the Confederacy. But he
destroyed any possibility of such support by holding businesses
for ransom, destroying commercial buildings, and looting local
treasuries, making no distinction between enemies and friends.
He was more successful in attaining his first objective; the raid
brought panic to the North, reinspired the flagging spirits of the
South, and delayed the fall of East Tennessee.

Morgan crossed the Cumberland River near Burkesville 2
July and began a series of running skirmishes with Federal
troops. He passed through Lebanon on the 5th, moved on to
Bardstown, then crossed the Ohio at Brandenburg and proceeded east through Lexington and north to Summansville.
From Summansville he marched through the suburbs of Cincinnati, completing the longest continuous march of the war
by covering 90 mi in 35 hours. He reached Pomeroy on the
18th, leaving in his wake a wide path of destruction and hundreds of stragglers who continued to terrorize the population.
During the raid Confederates captured 6,000 of the enemy,
pulled 14,000 Regulars from other duty, caused 120,000 militia to be mustered in 2 states, destroyed 34 bridges, demolished railroads to more than 60 locations, and damaged hun-

dreds of thousands of dollars' worth of property. The raiders
also made history by conducting the longest cavalry raid of the
war, traveling more than 700 mi in 25 days while almost
constantly in combat.

But the raid turned against Morgan on the 19th, when a
strong Union column under Brig. Gen. Edward H. Hobson
defeated his men at Buffington Island. Hobson pursued the
remnants of Morgan's troops relentlessly, capturing them and
their leader at New Lisbon on the 26th.

The Confederates' reward for their raid was confinement in
the OHIO PENITENTIARY as common criminals. The pillaging of
Morgan and his "Terrible Men" left an indelible mark in the
annals of warfare.   —WRB/DKS

Morgan's Second Kentucky Raid. 17 Oct.–1 Nov. 1862
After service in Confederate Gen. BRAXTON BRAGG'S KEN-
TUCKY CAMPAIGN and at the Battle of PERRYVILLE, Col. JOHN
HUNT MORGAN'S Kentucky cavalry joined Lt. Gen. E. KIRBY
SMITH's portion of the Army of Tennessee on its retreat out of
Kentucky. On 15 Oct. 1862, while the army sat 25 mi south-
east of Richmond, Ky., Morgan proposed to Smith that his
cavalry raid behind Union lines, disrupting railroads and supply
routes, thus hampering the Federals' timid pursuit of the main
Confederate force. Smith agreed.

Leaving their camp southeast of Richmond 17 Oct., Morgan's force traveled northwest, took the lightly defended town
of Lexington on the 18th, then left in early afternoon for Versailles to the west. For the next 12 days, passing west and south
in a wide arc, the raiders moved through Lawrenceburg,
Bloomfield, Bardstown, Elizabethville, and Litchfield; crossed
the Green River between Woodbury and Morgantown, and
the Muddy River south of Rochester; then rode toward
Greeneville and Hopkinsville, reaching the latter around 25
Oct. Union pursuit of Morgan was negligible after Lawrenceburg and Bloomfield, and ceased almost completely after the
Confederates crossed the Muddy. Morgan called a 3-day halt
at Hopkinsville, where his troops were feted by sympathetic
citizens and did minor damage to railroads and bridges before
setting out for Tennessee.

The men rode into Springfield in north-central Tennessee 1
Nov. Though they later pressed on to Gallatin in the east, the
raid effectively ended when they crossed the state line. The
raiding party, made up of the 2d Kentucky Cavalry, under the
subordinate command of Lt. Col. BASIL W. DUKE, Col. RICHARD
M. GANO's 3d Kentucky Cavalry, and a Kentucky cavalry battalion led by Maj. William C. Breckinridge, took and paroled
several prisoners and sustained few casualties. This minor operation served to keep Federals insecure in the Blue Grass
state.   —JES

Morgan's Third ("Christmas") Kentucky Raid. 21 Dec.
1862–2 Jan. 1863 Late in 1862 Maj. Gen. WILLIAM S. ROSE-
CRANS was preparing an unexpected assault on the Confederate army near Murfreesboro in an attempt to reverse the desperate Federal situation in the Tennessee theater of war.
Confederate Gen. BRAXTON BRAGG's countermove to impede
Rosecrans sent Brig. Gen. JOHN HUNT MORGAN on his third
cavalry raid into Kentucky to sever the long Union supply line
stretching from Louisville.

Morgan's 3,100-man cavalry division crossed the Cumberland River into Kentucky 22 Dec. 1862. Their objective was
to break up the Louisville & Nashville (L&N) Railroad, Rose-

crans' lifeline, by destroying 2 huge trestles near Muldraugh's Hill. Amid growing Union uncertainty about his purpose and movements, Morgan skirmished with Federals at Glasgow, crossed the Green River, and camped near Elizabethtown 26 Dec. He captured that town on the 27th and on the 28th decisively severed Rosecrans' railway supply line. By the 30th, despite their initial confusion and delay, Union forces were closing on the Confederates. Realizing his danger, Morgan raced through Campbellsville, Columbia, and Burkesville and crossed the Cumberland to safety 2 Jan. 1863.

During Morgan's 12-day raid his cavalry destroyed the trestles near Muldraugh's Hill, several bridges, 3 depots, 3 water stations, long sections of the L&N railway, and, by his own estimate, Union equipment and supplies worth $2 million. He captured more than 1,800 prisoners, killed or wounded many others, and pulled nearly 20,000 badly needed troops away from Rosecrans. Morgan's own losses were 2 killed, 24 wounded, and 64 missing.

In retrospect, however, Morgan's raid drew his cavalry away from Bragg when the latter met Rosecrans' Union army at STONE'S RIVER. His presence there might have been just enough to turn a monumental but indecisive battle into a Confederate victory and to alter the course of the war.   —WRB/DKS

Morrill (Land-Grant College) Act. The Land-Grant College Act, more commonly called the Morrill Act in honor of Vermont Sen. Justin S. Morrill, who sponsored the bill, was the most important educational legislation passed by the U.S. Congress between the Ordnance of 1787 and 1862. Jonathan B. Turner, a professor at the University of Illinois, began agitating for a nationally endowed college of agricultural and industrial arts in 1850. Morrill became interested in the idea in 1856, believing that the scientific study of farming would slow the wasteful use of farmland and that such a program would give farmers' sons a chance for an education generally unavailable to them because of the expense involved. The college land bill he introduced Dec. 1857 provided for the distribution of public lands to the states, with the understanding that the states would use profits from sales to establish at least one agricultural school in each state. Though the bill initially received little encouragement, by Feb. 1859 it had passed both houses of Congress. Pres. James Buchanan, however, vetoed the legislation because he questioned the constitutionality of giving public lands to the states for resale.

Morrill reintroduced the bill Dec. 1861, doubting it would pass among the more pressing wartime legislation. His fears seemed well founded when the Committee on Public Lands returned the bill 29 May, recommending that it not be passed. Nonetheless, Morrill had the support of powerful Republican Sen. BENJAMIN F. WADE, who presented the bill in the Senate a few days later. Nearly 2 months elapsed before the legislators voted on it. Western politicians objected to giving government lands, most of them located in the West, to Eastern states, but the proposals enjoyed wide popularity among the public, and numerous state legislators instructed their representatives to vote for the bill. On 10 June, many congressmen crossed party lines to pass the Morrill Act 32-to-7 in the Senate and 90-to-25 in the House. Abraham Lincoln added his signature to the legislation 2 July.

The act provided for every state participating in the program to receive 30,000 acres of land—10,000 more than provided for in the 1857 bill—for each senator and representative it sent

to Congress; the same terms were extended to Southern states after they returned to the Union. The schools struggled to get started, but Congress passed the Hatch Act in 1887 to give them additional financial assistance. In all, 13 million acres of government land were given away and 69 land-grant colleges established as a result of the Morrill Act.   —PLF

mortar. Mortars are among the oldest forms of artillery, and they had not changed much by the advent of the Civil War. Classified by bore size, 5.8-in., 8, 10, and 13 in., they threw a "bomb" or fused shell in a high arc over enemy walls and fortifications and sometimes lobbed shells over the heads of friendly troops as they charged the enemy. The coehorn mortar, among the smallest, had a 4.5-in. bore. Harold Peterson, author of *Round Shot and Rammers,* found 2.25- and 3.5-in. mortars mentioned in records, but not on official ordnance lists.

Made of iron, mounted on heavy wood and iron beds, mortars were usually intended for siege and garrison work. They performed well in Union Rear Adm. DAVID G. FARRAGUT's Mississippi River campaigns, floating on "mortar schooners," and are remembered for service at VICKSBURG and the Siege of PETERSBURG, where the "Dictator," a heavy 13-in. seacoast mortar mounted on a railroad flatcar, pounded Confederates. The 8-in. siege and garrison mortars had tubes 22.5 in. long, and threw a 44.5-lb shell. The 10-in. mortars had tubes 28 in. long and threw 87.5-lb shells. Seacoast mortars, 13-in. pieces, heaved a 220-lb bomb 4,325 yd at an elevation of 45° with a 20-lb powder charge.   —JES

Morton, James St. Clair. USA b. Philadelphia, Pa., 24 Sept. 1829, Morton was a talented military engineer. Following 4 years at the University of Pennsylvania, he entered West Point, graduating 2d in the class of 1851. Before the Civil War he worked on a series of coastal fortification projects, the Potomac River waterworks, the Washington, D.C., aqueduct, and took part in a Central American expedition.

USMHI

Until early 1862, Morton supervised construction of Fort Jefferson in the Dry Tortugas off Florida, then, as a captain of Regulars, on Maj. Gen. DON CARLOS BUELL's order he supervised construction of the Union defensive works at Nashville, Tenn. His Forts Negley, Morton, Houston, and Casino played critical roles in defending the city Dec. 1864. After Buell appointed him chief engineer of the Army of the Ohio, 9 June 1862, and gave him a troop command for the KENTUCKY CAMPAIGN, Maj. Gen. GEORGE H. THOMAS made him chief engineer for the Army of the Cumberland.

Though Morton was brave, he preferred engineering projects to infantry maneuvers. Given command of the XIV Corps pioneer brigade 3 Nov. 1862, he received promotion to brigadier general of volunteers 4 Apr. 1863, to date from 29 Nov. 1862; became a major in the Regulars 3 July 1863; then, at his request, was mustered out of volunteer service 7 Nov. 1863. During this period he served well at the Battles of STONE'S RIVER

Mortar "Dictator"

and CHICKAMAUGA, where he was wounded; worked in the defense of CHATTANOOGA; and was brevetted colonel of Regulars 20 Sept. 1863.

Through Jan. 1864 Morton superintended Tennessee garrison defenses, then went to Washington, D.C., as assistant to the chief of engineers. On 18 May he became chief engineer to the IX Corps for Virginia operations, and 17 June 1864, in a failed assault on PETERSBURG, was killed.

Morton wrote the distinguished engineering works *Memoir on the Dangers and Defenses of New York City* (1858), and *Memoir on American Fortifications* (1859), as well as the biography *Life and Services of Major John Sanders of the Engineers* (1861). He was posthumously promoted brigadier general of Regulars to date from his death.   —JES

Morton, Oliver Hazard Perry Throck. war governor b. Salisbury, Ind., 4 Aug. 1823. After the death of Morton's mother, his father sent him to live with 2 staunch Presbyterian aunts, who imbued in him a degree of inflexibility that marked his long career in politics. Morton had some formal elementary schooling and studied 1 year at Wayne County Seminary, though he acquired most of his education by reading. Dissatisfied with brief careers as a clerk and in the hatter's trade, he attended Miami University for 2 years, read law, and became a highly respected corporate lawyer whose services were in demand by the railroads.

In 1848 he failed in a bid to become prosecuting attorney on the Democratic ticket. Holding no elective office, he remained active in the party. Rather than see Democrats weakened by internal disagreement, he lent his support to the Wilmot Proviso, legislation that would have prohibited slavery in any territory won during the Mexican War. But in 1854 he took a firm stand against the KANSAS-NEBRASKA ACT and POPULAR SOVEREIGNTY, thereafter associating himself with the People's party, the forerunner of the Republicans in Indiana.

Republicans nominated Morton for governor in 1856, campaigning on a platform in favor of protectionism for U.S. industry and homestead legislation. Though he was not elected, he expected to win the nomination again in 1860. Instead, party leaders gave former Whig

Henry S. Lane the first slot on the ticket and Morton the second slot. When this moderate slate gave the Republicans a majority in the legislature, they elected Lane to the U.S. Senate and Morton succeeded to the governorship.

A skillful political opportunist, Morton emerged as the most powerful and, by some estimates, the best of the war governors. He answered ABRAHAM LINCOLN's call for troops by raising twice the number requested for Federal service. Certain the war would be brief, he labored to keep in uniform every Indianan who volunteered, so that none would be prevented from serving when the War Department began refusing troops it was unprepared to feed and equip. Largely because of his efforts to encourage volunteerism, Indiana provided 150,000 enlistments to the Federal army with little resort to the draft.

The governor generally backed Lincoln's war measures, though he complained about excessive military arrests, resisted the draft, and opposed freeing Southern slaves until the president issued his emancipation proclamation 1 Jan. 1863. Jealous for his state's prestige in the Union, he also clashed repeatedly with Federal authorities in his determination to prevent other states from being treated more favorably. He waged a bitter campaign against Copperheads (*see* PEACE DEMOCRATS) and when growing peace sentiment pitted him against a legislature threatening to limit his military powers, rather than call the hostile representatives into session Morton kept the state government running with loans from Washington, advances from the private sector, and profits from the state arsenal he had established. In 1864 he was reelected along with a Republican legislature, in part by arranging to have 9,000 sick and wounded Indiana soldiers furloughed home in time to vote.

Worn by long hours and stress, in summer 1865 Morton suffered a stroke that left him paralyzed. He nonetheless stayed in politics as an uncompromising foe of the Democrats. Initially a proponent of Lincoln's lenient plan for reconstructing the seceded states, in the postwar years he allied with Radical Republicans. After being elected to the U.S. Senate in 1867, he led the movement to pass the 14TH AMENDMENT providing for black suffrage.

Felled by a second stroke Aug. 1877, Morton traveled to Indiana to recuperate, dying at his home in Indianapolis 1 Nov. in the middle of his second congressional term. —PLF

Mosby, John Singleton. CSA b. near Richmond, Va., 6 Dec. 1833, Mosby attended the University of Virginia until imprisoned for shooting a fellow student. Becoming interested in law during his trial, he pursued the legal profession and was admitted to the bar.

USMHI

When the war began, he was practicing law in Bristol, Va. He quickly joined a local cavalry company, fought in the FIRST BATTLE OF BULL RUN, and then was assigned to Brig. Gen. J.E.B. STUART's cavalry as a scout. In the SEVEN DAYS' CAMPAIGN around Richmond, he originated the idea for Stuart's ride around Maj. Gen. GEORGE B. MCCLELLAN's Union army.

Desiring to lead an independent command under the Partisan Ranger Law (*see* PARTISAN RANGERS), he appealed to Stuart and was permitted to do so late in 1862. In his first major feat as a partisan, one night early in Mar. 1863 he and 29 men stole into Fairfax Court House, Va., and captured Union Brig. Gen. EDWIN H. STOUGHTON. Quickly Mosby became the bane of the Union, his activities in northern Virginia so successful that Lt. Gen. U. S. GRANT ordered him and his followers, when captured, hanged without trial.

Mosby was wounded 7 times. He kept his command—at its peak only 800 men—strictly disciplined, usually operating with bands of from 20 to 80, who quickly dispersed when overpowered.

Official records show that he was mentioned in Gen. ROBERT E. LEE's orders and reports more often than any other Southern officer. Stuart praised him highly. Grant, who later became a friend of Mosby, said that "there were probably but few men in the South who could have commanded successfully a separate detachment in the rear of an opposing army and so near

the border of hostilities as long as he did without losing his entire command."

Mosby estimated that he kept at least 30,000 Union soldiers away from the front. He believed cavalry was no strong offensive weapon but a fast-moving arm to upset enemy plans.

12 days after Lee surrendered, Mosby disbanded his organization and returned to the practice of law in Warrenton, Va., where he died 30 May 1916. —VCJ

Mosby's Rangers. CSA On 18 Jan. 1863, 16 Confederates rode toward Warrenton, Va., in a heavy rainstorm. For a few days they seemed to disappear into the countryside, then they attacked a series of Federal picket posts, capturing horses and men and throwing Union forces in the area into a state of fear. This band of raiders formed the core of Mosby's Rangers, a body of PARTISAN RANGERS led by JOHN S. MOSBY. Made up of volunteers or men on leave from regular army units, convalescents, and civilians unwilling to enlist in the Confederate army, the rangers operated out of Middleburg in Loudoun County. They boarded in private homes, lived with family or off the country rather than establish camps, and were called together by the grapevine when Mosby needed them.

Their guerrilla tactics—swift, night attacks by small groups of rangers, raids against trains and wagon trains—branded them the greatest menace to Union troops in northern Virginia. On one of their early forays, 29 rangers rode into Fairfax Court House and captured Brig. Gen. EDWIN H. STOUGHTON, 33 other men, and 58 horses from a Union encampment.

The command operated under the Partisan Ranger Act until 10 June 1863, when it was organized as Company A/43d Battalion/Partisan Rangers and mustered into the Regular Army. Though the men elected their officers in compliance with War Department regulations, the ticket they voted was selected by Mosby. His insistence on choosing officers for their merit, on weeding out ineffective men, and on strict discipline resulted in a unit of extraordinary ability and quality. By spring 1864 the 43d numbered about 240 mounted troopers (no accurate muster roster exists) in 4 companies. Men in Regular units called the rangers "spoiled darlings," "feather-bed soldiers," and "carpet knights." They were often commanded by Lt. William Chapman during Mosby's absences.

Late in 1864, Maj. Gen. PHILIP H. SHERIDAN authorized Capt. Richard Blazer to recruit and equip 100 men with Spencer repeating rifles to hunt and destroy Mosby's band. Blazer's Scouts failed in their mission. The rangers killed or wounded all but 2 of their pursuers and captured their Spencers near Kabletown, 18 November. Gen.-in-Chief ULYSSES S. GRANT tried to stop Mosby's Rangers by ordering the destruction of all forage and supplies in Loudoun County and the arrest of all men under 50 to keep them from being recruited into Confederate service. He also suggested taking the families of Mosby's men into custody and holding them as hostages to guarantee the rangers' good behavior. Captured rangers were to be hanged without trial, but Mosby's retaliation in kind ended the practice.

When Gen. ROBERT E. LEE surrendered at APPOMATTOX Court House 9 Apr., the rangers numbered about 800 effectives in 7 companies, including Company H, formed on the 5th of men fleeing the Army of Northern Virginia. Many of them stubbornly vowed to continue fighting in the mountains, but when Mosby learned of Gen. JOSEPH E. JOHNSTON's surrender, he called the rangers together at Salem, Va., 21 Apr. There he

NA

disbanded the unit to avoid surrendering it to Federal authorities. At his urging the men sought individual pardons.

—PLF

Mountain Department, Union. The Mountain Department, created 11 Mar. 1862 from the Department of Western Virginia, comprised the area of western Virginia, southwest Virginia, and eastern Kentucky. Brig. Gen. WILLIAM S. ROSECRANS briefly commanded the department until its appointed commander, Maj. Gen. JOHN C. FRÉMONT, reported 29 Mar.

Frémont's lackluster performance as a department commander was revealed during Confederate Maj. Gen. THOMAS J. "STONEWALL" JACKSON'S 1862 SHENANDOAH VALLEY CAMPAIGN. Jackson initiated his brilliant operation with a repulse of part of Frémont's command at MCDOWELL 8 May 1862. While Jackson rapidly marched northward down the valley, Frémont crawled eastward into the fertile region. After winning 2 more victories, the Confederates retreated up the valley as Frémont and 2 other Union commands attempted to crush the elusive Southerners. At CROSS KEYS, 8 June, Jackson turned and once more whipped Frémont, defeating another Union command at PORT REPUBLIC the next day.

On 26 June the War Department abolished the Mountain Department, relieved Frémont, and transferred his troops to Maj. Gen. JOHN POPE's newly created Army of Virginia.

—JDW

Mouton, Jean Jacques Alfred Alexander. CSA b. Opelousas, La., 18 Feb. 1829, the son of former governor and U.S. senator Alexander Mouton of Louisiana was educated at French-language schools in Vermillionville. Graduating 38th in the West Point class of 1850, he resigned from the Army 16 Sept. while on graduation leave.

While working as a railroad construction engineer for the New Orleans and Opelousas line, he became a brigadier general of the state militia and began recruiting in Lafayette Parish shortly after the war began. By October he had been elected colonel of the 18th Louisiana and in April 1862 re-

LC

ceived a near-fatal wound at the Battle of SHILOH. For his bravery he was commissioned a brigadier and fought under Maj. Gen. RICHARD TAYLOR, who constantly commended him for his leadership and bravery.

At MANSFIELD, where "almost every man in the direct attack . . . was struck with a bullet," Mouton's troopers pushed back the Federals despite their more than 700 casualties, including their commander. The fallen general, who had played such an important role in repulsing the Union's RED RIVER CAMPAIGN, died 8 Apr. 1864 and is buried in Lafayette, La. —FLS

Mower, Joseph Anthony. USA b. Woodstock, Vt., 22 Aug. 1827. Moving to Lowell, Mass., in his youth, Mower was educated there as well as in his native state, developing an interest in military and naval history. After attending college for

2 years, he practiced carpentry, with time out for service in the engineers during the Mexican War. In 1855 he entered the Regular Army as a 2d lieutenant of infantry. A few months after the outbreak of the Civil War, he was promoted to captain in his regiment, the 1st U.S.

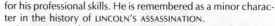

Mower proved adept at regimental, brigade, division, and corps command. From Mar. 1862 till early 1864 he received praise in a dozen reports by his superiors, winning 5 brevets

LC

during the war for gallantry in the Regular service, including that of major general, the full grade of which he obtained in the volunteers 12 Aug. 1864.

As colonel of the 11th Missouri Infantry early in May 1862, he fought conspicuously at Farmington, IUKA, and CORINTH. In the last battle he was wounded and taken prisoner, escaping from his guards only to be recaptured and held till paroled. He then received a brigade in the XV Corps/Army of the Tennessee, which he led adroitly throughout the VICKSBURG CAMPAIGN, being especially conspicuous during the engagement at JACKSON, Miss., 14 May 1863.

In 1864 he participated in the RED RIVER CAMPAIGN in Louisiana, performing notably during the attack on Fort De Russy, 14 Mar. At YELLOW BAYOU, 2 months later, he protected the rear of Maj. Gen. NATHANIEL P. BANKS's army. Elevated to division command soon afterward, he took part in opposing PRICE'S MISSOURI RAID, then accompanied Maj. Gen. WILLIAM T. SHERMAN on his MARCH TO THE SEA. Winning Sherman's praise several times during that operation, he rose to command the XX Corps as it began the CAROLINAS CAMPAIGN early in 1865.

Despite his 2-star brevet in the Regulars, Mower was dropped to captain on his muster-out of the volunteer army Feb. 1866. Soon, however, he was appointed colonel of the 39th and later of the 25th U.S. Infantry. He died of pneumonia in New Orleans 6 Jan. 1870, while commanding the Department of Louisiana, and was buried in Arlington National Cemetery.   —EGL

Mudd, Samuel Alexander. physician b. Charles Cty., Md., 20 Dec. 1833. The son of a prominent slaveholding family, Mudd was born and reared at "Oak Hill" farm, near Bryantown, Md. After being educated at public school and at home, he attended St. John's College in Frederick, Md., Georgetown College in the District of Columbia, and the University of Maryland, Baltimore, graduating in 1856 with a degree in medicine and a certificate of merit for a 1-year internship at the university hospital. Returning to the Bryantown area, he established his medical practice, married, and through the Civil War won a local reputation for antipathy toward the Lincoln administration as well as

LC

for his professional skills. He is remembered as a minor character in the history of LINCOLN'S ASSASSINATION.

Between 4 and 4:30 a.m. on 15 Apr. 1865, Lincoln assassin JOHN WILKES BOOTH and co-conspirator David Herold arrived at Mudd's home. Mudd set Booth's broken leg, gave both men lodging, a breakfast, and material assistance. Following a short ride into Bryantown with Herold, he is believed to have directed them toward a safe route to Virginia. Booth and Herold left the Mudd home later on the 15th. Several times during the next few days Union officers interviewed Mudd, asking if he had seen anyone suspicious, and on 21 Apr. they pressed him about his activities of 15 Apr. Mudd admitted that he knew Booth and produced the riding boot he had cut from the assassin's leg while treating him. Arrested on the spot, he was taken to Washington, tried by a military court, and, following his adamant denials that he had any part in Lincoln's murder, was convicted 30 June of complicity in the plot. He received a life prison sentence 6 July and shortly became an inmate at the Fort Jefferson military prison in the Dry Tortugas, off Florida.

Mudd's wife, Frances, repeatedly pled for mercy for her husband and, despite contrary circumstantial evidence, stated that he had met Booth only once before 15 Apr., in Nov. 1864. Meanwhile, the doctor made a poorly-thought-out escape attempt and was caught 25 Sept. 1865, hidden aboard the supply ship *Thomas A. Scott*. Held in irons until Jan. 1866, Mudd became a model prisoner, and during an 1867 yellow-fever epidemic in the prison tended the sick. After members of the garrison at Fort Jefferson petitioned Pres. ANDREW JOHNSON for Mudd's release in reward for his service, Johnson pardoned and released the doctor Feb. 1869.

Mudd returned to his home and resumed his medical practice, dying in Bryantown 10 Jan. 1883. In 1979 Pres. Jimmy Carter issued a proclamation absolving Mudd of any complicity in Lincoln's death.   —JES

"Mule Shoe," at Spotsylvania, Va. 12 May 1864 The fieldworks of the Army of Northern Virginia at SPOTSYLVANIA, May 1864, signaled an alteration in warfare—the use of tightly formed assault columns against entrenchments. Most of the entrenchments, which extended for miles, were carved from the ground in slightly more than 24 hours, expertly using the natural features of the terrain. The works contained ABATIS in front, infantry parapets, traverses, and entrenched batteries. In the center, along high ground, the Confederates constructed a salient that measured a mile deep and nearly half a mile across, dubbing it the "Mule Shoe" because of its shape. The salient invited attack, so 1 Confederate division and part of another, supported by 22 cannon, manned it.

Twice during the 12-day battle the Mule Shoe was attacked by the Union army. At twilight on 10 May, 12 Union regiments, tiered in 4 compact lines, charged the salient's western face. Planned and led by Col. EMORY UPTON, the massed Federal assault penetrated the Confederate works, routing a Southern brigade. When another Union division failed to support the attackers, Upton's force was dislodged by an overwhelming Confederate counterattack. The partial success of the tactical scheme convinced Lt. Gen. ULYSSES S. GRANT to attempt it again on a larger scale. Before daybreak on 12 May, 4 Union divisions stormed forward at the apex of the salient, crushing the works and destroying a Confederate division. A 20-hour battle ensued at the "BLOODY ANGLE," but the Mule Shoe was gone as the Southerners erected a new line along its base.

—JDW

Munford, Thomas Taylor. CSA b. Richmond, Va., 28
Mar. 1831. After graduating from the Virginia Military Institute
in 1852, Munford farmed in the Lynchburg area until the Civil
War. On 8 May 1861 he was appointed lieutenant colonel of
the 2d Virginia Cavalry, commanding the regiment as its colonel from 25 Apr. 1862.

Munford fought predominantly in the Shenandoah Valley
and in western Virginia on picket, rearguard, and raiding duty,
participating as well in most of the campaigns waged by the
Army of Northern Virginia. He served briefly in Brig. Gen.
GEORGE H. STEUART's brigade but requested and was granted a
transfer to Brig. Gen. TURNER ASHBY's command in spring 1862.
That June, after Ashby's death, Munford, senior brigade colonel, temporarily succeeded to brigade command. He returned
to the 2d when the War Department passed him over for
promotion and gave Ashby's troops, later reorganized as the
Laurel Brigade, to Brig. Gen. BEVERLY H. ROBERTSON.

That summer Munford led a spectacular charge at SECOND
BULL RUN in August and conducted an aggressive defense at
CRAMPTON'S GAP, 14 Sept., during the ANTIETAM CAMPAIGN. But
in October, when Robertson was transferred to North Caro-
lina, he was again slighted for promotion, this time in favor of
Brig. Gen. WILLIAM E. JONES.

Criticized for arriving late at BRANDY STATION, 9 June 1863,
in temporary command of Brig. Gen. FITZHUGH LEE's brigade,
Munford redeemed himself by conducting skillful operations at
Ashby's Gap as the Confederate army moved toward Pennsylvania during the GETTYSBURG CAMPAIGN. Yet he was denied
brigadiership and permanent brigade command a third time
when his rival, Col. THOMAS L. ROSSER of the 5th Virginia, was
promoted to replace Jones. Munford nonetheless frequently
commanded the brigade in Brig. Gen. WILLIAMS C. WICKHAM's
place after Rosser rose to divisional command, and toward the
end of the war led Fitz Lee's division during his absences.

Controversy flared between Munford and Rosser following
the Confederate defeat at Tom's Brook, 9 Oct. 1864, when the
2d Virginia broke after Rosser insisted, over Munford's objections, that they hold ground despite insurmountable disadvantage. Shortly thereafter he had Munford court-martialed for
failing to provide volunteers from the exhausted 2d Virginia to
conduct a winter foraging expedition; Munford, who had assembled the detachment from 2 better-equipped regiments,
was exonerated.

By Nov. 1864 the paperwork for Munford's promotion to
brigadier had been completed, though for some unexplained
reason his rank never was conferred officially. At SAYLER'S
CREEK, 6 Apr. 1865, the last major battle of the war in Virginia,
he had charge of Fitz Lee's division, still without commensurate rank. Learning of Gen. ROBERT E. LEE's decision to surrender
a few days later, he escaped with the 2d Virginia before the
formal laying down of arms, with hopes of reaching Gen.
JOSEPH E. JOHNSTON to continue the fight in the Carolinas. The
regiment traveled as far as Lynchburg and there dispersed
without being surrendered. Munford later claimed to have
been paroled about 10 May 1865.

During the postwar years he settled in Alabama, where he
became a cotton planter and businessman. For the remainder
of his life he signed himself "brigadier general" (as indeed he
had during the last months of war), the rank to which he felt

entitled and for which he had been recommended repeatedly.
A frequent contributor to postwar magazines, he wrote articles
for the SOUTHERN HISTORICAL SOCIETY PAPERS and for various
military journals that focus on criticism of Rosser and praise for
the Confederate cavalry. Munford's unpublished manuscript
memoirs are in the Duke University collection, Durham, N.C.
d. Uniontown, Ala., 27 Feb. 1918.   —PLF

Munfordville, Ky., Siege of. 14–17 Sept. 1862 After
Maj. Gen. E. KIRBY SMITH and Gen. BRAXTON BRAGG agreed to
cooperate loosely in an invasion of Kentucky, Kirby Smith's
10,000 men left Knoxville, Tenn., 14 Aug. 1862, and Bragg's
30,000 troops left Chattanooga, Tenn., on 28 August. On 13
Sept. Smith occupied Frankfort, roughly 60 mi southwest of
Cincinnati, Ohio. On 12 and 13 Sept., maneuvering away from
Union Maj. Gen. DON CARLOS BUELL's slowly pursuing army
from Nashville, Bragg approached Munfordville, Ky., a town
surrounding an important Louisville & Nashville Railroad
bridge crossing the Green River from the south. About 45 mi
north of the Tennessee state line, the Union garrison at Munfordville, commanded by Col. John T. Wilder, consisted of 3
Indiana regiments with 4 cannon secured in a heavy stockade
west of the railroad, a smaller blockhouse east of the tracks,
and a line of deep trenches connecting the 2 fortifications.
Determined to destroy the bridge and move north to threaten
Louisville, Bragg sent ahead Brig. Gen. JAMES R. CHALMERS'
Mississippi Brigade and Col. John S. Scott's 1st Louisiana Cavalry, detached from Smith's force, to secure the town's surrender.

Scott, riding ahead of Chalmers, sent in a surrender demand
to Wilder at 8 p.m., 13 Sept. Wilder refused. Chalmers arrived
that night, and at 5 a.m., 14 Sept., supported by Scott's artillery, sent 3 regiments against the western Union stockade and
2 regiments against the eastern blockhouse. Wilder's men
repulsed Chalmers' attack, the Federals losing 37 men in the
fight and the Confederates 228. At 9:30 a.m. Chalmers demanded surrender again, calling Wilder's position hopeless
and stating that, outnumbered, he would soon be surrounded.
Wilder declined. His telegraph line to Louisville remained
uncut.

Late on 14 Sept., 7 Indiana companies under Col. Cyrus L.
Dunham arrived from Louisville's small Federal garrison and
slipped into Munfordville from the north. The garrison, num-
bering 4,076, temporarily remained under Wilder's command.
Dunham, his superior, refused leadership for the moment since
Wilder had planned the coming fight.

Munfordville continued under stagnant siege 14 and 15
Sept. Late on the 14th a lengthy truce had been arranged for
the removal of dead and wounded. Buell's Federal army, reported to be at Bowling Green, neared Bragg's west flank. With
the bulk of his force at Glasgow, 40 mi west of Bowling Green,
Bragg felt an urgent need to take Munfordville and move on
to Louisville or join Smith. He moved his troops north, arrived
in front of Munfordville 15 Sept., prepared to attack, then was
dissuaded by division commander Maj. Gen. SIMON B.
BUCKNER, a native of the area who feared for the lives of civilian
friends in the town. Bragg conceded, sent corps commander
Maj. Gen. LEONIDAS POLK across the Green River to the Union
rear, positioned corps commander Maj. Gen. WILLIAM J. HAR-
DEE's men in front of the enemy works, and repeated Confederate surrender demands at 6 p.m., 16 Sept.

Dunham, now in command, vacillated, refused surrender,

then asked for an extension to consider the matter. Telegraphed instructions from Louisville soon came removing Dunham from leadership and replacing him with Wilder. Wilder, a volunteer soldier, remained unsure of Confederate claims of numerical superiority and whether duty required defense to the last man. Advised by local folk that Buckner was an honorable man, Wilder left Union lines under a flag of truce, secured an interview with the major general, and asked his advice. Buckner, amused, gave Wilder a partial tour of Confederate positions, pointed out superior gun emplacements and the extent of the besiegers' lines. Wilder capitulated.

Federals surrendered in formal ceremonies on the morning of 17 Sept.; disarmed and paroled, they were sent toward Buell's lines. Bragg's force remained at Munfordville through 20 Sept., then, informed that Buell's army had moved north to reinforce Louisville, marched northeast for Bardstown.

—JES

Murfreesboro, Tenn., Battle of. 31 Dec. 1862–2 Jan. 1863 *See* STONE'S RIVER, TENN., BATTLE OF.

Murrah, Pendleton. war governor   b. S.C., 1824. Unlike many of the men who became prominent Confederates, Murrah did not belong to the Southern planter class. During his youth his family moved to Alabama, where the Charitable Society of the Baptist Church provided for his education. In 1848 he graduated from Brown University in Rhode Island, studied law, and was admitted to the Alabama bar shortly before moving to Marshall, Tex., to establish a practice. He started his political career by winning a Democratic seat in the state legislature in 1857.

Ill health kept the ardent secessionist out of the army in 1861, though he served briefly as a regimental quartermaster early in the year. When he ran for governor in 1863, his supporters championed his "republican simplicity" and "noble impulses of the heart" to compensate for a lack of battlefield heroics. Elected in August, inaugurated that November, as a war governor Murrah proved marginally reliable at best to Confederate military authorities.

Despite repeated bursts of patriotic rhetoric, he lacked both the experience and the nationalistic vision critical to a Southern victory. He enthusiastically endorsed the idea of Confederate independence, but early pledges to cooperate with department commander Lt. Gen. E. KIRBY SMITH and the Jefferson Davis administration to keep the severed Trans-Mississippi under Confederate control quickly dissolved into rigid insistence on STATES RIGHTS. He hampered CONSCRIPTION by inviting all eligible Texans to enlist as state troops, then refused to transfer them to Confederate service until Maj. Gen. JOHN B. MAGRUDER threatened to withdraw all Confederate troops from the state. He also promoted a "state plan" designed to keep cotton from Confederate purchasing agents and impressment officers, endangering Smith's ability to trade abroad for army supplies until the commander threatened military takeover of the trade. Not until late summer 1864, when Murrah was pressured into abandoning the state plan and releasing state troops, was reasonably good will restored between civil and military authorities.

Murrah did not act entirely from arbitrary motives. Drained of men, Texas had lapsed into a lawlessness Confederate authorities could not control, nor could they spare soldiers to protect West Texans from a serious increase in Indian hostili-

ties. Much of Murrah's recalcitrance stemmed from concern for the citizens of Texas. To the end his loyalties were frustratingly divided: he insisted that the Southwest would deliver the Confederacy from defeat yet persisted in detailing soldiers to help plant civilian crops until Apr. 1865.

Midway into the night of 11 June Murrah fled to Mexico to avoid arrest by Federal occupation forces. His health broken by tuberculosis, he died in exile at Monterrey, 4 Aug. 1865.

—PLF

music. Civil War–era Americans preferred antebellum hymns, ballads, marches, and songs popularized by entertainers. According to studies by musicologist Dr. William Mahar, "The Last Rose of Summer" (1813), "Home, Sweet Home" (1823), "Annie Laurie" (1835), "Listen to the Mockingbird" (1855), "Lorena" (1857), and "Dixie" (1860) were the 6 most popular songs of the war years. All prewar favorites, 5 of them focused on sentimental themes. Only "DIXIE," written by Northern minstrel performer DANIEL D. EMMETT, made a regional reference. Ranking 7th in sales, entertainer Harry McCarthy's "THE BONNIE BLUE FLAG" (1861) was the most popular tune lyrically addressing the national political schism.

USMHI

A growing music-publishing industry molded Northern and Southern tastes. During the war 9,000 new songs were printed in the North and 750 in the South, many of them reproduced, for the entertainment of soldiers, in single-page broadsides or small, inexpensive songbooks called "songsters." Military bands played these favorites, as well as traditional or newly popular marches. Preserved arrangements used by the 26th North Carolina Regiment Band include waltzes, quicksteps, polkas, and ballads. The works of serious composers also received some attention. New Orleans–born pianist and composer Louis Moreau Gottschalk (1829–69), popular before the war, returned from an extended visit in the West Indies and toured the North in 1862, performing classical works and his own pieces employing hundreds of musicians.

Neither the Union nor the Confederacy had an official national anthem. Joseph Hopkinson's "Hail, Columbia!" (1798), played by Northern and Southern musicians, served as an informal anthem in antebellum years. "Dixie," "The Bonnie Blue Flag," "God Save the South" (1861) by Earnest Halphin and Charles Ellerbrock, and "The Virginia Marsellaise" (an anonymous adaptation c. 1863 of the French national anthem) were rejected by the Confederate Congress for use as anthems. "The Star-Spangled Banner" (1814), by Francis Scott Key, was popular during the war but did not become the national anthem until adopted by Congress in 1931. JULIA WARD HOWE's "Battle Hymn of the Republic" (1862), based on the tune of the more popular "John Brown's Body" (an anonymous composition first published in 1861), was outsold by GEORGE F. ROOT's "The Battle Cry of Freedom" (1862), but it is remembered as the song most closely associated with Union war aims.

Following tradition, bands saluted Pres. ABRAHAM LINCOLN with "Hail to the Chief." Its lyrics, written by Sir Walter Scott in 1810 for inclusion in his novel *Lady of the Lake,* were first set to the music of an unknown composer around 1812. The piece was played at Pres. James K. Polk's Mar. 1845 inauguration, and thereafter became associated with the presidential office. No musical composition similarly honored Confederate Pres. JEFFERSON DAVIS.

A second musical tradition began during the war. "Taps," the bugle composition played at the end of a soldier's day, was adapted from the "Tattoo" (1835) July 1862 by Union Maj. Gen. DANIEL BUTTERFIELD while in camp at Harrison's Landing, Va. Butterfield reworked the last 5¼ bars of the "Tattoo," itself adapted from a French bugle call, and with bugler O. W. Norton of the 83d Pennsylvania, polished the piece into what was later named "Taps." At Butterfield's own order it replaced the "Tattoo," previously played as a signal to extinguish lights in camp. Maj. Gen. EMORY UPTON's *Infantry Tactics* (1867) established "Taps" as the official "lights-out" call.   —JES

Myer, Albert James. USA b. Newburgh, N.Y., 20 Sept. 1829. Raised by an aunt in Buffalo, Myer graduated from Hobart College in 1847, receiving a degree from the Buffalo Medical College 4 years later.

His graduate thesis, "A Sign Language for Deaf Mutes," formed the basis of the military signal system he later devised. After 3 years in private medical practice, he joined the U.S. Army as an assistant surgeon.

Posted to the Southwest, Myer found his interest in SIGNAL COMMUNICATIONS heightened by the clear air on the Texas plains, which facilitated the sighting of objects at great distances. When transferred to New Mexico Territory, he was

LC

influenced by Indian smoke signals and other communications methods. In time he devised an improved method of signaling by motion, using flags in daytime and torches at night. His sytem of "WIGWAG" CROSS SIGNAL COMMUNICATIONS was an amalgam of the forms of visual communication he had studied, his work on a language for the deaf, and his long interest in Morse code and other telegraphy alphabets. He drafted a memorandum on his system in 1856; 2 years later a military board studied it. The board approved the method and recommended its usage, and in 1860 Myer was provided a staff position as signal officer, with the rank of major.

During the Civil War he applied his theories of communications to active campaigning, through service on the staffs of

commanders such as IRVIN MCDOWELL, BENJAMIN F. BUTLER, and GEORGE B. MCCLELLAN. His system proved its value on many fields, especially at ALLATOONA, Ga., Oct. 1864, where signal flags called in reinforcements that helped save a beleaguered Union garrison. Myer's most significant wartime achievement, however, was the formation of the U.S. Signal Corps, in which he became chief signal officer Mar. 1863. During the war he won 3 brevets, including that of brigadier general, which he gained Mar. 1865 when signal officer of the Division of West Mississippi.

After the conflict, Myer headed an enlarged and reorganized Signal Corps. In 1870 he helped form the U.S. Weather Bureau, whose operations he supervised for a decade. He was also partially responsible for the establishment of a uniform worldwide system of meteorological observations. Raised to the full rank of brigadier general in mid-1880, he died in Buffalo 24 Aug. of that year. His name survives in Fort Myer, Va.   —EGL

Myers, Abraham Charles. CSA b. Georgetown, S.C., May (?) 1811. A descendant of Moses Cohen, Charleston's first rabbi, Myers served as quartermaster general of the Confederacy through mid-1863. He entered West Point in 1828, but poor grades kept him from graduating until 5 years later, when he finished 32d in his class. He left the U.S. Military Academy as brevet 2d lieutenant in the 4th Infantry, with assignment to Baton Rouge, and fought in the Seminole Wars. During this time he entered the Quartermaster's Department with rank as captain, serving under Gens. Zachary Taylor and WINFIELD SCOTT in Mexico, where he was awarded 2 brevets for gallant and meritorious conduct. Until the Civil War he remained on duty with the Quartermaster's Department in the South, his last assignment being in New Orleans.

At the demand of THOMAS O. MOORE, governor of Louisiana, Myers surrendered the Federal supply depot to state troops 28 Jan. 1861, resigning his U.S. Army commission the same day. He entered the Confederate Quartermaster's Department as lieutenant colonel in April, was made quartermaster general in December, and was promoted to colonel 15 Feb. 1862.

Myers immediately began buying supplies from domestic and foreign manufacturers and established government factories to produce shoes, clothing, and military equipment. But he was never able to provide adequately for the army. To a great extent his effectiveness was hampered by poor transportation, depreciated currency, and insufficient appropriations, but his own inability to make long-range plans and manage inefficient subordinates drew severe criticism to his bureau. Nonetheless, by mid-1863 he had established an extensive supply network and become popular among congressmen, who had requested his promotion to brigadier general in April. Pres. JEFFERSON DAVIS, however, resented the congressional initiative as an infringement of his power of appointment, and Myers for calling Davis' wife "an old squaw" because of her dark complexion. In a bitter controversy with Congress, he replaced Myers with Brig. Gen. ALEXANDER R. LAWTON "in the interest of efficiency." When Congress confirmed the appointment 17 Feb. 1864, Myers refused to serve under Lawton and left the army.

Disgruntled, he moved to Georgia, living largely off the charity of friends. He seems to have traveled in Europe after the war, lived for a while in the town of Lake Roland, Md., then in Washington, D.C., where he died 20 June 1889, still believing Davis had treated him unfairly.   —PLF

N

Napoleon. The Napoleon, or Model 1857 gun howitzer, a 12-pounder smoothbore field artillery piece, was named for French emperor Louis Napoleon, a patron in its development. A lighter alternative to the 12-pounder gun, which had a tube weighing 1,757 lb, the Model 1857 (its tube weighing 1,227 lb) had a 66-in. length, just an inch longer than the 24-pounder howitzer, and fired antipersonnel rounds like a howitzer. But it had no chambered interior and did not arc its shells in the manner of a howitzer. With the same weight charge, it threw a 12.3-lb projectile as effectively as did a 12-pounder gun and was more maneuverable.

NA

Prior to the Civil War few Napoleons saw service in the U.S., but by the end of the conflict, states Harold Peterson in *Round Shot and Rammers,* these and rifled pieces had almost completely replaced guns in the Union Army of the Potomac. Generally made of bronze, Union models were identified by a slight muzzle swell. Richmond's TREDEGAR IRON WORKS developed an iron model with a tapered muzzle and band-reinforced breech. Napoleons were the most popular smoothbore field pieces in the Union and Confederate armies.   —JES

Nashville, Tenn., Battle of. 15–16 Dec. 1864 *See* FRANKLIN AND NASHVILLE CAMPAIGN.

Nashville Convention. 3–12 June and 11–18 Nov. 1850
Late in 1849 the prominent South Carolinian statesman JOHN C. CALHOUN urged Southerners to hold a convention of slaveholding states in Nashville, Tenn., the following June to make a display of Southern unity and develop a plan for resisting Northern efforts to exclude slavery from territory acquired as a result of the Mexican War. Although his colleagues were initially receptive to the idea, their enthusiasm diminished in spring when the compromise measures Henry Clay placed before Congress seemed to offer a solution to the sectional disagreement. Only 9 of the 15 slave states sent delegates to the June assembly; of these 175 delegates, 102 represented Tennessee.

Radical disunionists led by the South Carolina delegation demanded immediate secession by all the Southern states, but moderates with a better understanding of public opinion took control of the meeting. Of the 28 compromise resolutions the delegates approved, the most important called for the Federal government to open all territories to slavery and for the protection of slave property in territories without a slave code. In a gesture of cooperation they also agreed to accept the extension to the Pacific Ocean of the MISSOURI COMPROMISE line, which prohibited slavery above latitude 36° 30'.

The delegates adjourned to await the results of the congressional debate on Clay's proposals, passed as the COMPROMISE OF 1850 in September. Only 59 men reconvened in November to denounce the compromise and reassert the right of secession. These few represented a minority opinion. Most Southerners, still intensely loyal to the Union, believed that the recent legislation permanently ended the sectional conflict over slavery.

Though the Nashville Convention accomplished nothing of importance, it gave radical leaders from many parts of the South an opportunity to exchange ideas and retrench on the state level, where some thought the nascent movement toward Southern independence could best succeed. To the North, the convention served as a harbinger of an extremist Southern sentiment that could explode with any new crisis.   —PLF

Nassau, Bahamas. Nassau became second only to Bermuda as a center of blockade-running activities. Both British and Southern firms established agencies on the British island, and the large number of BLOCKADE RUNNERS in Nassau harbor became a matter of grave concern to U.S. authorities. During the war, 397 vessels entered Nassau harbor from Southern ports and 588 sailed from Nassau for Southern ports. These swift vessels, most flying English flags, sailed to Charleston, Wilmington, and the Florida coast carrying arms, medicine, and assorted cargo, returning to Nassau with cotton, turpentine, and tobacco for the European market. Enormous profits of up to 800% brought unprecedented prosperity to the residents of Nassau, as speculators purchased with gold, English pounds, and U.S. dollars.

In Mar. 1862 the steamer *Oreto* arrived at Nassau from Liverpool, England, prior to its commissioning as the CSS *FLORIDA,* causing British authorities there concern about violations of Britain's neutrality laws. On 6 May 1865, after the war had ended, the CSS *STONEWALL* stopped briefly at Nassau before proceeding on to Havana, Cuba.   —NCD

National Days of Prayer and Fasting.   The War for Southern Independence assumed the righteousness of a holy war for many Confederates. Pres. JEFFERSON DAVIS frequently declared a National Day of Prayer and Fasting, to invoke God's favor on the battlefield and to renew war-weary Confederate hopes in the cause of Southern nationhood. Though sincerely intended, the ritual had distinct propaganda value, if only to remind discouraged Confederates that Divine deliverance from a formidable foe exacted a cost in humility and suffering.

Occasionally ABRAHAM LINCOLN designated a day for similar purposes in the North, but his proclamations never matched in number or fervency those of the Southern president.
                                                              —PLF

National Union Party.   *See* UNION PARTY.

Navajo, removal of the.   1862–64 Public pressure for settlement and development of the Western frontier continued during the Civil War. With few troops in the Southwest to secure towns and ranches from Indian raids, Union officers changed their military tactics, becoming more aggressive. In Oct. 1862, Union Brig. Gen. JAMES H. CARLETON, commanding the Department of New Mexico, ordered Col. CHRISTOPHER "KIT" CARSON and 5 companies to the District of Arizona to begin operations against Mescalero Apache and Navajo tribesmen. Members of both tribes were to be captured and confined to the Bosque Redondo Reservation in eastern New Mexico Territory. Those resisting were to be killed. Carleton's order, approved by Gen.-in-Chief Maj. Gen. HENRY W. HALLECK, had the weight of official U.S. policy.

The Mescalero were subdued with comparative ease: 100 escaped to Mexico, and the remaining 400 had been secured at the Bosque Redondo by early 1863. During the round-up, a Navajo delegation parlayed with Carleton in Santa Fe Dec. 1862, sued for peace, was rebuffed, then vowed not to surrender. This began a running campaign with Carson's forces without set battles or engagements. A "scorched-earth policy" was pursued in 1863, as Indian settlements and crops were destroyed. Starving refugee Navajos surrendered individually or in small groups, and pressure by the army pushed fleeing survivors to the Canyon de Chelly area in present-day Arizona.

On 6 Jan. 1864, Carson and a 479-man force launched the final Canyon de Chelly Campaign, a 2-pronged maneuver that penned Navajos in the snow-filled canyon, killing 23 of them, capturing 34, and forcing the surrender of 200 by the 16th. This provoked the capitulation of remaining refugees. While only 3,000 were in U.S. hands by 28 Feb., 11,468 were even-

tually held at Fort Canby, then marched in large groups 425 mi to the Bosque Redondo. A tragic chapter in Navajo history called "The Long Walk," the march to the 40-sq-mi reservation may have claimed 3,000 lives from abuse and starvation. Another 2,000 Navajos died in captivity within 2 years of confinement to the reservation.   —JES

Naval Academy, Confederate States.   After authorizing an educational program for midshipmen late in 1861, the Confederate Congress began filling appointments to a new naval academy Apr. 1862. Cmdr. JOHN M. BROOKE and Lt. William H. Parker organized the academy, and Parker became its superintendent. The facility was unique: a vessel at Drewry's Bluff on the James River was converted into the school ship CSS *PATRICK HENRY.* Although 106 young men, ages 14 to 18, were initially appointed acting midshipmen, the *Patrick Henry* could accommodate only 52 of them, along with 20 officers, professors, and crew. Classes began officially Oct. 1863 and continued until the end of the war. In Dec. 1864, 29 former U.S. midshipmen and 30 others passed their promotion examinations and another 40 were expected to graduate Dec. 1865. While the academy's curriculum and discipline were similar to that of the U.S. Naval Academy, the *Patrick Henry* also offered firsthand experience in practical seamanship. Midshipmen were frequently required to respond to enemy fire directed at their ship. As active naval personnel, they received $500 annually, in addition to room and board and uniforms.

In Apr. 1865, following the evacuation of Richmond, Parker and about 50 of his midshipmen were specially chosen to escort Pres. JEFFERSON DAVIS south, along with the Confederate archives, specie, and bullion. The *Patrick Henry* was set afire to prevent its capture, and Parker was directed by Navy Sec. STEPHEN R. MALLORY to reestablish the academy in either North Carolina or Georgia, an order the end of the war made impossible to carry out.   —NCD

Naval Academy, United States.   Late in Apr. 1861 the U.S. Navy Department made the decision to move the Naval Academy from Annapolis, Md., to a more secure location in the North. The site chosen was Newport, R.I., and 9 May 1861 the USS *Constitution* and the chartered steamer *Baltic* arrived there with the academy's officer staff and midshipmen. The *Constitution,* which had been used as a training ship at Annapolis, and the hotel Atlantic House were utilized as dormitories and classrooms for the duration of the war. The vacated buildings and grounds at Annapolis were used as an army post and field hospital.

Capt. George S. Blake, superintendent of the Naval Academy, supported changes in the curriculum to meet the challenges of the new technical developments revolutionizing naval warfare in the 1860s. In addition to practical training in seamanship, Blake added more analytical geometry, calculus, mechanical drawing, and chemistry to the curriculum. As a result, some officers, Rear Adm. DAVID D. PORTER among them, became concerned that midshipmen were becoming "too scientific" at the expense of practical training.

In May 1865 Secretary GIDEON WELLES set up a board, headed by Vice-Adm. DAVID G. FARRAGUT, to investigate and review the academy and make any necessary recommendations for improving it. The board concluded that the move from Annapolis and the abrupt changes in curriculum had had a negative influence on training. With the academy once again at Annapolis in summer 1865, Porter became its new superintendent.   —NCD

Navy, Confederate States. In 1861 a Confederate naval captain prophesied that before the Southern navy could contend successfully with the Northern fleets "my bones will be white in the grave." The Confederate navy was the child of an agricultural nation locked in an industrialized war. With no seafaring tradition and few shipyards, the Confederacy began an innovative program to balance the odds. The water mine, the torpedo boat, the SUBMARINE, and the IRONCLAD warship were the weapons the South chose to fight the war afloat.

At Norfolk and New Orleans, in the backwaters of Mississippi and North Carolina, the South built armored ships. The first, the *VIRGINIA,* proved the validity of the concept when, 8 Mar. 1862, it smashed the blockading fleet of conventional wooden ships off Newport News, Va. But the next day, in a drawn battle at HAMPTON ROADS, the ship encountered a Union ironclad, the *MONITOR,* whose superior design and manufacture was increasingly evident as the war progressed.

The most deadly of the Confederate navy's innovations was the water mine, or TORPEDO. 37 Federal ships, including 9 ironclads, fell victim to those explosive devices, some pushed by small torpedo boats, most moored to float in ship channels.

Less effective, but more glamorous, were roving cruisers, mostly British-built, that flew the Confederate flag from the Arctic to South Africa. The *ALABAMA, FLORIDA, SHENANDOAH,* and others rarely engaged in combat, but preyed on U.S. merchant shipping, lighting the seas with burning hulks. (*See also* CRUISERS, CONFEDERATE.)

The Confederate navy met with remarkable success, except when the U.S. Navy massed a flotilla of ironclads for an attack, as at MOBILE BAY, 5 Aug. 1864.   —MM

Neale Publishing Co. Among the most desirable volumes sought by Civil War book collectors are those bearing the Neale Publishing Co. imprint. The opinionated, pretentious Walter Neale opened his first publishing house, The Neale Co., in Washington, D.C., in 1894, but few titles were issued before 1900. Thereafter, until 1916, he devoted himself to developing Southern authors, becoming the predominant publisher of books about the South and the Confederacy. Born in 1873, the son and brother of Confederate veterans, Neale considered the Civil War the "most interesting of all conflicts." He attempted unsuccessfully to launch several periodicals after moving his main office permanently to New York City in 1911, but his Confederate titles and those he published by his close friend Ambrose Bierce were his greatest pride. These he promoted astutely by advertising extensively to an ideal market, the subscribers of *CONFEDERATE VETERAN* magazine.

Neale Books: An Annotated Bibliography, by Robert K. Krick (Morningside Press, 1977), lists 579 Neale imprints. Krick breaks down the Civil War titles into 70 Confederate, 14 Federal, 29 Civil War fiction, 17 Civil War poetry, and 6 miscellaneous. Among these are some of the best books about the Confederacy ever published: *General Officers of the Confederate Army,* Gen. Marcus J. Wright (1911); *Mosby's Men,* John H. Alexander (1907); *One of Jackson's Foot Cavalry,* John H. Worsham (1912); *Four Years Under Marse Robert,* Robert Stiles (1903); *Three Years in the Confederate Horse Artillery,* George Michael Neese (1911); *Life of Turner Ashby,* Thomas A. Ashby (1914); *Morgan's Cavalry,* Basil W. Duke

(1906); and *Cleburne and his Command,* Irving A. Buck (1908).

After 1916 the quality and quantity of Neale books deteriorated sharply. Generally after 1927 Neale reverted to the imprint "Walter Neale, Publisher" or "Walter Neale, Publisher of General Literature." The last known Neale book issued is Ella Lonn's classic study *Salt as a Factor in the Confederacy,* 1933. No publisher since Neale, a man of vast energy and foresight, has provided students of the Confederacy with a greater treasure of original material.   —PLF

Nebraska Territory. In the decade before the war, the fight over the possible spread of slavery into Western territories focused on Nebraska and Kansas. The struggle between abolitionist and proslavery factions there generated the Republican party and in time brought the split in the Union, and the Civil War.

In the 1860 election of Nebraska's territorial delegate to Congress, the outcome between the Democratic and Republican candidate was so close that it was determined by Congress itself. After war came, the Federal HOMESTEAD ACT OF 1862 brought in many new residents and boosted Republican fortunes. Democrats, though called disloyal for their attacks on the Abraham Lincoln administration, fought doggedly and ran close in territorial elections until a Republican landslide in 1864.

Generally, the Civil War in its early stages was lukewarmly supported in Nebraska because Union military demands reduced garrisons at Fort Kearny and elsewhere on the Plains, leaving the frontier open to attacks by Indians. Still, Nebraskans responded promptly to Lincoln's call for volunteers, and Nebraska in time ranked second among the territories in numbers of recruits furnished to Federal forces. Nebraska units served with distinction at FORT DONELSON and SHILOH and later in cavalry campaigns in Tennessee and Alabama.

In late 1862 and 1863, however, local concerns prevailed. Local military companies were formed to guard key points along the Missouri River from depredations by Indians and later engaged in a preventive strike against the Sioux in Dakota and in a restraining action against the Cheyenne and Arapahoe along the Platte.

The other issue of concern to Nebraskans was that of statehood. In Apr. 1864 Congress authorized the formation of a state government. After much delay, a state constitution was approved and Nebraska finally entered the Union Mar. 1867.
                                                                          —DL

Neill, Thomas Hewson. USA b. Philadelphia, Pa., 9 Apr. 1826. After spending 2 years at the University of Pennsylvania, Neill entered West Point, graduating 27th in the class of 1847. Except for a 3-year tour as instructor at his alma mater, until the outbreak of the war he served mainly with the 5th Infantry on the frontier.

With the rank of captain, Neill joined the staff of Maj. Gen. George Cadwalader during the conflict's early months and Feb. 1862 was commissioned colonel of the 23d Pennsylvania. He led his Keystone State volunteers in the PENINSULA and SEVEN DAYS' campaigns as a part of the IV Corps. Shortly before the Battle of FREDERICKSBURG, Neill assumed command of a brigade, 2d Division/VI Corps, and was commissioned a brigadier general 15 Apr. 1863, to rank from 29 Nov. 1862. Neill led his brigade throughout the major campaigns of

1863 and 1864, eventually rising to division command. At
SALEM CHURCH in the CHANCEL-
LORSVILLE CAMPAIGN, May 1863,
the brigadier particularly distinguished himself. His brigade
saw heavy fighting at RAPPAHAN-
NOCK STATION, MINE RUN, and
the WILDERNESS. When his division commander fell wounded
in the last battle, Neill led the
division at SPOTSYLVANIA, NORTH
ANNA, COLD HARBOR, and the
early operations against PETERS-
BURG. He then served briefly on

GB

the staff of the XVIII Corps before joining the staff of Maj. Gen.
PHILIP H. SHERIDAN as acting inspector general.

As one of Sheridan's staff officers, he participated in the
victorious SHENANDOAH VALLEY CAMPAIGN of 1864. Neill left the
staff in December and apparently held no other assignment.
He was brevetted brigadier general in the Regular Army and
major general of volunteers for his service.

Neill remained in the army after the war, serving in the
infantry and then the cavalry before being appointed commandant of cadets at West Point. In 1879 he was promoted to
colonel of the 8th Cavalry, serving as its commander until his
retirement in 1883. d. Philadelphia, 12 Mar. 1885.   —JDW

Nelson, Allison. CSA. b. Fulton Cty., Ga., 11 Mar. 1822.
Before the Civil War, Nelson fought in the Mexican War and,
under Gen. Narcisco López, in the Cuban War of Independence, during which he attained
the rank of brigadier general,
appointed by López.

Though Nelson was born and
raised in Georgia, serving in the
state legislature 1848–49 and as
mayor of Atlanta in 1855, he
moved to Bosque Cty., Tex., in
1856 and adopted the state as
his home. In Texas he performed ably against hostile Indians and in 1861 became a
member of the state legislature
and the Texas secession convention.

GG

When the war began, Nel-
son's attention turned to the military, and he was instrumental
in forming the 10th Texas Infantry and became its colonel. By
the time his command answered a call to Arkansas by order
of Maj. Gen. THOMAS C. HINDMAN, his soldiers had acquired
Nelson's zeal, and Hindman was one of the first to say so. Still
a colonel, Nelson ordered his troops to entrench at Devall's
Bluff, Ark., June 1862, and harass Federal gunboats trying to
move up the White River toward Arkansas Post. For his service
that summer, at Holmes's request Nelson was commissioned
brigadier general to rank from 12 Sept. Less than a month later,
7 Oct. 1862, he died "of fever," in camp near Austin, Ark.
                                                                —FLS

Nelson, William. USA b. Maysville, Ky., 27 Sept. 1824.
Following 2 years at Norwich University in Vermont, William

"Bull" Nelson received a midshipman's appointment in
1840, spent 21 years in naval
service, saw action in the Mexican War, and rose to lieutenant.
From a politically prominent
Kentucky family allied with
ABRAHAM LINCOLN, he accepted
the president's commission to
organize Bluegrass State Unionists and 16 Sept. 1861 was
made a brigadier general.

NA

Nelson spent his first months
of the Civil War vying with
Confederates for Kentucky terri-
tory and residents' loyalties, which resulted in the engagement
at IVY MOUNTAIN, Ky. Attached to Maj. Gen. DON CARLOS
BUELL's Army of the Ohio, he led Buell's 4th Division at the
Battle of SHILOH 7 April 1862; took part in maneuvers to Corinth, Miss., and Chattanooga, Tenn.; was made major general
19 July 1862; and opposed Confederate Gen. BRAXTON
BRAGG's KENTUCKY CAMPAIGN. In his only independent battle,
he was wounded, outmaneuvered, and badly beaten at RICH-
MOND, Ky., 30 Aug., by Maj. Gen. E. KIRBY SMITH. Nelson
pulled back to Louisville to reorganize.

Making Louisville's Galt House hotel his headquarters, Nelson asked for help in recruitment and Brig. Gen. JEFFERSON C.
DAVIS was sent to assist him. After only 2 days, Nelson claimed
he was disappointed in Davis and told him so. As a Regular
officer, Davis believed he deserved more respect and said so,
but Nelson disagreed and relieved him from command. On the
morning of 29 Sept. 1862, Davis saw Nelson in the hotel's
lobby, demanded an apology, and was rebuffed. He flung a
wad of paper in Nelson's face; Nelson slapped his in return and
walked upstairs. Davis borrowed a pistol, followed the general,
called his name and, when Nelson faced him, shot him in the
chest from a distance of 3 ft. Nelson lingered for more than an
hour before he died.   —JES

Nelson's Cross Roads, Va., Battle of.   30 June 1862
See WHITE OAK SWAMP, VA., BATTLE OF.

Nevada. ABRAHAM LINCOLN, who became president 4 Mar.
1861, 2 days after the congressional bill creating the Territory
of Nevada became law, appointed as territorial governor
James W. Nye, a prominent New Yorker and one of Lincoln's
staunchest political supporters. By the time Nye reached
Nevada the Civil War was under way, and he made sure that
positions in the territorial government were filled with men
who were as eager as he to keep Nevada loyal to the Union.
Of the Confederate sympathizers in the territory, some were
aggressive, and there were a few clashes, but Nye and his
followers kept the opposition under control.

The mining of silver and gold in Nevada was of vital importance to the North. The $45 million of bullion the territory
produced during the Civil War years enabled the Union to
finance military operations and to maintain credit. In the view
of Congress, Nevada was admirably fulfilling its patriotic duty.
In 1863 a movement to give the territory statehood began, and
the next year, 31 Oct., Nevada was enthusiastically welcomed
into the Union, even though it had less than one-sixth of the
population required for a single representative in Congress.

Anxious to have the state's congressional support to assure passage of the 13th Amendment, President Lincoln had worked to have it admitted, prematurely or not.

Largely because of Indian hostilities in the area, the Department of the Pacific instructed Governor Nye to organize a regiment of infantry and a regiment of cavalry. 3 companies of cavalry and 1 of infantry were assigned to guard duty on the Overland Mail Route, providing for the safer passage of communications and merchandise from East to West. The remainder of the troops were stationed at forts throughout the state. Of the 1,080 men who served in Nevada's military units, 33 lost their lives from all causes. —PR

New Berne, N.C., capture of. 14 Mar. 1862 Following the capture of Roanoke Island, Feb. 1862, Maj. Gen. AMBROSE E. BURNSIDE moved to the North Carolina mainland with New Berne as his target. Confederate Brig. Gen. LAWRENCE O. BRANCH, plagued by inadequate forces, planned his major defense of the city some 6 mi below, by the Neuse River, across the road most likely to be taken by attacking forces. On 13 Mar. Burnside landed his troops without opposition 12 mi below New Berne and proceeded to move against the Confederate defenses. Branch had pulled his men out of the first line of fortifications and deployed them closer to the city.

Fighting opened on the morning of 14 Mar. The tenacious Confederate defense blunted the Federal advance for several hours, until its center gave way, precipitating a retreat. Some elements of Branch's command did not receive word to withdraw and were captured; others fled pell-mell. Those who managed to cross the Trent River and literally burn the bridge behind them were met by shells from Union gunboats as they arrived in New Berne. Branch realized the untenable nature of his position and moved his army to Kinston by rail. 5 days passed before he could effectively concentrate his demoralized command.

Federal troops occupied New Berne 14 Mar. The loss of the city was a severe blow to the Confederates, who had to reconsider the military situation in North Carolina and in fact dispatched reinforcements that might have made a difference weeks earlier. —JTH

New Berne, N.C., raid on. 1–2 Feb. 1864 Strategic New Berne, in Federal hands since Mar. 1862, was a thorn in Confederate flesh. Not till Jan. 1864 did Gen. Robert E. Lee feel able to detach from his army a force large enough to attempt to retake the coastal citadel. Jefferson Davis quickly approved the effort, which got under way on the 30th, supervised by Maj. Gen. GEORGE E. PICKETT.

The plan of attack, involving 13,000 troops, conformed to strategy proposed by Brig. Gen. ROBERT F. HOKE, Pickett's ranking subordinate. Brig. Gen. SETH M. BARTON, with parts of 3 infantry brigades, 14 guns, and 600 cavalry, would move below the Trent River, striking the city from the southwest. Meanwhile, Col. JAMES DEARING, commanding 3 regiments of foot soldiers, 3 cannon, and 300 horsemen, would move in from the northeast, seizing Fort Anderson, directly across the Neuse River from the city. Hoke's division, which Pickett would accompany, was to move on New Berne from the northwest via Batchelder's Creek, completing the 3-pronged offensive. In a supporting role, Cmdr. JOHN TAYLOR WOOD had been ordered to descend the Neuse in 14 cutters, capturing Union gunboats in the stream and aiding the land attack in any

way possible. By 1 Feb. the movement had made a promising start. Hoke crossed Batchelder's Creek above the town, despite burned bridges in his path, and repulsed Union forces between the stream and his objective. Meanwhile, Barton captured Union outposts below New Berne, moving with speed and secrecy until within view of the main defenses. Wood's seamen began their foray downriver, which the next morning resulted in their surprising, boarding, capturing, and scuttling the gunboat *Underwriter.*

Then Pickett's ambitious offensive collapsed. Barton found the enemy works too strong and intricate to crack and made no effort to attack, thereby incurring Pickett's wrath. Dearing likewise reported Fort Anderson too formidable to storm. With 2 prongs of his pincers broken, the Confederate leader withdrew Hoke's division early on the 2d, having inflicted what the commander at New Berne, Brig. Gen. INNIS N. PALMER, called "trifling" losses. Pickett took out his frustration on 22 former Confederates whom Hoke's men had captured in blue uniforms. After a drumhead court-martial at Kinston, Pickett hanged the luckless prisoners for DESERTION, creating a *cause célèbre* that would long endure. —EGL

Newburgh, Ind., raid on. 18 July 1862 Confederate raider ADAM R. JOHNSON took a 35-man force northeast about 10 mi from Henderson, Ky., on the night of 17 July. Crossing the Green River, a peninsula, and the Ohio River, at 10 a.m. the next day his unit split: 24 men led by scout Robert M. Martin crossed the Ohio into Indiana east of Newburgh to create a diversion; 8 waited at the river across from the town; Johnson and 2 others took a boat over and seized the lightly guarded 2-story brick Federal arsenal at the riverside. Martin's men set to work to ferry their way into town, cover the removal of arsenal guns to skiffs, then cross the whole force back into Kentucky before Union troops could arrive from nearby Evansville.

Townspeople, seeing the arsenal seized, ran to a nearby hotel and armed themselves. Confident of Martin's timely arrival, Johnson marched into the hotel's lobby, ordered all to disarm, took the local Union commander prisoner, and as Newburgh Home Guards gathered to run the Confederates off, he called on them to look across the river. The 8 raiders left behind 2 manned "cannon," actually lengths of stovepipe laid across wagon wheels and axles. Their appearance, at a distance, convinced outraged burghers to heed Johnson's threat to "shell this town to the ground." This escapade earned Johnson the nickname "Stovepipe."

As the last load of guns was being ferried across the Ohio, a Union gunboat and troop transport appeared unexpectedly. They intended to move downriver, round the peninsula, and, where the Green River empties into the Ohio, block the Confederate route to Kentucky. Johnson and 2 Confederates raced over the peninsula to the mouth of the Green River and fired on the vessels before they deployed to prevent the crossing. 2 Union soldiers hit by buckshot in this exchange constituted the only casualties on either side in the raid. Believing that a large number of Confederates faced them, the boats lobbed shells at the riverbank, then withdrew. Johnson's men passed over unmolested and returned to Henderson.

Indiana Gov. OLIVER P. MORTON, fearing more Southern incursions on home soil, wired Washington for reinforcements. Over the next few days Federal cavalry crossed into Kentucky, made piecemeal attacks on portions of Johnson's force, and occupied several border towns.   —JES

New England, Union Department of.

Established within the existing DEPARTMENT OF THE EAST 1 Oct. 1861, the Union Department of New England was commanded by Maj. Gen. BENJAMIN F. BUTLER of Massachusetts, with headquarters at Boston. Its mission entailed supervising and forwarding to Washington, D.C., state troops organized in Maine, Massachusetts, Vermont, New Hampshire, Rhode Island, and Connecticut. When the department was dissolved 20 Feb. 1862, its area fell under the direct responsibility of the War Department until reestablishment of the Department of the East Jan. 1863.

—JES

New Hampshire.

Antislavery sentiment had built up early in New Hampshire, where the Republican party found fertile ground in the late 1850s. Not surprisingly, in the 1860 presidential election, ABRAHAM LINCOLN carried the state with about 57% of the vote, approximately 37,500 to his opponents' combined total of 28,000. When war came in spring 1861, New Hampshire responded swiftly, sending to Washington the 1st New Hampshire regiment "armed and equipped and ready for the field" by 25 May.

In the years that followed, the state sent a flood of troops that fought in bloody engagements from the PENINSULA, ANTIETAM, FREDERICKSBURG, and CHANCELLORSVILLE to GETTYSBURG, VICKSBURG, the WILDERNESS, COLD HARBOR, PETERSBURG, and on to APPOMATTOX. All together, some 18 regiments of infantry, 1 of cavalry, a battery of light artillery, 3 companies of sharpshooters, and 3 special units for guard duty fought, while some 3,600 men served in the Marine Corps and some 3,100 in the navy. 36,000 New Hampshire men, half the men of military age, served at one time or another in the Federal forces.

Also contributing to ultimate Union victory were ships from New Hampshire ports and shipyards, manufactured goods from the many mills that bordered the state's rivers, and agricultural products from the state's farms.   —DL

New Hope Church, Ga., Battle of.   25–27 May 1864

After being flanked out of RESACA, Ga., 15 May 1864, Gen. JOSEPH E. JOHNSTON's Confederates retreated first to Calhoun, then to Adairsville, and finally to Cassville. Here on 19 May Johnston planned to ambush the left wing of Maj. Gen. WILLIAM T. SHERMAN's army as it advanced southward. However, the commander of the corps that was to execute the ambush, Lt. Gen. JOHN B. HOOD, failed to attack because a Federal force appeared in his rear. Johnston thereupon resumed his retreat, halting finally 22 May at Allatoona Pass, south of the Etowah River.

Sherman, rightly judging that a direct attack on Allatoona would produce nothing but heavy losses, tried to steal a march on Johnston by striking for Dallas in his left rear. But Johnston anticipated Sherman's move. Moving his army southwest, he confronted the Union vanguard at New Hope Church 25 May. Mistakenly assuming that the Confederates were in small force, Sherman ordered an attack by Maj. Gen. JOSEPH HOOKER's XX Corps. Maj. Gen. A. P. STEWART's division repelled it, inflicting 1,600 casualties while suffering lightly itself.

The next day both sides skirmished heavily while entrenching their lines. On 27 May Sherman sent Maj. Gen. OLIVER O. HOWARD's IV Corps to strike what was assumed to be Johnston's exposed right flank. The Confederates, however, detected the move, with the result that Maj. Gen. PATRICK R. CLEBURNE's division slaughtered more than 1,500 Union troops at Pickett's Mill while losing less than 500.

Sherman next began shifting eastward to the railroad at Acworth. Johnston counterattacked repeatedly in an attempt to pin him down, but during the first week of June the Union army reached the railroad. Johnston now had no choice but to assume a new defensive line south of Acworth. Although he had delayed the Federals and inflicted heavy losses, once more he had been maneuvered out of a strong position and forced to retreat, this time to within 30 mi of Atlanta.   —AC

New Ironsides, USS.

Built by Merrick & Sons in Philadelphia, Pa., the *New Ironsides* was launched 10 May 1862. Commissioned in August, it was a traditional broadside-type warship, classified as a steam frigate, but 170 out of 230 ft of the hull were covered with iron armor 4.5 in. thick. The armor belt covered the sides and deck, generally amidships, with bow and stern unarmored. The vessel carried a main battery of 16 11-in. Dahlgren guns.

The *New Ironsides* joined the SOUTH ATLANTIC BLOCKADING SQUADRON off Charleston 17 Jan. 1863, when it became the flagship of Rear Adm. SAMUEL F. DU PONT. In Apr. 1863 the armored warship joined Du Pont's other ironclads in an attack on the Confederate defensive works in Charleston harbor. During the engagement, which lasted approximately 2 hours, the *New Ironsides* was struck some 50 times by enemy fire but suffered no damage.

In the following months the ship remained off Charleston, guarding the wooden blockaders and joining occasional bombardments against Confederate positions. On the night of 5 Oct., the *DAVID,* a Confederate semisubmersible torpedo boat, exploded a spar torpedo against the Union warship's unarmored quarter. Although damaged, it remained on blockade duty until May 1864, then went back to Philadelphia for a lengthy overhaul.

In Aug. 1864 the *New Ironsides* joined the NORTH ATLANTIC BLOCKADING SQUADRON at Norfolk. In December it was part of the fleet assembled under Adm. DAVID D. PORTER's command to attack FORT FISHER at the entrance to the Cape Fear River in North Carolina. On Christmas Day it led the Union ironclads into the attack on the fort, but the land assault that followed failed. On 13 Jan. 1865, a second attack on the fort took place, and the *New Ironsides* again led the ironclad warships. 2 days later the fort surrendered.

For the remainder of the war the ship operated on the James River. It was decommissioned at League Island 6 Apr. 1865 and 9 months later was destroyed by fire.   —WNS

New Jersey.

A maverick among Northern states, New Jersey might be called the war's northernmost border state. Conservative, proslavery politics held sway in its populous, industrialized northern counties. Economic and social ties with the South led the state to flirt with secession and to promote peace movements in 1861. Throughout the war New Jersey tacitly sanctioned slavery and the Fugitive Slave Law (*see* FUGITIVE SLAVE ACT). Only in its southern counties, where a Quaker heritage abounded, did a cautious Republican (or Opposition) party and the Underground Railroad flourish.

New Jersey's political orientation is indicated by the dual defeats it dealt ABRAHAM LINCOLN. In 1860 he lost to STEPHEN A. DOUGLAS by some 4,500 votes and 4 years later, running

U.S.S. New Ironsides

OR

against the state's own GEORGE B. MCCLELLAN, he failed by 7,600 votes. While in office Lincoln was continually criticized by most of the state's newspapers; his EMANCIPATION PROCLAMATION and CONSCRIPTION program received particularly vocal opposition. Although many of his policies were promoted at the state level by opposition governor CHARLES S. OLDEN, 1859–62, and War Democrat governor JOEL PARKER, 1863–66, PEACE DEMOCRATS controlled the legislature and antiwar Copperheads exercised a powerful influence throughout the state.

At first lukewarm in responding to Lincoln's call for volunteers, New Jersey eventually contributed more than its share. By war's end 80,000 Jerseymen had served in 40 infantry and 3 cavalry regiments and 5 artillery batteries, 6,200 of them dying in battle. State militia helped suppress local draft riots and stood ready to oppose Confederate invasions in 1863–64. And several native or adopted sons became military leaders, including infantry generals PHILIP KEARNY, Charles G. Harker, and Gershom Mott; cavalry commanders H. JUDSON KILPATRICK and Joseph Kargé; and Adm. SAMUEL F. DU PONT and William N. Jeffers, second skipper of the ironclad *Monitor.* The state also furnished hundreds of men to the Confederacy, including Gens. SAMUEL COOPER and SAMUEL G. FRENCH.   —EGL

1st New Jersey Brigade. In May and June 1861 the 1st, 2d, and 3d New Jersey Infantry regiments were organized in Trenton, dispatched to Washington, D.C., then marched to Manassas for the Union defeat at FIRST BULL RUN. These core regiments of the 1st New Jersey Brigade fought in almost all the Army of the Potomac's battles and campaigned in the Shenandoah Valley under Maj. Gen. PHILIP H. SHERIDAN. They were joined by the 4th New Jersey, mustered in Aug. 1861; the 10th New Jersey, mustered in Oct. 1861; and the 15th New Jersey, mustered in Aug. 1862. Together they served as the 1st Brigade/1st Division/VI Corps/Army of the Potomac. The 23d New Jersey, a 9-month regiment mustered in Sept. 1862; the 40th New Jersey, mustered in Feb. 1865; the dismounted 1st Delaware Cavalry all temporarily bolstered the brigade's ranks.

Few Union brigades saw harder continuous combat service than the 1st New Jersey. Following the spring 1862 PENINSULA CAMPAIGN and the Siege of YORKTOWN, the SEVEN DAYS' CAMPAIGN, GAINES' MILL, and the other fights south to Harrison's Landing, Va., the brigade went north for Union Maj. Gen. JOHN POPE'S SECOND BULL RUN CAMPAIGN and nearly met destruction. Sent toward Manassas Junction by rail 27 Aug. 1862, the brigade inadvertently detrained in front of the bulk of Maj. Gen.

THOMAS J. "STONEWALL" JACKSON's force, declined surrender, and fought its way out, suffering heavy casualties and the loss of its commander, Brig. Gen. George W. Taylor.

After fighting through the ANTIETAM, FREDERICKSBURG, CHANCELLORSVILLE, GETTYSBURG, MINE RUN, and PETERSBURG campaigns, in 1864 it was detached for service with Sheridan in actions at WINCHESTER, FISHER'S HILL, and CEDAR CREEK. The brigade finished its part in the war fighting in the Siege of Petersburg and the campaign to APPOMATTOX, serving the last months as the 1st New Jersey Veteran Battalion, organized Dec. 1864. The 1st, 2d, 3d, 4th, 10th, and 15th New Jersey lost 900 officers and men killed in action and 595 to disease, for a total of 1,495 deaths.   —JES

12th New Jersey. Recruited throughout the southern half of the state, the 12th New Jersey went into camp at Woodbury in midsummer 1862. There, on 4 Sept., its 39 officers and 953 men entered Federal service. Under Col. Robert C. Johnson, a local politician, it was sent to Ellicott's Mills, Md., where for 3 months it guarded the nearby BALTIMORE & OHIO RAILROAD. In mid-December, under its new colonel, J. Howard Willets, it marched to Falmouth, Va., then joined the Army of the Potomac shortly after FREDERICKSBURG, assigned to the 2d Brigade/3d Division/II Corps.

The outfit saw its first battle action at CHANCELLORSVILLE, being lightly engaged 2 May 1863. Early the next day, it rushed to the support of the embattled III Corps near Fairview and held its ground despite suffering 179 casualties. Among the wounded was Colonel Willets, who lost an arm to amputation. 6 weeks later, Maj. John T. Hill led the Jerseymen northward to help Maj. Gen. GEORGE G. MEADE curtail the Confederate invasion of Pennsylvania. The 12th reached GETTYSBURG early on 2 July. That day and again the next, several companies, assisted by other troops, drove Confederate sharpshooters out of the Bliss barn, a strategic site about 600 yd west of the Union right flank along CEMETERY RIDGE. On the afternoon of the 3d, the regiment played a major role in repulsing PICKETT'S CHARGE. Breaking open their BUCK-AND-BALL cartridges and forming huge charges of buckshot, the men blew holes in the attack column of Pickett's supports, the division of Maj. Gen. ISAAC R. TRIMBLE.

Later that year the 12th participated conspicuously at Auburn Mills, where it repulsed a cavalry charge led by Maj. Gen. J.E.B. STUART, and at MINE RUN. Early in 1864, under Lt. Col. Thomas H. Davis, it was engaged at Morton's Ford and in the WILDERNESS. On 12 May, at Spotsylvania's "MULE SHOE," the 12th captured a line of Confederate entrenchments, losing heavily in the process, with Davis among those killed. The regiment also suffered greatly at COLD HARBOR and in the initial operations of the PETERSBURG CAMPAIGN.

From July 1864 to Apr. 1865 the 12th fought at DARBYTOWN, REAMS' STATION, BURGESS' MILL, HATCHER'S RUN, and in every engagement of the II Corps during the APPOMATTOX CAMPAIGN. By its muster-out, 15 July 1865, it had seen 276 of its officers and men die in combat or from disease, the second highest casualty rate among New Jersey regiments.   —EGL

New Madrid, Mo., Siege of. 3–14 Mar. 1862 The Federal capture of New Madrid in spring 1862 was part of a series of episodes that resulted in Union control on the Mississippi River as far south as Fort Pillow, Tenn. Confederate forces occupying New Madrid and Island No. 10 attempted to de-

fend an inverted S-bend in the river, thereby blocking access to the segment below. 18,000 troops under Federal Maj. Gen. JOHN POPE began an 11-day siege of New Madrid 3 Mar.

The besiegers fended off a sortie by troops under Confederate raider M. JEFF THOMPSON and then brought up heavy artillery. On 13 Mar. they hurled a long and severe cannonade. Confederate Capt. GEORGE N. HOLLINS elected to withdraw his gunboats and to have steamers evacuate the garrison to Island No. 10, just up the river.

On the next day Pope's men discovered the deserted positions and proceeded to occupy the empty Confederate earthworks. They secured supplies and guns the Confederates left behind and began to concentrate on the island and the fortifications across the river in Tennessee.

On 15 Mar. a flotilla under Federal Flag Officer ANDREW H. FOOTE arrived. 2 of the gunboats ran past the island at night, one on 4 Apr., the other 7 Apr.—the same day that the BATTLE OF SHILOH concluded. These vessels knocked out the Confederate artillery batteries located along the eastern shore. Pope's men crossed the river, destroyed the communications on the island, and blocked the only escape road. The Southerners surrendered, both on the mainland and at ISLAND NO. 10, yielding 6,000 prisoners. The loss of these troops and prodigious amounts of supplies was quite serious, as was the further crumbling of the Confederate defense of the Mississippi.   —HH

New Madrid Bend, Tenn. 7 Apr. 1862 *See* ISLAND NO. 10.

New Market, Va., Battle of. 15 May 1864 The SHENANDOAH VALLEY of Virginia was of major strategic importance to the Confederacy. Sprawling between the Allegheny and Blue Ridge mountains, angling from southwest to northeast, the great valley of Virginia supplied Confederates with livestock, while its numerous mills ground the lush harvests into food. During the war's initial 3 years both opponents battled among its farmlands and marched on its macadamized pike. To Southerners it was a favored route of invasion; to Northerners its control perhaps meant the end of the war in Virginia. In spring 1864 the Confederates once again faced the loss of its breadbasket.

The Union operation of May 1864 in the Shenandoah was only one segment of the massive Federal offensive undertaken in Virginia with the advent of warm weather. The Northerners came along 4 fronts: overland against Richmond; through BERMUDA HUNDRED toward the Confederate capital's southern defenses; into the Alleghenies against southwest Virginia; and up the Shenandoah Valley, a thrust to which Union Gen.-in-Chief ULYSSES S. GRANT committed Maj. Gen. FRANZ SIGEL, with 6,500 men.

Confederate General ROBERT E. LEE, his resources and manpower stretched to precarious limits, assigned to Maj. Gen. JOHN C. BRECKINRIDGE the task of stopping Sigel's army. The former vice-president of the U.S. rapidly scrapped together a command barely numbering 5,000. The Kentuckian mustered all the available militia and even summoned from Lexington the 258-strong cadet corps of the VIRGINIA MILITARY INSTITUTE. 2 infantry brigades, 1 brigade of cavalry, 14 cannon, the untrustworthy militia, and the teen-aged cadets composed Breckinridge's command by the second week in May.

The Confederate general's efforts to create an army were aided by Sigel's deliberate advance up the valley. On 2 May the Federals departed Winchester, marching south on the Valley Pike. Across their front stood Confederate Brig. Gen. JOHN IMBODEN's 1,500 horsemen, who harassed the Federal column, inflicting minor casualties while slowing the march. By 14 May Sigel had reached Mount Jackson, 7 mi north of New Market, a farming community 50 mi south of Winchester. A brisk cannonade ensued during the afternoon as the trailing Federal infantry arrived at Mount Jackson.

Sigel renewed his march at daylight on Sunday, 15 May. The Federals crossed the north fork of the Shenandoah River and halted 1 mi north of New Market astride the pike. Deploying his infantry division, cavalry division, and 28 cannon into line, Sigel waited for Breckinridge's advance. The Confederate general, meanwhile, formed his infantry, who had just arrived, into a defensive line. But once Breckinridge studied Sigel's position, he decided to assume the offensive.

A furious cannonade initiated the decisive little battle. Breckinridge then sent in his 2 infantry brigades and a regiment of dismounted cavalry. Passing through the town to the cheers of its residents, the Southerners drove forward. Sigel fell back half a mile, disposing his troops on the eastern sloping crest of a hillock. 17 Union guns, on the rise, slammed charges into the oncoming Confederates. To their rear came the cadets, nicknamed "Katydids" by the veterans. At this critical moment Breckinridge reluctantly said, "Put the boys in," and now the teen-agers, in dapper uniforms, filled a gap in the line and went into the attack. The Federal gunners unleashed sheets of canister against the boys, who refused to stop. Losing 20% of their numbers, the cadets, many shoeless after crossing a muddy gully, captured a cannon abandoned by the fleeing Northern troops.

The cadets' brave charge was part of a general advance by the other Confederate units. The Federal line gave way, and Breckinridge achieved a signal victory. Sigel, losing 831, withdrew across the river and burned the bridge spanning it. The Confederates suffered 577 casualties, including 10 cadets killed or mortally injured and 47 wounded. The courage of the cadets made the battle a legend but, more importantly, it temporarily ended a serious threat to the Shenandoah Valley. Sigel was relieved 19 May, and Breckinridge and his troops, minus the Katydids, were brought east to reinforce Lee's army.

—JDW

New Market Heights, Va., eng. at. 29 Sept. 1864 In the darkness of 28 Sept. 1864, 20,000 Federals, under the overall command of Maj. Gen. BENJAMIN F. BUTLER, crossed the James River at 2 locations. While most of Maj. Gen. E.O.C. ORD's XVIII Corps marched across a PONTOON BRIDGE at Aiken's Landing and advanced up the Varina road toward Forts Harrison and Gilmer, Maj. Gen. DAVID B. BIRNEY's X Corps moved over a pontoon bridge at Deep Bottom. The 2 wings shuffled through a heavy morning fog, Ord on the left, Birney on the right.

By 5 a.m. Birney's vanguard had halted before Confederate works on New Market Heights, a cliff dominating the terrain. Manning the parapet on the crest were Brig. Gen. JOHN GREGG's infantry brigade and Brig. Gen. MARTIN W. GARY's cavalry brigade. Earlier Federal expeditions during the Petersburg campaigning had endeavored to turn the Confederate left flank, but on this day Birney had orders to envelop the right, cutting off the Southerners from their main works at Forts Harrison and Gilmer.

Butler, one of the few Union generals who believed in the combat worth of black troops, suggested that Brig. Gen. CHARLES J. PAINE's division lead the attack. Paine chose Col. Samuel A. Duncan's brigade of U.S. Colored Troops, belonging to the XVIII Corps but attached to the X Corps for the operation, to initiate the Federal attack. Duncan's men, however, soon floundered before the swampy terrain and a creek crossing in front of the heights. Paine, moreover, had scattered his division and could give Duncan little assistance. The USCT brigade finally cleared the creek, scrambling up a sloping field. When the Federals reached an abatis, the Confederates unleashed a slicing volley, carving into pieces the helplessly caught black brigade. Enraged Southerners swarmed out, seizing some of the black troops as prisoners and murdering others.

Fighting slackened as the Federals regrouped. Though having suffered a bloody repulse, Birney persisted in the original scheme. Paine was ordered to renew his attack while Brig. Gen. ALFRED H. TERRY's division pressed the Confederate left more vigorously. Again, however, Paine attacked piecemeal. Col. Alonzo G. Draper's brigade of USCT soon followed Duncan's bloody route. Confederate artillery and infantry fire once more greeted the Union troops. Halted by the burning volleys, Draper's organization disintegrated. For 30 minutes the Federals endured the fury, replying with ineffectual fire. When Confederate fire slackened, the Federals resumed their attack, and the black volunteers poured over the parapet, seizing the summit. On their right Terry's skirmishers finally swept into the works. When the Federals reached the crest, they found that the main body of Confederates had withdrawn, having been pulled back when Ord's advance up the Varina road threatened Fort Harrison.

This engagement at New Market Heights revealed the valor of black soldiers and opened the way for Birney to support Ord in the latter's offensive against the Confederates' outer works guarding Richmond.   —JDW

New Market Road, Va., Battle of. 30 June 1862 *See* WHITE OAK SWAMP, VA., BATTLE OF.

New Market Road, Va., eng. at. 27 July 1864 *See* DARBYTOWN, VA., ENG. AT.

New Mexico, Confederate Army of ("Sibley's Arizona Brigade"). In summer 1861 Confederate leaders devised a plan to capture New Mexico Territory, which extended from Texas to California. The plan was designed to win the South mineral resources and cattle and to extend Confederate territory to the southern California coast.

Lt. Col. JOHN R. BAYLOR recruited the 2d Texas Mounted Rifles and occupied Fort Bliss, near El Paso, with about 300 men July 1861. Baylor then moved up the Rio Grande Valley, took Fort Fillmore, and 1 Aug. proclaimed the creation of the Confederate Territory of Arizona, with Mesilla, N.Mex., its capital and himself its governor.

In mid-Dec. 1861 Brig. Gen. HENRY HOPKINS SIBLEY arrived at Fort Bliss with his 3,700-man Confederate Army of New Mexico (4th, 5th, and 7th Texas Volunteer Cavalry, with support companies). Sibley marched his army northward up the Rio Grande and defeated a superior Union force commanded by Col. E.R.S. CANBY at the Battle of VALVERDE, New Mexico Territory.

The Southern plan for conquering the Southwest appeared

ready to succeed: Sibley's force took Albuquerque and Santa Fe, and seemed to control New Mexico by Mar. 1862; the Confederates sent Maj. Sherod Hunter with a small force to capture Tucson, which fell without a fight; and Southern loyalists in southern California worked to win their area for the Confederacy.

But Canby, bolstered by Colorado volunteers, rallied, defeating Sibley's army near Santa Fe at the Battle of LA GLORIETA PASS, often called the "Gettysburg of the West," 28 Mar. 1862. The Federals destroyed Sibley's entire supply train, virtually ending any hope for Southern success in the territory. The Army of New Mexico retreated to Fort Bliss, then fled all the way back to San Antonio, with Col. JAMES H. CARLETON's 2,500-man CALIFORNIA COLUMN in pursuit. New Mexico and Arizona remained in Union hands for the rest of the war.   —DS

New Mexico, Union Department of.   On 9 Nov. 1861 the Department of New Mexico, formerly part of the Western Department, was formed by General Orders No. 97. Initially coinciding with New Mexico Territory, the department was expanded 14 Feb. 1862 to include Fort Garland, Colo. Brig. Gen. JAMES H. CARLETON commanded the department as of 18 Sept. On 14 Jan. 1863 western Arizona was removed from the Department of the Pacific and added to Carleton's jurisdiction. 2 years later, after Arizona had been organized as a separate territory, it was removed from the Department of New Mexico and again became part of the Department of the Pacific. Carleton's department was discontinued 27 June 1865, the day Pres. ANDREW JOHNSON declared hostilities ended.   —PLF

New Mexico Territory.   New Mexico became a territory of the U.S. in 1850 as part of the legislation that included the COMPROMISE OF 1850. Though organized without restrictions on slavery, it never attracted slaveholders in significant numbers. The majority of its citizens were either pro-Union or indifferent to a civil war that was thousands of miles away and seemingly in another country.

The war came to New Mexico in 1861, however, and briefly occupied considerable attention. In July, Lt. Col. JOHN R. BAYLOR arrived with the 2d Texas Mounted Rifles and for a time claimed the southern portion of the territory for the South. On 1 Aug. he proclaimed the existence of the Confederate Territory of Arizona and himself military governor of the region. Though his expedition had not been authorized by the Confederate government, his presence there was significant as the Confederacy coveted the territory. (See also BAYLOR'S "BUFFALO HUNT.") In December the Confederacy sent Brig. Gen. HENRY HOPKINS SIBLEY into the New Mexican desert, and he expanded Baylor's proclamation (see also SIBLEY'S NEW MEXICO CAMPAIGN).

Although Sibley's campaign proved unsuccessful, New Mexico had not seen the last of warfare when the Confederates retreated to Texas May 1862. During the rest of the war Federal cavalry frequently conducted operations against hostile Indians in the region. On 24 Feb. 1864 Arizona was separated and organized as a territory in its own right.   —WCD

New Orleans, La., fall of.   18–25 Apr. 1862   See FORTS JACKSON AND ST. PHILIP, BATTLE OF.

Newport News, Va.   Newport News is located on the tip of the Virginia peninsula, where the James River flows into the

Chesapeake Bay at the expanse of waters known as HAMPTON ROADS. South from Newport News, across Hampton Roads, the Nansemond and Elizabeth rivers spill into the bay. Up the Elizabeth lie Norfolk, Portsmouth, and the Gosport Navy Yard. To the northeast at Old Point Comfort, on the peninsula, sits FORT MONROE. With the secession of Virginia Apr. 1861 and the coming of the war, this area encircling Hampton Roads became strategically important to both the North and the South.

The Old Dominion seceded 17 Apr. and 3 days later the Federals abandoned Norfolk. The Northerners partially destroyed Gosport Navy Yard, burning 5 vessels to the waterline and sinking 4 others, including the U.S.S. *Merrimack,* after burning them. This hasty departure gave Southerners an important naval base, including the dry dock, the machinery, some vessels, and more than a thousand guns. With the loss of Norfolk, Union authorities reinforced other points in the critical area. The 4th Massachusetts arrived at Fort Monroe on the day Norfolk was evacuated.

Activity quickened during May as both governments shifted troops to the region. On 21 May Col. JOHN B. MAGRUDER assumed command of the Confederate Department of the Peninsula, with headquarters at Yorktown. The next day Brig. Gen. BENJAMIN F. BUTLER arrived at Fort Monroe to establish headquarters of the Union Department of Virginia. Federal warships appeared, patrolling the waters as they blockaded the mouths of the 3 rivers.

Butler soon recognized the strategic importance of Newport News. About 7 a.m. on 27 May, the Union commander dispatched a force by transports to the tip of land overlooking the mouth of the James River. The Federals immediately began entrenching a camp at Newport News, christening the works Camp Butler. Butler subsequently reported that the defense line "will be able to hold itself against any force that may be brought against it." Additional troops and batteries, which swept both the land approach and the waters, eventually augmented the initial garrison.

The first serious clash between Magruder's and Butler's commands occurred 10 June at BIG BETHEL, about 10 mi up the peninsula from Newport News. Troops from Fort Monroe and Newport News composed the Union force, who were repulsed in confusing, hesitant attacks. After this Confederate victory, Magruder strengthened his defenses at Yorktown and probed Butler's works throughout the summer. Early in August the Southern troops approached Newport News, but the strong Union works dissuaded Magruder from any attack. The Confederates realized that even if they could take the town, they could hold it only briefly because Union warships could hammer the camp.

The Federals stationed at Newport News participated in the historic duel between the ironclads CSS *VIRGINIA* and USS *MONITOR* 9 Mar. 1862. The day before, the *Virginia* steamed into Hampton Roads seeking the wooden Union fleet. In an uneven battle it sank the *Cumberland* and ran aground the *Congress* and *Minnesota,* both of them near Newport News. Union gunners at the garrison skimmed the waters with artillery fire, which had no effect on the *Virginia.* On the 9th, while the 2 harbingers of a new type of naval warfare fought to a stalemate, the Federal land batteries once again added their firepower, again with no discernible damage. (See HAMPTON ROADS, VA., BATTLE OF.)

This classic duel was the highlight of the war for the Union garrison at Newport News. The vital point remained securely in Federal hands throughout the conflict. Activities in the town increased with the PENINSULA CAMPAIGN of 1862 and the PETERSBURG CAMPAIGN of 1864–65, and occasionally opposing ships clashed in the nearby waters. Having secured Fort Monroe and Newport News, the Union government maintained important footholds on the tip of the Virginia peninsula and the waters of Hampton Roads. —JDW

newspapers, soldiers'. Dozens of soldier-operated newspapers, Union and Confederate, were published during the war. The majority of them were turned out by Northern soldiers since most Union regiments included at least a few men with printing or journalism experience. When Federals occupied a Southern town, such men would invade the local newspaper office and appropriate presses, type, newsprint, and whatever other facilities they could use to inform, amuse, and inspirit their comrades. Other newspapers were the product of portable presses, such as the Army Press, manufactured by the Cincinnati Type Foundry Co. Still other papers, turned out in limited quantity, were handwritten, especially where presses were impossible to obtain, such as in hospitals and prison camps.

Many soldiers' papers were published by and for large organizations such as departments, armies, corps, divisions, and brigades; the majority, however, was produced by companies and regiments. Most carried military and political news of a general nature, heavily slanted to reflect the appropriate sectional bias. Popular features included poetry, military humor, and patriotic propaganda. Some papers ran regular columns written by unit officers, such as advice on health care from the regimental surgeon and lists of regulations from the provost marshal. —EGL

Newton, John. USA b. Norfolk, Va., 25 Aug. 1822, Newton graduated 2d in the West Point class of 1842, with assignment to the Corps of Engineers. He subsequently worked on the construction of fortifications, harbors, lighthouses, instructed at the Military Academy, and served as chief engineer in the 1858 Utah Expedition.

With the commencement of civil war, Newton, a captain since 1856, initially served as chief engineer of the Department of Pennsylvania, then in the same capacity for the Department of the Shenandoah. He was promoted to major 6 Aug. and brigadier general of volunteers 23 Sept. 1861. During winter 1862 he engaged in the construction of the defenses around Washington, D.C.

LC

In May 1862 Newton transferred to line duty, assuming command of a brigade in the VI Corps, which he led in the battles of the SEVEN DAYS, at SOUTH MOUNTAIN, and at ANTIETAM. In October he was assigned to the command of a division in the corps, directing it during the Battle of FREDERICKSBURG, 13 Dec. 1862.

In the aftermath of the Union defeat at Fredericksburg, 7 generals, including Newton, approached Pres. ABRAHAM LINCOLN directly to criticize the conduct of their commander,

Maj. Gen. AMBROSE E. BURNSIDE. Infuriated over this insubordination, Burnside requested their dismissal if he was to retain his command. The president relieved Burnside instead. Promoted to major general 30 Mar. 1863, Newton led his division with distinction at CHANCELLORSVILLE and directed the I Corps at GETTYSBURG after the death of Maj. Gen. JOHN F. REYNOLDS.

When the I Corps was broken up and reassigned, Newton transferred to the West. On 18 Apr. 1864, his rank of major general was revoked, probably because of his role in the Burnside affair. He led a division during the ATLANTA CAMPAIGN, once again proving his prowess as a combat officer. In October he assumed command of the District of West Florida, directing it until July 1865.

Newton returned to the Corps of Engineers after the war. On 6 Mar. 1884 the distinguished officer became chief of engineers with the rank of brigadier general. Retiring 2 years later, he died in New York City, 1 May 1895. —JDW

Newtonia, Mo., first eng. at. 30 Sept. 1862 On 29 Sept. 1862 Union Brig. Gen. Frederick Salomon ordered Col. Edward Lynde to take 150 men and 2 howitzers on a scout toward Newtonia, Mo., where 2 days earlier Confederates had established a 200-man outpost under Col. Tresevant C. Hawpe. Later that afternoon, in response to the sound of cannon fire, Salomon sent 2 companies of reinforcements and 3 additional howitzers to assist Lynde in front of Newtonia, 15 mi from the Federal headquarters at Sarcoxie. About 7 a.m. the next morning Salomon sent the 6th Kansas Cavalry and Col. William A. Phillips' 3d Indian Home Guard (Mounted) to the front; he followed at the head of infantry and more artillery, an aggregate force of about 4,500.

As Salomon hurried toward the fighting, Lynde's men drove Confederate pickets from a cornfield northeast of the town. His artillerists then began to duel with the Southerners' 2-gun battery, which responded until the Confederate gunners exhausted their supply of ammunition. The Federals advanced, pushing Hawpe's men back into the town. There the Confederates waged a stubborn defense for 2 hours before being heavily reinforced by Col. DOUGLAS H. COOPER. The fresh ranks dislodged Lynde's men, forcing them to withdraw about 3 mi. At that time Salomon reached the battlefield and immediately sent the 9th Wisconsin on a flanking maneuver to take Newtonia from the rear. Caught in a severe enfilading fire, the Confederates gave ground but rallied on the arrival of Col. JOSEPH O. SHELBY's 5th Missouri Cavalry, commanded during the engagement by Lt. Col. B. Frank Gordon. Salomon ordered his men out of Newtonia to form more secure lines on a wooded ridge a mile outside of the town.

Fighting slackened, and Cooper's troops massed for an attack. On the right of the Federal line the 6th Kansas wavered under a furious assault by Shelby's men. When expected reinforcements failed to arrive, Salomon's line could not hold against the onslaught of superior numbers. Phillips' Indians, hotly engaged in a fierce combat on the Federal left, broke in confusion when Lt. Col. Tandy Walker's 1st Choctaw and Chickasaw Mounted Rifles and Maj. J. M. Bryan's 1st Cherokee Cavalry Battalion charged headlong into the Union line. By 5:30 Salomon's army was in full retreat toward Sarcoxie.

Cooper's Confederates pursued the rear guard for 10 mi, shelling the defenders after dark with a few poorly placed artillery rounds. More than 400 Federal soldiers were reported killed, wounded, or missing in the fighting. Cooper, commanding a force numbering 6,000–7,000, reported his losses at 12 dead, 63 wounded, and 3 missing; Federal estimates placed Confederate casualties as high as 300.

After Salomon's defeat at Newtonia, Maj. Gen. JOHN M. SCHOFIELD, commander of the District of Southwest Missouri, led an offensive against Cooper's and Shelby's troops. Skirmishing continued for several days around Newtonia, but Cooper, the ranking Confederate officer, would not be drawn into battle. On 4 Oct. he retreated into Indian Territory with his Choctaws and Chickasaws, and Shelby withdrew to the Boston Mts., southwest of Fayetteville, Ark. Though the Confederacy later launched several expeditions into Missouri, for the moment Schofield had cleared the state of Confederate soldiers.   —PLF

Newtonia, Mo., second eng. at. 28 Oct. 1864 Early on the afternoon of 28 Oct. 1864 Confederate Maj. Gen. STERLING PRICE, in full retreat at the end of his disastrous raid into Missouri, halted his army a few miles south of Newtonia for a badly needed rest. The men had been encamped only a short time when 2 Union brigades belonging to Maj. Gen. JAMES G. BLUNT drove in Price's skirmish line. Taken by surprise, Brig. Gen. JOSEPH O. SHELBY quickly deployed his Iron Brigade (see SHELBY'S IRON BRIGADE) to shield the main body of Confederates as it fled toward Indian Territory. Sharp fighting continued for 2 hours, until Blunt, outnumbered and short of ammunition, began to fall back. Just as he yielded under threat of an assault against his weakened left flank, Brig. Gen. John B. Sanborn arrived on the field leading 3 brigades and 6 cannon. Within minutes Sanborn had his troopers dismounted and in position on Blunt's left. With the odds now against him, Shelby withdrew his men in an orderly retreat.

Though both sides claimed victory at Newtonia, tactically Shelby's rearguard defense gave the fight to the Confederates, since his successful stand allowed Price time to escape. Blunt, who failed to give pursuit, lost an opportunity to destroy the Confederate army, but the action at Newtonia ended Price's raid into the state and all military activities west of the Mississippi River. See also PRICE'S MISSOURI RAID.   —PLF

New York. Although New Yorkers generally supported the Union in the Civil War, there was also strong Democratic opposition in the state. In winter 1860–61 some New York City voices called for the state's secession. Political parties suffered factional splits: Some ardent WAR DEMOCRATS supported the Union (Republican) party, while other Democrats vehemently opposed the war. But most Democrats supported war to restore the Union, though they rejected the extreme measures of the administration. Among Republicans, moderates consistently supported the administration, but those more radical wanted immediate emancipation. At the outset Republicans controlled the governorship, with EDWIN D. MORGAN holding the office, but reaction and war-weariness in 1862 elected Democrat HORATIO SEYMOUR governor.

In time military failures and heavy casualty lists bred discouragement, and inflated prices compounded frustration. With military recruiting lagging, Congress in 1863 adopted conscription. When the draft began in New York, a violent protest erupted. Mobs ransacked the draft office, chased out the provost marshal, and rampaged through the streets in a mad spree, looting, lynching some blacks, and burning abolitionists' houses. These riots were partly inspired by workingmen who

refused to fight to emancipate blacks, their chief rivals for jobs. As military fortunes improved, Lincoln and the Republicans carried the state in 1864.

Militarily New York's contributions were large, providing the greatest number of soldiers, largest volume of supplies, and biggest financial support of any state. Some 474,701 New Yorkers served in Union forces, 50,000 of them giving up their lives. Economically the war produced diverse effects in the state. Manufacturing, finance, and transportation flourished, as did agriculture, despite a drop in farm population. The merchant fleet and foreign shipping suffered severely, but domestic commerce, notably by rail, boomed. While manufacturing and farm production increased, workers' real wages fell well behind inflation, spreading misery and discontent. War excitement and easy money bred more saloons, brothels, and gambling and increased graft and corruption in local government. At the end of the war New York's blacks found themselves not much better off than at its start.   —DL

69th New York. See IRISH BRIGADE.

121st New York. On 23 Aug. 1862 the 121st New York mustered into service at Herkimer, N.Y. Raised in Herkimer and Otsego counties and led by Col. Richard Franchot, it received just one week's training before being hurried to the Army of the Potomac for the ANTIETAM CAMPAIGN. In Maryland, its men witnessed the action at Crampton's Gap but were not engaged.

Known as the "Orange and Herkimer" regiment, the 121st came under the command of Col. EMORY UPTON 23 Oct. 1862, then fought its first battle at FREDERICKSBURG. Later it endured through BURNSIDE'S MUD MARCH and was bloodied in the fighting for SALEM CHURCH during the Chancellorsville Campaign, losing 97 men. Present, though not heavily engaged at Gettysburg, the regiment next fought at RAPPAHANNOCK STATION, Va., Nov. 1863; served in the MINE RUN CAMPAIGN; at the WILDERNESS in 1864; and on Upton's order took the lead in his assault on the "BLOODY ANGLE" at SPOTSYLVANIA. The success of this assault cost the regiment 60 dead and won Upton immediate promotion.

Next led by Col. Egbert W. Olcott, the 121st campaigned to Petersburg, was rushed north for the defense of Washington during Confederate Lt. Gen. Jubal A. EARLY'S WASHINGTON RAID, then on 7 Aug. 1864 joined Maj. Gen. PHILIP H. SHERIDAN for operations in the SHENANDOAH VALLEY. It saw action at WINCHESTER and FISHER'S HILL, fought desperately at CEDAR CREEK, and campaigned in the Shenandoah until December, when it returned to siege duty at PETERSBURG. Following the collapse of the town's defenses, the regiment fought its last battle at SAYLER'S CREEK, capturing 2 Confederate battle flags. Present at Appomattox Court House 9 Apr. 1865, it marched to Danville and Richmond, securing areas under Federal control. The regiment missed the Grand Review, but as members of the 2d Brigade/1st Division/VI Corps during their entire service, the men of the 121st were sent to Washington, D.C., for a corps review 8 June, before mustering out 25 June.

Of the 1,897 men enrolled in the 121st in Aug. 1862, 226 died in battle and 121 of disease during 2 years and 10 months of service. Its losses were among the heaviest suffered by New York regiments.   —JES

New York, Union Department of. From the war's earliest days, ABRAHAM LINCOLN's administration considered the industrial, financial, and manpower resources of New York State crucial to the war effort. The government was alarmed, therefore, when Gov. EDWIN D. MORGAN's ability to support that effort was jeopardized by the interference of a state military board and a Union Defense Committee in Manhattan. To give the governor personal power to raise, arm, and equip troops and to appoint their senior officers, the War Department on 26 Oct. 1861 issued General Orders No. 92. The decree assigned Morgan, recently appointed a major general of volunteers, to command the Department of New York, giving him both civil and military authority.

Headquartered at Albany, the department encompassed a force that ranged from 8,874 officers and men present for duty in Dec. 1861 to 812 by June 1862. It remained in existence until 3 Jan. 1863, when merged into Maj. Gen. JOHN E. WOOL's Department of the East. The merger coincided with Morgan's resignation as governor to take his recently won seat in the U.S. Senate.   —EGL

New York City, attempt to burn.

25 Nov. 1864   In retribution for Federal depravities committed during the ATLANTA and SHENANDOAH VALLEY campaigns, Confederate agents planned to burn New York City. Col. Robert M. Martin obtained permission from Confederate Secret Service headquarters to fire all the city's hotels with GREEK FIRE, a highly flammable substance, in hopes of causing a general conflagration.

None of the 8 agents involved in the plot was familiar with the substance; however an elderly chemist agreed to supply them with a large batch. On the night of 25 Nov. 1864, the raiders, toting 402 bottles of the mixture, checked into various hotels and set to work. Flammables such as rubbish and clothing were set ablaze within an hour but did not burn as expected. The arsonists had failed to open windows to ensure a proper draft, and by midnight nearly all the fires were out. Many fires, confined to 1 or 2 rooms, were quickly extinguished by residents. Martin and his men did create a spectacular blaze at Barnum's Museum, where stacked bales of hay and straw burned readily; although the fire caused a panic among the 2,500 people who had gathered there for a lecture, no one was harmed.

Naturally, New Yorkers were outraged. Maj. Gen. JOHN A. DIX, commander of the Department of the East, hurriedly issued a proclamation ordering the raiders hanged if caught. The agents quietly and quickly made their way to Toronto, where they went into hiding. Colonel Martin blamed their failure on faulty Greek fire. He believed the chemist had skimped on the ingredients, either to increase profit or out of fear that the agents might succeed in their mission.   —MTC

New York Fire Zouaves.   See ELLSWORTH'S ZOUAVES.

New York Times.

HENRY JARVIS RAYMOND and George Jones launched the first issue of the New York Daily Times 18 Sept. 1851. Rejecting the partisan excesses of mid-19th-century journalism, they sought to produce a newspaper filled with impartial reportage. Jones ran business affairs; Raymond, a 31-year-old editor and reporter, served as editor-in-chief and the voice and personality of the paper. In 1857 Daily was dropped from the Times logo.

By the eve of the Civil War, the New York Times was the second leading New York City daily, had some experience

with war reporting (Raymond having covered the 1859 Austrian-Sardinian War), and was using its editorial columns to back the newly elected administration of Abraham Lincoln. The Times competed with James Gordon Bennett's wealthier and more widely read New York Herald and HORACE GREELEY's morally strident NEW YORK TRIBUNE for leadership in serious, reliable Northern news coverage. Raymond personally took the field, helping report the FIRST BATTLE OF BULL RUN and the PENINSULA CAMPAIGN, while managing editor Alexander Wilson or James Spalding ran the New York editorial offices. Among the paper's wartime coups were the first reliable reports of the Battles of CHANCELLORSVILLE and MONOCACY in 1863 and 1864, respectively; in each instance, it printed reports at least 24 hours before the competition.

The Times numbered some of the most dedicated and talented writers among its correspondents. Reporter Franc B. Wilkie allowed himself to be taken prisoner by Confederates so he might better cover the Siege of Lexington, Mo. The American poet WALT WHITMAN, then a nursing volunteer, was a free-lance writer for the paper.

The Times withstood its share of Civil War embarrassments. Its administrators quarreled with other newspapers over use of telegraph lines. Caught eavesdropping on a private conversation between Lt. Gen. U. S. GRANT and Maj. Gen. GEORGE G. MEADE, reporter James Swinton was banned from the Army of the Potomac. After chiding other newspapers for publishing inaccurate stories, the Times committed to print several factual errors.

Through the war the Times prospered at a daily price of 2 cents a copy, rivaling the Herald in circulation. In immediate postwar years, its prestige suffered with Raymond as editor. Elected to the U.S. Congress in 1864, the partisan of ANDREW JOHNSON was vilified along with the president. The circulation of the Times fell below Greeley's third-ranked Tribune but recovered. Though not the inventor of journalistic objectivity, the Times used the Civil War to pioneer its use.   —JES

New York Tribune.

A daily newspaper allied with Whig, then Republican, party interests, the Tribune began publication 10 Apr. 1841. Founded by HORACE GREELEY, it served as a forum for liberal thought, backing wage, land, and labor reforms and damning slavery. Though closely associated with Greeley's thought and personality, and regularly featuring signed editorials by him, from 1847 Charles A. Dana, from 1862 Sydney Howard Gay, from 1866 JOHN RUSSELL YOUNG, and from 1869 Whitelaw Reid, as managing editors, were the paper's editorial stewards.

Prior to the Civil War the Tribune maintained lukewarm allegiance to the positions of Republican presidential candidates JOHN C. FRÉMONT and ABRAHAM LINCOLN on sectionalism and secession. But from the fall of FORT SUMTER to Greeley's death in 1872, it departed often from party lines, advocating some Radical Republican aims, some peace initiatives toward the South, some liberal Democratic aims, and, after the war, a conciliatory policy toward former Confederates.

Its mercurial political opinions were Greeley's. Dana and Gay supervised war coverage reported by 56 full- and part-time combat field correspondents. Samuel Wilkeson, HENRY VILLARD, GEORGE SMALLEY, and Whitelaw Reid became nationally known Tribune reporters during the Civil War. Upholding the liberal Tribune standard, Washington, D.C., was covered by newswomen Jane Grey Swisshelm, a woman's rights advocate, and Sara Jane Lippencott, who wrote under the name Grace Greenwood.

Suffering from periodic losses of public confidence in Greeley, the *Tribune* surrendered to the NEW YORK *TIMES* its second-rank prewar position among New York City newspapers (with a national circulation of 287,750). James Gordon Bennett's New York *Herald* held circulation leadership throughout the war.

Just as Greeley's supposed prewar editorial phrase "Go West, young man" became public property, so did Dana's wartime editorial declaration "Forward to Richmond!" *Tribune* editorials had impact on public policy, and individual columns, such as the "PRAYER OF TWENTY MILLIONS" urging manumission, were touted for their literary qualities.

Following the Civil War, the *Tribune*'s fortunes wavered along with Greeley's personal and political misadventures. On Greeley's defeat in the 1872 presidential election, Reid seized financial and editorial control of the paper, causing, some critics said, Greeley's breakdown and death. The newspaper continued until merging with the *Herald* in 1924. As the *Herald-Tribune* it ceased publication Aug. 1966. —JES

Nicholls, Francis Redding Tillou. CSA b. Donaldsonville, La., 20 Aug. 1834. Graduating 12th in the West Point class of 1855, Nicholls served only a year in the army before resigning his commission to study law at the University of Louisiana. Until the outbreak of the war, he practiced law in Napoleonville.

Nicholls entered Confederate service as captain of the Phoenix Guards. Elected lieutenant colonel 8 June 1861, he fought at FIRST BULL RUN. In spring 1862 his regiment participated in Maj. Gen. THOMAS J. "STONEWALL" JACKSON's Shenandoah Valley Campaign. At Winchester, 25 May, Nicholls was wounded in the elbow, which necessitated

USMHI

the amputation of his left arm. Less than a month later, 24 June, he was commissioned colonel of the 15th Louisiana and 14 Oct. received his promotion to brigadier general.

Nicholls then commanded the District of Lynchburg until early in 1863. During the CHANCELLORSVILLE Campaign in May he led a brigade of Louisiana troops and suffered another severe wound in the battle, having his left foot ripped off by a shell. Disabled from further combat duty, he was transferred to the Tran-Mississippi Department, where he directed the Volunteer and Conscript Bureau until the end of the war.

The veteran then resumed his legal practice. In 1876 he ran for governor, refusing to accept defeat by his Republican opponent. A period of dual administration followed until Federal authorities recognized Nicholls' election. Reelected governor in 1888, he served another 4 years. Appointed to the state supreme court in 1892, he served either as associate or chief justice until 1911. d. on his plantation near Thibodeaux, La., 4 Jan. 1912. —JDW

Nicolay, John George. USP b. Essingen, Bavaria, 26 Feb. 1832. After immigrating with his family to the U.S. in 1838,

Nicolay lived in Ohio, Indiana, Missouri, then settled in Pike Cty., Ill. Orphaned, he briefly clerked in a store before joining the Pittsfield *Free Press.* At about age 20 he befriended young JOHN M. HAY, a teen-age student in a Pittsfield preparatory school. Maintaining his relationship with Hay, Nicolay advanced to the ownership of the *Free Press* in 1854, sold the newspaper in 1856, became a state clerk in Springfield, and was employed as a personal sec-

USMHI

retary by attorney and Republican presidential aspirant ABRAHAM LINCOLN. In 1860 he secured for Hay the position of assistant secretary to Lincoln, and both followed the lawyer to the executive mansion.

Nicolay, the more thorough and methodical of the secretaries, held Lincoln's personal and political trust, supervised the president's daily schedule, and worked for his consolidation of Republican party power, serving as a liaison with congressional and national party Republicans. He attended the 1864 Republican convention, working to secure Lincoln's renomination. Realizing the gravity of the times and the uniqueness of his position, in 1861 he proposed to Hay that they write a history of Lincoln's presidency. Nicolay's preparation for *Abraham Lincoln: A History* (1890) began at that time.

In spring 1865 Lincoln appointed him U.S. consul to Paris, France. Nicolay served abroad until 1869, received appointment as marshal of the U.S. Supreme Court in 1872, then retired in 1887 to pursue his writing. Using the OFFICIAL RECORDS and other government sources he completed *The Outbreak of Rebellion* (1881), a history of the beginnings of the Civil War; edited the multivolume *Works of Abraham Lincoln* (1894); and wrote the brief biography *A Short Life of Abraham Lincoln* (1902). With Hay, his best-remembered literary achievement was writing the 1890 biography of Lincoln. Published in 10 volumes, it culminated 15 years of serious effort, received the personal support of the Lincoln family, and through sale of serialization rights to *Century* magazine netted Nicolay, never a wealthy man, a share of a 50-thousand-dollar publishing contract. d. Washington, D.C., 26 Sept. 1901. —JES

Niter and Mining Bureau. On 11 Apr. 1862 the Confederate Congress passed legislation authorizing "the organization of a corps of officers for the working of niter caves." This was the informal beginning of what was also called the Niter and Mining Corps. By a 16 June 1863 act of Congress it became an independent office of the Confederate War Department, officially known as the Niter and Mining Bureau.

The bureau, first loosely organized under engineer Maj. ISAAC M. ST. JOHN, mined, manufactured, and procured nitrates, saltpeter, lead, coal, and iron for the Confederacy's domestic production of gunpowder and munitions. Its 20 officers, led by St. John until Feb. 1865, surveyed niter and sulfur caves, superintended mining operations and foundry furnaces, requisitioned the purchase of foreign-made raw materials, and in a crisis organized miners or workmen for the military defense of the work site. St. John and others also worked with

Ordnance Department officers in the development of incendiary and armor-punching artillery shells.

Receiving pay equal to a cavalry officer's, bureau officer appointments, by order, were given the same status as line officer appointments. Adjutant general's office directives stressed that the bureau's service was "second to no other engaged in the public defense," and general orders permitted its personnel to impress mines, foundries, and black labor in select circumstances to ensure that national production levels met bureau-imposed daily quotas. The Federal BLOCKADE and Union seizures of niter and sulfur mines and caves in border states reduced bureau procurement and production of all important nitrates from an estimated Dec. 1862 peak of 500,000 lb per year to under 180,000 lb per year at the war's end. This necessitated the expedient of collecting the contents of Confederate chamber pots for deposit in specially prepared "beds" outside certain communities, where excess human nitrate content would be filtered out and cured in the soil.

On St. John's promotion to brigadier general and transfer to the post of commissary general Feb. 1865, second-in-command Lt. Col. Richard Morton became bureau chief, serving until the Confederate surrender. —JES

noncombatants. In 1861 neither the regulations nor Articles of War adopted by the Union and Confederate armed forces specifically addressed the status of noncombatants. Surgeons, nurses, CHAPLAINS, SUTLERS, and civilian employees traveling with armies, wives and families of service personnel living on military posts, and civilians of both sexes in the enemy's country (by recent tradition considered noncombatants in European wars) found that the bitter nature of American civil war placed their lives in jeopardy. Individual European forces had established codes for their military, but no American or international standard was agreed upon that governed definitions and treatment of noncombatants.

Francis Lieber, a Prussian-born veteran of the Napoleonic Wars, famed political theorist and philosopher, and a professor at Columbia College in New York City, produced 2 important works affecting noncombatants and the conduct of war. Working as a paid consultant to the Union government, he wrote *Guerilla Parties Considered with Reference to the Laws and Usages of War* (1862) and *A Code for the Government of America* (1863). At the head of a board of officers, Lieber helped write General Orders No. 100. Issued 24 Apr. 1863, this long document helped establish a standard for American troops in the field, committing to print and force of military law rules unspoken but usually accepted by Union and Confederate combatants. All parties traditionally accepted as noncombatants found themselves referred to in some fashion in General Orders No. 100.

Late in the war, Confederate army surgeon HUNTER H. MCGUIRE helped formalize the medical arm's noncombatant status by arranging for the immediate, unilateral exchange of captured medical personnel. And Confederate regulations, adopted in early war years, helped distinguish between public and private persons and property and their respective treatment in time of war. —JES

Norfleet house, Va., engs. at the. 14–15 Apr. 1863 Operations in the region in Virginia south of the James River and in the corresponding part of North Carolina intensified during winter 1863. This area between the James and Cape Fear, N.C., was a fertile country of corn and livestock drained by several rivers: the Nansemond, Chowan, Blackwater, and Neuse. Through it ran the Petersburg & Weldon Railroad, the sole rail supply line east of the Blue Ridge Mts. for the Confederate Army of Northern Virginia.

Union forces already occupied Suffolk, Va., on the Nansemond, 16 mi west of Norfolk, and New Berne, N.C., on the Neuse, which flows into Pamlico Sound. Federal gunboats prowled the waterways, providing heavy ordnance and mobility for the garrisons. The Northerners also used these points as bases for raids against vital Confederate installations. On 17 Dec. 1862, Federals burned the bridge over the Neuse at Goldsborough, and operated against the railroad linking Petersburg, Va., and Wilmington, N.C., the major Confederate supply line in the East, with points farther south.

When Gen. ROBERT E. LEE learned in Feb. 1863 of the dispatch of the Union IX Corps from the Army of the Potomac down the Potomac River to Hampton Roads, he sent 2 of his best combat divisions southward. Lt. Gen. JAMES LONGSTREET, with the I Corps divisions of Maj. Gen. JOHN B. HOOD and GEORGE E. PICKETT, arrived in the area in the latter part of the month. On 25 Feb. Longstreet was appointed commander of the Department of Virginia and North Carolina, in reality 3 departments extending from Richmond to the Cape Fear River.

Longstreet's operations eventually focused on the Union garrisons at New Berne and Suffolk and the garnering of badly needed foodstuffs and livestock. His initial campaign was against New Berne, where, 13–15 Mar., the Confederates made some feeble thrusts. Union gunboats easily repulsed the advances, which were little more than reconnaissances in force. For the next month the Confederates scoured the countryside, filling their wagons with the area's hogs and lush harvests.

Early in April the Confederate commander developed a plan for a demonstration in force against Suffolk. Though only 1 division of the IX Corps had been sent to Suffolk, the garrison by mid-April numbered 25,000 troops, with Maj. Gen. JOHN J. PECK commanding. On 11 Apr. the 2 Confederate divisions, with cavalry and several artillery batteries, appeared in front of the river town. Skirmishing flared between the 2 forces, continuing and increasing on the 12th and 13th.

On the next day the heaviest fighting occurred at the confluence of the west branch of the Nansemond with the larger stream. Confederate artillerists, positioned near the Norfleet house, engaged Union gunboats under the command of Lt. WILLIAM B. CUSHING. The navy crews suffered severe losses in the heavy exchange but disabled some Confederate cannon. Union land batteries assisted, crippling 1 Southern battery. Skirmishing and artillery duels also characterized the action on other sectors of the lines.

The artillery crews on both sides renewed the struggle on the 15th. At about noon, Union batteries across the river from the Norfleet house silenced 4 Confederate guns. By afternoon only periodic duels flared before the engagement subsided. For 3 days the antagonists stalked each other. Late on 19 Apr. a Union attack force overran FORT HUGER near the Norfleet house. This successful raid ended Longstreet's operations against Suffolk. With the siege over, in a few weeks activity in the region once again became routine. Longstreet's divisions rejoined Lee's army and the Federals maintained their garrisons. —JDW

Norfolk, Va., fall of. On 20 Apr. 1861, 3 days after the secession of Virginia, Federal troops abandoned Norfolk, that state's principal port.

Commandant CHARLES S. MCCAULEY had incorrectly determined that Norfolk's Gosport Navy Yard, the nation's most important naval base, was in danger of imminent attack. Soon after dark on the 19th, Federals began applying the torch liberally to prevent capture of the navy yard's many holdings. 5 vessels were burned to the waterline; 4 others, including the *Merrimack,* were scuttled; and the illustrious *United States* was skeletonized. Only 3 Federal vessels escaped northward. The loss of 10 ships of the line, antiquated though they were, caused a serious delay in the implementation of ABRAHAM LINCOLN's blockade of the South.

Federals also burned various waterfront buildings and barracks. Fortunately for the Confederacy, the dry dock and several valuable structures were not damaged. On 21 Apr. Virginia militia marched into the smoldering yard, confiscating 1,200 heavy-duty cannon that would strengthen forts all the way to Vicksburg, Miss. They also seized 2,800 barrels of gunpowder. Southerners then began fortifying Norfolk and neighboring Portsmouth.

The navy yard itself became of prime importance to the Confederacy. In addition to providing a dry dock and industrial plant for manufacturing critically needed items of war, the Norfolk complex became a major naval base less than a day's cruise from the enemy capital of Washington. Moreover, Virginia naval engineers were able to raise the *Merrimack.* Rebuilt, encased with iron sheets, and rechristened the CSS *VIRGINIA,* it became one of the first ironclad warships.

For the Federals, the loss of Norfolk and its naval stores was a humiliating disaster that would have far-ranging consequences.   —JIR

North Anna River, Va., Battle of the.   23–26 May 1864
The North Anna portion of Lt. Gen. U. S. Grant's southward drive in May 1864 occurred because of the importance of Hanover Junction. At the junction, 24 mi north of Richmond and 2 mi south of the North Anna River, the Virginia Central Railroad, a major Confederate supply line from the Shenandoah Valley area, connected with the Richmond, Fredericksburg, & Potomac Railroad, a major north-south Confederate supply route.

After his failure to break Gen. R. E. Lee's lines at SPOTSYLVANIA, Grant moved south and east toward Hanover Junction. Lee's troops also moved in that direction and by 23 May had set up strong defenses running from east of the junction north to the river for several miles, then south again to the Virginia Central. Lt. Gen. Richard S. Ewell's II Corps held the right, Lt. Gen. James Longstreet's I Corps the center, and Lt. Gen. Ambrose P. Hill's III the left. Lee was reinforced during this period by Maj. Gen. Robert F. Hoke's brigade and Maj. Gen. George E. Pickett's division, both coming from Petersburg, and Maj. Gen. John C. Breckinridge's division from the valley.

The Federals moved 23 May: the II Corps, under Maj. Gen. Winfield S. Hancock, against Chesterfield Ford, near the RF&P railroad bridge; the IX, led by Maj. Gen. Ambrose E. Burnside, to Jericho Mills, west of Hancock; and the V, under Maj. Gen. Gouverneur K. Warren, to the west of Jericho Mills, with the VI, led by Maj. Gen. Horatio G. Wright, following the V.

At Chesterfield Bridge the Federals took advanced Confederate works on the north side of the river, while at Jericho Mills the V Corps moved about a half-mile south of the river before being attacked by Lt. Gen. Daniel H. Hill's corps. The Confederates were repulsed and the Federals dug in while the VI Corps crossed the river in support of the V.

On the 24th the Confederates abandoned advance works on the south side of the river at Chesterfield Bridge; Hancock crossed and took them. Burnside's IX Corps probed against Confederate positions at Ox Ford but found them too strong to mount an attack. Other probes by Federal troops along the line produced the same result.

Lee's army was in a concentrated position south of the river, behind strong breastworks. The Federals were scattered and would have to cross the river twice to reinforce each other. The result was a stalemate, and 26 May Grant abandoned his effort, moving east toward COLD HARBOR.   —LDJ

North Atlantic Blockading Squadron. Late in July 1861 the U.S. Navy Blockade Strategy Board recommended that the blockade of the Confederate states along the Atlantic coast be divided into 2 areas, with the dividing line the border between North and South Carolina. The North Atlantic Blockading Squadron was created with the responsibility of blockading the coast north of the line, and 18 Sept. 1861 Capt. LOUIS M. GOLDSBOROUGH was ordered to its command. On assuming the command less than a week later he discovered that he had 13 vessels to cover the waters of North Carolina, and Virginia, exclusive of the Potomac.

The squadron, however, was rapidly increased and by the beginning of Feb. 1862 comprised more than 50 vessels on blockade duty. In addition to blockading ports and inlets, units of the squadron participated in combined operations to secure control of the North Carolina sounds. Goldsborough's warships also cooperated with Maj. Gen. George B. McClellan's military forces in the Peninsula Campaign. During the initial stages of that campaign units of the squadron, including the newly arrived *Monitor,* engaged Confederate naval forces in the Battle of Hampton Roads.

In Sept. 1862 Goldsborough was relieved by Rear Adm. Samuel P. Lee. The squadron was approximately the same size as in February but had been made stronger by the addition of ironclads. During the 2 years under Lee's command, it grew steadily in numbers and strength. In Oct. 1864 there were nearly 100 vessels divided into 3 divisions. One division was concentrated in Hampton Roads and the James River; the other 2 operated in the sounds and along the coast of North Carolina. The larger of these two was concentrated off the Cape Fear River, the entrance to the important port of Wilmington, N.C. During these months under Lee's command, more than 50 blockade runners were captured or sunk by the squadron.

In Oct. 1864 Adm. DAVID D. PORTER relieved Lee in command of the squadron. With orders to reduce FORT FISHER and take Wilmington, Porter assembled a powerful fleet of more than 40 warships. The first attack on the fort Dec. 1864 failed, but a second attempt Jan. 1865 was successful, and Wilmington surrendered shortly afterward.

This was the final major operation of the North Atlantic Blockading Squadron. It was gradually reduced in numbers during spring 1865 and in July was consolidated with the South Atlantic Blockading Squadron to form the Atlantic Squadron.   —WNS

North Carolina. North Carolina played only a minor role in the secession drama of 1860 and early 1861 and was not a party to the organization of the Confederacy in Montgomery Feb. 1861. Union sentiment was strong in the state and the general populace favored a watch-and-wait policy. But the masses did not approve of the use of force to bring the seceded states back into the Union, and, mid-Apr. 1861, when Pres. Abraham Lincoln asked for troops to fight the Confederacy, the great majority of North Carolina's "Unionists or conservatives" turned into "secessionists or radicals."

U.S. Sec. of War Simon Cameron wired a state troop requisition to North Carolina Gov. John W. Ellis: "two regiments of militia for immediate service." Governor Ellis fired back his answer: "I regard the levy of troops made by the administration for the purpose of subjugating the states of the South, as in violation of the Constitution, and as a gross usurpation of power. I can be no party to this wicked violation of the laws of the country and to this war upon the liberties of a free people. You can get no troops from North Carolina." The state seceded 20 May and joined the Confederacy. With announcement of the secession in Raleigh, the state capital, "STEPHEN RAMSEUR's Battery fired a salute of a hundred guns . . . and everybody congratulated everybody else."

North Carolina contributed between 120,000 and 125,000 men to the Confederate services, fed and clothed its own soldiers, and sustained about one-quarter of all Confederate losses; but it had more deserters than any other Southern state, with 23,694. North Carolinians led the Southerners in blockade running, and it was largely their success at Wilmington that enabled Gen. Robert E. Lee to remain in the field as long as he did. There were 11 battles and 73 skirmishes fought in the state.
—PR

North Carolina, Confederate Department of. The Department of North Carolina had its origins in the Department of Norfolk, created 23 May 1861 under Brig. Gen. BENJAMIN HUGER, and in the defenses of North Carolina, a coastal command established under Brig. Gen. RICHARD C. GATLIN 20 Aug. of that year. On 12 Mar. 1862, Brig. Gen. JOSEPH R. ANDERSON succeeded Gatlin as head of what had become known officially as the Department of North Carolina, embracing troops and installations throughout the state. 12 days later, Maj. Gen. THEOPHILUS H. HOLMES replaced Anderson at departmental headquarters in Goldsborough. By late April Holmes commanded 22,068 officers and men present for duty, embracing 5 field brigades and the garrison of Fort Macon.

On 21 June 1862, the Department of North Carolina was extended to the south bank of the James River, taking in Petersburg, Va., to which Holmes transferred his headquarters. On 17 July Maj. Gen. DANIEL H. HILL received charge of the department, its 21,196 officers and men and 141 field and siege cannon. On 18 Aug. Brig. Gen. JAMES G. MARTIN succeeded him, taking over a command now named the District of North Carolina, extending from the right banks of the Roanoke River to the South Carolina line.

Martin's command was merged into the CONFEDERATE DEPARTMENT OF NORTH CAROLINA AND SOUTHERN VIRGINIA, headed by Maj. Gen. GUSTAVUS W. SMITH, 19 Sept. 1862. It remained a component of this larger command until May 1863, when it absorbed the whole of southern Virginia. Again known as the Department of North Carolina, during its 1-year existence it was commanded successively by Maj. Gens. D. H. Hill, WILLIAM H. C. WHITING, and GEORGE E. PICKETT.

Early in May 1864 the domain again became a part of the revived Department of North Carolina and Southern Virginia, headed by Gen. P.G.T. BEAUREGARD. It reemerged as the Department of North Carolina 11 Nov., when Gen. BRAXTON BRAGG received command of troops near Wilmington during the Union offensive against FORT FISHER. Bragg's force theoretically retained its departmental identity during Gen. JOSEPH E. JOHNSTON's tenure in command of all Confederate units involved in the Carolinas Campaign. By then, however, chaotic conditions in that part of the Confederacy had blurred departmental distinctions beyond recognition.
—EGL

North Carolina, Union Department of. Established 7 Jan. 1862, the Department of North Carolina was created as a result of Maj. Gen. AMBROSE E. BURNSIDE's invasion of the state's lower coast and embraced North Carolina in its entirety. Originally it comprised the 4 brigades led by Burnside's subordinates—Brig. Gens. JOHN G. FOSTER, JESSE L. RENO, JOHN G. PARKE, and THOMAS WILLIAMS—an aggregate of 12,829 officers and men present for duty.

Steadily reinforced, Burnside led 15,782 troops by June 1862, shortly before he was sent to Virginia with more than half this force. The rest remained in North Carolina under his successor, Foster, garrisoning Beaufort, Fort Macon, Hatteras Inlet, New Berne, Newport Barracks, and Plymouth. At intervals troops were added to and subtracted from Foster's original complement. Designated the XVIII Army Corps Dec. 1862, his force reached a plateau of 29,917 present for duty that month. On 15 July 1863, the XVIII Corps united with the troops of Maj. Gen. John A. Dix's DEPARTMENT OF VIRGINIA (the VII Corps) to form the DEPARTMENT OF VIRGINIA AND NORTH CAROLINA. Foster held the combined command till replaced that November by Maj. Gen. Benjamin F. Butler.

Within the Department of Virginia, Butler conducted active operations during the 1864 PETERSBURG and RICHMOND campaigns; his field force, more than half of which was composed of the XVIII Corps, was known as the ARMY OF THE JAMES. The troops that remained in North Carolina, under his remote command, were also considered members of the XVIII Corps.

The Department of North Carolina reemerged as a separate command 31 Jan. 1865. It now comprised the X Corps—troops detached from the Army of the James under Maj. Gen. ALFRED H. TERRY for the FORT FISHER campaign—and the XXIII Corps, recently transferred from Tennessee under Maj. Gen. JOHN M. SCHOFIELD. As senior officer, Schofield took the departmental command, though subject to the orders of Maj. Gen. WILLIAM T. SHERMAN during the latter's CAROLINAS CAMPAIGN. By war's end, Schofield commanded not only the 2 corps but also forces at Wilmington and Beaufort and the cavalry division of Brig. Gen. H. JUDSON KILPATRICK, formerly under Sherman's direct authority—a total of 46,832 officers and men.

On 27 June the department became a RECONSTRUCTION command under Schofield, headquartered at Raleigh. Later Maj. Gen. Jacob D. Cox administered it, followed by Bvt. Maj. Gen. THOMAS H. RUGER. The department passed out of existence 19 May 1866 when merged into the Department of the Carolinas.
—EGL

North Carolina and Southern Virginia, Confederate Department of. Created under Maj. Gen. GUSTAVUS W. SMITH 19 Sept. 1862, the Department of North Carolina and Southern Virginia, by the end of that year, consisted of some

40,500 troops present for duty. These were spread among the DEPARTMENT OF RICHMOND, under Maj. Gen. Arnold Elzey, the DEPARTMENT OF SOUTHERN VIRGINIA, commanded by Maj. Gen. Samuel G. French, and Maj. Gen. William H. C. Whiting's DEPARTMENT OF NORTH CAROLINA. For a time, the name of Smith's domain was changed to the Department of the James and North Carolina; by Jan. 1863 massive troop transfers had left it with 18,200 effectives.

On 26 Feb. 1863 Smith was succeeded by Lt. Gen. James Longstreet, whose corps Gen. Robert E. Lee had detached from the ARMY OF NORTHERN VIRGINIA to protect Confederate supply regions and communication lines near Suffolk, Va. The same system of subordinate commands prevailed under Longstreet, although Maj. Gen. Daniel H. Hill replaced Whiting as subdepartmental commander 25 Feb. 1863.

Late in Apr. 1863, when Longstreet ended his Suffolk campaign and rejoined Lee, Hill succeeded him, remaining at the head of the Department of North Carolina after it absorbed the Department of Southern Virginia late in May. On 1 July Hill was sent to Richmond to supersede Elzey during a Federal movement against the capital; apparently no one replaced Hill at his former post. Once the crisis passed, however, he was transferred to Mississippi, and on his departure Elzey resumed the post at Richmond and Whiting succeeded to the command of the Department of North Carolina. Whiting was himself replaced 23 Sept. by Maj. Gen. George E. Pickett.

Pickett remained in command until felled by ill health during another enemy offensive against Richmond, May 1864. On the 10th of that month he gave way to Gen. P.G.T. Beauregard, who assumed command of a domain again known as the Department of North Carolina and Southern Virginia. The command now encompassed that part of Virginia south of the James and Appomattox rivers, plus North Carolina east of the Blue Ridge Mts. Divided into 3 districts, the department was manned by almost 8,000 troops, most of them concentrated about Richmond and Petersburg.

When the Army of Northern Virginia reached Petersburg in the third week of June 1864, Beauregard's department was merged into it. Part of the department was revived in November when Gen. Braxton Bragg received command of a rejuvenated Department of North Carolina, which he led till war's end. —EGL

Northeastern Virginia, Union Department of.
Federal units crossed the Potomac River and seized Alexandria 24 May 1861. 3 days later Brig. Gen. IRVIN MCDOWELL assumed command of the newly constituted Department of Northeastern Virginia. The department consisted of that part of the state east of the Allegheny Mts., south of the Potomac River, and north of the James River, excluding Fort Monroe and the area within a 60-mi radius of the bastion at Old Point Comfort.

McDowell's primary responsibility as department commander was to forge into an army the thousands of raw volunteers. On the Virginia hills south of the Potomac the Union Army of Northeastern Virginia took shape throughout June and early July. Still little more than an armed mob, the command advanced against the Confederates behind Bull Run. The FIRST BATTLE OF BULL RUN, 21 July, was the initial major engagement of the war and the only significant encounter in the department.

4 days after the Union defeat, 25 July, the Department of Northeastern Virginia was abolished and merged into the

short-lived Military District of the Potomac. On 15 Aug. this district became part of the DEPARTMENT and ARMY OF THE POTOMAC, with Maj. Gen. George B. McClellan commanding. —JDW

Northern Department, Union.
Drawing territory from 5 other departments, the Northern Department came into being 12 Jan. 1864. Composed of Michigan, Ohio, Indiana, and Illinois, it was headquartered at Columbus, Ohio. 8 days later, General Orders No. 17 placed in command Maj. Gen. SAMUEL P. HEINTZELMAN, a former commander of the III Corps considered too old for field command. Subsequently, his domain underwent 3 changes. On 8 Feb. the areas encompassing Jeffersonville, Ind., and Cairo, Ill., were removed from his authority. A week later, the Alton, Ill., vicinity was transferred to the DEPARTMENT OF THE MISSOURI. And on 25 June Covington, Ky., including the country around it within a radius of 10 mi, was added to the department.

Late in Sept. 1864, the War Department replaced Heintzelman with Maj. Gen. Joseph Hooker, former commander of the ARMY OF THE POTOMAC. Sec. of War EDWIN M. STANTON informed Hooker that his principal objectives were providing security at prisoner-of-war camps in Illinois and Ohio, guarding the northern frontier against spies based in Canada, blocking Confederate army incursions from West Virginia and Kentucky, and enforcing CONSCRIPTION throughout his territory.

During Hooker's term his department, now headquartered at Cincinnati, encompassed 12,000 to 13,000 federal troops present for duty and 13 to 17 field and heavy cannon. 3 territorial changes took place during his regime. On 28 Nov. 1864, Cairo, Ill., reverted to the Northern Department. On 10 Feb. 1865, Jeffersonville, Ind., was returned to the department, while Covington, Ky., was transferred to the Department of Kentucky, as were Jeffersonville and New Albany, Ind., 24 Mar. The Northern Department passed out of existence when it merged into the DEPARTMENT OF THE OHIO, 27 June 1865, at which time all departments were realigned for the Reconstruction. —EGL

Northern Virginia, Confederate Army of.
Called the Army of the Potomac until about the time Gen. ROBERT E. LEE assumed command 1 June 1862, the Army of Northern Virginia won an enviable reputation. Its first campaign under Lee, the SEVEN DAYS', 25 June–1 July, was disappointing, but Lee profited from his errors and at SECOND BULL RUN, 29–30 Aug., the army won a smashing victory. In the glow of this triumph, Lee invaded Maryland (see ANTIETAM CAMPAIGN).

At Sharpsburg, 17 Sept., he withstood repeated enemy onslaughts but at a cost so great his troops had to withdraw into Virginia. Lee now divided his army into 2 corps, the first commanded by Maj. Gen. JAMES LONGSTREET and the second by Maj. Gen. THOMAS J. "STONEWALL" JACKSON. At FREDERICKSBURG, 13 Dec., his position an enormous advantage, Lee won an easy victory over Maj. Gen. Ambrose E. Burnside. CHANCELLORSVILLE, 1–4 May 1863, marked the peak performance of the army and its leaders, but the mortal wounding of Jackson proved an irreparable loss. After reorganizing the army into 3 corps, headed by Longstreet and Lt. Gens. RICHARD S. EWELL and AMBROSE P. HILL, and with a strength of about 75,000—including 10,000 cavalry led by Maj. Gen. J.E.B. STUART—Lee invaded Pennsylvania (see GETTYSBURG CAMPAIGN).

At Gettysburg, 1–3 July, Lee's deficiencies in position,

reconnaissance, and coordination, combined with superior performance by the Federals, resulted in a costly defeat. Heavy bloodshed continued in the WILDERNESS–SPOTSYLVANIA–COLD HARBOR fights against Lt. Gen. Ulysses S. Grant and Maj. Gen. George G. Meade, May–June 1864. In 1 month the army suffered about 30,000 casualties, including 37 generals, a loss from which it never recovered.

During the last 9 months of the war, Lee's army, bedeviled by disease, exposure, and desertion, so shrank that those surrendering at APPOMATTOX numbered only 27,805. Shortly after Chancellorsville Lee had written: "There were never such men in an army before. They will go anywhere and do anything if properly led." —BIW

Northern Virginia, Confederate Department of. The Confederate Department of Northern Virginia was constituted 22 Oct. 1861, comprising the Districts of the Potomac, the Aquia, and the Valley. Gen. JOSEPH E. JOHNSTON, commanding the Department of the Potomac, assumed command of the new department, with headquarters at Manassas Junction. On 12 Apr. 1862, during the preliminary phases of the Peninsula Campaign, the Departments of Norfolk and of the Peninsula were included in Johnston's department.

Johnston continued to refer to his command as the Army of the Potomac, while Pres. Jefferson Davis called it the Army of the North or the Army of Richmond. When Johnston fell wounded at Seven Pines, Gen. ROBERT E. LEE assumed command of the department 1 June 1862. His initial order referred to the units as the ARMY OF NORTHERN VIRGINIA. This historic designation rested on Lee's continued usage rather than an authorized adoption.

Lee commanded the department and its army until his surrender at Appomattox 9 Apr. 1865. In their nearly 3 years together both he and his veterans won enduring renown. All the major battles in the East were fought by the Army of Northern Virginia or detached parts of other commands in the districts composing the department. Lee was appointed general-in-chief of the armies of the Confederate states 6 Feb. 1865, while still maintaining command of the department. His final act as department and army commander was his farewell address to his veterans, 10 Apr. 1865. —JDW

Northrop, Lucius Bellinger. CSA b. Charleston, S.C., 8 Sept. 1811, Northrop attended West Point, from which he graduated 22d of 33 in the class of 1831. He fought in the Seminole War, sustaining a wound in 1839 that permanently curtailed his physical activity. While on long-term sick leave, he studied medicine, then built up a lucrative practice in Charleston, retaining his army commission until he resigned in 1861 to side with the Confederacy.

GG

He was a lifelong friend, and, according to many, a "pet" of Jefferson Davis. In 1835 Northrop testified in behalf of Davis at a court-martial; during the Civil War Davis appointed Northrop a colonel in and commissary general of the Confed-

eracy. But Northrop's personality hindered his popularity: he was peevish, obstinate, condescending, fault-finding, secretive, indirect, and intolerant of suggestion. Vast numbers of irate citizens and soldiers believed him incompetent. Early in 1864 the Senate considered but defeated a measure calling for his removal.

Certainly Davis could have chosen a less cantankerous man, but anyone would have faced the same impossible circumstances. Northrop's office lacked sufficient funds, the currency depreciated in value, and both supplies and supply-producing areas fell into enemy hands. In truth, Northrop did rather well, but the administration of his department was inefficient and transportation capabilities inadequate. Late in 1864 Davis ordered him promoted to brigadier general but did not forward the nomination to the Senate, where it almost certainly would have been rejected. The continuing calls for Northrop's dismissal prevailed at last, and 15 Feb. 1865 he was removed.

Soon arrested by Federal authorities and imprisoned for several months on suspicion of having willfully starved prisoners, he quickly gained his freedom and spent the next 25 years on a farm near Charlottesville, Va. d. 9 Feb. 1894 in a Confederate home at Pikesville, Md. —HH

Northwest, Confederate Army of the. One of the first Confederate armies to go into battle, the Army of the Northwest operated in western Virginia June 1861–Feb. 1862. On 8 June 1861, the Army of the Northwest was established under command of Brig. Gen. ROBERT S. GARNETT, a West Point graduate. Garnett was given some eastern Virginia regiments and the 1st Georgia, nearly 5,000 men in all, and was ordered to recruit vigorously in western Virginia; since that region was Union country, the effort resulted in only 23 recruits.

Garnett became the first general on either side to lose his life in battle, falling 13 July 1861 at Corrick's Ford while leading the Confederate retreat from Laurel Hill. Gen. Henry R. Jackson temporarily replaced Garnett as commander of the army until Maj. Gen. WILLIAM WING LORING assumed command 21 July.

Led by Loring, the army attempted to regain lost western Virginia territory. But Gen. Robert E. Lee, in his first Civil War battle, was defeated by Union Brig. Gen. Joseph J. Reynolds at the Battle of CHEAT MOUNTAIN, 12–13 Sept. 1861, leaving western Virginia firmly in Union hands.

Loring then took his small army to Winchester, Va., where it joined with Maj. Gen. Thomas J. "Stonewall" Jackson's command, although still retaining its identity as the Army of the Northwest. Loring feuded with Jackson Jan. 1862, and when Jackson assigned Loring to hold the town of Romney, Va., Loring protested to Sec. of War Judah P. Benjamin. Benjamin's support of Loring led Jackson to submit his resignation, which he soon withdrew.

Loring was transferred to southern Virginia 9 Feb. 1862, and the Army of the Northwest lost its separate identity, merging with the ARMY OF NORTHERN VIRGINIA. —DS

Northwest, Union Department of the. Established by General Order No. 128, 6 Sept. 1862, the Department of the Northwest was composed of Wisconsin, Iowa, and Minnesota, and Nebraska and Dakota territories. Maj. Gen. JOHN POPE, recently defeated at Second Bull Run, assumed command of the department at St. Paul, Minn., 11 Oct. Nebraska Territory was later transferred to the DEPARTMENT OF THE MISSOURI.

Department headquarters were moved twice between 28 Nov. 1862 and 7 Feb. 1863: first to Madison, Wis., when Brig. Gen. William L. Elliott temporarily replaced Pope, then to Milwaukee 6 days before Pope resumed command 13 Feb. During summer 1862 Santee Sioux Indians killed nearly 800 white settlers in an uprising along the Minnesota River, drawing troops from the front (*see* SIOUX UPRISING OF 1862). Hostilities were quelled by 23 Sept. and the department became largely an administrative command. It was attached to the Division of the Missouri 30 Jan. 1865, Maj. Gen. Samuel R. Curtis commanding. General Order No. 23, 17 Feb. 1865, transferred Dakota west of the 27th longitude to the Department of the Missouri, which absorbed the entire Department of the Northwest 27 June.   —PLF

Northwest Conspiracy. In 1864 Confederate military reverses led to a plan for insurrection in the Northwest, the region known today as the Midwest. Confederate agents in Canada were to contact Southern sympathizers in Indiana, Illinois, and Ohio, overthrow the governments of those states, and form a Northwestern Confederacy allied to the Confederate States that would dismember the North and encourage it to accept peace terms.

The nucleus of the plan was to liberate Confederate prisoners at Camp Douglas in Chicago and arm them from Federal arsenals that were to be seized. Aid was expected from the Sons of Liberty, a secret order strongest in the Northwest, its 300,000 members "sworn to oppose the unconstitutional acts of the Federal Government and to support states' rights principles." But only the extremists of the order, which largely advocated restoring the Union by negotiation rather than violence, accepted Confederate funds and promised cooperation in the plot.

Uprisings planned for 20 July and mid-August were postponed because factions were not coordinated; the new date for the insurrection was 29 August, during the Democratic national convention in Chicago. While the city was busy with politics, the first blow was to be against Camp Douglas, from which some 5,000 of the 10,000 prisoners would be freed. Capt. Thomas Hines, one of Morgan's Raiders who had escaped from a Federal prison, and 60 other Confederate fugitives filtered into Chicago to lead the uprising.

Some days before the date of insurrection, Col. Benjamin J. Sweet, the Union officer in command of Camp Douglas, heard rumors that there were 5,000 armed Confederates in Chicago with plans to release prisoners and arm them with muskets; the city was to be burned, the flames to be the signal for a general uprising throughout the Midwest. The Federals immediately reinforced the Camp Douglas garrison and, by following Confederate prisoner John T. Shanks, who had been allowed to escape, located and arrested many of the leaders of the planned insurrection.   —PR

Norwich University. In 1819 Alden Partridge established in Norwich, Vt., the American Literary, Scientific, and Military Academy (known as Norwich University from 1834), the first private educational institution in the U.S. to be operated in a military mode. The Vermont institution served as a model for almost a score of private military academies and colleges founded by Partridge, or his students, before his death in 1854, and is regarded as the birthplace of the concept from which the Reserve Officers Training Corps is derived.

Partridge, convinced that a citizen-soldiery is the most important element in a satisfactory system of national defense, felt that military instruction is essential to a complete, truly liberal, system of education. Military science and physical education, along with engineering, modern languages, and political economy, constituted Partridge's highly innovative plan of education—a system replicated in Southern, as well as Northern, schools. More than 30 Norwich alumni served as preceptors at these schools before 1860, and many former cadets at these institutions provided military service during the Civil War.

Of the 1,013 cadets who attended Norwich University 1835–65, two-thirds served in the war, a majority as commissioned officers. Of graduates fighting for the Union, 7 became major generals, 16 brigadier generals, 6 commodores, and 1 a rear admiral; 5 were brevetted major general and 19 brigadier general, and 4 were awarded a MEDAL OF HONOR. In addition, 4 alumni served as generals or flag officers for the Confederate States. Sec. of the U.S. Navy GIDEON WELLES was also educated at Norwich. About 50 alumni became drillmasters and military instructors for various Federal units. A unique Civil War organization, a Union cavalry troop composed primarily of students and known as the College Cavaliers, was filled largely by Norwich University and Dartmouth College men. Perhaps only the national military academies at West Point and Annapolis rivaled Norwich as a school for Union Civil War officers.   —RJS

Norwood's Plantation, La., eng. at. 18 May 1864 *See* YELLOW BAYOU, LA., ENG. AT.

Nueces River, Tex., affair at the. 10 Aug. 1862 Large German settlements in central and northeastern Texas were enclaves of Unionist opposition to STATES RIGHTS and SLAVERY. Many Germans fled the state after the secession ordinance passed, and those who stayed resisted conscription into the Confederate army. Texas military authorities considered them a serious threat to internal security, fearing they would organize and arm themselves to open a corridor for invasion by Federal troops in Kansas and Missouri. Already short of manpower, the Confederacy could not defend another major front in the Trans-Mississippi.

The Germans had been holding Unionist meetings since June 1861, and 4 July 1862 several hundred of them met at Bear Creek near Fredericksburg. They organized into 3 military companies under Fritz Teneger to protect themselves against harassment by Capt. James Duff, an officer whose own men commented on the harshness of his reprisals against disloyal civilians. Within weeks Teneger disbanded his battalion in deference to the military authorities, but he also spread the word that a party would meet at Turtle Creek 1 Aug., strike out to cross the Rio Grande at its junction with Devil's River, and book passage from Mexico to New Orleans to join the Union army. 65 men decided to accompany Teneger.

Duff learned of the plan from a traitor and sent Lt. C. D. McRae with 94 men to intercept the refugees. The Confederates started trailing them on the 3d. Certain they were not being followed, Teneger's group traveled at a relaxed pace, on the 9th reaching a small prairie surrounded by cottonwood beside the Nueces River, about a day's ride from the Rio Grande. Some of the men wanted to continue toward Mexico, but Teneger, feeling safe, ordered a halt for the night.

McRae's scouts sighted the Germans on the same day and

planned to attack at dawn on the 10th. About 1 a.m. they moved to within 300 yd of the Germans' camp. McRae divided his command into 2 parts, planning to take the camp in a crossfire. An hour later the Confederates killed 2 German guards, the shots alerting the camp to the soldiers' presence.

The night passed in disorganized skirmishing, and at first light the Texans charged in earnest. Briefly the Germans held their ground, but in a poor defensive position and with inadequate guns, they were soon overrun by McRae's men. The Germans scattered, some seeking safety on a nearby hill, others helping the slightly wounded to Sycamore Creek, a half-mile distant.

19 Germans had been killed outright; 9 others were wounded and captured. Though initially cared for, all 9 were removed from the camp and shot in the back of the head. McRae, himself severely wounded early in the fighting, claimed to know nothing of the murders. Some Confederates blamed the killings on Lt. Edwin Lilly. The Texans lost 2 killed and 18 wounded in the affair, burying their own but not the German dead before leaving the site 12 or 13 Aug.

The engagement at the Nueces marked the end of most open disaffection among Texas Germans. While some continued to leave the state and others lived in hiding for the duration of the war, many, though still resisting the draft, took a loyalty oath and tried to live out the war quietly. Fearing reprisals, the German community did not retrieve the bodies of its dead from the battle site until Aug. 1865, when they interred them in a common grave in Comfort, Tex.   —PLF

nullification. Through the early national and antebellum years, states occasionally claimed the right to declare null and void within their boundaries Federal legislation that state officials judged unconstitutional or detrimental to state interests. South Carolinian JOHN C. CALHOUN perfected the theory of nullification as a means to combat what he and discontented Southerners foresaw as a powerful industrial North displacing the Southern stronghold in Congress.

Though talk of nullification occasionally colored radical secessionist rhetoric as the nation approached civil war, the great Nullification Crisis of 1832 ended serious threats of disunion on such flimsy grounds. The crisis peaked when South Carolina nullified a set of protective tariff acts that benefited Northern industry at the expense of the Southern agricultural economy. South Carolina threatened to secede, but Pres. An-drew Jackson was prepared to send Federal troops to keep the state in the Union by force. Other Southern states had not yet developed a sense of Southern nationhood, so South Carolina demurred. The crisis passed, but the belief in nullification formed an important part of the STATES RIGHTS theory leading to the Southern disunion movement that climaxed during the secession winter of 1860–61.   —PLF

numbers engaged. One of the puzzles of the Civil War never fully resolved is the actual number of troops in the Union and Confederate armies. In 1900, in Thomas L. LIVERMORE'S *NUMBERS AND LOSSES IN THE CIVIL WAR,* Livermore said that only someone who examined the muster rolls on file in the War Department and then transcribed the names of the men who originally composed the different military units would be able to provide fairly accurate numbers. States that raised troops during the war might contribute to producing such figures by emulating North Carolina, which has published a 12-volume roster of North Carolinians who served in the Confederate and Union forces.

But since no other state has followed North Carolina's lead, estimates of total forces vary from Livermore's 1,556,678 Federals and 1,077,384 Confederates to Woodrow Wilson's figures of 1.7 million for the Union and 900,000 for the Confederates in his *History of the American People* (1902), Cazenove G. Lee's generous estimate of 2,778,304 Union troops held off by 600,000 Confederates, and the *Encyclopaedia Britannica's* (1958) total of approximately 4 million troops for both sides.

Livermore estimated that there were 978,664 men in service in the Confederate army and further surmised that those serving in irregular organizations such as the militia totaled 98,720. If the North Carolina roster is used as a guide, the figure becomes 1,307,460, against Livermore's total of 1,077,384.

The estimates in the 1860 census of those subject to conscription come to 1,141,000 for the Confederacy, contrasting with the 2,778,304 actual enlistments in the Union army during the war. The disparity between the 1,141,000 men of military age the Confederacy had to draw on and the manpower the North had available should have given Jefferson Davis cause for serious reflection. Historian Francis Parkman wrote that the Confederacy, even though "ill-jointed, starved, attenuated," was able to hold the Union forces at bay for 4 years because it had "a head full of fire."   —AG

O

Oak Grove (French's Field; King's School House; the Orchard), Va., eng. at. 25 June 1862 The lines of Maj. Gen. GEORGE B. MCCLELLAN's Army of the Potomac sprawled, at some points, to within 6 mi of Richmond by the final week of June 1862. The bulk of the Federal army lay south of the Chickahominy River with Maj. Gen. FITZ JOHN PORTER's V Corps north of the stream. On 24 June McClellan ordered an advance of Maj. Gen. SAMUEL P. HEINTZELMAN's III Corps along the Williamsburg road. South of this road, at the western edge of White Oak Swamp, lay a boggy wooded stretch of land occupied by neither army. McClellan wanted this swampy ground seized, thus removing it from his front preparatory to a general advance by his entire army.

At 8 a.m. on the 25th, Brig. Gen. JOSEPH HOOKER's division of 3 brigades initiated McClellan's limited movement. On Hooker's left Brig. Gen. PHILIP KEARNEY shoved the pickets of his division forward as support, while Brig. Gen. ISRAEL B. RICHARDSON, commanding a II Corps division, supported Kearney. Hooker's leading brigade, under Brig. Gen. DANIEL E. SICKLES, soon encountered the pickets of Maj. Gen. BENJAMIN HUGER's Confederate division. The action quickly accelerated into a sharp fire fight.

Huger's 3 brigades of 6,000 effectives had been reinforced that morning by Brig. Gen. ROBERT RANSOM's brigade of 3,000. These Confederates easily stopped Hooker, who then requested reinforcements from Kearney. Brig. Gen. DAVID B. BIRNEY's brigade came in on Hooker's left, but the Confederates clung to the marshy terrain. Late in the morning McClellan's chief of staff, Brig. Gen. Randolph B. Marcy, ordered a withdrawal. McClellan, however, appeared and countermanded Marcy's action, ordering a renewal of the attack.

Hooker's and Kearney's solid combat veterans, supported by a brigade of the II Corps and an artillery battery, drove forward once more. The Federal artillerists scorched the ground with canister and the blue-clad infantry cleared the area of the stubborn Confederates, who withdrew to their main fieldworks. Behind these strong lines, the Southerners held firm and, with darkness enveloping the field, the action quickly subsided.

This engagement at Oak Grove was the initial action of the SEVEN DAYS' CAMPAIGN. Federal casualties amounted to at least 51 killed, 401 wounded, and 64 missing for a total of 516; Confederate losses comprised 40 killed, 263 wounded, and 13 missing—in all, 316 men. Though McClellan's probe briefly worried Gen. Robert E. Lee, the engagement did not alter the Confederate plan. The next day Lee, not McClellan, assumed the offensive, and the serious fighting of the week-long campaign began at Mechanicsville.   —JDW

Oak Hills, Mo., Battle of. *See* WILSON'S CREEK.

oblique. When Union or Confederate troops were directed to attack in oblique order, they were expected to cross the battlefield in a diagonal line and hit the enemy position at one end. As more attacking troops reached the point of contact, the enemy line, in theory, would roll up. This tactic was supposedly first used successfully over 300 years before the birth of Christ, and unfortunately for Civil War generals, it had not worked too well since. Though oblique attacks were tried intermittently, rifled 19th-century small arms made a diagonal crossing of a battlefield extremely hazardous.   —JES

Ocean Pond, Fla., Battle of. 20 Feb. 1864 *See* OLUSTEE, FLA., BATTLE OF.

Odell, Moses Fowler. USP b. Tarrytown, N.Y., 24 Feb. 1818. Following a public education, Odell pursued a brief business career and Democratic politics. A partisan of Pres. James K. Polk, he won patronage appointment to a clerkship in the New York custom house in 1845; under Democratic Pres. Franklin Buchanan was appointed a public appraiser, then won election to the 37th Congress in 1860, serving as Treasury Department Committee chairman and on the Indian Affairs Committee.

On 10 Dec. 1861, as a WAR DEMOCRAT, he accepted an important seat on the joint COMMITTEE ON THE CONDUCT OF THE WAR, a body dominated by RADICAL REPUBLICANS. Reelected to the 38th Congress, he also joined the Military Affairs Committee; on this and the Joint Committee he exerted unusual Democratic influence in investigation of Union military personalities and operations.

NA

Declining a third congressional term, Odell accepted appointment as naval agent for the port of New York from former Joint Committee member Pres. ANDREW JOHNSON in 1865. Stricken by cancer, he died in Brooklyn, N.Y., 13 June 1866.   —JES

Official Records. *See* WAR OF THE REBELLION OFFICIAL RECORDS OF THE UNION AND CONFEDERATE ARMIES *AND* OFFICIAL RECORDS OF THE UNION AND CONFEDERATE NAVIES IN THE WAR OF THE REBELLION.

Ohio. Despite divided opinions among its people—some giving all-out Union support, others yearning for a quick end to the fighting—Ohio played a critically important part in the war. Politically, Republicans largely controlled the state government but not always the congressional delegation. Democrats, in vocal opposition throughout the war, supported dissident CLEMENT L. VALLANDIGHAM in his failed attempt to become governor in 1863, even after his exile to Canada for having denounced the draft and arbitrary military arrests.

Direct military action touched Ohio only briefly. In 1862 a Confederate thrust into upper Kentucky roused Ohio's volunteer militia to man Cincinnati's defenses against attack. In summer 1863 Gen. John Hunt Morgan's raiding cavalry swept across southern Ohio only to be captured after a final fight at Salineville.

Ohio played a large part in the Union's military success. In economic terms Ohio farms, mines, manufacturing shops, and railroads contributed heavily in support of Federal forces. The response of military recruits, initially enthusiastic, waned in 1862–63, when open draft resistance erupted in Noble and Holmes counties, but picked up again in 1864. All together, more than 364,000 Ohioans served in Union units, of whom almost 25,000 lost their lives. Among those generals of Ohio birth or residence were Ulysses S. Grant, William T. Sherman, Philip H. Sheridan, George B. McClellan, Irvin McDowell, and George A. Custer. The "FIGHTING MCCOOKS" also saw service. War records added luster to the later political careers of Rutherford B. Hayes, James A. Garfield, and William McKinley. Within the Lincoln administration, Ohioan EDWIN M. STANTON, secretary of war, and SALMON P. CHASE, secretary of the treasury, furthered the Union cause, while in Congress Republicans BENJAMIN F. WADE and JOHN SHERMAN and Democrats Samuel S. "Sunset" Cox and George H. Pendleton were outspoken leaders. —DL

Ohio, Union Army of the. To liberate East Tennessee Unionists, Maj. Gen. AMBROSE E. BURNSIDE's mobile Army of the Ohio was formed in mid-1863 from the IX and XXIII corps in Kentucky. (This army was distinct from Maj. Gen. Don Carlos Buell's Army of the Ohio.) The XXIII Corps easily overran most of East Tennessee by early September, the IX Corps joined it there.

When Burnside belatedly headed for Chattanooga, he barely escaped a Confederate assault at CAMPBELL'S STATION, then withstood siege in KNOXVILLE. The reinforced Federals (the IV, IX, XXIII, and cavalry corps)—first under Maj. Gens. JOHN G. FOSTER and JOHN G. PARKE, then under Maj. Gen. JOHN M. SCHOFIELD—thereafter sparred inconclusively with Lt. Gen. James Longstreet, Dec. 1863–Mar. 1864.

That spring the IV and IX corps transferred elsewhere, and the cavalry corps shrank to 1 division. The Army of the Ohio thus entered the ATLANTA CAMPAIGN with just the XXIII Corps, soon reduced to 2 divisions, and Maj. Gen. George Stoneman's often-detached cavalry division. First on the left, subsequently on the right and center, Schofield's reduced army participated in Maj. Gen. WILLIAM T. SHERMAN's advance. At Utoy Creek, Maj. Gen. JOHN M. PALMER was relieved of XIV Corps command for refusing to serve under Schofield, his junior in rank but senior in office.

To give ambitious Schofield larger command, use his troops actively, and support Sherman, Lt. Gen. U.S. Grant moved the XXIII Corps through Cincinnati and Washington to North Carolina, Jan.–Feb. 1865. With 3 reinforced X (re-created from Terry's Provisional Corps) and XXIII corps divisions, Schofield

took WILMINGTON, N.C., 22 Feb. With Maj. Gen. Jacob D. Cox's provisional corps from New Berne, later bolstered by the XXIII Corps from Wilmington, Schofield countered heavy resistance at KINSTON and occupied Goldsborough 21 Mar. On the next day the X Corps from Wilmington joined Sherman, who united with Schofield at Goldsborough 23 Mar. In the ensuing drive on Raleigh, Schofield's Army of the Ohio (X and XXIII corps) constituted Sherman's center. Following Confederate Gen. Joseph E. Johnston's surrender, that army occupied North Carolina until discontinued 27 June 1865. —RJS

Ohio, Union Department of the. General Orders No. 14 from the Federal adjutant general's office established the Department of the Ohio 3 May 1861 and named Maj. Gen. GEORGE B. MCCLELLAN its commander. The general order stated parenthetically that the department, made up of Ohio, Indiana, and Illinois, was soon to be subdivided into several other departments. General Orders No. 19, dated 9 May, expanded the department "to embrace so much of Western Virginia and Pennsylvania as lies north of the Great Kanawha, north and west of the Greenbriar, thence northward to the southwest corner of Maryland, thence along the Western Maryland line to the Pennsylvania line." The new boundaries extended even farther north, embracing McKean County in eastern Pennsylvania.

Following his success at the Battles of PHILIPPI, RICH MOUNTAIN, and CORRICK'S FORD, McClellan won assignment to Washington, D.C., his subordinate Brig. Gen. WILLIAM S. ROSECRANS assuming temporary departmental command until relieved by Brig. Gen. ORMSBY M. MITCHEL 21 Sept. On 9 Nov., following rumors of Brig. Gen. WILLIAM T. SHERMAN's nervous breakdown, his Department of the Cumberland merged with the Department of the Ohio, and on 15 Nov. Maj. Gen. DON CARLOS BUELL assumed command of the restructured organization, encompassing Ohio, Michigan, Indiana, and that portion of Kentucky east of the Union Department of Missouri's Cumberland River boundary. On 11 Mar. 1862, Buell's troops and responsibility were briefly acquired for the newly formed Union Department of the Mississippi. But on 19 Aug. the Department of the Ohio was created anew and Maj. Gen. HORATIO G. WRIGHT named to command of an area including Ohio, Indiana, Illinois, Michigan, Wisconsin, the Cumberland Gap, and all Kentucky east of the Tennessee River. Headquarters were established at Cincinnati, Ohio.

Maj. Gen. AMBROSE E. BURNSIDE relieved Wright 25 Mar. 1863, then came under Maj. Gen. U. S. GRANT's command when the department was absorbed into the Military Division of the Mississippi 16 Oct. 1863. Within this division the department and its commanders assumed a role more administrative than military. On Burnside's departure 9 Dec., Maj. Gen. JOHN G. FOSTER took command, was replaced by Maj. Gen. JOHN M. SCHOFIELD 9 Feb. 1864, and he by Maj. Gen. GEORGE STONEMAN 17 Nov. Stoneman, an active combat commander, filled the post until 17 Jan. 1865, when for administrative purposes the department was annexed to the Department of the Cumberland. Following his 12 Mar. 1864 promotion, division commander Major General Sherman became nominal administrative department head when Schofield and Stoneman were involved with campaigning. The burden of these chores and the necessity of maintaining headquarters in the field prompted the department's annexation. At the head of the Department of the Cumberland, Maj. Gen. GEORGE H.

THOMAS oversaw the Department of the Ohio's former area until all departments were realigned 27 June 1865.

Having 2 armies—the Army of the Cumberland and the Army of the Ohio—both closely associated with the Department of the Ohio throughout the war created bureaucratic confusion within the organization when campaigns, commanders, and areas of responsibility overlapped or were duplicated at department level.   —JES

Ohio Penitentiary. On 30 July 1863, Ohio Gov. DAVID TOD wrote to Nathaniel Merion, warden of the Ohio Penitentiary, advising him of the impending arrival of Confederate Brig. Gen. JOHN HUNT MORGAN and 30 of his raiders recently captured at New Lisbon, Ohio. The Ohio Penitentiary, a stone prewar structure in Columbus, previously housed only hardened convicts, not prisoners of war. CAMP CHASE, on the outskirts of Columbus, Tod believed insufficiently secure to hold the desperate raiders. This began the penitentiary's brief career as a Civil War prisoner facility.

At no time did Merion oversee as many as 100 prisoners of war. Surviving prisoner reports for Feb. and Mar. 1864 show 66 Confederates in the entire facility. Similar to some modern penal institutions, the penitentiary, 3 stories tall, was divided into cell blocks and featured heavy iron bars at its windows. Confederates were first kept with the general prison population, and in summer 1863 were subjected to the same harsh rules governing convicts. Throughout the next year, prisoners of war there were occasionally punished with solitary confinement in unlighted, poorly ventilated dungeon cells in the penitentiary basement and placed on a bread-and-water diet. Morgan wrote to Governor Tod, complaining that Confederates were not treated according to rules governing confinement of prisoners of war. Tod visited the facility, certain rules were relaxed, and Confederates were permitted packages from relatives and friends and allowed to purchase some items with their own funds.

Col. William Hoffman, commissary general of prisoners, and later Maj. Gen. Samuel P. Heintzelman, commander of the Union's Northern Department headquartered at Columbus, had difficulty dealing with Merion and other state prison officials. Reports to military officials charged with prisoner care were not regularly completed, and Merion complained of the extra expense incurred in holding Confederates. Many were not permanently incarcerated in the penitentiary but were transfers to other facilities, only briefly held there in transit.

On the night of 27 Nov. 1863, Morgan and 6 other officers escaped after 23 days of tunneling through the cement floor of a ground-level cell into a 4-ft-high air chamber that extended to the outer prison walls. The officers scaled the 25-ft outer penitentiary wall with a rope made of bed sheets, then scattered through Columbus. 3 were recaptured several days later, but Morgan arrived safely in Franklin, Tenn., 23 Dec.

Following the escape, rules changed. Penitentiary Confederates were separated from other prisoners, confined to the third story, attended day and night by 4 military guards, and fed in their cells instead of the prison dining hall. On 18 Mar. 1864, Sec. of War Edwin M. Stanton ordered all Confederates transferred from the prison to FORT DELAWARE, ending the Ohio Penitentiary's involvement with the Civil War.   —JES

Okolona, Miss., eng. at. 22 Feb. 1864 *See* SOOY SMITH EXPEDITION.

LC

"Old Abe." Most notable Civil War animals were horses, but one of the most famous, indeed legendary, was "the war eagle," Old Abe. For most of 4 years, through 42 battles and skirmishes, he served as mascot for Company C/8th Regiment Wisconsin Volunteers, known during the war as the "Eagle Regiment."

Early in 1861 a party of Flambeau Indians (part of the Chippewa tribe) found the young bird nesting near the mouth of the Jump River. They later paddled down the Chippewa River to trade with the settlers on its banks. After offering an unknown measure of corn in return for the bird, Mrs. Dan McCann quickly became the owner of what was to be the symbol of a regiment, a state, and a nation.

The eagle first served as a family pet before the McCanns offered him to the 8th Wisconsin, then recruiting in Eau Claire. The regiment received the strange gift with some skepticism, but the men finally adopted "Old Abe," swore him in as their mascot, and built him a shield perch attached to a wooden pole. There he would sit in marches and on parade, a mascot, a symbol, and an effective morale booster.

When the 8th Wisconsin went into battle, the bird would fly over the fighting, screech at the enemy, and return to his perch as the shooting stopped. To the Southerners he was "the Yankee buzzard." Realizing Old Abe's importance to the regiment, they constantly made attempts to shoot or capture him but were never successful.

The eagle's military career ended 28 Sept. 1864, as the captain of Company C presented him to the state of Wisconsin, where he was displayed in a cage in the state capitol. Old Abe made countless public appearances and drew hundreds of visitors. On 28 June 1865, he appeared at the Soldiers' Home Fair in Madison for the benefit of children made orphans by the war; thousands of Old Abe photographs were sold.

On 28 Mar. 1881, he succumbed to smoke inhalation suffered when the capitol caught fire in February. State officials immediately had him mounted and again placed his body on display in the capitol's Memorial Hall. But again fire raged through the building and Old Abe burned up in it. Today, a replica of the famous war eagle overlooks both the Memorial Hall and the Assembly Chamber in Madison. —FLS

Old Capitol Prison. After the destruction of the Capitol during the War of 1812, a brick building for temporary use was built on 1st St. When Congress moved back to its permanent location, the building became known as the Old Capitol. By 1861 it was dilapidated, with decayed walls, creaking doors and stairways, wooden slats nailed across its windows, and high board fences around it. That year it became a prison for Confederates ranging from soldiers to known spies and persons vaguely suspected of sentiments disloyal to the Union. In 6 months it was full. Though the wooden slats had been replaced by iron bars, the real obstacles to escape were the military guards who constantly paced around the building.

Old Capitol "belonged to an ancient tradition in its gloom, filth, and discomfort"; lice, bedbugs, and spiders abounded; "half-spoiled beef and pork, half-cooked beans, and musty rice" made up the meals. Prisoners who had funds, however, had the privilege of buying—at profiteering prices—better food, tobacco, and other luxuries from the prison commissary. Some were allowed to receive gifts from outside, and a few were admitted, by purchased card, to the sinks used by officials—the only sinks that were clean and enclosed.

Old Capitol held many prominent Confederate generals, along with smugglers, BLOCKADE RUNNERS, and mail carriers. But its most noted inmates were its women spies. They included BELLE BOYD, "Heroine of the Shenandoah," who yelled taunts at the Federal guards and sang Confederate songs at her window, and ROSE O'NEAL GREENHOW, whose famous cipher message to Gen. P.G.T. Beauregard, "Order issued for McDowell to move on Manassas tonight," was largely responsible for the Federal rout at Bull Run. After the war HEINRICH WIRZ, commandant of Andersonville Prison, was confined at Old Capitol and hanged on a gallows in the yard.

William P. Wood, superintendent of Old Capitol, was a special secret agent of the War Department and managed to gain much valuable information by persistently questioning prisoners. —PR

Olden, Charles Smith. war governor b. Princeton, N.J., 19 Feb. 1799, into a Quaker family, Olden was educated in Lawrenceville, N.J., and worked in his father's store until 1823, when he accepted a clerkship in Philadelphia. In 1826 he opened his own business in New Orleans, prospering sufficiently to retire to Princeton after 8 years. There he farmed and served on the board of directors of the Trenton Banking Co., entering politics as a state senator 1845–51. Politically conservative and highly respected, he was nominated by the state Republican party for the governorship in 1859, defeated the Democratic candidate in a close race, and was inaugurated 17 Jan. 1860.

USMHI

Olden's Quaker background did not prevent him from expanding the state militia as sectional tensions escalated. Though he favored compromise once the Southern states began seceding, he rallied solidly behind the war effort after the firing on FORT SUMTER Apr. 1861. Shortly after Maj. Robert Anderson surrendered the garrison to South Carolina militia, Olden used his influence to raise $500,000 in war funds from New Jersey banks, and he

LC

received from the state legislature full cooperation in his efforts to support the Federal government. He publicly denounced traitors to the Union and responded quickly to Pres. Abraham Lincoln's call for troops. He opposed the administration strenuously only when the suspension of the writ of *HABEAS CORPUS* threatened the citizens of New Jersey, and he interfered with Federal authorities to prevent arbitrary arrests.

Unable to succeed himself under the provisions of the state constitution of 1844, Olden left office 20 Jan. 1863. He remained active in public life, serving as a judge on the state Court of Errors and Appeals, as a member of the Court of Pardons, and as leader of the New Jersey electors for the presidential election in 1872. d. Princeton, 7 Apr. 1876.

—PLF

"Old Gentlemen's Convention." *See* WASHINGTON PEACE CONFERENCE.

Old Oaks, La., eng. at. 18 May 1864 *See* YELLOW BAYOU, LA., ENG. AT.

***Olustee*, CSS.** *See TALLAHASSEE, CSS.*

Olustee (Ocean Pond), Fla., Battle of. 20 Feb. 1864 Late in 1863 Abraham Lincoln announced an AMNESTY PROCLAMATION for Southerners wishing to return to the Union. The plan also detailed ways in which Reconstruction governments might be established in occupied Confederate states. One who saw political profit in Lincoln's gesture was his Treasury secretary, SALMON P. CHASE, an aspirant for the 1864 Republican presidential nomination. A group of Unionists in Florida, led by Federal tax commissioners in the secretary's employ, helped him plot to bring that state back into the Union so that it might send to the Republican national convention delegates in Chase's support.

Chase's backers enlisted the support of Maj. Gen. QUINCY A. GILLMORE, head of the Department of the South, a command that included Florida. In mid-December, at their urging, Gillmore suggested to the War Department that an expedition be launched from his South Carolina headquarters into east Florida, securing Unionist enclaves, severing supply routes to the upper Confederacy, and recruiting BLACK SOLDIERS among local slaves. For these and other reasons, the government approved the venture, and on 7 Feb. 1864, a division of Gillmore's troops, under Brig. Gen. TRUMAN SEYMOUR, debarked from transports at Jacksonville and moved westward toward the Suwannee River.

Seymour's route carried him across a sparsely inhabited region toward a strategic railroad he wished to destroy. This effort to enlarge his incursion into the state ran counter to the wishes of the more cautious Gillmore. Regardless, Seymour pushed deep into the Florida interior, occupying towns, freeing slaves, burning Confederate camps, and torching supply caches. Not until the 20th, however, did he encounter a large enemy force. Late that morning he approached Olustee, a depot on the Florida, Atlantic & Gulf Railroad, almost 50 mi southwest of Jacksonville. Awaiting him were some 5,000 Confederates, mostly infantry, plus a small mounted force and 12 cannon, under Brig. Gen. JOSEPH FINEGAN, commander of the District of East Florida.

Finegan had placed his troops behind breastworks but, impatient with the enemy's wary approach, pushed 1 of his 2 infantry brigades, Brig. Gen. ALFRED H. COLQUITT's, a mile to the east. Colquitt met the advance contingent of Seymour's 5,500 effectives on open, pine-bordered ground along the railroad and southeast of a large lake known as Ocean Pond. The Union leader quickly took the initiative by sending his advance brigade, under Col. Joseph R. Hawley, to capture artillery in Colquitt's center. The effort was soundly repulsed. Falling prey to an enfilading fire, 2 of Hawley's regiments, the 7th New Hampshire and 8th U.S. Colored Troops, were cut up so badly that they fled to the rear in confusion, resulting in the capture of 2 cannon from a battery of Regular artillery.

After hours of fighting, Colquitt's troops, now reinforced by the bulk of Col. George P. Harrison's brigade, ran low on ammunition. However, when Seymour sought to exploit this opportunity by sending up Col. William Barton's brigade, two Confederate regiments, their cartridge boxes replenished, laced Barton's right and captured 3 more cannon.

Finegan's last reserves came up soon afterward, forcing the entire Union line to give way. By dusk Seymour had left Olustee in full retreat, having lost more than 1,860 casualties (34% of his force) compared to 946 troops of Finegan's. Through the apparent timidity of the Confederate leader and the incompetence of his cavalry chief, a pursuit was bungled; the vanquished invaders were permitted to reach Jacksonville on the 23d. Most soon returned to Gillmore's headquarters, ending the only large campaign waged in Florida.   —EGL

O'Neal, Edward Asbury. CSA b. Madison Cty., Alabama Territory, 20 Sept. 1818, O'Neal received a local secondary education and graduated from LaGrange College in 1836. In 1840, he began practicing law in Florence, Ala., became active in local politics and the secession movement, and lost a bid for a U.S. congressional seat in 1848. At the outbreak of the Civil War he joined the 9th Alabama Infantry, was elected major, then lieutenant colonel.

In 1862 O'Neal received a commission as colonel of the 26th Alabama Infantry and through 1863 fought in the Virginia theater in the PENINSULA, ANTIETAM, CHANCELLORSVILLE, and GETTYSBURG campaigns. A

LC

member of the II Corps/Army of Northern Virginia, he took

brigade command early in 1863 when Brig. Gen. Robert E. Rodes rose to divisional command. His performance did not recommend him for promotion; on the first day of fighting at Gettysburg he hung back with his old regiment, leaving the others in the brigade floundering. O'Neal's brigadier general's commission, first submitted for Senate confirmation when he assumed command, was delayed. During the delay Gen. Robert E. Lee made Brig. Gen. Cullen A. Battle brigade commander, angering O'Neal, who requested transfer to the Western theater. Though briefly pulled from the field, the 26th returned to Lee early in 1864, only to have Lee return O'Neal's commission unendorsed. Pres. Jefferson Davis canceled the promotion and transferred O'Neal and his regiment to the Atlanta front. After the fall of Atlanta O'Neal was relieved, sent to duty with the Conscription Bureau in Alabama, and served out the war there.

O'Neal resumed his legal and political activity during the Reconstruction period, was elected governor of Alabama in 1882 and 1884, then retired to Florence, Ala., dying there 7 Nov. 1890. —JES

Onondaga, USS. A double-turreted iron monitor, the *Onondaga* was built by George W. Quintard for the U.S. government in 1863. It was launched at Green Point, N.Y., 29 July 1863 and commissioned at the New York Navy Yard 24 Mar. 1864. The *Onondaga* weighed 1,250 tons and had a draft of 12 ft 10 in. and an average speed of 6 knots. Its battery consisted of 2 25-in. Dahlgren smoothbores and 2 15-pounder Parrott guns.

Beginning May 1864 the *Onondaga* participated in action against Confederate ironclads and shore batteries on the James River. On 29 Nov. 1864, Cmdr. William A. Parker engaged the monitor against Howlett's Battery for 3 hours. Then, 23 Jan. 1865, 2 Confederate ironclads—*Virginia No. 2* and *Richmond* —ran aground at Trent's Reach. The next morning Parker arrived on the *Onondaga* and joined in the shelling of the stranded ironclads. Nevertheless, both vessels were able to refloat and withdraw to safety. Secretary of the Navy GIDEON WELLES's displeasure with Parker cost him his command, and he was replaced by Lt. Commander Homer C. Blake.

After the evacuation of Richmond, sailors from the *Onondaga* participated in the seizure of Confederate naval property there. At war's end a broken propeller had so disabled the ship that it had to be towed to the New York Navy Yard. It was decommissioned there 8 June 1865. Returned to its builder at purchase price in 1867, the *Onondaga* was sold to the French navy and served the French as a coast defense battleship until 1903. —NCD

Opdycke, Emerson. USA b. Trumbull Cty., Ohio, 7 Jan. 1830. A descendant of soldiers in the Revolution and the War of 1812, Opdycke was raised in Williams Cty., Ohio, returning to his native region as a teenager. In the late 1840s he migrated to California and prospected for gold, then returned to Trumbull County, where he joined a mercantile firm.

Enlisting soon after the shelling of FORT SUMTER, Opdycke was commissioned a lieutenant in the 41st Ohio Infantry 26 Aug. 1861. From the first he displayed a fitness for high command; as one historian has remarked, he "proved to be one of those rare volunteer officers plucked from civilian life who

LC

worked at his new profession." By Jan. 1862 he was leading a company of the 41st. At SHILOH, 7 Apr., he won notice by grabbing the colors after the standard-bearer fell and carrying them to the head of his charging regiment. The movement spearheaded a counterattack by WILLIAM B. HAZEN's brigade, which captured a Confederate battery and broke its infantry support.

That September Opdycke resigned his commission to accept the lieutenant colonelcy of a new outfit, the 125th Ohio, which he whipped into excellent fighting shape. As colonel he led the regiment at CHICKAMAUGA, where it stubbornly held its

USMHI

part of the line along the Union right. That November the 125th and another Ohio regiment under Opdycke's command led the way up the slopes of MISSIONARY RIDGE, driving entrenched Confederates from the summit.

Opdycke also played a leading part in the ATLANTA CAMPAIGN of 1864. That May he was badly wounded at RESACA but recuperated to head a IV Corps brigade at KENNESAW MOUNTAIN, 27 June. 5 months later, at FRANKLIN, he rushed his command into a gap in Maj. Gen. JOHN M. SCHOFIELD's line at a critical juncture. His men then repulsed parts of 2 enemy divisions, a feat that brought him the brevet of major general of volunteers. Not till July 1865, however, did he attain a full-grade brigadier generalship.

In postwar years, Opdycke resided in New York City, worked in the dry-goods business, and wrote extensively on the conflict. d. New York City, 22 Apr. 1884, following a pistol-cleaning accident.   —EGL

Opequon Creek, Va., Battle of. 19 Sept. 1864 *See* WINCHESTER, VA., THIRD BATTLE OF.

Orange & Alexandria Railroad. More than a dozen railroads crisscrossed Virginia in 1861, with few more important to the fledgling Confederacy than the Orange & Alexandria. This 4 ft-8.5 in.-gauge track stretched for 170 mi from Alexandria on the Potomac River, through the Virginia Piedmont, to Lynchburg on the upper reaches of the James River. Nearly 70 mi south of Alexandria, at Gordonsville, the railroad intersected with the Virginia Central Railroad, whose iron rails connected Richmond with Staunton in the fertile SHENANDOAH VALLEY. From Gordonsville to Charlottesville trains of the Orange & Alexandria utilized the track of the Virginia Central. Beyond Charlottesville the rails were the property of the Orange & Alexandria to its terminus at Lynchburg, where it, the Virginia & Tennessee, and the Southside railroads converged.

The single-track Orange & Alexandria line figured prominently in most major campaigns in Virginia. From the outset the Orange & Alexandria–Virginia Central connection was vital to Confederate operations in northern and central Virginia. From First Bull Run to the war's final weeks, the two railroads affected the strategies of both North and South, and the tracks of the Orange & Alexandria eventually served both Union and Confederate armies. During the Second Bull Run Campaign, in the operations in fall 1862, fall 1863, and winter 1864, Union armies relied upon the railroad to supply them in their positions along the Rappahannock River. Using locomotives of the U.S. Military Railroads, the Federals supplied the troops' gargantuan needs. The Union's railroading genius, Brig. Gen. HERMAN HAUPT, subsequently asserted that the railroad, "under intelligent management," could supply an army of 200,000.

For the Confederates, the Orange & Alexandria never approached Haupt's assessment. By spring 1862 the demands of the Southern forces and the lack of rails, ties, and parts clogged the line into near-rigidity. A train trip between Gordonsville and Manassas Junction, 51 mi, took 36 hours. Gen. Joseph E. Johnston described the line's management as "wretched." But Confederate authorities, throughout the conflict, wrestled to keep the railroad operating. In June 1864 hissing engines and ragged cars carried the II Corps/Army of Northern Virginia, to Lynchburg to save that threatened vital junction, and by war's end trains still shuttled on the Orange & Alexandria.   —JDW

Orchard, the, Va., eng. at. 25 June 1862 *See* OAK GROVE, VA., ENG. AT.

Orchard Knob, Tenn., Battle of. 23 Nov. 1863 Maj. Gen. U. S. Grant, before his planned offensive on Confederate Gen. Braxton Bragg's lines overlooking Chattanooga, asked that elements of Maj. Gen. George H. Thomas' Army of the Cumberland probe the enemy center. Through late morning, 23 Nov., Brig. Gen. Philip H. Sheridan's and Thomas J. Wood's divisions of Maj. Gen. Gordon Granger's IV Corps assembled in full uniform along the center of the Union lines and gave the impression of preparing for a formal review of troops. It was a ruse. Without artillery support they were to make a reconnaissance in force on Orchard Knob, a 100-ft high, lightly wooded foothill of the Missionary Ridge range occupied by Bragg's troops. The Confederates' forward position, it sat a mile in front of the Union center, midway between the main Federal and Southern lines.

At about 12:30 p.m., the 2 divisions marched out of their lines to the open plain in front and assembled in formal fashion. Grant, Thomas, Granger, Maj. Gens. Joseph Hooker and Oliver O. Howard, and Asst. Sec. of War Charles A. Dana all watched from Fort Wood in the divisions' rear. Brig. Gen. Richard W. Johnson's troops guarded the divisions' left flank; Brig. Gen. Absalom Baird's XIV Corps division guarded their right. Southerners on Orchard Knob and Missionary Ridge left their rifle pit and tents to watch what witnesses called "a military pageant." For an hour Sheridan's and Wood's men marched back and forth, unmolested, positioning themselves for their push while appearing to be drilling.

At 1:30 a signal cannon fired in Fort Wood and they rushed forward, elements of Wood's troops in the lead. Confederates on the knob rushed back to their defenses; pickets in a belt of timber west of the hill were driven out. Within the hour each succeeding Southern line fell back on the next, Federals drove into hilltop ramparts, surviving Confederates ran for the lines on Missionary Ridge, and the Union flag was planted at the crest of the knob. Surprised at the success of the probe, Thomas signaled Wood, "You have gained too much to withdraw. Hold your position and I will support you." Blair's division and Howard's XI Corps troops moved to the attackers' left and right, secured the front, and the entire Federal army moved its lines forward. This was the easiest Union victory in the battles for CHATTANOOGA.

This unexpected success changed Grant's plans. His objective at Chattanooga was to turn Bragg's right, the north end of Missionary Ridge. Maj. Gen. William T. Sherman's troops were maneuvering to assault this position the next day. Meanwhile, Hooker's force was to make a demonstration on Bragg's left at LOOKOUT MOUNTAIN. Because of their surprise victory at Orchard Knob, Grant and Thomas instructed Hooker to press ahead at Lookout if his demonstration proved successful.

Reliable casualty figures for Federals and Confederates in the Orchard Knob fighting are not available; reports and estimates vary. Both armies added these casualties to their aggregates for the fighting 23, 24, and 25 Nov. Union troops did take approximately 200 prisoners 23 Nov.   —JES

Ord, Edward Otho Cresap. USA b. Cumberland, Md., 18 Oct. 1818. Shortly after Ord's birth, his family moved to Washington, D.C. He secured an appointment to the U.S. Military Academy at West Point, graduating 17th in his class

in 1839. During the Mexican
War, he served mainly in California, but his most notable prewar service was his participation in the expedition that led to
the capture of JOHN BROWN at
HARPERS FERRY, Va., in 1859.

USMHI

At the outbreak of the Civil
War Ord was appointed a brigadier general of volunteers as of
14 Sept. 1861 and assigned to
the command of a brigade in the
defenses of Washington. On 20
Dec. he fought a successful engagement against Confederate
forces at Dranesville, Va. Promoted to major general as of 2
May 1862, he participated in the Battles of Iuka and Corinth
in September and October and was severely wounded while
pursuing Confederate forces retreating from Corinth. Returning
to duty during the Siege of Vicksburg, he commanded the XIII
Corps after the relief of Maj. Gen. John A. McClernand and led
the corps during the Siege of Jackson, Miss., July 1863.

Commanding the XVIII Corps during the operations against
Richmond, he was again severely wounded during the assault
and capture of Fort Harrison, 29 Sept. 1864. Given command
of the ARMY OF THE JAMES and the DEPARTMENT OF NORTH CARO-
LINA as of 8 Jan. 1865, he assisted in the final destruction of
Gen. Robert E. Lee's Army of Northern Virginia and was present at Lee's surrender at Appomattox 9 Apr.

Ord, a favorite of Ulysses S. Grant, proved himself to be an
aggressive corps and army commander during the war. His
tactical abilities, however, were not outstanding. He remained
in the Regular Army and was promoted to brigadier general as
of 26 July 1866. d. Havana, Cuba, 22 July 1883.   —DLW

order of battle.   This term has 2 distinct meanings in mod-
ern-day military parlance, only one of which was common
usage during the Civil War. Today it is defined as 1) a particular
disposition of troops and other military resources in preparation for combat and 2) a tabular compilation of units, displaying information such as organization, commanding officers,
and casualty figures. During the 1860s, however, only the first
definition was operative, the term *table of organization* being
used to cover the second.   —EGL

Oregon.   On 4 occasions after Oregon was organized as a
territory in 1848, its voters were asked to decide whether the
territory should petition Congress for statehood. 3 times the
answer was no; the fourth time, in 1857, voters overwhelmingly decided in favor of drafting and submitting a state constitution. Congress did not act favorably on Oregon's petition
until Feb. 1859, but by that time a provisional state government had been in place for more than a year and Oregon's
Democratic legislature had chosen a congressman and 2 U.S.
senators, all 3 staunch supporters of slavery.

When they voted for statehood, Oregonians also voted
strongly against slavery and even more strongly against admitting free blacks to the state. In 1860 Oregon's Sen. Joseph Lane
sought the Democratic presidential nomination. When that
plum fell to Stephen A. Douglas, Lane accepted a bid to become John C. Breckinridge's running mate on the Charleston
Democratic ticket. When the ballots were counted, Lincoln

and Douglas together had nearly twice as many votes in Oregon as Breckinridge and Lane.

Edward D. Baker, a friend of Lincoln in Illinois, joined the
gold rush to California and came to Oregon in 1859 to campaign for Republicans. A brilliant orator, Baker so impressed
Oregonians with his strong antislavery views that they elected
him to fill a vacant U.S. Senate seat in 1860. Baker's career in
Washington was brilliant but brief. Retiring from the Senate to
lead a regiment of Union volunteers, he was shot and killed
while leading a charge at BALL'S BLUFF, Va., Oct. 1861.

At home, loyal Oregonians volunteered to protect the frontier from marauding Indians and to strengthen army posts
weakened by the departure of Regular troops. Some secessionist sentiment persisted throughout the war, but the coalescence
of Republicans and Douglas Democrats into the Union party
and the vigilance of Oregon's volunteer soldiers prevented
Southern sympathizers from taking any overt action to advance their cause in the state.   —BMcG

Oregon, Union Department of.   *See* PACIFIC, UNION DE-
PARTMENT OF THE.

***Oreto,* CSS.**   *See* FLORIDA, CSS.

Orme, William Ward.   USA   b. District of Columbia, 17
Feb. 1832. After graduation from Mount St. Mary's College in
Maryland, Orme moved to Chicago, then to Bloomington, Ill.,
where he was admitted to the
bar and became a law partner
of Leonard Swet, gaining the
respect of future president
Abraham Lincoln. He attended
the 1861 Illinois constitutional
convention, then answered the
call to fight; on 20 Aug. 1862 he
joined the 94th Illinois Infantry
as its colonel.

Orme joined the army just in
time to command a brigade in
the costly Dec. 1862 battle at
PRAIRIE GROVE, Ark. There he
took part in Brig. Gen. Francis J.
Herron's exhaustive race against

LC

the troops of Maj. Gen. Thomas C. Hindman and was victorious
in the thickest of the fighting. For his performance in this battle
he was promoted to brigadier general to rank from 19 Nov.

In 1863 Orme joined Herron again in Maj. Gen. Ulysses S.
Grant's Siege of Vicksburg 11 June; contracting tuberculosis,
he was forced to retire from the battlefield, becoming a Union
prison inspector in the Northern states. By December he had
settled in Chicago as the supervisor of the Camp Douglas
prison, but his health forced him to resign from the army Apr.
1864 and accept an appointment from his friend Lincoln to the
U.S. Treasury Department as a supervising special agent.

As Orme's health declined steadily he resigned the Treasury
post Nov. 1865 to live his last days at his home in Bloomington, where he died 13 Sept. 1866.   —FLS

"Orphan Brigade."   CSA   In a war of unusual military
commands, the 1st Kentucky ("Orphan") Brigade was one of
the most distinctive. The Confederate unit's roots lay in Kentucky, which remained a Union state throughout the war.

Since the regiments composing it were not recognized by their own state, in summer and fall 1861 they had to train and organize in Tennessee.

When the Confederate army was forced out of Kentucky, Feb. 1862, the 1st Kentucky Brigade went with it, never to return to its native soil during the war. Its exile made the later nickname "Orphan Brigade" appropriate. The unit fought at Shiloh, Corinth, Vicksburg, Baton Rouge, Stone's River, Jackson, Chickamauga, Missionary Ridge, and all through the Atlanta Campaign, and opposed Sherman's March to the Sea. Cut off from Kentucky, and unable to recruit its depleted ranks, it finished the war with only about 500 of the 4,000 original members of the unit. Yet it covered itself in glory repeatedly with the Army of Tennessee, most often being given the dangerous assignment as rear guard after a battle. Desertions were few and enthusiasm high. Commanded first by Brig. Gen. SIMON B. BUCKNER, then by former U.S. vice-president JOHN C. BRECKINRIDGE, the Orphans lost 2 of their generals in battle: ROGER W. HANSON died at Stone's River and BEN HARDIN HELM, Lincoln's brother-in-law, was killed at Chickamauga.

The brigade was mounted as cavalry in the final months of the war under its last commander, Brig. Gen. JOSEPH H. LEWIS, and surrendered at Washington, Ga., in the first week of May 1865, one of the last Confederate units in the East to lay down its arms. Gens. Joseph E. Johnston, John B. Hood, and others repeatedly declared that this was the best brigade in their army.   —WCD

Orr, James Lawrence. CSP/CSA b. Craytonville, S.C., 12 May 1822, Orr attended local schools and clerked in his father's store before entering the University of Virginia in 1839 as a law student. He completed

his studies with a South Carolina attorney and passed his bar examinations at age 21. For the next 2 years he edited the Anderson, S.C., *Gazette,* but abandoned journalism for successful careers in law and politics. He was first elected to the state legislature, 1844–48, promoting public-school reform, internal improvements, and the popular election of presidential electors. During his 11 years as a Democratic U.S. congressman, 1848–59, he tried to temper radical secessionists in his state, though he himself believed in the right of secession.

LC

His support of STEPHEN A. DOUGLAS and his opposition to the Know Nothing (American) party contributed to his popularity in the North. His colleagues in the 35th Congress elected him Speaker of the House in 1857. As president of the 1860 state secession convention, Orr assumed a pro-Union stance, but, a shrewd political opportunist, he conformed to the feelings of the majority in his state and became an ardent secessionist. After signing the ordinance of secession, he, along with 2 other commissioners, traveled to Washington to negotiate (unsuccessfully) state take-over of the forts at Charleston.

On his return to Charleston, he organized Orr's Rifles, serving briefly with the army. More in keeping with his abilities, he was then elected to the 2 Regular CONFEDERATE CONGRESSES. Initially he displayed liberal tolerance for Pres. Jefferson Davis' broad assumption of war powers but soon reverted to the hard-line states-rights position favored by his constituents. Certain the Confederacy could not win the war, he urged Davis to prepare for Reconstruction. By 1864, he belonged to the faction advocating negotiated peace to achieve independence.

On Confederate defeat, Orr participated in the South Carolina constitutional convention and was elected governor. Ever the pragmatist, he promoted a compromise policy, recommending moderation of the BLACK CODES and limited black franchise. However, when U.S. congressional Radicals pressed a punitive Reconstruction, Orr urged the state legislature not to pass the 14TH AMENDMENT. Public confidence in him waned when he again began to cooperate with military authorities in an effort to mitigate some of the harsh Reconstruction policies. He finally joined the Republicans, who rewarded him with an appointment on the circuit bench, 1868–70, and the U.S. ministry to Russia in 1873.

Orr died of pneumonia in St. Petersburg, Russia, 5 May 1873. An amicable man, he had been well liked during his career, even by political opponents. Though not a dynamic politician, he had one ability most of his fellow Southerners lacked: he could read Northern public opinion and knew when to accommodate it.   —PLF

Osage, USS. In Apr. 1862 the Union called on experienced shipbuilder James B. Eads for IRONCLADS with draft light enough to enable them to go up the nation's rivers. He responded with drawings for a vessel featuring a rotating turret, 2 11-in. guns, and a deck covered with iron that rose from 6 in. at water's edge to 4 ft in the center. The plating extended 2.5 ft under water.

First of these ironclads was the 523-ton *Osage,* built at St. Louis, Mo., for $119,678.37 and launched 11 Jan. 1863. On 23 Apr. it was ordered to Cape Girardeau, then to Cairo, Ill. Before the month was over it had grounded on a bar in the Mississippi River and was returned to Cairo for repairs. In July it was ordered to the Mississippi Squadron. Going up the river above Memphis, the *Osage* failed to answer its helm and was driven by the current into a tree protruding from the bank. Several days passed before the damage was repaired.

On 27 Feb. 1864, the vessel left the Mississippi to take part in the RED RIVER CAMPAIGN, an expedition to control Louisiana and eastern Texas. Its turret wheel broke the following month, but it was quickly repaired, and the ship was able to participate in the entire enterprise, becoming one of the first vessels to get up the Red despite the river's unseasonably low water level. On the way back down, however, the ironclad once more ran aground. Confederate bullets peppered it and wounded 7 crew members before the ship could get away.

On 1 Feb. 1865, armed with another gun, a 12-pounder rifle, it was ordered to New Orleans to take part in the West Gulf Squadron's operations around Mobile Bay. Some of the worst destruction at the war's conclusion occurred in this area. On 29 Mar., while moving up the Blakely River in Alabama, the *Osage* struck a torpedo and was sunk, with 2 killed and 10 wounded. The ironclad's career still had not ended. In 1867 it was raised and sold at auction for $20,467.10 in New Orleans, along with the *Calhoun, Nashville,* and *Tennessee.*

—VCJ

Osterhaus, Peter Joseph. USA b. Coblenz, Prussia, 4 Jan. 1823. Of the 3 German-born Americans to achieve general rank in the Union army, Osterhaus stood out as the best military commander and the one best accepted by his native-born comrades. He attended military school in Berlin and served as a volunteer in the 29th Infantry Regiment of the Prussian army before his involvement in the revolutions of 1848 forced his emigration to the U.S. Between his arrival in 1849 and the outbreak of civil war, he engaged in business in Belleville and Lebanon, Ill., and in St. Louis, Mo., successively.

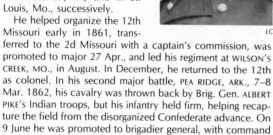

LC

He helped organize the 12th Missouri early in 1861, transferred to the 2d Missouri with a captain's commission, was promoted to major 27 Apr., and led his regiment at WILSON'S CREEK, MO., in August. In December, he returned to the 12th as colonel. In his second major battle, PEA RIDGE, ARK., 7–8 Mar. 1862, his cavalry was thrown back by Brig. Gen. ALBERT PIKE's Indian troops, but his infantry held firm, helping recapture the field from the disorganized Confederate advance. On 9 June he was promoted to brigadier general, with command of the 1st Division in Maj. Gen. Samuel Curtis' ARMY OF THE SOUTHWEST.

His division was ordered to support Maj. Gen. Ulysses S. Grant in 1863 during the Vicksburg Campaign by keeping supplies from reaching Confederates in the city. In the fighting at CHAMPION'S HILL, MISS., 16 May, his troops skirmished with Confederate pickets in the opening hours of battle. The next day, Osterhaus fell wounded by a shell fragment in the BIG BLACK RIVER engagement. At Chattanooga in November he led the advance from Lookout Mountain to attack MISSIONARY RIDGE, and in the hard fighting drove the southern wing of the Confederate line from the crest.

Assigned to Maj. Gen. William T. Sherman for the Atlanta Campaign, Osterhaus fought prominently in temporary command of the XV Corps and was advanced to major general 23 July 1864, over the objections of Sherman, who accused Osterhaus of absenting himself to lobby for promotion. He nonetheless remained with Sherman on the march through the Carolinas before being transferred west. It was to Osterhaus that Lt. Gen. SIMON B. BUCKNER surrendered Gen. E. Kirby Smith's Trans-Mississippi command 26 May. From then until being mustered out Jan. 1866, Osterhaus held departmental commands in the West.

Within a few months of his discharge, he received an appointment as U.S. consul to France, a post he kept for 11 years. Returning to the U.S., Osterhaus opened a hardware factory and export business. In Mar. 1898 he again accepted a diplomatic post as U.S. deputy consul at Mannheim, Germany. He resigned Nov. 1900 to spend his last years with his family.

On 3 Mar. 1905, in recognition of his long service to the U.S., Congress passed a special act appointing Osterhaus brigadier general in the Regular Army. He was placed on the retired list a few days later. Osterhaus died 2 Jan. 1917, in Duisburg, Germany, and was buried at Coblenz.   —PLF

O'Sullivan, Timothy. photographer b. Ireland, 1840. Records of the specifics of Timothy O'Sullivan's personal life are lost, among them the exact place and date of his birth. He immigrated to the U.S. with his parents at age 2 and grew up on Staten Island, N.Y. A letter of reference filed by MATHEW BRADY in 1880, supporting O'Sullivan's application for employment as official photographer for the U.S. Treasury Department, shows that the photographic entrepreneur had known O'Sullivan as a boy. O'Sullivan biographer James D. Horan believes that he may have learned photography from Brady at an early age. By the mid-1850s he was working in Brady's New York City gallery. He joined immigrant photographer ALEXANDER GARDNER at Brady's Washington, D.C., gallery about 1858, working under his direction.

With Gardner, O'Sullivan proved to be one of Brady's ablest field photographers during the Civil War. For a time attached to Brig. Gen. Egbert L. Viele's topographical engineers copying charts and maps, he carried a purely honorary rank of 1st

U.S.S. Osage

USMHI

lieutenant and never entered U.S. service. In Nov. and Dec. 1861 and Mar. and Apr. 1862 he photographed Union naval and army operations along the South Carolina coast, recording Forts Beauregard and Walker, Port Royal Island, Beaufort, and Hilton Head. Then, operating out of Washington, he photographed the old Bull Run battlefield and sites of the Antietam and Fredericksburg campaigns.

At about this time Gardner established his own studio and O'Sullivan left Brady's employ to join him. Under Brady he had received no personal credit for his work. Gardner followed a policy of crediting his operatives and made O'Sullivan his chief of field operations. Subsequently, O'Sullivan photographed Union army life before the Chancellorsville Campaign, shocking scenes of Gettysburg battlefield carnage, the aftermath of Spotsylvania and the Wilderness, and the Petersburg siege. He briefly followed Maj. Gen. Philip H. Sheridan's troops to the fight at Yellow Tavern, Va., and Jan. 1865 joined the Union expeditionary force that reduced Fort Fisher, N.C. Returning to Petersburg, he followed Union forces into Richmond when the city fell, and photographed the burned and conquered Confederate capital.

In postwar years O'Sullivan continued field photography, accompanying 3 expeditions to the Far West under Clarence King and John Montague Wheeler and an exploration of the Panamanian Isthmus of Darien under U.S. Navy Lt. Cmdr. THOMAS O. SELFRIDGE. The subject of a photograph long thought to show O'Sullivan at his camera in a Panamanian village has recently been identified as another photographer on the expedition; only 2 Civil War–era portraits of O'Sullivan are known to exist. O'Sullivan returned to New York in 1875. Suffering from tuberculosis, he worked intermittently, won appointment as official photographer for the U.S. Treasury Department 6 Nov. 1880, then declined rapidly in health. He died at his father's Staten Island home 14 Jan. 1882 and was buried in an unmarked grave in the island's St. Peter's Cemetery.

O'Sullivan's photographic work is scattered among the following repositories: the American Geographic Society, the Boston Public Library, the Bancroft Library of California, the Art Institute of Chicago, Harvard University, the George Eastman House, the Museum of New Mexico, the New Orleans Museum of Art, the New York Historical Society, Princeton University, UCLA, the National Gallery of Canada, the Library of Congress, and the National Archives. —JES

Overland Campaign. 4 May–12 June 1864 On 4 May 1864, Union Maj. Gen. GEORGE G. MEADE'S ARMY OF THE POTOMAC, 120,000 strong, crossed the Rapidan River into familiar territory, the war-scarred region between Fredericksburg and Richmond, Va. South of the river, waiting, was Gen. ROBERT E. LEE'S ARMY OF NORTHERN VIRGINIA, numbering slightly over 60,-000 effectives. From then until 12 June, for 40 days, without respite, the armies bled each other in some of the most savage combat of the Civil War. The Overland Campaign became a consuming, relentless war of attrition as Lt. Gen. ULYSSES S. GRANT, directing Federal operations, indicated when he proposed "to fight it out on this line if it takes all summer."

The initial clash of this classic confrontation between Grant and Lee occurred in the WILDERNESS, 5–7 May. When the Federals crossed the Rapidan, Lee reacted swiftly, catching his opponent in a landscape of vines, brambles, scrub oak, and pine trees. The terrain negated Grant's superior numbers, and in blinding, fearful fighting the Confederates inflicted more than twice as many casualties as they suffered. But, during the night of 7–8 May, Grant, instead of retreating, marched his veterans southward around Lee's right toward Spotsylvania Court House. With this crossroads village in Federal hands, RICHMOND would be threatened. Learning of Grant's march, Lee dispatched to the village Maj. Gen. RICHARD H. ANDERSON'S corps. On the 8th the Southerners won the race, bringing the Northerners to battle again.

The SPOTSYLVANIA COURT HOUSE CAMPAIGN lasted nearly 2 weeks. The tactical pattern of the Overland Campaign emerged as Grant sidled leftward and Lee, utilizing interior lines, parried each thrust. A new pattern of warfare also emerged as Lee's veterans constructed fieldworks that were more extensive and formidable than ever before seen. Twice, on the 10th and 12th, Grant launched major attacks on the entrenchments. On the latter date, the Federals crushed a SALIENT, only to be stopped by Confederate counterattacks. For 20 hours the opponents engaged in the war's most vicious fighting, around the "BLOODY ANGLE."

While at Spotsylvania, Grant sent his cavalry, under Maj. Gen. PHILIP H. SHERIDAN, on a raid toward Richmond. On 11 May Sheridan's troopers clashed with Maj. Gen. J.E.B. STUART'S horsemen at YELLOW TAVERN. In the action, the irreplaceable Stuart was mortally wounded.

10 days later Grant abandoned his lines at Spotsylvania, attempting to move once more southeastward beyond Lee's right. Lee countered and, on the 23d, intercepted the Federal movement along the NORTH ANNA RIVER. Stalemated, Grant resumed his sidling movement 26 May, heading toward the peninsula. Operating on interior lines, Lee barred Grant's route again at COLD HARBOR. The Confederates once more erected fieldworks, creating one of the strongest positions they ever defended. The Union commander, frustrated by Lee's brilliant countermoves, unwisely ordered a frontal attack against the Southern lines 3 June. The Confederates erased Grant's attack in 30 minutes, inflicting nearly 7,000 casualties.

This defeat ended the major fighting of the campaign. Sheridan undertook a second raid 7 June, this time against the Virginia Central Railroad and the James River Canal. Maj. Gen. WADE HAMPTON, Stuart's successor, intercepted Sheridan at TREVILIAN STATION, where the Confederates defeated the Federals 11–12 June. But, as Sheridan and Hampton battled, Grant started his army toward the James River and PETERSBURG, and a siege that would doom the Confederates.

Grant failed in the Overland Campaign either to destroy Lee's army or capture his capital. Grant's casualties averaged 2,000 daily, but unlike any previous Union commander, he had limited the offensive prowess of his opponent. With the Overland Campaign, the Army of the Potomac would never retreat again. —JDW

Overland Vicksburg Campaign. See VICKSBURG CAMPAIGN, FIRST.

Ox Hill, Va., Battle of. 1 Sept. 1862 See CHANTILLY, VA., BATTLE OF.

P

Pacific, Union Department of the.   Prior to the Civil War, West Coast military responsibilities were divided between the Departments of California and Oregon. The Department of California, its headquarters in San Francisco, encompassed the present state and southwest Oregon, and retained military authority over eastern New Mexico Territory, today Arizona. The Department of Oregon, its headquarters at Vancouver, Washington Territory, held responsibility for Oregon and what later became Washington and Idaho. On 1 Jan. 1861 these departments were combined to form the Department of the Pacific, with headquarters in Los Angeles and Brig. Gen. ALBERT SIDNEY JOHNSTON commander.

Johnston resigned his commission in April and left Los Angeles to join the Confederacy. Col. EDWIN V. SUMNER assumed command 25 Apr. until relieved by Col. GEORGE WRIGHT 30 Oct. On 27 July Utah and all but the southernmost portion of Nevada were added to the department; on 9 Nov. eastern New Mexico Territory became the responsibility of the Department of New Mexico, an organization previously responsible for what is today southern Colorado and the state of New Mexico.

On 1 July 1864, Maj. Gen. IRVIN MCDOWELL, veteran of Eastern combat, took command, and 20 Jan. 1865, given territorial autonomy, Arizona Territory became his responsibility.

Brig. Gen. JAMES H. CARLETON led a column of volunteers out of southern California in spring 1862 to oppose Confederate Brig. Gen. HENRY H. SIBLEY'S NEW MEXICO CAMPAIGN. No other Confederate threats to the department occurred during the war. Maj. Gen. HENRY W. HALLECK relieved McDowell when the department was dissolved and replaced by the Military Division of the Pacific 27 June 1865. This organization, established in General Orders No. 118 from the Adjutant General's Office, comprised the reconstituted Department of California and the newly formed Department of Columbia, an area encompassing the state of Oregon, and Washington and Idaho territories.

—JES

Pacific, Union Military Division of the.   *See* PACIFIC, UNION DEPARTMENT OF THE.

Paducah, Ky., Battle of.   25 Mar. 1864   In Mar. 1864 Confederate Maj. Gen. NATHAN B. FORREST had 5,000 men in his command at Columbus, Miss. Ordered to make a short campaign in West Tennessee, he took about 2,800 men, among them Brig. Gen. ABRAHAM BUFORD's 2d Division and the 7th Tennessee Cavalry. In addition to striking Federal forces, Forrest wanted to break up guerrilla bands, recover deserters, gain recruits, and allow his men to reoutfit.

While part of his command defeated the garrison at Union City, Tenn., Forrest hastened to Paducah, Ky., which had been

under Union control since Brig. Gen. U. S. Grant occupied it Sept. 1861. He arrived there shortly after noon on 25 Mar. after covering 100 mi in 50 hours. The Confederates quickly seized the town, but Col. Stephen G. Hicks retreated into Fort Anderson, a strong earthwork located in the west end of town. Hicks had 665 men from the 127th Illinois Infantry, 16th Kentucky Cavalry, and 1st Kentucky Heavy Artillery (Colored), the support of 2 gunboats, and determination. He refused to surrender, and his guns raked the streets. Forrest, after horses and supplies, had no intention of assaulting the strong position, but Col. Albert P. Thompson ignored orders and led the 3d and 7th Kentucky regiments in a rash attack that resulted in several casualties, including Thompson, who died within sight of his home.

After burning some cotton and a steamer in drydock, Forrest withdrew, carrying with him 50 prisoners, 400 horses and mules, and a considerable quantity of supplies. At Mayfield most of the Kentucky and Tennessee troops were furloughed until 3 Apr., when they were to report at Trenton. Forrest reported his casualties as 25; with Buford's report the total was raised to 10 killed and 40 wounded. Hicks listed 14 killed and 46 wounded but estimated Confederate losses at 1,500.

Union papers reported that Forrest had stolen mounts belonging to civilians and had missed 140 excellent army horses concealed in a foundry. The news sent Buford back to Paducah, where he arrived about noon 14 Apr. Hicks retreated again into Fort Anderson, and the Confederates rounded up the horses and their equipment, then rode southward to join Forrest.

—LHH

Page, Charles Anderson.   journalist b. Lee Cty., Ill., 1838, Page spent the late 1850s as a reporter and editor for the Mt. Vernon, Ill., *News* and as a tireless Republican partisan. He traveled to Washington, D.C., in 1861 for Abraham Lincoln's presidential inauguration, won a patronage appointment as a clerk in the Auditor's Office of the U.S. Treasury Department, and worked in the capital until hired as a reporter by ADAMS SHERMAN HILL of the New York *Tribune* in spring 1862. Page won a leave of absence from his clerkship, and 27 June 1862 reported the Battle of GAINES' MILL, Va.

Page's first stories earned him the notice of *Tribune* publisher HORACE GREELEY and the privilege of a byline, rare at the time. He covered the SEVEN DAYS' CAMPAIGN and the end of the PENINSULA CAMPAIGN, then joined Maj. Gen. John Pope's Army of Virginia for the SECOND BULL RUN CAMPAIGN. When Pope banned reporters from his army, Page became a hospital assistant for the coming Second Battle of Bull Run, then traveled to the *Tribune*'s New York offices following the fight, writing his story in transit. His speedy report of the battle bested the efforts of his rivals, men denied use of the telegraph for reasons of military security and content to wait for the easement of telegraphic censorship.

With the Army of the Potomac for the rest of the war, Page needed to stay close to the *Tribune*'s Washington office. He retained his Treasury post until 1865, fulfilling his duties as war correspondent during frequent leaves of absence. Unable to attain a leave, he missed covering Abraham Lincoln's Gettysburg Address, but in spring 1864 resumed field duties, reporting the BATTLE OF THE WILDERNESS, the Siege of PETERSBURG, and Lincoln's triumphal tour of Richmond, Va.

In 1865, in consideration of his active support of the administration, his Treasury duties, and articles written in 1864 demeaning Democratic presidential candidate George B. McClellan, Pres. Andrew Johnson appointed Page U.S. consul to Switzerland. Later that year he began the Anglo-Swiss Company at Cham, Switzerland, an evaporated-milk business known today as the Nestlé Company. While attending to business concerns, he died in London, England, in 1873.   —JES

Page, Richard Lucien. CSN/CSA b. Clarke Cty., Va., 20 Dec. 1807. Page had behind him 37 years of service in the U.S. Navy when the Civil War began. Becoming a midshipman in 1824, he rose to the rank of commander in 1855 and did sea duty all over the world, serving 3 tours of ordnance duty and 1 as executive officer of the Norfolk Navy Yard. A popular officer during the war, nicknamed "Ramrod" and "Bombast Page," he was gray-haired and wore a gray beard that made him resemble his first cousin ROBERT E. LEE.

When Virginia seceded, he resigned his commission and, as naval aide to the governor of his home state, supervised the construction of fortifications along the James and Nansemond rivers. In June 1861 he was made a commander in the Confederate States Navy and was assigned as ordnance officer at Norfolk. Promoted to captain, he established a naval construction bureau at Charlotte, N.C., early in 1862 and remained on duty there for 2 years.

On 1 Mar. 1864 Page became a brigadier general in the PROVISIONAL ARMY OF THE CONFEDERATE STATES and was assigned to command the outer defenses of Mobile Bay, with headquarters at FORT MORGAN, the principal bastion. When the combined Federal sea-and-land attack was launched early in Aug. 1864, he waged a gallant defense.

Early in the engagement, an old friend, Union naval leader Rear Adm. DAVID G. FARRAGUT, sent him a message under flag of truce: "To prevent the unnecessary sacrifice of human life . . . we demand the unconditional surrender of Fort Morgan." Page replied: "I am prepared to sacrifice life, and will only surrender when I have no means of defense." After 2 weeks of bombardment, however, he was forced to surrender and was held a prisoner of war at FORT DELAWARE until 24 July 1865.

After his release, Page settled in Norfolk as a businessman and 1875–83 was that city's superintendent of schools. He died, age 94, at Blue Ridge Summit, Pa., 9 Aug. 1901, and is buried in Norfolk.   —VCJ

Paine, Charles Jackson. USA b. Boston, Mass., 26 Aug. 1833. Although Paine was a Boston aristocrat, he was a shy, unobtrusive man in both military and public circles. He attended the prestigious Boston Latin School and graduated from Harvard University in 1853. After studying in the law office of lawyer and statesman Rufus Choate he was admitted to the bar 15 Sept. 1856 and opened an office in Boston, where he worked until 1861.

PHCW

From 5 Sept. to 8 Oct. 1861, Paine recruited a company attached to the 22d Massachusetts Infantry, a regiment that traveled to Washington, D.C., and joined the defense forces there for the winter. Paine was commissioned major 16 Jan. 1862 and was mustered out of the regiment in March to join the DEPARTMENT OF THE GULF, where he was promoted to colonel of the 2d Louisiana Volunteers 23 Oct. Under Maj. Gen. NATHANIEL P. BANKS, the following spring Paine and his command fought at PORT HUDSON, La. On 7 Nov. 1863, he was elected commander of his brigade but resigned to join Maj. Gen. BENJAMIN F. BUTLER's staff in the East as a brigadier general as of 4 July 1864.

With Butler he fought at Drewry's Bluff and New Market Heights, Va., and Fort Fisher, N.C., before accepting the command of a black division under Maj. Gen. William T. Sherman in North Carolina until the close of the war. For his war service Paine was brevetted major general 15 Jan. 1865 and mustered out exactly 1 year later.

Postwar he entered the railroad business, playing a prominent role in the management of the Atchison, Topeka, & Santa Fe; the Chicago, Burlington, & Quincy; and the Mexican Central. In 1897 he traveled to Europe as a member of a commission on bimetallism, representing the U.S.

In his spare time, Paine was a yachtsman. His business ventures had treated him well, and he was able to finance several crafts in many America's Cup races until 1893. He pursued his maritime interests into his final years, dying in Weston, Mass., 12 Aug. 1916.   —FLS

Paine, Halbert Eleazer. USA b. Chardon, Ohio, 4 Feb. 1826, Paine received a local education, graduated from Western Reserve College in 1845, briefly worked as a schoolmaster in Mississippi, then returned to Ohio to study law, practicing in Cleveland from 1848. Interested in expanding his opportunities, Paine migrated to Milwaukee, Wis., in 1857. Sharing the political goals of local attorney CARL SCHURZ, he worked as his law partner until the Civil War, when, as its colonel, he mustered in with the 4th Wisconsin Cavalry at Racine, 2 July 1861.

With the 4th Wisconsin, Paine served on railroad guard duty out of Baltimore, Md., until Feb. 1862, when he joined the Federal expedition to capture New Orleans, La. Most of his combat service was in the Department of the Gulf, where he fought at Fort St. Philip, took part in the seizures of New Orleans and Baton Rouge, and under Brig. Gen. THOMAS WILLIAMS went on an expedition against Vicksburg, Miss., and fought in the Battle of BATON ROUGE. From 3 Jan. 1863, he commanded the 2d Brigade/3d Division/XIX Corps, then received promotion to brigadier general 9 Apr. 1863 to rank from 13 Mar. Paine served in operations against PORT HUDSON and took part in Maj. Gen. Nathaniel P. Banks's Bayou Teche maneuvers and the engagement at FORT BISLAND. In the failed 14 June 1863 assault on the PORT HUDSON works, he lost a leg. During convalescence he worked on various army commissions until Confederate Lt. Gen. Jubal A. Early's July 1864 Raid on Washington. Pressed into service, during the crisis the

LC

one-legged brigadier general commanded the infantry lines between Union Forts Stevens and Totten. Shortly afterward he was appointed commander of the District of Illinois, on 13 Mar. 1865 was brevetted major general for past gallantry, then resigned his commission 15 May 1865.

Paine was noted for independent thought and RADICAL REPUBLICAN leanings. He followed Union Maj. Gen. BENJAMIN F. BUTLER's example by refusing to return escaped slaves to their masters during the early months of the war. But he disobeyed Butler's vengeful order to burn Baton Rouge while he directed the Aug. 1862 evacuation of its Union garrison. In postwar years, Paine maintained this independent posture as a moderate member of the Radical Republican wing in Congress. Elected to the House in autumn 1865, he served until 1871, during his last term chairing the Committee on Elections, which was charged with seating members of Congress elected from districts in the occupied South.

Paine practiced law in Washington, D.C., from 1871; at the insistence of Schurz, now secretary of the interior, served as U.S. commissioner of patents 1878–80; then resumed work as an attorney, dying in the capital 14 Apr. 1905. Drawing on his experience as elections committee chairman, he had written *A Treatise on the Law of Elections to Public Office* (1888), long a standard in the field of election law.   —JES

Palmer, Innis Newton.

USA b. Buffalo, N.Y., 30 Mar. 1824. After receiving a common-school education, Palmer entered West Point, graduating 38th of 59 in the class of 1846. He went directly from the classroom to the battlefields of the Mexican War, seeing action at Cerro Gordo, Contreras, Churubusco, and Chapultepec. In the last battle he was wounded and received the brevet of captain for gallantry. After the war, he served in numerous garrisons, most of them on the frontier; by April 1861 he was a major in the 2d U.S. Cavalry.

Early in the Civil War, Palmer was stationed in the defenses of Washington. He then took command of a battalion of Regular

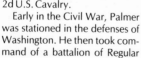

LC

cavalry, which he led at FIRST BULL RUN. In that battle he won the brevet of lieutenant colonel and 23 Sept. 1861 was raised to brigadier general of volunteers. In March of the following year

he was assigned an infantry brigade in the IV Corps/Army of the Potomac, which fought under him on the Virginia peninsula. Though never demonstrating brilliance, Palmer served competently at WILLIAMSBURG, SEVEN PINES, WHITE OAK SWAMP, and MALVERN HILL. Following the Seven Days' Campaign, he forsook field service to help organize volunteer regiments in New Jersey and Delaware and to superintend the draft center in Philadelphia.

From Dec. 1862 until summer 1865, he served in North Carolina. By mid-July 1863 he was in command of the XVIII Corps, and at intervals between Aug. 1863 and Jan. 1864 commanded troops occupying coastal garrisons. Thereafter he headed administrative commands, including the strategic Sub-District of New Berne. Early in Mar. 1865 he returned to the field at the head of a division under Maj. Gen. JACOB D. COX, which near KINSTON helped defeat a Confederate force under Gen. BRAXTON BRAGG and Maj. Gen. ROBERT F. HOKE. This success secured a base of supplies for Maj. Gen. WILLIAM T. SHERMAN during the CAROLINAS CAMPAIGN.

The end of the war found Palmer a brevet major general of volunteers and a brevet brigadier of Regulars. He remained in the army, rising to colonel of the 2d Cavalry June 1868. He left the service at that rank 11 years later and spent an additional 21 years in retirement, dying 9 Sept. 1900 in Chevy Chase, Md.   —EGL

Palmer, John McCauley.

USA b. Scott Cty., Ky., 13 Sept. 1817, Palmer, son of an antislavery family, moved to Alton, Ill., at age 14 and attended Shurtleff College in Upper Alton 1834–36. After holding odd jobs, in 1839 he studied law privately in Carlinville, then became an attorney and Free Soil Democrat, served as a county judge, state senator, organizer of the Illinois Republican party, and in 1859 was a failed Republican candidate for U.S. Congress. A strong antislavery Unionist, he also appreciated some STATES-RIGHTS arguments. Palmer, a delegate to the 1860 Republican national convention and the 1861 WASHINGTON PEACE CONFERENCE,

LC

finally despaired of national compromise and mustered in with the 14th Illinois Infantry as its colonel 25 May 1861.

His political prominence ensured quick promotion when he was sent to duty in Missouri. Commissioned brigadier general 20 Dec. 1861, he was given command of troops at La Mine Crossing, Mo., 28 Dec., took command of Brig. Gen. John Pope's 2d Division in the Army of the Mississippi 23 Feb. 1862, led it in attacks on New Madrid and Island Number 10 in March and April, commanded a brigade during Union Maj. Gen. Henry W. Halleck's advance on Corinth, Miss., and 31 Aug.–29 Sept. led the 1st Division/Army of the Mississippi. Sent to Nashville, Tenn., Palmer joined the XIV Corps/Army of the Cumberland, assumed command of its 2d Division 10 Dec., and, fighting with the left wing, survived the Battle of Stone's River. He received a transfer to command the 2d Division/XXI Corps, 9 Jan. 1863, won promotion to major general 16 Mar. to date from 29 Nov. 1862, led his men at

Chickamauga in September, then took over leadership of the XIV Corps 28 Oct. for the Siege of Chattanooga and the summer 1864 campaign on Atlanta, Ga. During this campaign he refused temporary subordination to Maj. Gen. John M. Schofield, a Regular Army officer whose major general's commission had received Senate confirmation later than Palmer's. A petty squabble, it ended with Palmer's request, granted 7 Aug. 1864, to be relieved and transferred out of combat to command of the Department of Kentucky. He resigned from volunteer service 1 Sept. 1866.

Palmer's postbellum career was distinguished by its political variety. After practicing law in Springfield, Ill., he won election as governor in 1868, took part in states-rights arguments with the Federal government, supported HORACE GREELEY's presidential campaign, then returned to the Democratic party, attending its 1884 national convention and in 1888 serving as its unsuccessful candidate for governor of Illinois. Elected to the U.S. Senate in 1891, he opposed Democratic leader William Jennings Bryan's position on a silver monetary standard and in 1896 ran for U.S. president on the splinter Gold Democrat ticket. His running mate was former Confederate Lt. Gen. SIMON B. BUCKNER, a man he had fought at Chickamauga. At age 80 he returned to his law practice, edited *The Bench and Bar of Illinois,* and wrote *Personal Recollections of John M. Palmer: The Story of an Earnest Life,* published posthumously in 1901. d. Springfield, 25 Sept. 1900. The historically valuable John M. Palmer papers are retained by the Illinois State Historical Library, Springfield.   —JES

Palmer, Joseph Benjamin. CSA b. Rutherford Cty., Tenn., 1 Nov. 1825. Raised by his grandparents, the orphaned Palmer received a local education, studied at Union University in Murfreesboro, and passed the

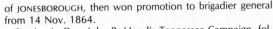

state bar in 1848. Interested in politics, he won election to the state legislature in 1849 and 1851, served as mayor of Murfreesboro 1855–59, and, as the secession crisis approached, urged compromise. With the failure of conciliation, Palmer raised a company for Confederate service with the 18th Tennessee and in spring 1861 was elected regimental colonel.

Palmer and his regiment helped garrison FORT DONELSON, were taken prisoner following its

LC

surrender, then exchanged. Promoted to brigade command without commensurate rank Dec. 1862, he led the 18th, 26th, 28th, 32d, and 45th Tennessee regiments and Moses' Georgia battery at the Battle of Stone's River as the 2d Brigade in Maj. Gen. John C. Breckinridge's 1st Division of Lt. Gen. William J. Hardee's corps. Palmer's men took part in the vicious fighting at the Round Forest, where the colonel received 3 serious wounds.

After lengthy convalescence, he resumed regimental command in Brig. Gen. John C. Brown's brigade in Maj. Gen. Simon B. Buckner's corps in the Confederate left wing at Chickamauga Sept. 1863. Seriously wounded again, he went on recuperative leave until the ATLANTA CAMPAIGN in summer 1864, with unerring bad luck was badly wounded at the Battle

of JONESBOROUGH, then won promotion to brigadier general from 14 Nov. 1864.

Serving in Gen. John B. Hood's Tennessee Campaign, following the Battle of Franklin he commanded a brigade consolidating Brown's and Brig. Gen. Alexander W. Reynolds' troops for detached service in front of Murfreesboro. Following Confederate defeat in the Battle of NASHVILLE, as a part of Maj. Gen. Carter L. Stevenson's division, Palmer's brigade fought in the rear guard during the army's retreat to Alabama. Palmer joined the remnants of the Army of Tennessee for the CAROLINAS CAMPAIGN. Leading a force made up of combined understrength Tennessee regiments, he fought the Battle of BENTONVILLE, then was surrendered at Greensborough, N.C.

In postwar years Palmer did not seek public office, taking an active part in the Southern Historical Society (*see* SOUTHERN HISTORICAL SOCIETY PAPERS) and practicing law in Murfreesboro, where he died 4 Nov. 1890.   —JES

Palmetto Armory. South Carolina prepared for war throughout the decade preceding the firing on FORT SUMTER. In 1850 the state legislature passed a defense act appropriating $300,000 to furnish arms, and an ordnance board was formed to dispense the weapons among South Carolina's 15,000 militiamen. One contract resulting from this legislation, dated 15 Apr. 1851, went to the Palmetto Iron Works at Columbia for the manufacture of 6,000 muskets, 2,000 pistols, 2,000 swords, and 1,000 rifles.

On receipt of this order, one of the owners, William Glaze, converted the works into the Palmetto Armory. Purchasing ordnance-construction equipment from Northern foundries, Glaze and his partners spent 2 years manufacturing weapons based on U.S. Army patterns, including thousands of .69-caliber muskets. These enabled South Carolina to attain a war footing in 1861 more quickly than any other state, North or South. During the Civil War, the armory changed its product line to turn out shells, bullets, and heavy equipment used to manufacture gunpowder. It also repaired and reconditioned small arms and produced some types of cannon—none of which proved satisfactory for field use. In 1865 Federals gutted the armory during the CAROLINAS CAMPAIGN, but the business later reopened.   —EGL

Palmetto State, CSS. An ironclad ram, the *Palmetto State* was built by Cameron & Co. at Charleston, S.C., Jan. 1862. Flag Officer Duncan N. Ingraham initially supervised the construction, and Lt. Alexander F. Warley completed the ram for service. The *Palmetto State* was 150 ft long, had a 14-ft draft, and was armored with 4-in. plates on its shield that were backed by 22 in. of wood. Its other plates were 2 in. thick. The vessel's battery consisted of several 7-in. rifles. Despite a formidable appearance, the ram had a serious defect: lack of power. Its inadequate engine had been taken from a small steamer.

Early on the morning of 3 Jan. 1863 the *Palmetto State,* along with the ram *CHICORA* and 3 tenders, made a surprise attack on the Federal blockading fleet off Charleston. The ship rammed and fired into the *Mercedita,* forcing surrender. Meanwhile, the *Chicora* inflicted such severe damage to the *Keystone State* that it had to be towed to safety by other Federal vessels. The rams withdrew after failing to destroy or disable other blockaders.

The *Palmetto State* played a vital role in the defense of

Charleston until the evacuation of that city 18 Feb. 1865. Then, it and the other ironclads there were destroyed in order to prevent their capture by the Federals. —NCD

Palmito ranch, Tex., eng. at. 12–13 May 1865 Palmito Ranch is a small rise dominating the approach to Brownsville from Brazos Island off the Texas coast. Although Union and Confederate forces in the area, sensing that the war was winding down, had been observing an unofficial truce since Mar. 1865, the situation changed with the arrival at Brazos Island of Union Col. Theodore H. Barrett, an inexperienced and ambitious officer. His coming led to the last engagement of the Civil War, fought 12–13 May 1865.

Disregarding direct orders not to initiate any military action, Barrett struck the Confederates near Brownsville 12 May. His attack force, numbering about 800, included soldiers from the 62d Colored Infantry, the 2d Texas Cavalry (Union), and 2 veteran Indiana and New York regiments. As this force moved to within 12 mi of Brownsville, they encountered at Palmito Ranch, 13 May, the Cavalry of the West, a ragtag force of about 350 determined Confederates commanded by the intrepid former Texas Ranger John S. "Rest in Peace" Ford.

The Confederates fired their 12-pounder guns; then Ford's cavalry charged. Their persistent attacks caused Barrett to order a retreat, and the Confederate horsemen pursued the Federals in their haphazard flight toward Brazos Island. Finally, anticipating the arrival of Federal reinforcements and concerned over the fatigue of his horses, Ford broke off the action.

Although the Confederates themselves had done nothing to precipitate the battle, which was clearly the result of Barrett's provocation, the engagement at Palmito Ranch was their victory. 30 Federals were killed and wounded and another 113 were taken prisoner; some had drowned while attempting to swim to safety. Ford gave his own casualties as only 5 suffering from minor wounds. Although he later insisted that he had treated his black and Texas prisoners well, contradictory reports tell of some of these men being shot while trying to surrender.

13 days after the engagement at Palmito Ranch, Ford, who had learned that the war was over, disbanded his Cavalry of the West in order to avoid a formal surrender. —NCD

panada. A concoction of crumbled hardtack and medicinal whiskey or water, popular in Mexican War field hospitals, panada was given to weak patients. It made its way into the Civil War on veterans' recommendations. MARY ANNE "MOTHER" BICKERDYKE, Union volunteer nurse, was noted for dispensing it in the underequipped facilities in which she worked. —JES

Parke, John Grubb. USA b. Chester Cty., Pa., 22 Sept. 1827. As a young boy Parke moved to Philadelphia with his family, then attended a private academy and the University of Pennsylvania, and entered West Point, graduating 2d in the class of 1849. Until the Civil War, Parke surveyed in Minnesota, New Mexico Territory, California, and Washington Territory as a lieutenant of engineers. He declined the captaincy of the 13th U.S. Infantry 14 May 1861, became captain of engineers 9 Sept., joined Union forces in the East in October, and 23 Nov. 1861 won appointment as brigadier general of volunteers.

Parke served in Brig. Gen. Ambrose E. Burnside's 1862 North Carolina expedition, fought at ROANOKE ISLAND and NEW

BERNE, N.C., Feb. and Mar. 1862, won promotion to major general 18 July, served in minor Virginia operations in summer, then as Burnside's chief of staff saw action at the Battles of SOUTH MOUNTAIN, ANTIETAM, and FREDERICKSBURG. He assumed command of the IX Corps, leading it in Kentucky and during the 1863 Siege of Vicksburg. Under Maj. Gen. William T. Sherman, Parke distinguished himself in the capture of Jackson, Miss., and won a

LC

brevet colonelcy in the Regulars to date from 12 July 1863.

Reassigned to Burnside's staff, with the Army of the Ohio he fought in East Tennessee at the engagement at BLUE SPRINGS and in the Siege of KNOXVILLE, was transferred to Virginia with the IX Corps spring 1864, and again as Burnside's chief of staff fought at the WILDERNESS, Spotsylvania, and in the Siege of Petersburg.

Following Burnside's relief from command, Parke reassumed leadership of the IX Corps, fought at HATCHER'S RUN, coordinated the Union defense of FORT STEDMAN, and took part in the brief APPOMATTOX CAMPAIGN. For gallantry at Knoxville and Fort Stedman, in the omnibus promotions of 13 Mar. 1865 Parke won brevets of brigadier and major general in the Regulars. After stints commanding the Districts of Alexandria and Southern New York he was mustered out of volunteer service 15 Jan. 1866 and resumed surveying duties in the Northwest.

He remained an engineer throughout the postwar years, earning promotion to lieutenant colonel in the Regulars 4 Mar. 1879 and colonel 17 Mar. 1884. From 1887 until his retirement 2 July 1889, Parke served as commandant of West Point, then resided in the District of Columbia, dying there 16 Dec. 1900. —JES

Parker, Ely Samuel. USA b. Genesee Cty., N.Y., 1828. Introduced to Col. Ely S. Parker in the parlor of the McLean house at Appomattox, Gen. Robert E. Lee looked startled, apparently thinking Lt. Gen. Ulysses S. Grant had brought a black to the surrender. But Lee soon realized that Parker was an Indian and said, "I am glad to see one real American here." "We are all Americans," Parker replied. Writing out the terms of surrender for Grant's signature, Parker had reached the height of his military career.

Born a Seneca, educated in 2 cultures, Parker was a trained lawyer, barred from practicing in New York because of his race, and a self-taught engineer who met Grant before the Civil War in Galena, Ill. Eager to join the army, Parker was once rejected for military service because he was an Indian. In 1863, with Grant's support, he was commissioned as a staff officer for another friend from Galena, Brig. Gen. JOHN E. SMITH, and later joined Grant's staff as military secretary. His commission as brigadier general was backdated to the day of Lee's surrender.

After the war Parker continued as Grant's secretary, holding rank in the army. In 1869 President Grant astounded the nation by appointing him commissioner of Indian affairs, a post never before deemed suitable for an Indian. Beset both by corrupt profiteers and overzealous churchmen, Parker was investigated by the House of Representatives. Exonerated, he resigned in sorrow and attempted a career in business, in which he was not successful.

Before his death in Fairfield, Conn., 31 Aug. 1895, Parker sank into poverty and left his widow with no income and few possessions; those few included, however, one of the valuable manifold (carbon) copies of the letter Parker had written at Appomattox.   —JYS

Parker, Joel. war governor b. near Freehold, N.J., 24 Nov. 1816. Son of a New Jersey state treasurer and a librarian, Parker was graduated in 1839 from the College of New Jersey. He studied law, passed the bar in 1842, and established a prosperous practice in his native city. Soon he became active in the Democratic party, was elected to the New Jersey assembly in 1847, and spent a term as a county prosecutor. As a militia officer, he rose to major general by 1861 and gained statewide prominence in the years immediately preceding the Civil War.

In 1860 Parker for a time supported a "fusion" ticket within the Democratic party but at the national convention in Charleston backed STEPHEN A. DOUGLAS for the presidential nomination. The November election of ABRAHAM LINCOLN troubled him, for he saw in it the coming of disunion. Though emphatically opposed to many of the new president's policies, he rallied to Lincoln's support after the Apr. 1861 firing on FORT SUMTER.

As an influential member of the conservative, centrist wing of the New Jersey Democracy, Parker was a dark-horse candidate at the Sept. 1862 gubernatorial convention. He won the nomination on the fourth ballot and that fall, thanks to his dramatic criticism of the Lincoln administration's abuse of civil rights, he defeated Republican Marcus L. Ward by nearly 15,000 votes. In his Jan. 1863 inaugural speech Parker enunciated Democratic orthodoxy, declaring the war a necessity but calling abolitionism "the parent of Secession." He particularly castigated Lincoln's EMANCIPATION PROCLAMATION and his suspension of *HABEAS CORPUS.*

Despite his opposition to the administration, Parker remained a confirmed Unionist, resisting the blandishments of Copperheads (*see* PEACE DEMOCRATS) who had gained control of the state's legislative machinery. He often spoke on behalf of the war and made strenuous efforts to meet state recruiting quotas, rendering CONSCRIPTION unnecessary. Early in the GETTYSBURG CAMPAIGN, he rushed militia to the aid of invaded Pennsylvania, something no Republican governor did. Outside his state, however, as one historian has it, "neither his personality nor his intellect attracted notice."

Parker's firm pro-war stance did not prevent his defeat by his old opponent, Ward, in 1865. He regained the governor's chair in 1873, however, and in later years was state attorney general and a justice of New Jersey's supreme court. He died of a stroke in Philadelphia, 2 Jan. 1888.   —EGL

Parker's Cross Roads, Tenn., Battle of.   31 Dec. 1862 Fought at Red Mound, Tenn., by Union Brig. Gen. JEREMIAH C. SULLIVAN's 2d and 3d brigades under Cols. Cyrus L. Dunham

and John W. Fuller, the Battle of Parker's Cross Roads was a part of Confederate Brig. Gen. NATHAN B. FORREST's Second Raid.

On 29 and 30 Dec. Forrest's cavalry force, about 2,000 men, were east of the Mobile & Ohio Railroad near McLemoresville and had dodged Fuller's troops scouting east toward Huntingdon. On 30 Dec., responding to intelligence that Forrest's route would take him south to Red Mound and the road to Lexington, Dunham's force at Huntingdon also moved south. Forrest, following a parallel road to the west, dispatched 4 companies east to Clarksville, a town 7 mi north of Red Mound, and ordered them to warn him of Union movements. Late on the 30th Dunham's advance skirmished with elements of this group and bivouacked around Clarksville. For unrecorded reasons these Confederates did not report this action and subsequent movements 31 Dec. Forrest's report of 3 Jan. 1863 lists them as missing; they may have deserted.

Dunham's 2d Brigade marched out of Clarksville in predawn hours and before 9 a.m. 31 Dec. its skirmishers collided with Forrest's at the Red Mound crossroads, a north-south, east-west intersection named for nearby Parker's Store. Woods covered the terrain northwest and southeast of the intersection, with slight rises and small hills dotting the area around the woods. Northeast of the crossroads lay a large open field with a ridge behind it. Dunham left his force waiting in column south of the intersection, Confederates fell back to the northwest woods and opened with artillery, and 3 Union cannon deployed on hills to the southeast responded with ineffective counterbattery fire. On Dunham's order, Federals fell back a half-mile and deployed in the southeast woods while Confederates occupied them with skirmishing and artillery fire until after noon. Between 12 and 1 p.m. mounted and dismounted Confederates charged Dunham's front. As Federals repulsed this attack, they were hit on the right flank by troops sent by Forrest in rear of the ridge to the north. With the ridge concealing their march, the Southerners were able to charge across the open field to the north of Dunham's position, forcing the Federals to change their front. Confederate artillery moved to the ridge and supported this attack. Fighting continued until near 2:30 p.m.

Meanwhile, another Confederate detachment had marched south and hit Dunham in the rear of his new line. With his enemy hemmed in on 3 sides, Forrest sent in a demand for unconditional surrender. Dunham refused and was preparing to meet the next assault when Fuller's 3d Brigade arrived from the north and attacked Forrest's rear. Accompanied by Sullivan, this force had left Huntingdon before daybreak on the 31st and marched south 17 mi for the fight, covering the last 7 mi in an hour and a half. Forrest was surprised and confused, and in reports expressed incredulity at not being warned by his detachments to Clarksville.

During the battle Forrest's men captured Dunham's ammunition train, 3 cannon, and 300 prisoners. Hit in rear by Fuller's troops, the Confederates abandoned the ammunition and their own and captured cannon, reversed front, briefly repelled the new attack, then pushed past Dunham's demoralized force and withdrew south on the road to Lexington. Federals gave no immediate pursuit, allowing Forrest to take his prisoners with him. These men were paroled in Lexington. Forrest lost 300 dismounted troopers of his own, taken prisoner when their tethered horses were stampeded by Fuller's attack. No official Confederate casualty list exists, but Forrest estimated a loss of 60 killed and wounded out of the 1,800 engaged. Federals lost 27 killed and 140 wounded.   —JES

parole. Lacking a means for dealing with large numbers of captured troops early in the war, the U.S. and Confederate governments relied on the traditional European system of parole and exchange of prisoners. The terms called for prisoners to give their word not to take up arms against their captors until they were formally exchanged for an enemy captive of equal rank. Parole was supposed to take place within 10 days of capture. Generally it was granted within a few days, especially after a major battle where thousands of troops were involved. Sometimes parolees went home to await notice of their exchange; sometimes they waited near their commands until the paperwork was processed.

The system grew increasingly complex, cumbersome, and expensive as the war progressed and the number of parolees soared. The prospect of being sent home encouraged many men to allow themselves to be captured in battle or by straggling. Some parolees were permanently lost to the army when they failed to return to their units. Detention camps established by Federal authorities angered parolees, as did attempts to use them as guards, send them west to fight Indians, or give them noncombat assignments. Technically, paroled troops could not be given any duty that would free other soldiers for combat, an interpretation upheld by military courts.

While paroling was in force, many inequities surfaced in the system. Soldiers assigned to detention camps frequently suffered from shortages of food and clothing and poor sanitation and were victimized by a criminal element among them. The men often became pawns for the governments, officers at one point being denied parole until formally exchanged. Union authorities generally withheld parole and exchange from guerrillas, bushwhackers, and BLOCKADE RUNNERS, which resulted in retaliatory action by the Confederacy.

Finally admitting that the war was being prolonged by returning men to the ranks through parole and exchange—which by 1863 was the Confederate army's principal means of maintaining troop strength—Federal authorities severely restricted the program. The alternative, confining captured enemy troops to prison camps, became policy for the 2 belligerents.

—PLF

Parrott, Robert Parker. USA b. Lee, N.H., 5 Oct. 1804, Parrott is remembered for his contribution to Civil War ordnance, the PARROTT GUN. Following a private education in Portsmouth, N.H., he entered West Point, graduated 3d in the class of 1824, was commissioned 2d lieutenant in the 3d U.S. Artillery, served in the East and on duty against the Creek Indians, then worked as assistant to the chief of the Ordnance Bureau until assignment as an inspector of ordnance at the civilian-run WEST POINT FOUNDRY at Cold Spring, N.Y. The foundry chairman offered Parrott a position as superintendent; he accepted, and resigned his rank of captain 31 Oct. 1836.

In the next 41 years Parrott experimented with artillery manufacture at Cold Spring, became lessee and operator of the foundry, and perfected a rifled cannon and corresponding projectile called the Parrott gun and Parrott shell, both patented in 1861. In the Civil War years he developed a Parrott sight and a Parrott fuse, and though the West Point Foundry had manufactured all types of cannon in the antebellum period, he placed the factory's efforts behind construction of rifled Parrott guns, all of which bore the initials WPF (West Point Foundry) and RPP (Robert Parker Parrott).

Parrott stopped gun manufacture at the foundry in 1867, turned its operation over to others, and until his death at Cold Spring 24 Dec. 1877 continued personal experiments with artillery projectiles and fuses.

—JES

Parrott gun. The Parrott gun, an iron artillery piece distinguished by its single reinforcing band on the breech, was perhaps one of the most widely used rifles of the Civil War. It was developed by ROBERT PARKER PARROTT, an 1824 graduate of West Point who had served in the artillery and the ordnance service and had been an inspector of cannon 1834–35. In 1836 Parrott resigned from the army to become the superintendent of the WEST POINT FOUNDRY in Cold Spring, N.Y., a post he held until 1867.

The West Point Foundry was a private firm able to experiment with rifled cannon without having to deal with government red tape. Parrott turned out his first piece under his own design, a 10-pounder, in 1860, and by the next year had developed the 20- and 30-pounder versions.

Parrott made no claim to being the first to band a rifle. Instead, his patent centered on the method of attaching the band. On most guns of the period, the band was heated, slipped on the gun, and allowed to cool. Sometimes the band and tube were threaded, and in some instances tapered, but in all cases the tube itself remained stationary. Parrott rotated the tube horizontally on rollers and had water sprayed inside to keep it cool. The band was slipped on hot, but because of the rotation of the tube it clamped itself in place uniformly, rather than in one or two places.

Parrott guns, ranging in caliber from 10-pounders to 300-pounders, saw service in all theaters of the war and were used by the Union army and navy. They drew mixed reviews. Critics complained they were not always as accurate as they might have been and the heavier rifles had a tendency to burst. Defenders maintained that while the Parrott was not ideal, it was cheap, could be produced quickly and in quantity, was easily operated by inexperienced crews, and was tough. If a piece of the muzzle broke off, it could be sawed smooth and put back into service. Parrott himself admitted that the gun was not perfect, but it was practical, and that tended to be more important than perfection in a war where the need for rifled artillery was great.

—LDJ

Parsons, Lewis Baldwin. USA b. Perry, N.Y., 5 Apr. 1818, Parsons moved with his family from his boyhood home in Homer, N.Y., to St. Lawrence County, where he attended local schools. For 2 years he taught in country schools, then entered Yale, graduating in 1840. 4 years later he earned an LL.B. from Harvard Law School. Relocating in Alton, Ill., he opened his practice, served as city attorney 1846–49, and worked for the Ohio & Mississippi Railroad 1854–60.

At the outbreak of war, Parsons volunteered as aide to FRANCIS P. BLAIR, JR., participating in the capture of Camp Jackson. In October, his friend Maj. Gen. George B. McClellan procured Parsons a captain's commission, assigning him to the Quartermaster's Department. Though he requested field command, the army took advantage of his administrative talents by keeping him in important noncombatant posts with the commissary department throughout the war. He reported in December to St. Louis and was placed in charge of river and rail transport in the Department of Mississippi, a territory that stretched from Montana to Pittsburgh to New Orleans. Promoted to colonel

USMHI

300-pound Parrott gun

NA

200-pound Parrott gun

100-pound Parrott guns   USMHI

Feb. 1862 and assigned as aide to Maj. Gen. HENRY W. HALLECK, he continued as chief of transportation in the West until Aug. 1864, when transferred to Washington with the same responsibilities for all Federal armies.

LC

Parsons brought order out of chaos in the first war ever to use railroads as a major means of moving troops. His regulations for rail transportation in the West eventually shaped the system applied to army transportation in general, and he succeeded effectively in organizing river transport as well. One of his greatest accomplishments occurred Jan. 1865, when he moved Maj. Gen. John A. Schofield's army and equipment from Mississippi to the Potomac in 17 days. The government recognized his achievement by promoting him to brigadier general 11 May 1865. He was kept in the army until 30 Apr. 1866 to oversee the transportation of discharged soldiers, and mustered out with rank as brevet major general.

After 2 years abroad to regain his health, Parsons returned to St. Louis in 1869. 6 years later he bought a farm in Flora, Ill., working as an executive for railroads and in business. In 1880 he ran unsuccessfully for lieutenant governor on the Democratic ticket. d. Flora, 16 Mar. 1907.   —PLF

Parsons, Mosby Monroe. CSA b. Charlottesville, Va., 21 May 1822. As a youth Parsons moved to Cole City, Mo., passed the state bar, and in the Mexican War commanded a company of mounted volunteers. From 1853 to 1857 he served as Missouri's attorney general, subsequently being elected to the state senate.

LC

During the secession crisis he allied with Gov. CLAIBORNE F. JACKSON to take Missouri out of the Union, commanding the 6th Division/Missouri State Guard until commissioned brigadier general in Confederate service 5 Nov. 1862. Through 1862 he fought at Carthage, Springfield, Pea Ridge, and in the Arkansas campaigning. Assigned thereafter to Maj. Gen. Richard Taylor's command in the District of West Louisiana, Parsons participated in the RED RIVER CAMPAIGN of spring 1864, being heavily engaged at Pleasant Hill, La., and at Marks' Mills and Jenkins' Ferry against Brig. Gen. Frederick Steele during the CAMDEN EXPEDITION. He was transferred to Maj. Gen. Sterling Price's army for Price's 1864 raid into Missouri.

Gen. E. Kirby Smith named Parsons major general as of 30 Apr. 1864; though he was paroled at that rank, the promotion was never confirmed by Pres. Jefferson Davis. After Smith surrendered, Parsons fled to Mexico. Details of his death there are sketchy, but he apparently joined Imperialist forces and was killed by Republican irregulars along with 5 other Americans about 15 Aug. 1865. He is probably buried in the Mexican state of Nuevo León.   —PLF

Partisan Rangers. As the war progressed, the South settled on a system of partisan warfare. An act adopted Apr. 1862 authorized organization of partisan bands for the purpose of making inroads into enemy territory. Recruits were to wear uniforms similar to the army's, were to be regularly received into the service, and paid for arms and munitions of war they captured and turned over to the government.

Bands sprang up rapidly. Those best recognized in the Eastern theater were led by JOHN S. MOSBY, J. H. MCNEILL, HARRY GILMOR, and Elijah V. White. They fought a commendable style of independent warfare, unlike the bloodbath WILLIAM CLARKE QUANTRILL waged in Missouri and Kansas.

But partisan service drew criticism, mainly because men in the ranks were jealous of the freedom allowed irregulars and because of the pay for captured goods. The greatest blow against partisans came Jan. 1864 when Brig. Gen. THOMAS L. ROSSER, commanding the Shenandoah Valley District, wrote to Gen. Robert E. Lee that they were "a nuisance and an evil to the service." Lee and cavalry leader Lt. Gen. J.E.B. STUART agreed, the latter stating that Mosby's command was "the only efficient band of rangers I know of."

The CONFEDERATE CONGRESS quickly repealed the Partisan Ranger Law, but gave the secretary of war authority to except such bands as he chose, enabling most organizations to carry on without interruption.

Their value to the Confederacy has been disputed, but they may have delayed the end of the war for nearly a year. When Lt. Gen. U. S. Grant took command of the Federal armies early in 1864, he announced plans to end hostilities in 90 days. One phase of his tactics called for the army fighting in the Shenandoah Valley to join forces with him around Richmond. This the partisans, in particular, prevented until spring 1865. In his memoirs, Philip H. Sheridan, last Union officer to command in the valley, wrote that partisans made it necessary for him to detach so many soldiers to protect his trains that "my excess in numbers was almost canceled."   —VCJ

Patrick, Marsena Rudolph. USA b. near Watertown, N.Y., 11 Mar. 1811, Patrick worked on the Erie Canal, taught school, and studied medicine before entering West Point, graduating 48th of 56 in the class of 1835. Resigning from the army in 1850, he practiced scientific agriculture and held the presidency of New York State Agricultural College at Ovid when the Civil War began.

First serving as inspector of the New York volunteers, he was appointed brigadier general 20 Mar. 1862. His disciplinarian approach to his brigade was not appreciated by his troops until they went into battle. More successful as military governor of Fredericksburg than as field commander, he was an obvious

USMHI

choice for provost marshal general, ARMY OF THE POTOMAC. His appointment, Oct. 1862, brought to the position a man so well qualified that he continued under all the successors of Maj. Gen. George B. McClellan. Lt. Gen. Ulysses S. Grant expanded his authority to include all armies operating against Richmond.

Patrick's responsibilities included preserving order among the troops, protecting civilians, regulating trade, guarding prisoners and deserters, and gathering information. A professional soldier, experienced educator, and ardent Christian, Patrick administered by combining firmness and fairness, discipline and discretion. His delightfully gossipy diary, *Inside Lincoln's Army,* published in 1964, shows him frequently discouraged by the multitudinous problems of maintaining discipline and outraged by the corruption he encountered daily, but never moving from the path of duty. When the war ended and Patrick was serving as provost at Richmond, Grant expressed concern that Patrick's "kindness of heart" might interfere with the government of the conquered Confederate capital. Surely no military policeman could have received a finer tribute. Patrick died 27 July 1888, in Dayton, Ohio, where he was employed as governor at the Soldiers' Home.   —JYS

***Patrick Henry,* CSS.** The *Patrick Henry* was one of the first ships to go into action for the Confederacy along the James River in Virginia. Formerly known as the *Yorktown,* a sidewheel merchant steamer of the New York & Old Dominion Steamship Line, it was seized by the state of Virginia and later sold to the Confederate States government.

Since the vessel was not at all equipped for fighting, its cabins were removed, decks strengthened, and 1-inch iron plates and shields placed to protect its engines and boilers. The ship was fitted with 12 guns and became a part of the James River Squadron, commanded by Capt. John R. Tucker.

Its first appearance against the enemy was 13 Sept. 1861, when Tucker took the *Patrick Henry* to NEWPORT NEWS, along with the *Jamestown* and the *Teaser,* to discourage Union excursions up the river. Another such raid was made in December, the vessels shelling 4 Federal steamers for about 2 hours.

When the ironclad VIRGINIA, formerly the *Merrimack,* steamed down to meet the Union ironclad *MONITOR* in Hampton Roads 9 Mar. 1862, the *Patrick Henry* accompanied it and was struck by a rifled shell that went through its boiler, scalding to death 4 persons. The ship was towed out of action and, as soon as damages were repaired, returned to its station.

In July 1863, when the Confederate States NAVAL ACADEMY was opened, the *Patrick Henry* was chosen as the school ship. From then until the end of the war, it was stationed at Drewry's Bluff, where on several occasions it aided in repulsing Union ships trying to get up the river. This gave students experience in war as well as the theory of war, and many of them gave a good account of themselves when they later went into service.

As the Union army made its final assault on Richmond, the *Patrick Henry* was sunk, along with the *Jamestown* and the *Virginia,* 4 Apr. 1865, to block the James River channel at Drewry's Bluff. There it remained until it was dredged up in pieces by the U.S. Navy in 1939, to clear the channel for navigation.   —VCJ

Patterson, Robert. USA b. Cty. Tyrone, Ireland, 12 Jan. 1792. Immigrating to Delaware Cty., Pa., in 1798 with his father, an Irish insurrectionist banished from his country, Patterson entered a Philadelphia banking business as a young man, fought in the War of 1812, won successive promotions to colonel of Pennsylvania militia and captain of the 32d U.S. Infantry, then mustered out June 1815 to start a wholesale business in eastern Pennsylvania. He was an active Jacksonian Democrat, traveled to the Iowa frontier, extended business interests in the West and South, and became a power in Pennsylvania politics.

USMHI

Patterson received commission as major general of volunteers for the Mexican War 7 July 1846. Performing ably at Cerro Gordo and seizing the town of Jalapa, he won praise from Maj. Gen. WINFIELD SCOTT and joined his staff, mustering out 20 July 1848. Until the Civil War he concentrated on his business interests, becoming owner of a Louisiana sugar plantation and 30 Pennsylvania cotton mills. When the war began, Scott mustered Patterson into Federal volunteer service for 3 months 19 Apr. 1861 (to date from 15 Apr.) and commissioned him major general of Pennsylvania volunteers. Appointed commander of the DEPARTMENT OF PENNSYLVANIA, he was to muster volunteers and defend state borders.

At age 69 Patterson was unable to respond effectively to an emergency call for active field service when, 24 May, Scott ordered him to advance his combined force of state volunteers and U.S. Regulars from Chambersburg, Pa., south through Maryland to Harpers Ferry. He was to retake the captured U.S. arsenal there and prevent enemy troops in the Shenandoah Valley from joining a larger force gathering near Washington, D.C. Timid and confused, Patterson did not leave the state until 14 June. Meanwhile, Confederates under Gen. Joseph E. Johnston used Harpers Ferry as a training center. Aware of Patterson's departure, they torched arsenal buildings, evacuated the town, for 3 weeks eluded Federals, then successfully joined the main Confederate army assembled at Manassas. Disgusted, Scott ordered Patterson relieved of command 19 July. He received an honorable discharge 27 July, the end of his 3-month commission.

After the Civil War, Patterson defended his conduct in a booklet, *A Narrative of the Campaign in the Valley of the Shenandoah in 1861* (1865), and pursued his business interests. d. Philadelphia, 7 Aug. 1881. —JES

Pattersonville, La., eng. at.

Pattersonville, La., eng. at. 28 Mar. 1863 During Maj. Gen. NATHANIEL P. BANKS's Teche River Campaign, spring 1863, Brig. Gen. GODFREY WEITZEL ordered Capt. Thomas L. Peterson to take the TINCLAD gunboat *Diana* on a reconnaissance up the Teche by way of Grand Lake. On board were 2 companies of infantry from the 160th New York and the 12th Connecticut, sent along to protect the naval crew. In violation of orders, Peterson sailed through the foot of Grant Lake into the narrower channel of the Atchafalaya River and directly into an enemy ambush a few miles from Pattersonville.

About 500 Confederates lined the riverbanks, including the 5-gun Valverde Battery, a few men from the 28th Louisiana, and the 13th Battalion Texas Cavalry (detached from Brig. Gen. HENRY HOPKINS SIBLEY's Texas Brigade) under Maj. Hannibal H. Boone. The cavalrymen raced alongside the *Diana*,

firing at the men on board until a shot from 1 of the boat's 3 guns felled several of their number and they scattered into the woods. Confederate artillerymen then opened up with a heavy barrage and sharpshooters raked the ship, killing Peterson and all officers on board except Lt. Henry Weston, Jr., and forcing the infantrymen to seek shelter below deck. In vain the crew tried to withdraw, but with the *Diana*'s steering mechanism shot away, the vessel was unmanageable and quickly went aground. At the sound of artillery fire, the USS *Calhoun* was ordered from Fort Buchanan at Berwick Bay to the *Diana*'s relief, but it went aground at the mouth of the Atchafalaya and withdrew after being freed by its crew.

At 4:30, after nearly 3 hours of futile defense, Weston surrendered to Boone. A few of the *Diana*'s crew had escaped in a skiff early in the fighting, but 33 Federals were killed or wounded and another 120 were captured. The Confederates suffered only slight casualties. Added to their victory was the satisfaction of having recovered the *Diana*, which had been taken by U.S. forces when Flag Officer DAVID G. FARRAGUT captured New Orleans Apr. 1862 (*see* FORTS JACKSON AND ST. PHILIP, LA., BATTLE OF). Repaired and added to Maj. Gen. RICHARD TAYLOR's fleet on the Teche, the vessel operated against Federal troops during the last 2 years of war. —PLF

Paulding, Hiram.

Paulding, Hiram. USN b. Westchester Cty., N.Y., 11 Dec. 1797. Paulding's long and distinguished naval service began with his appointment as midshipman 1 Sept. 1811.

During the War of 1812 he served as acting lieutenant aboard the USS *Ticonderoga* during the Battle of Lake Erie. By the beginning of the Civil War, he was one of the navy's senior captains and head of the important Bureau of Detail. On 18 Apr. 1861, Navy Sec. GIDEON WELLES assigned him command of a relief expedition to reinforce the Norfolk Navy Yard. Paulding was instructed to take all measures to prevent the vessels and equipment there from capture by the Secessionists. It

NA

was Paulding's decision, 20 Apr., to destroy and evacuate the yard and the vessels there, and this was partially accomplished before his withdrawal aboard the USS *Pawnee*.

On 8 Aug. 1861, Paulding and 2 other veteran officers were appointed to an ironclad board, which was authorized by Congress to consider designs for ironclad ships (*see* IRONCLADS) to be built for the navy. The board eventually decided on JOHN ERICSSON's *Monitor* design.

In fall 1861 Paulding became commandant of the New York Navy Yard, a position he held until the end of the war despite his official retirement Dec. 1861. As head of the yard, he contributed much to the success of the BLOCKADE by supplying and repairing vessels of the blockading squadrons. In July 1862 he became a rear admiral on the retired list. During the New York DRAFT RIOTS, July 1863, Paulding acted to save lives and property by stationing gunboats off Manhattan. In Aug. 1864 he detailed 3 vessels from the yard to join in the search for the Confederate commerce destroyer *TALLAHASSEE*, operating off the northeast coast.

From 1866 to 1869 Paulding headed the Naval Asylum at Philadelphia, then served as port admiral at Boston until 1870. He died at his Long Island, N.Y., home, 20 Oct. 1878.

—NCD

Paxton, Elisha Franklin. CSA b. Rockbridge Cty., Va., 4 Mar. 1828. A graduate of Washington College, Va., and Yale University, Paxton studied law at the University of Virginia, ranking 1st in his class. He began his legal practice in Ohio before settling in Lexington, Va., in 1854. 5 years later he abandoned his profession because of failing eyesight. When Virginia seceded, Paxton enlisted as a lieutenant in the Rockbridge Rifles, which became a company of the 27th Virginia.

This regiment of Shenandoah Valley volunteers and 4 other Virginia regiments were brigaded under the command of Brig. Gen. THOMAS J. JACKSON. At FIRST BULL RUN Jackson and his command earned enduring fame as "Stonewall" and the "Stonewall Brigade." In Oct. 1861 Paxton was elected major of the 27th. Nicknamed "Bull," he lacked the ability to ingratiate himself to his men and in spring 1862 failed reelection. Jackson, who liked his fellow townsman from Lexington, appointed Paxton to his staff as assistant adjutant general with the rank of major.

LC

Paxton served "Old Jack" during the campaigns of 1862, temporarily acting as chief of staff. On 1 Nov., with Jackson's endorsement, the staff officer was promoted to brigadier general and assigned to the command of the Stonewall Brigade. Jackson advanced him over all the regimental commanders, whom Stonewall believed were not qualified for the post. The officers and enlisted men vehemently protested the appointment; Col. Andrew Jackson Grigsby, commander of the 27th, led the protest, eventually resigning in disgust.

Paxton never had the opportunity to vindicate his selection by Jackson. The Stonewall Brigade held a reserve position at Fredericksburg Dec. 1862. At Chancellorsville, 2 May 1863, when Jackson's Corps routed the Union XI Corps in a surprise attack, Paxton's brigade again acted as support. The next morning, 3 May, as the brigade prepared to attack in the early light, Paxton was killed instantly by a minié ball. Today Frank "Bull" Paxton lies a few feet from "Old Jack" in a Lexington, Va., cemetery.

—JDW

Payne, William Henry Fitzhugh. CSA b. Fauquier Cty., Va., 27 Jan. 1830. A graduate of the VIRGINIA MILITARY INSTITUTE and the University of Virginia, Payne practiced law during the 1850s, serving as a commonwealth attorney after 1856. When Virginia seceded, he immediately enlisted as a private and participated in the occupation of Harpers Ferry, Va.

Payne was commissioned a captain of the Black Horse Cavalry 26 Apr. 1861; 5 months later, 27 Sept., he received an appointment as major of the 4th Virginia Cavalry. During the early stages of the 1862 PENINSULA CAMPAIGN, he commanded the regiment. At Williamsburg, 4 May, he fell severely wounded and was captured. Exchanged that summer, Payne returned to

duty in September, with the rank of lieutenant colonel and temporary command of the 2d North Carolina Cavalry. The next month he was ordered to a hospital in Lynchburg, Va.

Following his hospitalization he rejoined the 4th Virginia Cavalry as its temporary commander. On 20 Mar. 1863, Payne again transferred to the 2d North Carolina Cavalry, leading it at CHANCELLORSVILLE and at GETTYSBURG. In the latter campaign he suffered a saber cut in the side and was captured once more. After imprisonment at JOHNSON'S ISLAND, Ohio, for nearly a year, Payne returned to duty, commanding a brigade in the 1864 SHENANDOAH VALLEY CAMPAIGN. After his promotion to brigadier general 1 Nov. 1864, his brigade led the successful surprise attack on the Union garrison at New Creek, W. Va., later that month. During the final weeks of the war Payne fought at PETERSBURG, where 1 Apr. 1865 he was again wounded. Federal soldiers seized him for a third time 14 Apr., the night of Abraham Lincoln's assassination, while he was recuperating at his home in Warrenton, Va.

LC

Released 29 May 1865, he returned to Warrenton and resumed his legal practice. He served 1 term in the Virginia legislature before moving to Washington, D.C., where he acted as general counsel for the Southern Railway. The Confederate cavalry general died in the nation's capital 29 Mar. 1904.

—JDW

Payne's Farm, Va., eng. at. 27 Nov. 1863 A half-hour before sunrise, 26 Nov. 1863, the leading elements of the Army of the Potomac splashed across the Rapidan River at Ely's, Germanna, and Jacob's fords. 5 Union corps, 85,000 troops, marched in the early light on their first major offensive in Virginia since the conclusion of the Gettysburg Campaign in July. Except for the Bristoe Campaign in mid-October and a Union thrust across the Rappahannock River early in November, little fighting had occurred between the Federals and their opponent, the Army of Northern Virginia, during this span of 4 months.

This resumption of Union activity came about for various reasons. Administration officials in Washington, D.C., had been urging Maj. Gen. George G. Meade, commander of the army, to make an offensive in the Old Dominion before the onset of winter. Meade, however, reacted cautiously to the suggestions until he learned, 21 Nov., in a detailed intelligence report that Gen. Robert E. Lee's Confederate legions numbered less than 40,000 effectives. With a 2-to-1 advantage in numbers and a confidence resulting from the victories at BRISTOE STATION and Rappahannock Bridge, Meade decided to act.

The Union commander's plan called for a wide envelopment of the Confederate right flank. With Lee's 2 corps—which actually totaled 48,500—strung out on a 30-mi front on the Rapidan's south bank, Meade intended to cross the river, march swiftly on the Orange Turnpike, and crush Lee's right corps before the Confederates could concentrate. On the night of the 25th Meade outlined his scheme to his 5 corps commanders, emphasizing the need for speed.

The Federals, carrying 8 days' rations and shielded by a heavy morning fog, forded the river on the 26th. Confederate cavalry VIDETTES offered minimal resistance before galloping westward to sound the alarm. But the carefully planned Federal march soon encountered difficulties. Corps arrived late, commanders shifted units without authorization to other crossings, and soon wagons, caissons, and troops clogged the fords. By nightfall the Federals lay just across the river.

The march resumed briskly on the 27th. Maj. Gen. WILLIAM H. FRENCH, whom Meade blamed for most of the previous day's troubles, and his III Corps led the advance. But French took the wrong road, then countermarched; it was afternoon before he encountered Confederate infantry. The Southerners belonged to Maj. Gen. EDWARD JOHNSON's division of the II Corps. 2 other Southern divisions stretched beyond Johnson's right, directly across Meade's path. The tardy Federal march had given Lee ample time to react. Initially uncertain whether Richmond or his army was Meade's objective, Lee decided to meet the Federals head-on. He ordered Lt. Gen. AMBROSE P. HILL's III Corps eastward on the 26th while he prepared his right corps, Maj. Gen. JUBAL A. EARLY's II, to delay the Union advance.

When French finally met the Confederates, the latter were ready near Payne's farm. Heavy skirmishing erupted and Brig. Gen. Joseph B. Carr's Union division soon charged. Johnson's Confederates repulsed Carr's first attack and then a second. Johnson ordered a counterattack into the woods in his front. The Confederates stormed into the difficult terrain, with brigades, even regiments, becoming separated. Carr's troops, supported by French's 2 other divisions, scorched the woods. The confused fighting raged as Confederate regiments advanced, recoiled, and came on again. Johnson eventually halted the disjointed attacks, withdrawing his brigades to a fence, where they repulsed weak Federal counterattacks until darkness.

Johnson lost 545 men, including 2 wounded brigadiers (George H. Steuart and John M. Jones), in this engagement at Payne's farm, the first and heaviest clash of the MINE RUN CAMPAIGN. Neither French nor his division commanders delineated their losses in this action but totaled them for the entire campaign. Meade's offensive was fatally crippled by this engagement.   —JDW

Peace Convention of 1861. *See* WASHINGTON PEACE CONFERENCE.

Peace Democrats (Copperheads). Although the Democratic party had broken apart in 1860, during the secession crisis Democrats in the North were generally more conciliatory toward the South than were Republicans. They called themselves Peace Democrats; their opponents called them Copperheads because some wore copper pennies as identifying badges.

A majority of Peace Democrats supported war to save the Union, but a strong and active minority asserted that the Republicans had provoked the South into secession; that the Republicans were waging the war in order to establish their own domination, suppress civil and states rights, and impose "racial equality"; and that military means had failed and would never restore the Union.

Peace Democrats were most numerous in the Midwest, a region that had traditionally distrusted the Northeast, where the Republican party was strongest, and that had economic and

cultural ties with the South. The Lincoln administration's arbitrary treatment of dissenters caused great bitterness there. Above all, anti-abolitionist Midwesterners feared that emancipation would result in a great migration of blacks into their states.

As was true of the Democratic party as a whole, the influence of Peace Democrats varied with the fortunes of war. When things were going badly for the Union on the battlefield, larger numbers of people were willing to entertain the notion of making peace with the Confederacy. When things were going well, Peace Democrats could more easily be dismissed as defeatists. But no matter how the war progressed, Peace Democrats constantly had to defend themselves against charges of disloyalty. Revelations that a few had ties with secret organizations such as the KNIGHTS OF THE GOLDEN CIRCLE helped smear the rest.

The most prominent Copperhead leader was CLEMENT L. VALLANDIGHAM of Ohio, who headed the secret antiwar organization known as the Sons of Liberty. At the Democratic convention of 1864, where the influence of Peace Democrats reached its high point, Vallandigham persuaded the party to adopt a platform branding the war a failure, and some extreme Copperheads plotted armed uprisings. However, the Democratic presidential candidate, GEORGE B. MCCLELLAN, repudiated the Vallandigham platform, victories by Maj. Gen. WILLIAM T. SHERMAN and PHILIP H. SHERIDAN assured Lincoln's reelection, and the plots came to nothing.

With the conclusion of the war in 1865 the Peace Democrats were thoroughly discredited. Most Northerners believed, not without reason, that Peace Democrats had prolonged war by encouraging the South to continue fighting in the hope that the North would abandon the struggle.   —RJM/AC

peace societies. Soon after the war started, peace societies organized by disloyalists began appearing in the Confederacy. 3—the Peace and Constitutional Society, the Peace Society, and the Order of the Heroes of America—grew into well-developed disruptive forces that seriously undermined the Confederate war effort.

Disloyalists opposed the suspension of HABEAS CORPUS, IMPRESSMENT, TAX-IN-KIND legislation, and CONSCRIPTION, denouncing these laws as unjust and unconstitutional. When possible they evaded or refused to obey them. Conscription in particular invited defiance that the Conscript Bureau countered with harsh retaliatory measures and made banding together necessary for self-protection. Because of the danger of being exposed and arrested by Confederate authorities, disloyalists operated clandestinely, with secret oaths, handshakes, and passwords. Initially dominated by Unionists and others who had opposed secession, the number of those disaffected grew as dissatisfaction with the government and suffering caused by the war increased.

The Peace and Constitutional Society, the smallest of the organized opposition groups, was founded by staunch Unionists in Van Buren Cty., Ark. Its existence was discovered in fall 1861 when civil authorities arrested and tried 27 men for refusing to support the Confederacy. During their trials, the men were exposed as members of the society, which was pledged to encourage desertion and support the Federal army when it reached Arkansas.

The Peace Society, a powerful subversive group in Alabama, extended its influence to East Tennessee, Mississippi, Georgia, and possibly Florida. Confederate officials suspected its existence in 1862 and believed it had originated within Union lines. They did not investigate until the society successfully influenced the Aug. 1863 elections and sent to the Confederate Congress 6 officials who advocated ending the war and returning to the Union. During this time, to subvert the Confederacy's war effort in every way possible, prominent members traveled through the Southwest recruiting support for the society's doctrine. Their success in carrying their activities into the army became evident Dec. 1863, when some 60 Peace Society members in Brig. Gen. JAMES H. CLANTON's brigade attempted to mutiny, betraying a plan to lay down arms and go home on Christmas Day.

The best developed of the peace societies, the Order of the Heroes of America, may have been organized as early as Dec. 1861, though by whom and where is uncertain. Active in North Carolina, southwestern Virginia, and eastern Tennessee, the Heroes protected deserters, aided spies and escaped prisoners, and supplied Federal authorities with information about Confederate troop movements and strength to bring about a Confederate defeat. Brig. Gen. JOHN ECHOLS, who investigated the order in Virginia when it was discovered there in 1864, believed it had been formed at the suggestion of Federal authorities. Union civilian and military officials cooperated with the order by assuring its members safe passage through the lines and by offering them exemption from military service if they deserted, protection for their property, and a share of confiscated Confederate estates after the war. Both Lt. Gen. ULYSSES S. GRANT and Pres. ABRAHAM LINCOLN belonged to the order. In addition to their signs and passwords, the Heroes identified themselves by wearing a red string on their lapels and thus were nicknamed the "Red Strings" and the "Red-String Band."

As Confederate morale declined, the strength of the peace parties increased despite efforts by the military to suppress them. Their influence played a strong role in the Confederate Congress' reluctance to suspend *habeas corpus* for extended periods and boosted support for peace advocates in government. Protection of deserters and conscripts denied the army thousands of able-bodied men when they were critically needed. Faced with severe shortages of men and matériel and a hastily organized central government, the Confederacy suffered more disruption from the peace societies than the Union did from Copperheads (*see* PEACE DEMOCRATS).   —PLF

Peach Orchard, at Gettysburg, Pa. 2 July 1863
Sherfy's Peach Orchard was on the high point of ground in the shallow valley between CEMETERY RIDGE and Seminary Ridge. Formed by the intersection of the 2 ridges, the first leading north along the Emmitsburg road, the second angling east to DEVIL'S DEN, the rise loomed over the southern portion of the battlefield. At 3 p.m., 2 July 1863, Union Maj. Gen. DANIEL E. SICKLES, without precise instructions and on his own initiative, abandoned his position on Cemetery Ridge, occupying the lower ridges with his 2 divisions. Federal Brig. Gen. ANDREW A. HUMPHREYS' division filed on the ground along the Emmitsburg road while Brig. Gen. DAVID B. BIRNEY stretched his ranks the 1,000 yd to Devil's Den. The 2 divisions met at the Peach Orchard, forming a salient that invited attack.

At 4 p.m. 2 Confederate divisions of Lt. Gen. JAMES LONGSTREET's I Corps assaulted Sickles' line. The brigades of Maj. Gen. LAFAYETTE MCLAWS' division stormed toward the Peach

Orchard. Birney's veterans, supported by artillery, responded. Longstreet concentrated his attack on the Peach Orchard, the keystone of Sickles' front. The terrific combat cost both sides many casualties but the Confederates prevailed, wrenching the high ground from the Federals. Sickles' controversial move unhinged the Union left and threatened the army's position. The fighting then shifted to the east, to the WHEATFIELD and Devil's Den.   —JDW

Peach Orchard, Va., eng. at. 29 June 1862 *See* ALLEN'S FARM, VA., ENG. AT.

Peachtree Creek, Ga., Battle of (Hood's First Sortie).
20 July 1864 On 4 July, after evacuating its Kennesaw Mountain line, Confederate Gen. Joseph E. Johnston's army occupied a new and previously prepared position astride the railroad on the north bank of the Chattahoochee River. This surprised Maj. Gen. WILLIAM T. SHERMAN, who had expected the Confederates to retire to the south bank of that river. However, Sherman moved quickly to outflank Johnston. On 8 and 9 July portions of his army crossed the Chattahoochee above the Confederate position, whereupon Johnston fell back from that river to the south side of Peachtree Creek, barely 3 mi north of Atlanta.

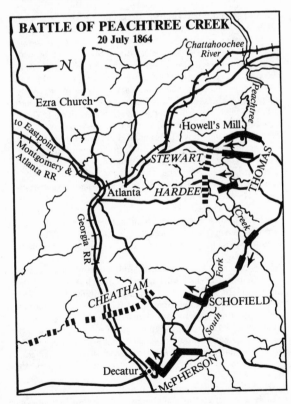

The Federals, as soon as their entire force had crossed the Chattahoochee, advanced on Atlanta in 3 separate columns: Maj. Gen. George H. Thomas' Army of the Cumberland from the north and Maj. Gen. John M. Schofield's Army of the Ohio

and Lt. Gen. James B. McPherson's Army of the Tennessee from the east. Johnston, seeing a chance to deliver a crippling blow, made plans to attack Thomas with the bulk of his army when Thomas crossed Peachtree Creek. But on 17 July Pres. Jefferson Davis, having concluded, probably rightly, that Johnston could not be relied on to make an all-out effort to hold Atlanta, replaced him with Gen. JOHN B. HOOD, who had a well-deserved reputation for aggressiveness.

Adopting Johnston's basic plan, Hood on 20 July assailed Thomas at Peachtree Creek with Lt. Gens. William J. Hardee's and Alexander P. Stewart's corps, while Maj. Gen. Benjamin F. Cheatham's corps and Georgia militia manned Atlanta's fortifications. The Confederate infantry charged with vigor and threatened at several points to overrun Federal units. In the end, however, the attack failed owing to stubborn Union resistance, poor coordination on the part of the Confederates, and the need to withdraw Maj. Gen. Patrick R. Cleburne's crack division from Hardee's Corps in order to bolster the forces defending against McPherson's column.

Of 20,000 Union troops engaged, 1,779 were killed, wounded, and missing, whereas Hood lost 4,796 of the almost 19,000 men who took part in what proved to be the first of his futile efforts to reverse the tide of the war in Georgia.

—AC

Pea Ridge (Elkhorn Tavern), Ark., Battle of. 7–8 Mar. 1862 On 10 Feb. 1862, Union Maj. Gen. SAMUEL R. CURTIS undertook a campaign designed to drive the Confederate forces of Brig. Gen. STERLING PRICE out of Missouri. Price, with 8,000 Missourians, offered little resistance to Curtis' 11,000 Federals and withdrew into northwestern Arkansas. Once in Arkansas, Price combined his troops with those of Brig. Gen. BEN MCCULLOCH, and together they retired to a position south of Fayetteville. The Confederates were halted there by Maj. Gen. EARL VAN DORN, commander of the TRANS-MISSISSIPPI DISTRICT, who assumed overall command of the Southern troops.

An aggressive officer, Van Dorn decided to retake the initiative by attacking the Federals. He started Price and McCulloch northward and ordered Brig. Gen. ALBERT PIKE to advance his command, composed primarily of 3 Cherokee Indian regiments. The weather turned cold; wet snow fell heavily as the Confederates slogged toward the Northerners. When Curtis learned of Van Dorn's approach, he concentrated his 4 infantry divisions, supported by artillery and cavalry, in a defensive position on Pea Ridge, approximately 10 mi northeast of Bentonville.

On 6 Mar. the van of the Confederate army engaged the Union rear guard, which fell back on its main line. By nightfall, Van Dorn had 17,000 troops at hand, including Pike's Cherokees. The Confederate commander, who was ill and would direct operations from an ambulance, fashioned a battle plan. While McCulloch and Pike feinted against the Union right and center, Price would assault Curtis' left near Elkhorn Tavern. To reach his attack position, Price marched his men all night. Behind them, to deceive the Federals, campfires flickered in the dark.

Skirmishing erupted between 6 and 7 a.m. 7 Mar. as the Confederates tested the Union lines. But the development of Price's attack was slow, and it was not until 10:30 that his Missourians charged. Union cannon and Col. EUGENE A. CARR's infantry division met the attackers. Twice the Federals repulsed the Missourians, but Price's third charge, delivered with a fury,

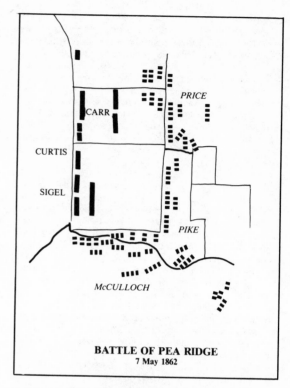

BATTLE OF PEA RIDGE
7 May 1862

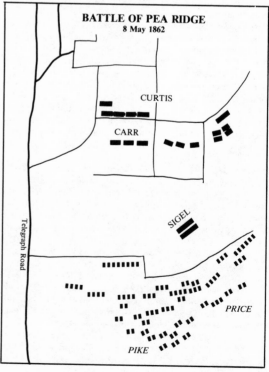

BATTLE OF PEA RIDGE
8 May 1862

swept Carr's division beyond the tavern. At the opposite end of the line, Pike's Cherokees, under Col. STAND WATIE, broke another Union division, but a counterattack retook the lost ground. McCulloch, on Pike's left, was killed by a SHARP-SHOOTER and the spirit went out of his men. Before darkness, the Missourians launched a fourth attack on Carr, driving that officer's division farther westward. Union reserves, however, stabilized Carr's ranks, and the fierce combat finally subsided.

The next morning, Curtis, who correctly surmised that the Confederates were running out of ammunition, assailed Price's Missourians around the tavern with 2 divisions under Brig. Gen. FRANZ SIGEL. Union batteries scorched the Confederate line, silencing one Southern battery after another. Sigel's men, cheering wildly, stormed toward the tavern, scattering the Missourians. On the Union right, Carr's division and another drove back Van Dorn's left wing in confusion. With his entire line broken, Van Dorn ordered a retreat.

Confronting superior numbers, Curtis had won a decisive victory. His casualties amounted to 1,384; Confederate losses reached approximately 1,300, with 300 listed as captured. The Battle of Pea Ridge secured Missouri for the Union for more than 2 years.   —JDW

Peck, John James. USA b. Manlius, N.Y., 4 Jan. 1821, Peck graduated 8th of 39 in the West Point class of 1843, which included 13 future Civil War generals, among whom was Ulysses S. Grant. He served on garrison duty, fought in the Mexican War, earning the brevets of captain and major for gallantry and meritorious service, and was stationed on the frontier. In 1853 Peck resigned his commission to engage in railroading and banking in Syracuse, N.Y. Actively involved in the Democratic party, the prosperous businessman was also a delegate to the 1856 and 1860 Democratic national conventions.

USMHI

Peck was appointed a brigadier general of volunteers 9 Aug. 1861, with the command of a brigade in the Department of the Potomac. He served in the defenses of Washington until spring 1862, when the Union army undertook the PENINSULA CAMPAIGN, during which his brigade fought at Yorktown, Williamsburg, and Seven Pines. The New Yorker commanded the 2d Division/IV Corps in the SEVEN DAYS' CAMPAIGN and received his promotion to major general 25 July, to rank from 4 July.

The War Department then assigned Peck to command of Union troops in southeastern Virginia south of the James River. During Apr. 1863 his command repulsed the Confederate offensive under Lt. Gen. James Longstreet against Suffolk on the Nansemond River. In engagements at the NORFLEET HOUSE on the 14th and 15th the Federals successfully outdueled Confederate artillery batteries and on the 19th captured Fort Huger. Peck was severely injured in the operation and was disabled for several months. In August he assumed command of the District of North Carolina, followed by command of the Department of Virginia and North Carolina. From July 1864 until he mustered out 25 Aug. 1865, he was in charge of the Department of the East along the Canadian border.

Peck organized the New York State Life Insurance Co. during the postwar years and served as its president until his death. His health impaired for years by an illness and wartime injuries, he died in Syracuse, N.Y., 21 Apr. 1878.   —JDW

Peck, William Raine. CSA b. Jefferson Cty., Tenn., 31 Jan. 1818, Peck moved to Louisiana in the 1840s, bought a plantation across the Mississippi River from Vicksburg, Miss., and prospered. When the war began, he enlisted as a private in the 9th Louisiana.

The regiment soon transferred to Virginia, arriving at Manassas Junction during the final moments of the Confederate victory at First Bull Run 21 July 1861. In the fall the 9th joined the 6th and 7th Louisiana and the battalion of "Louisiana Tigers" to form the Louisiana Brigade of Brig. Gen. RICHARD TAYLOR, who was the 9th's first colonel. Peck and the brigade participated in Maj. Gen.

LC

Thomas J. "Stonewall" Jackson's 1862 Shenandoah Valley Campaign and the Seven Days' Campaign. In July the 9th transferred to another brigade, fighting at Second Bull Run, Antietam, and Fredericksburg that year and at Chancellorsville and Gettysburg in 1863.

Standing nearly 6 ft 6 in., with a large frame, Peck went through these bloody battles unscathed while rising in rank. On 8 Oct. 1863 he was appointed colonel of the regiment. Under his leadership the 9th fought at the Wilderness, Spotsylvania, and Cold Harbor May–June 1864. As a colonel Peck often assumed temporary command of the brigade. His performance as a brigade commander during the Battle of Monocacy, Md., 9 July, drew particular praise from his division commander, Maj. Gen. John B. Gordon, one of the army's most redoubtable fighters. Peck received his appointment to brigadier general 18 Feb. 1865. Not present with the 9th at Appomattox 9 Apr., he was paroled at Vicksburg 6 June.

The veteran officer returned to his plantation, "The Mountain," after the war, dying there 22 Jan. 1871.   —JDW

Peebles' Farm (Poplar Spring Church), Va., Battle of.
30 Sept.–2 Oct. 1864 On 30 Sept. 1864, while Maj. Gen. BENJAMIN F. BUTLER's ARMY OF THE JAMES attacked below Richmond, Lt. Gen. U. S. Grant sent part of Maj. Gen. GEORGE G. MEADE's ARMY OF THE POTOMAC against the opposite end of the Confederate line, some 4 mi southwest of Petersburg. Grant knew that Gen. R. E. Lee had rushed reinforcements north to oppose Butler, and he hoped to find Lee's lower flank weakened. By attacking he also hoped to prevent Lee from detaching additional supports.

That morning part of Maj. Gen. GOUVERNEUR K. WARREN's V Corps moved west of Poplar Spring Church, with the IX Corps of Maj. Gen. JOHN G. PARKE and the cavalry of Brig. Gen. DAVID M. GREGG guarding the southern flank. In a midmorning assault across Peebles' farm, the leading division, Brig. Gen. CHARLES GRIFFIN's, captured a Confederate fort, a supporting line of trenches, and 100 prisoners. Later that day the IX Corps division of Brig. Gen. ROBERT B. POTTER moved past Griffin's left toward the Pegram house, where it was struck by Confederate infantry under Maj. Gens. HENRY HETH and CADMUS M. WILCOX. When Griffin's troops failed to support his right as anticipated, Potter saw his counterattack checked and his men tossed eastward in confusion. Aided by another IX Corps division, Potter disengaged and retained a position at Peebles' farm. A second assault by Heth and Wilcox was foiled when Griffin finally came on the scene.

The next day the Federals strengthened their foothold on Peebles' farm and dueled with the enemy at long range. Early on 2 Oct. Gregg's troopers repulsed attacks along the Vaughan road, below the infantry positions. Similar stands were made farther north on the V Corps' line, while portions of the IX Corps pushed past Pegram's house to within sight of Lee's new defenses.

Temporarily attached to the IX Corps, the II Corps division of Brig. Gen. Gershom Mott came up to probe the works before retiring to end the 3 days of fighting. Grant's latest gains had been made at a cost of more than 3,000 casualties (Confederate losses are unknown), and Lee's lower flank remained intact.
—EGL

Pegram, John. CSA b. Petersburg, Va., 24 Jan. 1832. From one of Richmond's most prominent families, Pegram, like his father, made the military a career. He graduated 10th in the West Point class of 1854 and, following service at various Western posts, became adjutant of the 2d U.S. Dragoons.

On 10 May 1861, Pegram resigned from the army and soon became lieutenant colonel of the 20th Virginia Infantry. At the 11 July 1861 engagement at RICH MOUNTAIN, western Va., he commanded half of the Southern lines. When Federals used an unguarded mountain pass to encircle the Confederate position, Pegram and 554 Southerners were forced to surrender. Soon exchanged, Pegram had to fight to overcome the stigma of early defeat.

He served as chief engineer on the staffs of Gens. P.G.T. Beauregard and Braxton Bragg before becoming chief of staff to Maj. Gen. E. Kirby Smith. On 7 Nov. 1862, Pegram received promotion to brigadier. He led a cavalry brigade at the Battle of Stone's River and temporarily commanded a division at Chickamauga. He then returned to Virginia to serve in Gen. R. E. Lee's army. Leading an infantry brigade at the Wilderness, he was shot in the leg and disabled for several months, recovering in time to take charge of Maj. Gen. Robert E. Rodes's division in the later stages of Maj. Gen. Philip H. Sheridan's 1864 Shenandoah Valley Campaign.

In Jan. 1865 Pegram's marriage to Hetty Cary was the gala social event of the year in Richmond. Exactly 3 weeks later, his bride returned to St. Paul's Church for her husband's funeral. Pegram was killed in a 6 Feb. battle at HATCHER'S RUN. —JIR

Pelham, John. CSA b. Benton Cty., Ala., 14 Sept. 1838, Pelham, son of an Alabama planter and descendant of American painter Peter Pelham, entered West Point in 1856. Enrolled in an experimental 5-year curriculum, he excelled in artillery studies under Maj. Henry J. Hunt. On 22 Apr. 1861, within weeks of graduation, he resigned from the academy and entered Confederate service as a lieutenant and ordnance officer posted to Lynchburg, Va.

Under Gen. Joseph E. Johnston at First Bull Run, Pelham demonstrated consummate gunnery skill on Henry Hill. On Johnston's recommendation he won promotion to captain, then assignment to Brig. Gen. J.E.B. Stuart's cavalry as the

NA

commander of an 8-gun battery of HORSE ARTILLERY, 29 Nov. 1861. Pelham fought in more than 60 engagements during his brief career and refined the concept of FLYING BATTERY. At the Battles of Williamsburg, the Seven Days', Malvern Hill, Groveton, Second Bull Run, Antietam, and Fredericksburg, his men and guns won the respect of Confederate superiors and earned him the sobriquet "The Gallant Pelham" from Gen. Robert E. Lee and Stuart. Following Second Bull Run he received promotion to major and command of a battalion of horse artillery, and at Antietam and Fredericksburg had the privilege of dueling with former mentor Hunt.

In artillery tactics Pelham improved the speed of movement, fire, and accuracy. At Antietam he moved his guns along the Federal flank, giving the impression of commanding a larger force, and at Fredericksburg, with enfilading fire from 2 guns, held up the Union advance for 2 hours, convincing opponents they faced 2 batteries. His horse artillery, most often operating with Stuart, kept pace with fast-moving cavalry columns on raiding expeditions and proved adept in operations against railroads and Union gunboats on Virginia's tidal rivers.

His contribution to Confederate folklore was as great. Loved by his men, noted for his extreme youth and courage, and distinguished for his service among Stuart's colorful entourage, he became a contemporary hero. On 17 Mar. 1863, away from his troops on personal business, out of curiosity he joined Stuart in observing the Confederate cavalry engagement at Kelly's Ford, Va. With youthful impetuosity he joined in a charge with the 3d Virginia Cavalry, was struck in the neck by a piece of an exploding shell, and was taken to the Culpeper home of his fiancée, Bessie Shackelford, where he died the same day. Grieving, Stuart ordered Pelham's body laid in state at the George Washington monument in Richmond.

The postwar writings of former Confederate JOHN ESTEN COOKE revived the Pelham legend and established him as a hero of the LOST CAUSE. —JES

Pember, Phoebe Yates Levy. nurse b. Charleston, S.C., 18 Aug. 1823. Nothing is known about Phoebe Yates Levy's schooling, but her postwar writings indicate that she was well educated. Her family moved from Charleston to Savannah, Ga., in 1850. There she met and married Thomas Pember of Boston, where the couple made their home until Pember died July 1861. The young widow returned to her family and by 1862 had accompanied them to Marietta, Ga.

Disheartened by inactivity and eager to serve the Confederate cause, late that year Pember used her friendship with the wife of Sec. of War George W. Randolph to secure a position as chief matron of Hospital No. 2 at Chimborazo Hospital in Richmond. She began working 1 Dec., staying in the Confederate capital to care for her patients after the surrender Apr. 1865.

With the return of peace Pember made her home in Georgia but traveled extensively in the U.S. and abroad. She died in Pittsburgh, Pa., 4 Mar. 1913.

In 1879 Pember had published her memoirs, *A Southern*

Woman's Story, a straightforward, detailed description of hospital life in Confederate Richmond. Though born into a well-to-do family, in her writing Pember focused on the common soldier from the lower levels of Southern society, expressing not only compassion for the sick and wounded, but a respect for the rank and file. Especially interesting are her accounts of the sometimes bitter friction between the soldiers of the various Confederate states. Few other memoirs show so explicitly the fierce localism that contributed heavily to the South's failed experiment with nationhood. Her criticism of bureaucratic incompetence, unqualified doctors, and inadequate supplies provides one of the best pictures of Southern medical care. A 1959 reissue of the memoir, edited by Bell I. Wiley, contains previously unpublished letters and a valuable sketch of Pember's life. —PLF

Pemberton, John Clifford. CSA b. Philadelphia, Pa., 10 Aug. 1814. The "Defender of Vicksburg" entered West Point in 1833 and promptly displayed a deep love of the South, advocating states rights philosophies and forming friendships mostly with Southern cadets. Graduating 27th of 50 in the class of 1837, Pemberton entered the cavalry service and was twice brevetted for gallantry in the Mexican War. In 1848 he married Martha Thompson, a native of Norfolk, Va., who further influenced his Southern leanings.

USMHI

On 24 Apr. 1861, Pemberton resigned from the army to join the Confederacy, while 2 of his brothers remained with the Union army. Given a brigadier general's commission by Pres. Jefferson Davis 17 June 1861, Pemberton took command of the DEPARTMENT OF SOUTH CAROLINA, GEORGIA, AND FLORIDA. This relatively minor assignment nevertheless brought him promotion to major general Jan. 1862 and to lieutenant general 10 Oct.

On 14 Oct. Pemberton took charge of the DEPARTMENT OF MISSISSIPPI AND EAST LOUISIANA, quickly discovering that all the affairs of his district centered on the besieged river fortress of VICKSBURG, Miss. The general soon became caught between the conflicting military plans of his 2 superiors, Gen. Joseph E. Johnston and President Davis. Trying to follow both plans, he was finally unable to follow either, and 4 July 1863 surrendered Vicksburg and 29,000 Confederate soldiers to Maj. Gen. Gen. U. S. Grant.

When no subsequent assignment could be found for his high rank, Pemberton resigned his lieutenant generalcy and accepted appointment as a colonel of artillery. He performed commendably at that level until war's end. Diligent and efficient, Pemberton was also a good administrator but was criticized for being an uninspiring officer.

After the war he settled on a farm near Warrenton, Va., and eventually returned to his native Pennsylvania, where he died 13 July 1881, in the village of Penllyn. —JIR

Pender, William Dorsey. CSA b. Edgecomb Cty., N.C., 6 Feb. 1834. One of the few advantages that the Confederacy enjoyed was an abundance of excellent fighting generals.

USMHI

Pender was illustrative of that group. He entered West Point at age 16, graduating 19th of 46 in the class of 1854, famous because it produced so many officers who achieved high rank. He then served, mostly on the Pacific Coast, with the 1st U.S. Dragoons.

Pender was among the first Southerners to offer his sword to his homeland, resigning his army commission Mar. 1861 to become colonel of the 3d North Carolina Infantry. The young officer quickly gained a reputation as a hard-hitting commander. Gallant conduct in the PENINSULA CAMPAIGN, notably at SEVEN PINES, earned him a brigadier's rank as of 3 June 1862. As a brigade commander in Lt. Gen. Ambrose P. Hill's Light Division, Pender was in the thick of fighting at Cedar Mountain, Harpers Ferry, Antietam, Fredericksburg, and Chancellorsville. 3 times he was wounded in action. On 27 May 1863 he was promoted to major general.

During the second day of combat at GETTYSBURG, Pender was reconnoitering when struck in the thigh by a 2-in.-sq shell fragment. He dismissed the injury as trivial and did not seek medical attention until Gen. R. E. Lee's army was back in Virginia. By then, massive infection had spread through his leg. Amputation followed, and Pender did not survive the surgery. The 29-year-old general died 8 July 1863 at Staunton, Va. His remains were interred at Tarborough, N.C.

A. P. Hill wrote of Pender: "No man fell during the bloody battle of Gettysburg more regretted than he, nor around whose youthful brow were clustered brighter rays of glory." The supreme compliment to Pender came from Robert E. Lee: "His promise and usefulness as an officer were only equaled by the purity and excellence of his private life." —JIR

Pendleton, Alexander Swift. CSA b. near Alexandria, Va., 28 Sept. 1840. "Sandie" Pendleton's father, WILLIAM N. PENDLETON, a minister and future Confederate general, settled his family in Maryland 1844–53. Educated at home and in a private school, at age 13 the younger Pendleton enrolled in Washington College at Lexington, Va., where his father had accepted a parish. An excellent student, he belonged to the same literary society as THOMAS J. JACKSON, then on the faculty of the VIRGINIA MILITARY INSTITUTE. Following his graduation in 1857, Pendleton taught at Washington College for 2 years. At that time he enrolled at the University of Virginia to earn a

LC

Master's degree. After entering the Provisional Army of Virginia as 2d lieutenant in the Corps of Engineers 17 May 1861, he left school without completing his studies. A week later he reported to Jackson, then a colonel in the Confederate army, at Harpers Ferry. In July Jackson requested Pendleton for his ordnance officer, and from the 19th of that month until his death Pendleton served as a capable, well-liked, and highly respected staff officer to Jackson and his successors.

Described by friends as determined, bold, self-reliant, and consistently good-humored, Pendleton enjoyed a close relationship with Jackson, whose intensely religious nature he shared. When the young officer's commission in the Virginia militia expired, Jackson arranged to have him appointed 1st lieutenant in Confederate service, 30 Nov. He served at that rank through the SHENANDOAH VALLEY CAMPAIGN of 1862, winning Jackson's approval for manning a field piece at KERNSTOWN when he saw its gun crew killed as he returned from carrying orders to Jackson's subordinates. Again Jackson interceded on Pendleton's behalf, securing for him a promotion to captain, June 1862. Illness kept him out of the SECOND BULL RUN CAMPAIGN, but he returned to duty in late summer holding a temporary appointment as assistant adjutant general of Jackson's II Corps.

Jackson depended on Pendleton's ability to convey his orders clearly and concisely, in routine paperwork and under battlefield conditions. Most of Jackson's battle reports after FIRST BULL RUN were written by Pendleton, whose efficiency resulted in a promotion to major and permanent assignment to the adjutant generalship 4 Dec. 1862. The two men became almost inseparable. It was Pendleton who dressed Jackson's body for burial after the latter's death from wounds received at CHANCELLORSVILLE, and he was one of the pallbearers at Jackson's funeral.

On succeeding Jackson as commander of the II Corps, Lt. Gen. RICHARD S. EWELL advanced Pendleton to chief of staff with rank of lieutenant colonel as of 23 July 1863. Lt. Gen. JUBAL A. EARLY requested him for detached duty in the Shenandoah Valley Dec. 1863 and again the following June.

On 22 Sept. 1864, 3 days after the third battle at WINCHESTER, Pendleton received a mortal gunshot wound to the abdomen at FISHER'S HILL as he tried to check an advance on the Confederate front. Buried near the battlefield, his body was later exhumed and sent to his family in Lexington, Va. On 24 Oct. his parents and his wife of 9 months attended his reburial at Lexington Cemetery near Jackson's grave.   —PLF

Pendleton, William Nelson.

CSA b. Richmond, Va., 26 Dec. 1809, Pendleton received his early education from private tutors. In 1826 he entered West Point, graduating 5th of 40 cadets in the class of 1830. Following 3 years in the army, Pendleton resigned to go into teaching. In 1838 he received ordination as an Episcopal rector and 15 years later accepted a call to become the minister of Grace Church in Lexington, Va. This post he held for the remainder of his life.

LC

Pendleton was 51 when civil war began. Despite his age, he was elected captain of the Rockbridge Artillery in Lexington, naming his 4 cannon Matthew, Mark, Luke, and John. He was quickly promoted to colonel and chief of artillery on the staff of Gen. Joseph E. Johnston, who called him "that model of a Christian soldier."

On 26 Mar. 1862, Pendleton was elevated to brigadier general. He served with the Army of Northern Virginia for the rest of the war and for much of the time was nominal chief of artillery. A good organizer, he was often given to long-windedness. His field performance was at best average, and in the last 2 years of war his duties were largely administrative, confined to command of the reserve ordnance. Pendleton never lost sight of his religious calling and often preached to large gatherings of soldiers.

Following Appomattox, he returned to his church and labored to rebuild his shattered community. Robert E. Lee served on his vestry for a short time. Pendleton died 15 Jan. 1883 and is buried in Lexington beside his son ALEXANDER, one of the Confederacy's most famous staff officers.   —JIR

Peninsula, Confederate Army of the.

On 21 May 1861 Col. JOHN B. MAGRUDER was given command of Confederate troops on Virginia's lower peninsula. A force had to be kept in the area to oppose the potential threat to Richmond from Union soldiers at FORT MONROE. On 26 May the DEPARTMENT OF THE PENINSULA was ordered into existence under Magruder's command. The small force that blunted a Union attack at Big Bethel, Va., 10 June 1861, thus became known as the Army of the Peninsula. The first land battle of the war, the skirmish made Magruder a Southern hero; he was rewarded with a promotion to brigadier general 17 June 1861.

Throughout the summer and fall the new army continued to fight occasional skirmishes with Union raiding parties. But Magruder concentrated efforts on preparing 3 defensive lines: one near Hampton, which he later decided could be outflanked; one on the Warwick River, including water batteries at Yorktown, Gloucester Point, and Mulberry Island; and a third covering the Williamsburg area. Obviously, Magruder intended a defense in more depth than his meager force would allow, hoping to fill out his works with the help of local militia units. The War Department did its best to fill his needs but became annoyed when Magruder's shrill demands grew frantic.

An invasion finally did come. On 17 Mar. 1862, Union Maj. Gen. George B. McClellan began moving his army amphibiously from Alexandria to Fort Monroe for its advance on Richmond. By April Magruder's force had risen to 17,000 along an 8-mi front, but he was opposed by the lead Union corps, numbering 60,000. The Union force should have been able to push aside the badly outnumbered Magruder, but he successfully resisted McClellan's army at Lee's Mill, along the Warwick River line, 16 Apr.

The amphibious move by McClellan had taken Confederate authorities by surprise, and Gen. Joseph E. Johnston needed time to gather forces to save Richmond. Time was provided by the Army of the Peninsula's unexpected opposition, which convinced McClellan he must lay formal siege to the Confederate lines at Yorktown. Although the Army of the Peninsula was absorbed into the main force in April and its defenses abandoned, its resistance saved Richmond.   —CMS

Peninsula, Confederate Department of the.

Virginia seceded from the Union 17 Apr. 1861, its withdrawal creating immediate defense problems for state and then Confederate authorities. No area of the Old Dominion was more vulnerable or critical than the peninsula, the large neck of land between the York and James rivers. At the peninsula's eastern tip the Union bastion of Fort Monroe stood, with the nearby waters of Hampton Roads patrolled by Union warships. The defense of this river and land approach to Richmond received early attention from the Confederates.

Col. JOHN B. MAGRUDER was assigned 21 May to command the operations on the peninsula. On the 26th the Department of the Peninsula was formally created with headquarters at Yorktown. Magruder's authority and responsibility covered the land and the 2 rivers. With volunteers arriving almost daily, the department commander faced the dual problem of organizing the raw levies and erecting fortifications. Magruder's opponents were Maj. Gen. BENJAMIN F. BUTLER's Federals composing the Union Department of Virginia with garrisons at FORT MONROE and NEWPORT NEWS.

Sporadic skirmishing occurred between the antagonists for 2 weeks. On 10 June Butler advanced in force, resulting in the Battle of BIG BETHEL, the first land battle of the war. After the Confederates repulsed the piecemeal Union assaults in this engagement, a stalemate settled over the lower peninsula, stretching for months. By the end of 1861 Confederate authorities had stationed 13,000 soldiers in Magruder's department.

In spring 1862 the major focus of the war in Virginia shifted from the defense of Richmond to the peninsula. Gen. JOSEPH E. JOHNSTON on 26 Apr. assumed control over Magruder's ARMY OF THE PENINSULA. Magruder, now with the rank of major general, commanded the redesignated right wing of Johnston's army. But Magruder's efforts as a department commander proved valuable as his works at Yorktown and his bluffing tactics delayed the huge Union Army of the Potomac for a month in the opening phase of the PENINSULA CAMPAIGN.

—JDW

Peninsula Campaign.

Peninsula Campaign. Mar.–Aug. 1862 During Mar. 1862 Union Maj. Gen. George B. McClellan transported his massive army of about 105,000 men from the vicinity of Washington to Fort Monroe on the tip of the Virginia peninsula between the York and James rivers. McClellan planned to move from the east against Richmond and its Confederate defenders, and by 4 Apr. he was ready to begin his assault on the capital.

Between the Federal host and Richmond stood only about 17,000 Southern troops commanded by Maj. Gen. JOHN B. MAGRUDER. The thin Confederate defense line stretched from Yorktown across the peninsula to the Warwick River. Yet when McClellan probed Magruder's works, he pronounced them too strong to carry with a single thrust. Consequently the Federals spent a month laying siege to the Yorktown line, and Gen. Joseph E. Johnston's Confederate army reinforced Magruder's troops. Finally, on 4 May McClellan began his grand assault on the Southern defenses, and found them unoccupied. Johnston had withdrawn his army up the peninsula.

The Federals plunged after the retreating Southerners, and both armies became mired in the mud created by excessively heavy spring rains. On 5 May the Union vanguard overtook the Confederate rear guard, and an action followed at WILLIAMSBURG. Johnston, however, made good his escape, although in doing so he abandoned eastern Virginia to Federal occupation. When the Union took Norfolk 9 May, the Confederate ironclad VIRGINIA (Merrimack) was left without a port and had to be destroyed. This opened the James to the Union navy. On 15 May, at DREWRY'S BLUFF, only 7 mi from Richmond, the Confederates were able to employ river obstructions and guns to halt a Federal flotilla led by the ironclad MONITOR.

Johnston took his Confederates into the suburbs of Richmond; on 31 May McClellan and nature offered Johnston a chance to make some counterstroke. Rains washed away bridges over the Chickahominy River and isolated 2 Union corps near the villages of SEVEN PINES and Fair Oaks Station. The Confederate attack proved indecisive, however, and Johnston suffered a severe wound. Pres. Jefferson Davis then installed Gen. Robert E. Lee in command.

Lee shored up Richmond's defenses while McClellan cautiously approached. Meanwhile, Maj. Gen. J.E.B. Stuart's Confederate cavalry rode completely around the Union army (see STUART'S RIDE AROUND MCCLELLAN), confirmed the fact that McClellan's right flank was unsecured, and further convinced the Federal general that he was outnumbered. Lee stationed only 25,000 troops between Richmond and the Federals and 26 June struck the exposed right with 47,000. Lee also planned for Maj. Gen. Thomas J. "Stonewall" Jackson's Army of the Confederate VALLEY DISTRICT to attack the Union rear, but Jackson was late and uncharacteristically unaggressive. On the night of 27 June, after a Confederate breakthrough at GAINES' MILL, McClellan, believing he was outnumbered, determined to "save this army" and ordered a withdrawal to the James. Lee pursued in vain and suffered a bloody repulse at MALVERN HILL 1 July before the Federals reached the relative safety of Harrison's Landing. Consequently, the fierce fighting of the SEVEN DAYS' CAMPAIGN drove McClellan from Richmond but did not destroy his army as Lee had hoped.   —EMT

Pennsylvania. Caught unprepared with a militia system fallen into decay, and with Quaker and Mennonite influences widespread, Pennsylvania was nevertheless the first state to respond to Pres. Abraham Lincoln's call for 75,000 volunteers by dispatching 5 unarmed companies to the defenseless national capital, an act that received a congressional vote of thanks. The same day, 18 Apr. 1861, Camp Curtin, the state training center, was established. Altogether, 427,000 Pennsylvania enlistments were recorded and 270 regiments furnished to the army. Among the unique and distinguished units were the PHILADELPHIA BRIGADE, which bore the brunt of PICKETT'S CHARGE; the Pennsylvania Reserves, an entire infantry division raised, trained, and equipped at state expense in excess of the Federal quota; the trophy-sporting "PENNSYLVANIA BUCKTAILS" of the 13th Reserves; and the coal miners of the 48th Regiment, who dug the Petersburg mine.

The state's loyalty never faltered, largely due to the leadership of Republican Gov. ANDREW G. CURTIN, who took office in 1861 and from the onset expected a long, bitter struggle. He called out 25,000 state militia during the 1862 invasion of Maryland and initiated the Altoona Conference, 24 Sept. 1862, which pledged the Northern governors' support during the Union's darkest hours. "The soldiers' friend," Curtin took exceptional care of their dependents.

War came to Pennsylvania in summer 1863, when Gen. R. E. Lee's seemingly invincible army invaded the state. After foraging in the Cumberland Valley and threatening Harrisburg, Lee concentrated at GETTYSBURG to face the Union army, commanded by Pennsylvanian Maj. Gen. GEORGE G. MEADE. Maj. Gens. JOHN F. REYNOLDS and WINFIELD S. HANCOCK and Brig. Gen. DAVID M. GREGG were other prominent Pennsylvanians who took part in the epic battle. At the dedication of the National Cemetery, 19 Nov. 1863, Pres. Abraham Lincoln delivered his immortal 5-minute GETTYSBURG ADDRESS.

On 30 July 1864, two-thirds of CHAMBERSBURG was burned by Confederate cavalry in reprisal for Union depredations in Virginia. It was the only Northern town to be destroyed.

—DPK

6th Pennsylvania Cavalry. *See* RUSH'S LANCERS.

11th Pennsylvania Reserves. Recruited in the western counties of the state, the 11th Pennsylvania Reserves was one of 13 regiments designated Pennsylvania Reserves. Organized, trained, and equipped at state expense by the order of Gov. Andrew G. Curtin, the regiments eventually constituted the Pennsylvania Reserves division/V Corps/ARMY OF THE POTOMAC. The 11th Pennsylvania Reserves were commanded successively by Cols. Thomas F. Gallagher and Samuel M. Jackson.

The unit sustained the heaviest losses of any regiment in the Pennsylvania Reserves, ranking 8th among all Federal regiments in percentage of men killed in action. Also designated the 40th Pennsylvania Volunteers, the 11th formed part of the division's 2d Brigade. At GAINES' MILL, 27 June 1862, almost the entire regiment surrendered after being cut off from the division. Exchanged 5 Aug., the unit fought at SECOND BULL RUN and SOUTH MOUNTAIN. It took only 200 into battle at ANTIETAM, but, with recruits and the return of wounded, the 11th sent 394 into action at FREDERICKSBURG, where it lost 211. The division, because of heavy losses, was rested during winter 1863. The 11th fought at GETTYSBURG in July, at BRISTOE STATION in October, and at the WILDERNESS and SPOTSYLVANIA May 1864. On 30 May 1864, the unit was mustered out of service.

—JDW

83d Pennsylvania. Raised in Erie, the 83d Pennsylvania mustered in 8 Sept. 1861, traveled to Washington, D.C., and went on to fight in every major battle of the Army of the Potomac. Serving first in Maj. Gen. FITZ JOHN PORTER's division, it joined the 1st Division/III Corps Mar. 1862 and in May entered the 3d Brigade/1st Division/V Corps, remaining there until the Confederate surrender at Appomattox. Arduous service assured it the distinction of suffering the second highest combat death rate of any Union regiment. With 1,808 men on its rolls late in 1861, the 83d tallied 282 battle deaths at war's end. Only the 5th New Hampshire lost more.

Under Maj. Gen. GEORGE B. MCCLELLAN, the unit served through the Siege of YORKTOWN, the SEVEN DAYS' CAMPAIGN, all other major fighting during the PENINSULA CAMPAIGN, the SECOND BATTLE OF BULL RUN, and ANTIETAM. After FREDERICKSBURG, CHANCELLORSVILLE, GETTYSBURG, SPOTSYLVANIA, the WILDERNESS and the Battle of the Crater at Petersburg, the regiment's original enlistment expired and all members mustered out in Harrisburg, Pa., 7 Sept. 1864. At that time enough veterans reenlisted to form 6 companies, which returned to action around Petersburg and, following the Battle of FIVE FORKS and the APPOMATTOX CAMPAIGN, took a place of honor in the GRAND REVIEW 23 May 1865. The regiment disbanded 4 July 1865.

Indicative of the regiment's bravery, its first 2 colonels, John W. McLane and Strong Vincent, were killed in combat. McLane fell at GAINES' MILL with 60 other men of the 83d, and Vincent died while the unit fought for LITTLE ROUND TOP at Gettysburg. William F. Fox's *Regimental Losses in the American Civil War* notes that the 83d's dead "always lay with their faces to the enemy."

—JES

140th Pennsylvania. Men from Pittsburgh made up the 140th Pennsylvania, mustered into service 8 Sept. 1862 with 1,132 members. Led by Col. Richard P. Roberts, through December its sole duty lay in guarding the Northern Central Railroad's line in Maryland. Ordered into winter quarters with the Army of the Potomac, the 140th did not fight its first battle until CHANCELLORSVILLE, May 1863. The GETTYSBURG, MINE RUN, WILDERNESS, and SPOTSYLVANIA campaigns followed, with the regiment losing 147 members killed in combat. Fighting in the WHEATFIELD on the second day at Gettysburg, Colonel Roberts fell with 60 other men of the unit. At Spotsylvania, 52 members died during the 12 May 1864 charge on the "BLOODY ANGLE" and other fighting.

Roberts was replaced by Col. John Fraser, who commanded the regiment from Mine Run through COLD HARBOR, the Siege of PETERSBURG, and the APPOMATTOX CAMPAIGN. At Cold Harbor, where other Union units were destroyed, the 140th escaped with comparatively light losses. But in the last days of the war 6 members died at SAYLER'S CREEK and in an engagement at Farmville, Va.

First a part of the VIII Corps, in Dec. 1861 the regiment joined in the II Corps, from Sept. 1863 serving as a part of its 1st Brigade/1st Division. After Farmville, it was present for the Confederate surrender at Appomattox, marched in the GRAND REVIEW, then mustered out 31 May 1865. William F. Fox's *Regimental Losses in the American Civil War* states that its battle dead numbered 198, approximately 17% of its original force. Adding to this figure the number of men and officers killed by disease, the 140th Pennsylvania sustained 326 deaths in less than 3 years of service.

—JES

141st Pennsylvania. Organized at Harrisburg under Col. Henry J. Madill in summer 1862, the 141st Pennsylvania, after serving in the defenses of Washington, joined the ARMY OF THE POTOMAC in October and was assigned to the 1st Brigade/1st Division/III Corps. It remained in that command until the corps' dissolution Mar. 1864, after which it became part of the 1st (later the 2d) Brigade/3d Division/II Corps.

Under Colonel Madill, the 141st saw action at FREDERICKSBURG, CHANCELLORSVILLE, GETTYSBURG, BRISTOE STATION, MINE RUN, the WILDERNESS, SPOTSYLVANIA, the NORTH ANNA RIVER, COLD HARBOR, the siege of PETERSBURG, and the battles of the APPOMATTOX CAMPAIGN. Altogether, it lost 6 officers and 161 enlisted men to battle deaths, hundreds of its officers and men being wounded. It suffered most at Chancellorsville, where, during a crucial counterattack, its 419 effectives absorbed 235 casualties. It lost three-quarters of its remaining men during the second day at Gettysburg, when it came under a heavy shelling in the PEACH ORCHARD. By its tenacity on that field, the regiment enabled its brigade to hold the line for some time after supporting units gave way, winning the admiration of participants and observers on both sides.

—EGL

142d Pennsylvania. Mustered in at Harrisburg 1 Sept. 1862, the regiment saw duty in the defenses of Washington and at Frederick, Md., before joining the I Corps/ARMY OF THE POTOMAC after Antietam. It was heavily engaged at FREDERICKSBURG, its first battle, losing half its men during an assault by Maj. Gen. George G. Meade's division against the Confederate right. It then participated in BURNSIDE'S MUD MARCH and was lightly engaged at CHANCELLORSVILLE. The 142d helped begin the Battle of GETTYSBURG from atop McPherson's Ridge, north-

573

west of the village, where it absorbed the initial Confederate assault of 1 July 1863. There Col. Robert P. Cummings was killed, and the regiment lost 211 officers and men before being forced to retreat south of Gettysburg.

Recruited back to strength, the unit, now under Col. Alfred B. McCalmont, fought in the V Corps at BRISTOE STATION, MINE RUN, the WILDERNESS, SPOTSYLVANIA, the NORTH ANNA RIVER, COLD HARBOR, PETERSBURG, and in the APPOMATTOX CAMPAIGN. By its muster-out, 29 May 1865, it had lost 7 officers and 148 enlisted men killed or mortally wounded; 72 others had succumbed to disease. —EGL

148th Pennsylvania. One of the regiments formed under Pres. Abraham Lincoln's call of July 1862, the 148th was sent from Camp Curtin, Harrisburg, to Cockeysville, Md., early in September. It guarded the line of the Northern Central Railroad, then occupied the Baltimore defenses. Joining the II Corps/ARMY OF THE POTOMAC shortly after Fredericksburg, the regiment saw its first battle action at CHANCELLORSVILLE. There it absorbed heavy losses, including the severe wounding of Col. James A. Beaver. At GETTYSBURG, 2 July 1863, it again suffered considerably, this time helping to plug gaps in the Union left caused by the III Corps's foray west of CEMETERY RIDGE.

After participating at BRISTOE STATION and MINE RUN, the 148th fought in the WILDERNESS. On 12 May 1864, it was depleted during an assault against the "MULE SHOE" salient at SPOTSYLVANIA. Despite its great loss, the outfit served on the NORTH ANNA RIVER and at COLD HARBOR, as well as in numerous actions during the Siege of PETERSBURG, where Colonel Beaver was twice wounded. The 148th left Union service 1 June 1865 at Alexandria, Va., having lost more than 200 men dead of battle wounds and nearly as many from illness. —EGL

149th and 150th Pennsylvania. One of the most renowned regiments in the ARMY OF THE POTOMAC was the "PENNSYLVANIA BUCKTAILS" (13th Pennsylvania Reserves). Organized Apr. 1861, the regiment was composed of excellent marksmen who wore a buck's tail on their hats to identify their unit. During the war's first year, the Bucktails distinguished themselves as skirmishers and SHARPSHOOTERS. As a consequence of the 13th's record, Sec. of War EDWIN M. STANTON in July 1862 directed one of its officers, Maj. Roy Stone, to enlist an additional brigade of Bucktails.

Stone performed his assignment efficiently and rapidly, raising 20 companies of recruits by the end of August. Sent to Harrisburg, the state capital, the companies were soon officially organized and designated the 149th and 150th Pennsylvania regiments, with Stone appointed colonel of the 149th and Langhorne Wister colonel of the 150th. These novice volunteers proudly adopted the distinctive badge and appellation of the original Bucktails.

Within days of their formation, the 149th and 150th were rushed to Washington, D.C., because of the Confederate invasion of Maryland. The regiments served in the capital's defenses until Feb. 1863, when they joined the Army of the Potomac in Virginia. Before their departure from Washington, Company K of the 150th was assigned to the soldiers' home as bodyguards for Pres. ABRAHAM LINCOLN, a duty the company performed until LINCOLN'S ASSASSINATION Apr. 1865.

On the assignment of the 149th and 150th to the army, authorities formed them and the 143d Pennsylvania into the 2d Brigade/3d Division/I Corps, with Stone as commander of

"Pennsylvania Bucktails" (13th Pennsylvania Reserves)

the brigade. The 3 regiments served with the army until the end of the war, participating in the major campaigns in the East from CHANCELLORSVILLE to PETERSBURG. On 1 July 1863, at GETTYSBURG, they fought with particular skill and courage. Stone suffered a wound, but his performance earned him a brigadier's star. With the dissolution of the I Corps Mar. 1864, the regiments were merged with others to form the 3d Brigade/4th Division/V Corps. At war's end, the 149th and 150th Pennsylvania were acting as guards at the ELMIRA PRISON in New York. Authorities disbanded these Bucktails June 1865. —JDW

Pennsylvania, Union Department of. Created 27 Apr. 1861, the Union Department of Pennsylvania consisted of the states of Pennsylvania and Delaware, and all of Maryland not covered by the Departments of Washington and Annapolis. Maj. Gen. ROBERT PATTERSON, a 60-year-old veteran of the War of 1812 and the Mexican War, assumed command of the department, with headquarters in Philadelphia.

Patterson slowly created an army, often imploring the War Department for more men, arms, uniforms, and supplies. By 1 June his army contained 16 regiments of infantry and 5 companies of cavalry. Patterson's primary responsibility as department commander, however, was to advance into western Maryland, threaten Confederate-held Harpers Ferry, Va., and support Union sentiment in western Virginia.

The old general's campaign, undertaken in a series of fitful starts throughout June, ended as a dismal failure. On 2 July, after long delays and many excuses, Patterson's 13,000-man Army of Pennsylvania forded the Potomac River, immediately engaging a brigade of Gen. Joseph E. Johnston's Confederate army. This engagement at Falling Waters lasted less than an hour and was the major battle of the campaign. For another 2 weeks the opponents stalked each other, but in the morning darkness of 19 July Johnston abandoned his position, marching eastward to join a Confederate army at Manassas Junction. Johnston's command was the decisive difference in the Southern victory at First Bull Run on the 21st.

Patterson, who had failed to keep Johnston in the Shenandoah Valley, read in a newspaper 23 July that he had been relieved of command. On 24 Aug. the Department of Pennsylvania was merged into the DEPARTMENT OF THE POTOMAC. On 1 Dec. 1864 the department was reconstituted as a part of the MIDDLE MILITARY DIVISION. —JDW

"Pennsylvania Bucktails" (13th Pennsylvania Reserves). In Apr. 1861 the Pennsylvania Volunteer Reserve Corps was created from companies in excess of those required to fill the state's first quota of men. Some of these companies from the northern part of the state became the 13th Pennsylvania Reserves (also designated the 42d Pennsylvania when the Reserve Corps regiments were given volunteer numbers). Because the 13th Pennsylvania Reserves adopted the custom of having each of its men wear on his hat the tail of a deer he had shot, it became known as the "Bucktails." The conduct of some of the men soon led to the designation "Bucktailed Wildcats."

The first colonel of the regiment was Charles J. Biddle, who was followed by Hugh W. McNeil (killed at Antietam), Charles F. Taylor (killed at Gettysburg), and W. R. Hartshorn. The regiment served in both the I and V corps in the Army of the Potomac.

In spring 1862 4 companies of the regiment were in the

SHENANDOAH VALLEY CAMPAIGN while the rest of the unit was with the army in the PENINSULA CAMPAIGN. The regiment fought at MECHANICSVILLE, WHITE OAK SWAMP, SECOND BULL RUN, ANTIETAM, FREDERICKSBURG (where it lost 19 killed, 113 wounded, and 29 captured or missing), GETTYSBURG (where it was prominent in the second day's battle on the Union left), the WILDERNESS, and SPOTSYLVANIA.

The term for which the regiment had enlisted expired, and it was mustered out of service June 1864. However, many reenlistees and latecomers with unexpired personal terms of enlistment were transferred to the 190th Pennsylvania. During its term of service the regiment lost 162 killed or mortally wounded and 90 who died from disease.

The 149TH AND 150TH PENNSYLVANIA regiments, both organized in late summer 1862, were sometimes called the "New Bucktails" because some of their officers came from the original Bucktail regiment.   —RMcM

Pennypacker, Galusha. USA b. Chester Cty., Pa., 1 June 1844. One of the neglected personalities of the Civil War had an improbable name and carved out an improbable military record as the war's youngest general.
Born near Valley Forge, Pennypacker grew up in the house used as headquarters by George Washington when his men wintered there. Pennypacker's mother died when he was 4, and his father went to California, leaving the boy with his grandmother, who saw that he received a good English and classical education.

LC

Pennypacker's grandfather had fought in the Revolution and his father had been an officer in the Mexican War. Pennypacker himself early acquired a reputation for "reliability in whatever depended upon his care." He was also described as being intelligent and "ever genial, cheerful, correct and manly in all respects."

In 1861, at age 16, Pennypacker enlisted for 3 months in Captain Henry R. Guss's company of the National Guard. On 22 Aug. 1861, he was elected captain of the 97th Pennsylvania Volunteers and that October was promoted to major.

For some time he was in the Department of the South, serving with distinction at Fort Wagner, DREWRY'S BLUFF, COLD HARBOR, PETERSBURG, and Green Plains. In 1864 his regiment joined Maj. Gen. Benjamin F. Butler's Army of the James, and on 15 Aug., at the age of 20, he was commissioned a colonel.

At FORT FISHER, 15 Jan. 1865, he led his brigade in a charge across a traverse and, having planted the colors of one of his regiments, fell wounded. After the battle he was hospitalized for 10 months at Fort Monroe. Brig. Gen. Alfred H. Terry called Pennypacker "the real hero of Fort Fisher," adding that without his bravery the fort would not have been taken. He was awarded the MEDAL OF HONOR for this act.

Just before his 21st birthday Pennypacker was made a brigadier general to rank from 18 Feb. and brevetted major general as of 13 Mar. 1865. He resigned from the army in 1866 but returned to the service as a colonel in the Regular Army, serving in the 34th Infantry, then in the 16th Infantry, in the South

during Reconstruction, and on frontier duty in Indian country. He retired in 1883, at the age of 39, and died a bachelor in Philadelphia, 1 Oct. 1916.   —AG

Pensacola, Fla., Union occupies. 10 May 1862 The loss of FORTS HENRY AND DONELSON early in 1862 threatened the safety of the western Confederacy. In response, officials in Florida decided to relinquish their hold on parts of the state's gulf coast, stripping local works in order to reinforce troops in Tennessee and Kentucky. In mid-February, Maj. Gen. BRAXTON BRAGG called for the evacuation of all state defenses, including his own post at Pensacola. Bragg himself was ordered west soon afterward and in his absence troop withdrawals from Pensacola began under the supervision of Col. Thomas M. Jones, 27th Mississippi Infantry.

Begun early in March, the evacuation took almost 2 months. It was done gradually to avoid alerting Union troops on Santa Rosa Island, across Pensacola Bay. By the first week in May troops and slave laborers had removed the post's heavy guns as well as most of its light cannon. Gone too were its ammunition and commissary stores, carried off at night.

On 7 Mar. Colonel Jones was informed by his superior, Brig. Gen. John H. Forney, commander of the DEPARTMENT OF ALABAMA AND WEST FLORIDA, that an enemy fleet was steaming down the Alabama coast, perhaps heading for Mobile. Following existing instructions, Jones prepared to lead his remaining troops to the threatened point. He was left with one large, final task: "the destruction of the beautiful place which I had labored so hard night and day for over two months to defend, and which I had fondly hoped could be held from the polluting grasp of our insatiate enemies." Under his direction, the troops torched Fort McRee; the Pensacola Navy Yard; the marine hospital and barracks; a large number of sawmills, planing mills, and window-sash factories; numerous lumber and cotton stores; and a quantity of boats. By the evening of the 9th $764,500 worth of Confederate property was ablaze.

The Federals across the bay noticed the flames and realized that a withdrawal was under way. Just after midnight their commander, Brig. Gen. Lewis G. Arnold, head of the Western District of the Department of the South, ferried across his chief of staff to receive the city's surrender. At dawn on the 10th Arnold occupied the Confederate position in force, salvaging what he could from the flames. By the 12th, some 1,000 troops had reached the city without encountering sustained opposition.   —EGL

percussion cap. The Rev. Alexander John Forsyth, a Scotsman, developed a percussion cap in 1805 and secured an English patent on a detonating lock of his design in 1807. Forsyth's cap, a crimped metal disc filled with fulminate of mercury and fitted over a nipple on the lock, eventually replaced the flintlock and powder-pan detonating system on smoothbore firearms. English regiments adopted the percussion system for Indian service in the 1830s and the percussion cap was widely used in the Crimean War. The U.S. Army adopted its first percussion weapons when it accepted designs for the U.S. carbine, Model 1840, and the U.S. cadet musket, Model 1841. At the start of the Civil War, caps, then filled with guncotton, were not in sufficient supply. U.S. and state armories fell back on their inventory of flintlock weapons until enough caps and percussion weapons could be procured and produced.   —JES

Perrin, Abner Monroe. CSA b. Edgefield District, S.C., 2 Feb. 1827, Perrin fought in the Mexican War as an infantry lieutenant in the Regular Army. Returning to South Carolina, he entered law school, passed the bar in Columbia in 1854, and practiced there until the outbreak of the Civil War.

USMHI

Commissioned a captain in the 14th South Carolina Regiment, he arrived at Port Royal, S.C., 1 Jan. 1862. By spring Perrin's regiment had been called to the Virginia peninsula in defense of the Confederate capital, Richmond. Throughout that year he fought commendably in the Seven Days' Campaign, and at Cedar Mountain, Second Bull Run, Harpers Ferry, Antietam, and Fredericksburg. After Brig. Gen. Samuel McGowan received a debilitating wound at Chancellorsville in spring 1863, Perrin took over his brigade, which he led in Maj. Gen. William D. Pender's division at the Battle of Gettysburg. At Falling Waters his men served as rear guard. For his service in 1863 he was promoted to brigadier general 10 Sept.

The following spring Perrin headed his brigade in a gallant stand in the Wilderness Campaign. His command consisted of the former brigade of Brig. Gen. Cadmus M. Wilcox, a part of Maj. Gen. James P. Anderson's division of Lt. Gen. Ambrose P. Hill's III Corps.

Before the Battle of SPOTSYLVANIA, which began 8 May 1864, Perrin made a prophetic remark: "I shall come out of this fight a live major general or a dead brigadier." He was killed in action near the "MULE SHOE" on the 12th. —FLS

Perry, Edward Aylesworth. CSA b. Richmond, Mass., 15 Mar. 1831. Though he was born, raised, and educated in New England, Perry became a Confederate commander, a staunch Southern Democrat, and governor of Florida.

He completed his primary education at the Richmond Academy before attending Yale in 1850. After 1 year there, Perry traveled south to Alabama, where he taught while studying law. In 1857 he moved to Pensacola, Fla., and established a law practice on his admission to the bar.

Because he sympathized completely with Secessionist Florida, particularly over STATES RIGHTS, at the start of civil war Perry closed his offices and organized a company of Florida natives to fight for the South. Elected captain of Company A/2d Florida Infantry, in May 1862 he accepted a promotion to colonel and commander of the regiment, soon answering a call to Virginia as a part of Lt. Gen. James Longstreet's division.

The Floridians' first fight came 31 May in the failed Confederate attack at Seven Pines, followed by the Seven Days' battles for Richmond. At WHITE OAK SWAMP, 30 June, Perry was severely wounded during Longstreet's attempt to break the Union lines. Though the assault failed, Longstreet praised Perry for his gallantry. On 28 Aug. Perry was commissioned a brigadier general in charge of the newly formed Florida Brigade.

He led his command in the victory at Chancellorsville, and at Gettysburg, 2 July 1863, he and his men broke through the Union lines in a brilliant but unsupported advance. His brigade and 2 others consequently withdrew, with his command sustaining some of the heaviest losses of the battle.

In 1864 Perry led his troops in the confusion at the Wilderness and was struck down by a serious wound for the second time in his short career. After months of convalescence he served in reserve in Alabama until the end of the war.

After the surrender Perry returned to his law practice in Pensacola, and his reputation as an attorney grew rapidly. So popular was he by 1884 that he was elected governor of Florida on the Democratic ticket. Within a year after his term ended, he died, 15 Oct. 1889, in Kerrville, Tex. He is buried in Pensacola. —FLS

Perry, Madison Starke. war governor b. S.C., 1814. Emigrating to Florida as a young man, Perry became one of the most prosperous planters in Alachua County and a prominent local political figure. In 1849 he was elected to the state legislature, the following year to the Florida senate, and in 1856 he became the Democratic gubernatorial candidate. Riding to victory on the wave of his party's national triumph, he defeated David S. Walker, the American Party candidate, by a scant 400 votes.

As Florida's 4th governor, Perry presided over a period of economic expansion, which featured the rise of state railroads and industries, particularly along the Atlantic and gulf coasts. Through improved transportation facilities, many previously inaccessible regions opened up to settlement, and the state's population climbed. Perry also presided over the negotiation of a long-standing border dispute with Georgia.

An avowed secessionist, he urged the reorganization and rearming of the state militia following JOHN BROWN'S 1859 RAID ON HARPERS FERRY. At the same time, Perry called for an "eternal separation from those whose wickedness and fanaticism forbid us longer to live with them in peace and safety." Such traits he ascribed to "black Republicans." In 1860, foreseeing the rise of a Northern sectional candidate, he warned his constituents to prepare for the "emergency of the approaching Presidential election." 20 days after Abraham Lincoln was elected, the governor sent a message to the Florida legislature declaring that the state's only acceptable course was a hasty departure from the Union. Even before South Carolina seceded, Perry announced Florida's readiness to "wheel into line with the gallant Palmetto State, or any other Cotton State. . . ."

By 1861 he was a lame duck; JOHN MILTON, a Jackson County planter, had won the Democratic nomination and the gubernatorial race. Perry's term, however, did not end until October. In the interim, he supported his state's secession convention, supervised the seizure of Federal arsenals and forts, made efforts to defend port cities on both coasts, and urged the recruiting, arming, and equipping of state troops for Confederate service. He proved inefficient as a wartime administrator, and his difficult workload, as well as numerous clashes with Milton and other political rivals, sapped his strength. After leaving office, he attempted to take command of the 7th Florida Infantry, but physical infirmities compelled him to resign and led to his death Mar. 1865. —EGL

Perry, William Flank. CSA b. Jackson Cty., Ga., 12 Mar. 1823. Perry's family moved to Chambers Cty., Ala., in 1833. With little or no formal education he taught in country schools in Talladega County 1848–53, studying law at the same time. Though admitted to the bar in 1854 he never established a practice and devoted the next several years to improving educational facilities in the state. Elected twice as state superintendent of education, 1854–58, he laid the basis for the free public-school system in Alabama. In 1858 he resigned to accept the presidency of East Alabama Female College at Tuskeegee.

A year into the war he enlisted as a private in the 44th Alabama Infantry. Elected major within weeks, Perry rose rapidly through the ranks, becoming lieutenant after Second Bull Run and colonel after Antietam. Assigned to Brig. Gen. EVANDER M. LAW's brigade at Gettysburg, he led the 44th in the assault on LITTLE ROUND TOP, was cited for gallantry at CHICKAMAUGA by Lt. Gen. James Longstreet, and fought at the WILDERNESS and SPOTSYLVANIA. He assumed command of Law's brigade after Cold Harbor, leading his men until they were paroled at Appomattox. His commission as brigadier general is dated 21 Feb. 1865.

After the war, Perry farmed for 2 years in Alabama before resuming his career as an educator. He was a professor of English and philosophy at Ogden College in Bowling Green, Ky., at the time of his death there, 18 Dec. 1901. —PLF

Perryville (Chaplin Hills), Ky., Battle of. 8 Oct. 1862 Confederate Gen. BRAXTON BRAGG and Maj. Gen. E. KIRBY SMITH met in Chattanooga, Tenn., 31 July 1862 and agreed to invade Kentucky. From Knoxville, Tenn., Smith marched north with 10,000 men 14 Aug.; won the Battle of RICHMOND, Ky., 30 Aug.; and by 3 Sept. had occupied the provisional Confederate capital, Frankfort. Bragg's 30,000 troops left Chattanooga 8 Aug.; besieged MUNFORDVILLE, Ky., 15, 16, 17 Sept.; moved north toward Louisville; then veered east, occupying Bardstown 21 Sept. 2 of Bragg's subordinates, Maj. Gens. LEONIDAS POLK and WILLIAM J. HARDEE, screened the area southeast of Louisville, while their commander went to Frankfort to supervise the installation of the Confederate state government. Union Maj. Gen. DON CARLOS BUELL's Nashville, Tenn., force timidly pursued Bragg through September, then entered Louisville on the 25th.

On 1 Oct., in the middle of the worst drought in years, Buell left Louisville with more than 50,000 men. Divided into 4 columns, they fanned out east and south. Following separate routes, Maj. Gen. ALEXANDER M. MCCOOK's I Corps on the left, Maj. Gen. THOMAS L. CRITTENDEN's II Corps at the center, and Brig. Gen. CHARLES C. GILBERT's on the right all headed for Bardstown and Harrodsburg, towns southwest of Frankfort. Buell's second-in-command, Maj. Gen. GEORGE H. THOMAS, traveled with Crittenden. Brig. Gen. Ebenezer Dumont, at the

head of the fourth column, led a large division directly east for a demonstration against Frankfort.

Poor intelligence convinced Bragg that Federals would attack Frankfort or Versailles to its south. Believing Dumont's column to be Buell's vanguard, he concentrated Kirby Smith's force around Frankfort. Unaware of the 3 intervening Union columns, he ordered Polk to attack Dumont's south flank.

Cavalry informed Polk of a growing force to his north. Advising Bragg of his movements, Polk sent Hardee to Perryville, southwest of Harrodsburg and 70 mi southeast of Louisville. His own troops concentrated at Harrodsburg, where Bragg joined him 5 Oct., urging that he and Hardee hurry north to the defense of Frankfort or Versailles. Hardee expressed concern about advance Union elements appearing west of Perryville, feared being attacked in flank if he moved north, and 6 Oct. requested reinforcements. Persuaded that Hardee faced only a large Union demonstration, Bragg testily agreed that Polk and Brig. Gen. JAMES P. ANDERSON's division could move south to Perryville. He said the force should "give the enemy battle immediately; rout him, and then move to our support of Versailles."

The 3 main Union columns suffered in unusual autumn heat, and, desperate for water, advance elements moved 6 and 7 Oct. toward Perryville, where shallow pools were reported in the bed of Doctor's Fork, a tributary of the Chaplin River 1.75 mi northwest of the town. Buell ordered all corps to concentrate there 7 Oct., but only Gilbert's men arrived that day, near dusk. His vanguard and advance skirmishers of the other 2

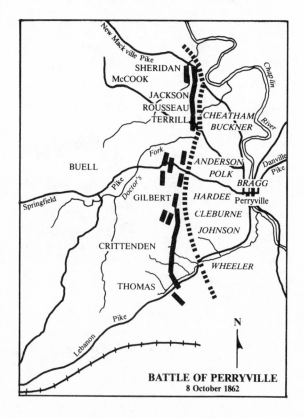

BATTLE OF PERRYVILLE
8 October 1862

columns had had sharp fights for 2 days with Confederate pickets guarding the little water remaining in Doctor's Fork. All columns had passed through Bardstown or south of Harrodsburg and did not know Polk's position or the number of troops in Perryville. Polk, with Anderson's division, had joined Hardee, and the night of 7 Oct., in council, the commanders decided to let the enemy make the first move. The Confederates mustered just 16,000 men.

Bragg, hearing that no attack had begun, arrived in Perryville early 8 Oct., hurried troops to the Doctor's Fork region to bring on a quick decisive engagement, and ordered Maj. Gens. BENJAMIN F. CHEATHAM's and SIMON B. BUCKNER's divisions to hit the left flank and left center of the force forming west of the mouth of the tributary. Buell pressed McCook and Crittenden forward and, uncertain of the size of the enemy force, urged Gilbert to show restraint. Brig. Gen. PHILIP H. SHERIDAN, Gilbert's subordinate, interpreting Buell's order loosely, brought on a brisk combat that morning to gain possession, he said, of only the pools of water. Fighting escalated near midday. Crittenden and Thomas took position on Gilbert's right at 11 a.m. McCook arrived near 12, throwing out a battle line far left of the III Corps. An unguarded ravine, formed by Doctor's Fork, separated him from Gilbert's left wing. Neither corps commander had his troops cover it.

Polk pressed forward Cheatham, Buckner, and 2 of Anderson's brigades as McCook was taking up position. The simple frontal assault became a desperate, close-quarters fight as Confederates exploited the unguarded ravine and rushed in on McCook's subordinates Brig. Gens. James S. Jackson, LOVELL H. ROUSSEAU, and WILLIAM R. TERRILL. Hardee, facing Gilbert, pressed forward Anderson's remaining men and Brig. Gens. PATRICK R. CLEBURNE and BUSHROD R. JOHNSON. Crittenden's troops, arched backward in a thin 3-mi line southwest of Perryville, never came into heavy combat. Confederate Col. JOSEPH WHEELER's 1,200 cavalry, with the aid of 2 cannon, kept the corps commander off-balance and unsure of how to proceed. Buell, several miles in the rear, did not hear the fighting because of an ACOUSTIC SHADOW and did not ride forward until notified of the action at 4 p.m.

The battle ended at dark. McCook's men had been shoved back more than a mile. Gilbert's had held on well but made no effort to reinforce McCook until late in the day. Buell determined to resume the battle 9 Oct., but the Confederates retired to Harrodsburg before morning. Federal losses totaled 4,211 in killed, wounded, and captured. Confederates lost 251 missing, 2,635 wounded, and 510 killed, Brig. Gens. Jackson and Terrill among the fatalities.   —JES

Petersburg Campaign. 15 June 1864–3 Apr. 1865 The Petersburg Campaign was the longest sustained operation of the Civil War. For 10 months, the Union Army of the Potomac besieged the vital railroad center 20 mi south of Richmond. Trench warfare and maneuvers for limited objectives replaced the strategic and tactical mobility that had characterized 3 years of warfare in Virginia. Throughout the campaign the Union army sidled toward the west to sever roads and railroads, the lifelines connecting the Confederate capital and its army to the Southern heartland and Atlantic coast. Miles of elaborate trenches, forts, redans, and ABATIS scarred the countryside. The Federals finally fixed in place the Confederate Army of Northern Virginia and eventually ground it down until the army broke.

The major Union offensive against Petersburg began in the darkness of 12–13 June when Maj. Gen. GEORGE G. MEADE's army, under the direction of Gen.-in-Chief ULYSSES S. GRANT, abandoned its trenches near COLD HARBOR. The previous 40 days of bloody combat from the Rapidan River to the James River had resolved little except for appalling casualties and Union repulses. While Grant and Gen. ROBERT E. LEE dueled, Maj. Gen. BENJAMIN F. BUTLER advanced from BERMUDA HUNDRED against Petersburg, only to display a remarkable operational incompetence. With Butler effectively bottled up by Confederates on the Bermuda Hundred peninsula, Grant decided to maintain the initiative and shift the campaign south of the James.

Grant's deep turning movement from Cold Harbor proceeded flawlessly. Screened by a cavalry division, the Federals secretly withdrew from Lee's front. After crossing the river on a specially constructed PONTOON BRIDGE, the Union troops marched on Petersburg, where only 2,500 defenders, under Gen. P.G.T. BEAUREGARD, manned the works. On 15 June Grant ordered Maj. Gen. WILLIAM F. SMITH's XVIII Corps and Maj. Gen. WINFIELD S. HANCOCK's II Corps to attack the Confederate lines. But the 2 corps commanders fumbled the opportunity. Smith advanced overcautiously and Hancock, without adequate orders, did not support Smith's feeble efforts. By nightfall Smith merely held a few outer lines. It was a bitter disappointment for Grant.

Other Union commanders repeated Smith's and Hancock's failure over the next 3 days. Petersburg remained vulnerable, but lack of coordination, contradictory orders, shoddy staff

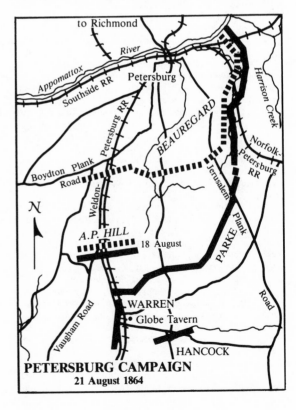

PETERSBURG CAMPAIGN
21 August 1864

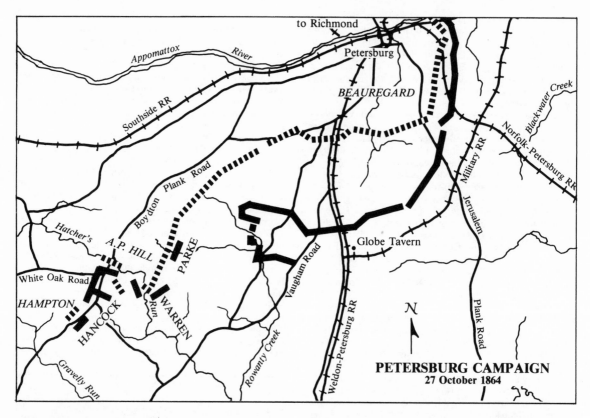

PETERSBURG CAMPAIGN
27 October 1864

work, and poor leadership resulted in a series of costly Union repulses. Beauregard may have rendered the Confederacy his greatest service by skillfully shifting his thin ranks, thus preventing a Federal breakthrough. Lee, who had been deceived by the scope of Grant's shift, finally responded to Beauregard's urgent requests for troops. By the 17th the vanguard of Lee's army had reached Petersburg, assisting in the repulse of the Northern charges. Lee had arrived by the next day, with most of his army close behind, and the works soon bristled with Confederate bayonets. In 4 days of combat Grant lost more than 11,000 men while only securing a few lines east of the city.

The antagonists then settled into a siege neither wanted. Grant had watched the army bungle an opportunity that might have ended the war. Within his grasp, victory seemingly exceeded the army's reach. Grant still held the initiative, yet a lengthy deadlock could sap his army's strength and adversely affect the forthcoming presidential election. For Lee, the siege meant a restriction in his renowned offensives and the burden of manning works that stretched from Richmond to west of Petersburg. The Confederate chieftain had to defend tenuous, but critical, supply lines while seeking an opportunity to attack a weakened section of the Union stranglehold. The conflict became an inexorable death struggle for the Southerners, who fought the enemy, disease, starvation, and desertion.

The pattern of the campaign soon emerged. The keys to Petersburg and ultimately Richmond were the roads and railroads supplying the 2 cities and their defenders. Grant moved

against these lifelines within days after his initial failure. From 22–24 June 2 Union corps attempted to sever the Weldon Railroad (see WELDON RAILROAD OPERATIONS) connecting Petersburg with North Carolina and points south. Confederate counterattacks secured the track. Grant, however, relentlessly extended his entrenchments south and west, forcing Lee to stretch further his lines. Between 18 and 21 Aug. the Federals seized the Weldon Railroad, denying its use to the Confederates for the remainder of the campaign.

The Union commander also attempted a sudden breakthrough and simultaneous operations north and south of the James River. The army's greatest fiasco occurred 30 July, when a regiment of Pennsylvania coal miners exploded a mine under a portion of the Confederate works (see Battle of the CRATER). The ensuing Federal attack into the huge crater resulted in a bloody disaster, illustrating the incompetency of Union officers and the ill luck that plagued their army. Grant's offensives north of the river against Richmond's works were intended to make Lee shift troops, thus weakening a sector of his lines so that Federal troops could penetrate it. Twice, when the mine exploded and in late September and early October, the Federals assaulted on the north side, but Lee brilliantly shuffled units to meet these threats, and, though he lost some works, his main lines held firm. By late fall the Union lines extended west of the Weldon Railroad and opposite the capital.

The suffering in the trenches increased during the winter. Scores of Confederates, unable to endure the hunger and deprivation, nightly entered Union lines and surrendered. The

Federals, moreover, continued their leftward shift, increasing Lee's losses. Early in February Union troops advanced against the Boydton Plank Road (see Battle of HATCHER'S RUN). Lee counterattacked, sustaining heavy losses, but temporarily kept the road open. Then late in March he attacked in a bold gamble to force Grant to retract his lines. Early on the 25th Maj. Gen. John B. Gordon's Confederates seized FORT STEDMAN east of the city. But the Federals counterattacked, wrenching the works from the Southerners, who lost 3,500 in the abortive attack.

The fall of Petersburg came a week after the engagement at Fort Stedman. On 1 Apr. Union infantry and cavalry crushed and routed a Confederate force at FIVE FORKS, a crossroads beyond Lee's western lines. The next day, at 4:30 a.m., Grant unleashed a massive assault on the Petersburg trenches. Lee's thinly held works dissolved under the onslaught. Lee extricated the remnant of his army but the fiercely defended city was in Union hands by nightfall. The next day Confederate authorities evacuated Richmond. On 9 Apr. Lee surrendered to Grant at Appomattox (*see* APPOMATTOX CAMPAIGN).

The Petersburg Campaign exacted approximately 42,000 Union casualties and 28,000 Confederate. The seemingly invincible Army of Northern Virginia was bled to exhaustion by the siege. When the final Union attack came, there were too few Southerners left to repel it. Grant's resources, manpower, and inexorable strategy overcame Lee's brilliant defense. Confined to trenches, the Confederates were doomed by attrition.   —JDW

Petersburg, Va., mine explosion. 30 July 1864 *See* CRATER, BATTLE OF THE.

Pettigrew, James Johnston. CSA   b. Tyrrell Cty., N.C., 4 July 1828, Pettigrew, commonly called by his middle name, Johnston, enrolled at the University of North Carolina at age 15. Graduating in 1847 after a brilliant scholastic career, he received an appointment from Pres. James K. Polk as assistant professor at the Naval Observatory in Washington, D.C. After holding the position for 2 years, he traveled to Germany, where he studied Roman law. Settling in Charleston, S.C., he practiced law, served in the state legislature, and attained the rank of colonel in the militia.

Pettigrew participated in the reduction of FORT SUMTER, Apr. 1861. After the outbreak of hostilities, he enlisted in the Hampton Legion and in May was elected colonel of the 12th South Carolina. The regiment went to Virginia but was little engaged. On 26 Feb. 1862, the Carolinian accepted a commission as brigadier general. Assigned command of a brigade in Maj. Gen. Gustavus W. Smith's division, Pettigrew led it at Seven Pines, where he was wounded and captured 1 June. Exchanged 2 months later, he served for nearly a year at Petersburg, Va., and in North Carolina.

Pettigrew returned to the Army of Northern Virginia May 1863 as a commander of a brigade in Maj. Gen. Henry Heth's newly created division, which led the Confederate advance and attack at Gettysburg 1 July. When Heth suffered a head wound in the action, Pettigrew assumed command of the division. He led it on the 3d in PICKETT'S CHARGE, and, though wounded in the hand, he refused to leave the field until the assault ended. During the retreat he resumed brigade command. On 14 July in the rearguard engagement at FALLING WATERS, Md., he was mortally wounded in the abdomen. He

lingered for 3 days, dying 17 July. Gen. Robert E. Lee said of Pettigrew's death that "the Army has lost a brave soldier and the Confederacy an accomplished officer."   —JDW

Pettus, Edmund Winston. CSA   b. Limestone Cty., Ala., 6 July 1821. After receiving his basic education at local common schools, Pettus studied at Clinton College in Tennessee and read law in Tuscumbia, Ala., gaining admittance to the bar in 1842. He established a practice at Gainesville and 2 years later was elected solicitor for the 7th Circuit Court. On being discharged from the army at the end of the Mexican War, Pettus traveled to California, staying there 2 years before returning to Alabama. Sometime in 1858 he moved to Cahaba. During the secession crisis, he was appointed a commissioner to Mississippi, where his brother, JOHN J. PETTUS, was governor, to discuss that state's plans to withdraw from the Union.

With future general ISHAM W. GARROTT, Pettus helped raise the 20th Arkansas Infantry, of which he was elected major, then lieutenant colonel 8 Oct. 1861. The 20th was initially part of Brig. Gen. E. KIRBY SMITH'S command in East Tennessee, marching into Mississippi to participate in the defense of PORT GIBSON. Pettus was captured when the garrison capitulated but escaped before he could be exchanged. On returning to the 20th, he distinguished himself during the Siege of VICKSBURG, was taken prisoner again when the city was surrendered, and was exchanged shortly thereafter. He returned to duty with a colonelcy, replacing Garrott, who had been killed in June. Taking the regiment east to Chattanooga, he fought at LOOKOUT MOUNTAIN and MISSIONARY RIDGE with a conspicuousness that brought him a promotion to brigadier general as of 18 Sept.

Through 1864 Pettus participated in all the campaigns involving the Army of Tennessee, at Nashville drawing praise from Lt. Gen. STEPHEN D. LEE for giving stiff resistance in the rearguard defense as the Confederacy's shattered Western army retreated. With Gen. JOSEPH E. JOHNSTON, Pettus fell back through the Carolinas, making last-ditch stands at KINSTON and BENTONVILLE, where he was wounded. Surrendered by Johnston at Durham Station, he returned home.

Settling in Selma, he reestablished his legal practice. Pettus represented his state at the national Democratic convention consistently 1876–96, the year he was elected to the U.S. Senate. Reelected to a second term, he served until his death in Hot Springs, N.C., 27 July 1907.   —PLF

Pettus, John Jones. war governor   b. Wilson Cty., Tenn., 9 Oct. 1813. The brother of future Confederate Brig. Gen. EDMUND W. PETTUS, John migrated with his family in 1814 to Alabama, where he received a rudimentary education. At age 22 he relocated in Mississippi, establishing himself as a prosperous cotton planter and slaveowner in Scooba. A prominent Democratic politician at the state level, he served 2 terms in the Mississippi house of representatives, 1844–46, and was elected to the state senate consistently 1848–58. Through the antebellum years, Pettus urged unity among the Southern states in the face of sectional dissension. An outspoken secessionist, he refused to attend the NASHVILLE CONVENTION in 1850, believing the time for compromise on the slavery issue had passed.

After his election to the governorship Nov. 1859, Pettus began preparing Mississippi for war by recruiting militia and calling for increased appropriations for military supplies and ordnance. Shortly after South Carolina seceded in December he called for a secession convention, which voted to take Mississippi out of the Union 9 Jan. By the middle of the month Pettus had sent several militia companies to Pensacola to assist in the siege of FORT PICKENS. Through the early months of 1861 he supplied the Confederate army generously with troops and tried to get the legislature to support COTTON DIPLOMACY by restricting cotton cultivation.

CWTI

Often his efforts to equip troops were frustrated by the 5-member military board that controlled the state's military spending. Despite some opposition to his war measures, Pettus won reelection by a comfortable margin in November.

Pettus' relations with Richmond became strained early in 1862 when war fever subsided as Mississippians began to suffer from war-induced shortages and the threat of invasion. The governor favored some form of conscription to fill the state's quota of troops but disagreed with Richmond over who had prior claim on the draftees. His attitude shifted from frustration to distrust and suspicion when troops were withdrawn from the state after Maj. Gen. Ulysses S. Grant's first unsuccessful assault on Vicksburg in July. Over the next year he invested heavily in fortifying the city, contended with strong pro-Union sentiment in the northeastern part of the state, and in May was forced to flee Jackson before Federal troops captured and burned the capital (*see* JACKSON, MISS., ENG. AT).

Mississippi's constitution prevented Pettus from serving a third term and Brig. Gen. CHARLES CLARK replaced him as governor that November. Unwilling to be inactive, Pettus enrolled as a private in the 1st Mississippi Infantry in summer 1864. He finished the war on staff duty with the rank of colonel.

Pettus signed a loyalty oath in Bolivar Cty., Miss., 4 Sept. 1865. On hearing rumors of his impending arrest he sought refuge on the farm of a cousin in Pulaski Cty., Ark. He took the oath again early in 1866 and friends tried to secure a pardon for him, but to no avail. He returned to his cousin's home, dying there of pneumonia either 25, 26, or 28 Jan. or 6 Feb. 1867. —PLF

Phelps, John Smith. war governor b. Simsbury, Conn., 22 Dec. 1814, Phelps received his elementary education at local schools and attended Washington (now Trinity) College in Hartford. He studied law under his father, being admitted to the bar in 1835. 2 years later he migrated to the frontier town of Springfield, Mo., establishing a prosperous legal practice. Elected as a Democrat to the state legislature in 1840, and to the U.S. House of Representatives in 1844, he developed a reputation as a skillful debater. During his 18 consecutive years in the national Congress, Phelps championed Federal funding for the building of railroads, the establishment of an overland mail line, and reduced postal rates. He was among the earliest proponents of admitting California and Oregon to the Union as free states.

After the firing on FORT SUMTER, Apr. 1861, Phelps returned to Missouri from Washington, D.C., and organized Phelps's Regiment, a 6-month unit he led in heavy fighting on the

second day of battle at PEA RIDGE, 8 Mar. 1862. His brief military career ended in July when ABRAHAM LINCOLN appointed him military governor of Missouri. On 29 Nov. Lincoln also appointed him brigadier general to rank from 19 July, but his commission expired Mar. 1863 when Congress failed to confirm the appointment.

Ill health forced Phelps to resign the governorship, and by 1864 he was once again practicing law. Better known as an efficient, personable politician than a soldier, he reentered public life as the Democratic candidate for governor in 1868, but was defeated because so many former Confederates within the party had been disenfranchised by Reconstruction legislation pushed through Congress by RADICAL REPUBLICANS. Over the next several years he labored successfully to ease war-related antipathies within the state Democratic party, which he led to victory in the gubernatorial election of 1876. After completing his 4-year term of office, he pursued his legal career until his death in St. Louis, 20 Nov. 1886. —PLF

Philadelphia Brigade. Though recruited in Philadelphia, this unit was made up of 4 regiments mustered into the Union army as the 1st, 2d, 3d, and 5th California at the insistence of California Sen. James A. McDougall, who paid to equip the 1st rather than have his state, too distant to provide troops for a conflict many believed would end quickly, unrepresented in the war. Organized by EDWARD D. BAKER, the other senator representing California, the 1st was recruited by Isaac J. Wistar in spring 1861, with Baker its colonel and Wistar lieutenant colonel.

Baker transported the 1st to New York for its training and 29 June the regiment passed through Philadelphia en route to Washington. By October the 1st had been joined by the 2d (Fire ZOUAVES), raised by Lt. Col. DeWitt Clinton Baxter from among the city's fire departments; the 3d, an almost all-Irish regiment recruited by Col. Joshua T. Owen; and the 5th, reorganized militia and 90-day men led by Col. Turner G. Morehead. Baker assumed command of the brigade, leaving Wistar in charge of the 1st.

Initially posted to the defenses of Washington, the brigade was first engaged in combat 21 Oct. at BALL'S BLUFF, where the men broke in confusion, the result of inadequate training and poor leadership from Baker, who was killed in the battle. With Baker dead, the unit assumed its identity as the Philadelphia Brigade, the 1st California being redesignated the 71st Pennsylvania. The 2d California became the 72d Pennsylvania, the 3d California the 69th Pennsylvania, and the 5th California the 106th Pennsylvania.

In Mar. 1862 Brig. Gen. WILLIAM W. BURNS, an experienced, competent Regular Army officer, took over the brigade. Designated the 2d Brigade/2d Division/II Corps, it fought 29 June at SAVAGE'S STATION during the PENINSULA CAMPAIGN. That September, under Maj. Gen. OLIVER O. HOWARD, the brigade formed the third line in Maj. Gen. JOHN SEDGWICK's division during the charge across the Cornfield at ANTIETAM. In that disastrous assault the Philadelphians were mowed down by a raking gunfire from the Confederate ranks, the 71st losing nearly 150 men and the Fire Zouaves counting 220 casualties.

Sent to garrison Harpers Ferry and recuperate, the brigade returned to the line in December and was the first unit to cross the Rappahannock River as Maj. Gen. AMBROSE E. BURNSIDE moved south to check Gen. Robert E. Lee's invasion of Maryland. Ordered to cover the right flank of the Federal column during the attack on Marye's Heights at FREDERICKSBURG, the brigade became an easy target for Confederate sharpshooters but was spared from Burnside's devastating attack on Lee's line.

In June 1863 the brigade marched into Pennsylvania when Lee again invaded the North, and fought on the Federal right on CEMETERY RIDGE at GETTYSBURG. Pitted against Lt. Gen. JAMES LONGSTREET's troops 2 July, the unit pushed back the Confederate assault, and on the 3d held its line against the furious onslaught of PICKETT'S CHARGE, the 69th losing all its field officers and about half of the 258 men engaged, the 72d counting 189 dead and wounded, and the 71st tallying losses of 25%. In the 2 days the Philadelphia Brigade captured 750 prisoners and 3 stands of enemy colors.

The fighting at Gettysburg destroyed the brigade as a unit. Brigaded briefly Mar. 1864 with the 152d New York, a heavy artillery regiment, the 71st and 72d were mustered out of service the next month when their enlistments expired. The 106th and the 69th merged with other depleted regiments and served until the war ended. In May 1865 they marched in the GRAND REVIEW of troops in Washington, D.C. The Philadelphia Brigade was the only Federal unit named for its home city. —PLF

Philippi ("Philippi Races"), western Va., Battle of. 3 June 1861

At dawn, 3 June 1861, an artillery shell exploded in the camp of raw Virginia troops at Philippi, in the northwestern section of Virginia. The explosion signaled a Federal attack by 5 regiments. The Confederates, taken by surprise, fled the field.

The "Battle" of Philippi became a tiny but well-publicized incident in Maj. Gen. GEORGE B. MCCLELLAN's drive to secure the BALTIMORE & OHIO RAILROAD and establish permanent Federal control of that largely Unionist portion of the state (today West Virginia). The immediate commander of the expedition, Brig. Gen. T. A. Morris, strove to mask his movement by encouraging the impression that he was about to descend on Harpers Ferry. The result of the clash, however, was determined by a meeting of officers called by Confederate commander Col. George A. Porterfield that opted for immediate retreat. Without cannon, experienced officers, or reliable ammunitions, Porterfield felt fortunate when the bulk of his men were able to escape in safety.

As the smoke settled, Col. BENJAMIN F. KELLEY of the Union 1st Virginia Volunteers lay severely wounded, but none of his comrades had been killed and only one other wounded. Porterfield's command had numbered around 1,000, though its officers were so ignorant of reporting procedures that no one knew precisely what the numbers were. Beyond sorely damaged pride, it sustained only 15 casualties. The Federals were able to make off with several Confederate flags, as well as a quantity of knapsacks, baggage, and munitions, but bemoaned the absence of Union cavalry, preventing captures *en masse*. An inquiry demanded by Porterfield praised his coolness under fire but chided him for failure to take precautions against surprise attack. —MPM

Philippoteaux, Paul. artist b. Paris, France, 1846.

A noted minor painter of historical scenes, Philippoteaux is remembered in America for his mammoth cyclorama, *The Battle of Gettysburg.*

Son of military artist Felix Philippoteaux, Paul began to study art seriously at 16, attended L'École des Beaux Arts in Paris, then, following the Franco-Prussian War, collaborated with his father on his first cyclorama, *The Defense of the Fort d'Issy* (1871). Displayed "in the round," providing paying customers with a full panoramic view of this Franco-Prussian War scene, *Fort d'Issy* was a commercial success. In the next decade Philippoteaux completed 6 more cycloramas depicting war in Europe, the Balkans, and North Africa and in 1881 traveled to Gettysburg, Pa., to sketch and photograph the battlefield. Calling *The Battle of Gettysburg* the greatest effort of his life, with the help of 5 assistants he completed this painting in Paris in 1884, then opened it for commercial exhibition in Boston, Mass., in 1885. Financial success there induced the artist to make 3 exact, full-scale copies of the work in the next several years for display in other cities.

For *The Battle of Gettysburg* New York City awarded Philippoteaux its Fine Arts Prize in 1910, and in 1913, for the 50th anniversary of the battle, his Boston cyclorama was permanently relocated in Gettysburg. The artist died in Paris, 2 July 1923, and 19 years later the U.S. government purchased his masterwork. The painting, done on individual panels 27 ft high, and the whole measuring 360 ft in circumference, has been restored and is displayed at the Gettysburg National Battlefield Park. One full-scale copy, privately owned, is known to survive in storage in the U.S. —JES

Phillips' Legion. CSA

In spring 1861 William Phillips, wealthy native of Marietta, Ga., organized 10,000 local volunteers into an infantry battalion, a cavalry battalion, and an artillery battalion. Known collectively as Phillips' Legion and intended to serve as a combined arms force, the units trained through June 1861, were reviewed and accepted into state service by Gov. JOSEPH E. BROWN 2 July at Big Shanty, and 12 Sept., at the insistence of the Confederate government, were assigned to duty in Brig. Gen. John B. Floyd's ARMY OF THE KANAWHA in Virginia.

The artillery battalion, broken up into individual batteries, was scattered throughout the Confederate army for the remainder of the war. Phillips, commissioned a colonel, led the remaining legionnaires until losing an eye early in winter. In November Governor Brown, a states-rights zealot, demanded the legion's return to Georgia for the defense of Savannah, claiming it had been armed and trained at state expense. Instead, it was assigned to Gen. Robert E. Lee's South Carolina command Dec. 1861 and remained in the state, quartered at Hardeeville, until late 1862.

Reassigned to Virginia, the legion guarded lines along the Rapidan and Rappahannock rivers, then fought at Fredericksburg in December and at Chancellorsville May 1863. At both battles the infantry and cavalry were separated: the cavalry served under Brig. Gen. J.E.B. Stuart; at Fredericksburg the infantry fought under Brig. Gen. Thomas R.R. Cobb and at Chancellorsville under Brig. Gen. William T. Wofford as a part of Maj. Gen. Lafayette McLaws' division of the I Corps.

By Lee's spring 1863 Special Orders No. 103, legion cavalry and infantry were permanently detached from one another. Until the Confederate surrender the legion cavalry served with Stuart, then with Maj. Gen. Wade Hampton, fighting all major cavalry engagements with the Army of Northern Virginia and, on Hampton's reassignment to the Carolinas Jan. 1865, all the last combats of the Army of Tennessee. The cavalry particularly distinguished itself at the 11–12 June 1864 engagement at TREVILIAN STATION, Va. Infantry legionnaires fought with the Army of Northern Virginia under McLaws from Gettysburg to Appomattox, except from late summer 1863 to spring 1864, when, as a part of Lt. Gen. James Longstreet's detached I Corps, they served in Tennessee. Delayed in transit, the infantry missed the Battle of Chickamauga but served in the Siege of Chattanooga and led the assault on the Union works at Knoxville.

Both battalions became badly depleted, and long before the end of the war neither could muster a regimental-size force. At no time following the Battle of Fredericksburg were they under the immediate command of an officer ranking higher than lieutenant colonel. Legion survivors and Marietta citizens erected a monument to Colonel Phillips and his efforts 17 May 1931. —JES

photography. MATHEW BRADY, America's foremost photographic entrepreneur, made an antebellum vow to photograph all his famous countrymen. Among his well-known subjects was former president Andrew Jackson. With the start of the Civil War, 2,000 photographers North and South embraced and expanded on Brady's historic decision. Seizing the moment, in Apr. 1861 the Charleston, S.C., photographic firm Osborn & Durbec made stereoscopic images of FORT SUMTER in Confederate hands, 3 days after the evacuation of the Union garrison. From that moment to the end of the Civil War, perhaps more than 1 million war photographs were taken. According to photographic historian William C. Davis, most were portraits. However, Brady and others fielded corps of photographers to make images in the countryside. Previously photographers had had some success with this: an unknown daguerreotypist made images of American troops in Saltillo, Mexico, in the late 1840s and photographers had made portraits of English and French troops in the Crimea in the 1850s.

James and ALEXANDER GARDNER, TIMOTHY O'SULLIVAN, and GEORGE N. BARNARD were Brady's best-known field operatives early in the Civil War. Northern firms other than Brady's gained prominence in later war years, among them Levy & Cohen of Philadelphia and Gardner's own enterprise, based in Washington, D.C. The firm of Haas & Peale made many views of Union troops in the Carolinas, and Confederate photographer Jay D. Edwards contributed to history by making about 100 images of Southern troops occupying Pensacola, Fla., during the FORT PICKENS crisis.

Edwards' Pensacola photographs, of which about 30 survive, are significant for showing Confederates in the field. The Union blockade of Southern ports made imported photographic chemicals hard to obtain in the Confederacy. Subsequently most Southern war photography consisted of studio portraits, pictures taken under conditions that economized on materials. Only one photograph taken of Confederates during active operations is known to be extant: an 1862 scene of Gen. Robert E. Lee's army marching through Frederick, Md., a photograph taken from the second story of a dry-goods store.

Rare were the photographs that successfully captured action. Louis Jacques Mandé Daguerre perfected a practical photographic process in France early in 1837. In ensuing years the collodion wet-plate process, requiring chemical-plate preparation and faster exposure time, replaced Daguerre's method. But wet plates, while allowing a subject to pose for a brief period, still could not capture physical movement, and their use required field photographers to travel in darkroom wagons filled with chemicals, colloquially called "what is it" wagons. In many pictures the blurred image of a horse tossing his head or a passerby moving through the background demonstrated this method's limitations.

Photographer's camp

USMHI

Once the image was "fixed" on a plate, commercial cameramen made prints for sale. These came in different formats. *CARTES DE VISITE*, portraits the size of calling cards, were popular, as were cabinet-size "Imperial" prints and stereo views, photographs taken with a binocular-lens camera that provided a 3-dimensional image when viewed through a stereoscope.

Alexander Gardner was believed to have come closest to capturing combat with a camera. On 17 Sept. 1862, at a great distance, while taking a landscape photograph of the Sharpsburg, Md., area during the Antietam Campaign, he made an image of what appeared to be troops in action. But through modern magnification methods, clouds of what had been believed to be gunsmoke are now shown to be either dust raised by distant troops, campfires, or haze drifting in from the main battleground.

Portraits and most views of armies in the field were taken for commercial use. Both Union and Confederate governments kept photographers on staff or hired independent cameramen for government work. The topographical departments of both armies used photographers as an aid to cartography, and the Confederate administration is known to have photographed sensitive documents. Capt. Andrew J. Russell, 141st New York Volunteers, under Brig. Gen. Herman Haupt served as the Union army's sole official photographer, taking photographs of railroad construction, bridges, and landscapes. Accompanying Maj. Gen. Joseph Hooker to Chancellorsville, Russell made some of the conflict's most famous photographs, images of Confederate dead at the Stone Wall on Marye's Heights at Fredericksburg, Va., and wreckage on the ground before it. George N. Barnard, an independent, was hired to photograph Union and Confederate fortifications around Atlanta for study by U.S. Army engineers.

In postwar years the work of Brady, Gardner, and O'Sullivan came into possession of the U.S. government. Today the National Archives, Library of Congress, and the U.S. Army Military History Institute, Carlisle, Pa., house the largest collections of Civil War photography.   —JES

Pickens, Francis Wilkinson. war governor b. St. Paul's Parish, S.C., 7 Apr. 1805. Pickens was the son of Gov. Andrew Pickens and grandson of Revolutionary War Gen. Andrew Pickens. He served in the state legislature 1832–34, in the U.S. House of Representatives 1834–43, and in the Senate 1844–46. He was minister to Russia for 2 years during the Buchanan administration and returned to South Carolina in 1860.

A member of South Carolina's ruling class, Pickens favored NULLIFICATION in the 1830s and was a lukewarm secessionist who appeared to be playing both sides. He was described as overbearing, impulsive, proud of his lineage, haughty, and rude and was frequently accused of giving offense.

On 16 Dec. 1860, after campaigning against ROBERT B. RHETT, Pickens took office as governor; 2 days later South Carolina seceded from the Union. 10 days after that, Maj. ROBERT ANDERSON moved his small force into FORT SUMTER.

Governor Pickens' hour of glory, however, was the period of almost 4 months when he tried to extricate Anderson from Sumter. Respectful of what guns Sumter had and conscious of his untrained forces, Pickens tried cajoling, threatening, and sending commissioners to Washington. On 9 Jan. 1861, Pickens sanctioned the firing on the *STAR OF THE WEST*, the ship Washington had sent down to bring supplies to the fort. Though the ship withdrew, there were no signs of any weakening of Anderson's resolve. And as indecisive weeks dragged along, constituents lost patience with the governor. Some called him a "peace-at-any-price" man.

Pickens' role in the drama was over when, 12 Apr., the newly formed Confederate government took matters into its own hands. Gen. P.G.T. Beauregard shelled the fort, and 14 Apr. Anderson capitulated.

Pickens' term as governor ended in 1862. He returned to his plantation to see the fortunes of the war go against the Confederacy, watch his slaves leave, and face his last years in debt. d. Edgefield, S.C., 25 Jan. 1869.   —AG

picket. An advance outpost or guard for a large force was called a picket. Ordered to form a scattered line far in advance of the main army's encampment, but within supporting distance, a picket guard was made up of a lieutenant, 2 sergeants, 4 corporals, and 40 privates from each regiment. Picket duty constituted the most hazardous work of infantrymen in the field. Being the first to feel any major enemy movement, they were also the first liable to be killed, wounded, or captured, and the most likely targets of snipers. Picket duty, by regulation, was rotated regularly in a regiment.   —JES

Pickett, George Edward. CSA b. Richmond, Va., 28 Jan. 1825, Pickett graduated from West Point in 1846, last in a class of 59. Among his several classmates who became generals were George B. McClellan and Thomas J. Jackson. In the war with Mexico Pickett was brevetted lieutenant and captain for his service in the Siege of Vera Cruz and during the subsequent advance on Mexico City. He served in Texas, Virginia, and Washington Territory until 1861, when he resigned his commission to enter the Confederate army.

LC

First a colonel, then a brigadier general, as of 14 Jan. 1862, he served under Maj. Gen. James Longstreet during the Seven Days' Campaign and was wounded at Gaines' Mill. As a major general, 10 Oct. 1862, commanding a division, he was at Fredericksburg. His name in Civil War history was secured in a losing cause, the charge against the Federal center on the third day at Gettysburg. Following bloody but inconclusive movements 1–2 July, Lee ordered the massive assault, which followed an intensive but basically ineffectual cannonade. Under Pickett's immediate command were the brigades of Brig. Gens. James L. Kemper, Richard B. Garnett, and Lewis A. Armistead. According to reports, Pickett was in excellent spirits and expected to carry the Union defenses. At midafternoon the forward movement began with the troops dressed as if on parade as they marched into the Federal guns. Pickett, as division commander, attempted to coordinate the ill-fated movement and, contrary to the view of some critics, acquitted himself bravely and well. But the task was impossible, and he ordered his men to withdraw when clearly they could not break the Union center. (*See* PICKETT'S CHARGE.)

Notwithstanding the bravery of his troops and his own efforts on the field, Pickett's military reputation was afterward in decline. He fought in battles at New Berne, Petersburg, and Five Forks. Gen. R. E. Lee relieved him of his command after Sayler's Creek, only days before the final surrender at Appomattox. Following the war he was an insurance salesman in Richmond and died in Norfolk, 30 July 1875.   —JTH

Pickett Papers. On 28 Mar. 1865, Confederate State Department clerk William J. Bromwell left Richmond, Va., entrusted by Sec. of State JUDAH P. BENJAMIN with the safe transfer of all state papers to Charlotte, N.C. Following Confederate military defeat and the flight of Confederate cabinet members, Bromwell took personal possession of the documents, moved to Washington, D.C., hid the papers in a suburban barn, and retained Washington attorney John T. Pickett to represent him in offering the material for sale. Advising Bromwell to remain anonymous, Pickett approached the U.S. government in 1868, 1869, and 1871, asking that they buy the records. Congress finally appropriated $75,000 for their purchase in 1871, on the condition that they were first authenticated by a government representative. Pickett, claiming the papers were hidden in Canada, then took them to Ontario, where they were appraised and approved by U.S. Navy Lt. THOMAS O. SELFRIDGE. Delivered to the U.S. government 3 July 1872, they were first used to assess war-damage claims brought against it by civilians. They were called the Pickett Papers because of the attorney's involvement, and their true owner was revealed only after the sale. Southern friends rejected Bromwell, who traveled to England to escape criticism and died there in 1875.   —JES

Pickett's Charge, at Gettysburg, Pa. 3 July 1863 A foreboding stillness pervaded the battlefield at GETTYSBURG at 3 p.m., 3 July 1863. For the 2 previous hours Confederate artillerists had hurled shells and balls into the center of the Union line on CEMETERY RIDGE near a small clump of trees. Then the Army of Northern Virginia (50 regiments, 11 brigades from 4 divisions—over 13,000 Confederates) emerged from the woods on Seminary Ridge. It was an amazing sight, a mile-long line, perfectly aligned, flags unfurled, all field officers mounted, war's pageantry and horror merged into one, as Gen. ROBERT E. LEE gambled at Gettysburg with the last doomed charge of the Confederacy.

With parade-ground precision the Southerners advanced across the nearly mile-wide open ground. Union artillery crews waited patiently and then unleashed their fury. Exploding shells toppled Confederates in clusters but others shifted, filling the gaps. Through the firestorm the Confederates marched, across the Emmitsburg road, then up the slope. Maj. Gen. GEORGE E. PICKETT's division of all-Virginia regiments spearheaded the assault, knifing toward the clump of trees. Union infantry finally fired, supported by sheets of artillery canister. Entire segments of the Southerners' line vanished under the searing discharges. The bravest Confederates—only a handful of the force—poured over a stone wall, disappearing under a blue wave of Federal reinforcements. Along the attackers' flanks, Union infantry and artillery enfiladed the line. On the Confederate left, North Carolinians penetrated the farthest, but Federal firepower ravaged the attackers, shoving them back. It was over in less than an hour, and the price paid was fearful. "The task was too great," Lee told the survivors.   —JDW

Piedmont, Augusta Cty., Va., eng. at. 5 June 1864 The Confederate victory at New Market, Va., 15 May 1864, tem-

porarily removed a Federal threat to the upper Shenandoah Valley. Gen. ROBERT E. LEE consequently transferred Maj. Gen. JOHN C. BRECKINRIDGE's infantry from the valley to Richmond. The defense of the valley shifted to Brig. Gen. WILLIAM E. "GRUMBLE" JONES and a combined infantry and cavalry force of about 8,500 effectives. The capable Jones was primarily responsible for the security of Staunton, with its warehouses and track of the vital Virginia Central Railroad.

To Union authorities the 15 May defeat required a change of command and the commitment of a larger force to the capture of Staunton. 6 days after the battle Maj. Gen. DAVID HUNTER replaced the discredited Maj. Gen. FRANZ SIGEL. Hunter's orders specified an immediate advance on the railroad center, then an operation across the Blue Ridge Mts. against Gordonsville or Charlottesville. To augment Hunter's army, Gen.-in-Chief ULYSSES S. GRANT directed Brig. Gen. GEORGE CROOK, who was stationed in the Allegheny Mts., to march his force into the valley and combine with Hunter. These 2 Union commands numbered nearly 20,000.

Hunter began his advance southward 26 May, Crook 5 days later. Hunter's troops followed the Valley Pike to Harrisonburg, where they turned eastward. Jones, confronting the 2 forces, detached 2 cavalry brigades to delay Crook while he, with 5,000 men, deployed across Hunter's line of march. Soon after daylight, 5 June, the Federals encountered Jones's pickets near Piedmont, 7 mi south of Port Republic.

The Confederate skirmishers withdrew to Jones's main line drawn closer to the town. About 9 o'clock Hunter's artillery opened fire; an hour later Col. Augustus Moor's Federal brigade drove against the Confederate left. The Confederates grudgingly fell back as Col. Joseph Thoburn's brigade moved against their other flank. The battle sputtered until about 1 p.m., when Moor charged, only to be repulsed. Jones counterattacked, but Thoburn's soldiers stopped the Confederates. Moor then renewed his attack, assisted by a cavalry brigade charging on the Southern right. The outnumbered Confederates buckled and finally broke into a stampede. While rallying his fleeing troops, Jones was killed.

The Federals captured nearly 1,000 and killed or wounded another 600. Hunter's decisive victory cost him 780 casualties. The next day Union troops entered Staunton, where destruction began immediately. Crook arrived on the 8th and 2 days later the Federals headed south into the vitals of the upper valley.   —JDW

Pierpont, Francis Harrison. war governor b. Monongalia Cty., western Va., 25 Jan. 1814. On graduating from Allegheny College in Meadville, Pa., Pierpont taught school in Virginia, then in Mississippi. His father's poor health brought him back to Virginia, where he read law and amassed a substantial fortune as an attorney for the Baltimore & Ohio Railroad and in the coal-mining business. Though a presidential elector for the Whig party, 1844–60, Pierpont did not hold elective office before the Civil War. In 1860 he was a hardline antislavery Unionist and a supporter of Abraham Lincoln.

Pierpont and a majority of the residents in the western counties of the state refused to accept the ordinance of secession passed by the Virginia legislature Apr. 1861. Pierpont organized a rump session of representatives from the pro-Union counties, and at Wheeling the next month they seceded from Virginia, wrote a constitution, renamed their state West Virginia, and elected Pierpont governor. When Congress formally admitted West Virginia to the Union in 1863, a new governor was elected and Pierpont moved his headquarters to Alexandria to finish out the war as governor of the restored state of Virginia in those few northern counties occupied by Federal troops. Following the Federal army into Richmond Apr. 1865, he tried unsuccessfully to ease tensions between the people of Virginia and West Virginia.

The Reconstruction Act of 1868 replaced him with a military governor, allowing Pierpont, whose asset was determined loyalty to the Union rather than political genius, to retire to his legal practice. He served once in the state legislature in 1870 and as collector of internal revenue under Pres. James A. Garfield. d. Pittsburgh, Pa., 24 Mar. 1899.   —PLF

Pigeon's Ranch, New Mexico Territory, Battle of.
26–28 Mar. 1862   *See* LA GLORIETA PASS, NEW MEXICO TERRITORY, BATTLE OF.

Pike, Albert.
CSA   b. Boston, Mass., 29 Dec. 1809. Pike's family moved soon after his birth to Newburyport, Mass., where he received his early education. He spent 1824–31 teaching, affiliated with schools in Gloucester, Fairhaven, and Newburyport, and in private study. In Mar. 1831 Pike started west, finally reaching Independence, Mo., where he joined a group of hunters and traders going to Santa Fe in New Mexico. After some time there, he accompanied another expedition into the Staked Plain of New Mexico and Texas. By 1833 he had arrived in Arkansas and was teaching school in Pope County. The 300-lb Pike became a poet of considerable reputation; a successful lawyer, planter, and newspaper publisher; and a not-so-successful Confederate brigadier general.

USMHI

A Whig, Pike opposed Arkansas' secession until the last moment, but once the Confederacy became a reality, he used his long familiarity with Indian tribal leaders to convert their tribes to the Confederate cause. Having gained $800,000 for the Creeks and others in a long court fight with the Federal government, he was an ideal envoy to Indian Territory. On 15 Aug. 1861, Pike was commissioned a brigadier general in the Confederate army. He began the military training of Indian men and assured Maj. Gen. Earl Van Dorn Jan. 1862 that he would have 7,000 ferocious warriors ready for action; the 3 Indian regiments he led to northern Arkansas Feb. 1862 numbered only one-third of that total.

On 7–8 Mar. they were sent into action as part of Van Dorn's army in the Battle of PEA RIDGE. Pike's warriors rashly attacked a Federal artillery battery under Col. PETER J. OSTERHAUS 7 Mar. and scared the gunners into a headlong retreat.

But the Indians stopped to celebrate victory and were routed in a Federal counterattack. Pike never was able to reassemble his troops, thus contributing to the Confederate defeat, and the angry Van Dorn pointedly ignored Pike's presence in his reports of the battle.

Pike's troubles were magnified by Federal claims that his Indians had scalped a number of dead or wounded soldiers on the field. Northern newspapers condemned the unlucky general. Then came an acrimonious exchange of charges between Pike and the new commander of the Trans-Mississippi District, Maj. Gen. Thomas C. Hindman, over the handling of money and material. Hindman ordered Pike's arrest, but he disappeared into the Arkansas hills and was never court-martialed. His resignation was accepted 11 Nov. 1862.

After the war, he returned to his law practice and became a national spokesman for Freemasonry in his later years. d. District of Columbia, 2 Apr. 1891.   —DS

Pillow, Gideon Johnson.
CSA   b. Williamson Cty., Tenn., 8 June 1806. After graduating from the University of Nashville in 1827, Pillow became a successful lawyer in Columbia, Tenn., in partnership with James K. Polk. A staunch Democrat, he played a significant role in engineering Polk's 1844 presidential nomination. 8 years later he was active in the convention that nominated Franklin Pierce and was an unsuccessful aspirant for the vice-presidential nomination at the 1852 and 1856 conventions.

In 1846, Pres. Polk appointed Pillow brigadier general of volunteers and later made him major general. Pillow, who communicated frequently with Polk, led a division in Gen. WINFIELD SCOTT's army on its campaign from Veracruz to Mexico City. He was twice wounded and engaged in an acrimonious and disruptive quarrel with Scott.

Although Pillow, supporting Democrat STEPHEN A. DOUGLAS in 1860, opposed secession, he cast his lot with Tennessee when it left the Union. Gov. ISHAM G. HARRIS named him senior major general in Tennessee's provisional army, and 9 July 1861 he entered Confederate service a brigadier general. He led a division at BELMONT, Mo., 7 Nov. 1861 and rushed to FORT DONELSON in the second week of Feb. 1862. As second-in-command to Brig. Gen. JOHN B. FLOYD, he urged and led the Confederate attack on the 15th that rolled back the Federals. Losing his nerve, he yielded initiative and recalled troops. That night the Confederate leaders met and agreed that their only option was surrender. Floyd relinquished the command to Pillow, who passed it to Brig. Gen. SIMON B. BUCKNER. The two senior officers escaped before the surrender was consummated.

Pillow was suspended from command by the War Department Mar.–Aug. 1862. On 2 Jan. 1863 he led a brigade at Stone's River. Other assignments, most of them administrative, followed.

After the war Pillow and former governor Harris established a successful law partnership in Memphis. d. Helena, Ark., 8 Oct. 1878.   —ECB

Pinkerton, Allan. secret service b. Glasgow, Scotland, 25 Aug. 1819. Though Pinkerton liked to think of himself as the Union's greatest spy-master, few of its servants were more bitterly criticized or derided. Far from aiding the Union, Pinkerton probably helped its army lose the PENINSULA CAMPAIGN in 1862 by feeding Maj. Gen. GEORGE B. MCCLELLAN vastly overrated estimates of Confederate strength, causing McClellan to hesitate and stumble in his attack on Richmond.

Pinkerton had great abilities, but not as a spy. He came to the U.S. in 1842, gaining quick success in police work when he caught a gang of counterfeiters, and rapidly rose to deputy sheriff of Cook County, Ill. By 1850 he had organized his own Pinkerton National Detective Agency, and in 1861 he guarded president-elect ABRAHAM LINCOLN on his way to Washington.

LC

Allan Pinkerton, seated left

Pinkerton was selected to organize the Federal Secret Service and to conduct intelligence operations for McClellan, then in command of the Department of the Ohio. When the general moved to attack Richmond by way of the James River peninsula in 1862, he used Pinkerton and his detectives to spy out Confederate troop strengths in Virginia. But Pinkerton's men were untrained to spy on armies and relied too heavily on the reports of frantic civilians and illiterate escaped slaves. In a series of reports signed with his pseudonym, "Major E. J. Allen," Pinkerton warned that the Confederates ranged from 180,000 to 200,000 when they had hardly a third of that number. McClellan, overcautious to begin with, frittered away one opportunity after another because of Pinkerton's information, and the Peninsula Campaign ended in failure.

When McClellan was relieved of command after the battle at ANTIETAM, Pinkerton's stock fell flat. He returned to his detective agency and continued to be the most famous American detective, even if his agency is best remembered for breaking up strikes and labor unions in the 1870s. Melodramatic and pompous to the end, he wrote several popular books about his adventures before his death 1 July 1884.   —ACG

Pioneer, **CSS.** The Confederacy realized that, to make its sea power equal to that of the North, it had to adopt naval machinery so improved and advanced as to render existing ships obsolete. From this realization came the *Pioneer,* built at New Orleans during winter 1861–62 by 2 munitions and steam-gauge engineers, John McClintock and Baxter Watson, who operated a local machine shop with private capital.

The submarine was completed Feb. 1862. Fabricated of ¼-in. sheet iron fastened with ⅝-in. countersunk rivets, it was 34 ft long overall, with a 4-ft beam and 6-ft depth, conical ends, and was painted black. Entrance was gained by a single hatchway at the center. The propeller was turned by cranks operated by 2 men seated facing each other on iron brackets fastened directly below the hatchway. The station of the pilot was well forward within reach of the diving lever, rudder control, depth gauge, and air cock. The vessel was armed with a powder magazine fastened to a towline.

During tests the vessel sank a barge placed as a target and was immediately declared a success. Application was made 29 Mar. for a letter of marque, listing it as a 4-ton submarine propeller, with John K. Scott of New Orleans as commander. It was to begin operations 12 Apr. under the appropriate name *Pioneer.*

But *Pioneer* never had an opportunity to face the enemy. Before it could be cleared for action, New Orleans was besieged by the Union, forcing the vessel to be scuttled in Bayou St. John to keep it from falling into Union hands.

In 1868 a dredge deepening the bayou accidentally struck the *Pioneer.* Raised to the surface and placed on the bank, it remained there until 1908, when the Sons of Confederate Veterans had it moved to the Louisiana State Home for Confederate Soldiers and placed on display on a concrete base, unprotected from the weather. The *Pioneer* later was moved to the Louisiana State Museum.   —VCJ

pioneers. Pioneers were, usually, skilled soldiers detached from their regular units to clear roads, construct bridges, dig trenches, and erect fortifications; sometimes civilians were hired or impressed for such service. Typical pioneer tools were billhooks, spades, pickaxes, saws, mattocks, and felling axes.

The Federal army periodically organized pioneer units, usually informally. When the Civil War began, such units volunteered for service in the Union army and others were formed in the U.S. Veteran Reserve Corps and the U.S. Colored Troops. Nevertheless, additional pioneers were needed but not always available. One officer complained that the manner of detail and number of pioneers per division or corps had not been provided for, although the type and number of pioneer tools had been announced in orders.

Maj. Gen. WILLIAM S. ROSECRANS attempted to remedy the situation. On 3 Nov. 1862, he ordered 2 men detached from each infantry company in his army. The 3,000 men became the Pioneer Corps of the ARMY OF THE CUMBERLAND.

Few, if any, pioneer units volunteered for service in the Confederate army. Also, the Confederates lacked orders regulating the organization of pioneers, though one issued in 1863 required the formation of engineer regiments. Gen. ROBERT E. LEE suspended this order within his command because he felt it would restrict operations of the pioneers.

The duties of pioneers and engineers were similar. Attempting to clarify the roles of each, a Civil War officer wrote that pioneers "move with the advance of the army" and engineers are "chiefly employed on the lines of communication."

The pioneers were an important adjunct to the Civil War armies. Perhaps Rosecrans most aptly appraised their worth when he wrote that the loss of his pioneers' services for one day would cost the government $200,000.   —DEF

Pittsburg Landing, Tenn., Battle of. 6–7 Apr. 1862 *See* SHILOH, TENN., BATTLE OF.

Pleasant Grove, La., Battle of. 8 Apr. 1864 *See* MANSFIELD, LA., BATTLE OF.

Pleasant Hill, La., eng. at. 9 Apr. 1864 Early on the morning of 9 Apr. 1864 Confederate Maj. Gen. RICHARD TAYLOR set forth to complete what he was confident he had begun the day before in the BATTLE OF MANSFIELD—the destruction of Maj. Gen. NATHANIEL P. BANKS's army. His force numbered about 13,000 effective troops, having been reinforced during the night by Brig. Gen. THOMAS J. CHURCHILL's 5,000 infantry from Arkansas.

In contrast to Taylor, Banks was apprehensive as he awaited the Confederates at Pleasant Hill. Although he had more than 18,000 men, many of them were still half demoralized by the previous day's humiliating defeat. He placed his main reliance on Brig. Gen. ANDREW J. SMITH's 2 veteran divisions, which had not participated at Mansfield.

At midafternoon Taylor came within striking distance. After resting his road-weary men for a couple of hours, he deployed them for the attack: Churchill was to swing around to the west and hit the Federal left flank, the rest of the infantry was to move against the enemy's front, and the cavalry was to slip around Banks's right and cut off his retreat.

At 5 p.m. Churchill struck. Caught by surprise, the Federal left wing, composed of troops routed at Mansfield, crumpled. Cheering triumphantly, Churchill's men pushed on with the intention of assailing the Union center from the rear. However, Smith, perceiving not only the peril but also the opportunity, brought up troops from the Federal reserve and right, then hit Churchill's right flank and drove it back. In turn the rest of Taylor's army broke and fled. Thus, when seemingly on the verge of a great victory, the Confederates suffered a resounding defeat, losing 1,621 casualties to the Federals' 1,369.

Despite the victory, Banks the following day resumed his retreat, wishing only to escape from the wilds of west Louisiana. On the other hand, Taylor, despite his defeat, wished to resume the pursuit of Banks. However, his departmental commander, Gen. E. KIRBY SMITH, instead sent most of Taylor's infantry to counter the Union thrust from Arkansas. Hence the Battle of Pleasant Hill proved to be the last major encounter of Banks's RED RIVER EXPEDITION.   —AC

Pleasant Hill Landing, La., eng. at. *See* BLAIR'S LANDING.

Pleasonton, Alfred. USA b. District of Columbia, 7 July 1824, Pleasonton graduated 7th in the class of 1844 at the U.S. Military Academy. After graduation he received regular promotions for meritorious and gallant service in the Mexican War and for his performance in various frontier areas.

During the Civil War, Pleasonton, promoted to brigadier general as of 16 July 1862, served as a cavalry officer and assisted in the reorganization of the often maligned Cavalry Corps of the Army of the Potomac. In the largest cavalry battle

of the war, at BRANDY STATION, Va., 9 June 1863, the Union cavalry gave notice of its growing ability to match Confederate cavalry. Confederate Maj. Gen. J.E.B. STUART was assembling his cavalry at Brandy Station to screen Gen. ROBERT E. LEE's invasion of Pennsylvania. Pleasonton's force of 3 cavalry divisions and 2 infantry brigades came very close to discovering Lee's army at Culpeper and wrecking the cavalry screen under Stuart. On 22 June Pleasonton was promoted to major general.

USMHI

In Mar. 1864 he was transferred to the DEPARTMENT OF THE MISSOURI to command the cavalry forces of Maj. Gen. WILLIAM S. ROSECRANS. In Oct. 1864 Confederate Maj. Gen. STERLING PRICE invaded Missouri with an army of almost 10,000. Taking command in the field, Pleasonton repulsed Price at Jefferson City, Mo., then pressed hard on Price's rear until Maj. Gen. SAMUEL R. CURTIS could organize his forces to confront Price. Battles were fought at the Little Blue and Big Blue rivers and at the Marais des Cygnes River, all in eastern Kansas. Pleasonton forced a passage across the Blue rivers to turn Price's right flank, thus requiring the Confederates to fight on Union terms. The result of this campaign was the virtual destruction of the best of Price's cavalry and the defeat of his expedition. Had Pleasonton and Curtis pursued Price closely, they could have inflicted even more damage; but they delayed, arguing over who should receive credit for the victory.

In the Mar. 1864 reorganization of the army, Maj. Gen. PHILIP H. SHERIDAN replaced Pleasonton as Cavalry Corps commander. Embittered at finding himself junior to men he had outranked and sometimes even commanded, Pleasonton resigned his commission Jan. 1868. d. District of Columbia, 17 Feb. 1897.   —PMMcC

Plum Point Bend, Tenn., eng. at. 10 May 1862 *See* PLUM RUN BEND, TENN., ENG. AT.

Plum Run Bend (Plum Point Bend), Tenn., eng. at. 10 May 1862 In spring 1862 Union Maj. Gen. JOHN POPE and Flag Officer ANDREW H. FOOTE had taken ISLAND NO. 10 on the upper Mississippi River. Now only Confederate Fort Pillow, 40 mi north of Memphis, Tenn., and a Confederate gunboat fleet provided effective protection of the river. Pope and Foote had planned to take the fort, destroy the fleet, and capture Memphis, but before their plans could be put into effect most of Pope's troops were ordered to join Maj. Gen. HENRY W. HALLECK's army at Pittsburg Landing. Foote could only threaten Fort Pillow. On 9 May Foote went on sick leave, his 7 ironclads, 16 mortar boats, 1 wooden gunboat, and 2 army regiments coming under the command of Capt. Charles H. Davis.

In response to the threat, Col. M. JEFF THOMPSON'S CONFEDERATE RIVER DEFENSE FLEET, 8 converted steamers commanded by Capt. James E. Montgomery, planned to attack the Federal fleet. The Confederate vessels, lacking heavy armament and armor, would rely on wood and cotton-bale armor, their rams, and their relatively high speed. Each carried only 1 or 2 guns.

On 10 May the Confederate ships moved upriver against

Union mortar boat No. 16, which was guarded by the Union ironclad *Cincinnati.* When the ironclad was caught by surprise, the rest of the Union fleet began to react. The Confederate ram *General Bragg,* after taking fire from the mortar boat, rammed the *Cincinnati,* then recoiled in the face of a Union broadside. The CSS *Sterling Price* rammed the *Cincinnati* a second time while the CSS *Sumter,* coming at full speed, struck it again. The *Cincinnati* rolled and sank in 11 ft of water.

Meanwhile, the CSS *General Earl Van Dorn* moved past the *Bragg* and against the oncoming ironclad *Mound City.* The ship rammed the Union gunboat and sank it on a sandbar. The remaining Confederate boats did not come within ramming distance but used their guns and sharpshooters. After 30 minutes, the Confederate fleet withdrew.

Confederate casualties were light, 2 men killed and 1 wounded. None of their craft was seriously damaged, whereas 2 Union gunboats were sunk, both later put back into commission. On 5 June Fort Pillow was discovered abandoned. The next day, in the Battle of Memphis, the Confederate fleet was effectively destroyed. The engagement at Plum Run Bend delayed but did not stop Union control of the upper Mississippi.   —LDJ

Poe, Orlando Metcalfe. USA b. Navarre, Ohio, 7 Mar. 1832. A descendant of Germans who settled in Maryland in the mid-18th century, Poe entered West Point in 1852 and graduated 4 years later 6th in his class. As a lieutenant of topographical engineers, he helped survey the northern lakes, a project completed just before the outbreak of the Civil War.

In June 1861 Poe helped raise units of Ohio volunteers, then served in Maj. Gen. GEORGE B. MCCLELLAN'S DEPARTMENT OF THE OHIO as a topographical engineer, accompanying "Little Mac" to western Virginia for that summer's campaigning. When McClellan went east as commander of the ARMY OF THE

USMHI

POTOMAC, Poe followed him and assisted in organizing the DEFENSES OF WASHINGTON.

Poe left staff duties for field command Sept. 1861 when named colonel of the 2d Michigan Infantry. He led the regiment during McClellan's PENINSULA CAMPAIGN, being conspicuous for gallantry at WILLIAMSBURG and SEVEN PINES. On sick leave during the SEVEN DAYS' CAMPAIGN, he later received a brigade in the III Corps. At the head of his new command he saw considerable action at SECOND BULL RUN, but during the ANTIETAM CAMPAIGN he remained idle in the capital defenses. He returned to the field in time for the debacle at FREDERICKSBURG, leading a brigade in the IX Corps that was only lightly engaged.

Though Poe had been appointed a brigadier general of volunteers prior to Fredericksburg, the Senate failed to confirm his promotion, and his commission in the volunteers expired early Mar. 1863. As a result, he reverted to his Regular Army rank of captain of engineers, at which grade he went to Tennessee as chief engineer of the XXIII Corps. There he helped construct the defenses of Knoxville and assisted in their

defense during Lt. Gen. JAMES LONGSTREET's siege.

In spring 1864, Poe was named chief engineer of Maj. Gen. WILLIAM T. SHERMAN's Military Division of the Mississippi. He rendered Sherman varied and valuable service during the ATLANTA CAMPAIGN, the MARCH TO THE SEA, and the CAROLINAS CAMPAIGN. By war's close he had attained the brevet of brigadier general of Regulars.

In postwar years he was an aide to Sherman, served on the Lighthouse Board, and supervised engineering projects on the Great Lakes. An injury received on the lakes led to his death in Detroit, 2 Oct. 1895.   —EGL

Poindexter's Farm, Va., Battle of. 1 July 1862 *See* MALVERN HILL, VA., BATTLE OF.

point d'appui. A fortified or secure point that anchored or strengthened an army's position was called a *point d'appui.* The Sunken Road and Stone Wall at Marye's Heights, Fredericksburg, Va., are examples of this. Civil War lexicographer Mark Boatner cites its original meaning as a "support" or "fulcrum."   —JES

Point Lookout. The largest prison in the North was established 1 Aug. 1863, at Point Lookout, Md., on the low peninsula where the Potomac runs into the Chesapeake Bay. It consisted of "two enclosures of flat sand, one about thirty and the other about ten acres, each surrounded by a fence fifteen feet high, all utterly innocent of tree or shrub." There were no barracks within the prison enclosures; prisoners, enlisted men, lived in tents. At times there were nearly 20,000 inmates, and the tents were overcrowded. Water was scarce, particularly when the shallow wells became polluted and it had to be imported. Black troops formed a large part of the guard, and there was much animosity between them and the prisoners. A Confederate soldier who had been confined at Point Lookout wrote: "Murder was not only scrupled at, but opportunities sought for its commission by the guards, who are known to have been offered by the officer of the day as much as ten and fifteen dollars apiece for every prisoner they could shoot in the discharge of their duty." That soldier and several others purchased their freedom from Point Lookout.

Anthony M. Keiley, a prominent citizen of Petersburg, Va., who was taken prisoner early in 1864 and spent several months at Point Lookout, recalled that the tent camp was

but a few inches above ordinary high tide, and was visited in winter by blasts whose severity caused death. . . . The case of the prisoners was pitiable indeed. The supply of wood issued to them during the winter was not enough to keep up the most moderate fires for two hours out of the twenty-four, and the only possible way of avoiding freezing was by unremitting devotion to the blankets. This, however, became impossible when everything was afloat.

Of the prisoners' meals Keiley wrote: "I never saw anyone get enough of anything to eat at Point Lookout, except the soup, and even a teaspoonful of that was *too much* for ordinary digestion." Several accounts of life in the prison refer to rat catching as both a sport and a source of meat.   —PR

Poison Springs, Ark., eng. at. 18 Apr. 1864 On 15 Apr. 1864, Union Maj. Gen. FREDERICK STEELE, with 14,000 troops, occupied Camden, Ark., until that time the Confederate

Point Lookout prison

stronghold in the state. Under orders to proceed to Shreveport, La., he expected to link up with Maj. Gen. NATHANIEL P. BANKS for joint operations in Louisiana during the RED RIVER CAMPAIGN. On reaching Camden, Steele learned that Banks was in retreat after PLEASANT HILL, ending his participation in the expedition. Rather than withdraw immediately, Steele remained at Camden to await developments. But an accident that seriously damaged 2 steamers carrying supplies to Camden left Steele dangerously short of provisions. To relieve the hunger of soldiers and civilians dependent on him, the commander ordered a forage party into the countryside to gather corn the Confederates had stored at several outlying farms.

On 17 Apr. Col. James M. Williams left Camden with 695 men—438 of them black troopers from the 1st Kansas Colored Volunteers—2 guns, and 198 empty wagons. By late afternoon the detachment had traveled 14 mi on the Prairie D'Ane–Camden road. There Williams bivouacked, sending half the wagons to retrieve the largest cache of corn from its storage area 6 mi distant. By midnight they had returned safely with the forage.

At dawn on the 18th, Williams started the train back to Camden, sending out details to collect the remaining corn from scattered depots along the return route. 4 mi out of camp he was reinforced by nearly 500 men and 2 additional guns, increasing his force to 1,170.

Meanwhile, Confederate scouts in the area reported Williams' movements to Brig. Gen. JOHN S. MARMADUKE, who moved toward the Lee plantation, 10 mi from Camden, dismounted 1,700 of his men, and deployed them across the

road. Shortly before 9:30 a.m. Maj. Gen. SAMUEL B. MAXEY arrived with his division from Confederate headquarters at Woodlawn, bringing Confederate strength to 3,335. Though he outranked Marmaduke, Maxey deferred to the Missourian, at his direction taking position behind a wooded ravine parallel to the road on the left of the Confederate line. Marmaduke's own men held the right, those of Brig. Gen. WILLIAM L. CABELL and Col. William Crawford, the center. Col. Colton Greene's 300 mounted troopers waited in reserve.

At 10 a.m. the Federal advance encountered Confederate skirmishers a mile east of Williams' main column. The gunfire brought his detachments back to the supply train. Williams hastily formed a defense, deploying the 1st Kansas in a battle line with cavalry on both flanks. A battery opened fire on the Confederates to provoke a response that would indicate the enemy's strength; but the Southerners' 12 guns remained silent. The Confederates lunged forward at 10:45, delivering a terrific fire on the Union defenders. A fierce counterassault compelled one part of the Southern line to fall back, but before Williams could exploit the gap, Greene's reserves charged into the hole.

For three-quarters of an hour the Union commander held firm. Desperately outnumbered, he tried stubbornly to protect the supply train, hoping the sound of battle would bring help from Camden. Then the Confederates slammed into the Union rear as 6 of Marmaduke's guns opened up, catching Williams' men in a devastating crossfire. Before Williams could form a second line, the remnants of the 1st Kansas fled to the rear. His shattered command rallied long enough for most of the unhurt survivors and walking wounded to reach the protection of a marsh nearby, but by 2 p.m. the fighting had ended, with 26% of Williams' force fallen on the field. His men dispersed and began making their way back to Camden, the last of them reaching the Union garrison on the morning of the 19th.

Williams' casualties amounted to 204 killed and missing and 97 wounded. Of these, 117 blacks died and 65 were wounded. Intent on getting the wagons to safety before Steele could pursue from Camden, Maxey assumed command after the rout and countermanded Marmaduke's order for a full-scale pursuit. Had he not, the losses would have been even higher. Witnesses claimed that the Confederates had ruthlessly murdered black soldiers who had been wounded and captured. The Southerners denied the charges, claiming the blacks died in great numbers because they had done most of the heavy fighting, or had refused to throw down their arms when captured; but their animosity toward blacks and brutal treatment of them on other battlefields support evidence of a massacre at Poison Springs.

Confederate losses were much lower: 114 to all causes; in exchange they captured the 198 supply wagons and the 4 Union guns. More important, the victory, the Confederates' first since Steele had departed his base in Little Rock a month earlier, provided a much-needed boost in morale for an army that had suffered a series of defeats in its own territory.   —PLF

Polignac, Camille Armand Jules Marie, Prince de. CSA

b. Millemont, Seine-et-Oise, France, 16 Feb. 1832. A member of one of the most distinguished families in French history, Polignac served with honor in the French army during the Crimean War and in 1859 resigned his commission to explore and study plant life in Central America, where he was living when the American Civil War began. 29 years old at the time, he immediately offered his services to the Confederacy and was accepted. On 16 July 1861 he received the rank of lieutenant colonel of infantry and began his service as chief of staff to Gen. P.G.T. BEAUREGARD. Polignac fought bravely at SHILOH and CORINTH and served on Beauregard's staff during the reorganization of the general's army in the area around Corinth. But the Frenchman's greatest contribution to the Confederacy came west of the Mississippi.

By 10 Jan. 1863 Polignac was a brigadier general serving with the command of Maj. Gen. RICHARD TAYLOR, operating in Louisiana under Lt. Gen. E. KIRBY SMITH. Polignac particularly distinguished himself in spring 1864 during the Confederates' defense against Union Maj. Gen. NATHANIEL P. BANKS'S RED RIVER CAMPAIGN. At the start of the campaign, Polignac's brigade was a unit of Brig. Gen. ALFRED A. MOUTON's division; when Mouton was killed in the bloody charge against the Federals near MANSFIELD, 8 Apr., Polignac rushed forward and assumed command, winning a spectacular victory. General Taylor wrote: "The gallant Polignac pressed the shattered division stubbornly and steadily onward after Mouton fell." On 13 June the Frenchman was appointed major general, with rank dating from the day of the battle, and he retained command of the division for as long as he was in Louisiana.

In Mar. 1865 Polignac went to France to seek aid for the Confederacy from Emperor Napoleon III. Before he could get any definite promises, news reached France of Gen. Robert E. Lee's SURRENDER, which doomed his mission. He decided against returning to the U.S. and retired to his French estate, where he wrote many articles about the Civil War. The last

surviving Confederate major general, Polignac died in Paris, 15 Nov. 1913 and was buried in Germany.   —PR

Polk, Leonidas. CSA b. Raleigh, N.C., 10 Apr. 1806, Polk
attended the University of North Carolina before his appointment to West Point, where he became a close friend of JEFFERSON DAVIS and graduated 8th in the class of 1827. Deeply influenced by the academy chaplain, Polk resigned his 2d lieutenant's commission soon after graduation to enter the Virginia Theological Seminary. He was ordained a deacon in the Episcopal Church in 1830 and 6 years later was appointed missionary bishop to the Southwest. In 1841 he was named bishop of Louisiana and spearheaded a long but successful campaign to establish "a great Episcopal university in the South." On 9 Oct. 1860 Bishop Polk laid the cornerstone for the University of the South (Sewanee).

USMHI

During the secession crisis, Polk felt the South was fighting for a sacred cause and, like many medieval bishops, exchanged his clerical vestments for a soldier's garb. On 25 June 1861, President Davis appointed Polk major general in the Provisional Confederate Army. Placed in command of DEPARTMENT NO. 2, including forces charged with defense of the Mississippi River approaches to the Southern heartland, Polk sent a column to take possession of and fortify Columbus, Ky.

On 15 Sept. 1861, he was succeeded as commander of the department by his West Point roommate Gen. ALBERT SIDNEY JOHNSTON. Polk served Johnston as a loyal subordinate, defeating Brig. Gen. U. S. GRANT at BELMONT and serving at SHILOH as a corps commander. During the thrust deep into Kentucky, he led a corps under Gen. BRAXTON BRAGG, who commended him at PERRYVILLE. Polk was promoted to lieutenant general to rank from 10 Oct. 1862.

Relations between Polk and Bragg, strained during the Kentucky Campaign, were exacerbated following the Confederate defeat at STONE'S RIVER 31 Dec. 1862–2 Jan. 1863. In 1863 they reached a breaking point after CHICKAMAUGA, when Bragg ordered Polk to face a court-martial because Polk had failed to attack at daybreak 20 Sept. as ordered.

President Davis sought to pacify the situation, and Polk was detached from the ARMY OF TENNESSEE and placed in command of the DEPARTMENT OF ALABAMA, MISSISSIPPI, AND EAST LOUISIANA, where he failed to distinguish himself in opposing the march of Maj. Gen. WILLIAM T. SHERMAN's columns from Vicksburg to Meridian. In mid-May 1864 Polk and his Army of Mississippi reinforced the Army of Tennessee, now led by Gen. JOSEPH E. JOHNSTON, in northwest Georgia. On 14 June 1864, while reconnoitering the Union positions from atop Pine Mountain, he was killed by an artillery shell. Polk was the uncle of Brig. Gen. LUCIUS E. POLK.   —ECB

Polk, Lucius Eugene. CSA b. Salisbury, N.C., 10 July
1833. Polk's family, members of the Southern aristocracy, moved to Columbia, Tenn., in 1835. Having received a basic education there, he attended the University of Virginia 1850–

51. Shortly thereafter he settled near Helena, Ark., establishing a prosperous plantation. At the onset of civil war he enlisted as a private in the "Yell Rifles," whose captain was the future Confederate general PATRICK R. CLEBURNE. The company mustered into Confederate service as part of the 15th Arkansas, and Polk advanced to 2d lieutenant.

Assigned to Cleburne's command, the 15th fought its first battle at SHILOH Apr. 1862, where Polk was wounded. Shortly after returning to the field, he was advanced to colonel and led the regiment aggressively at RICHMOND, Ky., in August and at PERRYVILLE in October. Cleburne commended his leadership frequently in reports, and 13 Dec. Polk was rewarded with a brigadier's star.

Through 1863 he fought in all the battles involving Maj. Gen. CARTER L. STEVENSON's division. He was prominent at STONE'S RIVER, led a gallant but futile unsupported charge on Maj. Gen. GEORGE H. THOMAS' well-fortified breastworks at CHICKAMAUGA, and withstood the unswerving Union attack on MISSIONARY RIDGE until the Confederate supply wagons were withdrawn to safety. Under Cleburne he opposed Maj. Gen. WILLIAM T. SHERMAN's thrust toward ATLANTA, until being critically wounded by artillery fire at KENNESAW MOUNTAIN. Rendered permanently unfit for duty, Polk left the army to recuperate at his father's plantation near Columbia.

Polk has received far less attention for his distinguished Confederate army career than has been accorded the service rendered by his uncle, Lt. Gen. LEONIDAS POLK, who achieved high rank because of his position in antebellum Southern society rather than because of any talent as a military leader.

Despite the severity of his wounding, Lucius Polk survived the war by 27 years. In 1884 he represented Tennessee at the Democratic national convention and 3 years later was elected to the state senate. d. Columbia, Tenn., 1 Dec. 1892.

—PLF

Pollard, Edward Alfred. journalist, author b. Nelson Cty., Va., 27 Feb. 1832. Following his graduation from Hampton-Sydney College in 1846, Pollard attended the University of Virginia 1847–49, studied law in Baltimore, and early in the 1850s worked as a journalist in the California gold fields. In 1856 he traveled to Asia, returning to Virginia 2 years later.

An avid secessionist who defended slavery as the foundation of Southern society, Pollard was hired as an editor of the RICHMOND *EXAMINER* in spring 1861, helping to turn it into an anti-administration newspaper. Until Federal troops entered Richmond Apr. 1865, he championed Confederate success, but strenuously opposed JEFFERSON DAVIS, accusing the president of being an obstinate, conceited intellectual who was mismanaging the government.

One of the most talented and prolific writers in the South, Pollard produced a 4-volume history of the war between 1862 and 1866. He was captured in 1864 while running the blockade to England to promote his books and imprisoned for 8 months in FORT MONROE and FORT WARREN before being exchanged and sent south Jan. 1865.

In the immediate postwar years, Pollard was the main Confederate apologist, even praising Davis, whom he blamed for the South's defeat, to preserve the memory of the Southern bid for independence. His best-known work, *The Lost Cause* (1866), was a condensed version of his four-volume Confederate history. It introduced the phrase LOST CAUSE and defined it for a war generation struggling to live with defeat.

Pollard left the *Examiner* in 1867 and edited 2 unsuccessful newspapers, *Southern Opinion* (1867) and *The Political Pamphlet* (1868). His writings after 1866 assumed a more conservative, nationalistic tone, and in 1868 he took the IRON-CLAD OATH. Shortly thereafter he moved to New York City, where he lived the last few years of his life. d. Lynchburg, Va., 16 Dec. 1872.

—PLF

Pomeroy Circular. In late 1863 and early 1864 Sec. of the Treasury SALMON P. CHASE, an Ohioan, campaigned quietly for the Republican presidential nomination. Sensing national party leaders' dissatisfaction with ABRAHAM LINCOLN and believing himself the better candidate, he courted the favor of senators and congressmen and established an informal campaign organization. Chase supporter Kansas Sen. Samuel C. Pomeroy wrote, or caused to be written, an anti-Lincoln letter that denigrated the president's leadership and promoted Chase's qualities. Circulated privately, it won Chase some congressional support; on 22 Feb. 1864 it appeared in several Washington newspapers.

Mortified by the crude circular, and disavowing any connection with it, Chase offered Lincoln his resignation. Lincoln refused to accept it, saying he felt Chase was not responsible for Pomeroy's action. The circular prompted state Republican leaders to rise to Lincoln's defense. Ohio Republicans repudiated Chase, and 5 Mar. the secretary ended his campaign.

—JES

Pon Pon River, S.C., eng. at. 10 July 1863 *See* WILLS-TOWN BLUFF, S.C., ENG. AT.

pontoon bridge. The pontoon bridge was a floating causeway that facilitated the rapid transportation of men and equipment across water barriers. Developed by the French and Russians, the pontoon bridge was used extensively in the Civil War under the jurisdiction of the U.S. Army Corps of Engineers and by Confederate PIONEERS. In addition to military bridges, pontoons were employed as wharves, loading docks, and railroad bridges.

The essential component was a flat-bottomed boat, or pontoon, available in wooden or canvas models. The cumbersome, 31-ft-long wooden type was used more frequently because of its durability. Canvas pontoons, 10 ft shorter and considerably lighter, enjoyed the advantage of easy handling and transportation. Specifically designed army wagons carried the pontoons with their full complement of balks (crossties) and chess (flooring).

Laying a pontoon bridge began with a single boat rowed upstream, its anchor secured, and the lead rope played out until properly positioned. Then a second one followed the same process, aligning itself with the first. As additional pontoons were placed, each was secured by interlocking the balks with the gunwales. The chess was laid on top and held down by side rails lashed to the balk. As a final measure, the chess received a layer of dirt to quiet the sounds of crossing and preserve the flooring.

Pontoon bridges were crucial to numerous campaigns. At FREDERICKSBURG, Dec. 1862, they provided the only avenue of attack for the Federal army. 6 months later a single floating bridge carried the retreating Confederates across the flooded Potomac River to safety. Probably the most spectacular use of these bridges occurred 15 June 1864, when Union engineers

erected a 2,200-ft span in just 5 hours, enabling Lt. Gen. U.S. GRANT to cross the James River ahead of Gen. R. E. LEE.
—MJO

USMHI

USMHI

"Pook Turtles." "Pook Turtles" was the name given to 7 Federal ironclad gunboats—the *Cairo, Carondelet, Cincinnati, Louisville, Mound City, Pittsburg,* and *St. Louis* (later renamed the *Baron De Kalb*)—after their designer, Samuel M. Pook. Pook and engine designer Thomas Merritt were employed by John B. Eads, who Aug. 1861 was contracted by the War Department to build armored vessels for use on Western rivers. Because they were named after Western river ports, they were also referred to as "city class." 4 of the gunboats were built near St. Louis and the other 3 at Mound City, Ill.

Round-nosed and flat-bottomed, each Turtle weighed 512 tons, was 175 ft long, and had a draft of 6 ft. Their slanted casements were protected by 2.5 in. of iron-plate armor. Armed with smoothbore and rifled cannon, the Turtles were manned by Regular Navy men, volunteers, detailed army personnel, and contract civilians. Despite serious defects in their design, the Pook Turtles contributed much to Federal successes in the RIVER WAR on Western waters 1862–63.

—NCD

USMHI

Pope, John. USA b. Louisville, Ky., 16 Mar. 1822. Raised in Illinois, Pope entered the U.S. Military Academy at age 16. Assigned to the engineers after graduating 17th in a class of 56 in 1842, he was brevetted captain for gallantry in the Mexican War. An excellent horseman, in 1853 he became a 1st lieutenant and 3 years later was a captain. That he was sociable, courageous, and energetic could not be disputed, but he was also impetuous and a loud-mouthed braggart with an abrasive personality that offended many people. As another Western general stated, "I don't care for John Pope one pinch of owl dung."

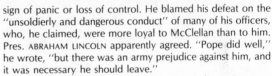

LC

In July 1861, shortly after the outbreak of the Civil War, Pope was appointed brigadier general of volunteers. Early in 1862 he commanded the Army of the Mississippi in the campaign to open up the Mississippi River and was successful in capturing NEW MADRID, Mo., and ISLAND NO. 10, thus opening up all of the upper half of the Mississippi. For this he was promoted to major general 22 Mar. and called east. Although decisively defeated by Gen. ROBERT E. LEE'S ARMY OF NORTHERN VIRGINIA at SECOND BULL RUN, Pope withdrew into the fortifications around Washington with no

sign of panic or loss of control. He blamed his defeat on the "unsoldierly and dangerous conduct" of many of his officers, who, he claimed, were more loyal to McClellan than to him. Pres. ABRAHAM LINCOLN apparently agreed. "Pope did well," he wrote, "but there was an army prejudice against him, and it was necessary he should leave."

Sent to the West to campaign against Indians, Pope remained a top frontier commander in various positions until his retirement in 1886, a period in which he became a respected, though controversial, commentator on frontier conditions and Indian problems. He died at the Old Soldiers' and Sailors' Home in Sandusky, Ohio, 23 Sept. 1892, at the age of 70.

—JPC

Poplar Spring Church, Va., Battle of. 30 Sept.–2 Oct. 1864 *See* PEEBLES' FARM, VA., BATTLE OF.

popular sovereignty. First known as territorial sovereignty, popular sovereignty is most often associated with STEPHEN A. DOUGLAS, but originated in 1848 as an alternative to the Wilmot Proviso, a measure that would have excluded slavery from any territory acquired in the Mexican War. Proposed by Democratic Vice-Pres. George M. Dallas and formally introduced in Congress by New York Sen. Daniel S. Dickinson, the concept supported local self-determination of the slavery issue, calling on the Federal government to neither establish nor prohibit slavery by national action, but to allow the people in each territory to decide for themselves whether they would enter the Union slave or free.

Michigan Democratic senator and presidential candidate Lewis Cass gave territorial sovereignty strong support, questioning Congress' authority to enact legislation for a territory, a power he claimed compromised the right of territorial residents to determine their internal affairs "under the general principles of the Constitution." The idea was ambiguous enough to appeal to both Northerners and Southerners, particularly since none of the proponents of territorial sovereignty defined the term "general principles." Compounding the vagueness was the unresolved question of when the people of a territory should decide to accept or reject slavery. Northerners claimed the decision could be made at any time by a territorial legislature, but Southerners insisted a territory had to be open to slavery when it was organized, allowing both slaveholders and free-soilers to settle the land, and the decision made when the residents sought statehood.

Unlike proslavery and free-soil factions, the later advocates of popular sovereignty optimistically believed slavery could not exist outside the South, where climate and geography permitted labor-intensive agriculture. They were able to apply their principles to the article organizing New Mexico and Utah as territories under the COMPROMISE OF 1850 without rescinding the MISSOURI COMPROMISE, but in 1854 Douglas, as chairman of the Committee on Territories, invoked popular sovereignty in the KANSAS-NEBRASKA ACT, which repealed the Missouri Compromise and infuriated the Northern public by opening the territories to slavery. —PLF

Porter, David Dixon. USN b. Chester, Pa., 8 June 1813. Union Sec. of the Navy GIDEON WELLES once qualified his generous praise of Porter with the observation that he was "given to Cliquism." Small wonder—
Porter's family was a powerful clique in itself. His father, David, was a distinguished naval officer and diplomat, his brother was Commodore WILLIAM D. PORTER, his adopted brother was Adm. DAVID G. FARRAGUT, and his cousin was Gen. FITZ JOHN PORTER.

Porter first went to sea with his father at age 10. After junior service in the Mexican navy and a stint as a prisoner of war of the Spanish, Porter returned to the U.S. in 1829 and joined the

USMHI

navy. His assignments were varied, but advancement was slow in peacetime service. Porter had mastered his profession and chafed for action; indeed, the energetic officer made no secret of his intent to leave the navy and seek an outlet for his talents elsewhere.

The secession crisis changed his plans. On 1 Apr. 1861, Cmdr. Porter eagerly accepted command of the *Powhatan* and of the naval portion of an expedition to relieve Florida's FORT PICKENS. Porter and the *Powhatan* remained in the Gulf of Mexico during the first year of the war. Early in 1862 he began preliminary plans for the capture of New Orleans and assumed command of a mortar flotilla during the assault on the city. Porter also received the surrender of FORTS JACKSON

AND ST. PHILIP after the fleet had run by them.

In Oct. 1862 he took command of the Mississippi Squadron and assumed responsibility for the Mississippi and its tributaries north of Vicksburg. In cooperation with the Federal army he was involved in the capture of ARKANSAS POST Jan. 1863 and then VICKSBURG in July. For the latter action he was promoted to rear admiral. With increased rank came increased responsibility—the Mississippi River system north of New Orleans.

After a courageous performance in the abortive RED RIVER CAMPAIGN of spring 1864, Porter went east to command the NORTH ATLANTIC BLOCKADING SQUADRON. In subsequent assaults on FORT FISHER he commanded the largest American fleet ever before assembled. The capture of the fort and defenses of Wilmington closed Porter's combat service in the war.

Immediately after the war Porter became superintendent of the Naval Academy. In this service and later with the Navy Department, he stressed professionalism and rewarded active service. Made admiral in 1870, Porter was himself active to the end of his life, dying in the District of Columbia, 13 Feb. 1891. —EMT

Porter, Fitz John. USA b. Portsmouth, N.H., 31 Aug. 1822, Porter began the war as one of the Union's most promising officers and finished in controversy. Born the son of a naval captain, and cousin of future Adm. DAVID D. PORTER and Commodore WILLIAM D. PORTER, he graduated 8th in the West Point class of 1845 and earned 2 brevets for gallantry in the Mexican War. After 6 years as an artillery instructor at the Academy, he was assigned as adjutant to Col. ALBERT SIDNEY JOHNSTON during the Utah Expedition.

In Aug. 1861 Porter was appointed brigadier general of volunteers to rank from 17 May. A loyal supporter of Maj. Gen.

USMHI

GEORGE B. MCCLELLAN, he fought with distinction through the PENINSULA CAMPAIGN of 1862, particularly at MECHANICSVILLE, and GAINES' MILL during the SEVEN DAYS' CAMPAIGN. For skillfully covering the army's retreat at MALVERN HILL, he received a promotion to major general, 4 July 1862.

That same summer McClellan's star faded and most of his troops were transferred to Maj. Gen. JOHN POPE's Army of Virginia. Like most of McClellan's officers, Porter despised Pope; unlike most of them, he said so openly. After Pope's humiliating debacle at SECOND BULL RUN in August, Pope charged Porter with disloyalty, disobedience, and misconduct in the face of the enemy. Meanwhile, Porter served again with McClellan at the Battle of ANTIETAM.

Relieved of command Nov. 1862, Porter saw his career swallowed by political vendettas. His court-martial was presided over by officers loyal to Sec. of War EDWIN M. STANTON, who loathed McClellan and any of his followers. After a controversial trial Porter was found guilty and cashiered from the army 21 Jan. 1863. He spent the remainder of his life struggling to clear his name. Not until 1878 did a board headed by Gen. JOHN M. SCHOFIELD exonerate Porter of all charges. But again politics intervened and it was not until 1886 that Pres. Grover

Cleveland signed a bill restoring Porter to the rank of colonel, without awarding him back pay.

The controversy over Porter's guilt or innocence has continued among historians, most of whom conclude that the only offense committed by that talented officer was indiscretion. d. Morristown, N.J., 21 May 1901. —MK

Porter, John Luke. CSN b. Portsmouth, Va., 19 Sept. 1813. Porter, a co-designer of the CSS VIRGINIA (Merrimack), learned the shipbuilding craft at his father's shipyard. As early as 1846 he conceived the idea of an IRONCLAD warship, but his plans were not acted upon by the Navy Department. In 1847 he failed his examination for appointment as U.S. naval constructor but in 1857 passed and was appointed. In 1860 he was tried by court-martial and exonerated of charges that he had contributed to construction defects found in the USS *Seminole.* At the time Virginia seceded, Porter was naval constructor at Pensacola, Fla. He resigned his commission and served briefly in Virginia naval service before being commissioned naval constructor in the Confederate navy and assigned to the Norfolk Navy Yard.

On 22 June 1861 Porter, along with Lt. JOHN M. BROOKE and Chief Engineer William P. Williamson, began converting the hulk of the scuttled *Merrimack* into an ironclad warship. Williamson was responsible for refitting her engines, Brooke for her armor and guns, while Porter was in charge of overall construction. The result of their efforts was the CSS *Virginia.* Later, Porter and Brooke each claimed sole credit for the concept of the ship, but both contributed much to her design. The *Virginia's* success brought Porter to Richmond as advisor to Navy Sec. STEPHEN R. MALLORY.

In Apr. 1863 Porter became chief naval constructor, the only person to hold that office. For each ironclad produced by the South he was responsible for the hull form, the steering apparatus, decks, interior furnishings, small boats, and the general supervision of construction. Although the South built or converted 21 ironclads during the war, inadequate engines and a shortage of iron and mechanics proved major obstacles to Porter's labors. In Nov. 1864 12 ironclads were complete except for iron to armor them with.

After the war, Porter worked for 2 Virginia shipyards before becoming superintendent of Norfolk and Portsmouth ferries. d. Portsmouth, Va., 14 Dec. 1893. —NCD

Porter, William D. USN b. New Orleans, La., 1809. A worthy member of a distinguished military family, William was the son of naval captain David Porter, brother of Adm. DAVID D. PORTER, cousin of Gen. FITZ JOHN PORTER, and adoptive brother of Adm. DAVID G. FARRAGUT.

Porter went to sea as a naval midshipman in 1823. Before the Civil War he established a lighthouse system and served with distinction in the Mexican War. When civil war began, Porter's family split; although he and his brother, adoptive brother, and cousin remained with the Union, 2 of his sons served the Confederacy.

USMHI

Sent to St. Louis to oversee the construction of the *Essex,* named for his father's ship, Porter commanded her and assisted Flag Officer ANDREW H. FOOTE in the campaign up the Tennessee River early in 1862. Porter was scalded by escaping steam during the attack on FORT HENRY; nevertheless he retained command of the *Essex* and participated in the fighting at FORT DONELSON Feb. 1862.

Later Porter took the *Essex* past all the Confederate batteries on the Mississippi River from Cairo to New Orleans. Appointed commodore July 1862, he took part in the shelling of Natchez, Vicksburg, and Port Hudson. From the fall of 1862, however, his health deteriorated, curtailing his service to sitting on boards and commissions. He died of heart disease in New York City, 1 May 1864. —EMT

Port Gibson, Miss., Battle of. 1 May 1863 On 30 Apr. 1863, Maj. Gen. U. S. GRANT ferried Maj. Gens. JOHN A. MCCLERNAND'S and JAMES B. MCPHERSON'S corps to the east bank of the Mississippi River at Bruinsburg, beginning overland operations for the SECOND VICKSBURG CAMPAIGN. With 24,000 troops, his first objective was Port Gibson, a crossroads village 10.5 mi east of the river and 22 land miles southwest of Vicksburg. Confederate Brig. Gen. JOHN S. BOWEN, at Grand Gulf, 6 mi northeast of Port Gibson, dispatched Brig. Gen. MARTIN E. GREEN 30 Apr. to oppose the invasion. Only 5,164 Southern troops took part in Port Gibson's defense.

McClernand's Federals, the first ashore, marched inland 7 mi late on 30 Apr., halting after dark when difficult terrain complicated maneuvers. At dawn McClernand rode to the head of his column and discovered that the road forked north and south. Both routes led to Port Gibson, but ridges and overgrown ravines necessitated 2 separate byways around them. Brig. Gen. PETER J. OSTERHAUS' division took the northerly road, and the divisions of Brig. Gens. EUGENE A. CARR, ALVIN P. HOVEY, and ANDREW J. SMITH followed the one south. Confederates established positions covering both routes. Green established a line across the southern road at Magnolia Church, about ¾ mile from the town. Confederate Brig. Gen. EDWARD D. TRACY, on the northern road, commanded a line nearer the fork; giving stiff resistance, he was killed by Osterhaus' men between 8 and 10 a.m. Col. ISHAM W. GARROTT took command and by 11 had fallen back less than 1,000 yd. Bowen had arrived at Port Gibson at 8 a.m. and assumed overall command.

Carr, in the lead on the southern route, pressed men into the overgrown off-road terrain. Gaps developed in his line. McClernand moved Hovey's troops forward to fill them, and at 10 a.m. a successful general assault knocked Green from his Magnolia Church position back to a point just over a half-mi from Port Gibson. Bowen assigned Brig. Gen. WILLIAM E. BALDWIN command of this new line and directed Green west to aid Garrott. 2 Confederate brigades and a few regiments arrived from Grand Gulf and Vicksburg through the morning, the majority used to bolster strength in Carr's front. Both Confederate positions gave resistance until a flanking movement against Carr's right failed near 4 p.m. Within the next hour and a half, troops of Maj. Gen. JOHN A. LOGAN's division of McPherson's corps reinforced both Union fronts, and a concentrated thrust was made at Green's and Garrott's positions. The Confederates' defense of the north road collapsed and a general retreat began toward Grand Gulf. Baldwin's front fell shortly afterward, his men falling back through the town, then turning north toward Vicksburg. Retreating Southern forces crossed Bayou Pierre and Little Bayou Pierre, burning bridges behind them. Grant's forces bivouacked outside Port Gibson and began bayou crossings 2 May.

Federals lost 131 killed, 719 wounded, and 25 missing in this small battle. To the Confederates' credit, according to Bowen's 4 June 1863 report, Southerners sustained a loss of 68 killed, 380 wounded, and 384 missing and presumed captured.
—JES

Port Hudson, La. 14 Mar.–8 July 1863 Located about 25 mi north of Baton Rouge, Port Hudson, La., was a formidable bastion on the Mississippi River. In spring 1863 the Confederacy exercised effective control of only that segment of the Mississippi that flowed between Vicksburg and Port Hudson, approximately 110 mi. Consequently Port Hudson was a critical objective in the Union strategy to seize the river and divide the Confederacy.

The partially successful passage of Port Hudson by Rear Adm. DAVID G. FARRAGUT's Union warships 14 Mar. 1863 demonstrated the strength of the Confederate position on the Mississippi and proved that reduction of the Southern batteries would require action on land. Accordingly, Maj. Gen. NATHANIEL P. BANKS's Army of the Gulf moved on Port Hudson and its garrison commanded by Maj. Gen. FRANKLIN GARDNER.

Banks tried twice to capture Port Hudson by storm, encircling the Confederate position 23 May 1863, while Union warships stood ready on the Mississippi to lend support from their heavy guns. On the night of 26 May Banks called a council of war and issued his orders. He envisioned a massive barrage from both army and navy guns and a simultaneous massed infantry assault on the defenders. Unfortunately for Banks, his orders did not make his intentions clear to his subordinates and few of them saw his vision in their instructions. Nevertheless, in the early morning hours of 27 May Banks proclaimed, "Port Hudson will be ours today."

At dawn on the 27th the battle opened as planned with a heavy bombardment of the Confederate lines. On the Union right assaulting troops charged across rugged ground into a hail of Southern shot and shell. During the morning the battle raged north of Port Hudson, and Banks wondered what had happened to the remainder of his army. Finally the attackers on the Union right spent themselves; the Confederate left held.

About 2:15 the Federals on the left began their assault. Again the fighting was fierce, but again the Southerners held their ground. Still later, the Union center charged, only to meet the same fate as their comrades. Although the battle raged from 6 a.m. until 6 p.m., Banks had not been able to coordinate his attacks, and though the Federals had displayed considerable valor, it had been valor in vain. The first assault on Port Hudson marked the first large-scale use of black troops by the Union. 2 regiments of Louisiana Native Guards participated in the assaults on the Confederate lines.

It is impossible to determine how many troops fought at Port Hudson 27 May. Gardner had about 7,000 in his garrison at the time. Banks had up to 30,000 at his disposal but committed nowhere near that many. The Confederates suffered about 250–275 casualties compared with nearly 2,000 for the attacking Federals. When the day was over Banks pronounced, "My force is too weak for the work it had to do."

On the morning of 13 June Banks and a Federal naval flotilla again opened fire upon Port Hudson. For an hour shells rained down at the rate of 1 per second on the besieged Confederates. Banks was determined to blast, drive, or starve them from their bastion on the Mississippi. After the shelling ceased, the Union commander sent a note through the lines to Gardner, who exclaimed to his staff, "What do you think? Why, Banks has notified me that to avoid unnecessary slaughter he demands the immediate surrender of my forces." He replied, "My duty requires me to defend this position, and therefore I decline to surrender."

When Banks received the answer, he ordered the bombardment resumed and prepared to launch a general assault the next day. Following more artillery shelling, Federals were to probe the extreme right of the Confederate works, then attack in strength in the center at a large fort known as the Priest Cap. Banks ordered his cavalry to stand ready to block any Southerners attempting to escape.

The Confederate defenders were unable to respond to the artillery shelling; their ammunition was quite low. They were hungry, as well. But Gardner's command was as determined as he to hold Port Hudson.

The battle began as planned about 4 a.m. 14 June. An entire Union division surged forward against the Priest Cap. A few of the attackers breached the Southern lines, but their comrades were unable to exploit the advantage. The Confederates repulsed each charge in fierce fighting. Federal units continued attacking throughout the morning, though with decreased intensity. By late morning many of Banks's subordinate commanders had determined further attacks to be suicidal, and the troops seemed to agree.

On the next day Banks proclaimed, "One more advance and they are ours!" But the Federal troops were weary and demoralized to the point of threatening mutiny after suffering 1,805 casualties 14 June. The battle for Port Hudson continued as a siege, and Banks never made "one more advance."

The Southerners were cut off from resupply. Food especially was in short supply. The Federals were digging zigzag trenches (saps) that brought them ever closer to the works. They attempted to tunnel under the Southern lines only to be foiled by a countermine dug by the Confederates. The defenders planted a powder charge in their shaft and, when it exploded, the Union tunnel collapsed. Both sides hurled makeshift hand grenades (artillery shells) at each other, and sharpshooters were deadly at the closing ranges.

By 8 July 1863, the Confederate garrison at Port Hudson had been under siege for 47 days. The Federals could afford to be patient. Nevertheless, Banks had reason to be nervous about his circumstance. His 30,000 troops were well fed, equipped, and armed; but their spirits were low. The abortive attacks of 27 May and 14 June had been mismanaged and costly. About 4,500 Federals had become casualties in this campaign, and grumbling among the ranks exceeded healthy proportions. Union officers, too, divided sharply in their opinions of Banks's competence to command.

Banks had planned another assault for 7 July but postponed it because of bad weather. And in the interim news arrived of the fall of VICKSBURG. In the Union camps celebrations broke out, while the Confederates suspected that the news had been planted to induce their surrender. Finally Banks complied with Gardner's request for proof, and the Southern commander decided his duty had been done.

Officers from both sides met at 9 a.m. 8 July and concluded their deliberations at 2 p.m. Formal surrender would take place the following day. During the night some Confederates made their way through the Union lines and escaped. The rest stood in formation on the morning of 9 July to watch Banks offer his sword to Brig. Gen. George L. Andrews, whom Banks had sent to receive the surrender. Andrews handed the sword back to Gardner in token of the gallantry of the Southern defense. The Confederates laid down their arms, and the Port Hudson siege was over. The Confederacy had suffered almost 900 casualties and lost most of the garrison as prisoners. The Union had lost more than 4,500 battle casualties and almost as many to disease and sunstroke.   —EMT

Port Republic, Va., Battle of. 9 June 1862 Along with CROSS KEYS, the Battle of Port Republic climaxed Maj. Gen. THOMAS J. "STONEWALL" JACKSON'S SHENANDOAH VALLEY CAMPAIGN. Union Brig. Gen. JAMES SHIELDS's division, located east of the Blue Ridge Mts., was ordered to the Luray Valley to attack Jackson. Learning of Shield's approach, Jackson sent his cavalry to burn the bridges over the Shenandoah River as far south as Port Republic. This forced Shields to move by a longer route, giving Jackson time to prepare defenses against his other antagonist, Maj. Gen. JOHN C. FRÉMONT, who was approaching from the west.

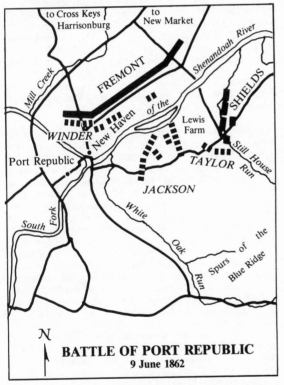

BATTLE OF PORT REPUBLIC
9 June 1862

On 8 June, as Jackson was engaging Frémont at Cross Keys, Shields made a halfhearted attack against the bridge at Port Republic. It was beaten back. On the morning of 9 June Jackson sent Brig. Gen. CHARLES S. WINDER's brigade (the STONEWALL BRIGADE) across the bridge and against Shields. Meanwhile, Brig. Gen. RICHARD TAYLOR's Louisiana brigade was to cross the

river and attack the Federal left, while Col. JOHN D. IMBODEN readied his mountain howitzers for use against an anticipated rally by Shields's troops in a defile Jackson had spotted.

As Winder's brigade moved across the Lewis farm toward the Union lines, it came under heavy fire. The brigade halted, and some of the men began moving toward the rear; Jackson personally rallied the troops. For some time, Confederate nerves were on edge. Taylor was not yet to be seen and the Stonewall Brigade was taking the brunt of the Federal fire. By 9:30 a.m., however, Taylor's troops were attacking the Union left. They took a Federal battery, lost it, took it again, lost it a second time, but held it on the third try. Shields's troops, under pressure from Winder and Taylor, yielded the field and were soon in full retreat. There was no Federal rally at the defile.

Jackson did not pursue Shields after the battle because of Frémont's presence in his rear at Cross Keys. However, as soon as he was satisfied that Frémont was no longer a threat, he took his army out of the valley and put it on trains to Richmond to help Gen. ROBERT E. LEE on the peninsula.   —LDJ

Port Royal, S.C., Battle of. 7 Nov. 1861 To sustain its BLOCKADE of Southern ports, the U.S. Navy needed a coaling, refitting, and supply station on the southeast coast. The best site seemed to be Port Royal, S.C., between Charleston and Savannah.

At the end of Oct. 1861 Flag Officer SAMUEL F. DU PONT assembled a fleet of about 75 warships with 12,000 troops in transport. Their objective, Port Royal Sound, was guarded by an earthwork on each side of the harbor entrance: Fort Beauregard at Bay Point and Fort Walker on Hilton Head. They were strong and seemed well armed, but few of their 41 guns were big enough to match the guns of Du Pont's squadron. The garrisons were spirited, but untrained, undermanned, and short of ammunition.

At 9 a.m., 7 Nov., Du Pont's fleet steamed into Port Royal Sound. His large ships began a steady circling movement between the two forts, firing broadsides first at one, then at the other. The inexperienced Confederate gunners found it hard to hit a moving target, while the U.S. Navy's professionals planted shot after shot into the forts. Federal gunboats took positions on Fort Walker's flank and enfiladed the work, dismounting guns one by one. Still, the Confederates fought on through the morning and into the afternoon.

At 2 p.m. the Southerners, ammunition running out, abandoned Fort Walker. At 3:30 they gave up Fort Beauregard, and Port Royal Sound belonged to Du Pont. Until the end of the war it provided a refuge for the keepers of the South Atlantic blockade.   —MM

Posey, Carnot. CSA b. Wilkinson Cty., Miss., 5 Aug. 1818, Posey attended college in Jackson, La., and law school at the University of Virginia before returning home to Mississippi. There he worked as a planter and established a law practice in Woodville. When the Mexican War broke out in 1846, he joined Col. Jefferson Davis' Mississippi Rifles as a 1st lieutenant and was wounded in the Battle of Buena Vista.

After the war Posey again returned home. Until 1861 he served as U.S. district attorney for southern Mississippi under Pres. James Buchanan. When the Civil War started, he organized the Wilkinson Rifles but officially entered the Confederate service in Corinth, attached to the 16th Mississippi Infantry as a colonel.

With this regiment he served honorably in the Battles of BULL RUN, BALL'S BLUFF, SECOND BULL RUN, HARPERS FERRY, and ANTIETAM, after which he was promoted to brigadier general 1 Nov. 1862 and then fought at FREDERICKSBURG. As commander of 4 Mississippi regiments, a part of Brig. Gen. Richard H. Anderson's division of Lt. Gen. Ambrose P. Hill's corps, Posey "conducted himself with the gallantry for which he had always been distinguished" at the Battles of Chancellorsville and Gettysburg.

LC

One of thousands who died of infected wounds during the war, Posey took a shell fragment in his thigh at BRISTOE STATION, Va., 14 Oct. 1863. After the engagement, members of Posey's command transported him to Charlottesville, to a Dr. Davis' residence, where he died 13 Nov. He is buried nearby on the University of Virginia grounds.   —FLS

Potomac, Confederate Army of the. In spring 1861 Southern troops stationed in northern Virginia on the ALEXANDRIA LINE were sometimes designated as belonging to the DEPARTMENT OF ALEXANDRIA and also to the Potomac Department. On 21 May 1861 they were put under the command of Brig. Gen. MILLEDGE L. BONHAM. After Gen. P.G.T. BEAUREGARD took command 2 June 1861, the force became known as the Army of the Potomac.

In preparation for the FIRST BATTLE OF BULL RUN, July 1861, Gen. JOSEPH E. JOHNSTON brought his Army of the Shenandoah eastward and merged with Beauregard's force under the Army of the Potomac. When, 3 months later, 22 Oct. 1861, the DEPARTMENT OF NORTHERN VIRGINIA was created under Johnston's command, Beauregard was assigned to head its Potomac District, a post he held until his transfer to Kentucky, 26 Jan. 1862. In spring 1862 Johnston's troops opposing Maj. Gen. GEORGE B. MCCLELLAN's force on the peninsula (see PENINSULA CAMPAIGN) were still called the Army of the Potomac, while Pres. JEFFERSON DAVIS referred to Confederate units along the Rappahannock and in the Shenandoah Valley as the Army of the North.

After Johnston was wounded, the command passed 1 June 1862 to Gen. ROBERT E. LEE, who unofficially bestowed on the force the name ARMY OF NORTHERN VIRGINIA. It made obvious sense to officially rename the Confederate force facing a Union Army of the Potomac that was at the moment pressing close to Richmond.   —DL

Potomac, Union Army of the. To wage civil war, the Federal Departments of Northeastern Virginia and Washington formed the DIVISION OF THE POTOMAC 25 July 1861, expanded into the DEPARTMENT OF THE POTOMAC 17 Aug. 1861. Department/Army of the Potomac commanders were Maj. Gens. GEORGE B. MCCLELLAN, Aug. 1861–Nov. 1862; AMBROSE E. BURNSIDE, Nov. 1862–Jan. 1863; JOSEPH HOOKER, Jan.–June 1863; and GEORGE G. MEADE, June 1863–June 1865.

The army initially contained 22 brigades. From Oct. 1861 McClellan formed 18 divisions. Over his objections Pres. ABRAHAM LINCOLN combined 14 divisions into the I–V corps 8

Mar. 1862. The I and V corps became independent departments Apr. 1862. A new V Corps and a VI Corps were created May 1862. The V and III reinforced the Army of Virginia Aug. 1862, rejoining the Army of the Potomac Sept. and Oct.–Nov. 1862, respectively. The I returned Sept. 1862; it and the III were discontinued Mar. 1864. The XII Corps joined during Sept.–Nov. 1862 and Jan.–Sept. 1863 and the XI Corps Dec. 1862–Sept. 1863. The IX Corps reinforced the army Sept. 1862–Feb. 1863 and May 1864–June 1865. The IV Corps's remnants left Aug. 1862. The cavalry division tripled into the Cavalry Corps Feb. 1863. 2 cavalry divisions and the VI Corps transferred to the Army of the Shenandoah Aug. 1864–Mar. 1865 and July–Dec. 1864, respectively. Only the II Corps stayed in the Army of the Potomac throughout the Civil War.

As the principal Federal force in the Eastern theater, the Army of the Potomac was to defend Washington and the North, capture Richmond, and destroy the ARMY OF NORTHERN VIRGINIA. It waged the PENINSULA, ANTIETAM, Loudoun, FREDERICKSBURG, CHANCELLORSVILLE, GETTYSBURG, Second Bristoe, MINE RUN, OVERLAND, PETERSBURG, and APPOMATTOX campaigns. Most of its early operations failed strategically and/or tactically; prior to 1864 only Gettysburg was a clear victory. Yet the discipline and character stamped by McClellan, the stalwart determination instilled by war's rigor, and eventually the combat effectiveness forged in battle sustained it through adversity. Finally, the consolidated army under the able Meade and overall direction of Gen.-in-Chief U. S. Grant overcame the enemy, doomed Richmond and Petersburg, and captured Gen. R. E. Lee's army. 5 days after the GRAND REVIEW, 23 May 1865, Meade's army was discontinued.

The Army of the Potomac was the North's greatest. Initially, it prevented the war in the East from being lost; ultimately, it won that war.   —RJS

Potomac, Union Department of the. On 22 July 1861, as the defeated remnants of Brig. Gen. IRVIN MCDOWELL's army streamed into Washington after FIRST BULL RUN, Pres. ABRAHAM LINCOLN ordered Maj. Gen. GEORGE B. MCCLELLAN to report to the capital. McClellan, 34-year-old victor in western Virginia, was directed to reorganize the army. "Little Mac" arrived on the 27th, assuming command of the MILITARY DIVISION OF THE POTOMAC, created on the 25th. On 15 Aug. the Department and Army of the Potomac replaced the short-lived Military Division.

McClellan's army was designated the ARMY OF THE POTOMAC, a name it retained until the end of the war. This army became the main Union fighting force in the East; on its flags would be stitched all the major campaigns in this theater from the Virginia peninsula to Appomattox. Its purpose was to defend Washington and destroy the Confederate ARMY OF NORTHERN VIRGINIA.

Sacrificed by incompetent officers, plagued by bad luck, the Army of the Potomac, under 4 different commanders and Gen.-in-Chief ULYSSES S. GRANT, ultimately brought to bay the Confederate army of Gen. ROBERT E. LEE. McClellan, commanding 15 Aug.–9 Nov. 1862, organized it, drilled it, and forged it into a solid command, but never fully committed it to battle. Maj. Gen. AMBROSE E. BURNSIDE replaced the popular "Little Mac" 9 Nov. and nearly destroyed the army before a stone wall at FREDERICKSBURG. The boastful Maj. Gen. JOSEPH "FIGHTING JOE" HOOKER superseded Burnside 26 Jan. 1863 but lost his nerve at CHANCELLORSVILLE, and the army suffered its most embarrassing defeat. 3 days before GETTYSBURG, 28 June 1863, the solid, capable Maj. Gen. GEORGE G. MEADE replaced Hooker. Meade and the veterans won at Gettysburg, and Meade retained the command until 27 June 1865. In the bloody campaigns of 1864 and 1865 General-in-Chief Grant personally directed the army's operations, with Meade acting basically as his chief executive officer.

On 12 Apr. 1865, 3 days after Lee surrendered to Grant at APPOMATTOX, the Confederate army formally laid down its weapons. As the proud Southerners passed by, the much-maligned, but victorious, veterans of the Army of the Potomac stiffened in a salute. It was an act that silently spoke of a shared bond between 2 formidable opponents.   —JDW

Potomac, Union Military Division of the.   4 days after the Union defeat at FIRST BULL RUN, 21 July 1861, the Military Division of the Potomac was created by the consolidation of the Department of Northeastern Virginia and the Department of Washington. Maj. Gen. GEORGE B. MCCLELLAN, hero of the successful Union operations in western Virginia, had been summoned to Washington by Pres. ABRAHAM LINCOLN and assumed command of the Military Division of the Potomac 27 July. On 15 Aug. McClellan's command was merged into the DEPARTMENT and ARMY OF THE POTOMAC, with "Little Mac" retaining his position.   —JDW

Potomac Department, Confederate.   See ALEXANDRIA, CONFEDERATE DEPARTMENT OF.

Potter, Robert Brown.   USA b. Schenectady, N.Y., 16 July 1829, Potter, son of Episcopal Bishop Alonzo Potter and grandson of Union College President Eliphalet Nott, studied at

LC

his grandfather's school, then left to pursue a law career. He passed the bar and had a brief, tragic marriage. At the start of the Civil War, with his wife dead, and with a young daughter, Potter, now a New York City attorney, joined the New York Rifles militia as a private. On 14 Oct. 1861 he received appointment as major of the 51st New York and in November became the regiment's lieutenant colonel.

With Brig. Gen. AMBROSE E. BURNSIDE's 1862 expedition to North Carolina, Potter fought at ROANOKE ISLAND and NEW BERNE, received a wound in the latter fight, took part in the Battle of CEDAR MOUNTAIN in August, won promotion to colonel 10 Sept., then fought at ANTIETAM, where he distinguished himself by helping break the bottleneck at Burnside Bridge.

Potter served in the IX Corps throughout the war, fighting at FREDERICKSBURG, serving in garrison at Cincinnati, Ohio, receiving commission to brigadier general 13 Mar. 1863, and, under Maj. Gen. JOHN G. PARKE, taking part in summer victories at Vicksburg and Jackson, Miss. From 25 Aug. 1863 to 17 Jan. 1864, he held nominal command of the IX Corps, fighting under Parke and Burnside in East Tennessee and being besieged at Knoxville. From 1 May 1864 to 2 Apr. 1865, he led the IX Corps's 2d Division in the Battles of the WILDERNESS and

Spotsylvania and the Siege of Petersburg. Men of the 48th Pennsylvania of Potter's division were the former coal miners responsible for digging the mine that led to the BATTLE OF THE CRATER at Petersburg. Potter was the only division commander present with his men for that disaster. On 1 Aug. 1864 he won a brevet to major general. In the last assault on the Petersburg lines, 2 Apr. 1865, Potter received a debilitating wound. On 29 Sept. he was given a full major generalcy, then mustered out of service 15 Jan. 1866.

Potter spent his remaining years in poor health. He served as receiver of the Atlantic & Great Western Railroad 1866–69, then went into semiretirement, living in England until 1873 and on his Newport, R.I., estate until his death 19 Feb. 1887. He was buried in Greenwood Cemetery, Brooklyn, N.Y.   —JES

Prairie Grove, Ark., Battle of.   7 Dec. 1862   Control of northwest Arkansas and southwest Missouri was being hotly contested in the bitter cold of early Dec. 1862 by Brig. Gen. JAMES G. BLUNT of the Union and Maj. Gen. THOMAS C. HINDMAN of the Confederacy. Although Hindman had been ordered to give up his Missouri mission and go to the aid of threatened Vicksburg, he was determined to make one last effort to destroy Blunt.

On 3 Dec. Hindman moved north from Van Buren, Ark., with 11,000 men. Blunt, near Fayetteville with only 7,000, called for help from Maj. Gen. SAMUEL R. CURTIS, commander of the DEPARTMENT OF THE MISSOURI. Curtis ordered to Blunt's aid Brig. Gen. FRANCIS J. HERRON, at that moment 110 mi away in Springfield, Mo.

Herron's 4,000 infantry and 2,000 cavalry covered the 110 mi in a nonstop 3-day march, arriving exhausted at Fayetteville on the night of 6 Dec. Hindman saw an opportunity to move between the 2 Union forces before they could unite. He could, with bold execution, defeat Herron's tired force and then smash Blunt.

In the predawn of 7 Dec., Hindman left Col. J. C. Monroe's small cavalry force to demonstrate before Blunt, while Hindman's force drove against Herron near the Prairie Grove Church, southwest of Fayetteville. Brig. Gen. JOHN S. MARMADUKE's cavalry and WILLIAM C. QUANTRILL's bushwhackers were in the advance of the Confederate attack, which drove back Herron's lead units.

Hindman had victory within his grasp, but, failing to follow up his advantage, he instead took a defensive position. Herron was able to form a battle line and launch an attack. 8 mi away, Blunt heard the guns and moved immediately to Prairie Grove to join the battle.

Hindman, meanwhile, engaged Herron with his main force but was weakened by the desertion of a newly recruited Arkansas regiment. In the afternoon Blunt arrived and opened an enfiladed fire, rolling up Hindman's flank. He was driven back by Brig. Gen. JOSEPH O. SHELBY's Confederate cavalry but recovered and counterattacked.

The fighting continued until dark, with some 1,300 casualties on each side. During the night the Confederates withdrew toward Van Buren, undetected by the Union commanders. Burial parties found many unwounded men frozen to death on the field. They learned, too, that scores of Hindman's unwilling conscripts had removed the bullets from their cartridges and fired blanks.

Blunt pursued Hindman the day following Prairie Grove,

captured Van Buren, and secured northwest Arkansas and western Missouri for the Union. —DS

"Prayer of Twenty Millions, The." 20 Aug. 1862 In summer 1862 Pres. ABRAHAM LINCOLN made a rough draft of his EMANCIPATION PROCLAMATION. Advised by cabinet members to withhold it until the most political leverage could be gained by its release, he came under tremendous pressure to issue the proclamation following the 17 July passage of the second CONFISCATION ACT. HORACE GREELEY, abolitionist editor of the NEW YORK TRIBUNE, believed Lincoln should use the second Confiscation Act as a tool for the general emancipation of slaves and became disappointed when the president did not make a liberal, sweeping interpretation of the new law. Through a signed 20 Aug. Tribune editorial, in the name of 20 million concerned Northerners, he made a passionate 9-point argument for Lincoln to end bondage. Titled "The Prayer of Twenty Millions," Greeley's editorial called for Lincoln to enforce the law, freeing slaves that came within Federal lines and punishing Confederate slaveholders that came under Federal jurisdiction. Speaking for other abolitionists, he wrote, "We think you are strangely and disastrously remiss in the discharge of your official and imperative duty. . . ." The editorial moved many readers and pained the president.

Lincoln replied to Greeley in a letter published in the Tribune 25 Aug. First mildly rebuking the editor and his "Prayer," he wrote, "If there be perceptible in it an impatient and dictatorial tone, I waive it in deference to an old friend, whose heart I have always supposed to be right." Lincoln then said he would not be pushed in any particular direction, his objective being to save the Union "not either to save or to destroy slavery." This, he explained, was his official duty, not his personal desire.

In some political quarters many erroneously believed Greeley's editorial provoked Lincoln to write his Emancipation Proclamation. Greeley maintained it was never his purpose to do so. The political strategy behind Lincoln's delay was not generally appreciated until after his death. —JES

Preble, George Henry. USN b. Portland, Maine, 25 Feb. 1816, Preble, a son and nephew of distinguished naval officers, received his appointment as midshipman Oct. 1835. He was promoted to passed midshipman in 1841, was a lieutenant when he participated in the Perry Expedition to Japan, 1853–54, and was promoted to commander 16 July 1862.

When the Civil War broke out, Preble was executive officer of the *Narragansett*. He commanded the *Katahdin* during the operations against New Orleans, April and May 1862. In August Preble was assigned to the BLOCKADE of Mobile as commander of the *Oneida*. He was on that station when, 4 Sept.

USMHI

1862, an unidentified vessel was seen approaching. Although Preble believed the ship to be British, it was actually the CSS *FLORIDA*, commanded by Lt. JOHN N. MAFFITT. Preble had no way of knowing this or that her captain and most of her crew

were stricken with yellow fever, nor could he have known that the *Florida*'s guns were inoperable.

Maffitt was relying on speed and deception to get the *Florida* past the blockaders to the safety of FORT MORGAN. Preble fired 3 warning shots before he began combat. Although his shot struck the *Florida*, inflicting casualties and heavy damage, the *Florida* with its greater speed, reached the safety of the harbor. Enraged, Navy Sec. GIDEON WELLES blamed Preble for allowing the vessel to escape and relieved him from duty.

It was not until 1872 that a naval court of inquiry exonerated Preble for his conduct at Mobile. He had been restored to his rank Feb. 1863 but was passed over for promotion to commodore because of the one blot on his record. When finally promoted in 1874, the new rank was made retroactive to 1871.

Ironically, Preble encountered the *Florida* a second time, at Funchal, Madeira, 1 Mar. 1864. This time he commanded the sloop *ST. LOUIS* in search of CONFEDERATE CRUISERS. Again the *Florida* got away, because of her superior speed and Preble's strict adherence to Portugal's neutrality.

In fall 1864 Preble became head of a 500-man naval brigade that cooperated with U.S. Army units along the coasts of South Carolina and Georgia. The brigade was involved in heavy fighting at HONEY HILL, near Grahamville, S.C., 30 Nov. 1864 and near Tulifinny Cross Roads, Ga., 5–9 Dec. 1864. Its action diverted Confederate forces opposing Sherman's MARCH TO THE SEA.

From Mar. to Aug. 1865 Preble commanded the *State of Georgia* and was assigned to protect U.S. commercial interests at Panama. In June the vessel rescued more than 600 passengers of a steamer shipwrecked on Roncador Reef in the Caribbean.

Preble was promoted to rear admiral in 1876, the same year he retired to Boston. d. 1 Mar. 1885. —NCD

Prentiss, Benjamin Mayberry. USA b. Belleville, Va., 23 Nov. 1819. As a teen-ager Prentiss, a descendant of the *Mayflower*'s William Brewster, migrated to Missouri with his parents, manufactured rope, then moved to Quincy, Ill., with a family of his own. Prentiss served with the local militia against Joseph Smith's Mormons in Illinois, 1844 and 1845, then as captain of the 1st Illinois fought in the Mexican War until honorably discharged Feb. 1847. Prior to the Civil War, Prentiss took up a law career, maintained a post with the state militia, and was an unsuccessful Republican candidate for U.S. Congress in 1860.

As a colonel of state militia

USMHI

Prentiss spent the first days of the Civil War intercepting southbound river traffic and seizing armaments smuggled to secessionists. He received commission as colonel of the 10th Illinois Infantry 29 Apr. 1861, and on assignment to duty at Cairo, Ill., began a feud with Col. ULYSSES S. GRANT over relative rank and the right of command. Appointed brigadier general 9 Aug., to rank from 17 May, he was assigned to duty in north Missouri and remained there fighting guerrillas until the following spring.

On 1 Apr. 1862, he won assignment as commander of the 6th Division/Army of the Tennessee, under Grant, now a major general. Camped at Pittsburg Landing, Tenn., Prentiss' troops held the most isolated ground, southeast of Shiloh Church. At the urging of Col. Everett Peabody, Prentiss ordered probes outside the Union perimeter. His troops were the first attacked by Confederates 6 Apr. and ended their day holding a desperately contested line called the "HORNETS' NEST" for 6 hours. Compelled to surrender, Prentiss remained a prisoner until exchanged in October, then served on the court-martial of Brig. Gen. FITZ JOHN PORTER and was sent to command the District of Eastern Arkansas. He received promotion to major general 13 Mar. 1863, to rank from 29 Nov. 1862.

Except for defending Helena from attack, July 1863, Prentiss' post remained relatively quiet. Grant and Maj. Gen. HENRY W. HALLECK claimed to have no appropriate combat command for him. Prentiss resigned his commission 28 Oct., citing health and personal concerns and tacitly acknowledging the unavailability of a suitable post. He practiced law in Quincy and, on Pres. U. S. Grant's patronage appointment, served as town pension agent until moving to Missouri in 1878. After practicing law in Kirksville and Bethany, and a brief period working for the Federal land office in Colorado, he won appointment as postmaster at Bethany, retaining that post until his death there 8 Feb. 1901.   —JES

President's General War Orders No. 1, Lincoln's.

In July 1861, by naming GEORGE B. MCCLELLAN his principal commander in the East, ABRAHAM LINCOLN expressed the utmost faith in the callow general's ability. "Little Mac" repaid his trust by organizing, drilling, disciplining, arming, and equipping the ARMY OF THE POTOMAC until it was a match for any troops the Confederacy could field against it. But when the year ended with no sign of an advance by McClellan's army, Lincoln's confidence began to fade.

For his part, McClellan thought Lincoln a good man but a poor commander in chief, too weak to prevent political considerations from dictating strategy. Believing also that the president could not keep a secret, McClellan, who in November had become the Union's general-in-chief, refused to divulge his plan of operations for any theater of the war. When he fell ill with typhoid fever in winter 1861, his insistence on bed rest prevented him from seeing the president altogether.

Harassed by a public and press anxious for action, Lincoln held a series of strategy meetings with members of his cabinet as well as with a few of McClellan's ranking subordinates. Fearing that a cabal was intriguing against him, the general rose from his sickbed to attend the conference of 12 Jan. 1862. Even then he refused to reveal his plans, but he did promise an early advance in Kentucky. Grasping at this hint of activity, Lincoln gave McClellan a few more weeks to prove his sincerity, but by the end of that period no offensive had commenced and the Chief Executive had lost his patience.

The result was his President's General War Orders No. 1, issued 27 Jan. In this remarkable document Lincoln announced that by 22 Feb. 1862 not only would the army in upper Virginia move against its enemy, but it also would land forces at FORT MONROE, in western Virginia, in southern Kentucky, and along the Mississippi River; meanwhile, Union flotillas on the Mississippi and the Gulf of Mexico would stand ready for action. Lincoln's President's Special War Orders No. 1, published 4 days later, revealed that he preferred McClellan personally to lead the Army of the Potomac in an overland movement against the Confederates near Manassas Junction, Va.

Lincoln's orders appeared an amateurish effort at assuming tactical command. Not surprisingly, few of his objectives were realized. Yet his dramatic intervention achieved its main purpose: thereafter Little Mac cooperated more fully with the administration, taking it into his confidence and working with it to formulate strategy.   —EGL

Preston, John Smith.

CSA   b. Abingdon, Va., 20 Apr. 1809, Preston attended Hampton-Sidney College, the University of Virginia, and Harvard University Law School, opening a legal practice in Abingdon. In 1840 he moved to Columbia, S.C., living there a short time, then migrating to Louisiana. There he owned a successful sugar plantation from which he made a sizable fortune. He returned to South Carolina in 1848 and entered politics as a vocal STATES-RIGHTS Democrat. His commitment to the doctrine won him a seat in the state senate that year, an office he retained until 1856. The next 4 years he lived abroad, returning in time to be elected to the South Carolina secession convention.

LC

Preston was chosen Feb. 1861 to travel to Virginia to urge that state to secede. When the fighting started he volunteered as an aide-de-camp to Gen. P.G.T. BEAUREGARD, but he held the post only until 13 Aug., at which time Pres. JEFFERSON DAVIS appointed him assistant adjutant general with the rank of lieutenant colonel. In October he was ordered to Charleston to muster troops into the Confederate army, an assignment he fulfilled with great efficiency. His abilities as an administrator were again displayed when he assumed command of the prison camp at Columbia, 28 Jan. 1862, and of the conscript camp opened there in April. But his inability to get along with people drew sharp criticism. He enjoyed controversy and frequently provoked arguments needlessly, but Davis, admiring his independence and initiative, refused to dispose of him. Instead, he promoted him to colonel 23 Apr. 1863 and in July appointed him superintendent of the Bureau of Conscription.

Though conscription never yielded large numbers of recruits, Preston enforced the unpopular draft law in an orderly if heavy-handed fashion. In December, Davis extended his control to overseeing conscription in the West, where the draft had been administered independently. Promoted to brigadier general 10 June 1864, Preston continued to administer the conscript program until the bureau was discontinued Mar. 1865.

Preston lived in Europe for a short time following the Confederates' defeat. Returning to Columbia, he became popular as an outspoken defender of states rights and the Confederacy. He remained UNRECONSTRUCTED until his death in Columbia, 1 May 1881.   —PLF

Preston, William.

CSA   b. Louisville, Ky., 16 Oct. 1816, Preston studied at Augusta and St. Joseph's colleges in Kentucky and in 1836 entered Harvard, where he received a law degree in 1838. He established a law practice in Louisville, and, when the Mexican War began, joined the 4th Kentucky Volunteers as a lieutenant colonel. Returning to Kentucky, he took part in the 1849 constitutional convention, won successive elections to the state legislature and senate, and in 1852 took a seat in the U.S. House of Representatives for 2 terms before being defeated by future Confederate Gen. Humphrey Marshall. Formerly a Whig, Preston

USMHI

became an active Democrat, a supporter of Pres. Franklin Buchanan, and minister to Spain in 1858, serving abroad until the secession crisis compelled his return to Kentucky to campaign for the state's removal from the Union.

Preston, whose late sister had been Gen. Albert Sidney Johnston's first wife, served on the general's staff as an aide without commission until Johnston's death in the Battle of SHILOH. On 14 Apr. 1862 Preston received appointment to brigadier general and, as a part of Maj. Gen. John C. Breckinridge's division, commanded the 3d Brigade. Leading the 1st, 3d, and 4th Florida, the 20th Tennessee, the 60th North Carolina, and Mebane's Light Battery, he fought at CORINTH, STONE'S RIVER, CHICKAMAUGA, and in the Siege of Chattanooga, where he won praise from Lt. Gen. James Longstreet.

After Preston briefly commanded troops in southwest Virginia, on 7 Jan. 1864 Pres. Jefferson Davis appointed him his diplomatic representative to the court of Maximilian, named emperor of Mexico. Charged with negotiating a mutual aid and commerce treaty with the Mexican government, Preston first went to Europe, by way of Cuba, to establish contacts with the Austrian archduke. Unsuccessful, he returned to the Confederacy by traveling through Matamoros, Mexico, to Texas, where he served under Gen. E. Kirby Smith until the Confederate surrender.

Historian Ezra Warner, in his *Generals in Gray,* states that Preston's rumored promotion to major general is unverifiable. The records of the SOUTHERN HISTORICAL SOCIETY list that promotion, dating it 1 Jan. 1865. However, according to Society researchers, in his last duties Preston was responsible for troops in the Richmond, Va., area, bringing into question the accuracy of their records in this instance.

Preston lived as a refugee in Mexico, England, and Canada until 1866, when he returned to Kentucky. Reestablishing his law practice, he served in the state legislature 1868–69 and remained active in the Democratic party national leadership until his death in Lexington, 21 Sept. 1887. —JES

Price, Sterling. CSA b. Prince Edward Cty., Va., 20 Sept. 1809, Price launched his Civil War career fighting to hold Missouri for the Confederacy, and he never stopped pursuing that elusive goal throughout the conflict. In the process he alienated Southern leaders, including Jefferson Davis.

Price migrated to the Missouri frontier with his family at 21 and soon became a prominent slaveowning tobacco planter and political leader. During the Mexican War he was military governor of New Mexico and earned a brigadier general's star.

Tall, portly, handsome, and commanding of manner, Price

LC

was the embodiment of Missouri rural aristocracy. Missouri gave him its highest honors—legislator, 1836–38 and 1840–44; congressman, 1844–46; governor, 1852–56; and commander of state troops—and Price served devotedly in return.

Price at first opposed Missouri's secession but May 1861 became so outraged at the takeover of Camp Jackson, St. Louis, by FRANCIS P. BLAIR, JR. and Brig. Gen. NATHANIEL LYON that he offered his sword to the South as commander of state troops. In uneasy concert with Brig. Gen. BEN MCCULLOCH, he defeated Lyon at WILSON'S CREEK, Mo., and soon captured the large Union garrison at Lexington. Price was commissioned major general from 6 Mar. 1862.

But he was to win no more major victories. He feuded with McCulloch, with whom he was teamed again in the Confederate defeat at PEA RIDGE, Ark., then commanded the ill-fated ARMY OF THE WEST at IUKA, CORINTH, and Helena, Ark., in 1862–63. Early in 1864 he helped repulse Union Maj. Gen. Frederick Steele's CAMDEN EXPEDITION.

Price's final bid for fame came late in 1864 when he was chosen by Gen. E. Kirby Smith to lead the Army of Missouri in the expedition now known as PRICE'S MISSOURI RAID. After driving spectacularly from southeast to northwest Missouri, Price's depleted force was driven back into Arkansas.

After the Confederacy fell, Price went to Mexico, returning to St. Louis Jan. 1867 impoverished and broken in health. He died there 8 months later, 29 Sept. —DS

Price's Missouri Raid of 1864. In fall 1864 the Confederate high command sent into Missouri a motley force of 12,000 men; while only a third of them were supplied with firearms, the troops were augmented with 14 pieces of artillery. Led northeast by Maj. Gen. STERLING PRICE from Princeton, Ark., their primary goal was to take St. Louis, then cross the Mississippi River to invade Illinois. The arrival in St. Louis of 6,000 Federals forced the adoption of a secondary plan: an attempt to recapture Missouri.

Turning west from the city, Price proceeded along the south bank of the Missouri River, destroying sections of railroad. With 2 Federal forces distantly in pursuit, Price's men occupied Herman, Mo., 5 Oct., bypassed the capital, Jefferson City, and took Boonville on the 9th and Glasgow on the 15th.

Thousands of state militia mobilized, but Price continued westward, skirmishing daily. At Waverly, a militia force engaged and slowed Price. Actions flared at Lexington 19 Oct., Little Blue River on the 20th, and on the 22d at Independence and Big Blue River (Byram's Ford). Federals in position along the Big Blue organized a new defense just south of Brush Creek near the Kansas-Missouri border, and Price now had Federals to his front and rear. Despite an open route of retreat to the South, he chose to attack, hoping to defeat both enemy forces in successive operations. On 23 Oct. the Confederates suffered a decisive repulse in an engagement at WESTPORT, near the Kansas border, marking the end of Price's raid.

Price retreated 61 mi in 2 days, halting to fight a rearguard action 25 Oct. at MARAIS DES CYGNES RIVER, then continuing his withdrawal without further incident. He had fought 43 engagements and lost half his command. His return marked the end of organized Confederate operations in the trans-Mississippi region, although guerrilla activity persisted.   —HH

Prince, Henry. USA b. Eastport, Maine, 19 June 1811, Prince graduated from West Point 30th in the class of 1835. As a 2d lieutenant with the 4th U.S. Infantry he was seriously wounded fighting Seminoles in 1836, went on frontier duty, won a brevet to captain for gallantry at Contreras and Churubusco during the Mexican War, and, following another severe wound at Molino del Rey, was brevetted major and given 3 years' recuperative leave. Until spring 1862, either on the frontier or in Washington, D.C., he served on paymaster or staff duty. He would live his life in pain, never fully recovered from his early war wounds or deprivations suffered during Civil War service.

GB

Commissioned brigadier general of volunteers 28 Apr. 1862, Prince assumed command of the 2d Brigade/2d Division/II Corps/Army of Virginia 16 July, then took command of the 2d Division 9 Aug. for the Battle of CEDAR MOUNTAIN. Captured in this fight, he was held until December, and the next summer, following the Battle of GETTYSBURG, led the 2d Division/III Corps/Army of the Potomac in a number of sharp affairs and engagements against elements of the retiring Confederate army in the vicinity of Harpers Ferry and western Maryland. His last active combat service came that autumn in the unproductive BRISTOE and MINE RUN campaigns. Prince's performance as commander of the 2d Division dissatisfied Maj. Gen. GEORGE G. MEADE, and Prince was implicated by corps commander Maj. Gen. WILLIAM H. FRENCH in the division's failure to have engaged Confederate Gen. ROBERT E. LEE's troops 26 Nov. 1863, the opening day of the Mine Run Campaign.

Prince next commanded garrison troops in the Districts of Cairo, Ill.; Pamlico, N.C.; and Columbus, Ga.; and briefly the 5th Division/XVIII Corps in the DEPARTMENT OF NORTH CAROLINA. Brevetted colonel and brigadier general of Regulars 13 Mar. 1865 for faithful service, he mustered out of the volunteers 30 Apr. 1866 and resumed paymaster duties.

Prince received promotion to lieutenant colonel of Regulars in the paymaster's department 3 Mar. 1877 and was retired 31 Dec. 1879. Despondent over his health, on 19 Aug. 1892, he committed suicide in a hotel in London, England.   —JES

prisoners.   During the Civil War the Federals captured 215,-000–220,000 prisoners, not including Confederate armies that surrendered at war's end, and the Confederates 200,000–211,000. Close to 26,500 Southerners and 22,600 Northerners died in prison camps. Their suffering became legendary.

At the very beginning of the war, because there were no places to detain prisoners, both sides released them on parole,

on oath to take up arms no more. Many prisoner exchanges took place in the field without much technical negotiation. The first Federals retained by the Confederates were confined in converted tobacco warehouses in Virginia. Soon both North and South were turning training camps, state penitentiaries, college buildings, and various public facilities into military prisons; even an old slave market in St. Louis served as a prison.

The public demanded that prisoners be exchanged, but it took more than a year to agree on a system of exchange. By a cartel signed 22 July 1862, captives were to be paroled and exchanged 1 general for 1 general, 1 private for 1 private, etc., with 60 privates equal to 1 general. The commissioners of exchange failed to agree on procedure in executing the cartel, and violations and arguments were frequent, with major problems arising over the exchange of former slaves captured while serving as Union soldiers. The South claimed they were runaways who should be returned to their owners, whereas the North demanded they be considered in the same manner as other prisoners of war.

Lt. Gen. U. S. GRANT strongly believed that the exchange of prisoners was of great disadvantage to the North, which did not suffer the manpower shortage characteristic of the South. He wrote: "Every man we hold, when released on parole or otherwise, becomes an active soldier against us. . . . If a system of exchange liberates all prisoners taken, we will have to fight on until the whole South is exterminated."

On 17 Apr. 1863 Grant ordered that prisoner exchanges cease. They were not resumed until the exchange of sick prisoners Feb. 1865. *See also* ALTON PRISON; ANDERSONVILLE PRISON; BELLE ISLE PRISON; CAMP CHASE; CAMP FORD; CAMP MORTON; CASTLE PINCKNEY; CASTLE THUNDER; FORT DELAWARE; FORT LAFAYETTE; FORT WARREN; OHIO PENITENTIARY; OLD CAPITAL PRISON; POINT LOOKOUT; ROCK ISLAND PRISON; SALISBURY PRISON. —PR

privateers. On 17 Apr. 1861 JEFFERSON DAVIS issued a proclamation offering letters of marque and reprisal allowing privately owned vessels to prey upon the North's ocean commerce. The Confederate Congress approved Davis' action 6 May 1861. Applications were sent from almost every Southern port but principally from New Orleans and Charleston. From 1861 to 1864 at least 52 vessels were granted letters of marque, but there is no evidence that 28 of these actually served as privateers.

Various types of vessels—pilot and fishing boats and merchant craft—were converted into armed privateers, their owners motivated by a combination of patriotism and pecuniary interest. They ranged in size from the small *Sea Hawk*, carrying a 9-man crew, to the steamer *Isabella* with its crew of 175 sailors and 50 marines.

The most successful and notorious of the privateers was the *Jefferson Davis,* commanded by Capt. LOUIS M. COXETTER; during a 7-week period in summer 1861, the vessel took 9 prizes. However, with the fall of New Orleans and the tightening of the Federal BLOCKADE, privateering became a risky business and the number of privateers steadily declined. Some became BLOCKADE RUNNERS and others were commissioned as Confederate men-of-war. Still others fell into Federal hands or were destroyed to prevent capture.

Soon after Davis' 1861 proclamation, Pres. ABRAHAM LINCOLN announced that the captured crews of privateers would be hanged as pirates. Davis countered by warning that if any

such execution occurred, reprisals would follow. These threats were tested when the crew of the captured privateer *Enchantress (see ENCHANTRESS AFFAIR)* was tried, convicted, and sentenced to death. Davis prepared to act on his threat, until Lincoln relented and the sentence was not carried out.

Lincoln also attempted to discredit privateering by agreeing to support the 1856 DECLARATION OF PARIS, which condemned the practice, even though the U.S. was not a signatory. The Lincoln administration issued no letters of marque but nevertheless accepted and utilized vessels owned or chartered by private citizens. Such a vessel was the *Quaker City* of New York, chartered for 2 months by private subscription before being purchased by the U.S. Navy. While in civilian control, it cruised the Chesapeake Bay waters, taking several prizes.

Although some Confederate privateers achieved individual successes, their overall value was extremely limited. Far more successful in inflicting damage to the North's ocean commerce were the CONFEDERATE CRUISERS. —NCD

prolonge. An 18-ft length of hemp rope 3.5 in. in diameter, a prolonge was wound between 2 hooks on a gun carriage trail and kept there for use in maneuvering an unlimbered gun. It had an iron hook on one end, a metal eye in the center, and 3 chain links and a toggle on the other end. —JES

Provisional Army of the Confederate States. Because of its political philosophy, the Confederacy could not easily form an effective field army. Confederate officials, though supporting state sovereignty, believed the new nation required a military establishment controlled by the central government to ensure organizational stability and facilitate recruitment, supply, and training. Even before war broke out, they sought a small army of about 10,000, roughly equivalent to the REGULAR ARMY OF THE U.S., to be raised, maintained, and employed by the authorities in Richmond. Soon, however, it became clear that war would come before so complex a force could be formed. Therefore, on 6 Mar. 1861, the CONFEDERATE CONGRESS set up a provisional army, comprised of militia enlisting for 12 months' service; later, nonmilitia volunteers made up the bulk of this force.

Officially, the troops composing the Provisional Army of the Confederate States were made available to the government by consent of the Southern governors, who retained authority over the raising, organizing, and maintaining of units, including the appointment of their officers. But in May 1861 Pres. JEFFERSON DAVIS was granted the authority to accept volunteer units without state consent, to appoint their field officers, and to form and staff brigades and larger formations. Additional legislation, increasing the central government's authority over the army, lengthened enlistment terms to cover the duration of the war, implemented CONSCRIPTION, and organized government bureaus that effectively transferred unit recruiting and organization from the state capitals to Richmond.

Early in 1861 the Congress also provided for the establishment of a regular Confederate army. This force, however, never attained the number of units and troops envisioned by the lawmakers (*see* REGULAR ARMY, CONFEDERATE STATES). Confederate Regulars constituted a meager portion of the total number of Southerners in uniform, variously estimated at 850,-000–1.1 million. In effect, an army designed to be an interim expedient became virtually the sole Confederate fighting force. —EGL

Pryor, Roger Atkinson. CSA b. Dinwiddie Cty., Va., 19 July 1828. Reared in Nottoway County, schooled at the Petersburg, Va., Classical Academy and at Hampton-Sydney College, Pryor graduated in 1845, valedictorian of his class. After studying law at the University of Virginia 1846–47, in 1849 he opened a law practice while editing the *Southside Democrat.* Interested in politics, oratory, and journalism, while maintaining his legal practice he began editing the Richmond *Enquirer* in 1853, founded the sectionalist Washington, D.C., newspaper *The South* in 1857, and wrote for a similar capital paper, *The States.* In 1855 he traveled to Greece on legal business,

LC

then campaigned for HENRY A. WISE, successful Democratic candidate for governor of Virginia. As a Democrat, Pryor won election to the U.S. House of Representatives in 1859, and, until the outbreak of civil war, he served as a spokesman for conservative and secessionist interests at regional congresses and conventions.

Pryor was a secessionist political theorist and agitator. In Charleston, S.C., Dec. 1860, he lobbied daily for passage of that state's secession ordinance, took a place of honor in Charleston's Secession Hall for the ceremonial signing of the legislation, resigned his seat in Congress 3 Mar. 1861, and in April roamed Charleston urging authorities to open fire on Fort Sumter. At 12:45 a.m., 12 Apr. 1861, Pryor accompanied the party of Confederate officers delivering Brig. Gen. P.G.T. Beauregard's ultimatum to the Union garrison at the fort. Later, after Federals declined to surrender, Pryor refused South Carolina Capt. George S. James's offer to fire the FIRST SHOT of the war.

After Virginia seceded, he entered the Provisional Confederate Congress, resigning to become colonel of the 3d Virginia Infantry. Pryor's service was routine until the 5 May 1862 BATTLE OF WILLIAMSBURG. Distinguished for gallantry there, he won promotion to brigadier general to date from 16 Apr. 1862. He fought through the SEVEN DAYS' CAMPAIGN, SECOND BULL RUN, and the ANTIETAM CAMPAIGN commanding the 5th and 8th Florida, 3d Virginia, and 14th Alabama regiments. After severe losses in the Army of Northern Virginia, his brigade was dismantled Nov. 1862.

Pryor then tried, unsuccessfully, to establish an independent brigade for service along Virginia's Blackwater River. He received temporary assignment to Lt. Gen. Thomas J. "Stonewall" Jackson's forces 17 Nov. and in 1863 took part in intelligence and scouting operations on the Virginia peninsula and in the Chancellorsville area. Following the Battle of CHANCELLORSVILLE he went without assignment, tendered his resignation 18 Aug. 1863, and took on solitary scouting and intelligence duties with Maj. Gen. Fitzhugh Lee's cavalry until captured 27 Nov. 1864. Held prisoner in Fort Lafayette, he was exchanged in spring 1865, prior to the surrender of the Army of Northern Virginia.

Pryor migrated to New York City in the immediate postwar period, wrote anonymously for the New York *Daily News* through 1866, practiced law until appointed to the New York Court of Common Pleas in 1890, and became a justice for the New York State Supreme Court in 1896. From 1899 until his death in New York City, 14 Mar. 1919, he served as a referee in the State Supreme Court's appellate division. His wife, Sara, recounted their war experiences in *Reminiscences of Peace and War* (1904).   —JES

Q

"Quaker guns." When faced with a shortage of artillery pieces, Southern defenders frequently resorted to "Quaker guns" as a defensive strategy. These were logs hewn to resemble cannon, painted black on the "firing" end, then positioned behind fortifications. Sometimes real gun carriages were used. This deception often delayed Federal attacks on "strongly held" Confederate positions.   —NCD

USMHI

Quantrill, William Clarke. CSA b. Canal Dover, Ohio, 31 July 1837. As a young man, Quantrill went west to teach school but became an outlaw and gambler, drawing charges of murder and petty thievery. When the Civil War broke out in 1861, he became involved in the border disturbances in Missouri and Kansas and soon was using the turmoil in the area for his own purposes, robbing and sacking communities with Union sympathies.

Known variously as "Charley Hart" and "Billy Quantrill," he fought with the Confederacy at WILSON'S CREEK Aug. 1861 and in 1862 began guerrilla operations in Missouri, capturing Independence in August. Commissioned a captain in the Confederate army shortly thereafter, he showed ability as a leader, but his unsavory lifestyle kept him from an honorable career.

Early in Nov. 1862 he and his band captured a wagon train. Of the 12 unarmed teamsters killed in the raid, all but 1 was found shot through the head, indicating that they had been murdered after being taken prisoners. Quantrill subsequently went to Richmond, hoping to get a command under the Partisan Ranger Law (*see* PARTISAN RANGERS), but reports of his atrocities had preceded him, and the best the South would do was promote him to colonel.

Early in 1863 he returned to his command and continued his style of warfare, soon branded as "little removed from that of the wildest savage." On several occasions, he was reported killed or captured.

On 21 Aug. 1863, with a band of about 400 men, he stormed LAWRENCE, Kans., and began a slaughter that lasted 3 hours. His men pillaged and burned, killing more than 150 men, women, and children. After the raid, the uproar against Quantrill soared. "No fiend in human shape could have acted with more savage barbarity," wrote Kansas Gov. Thomas Carney.

Quantrill continued his activities, occasionally drawing criticism from Confederate officers because he would not obey their orders. In May 1865 he was fatally wounded by Union troops while raiding in Kentucky, dying in Louisville 6 June.   —VCJ

Quarles, William Andrew. CSA b. James City Cty., Va., 4 July 1825. Moving to Kentucky with his family when he was 5, Quarles studied law at the University of Virginia, afterward practicing his profession in Clarksville, Tenn. He also became a circuit court judge, supervisor of Tennessee banks, and president of the Memphis, Clarksville, & Louisville Railroad.

LC

Soon after the outbreak of the Civil War, Quarles was elected colonel of the 42d Tennessee Infantry, a regiment assigned to Gen. ALBERT SIDNEY JOHNSTON. On 12 Feb. 1862 the outfit broke camp in Clarksville and reported to Brig. Gen. GIDEON J. PILLOW at nearby FORT DONELSON. A few days later Quarles and his men fought gallantly though futilely in the defense of that Cumberland River bastion, their participation, according to Brig. Gen. BUSHROD R. JOHNSON, being worthy of "particular notice." Captured there on the 16th, Quarles on his exchange was assigned a brigade composed of 5 Tennessee infantry units, 4 regiments and a battalion.

At the head of his new force, the colonel was sent to serve under Brig. Gen. SAMUEL B. MAXEY at Port Hudson, La., early in 1863. From there he was transferred to Gen. JOSEPH E. JOHNSTON's command during the Vicksburg Operations, then to Maj. Gen. DABNEY H. MAURY's DISTRICT OF THE GULF. As a newly commissioned brigadier general, from 25 Aug., Quarles was sent to Chattanooga in fall 1863 but failed to reach Gen. BRAXTON BRAGG in time to participate at MISSIONARY RIDGE. Afterward his much-traveled brigade was returned to Mississippi but was subsequently attached to Johnston's ARMY OF TENNESSEE for the ATLANTA CAMPAIGN. During that period, one biographer notes, Quarles and his men "exhibited a steady bearing," especially at Pickett's Mills, 27 July 1864, when they gave timely aid to comrades embattled by Federal attackers.

That fall, Quarles reentered Tennessee as part of the army of Gen. JOHN B. HOOD and was severely wounded while leading a charge that almost reached the main Union line at FRANKLIN. Again captured, he did not regain his freedom until 25 May 1865, when he went back to Clarksville and his law practice. In 1875 he won a seat in the Tennessee senate and was a delegate to the Democratic national conventions of 1880 and 1884. d. Logan Cty., Ky., 28 Dec. 1893.   —EGL

Queen of the West, **USS.** Used first by the North, then by the South, the *Queen of the West* was one of a fleet of RAMS that can be traced directly to CHARLES ELLET, a distinguished civil engineer without military background. For years he had urged adoption of a tactic dating back to the ancient galley—ramming enemy ships with vessels fitted with a prow carrying an iron ram. After the appearance of the *VIRGINIA* and other Confederate rams, he was commissioned to equip several such vessels at Cincinnati.

Within 40 days, he had procured 9 steamers and altered them into rams at a cost of less than $300,000. One of the first acquired was the *Queen,* a freight boat recognized for its speed and strength.

The ram fleet's initiation came at Memphis, 6 June 1862. Using the *Queen* as flagship, Ellet scattered the Confederate fleet and captured the city, but, wounded, he paid for it with his life.

With the fleet under command of his younger brother, Lt. Col. Alfred W. Ellet, the *Queen*'s first embarrassment came near Vicksburg, 15 July 1862, when the CSS *ARKANSAS* appeared in the Yazoo River and put the Federal vessel to flight. On 22 July the *Queen* attacked the *Arkansas* at Vicksburg and was so badly damaged it had to be sent north for repairs.

On 2 Feb. 1863 the ram was back in service and ran past Vicksburg. So active was the ship that the Union was able to report on 11 Feb. that it had already destroyed 4 Confederate steamers and more than $200,000 in Confederate property. 3 days later, it ran aground near Gordon's Landing on the Red River and was captured, a development blamed on the disloyalty of its pilot. The Confederates quickly repaired the *Queen,* and on 24 Feb. it aided in the capture of the Federal vessel *Indianola.*

After a concerted drive, the *Queen* was recaptured 14 Apr. in a battle with 3 Federal vessels on the Atchafalaya River, where the ram was surrounded and destroyed.   —VCJ

R

Radford, William. USN b. Fincastle, Va., 9 Sept. 1809, Radford was appointed midshipman 1 Mar. 1825, promoted to lieutenant in 1837 and commander in 1855. In 1861 he commanded the steam sloop USS *Dacotah* cruising in Far Eastern waters. Distrusting the loyalty of Southern officers, Sec. of the Navy GIDEON WELLES relieved Radford of his command and ordered him to return to the U.S. There Radford served as a lighthouse inspector until Feb. 1862. Finally convinced of Radford's loyalty, Welles gave him command of the *Cumberland* at HAMPTON ROADS. Shortly after assuming his new command, Radford was detailed to serve on a court-martial board, and thus

LC

was absent from Hampton Roads when the CSS *VIRGINIA* (*Merrimack*) made its appearance 8 Mar. 1862. When the vessel was sighted, he returned immediately, only to witness the *Cumberland* sinking from damage inflicted by the ironclad.

Promoted to captain July 1862 and commodore Apr. 1863, Radford next became commandant of the New York Navy Yard. In Mar. 1864 he was given command of the ironclad *NEW IRONSIDES.* He served as flag officer during the army/navy operations against FORT FISHER Dec. 1864–Jan. 1865, contributing greatly to the final victory. After the capture of Fort Fisher, he became head of the James River Squadron and cooperated with Lt. Gen. ULYSSES S. GRANT's forces on shore in final operations from Grant's base at CITY POINT. Radford commanded the Atlantic Squadron until Oct. 1865, became commandant of the Washington Navy Yard, and was promoted to rear admiral in 1866. His final command was the European Squadron, after which he retired in 1870. d. District of Columbia, 8 Jan. 1890. —NCD

Radical Republicans. The Republican party in 1861 was a coalition of disparate elements. Formed only 7 years earlier, it contained men who had been Whigs, antislavery Democrats, FREE-SOILERS, Know-Nothings, and abolitionists. By the outbreak of the war, these fragments had coalesced into 3 basic factions: conservatives, moderates, and radicals. Pres. ABRAHAM LINCOLN's task was to mold these factions into a government that could win the war without destroying the South politically and economically.

The most aggressive and, eventually, most influential of the three was the Radical Republican faction. All Republicans were against SLAVERY, but this group was the most "radical,"

in its opposition to the "peculiar institution." While conservatives favored gradual emancipation combined with colonization of FREEDMEN, and while moderates favored emancipation but with reservations, Radicals favored immediate eradication of an institution they viewed as iniquitous, and saw the war as a crusade for ABOLITION.

Never a majority within the party, the Radicals dominated the other factions because of their commitment to their cause and the talent of their members, some of whom chaired key committees in Congress. In the House, their ranks included the Speaker, GALUSHA A. GROW, the chairman of the Ways and Means Committee, THADDEUS STEVENS, and influential members like Owen Lovejoy, Joshua Giddings, and GEORGE W. JULIAN. In the Senate, CHARLES SUMNER, HENRY WILSON, John P. Hale, ZACHARIAH CHANDLER and BENJAMIN F. WADE chaired committees. Within Lincoln's cabinet, the secretaries of Treasury and War, SALMON P. CHASE and EDWIN M. STANTON, respectively, were Radicals. The center of Radical strength in the North was New England.

Men of little patience and less tolerance, the Radicals advocated an implacable, uncompromising prosecution of the war against the Southern rebellion, and were in the forefront of such issues and legislation as the CONFISCATION ACTS, emancipation, the enlistment of blacks (*see* BLACK SOLDIERS), the 13th Amendment, and RECONSTRUCTION policies. Though Lincoln, a moderate, eventually sided with the Radicals on a number of key issues, such as emancipation, many Radicals opposed his renomination in 1864 primarily because of their differences regarding Reconstruction. Certain generals also faced Radical opposition, not because of the officers' military abilities but because of their political views. Radicals dominated the COMMITTEE ON THE CONDUCT OF THE WAR, which investigated military matters. Gen. GEORGE B. MCCLELLAN, in particular, was an anathema to Radicals.

The Union victory and the destruction of slavery did not conclude the Radicals' program. With LINCOLN'S ASSASSINATION and ANDREW JOHNSON's succession, the Radicals' domination of the party and Congress increased. These committed politicians would shape the reconstruction of the nation.

—JDW

raid. A column of horsemen, stretching for miles along some country road, 4 troopers riding abreast, characterized a typical Civil War raid. Cavalry, moving swiftly, executed these daring operations behind enemy lines. Railroads, rolling stock and depots, warehouses, wagon trains, headquarters, and certain communities were the targets of a raid. Descending with lightning speed, hoping to surprise the enemy, the troopers burned, wrecked, and confiscated, before riding away in a race to outdistance an almost certain pursuit.

The reputations of various Civil War horsemen have been assured by their raids. Such notable Union cavalry officers as BENJAMIN H. GRIERSON, JAMES H. WILSON and PHILIP H. SHERIDAN conducted either remarkably successful thrusts or operations that crippled the Confederate war effort. GEORGE STONEMAN and H. JUDSON KILPATRICK led Union raids that ended in failure and tragedy, respectively.

Confederates, battling against Northern industrial strength and military manpower, utilized raids more frequently. EARL VAN DORN, JOHN HUNT MORGAN, NATHAN B. FORREST, J.E.B. STUART, WILLIAM E. JONES, and THOMAS L. ROSSER became renowned leaders of often dramatic, damaging raids that even penetrated into Northern territory.   —JDW

Railroad Act. Efforts to build America's first transcontinental railroad, including government surveys to determine its most practicable route, long predated the Civil War. But only after the REPUBLICAN PARTY, which was publicly committed to the project, gained the White House, did these preparations bear fruit. In Jan. 1862, the party's congressmen introduced a measure promoting construction of a Pacific Railroad. The result, House Bill 364, based on earlier efforts by Sen. James S. Rollins of Missouri and Iowa Congressman (later Gen.) SAMUEL R. CURTIS, was chiefly promoted by Representative Aaron A. Sargent of California. Iowa Sen. JAMES HARLAN was instrumental in adapting it to the preferences of the upper house of Congress. As amended, the bill passed the Senate 20 June 1862, the House 4 days later, and was signed into law by ABRAHAM LINCOLN 1 July.

The Railroad Act, in its final version, was designed "to aid in the construction of a railroad and telegraph line from the Missouri River to the Pacific Coast, and to secure to the Government the use of the same for postal, military and other purposes." The act incorporated the Union Pacific Co., at an authorized capital of $100 million and with a 162-man board of commissioners, and empowered it to build a branch line from Iowa to Omaha, NEBRASKA TERRITORY, as well as a main line westward from Omaha to the California border. The act authorized the Central Pacific, chartered in 1861, to lay that portion of the main line that crossed California. Whichever company reached Nevada first, however, was to continue building until it met the other. The legislation also authorized the issuance of land grants to the companies, of 10, later 20, alternate sections (640 acres) per mile on either side of the right-of-way for the length of the line. The government would loan the construction companies up to $50 million in 6% bonds, ranging from $16,000 to $48,000 per mile, according to the terrain built upon.

As a result of the legislation, the Central Pacific began construction at Sacramento 8 Jan. 1863, though not till 2 Dec. of that year did the fledgling Union Pacific break ground at Omaha. Scarcity of labor and other war-related problems prevented major construction east or west until after Appomattox, and the 2 lines did not link at Promontory Point, Utah, until 10 May 1869. *See also* RAILROADS, U.S. MILITARY.   —EGL

Railroads, Confederate States. Throughout the Civil War, railroads figured vitally in many campaigns. They hauled troops, carried arms, equipment, clothing, and foodstuffs from factories and farms, and often served as the only supply link for a marching army in the field. For Southerners, the war placed insurmountable demands on their railroads.

By 1861 the Confederate states claimed an estimated railroad mileage of 8,783, compared to the North's 22,385. The South's railroad network consisted of little more than feeder lines to depots for the exportation of cotton; of these lines, 35 were interstate links. Differing gauges, poorly constructed roadbeds and trestles, and inadequate rolling stock characterized many of the 112 railroad companies.

Initially Confederate authorities hesitated to harness and control the vital railroads. The government even hampered efforts of the companies as it limited their profits and provided no means for the return of confiscated rolling stock. Not a single mile of new track was laid in the Confederacy during the war. When Federal armies or raiders destroyed rails and tracks, Southerners replaced them by ripping up portions of little-used or abandoned lines.

Southern railways nevertheless operated, for most of the war, under the increasing burdens. Erratic schedules and soaring rates to offset inflation characterized their daily operations. Some lines became the focus or critical factor in several military campaigns. In the East, the MANASSAS GAP, ORANGE & ALEXANDRIA, Virginia Central, VIRGINIA & TENNESSEE, and RICHMOND & PETERSBURG affected, sometimes decisively, military operations. Gen. Robert E. Lee endured a 10-month siege at Petersburg, Va., to protect that rail center. In the West, in the Confederacy's heartland, both opponents utilized the region's rail lines, often as their only supply routes. In campaigns such as VICKSBURG, CHATTANOOGA, and ATLANTA, railroads assumed primary importance.

During the war's final year the railroads of the Confederacy collapsed completely. Union armies, penetrating deeper into Southern territory, routinely destroyed the tracks. Union soldiers piled the ties, set them on fire, then heated the rails until they could be wrapped around trees. These so-called "Sherman neckties," or "SHERMAN'S HAIRPINS," effectively ruined the rails. When the Confederates surrendered, their railroads lay in shambles. In such a conflict, Southern railways managed some remarkable achievements in a doomed struggle.   —JDW

Railroads, United States Military. The U.S. Military Railroads (USMRR) system came into being following passage of the U.S. Congress' Railways and Telegraph Act 31 Jan. 1862. Antebellum Northern railroads, all in private hands, consisted of over 22,000 mi of track, thousands of pieces of rolling stock, and a 1-billion-dollar investment inadequate to war needs and subject to corruption. Lines connecting Washington, D.C., and the Eastern and Western war theaters with supply sources farther north were susceptible to Confederate attack. Different track gauges and insufficient connecting lines prevented speedy troop movement. Sec. of War SIMON CAMERON, vice-president of the Pennsylvania Railroad, scandalized even hard-boiled politicians by charging his own administration 2¢ per mi per soldier, for transportation on PRR boxcars. Other railroad owners charged equally heavy, widely varied tariffs and abused U.S. Treasury resources.

Fearing punitive legislation, railway owners met privately prior to passage of the Railways and Telegraph Act and agreed on uniform tariffs for government passage and freight. On passage of the act, Pres. ABRAHAM LINCOLN was empowered to impress any telegraph or railroad and all equipage, make regulations for the maintainance and security of these lines, and subject all railroad and telegraph company officers and employees to military authority. On 11 Feb. 1862 Lincoln issued

U.S. military railroad at City Point USMHI

an executive order delegating this authority and appointing Daniel C. McCallum military director and superintendent of railroads in the U.S. McCallum, former general supervisor of the New York & Erie Railroad's Susquehanna division, established headquarters at 250 G Street in Washington and was directed to report to Maj. Gen. MONTGOMERY C. MEIGS for all fiscal assistance. In other matters he was to exercise autonomous authority over U.S. railways serving the military, impressing any lines, rolling stock, and property necessary to ensure what Lincoln's order called the "safe and speedy transport" of men and supplies. On 25 May 1862, Lincoln expanded McCallum's authority to all U.S. railways.

McCallum's appointment established the USMRR. In practice this network extended only to privately owned railroads operating in hostile or occupied Southern territory. However, the USMRR also constructed 2 lines of its own: a 7-mi track from Washington, D.C., to ALEXANDRIA, Va., and, late in the war, the City Point & Army Line, a supply road for the PETERSBURG siege. Historian Francis A. Lord estimates that at the close of hostilities McCallum's system comprised 2,100 mi of track with an inventory of 6,330 cars and 419 engines.

The USMRR's chief of construction and maintenance was Col. HERMAN HAUPT, a West Point–trained civil engineer and civilian railroad construction expert. Assigned to support Maj. Gen. IRVIN MCDOWELL's forces in Virginia Apr. 1862, Haupt assembled levies from various regiments to reconstruct destroyed sections of the Richmond, Fredericksburg, & Potomac Railroad. This was the informal beginning of the USMRR Construction Corps. By Apr. 1865 this unit had laid or rebuilt approximately 650 mi of track and 26 mi of bridges, and reworked several lines to a uniform track gauge of 4 ft, 8.5 in.

Union conscription laws exempted locomotive engineers from military service, but those assigned to USMRR engines often came under fire. Federal troop trains were attacked as early as spring 1861, and locomotives operating on the City Point & Army Line 1864–65 were regularly subjected to Confederate artillery fire at each stop. Aggregate statistics on casualties among USMRR personnel are undocumented.

At a cost of $30 million the USMRR maintained 16 railways in the Eastern theater and 19 shorter lines in Tennessee, Mississippi, and Georgia. The most prominent of these lines were: the Alexandria & Washington; the ORANGE & ALEXANDRIA; the MANASSAS GAP; the Richmond, Fredericksburg & Potomac; the Richmond & York River; the Richmond & Danville; the South Side; the Norfolk & Petersburg; the Nashville & Chattanooga; the Nashville, Decatur & Stevenson; the Chattanooga & Knoxville; the Knoxville & Bristol; the Chattanooga & Atlanta; and sections of the MEMPHIS & CHARLESTON. From the cessation of hostilities Apr. 1865 through early 1866, McCallum directed the return of these lines to civilian ownership and the repair of war damages. The USMRR's Washington & Alexandria line was sold to the Washington & Georgetown Railway Co. and the City Point & Army Line became the property of the South Side Railroad. *See also* RAILROAD ACT. —JES

Rains, Gabriel James. CSA b. Craven Cty., N.C., 4 June 1803. An 1827 graduate of West Point, 13th in his class, Rains had a distinguished career in the antebellum Regular Army. After being wounded and brevetted for gallantry in the Seminole War and serving in the Mexican conflict, he held the rank of lieutenant colonel of the 5th Infantry when he resigned from the army 31 July 1861.

Rains was appointed a brigadier general 23 Sept. 1861 and assigned to the command of a brigade in Maj. Gen. Daniel H. Hill's division. His brigade served in the DEPARTMENT OF THE PENINSULA, where in spring 1862 the command opposed the

advance of the Union ARMY OF
THE POTOMAC. During the Confederate withdrawal, Rains
originated land mines, burying
8- or 10-in. Columbiad artillery
shells a few inches under
ground level; these exploded
when stepped on or moved. His
devices angered officers in both
armies who considered the
mines unethical weapons.

LC

Rains led his brigade at SEVEN
PINES, where his failure to attack
drew severe criticism from Hill.
He held no other field com-
mand during the war. In December Rains became the first
superintendent of the volunteer and conscript bureau, serving
until May 1863. In June 1864 he assumed command of the
Torpedo Bureau.

Like his brother, Brig. Gen. GEORGE W. RAINS, who manufactured gunpowder in Georgia, the bureau head rendered the
Confederacy his greatest service in ordnance. Over protests
from officers, he secured permission to plant his mines in the
approaches to Richmond, Mobile, Charleston, and in the
James River.

During the postwar years Rains resided in Atlanta, Ga., and
Charleston, S.C., where he served 1877–80 as a clerk in the
U.S. Quartermaster Department. d. Aiken, S.C., 6 Aug. 1881.
—JDW

Rains, George Washington. CSA b. Craven Cty., N.C.,
1817. After attending New Berne Academy near his home,
Rains entered West Point, graduating 3d in his class in 1842.
Commissioned 2d lieutenant in the Corps of Engineers, he
requested a transfer to the artillery and was assigned to the 4th
Artillery, with orders sending him to Fort Monroe in Virginia.
In 1844 he reported to West Point for a tour of duty as assistant
professor of chemistry. He won 2 brevets for bravery in the
Mexican War, 1846–48, and a promotion to 1st lieutenant
Mar. 1847. Stationed at various garrisons in the South until
1850, he was at that time shifted to a series of assignments at
Northern forts. He resigned from the army Oct. 1856 to be-
come president of the Washington Iron Works at Newburgh,
N.Y., a position he retained until returning to the South at the
beginning of hostilities in 1861.

Rains, brother of Confederate Gen. GABRIEL J. RAINS, was
commissioned major in the Confederate artillery 10 July 1861
and immediately assigned to the Ordnance Bureau. There he
was placed in charge of procuring gunpowder and quickly
became the Confederacy's leading expert in gunpowder manufacture. In search of a suitable location for a powder works
and arsenal, he made a quick tour of the Confederate states in
fall 1861, selecting Augusta, Ga. As the BLOCKADE forced the
South to become self-sufficient, Rains's mission assumed critical importance. He created the NITER AND MINING BUREAU to
collect niter from limestone in the caves of the Lower South,
developed highly efficient production methods from facilities
of his own design, and used his experience as a chemist to
introduce numerous improvements in the processing of gunpowder. By the end of the war he had produced 2.75 million
lb of the most dependable powder made in the Confederacy
(*see* AUGUSTA POWDER WORKS).

Rains was promoted to lieutenant colonel 22 May 1862 and
to colonel 12 July 1863. He had charge of all munitions operations and general command of troops in Augusta until fall
1864, when reinforcements arrived to defend the powder
works against Maj. Gen. WILLIAM T. SHERMAN's advance.

After the war Rains taught chemistry at the Medical College
of Georgia in Augusta, becoming dean of the school in 1867.
In 1882 he published a 22-page pamphlet describing operations at the Augusta plant. Titled *The History of the Confederate Powder Works,* it is a detailed technical treatise on gunpowder production in the wartime South. Rains retired to
Newburgh, N.Y., dying there 21 Mar. 1898.   —PLF

Rains, James Edward. CSA b. Nashville, Tenn., 10 Apr.
1833, Rains graduated from Yale Law School in 1854, opened
a practice in Nashville, and in 1858 was elected city attorney.
Popular in his hometown, politi-
cal ally of Nashville *Republican
Banner* editor FELIX K. ZOLLICOF-
FER, Rains became associate editor of the *Banner* and in 1860
won the office of district attorney for Davidson, Williamson,
and Sumner counties. When the
Confederate 11th Tennessee Infantry organized May 1861,
Rains joined as a private, was
elected colonel, and with his
regiment mustered into Zollicoffer's brigade in midsummer.

Rains fought in his first skirmish in Laurel Cty., Ky., 26 Sept.
1861, north of Cumberland Gap, and in November occupied
the gap with 2 regiments and 7 cannon. He held this position
until confronted by Union Brig. Gen. GEORGE W. MORGAN's
force June 1862, then, on orders, retired to Tennessee. The next
month he returned with elements of Maj. Gen. E. KIRBY SMITH's
force, pressed Morgan from the gap, and in Maj. Gen. CARTER L.
STEVENSON's division soldiered through the KENTUCKY CAM-
PAIGN. For this service he was promoted brigadier general 4
Nov. 1862 and assigned command of the 2d Brigade in Maj.
Gen. JOHN P. MCCOWN's division for the Battle of STONE'S RIVER.

There, 31 Dec. 1862, leading his brigade in a sweeping
maneuver against the Federal right flank, Rains was killed.
Following the battle, a clergyman received Union Maj. Gen.
WILLIAM S. ROSECRANS' permission to move Rains's body
through Union lines for burial at Nashville on the condition that
the funeral did not become a Confederate propaganda event.
It did, however, and Rains, young and talented, briefly
achieved the status of Confederate martyr.   —JES

Raleigh, N.C., Union occupation of. 13 Apr. 1865
Made jubilant by the recently received news of Gen. Robert
E. LEE'S SURRENDER to Lt. Gen. ULYSSES S. GRANT, the troops of
Maj. Gen. WILLIAM T. SHERMAN marched buoyantly through
eastern North Carolina during the second week of Apr. 1865.
Their joy was enhanced by the lack of opposition they encountered on the road to Raleigh from the troops of Lt. Gen. WADE
HAMPTON and Maj. Gen. JOSEPH WHEELER. Sherman's BUMMERS
were in especially high spirits; they anticipated adding the state
capital to the list of towns they had looted and torched since
departing Atlanta the previous November.

If 2 elderly citizens of this area had their way, the bummers would be disappointed. On the afternoon of the 12th, former North Carolina governors WILLIAM A. GRAHAM and David L. Swain, the latter now president of the state university, were brought under guard to Sherman's headquarters at Gulley's Station, several miles south of the capital. Sherman found the old men—incongruously dressed in top hats and waistcoats—straining to maintain decorum, although recent events had left them "dreadfully excited." That morning, at the pair's urging, North Carolina Gov. ZEBULON B. VANCE had named them peace commissioners to the advancing enemy and had empowered them to seek of Sherman a pledge to refrain from sacking Raleigh. Already the pair, with 3 other envoys from Vance, had been twice detained, first by Confederates who objected to an armistice, then by outriders of Union Brig. Gen. H. JUDSON KILPATRICK's cavalry division. Before being conveyed under guard to Sherman, the peace party had been caught in the middle of a fire fight between opposing troopers.

Impressed by his visitors' composure under pressure and by their sincere desire to avoid bloodshed and destruction, Sherman agreed to spare the city unless its inhabitants fired on his people. Early the next morning, when Kilpatrick's outriders splashed into rainswept Raleigh, they dodged shots from one of Wheeler's stragglers, who had been looting the city. Capturing the assailant, an enraged Kilpatrick hanged him on the spot for violating truce terms. Mindful of Sherman's instructions, however, "Kill-Cavalry" did not retaliate against the local populace.

By the time Sherman entered Raleigh, about 7:30 a.m., a cordon of military police had secured the town. During their lengthy stay in the area his troops plundered some outlying districts, but the city itself escaped molestation—thanks largely to the efforts of 2 old men dedicated to peace. —EGL

rams. In the naval war both North and South used rams, so called because of the iron ram each ship carried by its massively built prow. In 1861 Confederate Navy Sec. STEPHEN R. MALLORY insisted that the *VIRGINIA* be made into a ram as well as an IRONCLAD. The vessel was provided with an iron prow, which was not fastened securely and came loose after the ironclad rammed and sank the *Cumberland* at HAMPTON ROADS, Mar. 1862. Nevertheless, the effectiveness of the ironclad ram had been proven.

Early in 1862 the Confederate War Department purchased 14 riverboats, and 7 of these (the *General Beauregard, General Earl van Dorn, General M. Jeff Thompson, GENERAL STERLING PRICE, General Sumter, Colonel Lovell,* and *Little Rebel*) were converted into cotton-clad rams of the River Defense Fleet. They were commanded by Capt. James E. Montgomery and manned by Confederate army personnel. On 10 May 1862 the rams attacked the ironclad gunboats of the Federal Mississippi Flotilla near Fort Pillow and were able to hold them off until after the fort was evacuated by the Confederates 1 June. The rams then withdrew to above Memphis.

In the meantime, during spring 1862, Union Col. CHARLES ELLET had been hastily converting several river steamers into rams, and these were incorporated into Flag Officer CHARLES H. DAVIS' flotilla. On 6 June 1862, opposing forces, which included Ellet's *Monarch* and QUEEN OF THE WEST, met near Memphis. The surrender of Memphis followed the Confederate naval defeat. All of the Confederate rams were either sunk or captured except the *General Earl Van Dorn,* which managed to escape to the Yazoo River.

In the South, Mallory concentrated on providing bigger and more powerful rams, and several of these saw action despite serious deficiencies in their design. The *ALBEMARLE* at Plymouth, N.C., Apr. 1864; the *CHICORA* and *PALMETTO STATE* outside Charleston harbor, Jan. 1863; the *William H. Webb,* the *Queen of the West* (originally one of the Ellet rams), and the CSS *Beatty,* below Warrenton, Miss.: All took on Federal vessels with some success. The CSS *ARKANSAS,* with an 18,000-lb iron beak for a rammer, never had the opportunity to use it while engaging the *CARONDELET* and the *TYLER* on the Yazoo River July 1862. The USS *TENNESSEE,* Adm. FRANKLIN BUCHANAN's flagship at the Battle of MOBILE BAY, Aug. 1864, lacked only speed to strike at its swifter adversaries. The *Tennessee* was itself rammed repeatedly until Buchanan was compelled to surrender the battered and helpless vessel.

Mallory was also determined to procure powerful seagoing rams that would break the North's BLOCKADE. Early in the war he sent JAMES D. BULLOCH, Confederate purchasing agent, to England, and Bulloch commissioned John Laird & Sons, shipbuilders at Birkenhead, to build 2 such vessels. But Mallory and Bulloch were frustrated by the British government's seizure of the LAIRD RAMS on the grounds that they violated that nation's neutrality. A final glimmer of hope for believers in a Southern naval miracle fell upon the formidable-appearing ram *STONEWALL,* which Bulloch built in France. Although it succeeded in crossing the Atlantic as a Confederate warship, the war was over before the vessel's potential could be tested. —NCD

Ramsay, George Douglas. USA b. Dumfries, Va., 21 Feb. 1802. Ramsay's family moved to Washington, D.C., in his youth; from there he was appointed to the U.S. Military Academy at age 14. Graduating 26th in the 30-man class of 1820, he was commissioned in the artillery and became a 1st lieutenant in 1826, switching to staff duties as regimental adjutant. In 1835, after serving on garrison duty in Virginia and New England, he joined the Ordnance Department as a captain and commanded arsenals in several seaboard states. He then served under Gen. Zachary Taylor in Mexico, winning the brevet of major in the Monterrey campaigning and June 1847–May

1848 acting as Taylor's ordnance chief. Afterward he returned to the command of arsenals in Pennsylvania, Virginia, and Missouri. He was on duty in the nation's capital when the Civil War erupted.

From early 1861 to May 1863 Ramsay commanded the Washington Arsenal, the most important installation his department administered. On 1 June 1863 he was named colonel and 3 months later brigadier general and chief of ordnance, a position he had neither sought nor desired. Nevertheless, he served diligently as successor to Brig. Gen. JAMES W. RIPLEY, promoting new weaponry of promise such as the breech-loading rifle, an arm his predecessor had blindly opposed, and rejecting impractical or overly costly inventions.

His tenure lasted less than a year, thanks to a feud with Sec. of War EDWIN M. STANTON. When Stanton installed as Ramsay's principal assistant an ambitious officer who continually undermined and criticized his superior, the latter bitterly protested his situation. On 12 Sept. 1864, Stanton relieved him from active service, and in 1870 a disgruntled Ramsay retired from all public duty, with the brevet of major general. He died at his residence in the capital 23 May 1882, survived by a son who later became a rear admiral in the U.S. Navy.   —EGL

Ramseur, Stephen Dodson. CSA b. Lincolnton, N.C., 31 May 1837, Ramseur graduated 14th in the West Point class of 1860 and served as a 2d lieutenant in the artillery before resigning his commission 6 Apr. 1861, a few weeks before North Carolina seceded. During the war's first year, he commanded an artillery battery. Appointed colonel of the 49th North Carolina Infantry in spring 1862, he led the regiment in the charge at MALVERN HILL, Va., where he fell with a severe wound in his right arm. While recuperating, he was promoted to brigadier general, 1 Nov. 1862, and assigned to a brigade of 4 North Carolina regiments.

LC

The North Carolinian led his command in a searing charge 3 May 1863 in the woods west of CHANCELLORSVILLE. Again wounded, Ramseur ruptured the Federal lines where others had failed. At Spotsylvania Court House a year later, his seasoned veterans, in a furious counterattack, assisted in repulsing the massive Federal assault. Gen. Robert E. Lee personally thanked Ramseur—the highest compliment afforded an officer in the Confederate States Army.

Lee promoted him to major general 1 June 1864 and assigned him a division he commanded during the SHENANDOAH VALLEY CAMPAIGN. At 27, the youngest West Pointer to attain the rank of major general in the Confederate army, he possessed a reputation for battlefield prowess rivaled by few other generals in the Army of Northern Virginia. Amid the staggering confusion and the nearly impossible coordination of offensive combat, Ramseur excelled. He again distinguished himself at WINCHESTER, FISHER'S HILL, and CEDAR CREEK. In this last battle, while rallying his broken troops, he fell mortally wounded. He died the next morning, 20 Oct. 1864.   —JDW

Ramsey, Alexander. war governor b. Harrisburg, Pa., 8 Sept. 1815. Orphaned at age 10, Ramsey entered Lafayette College in 1833, left school to study law privately, and passed the Pennsylvania bar in 1839. First representing Pennsylvania in the U.S. House of Representatives 1843–47, he served as appointed governor of Minnesota Territory 1849–53, mayor of St. Paul, Minn., in 1855, was the failed Republican candidate in Minnesota's first gubernatorial election in 1857, then won the governorship in 1859 and in 1861.

Ramsey's Civil War gubernatorial tenure presented him with problems not afflicting

LC

other Union governors. Visiting Washington, D.C., during the Fort Sumter crisis, he was the first governor to offer his state's troops for national service. Though Minnesota troops committed themselves honorably during the war, the state's comparatively small population and distance from active Confederate fronts allowed Ramsey to muster less than 20 regiments for field service. The SIOUX UPRISING OF 1862 required that he raise additional militia levies and request U.S. Army aid to protect settlers in the state. Indian depredations in Minnesota also affected his state's economy, creating problems in land speculation and resulting in rising taxes. Ramsey addressed these problems through state legislation and garnered sufficient public support to win election to the U.S. Senate, taking his seat July 1863. As a junior member, he exerted no great effect on Civil War policy issues.

His postwar career was extensive. Serving in the Senate until 1875, he became Pres. RUTHERFORD B. HAYES's secretary of war in 1879, leaving this post in 1881. The next year he joined the Edmunds Commission to investigate polygamy in Utah. From 1886 he pursued personal interests, supervised extensive Minnesota land holdings, and worked on the Minnesota Historical Collections. d. St. Paul, 22 Apr. 1903.   —JES

Randolph, George Wythe. CSA/CSP b. "Monticello," near Charlottesville, Va., 10 Mar. 1818. A grandson of Thomas Jefferson, Randolph served in the U.S. Navy, graduated from the University of Virginia, and practiced law near Charlottesville. In 1850 he moved his practice to Richmond, where, though suffering from pulmonary tuberculosis, he became involved in civic affairs and organized a howitzer company in the Virginia militia. Randolph was elected in 1861 to Virginia's state secession convention as a secessionist delegate.

When his company was called to service, it was expanded to a battalion with Randolph as major. He was promoted to colonel and later to brigadier general, from 12 Feb. 1862, as a result of his gallantry and skill as an artillerist under Maj. Gen. JOHN B. MAGRUDER at BIG BETHEL and on the peninsula. Randolph resigned due to poor health and his desire to serve the South politically.

Having lost a bid for the CONFEDERATE CONGRESS, he was appointed secretary of war by JEFFERSON DAVIS, 17 Mar. 1862. Facing manpower problems caused by a volunteer army of 1-year enlistments, most of which were to expire in April, Randolph convinced Davis that the only answer was CONSCRIPTION. Shepherding a bill through Congress, he persuaded Davis to sign it, despite the president's objections to holding 1-year volunteers in service for 3 years. The result was a strong conscription law that helped keep the Confederate armies in existence until 1865 by drafting all eligible white males between 18 and 45. Randolph also tried to bring attention to the Western theater, where he arranged the president's departmental system so that it would concentrate troops to the Confederacy's best benefit. He finally advocated a theater command in the West.

Davis constantly interfered with Randolph's administration

of the war effort and rebuked him for giving orders independently. On 15 Nov. 1862, Randolph resigned to return to his law practice. Late in 1864 he moved his family to Europe in hopes of improving his health. After the war he returned to Virginia and died near Charlottesville, 3 Apr. 1867.

—CMS

Ransom, Matt Whitaker. CSA b. Warren Cty., N.C., 8 Oct. 1826. An 1847 graduate of the University of North Carolina, an attorney, a Whig presidential elector, and a state legislator, Ransom served as 1 of 3 North Carolina commissioners to the Confederate government at Montgomery, Ala. When his state seceded, he immediately enlisted as a private in the 1st North Carolina and was soon commissioned its lieutenant colonel.

LC

Ransom fought with his regiment in the 1862 PENINSULA and SEVEN DAYS' campaigns. At MALVERN HILL, 1 July, he fell with 2 wounds. Later that year he assumed command of the 35th North Carolina, serving in the brigade of his younger brother, Brig. Gen. ROBERT RANSOM. He fought at ANTIETAM and FREDERICKSBURG and 13 June 1863 was promoted to brigadier general, succeeding his brother in command of the brigade.

During the conflict's final year Ransom's brigade participated in campaigns in North Carolina and Virginia, and Ransom led his command in his home state in the operations at Plymouth and Weldon. In the Old Dominion, he fought at Suffolk and in the PETERSBURG CAMPAIGN. Wounded at SECOND DREWRY'S BLUFF, he also was engaged at FORT STEDMAN and FIVE FORKS. Ransom and his brigade surrendered with the army at Appomattox.

The Confederate brigadier returned to North Carolina after the war, resuming his legal practice, farming his wife's plantation on the Roanoke River and reentering politics in 1870. 2 years later the gifted orator was elected to the U.S. Senate, serving until 1895, when he was appointed minister to Mexico. He retired in 1897 and died near Garysburg, N.C., 8 Oct. 1904.

—JDW

Ransom, Robert, Jr. CSA b. Warren Cty., N.C., 12 Feb. 1828. Graduating 18th in the 44-man West Point class of 1850, Ransom, brother of future Brig. Gen. MATT RANSOM, was posted to dragoon service. An excellent horseman, drillmaster, and combat officer, he became a captain in the 1st U.S. Cavalry 31 Jan. 1861, following service in the West and Southwest as well as at Carlisle Barracks, Pa. When his state seceded, Ransom hastened to accept a captaincy in the CONFEDERATE REGULAR ARMY. By late 1861 he was the colonel of the 1st North Carolina Cavalry.

Ransom's strict notions of discipline kept him from being popular with his men. Still, from his initial combat service, 26 Nov. 1861, he compiled an enviable record in command, winning repeated praise from his superiors. Named a brigadier general to rank from 1 Mar. 1862, he was selected to help organize Confederate cavalry in the West but was shifted to

USMHI

eastern North Carolina instead. As a member of Maj. Gen. BENJAMIN HUGER's division, he served on the Virginia peninsula, fighting 1 July with great valor at MALVERN HILL, where his infantry brigade was shattered at close range by Union cannon. He fought less conspicuously in the ANTIETAM CAMPAIGN but that December was prominent in division command, holding Gen. ROBERT E. LEE's center atop Marye's Hill at FREDERICKSBURG. His performance on that field helped him become a major general as of 26 May 1863. By then he was in charge of the military district encompassing southeastern Virginia. Thereafter he commanded at Richmond, was laid up for months by illness (his health failed him periodically throughout the war), and in October and November served bravely under Lt. Gen. JAMES LONGSTREET in East Tennessee.

Early in 1864 Ransom was back in Richmond. In mid-May he commanded the division under Gen. P.G.T. BEAUREGARD that broke the right flank of the ARMY OF THE JAMES at SECOND DREWRY'S BLUFF. Beauregard, however, criticized Ransom's performance as slow and uncertain, making him the scapegoat for the enemy's escape to BERMUDA HUNDRED. Later that year Ransom commanded cavalry under Maj. Gen. JOHN C. BRECKINRIDGE and Lt. Gen. JUBAL A. EARLY in the Shenandoah Valley, went on sick leave in August, and that November was assigned to head the 1st Military District of South Carolina. When hostilities ended he returned to North Carolina, where he became express agent and city marshal of Wilmington, a farmer in Warren County, and the engineer in charge of river and harbor improvements at New Berne, where he died 14 Jan. 1892.

—EGL

Ransom, Thomas Edward Greenfield. USA b. Norwich, Vt., 29 Nov. 1834, Ransom attended the military school at NORWICH UNIVERSITY, of which his father was president, his education being interrupted briefly when he went to work for the Rutland & Burlington Railroad. In 1851 he received a degree in civil engineering from Norwich, almost immediately went to Illinois as an engineer, then entered the real-estate business.

LC

From Fayette Cty., Ill., he organized an infantry company attached to the 11th Illinois in time for the sneak attack at Charleston, Mo. On 19 Aug. 1861, he and a Confederate officer exchanged blows in the heat of battle and Ransom, though wounded, killed his antagonist.

With little time to recover from his first wound, he received a second, severe wound, at FORT DONELSON. There his regiment lost more than half its men as the wounded Ransom remained on the field in command.

Promoted to colonel for this display of bravery, Ransom

repeated the act at SHILOH. So seriously was he wounded there that his men carried him behind battle lines late in the afternoon in spite of his protests. After a short period of convalescence he served with Maj. Gen. JOHN A. MCCLERNAND as his chief of staff and was appointed brigadier general 15 Apr. 1863, in command of a brigade at Vicksburg, Miss. His conduct during and after the siege prompted Lt. Gen. U.S. GRANT to write, for the *Official Records,* that Ransom was "the best man I have ever had to send on expeditions. He is a live man and of good judgment."

After a successful expedition along the gulf coast of Texas, he accepted command of the XIII Corps in Maj. Gen. NATHANIEL P. BANKS'S RED RIVER CAMPAIGN. In advance near MANSFIELD, La., at Sabine Cross Roads, outnumbered 3 divisions to 1, his command took the brunt of the Confederate assault. While rallying his troops, Ransom took his last wound on the field. Soon after Mansfield, he reported for duty, still in poor physical condition. But in the next few months he managed to command the 4th Division of the XVI Corps at Atlanta, forcing Gen. JOHN B. HOOD from the city into Alabama. After the pursuit ended near Gaylesville, 21 Oct., Ransom was put on a litter and carried with his troops as they marched back to Georgia. Wounded, and with typhoid, his condition worsened. He died on the stretcher at a house 6 mi from Rome, Ga., 29 Oct., 1864.   —FLS

Rappahannock, **CSS.** 1 of 5 vessels the Confederacy managed to obtain from England, this ship, a screw steamer with 3 masts, was supposed to be suitable for conversion into a cruiser. Originally the dispatch boat *Victor* of the British navy, it was sold at auction in 1863 near the mouth of the Thames River and purchased by intermediaries, acting on behalf of the Confederacy, under the pretense of being engaged in China trade.

Painted black and pierced for 8 guns, the vessel was renamed the *Rappahannock.* After repair work was fully in progress, the British became suspicious and made plans to delay the ship's departure, but it slipped out of port one night Nov. 1863. The *Rappahannock's* machinery soon became defective, and the ship was drifted across the English Channel to Calais, France, where it was permitted to stay. Repairmen still on board continued their work.

The crew soon discovered that the ship's greatest fault was lack of space. Its machinery took up so much room that only a few days' supply of coal and provisions could be carried on board. Its sailing capacity, moreover, was limited by low masts, so the sails had no great spread.

But the Confederacy proceeded with plans to put the *Rappahannock* into operation, instructing Lt. CHARLES M. FAUNTLEROY, appointed commander, to sail the refitted ship toward the Western Islands in search of whalers, then across the equator to intercept vessels on their way from the East Indies, and finally against Union commerce off the New England coast.

Work on the vessel progressed slowly. Fauntleroy expected to sail several times during winter 1863–64 but was delayed in port. At last, when he decided the ship was fit to sail, the French government would not permit its departure.

Held at Calais until spring 1865, then turned over to the U.S., the *Rappahannock's* only value to the Confederacy was to keep 1 or 2 Union vessels off the French coast to watch it.   —VCJ

Rappahannock, Union Department of the.   Maj. Gen. GEORGE B. MCCLELLAN'S long-delayed offensive against Confederate forces in Virginia began 17 Mar. 1862 with the movement of the ARMY OF THE POTOMAC to Fort Monroe, at the tip of the Virginia peninsula. McClellan had secured permission from Pres. ABRAHAM LINCOLN to advance by water against Richmond, Va., if the Union capital was adequately protected. Lincoln soon concluded that the troops left behind were insufficient and ordered Maj. Gen. IRVIN MCDOWELL'S 40,000-man I Corps detached from McClellan's army.

On 4 Apr. McDowell's command was formally constituted into the Department of the Rappahannock, with headquarters at Fredericksburg, Va. The department embraced the area of the Old Dominion east of the Blue Ridge Mts. and south and west of the Potomac River. It also encompassed the region crossed by the Fredericksburg & Richmond Railroad, including the District of Columbia and the country between the Patuxent and Potomac rivers.

McDowell's large command figured prominently in McClellan's PENINSULA CAMPAIGN. "Little Mac" constantly wired Washington, D.C., requesting McDowell's advance overland against the Confederate northern defenses encircling their capital. McDowell waited at Fredericksburg while Lincoln, Sec. of War EDWIN M. STANTON, and McClellan exchanged opinions on the disposition of his corps. The decision to keep McDowell at Fredericksburg occurred in the last week of May when Maj. Gen. THOMAS J. "STONEWALL" JACKSON'S legions routed Maj. Gen. NATHANIEL P. BANKS'S Union command at the FIRST BATTLE OF WINCHESTER.

Union authorities reacted swiftly to Jackson's occupation of the lower Shenandoah Valley, ordering Maj. Gen. JOHN C. FRÉMONT from the west and McDowell to detach a force from the east to crush the Confederates. Jackson, however, eluded the trap, repulsed Frémont at CROSS KEYS, 8 June, and defeated McDowell's force, under Brig. Gen. JAMES SHIELDS, at PORT REPUBLIC the next day. 17 days later, 26 June, the Department of the Rappahannock was merged into Maj. Gen. JOHN POPE'S newly created Army of Virginia.   —JDW

Rappahannock Station, Va., eng. at.   7 Nov. 1863   Assuming that Maj. Gen. GEORGE G. MEADE would renew his offensive after the engagement at BRISTOE STATION, 14 Oct. 1863, Gen. ROBERT E. LEE removed his army south of the Rappahannock River. Meade planned to retake the ground between the Rappahannock and the Rapidan, the administration having vetoed a larger movement toward Fredericksburg. Lee, fortifying the Rappahannock's major crossings at Rappahannock Station and at KELLY'S FORD a few miles below, planned to let Meade cross at Kelly's Ford, then attack him in force while holding the main crossing at Rappahannock Station.

On 7 Nov. the Federal left, under Maj. Gen. WILLIAM H. FRENCH, effected a crossing and lodgment at Kelly's Ford while the right, under Maj. Gen. JOHN SEDGWICK, advanced on Rappahannock Station and the crossings there. When dusk fell, Lee expected no more fighting. But he soon learned that French had crossed the river in force and that a night assault ordered by Sedgwick had captured the Confederate detachment on the north side of the Rappahannock, a loss of some 1,500 men and all their guns. Lee then ordered a general withdrawal and by 10 Nov. was south of the Rapidan.   —JTH

rations.   The rations provided to Union and Confederate soldiers alike probably have been among the most maligned aspects of soldier life, having been attacked as insufficient in quantity and abysmal in quality. Though to an extent this is true, most troops fared reasonably well during the war, considering the scanty knowledge about diet and nutrition at the time.

According to the army regulations for camp rations, a Union soldier was entitled to receive daily 12 oz of pork or bacon or 1 lb 4 oz of fresh or salt beef; 1 lb 6 oz of soft bread or flour, 1 lb of hard bread, or 1 lb 4 oz of cornmeal. Per every 100 rations there was issued 1 peck of beans or peas; 10 lb of rice or hominy; 10 lb of green coffee, 8 lb of roasted and ground coffee, or 1 lb 8 oz of tea; 15 lb of sugar; 1 lb 4 oz of candles; 4 lb of soap; 2 qt of salt; 4 qt of vinegar; 4 oz of pepper; ½ bu of potatoes; and 1 qt of molasses. In addition to or as substitutes for other items, desiccated vegetables, dried fruits, pickles, or pickled cabbage might be issued.

The marching ration consisted of 1 lb of hard bread, ¾ lb of salt pork or 1¼ lb of fresh meat, plus the sugar, coffee, and salt. The ration lacked variety, but John Billings in his classic memoir, *Hardtack and Coffee* (1887), felt that the complaints of starvation by old Union soldiers were largely exaggerated. A few Confederates echoed his sentiments from their side. Yet many former soldiers complained almost constantly about both the quality and the quantity of the food they had been issued. Perhaps the almost universal abhorrence of army food during wartime was a factor in such pronouncements.

Generally, the Confederate ration, though smaller in quantity and tending to substitute cornmeal for wheat flour, was little different. But the Confederate commissary system had problems keeping rations flowing to the troops at a steady rate, thus alternating abundance and scarcity in its issuances. On an active campaign each army was likely to outrun its supply trains and thus face the enemy on empty stomachs.   —LDJ

Rawlins, John Aaron.   USA   b. Galena, Ill., 13 Feb. 1831. Though Rawlins received little education early in his life, he studied in a local law office and was admitted to the Illinois bar in 1854. He practiced in partnership in Galena, became city attorney in 1857, and in 1860 was nominated as presidential elector for STEPHEN A. DOUGLAS. At the outbreak of war, Rawlins supported the armed defense of the Union and so impressed fellow townsman ULYSSES S. GRANT that when Grant learned of his appointment as brigadier general Aug. 1861, he invited Rawlins to join his staff. The Galena lawyer, a staunch Democrat, accepted Grant's offer and served as his adjutant through

NA

the war, emerging with a brigadier's star of his own 11 Aug. 1863 and the newly created title of chief of staff of the army 3 Mar. 1865.

As adjutant, Rawlins issued orders for Grant and assisted with correspondence. By far the better writer, Grant sometimes drafted orders for Rawlins to sign, reversing the process indicated by military efficiency. Grant also drafted his own reports, allowing Rawlins to insert relevant correspondence and to verify facts and dates. As he advanced in rank, Grant

might have acquired a better adjutant, but his sense of loyalty did not permit him to consider such a step.

Rawlins headed Grant's military household, providing him with companionship and support. Irascible and profane, Rawlins guarded Grant's privacy, looked to his comfort, and warned him frequently against drink. His own father's drinking had kept the family in poverty and left Rawlins with a lifelong hatred of liquor. Whether or not such warnings to Grant were needed is disputed, but clearly Rawlins did his superior a disservice by dramatizing his role to suggest that only his faithful guardianship kept Grant from excessive drink.

In the latter days of the war, Rawlins frequently overstepped his position, even trying to interfere with Maj. Gen. WILLIAM T. SHERMAN's campaign in Georgia, but his hold on Grant's loyalty remained firm. After election as president, Grant planned to send the tubercular Rawlins to a post with a suitable climate. But Grant acquiesced when Rawlins insisted on being secretary of war. Rawlins died in Washington, 6 Sept. 1869, within 6 months of his appointment.   —JYS

Raymond, Henry Jarvis.   journalist   b. Lima, N.Y., 24 Jan. 1820. After a brief stint as a schoolteacher and graduation from the University of Vermont in 1840, Raymond moved to New York City. At first a free-lance writer for HORACE GREELEY's *New Yorker,* he joined the staff of Greeley's new NEW YORK *TRIBUNE* in 1841. Raymond left the *Tribune* in 1843, joined the Whig party newspaper, *Morning Courier and New York Enquirer,* won election to the New York legislature in 1849, accepted the editorship of *Harper's New Monthly Magazine* in 1850, and in 1851 founded the New York *Daily Times* with his friend George Jones *(see* NEW YORK *TIMES).*

An indefatigable man, Raymond, elected speaker of the New York house of representatives in 1851, simultaneously held this post, edited *Harper's,* and ran the *Times.* Continuing his editing chores, he won election as lieutenant governor of New York in 1854. Giving up his duties at *Harper's* in 1856, that same year he joined the Republican party. The word *Daily* was dropped from the newspaper's title in 1857, and from this period through the rest of Raymond's career he and his newspaper hewed to the principles of the Republican party.

The *Times*'s partisanship was confined to its editorial columns, Raymond preferring a straightforward, nonflamboyant news style. Throughout the Civil War his politics and his newspaper's usurpation of the New York *Tribune*'s prominence in public life and newspaper sales made Horace Greeley the publisher's bitter critic. In 1859 Raymond personally had reported Italian combat in the Austrian-Sardinian War. He applied this same energy to the domestic conflict, traveling to Virginia's Civil War theater many times and maintaining a large staff of war correspondents. Greeley's *Tribune* and James Gordon Bennett's New York *Herald* gave Raymond active competition through 1865. The 3 newsmen had treated New Yorkers to a 4-year "circulation war" that saw the *Times* rise to second place prewar, after the *Herald.*

Raymond reentered the New York legislature in 1861, was its speaker in 1862, and failed in a bid for the U.S. Senate in 1863. In 1864 he helped shape the Republican presidential platform and won election to the U.S. House of Representatives. A moderate among RADICAL REPUBLICANS, he served ineffectively, was removed from influential committees, and labeled a COPPERHEAD by detractors. This 1 congressional term ended his political career.

Raymond thereafter confined most of his activities to *Times* editorial work, dying in New York City 18 June 1869. As well as many political tracts and pamphlets, Raymond wrote *Disunion and Slavery* (1860) and *The Life and Public Services of Abraham Lincoln* (1865). —JES

Raymond, Miss., eng. at. 12 May 1863 On 11 May Confederate Brig. Gen. JOHN GREGG and his brigade, having reached Jackson from Port Hudson, La., marched to Raymond. Gregg was alerted by Lt. Gen. JOHN C. PEMBERTON, then at Vicksburg, to look out for the advance of thousands of Federals (*see* VICKSBURG, MISS., SECOND CAMPAIGN). The force proved to be 2 divisions of Union Maj. Gen. JAMES B. MCPHERSON's XVII Corps, 12,000 strong. McPherson had his column on the road before daylight on the 12th, and by 10 o'clock his vanguard was ascending a ridge 3 mi southwest of Raymond.

Alerted to the Federals' approach by scouts, Gregg posted 3 infantry units north of Fourteen Mile Creek, to dispute the nearby Utica road crossing. Cannoneers of (H. M.) Bledsoe's Missouri battery unlimbered their 3 guns while Gregg's other regiments marched out the Gallatin road, taking a position from which they could sweep cross-country and envelop the Federals' right.

As McPherson's skirmishers came down the slope, Bledsoe's gunners opened fire. Union brigades deployed into line of battle, descended the grade, and entered the woods bounding Fourteen Mile Creek. Smoke and dust kept Gregg from seeing he was outnumbered, and he hurled troops against the Federals. Bewildered by junglelike growth, some Union troops broke, but Maj. Gen. JOHN A. LOGAN galloped up and rallied them to hold their line. Meanwhile, 2 of Gregg's regiments forded Fourteen Mile Creek, to be opposed by overwhelming numbers. After being fired upon, they withdrew.

By 1:30 p.m. a brigade of Brig. Gen. MARCELLUS M. CROCKER's division had arrived and filed into position on Logan's left. Supported by the fire of 22 cannon, McPherson counterattacked and seized the initiative. For the next several hours, McPherson's and Gregg's regiments generally acted on their own, in a confused affair in which smoke and undergrowth kept the senior officers from knowing where their units were and what they were accomplishing.

After the collapse of his right wing, Gregg ordered the fight abandoned. Disengaging, the Confederates retired toward Jackson. Union losses in the battle were 66 killed, 339 wounded, and 37 missing. Gregg listed 72 killed, 252 wounded, and 190 missing. —ECB

Reagan, John Henninger. CSP b. Sevier Cty., Tenn., 8 Oct. 1818. Moving to Texas in 1839, Reagan fought Indians, surveyed, farmed, practiced law, and was elected Henderson County judge. After serving in the state legislature he was elected district judge in 1852; reelected in 1856, he resigned to accept a seat in the U.S. House of Representatives 1857–61.

Reagan held moderate Southern views but voted for secession at the 1861 Texas convention. Elected to the Provisional Confederate Congress, he reluctantly agreed to accept the position of postmaster general Mar. 1861. He acquired samples of Federal postal materials and secured the services of a number of former Federal employees. The Constitution required the department to be self-supporting after 1 Mar. 1863, a goal he met by eliminating some routes and offices, increas-

ing rates, and securing a sharp reduction in railroad costs. Draft exemptions for postal workers eased personnel problems but led to clashes with the War Department. Stung by criticism, Reagan tried to resign early in 1862 but was persuaded to remain in office. Respect for the postmaster increased as the war wore on.

Within the cabinet Reagan aggressively pressed his views, but he was devoted to Pres. JEFFERSON DAVIS and won his confi-

LC

dence, and when Davis was captured in 1865 Reagan was the only cabinet member with him. Imprisoned at FORT WARREN for several months, Reagan appealed to Pres. ANDREW JOHNSON to adopt a lenient policy toward the South and to Texans to accept the results of the war, including civil rights for blacks.

After his release Reagan resumed his political career. In 1875 he helped write a new state constitution. An active member of the U.S. House 1875–87, he was elected in 1887 to the Senate, where he was instrumental in establishing the Interstate Commerce Commission. In 1891 Gov. James S. Hogg persuaded him to head the powerful Texas Railroad Commission. He retired in 1903 and died in Palestine, Tex., 6 Mar. 1905, the last survivor of the Confederate cabinet. —LHH

Reams' Station, Va., Battle of. 25 Aug. 1864 By the morning of 21 Aug. 1864, following a week of fighting above the James River and an arduous march to Petersburg, Union Maj. Gen. WINFIELD S. HANCOCK's II Corps/Army of the Potomac was worn and weary. That day the divisions of Maj. Gen. JOHN GIBBON and Brig. Gen. NELSON A. MILES were put on fatigue duty in the Union rear. At noon on the 22d, Miles's men were sent south of Petersburg to continue a track-wrecking project along the Weldon Railroad begun on the 18th by Maj. Gen. GOUVERNEUR K. WARREN's V Corps. Passing south of Warren's position, Miles destroyed 2 mi of trackage and halted at Reams' Station, about 7 mi below Petersburg. A mounted force under Brig. Gen. DAIVD M. GREGG and Col. Samuel P. Spear guarded the infantry's front and flanks.

Early on the 24th Hancock had Gibbon's division come down and occupy trenches that Miles's men had held near the depot. When relieved, Miles wrecked 3 more miles of track, forcing the enemy to supply Petersburg by way of roundabout wagon-train routes. That evening, however, Hancock learned of the approach of Confederates under Lt. Gen. AMBROSE P. HILL, estimated at 8,000–10,000 infantry, and made ready to fight.

On the next day the Confederates launched 2 attacks against Miles and Gregg that were speedily repulsed. During a third attack, part of Miles's line held by inexperienced regiments caved in. Rushing through the breach, the attackers captured hundreds of men and 9 cannon. When ordered to plug the gap, Gibbon's tired division responded feebly before breaking and fleeing. Though the remainder of Miles's command stood firm, as did Gregg's and Spear's, Gibbon's troops were driven from their entrenchments with an ease that surprised even the Confederates.

That evening the Federals withdrew toward Petersburg

under cover of support troops hurriedly collected. Hancock's losses amounted to 2,372, including nearly 2,000 captured or missing, whereas Hill had suffered one-third as many.

—EGL

reconnaissance. Small parties of cavalry and/or infantry conducted reconnaissance to examine the terrain, locate enemy positions, and discover any indication of movements. According to regulations used by Civil War officers, a reconnaissance was to be conducted daily when near an opposing force. Cavalry usually reconnoitered on open ground, while infantry, with a handful of cavalrymen to relay the intelligence, operated in mountainous terrain. A reconnoitering party generally had orders to advance cautiously and to avoid combat.

A reconnaissance in force designated an offensive thrust intended to ascertain with certainty an opponent's position or strength. Such an operation usually was conducted by a brigade but often a division was used. Sometimes a reconnaissance-in-force preceded a real engagement or sometimes served only as a demonstration. The reconnoitering force engaged the enemy, driving in outposts and perhaps actually attacking a portion of the line. Most Civil War veterans participated in a reconnaissance at some time during their military careers.

—JDW

Reconstruction. On 8 Dec. 1863, Union Pres. ABRAHAM LINCOLN issued a Proclamation of Amnesty and Reconstruction. By its terms, he offered "full pardon" and restoration of property "except as to slaves" to Confederates who swore an oath of allegiance to the U.S. and its law. Additionally, if in any state 10% of the adult white males who had voted in 1860 took the oath, those loyal citizens could reestablish a state government. This 10% plan formed the basis of Lincoln's Reconstruction policy and ignited a divisive political struggle within the Republican Party.

Lincoln adhered to the theory of the indissoluble Union. In his view, states could not legally secede and, consequently, the 11 Confederate states were still in the Union. He believed that a policy of Reconstruction should bring Southern Unionists back into control of the state governments. A magnanimous policy, it viewed Reconstruction as a restoration, not a revolution.

Congressional Republicans, however, distrusted former Confederates and wanted to guarantee the freedom and civil rights of blacks. To them, especially to the influential RADICAL REPUBLICANS, Lincoln's policy fell far short of a revolution that would stamp Northern values and institutions on the seceded states. Radicals, moreover, advocated land reform in the South and black suffrage.

Lincoln implemented his 10% plan early in 1864 in the Union-occupied portions of Louisiana and Arkansas. By executive order he recognized these restored state governments, but Congress excluded the newly elected representatives and senators. On 2 July 1864, Congress passed a bill, sponsored by Rep. HENRY W. DAVIS and Sen. BENJAMIN F. WADE, that required an oath from the majority of the 1860 electorate, mandated a constitutional convention in each state, and provided legal safeguards for FREEDMEN. But Lincoln killed the bill with a pocket veto. (*See* WADE-DAVIS BILL.)

The divisiveness among Republicans over Reconstruction policy nearly split the party in 1864 when Radical Republicans launched a campaign to deny Lincoln renomination, support-

ing Treasury Sec. SALMON P. CHASE. But Lincoln, a masterful politician, using patronage, secured his nomination before the Republicans met in convention in June. His reelection in the fall resulted in a compromise between him and Congress over Reconstruction.

Lincoln and House Republican leaders agreed that in return for congressional recognition of the governments in Louisiana and Arkansas, the president would approve legislation similar to the Wade-Davis Bill for the remaining Southern states. The legislation never secured passage primarily because of the issue of black suffrage, and the question of Reconstruction was postponed until the war's conclusion. The governments in Louisiana and Arkansas functioned under Lincoln's policy, and a third was forming in Tennessee.

After LINCOLN'S ASSASSINATION, Vice-Pres. ANDREW JOHNSON assumed the presidency, with his own ideas about Reconstruction. In May 1865, after war's end, Johnson issued proclamations pardoning most Confederates and authorizing governors of Southern states to proceed with governmental reorganization. In each state, voters who pledged future loyalty to the U.S. were to appoint a constitutional convention expected to repeal ordinances of secession, disavow the Confederate debt, and accept the 13TH AMENDMENT, which abolished slavery. Johnson's policy conflicted with the Republican faction in Congress on 2 counts: it was, like Lincoln's plan, nonpunitive; and it made no provision to guarantee the rights of blacks.

In the 1865–66 congressional session, Republicans tried to formulate a plan for Reconstruction. The result was the 14TH AMENDMENT, which guaranteed the basic civil rights of all citizens regardless of color, and diminished representation in Congress of those Southern states that refused to enfranchise blacks. In opposition, Johnson toured major cities Aug.–Sept. 1866, just prior to that year's elections, to explain and gain support for his own Reconstruction program. As a result, every Southern state but Tennessee rejected the 14th Amendment; but the president was not so successful in non-Southern states, where Republican candidates dominated the fall elections.

In the next congressional session the victorious Republicans passed, over Johnson's veto, a series of Reconstruction acts that replaced with Federal military governments those set up under Johnson's 1865 proclamations, and that required new constitutional conventions mandated to adopt both black suffrage and a ban on officeholding by former Confederate leaders. Radical Republicans had finally succeeded in establishing their regime. Though increasingly weak through the 2 administrations of U. S. Grant, 1869–77, as the country tired of Reconstruction issues and Radicals lost their influence, it lasted until Pres. Rutherford B. Hayes restored home rule to the South in 1877.

—JDW

Rector, Henry Massey. war governor b. Louisville, Ky., 1 May 1816, Rector migrated with his family to St. Louis, Mo., during his youth. With the exception of 1 year of formal schooling in Louisville, he was educated by his widowed mother. For 6 years after she remarried, he drove freight wagons for his stepfather's salt mills, moving to Arkansas in 1835 to manage land he had inherited from his father. After working as a bank teller for 18 months, he settled into farming and local politics near Collegeville.

During this time he read law and passed the bar, opening a profitable criminal practice in Little Rock. He served as U.S. marshal 1842–43, was elected to the state senate in 1848, and held an appointment as U.S. surveyor general of Arkansas. The Democratic party backed him successfully for the legislature in 1855, a judgeship on the supreme court in 1859, and the next year nominated him for governor. The campaign, one of the most bitter in the state's history, gave Rector the election by a large majority.

A longtime secessionist, Rector defended slavery in his 1861 inaugural address and called a secession convention. But when the delegates met in March, they voted against seceding, hoping compromise could be achieved. While they continued to debate taking Arkansas out of the Union, Rector seized the Federal arsenal at Little Rock, occupied FORT SMITH for the Confederacy, and sent a regiment of volunteers to help defend Virginia after that state seceded.

A secession ordnance finally passed 6 May, but the convention also voted to stay in session to direct the state war effort. Rector tried in vain to bring stability to Arkansas, still a poor frontier state with a large pro-Union population in many sections. Unable to ease economic hardships or opposition to conscription, Rector saw his lukewarm relationship with the convention deteriorate. The new constitution framed by the delegates failed to confirm Rector as governor and they refused to call a gubernatorial election. Eager to remove him from office, the supreme court declared it vacant and Rector became a private citizen 2 years before his term expired. He retired to his law practice, returning to public life to participate in the constitutional convention in 1874. d. Little Rock, 12 Aug. 1899.   —PLF

redoubt. A many-sided extension of a permanent fortress or fieldwork, or a detached defensive work supporting a main fort or fortified line was called a redoubt. Ostensibly capable of self-defense, often holding cannon, redoubts were frequently made of earth and logs, and ringed cities or positions under threat of imminent attack.   —JES

Red River Campaign. Mar.–May 1864 Following the Federal victories at VICKSBURG and PORT HUDSON, 4 and 8 July 1863, Maj. Gen. ULYSSES S. GRANT focused on Mobile as the next major target in the West. However, before a campaign could be launched, Pres. ABRAHAM LINCOLN authorized an expedition against Shreveport, La.—the headquarters of Lt. Gen. E. KIRBY SMITH, the temporary capital of Confederate Louisiana, and a major supply depot and gateway to Texas. Politically, Lincoln hoped to win pledges of loyalty from the planters along the river in exchange for the military's willingness to purchase cotton.

The plan called for a large combined naval/military force under Adm. DAVID D. PORTER and Maj. Gen. NATHANIEL P. BANKS moving up the Red River to Shreveport. Porter's gunboats would provide artillery support and serve as troop transports for a 10,000-man contingent sent by Maj. Gen. WILLIAM T. SHERMAN and commanded by Brig. Gen. ANDREW J. SMITH. An additional 15,000 men under Maj. Gen. FREDERICK STEELE, coming from Little Rock, were to join the main force before the attack on Shreveport. Neither Grant nor Porter was optimistic about the plan, and Porter felt concern over the falling level of the Red

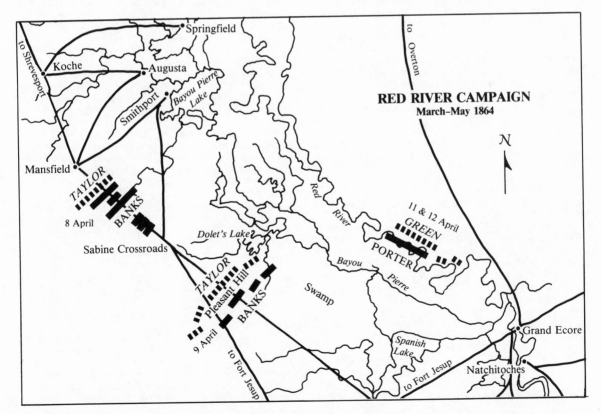

River, which could adversely affect his fleet of 12 ironclad gunboats, 2 large wooden steamers, and 4 smaller steamers.

The campaign began early in Mar. 1864 and brought initial success for the Federals. After removing the obstructions that the Confederates had placed in the Red River, Porter's and Smith's force captured Fort De Russy, which the Confederates had depended on to defend the river. The Federals continued upriver to Alexandria, La., which they occupied on 19 Mar. Banks, having missed the scheduled date of departure, caught up with Porter and Smith at Alexandria 25 Mar., a week late. At Alexandria, dispatches arrived from Grant ordering Banks to return to New Orleans as soon as possible after Shreveport was taken to participate in the campaign against Mobile. Grant also ordered Smith to return his command to Sherman by 25 Apr. for participation in the ATLANTA CAMPAIGN. Frustrating delays put the Federals still further behind schedule. Not until 3 Apr. did Porter get Smith's division past the rapids above Alexandria for rendezvous with Banks's force, which was traveling overland to Shreveport. In the process Porter lost his hospital ship on the rocks.

After arriving at Grand Ecore, most of Smith's command left to rejoin Banks's army at Natchitoches for the planned assault on Shreveport. But the situation changed abruptly 8 Apr. when Banks was defeated at MANSFIELD (40 mi south of Shreveport) by 8,000 Confederate troops commanded by Maj. Gen. RICHARD TAYLOR. The following day the retreating Federal army made a stand at Pleasant Hill and won, but Banks continued his retreat nonetheless. Any further move against Shreveport was now out of the question, and Smith's command rejoined Porter. The gunboats retraced their course down the Red River, subjected to artillery and rifle fire from Taylor's men following along the banks. At BLAIR'S LANDING dismounted Confederate cavalry, supported by artillery, attacked the Federals but withdrew after suffering heavy losses. Confederate Brig. Gen. THOMAS GREEN was among the slain.

Porter's situation was becoming critical. The Red River continued falling, while the Confederates intensified their harassment from the banks. Porter's squadron was the target of their well-aimed shells, and Porter was compelled to destroy one of his gunboats and a pump steamer after both were severely damaged. A second pump steamer was captured by the Confederates. When the squadron reached Alexandria, Porter was dismayed to find that the water at the rapids had fallen to only 3 ft, while his vessels required at least 7 ft to pass. He was faced with the agonizing decision of whether or not to destroy his own squadron to prevent its capture, as there was little likelihood of a rise in the river.

Fortunately for the Federals, one of the engineer officers with the army was Lt. Col. JOSEPH BAILEY, a former Wisconsin lumberjack. Bailey proposed building a dam to back up the water to the required 7-ft level. Porter accepted the plan, and work began 30 Apr. After 8 days of hard labor, the almost completed dam broke as 2 stone-filled sunken barges gave way under pressure. Although the water fell rapidly, 4 of the light-draft gunboats managed to pass over the rapids. Bailey and his men then renewed their work, and by 13 May the remaining vessels of the squadron had succeeded in passing the rapids through 2 wing dams.

A week later the gunboats were back on the Mississippi, and the ill-fated Red River Expedition was ended. It had accomplished nothing and had even antagonized most of the planters the Federals had encountered along the river. Porter's officers

had seized cotton without reimbursement, causing other planters to burn theirs rather than have it taken. Moreover, the expedition had delayed the more important campaign against Mobile that Grant had planned.   —NCD

Red Rover, USS. Before fleeing from ISLAND NO. 10, Apr. 1862, Confederates sank 6 Federal transports, inadvertently providing the Union with one of its finest hospital ships. One of these vessels, a sidewheel steamer purchased at New Orleans the previous November for $40,000, was damaged by a shell that went through its decks and bottom. With the aid of the Western Sanitation Association, which contributed $3,500 toward the cost, the Federals raised the vessel May 1862 and sent it to St. Louis to be converted to a hospital ship.

The converted vessel was taken to Cairo, Ill., early in June and was later officially commissioned the hospital ship of the Mississippi Squadron. An entry in the log of the USS *Richmond* for 12 July 1862 recorded: "At 9 a.m., the steamer *Red Rover* came down the river; . . . she is one of the largest and most beautiful steamers on the river, and has splendid accommodations for the sick."

The vessel had bathrooms, a laundry, an elevator between decks, an amputating room, 2 kitchens, gauze-covered windows, and a corps of nurses aboard. Its icebox held 300 tons, and there were on board enough stores and medical supplies to last 200 men 3 months, as well as delicacies for the sick. "Out on the bosom of the river," the log continued, "the fever-stricken men on the shady decks grasped that chance of life which would have been denied them tossing in tents on shore, where the beating sun by day and the miasma from the bottom-lands by night, coupled with imperfect draining, made recovery almost impossible."

The *Red Rover* served the Mississippi Squadron throughout the remainder of the war. General orders specified that only those who were expected to be sick for a long time were to be sent aboard. With the Confederacy's surrender, the ship no longer had a reason to exist, and 27 Nov. 1865 was sold at public auction at Mound City, Ill., for $4,500.   —VCJ

Redwood, Allen Christian. artist b. Lancaster Cty., Va., 19 June 1844. Redwood received an academy education in Baltimore, Md., then attended the Polytechnic Institute of Brooklyn, N.Y. At the start of the Civil War he returned to the South, enlisted in the 1st Maryland Cavalry at age 17, and transferred to the 55th Virginia Infantry.

As a common soldier with the ARMY OF NORTHERN VIRGINIA, Redwood was captured at the SECOND BATTLE OF BULL RUN and was exchanged within 10 days; fought at CHANCELLORSVILLE, where he witnessed Gen. ROBERT E. LEE and Lt. Gen. THOMAS J. "STONEWALL" JACKSON's last meeting; and served at GETTYSBURG. Through the war he remained with that quick-marching group of regiments known colloquially as Jackson's "FOOT CAVALRY." Though he briefly served as secretary and courier to Brig. Gen. LUNSFORD L. LOMAX, he saw much combat, received 3 wounds, and was captured a final time at Somerton, Va., Apr. 1865.

Redwood is best remembered as an artist who recorded history. In postwar years he traveled abroad, sketched Franco-Prussian War scenes, and as a free-lance writer and illustrator worked for the *Century Magazine, Harper's Monthly,* and various lithographers in Baltimore. He specialized in Civil War scenes, illustrating *Century*'s series of war articles later repro-

U.S.S. Red Rover

duced as the 4-volume history *Battles and Leaders of the Civil War* (1887). His illustrations also appeared in the books *The Maryland Line in the Confederate Army* (1869), *Two Little Confederates* (1888), and *A Rebel of '61* (1899). In his work Redwood drew from personal experience at home, in the field, in combat, and in prisoner-of-war camps. The blunt violence, accuracy, and detail of his illustrations made him popular with the postwar Northern and Southern public and expanded the visual record of the war.

Many of his illustrations were based on well-known photographs. Union Capt. Andrew J. Russell's photograph of Confederate dead along the Stone Wall at Fredericksburg, taken during the 1863 Chancellorsville Campaign, was Redwood's model for his illustration of the 1862 Battle of Fredericksburg. A dead Confederate in the far left of Russell's 1863 photograph appears in Redwood's drawing of 1862 fighting along the Stone Wall.

Redwood died in his brother's home in Asheville, N.C., 24 Dec. 1922. Through the bequest of collateral descendants, the bulk of his unpublished work was donated to the Museum of the Confederacy in Richmond, Va., in 1982.   —JES

Reed projectile. First produced for rifled Parrott artillery, the Reed projectile had a soft, hollow cupped base that expanded on firing to fit the rifling of the weapon. Though it was supplanted by the more sophisticated Parrott shell in the North, Confederates continued manufacturing the simpler Reed model, which was easily produced and adaptable to many rifled field pieces.   —JES

regiment. The Civil War soldier reserved his greatest attachment and pride for his regiment. Though some soldiers were part of renowned brigades and divisions, they identified most

with their regiments. Composed of men usually from the same area and acquainted with each other in civilian life, the regiment became their wartime home.

The volunteer infantry regiment, as prescribed by U.S. Army regulations, consisted at full strength of 10 companies, each of 97 men and 3 officers. Heavy artillery and cavalry regiments were each composed of 12 companies, all lettered in alphabetical order with the letter J omitted. A colonel commanded a regiment, assisted by a lieutenant colonel and a major. Because of absenteeism, the actual strength of a regiment usually numbered only about half of the prescribed strength.

Union authorities during the war organized 2,144 infantry regiments, 61 of heavy artillery, 272 of cavalry, 13 of engineers, 9 light infantry battalions, and 432 artillery batteries. The Confederate government raised 642 infantry regiments, 137 of cavalry, 16 of artillery, and 227 batteries. State governments were responsible for recruiting, organizing, and often rudimentary training. State authorities designated each regiment, once organized, by number: i.e., 1st Virginia Volunteer Infantry.

The war attested to the fighting prowess of these volunteer regiments, their casualty lists to the fury of that prowess. The 5th New Hampshire earned the grievous distinction of suffering more total casualties than any Union infantry regiment, whereas the 1ST MAINE HEAVY ARTILLERY suffered the largest loss in a single engagement: 635 killed and wounded at Petersburg, 18 June 1864. For the Confederates the 1st Texas lost the largest percentage of men, 82.3, at Antietam. In the end, the tattered regimental flags symbolized searing combat and unwavering devotion.   —JDW

Regular Army, Confederate States. A month before the Civil War broke out, the Confederate government took steps to raise 3 distinct armies. In time, 2 of these—militia enlisted for 12 months' service and volunteers recruited for the duration of the conflict—became inextricably entwined, organizationally and administratively. Although only the militia was originally designated by the term, both forces became known as the PROVISIONAL ARMY OF THE CONFEDERATE STATES. The act of 6 Mar. 1861 that organized these forces also provided for the establishment of the Army of the Confederate States of America, a counterpart to the U.S. REGULAR ARMY.

At the outset, Confederate officials projected this Regular force to number about 10,000 officers and men, a figure that Pres. JEFFERSON DAVIS later cited as proof that "the wish and policy" of his government "was peace." Early legislation called for this force to consist of a corps of engineers, 1 regiment of cavalry, 6 regiments of infantry, a corps of artillery (which would also handle ordnance duties), and 4 staff bureaus: the adjutant and inspector general's, the quartermaster general's, the commissary general's, and the medical department's. Later laws increased the number of cavalry and infantry regiments, one of the foot units being designated a ZOUAVE outfit, as well as the size of the engineer corps and each staff bureau. No officer above the rank of brigadier general would be assigned to the combat arms, while each staff department was to be headed by a colonel.

The chief value of this force was as an administrative arm into which former U.S. Army officers were accepted just before the shooting started. Intended as a peacetime establishment, it lost much of its utility once it became evident that militia and volunteers would carry the bulk of the South's combat burden and when new laws permitted Regular officers to hold rank in the Provisional Army as well. When money appropriated for the raising, organizing, and equipping of Regular units was diverted to the Provisional Army, the recruiting of Regulars declined sharply. In consequence, that army attained a fraction of its intended size. Although the OFFICIAL RECORDS mention numerous Regular units (1 battery, 12 cavalry and 7 infantry regiments, and various independent companies of line and support troops), other sources indicate that only 750 officers and 1,000 enlisted men served in the Confederate States Regular Army and that only 5 companies remained in existence through most of the war.   —EGL

Regular Army, United States. When the Civil War began, the Regular Army of the United States numbered 16,367 officers and men comprising 198 line companies distributed among 4 artillery regiments, 5 mounted regiments, and 10 regiments of infantry. The army also embraced 8 staff bureaus —the Adjutant General's, Inspector General's, Judge Advocate General's, Quartermaster General's, Subsistence, Medical, Pay, and Ordnance departments—a Corps of Engineers, and a Corps of Topographical Engineers (see ENGINEERS).

Dozens of Regular officers resigned their commissions in 1861 to serve with the Confederacy, although few enlisted men followed their lead. Instead of using the remainder as a nucleus of professionalism within the volunteer forces of the North, the government kept the Regular Army a separate service, and Regulars were parceled out to various armies according to need. Numerous officers and men, however, were granted leave from their units to accept higher rank in the volunteers. At war's end, each returned to his original rank and unit; more than one major general of volunteers reverted to a captaincy in the Regular establishment.

Various administrative changes took place in the Regulars

during the conflict. Two that occurred in 1863 affected the staff departments: the Corps of Topographical Engineers and the Corps of Engineers, previously separate entities, joined under a common organization; and the Signal Corps was established as a permanent bureau. Other organizational changes affected the line arms. In May 1861 a sixth mounted regiment was formed and 3 months later a reorganization resulted in the 1st U.S. Dragoons being redesignated the 1st U.S. Cavalry, the 2d Dragoons becoming the 2d Cavalry, the Regiment of Mounted Rifles being renamed the 3d Cavalry, the old 1st and 2d Cavalry becoming the 4th and 5th Cavalry respectively (to the detriment of unit morale), and the newest regiment being christened the 6th U.S. Cavalry. Also in May 1861, a fifth artillery regiment was authorized and was the first to be composed exclusively of light field batteries. That same month, 9 new infantry regiments were ordered recruited. Unlike the older outfits, composed of 10 companies apiece, each of these units comprised three 8-company battalions.

The Regulars served in every theater of operations. The artillery regiments were broken up, each sending some companies to serve in the East, others in the West. Centralized administration suffered because, as one artillery officer lamented, "regimental organization simply went to pieces." Of the cavalry regiments, the 1st, 2d, 5th, and 6th served prominently in the ARMY OF THE POTOMAC. Most heavily engaged were the 5th and 6th, a battalion of the former losing all but one of its officers during a dramatic charge against Confederate infantry and artillery at GAINES' MILL and the latter participating in 57 engagements from Williamsburg to Appomattox. The 3d Cavalry served entirely in the West, as did most of the 4th Cavalry. A mainstay of the ARMY OF THE CUMBERLAND, the latter for a time lacked 2 companies, which formed a headquarters escort unit in the Army of the Potomac.

Among the infantry regiments, the 1st and 2d were broken up, serving in both the East and the West. The 3d, 4th, 6th, 7th, 8th, 10th, 11th, 12th, 14th, and 17th infantry saw action mostly in the Army of the Potomac. The 5th Infantry remained in the Southwest and the 9th in California throughout the conflict, while the 13th, 15th, 16th, 18th, and 19th regiments fought in the Western armies. Portions of the latter 4 outfits formed the Regular Brigade of the West, a counterpart to the brigade that included most of the Regular infantry serving in the Army of the Potomac.   —EGL

Reid, Hugh Thompson. USA   b. Union Cty., Indiana, 18 Oct. 1811. A farmer's son, Reid graduated from Bloomington College, Indiana, in the 1830s. He started a law practice, moved to Fort Madison, Iowa, in 1839, and for 3 years served as district attorney for southeast Iowa. Making his residence in Keokuk in 1849, he assumed the presidency of the Des Moines Valley Railroad, holding this position through the first year of the Civil War.

Reid personally raised the 15th Iowa Infantry in Keokuk and 22 Feb. 1862 was commissioned its colonel. He led it to St. Louis in March, then joined the Army of the Tennessee at Pittsburg Landing, Tenn., for the Battle of SHILOH. Although shot through the neck, Reid survived the 6 Apr. 1862 fighting and took recuperative leave. He rejoined the 15th in garrison at Corinth, Miss., but illness kept him from the field during the October Battle of CORINTH. He joined in central Mississippi operations, then was transferred to brigade command at Lake Providence, La., 18 Jan. 1863, preparatory to the SECOND VICKS-

BURG CAMPAIGN. Promoted brigadier general to date from 13 Mar. 1863, he commanded the 1st Brigade/6th Division/XVII Corps, an organization made up of Illinois, Wisconsin, Kansas, and black Louisiana troops. Reid's force next opposed Confederate Maj. Gen. RICHARD TAYLOR's operations to relieve Union pressure on Vicksburg, Miss., fighting several sharp actions around Lake Providence June 1863. On 3 Oct. Maj. Gen. U.S. GRANT dispatched him to

command the District of Cairo, with headquarters at Paducah, Ky. Poor conditions there kept his command small and ineffective.

He resigned his commission 4 Apr. 1864, returned to the presidency of the Des Moines Valley Railroad, and died in his Keokuk home 21 Aug. 1874.   —JES

Reilly, James William. USA b. Akron, Ohio, 20 May 1828. On graduation from Mount St. Mary's College in Emmitsburg, Md., Reilly studied law and was subsequently admitted to the bar in Ohio. In 1861 he represented his own Columbiana County in the state legislature.

Reilly's Civil War service started in 1862 as colonel of the 104th Ohio, organized 30 Aug. He and his regiment served on garrison duty in Kentucky through the rest of that year and half of the next. Reilly led a brigade at Knoxville and in spring 1864 joined Maj. Gen. WILLIAM T. SHERMAN's campaign against Atlanta, Ga. He rose to the rank

of brigadier general of volunteers 30 July 1864 under Maj. Gen. GEORGE H. THOMAS in the Federal attempt to stem Confederate Gen. JOHN BELL HOOD's invasion of Tennessee, which included the Battle of FRANKLIN early in winter 1864. There, as a temporary commander of the 3d Division/XXIII Corps, Reilly emerged from the fighting with 1,000 prisoners and 22 Confederate battle flags. His final achievement was to lead a division in the union of troops under Maj. Gen. JOHN M. SCHOFIELD with those of Maj. Gen. William T. Sherman in the CAROLINAS CAMPAIGN.

He resigned from the army 20 Apr. 1865. On his return to Ohio, he resumed his Wellsville law practice and later became president of the First National Bank of Wellsville. d. in that city 6 Nov. 1905.   —FLS

Remington carbine. The Remington carbine, a single-shot weapon, patented 23 Dec. 1863, fired a .56–.50 rimfire cartridge. It featured a rolling-block breech that rose to accept 1 round of fixed ammunition. The Union War Department contracted with the Remington Arms Co. for 15,000 of these carbines. A less expensive arm than the multishot SPENCER rifle or carbine, it accepted Spencer ammunition.   —JES

Remington revolver. Remington revolvers were produced in several models and 2 calibers during the war, and 1 model in particular, the New Model 1863, was purchased in greater quantity by the U.S. government than any other handgun except the COLT. In fact, by 1863 Remington's prices were so favorable and the weapons so good that Colt, whose prices were higher, no longer received government contracts.

The direct descendant of the Beals-Remington revolver Remington had just finished producing, the Remington Model 1861 revolver was manufactured in both army and navy calibers, .44 and .36 respectively. The distinctive feature of this model was the use of a loading lever based on William H. Elliott's patent, in which the cylinder arbor could be drawn forward without lowering the loading lever. The transition between this model and the New Model 1863 is difficult to trace for several reasons. First, the 1861 model directly followed production of the Beals-Remington, and the serial numbers were continued in sequence, beginning at about 2,000. A change in the frame design occurred at about 7,075, and between serial numbers 10,500 and about 22,000 more or less standard revolvers were produced using old and new parts, but generally using the old, longer Beals frame. It was not until about serial number 22,000 that the New Model 1863 began to emerge, and even then another 12,000 transition revolvers were produced before all the features of the New Model were in place.

The New Model featured a slightly different frame, a refined cylinder arbor patented by Samuel Remington 17 Mar. 1863, and safety notches between the cylinder wells. Between 1863 and 1875, roughly 126,000 New Model Army revolvers were produced. In addition, the government purchased probably as many as 6,000 navy revolvers.

Remington also produced a New Model percussion-belt revolver beginning in 1863, a Remington-Rider percussion-belt revolver in double action, and a New Model police revolver.
                                                                                                      —LDJ

Reno, Jesse Lee. USA b. Wheeling, western Va., 20 June 1823. 9 years after his birth, Reno, a name adapted from the French "Renault," moved with his family to Venango Cty., Pa. From that state he was appointed to attend the U.S. Military Academy, graduating 8th in his class in 1846. In Mexican War service he distinguished himself with "gallant and meritorious conduct" at Cerro Gordo and Chapultepec, where he earned the brevets of 1st lieutenant and captain, respectively.

After a year's assistant professorship at West Point in 1849, he became secretary of a board on artillery technique, then assistant to the Ordnance Board at the Washington Arsenal. He went on to command arsenals at Mount Vernon, Ala., and Leavenworth, Kans., until the Civil War began in 1861. On 12 Nov. that year he accepted a brigadier general's commission and took command of a brigade under Brig. Gen. AMBROSE E. BURNSIDE in the expedition through North Carolina during the winter of 1861–62.

In Apr. 1862 he took the reins of a division in the Department of North Carolina and went on to Virginia in August in time for the SECOND BULL RUN CAMPAIGN. Throughout the campaign he retained command of the IX Corps and took part in the pursuit of Maj. Gen. THOMAS J. "STONEWALL" JACKSON's crack cavalry through Maryland.

Allegedly Reno met Barbara Fritchie in Frederick, offering to purchase the flag she was said to have waved at Jackson as he marched through the town; apparently, Fritchie had not even seen Jackson. She did present Reno with a homemade bunting flag that he tucked carefully away in his saddlebag.

In the dusk light of 14 Sept. 1862 the Union IX Corps, near Fox's Gap in the shadow of South Mountain, Md., was trying to scale the slopes and push the Confederates from the gap. The entire afternoon Reno's corps had been in the heavy fighting on the Union left flank. As Reno rushed up and down the line of his command, shouting words of encouragement, Confederate rifle fire cut him down. The Battle of SOUTH MOUNTAIN was over, and the Union army had lost a respected commander.

On Reno's death, Burnside referred to him as "one of the country's best defenders." His brother took his remains to Baltimore, and they were then transferred to Trinity Church in Boston, Mass., where he was buried 20 Sept. with his casket covered by the Fritchie flag.   —FLS

Republican party.   Until the 1850s the 2 major political parties were the Whigs and the Democrats. Sectional antagonisms fomented by the COMPROMISE OF 1850 and the KANSAS-NEBRASKA ACT of 1854 tore the Whigs apart. By 1854 mass meetings were being held in Michigan, Wisconsin, and other Midwestern states, and the Republican party was born. A coalition made up principally of former Whigs and disgruntled Democrats, the movement spread to other Northern states. In 1856 the Republicans nominated JOHN C. FRÉMONT for the presidency and did well in their first campaign. Because the party was purely sectional, Southerners viewed its growth with dismay. A Republican victory, many warned, would so endanger Southern interests as to warrant secession from the Union. When ABRAHAM LINCOLN won in 1860, the threat became a reality.

Southerners were wrong to view the party as abolitionist at the time. Though some members were abolitionists, the majority cared little about slavery where it existed. They were against the spread of slavery into the territories because they wanted the land reserved for free labor. Despite Lincoln's assurances that he would not interfere with Southern institutions, pro-secessionists believed that eventually slavery would be jeopardized. Almost as important, the Republican party stood for high tariffs, internal improvements decided upon at the national level, and other measures most Southerners found repugnant.

The coalition was at first unwieldy, and as the war ground on, internal divisions became more pronounced. The abolitionist element became stronger, while other Republicans wanted to make peace with the South. By 1864 Lincoln's popularity in the North had sagged. To help rectify the damage the Republicans renamed themselves the "Union Party" and added "WAR DEMOCRAT" ANDREW JOHNSON to the ticket. The fall of Atlanta in September gave an enormous boost to Northern morale and to Lincoln's prestige. He won the 1864 election handily. Under Lincoln the goal of the war changed from merely preserving the Union to ending slavery, and the Republicans enacted the tariffs, land grants, and internal improvements Southerners op-

posed. *See also* RADICAL REPUBLICANS.   —RJM

Resaca, Ga., Battle of. 14–15 May 1864   During action early in May at Rocky Face Ridge in Georgia, Union Maj. Gen. WILLIAM T. SHERMAN attempted to force Gen. JOSEPH E. JOHNSTON's army from its impregnable position along the ridge by sending Maj. Gen. JAMES B. MCPHERSON's Army of the Tennessee through SNAKE CREEK GAP to cut the railroad in the Confederate rear. On 10 May 1864, learning that Johnston had not retreated, Sherman began moving his entire army through Snake Creek Gap to capture Resaca and trap Johnston north of the Oostenaula River. Perceiving Sherman's intent, Johnston countered by likewise shifting all of his forces to Resaca.

On 14 May the 2 armies confronted each other in full strength on a north-south line west of Resaca. Sherman had 100,000 men; Johnston about 70,000, reinforced recently by Lt. Gen. LEONIDAS POLK's corps from Mississippi. That afternoon Sherman attacked Johnston's center but was beaten back with heavy losses. Johnston in turn struck the exposed left flank of the Union army with Lt. Gen. JOHN B. HOOD's corps. Hood seemed about to gain an important success when the arrival of a Union division sent by Maj. Gen. GEORGE H. THOMAS stopped his drive. Meanwhile, at the other end of the battlefront, Sherman's troops captured a hill that commanded the railroad bridge over the Oostenaula and put them in position to drive a wedge between the bridge and Resaca, thus trapping Johnston. Fortunately for the Confederates, Sherman did not realize this and failed to exploit his advantage.

15 May saw more heavy fighting, with both sides gaining little and losing heavily. Concluding that it was useless to assault the Confederates straight on, Sherman sent a division across the Oostenaula, thereby threatening Johnston's railroad supply line. After vainly trying to eliminate the Federal bridgehead, Johnston evacuated his Resaca position during the night by means of a PONTOON BRIDGE over the Oostenaula.

Johnston's losses at Resaca were approximately 5,000, Sherman's 6,000. Tactically the battle was a Confederate victory, but strategically the Federals gained the advantage in the Snake Creek Gap–Resaca operations by forcing Johnston to abandon his Rocky Face stronghold and retreat deeper into Georgia.

—AC

revenue cutters.   The fleet of revenue cutters was the forerunner of the U.S. Coast Guard, patrolling waters against smuggling activity that would have deprived the U.S. of customs fees and importation taxes. In Apr. 1861 the U.S. Revenue Service had only 28 cutters for duty. 4 of these were sailing off the Pacific Coast, 6 on the Great Lakes, and 18 were at North Atlantic ports. 5 other cutters had either been seized by Southern states after secession or turned over to state authorities by pro-Southern revenue captains. These vessels served the Confederacy as PRIVATEERS, BLOCKADE RUNNERS, and warships. Pres. ABRAHAM LINCOLN invoked an act of 1799 authorizing that revenue cutters be used to assist the navy. Sec. of the Treasury SALMON P. CHASE ordered all customs collectors and revenue captains to be vigilant in halting commerce to and from "all persons or parties in armed insurrection against the Union." He also ordered 5 of the Great Lakes cutters to the Atlantic Coast and began acquiring additional vessels. Several vessels, originally used as cutters, were returned by the U.S. Coast Survey, while additional vessels were built or purchased. A few private citizens sold or donated their yachts for use as cutters.

Even as revenue cutters were helping to win the war, they also carried out their regular duties, assisting vessels in distress. In June 1863 several were involved in the search for the Confederate raider *Tacony* off the northeast coast. Confederate Lt. Charles W. Read created a crisis to shipping along the coast as he captured and destroyed merchant and fishing vessels alike. Read's raid culminated in the destruction of the revenue cutter *Caleb Cushing* outside Portland harbor on the morning of 27 June 1863.

The revenue cutter *HARRIET LANE* played an especially important role in the naval war. The only steam cutter in revenue service in 1861, it participated in the expedition to relieve FORT SUMTER in April of that year. Assigned to the navy, it was part of the HATTERAS INLET expedition, Aug. 1861, then served on the Mississippi. On 1 Jan. 1863 it was captured during the battles for GALVESTON and became the CSS *Harriet Lane* and later a blockade runner. —NCD

revetment. A support or reinforcing wall of earthworks or permanent fortifications was called a revetment. Sandbags, GABIONS, or FASCINES revetted fieldworks; masonry revetments supported stone or brick forts. —JES

Reynolds, Alexander Welch. CSA b. Frederick Cty., Va., Apr. 1816. No extant records agree on Reynolds' exact birthdate or early life and education. He entered West Point 1 July 1833, giving his age as 17 years and 3 months, and graduated in 1838, ranking 35th in his class. Commissioned a 2d lieutenant in the 1st U.S. Infantry, he served in garrison and Seminole War operations, became a captain in the Quartermaster Department 5 Aug. 1847, and was dismissed from the army 8 Oct. 1855, unable to explain money missing from army accounts. Facts on this embarrassing incident and Reynolds' next years are unclear, but army authorities reappointed him to the

USMHI

service 29 Mar. 1858 without loss of rank or seniority.

Reynolds absented himself from U.S. Army duties early in 1861. National Archives records indicate that he secured a Confederate captaincy about March, then won commission as colonel of the 50th Virginia Infantry 10 July. Reynolds' son Frank, a recent West Point graduate dismissed from Federal service July 1861, entered Confederate service that summer. Alexander Reynolds was dropped from U.S. Army rolls 4 Oct. 1861 for being absent without leave. A few contemporary sources confuse these officers' records.

With Brig. Gen. JOHN B. FLOYD'S ARMY OF THE KANAWHA through early 1862, Reynolds transferred to north Alabama, led a 450-man brigade under Brig. Gen. DANVILLE LEADBETTER, garrisoned Knoxville, Tenn., then joined Confederate forces at VICKSBURG, Miss. Surrendered 4 July 1863 and exchanged, he won a brigadier general's commission 14 Sept. 1863 and in Maj. Gen. CARTER L. STEVENSON's division led the 58th and 60th North Carolina and 54th and 63d Virginia regiments in the battles for CHATTANOOGA and the early ATLANTA CAMPAIGN.

In the May 1864 Battle of NEW HOPE CHURCH, Ga., Reynolds

was severely wounded. On recovery he assumed district command in northeast Georgia with headquarters at Athens. His poor performance in this assignment led to his relief by Brig. Gen. WILLIAM T. WOFFORD Jan. 1865. At the time of the Confederate surrender he is believed to have been awaiting orders.

Until 1869 Reynolds' postwar movements are undocumented. In that year he accepted a commission as a colonel in the army of the khedive of Egypt, serving as a staff officer under former Confederate Maj. Gen. WILLIAM WING LORING. Son Frank also entered Egyptian service. The elder Reynolds died in Alexandria, Egypt, 26 May 1876. —JES

Reynolds, Daniel Harris. CSA b. Centerburg, Ohio, 14 Dec. 1832. Educated at Ohio Wesleyan University, Reynolds moved to Somerville, Tenn., attended law school there, and gained admission to the bar in 1858. That May he settled in Lake Village, Ark., where he established his practice. By the time the Civil War came, he was sure of his sectional allegiance. About the time his adopted state seceded, he raised a company for Confederate service that became a part of the 1st Arkansas Mounted Rifles. He was elected its captain 25 May 1861, his rank being confirmed by the Confederate government 3 weeks later.

LC

Under his regimental commander, THOMAS J. CHURCHILL, Reynolds served prominently in the Battle of WILSON'S CREEK, 10 Aug. 1861. Afterward his company took part in numerous skirmishes and engagements in Missouri and Arkansas until early spring 1862, when it was transferred with the army of Maj. Gen. EARL VAN DORN to the east side of the Mississippi River. In that theater, Reynolds rose swiftly in rank, reaching major in April and lieutenant colonel the following month. Under Lt. Gen. EDMUND KIRBY SMITH, the 1st Arkansas, now serving afoot, fought in East Tennessee and Kentucky throughout 1862. After CHICKAMAUGA—in which his regiment fought tenaciously along the Confederate left flank—Reynolds was appointed colonel of his outfit. In that battle, Brig. Gen. BUSHROD R. JOHNSON, another native Ohioan in Confederate service, praised Reynolds' "faithful toil and heroic conduct," especially "his efforts to preserve our lines and encourage and press on our men."

Thanks to such encomiums, Reynolds was named a brigadier general to rank from 5 Mar. 1864. At that rank he led a brigade serving with the ARMY OF TENNESSEE through the ATLANTA and CAROLINAS campaigns; it was especially prominent in guarding the retreat of Gen. JOHN B. HOOD from Nashville. Under Gen. JOSEPH E. JOHNSTON at BENTONVILLE, 19 Mar. 1865, Reynolds was so badly wounded that he lost a leg to amputation. Captured, he was paroled 2 months later at Charlottesville, Va., thereafter returning to Arkansas and his legal practice. In postwar life he served a term in the state senate. He died in Lake Village, 14 Mar. 1902. —EGL

Reynolds, John Fulton. USA b. Lancaster, Pa., 20 Sept. 1820. Few general officers in the ARMY OF THE POTOMAC earned greater respect from their soldiers and were more lamented than Reynolds, who possessed courage, reliability, and superb tactical skill. He was also an excellent horseman and was skilled in the use of expletives.

USMHI

The son of a newspaper editor and friend of James Buchanan, Reynolds attended various academies before entering West Point in 1837. He graduated 26th in his class 4 years later and spent the next 5 years on garrison duty and in Texas. During the Mexican War, he earned brevet promotions of captain and major. After more tedious garrison duty, the Pennsylvanian became commandant of cadets and instructor of TACTICS at West Point Sept. 1860, a post he held until the outbreak of war.

Reynolds was initially promoted to lieutenant colonel of the 14th U.S. Infantry 14 May 1861, then to brigadier general 26 Aug., to date from the 20th. He served in the defenses of the capital and as temporary military governor of Fredericksburg, Va., during the war's first year. He joined the Army of the Potomac June 1862 as a brigade commander. Captured after the Battle of GAINES' MILL, he spent several weeks in LIBBY PRISON before being exchanged 13 Aug.

Reynolds led the 3d Division/Pennsylvania Reserves at SECOND BULL RUN and commanded the Pennsylvania militia, which was mustered in to repel an expected Confederate invasion during the ANTIETAM CAMPAIGN, Sept. 1862. Promoted to major general 29 Nov., he directed the I Corps at FREDERICKSBURG 13 Dec.

His corps fought at CHANCELLORSVILLE, where the Union army suffered a humiliating defeat under Maj. Gen. JOSEPH HOOKER. In the aftermath of this debacle, Pres. ABRAHAM LINCOLN tendered Reynolds command of the army. Regarding politicians with deep suspicion, he apparently declined the offer when Lincoln could not guarantee him a free rein. His junior, Maj. Gen. GEORGE G. MEADE, subsequently replaced Hooker 3 days before the BATTLE OF GETTYSBURG.

On 1 July 1863, Reynolds, commanding the I, III, and XI corps, reached the southern Pennsylvania village about midmorning. He hurriedly shuffled his leading infantry units forward to replace Union cavalry, who were fighting Confederate infantry. Entering some woods, the general turned in his saddle to look for more troops. He suddenly toppled to the ground, dying almost instantly from a bullet in the back of his neck.

—JDW

Reynolds, Joseph Jones. USA b. Flemingsburg, Ky., 4 Jan. 1822. In 1837 Reynolds entered Wabash College, Ind., having moved with his family to that state. He soon secured a U.S. Military Academy appointment and was graduated 10th in the class of 1843, which included his close friend ULYSSES S. GRANT. After service in the 4th U.S. Artillery in Virginia, Pennsylvania, and Texas, he was an instructor at West Point 1846–55. Enjoying the classroom, he resigned his 1st lieutenant's commission in 1857 and from then until 1860 was professor of mechanics and engineering at Washington University, St. Louis, Mo.

When hostilities began in spring 1861, Reynolds became commander of an Indiana militia regiment. His military background resulted in his appointment as a brigadier general of volunteers to rank from 17 May and in his assignment to command a brigade in northwestern Virginia. In September he repulsed a Confederate incursion near CHEAT MOUNTAIN, securing that portion of the state for the Union.

LC

On his brother's death, Reynolds again resigned his commission and Jan. 1862 returned to Indiana to oversee the family's grocery business. In his free time he helped organize state units. In August he reentered the volunteer service as colonel of the 75th Indiana Infantry and a month later was recommissioned brigadier. On 29 Nov. he rose to major general, at which rank he supervised a division in the XIV Corps/Army of the Cumberland at Hoover's Gap, 24 June 1863, and at CHICKAMAUGA. He then became army chief of staff, serving Maj. Gen. GEORGE H. THOMAS throughout the Siege of CHATTANOOGA.

In Jan. 1864 Reynolds was sent to command the defenses of New Orleans. 6 months later he took charge of the XIX Corps/Army of the Gulf and helped Maj. Gen. E.R.S. CANBY organize the expedition that captured MOBILE, Ala., the following spring. At the end of the war, Reynolds commanded along the Mississippi from Memphis to the river's mouth. During RECONSTRUCTION, he headed the DEPARTMENT OF ARKANSAS, then commanded occupation forces in Texas and Louisiana and frontier units in Nebraska and Wyoming. For a brief period in 1871 he was U.S. senator from Texas, losing his seat when the election was contested. His tenure as colonel of the 3d Cavalry ended with his resignation 25 June 1877, following a court-martial inquiry into his conduct during the Powder River campaigning against the Sioux. He spent his retirement years in Washington, D.C., where he died 25 Feb. 1899.   —EGL

Reynolds, Thomas C. war governor b. Charleston, S.C., 11 Oct. 1821, Reynolds moved with his family to Virginia, where he attended the University of Virginia. After graduating in 1842, he traveled extensively in Europe and learned to speak French and Spanish proficiently. On returning to the U.S. he read law, being admitted to the bar in 1844. 2 years later he again went abroad, to work as secretary for the U.S. legation in Madrid.

Rather than settle in Virginia when his appointment expired, Reynolds opened a law office in St. Louis, Mo., a city that offered an ambitious attorney better opportunities than existed in the East. A hardline secessionist Democrat, he endorsed the nativism of the Know Nothing movement and served 1853–57 as U.S. district attorney for Missouri. He allied himself politically with CLAIBORNE F. JACKSON, a pro-slavery Democrat also in favor of secession, who chose Reynolds to be his running mate in the 1860 gubernatorial election. Their successful campaign gave Reynolds the lieutenant governorship. Immediately he began using his influence to take Missouri out of the Union, in part by circulating a strongly argued pro-secession pamphlet published at his own expense Feb. 1861. He also labored to organize state troops for the Confederacy despite the presence of a strong Federal garrison in St. Louis.

When the Missouri secession convention refused to withdraw from the Union, Reynolds fled with Jackson from Jefferson City to Neosho, gathered together pro-Confederate delegates into a rump session, and passed an ordinance of secession. On Jackson's death Dec. 1862, Reynolds succeeded to the governorship-in-exile, but the control Federal troops exercised over vast sections of the state restricted him to an office with little power.

Eager to see Southern nationhood achieved, he gave Confederate officials control over those state troops and supplies at his disposal and, over the objections of military authorities in the TRANS-MISSISSIPPI DEPARTMENT, sanctioned Col. JOSEPH O. SHELBY's summer 1863 raid into Missouri. In 1864 Reynolds joined Shelby as a volunteer aid during Maj. Gen. STERLING PRICE's raid into the state (*see* PRICE'S MISSOURI RAID OF 1864). Of the Trans-Mississippi governors who met in Marshall, Tex., May 1865 to discuss the prospects of continuing the war, Reynolds was the only one who refused to send Gen. E. KIRBY SMITH a telegraph with instructions to surrender the Trans-Mississippi Department.

After the war ended, Reynolds fled across Texas into Mexico with Shelby and the troopers of the Confederacy's Iron Brigade (*see* SHELBY'S IRON BRIGADE), his knowledge of languages and foreign protocol assisting Shelby during the journey through the war-torn country. Once they arrived in Mexico City, the Emperor Maximilian refused to hire the troopers as mercenaries. Reynolds then persuaded Marshal François-Achille Bazaine to give each of Shelby's men $50 in gold to finance their return to the U.S. Employed briefly as Maximilian's counselor, Reynolds returned to Missouri in 1868, after Benito Juárez overthrew the French regime.

Except for a term in the state legislature in 1874 and an appointment in 1886 to a U.S. commission to South and Central America, Reynolds directed his energies toward his law practice until his death in St. Louis, 30 Mar. 1887. —PLF

Rhett, Robert Barnwell.

CSP b. Beaufort, S.C., 21 Dec. 1800. Born to an aristocratic South Carolina family that had changed its name from Smith to that of a distinguished ancestor, Rhett became the "Father of Secession." Nervous, energetic, fiery, a curious mixture of idealist, revolutionary, states righter, Southern nationalist, constitutionalist, aristocrat, and democrat, he labored to bring the Union's disruption.

Rhett began his political career as a state legislator, enjoying such loyalty from his constituents that South Carolina later was dubbed "Rhettsylvania." In Dec. 1832 he became attorney general of the state, and 1837–49 served in the U.S. House of Representatives.

LC

A follower of JOHN C. CALHOUN, Rhett broke with him in 1844. In 1850 he attended the NASHVILLE CONVENTION to consider secession but returned disillusioned. After Calhoun died, Rhett won his Senate seat, serving 1850–52. Through the 1850s he called upon South Carolina to leave the Union, and early expressed his belief that although the state could survive as an independent nation, its real hope lay in the formation of a Southern confederacy.

In 1857 his son became editor of the Charleston *Mercury,* and Rhett joined the staff, where he vigorously asserted his ideas. In 1858 he and a number of radicals met in Montgomery, Ala., to discuss strategy that would effect secession, but concluded that the only hope for success lay in an 1860 Republican presidential victory. Rhett and other "fire eaters," as extremist secession advocates were called, maneuvered persistently to bring it about.

Though he wanted a job in the Confederate government, he was rebuffed in each of several attempts to secure one. Disillusioned, he became a bitter, potent critic of the JEFFERSON DAVIS administration and a defender of "Southern civilization," which he perceived as being sacrificed to the war effort. After the war he wrote an apologetic history. He died at his son-in-law's home in St. James Parish, La., 14 Sept. 1876. —HH

Rhode Island.

After the firing on FORT SUMTER, S.C., 12 Apr. 1861, Rhode Island responded quickly to the call for arms. Within a week the hastily organized 1st Rhode Island departed for Washington to relieve that city's anxiety. A second regiment, along with its battery of artillery, joined the 1st in time to participate in FIRST BULL RUN. During that fight, the 1st Rhode Island broke and led the headlong flight back to Washington. The 2d and its artillery fought superbly but were swallowed up in the Union rout.

In all, Rhode Island provided the Union army with 10 regiments of infantry, 3 regiments and a battalion of cavalry, 3 regiments of heavy artillery, 10 batteries of light artillery, and a company of hospital guards. Its contribution of 23,236 troops was about 5,000 above the quotas called for by the War Department and included 1,837 black troops and 1,878 sailors. Of the infantry units, the 2d, 4th, and 7th regiments saw extensive service and were the only ones to lose more than 50 men killed in action. The state lost a total of 1,321 men, two-thirds of them from disease.

Light artillery brought Rhode Island its chief military glory. All 8 batteries of the 1st Regiment served until the war's end. Capt. John Hazard of Battery B rose to command all the artillery of the II Corps. Other batteries achieved distinction during battles that included ANTIETAM and FREDERICKSBURG.

7 Rhode Islanders attained the rank of general. The only one of them to achieve national prominence, AMBROSE E. BURNSIDE, was known more for his failures than his successes. Isaac P. Rodman was shot dead at Antietam; Thomas W. Sherman lost a leg at Port Hudson; and George S. Greene, at 60 one of the Union's oldest field commanders, suffered a severe face wound Oct. 1863. 2 West Pointers, Richard Arnold and Silas Casey, saw limited action while Frank Wheaton, an efficient but unspectacular soldier, rose to the rank of major general.

The best-known Rhode Islander during the war was its governor, WILLIAM SPRAGUE. Handsome, wealthy, energetic, and only 30 years old when the war began, he used his own money to lavishly outfit the 1st Rhode Island and dreamed of finding military glory at its head. That dream crumbled when the 1st disgraced itself at Bull Run, and Sprague returned to politics. —MK

Rhode Island, USS.

A sidewheel steamer 236 ft long, with a 36-ft beam, a cargo capacity of 1,517 tons, and a speed of

14 knots, this vessel was completed at the start of the war for the Charleston Line and was named the *Eagle*. The Union navy bought the steamer for $185,000 and changed its name to *Rhode Island*.

Its first and only commander, Lt. Stephen D. Trenchard, later a rear admiral, shoved off on his first trip 31 July 1861. Soon known as "Little Rhody," the *Rhode Island* was used as a dispatch boat and was loaded with provisions, newspapers, cigars, medicines, and numerous other items.

As one of the few Federal cruisers swift enough to overtake the fast BLOCKADE RUNNERS, in Nov. 1862 the *Rhode Island* was equipped with 12 guns and fitted with heavy iron plating on its bow so the steamer could be used as a RAM. At HAMPTON ROADS, its first assignment was to tow the ironclad *MONITOR* to Port Royal, S.C. En route, the vessel ran into stormy weather and was unable to keep the ironclad from sinking off the North Carolina coast.

The *Rhode Island* was next sent to West Indian waters to search for Confederate privateers and blockade runners and took numerous prizes there.

Transferred to the SOUTH ATLANTIC BLOCKADING SQUADRON, the steamer took part in the 2 final attacks on FORT FISHER, N.C. It was one of the last Federal ships to go out of service.   —VCJ

Rice, Elliott Warren. USA b. Allegheny City, Pa., 16 Nov. 1835. Born in a community that is today the North Side of Pittsburgh, Pa., Rice was taken to Belmont, Ohio, in 1836, reared there, and given a varied education. He attended school in Wheeling, western Va.; and Franklin College at Athens, Ohio, then traveled to Oskaloosa, Iowa, in 1855 to study law under his older brother, SAMUEL A. RICE, graduating from the University of Albany Law School in 1858.

He practiced law in Oskaloosa with his brother until joining the 7th Iowa Infantry as a corporal 24 July 1861. Promoted major 30 Aug. and attached to the District of Cairo,

NA

he fought in the Battle of BELMONT in November, assumed regimental command on the death and wounding of his superiors, then received a bullet wound to the lower extremities. While recuperating he took a minor part in the campaigns for FORTS HENRY AND DONELSON, then held regimental command during the Battle of SHILOH, receiving promotion to colonel to date from the second day of the battle, 7 Apr. 1862. He next joined the Corinth, Miss., garrison; fought in the Oct. 1862 Battle of CORINTH; and commanded the posts at Bethel and La Grange, Tenn., leading the 1st Brigade/2d Division/XVI Corps without commensurate rank.

At the head of his brigade he saw action at RESACA, NEW HOPE CHURCH, and KENNESAW MOUNTAIN, Ga.; received promotion to brigadier general 22 June 1864; briefly led the 2d Division; weathered the Siege of Atlanta; and, transferred to the XV Corps, served through the MARCH TO THE SEA and the CAROLINAS CAMPAIGN. Brevetted major general for war service 13 Mar. 1865, he mustered out of Federal service 24 Aug., having been wounded 7 times in 4 years.

Rice practiced law in Washington, D.C., until retiring in poor health to his sister's home in Sioux City, Iowa, in 1885. He died there 22 June 1887.   —JES

Rice, Samuel Allen. USA b. Cattaraugus Cty., N.Y., 27 Jan. 1828. As a boy Rice migrated with his family to Allegheny City, Pa., and Belmont, Ohio, then attended Franklin College at Athens, Ohio, and graduated from Union College at Schenectady, N.Y., in 1849. He continued law studies at Union in 1850, moved to Oskaloosa, Iowa, in 1851, and maintained a private law practice there until elected county attorney in 1853. In 1855 he was joined in Oskaloosa by his younger brother, future Brig. Gen. ELLIOTT W. RICE. Elected state attorney general in 1856 and 1858, the elder Rice remained a Unionist partisan of Gov. SAMUEL J. KIRKWOOD through the outset of the Civil War.

Rice organized the 33d Iowa Infantry in Oskaloosa in summer and early autumn 1862. After his commission as colonel of the 33d, 10 Aug. 1862, his regiment was accepted for Federal service 1 Oct. 1862 and went on duty in St. Louis, Mo., remaining there into December. Assigned to garrison duty in Helena, Ark., Jan. 1863, he participated in the YAZOO PASS EXPEDITION in February and April, fought in the July battle at Helena, won promotion to brigadier general 4 Aug. 1863, and, under Maj. Gen. FREDERICK STEELE, joined in the occupation of Little Rock, Ark., in September.

In spring 1864 Steele supported Maj. Gen. NATHANIEL P. BANKS'S RED RIVER CAMPAIGN by marching south from Little Rock, intending to join him near Shreveport, La. Rice served with Steele's force, in Brig. Gen. Frederick Salomon's 3d Division, commanding a brigade composed of the 33d and 29th Iowa, the 50th Indiana, and the 9th Wisconsin. Steele failed to meet Banks, and on the retreat to Little Rock, Rice served in rearguard action. At the Battle of JENKINS' FERRY, Ark., 30 Apr. 1864, while rushing to organize resistance on the Union left, Rice was badly wounded in the right ankle when a bullet struck his spur, driving fragments of it through his boot. Sent home to Oskaloosa, he died in surgery 6 July 1864.   —JES

Richardson, Albert Deane. journalist b. Franklin, Mass., 6 Oct. 1833. Born to a farming family and educated in public schools and at Holliston Academy, Richardson was 27 at the beginning of the Civil War; for 9 years he had worked on newspapers in various cities. In 1859 he went with HORACE GREELEY to Pike's Peak; it was the start of a warm friendship between the two. Through the remainder of his life Richardson was employed by Greeley's NEW YORK TRIBUNE.

In 1860 he volunteered for the dangerous assignment of going into the South and reporting on the secession movement. The dispatches he sent back, particularly those from New Orleans, provided the North with astute inside views of the tumultuous Southern scene. After many narrow escapes—he barely missed being lynched several times, he said—he returned safely to *Tribune* headquarters in New York just before the bombardment of FORT SUMTER Apr. 1861.

Richardson then became the *Tribune*'s chief war correspondent. On 3 May 1863, while attempting with *Tribune* reporter Junius H. Browne to run a tugboat past the Confederate batteries at Vicksburg, the two were captured. They spent more than 19 months in various Confederate prisons, making their escape from SALISBURY PRISON, N.C., 18 Dec. 1864 by visiting the prison hospital, casually walking around the hospital enclosure until no one noticed them, then slipping out the gate and hiding in a barn until the search for them was abandoned. They walked 400 mi to Strawberry Springs, near Knoxville, Tenn., helped along the way by the Sons of America, an organization formed to assist escaping Union prisoners. Soon they were safely behind Union lines.

Richardson drew on his wartime experiences to write 3 books: *The Secret Service, the Field, the Dungeon, and the Escape* (1865); *Beyond the Mississippi* (1866); and *Personal History of Ulysses S. Grant* (1868). On 25 Nov. 1869 the former husband of his fiancée shot Richardson at the *Tribune* offices. He died in New York City a week later, 2 Dec.   —PR

Richardson, Israel Bush. USA b. Fairfax, Vt., 26 Dec. 1815, Richardson was a man of absolute fearlessness in combat, earning the nicknames "Fighting Dick" and "Greasy Dick."

A descendant of Revolutionary War Gen. Israel Putnam, Richardson graduated 38th in his class at the U.S. Military Academy in 1841. He fought in the Seminole War, then earned the brevets of captain and major for gallantry in Mexico. He resigned in 1855 to farm in Michigan.

USMHI

With the outbreak of civil war, the veteran officer recruited and organized the 2d Michigan, mustering in as its colonel. He commanded a brigade at FIRST BULL RUN and was promoted to brigadier general 9 Aug. 1861. Until spring 1862 he commanded a brigade in the ARMY OF THE POTOMAC. An able organizer and firm disciplinarian, Richardson led a division of the II Corps during the PENINSULA and SEVEN DAYS' campaigns. On 5 July 1862, to date from the 4th, the New Englander was promoted to major general and assigned to a division in the I Corps.

Before SECOND BULL RUN, Richardson transferred back into the II Corps, leading his division there and at SOUTH MOUNTAIN and ANTIETAM. In this last battle, his division spearheaded the savage Union attacks against the Confederates in the "BLOODY LANE." While directing the fire of a Union battery, Richardson fell wounded by a ball from a spherical case shot fired by Southern artillerists. The general lingered until 3 Nov. 1862, dying in the Pry house, the army's headquarters. He was buried in Pontiac, Mich.   —JDW

Richardson, Robert Vinkler. CSA b. Granville Cty., N.C., 4 Nov. 1820. Reared and schooled in Hardeman Cty., Tenn., Richardson studied law privately, passed the Tennessee bar, and in 1847 established a legal practice in Memphis. Until the Civil War he followed a legal career and invested heavily in Southern industrial development.

Early in 1861 Richardson entered Confederate service under Brig. Gen. GIDEON J. PILLOW, saw service in Missouri, at SHILOH, and in 1862 organized the 1st Tennessee Partisan Ranger Regiment. His early war rank, service, and the date of his organization of the 1st Tennessee Partisans are all arguable. In Aug. 1861 correspondence with Brig. Gen. M. Jeff Thompson he is addressed as "General." However, most primary sources

GG

agree that he did not represent himself as a brigadier general until late in 1863. According to several sources, he organized the 1st Tennessee 14 Feb. 1863, but in correspondence dated 13 Mar. 1863, Richardson, signing himself "Colonel R.V. Richardson," stated that he received War Department authorization to organize his regiment 6 Sept. 1862, spent 4 months assembling it, and did not hold election of officers until 14 Feb.

Richardson and his command were accused by Unionists in West Tennessee of depredations, operating without authority, and being no better than bandits. Confederate Adj. Gen. SAMUEL COOPER ordered Richardson's authority revoked 16 Mar. 1863 and his men mustered into regular Confederate service. Before this order could be acted on, the 1st Tennessee was mauled by Federals near Bolivar, Tenn., late in March. Richardson was separated from his men, and second-in-command Lt. Col. J. U. Green temporarily disbanded the unit 1 Apr.

As acting agent for the Bureau of Conscription in West Tennessee, Richardson reorganized his men in Mississippi in summer 1863, on 10 Aug. assembled a unit incorporating the 12th Tennessee, and joined the command of Maj. Gen. NATHAN B. FORREST, an antebellum business associate. After participating in the Feb.–Mar. 1864 MERIDIAN CAMPAIGN, fighting Union Brig. Gen. WILLIAM SOOY SMITH's cavalry, Richardson was temporarily removed from Forrest's command in a disciplinary dispute, on 19 July divested of authority in the reorganization of Forrest's cavalry, and on 30 Aug. given leadership of the restructured 12th Tennessee, leading it in the FRANKLIN AND NASHVILLE CAMPAIGN. Though he was appointed brigadier general 3 Dec. 1863, Pres. Jefferson Davis rejected his commission 9 Feb. 1864.

Briefly leading a brigade Jan. 1865, he lost command in Forrest's February reorganization of Mississippi, Alabama, and Tennessee forces. The 12th Tennessee was paroled at Gainesville, Ala., May 1865, but whether Richardson led it at that time is undocumented.

Resuming his legal and business career after a brief trip abroad, Richardson became involved with the Selma, Marion & Memphis Railroad. On 5 Jan. 1870, under mysterious circumstances, he was murdered in Clarkton, Mo., while on a business trip.   —JES

Richmond, Ky., Battle of. 29–30 Aug. 1862 Confederate Brig. Gen. PATRICK R. CLEBURNE led a small division in the van of Maj. Gen. E. KIRBY SMITH's advance into Kentucky at the outset of the 1862 Kentucky Campaign. Col. John Scott's Confederate cavalry rode ahead of Cleburne's infantry, scouting for the enemy. On 29 Aug. 1862, Cleburne's division descended Big Hill, more than 60 mi north of the Tennessee state line, and marched north-northwest on the road to Richmond, Ky. Union Brig. Gen. Mahlon D. Manson, commanding troops in front of Richmond, learned near midday that his cavalry had met Scott's horsemen between Rogersville and Kingston, about 8¾ mi south. He sent more cavalry forward and began marching elements of his 1st Brigade/Army of Kentucky forward to

Rogersville. Scott's cavalry engaged the Union horsemen and some infantry and artillery late in the afternoon, was driven through Kingston, and joined Cleburne's troops 3 mi south of that village. After a brief scuffle with pursuing Union elements, the Confederates bivouacked and the Federals retired to Rogersville.

At 11 p.m., hearing of Smith's rapid approach behind Cleburne, from his Rogersville command post Manson sent word of his situation to area commander Maj. Gen. WILLIAM NELSON at Louisville and directed Brig. Gen. Charles Cruft to position his 2d Brigade/Army of Kentucky on the Lancaster Turnpike, covering the eastern approach to Richmond. Cruft was to march to his support on a moment's notice. That same night Smith sent ahead orders for Cleburne to engage Manson at daylight; Confederate Brig. Gen. THOMAS J. CHURCHILL's division, far south, was marching to his support.

Cleburne's division and 2 artillery batteries advanced at daybreak, passed through Kingston, drove in Manson's skirmishers, and confronted the Union battle line a half-mile in front of Rogersville. Informed of Cleburne's advance, Manson sent for Cruft's troops at 6 a.m. Facing south, he deployed a regiment behind a fence on the left of the Richmond road, established a masked artillery position on a rise to its left, placed a regiment behind the battery in reserve, then deployed a regiment on the right of the road. A late-arriving Union regiment extended the Federal left, and inside minutes the battle began. Cleburne set up 1 battery on a low hilltop 500 yd in front of Manson's line, held a regiment in reserve behind it, threw out the rest of his troops to his right opposite the Federals, then set up his second battery on a rise behind the midpoint of his infantry line.

After some rapid artillery fire from both sides, Cleburne received news of Churchill's imminent arrival. Ordering his artillery to assume a slower pace, he began a 2-hour small-arms fight with Manson's troops. Meanwhile, Cruft's troops began arriving and were deployed by Manson against Cleburne's right. Cleburne, in turn, reinforced his right and waited for Churchill. At the end of 2 hours, with pressure on the right reaching harsh intensity, and expecting Churchill at any moment, Cleburne sent Col. PRESTON SMITH with the last of his reserves to the right and, believing the Federal right weakened by the detachment of troops to the area of heaviest fighting, decided to attack it with his left and roll up Manson's line. As he checked his dispositions for the assault, Cleburne was shot through the left cheek, and, unable to speak, was forced to pass command to Preston Smith. At that moment Kirby Smith arrived with Churchill's division, the attack went forward, and Manson's and Cruft's troops were driven back to Rogersville.

Meanwhile, Nelson, concerned about Manson's ability to defend his position, had arrived from Louisville and took command in front of Richmond. Manson's and Cruft's troops, after trying to rally at their old Rogersville bivouac, were routed by Smith's fresh division. Running for Richmond, approximately 2,500 of them were personally rallied by Nelson and deployed on a hill on the town's southern outskirts. Nelson later said that these men, hit in front and on both flanks, withstood just 3 volleys before they broke. Nelson was wounded through the leg but escaped with his staff to Lexington, Ky. Trying to make the same escape Manson was captured by cavalry that evening.

The Federal loss in the 3 engagements comprising the Battle of Richmond amounted to 206 killed, 844 wounded, and 4,303 missing, most of the last being captured. Cleburne's

skillful handling of troops and Churchill's timely arrival kept Southern losses to 78 dead, 372 wounded, and an insignificant number missing.

—JES

Richmond, Va. Established in 1737 at the falls of the James River, Richmond had slowly aged from an old town into a young city by spring 1861. Its population of 38,000 whites, free blacks, and slaves ranked it 25th among all cities in the U.S. and 3d among Southern cities. Throughout its existence the city's mercantile economy, linking the Piedmont to the commercial world, brought prosperity to its citizens. More distinctively, Richmond led the South in manufacturing—flour, meal, tobacco, and iron. The TREDEGAR IRON WORKS possessed the South's only facilities for making cannon and railroad rails. Richmond ranked 1st in value of manufactures among Southern cities and 13th in the country as a whole.

The firing on FORT SUMTER, S.C., and the Federal government's immediate call for volunteers to suppress the rebellion, propelled Virginia into the Confederacy. On 17 Apr. 1861, a convention of Virginians passed an ordinance of secession, and within a week Confederate Vice-Pres. ALEXANDER H. STEPHENS arrived in Richmond to negotiate a military alliance between the fledgling Southern nation and the Old Dominion. After Stephens alluded to the possibility of Richmond becoming the Confederate capital, the Virginia delegates reached an agreement with him and formally invited the Confederate government to relocate in Richmond.

During May the Confederate government dismantled its offices in its first capital, MONTGOMERY, Ala., and moved to Richmond, the beginning of a human and bureaucratic flood that transformed the city. Confederate authorities selected Richmond primarily because of its proximity to the developing conflict. The decision has since been criticized, for the government, preoccupied with Richmond's defense, sometimes ignored the Confederacy's vital heartland. The capital attracted Federal armies for 4 years, and the 100 mi between Richmond and WASHINGTON, D.C., became the bloodiest stretch of ground in America. In the end, Richmond's prime defender, the ARMY OF NORTHERN VIRGINIA, was destroyed trying to protect it.

The war rapidly governed the city's life. Besides the influx of civilians, thousands of Confederate soldiers poured into and out of the capital. Earthworks and heavy ordnance eventually rimmed the city, while its huge Chimborazo Hospital mended the wounded and its LIBBY and BELLE ISLE prisons housed Union officers and soldiers. The approach of Federal forces, as during the PENINSULA CAMPAIGN, Mar.–Aug. 1862, and the KILPATRICK-DAHLGREN RAID, Feb.–Mar. 1864, periodically alarmed Richmonders and brought increases in local defense forces.

The transformation inundated all aspects of Richmond's society. Crime soared as gambling houses, called "hells," saloons, and prostitution proliferated. Provost Marshal Brig. Gen. JOHN H. WINDER and his "Plug Uglies" fought vainly against the sordid businesses. The war brought prosperity to nearly everyone, but the economic boom could not compensate for the spiraling inflation and the scarcity of necessities. Starvation and privation hung constantly over the city's citizens. In spring 1863, women, angered over higher prices and the scarcity of food, stormed through the city in a so-called BREAD RIOT. Confederate Pres. JEFFERSON DAVIS personally interceded to calm the mob.

During fall 1864 and winter 1865, the suffering of Richmond

Top: *Richmond, Va., ruins*   Bottom: *Richmond armory and arsenal*

residents reached its worst. On all fronts, Union armies hammered at weakening Confederate forces. 20 mi south of the capital, at Petersburg, the Army of Northern Virginia clung to its trenches, protecting the railroad center and Richmond, but on 2 Apr. 1865, the Federals wrenched the earthworks from Petersburg's defenders and opened the road to Richmond.

The end of the Confederate capital came swiftly and in a firestorm. Throughout the 2d and into the early hours of 3 Apr., government officials, defense troops, and some civilians fled the city. About 3 a.m. a fire began that soon raged out of control, destroying a large area from the James River to Capitol Square. 5 hours later, Union troops entered Richmond. The symbol of the Confederacy had become a smoldering ruin.

—JDW

Richmond, Confederate Department of. The Confederate Department of Richmond encompassed what was officially described as "the defenses of Richmond, etc." Maj. Gen. GUSTAVUS W. SMITH assumed command of these defenses 30 Aug. 1862, though responsibility for the Confederate capital had been formally placed since Dec. 1861 in the DEPARTMENT OF HENRICO, under Brig. Gen. JOHN H. WINDER. Smith relinquished his post 19 Sept., succeeded eventually by Maj. Gen. ARNOLD ELZEY, who commanded 12 Dec. 1862–25 Apr. 1864. On 1 Apr. 1863, the Department of Richmond was formally authorized as a part of Lt. Gen. JAMES LONGSTREET'S DEPARTMENT OF NORTH CAROLINA AND SOUTHERN VIRGINIA.

Elzey's primary responsibility was the erection and manning of the defenses that encircled Richmond. An artillery force, known as the Richmond Defenses, was authorized to protect the capital. 4 battalions of Virginia Heavy Artillery—the 10th, 18th, 19th, and 20th—the Louisiana Guard Artillery, and the Engineer Company composed this force under Col. WALTER H. STEVENS. During the CHANCELLORSVILLE CAMPAIGN, May 1863, when Federal cavalry skirted the defenses, Confederate authorities organized a "local defenses, special service" force to augment the artillery battalions. On 21 Apr. 1864, this new command numbered 3,000 men drawn from the War, Navy, Treasury, and Postmaster General departments. During the KILPATRICK-DAHLGREN RAID by Federal cavalry in winter 1864, these clerks-turned-soldiers successfully defended the capital.

Lt. Gen. RICHARD S. EWELL, kept from field command by wounds and health problems, replaced Elzey 29 May 1864 and commanded until the capital fell Apr. 1865. His units became of increasing importance to the Confederacy during 1864 as the Federal grip on Petersburg tightened, then extended north against Richmond's Inner and Outer Defenses. The novice soldiers repeatedly manned the earthworks as Federals hammered against the entrenchments north of the James River. The Department of Richmond ceased to exist 3 Apr. 1865, when the Union army captured the capital. Most of the city's defenders had already fled to join the Army of Northern Virginia in its flight toward Appomattox. —JDW

Richmond & Petersburg Railroad. Constructed in summer 1861, financed by Confederate bonds, the 22.5-mi-long, single-track Richmond & Petersburg Railroad connected the Confederate capital with the rail center of Petersburg, Va. Into Petersburg came the tracks and rolling stock of the Southside Railroad, the Wilmington & Weldon Railroad, and others. The Richmond & Petersburg was built to close the transportation gap between the railhead and Richmond.

No comparable extent of track was more valuable to the South. On its rails rolled foodstuffs and matériel from the heartland of the Confederacy. Thousands of troops coming north to Virginia rode in its cars as did those shifted from the Old Dominion to coastal defenses. As the war lengthened and its demands increased, the railroad's trains crawled under the congestion. To meet these demands, the line bought, or received from abandoned railroads, additional engines and rolling stock.

Defense of the railroad was crucial in spring 1864. In May nearly 39,000 Federals under Union Maj. Gen. BENJAMIN F. BUTLER disembarked at BERMUDA HUNDRED, directly east of the track. Butler's command temporarily severed the line, but Confederate defenders halted the Union advance at SWIFT CREEK on the 9th.

To counter Union thrusts during the PETERSBURG CAMPAIGN, Gen. ROBERT E. LEE used this railroad to shuttle his outnumbered defenders from around the James River. The railroad also hauled the ever-diminishing supplies brought into Petersburg by the other lines. The Richmond & Petersburg ceased operations when Petersburg and the capital fell into Union hands 2 and 3 Apr. 1865. —JDW

Richmond Blues. The martial spirit pervaded antebellum Southern society, and militia companies proliferated in towns and cities. One of the most renowned of these units was the Richmond Light Infantry Blues, made up of sons of Virginia's leading families. With the Grays and Howitzers, the Blues were the pride of the citizens of Richmond, marching at various civic and state functions.

When Virginia seceded, 17 Apr. 1861, these militia units embraced the Confederate cause. The Blues soon became Company A/46th Virginia, with O. Jennings Wise, son of former governor HENRY A. WISE, elected its captain. The 46th was ordered into western Virginia, where it fought under Brig. Gen. ROBERT S. GARNETT in his disastrous campaign. Former governor Wise, now a brigadier general, replaced Garnett but Confederate fortunes did not improve. In fall the 46th was transferred to ROANOKE ISLAND, N.C. During successful Federal attacks early in Feb. 1862, Jennings Wise fell mortally wounded at the head of the Blues; his men marched in his state funeral in Richmond.

The Blues remained in the Confederate capital, with an assignment to aid the provost guard. The war had brought unparalleled crime to Richmond, and saloons, gambling houses, and prostitutes taxed the police force. The Blues performed their duties well.

The 46th Virginia, remaining in General Wise's brigade, stayed in the defenses of the capital for the rest of the war. During the 10-month PETERSBURG CAMPAIGN in 1864 and 1865, the Blues often manned the works, defending their homes. When the Confederates abandoned Richmond, 2–3 Apr. 1865, the Blues are believed to have formed part of the fleeing column. —JDW

Richmond Campaign. *See* OVERLAND CAMPAIGN.

Richmond *Enquirer*. One of the oldest Southern newspapers, the Richmond *Enquirer* was founded by Thomas Ritchie in 1804 and was among the most influential Democratic organs in the state. During the controversy over slavery in the 1850s it criticized extremists in secessionist and abolitionist camps but championed Confederate nationhood after Virginia seceded Apr. 1861. The first wartime editors, Bennett M. De-Witt and Richard M. Smith, supported JEFFERSON DAVIS' war policies with a consistency that earned the newspaper a reputation for being the official organ of the administration. Rumor attributed to Davis and Sec. of State JUDAH P. BENJAMIN some of the articles published in the paper, but these claims are unsubstantiated.

As in the antebellum years, the *Enquirer* enjoyed a broad-based circulation outside Virginia, and was known for its literary quality as well as its editors' insistence on verifying information before it was printed. Toward the end of the war the paper was edited by Nathaniel Tyler, who had purchased the paper in partnership with O. Jennings Wise and W. B. Allegre Aug. 1860. Under the leadership of Tyler, a former officer whose regiment had disbanded Dec. 1862, the *Enquirer* became critical of the Confederate government but remained friendlier than other Southern newspapers. In 1867 the *Enquirer* merged with the RICHMOND *EXAMINER*.   —PLF

Richmond *Examiner*. Founded in 1847 at the encouragement of Democratic politicians, the *Examiner* joined the RICHMOND *ENQUIRER* in opposing the influence of the RICHMOND *WHIG*. Except for a few years during the antebellum era and 2 brief periods during the war, the *Examiner* was edited by John M. Daniel, owner of the newspaper since 1848. During Daniel's wartime absences from the *Examiner*—both times to serve in the army—he assigned the dynamic journalist and contemporary anti-administration Confederate historian EDWARD A. POLLARD to oversee the editorial desk.

Daniel insisted on editorial excellence, a quality that continued through the war years. A man of as many peculiarities as talents, he was cynical, fond of sensationalism, and prone to invite controversy. Although he encouraged secession, his editorials indicating a deep admiration for the great STATES RIGHTS theorist JOHN C. CALHOUN, he did not lend journalistic support to the Confederate government, lashing out with sarcastic, invective criticism of JEFFERSON DAVIS and his war policies. Among his strongest editorials are those refusing even to consider the possibility of enlisting blacks in the Confederate army during the desperate final days of the war (*see* BLACK TROOPS, CONFEDERACY APPROVES USE OF). Widely circulated and financially successful despite the war, the *Examiner* at times had more subscribers in distant Confederate states than in Virginia.   —PLF

Richmond *Whig*. A competitor of the Democratic RICHMOND *EXAMINER* and the RICHMOND *ENQUIRER*, and in its early years the organ of the Whig party, the *Whig* was founded by John H. Pleasants in 1824. Projecting a strong nationalistic bias, the paper opposed POPULAR SOVEREIGNTY and secession in the 1850s but, as the sectional crisis over slavery heightened, warned Republican politicians that coercion of the seceded states would unite the South. With the firing on FORT SUMTER and ABRAHAM LINCOLN's call for troops Apr. 1861, the *Whig* reversed its position, throwing its support zealously behind the war effort.

Once the early enthusiasm for war waned, the newspaper's editor, Alexander Mosely, maintained a cautious distrust of JEFFERSON DAVIS' administration. After Mosely retired Mar. 1863, his successor, James McDonald, turned the *Whig* into a vigorous critic of Davis' war policies and the newspaper offices into a meeting place for anti-administration congressmen.   —PLF

Rich Mountain, western Va., eng. at. 11 July 1861 When Virginia seceded from the Union 17 Apr. 1861, the mountainous western counties of the state contained few slaves and many pro-Union men. On 11 June those counties defied the state government and seceded from Virginia in order to rejoin the Union. To support pro-Union counties, the new commander of the DEPARTMENT OF THE OHIO, Maj. Gen. GEORGE B. MCCLELLAN, moved into western Virginia with 20,000 Federal soldiers. To hold off McClellan's advance, the Virginia state government sent Confederate Brig. Gen. ROBERT S. GARNETT and 4,500 men to the vital turnpike crossroads at Beverly, 50 mi west of the SHENANDOAH VALLEY.

Unable to get reinforcements or recruits from the pro-Union population, Garnett was reduced to staging nuisance raids against Federal supply lines. Fighting by means of "marauding parties" angered McClellan, who moved on Beverly to wipe out Garnett's guerrilla war. When he arrived 9 July, he found that Garnett had entrenched his troops on the heights of Rich Mountain and Laurel Mountain, protecting Beverly on the west and north, respectively. Still, McClellan decided to attack. On 11 July he sent Brig. Gen. WILLIAM S. ROSECRANS and a brigade scrambling up the steep sides of Rich Mountain in pouring rain. Fortunately for Rosecrans, Garnett had thought Rich Mountain too strong to be attacked and had left only 1,300 Confederates to hold it. With few defenders, Rosecrans' men quickly overran the position.

The loss of Rich Mountain put the Federals squarely across Garnett's line of retreat from Laurel Mountain to Beverly. He tried to slip his men between Rosecrans and McClellan, but 13 July McClellan caught them at Carrick's Ford, routing the Confederate troops and killing Garnett.

The Rich Mountain victory secured western Virginia for the Union and brought McClellan instant fame in Washington.
          —ACG

Ricketts, James Brewerton. USA b. New York, N.Y., 21 June 1817, Ricketts spent almost 3 decades in the U.S. Army. After graduating 16th in the West Point class of 1839, he fought in the Mexican and Seminole wars and served in various garrisons in the antebellum army. Promoted to captain in 1852, he held that rank at the outbreak of the Civil War.

Ricketts commanded an artillery battery at FIRST BULL RUN 21 July 1861. Shot 4 times during the battle, he fell into Confederate hands. He was exchanged Jan. 1862 and 30 Apr. received his commission as brigadier general, to date from First Bull Run. Initially assigned to command of a brigade in the Army of the Rappahannock, Ricketts succeeded to division command 10 June.

KA

He led his division, a part of Maj. Gen. John Pope's Army of Virginia, at CEDAR MOUNTAIN and SECOND BULL RUN. At the former his men covered the Union retreat, while at the latter he spent much of the time marching and countermarching. He was then given a division in the I Corps, leading it during the ANTIETAM CAMPAIGN. There Ricketts had 2 horses killed under him, suffering serious injury when the second fell on him.

Ricketts did not return to field command for more than 19

months. He served on commissions and on courts-martial, including the one that cashiered Maj. Gen. FITZ JOHN PORTER for the officer's performance at Second Bull Run. On 4 Apr. 1864, Ricketts assumed command of a division in the VI Corps, leading this veteran unit in the battles of the WILDERNESS, SPOTSYLVANIA, NORTH ANNA, COLD HARBOR, and PETERSBURG.

Early in July Ricketts' division was hurriedly sent north to Washington, D.C., to intercept Lt. Gen. Jubal A. Early's approaching Confederates. At MONOCACY, Md., 9 July, Ricketts' soldiers bore the brunt of the battle that delayed the Confederates for 24 vital hours. His command suffered 595 casualties out of a total Union loss of 677. The remainder of the VI Corps soon joined Ricketts, and the entire command participated in the SHENANDOAH VALLEY CAMPAIGN of 1864. At CEDAR CREEK, 19 Oct., Ricketts, a major general since 1 Aug., temporarily commanded the corps and suffered a disabling wound in the chest. He returned to duty only 2 days before the Confederates surrendered at Appomattox.

Brevetted a major general in the Regular Army, Ricketts remained in the service until 3 Jan. 1867, when he retired because of his wounds. He performed court-martial duty until 1869. d. District of Columbia, 22 Sept. 1887.   —JDW

Ride Around McClellan.   12–16 June 1862   *See* STUART'S RIDE AROUND MCCLELLAN.

rifle. Both artillery and infantry shoulder weapons with a "rifled" or grooved barrel interior were classified as rifles during the Civil War. In large and small arms rifling allowed a fired projectile to travel a true course to its target. PARROTT GUNS, 3-in. ordnance rifles, similar field artillery pieces, and some seacoast artillery fell under this generic classification. Though varying widely in mechanical sophistication and projectile type, the infantry's muzzle-loading rifle-musket, the HARPERS FERRY RIFLE, the breech-loading SHARPS, a COLT model featuring a revolving 6-shot cylinder, and the lever-action HENRY are all grouped under the general description "rifles."   —JES

rifle-musket. In this muzzle-loading shoulder arm with rifled barrel interior, the exterior resembled the smooth-bore musket in size and general detail. Approved by Sec. of War Jefferson Davis in 1855, the rifle-musket barrel measured 40 in., with a percussion cap fired a .58-caliber projectile, and carried a simple pointed iron "tent peg" or musket bayonet. In some sources, the HARPERS FERRY RIFLE is confused with the rifle-musket: the former had a slightly shorter barrel and, since it was designed in the 1850s, was equipped to carry a sword bayonet. James B. Edwards' *Civil War Guns* (1962) notes this confusion, pointing to drawings in the U.S. government's *Official Records Atlas* that label the Harpers Ferry model weapon a rifle-musket.   —JES

rifle pit. A rifle pit, most often described as a Civil War soldier's foxhole, varied from its 20th-century successor. Paintings and drawings from the Civil War era show a shallow, body-length trench facing the enemy, with the earth from the trench mounded in front of the soldier, who is lying in a prone firing position.   —JES

Ripley, James Wolfe. USA   b. Windham Cty., Conn., 10 Dec. 1794. Descended from an Englishman who settled in Massachusetts early in the 17th century, Ripley received a

county-school education and entered West Point May 1813. Because of a military emergency stemming from America's second war with Great Britain, he was graduated 12th in his class the following June in order to hold an artillery command at Sackett's Harbor, N.Y. After the conflict he fought Creek and Seminole Indians under Gen. Andrew Jackson, served at numerous garrisons, did surveying work in Florida, garrisoned Charleston harbor during the

LC

1832 nullification crisis in South Carolina, served meritoriously in the Mexican War, and 1841–54 commanded Massachusetts' SPRINGFIELD ARMORY.

When the Civil War broke out, Ripley was a lieutenant colonel of ordnance and a veteran of 47 years' service. On 23 Apr. 1861, he was promoted colonel and chief of ordnance; 4 months later he received a brigadier's star. As head of one of the War Department's most important bureaus, he strongly influenced the Union's conduct of the war. He brought to his new position varied experience, professional integrity, and an unswerving faith in his own judgment. While in office he accomplished several notable feats, helping to restore administrative order to a department stultified by disorganization and mired in red tape; protecting the government from unscrupulous contractors, visionary inventors, and their impractical contraptions; increasing the output of government armories; laboring to standardize weaponry and ammunition; and championing the use of breech-loading carbines by the cavalry.

On balance, however, Ripley's weaknesses outweighed his strengths. He was short-tempered, imperious, and rude with his subordinates as well as with businessmen. He sometimes let contracts without advertising for bids or requiring written proposals, to the detriment of government economy. Above all, he was resistant to new ideas and habitually snubbed inventors, even when their offerings had merit. He was especially obstinate in disapproving contracts for breech-loading infantry rifles and repeating carbines. It has been said that "instead of seeking out better designs, he applied his ingenuity, which was considerable, to fighting them off."

After repeated clashes with Pres. ABRAHAM LINCOLN and Sec. of War EDWIN M. STANTON regarding his opposition to innovation, Ripley was replaced 15 Sept. 1863 by Col. GEORGE D. RAMSAY. In later years he was inspector of government armaments, with the brevet of major general. On 15 Mar. 1870, he died at his home in Hartford, Conn. Ripley was the uncle of Confederate Brig. Gen. ROSWELL S. RIPLEY.   —EGL

Ripley, Roswell Sabine. CSA   b. Worthington, Ohio, 14 Mar. 1823. The son of a captain in the War of 1812 and nephew of Union Brig. Gen. JAMES W. RIPLEY, Roswell graduated from West Point in 1843, ranking 7th of 39 cadets. Thereafter he served in the 2d and 3d Artillery. During the Mexican War, about which he wrote a 2-volume history, *The War with Mexico* (1849), he was on the staffs of Gens. Zachary Taylor and GIDEON PILLOW, winning 2 brevets for gallantry at Cerro Gordo and Chapultepec. Later he fought the Seminoles in Florida and served in numerous Southern forts. In 1852 he married a

Charleston woman and the following year resigned from the army to settle in his wife's state.

Ripley took an avid interest in the South Carolina militia and by 1860 was a major of ordnance. The next year, as a lieutenant colonel, he commanded 30 cannon inside Fort Moultrie as well as 22 guns and mortars on Sullivan's Island during the 12–13 Apr. bombardment of FORT SUMTER. Afterward, despairing of further promotion in the Confederate ranks, he nearly resigned prior to receiving a brigadier generalship 15 Aug. For several months he commanded the DEPARTMENT OF SOUTH CAROLINA, where he proved adept at artillery defense, though he quarreled with Gens. ROBERT E. LEE, JOHN C. PEMBERTON, P.G.T. BEAUREGARD, and other Confederate stalwarts.

LC

Despite his contentiousness, Ripley joined Lee's ARMY OF NORTHERN VIRGINIA June 1862 and fought through the PENINSULA CAMPAIGN. His brigade of Georgians and North Carolinians suffered heavy losses at MECHANICSVILLE and MALVERN HILL, while his leadership at GAINES' MILL drew much criticism. That September he again performed less than masterfully at Fox's Gap, during Lee's invasion of Maryland; 3 days later he was severely wounded in the neck while holding the Confederate center at ANTIETAM.

Soon afterward recalled to his home state by Gov. FRANCIS W. PICKENS, Ripley commanded South Carolina's 1st Artillery District, then held various other posts in Charleston, until joining Gen. JOSEPH E. JOHNSTON in North Carolina Mar. 1865.

In postbellum life he engaged in business ventures in his home state and abroad, lived for a period in London, and wrote articles and pamphlets about the war. Late in life he spent an increasing amount of time in New York City, dying there 29 Mar. 1887.   —EGL

river war. From early 1862 until Apr. 1864, combined U.S. army and navy forces fought to gain control of strategic Western rivers. On these waterways—the Mississippi, Cumberland, Tennessee, Arkansas, Yazoo, and Red rivers—former riverboats served as IRONCLAD, "TINCLAD," and cotton-clad gunboats, and conventional wooden ships were replaced with formidable iron RAMS. Arrayed against these vessels were the torpedoes used by Confederates to mine the rivers. Despite the Confederates' defense, by July 1863 the North had accomplished a major objective by gaining complete control of the Mississippi and splitting the Confederacy, culminating in the capture of VICKSBURG and PORT HUDSON July 1863.

In January 1862 7 newly converted ironclad gunboats were assigned to Flag Officer ANDREW H. FOOTE. These cumbersome yet deadly vessels alone brought about the surrender of FORT HENRY on the Tennessee River 6 Feb. 1862, before the arrival of the army. The same gunboats contributed to the capture of FORT DONELSON on the Cumberland River 16 Feb. 1862, this time with major support from land forces commanded by Brig. Gen. ULYSSES S. GRANT. On the Mississippi, Confederate forces fell back on ISLAND NO. 10, located near the junction of Kentucky, Tennessee, and Missouri. This important post was surrendered 8 Apr. 1862, after 2 Federal gunboats, successfully

passing the fort, provided support for the army of Maj. Gen. JOHN POPE.

Naval operations farther south on the lower Mississippi involved the fleet commanded by Union Flag Officer DAVID G. FARRAGUT. On 24 Apr. 1862, Farragut ran his ships past Confederate FORTS JACKSON AND ST. PHILIP, defeated an enemy flotilla below New Orleans, and went ashore to receive the surrender of the city 25 Apr. The 2 forts surrendered 3 days later. The impressive victory was a disaster for the South, costing them their largest and wealthiest city.

On 6 June 1862, U.S. gunboats under Capt. Charles H. Davis and rams under Col. CHARLES ELLET destroyed or captured the same CONFEDERATE RIVER DEFENSE FLEET that had earlier checked another U.S. naval force near FORT PILLOW, Tenn. This defeat cost the Confederates the loss of yet another important city: Memphis. Later in June, Farragut's fleet passed the Vicksburg batteries and joined with that of Davis 1 July 1862. The Federals then began operations against Vicksburg, which would continue for the next year. To defend Vicksburg the Confederates introduced the powerful iron ram ARKANSAS. On 15 July 1862, the vessel engaged the Federal fleet above Vicksburg, inflicting damage on 2 of the gunboats. Although it reached the safety of Vicksburg, the *Arkansas* was destroyed by its own crew during a Confederate attack on BATON ROUGE 6 Aug. Engine failure had made the vessel unmanageable.

The year 1863 brought continuing Federal successes in the river war, with Rear Adm. DAVID D. PORTER commanding the upper Mississippi fleet. ARKANSAS POST was taken by a combined army/navy assault 10–11 Jan. 1863. During February and March, Porter attempted to cut off Vicksburg from the rear, but he was unsuccessful. Farragut, however, succeeded in getting a squadron past enemy batteries at Port Hudson and tightening a blockade of Confederate supply lines on the Red River.

In Apr. 1863 Porter's gunboats escorted army transports past Vicksburg for an attack on Grand Gulf, and 3 May the Confederates abandoned their positions there. Then, after months of bombardment and siege from land and river, Vicksburg fell. Finally, with the capture of Port Hudson 5 days later, the Federals held complete control of the Mississippi. They had won the river war.

Although the South was now severed, the North made an attempt to gain a foothold in the interior of Texas during spring 1864. This was the ill-fated RED RIVER CAMPAIGN, in which Porter and his gunboats supported Maj. Gen. NATHANIEL P. BANKS in an upriver advance from Alexandria toward Shreveport, La. However, after Banks's army was defeated and in retreat, Porter's gunboats were compelled to return down a shallow and falling river that was strongly defended by enemy artillery and riflemen.   —NCD

Roane, John Seldon. CSA b. Wilson Cty., Tenn., 8 Jan. 1817. After receiving an education at Cumberland College, Ky., Roane settled in Arkansas. In 1844 he was elected to the state legislature, and became its speaker. 2 years later the adopted Arkansan joined a regiment of volunteers as its lieutenant colonel in the conflict with Mexico, succeeding to command when the regiment's colonel, Archibald Yell, was killed at Buena Vista. Roane then fought a duel with future Confederate general ALBERT PIKE, who had criticized the regiment's conduct at Buena Vista. Both escaped unscathed.

In 1849 Arkansas elected Roane governor, an office he held until 1852. An opponent of secession, he belatedly joined the

Confederate cause. On 20 Mar. 1862, he received an appointment as brigadier general, then, 11 May, assumed command of all Confederate forces in Arkansas. Succeeded by Maj. Gen. THOMAS C. HINDMAN, Roane fought under the new commander at PRAIRIE GROVE, Ark., 7 Dec. 1862. For the duration of the war he served principally in garrison and on detached duty in the TRANS-MISSISSIPPI DEPARTMENT. He was finally paroled at Shreveport, La., 11 June 1865.

Roane returned to his home in Pine Bluff, where he died 8 Apr. 1867.　　　　　　　　　　　　　　　　　　—JDW

Roanoke Island, N.C., Battle of.

8 Feb. 1862　Steaming down Croatan Sound 7 Feb. 1862, a Union flotilla of nearly 100 ships was about to take part in a Civil War rarity: the amphibious landing of 15,000 troops under enemy fire. The invaders, commanded by Brig. Gen. AMBROSE E. BURNSIDE and transported by Flag Officer LOUIS M. GOLDSBOROUGH, were to seize North Carolina's Roanoke Island.

Fewer than 3,000 Confederates could be mustered to repel the Federals. Led by Col. Henry M. Shaw, they were supported by only 7 gunboats, commanded by Flag Officer William F. Lynch. Long thought indefensible, the island had 3 forts on its northwestern shore, but all were poorly positioned to oppose invaders.

After Goldsborough's fleet brushed aside Lynch's assaults, at about 4 p.m. Burnside's men, in small boats, hit the Roanoke beachhead at Ashby's Harbor. Shaw assigned 450 men to fire on the Federals to delay them. Observing the landing from forest cover, the intimidated Confederates withdrew, allowing all the Union troops to reach the beach by midnight.

At 8 a.m., 8 Feb., the Federals set out after the enemy, traveling north on the causeway traversing Roanoke's great interior swamp. Leading units met no serious resistance until reaching a clearing midway up the 12-mi-long island. There 1,500 Confederates and a 3-gun battery opposed them.

Leaving a midshipman to command troops at the center of their line, Federal commanders sent 2 flanking parties on a 3-hour march through the swamp to assault the Confederate position. Once ready, the Federals rushed the Southerners on left and right and sent the 9th New York Zouaves charging up the causeway with fixed bayonets. Enveloped, the Confederates broke and rushed for Roanoke's northern tip with the Federals pursuing. Outnumbered, with no escape avenues, Shaw unconditionally surrendered his remaining 2,500 troops when their backs were to the sea.

A small victory, Burnside's conquest of Roanoke provided a morale boost for a country that still had not recovered from its defeat at FIRST BULL RUN.　　　　　　　　　—JES

Roberts, Benjamin Stone.

USA　b. Manchester, Vt., 18 Nov. 1810. The son and grandson of generals, Roberts graduated from West Point in 1835, ranking 53rd in his class. Despite his low academic standing, he possessed varied interests and talents, as indicated by his antebellum civil and military career. In 1839, following dragoon service on the frontier, he resigned his commission to accept a position as chief engineer of a railroad in upstate New York; 2 years later he became that state's chief geologist. He went to Russia in 1842 to help construct a railroad from St. Petersburg to Moscow and the next year returned to the U.S., opening a law practice in Iowa. Subsequently he became a lieutenant colonel of militia and an officer of mounted rifles during the Mexican War, winning the

NA

brevet of lieutenant colonel for gallantry in action and remaining in the army when peace returned.

Roberts' Civil War service was no less varied. Promoted to major, 3d U.S. Cavalry, May 1861, he was sent to NEW MEXICO TERRITORY to command its southern district. Leaving the Regulars, he became colonel of the 5th New Mexico Volunteers in December and until May 1862 fought at Fort Craig, Albuquerque, VALVERDE, and Peralta. He was named a brigadier general of volunteers 16 June 1862 and served as inspector general and chief of cavalry to Maj. Gen. JOHN POPE during the SECOND BULL RUN CAMPAIGN. As inspector general, Roberts officially preferred charges against Maj. Gen. FITZ JOHN PORTER in the latter's court-martial. That fall Roberts was detached to Minnesota, where he led a punitive expedition against hostile Chippewas. He returned east Mar. 1863, this time to command a brigade and briefly a division in the MIDDLE DEPARTMENT. The following month he unsuccessfully opposed a cavalry raid by Brig. Gens. WILLIAM E. JONES and JOHN D. IMBODEN through western Virginia.

In 1864 Roberts again went west, for a time commanding the XIX Corps, then the DISTRICT OF WEST TENNESSEE and the cavalry of the DEPARTMENT OF THE GULF. By the end of hostilities he was a brevet major general of volunteers. Discharged from the latter service Jan. 1866, he served with the 3d U.S. Cavalry in New Mexico, then taught military science at Yale. He retired from the Regular Army in 1870 to practice law in Washington, D.C., while directing the manufacture and sale of firearms of his own invention. He died of pneumonia in the nation's capital 29 Jan. 1875.　　　　　　　　　　　　　　　—EGL

Roberts, William Paul.

CSA　b. Gates Cty., N.C., 11 July 1841, Roberts was the youngest Confederate general officer, securing his brigadiership at age 23. It has been asserted, but not verified, that Gen. Robert E. Lee presented Roberts with his own gauntlets in recognition of the officer's promotion.

Roberts enlisted in 1861 at age 19 in the 19th North Carolina, subsequently the 2d North Carolina Cavalry. Promoted to 2d lieutenant 30 Aug., he served in his native state until autumn 1862, when his regiment was transferred to Virginia. With the rank of 1st lieutenant, Roberts fought at FREDERICKSBURG, Suffolk, and BRANDY STATION. With no formal military training he performed with increasing prowess.

USMHI

Promoted to captain 19 Nov. 1863, major a short time later, and colonel June 1864, he commanded the regiment during the PETERSBURG CAMPAIGN. At REAMS' STATION, 25 Aug., Roberts' dismounted command gallantly attacked Federal entrenchments. On 23 Feb. 1865, to date from the 21st, he was appointed brigadier general. During the war's final weeks, he commanded a brigade in Maj. Gen. W.H.F. "Rooney" Lee's division. At FIVE FORKS, 1 Apr., Federals overwhelmed Roberts' thin ranks. He surrendered at Appomattox.

Returning home, Roberts served in the state legislature and 1880–88 as state auditor. d. Norfolk, Va., 28 Mar. 1910.

—JDW

Robertson, Beverly Holcombe.

CSA b. Amelia Cty., Va., 5 June 1827. Graduating 25th in the West Point class of 1849, Robertson spent his prewar career in the 2d Dragoons, the last 7 months of his service as regimental adjutant. On 8 Aug. 1861, he was dismissed from the army, having been tendered a captaincy in the Confederate Adjutant General's Department. Late in 1861, he became colonel of the 4th Virginia Cavalry.

USMHI

In contrast to his distinguished service in the prewar army, Robertson's Confederate career was marred by controversy, criticism, and charges of incompetence. His first superior, Brig. Gen. J.E.B. STUART, called him "by far the most troublesome man I have to deal with." One of Stuart's aides voiced the prevalent belief that, while Robertson was a formidable disciplinarian and drillmaster, "in the presence of the enemy, he lost all self-possession, and was perfectly unreliable."

Despite such pronouncements, Robertson became a Confederate brigadier 9 June 1862. That summer he commanded the late Brig. Gen. TURNER ASHBY's cavalry under Maj. Gen. THOMAS J. "STONEWALL" JACKSON during the SHENANDOAH VALLEY and SECOND BULL RUN campaigns. Displeased by his sluggishness before and during CEDAR MOUNTAIN, Jackson sought his transfer. That August, however, Stuart praised Robertson's troopers for their service in a skirmish at Brandy Station. Only a month later Robertson was sent to North Carolina, where he fought competently at Kinston, Goldsborough, and New Berne. Despite these efforts, his new commander, Maj. Gen. DANIEL H. HILL, complained repeatedly about the Virginian's "wonderfully inefficient Brigade."

In May 1863 Hill returned Robertson, with 2 of his regiments, to Virginia. Placed again under Stuart, he failed to guard the Confederate south flank against Federal horsemen at the Battle of BRANDY STATION, 9 June, and 12 days later he saw much of his demibrigade routed at Upperville. Temporarily left in Virginia during Stuart's GETTYSBURG CAMPAIGN expedition, Robertson did not keep in contact with Gen. Robert E. Lee's main army as ordered. On the retreat from Pennsylvania, he failed to hold a South Mountain pass assigned him by Stuart. Consequently, that October he was again transferred, this time to South Carolina.

In command of that state's 2d Military District, Robertson helped defend Charleston against enemy incursions and Feb. 1865 covered Lt. Gen. WILLIAM J. HARDEE's retreat from that city. Surrendering a month later under Gen. JOSEPH E. JOHNSTON, he subsequently moved to Washington, D.C., where he was an insurance broker. He died in the capital 12 Nov. 1910.   —EGL

Robertson, Felix Huston.

CSA b. Washington, Tex., 9 Mar. 1839. Late in Jan. 1861, shortly before his West Point graduation, Robertson left the academy to take a commission as a Confederate 2d lieutenant of artillery. With Brig. Gen. P.G.T. BEAUREGARD's guns, he participated in the shelling of FORT SUMTER, then was assigned briefly to Florida. Promoted to captain of artillery, he was ordered north to Tennessee shortly before the Battle of SHILOH.

LC

During combat at Shiloh, 6 Apr. 1862, Robertson's battery took part in heavy fighting. Distinguished for workmanlike performance there, he went to another bloody field, STONE'S RIVER. His work there won him promotion to major and eventually a battalion command for the fight at CHICKAMAUGA. In Jan. 1864 he was made lieutenant colonel in charge of artillery in Maj. Gen. JOSEPH WHEELER's cavalry command.

In a highly visible post he fought on through the ATLANTA CAMPAIGN, dueling with Maj. Gen. WILLIAM T. SHERMAN's inept cavalry. This brought him promotion to brigadier general, 26 July 1864, and command of a division of horse soldiers. But in a clash with Union troops at BUCK HEAD CREEK, Ga., he received a debilitating wound, which resulted in retirement from active field command and the end of the fighting for Robertson, though he remained with the army in command of a small brigade that participated in the SALTVILLE MASSACRE 2 Oct. 1864.

When, at the end of the war, Union raider Maj. Gen. JAMES H. WILSON rode up before Macon, Ga., and demanded its surrender, his troops were met by Robertson carrying a white flag. The brigadier, on sick leave in that city, had been asked by Brig. Gen. HOWELL COBB to go out and ask for a truce from Robertson's West Point classmate, Wilson. Dutifully, Robertson went, and was told he would be "given five minutes to clear the road before the Seventeenth Indiana rode on."

After Wilson seized Macon, he arrested and briefly held Robertson, but on his release no other action was taken against him, and he returned to his native Texas to become a fixture in the state legal community. The last surviving Confederate general, Robertson died in Waco, Tex., 20 Apr. 1928. His death attracted national headlines, giving the old soldier more public attention than he had received during his 4 years in the army. Robertson was the son of Confederate Brig. Gen. JEROME B. ROBERTSON.

—JES

Robertson, Jerome Bonaparte.

CSA b. Woodford Cty., Ky., 14 Mar. 1815. Apprenticed as a youth to a hatter by his widowed and penniless mother, Robertson managed to study medicine at Transylvania University. Graduating in 1835, he moved to Texas the next year and served in the revolution that overthrew the Mexican forces. He then settled in Washington County, practiced medicine, and became a renowned Indian fighter and a member of both houses of the state legislature. In Jan. 1861 he was a delegate to the secession convention.

Robertson and his son, future general FELIX H. ROBERTSON, entered Confederate service that spring. The elder Robertson, familiarly called "Polly," joined the 5th Texas as a captain. The regiment transferred to Virginia, where it became a part of the famous Texas Brigade of Brig. Gen. John B. Hood (*see* HOOD'S TEXAS BRIGADE). Promoted to lieutenant colonel Nov. 1861, Robertson assumed command of the 5th Texas 1 June 1862 with the rank of colonel, leading his regiment during the SEVEN DAYS' CAMPAIGN. At GAINES' MILL, 27 June, the Texans and another brigade ruptured the Union center in a riveting attack that resulted in a Confederate victory.

USMHI

After being wounded at SECOND BULL RUN and at SOUTH MOUNTAIN, Md., during the ANTIETAM CAMPAIGN, Robertson collapsed from exhaustion.

Promoted to brigadier general 1 Nov. 1862, Robertson succeeded Hood as commander of the brigade. He directed it at FREDERICKSBURG and GETTYSBURG, where he suffered a slight wound. In Sept. 1863 the brigade went west with Lt. Gen. JAMES LONGSTREET's I Corps, fighting at CHICKAMAUGA. During the KNOXVILLE CAMPAIGN, Robertson incurred the displeasure of Longstreet and Brig. Gen. MICAH JENKINS, who had succeeded the wounded Hood as division commander. On 26 Jan. 1864, Longstreet filed court-martial charges against Robertson for alleged delinquency and pessimistic remarks during the campaign. The brigadier was apparently never brought to trial but was transferred to Texas, where he commanded the state's reserve forces for the remainder of the war.

After the Confederate surrender, Robertson returned to his home and practiced medicine until 1874. He then served as superintendent of the state bureau of immigration. 5 years later he moved to Waco, engaging in railroad construction. The veteran died there 7 Jan. 1891. —JDW

Robinson, Charles. war governor b. Hardwick, Mass., 21 July 1818. Robinson's early education at private schools prepared him to study medicine. He first opened a private practice, then founded and operated a hospital in Fitchburg, Mass. In 1849 Robinson, widowed a few years earlier, migrated to California. There he mined for a couple of weeks, but left the gold fields to run a restaurant in Sacramento and co-edit the Sacramento *Settlers' and Miners' Tribune.* Easily attracted to a cause, he used the paper to champion settlers' rights against land speculators. A free-soiler, Robinson supported JOHN C. FRÉMONT for the California senate and himself served in the state assembly 1850–51.

At the end of his term he returned to his medical practice in Massachusetts, at the same time editing the Fitchburg *News.* As a result of his antislavery convictions and his experience in the Western country en route to California, in 1854 Robinson was appointed resident agent in Kansas for the New England Emigrant Aid Company. At once he began conducting parties of settlers to the territory and working to unite antislavery factions there. As a leader of the Free-State party he denounced POPULAR SOVEREIGNTY and was named commander-in-chief of the free-soilers when proslavery forces threatened Wakarusa Dec. 1855. Never exceedingly popular, Robinson was efficient, cautious, shrewd, an exceptional debater, and was highly respected for his pragmatic approach to territorial difficulties.

Chosen governor in 1856 under the abortive Topeka constitution, 1 of 6 submitted before Kansas attained statehood, he was again elected in 1859 under the successful Wyandotte constitution and inaugurated 9 Feb. 1861. On 26 Mar. he convened the legislature and began preparing the divided state for war. His effectiveness waned when his efforts clashed with JAMES H. LANE's military plans for the state. A man of extraordinary power within the state, Lane spearheaded a movement to oust Robinson from office. Though Robinson was acquitted of impeachment charges involving irregularities in the sale of state bonds, he was defeated in the 1862 elections.

Retiring to "Oakridge," his home near Lawrence, Robinson joined the Liberal Republicans during the postwar years, winning a seat in the state senate in 1874 and 1876. A decade later he was defeated in a second bid for the governorship, on the Democratic ticket, and in 1890 failed in a third attempt. He continued his longtime activities in behalf of public education, served as president of the Kansas Historical Society 1879–80, and wrote *The Kansas Conflict* (1892), devoted to the prewar conflict in the state. d. Lawrence, 17 Aug. 1894. —PLF

Robinson, John Cleveland. USA b. Binghamton, N.Y., 10 Apr. 1817. After a private education and study at Oxford Academy, Oxford, N.Y., Robinson entered West Point 1 July 1835. Dismissed from the school in a disciplinary dispute 14 Mar. 1838, he wrangled an appointment to the Regular Army, joining the 5th U.S. Infantry as a 2d lieutenant 27 Oct. 1839. He served through the Mexican War in the Quartermaster's Department and saw action at Palo Alto, Resaca de la Palma, Monterrey, and Mexico City. After duty in Texas, promotion to captain in 1850, and service in the Seminole Wars and the 1857 Utah Expedition, Robinson assumed command of Fort McHenry, Baltimore, Md.

LC

At the head of McHenry's 60-man garrison Robinson made a show of force against Maryland secessionists during the 19 Apr. 1861 BALTIMORE RIOTS, preventing the fort's seizure. In Sept. 1861 Robinson was sent on recruiting duty in the Midwest, raised the 1st Michigan Volunteers, and was elected its colonel. On railroad guard duty in Maryland until Mar. 1862, he won appointment to brigadier general 28 Apr. 1862 and joined Maj. Gen. George B. McClellan's army for the PENINSULA CAMPAIGN as a member of the III Corps. Leading the 1st Brigade/1st Division, he fought through SECOND BULL RUN and FREDERICKSBURG, assumed leadership of the 2d Division/I Corps for the Battle of CHANCELLORSVILLE, and 1 July 1863, with 2,500 men, held off more than twice that number of Confederates for 4 hours at GETTYSBURG.

Next commanding the 2d Division/V Corps in the 8 May 1864 combat at Laurel Hill, Va., Robinson followed orders to lead his scattered force against massed Confederates preparing for the Battle of SPOTSYLVANIA. His charge was repulsed and, severely wounded in the left knee, he lost his leg to amputation. Brevetted major general of volunteers 27 June 1864, he assumed district command in New York State, then was awarded brevets to brigadier and major general in the Regulars for his action at Laurel Hill and his war service.

Robinson ran the FREEDMEN'S BUREAU in North Carolina in 1866, the DEPARTMENT OF THE SOUTH in 1867, the Department of the Lakes in 1868, and received disability retirement 6 May 1869 as a full major general of Regulars. Elected lieutenant governor of New York in 1872, he served until 1874, and became active in the leadership of the Society of the Army of the Potomac and the Grand Army of the Republic until overtaken by blindness in 1893. In Mar. 1894 he received the Congressional Medal of Honor for his actions at Laurel Hill. d. Binghamton, N.Y., 18 Feb. 1897. In Apr. 1917 his valiant stand on the first day of fighting at Gettysburg was commemorated with a statue on the battlefield.   —JES

Rock Island Prison. Built by the Union to confine Confederates, Rock Island Prison was located in the Mississippi River between the cities of Rock Island, Ill., and Davenport, Iowa. The island, about 3 mi long and a half-mile wide, had the disadvantage of poor drainage and was partly swampy.

Federals approved construction of the prison July 1863, and in mid-August the quartermaster general instructed the builder that "barracks for prisoners on Rock Island should be put up in the roughest and cheapest manner, mere shanties, with no fine work about them." The 84 barracks, each 82 ft $\times$ 22 ft $\times$ 12 ft, were lined up in 6 rows of 14 each, all enclosed by a high fence. A cookhouse was at the end of each barrack. All barracks were poorly ventilated and inadequately heated, with only 2 stoves in each. An artesian well on the island supplied some of the water for the prison but most was drawn from the river with a steam pump. Inside the prison, water was always scarce and, when the pump failed, nonexistent.

In Dec. 1863 about 5,000 prisoners were sent to Rock Island, though the installation was not ready. Until the end of the war it held between 5,000 and 8,000 prisoners. Many of the first to arrive had been exposed to smallpox at Camp Douglas, and the disease spread rapidly. In January 1864, of 7,149 prisoners, 173 died; in February 331 died; in March 132. Thousands of others were ill but survived.

Commandants of Federal military prisoners had been authorized, at their discretion, to reduce prisoners' rations and to use the money saved on improvements deemed necessary for the prisoners' health. At Rock Island a thirty-thousand-dollar hospital was paid for out of funds issued for rations. Though there were complaints about the food—mainly about the scarcity of vegetables—the hospital was needed.

After the war ended in 1865, Rock Island Prison barracks were emptied of prisoners by 11 July. Buildings were turned over to the Ordnance Department 7 Aug. for $89,113, about one-third of their original cost, and were used as storehouses, barracks, and officers' quarters. The hospital remained in use until 1909. Nothing is left of the prison buildings today.   —PR

"Rock of Chickamauga." *See* THOMAS, GEORGE HENRY.

Rockville Expedition, Md. 10 June–7 July 1861 On 8 June 1861, U.S. Gen.-in-Chief WINFIELD SCOTT ordered Col. CHARLES P. STONE, 14th U.S. Infantry, to lead a column of volunteers northwestward from Washington, D.C. Stone was instructed to cover the upper Potomac against Confederate incursions, to staunch the flow of enemy supplies from Baltimore to Virginia, to open the obstructed Chesapeake & Ohio Canal near Leesburg, Va., and to "give countenance to our friends in Maryland and Virginia." If possible, he was also to

link with the army of Maj. Gen. ROBERT PATTERSON, about to leave Pennsylvania for operations in western Virginia near Harpers Ferry.

Stone started from the capital's suburbs 2 days later, marching up the Maryland side of the Potomac with 2,500 troops of all arms—3 regiments and 4 battalions of infantry, 2 mounted companies, and 2 cannon. The movement proceeded smoothly to Tennallytown and Rockville, Md., which his troops occupied on the 11th, sending waves of alarm through Confederate enclaves as far west as Harpers Ferry. From Rockville, where Stone established his headquarters, detachments fanned out to numerous towns along the river, including Seneca Mills (where they skirmished with local Confederates on the 14th), Great Falls, and Darnestown. By these movements, the Federals secured the C&O Canal almost as far north as Edwards' Ferry and protected the property of numerous Unionists. On the 15th, the expedition reached Edwards' and Conrad's ferries, the main approaches to strategic Leesburg.

The next day, Stone found Confederate forces of undetermined size moving against him from Leesburg, and on the 17th a skirmish, primarily a long-range artillery duel, broke out in that sector. When some of the enemy attempted to cross at Edwards' Ferry, Stone's cannon blasted them into retreat. Hesitating to occupy Leesburg against unknown opposition, Stone marked time at Poolesville, between Edwards' and Conrad's ferries, till on the 30th Scott ordered him to join Patterson near Martinsburg, Va., northwest of Harpers Ferry.

Leaving a rear guard to secure the canal and the ferries for as long as possible, the colonel moved upriver. On Independence Day, Stone crossed the Potomac at Harpers Ferry, where he had a long-range clash with the rear guard of Gen. JOSEPH E. JOHNSTON's army, which had recently evacuated the town. Reaching Martinsburg on the 7th, he assumed command of a brigade in Patterson's army. Though Stone's expedition was of only moderate strategic significance, General Scott reported himself "highly pleased" by its conduct.   —EGL

Rocky Gap (White Sulphur Springs), W.Va., eng. at.
26 Aug. 1863 Union Brig. Gen. WILLIAM W. AVERELL, with 4 regiments of cavalry and mounted infantry and 2 artillery batteries, left Winchester, Va., 5 Aug. 1863, marching westward toward the Allegheny Mts. The Federals were on another in a series of raids that plagued this backwater area throughout the war. Averell's mission was to destroy Confederate saltpeter and gunpowder works near Franklin, W.Va., and attack Col. WILLIAM L. JACKSON's Confederate cavalry brigade, reportedly located at Huntersville.

Averell's command, numbering about 2,000, covered 58 mi the first 2 days, reaching Moorefield, W.Va., late on the 6th. Nearby, advanced Confederate outposts skirmished with the Federals before disappearing into the rugged terrain. The Northerners resumed their march on the 9th, heading southward, deeper into the mountain fastnesses, a lack of supplies, horseshoes, and nails and insufficient ammunition hampering their progress. By 22 Aug. the Union force had dislodged Jackson from Huntersville, with the Confederates eventually retreating to Warm Springs.

Averell trailed Jackson on the 24th, shoving the Southerners eastward and occupying Warm Springs. The Federals marched to Callaghan's Station the next day, destroyed the saltpeter works on Jackson's River, and prepared to move to White Sulphur Springs on the 26th. The Union advance resumed at 4 a.m., 26 Aug., moving westward. At Rocky Gap in the Allegheny Mts., about 2 mi from White Sulphur Springs, the Northerners encountered 4 regiments of Virginia infantry and an artillery battery, numbering 1,900, under Col. George S. Patton.

Patton, directed by department commander Maj. Gen. SAMUEL JONES to intercept Averell, arrived at the mountain defile at about 9:30 a.m. Averell quickly shook out a battle line and charged the waiting Confederates, who had deployed across the road. The musketry quickly escalated as the Federals, most of them dismounted, assaulted the Virginians. The battle raged all day as one Union attack after another was repulsed in the heavily wooded terrain.

Expecting reinforcements that never arrived, Averell did not withdraw during the night. Resuming his attacks the next morning, he again made little headway against Patton's veterans. By noon the Union force had abandoned the field, countermarching toward Callaghan's Station. Averell's casualties amounted to 26 killed, 125 wounded, and 67 captured or missing; Patton suffered 20 killed, 129 wounded, and 13 missing.

For the next 3 days Averell retreated northward, arriving at Beverly, W.Va., on the 31st. Except for the engagement at Rocky Gap, he had inflicted few casualties, captured only a handful of Confederates, destroyed 2 saltpeter works, and seized some cattle. —JDW

Roddey, Philip Dale. CSA b. Moulton, Ala., 2 Apr. 1826, Roddey received little education, became a tailor in Moulton, served 3 years as sheriff there, then worked as a steamboat deckhand until the Civil War.

The several brief biographies of Roddey give few facts and dates about his early war experience. At an unspecified date in 1861 he organized the Tishomingo Rangers, a unit made up of Mississippians and Alabamans who served as excellent scouts in the Western theater, providing intelligence prior to the SHILOH campaigning and, by some accounts, acting as Gen. BRAXTON BRAGG's personal escort during the Battle of Shiloh.

LC

Roddey served under Brig. Gen. JAMES R. CHALMERS during the retreat to Corinth, Miss., was active in the IUKA and CORINTH campaigning in autumn 1862, and in December won commission as colonel of the 4th Alabama. Commanding the post at Tuscumbia, Ala., with a force of 1,400 men in winter 1862–63, he confronted the Union cavalry of Col. ABEL D. STREIGHT in April, and under Brig. Gen. NATHAN B. FORREST pursued the Federal raider.

On 3 Aug. 1863 he won promotion to brigadier general and, in Brig. Gen. WILLIAM T. MARTIN's division, fought through the Battle of CHICKAMAUGA and the CHATTANOOGA CAMPAIGN as a part of Brig. Gen. JOSEPH WHEELER's cavalry. Next attached to Forrest's command, he distinguished himself in the Battle of BRICE'S CROSS ROADS and the FRANKLIN AND NASHVILLE CAMPAIGN, and in the Feb. 1865 reorganization of Forrest's cavalry, during which several officers were dismissed for want of appropriate commands, he was retained as a brigade leader. Roddey fought through Forrest's last campaign in Alabama,

joined in the retreat from Selma, and surrendered with his men May 1865. Throughout the war he won recognition as a raider in northern Alabama and along the line of the Tennessee River.

In postwar years, Roddey moved to New York City and, with the same brash confidence that made him a good steamboatman and cavalry leader, entered the business world. Later an investor in a new pump design, he traveled to Britain to negotiate the sale of its patent and died of uremia in London, 20 July 1897. His body was returned to Tuscaloosa for burial. —JES

Rodes, Robert Emmett. CSA b. Lynchburg, Va., 29 Mar. 1829. One of the finest of Robert E. Lee's officers, Rodes graduated from the VIRGINIA MILITARY INSTITUTE in 1848, serving there as an instructor until 1851, when he went to Alabama to begin a career as a civil engineer. During the next 9 years he married, became chief engineer for the Northeast & Southwest Alabama Railroad, and, just before war began, accepted a professorship at VMI.

From colonel of the 5th Alabama at FIRST BULL RUN, Rodes was commissioned brigadier general 21 Oct. 1861. As part of Maj. Gen. DANIEL H. HILL's division, during the PENINSULA CAMPAIGN his brigade performed

USMHI

courageously at SEVEN PINES (where Rodes was wounded), GAINES' MILL, and MALVERN HILL, suffering 50% casualties. Not present at Malvern Hill, Rodes recovered to lead his brigade in rearguard action at SOUTH MOUNTAIN, Md. At the Battle of ANTIETAM, his battered regiments helped hold the Confederate center at "BLOODY LANE," where he was again wounded. The fighting in Maryland brought severe losses to the brigade, but it was not actively engaged at Fredericksburg, and fall and winter enlistments restored the ranks. Made division commander when Hill was sent to North Carolina, Rodes led Lt. Gen. THOMAS J. "STONEWALL" JACKSON's famous flank attack on the Union XI Corps at CHANCELLORSVILLE; it gained him his major generalcy.

GETTYSBURG was Rodes's poorest battle. Failure to reconnoiter cost him heavily 1 July; on the next day the same failure left Maj. Gen. JUBAL A. EARLY's dusk attack unsupported. But at the "BLOODY ANGLE" at Spotsylvania he brilliantly led the counterattack along the "MULE SHOE." 4 months later, 19 Sept. 1864, at the Third Battle of Winchester, he was killed as he directed the counterattack that allowed Early's beaten army to retreat safely.

Modest, soldierly, an inspiring leader in attack, Rodes has been overshadowed by more colorful, but not more capable, figures. —RDH

Rodgers, John. USN b. Havre de Grace, Md., 8 Aug. 1812. Son of an American naval hero of the same name, Rodgers won a midshipman's appointment 18 Apr. 1828 and remained in naval service until his death. He cruised the Mediterranean aboard the *Constellation* and the *Concord,* attended the naval school at Norfolk, Va., attained passed midshipman's rank in 1834, attended the University of Virginia for a year, then returned to sea duty. At sea he served in the Coast Survey, the Brazil Squadron, fought in the Seminole War, saw duty in the Home Squadron, in the Mediterranean and off the African coast, and in the North Pacific and Surveying Expedition cruising Hawaii, Japan, other Pacific Islands, and the Arctic Ocean. During this period he was promoted to lieutenant 28 Jan. 1840, supervised construction of the *Alleghany* at Pittsburgh, Pa., in 1845, and won promotion to commander 14 Sept. 1855.

USMHI

Ordered to Cincinnati, Ohio, at Maj. Gen. GEORGE B. MCCLELLAN's direction, on 16 May 1861 he began converting 3 steamers into gunboats for service on the Mississippi River, was superseded by Capt. ANDREW H. FOOTE, then traveled east, assuming command of the *Flag* 17 Oct. for duty in Flag Officer SAMUEL F. DU PONT's Port Royal Expedition (*see* BATTLE OF PORT ROYAL). In fighting at Hilton Head, S.C., 7 Nov., Rodgers acted as Du Pont's aide, took an active part in obtaining the surrender of Forts Walker and Beauregard, and was allowed the privilege of hoisting the first Union flag on hostile South Carolina soil.

After briefly commanding a gunboat flotilla near Savannah, Ga., he received assignment to the new ironclad *GALENA* 21 Apr. 1862, and at Pres. ABRAHAM LINCOLN's direction led 4 other vessels up Virginia's James River 15 May to secure McClellan's flank during the PENINSULA CAMPAIGN. Unable to pass Confederate batteries atop Drewry's Bluff, he suffered under severe enemy fire for 4 hours, lost 13 *Galena* crewmen, and was forced to retire to the mouth of the James. Despite this loss, he became a captain 16 July 1862, assumed command of the monitor *Weehawken,* joined in the blockade of Charleston, S.C., and in Du Pont's 7 Apr. 1863 attack on the city's harbor forts cruised in the van, pushing a torpedo-sweeping device. In less than an hour Rodgers' *Weehawken* took 53 hits from enemy fire before withdrawing.

Supervising the *Weehawken*'s repair, he took it to the flotilla at Wassaw Sound, Ga., and 17 June, in a short duel, directed the sinking of the feared Confederate ironclad *ATLANTA*. At Lincoln's order, Rodgers' gallant service was rewarded with the THANKS OF CONGRESS and advancement to commodore to date from the fight with the *Atlanta.* He next served on the *Canonicus* and the *Dictator* in blockading service through 1863, then assumed administrative duties until the war's end.

In autumn 1865, Rodgers commanded an American squadron off Chile, in 1869 ran the Boston Navy Yard, was raised to rear admiral 31 Dec. 1869, then commanded the Asiatic Squadron leading a punitive expedition in Korea in 1871. He retired from sea duty in 1872 to head successively several naval examining boards and San Francisco's Mare Island shipyard, and assume superintendency of the Naval Observatory. d. District of Columbia 5 May 1882, the U.S. Navy's oldest active rear admiral.   —JES

Rodman, Thomas Jackson. USA b. Salem, Ind., 30 July 1815. Privately educated in Indiana, Rodman graduated 7th in

the West Point class of 1841, the same class in which JOSIAH GORGAS, future chief of Confederate ordnance, graduated 6th. Rodman entered the Ordnance Department as a brevet 2d lieutenant. He is best known for his patented method of gun casting and the generic association of his name with the ROD-MAN SMOOTHBORE.

First assigned to the Allegheny Arsenal in Pennsylvania, until the Mexican War Rodman worked in gun manufacture and testing in Richmond, Boston, and Pittsburgh, perfecting his idea of cooling cast cannon tubes from the inside out with water circulating through the casting core. Rough casting methods previously rendered large weapons such as the 1844 COLUMBIAD structurally weak. Following Mexican War service in arsenals at Camargo and Point Isabel, Rodman secured permission for the owner of Fort Pitt Foundry, Pittsburgh, to register process patents on his cooling process, and in 1847 pursued private testing. Successful, his method was used by private firms until adopted by the U.S. Army in 1857. Rodman then designed 1858 and 1861 models of the Columbiad that saw heavy Civil War service in seacoast batteries and fortifications.

Promoted captain 1 July 1855, Rodman spent the years prior to the Civil War at the Allegheny Arsenal; Iron Mountain and Pilot Knob, Mo.; the Baton Rouge, La., Arsenal; Pittsburgh; and the Watertown, N.Y., Arsenal pursuing further gun-casting experiments and developing a gunpowder for use with heavy ordnance. His *Reports of Experiments on the Properties of Metals for Cannon, and the Qualities of Cannon Powder* was published in 1861. Rodman assumed command of the Watertown Arsenal 12 Apr. 1861, remained there until 3 Aug. 1865, and from 27 Sept. 1864 extended his casting methods to the manufacture of heavy ordnance projectiles. Advanced to major 1 June 1863, on 13 Mar. 1865, in appreciation for his technical contributions to the Union war effort he won brevets to lieutenant colonel, colonel, and brigadier general.

After a lengthy illness he transferred to command of the Rock Island, Ill., Arsenal, planned construction of a new armory and arsenal there, won promotion to lieutenant colonel in the Regulars 7 Mar. 1867, then suffered a permanent deterioration in health. d. Rock Island 7 June 1871.

It is important to note that in contemporary Civil War literature volunteer artillerymen frequently referred to 3-IN. ORDNANCE GUNS as Rodmans, though the ordnance officer was not its inventor. The ordnance guns' tapered, smooth lines approximate those on Columbiads made by Rodman's method.
                                                                                          —JES

Rodman smoothbore. The Rodman gun was actually a Model 1861 COLUMBIAD cast by a process that allowed larger guns to be fabricated. Lt. THOMAS J. RODMAN of the U.S. Ordnance Department developed the process in 1844–45. At that time, the forming of large guns depended on casting a large solid block in the general shape of the gun, then boring out and finishing the piece by drill and lathe. Large castings tended to develop cracks and weak spots. Rodman believed the trouble was caused by the gun cooling from the outside inward. He reversed the process by casting the gun tube around a hollow pipe the size of the bore, closed at the bottom. A second pipe was inserted within a few inches of the base of the first pipe. When molten metal was poured into the mold, water was poured into the smaller pipe. It flowed out the bottom, through the larger pipe, and ran out the top. Coals were heaped around

LC

the exterior of the casting to make sure that the gun cooled from the inside out.

Rodman patented his process and contracted with the Fort Pitt Foundry to build his guns. They proved capable of outlasting those cast by conventional means, and the 1861 Columbiad was cast by his process.

A smoothbore weapon intended for use in seacoast fortifications, the Rodman Columbiad was made in calibers of 8, 10, 13, 15, and even 20 in. Although they were widely publicized, most saw no action.

The Confederates made very few guns by the Rodman process, though there is evidence that the TREDEGAR IRON WORKS in Richmond cast a pair of 12-in. Columbiads by Rodman's method late in the war. Both guns were captured at the ironworks and never saw service. —LDJ

roll of honor. Confederate authorities, seeking to stimulate the morale and performance of its soldiers, authorized medals and badges for those men cited in official battle reports. When the emblems could not be supplied, the Confederate Congress, 13 Oct. 1862, authorized a roll of honor. Any officer, noncommissioned officer, or private, who was "conspicuous for courage and good conduct on the field of battle," would have his name inscribed on the roll.

The act also specified that after every battle the names of those placed on the list were to be read at dress parades, published in at least 1 newspaper in each state, and filed in the offices of the adjutant and inspector generals. The Confederacy maintained a roll of honor for the duration of the conflict. —JDW

Root, George Frederick. composer b. Sheffield, Mass., 30 Aug. 1820. Before the Civil War, Root established his reputation as a leading music educator and composer. In 1860 he moved to Chicago to take up part ownership in the music firm of Root & Cady, founded a year earlier by his brother. Shortly after the firing on FORT SUMTER, Apr. 1861, his first effort to furnish the public with a war song produced "The First Gun Is Fired! May God Protect the Right!," which enjoyed only moderate success. In all, Root wrote 28 wartime songs, among them such hits as "Tramp, Tramp, Tramp, the Boys are Marching," "The Vacant Chair," and "Just Before the Battle, Mother," but none matched "The Battle Cry of Freedom." When it was released Aug. 1862, its dramatic words and rousing marching tune appealed to the nation's patriotic spirit, its popularity spreading rapidly through the troops and among the civilian population. The New York *Tribune* reported 18 Nov. 1862 that sheet-music sales of the rallying song had reached 12,000. 2 years after the war Root & Cady claimed sales of 350,000. "The Battle Cry of Freedom" was played at Fort Sumter, 14 Apr. 1865, when Brig. Gen. Robert Anderson raised the Union flag over the recaptured fort. Confederate Gen. George E. Pickett claimed it was also popular among Southern troops.

Root's autobiography, *The Story of a Musical Life* (1891), gives a full account of his wartime songs. He continued working as a composer, publisher, and teacher until his death in Chicago, 6 Aug. 1895. —PLF

Rosecrans, William Starke. USA b. Delaware Cty., Ohio, 6 Sept. 1819, Rosecrans secured an appointment to the U.S. Military Academy at West Point in 1838, graduating 5th in his class. He received a coveted appointment as 2d lieutenant, Corps of Engineers, as of 1 July 1842 and resigned from the army in 1854 to enter business as an architect and civil engineer.

At the outbreak of the Civil War, Rosecrans served as a volunteer aide, organizing and training Union volunteer troops. A promising officer, a Democrat, and a Catholic, he was an ideal choice for a Republican administration seeking broad support to appoint brigadier general in the Regular Army; he received his commission from 16 May 1861. Rosecrans served with distinction in western Virginia, winning the Battle of RICH MOUNTAIN 11 July. He commanded a division of the Army of the Mississippi during the Siege of Corinth, Miss., 22–30 May 1862, and commanded that army 11 June–20 Oct. He fought 2 partially successful actions at IUKA 19 Sept. and CORINTH 3–4 Oct.

USMHI

Given command of the ARMY OF THE CUMBERLAND 27 Oct., Rosecrans fought the Battle of STONE'S RIVER 31 Dec. Although the Confederate attack on his army was tactically successful, Rosecrans claimed victory by virtue of possession of the field once the Confederates had withdrawn. After numerous delays, he opened a brilliant campaign 24 June 1863, maneuvering Confederate forces out of Chattanooga 9 Sept. During the Battle of CHICKAMAUGA, 19–20 Sept., he blundered by moving a division, thus creating a gap in his line. The attacking Confederates exploited the gap with disastrous effect, and only the heroic stand of Maj. Gen. GEORGE H. THOMAS saved the Union army from complete destruction. Inexplicably permitting the Confederates to occupy the high ground around CHATTANOOGA, Rosecrans allowed his army to be besieged, and he was relieved from command 19 Oct. His last active command was the DEPARTMENT OF MISSOURI, 28 Jan.–9 Dec. 1864.

Rosecrans was an excellent organizer and planner who worked well with volunteer troops. At times he exhibited flashes of strategic genius. But as a field commander he proved to be a disastrous failure. After more than 2 years without receiving a command, he resigned from the army 28 Mar. 1867.

Pres. Andrew Johnson appointed Rosecrans minister to Mexico in 1868. Removed from the post the following year by newly elected Pres. Ulysses S. Grant, he retired to his ranch in California until his election to the U.S. House of Representatives in 1880. When his second congressional term ended in 1885, he accepted an appointment as register of the treasury, a position he held until 1893. Rosecrans died at his ranch in Redondo, Calif., 11 Mar. 1898.   —DLW

Ross, Lawrence Sullivan. CSA b. Bentonsport, Iowa, 27 Sept. 1838. Taken to Texas by his parents as an infant, Ross had earned by age 21 an enduring reputation as an Indian fighter on the state's frontier. An 1859 graduate of Wesleyan University in Alabama, he spent his vacations in operations against the Comanches. He rescued the celebrated Cynthia Ann Parker, mother of Quanah, who became chief of the Comanches; killed in single combat chief Peta Necona; was appointed by Sam Houston as a captain of a company of Texas Rangers; and declined a commission in the U.S. Army offered by Gen. WINFIELD SCOTT.

LC

When Texas seceded, Ross entered Confederate service as a private. Named major of the

6th Texas Cavalry Sept. 1861, he was promoted to colonel 14 May 1862. In October he distinguished himself covering the retreat of the Confederate army after the Battle of CORINTH, Miss. His prowess as a cavalry officer earned him numerous commendations from various superiors and, 21 Dec. 1863, he was promoted to brigadier general. He subsequently commanded a brigade under Maj. Gen. JOSEPH WHEELER during the ATLANTA CAMPAIGN. During the course of the war Ross had 5 horses shot under him and participated in 135 battles and engagements.

After the war, "Sul" Ross returned penniless to Texas, where he engaged in farming in Brazos Bottom. His plantation eventually made him wealthy. After serving as sheriff of McLennan County, he became a member of the constitutional convention and 1881–85 a state senator. In 1887 he was elected governor and was overwhelmingly reelected 2 years later. From 1891 to 1898 he was president of Texas Agricultural & Mechanical College. Endeared to many Texans, Ross died from exposure while hunting along the Trinity River 3 Jan. 1898. He is buried in Waco, Tex.   —JDW

Rosser, Thomas Lafayette. CSA b. Campbell Cty., Va., 15 Oct. 1836, Rosser moved with his family to Texas in 1849. 2 weeks before his graduation from West Point, where he was an intimate friend of GEORGE A. CUSTER, he resigned and hurried south to serve as an artillery officer at FIRST BULL RUN. One of a small group of Southern cavalry commanders who made war seem glorious and noble, Rosser fought with honor in numerous engagements, frequently receiving high praise from his superiors. When he returned to the field after recovering from severe wounds sustained in the PENINSULA CAMPAIGN, Maj. Gen. J.E.B. STUART appointed him colonel of the

USMHI

5th Virginia Cavalry, which he commanded brilliantly for 15 months. On 28 Sept. 1863 he was promoted to brigadier general and assumed command of the Laurel Brigade, leading it with distinction in frequent encounters with his old friend Custer. Though he did not live up to his epithet of "Savior of the Valley," a title prematurely bestowed on him in 1864, his bravery and audacity were widely admired. Even after Custer soundly defeated him in the Shenandoah Valley Oct. 1864, Rosser was promoted to major general from 1 Nov.

In the waning months of the war he continued to enhance his reputation, successfully staging a series of daring raids into West Virginia (see ROSSER'S BEVERLY, W.VA., RAID; ROSSER'S NEW CREEK, W.VA., RAID; see also ROSSER'S RAID TO MOOREFIELD, W.VA.). Although he was with Gen. ROBERT E. LEE at Appomattox, Rosser managed to evade surrender by breaking through the Union lines with 2 regiments of cavalry and fought on until his capture 2 May.

After the war Rosser became chief engineer on both the Northern Pacific and Canadian Pacific railroads, where he renewed his friendship with Custer, whose troops frequently guarded his surveying parties. At the outbreak of the Spanish-American War, Pres. William McKinley commissioned him brigadier general and gave him command of a brigade of U.S. Volunteers. d. Charlottesville, Va., 29 Mar. 1910.   —PRR

Rosser's Beverly, W.Va., raid. 6–11 Jan. 1865 By winter 1865 hunger and defeat stalked the armies of the Confederacy. In the SHENANDOAH VALLEY of Virginia, where Maj. Gen. PHILIP H. SHERIDAN's command had wrecked Lt. Gen. JUBAL A. EARLY's Confederate legions and ravaged the fertile valley, the suffering was particularly acute. Entire regiments had been temporarily sent home to relieve the critical shortages in rations and forage. Only a remnant of Early's infantry and Brig. Gen. THOMAS L. ROSSER's half-clothed and badly mounted cavalry division remained.

Early in January Rosser learned that at Beverly, W.Va., more than 75 mi from his camp near Staunton, Va., a Federal depot, guarded by 1,000 troops, bulged with supplies. Though fierce cold and heavy snow blanketed the region, Rosser determined to undertake a raid. Securing permission, he asked for volunteers and organized a force of 300. Dividing it into 2 detachments of 150 men each, commanded respectively by Cols. Alphonso F. Cook and William A. Morgan, Rosser marched about 7 or 8 Jan.

The Confederates struggled through the deep drifts, their suffering intensifying with each mile. On the night of the 10th, the raiders bivouacked on a mountainside near a road that intersected the Philippi Turnpike north of Beverly. Before daylight, the Confederates, most of them dismounted, advanced over the frozen snow. A mounted detachment, sweeping ahead, galloped into the camps of the 34th Ohio and 8th Ohio Cavalry. The sleeping Federals, completely surprised, scattered under the onslaught. Handfuls of Union troops offered slight resistance before surrendering to the charging Southerners.

The Confederates killed 6 and wounded 32 Northerners while losing 1 killed and a few wounded, including Colonel Cook, whose left leg was amputated that night. Rosser's men seized 580 prisoners, 100 horses, about 600 arms and equipment, and 10,000 rations, which the famished Confederates immediately enjoyed. Rosser then returned to the valley, where the stores temporarily relieved the hunger of his command.   —JDW

Rosser's New Creek, W.Va., raid. 28 Nov. 1864 A series of Union forts and depots in Maryland and West Virginia guarded the vital BALTIMORE & OHIO RAILROAD. Garrisoned by thousands of Federal soldiers, these installations, clustered at strategic points, protected repair crews and bulging warehouses from Confederate raiders and guerrillas. The protection of the garrisons and railroad was a constant problem for Union authorities throughout the war.

No place along the railroad seemed more secure than New Creek, W.Va., a supply depot described as the finest in the department. Located at the intersection of New Creek Valley and the Potomac River Valley, New Creek sat on a ridge at the northern end of a narrow valley between 2 mountains. Its Fort Kelley, with a garrison of nearly 800 men and 5 cannon, had defied any Confederate attempts at capture. With the confining New Creek Valley as the only route of approach, Southerners considered the depot and fort impregnable.

On 26 Nov. 1864, Brig. Gen. THOMAS L. ROSSER and 2 brigades of cavalrymen abandoned their camps in the Shenandoah Valley for another Confederate raid against New Creek.

Reaching Moorefield, W.Va., the next morning, Rosser's command, numbering between 500 and 600, encountered a detachment from New Creek. The Confederates scattered the Federals in a running fight, but most of the Northerners escaped to sound the alarm. Rosser, who had been told earlier by 2 scouts that success depended on secrecy and surprise, rode with his men all night.

The Confederates halted at dawn 6 mi from New Creek, near Harrison's Gap, where Rosser convened a council of war. The gray-clad officers decided to attack the garrison, and the entire command soon remounted. Cautiously the Confederates advanced at a walk, led by 20 troopers in blue Federal overcoats. Encountering a Union picket, the Southerners claimed that they were a returning Union scouting party. The surprised Federals were quickly captured along with a second post only 2 mi from the fort. With the road cleared, the raiders slowly approached the base of the ridge when the charge was sounded.

The Confederates galloped toward Fort Kelley. Unbelievably, only a few sentinels manned their posts; most of the Northerners either were eating lunch or resting in the camp area. The garrison's commander, Col. George R. Latham, though forewarned of Rosser's presence at Moorefield, had failed disgracefully to place his command on alert. Within 30 minutes the Southerners had seized the fort and captured more than 700 Federals.

The Confederates ransacked the warehouses, indulging in the tons of foodstuffs before burning the buildings. Rosser inexplicably did not wreck the railroad or destroy a bridge. Late in the afternoon the Southerners retraced their route, disappearing into the woodlands. Pursuing Federals never caught up to Rosser's troopers, who arrived at their camp 2 Dec. In Jan. 1865 Latham was found guilty of neglect of duty and dishonorably discharged. 2 months later, however, Latham, now a Republican congressman, had his dismissal revoked and was honorably mustered out of the service.   —JDW

Rosser's raid to Moorefield, W.Va. 29 Jan. 1864 On 28 Jan. 1864 a Confederate raiding force, composed of Brig. Gen. THOMAS L. ROSSER's cavalry brigade, Brig. Gen. EDWARD L. THOMAS' infantry brigade, and a battery of artillery, abandoned its camps near New Market, Va., angling westward toward the Allegheny Mts. Maj. Gen. JUBAL A. EARLY, commanding the Valley District, accompanied the column of raiders on a foraging and cattle-stealing operation.

Rosser's Laurel Brigade, leading the advance, entered Moorefield, W.Va., on the 29th. Early and the cavalry officer learned from scouts that a Federal wagon train was moving south toward Petersburg, W.Va. Early ordered Rosser to cross the Branch Mountain and intercept the train.

The Confederate horsemen left Moorefield the next morning. Snaking up the mountainside, they entered the gap, where a Federal infantry regiment blocked the road. Rosser rapidly charged with the 12th Virginia Cavalry, routing the Union troops, who fell back to Medley. The Southerners found the wagon train at the latter town, guarded by 4 infantry regiments and a detachment of cavalry. Rosser deployed his 400 troopers for an attack, directing the 12th to move beyond the Union flank toward its rear.

The Confederate officer hurled his 3 remaining regiments, dismounted, against the Federals. The initial charge faltered before the fire of the Northerners. Supported by an artillery piece, the Confederates renewed the attack. The 35th Battalion of Virginia Cavalry drove in a mounted charge toward the Federal front while the 2 dismounted regiments stormed the Northerners' left flank. The Federals broke under the assault, fleeing in disorder and abandoning 95 wagons loaded with supplies.

The next day Rosser and Thomas marched to Petersburg, where they found additional stores of ammunition and commissary supplies. Leaving Thomas at Petersburg, Rosser moved northward down Patterson's Creek, his troopers searching for cattle and sheep. Learning of the approach of Federal reinforcements, Rosser returned to Moorefield, rejoined Thomas, and marched eastward toward the Shenandoah Valley. At a cost of 25 casualties, the Confederates had captured 80 Federals, 95 wagons, 1,200 cattle, and 500 sheep. The jubilant members of the Laurel Brigade all reenlisted after the raid, an endorsement of Rosser's admirable performance.   —JDW

Rost, Pierre Adolph. diplomat b. France, 1797. A student at the Lycée Napoléon and the École Polytechnique in Paris, Rost fought in the unsuccessful defense of the city in 1813. He applied for a commission in the French army on Napoleon's return from Elba, but the emperor was defeated at Waterloo before it could be approved. Unwilling to remain in France, Rost emigrated to Louisiana, then settled in Natchez, Miss., where he read law with JOSEPH R. DAVIS, brother of JEFFERSON DAVIS. On passing the bar he established a practice in Natchitoches, La., and served 1 term in the state senate before relocating to New Orleans in 1828. Following a visit to Europe a decade later, he sat for 4 months on the state supreme court but resigned to manage his plantation near St. Charles. Reappointed to the bench in 1846, he retained the position for 6 years.

Rost had no political experience and was unknown outside of Louisiana when the Civil War started, but his French birth, his connection with Joseph Davis, and his acquaintance with JUDAH P. BENJAMIN induced Jefferson Davis to appoint him, along with A. DUDLEY MANN and WILLIAM L. YANCEY, commissioner to Europe in 1861. They arrived in London 29 Apr. to a cool reception from the British diplomatic office. Ineffectual in helping secure recognition for the Confederacy, Rost moved on to Paris, where he found French officials no friendlier. Further, the French disliked Rost, taking offense at his ineptitude and lack of diplomatic experience and at the illiterate use of their language by a man who had placed himself in self-imposed exile 45 years earlier. He had no grasp of the deteriorating state of Confederate affairs, and his unrealistically buoyant response of *"tout va bien"* to queries about the war's progress attracted ridicule, particularly after his own plantation was confiscated by Federal authorities.

In 1862 he was named minister to Spain, where he would be less of an embarrassment to the Confederate administration. Soon after his arrival he reported the hopelessness of receiving aid from the Spaniards, but he stayed at his post until the Confederate surrender.

Rost returned to New Orleans after the war, dying there 6 Sept. 1868.   —PLF

Rousseau, Lovell Harrison. USA b. Lincoln Cty., Ky., 4 Aug. 1818. Born near Stanford, Ky., Rousseau attended local schools before his father died of cholera. On his father's death, he dropped out of school and joined a road crew in the con-

struction of a turnpike. After concentrating on law studies in Lexington, he gained admission to the bar in Bloomfield, Ind. Turning to politics, he was elected to the Indiana legislature as a Whig in 1844.

In the Mexican War, as a captain in the 2d Indiana Infantry, he fought at the Battle of Buena Vista and was cited for gallantry in that engagement. 4 days after he returned to Indiana he was elected to the state senate but moved back to Louisville, Ky., before his term expired.

USMHI

Back in his home state he was a successful criminal lawyer, and by 1860 he had returned to politics, this time elected to the Kentucky senate. With secession threatening, he resigned and raised troops for the Union. Mustered in as colonel of the 3d Kentucky Infantry, September 1861, Rousseau attained the rank of brigadier general of volunteers 1 Oct., less than a month after he officially entered Union service.

Rousseau fought at SHILOH and performed so brilliantly at PERRYVILLE that he rose to major general 8 Oct. 1862. Though he had little experience as a horseman, Rousseau is responsible for one of the most successful Federal cavalry operations of the Civil War, covering nearly 400 mi through northern Alabama 10–22 July 1864 (*see* ROUSSEAU'S ALABAMA RAID). Besides his foray through Alabama, he participated in similar expeditions across Mississippi and western Tennessee.

Defeated for a seat in the U.S. Senate in 1865, he won election to the U.S. House of Representatives and resigned from the army shortly before traveling to Washington for the opening session 30 Nov. It was the beginning of a fiery congressional career. He entered the House as a RADICAL REPUBLICAN, but harsh talk from fellow congressmen about RECONSTRUCTION and the FREEDMEN'S BUREAU made his views less extreme. Moderate as he became, he was forced to resign his seat for losing his temper and beating Iowa Congressman Josiah Grinnell with a cane in the Capitol. Kentucky voters reinstated him, and he served until July 1866.

Rousseau then reentered the army and served in Alaska, testified in Washington at the impeachment trial of Pres. Andrew Johnson, and served his final days in Louisiana, where he died in New Orleans 7 Jan. 1869.   —FLS

Rousseau's Alabama raid. 10–22 July 1864 Maj. Gen. LOVELL H. ROUSSEAU was commanding the District of Tennessee in summer 1864 when he received orders from Maj. Gen. WILLIAM T. SHERMAN to organize a cavalry expedition to Alabama. The main target would be the Montgomery & West Point Railroad, which the raiders were to destroy, "doing all the mischief possible" on the way. By 22 July, Rousseau's raid had become one of the most successful Union cavalry operations in the Civil War.

Even though he was no horseman, Rousseau volunteered in June for the job of leading the raid, which Sherman authorized after modifying Rousseau's master plan. It would concentrate between Montgomery and Opelika, but if successful, Rousseau was ordered to meet Sherman in Georgia. The cavalrymen were to destroy the railroad by heating and bending the rails over open fires, severing "the channels of trade and travel between Georgia, Alabama, and Mississippi." Pursuing Rousseau was the DEPARTMENT OF ALABAMA, MISSISSIPPI, AND EAST LOUISIANA commander, Lt. Gen. STEPHEN D. LEE, but the Confederate never quite caught up.

Rousseau's raid cost him only 12 killed, 30 wounded, and 1 piece of artillery. The amount of wares and supplies destroyed by the raiders was impossible to calculate; however, in Opelika alone they destroyed or confiscated approximately 42,000 lb of bacon, flour, and sugar. 6 railroad freight cars filled with leather also fell into Federal hands. But in the 400 mi Rousseau covered, his major accomplishment was the destruction of the railroad. The defiant raid into the South also had a more far-reaching effect. Rousseau had shown the confused state of the Confederate command and put a scare into the people of Alabama. They were no longer safe.   —FLS

Rowan, Stephen Clegg. USN b. near Dublin, Ireland, 25 Dec. 1808, Rowan settled in Piqua, Ohio, in 1818 and was appointed a midshipman from that state in 1826. He was promoted to lieutenant in 1837 and commander in 1855. During the Mexican War, he was executive officer of the *Cyane* and commanded a battalion of sailors and marines in several shore engagements in California. When the Civil War began, Rowan commanded the *Pawnee* and helped defend Washington during ABRAHAM LINCOLN's inauguration. He participated in the attempt to relieve FORT SUMTER and in the evacuation of the Norfolk Navy Yard.

In May 1861 he commanded a naval expedition that seized ALEXANDRIA, Va., in the first amphibious assault of the war. In Aug. 1861 he participated in the expedition against HATTERAS INLET, N.C. Then, aboard the *Delaware,* he commanded a squadron that cooperated with Maj. Gen. AMBROSE E. BURNSIDE in a campaign resulting in the capture of ROANOKE ISLAND, Elizabeth City, Edenton, and NEW BERNE. These impressive victories resulted in Rowan's promotion to captain and commodore on the same day, 16 July 1862.

Commanding the *NEW IRONSIDES* of the SOUTH ATLANTIC BLOCKADING SQUADRON, Rowan saw heavy action against the forts defending Charleston. From July to Sept. 1863 the *New Ironsides* came under fire 14 times and was struck 164 times. In fall 1864, Rowan was placed on waiting orders after having commanded all naval forces in North Carolina sounds.

In 1866 he was promoted to rear admiral and to vice-admiral in 1870, when he left active command at sea for shore duty until his retirement in 1889. d. District of Columbia, 31 Mar. 1890.   —NCD

Ruffin, Edmund. writer/editor/agriculturist b. Prince George Cty., Va., 5 Jan. 1794. Sickly at birth, Ruffin surprised his family by surviving childhood and himself by living to old age. He received his education from private tutors and was an indifferent student during his 1 term at William and Mary College in 1810. When his father died that year, Ruffin inherited a rundown farm. Intent on making it profitable, he immersed himself in a study of scientific farming. His successful use of marl as a fertilizer to replenish the exhausted Virginia soil increased his own crop yields dramatically and attracted a substantial body of followers from among neighbors who had initially ridiculed him. By the 1840s Ruffin was recognized as the leading Southern agriculturist of the era.

An ambitious, stubborn man given to fits of sulking and

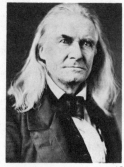

LC

depression when public appreciation of his theories did not match his expectations, Ruffin became well known for his dogmatic defense of slavery. In the prewar era, he wrote many articles spreading the gospel of SOUTHERN NATIONALISM and traveled to several Southern states to promote secession. When Virginia refused to follow South Carolina out of the Union Dec. 1860, Ruffin placed himself in voluntary exile in the Palmetto State, there joining the Palmetto Guard in anticipation of hostilities. To honor the 67-year-old zealot, the Guard permitted Ruffin to fire the FIRST SHOT on FORT SUMTER from a battery emplacement on Cummings Point on the tip of Morris Island 12 Apr. 1861.

When Virginia seceded a few days later, Ruffin returned home. He rejoined the Palmetto Guard for the FIRST BATTLE OF BULL RUN, but age kept him safely out of the fighting. The remainder of the war he spent in the Richmond area, returning with his family to "Marlbourne," his own estate near the city, after the Confederate surrender.

Ruffin expected to be arrested by Federal authorities and was disappointed when they ignored him. Despondent over the South's defeat and defiantly refusing to live under the Yankee government he bitterly hated, Ruffin retired to his room 17 June 1865, wrote a final diary entry condemning his enemies, and committed suicide.   —PLF

Ruger, Thomas Howard. USA b. Lima, N.Y., 2 Apr. 1833. The son of an Episcopal minister, at 13 Ruger moved with his family to Janesville, Wis. After a preparatory education, he entered the U.S. Military Academy, graduating 3d in the class of 1854, which produced 12 Civil War generals. Only 9 months later, he resigned from the Corps of Engineers to open a law office in his hometown.

On 29 June 1861, Ruger reentered the army as executive officer of a volunteer infantry regiment, the 3d Wisconsin. On 1 Sept. he became the outfit's colonel. By then he was serving under Maj. Gen. NATHANIEL P. BANKS in Virginia's SHENANDOAH

LC

VALLEY, where early in 1862 the Federals waged a frustrating campaign against Maj. Gen. THOMAS J. "STONEWALL" JACKSON's FOOT CAVALRY. Subsequently, Ruger suffered through Maj. Gen. JOHN POPE'S SECOND BULL RUN CAMPAIGN, serving conspicuously at CEDAR MOUNTAIN 9 Aug. 1862. 5 weeks later, at ANTIETAM, he led the 3d Brigade/1st Division/XII Corps/Army of the Potomac, taking a wound while fighting near the West Woods.

Back on his feet, he was named a brigadier general to rank from 29 Nov. At CHANCELLORSVILLE, he labored to stem the rout of the XII Corps following Jackson's flank offensive of 2 May 1863. His efforts on this field and others so impressed his immediate superior, Brig. Gen. Alpheus S. Williams, that at GETTYSBURG the latter gave his division to Ruger, who was not his senior subordinate, when moving up to corps command. On 2 July 1863, Ruger justified such faith by his judicious placement of troops along CULP'S HILL, ensuring that the next day's attack on the far Federal right would fail.

Following Gettysburg, Ruger was sent to New York City to help suppress the DRAFT RIOTS. That October his troops moved west, and in 1864 he participated in Maj. Gen. WILLIAM T. SHERMAN's Georgia campaigning as a brigade and later a division commander. Accompanying Maj. Gen. GEORGE H. THOMAS to Tennessee that fall, Ruger fought expertly at FRANKLIN and Nashville in command of a XXIII Corps division. Early in 1865 he led that division under Maj. Gen. JOHN M. SCHOFIELD in North Carolina, notably at KINSTON and during the occupation of WILMINGTON.

After the war he became colonel of the 33d and later the 18th U.S. Infantry, headed 2 RECONSTRUCTION departments, opposed Indians and railway rioters on the West Coast, was superintendent of West Point 1871–76, and retired Apr. 1897 as a major general. d. Stamford, Conn., 3 June 1907.

—EGL

Ruggles, Daniel. CSA b. Barre, Mass., 31 Jan. 1810, Ruggles married into a wealthy Virginia family and made the South his home. Graduating 34th out of 43 in the West Point class of 1833, he saw action in the Seminole and Mexican wars. For outstanding service in the latter conflict, he was brevetted lieutenant colonel.

When war broke out, Ruggles resigned his commission and joined the Confederate forces May 1861. On 9 Aug. he received a commission as brigadier general in the Confederate army and was appointed commander of the 1st Division/II Corps in Gen. ALBERT SIDNEY JOHNSTON'S ARMY OF TENNESSEE.

LC

On 4 and 5 Apr. 1862, prior to the Battle of SHILOH, Tenn., Ruggles was slow in positioning his troops for battle. The general cited conflicting orders and poor roads for the delay, much to the dismay and ire of Johnston. When the attack began 6 Apr., Ruggles' men took part in the initial assault on Maj. Gen. WILLIAM T. SHERMAN's camp. Later in the day, they attacked the "HORNETS' NEST." The general massed 62 cannon and finally smashed the position, taking 2,200 Federal prisoners in the process. The next day, Ruggles' troops help stave off Union attacks against the demoralized Confederate army. Shiloh proved to be the high point in Ruggles' military career.

After the battle, the general found himself shuffled into a series of purely administrative posts. In May 1862, he was ordered by Gen. BRAXTON BRAGG to handle the army's logistics and rear guard. In June, Ruggles was appointed commander of eastern Louisiana but was replaced within 6 months. In Aug. 1863 he was assigned to the staff of Maj. Gen. JOSEPH E. JOHNSTON. Dismayed by these assignments, the general was finally appointed head of the Confederate prison system during the last month of the war.

Ruggles returned to Fredericksburg, Va., at the end of hostilities and went into real-estate management and farming. He was appointed to the U.S. Military Academy's Board of Visitors in 1884 and died in Fredericksburg 13 years later, 1 June 1897.

—MTC

running the guard. "Running the guard" or "flanking the sentinel" meant, in the slang of Civil War soldiers, taking an unauthorized absence, or desertion. This practice of the independently minded citizens turned soldiers plagued both armies throughout the conflict. The Confederacy, with its limited manpower, suffered more than the Union. "Running the guard" generally increased significantly when Confederate regiments were stationed or campaigned closer to their homes.

—JDW

Rush's Lancers (6th Pennsylvania Cavalry). Among all mounted units, Union and Confederate, the 6th Pennsylvania Cavalry was unique both in personnel and weaponry. Composed of the social, military, and athletic elite of Philadelphia, the regiment was formed in summer 1861 by Col. Richard H. Rush, a West Pointer, the son of a prominent diplomat, and the descendant of a founding father. To complement its singular origins, the unit adopted as its primary arm a 9-ft-long lance with an 11-in., 3-edged blade, a scarlet swallow-tailed pennant attached. Not until June 1863 were these anachronistic weapons discarded as unsuited for American service and replaced by carbines.

Col. Richard H. Rush   USMHI

Rush's Lancers   USMHI

Attached to the ARMY OF THE POTOMAC for the 1862 PENIN-SULA CAMPAIGN, the 6th Pennsylvania made a successful show-ing in its first battle, Hanover Court House, pursuing and cap-turing numerous Confederate foot soldiers. In their next engagement, GAINES' MILL, however, the lancers were over-whelmed and forced to retreat through artillery units guarding Brig. Gen. FITZ JOHN PORTER's V Corps. During the balance of the campaign Rush's men redeemed themselves, serving effi-ciently as escort units, couriers, and skirmishers.

At BRANDY STATION, 9 June 1863, the regiment gave its most memorable performance. In 2 determined charges against Maj. Gen. J.E.B. STUART's cavalry it suffered dozens of casual-ties, including the wounding and capture of Maj. Robert Mor-ris, Jr., grandson and namesake of the "Financier of the Ameri-can Revolution."

In the campaigns of 1864 the unit often rendered excep-tional service: in its role in the advance of the Reserve Cavalry Brigade at Todd's Tavern, 7 May; its protection of the cavalry's center at COLD HARBOR, 1 June; and its near-suicidal stand against a Confederate brigade, 12 June, during the engagement at TREVILIAN STATION.

By war's end the erstwhile lancers had seen 24 officers and 498 men killed, wounded, or captured. They had also achieved a record befitting their elite status. Wrote Maj. Gen. PHILIP H. SHERIDAN: "No organization in either the regular or volunteer service enjoyed a more enviable reputation in every respect."

—EGL

Russell, David Allen. USA b. Salem, N.Y., 10 Dec. 1820. A career soldier, Russell graduated from West Point in 1845, 38th in a class of 45. He fought in the Mexican War and soldiered on lonely outposts in the Pacific Northwest, rising to the rank of captain by the outbreak of war.

Made colonel of the 7th Massachusetts Volunteers 31 Jan. 1862, Russell fought with his unit during the PENINSULA CAM-

PAIGN as part of Brig. Gen. DARIUS N. COUCH's division/IV Corps. Serving with distinction, he was promoted to brigadier general of volunteers 29 Nov. 1862. Commanding the 3d Brigade/1st Division/VI Corps, Russell led his troops at FRED-ERICKSBURG, where they were lightly engaged. The following year his soldiers participated in Maj. Gen. JOHN SEDGWICK's as-sault on Marye's Heights during the CHANCELLORSVILLE CAM-PAIGN, suffering heavy casual-ties.

LC

Russell next saw action 7 Nov. during an engagement at RAPPAHANNOCK STATION, where, temporarily in command of the 1st Division, he personally led a charge that crushed a Confederate bridgehead over the river. Though Russell was wounded in the melee, his troops captured more than 1,600 prisoners, ordnance, and assorted trophies. The Lincoln ad-ministration applauded this performance and Russell was placed in permanent command of the 1st Division.

During the Wilderness and PETERSBURG campaigns, at Spot-sylvania, Va., Russell had as a subordinate Col. EMORY UPTON, who tendered an idea for breaching the formidable Confeder-ate trenches. The brigadier endorsed Upton's plan and referred it to headquarters for approval. Upton's subsequent mad dash sundered the Confederate line.

While at Petersburg, Russell was part of the VI Corps's his-toric transfer to Washington, D.C., to counter Confederate Lt. Gen. Jubal A. Early's II Corps, who threatened capture of the capital (see EARLY'S WASHINGTON RAID). During this campaign, at the BATTLE OF WINCHESTER, 19 Sept. 1864, Russell was killed instantly by a piece of shrapnel. For his outstanding war record he was posthumously brevetted major general in the Regular Army, dating to 19 Sept. 1864. —MTC

Russell, William Howard. journalist b. Ireland, 28 Mar. 1820. In the first months of the Civil War, probably no individual did more to alienate North and South alike than William Howard Russell. Yet his barbed commentaries on the American conflict remain a basic source on the initial 6 months of the war.

Russell was a product of British aristocracy. He attended Trinity College, then embarked on a journalistic career as a special correspondent for the London *Times.* In the 1850s he covered wars in Denmark, the Crimea, and India. His unrestrained, penetrating dispatches brought him knighthood and a reputation as the most prominent British reporter of his day.

LC

He arrived in New York City Mar. 1861 to cover the American struggle. For 2 months the portly, graying, rather dandified Britisher traveled through the Confederacy. He infuriated Southerners with his criticisms of slave society, then returned to the North to continue his coverage. His subsequent dispatches, especially his accounts of the BATTLE OF FIRST BULL RUN, in which he bantered the Federals unmercifully, created widespread anger through the Union. Despite the fact that he was generally regarded abroad as the most authoritative commentator on the Civil War, American resentment led to his virtual expulsion from the country in spring 1862.

Thereafter, Russell continued as England's foremost battlefield reporter. He covered wars in Europe and Africa, married twice, and traveled for a time on the staff of the Prince of Wales. He spent his last years as editor of the *Army and Navy Gazette.* d. London, England, 10 Feb. 1907.

Many Americans of a century ago agreed with diarist Mary Chesnut, who dismissed Russell as "a typical English writer with three P's: Pen, Paper, and Prejudices." His extensive writings on the Union and the Confederacy are embodied in 2 volumes: *The Civil War in America* (1861) and *My Diary North and South* (1863). —JIR

Rust, Albert. CSA b. Fauquier Cty., Va., 1818. Though born in Virginia, about 1837 Rust settled in Union Cty., Ark. Within 5 years, he studied law, was admitted to the bar, and in 1842 was elected to the state legislature. He held his seat for 6 years, then again 1852–54. In the latter year he was elected to the U.S. House of Representatives. Defeated for reelection in 1856, he returned to Congress in 1858, serving until he resigned 3 Mar. 1861.

Rust entered Confederate service 5 July 1861 with a commission of colonel of the 3d Arkansas, a regiment he had recruited. His initial duty was in western Virginia, where he participated in the Battle of CHEAT MOUNTAIN under Gen. ROBERT E. LEE. He remained in Virginia during winter 1862 and, 4 Mar. 1862, was appointed brigadier general. Transferring to the West, Rust fought at CORINTH, Miss., in October. The fol-

lowing spring, Apr. 1863, he reported to Maj. Gen. STERLING PRICE in the TRANS-MISSISSIPPI DEPARTMENT.

For the next 2 years Rust served successively under Maj. Gens. THOMAS C. HINDMAN and JOHN C. PEMBERTON and Lt. Gen. RICHARD TAYLOR. His assignments carried him from Arkansas to Louisiana, where he was serving when the war concluded.

The conflict ruined Rust financially. He settled on a farm

LC

on the Arkansas River near Little Rock, dying at his home 4 Apr. 1870. —JDW

Ryan, Abram Joseph. poet b. Hagerstown, Md., 5 Feb. 1838. The son of Irish immigrants who moved from Maryland to St. Louis, Mo., during his childhood, Ryan was educated at the Christian Brothers Cathedral in St. Louis and at Niagara University, operated by the Vincentian Fathers at Niagara Falls, N.Y. He took his final vows for the priesthood at the Vincentian seminary in Philadelphia in 1856 and was ordained 4 years later.

An avid proponent of Southern nationhood, Ryan temporarily abandoned his teaching career to join the Confederate army 1 Sept. 1862. Unable to secure a commission, he attached himself to the service as a free-lance chaplain, and worked gallantly on the battlefields removing the wounded and administering to the dying.

The death of a younger brother in the Confederate ranks moved Ryan to write 2 poems, "In Memory of My Brother" and "In Memoriam," but he wrote the verse resulting in his recognition as the "Poet-Priest of the Confederacy" after the war had ended. The intensely spiritual poem "The Conquered Banner" first appeared in the *Freeman's Journal* (N.Y.), 19 May 1866, and was soon being sung throughout the South to the tune of a hymn. This he followed with "The Sword of Robert E. Lee" and a series of emotionally patriotic verses popular from Virginia to Texas. For many years Southern schoolchildren recited Ryan's lyrical eulogies to the Confederacy as a routine part of their lessons.

Ryan claimed to compose his poems on impulse and purely from deep-seated reverence for the LOST CAUSE. UNRECONSTRUCTED until his resistance was softened in 1878 by Northern relief workers who donated money, labor, and supplies to the South during a severe outbreak of cholera, he wrote his poem of forgiveness, "Reunited," to acknowledge the passing of sectional bitterness. A collection of Ryan's Confederate verse, *Father Ryan's Poems,* was published in 1879.

Ryan filled pastorates and teaching positions in several Southern cities through the postwar years and edited 3 publications: the *Pacificator, The Banner of the South,* and *The Star,* the last a Catholic weekly issued in New Orleans. Popular on the lecture circuit, he often donated the proceeds from his tours to be used for the relief of Southern widows and orphans. d. at the Franciscan monastery in Louisville, Ky., 22 Apr. 1886. —PLF

S

saber. A sword with a curved blade, the saber was used extensively during the Civil War at the same time that developing tactics were making it obsolete. Most sabers were cavalry weapons, although the U.S. Model 1840 light artillery saber or Confederate copies of it did see some service. In general, however, the most widely used sabers were the U.S. 1840 cavalry model and the 1860 light cavalry model, which was slightly lighter and shorter. Both had 3-branch brass guards and long curved blades and were carried in steel scabbards; the Confederates copied both models extensively. Some French and English cavalry sabers also saw service during the war.

At the beginning of the war, the saber was considered the standard arm for cavalry. In line with the concepts of battle TACTICS developed during the 18th century and the Napoleonic Wars, most commanders considered cavalry to be useful mainly for scouting missions or for pursuing a fleeing enemy after the infantry had broken their lines. In such a situation the cavalry was expected to move in and cut down the fugitives with their sabers. Also anticipated were cavalry charges met by enemy cavalry in which massive saber duels would occur. The pistol and carbine were considered secondary weapons. While a few situations like those expected did occur, including the classic cavalry battles at BRANDY STATION and GETTYSBURG, in time it was found that firepower was a more important factor in combat than the shock of a saber charge.

As cavalry began more and more to fight dismounted as skirmishers and to be armed with repeating weapons like the Spencer, many units began to consider the saber a useless encumbrance. Many Confederates placed their faith in pistols, carbines, and shotguns, and either discarded their sabers altogether or strapped them to their saddles. Still, the possibility that a classic cavalry encounter might occur caused most troops to retain the saber, despite its disadvantages, until the end of the war. —LDJ

Sabine Cross Roads, La., Battle of. 8 Apr. 1864 *See* MANSFIELD, LA., BATTLE OF.

Sabine Pass, Tex., Battle of. 8 Sept. 1863 Pres. JEFFERSON DAVIS called the Battle of Sabine Pass the ''Thermopylae of the Civil War,'' but to Lt. RICHARD W. DOWLING, a young Houston, Tex., saloonkeeper, the battle was a defense of his pride.

Dowling, an artillerist commanding 43 of the Texan Davis Guards, was charged with the defense of small Fort Griffin at Sabine Pass, Tex., near the mouth of the Sabine River. Dowling and the rowdy Guards had had checkered military careers until posted in shame to quiet Griffin, which they helped construct. To stay out of trouble, between daily work periods on the fort they practiced with their 6 artillery pieces, firing at range markers placed in the river.

On 8 Sept. 1863, Union Maj. Gen. NATHANIEL P. BANKS decided to launch his invasion of southern Texas by having the Federal gunboats *Clifton, Sachem, Granite City,* and *Arizona* and 7 troop transports cross the bar from the Gulf of Mexico, move up the Sabine, reduce Griffin, and make a landing. But the previous evening Dowling had been warned of the invasion by observing Union signal lights and was prepared for attack. As the Federal gunboats moved up the shallow channel, circumnavigating a mid-river reef, they passed long white poles rising from the river bottom. Those poles were the Guards' range markers. With just their 6 cannon and the poles for guides, Dowling and the now expert Guards disabled or repelled all Union craft in front of them and stalled Banks's Texas invasion by a month. On the afternoon of the 8th, Dowling accepted the *Clifton*'s surrender and took charge of more than 400 Federal prisoners.

For all these feats Dowling and the Guards were praised and each was awarded the only official Southern medal for valor, the DAVIS GUARD MEDAL. —JES

Safford, Mary Jane. nurse b. Hyde Park, Vt., 1831, Safford lived in Crete, Ill., from age 3. In 1849, following her parents' death, family members secured her education at an academy in Bakersfield, Vt., then allowed her to travel in Canada to learn French and act as governess to a German-speaking family to acquire skill in German. Unmarried, she took up residence with her elder brother Alfred Safford, a Joliet, Ill., businessman, then moved with him to Shawneetown, and in 1858 to Cairo, Ill. Safford's exact birthdate is unknown, but she is thought to have been 29 at the outbreak of the Civil War.

On the arrival of nurse MARY ANN ''Mother'' BICKERDYKE in Cairo in summer 1861, Safford volunteered to work with her as a nursing aide, showed talent, and was pressed into full-time nursing. With Bickerdyke, she cared for troops succumbing to camp diseases and the large numbers of wounded from the Battles of BELMONT and FORT DONELSON. Though based at the large field hospital in Cairo, she often left the facilities to care for the sick in surrounding camps, and is remembered for walking the Belmont battlefield under her own flag of truce searching out the wounded. After the Battle of Fort Donelson, Bickerdyke recalled that Safford worked 10 days in the Cairo hospital with little sleep, neared collapse, then accepted nursing duties aboard the transport boat *City of Memphis.* These exertions forced her to retire to her brother's home in poor health.

Safford returned to nursing for the Battle of SHILOH, working aboard the transport boat *Hazel Dell* and with Bickerdyke in Savannah, Tenn., field hospitals. An attractive, polished, compassionate woman, she impressed her patients aboard the *Hazel Dell* and won the sobriquet ''Angel of Cairo.'' However, overworked and weak, she suffered a breakdown after caring for the Shiloh wounded, was confined to bed for several months, then, at her brother's urging, accompanied the family of former Illinois governor Joel Matteson on a lengthy European tour to recuperate. She did not return to the U.S. until autumn 1866.

Interested in resuming medical work, Safford entered the New York Medical College for Women in 1867; graduated in 1869; studied surgery at the General Hospital of Vienna, Austria, through 1871; continued studies at the University of Breslau, Germany, for several months, performing there the first ovariotomy ever done by a woman; returned to the U.S. late in 1872; and in 1873 opened a private practice in Chicago. In 1872 she married James Blake. When the marriage proved unworkable, Safford joined the Boston University School of Medicine faculty, divorced Blake in 1880, then retired from the school in poor health in 1886. She took up residence in Tarpon Springs, Fla., where she died in 1891.   —JES

St. Albans, Vt., raid on.

19 Oct. 1864 The northernmost engagement of the Civil War was fought far from the usual battlefields, in the little Vermont town of St. Albans near the Canadian border.

Hoping to divert Union soldiers from Southern fronts, the Confederate government authorized a daring young Kentuckian, Bennett H. Young, to recruit for the raid a band of prisoners who had escaped to Canada. Young and 20 fellow raiders, posing as vacationers and hunters, converged on St. Albans over a period of several days. Just before 3 p.m., 19 Oct., while some of the Confederates began herding citizens onto the town common and taking their horses, others burst into the 3 local banks and began scooping up cash, securing a total of $20,000. Several of the townspeople resisted; while 2 of these were wounded, the only fatality was a Southern sympathizer who stepped into the line of fire.

As word of the raid spread, local workmen and 2 Federal soldiers on leave organized a posse, and the raiders hurriedly rode out of town to reach the Canadian border just after dark. There Young split his men into small groups. The posse overtook a few only to have them taken over by Canadian authorities, who ultimately arrested the others. Ignoring Federal requests for extradition, Canadian courts ruled that Young and his men were soldiers under military orders and released them on bond as internees.

The raid attracted much attention, but no Union soldiers were diverted to guard border towns. If anything, the will of the Northern public was made stronger.   —RHF

St. John, Isaac Munroe.

CSA b. Augusta, Ga., 19 Nov. 1827. Raised in New York City, St. John graduated from Yale in 1845. After a brief interest in law, he became assistant editor of the Baltimore *Patriot*. In 1848 he turned to the profession for which he was best suited, civil engineering, and for the next 7 years worked on the engineering staff of the BALTIMORE & OHIO RAILROAD. In 1855 he moved to Georgia and later to South Carolina as chief of construction for the Blue Ridge Railroad.

When the Civil War began, St. John enlisted in the South Carolina militia, and his engineering abilities soon brought him to Richmond. As a civilian he became chief engineer for Maj. Gen. John B. Magruder's army on the peninsula. In Feb. 1862 he was appointed a captain of engineers. Advancing to major

later that year, he reported to Col. JOSIAH GORGAS and was assigned to the Niter and Mining Corps in Richmond. Blockaded on all sides, the Confederacy, short of gunpowder and metals, was desperate for these materials. St. John soon efficiently organized the vital supply operations that provided them. His success was recognized by promotion to lieutenant colonel, then to colonel in 1863.

USMHI

As the circumstances of the Confederate armies worsened, it became evident that the ailing commissary general, Col. LUCIUS B. NORTHROP, would have to be relieved. St. John was the obvious choice, and he accepted this difficult assignment 16 Feb. 1865 with the rank of brigadier general.

St. John accompanied Pres. Jefferson Davis and other Confederate officials when Richmond was evacuated 2 Apr. 1865. He surrendered at Thomasville, Ga., 23 May and returned to Richmond, where he took the amnesty oath 18 June.

After the war, St. John resumed his civil-engineering work. From 1866 to 1869 he was chief engineer for the Louisville, Cincinnati, & Lexington Railroad. He then served as city engineer in Louisville. At the time of his death, 7 Apr. 1880 at "Greenbriar," White Sulphur Springs, W. Va., he was in charge of the mining and engineering department of the Chesapeake & Ohio Railroad. He was buried in Hollywood Cemetery, Richmond.   —JOH

St. Louis, USS.

The USS *St. Louis* was one of 7 IRONCLADS called "POOK TURTLES" after their designer, Samuel M. Pook. Built for the War Department by James B. Eads at Carondelet, Mo., and launched 12 Oct. 1861, the *St. Louis* was a flat-bottom light-draft stern-wheeler measuring 175 ft in length and 51 ft 2 in. in beam, and carrying a complement of 251 officers and men. Its battery consisted of 4 42-pounders and 7 32-pounders.

For approximately a year, 12 Oct. 1861–1 Oct. 1862, the *St. Louis* was a unit of the Western Gunboat Fleet, under the control of the Union army, though commanded by a naval officer, Lt. L. Paulding. It participated in the attacks on FORTS HENRY AND DONELSON Feb. 1862 and April–June operated against Fort Pillow, Tenn. During the Fort Pillow campaigning the ship successfully rammed and sank a Confederate vessel. In June the ironclad also fought in the naval engagement off Memphis, Tenn., that resulted in the destruction of the CONFEDERATE RIVER DEFENSE FLEET. Shortly afterward it engaged Confederate batteries in a sortie up the White River in Arkansas.

In Sept. 1862 the *St. Louis* was renamed the *Baron De Kalb,* and a month later it and all other Union river gunboats were transferred to the Navy Department. Under the flag of Rear Adm. DAVID D. PORTER the ironclad continued to be heavily involved in combat on the Western rivers.

From 21 to 28 Dec. it took part in the Yazoo River Expedition, followed Jan. 1863 by the combined operation that led to the capture of ARKANSAS POST. Throughout winter and spring 1863 it participated in a number of expeditions and actions that centered on Brig. Gen. U. S. Grant's efforts to take Vicksburg, Miss.

On 13 July 1863, 9 days after Vicksburg surrendered, the *Baron De Kalb,* along with 3 other vessels, ascended the Yazoo River to locate and destroy a reported Confederate battery. While maneuvering into position approximately 20 mi from the river's mouth, it was sunk by 2 torpedoes.

—WNS

Salem Church (Salem Heights), Va., Battle of. 3 May 1863 As Lt. Gen. Thomas J. "Stonewall" Jackson's men renewed the attack at Chancellorsville 3 May, Brig. Gen. JOHN SEDGWICK's Federals pushed across the Rappahannock at Fredericksburg and seized the old Confederate works at the Sunken Road and along Marye's Heights. The Northern troops then rapidly moved westward to reinforce Maj. Gen. JOSEPH HOOKER. 6 mi east of Chancellorsville the Federals came to a low ridgeline on which stood Salem Church, a Baptist sanctuary dating from 1844. Confederates under Maj. Gen. LAFAYETTE MCLAWS were posted along the ridge, which provided a commanding view of the surrounding countryside.

2 heavy Federal divisions under Brig. Gen. WILLIAM T. H. BROOKS and Maj. Gen. JOHN NEWTON surged forward, only to run into volleys of concentrated musketry from the high ground. Federal artillery pounded the Confederate position as the Northerners struggled through underbrush to within a few yards of the ridge. Then a Southern counterattack from front and rear sent them reeling back down onto the plain. Darkness prevented Gen. Robert E. Lee's men from driving Sedgwick completely from the field, but Hooker made no attempt to come to Sedgwick's aid. The next day, when Confederates sought to renew the struggle, they discovered that the Federals had fallen back across the river.

Salem Church cost the Federals 4,700 casualties and did little more than divert Lee's attention from Hooker for 36 hours. The church building became a field hospital for the human debris of the battle. In the words of one eyewitness, "the floors, the benches, even the chancel and pulpit were all packed almost to suffocation" with wounded and dying soldiers.

In Apr. 1865 Maj. Gen. William T. Sherman's victorious army passed through the area en route to Washington. When the general beheld many dead soldiers still improperly buried at Salem Church, he filed a strong protest to Federal authorities. The result was the establishment of the Fredericksburg National Cemetery.

—JIR

salient. A salient is an area of a defensive line or fortification that protrudes beyond the main works. In the Civil War, it extended closest to an enemy's position and usually invited an attack. Generals erected salients primarily to cover dominating ground beyond their entrenchments. The most famous salient of the Civil War was the "MULE SHOE" at SPOTSYLVANIA, Va., which was the scene of savage combat 12 May 1864.

—JDW

Salisbury, N.C., eng. at. 12 Apr. 1865 By Mar. 1865, the Confederacy was dying but Union forces in the West sought to speed up the process. Their efforts included a raid east from Morristown, Tenn., by Maj. Gen. GEORGE STONEMAN, begun on the 23d. Backed by the 6,000-man cavalry division of Brig. Gen. ALVAN C. GILLEM, Stoneman intended to sever strategic portions of the nearby VIRGINIA & TENNESSEE RAILROAD and, in western North Carolina, the Piedmont and North Carolina railroads. His raiders were to return home through Salisbury, after liberating the thousands of Federal prisoners held there.

Stoneman and his 3 veteran brigades did much damage to their objectives during the first 2 weeks of the expedition, while also capturing North Carolina towns including Boone, Patterson, Danbury, Salem, and Mocksville. Then, 12 Apr., the invaders descended on Salisbury, whose military importance included not only its prison camp but also its many warehouses, bulging with supplies sent there to evade the advance of Maj. Gen. WILLIAM T. SHERMAN's troops. Stoneman found the place defended by fewer than 800 Confederates under Brig. Gen. WILLIAM M. GARDNER. Available as an unofficial adviser to the latter was former lieutenant general JOHN C. PEMBERTON, now—almost 2 years after his surrender at VICKSBURG—doing duty as an ordnance inspector, with the rank of colonel.

Reaching Grant's Creek, just north of Salisbury, Stoneman and Gillem found their advance halted by an unplanked bridge, several cannon, and formidable-looking works along the road into town. Making a frontal demonstration with his 12th Kentucky Cavalry, Gillem sent detachments of the 11th Kentucky and 13th Tennessee to gain the Confederate rear by way of fords above and below the span. When the detachments struck, the enemy flanks collapsed; soon afterward, the 8th Tennessee captured much of Gardner's artillery in a dashing saber charge. The bulk of Col. John K. Miller's brigade then rushed forward, crossing a bridge on planks that his troopers had replaced under fire, and routing Gardner, Pemberton, and most of their troops.

Entering Salisbury without further difficulty, Stoneman enforced strict prohibitions against looting. He did, however, raze the empty prison, whose inmates had been removed shortly before the raiders' arrival, and his men torched millions of dollars' worth of military stores and public property. Moving out of town on the next day, Stoneman left behind, in the words of one resident, "a destruction that promised a future resultant poverty, bitter indeed. . . ."

—EGL

Salisbury Prison. On 2 Nov. 1861, the Confederate government purchased an abandoned cotton factory in Salisbury, N.C., for use as a prison to confine Confederate soldiers under sentence of court-martial, deserters, disloyal citizens, suspected spies, and prisoners of war. The first Union prisoners arrived in mid-December; by Mar. 1862 Salisbury housed 1,500. Until the end of 1863, conditions at the prison were favorable. In Mar. 1862, only 1 inmate died. Food was plentiful, quarters were roomy, and the weather pleasant; the prisoners enjoyed various sports, particularly baseball.

Early in 1864 the prison's capacity of 2,000 was reached, but prisoners continued to arrive until, Oct. 1864, there were more than 10,000. Many old tents had been raised on the 11 acres of the prison grounds, but still there were inmates without shelter; a number burrowed into the earth and others built mud huts. The hospital was small and poorly equipped, and hundreds of prisoners died in whatever quarters they occupied. Sanitary conditions were wretched. There was a shortage of clothing, and food became scarcer, until inmates were eagerly eating the acorns from the oaks in the yard to supplement the daily ration of soup and 20 oz of bread—the same ration issued to the guards.

To make matters worse, desperate men among the prisoners robbed and even murdered to get a bit of food or bunk straw.

NA

The guards, boys under 17 and men too old for army service, could not maintain order. From Oct. 1864 through Feb. 1865, 3,419 prisoners died. Since there was no lumber for coffins, they were buried nearby in an abandoned field in long pits. In March all the prisoners able to travel were sent to Wilmington to be exchanged. Since there was not transportation for all, thousands started to march, and many were left along the way, sick or dead.

When Salisbury was captured by Maj. Gen. George Stoneman, Apr. 1865, he gave the men of the 12th Ohio the "grateful duty" of burning the prison.   —PR

Salm-Salm, Agnes Elisabeth Winona Leclerq Joy, Princess. nurse b. Franklin Cty., Vt., or Philipsburg, Quebec, Canada, 25 Dec. 1840. Though the place of Agnes Joy's birth is uncertain, she was reared and educated in Philipsburg. She arrived in Washington, D.C., in 1861, attracted by the excitement and drama of war and 20 Aug. 1862 married FELIX CONSTANTIN ALEXANDER JOHANN NEPOMUK, PRINCE SALM-SALM, a German soldier of fortune on Brig. Gen. LOUIS BLENKER's staff. An ambitious, attractive woman, she lobbied to secure a better command for her husband and succeeded in getting him a colonelcy first of the 8th and later of the 68th New York Infantry. During the war Princess Salm-Salm lived in the field with her husband, working industriously as a nurse and with the various organizations involved in soldiers' relief. Her high-

spiritedness was legendary throughout the Army of the Potomac and she became a favorite both of officers and enlisted men.

After the Confederate surrender Prince Salm-Salm was employed by Mexican Emperor Maximilian as his aide-de-camp. When the government fell to Benito Juárez, and her husband and the emperor were condemned to death, the princess schemed to raise money and recruit accomplices to free the prince and smuggle Maximilian out of the country. Her attempts failed and in desperation she pleaded directly to Juárez for their lives; many accounts say she fell to the floor and threw her arms around his knees in a great dramatic scene that frequently has been re-created in novels and reenacted in the theater. Salm-Salm was released. Maximilian was not, but before he faced the firing squad he presented the princess with the Grand Cordon of the Order of San Carlos in appreciation of her efforts.

The Salm-Salms went from Mexico to Europe, where the prince was killed in the Franco-Prussian War and the princess won a Prussian Medal of Honor for her relief work among the soldiers. She remarried in 1876, that year in London publishing *Ten Years of My Life,* which deals in part with her American Civil War career. Twice in 1899–1900, during the South African War, she visited the U. S. to raise funds to improve the Boer ambulance corps. d. Karlsruhe, Germany, 21 Dec. 1912.
—PLF

Salm-Salm, Felix Constantin Alexander Johann Nepomuk, Prince.

USA b. Anhalt, Prussia, 25 Dec. 1828. Salm-Salm attended the Cadet School in Berlin and was commissioned into the Prussian cavalry. He saw action during the Schleswig-Holstein War of 1848 and at Aarhuis, was wounded 7 times and taken prisoner. For his bravery, future Kaiser Wilhelm I awarded the prince a sword of honor.

LC

In 1861 the Prussian tendered his services to the Union cause. Salm-Salm could not speak English, but did possess testimonials from the crown prince of Prussia and Prussia's minister to Washington, D.C. The prince obtained an audience with Abraham Lincoln, who liked the young man and appointed him colonel and chief of staff to Brig. Gen. LOUIS BLENKER, commander of the 1st Brigade/5th Division/Army of the Potomac. Salm-Salm was appointed colonel, 8th New York Infantry, 21 Oct. 1862. The regiment saw little service and was disbanded Apr. 1863. On 8 June 1864, the Prussian was placed in command of the 68th New York Infantry and sent to the Western theater. There his unit was attached to the command of Maj. Gen. JAMES B. STEEDMAN. Salm-Salm saw action fighting guerrillas in Tennessee and took part in the Battle of NASHVILLE Dec. 1864. For his part in the conflict, he was brevetted a brigadier general of volunteers 13 Apr. 1865. At war's end, he was appointed military governor of Atlanta, Ga.

Throughout Salm-Salm's career he was abetted by his pretty and ambitious wife, AGNES, who accompanied her husband in the field and wangled important commissions and assignments for him. When the war ended, Salm-Salm went to Mexico to serve as aide-de-camp to Emperor Maximilian. He was captured by Juarista forces in 1866 and condemned to death. Agnes made many personal appeals to President Juárez, and Salm-Salm was spared the firing squad. The prince returned to Germany and enlisted in the Grenadier Guards. He was killed during the Franco-Prussian War at the battle for Gravelotte, 18 Aug. 1870.

—MTC

Salomon, Edwards.

war governor b. Stroebeck, Prussia, 11 Aug. 1828. Growing up in urban Prussia, Salomon received degrees in natural history and philosophy from the University of Berlin in 1849. That same year, he immigrated to America and settled in Wisconsin, where he taught school and entered politics. Passing the bar in 1855, he set up a lucrative practice within the German community.

Formally a Democrat, Salomon supported Abraham Lincoln in the 1860 elections. A year later, at the Wisconsin Republican convention, LOUIS P. HARVEY was nominated for the governorship and Salomon as lieutenant governor; they were elected Jan. 1862. 4 months later, Harvey traveled with a relief expedition he had organized to aid Wisconsin troops wounded at Shiloh. On his way there, 19 Apr., he lost his footing while transferring from one boat to another, fell into the Tennessee River, and drowned.

The draft proved to be the new governor's biggest problem. Lincoln's call for troops June 1862 was met with disfavor in

LC

Wisconsin, particularly among immigrants, many of whom resented intensely Yankee exploitation and felt less strongly about abolition. Feelings ran so high that resisters attacked homes of Federal officials and wealthy Republicans. Salomon responded quickly, issuing a proclamation declaring that the draft would be enforced at any cost and arresting 100 protesters.

Salomon sought reelection in 1863, but his problems with the draft and an abrasive personality had soured Republican committeemen, who instead ran wealthy lawyer James Taylor Lewis on the Union ticket. Turned out of office, Salomon continued his humanitarian work with Wisconsin troops serving in the armies. He stumped for Lincoln in the 1864 presidential campaign and ran unsuccessfully for the U.S. Senate 5 years later. After this defeat, he moved to New York City to start a law practice within the German community there. Failing in his bid for a seat on the New York supreme court in 1882, he returned to Germany, dying in Frankfurt am Main 21 Apr. 1909.

—MTC

salt beef.

A standard ration in field operations, pickled beef, called "salt beef" or "salt horse," was beef preserved in brine. The daily ration for Union forces was 1 lb 4 oz per man.

—JES

Saltville, Va., massacre at.

2 Oct. 1864   One of the most brutal acts of the Civil War occurred at Saltville, a village isolated in the mountains of Virginia's southwestern peninsula and lying alongside the VIRGINIA & TENNESSEE RAILROAD, a major link between the Eastern and Western military theaters. The hamlet was named for the vital substance it produced for the Confederacy; without salt, beef could not be preserved for army rations.

Late in the war Federal Brig. Gen. STEPHEN G. BURBRIDGE launched a raid with the capture of Saltville as its major objective. Included in the Federal force were 400 black soldiers of the 5th U.S. Colored Cavalry. At mid-morning, 2 Oct. 1864, Burbridge's 3,600 men attacked a hodgepodge Confederate army of 2,800 troops who had hastily prepared stone and log barricades at Saltville. The Southern command included a company of bushwhackers under Capt. Champ Ferguson and rowdies in the small brigade of Brig. Gen. FELIX H. ROBERTSON. Repeated Federal attacks failed. At sundown, with 350 Union casualties sprawled on the ground, Burbridge pulled his men from the field.

The next morning, Confederates advanced cautiously over the battleground. Shooting began as men under Ferguson and Robertson moved among the wounded, killing helpless blacks. The exact number of Federal soldiers thus murdered is unknown, yet from accounts by men on both sides the figure unquestionably was in excess of 100.

The Federals occupied and destroyed much of Saltville 2 months later. Ferguson was eventually captured, arraigned on charges of murder, and, 20 Oct. 1865, hanged. Robertson not only escaped punishment but lived until 20 Apr. 1928 and was at the time of his death the last surviving Confederate general.

—JIR

Sand Creek Massacre, Colorado Territory. 29 Nov. 1864 Early in Sept. 1864 Maj. Edward W. Wynkoop arranged a peace meeting between Gov. John Evans of Colorado Territory and several chiefs from the Arapaho and Cheyenne tribes, whose warriors had been harassing whites. When he received word of Wynkoop's plans, commanding general SAMUEL R. CURTIS sent word that no peace could be made until he approved the terms and until the Indians first were punished for their depredations.

While the Indians waited for negotiations to begin, they camped at Sand Creek, 40 mi northeast of Fort Lyon, believing they were safe, having complied with the white man's demands to lay down arms. Against the advice of military officers and civilians, Col. JOHN M. CHIVINGTON, commanding the District of Colorado under Curtis, led the 950 100-day men of the 3d Colorado Cavalry, the 1st Colorado with its 2 howitzers, and a detachment of the 1st New Mexico Infantry in reprisal against the Indians. The men of the 3d had been recruited to put down the outbreak of hostilities that had begun after the Regular Army was transferred east in 1861. With their enlistments about to expire, they were eager for revenge.

At sunrise on the morning of 29 Nov., Chivington's troops reached the Indian village. To prevent escape, they seized the Indians' ponies and unlimbered the howitzers, training them on the still-sleeping Cheyenne and Arapaho. Soldiers attacked the village from 3 sides. When he saw the troops approaching, Black Kettle, chief of the Cheyenne, raised the U.S. flag over his lodge as a gesture of peace. Chivington also ignored the pleas of interpreter John Smith to break off the attack, and his men began shooting indiscriminately, following his orders to take no prisoners.

Some of the warriors seized their weapons and formed a battle line one-half mile above the camp at Sand Creek, but their defense collapsed before overwhelming odds. The Indians contested the soldiers' pursuit for 5 mi before dispersing into the countryside.

Estimates of the number of Indians at the encampment range between 500 and 1000; 400 to 600 were killed, many of them women and children whose bodies had been mutilated. 8 to 10 soldiers died in the fighting, and 40 others lay wounded when the butchery finally ended.

Public reaction to the brutal massacre ranged from approval to condemnation, but many blamed Chivington for having committed an unpardonable act of violence that resulted in a renewed outburst of hostilities. In 1865 Sen. James R. Doolittle headed a congressional committee investigating the massacre. The proceedings ended in a denunciation of Chivington, ruining his military career. The Indians were not checked until the Confederate surrender freed Regular Army troops to return to duty on the frontier.

—PLF

Sanders, John Caldwell Calhoun. CSA b. Tuscaloosa, Ala., 4 Apr. 1840. At age 18, Sanders entered the University of Alabama, where he studied until early 1861, when his state seceded. Enlisting in the 11th Alabama, he was soon elected captain of a company.

The 11th saw no action during the first year of war, receiving its baptism in combat at SEVEN PINES 31 May–1 June 1862. During the SEVEN DAYS' CAMPAIGN, Sanders fell severely

wounded at White Oak Swamp 30 June. He returned to duty 11 Aug., assuming command of the regiment. He led his Alabamians at ANTIETAM and was formally promoted to colonel after the battle. At FREDERICKSBURG, in December, Sanders again commanded his unit with skill and bravery.

Throughout the Army of Northern Virginia's campaigns in 1863 and 1864, he continued to perform conspicuously, fighting with gallantry at CHANCELLORSVILLE and at GETTYSBURG, where he was wounded in the knee. While recovering, he served as president of the division court-martial. Sanders returned to regimental command in spring 1864, leading his veterans in the WILDERNESS and at SPOTSYLVANIA. In the latter battle, he temporarily assumed command of Brig. Gen. Abner M. Perrin's brigade when that officer was killed during the Federal assault on the "MULE SHOE." His performance earned him his commission of brigadier general, to date from May 31.

During the PETERSBURG CAMPAIGN, Sanders commanded Brig. Gen. Cadmus M. Wilcox's veteran brigade of Alabama regiments, leading them brilliantly 30 July in the Confederate counterattack in the Battle of the CRATER. On 21 Aug., while engaged along the Weldon Railroad, Sanders was mortally wounded. A minié bullet passed through his thighs, severing both femoral arteries, and he bled to death in a few minutes. He was buried with other fallen Confederates in an unmarked grave in Hollywood Cemetery, Richmond.

—JDW

Sands, Benjamin Franklin. USN b. Baltimore, Md., 11 Feb. 1812, Sands was appointed a midshipman 1 Apr. 1828, and was promoted to passed midshipman in 1834, to lieutenant in 1840, and to commander in 1855. He demonstrated a special aptitude for naval surveying and hydrography, and among his inventions was a device for deep-sea sounding. From 1850 to 1861 he served as head of the Navy's Bureau of Construction.

Following the secession of Virginia, Sands participated in the expedition sent by Navy Sec. GIDEON WELLES to reinforce the Norfolk Navy Yard. When the decision was made to evacuate the yard, he supervised the hasty attempt to destroy vessels and buildings. Sands's next assignment was far from the war, as he performed coast survey duty along the Pacific Coast of the U.S. Promotion to captain came July 1862. Sands then became ranking officer on the BLOCKADE of the North Carolina coast, from Wilmington to the Cape Fear River. His command ship was the *Dacotah* and, later, the *Fort Jackson*. An active and resourceful commander, he originated the practice of using an additional outer line of blockaders. The vessels under his command accounted for the capture of more than 50 BLOCKADE RUNNERS.

Sands took an active part in the naval attack on FORT FISHER, Dec. 1864 and Jan. 1865. After the fort's capture, he commanded a division of the West Gulf Squadron and was off Galveston aboard the *Fort Jackson* to receive the surrender of the city 2 June 1865.

Sands was promoted to rear admiral in 1871. From 1867 to

1874 he was head of the Naval Observatory, despite his official retirement in 1871. d. District of Columbia, 30 June 1883.
—NCD

Sanitary Commission, United States. The U.S. Sanitary Commission was organized by civilians June 1861 to assist the army, specifically to provide care for sick and wounded soldiers and to protect their dependent families. Dr. Henry W. Bellows, pastor of All Souls Unitarian Church in New York City and president of the Sanitary Commission, said the organization would attempt to do those things to improve life for soldiers that the government felt unable to do. After developing an enormous operational structure that at times employed 500 agents, the commission became involved in aid that ranged from field ambulance, nursing, and hospital service to the care and protection of discharged soldiers (which included helping solve problems with pension claims and collecting more than $2.5 million in soldiers' wages).

The mark of the organization's determined "inquiry, advice and supply" efforts could be seen everywhere, from the bat-tlefields to the lodges established near railway stations to give soldiers temporary shelter. The commission supplied more than 1 million nights' lodgings during the war. It not only maintained convalescent camps offering soldiers' special diets and attention but also furnished paper and stamps, had letters written for the men, and telegraphed relatives of the very sick.

The commission's members, among them some of the country's best-known doctors and most prominent business, government, and civic leaders, served without pay. Hired workers —field inspectors, nurses, cooks, teamsters—received small salaries. With its central office in Washington, D.C., the commission formed more than 7,000 aid societies and had main branches in 10 of the North's largest cities. From the branches, whatever soldiers needed—medicine, clothing, food, personal items—was transported to them, usually by Sanitary Commission wagons. All this was financed by donations and by SANITARY FAIRS; those in New York and Philadelphia realized more than $1 million each. During the war the commission and its branches raised and spent more than $7 million and distributed donated supplies valued at $15 million.   —PR

LC

sanitary fairs. The first sanitary fair was held in Chicago, 27 Oct.–7 Nov. 1863, to replenish the treasury of the Northwestern branch of the U.S. SANITARY COMMISSION. Lavish, popular, and profitable, the Chicago fair, organized by MARY A. LIVERMORE and JANE HOGE, set the tone for those that followed. Schools, businesses, and courts closed for opening day. Spectators lined the streets to watch the parade, then crowded into the fairgrounds buildings to see exhibits, dine, be entertained, and purchase donated merchandise ranging from turnips to handmade lace and homemade preserves to farm machinery. The auction of Pres. Abraham Lincoln's contribution, the original draft of the Emancipation Proclamation, generated more excitement than other activities. T. B. Bryan purchased the document for $3,000, then donated it to the Chicago Soldiers'

Home. The organizers reported a net profit of $75,682.89, with the total income reaching nearly $100,000 a few months later, after leftover goods had been sold.

From Chicago, the sanitary fairs spread east, every larger city in the North and many smaller communities staging their own shows during 1864. Usually an important military personality was named president of the fair, and attendees were invited to participate in "sword-voting" contests to elect at $1 per vote their favorite hero as general-in-chief of the Federal armies. Profits for gate receipts, sales of food and merchandise, and donations ranged from a low of $200 at the Bridgeport, Conn., fair to a high of $1,183,506.23 at the New York City fair, which offered for sale contributions from foreign powers in sympathy with the Union and fans and rings crafted by

NA

Confederate prisoners at Point Lookout Prison.

Though the fairs provided the Sanitary Commission with its greatest source of income in 1864–65, they also incurred increased expenses. Women who once made supplies for the commission now spent their time producing needlework for sale. The commission was forced into purchasing at high prices on the open market and was saddled with increased costs for storage and distribution of goods for the troops. The fairs also sparked disagreement over the percentage of profit to be turned over to national headquarters by local Sanitary Commission branches, since many fairs were held to benefit regional treasuries and a particular local beneficiary, such as the Chicago Soldiers' Home. Some of the fairs were operated as cooperative ventures with the U.S. CHRISTIAN COMMISSION, which caused friction since the 2 agencies competed for funds and public support.

In all, the sanitary fairs for which there are records raised approximately $4,392,980.92. Of this amount, $2,736,-868.84 reached the U.S. Sanitary Commission's central treasury, the remainder going to co-sponsoring organizations. More important than their net proceeds, the fairs provided a public expression of unity and patriotism at a time when war-weariness and disappointments on the battlefield weighed heavily on national morale.   —PLF

San Jacinto, USS. A 1,567-ton wooden steam sloop of war, the *San Jacinto* was built in 1850 at the New York Navy Yard. Its 2 engines and single boiler were manufactured by Merrick & Sons at Philadelphia. Known as "Saucy Jack" by officers and crew, the formidable warship was armed with 1 11-in. and 10 9-in. DAHLGRENS and 1 12-pounder PARROTT rifle gun. In 1863 the 11-in. gun was replaced by a 100-pounder Parrott rifle gun, and additional guns were added.

The *San Jacinto* and its commander, Capt. CHARLES WILKES, achieved fame and notoriety in 1861 over the so-called TRENT AFFAIR. Wilkes deliberately stopped the British mail steamer *Trent* at sea and removed to the *San Jacinto* passengers JAMES M. MASON and JOHN SLIDELL, both Confederate commissioners. After the 2 men were brought to the U.S., the *San Jacinto* was decommissioned and received a complete overhaul at the Boston Navy Yard. Recommissioned 1 Mar. 1862, the vessel was subsequently commanded by Cmdr. William Ronckendorff, Lt. Cmdr. Ralph Chandler, Cmdr. James F. Armstrong, Lt. Cmdr. John N. Quackenbush, and Capt. Richard W. Meade.

While searching for CONFEDERATE CRUISERS off the Florida coast and in the Caribbean, the *San Jacinto* captured several BLOCKADE RUNNERS. In Nov. 1862 Ronckendorff discovered the CSS *ALABAMA* at Martinique, but the raider took advantage of darkness and stormy weather to escape. On 1 Jan. 1865, the

San Jacinto ran onto a reef by the Abaco Islands in the Bahamas. All hands reached shore safely and Meade was able to salvage the vessel's guns and equipment; but the ship was lost. A court-martial found Meade guilty of negligence and "culpable inefficiency in the discharge of his duty."   —NCD

sap roller. A large wicker basket similar to a GABION, a sap roller was filled with stones and planks and rolled in front of lead sappers working on assault trenches in the face of the enemy. It deflected some small-arms fire and partially obscured a view of sappers at work.   —JES

Saugus, USS. The *Saugus* was one of many new ironclad monitors used by the North during the latter half of the war. Built at Wilmington, Del., at a cost of $524,817, and completed Dec. 1863, it was commissioned at the Philadelphia Navy Yard 7 Apr. 1864. Single-turreted, weighing 1,034 tons, and armed with 2 15-in. guns, the *Saugus* could steam at speeds up to 8 knots but was difficult to maneuver and, when towed in rough seas, leaked considerably through the bow.

Under Cmdr. Edmund R. Colhoun, the vessel first saw action on the James River against Confederate shore batteries June 1864. Its first engagement was at Howlett's Bluff, near Trent's Reach, 21 June, an encounter demonstrating that not even a monitor was invulnerable: both deck and turret of the *Saugus* were damaged by 1 10-in. shot. On 29–30 June the *Saugus* and another monitor shelled an enemy battery at Four-Mile Creek, forcing the Confederates to withdraw with their guns. On 5–6 Dec. another attack was made on the Confederate battery at Howlett's Bluff. For the second time the *Saugus* was struck, but, despite severe damage to its turret, the vessel remained in the action.

USMHI

From Dec. 1864 to Jan. 1865 the *Saugus* was a part of the great naval force that attacked FORT FISHER, N.C. It participated in the action of 25 Dec. and played an important role in the bombardment of 13 Jan., which helped bring Federal victory 2 days later. The *Saugus* and other monitors approached within 1,000 yd of the fort. Struck eleven times by enemy shells, the vessel recorded 1 casualty—a seaman severely wounded by the explosion of one of its own guns.

In Apr. 1865 the ship, then at the Washington Navy Yard, served briefly as a prison for some of the alleged conspirators in Pres. ABRAHAM LINCOLN's assassination. The vessel was decommissioned 2 months later. Unsuited to the needs of the

post–Civil War American navy, the *Saugus* was scrapped in 1889.   —NCD

Savage revolver. Patented by Edward Savage 15 May 1860, the Savage revolver featured 2 triggers and a gas-tight seal formed between the cylinder and barrel when the weapon was cocked. Pulled with the middle finger, the first or ring trigger revolved the cylinder, sealed it against the barrel and cocked the weapon. The index finger pulled the firing trigger. The cap nipples sat on the cylinder exterior of this percussion-cap weapon. Inventor Henry S. North contributed to the revolver's mechanical design and was a partner in its early manufacture.

The frame and trigger guard were modified on subsequent models, but this .36-caliber revolver, unpopular with the War Department, was never widely distributed. Army arms buyers took delivery on 10,000 at $19 each by 10 June 1862 and did not renew their order. Undistributed Savages were sold by the government as surplus for 25 cents each at the close of the war.   —JES

Savage's Station, Va., Battle of.   29 June 1862   On 29 June 1862, Gen. ROBERT E. LEE planned to follow and destroy Maj. Gen. GEORGE B. MCCLELLAN's Federal army as it withdrew to the James River from its position before Richmond. Lee took a characteristic risk and ordered an all-out pursuit. He ordered the divisions of Maj. Gens. JOHN B. MAGRUDER and BENJAMIN HUGER, men who had been screening Richmond from the bulk of the Federal army for several days, to move forward, to the east, and attempt to strike the retreating column on the flank. To Maj. Gen. THOMAS J. "STONEWALL" JACKSON, a disappointment so far in the SEVEN DAYS' CAMPAIGN, Lee gave Maj. Gen. DANIEL H. HILL's division and orders to press directly on McClellan's rear with his entire force.

At 3:30 a.m., Magruder began his march along the axis of the Richmond & York River Railroad down the Nine Mile and Williamsburg roads. He realized that his troops would be first to strike, but he depended on Jackson to cross Grapevine Bridge over the Chickahominy and support his left. And he depended on Huger, proceeding down Charles City Road, to support his right. Huger was slow, and Jackson spent the day rebuilding Grapevine Bridge.

Magruder moved cautiously. Nearing the old battlefields at Fair Oaks, he slowed his advance, then stopped. Anxiously he inquired of Jackson's movements and of Huger's. Convinced that the Federals to his front were about to attack with superior force, he requested and received 2 brigades of Huger's division and began preparing a defensive position from which to receive the attack. By this time many hours had slipped away.

Finally, prodded by Lee, Magruder ordered a general assault, yet of 6 brigades on hand, he employed only 2½. The advance sputtered near Savage's Station. The Confederates sustained 354 casualties before darkness and a thunderstorm combined to close the action.

In the aftermath Lee wrote to Magruder, "I regret very much that you have made so little progress today in pursuit of the enemy. In order to reap the fruits of victory the pursuit should be most vigorous."   —EMT

Savannah, Ga., Siege of.   9–21 Dec. 1864   Savannah, the objective of Maj. Gen. William T. Sherman's MARCH TO THE SEA, was Georgia's largest city and one of the South's main ports. To defend it the Confederates early in Dec. 1864 mustered a garrison of 10,000 Regulars and militia commanded by Lt. Gen. WILLIAM J. HARDEE. These troops occupied formidable fortifications covering all sides of the city, which was surrounded by swamps, rivers, and rice fields.

On 9–10 Dec. Sherman's 62,000-man army moved into positions north, west, and south of Savannah. Perceiving that the city was strongly defended, Sherman first opened communications with the Union fleet to obtain badly needed supplies. On 13 Dec. one of his divisions assaulted and captured FORT MCALLISTER on the Ogeechee River south of Savannah. 3 days later ships steaming up the Ogeechee delivered food, siege guns, and other equipment to Sherman.

On 17 Dec. Sherman called on Hardee to surrender, threatening otherwise to destroy Savannah. Hardee, however, refused. Sherman thereupon ordered his troops to prepare to storm the Confederate fort. But at the same time he went to the headquarters of Maj. Gen. JOHN G. FOSTER, commanding Union forces in South Carolina, and arranged for Foster to seal off Savannah from the east. In this way Sherman hoped to trap Hardee and so make it unnecessary to carry out a costly assault on Savannah.

But before this plan could be executed, Hardee—more concerned with preserving his army than attempting a hopeless defense of Savannah—constructed a makeshift PONTOON BRIDGE across the Savannah River, over which his troops escaped into South Carolina on the night of 20 Dec. On 21 Dec. a Union division occupied Savannah, bringing the March to the Sea to a triumphant conclusion. —AC

"Saviour of the Valley." *See* ROSSER, THOMAS L.

Sawyer gun and shell. An unsuccessful piece of heavy rifled artillery invented by Sylvanus Sawyer in the mid-1850s, the Sawyer gun came in 6-, 24-, and 30-pounder models with, respectively, bore diameters of 3.67, 4.62, and 5.862 in. and fired a lead-coated shell with 6 ribs cast to its exterior to fit the weapon's rifling. The lead coating on the shell was intended to expand on firing to help the shell mate with the barrel rifling. Prone to bursting and sometimes clumsy to load, it saw extensive service only during the PENINSULA CAMPAIGN. Most successful in the largest caliber, a Sawyer often served as seacoast artillery. One with a 5.862-in. bore installed on Rips Raps Island at the mouth of the James River, Va., was involved in frequent duels with inland Confederates and Southern vessels. Records rarely mention this weapon after 1862. —JES

Saxton, Rufus. USA b. Greenfield, Mass., 19 Sept. 1824, Saxton graduated from the U.S. Military Academy 18th in the class of 1849. He served in Florida against the Seminoles 1849–50, receiving his commission as 2d lieutenant 12 Sept. 1850. Over the next decade he drew frontier duty, participated in the Northern Pacific Railroad survey, and, after being promoted to 1st lieutenant 2 Mar. 1855, held various assignments involving coastal survey and fortification.

After teaching artillery tactics at West Point for a year and following several months on duty in Europe, Saxton early in 1861 commanded a detachment of artillery at the St. Louis arsenal in Missouri, assisting Brig. Gen. NATHANIEL LYON in disbanding seccessionists training at Camp Jackson. Promoted to captain 13 May, he served briefly as quartermaster to Lyon and to Maj. Gen. GEORGE B. MCCLELLAN in western Virginia, and

he participated in the expedition to PORT ROYAL, S.C. Advanced to brigadier general 15 Apr. 1862, he commanded the defenses at Harpers Ferry during Maj. Gen. THOMAS J. "STONEWALL" JACKSON's SHENANDOAH VALLEY CAMPAIGN of 1862.

From July 1862 until Jan. 1865 Saxton held various commands and titles within the Department of the South, the most important being the independent military governorship of the coastal islands off South Carolina and Georgia. With the assignment came orders for which he was well suited: the first orders issued by the War Department authorizing the recruitment and organization of up to 5,000 black soldiers for Federal service.

A reasoned, practical man opposed to slavery, but no abolitionist, Saxton labored diligently at Beaufort, S.C., to recruit and train the 1st South Carolina Colored Volunteers. The unit, begun by former Department of the South commander Maj. Gen. DAVID HUNTER on his own initiative, had been seriously undermined by his rude treatment of blacks and his radical abolitionism. Saxton, by insisting on treating them with respect and insisting they be enlisted on an equal basis with whites, became trusted by blacks reluctant to fight for a government that discriminated against them.

To help combat the prejudice he found among whites in the army, he gave the black recruits their first opportunity to prove themselves as combat troops by sending a company to operate from aboard a steamer and raid along the coast of Georgia and Florida 3–10 Nov. Elated by their success and by the public support it brought, he was able to shape the 1st South Carolina Colored Volunteers into the first full-strength officially mandated black regiment in the Federal army. Once ABRAHAM LINCOLN issued the EMANCIPATION PROCLAMATION, 1 Jan. 1863, the aggressive recruitment of blacks began throughout the army. (*See also* BLACK SOLDIERS.)

Concerned with black civilians as well, Saxton tried to reduce the hardships of CONTRABANDS by assigning to them parcels of land on Sea Islands estates abandoned by Confederate plantation owners. The former slaves, supplied by the government with seed and tools, were to grow enough food for their own support and were encouraged by Saxton to market surpluses as a means of becoming independent. In exchange for the opportunity, each farmer was obliged to raise an allotment of cotton for use by the Federal government.

When Maj. Gen. WILLIAM T. SHERMAN's forces occupied Georgia and moved into the Carolinas, Saxton transferred to the FREEDMEN'S BUREAU as assistant commissioner in South Carolina, Georgia, and Florida. Hoping Congress would pass legislation permitting the distribution of confiscated estates to former slaves, he delayed restoring to former owners plantations being farmed by freedmen. Pres. ANDREW JOHNSON removed him from his post Jan. 1866, ending his ambitious efforts to help former slaves adjust to the self-sufficiency freedom required.

Saxton continued his military career in the Quartermaster Department of the Regular Army, receiving promotions to major 29 July 1866, to lieutenant colonel and deputy quartermaster general 6 June 1872, and to his highest rank, colonel, 10 Mar. 1882, the year he was named assistant quartermaster general. He retired from active duty 10 Oct. 1888 at the end of 5 years as head of the supply depot at Jeffersonville, Ky. d. at his home in the District of Columbia, 23 Feb. 1908. —PLF

Sayler's Creek, Va., Battle of. 6 Apr. 1865 Every man

in Gen. Robert E. Lee's retreating army remembered 6 Apr. 1865 as "Black Thursday." For the better part of 4 days impoverished Confederate forces had struggled westward from the Richmond-Petersburg lines. Massed Federal troops kept in hot pursuit. To gain speed, Lee on 5 Apr. rearranged the order of march. The bulk of his infantry led the way, followed by the wagon trains and the rearguard divisions of Maj. Gen. JOHN B. GORDON. All seemed to be well until the Southern army began passing through the bottomlands of Sayler's Creek, where a gap developed midway in the long Confederate column. Gordon and the wagons veered to the north in search of safety. The isolated corps of Lt. Gens. RICHARD H. ANDERSON and RICHARD S. EWELL turned around and promptly came under heavy attack.

Fighting desperately, Confederates managed to repel a Federal advance against their center. Exuberant Southerners, many of whom had defended Richmond for most of the war and thus were green to the ways of battle, launched a disorganized counterattack. Federal artillery shredded the gray ranks, and Union infantry assailed the buckling columns. Entire brigades began laying down their arms. Meanwhile, Lee's wagon trains had bogged down along the creek bed. Making a stand, Gordon's men were overwhelmed by Federal forces. By day's end nearly 8,000 Confederates had been captured—the largest number of American soldiers ever captured in combat on the North American continent. Included in the number were Gens. Ewell, DUDLEY M. DUBOSE, MONTGOMERY D. CORSE, EPPA HUNTON, JOSEPH B. KERSHAW, and G. W. C. LEE.

One-fourth of the Army of Northern Virginia had melted away in an afternoon, and the stunned Robert E. Lee moaned: "My God! Has the army dissolved?"   —JIR

scalawags. Southern Republicans, called "scalawags," emerged as a force in postwar politics almost immediately following the Confederate surrender. Some had advocated peace during the war, even at the cost of independence. Others were Unionists who had never supported the Confederacy and now hoped to have their loyalty rewarded. Though Southern Republicans were characterized as vindictive, unprincipled opportunists, traitorous to their own people, many believed that the acceptance of Congressional Reconstruction, especially the 14TH AMENDMENT, was the only way to restore the Southern states to the Union quickly.

Though some Southern Republicans proved the stereotype of the despicable scalawag in alliance with Northern Carpetbaggers, the majority supported progressive though unpopular political and economic reforms as a way to help the South recover from the devastation brought on by the war. Deep-seated opposition to social equality caused many to defect to the Democratic party as RADICAL REPUBLICANS advocated, along with punitive legislation, immediate emancipation of slaves, in the defeated South. Those who remained in the Republican party after passage of the supplementary Reconstruction Act of 27 Mar. 1867, which provided for military occupation to enforce suffrage, bore the full force of the detested label *scalawag* for many years after Reconstruction ended in 1877. 2 prominent Confederates who became postwar Republicans were Lt. Gen. JAMES LONGSTREET and Col. JOHN S. MOSBY.   —PLF

Scales, Alfred Moore. CSA b. Reidsville, N.C., 26 Nov. 1827. Educated at Caldwell Institute in Greensborough and at the state university in Chapel Hill, Scales opened a law practice

in Madison, N.C. After serving as solicitor of Rockingham County, he was a 4-term member of the state legislature and in 1856 was elected to the U.S. House of Representatives. 4 years later he was a presidential elector for JOHN C. BRECKINRIDGE.

At the outbreak of the Civil War, Scales enlisted as a private soldier in Company H/13th North Carolina Infantry. His political prominence resulted in his immediate promotion to command the company. By October he had succeeded WILLIAM D. PENDER as colonel of the 13th, which he led with distinction spring and summer 1862 at YORKTOWN and WILLIAMSBURG and during the SEVEN DAYS' CAMPAIGN. At FREDERICKSBURG that December, his gallant service along the Confederate right flank above Hamilton's Crossing temporarily won him brigade command. He was named a brigadier general to rank from mid-June 1863, 6 weeks after being severely wounded through the thigh while distinguishing himself in regimental command at CHANCELLORSVILLE. His leadership on that field prompted his brigade leader, Pender, to hold up Scales and his unit "as models in duty, courage and daring."

On the first day at GETTYSBURG, Scales led Pender's brigade down the Cashtown road against Union infantry along Seminary Ridge. Subjected to a murderous artillery barrage, his command suffered more than 540 casualties, including 55 officers. Again, Scales was severely wounded, this time by a shell fragment in the leg. Carried from Pennsylvania in an ambulance during Gen. ROBERT E. LEE's retreat, he was left to convalesce at Winchester, Va. He recovered to lead his brigade, now part of Maj. Gen. CADMUS M. WILCOX's division, through most of the 1864 campaigning, being conspicuous in the WILDERNESS and in several of the engagements around PETERSBURG. He took an extended sick leave early in 1865 and thus missed Lee's surrender at Appomattox.

Returning to his native state, he settled in Greensborough, where he resumed his law practice. From 1866 to 1869 he was again a state legislator and 1875–84 reoccupied his old seat in the House of Representatives. He was also governor of North Carolina 1884–88, and from 1888 till his death, 8 Feb 1892, served as president of a Greensborough bank.   —EGL

Schenck, Robert Cumming. USA b. Franklin, Ohio, 4 Oct. 1809. A lawyer, state legislator, congressman, diplomat, general, and renowned authority on draw poker, Schenck had a distinguished career. The 1827 graduate of Miami University practiced law in Dayton, Ohio, before his election to the Ohio legislature in 1840. 2 years later he was elected to the U.S. House of Representatives, serving 4 terms. Resigning in 1851, Schenck accepted, for 2 years, the position of minister to Brazil. A former Whig, he enthusiastically supported Abraham Lincoln's campaign for the presidency in 1860.

With the outbreak of civil war, Schenck, a military novice with political power, secured a commission as brigadier general of volunteers 5 June 1861, to rank from 17 May. He led a brigade at FIRST BULL RUN and was transferred to Brig. Gen. William S. Rosecrans' command in Western Virginia. Briefly in spring of 1862 he commanded at Cumberland, Md., before being reassigned to the Union forces in western Virginia, under Maj. Gen. Charles C. Frémont. Schenck fought with "The Pathfinder" against Maj. Gen. Thomas J. "Stonewall" Jackson in the SHENANDOAH VALLEY CAMPAIGN of 1862, commanding Frémont's right flank at the Battle of CROSS KEYS in June.

LC

When Frémont was relieved at his own request in July, Schenck briefly commanded the I Corps/Army of Virginia, until Maj. Gen. Franz Sigel arrived to relieve him. Schenck led Sigel's 1st Division at SECOND BULL RUN, suffering a disabling wound, and for his services in that battle was promoted to major general, to date from 30 Aug. 1862. He commanded the Middle Department and VIII Corps, with headquarters at Baltimore, Md., until 5 Dec. 1863, when he resigned from the army to return to Congress.

Schenck served an additional 4 terms in the lower House. He chaired the powerful Committee on Military Affairs and later the Ways and Means Committee. Defeated for reelection in 1870, he became minister to Great Britain and a member of the ALABAMA CLAIMS Commission. He returned to the U.S. in 1876, practiced law in the nation's capital and wrote a treatise on draw poker. d. District of Columbia, 23 Mar. 1890.   —JDW

Schimmelfenning, Alexander. USA b. Lithauen, Prussia, 20 July 1824, Schimmelfenning was among those German expatriates who held positions of command in the Union army.
A former officer of engineers in the Prussian army, he supported the revolution of 1848 in Baden, which was crushed by the Prussian forces. Fleeing his native land, he came to the U.S. in 1853. He settled in Philadelphia, wrote a book predicting the Crimean War, and worked as an engineer and draftsman. By 1860 he was apparently employed in the latter capacity by the War Department.
When the Civil War began, Schimmelfenning volunteered his services to the Federal government, on 30 Sept. 1861 receiving a commission as colonel of the 74th Pennsylvania. Injured in a fall with his horse, then suffering from a case of smallpox, he saw no active field duty until the SECOND BULL RUN CAMPAIGN. There he commanded a brigade in the division of fellow Prussian Brig. Gen. CARL SCHURZ. He was promoted to brigadier general 29 Nov. 1862, commanding a brigade in the overwhelmingly German XI Corps.

The corps suffered heavy losses in 1863. On 2 May Lt. Gen. Thomas J. "Stonewall" Jackson's Confederates routed it at CHANCELLORSVILLE. At GETTYSBURG, 1 July, the luckless corps broke again under Confederate assaults, and Schimmelfenning, temporarily commanding Schurz's division, fell "by the blow

USMHI

of a gun." Regaining consciousness within the Confederate lines, the brigadier hid in a pigsty, where he stayed until the Southerners retreated on the 4th. He then requested a transfer but before it could be effected, he was afflicted with malaria.

Schimmelfenning returned to duty early in 1865, participating in the operations against Charleston, S.C. Granted sick-leave 8 April, he became a victim of virulent tuberculosis. While seeking medical treatment near Wernersville, Pa., Schimmelfenning died, 5 Sept. 1865.   —JDW

Schofield, John McAllister. USA b. Gerry, N.Y., 29 Sept. 1831, Schofield graduated 7th in the West Point class of 1853. After 2 years of service with the 1st Artillery in Florida, he was ordered back to West Point, where he taught philosophy until 1860. War erupted while he was on leave teaching physics at Washington University, St. Louis, Mo., and he remained in the West, on the staff of Brig. Gen. NATHANIEL LYON. At WILSON'S CREEK, Mo., Schofield counseled retreat for the outnumbered Union forces but was not heeded, and the resulting defeat cost many Federal lives, including Lyon's. On 21 Nov. 1861, Schofield became a brigadier general, and Oct. 1862–

LC

Apr. 1863 was assigned to primarily organizational duties as commander of the Army of the Frontier and the District of Southwest Missouri, while operating against guerrilla forces in Kansas and Missouri and lobbying for a more important position.

Named major general of volunteers 12 May 1863, Schofield in Feb. 1864 was appointed to command the Department and Army of the Ohio, then took part in Maj. Gen. William T. Sherman's campaign against ATLANTA. Confederate Gen. JOHN B. HOOD, driven from the city, was making a desperate attempt to rekindle Confederate spirits by invading Tennessee. Hood attempted to cut off Schofield's troops from Nashville but, through a combination of Schofield's ability and Hood's blunders, the Union forces eluded the Confederates and entrenched at FRANKLIN. On 30 Nov. Schofield's troops destroyed Hood's attacking forces, substantially contributing to Hood's crushing defeat at NASHVILLE in December by Maj. Gen. GEORGE H. THOMAS.

In command of the Department of North Carolina, Schofield cooperated with Sherman in final operations against Confederate Gen. JOSEPH E. JOHNSTON.

A competent, ambitious subordinate officer in the Civil War, Schofield proved to be an able administrator in the peacetime army. In addition to commanding the First Military District in Virginia, he journeyed to France to confidentially negotiate the removal of French troops from Mexico and in 1868 served briefly as secretary of war under Pres. Andrew Johnson. For 5 years, Schofield was superintendent of West Point, and succeeded Philip H. Sheridan as commanding general of the army in 1888. He retired as lieutenant general in 1895, dying in St. Augustine, Fla., 4 Mar. 1906.   —TMM

Schurz, Carl. USA b. Liblar, Prussia, 2 Mar. 1829. A journalist, statesman, and soldier who was part of the German revolutionary movement, Schurz arrived in Philadelphia in 1852 as a political refugee. For a few years he traveled in the East and Midwest, then settled in Wisconsin and entered politics. The idealism of the newly formed Republican party attracted the liberal, who quickly became influential among the German population.

USMHI

Actively supporting JOHN C. FRÉMONT for the presidency in 1856, Schurz urged fellow Germans to desert Democratic ranks in favor of the Republican free-soil platform. Many did, sending Schurz to the 1860 Republican national convention as chairman of the Wisconsin delegation. Appointed to lead the foreign department of the Republican national committee, Schurz supported Abraham Lincoln's nomination, then delivered German votes in the fall election.

As a reward Lincoln appointed him minister to Spain when the Civil War started, but Schurz wanted a military commission; returning to the U.S. Jan. 1862, he resigned the diplomatic post. Lincoln awarded him a commission as brigadier of volunteers, from 15 Apr. 1862, then a major generalship 17 Mar. 1863. Schurz proved to be a competent officer, winning respect from professional army men and great popularity among German troops.

At SECOND BULL RUN his division covered the final retreat of Frémont's I Corps, and at GETTYSBURG he commanded a division of the XI Corps. In fall 1863 Schurz was transferred to the Western theater, arriving in time to fight at CHATTANOOGA. He remained in the West until mid-1864, when he took a leave of absence to help Lincoln win reelection.

Schurz resigned his commission after Gen. Robert E. Lee's surrender. A Liberal Republican, he was elected senator from Missouri in 1868, served as secretary of the interior in Pres. Rutherford B. Hayes's cabinet in 1877, then resumed a career in journalism. He distinguished himself as a writer, winning admiration for his willingness to stand by his principles. He died at his home in New York City, 14 May 1906.   —PLF

Scott, Thomas Moore. CSA b. Athens, Ga., 1829. Details of Scott's personal life are obscure, since fire destroyed family records in postwar years; but historian Ezra Warner reconstructed some details of Scott's civilian career by corresponding with surviving family members.

The son of an agricultural family in the Athens, Ga., area, Scott is presumed to have been born there and followed the family occupation. Frequently traveling to New Orleans on business, he entered a New Orleans Masonic lodge in 1852, then married in La Grange, Ga., in 1854. Next a farmer in Claiborne Parish, La., according to 1860 census records, he prospered there. Early in the Civil War Scott organized the 12th Louisiana Infantry, which was accepted into Confederate service 13 Aug. 1861. He was elected colonel and given a commission to date from 9 Aug., then was assigned to duty at Columbus, Ky. Serving behind the lines at the Battle of BELMONT, Mo., then in garrison at Island No. 10 and Fort Pillow,

he next saw duty in the Port Hudson, La., area through winter 1862–63; under Maj. Gen. William Wing Loring took part in the early maneuvering for Vicksburg; and clashed with Union Maj. Gen. Andrew J. Smith's forces in the May 1863 Battle of CHAMPION'S HILL, Miss.

NA

Escaping containment in Vicksburg, Scott served with Gen. Joseph E. Johnston in Mississippi, but may have been briefly separated from his command while pursuing other duties. Transferred to Georgia, he fought in the early stages of the ATLANTA CAMPAIGN, won promotion to brigadier general 24 May 1864, to date from 10 May, and assumed leadership of the 22nd, 35th, 49th, 55th, and 57th Alabama regiments, as well as the 12th Louisiana. In Gen. John B. Hood's Tennessee campaigning that autumn he was disabled by an artillery wound in the Battle of FRANKLIN and saw no further field service.

Scott farmed near Homer, La., in postwar years and ran a gulf-coast sugar plantation. d. New Orleans, 21 Apr. 1876.

—JES

Scott, Winfield. USA b. near Petersburg, Va., 13 June 1786. Before FORT SUMTER fell to Southern assault, Gen. Winfield Scott complained that his Regular Army was inadequate to handle even peacetime troubles with Indians. With sectional war imminent, the 75-year-old Mexican War hero urged an unheeding Pres. James Buchanan to strengthen Federal forts in the South. Months later, Apr. 1861, Pres. Abraham Lincoln disagreed when Scott, his highest-ranking officer and chief military adviser, pointed out the futility of trying to hold Sumter, and Congress balked when the general asked for 300,000 3-year soldiers instead of 90-day volunteers.

USMHI

A professional, dubbed "Old Fuss and Feathers" for his meticulous dress and insistence on military protocol, Scott was a veteran of every U.S. war since 1812. He refused a Confederate commission to retain command of the Union forces, successfully directing Washington's defense Oct. 1861. But Scott's small-army experience ill prepared him to organize the unwieldy collection of raw recruits, and his subordinates deemed him a superannuated bureaucrat and increasingly disregarded his advice.

He requested as field commander Maj. Gen. GEORGE B. MCCLELLAN, whose flamboyant ego surpassed his own, but questions over policy and command led to clashes between them. A morale-crushing defeat at FIRST BULL RUN and the subsequent rout at BALL'S BLUFF cast more doubt on his military capabilities, which some thought had been replaced by senility. The latter episode led to his resignation 1 Nov. 1861.

Scott foresaw a long, costly war and developed the battle

strategy that ultimately led to Union victory. His famous ANA-CONDA PLAN, designed to envelop and strangle the Confederacy, called for strong offensive action in the West to divide the South, establishing the unreliable border states as a buffer zone, and blockading the coast from Norfolk, Va., to Galveston, Tex.

Scott lived to see the South defeated, dying in West Point, N.Y., 29 May 1866.   —PLF

scout. A Civil War scout operated on the fringes of an army with the purpose of obtaining enemy locations, movements, and strength. Individual soldiers or small groups acted as scouts, often operating at or even behind enemy lines. Scouts provided crucial daily contact with the enemy in terrain that often shielded one army from another.   —JDW

USMHI

Scouts and guides of the Army of the Potomac

Scurry, William Read. CSA b. Gallatin, Tenn., 10 Feb. 1821, Scurry, at age 16, migrated to Texas, settling in San Augustine. When the Mexican War broke out in 1846, he enlisted as a private in the 2nd Texas Mounted Volunteers. Rendering distinguished service, he mustered out as major of the regiment. Scurry served in 1859 as a Texas commissioner delegated to adjust the Texas–New Mexico boundary and in 1861 as a member of Texas' secession convention.

LC

Joining the Confederate army as lieutenant colonel of the 4th Texas cavalry, early in 1862 Scurry participated in Brig. Gen. HENRY HOPKINS SIBLEY's expedition into New Mexico. He fought at VALVERDE 21 Feb. and at LA GLORIETA PASS 26–28 Mar., in the latter engagement rendering important service when Sibley was absent, allegedly for medical reasons. Scurry's performance in the unsuccessful campaign resulted in his promotion to brigadier general, to rank from 12 Sept.

During Maj. Gen. John B. Magruder's recapture of GALVES-

TON, Tex., Jan. 1863, Scurry commanded the land forces and a year later led his brigade in the RED RIVER CAMPAIGN. Under Lt. Gen. Richard Taylor his brigade fought at MANSFIELD and PLEASANT HILL 8–9 Apr. 1864. When the Federals retreated, Taylor sent Scurry's brigade to oppose the advance of Maj. Gen. Frederick Steele's Union column. On 30 Apr., at Jenkins' Ferry, the opponents collided. Scurry was wounded, refused to leave the field for medical help, and bled to death while the combat raged.   —JDW

seacoast guns. Columbiads, Parrott rifles, and Whitworth, Armstrong, and Blakely rifles were all seacoast guns, designed for coastal and harbor defense; their bores ranged from 8 to 12.75 in. 8-, 10-, and 15-in. Columbiads fired projectiles weighing, respectively, 65, 128, and 302 lb. Parrotts with 6.4-, 8-, and 10-in. bores threw 100-, 175-, and 250-lb projectiles. The Whitworth, with a 5-in. bore; Armstrongs, with 6.4- and 8.5-in. bores; and Blakeleys, having 8- and 12.75-in. bores, fired rounds weighing 70, 71.7, 150, 200, and an amazing 700 lb. The range of the heaviest of these weapons is undocumented, but a 5-in. Whitworth was known to heave a projectile 7,722 yd and a 100-lb Parrott shell was recorded traveling more than 8,400 yd on a heavy charge.

These enormous pieces, with tubes weighing from 9,210 lb (the smallest Columbiad) to 54,000 lb (the largest Blakely), were usually mounted on barbette platforms or swiveling casemate carriages and used in permanent masonry fortifications. Some heavy cannon were mounted on iron carriages, and remarkably, in both contending forces, were occasionally transported by rail and sea to take on specific opponents. Union Maj. Gen. QUINCY A. GILLMORE transported seacoast guns to assault Fort Pulaski, off Savannah, Ga., and installed them on Morris Island to bombard Charleston, S. C. Blakelys installed in Confederate Fort Fisher, N. C., held off Federal warships until Southern troops succumbed to a combined land/sea assault Jan. 1865.

Columbiads designed by THOMAS J. RODMAN in the late 1850s brought about the rise of truly heavy seacoast guns. Previously, 32-pounder and 42-pounder guns and the first Columbiads designed in the 1840s had made up America's coastal arsenal. Though they were quickly loaded and fired, their projectiles averaged a flight of much less than 2,000 yd and, even with the early Columbiads, usually only fired solid shot. The new weapons accommodated shells, and though a crew had to spend several minutes loading and aiming them (on the largest weapons with the aid of a block and tackle), they made up in distance, accuracy, and destructive power what they lacked in speed.   —JES

Sears, Claudius Wistar. CSA b. Peru, Mass., 8 Nov. 1817. A member of the West Point class of 1841, Sears resigned from the army after 1 year's service to become an educator in the South. He taught in Holly Springs, Miss., then in New Orleans at what became Tulane University. He quit his professorship in mathematics and engineering in 1859 to return to the academy at Holly Springs as an administrator. A confirmed secessionist, in 1861 he entered Confederate service as an enlisted member of the 17th Mississippi Infantry but quickly rose to captain of Company G of the regiment.

On 11 Dec. 1862, Sears became colonel of the 46th Mississippi, which he led 2 weeks later at CHICKASAW BLUFFS in repulsing a movement against Vicksburg under Maj. Gen. WILLIAM T.

SHERMAN. In the VICKSBURG CAMPAIGN, he was in garrison service along the Yazoo River, then fought adeptly at PORT GIBSON, CHAMPION'S HILL, and during the siege of the river citadel. Captured at Vicksburg 4 July 1863, he was quickly paroled but was not exchanged, and thus could not retake the field, for several months.

He returned to active campaigning in spring of 1864. As a brigadier general, to rank from 1 Mar., he was assigned 5 regiments and a battalion of Mississippi infantry, which he commanded at Rome and later at Resaca, Ga. During the ATLANTA CAMPAIGN, Sears earned a reputation as one of the more combative brigade leaders in the ARMY OF TENNESSEE. In September he became severely ill and for a time relinquished his command. He rebounded to fight at ALLATOONA under Maj. Gen. SAMUEL G. FRENCH, who praised his bravery and tactical skill.

Accompanying Gen. JOHN B. HOOD into Tennessee in fall 1864, Sears won new fame at FRANKLIN, where part of his command briefly seized the main Union line. Subsequently he cooperated in the attack on Murfreesboro, before losing a leg to an artillery shell at Nashville 15 Dec. Falling into Federal hands, he was not paroled until 23 June 1865; by then his brigade had been surrendered at Mobile, Ala.

In postbellum years, Sears returned to teaching, occupying the chair of mathematics at the University of Mississippi until 1899. d. Oxford, Miss., 15 Feb. 1891.   —EGL

secession conventions. *See* individual Southern states.

Secessionville, S.C., Battle of. 16 June 1862 Union Brig. Gen. Henry W. Benham temporarily commanded the troops of Brig. Gens. HORATIO G. WRIGHT and ISSAC I. STEVENS at camps to the west-southwest of James Island, a swampy neck of land south of Charleston, S.C. Wright's camp, with its back to the Stono River, sat at Grimball's plantation, north of Stevens' camp in a clearing more inland. East of Wright's camp and northeast of Stevens', in the hamlet of Secessionville, was a Confederate fort with a floating battery in the inlet next to it. The guns of the floating battery and the fort's forward batteries were within range to shell the forwardmost positions in Stevens' camp. These Confederates were commanded by Brig. Gen. NATHAN G. EVANS.

Early in June 1862 Union Maj. Gen. DAVID HUNTER, commanding the Department of the South, headquartered at Hilton Head Island, S.C., permitted Benham to set up a battery forward of Stevens' camp to silence Evans' artillery. These Federal guns incapacitated the floating battery but could not stop the fort's cannon. Responding to correspondence with Hunter (dated 11 June) that sanctioned a reconnaissance in force, Benham started 3,500 of Stevens' troops and 3,100 of Wright's from their respective camps between 2 and 3:30 a.m., 16 June. The movements appear to have been ordered to bring on a general engagement, though when left in command at James Island, Benham had been instructed to initiate no battles. Later, Benham vehemently denied this was his intent.

Evans' overall responsibility was the Second Military District

of South Carolina. The resident commander of the fort at Secessionville was Col. Thomas G. Lamar. Activity in the Federal camps to the west convinced Lamar that attack was imminent the night of 15 June or the morning of 16 June; he informed Evans of his suspicions at 2 p.m., 15 June. At 2 a.m. on the 16th Evans, at his nearby Adams Run headquarters, got word from Lamar that attack was expected at any time, forces were being deployed, and guns sighted. Evans headed for the fort with reinforcements.

Between 3 and 3:30 Stevens' advance captured Lamar's pickets as quietly as possible and were formed for attack within rifle range of the Secessionville works. They were to lead the attack; Wright's troops, personally commanded by Benham, would follow. Firing first grape, then canister, Lamar's guns splintered the first assault at 4 a.m., repelling it within 15 minutes. Evans arrived with reinforcements at 4:15, bringing the garrison strength to 2,000. With some field artillery behind him, and 2 long, high hedgerows covering his troops' approach, Benham tried a second and third frontal assault later in the morning; during both attempts, some Federals reached Lamar's parapets, but the attacks were repulsed. Between 9:30 and 10 a.m., Benham ordered a retreat.

Subsequently, Evans praised Lamar in reports, and the Secessionville fort was named Fort Lamar in his honor. Total Confederate losses in the fort's defense were reported at 204 killed, wounded, and captured. Benham was detained, informally charged with disobedience of orders, and his brigadier general's commission (then awaiting Senate confirmation) was revoked by Pres. Abraham Lincoln. In statements to the War Department Stevens and Wright claimed that in a 15 June council of war they had warned Benham he was bringing on a battle in violation of orders, and in a published letter to the editor of the New York *Times* Stevens stated that Wright had warned Benham the latter's orders "were, in fact, orders to fight a battle." Though Benham pled for an opportunity to clear his name, Federal losses of 107 dead, 487 wounded, and 89 captured at Secessionville suggested the results of a lost battle more than those of a permissible reconnaissance in force. Benham was quietly mustered out of service 7 Aug. 1862.
          —JES

Second Confiscation Act. *See* CONFISCATION ACT OF 1862.

Seddon, James Alexander. CSP b. Fredericksburg, Va., 13 July 1815. Born to a distinguished plantation family from Goochland Cty., Va., Seddon was a graduate of the University of Virginia's law school, a man of great cultural acquirements, and an ardent states-rights advocate. A member of the House of Representatives 1845–47 and 1849–51, he remained active in government until 1851, when his health failed and he retired to his "Sabot Hill" plantation.

The 1860 secession crisis pressed the ailing aristocrat into public service again, and he took part in the WASHINGTON PEACE CONFERENCE. Disregarding his 9 years of civic inactivity and poor health that made him look

LC

like "a man who has been in his grave a full month," Seddon gave himself to the cause of the Confederate states. When offered the post of secretary of war Nov. 1862, he accepted, giving the task all the energy he had at his command.

The 4 opinionated men who preceded Seddon in office had felt frustrated when Pres. JEFFERSON DAVIS subordinated their efforts and policies to his own. The fifth secretary of war held that post longest because, in the estimate of many historians, he acquiesced in most cases to Davis' authority as commander-in-chief and adopted his president's quarrels as his own. From the time of his appointment until his resignation 1 Feb. 1865, Seddon functioned as the War Department's top bureaucrat and administrator, but most serious matters were left to the Confederate chief executive. Seddon took up his superior's fights with anti-Davis Confederates, and was a partial referee in bouts between Davis and his dissenting generals JOSEPH E. JOHNSTON and P.G.T. BEAUREGARD. Only his resignation may have been an independent act.

Early in 1865 the president, though threatened by Congress with a vote of "no confidence" if he did not replace his CABINET, urged Seddon not to retire. But stung by the insult from Congress, Seddon promptly left his post, indicating he would not "abrogate his constitutional prerogatives."

After the Confederate collapse, Federal authorities arrested Seddon, imprisoning him for several months at FORT MONROE. Following his release, he retired to his estate, where he died 19 Aug. 1880. —JES

Sedgwick, John. USA b. Cornwall Hollow, Conn., 13 Sept. 1813, Sedgwick attended Sharon Academy briefly and taught school for 2 winters before entering West Point. Graduating 24th in the class of 1837, he won distinction in the army of Gen. WINFIELD SCOTT in the Mexican War, from which he emerged with the brevet rank of major. At the opening of the Civil War he held the rank of major, having spent the preceding 6 years in Indian campaigns with the 1st Cavalry.

Appointed brigadier general as of 31 Aug. 1861, Sedgwick commanded a division during the PENINSULA CAMPAIGN and advanced to major general at its conclusion, to rank from 4 July.

LC

Badly wounded at ANTIETAM, he assumed corps command after recovery. As commander of the VI Corps, he achieved a reputation as a solid and dependable leader, and his forced march to GETTYSBURG brought special recognition. His achievements fueled rumors that he might be given command of the Army of the Potomac, while his modesty inspired reports that he had declined it.

Superintending the placement of artillery 9 May 1864, just before the Battle of SPOTSYLVANIA, Sedgwick was struck in the head by a fatal bullet. He was buried in his native village. —JYS

Selfridge, Thomas Oliver. USN b. Charleston, Mass., 6 Feb. 1836, Selfridge was appointed to the U.S. Naval Academy 3 Oct. 1851 and graduated in 1854. He was promoted

to passed midshipman in 1856, master in 1858, and lieutenant in 1860. Assigned to the *Cumberland,* he participated in the expedition that evacuated the Norfolk Navy Yard Apr. 1861 and another that captured the forts at HATTERAS INLET, N.C., Aug. 1861. Selfridge demonstrated courageous leadership during the encounter between the *Cumberland* and the CSS *VIRGINIA (Merrimack)* at HAMPTON ROADS 8 Mar. 1862, commanding the *Cumberland's* forward battery until his ship, rammed by the ironclad, sank.

USMHI

Selfridge served briefly on the torpedo boat *ALLIGATOR.* Following his promotion to lieutenant commander July 1862, he was assigned to the gunboat *CAIRO* of the Mississippi Squadron. On 12 Dec. 1862 the *Cairo* struck a torpedo and sank while searching for enemy torpedoes on the Yazoo River. Selfridge's next command, the *Conestoga,* became the third casualty of the vessels he served aboard. On 8 Mar. 1864, it sank after a collision with the USS *General Price.*

As commander of the *OSAGE,* Selfridge contributed to the RED RIVER CAMPAIGN. His courage and initiative impressed his superiors, and he was chosen by Rear Adm. DAVID D. PORTER to command the *Huron* in the assaults on FORT FISHER Dec. 1864 and Jan. 1865. On 15 Jan. Selfridge and some 60 sailors and marines stormed the fort's palisade but were driven back under heavy fire. Nevertheless, their effort contributed much to the final victory.

After the war Selfridge was involved in exploration and surveying expeditions in Panama and along sections of the Amazon and Madeira rivers in Brazil. After promotion to captain in 1881, he served as chief of the Naval Torpedo Station at Newport, R.I. He was promoted to rear admiral in 1896 before retiring in 1898. d. District of Columbia, 4 Feb. 1924. —NCD

Selma, Ala., capture of. 2 Apr. 1865 Late in the afternoon of 2 Apr. 1865, 2 divisions of Federal cavalry under Brig. Gen. JAMES H. WILSON—the main body of the largest mounted force ever assembled in North America—halted north of Selma, Ala. Having come 300 mi into the Deep South since 22 Mar., besting Lt. Gen. NATHAN B. FORREST's vaunted cavalrymen several times along the way, the Northern troops now prepared to demonstrate the ability of a massive, highly mobile strike force to capture a well-defended position.

A major Confederate munitions and manufacturing center, Selma had long anticipated Wilson's coming. The city was guarded by 5,000 troops of all arms under Forrest; by several heavy guns; by a complex of redans, REDOUBTS, ABATIS, palisades, and ditches; and by the nearby Alabama River. Though Wilson had obtained a sketch of the works, the Confederate position should have proved unassailable to the Federal horsemen.

But Wilson's troopers knew how to fight afoot when required. Shortly before evening, one of his division leaders, Brig. Gen. Eli Long, led an assault against the right of the line along a treacherous 600-yd approach. Long and several of his subordinates fell wounded, but their 1,500 men scrambled up and over the parapets, driving back defenders. Meanwhile, Brig.

Gen. EMORY UPTON led his division across a swamp and through gaps in the left flank, while Wilson and his escort unit galloped down the main Selma road in Long's rear. The combined strikes placed unbearable pressure on the garrison, despite Forrest's frantic efforts to hold firm. By mid-evening Selma was in Union hands, 2,700 prisoners, 102 cannon, and an immense number of supplies having been captured.

Though Forrest and many others escaped, Selma's fall signaled the collapse of the interior of the Confederacy. During the next 3 weeks Wilson ranged into middle Georgia with unstoppable momentum, capturing other cities, thousands of prisoners (including fleeing Confederate Pres. JEFFERSON DAVIS), and untold spoils. But none of his subsequent successes equaled the magnitude of Selma's capture. —EGL

Semmes, Paul Jones. CSA b. Wilkes Cty., Ga., 4 June 1815. A brother of Confederate naval officer RAPHAEL SEMMES, Paul Jones Semmes attended the University of Virginia before

becoming a banker and planter near Columbus, Ga. Active in the state militia, he served as captain of the Columbus Guards from 1846 until the outbreak of the Civil War.

Semmes was immediately named colonel of the 2d Georgia Infantry, which, transferred to Virginia, missed the major fighting of the war's first year. Semmes was subsequently promoted to brigadier general, to rank from 11 Mar. 1862, and given command of a brigade in Maj. Gen. John B. Magruder's

LC

division. His brigade fought under Magruder in the PENINSULA CAMPAIGN at YORKTOWN, WILLIAMSBURG, and SEVEN PINES. Before the SEVEN DAYS' CAMPAIGN, Semmes was transferred to command of a brigade in Maj. Gen. Lafayette McLaws' division that fought at SAVAGE'S STATION and MALVERN HILL.

The Georgia brigadier served under McLaws for the remainder of 1862 and during 1863. He fought with notable distinction at CRAMPTON'S GAP, Md., and at ANTIETAM. Semmes's brigade of 4 Georgia regiments assisted in the defense of Marye's Heights during the Battle of FREDERICKSBURG Dec. 1862. During the CHANCELLORSVILLE CAMPAIGN, May 1863, Semmes fought at SALEM CHURCH.

The Battle of GETTYSBURG was his final engagement. Late on the afternoon of 2 July, his brigade, as a part of the Confederate assault on the Union left, charged into the WHEATFIELD. Semmes fell mortally wounded at the first fire. He was returned in an ambulance to Martinsburg, Va., where he died 10 July. His remains were returned to Georgia. —JDW

Semmes, Raphael. CSN b. Charles Cty., Md., 27 Sept. 1809. A brother of future Brig. Gen. PAUL JONES SEMMES, Raphael was appointed a midshipman 1 Apr. 1826, promoted to lieutenant in 1837, and to commander in 1855. Between cruises he studied law and in 1834 was admitted to the bar. During the Mexican War he narrowly escaped drowning when his ship, the *Somers,* capsized in a gale while blockading Vera Cruz. In 1849 he settled in Mobile, Ala., and wrote of his war experiences in *Service Afloat and Ashore During*

the Mexican War.

LC

When Alabama seceded, Semmes resigned his commission to become a commander in the Confederate States Navy. Before the outbreak of war, he was sent north to purchase ships and military supplies. He was then appointed head of the Confederate Lighthouse Service. But Semmes had other work in mind: he strongly believed that the South's small navy should include commerce destroyers to weaken the North's overseas trade, and he wanted to command one of these CRUISERS. Supported by Sec. of the Navy STEPHEN R. MALLORY, Semmes obtained a steamer at New Orleans and converted it into a cruiser, the *SUMTER,* the first of the South's commerce destroyers. During 6 months at sea, Semmes captured 17 American merchant ships before the vessel was decommissioned and sold at Gibraltar early in 1862.

Anxious to acquire more and better cruisers, Mallory had authorized JAMES D. BULLOCH to obtain them in Europe. One of Bulloch's ships built in England, the CSS *ALABAMA,* was assigned to Semmes, now a captain, who took command at Terceira in the Azores. During the next 22 months, Aug. 1862–June 1864, the *Alabama* was responsible for 55 prizes captured and sunk —more than any other Confederate cruiser. But as Semmes's actions made him a hero in the South, he became a hated "pirate" in the North, and stopping him became a paramount objective of U.S. Sec. of the Navy GIDEON WELLES. To Northerners Semmes appeared to relish his role as destroyer, and indeed he was relentless in his mission. For nearly 2 years he succeeded in evading his pursuers, even sinking a U.S. warship, the *HATTERAS,* in a 13-minute battle off Galveston 11 Jan. 1863.

By late 1863 Semmes was encountering fewer U.S. merchantmen, an indication of his success. The *Alabama* and the *FLORIDA* had caused hundreds of U.S. vessels either to remain in port or be transferred to foreign ownership. Semmes's success, however, was not without cost to his health. In addition to the demands of constant vigilance during months at sea, Semmes was disgusted by a lack of discipline in his largely mercenary crew. In June 1864 he brought the *Alabama* to Cherbourg, France, for major repairs, expecting to be replaced. But, after the arrival of the USS *KEARSARGE* off Cherbourg, Semmes sent a challenge to its captain, JOHN A. WINSLOW, believing that the 2 wooden vessels were evenly matched. The battle was fought outside Cherbourg harbor 19 June 1864, and the *Kearsarge*'s heavy pivot guns and well-trained gun crews made the difference. After just over an hour, the *Alabama* was beaten and 19 of the men aboard it killed or drowned. Semmes was rescued from drowning by the yacht *Deerhound,* aboard which he was brought to England. Stung by his defeat, he returned to the Confederacy, where he was promoted to rear admiral.

In Feb. 1865 Semmes took command of the James River Squadron (3 ironclad rams and 3 wooden steamers), but there was little action until the evacuation of Richmond 2 Apr., when he destroyed his ships to prevent their capture and organized his sailors and naval cadets into a brigade. At Danville, Va., he was made a brigadier general by Pres. JEFFERSON DAVIS, although the appointment was never made official. A few weeks later Semmes and his sailors were with Maj. Gen. JOSEPH E. JOHNSTON when that officer surrendered his army at Durham, N.C.

On 15 Dec. 1865, Semmes was arrested and brought to Washington to be tried for treason and piracy. The U.S. government also investigated charges that he had mistreated prisoners and had violated the rules of war. All charges were eventually dropped, however, and after 3 months' detainment he was released. Harassment from the government continued, however, and Semmes was unable to keep positions he had obtained as a college professor and newspaper editor. He finally returned to Mobile to practice law. In 1869 he published his *Memoirs of Service Afloat During the War Between the States.* d. Mobile, Ala., 30 Aug. 1877.   —NCD

Seven Days' Campaign, Va.

Seven Days' Campaign, Va.   25 June–1 July 1862   Gen. ROBERT E. LEE assumed command of the Army of Northern Virginia 1 June 1862. For the next 2 weeks, in the shadow of the capital of the Confederacy, Richmond, Va., his men dug field fortifications to strengthen the city's defenses. To the east, across the fields and bottomlands, lay Maj. Gen. GEORGE B. MCCLELLAN's huge Army of the Potomac. While the Confederates spaded, the Federals dragged up heavy artillery to blast the defenders out of their capital. Lee, though outnumbered, decided to seize the initiative and attack McClellan before he could bring his ordnance to bear.

The position of the Union army gave the Confederate commander the opportunity to undertake an offensive. McClellan, after the Battle of SEVEN PINES, had moved the bulk of the army, 70,000 effectives, south of the Chickahominy River, while keeping Maj. Gen. FITZ JOHN PORTER's reinforced V Corps, numbering about 30,000, north of the stream. "Little Mac" maintained this deployment in the expectation of an overland advance from Fredericksburg, Va., by Maj. Gen. IRVIN MCDOWELL's corps.

On 12 June Lee dispatched Brig. Gen. J.E.B. STUART and the cavalry on a reconnaissance to locate McClellan's exact position. The dashing Stuart boldly encircled the Union army in a 3-day ride, seizing prisoners and destroying supplies (*see* STUART'S RIDE AROUND MCCLELLAN). Stuart reported to Lee that the Federal army's right (northern) flank was vulnerable to an envelopment.

The Southern commander, in what would become the hallmark of his generalship, fashioned a bold plan. Leaving only 25,000 men south of the Chickahominy to confront McClellan's 70,000, Lee prepared to strike Porter with 47,000. To deceive the Federals, he sent 1 division westward toward the Shenandoah Valley, while at the same time recalling Maj. Gen. THOMAS J. "STONEWALL" JACKSON and his 18,000 troops from the valley to a point north of Porter's unsupported right flank. Jackson, riding ahead of his men, conferred with Lee and other generals. The Confederate officers scheduled the offensive for 26 June.

McClellan, meanwhile, completed the necessary preliminaries for his long-promised assault on Richmond. Cautious by temperament, the Union commander believed his miserable intelligence, which reported that the Confederates outnumbered him 2-to-1. On 25 June, the day before Lee's scheduled advance, McClellan ordered a reconnaissance in force south of the Chickahominy. The Confederate defenders met the Federals at OAK GROVE in a brief, lively engagement. The Seven Days' Campaign had begun.

The next day, the 26th, Lee seized the initiative, launching his offensive across the Chickahominy. 3 Confederate divisions, those of Maj. Gens. AMBROSE P. HILL, DANIEL H. HILL, and JAMES LONGSTREET, sat poised to strike, awaiting the arrival of Jackson from the north. Jackson, however, never reached the field on this day, and his strange performance throughout the campaign seriously hampered Confederate operations. His failures have been attributed, most persuasively, to lethargy and exhaustion from his SHENANDOAH VALLEY CAMPAIGN and several near-sleepless nights.

A.P. Hill, an impetuous officer, waited for Jackson until midafternoon, then crossed the river at Meadow Bridge and assaulted Porter's troops. The Federals, aligned behind Beaver Dam Creek in a strong position, wrecked Hill's charging brigades with musketry and artillery fire. D.H. Hill brought up some of his brigades, but they fared no better against the entrenched Federals. Porter withdrew after dark to another prepared position behind Boatswain Swamp, near Gaines' Mill. This Battle of MECHANICSVILLE cost the Southerners 1,484 casualties to 361 for Porter.

Lee, with most of his army now away from Richmond, had to strike Porter again on the 27th. By late morning the leading Confederates found Porter waiting at Gaines' Mill. The Union corps commander, under orders from McClellan to hold his position at any cost, maintained a strong semicircle defense. Lee's divisions in midafternoon launched a series of attacks. The stalwart defenders, clinging to the bluff, repulsed them with heavy losses. Finally, at dark, 2 Confederate brigades pierced the Union center and Porter withdrew. This Battle of GAINES' MILL, costing both sides more than 15,000 men, bought for McClellan a crucial day.

The Union commander, surprised by Lee's boldness, had become a beaten man, ordering a change of base from the York River to the James River. McClellan described it as a strategic withdrawal, while others, less generous, called it a "great skedaddle." Once Lee took the initiative 26 June, he never relinquished it during the campaign.

For the next 3 days, 28 June–1 July, Lee endeavored to destroy in detail McClellan's retreating army, with its ponderous wagon train and cattle herd. His complicated plans miscarried, however, plagued by faulty staff work and lack of coordination between the attacking divisions. At ALLEN'S FARM, on the 29th, and at WHITE OAK SWAMP, on the 30th, the Federal rearguard repulsed the Confederate thrusts. McClellan halted at a strong position on MALVERN HILL, where 1 July Lee ordered a final attack in an effort to crush the Federals. Union artillery erased the Southern charges in shellfire and canister.

Lee's bloody defeat 1 July concluded the campaign. His casualties for the week were an appalling 3,286 killed, 15,909 wounded, and 946 missing, for a total of 20,141. The Federals, on the defensive, suffered 1,734 killed, 8,062 wounded, and 6,053 missing, for a total of 15,849.

The Seven Days' Campaign changed the course of the war in Virginia. Lee had relieved the Confederate capital and had seized the initiative in the East, which he maintained until the Battle of ANTIETAM in September. Lee corrected problems plaguing his army during their initial campaign together by strengthening his staff, relieving some generals, and grouping his divisions into 2 corps under Longstreet and Jackson. Within weeks, the reorganized Army of Northern Virginia turned north toward a new opponent. McClellan remained on the

James River, blaming the Union administration for his defeat and asking for more reinforcements.   —JDW

Seven Pines (Fair Oaks), Va., Battle of.

31 May–1 June 1862   The Union Army of the Potomac, crawling up the Virginia peninsula between the York and James rivers, reached the outskirts of Richmond during the final days of May 1862. The Federal soldiers could see the spires of Richmond churches 6 mi away. Maj. Gen. GEORGE B. MCCLELLAN divided his Union army, placing 2 corps south of the Chickahominy River and 3 to the north. Though this was a dangerous disposition, McClellan argued that his northern wing could hook up with Maj. Gen. IRVIN MCDOWELL's command, expected to be moving south from Fredericksburg.

During the month, rains had swollen the Chickahominy and, when a howling storm 30 May deluged the area, the river became a raging torrent. Confederate Gen. JOSEPH E. JOHNSTON seized this opportunity, rapidly devising a complicated plan of attack against McClellan's 2 isolated corps, the III and IV, under Maj. Gens. SAMUEL P. HEINTZELMAN and ERASMUS D. KEYES, respectively.

Johnston's scheme assigned two-thirds of his army to the attack. While 2 divisions screened along the line north of the river, 3 Confederate commands were ordered to charge from 3 separate directions. Maj. Gen. JAMES LONGSTREET's corps, reinforced by Brig. Gen. WILLIAM H. C. WHITING's division, was directed to envelop Keyes's right flank at Seven Pines by the Nine Mile road. Maj. Gen. DANIEL H. HILL's division was ordered to attack along the Williamsburg road, while Maj. Gen. BENJAMIN HUGER's division, protecting the Confederate right, advanced along the Charles City road.

The intricate battle plan floundered immediately on the morning of 31 May. Johnston had issued verbal, not written, orders and confusion resulted as Longstreet marched along the roads assigned to Hill and Huger. Longstreet's error entangled the Confederate commands, delaying the attack for several hours. The battle finally began at 1 p.m. when Hill charged alone at Seven Pines.

Hill's 4 brigades stormed through the swampy, wooded terrain, pushing back Keyes's Federals. In the heavy fighting Brig. Gen. ROBERT E. RODES's Confederate brigade lost more than half its numbers. Brig. Gen. Henry M. Naglee, though wounded, led his Union brigade in a spirited bayonet charge that saved Union artillery and permitted the formation of a new line. Keyes's subordinates shifted troops while Heintzelman sent reinforcements. The Confederates crushed the Union right, forcing some Federals north to Fair Oaks. Late in the day one of Longstreet's brigades bolstered Hill's forces and the Southerners swept forward again. The Federals withdrew to a third line after their counterattack was repulsed. By 6 o'clock the action had subsided at Seven Pines.

At Fair Oaks, meanwhile, Whiting finally charged at about 4 o'clock. His assault struck elements of the Union II Corps, whose commander, Maj. Gen. EDWIN V. SUMNER, had brought them across the flooded Chickahominy less than an hour before. Sumner's soldiers repulsed the attack and, in the twilight, Johnston, riding along the lines, fell severely wounded. Maj. Gen. GUSTAVUS W. SMITH temporarily replaced him, ordering a renewal of attacks at dawn.

Longstreet, as on the day before, failed his assignment 1 June. He attacked tentatively with only 2 brigades, believing that the Federals were about to assault him. The weak Confed-

erate charge was easily repulsed and no other serious action occurred. Gen. ROBERT E. LEE, formally replacing Johnston, ordered a withdrawal to the original positions at 2 p.m.

McClellan's soldiers prevented a possible disaster, holding the field in a tactical victory. Each opponent had nearly 42,000 troops engaged, with the Federals suffering 5,031 casualties and the Confederates 6,134. The Battle of Seven Pines had significant results, however. The "mangled corpses" unnerved McClellan, reinforcing his natural caution to avoid battle. Johnston's fall elevated Lee to command, a turning point in Confederate fortunes in Virginia.   —JDW

XVII Corps Medal.

Designed by corps commander Maj. Gen. JAMES B. MCPHERSON, the XVII Corps Medal was intended, according to McPherson 2 Oct. 1863, "to encourage and reward the meritorious and faithful officers and men of this corps . . . who, by their gallantry in action and other soldier-like qualities, have most distinguished themselves or who may hereafter most distinguish themselves during the war."

Crafted by Tiffany & Co. of New York City, the medal was made available in both gold and silver. It consisted of a star emblem, bearing the corps numeral, suspended from an arm fastened to a metal clasp; an enwreathed shield-of-Union was likewise affixed to the clasp. A red, white, and blue ribbon provided a background for star, arm, and shield. The arm of the medal carried a personalized inscription denoting the action and date for which the medal was awarded, such as *Vicksburg, July 4, 1863.*

One of the recipients of this decoration was Pvt. George J. Reynolds of Company D/15th Iowa Infantry, to whom it was presented on 26 July 1864. Reynolds had distinguished himself 4 days before, during the Battle of ATLANTA, by his heroic attempt to rescue the mortally wounded McPherson.

          —EGL

79th U.S. Colored Troops.

A total of 178,895 blacks served as Union soldiers during the Civil War. Organized into 139 regiments and 10 batteries, they fought in at least 39 major battles and 410 minor engagements, sustaining casualties of 68,178. The 79th U.S. Colored Troops, or 1st Kansas Colored Volunteers, had the distinction at Island Mount, Mo., 29 Oct. 1862, of being the first black regiment to fight in combat in the war.

Recruiting for the regiment began Aug. 1862, progressing slowly until Jan. 1863, when 6 companies organized to form the 1st Kansas Colored Volunteers. The unit retained its original designation until 13 Dec. 1864, when it became the 79th U.S. Colored Volunteers. 4 additional companies joined the original, 6 May 1863. The commander was Col. James M. Williams.

The 79th spent its entire existence west of the Mississippi River. After Jan. 1864 it was in the Department of Arkansas. The black volunteers fought in 12 engagements and several minor actions. Mustered out 1 Oct. 1865, the 79th U.S. Colored Volunteers ranked 21st among all Union regiments in the percentage of total enrollment killed in battle.   —JDW

Seward, William Henry.

USP   b. Florida, N.Y., 16 May 1801. Of Welsh and Irish descent, Seward attended local schools and in 1820 graduated from Union College in Schenectady. Precocious and hardworking, he was admitted to the state bar at 21 and the next year began practicing law in the village of Auburn, his home for the remainder of his life. He quickly developed a love for the political arena, which he entered in 1830 as a state senator. A staunch Whig, he served in Albany until 1834. Defeated in a bid for the governorship that year, he won the office in 1838 and was reelected in 1840.

NA

As legislator and governor, Seward sought reforms in state education, promoted internal improvements and a national banking system, and vociferously advocated safeguards on civil rights, including jury trials for fugitives white and black. His failure to slash state spending during depressions hastened his return to private life in 1842. However, he continued to speak out on issues of state and national importance, and his continued prominence in Whig circles propelled him into the U.S. Senate in 1849 and secured his reelection in 1855.

As senator, Seward often railed against slavery's expansion into the Western territories; in Mar. 1850 he urged fellow free-soldiers to remain true to a "higher law" than the Constitution. In an equally well publicized speech Oct. 1858, he predicted an "irrepressible conflict" over slavery. Such inflammatory remarks embroiled him in controversy and impelled him to equivocate on these and other stands; ultimately he supported the POPULAR SOVEREIGNTY doctrine of STEPHEN A. DOUGLAS.

Despite his vacillating idealism, Seward was the front-runner for the Republican presidential nomination in 1860, a prize that powerful foes snatched from him. When ABRAHAM LINCOLN gained the White House, he offered Seward the State Department, a post the New Yorker accepted with some misgivings. Considering himself the rightful head of the new administration, he tried at first to overawe Lincoln, presuming to dictate presidential policy and meddling in military affairs during the SEWARD-MEIGS-PORTER AFFAIR. Early in 1861 he appeared eager to provoke a war with European nations who threatened to interfere with the blockading of Southern ports, viewing the crisis as a means of reunifying the Union. Late that year, however, Seward's deft and prudent statesmanship enabled the Union to avoid a military confrontation with England in the wake of the TRENT AFFAIR.

Throughout the war Seward displayed the strengths and weaknesses of his approach to statesmanship, which, as one biographer observes, "combined devotion to principle, and flexibility as to means." Sometimes blustering and heavy-handed toward foreign powers, he often conducted diplomacy with an eye on public opinion. For a time in 1862 he nearly resigned over widespread charges that he was responsible for the long series of Union military defeats. But he rose above his critics when preventing foreign nations from intervening on behalf of the South, influencing the British to keep the LAIRD RAMS off the seas, laying the basis for the postwar ALABAMA CLAIMS, and fending off the French threat in Mexico. On the whole, his wartime supervision of state affairs appears judicious, able, and effective.

After the war Seward supported Pres. ANDREW JOHNSON, urged conciliation toward the South, and drifted ever farther

from the mainstream of his party. His most memorable postwar achievement was the purchase of Alaska from Russia in 1867 for a mere $7.2 million. Leaving the State Department Mar. 1869, he toured the world before returning to Auburn, where he died 10 Oct. 1872.   —EGL

Seward-Meigs-Porter Affair. By the first week in Apr. 1861, Pres. ABRAHAM LINCOLN had authorized 2 seaborne expeditions to relieve U.S. garrisons in Confederate territory. The first, organized by his navy secretary, GIDEON WELLES, would sail to beleaguered FORT SUMTER, Charleston harbor. The second, a covert operation unknown even to Welles, would reinforce FORT PICKENS, at Pensacola, Fla. The latter project was sponsored by WILLIAM H. SEWARD, Lincoln's secretary of state, who viewed it as a more prudent alternative to the Charleston expedition, which he feared would precipitate war.

Confusion resulted when Lincoln extended overlapping instructions to Welles and Seward. At the latter's urging, he assigned the powerful warship *Powhatan* to the fleet bound for Florida, forgetting that he had given Welles authority to use the same ship for his expedition. This complicated the efforts of army Capt. MONTGOMERY C. MEIGS (later the U.S. quartermaster general), whom Seward sent to New York City to outfit the Florida fleet. When, late on the 5th, Meigs telegraphed Seward about the confusion, the latter explained the situation to Welles and accompanied him to the White House. That evening a weary Lincoln met with both men, listened to their arguments, and decided in favor of the irate and indignant Welles, who considered the *Powhatan*'s presence crucial to the success of his mission. To mollify the navy secretary, Seward agreed thereafter to confine himself to the affairs of his own department.

The meeting came too late, however, to prevent the warship from accompanying the Florida fleet. At Lincoln's direction, Seward telegraphed Meigs and the naval authorities at New York to hand the warship over to Welles's subordinate in the city. But by the time the cable arrived on the 6th, the *Powhatan* had set sail down New York bay. A fast tug sped the message to the officer Seward had chosen to command the warship, Lt. (and future Rear Adm.) DAVID D. PORTER. Considering himself protected by Lincoln's earlier authority, which a cabinet official could not rescind, the brash Porter ignored Seward's order and continued on to Pensacola harbor. He arrived there 17 Apr., 4 days after Sumter's surrender, but in time to save Pickens.   —EGL

Seymour, Horatio. war governor b. Onondaga, N.Y., 31 May 1810. Educated at local schools in Utica and at Alden Partridge's military academy at Middletown, Conn., Seymour settled in Utica in 1826 to study law. He was admitted to the bar in 1832. The next year Democratic politician William L. Marcy hired Seymour to be his secretary. At the state capitol in Albany, the ambitious young lawyer emerged as a leader among conservative Democrats, serving in the assembly in 1841, 1844, and 1845, and as mayor of Utica in 1842. Given to intellectualism and persuasive oratory, Seymour promoted the development of internal waterways and came to prominence in the party for reconciling differences between the Barnburners and the Hunkers factions 1844–46. Nominated for governor in 1852, he campaigned successfully on a platform denouncing abolitionism, prohibition, and nativism.

Once his term ended, Seymour retired briefly from public

life, then backed STEPHEN A. DOUGLAS in the 1860 presidential race, taking a firm stand in support of compromise with Southern interests. Seymour opposed nearly all of Abraham Lincoln's war measures, but when the Democrats chose him as their gubernatorial candidate in 1862, he carried the election by championing the president and the Union under the Constitution. Once in office he quickly became the leader of Northern proponents of STATES RIGHTS and

LC

the most influential of the anti-administration governors. Suspicious of any concentration of power in the Federal government, Seymour challenged the constitutionality of CONSCRIPTION, suspension of the writ of *HABEAS CORPUS*, and emancipation (see EMANCIPATION PROCLAMATION), stating forcefully in his inaugural address his intention "to maintain and defend the sovereignty and jurisdiction of New York."

He resisted using state troops to enforce the draft and protested the partisan practices of enlistment officers after the DRAFT RIOTS in New York City July 1863, but he also labored diligently to fulfill the state's quotas under the calls for troops in 1863 and 1864.

Recognizing Seymour's powerful position as head of the North's most populous state, Lincoln used tact in dealing with his political foe but remained firm with him. His skillful handling and Seymour's own deep commitment to the Union kept New York firmly behind the war effort despite the governor's partisan opposition.

By 1864 Seymour's unwavering insistence on protecting what he called "the supreme importance of local government" proved a liability rather than an asset to the Democrats, who were being charged with Copperheadism (see PEACE DEMOCRATS). Though the party nominated Seymour for reelection, he lost due to his hardline rhetoric and his refusal to support a bill that would have allowed New York troops to vote in the 1864 elections by absentee ballot.

On leaving office Seymour retired to his home at Deerfield, where he farmed and worked toward rebuilding the Democratic party. Still a formidable political figure, he helped oust William M. "Boss" Tweed from power in Tammany Hall in the 1870s, and in the last decade of his life declined his sixth nomination for governor in 1876 and a senatorial candidacy. d. Deerfield, N.Y., 12 Feb. 1886. —PLF

Seymour, Truman. USA b. Burlington, Vt., 24 Sept. 1824, Seymour had the dubious distinction of being the Union commander at the only battle on Florida soil, the Battle of OLUSTEE. A Federal invasion of east Florida, launched by Seymour 4 Feb. 1864, ended in disaster, but it could have been worse had Confederates pursued the retreating Northerners. The defeat was sufficient, however, to cause Seymour the embarrassment of being relieved of his command. Although he fought gallantly in other engagements, Seymour will always be remembered as the commander who blundered blindly into a major battle, one brigade after another falling against the enemy.

The capable commander attended NORWICH UNIVERSITY, the

USMHI

military school headed by the father of Gen. Thomas E. G. Ransom. After 2 years he withdrew from the university to accept an appointment to West Point. On 1 July 1846, Seymour graduated from the academy 19th in a class of 59, then served in the Mexican War as a 2d lieutenant in the 1st Artillery. He fought admirably and received 2 brevets for gallantry and merit at Cerro Gordo, Contreras, and Churubusco. Seymour returned to West Point as a drawing instructor, then rejoined the 1st Artillery at Fort Moultrie, S.C., fighting in Florida against the Seminole Indians.

At the beginning of the war Seymour was brevetted for his gallantry in the defense of FORT SUMTER. Later that year he commanded Camp Curtin, a training center in Harrisburg, Pa., but soon transferred to Washington and the defensive actions around the city. On 28 Apr. 1862 he accepted an appointment to brigadier general of volunteers.

Seymour distinguished himself at MECHANICSVILLE, GAINES' MILL, MALVERN HILL, SECOND BULL RUN, SOUTH MOUNTAIN, ANTIETAM, PETERSBURG, SAYLER'S CREEK, and APPOMATTOX. He was less successful at Olustee and in 2 other battles: On 18 July 1863, he led an unsuccessful assault on BATTERY WAGNER in the Charleston, S.C., harbor, taking a serious wound. Less than a year later he was imprisoned after the Battle of the WILDERNESS. On his return after a prisoner exchange, he commanded a division in the VI Corps in Virginia's Shenandoah Valley.

Seymour stayed in the army until 1876, when he journeyed to Florence, Italy. There he died 30 Oct. 1891.   —FLS

Shackelford, James Murrell. USA b. Lincoln Cty., Ky., 7 July 1827. Growing up in rural Kentucky, Shackelford attended local schools. Having no formal military education, he joined the 4th Kentucky Volunteers at the outbreak of the Mexican War and was elected 1st lieutenant by his company. When the war ended, he returned home and became a lawyer, setting up a successful practice in Louisville.

In Sept. 1861 the wealthy attorney raised the 25th Kentucky Infantry and was appointed its colonel. The unit first saw action at FORT DONELSON, Tenn., as part of 1st Brigade/3d Division. After the battle, Shackelford resigned his commission and returned

LC

home to raise another regiment, the 8th Kentucky Cavalry. Mustered into service Sept. 1862 the 8th fought its first action several days later at Geiger's Lake, Ky. On 17 Mar. 1863, the colonel was promoted to brigadier general of volunteers. 3 months later, he was instrumental in capturing the legendary Brig. Gen. JOHN HUNT MORGAN and his Kentucky cavalry near New Lisbon, Ohio.

In September, Shackelford, now in command of 3d and 4th

brigades/XXIII Corps, participated in Maj. Gen. Ambrose E. Burnside's invasion of East Tennessee. At Cumberland Gap, the general's troopers helped capture the Confederate garrison. In appreciation of his efforts, Shackelford was given command of the cavalry corps/Department of the Ohio Aug. 1863. On 7 Oct. his cavalry and units of the IX Corps skirmished sharply with Maj. Gen. Joseph Wheeler's troopers at BLUE SPRINGS, Tenn. 2 months later, at BEAN'S STATION, Tenn., Shackelford's command was attacked by Lt. Gen. James Longstreet's I Corps. In this vicious engagement Shackelford was forced to withdraw after 2 days of fighting.

On 18 Jan. 1864, in poor health, Shackelford left the army and resumed his law practice. In later years he was appointed Federal judge of the Indian Territory. He died in Port Huron, Mich., 7 Sept. 1909 and was buried in Louisville, Ky.   —MTC

Shaler, Alexander. USA b. Haddam, Conn., 19 Mar. 1827. Educated at private schools in Manhattan, Shaler joined the New York militia at 18, eventually serving in the celebrated 7th Militia Regiment. His tactical expertise enabled him to rise steadily through the ranks, attaining a majority by Dec. 1860. A year later he wrote *Manual of Arms for Light Infantry Using the Rifle Musket.*

LC

When the Civil War erupted, Shaler joined the 65th New York Volunteers; in June 1861 he was appointed its lieutenant colonel. He served competently enough in the PENINSULA CAMPAIGN to become colonel of the 65th July 1862. A year later he distinguished himself in command of the 1st Brigade/3d Division/VI Corps at both CHANCELLORSVILLE and GETTYSBURG. In the former battle, his troops helped break through the Confederate position atop Marye's Heights, a feat for which he was awarded, 30 years later, the MEDAL OF HONOR. At Gettysburg, his command reinforced the XII Corps on CULP'S HILL, 3 July 1863, helping hold that crucial position for the ARMY OF THE POTOMAC.

Having been promoted to brigadier general of volunteers 26 May 1863, Shaler left the field that autumn to command the prison camp on JOHNSON'S ISLAND, Ohio. Returning to Virginia, he himself became a prisoner of war 5 May 1864, when his VI Corps brigade was flanked and rolled up by Confederate forces in the WILDERNESS. His captors sent him to prisons first in Georgia, then in South Carolina. That summer he was confined in a part of Charleston shelled by Union siege batteries.

After his exchange and parole, Shaler went west. At first he led a brigade in the XIX Corps/Army of the Gulf, then, Dec. 1864–Aug. 1865, the 2d Division/VII Corps/Department of Arkansas. He also commanded for a time the White River District of Arkansas and the post at Devall's Bluff. By his muster-out, 24 Aug. 1865, he was a brevet major general of volunteers.

After the conflict, he held numerous public offices, including those of fire commissioner of New York City and consultant to the Chicago fire department. He headed the New York commandery of the MILITARY ORDER OF THE LOYAL LEGION, was a major general in the New York National Guard 1867–86, and served as president of the National Rifle Association, which he helped found. d. New York City, 28 Dec. 1911.   —EGL

Sharp, Jacob Hunter. CSA b. Pickensville, Ala., 6 Feb. 1833. Moving in his youth to Lowndes Cty., Miss., Sharp attended the University of Alabama, then returned to Mississippi to practice law. When his adopted state seceded, he was elected captain in the 1st Battalion Mississippi Infantry, later an element of the 44th Mississippi Regiment.

LC

As a part of the Army of Mississippi, Sharp's unit was engaged at SHILOH and PERRYVILLE, as well as at STONE'S RIVER as a part of the ARMY OF TENNESSEE. Shortly before CHICKAMAUGA, Sharp was promoted to colonel of the 44th Mississippi, which he led through the battle of 19–20 Sept. 1863. On the second day of that struggle, as a member of Brig. Gen. J. PATTON ANDERSON's brigade of Maj. Gen. THOMAS C. HINDMAN's division, he played a role in repulsing the Union right wing. Before the end of the fight, Sharp was placed in brigade command, as Anderson replaced the wounded Hindman. He reverted to regimental leadership during the siege of CHATTANOOGA, although for part of that period he was incapacitated, his outfit being led by Col. James Barr of the 10th Mississippi.

At the outset of the ATLANTA CAMPAIGN, Sharp came into his own as a brigade leader in the Army of Tennessee, succeeding the disabled Brig. Gen. WILLIAM F. TUCKER. Thereafter he led 6 Mississippi infantry units, 5 regiments, and 1 sharpshooter battalion. His tactical skill and ability to inspire troops led to his elevation to brigadier general 26 July 1864, 2 days before he distinguished himself at EZRA CHURCH. At campaign's end, he served adroitly during Gen. JOHN B. HOOD's Tennessee invasion and Gen. JOSEPH E. JOHNSTON's CAROLINAS CAMPAIGN, finishing his active career with a spirited performance at BENTONVILLE. Typical of the praise he received from superiors is a comment from his division leader, Anderson, calling attention to Sharp's "prompt obedience to every order and cheerful co-operation in everything tending to promote the efficiency" of the division.

After surrendering with Johnston in North Carolina, Sharp resumed his legal career in Mississippi. He also purchased a newspaper and served as a member of the state legislature 1886–90. d. Columbus, Miss., 15 Sept. 1907.   —EGL

Sharpsburg, Md., Battle of. 17 Sept. 1862 *See* ANTIETAM, MD., BATTLE OF.

sharpshooters. Sniping, or sharpshooting, was a recognized psychological weapon at the outset of the Civil War. Champion marksman HIRAM G. BERDAN of New York, authorized to raise a regiment of sharpshooters for Federal service, began recruiting competitions in summer 1861. Qualified recruits had to place 10 shots in a 10-in. circle at 200 yd, firing any rifle they chose from any position they preferred. In this way Berdan organized companies in New York City, Albany, New York, and in the states of New Hampshire, Vermont,

Fallen sharpshooters in Devil's Den at Gettysburg   *LC*

Michigan, and Wisconsin. Mustered in as the 1st Regiment Sharpshooters/U.S. Volunteers 29 Nov. 1861, the unit saw service in every Eastern campaign through autumn 1864. The 2d Regiment Sharpshooters/U.S. Volunteers was raised similarly, its companies mustered in individually autumn 1861, and its men drawn from New Hampshire, Maine, Pennsylvania, Michigan, Minnesota, and Vermont. It too served in the Eastern theater and Dec. 1864 its veteran volunteers were briefly consolidated with reenlisted veterans of the 1st Regiment.

While the history of BERDAN'S SHARPSHOOTERS is well documented, many other Union marksmen also saw action in the Eastern and Western campaigns, and, though no records have been preserved, a Confederate sharpshooter unit similar to Berdan's was authorized by act of Confederate Congress in 1862.

But the formal muster of entire sharpshooting regiments in the North and South was found to be unwieldy. In correspondence with Rhode Island Gov. William Sprague 19 Sept. 1862, Union Sec. of War Edwin M. Stanton expressed the view of the general staff that snipers were best organized in units no larger than companies and attached to regular regiments for special deployment at a field general's order in a specific action. An approximation of this system was adopted in both Union and Confederate armies.

Armed with SHARPS RIFLES, WHITWORTH RIFLES, sporting arms, and custom-made, privately owned target weapons (some weighing over 30 lb) Northern and Southern marksmen performed efficient service at Yorktown, Gettysburg, Vicksburg, Chattanooga, Atlanta, Spotsylvania, the Wilderness, and Petersburg, and were valued in any protracted battle or small combat. The unpleasant results of this service and the moral climate of the day make finding specific records of sharpshooting duty a rarity, but the efficiency of Confederate sharpshoot-

ers in DEVIL'S DEN at Gettysburg and the demoralizing effects of the sniping deaths of such prominent soldiers as Union Maj. Gen. JOHN SEDGWICK demonstrate the sharpshooter's worth.

—JES

Sharps rifle. The breech-loading rifle was designed by Christian Sharps, who patented his first such military arm in 1848. It was a single-shot percussion weapon with an open-sighted barrel 30 in. long. The overall length of the weapon was 47 in. The rifle used both linen and skin combustible cartridges of .52-caliber conical ball and could be fired 8 to 10 times per minute. Its companion bayonet was of the socket, or angular, style common in that era. However, Sharps also offered the sword bayonet, which could be used after soldering a stud beneath the muzzle to lock on the bayonet handle clip.

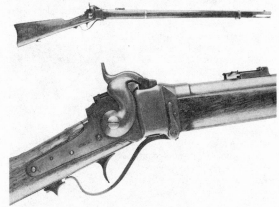

HTIC

Records indicate that the Federal government purchased 9,141 of these rifles from the Sharps Rifle Manufacturing Co. during the war at an average cost of $36.15 each. Many others were carried by Federal soldiers as a result of private, state, and independent militia purchases.

Federal military distribution was generally restricted to units such as BERDAN'S SHARPSHOOTERS, with whom the weapons' accuracy and rapidity of fire were put to best advantage.

This breech-loading rifle was 1 of 3 types of long arms supplied to the Union forces by Sharps. Rarest of these was the Model 1859 rifle musket with a 36-in. barrel, no patchbox, and an overall measurement of 53 in. These were sometimes issued to artillery when adapted for taking the sword bayonet. The third type of shoulder arm produced was the 22-in. barrel breech-loading carbine, a popular weapon for cavalry. Federals had purchased 80,512 of them by the war's end.

In 1863 Sharps introduced the New Model 1863 for both the rifle and the carbine. Slight improvements had been performed on the old models, but the parts for each, old and new, were interchangeable.

Use of the percussion Sharps declined with the advent of the metallic cartridge used by the Henry, Spencer, and others, but it remained a popular weapon until the close of the war.

—SWS

Shaw, Robert Gould. USA   b. Boston, Mass., 10 Oct. 1837. The son of a well-to-do Boston abolitionist, Shaw entered Harvard in 1856, abandoning his studies during his third year. Moving to New York, he joined the 7th New York National Guard. When the Civil War began, he accepted a commission as 2d lieutenant of the 2d Massachusetts, rising to the rank of captain.

On 26 Jan. 1863, Massachusetts Gov. JOHN A. ANDREW, a long-time abolitionist, secured permission to raise black regiments. The War Department's approval resulted in the recruitment of the 54TH MASSACHUSETTS COLORED REGIMENT, the first black regiment from a

USMHI

Northern state. To lead them, Andrew selected Shaw, one of a small group of Union officers who believed that black troops could be trained to match the fighting quality of white soldiers. Feeling he had an obligation to prove this, Shaw accepted the colonelcy of the 54th. By May the regiment had been organized, equipped, and drilled under his guidance. When they paraded through Boston, the youthful colonel's mother, watching in the crowd, exclaimed, "What have I done, that God has been so good to me."

The 54th departed Boston, bound for the South Carolina coast. Routine garrison duty followed until mid-July, when Maj. Gen. Quincy A. Gillmore decided to attack the several Confederate forts on Morris Island that guarded the main ship's channel to Charleston, S.C. Shaw's regiment moved against James Island in a diversionary attack. On 16 July the Confederates charged the Union position on James Island, and in the ensuing combat, the 54th lost 46 men.

On 18 July the regiment was transported to Morris Island, where Shaw received an offer to lead the Federal assault on BATTERY WAGNER. He accepted and at 7:45 p.m. the black volunteers stormed across the beach. Confederate musketry and artillery fire scorched the charging Federals. Into a ditch and up toward a palmetto log parapet they scrambled, with Shaw in the lead. The young colonel, reaching the top first, stood, turned, and shouted, "Onward, Fifty-fourth." He suddenly lurched and fell, killed by a ball in the chest. Today, a monument, sculpted by Augustus Saint-Gaudens, stands in Boston's Public Garden, honoring Shaw and his black soldiers.
—JDW

Shelby, Joseph Orville. CSA b. Lexington, Ky., 12 Dec. 1830, Shelby received his early education from his stepfather, and at Transylvania University 1845–48. After an additional year of study in Philadelphia, he returned to Lexington, where he engaged in the manufacture of rope. Relocating in Berlin, Mo., in 1852, he finally moved to Waverly, there establishing a rope factory. A businessman and also a prosperous planter favoring slavery, "Jo" Shelby led pro-Southern forces in the Missouri-Kansas border conflict of the late 1850s. When the Civil War erupted, the 30-year-old declined a Union army commission, becoming instead a captain of Confederate cavalry. He rapidly displayed the ability that eventually led Federal Maj. Gen. ALFRED PLEASONTON to call Shelby the South's finest cavalryman.

Wearing a black plume in his hat, Shelby fought in every

major campaign in Missouri and Arkansas, beginning at WILSON'S CREEK in 1861. His talents earned him a colonelcy June 1862, and he led a cavalry brigade at Cane Hill and PRAIRIE GROVE in Maj. Gen. Thomas C. Hindman's Missouri campaigning of late 1862. Throughout 1863 Shelby continued to lead his brigade in the numerous engagements of the Missouri-Kansas theater. Wounded at Helena, Ark., July 1863, he

LC

nonetheless launched in September what became the longest cavalry raid of the war. From 22 Sept. until 3 Nov. the colonel slashed his way across Missouri. Despite being heavily outnumbered, Shelby in 1,500 hard miles inflicted more than 1,000 casualties on Union forces while destroying army and public property worth approximately $2 million. He was able to return with several hundred new recruits and a completely reequipped command. Shelby received a long overdue brigadier general's commission to rank from 15 Dec.

Leading a cavalry division during Maj. Gen. Sterling Price's unsuccessful 1864 Missouri Raid, Shelby fought many desperate rearguard actions, with Confederate survival often hinging on his success. Price's eventual escape was due largely to Shelby's tenacity and tactical skills.

Although Confederate defeat now seemed inevitable, Shelby vowed never to surrender, and June 1865 he led several hundred men into Mexico to offer their services to Maximilian. The emperor declined Shelby's sword but offered him land, which Shelby occupied until Maximilian's fall. Returning to Missouri in 1867, Shelby resumed farming until his death in Adrian, 13 Feb. 1897.
—BNO

Shelby's Iron Brigade. CSA With a few hand-picked men as the core of a new regiment, Capt. JOSEPH O. SHELBY moved into Missouri on a recruiting expedition in spring 1862. Promised a colonel's commission if he succeeded, he raised 1,000 men in 4 days at Waverly. On Shelby's return to the Trans-Mississippi Department's headquarters at Little Rock, Ark., Maj. Gen. THOMAS C. HINDMAN gave him his rank and mustered the recruits into Confederate service as the 4th Missouri Cavalry. Hindman also organized the 4th, Col. Upton Hays's 12th Missouri Cavalry, Col. John T. Coffee's 6th Missouri Cavalry, and Capt. Richard A. Collins' battery into Shelby's Missouri Brigade and assigned the 2,500-man command to Maj. Gen. JOHN S. MARMADUKE's cavalry division.

Shelby's men quickly earned a reputation rivaling that of Maj. Gen. J.E.B. STUART's horse soldiers in the East, and with it the nickname "Iron Brigade of the West." Rugged and undisciplined by military standards, they fought Indian-style, using hit-and-run tactics well suited to the rugged Western terrain. Their daring raids into Missouri served the twofold purpose of keeping the brigade provisioned, which the Confederate commissary could not, and harassing Union adversaries in lightning assaults deep behind enemy lines. Devoted to the Confederate cause and to Shelby, the men of the Iron Brigade wore red sumac in their hats as a badge of pride.

Heavily engaged at Cane Hill 8 Nov. 1862, the Iron Brigade

covered Marmaduke's rear while he withdrew to a better defensive position in the Boston Mts. Outnumbered by nearly 5-to-1, Shelby ordered his men to form 2 columns, 1 along each side of the road. At his command, the first 2 companies in each line opened fire, then raced to the tail of the column to reload while successive companies kept up a steady fire on the enemy.

The Iron Brigade fought at PRAIRIE GROVE 7 Dec., inflicted heavy damages on Federal property during Marmaduke's Dec. 1862–Jan. 1863 raid to Springfield, and skillfully covered his retreat in poorly organized operations against Cape Girardeau, April–May. In September and October Shelby's men struck a series of blows against reinforcements en route to the Federal army besieged at CHATTANOOGA, routed Union forces at Neosho 4 Oct., and 3 days later staged a spectacular raid against the supply depot at Warsaw, capturing 30 wagons and destroying the telegraph wires and about 30 mi of railroad track. In 41 days they covered 1,500 mi, killed or wounded 600 Federal troops, captured as many more, destroyed nearly $800,000 in property and $1 million in supplies, and recruited several hundred men. During Maj. Gen. STERLING PRICE'S MISSOURI RAID of 1864, the Iron Brigade was commanded by Col. David Shanks. Col. M. JEFF THOMPSON replaced Shanks after the latter's death at Moreau Creek, 7 Oct.

Some troops of the Iron Brigade refused to surrender when the war ended. These followed Shelby across Texas and fought their way to Mexico City to offer their services to Maximilian. The Iron Brigade disbanded when the emperor refused its service for political reasons, each man receiving a generous travel allowance from Maximilian out of respect for their wartime achievements. —PLF

shell. Artillery shells, distinct from solid-shot, shrapnel, grape, and canister, were the major explosive round used during the Civil War. They were made for virtually every type of artillery piece in use, from mortars to heavy guns, both smoothbore and rifled. Though their exterior configurations varied, they all consisted of a hollow casing in which powder was placed and to which a fuse was attached. When fired, the fuse lit and exploded the shell at the prescribed distance, causing long-range destruction. Within these limits, however, the variations of shell and fuse types were almost endless.

Mortar shells were round and, because they were fired with a relatively light charge, had fairly thin walls to reduce their weight. Round shells for smoothbore artillery tended to have thicker walls and were often reinforced around the fuse hole, thus increasing their weight. All types of round shell had to be handled with some care, primarily to make sure that, when they were loaded into the gun, the fuse faced outward.

Rifled shells varied considerably in their outer configuration. Many were experimental, and others were made for artillery pieces that saw only limited use. The main reason for the variation was the need to develop projectiles that would slip down the bore of the rifled gun easily when loading but that would also grip the rifling grooves when the gun was fired. To accomplish both, some projectiles were covered with paper or lead to grip the bore; others were in 2 parts with a soft metal band between that caught the rifling. Some had flanges to follow the bore grooves, and some were cast in a special shape to mate with equally special rifling. The most successful types employed had an iron, brass, lead, or copper ring affixed to the base.

Internally, rifle shells also varied. Most were smooth, but a

few, including some Confederate types, were segmented to help break the casing when the shell burst. Numerous fuse types were used, ranging from simple powder trails encased in a wood plug to time and percussion fuses. The major types of shells were successful, but many of the experimental ones proved worthless. —LDJ

Shelley, Charles Miller. CSA b. Sullivan Cty., Tenn., 28 Dec. 1833. Migrating to Talladega, Ala., with his parents in 1836, Shelley studied architecture under his father, and prior to the Civil War pursued a career in the building and construction business.

Early in 1861, as a member of the volunteer Talladega Artillery, he served in garrison at Fort Morgan in Mobile Bay. His unit, reorganized as infantry and combined with other small Alabama units, became the 5th Alabama. Shelley, elected captain, served in the FIRST BULL RUN CAMPAIGN under Col. Robert E. Rodes, winning praise from Gen. P.G.T. Beauregard for his bravery in skirmishing at Fairfax

LC

Court House, Va., 17 July 1861, and in the great battle days later.

Returning to Alabama, he organized the 30th Alabama early in 1862, received a Confederate colonel's commission 22 Mar., and as a member of Brig. Gen. Seth M. Barton's brigade in Maj. Gen. Carter L. Stevenson's division served through the autumn KENTUCKY CAMPAIGN. After service at PORT GIBSON, Miss., and capture and exchange following the fall of VICKSBURG in summer 1863, he led the 30th Alabama in the Siege of CHATTANOOGA, fought in the ATLANTA CAMPAIGN, and as a colonel commanded a brigade in Maj. Gen. Edward C. Walthall's division in summer 1864. Promoted brigadier general to date from 17 Sept., he commanded the 17th, 26th, and 29th Alabama and the 37th Mississippi in the autumn FRANKLIN AND NASHVILLE CAMPAIGN, losing more than a third of his force in combat. Shelley campaigned through the Carolinas with the remnants of the Army of Tennessee and was surrendered with it Apr. 1865.

After the war, Shelley first settled in Louisiana, then moved to Dallas Cty., Ala., became active in politics of the "New South," was elected sheriff of the county in 1874, and won the first of 4 consecutive elections to the U.S. Congress in 1876. Opposed to political Reconstruction and a supporter of veterans' organizations, he voted with other Democrats and former brigadier generals in Congress for the South's economic revitalization. He served as fourth auditor of the U.S. Treasury 1885–88 during the Cleveland administration, then retired to Alabama, dying in Birmingham 20 Jan. 1907. —JES

Shelton Laurel, N.C., massacre at. Jan. 1863 Throughout the conflict, western North Carolina, an area of bitterly divided loyalties, experienced a civil war all its own. On numerous occasions, the Unionists who predominated in that remote, mountainous region—many of them self-proclaimed bushwhackers—raided local Confederate outposts and supply depots, waylaid Southern troops, and brutalized the families of leading secessionists. Confederates in and out of uniform retaliated with equal violence, beating, torturing, and killing local "tories" and sacking their property.

The feud reached its height in the first month of 1863, when a band of about 50 Union men, including several deserters from the 64th North Carolina Infantry, terrorized Confederate sympathizers living near Marshall, a village nestled in a secluded valley known as Shelton Laurel. The raiders—who sought booty, especially salt, a staple commodity in scarce supply that winter—plundered with such abandon that the local Confederate commander, Brig. Gen. HENRY HETH, demanded that Shelton Laurel be cleared of guerrillas once and for all. From his headquarters in East Tennessee, he assigned the task to the ranking officers of the deserters' regiment, Col. Lawrence M. Allen and Lt. Col. James A. Keith. Since Allen's home had been among the guerrillas' targets, he was not displeased when Heth stated: "I do not want to be troubled with any prisoners and the last one of them should be killed."

Quickly marching east, the 64th North Carolina swept through Shelton Laurel with a vengeance, sacking the homes of Unionists, beating and whipping their inhabitants (including women and children), and rounding up 15 male prisoners, aged 13 to 59. At least 8 had not been involved in the raid on Marshall. After 2 captives escaped, a detachment under Keith massed the others near a mountain gorge early on 18 Jan., then drew pistols and rifles. Ignoring the prisoners' pleas for mercy, the soldiers shot them down as they knelt in the road. 13 bodies were buried in a single shallow grave.

When the news leaked out, it rocked the Confederacy. Political officials including Sec. of War JAMES A. SEDDON and North Carolina Gov. ZEBULON B. VANCE demanded an investigation and the punishment of all found guilty. The army, however, impeded the inquiry; the only tangible results were the forced resignation of Keith, who was jailed for a time after the war, and 4 of his officers. Colonel Allen remained in the army and General Heth went east, where he won renown as a combat commander.   —EGL

Shenandoah, Confederate Army of the. Virginia militia reporting to training camps near Harpers Ferry mid–Apr. 1861 formed the nucleus of the Army of the Shenandoah. By the first week in May, when Brig. Gen. THOMAS J. "STONEWALL" JACKSON arrived to command the garrison, a few thousand volunteers had also assembled. Jackson, a former instructor at the Virginia Military Institute, helped whip them into shape before relinquishing command 23 May to Gen. JOSEPH E. JOHNSTON.

Eventually Johnston commanded some 10,000 troops of all arms, representing nearly every Southern state. Nevertheless, he felt the force insufficient to hold Harpers Ferry, although the Confederate War Department considered the town a door to the Shenandoah Valley that must be kept closed to the enemy. When, early in June, a larger Union force under Gen. ROBERT PATTERSON poised to invade the valley, Johnston demanded the right to abandon his post. Receiving what he considered ample authority, he destroyed excess matériel, then withdrew south to Winchester on the 15th. Patterson immediately occupied the town but advanced no farther, finally retreating back across the Potomac River. On 2 July his troops returned to the valley, outmaneuvered a force under Jackson at Falling Waters, and tossed it back on Johnston's unified command.

On 18 July Johnston received orders to move to Manassas Junction, 65 mi to the east, and join a smaller army under Gen. P.G.T. BEAUREGARD, hard-pressed by a Federal invasion force.

Brilliantly screened by the cavalry of Col. J.E.B. STUART, Johnston left Winchester that day and soon had 4 brigades (some 8,300 men) aboard eastbound trains. The troops began to arrive in Manassas early on the 20th and on the next day helped Beauregard crush the right flank of Maj. Gen. IRVIN MCDOWELL's forces along BULL RUN. Following this dramatic victory, the Confederate armies merged, becoming known as the Confederate Army of the Potomac, and Johnston assumed overall command.   —EGL

Shenandoah, CSS. Built in Scotland in 1864 for use as a British transport, the *Shenandoah* was the last Confederate commerce destroyer to operate on the seas. After its purchase by Confederate agent JAMES D. BULLOCH, the vessel was placed under the command of Lt. JAMES I. WADDELL, who was ordered to cruising grounds neglected by earlier raiders. The *Shenandoah* left London 8 Oct. 1864 disguised as a British merchant ship, the *Sea King*. At Funchal, Madeira, the ship was converted to an armed cruiser and commissioned CSS *Shenandoah* 19 Oct., then began a year's cruise that would take it 58,000 mi around the globe.

Most of the 38 prizes taken by the *Shenandoah* were Yankee whalers, and two-thirds of these were captured after the war had ended. 20 whaling ships in the Arctic Ocean were burned by Waddell despite rumors of the war's end. Finally convinced of the Confederacy's defeat through communication with a British vessel 2 Aug. 1865, Waddell disarmed the *Shenandoah* and sailed it to England disguised as a merchant ship. At Liverpool, 6 Nov. 1865, the cruiser was surrendered to British authorities.

The *Shenandoah*, iron-framed and teak-plated, was rigged as a clipper, with a 250-horsepower engine and a propeller that could be raised out of the water when not in use. It weighed 1,018 tons, had a breadth of 32 ft 5 in., a depth of 20 ft 5 in., and a length of 220 ft. The cruiser's top speed was about 8 knots, but that could be doubled in a favorable wind. It was armed with 6 68-pounders and 2 32-pounders.

Sold after the war, the *Shenandoah* was being used for trade when lost in the Indian Ocean in 1879. At the time it was owned by the sultan of Zanzibar.   —NCD

Shenandoah, Union Army of the. This particular designation properly belongs only to those forces that served under Maj. Gen. PHILIP H. SHERIDAN and his successors in the Shenandoah Valley of Virginia 1864–65 and not to the small force that served in the same general area under Gen. Robert Patterson in 1861.

Organized early in Aug. 1864, Sheridan's command, also known as the Middle Military Division/Department of the Shenandoah, consisted of units of the VI Corps/Army of the Potomac under Maj. Gen. HORATIO G. WRIGHT; the 1st and 2d divisions of the original XIX Corps/Army of the Gulf under Brig. Gen. WILLIAM H. EMORY; the 1st and 3d cavalry divisions of the Cavalry Corps/Army of the Potomac under Brig. Gens. ALFRED T. A. TORBERT and WESLEY MERRITT; and the Army of West Virginia, under Maj. Gen. GEORGE CROOK—some 60,000 troops altogether.

Formed because of a Confederate raid that penetrated the suburbs of Washington, D.C., the Army of the Shenandoah had as its sole mission driving from the valley, or destroying, Confederate Lt. Gen. Jubal A. Early and his 2 corps. The campaign was called Sheridan's SHENANDOAH VALLEY CAMPAIGN and was headquartered at Harpers Ferry. Its engagements at

WINCHESTER, FISHER'S HILL, Tom's Brook, and CEDAR CREEK ended the Southern military threat in the valley. Subsequently, Sheridan and the Army of the Shenandoah devastated the valley, methodically seizing or destroying every animal, crop, and building in the area.

The army began its dissolution as Wright's VI Corps returned to the Army of the Potomac as of 6 Dec. 1864, and the XIX Corps units joined Sherman at Savannah Jan. 1865. Torbert succeeded Sheridan in command of the greatly depleted force and was in turn replaced 7 Mar. 1865 by Maj. Gen. WINFIELD S. HANCOCK, who commanded the army of occupation until it was abolished 27 June 1865.   —RAP

Shenandoah, Union Department of the.   Constituted 19 July 1861, the Union Department of the Shenandoah comprised the Shenandoah Valley and the Maryland counties of Washington and Allegheny. Federal authorities discontinued the department 17 Aug., when it was merged into the Department of the Potomac.

On 4 Apr. 1862, the War Department reauthorized the department, re-creating the command because of Confederate Maj. Gen. THOMAS J. "STONEWALL" JACKSON's attack on Federal forces at the FIRST BATTLE OF KERNSTOWN, Va., 23 Mar. Though defeated, Jackson altered Union STRATEGY by preventing Maj. Gen. NATHANIEL P. BANKS and his corps from reinforcing the Army of the Potomac. Banks assumed command of the department and maintained his position near Winchester, Va.

After being placed in departmental command, Banks cautiously advanced southward up the valley. Jackson reacted swiftly during the first week of May, initiating his brilliant 1862 SHENANDOAH VALLEY CAMPAIGN. On 8 May the Confederate general attacked and defeated 1 Federal force at MCDOWELL. Returning to the valley, he moved against Banks, who withdrew northward. The Confederates on the 23d nearly destroyed a 1,000-man Union force at FRONT ROYAL. 2 days later, Jackson, in a skillful attack, defeated Banks at FIRST WINCHESTER. The Northerners crossed the Potomac River on the 26th and, a month later, 26 June, the department was again discontinued when Banks's Corps became part of the Union Army of Virginia.   —JDW

C.S.S. Shenandoah   USN

Shenandoah Valley. The great valley of Virginia, the Shenandoah, was second only to the Mississippi River Valley in its strategic importance to the Confederacy. Flanked on the west by the Allegheny Mts. and on the east by the Blue Ridge Mts., the valley stretched for nearly 150 mi from the Potomac River in the north to the James in the south. Its fertile farms and abundant mills made it the granary of the Confederacy. Angling from the southwest to the northeast, it was a giant arrow thrust at the Union's heart, Washington, D.C., a natural invasion route for Southern armies.

Much of the drama and legend of the Civil War in Virginia centered on the Shenandoah, and, from the war's outset, it was one of the most hotly contested areas of the conflict. 4 major campaigns and several lesser struggles occurred within this historic corridor. The town of WINCHESTER exchanged hands more than 70 times during the 4 years of warfare.

During the conflict's initial 3 years, Union forces suffered constant defeat and embarrassment in the Shenandoah. The lush fields became a green and golden deathtrap for Federals as the Confederates routed Union commands and used the area for invasions into Northern soil. The valley seemingly belonged to 1 man in those early years—Maj. Gen. THOMAS J. "STONEWALL" JACKSON, whose brilliant SHENANDOAH VALLEY CAMPAIGN of May–June 1862 forever linked him and his FOOT CAVALRY to the Shenandoah. A year later Gen. ROBERT E. LEE used the natural avenue as his route of invasion into Pennsylvania.

In 1864 Union fortunes finally changed. Twice in the spring and early summer, the Northerners launched invasions into the heart of the valley and twice, at NEW MARKET and at Lynchburg, the Confederates repulsed them. After Lt. Gen. JUBAL A. EARLY moved northward down the valley and threatened Washington, D.C., in an audacious July raid, Union authorities brought a solid army and an aggressive commander to the area. In September and October Maj. Gen. PHILIP H. SHERIDAN and his Federals inflicted 4 defeats on Early—at THIRD WINCHESTER, FISHER'S HILL, Tom's Brook, and CEDAR CREEK—and systematically destroyed the granary. Sheridan's 1864 SHENANDOAH VALLEY CAMPAIGN secured the region and marked the beginning of the end of the war in Virginia.   —JDW

Shenandoah Valley Campaign, Jackson's. May–June 1862 Ordered to conduct "diversionary" operations in the SHENANDOAH VALLEY, Confederate Maj. Gen. THOMAS J. "STONEWALL" JACKSON advanced on Kernstown, Va. Though the FIRST BATTLE OF KERNSTOWN, 23 Mar. 1862, resulted in a tactical defeat for the Confederates, Union authorities in Washington, D.C., were alarmed and withheld troops from the planned Union offensive against Richmond, Va. At the same time, Jackson recruited new troops while receiving the division of Maj. Gen. RICHARD S. EWELL, and by late April commanded 17,000 Confederates in the valley.

Union Maj. Gen. GEORGE B. MCCLELLAN's Army of the Potomac had been moving slowly up the Virginia peninsula toward the Confederate capital since early April. From Richmond, Gen. ROBERT E. LEE, military adviser to Pres. Jefferson Davis, suggested to Jackson another diversionary offensive in the valley to prevent McClellan from obtaining additional reinforcements. Jackson immediately seized the opportunity. Obsessed with secrecy, "Old Jack" confided in no one, which drove the frustrated Ewell to conclude that his superior was insane. But Jackson planned carefully and 3 May marched half his command eastward out of the valley. This baffling movement began one of the most brilliant strategic campaigns in military history.

Beyond the Blue Ridge Mts., near Charlottesville, Jackson herded his amazed veterans onto railroad cars for a return trip to the Shenandoah. The Confederates rolled into Staunton, got off, and marched toward the Allegheny Mts., where Union Maj. Gen. JOHN C. FRÉMONT's army was located. On 8 May, at the Battle of MCDOWELL, Jackson defeated part of the Federal command, sending it westward. Turning back toward the valley, he pushed his marching columns toward another Union force under Maj. Gen. NATHANIEL P. BANKS.

Learning that Banks had been ordered to move to join McClellan, Jackson decided to advance immediately against these Federals. He ordered Ewell to move northward down the Luray Valley, while he drove forward in the Shenandoah on the other side of Massanutten Mountain. Reaching New Market, south of Banks's position at Strasburg, Jackson swerved eastward, passing through a gap in the ridge to unite with Ewell. The combined Confederate forces then knived down the Luray Valley. On 23 May, the Southerners overwhelmed a small detachment of Banks's at Front Royal.

With the unpredictable Jackson between him and Washington, Banks quickly retreated northward. Planning to cut off Banks, the Confederate general urged his weary men forward all day on the 24th and through the night. At dawn, 25 May, he attacked Banks, who had halted at Winchester. The Federals briefly resisted the Confederate charges before breaking and scampering northward. "Old Jack" ordered an immediate pursuit, but his infantry was exhausted and Brig. Gen. TURNER ASHBY's ill-disciplined cavalry abandoned the action to loot the Federal camps. Banks retreated across the Potomac River into Maryland.

Banks's defeat at the FIRST BATTLE OF WINCHESTER caused panic in some parts of the North. Pres. Abraham Lincoln, wanting to trap and destroy the Confederates, ordered Frémont to advance from the south, told Banks to rally and pursue from the rear, and directed Maj. Gen. IRVIN MCDOWELL, at Fredericksburg, to suspend his move on Richmond and detach 20,000 men toward the valley from the east. Lincoln formulated a sound plan, but it required aggressiveness and coordination from officers not known for either.

Jackson, meanwhile, threatened Harpers Ferry, before turning south in a race to elude the converging Union commands. He pushed his men relentlessly, constantly riding along the ranks, saying, "Close up, men, close up. Press on, press on. Close up, men, close up." By their long, swift marches, his rugged veterans earned the sobriquet "FOOT CAVALRY." Jackson's efforts foiled the Union trap. At CROSS KEYS, 8 June, Ewell defeated Frémont. The next day, at PORT REPUBLIC, Jackson and Ewell hammered McDowell's troops under Brig. Gen. JAMES SHIELDS. This engagement concluded the campaign.

In 30 days Jackson had achieved immortal fame with this classic offensive. His foot cavalry had marched 350 mi; defeated 3 separate Union armies, numbering twice its strength, in 5 battles; inflicted twice its casualties; seized numerous supplies; and immobilized an additional 60,000 Federals. Using the terrain and mobility to achieve numerical battlefield superiority, Jackson became a legend in the Shenandoah Valley and the Confederacy's foremost hero.   —JDW

Shenandoah Valley Campaign, Sheridan's. 7 Aug.

1864–2 Mar. 1865   On the night of 12–13 July 1864, Lt. Gen. JUBAL A. EARLY's Confederate troops slipped into the darkness away from their lines outside Washington, D.C. In this fourth summer of the war, Early's troopers had again penetrated Northern territory in an audacious raid (see EARLY'S WASHINGTON RAID). The Union government launched a pursuit the next day, but the Confederates eluded the Federals and returned to the SHENANDOAH VALLEY. Most of the pursuers turned back toward the capital 20 July. On the 24th Early attacked the Federals assigned to watch him and routed the Northerners in the SECOND BATTLE OF KERNSTOWN. "Old Jube" then dispatched a cavalry force to Pennsylvania, where on the 30th it burned the community of CHAMBERSBURG.

This series of lightning Confederate movements and victorious engagements embarrassed Northern authorities. Since 1861 the Shenandoah Valley, the fertile granary of the Confederacy, had been a valley of humiliation and death for Union armies. Confederates in Virginia supplied themselves from the region's farms and had twice used the corridor for an invasion of Northern soil. Early's recent offensive, swiftly and boldly executed, increased the frustration of the Union administration.

The man ultimately responsible for Federal operations in the valley and the defense of the capital in 1864 was Lt. Gen. ULYSSES S. GRANT, general-in-chief of all Union armies. As a part of his spring offensive in the East and West, Grant had sent Maj. Gen. FRANZ SIGEL southward up the Shenandoah. Sigel, however, had met defeat at NEW MARKET 15 May and retreated. Maj. Gen. DAVID HUNTER, replacing Sigel, launched a second thrust within 2 weeks. Hunter penetrated into the heart of the upper valley, reaching Lynchburg, where in June Early, ordered to the area by Gen. ROBERT E. LEE, arrived and chased Hunter into the Allegheny Mts. The Confederate corps commander, under Lee's orders to divert the pressure brought by Grant in besieging PETERSBURG, then turned north toward the Union capital.

Early's descent on the capital finally made Grant realize that a successful resolution of the war in Virginia depended on victory in the valley and destruction of the region. During the first week of August Grant combined 4 overlapping Union departments into the Middle Military District and, on the 6th, replaced Hunter with Maj. Gen. PHILIP H. SHERIDAN. The Federal commander's selection of his 33-year-old cavalry commander was made over the doubts of Pres. Abraham Lincoln and Sec. of War Edwin M. Stanton. Grant wanted an aggressive officer he could trust to head the new district; the forthcoming campaign vindicated him.

"Little Phil" immediately organized the newly formed Army of the Shenandoah. Numbering more than 40,000, the army included the VI Corps, 2 divisions of the XIX Corps, the Army of West Virginia, and 3 cavalry divisions, 2 of which were splendid commands released by Grant from the Petersburg area. Early's Army of the Valley consisted of 4 infantry divisions, 2 artillery battalions, and eventually 2 cavalry divisions, totaling about 12,000. The Confederate general had 3 of the best infantry divisions in the Confederacy: the famed II Corps, the FOOT CAVALRY of Lt. Gen. THOMAS J. "STONEWALL" JACKSON. Though now bled by 3 months of battles and marches, these veterans had never been driven from a field they defended.

Within a week of assuming command, Sheridan advanced his army up the valley. Early withdrew to a naturally strong position at Fisher's Hill. For 3 days the opponents skirmished

indecisively until Sheridan ordered a withdrawal. Hoping to force Grant to dispatch more troops from Petersburg or attack Early again, Lee sent his general an infantry and a cavalry division with an additional artillery battalion. When the Confederates arrived opposite Sheridan's left flank, the Union army retreated northward.

For the next month the 2 forces maneuvered, skirmished, and probed along Opequon Creek, which flowed into the Potomac River. It was 30 days of "backing and filling," as one Federal said. Sheridan pursued this cautious strategy, constrained by the Republican administration's fears that another defeat would adversely affect Lincoln's reelection campaign. But the Union capture of ATLANTA, Ga., 2 Sept. 1864, reversed the president's political fortunes and allowed Sheridan to advance. Grant then personally visited Sheridan, who confidently outlined an offensive operation. Grant listened and, in his briefest order of the war, simply said, "Go in."

The Federals advanced before daylight, 19 Sept. 1864, against Early's Confederates behind Opequon Creek, near Winchester. All day in cornfields and woodlands the 2 armies hammered at each other in a vicious stand-up fight. Sheridan made a number of tactical errors that nearly proved disastrous, but his overwhelming numbers prevailed. The Federals, as Sheridan telegraphed Lincoln, sent the Confederates "whirling through Winchester." Sheridan lost more than 5,000 men, Early more than 3,500 in this THIRD BATTLE OF WINCHESTER.

The Southerners again withdrew to Fisher's Hill, a position a Union officer described as "the bugbear of the Valley." For 2 days Sheridan probed Early's lines. On the 22d Brig. Gen. GEORGE CROOK moved his command beyond the Confederate left and charged. The rest of the Federal army hit the front of the works and the Southerners broke under the onslaught. The Battle of FISHER'S HILL was another signal victory for Sheridan.

The Federals advanced up the valley to near Harrisonburg. Early halted and regrouped to the east at the Blue Ridge Mts. After 2 weeks the Union troops headed back down the Shenandoah. From 6–8 Oct. the Federal cavalry systematically destroyed the farms, mills, crops, and livestock of the residents. These 3 days were remembered in the area simply as "The Burning." Confederate horsemen pursued vigorously and, on the 9th, the Federal troopers turned and routed them in the Battle of Tom's Brook, or the "Woodstock Races."

The Union army halted at Middletown, behind Cedar Creek. Sheridan went on to Washington, D.C., to confer with Stanton on the disposition of his army. On 19 Oct. Early launched a brilliant surprise attack at dawn. The Confederates crushed two-thirds of the Union infantry, sending them north beyond Middletown. Sheridan, on his way back to the front, arrived about 10:30 a.m. He rallied his army and at 4 p.m. counterattacked and routed the Confederates for a fourth time. The Battle of CEDAR CREEK ended the campaign's major action.

Throughout the fall and winter Sheridan and Early returned most of their armies to their respective commanders at Petersburg. Sheridan, keeping his cavalry, finally advanced late in Feb. 1865. On 2 Mar. his horsemen dispersed the last pitiful remnant of Early's command in an engagement at WAYNESBOROUGH. "Little Phil," moving east, then rejoined Grant for the war's final campaign.

The Shenandoah Valley Campaign of summer and autumn 1864 marked the beginning of the end of the Confederacy in Virginia. Sheridan's 4 major victories in a span of 30 days brought Lincoln's campaign timely successes, and his destruction of the valley ensured that the Confederates could no longer garner its lush harvests. The campaign was one of the most decisive of the war.   —JDW

Shepherdstown, western Va., eng. at.   20 Sept. 1862

The Confederate Army of Northern Virginia, during the night of 18–19 Sept. 1862, abandoned its lines on the ANTIETAM, Md., battlefield and crossed the Potomac River back into Virginia. Covered by the darkness, the Southerners withdrew safely. To protect the army's rear from an expected Federal pursuit, Gen. ROBERT E. LEE assigned 2 battered brigades and 45 cannon under the command of Brig. Gen. WILLIAM N. PENDLETON, the army's chief of artillery. Lee directed Pendleton to hold the crossing at Boteler's Ford, near Shepherdstown, all day and for the night of the 19th–20th unless Federal pressure became too great.

The Union pursuers, Federal cavalry, came with the sunrise. As the troopers rode into view, Pendleton's gunners reacted. 3 batteries of Federal horse artillery soon arrived, and the foes dueled for 2 hours. Maj. Gen. FITZ JOHN PORTER's V Corps replaced the Union horsemen, who withdrew with their cannon to their camp. Porter's gun crews resumed the artillery barrage, which lasted throughout the afternoon. Union sharpshooters sniped at Confederate artillerists as Southern infantrymen joined the fray.

At sunset 500 volunteers, led by Brig. Gen. CHARLES GRIFFIN, waded across the river under fire, storming the Southern position. The undermanned Confederate brigades immediately broke under the assault and abandoned their steep 80-ft bluffs. Pendleton, uncertain what had occurred in the twilight, galloped to the rear, searching for Confederate reinforcements. He eventually found Lee and told the shocked commander that all 45 cannon had been seized by the charging Federals. Lee maintained his composure while Maj. Gen. THOMAS J. "STONEWALL" JACKSON, learning of Pendleton's bungled affair, immediately ordered his 3 divisions forward to drive the Northerners back into Maryland.

By 9 a.m. on the 20th, Maj. Gen. Ambrose P. Hill's LIGHT DIVISION, deployed in 2 lines, 3 brigades in each line, was advancing through a cornfield toward the Federal line on the bluffs. As Hill's front line surged forward, the Federals buckled under the riveting charge, then cracked. Caught in the middle, the 118th Pennsylvania, the "Corn Exchange Regiment," armed with defective muskets, was riddled by the Confederates. A panic seized the Federals, who plunged into the river. Hill's troops, lining the bluffs, killed or wounded many of them as they swam toward the opposite bank.

Jackson's quick reaction and Hill's brilliant assault secured Lee's rear. Pendleton, however, had been mistaken: only 4 of his cannon had fallen into Union hands. After Shepherdstown, Lee mainly confined Pendleton to administrative duties.
                                                                                       —JDW

Sheridan, Philip Henry.   USA   b. Albany, N.Y., 6 Mar. 1831.

The son of Irish immigrants, Sheridan received his basic education in Somerset, Ohio, where his parents had moved shortly after his birth. Unlike many of his future colleagues, Sheridan was too young to serve in the Mexican War. Eager to pursue a military career, in 1848 he falsified his birthdate by 1 year to gain early admittance to the U.S. Military Academy. Shortly after his arrival, during a military formation he broke ranks in a fit of anger and chased a cadet officer with fixed

USMHI

bayonet, which resulted in his suspension for a year. Returning to the academy, the temperamental Sheridan graduated in 1853, 34th in a class of 49. As brevet 2d lieutenant in the 1st Infantry he was assigned to frontier duty along the Rio Grande, then to the 4th Infantry in the Northwest to combat hostile Indians.

In 1861 Sheridan was called to war duty as a captain in the 13th Infantry in southwest Missouri. He served as quartermaster and commissary for the regiment, then as quartermaster for Maj. Gen. Henry W. Halleck's troops during the campaigning for CORINTH. Dissatisfied with staff duty, Sheridan exhibited his displeasure in his relations with others. With a sense of relief for all concerned, he was appointed colonel of the 2d Michigan Cavalry 25 May 1862. The transfer marked the turning point of his army career. Within the first month of his new assignment, his victory at BOONEVILLE, Miss., at the command of a brigade, earned him the rank of brigadier of volunteers, 13 Sept. Within 6 months he had distinguished himself at PERRYVILLE as commander of an infantry division, and at STONE'S RIVER he was credited with saving Maj. Gen. William S. Rosecrans' army by offering stiff opposition to the Confederates. On 16 Mar. 1863, he was promoted to major general of volunteers to rank from 31 Dec. 1862.

At CHICKAMAUGA in fall 1863 Sheridan again distinguished himself, as commander of the XX Corps/Army of the Cumberland. At the Battle of CHATTANOOGA his forces charged up the steep, rough terrain of MISSIONARY RIDGE, contributing substantially to the defeat of Gen. Braxton Bragg in an action that brought Sheridan to Maj. Gen. Ulysses S. Grant's attention. When Grant was promoted to lieutenant general, he gave Sheridan command of all cavalry in the Army of the Potomac. Sheridan's new command included 3 divisions of about 10,-000 men.

"Little Phil's" meteoric rise is attributed to 2 traits he himself recognized: a willingness to take the offensive wherever possible and as aggressively as possible, and a willingness to exploit every edge over an opponent. These 2 principles, carried out against the weakened and diminished Confederates of 1864–65, yielded a string of victories.

Sheridan reorganized the cavalry with speed and fervor. Within a month his units were ready for the battles at the WILDERNESS, Todd's Tavern, SPOTSYLVANIA COURT HOUSE, and COLD HARBOR. Between 9 May and 25 May, his forces severed many vital communication lines around Richmond, causing great fear in the capital. The destruction included 10 mi of railroad track on 3 different lines, the telegraph system, and an extensive capture of stores and supplies (see SHERIDAN'S RICHMOND RAID). Though his men were defeated at TREVILIAN STATION, 11–12 June, a month earlier they had been responsible for the death of Lt. Gen. J.E.B. Stuart at YELLOW TAVERN, an irreplaceable loss to the Confederates.

In Aug. 1864 Grant made Sheridan commander of the Army of the Shenandoah with specific instructions to move the Confederates south and to destroy all supplies that would aid the enemy. The fertile SHENANDOAH VALLEY had been a place of supply and food for the Confederates throughout the war. Sheridan made careful preparation, appearing to his superiors in Washington to be somewhat slow. He justified the preparation 19 Sept. by advancing against Lt. Gen. Jubal A. Early and defeating him at THIRD WINCHESTER and again at FISHER'S HILL several days later. For this victory Sheridan was advanced to brigadier general in the Regular Army. Southerners hated him for laying waste to the land and reducing the populace to starvation, a "scorched earth" policy Sheridan defended as a military necessity to cut the Confederate source of foodstuffs and end the war.

Early's forces regrouped and assaulted Sheridan at CEDAR CREEK, 19 Oct. 1864. This surprise action caught the Federal troops unprepared and almost resulted in their defeat. Sheridan made his famous ride to the front and rallied his troops, turning near defeat into victory. He was rewarded with the THANKS OF CONGRESS and promoted to major general in the Regular Army, to date from 8 Nov. (*See also* SHERIDAN'S SHENANDOAH VALLEY CAMPAIGN.)

With undiminished energy he continued to strike Confederate lines of supply, 27 Feb.–24 Mar. 1865, raiding enemy locations from Winchester to Petersburg (*see* SHERIDAN'S VIRGINIA RAID). At WAYNESBOROUGH, 2 Mar., he again defeated Early, effectively destroying the Confederate army in the valley. Sheridan cut 3 railroad lines and 2 canals, leaving Gen. Robert E. Lee with only 1 open rail line to the south. The buildup of his forces at FIVE FORKS gave him the means to turn the Confederate flank and force it to evacuate Petersburg 1 Apr. Sheridan pursued the retreating Confederates and defeated them at SAYLER'S CREEK. He and his troops were at Appomattox when Lee surrendered the Confederate army to Grant.

Sheridan's postwar career included assignment to the Military Division of the Gulf—where he dealt with sensitive conditions along the Mexican border, the result of conflict between Mexican liberals and French-supported Maximilian—and in 1867 his assignment as commander of the Fifth Military District (Texas and Louisiana) during Reconstruction. His harsh policies in the latter role resulted in his removal after 6 months. In 1869 he was promoted to lieutenant general when William T. Sherman was advanced to full general and commander-in-chief of the army following Grant's election to the presidency. He served in several different posts until succeeding Sherman as commander-in-chief in 1884. He was promoted to full general as of 1 June 1888. Sheridan completed his 2-volume *Personal Memoirs* three days before his death in Nosquitt, Mass., 5 Aug. 1888.   —JDK

Sheridan's Richmond raid. 9–24 May 1864 On 9 May 1864, 3 Federal cavalry divisions (12,000 troopers) and 32 cannon, riding in a column stretching 13 mi, abandoned the army's lines around Spotsylvania Court House. Ordered by Lt. Gen. ULYSSES S. GRANT to pass around Gen. ROBERT E. LEE's army and attack his cavalry and communications, the commander, Maj. Gen. PHILIP H. SHERIDAN, marched at a leisurely pace. Sheridan's purpose, as he said, was to whip Maj. Gen. J.E.B. STUART out of his boots.

Before dusk the powerful force reached the North Anna River, where 2 divisions camped while a third rode to Beaver Dam Station, Lee's advance supply base on the Virginia Central Railroad. The night sky glowed with the flames of a burning depot, torched by Confederate guards, and 100 railway cars

and 2 locomotives destroyed by the Federal troopers. The cavalrymen also freed nearly 400 Union soldiers. On the 10th Sheridan resumed his deliberate pace, halting at night along the banks of the South Anna River.

The confrontation Sheridan sought came the next day when Stuart, who had pushed his horsemen for 2 days, intercepted the Federal command at YELLOW TAVERN, 6 mi north of Richmond. In the swirling engagement the Confederates stubbornly held against Sheridan's superior numbers and armament. During one of the Federal assaults late in the day, Stuart fell mortally wounded. "Little Phil" finally broke off the action, advanced toward Richmond, and passed the capital's outer works that evening.

Sheridan considered attacking Richmond, then abandoned the audacious scheme, swinging eastward. Passing across the peninsula, the Northerners reached Maj. Gen. BENJAMIN F. BUTLER's lines at Haxall's Landing 14 May. 10 days later they rejoined the Army south of Spotsylvania. Sheridan's raid supplied additional proof of the rising superiority of Federal cavalry, now augmented by the irreplaceable loss of "Jeb" Stuart.
                                                              —JDW

Sheridan's Virginia raid. 27 Feb.–24 Mar. 1865 On 27 Feb. 1865, 10,000 Union cavalrymen under Maj. Gen. PHILIP H. SHERIDAN left Winchester, Va., and advanced southward through the Shenandoah Valley toward Staunton and Lynchburg. Gen.-in-Chief ULYSSES S. GRANT had ordered "Little Phil" to wreck Confederate railroads and canals near the latter town before turning east to join other Federal commands. Near Staunton stood the only barrier to Sheridan's progress: Lt. Gen. JUBAL A. EARLY's 1,800-man army, the pitiful remnant of a once-proud force that Sheridan had virtually annihilated the previous September and October at THIRD WINCHESTER, FISHER'S HILL, and CEDAR CREEK.

During the first days of the march the Federals confiscated enemy supplies, secured some bridges above Staunton, burned others, and bested Early's cavalry. On 1 Mar. the Federals occupied Staunton, forcing Early to relocate at Waynesborough, about a dozen miles to the east. There, at the foot of Rockfish Gap, a strategic defile through the Blue Ridge Mts., "Old Jube" attempted to make a stand with 2 infantry brigades and an artillery battalion.

On the rainy morning of 2 Mar., Sheridan's advance, under Maj. Gen. GEORGE A. CUSTER, probed the Confederate line and found a wide gap between its left flank and the South River. About 3:30 p.m. 3 of Custer's dismounted regiments, having slipped into position under cover of woods, struck Early's left, while Sheridan's cannon and the rest of his command battered Early's center and right. The result was a headlong stampede by the enemy. Sheridan captured 1,600 troops, a dozen cannon, and 200 supply wagons. Early and other survivors fled in several directions, uncovering Rockfish Gap and the previously unspoiled territory above the James River.

With the valley Confederates dispersed, Sheridan spent 4 weeks destroying barns, mills, the Virginia Central Railroad, and the James River Canal. Electing not to attack heavily guarded Lynchburg, he turned in triumph toward the Petersburg front, where on the 28th he joined Grant and the Army of the Potomac just in time to participate in the APPOMATTOX CAMPAIGN.   —EGL

Sherman, John. USP b. Lancaster, Ohio, 10 May 1823. A

younger brother of future Union Gen. WILLIAM T. SHERMAN, John was descended from Englishmen who settled in Boston in the 1630s. The early death of his father, a justice of the Ohio supreme court, resulted in John's growing up in the family of a relative, a Mount Vernon, Ohio, merchant. An indifferent student, he opted for work instead of education. At 14 he became a laborer on the Muskingum River Canal, a position he lost 2 years later when the state's Democratic administration learned of his Whig affiliation. The firing deepened his political awareness.

In 1840 Sherman began the study of law under the tutelage of his brother Charles, an attorney in Mansfield; 4 years later he was admitted to the bar, proving highly successful as a trial lawyer and learning to win cases more "by plain talk than by rhetoric." In 1854 he applied this philosophy to the political canvas, and his prominent opposition to the KANSAS-NEBRASKA ACT swept him into the U.S. House of Representatives. In Washington he made a reputation as an opponent of the expansion of slavery into the Western territories and for his sober, moderate views on other governmental, economic, and social issues. Elected as a Whig, he was 3 times returned to the House as a Republican and by 1861 was almost assured of gaining the speakership. By now a staunch ally of ABRAHAM LINCOLN, Sherman was persuaded by the president and other associates to run instead for the senate. That March he was chosen to succeed Sen. (now Treasury Sec.) SALMON P. CHASE. He held his seat until 1877 and again 1881–97.

During the war, Sherman acquired a reputation as an expert on financial matters as well as on military affairs (the value of his advice on and support of army legislation seemed to grow with his brother's rise to fame). Despite his conservative orientation, he supported liberal measures such as the LEGAL TENDER ACTS, the FEDERAL INCOME TAX, a national banking system, and emancipation.

After the conflict, Sherman strengthened the value of Federal currency as Pres. RUTHERFORD B. HAYES's Sec. of the Treasury. He was 3 times a presidential candidate, in 1888 coming within a handful of ballots of receiving the Republican nomination. He lent his name, with some misgivings, to the Anti-Trust and Silver Purchase laws of 1890. From Mar. 1897 to Apr. 1898 he was secretary of state in Pres. WILLIAM MCKINLEY's administration. Resigning the office due to failing health, he died in the capital 22 Oct. 1900.   —EGL

Sherman, Thomas West. USA b. Newport, R.I., 26 Mar. 1813, Sherman is best remembered, not for his service in the Civil War, but for a feat he accomplished at age 18. Bored with the educational prospects in his home state affordable on his family's scant income, Sherman walked to Washington, D.C., nearly 400 mi from home, for an interview with Pres. Andrew Jackson. For his efforts, Jackson rewarded him with an appointment to West Point, the prize for which he had left home against his father's wishes.

Having attended public schools in Newport, Sherman graduated from the U.S. Military Academy 18th in the class of 1836 as a 2d lieutenant in the 3d U.S. Artillery. From 1836 through 1859 he had a varied military career: he served in the Florida War; in Indian Territory, assisting with the Cherokee transfer; at Fort Moultrie, S.C., and as a recruiter. He fought with Gen. Zachary Taylor in the Mexican War and later served at Fort Trumbull, Conn., and Fort Adams, R.I. He then traveled west on an assignment to the frontier of Minnesota, down to Kansas,

USMHI

and back to Minnesota, in command of his own expedition to quell a Sioux uprising at Kettle Creek.

Sherman's first Civil War service came in the defense of Washington, D.C., in 1861. He quickly attained the ranks of lieutenant colonel in the Regular Army and brigadier general of volunteers before he journeyed south to seize and hold bases on the coast for the Union blockading squadron. Because of his abrasive personality, his service with Maj. Gen. Henry W. Halleck was cut short, and he was assigned to the Department of the Gulf.

For the remainder of the war, he took part in actions in Louisiana, including the battle at PORT HUDSON, where he sustained wounds requiring amputation of his right leg.

After the war, Sherman served at various commands on the Atlantic Coast and retired from military service in 1870 as a major general. On 16 Mar. 1879 he died in his Newport home, remembered as a tactless commander; but one with unquestioned ability.   —FLS

Sherman, William Tecumseh. USA b. Lancaster, Ohio, 8 Feb. 1820. Sherman's ancestors arrived in America about 1634. His father, a lawyer and jurist, died suddenly in 1829, leaving 11 children, among them future politician JOHN SHERMAN. William was sent to the family of Thomas Ewing, a U.S. senator and a cabinet member, for upbringing. After receiving his early education in Ohio, Sherman, called "Chump" by his friends, obtained an appointment to West Point through the efforts of his foster father. In 1840 he graduated 6th in a class of 42 and was assigned to the 3d Artillery as a 2d lieutenant. A year later, on duty in Florida, he advanced to

USMHI

1st lieutenant and in 1842 was assigned to Fort Moultrie, S.C.

Sherman took his first leave in 1843, returned to Lancaster, and became engaged to Ellen Ewing, the daughter of his foster parents. On his return to South Carolina he traveled down the Mississippi River and across Georgia. The next year he toured the Southern states for 3 months and in 1845 inspected the Federal arsenal at Augusta, accumulating a knowledge of Southern geography that would be valuable to him later in his career.

During the Mexican War Sherman served as an aide to Capt. Philip Kearny and then as adjutant to Col. Richard B. Mason. Seeing little action, he wanted to resign but was convinced to remain in the army by Gen. Persifor Frazer Smith, commanding the newly created Pacific Division. Smith established his headquarters in San Francisco and made Sherman his adjutant general. In 1850 the young officer was relieved to carry dispatches to the East for Gen. Winfield Scott, marrying Ellen

Ewing in Washington, D.C., on the same trip. 3 years later he resigned his commission as captain and returned to San Francisco to work as the local agent for a St. Louis–based banking firm. As a businessman he managed the company's funds skillfully through the financial crisis of 1857, but the parent bank failed, and Sherman moved to Fort Leavenworth, Kans., to open a law and real-estate office.

Moderately successful in the venture, in Oct. 1859 Sherman accepted the superintendency of the Louisiana State Seminary of Learning and Military Academy near Alexandria, La., the forerunner of Louisiana State University at Baton Rouge. He continued there until the state seceded from the Union in 1861. Offered a commission in the Confederate army, Sherman declined, accepting instead the presidency of a St. Louis streetcar company. After the firing on Fort Sumter, he returned to the army with an appointment as colonel in the new 13th Infantry (Regulars) 14 May. By July Sherman had been given command of a brigade in Brig. Gen. Irvin McDowell's army, which was defeated at BULL RUN in the first major battle of the war.

Sherman was advanced to brigadier general of volunteers 2 Aug., to date from 17 May, and sent to Kentucky as second-in-command to Brig. Gen. Robert Anderson. When Anderson became ill, he succeeded to command under orders to hold the state aided only by the home guard. Throughout the war Sherman felt the sting of the press. Now the strain of expecting a long war and the frustration of conducting a defense with untrained local troops unleashed his volatile temper, causing journalists to print stories claiming that his mind was being affected by the weight of responsibility. Replaced by the War Department, he was ordered to report to Maj. Gen. Henry W. Halleck in Missouri. Sherman assumed command of the District of Cairo, Brig. Gen. Ulysses S. Grant's former command, fighting vigorously at SHILOH and during the advance to CORINTH. Though his brigade was routed at Shiloh, Sherman's effective leadership earned him a promotion to major general of volunteers to rank from 1 May.

When Grant replaced Halleck and assumed command of the Western armies July 1862, he sent Sherman to Memphis to maintain its defense. There Sherman did an admirable job of suppressing guerrillas and establishing a strong civil authority. When Grant began his second advance against VICKSBURG late in 1862, he sent Sherman against CHICKASAW BLUFFS, 27–29 Dec. Defeated when Grant's support troops were unable to advance, Sherman pulled back his men and relinquished command of forces on the river to Maj. Gen. John A. McClernand by order of Pres. Abraham Lincoln. McClernand organized his troops as the Army of the Mississippi, dividing them into 2 corps and assigning 1 to Sherman. At Sherman's suggestion the command moved successfully against ARKANSAS POST. During the campaign, 16 Dec., Grant organized the Army of the Tennessee, which included McClernand's troops at the conclusion of the expedition to Arkansas Post. Now part of the Army of the Tennessee, Sherman's XV Corps participated in the land/sea operations that led to the surrender of Vicksburg 4 July 1863.

In September Sherman was ordered back to Memphis and sent to the relief of CHATTANOOGA. When Grant was given supreme command in the West, he assigned Sherman command of the Army of the Tennessee. In Mar. 1864 Grant went east as the newly appointed general-in-chief of the Federal armies, leaving Sherman in command of all Western troops. Grant's grand strategy called for Maj. Gen. George G. Meade's Army of the Potomac to move against Gen. Robert E. Lee and take Richmond while Sherman launched his ATLANTA CAMPAIGN against Gen. Joseph E. Johnston to capture the Confederacy's last major rail center.

Sherman planned to push into Georgia with the Armies of the Cumberland, the Tennessee, and the Ohio under the command of Maj. Gens. George H. Thomas, James B. McPherson, and John M. Schofield respectively. Operations were headquartered in Chattanooga by late Apr. 1864. All together the forces numbered about 100,000 men to oppose the 60,000 Confederates under Johnston. Sherman assured his lines of supply by taking the railroads out of civilian control, stockpiling certain critical supplies, and discarding all nonessential equipment he thought might slow his advance. Early in May he deployed Thomas and Schofield against Johnston at Dalton, Ga., holding Buzzard Roost Gap near the railroad line. Sherman directed McPherson to proceed around the Confederate left by way of SNAKE CREEK GAP to take RESACA and sever the rail line. McPherson advanced through the gap 9 May but was unsuccessful because of Johnston's movements in the area. On 15 May Sherman advanced over McPherson's route and took Resaca, secured the East Tennessee & Georgia Railroad as far as Kingston, and drove Johnston back to ALLATOONA Pass. Sherman's advance was slowed by the Confederates' favorable position near KENNESAW MOUNTAIN. After several unsuccessful attempts to dislodge Johnston by direct assault, Sherman extended his right to overcome the Confederate position. Johnston retreated to the Chattahoochee River. On 9 June Schofield crossed the river in advance of Sherman's right, causing Johnston to drop back to PEACHTREE CREEK in front of Atlanta.

Dissatisfied with Johnston's performance, Confederate Pres. Jefferson Davis relieved him of command and placed Lt. Gen. John B. Hood at the head of the Army of Tennessee. Sherman advanced on Atlanta from the north and the east but encountered fierce opposition from Hood. Unable to take the city by assault, he besieged Atlanta and cut the railroads to Montgomery, Ala., and Macon, Ga. On 1 Sept. Hood evacuated Southern troops from Atlanta under cover of night. The victorious Sherman was promoted to major general in the Regular Army to rank from 12 Aug. After negotiating with Hood, who accused him of barbarism, Sherman evacuated the civilian population from Atlanta. He sent Thomas' and Schofield's armies west to restrain Hood and defend Tennessee. The balance of Sherman's forces, about 62,000 men, destroyed the military resources in Atlanta, abandoned the city, and moved across Georgia on the famous MARCH TO THE SEA to cut off Confederate communications with the state, the last line of supply for the Eastern Confederate armies.

The devastation and wanton destruction of property by BUMMERS alienated the Southern people, but Sherman contended that the war could be brought to a halt sooner with a firm hand and that the loss of property was less odious than the continued wasting of lives. This earned for Sherman a reputation as one of the first modern military leaders. Twice Sherman's aggressive warfare won him the THANKS OF CONGRESS.

Hostilities in the Carolinas (see CAROLINAS CAMPAIGN) ended 17 Apr. when Sherman and Johnston, once again commanding the Army of Tennessee, met under truce to discuss surrender terms 8 days after Gen. Robert E. Lee surrendered at Appomattox (see SHERMAN'S PEACE PROPOSALS).

Sherman's postwar military career included command of the Division of the Mississippi, military assistance to the construction of the transcontinental railroad, and campaigning against hostile Indians. On 25 July 1866, when Grant was promoted to full general, Sherman was advanced to lieutenant general and moved to Washington to take temporary command of the army. On Grant's inauguration as president in 1869, Sherman became full general and general-in-chief of the army. He retired 1 Nov. 1883, in 1886 settling in New York City, where he died 14 Feb. 1891. The *Memoirs of General William T. Sherman,* direct and forceful like the man who wrote them, were first published in a 2-volume edition in 1875.   —JDK

"Sherman's bowties." *See* "SHERMAN'S HAIRPINS."

"Sherman's hairpins." During the ATLANTA CAMPAIGN, and especially on their MARCH TO THE SEA and in the CAROLINAS CAMPAIGN, Maj. Gen. WILLIAM T. SHERMAN's invaders laid waste to mile upon mile of railroad track. To ensure the destruction of these Confederate communications lines, the mere displacement of rails and ties would not suffice. Encouraged and inspired by Sherman and his generals, the men of the ARMY OF THE CUMBERLAND, the ARMY OF THE TENNESSEE, and the Army of the Ohio became adept at prying rails loose, setting fire to stacks of ties, warping rails over the flames, and bending the hot steel around tree trunks until hairpin-shaped.

Even this was not enough, according to one of Sherman's senior lieutenants. Writing after the war, Maj. Gen. HENRY W. SLOCUM noted that "a rail which is bent can easily be restored to its original shape. No rail should be regarded as properly treated till it has assumed the shape of a doughnut; it must not only be bent but twisted. To do the twisting Poe's [Capt. ORLANDO M. POE, Sherman's chief engineer] railroad hooks are necessary. . . . With Poe's hooks a double twist can be given to a rail, which precludes all hope of restoring it to its former shape except by re-rolling."   —EGL

Sherman's land grants.   Early in Jan. 1865 Maj. Gen. WILLIAM T. SHERMAN, resting in Savannah after his MARCH TO THE SEA, received a visit from Washington notables including Sec. of War EDWIN M. STANTON. Conferring with the Union commander, Stanton turned Sherman's attention to recruiting BLACK SOLDIERS for his armies and providing for former slaves living in areas occupied by his and other forces. After meeting with a delegation of local black leaders, Sherman agreed to put his suggestions for solving the "Negro question" on paper.

The result was his Special Field Order No. 15, published 16 Jan. In addition to providing for the enlistment of blacks, the order set aside for black colonization the coastline and riverbanks 30 mi inland from Charleston, S.C., to Jacksonville, Fla., each resettled family to receive 40 acres of land. The measure was based on the CONFISCATION ACT OF 1862, which held that land owned by certain classes of Secessionists could be seized and redistributed by the Federal government. Sherman's order went into effect immediately, and within 5 months the army had settled more than 40,000 freedmen in the designated areas. In 1866, however, Pres. ANDREW JOHNSON vetoed congressional efforts to convert these "possessory titles" into legal ownership.   —EGL

Sherman's peace proposals.   After the surrender of Gen. ROBERT E. LEE, Maj. Gen. WILLIAM T. SHERMAN, headquartered

at Raleigh, N.C., received a message from Confederate Gen. JOSEPH E. JOHNSTON requesting a "temporary suspension of active operations." On the 17th, 3 days after ABRAHAM LINCOLN was assassinated, the 2 generals met in the Bennett house near Durham's Station to discuss terms. The next day Sherman and Johnston met again and signed a "Memorandum on basis of agreements."

Sherman later wrote, "I sat down at the table, and wrote off the terms which I thought concisely expressed [Lincoln's] views and wishes." The document called for an armistice and general amnesty, Confederate forces to be disbanded, arms to be deposited in state arsenals, men to abide by state and Federal authority, state governments to be reorganized by the president, Federal courts to be reestablished, and all citizens to be guaranteed rights of person and property.

The day Sherman's peace proposals reached Washington, Pres. ANDREW JOHNSON called a meeting of his cabinet, which promptly rejected them. Official Washington fumed over what was called Sherman's "treaty of peace." Statements given to the newspapers by a furious Sec. of War EDWIN M. STANTON fanned the criticism. Newspapers called Sherman a "traitor" with "corrupt motives."

Stanton then sent Lt. Gen. ULYSSES S. GRANT to see Sherman, who took the news calmly and renewed negotiations with Johnston 26 Apr. This time they signed terms that followed those Grant had given Gen. ROBERT E. LEE at APPOMATTOX (*see also* SURRENDERS: Lee and SURRENDERS: Johnston). At about the same time Sherman was able to read Stanton's attacks in 5-day-old newspapers that finally reached his headquarters. His staff stared in disbelief as Sherman paced "like a caged lion, talking to the whole room with furious invective." In his estimate Stanton was "a mean, scheming, vindictive politician." Though Sherman had agreed to renegotiate, he always held that his original terms had been "right, honest, and good."
                                                                                       —AG

Shields, James.   USA b. Cty. Tyrone, Ireland, 10 May 1810, Shields had a remarkably varied, if not distinguished, career. The recipient of an excellent classical education in Ireland, fluent in 4 languages, Shields became an attorney and state supreme-court justice, challenged Abraham Lincoln to a duel, fought in 3 wars, and represented 3 different states in the U.S. Senate.

Shields immigrated to the U.S. in 1826, settling first in Kaskaskia, Ill., where he became a lawyer and an active member of the Democratic party. He participated in the Black Hawk War in 1832. In 1836 Shields was elected to the state legislature, later serving as state auditor and

LC

justice of the Illinois supreme court. He challenged Lincoln after the latter accepted partial responsibility for having criticized in the Whig press Shields's activities as auditor; but the matter was resolved and the 2 lawyers became good friends. During the Mexican War, he was a brigadier general of Illinois volunteers, earning the brevet of major general. A modest war hero, he served in the U.S. Senate 1849–55 but was not reelected. Settling in Minnesota, he returned to the senate in 1858 as a representative of the new state.

With the advent of the war, Shields secured from his old friend Lincoln a commission of brigadier general 19 Aug. 1861. During the 1862 Shenandoah Valley Campaign he commanded a division under Maj. Gen. Irvin McDowell. At PORT REPUBLIC, Va., 9 June 1862, Maj. Gen. Thomas J. "Stonewall" Jackson's Confederate forces attacked and defeated Shields's division. What additional commands he held or duties he performed are unknown.

Shields resigned from the army 28 Mar. 1863, then moved to San Francisco, Calif., where he held a state railroad post. By 1866 he had settled in Missouri. 6 years later he ran unsuccessfully for Congress but in 1879 was chosen to serve an unexpired term in the Senate. He did not stand for reelection because of poor health. He died while on a lecture tour in Iowa, at Ottumwa, 1 June 1879.   —JDW

Shiloh (Pittsburg Landing), Tenn., Battle of. 6–7 Apr.
1862   The capture of FORTS HENRY and DONELSON Feb. 1862 opened Middle Tennessee to invasion by Union forces. Maj. Gen. DON CARLOS BUELL's army occupied Nashville while Maj. Gen. ULYSSES S. GRANT's army penetrated as far south as Pittsburg Landing on the west bank of the Tennessee River, about 23 mi from the Confederate railroad center of Corinth, Miss. During the third week of March, Maj. Gen. HENRY W. HALLECK, theater commander, ordered Buell to join Grant for a joint offensive against Corinth.

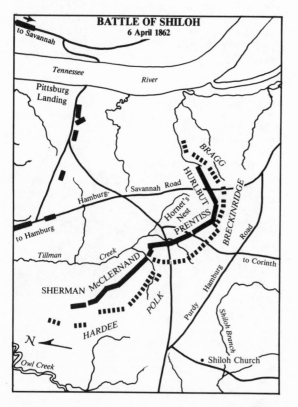

Confederate Gen. ALBERT SIDNEY JOHNSTON, meanwhile, had concentrated his scattered forces at Corinth to oppose such a thrust by the Federals. By the end of March he had 44,000 troops and proposed an attack on Grant's 39,000-man command before Buell, who was delayed by flooded rivers, arrived with his 36,000 soldiers. The Southerners left Corinth 3 Apr., but rain, the wooded countryside, and the troops' inexperience turned the 1-day march into a 3-day crawl. The Confederates were not in position to strike until the afternoon of the 5th. Because of the delay, Gen. P.G.T. BEAUREGARD, second-in-command, protested against an assault, arguing for a withdrawal. But Johnston, supported by the corps commanders, ordered an advance at daylight, stating, "I would fight them if they were a million."

Confederate skirmishers, preceding 3 successive battle lines, collided with Union patrols about 5 a.m. on Sunday, 6 Apr. The Federals, reinforced by a brigade, fought a delaying action for nearly 3 hours, but at 8 o'clock the first gray-coated wave hit Brig. Gen. WILLIAM T. SHERMAN's division near a small log church named Shiloh. Though warned of the onslaught, Sherman had not prepared for it, and his inexperienced troops were driven back. The attackers then struck the division of Brig. Gen. BENJAMIN M. PRENTISS and Maj. Gen. JOHN A. MCCLERNAND. These troops, plus Sherman's re-formed command, fought stubbornly for 3 hours, both sides suffering appalling casualties in the vicious combat. Confederate numbers finally prevailed, and the 3 Union divisions were overrun.

The momentum of the Southern offensive, however, slowed. Coordination had been lost; unit organizations had evaporated. Brigades, divisions, even corps were so badly intermingled that the commanders directed portions of the line, not units. Johnston ordered a ponderous shift, which further impeded the advance. Meanwhile, the Northerners, under Prentiss' direction, rallied along a sunken road in a densely wooded thicket. Grant, who had been at his headquarters 7 mi from the field when the battle started, ordered Prentiss to hold his position at all costs.

Prentiss' soldiers were ready when the Southerners attacked, the Union fire erasing charge after charge, perhaps as many as a dozen. The bloodied Confederates described the place as "a hornets' nest," and the name stuck. About 2:30 p.m. Johnston, directing the attacks, was fatally wounded. Beauregard assumed command and, as the "Hornets' Nest" stood unconquered, he brought 62 cannon to bear on the Union stronghold. For 2 hours the gray-clad gunners raked the thicket, hammering the Federal line into the shape of a horseshoe. Finally, at 5:30, Prentiss, who knew his men could endure no more, surrendered approximately 2,000 survivors.

The defenders of the "Hornets' Nest," however, gave Grant time to fashion a line on the ridge overlooking the landing. Bolstered by artillery and 2 gunboats, this position was strong. As twilight settled across the field, Beauregard wisely suspended a final assault on the waiting Federals. During the night, Maj. Gen. LEW WALLACE's division and all but 1 division of Buell's army joined Grant, who decided to assume the offensive on the 7th.

The Union forces rolled forward about 7:30 a.m., and the outnumbered Confederates fought doggedly throughout most of the day. The combat was again bloody, but the Federals steadily pushed back the Southerners. Late in the afternoon, Beauregard ordered a withdrawal to Corinth.

Shiloh was the first great bloody battle of the war. The

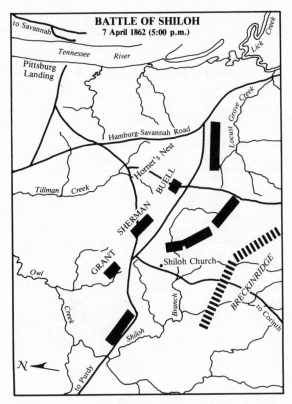

BATTLE OF SHILOH
7 April 1862 (5:00 p.m.)

casualty totals staggered both the North and the South. Union losses were 1,754 killed, 8,408 wounded, and 2,885 captured, for a total of 13,047, while Confederate casualties reached 10,694—1,723 killed, 8,012 wounded, and 959 missing. Although the Federals had paid a fearful price, Shiloh was decisive. Grant perhaps salvaged his career by attacking on the second day, and the defeat doomed the Confederates in the West.   —JDW

Shimonoseki, Japan, Battle of. 16 July 1863 During the 1860s Japan was experiencing serious internal unrest and an extreme reaction against foreigners. The prince of the Choshiu clan began his own private war against the "foreign barbarians" in 1863. In addition to fortifying the Straits of Shimonoseki with artillery, he purchased and armed 3 vessels —the steamer *Lancefield,* the brig *Lanrick,* and the bark *Daniel Webster*—and began shelling foreign ships using the straits. On 26 June 1863 the American ship *Pembroke* was fired upon but got away with no lives lost.

Commander David S. McDougal of the USS *Wyoming* was at Yokohama when he learned 13 July 1863 that the *Pembroke* had been attacked. He immediately steamed the *Wyoming* for the straits, entering early on the morning of 16 July. The *Wyoming* was fired upon as soon as it was sighted, but McDougal steered the ship directly toward shore and the 3 ships of the Choshiu. After passing directly between 2 of the vessels, he fired his heavy guns at close range. The battle lasted about an hour. According to McDougal, the *Wyoming* sank both the steamer and brig, severely damaged the bark, and inflicted

considerable damage on shore. The *Wyoming* returned to Yokohama with 4 sailors dead and another 7 wounded and the ship's smokestack and rigging severely damaged.

The next year 5–8 Sept. 1864, at Yokohama, Capt. Cicero Price and Robert H. Pruyn, U.S. minister to Japan, chartered a steamer that participated in a punitive shelling of Shimonoseki along with British, French, and Dutch warships. Japan eventually paid an indemnity of $3 million, but the U.S. returned its share ($750,000) in 1883.   —NCD

shoddy. An inferior wool cloth used in the manufacture of Federal soldiers' uniforms early in the war, shoddy was of such poor quality that clothing literally fell apart within weeks of being issued. *Shoddy* quickly became the word used to describe any inferior government equipment. Civil War veteran and novelist Henry Morford titled his book about the first year of the war *The Days of Shoddy* (1863).   —PLF

Shorter, John Gill. war governor b. Monticello, Ga., 23 Apr. 1818. From a wealthy family, Shorter graduated from the University of Georgia in 1837. He passed the bar a year later and moved to Eufaula, Ala. After practicing law for 4 years, he was appointed solicitor for his home district. Shorter entered politics in 1845, when he ran successfully for the state senate. After serving 2 short terms in the Alabama congress, he was appointed a circuit court judge, serving in this office for 9 years.

In 1861, prior to the outbreak of war, Shorter was sent as a state commissioner to the Georgia secession convention. An ardent secessionist, he was elected by his district to the Provisional Confederate Congress that same year. In Congress, he supported all of Pres. Jefferson Davis' war measures and took a hand in writing the CONFEDERATE CONSTITUTION.

In Aug. 1861 Shorter was elected governor of Alabama by an enthusiastic populace, defeating Whig candidate THOMAS H. WATTS. Taking office 4 months later, the new governor used all his resources to fortify the state, especially Mobile, and worked hard to provide aid for families of Confederate soldiers. In Apr. 1862 northern Alabama was invaded by Union troops commanded by Brig. Gen. Ormsby M. Mitchel. The Federals proceeded to destroy railroads and anything else of military value. This occupation severely hampered Alabama's contribution to the war effort and brought new hardships to the population, who came to blame Shorter for their misery. The governor's unpopularity was compounded by increased taxes and the institution of the draft.

In the election of 1863, Shorter was overwhelmingly defeated by Watts, former attorney general of the Confederacy. When his term expired 1 Dec. 1863, he returned to his law practice in Eufaula, never again running for public office. Arrested after the war by Federal authorities, he was imprisoned for a time. d. Eufaula, 29 May 1872.   —MTC

Shoup, Francis Asbury. CSA b. Laurel, Ind., 22 Mar. 1834. The eldest son of 9 children born to a wealthy merchant, Shoup graduated from West Point in 1855, ranking 15th of 34 cadets, and was assigned to the 1st U.S. Artillery. As a 2d lieutenant he served in Florida against the Seminoles, then resigned to practice law and lead a militia unit in his native state. Motivated by "aristocratic inclinations and admiration for the South," he returned to Florida, was admitted to the bar at St. Augustine, and when the Civil War began offered his services to Gov. MADISON S. PERRY.

Named a lieutenant of state artillery, Shoup erected and commanded a battery at Fernandina. In Oct. 1861 he was promoted to major in the Confederate ranks and was sent to the TRANS-MISSISSIPPI DEPARTMENT, then to Kentucky to lead a 12-gun battalion of Arkansas artillery. As chief of artillery to Maj. Gen. WILLIAM J. HARDEE, he served brilliantly at SHILOH, where his massed cannon laced

LC

the Union salient known as the "HORNETS' NEST." For his participation he was named a brigadier general as of 12 Sept. 1862. Later he joined the staff of Maj. Gen. THOMAS C. HINDMAN, under whom he fought at PRAIRIE GROVE, Ark., that December.

Early the next year Shoup served at Mobile, Ala., as artillery chief to Brig. Gen. SIMON B. BUCKNER, then shifted to infantry service, leading a Louisiana brigade under Lt. Gen. JOHN C. PEMBERTON at VICKSBURG. Captured in that city July 1863, he was paroled in time to serve as artillery chief to Gen. JOSEPH E. JOHNSTON during the Georgia campaigning of 1864. As 1 biographer notes, "it was in a great measure due to his skillful management of the artillery that not a gun was lost in the several retreats of the Army of Tennessee from Dalton to Atlanta." Shoup also won acclaim for the defensive works constructed under his supervision along the CHATTAHOOCHEE RIVER.

Following Johnston's relief, Shoup served as chief of staff to Gen. JOHN B. HOOD, meanwhile promoting the Confederate authorization of BLACK SOLDIERS, a proposal Pres. JEFFERSON DAVIS studied carefully.

After the war he became an Episcopal rector and joined the faculty of the University of Mississippi and the University of the South. The author of wartime texts on infantry and artillery drill and postwar treatises on mathematics and metaphysics, Shoup died in Columbia, Tenn., 4 Sept. 1896. —EGL

shrapnel. More commonly known in the Civil War as "spherical case shot," shrapnel was one of the most common types of smoothbore artillery ammunition used during the war. Gen. Henry Shrapnel of the British army developed shrapnel during the Napoleonic Wars in an effort to extend the range of bursting, multishotted projectiles such as grape and canister. Basically, the shell consisted of a hollow, thin-walled iron ball filled with smaller lead or iron balls with a bursting charge in the center. The whole was set off by a time fuse.

The BORMANN FUSE was the standard type attached to spherical case during the war. Because the time was limited to 5 seconds, the maximum range of the shell was the distance it could travel in that time—in most cases, about 1,200 yd. Since the bursting charge was only sufficient to rupture the casing, the balls did not scatter laterally as the shell burst but continued on the original trajectory of the shell. The effect was as intended: an extension of grape or canister without the scattering of balls that would have normally occurred at long ranges.

The most common type of spherical case was the 12-pounder size, used in the Napoleon gun howitzer, Model 1857. Other sizes were also used, extending upward officially to an 8-in. shell and experimentally to a 10-in. Originally,

spherical case was loaded by pouring the balls in through the fuse hole and filling the casing with powder. However, the powder tended to be ground fine by the balls and became so dispersed that the case often failed to break. By the time of the Civil War, a mandrel was used to push the balls to the side and molten sulfur or rosin was poured in to hold the balls in place and form a cavity for the powder. The Confederates were forced to use wooden plug fuses because of the failure of their Bormanns, and at times they used asphalt instead of sulfur or rosin. Both of these ideas resulted in inferior shells. —LDJ

Sibley, Henry Hastings. USA b. Detroit, Mich., 29 Feb. 1811. Educated in a common school in the Michigan wilderness, Sibley was a clerk and fur trapper with the American Fur Co. and in 1835 built the first private residence in Minnesota, and in 1849 was elected as a territorial delegate to Congress, actively pursuing the establishment of Minnesota Territory. In 1858 he became the state's first elected governor. Choosing not to run again in 1859, the 50-year-old Sibley was in private life when the Civil War began.

LC

Sibley's contribution to the Union cause was his suppression of the SIOUX UPRISING OF 1862 in Minnesota. That summer the Santee Sioux, encouraged by the removal of Federal soldiers to the East, rebelled against the white settlers in Minnesota. Led by Chief Little Crow, they rampaged up and down the Minnesota River Valley, killing more than 800 whites. The governor commissioned Sibley colonel in the state militia and assigned him to command 1,400 volunteers. On 23 Sept., at the Battle of Wood Lake, Sibley's troops defeated Little Crow's warriors, who fled into the Dakotas. For his services Sibley was promoted to brigadier general 29 Sept. but the Senate failed to confirm his commission, which expired 4 Mar. 1863. He was then reappointed and confirmed 20 Mar. Though Sibley held no other command, he was brevetted major general for "efficient and meritorious service" 29 Nov. 1865 and mustered out 30 Apr. 1866.

Sibley prospered in postwar Minnesota. An active businessman, he successively headed a gas company, an insurance company, and a bank. He served in the state legislature, was president of the St. Paul Chamber of Commerce, held a seat on the Board of Regents of the University of Minnesota, and served as president of the state historical society. d. St. Paul, 18 Feb. 1891. —JDW

Sibley, Henry Hopkins. CSA b. Natchitoches, La., 25 May 1816, Sibley, who graduated 31st in the West Point class of 1838, was stationed in New Mexico Territory when the war began. Resigning from the U.S. Army on the same day he was promoted to major, he accepted a Confederate colonel's commission and hurried to Richmond to promote a grandiose plan for Southwest conquest. Pres. Jefferson Davis promoted Sibley to brigadier general 17 June 1861 and directed him to recruit a Texas brigade that was to sweep the Federals from what is today New Mexico and Arizona and open the door to California for the Confederates.

Sibley had solid credentials: experience in the Seminole War and the expedition against the Utah Mormons, along with a brevet for bravery in the Mexican War. He was also the inventor of the SIBLEY TENT. But he believed unrealistically that his men could live off the land in barren New Mexico Territory and that the Union would offer little resistance to a Confederate invasion.

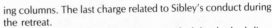

LC

Arriving at Mesilla Dec. 1861 with a command of eager Texans, he charged up the Rio Grande Valley early in 1862. He defeated Union Col. E.R.S. CANBY at VALVERDE and captured Albuquerque, Santa Fe, and other strong points in New Mexico Territory.

When Sibley's Army of New Mexico apparently triumphed in the bloody Battle of LA GLORIETA PASS 26–28 Mar. 1862, Confederate success seemed assured. But Sibley lost his provision and ammunition train in a Union counterattack and was left helpless in the face of growing Union strength in the territory. He withdrew to Fort Bliss, Tex., with his force reduced to 1,500, then retreated all the way to San Antonio to escape the oncoming CALIFORNIA COLUMN under Brig. Gen. JAMES H. CARLETON. (*See also* SIBLEY'S NEW MEXICO CAMPAIGN.)

Sibley's greatest achievements were over. He was assigned to minor commands in Louisiana but never achieved much success. Plagued by chronic illness and worsening alcoholism, he proved ineffective as a leader during the Teche River Campaign of 1863. Court-martialed and censured by Maj. Gen. Richard Taylor (*see* SIBLEY AND GRANT COURT-MARTIAL) for his failures at IRISH BEND AND FORT BISLAND, 13–14 Apr. 1863, Sibley was later listed by Gen. E. Kirby Smith as having no command.

In 1869 he became general of artillery for the khedive of Egypt. He returned to the U.S. in 1874, lectured for a time, and died in poverty at Fredericksburg, Va., 23 Aug. 1886.   —DS

Sibley and Grant court-martial.   In Apr. 1863 Union Maj. Gen. NATHANIEL P. BANKS advanced toward Alexandria, La., to clear Confederates from the west bank of the Mississippi River and to turn their Port Hudson, La., defenses. Confederate Maj. Gen. RICHARD TAYLOR reacted immediately to this threat, and the opponents collided at IRISH BEND AND FORT BISLAND 13–14 Apr. Banks, with 15,000 troops, defeated Taylor's 5,000 Confederates, who abandoned Fort Bisland and extricated themselves from a trap. In the aftermath of the defeat, Taylor charged Brig. Gen. HENRY HOPKINS SIBLEY with disobedience of orders and unofficerlike conduct. The Confederate commander also charged Capt. Alexander Grant, commanding the gunboat *Cotton,* with disobedience of orders.

On 25 Sept. 1863, a court-martial, with Maj. Gen. JOHN G. WALKER presiding, convened to try Sibley and Grant. Taylor's first charge, with 3 specifications, against Sibley resulted from the brigadier's failure to organize and deliver, as ordered, an attack against the Federals 13 Apr. below Fort Bisland. Taylor also alleged that Sibley had failed to protect a steamboat loaded with wounded that was subsequently captured by the Federals and had abandoned his post at the head of the retreat-ing columns. The last charge related to Sibley's conduct during the retreat.

The single charge against Grant specified that he had disobeyed repeated orders to assist in the defense of Fort Burton and to remove the garrison guns and stores if the fort had to be evacuated. Grant, however, abandoned the fort 20 Apr. "without rendering suitable assistance in its defense."

Walker's court declared both officers not guilty of the charges. In Sibley's case, the tribunal's officers asserted that the brigadier "did not display that promptness" in preparing an attack and "is to that extent censurable." The court exonerated him because of "a train of circumstances." What these were, the court never stated, but Taylor, in his report, claimed Sibley had asserted that he was sick. The court simply ruled Grant not guilty, with no explanation given. Both officers returned to their commands.   —JDW

Sibley's Arizona Brigade.   *See* NEW MEXICO, CONFEDERATE ARMY OF.

Sibley's New Mexico Campaign.   Nov. 1861–May 1862 Late in spring 1861, HENRY HOPKINS SIBLEY, who had just resigned from the U.S. Army, proposed that the Confederate government send an army of Texans into New Mexico from El Paso and press through Arizona gathering supplies and recruits until reaching and subduing California. Certain of much Confederate sentiment and cooperation in the sparsely defended deserts, Confederate officials gave Sibley a brigadier's commission and approval for his plan.

Sibley's 3,700-man Army of New Mexico left San Antonio Nov. 1861, stopping in El Paso to proclaim to the New Mexicans that they came as liberators. Then they moved to their first objective, Fort Craig, under command of Col. E.R.S. CANBY. This southern New Mexico stronghold and nearby VALVERDE saw several days' inconclusive fighting that left Canby victor by default; Sibley lost too many men and supplies to continue besieging the Federals. Desperate for food and material, the Texans went north around Fort Craig to Albuquerque, where the Federals had stored $250,000 worth of goods. Attacking, the Confederates found the defenders gone and the supplies destroyed.

Sibley detached 600 men to try plundering Santa Fe, but they met similar Federal tactics. Worse, holding a barren prize, the small force had to fend off 1,300 of the enemy attacking from nearby Fort Union. Although this Battle of LA GLORIETA PASS culminated in a miraculous Confederate victory, the Texans' few supplies were captured in the fight, leaving them destitute. The detached force retreated to Albuquerque only to find Canby, recently promoted to brigadier general, outside the town with 1,200 men. Facing defeat and starvation, Sibley retreated to Texas.

Dogged almost all the way to Fort Craig by Canby's men, the weakening Confederate troops finally slipped from Federal sight in a night maneuver that took them home by a circuitous route. Nearly dead of thirst and starvation, 1,700 Confederate survivors eventually reached safety in El Paso 4 May 1862.

—JES

Sibley tent.   Maj. Henry Hopkins Sibley of the 1st U.S. Dragoons patented a conical canvas tent 22 Apr. 1856. Able to accommodate 20 soldiers and their personal gear with a minimum of discomfort, it also allowed a stove or fire to be used inside. 2 doors or flaps on its sides and an adjustable skirt at its peak ensured ventilation. Raised on an iron tripod and supported by a center pole, a Sibley tent was easily erected by 2 men within minutes.

The U.S. Army adopted the Sibley for general field use in the antebellum period, but standing 12 ft tall, with an 18.5-ft diameter at its base, and weighing 73 lb, it proved ungainly during rapid Civil War campaigning. A shelter half ("dog" or "pup") tent replaced it in the field and relegated Sibleys to permanent camp and garrison use. First designed for shelter on the Plains, it remained a regular U.S. Army issue through the 1890s. More than 43,000 are believed to have been used by Union and Confederate forces during the Civil War. —JES

Sickles, Daniel Edgar.

USA b. New York City, N.Y., 20 Oct. 1819. One of the most competent and yet one of the most controversial of Civil War generals, Sickles studied law at New York University and was active in Democratic politics at the city, state, and national levels, serving in the U.S. Congress 1857–61. He also achieved public notice when in 1859 he shot his wife's lover, the son of Francis Scott Key. He was acquitted on the grounds that he was in effect defending home and family. In Sept. 1861 he became a brigadier general of volunteers, a reward for his support of Pres. Abraham Lincoln's war policy and for raising a brigade of soldiers from New York.

USMHI

He advanced to major general and division command 29 Nov. 1862, in which capacity he fought in the PENINSULA CAMPAIGN, at Antietam, and at FREDERICKSBURG. In command of the III Corps at CHANCELLORSVILLE, he was sent to pursue Lt. Gen. THOMAS J. "STONEWALL" JACKSON's command, mistakenly reported to be retreating. The gap left in the Union lines by the absent two-thirds of his corps contributed to the success of Jackson's movement, actually a brilliant flank march that gave the Confederates the battle.

One of the most acrimonious controversies of the war stemmed from Sickles' actions at GETTYSBURG. The III Corps was ordered to cover the Union left near the Round Tops. On his own initiative he advanced his corps to an exposed position that bore the brunt of Lt. Gen. JAMES LONGSTREET's assault. In the fighting Sickles was severely wounded in the right leg. He lost not only his leg but his command and some of his reputation. During the course of his long life he blamed Maj. Gen. GEORGE G. MEADE for the unfortunate results of his ill-considered advance. He also, groundlessly, charged Meade with incompetence as an army commander.

Sickles retired in 1869 as a major general in the Regular Army, then filled various public offices, including U.S. minister to Spain 1869–75 and U.S. congressman 1893–95. Sickles was a capable man, a leader, and possessed of great personal courage; even his misstep at Gettysburg could have been excused had he not made a public debate of his differences with Meade. His proclivity for controversy with his fellow officers and his combative attitude toward his superiors detracted from an otherwise admirable military record. d. New York City, 3 May 1914. —JTH

Sigel, Franz.

USA b. Baden, Germany, 18 Nov. 1824. When Sigel arrived in the U.S. from Germany in 1852, he brought a reputation as a fighter and a liberal. A graduate of Karlsruhe Military Academy, he retired from the German army in 1847 and was minister of war for the unsuccessful Revolution of 1848 against Prussia. He fled Germany, finally arriving (by way of Switzerland and England) in St. Louis, Mo., where he taught school until 1861. There he became an influential leader among the area's large German population; as part of Pres. Abraham Lincoln's plan of courting antislavery, Unionist immigrants, Sigel was commissioned brigadier 7 Aug. 1861, then major general in less than a year, 22 Mar. 1862.

USMHI

He served under Brig. Gen. NATHANIEL LYON in the capture of the secessionist Camp Jackson in St. Louis and at WILSON'S CREEK. His finest performance came 8 Mar. 1862 at PEA RIDGE, where, under Maj. Gen. Samuel R. Curtis, he commanded 2 divisions and personally directed the Union artillery in the demoralizing slaughter of Maj. Gen. Earl Van Dorn's Confederates. Transferred to the East, he served in the SHENANDOAH VALLEY against Maj. Gen. Thomas J. "Stonewall" Jackson and commanded the I Corps in Maj. Gen. John Pope's Army of Virginia at SECOND BULL RUN; he also briefly led the XI Corps. But his military usefulness ended when, as commander of the Department of West Virginia, he was defeated 15 May 1864 at NEW MARKET, Va., in the battle made famous by the charge of the VIRGINIA MILITARY INSTITUTE cadets. Relieved of field command shortly thereafter, he resigned his commission 4 May 1865 and reentered civilian life. d. New York City, 21 Aug. 1902.

Sigel was an odd combination of ineptitude and ability. On the record his military performance, aside from Pea Ridge, was little better than mediocre. But he unquestionably helped the Union cause by rallying German-Americans to the flag, and he held their loyalty to the end. —RDH

signal communications.

During the Civil War signal communications were of 2 types, visual and electrical. The former was the province of the signal corps of the Union and Confederate armies, while electrical communications, in the North, were handled by the U.S. Military Telegraph. In both areas, the Confederacy generally enjoyed fewer resources than its enemy, although in the number of signalmen it matched the Union, both armies employing about 1,500 officers and enlisted men. In regard to electrical telegraphy, the South's strength in operators, equipment, and expertise never approached that of the North. As one authority in the field states: "the story of Civil War signal communications is the story of two organizations—the United States Army Signal Corps and the United States Military Telegraph."

Those organizations conducted a running feud over mission prerogatives for more than half the war. Established June 1860, the Signal Corps enjoyed an early administrative advantage over the Military Telegraph, which did not come into being until Feb. 1862. Under the aggressive leadership of Maj. (later Col.) ALBERT J. MYER, the Signal Corps was not content to employ visual communication devices such as signal pistols, flags,

Signal Tower, Chain Bridge on the Potomac River   USMHI

Signal Tower, Elk Mountain (Antietam), Md.   USMHI

rockets, and torches. Early in 1862 Myer formed a corps of operators who took the field with "FLYING TELEGRAPH TRAINS" that carried magneto-powered BEARDSLEE TELEGRAPH machines. Soon Myer's telegraphers were vying for position with the fledgling War Department agency, which employed civilian telegraphers and Morse sounders powered by 100-cell, 150-watt batteries carried aboard Quartermaster Department ambulances. An attempt by Myer late in 1863 to gain control of all field telegraphy resulted in his removal to Memphis, Tenn., after Sec. of War EDWIN M. STANTON supported Myer's chief rival, Col. ANSON STAGER, head of the Military Telegraph. Thereafter all field telegraphy was handled by the latter agency. Yet Stager himself pointed out that on numerous occasions the rival organizations cooperated "by diffusing information from advanced signal stations simultaneously" to various Union field headquarters.

It is difficult to determine the relative effectiveness of the competing agencies in facilitating Union army communications. But during the conflict, the Military Telegraph laid 15,000 mi of wire and transmitted an estimated 6.5 million messages—an average of more than 5,000 daily, at a cost of $2,655,500 (about 40 cents apiece). The Signal Corps, which at its height employed 5,000 fewer operators than its rival, sent countless messages, costing the government $1,595,257 by the close of fiscal year 1865.
                                                                                —EGL

"silent battle." *See* ACOUSTIC SHADOW.

Sill, Joshua Woodrow. USA b. Chillicothe, Ohio, 6 Dec. 1831. The son of a prominent lawyer, Sill proved to be a brilliant student at West Point, ranking 3d of 52 in his 1853 graduating class. Prior to the war, he served as an ordnance expert and for a time taught at the academy. In Jan. 1861 he quit the army to teach mathematics and civil engineering. At the outbreak of war, Sill was commissioned assistant adjutant general of Ohio by the state's governor.

He first saw action July 1861 at an engagement at RICH MOUNTAIN, Western Va., serving under Maj. Gen. George B. McClellan. There the Union forces won a decisive victory

LC

that effectively ended Confederate influence in the region. Sill was commissioned colonel of the 33d Ohio Regiment for his part in the battle. By November, he was commanding the 9th Brigade/3d Division in Maj. Gen. Don Carlos Buell's Department of the Ohio. On 16 July 1862, Sill was made a brigadier general of volunteers. He now commanded the 2d Division of Maj. Gen. Alexander M. McCook's I Corps/Army of the Ohio. In October Sill's division took part in the campaign to drive Gen. Braxton Bragg's Confederate Army of Tennessee from Kentucky. His feint toward Frankfort, Ky., forced Bragg to withdraw and fight the bloody Battle of PERRYVILLE.

31 Dec. 1862 found Sill commanding a brigade in Sheridan's 3d Division/XVI Corps of Maj. Gen. William S. Rosecrans' reorganized Army of the Cumberland. Rosecrans planned to attack Bragg and drive the Confederates out of Tennessee. As the cold mist rose off Stone's River, Sill's men

were cooking breakfast. Suddenly wave upon wave of Confederate troops under Maj. Gens. William J. Hardee and Leonidas Polk struck the Union right wing and the 3d Division. After making a temporary stand, Sill's troops began to break and run for the rear. Sill, desperate to halt a rout of his men, was killed trying to repulse another Confederate attack. He was buried near his hometown of Chillicothe. After the war, his friend Maj. Gen. Philip H. Sheridan named Fort Sill in his memory.

—MTC

Simms, James Phillip. CSA b. Covington, Ga., 16 Jan. 1837. The antebellum background, education, legal history, and entry into Confederate service of this Georgia attorney are undocumented. Georgia archival records list a James P. Simms's appointment as assistant quartermaster of the 42d Georgia Aug. 1862. However, this unit served in the Western theater, and Simms's recorded military career places him in the East.

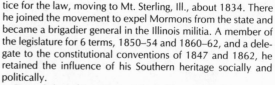

LC

Sources list no transfer or appointment of Simms until his nomination 24 Sept. 1862 to major of the 53d Georgia, a unit previously serving on the Virginia peninsula in Maj. Gen. Lafayette McLaws' division. On the resignation of Leonard T. Doyal as colonel of the 53d, Simms won commission as colonel of the regiment, 8 Oct. 1862. His Civil War service is documented from this date.

Through spring 1864, as a member of the I Corps/McLaws' division, Simms fought at FREDERICKSBURG, SALEM CHURCH, and GETTYSBURG; besieged CHATTANOOGA; served in the KNOXVILLE CAMPAIGN; wintered in East Tennessee; and fought at SPOTSYLVANIA and the WILDERNESS. Distinguished for his service at Salem Church, where the 53d captured the flag of the 2d Rhode Island Infantry, and for leading his men in the assault against Knoxville's Fort Sanders, where he was wounded, Simms became Brig. Gen. Goode Bryan's valued subordinate. Bryan's brigade joined Maj. Gen. Joseph B. Kershaw's division in summer 1864 for service in the Shenandoah Valley. When Bryan resigned in poor health in September, Simms assumed brigade leadership. He commanded the 10th, 50th, 51st, and 53d Georgia regiments in Shenandoah fighting, won recognition for his part in the Battle of CEDAR CREEK, and received promotion to brigadier general 8 Dec. 1864, to rank from November.

Fighting through the PETERSBURG siege, he remained under Kershaw's command, and with his major general was captured during the Battle of SAYLER'S CREEK, then imprisoned at Fort Warren, Boston harbor, until 24 July 1865.

Returning to Covington, Ga., Simms served in the state legislature in 1865 and 1866, practiced law, then returned to the state house in 1877. d. Covington, 30 May 1887.   —JES

Singleton, James Washington. USP b. Frederick Cty., Va., 23 Nov. 1811. The son of Revolutionary War Gen. James Singleton, James Washington was born at "Paxton," his father's estate in northern Virginia, and educated at the academy in Winchester. He studied medicine but abandoned his prac-

tice for the law, moving to Mt. Sterling, Ill., about 1834. There he joined the movement to expel Mormons from the state and became a brigadier general in the Illinois militia. A member of the legislature for 6 terms, 1850–54 and 1860–62, and a delegate to the constitutional conventions of 1847 and 1862, he retained the influence of his Southern heritage socially and politically.

One of the more vocal of the Midwestern advocates of peace during the Civil War and a prominent member of the Sons of Liberty, Singleton consistently defended slavery as a legal institution and condemned the war as unconstitutional. On several occasions he approached Abraham Lincoln offering plans to achieve negotiated peace and reunion with the Confederacy, at the same time severely criticizing the president's war measures as arbitrary and extreme. His Copperheadism (see PEACE DEMOCRATS) resulted in the loss of his seat in the legislature, but he continued to promote a negotiated end to the war. Hardline Unionists burned the outbuildings on his farm Aug. 1864 while he was attending a peace convention in Peoria. That same month he was among the peace advocates who bolted from the Democratic national convention in Chicago and reconvened in Cincinnati to protest the presidential candidacy of Maj. Gen. GEORGE B. MCCLELLAN, who, like Lincoln, believed the war would have to be won by inflicting military defeat on the Confederacy.

In Nov. 1864 Singleton met informally in Canada with Confederate commissioner CASSIUS M. CLAY to investigate peace terms, and over the next months traveled several times to Richmond for the same purpose. Though aware of the visits, Lincoln did not give them official sanction. One plan the president considered but did not adopt involved Singleton's proposal to purchase Southern goods with GREENBACKS, in the hope that introducing Federal dollars into the devastated Confederate economy would shorten the war by creating a widespread demand for peace among Southerners eager to market their products in the North.

Despite the unpopularity of his wartime Copperhead activities, Singleton regained his political influence in the postbellum years, serving in the U.S. House of Representatives 1879–83. Acutely aware of the economic advantages a good system of transportation would bring to Illinois, he invested much of his energy in promoting railroads within the state. He lived in comfort and entertained lavishly at "Boscobel," the home he had built in Quincy early in his career, until 1891. That year he moved to Baltimore, Md., dying there 4 Apr. 1892.

—PLF

Sioux Uprising of 1862. After the start of the Civil War, the Federal government withdrew most Regular Army units from its Western outposts to the East, leaving the frontier virtually undefended. Minnesota, home of the Santee Sioux, had been relatively quiet for several years despite the fact that by 1861 about 200,000 whites had moved into the state. With the withdrawal of the army, the Sioux had expected the white influx to cease, but when settlers and immigrants continued to pour into the area despite the Civil War, the Sioux decided it was an opportunity to attack. Led by Chief Little Crow, in summer 1862 they raided up and down the Minnesota River Valley, killing more than 800 whites. For protection, refugees from the raids poured into Fort Ridgely, which Little Crow attacked 20 and 22 Aug. with about 800 men but failed to capture. He then attacked New Ulm, a German settlement a few miles down the valley, but the poorly armed settlers successfully defended themselves and drove off the Sioux.

Learning of the uprising, Minnesota's governor commissioned HENRY HASTINGS SIBLEY a colonel in the state militia, with orders to quell the uprising. Sibley assembled about 1,400 volunteers, who would have normally been sent east to fight, and 18 Sept. moved up the valley after the marauding Sioux. At the Battle of Wood Lake, 23 Sept., Little Crow was decisively defeated and, rather than surrender, fled to Dakota with many of his followers, thus ending the uprising. Sibley captured about 1,500 Sioux, who were tried before a military court that sentenced 307 to die. Pres. Abraham Lincoln pardoned all but 38, who were publicly hanged in December, resulting in a temporary peace with the proud Sioux, who would attack again the following spring.   —JPC

skirmish. Of the various terms applied to Civil War military actions, "skirmish" denoted a clash of the smallest scope. In general, a skirmish was a limited combat, involving troops other than those of the main body; when the latter participated, the fight was known as an ENGAGEMENT, affair, or battle, depending on its scale. More specifically, a skirmish denoted an encounter between opposing SKIRMISH LINES, composed of troops assigned to protect the head and/or flanks of an army in motion.   —EGL

skirmish line. A Civil War army on the march protected itself with lines of skirmishers, troops deployed in loose formation in advance and/or on the flanks of the main body. These troops drew the enemy's fire, developed his position, and warned comrades of an imminent clash. Infantry manuals in use during the war devoted much coverage to skirmisher TACTICS, made popular by Napoleon's heavy reliance on them during the Continental warfare of the early 19th century.   —EGL

Slack, William Yarnell. CSA b. Mason Cty., Ky., 1 Aug. 1816, Slack, at age 3, moved with his family to Missouri, settling near Columbia. After studying law he opened an office in Chillicothe, Mo. During the

Mexican War, he served as captain of the 2d Missouri Volunteers. Returning home, he was practicing law when the Civil War erupted.

In the tragically divided state, Slack chose the Confederate cause. Missouri Gov. Claiborne F. Jackson appointed him brigadier general of the State Guard, of which Slack commanded a division at CARTHAGE 5 July 1861 and at WILSON'S CREEK 10 Aug. In the latter battle he was wounded in the hip while directing an attack.

LC

Having recovered from his wound by October, Slack rejoined his division. At the Battle of PEA RIDGE, Ark., 7 Mar. 1862, he suffered a second wound, being struck by a minié bullet only an inch from his old scar. Removed to a house near the battlefield, he seemingly rallied. Surgeons, however, fearful of his possible capture, transported him 7 mi to Moore's Mill. His condition quickly deteriorated and he died there 21 Mar.

Confederate authorities posthumously promoted Slack to brigadier general 17 Apr., to rank from 12 Apr.   —JDW

Slaughter, James Edwin. CSA b. Slaughter's (Cedar) Mountain, Va., June 1827. A great-nephew of Pres. James Madison, Slaughter attended VIRGINIA MILITARY INSTITUTE before withdrawing in 1846 to accept a commission in the U.S. Army. He fought in Mexico, then remained in the antebellum army until the outbreak of civil war, having risen in rank to 1st lieutenant of the 1st Artillery. Dismissed from the service 14 May 1861, Slaughter joined the Confederate army as an artillery captain.

USMHI

The Virginian served initially on the staff of Brig. Gen. BRAXTON BRAGG at Pensacola, Fla. In November he was promoted to major and 8 Mar. 1862 jumped in rank to brigadier general. He then acted as Gen. ALBERT SIDNEY JOHNSTON's assistant inspector general at SHILOH, continuing in that assignment with Johnston's successors, Gen. P.G.T. BEAUREGARD and Bragg. In Apr. 1863 he joined the staff of Maj. Gen. JOHN B. MAGRUDER as chief of artillery and later was chief of staff. He served with Magruder in Texas for the remainder of the war.

With the collapse of the Confederacy, Slaughter emigrated to Mexico. He lived there several years before returning to the U.S. and residing in Mobile, Ala., to work as a civil engineer and subsequently postmaster. He moved to New Orleans and, while on a visit to Mexico City, died 1 Jan. 1901 and was buried in the Mexican capital.   —JDW

Slaughter Mountain, Va., Battle of. 9 Aug. 1862 *See* CEDAR MOUNTAIN, VA., BATTLE OF.

slavery. African slavery was introduced to America early in the 17th century. Many believed it would be temporary, and by the end of the American Revolution its growth was confined to the South. Millions of Africans were bought or kidnapped to be shipped to the New World under barbaric conditions. In 1807 the U.S. outlawed the international slave trade, but illegal importing of slaves continued, as did the selling of slaves within the nation.

Slaves labored on plantations, small farms, and wherever heavy work was required. Some were highly trained artisans. In America they adopted the language, manner, and religion of their masters, but they retained much of their African culture as well. In turn, they influenced the language, dance, and music of their masters.

Slaveowners drew on many arguments to justify slavery, picturing it as a benevolent institution. Yet mistreatment of slaves was widespread, families were separated by sales, and punishment by whipping was not unusual. The most humane master denied the humanity of his slaves. "It was a great heaviness on a person's mind to be a slave," said a former bondsman. Slaves hid their true feelings behind masks. There were few open rebellions, but slaves would pretend illness, organize slowdowns, sabotage farm machinery, and sometimes commit arson or murder. Running away was common, usually for short periods, but sometimes for permanent freedom in the North or Canada.

Young Southerners aspired to own large plantations with a huge labor force, yet such holdings were the exception. By 1860 only 10,000 families owned more than 50 slaves each, and three-fourths of Southern families owned none at all. The typical plantation included 10 to 20 slaves; other slaves worked in the cities or hired out their time elsewhere.

Slavery, which its defenders labeled "the peculiar institution," came to dominate Southern life even when virtually all of the civilized world had abandoned it. It was to have been the cornerstone of the Confederacy. Slavery itself did not cause the Civil War, but it was intertwined with every sectional confrontation.

—LG

Slidell, John. diplomat b. New York City, N.Y., 1793, the Northern-born Slidell rose to prominence as a Louisiana politician in the decades before the Civil War. A lawyer who began his career as a businessman, he moved to New Orleans in 1819 after his mercantile interests failed during the War of 1812.

Slidell lost a bid for Congress in 1828 and was frustrated in his political ambitions until 1843, when he was elected to the U.S. House of Representatives. As a states-rights Democrat he supported James K. Polk for the presidency in 1844 and used questionable legal means to assure him a Louisiana majority in the presidential election. Polk appointed Slidell commissioner to Mexico, with instructions to settle the Texas-Mexico boundary dispute and purchase New Mexico and California. The mission failed when the Mexican government refused to accept his credentials.

Slidell was elected to the Senate in 1853 and cast his lot with other pro-Southern congressmen to repeal the MISSOURI COMPROMISE, acquire Cuba, and admit Kansas under the Lecompton constitution. In the 1860 campaign Slidell supported Democratic presidential candidate JOHN C. BRECKINRIDGE, but remained a pro-Union moderate until ABRAHAM LINCOLN's election pushed the Southern states into seceding. Siding with the South, Slidell accepted a diplomatic appointment to represent the Confederacy in France.

His arrival in Europe was delayed by the *TRENT* AFFAIR, when he and fellow diplomat JAMES M. MASON were removed from their British-registered ship by the commander of a Federal vessel. Once there, he found the French sympathetic to the Confederate cause, but met with little success in securing extensive military aid or the Franco-Confederate treaty of alliance he sought. Slidell remained in France lobbying throughout the war. Though he was never able to accomplish a Franco-Confederate liaison, and though many of his Confederate colleagues distrusted him, Slidell, through his political abilities and bolstered by his marriage to a Louisiana Creole woman, arranged some Confederate financing through private French interests.

Uncertain of his safety at home after the war, Slidell and his family stayed in Paris. He never sought pardon from the Federal government for his Confederate service, dying in London, England, 29 July 1871.

—PLF

Slocum, Henry Warner. USA b. Delphi, N.Y., 24 Sept. 1827, Slocum attended Cazenovia Seminary in New York and taught school until admitted to West Point, from which he

graduated 7th in the class of 1852. Commissioned 2d lieutenant of the 1st Artillery, he saw action against the Seminoles, then was stationed at Ft. Moultrie, S.C., but resigned to practice law in Syracuse, N.Y. Before the Civil War he was county treasurer, a state legislator, and an officer in the state militia.

USMHI

After the fall of FORT SUMTER, Slocum was appointed colonel of the 27th New York Infantry and fought in Brig. Gen. David Hunter's division at FIRST BULL RUN, where he was severely wounded. After recovering he commanded a brigade in Brig. Gen. William B. Franklin's division, which became part of the VI Corps. When Franklin was assigned to command the corps, Slocum was commissioned major general of volunteers from 4 July 1862 and succeeded Franklin as commander of the division. Slocum assisted in covering Maj. Gen. John Pope's withdrawal after SECOND BULL RUN and fought in the Battles of SOUTH MOUNTAIN and ANTIETAM. He commanded the XII Corps in reserve during the FREDERICKSBURG CAMPAIGN, fought at CHANCELLORSVILLE, and at GETTYSBURG commanded the Union army's extreme right.

After the Battle of CHICKAMAUGA Slocum's XII Corps and Maj. Gen. Oliver O. Howard's XI Corps were sent south as the ARMY OF THE TENNESSEE with Maj. Gen. Joseph Hooker in command. Slocum refused to serve under Hooker and offered his resignation, which was not accepted. The XI and XII corps were consolidated as the XX Corps under Hooker, and Slocum was appointed commander of the District of Vicksburg. When Maj. Gen. John B. McPherson was killed, Howard took command of the Army of the Tennessee. Hooker, believing himself senior to Howard, angrily asked to be relieved, and Slocum returned east to command the XX Corps. In 1864 he took over the ARMY OF GEORGIA for the MARCH TO THE SEA.

In Sept. 1865 Slocum resigned, returned to Syracuse, and ran for secretary of the state of New York. Defeated, he moved to Brooklyn, where he practiced law; served 3 terms in the U.S. House of Representatives, 1869–73 and 1883–85; and was a member of the board of the Gettysburg Monument Commission. d. Brooklyn, N.Y., 14 Apr. 1894.   —DBS

Slough, John Potts. USA b. Cincinnati, Ohio, 1 Feb. 1829. Early in life Slough decided on a legal career and at 21 was elected a state legislator. Though he pronounced his name "slow," he was quick to anger and impulsive in his actions; that same year he was expelled from the legislature following a fistfight with a political rival. Despite the unfortunate incident, 2 years later he became secretary of the Ohio Democratic committee, a position he relinquished to migrate to Kansas, then farther west. By 1860 he was residing in Denver, Colorado Territory.

Slough's outspoken Democratic views made his Unionism suspect until mid-1861, when he raised a company of Federal volunteers. Later he assumed command of Fort Garland, Colorado Territory, and 26 Aug. became colonel of the 1st Colorado Volunteer Infantry, which he whipped into military trim at Denver.

In Mar. 1862 the 1st Colorado became a part of Brig. Gen. E.

R. S. CANBY's New Mexico column, which opposed Confederate invaders under Brig. Gen. HENRY HOPKINS SIBLEY. Placed at the head of a 1,340-man force detached from Canby's main body, Slough led an expedition from Fort Union toward LA GLORIETA PASS, where, 28 Mar., he clashed with Sibley's force, despite Canby's order that no engagement be brought on in that sector. At first the Confederates enjoyed the upper hand. On the brink of defeat, Slough was

LC

saved by a flanking column that gained Sibley's rear, captured his baggage and ammunition trains, spread panic through the ranks, and forced the Southerners to withdraw into Texas.

Slough parlayed the publicity this victory brought him into a brigadier generalship, to rank from 25 Aug. His field career, however, was nearly over. Following a trip east to command a brigade in the Shenandoah Valley and then in Maj. Gen. JOHN POPE's Army of Virginia, he spent the remainder of the war as military governor of ALEXANDRIA, VA. He also sat on the tribunal that in Jan. 1863 convicted Maj. Gen. FITZ JOHN PORTER of dereliction of duty at SECOND BULL RUN.

Mustered out 24 Aug. 1865, Slough was appointed chief justice of NEW MEXICO TERRITORY, where he feuded with officials who objected to his "manner and irritable temper." Ultimately the legislature passed a series of resolutions advocating his removal. On 15 Dec. 1867 Slough had an altercation in Sante Fe with a lawmaker who had sponsored the legislation, receiving a mortal wound from which he died 2 days later.
—EGL

small arms. The personal firearm of the soldier or sailor is a small arm. During the Civil War this included muskets, rifles, pistols, carbines, and shotguns. Standard infantry weapons were the .69-caliber HARPERS FERRY RIFLE, the .58-caliber RIFLE MUSKET, and .44- or .36-caliber revolvers after the Colt or Remington patterns. Whether supplied by U.S. arsenals or large New England factories, or produced in small shops in Virginia, Georgia, or Alabama, the majority of Union or Confederate small arms found on any battlefield were of these types. However, imported weapons, antique weapons, and experimental weapons were scattered through every Northern and Southern division, and have proved the most interesting to historians and collectors.

HENRY and Spencer repeating rifles, SPENCER CARBINES, a few imported pistols, and some Union and Confederate single-shot carbines constructed to accept Spencer ammunition used fixed rimfire cartridges made of metal. Most other small arms were percussion-cap weapons, though some single-shot Maynard carbines using a roll of caps in a magazine and a few flintlocks saw service early in the war.

The standard long-range small arm of the cavalry was the carbine. Aside from the unusual Maynard and the coveted and feared Spencer, the most common makes were Sharps, REMINGTON, Joslyn, BURNSIDE, Starr, and Confederate models called Tarpley, Cook, Perry, and Richmond. Breechloaders, whether using a rolling block and lever or a broken breech (like a modern shotgun), were the preferred carbines, allowing

quick, efficient loading on horseback. But some muzzle-loading carbines remained in use. More than 30 types of the weapon saw service. Usually taking .52- or .54-caliber ammunition, they ranged on average from 38 to 40 in. in length.

After the carbine, the favorite shoulder arm of Confederate horse soldiers was the shotgun. They abounded in poorly supplied Western regiments, but were preferred by many in the Eastern theater as well. Privately owned, they were found in all gauges and were frequently sawed-off. Virginia partisan JOHN H. MCNEILL claimed that it was the best weapon at close range.

Pistols were found in a bewildering variety of designs, sizes, and calibers, and were supplied by American and European makers. Many soldiers brought with them family dueling pistols, derringers, or small multibarreled "pepperbox" models for personal protection. But the Union and Confederate governments concentrated on purchasing revolvers. Aside from COLTS and REMINGTONS, revolvers ranging from .32 to .44 caliber were purchased by the hundreds of thousands. The most common makes were STARR, Deane and Adams, Lefaucheaux, SAVAGE, Whitney, Allen, LEECH & RIGDON, Spiller & Burr, and GRISWOLD & GUNNISON. These weapons often became associated with individuals. A Lefaucheaux, a French arm firing a fixed, metallic cartridge, was carried by Lt. Gen. THOMAS J. "STONEWALL" JACKSON. The LEMAT REVOLVER, an import with a second barrel for firing a shotgun round, was made famous by Maj. Gen. J.E.B. STUART and Gen. P.G.T. BEAUREGARD.

French, Belgian, and English gunmakers were among the Confederacy's most reliable small-arms suppliers. Of all their products, the English ENFIELD RIFLE, noted for accuracy and dependability, is best remembered. Thousands of them saw Southern service, impressed Union buyers, then came into the Federal arsenal. Supplementing the rifle-musket in both armies, the average model fired a .577-caliber projectile and had 3 barrel bands, a "crown" or "tower" stamped on the lockplate, and a barrel measuring 39 in. Later produced in the North, about 700,000 were imported from Britain for American belligerents.
—JES

Smalley, George Washburn. journalist b. Franklin, Mass., 2 June 1833, Smalley was raised in Worcester, Mass., graduated from Yale University in 1854, attended Harvard Law School in 1855, then worked as a Boston attorney until the Civil War. He was an antebellum associate of abolitionists William Lloyd Garrison and Wendell Phillips and a strong Unionist. Poor eyesight adversely affected his legal career and kept him from military service.

Phillips introduced Smalley to NEW YORK *TRIBUNE* managing editor Sydney Howard Gay in fall 1861. Assessing Smalley's abolitionist interests, Gay hired him as a *Tribune* correspondent, assigned him to write about the lives of blacks in Port Royal, S.C., then assigned him to Maj. Gen. John C. Frémont's Union army in the Shenandoah Valley in spring 1862. Smalley recounted each of Frémont's successive defeats and, following the Battle of PORT REPUBLIC, attributed the Union loss to Brig. Gen. James Shields. Vilified by Shields and his partisans in the press, Smalley next covered the Antietam Campaign, where he witnessed the Battle of SOUTH MOUNTAIN at Maj. Gen. George B. McClellan's side. As a volunteer aide to Maj. Gen. Joseph Hooker, he capped his journalistic career with his coverage of the Battle of ANTIETAM.

With Hooker from the battle's outset until that officer's

wounding at 9 a.m., 17 Sept., Smalley rode over the battlefield delivering orders and getting a comprehensive view of the fight. That night, riding to Frederick, Md., he telegraphed a brief story to the *Tribune,* then took a succession of railroad trains to New York City, writing his full story en route. With the first complete account of Antietam published, Smalley had scooped all other reporters.

For his efforts, he was given a *Tribune* editorial job and remained in New York for much of the rest of the Civil War. Though he traveled to interview Hooker, Maj. Gen. George G. Meade, and other Federal officers after the Union defeat at CHANCELLORSVILLE, his story of the army's poor condition was suppressed. During the New York City DRAFT RIOTS of July 1863, Smalley armed several *Tribune* staffers and defended the newspaper offices from rioters who had singled out the abolitionist newspaper for vandalism.

In postbellum years he reported the 1866 Austro-Prussian War, in 1867 established the *Tribune*'s London bureau, coordinated his paper's reportage of the 1870 Franco-Prussian War, and served as *Tribune* European bureau chief until accepting a job as the London *Times* American correspondent in 1895. Working in New York and the English capital, he retired from the *Times* in 1905, moved to London, and died there 4 Apr. 1916. He published several books in postwar years, the most notable being his autobiographical 2-volume *Anglo-American Memories* (1911 and 1912).   —JES

Smith, Andrew Jackson. USA b. Bucks Cty., Pa., 28 Apr. 1815, Smith grew up on a farm in Buckingham Township in southeastern Pennsylvania. The youngest son of Revolutionary War and War of 1812 veteran Samuel Smith, Andrew was named after his father's commander at the Battle of New Orleans. Andrew also pursued a military career, entering West Point in 1834 and graduating 36th in his class 4 years later as a 2d lieutenant in the 1st Dragoons. During the next 23 years he attained the rank of major, having served almost exclusively in the West against the Indians.

Smith began his Civil War service in California as colonel of the 2d Cavalry from that state. In Nov. 1861 he resigned his California post in favor of a position as chief of cavalry with Maj. Gen. Henry W. Halleck in Missouri. After the Corinth Campaign in 1862 he was appointed brigadier general of volunteers, to rank from 17 Mar. As a division commander, Smith took part in the expeditions to CHICKASAW BLUFFS and ARKANSAS POST.

In 1863 he led a division in the VICKSBURG CAMPAIGN and the following year commanded parts of 2 Union corps in Maj. Gen. Nathaniel P. Banks's RED RIVER CAMPAIGN. On 14 May 1864 he accepted an appointment to major general of volunteers. Serving in Tennessee and Mississippi during the next few months, Smith became one of only 2 Union generals to defeat Nathan B. Forrest when, 14 July, he and his XVI Corps overwhelmed the Confederate defenders in the Battle of TUPELO.

After Tupelo, Smith was transferred to Missouri, but he came back to Tennessee to reinforce Maj. Gen. George H. Thomas

in the Battle of Nashville. The campaign against MOBILE, Ala., in 1865 was Smith's last engagement in the Civil War.

Smith stayed in the army for 4 years after the war, in 1869 resigning and moving to St. Louis, Mo. There he served as postmaster of the city, city auditor, and commander of a Missouri militia brigade before he died at his home 30 Jan. 1897.
                                                              —FLS

Smith, Caleb Blood. USP b. Boston, Mass., 16 Apr. 1808. Early in life, Smith's family moved to Ohio, where the young man attended Cincinnati College and Miami University. Passing the bar in 1828, Smith set up a practice in Connersville, Ind. 4 years later, he founded the Indiana *Sentinel,* a newspaper serving the Whig party. Elected to the Indiana house of representatives in 1833, he labored in that body throughout most of the decade. In 1843, he won a seat in the U.S. House and for the next 7 years furthered Whig interests there. He returned to Cincinnati in 1851, resuming his practice and managing the Cincinnati & Chicago Railroad.

USMHI

An influential member of the Indiana delegation to the Republican national convention of 1860, Smith was catered to by David Davis, Abraham Lincoln's political manager. The Lincoln faction needed the Indiana votes to ensure their candidate's nomination, and to keep these votes in their camp, Davis promised Smith a cabinet post in the new administration. Lincoln, unaware of Davis' deal, later agreed to it, stating that Smith would add a conservative touch to his cabinet.

Smith's term as Lincoln's secretary of the interior was undistinguished. A machine politician of the old school, the secretary looked out for his own interests first. He appointed his son to a post in the Interior Department and caused Lincoln other problems with patronage. He argued against the resupply of besieged FORT SUMTER, advising that the decision could be explained away if public outcry resulted. In July 1862 the secretary also signed a memorandum to Lincoln calling for the removal of Maj. Gen. GEORGE B. MCCLELLAN. A few weeks later, he defended Maj. Gen. JOHN POPE prior to the debacle at the Battle of SECOND BULL RUN Aug. 1862.

In Dec. 1862, Smith, in poor health, submitted his resignation to the president. The secretary had been offered a Federal judgeship in Indiana and wanted the appointment for security's sake. On 7 Jan. 1864, while in Indianapolis for a court session, he was suddenly taken ill and died.   —MTC

Smith, Charles Ferguson. USA b. Philadelphia, Pa., 24 Apr. 1807. Graduating from West Point in 1825, ranking 19th in a class of 37, Smith saw service in the Mexican War and rose to the rank of lieutenant colonel by war's end. After serving on the frontier, he took part in the Red River expedition of 1856 and the suppression of the Mormons in Utah a year later.

Smith returned to Washington, D.C., at the outbreak of war and soon became involved in politics. Speaking freely, the colonel angered some influential politicians and, under a cloud, was relegated to recruiting duties in New York. He was saved from oblivion by Maj. Gen. JOHN C. FRÉMONT, who used his political influence to have Smith promoted to brigadier general of volunteers 30 Aug. 1861 and transferred to his Western command.

In Jan. 1862 Smith's troops joined Maj. Gen. Ulysses S. Grant's Army of the Mississippi in the historic campaign to capture FORTS HENRY AND DONELSON. During the siege of Fort Donelson, 15 Feb., the Confederates attempted a breakout, striking the Federal right. Success was within their grasp when Grant ordered Smith to attack the right side of the fort's works. At the head of his 3d Division, Smith led a charge that breached the defenses and forced the Confederates to surrender. When they asked for terms of capitulation, Smith counseled his chief to offer no terms save unconditional surrender (*see* TERMS OF SURRENDER). Consequently, Grant drafted this term into his famous dispatch.

LC

On 21 Mar. Smith was promoted to major general of volunteers. That month, he was placed in temporary charge of the army, when Major General Grant was accused of drunkenness. During this interval, Smith moved the army to Pittsburg Landing, Tenn. While jumping into a small boat, he slipped and badly scraped his shin. The wound became septic and the general was bedridden. He was moved to Savannah, Tenn., to recover, but the wound grew worse and he died there 25 Apr. 1862. His body was returned to Philadelphia for burial.   —MTC

Smith, Edmund Kirby. CSA b. St. Augustine, Fla., 16 May 1824, Smith received his early education at a preparatory school in Alexandria, Va., then graduated 25th in the West

Point class of 1845. Less than a year later he was taking part in the first battles of the Mexican War and was cited for bravery at Cerro Gordo.

In 1855 Smith was assigned as a captain to the 2d Cavalry Regiment, where his fellow officers included ALBERT SIDNEY JOHNSTON, ROBERT E. LEE, GEORGE H. THOMAS, JOHN B. HOOD, and FITZHUGH LEE, all destined for fame as Civil War generals.

When Florida seceded from the Union in 1861, Smith accepted a commission as brigadier general in the Confederate army. His timely arrival on the battlefield at FIRST BULL RUN turned the tide and gave the Confederacy victory in the first clash of the Civil War. Wounded in the battle, Smith later led a Southern advance into Kentucky, winning a crucial battle at RICHMOND, Ky., Aug. 1862. In Oct. 1862 he was promoted to lieutenant general and placed in command of the TRANS-MISSISSIPPI DEPARTMENT. A devout Christian, Smith almost resigned his commission in fall 1863 to enter the ministry, but he remained in the army, waging a well-planned defensive campaign to keep the Federals from taking western Louisiana and Texas 1863–65. Though he had few resources and was unable

LC

to please his superiors in Richmond, his Trans-Mississippi command was the last Southern army to stay on the field.

After his surrender to Brig. Gen. E.R.S. Canby 26 May 1865 (*see* SURRENDERS: Kirby Smith), Smith served as president of the University of Nashville (now George Peabody College for Teachers) and taught at the University of the South, Sewanee, Tenn., where he died 28 Mar. 1893.   —DS

Smith, Giles Alexander. USA b. Jefferson Cty., N.Y., 29 Sept. 1829. Descended from 18th-century settlers of Massachusetts, Giles was the younger brother of Union Gen. Morgan L. Smith. In his teens, he migrated to Ohio, eventually working in a dry-goods firm in Cincinnati. Later he moved to Bloomington, Ill., where he was the proprietor of a hotel at the outbreak of the Civil War.

When his brother formed the 8th Missouri Infantry in summer 1861, Giles Smith served under him, initially as commander of Company D. He demonstrated conspicuous ability in such campaigns as FORTS HENRY AND DONELSON, SHILOH (where the 8th Missouri was a part of Maj.

LC

Gen. LEW WALLACE's division, which shored up the Union rear 7 Apr.), and CORINTH. These performances helped him rise in rank along with his brother. Named lieutenant colonel 12 June 1862, he was jumped to colonel 18 days later, on Morgan Smith's elevation to brigadier general.

Giles Smith attained brigade command that December while participating in Maj. Gen. WILLIAM T. SHERMAN's ill-starred offensive at CHICKASAW BLUFFS. He retained that position during the operations that led to the capture of ARKANSAS POST the following January. During the VICKSBURG CAMPAIGN, he distinguished himself on a number of occasions, especially by helping rescue a gunboat fleet trapped in Steele's Bayou, Miss., Mar. 1863. At the close of those operations, he was named a brigadier general of volunteers.

In the Siege of CHATTANOOGA, he helped cover the crossing of the Tennessee River by Sherman's corps 24 Nov. 1863 and later that day was severely wounded during the first assault on MISSIONARY RIDGE. He recovered to participate in the ATLANTA CAMPAIGN, leading a XV Corps brigade, then a division in the XVII Corps. In brigade command he served at RESACA and along the CHATTAHOOCHEE RIVER; as a divisional leader, he saw action at LEGGETT'S HILL and in the Battle of ATLANTA, as well as during Sherman's MARCH TO THE SEA and CAROLINAS CAMPAIGN.

With hostilities ended, Smith led a division of black troops on occupation duty in the Southwest. As a major general of volunteers he was mustered out of the service 24 Nov. 1865, having refused a colonelcy in the Regulars. Named assistant postmaster general in 1869, he resigned 3 years later due to failing health. After living in California for 2 years, he returned to Bloomington shortly before his death there 5 Nov. 1876.   —EGL

Smith, Gustavus Woodson. CSA b. Georgetown, Ky., 30 Nov. or 1 Dec. 1821, Smith graduated 8th in the class of 1842 at West Point and entered the U.S. Army as an engineer. He taught engineering at the military academy and served in the Mexican War, resigning in 1854 to go into civil engineering. Smith was street commissioner for New York City 1858–61 and a member of a curriculum committee for West Point when the war began. He was commissioned a major general in the Confederate army 19 Sept. 1861, serving under Gen. JOSEPH E. JOHNSTON in Virginia.

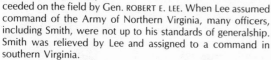

LC

When Johnston was seriously wounded at SEVEN PINES in 1862, Smith took temporary command of the army until succeeded on the field by Gen. ROBERT E. LEE. When Lee assumed command of the Army of Northern Virginia, many officers, including Smith, were not up to his standards of generalship. Smith was relieved by Lee and assigned to a command in southern Virginia.

He served as interim secretary of war for a few days Nov. 1862, between GEORGE W. RANDOLPH and JAMES A. SEDDON. In Feb. 1863, when 6 men commissioned after him were promoted to lieutenant general, Smith resigned his commission. He became a major general in the GEORGIA MILITIA, and was appointed by Gov. JOSEPH E. BROWN to help defend the state against Maj. Gen. WILLIAM T. SHERMAN in summer 1864. Smith fought at the CHATTAHOOCHEE RIVER and around Atlanta and Savannah, and surrendered his small force at Macon 20 Apr. 1865.

After the war he ran an iron works in Chattanooga, Tenn., was insurance commissioner of Kentucky, and wrote *Confederate War Papers* (1884) and *The Battle of Seven Pines* (1891) as well as a book on his Mexican War experiences, *Company "A," Corps of Engineers, U.S.A., in the Mexican War* (1896). d. New York City, 24 June 1896. —JTP

Smith, James Argyle. CSA b. Maury Cty., Tenn., 1 July 1831. The 45th-ranked graduate in the West Point class of 1853, Smith had risen to 1st lieutenant in the 6th U.S. Infantry by the outbreak of the Civil War. By that time he had served in garrisons in Kansas and Missouri, in the Sioux campaigning of 1855, during the "BLEEDING KANSAS" troubles 1856–58, and on the Utah Expedition of 1858. "Being a Southern man in sympathy as well as by birth," he resigned from Federal service early in May 1861 to accept a captaincy of Confederate infantry.

In Mar. 1862 Smith was elevated to major and tendered a position on the staff of Maj.

LC

Gen. LEONIDAS POLK. He accepted a field command a few weeks afterward and at SHILOH served as lieutenant colonel of the 2d Tennessee Infantry, a regiment that helped batter the Union right wing 6 Apr. 1862. Extensively praised for his performance on that field, he was soon promoted to colonel of a CONFEDERATE REGULAR ARMY regiment, the 5th Infantry. Lead-

ing the outfit at PERRYVILLE, Smith won commendation for his celerity of movement and the destructive fire his troops generated, which "utterly whipped" part of Brig. Gen. LOVELL H. ROUSSEAU's division. Smith's Regulars were also lauded for their services at STONE'S RIVER and CHICKAMAUGA. After the latter battle, their leader was commissioned a brigadier general, to rank from 30 Sept. 1863.

Succeeding to the command of Brig. Gen. HIRAM B. GRANBURY's brigade of Texas infantry and dismounted cavalry, Smith made it a potent element of Maj. Gen. PATRICK R. CLEBURNE's division/Army of Tennessee during the ATLANTA CAMPAIGN. On 21 July at LEGGETT'S HILL and the next day in the Battle of ATLANTA, however, his command suffered heavy casualties, Smith himself falling wounded on the 22d. He nevertheless commanded another of Cleburne's brigades during the balance of the campaign and the entire division following Cleburne's death at FRANKLIN. Early in 1865 he led half of Maj. Gen. BENJAMIN F. CHEATHAM's corps in North Carolina, winning high praise at BENTONVILLE 19 Mar.

Subsequently paroled at Greensborough, N.C., Smith eventually settled in Mississippi, where he farmed for a dozen years before being elected state superintendent of public education. d. Jackson, Miss., 6 Dec. 1901. —EGL

Smith, James Youngs. war governor b. Groton, Conn., 15 Sept. 1809. After an elementary public education, Smith clerked in a general store, moved to Providence, R.I., learned the lumber business, became proprietor of the Asborn & Smith Lumber Co., then became prominent in the cotton-mill and merchandising business and a leader of the state Republican party. A member of the Providence school committee, he won election to a 2-year term as mayor of the city in 1855, then lost a bid for the governorship in 1861.

Smith succeeded in winning the governorship in 1863, but because of Rhode Island's small population had difficulty meeting manpower quotas for the Civil War. While Rhode Island industry prospered during the war years, Smith backed opposition to the military draft, urged the employment of a bounty system, and received harsh criticism from national and state War Democrats for perceived mercenary conduct. Personally exonerated in investigations of corrupt state military recruiting practices, he declined reelection in 1866.

Retiring from public life, Smith pursued his business interests and died in Providence 26 March 1876. —JES

Smith, John Eugene. USA b. Berne, Switzerland, 3 Aug. 1816. Smith's family immigrated to Philadelphia, Pa., during his childhood. There he received a basic education and training to be a jeweler. Moving first to St. Louis, Mo., then to Galena, Ill., in 1836, he practiced his craft and became active in local affairs. In 1860 he was elected county treasurer.

When Gov. RICHARD YATES began mobilizing Illinois for war, Smith recommended ULYSSES S. GRANT to him as someone well qualified to train a regiment. Smith served briefly on the governor's staff but left to recruit the 45th Illinois, of which he was commissioned colonel 23 July 1861.

Assigned to field duty, he participated in the fighting at FORTS HENRY AND DONELSON, and at SHILOH temporarily held brigade command. He was promoted to brigadier general 29 Nov. 1862, commanding a brigade in the XVII Corps at PORT GIBSON, RAYMOND, JACKSON, CHAMPION'S HILL, and BIG BLACK RIVER BRIDGE during the VICKSBURG CAMPAIGN. He stayed in the Western theater through the fighting around CHATTANOOGA, was assigned to the advance as Maj. Gen. WILLIAM T. SHERMAN moved toward Atlanta in spring 1864, and remained in the East for the MARCH TO THE SEA and most of the CAROLINAS CAMPAIGN. During the last months of war, he commanded the DISTRICT OF WEST TENNESSEE.

Smith was mustered out of volunteer service Apr. 1866. Instead of returning to civilian life, in July he accepted the colonelcy of the 27th Infantry/Regular Army, serving at frontier garrisons until his retirement 19 May 1881. d. Galena, Ill., 29 Jan. 1897.   —PLF

LC

Smith, Joseph Bryant.

USN b. Nobleboro, Maine, 29 Dec. 1826, Smith was the son of Adm. Joseph Smith, who had been awarded the THANKS OF CONGRESS for gallant service during the War of 1812. Desiring to emulate his father, the young man secured a U.S. NAVAL ACADEMY appointment Oct. 1841 and graduated 10 Aug. 1847. On active duty, he earned a reputation for affability as well as for "rare courage," and, after a slow start, quickly advanced in rank. Named a ship's master Aug. 1855, he was promoted to lieutenant less than a month later.

Early in Mar. 1862, following a series of minor assignments, Smith succeeded Cmdr. William

USMHI

Smith (no relation) in command of the warship *Congress,* in Hampton Roads, Va., near FORT MONROE. The 50-gun frigate, part of the Atlantic Blockading Squadron, was lying off Newport News Point, where it guarded Union shipping and land installations against the reported threat of a Confederate ironclad. That threat proved real: early on the afternoon of 8 Mar. Smith found himself facing the *VIRGINIA,* an iron-plated reincarnation of the old U.S.S. *Merrimack.* Having steamed up from Norfolk, the ironclad attacked the sloop *Cumberland,* which lay west of Smith's station. After ramming and sinking the sloop, the vessel turned against the *Congress,* silencing the latter's stern guns and bearing down on it with intimidating speed.

Seeing the uselessness of a fight, Smith ordered his ship towed to shore. Just before running aground, the frigate took several direct hits from the ironclad's cannon, suffering heavy casualties. About 4:20 p.m., while rushing from the quarterdeck to the main deck of his vessel, Smith was struck by a shell fragment that carried away his head. His successor promptly surrendered the ship. Word of the lieutenant's death was slow to reach the North, but when his father, then on duty in the Navy Department, learned that the *Congress* had run up a white flag, he observed prophetically: "Then Joe is dead."
                                                                                        —EGL

Smith, Martin Luther.

CSA b. Danby, N.Y., 9 Sept. 1819, Smith graduated 16th in the West Point class of 1842 and, commissioned a brevet 2d lieutenant of engineers, went on duty in Florida. Until the Mexican War he surveyed the coasts and rivers of Florida and Georgia, in 1848 won a brevet to 1st lieutenant for making a reconnaissance in the enemy's country and mapping the area around Mexico City, then returned to duty in Georgia and Texas. Relocating to Florida, presumably on leave of absence, he took a civilian job, serving as chief engineer for the Fernandina & Cedar Key Railroad until resigning from the U.S. Army 1 Apr. 1861. Prior to

LC

his resignation he accepted a Confederate commission as major of engineers, 16 Mar. 1861. Though from an old Northern family, he had lived in the South since age 22, married a woman from Athens, Ga., in 1846, and had his business interests in the Confederacy. He stated these associations as his reason for serving the South.

Smith was assigned to Maj. Gen. DAVID E. TWIGGS's command in New Orleans in summer 1861, worked on the city's defenses, then assumed the colonelcy of the 21st Louisiana Infantry Feb. 1862. Promoted to brigadier general 11 Apr. 1862 for the defense of New Orleans, he was assigned to command of the Third District of the Department of Southern Mississippi and East Louisiana, then was assigned to a command at Vicksburg, won promotion to major general 4 Nov. 1862, and supervised construction of the city's defensive works until captured July 1863.

Paroled, he was not exchanged until Mar. 1864. He requested a divisional command with the Army of Northern Virginia, but with no appropriate openings available, he accepted a post as Gen. ROBERT E. LEE's chief engineer until assigned to the Army of the Tennessee at Atlanta in July. Smith served as Gen. JOHN B. HOOD's chief engineer until October, then assumed the same post with the Department of Alabama, Mississippi, and East Louisiana, constructing defenses for Maj. Gen. DABNEY H. MAURY at Mobile, Ala. He remained with Maury until the fall of that city, then surrendered at Athens, Ga., May 1865.

Smith briefly established a civil-engineering firm in Savannah, Ga., dying there suddenly 29 July 1866.   —JES

Smith, Preston.

CSA b. Giles Cty., Tenn., 25 Dec. 1823. After attending rural schools, Smith went to Jackson College, Tenn., and, after passing the bar, became a successful lawyer in Memphis. When war was declared, he obtained a commission as colonel of the 154th Tennessee infantry regiment.

On 6 Apr. 1862, at the Battle of SHILOH, Smith was wounded while leading his regiment. Recovered, the colonel was assigned command of the 1st Brigade in Maj. Gen. Patrick R. Cleburne's 2d Division. Smith took part in Maj. Gen. E. Kirby Smith's invasion of Kentucky Aug. 1862. At the Battle of RICHMOND, 30 Aug., Cleburne's division crushed a hastily assembled group of raw Union recruits. During the fighting, Cleburne was shot through the mouth and Smith assumed command, capturing 4,000 prisoners and a Union wagon train. In appreciation of his splendid victory, the government awarded Smith a brigadier's commission 27 Oct. 1862.

In Sept. 1863, Smith's brigade took part in Confederate attempts to annihilate Maj. Gen. William S. Rosecrans' ARMY OF THE CUMBERLAND, which was advancing toward Chattanooga, Tenn. Although the army was dispersed over a wide area, Gen. BRAXTON BRAGG fumbled

LC

any chance to destroy the enemy in detail. On 19 Sept. he finally brought the Federals to bay around Chickamauga Creek. Throughout the day, Smith's brigade fought a running battle with Union troops in the woods around the Brock house. The fighting gained little for either side but more casualties. Toward evening, Smith's men were part of Cleburne's general assault on the Union left. Bragg had hoped to envelop the Federal line, but Maj. Gen. GEORGE H. THOMAS anticipated the move and placed his soldiers in strong defensive positions. Eventually the Confederate attack subsided and the woods became quiet as darkness fell. While inspecting his lines that night, Smith lost his way and rode into an enemy unit. The Federals unleashed a volley, striking the general. Taken to an aid station, he died shortly thereafter. Smith was buried in Memphis. —MTC

Smith, Thomas Benton. CSA b. Mechanicsville, Tenn., 24 Feb. 1838. Educated locally, then at Nashville Military Institute, Smith also, reportedly, attended West Point briefly. After working for the Nashville & Decatur Railroad, he entered Confederate service as a lieutenant of Company B/20th Tennessee Infantry. As a subaltern he fought at MILL SPRINGS Jan. 1862 and 3 months later at SHILOH, where his regiment struck the Union left below the Peach Orchard. In May 1862, on the 20th Tennessee's reorganization, he became its colonel.

That August Smith participated in Maj. Gen. JOHN C. BRECKINRIDGE'S unsuccessful

LC

offensive against the Union post at BATON ROUGE, La. On that field, he was placed in temporary command of a brigade in the division of Brig. Gen. (later Gov.) Charles Clark. Breckinridge praised his efforts, noting that despite heavy fire from a naval fleet as well as from the garrison, the colonel "moved against the enemy in fine style." Smith also earned plaudits for his performance at STONE'S RIVER, where he was severely wounded 2 Jan. 1863 while participating in an assault by Brig. Gen. WILLIAM PRESTON's brigade against the far Union left.

Smith recovered only to be wounded again during the operations of Brig. Gen. WILLIAM B. BATE's brigade at CHICKAMAUGA. He retook the field for the ATLANTA CAMPAIGN, succeeding to the command of Brig. Gen. ROBERT C. TYLER's brigade and being

promoted to brigadier himself 29 July 1864. From Dalton to JONESBOROUGH, Smith won a reputation as one of the most stalwart brigade leaders of the ARMY OF TENNESSEE. He further enhanced this reputation in the battles at FRANKLIN and Nashville and during the attack on Murfreesboro, Tenn., late in 1864 (see also FRANKLIN AND NASHVILLE CAMPAIGN).

His combativeness cost him his sanity and threatened his life. Captured at Nashville, 16 Dec., after a tenacious stand against superior numbers, he was led to the rear along with many of his troops. While under guard, he was accosted by the colonel of an Ohio regiment whose men had suffered heavily in opposing Smith's brigade. The enraged officer repeatedly struck his captive across the head with his saber, laying open his brain. Though Smith recovered sufficiently to return to postwar railroad work, he spent his last 47 years in an insane asylum at Nashville, where he died 21 May 1923. —EGL

Smith, William. CSA/war governor b. King George Cty., Va., 6 Sept. 1797. William Smith, nicknamed "Extra Billy," was so designated for the frequent extra payments he received from the Post Office Department for the mileage covered while operating a mail-coach service from Washington, D.C., to Milledgeville, Ga., 1827–36. After 1836, Smith served 5 years in the Virginia senate, 5 terms in the U.S. House of Representatives 1841–43 and 1853–61, and 1 full term as governor of his state 1846–49.

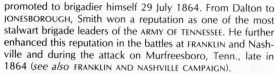

When the war broke out, Smith was 63 years old and so impressed Virginia Gov. JOHN LETCHER that he commissioned Smith a colonel. In fall 1861 he

LC

was elected to the Confederate House of Representatives and served both as congressman and military officer until May 1862. At FIRST BULL RUN he commanded the 49th Virginia Infantry. In the reports of the battle, Brig. Gen. P.G.T. Beauregard said Smith was "efficient and self-possessed and brave."

At SEVEN PINES, when his men protested that they could no longer stand the intense fire from the Union forces, Smith agreed, said it was "West P'nt tomfoolery," but then urged them to "fire, and flush the game."

In Sept. 1862 Smith's regiment held the right of Brig. Gen. Jubal A. Early's line at ANTIETAM. In the fighting Smith was wounded 3 times and incapacitated for several months. On his return to duty he was promoted to brigadier general, 31 Jan. 1863, and given command of Early's old brigade.

At GETTYSBURG, Smith's spirit to fight was not enough. In the course of this battle his superiors and men realized that he had valor in abundance but lacked tactical skill. At this crucial moment Smith was reelected governor of Virginia and left the field to assume his executive duties during the last year of the war. He was promoted to major general 12 Aug. 1863, and the following January was inaugurated governor.

When the war ended the Federal government posted a reward for Smith, but when he surrendered he was promptly paroled. He returned to farming on his estate near Warrenton, Va., where he died 18 May 1887 at the age of 89. —AG

Smith, William Duncan.

CSA b. Augusta, Ga., 28 July 1825. An 1846 graduate of the U.S. Military Academy, ranking 35th in his class, Smith immediately entered the Mexican War as an officer of dragoons. He fought at Vera Cruz, Cerro Gordo, Contreras, and Churubusco, and was seriously wounded at Molino del Rey. After recuperating, he engaged in frontier garrison duty, rising to 1st lieutenant Aug. 1851 and to captain June 1858. From 1859 to 1861 he was on leave in Europe and on his return resigned his commission to accept a captaincy in Confederate service to date from 16 Mar. 1861. On 14 July of that year he became colonel of the 20th Georgia Infantry.

USMHI

Even before entering active campaigning, Smith enjoyed such favor with Richmond that he was promoted to brigadier general to rank from 7 Mar. 1862. Reporting for duty in the DEPARTMENT OF SOUTH CAROLINA, GEORGIA, AND FLORIDA, he was placed in command of a district in South Carolina that June. As commander of troops and works on James Island, south of Charleston Harbor, he led a part of the force under Brig. Gen. NATHAN G. EVANS that held the fortified camp at SECESSIONVILLE. Thanks to Smith's support, Evans repulsed a Union assault on that camp 16 June 1862, inflicting almost 700 enemy casualties compared to only 200 among the defenders. Charleston remained secure from Federal encroachment for several months.

Though Rep. WILLIAM P. MILES urged his promotion to replace Maj. Gen. JOHN C. PEMBERTON in command of the 3-state department, Smith contracted yellow fever in fall 1862 and 4 Oct. succumbed to the disease in Charleston. His remains were carried to his birthplace for burial.   —EGL

Smith, William Farrar.

USA b. St. Albans, Vt., 17 Feb. 1824, Smith graduated from West Point 4th in the class of 1845, then served as a topographical engineer before the Civil War. Appointed colonel of the 3d Vermont as of 16 July 1861, then brigadier general as of 13 Aug., he commanded a division in the PENINSULA CAMPAIGN, at ANTIETAM, and at FREDERICKSBURG. After this last battle his public criticism of Maj. Gen. Ambrose E. Burnside cost him both his command and confirmation as major general.

In Oct. 1863 Smith, acting as chief engineer of the Department of the Cumberland, opened the famous CRACKER LINE to supply the U.S. Army besieged in CHATTANOOGA. This notable engineering achievement won for Smith the admiration of Maj. Gen. ULYSSES S. GRANT and his subordinates and could have given Smith the honors and recognition he craved had he not persisted in

USMHI

claiming credit for originating as well as executing the plan. Asking too much diminished the value of his accomplishment and offers the key to his personality, a mixture of brilliance and shortsighted quarrelsomeness.

Winning Grant's favor at Chattanooga revitalized Smith's military career and even led to speculation that he might command the Army of the Potomac. In the spring campaign of 1864 he commanded the XVIII Corps/Army of the James under Maj. Gen. Benjamin F. Butler. Smith's failure to attack Petersburg vigorously 15 June was a blunder that may have prolonged the Civil War by months. Grant could have forgiven Smith if Smith had not quarreled with Butler to the point where one had to be removed. The decision is difficult; Smith made it easier by criticizing Maj. Gen. George G. Meade in a manner that reflected on Grant. Removed from command 19 July, he launched a campaign on his own behalf that made reinstatement impossible.

Smith spent the rest of his life in acrimonious dispute over his Civil War record, apparently never recognizing that he was his own worst enemy. d. Philadelphia, Pa., 28 Feb. 1903.
                                                                              —JYS

Smith, William Sooy.

USA b. Tarlton, Ohio, 22 July 1830, Smith, son of Justice of the Peace Sooy Smith, supported himself through the University of Ohio, graduated there in 1849, then entered West Point for his engineering education, graduating 6th in the class of 1853. A man of high technological and intellectual ability, he resigned from the U.S. Army 19 June 1854 to work as an engineer on the Illinois Central Railroad. He lost the job due to poor health, but after 2 years as a teacher in Buffalo, N.Y., in 1857 he established the private engineering firm Parkinson & Smith, working on the International Bridge at Niagara Falls, N.Y., and, utilizing *avant garde* engineering techniques, the Charleston & Savannah Railroad Bridge near Savannah, Ga.

LC

Smith left the South at the start of the Civil War, joining the 13th Ohio Infantry and winning commission as its colonel 26 June 1861. After early service in western Virginia and assignment to the Army of the Ohio, he won commission as brigadier general 15 Apr. 1862 for his services at the Battle of SHILOH, where, as a colonel, he led the 14th Brigade/5th Division in Maj. Gen. Don Carlos Buell's force. Remaining with the Army of the Ohio, later commanding its 4th Division, Smith served in reserve at the Battle of PERRYVILLE, then assumed command of the 2d Division/XVI Corps 22 Mar. 1863 for the SECOND VICKSBURG CAMPAIGN. On 20 July, he became chief of cavalry of the Department of Tennessee, and in October exercised this office for the Military Division of the Mississippi. For Maj. Gen. William T. Sherman's MERIDIAN CAMPAIGN, Feb. 1864, he led a large cavalry force from Tennessee south toward Meridian, Miss. Known as the SOOY SMITH EXPEDITION, it failed miserably, angering Sherman and bringing embarrassment to Smith, who had been beaten back in engagements at West Point and Okolona, Miss., by an inferior force under Maj. Gen. Nathan B. Forrest. Smith then served in administrative duties at Nashville, Tenn., until resigning in poor health 15 July 1864.

Smith suffered from rheumatoid arthritis and after the war lived as a gentleman farmer in Cook Cty., Ill., until reestablishing his private engineering practice in 1866. He became an internationally known expert on bridges and foundations, and was responsible for several Missouri River railroad bridges, the first all-steel bridge (constructed at Glasgow, Mo.), the refinement of pneumatic caissons in construction, and the unusual techniques required for successfully constructing tall buildings in Chicago, Ill., where the low-lying bedrock makes foundation construction difficult. Awarded an American Centennial Exposition prize in 1876 for his bridge designs, from 1890 to 1910 he remained in the Chicago area, then retired to Medford, Ore., dying there 4 Mar. 1916.

Smith named a son Charles Sooysmith, adopting Sooysmith as a last name for the boy. This child also became internationally known for his civil engineering. His career overlapped his father's postbellum work, and he also died in 1916. In some sources, these men are confused with one another.   —JES

Smyth, Thomas Alfred. USA b. Ballyhooley, Cty. Cork, Ireland, 25 Dec. 1832. The son of an Irish farmer, Smyth immigrated to the U.S. in 1854, settling initially in Philadelphia, Pa. He volunteered to accompany adventurer William Walker's expedition to Nicaragua before establishing himself as a coachmaker in Wilmington, Del.

LC

On the outbreak of hostilities in 1861, Smyth immediately volunteered, recruiting a company of infantry that became part of the all-Irish 24th Pennsylvania, a 3-month regiment. When the 24th disbanded, Smyth secured the appointment of major of the 1st Delaware. The regiment participated in operations around Suffolk, Va., July 1862, then fought in its first major battle at ANTIETAM, Md., where it lost nearly one-third of its members. The unit fought at FREDERICKSBURG 13 Dec., and Smyth was promoted to lieutenant colonel on the 30th. On 7 Feb. 1863 he was named colonel and given command of the regiment, leading it at CHANCELLORSVILLE in May.

During the Battle of GETTYSBURG, Smyth commanded a brigade in the II Corps that participated in the repulse of PICKETT'S CHARGE 3 July. He then rendered distinguished service as a brigade commander throughout the remainder of 1863 and during the OVERLAND CAMPAIGN in spring 1864. For his gallant performance at COLD HARBOR in June, Smyth was promoted to brigadier general 1 Oct. 1864 and led his command during the entire PETERSBURG CAMPAIGN.

Smyth commanded a division in the APPOMATTOX CAMPAIGN. On 7 Apr. 1865, in a skirmish near Farmville, Va., he fell mortally wounded, shot through the mouth by a Confederate sniper. The minié bullet shattered a cervical vertebra, and Smyth lingered only for 2 days, dying 9 Apr., the day his army accepted the surrender of the Confederates. Smyth was the last Union general to be killed in the Civil War.   —JDW

Snake Creek Gap, Ga., maneuvers around. 7–12 May 1864 Backed by the 98,000 veterans of Maj. Gen. GEORGE H. THOMAS' ARMY OF THE CUMBERLAND, Maj. Gen. JAMES B. MCPHERSON'S ARMY OF THE TENNESSEE, and the Army of the Ohio under Maj. Gen. JOHN M. SCHOFIELD, Union Maj. Gen. WILLIAM T. SHERMAN moved southeastward toward Dalton, Ga., in the first week of May 1864. Just above Dalton, atop a 500-ft wall of stone and earth known as Rocky Face Ridge, the 53,000 troops of the ARMY OF TENNESSEE, under Confederate Gen. JOSEPH E. JOHNSTON, awaited the Union advance. The ATLANTA CAMPAIGN—the most crucial series of operations in the West —was under way.

Although Sherman held a heavy advantage in numbers, his enemy's formidable position prevented him from relying on a frontal assault. Accordingly, he sent Thomas, with Schofield on his left and the cavalry division of Brig. Gen. H. JUDSON KILPATRICK on his right, to hold the enemy's attention along the northern shelf of the ridge. Meanwhile, the Army of the Tennessee was to pass down the far side of Taylor's Ridge, which paralleled Rocky Face on the west, and forge eastward through the mountains to cut Johnston's rail line to Resaca, 13 mi below Dalton. Sherman's strategic acuity was never better displayed: his diversionary maneuvers proved so effective that for several days Johnston remained unaware of the Union flanking drive.

On 7 May, as McPherson headed south, preceded by mounted infantry, Thomas' XIV Corps, under Maj. Gen. JOHN M. PALMER, struck Confederate cavalry and artillery atop Tunnel Hill, a northwestern spur of Rocky Face Ridge. The enemy resisted valiantly until the arrival on Palmer's left of Maj. Gen. OLIVER O. HOWARD's IV Corps, whereupon the Confederates fled south into a gaping defile in Rocky Face called Buzzard Roost, where strong works had been erected. The balance of Thomas' command, the XX Corps of Maj. Gen. JOSEPH HOOKER, moved into position farther to the right to menace the new Confederate position. Early on the 8th, part of Brig. Gen. JOHN NEWTON's IV Corps division pressed the Confederates along the northern crest of the ridge, while Howard, Palmer, and Hooker each sent skirmishers to press Buzzard Roost. Some of these forces seized the mouth of the gap. The day's fighting closed with Brig. Gen. JOHN W. GEARY's XX Corps launching a strong offensive against Dug Gap, south of Buzzard Roost. 3 times Geary's troops clawed their way up the craggy wall, each time holding the crest briefly before retreating. Their efforts cost them more than 350 casualties.

On 9 May the IV, XIV, and XX corps made new drives against Buzzard Roost and its southern environs. Though failing to disperse the Confederates—the infantry divisions of Maj. Gens. ALEXANDER P. STEWART, BENJAMIN F. CHEATHAM, and WILLIAM B. BATE, supported by those of Maj. Gens. CARTER L. STEVENSON and THOMAS C. HINDMAN—they won the admiration of their enemy. Johnston later termed their great losses "proportionate to their courage." On this day, too, Schofield's army demonstrated through the valley east of Rocky Face Ridge. Reconnoitering on the left of this force, a brigade from the cavalry division of Brig. Gen. Edward M. McCook tangled with part of Johnston's mounted force under Maj. Gen. JOSEPH WHEELER. Fighting ranged south from Varnell's Station, on the railway to Dalton, until the hard-pressed Confederates made a stand near Poplar Place and repulsed their assailants with heavy loss.

Having moved without hindrance along Taylor's Ridge,

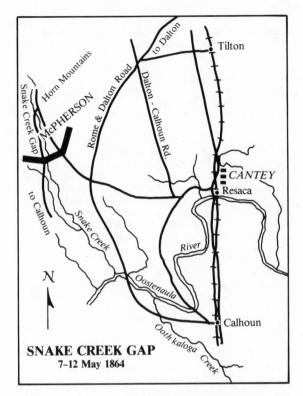

SNAKE CREEK GAP
7–12 May 1864

McPherson's troops pressed eastward, through Ship's Gap, to the town of Villanow, then through a strategic defile in the Horn Mts., Snake Creek Gap, which opened on Resaca. Though Johnston's scouts had failed to apprise him of the Federals' approach (a miscue attributable to Wheeler's laxity), the Northerners did encounter a mounted brigade, under Col. J. Warren Grigsby, when debouching from Snake Creek Gap near dawn on the 9th. Hurling Grigsby aside, McPherson started on the last leg of his circuitous journey into the Confederate rear. Early that afternoon he dispatched a division from Maj. Gen. GRENVILLE M. DODGE's XVI Corps, supported by the XV Corps of Maj. Gen. JOHN A. LOGAN, to reach the railroad above Resaca, only 5 mi off. Learning of this movement, Sherman exclaimed: "I've got Joe Johnston dead!"

He was wrong. With untold opportunity at hand, McPherson hesitated, then pulled back, recalling Dodge and Logan and fortifying near Snake Creek Gap on the 10th. Unexpectedly, his scouts had found the Resaca vicinity occupied by Confederates of all arms—the brigade of Brig. Gen. JAMES CANTEY, recently dispatched to Johnston's aid from Mobile, Ala. Cantey's troops were too few to have posed a serious obstacle to McPherson. Nevertheless, cut off from Sherman, fearing for the security of his left flank and rear, and aware that Johnston might suddenly turn against him, the army leader remained west of his main objective. Sherman's exultation turned to gloom. Though admitting that McPherson had exercised permissible discretion, he groaned, "Such an opportunity does not occur twice in a single life!"

On the 11th, the disappointed commander decided to send his remaining troops along McPherson's route. Leaving the IV

Corps and 2 mounted divisions to face Johnston's entire army atop Rocky Face, an assignment that "terrified" Howard, Sherman led Schofield's army and the remainder of Thomas' down the valley beyond Taylor's Ridge toward Snake Creek Gap. The march, forced to proceed over a single road, was so slow that not till early on the 13th did the head of the Federal column clear the gap.

As Sherman feared, the delay proved fatal to his plans. Though the force Johnston had initially dispatched toward Snake Creek—3 divisions under Lt. Gen. JOHN B. HOOD—failed to alert him to the danger there, reports of scouts 11–12 May brought definitive word of Sherman's movements. In response, late on the 12th the Army of Tennessee dropped down to Resaca, arriving just in time to choke off the Federal advance toward the town. Thus ended the initial confrontation of the crucial campaign in northwestern Georgia.   —EGL

Snodgrass Hill, at Chickamauga, Ga.   20 Sept. 1863
See HORSESHOE RIDGE (SNODGRASS HILL), AT CHICKAMAUGA, GA.

Society of the Army of the Potomac.   Within days after the surrender of the Confederates, Apr. 1865, officers of the Union Army of the Tennessee met to form a society. During the next 5 years, veterans of other Union armies created similar societies. One of the last, surprisingly, was that of the veterans of the most famous Union army, the Army of the Potomac. These former opponents of the Confederate Army of Northern Virginia met 5 July 1869 in New York City to organize the Society of the Army of the Potomac.

The organizers opened membership in the society to all officers and soldiers who had served in the army and in the X and XVIII corps/Army of the James. The society's constitution provided for a president elected at large and a vice-president from each army, artillery, cavalry, and signal corps, and each general staff. Such notable former commanders or corps commanders as IRVIN MCDOWELL, AMBROSE E. BURNSIDE, JOSEPH HOOKER, GEORGE G. MEADE, WINFIELD S. HANCOCK and PHILIP H. SHERIDAN served as presidents of the society. This organization of veterans, like the many others, existed to maintain the associations of those who fought in the army's ranks.

—JDW

soldiers' battle.   The outcome of a number of Civil War engagements ultimately rested with the courage and combat prowess of individual soldiers or regiments and their officers. Because of terrain, surprise attacks, or the determination of the soldiers, these battles raged without the strategic and tactical leadership of the generals and commanders. Such struggles were called "soldiers' battles."

A few notable soldiers' battles were fought in both the Western and Eastern theaters during the war. At SHILOH, 6 Apr. 1862, Confederates unleashed a massive surprise attack on the Union army. But Union regiments and brigades, forming pockets of resistance in places like the "HORNETS' NEST," eventually repulsed the serried Confederate attacks and saved their army. On 25 Nov. 1863, at MISSIONARY RIDGE, Union soldiers, ordered to seize the base of the ridge, stormed up the heights on their own initiative, routing the Confederate defenders.

Perhaps the best example of a soldiers' battle was the furious struggle in the WILDERNESS, 5–7 May 1864. There the opposing armies slaughtered each other blindly in a landscape of scrub brush and trees. With visibility reduced to paces in the dense terrain, Federals and Confederates hammered each other in a battle no one could direct and few could even see except for the flashing musketry and choking smoke.　　　—JDW

Somerset, Ky., Battle of. 19 Jan. 1862　*See* MILL SPRINGS, KY., BATTLE OF.

Sooy Smith Expedition, Miss. 11–26 Feb. 1864　To support the MERIDIAN CAMPAIGN, Union Maj. Gen. WILLIAM T. SHERMAN ordered Brig. Gen. WILLIAM SOOY SMITH to leave Colliersville, Tenn., west of Memphis, 1 Feb., raid from Pontotoc, Miss., to the Memphis & Ohio Railroad, then strike south through Okolona to unite with Sherman's force at Meridian 10 Feb. Contrary to instructions to push ahead with a smaller force and maintain the schedule, Smith waited until 11 Feb., when he was joined by Col. George E. Waring and 2,000 cavalry reinforcements from Columbus, Ky. On 11 Feb., far behind schedule, Smith, 7,000 cavalry, 20 artillery pieces, and a pack and ambulance train left Collierville, moving southwest for Pontotoc, with Brig. Gen. BENJAMIN H. GRIERSON second-in-command.

Burning corn and cotton, tearing up Memphis & Ohio Railroad track, Smith's column pushed aside 600 Mississippi militia under Col. Samuel Gholson and pressed south almost unimpeded. En route the Federals attracted more than 1,000 slaves seeking protection and passage to freedom.

Confederate Maj. Gen. NATHAN B. FORREST had a force of 2,500 cavalry scattered north of Meridian. After a week of raiding, Smith's troops made numerous contacts with Forrest's advance elements. On 20 Feb. Smith's main column skirmished with Forrest's men at Prairie Station, 15 mi north of West Point, and a Federal flank column collided with a Confederate brigade led by Col. Jeffrey E. Forrest at Aberdeen, northeast of West Point along the west fork of the Tombigbee River. Daunted by Nathan Forrest's reputation, uncertain of the number of enemy troops he faced, and worried over the fate of the escaped slaves, Smith ordered his men to concentrate at Prairie Station, then rode for West Point at dawn 21 Feb.

At 2 a.m. 21 Feb., Jeffrey Forrest pulled his brigade from Aberdeen and rode southwest, intercepting Smith's column shortly after its dawn departure. Fighting and withdrawing steadily, he drew the Union force 4 mi south of West Point onto swampy ground with the Tombigbee River on its left, the Okitbbeha Creek on its right, and the Sakatonchee Creek on its front. At Major General Forrest's order, Brig. Gen. JAMES R. CHALMERS' small division and Col. Robert A. McCulloch's brigade arrived on the south bank of the Sakatonchee and crossed at early morning to reinforce Jeffrey Forrest and bring on a general engagement.

Smith, rationalizing the raid's accomplishments and difficulties and believing the enemy his superior in numbers, claimed the West Point confrontation was a "trap set for me by the rebels" and ordered retreat to Tennessee. He designated his advance to form a rear guard, then ordered the bulk of his column to press north. The Federal rear guard, though unnerved by the swampy conditions, were protected on their flanks by the Sakatonchee and the Tombigbee. They held the Confederates at the Okitbbeha crossing for 2 hours, then withdrew. Nathan Forrest arrived on the scene and ordered pursuit. This ended the engagement at West Point.

Through the rest of 21 Feb. Confederates skirmished with

the Union column, sniping at one another for 25 mi and engaging in several minor clashes. At dawn 22 Feb., 4 mi south of Okolona, Confederate advance elements attacked Smith in an open area locally called "the prairie."

Additional Southern units arriving on the field broke the Federal lines in an enthusiastic charge, initiating an 11-mi running skirmish. Union troops tried twice to make a stand, first 1 mi, then 2 mi north of Okolona. After losing 6 artillery pieces in the retreat, Smith's men organized a defense in wooded hills and around buildings at the Ivey's Farm plantation, 7 mi northwest of Okolona. A general Confederate charge was repulsed in which Jeffrey Forrest died. A second charge and a Confederate move on Smith's right flank and rear failed. Federals organized 2 countercharges. Nathan Forrest's men, fighting dismounted in the open, and in inferior numbers, miraculously repelled both. Federals broke off the engagement and continued a retreat to Pontotoc. Forrest, his men nearly out of ammunition, ordered a halt. This ended the engagement at Okolona. Mississippi militia picked up the pursuit and harassed the Federals to the Tennessee line. Smith's column arrived at Collierville, Tenn., 26 Feb.

For the fighting of 20–22 Feb., Forrest reported a total of 144 casualties and gave no specific count for the individual engagements. Similarly, Smith reported 700 casualties for his entire raid but gave no clear count for West Point or Okolona. The majority of Union casualties are believed to have occurred 20 Feb.　　　—JES

Sorrel, Gilbert Moxley. CSA　b. Savannah, Ga., 23 Feb. 1838. At the outbreak of the Civil War, Sorrel was a clerk for a railroad and a private in the Georgia Hussars, a militia company. After witnessing the reduction of Fort Sumter, S.C., he participated in the capture of Fort Pulaski, Ga., then went to Virginia, where, before FIRST BULL RUN, he secured a position on Lt. Gen. JAMES LONGSTREET'S staff as captain and volunteer aide-de-camp. From that battle until the Wilderness, Sorrel's Civil War career was inextricably linked to that of Longstreet. As Longstreet rose in rank to command of the I Corps, Sorrel's duties increased, and he eventually became the I Corps's

VM

chief of staff. Rising to the rank of colonel, the Georgia officer participated with Longstreet in every major campaign in the East and went with his commander to the West during the CHICKAMAUGA and KNOXVILLE campaigns.

During the Battle of the WILDERNESS, where Longstreet was critically wounded, Sorrel personally led 4 brigades in a successful envelopment of the Union left. On 27 Oct. 1864 he was promoted to brigadier general and assigned to command of a brigade in Maj. Gen. William Mahone's division. Later that autumn he sustained a leg wound in the battles around PETERSBURG, Va. On 7 Feb. 1865 Sorrel fell with a severe chest wound in an engagement at HATCHER'S RUN. He was returning to his command when the Confederate army was surrendered 9 Apr. at Appomattox.

After the war Sorrel returned to Savannah. A merchant, he

was also connected with a steamship company. In 1905 he published his *Recollections of a Confederate Staff Officer,* one of the most valuable and perceptive memoirs of an aide. d. near Roanoke, Va., 10 Aug. 1901.   —JDW

South, Union Department of the. The Department of the South was organized 15 Mar. 1862 before most of the territory within its boundaries had been invaded and captured from the Confederacy. Consisting of South Carolina, Georgia, and Florida, the department was commanded by Maj. Gen. DAVID HUNTER from headquarters at Hilton Head, Port Royal, S.C. On 9 May Hunter, a radical abolitionist, declared martial law and proclaimed all slaves in the 3 states free, but ABRAHAM LINCOLN repudiated the emancipation order on the 19th rather than alienate the BORDER STATES.

On 8 Aug. the District of West Florida was removed from Hunter's jurisdiction and attached to the Department of the Gulf. On 5 Sept. Brig Gen. JOHN M. BRANNAN replaced Hunter for 12 days until Maj. Gen. ORMSBY M. MITCHEL assumed command. During Brannan's brief tenure, part of southern Georgia was transferred to the Department of the Cumberland. When Mitchell died from yellow fever in October, Brannan again took over the department, heading it until Hunter resumed command 20 Jan. 1863. In mid-March Key West and the Tortugas were transferred to the Department of the Gulf, and parts of northern Georgia were designated to be transferred to the Department of the Cumberland as they were occupied by troops from that military jurisdiction.

Maj. Gen. QUINCY A. GILLMORE assumed command of the department 12 June, and during the next 10 and a half months made his most significant contributions to the Union cause. Under his direction, the formidable Batteries Wagner and Gregg were captured, and from his fortification on Morris Island he carried out the long-range bombardment of Charleston (*see also* "SWAMP ANGEL" and BATTERY (FORT) WAGNER, SIEGE AND EVACUATION OF). When Gillmore and his X Corps, created 3 Sept. 1862 to operate in the department, were transferred to the Army of the James May 1864, command passed temporarily to Brig. Gen. JOHN P. HATCH and on the 26th to Maj. Gen. JOHN G. FOSTER.

For 2 weeks after the capture of FORT FISHER, N.C., Jan. 1865, North Carolina was added to the department with Gillmore again commanding. Florida was removed from his jurisdiction 17 May. The major military geographical redistribution of 27 June terminated the Civil War–era Department of the South, dividing its territory into the Departments of South Carolina and Georgia, with Gillmore being assigned to the former. The department was reinstated 19 May 1866, remaining in existence with numerous redefinitions and commanders during the postwar years.   —PLF

South Atlantic Blockading Squadron. Late in July 1861 the U.S. Navy's Blockade Strategy Board recommended that the South Atlantic Blockading Squadron have responsibility for conducting naval operations along the coast south of the North Carolina border. On 18 Sept. 1861 Capt. SAMUEL F. DU PONT was appointed to command the squadron and ordered not only to enforce the BLOCKADE but to seize, with the support of the army, PORT ROYAL, S.C., as a base of operations. With 8 warships already on blockade duty along the coast, Du Pont assembled some 75 vessels in Hampton Roads and 7 Nov. 1861 successfully attacked Confederate forces at Port Royal.

During the following months the squadron continued to cooperate with army units in the occupation of various islands and coastal areas along South Carolina, Georgia, and Florida. At the same time the effectiveness of the blockade gradually improved as more vessels were added to the squadron. In June 1862 some 24 warships were distributed along the coast, and by the end of the year the number had nearly doubled, with 13 of them guarding Charleston, S.C.

The Navy Department considered Charleston the weak link in the blockade along the South Atlantic coast and ordered Du Pont to attack and reduce the forts guarding the port. On 7 Apr. 1863, 7 monitors, an armored gunboat, and the *NEW IRONSIDES,* added to the squadron for this purpose, attacked the forts but were repulsed. The defeat resulted in public criticism, and in July Du Pont asked to be relieved of the command. (*See also* CHARLESTON, S.C., DU PONT'S ATTACK ON.)

At the time Rear Adm. JOHN A. DAHLGREN replaced Du Pont, the squadron comprised some 70 vessels. The number continued to increase as Dahlgren attempted to tighten the blockade as well as cooperate with the army in military operations. In 1863 attacks were launched against Morris and Sullivan islands and Forts Sumter and Wagner, but with the exception of Morris Island, which was taken by Union forces, the Charleston defenses remained strong.

The squadron had little more success in operations against the Savannah defenses. The Confederate ironclad *Atlanta* was captured in summer 1863 after a brief action with the monitor *Weehawken,* but Union forces were unable to move up the Savannah River and take the city. Savannah as well as Charleston was finally taken as a result of Maj. Gen. William T. Sherman's campaign through Georgia and the Carolinas. Dahlgren's units cooperated with Sherman's troops as they moved up the coast and approached Charleston. On 15 Jan. 1865, the monitor *Patapsco* struck a mine in Charleston harbor and sank, the last operational loss suffered by the South Atlantic Blockading Squadron.

During spring 1865 the squadron was reduced in numbers, and in July was consolidated with the North Atlantic Blockading Squadron to form the Atlantic Squadron.   —WNS

South Carolina. South Carolina seceded 20 Dec. 1860 at a convention in Charleston, the fulfillment of a pledge made by many of its leaders that the election of a Republican president would bring the state's separation from the Union. The first state to secede, South Carolina was soon joined by others, and early in 1861, 11 Southern states formed the Confederate States of America, with hopes that their independence might be maintained peaceably.

Confederate sympathizers and soldiers under Brig. Gen. P.G.T. Beauregard, fearing that FORT SUMTER in Charleston harbor might receive Union reinforcements, bombarded the installation, causing the small garrison to surrender 13 Apr. 1861. The attack on the U.S. flag and Federal troops led Pres. Abraham Lincoln to call for 75,000 volunteers to suppress rebellion.

During the war, Charleston was blockaded by ships of the Union navy but was not captured until the city surrendered Feb. 1865. Union forces took 2 Confederate forts in PORT ROYAL SOUND Nov. 1861, providing a useful base for U.S. Navy operations along the coast.

South Carolina did not suffer enemy invasion until 1865 during the CAROLINAS CAMPAIGN. In February, Maj. Gen. WIL-

LIAM T. SHERMAN's army moved north from Savannah over soggy roads and through endless swamps, to the state capital, COLUMBIA. There was no major Confederate force to oppose the Union army, and the city was surrendered by the mayor. Shortly after Sherman's arrival, a destructive fire broke out and ruined much of the city before it could be extinguished. The fire may have spread from supplies burned by departing Confederates or it may have been spread by Union soldiers resenting the state for Fort Sumter and the first act of secession. Sherman denied any official responsibility, but there was much lawlessness in the open city. *See also* CHARLESTON, S.C., DU PONT'S ATTACK ON; CHARLESTON, S.C., EVACUATION OF; CHARLESTON, S.C., SIEGE OF.   —FSK

South Carolina, Confederate Department of. In existence for barely 2 and a half months early in the war, the Department of South Carolina was established 21 Aug. 1861 to consist of the entire state, including its coastal defenses, and was placed under Brig. Gen. ROSWELL S. RIPLEY. During its brief life, the department comprised approximately 8,300 troops of all arms, present and absent, with an aggregate present of only 5,300. It embraced the defensive works at and near Charleston (including those on Sullivan's Island and along the Stono River and the North and South Edisto rivers), Georgetown, Aiken, Field's Point, Port Royal Sound (including Fort Walker), Sam's Point, Braddock's Point, Camp Lookout, Columbia, and Lightwood Knot Spring. The department passed out of existence 5 Nov. 1861, 2 days before the loss of PORT ROYAL, when it was absorbed into Gen. ROBERT E. LEE's DEPARTMENT OF SOUTH CAROLINA AND GEORGIA.   —EGL

South Carolina, Union Department of. One of 18 postwar military departments created by the War Department 27 June 1865, the Department of South Carolina consisted of the Palmetto State in its entirety, with headquarters at Hilton Head Island. It was assigned to Maj. Gen. QUINCY A. GILLMORE, who June 1862–May 1864 had commanded Union troops operating against Charleston. The department was attached to the DIVISION OF THE ATLANTIC, which, under Maj. Gen. GEORGE G. MEADE, embraced all seaboard states from South Carolina to Maine, plus Pennsylvania and the rest of New England.

Gillmore took command on Hilton Head 18 July 1865 and served until relieved by Maj. Gen. DANIEL E. SICKLES 18 Nov. of that year. Moving his headquarters to Charleston, Sickles retained the department after its merger with the Department of the Carolinas 19 May 1866.   —EGL

South Carolina and Georgia, Confederate Department of. Established 5 Nov. 1861, the Department of South Carolina and Georgia consisted of the coasts of South Carolina, Georgia, and east Florida. Formed from existing military departments in the first 2 states, it was assigned to Gen. ROBERT E. LEE. This action, coming in the wake of the Union landing at PORT ROYAL Sound, S.C., was taken (in the words of Confederate War Sec. JUDAH P. BENJAMIN) to "enable him [Lee] to concentrate all our forces at any point that might be attacked." Originally, the command was divided into 6 military districts. 5 of these—later increased to 6, later still reduced to 3—were located in South Carolina; the remaining district took in Georgia and the Florida coast, though it was known only as the Military District of Georgia.

The former head of the Fourth Military District of South

Carolina, Maj. Gen. JOHN C. PEMBERTON, replaced Lee in departmental command 19 Mar. 1862, following the latter's reassignment to Richmond. Pemberton's realm was temporarily expanded when the DEPARTMENT OF MIDDLE AND EASTERN FLORIDA merged with it 7 Apr., 2 days before Florida was again declared a separate department. From his headquarters at Charleston, Pemberton administered a domain that embraced, by mid-1862, 1,436 officers and 21,939 enlisted men present for duty. Most were concentrated about large coastal cities such as Charleston and Savannah, both of which the departmental leader fortified against enemy assault by land or sea.

Gen. P.G.T. BEAUREGARD succeeded Pemberton 29 Aug. 1862. A month later the command consisted of an aggregate present and absent total of 27,093 troops. Under Beauregard's regime the department expanded 7 Oct., reacquiring the Department of Middle and Eastern Florida. The latter was composed of 2 districts, which Beauregard added to the 3 existing in South Carolina and the single district in Georgia. To reflect the expansion, the whole became known as the DEPARTMENT OF SOUTH CAROLINA, GEORGIA, AND FLORIDA.   —EGL

South Carolina, Georgia, and Florida, Confederate Department of. This department came into existence 7 Oct. 1862, when Gen. P.G.T. BEAUREGARD'S DEPARTMENT OF SOUTH CAROLINA AND GEORGIA expanded to take in the DEPARTMENT OF MIDDLE AND EASTERN FLORIDA. For the next 16 months the latter was divided into 2 separate districts, which during most of that period encompassed all of Florida east of the Choctawatchie River. Beauregard thus administered a total of 6 military districts, including 3 in South Carolina and 1 in Georgia—the last taking in all but the northwestern corner of its state, which remained a part of the DEPARTMENT OF THE WEST. By the end of 1863, 4 more districts had been added in the Palmetto State, scene of intense activity around Charleston. 2 of these, however, were dropped before war's close, while in Feb. 1864 the Florida districts merged into one.

At the time of the department's inception, it comprised approximately 35,000 officers and men present for duty. From Charleston, Beauregard repeatedly complained to Confederate officials that his effective force was far less than this figure, at times no more than 15,000 infantrymen. He received additions at various points during his tenure, but in Jan. 1864 his force peaked at 38,227 present.

Beauregard was transferred north late in Apr. 1864 and was succeeded by Maj. Gen. SAMUEL JONES. On 5 Oct. 1864, Jones was replaced by Lt. Gen. WILLIAM J. HARDEE, who moved departmental headquarters to Georgia for the Siege of SAVANNAH. By 20 Nov. the department's resources had dwindled to 14,680 officers and men and 100 cannon.

Late in December, Pres. JEFFERSON DAVIS reinstated Beauregard to the command of that portion of the department west of Augusta, Ga., which concurrently became a segment of the DEPARTMENT OF TENNESSEE AND GEORGIA. Hardee retained the rest of his domain, still known as the Department of South Carolina, Georgia, and Florida. This arrangement remained in effect at the outset of the CAROLINAS CAMPAIGN, but on 25 Feb. 1865, Gen. JOSEPH E. JOHNSTON replaced both officers, combining their departments while regaining field leadership of his old ARMY OF TENNESSEE. Beauregard became his second-in-command, while Hardee returned to corps command in the army, posts both men retained till war's end.   —EGL

South Carolina military academies. The Citadel in Charleston, S.C., and the Arsenal in Columbia, S.C., were 2 state military colleges begun in antebellum years to supply officers for state and national defense, similar to the better-known VIRGINIA MILITARY INSTITUTE. The collective enrollment of both institutions, about 200 cadets, was organized into Companies A and B of the South Carolina Cadet Battalion and mustered into the South Carolina state militia Nov. 1861. Both units saw periodic service around Charleston in the early war years.

The Arsenal was destroyed in the fire that consumed Columbia in 1865. The Citadel was permitted to operate as a nonmilitary college in postwar years and resumed a military curriculum in 1882.   —JES

Southern Bivouac: A Monthly Literary and Historical Magazine. One of the best of the veterans' magazines, _Southern Bivouac_ was published in Louisville as an endeavor of the Kentucky branch of the Southern Historical Society, and was written for former Confederates and Southern sympathizers. The society issued the magazine Sept. 1882–Aug. 1883, when E. H. and W. N. McDonald acquired it. B. F. Avery & Sons, publishers of _Home and Farm_ magazine, bought _Southern Bivouac_ in June 1885, hiring former Confederate cavalryman BASIL W. DUKE and R. W. Knott as its editors. The two men continued to produce a periodical aimed at veterans through the publication of memoirs and war papers, but their expanded format included more literary features and articles concerning Southern life in general. Among the prominent contributors to _Bivouac_ was the popular author JOHN ESTEN COOKE, who wrote nostalgically of a gracious antebellum plantation society destroyed by the war.

In 1887 the magazine was taken over by _Century_ magazine, an aggressive competitor for the Civil War market. The last issue of _Southern Bivouac_ appeared in May.   —PLF

Southern Historical Society Papers. Publication of the _Southern Historical Society Papers_ was begun in 1876 by members of the Southern Historical Society, which had been founded 6 and a half years earlier by former Confederate leaders. Intent on providing future historians with "a complete weapon from which defenders of our cause may draw any desired weapon," the society began collecting, classifying, and preserving all manuscript and printed material concerning the wartime South. The ambitious program was spurred by the Federal government's plans to begin publishing the _WAR OF THE REBELLION: OFFICIAL RECORDS OF THE UNION AND CONFEDERATE ARMIES_ and _OFFICIAL RECORDS OF THE UNION AND CONFEDERATE NAVIES IN THE WAR OF THE REBELLION_, which many Southerners suspected would be biased against the Confederacy in quantity of material presented and would include documents that had been altered unfavorably as they were copied from the original Confederate records. Their apprehensions deepened when the government purchased 5 trunksful of important Confederate papers in 1871 (_see_ PICKETT PAPERS) and when the secretary of war refused to give the society access to the Confederate archives confiscated at the cessation of hostilities. (This restriction was removed in 1878.)

The Southern public responded generously to the appeal for material, and an invaluable collection of military reports, memoirs, maps, newspapers, books, rosters, correspondence, and speeches began arriving at the society's headquarters in Richmond, Va. Publication began Jan. 1874 in the Baltimore-based _Southern Magazine,_ which gave 20 pages to the printing of the Confederate documents in each issue through July 1875. The following January, newly elected Southern Historical Society secretary-treasurer Rev. J. William Jones initiated independent serialization of the documents published under the title _Southern Historical Society Papers._

The project was funded by annual membership dues of $3, a yearly donation of $500 from banker and philanthropist W. W. Corcoran, smaller private gifts, and moneys raised by former Confederate leaders who in the 1880s gave fund-raising lectures to establish an endowment that saved the society from bankruptcy. Until 1890 the _Southern Historical Society Papers_ were distributed monthly; for several years thereafter they were issued annually; but by the 1920s new volumes had begun appearing only occasionally. Volumes 44–52, covering the journals of the Confederate Senate and House of Representatives and newspaper reports of the congressional proceedings, were issued over a period of 30 years beginning in 1923 under the direction of Douglas Southall Freeman. On Freeman's death in 1953, the last surviving member of the Southern Historical Society turned over to the Virginia Historical Society all manuscripts not given previously to the Confederate Memorial Literary Society (Museum of the Confederacy). Later that year the Virginia Historical Society published the 3 volumes unprinted at the time of Freeman's death.

Though some of the memoirs are unsubstantiated, the _Southern Historical Society Papers_ are second in value only to the _Official Records_ as research tools for students of the Confederacy. The papers were originally issued unbound in wraps or bound in volumes in a choice of cloth, half morocco, or half calf. A reprint of the series was issued in unmatched bindings 1977–80.   —PLF

Southern Manifesto. Co-written by Senators LOUIS T. WIGFALL (Tex.) and James L. Pugh (Ala.), the Southern Manifesto was issued 14 Dec. 1860, at a time when disunionists throughout the South were calling for their states to secede immediately. The document declared that Northern politicians had refused to make acceptable guarantees for the protection of Southern rights within the Union. The aggrieved states, continued the authors, had no choice but to form an independent Southern confederacy. Signed by 6 senators and 23 representatives, the manifesto convinced moderates that further efforts toward conciliation would be fruitless.   —PLF

Southern Mississippi and East Louisiana, Confederate Department of. On 20 June 1862, Maj. Gen. EARL VAN DORN assumed command of the newly created Department of Southern Mississippi and East Louisiana. Essentially a subdepartment created out of the larger Confederate Department No. 2, it encompassed all Louisiana east of the Mississippi River, and that part of Mississippi bordered on the east, south of Jackson, by the Pearl River and, north of Jackson, by the Mississippi Central Railroad to the state's northern border. In his General Orders No. 89, 2 July 1862, commanding Gen. BRAXTON BRAGG refers to Van Dorn's geographic area of responsibility as a "district." Van Dorn himself divided his department into Districts 1, 2, and 3, and delegated their respective commands to Brig. Gens. DANIEL RUGGLES, MARTIN L. SMITH, and WILLIAM N. R. BEALL. On 1 Oct. 1862, this organization was absorbed into the new DEPARTMENT OF MISSISSIPPI AND

EAST LOUISIANA, commanded by Lt. Gen. JOHN C. PEMBERTON. Pemberton kept Van Dorn's district commanders, readjusting their areas of responsibility.   —JES

Southern nationalism. Gradually over the 40 years preceding the Civil War, Southerners came to see themselves as guardians of a civilization within a civilization. Theirs was an agricultural economy dependent on cotton and slave labor. Northerners, they said, had betrayed Thomas Jefferson's dream of an agrarian republic by moving steadily toward an economy based on industrialization and commerce. As the North grew populous through immigration, and Northern banks accumulated the nation's wealth, Southern politicians saw the shifting balance of power in Congress as a threat to their section's long-standing dominance in national affairs.

With alarming frequency, politics divided along geographical lines over such issues as protectionism, tariffs, the Mexican War, and extending slavery into the territories. More threatening, the South seemed to lose ground to aggressive antislavery factions. As abolitionists railed against the immorality of slaveholding and lobbied to prevent its expansion, Southerners rushed to defend their way of life. Ultimately, this impassioned defense of slavery became the cornerstone of a nascent Southern nationalism.

To South Carolinian JOHN C. CALHOUN, the MISSOURI COMPROMISE promised nothing but evil for his region. He spent 30 years perfecting the STATES RIGHTS theory that eventually carried his beloved South through the secession crisis. While Calhoun waged political war against Northern domination, romantic novelists William Gilmore Simms and John Pendleton Kennedy glamorized Southern plantation life and the cavalier tradition. From pulpit, newspaper, and political platform, Southern leaders denounced Yankees as money-grubbing, abrupt, self-interested aggressors, while stressing the hospitality, independence, and genteel characteristics that distinguished the democracy-loving South.

Fearing that their society faced destruction, Southerners retreated into the romanticized image they had created for themselves, convinced that the South alone guarded the revolutionary principles of 1776. The basis for Southern nationhood had been well established before the Confederate Congress met in Montgomery, Ala., Feb. 1861.   —PLF

Southern Virginia, Confederate Department of. The Confederate Department of North Carolina and Southern Virginia was reorganized 1 Apr. 1863 into 3 departments: the DEPARTMENT OF RICHMOND, the Department of Southern Virginia, and the DEPARTMENT OF NORTH CAROLINA. Though these 3 departments existed prior to this date, they were not formally constituted until then.

The Department of Southern Virginia covered the area in the Old Dominion south of the James River and east of the county of Powhatan. Maj. Gen. SAMUEL G. FRENCH commanded the department, under the overall authority of Lt. Gen. JAMES LONGSTREET. On 28 May Confederate authorities merged the Department of Southern Virginia into the Department of North Carolina, which now included Petersburg, Va., and its environs. French was transferred and Maj. Gen. DANIEL H. HILL assumed command of the newly constituted department.   —JDW

South Mountain, Md., Battle of. 14 Sept. 1862 On the morning of 14 Sept. 1862, the outcome of the Confederate

invasion of Maryland hinged on the passes through South Mountain, Md. Gen. ROBERT E. LEE's Army of Northern Virginia lay west of the mountains in 5 widely scattered increments. To the east, Union Maj. Gen. GEORGE B. MCCLELLAN's powerful Army of the Potomac, spurred into action by the discovery of a lost copy of Lee's orders (see LEE'S LOST ORDER), was moving toward the defiles. If the Federals penetrated South Mountain, Lee's army faced the possibility of being carved into pieces.

The Federal army advanced in 2 wings. The left segment, under Maj. Gen. WILLIAM B. FRANKLIN, angled to the southwest toward Crampton's Gap. Franklin, with orders to relieve the Harpers Ferry garrison and to cut off the surrounding Confederates, moved into the pass and engaged the Southerners in the Battle of CRAMPTON'S GAP.

McClellan's right wing, numbering nearly 30,000, marched on the National road, the road that passed through the mountain at Turner's Gap. A mile to the south of Turner's Gap, a smaller road snaked through South Mountain at Fox's Gap. These 2 gaps and a network of trails were crucial to Lee's army and his wagon train. As the Federals approached, only 1 Confederate brigade of Maj. Gen. DANIEL H. HILL's division manned Turner's Gap.

Brig. Gen. ALFRED PLEASANTON's Union cavalry opened the battle, engaging Hill's lone brigade. As the opponents skirmished, Hill brought up one of his remaining 4 brigades and deployed it. Maj. Gen. AMBROSE E. BURNSIDE, directing the Federal wing, then sent Maj. Gen. JESSE L. RENO with the IX Corps against Fox's Gap. Brig. Gen. JACOB D. COX's leading division replaced the Union horsemen about 9 a.m., and the fighting intensified. Cox's division charged through the open pastures below Fox's Gap. Brig. Gen. SAMUEL GARLAND's brigade of North Carolinians responded. In a jumbled, confusing battle the Federals broke one of Garland's regiments. Garland was killed, as was Reno. By noon the remainder of the IX Corps had arrived, pressing the attack through the gap. But then the Federal attack stalled and a 2-hour lull ensued.

These 2 hours probably saved Hill. By 2 o'clock Brig. Gen. GEORGE B. ANDERSON's brigade had reached the crest and moved to support the North Carolinians at Fox's Gap. Brig. Gen. ROBERT E. RODES arrived with his Alabamians, extending Hill's left beyond Turner's Gap. Brig. Gen. ROSWELL S. RIPLEY's Georgians also soon came up the mountainside and moved into position on Anderson's left. Down in the valley, behind Hill, the divisions of Maj. Gen. DAVID R. JONES and Brig. Gen. JOHN B. HOOD were racing toward the gaps through dust-choked roads.

Late in the afternoon the ponderous Union command resumed its advance on Fox's Gap and launched a long-overdue assault at Turner's Gap. Maj. Gen. JOSEPH HOOKER's I Corps climbed toward Hill's main position across the National road. Musketry cascaded along the mountainside as Federal hammered at Confederate. The Southerners stubbornly defended open knolls and patches of dense woodland. Jones's and Hood's veterans arrived, bolstering the Confederate line. Through the evening the battle raged in the darkening woods. One Confederate brigade delivered a spirited counterattack down the wrong side of the mountain.

By 10 p.m. the Federals had seized the high ground commanding Turner's Gap. The exhausted Confederates began withdrawing about midnight and marched toward Sharpsburg, Md., where Lee had ordered a reconcentration of his army along Antietam Creek. The Federals lost 325 killed, 1,403 wounded, and 85 missing, for a total of 1,813. An aggregate of 2,685 Confederates were listed as casualties, with 325 killed, 1,560 wounded, and 800 missing. But Hill's, then Jones's and Hood's veterans had given Lee crucial time to regroup and saved the army's supply train.   —JDW

Southwest, Confederate Department of the.
On 23 Dec. 1863, Lt. Gen. LEONIDAS POLK assumed command of the Confederate DEPARTMENT OF MISSISSIPPI AND EAST LOUISIANA, which was immediately designated the Department of the Southwest. Polk commanded 2 cavalry divisions, which during winter 1863 and spring 1864 opposed the operations of Union Maj. Gen. WILLIAM T. SHERMAN in Mississippi.

Confederate officials created the DEPARTMENT OF ALABAMA, MISSISSIPPI AND EAST LOUISIANA 9 May 1864, superseding the Department of the Southwest. 3 days later, Polk moved with his command to rejoin the Army of Tennessee for the ATLANTA CAMPAIGN.   —JDW

Southwest, Union Army of the.
The Union Army of the Southwest, also known as the Army of the Southwest Missouri, was a command whose primary mission was territorial occupation. Created 25 Dec. 1861, the force existed less than a year, being merged into the District of Eastern Arkansas, DEPARTMENT OF THE TENNESSEE, 12 Dec. 1862. During its lifetime the army of about 15,000 troops was commanded by Brig. Gens. SAMUEL R. CURTIS, 25 Dec. 1861–29 Aug. 1862; FREDERICK STEELE, 29 Aug.–7 Oct. 1862; EUGENE A. CARR, 7 Oct.–12 Nov. 1862; and Willis A. Gorman, 12 Nov. until termination.

Under Curtis' command the army fought in the Battle of PEA RIDGE, one of the major engagements of the early part of the war, particularly in the Western theater. There Curtis defeated Confederate Maj. Gen. EARL VAN DORN and his TRANS-MISSISSIPPI ARMY of about 17,000 troops 7–8 Mar. 1862 and preserved for the Union a portion of nearby southern Missouri and northern Arkansas. Carr, a subsequent commander, was the recipient of the Medal of Honor for his gallant performance in this action. At this remote place in northwest Arkansas the Army of the Southwest achieved its place in history.

After the army was assimilated into the Department of the Tennessee, some units went on to perform conspicuously in the VICKSBURG CAMPAIGN and Maj. Gen. William T. Sherman's subsequent ATLANTA CAMPAIGN and the MARCH TO THE SEA.
          —RAP

Southwest, Union Military Division of the.
The Union Military Division of the Southwest was constituted 25 Dec. 1861 from troops in portions of the Department of Missouri. Numbering 15,000, the troops were concentrated generally in the southwestern part of the state. Brig. Gen. SAMUEL R. CURTIS assumed command of the division and 10 Feb. 1862 advanced his force, which he had redesignated the Army of the Southwest, on Springfield, Mo. Brig. Gen. STERLING PRICE's 8,000-man Confederate army withdrew before the Federals, retreating into northwestern Arkansas, where Maj. Gen. EARL VAN DORN joined him with reinforcements. On 7–8 Mar. the opponents collided in the Battle of PEA RIDGE. In bloody fighting Curtis' Federals held the field.

Curtis eventually withdrew to Missouri, only to undertake another offensive into Arkansas during July and August. On 29 Aug. Brig. Gen. FREDERICK STEELE replaced Curtis as commander of the division. Steele retained the post until 7 Oct., when Brig.

Gen. EUGENE A. CARR succeeded him, commanding the district for slightly more than a month. Brig. Gen. Willis A. Gorman replaced Carr 13 Nov. as the district's final commander. A month later, 13 Dec. 1862, the district was merged into the District of Eastern Arkansas of the DEPARTMENT OF TENNESSEE.
          —JDW

Southwestern Army, Confederate.
Pres. Jefferson Davis established the DEPARTMENT OF MISSISSIPPI AND EAST LOUISIANA 1 Oct. 1862 and placed Lt. Gen. JOHN C. PEMBERTON in command of the second Army of Mississippi. Gen. JOSEPH E. JOHNSTON was sent to Pemberton's aid when Grant threatened Vicksburg May 1863. After Vicksburg fell, 4 July, Johnston commanded the department.

Seeking a new command for Lt. Gen. LEONIDAS POLK after Chickamauga, President Davis assigned Polk to Johnston's department in Mississippi 23 Oct. 1863. Polk succeeded Johnston as commander in the Southwest 23 Dec. when Johnston was sent to replace Gen. BRAXTON BRAGG as Army of Tennessee commander.

In his first general order, issued at Enterprise, Miss., Polk christened his command "The Department (and Army) of the Southwest." It consisted of only 2 infantry divisions, commanded by Maj. Gens. WILLIAM WING LORING and SAMUEL G. FRENCH, and cavalry units under Maj. Gens. NATHAN B. FORREST and STEPHEN D. LEE.

The Southwestern Army, in the renamed DEPARTMENT OF ALABAMA, MISSISSIPPI, AND EAST LOUISIANA, faced 2 major threats: to Mobile by Rear Adm. DAVID G. FARRAGUT's Federal naval force and to northern Mississippi by Maj. Gen. WILLIAM T. SHERMAN's army. But Polk worked feverishly with Maj. Gen. DABNEY H. MAURY, Mobile's defender, to bolster defensive positions there while harassing Sherman to the north.

Polk's aide, William Gale, praised his general's skill in foiling Sherman: "the country breathes free again. The Yankee army, baffled and whipped, almost without a battle, has retired."

By 1 May 1864, when Polk and his army were ordered to join in the Atlanta defense, the Southwestern Army had 10,000 infantry and 4,000 cavalry. S. D. Lee became commander of the Department of Alabama, Mississippi, and East Louisiana after Polk's departure. Forrest commanded the department from 24 Jan. 1865 until the end of the war.   —DS

Southwestern Virginia, Confederate Department of.
The Confederate Department of Southwestern Virginia, formed 8 May 1862, comprised that area of Virginia extending "west to the eastern boundary of Kentucky and as far west of that boundary as circumstances may allow." During the course of the war, this department was designated at various times the Department of Western Virginia, the Department of Southwestern Virginia and East Tennessee, and the Department of Western Virginia and East Tennessee.

A series of Confederate generals commanded the department and the Army of Southwest Virginia. Maj. Gen. WILLIAM WING LORING assumed initial command 8 May 1862. Brig. Gen. JOHN ECHOLS replaced Loring 16 Oct., and Echols was succeeded within 4 weeks by Brig. Gen. JOHN S. WILLIAMS. On 25 Nov. Brig. Gen. SAMUEL JONES replaced Williams. A capable officer, Jones held the post for more than a year, succeeded on 25 Feb. 1864 by Maj. Gen. JOHN C. BRECKINRIDGE. Brig. Gen. JOHN H. MORGAN followed Breckinridge in command. When Morgan was killed 4 Sept. Breckinridge returned to the post. 25 Feb. 1865 the Confederate Valley District was extended to include the department.

Several notable engagements occurred within the department or were fought by Confederate troops from the department. Most of these battles resulted from Union thrusts into the department against the East Tennessee and Virginia Railroad. On 6 Nov. 1863, Confederates under Echols suffered a defeat at DROOP MOUNTAIN, but the Federals abandoned their raid. In a battle at CLOYD'S MOUNTAIN 9 May 1864, another Union command routed the Confederate defenders. Breckinridge, however, scored a strategically significant victory at NEW MARKET 15 May, repulsing a major Union advance up the Shenandoah Valley. During the 1864 SHENANDOAH VALLEY CAMPAIGN many of the department's troops fought with the Confederate Army of the Valley. —JDW

Southwestern Virginia and East Tennessee, Confederate Department of. *See* WESTERN VIRGINIA AND EAST TENNESSEE, CONFEDERATE DEPARTMENT OF.

Southwest Mountain, Va., Battle of. 9 Aug. 1862 *See* CEDAR MOUNTAIN, VA., BATTLE OF.

Spangler's Spring, at Gettysburg, Pa. 1 and 3 July 1863

Part of the fascination for Americans with the Battle of GETTYSBURG are such places as LITTLE ROUND TOP, DEVIL'S DEN, the WHEATFIELD, CULP'S HILL, and Spangler's Spring. This last spot, located at the eastern base of Culp's Hill, has attracted interest because of an alleged truce on the night of 2 July when Union and Confederate soldiers shared the spring's cool waters. This story cannot be verified and is probably more legend than fact.

If the 2 opponents never enjoyed a peaceful truce around the spring, they did kill each other there 3 July. At 10 a.m. the 2d Massachusetts and the 27th Indiana charged across the boggy ground next to the spring known as Spangler's Meadow. 4 Virginia regiments, aligned in the woods of Culp's Hill, ravaged the 2 Union regiments with a withering fire. The 27th Indiana barely made it halfway across before turning back, while the 2d Massachusetts momentarily reached the Confederate works. Losing nearly half its members, that regiment also retreated. It had been "murder," as one officer accurately predicted when given the order to charge. —JDW

Special Orders No. 191. 9 Sept. 1862 *See* LEE'S LOST ORDER.

Speed, James. USP b. Jefferson Cty., Ky., 11 Mar. 1812. After attending local schools, Speed entered St. Joseph's College and Transylvania University, studying law at the latter. Passing the bar in 1833, he set up a practice in Louisville. Elected to the state legislature in 1847, he served only 1 term, primarily due to his strong antislavery views. Prior to the start of war, he spoke out against secession and the need for Kentucky to remain neutral in the coming conflict.

At the outbreak of hostilities, Speed dropped any notion of neutrality and wholeheartedly supported the Union cause. Elected to the Kentucky senate in 1861, he and others worked, first in secret, then openly, with Abraham Lincoln to arm pro-Federal sympathizers. As the war progressed, Speed spoke out for emancipation and sponsored a bill calling for seizure of Confederate property, including slaves.

At the end of his term, July 1863, he became a personal adviser to Lincoln on the political climate in Kentucky. When EDWARD BATES resigned as attorney general Nov. 1864, the president appointed Speed to the post. Supporting Lincoln's policy of moderation toward the South, he drew high praise from the president as "an honest man and a gentleman, and one of those well-poised men, not too common here, who are not spoiled by big office." After Lincoln's death, Speed joined the RADICAL REPUBLICANS and

LC

consequently advocated black suffrage and harsher treatment toward the South. When Pres. ANDREW JOHNSON vetoed the Freedmen's Bill, he resigned in protest 17 July 1866.

Speed subsequently returned to Louisville to practice law and further Radical Republican ambitions in the South. He ran unsuccessfully for the U.S. Senate in 1867 and for the U.S. House of Representatives 3 years later. He attended the national Republican conventions of 1872 and 1876 and served on their resolutions committee. During this period, he also taught law at Louisville University. The former attorney general died in Louisville 25 June 1887 and was buried there.

—MTC

Spencer carbine. On 6 Mar. 1860, Christopher M. Spencer patented the repeating carbine that bore his name. Stamped on the top of each breech was *Spencer Repeating Rifle Co. Boston, Mass./Pat'd March 6, 1860.* 7 rimfire copper cartridges, positioned end on end in a metal tube, were loaded through the buttstock. A depressed lever passed the .52-caliber cartridges into the chamber, where they were struck by a side hammer and fired down a 22-in. barrel. Anywhere from 10 to 13 bullet tubes were carried in the hexagonal cartridge box made of leather-covered wood, designed specifically for the Spencer.

CWTI

Although Spencer carbines (and rifles) were available at the outset of the war, substantial quantities were not issued to Federal cavalrymen until late in 1863. In August of that year Pres. Abraham Lincoln agreed to have Spencer's weapon tested. Results were satisfactory enough to elicit large purchases by the U.S. Ordnance Department. Several individual units, equally impressed with the Spencer's capabilities, raised the money to equip themselves. By the war's end, it was the most widely used carbine in the service.

Large-scale employment of Spencer carbines gave the Union cavalry an edge over their Confederate counterparts, thereby shortening the war. The day of the single-shot muzzleloader was over. Military tacticians were forced to reconsider traditional strategies in light of the destructiveness of repeating weapons. A few generals, concerned about the potential waste of ammunition, questioned the value of these new arms. But according to a popular adage of the day, it was "far easier to carry extra bullets than a stretcher."

An estimated 200,000 Spencer carbines were used in the Civil War. However, the weapon was overproduced and sales declined sharply after Appomattox. The Spencer Repeating Rifle Co. filed for bankruptcy in 1869 and its plant, located in Boston, was sold at auction to the Winchester Repeating Arms Co.   —MJO'D

spies. *See* ESPIONAGE.

Spotsylvania Court House Campaign. 7–19 May 1864

Spotsylvania Court House, a tiny crossroads village in Virginia, was southeast of the WILDERNESS, where a major battle had been fought 5–7 May 1864. Throughout the night of 7–8 May, the Union and Confederate armies moved toward the settlement. Lt. Gen. ULYSSES S. GRANT intended to interpose his army between Gen. ROBERT E. LEE's and Richmond to force the Confederate leader to attack the powerful Union command. Lee anticipated the maneuver and advanced to intercept the threat.

Maj. Gen. RICHARD H. ANDERSON's Confederate corps won the race on the 8th, repulsing the leading Federal units. Both commanders funneled troops into action west of the village, where Lee's veterans stubbornly defended their position. That night and throughout the next day the Confederates erected forbidding fieldworks. A determined Grant sent 3 corps against the Southern entrenchments 10 May. The Federals reeled before the crippling fire. At 6 p.m. at the "MULE SHOE" salient in the center of Lee's line, Col. EMORY UPTON, massing 12 regiments on a narrow front, breached the Confederate works but could not expand the penetration.

Upton's success persuaded Grant to use similar tactics but with a corps. At 4:30 a.m., 12 May, Maj. Gen. WINFIELD S. HANCOCK's corps struck the tip of the salient. Almost an entire Confederate division was captured but additional units blunted the breakthrough. For 20 hours the opponents, in a severe rainstorm, engaged in some of the war's most vicious fighting. Lee erected a new line at the base of the salient and withdrew to it. Grant assaulted these new works 6 days later, only to be repulsed at a fearful loss.

The next day, 19 May, Lee's demonstration against Grant's right resulted in severe fighting. Grant withdrew 2 days later, once more endeavoring to move beyond Lee's right. "We have met a man, this time," a Confederate wrote of Grant, "who either does not know when he is whipped, or who cares not if he loses his whole Army."   —JDW

Sprague, Kate Chase. b. Cincinnati, Ohio, 13 Aug. 1840

The well-educated, beautiful, politically astute daughter of widowed Sec. of the Treasury SALMON P. CHASE dominated Washington society from the time she assumed the role of her father's hostess at age 16. Her clothes, her parties, her friendships were reported widely in the newspapers, and her marriage to the wealthy WILLIAM SPRAGUE, 12 Nov. 1863, was described as the grandest social event of the war years. Sprague's money supported her extravagances and provided her with the means to move freely in circles where her charm and influence could benefit his career. Supporting her father's ambition for the presidency, she harbored an intense dislike of ABRAHAM LINCOLN and may have known about the POMEROY CIRCULAR before her father saw it in print. At the 1868 Demo-

cratic national convention she campaigned tirelessly for Chase's nomination.

The Spragues' marriage deteriorated steadily after the financial panic of 1873 reduced the family fortune, finally ending in scandal involving ROSCOE CONKLING and divorce in 1882. After traveling in Europe for several years, from 1886 Kate lived in increasing poverty at "Edgemont," her father's home in Washington. During her last years she supported herself by selling chickens and milk at the doors of mansions where she had once reigned as a society queen. d. District of Columbia, 31 July 1899.   —PLF

Sprague, William.

war governor b. Cranston, R.I., 12 Sept. 1830. Sprague, whose father had made a fortune in the textile industry, attended private academies but showed neither interest nor aptitude in studying. At 15 he began working in the family business, and 11 years later took over the enterprise with his brothers. His wealth and handsome features brought prominence within the state. Republicans seeking a popular, inoffensive candidate nominated him for governor in 1859. In Europe at the time, Sprague returned to win the election by a large majority that some opponents believed had been bought with bribes. Reelected in 1861, he used his

LC

money to outfit one of the first regiments to reach Washington. Arriving in the capital with the troops, he served as aide to Brig. Gen. AMBROSE E. BURNSIDE and participated in the FIRST BATTLE OF BULL RUN.

In Washington Sprague's popularity flourished, but few in government circles regarded him seriously. Shallow, erratic, and irresponsible, he tried to secure a major generalship from Sec. of War SIMON CAMERON in exchange for having the Rhode Island legislature repeal a state law limiting volunteer enlistments to 3 months. ABRAHAM LINCOLN overruled the plan, and Sprague refused the brigadier generalship offered, claiming that the people of his state would consider the lower rank an insult. Sprague attended but took little active part in the governors' conference at Altoona, Pa., in 1862. So politically moderate was he that Democrats considered his election to a third term in office that year a victory over RADICAL REPUBLICANISM.

Though Sprague won the election, he resigned the governorship to become a U.S. senator, an office he held Mar. 1863–Mar. 1875. In Nov. 1863 he married the vivacious KATE CHASE, daughter of Sec. of the Treasury SALMON P. CHASE. He played only a minor role in legislative debate until 1869, when colleagues challenged his loyalty for having delivered a series of speeches attacking the power that capitalists and industrialists exerted over the Federal government.

The Panic of 1873 nearly destroyed Sprague's fortune, and he grew increasingly unstable. After a marital scandal that ended in divorce in 1882, he again ran for governor but was defeated. When fire destroyed "Canonchet," the opulent home he had built at Narragansett Pier, he moved with his new wife to Paris, France, dying there 11 Sept. 1915.   —PLF

Springfield, Mo., Battle of.

Springfield, Mo., Battle of. 10 Aug. 1861 *See* WILSON'S CREEK, MO., BATTLE OF.

Springfield Armory. Located in Springfield, Mass., the Springfield Armory, producing weapons for the U.S. since the 1790s, manufactured the principal shoulder weapon of the Civil War, the famous SPRINGFIELD RIFLE. In 1861, after the Federals abandoned the Harpers Ferry Arsenal, the armory became the major small-arms factory in the North, expanding from a capacity of 1,200 rifles annually to 300,000 in 1864.
—JDW

Springfield rifle-musket. The .58-caliber Springfield percussion rifle-musket was the most widely used shoulder arm of the Civil War. A modern weapon for its time, the Springfield was acclaimed for its innovations, overall quality of design and construction, and performance. Adopted in 1861, the weapon became the principal longarm of the U.S. infantry, with the Federal government purchasing more than 1.5 million Springfield rifles during the war.

The most profound innovations incorporated into the weapon's design were the rifled bore, interchangeable parts, and conical ammunition. Although these developments were achieved prior to the war, their application by the military in full-scale warfare was unprecedented. While the age of the smoothbore musket and round-ball ammunition had not yet passed, the Springfield rifle and its counterparts would bring that age to a rapid close by 1865.

WPC

Specifications for the Model 1861 Springfield called for a 40-in. round barrel secured to a sturdy oil-finished black walnut stock by 3 iron barrel bands. Total length of the piece was 58.5 in.; its weight was 9¼ lb. Black powder (60 grains) propelled a .58-caliber 3-ring lead minié bullet weighing 500 grains. The bright finished lockplate was 5⁷/₁₆ in. long, flat with beveled edges. *U.S.* and *Springfield* were stamped into the face of the plate in 2 horizontal lines. To the rear of the hammer was stamped the year of manufacture. Barrels were stamped near the breech with proofmarks *V, P,* and an eagle head. In addition, the weapon was equipped with a ramrod and a 21-in. socket bayonet that fit on the barrel by a clamping band.

There were 2 subsequent models of 1863, types I and II, which featured slight improvements. However, most of the Federal contract arms were based on the Model 1861, and it was this weapon that saw service on all fronts and participated in every major battle of the War Between the States. —SWS

Spring Hill, Tenn., eng. at. 29 Nov. 1864 On 28 Nov. 1864, Gen. JOHN B. HOOD's Confederate Army of Tennessee faced a Federal force under Maj. Gen. JOHN M. SCHOFIELD at Columbia, Tenn. Hood's army was south of the Duck River, Schofield's men north of the stream.

Hood planned to get around Schofield by crossing the river east of Columbia and advancing northwest to Spring Hill, where he would be on the road to Nashville. Hood's objective is uncertain. He later claimed that he intended to cut Schofield off from other Federals in Nashville and destroy him. Recent historians have speculated that Hood, probably unaware of the Northerners at Nashville, intended only to get around Schofield so he could continue northward.

Hood's cavalry crossed the river and drove away Schofield's horsemen. Confederate infantry followed early 29 Nov. Meanwhile, Schofield, learning of the crossing, sent reinforcements to Spring Hill.

Late in the afternoon Hood's army arrived a few miles east of Spring Hill. In a series of uncoordinated moves Hood sent 3 of his divisions west toward the town. The Southerners struck the Northerners posted nearby, and confused skirmishing continued into the night. Hood withdrew to his headquarters several miles away, thinking that his men held the road at or near Spring Hill.

During the night Schofield drove his men north through the town and on to Franklin. Several reports of his march reached Hood, who either ignored them or sent ineffective orders to block the road. Hood was confused, exhausted, and probably in pain from wounds suffered in earlier battles. He appears simply not to have known what was going on.

On the morning of 1 Dec. Hood discovered that Schofield had gotten past him during the night and was posted several miles to the north at Franklin, again blocking the road to Nashville. —RMcM

"Spy of the Cumberland." *See* CUSHMAN, PAULINE.

Stafford, Leroy Augustus. CSA b. at "Greenwood," near Cheneyville, La., 13 Apr. 1822. After receiving an education in Kentucky and Tennessee, Stafford became one of the most wealthy planters in Louisiana. Elected sheriff of Rapides Parish in 1845, a year later he served as a private in the Rapides Volunteers in the Mexican War.

GG

With the advent of the Civil War, Stafford, a captain of the Stafford Guards, a militia unit, entered Confederate service as lieutenant colonel of the 9th Louisiana. In Oct. 1861 he was promoted to colonel and command of the regiment, succeeding Brig. Gen. Richard Taylor, who now commanded the Louisiana Brigade, of which the 9th was a part. Under Taylor, Stafford and the Louisianans fought in the 1862 SHENANDOAH VALLEY CAMPAIGN. Stafford briefly commanded the brigade during the latter stages of the SEVEN DAYS' CAMPAIGN.

Returning to command of the 9th, Stafford led it at ANTIETAM, where he suffered a foot wound. The regiment transferred to Brig. Gen. Harry T. Hays's brigade Oct. 1862, and Stafford fought under Hays at FREDERICKSBURG, CHANCELLORSVILLE, and GETTYSBURG. In this last battle, the Louisianans stormed up CEMETERY HILL in the twilight of 2 July 1863, momentarily seizing the vital Union position. Stafford received his promotion to brigadier general 8 Oct. 1863 and command of the 2d Louisiana Brigade.

He led this unit at Mine Run Nov. 1863 and at the Wilderness May 1864. There, 5 May, during the battle's first day, he fell mortally wounded at the head of his brigade. Stafford died 8 May in Richmond and was buried in Hollywood Cemetery. A year later his remains were removed to his plantation in Louisiana.   —JDW

Stager, Anson. USA b. Ontario Cty., N. Y., 20 Apr. 1825. Raised in Rochester, N. Y., the son of a toolmaker, Stager began work as a printer's assistant and bookkeeper in the office of the Rochester *Daily Adver-*

tiser. In mid-1845 he entered into business with the newspaper's publisher, Henry O'Reilly, who had contracted with Samuel F. B. Morse to build a telegraph network from Philadelphia to the Great Lakes. During the line's construction period, the young man learned telegraphy; in 1846, when the first leg of the network reached central Pennsylvania, he became the telegrapher at Lancaster, and later at Chambersburg, then Pittsburgh.

LC

Late in 1847, when the line had been strung as far as Cincinnati, Stager became manager of the operating department of O'Reilly's Pittsburgh, Cincinnati & Louisville Telegraph Co. As his new supervisor, James Reid, recalled: "he at once infused efficiency into the working of the line, and was, confessedly, the most skillful operator in the service at that time." In 1856, after devising a system to connect various wires to a single closed-circuit battery, Stager moved to Cleveland as general superintendent of the fledgling Western Union Co. For this firm he negotiated contracts that gave it a monopoly on stringing wires along railroad rights-of-way.

In 1861 his communications expertise made him invaluable to the U.S. Army (*see* TELEGRAPH). On 11 Nov. he became a quartermaster captain on the staff of Maj. Gen. GEORGE B. MCCLELLAN in western Virginia. Later he was placed in charge of the U.S. Military Telegraph in Washington. In Feb. 1862 he received a colonelcy as aide to Gen.-in-Chief HENRY W. HALLECK. Given control of the cipher correspondence of War Sec. EDWIN M. STANTON, he devised a cryptographic system that the enemy was unable to translate. For these and other services, he was brevetted a brigadier general of volunteers 13 Mar. 1865.

After the war, Stager became superintendent of the central branch of the reorganized Western Union system. Moving to Chicago, he helped found the Western Electric Manufacturing Co. He died in that city 26 Mar. 1885.   —EGL

Stahel, Julius. USA b. Szeged, Hungary, 5 Nov. 1825, Stahel, educated in his birthplace and in Budapest, enlisted in the Austrian army as a private, eventually rising to the rank of lieutenant. Embracing the cause of Hungarian independence, he fought in the revolutionary army. After suppression of the revolt in 1848, Stahel fled, settling in London and then Berlin as a teacher and journalist. He immigrated to the U.S. in 1859,

working for a New York City newspaper.

USMHI

Stahel and LOUIS BLENKER, a revolutionary expatriate from Germany, recruited the 8th New York (1st German Rifles) when the war began. Commissioned its lieutenant colonel, Stahel fought with the regiment at FIRST BULL RUN. On 11 Aug. he succeeded Blenker as colonel and was promoted to brigadier general 12 Nov.

During the operations of 1862, Stahel commanded a brigade in Maj. Gen. Thomas J. "Stonewall" Jackson's SHENANDOAH VALLEY CAMPAIGN and a division in Maj. Gen. FRANZ SIGEL's corps at SECOND BULL RUN. Promoted to major general 17 Mar. 1863, he then commanded the cavalry in the defenses of Washington, D.C.

In spring 1864 Stahel returned to Sigel's command as commander of a cavalry division. He led his unit in Sigel's defeat at NEW MARKET, Va., 15 May. Maj. Gen. David Hunter replaced Sigel, and soon reported that "it would be impossible to exaggerate the inefficiency of General Stahel." At PIEDMONT, 5 June, however, Stahel fought with distinction, fell wounded, and in 1893 received the MEDAL OF HONOR for his performance there. He then served on courts-martial until his resignation 8 Feb. 1865.

After the war, Stahel spent nearly 20 years in the consular

Stand of arms

LC

service in Japan and China. Resigning because of poor health, he returned to the U.S. in 1885 and became associated with the Equitable Insurance Co. of New York. d. New York City, 4 Dec. 1912. —JDW

Stainless Banner. *See* FLAGS, CONFEDERATE.

stand of arms. A stand of arms designated a complete set of equipment for 1 Civil War soldier. It included a rifle, bayonet, cartridge belt, and ammunition box. From common usage, the term frequently came to mean only the rifle and cartridge belt. —JDW

stand of colors. A stand of colors was a single color or flag. A Union infantry regiment carried 2 silken flags, or 2 stands of colors. The first was the national banner, with the regiment's number or name embroidered in silver thread on the center stripe. The second, or regimental, color had a blue field with the arms of the U.S. embroidered in silk on the center. A typical Confederate infantry regiment possessed only 1 stand of colors. —JDW

Stanley, David Sloane. USA b. Cedar Valley, Ohio, 1 June 1828. A farmboy, Stanley was apprenticed to a physician at age 14. Attracted to military life, he eagerly accepted a West Point berth in 1848. A diligent student, he graduated 4 years later 9th in a class that included 15 future generals.

As an officer in the 2d U.S. Dragoons, and later in the 1st Cavalry, Stanley spent his prewar years at frontier garrisons in Arkansas, California, Texas, and Kansas. Refusing a commission in the Confederate army early in 1861, he joined Brig. Gen. NATHANIEL LYON in Missouri and participated at WILSON'S CREEK. After Lyon's defeat and death, Stanley served for a time under

Maj. Gen. JOHN C. FRÉMONT, whose posturing and extravagance appalled him but under whose regime he became a brigadier general of volunteers 28 Sept. 1861. Early the next year, he fought conspicuously under Maj. Gen. JOHN POPE at NEW MADRID and ISLAND NO. 10, then accompanied Maj. Gen. WILLIAM S. ROSECRANS against CORINTH, Miss., a campaign Stanley considered strategically senseless.

In Nov. 1862 Rosecrans made Stanley chief of cavalry of his ARMY OF THE CUMBERLAND. During his tenure, after Apr. 1863 as a major general, Stanley massed the scattered command, greatly enhanced its effectiveness, and tripled its strength. He left mounted service that September to command the 1st Division/IV Corps, which he led through much of the ATLANTA CAMPAIGN, including SNAKE CREEK GAP, RESACA, KENNESAW MOUNTAIN, and VINING'S STATION. Promoted to corps leadership 27 July 1864, he was criticized by Maj. Gen. WILLIAM T. SHERMAN for slowness at JONESBOROUGH, 1 Sept. Stanley attributed his delay to Sherman's having ordered the IV Corps to wait to advance until it had wrecked the railroad above the town. His reputation was regained when he was sent west in November to oppose Gen. JOHN B. HOOD'S TENNESSEE CAM-

PAIGN. He received praise at Columbia, SPRING HILL, and especially at FRANKLIN, where he was severely wounded while leading Col. EMERSON OPDYCKE's brigade in a charge that staved off Union disaster.

Following the war, Stanley commanded the 22d U.S. Infantry. He served in Texas during the French occupation of Mexico and at various frontier posts, and led the Yellowstone Expedition of 1873. He retired from the service June 1892, after 8 years as a brigadier general, U.S. Army. Later governor of the soldiers' home in Washington, D.C., he died in the capital 13 Mar. 1902. —EGL

Stanley, Henry Morton. CSA/USN b. Denbigh, Wales, 28 Jan. 1828. Born John Rowlands, an illegitimate child, Stanley spent his early youth with indigent relatives and as an inmate of the St. Asaph Union Workhouse. Sailing for New Orleans, La., as a cabin boy in 1859, in the American South he was befriended and adopted by businessman Henry Morton Stanley. He took Stanley's name, entered his business, and in 1860 traveled to Arkansas to manage one of his stores.

In 1861 Stanley joined the 6th Arkansas Infantry. Known as the "Dixie Grays," it served at SHILOH, and in this battle Stanley became a prisoner. Sent to Camp Douglas, Chicago, Ill., after 2 months confinement he volunteered for Federal military service in exchange for his freedom. Stanley was enrolled as a Union artilleryman for less than a month, then given a medical discharge. He returned to Wales, briefly, then came back to the U.S. in 1863, enlisted in the U.S. Navy in 1864, and as a Federal seaman took part in the Jan. 1865 assault on FORT FISHER, N.C.

Stanley's long postwar career made him world-famous. As a journalist on James Gordon Bennett's New York *Herald,* he discovered the missing missionary David Livingstone near Lake Tanganyika in Central Africa Nov. 1871, explored the African Congo, went on a military expedition through Egypt, became a member of Britain's Parliament, and was decorated by the British crown. d. London, 10 May 1904. Best remembered for the quote "Dr. Livingstone, I presume," in American Civil War history he is recognized as the most prominent GALVANIZED YANKEE. —JES

Stanton, Edwin McMasters. USP b. Steubenville, Ohio, 19 Dec. 1814. In 1827 Stanton's father died, forcing the 13-year-old to leave school and work in a Steubenville bookstore to supplement the family's income. Keeping up with his studies in his spare time, in 1831 he was able to enter Kenyon College, where he attended for 2 years until his funds were depleted. In Columbus he completed his studies in law in the office of his guardian and was admitted to the bar in 1836. From 1849 to 1856 he was counsel for the state of Pennsylvania, establishing a national reputation. Afterward his most important work was as special counsel for the U.S. government in 1858 litigating fraudulent land claims in California. His success there won for him the appointment of attorney general 20 Dec. 1860 under Pres. James Buchanan.

After ABRAHAM LINCOLN was inaugurated as president, Stanton returned to private life. With his nomination as secretary of war confirmed 15 Jan. 1862, he again became member of a presidential cabinet. Stanton sacrificed a yearly income of $40,000–$50,000 as a successful lawyer for a cabinet salary of $8,000. His bluntness made him enemies among the many who sought contracts to supply poor food and shoddy material to the army. To preserve and protect that army, he enforced the unpopular draft laws and restricted the liberty of a press that too often gave as much information to the enemy as Stanton's best spies could obtain from the South. He had great administrative abilities: the transfer by rail of more than 20,000 men with equipment to the relief of Chattanooga in little over a week was due to Stanton's planning, organization, and drive.

A patriot whose consuming passion was the preservation of the Union at any cost, he frequently quarreled with Lincoln and abused him behind his back for what he thought was weakness or compromise in carrying on the war. Yet the two worked together as a team in serving a common cause, the strength of each complementing the deficiencies of the other. Lincoln understood him: during the war he told a friend that Stanton "is utterly misjudged . . . at present, the man's public character is a public mistake."

The crowning calumny has been the suggestion that Stanton was associated with the Lincoln assassination conspiracy. However, JOHN HAY, Lincoln's personal secretary, wrote to Stanton soon after the war ended: "Not everyone knows, as I do, how close you stood to our . . . leader, how he loved you and trusted you, and how vain were all the efforts to shake that trust and confidence, not lightly given and never withdrawn. All this will be known some time, of course, to his honor and yours."

At Pres. ANDREW JOHNSON's request, Stanton kept his cabinet post until he resigned 26 May 1868, after a struggle between Congress and the president over his tenure forced him out of office. Worn by his hard work during the war and as an ardent Radical reconstructionist afterward, Stanton refused several opportunities to run for public office in order to recover his strength. On ULYSSES S. GRANT's election to the presidency, he offered Stanton a seat on the U.S. Supreme Court. Stanton died 24 Dec. 1869, 4 days after Congress confirmed the nomination.   —RDH

Starke, Peter Burwell. CSA b. Brunswick Cty., Va., 1815. Starke's exact birthdate is unknown, the year of birth determined from information Starke supplied Feb. 1865, now on file in the National Archives. The brother of future Confederate Brig. Gen. WILLIAM E. STARKE, Peter worked in the family stagecoach business until migrating to Bolivar, Miss., in the early 1840s and entering politics. An unsuccessful candidate for U.S. Congress in 1846, he won election to the state house of representatives in 1850, entered the state senate in 1856, and served there through the first year of the Civil War.

Starke won commission as colonel of the 28th Mississippi Cavalry 24 Feb. 1862, as a member of Maj. Gen. Earl Van Dorn's forces took part in operations in central and northern Mississippi, rode in Brig. Gen. William H. Jackson's cavalry division during VICKSBURG operations, and 23 December 1863, without commensurate rank, assumed command of Jackson's 1st Brigade. Next serving under Maj. Gen. Stephen D. Lee,

LC

Starke opposed Union Maj. Gen. William T. Sherman's advance on MERIDIAN, Miss., Feb. 1864. A reorganization of the brigade followed, and Starke reverted to command of the 28th Mississippi Cavalry, serving in the ATLANTA CAMPAIGN under Brig. Gen. Frank C. Armstrong in Jackson's division. He won promotion to brigadier general 4 Nov. 1864, under Maj. Gen. Nathan B. Forrest joined in the FRANKLIN AND NASHVILLE CAMPAIGN, and to his credit, during Forrest's reorganization of command and dismissal of officers early in 1865, retained his rank, serving out the last months of the war in Brig. Gen. James R. Chalmers' division opposing Union Brig. Gen. James H. Wilson in Alabama.

Starke spent the immediate postwar years in public appointments, serving on the board of Mississippi levee commissioners and a term as sheriff of Bolivar County. Retiring to a farm near Lawrenceville, Va., in 1873, he died there 13 July 1888.
                                                                                              —JES

Starke, William Edwin. CSA b. Brunswick Cty., Va., 1814. Starke and his brothers, including future Confederate Gen. PETER B. STARKE, operated a stage line from Lawrenceville to Petersburg, Va. Starke then moved to Mobile, Ala., and eventually to New Orleans, La., where he became a successful cotton broker. He was living in the Crescent City when the Civil War erupted.

Starke returned to his native state, serving as an aide-decamp to Brig. Gen. ROBERT S. GARNETT in the latter's disastrous 1861 western Virginia campaigning before being commissioned colonel of the 60th Virginia. After additional duty in western Virginia, Starke's regiment was assigned to Brig. Gen. Charles W. Field's brigade in Maj. Gen. Ambrose P. Hill's division. The regiment fought under Field in the SEVEN DAYS' CAMPAIGN, where Starke was commended twice for his gallant performance.

LC

Promoted to brigadier general 6 Aug. 1862, Starke assumed command of Brig. Gen. William B. Taliaferro's division during the SECOND BATTLE OF BULL RUN after Taliaferro fell wounded. On 17 Sept. 1862, at ANTIETAM, Md., Starke again commanded the division. In the furious combat around the Cornfield and East and West Woods, Starke was hit 3 times, dying within an hour. He was buried in Hollywood Cemetery in Richmond.
                                                                                              —JDW

***Star of the West,* USS.** On 5 Jan. 1861, the USS *Star of the West* sailed with cargo from New York, ostensibly to New Orleans. In truth the sidewheel steamer was bound for Charleston, S.C., carrying supplies and reinforcements for FORT SUMTER.

The voyage of the *Star of the West* represented a compromise on the part of Pres. James Buchanan between the necessity to shore up Sumter and the reluctance to provoke civil war. The U.S. government chartered the merchant vessel for $1,250 a day and went to some lengths to keep its mission and cargo secret. Thus civilian JOHN MCGOWAN was master of the vessel, and 1st Lt. Charles R. Woods kept his detachment of soldiers below decks.

On the same day that the ship sailed, the Buchanan government dispatched instructions to Maj. ROBERT ANDERSON, who commanded at Sumter, to open fire on any of the South Carolina batteries that might fire on the ship. However, the message to Anderson traveled by regular mail and reached Charleston after the *Star of the West* had arrived, and the government's attempted secrecy evaporated when Northern newspapers reported details of the mission for all to read.

The vessel reached the entrance to Charleston harbor during the night of 8 Jan., and very early on the morning of the 9th McGowan began his passage into the harbor toward Sumter. The forewarned Southerners were ready, and the first shot was fired from Morris Island. At Fort Sumter Anderson, without instructions, chose to withhold his fire, if not his fury. The *Star of the West* continued its course and came under fire from batteries at Fort Moultrie. Then McGowan turned the ship about and headed back out to sea. The immediate crisis had passed, while the ultimate crisis deepened.

During the war the *Star of the West* served the Union navy until captured by Confederates at Indianola, Tex., Apr. 1861. The Southerners sank it Mar. 1863 in an effort to block the Tallahatchie River. —EMT

Starr revolver. After the Colt and Remington, the Starr revolver was the most popular handgun supplied to Union troops. Patented by Eben T. Starr, son of the famous Connecticut arms maker Nathan Starr, the revolver was produced in 3 models in factories at Yonkers, Binghamton, and Morrisania, N.Y.

The Model 1858 Navy revolver was a double-action, .36-caliber, 6-shot weapon produced in 1859 and 1860. What appears to be the trigger is actually a cocking lever. When pulled, the cylinder rotates and the hammer is pulled back. The

USA

real trigger is concealed on the inside rear of the trigger guard. It is fired either in the conventional manner with the index finger or by the use of an adjustable stud located on the back of the cocking lever. Approximately 3,000 of these navy revolvers were produced. Of these, 100 were ordered by the

U.S. Navy but were rejected and returned to the factory. The army purchased 1,402. The remainder were sold commercially.

The 1858 Army revolver was essentially the same as the navy model but in .44 caliber. About 16,000 of the guns were purchased by the government between Jan. 1862 and May 1865 at $25 each.

The Model 1863 Army revolver eliminated the double-action system in favor of single action. The primary reason for the change was that Remington and Whitney were supplying first-class single-action revolvers to the government at $15 each, and it was obvious that Starr's more expensive weapons would price themselves out of the market. The new version was produced at $12 each, and Starr sold about 31,000 of them to the government. Many were supplied to the Western theater. —LDJ

Stars and Bars. *See* FLAGS, CONFEDERATE.

states rights. In the decades preceding civil war the states-rights issue hung over the nation like a saber. The doctrine held that certain rights and powers remained the sovereignty of the state, and that the exercise of that sovereignty lay in the will of its citizens. Through elected delegates the people bestowed on the central government certain powers, among them the right to declare war and conduct diplomacy, with all those left unspecified remaining in state control. Those who adhered to the doctrine felt the Constitution was not binding since it represented a contractual agreement that could be invalidated as public sentiment dictated.

In the antebellum years, authority granted the Federal government during the Constitutional Convention in 1787 was held to be vague, and conflicting interpretations escalated into rigid sectional differences over the slavery issue. As the Northern economy and population grew, Southerners' political edge in Congress seemed to erode. They rallied to the states-rights banner, seceded, and patterned the Confederacy around the doctrine.

But states rights destroyed the Confederate nation it created. Citing the sovereignty of their states, Confederate governors refused to comply with the centralizing measures Pres. JEFFERSON DAVIS passed to meet the civil-war crisis. They withheld the taxes and cotton Richmond needed to finance the war, denied Davis' power to suspend the writ of *HABEAS CORPUS,* kept control of Federal military installations within state borders, and rejected impressment and enforced currency devaluation. With devastating effects, unyielding Secessionists like JOSEPH E. BROWN and ZEBULON B. VANCE opposed CONSCRIPTION, arming slaves, and giving Richmond sorely needed use of state militias.

Occasionally the North cried states rights, but for Southern states it was a defiant, defensive extreme. Jealousy, pride, and obsessive self-interest rendered them incapable of winning a common victory. State leaders turned against Davis and each other so completely that the states-rights weapon they had turned northward destroyed any chance of Confederate nationhood. —PLF

Steedman, James Blair. USA b. Northumberland Cty., Pa., 29 July 1817. Orphaned at an early age, and with little formal education, Steedman learned printing; worked on newspapers in Lewisburg, Pa., and Louisville, Ky.; saw military

service in Texas; then moved to
Ohio. Popular there, he won
election to 2 terms in the state
legislature in 1847 and 1848,
joined in the gold rush in 1849,
worked as proprietor of the
Toledo, Ohio, *Times,* and became active in Democratic politics. His political activity won
him appointment as U.S. government public printer in 1857,
a seat in the 1860 Charleston
and Baltimore Democratic conventions, and nomination for a
U.S. congressional seat in 1860.

LC

Losing to the Republican candidate, Steedman raised the 14th
Ohio Infantry for 90 days' Civil War service and was elected
its colonel 27 Apr. 1861.

With the 14th Ohio he fought the Battle of PHILIPPI and saw
other western Virginia service, then, on expiration of its enlistment, reorganized the regiment 1 Sept. 1861. Sent to Kentucky, under Brig. Gen. George H. Thomas he fought the Jan.
1862 Battle of MILL SPRINGS; under Maj. Gen. Henry W. Halleck marched on CORINTH, Miss., in April; won promotion to
brigadier general 17 July; then led the 2d Brigade/1st Division/
III Corps in the Battle of PERRYVILLE in October. Leading
Thomas' 3d Brigade/3d Division, Steedman was not engaged
at the Battle of Stone's River, but, at the head of the 1st Division in Maj. Gen. Gordon Granger's reserve corps, he distinguished himself in the TULLAHOMA CAMPAIGN and at the Battle
of CHICKAMAUGA.

With Granger at Chickamauga, he rode to Snodgrass Hill,
rallied his men in a desperate defense, and was hurt in the fall
when his horse was shot beneath him. On the portion of the
hill called HORSESHOE RIDGE, he led his men while carrying a
regimental standard and admonished a subordinate to ensure
his name be spelled correctly in the obituaries. Miraculously
escaping death, along with Thomas and Granger, he emerged
a hero from the battle.

A forthcoming major general's appointment was delayed
because Steedman's Democratic Ohio newspaper had editorialized against emancipation policies of the Lincoln administration. After weathering the CHATTANOOGA siege, he took an
early part in the ATLANTA CAMPAIGN, received his major generalcy 20 Apr. 1864, then joined Thomas' command at Nashville. In the December Battle of NASHVILLE, commanding a
temporary division-sized organization, he fought the Union
left, on the first day pushing across the Murfreesboro Pike, and
on the second day embroiling himself in the Peach Orchard
Hill combat with Lt. Gen. Stephen D. Lee's force. Thereafter,
Steedman served in garrison and district command, resigning
his volunteer commission 18 Aug. 1866.

Until 1869 he served as collector of Internal Revenue at
New Orleans, then returned to Toledo, editing the *Northern
Ohio Democrat* and serving in the state senate. He was
elected chief of police of Toledo May 1883 and died in that
city 18 Oct.   —JES

Steele, Frederick. USA b. Delhi, N.Y., 14 Jan. 1819.
Graduating 30th in the West Point class of 1843, Steele distinguished himself in the Mexican War, earning 2 brevets. For the
next 15 years, he served in garrisons in the Western U.S. and

earned promotion to captain,
then major. When civil war
began, Steele was stationed at
Fort Leavenworth, Kansas.

His first combat in the war
came 10 Aug. 1861, at WILSON'S
CREEK, Mo., where he com-
manded a brigade of Regulars.
Appointed colonel of the 8th
Iowa 23 Sept., he led the regiment until his promotion to brigadier general 29 Jan. 1862. He
then commanded the District of
Southwest Missouri until May,
when he received a division in

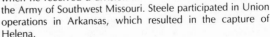

LC

the Army of Southwest Missouri. Steele participated in Union
operations in Arkansas, which resulted in the capture of
Helena.

In Dec. 1862 Steele transferred to divisional command in
Maj. Gen. William T. Sherman's Army of the Tennessee, leading his unit at CHICKASAW BLUFFS and in the capture of ARKANSAS
POST. Promoted to major general 17 Mar. 1863, to rank from
29 Nov. 1862, he commanded a division in the XV Corps
during the VICKSBURG CAMPAIGN.

Steele was then assigned to command of the Department of
Arkansas, or VII Corps. Directed to clear the state of organized
Confederates, he advanced his corps across the state, capturing the capital Sept. 1863. The following spring, the department commander again marched into southwest Arkansas, to
prevent Confederates from opposing Maj. Gen. Nathaniel P.
Banks's advance in the RED RIVER CAMPAIGN. From March to
May Steele operated in this CAMDEN EXPEDITION, and was ultimately defeated at JENKINS' FERRY 30 Apr. In Feb. 1865 he was
transferred to the Department of the Gulf and led a division in
Union operations against Mobile, Ala.

A veteran of more than 2 decades, Steele remained in the
postwar Regular Army. Appointed colonel of the 20th Infantry,
he commanded the Department of Columbia. While on leave
in California, he suffered an attack of apoplexy and fell from
a carriage he was driving. As a result of the accident he died
in San Mateo, Calif., 12 Jan. 1868.   —JDW

Steele, William. CSA b. Albany, N.Y., 1 May 1819.
Graduating 31st in the West Point class of 1840, Steele served
for more than 2 decades in the antebellum U.S. Army. He

fought in the Seminole War and
earned the brevet of captain for
gallantry in the Mexican conflict. Promoted in 1851 to the
Regular rank of captain, he
served for the next decade with
the 2d Dragoons in Texas. Having spent most of his duty in the
South and having married a
woman from Texas, the native
New Yorker resigned his commission 30 May 1861 and
joined the Confederacy.

Steele immediately was appointed colonel of the 7th Texas
Cavalry. His regiment par-
ticipated in Brig. Gen. HENRY HOPKINS SIBLEY's operations to

LC

recover New Mexico Territory 1861–62. During the campaign, Steele temporarily acted as commander of Southern forces in the Mesilla area. He received his promotion to brigadier general 12 Sept. 1862. In Jan. 1863 he assumed command of Indian Territory, serving there until Mar. 1864, when he was placed in charge of the defenses of Galveston, Tex. Within a month, however, he joined Lt. Gen. Richard Taylor's army in the RED RIVER CAMPAIGN. Taylor commended the brigadier's performance at PLEASANT HILL 9 Apr. 3 days later Brig. Gen. Thomas Green was killed, and Steele replaced him as commander of a cavalry division, leading it until superseded by a senior officer. Steele then reverted to brigade command, remaining in the Trans-Mississippi Department until the end of the war.

Immediately after the war, the Confederate veteran became a commission merchant in San Antonio. In 1873 he moved to Austin and accepted the appointment of adjutant general of Texas. He eventually returned to San Antonio, where he died 12 Jan. 1885.   —JDW

Steele's Bayou Expedition, Miss. 14–25 Mar. 1863

During the ill-fated YAZOO PASS EXPEDITION, Rear Adm. DAVID D. PORTER hit on a separate idea for reaching the Yazoo River and approaching Vicksburg, Miss., from the northeast. A little more than 6 mi up the Yazoo from its mouth, on its north bank, was the entrance to Steele's Bayou. Porter suspected that Steele's Bayou, Black Bayou beyond it, and Deer Creek to the north were all connected, navigable at high water, and could connect with the Big Sunflower River and the Yazoo, bringing a naval expedition almost full circle from its starting point to attack Confederate batteries on the Yazoo at Haynes' and Drumgould's bluffs, points 10 and 12 mi northeast of the mouth of Steele's Bayou. Troops might also be landed behind these batteries and approach Vicksburg from the northeast. The Steele's Bayou entrance lay 7 mi overland north of Vicksburg.

Ill-advised in pursuing this plan, particularly in light of the failure on the Yazoo the previous December at CHICKASAW BLUFFS, Porter exhibited a boyish sense of adventure and personally scouted the Yazoo and several miles of Steele's Bayou with a local guide. On 14 Mar. he entered the bayou with the ironclads *Mound City, Louisville, CARONDELET, Cincinnati,* and *Pittsburgh,* 4 mortars, and 4 tugboats. These waters were heavily overgrown, normally shallow at many points, obstructed by fallen timber, and had not been navigated by any vessel larger than a skiff or pirogue. Pledging cooperation, Maj. Gen. William T. Sherman sent 50 army pioneers aboard the steamer *Diligent* 16 Mar., and followed behind with Maj. Gen. U. S. Grant, meeting Porter at Hill's Plantation at the head of Black Bayou on the same day. Having encountered no armed resistance and having traveled more than 30 mi in 2 days, Porter pressed on up Deer Creek on the 16th with his 5 ironclads. Sherman remained at Hill's Plantation administering the transport of the 2d Division/XV Corps to Black Bayou, and Grant returned to camp in front of Vicksburg.

North then east on Deer Creek, 32 water mi from Hill's Plantation, sat the Rolling Fork, a spot Porter believed was unobstructed. From there he expected clear sailing to the Yazoo. But obstructions slowed travel through Deer Creek, the ironclads making a top speed of half a mile an hour. On 19 Mar., within 7 mi of Rolling Fork, advance Confederate elements from the Haynes' Bluff garrison arrived, impressed slaves, and put them to work felling trees into Deer Creek and

the Sunflower beyond Rolling Fork. Porter dispatched 300 seamen and pioneers ahead to hold Rolling Fork and suffered under sniper fire through the 20th, at that time passing Rolling Fork and hitting willows growing directly out of the stream bed. Confederates began felling trees behind the flotilla and intended on bottling it up until sufficient force arrived from Haynes' Bluff to take it.

3 regiments of the Federal 2d Division arrived at Hill's Plantation early on the 21st. Sherman dispatched them to Porter's assistance, 12 mi overland at Rolling Fork. Other troops arrived on 3 steamboats at Hill's Plantation that night, and Sherman personally led them on a quick march to Porter's aid early on the 22d.

On the 21st a Confederate force, estimated at 2,000–3,000 men, began marching on Porter from the east. The first 3 Union regiments, under Col. GILES A. SMITH, reached Porter's boats later that day in time to stall the Confederate advance. Troops with Sherman arrived on the 22d, skirmished again with Confederates, then helped Porter return to Hill's Plantation. Sherman and the ironclads reached Black Bayou again 24 Mar., skirmishing that day and the next with 3 Confederate regiments that had pursued them. This ended the expedition.

Though Porter's cannon were used and some skirmishing took place, the number of Confederate casualties in this episode are unknown. Porter lost 4 seamen wounded and an engineer killed by sniper fire. The Federal infantry lost only 2 men killed.   —JES

Steele's Expedition, Ark. 23 Mar.–3 May 1864 *See* CAMDEN EXPEDITION, ARK.

Stephens, Alexander Hamilton. CSP b. 11 Feb. 1812, Taliaferro Cty., Ga.

Orphaned at the age of 12, Stephens lived with an uncle, who provided him with educational opportunities. In 1832 he graduated, from the University of Georgia, ranking 1st in his class. After teaching briefly, he studied law and was admitted to the bar. Politics soon attracted him and, in 1836, he was elected to Georgia's legislature, serving every year except one until 1843. He was respected by his colleagues and was popular with his constituents, who dubbed him "Little Aleck" because of his physical stature.

Stephens entered the U.S. House of Representatives in

NA

1843. For the next decade and a half, first as a Whig, then as a Democrat, he advocated states rights and defended slavery. But he opposed the idea of secession, and he, ROBERT A. TOOMBS, and HOWELL COBB tried unsuccessfully in the early 1850s to form a party dedicated to the principles of union. By 1860, however, Toombs and Cobb had embraced secession while Stephens supported STEPHEN A. DOUGLAS in the presidential election. The electoral victory of ABRAHAM LINCOLN, an old friend of Stephens, resulted in secession, and Stephens, though arguing in the Georgia convention against the dissolution of the union, signed the ordinance after its adoption by the delegates. On 9 Feb. 1861, JEFFERSON DAVIS and Stephens were elected president and vice-president, respectively, of the new Southern nation.

The war was hardly a year old before Stephens broke with Davis over the latter's policies of CONSCRIPTION, the suspension of *HABEAS CORPUS,* and the establishment of military governments in certain areas of the South. For 18 months Stephens lived in Georgia in a self-imposed exile from Richmond, participating in only 2 official missions as vice-president: as a commissioner to Virginia's secession convention in 1861 and as a representative at the HAMPTON ROADS CONFERENCE in 1865. He centered his official duties on the plight of the wounded and prisoners, visiting hospitals and prison camps while promoting rapid exchange of prisoners. With the defeat of the Confederacy, Federal officials imprisoned him at Fort Warren in Boston harbor.

Paroled Oct. 1865, Stephens returned to Georgia, where he was elected to the U.S. Senate Jan. 1866. Republicans, however, refused all Southern delegates their seats, so Stephens resumed his legal practice. In 1872 he returned to his seat in the House, wrote a number of books, including the 2-volume *A Constitutional View of the Late War Between the States* (1868, 1870), and was elected governor of Georgia in 1882. He died in Atlanta 4 Mar. 1883, a few months after his inauguration.
—JDW

Steuart, George Hume. CSA b. Baltimore, Md., 24 Aug. 1828, Steuart, at age 19, was graduated from West Point in 1848, ranking 37th, next to last, in his class. He served during the antebellum period on the frontier, fighting Indians and participating in the Utah Expedition. Resigning his commission 22 Apr. 1861, he entered Confederate service as a captain of cavalry.

With the formation of the 1st Maryland, Steuart became its lieutenant colonel. The regiment fought at FIRST BULL RUN, after which Steuart succeeded Col. Arnold Elzey as regimental commander, his commission dated the day of the battle, 21 July 1861. On 6 Mar. 1862, he received his promotion to brigadier general and command of a brigade in the division of Maj. Gen. Richard S. Ewell.

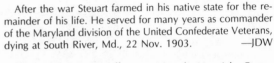

LC

During the 1862 SHENANDOAH VALLEY CAMPAIGN, "Maryland" Steuart commanded both cavalry and infantry, but his performance with the mounted arm displeased Maj. Gen. Thomas J. "Stonewall" Jackson. Returned to command of his brigade during the campaign's final week, Steuart was severely wounded in the shoulder at CROSS KEYS 8 June. Disabled for nearly a year, he returned to duty May 1863 and assumed command of a brigade in the division of Maj. Gen. Edward Johnson. At GETTYSBURG he led his veterans with distinction and courage.

On 12 May 1864, at SPOTSYLVANIA, Steuart and most of Johnson's division were captured when the Federals crushed the "MULE SHOE" salient. Subsequently exchanged, he commanded a brigade under Maj. Gen. George E. Pickett during the PETERSBURG CAMPAIGN. His brigade fought at FIVE FORKS and surrendered with the army at Appomattox.

After the war Steuart farmed in his native state for the remainder of his life. He served for many years as commander of the Maryland division of the United Confederate Veterans, dying at South River, Md., 22 Nov. 1903.
—JDW

Stevens, Clement Hoffman. CSA b. Norwich, Conn., 14 Aug. 1821. The son of a Southern-born naval officer, Stevens relocated with his family to South Carolina in 1836. In his youth he enjoyed several years of travel and adventure as a secretary to a pair of relatives, both naval commodores. By 1842 he had settled down to a career as the cashier for a Charleston bank, and was a member of a railroad construction firm when South Carolina seceded Dec. 1860.

With the coming of war, Stevens achieved notability by designing and constructing on Morris Island, below Charleston, an iron-plated battery—conceivably the first armored fortification in military history. Later he invented a portable oven with which to supply troops fresh bread, an invention that, like the ironclad battery, saw limited application during the conflict.

Stevens' combat services to the Confederacy had longer-lived effects. As a volunteer aide, he accompanied his brother-in-law, Brig. Gen. BARNARD E. BEE, at FIRST BULL RUN. There Stevens was wounded and Bee killed (the latter soon after giving Brig. Gen. THOMAS J. JACKSON and his brigade the nickname "Stonewall"—an appellation that Stevens insisted characterized Jackson's inertia, not his tenacity). When he was able to return to the field, Stevens took charge of a militia regiment at Charleston, then the 24th South Carolina Infantry. He led the 24th with precision 16 June 1862 at SECESSIONVILLE, helping repulse an assault on that James Island position by Brig. Gen. Henry W. Benham.

Sent to Mississippi early in 1863, Stevens fought as a member of Brig. Gen. States Rights Gist's brigade/Joseph E. Johnston's army in the VICKSBURG CAMPAIGN. That September he was again severely wounded, this time while leading his South Carolinians "with reckless bravery" at CHICKAMAUGA. His performance was described in one superior's after-action report as "iron-nerved."

Promoted brigadier general as of 20 Jan. 1864, he rejoined the ARMY OF TENNESSEE, though not fully recovered from his wound, for the ATLANTA CAMPAIGN. He was killed at PEACHTREE CREEK, late on the evening of 20 July, while leading his troops in another headlong attack against superior forces. By then his courage and steadfastness had won him the nickname "Rock."
—EGL

Stevens, Isaac Ingalls. USA b. Andover, Mass., 25 Mar. 1818. Descended from Puritans who had settled in New England in 1638, Stevens grew up sickly and slight (barely 5 ft tall) but with a towering intellect and an energetic disposition. He spent 16 months at Phillips Academy, then entered West Point, from which he graduated in 1839, 1st in his class. As a lieutenant in the construction engineers, he spent several years building and repairing fortifications along the Eastern Seaboard; at one point he was responsible for engineering projects at 5 garrisons. For his hard work he won high praise from his superiors, including Brig. Gen. JOSEPH G. TOTTEN, chief of his corps.

During the Mexican War Stevens served on the staff of Maj. Gen. WINFIELD SCOTT, seeing action at Cerro Gordo, Churubusco, and Contreras and winning the brevets of captain and major. After a slow recuperation from a foot wound received at the San Cosme Gate outside Mexico City, an injury that nearly took his life when blood poisoning resulted, he returned to active duty in the U.S. Meanwhile, he wrote *Campaigns of the Rio Grande and of Mexico,* published in 1851.

USMHI

Late in 1849 Stevens became an assistant to Alexander D. Bache, director of the U.S. Coast Survey, in which position he spent 4 years in the War Department. In 1852 he entered politics as a supporter of future president Franklin Pierce. His speechmaking and literary efforts in Pierce's behalf brought him the governorship of WASHINGTON TERRITORY in 1853, prompting him to resign his commission that March. Traveling to his new post, he filled another recently proffered position by directing a 120-man party in surveying the proposed northern route of the transcontinental railroad.

As a governor in the Northwest, Stevens worked honestly and tirelessly to negotiate peace treaties with numerous Indian tribes. But in his dealings with white men and red he displayed egotism and a dictatorial bent as well as impatience and imprudence. His latest biographer notes that "he often reacted more to the contingencies of the moment than to sober thought or calm reflection." His reputation was damaged when, despite his efforts, hostilities broke out between some tribes and white settlers late in 1855 and when he ill-advisedly declared martial law in part of his realm for 2 months in 1856. He retained enough popularity, however, to gain his territory's seat in the House of Representatives in 1856 and to win reelection 2 years later.

When civil war came, Stevens sought to return to uniform. His staunch Democratic leanings and friendships among pro-Southern politicians such as Joseph Lane at first denied him the rank he desired, but July 1861 he accepted the colonelcy of the 79th New York Infantry. Restoring order to this mutinous outfit, he led it in Virginia and later in South Carolina, following PORT ROYAL Sound. A brigadier general of volunteers as of 28 Sept. 1861, he commanded the post at Beaufort and June 1862 led a division of infantry in an unsuccessful assault on SECESSIONVILLE, below Charleston.

Sent with the IX Corps to link with the Army of Virginia, Stevens subsequently fought at SECOND BULL RUN under Maj. Gen. JOHN POPE. Following the army's drubbing 29–30 Aug., he brought up Pope's rear during the retreat to Washington, D.C. On 1 Sept. Stevens' command was attacked outside CHANTILLY, Va., by troops under Maj. Gen. THOMAS J. "STONEWALL" JACKSON. In the act of repulsing the enemy, Stevens fell dead, a rifle ball in his temple. He was posthumously raised to major general of volunteers. —EGL

Stevens, Thaddeus. USP b. Danville, Vt., 4 Apr. 1792. As a young man Stevens learned to despise class distinctions and privileges that fell to the moneyed few. It was a prejudice he never overcame.

A lawyer, Stevens moved to Gettysburg, Pa., in 1816 and opened practice there. Outraged by the conditions slaves suf-

fered across the border in Maryland, he soon began defending runaways at no charge. Although he advocated public education and strong protective tariffs throughout his career, he became best known for his opposition to slavery and later insistence on Military Reconstruction.

LC

Stevens, one of the most powerful politicians in Pennsylvania, was elected to the U.S. House of Representatives on the Whig ticket in 1848. Soon disillusioned with Whig conservatism, he used his influence to organize the Republican party in his state. In 1858 he returned to the House as a Republican. A supporter of ABRAHAM LINCOLN in the 1860 presidential campaign, he expected but lost a cabinet appointment, partly because of his sharp tongue and blatant anti-Southern position.

Instead, as Ways and Means Committee chairman, he used his power to speed through legislation he thought necessary to end the rebellion. Convinced the Confederacy was willing to sustain extended war, he defended Lincoln's broad interpretation of the Constitution under the guise of war powers. The president, however, frustrated Stevens' ambitions to win equality for blacks. Bitter and uncompromising, Stevens agitated for the enlistment of BLACK TROOPS and uncompensated emancipation, and expedited bills abolishing slavery in the territories and forbidding the army to turn away refugee slaves. Aware of Northern racism, he worked to prepare the North to accept the 13TH AMENDMENT.

Most unrelenting of RADICAL REPUBLICANS, Stevens secured approval of the Civil Rights Bill and Freedmen's Bureau Bill over Pres. ANDREW JOHNSON's vetoes and made ratification of the 15th Amendment a condition for Southern states reentering the Union.

The indefatigable egalitarian once remarked bitterly that he would never see "merit balance the crime of color," and he did not. Southerners hated him for his vindictiveness and many colleagues resented the biting sarcasm he used against them on the House floor. But when he died in Washington, D.C., 11 Aug. 1868, many acknowledged him admiringly as the "Great Commoner." —PLF

Stevens, Walter Husted. CSA b. Penn Yan, N.Y., 24 Aug. 1827. An 1848 graduate of the U.S. Military Academy, standing 4th in his class, Stevens entered the Corps of Engineers, and for nearly 13 years performed engineering duties in Louisiana and Texas. His tour in the South and his marriage to the sister of future Confederate general Louis Hébert made Stevens an avowed Southerner in sentiment. After Texas seceded, he submitted his resignation 2 Mar. 1861. The War Department refused to accept it, and Stevens was eventually dismissed on a technicality 2 May.

Appointed a captain of engineers in the Confederate army, Stevens acted as Gen. P.G.T. Beauregard's engineer officer at FIRST BULL RUN. When Gen. Joseph E. Johnston replaced Beauregard, Stevens remained as chief engineer of the Army of Virginia. He performed his duties during the 1862 PENINSULA CAMPAIGN until Johnston's wounding at SEVEN PINES 31 May.

Johnston's successor, Gen. Robert E. Lee, gave Stevens, now a colonel, command of the defenses of Richmond, Va., and for the next 2 years Stevens expanded and strengthened the earthworks rimming the Confederate capital.

In summer 1864 Lee appointed him chief engineer of the Army of Northern Virginia. Promoted to brigadier general to rank from 28 Aug., Stevens supervised the Confederate defenses at Petersburg, Va., works

LC

that defied the Union army for nearly 10 months. When Richmond fell, 2 Apr. 1865, Stevens was supposedly the final uniformed man to abandon the city. He surrendered with the army at Appomattox.

Stevens then emigrated to Mexico, where he became engineer and superintendent of the Imperial Railroad. d. Vera Cruz, 12 Nov. 1867. —JDW

Stevenson, Carter Littlepage. CSA b. Fredericksburg, Va., 21 Sept. 1817. Graduating 42d of 45 in the West Point class of 1838, Stevenson saw action during the Mexican War and later fought Indians on the frontier and Mormons in Utah.

Commissioned colonel of the 53d Virginia Infantry July 1861, Stevenson was promoted to brigadier general 27 Feb. 1862 and ordered to the Western theater, where he took part in Maj. Gen. E. Kirby Smith's invasion of Kentucky in August. Advanced to the rank of major general from 10 Oct., Stevenson was sent to Vicksburg, Miss., to command a division in Lt. Gen. John C. Pemberton's army. On 16 May 1863, the division was outflanked at the Battle of CHAMPION'S HILL and was forced to retreat. 2 months later, Stevenson and others counseled Pemberton to surrender the city.

Stevenson was exchanged in time for the CHATTANOOGA CAMPAIGN. In Sept. 1863 he and his old division were stationed on LOOKOUT MOUNTAIN, Tenn., and 24 Nov. were attacked by Union troops under the command of Maj. Gen. Joseph Hooker. Heavily outnumbered, Stevenson's men were assaulted on the front and flank and finally had to withdraw to the sanctuary of the main Confederate line on MISSIONARY RIDGE.

Stevenson subsequently served under Gen. Joseph E. Johnston during the ATLANTA CAMPAIGN, his division being heavily engaged at the Battle of RESACA 15 May, and at KENNESAW MOUNTAIN 27 June 1864. During the FRANKLIN AND NASHVILLE CAMPAIGN, in December, the division stoutly defended Overton Hill, Tenn., until forced to retreat in the face of overwhelming numbers. On 17 Dec. Lt. Gen. Stephen D. Lee was wounded at Winstead Hill, Ga., and Stevenson was placed in temporary command of his corps.

In the closing months of the war, the general served in the Carolinas against Maj. Gen. William T. Sherman's army. He fought his last major engagement at BENTONVILLE, N.C., 19–21 Mar. 1865. After the war, Stevenson turned to engineering. He died in Caroline Cty., Va., 15 Aug. 1888 and was buried in Fredericksburg, Va. —MTC

Stewart, Alexander Peter. CSA b. Rogersville, Tenn., 2 Oct. 1821. At age 17 Stewart was appointed to the U.S. Military Academy, from which he graduated 12th in the class of 1842. From Aug. 1843 until May 1845, when he resigned from the army, he taught mathematics on the West Point faculty. Afterward he taught at Cumberland University in Lebanon, Tenn., then at Nashville University.

Although a Whig opposed to secession, Stewart volunteered for Confederate service and 17 May 1861 was commissioned a major in the Artillery Corps of Tennessee. He spent the next several months at Forts Randolph and Pillow and Island No.

NA

10, guarding the Tennessee River approaches to Memphis, drilling his heavy artillery battalion, and instructing personnel in handling big guns. On 15 Aug. Stewart and his battalion were mustered into Confederate service. Soon thereafter they took position at Columbus, Ky., and at the 7 Nov. Battle of BELMONT, Mo., Stewart commanded heavy batteries that dueled with Union gunboats and shelled Brig. Gen. U. S. Grant's troops on the Mississippi's western shore.

Stewart was named a brigadier general to rank from 8 Nov. 1861 and placed in command of an infantry brigade in what became Lt. Gen. Leonidas Polk's corps. He battered the enemy at Shiloh's "HORNETS' NEST" and participated in the Siege of CORINTH and the invasion of Kentucky. At STONE'S RIVER, he and his 6 Tennessee regiments and Mississippi battery helped drive Maj. Gen. George H. Thomas' 2 divisions from the cedar woods north of the Wilkinson Pike.

On 2 June 1863 he was made a major general and at CHICKAMAUGA led a division in Maj. Gen. Simon B. Buckner's corps. Known as "Old Straight" by his men, Stewart led his division at MISSIONARY RIDGE and in the ATLANTA CAMPAIGN of 1864 from Dalton to the CHATTAHOOCHEE River. Promoted lieutenant general to rank from 23 June 1864, Stewart succeeded to command of Polk's Corps 6 July, leading it through the Army of Tennessee's remaining marches and battles. He was wounded at EZRA CHURCH 28 July and was paroled at Greensborough, N.C., Apr. 1865.

After the return of peace, Stewart served successively as a professor at Cumberland University, secretary of the St. Louis Mutual Life Insurance Co., chancellor of the University of Mississippi, and commissioner of the Chickamauga and Chattanooga National Military Park. d. Biloxi, Miss., 30 Aug. 1908. —ECB

Stohlbrand, Charles John Meuller. USA b. near Kristianstad, Sweden, 11 May 1821. A graduate of his country's military academy, Stohlbrand joined the Royal Vendes Artillery at 18, and 9 years later participated in the Schleswig-Holstein campaign during the Danish-Prussian War. Having defended Denmark from invasion, he immigrated to the U.S., ultimately settling in Chicago. In July 1861, with the assistance of the city's Swedish consul, he organized a local artillery company composed largely of immigrant Scandinavians. Though this unit was not accepted for Federal service, since Illinois had filled its original quota, he recruited a second company of light artillery, of which he was commissioned captain 5 Oct.

NA

That December, Stohlbrand's Continental military background enabled him to become major of his battery's parent unit, the 2d Illinois Light Artillery. In 1862 he was installed as artillery chief to Brig. Gen. JOHN A. LOGAN, then leading a brigade in the ARMY OF THE TENNESSEE and commanding the District of Jackson. The following year, Stohlbrand served Logan in the VICKSBURG and CHATTANOOGA campaigns, and by spring 1864 was commanding the artillery brigade of the XV Corps. Early in the ATLANTA CAMPAIGN, he served notably at RESACA, 14–15 May, but on the 19th was captured near Kingston, Ga. Sent to ANDERSONVILLE, he soon escaped from the infamous prison camp and in October rejoined his command.

During the MARCH TO THE SEA and the first months of the CAROLINAS CAMPAIGN, Stohlbrand's obvious abilities attracted the attention of Maj. Gen. WILLIAM T. SHERMAN. In Jan. 1865, learning that the Swede was considering resigning from the army due to his inability to rise above major, Sherman sent him to Washington, D.C., with dispatches. One, which Stohlbrand delivered personally to Pres. ABRAHAM LINCOLN, carried Sherman's strong recommendation that Stohlbrand be elevated to brigadier general—a promotion Lincoln conferred that same day, 18 Feb. 1865. Returning to the Carolinas, the new general led an Illinois infantry brigade in the XVII Corps till his muster-out Jan. 1866.

In postwar years Stohlbrand was a political power in South Carolina. Until his death in Charleston, 3 Feb. 1894, he was secretary of the state constitutional convention, Republican presidential elector, warden of the state penitentiary, and superintendent of Federal buildings in Charleston. In his free time, he worked at steam engineering and tinkered with industrial inventions. —EGL

Stone, Charles Pomeroy. USA b. Greenfield, Mass., 30 Sept. 1824. The son of a New England doctor, Stone attended West Point, graduating 7th in the class of 1845 in time to serve with Gen. WINFIELD SCOTT's siege train in the Mexican War. In 1856 he was employed privately as chief commissioner for the exploration of the state of Sonora, Mexico. He started Civil War service Apr. 1861 as a colonel for the District of Columbia Volunteers, in charge of the safety of the national capital and Pres. Abraham Lincoln.

Stone's is the unfortunate story of a man in the wrong place at the wrong time. At the outset of the war he fought in the Shenandoah Valley and on the ROCKVILLE EXPEDITION. 2 months after his promotion to brigadier general of volunteers 6 Aug.

1861, to rank from 17 May, a small battle at BALL'S BLUFF, near Leesburg, Va., ended in a Union disaster. With a brigade of Stone's command, spirited Col. and Sen. EDWARD D. BAKER engaged Confederates under Col. Nathan G. Evans 21 Oct. 1861. The popular Baker fell with a mortal wound in the fighting, and in the subsequent public outcry, the sole blame for the Federal debacle fell on Stone.

After considering several pieces of questionable testimony, the COMMITTEE ON THE CONDUCT OF THE WAR had Stone arrested at midnight, 8 Feb. 1862. Without explanation he was thrown into solitary confinement for 50 days in New York's Fort Lafayette prison. He was then sent to Fort Hamilton and, after a total of 189 days behind bars, was released 16 Aug., still with no idea of what charges had been leveled against him.

NA

The remainder of Stone's Civil War career included service with Maj. Gen. Nathaniel P. Banks at PORT HUDSON and in the RED RIVER CAMPAIGN. Tired of the treatment he received, Stone resigned from the Regular Army 13 Sept. 1864.

After the war he served as superintendent for a Virginia mining company, as chief of staff in the Egyptian army for 13 years, and as engineer for the Florida Ship Canal Co. He then moved to New York City, where, as an engineer, he helped build the foundations of the Statue of Liberty. He died in New York City, 24 Jan. 1887, and is buried where his bitter military career began, West Point. —FLS

"stone fleets." On 16 July 1861, the U.S. Navy's Blockade Strategy Board suggested a plan to help implement the BLOCKADE of Southern ports: the navy would acquire a number of old vessels of not less than 250 tons each, load them with heavy stones, and scuttle them at entrances to Southern harbors. The idea was apparently taken from the Confederates, who, 11 Jan. 1861, had sunk 4 hulks in Charleston's Main Ship Channel to prevent the Federals from reinforcing FORT SUMTER. Sec. of the Navy GIDEON WELLES approved the plan, and 25 whaling ships were purchased and loaded with 7,500 tons of stone. Captains, mates, stewards, and seamen were specially recruited for these vessels, which left Northern ports 20 Nov. 1861. 15 were sunk in Charleston's Main Ship Channel 19–20 Dec. A second "stone fleet" of 20 old whaling and merchant ships was sunk in Maffitt's Channel, also leading into Charleston harbor, 25–26 Jan. 1862.

These attempts to increase the effectiveness of the blockade proved a failure. Marine worms caused the hulks to break up in less than 3 months, and the water flowing around the stones created a passage in the Main Ship Channel that was several feet deeper than the one that had previously existed.

—NCD

Stoneman, George. USA b. Busti, N.Y., 22 Aug. 1822, Stoneman, who graduated 33d in the West Point class of 1842, was a veteran of the Mexican and Indian wars. On 13 Aug. 1861, he became a brigadier general with command of a division in the PENINSULA CAMPAIGN. As a major general, to rank from 29 Nov. 1862, he led a corps at FREDERICKSBURG.

Stoneman was relieved of command for his lackluster leadership of the Army of the Potomac's cavalry in the CHAN-CELLORSVILLE CAMPAIGN (see STONEMAN'S RAID, CHANCELLORS-VILLE CAMPAIGN) and relegated to the Cavalry Bureau in Washington until 1864, when he was sent to Maj. Gen. William T. Sherman to head a division in the ATLANTA CAMPAIGN. He and 700 of his men were captured in a joint raid with Brig. Gen. Edward M. McCook against

USMHI

Macon (see STONEMAN'S AND MCCOOK'S RAID, ATLANTA CAMPAIGN) but Stoneman was released in time to lead a successful raid through southwestern Virginia Dec. 1864 (see STONEMAN'S RAID, SOUTHWESTERN VIRGINIA). In Mar. 1865 he raided across southern Virginia and western North Carolina, through the last bastion of the shrinking Confederacy (see STONEMAN'S RAID, NORTH CAROLINA AND VIRGINIA).

Despite his uneven military career, he remained in the Regular Army until 1871, then retired to California, where he served as governor 1883–87. d. Buffalo, N.Y., 5 Sept. 1894.

—RDH

Stoneman's and McCook's Raid, Atlanta Campaign.

26–31 July 1864   After 3 years of war, the Union cavalry remained inferior to the Confederate in every respect but weapons. Thus in ATLANTA CAMPAIGN operations between Dalton and the CHATTAHOOCHEE RIVER, the Federal cavalry lost every major engagement, and Maj. Gen. WILLIAM T. SHERMAN relegated them to the role of substitute infantry. However, after reaching the outskirts of Atlanta, Sherman decided to give his cavalry a significant opportunity. On 27 July Maj. Gen. GEORGE STONEMAN, with 6,500 troopers, swung east and Brig. Gen. Edward M. McCook, with 3,500 sabers, rode west of Atlanta. To compel the Confederates to evacuate Atlanta, they were to join forces at Lovejoy Station and destroy the last remaining railroad supplying Gen. JOHN B. HOOD's army. Sherman also authorized Stoneman, at the latter's behest, to march farther south and release the more than 30,000 Union prisoners at Macon and ANDERSONVILLE—but only after the railroad had been cut.

Stoneman ignored this proviso, heading for Macon instead of Lovejoy Station and leaving Brig. Gen. KENNER GARRARD's division to cover the move. As a consequence Maj. Gen. JOSEPH WHEELER's Confederate cavalry, 10,000 strong, was able to isolate the 3 Union columns and deal with them in succession. On 28 July they routed Garrard's division, on the 29th they captured Stoneman and 700 of his men near Macon, and on the 30th they scattered McCook's command. All together the Federal raiders lost more than 2,000 men and failed utterly in their mission. Hood's hard-riding cavaliers achieved one of the greatest cavalry victories of the war and boosted the sagging morale of his army.

The outcome of the July raids confirmed Confederate superiority in cavalry. It also confirmed Sherman in his low opinion of his mounted arm. Cavalry, he concluded, "could not, nor would not make a sufficient lodgement on the railroad below Atlanta. . . ." Infantry would have to force the Confederates from that city, and he now planned accordingly.   —AC

Stoneman's Raid, Chancellorsville Campaign.

29 Apr.–8 May 1863   Maj. Gen. Joseph Hooker, in his plans for the CHANCELLORSVILLE CAMPAIGN, Apr.–May 1863, ordered some 10,000 Federal troopers on a mounted raid against the communication and supply lines of Gen. Robert E. Lee's Army of Northern Virginia. This raid was to take place before the main body of the army attempted a turning movement on the Confederate flank, and comprised nearly all of the cavalry of the Army of the Potomac. Leading the newly established Cavalry Corps of the army was Maj. Gen. GEORGE STONEMAN.

Stoneman was originally scheduled to start from Falmouth, Va., 13 Apr. and cross the Rappahannock River the next day, but a heavy storm flooded the river and made fording impossible for 2 weeks. As a result of this delay, on 29 Apr. the cavalry crossed the Rappahannock with the rest of the army. The command was split into 2 columns, 1 commanded by Brig. Gen. WILLIAM W. AVERELL and the other by Brig. Gen. JOHN BUFORD. Stoneman rode with Buford's command, which was the main force of the Union cavalry. Averell was intended to ride toward Gordonsville and the ORANGE & ALEXANDRIA RAILROAD and to mask the movements of the larger column, which was to strike the Richmond, Fredericksburg, & Potomac Railroad.

The raid was an unrelieved failure. Averell spent most of his time at Rapidan Station worrying about phantom Confederate cavalrymen and was recalled by Hooker 2 May. He was subsequently relieved and replaced by Brig. Gen. ALFRED PLEASONTON. Stoneman, with Buford and Brig. Gen. DAVID M. GREGG, destroyed some railroad track and other property around the Virginia countryside, but their efforts had no lasting effect. Stoneman's raid was one of Hooker's worst mistakes in the campaign.   —JTP

Stoneman's Raid, North Carolina and Virginia.

20 Mar.–23 Apr. 1865   Early in 1865, while Maj. Gen. WILLIAM T. SHERMAN was marching through the Carolinas attempting to join forces with Lt. Gen. ULYSSES S. GRANT in Virginia and crush the Confederacy between them, Maj. Gen. GEORGE H. THOMAS at Nashville was ordered to send some of his troopers on a raid into the Carolinas as a diversion. There were few organized bodies of Confederates left to divert the Federals from anything at this late date, and the raid, under Maj. Gen. GEORGE STONEMAN, was intended to destroy property more than armies.

Originally the plan had been for Stoneman to threaten Columbia, the South Carolina capital, but Sherman had already burned and passed through that city and had reached Goldsborough, N.C., before the Federal cavalry was ready to move 20 Mar. 1865. Leaving Tennessee, the troopers rode into the western North Carolina mountains, wrecking parts of the VIRGINIA & TENNESSEE RAILROAD around Salem and Wytheville, Va., and the Piedmont Railroad between Danville, Va., and Greensborough, N.C. Stoneman marched through Asheville and stopped at Hendersonville when he learned of the surrender of the Army of Tennessee under Gen. Joseph E. Johnston to the Union forces under Sherman.

Stoneman was then ordered to Raleigh by Sherman to place his cavalrymen along the supposed escape route of Pres. JEFFERSON DAVIS and the CONFEDERATE CABINET into North Carolina from Virginia, but he achieved no success.

Only a few scattered remnants of Confederate cavalry and militia had opposed the raid, and Federals captured about 2,000 prisoners. Since the raid started about 2 weeks before the end of the war, the railroad track and other property destroyed were of no military advantage to the South, making the raid an exercise in military waste. —JTP

Stoneman's Raid, southwestern Virginia.

1 Dec. 1864–1 Jan. 1865 In mid-Nov. 1864 Maj. Gen. GEORGE STONEMAN, a recently released prisoner of war, was sent to command Union cavalry in East Tennessee. Immediately he mapped an expedition against long-coveted nearby resources: Confederate iron mines and saltworks. Within 2 weeks he had massed some 4,200 Kentucky cavalry and HORSE ARTILLERY under Richard G. Burbridge, plus 1,500 Tennessee horsemen led by Brig. Gen. Alvan C. Gillem. On 1 Dec., despite bad weather, all moved east from Knoxville in the direction of Wytheville and Saltville, Va.

At Kingsport, Tenn., 4 Dec., Stoneman's command struck and routed an understrength cavalry brigade under Brig. Gen. BASIL W. DUKE, part of Maj. Gen. JOHN C. BRECKINRIDGE's Confederate Department of Western Virginia and Eastern Tennessee. 2 days later, near Bristol, 20 mi farther east, Stoneman dispersed a mounted command under Brig. Gen. JOHN C. VAUGHN, preventing it from linking with Breckinridge outside Saltville. Pursuing Vaughn's escapees through Marion and into Virginia, the raiders halted near Wytheville long enough to damage several mines and foundries.

Resuming his advance, Stoneman on the 8th attacked Breckinridge's main force, 6,000 strong, and cut it off from Saltville. Overwhelmed, the Confederate commander fled across the mountains into North Carolina, leaving 700 Virginia home guards to defend the saltworks. The Federals made short work of such opposition, then thoroughly destroyed the works, including 50,000–100,000 bushels of salt. Facing no major opposition, Burbridge returned to Kentucky and Gillem to Tennessee.

On this, the most successful of his several cavalry raids, Stoneman suffered minimal losses while capturing 4 enemy-held towns, almost 900 prisoners, 19 cannon, 3,000 horses and mules, 3,000 muskets, and 25,000 rounds of artillery ammunition. He had also laid waste to every factory, train, bridge, supply depot, mill, and warehouse along his route, and had confiscated what he called "four pestiferous secession printing-presses." —EGL

Stone's River (Murfreesboro), Tenn., Battle of.

31 Dec. 1862–2 Jan. 1863 The day after Christmas 1862, with over half his Army of the Cumberland, Maj. Gen. WILLIAM S. ROSECRANS advanced southeast from Nashville, Tenn. His 47,-000 men were divided into 3 units: the right wing, commanded by Maj. Gen. ALEXANDER M. MCCOOK; the center, commanded by Maj. Gen. GEORGE H. THOMAS; and the left wing, commanded by Maj. Gen. THOMAS L. CRITTENDEN. From 26 Dec. to 30 Dec. they moved ahead in separate columns roughly 30 mi to Confederate Gen. BRAXTON BRAGG's position in front of Murfreesboro. With 38,000 men from his Army of Tennessee, Bragg was deployed along a 4-mi front arching inward. About 1.5 mi west and northwest of Murfreesboro, his lines covered the Nashville Pike, running northwest, and the winding Stone's River, which passed behind his men, under the pike, then meandered northwest along the east of the pike. Recent heavy rains had raised the level of the river.

Rosecrans' troops skirmished daily with Bragg's cavalry and advance infantry until arriving before Bragg's position.

The Federal commander believed that if he could push Bragg from Murfreesboro, he could secure Nashville's supply lines and eliminate threats from the Army of Tennessee until spring. Bragg hoped to do the opposite, and used the days of Rosecrans' slow advance to plan the coming battle. By late on the 30th of December, from the Confederate right to left, he had deployed Maj. Gen. John C. Breckinridge's division (east of the pike and the river), Lt. Gen. Leonidas Polk's corps (from the pike river crossing to a point about 1¼ mi west), and Lt. Gen. William J. Hardee's corps (from Polk's left, west about 1¾ mi). He planned on assaulting Rosecrans' right with Hardee's Corps and turning the entire Union force, putting its back to the Stone's River, and, ideally, cutting off its northwest line of retreat on the Nashville Pike. A second road, the Wilkinson Pike, traveling west-northwest, cut the intervening ground between the Confederate left and the Nashville Pike, and intersected and ended at the Nashville Pike about a quarter of a mile behind Southern lines. Bragg established headquarters at the intersection and ordered an attack for daylight 31 Dec.

Rosecrans' plan of battle was for McCook to hold the right, Thomas' center troops to begin with skirmishing, and Crittenden's left wing to maneuver to Stone's River, cross 2 divisions, and assail Bragg's right. Rosecrans' intelligence revealed that Breckinridge's lone division held the Confederate line east of the river. With 2 divisions to Breckinridge's 1, he would thrust the Confederates back, get in Bragg's rear and flank, and, with the Union line wheeling to its left, push the Confederates west and southwest, out and away from Murfreesboro. To ensure an overextension of Confederate lines, he ordered McCook to send detachments farther to the left after dark, 30 Dec., and

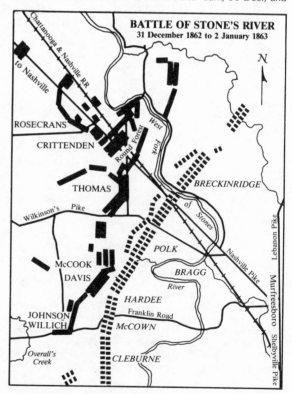

BATTLE OF STONE'S RIVER
31 December 1862 to 2 January 1863

build campfires, giving the illusion of a longer Union line. He then ordered an attack for 7 a.m. 31 Dec.

Deceived by the false extension of Rosecrans' lines in the dark, Bragg pulled his lone reserve division, commanded by Maj. Gen. John P. McCown, and a second line division of Hardee's, led by Maj. Gen. Patrick R. Cleburne, and threw them out on his left against McCook's phantom troops. Bragg's daylight assault caught the Federals unprepared and, weighted against McCook's right wing, pushed McCook's troops back on Thomas. Polk pushed ahead, startling more Federals, and Confederate cavalry rode far around the Union right and harassed Rosecrans' rear. Union Brig. Gen. August Willich was captured and Brig. Gen. Edward N. Kirk horribly wounded. Union Brig. Gen. Richard W. Johnson's routed division crossed the Wilkinson Pike, driving Union Brig. Gen. Jefferson C. Davis' division into confusion and back to the Nashville Pike. Brig. Gen. Philip H. Sheridan, commanding a division under McCook, had his men make a stand in front of the Wilkinson Pike, repelled 3 assaults, then executed a slow, fighting retreat.

As Federals fell back on the Nashville Pike, the first Union division sent across Stone's River to assault Breckinridge was recalled. Rosecrans formed it and another division in front of massed artillery at the Nashville Pike. The Chattanooga & Nashville Railroad ran parallel to the pike on the east, and around it sat a 4-acre wood called the Round Forest, dubbed by soldiers ''Hell's Half-Acre.'' Rosecrans pulled his artillery to an elevation behind the woods. Now protected from attacks from the south by Union Maj. Gen. James S. Negley's division, Sheridan's division held the Federal center. The Union line resembled a narrow *V*, its right and left being pressed back on one another. Sheridan's troops fell back about 11 a.m., Negley's following suit quickly, and a new line was created, with the Round Forest forming a sharp salient. The forest itself was held by 5 brigades. Supported by the massed artillery in their rear, they withstood repeated Confederate attacks until nightfall. A thin line of Union divisions held the road to Nashville, and additional troops stretched around to the east of the Round Forest, facing Stone's River and Breckinridge's Confederates. This situation held until fighting ceased at dark.

On 1 Jan. 1863, neither side renewed the battle. Rosecrans had pulled his troops from the Round Forest salient during the night, establishing a new line to the north. Still retaining some of its V shape, it covered both the Nashville Pike and the river. Bragg expected Rosecrans to retreat and, north on the pike had his cavalry disrupt attempts at resupply. After dark, 1 Jan., Union Col. Samuel Beatty led Crittenden's 3d Division across Stone's River and established it on a ridge facing Breckinridge.

On 2 Jan. the Federals remained in place until after 4 p.m., when Bragg ordered Breckinridge to assault Beatty's position. After protesting that the assignment was impossible, Breckinridge obeyed. As he massed his 4,500 men for assault, he was observed by Crittenden at a distance. Crittenden ordered his artillery chief, Maj. John Mendenhall, to mass his guns at the ford where Beatty had crossed. Breckinridge attacked, knocking Beatty from the ridge and across the river and pursuing the Federals to its banks. At 4:45 p.m. Mendenhall opened on Breckinridge with the concentrated fire of 57 cannon. The Confederates were cut up badly. Fresh Union troops charged across the ford and by nightfall had driven Breckinridge back to his original position.

Confederate Maj. Gens. Benjamin F. Cheatham and Jones M. Withers, commanders of divisions that had suffered greatly

31 Dec., wrote a memorandum to Bragg the night of 2 Jan. asking for retreat. Endorsed by Polk, the memorandum first angered Bragg, who rejected the idea. He reconsidered at 10 a.m. 3 Jan. and ordered retreat for that evening, believing, falsely, that Rosecrans had been reinforced. Left in possession of the field, Rosecrans declared Stone's River a Union victory. The stalemated fight cost him 1,730 dead, 7,802 wounded, and 3,717 missing. Bragg fared little better, sustaining a loss of 1,294 dead, 7,945 wounded, and 1,027 missing. His troops withdrew toward Shelbyville, Tenn. Rosecrans declined pursuit, occupying Murfreesboro instead.   —JES

***Stonewall*, CSS.** The *Stonewall* was one of 2 RAMS built for the Confederacy by L. Arman, Bordeaux, France, in 1864 and the only European-built ram to actually reach Confederate hands. 172 ft long and 33 ft wide, the *Stonewall* was covered by 3.5 in. of iron, backed by 3 in. of teak, and lined with 1 in. of iron. Its most unusual and important offensive weapon was an iron ram, extending 20 ft beyond the bow and ending in a sharp steel point.

The vessel was first sold to Denmark, but the Danes, dissatisfied with its performance, returned it to the builders. Then, through an elaborate subterfuge, the ram was sold to the Confederacy and brought from Copenhagen to Quiberon Bay, France. When the transfer was completed, Dec. 1864, the *Stonewall* offered a dying Confederacy hope for a miracle. It was expected to raise the BLOCKADE of WILMINGTON, N.C., intercept California gold steamers, attack New England ports, and destroy the Northern fishing fleet.

From the beginning, serious sailing problems caused delays, and Capt. Thomas J. Page brought the *Stonewall* to Ferrol, Spain, for repairs. Blockaded there by the U.S. steamers *Sacramento* and *Niagara*, the vessel left port; Page expected a fight, but Commodore THOMAS T. CRAVEN believed his wooden ships no match for the ram and declined combat.

When the *Stonewall* reached Havana, Page, learning of the war's end, surrendered his vessel to Spanish authorities, who turned it over to the U.S. Finally, it was sold to Japan and, renamed the *Azuma*, served from 1867 until scrapped in 1908.

Since the *Stonewall* never engaged Northern ships in combat, its effectiveness in battle is not known. But its own officers

LC

considered the ship to be unreliable and unseaworthy, and Page reported that it leaked badly, had serious structural defects, and lacked speed and maneuverability. Nevertheless, the *Stonewall* panicked many in the U.S. into believing that they were about to be attacked by an invincible armored monster. —NCD

Stonewall Brigade. CSA When Col. THOMAS J. JACKSON assumed command of the 1st Brigade/Virginia Volunteers at Harpers Ferry, Va., May 1861, there was little reason to suspect that the organization would become one of the most renowned in American history. But this inexperienced collection of citizen-soldiers from the Shenandoah Valley was molded by Jackson and subsequent commanders into a bulwark of the Army of Northern Virginia, distinguished by its well-justified pride and élan in battle.

The men composing this celebrated unit, in large part the descendants of non-English foreign-born, were formed into the 2d, 4th, 5th, 27th, and 33d Virginia Infantry regiments. Affiliated with the brigade until 20 Oct. 1862 was the elite Rockbridge Artillery. Originally numbering 2,611 men, the brigade in the course of its battle-scarred career shrank to as few as 635 (after Second Bull Run) and grew as large as 3,681 (at Chancellorsville). The mettle of its members is suggested by the fact that 8 of their number attained the rank of general.

The firm stand of the brigade at FIRST BULL RUN prompted Brig. Gen. BARNARD E. BEE to exclaim, "There stands Jackson like a stone wall! Rally behind the Virginians!," bestowing an undying appellation on both the outfit and its leader.

Of the 8 men who commanded the brigade, only 3 survived the war. Heavy casualties led to the official end of the brigade after the Battle of SPOTSYLVANIA, when it was merged with 2 other brigades. At Appomattox 210 men of the original units were paroled. The brigade never recovered from the loss of Jackson at CHANCELLORSVILLE, for the devotion of the original commander to them, and of them to him, infused the unit with a special character. That character was shown at the Battle of PORT REPUBLIC when Jackson, perceiving disarray, cried, "The Stonewall Brigade never retreats! Follow me!" —MPM

Stoughton, Edwin Henry. USA b. Chester, Vt., 23 June 1838, Stoughton graduated from West Point in 1859, 17th in the academy's first 5-year class, and traveled to New York City for garrison duty. He then took a leave of absence until 25 Sept. 1861, when the governor of Vermont appointed him colonel of that state's 4th Infantry. After spending the winter in the defenses of Washington, D.C., his regiment joined Brig. Gen. William T. H. Brooks's division in Maj. Gen. George B. McClellan's campaign up the Virginia peninsula. Stoughton again took leave, July–Nov. 1862. He was promoted to brigadier general 5 Nov., up to that time the youngest brigadier in the Union army.

LC

Throughout the winter he again served on garrison duty around the Federal capital before setting up his headquarters at Fairfax Court House. There, 8 Mar. 1863, the most memora-

ble event in Stoughton's military service occurred when Confederate Lt. JOHN S. MOSBY led 29 men into the center of the Union encampment. An unverified story claims that a young woman saw to it that Stoughton was drunk on champagne when Mosby arrived. Supposedly, after penetrating Union picket lines at weak spots disclosed to him by the woman, Mosby found Stoughton surrounded by empty bottles. Amid the thousands of sleeping Federals, Mosby captured 39 men, including Stoughton, and rode out with 58 horses.

Stoughton gained his release in May that year in a prisoner exchange, but found himself without an assignment on his return. He immediately picked up the pieces of his less than noteworthy career and moved to New York City, where he established a law practice with his uncle. He died there 25 Dec. 1868, and his body was transported to Vermont for burial. —FLS

Stovall, Marcellus Augustus. CSA b. Sparta, Ga., 18 Sept. 1818. The grandson of 2 Revolutionary War officers, Stovall was sent to school in Massachusetts by his father, an Augusta merchant. At 17 he returned to Georgia and became the youngest member of the Richmond Blues, a unit that served in Florida during the Seminole uprising of 1836. That year he received an appointment to West Point, which illness forced him to relinquish in 1837. Thereafter he toured Europe, returned to settle in Augusta (where he engaged in the mercantile trade and was prominent in militia affairs), and in 1846 settled on an estate near Rome, Ga. By Apr. 1861 he was captain of a local artillery company.

NA

Stovall's military education and experience quickly gained him a colonelcy in the Georgia state artillery. After months of local service, he entered the Confederate ranks Oct. 1861 as lieutenant colonel of the 3d Georgia Battalion. From the first, his unit exhibited the benefits of his organizational skill. As one historian notes: "Though a battalion of only seven companies it always had more muskets [present] for service than any of the regiments with which it was associated, while its discipline and morale were equaled by few and surpassed by none."

Following service in Virginia, North Carolina, East Tennessee, and southern Kentucky, 1861–62, Stovall led his cohesive, well-trained Georgians at STONE'S RIVER as part of Gen. BRAXTON BRAGG'S ARMY OF TENNESSEE. Early on 31 Dec. 1862, they helped drive back a part of the Union right flank, although hindered by a dense cedar thicket; for his part in this feat, Stovall was promoted brigadier general as of 20 Jan. 1863. That September, at CHICKAMAUGA, his brigade of Georgia and Mississippi infantry gained the left flank and rear of the ARMY OF THE CUMBERLAND, helping Bragg to his only sustained battlefield triumph. Stovall was also conspicuous in many of the engagements of the ATLANTA CAMPAIGN, especially 22 July 1864 at the Battle of ATLANTA. He led his Georgians with equal success under Gen. JOHN B. HOOD in Tennessee late in 1864 and under Gen. JOSEPH E. JOHNSTON in the CAROLINAS CAMPAIGN of 1865.

Surrendering with Johnston that April, Stovall went back to Augusta. There he brokered cotton, manufactured fertilizers, and organized and operated the Georgia Chemical Works. d. Augusta, 4 Aug. 1895.   —EGL

Stowe, Harriet Beecher. author b. Litchfield, Conn., 14 June 1811. The daughter of a prominent minister, Beecher moved to Cincinnati in 1832. 4 years later she married Calvin Stowe, eventually becoming the mother of 7 children. In 1850 her husband accepted a professorship at Bowdoin College and moved his family to Maine. There Stowe produced in 1852 the novel that thrust her into national prominence, *Uncle Tom's Cabin.*

NA

A Victorian tearjerker of slight literary value, the novel stirred emotions and aroused passions with its vivid characterizations. In an age convulsed by the question of slavery, Stowe provided Northerners with potent stereotypes that defined for them what Southerners, slaves, and slavery really were about. She knew little of these things firsthand; most of the material was drawn from abolitionist tracts and her own imagination. Her indictment was not aimed at the South or Southerners, rather at slavery itself. But Southerners misread the book as an attack on their way of life and denounced it angrily. As *Uncle Tom's Cabin* became fuel in the sectional controversy, it outsold all other books of the century and spawned countless stage versions. Distressed by misinterpretations of her work, Stowe published *A Key to Uncle Tom's Cabin* in 1853, but to no avail.

It is doubtful that Pres. ABRAHAM LINCOLN, when introduced to her, remarked, "So this is the little lady who made this big war," but her novel had an undeniable impact on the slavery debate. During her long life Stowe wrote numerous works. Many of them excelled *Uncle Tom's Cabin* in literary merit, but none even approached the sensation created by it. She died 1 July 1896 in Hartford, Conn., having said of the book that made her world-famous, "God wrote it!"   —MK

Strahl, Otho French. CSA b. McConnelsville, Ohio, 3 June 1831. After graduating from Ohio Wesleyan University, Strahl studied law. Passing the bar in 1858, he set up practice in a succession of small Tennessee towns.

When war broke out, the successful lawyer was appointed captain of the 4th Tennessee Infantry May 1861 and first saw action at SHILOH. Assigned to Brig. Gen. Alexander P. Stewart's 2d Brigade/1st Division/I Corps, the 4th was involved in heavy fighting 6 Apr. 1862. In Jan. 1863 Strahl was promoted to full colonel and 7 months later, 28 July, to brigadier general. In September he led his bri-

USMHI

gade with distinction during the Battle of CHICKAMAUGA. Serving in Maj. Gen. Benjamin F. Cheatham's division, his men made repeated assaults against the Union center 19 Sept. and next saw action 2 months later during the CHATTANOOGA CAMPAIGN. Again assigned to Stewart's division, Strahl was stationed on the Confederate left at the Battle of MISSIONARY RIDGE. His unit, along with the rest of the Confederate line, gave way and retreated as a result of the Federal assault.

Strahl's brigade gave valuable service throughout the ATLANTA CAMPAIGN in 1864. When Gen. JOHN B. HOOD invaded Tennessee Nov. 1864, Strahl served in Maj. Gen. John C. Brown's division. At the Battle of FRANKLIN, 30 Nov., Brown's and Maj. Gen. Patrick R. Cleburne's divisions were ordered to make a frontal assault on the forbidding entrenchments surrounding the town. Before the fight, Strahl cautioned his men that the work "would be short but desperate." Attacking along the Columbia Turnpike, the Confederates drove a force of Union troops into the breastworks and entered after them. The opposing lines, at most a few paces apart, engaged in vicious fighting, but Strahl, when asked if his brigade should withdraw, told his men to "keep on firing." The general was passing reloaded rifles to his soldiers on the ramparts when a bullet found and killed him. He was buried in Dyersburg, Tenn.
                                                                      —MTC

strategy. In this military art, troops are maneuvered outside the battlefield to achieve success in a large geographic area. That geographic expanse can be a "front" (in the Civil War, part or all of one state) or a "theater" (several contiguous states possessing geographical, geopolitical, or military unity). When the expanse encompasses an entire country, the corresponding waging of war on the largest scale to secure national objectives is called "grand strategy."

"Offensive strategy" carries war to the enemy, either directly by challenging his strength or indirectly by penetrating his weakness. "Defensive strategy" protects against enemy strategic offensives. And "defensive-offensive strategy" (which Confederates often practiced) uses offensive maneuvers for defensive strategic results (*e.g.*, Gen. R. E. Lee and Maj. Gen. Thomas J. "Stonewall" Jackson took the *offensive* May–June 1862 to *defend* Richmond and Virginia).

Strategic objectives include defeating, destroying, or forcing enemy armies to retreat; seizing enemy strategic sites (supply lines, depots, arsenals, communications centers, and industry) crucial to his military effort; capturing the enemy capital; disrupting his economy; and demoralizing his will to wage war. While seeking such goals, the strategist must correspondingly protect his own army, strategic sites, capital, economy, and populace. He must strike proper balance between securing his rear and campaigning in his front. Supply lines and homelands must be guarded; especially in war between 2 republics, which the Civil War really was, the compelling necessity of protecting the political base cannot be ignored. Yet if too many troops are left in the rear, too few remain to attack or even defend against enemy armies at the front.

Of these objectives, European experience, from which Civil War strategic doctrine derived, emphasized 3 strategies: destroying the enemy's army in 1 battle, seizing strategic sites, and capturing the enemy's capital. In the Civil War, attacking and defending Richmond and Washington consumed much effort, but their actual strategic importance, though great, was more symbolic than substantial, since neither was its country's nerve center, as European capitals were. Also illusory were quests for victory through seizing strategic sites and cutting "lines of communication" (supply lines); only a few Civil War campaigns, such as HOLLY SPRINGS and SECOND BULL RUN, were decided or even significantly affected by such captures. Most chimerical of all were hopes of annihilating the enemy's army in 1 great Napoleonic victory (see TACTICS).

Rather, Civil War strategists used a series of battles—each of them indecisive but cumulatively effective—to cripple the enemy, drive him back, and overrun or protect territory. Some strategies aimed directly at such battles. Other strategies sought first to maneuver so as to gain advantage of ground or numbers and only then to give battle under such favorable conditions. Whatever the overall numbers in the theater, strategy strove to assure numerical superiority on the battlefield; this principle was called "concentrating masses against fractions." Both sides practiced it, but it was especially important to the overall weaker Secessionists, as when Jackson performed it so effectively in the SHENANDOAH VALLEY.

Again, each side, particularly the Confederates, used "interior lines" to move forces from quiet fronts through the interior to threatened fronts more quickly than the enemy could move around the military border. But, in practice, Southern supply lines were so primitive and Federal supply lines were so good that, despite longer distance, Northerners often moved in shorter time due to their "superior lateral communications." Even more effective against Confederate reliance on interior lines was Ulysses S. Grant's grand strategy of concerting the armed might of the Union for simultaneous advances to pin and defeat Confederate troops on all major fronts.

Besides these approaches, Civil War strategists, especially Union commanders such as WILLIAM T. SHERMAN and PHILIP H. SHERIDAN, usually reluctantly but increasingly came to make the enemy's economy and populace suffer. For the first time since the Thirty Years' War, those 2 targets regained legitimacy. While free from the brutality of 1618–48, Federal strategy eventually crippled Southern capability and will to wage war—though, to be effective, such strategy could only complement Northern success in maneuver and battle.

Long-range strategic cavalry raids—in brigade to corps strength—played some role in such crippling, but those raids rarely had much military effect before collapse became imminent in 1865. Instead, the principal unit of strategic maneuver was the infantry corps, and the basic element of strategic control was the army. And in theaters where 1 side had several armies, those armies themselves became maneuver units, and control resided at military division headquarters or with the general-in-chief himself.

Whatever the elements and whatever the means, the fundamental goal of strategy remains the same: the overall use of force to accomplish broad military and political objectives.

—RJS

Strawberry Plains, Va., eng. at. 27 July 1864 *See* DARBYTOWN, VA., ENG. AT.

Streight, Abel D. USA b. Wheeler, N.Y., 17 June 1828. By 9 Feb. 1864, 109 prisoners had tunneled under the walls of LIBBY PRISON and onto Richmond's 20th St. Through the winter each man had taken his turn, digging relentlessly and secretly. Under the direction of Col. Thomas E. Rose the break commenced, and all eventually made the initial escape. The

LC

group consisted of captured soldiers from various engagements, among them a few who had surrendered to Brig. Gen. Nathan B. Forrest in his repulse of STREIGHT'S RAID through Alabama the previous spring. After emerging from the narrow tunnel, 2 escapees drowned, attempting to swim the nearby James River, and 48 fell back into the hands of their captors. But 59 successfully eluded the Confederate pursuers. One of the fugitives was the leader of the ill-fated raid that carried his name, Col. Abel Streight.

Despite his sparse education, Streight became a successful businessman and an able, respected Civil War commander. He was born into a rural farm family but decided on a more profitable career, opening a mill at age 19 and another soon after. His early love of carpentry influenced his decision to concentrate on the lumber industry. After 10 years in business he moved to Cincinnati, Ohio, and the following year continued west to Indianapolis, Ind.

As national hostilities increased, Streight started a brief publishing career, compiling a staunch pro-Union pamphlet. In it he revealed his "indomitable spirit" so vividly that he was appointed colonel of the 51st Indiana Volunteers 4 Sept. 1861. He participated in the battles of SHILOH, PERRYVILLE, and STONE'S RIVER, and other engagements in Tennessee and Alabama. After one of the boldest mounted raids of the war, commonly called Streight's Raid, the colonel surrendered his troops, most of them astride army mules, to Forrest 3 May 1863. For the best part of a year the raiders stood behind bars in various prisons throughout the South.

Following Streight's escape from Libby Prison and a period of rest, he returned to active duty and served until 1865, when he retired with a brevet rank of brigadier general.

After the war he resumed his publishing ventures and his career in lumbering, and ultimately headed the Indianapolis Chair Co. In 1876 Streight turned to politics and won a seat in the Indiana senate. In 1880 he made an unsuccessful bid for the Republican candidacy in the state gubernatorial election. He then returned to his businesses and died in Indianapolis, 27 May 1892.

—FLS

Streight's Raid. 11 Apr.–3 May 1863 From Nashville, Tenn., Federal Col. ABEL D. STREIGHT led what became known as his "Mule Brigade" on a 17-day raid through the hills of northern Alabama. Although the purpose of the move toward Georgia was to destroy Southern railroads, the raid was fraught with problems from the start.

First, Streight was forced to contend with a formidable foe in brilliant cavalryman Brig. Gen. NATHAN B. FORREST. But immediate problems forced him to overlook the enemy for several days. Streight and his 2,000 troopers were infantrymen, but they needed horses for the rough terrain of the Alabama mountains. An army expert convinced authorities in Nashville that 800 mules would be better suited to the task.

The mules presented more problems than they alleviated. 50 or 60 were either left behind because they were "too near dead" for such an expedition or died before it started. It also took a day and half for the animals and men to become acquainted. Streight was scheduled to meet Brig. Gen. Grenville M. Dodge 16 Apr., but the cantankerous mules made him late. Dodge had reached the rendezvous point at Eastport and met Confederate cavalryman Col. Philip D. Roddey, who pushed him 23 mi to Bear Creek. On arriving in Eastport, Streight left for Bear Creek and a conference with Dodge. Back in Eastport, Roddey's cavalrymen, tipped off by the constant braying of the mules, stole into the Federal corrals and stampeded 400 of them; only 200 mules were recovered.

After receiving 200 mules as replacements at Tuscumbia, and with 1,500 of his best men, Streight was ready to concentrate on the enemy, General Forrest. In the next week Streight and his entire command traveled across the Alabama hills, clashing with Roddey and Forrest at Day's Gap, Hog Mountain, and, finally, Lawrence.

With only 600 men, creatively deployed to look like thousands, Forrest called for Streight's surrender 3 May. Streight's men eventually handed down their guns, only to find they had been tricked. That which appeared to be a continuous train of guns was a mere section of artillery, ordered to move in circles. Forrest's orders to imaginary units completed the ruse resoundingly. Streight had been stopped, and once again Forrest emerged a hero. —FLS

Stringham, Silas Horton. USN b. Middletown, N.Y., 7 Nov. 1797, Stringham became a midshipman in the U.S. Navy in 1809 at age 11 and served in the War of 1812 and later on the Mediterranean during the Algerian war. He also put in duty along the coast of Africa and in the West Indies.

Commissioned lieutenant in 1814, he was promoted to commander in 1831 and captain in 1841. He served as commandant of the New York Navy Yard 1844–46; took part in the bombardment of Vera Cruz in 1847; was in charge f the Norfolk Navy Yard 1848–52; was flag officer of the Mediterranean Squadron 1853–56; and 1856–61 commanded the Boston Navy Yard.

LC

With 52 years of outstanding naval service behind him, the 63-year-old Stringham seemed a natural choice when in 1861 he was called to Washington to serve as consultant to Pres. James Buchanan. One of his first bits of advice to Buchanan was to reinforce FORT SUMTER. Although the suggestion came before the outbreak of war, no attempt was made to carry it out until too late to be feasible.

On 1 May 1861, Stringham was made flag officer of the NORTH ATLANTIC BLOCKADING SQUADRON. In this capacity he helped plan and commanded the first naval expedition of the war—the capture of HATTERAS INLET, a nest for BLOCKADE RUNNERS, on the coast of North Carolina Aug. 1861. It was the first time during the war that batteries on shore were bombarded by the broadsides of wooden vessels; the 7 ships in his fleet were kept in constant motion and so adroitly handled that they received virtually no damage. Stringham received little recognition for introducing a style of warfare that later brought great

credit to other naval commanders. Some thought this was the reason he asked on 16 Sept. 1861 to be relieved of command.

In 1862 he became an admiral on the retired list but did not long remain inactive. He soon resumed his post at the Boston Navy Yard and served there until the end of the war. For a time before his death, 7 Feb. 1876, he was Port Admiral at New York City. —VCJ

Strong, George Crockett. USA b. Stockbridge, Vt., 16 Oct. 1832. Raised in Easthampton, Mass., by an uncle, Strong entered the U.S. Military Academy in 1853, graduating 5th in his class. Prior to the outbreak of the Civil War, he served as a 2d lieutenant of ordnance at arsenals in the East and South, in 1859 becoming assistant superintendent of New York's Watervliet Arsenal.

Promoted to 1st lieutenant Jan. 1861, Strong began his war career as chief of ordnance in Brig. Gen. IRVIN MCDOWELL'S DEPARTMENT OF NORTHEASTERN VIRGINIA. Following service during the FIRST BULL RUN CAMPAIGN, he was briefly assistant ordnance chief to McDowell's successor,

LC

Maj. Gen. GEORGE B. MCCLELLAN. In Sept. 1861 Strong transferred to the staff of Maj. Gen. BENJAMIN F. BUTLER, whom he served as adjutant general, with the rank of major of volunteers. He helped organize and outfit Butler's expedition to New Orleans early the next year and while on duty in Louisiana became chief of staff to the Massachusetts political general.

In Louisiana, Strong was given assignments in field command. On 3–4 Apr. 1862, he led an expedition from Ship Island to Biloxi and Pass Christian, Miss., and 13 Sept. a force under his command destroyed enemy supply depots at Ponchatoula, La. His performance on these occasions indicated a fitness for higher rank; accordingly, he was appointed a brigadier general of volunteers 23 Mar. 1863, antedated to 29 Nov. of the previous year.

In spring 1863 the new general was sent to Charleston Harbor, S.C., as a subordinate to Maj. Gen. QUINCY A. GILLMORE, commander of the DEPARTMENT OF THE SOUTH. On 10 July Strong led a brigade of infantry up Folly River to Morris Island, below Charleston, covered by the fire of 47 cannon and mortars on Little Folly Island. Almost drowned on landing, he quickly led his brigade toward BATTERY WAGNER, the main Confederate work on Morris Island. His attack on the 11th, however, was beaten back with heavy loss. A second assault 7 days later, with Strong commanding one of 3 columns under the overall leadership of Brig. Gen. TRUMAN SEYMOUR, proved another bloody failure. Wounded in the thigh during this second effort, Strong contracted tetanus on his way to New York City for medical treatment. He died there 20 July, 1 day before the U.S. Senate confirmed his nomination as major general. —EGL

Stuart, James Ewell Brown. CSA b. "Laurel Hill," Patrick Cty., Va., Stuart received his primary education at home and later at Wytheville, Va. From 1848 to 1850 he attended Emory and Henry College, then entered the U.S. Military

Academy in 1850, graduating 13th in his class.

On graduation Stuart was appointed brevet 2d lieutenant in the Mounted Rifles. In October he received his commission and by December was assigned to Texas. Transferred to the 1st U.S. Cavalry Mar. 1853, he spent most of the next 6 years in Kansas on frontier duty. There, 14 Nov. 1855, he married Flora Cooke, the daughter of Col. (and future Union Maj. Gen.) PHILIP ST. GEORGE COOKE. He was promoted to 1st lieutenant 20 Dec.

USMHI

Stuart traveled east in summer 1859 to sell the War Department the rights to an invention of his, a device to hold a cavalry saber to the belt. During the visit Col. Robert E. Lee, superintendent at West Point during Stuart's studies at the academy, requested him as his aide when Lee was ordered to Harpers Ferry to subdue abolitionist John Brown after his 1859 raid on the Federal arsenal at the town (see HARPERS FERRY, WESTERN VA., JOHN BROWN'S RAID ON).

Stuart returned to Kansas until Virginia seceded Apr. 1861. On 10 May he resigned his U.S. Army commission, having been promoted to captain just 3 weeks earlier, and on that day accepted a commission as lieutenant colonel in the Virginia infantry. On 24 May he became a colonel in the Confederate cavalry, organizing 300 men, the beginning of the 1st Virginia Cavalry, at Harpers Ferry. At FIRST BULL RUN he defended the Confederate left and led a charge that aided the Southern victory. His bravery and good timing resulted in his appointment as brigadier general 24 Sept. By the end of 1861 Stuart had built his cavalry into a highly trained, efficient fighting unit.

In the PENINSULA CAMPAIGN Stuart was assigned to scouting duty to discover whether Union forces occupied the watershed area between the Chickahominy and Totopotomoy rivers. Once he had learned that Maj. Gen. George B. McClellan's forces were not occupying the area, his mission was complete, but rather than return to camp he rode around the entire Union line (see STUART'S RIDE AROUND MCCLELLAN).

Stuart commanded an enlarged force during the SEVEN DAYS' CAMPAIGN, pursuing McClellan as the latter was abandoning his position. Advancing to MALVERN HILL, Stuart positioned his men on Evelington Heights, which overlooked the Federal troops encamped at Harrison's Landing. He impetuously threw away his advantage by opening fire with his 1 howitzer, alerting the Federals to his presence. Federal Brig. Gen. WILLIAM B. FRANKLIN ordered his troops to safety, denying the Confederates victory. This event did not interfere with Stuart's promotion to major general 25 July 1862.

Immediately prior to SECOND BULL RUN Stuart was given command of all the cavalry in the Army of Northern Virginia. During the campaigning he raided Maj. Gen. John Pope's headquarters at CATLETT'S STATION, covered Maj. Gen. Thomas J. "Stonewall" Jackson's movements to Bristoe Station and Manassas Junction, and aided him at GROVETON. Throughout the Bull Run and ANTIETAM campaigns Stuart turned in superior performances, winning praise from General Lee. When Lee returned to Virginia at the end of his invasion of Maryland, Stuart moved north to Chambersburg with 1,800 men and 4

guns, attempting unsuccessfully to destroy an iron bridge over the Conococheague Creek (see CHAMBERSBURG, PA., RAID, STUART'S).

Stuart served creditably at FREDERICKSBURG, directing the artillery on the Confederate right. His men held the line along the Rappahannock River during the winter of 1862–63 and gave Lee timely information on Maj. Gen. Joseph Hooker's crossing of the river at the beginning of the CHANCELLORSVILLE CAMPAIGN. He held firm against Brig. Gen. George Stoneman's raiders (see STONEMAN'S RAID, CHANCELLORSVILLE CAMPAIGN), protected the path of Jackson's march, and temporarily but ably commanded the II Corps when Jackson was wounded and Maj. Gen. Ambrose P. Hill, also wounded, was unable to succeed him. On 9 June 1863, Stuart's cavalry engaged Maj. Gen. Alfred Pleasonton's cavalry at the Battle of BRANDY STATION, which, costly in lives and inconclusive, was the largest cavalry battle fought in America.

Lee planned to have Stuart hold the South Mountain passes later that month until the Confederate army moved through them on its northward march into Pennsylvania. Stuart was then to cross the Potomac River and make contact with Lt. Gen. Richard S. Ewell's army to gather advance information and obtain supplies. Stuart sought Lee's permission to cut off Federal forces moving out of Washington. Lee gave him a discretionary order allowing him to strike the Federals, assuming Stuart understood that the cavalry should be prepared to return to the defense of Ewell's flank whenever needed. But a heavy concentration of Union columns prevented Stuart from crossing the Potomac until 27–28 June, cutting him off from Ewell. Rather than make an effort to close the distance between his men and the infantry, Stuart followed his own plans, trusting that he could catch up with Ewell's men. After attacking some Federal supply and communications lines, he moved into Pennsylvania, to Dover, where he found no Federals, then to Carlisle, where 1 July he received urgent orders from Lee to go to GETTYSBURG. Arriving on the second day of the battle, Stuart had by his lateness deprived the Confederate army of support from the cavalry. (See GETTYSBURG, PA., RAID, STUART'S.)

For the remainder of his career he heeded the hard-learned lesson of Gettysburg and kept in close communication with the army, continuing his scouting activities. In spring 1864, when Lt. Gen. Ulysses S. Grant crossed the Rapidan River, Stuart was at his finest, bringing Lee valuable information on Federal movements.

On 9 May 1864, Maj. Gen. Philip H. Sheridan began moving from Spotsylvania to Richmond with 12,000 cavalrymen. Stuart mounted a force of 4,500 fatigued Confederate horsemen to oppose the Federal troops. Stuart's forces clashed with Sheridan's at YELLOW TAVERN 11 May. During the battle Stuart was mortally wounded by a dismounted Federal cavalryman. On 12 May 1864, the "Cavalier of Dixie" died, and was buried in Hollywood Cemetery, Richmond. On learning of his death, Lee, who considered Stuart the "eyes of the army," said of his trusted officer, "He never brought me a piece of false information." See also DUMFRIES, VA., RAID, STUART'S.   —JDK

Stuart's Ride Around McClellan. 12–16 June 1862 At 2 o'clock on the morning of 12 June 1862, Confederate Maj. Gen. J.E.B. STUART awakened his staff and announced cheerfully, "Gentlemen, in ten minutes every man must be in the saddle." That day Stuart's 1,200 cavalrymen rode 22 mi north from Richmond to the North Anna River. Before dawn the next day the troopers were again in their saddles, riding eastward toward the flank of Union Maj. Gen. GEORGE B. MCCLELLAN's army, which lay before Richmond.

The Confederates met little resistance as they rode past Hanover Court House and Haw's Shop. At Old Church Stuart knew that he might encounter his father-in-law, Federal Brig. Gen. PHILIP ST. GEORGE COOKE, who commanded rival cavalry, but Cooke was not present. Some of his troopers were, and there was a spirited clash. The Southerners prevailed, but Capt. William Latané, who led the charge, was killed.

At this point Stuart had fulfilled his mission: he knew that the Federal right flank was unsecured. Pondering the best way to return to Richmond and inform Gen. Robert E. Lee, he decided not to retrace his route but to continue the march completely around the Union army. Accordingly, he set out for Tunstall's Station, thence to Forge Bridge over the Chickahominy, where there were anxious moments while the men stopped to repair the span.

From the Chickahominy, Stuart pressed on alone. He clattered into Richmond from the south on the morning of 15 June; the rest of the column arrived the same day. The Confederate cavalrymen had ridden 100 mi around an army of more than 100,000 men and lost only 1 of their number. Stuart's ride gave Lee the information he required about the Federal flank and provided the Confederacy with a new hero. Stuart had lifted Southern spirits in an uncertain hour and had reinforced McClellan's natural caution.   —EMT

Sturgis, Samuel Davis. USA b. Shippensburg, Pa., 11 June 1822. Graduating 32d in the West Point class of 1846, Sturgis devoted 4 decades of service to the U.S. Army. Fighting in the Mexican War, he was captured near Buena Vista. During the 1850s he served on the frontier against Indians, rising in rank to captain. In command of FORT SMITH, Ark., when the Civil War began, Sturgis, refusing to surrender, extricated his men and much of the property to Fort Leavenworth, Kans.

LC

Promoted to major 3 May 1861, he fought at WILSON'S CREEK, Mo., 10 Aug., succeeding to command of the Union forces after the fall of Brig. Gen. Nathaniel Lyon. He then served as Brig. Gen. David Hunter's chief of staff. In Mar. 1862 he was promoted to brigadier general, to date from the engagement at Wilson's Creek. Transferred to Virginia, Sturgis briefly commanded a brigade in the defenses of Washington, D.C.

In Aug. 1862 the Pennsylvanian, now commanding a division, was ordered to join Maj. Gen. John Pope's Army of Virginia in preparation for SECOND BULL RUN. Delayed in boarding railroad cars by other troops also ordered to the front in

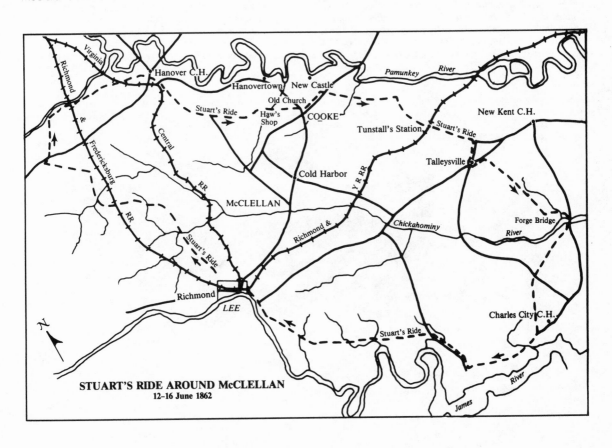

STUART'S RIDE AROUND McCLELLAN
12–16 June 1862

support of Pope, Sturgis made the famous observation "I don't care for John Pope one pinch of owl dung!" He subsequently led a division of the IX Corps at SOUTH MOUNTAIN, ANTIETAM, and FREDERICKSBURG.

In 1863 the IX Corps transferred to the Western theater, with Sturgis commanding a division in the Army of the Ohio. On 8 July he was made the army's chief of cavalry, serving until 15 Apr. 1864. At BRICE'S CROSS ROADS, Miss., 10 June, Sturgis' troopers were routed by Maj. Gen. Nathan B. Forrest's Confederate horsemen. A board investigated the decisive Union defeat, and Sturgis spent the remainder of the war "awaiting orders." He was nevertheless brevetted brigadier and major general, U.S. Army, Mar. 1865.

Mustering out of the volunteers in August, Sturgis stayed in the army, reverting to his Regular Army rank of lieutenant colonel. For the next 2 decades he again fought Indians in the West. Promoted to colonel in 1869, he commanded the 7th Cavalry for a time. He resigned in 1886, dying in St. Paul, Minn., 28 Sept. 1889.   —JDW

submarines. A few ingenious designers and private contractors in both the North and South produced several submersible torpedo boats during the war. These vessels were slow, difficult to maneuver, and extremely dangerous to their crews. Only 1, the *H. L. HUNLEY*, by becoming the first submarine to sink an enemy vessel in combat, can be credited with success.

In Nov. 1861 concern over the CSS *VIRGINIA (Merrimack)* prompted the U.S. Navy to contract for the building of a submarine, the USS *ALLIGATOR*. This boat, ready for use June 1862, was to be propelled underwater by manually operated oars. A special exit would allow divers to attach mines to the bottoms

of enemy vessels. After being brought to the James River, the *Alligator* was found to be unsuited for operating there and was returned North for alterations. The navy planned to use the vessel at Charleston, but it was lost in a gale while under tow 2 Apr. 1863. In Apr. 1864 the American Submarine Co. was formed, and building began on another submarine, the *Intelligent Whale*. The navy was impressed enough to purchase it, but the ship did not become operational until 1872.

The South also recognized the potential usefulness of this type of vessel. In 1861 a 2-man submarine was built at New Orleans and was commissioned the CSS *PIONEER* Mar. 1862. A torpedo carried on its top could be screwed into the bottom of an enemy ship. Although the *Pioneer* is believed to have destroyed a small craft and rafts during experiments on Lake Pontchartrain, it never faced a test in battle. After New Orleans was captured by the Federals, Apr. 1862, the ship was scuttled by the Confederates. An unnamed successor to the *Pioneer* (sometimes referred to as the "*Pioneer II*") was a 5-man submarine built at Mobile. In Feb. 1863 it was towed off FORT MORGAN for an attack on the Federal fleet, but foul weather and rough seas swamped it, without loss of life.

The *H.L. Hunley* was Horace L. Hunley's second attempt to build a submarine for the Confederacy. His ship was built at Mobile, then brought to Charleston. Manually operated by an 8-man crew, it was equipped with a barbed spike for ramming and armed with a spar torpedo that held 90 lb of gunpowder. 2 disastrous trial runs at Charleston caused Gen. P.G.T. BEAUREGARD to order no further diving. The ship then operated as a surface gunboat and ventured into Charleston harbor several times at night from its base at Sullivan's Island. Finally, on the night of 17 Feb. 1864, the *Hunley* rammed the USS *Housatonic*. However, the submarine and all those aboard were lost,

H. L. Hunley

either from the explosion or from being unable to disengage from the wooden adversary as it sank. Still another Confederate submarine, the 5-man *St. Patrick,* was built at Selma, Ala., and taken to Mobile late in 1864. On 28 Jan. 1865, it attacked the USS *Octorara,* but its spar torpedo failed to explode. The *St. Patrick* returned safely to Mobile, and there is no record of its being further engaged.   —NCD

substitutes. Draft evasion during the war flourished under the legalities of substitution. Theoretically, the system freed skilled labor and businessmen to develop crucial war industries and kept CONSCRIPTION to a minimum, but it bred opportunism and fraud that ended in scandal.

Under the system's provisions, a man subject to military service could avoid it by supplying an able-bodied replacement. Supply and demand determined fees for substitutes. Newspaper advertisements early in the war offered a few hundred dollars for a service-worthy male; the price jumped to several thousand in Richmond when the manpower shortage hit the Confederacy hard.

Professional substitute brokers quickly displaced bankers and dominated the trade; profit dictated the quality of men they produced. Some were physically defective. Many, attracted by money, lined their pockets with fees and bounties, then deserted to repeat the swindle elsewhere. Brokers also supplied forged papers to men buying substitutes, without providing the replacements.

Young boys, often war-struck runaways, were easy prey for brokers. Particularly in Northern port cities, kidnapping rings sought out foreigners: an amiable-looking gang member treated an immigrant or sailor to whiskey, knocked him unconscious, and the victim came to, wearing a uniform in some army camp on the Potomac. Enough sued for their release to raise public indignation and cause protest from foreign governments.

Enraged civilians complained that men who could afford substitutes turned into the worst offenders. In the South, healthy men out of uniform when the army needed them drew criticism, forcing an 1863 law making substitution illegal in the Confederacy.

Substitution devastated army morale. As the war dragged on, soldiers' resentment toward the system festered. Discouraged, bored when not in battle, soldiers saw profiteers making fortunes while they bled for $16 a month. To them, substitution was a biting confirmation that this was a rich man's war and a poor man's fight.   —PLF

Sullivan, Jeremiah Cutler. USA b. Madison, Ind., 1 Oct. 1830, Sullivan entered the U.S. Navy as a midshipman in 1848, serving on 4 different vessels before resigning 6 years later. The son of a justice of the Indiana supreme court, he studied law and practiced his profession until the outbreak of hostilities in 1861.

The attorney helped recruit and organize the 6th Indiana. Commissioned a captain, he fought with his unit at PHILIPPI, in western Virginia, 3 June. When his 3-month regiment mustered out, he became, 19 June, colonel of the 13th Indiana, leading his new command at CHEAT MOUNTAIN and RICH MOUNTAIN, Western Virginia, later that year. In spring 1862 the colonel commanded a brigade in the Shenandoah Valley, fighting with it at FIRST KERNSTOWN 23 Mar. He was then commissioned brigadier general to rank from 28 Apr.

In June Sullivan was sent to the West, assuming command of a brigade in the Army of the Mississippi. He fought at IUKA and CORINTH, Miss., before being appointed commander of the District of Jackson, Tenn. There his garrison forces unsuccessfully battled Brig. Gen. Nathan B. Forrest's Confederate cavalry. During the early phases of the VICKSBURG CAMPAIGN in 1863, Sullivan served as acting inspector general on the staff of Maj. Gen. ULYSSES S. GRANT. From July to September he was Maj. Gen. James B. McPherson's chief of staff.

In autumn 1863 Sullivan returned from the Western theater, serving under his father-in-law, Brig. Gen. BENJAMIN F. KELLEY, in Western Virginia. His division guarded the BALTIMORE & OHIO RAILROAD in western Maryland. As a result of his poor performance against Lt. Gen. Jubal A. Early's Confederate raiders, he was succeeded 16 July 1864 by Brig. Gen. George Crook. Sullivan held no important post for the remainder of the war, resigning his commission 11 May 1865.

After the war he resided in Maryland, moving in 1878 to California. He did not practice law but held a few minor clerical jobs. d. Oakland, Calif., 21 Oct. 1890.   —JDW

***Sultana* disaster.** 27 Apr. 1865 Perhaps the busiest spot along the Mississippi River 27 Apr. 1865, not quite 3 weeks after the end of the war, was Camp Fisk near Vicksburg, established for the general exchange of prisoners captured during the operations of the armies in the West.

Boats arrived one after another to transport the Union exchangees to the North. First to depart on the 27th was the *Henry Adams,* with about 1,300. Scheduled next was the *Olive Branch,* with 700, but it was mysteriously detained. Then came the *Sultana,* fresh from St. Louis and held up en route by boiler trouble. The *Pauline Carroll* was last.

The Federal government had established a set fee for the soldiers' passage: $5 for each enlisted man, $10 for each officer. Rumors soon spread that some of the boat owners, eager to make the largest profit possible, were offering bribes to increase the number of parolees assigned to their boats. Developments were indeed puzzling. Rolls for only 300 had been prepared for the *Sultana,* and its captain complained that proper steps were not being taken to get the men aboard.

As the day wore on, men came onto the *Sultana* in 3 batches. When the ship left, it had on board 1,866 troops, 75 cabin passengers, 85 crew members, 60 horses and mules, and more than 100 hogs. It was almost impossible to move about. Cooking was done either with hot water taken from the boilers or at a small stove on the main deck.

Shortly after 3 a.m., when the *Sultana* was about 90 mi from Memphis, its boilers exploded. About one-third of those on board were lost. The exact cause of the trouble was never determined. Possible reasons cited were water shortage in the boilers, perhaps due to the demands placed upon them by cooking; faulty metal used in repairing the boilers; and overloading of the ship.

Blame for the overloading was placed on Capt. Frederic

U.S.S. Sultana

LC

Speed, who had been in charge of transferring the paroled prisoners from Camp Fisk. He was dismissed from the service after a trial that lasted nearly 5 months. —VCJ

Sumner, Charles. USP b. Boston, Mass., 6 Jan. 1811. Graduated from Harvard Law School in 1833 and admitted to the bar the next year, Sumner worked as a reporter for the U.S. circuit court and lectured at Harvard 1835–37. He then traveled abroad for several years, learning much about European governments and making many prestigious friends in high political circles. Returning to Boston in 1840, he practiced law and developed into a forceful antislavery lecturer given to arguing his principles to the extreme.

USMHI

Sumner opposed the annexation of Texas and the COMPROMISE OF 1850 as schemes by Southern politicians to spread slavery into the territories. After his election to the U.S. Senate in 1851 by a coalition of Free-Soilers and Democrats, he tried unsuccessfully to have those funds allotted to enforce the FUGITIVE SLAVE ACT removed from an impending appropriations bill. In 1854 he opposed the KANSAS-NEBRASKA ACT and condemned

POPULAR SOVEREIGNTY as deceiving the American public. In his "The Crime Against Kansas" speech, delivered 19–20 May 1856, he denounced the act as a swindle, spoke critically of several prominent congressmen, and accused Sen. STEPHEN A. DOUGLAS of selling out the country to slaveowners. The inflammatory harangue infuriated South Carolina Sen. Preston S. Brooks into caning Sumner senseless on the Senate floor. Indignation over the beating strengthened Northern public opinion against slavery, and Sumner was returned to the Senate as a Republican in 1857.

After ABRAHAM LINCOLN's election to the presidency Nov. 1860, Sumner refused to support any compromise measures to appease disunionist Southerners. Once hostilities began, he urged the president to adopt emancipation as a war measure. Though Lincoln would not be rushed into abolishing slavery, he appointed Sumner chairman of the Senate Foreign Relations Committee and heeded his advice by releasing Confederate diplomats JOHN SLIDELL and JAMES M. MASON to avert war with England over the *TRENT* AFFAIR.

By Feb. 1862 Sumner, a leading RADICAL REPUBLICAN, was advancing his theory of "Southern suicide," in which he argued that, by seceding, the Southern states had abdicated their constitutional rights under statehood. He opposed Lincoln's mild terms for restoring the South to the Union, insisting on Congress's right to control RECONSTRUCTION. In addition to his goal of legislating equal rights for freedmen, Sumner agitated for free schools for blacks and was prominent among those Radicals calling for the permanent confiscation of Confederate estates in occupied territory for distribution to former slaves. At his insistence readmission to the Union was made contingent on equal-suffrage clauses written into the new constitutions submitted by the former Confederate states for approval by Congress.

Sumner's harsh stance toward the South softened when he toured the devastated region shortly after the war, and he exerted a moderating influence on some of the more severe retaliatory measures proposed by his Radical colleagues. He nonetheless led the Radicals in pressing impeachment proceedings against ANDREW JOHNSON May 1868 and was embittered when the Senate failed to remove him from office. After being reelected again in 1869, he came into conflict with Pres. ULYSSES S. GRANT and Sec. of State Hamilton Fish over his extreme views on the ALABAMA CLAIMS, and the president removed him from the chairmanship of the Foreign Relations Committee.

Sumner's health, erratic for many years, deteriorated sharply after the war. On 10 Mar. 1874, before the civil rights act for which he had been working tirelessly was passed, he suffered a heart attack in the Senate chamber, dying the next day. His body lay in state in the Capitol rotunda for several days before being returned to Cambridge, Mass., for burial.   —PLF

Sumner, Edwin Vose.
USA b. Boston, Mass., 30 Jan. 1797, Sumner was the oldest active corps commander serving in the Civil War. When war began, the 64-year-old was a veteran of 42 years of military service. Intensely patriotic and courageous, he was also said to lack imagination.

In 1819, at age 22, he was commissioned a 2d lieutenant in the Regular Army's 2d Infantry and promoted to 1st lieutenant in 1823 and captain of the 1st Dragoons (later the 1st Cavalry) in 1833. He saw service on the frontier until the start of the Mexican War, when he moved up to major of the 2d Dragoons and joined Gen. WINFIELD SCOTT's army.

USMHI

Sumner was wounded at Cerro Gordo and brevetted there and at Molino del Rey to lieutenant colonel of the 1st Dragoons and colonel of the 1st Cavalry, respectively. He also served as acting governor of New Mexico Territory. He then commanded Fort Leavenworth in 1856, campaigned against the Cheyennes in 1857, and assumed command of the Department of the West in 1858. In 1861 Colonel Sumner was selected by Scott to accompany president-elect Abraham Lincoln from Springfield to Washington, D.C. On 16 Mar. 1861, he was appointed brigadier general.

During the PENINSULA CAMPAIGN Sumner commanded the II Corps, as he did at SOUTH MOUNTAIN and at ANTIETAM. Maj. Gen. George B. McClellan praised his gallantry, judgment, and energy at the Battle of SEVEN PINES. As a major general, to rank from 5 July 1862, he commanded the Right Grand Division at the Battle of FREDERICKSBURG.

Following the battle of Antietam Sumner was criticized for committing his men to battle one division at a time and for leading his main division "like a colonel of cavalry" instead of handling his entire army from a more strategic rear position. Upset by the criticism and exhausted physically, Sumner asked to be relieved from duty. He was assigned to the Department of Missouri but fell ill of pneumonia on his way west and died in Syracuse, N.Y., 21 Mar. 1863. On his deathbed he drank a toast to the U.S.   —AG

Sumter, CSS.
At the start of the war, the South found it difficult to obtain ships with which to build a navy. One the Confederates managed to buy was the screw steamer *Habana,* running regularly between Havana, Cuba, and New Orleans. The purchase was made on the recommendation of RAPHAEL SEMMES, a former U.S. Navy lieutenant who had fought in the Mexican War.

On 18 Apr. Semmes was assigned to command the 520-ton vessel and immediately set to work at New Orleans to convert it into a sloop of war, fitting it with 5 guns and large sails. The ship's name was changed to *Sumter,* after the first fort to fall into Confederate hands. By mid-June, it was ready for sea. Semmes watched his opportunity and, 30 June, managed to run through Pass à l'Outre to the Gulf of Mexico, eluding the USS *Brooklyn,* on BLOCKADE at the mouth of the Mississippi River.

Semmes's instructions were "to do the enemy's commerce the greatest injury in the shortest time." On 3 July, off the Cuban coast, he made his first capture, a bark from Maine. In the next few days, he captured 5 more vessels and took them into Cienfuegos, Cuba, but Spain would not permit him to leave them there.

He next sailed for Martinique, taking more prizes along the way. There he was blockaded by the USS *Iroquois,* stationed outside the 3-mi limit. Suspecting that the Federal captain was communicating with contacts on shore, he ran southward until he saw signal lights warning of his departure, then abruptly reversed his course.

By 4 Jan. 1862, he was at Cádiz, Spain, but was ordered away before he could make necessary repairs to the boilers of his ship. He went on to Gibraltar, where he was blockaded by 3 Union ships. Unable to obtain coal, he finally paid off his crew.

The *Sumter* was sold to a British buyer for $19,500. Its career had lasted 6 months, during which time it made 18 captures, some of which were burned and the remainder released or bonded. Semmes later improved that record as commander of the CSS ALABAMA.   —VCJ

supply.
Supply involves not only the procurement of everything an army or a navy requires in food, clothing, equipment, ordnance, and ordnance stores, but also its distribution to the forces, wherever they may be. During the Civil War, the North and South differed widely in both aspects of supply. The North was strong in both industry and agriculture, with the capacity to supply practically all its military needs; the South, on the other hand, although its agricultural capacity was adequate, was woefully lacking industrially, especially in vitally needed iron works and machine shops. Moreover, the North's rail system was immensely superior, and the gap widened as the war went on; Confederate armies were often on semistarvation rations when their worn-out railroads could not deliver the food supplies that were available. And the South had no SUTLERS' stores.

Pennsylvania-born JOSIAH GORGAS' Confederate Ordnance

Bureau, after a slow start, was functioning efficiently by 1863, but by then the Southern armies' situation was aggravated by the inefficiency of their "peevish, obstinate, condescending, and fault-finding" commissary general of subsistence, LUCIUS B. NORTHROP. His Northern counterpart, Q.M. Gen. MONTGOMERY C. MEIGS, organized a system so efficient that Union forces were usually well supplied.

Both sides sought supplies in Europe, the South more extensively than the North. Capt. JAMES D. BULLOCH, as the Confederate navy's civilian agent, secured and outfitted, among other ships, the raiders *ALABAMA, FLORIDA, STONEWALL,* and *SHENANDOAH.* Massachusetts-born Maj. CALEB HUSE was a highly successful purchaser of European equipment and ordnance, shipped across the Atlantic in BLOCKADE RUNNERS.

In the end, the crucial factor was the availability of supplies when and where they were needed, and here the Union's miles-long, mule-drawn wagon trains and HERMAN HAUPT'S U.S. Military Railroad far outclassed the South's patched-up wagon transport and broken-down railroads.   —RDH

Supreme Court, Confederate States. Article III of the Provisional CONFEDERATE CONSTITUTION, passed in Montgomery, Ala., 16 Mar. 1861, provided for the establishment of a supreme court identical to the one that existed under the old Union. Through Jan. 1863 the representatives engaged in heated debates over the extent of authority the Supreme Court should be permitted to hold over state courts. Georgia Sen. BENJAMIN H. HILL stressed the danger to national stability if each state was permitted to interpret Federal laws as it chose without a supreme court to ensure the uniform application of congressional legislation. The opposition, led by Sen. WILLIAM L. YANCEY, argued for the repeal of those sections of Article III that would give the Supreme Court appellate jurisdiction over state courts.

At the heart of the disagreement lay the issue of STATES RIGHTS. Most of the legislators blamed the U.S. Supreme Court for undermining state sovereignty through its antebellum rulings; many also believed that both the Confederate and the U.S. constitutions reserved appellate jurisdiction for the states because it was not specifically granted to the Federal judiciary.

The Senate passed an amendment denying the Supreme Court authority to rule on appeals, but the House of Representatives voted against it, and the issue was dropped after Jan. 1863. No enabling act to organize a supreme court was ever passed. For the duration of the war, the Confederacy prosecuted its cases in state courts, which enjoyed greater respect and less distrust than the central government.   —PLF

Supreme Court, United States. While Americans grappled with the military, economic, and social problems engendered by the Civil War, questions about the conflict's very nature, its legality, and its prosecution arose. What were the war powers of the Union government? What was the status of the rebellious Southerners? What were the Constitutional rights of these Northerners who opposed the Federal administration? What were the Constitutional limitations on the president of the U.S. and his powers?

The answers to these legal questions ultimately had to be confronted by the U.S. Supreme Court, which rendered significant decisions during the war and the years immediately after, defining the most difficult Constitutional questions. For instance, it compiled an admirable record in defending civil

liberties. It could not, however, when confronting the military, enforce its decrees.

Chief Justice ROGER B. TANEY, 84 years old in 1861, scion of an old Maryland family, presided over the Court until his death, 12 Oct. 1864. Pres. ABRAHAM LINCOLN then nominated SALMON P. CHASE, former secretary of the treasury, to replace Taney. Lincoln also placed 4 associate justices on the Court—Noah H. Swayne, Samuel F. Miller, his old friend David Davis, and Stephen J. Field. This final appointment, made in 1863, expanded the court to 10 members, with a strongly pro-Union bent.

Under Taney, the Court wrestled with many timely issues. In *Miller v. U.S.,* it gave an orthodox opinion concerning the legal status of the rebellious Southerners. The justices declared that the U.S. possessed toward the Southerners "the double character of a belligerent and a sovereign, and had the rights of both." In theory the Confederates were traitors, but throughout the conflict they enjoyed belligerent rights accorded a recognized government conducting a war.

The Court's gravest Constitutional questions dealt with the civil rights and the wartime powers of the president. Lincoln probably carried presidential power, independently of Congress, further than any chief executive in the nation's history. From 15 Apr. 1861 until 13 July 1861, when Congress convened, Lincoln committed the government to a definite theory of the nature of the conflict. Without a declaration of war, he prosecuted it as a regular war between 2 independent nations. His expansive view of his own war powers led to the suspension of the writ of *HABEAS CORPUS* and the eventual imprisonment, without trial, of more than 13,000 persons. He also sanctioned the trial of civilians before military tribunals.

The Supreme Court supported Lincoln's action in the war's initial months in the so-called Prize Cases of 1863. The defendants argued that the seizure of certain ships for violation of the BLOCKADE proclamations were illegal. Lincoln had acted, they argued, without authority in the absence of a Congressional declaration. In a 5-to-4 decision the Court upheld Lincoln's measures, declaring that a domestic war may begin without a declaration, and the president was empowered to confront it. The 4 dissenting members, including Taney, argued that an insurrection was not tantamount to the initiation of a legal state of war and Lincoln had overreached his authority.

The problem of civil rights of citizens was never resolved during the war. In *Ex parte Merryman,* 1861, the Court declared Maj. Gen. George Cadwalader in contempt for not producing a prisoner for trial when directed to do so. Cadwalader, however, went unpunished, and the unfortunate prisoner remained incarcerated. Finally, in 1866, in *Ex parte Milligan,* the Court, under Chase, in a ringing proclamation, declared illegal the military trials of civilians in areas where regular courts were functioning. This affirmation has become famous as one of the bulwarks of civil liberties in America. The *Milligan* decision was a fitting conclusion to the record of the Supreme Court during the Civil War.   —JDW

Surratt, John Harrison. b. Prince George's Cty., Md., 13 Apr. 1844. The son of John H. Surratt and MARY ELIZABETH JENKINS SURRATT, John Harrison Surratt attended the St. Charles College Catholic seminary school in Howard Cty., Md., 5 Sept. 1859–autumn 1862. Assuming his late father's duties as postmaster and innkeeper at the family tavern in September, in what is now Clinton, Md., he associated with Confederate sympathizers. Authorities removed him from his postmaster's appointment 17 Nov. 1863 for what Surratt claimed were accusations of disloyalty.

In 1862, long before his removal as postmaster, Surratt had become a courier for the Confederate government, operating in southern Maryland and the national capital. As an agent his movements are impossible to document, but he was known to have later made several trips to Canada and New York State on Confederate business.

On 23 Dec. 1864, in front of the National Hotel in Washington, he was introduced to actor JOHN WILKES BOOTH, fomenter of the Lincoln kidnap plot and future assassin of ABRAHAM LINCOLN. Recommended to Booth as a reliable man by Thomas H. Harbin of Maryland, Surratt in turn enlisted in Booth's schemes pharmacist David E. Herold. Surratt's part in the kidnap plot was minimal. He traveled for Booth and arranged Confederate connections for him. At the time of Lincoln's murder he was in the Elmira, N.Y., area, recently returned from a courier assignment in Canada and a meeting with Confederate commissioner JACOB THOMPSON and Brig. Gen. EDWIN G. LEE. As "John Harrison," an alias he used frequently, he registered in a Canandaigua, N.Y., hotel 15 Apr. 1865. But his associations with Booth and other plotters implicated his mother, a Washington, D.C., boardinghouse owner whose home had sometimes served as a rendezvous for the conspirators. In the manhunt following LINCOLN'S ASSASSINATION, she was arrested, tried, and hanged.

Wanted by the Federal government, Surratt hid with a Canadian priest until smuggled from Canada 16 Sept. on a ship bound for Britain. Recognized there, he escaped to Italy, enlisted in the Papal Zouaves, a Vatican regiment, under the alias "Watson." After Surratt fought in the Italian wars, opposing Giuseppe Garibaldi, an informer told his story to Pope Pius IX, who directed his arrest. Surratt escaped prison in Italy while awaiting extradition and arrived in Alexandria, Egypt, 23 Nov. 1866. Rearrested there 27 Nov., he was extradited to the U.S., to be tried 10 June 1867. After a 62-day trial he was acquitted of having taken an active part in Lincoln's assasination.

Settling in Baltimore, Md., in 1872 Surratt married, then took employment with the Old Bay Line, a Chesapeake Bay waterborne freight company. He retired Aug. 1915 and died in Baltimore, 2 Apr. 1916.   —JES

Surratt, Mary Elizabeth Jenkins. b. Prince George's Cty., Md., 1823. The daughter of Maryland farmer Archibald Jenkins, Mary attended St. Mary's Church school in Alexandria, Va., in the 1830s, accepted the Catholic faith under the Sisters of Charity, and received a marriage license 6 Aug. 1840 for her wedding to John H. Surratt, also of Prince George's County. The dates of her birth and wedding are unknown, but Surratt scholar James O. Hall believes she was born May 1823.

Mary Surratt lived on her husband's Maryland acreage through the early 1860s, bore 3 children—Isaac Douglas Surratt, Elizabeth Susanna Surratt, and JOHN HARRISON SURRATT—and helped tend a tavern erected by her husband in 1852 in what is today Clinton, Md. The tavern and post office within it were called Surrattsville. Mary's husband, deeply in debt, died Aug. 1862. Unable to meet financial obligations, in autumn 1864 she relocated to her sole debt-free property, purchased in 1853, 541 H St., Washington, D.C., and opened a boardinghouse. Her son John (a Confederate courier), actor JOHN WILKES BOOTH, some ladies of doubtful virtue, and several

Southern sympathizers frequented the H St. home. Following the assassination of ABRAHAM LINCOLN, her boardinghouse and former tavern were searched, several boarders arrested, and she was taken into Federal custody 17 Apr. 1865, charged with complicity in the murder of the president.

Convicted by a military court and condemned to death, she appealed for clemency. Her appeals were denied, and she was hanged at the Old Capitol Prison, Washington, D.C., 7 July 1865, the first woman ever executed by the Federal government. She is now widely believed to have been an innocent convicted by association and circumstantial evidence. Her Maryland tavern and memory are preserved by the Surratt Society.   —JES

surrender, terms of. Many of the surrenders of Civil War troops, posts, and positions took place under terms worked out in advance under a flag of truce, a gesture of chivalry to which Victorian-era generals paid homage. One frequently imposed condition was that the surrendered personnel would receive PAROLES and be sent home to await exchange, rather than be held in prison camps. Less frequently, commanders were unwilling to surrender unless they received proof that the opposing forces outnumbered their own. In at least one case, the leader of a surrounded force declined to capitulate unless advised to do so by an opponent whose judgment and integrity he respected.

Generals who held overwhelmingly superior positions usually refused to negotiate surrender terms under a flag of truce, during which time the enemy might reconsolidate his position or regroup to offer further resistance. One such leader was Brig. Gen. ULYSSES S. GRANT, who on 16 Feb. 1862 spurned a request for an armistice by the commander of FORT DONELSON; Grant refused to consider anything except "unconditional and immediate surrender." Though his adversary considered the ultimatum "ungenerous and unchivalrous," it made "Unconditional Surrender" Grant a household name throughout the North.   —EGL

surrenders.

Gen. Robert E. Lee

9 Apr. 1865   Having arranged a truce and sent notes to Lt. Gen. ULYSSES S. GRANT requesting a meeting, Confederate Gen. ROBERT E. LEE awaited his response. Shortly after noon, 9 Apr. 1865, Grant's reply came and Lee rode into the village of Appomattox to prepare for Grant's arrival. Lee's aide selected the home of WILMER MCLEAN. Lee waited in the parlor.

At about 1:30 p.m. Grant arrived with his staff. The 2 generals exchanged greetings and small talk, then Lee brought up the object of the meeting. Grant wrote out the surrender terms himself in an order book and handed it to Lee to read.

The terms, proposed in an exchange of notes the previous day, were honorable: Surrendered officers and their troops were to be paroled and prohibited from taking up arms until properly exchanged, and arms and supplies were to be given over as captured property. After Lee had read the terms and added an omitted word, he ordered his aide to write a letter of acceptance. This done, at about 3:45 p.m. the generals exchanged documents.

Riding back to his lines, Lee was swarmed by his adoring troops, many nearly hysterical with grief. Trying to soothe them with quiet phrases—"You have done all your duty. Leave the results to God . . ."—he rode slowly on, followed by many who wept and implored him to say that they should fight on. The next day he issued his eloquent farewell to his army (see LEE'S FAREWELL TO THE ARMY OF NORTHERN VIRGINIA).

On the morning of 11 Apr., following a spartan breakfast and tearful good-byes from his staff, the general mounted his warhorse, Traveler, and with a Union honor guard left Appomattox for home. —EMT

Gen. Joseph E. Johnston

26 Apr. 1865   Following its strategic defeat at BENTONVILLE, N.C., 21 Mar. 1865, the Confederate army of Gen. JOSEPH E. JOHNSTON was reduced to perhaps 30,000 effectives, less than half the size of Union Maj. Gen. WILLIAM T. SHERMAN's Federal command. Though the Confederates had fought well at Bentonville, their leader had no illusions about stopping his adversary's inexorable march through North Carolina. When Maj. Gen. JOHN M. SCHOFIELD's force, joining Sherman at Goldsborough 24 Mar., swelled the Union ranks to 80,000, Johnston saw the end approaching. Dutifully, however, he followed Sherman's resumed march northward 10 Apr. En route the Confederate commander learned of the evacuation of Petersburg and Richmond and of Gen. ROBERT E. LEE'S SURRENDER at Appomattox. This ended his long-held hope of joining Lee to oppose the invaders of the Carolinas.

Arriving near Raleigh, Johnston at first attempted to have North Carolina Gov. ZEBULON B. VANCE broach surrender terms to Sherman. On 12 Apr. Johnston went to Greensborough to meet with fugitive Confederate Pres. JEFFERSON DAVIS, whom he persuaded to authorize a peace initiative. Sherman was immediately receptive to peace negotiations, and on the 17th, under a flag of truce near Durham Station, met General Johnston for the first time "although we had been interchanging shots constantly since May, 1863."

The 2-day conference at the James Bennett home produced peace terms acceptable to both generals. But since these intruded on matters of civil policy (for example, recognition of the existing Southern state governments), officials in Washington quickly rejected the agreement and criticized Sherman's imprudence (see SHERMAN'S PEACE PROPOSALS).

Disappointed, the Federal leader informed Johnston that unless more widely acceptable terms were reached, a 4-day armistice would end on the 26th. That day, however, the war-weary commanders met again at the Bennett home and thrashed out an agreement confined to military matters. At once Gen.-in-Chief ULYSSES S. GRANT wired his approval, and 3 May Johnston's once-proud army laid down its arms, closing hostilities east of the Mississippi River. —EGL

Lt. Gen. Richard Taylor

4 May 1865   At the war's end Confederate Lt. Gen. RICHARD TAYLOR, son of former U.S. president Zachary Taylor, held command of the administrative entity called the Department of Alabama, Mississippi, and East Louisiana, with some 12,000 troops.

By the end of Apr. 1865 Mobile, Ala., had fallen and news had reached Taylor of the meetings between Gen. Joseph E. Johnston and Maj. Gen. William T. Sherman. Taylor agreed to meet Maj. Gen. E.R.S. CANBY for a conference a few miles north of Mobile. On 30 Apr. the 2 officers established a truce, terminable after 48 hours' notice by either party, then partook of a "bountiful luncheon . . . with joyous poppings of champagne

corks . . . the first agreeable explosive sounds," Taylor wrote, "I had heard for years." A band played "Hail Columbia" and a few bars of "Dixie."

The party separated: Canby went to Mobile and Taylor to his headquarters at Meridian, Miss. 2 days later Taylor received news of Johnston's surrender, of Pres. JEFFERSON DAVIS' capture, and of Canby's insistence that the truce terminate. Taylor elected to surrender, which he did 4 May 1865 at Citronelle, Ala., some 40 mi north of Mobile. "At the time, no doubts as to the propriety of my course entered my mind," Taylor later asserted, "but such have since crept in." He grew to regret not having tried a last-ditch guerrilla struggle.

Under the terms, officers retained their sidearms, mounted men their horses. All property and equipment was to be turned over to the Federals, but receipts were issued. The men were paroled. Taylor retained control of the railways and river steamers to transport the troops as near as possible to their homes. He stayed with several staff officers at Meridian until the last man was gone, then went to Mobile, joining Canby, who took Taylor by boat to the latter's home in New Orleans. —HH

Lt. Gen. E. Kirby Smith

26 May 1865   From 1862 until the war's end Confederate Lt. Gen. E. KIRBY SMITH commanded the Trans-Mississippi Department. By early May 1865 no regular Confederate forces remained east of the Mississippi River. Smith received official proposals that the surrender of his department be negotiated.

The Federals intimated that terms could be loose, but Smith's demands were unrealistic. Smith then began planning to continue the fight. Lt. Gen. U. S. Grant took preliminary steps to prepare a force to invade West Texas should that prove necessary. It did not.

The war's last land fight occurred 12–13 May at PALMITO RANCH, where 350 Confederates under Col. John S. "Rest in Peace" Ford scored a victory over 800 overconfident Federals under Col. Theodore H. Barrett. But afterward the Confederates learned that Richmond had fallen and Gen. Robert E. Lee had surrendered more than a month earlier. The news devastated their morale, and they abandoned their lines.

A similar decay in morale occurred all over the department. On 18 May Smith left by stagecoach for Houston with plans to rally the remnants of the department's troops. While he traveled, the last of the department's army dissolved. On 26 May, at New Orleans, Lt. Gen. Simon B. Buckner, acting in Smith's name, surrendered the department. Smith reached Houston 27 May and learned that he had no troops.

Not all of the Trans-Mississippi Confederates went home. Some 2,000 fled into Mexico; most of them went alone or in squad-sized groups, but 1 body numbered 300. With them, mounted on a mule, wearing a calico shirt and silk kerchief, sporting a revolver strapped to his hip and a shotgun on his saddle, was Smith. —HH

Brig. Gen. Stand Watie

23 June 1865   When the leaders of the CONFEDERATE INDIANS learned that the government in Richmond had fallen and the Eastern armies had been surrendered, they, too, began making their plans to seek peace with the Federal government. The chiefs convened the Grand Council 15 June and passed resolutions calling for Indian commanders to lay down their

arms and for emissaries to approach Federal authorities for peace terms.

The largest force in Indian Territory was commanded by Confederate Brig. Gen. STAND WATIE, who was also a chief of the Cherokee Nation. Dedicated to the Confederate cause and unwilling to admit defeat, he kept his troops in the field for nearly a month after Lt. Gen. E. KIRBY SMITH surrendered the Trans-Mississippi 26 May. Finally accepting the futility of continued resistance, on 23 June Watie rode into Doaksville near Fort Towson in Indian Territory and surrendered his battalion of Creek, Seminole, Cherokee, and Osage Indians to Lt. Col. Asa C. Matthews, appointed a few weeks earlier to negotiate a peace with the Indians. Watie was the last Confederate general officer to surrender his command.   —PLF

Susquehanna, Union Department of the. Alarmed by the northward movement of Confederate Maj. Gen. J.E.B. STUART's cavalry and expecting an invasion of Pennsylvania by the ARMY OF NORTHERN VIRGINIA, Union Sec. of War EDWIN M. STANTON issued orders 9 June 1863 dividing the state into 2 military departments. On 10 June he issued General Orders No. 172, creating the Union Military Department of the Susquehanna and naming Maj. Gen. DARIUS N. COUCH its commander. The department constituted all Pennsylvania east of Johnstown and the Laurel Mts., with its headquarters at Chambersburg, southwest of Harrisburg and Carlisle. Couch accepted command 11 June and issued orders for the organization of a corps of volunteers for state defense. A number of companies were raised, most serving only 100 days.

After the Gettysburg crisis passed, the department assumed a more administrative nature. On 4 Apr. 1864, the Department of the Susquehanna expanded to embrace the short-lived western Pennsylvania DEPARTMENT OF THE MONONGAHELA and that department's responsibility for Ohio and West Virginia counties on Pennsylvania's southwest border. With Couch retaining command, on 1 Dec. 1864 this organization was dissolved and the DEPARTMENT OF PENNSYLVANIA re-created, its headquarters at Philadelphia.   —JES

Sutherland's Station, Va., eng. at. 2 Apr. 1865 The Union Army of the Potomac launched a massive assault at 4:30 a.m., 2 Apr. 1865, on the Confederate earthworks west of Petersburg, Va. For 10 months the Army of Northern Virginia had repulsed the Federals, but not on this day. 4 Union corps advanced against the thinly held Southern entrenchments, with the VI Corps making the decisive breakthrough. The Confederate line began to unhinge, and from Hatcher's Run to the Boydton Plank Road, the Northerners gained the works.

Gen. ROBERT E. LEE, with his front crushed, issued orders for an evacuation of Petersburg, but he needed time to regroup and undertake the retreat. At FORT GREGG, 500 Confederate defenders ferociously repulsed Federal attacks, giving Lee time to erect an inner line to protect the army's rear. The Federal assault stalled after the bloody capture of the fort.

To the west, along the Southside Railroad, toward Five Forks, Union Maj. Gen. ANDREW A. HUMPHREYS' II Corps seized the Crow salient and pursued up the Clairborne road. While the battle raged around Fort Gregg, Maj. Gen. NELSON A. MILES's division of Humphreys' corps moved on Sutherland's

Sutlers

Station, where Maj. Gen. HENRY HETH's Confederate division had regrouped. Gen.-in-Chief ULYSSES S. GRANT, directing the operations, had specifically ordered only Miles to press Humphreys' breakthrough.

Miles charged Heth about 3 p.m. The Confederates buckled under the assault, then broke. The oncoming Federals captured nearly 1,000 prisoners and 2 cannon. Grant delayed the final attack on the fort while he awaited the outcome of Miles's operation, apparently exaggerating the importance of this minor engagement. The defense of Fort Gregg and Grant's hesitation permitted Lee to evacuate his army that night.

—JDW

sutlers. A common sight in the camps of Civil War soldiers was a string of huts or tents bulging with various items for sale. These business establishments belonged to sutlers, civilians officially appointed to supply soldiers with a long list of approved items. In both the Union and Confederate armies each regiment was allowed 1 sutler. From these camp vendors a soldier could purchase such items as food, newspapers, books, tobacco, razors, tin plates, cups, cutlery, and illegal alcohol—all at prescribed prices.

As the war progressed, sutlers virtually monopolized the soldiers' business. The veterans either bought from sutlers or went without. These shrewd businessmen inevitably profited from the arrangement, extending credit and inflating prices. Soldiers frequently complained of being cheated and, often, a group of infuriated troops would raid a sutler's tent and clean him out. A Union veteran stated the accepted view of these civilians when he said that "these gentlemen sutlers skin the soldiers unmercifully." —JDW

"Swamp Angel." On 2 Aug. 1863, following his engineers' thorough study of the marshes on Morris Island, at the entrance to Charleston harbor, Union Maj. Gen. QUINCY A. GILL-MORE ordered the construction of a battery in the swampy

USMHI

earth. When the platform and parapet were completed, the troops dragged an 8-in., 200-pounder Parrott rifle across the marshes and mounted it under heavy fire from Confederate

artillery on James Island. The men promptly named the battery "Swamp Angel."

Artillerists trained the gun on Charleston, 7,900 yd across the harbor. At 1:30 a.m., 22 Aug., the first shot was fired into the city and was quickly followed by 15 more. The next day the Federals resumed the barrage, firing 20 additional shells toward Charleston. On the last shot the force of the discharge disabled the Parrott, and the gun crew withdrew. Of the 36 shells fired, 12 had been manufactured by the inventor of the Parrott rifle, Robert P. Parrott, at the West Point Foundry at Cold Spring, N.Y. The others had been filled with GREEK FIRE, an unstable combustible noted for exploding prematurely.

The Swamp Angel was purchased as scrap metal after the war and shipped to Trenton, N.J. Before the gun could be melted down, someone identified it; city officials decided to mount the barrel atop a granite monument, where it stands today. —PLF

Sweeny, Thomas William. USA b. Cty. Cork, Ireland, 25 Dec. 1820. At age 12 Sweeny followed his widowed mother to America, eventually settling in New York City. There he worked for a law publisher and about 1843 joined a militia company known as the Baxter Blues. This unit fought in the Mexican War as Company A/2d New York Volunteers, with Sweeny its 2d lieutenant. At Churubusco he took a wound that led to the amputation of his right arm. By 3 Mar. 1848, he had recuperated sufficiently to accept a lieutenant's commission in the 2d U.S. Infantry. In that regiment he fought Indians in the Southwest and on the Great Plains until the start of the Civil War.

LC

In May 1861, while stationed at St. Louis, Mo., Sweeny traded his Regular Army captaincy for a brigadier generalship of Missouri short-term volunteers. 3 months later he fought under Brig. Gen. NATHANIEL LYON at WILSON'S CREEK, where he fell wounded and was carried from the field. Within days he was mustered out of volunteer service but reentered it the following January as colonel of the 52d Illinois Infantry. He led the outfit at FORT DONELSON and expertly commanded a brigade at SHILOH, where he was again wounded, and CORINTH. On 16 Mar. 1863, he was raised to brigadier general of volunteers and by the outset of the ATLANTA CAMPAIGN was leading a division in Maj. Gen. GRENVILLE M. DODGE's XVI Corps/Army of the Tennessee.

In the early part of the campaign, Sweeny distinguished himself at Shiloh, Corinth, Kennesaw Mountain, and in the Battle of ATLANTA. On 25 July 1864, he brought to a climax a long-lived feud with Dodge and another politician-commander he resented, Brig. Gen. John W. Fuller. Entertaining both officers at his headquarters, supposedly while under the influence of liquor, Sweeny called Dodge a "God-damned liar" and a "cowardly son of a bitch," struck him, then wrestled his fellow division leader, Fuller, to the ground. Dodge at once arrested his assailant on numerous charges, including conduct unbecoming an officer, but Jan. 1865 a military court acquitted him.

Sweeny remained in the army until May 1870, despite controversial service that included active participation in the Fenian movement. In summer 1866 he led a force of Irish-Americans in an effort to capture Canada from the British. Thwarted by U.S. officials, he was arrested but later released. After his retirement as a brigadier general of Regulars, he lived in Astoria, Long Island, N.Y., till his death there 10 Apr. 1892.
— EGL

Swift Creek, Va., eng. at. 9 May 1864 The advance elements of Union Maj. Gen. BENJAMIN F. BUTLER's 39,000-man Army of the James disembarked from transports at BERMUDA HUNDRED, Va., 5 May 1864. Butler, ordered to operate against Richmond and Petersburg, occupied the peninsula between the James and Appomattox rivers. The Federals' presence in force on Bermuda Hundred endangered the vital RICHMOND & PETERSBURG RAILROAD, the lifeline connecting the Confederate capital to Petersburg and points south.

Confederate authorities reacted swiftly to Butler's occupation. Too ill to lead, the department commander, Gen. P.G.T. BEAUREGARD, gave control of the defense to Maj. Gen. GEORGE E. PICKETT. Pickett and authorities in Richmond funneled reinforcements to the peninsula, and 2 days after Butler landed, 3,500 Confederates manned the works, opposing an army 10 times their size.

Butler aided the Southern concentration by advancing with deliberate caution. He constructed a 3-mile-long line of entrenchments across the peninsula's neck, only 2 mi east of the railroad. He advanced some troops in a reconnaissance on the 6th, but a heavy screen of Confederate skirmishers halted the Federal probe. The next day, near Port Walthall Junction, the Federals launched an attack, seizing a section of the railroad, destroying the tracks, and cutting the telegraph line.

Apparently satisfied with his work on the 7th, Butler remained inactive the next day. Finally, 9 May, the Union army lumbered toward Petersburg, the movement feared by the Confederates. In front of the Federals, on the strongly defended southern bank of Swift Creek, lay Brig. Gen. BUSHROD R. JOHNSON's Confederate division. Johnson initiated the engagement, sending 1 brigade forward in a reconnaissance in force. The Federals responded and the action flared. Butler ordered a strong demonstration later in the afternoon, but the Confederates repulsed it.

Maj. Gens. WILLIAM F. SMITH and QUINCY A. GILLMORE, Butler's corps commanders, proposed a turning movement around Johnson's position by erecting a PONTOON BRIDGE over the Appomattox River. A sound plan, which might have resulted in the capture of Petersburg, it was rejected by Butler, who limited his orders to additional destruction of the railroad. After suffering minor casualties, Butler withdrew from Johnson's front about noon on the 10th. On 12 May the Union army moved on the Confederate defenses at DREWRY'S BLUFF.   —JDW

Sykes, George. USA b. Dover, Del., 9 Oct. 1822, Sykes graduated 39th in the West Point class of 1842, which contributed a dozen corps and army commanders to Union and Confederate forces. He fought against the Seminoles in Florida, served at various posts in the South and West, earned a captain's brevet for gallantry in the Mexican conflict, and participated in Western campaigns.

USMHI

Soon after the Civil War began, Sykes was promoted to major, 14th U.S. Infantry. He commanded a battalion of Regulars, nicknamed "Sykes's Regulars," at FIRST BULL RUN, where his command covered the rout of the Union volunteers. His commendable performance earned him promotion to brigadier general 28 Sept. 1861. He then commanded the Regular Infantry Brigade in the defenses of Washington, D.C., until Mar. 1862.

During the 1862 PENINSULA and SEVEN DAYS' campaigns, he initially commanded a brigade, then a division, in Maj. Gen. Fitz John Porter's V Corps. A tough division of Regulars, the men fought with particular distinction at GAINES' MILL 27 June and MALVERN HILL 1 July. The command was heavily engaged again at SECOND BULL RUN but saw only limited action at ANTIETAM and was in reserve at Fredericksburg.

Shortly before this last engagement, on 29 Nov. 1862, Sykes received his promotion to major general. His division was once again only lightly engaged at CHANCELLORSVILLE May 1863. When the V Corps commander, Maj. Gen. George G. Meade, assumed control of the Army of the Potomac 28 June, Sykes succeeded Meade. His corps at GETTYSBURG fought valiantly on the Union left 2 July, when 2 Confederate divisions crushed the III Corps. Troops from the V Corps also secured LITTLE ROUND TOP for Meade's army.

Sykes retained command of the corps in the operations during autumn 1863. At Mine Run in November, Meade believed that Sykes acted with too much deliberation when aggressive action was demanded. In December the army commander relieved Sykes, who had been nicknamed "Tardy George" in the antebellum army. On 20 Apr. 1864, Sykes assumed command of the Department of Kansas, a post he held until the war's end.

The veteran officer remained in the postwar army, serving at posts from Minnesota to Texas and eventually attaining the rank of colonel, U.S. Army. He died at Fort Brown, Tex., 8 Feb. 1880, and was buried at the Military Academy.   —JDW

T

tactics Tactics is the military art of maneuvering troops on the field of battle to achieve victory in combat. "Offensive tactics" seek success through attacking; "defensive tactics" aim at defeating enemy attacks.

In Civil War tactics, the principal combat arm was infantry. Its most common deployment was a long "line of battle," 2 ranks deep. More massed was the "column," varying from 1 to 10 or more companies wide and from 8 to 20 or more ranks deep. Less compact than column or line was "open-order" deployment: a strung-out, irregular single line.

Battle lines delivered the most firepower defensively and offensively. Offensive firepower alone would not ensure success. Attackers had to charge, and massed columns, with their greater depth, were often preferable to battle lines for making frontal assaults. Better yet were flank attacks, to "roll up" thin battle lines lengthwise. Offensive tacticians sought opportunity for such effective flank attacks; defensive tacticians countered by "refusing" these flanks on impassable barriers. In either posture, tacticians attempted to coordinate all their troops to deliver maximum force and firepower and to avoid being beaten "in detail" (piecemeal). Throughout, they relied on open-order deployment to cover their front and flanks with skirmishers, who developed the enemy position and screened their own troops.

Open order, moreover, was best suited for moving through the wooded countryside of America. That wooded terrain, so different from Europe's open fields, for which tactical doctrine was aimed, also affected tactical control. Army commanders, even corps commanders, could not control large, far-flung forces. Instead, army commanders concentrated on STRATEGY. And corps commanders handled "grand tactics": the medium for translating theater strategy into battlefield tactics, the art of maneuvering large forces just outside the battlefield and bringing them onto that field. Once on the field, corps commanders provided overall tactical direction, but their largest practical units of tactical maneuver were divisions. More often, brigades, even regiments, formed those maneuver elements. Essentially, brigades did the fighting in the Civil War.

Besides affecting organization, difficult terrain helped relegate cavalry and artillery to lesser tactical roles. More influential there was the widespread use of long-range rifled shoulder arms. As recently as the Mexican War, when most infantry fired smoothbore muskets, cavalry and artillery had been key attacking arms. Attempting to continue such tactics in the Civil War proved disastrous, as infantry rifle power soon drove horsemen virtually off the battlefield and relegated artillery to defensive support. Rifle power devastated offensive infantry assaults, too, but senior commanders, who were so quick to understand its impact on cannon and cavalry, rarely grasped its effect on infantry. By 1864, infantry customarily did erect light field fortifications to strengthen its defensive battlefield positions and protect itself from enemy rifle power; but when attacking, whether against battle lines or fortifications, infantry continued suffering heavy casualties through clinging to tactical formations outmoded by technology.

But if infantry was slow to learn, other arms swiftly found new tactical roles. The new mission of the artillery was to bolster the defensive, sometimes with 1 battery assigned to each infantry brigade, but more often with 1 battalion assigned to a Confederate infantry division and 1 brigade to a Federal infantry corps. With long-range shells and close-in canister, artillery became crucial in repulsing enemy attacks. But long-range shelling to support one's own attack had minimal effect, and artillery assaults were soon abandoned as suicidal. Throughout, artillery depended almost entirely on direct fire against visible targets.

Cavalry, in the meantime, served most usefully in scouting for tactical intelligence and in screening such intelligence from the foe. By midwar, moreover, cavalry was using its mobility to seize key spots, where it dismounted and fought afoot. Armed with breech-loading carbines, including Federal repeaters by 1864–65, these foot cavalry fought well even against infantry. Only rarely did mounted cavalry battle with saber and pistol. Rarer still were mounted pursuits of routed enemies.

Cavalry so infrequently undertook such pursuits chiefly because defeated armies were rarely routed. Size of armies, commitment to their respective causes by individual citizen-soldiers, difficult terrain, and impact of fortifications and technology all militated against the Napoleonic triumph, which could destroy an enemy army—and an enemy country—in just 1 battle. Raised in the aura of Napoleon, most Civil War commanders sought the Napoleonic victory, but few came close to achieving it. 60 years after Marengo and Austerlitz, warfare had so changed that victory in the Civil War would instead come through strategy. Yet within that domain of strategy, not just 1 battle but *series* of them—and the tactics through which they were fought—were the crucial elements in deciding the outcome of the Civil War. —RJS

Taliaferro, William Booth. CSA b. Gloucester Cty., Va., 28 Dec. 1822. In 1841 Taliaferro was graduated from the College of William and Mary, and later studied law at Harvard. In Feb. 1847, he entered the Regular Army, fighting in Mexico as a captain in the 11th and major of the 9th U.S. Infantry. From 1850 to 1853 he served in the Virginia legislature, was a Democratic presidential elector in 1856, and commanded the militia at Harpers Ferry following JOHN BROWN'S RAID of Nov. 1859.

Early in the Civil War, Taliaferro (pronounced Tarl'-iver), was the major general in command of Virginia militia at Norfolk and Gloucester Point. Later made colonel of the 23d Virginia Infantry, he gained a reputation as a disciplinarian, so alienating his men that at least one physically assaulted him. After serving under Brig. Gen. ROBERT S. GARNETT at RICH MOUNTAIN and CORRICK'S FORD, he also made an enemy of his new superior, Maj. Gen. THOMAS J. "STONEWALL" JACKSON. In Jan. 1862 Taliaferro joined Brig. Gen. WILLIAM WING LORING and other officers in pro-

CWTI

testing the squalid winter quarters Jackson had assigned them at Romney, Va. Later he wrote friends in Richmond about Jackson's "bad marches and bad management"; later still, he personally intrigued against Jackson in the Confederate capital.

For a time on detached service, Taliaferro returned to Jackson's army Apr. 1862 as a brigadier general, over Stonewall's protests. Nevertheless, he served with distinction during the latter's spring campaign in the Shenandoah Valley. He engineered an effective holding action that saved the day at MCDOWELL, 8 May, and 17 days later safeguarded the Confederate left at FIRST WINCHESTER. He also fought well at PORT REPUBLIC, CEDAR MOUNTAIN (where he succeeded to the command of Jackson's old division), GROVETON (where he was 3 times wounded), and FREDERICKSBURG. Failing to become a major general, however, he left Jackson's army Feb. 1863.

Thereafter he commanded at Savannah, then at Charleston under Gen. P.G.T. BEAUREGARD. That July his 1,200 troops held BATTERY WAGNER on Morris Island against 2 assaults by 6,000 Federals. Subsequently he led troops on James Island and in eastern Florida, and Dec. 1864 he safeguarded Lt. Gen. WILLIAM J. HARDEE's evacuation of SAVANNAH. The following March he led a division at BENTONVILLE.

In postbellum life Taliaferro again became a state legislator, as well as a county judge and a member of the boards of visitors of William and Mary and the Virginia Military Institute. On 27 Feb. 1898, he died at "Dunham Massie," his Gloucester County estate.   —EGL

Tallahassee, CSS. Although the *Tallahassee* is less well known than other CONFEDERATE CRUISERS, its brief career was nonetheless remarkable. Unlike the *ALABAMA, FLORIDA*, and *SHENANDOAH*, which sailed originally from England, the *Tallahassee*, although built in England, operated from a Southern port and was manned by an all-Southern volunteer crew.

The sinking of the *Alabama* June 1864 left only the *Florida* to continue the destruction of the North's ocean commerce. Confederate Navy Sec. STEPHEN R. MALLORY ordered that more cruisers be obtained, and the BLOCKADE RUNNER *Atlanta*, renamed the *Tallahassee*, was purchased at Wilmington, N.C., July 1864 for this purpose. The vessel's twin-screw propeller system and 2 engines, enabling the ship to turn on its center, contributed to the *Tallahassee*'s speed and maneuverability. It was, however, vulnerable, with facilities providing for storage of only a very limited supply of coal, and its engines were unprotected. Cmdr. JOHN T. WOOD, the resourceful officer assigned to the *Tallahassee*, compensated for these limitations by storing coal on deck and stacking cotton bales to protect his

engines. His battery consisted of a rifled 100-pounder, a rifled 32-pounder, and a Parrott gun.

After a daring escape from Wilmington 6 Aug. 1864, Wood headed the *Tallahassee* northward. In less than 3 weeks at sea, the Confederate destroyed 26 merchant and fishing vessels and released 7 others on bond. The activities of the raider in Northern waters caused the disruption and panic that Mallory had intended. Unable to secure coal from his prizes, Wood brought the *Tallahassee* into the harbor of Halifax, Nova Scotia. However, hounded by Federal warships and frustrated by Nova Scotia's strict enforcement of England's neutrality laws, Wood returned the *Tallahassee* to Wilmington 26 Aug.

Renamed the *Olustee* and then the *Chameleon,* the vessel continued to serve the South under different commanders. As the *Chameleon,* it was surrendered to British authorities 9 Apr. 1865, and was turned over to the U.S. the following year.
                                                          —NCD

Taney, Roger Brooke. jurist b. Calvert Cty., Md., 17 Mar. 1777. The second son of a plantation owner in Maryland, Taney graduated from Dickinson College in 1795, read law, and was admitted to the bar 4 years later.

Through the influence of family and friends he was elected to the state legislature in 1799. When the 1-year term expired, he stayed politically active without holding elective office. A masterful orator with an exceptional ability for analyzing legal technicalities, he took a special interest in promoting legislation to protect the rights of blacks, free and slave, within the state, and he assumed leadership of the minority faction among the

LC

Federalists in supporting the government during the War of 1812. Elected to a 5-year term in the state legislature in 1816, he concerned himself with shaping banking and currency policies. When the Federalist party dissolved, he joined the Jacksonian Democrats, serving as Pres. Andrew Jackson's attorney general 1831–33 and as Sec. of Treasury 1833–34. In Dec. 1835 Taney was nominated as chief justice of the SUPREME COURT and was confirmed 15 Mar. 1836.

Taney's Southern background invited charges of favoritism toward the slave states, but he based his judicial opinions on Constitutional interpretations that he felt reduced the threat to the Union in the tense antebellum years. On issues such as control of inland waters, he supported extending federal authority, but he did not believe that the U.S. Constitution gave Congress the power to exclude slavery from the territories. Early in his career Taney had manumitted his own slaves and supported the colonization movement (*see also* AMERICAN COLONIZATION SOCIETY), believing that blacks and whites could not live together as equals. Though preferring some form of compensated emancipation, he felt that slavery must exist in the U.S. as long as blacks remained in the country, and he opposed Northern interference with the South's "peculiar institution."

In 1857 he delivered the majority opinion in the *DRED SCOTT CASE*, overturning a Missouri state court decision granting freedom to Scott, whose former master had taken him to free territory. In reversing the lower court's ruling, Taney argued that as a slave, Scott was not a citizen and therefore could not sue for his freedom in a Federal court. He also took his opinion beyond the concerns of the case by declaring unconstitutional the prohibition on slavery in U.S. territories. Republicans and abolitionists were embittered by the decision, which nullified the MISSOURI COMPROMISE and stripped black slaves of all rights.

Dred Scott became one of the principal causes of the Civil War, yet during the conflict itself the chief justice often opposed the Lincoln administration by defending the rights of citizens arrested for disloyalty during wartime. On Taney's death in Washington, 12 Oct. 1864, Lincoln appointed former secretary of the treasury and RADICAL REPUBLICAN SALMON P. CHASE to replace him.   —PLF

Tappan, James Camp. CSA b. Franklin, Tenn., 9 Sept. 1825. The son of transplanted New Englanders, Tappan went back to the region for his education. After attending Exeter Academy in New Hampshire, he graduated from Yale in 1845. Returning to the South, he studied law in Vicksburg, Miss., before practicing the profession in Helena, Ark. He served 2 terms in the Arkansas legislature and as a circuit-court judge until the outbreak of the Civil War.

Tappan immediately embraced the Confederate cause and was commissioned colonel of the 13th Arkansas May 1861. He led his regiment at BELMONT, Mo., 7 Nov., earning praise from his commander, Gen.

LC

Leonidas Polk. At the Battle of SHILOH, 6 Apr. 1862, his Arkansans participated in the repeated bloody assaults on the famous "HORNETS' NEST." During that autumn he fought at RICHMOND and PERRYVILLE, Ky., in the Confederate invasion of the Blue Grass state. On 5 Nov. 1862, he was promoted to brigadier general and transferred to the Trans-Mississippi Department.

Tappan served in this department as a brigade commander for the remainder of the war. During 1863 he commanded a brigade under Maj. Gen. STERLING PRICE in Arkansas, and the following spring his brigade fought in the RED RIVER CAMPAIGN. At PLEASANT HILL, La., 9 Apr., he rendered distinguished service. His brigade then was immediately sent north toward Arkansas to stop the advance of Union Maj. Gen. FREDERICK STEELE. The Confederates encountered Steele at JENKINS' FERRY 30 Apr. Tappan subsequently returned to Price's command, participating in his raid into Missouri, which extended from August to December.

When the Confederates surrendered in spring 1865, Tappan returned to Helena and resumed his legal practice. He was again elected to the state legislature and twice declined the Democratic nomination for governor. He was also dean of the state bar for many years, holding that honor when he died in Helena 19 Mar. 1906.   —JDW

"Taps." *See* MUSIC.

Tarheel. Tarheel was the nickname for a Confederate soldier from North Carolina. The sobriquet came from the state's

colonial past, when its citizens made pine tar and pitch for export. During the Civil War, more Tarheels fell in behalf of the Confederate cause than soldiers from any other Southern state. It was a Tarheel's proud boast that he was "First at Bethel, last at Appomattox."   —JDW

Tattnall, Josiah. CSN b. "Bonaventure," near Savannah, Ga., 9 Nov. 1795. Educated in England, Tattnall went to sea in 1812 as a midshipman in the U.S. Navy. His service included participation in the War of 1812, in the action against Algiers, and in the Mexican War. In 1859 he generated a minor diplomatic incident by assisting a British fleet in China, thus violating American neutrality.

During the secession crisis, Tattnall resigned his U.S. commission, 20 Feb. 1861, and accepted appointment as senior flag officer in the Georgia navy. Soon after, he became a captain in the Confederate service and assumed the duties of defending the Georgia–South Carolina coast. Lacking ships, guns, and men, he could manage only feeble resistance to the Union capture of PORT ROYAL Nov. 1861.

In Mar. 1862 Tattnall succeeded the wounded Capt. FRANKLIN BUCHANAN in command of the naval defense of Virginia and of the ironclad *VIRGINIA (Merrimack)*. During Apr. 1862 he attempted to lure the Union ironclad *MONITOR* into combat under circumstances favorable to the *Virginia*. The effect was a long-range sparring match in which neither vessel renewed the duel of 9 Mar (*see* HAMPTON ROADS, VA., BATTLE OF). When Norfolk fell to Federal forces 9 May, the *Virginia* became a ship without a port. Tattnall tried unsuccessfully to lighten the vessel enough to retire up the James River, then, 11 May, ordered the ironclad blown up to prevent its capture.

Eventually exonerated by a court-martial for his decision to destroy the *Virginia,* Tattnall returned to command in Savannah. There he was able to deny the Savannah River to the Federals, but little else. Tattnall left Savannah when the city fell to Maj. Gen. William T. Sherman's army Dec. 1864, and served in Gen. Joseph E. Johnston's army until Johnston surrendered.

After the war Tattnall lived in Nova Scotia for 4 years, then returned to Savannah as inspector of the port. d. Savannah, 14 June 1871.   —EMT

tax in kind. The CONFEDERATE CONGRESS passed the tax-in-kind law 24 Apr. 1863, levying a 10% assessment on all agricultural products and livestock raised for slaughter that were in the hands of producers. Legislators expected this first major tax on farm goods to fund about one-third of the cost of waging war, to feed the armies, and to allow the government to market surpluses to the public. To encourage cooperation, the government imposed a 50% penalty on any undelivered payment, and placed a heavy penalty on stockpiled produce in hopes of ending agricultural speculation.

In May Asst. Q.M. Gen. Larkin Smith assigned 1 quartermaster to each Confederate congressional district to oversee collection. Subagents within the districts assessed each farmer's crops to establish the quantities of good to be delivered to collection depots. The government supplied grain sacks and molasses barrels and paid freight charges for distances exceeding 8 mi. 10 months after the tax went into effect, the quartermaster general's department reported having collected $40 million in goods.

Lack of transportation and the scale of the operation led to large stockpiles of food that often spoiled in warehouses before it reached the marketplace or the armies. In Dec. 1863 Congress attempted to solve the problems of waste by revising the law to permit payment in cash equivalent to the value of the tithe at impressment prices. In response to complaints that the tax in kind placed an unfair burden on farmers, in Feb. 1864 the legislators made the agricultural tax deductible from a 5% tax on real and personal property and enacted exemptions for families struggling to feed themselves with their crops. Little could be done to prevent hungry troops from collecting payments themselves and leaving angry farmers with worthless vouchers, though commissary general Col. LUCIUS B. NORTHROP issued warnings against relinquishing goods to anyone except official collection agents.

Despite its faults, the tax in kind provided the Confederate government with a valuable source of income. Authorities in Richmond claimed they had collected $150 million in goods and cash by Nov. 1864, though critics of the administration cited more conservative receipts. Of the goods collected, two-thirds came from North Carolina, Georgia, and Alabama. Georgia Sen. BENJAMIN H. HILL credited the tax in kind with preventing the Confederate armies from starving.   —PLF

Taylor, Benjamin Franklin. journalist b. Lowville, N.Y., 18 July 1819. Taylor's father, principal of the private Lowville Academy, took a position as a professor of mathematics at Madison (now Colgate) University in Hamilton, N.Y. Young Taylor grew up in Hamilton, graduated from the University (then known as the Hamilton Literary and Theological Institute) in the class of 1838, served as principal of the Norwich Academy in Vermont, then joined the staff of the Chicago, Ill., *Evening Journal* in 1845, over the years advancing from reporter to literary editor.

From the start of the Civil War until late summer 1863 Taylor worked on the *Evening Journal* editorial desk, then secured permission to join Maj. Gen. William S. Rosecrans' army maneuvering between Chattanooga, Tenn., and Chickamauga Creek, Ga. Having neither visited the South nor reported combat before, Taylor brought a fresh perspective to his correspondence. His reportage is not remembered for its content, but for its literary merit.

Taylor covered the Battle of CHICKAMAUGA, the Siege of CHATTANOOGA, the Battles of LOOKOUT MOUNTAIN and MISSIONARY RIDGE, and the early part of the ATLANTA CAMPAIGN. In spring 1864 he reported to the *Evening Journal* that "our lines now extend from Knoxville to Huntsville." Maj. Gen. William T. Sherman, considering this dissemination of secret intelligence, ordered Taylor's arrest and court-martial on espionage charges. In May, Taylor left the army rather than face the charges and assumed the post of Washington, D.C., correspondent for the *Evening Journal*. In this capacity he reported political news, but, as in the Western theater, won notice for his army reportage, covering Confederate Lt. Gen. Jubal A. EARLY'S WASHINGTON RAID and the panic it caused within the city.

Taylor left the *Evening Journal* in 1865, traveled in the West, Mexico, and the Pacific, lectured, and pursued a career as a free-lance writer and poet. Best known in his day for his poetry, he published several volumes and a Civil War narrative, *Mission Ridge and Lookout Mountain, with Pictures in Camp and Field* (1872). d. Columbus, Ohio, 24 Feb. 1887.   —JES

Taylor, Joseph Pannell. USA b. Louisville, Ky., 4 May 1796. Brother of U.S. Pres. Zachary Taylor and uncle of Confederate Lt. Gen. RICHARD TAYLOR, Joseph P. Taylor enlisted as a private in the U.S. Army volunteers in 1812; won a commission as lieutenant 20 May 1813; was discharged at the end of the War of 1812, 15 June 1815; and was reinstated in the U.S. Regulars 17 May 1816 as a lieutenant of artillery. Promoted to captain 6 July 1825, he left the artillery for the army commissary department in 1829, remaining in that branch of service until his death. Brevetted colonel 30 May 1848 for his performance in supply during the Mexican War, he received a full colonelcy 29 Sept. 1861.

LC

Taylor's age and training kept him from field duty during the Civil War. Under commissary general Col. George Gibson, he supplied Union forces in both the Eastern and Western theaters and fulfilled administrative duties. On Gibson's death in office, Taylor assumed the post of commissary general, and by act of Congress was promoted to brigadier general 9 Feb. 1863.

He died 29 June 1864 at his post in Washington, D.C., remembered in Civil War history for his family associations and as the first commissary general to attain the rank of brigadier general. The act of Congress from which his commission was dated provided that the holder of that post be elevated to the rank of brigadier.   —JES

Taylor, Richard. CSA b. "Springfields," near Louisville, Ky., 27 Jan. 1826. Although he had almost no previous military training, Taylor took command of the 9th Louisiana Infantry Regiment July 1861 with glittering credentials: son of former president Zachary Taylor; nephew of future Union Brig. Gen. JOSEPH P. TAYLOR; educated in Europe, at Harvard, and at Yale; former brother-in-law of Jefferson Davis; influential planter and Louisiana state senator. And he soon became an outstanding combat commander, earning rank as brigadier general 21 Oct. 1861, major general 28 July 1862, and lieutenant general to rank from 8 Apr. 1864. A veteran of campaigns in Virginia, Mississippi, and Louisiana, he achieved his

LC

most notable victory Apr. 1864, when, with an inferior force, he defeated Union Maj. Gen. NATHANIEL P. BANKS at MANSFIELD, La., and repulsed the Federal RED RIVER CAMPAIGN.

In his excellent postwar memoir, *Destruction and Reconstruction* (1879), Taylor wrote "We could have captured [Rear Adm. DAVID D.] PORTER's fleet and with it would have at once recovered possession of the Mississippi." His men could have "undone all the work of the Federals since the winter of 1861." But it was not to be. Taylor's superior, Gen. E. KIRBY

SMITH, detached much of Taylor's force and let Banks and Porter escape. Enraged, Taylor wanted to quit his command and called Kirby Smith "stupid, pig-headed and obstinate." Despite almost unprecedented vituperation directed toward a superior, he was promoted to lieutenant general and given command of the Department of East Louisiana, Mississippi, and Alabama.

Taylor directed daring delaying actions in Alabama and held off Union efforts to capture Mobile until Apr. 1865. When the surrender of Gens. Robert E. Lee and Joseph E. Johnston effectively ended Confederate resistance, Taylor turned over his command to Maj. Gen. E.R.S. Canby 4 May 1865 (see SURRENDERS: Lt. Gen. Richard Taylor). It was the last major surrender of Confederate forces east of the Mississippi River.

From the 1862 Shenandoah Valley and Seven Days' campaigns to the Louisiana and Mississippi campaigns of 1863 and the Red River operations of 1864, Taylor proved himself an able and courageous battler against superior forces. Later, during Reconstruction, he was an effective advocate of Southern rights.

Historian Douglas Southall Freeman had high praise for Taylor's memoirs, calling Taylor "the only Confederate general with literary art approaching the first rank." Taylor's book was published only a week before his death in New York City, 12 Apr. 1879   —DS

Taylor, Thomas Hart. CSA b. Frankfort, Ky., 31 July 1825, Taylor attended college in the North, at Kenyon College in Ohio, then at Centre College in Kentucky. He served in the Mexican War as a 1st lieutenant before engaging in various business enterprises, and in the years immediately preceding the war worked as a cattle drover in the West.

On enlisting, he accepted an appointment as captain of infantry in the Confederate army and lieutenant colonel of the 1st Kentucky Infantry. Taylor fought with his regiment against Maj. Gen. George B. McClellan in the PENINSULA CAMPAIGN in 1862 until the 1st Kentucky was officially mustered out of service that summer. He next served under Maj. Gen. E. Kirby Smith at Cumberland Gap in Tennessee and in various other actions in Kentucky, with promotion to brigadier general 4 Nov.

In 1863 at VICKSBURG Taylor was captured while serving as Lt. Gen. John C. Pemberton's provost marshal, but was soon paroled. He returned to duty in command of the District of South Mississippi and East Louisiana before becoming a provost marshal under Lt. Gen. Stephen D. Lee. His last service in the Confederate army came as commander of the forces at MOBILE, Ala.

After the war, Taylor engaged in business in Mobile until 1870, when he became a deputy U.S. marshal and chief of police in Louisville, Ky. He died in that city 12 April 1901.
                                   —FLS

Taylor's Ridge, Ga., eng. at. 27 Nov. 1863 Confederate Gen. BRAXTON BRAGG's retreat from Chattanooga carried his ARMY OF TENNESSEE through Missionary Ridge to Ringgold, Ga. On 26 Nov. 1863, he continued his southeastward withdrawal toward Dalton, leaving outside Ringgold a strong force, the division of Maj. Gen. PATRICK R. CLEBURNE.

Leading Lt. Gen. ULYSSES S. GRANT's pursuit was Maj. Gen. GEORGE H. THOMAS' ARMY OF THE CUMBERLAND. That army's XII Corps, under Maj. Gen. JOSEPH HOOKER, drove toward Cleburne's position by way of Rossville. While elements of Maj. Gen. WILLIAM T. SHERMAN's ARMY OF THE TENNESSEE operated northeast of Ringgold against enemy communications, part of Sherman's XV Corps marched to Ringgold to dislodge Bragg's rear guard and reopen the road to Dalton.

First to reach Ringgold, about 8 a.m. on the 27th, was the 1st Division/XV Corps of Brig. Gen. PETER J. OSTERHAUS. Finding his enemy strongly entrenched on Taylor's Ridge, below the town, the Prussian-born commander promptly attacked, driving in the skirmishers of Brig. Gen. MARK P. LOWREY's brigade. After an unsuccessful attempt to skirt the Confederate north flank, Osterhaus launched an offensive against the left, his men clambering up the steep ridge although doused by rifle and cannon fire. A Confederate counterattack finally halted the effort.

While the fighting raged, Hooker arrived and dispatched the division of Brig. Gen. JOHN W. GEARY to Osterhaus' aid. Geary in turn sent Col. William R. Creighton's brigade to the Prussian's left in another attempt to flank Cleburne from above. Bereft of artillery support, Creighton was mortally wounded and most of his men became casualties or fled. Soon afterward, another of Geary's brigades, under Col. George A. Cobham, formed behind Osterhaus' right, steadying the Union south flank. When that sector still seemed endangered, Geary threw in Col. David Ireland's brigade, which, in the division leader's words, compelled Cleburne "to recoil in the zenith of [Ireland's] audacious charge. . . ."

The battle was decided early in the afternoon when several Union batteries, delayed in crossing West Chickamauga Creek, reached the field. Concentrating their fire against the Confederate left, the cannon swept the ridge and cleared the gorge outside Ringgold through which ran the Western & Atlantic Railroad. About 1 o'clock Cleburne's men began to waver. Soon afterward Osterhaus' troops scaled the heights and Ireland's occupied the gorge, precipitating a general retreat.

The resumption of the Federals' pursuit of Bragg's forces proved short-lived. No longer considering Bragg's army a threat to Tennessee, Grant soon shifted his attention to raising the Siege of KNOXVILLE.   —EGL

Tebe, Marie. vivandière Marie Tebe was the VIVANDIÈRE of the 114th Pennsylvania Volunteers, a zouave regiment of wealthy and prominent young Philadelphians, who provided her uniform and pay. Her war career is documented in the history of the regiment's band, *Music on the March* (1892), but this sole source of biographical information about her states neither her age nor birthplace. The regimental roster implies that she was a resident of Philadelphia. From pictorial evidence, she was probably in her mid-twenties during the war.

Technically a CAMP FOLLOWER, Tebe joined the regiment at its mustering-in 17 Aug. 1862, served with it through all the campaigns in the Eastern theater, and was awarded a medal by Maj. Gen. David B. Birney for gallantry at CHANCELLORSVILLE, where she went among the thirsty troops with a canteen, her uniform riddled by bullets. Described as a crusty young woman concerned with financial advancement, Tebe disdained her medal, saying she would have valued it more were it made of gold. She also briefly participated in the gambling craze sweeping the Army of the Potomac and subsequently suffered financial losses.

Tebe's service is significant in that its record substantiates the duties and uniform of vivandières. It is believed that as a noncombatant she wore the pistol provided by the 114th only on parade occasions. Though following a regiment of foot soldiers, occasionally she was allowed to ride a mule. Her behavior, as described, implies that she came from a lower class than most members of the regiment. There is no known record of Tebe's life following the 114th's mustering out 29 May 1865. —JES

***Tecumseh*, USS.** A single-turreted monitor built at Jersey City, N.J., by Secor & Co. of New York, the *Tecumseh* and other monitors of the same class represented a major advance in design over the USS *MONITOR*. Their turrets and side armor were strengthened, propellers made more efficient, and ventilation improved. The *Tecumseh* was 223 ft long, weighed 1,034 tons, and had a 14-ft draft when loaded. Its turret armor was 10 in. thick, and the 5-in. armor on its sides was strengthened by the addition of 2 4-in. stringers. A protective glacis 5 in. thick and 15 in. high was placed around the base of the turret as added protection. The *Tecumseh* was armed with 2 15-inch DAHLGREN smoothbore turret guns. It was launched 12 Sept. 1863 and commissioned 19 Apr. 1864. The vessel's captain during its brief length of service, Apr.–Aug. 1864, was Cmdr. TUNIS A. M. CRAVEN.

From April to June the *Tecumseh* served with the James River Squadron. Then it was towed to Pensacola and from there to outside Mobile Bay, where it became part of Adm. DAVID G. FARRAGUT's naval force to capture MOBILE. The battle began early on the morning of 5 Aug. Moving ahead with the other monitors, the *Tecumseh* struck a TORPEDO and was blown out of the water. It sank rapidly, carrying with it Craven and about 100 others. —NCD

telegraph. The solitary wire of the transcontinental telegraph reached the Pacific Coast in 1861, just as the Civil War was beginning. Both armies used the telegraph extensively. Although it did not entirely eliminate the "WIGWAG" signal system (flags by day, torches by night), by 1864 the U.S. Military Telegraph Service was using more than 6,500 mi of wire, 76 mi of which were underwater cables. Confederate records are few.

Official U.S. use of the telegraph began after FIRST BULL RUN when Asst. Sec. of War Thomas A. Scott took charge of the commercial telegraph systems around Washington, D.C. The first wire used in field service was bare and had to be strung on poles through insulators. Insulated wire came next, protected enough to withstand wagon and artillery traffic when laid on the ground. Linemen using a wire reel on a stretcherlike frame that could be carried by 2 men could lay 2 mi of wire in an hour. Ambulances converted into "battery wagons" transported the heavy 100-cell, 150-volt wet batteries, along with regular sending and receiving apparatus. Portable signal-coding machines recommended by Maj. ALBERT J. MYER were found unreliable.

Operators acted as censors. Col. Edward S. Sanford, as chief censor of the Military Telegraph Service, withheld 2 bitter sentences in Maj. Gen. GEORGE B. MCCLELLAN's dispatch to Sec. of War EDWIN M. STANTON after SAVAGE'S STATION: "If I save this army now, I tell you plainly that I owe no thanks to you or to any other persons in Washington. You have done your best to sacrifice this army." Maj. Thomas T. Eckert at the Washington office suppressed Lt. Gen. U.S. Grant's order for Maj. Gen. GEORGE H. THOMAS' removal, allowing that general time to win the Battle of Nashville (see FRANKLIN AND NASHVILLE CAMPAIGN).

Each side tapped the other's lines; each used code. Union telegraphers broke the enemy's code to learn vital Confederate plans; the South never solved the Union cipher. Often close to the front, operators suffered casualties of nearly 10%, about the same as combat troops. —RDH

Tennessee. Secession and civil war sharply divided Tennesseans. The split was largely regional, East Tennessee standing by the Union, central and West Tennessee favoring secession. Having favored the Constitutional Unionist candidate, John Bell, in the 1860 presidential election, voters in Jan. 1861 rejected secession by a 4–1 vote and turned down a legislative call for a convention to consider secession.

After the firing on FORT SUMTER, Tennessee's governor, ISHAM G. HARRIS, had the legislature approve a military liaison with the Confederacy and begin recruiting. In June 1861 a plebiscite of Tennesseans upheld the measure. East Tennessee counties maneuvered to leave Tennessee and adhere to the Union, but Confederate military occupation there squelched the effort. The state's secessionist government would not last long: Union success at FORT DONELSON and SHILOH forced Confederate abandonment of the capital, Nashville, and Pres. ABRAHAM LINCOLN installed Tennessean ANDREW JOHNSON as military governor with instructions to restore the state to the Union. Paradoxically, while Confederate military forces were driven from heavily pro-Confederate West and central Tennessee, Southern military control long remained in pro-Union East Tennessee, which contributed more volunteers to Federal than to Confederate armies.

Although Federal troops captured Chattanooga in East Tennessee Sept. 1863, Confederates held them there until the Union breakout at MISSIONARY RIDGE 25 Nov. 1863. By then most Southern forces, other than raiding cavalry and irregular bands, had been cleared from the state. The war caused greater suffering in Tennessee than elsewhere, except Virginia. As a major battleground, the state endured long campaigns, marching, countermarching, Federal foraging, and much guerrilla activity that spread destruction and distress. Relatives, neighbors, and friends often espoused opposite sides and fought each other. Casualties among Tennesseans were high. Hoping to put the war behind it, Tennessee early ratified the 13TH AMENDMENT, ending slavery. —DL

Tennessee, Confederate Army of. The Army of Tennessee, though not designated as such until Nov. 1862, really came into being when Gen. ALBERT SIDNEY JOHNSTON assembled a force of 42,000 at Corinth, Miss., Mar. 1862. It was a hard-luck army. At SHILOH, 6–7 Apr., its first major battle, success on the first day turned into defeat on the second, and casualties exceeded 10,000. Gen. P.G.T. BEAUREGARD, Johnston's successor, fell into disfavor with Pres. Jefferson Davis June 1862 and was replaced by Gen. BRAXTON BRAGG.

Bragg won a tactical victory at PERRYVILLE, Ky., 8 Oct. 1862, then yielded the field to his foe. In his next battle, STONE'S RIVER, Tenn., 31 Dec.–2 Jan., success on the first day was nullified by Bragg's subsequent irresolution and mismanagement, and he again yielded the field to the Federals. In summer 1863 Bragg was forced back into Georgia by the skillful maneuvering of Maj. Gen. WILLIAM S. ROSECRANS. Instead of following up the victory won at CHICKAMAUGA, Tenn., 19–20 Sept., Bragg remained on the defensive while Maj. Gen. U. S. GRANT built up a force that defeated him in 3 days of fighting, 23–25 Nov. When on the third day Maj. Gen. GEORGE H. THOMAS' troops scaled MISSIONARY RIDGE, many of Bragg's troops fled in panic, partly because they had lost confidence in their commander.

Bragg's successor, Gen. JOSEPH E. JOHNSTON, built up the army's strength and morale, but instead of taking the offensive as Davis wished, he gradually fell back before Maj. Gen. WILLIAM T. SHERMAN's advance until he reached Atlanta (see ATLANTA CAMPAIGN). There, 17 July 1864, Davis replaced him with Gen. JOHN BELL HOOD, who fought 4 battles to save the city, but in vain. After Sherman's forces occupied Atlanta 2 Sept., Hood, hoping Sherman would follow him, headed for Tennessee. But Sherman left Hood to Thomas while he marched to the sea. Thomas decisively defeated Hood at Nashville, 15–16 Dec. (see FRANKLIN AND NASHVILLE CAMPAIGN).

The tattered remnants of the army, with Johnston again in command, fought 1 more battle, at BENTONVILLE, N.C., 19–21 Mar. 1865. They fought gallantly, but futilely. Surrender came 26 Apr. near Durham, N.C.   —BIW

Tennessee, Confederate Department of.

By Special Order No. 176 from the Confederate Adjutant and Inspector General's Office, on 25 July 1863 former Confederate Department No. 2 was eliminated and the Department of Tennessee created with Gen. BRAXTON BRAGG as commander. Bragg's geographic area of responsibility briefly created confusion within the Confederate army as the Department of Tennessee assumed administrative and military authority over the Confederate Department of East Tennessee, commanded by Maj. Gen. SIMON B. BUCKNER (see EAST TENNESSEE, CONFEDERATE ARMY AND DEPARTMENT OF). However, Buckner's command retained a semi-independent status within the larger organization of Bragg's department.

With Buckner's command included in Bragg's area of responsibility, the Department of Tennessee had an eastern border that ran along the western face of the Blue Ridge Mts. in North Carolina, entered Georgia, then followed the Georgia Railroad west from the Augusta area. In the south, the department's border continued west along the railroad to Atlanta, dipped southwest to West Point, Ga., followed a wavering line northwest taking in the Alabama counties of Franklin, Lawrence, Morgan, Blount, St. Clair, Calhoun, Cherokee, De Kalb, and Marshall, then followed the Tennessee River north to its mouth at the Mississippi River. The department's northern border was Tennessee's state line.

Gen. JOSEPH E. JOHNSTON replaced Bragg as department commander following the Confederate defeat at CHATTANOOGA Nov. 1863. Promoted to general, JOHN B. HOOD replaced Johnston as department commander July 1864. With command of the department also came Hood's command of the Army of Tennessee.

On 25 Mar. 1864, responding to a boundary dispute between the Departments of Tennessee and ALABAMA, MISSISSIPPI, and EAST LOUISIANA, the Department of Tennessee's southwestern boundary was extended south along the Chattahoochee River to Florida's northern border. On 15 Aug. 1864, the department was dissolved and replaced by the DEPARTMENT OF TENNESSEE AND GEORGIA.   —JES

Tennessee, CSS.

Adm. FRANKLIN BUCHANAN had 4 ships at Mobile, Ala., but the only one of significance was the great ironclad *Tennessee,* the pride of the Confederate squadron. 209 ft long, with a beam of 48 ft and a 14-ft draft, it was the biggest ironclad built in the Confederacy. The ship was framed with 13-in. yellow pine timbers and covered with 5.5 in. of pine, then 4 in. of oak. With 6 in. of armor forward, 2 in. of armor on the deck, and a battery of 6 powerful guns, the warship was one of the South's best.

Outside Mobile Bay, U.S. Rear Adm. DAVID G. FARRAGUT was mounting an assault on Buchanan's force. Farragut had 18 warships, 4 of these tough, deadly monitors, ready to brave the forts and fleet of MOBILE. The Federal fleet rode in on the flood tide the morning of 5 Aug. 1864. Fort Morgan opened for the defense, and Buchanan moved the *Tennessee* behind a line of TORPEDOES (water mines). Farragut's lead monitor, the *TECUMSEH,* turned directly for the *Tennessee,* struck a mine, and sank within 2 minutes. Farragut's flagship then took the lead and brought his fleet safely through the minefield.

Then Buchanan attacked. The quicker Union vessels evaded the *Tennessee*'s efforts to ram, but its guns damaged 6 of Farragut's ships, while Union shot bounced off the ironclad's armor. The *Tennessee* traded broadsides with the Federals until midmorning, then retired to the safety of Fort Morgan.

Farragut brought his ships to anchor and called his crews to breakfast, but Buchanan had decided to risk all in another attack. Again the *Tennessee* came on, and the Federals rushed to meet her. 1 ship rammed the Confederate vessel, then the entire fleet closed in, ringing the *Tennessee* in fire. For a mile around, Union ships rammed and fired, while the *Tennessee* replied with every gun.

Numbers soon began to tell. The monitor *Chickasaw*'s giant solid shot opened a hole in the ironclad's side. The storm of fire riddled its smokestack, and its engines lost power. Then its steering chains were shot away and the warship was out of control. Shot and shell ricocheted through open gunports, wounding Buchanan, killing others. With the ironclad dead in the water and its armor giving way, the Confederates surrendered. Farragut, the conqueror of New Orleans, had beaten the mighty *Tennessee.*   —MM

Tennessee, Union Army of the.

Created 16 Oct. 1862, the Army of the Tennessee was the best known of the Union Western armies. Although General Orders No. 168, from the Adjutant General's Office, dated 24 Oct. 1862, originally designated all troops to become the XIII Corps, the size of the force was too cumbersome, and the army was reorganized 18 Dec. 1862 into 4 corps, the new XIII, and the XV, XVI, and XVII.

The original XIII Corps was organized into the Districts of Memphis, Tenn., Corinth, Miss., and Jackson, Miss., with up to 11 divisions plus a cavalry command. When reorganized into 4 corps, each corps normally consisted of 2 or 3 brigades with attached artillery or cavalry.

The army was initially commanded by Maj. Gen. ULYSSES S.

C.S.S. Tennessee

GRANT, 16 Oct. 1862–24 Oct. 1863, and Maj. Gen. WILLIAM T. SHERMAN, 24 Oct. 1863–26 Mar. 1864. Maj. Gen. JAMES B. MCPHERSON commanded 26 Mar.–22 July 1864, when he was killed in front of Atlanta. Maj. Gen. JOHN A. LOGAN commanded briefly, 22–27 July 1864, and was replaced by Maj. Gen. OLIVER O. HOWARD, who commanded 27 July 1864–19 May 1865. Logan again assumed command until 1 Aug. 1865, when the army was mustered out of Federal service.

During its 2 years and 10 months of hard service the Army of the Tennessee participated in the winter campaigning of 1862 in northern Mississippi, the VICKSBURG CAMPAIGN of 1863, the ATLANTA CAMPAIGN of 1864, the CAROLINAS CAMPAIGN in 1865, and was at Gen. Joseph E. Johnston's surrender near Greensborough, N.C., Apr. 1865.

The army was constantly campaigning or in action and performed well throughout the war. It played a major role in the outcome of the conflict but was overshadowed by the Army of the Potomac, which received more extensive coverage in newspapers. —RAP

Tennessee, Union Department of the. At the behest of Pres. Abraham Lincoln, Maj. Gen. GEORGE H. THOMAS received General Orders No. 38, creating the Department of the Tennessee and naming him commander. Dated 23 Sept. 1862, the original order and command assignment were found unworkable and were canceled by Maj. Gen. Henry W. Halleck 29 Sept. On 16 Oct. 1862, Adj. Gen. Lorenzo Thomas informed Maj. Gen. U. S. GRANT of the creation of the department and his assignment to its command. The genesis of the department is dated from Adjutant General Thomas' order.

Defined as an area bordered on the north by Cairo, Ill., and Forts Henry and Donelson in Tennessee, the department was to include as much of northern Mississippi around Corinth and as much of Kentucky and Tennessee west of the Tennessee

River as could be controlled by Grant's troops. On creation of the Military Division of the Mississippi and Grant's elevation to its command 24 Oct. 1863, Maj. Gens. WILLIAM T. SHERMAN, JAMES B. MCPHERSON, JOHN A. LOGAN, and OLIVER O. HOWARD each in turn commanded the department. Sherman held leadership till 26 Mar. 1864, when he replaced Grant in command of the Military Division of the Mississippi; McPherson till his death 22 July; Logan only until 27 July; and Howard until 19 May 1865. Under the Military Division of the Mississippi, the department assumed a much more subordinate character, as most significant military decisions and planning were made and done by Grant and Sherman, the division commanders. Even so, command of the department was jealously sought following McPherson's death.

For RECONSTRUCTION and occupation duty, the division was dissolved 27 June 1865 in favor of the Department of the Tennessee, a command encompassing all of Tennessee, with headquarters at Knoxville. It was subordinate to the Military Division of the Tennessee (*see next entry*). —JES

Tennessee, Union Military Division of the. Following General Orders No. 118, 27 June 1865, the Military Division of the Tennessee was formally created, with headquarters at Nashville, and Maj. Gen. GEORGE H. THOMAS was named its commander. An administrative division, it oversaw the Departments of the Tennessee, Kentucky, Georgia, and Alabama —state commands for troops on occupation duty during RECONSTRUCTION. —JES

Tennessee and Georgia, Confederate Department of. The Confederate DEPARTMENT OF TENNESSEE was dissolved 15 Aug. 1864 by Special Orders No. 192 from the Adjutant and Inspector General's Office. By the same order the Confederate Department of Tennessee and Georgia was created and Gen.

JOHN B. HOOD named its commander. The new department expanded the limits of the former Confederate Department of Tennessee.

While the western and northern borders of the department were preserved, the eastern boundary changed at Augusta, Ga. The boundary arched southwest through Milledgeville and Macon, followed the western borders of the Georgia counties of Bulloch and Tattnall south, hewed to the south bank of the Ocmulgee River south to northeast Irwin County, then followed the Apalachicola River south through north Florida to the Gulf of Mexico. The southern border was simply the gulf coast from the mouth of the Apalachicola west to the mouth of the Chattahoochee River. The western border was amended 1 Oct. 1864 to follow the Chattahoochee River north and the Georgia and Alabama state lines to the Tennessee River, then to follow that stream north to the Mississippi River and that river to Tennessee's northern state line.

With Confederate fortunes waning, Gen. JOSEPH E. JOHNSTON was given command of the department 22 Feb. 1865, along with command of the DEPARTMENT OF SOUTH CAROLINA, GEORGIA, AND FLORIDA. He, in turn, delegated command of the Department of Tennessee and Georgia to Maj. Gen. HOWELL COBB 27 March. This change of command was the last and merely a formality. Organized Confederate resistance within the department had ceased weeks before.   —JES

Terrell's Texas Cavalry. CSA Alexander Watkins Terrell, a native Virginian, came in 1852 to Austin, Tex., to practice law. When the Civil War began, he received an appointment as major of the 1st Texas Cavalry of "Sibley's Arizona Brigade" (see NEW MEXICO, CONFEDERATE ARMY OF). Appointed lieutenant colonel, Terrell formed and commanded Terrell's Texas Cavalry Battalion. The officer was subsequently promoted to colonel and the battalion expanded to become Terrell's Texas Cavalry Regiment.

This regiment, sometimes incorrectly referred to as the 34th Texas Cavalry, fought primarily in Texas and Louisiana. On 11 Sept. 1863, while Terrell was absent, about 100 members of the regiment mutinied and deserted the service. Allegedly the uprising resulted from the regiment being dismounted and ordered to garrison duty at Galveston. During spring 1864 the unit fought in the RED RIVER CAMPAIGN. It was mustered out May 1865. Gen. Edmund Kirby Smith personally promoted Terrell to brigadier general shortly before the latter left the service. The appointment was, of course, never ratified.   —JDW

Terrill, James Barbour. CSA b. Bath Cty., Va., 20 Feb. 1838. An 1858 graduate of the VIRGINIA MILITARY INSTITUTE, Terrill was a practicing attorney in Warm Springs, Va., when the Civil War began in 1861. The sectional struggle divided the Terrill family, as it did so many households at that time. James accepted a commission as major in the 13th Virginia, while his older brother, WILLIAM R. TERRILL, remained loyal to the Union, becoming a brigadier general and losing his life at PERRYVILLE, Ky.

The 13th Virginia, commanded by Col. Ambrose P. Hill, fought at FIRST BULL RUN. In 1862 Terrill and the regiment participated in the SHENANDOAH VALLEY, SEVEN DAYS', CEDAR MOUNTAIN, SECOND BULL RUN, ANTIETAM, and FREDERICKSBURG campaigns. Performing capably during these battles, Terrill was promoted to lieutenant colonel and, 15 May 1863, after the Battle of CHANCELLORSVILLE, was given command of the

USMHI

regiment and his colonelcy. He led his veterans at GETTYSBURG in July and at MINE RUN in November.

Terrill continued in regimental command during the sanguinary battles of the WILDERNESS and SPOTSYLVANIA May 1864. On 30 May, during the early movements that resulted in the Battle of COLD HARBOR, Terrill was killed at Bethesda Church, Va. Federal soldiers buried the fallen officer near where he fell. The next day the Confederate Senate confirmed his previously submitted nomination to brigadier general, to rank from 1 June 1864.   —JDW

Terrill, William Rufus. USA b. Covington, Va., 21 Apr. 1834. The son of a Virginia lawyer and congressman, and brother of future Confederate Brig. Gen. JAMES B. TERRILL, William graduated 16th in the West Point class of 1853 and was assigned to the artillery. He fought in Florida against the Seminole Indians until being assigned to duty as a recruiter. Before going west to help quell the Kansas-Missouri border wars (see "BLEEDING KANSAS"), he served briefly as a mathematics instructor at his alma mater and took part in several coastal surveys conducted by the army.

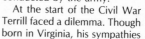

LC

At the start of the Civil War Terrill faced a dilemma. Though born in Virginia, his sympathies remained with the Union, and after a family conference, he decided to fight against the Confederacy, but only if he would not be forced to take arms against his home state.

On 14 May 1861, Terrill accepted an appointment as captain of the 5th Regular Artillery in Washington, D.C. After serving as a commandant of an instruction camp in Louisville, Ky., until the end of 1861, he became chief of artillery in the 2d Division of the Army of the Ohio. Terrill's artillery command fought with distinction at the Battle of SHILOH, and he played a major role in the Siege of CORINTH, Miss., in opposition to Gen. Braxton Bragg's Confederate invasion of Kentucky. Terrill was promoted to brigadier general of volunteers to rank from 9 Sept. 1862 after he fought in the Battle of RICHMOND, Ky.

On 8 Oct. 1862, Terrill, one of the Union army's top artillerymen, fought his last battle at PERRYVILLE. Late that afternoon, while rallying his men, he was mortally wounded by an enemy shell fragment. He died that night in the field and was transported to West Point for burial.   —FLS

Terry, Alfred Howe. USA b. Hartford, Conn., 10 Nov. 1827, Terry was one of relatively few non–West Pointers who became a major general of volunteers and went on to the same rank in the postwar Regular Army. He attended Yale Law School briefly in 1848, withdrew from the Connecticut bar a year later, then was clerk of the New Haven County Superior Court from 1854 until war began.

At FIRST BULL RUN he commanded the 2d Connecticut, a 90-day regiment, then recruited the 7th Connecticut for 3 years or the duration. With this regiment he shared in the capture of PORT ROYAL, S.C., which gave the Union a valuable base for both land and sea operations; his command also helped take FORT PULASKI, Ga. He was made

LC

brigadier general 26 Apr. 1862, and in fall 1863 assumed command of the X Corps in Maj. Gen. Benjamin F. Butler's Army of the James. During most of the next year his corps operated against Petersburg and Richmond. In Dec. 1864 he was part of Butler's force in the attempt to capture FORT FISHER, N.C. When Butler's "secret weapon"—a boat loaded with 235 tons of gunpowder—exploded harmlessly offshore, Butler called off his attack. Recalled, Butler was replaced by Terry, who, in a model amphibious operation, 15 Jan. 1865, captured the fort and sealed off Wilmington, the Confederacy's last port on the East Coast. For this he won the THANKS OF CONGRESS, a major generalcy of volunteers, and was made brigadier in the Regular Army, as of 15 Jan.

Terry's corps ended the war in the Carolinas as part of Maj. Gen. John M. Schofield's Army of the Ohio, under Maj. Gen. William T. Sherman. In the postwar years Terry commanded a department in the West, fighting Indians. He served in 1878 on the military board that reexamined the FITZ JOHN PORTER case. Regular Army major generalcy came in 1886. d. New Haven, Conn., 16 Dec. 1890.   —RDH

Terry, Henry Dwight. USA b. Hartford, Conn., 16 Mar. 1812. Though Terry had roots in New England, he moved west as a young man, establishing a law practice in Detroit and involving himself in Michigan militia affairs. When the Civil War came, he organized the 5th Michigan Infantry, becoming its colonel 10 June 1861.

During the war's first winter, Terry and his regiment served in the defenses of Washington, D.C. Throughout the 1862 PEN-INSULA CAMPAIGN, the 5th Michigan fought gamely in Brig. Gen. SAMUEL P. HEINTZELMAN's III Corps/Army of the Potomac. It absorbed heavy losses at both WILLIAMSBURG and SEVEN PINES, and in mid-July Terry was promoted to brigadier general of volunteers.

LC

Early in 1863, as a part of the VII Corps, Terry's brigade, composed of men from New York, Michigan, and Pennsylvania, was sent to Suffolk, Va. There, in April and May, it was besieged by Confederates under Lt. Gen. JAMES LONGSTREET. Once the siege was lifted, Terry reported to Maj. Gen. JOHN A. DIX, who late in June shipped his brigade up the York and

Pamunkey rivers to White House, Va. For the next 3 weeks Terry participated in an operation threatening Gen. ROBERT E. LEE's communications line to Richmond during the Confederate invasion of Pennsylvania. On 1 July 1863, while attached to Maj. Gen. ERASMUS D. KEYES's IV Corps, Terry's command marched to Baltimore Cross Roads, within striking distance of the Confederate capital, where it encountered a scratch force of defenders. Terry, however, fed Keyes's fear that enemy hordes were gathering in their rear, cutting their line of retreat. This helped persuade Keyes to retreat toward White House late on the 2d.

In the wake of the botched offensive, Dix and Keyes lost their field commands but Terry was returned to the Army of the Potomac, where that autumn he led a division in the VI Corps. His force supported Maj. Gen. GOUVERNEUR K. WAR-REN's V Corps during the abortive MINE RUN CAMPAIGN that November. Less than 2 months later, the division was sent to garrison the prison camp on JOHNSON'S ISLAND, Ohio; in May 1864, when it returned to Virginia for the spring campaign, Terry found himself superseded and left idle. He remained on inactive duty until he resigned from the volunteer service on 7 Feb. 1865. Thereafter he resumed his law practice in Washington, D.C., dying there 22 June 1869.   —EGL

Terry, William. CSA b. Amherst Cty., Va., 14 Aug. 1824, Terry graduated from the University of Virginia in 1848, taught school, practiced law, and periodically edited the Wytheville, Va., *Telegraph*. A lieutenant in a local militia company, he eventually entered Confederate service at the same rank in the 4th Virginia.

Terry and the regiment fought initially at FIRST BULL RUN, where the 4th and 4 other Virginia regiments achieved enduring fame for themselves and their commander, Brig. Gen. Thomas J. "Stonewall" Jackson. The STONEWALL BRIGADE then participated in all the major campaigns of 1862—SHENANDOAH VALLEY, SEVEN DAYS', SECOND

LC

BULL RUN, ANTIETAM, and FREDERICKSBURG. With the rank of major, Terry was wounded at Second Bull Run but returned to command the 4th Virginia at Fredericksburg.

Terry led the regiment throughout 1863 at CHANCELLORS-VILLE, GETTYSBURG, and MINE RUN. In September he received his well-deserved promotion to colonel. He commanded the regiment at the WILDERNESS May 1864 and at Spotsylvania, where the Stonewall Brigade was decimated 12 May in the Federal assault on the "MULE SHOE" salient. Promoted to brigadier general a week later, he assumed command of the merged remnants of the brigade.

Terry led the unit at COLD HARBOR, then in the 1864 SHENAN-DOAH VALLEY CAMPAIGN. At THIRD WINCHESTER, 19 Sept., he suffered his second wound. During the war's final months his brigade fought at Petersburg. On 25 Mar. 1865, in the Confederate assault on FORT STEDMAN, Terry fell severely wounded and was recovering when the army surrendered early in April.

He resumed his legal practice in Wytheville after the war; was twice elected to the U.S. House of Representatives,

1871–73 and 1875–77; and served as a delegate to the 1880 Democratic national convention. While trying to ford a creek near his home, the Confederate veteran drowned 5 Sept. 1888.　—JDW

Terry, William Richard. CSA b. Liberty, Va., 12 Mar. 1827. An 1850 graduate of the VIRGINIA MILITARY INSTITUTE, Terry then graduated from the University of Virginia. He farmed and became a merchant until the beginning of the Civil War. When Virginia seceded, he joined the Confederacy as captain of a company of cavalry.

Terry fought bravely at FIRST BULL RUN 21 July 1861, his performance earning him promotion in September to colonel and command of the 24th Virginia. He led his regiment in the 1862 PENINSULA CAMPAIGN. At WILLIAMSBURG, Va., 5 May, he suffered the first of 7 combat wounds. Returning to duty after the SEVEN DAYS' CAMPAIGN, he led the 24th at SECOND BULL RUN late in August, then temporarily commanded the brigade of Brig. Gen. James L. Kemper of Maj. Gen. George E. Pickett's division.

Terry resumed command of his regiment in 1863. At GETTYSBURG, 3 July, he fell in PICKETT'S CHARGE against the Union center. Kemper was grievously wounded in the assault, and Terry subsequently replaced the brigadier. Early in 1864 Pickett's division was sent to the Department of North Carolina and Southern Virginia, where it participated in operations against New Berne, N.C. After receiving his commission as brigadier general 31 May 1864, Terry led his brigade in the PETERSBURG CAMPAIGN. At DINWIDDIE COURT HOUSE, Va., 31 Mar. 1865, he was wounded for the final time but stayed with the army until its surrender at Appomattox.

During the postwar years, Terry served for 8 years as a Virginia state senator, then as superintendent of a penitentiary, and for 6 years as superintendent of the Confederate Soldiers' Home in Richmond, Va. The veteran died in Richmond 28 Mar. 1897. He rests with many Confederates in that city's Hollywood Cemetery.　—JDW

Terry's Expedition. 24 Dec. 1864–15 Jan. 1865 See FORT FISHER, N.C., EXPEDITION TO.

Terry's Texas Rangers (8th Texas). When Texas seceded from the Union, Benjamin Franklin Terry, a wealthy sugar planter, and Thomas S. Lubbock, a Houston commission merchant, went east to join the Confederate army. The 2 Texans subsequently served as aides at FIRST BULL RUN, received commissions, and were ordered to return to Texas and organize a cavalry regiment. Operating out of Houston, Terry and Lubbock recruited 10 companies, mustering them into service 9 Sept. 1861, a number of their officers with experience as former Texas Rangers.

The command immediately proceeded to Bowling Green, Ky., where it received horses and was formally organized into the 8th Texas Cavalry. In November the regiment's members elected Terry colonel and Lubbock lieutenant colonel. Excellent scouts, the Texans constantly patrolled the area in reconnaissance missions. At Woodsonville, Ky., 17 Dec. 1861, the regiment engaged a Federal force, and Terry, leading the initial charge, was killed. Lubbock succeeded the fallen officer, and the cavalrymen adopted the name Terry's Texas Rangers.

For the next 3 years the regiment earned a reputation as one of the hardest-fighting cavalry units of the war. A Union officer said of them that "the Texas Rangers are as quick as lightning. They ride like Arabs, shoot like archers at a mark, and fight like devils." Serving under such outstanding cavalry commanders as Maj. Gens. NATHAN B. FORREST and JOSEPH WHEELER, the regiment fought at SHILOH, PERRYVILLE, STONE'S RIVER, CHICKAMAUGA, Knoxville, and Atlanta. In a raid on Fort Donelson in winter 1863, a ranger, Sam Maverick, swam the frigid Cumberland River in a sleet storm and set fire to a number of Union transports.

Never well disciplined, Terry's troops fought with recklessness and courage. Their howling "Rebel yell" in combat soon became famous. Paroled at Greensborough, N.C., 28 Apr. 1865, Terry's Texas Rangers had a combat record among Texas troops second only to Gen. JOHN B. HOOD's famous Texas Brigade (see HOOD'S TEXAS BRIGADE).　—JDW

Texas. Most Texans favored secession after ABRAHAM LINCOLN's election. When Unionist Gov. SAM HOUSTON refused to convene the legislature or call for a secession convention, prominent secessionists published an address to the people that called for the election of delegates to a 28 Jan. 1861 convention. When Houston finally convened an emergency legislative session, its members authorized the convention but required a referendum on its decision.

A resolution of secession was passed 168–8, 1 Feb., and on 23 Feb. voters approved it 46,129–14,697, despite the opposition of some German and Northern immigrants. On 5 Mar. the convention voted to join the Confederacy, which had already admitted Texas. Houston was deposed in favor of Lt. Gov. EDWARD CLARK. Before secession was completed Union Brig. Gen. DAVID E. TWIGGS surrendered all Federal posts in Texas to Col. Ben McCulloch.

During the war Texas had great trouble with Indian raids on the frontier. Col. JOHN R. BAYLOR and Brig. Gen. HENRY HOPKINS SIBLEY led troops into New Mexico in 1861–62 but were not able to hold the territory. On 1 Jan. 1863, Maj. Gen. JOHN B. MAGRUDER recaptured GALVESTON, and on 18 Sept. Lt. RICHARD DOWLING's tiny command repulsed a Federal expedition at SABINE PASS. Federal Maj. Gen. NATHANIEL P. BANKS captured several ports late in 1863, but most of them were retaken in 1864. Banks's 1864 RED RIVER CAMPAIGN was checked in northwestern Louisiana, and he withdrew. During the latter part of the war, cut off from the Confederate government, Texas was a part of Gen. E. KIRBY SMITH's TRANS-MISSISSIPPI DEPARTMENT (often called the "Kingdom of Kirby Smith"). Smith's formal surrender was at Galveston 2 June 1865, but many Confederate soldiers had already gone to Mexico (see SURRENDERS: Gen. Kirby Smith).

Texas supplied 50,000–60,000 troops to the Confederacy. One-quarter or more of them fought east of the Mississippi; TERRY'S TEXAS RANGERS and HOOD'S TEXAS BRIGADE were the best-known units. State authorities clashed frequently with the Confederate government over such issues as CONSCRIPTION and cotton exportation. Severe shortages developed despite some trade through Mexico and a considerable expansion of industry within the state.　—LHH

8th Texas. See TERRY'S TEXAS RANGERS.

Texas, Confederate Department of. The Confederate War Department created the Department of Texas 21 Apr. 1861, assigning Maj. Gen. EARL VAN DORN to command in the

Lone Star State. Van Dorn transferred command of the department to Col. HENRY E. MCCULLOCH 4 Sept. and on the 18th Brig. Gen. PAUL O. HÉBERT replaced McCulloch as commander.

Hébert directed Confederate operations in Texas for more than a year. During this time Confederate authorities reconstituted the geographical size and administrative structure of the department. On 26 May 1862, the War Department created the TRANS-MISSISSIPPI DEPARTMENT, which encompassed Missouri, Arkansas, western Louisiana, Texas, and Indian Territory. 2 days later the District of West Louisiana and Texas was authorized, under Hébert's command. Hébert, however, continued to refer to his command as the Department of Texas. Maj. Gen. THEOPHILUS H. HOLMES, commanding the Trans-Mississippi Department, restructured it into 3 districts 20 Aug. The newly created District of Texas now embraced the entire state and the territory of Arizona.

Maj. Gen. JOHN B. MAGRUDER assumed command in Texas 10 Oct. 1862. On 29 Nov. the district was again reconstituted, as the DISTRICT OF TEXAS, NEW MEXICO, AND ARIZONA. Magruder, with headquarters at Houston, had barely 10,000 troops, absent and present, in his command. This new district permanently replaced the Department of Texas, which ceased to exist as a separate command for the state.   —JDW

Texas, Union Department of. Comprising the entire Lone Star State, with headquarters at San Antonio, the Union Department of Texas predated the Civil War. Brig. Gen. DAVID E. TWIGGS, a 70-year-old Georgian and veteran of 4 wars, commanded the department. Its Regular Army troops, mostly dragoons and cavalry, primarily guarded the state's frontier against Indian depredations.

Twiggs, a Southern sympathizer, surrendered the department's posts and property to Col. Ben McCulloch 18 Feb. 1861 before submitting his resignation from the army. With the secession of Texas, the department existed only on paper.

On 23 Feb. 1862, Union authorities placed the state in the newly organized Department of the Gulf (see GULF, UNION ARMY OF THE). Over 2 years later, 7 May 1864, the department became a part of the MILITARY DIVISION OF WEST MISSISSIPPI.
                                                           —JDW

Texas, New Mexico, and Arizona, Confederate District of. The Confederate District of Texas, New Mexico, and Arizona was officially constituted 29 Nov. 1862. Its organization resulted from the restructuring of the districts of the TRANS-MISSISSIPPI DEPARTMENT. The district's predecessor, the DEPARTMENT OF TEXAS, had undergone some alterations before Confederate authorities replaced it with the new district. The District of Texas, New Mexico, and Arizona existed until May 1865.

Maj. Gen. JOHN B. MAGRUDER assumed command of the district on the date of its creation. With headquarters at Houston, Magruder commanded 10,000 troops, most of whom were garrisoned in Texas. The actual operations of Magruder's command centered on Texas, for Federal soldiers, since early 1862, controlled the territories of New Mexico and Arizona.

The district's troops participated in a number of important engagements under Magruder's direction. On 1 Jan. 1863, in a surprise attack at dawn, the Confederates recaptured GALVESTON, holding the gulf port until 2 June 1865. Later in January, on the 29th, troops of the district, using 2 steamers, attacked and captured 2 Federal blockading ships at SABINE PASS, on the

Red River. In spring 1864, the district commander sent most of his troops to Lt. Gen. RICHARD TAYLOR for the RED RIVER CAMPAIGN. With the aid of the Texas soldiers, Taylor defeated the Union army of Maj. Gen. NATHANIEL P. BANKS.

Maj. Gen. JOHN G. WALKER replaced Magruder as district commander 10 June 1864, holding the post until 31 Mar. 1865, when Magruder returned, assuming command 4 Apr. The district ceased to exist with the surrender of the Confederates in Texas.   —JDW

Thanks of Congress, Confederate States. The Provisional Congress of the newly formed Confederacy passed its first Thanks of Congress 8 Feb. 1861, its second day of business. The citation thanked the state of Alabama for hosting the Confederate government at Montgomery and for voting a loan of $500,000 to the Confederacy. Thereafter, scarcely a month went by during the Civil War in which the Congress did not pass several resolutions thanking an officer, a military or naval unit, a state, or a civilian.

Although most Confederate Thanks of Congress went to army and navy commanders and their men for victories in the field, many went to units for reenlisting and to states for monetary support. A 19 June 1864 thanks went to "John Lancaster of England, for gallant and humane conduct in the rescue of Capt. Raphael Semmes and his men after the sinking of the *Alabama*."

The first military citation, published in the *Journal* of the Confederate Congress 6 May 1861, went to "General [Pierre] Gustave T. Beauregard and the army under his command for their conduct in the affair of Fort Sumter." The Confederate victory in the first major battle of the war, FIRST BULL RUN, brought congressional thanks "to Gen. Joseph E. Johnston and Gen. [Pierre] Gustave T. Beauregard and the men under their command."

Gen. ROBERT E. LEE received several Thanks of Congress. Some members of Congress, urging an invasion of the North Sept. 1862, tried to push their views by introducing a resolution thanking Lee for advancing north of the Potomac, but the citation was reworded after debate to thank Lee and his men only "for battles won." Among the many naval commanders thanked by the Confederate Congress were JOHN T. WOOD (Chesapeake Bay), Ebenezer Farrand (Drewry's Bluff), Issac N. Brown (Vicksburg), and RAPHAEL SEMMES and the officers of the *ALABAMA*.

The Confederate Congress published its thanks until the final days of the Confederacy. Its final citation, 17 Mar. 1865, went to Lt. Gen. WADE HAMPTON for the defense of Richmond.
                                                           —DS

Thanks of Congress, United States. Thanks of Congress citations were published in the *Congressional Record* to honor officers and enlisted men of the U.S. Army and Navy from late 1861 through May 1866. These citations were made sparingly —only 15 each for army and navy personnel during the entire war—although some honored more than 1 hero or military unit. The citation of 28 Jan. 1864, for example, thanked Maj. Gens. JOSEPH HOOKER, GEORGE G. MEADE, and OLIVER O. HOWARD for various actions; that of 7 Feb. 1863 thanked 5 naval officers for a variety of feats.

The first Thanks of Congress, published 24 Dec. 1861, recognized "the gallant and patriotic services of the late Brig. Gen. Nathaniel Lyon, and the officers and soldiers under his command at the Battle of WILSON'S CREEK, 10 Aug. 1861. On 22 Feb. 1862 came the most all-inclusive thanks: "To the officers, soldiers and seamen of the Army and Navy of the United States, for the heroic gallantry that . . . has won the recent series of brilliant victories over the enemies of the Union and constitution."

Among the more notable thanks to army officers were those to Maj. Gen. U. S. GRANT (along with a specially struck gold medal) for his victories of 1863; to Maj. Gen. WILLIAM T. SHERMAN (2 citations) for Tennessee and Georgia victories in 1863–64; and to Maj. Gen. WINFIELD S. HANCOCK for his conduct at Gettysburg (awarded in 1866, 3 years after the battle).

Navy heroes DAVID G. FARRAGUT and DAVID D. PORTER received 2 or more Thanks of Congress. Lt. JOHN L. WORDEN, commander of the *Monitor,* was thanked for his leadership in the epic duel with the CSS *Virginia (Merrimack),* and Capt. JOHN A. WINSLOW of the *Kearsarge* was thanked for sinking the Confederate raider *Alabama.*

Countless important victories and acts of heroism went unthanked. Whether thanks was given seems to have depended on the concern of a commander's friends and admirers in Congress. Highly prized, a Thanks of Congress citation was almost always included in any biographical sketch of a Union officer.   —DS

Thayer, John Milton. USA b. Bellingham, Mass., 24 Jan. 1820, Thayer, whose ancestors came to the Bay State in 1647, briefly taught school before graduating from Brown University in 1841. Studying law, he opened an office in Worcester, Mass., and in 1854 moved to Nebraska Territory, where he farmed near Omaha. A former lieutenant of a militia company in Worcester, Thayer was appointed the territory's first brigadier general of militia when the Pawnees staged an uprising. He performed capably in that post and the legislature elected him major general.

LC

When the Civil War began, Thayer became colonel of the 1st Nebraska 21 July 1861. By early 1862 he was commanding a brigade in the division of Maj. Gen. Lew Wallace, leading it at FORT DONELSON and SHILOH. He was promoted to brigadier general 4 Oct. 1862, but the Senate failed to confirm the nomination before it expired. Reappointed and confirmed 13 Mar. 1863, Thayer commanded a division in the XV Corps during the VICKSBURG CAMPAIGN.

Thayer then transferred to Arkansas. On 22 Feb. 1864, he was named commander of the District of the Frontier. That spring he participated in Maj. Gen. Frederick Steele's CAMDEN EXPEDITION in southwestern Arkansas. Relieved of his command of the district 27 Feb. 1865, he was stationed at St. Charles, Ark., until he resigned 19 July. For his war services, the War Department brevetted him major general.

Returning to Nebraska, Thayer engaged in politics for nearly 30 years, becoming one of Nebraska's first 2 senators in 1867. A Republican, he favored Radical Reconstruction and gave his political support to Pres. Ulysses S. Grant. When Thayer's

constituents failed to reelect him in 1871, Grant appointed him governor of Wyoming Territory. From 1886 to 1892 he served as governor of Nebraska, retiring from public life when his term expired. d. Lincoln, Neb., 19 Mar. 1906.   —JDW

13th Amendment. Though emancipation was not one of the original war issues, and only gradually became a major political issue, the Federal government made repeated efforts to interfere with the institution of slavery in the rebellious states. In 1861 and 1862 Congress enacted Confiscation Acts, by terms of which slaveholders forfeited the labor of all slaves employed in making arms or building fortifications, and Confederate-owned slaves found in captured territory or in military service to the Union were emancipated. In his EMANCIPATION PROCLAMATION of 1 Jan. 1863, Pres. ABRAHAM LINCOLN freed all persons held as slaves in states or parts of states then in rebellion. Though they were bitterly denounced by the Confederates, these measures still left vast numbers of slaves untouched. Lincoln himself regretted that his proclamation did not reach the children of freed slaves and slaves in uncaptured territory, and he entertained real fears that the SUPREME COURT might declare the entire measure unconstitutional.

To finally eradicate the hated institution, Republicans in Congress proposed a sweeping Constitutional amendment that would abolish slavery everywhere and for all time. On 8 Apr. 1864, the Senate adopted the resolution of amendment by a vote of 38–6. The same resolution was favored in the House, but not by the required two-thirds. After a summer of Union victories on the battlefield and the presidential election of 1864, the amendment was brought for a second time before the House, where, 31 Jan. 1865, it carried by a vote of 119–56 —just 3 votes more than the required two-thirds.

Though the U.S. Constitution does not require it, the amendment was submitted to Lincoln, who promptly added his signature. The measure was, Lincoln said, "a king's cure for all evils. It winds the whole thing up."

The constitutionality as well as the wisdom of the proposed 13th Amendment were the subjects of widespread and heated discussion. It was the first time a substantive reform had been the object of an amendment—the first time the amending power had been used for any purpose other than a change in the rules of elections or a limitation on the powers of the Federal government. Some argued that the proposed amendment was itself unconstitutional—that the amending power did not extend to interference in the domestic affairs of the states. The Constitution, these opponents argued, was a contract among the states; it could be amended so as to diminish the power of any state only if that state—if, in fact, *all* the states —consented to the diminution.

36 states existed when the amendment was proposed. The favorable vote of 27—three-fourths of the total—was required for ratification. Not counting the Confederate states, there were 25 that could consider the issue. 2 (Kentucky and Delaware) were slaveholding states and rejected the measure. If the amendment was to become part of the Constitution, at least 4 of the Confederate states would have to assent. After the Confederate surrender at Appomattox, Pres. ANDREW JOHNSON established RECONSTRUCTION governments in the former Confederate states. Radicals in Congress did not recognize these governments, though they were willing to accept their resolutions of ratification. When on 18 Dec. 1865 Sec. of State WILLIAM H. SEWARD counted the votes of 27 states in favor of

the 13th Amendment, 8 were past members of the Confederacy. The amendment had been ratified. Att. Gen. EDWARD BATES noted in his diary that 1 prominent Radical had frequently declared in the House: "The State of Tennessee is not known to this House or to Congress!" "And so it seems," Bates added, "they are not states in the Union, yet they can enact a Constitution for the United States!" —BMcG

Thomas, Allen.

Thomas, Allen. CSA b. Howard Cty., Md., 14 Dec. 1830. An 1850 graduate of the College of New Jersey, Thomas studied law in his home state and maintained a practice there until his marriage in 1857 to a woman from Louisiana, where he established himself as a planter. 2 of his brothers-in-law, DUNCAN F. KENNER and RICHARD TAYLOR, became prominent Confederates.

At the outbreak of Civil War Thomas organized a battalion of infantry, which was enlarged into the 29th Louisiana Infantry. He was later elected colonel of the regiment, to rank from 2 May 1862, and led the 29th in the fighting around Vicksburg, notably at Chickasaw Bluffs

LC

Dec. 1862. Having been pushed back into the city by advancing Federals, he and his command were among the troops surrendered by Maj. Gen. JOHN C. PEMBERTON 4 July 1863. Thomas was paroled quickly, and carried to Pres. JEFFERSON DAVIS in Richmond Pemberton's report of the surrender of Vicksburg. The War Department then assigned him to the Trans-Mississippi with orders to collect and reorganize parolees west of the Mississippi River.

On 4 Feb. 1864, Thomas was promoted to brigadier general and sent to Alexandria, La., to Maj. Gen. Richard Taylor's department. He took over Maj. Gen. Camille Polignac's division early in 1865, when that officer traveled to Europe to seek Napoleon's aid for the Confederacy. Thomas was paroled at Natchitoches, La., 8 June 1865, shortly after Taylor surrendered the last troops east of the Mississippi.

He then returned to his plantation, serving as a presidential elector in 1872 and 1880, on the board of supervisors of Louisiana State University in 1882, and as a professor of agriculture there 1882–84. From 1889 until 1907 Thomas lived in Florida, except for 3 years, 1894–97, during which he held the consulship in Venezuela. Shortly before his death 3 Dec. 1907, he moved to a plantation he had bought near Waveland, Miss. His remains were buried in his wife's family vault in Donaldsonville, La. —PLF

Thomas, Bryan Morel.

Thomas, Bryan Morel. CSA b. Milledgeville, Ga., 8 May 1836. After attending Oglethorpe University in Georgia, Thomas won appointment to West Point and graduated 22d in the class of 1858. Following garrison duty in New York State, he was stationed in Utah, served in New Mexico, then resigned his commission 6 Apr. 1861 to accept a lieutenant's position in the Confederate service.

Thomas joined Maj. Gen. Jones M. Withers' staff, fought at the Battle of SHILOH, and as acting adjutant and inspector general won praise for his action on the Confederate right on the

LC

first day of the fight. Advanced to captain, then major, he retained his staff position with Withers through the KENTUCKY CAMPAIGN of autumn 1862, briefly took sick leave, then rejoined his major general for the Battle of STONE'S RIVER.

Continuing as a staff officer until Mar. 1864, at Lt. Gen. Leonidas Polk's suggestion he recruited a cavalry brigade in Alabama. But the state's depleted manpower reserve limited him to a unit of 375 under-age boys and men over 45. Though addressed as colonel, he was not commissioned as such, and his "brigade" briefly served in Brig. Gen. James H. Clanton's Alabama cavalry with no state or national unit designation. Temporarily assigned to Brig. Gen. Gideon J. Pillow, Thomas' men were transferred to the Mobile, Ala., defenses.

Maj. Gen. DABNEY H. MAURY, commander of Mobile and the DISTRICT OF THE GULF, had serious need there of capable general officers and none could be transferred to him. Thomas, trained at West Point and experienced with military staff work, won promotion 4 Aug. 1864 from major to brigadier general at the urging of his superiors. He served capably through the last days of the Confederate defense of Mobile, refused surrender, was captured in a desperate attempt to hold FORT BLAKELY 9 Apr. 1865, then was released shortly afterward.

In postwar years Thomas farmed in Georgia, served as a deputy U.S. marshal, founded a private academy in 1884, and, settling in the Dalton area, became superintendent of the city's schools. d. Dalton, 16 July 1905. —JES

Thomas, Edward Lloyd.

Thomas, Edward Lloyd. CSA b. Clarke Cty., Ga., 23 Mar. 1825. A wealthy Georgia planter, without formal military training, Thomas became one of the better brigade commanders in the Army of Northern Virginia. For nearly 3 years, he led, with gallantry and distinction, 4 Georgia regiments in the rugged LIGHT DIVISION, participating in nearly every major campaign in the East from Seven Days' to Appomattox.

An 1846 graduate of Emory College in Georgia, Thomas served as a 2d lieutenant in a cavalry command during the Mexican War. Returning to his Georgia plantation, he prospered, becoming a prominent local leader. Thomas did not immediately volunteer after the dissolution of the Union but, 15 Oct. 1861, he was commissioned colonel of the 35th Georgia, a regiment he recruited with the authorization of Confederate Pres. Jefferson Davis.

GG

Thomas' initial engagement of the war was the Battle of SEVEN PINES, Va., where he temporarily commanded a brigade. A natural leader, he succeeded Brig. Gen. JOSEPH R. ANDERSON as brigade commander June 1862. He led his unit during the

SEVEN DAYS' battles, falling wounded at MECHANICSVILLE on the 26th but refusing to relinquish command. His brigade then fought at CEDAR MOUNTAIN early in August and with the other 5 brigades of Maj. Gen. Ambrose P. Hill's Light Division, savagely defended the unfinished railroad embankment line at SECOND BULL RUN. Paroling prisoners at Harpers Ferry, Va., Thomas' unit missed the division's timely counterattack at ANTIETAM, Md., 17 Sept.

On 1 Nov. 1862, Thomas secured his promotion to brigadier general. He commanded his Georgians at FREDERICKSBURG in December and at CHANCELLORSVILLE May 1863. After the latter battle, the Confederate army was reorganized, and Thomas' brigade and 3 other brigades of the Light Division were placed in a new division under Maj. Gen. WILLIAM D. PENDER. When Pender fell mortally wounded at Gettysburg, Gen. Robert E. Lee considered Thomas for the command but assigned another brigadier because the division contained 2 North Carolina brigades and 1 from South Carolina. Promoting the Georgian, Lee believed, might cause dissatisfaction among these Carolinians. Thomas remained a brigade commander, leading his Georgians during the struggles of 1864–65. He surrendered with his men at Appomattox.

After the surrender, Thomas returned to his plantation, remaining there until 1885, when Pres. Grover Cleveland appointed him to a post in the Land Department, then in the Indian Bureau. Thomas died in Indian Territory 8 Mar. 1898 and is buried in Oklahoma. —JDW

Thomas, George Henry. USA b. Southampton Cty., Va., 31 July 1816. A veteran officer of the antebellum army, Thomas, expected to leave Federal service for a Confederate commission when secession began, faced a personal crisis in 1861. His decision to stay in the uniform he had worn since youth alienated him from family and friends, and invited the distrust of the U.S. government.

Thomas began the Civil War with troops in the Shenandoah Valley during the FIRST BULL RUN CAMPAIGN. On 17 Aug. 1861, he was made a brigadier general and was transferred to Kentucky, where he handed the Union a victory at MILL SPRINGS Jan. 1862. In the next several

USMHI

months he served under Maj. Gens. Henry W. Halleck, Don Carlos Buell, and William S. Rosecrans; was promoted to major general 25 Apr. 1862; and fought in the Siege of CORINTH and the Battles of SHILOH, PERRYVILLE, and STONE'S RIVER.

At CHICKAMAUGA, on the second day of fighting, when the right of the Union line folded, Thomas and his men held their ground until support came. For resilience in that fight, the press and his troops acclaimed him the "Rock of Chickamauga."

After helping break the Confederate Siege of CHATTANOOGA, in Nov. 1863 Thomas' troops distinguished themselves at the Battles of LOOKOUT MOUNTAIN and MISSIONARY RIDGE. Added to previous successes, they won the Virginian the position of second-in-command on Maj. Gen. William T. Sherman's staff for the ATLANTA CAMPAIGN. Heading the Army of the Cumberland, he did yeoman service on the road to Georgia and acquit-

ted himself smartly against Gen. John B. Hood in the Battle of PEACHTREE CREEK.

Sherman seized Atlanta, Hood invaded Tennessee, and Thomas was hurried off to organize the defense of NASHVILLE. There he received little support from subordinates and superiors uncertain of his loyalties, but 2 days of hard battle and victory bought him respect from those in Washington who had doubted his patriotism and ability.

For his triumph at Nashville Thomas was made a major general in the U.S. Army Regulars, and given command of the Division of Tennessee and the Departments of Tennessee and the Cumberland. He completed the war in that post, receiving the THANKS OF CONGRESS 3 Mar. 1865.

In 1869 Thomas requested command of the Division of the Pacific, which he received. The following year, 28 Mar. 1870, he died at his office in San Francisco. —JES

Thomas, Lorenzo. USA b. New Castle, Del., 26 Oct. 1804, Thomas graduated from West Point in 1823, 17th in his class, and joined the 4th Infantry, apparently destined for a brilliant military career.

He served in the various campaigns against the Florida Seminoles, both in the Quartermaster Department and as chief of staff. In 1838 he was in Washington as assistant adjutant general with the rank of a brevet major, and during the Mexican War served as adjutant general in the volunteer division of Maj. Gen. William O. Butler. After he was brevetted lieutenant colonel for "gallant and meritorious conduct" at Monterrey, his army career consisted of long stretches of mediocre performance.

LC

Back in Washington after the war Thomas again settled down to the routines of an assistant adjutant general. In 1853 he became the chief of staff for Gen. WINFIELD SCOTT and 7 Mar. 1861 became the adjutant general of the Federal army. He was given the rank of brigadier general as of 3 Aug.

Early in the Civil War Thomas was criticized for being "too slow," "laxity and inefficiency," and being "lukewarm" about the war. But there is evidence the general was a vain, garrulous man who offended Sec. of War EDWIN M. STANTON. No-nonsense Stanton removed Thomas from Washington, sending him to the Mississippi Valley to organize black regiments and on inspection tours of the provost marshal general's offices and national cemeteries.

In the postwar controversy between Pres. ANDREW JOHNSON and Stanton, the president directed Thomas to take full charge of the adjutant general's office, then dismissed Stanton and appointed Thomas acting secretary of war. During Johnson's impeachment trial Thomas served the president well with testimony so naïve it dispelled any suspicion that he and the president had "conspired" to remove Stanton.

Thomas continued his inspection duties until he retired 22 Feb. 1869. d. District of Columbia, 2 Mar. 1875. —AG

Thompson, Jacob. CSP b. Leasburg, N.C., 15 May 1810, Thompson, the studious son of a wealthy Virginian, graduated from the University of North Carolina in 1831. He then studied law, remaining at the university as a tutor until being admitted to the bar in 1835. As much to escape his stern father as for any other reason, Thompson moved to Pontotoc, Miss., and later to Oxford, where he entered politics. A Democrat elected to 6 terms in the U.S. House of Representatives beginning in 1838, he was appointed secretary of the interior by Pres. James Buchanan in 1857. After he resigned his cabinet post to join the Confederacy, he became Gen. P.G.T. Beauregard's aide, later served consecutively under Gens. John C. Pemberton and Stephen D. Lee, and in 1863 held a seat in the Mississippi legislature.

A year later JEFFERSON DAVIS appointed him Confederate commissioner to Canada. A secret agent, Thompson was to free Confederate soldiers imprisoned in the Great Lakes region and attempt to weaken the financial strength of gold in the North. Initially entrusted with at least $200,000, by 1865 he had received an additional $330,000 from bank- and train-robbing Confederate raiders.

As the last of Davis' cabinet fled Richmond Apr. 1865, they were encouraged by the thought that Thompson had funds left over from his wartime mission. But through navy captain John T. Wood, Sec. of War JOHN C. BRECKINRIDGE learned that all Confederate accounts in Canada had been closed. After the assassination of ABRAHAM LINCOLN, Thompson had withdrawn all Confederate money from Toronto and Montreal banks and fled to France. For 4 years he lived in high style in the elegant Grand Hotel in Paris, refusing to turn over the money to former secretary of state JUDAH P. BENJAMIN, also a refugee, because he thought the government owed it to him for his crops, destroyed in Mississippi by Federal troops during the war.

Finally, Thompson, who 1 historian claims "may very well rank as the greatest scoundrel of the Civil War," agreed to turn over £12,000 if Benjamin would make no more claims against him and if Breckinridge would arrange for the return of $5,000 Thompson had contributed toward the postwar defense of Davis. To this day, the amount Thompson embezzled is undetermined, but his bequests reveal that he died a relatively rich man in Memphis, Tenn., 24 Mar. 1885.   —FLS

Thompson, Merriwether Jeff.
CSA b. Harpers Ferry, Va., 22 Jan. 1826, M. Jeff Thompson left Virginia after his applications to West Point and Lexington Military Academy were rejected. Frustrated in his attempts to be a professional soldier, he worked as a clerk, drifting from city to city, until he stopped in Liberty, Mo. He briefly worked as a fur trapper before settling in St. Joseph. During the antebellum years, he surveyed for a railroad and the county, organized a gas company, and dabbled in real estate. In 1859 citizens of St. Joseph elected the likable and prosperous Thompson mayor.

When the Civil War rent the border state, Thompson, an avowed secessionist, organized a battalion of volunteers and issued a statewide proclamation calling on fellow citizens to embrace the Confederate cause. When Gov. Clairborne F.

LC

Jackson rejected his battalion, Thompson rode south with his command. Calling themselves "Swamp Rats," these Missouri Confederates began raiding Union posts and towns.

Over the next 4 years Thompson, a natural leader, became feared as the "Swamp Fox of the Confederacy." He operated both as a part of Confederate armies and independently, fighting valiantly for the Southern cause in Missouri and Arkansas. On 10 May 1862, Thompson directed the Confederate rams in the action at PLUM RUN BEND, Tenn. In 1863 he offered his services to Lt. Gen. E. KIRBY SMITH in the Trans-Mississippi Department. While working on Smith's staff, he was surprised and captured by Missouri state cavalry 22 Aug. and was imprisoned until exchanged June 1864.

Returning to Missouri, Thompson, who called himself a general, participated in Maj. Gen. STERLING PRICE's raid into the state. He bravely led his brigade of cavalry at WESTPORT 23 Oct. After spending the war's final months in the swamps, he finally surrendered 9 May 1865.

Thompson drifted again after the war. He established a business in Memphis that failed within a year, then moved to New Orleans. d. St. Joseph, Mo., 5 Sept. 1876.   —JDW

3-in. ordnance gun.
The 3-in. rifled ordnance gun was one of the most common field pieces used in the Civil War. Adopted by the U.S. military in 1861, the weapon was maneuverable, accurate at long range, and capable of firing a variety of shells. As a result, it was popular among field artillery units and performed in nearly every major action of the war.

Rifled artillery was still in its infancy when the Civil War broke out. Developed in the mid-1850s, the concept commanded the attention of cannon builders and designers until the end of the war. The 3-in. ordnance gun was among the first family of rifled artillery whose virtues were quickly applied by Federal artillerists. In the Union army a division or brigade had at its disposal batteries of rifled guns (ordnance or Parrotts) for long range and smoothbores (Napoleons or howitzers) for close range. The combination was extremely effective.

The wrought-iron barrel of the ordnance gun, weighing approximately 820 lb, was constructed of sheets of boiler iron wrapped around a core. This sturdy tube, which was strong enough not to need breech reinforcement, tapered evenly from breech to muzzle in a distinctive, sleek fashion.

The bore was a full 3 in. and could fire elongated 10-lb Schenkl, Hotchkiss, and Parrott shells. As a rule, the powder charge weighed 1 lb and could propel a shell up to 2,000 yd accurately at an elevation of only 5°. Greater distances could be attained with higher elevations, but the level of accuracy decreased accordingly.

Artillerymen of the day often referred to the ordnance gun as a "Rodman," despite the fact that cannon designer Thomas J. Rodman had nothing to do with the building or design of the weapon.   —SWS

Tibbits, William Badger.
USA b. Hoosick Falls, N.Y., 31 Mar. 1837. An 1859 graduate of Union College in Schenectady, Tibbits studied law and engaged in manufacturing. When Pres. Abraham Lincoln, 15 Apr. 1861, called for volunteers to suppress the Southern rebellion, he recruited a company of the 2d New York, a 2-year command.

Commissioned captain 14 May, Tibbits fought initially at BIG BETHEL, Va., 10 June. The 2d New York then participated in the major campaigns of 1862: PENINSULA, SEVEN DAYS', SECOND

BULL RUN, and FREDERICKSBURG. Promoted to major 13 Oct. 1862, Tibbits fought at CHANCEL-LORSVILLE May 1863. The regiment, its term of service having expired, mustered out 26 May.

Tibbits reenlisted 5 Feb. 1864 as colonel of the 21st New York Cavalry and commanded a brigade of cavalry during the Union defeat at NEW MARKET, Va., 15 May. The next month he led his cavalrymen in the fighting at PIEDMONT, his performance earning him a strong

LC

recommendation for promotion from Maj. Gen. David Hunter, department commander. He was brevetted brigadier general 21 Oct. 1864. From Feb. to Apr. 1865, he commanded a cavalry division in the Middle Military Division, on 18 Oct. 1865 becoming one of the last officers commissioned to the full rank of brigadier general.

Mustering out in 1866, Tibbits moved to Troy, N.Y., residing there until his death on 10 Feb. 1880.   —JDW

Tilghman, Lloyd. CSA b. "Rich Neck Manor," near Claiborne, Md., 18 Jan. 1816, Tilghman attended West Point, from which he graduated 46th in the class of 1836. Deciding not to be a professional soldier, he re-signed from the army, but did serve during the Mexican War as a volunteer general's aide. After the war Tilghman worked as a construction engineer for a number of railroads in the South. He entered Confederate service from Kentucky, the state he had adopted in 1852, and acquired a brigadier generalcy 18 Oct. 1861.

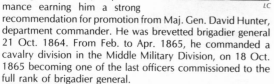

Tilghman was made inspector of FORTS HENRY and DONELSON in Tennessee and early began a series of warnings that those

NA

points were in a woeful state of unreadiness. Despite Tilghman's repeated pleas, Maj. Gen. Leonidas Polk, the district commander, sent no help. Worse, for many weeks various Confederate officers with responsibility for the forts engaged in petty spats, and inefficiencies blurred and hindered the preparation of defenses.

Tilghman took personal command at Fort Henry and did everything he could to make the place ready and to warn his superiors of an impending Federal onslaught. When Maj. Gen. Ulysses S. Grant's attack nearly encircled the fort, Tilghman, knowing that his 2,600 poorly armed troops could not match the 16,000 Federals, sent all but 80—a skeleton garrison—to Fort Donelson. He gallantly remained with the remnant of his men and 6 Feb. 1862 surrendered Fort Henry.

Taken prisoner, he was not exchanged until fall 1862. He then took command of a brigade in Maj. Gen. William Wing Loring's division/Army of the West and led the unit at COR-INTH, in the rear guard after HOLLY SPRINGS, and in the VICKS-BURG CAMPAIGN. On 16 May 1863, while directing artillery fire

during the Battle of CHAMPION'S HILL, he was struck in the chest by a shell fragment and killed.   —HH

Tillson, Davis. USA b. Rockland, Maine, 14 Apr. 1830. Tillson attended West Point for 2 years when an accident leaving him with 1 leg ended his career at the Military Academy. In the 10 years before the war he served in the state legislature, as Maine's adjutant general, then as his district's collector of customs.

Tillson began his Civil War service as captain of the 2d Battery/1st Mounted Artillery, mustered on 30 Nov. 1861. Although his war career cannot be considered distinguished, he performed creditably for the Federal Army at the Battles of CEDAR MOUNTAIN, 9 Aug. 1862, and SECOND BULL RUN, 29–30 Aug. 1862. As a lieutenant colo-

LC

nel in his first year of service, Tillson gained the trust of several Union officers who retained him as chief of artillery.

In spring 1863 he accepted an appointment as brigadier general of volunteers, to rank from 29 Nov. 1862. A few weeks later, in Cincinnati, Ohio, he was in charge of artillery for fortifications in the Department of the Ohio. While simultaneously commanding an infantry brigade, Tillson was placed in charge of the defensive works at Knoxville, Tenn.

He then commanded the District of East Tennessee until being appointed to lead a division in the Army of the Cumberland, a post held through the end of the war. As a director of the FREEDMEN'S BUREAU in Georgia and Tennessee, he stayed in the army until the end of 1866, when he remained in the South in an attempt to prosper at cotton farming in Georgia. 2 years later he moved back to Maine to enter into a stone-mining business. d. Rockland, Maine, 30 Apr. 1895.   —FLS

Timrod, Henry. poet b. Charleston, S.C., 8 Dec. 1828. From his father, a bookbinder and local poet of some note, Timrod inherited the literary talents that made him the finest of the Confederate poets. An absentminded romantic little inclined to serious study, he ended his formal education after 2 years at Franklin College, now the University of Georgia at Athens. His attempt to read law in the office of Charlestonian James L. Petigru revealed him unsuited to a legal career. For a few years he tutored on local plantations and wrote for various periodicals, including the *Southern Literary Messenger*. A small collection of nature poems he published in 1860 drew favorable reviews but failed to attract the attention of a public distracted by sectional conflict.

Secession inspired the poet to express his patriotism in verses celebrating the Southern cause, and Feb. 1861 he wrote "Ethnogenesis" to commemorate the formation of the Confederacy. The intense emotionalism of his poetry fed Southerners' war fervor. The best of his works, among them "A Cry to Arms," "Carolina," "Carmen Triumphale," and "Charleston," were widely reprinted in Confederate newspapers, winning for Timrod the title "Poet Laureate of the Confederacy."

Timrod delayed entering Confederate service because of ill health, and his military career was short-lived. On enlisting

Mar. 1862, he was sent to the West as a correspondent for the Charleston *Mercury,* arriving shortly after the battle at SHILOH. That December he was discharged as medically unfit and returned to South Carolina to work in Columbia as a reporter and editor until the end of the war. During his last 2 years he lived in poverty, suffering from the final stages of tuberculosis. "Ode," a postwar composition written as a eulogy to Confederates buried at Charleston's Magnolia Cemetery, is considered by many critics the best of his works.

Timrod died in Columbia, 6 Oct. 1867. In 1884 his close friend and fellow Southern poet, Paul Hamilton Hayne, published *The Poems of Henry Timrod.* —PLF

"tinclads." Also called "light drafts," these vessels were not tin at all, nor were they classified as ironclads. Instead, they were 4th-class U.S. gunboats designed for use by the navy on shallow Western and Southern rivers, lakes, and bayous. Because of continual harassment of U.S. naval forces by Confederate batteries and riflemen stationed along the riverbanks, Flag Officer CHARLES H. DAVIS recognized the urgency in acquiring and utilizing tinclad-type vessels. Late in 1862 the Navy Department began purchasing side- and stern-wheel river steamers and converting them into gunboats light enough to maintain a draft of 2 to 3 ft. The USS *Rattler* became tinclad No. 1, and more than 60 others followed. Iron plates one-half to three-quarters of an inch thick were attached along their lower hulls, up to 11 ft above waterlines. Boilers were also protected with iron. Although not strong enough to withstand heavier shells, the iron nevertheless offered adequate protection from rifle fire and light and medium artillery. These vessels were armed with howitzers, usually 2 bow guns. A heavier class of tinclads was armed with larger-caliber guns and had a somewhat heavier armor.

The tinclads played an important part in the RIVER WAR during 1863 and 1864. 2—the USS *Signal* and USS *Queen City* —were captured by Confederates in May and June 1864. Another tinclad, the USS *Cricket,* gained special renown for capturing 2 Confederate steamers on the White River, taking part in the final campaign against VICKSBURG, and enduring intense enemy fire while serving as Adm. DAVID D. PORTER's flagship during the RED RIVER CAMPAIGN. —NCD

Tishomingo Creek, Miss., Battle of. 10 June 1864 *See* BRICE'S CROSS ROADS, MISS., BATTLE OF.

Tod, David. war governor b. near Youngstown, Ohio, 21 Feb. 1805. The son of a noted judge, Tod attended Burton Academy in Ohio and passed the bar in 1827. Entering local politics, Tod, a Democrat, took a seat in the Ohio state senate in 1838. He was appointed minister to Brazil by Pres. James K. Polk in 1847. 10 years later he returned to Youngstown to oversee his growing coal and iron business. In Apr. 1860 he attended the Democratic national convention in Charleston, S.C. 2 years later, he was nominated Ohio's governor on the Union ticket and handily defeated Democrat Hugh J. Jewett.

Taking office Jan. 1862, Tod found growing antiwar sentiment his biggest problem. To supply Ohio's quota for the Federal army, the governor induced militia regiments to enter Regular service by paying high bounties. To finance the cost, stiff COMMUTATION fees were levied against draft evaders and resisters. During the Ohio gubernatorial race of 1864, the Democrats nominated U.S. Congressman CLEMENT L. VALLAN-

DIGHAM, a vocal anti-Lincoln activist who drew support in war-weary Ohio. Tod had threatened to arrest disloyal citizens. Unfortunately for the governor, an overly zealous Maj. Gen. AMBROSE E. BURNSIDE, head of the Military Department of the Ohio, arrested Vallandigham, causing a great uproar among Northern Democrats. Tod was nearly forced out of office before the din subsided.

At the Republican state convention in 1864, the governor was bitterly disappointed over not being renominated. The Vallandigham affair, arbitrary arrests, and high administrative expenses had diminished his popularity among the electorate. The governor had also run afoul of railroad interests intent on linking Ohio and the South.

As a private citizen, Tod continued to support Lincoln and the war effort. When SALMON P. CHASE resigned as secretary of the treasury 30 June 1864, Lincoln offered Tod the post. The former governor refused, citing poor health and pressing business interests. Elected a Republican presidential elector in 1868, Tod died the same year 13 Nov. —MTC

Tompkins, Sally Louisa. nurse b. "Poplar Grove," Mathews Cty., Va., 9 Nov. 1833. After her husband's death, Tompkins' mother moved the family to Richmond, where Sally lived at the outbreak of civil war.

MC

When the government asked the public to help care for the wounded of FIRST BULL RUN, Tompkins responded by opening a private hospital in a house donated for that purpose by Judge John Robertson. Robertson Hospital, subsidized by Tompkins' substantial inheritance, treated 1,333 Confederate soldiers from its opening until the last patients were discharged 13 June 1865.

Because the hospital returned more of its patients to the ranks than any other medical-care facility, officers tried to place their most seriously wounded men in Tompkins' care. She used her high rate of success to convince Pres. JEFFERSON DAVIS to allow her hospital to stay open even as his orders shut down other private hospitals in the city. To circumvent the regulation calling for all hospitals to be run by military personnel, on 9 Sept. 1861 Davis appointed Tompkins captain of cavalry, unassigned, making her the only woman to hold a commission in the Confederate States Army. Her military rank allowed her to draw government rations and a salary to help defray some of her operating costs. Only 73 deaths were recorded at Robertson Hospital during its 45-month existence.

Tompkins remained a beloved celebrity in postwar Richmond, active in the Episcopal church and a popular guest at veterans' reunions and Daughters of the Confederacy meetings. The war, her continued charity work, and her generous hospitality to veterans eventually exhausted her fortune. In 1905 "Captain Sally" moved into the Confederate Women's Home in Richmond as a lifetime guest, dying there 26 July 1916, in her 83d year. An honorary member of the R. E. Lee Camp of the Confederate Veterans, she was honored with a full military funeral. 4 chapters of the United Daughters of the Confederacy are named in Tompkins' honor. —PLF

Toombs, Robert Augustus. CSA/CSP b. Wilkes Cty., Ga., 2 July 1810. At the war's outset Toombs was a wealthy land and slave owner, a veteran Georgia politician known to constituents as "Bob" Toombs.

A graduate of Union College in Schenectady, N.Y., he began his political career as a state legislator 1837–43, went to the U.S. House of Representatives 1844–52 as a Whig, and to the Senate as a Democrat and Constitutional Unionist 1852–61. At the time a political ally of ALEXANDER H. STEPHENS and HOWELL COBB, he supported the COMPROMISE OF 1850.

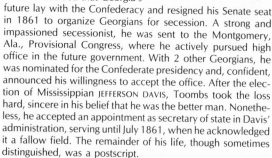

LC

With ABRAHAM LINCOLN'S election to the presidency, Toombs decided that Georgia's future lay with the Confederacy and resigned his Senate seat in 1861 to organize Georgians for secession. A strong and impassioned secessionist, he was sent to the Montgomery, Ala., Provisional Congress, where he actively pursued high office in the future government. With 2 other Georgians, he was nominated for the Confederate presidency and, confident, announced his willingness to accept the office. After the election of Mississippian JEFFERSON DAVIS, Toombs took the loss hard, sincere in his belief that he was the better man. Nonetheless, he accepted an appointment as secretary of state in Davis' administration, serving until July 1861, when he acknowledged it a fallow field. The remainder of his life, though sometimes distinguished, was a postscript.

Appointed brigadier general 19 July 1861, he fought aggressively in the SEVEN DAYS' CAMPAIGN on through to the Battle of ANTIETAM, where he was badly wounded. All this time he held a Confederate congressional seat and kept up criticism of Confederate military policy. Failing promotion in 1863, he resigned his brigadier's commission and spent the remaining war years harassing his government. He returned to uniform only once, in the state militia, to oppose Sherman in Georgia.

Toombs fled the country after Confederate defeat, returning in 1867 to reestablish himself as a powerful influence in Georgia politics, but he refused to apply for a pardon, thus never again held elected office. d. Washington, Ga., 15 Dec. 1885. —JES

Toon, Thomas Frentress. CSA b. Columbus Cty., N.C., 10 June 1840. When the Civil War exploded in spring 1861, Toon, a senior at Wake Forest College, left school and enlisted 20 May in a company that became a part of the 20th North Carolina. He returned to the school to graduate in June before being elected his company's 1st lieutenant, then its captain in July.

Toon fought in all the major engagements of the Army of Northern Virginia 1862–Mar. 1865, suffering 7 wounds. He performed conspicuously at SEVEN PINES, in the SEVEN DAYS' CAMPAIGN, at SOUTH MOUNTAIN, and at FREDERICKSBURG, being elected colonel of the 20th 26 Feb. 1863 when the senior officers in the regiment waived their rights to the command. Toon led the regiment at CHANCELLORSVILLE, at GETTYSBURG, and at MINE RUN in 1863.

During the bloody engagements of 1864, the young North

Carolinian continued to display solid leadership. When his brigade commander, Brig. Gen. ROBERT D. JOHNSTON, fell wounded at Spotsylvania in May, Toon succeeded to command of the unit. Promoted to brigadier general, to rank from 31 May, he led the brigade during Lt. Gen. Jubal A. Early's July raid on Washington, D.C. (see EARLY'S WASHINGTON RAID). In August Johnston returned, and Toon reverted to his former rank of colonel and command of the

GG

20th North Carolina. He directed his veteran regiments in the battles of the 1864 SHENANDOAH VALLEY CAMPAIGN and subsequently at Petersburg. On 25 Mar. 1865, he was severely wounded during the Confederate assault on FORT STEDMAN, incapacitating him for the remainder of the war.

During the postwar years, Toon resided in his native state. In 1901 he was elected superintendent of public instruction for North Carolina, dying in Raleigh 19 Feb. 1902. —JDW

Torbert, Alfred Thomas Archimedes. USA b. Georgetown, Del., 1 July 1833, Torbert had the distinction of being an officer in both the Union and Confederate armies at the same time. Graduating 21st in the West Point class of 1855, Torbert, a 1st lieutenant in the U.S. Army, was on a leave of absence 25 Feb.–17 Apr. 1861, when he was confirmed as a 1st lieutenant of artillery in the Confederate Army. Rather than accept the appointment, he remained loyal to the Union, rendering distinguished service and earning every brevet to major general in both the volunteer and Regular services.

KA

When Torbert returned from his leave, he mustered in New Jersey volunteers until September. On the 16th of that month he became colonel of the 1st New Jersey and for the next 2 years commanded his regiment, then a brigade, in all the major campaigns of the Army of the Potomac. From 29 Aug. 1862 he led a brigade in the VI Corps, earning commendations for his solid performances. On 29 Nov. 1862, he was promoted to brigadier general of volunteers.

In Apr. 1864, in the reorganization of the Army of the Potomac, Torbert received command of a cavalry division under Maj. Gen. Philip H. Sheridan. He participated in the battles of the OVERLAND CAMPAIGN and in Sheridan's raids on Richmond, Va., and the Virginia Central Railroad. Appointed commander of the Middle Military District in August, Sheridan selected Torbert to command his cavalry. In the 1864 SHENANDOAH VALLEY CAMPAIGN Torbert performed unevenly, failing Sheridan during the Battle of FISHER'S HILL but redeeming himself when his troopers routed Confederate cavalry at Tom's Brook. His horsemen also systematically destroyed the valley's farms and mills during the campaign. He retained his command until the war's end, briefly commanding the Army of the Shenandoah.

Torbert mustered out as brigadier general of volunteers 15 Jan. 1866. Reverting to his Regular Army rank of captain, he stayed in the army only until 31 Oct. 1866. From 1869 until 1878 the veteran officer held minor diplomatic posts in Central America, Cuba, and France. After 1878 he was a businessman in Mexico. He drowned 29 Aug. 1880 on a steamer that was wrecked off Cape Canaveral, Fla.   —JDW

torpedo. The torpedo, today called a mine, was the "infernal machine" of the Civil War. Torpedoes were developed in a variety of sizes for a multitude of uses, mostly by the Confederates.

USA

One of the first instances of Confederate use of torpedoes was during the withdrawal of Gen. Joseph E. Johnston's forces from YORKTOWN, Va., May 1862. Artillery shells were left buried in the roads, set to burst when stepped on. At the time, such a device was considered outside the bounds of civilized warfare, and Brig. Gen. GABRIEL J. RAINS, who had been experimenting with the use of explosives, was told to stop planting them.

However, the Confederates were soon using torpedoes widely, primarily as water defenses. Some built from scratch, others improvised using barrels as casings, the mines were floated in Southern harbors and rivers to protect them from Union naval incursions. Many mines were designed to be set off by the pressure of a ship moving over them; others were wired to batteries and set off by an observer on shore. A number of Union vessels were lost to torpedoes, including the ironclad *CAIRO*, sunk in the Yazoo River in Mississippi in 1863.

Torpedoes were also used as offensive weapons. Many of the Confederate semisubmersible "Davids" (*see DAVID*, CSS) had torpedoes attached to a spar mounted on the bow of the vessel. These were intended for ramming Union vessels, upon which they would explode. While the "Davids" never scored a hit, the Confederate submarine *H.L. HUNLEY* did sink the USS *Housatonic* off Charleston in 1864 with a spar torpedo, although the *Hunley* itself sank in the process.

A number of the Confederacy's best minds were involved in the design and perfection of torpedoes, among them MATTHEW F. MAURY, navigator and "pathfinder of the seas." Many experiments were carried out in the bathtub in his residence, only a block from the Confederate White House.

A few torpedoes were also used on the Union side, including one that sunk the Confederate ironclad *ALBEMARLE*.   —LDJ

Totten, Joseph Gilbert. USA b. New Haven, Conn., 17 Apr. 1788. Raised by his uncle, West Point's first professor of

mathematics, Totten was a member of that institution's inaugural class. Graduating 1 July 1805 with a record of academic excellence and "gentlemanly deportment," he was commissioned a 2d lieutenant of engineers. He left the army in 1806 to serve as secretary to his uncle, now the surveyor general of Northwestern Territory, but 2 years later was reinstated in the Corps of Engineers. He was promoted to captain in 1812, major 6 years later, lieutenant colonel in 1828, and colonel and chief of engineers Dec. 1838. Meanwhile, he served on the Niagara

PHCW

frontier during the War of 1812 and was Maj. Gen. WINFIELD SCOTT's chief engineer during the Mexican War, being brevetted brigadier general for meritorious conduct at Vera Cruz.

By 1860 Totten was recognized as among the foremost military engineers of his era. He was responsible for such premier engineering projects as the fortifications in New York City; Sag Harbor, Long Island; Newport, R.I.; and New Haven and New London, Conn. He also served on numerous engineering boards that not only supervised coast defense construction but also river and harbor improvements in aid of civil transportation. Perhaps his most notable advisory work was as a member of the Lighthouse Board 1851–58 and again 1860–64. In this capacity he helped establish a system of offshore lights that alleviated navigational hazards along the Atlantic Coast. The success that followed these efforts gained him membership in harbor improvement commissions in New York and Boston. He also served on the Board of Regents of the Smithsonian Institution and helped incorporate the National Academy of Sciences. He wrote numerous reports and essays on harbor engineering, the nation's defenses, and casemated ordnance. And for more than a quarter of a century he was inspector of the Military Academy as well as chief engineer of the army.

From 1859 to 1861 Totten reconnoitered coastal defenses in the Far West; later he supervised the construction and inspection of the DEFENSES OF WASHINGTON. He also served on boards to retire disabled officers and to fix ordnance standards. On 3 Mar. 1863, he became brigadier general of Regulars and was brevetted a major general 1 day before his death in the District of Columbia, 22 Apr. 1864.   —EGL

Townsend, George Alfred. journalist b. Georgetown, Del., 30 Jan. 1841. From the Civil War until the end of the century, Townsend was one of the most widely read newspaper writers. With his flair for words, his prose marched across the page, vivid, often flamboyant, and sometimes inaccurate.

Townsend worked for the Philadelphia *Inquirer,* then for that city's *Press.* When civil war came, the New York *Herald* sent him to cover Maj. Gen. George B. McClellan's PENINSULA CAMPAIGN. In Aug. 1862 he went to England, where his lectures and articles argued the Union cause. Returning to the U.S., he covered the final battles of the war for the New York *World.* These articles, and his perceptive insights into the events surrounding the assassination of Pres. ABRAHAM LINCOLN, brought him to national prominence.

After traveling to Europe for a few months in 1866 to report on the Austro-Prussian War for the *World,* he settled in Washington, D.C., in 1867. He wrote for the Chicago *Tribune,* the Cincinnati *Enquirer,* and the now familiar initials GAT appeared in a growing number of newspapers. At some point, Townsend added an *H* to GAT, becoming known to his readers as "Gath."

For the next 40 years his newspaper articles were widely published. He wrote historical books, biographies, novels, and reams of poetry, and lectured as well. His *Tales of the Chesapeake* (1880) and a novel, *The Entailed Hat* (1884), are considered his best literary efforts, although another novel, *Katy of Catoctin* (1886), is frequently consulted by researchers into LINCOLN'S ASSASSINATION. *The Life, Crime, and Capture of John Wilkes Booth,* published in 1865 as a 25-cent paperback, is now highly prized.

In 1884 Townsend purchased land in Maryland at Crampton's Gap on South Mountain, near the sites of bitter Civil War battles during the ANTIETAM CAMPAIGN, and invested heavily in construction on his estate, "Gapland." Today it is Gathland State Park.

Townsend suffered poor health in later years. He died 15 Apr. 1914 and was buried in Laurel Hill Cemetery, Philadelphia, Pa.   —JOH

Tracy, Edward Dorr. CSA b. Macon, Ga., 5 Nov. 1833, Tracy left his home state in the late 1850s to establish a law practice in Huntsville, Ala. With his involvement in law came an avid interest in politics, and in 1860 he worked unceasingly for presidential candidate JOHN C. BRECKINRIDGE, serving as alternate elector for the state of Alabama.

GG

Tracy began his Civil War service as captain of a company of the 4th Alabama. He turned down a promotion to major soon after he entered Confederate service in favor of fighting with his men at the FIRST BATTLE OF BULL RUN. In October of that year, he accepted a promotion to lieutenant colonel under Col. Joseph Wheeler, commander of the 19th Alabama.

He fought at SHILOH, where his horse was shot under him, and throughout East Tennessee under Maj. Gen. John P. McCown. On 16 Aug. 1862, Maj. Gen. E. Kirby Smith cited him for his past performance with a promotion to brigadier general.

Stationed at PORT GIBSON, Miss., Tracy's 5 regiments were largely responsible for defending against a corps of invading Federals under Maj. Gen. JOHN A. MCCLERNAND. After desperate fighting 1 May 1863, the Confederates broke in retreat and opened the way for Maj. Gen. Ulysses S. Grant's siege at Vicksburg, 30 mi to the north. Tracy was one of 272 casualties sustained by his 1,500-man brigade at Port Gibson. He "fell near the front line, pierced through the breast, and instantly died without uttering a word," recorded a subordinate, Col. Isham W. Garrott.   —FLS

Trans-Allegheny Department, Confederate. On 25 Nov. 1862, Confederate Sec. of War James A. Seddon's Spe-

cial Orders No. 276 appointed Maj. Gen. SAMUEL JONES to the command previously held by Brig. Gens. JOHN ECHOLS and JOHN S. WILLIAMS. Formerly the Confederate DEPARTMENT OF SOUTHWESTERN VIRGINIA, the area was renamed the Trans-Allegheny Department. Seddon's order, temporarily establishing Jones's headquarters at "The Narrows" on the New River, loosely defined the department as that area previously comprising the old department but with its western border extending to Kentucky or "as far west of that boundary as circumstances will allow."

Jones's instructions were to safeguard the East Tennessee & Virginia Railroad and cooperate with Brig. Gen. Humphrey Marshall's force at Abingdon, Va., near East Tennessee's northern border. Subsequent commanders were Maj. Gen. JOHN C. BRECKINRIDGE, 25 Feb. 1864–22 June 1864, and Brig. Gen. JOHN H. MORGAN, to 4 Sept. On Morgan's death, Breckinridge resumed command and 27 Sept. was informed that his departmental responsibility officially extended over Confederate reserves in East Tennessee. During this period the area was also known informally as the Department of Southwestern Virginia and East Tennessee, and first appears in the *Official Records* as such late in 1863. In 1865 its formal title was changed to the Department of Western Virginia and East Tennessee.   —JES

Trans-Mississippi, Confederate Department and Army of the. The Confederacy's Trans-Mississippi Department was created 26 May 1862, with Maj. Gen. THOMAS C. HINDMAN commanding. It encompassed the vast area west of the Mississippi River, which included Missouri, Arkansas, western Louisiana, Texas, and Indian Territory. On 6 July Maj. Gen. THEOPHILUS H. HOLMES was chosen to succeed Hindman.

The dominant figure of the Trans-Mississippi theater was Gen. E. KIRBY SMITH, who was given command of all Confederate forces west of the Mississippi 7 Mar. 1863. 4 months later VICKSBURG fell and Kirby Smith found his Army of the Trans-Mississippi, some 40,000 men in the department, cut off from Richmond. His was an almost impossible task—maintaining an army despite lack of communication from his superiors, waning enthusiasm in the ranks, lack of pay, and isolation from the main conflict.

But the officers of "Kirby Smithdom," as the Trans-Mississippi was often called, did what they could for the Southern cause. Lt. Gen. RICHARD TAYLOR kept pressure on New Orleans, and Holmes and Hindman fought several battles in western Arkansas. The biggest contribution made by the Trans-Mississippi army in the final year of the war was its thwarting of the Union's RED RIVER CAMPAIGN of 1864. In that campaign, Maj. Gen. NATHANIEL P. BANKS, determined to plant the Union flag in Texas, tied up tens of thousands of troops badly needed in the East. Taylor at last defeated Banks in the crucial battles at MANSFIELD and PLEASANT HILL, La., to end the threat to the Texas gulf coast.

There was little further action in the Trans-Mississippi. Acting in Kirby Smith's name, Lt. Gen. SIMON B. BUCKNER surrendered the Trans-Mississippi Department to Maj. Gen. PETER J. OSTERHAUS, representing Maj. Gen. E.R.S. CANBY, at New Orleans, 26 May 1865. Kirby Smith approved the terms 2 June at Galveston.   —DS

Trans-Mississippi District, Confederate. The Trans-Mississippi District was created within DEPARTMENT NO. 2, 10

Jan. 1862, to ease tension between Maj. Gen. STERLING PRICE, commanding the Missouri State Guard, and Maj. Gen. BEN MCCULLOCH, commanding troops in Arkansas and Louisiana. During its short existence it was headed by Maj. Gen. EARL VAN DORN, who arrived to assume leadership 29 Jan. After 4 Mar., troops within the district were designated the Army of the West. Only 1 major battle, at PEA RIDGE, Ark., 7–8 Mar., took place before the district became part of the newly created TRANS-MISSISSIPPI DEPARTMENT, 26 May 1862.   —PLF

Trans-Mississippi Division, Union. *See* WEST MISSISSIPPI, UNION MILITARY DIVISION OF.

Trapier, James Heyward. CSA b. near Georgetown, S.C., 24 Nov. 1815, Trapier graduated 3d in the West Point class of 1838, ranking directly behind P.G.T. BEAUREGARD, under whom he fought at Charleston 23 years later. As an officer of artillery and, later, of engineers, he served mostly in seacoast construction, helping build or repair Forts Macon, Pulaski, Caswell, Ontario, Niagara, and Porter; he also fought in Mexico in 1847. Resigning his commission a year later, he became a planter and a militia officer in his native state.

LC

In 1851–52 Trapier was South Carolina's chief of ordnance, with the rank of major. In this position he helped the state arm itself during the decade before it seceded. In 1851

he negotiated a contract with the TREDEGAR IRON WORKS of Richmond, Va., for the supply of fifty heavy ordnance pieces. This siege train, consisting of 4 8-in. Columbiads, 4 8-in. siege howitzers, 8 10-in. mortars, and 34 24-pounder cannon, was later deployed in various works about the harbor of Charleston, most of which Trapier had helped construct. On 12 Apr. 1861, many of the weapons, including a mortar unit on Morris Island known as Battery Trapier, inaugurated the Civil War by bombarding the Federals in FORT SUMTER.

Trapier began his career in Confederate service as engineer-in-chief of the Morris Island defenses. At first a captain on Beauregard's staff, he was sent south Oct. 1861 as the brigadier general in command of the DEPARTMENT OF MIDDLE AND EASTERN FLORIDA. Early in 1862, restive in administrative command, he sought field service. In March he was ordered to report to Alabama, where Gen. ALBERT SIDNEY JOHNSTON assigned him a division in the Army of the Mississippi. Trapier led his command that spring at CORINTH and later in the fighting at Farmington. With his lack of experience in infantry service, Trapier's field debut was inauspicious. Soon, in fact, superior officers were demanding his relief as unfit to command.

In Nov. 1862 Trapier returned to the DEPARTMENT OF SOUTH CAROLINA, where he took charge of the state's Fourth Military District, headquartered at Georgetown. The following spring he was in command on Sullivan's Island during Adm. SAMUEL F. DU PONT's unsuccessful naval assault on Charleston. Trapier then returned to his desk job at Georgetown, where he spent the balance of the war. d. near that city, 21 Dec. 1865.   —EGL

Treaty of Washington. *See* ALABAMA CLAIMS.

Tredegar Iron Works, Richmond, Va. One of the most formidable problems the Confederate States of America grap-

USMHI

pled with during the Civil War was the acquisition of artillery. Throughout the conflict, the government relied on purchasing European cannon, capturing Union pieces, and domestic production to fill the need. This last source proved to be the most reliable, eventually supplying Confederate armies with more than 2,200 cannon. Of this total, the Tredegar Iron Works in Richmond, Va., forged nearly 50%.

A private firm, Tredegar was the South's only major antebellum rolling mill capable of producing cannon and railroad rails. Since 1843 its proprietor was JOSEPH R. ANDERSON, a West Point graduate and ardent secessionist. Under Anderson, who managed the works like a plantation, Tredegar's foundries and machine shops developed into first-class operations, fabricating cannon and gun carriages for the U.S. government.

With Virginia's secession and the advent of war, Tredegar, employing 900 workers, was flooded with state and private contracts. The iron works concentrated initially on casting heavy-caliber seacoast and siege guns. It also rifled and rebored scores of antiquated field cannon from the Virginia State Armory, pieces that served Confederate forces in Virginia while new cannon were being made. Pig-iron supplies, however, diminished rapidly, were soon completely exhausted, and for nearly a month late in summer 1861, Tredegar produced not a single cannon.

Anderson accepted a commission of brigadier general 3 Sept. and assumed field command of a brigade, but agreed to return to the foundry if the need arose. He fell wounded during the SEVEN DAYS' CAMPAIGN and, resigning 19 July 1862, returned to direct Tredegar.

The cannon cast at Tredegar and other Southern foundries were initially all made of bronze or iron. These works lacked the facilities for forging steel and, more importantly, none adapted the superior Rodman method of casting (see RODMAN, THOMAS J.). Even Anderson at first failed to realize the value of this method, and though he hurried to install it at Tredegar late in the war, the foundry produced only 2 12-in. Rodmans using the method. The works led Confederate foundries in the manufacture of 3-IN. ORDNANCE GUNS, the highly effective 12-pounder NAPOLEONS, and the heavy cannon used for the defense of coastal cities.

By 1863 Tredegar had expanded its work force to 2,500, nearly 3 times its prewar number. The works also operated shoemaking shops, a firebrick factory, sawmill, tannery, and 9 canal boats. Anderson even dispatched agents into other states to purchase livestock, which he ordered slaughtered and sold to employees at cost to help relieve the problems they faced with food shortages in the Richmond area.

But the scarcity of skilled mechanics and raw materials plagued the foundry's operations throughout the war. By 1864 production of bronze Napoleons had ceased because a copper mine, the source of 90% of the Confederacy's copper, had been captured by Federals. Foundrymen, however, had developed an iron Napoleon that partially filled the need. To augment its dwindling supply of white mechanics, Tredegar and other works relied increasingly on slave labor, a source Anderson had exploited before the war.

The production of artillery pieces had all but ceased in the Confederacy by early 1865. Though the Southern foundries produced barely more than 25% of the cannon turned out by Northern companies, their record was remarkable. None approached that of the contribution of the Tredegar Iron Works, the Confederacy's most valuable manufacturer.   —JDW

Trenholm, George Alfred. CSP b. Charleston, S.C., 25 Feb. 1807, Trenholm, a well-known banker and businessman, was generally thought to be the wealthiest man in the Confederacy. He left school in 1823 at age 16 to work for John Fraser & Co., Charleston's leading cotton shippers; 30 years later he was the firm's head and chief owner. He had interests in steamships, railroads, banks, hotels, plantations, wharves, and cotton presses. Charming, handsome, and influential, he was a Democrat who served in the South Carolina legislature 1852–56 and who later strongly supported secession.

LC

During the Civil War, Trenholm devoted his financial skill and resources to the Confederacy, developing a foreign branch in Liverpool, FRASER, TRENHOLM, & CO., to act as the Confederacy's financial agent, and, with a fleet of some 60 ships, run the Federal BLOCKADE. He shipped out cotton, tobacco, and turpentine, and brought in coal, iron, salt, ammunition, and arms, including the South's first 40,000 ENFIELD RIFLES. JOSIAH GORGAS, chief of ordnance of the Confederate Army, in his 25 Mar. 1863 journal entry estimated that John Fraser & Co. of Charleston had already made $9 million in the blockade-running business.

From the beginning of the war Trenholm served as unofficial adviser to CHRISTOPHER G. MEMMINGER, Confederate treasury secretary, and July 1864 succeeded him in that post. But Trenholm was no more successful than his predecessor as he attempted to persuade Congress to pass his proposed money-making measures in a last-ditch stand to save the failing Confederacy.

Trenholm was captured Apr. 1865 and held by the Federals at Fort Pulaski, Ga., until October of that year. He returned to his family and business interests in Charleston. Bankrupt, he reorganized his cotton-brokerage firm and by 1868 was on his way to making another fortune. In 1874 he was returned to the South Carolina legislature, serving until his death in Charleston, 9 Dec. 1876.   —PR

Trent Affair. On 7 Nov. 1861, the British mail steamer *Trent* left Havana, Cuba, bound for the British West Indies. Aboard were 2 Southerners, JAMES M. MASON and JOHN SLIDELL, Confederate commissioners to Great Britain and France, respectively, en route to London and Paris to plead for, among other things, recognition of the Confederacy. Around noon, 8 Nov., the *Trent* encountered a Union warship, the *SAN JACINTO*, commanded by Capt. CHARLES WILKES. Wilkes, who had been waiting for the *Trent*, had 2 shots fired across that ship's bow and sent a boarding party to demand that Mason and Slidell be surrendered. When the British captain reluctantly acquiesced, the 2 men were transferred to the *San Jacinto*, which proceeded to Boston. Before this incident was resolved, it brought the Union to the verge of war with Great Britain.

Wilkes had acted without the approval or knowledge of his government. Yet, as news of his exploit spread, he became an instant hero to a people starved for some kind of victory.

Although boarding an unarmed mail vessel scarcely ranks as an heroic deed, most Northerners greeted it as such. A British ultimatum to release the prisoners placed Pres. ABRAHAM LINCOLN and Sec. of State WILLIAM H. SEWARD in a dilemma. To release the men might be politically disastrous at home, while to keep them risked conflict with Great Britain.

Seward devised a way out and persuaded Lincoln to go along. The secretary sent a message to the British in which he stated that although the U.S. had not acted illegally, it would release the prisoners anyway. He added that he was pleased by the protest because it seemed to indicate that at last the British were willing to follow America's traditional recognition of the rights of neutral vessels. Seward's scheme worked. He avoided war with Great Britain and at the same time soothed domestic opinion by converting an apparent defeat into a triumph for American principles. —RJM

Trevilian Station, Va., eng. at. 11–12 June 1864 On 7 June 1864, 6,000 Federal cavalrymen, under Maj. Gen. PHILIP H. SHERIDAN, traveled northwestward from their camps near Cold Harbor. Ordered to join forces with Maj. Gen. DAVID HUNTER, advancing from the Shenandoah Valley, then destroy the Virginia Central Railroad and the James River Canal, Sheridan led his troopers for 4 days toward Trevilian Station, a freight and water stop on the vital Confederate railroad. While the Federal troopers marched leisurely, Maj. Gen. WADE HAMPTON pushed his 5,000 Confederate cavalrymen to intercept the menace.

The 2 forces clashed about 5 a.m., 11 June, 2 mi northeast of the depot. Each commander committed a division to the dismounted fight, which took place among a tract of dense underbrush and trees. The opponents fought blindly in the thick growth, with troopers from each side stumbling into one another's lines. Late in the morning Sheridan attacked with his second division, smashing Hampton's front. At the depot the fleeing Confederates encountered Brig. Gen. GEORGE A. CUSTER's Michigan brigade, which had earlier surprised Hampton's wagon train and horses. Hampton's incensed troopers charged, and a furious struggle ensued. From 3 sides Confederate reinforcements closed in on Custer's beleaguered cavalrymen. For several hours, in stifling heat, the Federals parried the attacks, finally cracking a seam in the Confederate lines and escaping. The fighting ebbed through fatigue and lack of ammunition.

The next morning Sheridan's horsemen attacked the railroad, then renewed the action in the afternoon. A stunning Confederate counterattack nearly broke the entire Union line. Darkness ended the battle, and at dawn on the 13th the Federals began backtracking toward Cold Harbor. Burdened with wounded, prisoners, and runaway slaves, they crossed the James River to safety 29 June.

Sheridan had failed to seriously damage the railroad and canal, and to combine with Hunter's army. The cavalry expedition nevertheless succeeded in denying Gen. Robert E. Lee use of his main cavalry force in harassing the Army of the Potomac as it crossed the James River. The engagement at Trevilian Station also exemplified the Union cavalryman's mounting battlefield superiority over his worn opponent. —JDW

Trimble, Isaac Ridgeway. CSA b. Culpeper Cty., Va., 15 May 1802. Graduating 17th in the West Point class of 1822,

Trimble performed various ordnance and topographical duties before resigning from the army in 1832. For the next 29 years, he served as chief engineer and superintendent for several Eastern and Southern railroads. When the war began at FORT SUMTER, S.C., Apr. 1861, Trimble, who had adopted Maryland as his home state, burned bridges north of Baltimore to disrupt the passage of Union volunteers to Washington, D.C.

LC

In May he accepted a commission as colonel of engineers in the Virginia state forces. After assisting in the construction of the defenses at Norfolk, Va., he was appointed brigadier general in the Confederate army 9 Aug. 1861. He received a brigade in the division of Maj. Gen. RICHARD S. EWELL, forming a close association with that officer.

Trimble rendered distinguished service under Ewell in the 1862 SHENANDOAH VALLEY CAMPAIGN, in the SEVEN DAYS' CAMPAIGN, and at CEDAR MOUNTAIN. On 29 Aug. 1862, at SECOND BULL RUN, he suffered a wound from an exploding bullet, which kept him out of the war for nearly a year.

Trimble returned to duty 22 June 1863, as the Army of Northern Virginia moved north for its invasion of Pennsylvania. With no command available, he attached himself as a volunteer aide to Ewell, who now commanded the II Corps. At GETTYSBURG, on the evening of 1 July, Trimble urged Ewell to press his advantage and attack CEMETERY HILL. Ewell demurred and perhaps missed a decisive opportunity to win the battle. On the 3d, Trimble assumed command of the division of Maj. Gen. WILLIAM D. PENDER, who had been mortally wounded on the 2d. That afternoon, he led the command in PICKETT'S CHARGE, being wounded and captured in the assault. Federal surgeons subsequently amputated his leg.

Not exchanged until Feb. 1865, Trimble never rejoined the army. Promoted to major general, to rank from 17 Jan. 1863, he was one of Maryland's most distinguished Confederate officers. He lived in Baltimore after the war, earning a living as a consulting engineer. He died there 2 Jan. 1888. —JDW

Trumbull, Lyman. USP b. Colchester, Conn., 12 Oct. 1813. Educated locally, Trumbull taught school and studied law. Admitted to the bar in 1836, he subsequently set up a law practice with his brother, George, in Belleville, Ill. Elected to the state legislature in 1840, he resigned a year later to serve as Illinois' secretary of state. Removed from office in 1843, he returned to his law practice. 5 years later, he was elected a state supreme court justice, serving in that capacity until 1854.

LC

Appointed as a Democrat to the U.S. Senate the next year, he served there for 18 years. Trumbull held vehement antislavery beliefs and consequently split with the Democratic party over the KANSAS-NEBRASKA ACT. He became closely associated with the Radicals and in 1861 was reelected to the Senate as a Republican.

When the conflict began, Trumbull supported most of ABRAHAM LINCOLN's war measures but broke with the president over the growing powers of the executive branch. In Dec. 1861 he introduced into Congress the controversial Confiscation Bill, which provided for seizure of property and emancipation for slaves of disloyal citizens. By 1864 Trumbull was chairman of the Senate Judiciary Committee, and his support was instrumental in the passage of the 13th Amendment.

The senator tried to reach an accommodation with Pres. ANDREW JOHNSON's administration, but was alienated by party politics and presidential vetoes of important legislation. By 1866 Trumbull had moderated his views and resisted Radicals' attempts to subjugate the South. 16 May 1868, he voted against Johnson's impeachment. In 1872 he supported HORACE GREELEY for president and a year later resigned from the Senate, returning to his Chicago law practice. In 1880 Trumbull ran unsuccessfully as a Democrat for governor of Illinois. He then practiced law in Chicago until his death there 25 June 1896.
—MTC

trunnions. 2 cylindrical pivots cast on the exterior of a cannon or mortar at its center of gravity are called trunnions. They rest on the field carriage or platform carriage and allow the weapon to be elevated or depressed easily. —JES

Tucker, John Randolph. CSN b. Alexandria, Va., 31 Jan. 1812. A member of a prominent family, Tucker was educated in local schools. Appointed midshipman in the U.S. Navy 1 June 1826, he was commissioned lieutenant from 20 Dec. 1837. For the next 17 years he served, alternately with tours of duty at Norfolk Navy Yard, in the Home Squadron in the East Indies, aboard the *Stromboli* during the Mexican War, in the Home Squadron again, and in the Mediterranean Squadron. Promoted to commander from 14 Sept. 1855, he was serving as ordnance officer at the Norfolk yard when the war began.

Promptly resigning, he offered his services to his native state, which readily accepted them and put him in charge of the naval defenses of the James River. As commander of the *PATRICK HENRY*, he took part in the early fighting in the area, leading the Confederate fleet into action during the Battle of HAMPTON ROADS, demonstrating against Federal ships below Fort Monroe Apr. 1862, and commanding the fleet as it retired to Drewry's Bluff after the evacuation of Norfolk in May.

On 30 Aug. 1862, Tucker was transferred from Virginia to Charleston, S.C., to take command of the *PALMETTO STATE*. When an effort was made to break the BLOCKADE there 31 Jan. 1863, he took part as commander of the *CHICORA*, which damaged or destroyed several Union vessels.

Promoted to captain and placed in charge of the entire Confederate naval squadron at Charleston, he continued to defend the city until he was ordered to evacuate it 18 Feb. 1865. He left with 350 men, intending to join Confederate forces in North Carolina, but en route he received orders to move the entire naval command to Richmond.

At the Confederate capital Tucker was assigned command of Drewry's Bluff on the James River. On 2 Apr. hours passed before he learned that Richmond had been evacuated, where-

upon he promptly joined forces with the army retreating under Lt. Gen. RICHARD S. EWELL.

When Ewell's army was captured at SAYLER'S CREEK 6 Apr., Tucker's seamen continued to fight because he stubbornly refused to surrender, goading them into action. 15 minutes later he consented to give up his sword, thus ending the last of the great battles of the war.

In 1866 Tucker became a rear admiral in the navy of Peru, then was appointed to survey the upper reaches of the Amazon. He retired to Petersburg, Va., in 1877, dying there 12 June 1883. —VCJ

Tucker, William Feimster. CSA b. Iredell Cty., N.C., 9 May 1827, Tucker graduated from Emory and Henry College in Virginia in 1848 and moved to Houston, Miss., that year. His early occupation is unknown, but without training in law he was elected probate judge of Chickasaw Cty., Miss., in 1855, and only then studied law. He became a practicing attorney, pursuing this profession until the outset of the Civil War.

LC

Tucker joined the 11th Mississippi Infantry as captain, Company K, May 1861; trained at Harpers Ferry, Va., as a part of the 3d Brigade in Brig. Gen. Joseph E. Johnston's Army of the Shenandoah; maneuvered in the Shenandoah Valley in June and July; then fought in the FIRST BATTLE OF BULL RUN. Tucker's 11th was returned to Mississippi, melded with other units into the 41st Mississippi, and Tucker was commissioned its colonel 8 May 1862. In the 2d Brigade/2d Division of Lt. Gen. Leonidas Polk's corps, he served in the autumn KENTUCKY CAMPAIGN and the Battle of STONE'S RIVER, then transferred to the 1st Brigade of Maj. Gen. Thomas C. Hindman's division, fighting under Brig. Gen. J. Patton Anderson in the Battle of CHICKAMAUGA and the siege of and battles for CHATTANOOGA. In spring 1864 he was made commander of a brigade comprising the 7th, 9th, 10th, 41st, and 44th Mississippi regiments, and was commissioned brigadier general 11 May to date from 1 Mar. 1864. 3 days after his confirmation, he was wounded in fighting at RESACA, Ga., and was unable to return to combat duty. His brigade served without him in the FRANKLIN AND NASHVILLE CAMPAIGN. When sufficiently recovered, Tucker assumed command of the District of Southern Mississippi and East Louisiana in 1865, negotiating the end of hostilities in the area with Union Maj. Gen. Napoleon J. T. Dana in April and May.

After the war, he resumed his law practice in Chickasaw County. To end his prosecution of a trust-fund theft case, hired gunmen killed him at Okolona, Miss., 14 Sept. 1881.

—JES

Tullahoma Campaign. 23 June–3 July 1863 For 6 months following the Battle of STONE'S RIVER, Union Maj. Gen. WILLIAM S. ROSECRANS' Army of the Cumberland regrouped and built up around Murfreesboro, Tenn. Opposing him, Confederate Gen. BRAXTON BRAGG's Army of Tennessee covered the nearby Duck River with a fortified line running, left to right, from the town of Shelbyville to Wartrace on the Nashville & Chattanooga Railroad. Confederate infantry and cavalry under Lt. Gen. LEONIDAS POLK and Brig. Gen. NATHAN B. FORREST held the line's left; infantry and cavalry under Lt. Gen. WILLIAM J. HARDEE and Maj. Gen. JOSEPH WHEELER took the right. Approaches to the right were covered by infantry and artillery detachments at Liberty, Hoover's, and Bellbuckle gaps. Bragg's headquarters and depots were at Tullahoma, on the railroad 15 mi southeast of Wartrace.

Fearing that large elements of Bragg's command would be used to help break the Siege of Vicksburg to the southwest, Federal officials pressured Rosecrans to take the offensive. He yielded, alerting the troops to march on 24 June. He planned a feint against Shelbyville with Maj. Gen. GORDON GRANGER's corps, while 3 other corps massed against Bragg's right.

Federal Maj. Gen. ALEXANDER M. MCCOOK's corps, advancing on Wartrace, penetrated Liberty Gap, compelling Confederates to retire on Bellbuckle. Maj. Gen. GEORGE H. THOMAS' troops thrust toward Manchester, routing Confederates from Hoover's Gap. Maj. Gen. THOMAS L. CRITTENDEN's corps, on the Union left and rear, occupied Bradyville, while Granger's, on the right, felt its way toward Shelbyville. Union horse soldiers, screening Granger's corps, drove Confederate cavalry from Guy's Gap and into Shelbyville entrenchments.

The rain that had begun on the 24th continued for days, slowing the Federals' march. But on the 26th Thomas' columns pressed ahead and on the 27th occupied Manchester, flanking Bragg's Shelbyville-Wartrace line. The Confederates pulled back to Tullahoma. While his divisions converged on Manchester, Rosecrans sent a flying column, 28 June, to strike the railroad in Bragg's rear. It arrived too late to destroy the Elk River railroad bridge, but infantry tore up hundreds of yards of track at Decherd.

Satisfied that his position in Middle Tennessee was untenable, Bragg called retreat. After the Federals crossed the Elk on the 3d, the pursuit and the Tullahoma Campaign ended. Bragg's army moved across the Cumberland plateau and took position behind the Tennessee River. Rosecrans called a halt.

During the campaign Rosecrans' army, at a cost of 560 killed, wounded, and missing, had repeatedly outmaneuvered Bragg, compelling him to withdraw 85 mi and evacuate several formidable positions with the loss of 1,634 prisoners, 11 cannon, and large quantities of supplies.   —ECB

Tunnel Hill (Buzzard's Roost), Ga., eng. at.

24–25 Feb. 1864 Prodded into activity by Lt. Gen. ULYSSES S. GRANT, Maj. Gen. GEORGE H. THOMAS late in Feb. 1864 sent a portion of his ARMY OF THE CUMBERLAND southeastward from near Ringgold, Ga., toward Dalton. 4 divisions under Maj. Gen. JOHN M. PALMER had been ordered to reconnoiter the positions of Gen. JOSEPH E. JOHNSTON's ARMY OF TENNESSEE and to prevent it from detaching troops to more active theaters.

Palmer's reconnaissance began 22 Feb. and was well advanced by the 24th. On that morning the IV Corps division of Brig. Gen. Charles Cruft moved south from Varnell's Station toward Rocky Face Ridge, a steep natural barrier just west of Dalton. Advancing simultaneously from the northwest was Palmer, with the 3 divisions of his XIV Corps, under Brig. Gens. JEFFERSON C. DAVIS, Richard W. Johnson, and ABSALOM BAIRD. The 2 columns linked just above Tunnel Hill, a northwestern spur of Rocky Face Ridge, where they encountered Confederate outposts.

Covered by Johnson's division and an artillery barrage, Davis' troops clambered up the north slope of the hill. Skirmishers from the brigade of Brig. Gen. James D. Morgan then chased the outposts from the summit without difficulty. The Confederates, however, crossed to Rocky Face Ridge and atop it manned prepared positions near a wide defile named Buzzard Roost Gap. There they joined a part of Johnston's main line, 3 infantry brigades and 2 batteries under Maj. Gen. ALEXANDER P. STEWART, with 4 other brigades and another battery in close support.

Determined to press his reconnaissance, Palmer launched a 2-pronged offensive early on the 25th. His flanks guarded by Baird's division and a cavalry brigade under Col. Eli Long, Cruft assaulted the north side of the ridge at about 11:30 a.m. His 2 brigades, led by Cols. William Grose and Thomas E. Champion, scattered Confederate skirmishers, then drove their supports from a steep, timbered ridge. When about to attack a second enemy line, however, the Federals were halted by Palmer's order. Soon afterward, in an effort to relieve pressure on Cruft, Davis sent Morgan's brigade and that of Brig. Gen. Daniel McCook up the west side of the ridge toward Buzzard Roost Gap—only to see the columns sliced apart by frontal and flank fire.

Having suffered some 350 casualties, Palmer ordered a general withdrawal that evening. His reconnaissance had been effective: in response to it, Johnston had recalled much of Lt. Gen. WILLIAM J. HARDEE's corps, recently dispatched to Mississippi to oppose Maj. Gen. WILLIAM T. SHERMAN's MERIDIAN CAMPAIGN.   —EGL

Tupelo (Harrisburg), Miss., Battle of.

14–15 July 1864 On 5 July 1864, a Union army of 14,200 infantry and cavalry under Maj. Gen. ANDREW J. SMITH began moving south from La Grange, Tenn. Smith's mission, as assigned by Maj. Gen. WILLIAM T. SHERMAN, was to prevent Maj. Gen. NATHAN B. FORREST's cavalry in north Mississippi from striking the railroads supplying the Federal forces advancing on Atlanta.

Smith's column, devastating the countryside as it marched, reached Pontotoc, Miss., 11 July. Forrest concentrated his 6,000 troops south at Okolona, having been ordered by his commander, Lt. Gen. STEPHEN D. LEE, not to engage Smith until reinforced. On 13 July Smith, fearing ambush, swerved east toward Tupelo. That same day Lee reached Okolona with 2,000 men. Assuming personal command, he set out with Forrest in pursuit of Smith.

At nightfall the Confederates found the Federals in a strong line 2 mi west of Tupelo. Forrest proposed making hit-and-run attacks when Smith resumed his march, thereby wearing down the Federals. Lee, however, wished to dispose of Smith at once so that he could send reinforcements to Mobile, reportedly threatened by a Union advance from New Orleans. Hence he ordered an assault on the Federals in the morning.

Starting at 7:30 a.m., 14 July, the Confederates delivered a series of brave but uncoordinated charges. The veteran Federal infantry beat them back without difficulty and with heavy loss. After 2 hours Lee broke off the assault, having lost more than 1,300 men, compared with Union casualties of fewer than 700. Had Smith counterattacked, he probably would have smashed Lee's and Forrest's army. But short on rations, he headed back north 15 July.

Sherman criticized Smith for not having destroyed Forrest and ordered him to launch another expedition immediately.

However, Smith had badly crippled Forrest and thus accomplished his primary assignment of keeping the dreaded raider away from Sherman's railroad supply line.   —AC

Turchin, John Basil. USA b. province of the Don, Russia, 30 Jan. 1822, Ivan Vasilovitch Turchinoff graduated in 1841 from the Imperial Military School in St. Petersburg. He rose rapidly from ensign in the czar's
horse artillery to colonel of the Imperial Guard. During that time he served as a captain on the Russian general staff, fought in Hungary and the Crimea, and was hailed as an engineering genius for designing the coastal defenses of Finland. In 1856 he came to America with his wife, the daughter of a Russian officer, and settled in Chicago as an employee of the Illinois Central Railroad.

LC

When the Civil War broke out, Turchin (as he now spelled his name) offered his services to the Union. In June 1861 he was commissioned colonel of the 19th Illinois Volunteers, which he molded into a well-drilled and hard-fighting outfit. Accompanied by his wife, who served as nurse and mother figure to the regiment, he led the 19th during the early operations in Missouri, Kentucky, and Alabama. By Feb. 1862 his battlefield skill and courage had gained him brigade command in Maj. Gen. DON CARLOS BUELL's Army of the Ohio. For feats such as his capture of Huntsville, Ala., in April, he earned the nickname "Russian Thunderbolt."

For a time, however, his career seemed ruined. In May 1862 his European notions of total war led him to promote the razing of Athens, Ala., some of whose inhabitants had shot at his brigade. In broken English, he told his troops that he would "shut mine eyes for von hour" to whatever looting they did. When he learned the town had not been torched during that period, he said, "I shut mine eyes for von hour and a half." Finally, his soldiers got the message.

Incensed, Buell court-martialed Turchin and ordered him cashiered. Only a mission to Washington by his wife, who persuaded Pres. ABRAHAM LINCOLN to vacate Buell's verdict, kept him in uniform. In fact, so impressed was the president with Mme. Turchin that he made her husband a brigadier as of 17 July 1862.

Thereafter, the Russian served ably in the XV Corps at CHICK-AMAUGA, CHATTANOOGA (especially at MISSIONARY RIDGE), and during the ATLANTA CAMPAIGN. Ill health forced him to resign his commission 4 Oct. 1864. He then returned to Chicago as an engineer and a patent solicitor. Losing his sanity late in life, he died in an asylum in Anna, Ill., 19 June 1901.   —EGL

Turkey Bridge, Va., Battle of. 30 June 1862 *See* WHITE OAK SWAMP, BATTLE OF.

Turner, John Wesley. USA b. near Saratoga, N.Y., 19 July 1833. Appointed to the U.S. Military Academy in 1851 from Illinois, where his family had moved 8 years earlier, Turner graduated 14th in the class of 1855. For the next 6 years he served in Oregon Territory, against the Seminoles in

Florida, and at various garrisons.

On 3 Aug. 1861, Turner transferred to staff duty as captain of commissary and subsistence. 2 months later he was named chief of commissary for the army in western Missouri and subsequently for the Department of Kansas. He transferred to the Department of the South in spring 1862, then to the Department of the Gulf. Promoted to colonel 3 May, he served under Maj. Gens. Benjamin F. Butler and Nathaniel P.

USMHI

Banks for a year. On 13 June 1863, he accepted the post of chief of staff of the Department of the South.

Turner received his promotion to brigadier general 7 Sept. Besides his staff duties, he commanded the department's artillery in its operations against Charleston, S.C., and Forts Wagner and Sumter. In May 1864 Turner assumed command of a division in the X Corps, leading it in the battles at BERMUDA HUNDRED, SECOND DREWRY'S BLUFF, and Petersburg, Va. (*see* CRATER, BATTLE OF THE). He returned to staff command in November as chief of staff of the Department of Virginia and North Carolina and the Department of the James. During the war's final engagements in Virginia, he led a division of the XXIV Corps.

Brevetted brigadier and major general, U.S. Army, Mar. 1865, Turner commanded the District of Henrico, which included Richmond, Va., June 1865–Apr. 1866. He stayed in the Regular Army for 5 more years as colonel and depot commissary in St. Louis, Mo., where he resided after his resignation, prospering as a businessman. He also served as that city's street commissioner for a few years and as president and director of several corporations. d. St. Louis, 8 Apr. 1899.

—JDW

Turner's Gap, Md., Battle of. 14 Sept. 1862 *See* SOUTH MOUNTAIN, MD., BATTLE OF.

turning movement. In the lexicon of the Civil War, a turning movement meant a wide strategic ENVELOPMENT of an opponent's main position achieved by moving beyond it and threatening some vital point in his rear. Designed to avoid fighting, the movement turned the enemy out of his position. Turning movements were prominent in the TULLAHOMA, SECOND BULL RUN, and CHANCELLORSVILLE campaigns.   —JDW

Tuttle, James Madison. USA b. Summerfield, Ohio, 24 Sept. 1823. As a young man Tuttle migrated to Farmington, Iowa, and from 1846 worked as a farmer and merchant until being elected sheriff of Van Buren County in 1855. Elected county treasurer in 1857 and recorder of deeds in 1859, he joined the 2d Iowa Infantry as a lieutenant colonel 31 May 1861.

A modestly capable soldier, serving best in combat, Tuttle never set aside personal ambitions during his war service. Promoted colonel of the 2d Iowa 6 Sept. 1861, he saw duty at FORT DONELSON, then assumed command of the 1st Brigade/2d Division/Army of the Tennessee for the Battle of SHILOH. Following division commander Brig. Gen. William H.

L. Wallace's wounding in combat 6 Apr. 1862, Tuttle led 2d Division troops in fighting around the Shiloh "HORNETS' NEST," barely escaped capture, won promotion to brigadier general 9 June 1862, then successively led the 3d Division/XV Corps and the 1st Division/XVI Corps in Vicksburg and central Mississippi campaigning, and distinguished himself in the 14 May 1863 capture of JACKSON, Miss. During this year and the next he unsuccess-

LC

fully promoted his war record at home in bids for the governorship of Iowa while retaining his commission and participating in Maj. Gen. William T. Sherman's MERIDIAN CAMPAIGN.

Made commander of the post at Natchez, Miss., 7 Mar. 1864, Tuttle pillaged army financial accounts entrusted to him, extorted money from local citizens, took large bribes, and arrested citizens marginally suspected of Confederate sympathies, then ransomed them back to their families. In collusion with a Judge Hart, a U.S. Treasury official, he engaged in profiteering and in extracting tribute from residents in the area. Politicians and other volunteer officers, accustomed to some minor measure of corruption, were stunned at Tuttle's venality and aggressiveness. Maj. Gen. HENRY W. SLOCUM ordered his relief late in May, concurrent with a similar order from Sec. of War EDWIN M. STANTON 25 May. Before investigations could proceed, Tuttle resigned 14 June 1864, and hastily returned to Iowa. Judge Hart was apprehended, and a partial confession was extracted from him before he was released. Maj. Gen. Napoleon J. T. Dana inspected Tuttle's former command July 1864 and recommended pursuit and prosecution. For undisclosed reasons his suggestion was not followed.

Tuttle served in the Iowa legislature for several years after the war, engaged in the real-estate and meat-packing businesses, and in 1877 invested his money in mines in the Southwest. He died at one of his mine sites near Casa Grande, Arizona Territory, 24 Oct. 1892.   —JES

Twenty-Negro Law. The provision in the Confederacy's Conscription Act of 16 Apr. 1862 that exempted from military service the overseer or owner of any plantation with 20 or more slaves was called the Twenty-Negro Law. It applied only in states with laws requiring an adult white male in residence at all times on each plantation and was intended to leave an adequate police force among the civilian population.

Legislative opponents of the exemption claimed it showed favoritism to the planter class, a criticism that mirrored public opinion. As the manpower shortage in the South became acute and exemptions came under close scrutiny, legislators revised the law May 1863 to require payment of an exemption fee of $500 and affidavits from 2 witnesses swearing that the overseer had been employed before 16 April 1862.

Restrictions were tightened again Feb. 1864. Though the number of blacks required was reduced to 15, exemption was granted only if owners agreed to deliver to the government a specific quantity of meat and their surplus produce at impressment prices. In addition, a civil magistrate and 2 witnesses had to certify the overseer's services to be indispensable.   —PLF

Twiggs, David Emanuel. CSA b. Richmond Cty., Ga., 1790. The oldest and most senior officer of the U.S. Army to declare for the Confederacy, Twiggs had already rendered his nation long and distinguished service by the outbreak of the Civil War. The son of Revolutionary War Gen. John Twiggs, the "Savior of Georgia," he saw limited service in the War of 1812 as an officer. After 11 years of civilian life, he was recommissioned and rose through the ranks until brevetted major general for his gallant service in the Mexican War, for which he was also presented a sword by Congress. In 1856, after serving in various military capacities, he was given command of the De-

LC

partment of Texas, where he attempted to pacify the Comanches devastating the frontier.

In the turbulent days of early 1861, Twiggs, of strong Southern sympathies, repeatedly asked Washington for advice as to the disposition of his forces and government property should the state of Texas demand their surrender. Receiving no guidance from his superiors, he turned over all troops, supplies, forts, outposts, equipment, and army funds 18 Feb. to Col. BEN MCCULLOCH, commander of Texas troops.

Prior to his surrender, Twiggs had requested Gen. WINFIELD SCOTT to relieve him of his command, which Scott did 1 Mar. 1861. On 22 May Twiggs was appointed major general in the Confederate army, the senior officer of that grade, and although assigned command of the District of Louisiana, because of advancing age he was never active in that position.

He died 15 July 1862 and was buried near his birthplace. Although reviled by many Northerners for his small part in the great conflict, by surrendering his troops he undoubtedly prevented the first shots of the coming struggle from being fired for another 2 months.   —PRR

"290." See ALABAMA, CSS.

Tyler, Robert Charles. CSA b. about 1833. A soldier of fortune reputedly born in Baltimore, Md., Tyler served as a 1st lieutenant in American adventurer William Walker's private army during Walker's attempt to seize Nicaragua in 1856. Called "a stranger in Tennessee" by contemporary National Archives sources, Tyler, who had been staying in Memphis, joined Company D/15th Tennessee Infantry at Jackson, Tenn., 18 Apr. 1861, giving his age as 28. Nothing else is known of his life before the Civil War.

Rising from private to regimental quartermaster, Tyler is believed to have held the rank of captain, assuming regimental command for the autumn 1861 Battle of BELMONT. He won

LC

election to lieutenant colonel Dec. 1861 and led his regiment in Brig. Gen. Bushrod R. Johnson's 1st Brigade/2d Division/I Corps for the Battle of SHILOH. Badly wounded there, he retreated to Corinth, Miss., with his command and May 1862 was elected colonel. In the autumn 1862 KENTUCKY CAMPAIGN Tyler briefly served as Gen. Braxton Bragg's provost marshal, was later heavily engaged at the Battle of PERRYVILLE, served in garrison at TULLAHOMA, fought in the June 1863 engagement at Hoover's Gap, then assumed command of the consolidated 15th and 37th Tennessee regiments.

In Brig. Gen. William B. Bate's brigade he fought at CHICK-AMAUGA, then commanded the brigade for the Battle of MIS-SIONARY RIDGE, losing a leg in combat. Tyler's service there won him promotion to brigadier general to rank from 23 Feb. 1864 and command of the post at West Point, Ga.

During his last cavalry raid in spring 1865, Union Maj. Gen. James H. Wilson dispatched a column under Col. Oscar H. La Grange to assault West Point. At 2 p.m., 16 April, Tyler was killed by La Grange's troops while directing the defense of the post's Fort Tyler.   —JES

Tyler, USS. A 575-ton sidewheel steamer, the *Tyler* was one of 3 vessels bought at Cincinnati, Ohio, May 1861, that became the nucleus of the Union's river force. Its bottom was in bad condition, but was repaired, its frame strengthened, machinery lowered, and sides plated with oak lumber 5 in. thick. An unsuccessful attempt was made to have its name changed from *Tyler* to *Taylor* because former president John Tyler had remained faithful to his native state of Virginia.

Action came early. On 4 Sept. 1861, the *Tyler* exchanged shots on the Mississippi River with the Confederate gunboat *Yankee* and the batteries at Hickman, Ky. In November, in Brig. Gen. ULYSSES S. GRANT's attack on BELMONT, Mo., it closed in on the Confederates and drove them back from the river.

On 6 Feb. 1862, along with the *CONESTOGA* and the *LEXING-TON*, the *Tyler* participated in the attack on FORT HENRY, Tenn. When that fortification fell after a few hours of fighting, the 3 gunboats ran all the way up the Tennessee River to Florence, Ala., destroying craft along the way and capturing the partly finished Confederate gunboat *EASTPORT*. In the Battle of SHI-LOH, Tenn., 6–7 Apr. 1862, fire from the *Tyler* and *Lexington* kept the Confederates from turning the Union left.

The *Tyler*'s only embarrassing experience came 15 July 1862. That day it was part of the Union fleet, under Capt. DAVID G. FARRAGUT, that failed to stop the newly built Confederate ironclad *ARKANSAS* from reaching the safety of the guns at Vicksburg.

The *Tyler* had still another contribution to make to the Union cause. When Confederates stormed Helena, Ark., early on the morning of 4 July 1862, the gunboat fired 413 rounds at them during an 8-hour period and drove them back. Comdr. DAVID D. PORTER wrote its encomium: "First at Belmont, then at Pittsburg Landing, and now here [Helena], the Tyler has been of inestimable value, and has saved the fortunes of the day." In June 1864 Confederate Brig. Gen. JOSEPH O. SHELBY paid tribute to the ship, describing it as "the most formidable boat in the White River fleet."   —VCJ

Tyndale, Hector. USA b. Philadelphia, Pa., 24 Mar. 1821. The son of a china and crystal importer, Tyndale entered his father's business. In 1845, on his father's death, he began his own porcelain and crystal importing firm, achieving a national reputation for expertise in porcelain. A Free Soil Democrat, he joined the young Republican party, and in 1859 escorted Mrs. John Brown to Charlestown, Va., to visit her condemned abolitionist husband and help her return his body north following execution. Tyndale maintained that he did this out of charity, not from sympathy with Brown.

In Paris, France, on business at the outbreak of the Civil War, Tyndale returned to Philadelphia, entered the 28th Pennsylvania Infantry as a major 28 June 1861, and, under Col. John W. Geary, participated in several engagements in the Harpers Ferry area through autumn of that year. Promoted lieutenant colonel 25 Apr. 1862, he fought at FRONT ROYAL, CEDAR MOUNTAIN, SECOND BULL RUN, and CHANTILLY, and on the wounding of Col. Charles Candy as-

LC

sumed command of the 1st Brigade/2d Division/XII Corps at the Battle of ANTIETAM, fighting until felled by 2 wounds. Briefly believed dead, Tyndale was returned to Union lines, revived, and was sent home for a lengthy recuperation.

Advanced to brigadier general 9 Apr. 1863, he resumed duties in May and next fought in the campaign for CHATTANOOGA, distinguishing himself in coming to Geary's relief during the WAUHATCHIE NIGHT ATTACK and in service under Maj. Gen. Oliver O. Howard during the battles for CHATTANOOGA. He commanded the 3d Division/XI Corps during the winter of 1863–64, then reverted to brigade command for the beginning of the ATLANTA CAMPAIGN. In poor health, he obtained a leave of absence 2 May 1864, returned to Philadelphia, and resigned his commission 26 Aug. In the omnibus promotions of 13 Mar. 1865, Tyndale's record was honorarily amended to show promotion to major general, a promotion not recorded in postwar army reference works.

Returning to his import business and Republican politics, he ran unsuccessfully for mayor of Philadelphia in 1868, helped support several local educational institutions, and became a benefactor of the University of Pennsylvania. d. Philadelphia, 19 Mar. 1880.　　　　　　　　—JES

U

Uncle Tom's Cabin. *See* STOWE, HARRIET BEECHER.

unconditional surrender. *See* SURRENDER, TERMS OF.

uniforms, Confederate States military. Confederate army, navy, and marine uniforms closely resembled those of their Union counterparts. In the early war years a variety of garish militia uniforms were common in each of the Confederacy's armies. One New Orleans militia unit mustered for Confederate service wore Revolutionary War attire on parade. Another New Orleans unit, WHEAT'S TIGERS, adopted the style of the French ZOUAVE uniform. Several other Southern volunteer units wore dark blue outfits and were sometimes mistaken on the battlefield for the enemy. By 1863 all troops in national service were asked to adhere to Article 47 of the *Regulations for the Army of the Confederate States.* As with UNITED STATES UNIFORMS, the frock coat, hanging to midthigh, was prescribed for all infantry officers and enlisted men, and was to be double-breasted and colored cadet gray.

The use of buttons and insignia for identification was not as elaborate as in the Union service. On an upright collar generals, lieutenant generals, major generals, and brigadier generals wore 3 gold stars within a wreath, the center star larger than the others. Colonels wore 3 gold stars of the same size. Lieutenant colonels wore 2 stars on their collars; majors, 1 star; captains, 3 gold horizontal bars; 1st lieutenants, 2 bars; 2d lieutenants, 1 bar. Though various ratings and duties were indicated by cloth, silk, or worsted devices on a sergeant's chevrons, all sergeants wore 3 chevrons on their sleeves and corporals wore 2. A brigadier general's coat had 2 rows of 8 buttons, grouped in pairs. All other junior-officer grades wore 2 rows, 7 buttons each, equally spaced. Cavalrymen and artillerists followed the same designations and insignia but wore waist-length jackets.

Army officers indicated their affiliation with colored facing on their coats or jackets: red for artillery, yellow for cavalry, light blue for infantry, black for medical. Regimental officers wore these colors on the outer seam of their trousers on 1¼-in. stripes; generals wore 2⅝-in. stripes on each leg; adjutant, quartermaster, commissary, and engineer officers wore 1 gold 1¼-in. outer-seam stripe. Noncommissioned officers were expected to wear on their outer seams a 1¼-in. cotton stripe or braid of colors appropriate to their army branch. Privates wore no stripes or facing, but their trousers and those of noncommissioned and regimental officers were to be sky blue. All others were to wear dark blue trousers.

The ankle-high Jefferson boot was to be supplied to all officers and men. Taller boots were acquired personally. The KEPI was also standard issue to all army personnel, with dark blue crowns for generals, staff officers, and engineers; red for artillery officers; yellow for cavalry officers; and light or sky blue for infantry officers. The crowns of all other kepis were to be cadet gray. Overcoats were also cadet gray and designed the same as those in U.S. uniforms.

The proper wear and design of buttons, braids, knots, spurs, gloves, sashes, swords, cravats, and neck stocks are detailed in the Confederate *Regulations.*

Confederate naval and marine uniforms differed little from those of their Union opponents. Cadet gray was the predominant color, and, in the navy, white was accepted for summer or tropical wear.

As with weaponry and foodstuffs, the Confederate services were poorly supplied with uniforms. Servicemen actually wore combinations of uniform pieces and items of personal clothing; infantrymen sometimes went without shoes altogether; and broad felt hats were worn as often as kepis. From the middle war years many uniforms were homespun and dyed a yellow-brown with coloring from butternuts, giving rise to the name *butternut* to refer to Confederate army volunteers. In the main, Confederate service dress regulations were more honored in the breach than in the observance.   —JES

uniforms, United States military. The dress of U.S. infantry volunteers varied greatly at the start of the Civil War and no effort was made to enforce conformity until after the First Battle of Bull Run. In that battle Union troops fought in French ZOUAVE dress, tartan Scots caps and trousers, and cadet-gray outfits matching many Confederate designs. Several Northern prewar militias with strong ethnic rosters adopted military dress styles from their homeland. The Garibaldi Guard of New York City wore an Italian-style uniform featuring a broad flat hat adorned with chicken feathers. A unit made up mostly of French immigrants wore an Algerian campaign uniform. The 79th New York wore kilts on parade. This same variety was found in CONFEDERATE STATES UNIFORMS.

Though volunteer units were not forbidden distinctive dress in 1861 and 1862, by midwar field hardships had forced most to abandon their original uniforms and adopt the dress prescribed for U.S. Regulars. This allowed easier communication in the field, since Regular Army uniform regulations made rank and service affiliation recognizable at a distance.

Infantry officers and enlisted men wore dark blue frock coats hanging to midthigh; majors, lieutenant colonels, colonels, and all general officers' coats were double-breasted. Those ranking lower wore single-breasted frock coats. Major generals' coats were distinguished by 9 buttons in each row, the buttons grouped in threes. Brigadier generals wore 8 buttons to a row, grouped by twos. Colonels, lieutenant colonels, and majors each wore 2 rows of 7 buttons, equally spaced. All others wore a single row of 9 equally spaced buttons.

LC

Further distinctions of rank were indicated with shoulder boards for officers and sleeve chevrons on noncommissioned officers and enlisted men. On their shoulder boards major generals commanding armies wore 3 stars, the center star being larger than the others. Major generals wore 2 stars; brigadier generals, 1 star; colonels, an eagle; lieutenant colonels, 2 silver embroidered leaves; majors, 2 gold embroidered leaves; captains, 2 groups of 2 gold bars; a 1st lieutenant, a gold bar; and 2d lieutenants wore boards with no insignia. Sergeants wore 3 chevrons, corporals 2. Regular enlisted men were distinguished by 1 stripe on the lower sleeve for each 5 years of faithful service. Artillerymen and cavalrymen wore the same badges of rank on waist-length jackets. The different grades and duties of sergeants were distinguished by cloth or worsted devices on chevrons.

Infantry members and general officers wore Jefferson boots,

and in cold weather all soldiers wore dark blue overcoats with a short cape extending to the cuff on commissioned officers and mounted troops, and to the elbow on all others. General officers, ordnance officers, and all privates wore plain dark blue trousers, except in the light artillery, where trousers were sky blue. Staff officers wore a gold cord on the outer seam of each leg. Sergeants, ordnance sergeants, and hospital stewards wore a 1½-in. stripe down each outer seam; corporals wore a ½-in. stripe. The color of the stripe denoted an affiliation with a particular branch of the army: yellow for cavalry, scarlet for artillery, sky blue for infantry, emerald green for mounted riflemen, crimson for ordnance and hospital personnel. Individuals further identified their affiliations with CORPS BADGES.

Though the HARDEE HAT was popular at the outset of the war, it was widely replaced by the KEPI. Loose-fitting forage caps, some with the crown thrust far forward, and expansive fatigue blouses were the usual field wear. Cavalrymen and field artillerymen wore knee-high boots on campaign.

Uniform regulations were extensive and also addressed the proper design and wear of buttons, vests, sashes, gloves, cap insignia, spurs, knots, epaulettes, belts, swords, cravats, and neck stocks. Trimming, braiding, and design on many of these items denoted rank or affiliation. Proper wear and design are detailed in the *U.S. Army Regulations.*

Regulation uniforms of U.S. naval officers approximated those of the army. Dark blue, double-breasted frock coats were worn; vests were expected; trousers were white in summer or when sailing in the tropics; caps featured a round, flat crown; and straw boaters were permitted for summer or tropical wear. A fouled anchor insignia was worn on the cap. Epaulettes, appropriate knots, and a cocked hat were to be worn on formal occasions. In ascending rank, the shoulder boards for ensign, master, lieutenant, lieutenant commander, and commander were the same as those for army officers from 2d lieutenant to lieutenant colonel, except that each from master to commander also featured a silver eagle. A naval captain wore a silver eagle and fouled anchor, a commodore the eagle and a star, and rear and full admirals a fouled anchor and 2 stars. Uniforms of seamen and boswain mates approximated modern naval dress in the ranks; rank insignia was worn on the right sleeve among hands and on the left sleeve for those ranking boswain's mate and above. Petty officers wore waist-length jackets. Seamen and boswains wore black neckerchiefs under a long collar draping down the back and a cloth "square-rig" cap, with a ribbon around the outer headband that draped down the back of the neck; white was worn in summer or on tropical duty.

U.S. Marine uniforms were approximately the same as those for U.S. Army Regulars, except bandsmen wore brilliant red coats. The shako (discontinued for army artillery and cavalry units), regulation marine headgear in early war years, was replaced by the kepi. Marines were distinguished by their cap insignia, a bugle with an *M* in the center.   —JES

Union League of America. The Union League began forming in 1862 in the East and Midwest to combat defeatism and disloyalty in the North, to rally patriotism, and to encourage enlistments and support for the war policies of the Republican administration. In Eastern cities the league was an outgrowth of elitist Union League Clubs organized in major cities to oppose sedition and incompetent politicians. In the Midwest it had roots in Unionist secret societies operating in East

Tennessee and Kentucky. A bipartisan organization characterized by rituals, secret signs, and oaths, it received encouragement and financial support from the Republican party, which frequently acted as its militant arm. Though members denied any political affiliation, they championed Republican war aims, circulated campaign propaganda, and labored to educate voters on political issues. A grand national council was organized in summer 1862, and hundreds of thousands of patriotic citizens joined local leagues. In Apr. 1863 Joseph Medill, an aggressive promoter of the league employed by the Chicago *Tribune,* claimed 75,000 members in Illinois alone.

The league singled out PEACE DEMOCRATS as its principal enemy, using influence and force to have the peace advocates arrested, defeated at the polls, or intimidated into suppressing their opposition to Lincoln's war measures. Copperhead leaders accused the Union League of being the "Republican K.G.C." (KNIGHTS OF THE GOLDEN CIRCLE), and claimed the acronym ULA stood for "Uncle Lincoln's Asses." They tried to discredit Union League objectives by insisting that the organization was a new form of Know-Nothingism, the nativist, anti-Catholic movement that peaked in the mid-1850s. Despite these verbal attacks against it, the league wielded substantial power over public opinion and elections, continuing to grow in strength until the war ended.   —PLF

Union (National Union) party. Increasingly after mid-1863, Republicans concerned about retaining their recently achieved majority in the national government began identifying themselves as the Union party. Admirers of ABRAHAM LINCOLN and his war programs, they built a bipartisan coalition of moderate Republicans in favor of the Union, emancipation, and mild RECONSTRUCTION, and WAR DEMOCRATS advocating restoration of the Union with no other conditions attached. Directing their efforts against PEACE DEMOCRATS willing to acknowledge Confederate independence and RADICAL REPUBLICANS demanding a peace followed by prolonged, punitive measures for restoring the seceded states, Union party organizers held conventions and financially supported loyalty leagues (*see* UNION LEAGUE OF AMERICA) in those states where political contests were in doubt.

The strategy helped defeat Ohio Rep. CLEMENT L. VALLANDIGHAM in his bid for the governorship in 1863 and elect former Democrat JOHN BROUGH to the office, and it strengthened Republican Gov. OLIVER P. MORTON's political power in Indiana. The Unionism label put Democrats at a disadvantage throughout the North and was effective in discrediting copperheadism in the Midwest. The Detroit *Free Press,* a Democratic organ, accused Republicans of using Unionism as "a cloak with which they hope[d] to hide past wickedness and corruption from the eyes of the people."

In his effort to unite Republicans, Lincoln used the Union party label to ensure the presidential nomination at the national Union convention in Baltimore Aug. 1864. His shrewdness in selecting Democrat ANDREW JOHNSON as his vice-presidential candidate assured his renomination on the first ballot by a vote of 506–22. His enormous popularity among the electorate, particularly among soldiers voting by absentee ballot and on leaves conveniently arranged to have the men at home for the election, resulted in a comfortable victory over GEORGE B. MCCLELLAN at the polls in November.

Union party members held a second national convention in 1866, but with peace won, Unionism lost its political clout and its adherents returned to their respective parties.　　—PLF

Union Volunteer Refreshment Saloon.

Late in Apr. 1861 state governments responding to Abraham Lincoln's call for troops sent their recruits to Washington by way of Philadelphia. There large numbers of men passed through the railroad station on Otsego St., below Broad St. and Washington Ave. Women eager to show their patriotism met the volunteers at the trains and handed them cups of coffee as the cars moved slowly by. To support the women, William M. Cooper, who owned a warehouse nearby, convinced his partner, Hervey M. Pearce, to give them use of a large fireplace in the building. At the businessmen's urging, friends began to contribute supplies to feed the soldiers. Soon donations of cash and goods allowed the women to furnish meals and overnight accommodations to soldiers in transit and a hospital for sick and wounded men on their way home. An offshoot of the refreshment saloon was the Philadelphia Soldiers' Home, chartered 15 Feb. 1862.

The *History of the Cooper Shop Volunteer Refreshment Saloon* (1866) credits the organizers with being able to feed 1,000 men an hour if necessary. Soldiers praised the efficient, well-organized operation, which over the course of the war aided about 4 million men.　　—PLF

United Confederate Veterans.

Representatives from veterans' groups in several former Confederate states met in New Orleans June 1889 to establish the United Confederate Veterans, choosing JOHN B. GORDON as their first commanding general. Adopting an elaborate military structure, UCV members called their local units "camps," designated their national organization "general headquarters," and addressed their elected officers by military rank. At its peak, membership included 1,855 camps; a total of 160,000 veterans belonged to the UCV during its 62-year existence. All except 6 UCV camps were located within the former Confederate states.

UCV camps functioned most effectively at the local level, aiding disabled and indigent veterans through relief associations, establishing veterans' homes, lobbying for pensions from state governments, raising funds for Confederate monuments, and encouraging the study of history within communities. This last goal resulted from veterans' eagerness to keep Southern children from being taught the history of the war and of SLAVERY from textbooks they felt had been written with a Northern bias. The Historical Committee, appointed in 1892, addressed educational concerns at the national level, making sincere if not always successful attempts to offer objective appraisals of historical writings. The UCV itself entered the history-writing market in 1899, publishing the 12-volume *Confederate Military History,* edited by CLEMENT A. EVANS. In 1894 the UCV adopted as its official organ *CONFEDERATE VETERAN* magazine, a vehicle for publishing memoirs and social notices.

Differences of opinion sometimes resulted in friction with the powerful Union veterans' organization, the GRAND ARMY OF THE REPUBLIC, which initially interpreted UCV activities as a sign of continuing disloyalty. After the Spanish-American War pitted Northerners and Southerners together against a common enemy, tensions between the 2 largest veterans' groups eased. By the early years of the 20th century, they were staging joint reunions conciliatory in tone.

The UCV held its first reunion in Chattanooga in 1890, and thereafter Southern cities competed for the honor of hosting the annual encampments. UCV strength reached its zenith about 1904, then declined steadily as the old soldiers began dying in large numbers. Some 106,000 veterans and members of their families assembled in Little Rock, Ark., in 1911; 3 surviving veterans attended the last reunion in 1951.

　　—PLF

unreconstructed.

Into the 20th century, former Confederates who refused to accept defeat prided themselves on being "unreconstructed." Sometimes rooted in bitterness, the Lost Cause found popular expression in the postwar song "The Good Old Rebel," which declares, "I don't want no pardon;/ For what I was and am./And I won't be reconstructed,/And I do not give a damn."　　—PLF

Upton, Emory.

USA　b. near Batavia, N.Y., 27 Aug. 1839, into a highly disciplined family, Upton decided early on a military career. Entering West Point after 2 years of preparation at Oberlin College in Ohio, he graduated 8th in his class 6 May 1861 and 8 days later was promoted to 1st lieutenant, 5th U.S. Artillery.

LC

Wounded during the FIRST BULL RUN CAMPAIGN, where, at BLACKBURN'S FORD, he aimed and fired the opening gun of the battle, he served with distinction in the PENINSULA CAMPAIGN, earning promotion to command of an artillery brigade. His guns were at CRAMPTON'S GAP and ANTIETAM. In Oct. 1862, to avoid an assignment to instruct at West Point, he secured the colonelcy of the 121st New York Volunteers. This VI Corps regiment saw little action at Fredericksburg, Chancellorsville, and Gettysburg, but just before Gettysburg Upton received brigade command, exercising it brilliantly 7 Nov. 1863 at RAPPAHANNOCK STATION.

At Spotsylvania's "BLOODY ANGLE" he won his brigadier's star, to rank from 12 May 1864, for innovating a rushing assault by column instead of by the standard linear attack. When the VI Corps was sent from Petersburg to join Maj. Gen. PHILIP H. SHERIDAN'S SHENANDOAH VALLEY CAMPAIGN, 25-year-old Upton was given a divisional command at Opequon, was wounded, and the next day was brevetted major general. With his wound barely healed, he joined Maj. Gen. JAMES H. WILSON at Nashville to lead a division of the cavalry corps in the campaign against SELMA, Ala., and Columbus, Ga. By then, the war was over. He had commanded outstandingly in all 3 branches of the army.

Author of *Infantry Tactics* (1867) and *Military Policy of the United States* (1904), and an ardent advocate of reform in the country's military system, Upton, tormented by violent headaches, became increasingly discouraged and disillusioned in the postwar years. On 15 Mar. 1881, at his post at the Presidio in San Francisco, he shot himself.　　—RDH

Urbanna Plan, McClellan's.

The stalemate in northern Virginia after FIRST BULL RUN, July 1861, lengthened through summer and fall into winter. Gen. JOSEPH E. JOHNSTON's Confederate army maintained its position around Manassas Junction and Centreville. To the east, Maj. Gen. GEORGE B. MCCLEL-

LAN continued his extensive reorganization and drilling of the ARMY OF THE POTOMAC. The Union administration had been urging on the youthful commander some offensive operations against Johnston before the advent of winter, but "Little Mac" balked.

In mid-December McClellan evolved a campaign plan for an offensive thrust beyond Johnston's flank with the assistance of the navy. He decided to load his army on transports, steam down the Potomac River into Chesapeake Bay, then follow its coast to the mouth of the Rappahannock River and up that stream to Urbanna. At this landing on the Rappahannock's southern bank, McClellan would disembark, 50 mi from Richmond and in the rear of the Confederates along the Manassas line.

The Union commander soon found that implementing such a complex operation would require time, so he delayed until spring. Pres. ABRAHAM LINCOLN, unaware of McClellan's plan, lost patience with the general's inactivity. On 27 Jan. 1862, on his own initiative, Lincoln peremptorily ordered an advance of all Union armies to begin 22 Feb. According to Lincoln's instructions, McClellan's army would move against Johnston toward a point southwest of Manassas Junction.

Lincoln's order stunned McClellan, who immediately went to see the commander in chief. After the president was briefed, he objected to the plan because it would endanger Washington. McClellan requested permission to submit written objections to Lincoln's orders and reasons supporting his own proposal. After an exchange of questions and answers, Lincoln reluctantly agreed to the Urbanna Plan.

McClellan did not move 22 Feb., and Lincoln's doubts increased. On 8 Mar., at Lincoln's request, McClellan submitted the plan to his 12 division commanders, who listened and voted 8–4 in favor of the Urbanna route. Lincoln acceded, but only after specifying in an order that the capital must be sufficiently defended. On 9 Mar., however, Johnston abandoned the Manassas line, moving toward the Rappahannock River. McClellan's Urbanna Plan was now useless.   —JDW

Usher, John Palmer. USP b. Brookfield, N.Y., 9 Jan. 1816. The son of an established New England family, Usher attended local schools, then became a legal apprentice to Henry Bennett in New Berlin, N.Y. Admitted to the bar in 1839, he opened a practice in Terre Haute, Ind., and while on the judicial circuit met and became friends with ABRAHAM LINCOLN. Elected to the Indiana state legislature in 1850, Usher served 1 term. In 1856 he ran unsuccessfully for the U.S. House of Representatives on the Republican ticket. 5 years later he was appointed Indiana's attorney general, but soon resigned to accept the post as first assistant secretary of the U.S.

LC

Department of the Interior. When CALEB B. SMITH resigned his post as secretary Dec. 1862, Usher succeeded him.

During his term, Usher advocated several plans for the colonization of former slaves, believing that blacks should be reset-

tled away from white populations. Attempts at colonizing Central America failed, and Usher could not get support for the establishment of black reservations in the States. The secretary was also a large stockholder in the Union Pacific Railroad, which was completing its leg of the transcontinental railway. As secretary of the interior, he was in an excellent position to determine rights of way; consequently, entire Indian reservations were relocated to facilitate the railroad's completion. While in office, he also presented reports commenting on the benefits of the HOMESTEAD ACT OF 1862, increased appropriations for Indian reservations, and the taxation of gold and silver mines.

Usher supported Lincoln's policies until the latter's assassination. He then fell in with the Radicals (see RADICAL REPUBLICANS) and criticized Pres. ANDREW JOHNSON for his policies toward the South. On 15 May 1865, he resigned his post in protest and moved to Lawrence, Kans. There he accepted the position of chief counsel to the Union Pacific Railroad, serving until his death in Philadelphia, 13 Apr. 1889.   —MTC

Utah, Union Department of. The Department of Utah was formed by General Orders No. 12, 1 Jan. 1858, to consist of Utah Territory under the command of Col. ALBERT SIDNEY JOHNSTON. Command passed to several officers during the prewar years, falling to Col. PHILIP ST. GEORGE COOKE 20 Apr. 1860. With the approval of military authorities, Cooke marched the department's troops to the East 9 Aug. 1861. On their departure the department was effectively discontinued.   —PLF

Utah Territory. Following Spanish exploration in 1540 and 1776–77, later visits by trappers (among them Jed Smith and Jim Bridger), and U.S. Army exploration under Lt. JOHN C. FRÉMONT in 1842–43, first settlement of the land came July 1847. A party of 147 Mormons led by Brigham Young set up their homes near the Great Salt Lake, ending a journey from Nauvoo, Ill., where their leader, Joseph Smith, had been murdered. This pioneer party was joined before winter by 1,500 additional Mormons, all of whom claimed a territory covering all of the area (except California) ceded by Mexico at the close of the Mexican War. 3 years later they applied for statehood as the State of Deseret. By the terms of the COMPROMISE OF 1850, the government instead made Utah a territory with Brigham Young governor.

The Mormon practice of polygamy gave rise to rumors culminating in a report that the Latter-Day Saints were in rebellion against the laws of the U.S. As a result, in 1852 Pres. Franklin Pierce offered governorship of the territory to future Union Gen. JOHN W. GEARY, who rejected the offer. The Utah Expedition of 1857–58, under Col. ALBERT SIDNEY JOHNSTON, with Lt. Col. BARNARD E. BEE commanding the volunteer battalion, found the report false.

In 1862 Col. Patrick E. Connor established Fort Douglas near Salt Lake City to guard against Confederate invasion, to "watch" the Mormons, to keep open the mail route to California, and to put an end to Indian depredations. At Bear River he decisively defeated a coalition of Bannocks and Shoshones, ending for several years the Indian threat to Salt Lake Valley and ensuring Mormon support of the Union.

The territory became the 45th state in 1896.   —RDH

V

Vallandigham, Clement Laird. USP b. New Lisbon, Ohio, 29 July 1820, Vallandigham studied at the New Lisbon Academy, attended Jefferson College in Pennsylvania in 1837 and 1840, taught at a Maryland school in the intervening period, then privately pursued legal studies in Ohio, passing the state bar in 1842. A noted New Lisbon attorney, he won election to the state house of representatives in 1845 and 1846, moved to Dayton in 1847, bought a half-interest in the Dayton *Empire,* edited it until 1849, and was the defeated Democratic candidate in the 1852 and 1854 congressional elections. A candidate again in 1856, he contested his third de-

NA

feat and won his seat in the U.S. House May 1858. Narrowly reelected that autumn, Vallandigham made a national reputation as a conservative and as a contentious states-rights advocate. He became brigadier general of Ohio militia in 1857, met with the captured abolitionist JOHN BROWN in 1859, subsequently spread rumors of a national abolitionist conspiracy, then supported a moderate course in the secession crisis, backing Democratic presidential candidate STEPHEN A. DOUGLAS in 1860.

Vallandigham opposed the Federal government's prosecution of the Civil War, publishing a letter in the 20 Apr. 1861 Cincinnati *Daily Enquirer* stating his belief that the South could not be coerced into reentering the Union. Supported by vocal immigrant and farm constituencies in Ohio, he blamed the war on Pres. ABRAHAM LINCOLN and the REPUBLICAN PARTY, voted against national CONSCRIPTION, refused to cooperate with congressional war measures, and alienated the powers within his own political party. A COPPERHEAD, falsely believed to belong to the KNIGHTS OF THE GOLDEN CIRCLE, he was abandoned by the state's WAR DEMOCRATS in a fight to keep his original congressional district intact. It was gerrymandered to contain a minority of his supporters, and he was not reelected in 1862. Determined to run for the governorship in 1863, he began an unofficial campaign in spring 1862, following Democratic victories in Dayton, and tried to rally support for his candidacy over that of Democratic elder-statesman Hugh J. Jewett. The preliminary Ohio Democratic convention met 28 Apr. and rejected Vallandigham's bid for the gubernatorial nomination.

On 13 Apr. 1863, Maj. Gen. AMBROSE E. BURNSIDE, commander of the DEPARTMENT OF THE OHIO, had issued General Order No. 38, forbidding expression of sympathy for the

enemy. On 30 Apr. Vallandigham addressed a large audience in Columbus, made derogatory references to the president and the war effort, then hoped that he would be arrested under Burnside's order, thus gaining popular sympathy. Arrested at his home at 2 a.m., 5 May, by a company of troops, he was taken to Burnside's Cincinnati headquarters, tried by a military court 6–7 May, denied a writ of *habeas corpus,* and sentenced to 2 years' confinement in a military prison. Following a 19 May cabinet meeting, President Lincoln commuted Vallandigham's sentence to banishment to the Confederacy. On 26 May the Ohioan was taken to Confederates south of Murfreesboro, Tenn., and there entered Southern lines. Outraged at his treatment, by a vote of 411–11 state Democrats nominated Vallandigham for governor at their 11 June convention.

Vallandigham was escorted to Wilmington, N.C., and shipped out to Bermuda, arriving there 17 June. He traveled to Canada, arrived at Niagara Falls, Ontario, 5 July, and from there and Windsor, Ontario, conducted his campaign for the governorship. Candidate for lieutenant governor George Pugh represented Vallandigham's views at rallies and in the press. Lincoln interested himself in the election, endorsed Republican candidate JOHN BROUGH, downplayed the illegalities of a civilian's arrest and trial by military authorities, and claimed that a vote for the Democratic contender was "a discredit to the country." In the election of 13 Oct. 1863, Brough defeated Vallandigham 288,000–187,000.

With the election crisis passed, Lincoln and the military ignored Vallandigham's return to the U.S. in disguise 14 June 1864. He reestablished residence in Ohio, attended the August national Democratic convention in Chicago, and helped construct the disastrous "peace" plank in presidential candidate GEORGE B. MCCLELLAN's platform.

In postwar years the Democratic party declared him *persona non grata* at its 1866 Philadelphia convention, a meeting of old Federals and recently reconstructed Southern Democrats, where it was felt his presence was disruptive. After he lost a bid in 1867 for election to the state senate, he resumed his law practice. In a Lebanon, Ohio, hotel, 16 June 1871, a gun went off while he was demonstrating to other attorneys how a defendant's supposed victim may have accidentally shot himself. He died there the following day.

The Ohioan is best remembered for the Feb. 1864 Supreme Court decision, *Ex Parte Vallandigham,* which decreed that the Court could not issue a writ of *habeas corpus* in a military case, and for a Democratic campaign slogan he created May 1862: "The Constitution as it is, the Union as it was." Inspired by the story of Vallandigham's banishment and his remark at that time that he did not care to live in a country where Lincoln was president, Edward Everett Hale wrote "The Man Without a Country" (1863).   —JES

Valley District, Confederate.

Valley District, Confederate. When Confederate authorities created the DEPARTMENT OF NORTHERN VIRGINIA 22 Oct. 1861, they designated the SHENANDOAH VALLEY as the Valley District of the department. Maj. Gen. THOMAS J. "STONEWALL" JACKSON assumed initial command, and for the next 3 years Confederate forces, operating in the strategically vital area, enjoyed almost untarnished successes.

As district commander, Jackson achieved lasting fame in the Shenandoah Valley in 1862. Defeated at FIRST KERNSTOWN 23 Mar., he undertook his brilliant SHENANDOAH VALLEY CAMPAIGN in May, winning 5 battles and defeating 3 Union commands. His FOOT CAVALRY then rejoined the ARMY OF NORTHERN VIRGINIA for the summer campaigns.

On 29 Dec. 1862, Brig. Gen. WILLIAM E. "GRUMBLE" JONES succeeded Jackson as commander of the district, holding the post until May 1863, when Brig. Gen. ISAAC R. TRIMBLE replaced him. During the Confederate invasion of Pennsylvania, the Southerners defeated a Union force 14–15 June at the SECOND BATTLE OF WINCHESTER. Brig. Gen. JOHN D. IMBODEN succeeded Trimble 21 July, retaining the command until 15 Dec., when Maj. Gen. JUBAL A. EARLY assumed the post.

In spring 1864 Early was named commander of the II Corps. In June he arrived in the Shenandoah with his command, routed a Union army, and launched a spectacular raid on Washington, D.C. In August Union authorities created a new army to oppose Early and assigned Maj. Gen. PHILIP H. SHERIDAN as its commander. In a series of battles—THIRD WINCHESTER, FISHER'S HILL, Tom's Brook, and CEDAR CREEK—Sheridan crushed Early's army. On 29 Mar. 1865, Brig. Gen. LUNSFORD L. LOMAX became the district's last commander.   —JDW

Valverde, New Mexico Territory, eng. at.

Valverde, New Mexico Territory, eng. at.   21 Feb. 1862
On 19 Feb. 1862, Confederate Brig. Gen. HENRY HOPKINS SIBLEY ordered his 2,600 men across the Rio Grande to Valverde ford, 5 mi north of Fort Craig, hoping to isolate the Union garrison from its military headquarters at Santa Fe. To prevent the Confederates from crossing the river, Col. E.R.S. CANBY left Fort Craig and marched up the west bank of the Rio Grande with a force of 3,810. Early on the morning of the 21st Canby's troopers fired at the Confederates across the river, initiating a duel between artillery and small arms in which Sibley's Texans gave ground. Union cavalry crossed the river in pursuit and pushed the outnumbered Texans back to the old river channel of the Rio Grande, a stronger defensive position than they had occupied earlier. Canby followed about 3 p.m. with the rest of his army and his artillery.

Fearing that a direct assault would fail, the Union commander deployed his men to envelop the Confederate left flank, but the Confederates unexpectedly seized the offensive. The Federal forces repulsed a desperate cavalry charge against their left, led by Maj. Henry W. Raguet, sending the Texans reeling back to safety under withering small-arms fire and single artillery shell that exploded in the attackers' midst.

Just as the battered force was pulling back, the main body of Confederates, led by Col. THOMAS GREEN, stormed Canby's lines in a frontal attack. With double-barreled shotguns, muskets, and revolvers, the Texans poured a lethal volley on the battery commanded by Capt. Alexander McRae, killing McRae and capturing his 6 guns in hand-to-hand combat, then turning them against the Union troopers. Canby's unseasoned New Mexican volunteers and many of his Regulars broke, and when the right of his line collapsed, the Union commander was

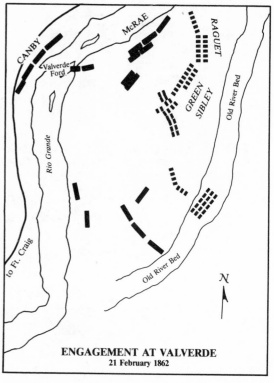

ENGAGEMENT AT VALVERDE
21 February 1862

forced to order retreat.

With the arrival of 5 fresh companies of cavalry, Green gave Col. WILLIAM R. SCURRY permission to pursue the enemy, but ordered him back to the Confederate lines when Canby raised a flag of truce to allow the removal of his dead and wounded from the field.

Sibley reported no more than 1,750 engaged at Valverde, giving losses as 36 killed, 150 wounded, and 1 missing. Most of the Federal casualties—68 killed, 160 wounded, and 35 missing—occurred during the attack on McRae's battery. Left in control of the battlefield, the Confederates could claim victory, but Sibley had learned that he would face stubborn opposition in the campaign to occupy New Mexico Territory for the Confederacy.

The Confederate invasion of the Southwest reached its peak 4 Mar., when Sibley occupied Santa Fe after Federal forces there, having learned of Canby's defeat at Valverde, withdrew northwest to Fort Union.   —PLF

Van Brunt, Gershom Jaques.

Van Brunt, Gershom Jaques.   USN   b. Monmouth Cty., N.J., 28 Aug. 1798, Van Brunt was appointed midshipman 1 Jan. 1818. His distinguished naval career included action against pirates in the Caribbean 1823–24 and further action at sea during the Mexican War. In 1848–49 he was a member of the U.S. commission that surveyed the boundary of California. At the onset of civil war Van Brunt was captain of the wooden steamer USS *Minnesota*. This vessel, with Van Brunt in command, served as Flag Officer SILAS H. STRINGHAM's flagship in operations at HAMPTON ROADS, Va., and during the joint army/navy expedition to capture HATTERAS INLET, N.C., Aug. 1861.

After the success there, the *Minnesota* returned to Hampton Roads, where it was on BLOCKADE duty when the newly launched ironclad CSS *VIRGINIA (Merrimack)* made its appearance 8 Mar. 1862. During the action the *Virginia* destroyed both the USS *Congress* and USS *Cumberland* and attempted to destroy the grounded *Minnesota*. Although Van Brunt vowed that he would fight to the end and destroy his ship rather than have it captured, such action

USMHI

proved unnecessary after the arrival of the USS *MONITOR* 9 Mar. (*see* HAMPTON ROADS, VA., BATTLE OF).

Van Brunt had proven himself a valiant officer, but age and illness brought his retirement 28 Apr. 1863. d. Dedham, Mass., 17 Dec. 1863.   —NCD

Vance, Robert Brank. CSA b. Buncombe Cty., N.C., 24 Apr. 1828. The elder brother of Confederate Gen. and Gov. ZEBULON B. VANCE, Robert received the standard education of

his day, thereafter engaging in commerce, farming, and clerking for his county court. When his state seceded, he organized and led the Buncombe Life Guards and later commanded the regiment to which the unit was assigned, the 29th North Carolina Infantry.

In Oct. 1861 Colonel Vance and his regiment were dispatched to Raleigh for further training and a month later to East Tennessee for their first field service. The outfit served principally as a railroad garrison

LC

until early in 1862, when transferred to Cumberland Gap, Tenn. After the Confederates abandoned that mountain position in June, Vance's outfit served under Brig. Gen. CARTER L. STEVENSON in the Aug. 1862 engagement at Tazewell, Tenn. Vance then commanded several regiments at Baptist Gap before accompanying Maj. Gen. E. KIRBY SMITH on his late summer campaign in Kentucky. After reaching Frankfort that September, Vance returned to Tennessee and 3 months later fought in the division of Maj. Gen. JOHN P. MCCOWN at STONE'S RIVER. On that field he moved up to brigade command on the death of his immediate superior, Brig. Gen. JAMES E. RAINS, and, in McCown's words, "bore himself gallantly." Following the fight, Vance was stricken with typhoid fever. While convalescing, he was appointed a brigadier general to rank from 4 Mar. 1863.

On recovery, he was dispatched to western North Carolina and given command of a local military district. His service in that region was brief and unhappy. That October, leading a 150-man expedition through Madison County, he was overwhelmed and routed by the enemy. On 14 Jan. 1864, a larger force under his supervision met a similar fate while forging into East Tennessee in support of Lt. Gen. JAMES LONGSTREET's army.

At Schultz's Mill, near Seviersville, Tenn., Federal cavalry surprised Vance's camp, capturing him and most of his men. He spent the next 14 months in Northern prisons.

After his release he went home; served a term in the state legislature and 6 more in the U.S. House of Representatives, 1873–85; was assistant U.S. commissioner of patents 1885–89; formed a national temperance organization; and was active in the Methodist Church. d. Asheville, N.C., 28 Nov. 1899.   —EGL

Vance, Zebulon Baird. war governor b. Buncombe Cty., N.C., 13 May 1830, Vance, younger brother of future Confederate Brig. Gen. ROBERT B. VANCE, was educated at Washington

College in eastern Tennessee and at the University of North Carolina Law School. In 1852 he opened a law office in Asheville, in 1853 served as county solicitor, and in 1854 was elected to the state legislature. In 1858 he ran for a seat in the U.S. House of Representatives and won. Vance was both a Democrat and a Unionist and in 1860 supported Constitutional Unionist John Bell for the presidency. When North Carolina seceded, Vance refused to be a candidate for the Confederate

LC

Congress and instead became colonel of the 26th North Carolina. His unit was engaged at NEW BERNE Mar. 1862 and again during the SEVEN DAYS' CAMPAIGN around Richmond in late June and early July. In Sept. 1862 he was elected governor, and was reelected in 1864.

As governor, Vance has often been portrayed as a selfish STATES-RIGHTS figure. While he often disagreed with the centralist tendencies of Jefferson Davis' administration, Vance in fact supported the Confederacy strongly. He worked to maintain North Carolina's fighting spirit and helped the state maintain and expand its considerable munitions and clothing factories. His state supplied more troops to the Confederacy than any other, and they were maintained largely at state expense, thus relieving the Confederate government of the burden. Vance initiated his own overseas supply purchases and often shared state supplies with Confederate troops of other states. Within North Carolina he championed individual rights and never allowed the suspension of *HABEAS CORPUS* during the war.

Imprisoned briefly after the war, Vance returned to his law practice July 1865. He was elected to the U.S. Senate in 1870 but was not allowed to take his seat. He lost a second race for the Senate in 1872, but in 1876 was once again elected governor. In 1879, he became a U.S. senator and maintained that position until his death in Washington, Ga., 14 Apr. 1894.   —LDJ

Van Dorn, Earl. CSA b. near Port Gibson, Miss., 17 Sept. 1820, Van Dorn graduated from West Point 52d in the class of 1842. Serving with distinction in the Mexican War, in 1855 he was appointed a captain of the 2d Cavalry and stationed in Texas, where he gained national recognition for his exploits against the Comanches. On 3 Jan. 1861, Van Dorn resigned his U.S. Army commission for a colonelcy in the Confederate army and was assigned to Texas, there helping to effect the bloodless surrender of U.S. troops. He was promoted to brigadier general 5 June, and 19 Sept. rose to the rank of major general, with which he was given command of the TRANS-MISSISSIPPI DEPARTMENT.

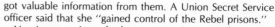

LC

Like so many other Confederate generals, Van Dorn never lived up to his country's early expectations. Zealous for personal glory, he was frequently the center of controversy, both for his military tactics and the conduct of his personal life. As an army commander Van Dorn lost his 2 major battles, PEA RIDGE and CORINTH, because of poor staff work and his inability to handle details. For the loss at Corinth he faced a court of inquiry, which exonerated him of any misconduct, including the charge of drunkenness on the battlefield; nevertheless, he did not command an army again.

Still believing he was a valuable asset, the Confederate War Department gave him a cavalry command that he used brilliantly at HOLLY SPRINGS, destroying so many supplies that Maj. Gen. ULYSSES S. GRANT's VICKSBURG CAMPAIGN had to be rescheduled. Again, at Thompson's Station, he proved his mastery of cavalry tactics. By spring 1863 he was being ranked with NATHAN B. FORREST, JOSEPH WHEELER, and JOHN HUNT MORGAN as one of the South's most outstanding Western cavalry commanders.

Described as handsome, trim, elegant in appearance, and a lady's man, Van Dorn was killed by an irate husband at his headquarters in Spring Hill, Tenn., 7 May 1863. While he had proved himself unsuited to handle a large army, as a commander of cavalry he had few peers.   —PRR

Van Lew, Elizabeth. spy b. New York, 1818, Van Lew differed from the traditional image of women spies in that she used neither charm nor beauty to acquire and relay military information. Instead, she used her natural odd behavior to help the North throughout the Civil War. Gen. George H. Sharpe of U.S. Army Intelligence said of Van Lew: "For a long, long time, she represented all that was left of the power of the United States government in Richmond."

An angular, sharp-nosed woman with eyes of "unearthly brilliance," Van Lew was educated in Philadelphia. A resident of Richmond most of her life, she was an ardent abolitionist. Locals believed that no sane Virginian could be so vocal in her sympathy with the North—an opinion that shielded Van Lew from suspicion of ESPIONAGE. Known as "Crazy Bet" by Richmond residents, she was regarded as a silly, hysterical woman. All the while, she was secretly writing to Federal officials, giving them valuable, accurate information about the Confederacy, and securing and financing fellow spies.

She helped Union prisoners escape from LIBBY PRISON, gave them money (left by her prosperous father, a hardware merchant), and hid them, along with espionage agents, in the upper rooms of the Van Lew mansion in Richmond or on the family farm outside the city. She carried clothes, bedding, food, and medicines to those prisoners unable to escape, and

got valuable information from them. A Union Secret Service officer said that she "gained control of the Rebel prisons."

Van Lew was in such close communication with Lt. Gen. ULYSSES S. GRANT during his Richmond campaign (see OVERLAND CAMPAIGN) that flowers from her garden often graced his dining table. When the Federals entered Richmond, Grant sent his aide-de-camp to protect the Van Lew property, and the general himself, along with many Union officials, soon called on the extraordinarily clever spy.

Through the postwar years Van Lew struggled financially, having spent all her convertible property in work for the Union cause. In 1869, Grant, now president, appointed her postmistress of Richmond, a position she held for 8 years. She was not reappointed when Grant's second term expired. With barely enough income to subsist, she eventually appealed for help to friends in New England, relatives of a former Union officer, Col. Paul J. Revere, whom she had helped in Libby Prison. Provided an ample annuity by them, Van Lew lived out her days in Richmond. d. place and date unknown. Her tombstone, placed by New England friends, reads, "She risked everything that was dear to her—friends, fortune, comfort, health, even life itself—all for one absorbing desire of her heart —that slavery might be abolished and the Union preserved."
—PLF

Vaughan, Alfred Jefferson, Jr. CSA b. Dinwiddie Cty., Va., 10 May 1830. In 1851 Vaughan graduated from the VIRGINIA MILITARY INSTITUTE as senior captain of cadets. Entering civil engineering, he migrated to California as a deputy U.S. surveyor, then served on the staff of an official of the fledgling Northern Pacific Railroad before settling in Marshall Cty., Miss., as a planter.

When both his native and adopted states seceded in 1861, Vaughan abandoned the Unionist views he had earlier espoused and raised a company of Mississippians. Finding the state unable to arm and equip his men, he led them north; they were mustered into Confederate service as part of the 13th Tennessee Infantry, with Vaughan their captain.

LC

Vaughan had a varied and active war career. Elected lieutenant colonel June 1861, he served in regimental or brigade command during almost every major contest in the Western theater, including BELMONT, SHILOH, PERRYVILLE, CHICKAMAUGA, and MISSIONARY RIDGE, and the first half of the ATLANTA CAMPAIGN. During that period he had no fewer than 8 horses shot under him, winning the reputation of a "fighting officer." Perhaps his most dramatic service came at Shiloh, where, 6 Apr. 1862, he led his troops in a charge against the Union right, routing an Ohio regiment and causing a nearby battery to abandon 3 of its guns.

For his able service in brigade command at Chickamauga, Vaughan was commissioned a brigadier as of 18 Nov. 1863. Thereafter he led 6 Tennessee regiments in the corps of Maj. Gen. JOHN C. BRECKINRIDGE and later in Lt. Gen. WILLIAM J. HARDEE's Corps/Army of Tennessee. It was under Hardee that he saw his last day of field service. On 4 July 1864, as the Confederates resisted the advance of Maj. Gen. WILLIAM T. SHERMAN's forces at VINING'S STATION, on the Western & Atlantic Railroad between Marietta and Atlanta, Vaughan was permanently disabled by an exploding shell that tore off his leg.

After recovering from the wound, he returned to farming in Mississippi. In later life he became active in the Grange movement, opened a mercantile firm in Memphis, and was twice elected clerk of the criminal court of Shelby Cty., Tenn. Until his death in Indianapolis, Ind., 1 Oct. 1899, he also headed the Tennessee chapter of the UNITED CONFEDERATE VETERANS.

—EGL

Vaughan Road, Va., Battle of. 5–7 Feb. 1865 *See* HATCHER'S RUN, VA., BATTLE OF.

Vaughn, John Crawford. CSA b. Roane Cty., Tenn., 24 Feb. 1824, Vaughn fought in the Mexican War as a captain in the 5th Tennessee and during the 1850s was a merchant. While visiting Charleston, S.C., Apr. 1861, he witnessed the reduction of FORT SUMTER. After returning home, he recruited a regiment in East Tennessee, a strong Union area, and 6 June mustered into Confederate service as colonel of the 3d Tennessee.

Vaughn and his regiment were ordered to Virginia, where they served under Gen. JOSEPH E. JOHNSTON at Harpers Ferry and at FIRST BULL RUN. In spring 1862, Vaughn transferred to his native state. On 22 Sept. he received his promotion to brigadier general and the command of a brigade with which he participated in the VICKSBURG CAMPAIGN and surrendered 4 July 1863.

Following his exchange, he commanded a cavalry brigade in eastern Tennessee and southwestern Virginia. His troopers fought at PIEDMONT, Va., 5 June 1864, opposing the advance of Maj. Gen. DAVID HUNTER's Union army. In July his brigade participated in Lt. Gen. JUBAL A. EARLY's raid on Washington, D.C. (*see* EARLY'S WASHINGTON RAID). During the 1864 SHENANDOAH VALLEY CAMPAIGN, Vaughn suffered a wound near Martinsburg, W. Va., which temporarily incapacitated him. When he recovered, he replaced Brig. Gen. JOHN HUNT MORGAN, who had been killed, as commander of Confederate forces in East Tennessee. After the surrender of Confederate forces in Virginia, he joined Johnston in North Carolina. His brigade formed part of the escort as Pres. JEFFERSON DAVIS fled. Vaughn was paroled at Washington, Ga.

During the postwar years, the Confederate general lived alternately in his native state and in Georgia. He served 1 term as presiding officer of the Tennessee senate, dying on his Georgia plantation near Thomasville, 10 Sept. 1875.

—JDW

Veatch, James Clifford. USA b. Elizabethtown, Ind., 19 Dec. 1819, Veatch studied law privately, passed the Indiana bar in 1840, established a legal practice in Rockport, Ind., in 1841, and that year was chosen auditor of Spencer County.

LC

Elected to serve in the state legislature in 1861, he instead joined the 25th Indiana Infantry at Evansville, and 19 Aug. was mustered in with the regiment as its colonel.

First detailed to Missouri, Veatch and the 25th served at FORT DONELSON. He assumed command of the 2d Brigade/4th Division/XVI Corps/Army of the Tennessee and, under Brig. Gen. Stephen A. Hurlbut, anchored the left of the Union line 6 Apr. 1862 in the Battle of SHILOH. He fought well there; was appointed brigadier general 28 Apr. 1862; took part in the campaigning around Corinth, the occupation of Memphis, Tenn., and the pursuit of Maj. Gen. EARL VAN DORN's army after the Oct. 1862 Battle of CORINTH; and Jan. 1863 briefly took command of the District of Memphis. Soon replaced by Brig. Gen. Ralph P. Buckland, Veatch resumed command at Memphis 31 Mar. 1863, serving there until 24 Jan. 1864, when he assumed leadership of the 4th Division/XVI Corps over the objections of Maj. Gen. OLIVER O. HOWARD, who deemed him less than industrious.

After service in the ATLANTA CAMPAIGN, Veatch went on sick leave 17 July 1864. On returning to duty in September he awaited orders in Memphis and fulfilled administrative duties, then took leadership of the 1st Division/XIII Corps/Army of the Gulf 18 Feb. 1865. He served with this division through the Mobile campaigning, was commander of the District of West Louisiana, then mustered out Aug. 1865. After leaving the volunteer service he was awarded a brevet to major general for his service at Mobile.

Veatch returned to his legal practice in Rockport and won appointments as adjutant general of Indiana in 1869 and collector of internal revenue 1870–83, dying in Rockport 22 Dec. 1895.

—JES

vedette. *see* VIDETTE.

Velazquez, Loreta Janeta. b. 26 June 1842, Havana, Cuba. About 1849 Velazquez's family settled in New Orleans. There Loreta Janeta was educated and in 1856 married a U.S. Army officer, who joined the Confederate army early in 1861. In the postbellum years Velazquez claimed that about this time she assumed the name Harry Buford and raised a company of cavalry in Arkansas, became lieutenant of the unit, temporarily commanded it under Brig. Gen. BARNARD E. BEE at FIRST BULL RUN, and fought again at BALL'S BLUFF in 1861 and at SHILOH Apr. 1862. After her husband died from an accidental gunshot wound, she stayed in the army until discovered in 1863. From then until the end of the war she was employed as a Confederate spy, frequently operating in Washington, D.C., as well as in Canada.

The book Velazquez wrote after the war chronicles an unbelievable series of adventures with more characteristics of fiction than of fact. Titled *The Woman in Battle: A Narrative of the Exploits, Adventures, and Travels of Madame Loreta Janeta Velazquez, Otherwise Known as Lieutenant Harry Buford, Confederate States of America* (1876), it is the least credible of the Civil War spy literature. What is known about

Velazquez is based almost exclusively on the information she gives in the book. During the postwar years she remarried and traveled extensively in South America.   —PLF

Vermont. Vermont had vigorously opposed SLAVERY for many years and responded quickly to Pres. ABRAHAM LINCOLN's call for volunteers. A total of 35,262 Vermont men formed 19 regiments, 3 batteries, and 1 company during the war. The Vermont Brigade in the VI Corps was made up exclusively of Vermont units throughout the entire conflict.

Vermont troops participated in most of the major battles in the East and suffered heavy losses. 5 companies of the 1ST VERMONT fought in the first battle of the war, 10 June 1861, at BIG BETHEL, Va. At GETTYSBURG, Brig. Gen. George J. Stannard's 14th Vermont Regiment took part in one of the most dramatic and significant exploits of the war. At the most critical period of PICKETT'S CHARGE, 3 July, Stannard saw an opportunity to move forward into a gap in the Confederate lines. He first delivered deadly flanking fire against 1 advancing line on his right, then made an about-face, destroying the enemy's advance on his left. An independent action, it deprived Confederate Maj. Gen. GEORGE E. PICKETT of valuable support.

The 5th Vermont Regiment performed significantly at SAVAGE'S STATION in 1862 when the rear of Maj. Gen. GEORGE B. MCCLELLAN's retreating army was being attacked by Confederate Maj. Gen. JOHN B. MAGRUDER and was in danger of being overrun. A sudden counterattack by the Vermont troops broke through the enemy advance and enabled the Union army to make a final stand later at MALVERN HILL. Vermont units suffered heavy casualties at the WILDERNESS and SPOTSYLVANIA and at CEDAR CREEK, where the 8th regiment lost a devastating 68% of its complement.

On 19 Oct. 1864, Vermont was "invaded" from Canada by a group of disguised Confederate soldiers who raided the town of ST. ALBANS and secured $200,000 for the Confederacy from local banks. The raiders fled back to Canada, where they were arrested and tried by Canadian authorities and discharged. Excitement in the North was high, but the raid was soon forgotten as the war neared its end.   —FSK

1st Vermont Brigade. Except for a brief period, the 1st Vermont Brigade, unlike most Federal brigades, throughout the war consisted of regiments from the same state. 2 of these regiments, the 2d and 3d Vermont, formed part of Vermonter Brig. Gen. WILLIAM F. SMITH's brigade Aug. 1861. When his brigade became a division that October, the 2d and 3d joined the new 4th, 5th, and 6th Vermont regiments as the 1st Vermont Brigade/Smith's Division/Army of the Potomac (later the 2d Brigade/2d Division/VI Corps). In May 1864 the 1st Vermont Heavy Artillery Regiment reinforced the brigade. 1 non-Vermont outfit, the 9-month 26th New Jersey Regiment, also served with it Oct. 1862–June 1863.

Throughout its long service, the unit had only 3 official commanders: Smith, Aug.–Oct. 1861; Brig. Gen. WILLIAM T. H. BROOKS, Oct. 1861–Oct. 1862; and Brig. Gen. LEWIS A. GRANT, Jan. 1864–June 1865. Between and during their tours, numerous regimental officers led it temporarily.

Its combat debut at Lee's Mill was inauspicious, as just 12 of the unit's 50 companies advanced piecemeal in brave but unsupported probes. Brooks's troops gained greater distinction at SAVAGE'S STATION, WHITE OAK SWAMP, and CRAMPTON'S GAP, and fought gallantly at CHANCELLORSVILLE. After helping over-

awe traitors in New York, Aug.–Sept. 1863, the brigade rejoined the Army of the Potomac to support the Federal victory at RAPPAHANNOCK STATION.

During 1864 the unit battled at the WILDERNESS, SPOTSYLVANIA, COLD HARBOR, and First Weldon Railroad. When the brigade rushed north to save Washington, some of its troops skirmished with Lt. Gen. JUBAL A. EARLY before Fort Stevens. The 1st Vermont subsequently helped defeat him at THIRD WINCHESTER, FISHER'S HILL, and CEDAR CREEK.

Returning to the Army of the Potomac Dec. 1864, the Vermonters spearheaded the onslaught that finally overran Petersburg's defenses 2 Apr. 1865 (see PETERSBURG CAMPAIGN). Lewis Grant's men also harried Maj. Gen. WILLIAM MAHONE's final line at SAYLER'S CREEK. After occupying southside Virginia that spring, the brigade participated in the VI Corps's Grand Review 8 June 1865. It was discontinued 28 June 1865, and its infantry regiments mustered out the following month. The 1st Vermont Heavy Artillery Regiment, which had remained at Fort Foote, went home in August.   —RJS

Veteran Reserve Corps. After a year of civil war the Union army was suffering from a shortage of manpower. Many of those not serving on the battle line for reasons of health became assistants to quartermasters or doctors, who sometimes inflated the numbers on sick lists to justify keeping the help. This practice caused much anger among army officers who believed the men so retained were shirkers.

In 1863 the War Department began to organize invalid detachments in which those unfit for regular combat duty were to serve in hospitals or as guards. The group, named the INVALID CORPS, was organized into 2 battalions, the first made up of men fit for limited armed service and garrison duty, and the second of the more disabled, who were to act as nurses and clerks.

Service in the corps, whose members were easily identified by distinctive sky-blue uniforms, was at first avoided by many wounded veterans willing to return to duty. The corps was not organized into units by state, nor did it encourage recruiting among men loyal first to their state; neither did it offer bounties for enlisting. Further, the corps's initials were the same as letters stamped on government equipment that had been "Inspected—Condemned." To eliminate this coincidence and to promote veterans' reenlistments, the War Department in March 1864 changed the hated corps name to Veteran Reserve Corps and had it adopt the uniforms of the Regular Army.

The Veteran Reserves saw duty mainly as noncombat and garrison troops, relieving able-bodied men for frontline service. Of a number of small engagements in which they served, the most famous was in July 1864, when they helped repulse Lt. Gen. Jubal A. EARLY's WASHINGTON RAID. The Veteran Reserves suffered only 16 killed in action throughout its existence during the war.

In addition to its principal functions, the corps provided a means by which those disabled veterans who desired to continue their military duty could do so.   —CMS

Veteran Volunteer Corps. By autumn 1864 at least 100,-000 discharged Union soldiers had returned home. Exempt from the draft, but physically able for service, these veterans were an important source of manpower to the Federal government. Sec. of War EDWIN M. STANTON proposed the organization of a new corps, the Veteran Volunteer Corps, composed entirely of these discharged veterans. On 28 Nov. Stanton authorized a special bounty and proposed to Maj. Gen. WINFIELD S. HANCOCK, the distinguished and popular commander of the II Corps/Army of the Potomac, that he direct recruitment and organization of the corps.

Hancock accepted, and, resigning his command of the II Corps, immediately went north. Throughout winter 1865, the general labored to bring the thousands back into the ranks. As an enticement, bounties were promised: a veteran from Philadelphia could expect to receive more than $1,100 from a year's pay and bounties if he would reenlist. But neither the enticement of bounties nor appeals to patriotism moved many veterans, and by 30 Apr. 1865, only 4,422 officers and men had reenlisted. The Veteran Volunteer Corps ended as a disappointing failure.   —JDW

Vicksburg, Confederate Army of. Lt. Gen. JOHN C. PEMBERTON, a Pennsylvania-born West Pointer, commanded the Confederate army entrusted with the defense of that vital Mississippi River strongpoint, Vicksburg. Pres. JEFFERSON DAVIS placed Pemberton in command of the DEPARTMENT OF MISSISSIPPI AND EAST LOUISIANA Oct. 1862. Within 6 months Maj. Gen. U.S. GRANT was beginning his encirclement of Vicksburg, and after the Federal victory of 16 May 1863 at CHAMPION'S HILL, Pemberton's troops were penned inside the city, enduring a terrible siege.

Pemberton's Vicksburg army was made up of Smith's Division, 3 brigades under Maj. Gen. MARTIN L. SMITH, primarily from Louisiana, Mississippi, and Tennessee, which manned the Vicksburg forts during the long campaign; Stevenson's Division, 4 brigades under Maj. Gen. CARTER L. STEVENSON, drawn from Louisiana, Georgia, Alabama, and Tennessee; Forney's Division, 2 brigades under Maj. Gen. JOHN H. FORNEY, from Louisiana, Mississippi, Arkansas, and Alabama; Bowen's Division, 2 brigades under Maj. Gen. JOHN S. BOWEN, primarily from Missouri and Arkansas, held in reserve to fill in where needed most; and Loring's (1st) Division, 3 brigades under Maj. Gen. WILLIAM WING LORING, mostly Mississippians and Alabamians, which was cut off from the main force at Champion's Hill and escaped the final siege. River batteries under Col. Edward Higgins and other small units were among the force that surrendered at Vicksburg.

From 1 May to 3 July, according to the *Official Records,* the Vicksburg defenders lost 1,260 killed, 3,572 wounded, and 4,227 captured or missing. Of the 20,000 troops that surrendered 4 July, fully half were too ill or too weak to continue resistance. Grant, whose army of 71,000 had kept Gen. JOSEPH E. JOHNSTON from coming to Pemberton's aid during the siege, paroled the Vicksburg army, and many of its officers and men fought in later battles.   —DS

Vicksburg Campaign, First (Overland Vicksburg Campaign). 16 Oct.–20 Dec. 1862 With his 16 Oct. 1862 appointment as commander of the Department of the Tennessee, Union Maj. Gen. ULYSSES S. GRANT laid immediate plans for a campaign south against Vicksburg, Miss.

On 20 Oct. Maj. Gen. JOHN A. MCCLERNAND secured command of the short-lived Army of the Mississippi, with the express mission of seizing Vicksburg. A dubious political appointment made by Pres. ABRAHAM LINCOLN, its effect was soon nullified by political pressure within the Regular Army. Grant proceeded with his campaign plans, never overtly acknowl-

edging McClernand's. Assuming departmental command 25 Oct., by 8 Nov. Grant had his troops gathered around La Grange, Tenn., north of the Mississippi state line, just a few miles west of Grand Junction, Tenn. His plan was to follow the line of the Mississippi Central Railroad south toward Vicksburg. Supplies were to come south from Columbus, Ky., by way of the Tennessee & Ohio Railroad and at Grand Junction switch onto the Mississippi Central track for the journey south. Maintaining lines of communication and supply along the railroads would prove to be the failure of this campaign.

With little force to oppose Grant, the Confederate commander at Vicksburg, Lt. Gen. JOHN C. PEMBERTON, had to rely on Maj. Gen. EARL VAN DORN's troops, recently defeated at CORINTH, and on action against the Union rear supplied by Brig. Gen. NATHAN B. FORREST. By 1 Dec. Grant's troops were facing Confederates, in shallow trenches, along the Tallahatchie River, north of Oxford, Miss., 35 mi south of Grand Junction. A large Union supply depot had been established at Holly Springs, Miss., a little over 15 mi north along the Mississippi Central. By 2 Dec. Federals had occupied Oxford and dispatched cavalry in pursuit. Van Dorn's cavalry, serving as rear guard, stopped these Federal horsemen at the engagement at COFFEEVILLE, Miss., 5 Dec., and forced their return to Oxford. But Federal troops continued probing southward during the next 2 weeks.

Pemberton was to rely on Gen. JOSEPH E. JOHNSTON for supervision in the defense of Vicksburg. Johnston had been given this task 24 Nov., but little advice had been forthcoming. When Pemberton requested aid from Gen. BRAXTON BRAGG in Tennessee, Bragg told Pemberton that he was preparing for his Murfreesboro campaigning (which would end in the Battle of STONE'S RIVER) and could offer no material assistance; but he could order Forrest's cavalry to hit Grant's supply lines. This was FORREST'S SECOND RAID. Begun 11 Dec., it destroyed great portions of Tennessee rail line and threatened Grant's Columbus, Ky., railhead. Grant responded by switching his base of supply to Memphis, sending matériel east on the Memphis & Charleston Railroad to Grand Junction. However, on 20 Dec. Van Dorn led 3,500 cavalry from Grenada, south of Grant's lines, and attacked the Union general's Holly Springs supply base. The HOLLY SPRINGS RAID resulted in the loss of more than $1.5 million in Union supplies. Col. BENJAMIN H. GRIERSON pursued Van Dorn in vain for days before the Confederates easily reentered Southern lines at Grenada.

Grant realized the error of trying to maintain his supply and communication along rail lines, and within a week of the Holly Springs raid withdrew most of his forces to La Grange. This ended his First Vicksburg Campaign. But determined to keep up relentless pressure on Vicksburg, he initiated the first of many waterborne invasion plans, which brought on the battle at CHICKASAW BLUFFS.   —JES

Vicksburg Campaign, Second. 1 Apr.–4 July 1863 From mid-Oct. 1862, Maj. Gen. ULYSSES S. GRANT made several attempts to take Vicksburg. Following failures in the FIRST VICKSBURG CAMPAIGN, the Battle of CHICKASAW BLUFFS, the YAZOO PASS EXPEDITION, and STEELE'S BAYOU EXPEDITION, in spring 1863 he prepared to cross his troops from the west bank of the Mississippi River to a point south of Vicksburg and drive against the city from the south and east. Commanding Confederate batteries at PORT HUDSON, La., farther south prevented the transportation of waterborne supply and any communica-

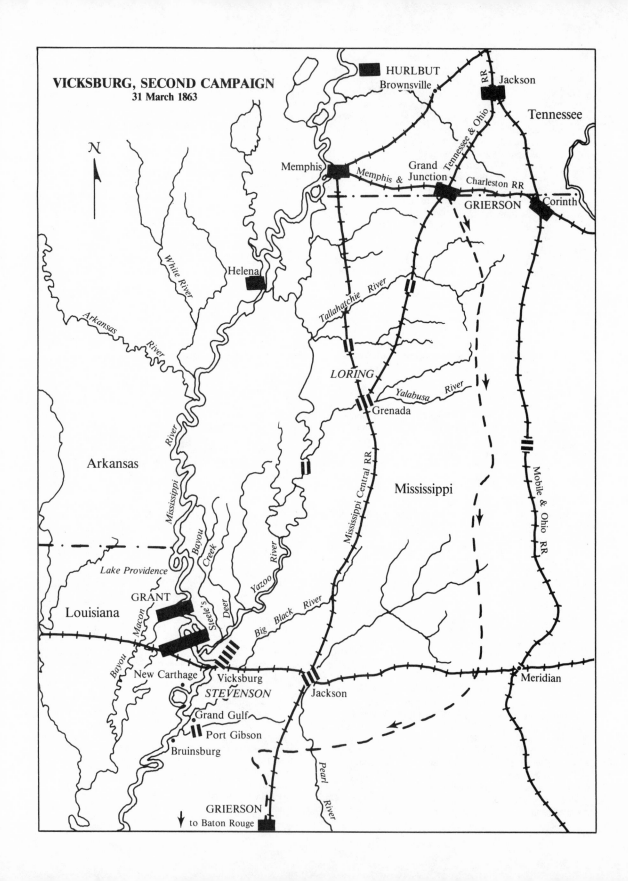

VICKSBURG, SECOND CAMPAIGN
31 March 1863

N

HURLBUT
Brownsville

RR   Jackson

Tennessee

Memphis   Grand Junction

Memphis &   Charleston RR   GRIERSON   Corinth

Tennessee & Ohio

Helena

Tallahatchie River

LORING

Yalabusa   River

Grenada

White River

Arkansas   River

Mississippi   River

Arkansas

Mississippi Central RR

Mississippi

Mobile & Ohio RR

Bayou   Creek

Lake Providence

GRANT

Louisiana

Steele's   Deer   Yazoo River

Big Black River

New Carthage

Vicksburg

STEVENSON   Jackson   Meridian

Macon   Bayou

Grand Gulf

Port Gibson

Bruinsburg

Pearl River

GRIERSON
to Baton Rouge

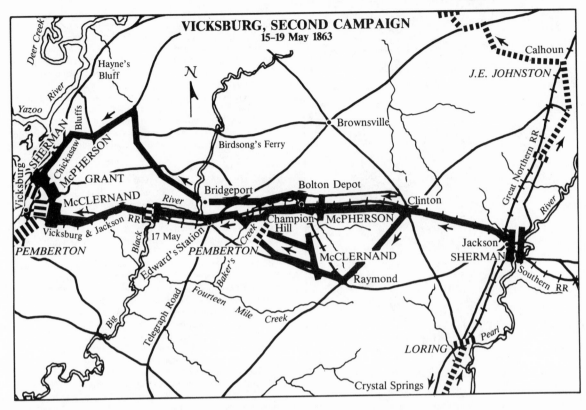

VICKSBURG, SECOND CAMPAIGN
15–19 May 1863

tion from Union forces in Baton Rouge and New Orleans. Naval support for his campaign would have to come from Rear Adm. DAVID D. PORTER's fleet north of Vicksburg. Running past the powerful Vicksburg batteries, Porter's vessels, once south of the city, could ferry Federals to the east bank. There infantry would face 2 Confederate forces, one under Lt. Gen. JOHN C. PEMBERTON at Vicksburg and another around Jackson, Miss., soon to be commanded by Gen. JOSEPH E. JOHNSTON.

In Jan. 1863 Grant organized his force into the XIII Corps under Maj. Gen. JOHN A. MCCLERNAND, the XV Corps under Maj. Gen. WILLIAM T. SHERMAN, the XVI Corps under Maj. Gen. STEPHEN A. HURLBUT, and the XVII Corps under Maj. Gen. JAMES B. MCPHERSON. Simultaneous with Grant's Vicksburg offensive, Maj. Gen. NATHANIEL P. BANKS began his maneuvering along the Red River in Louisiana. Hurlbut's corps was subsequently transferred to New Orleans. With his 3 remaining corps, Grant began operations late in March. On the 29th and 30th McClernand's and McPherson's men, at Milliken's Bend and Lake Providence, northwest of Vicksburg, began working their way south, building a military road to New Carthage, La., preparatory to a move south to Hard Times, La., a village opposite Bruinsburg, Miss.

On the night of 16 Apr., at Grant's request, Porter took 12 vessels south past the Vicksburg batteries, losing 1 to Confederate fire. On 17 Apr. GRIERSON'S RAID began. Led by Brig. Gen. BENJAMIN H. GRIERSON, Federal cavalry left La Grange, Tenn., for 16 days riding through central Mississippi to Baton Rouge, La., pulling away large units from Vicksburg's defense to pur-

sue them. Porter, encouraged by light losses on his first try, ran a large supply flotilla past the Vicksburg batteries the night of 22 Apr. Sherman's troops, many at work on a canal project at Duckport, abandoned this work, joined in a last action along the Yazoo River, northeast of Vicksburg, and 29–30 Apr. made a demonstration against Confederate works at Haynes' Bluff and Drumgould's Bluffs, diverting more of Pemberton's force. Also on 29 Apr., as McClernand's and McPherson's troops gathered near Hard Times, Porter's fleet assailed Confederate batteries at Grand Gulf, 33 mi southwest of Vicksburg, testing the Grand Gulf area as a landing site for Union troops. Though Porter found the guns there too strong, he had succeeded in further diverting Pemberton in Vicksburg.

Grant had originally determined that Rodney, Miss., would be the starting point of his invasion, but took the advice of a local slave and picked Bruinsburg instead. McClernand's and McPherson's corps were ferried east across the Mississippi from Hard Times 30 Apr. That day Grant sent word north for Sherman to follow McPherson's route south and join him.

On 1 May the Federal invasion force engaged the Confederates in the Battle of PORT GIBSON. Pemberton had just over 40,000 men assigned to the Vicksburg region. Since they were scattered throughout the area, chasing Grierson and wary of Sherman, few of them could be brought to bear against Grant on short notice. Defeated at Port Gibson, Pemberton's troops moved north. Grant, to Pemberton's confusion, pushed northeast. Sherman's corps joined him 8 May, and 12 May the engagement at RAYMOND was fought. Johnston took personal

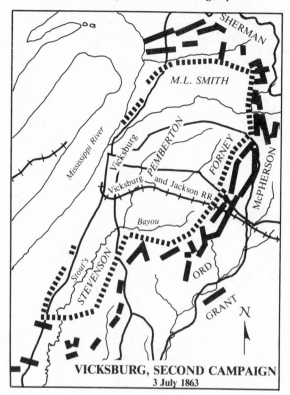

VICKSBURG, SECOND CAMPAIGN
3 July 1863

command of Confederates at Jackson, 15 mi northeast of Raymond, 13 May. On 14 May Federals quickly won an engagement at JACKSON, cut off Johnston from Pemberton, and ensured the latter's isolation for the rest of the campaign. In 2 weeks Grant's force had come well over 130 mi northeast from their Bruinsburg landing site.

Ordering Sherman to destroy Jackson's heavy industry and rail facilities, Grant turned west, roughly following the Southern Mississippi Railroad to Bolton, and 16 May fought the climactic combat of his field campaign, the Battle of CHAMPION'S HILL. With the largest force he had yet gathered to oppose Grant, Pemberton nevertheless took a beating there and pulled his army into the defenses of Vicksburg. In a delaying battle at BIG BLACK RIVER BRIDGE, 17 May, Confederates crossed the Big Black, destroying their river crossings behind them. Undeterred, Federals threw up their own bridges and continued pursuit the next day.

Approaching from the east and northeast, McClernand's, McPherson's, and Sherman's corps neared the Vicksburg defenses 18 May, Sherman's veering north to take the hills overlooking the Yazoo River. Possession of these heights assured Grant's reinforcement and supply from the North. The next day Federals made the failed first assault on Vicksburg. The second assault, 22 May, was a disaster for Union forces, showed the strength of the miles of Confederate works arching east around the city, and convinced Grant that Pemberton could only be defeated in a protracted siege.

The siege of Vicksburg began with the repulse of the 22 May assault and lasted until 4 July 1863. As the siege progressed, Pemberton's 20,000-man garrison was reduced by disease

and starvation, and the city's residents were forced to seek the refuge of caves and bombproofs in the surrounding hillsides. Hunger and daily bombardments by Grant's forces and Porter's gunboats compelled Pemberton to ask for surrender terms 3 July. Grant offered none, but on the garrison's capitulation immediately paroled the bulk of the force. Many of these same men would later oppose him at CHATTANOOGA.

Pemberton's surrender ended the Second Vicksburg Campaign. But during the siege, to the east Johnston had raised a 31,000-man force in the Jackson area. On 4 July, as Confederates were being paroled, Sherman moved his force to oppose this new threat. Sherman's march would result in the Siege of JACKSON. —JES

Vicksburg, Miss., Capt. David G. Farragut passes. 28 June 1862   Early in the war Union officials set as a major goal the capture of the Mississippi River, to cut the Confederacy in half and block the transfer of food from the West. In his 60th year, Capt. DAVID G. FARRAGUT, a Southern-born veteran who had served in the navy since he was 9, was chosen to lead the expedition.

By the middle of Feb. 1862 Farragut had assembled a fleet at Ship Island, near the mouth of the Mississippi. His first objective was to pass FORTS JACKSON AND ST. PHILIP, commanding the river a short distance above Head of Passes. This he did 24 Apr., captured them 4 days later, and 1 May took the city of New Orleans.

Vicksburg, the "key to the Mississippi," was next. Spread along the banks at a hairpin turn of the river, the city was protected from a naval attack by bluffs so high that ships' guns could not reach the batteries crowning them. Farragut realized at once that it could be taken only by an army force from the rear, but he bombarded it ineffectively for a day or two, then returned to New Orleans.

At the insistence of the Union high command, late in June Farragut returned to Vicksburg and resumed the bombardment. In the midst of it he ran past the city and joined a fleet that had come down from Cairo, Ill., under Capt. CHARLES H. DAVIS. Combined, they continued the siege, disturbed 15 July when the Confederate ironclad ARKANSAS blazed its way through them and safely reached Vicksburg. All Union efforts to destroy the vessel failed.

Farragut remained in front of Vicksburg for 67 days. During this time he wrote Navy Sec. GIDEON WELLES that the city could be taken only by land forces, but received no reply. As the water in the Mississippi began falling and sickness in the fleet increased, he was ordered back to New Orleans.

On 4 July 1863, Vicksburg fell—to an army under Maj. Gen. ULYSSES S. GRANT. —VCJ

Vicksburg, Miss., Rear Adm. David D. Porter passes. 16 Apr. 1863   On 29 Mar. 1863, Maj. Gen. ULYSSES S. GRANT, after 4 attempts to bypass Vicksburg had failed, sent Maj. Gen. JOHN A. McCLERNAND's corps to open a road from Milliken's Bend to New Carthage, Miss. The effort was successful, and by mid-April McClernand was massing his corps in the New Carthage area, 20 mi southwest of Vicksburg.

Confederate Lt. Gen. JOHN C. PEMBERTON misinterpreted Grant's intentions, having satisfied himself that the Federal troops were recoiling from Vicksburg. Following instructions from Gen. JOSEPH E. JOHNSTON, Pemberton moved to transfer 4 brigades to Middle Tennessee to replace the 10,000 troops

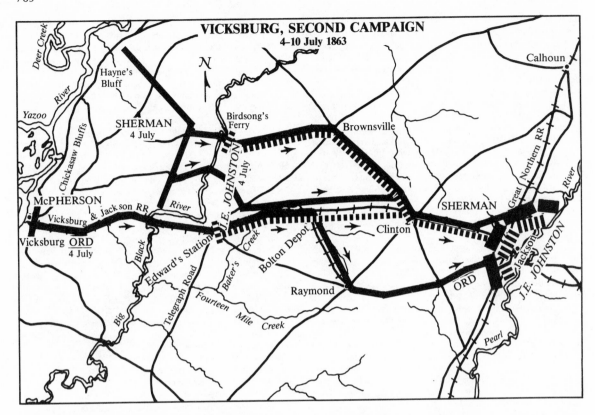

VICKSBURG, SECOND CAMPAIGN
4–10 July 1863

rushed to Mississippi 4 months earlier to oppose Grant.

Pemberton's illusion was shattered 16 Apr. That night Rear Adm. DAVID D. PORTER had his sailors prepare selected vessels of his Mississippi Squadron to run past Vicksburg's big guns. Long before casting off, lights were extinguished, portholes covered, and fires started—all in an effort to show as little smoke as possible. To muffle engine noises, steam was exhausted into the paddlewheel houses.

At 9:30 p.m., the 11-ship squadron departed the mouth of the Yazoo River and headed down the Mississippi River, Porter's flagship *BENTON* leading. The *Benton* rounded the toe of De Soto Point a few minutes after 11, taking by surprise Confederates manning the 31 great guns of the river batteries. After about 6 minutes the Southerners began to fire, slowly at first, then faster. The Confederates kindled fires on the De Soto shore to silhouette the boats as they battled their way downstream. Each vessel was under fire for about 30 minutes while running the Vicksburg batteries and for a few minutes passing Warrenton. All were hit repeatedly but, except for the transport *Henry Clay*, which was set afire and abandoned, they reached New Carthage.

On the 22d, 5 transports passed Vicksburg. The passage of the Vicksburg batteries by Porter's gunboats was vital to the success of Grant's campaign (*see* VICKSBURG CAMPAIGN, SECOND). He now had the means to cross the Mississippi.

—ECB

vidette. A mounted sentry on picket or guard duty was called a vidette. Also spelled "vedette," the word derives from the Latin meaning "to watch" or "see."

—JES

Villard, Henry. journalist b. Speyer, Bavaria, 10 Apr. 1835. The son of a prominent Bavarian jurist who threatened him with service in the Bavarian army, Ferdinand Heinrich Gustav Hilgard assumed the name Henry Villard and fled to the U.S. in 1853. He traveled from New York City to Belleville, Ill., settled with relatives, applied himself to mastering the English language, pursued odd jobs, dabbled in journalism, and in 1858 won a position as special correspondent to the New York German-language newspaper *Staats-Zeitung,* covering the Lincoln-Douglas debates. Joining the staff of the Cincinnati *Commercial* in 1859, he reported the gold rush to Pike's Peak, traveled in the West, published in English *The Past and Present of the Pike's Peak Gold Regions* (1860), covered the Republican national convention, and, following Abraham Lincoln's election, joined the New York *Herald* staff as its Springfield, Ill., correspondent.

After the fall of FORT SUMTER, the *Herald* installed Villard as a Washington correspondent. During the BALTIMORE RIOTS, when telegraphic communication with the North ceased, he established a courier service to keep news moving to New York and Chicago. On the commencement of military activity in Virginia, he covered the engagement at BLACKBURN'S FORD, filed the first story on the FIRST BATTLE OF BULL RUN, then traveled west to report operations in Kentucky and Tennessee. In Kentucky, he made an amiable acquaintance of Brig. Gen.

WILLIAM T. SHERMAN, but their relationship cooled when stories circulated that Villard was responsible for disseminating news of the general's nervous breakdown. Villard followed Union occupation forces into Nashville in 1862, then, with Maj. Gen. DON CARLOS BUELL's Army of the Ohio, joined Union troops late on 6 Apr. for the Battle of SHILOH.

Impressed by Villard's work, the NEW YORK *TRIBUNE* hired him and assigned him coverage of the Western theater. He reported Buell's maneuvers during the autumn 1862 KENTUCKY CAMPAIGN, the murder of Maj. Gen. WILLIAM "Bull" NELSON, and the Battle of PERRYVILLE, then transferred east in November as the *Tribune*'s chief correspondent with the ARMY OF THE POTOMAC. He covered the Battle of FREDERICKSBURG; traveled to Port Royal, S.C., and observed Rear Adm. SAMUEL F. DU PONT's assaults on Charleston; in summer 1863 visited Maj. Gen. WILLIAM S. ROSECRANS in Tennessee; then fell ill in June. Though he recovered sufficiently to report on the fighting at CHICKAMAUGA and CHATTANOOGA, his health forced him from field reportage soon after.

In Washington, D.C., with former *Tribune* bureau chief ADAMS S. HILL, he left the *Tribune*'s employ and began the Independent News Room news service. During the GOLD HOAX OF 1864 he was detained by the military for 2 days as a suspect in the failed swindle. Released, he finished out the Civil War as an independent journalist, then rejoined the *Tribune* staff.

Villard's postwar years were his most illustrious. He reported the Austro-Prussian War of 1866, left the *Tribune* again in 1868, covered the Franco-Prussian War as a free-lance journalist, then left newspaper work, serving as secretary of the American Social Science Association. Representing German nationals who were investors in the Oregon & California Railroad, from 1873 he became a power in Western railroading, eventually becoming president of the Northern Pacific Railroad and in 1881 purchasing a controlling interest in the New York *Evening Post*. A large investor in the Edison General Electric Co. in 1889, he died a wealthy man at his Dobbs Ferry, N.Y., home, 12 Nov. 1900.   —JES

Villepigue, John Bordenave. CSA b. Camden, S.C., 2 July 1830, Villepigue won appointment to West Point, graduating 22d in the class of 1854. Commissioned a 2d lieutenant in the dragoons, he served in Missouri and Kansas, Dakota and Nebraska territories, Utah, and Pennsylvania until resigning his commission 31 Mar. 1861 to accept a captaincy in the Confederate artillery.

Assigned to the Confederate defenses at Pensacola Harbor, Fla., by 30 Sept. 1861 he had been promoted to lieutenant colonel and, commanding the 1st Georgia Battalion (a unit made up of Georgia and Mississippi troops), assigned to the defense of Fort McRee at the har-

USMHI

bor's mouth. Promoted to colonel and made the city's chief of artillery, at Pensacola in November he fought a 2-day artillery duel with Federal ships and the FORT PICKENS batteries, was wounded, and won the praise of Maj. Gen. BRAXTON BRAGG. His troops were reorganized into the 36th Georgia Regiment

31 Jan. 1862, and as its colonel he briefly served as commander of Pensacola's garrison until transferred to Mobile, Ala. There he won promotion to brigadier general 13 Mar. 1862, then traveled to Corinth, where 25 Mar. 1862 he won assignment to command of Fort Pillow, Tenn. Federal naval superiority forced Gen. P.G.T. BEAUREGARD to withdraw him from there 4 June. Reassigned to Maj. Gen. EARL VAN DORN's troops, commanding the 2d Brigade in Maj. Gen. MANSFIELD LOVELL's 1st Division, he served in the October Battle of CORINTH. Following Van Dorn's retreat, ill-health forced his retirement to Port Hudson, La., where he died of fever 9 Nov. 1862.   —JES

Vincent, Strong. USA b. Waterford, Pa., 17 June 1837. After preparatory schooling, Vincent graduated from Harvard in 1859. He then studied law, entered the profession, and opened an office in Erie, Pa.

When the war exploded in South Carolina, he immediately volunteered, serving 21 Apr.–25 July 1861 as 1st lieutenant and adjutant of a 3-month Pennsylvania militia regiment. Reenlisting, he was commissioned lieutenant colonel of the 83d Pennsylvania 21 Sept.

LC

During the 1862 PENINSULA CAMPAIGN, he saw action at YORKTOWN before being stricken with malaria. Appointed colonel of the 83d on the death of its commander 27 June, he did not rejoin the regiment until the Battle of FREDERICKSBURG in December. His unit was only slightly engaged at CHANCELLORSVILLE May 1863. In the subsequent reorganization of the ARMY OF THE POTOMAC, Vincent became commander of the 1st Brigade/1st Division/V Corps.

Vincent's finest service to the Union cause came during the afternoon of 2 July at GETTYSBURG. The Union left flank, reeling under a massive Confederate onslaught, had become unhinged. In fields to the rear lay Vincent's brigade. When a messenger galloped up and requested troops, Vincent, on his own initiative, led his brigade up the slopes of unoccupied LITTLE ROUND TOP. Within minutes Confederates came storming up the rocky slope, and a searing fight ensued. Vincent's forthright action and his veterans' stalwart defense saved the Union army at Gettysburg but cost the 26-year-old his life. Shot while rallying his men, he died 5 days later, 7 July. His promotion to brigadier general, dated 3 July, probably came through after his death.   —JDW

Vining's Station, Ga., eng. at. 4 July 1864 Early on 3 July 1864, Confederate Gen. JOSEPH E. JOHNSTON led his Army of Tennessee toward the CHATTAHOOCHEE RIVER, ending 26 days of operations around Marietta. Fearing for the safety of his left flank, Johnston placed his troops behind prepared works 6 mi south of Marietta, adjacent to Smyrna Camp Ground and not far above the Western & Atlantic Railroad depot of Vining's Station.

The armies of Union Maj. Gen. WILLIAM T. SHERMAN followed in pursuit. Doubting that his adversary would stop short of the Chattahoochee, Sherman planned to strike Johnston's south flank during his crossing. On 4 July, closing up on

Smyrna, the Union leader sent the IV Corps/Army of the Cumberland, under Maj. Gen. OLIVER O. HOWARD, to attack down the railroad against Johnston's center, held by Lt. Gen. WILLIAM J. HARDEE's corps. Simultaneously, Maj. Gen. GRENVILLE M. DODGE's XVI Corps/Army of the Tennessee would menace the enemy left near the river.

Howard's offensive achieved limited success. Unable to convince his superior that a formidable line of works lay before him ("You are mistaken," Sherman told him, "there is no force in your front"), Howard dutifully advanced early on Independence Day. His 1st Division, under Maj. Gen. DAVID S. STANLEY, the brigade of Col. William Grose leading, gained some ground, capturing a line of skirmishers' rifle pits under fire. But even with support from the divisions of Brig. Gens. JOHN NEWTON and THOMAS J. WOOD, Stanley failed to reach the main enemy works. His troops reeled under what Stanley called "the severest and most continued cannonade the rebels had ever used upon us."

Dodge's turning movement proved more fruitful. At daybreak, the XVI Corps, led by the division of Brig. Gen. JAMES C. VEATCH, crossed Nickajack Creek near Ruff's Mills, then plowed into the corps of Gen. JOHN B. HOOD. Some Union troops met unexpectedly stiff resistance on the extreme left, held by the mounted division of Brig. Gen. WILLIAM H. JACKSON and GEORGIA MILITIA under Maj. Gen. GUSTAVUS W. SMITH, and the attackers fell back in disorder. But the bulk of Dodge's corps—aided by a XV Corps division, 2 XVII Corps regiments, plus an infantry brigade and the cavalry of the Army of the Ohio—secured a lodgment 1 mi beyond Nickajack Creek. With Federals now closer to the Chattahoochee than Johnston's main body, another Confederate retreat was inevitable.
—EGL

Virginia.   On seceding from the Union 17 Apr. 1861, Virginia became one of the most important states of the new Confederacy—perhaps its central state. When Virginia formally joined the Confederacy in May, RICHMOND was established as its new capital city. Virginia also gave the South its great trio of generals—ROBERT E. LEE, THOMAS J. "STONEWALL" JACKSON, and J.E.B. STUART—and was the major battleground of the Civil War in the East.

Place names familiar to Virginians would become well known to most Americans in the 4 years after 1861, as the 2 great armies in the East fought across the state. From BIG BETHEL and Manassas Junction (*see* BULL RUN) to PETERSBURG and the end at APPOMATTOX, the fierce battles and small skirmishes alike nearly destroyed the Virginia countryside.

The state contributed more than its share of soldiers to the armies, most notably the ARMY OF NORTHERN VIRGINIA. Along with Lee, Jackson, and Stuart, prominent Virginia generals included JOSEPH E. JOHNSTON, RICHARD S. EWELL, AMBROSE P. HILL, and JUBAL A. EARLY. The famed STONEWALL BRIGADE, to which Jackson gave his nickname, was made up of the 2d, 4th, 5th, 27th, and 33d Virginia regiments. The Rockbridge Artillery, with its guns named Matthew, Mark, Luke, and John, distinguished itself on many fields. The 1st Virginia Cavalry rode under Stuart and FITZHUGH LEE on numerous daring raids. Virginia furnished 63 infantry regiments and 26 cavalry regiments to the Southern cause.

In addition to the military, Virginia also provided leaders for the Confederate civil government. JOHN LETCHER and WILLIAM SMITH were capable war governors; ROBERT M. T. HUNTER was

secretary of state until 1862; GEORGE W. RANDOLPH became secretary of war in 1862; and his successor, JAMES A. SEDDON, served until 1865.

Virginia was also important industrially to the South's war effort, with Richmond's TREDEGAR IRON WORKS and the Richmond Armory and Arsenal providing most of the Confederacy's arms and ammunition; the railroads in the state were among the best in the South.
—JTP

Virginia, CSS.   In June 1861 Confederate Sec. of the Navy STEPHEN R. MALLORY told a joint congressional committee that the Confederacy needed armored warships. Heading a navy with few shipyards, shipbuilders, and sailors, Mallory planned to build several IRONCLADS that could challenge and defeat all the wooden frigates, sloops, and gunboats the U.S. could put afloat.

For the first of his ironclads, Mallory used the hull and engines of the USS *Merrimack,* a frigate burned to the waterline and left when the U.S. Navy had abandoned its Norfolk, Va., navy yard. Naval designers developed an armored gun casemate that seemed to float on the water, with the rest of the ship submerged below the waterline. 10 heavy guns nestled inside the casemate, and an iron ram on the bow completed the armament.

The ship was christened the CSS *Virginia,* and Capt. FRANKLIN BUCHANAN designated it flagship of the James River Squadron. On 8 Mar. 1862, he took the ironclad from the Norfolk area up toward HAMPTON ROADS to test its machinery and handling. Though Buchanan had been ordered to make a trial run, instead he put a boatload of workmen ashore and took the brand-new *Virginia* out to battle the entire Union blockading squadron.

The *Virginia* first attacked the *Cumberland,* which it rammed and sank. Then it turned to the frigate *Congress,* which had run aground trying to escape. Buchanan was wounded in the action against this ship, but when the *Virginia* retired for the night, the *Congress* was in flames and the rest of the blockading squadron awaited certain destruction the next day.

Lt. Cmdr. CATESBY AP R. JONES brought the *Virginia* out for combat 9 Mar. Facing his ship was the Federal ironclad *MONITOR,* which had arrived at the last moment to save the squadron. All day the 2 ships fought, retiring only when the *Monitor*'s captain was wounded and the falling tide threatened to ground the big *Virginia.* The rest of the Union's wooden ships were saved and the BLOCKADE was still intact, but the *Virginia* and its nemesis the *Monitor* had opened a new era in naval warfare.

Early in May, Maj. Gen. GEORGE B. MCCLELLAN'S ARMY OF THE POTOMAC forced the Confederates to abandon Norfolk. The *Virginia,* homeless, was burned.
—MM

Virginia, Union Army of.   To reorganize the fragmented command that had doomed Union efforts in northern Virginia Mar.–June 1862, the Mountain Department, Department of the Shenandoah, and Department of the Rappahannock became, respectively, the I, II, and III corps/Army of Virginia 26 June 1862. 2 IX Corps divisions, the Pennsylvania Reserve Division, the III and V corps, and 2 additional brigades subsequently reinforced the army, and 5 more divisions joined after 30 Aug.

A victorious Westerner, Maj. Gen. JOHN POPE, commanded

this army. Outsider, braggart, and oppressor, Pope forfeited his men's loyalty and outraged Southerners. Nor did success redeem these shortcomings as Pope was handicapped by logistic and strategic imperatives: maintaining divergent communications with Alexandria and Acquia Creek and relieving pressure on Maj. Gen. GEORGE B. MCCLELLAN without jeopardizing his own small army.

Pope's scattered forces initially converged on Culpeper County, where a rash van and tardy supports produced defeat at CEDAR MOUNTAIN 9 Aug. 1862. His concentrated army nevertheless held the Rapidan, then skillfully withdrew before being trapped by Gen. R. E. LEE. Aggressor no longer, Pope tried checking superior Confederate troops until reinforcements arrived. He ably defended the Rappahannock Station–Waterloo Bridge line but counterattacked ineffectively and vacillated between defense and offense.

Worse, he uncovered his Manassas Junction base to Maj. Gen. THOMAS J. "STONEWALL" JACKSON. Ironically, having chided predecessors for worrying about supply lines, Pope now found his lines severed. Nor could he trap the raiders, as his column and others merely brushed with Jackson and Maj. Gen. JAMES LONGSTREET at Bull Run Bridge, Bristoe Station, Groveton, and Thoroughfare Gap. Pope finally engaged Jackson at SECOND BULL RUN, only to be repeatedly repulsed 29–30 Aug. Frazzled cavalry and inept subordinates thwarted him, but the worst drawback was his own obliviousness to reality, causing him to ignore evidence of Longstreet's arrival until the Georgian's massive counterattack against his exposed left decisively defeated him.

Rallying at Centreville, Pope parried Jackson's thrust at CHANTILLY, then withdrew into Maj. Gen. George B. McClellan's Washington earthworks. Pope briefly served under "Little Mac" but was relieved 5 Sept. By 12 Sept. 1862, the ARMY OF THE POTOMAC had absorbed his forces.

Beset with an overconfident commander, mediocre or incompetent subordinates, great internal discord, and oft-beaten troops, the Army of Virginia coalesced only in hating Pope. It was the least successful Union army.   —RJS

Virginia, Union Department of. The Union Department of Virginia was created 22 May 1861 with Maj. Gen. BENJAMIN F. BUTLER in command. With its headquarters at FORT MONROE, the department encompassed the area around HAMPTON ROADS, Va., on the tip of the Virginia peninsula. It remained an independent command until 15 July 1863, when it merged with the DEPARTMENT OF NORTH CAROLINA to become the DEPARTMENT OF VIRGINIA AND NORTH CAROLINA. Re-created 18 Jan. 1865, it functioned until officially disbanded 28 June.

A series of officers, in addition to Butler, commanded the department and its troops during its existence. Maj. Gen. JOHN E. WOOL succeeded Butler, holding the post until 2 June 1862, when Maj. Gen. JOHN A. DIX replaced him. Dix commanded until the department was abolished. Brig. Gen. GEORGE W. GETTY was appointed commander for 5 days during the reorganization of the department. When it was re-created, Maj. Gen. E.O.C. ORD commanded until 16 Apr. 1865, his replacement being Maj. Gen. HENRY W. HALLECK. On 14 June Halleck was succeeded by Maj. Gen. ALFRED H. TERRY, who retained command until the department merged into the Department of the Potomac 6 Aug. 1866.

The 10,000 troops assigned to the department maintained garrisons at Fort Monroe, Camp Hamilton, and Newport

News. On 22 July 1862, they were organized into the VII Corps. When the department was re-created, they were also designated the ARMY OF THE JAMES. The department's command fought at BIG BETHEL 10 June 1861 and participated in the 1862 PENINSULA CAMPAIGN and in operations against Richmond in 1863.   —JDW

Virginia and North Carolina, Union Department of.
After failing to break Gen. ROBERT E. LEE's communications with Richmond during the GETTYSBURG CAMPAIGN, Maj. Gen. JOHN A. DIX was relieved as head of the DEPARTMENT OF VIRGINIA. On 15 July 1863, the latter merged with Maj. Gen. JOHN G. FOSTER'S DEPARTMENT OF NORTH CAROLINA, with Foster heading the consolidated command. His new domain embraced North Carolina and "so much of Virginia as lies within a radius of sixty miles from Fort Monroe, including the country south of the Rappahannock and east of the railroad from Fredericksburg to Richmond, Petersburg, and Weldon." On 1 Aug. Foster's XVIII Corps absorbed Dix's old IV and VII corps, resulting in a force of almost 42,000 officers and men "present and absent." Foster assigned these troops to Brig. Gen. INNIS N. PALMER.

Initially, Foster's command consisted of the District of Virginia, under Brig. Gen. Henry M. Naglee, and the District of North Carolina, headed by Maj. Gen. JOHN J. PECK. Naglee's district (discontinued with his transfer west late in September) encompassed posts at Norfolk, Portsmouth, and Yorktown and vicinity (the latter including Gloucester Point, Newport News, and Williamsburg), while Peck's command included the Sub-Districts of the Pamlico, the Albemarle, and Beaufort, as well as the defenses of New Berne. Foster's department added the District of St. Mary's Dec. 1863, after St. Mary's Cty., Md., and Northampton and Accomac counties, Va., came under his jurisdiction. That same month, the District of the Currituck joined the department, adding territory from southeastern Virginia. St. Mary's County was removed from Foster's realm the following June, and the district of that name was discontinued.

On 11 Nov. 1863, Maj. Gen. BENJAMIN F. BUTLER replaced Foster in departmental command. Butler's authority increased the following April when much of Maj. Gen. QUINCY A. GILLMORE's X Corps was transferred from South Carolina to join the XVIII Corps, now under Maj. Gen. WILLIAM F. SMITH, for the 1864 campaigning in Virginia. At its height, the field force comprising these troops, the ARMY OF THE JAMES, numbered approximately 50,000 officers and men.

On 3 Dec. 1864, after many changes in corps leadership, a reorganization resulted in the demise of the X and XVIII corps and the birth of the XXIV Corps, composed of the department's white troops, and the XXV Corps, consisting exclusively of its U.S. Colored Troops. A month later, Maj. Gen. E.O.C. ORD succeeded Butler, and 18 Jan. 1865 the War Department separated the Departments of Virginia and North Carolina, which took their former names.   —EGL

Virginia & Tennessee Railroad. The Virginia & Tennessee Railroad stretched 204 mi from Bristol, over the Tennessee border, to Lynchburg, in southwestern Virginia. Perhaps the most progressive company south of the Potomac River before the Civil War, the railroad possessed some of the largest engines and one of the best-constructed tracks in the South. With the advent of the war, the carrier became a vital supply line for the Confederacy.

The railroad's importance to the new nation rested in its location and its direct connection to other lines. The Virginia & Tennessee passed through southwestern Virginia, where salt and lead mines lay. The operation of these mines and the shipment of their ore were crucial concerns to the Confederacy. At its eastern terminal, Lynchburg, the railroad connected with the ORANGE & ALEXANDRIA and the Southside railroads. These latter lines crossed other regions of the Old Dominion. The Southside extended to Petersburg, Va., where it intersected with a direct line to Richmond. The Orange & Alexandria, running north to the Potomac, connected with the Virginia Central, which also terminated at the Confederate capital.

The strategic and logistic importance of the Virginia & Tennessee attracted the attention of Union commands, and throughout the war Federals launched raids against the railroad and the mines. Defense of the carrier rested primarily with Confederate soldiers stationed in the DEPARTMENT OF SOUTH-WESTERN VIRGINIA. These Union operations, though only modestly successful overall, resulted in such battles as DROOP MOUNTAIN, ROCKY GAP, CLOYD'S MOUNTAIN, and LYNCHBURG.

Engines and cars rumbled on the Virginia & Tennessee until the war's end. By Apr. 1865, however, only 1 of its depots still stood. Like other Southern lines, the railroad suffered heavily because of the war. —JDW

Virginia Military Institute. Founded in 1839, the Virginia Military Institute, located in Lexington, rendered the Confederacy almost unparalleled service. From Virginia's secession 17 Apr. 1861 until the end of the war, the institute's professors, alumni, and students drilled the raw volunteers and commanded regiments, brigades, divisions, and corps in numbers unequaled by any other military school. Of its 1,902 matriculates 1839–65, 1,781 served in the Confederate army; 17 rose to the rank of general.

VMI was consciously modeled after the U.S. MILITARY ACADEMY, combining standard college study with the discipline and professional military training of West Point. Francis H. Smith, a native Virginian and West Pointer, class of 1833, was its superintendent from its founding. Under his remarkable direction, VMI acquired a reputation second only to West Point.

When Virginia seceded, the institute's students and alumni provided the Confederacy with a reserve of trained officers. Professor THOMAS J. JACKSON took part of the student body with him. With other Virginia volunteers, these former cadets fought at FIRST BULL RUN under Jackson and earned enduring fame as the STONEWALL BRIGADE. Within 3 months, one-third of the field officers of Virginia volunteer regiments were VMI men. By the end of 1861, nearly one-third of Virginia's 76 regiments had institute graduates at their head. No school supplied the ARMY OF NORTHERN VIRGINIA with more field officers. Among graduates, Gens. ROBERT E. RODES, SAMUEL GARLAND, RALEIGH E. COLSTON, and JAMES H. LANE became distinguished combat commanders.

The institute continued to function during most of the war. In spring 1864, 229 of its students answered Virginia's call to repel a Union invasion in the SHENANDOAH VALLEY. At NEW MARKET, 15 May 1864, these boy soldiers valiantly advanced and helped rout the Union line. Their heroic feat is still honored annually at the institute. In June 1864, Union Maj. Gen. DAVID HUNTER, leading another invading force, burned the institute's buildings. Smith, however, managed to resume classes later that year. —JDW

Virginia Peace Conference. *See* WASHINGTON PEACE CONFERENCE.

vivandière. A woman unofficially attached to a regiment, performing various camp and nursing duties, was known as a vivandière. A CAMP FOLLOWER, unlike other women with a regiment she sometimes wore a stylized uniform. Hers was a respected position rising from a centuries-old European tradition and implied nothing sexual. BRIDGET DIVERS and MARIE TEBE were two well-known vivandières. —JES

Vizetelly, Frank. journalist b. London, England, 1830. In his early twenties Vizetelly became a correspondent and draftsman for the London *Pictorial Times.* In 1857, with his brother Henry, he founded *Le Monde Illustré,* becoming its editor and covering the war between Austria and Sardinia-Piedmont in 1859. As artist-correspondent for the *Illustrated London News,* he reported Garibaldi's expedition in Sicily and Italy.

LC

In May 1861, Vizetelly arrived in New York City on assignment for the *Illustrated London News.* He sketched in the vicinity of Washington and northern Virginia and was present at the Union disaster at FIRST BULL RUN.

In June of the following year, on the Mississippi with the Union gunboat flotilla, he sketched the Battle of MEMPHIS. Returning to Washington, and increasingly annoyed by official restrictions on his freedom of movement, he secretly passed through Federal lines and made his way to Richmond. At FREDERICKSBURG, Dec. 1862, he observed the battle in the company of Gens. ROBERT E. LEE and JAMES LONGSTREET.

In 1863 Vizetelly was in South Carolina when Rear Adm. SAMUEL F. DU PONT's ironclads attacked Charleston harbor (*see* CHARLESTON, S.C., DU PONT'S ATTACK ON). He sketched the Siege of VICKSBURG and was present during the Union assault on WILMINGTON, N.C. By Christmas 1863 he was back in northern Virginia with Maj. Gen. J.E.B. STUART's command. The gregarious Vizetelly was a great favorite in Stuart's camp—"the most interesting narrator I have ever listened to around a campfire," wrote a Confederate officer.

Early in 1864 Vizetelly sailed for England but was back in the Southern states by June, having run the Union BLOCKADE. He was an observer of the SHENANDOAH VALLEY CAMPAIGN (Sheridan's) and in December was present to sketch the bombardment and fall of FORT FISHER, N.C. ("Never has the world seen aught so fearful as the terrific concentration of fire brought to bear on the luckless sandwork," he wrote.) In Apr. 1865 he joined Pres. JEFFERSON DAVIS' party fleeing south after the fall of Richmond and sketched a unique record of the last days of the Confederacy.

Returning to England, he continued to cover battlefronts in Europe, and in 1883, while reporting the war in Egypt, he disappeared in the massacre of Hicks Pasha's army in the Sudan.

Woodcuts of Vizetelly's drawings appeared throughout the

Civil War years in the *Illustrated London News.* A number of his sketches, dispatched to England on BLOCKADE RUNNERS, were intercepted by Union warships and pirated by the Northern illustrated weeklies. The only existing original drawings are owned by the Harvard College Library; the balance of his work was destroyed in the London Blitz of World War II.   —FR

Vogdes, Israel. USA b. Willistown, Pa., 4 Aug. 1816. A graduate of the West Point class of 1837, Vogdes ranked 11th of 50 cadets. Immediately commissioned a 2d lieutenant in the 1st U.S. Artillery, he rose to 1st

lieutenant a year later. Subsequently he spent 12 years as a mathematics instructor at the Military Academy, fought the Seminoles in Florida, and served in frontier garrisons as well as at the Artillery School for Practice at Fort Monroe, Va.

Early in 1861, when hostilities seemed imminent at FORT PICKENS, Fla., Captain Vogdes was ordered there. On March 11 his company of the 1st Artillery was ordered to reinforce the Pensacola Bay garrison under Lt.

LC

Adam J. Slemmer. 8 months later Vogdes, still serving at Pensacola, was taken prisoner during a Confederate assault on Santa Rosa Island. Not exchanged till Aug. 1862, he then helped supervise the construction of artillery positions in the harbor of Charleston, after 29 Nov. as a brigadier general of volunteers.

For another year, he remained in Charleston and vicinity as a brigade and division commander in the DEPARTMENT OF THE SOUTH. In July and Aug. 1863 he led the 6 infantry regiments that composed the 1st Brigade/2d Division/X Corps; from August to December he was in charge of 3 brigades stationed on the northern end of Folly Island; and during the first half of 1864 he commanded all troops on that island. Several times during this period he was commended for his engineering skill and administrative expertise; even the enemy commander at Charleston, Gen. P.G.T. BEAUREGARD, called him "an officer of merit."

In May 1864 Vogdes was transferred to southeastern Virginia to supervise troops manning the defenses of Norfolk and Portsmouth. During the war's final month, he was a brigade and district commander in Florida. On 15 Jan. 1866, he was mustered out of the volunteers, then rejoined the 1st U.S. Artillery as a colonel and brevet brigadier of Regulars. He led the outfit in garrisons in New York, South Carolina, Rhode Island, and other seaboard states, guarding the Atlantic Coast, fighting the Fenian uprisings of 1866 and 1870, keeping peace in the South during the disputed presidential election of 1876, and opposing Pennsylvania labor rioters in 1877. Resigning from the army Jan. 1881, he resided in New York City until his death there 7 Dec. 1889.   —EGL

voltigeur. Originally organized in 1805, voltigeur companies were added to each French army infantry battalion to serve as skirmishers and were composed of drafted men shorter than the standard height. Over the years these voltigeur companies became elite units in the French army, and the men

serving in them were known for their courage as well as their short stature. Awarded the honor of leading the attack, voltigeurs were skirmishers who did not fight in close ranks and theoretically could run as fast as trotting cavalry.

The popularity of these famous units influenced the U.S. Regular Army to form a Regiment of Voltigeurs and Foot Riflemen Feb. 1847 for service in the Mexican War. Half of the regiment was to be mounted and paired with a foot rifleman who would ride double when speed was necessary. Actually, horses were never issued to the regiment, and the men served as irregular riflemen performing skirmish duties, including the clearing of woods. At the end of the Mexican War, Aug. 1848, the regiment was disbanded.

During the Civil War numerous volunteer units were organized in both the Union and Confederacy and many chose interesting names such as "avengers," "invincibles," "true blues," and "plow boys." Others adopted names of units in European armies, including chasseurs, fusileers, hussars, lancers, and voltigeurs. A few of the units performed duties similar to their European counterparts, but most did not.

In fact, many units, after being mustered into the Union or Confederate armies, had their names changed and often performed duties as necessity demanded. Voltigeur as well as artillery and cavalry units served as ordinary infantry. For instance, the 3 companies of Col. Albert C. Ramsey's U.S. Voltigeurs, or Rangers, were assigned to the 51st and 57th New York Infantry regiments and served as ordinary infantry throughout the war. Thus, although some volunteer units assumed the title, none are known to have performed primarily the duties of voltigeurs.   —DEF

volunteers. The Civil War began as a war of volunteers. The North's Regular Army (see REGULAR ARMY, U.S.) numbered fewer than 16,000 men, many of them at Western frontier forts guarding against Indian attack; the South started with no army at all. With the firing on FORT SUMTER, war enthusiasm swept the nation, especially the South. Unprepared to cope with the thousands of eager volunteers, both governments initially made the individual states responsible for their arms and equipment.

Each government enacted legislation for military service that in general paralleled the other. Both started with short ENLISTMENT terms for volunteers, lengthened them to 3 years or the duration, became unable to fill quotas with volunteers, and then were obliged to enact draft legislation, which provided means for men to buy their way out of service.

The volunteers of 1861 and 1862 were for the most part the cream of idealistic American youth. As the war progressed, the depleted ranks were filled with "bounty men" and unwilling draftees who often seized every opportunity to shirk camp duty and the dangers of battle. Veteran volunteers thus were saddled with the extra responsibility of instructing the new men and keeping them in line. The South could offer volunteers little special recognition, but Union 3-year men, on reenlisting, received a 30-day furlough, transportation home, and a bounty of $400.   —RDH

Von Borcke, Johann August Heinrich Heros. CSA b. Prussia, 1835. Few foreigners crossed the Atlantic Ocean during the Civil War to fight with the Confederacy. Of these, none achieved more contemporary renown or served the Confederacy more capably than Heros von Borcke. Scion of an aristo-

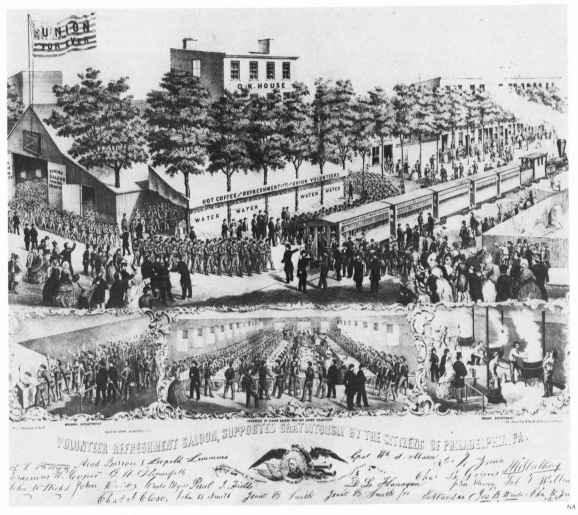

NA

Volunteer Refreshment Saloon

cratic Prussian family, son of an army officer and a former lieutenant in the 2d Brandenburg Dragoons, von Borcke arrived in Charleston, S.C., May 1862, on a BLOCKADE RUNNER. By the end of the month, he had joined the staff of Brig. Gen. J.E.B. STUART. Von Borcke immediately became devoted to the dashing Stuart, who found von Borcke to be a kindred spirit.

A trained professional, von Borcke reputedly carried the largest sword in the Confederacy, which earned him such nicknames as "Long Blade" and "Major Armstrong." His comrades most often called him simply "Von." Promoted to major Aug. 1862, he participated in all of Stuart's engagements from SECOND BULL RUN to CHANCELLORSVILLE, and in both Southern and Northern newspapers was repeatedly reported killed in battle. On 19 June 1863, at Upperville, Va., while he and Stuart were directing the rear guard, von Borcke fell grievously wounded with a bullet in the neck. A local doctor told him that

he could not survive the night, but he rallied. Von Borcke recovered slowly from the wound and never again fought in the field. In May 1864, he sat beside Stuart's deathbed, holding his friend's hand and weeping.

Later that year he agreed to undertake a diplomatic mission in England on behalf of the Confederacy. Promoted to colonel 24 Dec. 1864, he left for Europe the next day. When the Confederacy surrendered, von Borcke went back to Prussia, where he wrote his *Memoirs of the Confederate War for Independence* (1866), among the finest pieces of Confederate literature, and served on the staff of Prince Frederick Charles in the Austrian War.

Von Borcke returned to the U.S. once, in 1884, for a visit of more than 2 months. Never fully recovering from the wound he had received in 1863, he died in Berlin, 10 May 1895.

—JDW

von Steinwehr, Baron Adolph Wilhelm August Friedrich.

USA   b. Brunswick, Germany, 25 Sept. 1822, into a military family, von Steinwehr studied at the Brunswick Military Academy and entered the Prussian ducal service. He jour-

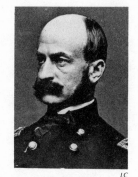

neyed to the U.S. during the Mexican War 1846–48, hoping to receive a commission in the Regular Army. Unsuccessful, he accepted service with a regiment of Alabama volunteers, and was appointed to a detachment of engineers assigned to survey the new border between Mexico and the U.S. About this time he married a woman from Mobile and became an American citizen. From 1849 to 1854 the family lived in Europe, re-

LC

turning to settle on a farm in Wallingford, Conn.

After the firing on FORT SUMTER von Steinwehr enlisted in the volunteer service and was commissioned colonel of the 29th New York, which was held in reserve at FIRST BULL RUN and helped cover the Federal retreat. A cautious but brave soldier, probably the best-trained of the German-born officers, von Steinwehr recruited extensively among his countrymen, earn-

ing a promotion to brigadier general 12 Oct. 1861. During Maj. Gen. JOHN C. FRÉMONT's operations against Maj. Gen. THOMAS J. "STONEWALL" JACKSON in the SHENANDOAH VALLEY in 1862, he commanded the 2d brigade in Brig. Gen. LOUIS BLENKER's division. During the SECOND BULL RUN CAMPAIGN he was given the 2d Division in Maj. Gen. FRANZ SIGEL's corps/Army of Virginia. When that army was discontinued, Sigel's corps was redesignated XI Corps/Army of the Potomac and placed under the command of Maj. Gen. OLIVER O. HOWARD. Under Howard, von Steinwehr led his division in the fighting at CHANCELLORSVILLE May 1863 and in the defense of CEMETERY HILL at GETTYSBURG in July.

Transferred to the West that autumn, von Steinwehr's division fought at CHATTANOOGA and in the WAUHATCHIE NIGHT ATTACK. Von Steinwehr lost divisional command to Brig. Gen. JOHN W. GEARY Apr. 1864, when the XI and XII corps were consolidated and redesignated the XX Corps, and he reverted to command of a brigade in the XIV Corps. Apparently he refused the assignment, angry over being demoted: he had received his brigadier's commission more than 6 months before Geary had. His resignation was accepted 8 July 1865.

Von Steinwehr lived in several cities during his postwar career. An accomplished cartographer and geographer, he taught at Yale University, worked for the Federal government, and wrote extensively, dying in Buffalo, N.Y., 25 Feb. 1877.

—PLF

W

Wachusett, USS. This wooden steamer, built and launched at the Boston Navy Yard in 1861, had machinery manufactured by the Morgan Iron Works of New York City. The *Wachusett* was 201 ft long, weighed 1,032 tons, and had a 14-ft draft. Although its 2 engines and 3 boilers were designed for speeds up to 11.5 knots, the steamer averaged only half that speed. When commissioned 3 Mar. 1862, it carried a battery of 2 11-in. DAHLGRENS, 2 30-pounder PARROTT rifles, and 1 20-pounder Parrott rifle.

Under Cmdr. William Smith, the *Wachusett* provided sea support for army troops engaged in Maj. Gen. GEORGE B. MCCLELLAN's PENINSULA CAMPAIGN. In Sept. 1862 it became part of Rear Adm. CHARLES WILKES's "flying squadron": 7 vessels sent in search of the commerce destroyers CSS *ALABAMA* and CSS *FLORIDA*. Although this mission was a failure, several BLOCKADE RUNNERS were apprehended, and the *Wachusett* accounted for 2 of these.

In 1864 Cmdr. NAPOLEON COLLINS was assigned the vessel and ordered to continue the search for the *Florida*. He finally found the cruiser at Bahia harbor, Brazil, 7 Oct. 1864. Determined either to capture or destroy the *Florida*, Collins violated Brazil's neutrality by deliberately ramming the ship after assuring authorities that he would take no action while in port. After subduing the *Florida*'s crew, he took the ship in tow to the U.S. Under Cmdr. Robert Townsend, the *Wachusett* next participated in the unsuccessful search for yet another commerce raider, the *SHENANDOAH*. Cruising Pacific waters at war's end, the *Wachusett* was incorporated into the East India Squadron. The vessel continued in active service until 1887, when it was sold for salvage. —NCD

Waddell, James Iredell. CSN b. Pittsboro, N.C., 13 July 1824, Waddell was appointed a midshipman 10 Sept. 1841 and graduated from the U.S. Naval Academy as a passed midshipman in 1847. A duel with another midshipman in 1842 left him with a permanent limp. Waddell was promoted to lieutenant in 1855. After returning from the Orient, where he had served with the East India Squadron, he resigned his commission and 27 Mar. 1862 was appointed a lieutenant in the Confederate States Navy.

OR

Waddell was assigned to the uncompleted ram *Mississippi,* but the unarmed vessel was destroyed to prevent its capture by the Federal squadron moving against New Orleans. He next commanded naval batteries at Drewry's Bluff, Va., and at Charleston until Mar. 1863. He was then ordered to Europe to await assignment to one of the LAIRD RAMS nearing completion in England. But the rams would never serve as Confederate warships, and Waddell spent

LC

months awaiting assignment to a cruiser or BLOCKADE RUNNER instead.

On 5 Sept. 1864, he was appointed a lieutenant commandant by Flag Officer SAMUEL BARRON, the South's chief naval officer in Europe. Confederate naval agent JAMES D. BULLOCH had secured a vessel, the *Sea King,* in England, and Waddell was assigned to command it. He was instructed by Barron to find and destroy the North's whaling fleet. On 19 Oct. 1864, off Madeira, the *Sea King* was commissioned the CSS SHENANDOAH. After a stopover at Melbourne, Australia, Waddell brought the vessel north to the Bering Sea and the Arctic Ocean, where he discovered a large number of the whaling ships he was searching for. Refusing to believe reports that Lee had surrendered, Waddell destroyed most of them April–June 1865. Not until 2 Aug., after he had left northern waters, did he become convinced that the South had lost the war. Believing that his destruction of so many vessels after war's end made him an outlaw in the U.S., Waddell disguised the *Shenandoah* and sailed it 17,000 mi to England without stopping at any port. At Liverpool, 5 Nov. 1865, he surrendered the vessel to English authorities. He remained in England until he was confident that he would not be prosecuted in the U.S.

In 1875 Waddell became a captain for the Pacific Mail Co. 2 years later the ship he commanded was wrecked off the coast of Mexico, but all lives were saved. Waddell then became commander of the Maryland State Fishery Force. d. Annapolis, Md., 15 Mar. 1886.   —NCD

Wade, Benjamin Franklin. USP b. Fleeting Hills, Mass., 27 Oct. 1800. Born into a respected but impoverished New England family, Wade knew hard times as a youth. In 1821 he moved with his parents to the Ohio frontier and worked variously as a farmer, drover, laborer, medical student, and schoolteacher. Finally he studied law, entered politics, and became one of the country's leading antislavery statesmen. Rising through positions as county prosecuting attorney, state senator, and circuit judge, in 1851 he won a seat in the U.S. Senate, where he served 3 terms, the first as a Whig, the latter 2 as a Republican.

Brash and outspoken, he clashed often with pro-slavery

LC

leaders. Once he accepted a challenge to a duel with an irate Southerner and, as the challenged party, exercised his right to choose the weapons: squirrel rifles at 20 paces. The abashed Southerner backed down. Wade became known thereafter as "Bluff Ben."

From the start of the Civil War, Wade belligerently called for swift and decisive military action. He was prominent in establishing the COMMITTEE ON THE CONDUCT OF THE WAR, which ferreted out inefficiency and agitated for the removal of unsuccessful generals. Always advocating harsh punishment of the South, he favored confiscating enemy property and total emancipation. He opposed both ABRAHAM LINCOLN's and ANDREW JOHNSON's conservative RECONSTRUCTION plans, which he characterized as "absurd, monarchical, and anti-American." (*See* WADE-DAVIS BILL.) Eventually turning completely against Johnson, Wade voted for his impeachment. In 1868 he unsuccessfully sought the vice-presidential nomination on ULYSSES S. GRANT's ticket.

On retirement from the Senate, Wade resumed law practice in Ohio, and worked in behalf of the Northern Pacific and the Union Pacific railroads. In 1871 he went to Santo Domingo as a member of a commission investigating possible annexation, which he favored. d. Jefferson, Ohio, 2 Mar. 1878.

—HH

Wade-Davis Bill. To the increasing dissatisfaction of RADICAL REPUBLICANS, Pres. ABRAHAM LINCOLN tried imposing a mild RECONSTRUCTION in Louisiana, Tennessee, and Arkansas after Union troops occupied large sections of those states through 1864. That spring, Rep. HENRY W. DAVIS, chairman of the House Committee on the Rebellious States, and Sen. BENJAMIN F. WADE, chairman of the corresponding body in the Senate, presented a bill in Congress making 3 preliminary demands for Reconstruction. The first required the president to appoint a provisional governor for each state in rebellion; the second called for the registration of each white male in those states, once military resistance had ceased, and required them to swear an oath of past allegiance; the third demanded that elections be held for delegates to state constitutional conventions, after a majority of the registered voters had taken the oath.

These provisions seemed reasonable to Lincoln, but he objected to the legislators' additional demands, which included prohibiting all high-placed civil and military officers from holding political office, and forbidding former Confederate officeholders from swearing the oath. They also insisted that each new state constitution abolish SLAVERY. Only if these provisions were enacted could the president, with congressional consent, recognize a reorganized state government.

Among Radical Republicans, Rep. THADDEUS STEVENS alone opposed the bill, and he thought it too lenient. Lincoln accurately read it as a retaliatory blow against the South and a refutation of his 10% Plan, which would permit the election of constitutional conventions when 10% of a Southern state's voting population had signed an oath of future allegiance. Both houses of Congress passed the bill in close votes, but Lincoln pocket-vetoed it 4 July. Sen. ZACHARIAH CHANDLER threatened the loss of Michigan and Ohio in the November elections because of Lincoln's veto, and Radicals in general denounced the president for insisting that the Federal government could not impose emancipation on individual states.

Lincoln would not retreat from his position. 4 days after his

795   **Walcutt, Charles Carroll**

veto, he issued a proclamation explaining his reasons for refusing to sign the bill. Davis responded in a scathing article first published by HORACE GREELEY in the NEW YORK *TIMES* 5 Aug. Also signed by Wade, the document, labeled the Wade-Davis Manifesto, called Lincoln's veto a statement against human rights, accused the president of "dictatorial usurpation" of legislative power, and warned him to "confine himself to his executive duties—to obey and execute, not to make, laws."

The public saw the manifesto as a vindictive attack on the president's authority to rebuild the nation by a Congress jealous of the wartime expansion of executive power, and rallied to support Lincoln. In 1867 several of the measures in the Wade-Davis Bill would become the basis for Congressional Reconstruction, but in summer 1864 Northerners wanted to win the war before concerning themselves with restoring the Southern states to the Union.   —PLF

Wadsworth, James Samuel. USA b. Geneseo, N.Y., 30 Oct. 1807, Wadsworth, son of one of the state's wealthiest landowners, received a private education, attended Harvard Law School, continued study at home, and passed the New York bar. He used his legal education to manage his estate and, first as a Democrat, made politics his avocation. A party power and policy maker, he did not run for office but led New York's FREE SOIL PARTY, then joined the Republican fold in 1856.

At the start of the Civil War he declined a major generalcy offered by the governor of New York, instead serving as a volunteer aide to Brig. Gen. IRVIN MCDOWELL. Impressed by Wadsworth's energy, McDowell helped secure his brigadier general's commission, effective 9 Aug. 1861. After administrative duty, Wadsworth took command of the 2d Brigade/McDowell's Division/Army of the Potomac 3 Oct. 1861, served until appointed military governor of Washington, D.C., 17 Mar. 1862, then allowed New York Republicans to enter him as a candidate in the governor's race in autumn. He remained in garrison, did not participate in the PENINSULA CAMPAIGN, lost the gubernatorial election, did not win a combat assignment for the Battle of FREDERICKSBURG, then took command of the 1st Division/I Corps/Army of the Potomac 27 Dec. 1862.

Though briefly in charge of the I Corps Jan. 1863, he served as 1st Division commander with few interruptions until 15 July 1863. Seeing little service at the Battle of CHANCELLORSVILLE, he took part in the heaviest action on the first day of the Battle of GETTYSBURG, and his division was effectively destroyed. Reassigned to command of the 4th Division/V Corps 25 Mar. 1864 for the OVERLAND CAMPAIGN, he served at SPOTSYLVANIA, then took a mortal wound 6 May 1864 in the Battle of the WILDERNESS, was made a prisoner, and died in a Confederate hospital behind the lines 8 May.   —JES

Wagner, George Day. USA b. Ross Cty., Ohio, 22 Sept. 1829. Migrating to Warren Cty., Ind., with his family in early youth, Wagner attended public school and farmed until win-

ning election to the state house of representatives as a Republican in 1856. He won a seat in the state senate in 1860 and served as president of the Indiana State Agricultural Society until the Civil War began.

Wagner mustered in as colonel of the 15th Indiana 14 June 1861, served on occupation duty in western Virginia, then returned west, assuming command of the 21st Brigade/6th Division/Army of the Ohio 11 Feb. 1862. Under Brig. Gen. THOMAS J. WOOD, on 7 Apr. 1862 at the Battle of SHILOH, Wagner's troops engaged the enemy midafternoon and took part in some of the last combat of the day. Commended by Wood for his service there, on 29 Sept. he was given command of the 2d Brigade of Wood's Division in the ARMY OF THE CUMBERLAND. At the Battle of STONE'S RIVER he anchored the Union left wing on the first day of fighting and saw some of the heaviest action of the day in the combat in the Round Forest.

Appointed brigadier general 4 Apr. 1863, to rank from 29 Nov. 1862, Wagner had been appointed commander of the 2d Brigade/2d Division/XXI Corps 9 Jan. 1863, and also briefly assumed leadership of the 1st Division 19 Feb. He returned to command of the 2d Division 13 Apr., joined in Maj. Gen. WILLIAM S. ROSECRANS' occupation of Chattanooga Sept. 1863, stayed there through the Battle of CHICKAMAUGA, then fought with distinction on MISSIONARY RIDGE, where his command took fearful losses.

Next commanding the 2d Brigade/2d Division/IX Corps, he served in the ATLANTA CAMPAIGN, joined Maj. Gen. JOHN M. SCHOFIELD's forces for the FRANKLIN AND NASHVILLE CAMPAIGN, and at the Battle of FRANKLIN ended his military career. Posted far in advance of the Carter house at the Union center, he did not follow instructions to retire to the main line should the enemy begin an advance. Instead he held until nearly overrun, then allowed his broken force to flee to the rear, blocking Federal fire. On the heels of Wagner's men, Confederates penetrated the Union center. On 9 Dec. 1864, Wagner requested relief from duty, stating concern for his wife's health. He returned to Indiana and awaited orders until mustered out 24 Aug. 1865.

Wagner established a law practice in Williamsport, Ind., in 1866 and resumed the presidency of the agricultural society, dying in Indianapolis, 13 Feb. 1869. When or where he acquired legal training is undocumented.   —JES

Walcutt, Charles Carroll. USA b. Columbus, Ohio, 12 Feb. 1838. The son of a veteran of the War of 1812 and grandson of a soldier who served in the Revolution, Walcutt graduated in 1858 from the Kentucky Military Institute. He devoted himself to civilian pursuits, principally as a county surveyor in central Ohio, until Apr. 1861, when he raised a company of Ohio volunteers—an ambition temporarily frustrated when the state, having filled its original enlistment quota, refused to accept his unit. For a time he had to be contented with the rank of major of state troops, but on 1 Oct. 1861, he entered Federal service as a field officer in the 46th Ohio Infantry.

Walcutt was wounded in his first battle, SHILOH, where his regiment was ravaged by a Confederate brigade that assaulted the far Union right. Though a minié bullet lodged in his left shoulder, he remained with his regiment, becoming its colonel 16 Oct. 1862 and fighting skillfully throughout the VICKSBURG CAMPAIGN. Late in 1863, at MISSIONARY RIDGE and during the relief of KNOXVILLE, he commanded a brigade in the XV Corps/Army of the Tennessee.

LC

He rendered his most conspicuous service during the ATLANTA CAMPAIGN and on Maj. Gen. WILLIAM T. SHERMAN'S MARCH TO THE SEA as a brigadier general of volunteers, effective 30 July 1864. He distinguished himself at Dallas, Ga., 28 May 1864, where his troops repulsed the charging brigade of Brig. Gen. FRANK C. ARMSTRONG on the Villa Rica road, killing or wounding almost 250 Confederates. 4 months later, Walcutt led the Union forces in the only pitched battle on the road from Atlanta to the sea. At Griswoldville, 22 Nov., his brigade, guarding Sherman's rear, destroyed a larger force comprising GEORGIA MILITIA and state troops. Among the few Federal casualties was Walcutt himself, wounded in the leg.

Recovered, he returned to his brigade Mar. 1865 and early the next month succeeded to the command of the 1st Division/XIV Corps. As a brevet major general, he was mustered out of the volunteers 15 Jan. 1866 to become warden of the Ohio Penitentiary. He briefly returned to uniform as lieutenant colonel of the 10th U.S. Cavalry, and in 1869 Pres. ULYSSES S. GRANT appointed him collector of internal revenue. Later a 2-term mayor of his native city, he died in Omaha, Neb., 2 May 1898.   —EGL

Walke, Henry. USN b. Princess Anne Cty., Va., 24 Dec. 1808, Walke was appointed a midshipman 1 Feb. 1827 and was promoted to lieutenant in 1839. Later promoted to commander, he was at Pensacola, Fla., aboard the U.S. storeship *Supply* Jan. 1861, when the Pensacola Navy Yard was seized by Florida secessionists. Walke arranged the removal of the U.S. garrison, then brought them to New York aboard the *Supply.* He was court-martialed and found guilty of leaving his station without permission, but received only a mild reprimand for his action.

In Sept. 1861 Walke was commanding the gunboat *TYLER* on the upper Mississippi under

USMHI

Flag Officer ANDREW H. FOOTE. As commander of the gunboat *CARONDELET*, he contributed to the capture of FORTS HENRY and DONELSON Feb. 1862. In running the *Carondelet* past enemy batteries on ISLAND NO. 10 on the night of 4 Apr. 1862, he demonstrated outstanding heroism. Lightning from a severe thunderstorm revealed his position to the enemy, and only the

Confederates' inability to lower the elevation of their guns allowed the vessel to pass. Because of Walke's action, the U.S. Army at New Madrid was able to cross the river and capture the enemy's position from the rear.

Walke next participated in operations against FORT PILLOW, Tenn., and during the Yazoo Expedition, May–July 1862. He was promoted to captain 16 July 1862. From Feb. to Aug. 1863 he commanded the ironclad *Lafayette* on the Mississippi, contributing to the Federals' capture of Vicksburg 4 July.

In Jan. 1864 Walke was assigned to the *Sacramento* and sent in search of CONFEDERATE CRUISERS in European waters. The CSS *STONEWALL* was located at Ferrol, Spain, but Commodore THOMAS T. CRAVEN declined to risk the *Sacramento* and the *Niagara* against what he considered an invincible opponent. Walke found the *RAPPAHANNOCK* in drydock at Calais and spent 15 months blockading the ship there.

Promoted to rear admiral in 1870, Walke retired in 1871. d. Brooklyn, N.Y., 8 Mar. 1896.   —NCD

Walker, Henry Harrison. CSA b. "Elmwood," Sussex Cty., Va., 15 Oct. 1832. Graduating 41st in the West Point class of 1853, Walker served on frontier garrison duty in the antebellum army. He also acted as aide-de-camp to the governor of Kansas during the warfare in that territory between pro- and anti-slavery groups. On 3 May 1861, soon after Virginia seceded, he resigned and was appointed captain in the Confederate army.

USMHI

Walker was subsequently elected lieutenant colonel of the 40th Virginia and June 1862 was promoted to colonel of the regiment, leading it in the SEVEN DAYS' CAMPAIGN. At GAINES' MILL on the 27th, he suffered 2 wounds. He then served as commander of a convalescent camp and in the defenses of Richmond, Va. On 1 July 1863, he was commissioned brigadier general.

Walker commanded a brigade during the BRISTOE and MINE RUN campaigns later that year, fighting in spring 1864 at the WILDERNESS and SPOTSYLVANIA. In the latter battle he was again wounded, and his foot was amputated. Thereafter he served on courts-martial and, in the war's final weeks, guarded the Richmond & Danville Railroad. Walker allegedly was the officer who informed Pres. JEFFERSON DAVIS at Danville, Va., of the surrender of Gen. ROBERT E. LEE's army. Davis ordered Walker and his troops to North Carolina, but the Virginia officer was paroled in Richmond 7 May 1865.

After the war Walker moved to Morristown, N.J. An investment broker, he worked and resided there until his death 22 Mar. 1912.   —JDW

Walker, James Alexander. CSA b. Mt. Sidney, Va., 27 Aug. 1832. During his senior year at the VIRGINIA MILITARY INSTITUTE, Walker was dismissed on charges preferred by a professor—Walker's future commander, THOMAS J. JACKSON. Although the cadet challenged him to a duel, the two did not meet. Walker then worked for the Carrington & Ohio Railway before studying law at the University of Virginia. Following his graduation, he practiced his profession in Pulaski Cty., Va. When Virginia seceded, he entered Confederate service as captain of the Pulaski Guard.

Walker initially served under Jackson at Harpers Ferry, Va., then became lieutenant colonel of the 13th Virginia. In Feb. 1862 he succeeded Brig. Gen. AMBROSE P. HILL as colonel of the regiment, leading it in the 1862 SHENANDOAH VALLEY, SEVEN DAYS' and SECOND BULL RUN campaigns. A skillful, ferocious

LC

combat officer, Walker commanded a brigade at ANTIETAM, where he suffered a wound.

He commanded another brigade at FREDERICKSBURG Dec. 1862 and at CHANCELLORSVILLE May 1863. His prowess as an officer so impressed Jackson that "Stonewall" specially requested Walker's promotion to brigadier general. Walker received his commission, to rank from 15 May 1863, and command of the STONEWALL BRIGADE, which he led at GETTYSBURG, BRISTOE, MINE RUN, the WILDERNESS, and SPOTSYLVANIA. In this last battle, the brigade was mowed down and Walker grievously wounded. On his return to duty, he commanded a division at PETERSBURG and at APPOMATTOX.

After the war, Walker returned to Pulaski County, farmed, and resumed his legal practice. He was elected to the state legislature as a Democrat in 1871 and became lieutenant governor in 1876. He eventually split with the party and, as a Republican, served 2 terms, 1895–99, in the U.S. House of Representatives. d. Wytheville, Va., 20 Oct. 1901.   —JDW

Walker, John George. CSA b. Cole Cty., Mo., 22 July 1822. After graduating from Jesuit College in St. Louis, Walker was commissioned directly into the Regular Army in 1846. He remained in the antebellum army following the Mexican War, rising to the rank of captain, and resigned 31 July 1861 to join the Confederacy.

Initially commissioned a major, Walker soon was appointed lieutenant colonel of the 8th Texas Cavalry. On 9 Jan. 1862, he received his commission as brigadier general. He then served in the District of Aquia and the DEPARTMENT OF NORTH CAROLINA before joining the ARMY OF NORTHERN VIRGINIA in September during the AN-

NA

TIETAM CAMPAIGN. Commanding a demidivision of 2 brigades, Walker seized Loudoun Heights in the operations against the Union garrison at Harpers Ferry, Va. At ANTIETAM, on the 17th, his 2 brigades fought gallantly in the savage combat around the West Woods and Miller's Cornfield. Walker's performance resulted in his promotion to major general 8 Nov. 1862.

With his new rank, Walker was transferred to the TRANS-MISSISSIPPI DEPARTMENT and assigned command of a division of Texas infantry. He led his veterans during the RED RIVER CAM-

PAIGN in spring 1864, briefly commanded the District of West Louisiana, and in June assumed direction of the DISTRICT OF TEXAS, NEW MEXICO, AND ARIZONA, holding this post until 31 Mar. 1865.

Walker briefly fled to Mexico at the war's conclusion. Returning to the U.S., he served as consul general at Bogotá, Colombia, and as a special commissioner to the Pan-American Convention. d. District of Columbia, 20 July 1893.   —JDW

Walker, Leroy Pope. CSP b. Huntsville, Ala., 7 Feb. 1817. Scion of a prominent north Alabama family, Walker attended the University of Alabama and studied law at the University of Virginia. Admitted to the bar in 1837, he began a law practice, served in several political offices, and became a leader of Southern-rights forces in Alabama. In 1860 he chaired the Alabama delegation to the Democratic national convention. When the convention refused to endorse protection of slave property in the territories, Walker led his delegation out, followed by other slave states. After the election of ABRAHAM LINCOLN, he worked for Alabama's secession.

LC

When the Confederate government was organized, Pres. JEFFERSON DAVIS desired a cabinet seat for each state. Leading Alabamians recommended Walker for their state's post. Walker would have been a logical choice for attorney general but, since that position was filled, became secretary of war. Though he played an important role in organizing the Southern army, his contributions have often been ignored.

Walker faced what he later called "a task of great labor, and, within the period allowed me, one of almost insuperable difficulties." He deserves credit for mobilizing 200,000 men in the first 6 months of the war, but he encountered difficulties equipping them with weapons and supplies, and made only limited progress dealing with such problems during his brief tenure.

A poor administrator, Walker was confronted with much detailed work. He also quarreled with state governors—a problem inherent in Confederate STATES-RIGHTS philosophy—as well as with disappointed office seekers and their politician friends. As criticism mounted, his health failed. After he and the president disagreed about the occupation of Columbus, Ky., by Confederate forces, he resigned 16 Sept. 1861.

Appointed brigadier general 17 Sept. 1861, Walker served as such for several months, then, late in the war, as a military court judge in north Alabama, with rank of colonel. After 1865 he resumed his law practice, dying in Huntsville, 23 Aug. 1884.   —RMcM

Walker, Lucius Marshall. CSA b. Columbia, Tenn., 18 Oct. 1829, Walker graduated from the U.S. Military Academy, 15th in the class of 1850. He remained in the army only 2 years, resigning his commission to engage in the mercantile business in Memphis. A nephew of former president James K. Polk, Walker joined the Confederate army in 1861 as lieutenant colonel of the 40th Tennessee.

Promoted to colonel 11 Nov. 1861, he assumed command

of the defenses of Memphis and 4 months later, 11 Mar. 1862, was commissioned a brigadier general. Because of poor health he missed the Battle of SHILOH, but joined the Army of Mississippi to participate in the actions at CORINTH and at Farmington, Miss. Sometime during summer or autumn 1862, Maj. Gen. BRAXTON BRAGG, commanding the Confederate army, asserted that Walker and another brigadier "were not safe men to be entrusted with any command."

LC

Though never brought before a board, Walker requested transfer to the TRANS-MISSISSIPPI DEPARTMENT, which Bragg readily approved.

Walker joined the command of Lt. Gen. E. KIRBY SMITH Mar. 1863. Assigned a brigade of cavalry, he fought under Maj. Gen. STERLING PRICE at Helena, Ark., in July. He then became embroiled in a personal dispute with Brig. Gen. JOHN S. MARMADUKE. The latter officer allegedly questioned Walker's courage, and Walker challenged him to a duel. Price interceded in vain, and at sunrise, 6 Sept. 1863, at Little Rock, Marmaduke mortally wounded Walker, who died the next day.   —JDW

Walker, Mary Edwards. physician b. Oswego, N.Y., 26 Nov. 1832. In 1919, when Federal authorities told Dr. Mary E. Walker that the MEDAL OF HONOR she had won for gallantry during her Civil War service had been revoked, she replied sharply, "You can have it over my dead body."

In the 1840s and 1850s, Dr. Walker worked against prejudice and criticism to become a physician. After graduating from Syracuse Medical College, she found little acceptance of a female doctor even among her own sex. To help fill the desperate need for medical personnel during the Civil War, Walker abandoned her struggling Cincinnati, Ohio, practice and spent 3 years working as a nurse for the Union army. In 1864 an Ohio regiment hired her as a contract surgeon for 6 months.

In a position to move back and forth across Union and Confederate lines, she became active as a spy. In Oct. 1864 the army commissioned her an assistant surgeon, a position she held until her resignation June 1865. She attended the wounded on both sides, and spent 4 months in a Confederate prison after she was captured while treating a Confederate soldier on the battlefield.

During her army career Walker adopted the uniform of her fellow officers and continued wearing male clothing in civilian life. But with strong pride in her own sex, she wore her hair in curls, so that people would know that she was a woman.

Although she actively supported several reform movements, including the popular election of senators, most of Walker's energies went into the woman's rights movement. She went so far as to establish a colony for women in 1897, calling it Adamless Eden. Because she rejected the boundaries set for women in her day, women scorned her, and even her family shunned her as a militant.

Walker died poor and alone near Oswego, 21 Feb. 1919, 6 days after the Board of Medals revoked her Medal of Honor. The award was officially reinstated in 1977.   —PLF

Walker, Reuben Lindsay. CSA b. Logan, Va., 29 May 1827. The Confederate ARMY OF NORTHERN VIRGINIA possessed several outstanding artillery commanders, among them Reuben L. Walker, who fought in 63 battles and engagements, was never wounded, and took only 1 brief leave of absence, due to illness. His record was matched by few, if any, officers in that command.

LC

Walker was an 1845 graduate of the VIRGINIA MILITARY INSTITUTE, then worked as a civil engineer before becoming a farmer. With the outbreak of the Civil War, he was commissioned captain and commander of the Purcell Battery, which reached the field at FIRST BULL RUN only in time to shell the retreating Union army.

In Mar. 1862 Walker was promoted to major and named chief of artillery of Brig. Gen. AMBROSE P. HILL's division. For the next 3 years he served under Hill, eventually as commander of the artillery of Hill's III Corps. He fought in every major campaign in the East—except the SEVEN DAYS', which he missed because of illness—until the surrender at Appomattox. Promoted to lieutenant colonel, then colonel, he received his commission of brigadier general 18 Feb. 1865.

Resuming farming after the war, in 1872 Walker moved to Selma, Ala., where he served for 2 years as superintendent of the Marine & Selma Railroad. Returning to Virginia in 1876, he worked for the Richmond street railways and as a construction engineer for the Richmond & Allegheny Railroad. He eventually supervised the construction of an addition to the Virginia State Penitentiary and the Texas state capitol. He died on his Virginia farm in Fluvanna County, 7 June 1890.   —JDW

Walker, William Henry Talbot. CSA b. Augusta, Ga., 26 Nov. 1816. The son of a former U.S. senator, Walker was educated in local schools before entering West Point at age 16. Though he graduated 46th in the 50-man class of 1837, he became one of Georgia's most esteemed soldiers; state officials presented him with a sword of honor in 1849. As a lieutenant in the 6th U.S. Infantry, he was severely wounded by Seminoles in 1837 and 10 years later by Mexicans at Molino del Rey. Not expected to recover from the second wound, he was placed on sick leave and light duty for the next 5 years. From 1854 to 1856 he was commandant of cadets and instructor of

LC

tactics at West Point. On 20 Dec. 1860, after serving briefly in Minnesota, he resigned his major's commission to enter the military service of Georgia.

Appointed a major general of state volunteers the following April, Walker became a Confederate brigadier a month later. That October, however, he relinquished the latter commission

—quite possibly to protest the military policies of Pres. JEFFER-
SON DAVIS—and was again commissioned a major general of
Georgia troops. In Mar. 1863 he reentered Confederate service as a brigadier, this time to stay. His conspicuous abilities
impelled Gen. JOSEPH E. JOHNSTON, in whose ARMY OF TENNES-
SEE Walker served, to secure for him a major generalship to
rank from 23 May. Walker justified his rapid rise by ably handling a brigade during Johnston's Mississippi campaigning and
by his gallant conduct that September at CHICKAMAUGA, where
he commanded the Reserve Corps of the army. On the second
day of the battle he attacked the Federal left wing, doing
considerable damage, although his command later became
disorganized. This Walker attributed to the poor tactics of his
superior, Maj. Gen. DANIEL H. HILL, with whom he subsequently
quarreled.

After Chickamauga, Walker fought under Johnston from
RESACA to the CHATTAHOOCHEE RIVER and under Gen. JOHN B.
HOOD at ATLANTA. On 22 July 1864, he led one of the divisions
that Hood hurled against Maj. Gen. WILLIAM T. SHERMAN's left,
east of the Confederate citadel. That afternoon he was instantly
killed by a volley from a XVI Corps picket line. His body was
removed to Augusta for burial.   —EGL

Walker, William Stephen. CSA b. Pittsburgh, Pa., 13
Apr. 1822. Raised by his uncle, Mississippi Sen. Robert J.
Walker, William attended school in the District of Columbia.
During the Mexican War he
served as a lieutenant of VOL-
TIGEURS and later as a staff
officer, and at Chapultepec won
a captain's brevet for gallant and
meritorious conduct. In Mar.
1855 he took command of a
troop of the 1st U.S. Cavalry,
resigning 6 years later for the
South. By then he had been
tendered a lieutenant's commission in the CONFEDERATE REGU-
LAR ARMY.

Walker's early war career included mustering chores and
inspection duties in the DEPART-
MENT OF SOUTH CAROLINA AND GEORGIA. While in administrative service in South Carolina, he was promoted to colonel,
then, 30 Oct. 1862, to brigadier general. He became a subordinate of Gen. P.G.T. BEAUREGARD, who early in 1863 gave him
command of the military district between the Ashepoo and
Savannah rivers.

After holding additional administrative posts in Georgia and
South Carolina, Walker was transferred to brigade command
at Kinston, N.C., early in 1864. In May he was sent to Virginia
and under Beauregard fought in defense of Richmond, then
under attack by Maj. Gen. BENJAMIN F. BUTLER's ARMY OF THE
JAMES. Arriving with his brigade shortly after the Second Battle
of DREWRY'S BLUFF, Walker immediately threatened the new
Union position at BERMUDA HUNDRED, 12 mi below the Confederate capital. On 20 May he led what Butler himself termed
"a very daring charge" against the Union right. In the melee
that followed, Walker blundered into the enemy line; attempting to flee, he received a volley from the 67th Ohio Infantry.
His horse was killed and Walker fell, his left arm pierced and
his right leg shattered above the ankle.

Captured and carried to a hospital at FORT MONROE, he
dictated deathbed letters to his wife, Beauregard, and others
close to him. However, through the skill of surgeon John J.
Craven, medical director of Butler's X Corps, who amputated
his leg, Walker survived and that October was exchanged.
Partially recovering, he retook the field; at the end of the
conflict he was serving at Weldon, N.C. With the return of
peace, he settled in Georgia, dying in Atlanta 7 June 1899.
                                                        —EGL

Wallace, Lewis. USA b. Brookville, Ind., 10 Apr. 1827,
Wallace, like many fellow officers, was raised to high military
rank because of his connections within government. This political general served in the Mexi-
can War, then left the army for
a legal and political career.
When Civil War broke out, he
raised the 11th Indiana Infantry
and was appointed brigadier
general of volunteers 3 Sept.
1861.

Wallace first saw action during the campaigning for FORT
HENRY and FORT DONELSON as a
division commander under Maj.
Gen. ULYSSES S. GRANT. He performed competently enough to
earn a major general's commission, to rank from 21 Mar.

USMHI

1862, just before the battle at SHILOH. Bivouacked 6 mi downstream from the battlefield, Wallace's division was ordered
into action with all possible speed. Wallace took an interior
road toward Brig. Gen. WILLIAM T. SHERMAN's camp, not knowing that it was 3 mi longer than the river route and would bring
him on the Confederate rear, where his division could be
encircled and destroyed. Early in the afternoon the general
realized his error and made a confused countermarch to Shiloh. The next day Wallace's cautious attack on the right flank
drew Grant's criticism.

Under a cloud after Shiloh, Wallace was subsequently
removed from combat duty. Appointed commander of the
MIDDLE DEPARTMENT, an administrative post comprising Mid-
western states, he organized the defense of Cincinnati when
Maj. Gen. E. KIRBY SMITH invaded Kentucky. Later, at
MONOCACY, Wallace led a patchwork force easily routed by Lt.
Gen. JUBAL A. EARLY during the 1864 SHENANDOAH VALLEY CAM-
PAIGN. At war's end Wallace sided with Mexican liberals in that
French-occupied country. There he hoped to find fame and
glory leading Republican troops, but he never saw action.

The general resigned from the army shortly after the war, but
his career was not over. He served as governor of New Mexico, minister to Turkey, and finally won immortality by writing
a novel titled *Ben Hur* (1880). d. Crawfordsville, Ind., 15 Feb.
1905.   —MTC

Wallace, William Harvey Lamb. USA b. Urbana, Ohio,
8 July 1821. As a boy Wallace moved with his family to La
Salle Cty., Ill., later studied law privately, passed the state bar
in 1846, then joined the 1st Illinois Infantry as a private for
Mexican War service. Active in combat, he rose to lieutenant
and adjutant, mustered out in 1848, practiced law in La Salle
County, and served as district attorney until the Civil War.

LC

On 30 Apr. 1861, Wallace mustered in as colonel of the 11th Illinois Infantry, a 3-month regiment. Reenlisting with its men 30 July, he served in the District of Cairo, Ill., being elevated to command of the district's 3d Brigade 14 Oct. 1861. He led the brigade at the Battle of FORT DONELSON, and won distinction there and promotion to brigadier general 21 Mar. 1862. He then took command of the 2d Division, and, ill with fever, went into camp with the ARMY

LC

OF THE TENNESSEE at Pittsburg Landing, Tenn.

As the Battle of SHILOH began 6 Apr. 1862, Wallace's division, fighting on the Federal right, far in the advance, suffered repeated Confederate assaults, then fell back, taking up a position on the right of Brig. Gen. BENJAMIN M. PRENTISS' 6th Division holding the "HORNETS' NEST." Late in the afternoon, as the "Hornets' Nest" position began breaking, Wallace agreed with Prentiss to hold out to the last man, then was suddenly struck in the head by a piece of shell. Prentiss was forced to surrender shortly afterward, and, mortally wounded, Wallace lay on the field inside Confederate lines. Found by Federals at 10 a.m. 7 Apr., he was taken to his wife, who had arrived at Pittsburg Landing the previous day, and was transported to Savannah, Tenn., where he died 10 Apr. 1862.   —JES

Wallace, William Henry. CSA b. Laurens District, S.C., 24 Mar. 1827. An 1849 graduate of South Carolina College, Wallace became a planter, newspaper publisher, and lawyer. Elected to the state legislature in 1860, he advocated calling for a secession convention. When his term expired, he enlisted as a private in the 18th South Carolina and was soon named the regiment's adjutant.

The regiment spent the first year of the war in South Carolina, and May 1862 Wallace was elected its lieutenant colonel. In July the unit transferred to Virginia. At SECOND BULL RUN, 30 Aug., Wallace succeeded the regiment's slain colonel as commander. His promotion to

USMHI

the rank was dated the 30th, though the Confederate Senate did not confirm it until 10 June 1864. After Second Bull Run he led the regiment at SOUTH MOUNTAIN and ANTIETAM in the ANTIETAM CAMPAIGN.

Wallace and the 18th returned to their native state later in 1862. After serving more than a year in the defenses of Charleston, the unit returned to Virginia. On 30 July 1864, at Petersburg, the explosion of the Federal mine at the CRATER blew up 4 companies of the 18th, and the Federal attack engulfed Wallace's regiment. On 20 Sept. he received his commission as brigadier general and command of a brigade. He surrendered with the army at Appomattox Apr. 1865.

Returning to South Carolina, Wallace ran his plantation and resumed his legal practice. He served 3 more terms in the legislature before being appointed a circuit-court judge in 1877. He retired from the bench in 1893, dying in Union, S.C., 20 Mar. 1901.   —JDW

Walnut Hills, Miss., Battle of.   27–29 Dec. 1862 *See* CHICKASAW BLUFFS, MISS., BATTLE OF.

Walthall, Edward Cary. CSA b. Richmond, Va., 4 Apr. 1831. At age 10 Walthall moved with his family to Holly Springs, Miss., then attended a private academy, St. Charles Hall; studied law privately in Pontotoc, Miss.; worked as a circuit-court deputy clerk; and passed the Mississippi bar in 1852. Establishing a legal practice in Coffeeville, Miss., he won election as attorney for the tenth judicial district of Mississippi in 1856 and 1859.

LC

In spring 1861 Walthall joined the Yalobusha Rifles, was elected lieutenant, and that summer, following the unit's incorporation with the 15th Mississippi, became regimental lieutenant colonel. With the 15th's colonel absent, Walthall led the regiment at the Jan. 1862 Battle of MILL SPRINGS, fighting on the Confederate right. Praised for his bravery there, on 11 Apr. 1862 he was elected colonel to fill a vacancy in the 29th Mississippi. He served in the 1862 KENTUCKY CAMPAIGN, fighting at MUNFORDVILLE, then fell ill, missing the Battle of STONE'S RIVER. He won promotion to brigadier general 23 Apr. 1863, to rank from 13 Dec. 1862, and from the Battle of CHICKAMAUGA fought in every major movement of the ARMY OF TENNESSEE until its surrender in 1865. In Maj. Gen. WILLIAM H. T. WALKER's division he served at Chickamauga, commanded the front at LOOKOUT MOUNTAIN, was wounded at MISSIONARY RIDGE, and took part in the ATLANTA, FRANKLIN AND NASHVILLE, and CAROLINA campaigns, gaining distinction for commanding the infantry rear guard on the retreat from Nashville. He was paroled at Greensborough, N.C., 1 May 1865.

A postwar friendship and brief law partnership with LUCIUS Q. LAMAR, later elected U.S. senator, led to Walthall's appointment to the U.S. Senate Mar. 1885 on Lamar's resignation to become secretary of interior. Walthall remained in the Senate, except during 13 months of poor health in 1894 and 1895, until his death in Washington, D.C., 21 Apr. 1898.   —JES

war correspondents. At the start of the Civil War, fewer than 12 newspapers kept regular correspondents in Washington, D.C., and only a handful had correspondents who had ever experienced or reported a war.

WILLIAM HOWARD RUSSELL of the London *Times* had covered the Crimean War (1853–56) for the English press and is often called the first war correspondent. Prior to the outbreak of hostilities in the U.S., his publishers sent him to North America. He toured the North and South, reporting war fever, then covered the FIRST BATTLE OF BULL RUN. Though his were not the best or first dispatches written of First Bull Run, they received the widest notice and, in America, the greatest vilification.

Russell criticized much, was consequently denied interviews, and soon returned home. Other reporters covering the FIRST BULL RUN CAMPAIGN were CHARLES COFFIN of the Boston *Journal,* ADAMS S. HILL of the New York *Tribune,* HENRY VILLARD of the New York *Herald,* JOHN RUSSELL YOUNG of the Philadelphia *Press,* and the publisher of the New York *Times,* HENRY RAYMOND. Of these men, only Raymond had previous war-reporting experience, having covered the conflict between Austria and Sardinia in 1859. Many times their number of Union war correspondents were on the field at First Bull Run, and reporters from the Richmond *Dispatch,* Charleston *Mercury,* Montgomery *Advertiser,* Columbus, Ga., *Times,* and 26 other Southern newspapers had passes to cover the battle. This was the last battle where so many Northern and Southern correspondents would be present.

The shortage of Confederate manpower and Southern commanders' reticence to allow reporters on the field kept the number of Southern war correspondents to fewer than 100 throughout the war. Only 2 were permitted to cover the SECOND BATTLE OF BULL RUN, one of whom was Felix G. DeFontaine. Formerly of the New York *Herald,* he covered the FORT SUMTER crisis, First Bull Run, operations on the PENINSULA, BALL'S BLUFF, SHILOH, the SEVEN DAYS' CAMPAIGN, Second Bull Run, the ANTIETAM, CHATTANOOGA, KNOXVILLE, and ATLANTA campaigns, and many smaller battles and operations. He worked for several Southern papers and the Confederate Press Association, and like many other Southern reporters frequently used a pen name. Because of CONSCRIPTION, most Confederate war correspondents were soldiers and wrote under pseudonyms to protect themselves from the interference of superiors or conviction under CENSORSHIP laws.

Conversely, the number of reporters covering the war for Northern newspapers exceeded 341, including parttime and soldier correspondents. Like Southerners, many used pen names. One of these was "Gath," GEORGE ALFRED TOWNSEND. During the war Townsend worked for both the New York *Herald* and New York *World,* covered the Eastern theater, and, after the war, erected near South Mountain, Md., the only known monument to war correspondents.

Townsend was a member of the "Bohemian Brigade," as Union war correspondents called themselves. Living on expense accounts, following the armies in packs, free from most army regulations, and with reputations as hard drinkers, they often banded together to pool reports and casualty statistics. CHARLES ANDERSON PAGE of the New York *Tribune* and Samuel Wilkeson of the New York *Times* and *Tribune* were members of this brigade who covered the Eastern theater. JOHN B. MCCULLAGH of the Cincinnati *Commercial* was one of the better known members in the Western theater. 2 correspondents who were not associated with the wilder aspects of the brigade were GEORGE WASHINGTON SMALLEY and BENJAMIN F. TAYLOR, who were also editors, for the New York *Times* and the Chicago *Journal,* respectively.

Associated with the Bohemian brotherhood were the war artists, among them Eugene Benson, EDWIN FORBES, Henry Mosler, FRANK VIZETELLY, and the brothers William and ALFRED WAUD. With the exception of Vizetelly, who sketched for English newspapers, these artists contributed illustrations to the Northern illustrated newspapers *HARPER'S WEEKLY* and *FRANK LESLIE'S ILLUSTRATED NEWSPAPER.* Vizetelly, a subject of the British crown, had neutral status and was permitted to sketch action with Southern troops. Traveling mostly with the ARMY OF NORTHERN VIRGINIA, he smuggled his sketches to Britain aboard BLOCKADE RUNNERS.

In the age before newspaper photography was possible, these men shared the same hardships as war correspondents, if not greater ones, often risking their safety by capturing under fire sketches that would later appear in their papers as woodcuts. —JES

Ward, James Harmon. USN b. Hartford, Conn., 25 Sept. 1806. The first naval officer to lose his life in the Civil war, Ward graduated in 1823 from the American Literary, Scientific, and Military Academy in Norwich, Vt. (*see* NORWICH UNIVERSITY). Entering the navy as a midshipman 4 Mar. 1823, he took a year's leave of absence in 1828 to study science at Washington (now Trinity) College in Hartford. He gained a reputation as a scholar and an authority on naval tactics and gunnery, and in 1852 the U.S. Naval Academy adopted his *An Elementary Course of Instruction on Ordnance and Gunnery* (1845) as its official text. Ward became the academy's first executive officer, while also serving as instructor of ordnance and gunnery. By 1861 he had risen to the rank of commander and was in command of the *North Carolina,* based at the Brooklyn Navy Yard.

LC

The secession of Virginia posed the threat of a Southern blockade of the Potomac River, which would isolate Washington from naval support. To counter this threat, Sec. of the Navy GIDEON WELLES placed Ward in command of a hastily improvised Potomac Flotilla of 7 vessels. Ward selected as his flagship the *Thomas Freeborn,* a converted sidewheel ferryboat. On 24 May 1861, his sailors and marines occupied ALEXANDRIA after its evacuation by the Confederates. On 31 May and 1 June the flotilla engaged enemy batteries at Aquia Creek, then moved against strategic Mathias Point. A small force of Federals landed near the point 27 June but came under heavy enemy fire. Attempting to cover their retreat, Ward, while sighting a bow gun aboard the *Thomas Freeborn,* received a mortal wound. His heroic efforts to keep open the Potomac failed, as Confederate batteries continued to threaten Federal vessels on the river until Mar. 1862. —NCD

Ward, William Thomas. USA b. Amelia Cty., Va., 9 Aug. 1808. Educated at Kentucky's St. Mary's College, Ward practiced law in the Bluegrass State, interrupting his career to serve as major of the 4th Kentucky Volunteers Oct. 1847–July 1848. On his return from the Mexican War he was elected to the state legislature and 1851–53 was a Whig member of the U.S. House of Representatives. Refusing to seek reelection, he returned to the legal profession and became a prominent citizen of Greensburg, Ky.

In Aug. 1861 Ward prepared to reenter military service by recruiting a brigade of Unionists in his home district. Within a brief time more than 20 companies of volunteers pledged to serve under him, and 18 Sept. the government conferred on him the rank of brigadier general. For a time his brigade was one of the few organized bodies of Brig. Gen. ROBERT ANDER-SON's Department of Kentucky.

LC

By spring 1862 Ward, called "Old Pap" by his men, was commanding the 2d Brigade/3d Division/Reserve Corps/Army of the Ohio. In this capacity he was drawn into the unsuccessful pursuit of Col. JOHN HUNT MORGAN's Kentucky Raid, July 1862. In November he took charge of the post at Gallatin, Tenn., a position he held until Aug. 1863. Early the next year he was given a division in the XI Corps/Army of the Cumberland.

Returned to brigade command at the outset of the ATLANTA CAMPAIGN, Ward drove his troops at RESACA, 14–15 May 1864, briefly seizing a sector of the Confederate works toward which Maj. Gen. WILLIAM T. SHERMAN had directed his attack. Severely wounded in the arm, he refused to quit the fight till its close. One of his soldiers saw him borne to the rear: the general passed "with his arm in a sling, and said, 'Old Pap got it this time, boys.' He was pretty drunk, and seemed to be proud of his wound."

Despite his alleged intemperance, Ward also distinguished himself at PEACHTREE CREEK, then led the 3d Division/XX Corps on Sherman's MARCH TO THE SEA and through the Carolinas. Brevetted a major general of volunteers 24 Feb. 1865, he was mustered out 6 months later. Thereafter he practiced law in Louisville until his death there 12 Oct. 1878.   —EGL

War Democrats. "War Democrats" refers to those members of the Democratic party who supported ABRAHAM LINCOLN's administration during the Civil War. The outbreak of war produced a political reversal in the U.S. CONGRESS. When all Southern senators and representatives except ANDREW JOHNSON left Congress, the Republicans, who had been in the minority, suddenly found themselves the majority party.

Northern Democrats faced a dilemma in 1861. If they opposed the administration's war policy, they risked being denounced as traitors to the Union. If they acquiesced meekly to Republican leadership, they risked losing their viability as a political party. Their dilemma over this was never satisfactorily resolved.

Most Democrats followed the lead of STEPHEN A. DOUGLAS, who supported the Union until his death June 1861. During the next 4 years the War Democrats remained staunchly loyal to the Union effort, differing with Republicans only over the issue of how best to achieve victory. As the war dragged on and gloom pervaded the North, the number of War Democrats diminished while the ranks of PEACE DEMOCRATS, or Copperheads, swelled steadily.

Nevertheless, the dwindling band of War Democrats provided the Lincoln administration with a crucial element of support until the war's end. Their presence enabled Lincoln to maintain the vital illusion that the Northern war effort was bipartisan and unified.   —MK

War of the Rebellion Official Records of the Union and Confederate Armies* and *Official Records of the Union and Confederate Navies in the War of the Rebellion.

In May 1864 the U.S. Congress passed a resolution authorizing the preservation of government papers related to the Civil War. Confederate files began arriving at the adjutant general's office in Washington May 1865 to be included in the massive, nonpartisan documentary history.

Several men, beginning with Franz Leiber in 1868, oversaw the sorting and selection of several tons of accumulated papers. Capt. Robert N. Scott took over the project as head of the newly created War Records Department in 1877; former Confederate general MARCUS J. WRIGHT was appointed in 1878 to gather Confederate materials; Col. H. M. Lazelle succeeded Scott temporarily in 1887; and the last army volumes were prepared by Brig. Gen. Fred C. Ainsworth and Joseph W. Kirkley. Wright's assignment resulted in the availability of many donations from former Confederates who had withheld private and public papers in their possession, believing that the work would be biased against the Confederacy.

By the time Scott's administration began, 37 Union and 10 Confederate volumes had been printed in an issue of 30 copies. Compilers had examined papers by the buildingful, but disagreement over what was and what was not an official document resulted in an uneven, undiscriminating selection. Scott established guidelines omitting such papers as contracts and muster records, and organized the material methodically, dividing the work into 4 series. Series I is arranged by campaigns and theaters of operation in chronological order; series II relates to prisoners of war and political prisoners; series III contains reports and correspondence of Federal and state officials; and series IV is the Confederate counterpart of series III. 25 volumes had been completed under this system when Scott died in 1887, and several additional volumes were in progress.

Between June 1880 and 1900, Congress appropriated funds for the publication of the *Official Records,* with distribution to be determined by the legislators. After 1882, 8,300 sets were allocated for individuals and institutions designated by Congress, 1,000 sets were distributed to army officers and people working on the project, and 1,000 sets were sent to the Executive Department. Additional volumes were sold to the public at 10% above cost. Designees continued to receive new volumes as they were issued. Ultimately the army *Official Records* numbered 128 volumes, with a separate atlas containing 1,006 maps and sketches. The last volume, an index and compendium of additions and corrections, was published in 1901.

The 31-volume naval *Official Records,* begun in 1884 by J. R. Soley, librarian for the Navy Department, was completed with the publication of its index in 1927. As with the army volumes, the naval compilers encountered a shortage of Confederate documents compensated for in part by contributions from former officers. Both sets of *Official Records* remain the mainstay for Civil War researchers. *See also* SOUTHERN HISTORICAL SOCIETY PAPERS.   —PLF

Warren, Fitz-Henry. USA b. Brimfield, Mass., 11 Jan. 1816. In his youth Warren served as a clerk in a mercantile house and 1835–43 manufactured leather goods in partnership with his father and brother. In 1844 he moved west, eventually settling in Iowa. There he reentered the mercantile business until taking over the editorship of an influential newspaper, the Burlington *Hawk-Eye.* He also entered local politics, rising to chair the Whig party in Iowa and being named

assistant postmaster general of
the U.S. in 1849. By 1860 he
was being considered for the
postmaster generalship itself.
The following year he headed
the NEW YORK TRIBUNE's Washington desk, where he helped
initiate the "On to Richmond"
clamor that led to the Union defeat at FIRST BULL RUN.

LC

On 13 June 1861, Warren
was named colonel of the 1st
Iowa Cavalry. Returning west to
lead the regiment, he spent more
than a year fighting Confederate
Regulars and guerrillas in middle and western Missouri. By the
close of 1862 he was a brigadier general, to rank from 16 July, in
command of the post at Houston, Mo. Early the next year he
took over the 2d Brigade/2d Division/Army of Southeastern
Missouri. That summer he was back east, briefly leading a
division in the DEPARTMENT OF THE SUSQUEHANNA, with headquarters at Scranton, Pa. In September, he reported for duty in
the Department of the Gulf. From Dec. 1863 until Apr. 1864 he
led a brigade in the XIII Corps, then commanded the 1st Division of that corps and later the District of Baton Rouge and U.S.
forces along the Texas side of the Rio Grande.

Late in Sept. 1864 Warren's health deteriorated. That month
he was ordered east once again, this time to assume an administrative post in New York City, where he remained till the
close of the conflict. On 24 Aug. 1865, he was mustered out
of the volunteer service as a brevet major general.

In peacetime, Warren returned to politics and diplomacy.
He served in the Iowa senate, became U.S. ambassador to
Guatemala, and in 1872 was an official of the Liberal party,
which nominated for president Warren's old employer, HOR-
ACE GREELEY. In 1875–76 he was a New York and Washington
correspondent for the New York *Sun.* Returning to Massachusetts, he died in his native town 21 June 1878.   —EGL

Warren, Gouverneur Kemble. USA b. Cold Spring,
N.Y., 8 Jan. 1830, Warren graduated from West Point in 1850,
2d in his class. Until the Civil War began he served in the Corps
of Topographical Engineers and
taught mathematics at the U.S.
MILITARY ACADEMY. He served as
colonel of the 5th New York,
and commanded a brigade in
the PENINSULA CAMPAIGN, at SEC-
OND BULL RUN, and at ANTIETAM,
being advanced to brigadier
general 26 Sept. 1862. At GET-
TYSBURG he was chief engineer
of the ARMY OF THE POTOMAC
and as such did not command
troops. However, he is credited,
as much as one man can be
credited, with saving the day for
the Union when 2 July 1863 he
realized that the Union left was in a precarious position should
the Confederates under Maj. Gen. JOHN B. HOOD seize the
unoccupied Round Tops. He urged elements of Maj. Gen.
GEORGE SYKES's corps to form a defensive line, advice that

USMHI

averted probable disaster. He was subsequently promoted to
major general in August, to rank from 3 May.

After temporary command of the II Corps, Warren was
named commander of the V Corps for the OVERLAND CAMPAIGN
of 1864 against Gen. ROBERT E. LEE and Richmond. Warren's
problem as a field commander was undue caution, according
to criticism leveled at him by Lt. Gen. ULYSSES S. GRANT and
later, and more directly, by Maj. Gen. PHILIP H. SHERIDAN. As
the Federals moved on FIVE FORKS, Sheridan was authorized by
Grant to relieve Warren, and Sheridan believed it necessary to
do so. Ironically, Warren had won this decisive battle, but he
had dragged his feet once too often. The V Corps had arrived
late, and Warren had also mishandled his troops. (*See* WARREN
COURT OF INQUIRY.)

Warren spent the rest of his army career as an engineer and
writer on military subjects. d. Newport, R.I., 8 Aug. 1882.
                                                                  —JTH

Warren Court of Inquiry.   Late on the afternoon of 1
Apr. 1865, as the battle of FIVE FORKS closed in Union victory,
Maj. Gen. PHILIP H. SHERIDAN, whom Lt. Gen. ULYSSES S. GRANT
had made an independent army commander, relieved from
duty Maj. Gen. GOUVERNEUR K. WARREN, leader of the V Corps/
Army of the Potomac. Sheridan's act stemmed from his displeasure over Warren's slowness in reaching nearby DINWID-
DIE COURT HOUSE the day before, his lateness in attacking the
troops of Maj. Gen. GEORGE E. PICKETT at Five Forks on the 1st,
and the failure of his initial assault against Pickett.

When, late on the 1st, a shocked and unhappy Warren
sought to learn the basis for Sheridan's move, "Little Phil"
refused his request. Later sent west on engineering duties,
Warren was unable to protest effectively the action that had
ended his long and distinguished career in disgrace. He frequently requested a hearing on his removal but a court of
inquiry was not set up for 14 years. Finally, 9 Dec. 1879, at
the urging of Warren's supporters in Congress, the army, and
civilian life, Pres. RUTHERFORD B. HAYES established a panel
composed of Bvt. Maj. Gens. CHRISTOPHER C. AUGUR and JOHN
NEWTON, with Bvt. Lt. Col. Loomis L. Langdon as recorder.

The Warren Court of Inquiry sat irregularly for almost 2
years. It took testimony from numerous witnesses on both
sides, including Grant, Sheridan, and former Confederate cavalry leader FITZHUGH LEE, and scrutinized a large volume of
evidence bearing on the operations during and prior to Five
Forks. The findings of the court were ordered published 21
Nov. 1882, at the behest of Pres. Chester A. Arthur. Though
mildly critical of Warren's lack of promptness 31 Mar. 1865,
the court rejected Grant's and Sheridan's contention that this
had jeopardized Union success that day and the next. It exonerated Warren of the 4 principal charges lodged against him:
that he moved against Pickett's line 31 Mar. with only a portion
of his corps, against orders; that he did so with unconscionable
slowness; that he was criminally late in attacking on the next
day as well; and that 1 Apr. part of his line gave way due to
his troops' "want of confidence" in his leadership. These
findings could not comfort the vindicated man, however, for
Warren had died, bitter and dispirited, 3 months before their
publication.   —EGL

Washburn, Cadwallader Colden.   USA b. Livermore,
Maine, 22 Apr. 1818, Washburn, brother of politicians ISRAEL
WASHBURN and ELIHU B. WASHBURNE, had a common-school

education. He left Maine in
1839, traveled to Iowa, Mississippi, and Illinois, held various
jobs, read law, then settled in
Mineral Point, Wisc., in 1842
and began a legal practice.
From 1844 he speculated in real
estate, founded the Mineral
Point Bank, and acquired lumber, water, railroad, and flour-
milling interests. Elected to the
U.S. House of Representatives
in 1854 as a Republican, he
served in Washington, D.C.,
through the first year of the Civil
War and was a delegate at the 1861 WASHINGTON PEACE CON-
FERENCE.

LC

Washburn raised the 2d Wisconsin Cavalry, mustered in as
its colonel 6 Feb. 1862, and went on duty with the ARMY OF
THE SOUTHWEST, serving in Missouri and the Helena, Ark., area.
Promoted to brigadier general 16 July 1862, he led the 3d
Cavalry Division in the District of Eastern Arkansas, transferred
to Tennessee early in 1863, led the YAZOO PASS EXPEDITION in
February, won promotion to major general 13 Mar. 1863, and
as commander of the 1st Cavalry Division/XVI Corps took part
in the operations around Vicksburg. Late in June he briefly
commanded the 3 XVI Corps cavalry divisions and, following
the surrender of Vicksburg, on 28 July assumed command of
the XIII Corps, transferring with it to the Department of the
Gulf.

Much of Washburn's remaining service was administrative.
On 17 Apr. 1864, he took command of the District of West
Tennessee, dispatched cavalry to duel with Confederate Maj.
Gen. NATHAN B. FORREST, took command of the District of
Vicksburg, then returned to West Tennessee Mar. 1865. He
resigned his commission 25 May 1865 and returned to his
considerable business interests.

In postwar years Washburn lived in La Crosse, Wisc.,
amassed a notable fortune, served in the U.S. House of Representatives 1867–71, won the Wisconsin governorship, serving
until 1873, and founded Washburn, Crosby & Co., which
became the General Mills Corporation. He suffered a severe
stroke in 1881, and on 14 May 1882 died while taking the
waters at Eureka Springs, Ark.   —JES

Washburn, Israel. war governor b. Livermore, Maine, 6
June 1813. After attending local schools, Washburn became a
legal apprentice to his uncle, Ruel Washburn. Passing the bar
in 1834, he practiced law in Orono, Maine, served 2 terms in
the Maine house of representatives, was elected to the U.S.
House Mar. 1851, and was reelected to 4 additional terms.
During this period, he became an outspoken critic of SLAVERY,
opposing the KANSAS-NEBRASKA ACT and other legislation aimed
at compromise and appeasement of the South.

In Sept. 1860 Washburn was elected governor of Maine on
the Republican ticket. Running again the following year, he
easily defeated 2 Democratic candidates and took office 2 Jan.
1861. When war broke out 3 months later, the governor began
filling the president's call for troops and received permission
from the Lincoln administration to raise 3,000 militia for home
defense. He established a coast guard and began building harbor fortifications. Concerned with growing Confederate senti-

ment in Canada, he requested defenses be built along the
border; however, the War Department refused him permission
for these.

During his time in office, Washburn also instituted a program
of state improvement, selling 1 million acres of land for the
completion of a railroad linking Maine and Nova Scotia and
authorizing a geological survey of the state.

Washburn refused to run for a third term and left office Jan.
1863. Appointed collector of customs in Portland, he held this
position until 1877, when he resigned to serve as president of
trustees at Tufts College in Massachusetts. In Mar. 1878 he was
made president of the Rumfield Falls & Buckfield Railroad. He
died in Philadelphia, Pa., 12 May 1883 and was buried in
Bangor, Maine. Washburn was the brother of Union Maj. Gen.
CADWALLADER C. WASHBURN and Union politician ELIHU B.
WASHBURNE.   —MTC

Washburne, Elihu Benjamin. USP b. Livermore, Maine,
23 Sept. 1816. Brother of ISRAEL and CADWALLADER WASHBURN,
Elihu B. Washburne left home at age 17, added an *e* to his last
name (after an old family spelling), and briefly pursued teaching and work in the printing trade before obtaining an education at Maine Wesleyan Seminary and Harvard Law School.
He left Harvard, passed the state bar in 1840, moved to
Galena, Ill., practiced law, and as a Whig was defeated in his
bid for the U.S. Congress in 1848.

Washburne won Galena's seat in the House of Representa-
tives in 1852, became a Republican, and at the outset of the
Civil War was chairman of the House Commerce Committee.
He served in Congress until 1869, a RADICAL REPUBLICAN ally
of THADDEUS STEVENS, a conservative guardian of the national
Treasury, a political supporter of Treasury Sec. SALMON P.
CHASE, and, in the early months of the Civil War, an adviser to
Pres. ABRAHAM LINCOLN on Illinois Republican affairs.

He is best remembered as ULYSSES S. GRANT's congressional
sponsor. Illinois authorities, who were allowed to appoint 4
brigadier generals in 1861, had named 3 and had given the
privilege of awarding the fourth to Washburne. A resident of
Galena, Grant had extensive military experience, and Washburne, disregarding Grant's personal difficulties, gave him the
commission. Later, in Congress he sponsored the revival of the
rank of lieutenant general and its award to Grant.

In postwar years, Washburne was one of Pres. ANDREW
JOHNSON's most vocal critics and worked arduously for his
impeachment. He then advised Grant during the latter's presidential campaign, won appointment as secretary of state to
Grant in 1869, and resigned after 1 week. Grant had made the
appointment to compliment Washburne and had expected the
resignation. Appointed U.S. minister to France, Washburne
served in Paris through autumn 1877, then retired to Illinois,
where he wrote *Recollections of a Minister to France, 1869–
1877* (1887), and served as president of the Chicago Historical
Society from 1884 until his death in Chicago, 23 Oct. 1887.
                                                  —JES

Washington, Union defenses of. Maj. Gen. GEORGE B.
MCCLELLAN is accorded much of the credit for creating the
system of defenses that made Washington, D.C., virtually impregnable. When McClellan assumed command of the ARMY
OF THE POTOMAC July 1861, the general, a superb organizer,
initiated an extensive training of the raw volunteers and the
erection of the city's defenses. "Little Mac" selected and en-

LC

trusted with most of the fortification work Maj. JOHN G. BAR-
NARD, a Regular engineer officer. Barnard, the "true father of
the defenses," directed the extensive work. By the end of
1861, 37 mi of unbroken lines encircled the Union capital.

The expansion and refinement of the fortifications continued
throughout the remainder of the conflict. Eventually 20 mi of
rifle pits intersected with the 60 enclosed forts and 93 batteries
of 762 heavy guns and 74 mortars.

Responsibility for garrisoning the forts, batteries, and rifle
pits ultimately belonged to the commander and troops in the
DEPARTMENT OF WASHINGTON. Reconstituted 2 Feb. 1863, this
department, also designated the XXII Corps, existed until 11
June 1866. During this period Maj. Gens. SAMUEL P. HEINTZEL-
MAN and CHRISTOPHER C. AUGUR commanded the department,
most of whose garrison troops were not combat-tested veterans.

The security of the capital and Pres. ABRAHAM LINCOLN'S
sensitivity over its safety affected some Eastern campaigns.
When McClellan undertook his 1862 PENINSULA CAMPAIGN, he
and Lincoln disagreed over the number of soldiers required to
protect the capital. The president prevailed and relations between the two soured. Any officer who commanded the Army
of the Potomac, which generally operated between the capital
and the Confederate ARMY OF NORTHERN VIRGINIA, had to assure, above all else, the safety of Washington.

The only serious threat to the capital occurred July 1864,
when Lt. Gen. JUBAL A. EARLY'S Confederates invaded Maryland
and arrived opposite the capital's defenses on the 11th. Early
probed the works near FORT STEVENS but, when veterans of the
VI Corps arrived to fill the entrenchments, the Confederate
general withdrew to Virginia. The work begun by McClellan
and Barnard had evolved into the most powerful fortifications
of any city in the U.S.   —JDW

Washington, Union Department of.   Lt. Gen. WINFIELD
SCOTT'S General Orders No. 3, dated 19 Apr. 1861, established the Union Department of Washington, originally conceived 9 Apr. 1861. Encompassing the District of Columbia
and the states of Maryland, Delaware, and Pennsylvania, the
department was immediately found to be ungainly. On 27 Apr.
Adj. Gen. LORENZO THOMAS' General Orders No. 12 redefined
the department to include Washington; Georgetown; Alexandria, Va.; Fort Washington and environs; and all of Maryland
south of Bladensburg. Col. JOSEPH K. F. MANSFIELD assumed
departmental command the same day, serving until the department was absorbed into the MILITARY DIVISION OF THE POTOMAC
25 July. The division was defined Mar. 1862 as comprising
Washington and Alexandria; its commander was Brig. Gen.
JAMES S. WADSWORTH.

Departmental status for the city returned 2 Feb. 1863, with

Washington artillerists   LC

Maj. Gen. SAMUEL P. HEINTZELMAN assuming command 7 Feb., and the XXII Corps manning its defenses. This structure remained, later under Maj. Gen. CHRISTOPHER C. AUGUR, until 27 June 1865, when it was redefined anew to include the District of Columbia, all surrounding Maryland counties and Fairfax Cty., Va.   —JES

Washington Artillery. CSA The Washington Artillery of New Orleans had several years' experience when the war broke out. Organized in 1838, and manned and led by the best of Creole society, the unit comprised 5 companies ready to fight when the firing began in 1861.

The unit's service in the war with Mexico could not compare with its wide-reaching activity during the Civil War. Accepted into the Confederate army May 1861, the first 4 companies went immediately to Virginia to take part in FIRST BULL RUN under the command of Col. James B. Walton. Thereafter the Washington Artillery remained with the ARMY OF NORTHERN VIRGINIA throughout all of its major campaigns. After leaving New Orleans, the Fifth company followed the ARMY OF TENNESSEE from SHILOH through to the Carolinas (see CAROLINAS CAMPAIGN).

Armed mostly with cannon captured from the Baton Rouge Arsenal early in 1861, the companies used them effectively in every major engagement of the war. The artillery was regarded as one of the premier volunteer artillery units in the Confederate army. Once the war was over, the organization continued to serve, first in the war with Spain in 1898 and later in both world wars.   —WCD

Washington, D.C. In 1861, nearly 70 years after it was begun, the capital of the U.S. remained incomplete—a raw, young city with much growth to accomplish. Shabby busi-

nesses, saloons, and boardinghouses shared the unpaved streets with imposing government buildings. The canals reeked of open sewage, the Capitol's dome stood uncapped, and the Washington Monument loomed as little more than an auspicious base. For decades the government had ceased to function during summer as presidents, congressmen, senators, justices, and hordes of workers and civilians fled from the city to escape the effects of its surrounding swamps. But the Civil War, as it did to much of America, transformed the capital that antebellum Americans called Washington City.

From the firing on FORT SUMTER, S.C., the war became the abiding, central fact of the city's life. During the conflict's early days, fear wrenched the capital as Southern sympathizers in Maryland attempted to isolate the city (see BALTIMORE RIOTS). Order and relief returned when the first of thousands of Union volunteers poured into the district, but in July the Union rout at FIRST BULL RUN produced near-panic. During the following months, tens of thousands of drilling soldiers and sprawling earthworks brought security to the city (see WASHINGTON, UNION DEFENSES OF). Washington, D.C., like its Confederate counterpart, RICHMOND, Va., 100 mi to the south, became a nation's symbol, the one place that could not be surrendered to the enemy.

The war brought unparalleled growth, bustle, and problems. The city's population quadrupled from 41,000 in 1860 to 160,000 at its wartime peak. With the advent of Northerners, the city's distinctive antebellum Southern atmosphere changed to that of a thriving city, riding the crest of the wartime wave. Besides the regiments of soldiers who daily marched through the streets, throngs of lobbyists, speculators, inventors, and job seekers poured in, each looking for a share of the money to be made in the wartime economy. Boardinghouses bulged, and at Willard's Hotel, a famous watering hole, officers, politicians, and civilians mingled day and night.

The influx generated vice and crime. JOHN HAY, Pres. ABRAHAM LINCOLN's personal secretary, said that "this miserable sprawling village imagines itself a city because it is wicked." Drunken soldiers and civilians filled the streets, seeking another thriving saloon or ever-present prostitutes. A reported 163 gambling houses fleeced their share of the wartime boom; one congressman, breaking the bank, left one gambling den on a single night with $100,000. But as the war progressed, the city became cleaner and better policed.

The mood of the city's inhabitants reflected the fortunes of Union armies: euphoria after a victory, despair following a defeat. The war was never far away. Numerous private residences, taken over by the Federal government, became hospitals, teeming with wounded young men. Crippled veterans, without arms or legs, daily reminded the populace of the war's cost.

Events within the capital also marked the mood of its residents: the death of Lincoln's son Willie, the marriage of Sec. of the Treasury SALMON P. CHASE's vivacious daughter Kate to Rhode Island's governor, WILLIAM SPRAGUE, which was the social event of the period. Workmen finally completed the Capitol's dome in time for Lincoln's second inaugural. Finally, late in May 1865, the country's 2 major armies marched in a GRAND REVIEW down Pennsylvania Avenue in a city irrevocably altered by 4 years of conflict.   —JDW

Washington Peace Conference. From 4 to 27 Feb. 1861, delegates from both North and South met in Washington's Willard Hotel in hope of averting war. The conference had been proposed by the Virginia legislature earlier that year as a means by which opposing factions might reach a compromise on the question of slavery. ABRAHAM LINCOLN expected nothing to come of it. And after it had ended, Gen. WINFIELD SCOTT called it a "collection of visionaries and fanatics"; Adam Gurowski, Washington gadfly, saw it as a "Southern plot"; and the New York *Herald* labeled many of the delegates "political fossils."

There was not enough spirit of compromise to make the conference a success. Discussions began with only two-thirds of the states represented; 6 from the Lower South sent no delegates, nor were Arkansas, California, Michigan, Minnesota, Oregon, Texas, or Wisconsin represented. The roster included such distinguished Americans as Joshua Bell, GEORGE S. BOUTWELL, Thomas Ewing, Stephen Logan, REVERDY JOHNSON, CALEB B. SMITH, and DAVID WILMOT. John Tyler, tenth president of the U.S., was president of the conference, JAMES A. SEDDON of Virginia its managing director.

With the 7 slave states outnumbered 2-to-1, their representatives were defensive and, at times, belligerent. Some Northern governors had given their delegates instructions so specific that they became obstacles to agreement. The intransigent attitudes taken by different factions long before the conference began could not be expected to change when brought together in one room.

After more than 20 days of interminable debate, accusations, and lengthy lectures, the conference drafted 7 proposals to be considered by Congress as Article 13 of the amendments to the Constitution. Though they satisfied no one, the proposals were submitted 27 Feb. to a Congress that was to adjourn in 3 days. The House and Senate rejected them, substantiating what Lincoln had thought would happen.   —AG

Washington Territory. Created by Congress in 1852, Washington Territory on the eve of the Civil War included the present-day states of Washington and Idaho and the northwestern corner of the present-day state of Montana. Far from the Eastern and Southern battlefields, the people of Washington Territory nevertheless took a keen interest in the conflict. Leading military figures on both sides had been stationed in Washington before the war (ULYSSES S. GRANT had served at Fort Vancouver in 1853), and the territory's leading Democratic politician, governor and later delegate to Congress ISAAC INGALLS STEVENS, joined the Northern army shortly after the attack on FORT SUMTER, losing his life at CHANTILLY in 1862.

There had never been much support for SLAVERY in Washington, and there was correspondingly little sympathy for the secessionists. JAMES I. WADDELL, captain of the Confederate raider *SHENANDOAH,*, did little to win the South more friends in the territory when he sailed his ship into the northern Pacific, capturing 38 American merchant ships and burning or scuttling all but 8.

There were, of course, a few Confederate supporters in Washington. Hoping to weaken the Union, they proposed that Washington and Oregon (and possibly California) be organized into an independent Pacific Republic with a government modeled after that of the Confederate States. The idea of the Pacific Republic was an old one, dating as far back as the 1840s, but there had never been much support for it. Revived during the war, the idea was again soundly squelched.

Though there was no fighting in Washington Territory, local residents did what they could to aid the Union cause. Women made and sent clothing and hospital supplies to the East, while men organized volunteer military units to provide protection against Indian attacks and garrison local forts left weakened when Regular Army units were called to more urgent duty in the East.   —BMcG

Waterhouse, Richard. CSA b. Rhea Cty., Tenn., 12 Jan. 1832, Waterhouse ran away from home to fight in the Mexican War. On his return, he moved with his parents in 1849 to San Augustine, Tex., working with his father in the family business until the Civil War. On 13 May 1862, he was commissioned colonel of the 19th Texas, a regiment he had helped recruit, and through 1863 he served in Arkansas and Louisiana. At Milliken's Bend, La., 18 Aug. 1862, he won high commendations from Brig. Gen. HENRY E. MCCULLOCH for leading a determined charge against Federal troops within artillery range of Union gunboats. Commanding a regiment in Brig.

LC

Gen. WILLIAM R. SCURRY's brigade/Maj. Gen. JOHN G. WALKER's division, Waterhouse participated in the battles at MANSFIELD and PLEASANT HILL during the RED RIVER CAMPAIGN in spring 1864, being singled out for praise by Lt. Gen. RICHARD TAYLOR.

Favorably impressed, Gen. E. KIRBY SMITH, commanding the TRANS-MISSISSIPPI DEPARTMENT, appointed Waterhouse brigadier general to rank from 30 Apr. 1864. The promotion was not confirmed by Pres. JEFFERSON DAVIS until 17 Mar. 1865 or by the Confederate Senate until the 18th, the last day the legislators were in session before the government collapsed.

In postwar years Waterhouse lived in San Antonio and in Jefferson, Tex., where he speculated in land. He died 20 Mar. 1876 from pneumonia contracted after falling down a set of hotel stairs on a trip to Waco. His body was returned to Jefferson for burial.   —PLF

Watie, Stand. CSA b. near present-day Rome, Ga., 12 Dec. 1806. The only Indian to become a brigadier general in the Confederate Army, Watie was one of the signers of the 1835 treaty in which Cherokees gave up their Georgia lands and moved to Oklahoma. Watie became a successful planter in his new home, and when the Cherokee Nation divided politically, he became the leader of the minority faction.

At the outbreak of the Civil War the Cherokees remained neutral, but after the Confederate victory at WILSON'S CREEK, Mo., in 1861, Watie influenced his followers to ally with the Confederacy. He raised a Cherokee volunteer regiment called the Cherokee Mounted Rifles and was appointed its colonel by the Confederate government.

A daring cavalry raider, Watie employed hit-and-run tactics so effectively that he became known as a genius at guerrilla warfare against Union forces, including pro-Union Indians, in Indian Territory. By summer 1864 the major part of the war waged by Confederates in the territory was guerrilla-style fighting under the command of Watie, a brigadier general since 6 May 1864. One of his successes was his capture of the Union steamer *J. R. Williams* in June. The Federals, attempting to ship provisions up the Arkansas River from FORT SMITH to Fort Blunt, loaded the steamer with $120,000 worth of supplies. At Pleasant Bluff, Watie and his Cherokees surprised the vessel and its escort of 26 soldiers, sweeping the *J. R. Williams* with artillery and musket fire. The steamer was beached across the river from Watie's force, and the Union soldiers retreated to Fort Smith, leaving the valuable cargo for the guerrillas. Watie's success in such raids bolstered the morale of Confederate forces in the West and brought praises to the Cherokee leader from the Confederacy's high command.

Watie was the last Confederate general to surrender his command (see SURRENDERS: Brig. Gen. Stand Watie). The war had been over for a month when he finally gave up his sword to the Federals 23 June 1865. d. Delaware Cty., Okla., 9 Sept. 1871.　　—PR

Watts, Thomas Hill. war governor　b. near present-day Greenville, Ala., 3 Jan. 1819, Watts, the most prolific of Confederate attorney generals, wrote 100 opinions on the interpretation of Confederate laws. He

graduated from the University of Virginia in 1840, then established a law practice in Alabama. Becoming involved in state politics, he represented Butler County in the state legislature until he moved his practice to the city of Montgomery in 1846 and was elected to represent Montgomery County. As a Whig, Watts opposed secession in 1850 and supported Constitutional Unionist John Bell in the 1860 election. After ABRAHAM LINCOLN's election

NA

Watts became a secessionist, an ally of Southern radical WILLIAM LOWNDES YANCEY, and played an important role in the Alabama secession convention.

He organized the 17th Alabama and served as its colonel at Pensacola and Corinth until called to the position of attorney general 17 Mar. 1862. Since the Confederate courts had been set up by his predecessor, THOMAS BRAGG, much of Watts's time was spent giving legal opinions and hearing claims against the government. His most important opinions were those given on the legal problems of enforcing the Conscription Act, which he held to be constitutional since complete power had been given the central government for the nation's defense. In most cases Pres. JEFFERSON DAVIS backed Watts's decisions, even though other cabinet members questioned them.

Though Watts felt the establishment of a CONFEDERATE SUPREME COURT was important, all attempts were scuttled by the Confederate Congress. Thus the Confederacy was forced to rely on state courts and the attorney general's opinion to decide the constitutionality of laws. Watts's deep regard for state

and local laws was reflected in his advice to the president that martial law should be used only in true emergencies. Watts had a high opinion of Davis, who hated to lose him when he resigned 8 Sept. 1863 after being elected governor of Alabama.

Although he had once supported CONSCRIPTION laws, as governor Watts considered them an encroachment by the Confederacy on the rights of individual states. He became angry when members of the state militia and administration were drafted although supposedly exempt. But he continued optimistically to support the cause and claimed in spring 1865 that the South was better off than the year before.

That same spring the war ended and Watts was sent to a Northern prison. On his release he returned to his law practice in Montgomery, Ala., where he died 16 Sept. 1892.

　　—CMS

Waud, Alfred Rodolph. artist　b. England, 1828. The most prolific of the Civil War combat artists, Waud migrated to America in 1850, worked as an illustrator of periodicals and books until, at the outbreak of war, he joined the staff of the New York *Illustrated News* as a field artist, or "special." With pencil and sketchbook he reported the opening months of the war and was present at FIRST BULL RUN, where, though caught up in the headlong Union rout, he was able to bring back his first battle sketches for reproduction as woodcuts in the *News*. In Oct. 1861 he accompanied the Union fleet in its attack on HATTERAS INLET.

LC

Early in 1862 Waud joined the staff of *HARPER'S WEEKLY* and remained throughout the war its most popular "special," following the ARMY OF THE POTOMAC on all its major campaigns. He was on the field at ANTIETAM, pictured Maj. Gen. AMBROSE E. BURNSIDE's debacle at FREDERICKSBURG, and was present at CHANCELLORSVILLE, SECOND BULL RUN, and GETTYSBURG. As the war ground on, Waud continued to be in the thick of the battle, in the WILDERNESS with Lt. Gen. ULYSSES S. GRANT's army and, with his brother, field artist William Waud, at the Siege of Petersburg, where he dodged snipers' bullets. At APPOMATTOX in 1865 he sketched Gen. ROBERT E. LEE leaving the McLean house after the final surrender.

Waud continued with *Harper's* as an artist-reporter during the latter 1860s, producing an historic series of drawings of the postwar South on a trip down the Mississippi to New Orleans.

While sketching the battlefields of Georgia in 1891 he was stricken by a heart attack and died in Marietta.　　—FR

Wauhatchie night attack, Tenn.　28–29 Oct. 1863　As a part of the CRACKER LINE OPERATION, the Brown's Ferry bridgehead on the Tennessee River, opposite Chattanooga, was established 27 Oct. Marching from Bridgeport, Ala., Union Maj. Gen. JOSEPH HOOKER's force passed through Lookout Valley 28 Oct. and that morning left behind Brig. Gen. JOHN W. GEARY's 2d Division/XII Corps at Wauhatchie Station, a stop in the valley along the Nashville & Chattanooga Railroad. At Wauhatchie, a little over 3 mi southwest of Brown's Ferry and the camps of Hooker's troops, Geary was to guard the line of communications south and a road west to Kelley's Ferry on the Tennessee River.

Confederates were surprised by the establishment of the Brown's Ferry bridge. Confederate Brig. Gen. EVANDER M. LAW's brigade was pulled from in front of Brown's Ferry Federals 27 Oct. and positioned on the west side of Lookout Mountain, and 28 Oct. Lt. Gen. JAMES LONGSTREET observed the passage of Hooker's troops below Law's brigade and Geary's detachment to Wauhatchie. Meeting with Gen. BRAXTON BRAGG that day, Longstreet determined to use Law's brigade and 3 others brought from the east face of Lookout Mountain to attack Geary that night and cut off Hooker's rear. The 4 brigades, from a division commanded by Brig. Gen. MICAH JENKINS, moved at dusk. Law's brigade descended the mountain and occupied a small hill overlooking the road running northeast from Wauhatchie. The brigades of Brig. Gens. HENRY L. BENNING and JEROME B. ROBERTSON and Col. JOHN BRATTON interposed themselves in the valley between the Wauhatchie Federals and Law's brigade. Robertson's troops joined Law's, facing northeast to oppose Union reinforcement. Benning's stood off to the east as reserve. Though the assault was scheduled to begin at 10 p.m., confusion resulting from the darkness delayed it until midnight, when Bratton's troops attacked Geary from the north and east.

Capturing Union pickets and killing sentries, the Confederates surprised Geary. Federal troops kicked out campfires and were formed in a V-shaped battle line, its right facing east along the railroad line, its left facing north. 1 regiment was sent west to cover the route to Kelley's Ferry, and (Joseph M.) Knap's battery was deployed in Geary's rear. A squad of Confederate sharpshooters worked in behind the Federals and fired on the artillerists throughout the fight. In the dark the muzzle flashes of small arms made the only targets as the moon was periodically covered by heavy clouds.

At Brown's Ferry Hooker heard the fighting and dispatched 2 of Maj. Gen. OLIVER O. HOWARD's divisions to Geary's aid. Marching to the sound of the firing, Union Brig. Gen. HECTOR TYNDALE's troops were the first to clash with Law's and Robertson's brigades. Benning joined the Confederate rear guard and the firing became general along the line. As more Federals arrived from Brown's Ferry, at 3 a.m. Jenkins, commanding on the field, ordered all to retire to Lookout Mountain. Elements of Robertson's brigade covered the withdrawal.

Descriptions of the Wauhatchie night attack are inconsistent, due to the confusion of the participants themselves. Displeased with 2 reinforcing brigades that claimed to have become lost on the way to Geary's relief, Hooker chastised division commander Maj. Gen. CARL SCHURZ, who requested a court of inquiry and was absolved of charges of incompetence. Similarly, Longstreet preferred charges against Law, claiming that he showed little enthusiasm and was the individual who ordered withdrawal. Law claimed he was ordered to retire. Longstreet also told War Department officials that the officers did not seem to appreciate the vigor required in a night attack and impugned the fighting quality of Jenkins' command. The charges against Law were dropped as there was no time for a formal court-martial.   —JES

Waul, Thomas Neville. CSA/CSP b. Sumter District, S.C., 5 Jan. 1813, Waul studied at South Carolina College for

3 years, leaving to teach school in Florence, Ala. He then moved to Vicksburg, Miss., where he read law and was admitted to the bar in 1835. Establishing himself in Gonzales Cty., Tex., he opened a practice and ran a successful plantation. An unsuccessful Democratic candidate for the U.S. House of Representatives in 1854, Waul championed secession in Texas as the sectional crisis intensified.

LC

After serving as a delegate to the state secession convention, he was elected to the Provisional Confederate Congress Jan. 1861. Waul backed the legislation proposed to establish the central government and deal with the military emergency, and he favored making provisions for local defense and free trade. Since the Confederacy wished to establish trade relations with Europe, and antislavery sentiments there were strong, Waul also favored as a compromise a provision that would allow slave importations from any country except Africa. He opposed the administration on all measures that would have restricted the cotton trade (see COTTON DIPLOMACY).

When he lost his bid for a seat in the Regular Confederate Congress, Waul recruited Waul's Texas Legion and was commissioned colonel of the unit 17 May 1862. He and his men were sent to Mississippi during the assault on Vicksburg and were surrendered there when the city fell. Maj. Gen. STEPHEN D. LEE commended Waul for his effective leadership during the campaign, praise contributing to his promotion to brigadier general 18 Sept. 1863, after his exchange. Sent to Louisiana in 1864, Waul held brigade command in Maj. Gen. JOHN G. WALKER's division during the RED RIVER CAMPAIGN. He ended the war in Arkansas opposing Federal Maj. Gen. FREDERICK STEELE in an engagement at JENKIN'S FERRY.

Waul was elected to the first Texas Reconstruction convention. He then practiced law in Galveston until retiring to his farm near Greenville, where he died 28 July 1908.   —PLF

Wayne, Henry Constantine. CSA b. Savannah, Ga., 18 Sept. 1815. The son of a former congressman and mayor of Savannah, Wayne was educated at Harvard 1832–34 before receiving an appointment to the U.S. MILITARY ACADEMY. He graduated from West Point in 1838, ranking 14th in his class. For some years he served in the 4th and 1st U.S. Artillery along the Canadian border, then taught TACTICS at his alma mater. An expert swordsman, in 1850 he published a text on saber exercises. In May 1846 he switched from line to staff, becoming a captain and assistant adjutant general and later a quartermaster officer. Nevertheless, in the Mexican War he won the brevet of major for gallant conduct at Contreras and Churubusco. On

LC

31 Dec. 1860, after studying the logistics of employing Egyptian camels as military mounts in the Southwest, he resigned his commission and offered his services to his native state.

Early in 1861 Wayne was appointed both adjutant general and inspector general of Georgia troops. For some months he served on the staff of Gov. JOSEPH E. BROWN until 16 Dec., when he was appointed a brigadier general in the CONFEDERATE PROVISIONAL ARMY. The next month, after receiving orders to report to Gen. JOSEPH E. JOHNSTON near Manassas Junction, Va., Wayne relinquished his newest commission and returned to state service. For the rest of the conflict he served as a major general of Georgia troops, discharging his adjutant general's duties with efficiency, economy, and precision. He also served creditably in the field during the first month of the ATLANTA CAMPAIGN, commanding 2 brigades of GEORGIA MILITIA and state troops called out for local defense. His principal job, in cooperation with Johnston's ARMY OF TENNESSEE, was to guard the crossing of the CHATTAHOOCHEE RIVER from Roswell to West Point, a distance of 100 mi.

On 1 June 1864, Maj. Gen. GUSTAVUS W. SMITH relieved Wayne in field command, enabling the latter to resume his administrative duties at Milledgeville, which he conducted throughout the remainder of the war. Later he returned to his residence in Savannah, worked in the lumber business 1866–75, and labored to restore the prewar prosperity of his native city. He died there 15 Mar. 1883. —EGL

Waynesborough, Ga., eng. at. 4 Dec. 1864 Following his encounter with the troopers of Confederate Maj. Gen. JOSEPH "Fighting Joe" WHEELER at BUCK HEAD CREEK, Ga., Brig. Gen. H. JUDSON KILPATRICK spent 2 days resting his 3d Cavalry Division/Military Division of the Mississippi in the village of Louisville. His respite ended 1 Dec. 1864 when Maj. Gen. WILLIAM T. SHERMAN ordered him to attack Wheeler at every opportunity. Sherman wanted the Confederates pressed toward Augusta to create the false impression that the Union infantry would march there too.

Happy to oblige, Kilpatrick joined some of Sherman's foot soldiers in a limited encounter with the Confederate horsemen the next day at Rocky Creek. At Thomas' Station, on the 3d, Wheeler struck Union infantrymen wrecking parts of the railroad between Millen and Augusta, withdrawing to Waynesborough, about 30 mi below Augusta, before Kilpatrick could punish him for his audacity. That night, Kilpatrick issued orders for a march to Waynesborough early 4 Dec., "to attack and rout the command of Wheeler."

About 7:30 a.m. on the appointed day, Kilpatrick's leading unit, Col. Smith D. Atkins' brigade, met the Confederate vanguard a few miles below the town. After driving in Wheeler's skirmishers, Atkins discovered hundreds of their comrades ensconced behind barricades just south of Waynesborough. When an initial attack failed to dislodge them, the colonel brought up his HORSE ARTILLERY (which soon silenced the enemy's guns), trained the carbines of his 92d Illinois Mounted Infantry on the barricades, then charged the Confederate right with his 9th Michigan and 10th Ohio cavalry and the left flank with his 9th Ohio. After stubborn resistance, the Confederates fled north.

A brisk pursuit, punctuated by charges and countercharges, brought the Federals to a second stretch of barricades inside the town. Since the elongated line prevented another flank drive, Kilpatrick called up Col. Eli H. Murray's brigade and

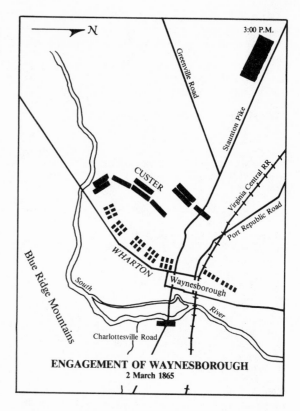

ENGAGEMENT OF WAYNESBOROUGH
2 March 1865

about midday threw it against Wheeler's front. Charged by Murray's 9th Pennsylvania and 2d, 3d, and 5th Kentucky cavalry, supported by the dismounted 8th Indiana, the Confederate line again crumbled. Within 20 minutes, Wheeler was fleeing across Brier Creek, 4 mi north of Waynesborough.

Wheeler later contended that he had bested Kilpatrick's troopers, falling back, and in good order, only because of the proximity of Sherman's infantry. By day's close, however, his opponents had inflicted more than 250 casualties (60 more than they absorbed), had burned several bridges over Brier Creek, and had thrust Wheeler's men toward Augusta. There they would remain until well after Sherman turned south toward Savannah. —EGL

Waynesborough, Va., eng. at. 2 Mar. 1865 On 27 Feb. 1865, 2 Federal cavalry divisions, numbering 10,000, cantered southward from Winchester. Directed by Lt. Gen. ULYSSES S. GRANT to destroy the Virginia Central Railroad and the James River Canal and capture Lynchburg, if possible, Maj. Gen. PHILIP H. SHERIDAN advanced, covering 30 mi the first day.

In Staunton, over 90 mi southward, Lt. Gen. JUBAL A. EARLY, commanding a remnant of his once-fearful army, endeavored to thwart Sheridan's movement. Throughout the 28th, fewer than 200 Confederate cavalry vainly sniped at the overpowering Union command. Only streams, swollen by winter freshets and icy rainstorms, hampered the Federal advance, which arrived at Staunton 1 Mar. The Federals found deserted streets and empty warehouses, their contents emptied by Early's troops.

Sheridan entered the town the next morning and ordered Maj. Gen. GEORGE A. CUSTER's horsemen in pursuit. Custer's troopers encountered Brig. Gen. GABRIEL C. WHARTON's 1,700 Confederates on a range of low hills in front of Waynesborough. With his back to a swollen river, Wharton stretched his line of troops to critical limits.

The enterprising Union cavalry officer carefully reconnoitered the Confederate position, discovering a gap of ⅛ mi between Wharton's left flank and the river. Shortly after 3:30 p.m., 3 dismounted Federal regiments knifed into the gap. The stunned Confederates managed to fire a few shots before running. A Federal brigade then galloped into Wharton's center, and the Confederate line dissolved. Early tried to rally his men before fleeing himself. In the rout, more than 1,600 Confederates were captured, along with nearly 200 wagons, 14 cannons, and 17 flags.

For the next 25 days Sheridan ravaged the area north of the James River before joining Grant at Petersburg. The engagement at Waynesborough closed the SHENANDOAH VALLEY chapter of the Civil War.   —JDW

Webb, Alexander Stewart. USA b. New York City, N.Y., 15 Feb. 1835. A son of James Watson Webb, renowned newspaper owner and diplomat, Alexander attended private schools before entering the U.S. MILITARY ACADEMY in 1851. Graduating 13th in the class of 1855, he fought against the Seminoles in Florida, then returned to West Point as instructor of mathematics. At the outbreak of the Civil War, Apr. 1861, Webb participated in the defense of FORT PICKENS, Fla.

LC

Assigned to Virginia, promoted to 1st lieutenant and subsequently captain, the New Yorker served as assistant to the chief of artillery of the ARMY OF THE POTOMAC, Brig. Gen. WILLIAM F. BARRY, during the FIRST BATTLE OF BULL RUN. He held this post until Apr. 1862, when Barry named him acting inspector general. During the ANTIETAM CAMPAIGN in September, Webb was chief of staff of the V Corps, and 2 months later was assigned to duty at Camp Barry in the DEFENSES OF WASHINGTON, D.C., as inspector of artillery. He returned to the V Corps as assistant inspector general Jan. 1863, participating in the CHANCELLORSVILLE CAMPAIGN in May.

Webb received his commission as brigadier general and command of a brigade in the II Corps 23 June 1863. On 3 July his 4 Pennsylvania regiments manned the angle formed by a stone wall north of a clump of trees in the center of the Union line. His position became the focal point of PICKETT'S CHARGE. In the savage action, Webb lost 451 men and was himself wounded. His conduct later earned him the MEDAL OF HONOR.

The brigadier temporarily commanded the 2d Division/II Corps during the operations at BRISTOE and MINE RUN, Va., and resumed command of his brigade in spring 1864, suffering a grievous wound at SPOTSYLVANIA in May. Returning to duty Jan. 1865, he served as Maj. Gen. GEORGE G. MEADE's chief of staff until the conclusion of hostilities.

Brevetted major general in the volunteer and Regular ser-

vices for his war record, Webb remained in the army until 1870. During his final tour of duty, he again instructed at West Point. After his honorable discharge, he became president of the College of the City of New York, a position he held for 33 years. d. Riverdale, N.Y., 11 Feb. 1911.   —JDW

Weed, Stephen Hinsdale. USA b. Potsdam, N.Y., 17 Nov. 1831. Graduating 27th in the West Point class of 1854, Weed served in the antebellum army on the frontier, in Florida and Kansas, and in the Utah Expedition. When the war began, he was promoted to captain of the 5th U.S. Artillery 14 May 1861 and assigned to Harrisburg, Pa.

LC

Weed joined the ARMY OF THE POTOMAC in spring 1862, commanding a battery during the PENINSULA and SEVEN DAYS' campaigns. At SECOND BULL RUN he directed the artillery of Brig. Gen. GEORGE SYKES's division. He returned to command of his battery at ANTIETAM, and was then named chief of artillery of the V Corps, supervising its batteries at FREDERICKSBURG and CHANCELLORSVILLE. On 6 June 1863, he was jumped in rank from captain to brigadier general and assigned an infantry brigade in the V Corps.

On the afternoon of 2 July, at GETTYSBURG, Pa., Weed's brigade received orders to move up the slopes of LITTLE ROUND TOP, where Col. STRONG VINCENT's brigade was clinging to the vital peak. His regiments stabilized Vincent's crumbling front and lengthened the line to the north. Weed personally saw to it that his men, by sheer strength, got a battery of 6 3-in. rifles up the rugged slope. A firestorm engulfed the summit as he directed the battery's fire. Like Vincent, he fell mortally wounded, a minié bullet passing through his arm into his chest. He died within a few hours.   —JDW

Weisiger, David Addison. CSA b. "The Grove," Chesterfield Cty., Va., 23 Dec. 1818. A veteran of the Mexican War, serving as a 2d lieutenant, 1st Virginia Volunteers, Weisiger became a businessman in Petersburg, Va., and a captain in the Virginia militia, acting as officer of the day at the execution of radical abolitionist JOHN BROWN Dec. 1859. On 9 May 1861, after his state seceded, Weisiger entered the Confederate army as colonel of the 12th Virginia.

During the war's first year the regiment served on the lower Peninsula, being assigned in spring 1862 to the brigade of Brig. Gen. WILLIAM MAHONE. Weisiger fought under Mahone

LC

at SEVEN PINES and in the SEVEN DAYS' and SECOND BULL RUN campaigns. Falling dangerously wounded in the latter fighting, he was out of the war until July 1863.

Weisiger again commanded the 12th Virginia, until 6 May 1864, when he succeeded Mahone as brigade commander during the Battle of the WILDERNESS. He then led the veteran unit at SPOTSYLVANIA and COLD HARBOR. Commissioned brigadier general with temporary rank from 31 May, he was in the lines at Petersburg, Va., 30 July when the Federals exploded their mine. He and Mahone directed the vicious Confederate counterattack that resulted in the Battle of the CRATER and a decisive Southern victory. Wounded in the charge, Weisiger received a battlefield promotion to permanent rank for his skillful performance. He ultimately surrendered with his brigade at Appomattox.

Weisiger returned after the war to Petersburg, the city he had so gallantly defended, and became a bank cashier. He eventually moved to Richmond, engaged in business, and died in the former Confederate capital 23 Feb. 1899.   —JDW

Weitzel, Godfrey. USA b. Cincinnati, Ohio, 1 Nov. 1835, Weitzel had a public-school education; won appointment to West Point, graduating 2d in the class of 1855; and, commissioned 2d lieutenant of engineers, worked on the defenses of New Orleans, La., until appointment to the West Point faculty as an assistant professor of engineering 2 Sept. 1859.

A 1st lieutenant at the outbreak of the Civil War, Weitzel worked as an engineer in the WASHINGTON, D.C., DEFENSES and joined the relief expedition to FORT PICKENS, Fla., Apr. 1861. Returning north in September, he was chief engineer of the fortifications of Cincinnati, then commanded an engineering

LC

company in Washington. On 23 Feb. 1862, for operations against New Orleans, he was appointed Maj. Gen. BENJAMIN F. BUTLER's chief engineer. On the city's capture, he briefly assumed mayoral duties, then won commission as brigadier general of Federal volunteers 29 Aug. 1862 and command of combat troops for the pacification of the Lafourche District in September.

At the head of the Reserve Brigade/Army of the Gulf, he took part in engagements at Labadieville and Thibodeaux, La., in October, then joined Maj. Gen. NATHANIEL P. BANKS's force for the Apr. 1863 Battle of FORT BISLAND and the reduction of PORT HUDSON in July. Briefly assuming command of the 1st Division/XIX Corps 15 July 1863, he led the failed Sept. 1863 assault on Sabine Pass, Tex., and campaigned in western Louisiana. He transferred to Butler's ARMY OF THE JAMES in spring 1864, led the 2d Division/XVIII Corps, and served as Butler's chief engineer. On 1 Oct. 1864, Weitzel took command of the XVIII Corps, with promotion to major general 17 Nov. 1864.

Given leadership of the all-black XXV Corps 3 Dec., he retained this command until being mustered out of volunteer service 1 Mar. 1866. During this period he took part in the Petersburg siege, the Dec. 1864 Fort Fisher operations, and the occupation of Richmond, Va., 3 Apr. 1865.

Weitzel's association with political generals Banks and Butler impeded his professional army career. In postwar years he reverted to the rank of captain of engineers in the Regulars, was

promoted to major Mar. 1866, worked on navigational projects in the Great Lakes region, and received his lieutenant colonelcy 23 June 1882. In poor health, he assumed light duties in Philadelphia, Pa., and died there 19 Mar. 1884.

—JES

Weldon Railroad Operations. 22 June–21 Aug. 1864
On 4 successive days, 15–18 June 1864, the Union ARMY OF THE POTOMAC launched assaults against Confederate defenses at Petersburg, Va. These bungled attacks failed, squandering an excellent opportunity to capture the railroad center and shorten the war. When Gen. ROBERT E. LEE's ARMY OF NORTHERN VIRGINIA arrived to man the works, Lt. Gen. ULYSSES S. GRANT, directing the Union army, concluded that the city could not be taken by assault. Petersburg would have to be invested by siege and its vital railroads severed. Grant's decision established the pattern of the 10-month-long PETERSBURG CAMPAIGN.

Grant decided almost immediately to advance on the railroads linking Petersburg to the Southern coast and heartland. The Weldon Railroad, connecting Petersburg to North Carolina, lay closest to the Union army's line, and Grant ordered an operation against it 4 days after the final Union assault recoiled before the city's defenders. The Northern commander committed a cavalry division and 2 infantry corps toward the success of the movement.

On 22 June Maj. Gens. DAVID B. BIRNEY's II Corps and HORATIO G. WRIGHT's VI Corps, rimmed by Brig. Gen. JAMES H. WILSON's horsemen, marched against the railroad. The Union infantry corps groped through the heavily wooded terrain, creating a dangerous gap between the 2 units. When Confederate Lt. Gen. AMBROSE P. HILL learned of the movement, he responded immediately. Discovering the gap between the 2 Union corps, Hill sent Maj. Gen. CADMUS M. WILCOX's division to occupy Wright on the Federal left while Maj. Gens. WILLIAM MAHONE's and BUSHROD R. JOHNSON's infantry divisions attacked Birney.

Their attack ripped into the exposed flank of the II Corps, as Maj. Gen. JOHN GIBBON's Union division staggered under the Confederate charge. The Southerners captured 1,600 Federals and shoved Gibbon back on the rest of the corps. The next day Birney and Wright recovered the lost ground, but the operation failed to sever the railroad. The 2 corps, losing 2,962 men in the 2 days, retained their position across the Jerusalem Plank Road.

Grant suspended efforts against the Weldon Railroad for 8 weeks. In mid-August the Union commander, hoping to draw Confederates from the SHENANDOAH VALLEY, ordered joint movements against the railroads north of the James River and against the Weldon. During the night of 14–15 Aug., Maj. Gen. GOUVERNEUR K. WARREN's V Corps abandoned its position in the Union lines and assembled behind the left, or western, flank of the army.

At 4 a.m., 18 Aug., Warren's 4 divisions advanced. Confronted only by a Confederate cavalry brigade, the Federals easily seized Globe Tavern on the railroad. While 1 division destroyed the track and another moved farther west, Warren moved Brig. Gen. ROMEYN B. AYRES's division north toward Petersburg. About 2 p.m. Maj. Gen. HENRY HETH's Confederate division slammed into Ayres's left flank, wrecking 1 brigade. Ayres regrouped and counterattacked, the 2 divisions fighting stubbornly in the dense woods during a heavy rain. Federal casualties amounted to 836 in the action.

During the night both Grant and Lee dispatched reinforcements to the vital railroad. Warren consolidated his position north of Globe Tavern throughout the morning and early afternoon. At 4:30 p.m. Hill hurled 5 infantry and 1 cavalry brigade against Ayres's and Maj. Gen. SAMUEL W. CRAWFORD's divisions. The Confederate assault pushed the Federals back. Warren rapidly counterattacked, recovered the ground, and the fighting subsided. He then withdrew from 1 to 2 mi to stronger defensive positions.

Skirmishing flared on the 20th as both opponents probed for weaknesses. The next day Hill attacked again but was repulsed by the new Federal works. Arriving that afternoon, Lee finally stopped the attacks against Warren, who had been reinforced by the IX Corps. The Battle of Weldon Railroad (Globe Tavern) cost the Federals 198 killed, 1,105 wounded and 3,152 missing, for a total of 4,455 of 20,289 engaged. About 14,000 Confederates were engaged, sustaining an estimated 1,600 casualties. The Federals, holding Globe Tavern, had permanently severed the railroad, an important supply artery for Lee's army and RICHMOND. —JDW

Welles, Gideon. USP b. Glastonbury, Conn., 1 July 1802, Welles completed studies at Norwich Academy in Vermont (*see* NORWICH UNIVERSITY) and turned to journalism and politics. A supporter of Andrew Jackson, he helped organize the Democratic party in Connecticut. Although a state legislator and later comptroller of public accounts, Welles failed in 3 attempts at higher elective office. In 1836 President Jackson appointed him postmaster of Hartford and, in 1846, Welles became head of the Naval Bureau of Provisions and Clothing. Strong antislavery feelings caused him to become a Republican in 1854, although years later he rejoined the Democrats. Thus Welles, a Republican moderate in 1860, was appointed navy secretary by Pres. ABRAHAM LINCOLN, serving in that post until 1869.

NA

Welles is rated an effective secretary of the navy despite his lack of naval background and some initial blunders. His able and energetic assistant, GUSTAVUS V. FOX, was a navy man, and together they revitalized the department. Welles was resourceful in securing a BLOCKADE fleet but slower to realize the potential of IRONCLADS. Once convinced of their value, however, he pushed for their construction. He also supported development of armored cruisers, heavy ordnance, and steam machinery. Quick to reprimand persons he believed negligent or incompetent, he thereby angered some high-ranking officers.

After retirement Welles continued speaking out on public issues and wrote articles and a book about the Lincoln administration. His most lasting contribution to Civil War historiography is the 3-volume *Diary of Gideon Welles* (1911). The diary is an opinionated, brilliant insider's account and analysis of events and personalities of the war years, but was edited by Welles to reflect favorably on himself. Although valuable, the diary must be read with care. d. Hartford, Conn., 11 Feb. 1878. —NCD

West, Confederate Army of the. On 2 Mar. 1862, Maj. Gen. EARL VAN DORN proclaimed the birth of the Confederacy's Army of the West. Van Dorn, whom Pres. JEFFERSON DAVIS reluctantly chose to command the TRANS-MISSISSIPPI DISTRICT, had grandiose plans. With Maj. Gen. STERLING PRICE's Missourians, Brig. Gen. BEN MCCULLOCH's Arkansas division, and Brig. Gen. ALBERT PIKE's Indian regiments, he intended to storm through Missouri, take St. Louis, and perhaps invade Illinois.

On 7 Mar. 1862, the Army of the West suffered a stinging defeat at PEA RIDGE, Ark., and the army retreated southward. That was but the first of setbacks that plagued this ill-starred army during its 9 months' existence.

Van Dorn took the army to Corinth, Miss., to aid in the defense of that key railroad junction, but Maj. Gen. HENRY W. HALLECK's Union army forced the Southerners out of Corinth, without a fight, on the night of 29–30 May 1862.

At that point Van Dorn's 20,000-man Army of the West was composed of Price's 1st Division, Maj. Gen. SAMUEL JONES's 2d Division, and Maj. Gen. JOHN P. MCCOWN's 3d Division. When Van Dorn was ordered to Vicksburg late in June, McCown assumed command for 2 weeks until Price was appointed commander of the army 3 July 1862 and took charge of operations in northern Mississippi and western Tennessee.

The army next saw action at IUKA, near Corinth, 19–20 Sept. 3 weeks later, 3–4 Oct. 1862, Price's Army of the West was the major element in Van Dorn's Army of West Tennessee, which clashed with Maj. Gen. WILLIAM S. ROSECRANS in the fierce Battle of CORINTH. Both of Price's divisions fought gallantly and with heavy losses: 505 killed, 2,150 wounded, and 4,838 captured or missing. The army retreated to Holly Springs, Miss., where, 26 Nov. 1862, it was merged with Maj. Gen. JOHN C. PEMBERTON's Vicksburg defenders and ceased to be a separate command. —DS

West, Confederate Department of the. Special Orders No. 235, dated 24 Nov. 1862, placed Gen. JOSEPH E. JOHNSTON in command of the newly created Department of the West. A geographical rather than an army command, the department included Gen. BRAXTON BRAGG's DEPARTMENT NO. 2, Lt. Gen. E. KIRBY SMITH's DEPARTMENT OF EAST TENNESSEE, Lt. Gen. JOHN C. PEMBERTON's DEPARTMENT OF MISSISSIPPI AND EAST LOUISIANA, northwestern Georgia, and a small section of northwestern South Carolina. Atlanta was added to Johnston's jurisdiction 29 Nov. 1862.

To halt Maj. Gen. ULYSSES S. GRANT's advances on VICKSBURG, the War Department ordered Johnston to coordinate operations of the 3 armies in his command; but the vastness of the territory, Johnston's uncertainty of his authority as commanding general, and his subordinates' unwillingness to cooperate ended in the surrender of Vicksburg and the loss of the Mississippi River to Federal forces 4 July 1863.

3 weeks later, 25 July, the Department of East Tennessee was added to the Department of the West. At the same time western North Carolina and Georgia west of the line running from Atlanta to West Point and south along the Chattahoochee River were added to the command. That September the battles for CHATTANOOGA were fought and lost by Bragg's ARMY OF TENNESSEE. Bragg was relieved of duty, replaced by Johnston in army command, and the Department of the West was discontinued 27 Dec. 1863. —PLF

West, Confederate Military Division of the.
Created 3 Oct. 1864, at the beginning of the FRANKLIN AND NASHVILLE CAMPAIGN, the Confederate Military Division of the West was composed of Gen. JOHN B. HOOD'S DEPARTMENT OF TENNESSEE AND GEORGIA and Lt. Gen. RICHARD TAYLOR'S DEPARTMENT OF ALABAMA, MISSISSIPPI, AND EAST LOUISIANA. It was placed under the command of Gen. P.G.T. BEAUREGARD, who was ordered to be available as an adviser during the Confederate invasion of Tennessee but not to interfere with the field commanders or to direct troops.

Twice in 1865 the division was expanded: first when the Department of Tennessee and Georgia was enlarged to include all of Georgia west of the line running from Augusta to Macon to Jacksonville, and again when all troops operating in South Carolina were added to Beauregard's command. The division continued to exist until the war ended, at which time Beauregard was serving as second-in-command to Gen. JOSEPH E. JOHNSTON.   —PLF

West, Joseph Rodman.
USA b. New Orleans, La., 19 Sept. 1822. Soon after his birth, West's family moved to Philadelphia, Pa., where he was educated at private schools and attended the University of Pennsylvania for 2 years. He returned to New Orleans in 1841, but served in the Mexican War as a captain of volunteers from Maryland and Washington, D.C. After the war he migrated to California, working there as a businessman and publisher.

LC

At the outbreak of Civil War, West was commissioned lieutenant colonel in the 1st California Volunteers, commanded by Col. JAMES H. CARLETON. In Oct. 1861 he led an expedition to occupy Fort Yuma and continued to operate under Carleton in the latter's campaign to regain New Mexico Territory for the Union (see SIBLEY'S NEW MEXICO CAMPAIGN and CALIFORNIA COLUMN). When Carleton was promoted to brigadier general, West replaced him as colonel of the 1st California, 1 June 1862, and was promoted to brigadier general 25 Oct. He led the Jan. 1863 expedition against the Gila Apaches in which the Apache chief Mangas Coloradas was killed. During that year he also commanded the District of Arizona.

Ordered to Arkansas Apr. 1864, West took command of the 2d Division/VII Corps and led it through the RED RIVER CAMPAIGN. In the fall, under Maj. Gen. FREDERICK STEELE, he was lightly engaged against Confederate Maj. Gen. STERLING PRICE. West finished the war commanding the cavalry in the Department of the Gulf, 15 May–12 June 1865. He was mustered out of the army in San Antonio 4 Jan. 1866.

Settling in New Orleans, he held appointments as deputy U.S. marshal and customs auditor, and was elected to the U.S. Senate on the Republican ticket Mar. 1871. His term expired in 1877, the year Military Reconstruction ended, and West retired from politics once local governments returned to civilian control. He remained in Washington, holding a series of political appointments, and died there 31 Oct. 1898.

—PLF

West, Union Department of the.
With headquarters at Fort Leavenworth, Kans., the Union Department of the West existed at the outbreak of the Civil War. The department comprised the portion of the U.S. west of the Mississippi River to the Rocky Mts., extended southward to Texas, and included the states of Arkansas and Louisiana. It was reduced when the latter 2 states seceded and Missouri was assigned to the DEPARTMENT OF THE OHIO 3 May 1861.

Brig. Gen. William S. Harney commanded the department 17 Nov. 1860–31 May 1861, and was succeeded by Brig. Gen. NATHANIEL LYON, who directed the command until 3 July, when it became part of the WESTERN DEPARTMENT.   —JDW

Western Department, Confederate.
The Western Department was the alternate designation for Confederate DEPARTMENT NO. 2. The order assigning Maj. Gen. BRAXTON BRAGG to temporary command 17 June 1862 referred to Department No. 2 "or Western Department." The atlas accompanying the *Official Records,* however, does not use the names synonymously. Department No. 2, not Western Department, was the accepted designation for the command that encompassed various parts of Mississippi, Arkansas, Louisiana, Alabama, and Tennessee at different times.   —JDW

Western Department, Union.
Union authorities constituted the Western Department 3 July 1861 by merging the state of Illinois with the DEPARTMENT OF THE WEST, which consisted of all states and territories west of the Mississippi River to the Rocky Mts. Headquarters were designated at Fort Leavenworth, Kans., and Maj. Gen. JOHN C. FRÉMONT was assigned to command.

The general's broad responsibilities included safeguarding Missouri and the Midwest and organizing, equipping, and leading an army down the Mississippi River to capture New Orleans. The immediate problem confronting him was the confusing and vicious struggle in the divided state of Missouri.

When Frémont moved his headquarters to St. Louis 25 July, he commanded about 23,000 troops, more than one-third of which were 3-month volunteers whose ENLISTMENTS were soon to expire. Brig. Gen. NATHANIEL LYON had earlier done valuable service for the Union cause in the state and now occupied a position in southwest Missouri. On 10 Aug. Confederates under Maj. Gen. STERLING PRICE defeated Lyon's force and killed its commander at WILSON'S CREEK. Frémont disclaimed responsibility for the disaster.

After Wilson's Creek, Frémont's grip on the department deteriorated. He surrounded himself with useless staff officers, and carelessly issued contracts for supplies to many dishonest contractors. He also feuded with the powerful Blair family, one of whose members, MONTGOMERY BLAIR, was ABRAHAM LINCOLN's postmaster general. On 30 Aug. Frémont proclaimed martial law in the state and emancipated all slaves owned by Confederates (see FRÉMONT'S EMANCIPATION PROCLAMATION). The action angered Lincoln, who asked the general to modify it. Frémont refused, and the president revoked the measure.

Late in Oct. 1861 Lincoln ordered Sec. of War SIMON CAMERON to St. Louis to remove the "Pathfinder." Frémont pleaded for time, but another removal order followed. The department commander then posted guards to prevent the delivery of the presidential directive. A captain of volunteers, disguised as a farmer, passed the sentries and handed Frémont the order 2 Nov.

Maj. Gen. DAVID HUNTER replaced Frémont, commanding the department for only a week. On 9 Nov. the Western Department became part of the newly created DEPARTMENT OF THE MISSOURI.   —JDW

Western Kentucky, Confederate Department of. On 6 Sept. 1864, the Confederate Adjutant and Inspector General's Office issued Special Orders No. 211, establishing the Department of Western Kentucky. The orders defined the department as an area bordered on the north by the Ohio River, from its mouth at the Mississippi River east to the mouth of the Salt River near West Point, Ky. From there its border ran south through Elizabethtown, Glasgow, and Tompkinsville, Ky., on to Carthage, Tenn., followed the Tennessee River west to Nashville, the Northwestern Railroad line northwest to Hickman, Ky., near the Missouri state line, and followed the Mississippi River north back to the mouth of the Ohio. Unaware that Brig. Gen. ADAM R. JOHNSON had been blinded in action 21 Aug., the Adjutant and Inspector General's Office appointed him department commander, to date from 6 Sept. Informed of Johnson's condition, superiors replaced him with Brig. Gen. HYLAN B. LYON 26 Sept.

This great circular department's central region had a small population and saw little military activity. Lyon was expected to enforce Confederate CONSCRIPTION laws there and curb depredations by Union guerrillas. He claimed some success at this, but 4 Feb. 1865 complained to the War Department of neighboring department commander Lt. Gen. RICHARD TAYLOR's intentions to absorb his area of geographic responsibility into the DEPARTMENT OF ALABAMA, MISSISSIPPI, AND EAST LOUISIANA. This change was not made and Lyon served out the war at his post.   —JES

Western Virginia, Confederate Department of. See TRANS-ALLEGHENY DEPARTMENT, CONFEDERATE.

Western Virginia, Union Department of. The Union Department of Western Virginia was created 19 Sept. 1861 from the Army of Occupation of Western Virginia/DEPARTMENT OF THE OHIO and encompassed that area of Virginia west of the Blue Ridge Mts. Brig. Gen. WILLIAM S. ROSECRANS, commanding the army, assumed the post of department commander. Rosecrans had 20,000 troops, organized into 8 brigades, stationed at various points in western Virginia. The department existed for only 6 months and was merged, 11 Mar. 1862, into the newly authorized MOUNTAIN DEPARTMENT.   —JDW

Western Virginia and East Tennessee, Confederate Department of. Previously known as the DEPARTMENT OF SOUTHWESTERN VIRGINIA, the TRANS-ALLEGHENY DEPARTMENT, and the Department of Southwestern Virginia and East Tennessee, on 20 Feb. 1865 Gen. ROBERT E. LEE's Special Orders No. 2 renamed this geographic area the Department of Western Virginia and East Tennessee and expanded Lt. Gen. JUBAL A. EARLY's command to encompass it.

On 27 Sept. 1864, Maj. Gen. JOHN C. BRECKINRIDGE, then commanding the department, was informed that his responsibilities would now embrace the activities of Confederate reserves in East Tennessee. Officially named the Trans-Allegheny Department, Breckinridge's command had long been informally known as the Department of Southwestern Virginia and

East Tennessee and appears in the *Official Records* under that title from late 1863. The department's prior involvements in the military affairs of East Tennessee and Breckinridge's instruction of 27 Sept. gave this latter name precedence over the former title, Trans-Allegheny Department. But this area of geographic command underwent no official change of name from 25 Nov. 1862, when the Trans-Allegheny Department was created, until Lee's order of 20 Feb. 1865, which was bluntly termed illegal by Confederate War Department officials. By law, a change in the name or area of a department could only be made, and a departmental command could only be assigned, by the secretary of war. Lee, only recently made commander of all Confederate armies believed that his new responsibilities embraced this authority. For this reason, on the same day, the Confederate War Department issued a duplicate order for changes in the department's name and command, to give Lee's wishes the force of law.

The Department of Western Virginia and East Tennessee was the last name given to this command. Confederate operations effectively ceased there within 60 days.   —JES

West Florida, Confederate Department of. An anomalous command, the Confederate Department of West Florida existed only in the mind of Brig. Gen. WILLIAM M. GARDNER. The area he commanded Oct. 1863–Feb. 1864 was regarded as the District of Middle Florida by Gen. P.G.T. BEAUREGARD, who headed the DEPARTMENT OF SOUTH CAROLINA, GEORGIA, AND FLORIDA, the military realm of which Gardner's command formed a part.

There was some basis for using the title Gardner preferred. His command did include the western reaches of the state and was headquartered at Quincy, well within the Florida panhandle. Moreover, the Confederate War Department referred to it as the Department of West Florida when assigning Gardner to command 6 Oct. 1863. In the same order, however, the War Department stated that Gardner was to assume the position formerly held by Maj. Gen. HOWELL COBB, and, while Cobb's area of command had included the panhandle, its title had been the District of Middle Florida. After Gardner's succession, the Confederate government consistently referred to it by the latter title, although Gardner and his subordinates adopted the name that seemed more geographically apt.

Questions of nomenclature aside, Gardner achieved much during his short rule. He revamped the organizational apparatus of a department that had been badly administered under Cobb, a political general. By revoking his predecessor's suspension of Confederate CONSCRIPTION throughout the command, Gardner also managed to upgrade his forces to a total of 3,794 officers and men present and absent as of 1 Dec. 1863, comprising 2 regiments and 3 separate companies of cavalry, 2 regiments and 2 battalions of infantry, and 3 batteries of artillery. Gardner rushed many of these units to the support of Brig. Gen. JOSEPH FINEGAN, commander of Confederate forces at the Battle of OLUSTEE, though most arrived too late to take part in the Southern victory of 20 Feb. 1864.

3 days after the battle, the title "Department of West Florida" disappeared when the Districts of Middle and Eastern Florida were combined to form the District of Florida, under Maj. Gen. J. PATTON ANDERSON. In March Anderson assigned Gardner to head the district's Sub-District No. 1, at Quincy.   —EGL

West Mississippi, Union Military Division of. Created 7 May 1864, the Union Military Division of West Mississippi embraced the Departments of ARKANSAS and the GULF, and included the states of Louisiana and Texas, eastern Arkansas, coastal Mississippi and Alabama, and northwest Florida. Maj. Gen. E.R.S. CANBY assumed formal command of the division 11 May and established his headquarters in New Orleans. On 27 June Canby's divisional responsibility was expanded to include the state and DEPARTMENT OF THE MISSOURI. The mission of his division was largely administrative, allowing him to coordinate tactical and logistical support for his gulf-coast operations, the most prominent of which was the capture of MOBILE, Ala. Sometimes referred to as the Military Division of the Gulf or the Trans-Mississippi Division in the *Official Records,* it was dissolved by the War Department 17 May 1865. The Department of the Missouri left the division early in 1865.   —JES

West Point, Miss., eng. at. 21 Feb. 1864 *See* SOOY SMITH EXPEDITION.

West Point, Va., eng. at. 7 May 1862 *See* ELTHAM'S LANDING, ENG. AT.

West Point Foundry at Cold Spring, N.Y. (Cold Spring Foundry). Located across the Hudson River from the U.S. MILITARY ACADEMY, the West Point Foundry produced one of the most widely used rifled cannon of the Civil War, the PARROTT GUN. The foundry's superintendent was the gun's inventor, ROBERT P. PARROTT, a graduate of the nearby academy who had resigned from the army in 1836 to direct the foundry's operations.

During the Civil War the foundry, a private firm, fabricated 10-, 20-, and 30-pounder calibers, reaching a weekly production of 25 guns and 7,000 projectiles. On 24 June 1862, Pres. ABRAHAM LINCOLN, who had an intense curiosity regarding ordnance, visited the foundry to witness its workings. By the end of the conflict, the West Point Foundry had produced more than 1,700 Parrott guns and 3 million projectiles.   —JDW

Westport, Mo., eng. at. 23 Oct. 1864 The engagement at Westport (now a part of Kansas City) marked the end of a disappointing but ambitious Confederate raid into Missouri. Confederate Maj. Gen. STERLING PRICE had led his 12,000 men from Arkansas. Only one-third of them were armed initially, but they were augmented by 14 pieces of artillery. Hoping to take St. Louis, then to invade Illinois, they were forced to adopt an alternative plan: to cut a swath westward across central Missouri. Taking a number of towns, they captured Federal garrisons and caches of arms and supplies.

The Federals countered by diverting Maj. Gen. ANDREW J. SMITH, with 6,000 men en route to Georgia, and by mobilizing thousands of militia. Union Brig. Gen. ALFRED PLEASANTON led about 7,000 men in a provisional cavalry division, supplemented by veteran Maj. Gen. SAMUEL R. CURTIS' "Army of the Border" from Kansas.

Faced with Curtis' troops approaching from his front and Pleasonton's from his rear, Price ignored an open route of retreat to the South. He planned first to attack Curtis, then to turn and attack Pleasonton, but his plans were thwarted by Curtis' strong defensive lines. Hurling themselves in fruitless frontal assaults, the Southerners charged valiantly. For some 4 hours, they fought, and failed. Each side lost about 1,500 men.

Retreating 61 mi in 2 days, Price halted 25 Oct. to fight a costly rear-guard action at Mine Creek in Kansas. He returned to Arkansas with only 6,000 survivors and had gained no material advantage for the Confederacy.   —HH

West Tennessee, Union District of. Maj. Gen. HENRY W. HALLECK issued General Orders No. 37 14 Feb. 1862, assigning Maj. Gen. ULYSSES S. GRANT command of the Union District of West Tennessee. Following Grant's victory at FORT DONELSON, this assignment did not limit his command geographically. Rather, with these orders Grant now headed the ARMY OF THE TENNESSEE, operating along the Tennessee River south of Forts Henry and Donelson, southwest of Nashville, and north of the Mississippi state line, all of it hostile territory.

On 21 Feb. Grant took command of the district (organized 17 Feb.) and later briefly established headquarters at Savannah, Tenn., north of Pittsburg Landing. By the time the district was absorbed into the newly created Union DEPARTMENT OF THE TENNESSEE, 16 Oct. 1862, the Battles of SHILOH and MEMPHIS had been fought in West Tennessee, and the Mississippi River, on the state's western border, had come under nominal Union control.   —JES

West Virginia. In Apr. 1861 the beginning of civil war convulsed the country, dividing state against state. In the South, secession also caused dissension within states as pro-Unionist citizens opposed the formation of the Confederacy. In no Confederate state did this divisiveness have more important political consequences than in Virginia.

When Virginia seceded 17 Apr. 1861, residents of its western counties beyond the Allegheny Mts. immediately called mass Unionist meetings to oppose the action. Decades of intrastate differences lay behind this movement. Few citizens of the region owned slaves, and they had little in common with the powerful landed gentry east of the Alleghenies. The region's major rivers and highways generally snaked northward, and its culture and economy were oriented toward Pennsylvania and Ohio.

Virginia's decision to join the Confederacy and the region's strategic importance to both the North and South exacerbated these longstanding differences. Within a month of secession, Virginia's western counties had become a battleground because of the vital BALTIMORE & OHIO RAILROAD and the Ohio River. In July Union Maj. Gen. GEORGE B. MCCLELLAN's series of victories over Confederate forces at LAUREL HILL, RICH MOUNTAIN, and CORRICK'S FORD secured much of the region for the Union.

These victories also accelerated the dissolution of the Old Dominion. While McClellan prepared for his campaign, pro-Union citizens had summoned a general convention to take political action for Virginia as a whole. On 11 June 1861, at Wheeling, delegates from 26 counties convened. After 2 months they passed ordinances reorganizing the government of Virginia and creating a new state, the state of Kanawha, to consist of 48 designated counties (2 were added later), with its capital at Wheeling.

The irregular and illegal processes begun by this convention ultimately created the state of West Virginia. The delegates authorized a reorganized legislature, elected Francis H. Pierpoint "Governor of Virginia" at Wheeling, and called for a constitutional convention. This convention met in November, formed a constitution for the state of West Virginia, and 3 Apr.

1862 saw it ratified by voters who had taken the oath of allegiance to the Union. The new state legislature, convening 13 May, requested admission to the U.S.

The Federal Congress approved the bill admitting West Virginia. Pres. ABRAHAM LINCOLN, however, disapproved of the bill and considered vetoing it, but eventually gave his reluctant consent. On 13 Dec. 1862, the bill became law with a proviso requiring the gradual abolition of SLAVERY within the new state. Lincoln signed the proclamation 20 Apr. 1863, and 2 months later, 20 June, West Virginia formally entered the Union.

The Civil War created West Virginia, but, like Missouri, the new state suffered from its own civil war during those 4 years of struggle. Regular troops, guerrillas, and bushwhackers engaged in bitter, deadly combat in the rugged mountains and valleys. West Virginia contributed about 25,000 men to the Union cause, while an estimated 15,000 of its residents fought for the Confederacy. The wounds engendered by the war and the official dismemberment of Virginia took decades to heal.
—JDW

West Virginia, Union Army and Department of. Authorized 24 June 1863, the Union Department of West Virginia resulted from a subdivision of the MIDDLE DEPARTMENT. The department comprised all of Maryland west of the Allegheny Mts. and the new state of West Virginia. Brig. Gen. BENJAMIN F. KELLEY assumed command of the department with its army of 23,000 troops drawn from the VIII Corps. His responsibility included the protection of the BALTIMORE & OHIO RAILROAD and its depots, operations against Confederate forces in the SHENANDOAH VALLEY and southwestern Virginia, and protection of property in the new Union state.

Maj. Gen. FRANZ SIGEL replaced Kelley 10 Mar. 1864, undertaking in April a campaign southward up the Shenandoah Valley. Confederate forces, under Maj. Gen. JOHN C. BRECKINRIDGE, defeated Sigel's army in the strategically decisive Battle of NEW MARKET 15 May. While Sigel operated in the valley, additional troops from the department, commanded by Brig. Gen. GEORGE CROOK, marched through the Alleghenies in a raid on the VIRGINIA & TENNESSEE RAILROAD. Crook defeated a Confederate force on the 9th at CLOYD'S MOUNTAIN, but accomplished little else.

6 days after Sigel's defeat at New Market, Maj. Gen. DAVID HUNTER succeeded to command of the department. Within a week, Hunter had launched a second invasion of the upper Shenandoah, defeating a Southern force at PIEDMONT 5 June and burning the VIRGINIA MILITARY INSTITUTE and parts of Lexington before combining his troops with those of Crook's. The Army of West Virginia then marched on Lynchburg, Va. Hunter, however, lost his nerve when Lt. Gen. JUBAL A. EARLY'S veterans of the II Corps arrived and ordered a hasty retreat into the Alleghenies. Hunter was replaced 8 Aug. by Crook.

Crook's Army of West Virginia served under Maj. Gen. PHILIP H. SHERIDAN in the successful 1864 SHENANDOAH VALLEY CAMPAIGN. Confederate guerrillas, Capt. John H. MCNEILL'S RANGERS, captured Crook along with Kelley at their headquarters in Cumberland, Md., 22 Feb. 1865. Crook was replaced until 27 Feb. by Brig. Gen. John D. Stevenson, who was succeeded by Brig. Gen. Samuel S. Carroll until 7 Mar. 1865. Maj. Gen. WINFIELD S. HANCOCK directed the department until its disbandment 27 June 1865.   —JDW

Wharton, Gabriel Colvin. CSA   b. Culpeper Cty., Va.,

23 July 1824, Wharton attended the VIRGINIA MILITARY INSTITUTE, graduating 2d in the class of 1847, and became a civil engineer. In the Southwest, he invested in mining and worked in western New Mexico Territory.

LC

Returning to Virginia before the start of the Civil War, he enlisted in the 45th Virginia Infantry, was elected its major July 1861, and transferred to the 51st Virginia, which elected him its colonel in August. With the 51st, first attached to Brig. Gen. JOHN B. FLOYD'S ARMY OF THE KANAWHA, then Floyd's FORT DONELSON garrison in Tennessee, Wharton served in southwestern Virginia, then commanded Floyd's 1st Brigade at Donelson. Made up of the 51st and 56th Virginia, the 1st Brigade escaped from Donelson 16 Feb. 1862, and, after brief service at Nashville, the 51st returned with Wharton to southwest Virginia, there serving under Maj. Gen. SAMUEL JONES through autumn 1863.

Wharton won promotion to brigadier general 8 July 1863, briefly assumed command of the Shenandoah Valley District, and during the CHICKAMAUGA CAMPAIGN went on a diversionary mission against targets in East Tennessee from Dublin Depot, Va. As a part of Maj. Gen. ROBERT RANSOM'S division, attached to Lt. Gen. JAMES LONGSTREET'S I Corps for the KNOXVILLE CAMPAIGN, he led Wharton's Brigade of Sharpshooters, made up of the 30th, 45th, and 51st Virginia Infantry regiments.

Returning to southwest Virginia again in spring 1864, he joined in Maj. Gen. JOHN C. BRECKINRIDGE'S campaign ending in the Battle of NEW MARKET, pursued the force of Union Maj. Gen. DAVID HUNTER in the Shenandoah Valley, then was given divisional command in the II Corps, under Lt. Gen. JUBAL A. EARLY. With Early he opposed Union Maj. Gen. PHILIP H. SHERIDAN at WINCHESTER, CEDAR CREEK, and FISHER'S HILL in autumn 1864, and in Early's final defeat in an engagement at WAYNESBOROUGH 2 Mar. 1865 had his command destroyed. He accepted Federal parole at Lynchburg, Va., 21 June 1865.

After the war Wharton made his home in Radford, Va., turned his antebellum experience in mine engineering to developing Virginia mines, and won election to the Virginia state house, serving 1871–74 and again 1897–98. d. Radford, 12 May 1906.   —JES

Wharton, John Austin. CSA b. near Nashville, Tenn., 3 July 1828. Educated in Texas, where he had moved with his father, and at South Carolina College, Wharton was admitted to the Texas bar and opened a law practice in Brazoria. In 1861 he was elected to the state secession convention. Enlisting in TERRY'S TEXAS RANGERS (8th Texas Cavalry) and commissioned a captain, he succeeded to the colonelcy on the death of Rangers' organizers Benjamin F. Terry and Thomas S. Lubbock. He led the regiment with distinction at SHILOH, where he was wounded.

After fighting through the KENTUCKY CAMPAIGN in 1862, Wharton was promoted to brigadier general 18 Nov. Though his neighbors in Texas wanted him to run for the Confederate Congress in the 1862 elections, he preferred to remain in active field service. At STONE'S RIVER, 31 Dec. 1862–2 Jan. 1863, he fought vigorously against the Union right wing, capturing 1,500 prisoners, a 4-gun battery, and several hundred wagons. Following the battle he was promoted to major general to rank from 10 Nov. Transferred to Lt. Gen. RICHARD TAYLOR's command in Louisiana, Wharton led the cavalry toward the end of the RED RIVER CAMPAIGN and for the duration of his war career operated in the Trans-Mississippi.

LC

On 6 Apr. 1865, Col. George W. Baylor, a longtime enemy, shot Wharton to death during a quarrel in a hotel room in Houston, Tex. No charges were brought against Baylor, though Wharton was found to have been unarmed at the time of his death. His body was taken to Austin for burial.　　—PLF

Wheat, Chatham Roberdeau. CSA b. 9 Apr. 1826, Alexandria, Va. The son of an Episcopal clergyman and member of a distinguished Maryland family, Wheat was a man of war. After graduating from the University of Nashville in 1845, he studied law for a year in Memphis, Tenn., before volunteering for service in the Mexican War. There he earned a captain's commission and, returning to civilian life, he settled in New Orleans, began a legal practice, entered politics, and was elected to the Louisiana legislature. He abandoned a promising career to join filibustering expeditions to Latin America, and by 1860 he was in Italy, fighting with English volunteers in Giuseppe Garibaldi's revolutionary forces.

When the Civil War began, Wheat returned to the U.S., organized the 1st Louisiana Special Battalion, and was appointed its commander, with the rank of major. One company of the battalion was composed of unsavory characters and former convicts from New Orleans who styled themselves the "Tiger Rifles." The name stuck to the entire battalion, and "WHEAT'S TIGERS" soon left Louisiana for Virginia.

The Tigers saw their initial action at FIRST BULL RUN. While leading the battalion in a charge, Wheat was shot through both lungs. A surgeon told him that the wound was fatal, but Wheat replied: "I don't feel like dying yet," and recovered. With an imposing presence and absolute fearlessness, only Wheat could maintain discipline in the battalion. In 1862 it served in Brig. Gen. RICHARD TAYLOR's Louisiana brigade, participating in the SHENANDOAH VALLEY and SEVEN DAYS' campaigns. In the latter, at GAINES' MILL, 27 June 1862, Wheat suffered a second wound. This time he could not will life, dying the same day. Soon after their commander's death, Wheat's Tigers were disbanded and the members assigned to other Louisiana commands.　　—JDW

Wheatfield, at Gettysburg. 2 July 1863 The massive Confederate assault against the Union left flank at GETTYSBURG exploded about 4 p.m. 2 July. For the next 4 hours, from the PEACH ORCHARD to LITTLE ROUND TOP, savage combat engulfed the area. Halfway between these 2 points lay the Wheatfield. As the battle ebbed and flowed, more and more soldiers were drawn into the fierce fighting.

When the Confederate attacks finally crushed the Union salient at the Peach Orchard, the fury shifted to the Wheatfield. For the next 2 or 3 hours, the opponents savaged each other in some of the war's bloodiest fighting. Confederates of Maj. Gens. JOHN B. HOOD's and LAFAYETTE MCLAWS' divisions captured the ground 6 times, only to be repulsed by Federals from the II, III, and V corps. The 1st Minnesota lost more than 80% of its members in 1 counterattack. At day's end 500 Confederates lay dead among the trampled wheat.　　—JDW

"Wheat's Tigers." CSA In 1861 CHATHAM R. WHEAT, a young soldier of fortune living in New Orleans, organized the 1st Louisiana Special Battalion. One of the companies that joined his battalion was the "Tiger Rifles," raised by Capt. Alex White from among the young Irishmen of the city.

White had served time in the penitentiary for pistol-whipping another man, and many of his Tigers—"the very dregs of the City," one writer called them; "the lowest scrapings of the Mississippi and New Orleans," observed another—had similar records. A. Keene Richards, a wealthy citizen, provided the company's ZOUAVE uniform, consisting of a scarlet skullcap with a long tassel, a red shirt, an open brown jacket, and baggy trousers of blue-and-white stripes tucked into white leggings. The Tigers gave their name and reputation to the entire battalion.

Wheat's 1st Special Battalion fought at FIRST BULL RUN, where it played an important role in holding the left of the Southern line. The Tigers were later assigned to the Louisiana brigade commanded by Brig. Gen. RICHARD TAYLOR. Under him they fought in the SHENANDOAH VALLEY CAMPAIGN of 1862, where they figured prominently in the Battle of PORT REPUBLIC.

Wheat was mortally wounded at GAINES' MILL 27 June 1862, and without his leadership the battalion was ineffective. In Aug. 1862 it was broken up and the men transferred to other Louisiana commands. Although they carried a banner depicting a lamb, with the motto *As Gentle As,* the Tigers had a well-deserved reputation as fierce fighters and troublemakers.　　—RMcM

Wheeler, Joseph. CSA b. Augusta, Ga., 10 Sept. 1836. Joseph "Fightin' Joe" Wheeler graduated 19th in the West Point class of 1859 and was assigned to the Mounted Dragoons. For 2 years he fought Indians on the frontier, then resigned to join the Confederate States Army. Commissioned colonel of the 19th Alabama Infantry, he fought with the regiment through SHILOH and, July 1862, took command of the cavalry of the Army of Mississippi. He commanded the cavalry in the Western theater for the rest of the war, rising from brigadier general, to rank from 30 Oct. 1862, to major general, dating from 20 Jan. 1863.

He covered Gen. BRAXTON

USMHI

BRAGG's advance on and the retreat from Kentucky, fought at STONE'S RIVER and CHICKAMAUGA, and bottled up Maj. Gen. WILLIAM S. ROSECRANS in CHATTANOOGA by a masterly executed raid on Union communications. During the KNOXVILLE siege, he fought with Lt. Gen. JAMES LONGSTREET. Wheeler's were practically the only troops contending Maj. Gen. WILLIAM T. SHERMAN'S MARCH TO THE SEA, and also opposed Sherman as far as Raleigh. Wheeler was captured near Atlanta after Gen. JOSEPH E. JOHNSTON'S surrender.

After the war Wheeler became a cotton planter in Wheeler, Ala. (which was named after him), entered politics, and served in the U.S. House of Representatives 1885–1900. During the Spanish-American War, when Pres. WILLIAM MCKINLEY appointed him major general of volunteers, the appointment was hailed throughout the country as a healing of the wounds of the Civil War. Wheeler commanded the cavalry division on the Santiago expedition and took part in the Battle of San Juan Hill. He was sent to the Philippines in command of a brigade but soon returned to the U.S. to be commissioned a brigadier general in the Regular Army, as of 10 Sept. 1900. He retired on his 64th birthday, living in Brooklyn, N.Y., until his death there 25 Jan. 1906. *See also* WHEELER'S RAIDS.   —DBS

Wheeler's Raid. 1–9 Oct. 1863   Thanks mainly to the confidence of Confederate Gen. BRAXTON BRAGG and the timidity of Maj. Gen. AMBROSE E. BURNSIDE, the Confederate siege of Union-held CHATTANOOGA was succeeding. Pushed back to the city after the disastrous Battle of CHICKAMAUGA, Maj. Gen. WILLIAM S. ROSECRANS and his hungry troopers were in desperate need of supplies and ammunition. Sending no relief, Burnside was content to stay on guard at Cumberland Gap, sidestepping any confrontations with cavalryman Maj. Gen. NATHAN B. FORREST. Only one alternative remained to Rosecrans: the Sequatchie Valley road, a winding, narrow swath through the south Tennessee woods and the only supply route open to the Federals.

On 27 Sept. 1863, Bragg decided to deliver a final blow to the starving Federals by cutting off Chattanooga's lifeline. To lead this raid he chose a reluctant Maj. Gen. JOSEPH WHEELER, who questioned the ability of his already depleted force to carry out the order. However, Wheeler assured his subordinates: "I have my orders, gentlemen, and I will attempt the work." That "attempt" turned out to be one of the most audacious cavalry raids of the war. Highlighted by a series of quick, sharp strikes, Wheeler's Raid left the Union army in the West a shambles.

As Union Maj. Gen. GEORGE CROOK peered across the Tennessee River at Wheeler's cavalrymen 1 Oct., the 27-year-old Wheeler suddenly ordered his troops to cross. Under heavy fire the men forded the river, leaving their dead and wounded in the water, intent on storming the Federal position. On the western bank they charged with abandon into Crook's 4th Ohio. It was the first in a series of Confederate successes and typical of Wheeler's actions in the future.

Joined by some of Forrest's brigades, Wheeler organized 3 divisions, ordering them to move out at dusk toward Walden's Ridge. In the night rain and mud the Southerners trudged up the slopes. Suddenly the advance guard ran into a Union patrol. Again, Wheeler immediately ordered a charge, scattering the enemy through the woods. The Confederates spent the next day plodding toward the ridge. That night Wheeler laid out his strategy, ordering Brig. Gen. JOHN A. WHARTON to proceed to McMinnville while he and Brig. Gen. WILLIAM T. MARTIN converged on the Sequatchie Valley and captured the Federal supply trains.

During the next week Wheeler galloped through the valley, destroying nearly everything in sight, with Crook's Federals in close pursuit. This raid inflicted 2,000 Federal casualties; 3,000 Confederates were either killed or wounded. Wheeler destroyed or captured more than 1,000 supply wagons, hundreds of draft animals, 2 towns in Tennessee, 5 critical bridges, miles of railroad, and millions of dollars in supplies. The Confederates suffered only 212 casualties and caused an upheaval in the entire Union command structure.   —FLS

Wheeler's Raid. 10 Aug.–10 Sept. 1864   Early in Aug. 1864 Gen. JOHN B. HOOD, commander of the Confederate forces defending Atlanta, Ga., was in a strategic predicament. Although he had repulsed attempts by Union cavalry and infantry to break his only remaining supply line, the Macon & Western Railroad, he lacked the strength to drive back Maj. Gen. WILLIAM T. SHERMAN'S army. It was only a matter of time before the far superior numbers of the Federals would enable them to reach the Macon & Western, thus compelling Hood to evacuate Atlanta (see ATLANTA CAMPAIGN).

Hood's solution to this problem was to send Maj. Gen. JOSEPH WHEELER with 4,000 cavalry on a raid against Sherman's supply line. He ordered Wheeler to attack the Western & Atlantic Railroad below Chattanooga, then to strike at the railroads south of Nashville, and finally to return to Atlanta with 2,800 of his men, again hitting the Western & Atlantic as he did so, while leaving the rest of his command in Tennessee to continue operations there. With these railroads out of commission, Sherman's army would be faced with starvation, and either be forced to retreat or make a suicidal frontal assault on Atlanta's strong fortifications.

Wheeler set out 10 Aug. At first he was successful, ripping up more than 30 mi of track near Marietta, Resaca, and Dalton. But heavy concentrations of Union infantry drove him away from the Western & Atlantic and caused him to ride, contrary to orders, into East Tennessee. From there he swerved westward, destroyed a few miles of track south of Nashville, then fled into Alabama with his command so exhausted and demoralized that it was not able to resume active operations until October.

The highly efficient Union repair crews speedily restored the tracks destroyed by Wheeler, Sherman's forces suffered no serious supply problems, and Hood was left in an even worse military situation, having in effect thrown away the cream of his cavalry. Yet, given his circumstances, he was justified in ordering the raid, for he had no other card to play in his desperate struggle to hold Atlanta.   —AC

Whipple, William Denison. USA   b. Nelson, N.Y., 2 Aug. 1826, Whipple won appointment to West Point, graduated 31st in the 37-man class of 1851, was brevetted 2d lieutenant in the 3d U.S. Infantry, served in garrison in Kentucky and at Fort Defiance, New Mexico Territory. He saw combat against Apache tribesmen, then became quartermaster at Indianola, Tex.

When Whipple's post was seized by Texas secessionists in spring 1861, he escaped east, received promotion to 1st lieutenant 14 May, and began a lifetime career in army administration. First an assistant in the adjutant general's office in Washington, D.C., he served as assistant adjutant general with Col. DAVID HUNTER'S division at the First Battle of BULL RUN, won promotion to captain in the Regulars 3 Aug. 1861, then served as aide-de-camp and assistant adjutant general in the DEPART-

The misidentified "Whistling Dick"   USMHI

LC

MENT OF PENNSYLVANIA, the DE-PARTMENT OF VIRGINIA, the MIDDLE DEPARTMENT, and in Philadelphia until commissioned brigadier general of volunteers 17 July 1863 and given command of the 2d Division/Lehigh District, Pa., 31 July.

Transferred west, on 12 Nov. he became assistant adjutant general of the ARMY AND DEPARTMENT OF THE CUMBERLAND, and on 5 Dec. became chief of staff to Maj. Gen. GEORGE H. THOMAS. He was present with his general at the Battles of MISSIONARY RIDGE, RESACA, NEW HOPE CHURCH, KENNESAW MOUNTAIN, JONESBOROUGH, and NASHVILLE. Brevetted to brigadier and major general in the Regulars 13 Mar. 1865, he became assistant adjutant general and chief of staff of the postwar Military Division of the Tennessee 27 June 1865–16 Aug. 1866, having mustered out of volunteer service 16 Jan. 1866.

After postwar occupation duty in Tennessee and Kentucky, Whipple transferred to San Francisco with Thomas in 1869, and in 1870, following Thomas' death, worked as assistant to the adjutant general in Washington, D.C. On 1 Jan. 1873, he joined Gen. WILLIAM T. SHERMAN as aide-de-camp, and from 1878 served as adjutant general of the Divisions of the Missouri, Atlantic, and the East. He retired as a colonel in 1890, settled in New York City, and died there 1 Apr. 1902.   —JES

"Whistling Dick." "Whistling Dick" was a rifled and banded 18-pounder cannon used by Confederates in the river defenses at Vicksburg. Originally cast as a smoothbore at the TREDEGAR IRON WORKS, the artillery piece was rifled by Southerners. This alteration gave the cannon's conical projectiles an erratic spin, which produced a distinctive whistling sound while in flight; thus the cannon's nickname. The cannon's most notable achievement occurred 27 May 1863, when its swirling projectiles sank the Union gunboat *Cincinnati.*

One of the cannon captured by the Federals when Vicksburg surrendered went on display at West Point after the war as "Whistling Dick." Not until the late 1950s was it established that an error had been made. What happened to "Whistling Dick" remains a mystery.   —JDW

White, Julius. USA b. Cazenovia, N.Y., 23 Sept. 1816, White moved to Illinois in 1837, migrated to Wisconsin, where he won election to the state legislature in 1849. He became an active Republican, in 1861 won a patronage appointment as collector of customs in Chicago, Ill., and that summer raised the 37th Illinois Infantry for Civil War service.

As colonel of the 37th, known as the "Frémont Rifles," White mustered in 18 Sept. 1861 and went on duty in Missouri, taking part in Maj. Gen. JOHN C. FRÉMONT's march on Springfield and in campaigning against Maj. Gen. STERLING PRICE's Confederates. Given command of the 2d Brigade/3d Division/Army of the Southwest, he fought well at the Mar. 1862 Battle of PEA RIDGE, Ark., assumed command of the post at Cassville, Mo., received promotion to brigadier general 9 June 1862, and transferred east in July.

In command of an Army of Virginia brigade garrisoning Winchester, Va., on 2 Sept. White received orders from Maj. Gen. HENRY W. HALLECK to evacuate the town and fall back on Col. Dixon S. Miles's force at Harpers Ferry. Arriving in Harpers Ferry 3 Sept., he was ordered to Martinsburg, then back to Harpers Ferry 12 Sept. to assist Miles in defending the town. Declining command, in deference to Miles's rank in the Regulars, White fought with the rest of the garrison until surrounded by Confederates led by Maj. Gen. THOMAS J. "STONEWALL" JACKSON. At Miles's direction White arranged the Federals' surrender 15 Sept. Miles was killed in the surrender, the Union prisoners paroled, and all Federal brigade commanders subjected to an investigation by a military commission.

Found blameless in evacuating Winchester and in his actions at Harpers Ferry, White was assigned to the DEPARTMENT OF THE OHIO Jan. 1863 and fought at CAMPBELL'S STATION and KNOXVILLE in East Tennessee that autumn. He became Maj. Gen. AMBROSE E. BURNSIDE's chief of staff early in 1864, served inside the PETERSBURG, Va., siege lines, and, after Burnside's relief from command, assumed leadership of the 1st Division/IX Corps 6 Aug. 1864. White took sick leave 28 Aug., then resigned his commission 19 Nov. 1864. Though he was out of Federal service, his record was amended to show a brevet to major general 13 Mar. 1865.

White returned to Illinois, settled in Evanston, and later served as commander of the Illinois State Commandery in the MILITARY ORDER OF THE LOYAL LEGION OF THE U.S. d. Evanston, 12 May 1890.   —JES

White Oak Road, Va., eng. at.   31 Mar. 1865 By the morning of 31 Mar. 1865, Union cavalry divisions and 2 infantry corps, ordered west to turn the Confederate right flank at Petersburg, Va., lay in the vicinity of Dinwiddie Court House. Commanded by Maj. Gen. PHILIP H. SHERIDAN, the Federals opposed nearly 19,000 Confederates under Maj. Gens. GEORGE E. PICKETT and FITZHUGH LEE. For 2 days the opponents had skirmished in the wooded terrain while a heavy rain slowed the movements.

Sheridan pressed his advance early on the 31st as his cavalry slogged northward toward Five Forks, while Maj. Gen. GOUVERNEUR K. WARREN and his V Corps probed the woods 3 mi east of the Union troopers. Sheridan's horsemen collided with Pickett's oncoming Confederates, resulting in the engagement at DINWIDDIE COURT HOUSE.

Warren, meanwhile, moving more slowly than the cavalry, pushed 1 division toward the White Oak road. Advancing through the woods, the Federals ran headlong into Lee's charging Southerners. The Confederate attack disrupted the Union line, shoving the division back in disorder through the camps of Warren's 2d Division. The corps commander then brought up his 3d Division, which recovered the lost ground in stubborn combat.

The engagements at Dinwiddie Court House and White Oak road were preliminary encounters; the next day Sheridan crushed the Confederate right flank in the decisive Battle of FIVE FORKS.   —JDW

White Oak Swamp (Charles City Cross Roads; Frayser's Farm; Glendale; Nelson's Cross Roads; New Market Road; Turkey Bridge; Willis' Church), Va., Battle of.
30 June 1862 On 30 June 1862, Gen. ROBERT E. LEE's planned convergence on Maj. Gen. GEORGE B. MCCLELLAN's

retreating army again miscarried. Again Maj. Gen. THOMAS J. "STONEWALL" JACKSON was slow and indecisive in his advance. Once again Maj. Gen. JOHN B. MAGRUDER vacillated, and Maj. Gen. BENJAMIN HUGER allowed felled trees across the Charles City road to block his advance. As a result Maj. Gens. JAMES LONGSTREET's and AMBROSE P. HILL's divisions were all but alone in the assault that began about 4 p.m. against the Federal division commanded by Brig. Gen. George A. McCall.

The Confederates were successful at first, breaking McCall's line and even capturing the general, who was attempting to rally support for his fleeing division. But Hill and Longstreet struck very near the center of the ARMY OF THE POTOMAC and Federal reinforcements were nearby. Brig. Gen. PHILIP KEARNY's and Maj. Gen. JOSEPH HOOKER's divisions, along with Brig. Gen. JOHN SEDGWICK's, closed the gap. In brutal, often hand-to-hand, fighting amid tangled undergrowth, the battle raged into the night. When it was over the Union line had held, and McClellan's escape was all but secure.

During the night, 4 Union corps took up positions on MALVERN HILL. McClellan's remaining corps, that of Brig. Gen. ERASMUS D. KEYES, occupied Harrison's Landing about 7 mi away. The huge wagon train of the Army of the Potomac was also at Harrison's Landing, safely under the guns of Federal warships on the James. The fighting on this the sixth day of the SEVEN DAYS' CAMPAIGN cost the Union 2,853 casualties; the Confederates lost 3,615.   —EMT

White Point, S.C., eng. at.   29 Apr. 1862 In Apr. 1862, Lt. Alexander C. Rhind was the senior naval officer serving with the Union forces on Edisto Island, below Charleston. An energetic and resourceful career officer, Rhind nevertheless had a black mark on his record: in 1855, on the recommendation of a Naval Efficiency Board, he had been dropped from the service. Though he had been reinstated 3 years later, the action still rankled. Now he was determined to show Flag Officer SAMUEL F. DU PONT, commanding the SOUTH ATLANTIC BLOCKADING SQUADRON and in 1855 a member of the efficiency board, that Du Pont had erred badly 7 years earlier.

On 29 Apr. Rhind left the island headquarters of the local commander, Brig. Gen. HORATIO G. WRIGHT, aboard Lt. James H. Gillis' *E. B. Hale,* a former freighter fitted with a pair of rifled cannon. He took the little gunboat up the Dawhoo River toward a strategically located Confederate land battery near Grimball's Plantation, 2 mi below the Dawhoo's confluence with the South Edisto River. Reaching the fort late in the day, the *Hale* made directly for it, under a shower of fire from 2 Confederate 32-pounder cannon on the north bank. Once within range, as Admiral Du Pont later noted, Rhind opened "with greater damage than he himself expected, when the rebels, a large force too, cleared out." Before enemy reinforcements could arrive, the lieutenant dispatched a landing party that spiked the guns, burned their platforms and carriages, and leveled their works.

His job well done, Rhind reembarked and early that evening retraced his route downriver. On the way, he sensed that enemy land troops were gathering to dispute his passage near White Point, where heavy timber could mask their presence. Before reaching the area, Rhind ordered Gillis and his crew to hug the deck of the ship, which enabled them to avoid the torrent of rifle and cannon fire that crashed forth from the trees. At an oblique angle to Evans' position, the *Hale* blasted the enemy into withdrawing. The leader of the ambush, Brig. Gen.

NATHAN G. EVANS, commander of South Carolina's Third Military District, boasted of killing and wounding several crewmen and crippling their vessel. Actually, Rhind's foresight had combined with gathering darkness to prevent the infliction of a single Union injury, which General Wright termed "almost a miracle." On returning to Edisto Island, Rhind received the sort of publicity he had sought: an admiring Du Pont wrote that "these things will really keep up the gunboat prestige." —EGL

White Sulphur Springs, W.Va., eng. at. 26 Aug. 1863
See ROCKY GAP, W.VA., ENG. AT.

Whitfield, John Wilkins. CSA b. Franklin, Tenn., 11 Mar. 1818. Reared and educated in Tennessee, Whitfield volunteered for military duty during the Mexican War, serving as captain, then lieutenant, of Tennessee regiments. In 1853 he moved to Independence, Mo., working as an Indian agent in Missouri and Arkansas. About a year later he relocated to Tecumseh in newly organized Kansas Territory. There the residents elected him territorial delegate to the 33d U.S. Congress, and he took his seat in Washington 20 Dec. 1854, 16 days into the second session. Though he was returned to the 34th Congress, the election was contested and his seat declared vacant 1 Aug. 1856.

LC

At the beginning of the Civil War Whitfield was employed as register of the land office at Doniphan, Kans. He entered Confederate service as major of the 4th Battalion Texas Cavalry and at PEA RIDGE, 7–8 Mar. 1862, commanded the 27th Texas (Whitfield's Texas Legion). That autumn his command, along with the 3d Louisiana, suffered heavy losses when they charged the Federal lines at IUKA and captured 9 cannon. Whitfield himself was severely wounded in the fighting.

Attached to Maj. Gen. EARL VAN DORN's command in Tennessee early in 1863, Whitfield was promoted to brigadier general 9 May. Through early summer he participated in the defense of VICKSBURG, operating under Brig. Gen. WILLIAM H. JACKSON in Mississippi later that year. He does not appear to have had a command at the time he was paroled at Columbus, Tex., 29 June 1865.

Whitfield stayed in Texas after the Confederate surrender, settling in Lavaca County and serving in the state legislature. d. near Hallettsville, Tex., 27 Oct. 1879. —PLF

Whiting, William Henry Chase. CSA b. Biloxi, Miss., 22 Mar. 1824. The son of a lieutenant colonel in the U.S. Army, Whiting graduated in engineering from West Point 1st in the class of 1845 with the highest scholastic record ever attained by a cadet until that time.

As a rising young captain in the Corps of Engineers, he was engaged in river and harbor improvements until he resigned 20 Feb. 1861 to fight for the Confederacy. Thus began a military career that showed him to be an outstanding engineer but a disappointment as a field commander, largely because of his pessimistic nature and his inability to get along with certain fellow officers.

LC

Whiting was assigned to duty as chief engineer with the Army of the Shenandoah, commanded by Gen. JOSEPH E. JOHNSTON. In Aug. 1861, after he had arranged the transfer of this army to Manassas, Va. (*see* BULL RUN, VA., FIRST BATTLE OF), he was promoted to brigadier general, to rank from 21 July.

One officer to whom Whiting took a dislike, perhaps jealously, was Maj. Gen. THOMAS J. "STONEWALL" JACKSON, who had ranked only 17th scholastically in the West Point class of 1846. Gen. ROBERT E. LEE, who succeeded Johnston, recognized Whiting's faults but realized that he was a good engineer. To avoid trouble in the field, Lee had him transferred to command of the military district at Wilmington, N.C. There Whiting put to good use his engineering abilities by erecting Fort Fisher, the South's strongest bastion. He was promoted to major general 22 Apr. 1863.

In May 1864 he was assigned to cooperate with Gen. P.G.T. BEAUREGARD in driving off Union troops besieging Richmond from the east. His failure to do so led to charges that at the time he was either drunk or under the influence of narcotics. At his own request, he was returned to the command at Wilmington, N.C.

In the successful Union attack on FORT FISHER 15 Jan. 1865, Whiting was wounded twice while leading a counterattack. Captured, he was imprisoned on Governor's Island in New York harbor, where he died of his injures 10 Mar. —VCJ

Whitman, Walter. poet, journalist b. West Hills, Long Island, N.Y., 31 May 1819. Born in a farming community, at age 4 Walt Whitman moved with his family to Brooklyn, N.Y. After a public-school education, at age 11 he became an office boy. When he was 14 his family returned to Long Island, but Whitman stayed in Brooklyn, worked as a printer's apprentice, then entered journalism. By the outbreak of the Civil War he had been the editor of several newspapers, most notably the Brooklyn *Eagle.* He established himself as a Free-Soiler in politics, traveled to New Orleans as a writer for the New Orleans *Crescent,* and became a minor literary personality following a poorly received first edition of 12 of his poems entitled *Leaves of Grass* (1855).

Until Dec. 1862 he wrote feature articles for the Brooklyn *Standard* and New York *Leader.* After his brother George, a member of the 51st New York Infantry, was wounded in the Battle of FREDERICKSBURG, Whitman traveled to Virginia to find him. Exposed to hospital work, in 1863 he established himself in Washington, D.C., as a volunteer nursing aide, raising funds for soldiers' relief and supporting himself as a part-time clerk. Connected with the U.S. CHRISTIAN COMMISSION, he traveled occasionally to the Virginia countryside and observed a few military operations, while seeking appointment to a government clerkship to sustain him in his charity work. On 1 Jan. 1865, he won appointment as a clerk in the Department of the Interior's Bureau of Indian Affairs, was dismissed from this position 30 June 1865, and 1 July became a clerk in the attorney general's office. He remained in government employ until disabled by a stroke 18 Jan. 1873.

Whitman's Civil War experience inspired him to write the

collection of poems *Drum-Taps* (1865) and the prose work *Memoranda During the War* (1875). Grieving over the assassination of Pres. ABRAHAM LINCOLN, he chose a phrase from contemporary author Herman Melville's *Moby-Dick* and wrote the poem "O Captain! My Captain!," first published in the New York *Saturday Press* in 1865. This poem is his best remembered work of the Civil War period and the only one to gain broad public acceptance during his lifetime. His regularly expanded and revised editions of *Leaves of Grass,* addressing sexual matters among many other things, gave him an ill-deserved national reputation as someone morally suspect, and resulted in his dismissal from his Interior Department clerkship. Residing in Camden, N.J., from 1873, he died there 26 Mar. 1892. —JES

Whitworth rifle. In the mid-1850s English engineer Sir Joseph Whitworth developed a rifle for the Royal Army that attained a deadly range of 1,500–1,800 yd. A percussion-cap weapon with a hexagonal bore of .45 in., it fired a long, grooved, hexagonal projectile made of hard lead and carried a telescopic sight mounted on the left of the stock. Approximating the size and dimensions of the familiar ENFIELD RIFLE, it saw only limited Royal Army service.

Confederates imported Whitworth rifles from the Enfield armory in unknown numbers. They were the preferred arm of Southern SHARPSHOOTERS, and were usually reserved for issue to men detailed for sniper duty. However, several Southern Whitworths were privately owned. This weapon, used to good effect in siege situations, was feared at PETERSBURG, where deadly results showed that at a range of just over a mile, one of its projectiles deviated less than 12 ft from its intended target. —JES

Wickham, Williams Carter. CSA b. Richmond, Va., 21 Sept. 1820. A graduate of the University of Virginia, Wickham enjoyed a varied antebellum career. He practiced law before turning to planting, served in both houses of the Virginia state legislature, and was presiding justice of the Hanover County court. When Virginia seceded Apr. 1861, Wickham, a Unionist in principle, and his militia company, the Hanover Dragoons, volunteered immediately for Confederate service.

LC

With the rank of captain, Wickham fought at FIRST BULL RUN. In September he was elected lieutenant colonel of the 4th Virginia Cavalry, serving for the next 3 years in the Cavalry Corps/Army of Northern Virginia. On 5 May 1862, at WILLIAMSBURG, he suffered a saber wound and, while recovering at his home, was captured by Federals. Exchanged shortly thereafter for a Union officer who was his wife's kinsman, Wickham was promoted to colonel in August. He led the 4th Virginia Cavalry at SECOND BULL RUN and at ANTIETAM. While temporarily commanding a brigade, he was wounded in the latter stages of the ANTIETAM CAMPAIGN.

He fought in nearly every major battle or cavalry engagement during 1863–64, commanding his regiment at CHANCELLORSVILLE and GETTYSBURG. Promoted to brigadier general 1

Sept. 1863, he directed a brigade for the remainder of his service. In Feb. 1864 his command helped repel Union Brig. Gen. H. JUDSON KILPATRICK's raid on Richmond. Wickham fought in the battles of the OVERLAND CAMPAIGN May–June 1864 and concluded his service in the 1864 SHENANDOAH VALLEY CAMPAIGN. On 9 Nov. the cavalry officer resigned to take his seat in the Confederate Congress, to which he had been elected in spring 1863, having postponed accepting the seat to remain in the field. He then participated in the unsuccessful HAMPTON ROADS CONFERENCE.

Wickham returned to his plantation after the war and soon left the Whigs to join the Republican party. Though considered apostasy by most former Confederates, his change of allegiance apparently had little effect on his career. He served with success as president of the Virginia Central Railroad and subsequently of the Chesapeake & Ohio, held some political offices, and rejected the secretaryship of the navy and the Republican gubernatorial nomination. He died 23 July 1888 while a state senator and chairman of the board of supervisors of Hanover County. —JDW

Widow Bixby letter. Massachusetts Gov. JOHN A. ANDREW, in Sept. 1864, wrote a memorandum to the War Department relating the tragic case of one of his state's citizens. William Schuler, the Massachusetts adjutant general, had informed Andrew that a widow, Mrs. Lydia Bixby, 15 Dover St., Boston, had lost 5 sons in the war. Mrs. Bixby had subsequently visited the governor, showing him 5 letters from 5 company commanders and claiming that each son had been killed in battle. Andrew then informed the War Department, adding that "this is a case so remarkable that I really wish a letter might be written her by the President of the United States."

The War Department requested an investigation by Schuler, who soon certified the deaths with names of the sons—Charles, Henry, Edward, Oliver, and George—regiments, and dates of death. With this information, the department forwarded the document to Pres. ABRAHAM LINCOLN in mid-October. In the midst of a reelection campaign, Lincoln held the letter for more than a month. The president had in the past written a few letters to bereaved parents and 21 Nov. wrote a letter to Mrs. Bixby.

Addressing it only "Mrs. Bixby, Boston, Massachusetts," Lincoln said:

> "I have been shown in the files of the War Department a statement of the Adjutant-General of Massachusetts that you are the mother of five sons who have died gloriously on the field of battle. I feel how weak and fruitless must be any words of mine which should attempt to beguile you from grief of a loss so overwhelming. But I cannot refrain from tendering to you the consolation that may be found in the thanks of the Republic they died to save. I pray that our heavenly Father may assuage the anguish of your bereavement, and leave you only the cherished memory of the loved and lost, and the solemn pride that must be yours to have laid so costly a sacrifice upon the altar of freedom."

He then signed it, "Abraham Lincoln."

Schuler copied the letter and distributed it to Boston newspapers, and Lincoln's words were soon read across the nation. Some critics called the letter "cheap sympathy," but most praised it. The government subsequently learned that only Charles and Oliver had been killed, that Henry had been captured, and Edward and George had deserted. But by that time

Lincoln's words had reached into thousands of Northern homes, where grieving parents, wives, and children understood individually the human agony of war.   —JDW

Wigfall, Louis Trezevant. CSP/CSA b. near Edgefield, S.C., 21 Apr. 1816, Wigfall attended the University of Virginia for a year, graduating from South Carolina College in 1837. A lawyer who espoused secession as early as 1844 in protest against the protective tariff and the defeat of Texas' annexation, Wigfall became an outspoken leader in the disunionist movement. He moved to Marshall, Tex., in 1848 and is identified with that state.

USMHI

The ambitious Democrat served in both houses of the Texas legislature. He entered the U.S. Senate in 1859, a leader among the Southern-rights faction that agitated for the Federal government to protect slave-owners' freedom to settle in the territories with their black slaves. Increasingly he preached SOUTHERN NATIONALISM, opposing all attempts at compromise during the secession crisis. In Dec. 1860 he wrote the SOUTHERN MANIFESTO, which declared conciliation hopeless and independent nationhood the only course open to the disaffected states. Along with 5 other Southern senators, he refused to vote on the CRITTENDEN COMPROMISE Jan. 1861, causing the defeat of the only measure that might have averted war. During these weeks he urged the Southern state governments to take over Federal military installations, stressing the importance of establishing control over FORT SUMTER and FORT PICKENS. Despite his vocal disloyalty, he stayed in the U.S. capital to keep abreast of the government's activities until 23 Mar., finally being expelled from the Senate in July.

Meanwhile, Wigfall had traveled to Charleston to become one of Brig. Gen. P.G.T. BEAUREGARD's several aides-de-camp, gaining notoriety and what little military experience he would ever possess by rowing across the harbor during the bombardment to present unauthorized terms for surrendering the garrison. Though he had already been appointed to the Provisional Congress, Texas commissioned him colonel of the 1st Texas Infantry 28 Aug., and Pres. JEFFERSON DAVIS rewarded his patriotism with a brigadiership in the Confederate army 21 Oct. His field service was fortuitously brief. On 18 Feb. 1862, he resigned to take his seat in the Confederate Senate.

The energetic, inflexible nationalist vigorously supported CONSCRIPTION, IMPRESSMENT, the suspension of *HABEAS CORPUS,* and the government takeover of railroads, all unpopular measures he believed necessary to Confederate success. He also relentlessly defended STATES RIGHTS whenever he believed the central government's policies infringed on private citizens' freedoms, and his opposition to a SUPREME COURT helped prevent Congress from enacting the Constitutional clause authorizing that judicial body.

A bitter opponent of Davis' military policies, Wigfall blamed the president for the loss of Vicksburg and led the movement to have him stripped of his powers as commander-in-chief of the army. His denunciation of Davis for removing Gen. JOSEPH

E. JOHNSTON from command of the Army of Tennessee further strained relations between the two politicians. Largely through Wigfall's efforts, Congress finally pressured Davis into naming Gen. ROBERT E. LEE general-in-chief of all Confederate armies Jan. 1865.

After the Confederate collapse Wigfall fled to Texas. Refusing to accept defeat, he hoped to continue the war there, but learned on his arrival that the army in that sector had already disbanded. Sought by Federal authorities, he went into hiding, finally escaping to England about Mar. 1866. He stayed abroad for 6 years, until friends in the U.S. sent word that he could return to the country without being arrested. His wife arrived first and purchased a house in Baltimore near his married daughter's residence. Wigfall soon followed, but he wanted to go home to Texas and did so Jan. 1874. On 17 Feb., within weeks of his arrival in Galveston, the 57-year-old secessionist died.   —PLF

"Wigwag" cross-signal communications. Prior to the mid-19th century, military information was transmitted across long distances by stationary flags, semaphores, heliostats, and other rudimentary communications devices. Modern SIGNAL COMMUNICATIONS began about 1854, with the work of army surgeon ALBERT J. MYER. Having studied deaf-mute alphabets, telegraphic codes, and Indian smoke signals, Myer by 1856 had developed a signal technique employing the waving of flags by day and torches by night.

Myer's system leaned heavily on the Bain and Morse TELEGRAPH alphabets. The former used 2 elements (dot and dash) to signify letters, the latter 4 elements (dot, short dash, long dash, and the interval between dashes). Combining these methods, Myer devised a 4-element code based on a 2-motion concept. Swings of a colored flag or torch (both to and from a vertical position) represented numbers, which, in combinations, spelled out the letters of the alphabet. Later he simplified his system by using 2 elements—numbers 1 and 2.

The process of transmittal was slow; even abbreviations failed to speed the pace beyond about 3 words per minute. But flags could send messages as far as 20 mi on a clear day, a much greater range than older signal devices had boasted. Myer's technique also required only a single, portable apparatus, in contrast to the varied and cumbersome equipment previously used by both army and navy. One of Myer's pupils, 2d Lt. E. PORTER ALEXANDER, later observed that "by the waving of anything to the left for dot, and to the right for dash, any letter could be indicated by a few waves."

The "wigwagging" of messages became one of the most visible features of Civil War communications. In June 1861 the U.S. Army established a signal school near Fort Monroe, Va., with Myer as instructor. 11 months later, a Signal Bureau was set up within the Confederate War Department in Richmond. Myer's system was first used to effect 21 July 1861, when Alexander, now chief signal officer to Confederate Brig. Gen. P.G.T. BEAUREGARD, used it to warn his commander of a turning movement at FIRST BULL RUN, thus thwarting Union victory. The signal corps of both armies grew with the scope of the conflict, and wigwagging played a prominent role in numerous battles, including HATTERAS INLET, FORT PULASKI, SECOND BULL RUN, ANTIETAM, CHANCELLORSVILLE, GETTYSBURG, PORT HUDSON, MOBILE BAY, ALLATOONA, and FORT FISHER.   —EGL

Wilcox, Cadmus Marcellus. CSA b. Wayne Cty., N.C.,

29 May 1824, Wilcox graduated from West Point 54th in the class of 1846, in time to win a brevet as 1st lieutenant in Mexico for gallantry at Chapultepec and Mexico City. Dur-
ing the 1850s he served at rou-
tine frontier posts and as an instructor at the Military Academy, where he wrote a text on rifle practice.

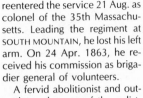

Wilcox entered Confederate service July 1861 as colonel, and by October he was com-
manding a brigade in Maj. Gen. JAMES LONGSTREET's division, his promotion to brigadier general dated 21 Oct. At SEVEN PINES and during the SEVEN DAYS' CAM-
PAIGN, he proved an able briga-

LC

dier; in the campaign his hard-fighting Alabama troops suffered the heaviest casualties in the Confederate army. Throughout the SECOND BULL RUN and FREDERICKSBURG campaigns, Wilcox continued to render reliable service, but his greatest day came in the CHANCELLORSVILLE CAMPAIGN.

3 May 1863 found him guarding Banks' Ford on the Rappahannock, well behind the main action raging at Chancellors-
ville. While disappointed over missing the fighting, Wilcox maintained his vigilance and soon discovered a Union attempt to strike Gen. ROBERT E. LEE from the rear with a corps moving toward Chancellorsville from Fredericksburg. In a classic holding action at SALEM CHURCH, Wilcox delayed the Federal ad-
vance, allowing Lee to take the offensive against Federals commanded by Maj. Gen. JOSEPH HOOKER, then turn to defeat the new threat.

Heavy losses sustained in futile support of PICKETT'S CHARGE at GETTYSBURG soured Wilcox's attitude toward Longstreet, his corps commander. On 3 Aug. 1863, Wilcox's overdue promotion to major general sent him to command a division in Lt. Gen. AMBROSE P. HILL's III Corps. As part of Hill's Corps, Wilcox was frequently in the heaviest fighting of 1864 at the WILDER-
NESS, SPOTSYLVANIA, and PETERSBURG. As the long Petersburg siege debilitated Lee's army, he held his division together. On 2 Apr. 1865, his men stubbornly held FORT GREGG, temporarily denying the Federals the streets of Petersburg. On 9 Apr. Wil-
COX, with the rest of the ARMY OF NORTHERN VIRGINIA, sur-
rendered, as he prepared to lead an assault against the encircling Union forces.

After the war, Wilcox lived in Washington, D.C. From 1886 until his death 2 Dec. 1890, he held the post of chief of the railroad division in the U.S. Government Land Office.

—BNO

Wild, Edward Augustus. USA b. Brookline, Mass., 25 Nov. 1825, Wild graduated from Harvard in 1844, then from Jefferson Medical College. He extended his medical studies in Paris, France, before serving as a medical officer in the Turkish army during the Crimean War. Returning to Massachusetts, he practiced his profession until the outbreak of the Civil War.

The doctor chose field duty, enlisted in the 1st Massachu-
setts, and became captain of a company 23 May 1861. The regiment suffered only 1 casualty at FIRST BULL RUN. During the 1862 PENINSULA CAMPAIGN, Wild fell severely wounded at SEVEN PINES. He mustered out with his regiment 23 July, but

reentered the service 21 Aug. as colonel of the 35th Massachu-
setts. Leading the regiment at SOUTH MOUNTAIN, he lost his left arm. On 24 Apr. 1863, he received his commission as briga-
dier general of volunteers.

A fervid abolitionist and outspoken advocate of the enlist-
ment of BLACK SOLDIERS, Wild returned to duty recruiting FREEDMEN and former slaves. On 30 June 1863, "Wild's African Brigade" was organized at New Berne, N.C. Initially the unit

LC

served in Charleston harbor, S.C., then transferred to south-
eastern Virginia, where Wild commanded all black troops in the area. During the PETERSBURG CAMPAIGN in 1864, his brigade served in the XVIII Corps, and, when the war ended, was part of the occupation force in Richmond, Va. Wild mustered out Jan. 1866.

Rather than resume his medical practice after the war, Wild became involved in silver mining, running a mine in Nevada before journeying to South America, where he pursued his business. He died in Medellín, Colombia, 28 Aug. 1891, and was buried there.

—JDW

Wilderness, Va., Battle of the. 5–7 May 1864 12 a.m., 4 May 1864, the Army of the Potomac began crossing the Rapidan River in an effort to turn the strategic right flank of the ARMY OF NORTHERN VIRGINIA. Within 36 hours the adversaries were locked in combat in an impenetrable, marshy tract of land known as the Wilderness. Though Maj. Gen. GEORGE G. MEADE commanded the ARMY OF THE POTOMAC, general-in-
chief Lt. Gen. ULYSSES S. GRANT would direct the battle. Gen. ROBERT E. LEE commanded the Confederate army.

The Federal army moved into the Wilderness 4 May, using the Germanna Plank Road and the Ely's Ford road. Confeder-
ate reaction to the advance was prompt, and by noon Lt. Gen. RICHARD S. EWELL's II Corps on the Orange Turnpike and Lt. Gen. AMBROSE P. HILL's III Corps on the Plank Road were moving toward the Union forces. In both armies the infantry was ineffectively screened by the cavalry command who were protecting its lines of supply.

On the morning of the 5th, Union V Corps pickets reported the Confederates' presence, and Meade at 7:30 a.m. ordered Maj. Gen. GOUVERNEUR K. WARREN to attack. The initial assault nearly broke the Confederate line, but Warren had delayed the attack until 1 p.m., allowing Ewell to bring up reinforcements. Counterattacking, Ewell pushed back the Union troops. Further Federal advances were repulsed, including an attempt by Maj. Gen. JOHN SEDGWICK's VI Corps to turn Ewell's left flank. The fighting continued until nightfall.

Meanwhile, Hill's III Corps had pushed forward, brushing aside 1 regiment of Union cavalry, until halted by Brig. Gen. GEORGE W. GETTY's division of the VI Corps, just short of the Brock road. At 4 p.m. Getty, supported by the II Corps, attacked the Confederates, but several Federal units performed badly and the assault failed. A later attempt by Maj. Gen. WINFIELD S. HANCOCK almost broke Hill's lines but was repulsed. The onset of darkness gave relief to the Southerners.

There was no significant cavalry action on the 5th, except

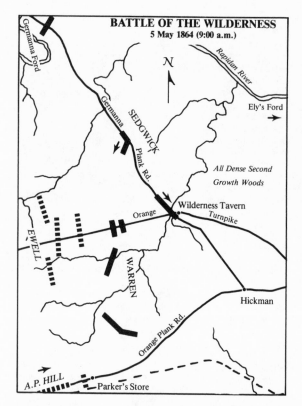

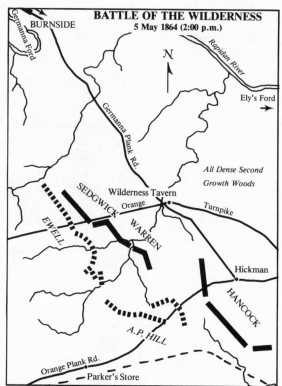

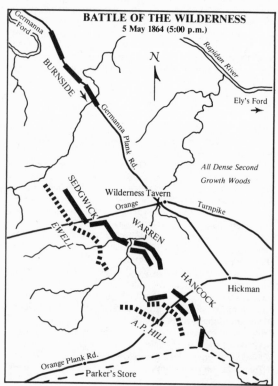

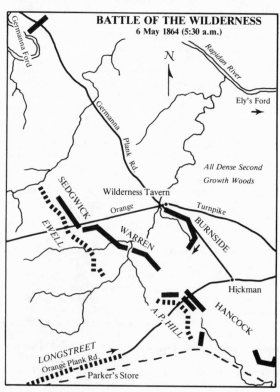

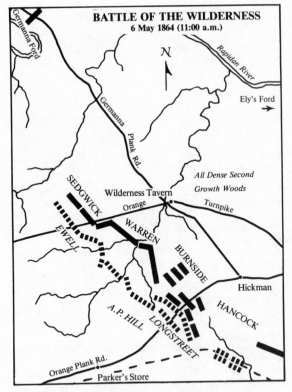

BATTLE OF THE WILDERNESS
6 May 1864 (11:00 a.m.)

for an encounter between Brig. Gen. THOMAS L. ROSSER's Confederate horsemen and Brig. Gen. JAMES H. WILSON's Union cavalrymen. The day ended with the opposing cavalries facing each other on the southern flanks of the armies.

On the 6th Grant ordered a 5 a.m. attack to throw the Union right against the Confederate left while Hancock completed his destruction of Hill. He also ordered Maj. Gen. AMBROSE E. BURNSIDE's IX Corps to advance between the Union concentrations and into a gap that separated Ewell and Hill. Though Lee had no definitive plans for the 6th, the Confederates delivered the first blow. At 4:30 a.m., Ewell attacked the VI Corps but was driven back by Federal forces preparing to launch their own offensive. Further Union attempts were not strong enough to defeat Ewell or to prevent him from sending reinforcements to other parts of the Southern line.

Hancock went forward against Hill as planned at 5 a.m., and, meeting little resistance, drove the Confederate III Corps from the field. However, Burnside was late, and instead of completing the destruction of the Confederate right, he ran into Ewell's reserve, which had been hurried forward, and was halted. By now, Confederate Lt. Gen. JAMES LONGSTREET's I Corps had arrived. With his men and reorganized units of the III Corps, he stopped Hancock's advance and closed the gap between Ewell and Hill. Further Southern attacks pushed Hancock back, and his efforts to resume the offensive were unsuccessful. By late morning, the fighting had reached a stalemate.

In fact, the Confederate defense was so strong that it enabled Longstreet to detach 4 brigades for a flanking maneuver against Hancock's left. A Southern reconnaissance had discovered a shielded approach to that position, and the flanking column led by Lt. Col. G. MOXLEY SORREL attacked it at 11:30 a.m., driving the Union forces in disorder from the south side

of the Plank Road. Simultaneously, Longstreet pushed forward his other divisions in a frontal attack. The combined assaults drove Hancock back to the Brock road.

Another Confederate reconnaissance determined that the left flank of the Brock road position was vulnerable. As the units were being assembled to attack, Longstreet and others were mistakenly fired upon by men from Sorrel's brigades. Lee then took command and, instead of the flank attack, launched a massive blow at Hancock's center at 4 p.m. The delay gave the Federals time to reorganize and strengthen their field works. Though they began to penetrate the Union position, by 5 p.m. the Confederates had been repulsed with the aid of Union artillery. Fighting in this section of the Wilderness ended.

Meanwhile, Ewell, learning that Sedgwick's right flank was exposed, attacked at 6 p.m. Initially the assault was successful, but with the arrival of reinforcements and nightfall, Federal soldiers were able to force the Confederates back to their lines. This action concluded the Battle of the Wilderness. The cavalry had engaged only lightly again on the 6th.

The effective strength of the Army of the Potomac was 115,-000; it suffered 17,500 casualties (15%). The effective strength of the Army of Northern Virginia was 60,000; its casualties have been estimated at 7,500 (12%). The battle ended in a tactical draw. However, it was a strategic victory for Grant, who turned south 7 May unimpeded by Lee. —MMul

Wilkes, Charles D. USN b. New York City, N.Y., 3 Apr. 1798. The son of a New York merchant, Wilkes early developed a love for the sea and joined the navy when he was 20. Though a brilliant student of navigation and naval technology, he was headstrong and almost constantly at odds with his superiors. His most notable post before the war was commander of a naval expedition in the Pacific 1838–42. Despite the very real accomplishments of the mission, it ended in controversy, and Wilkes was still only a captain at the onset of the Civil War.

Wilkes is best known for his part in the *TRENT* AFFAIR of Nov. 1861. Commanding a Union warship, he removed 2 Confederate envoys, JOHN SLIDELL and JAMES M. MASON, from the British mail packet *Trent*. Though he acted against orders and the British ship was unarmed, Wilkes quickly became a hero in the North. The incident embarrassed the Lincoln administration and raised the possibility of a confrontation with Great Britain. A rupture was avoided, but Wilkes continued to be a controversial figure until his removal from active duty June 1863.

USMHI

In Sept. 1862 Wilkes was given command of a "flying squadron" of 7 vessels in the West Indies and was ordered to harass Confederate trade. The appointment of this aggressive man was intended as a warning to the British that the U.S. meant to enforce vigorously its interpretations of maritime rules. Wilkes frequently exceeded his instructions and repeatedly clashed with the British. Because of growing domestic criticism of his conduct, and because Lincoln now wanted to placate the British, Wilkes was relieved in 1863. In Mar. 1864 he was court-martialed and received a public reprimand. He died embittered 8 Feb. 1877, in the District of Columbia. —RJM

Willcox, Orlando Bolivar. USA b. Detroit, Mich., 16 Apr. 1823. Graduating 8th in the West Point class of 1847, Willcox served in garrisons in Mexico, New Mexico Territory, Massachusetts, and Florida. In 1857 he resigned his commission, returned to Detroit, and became an attorney.

Reenlisting in military service 1 May 1861 as colonel of the 1st Michigan, he led his regiment at FIRST BULL RUN, where he was wounded and captured. In Confederate prisons for more than a year, Willcox was released 19 Aug. 1862 and on that day received his commission as brigadier general, to rank from 21 July 1861, the date of First Bull Run. Assigned a division of the IX Corps, he directed it at SOUTH MOUNTAIN and ANTIETAM. When Maj. Gen. AMBROSE E. BURNSIDE, the corps commander, succeeded to command of the army, Willcox led the corps at FREDERICKSBURG.

LC

Early in 1863 the IX Corps was transferred to the West, assigned to the Army of the Ohio. During 1863 and part of 1864, Willcox commanded the corps 3 times. He also served briefly as commander of the District of Central Kentucky. The IX Corps in spring 1864 returned to Virginia, where Willcox led his division at the WILDERNESS, SPOTSYLVANIA, COLD HARBOR, and PETERSBURG. When Burnside resigned after the disastrous Battle of the CRATER, 30 July, Maj. Gen. JOHN G. PARKE, the corps's chief of staff, not Willcox, assumed command. Despite his excellent record, Willcox had never been promoted to major general. He stayed at divisional command until the surrender at Appomattox.

Brevetted major general in the volunteer and Regular service, Willcox was mustered out Jan. 1866, returning to his legal practice in Detroit. In July, however, the army was enlarged, and he was reappointed as colonel of the 29th U.S. Infantry, remaining in the army for 21 years. Because of his performance as commander of the Department of Arizona, the town of Willcox, Ariz., was named after him. He retired in 1887 and, 8 years later, Congress awarded him the MEDAL OF HONOR for his performance at First Bull Run. Willcox died in Coburg, Ontario, Canada, 10 May 1907, and was buried in Arlington National Cemetery. —JDW

Williams, John Stuart. CSA b. Mt. Sterling, Ky., 10 July 1818, Williams graduated from Miami University in Oxford, Ohio, in 1839, passed the Kentucky bar, and established a legal practice in Paris, Ky., in 1840. During the Mexican War, as captain of a volunteer company of independent scouts, he campaigned with the 6th U.S. Infantry, then won election to colonel of the 4th Kentucky Volunteers. For distinction at the battle of the same name, his troops awarded him the sobriquet "Cerro Gordo." Returning to Kentucky, he resumed his law career, was elected to the state legislature in 1851 and 1853, and early advocated Kentucky's neutrality during the secession crisis.

With the onset of Union military activity in the state, Williams crossed southeast into Virginia, with Brig. Gen. HUMPHREY MARSHALL tried to organize a command, and in mid-October reentered Kentucky to raise a regiment. His recruitment camp was assaulted by Brig. Gen. WILLIAM NELSON, resulting in the engagement at IVY MOUNTAIN, Ky., 8 Nov. 1861. Returning to Virginia, Williams received formal commission as colonel of the 5th Kentucky Infantry 16 Nov.,

USMHI

and through winter 1861–62 dueled with Nelson in forays across the Kentucky-Virginia border. He was promoted to brigadier general 16 Apr. 1862, his brigade first consisting of the 8th Virginia Cavalry; the 22d, 36th, and 45th Virginia infantry; 2 small battalions; and a battery of light artillery. Williams next served in operations around Cumberland Gap in July, fought under Marshall in the autumn 1862 KENTUCKY CAMPAIGN, then led a combined force of Kentucky, Georgia, Tennessee, and Virginia cavalry in operations in southwestern Virginia until 6 Sept. 1863, when he assumed command of all troops in Tennessee east of Knoxville.

In this post he directed several brisk engagements with Union Maj. Gen. AMBROSE E. BURNSIDE's forces and fought a valiant delaying action at BLUE SPRINGS, Tenn., in October. Unhappy with the support he received there, he requested relief from duty in November, assumed limited duties around Abingdon and Saltville, Va., then joined Maj. Gen. ROBERT RANSOM's division in the Trans-Allegheny Department Jan. 1864. Assigned to Maj. Gen. JOSEPH WHEELER's cavalry for the ATLANTA CAMPAIGN, in Brig. Gen. JOHN H. KELLY's division from July 1864, he rode on WHEELER'S RAID of Aug.–Sept. 1864. In Tennessee he begged Wheeler to detach to him a portion of the raiding force for a strike on Union cavalry at Strawberry Plains. He did not reach his objective. Wheeler was denied the detached troops for the remainder of the raid and censured Williams in his report. Williams spent the remainder of the war in southwestern Virginia.

Settling in Winchester, Ky., in postbellum years, Williams turned to farming, was elected to the state legislature in 1873 and 1875, and was defeated in a bid for the governorship in 1875. He won election to the U.S. Senate in 1878, served until defeated in the election of 1883, then resumed farming. d. Mount Sterling, Ky., 17 July 1898. —JES

Williams, Thomas. USA b. Albany, N.Y., 10 Jan. 1815. Williams' military career before the Civil War was extensive. His father, a militia general, commanded young Williams as a private in the Black Hawk War. In 1837 Williams graduated from the U.S. Military Academy, ranking 12th in his class, then served consecutively against the Seminole Indians, on garrison duty in Florida, and as an instructor at West Point. In the Mexican War he fought under Gen. WINFIELD SCOTT as the general's aide-de-camp. After the war he served at various garrison posts and again fought the Seminoles, this time in the West.

Williams was attending artillery school at FORT MONROE, Va., when he officially entered Civil War service as major of the 5th

Artillery May 1861. By 28 Sept. he had been promoted brigadier general and assigned as inspector general of the DEPARTMENT OF VIRGINIA. Returning to his old regiment, he embarked with Brig. Gen. AMBROSE E. BURNSIDE on the North Carolina Expedition in October and later took command of Fort Hatteras.

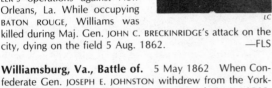

LC

He then journeyed south to join Maj. Gen. BENJAMIN F. BUTLER's operations against New Orleans, La. While occupying BATON ROUGE, Williams was killed during Maj. Gen. JOHN C. BRECKINRIDGE's attack on the city, dying on the field 5 Aug. 1862.   —FLS

Williamsburg, Va., Battle of. 5 May 1862 When Confederate Gen. JOSEPH E. JOHNSTON withdrew from the Yorktown line across the tip of the Virginia peninsula 3 May 1862, he did so in order to find more favorable circumstances in which to confront Maj. Gen. GEORGE B. MCCLELLAN's massive Federal army. McClellan, in turn, sent troops in pursuit to press his advantage, and his vanguard overtook Johnston's rear guard near Williamsburg.

Months earlier, Confederate Maj. Gen. JOHN B. MAGRUDER had established a crude line of field works about 2 mi east of Williamsburg. In the center of this line was Fort Magruder; smaller REDOUBTS flanked the fort and extended for about 4 mi. Maj. Gen. JAMES LONGSTREET's division took up positions in Fort Magruder and some of the redoubts on the night of 4 May. The next morning 2 full Union divisions, Maj. Gen. JOSEPH HOOKER's and Brig. Gen. WILLIAM F. SMITH's, challenged the Confederates. The Southerners repulsed an attack by Hooker's troops and counterattacked with limited success. Near noon Johnston arrived to survey the situation and recalled Maj. Gen. DANIEL H. HILL's division to support Longstreet.

Meanwhile, a brigade of Smith's division, commanded by Brig. Gen. WINFIELD S. HANCOCK, was making a long flank march. The Federals arrived behind the Southern left and seized 2 unoccupied redoubts from Magruder's line. When Hill's Confederates reached the field, Hancock's men were pouring artillery fire into Longstreet's flank and rear.

Leading Hill's division into the fighting was the brigade commanded by Brig. Gen. JUBAL A. EARLY, which arrived in a position to outflank Hancock. Hill and Early planned to attack. Because they prepared in haste, the Confederate units reached the Union position at different times and from different directions. Thus the attack was a ragged failure. Hancock reported, "No man . . . left the ground unhurt who had advanced within five hundred yards of our line." The Confederates were gallant but their gallantry was costly: some regiments lost as many as half their numbers, and no accurate count survived because most of the officers responsible for it did not survive. Throughout the confused day, the Federals lost about 2,200 men; the Confederates lost around 1,700, probably many more. In the darkness the Confederates quit the field and continued their withdrawal.   —EMT

Williams Rapid-Fire Gun. A Confederate invention, the Williams Rapid-Fire Gun saw service in both the Eastern and

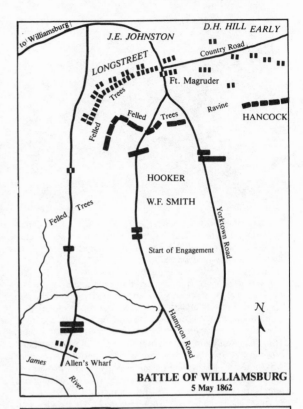

BATTLE OF WILLIAMSBURG
5 May 1862

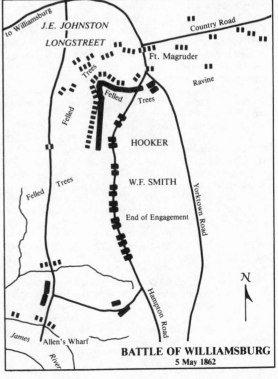

BATTLE OF WILLIAMSBURG
5 May 1862

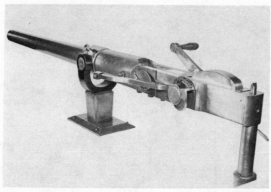

Western theaters. Although it was a hand-crank-operated weapon similar to the GATLING GUN, it was not a machine gun; rather, it was one of the first practical rapid-firing breech-loading artillery pieces used in battle.

The Williams gun was invented by Kentuckian R. S. Williams, who Sept. 1861 supervised the construction of the first of his guns at the TREDEGAR IRON WORKS in Richmond. The gun was used at the Battle of SEVEN PINES and so impressed the War Department that Williams was authorized to raise a battery armed with his weapons. Tredegar produced 20 of the guns 1862–63; 4 of them were sent to Maj. Gen. STERLING PRICE'S army in the TRANS-MISSISSIPPI DEPARTMENT and the remainder was turned over to Williams. Another Richmond firm, Samson and Pae, turned out 4 more of these guns, while 2 full batteries were produced in Lynchburg and another in Mobile, Ala.

The Williams gun was a 1-pounder steel breechloader with a barrel about 4 ft long and a bore of 2 in. It was mounted on a 2-wheel carriage pulled by 1 horse, and thus was light and particularly suited to cavalry operations. Its hand crank was attached to a revolving cam shaft that rotated a cylinder located beneath a hopper holding the ammunition. Cartridges were fired by a sliding hammer that automatically struck the percussion caps at each revolution of the cylinder. It took a crew of 3 to operate the gun, 1 man to place the cartridge in the breech, another to cap it, and a third to sight the gun and fire it. The rate of fire was about 20 rounds per minute, and it had a maximum range of 2,000 yd.

(James J.) Schoolfield's Battery, attached to the 4th Kentucky Cavalry, took the guns into action at BLUE SPRINGS, Tenn., Oct. 1863. The battery's opponent was the 7th Ohio Cavalry, one of whose members, Capt. Theodore V. Allen, noted: "We had heard artillery before, but we had never heard anything that made such a horrible noise as the shot from these breechloaders. . . ." The guns tended to jam when hot and eventually were abandoned. —LDJ

Willis' Church, Va., Battle of. 30 June 1862 *See* WHITE OAK SWAMP, BATTLE OF.

Willstown Bluff (Pon Pon River), S. C., eng. at. 10 July 1863 In preparation for an attack on BATTERY WAGNER, Morris Island, Maj. Gen. QUINCY A. GILLMORE, commanding Federal troops operating against CHARLESTON (*see* CHARLESTON, S.C., SIEGE OF), mapped 2 diversionary maneuvers. The first, which took place 9 July 1863, involved the shelling of and a landing

on James Island, west of Morris. The operation was executed as scheduled and without difficulty; the outnumbered Confederates proved unable to oppose it in force.

Gillmore's second diversion, an amphibious expedition against a railroad bridge on the South Edisto River below Morris Island, occurred on the 10th. On that dark, fog-shrouded morning, a small fleet out of Beaufort—a steamer, a tug, and a transport carrying 250 members of the 1st South Carolina Colored Infantry, plus 2 guns of the 1st Connecticut Battery—passed up the South Edisto under Col. Thomas Wentworth Higginson. The little flotilla had smooth sailing till about 4 a.m., when it reached Willstown Bluff, about 20 mi up the Edisto, at its confluence with the Pon Pon River. There Higginson found his way blocked by spiked timbers sunk across the river's neck, as well as by a 3-gun field battery, which withdrew when the colonel landed troops on the bluff and took possession of the area.

The obstructions posed greater difficulties. The expeditionary force worked till 1 p.m. to clear them, with the aid of high tide, and only after the tugboat, the *Governor Milton,* had run aground. After passing the spikes, Higginson's transport, the *Enoch Dean,* moved barely a mile before again encountering Confederate artillery and likewise running aground. Finally, early in the afternoon, the fleet cleared the shoals and ascended the river, moving to within 2 mi of its objective, before the *Dean* grounded a second time. Unable to free the vessel, Higginson dispatched the tug to attack the rail bridge on its own.

It did not get far. Under an intense shelling by gunners ashore—members of the WASHINGTON ARTILLERY of New Orleans and South Carolina's Chesnut and Marion batteries—the tug was forced to retreat soon after starting out. With the *Dean* free once again, both ships returned downriver, only to have the *Milton* become entangled in the same obstructions it had cleared earlier. When Higginson's steamer, the *John Adams,* failed to pry the vessel loose, the colonel set the tug afire, transferred its crew to the transport, and returned in disgust, his expedition a failure.

—EGL

Wilmington, N.C. 28 mi up the Cape Fear River, Wilmington, N.C., was the South's most active port for BLOCKADE RUNNERS operating from Nassau (570 mi away) and Bermuda (674 mi). Most of these vessels used New Inlet passage, which was guarded by FORT FISHER, while others used the lower passage, which was protected by shore batteries and by Forts Caswell, Campbell, and Holmes. Forts Johnston and Anderson, on the river's west bank, also protected Wilmington from attack by sea. The Federal blockading squadron patroling outside the 2 entrances had to cover a 50-mi arc while keeping out of range of Confederate shore batteries. Until late in the war, Wilmington had good road and railroad connections with Virginia and South Carolina.

After war began, many of its citizens left Wilmington, even as others, including foreigners, were drawn to the city by the prospect of quick wealth gained through blockade-running and speculation. The years 1863 and 1864 were the high point of this wartime maritime activity at Wilmington, as other Southern ports were either captured by the Federals or became increasingly isolated by the tightening BLOCKADE. These years brought riches to those connected with blockade-running and speculation, and public auctions of newly arrived goods included luxury items from the finest fashion shops of Europe.

But, although some individuals became rich, the average citizen suffered from the skyrocketing inflation that made it increasingly difficult for all but a few to purchase even basic commodities. Among the changes that war profiteering brought to Wilmington was a dramatic rise in acts of criminal violence caused by some of the newcomers. During summer 1862, the city also had to cope with a yellow-fever epidemic that cost almost 500 lives—10% of its native population.

By late 1864 the ARMY OF NORTHERN VIRGINIA was largely dependent on Wilmington for a major portion of its supplies, and Gen. ROBERT E. LEE regarded the defense of the city as critical to the survival of his army. The Federals, too, realized the importance of Wilmington to the Confederacy and had planned to capture the city as early as 1862. However, the defenses were formidable, and it was not until Nov. 1864 that a major campaign was launched. During that month and the next, 2 assaults were made by sea against Fort Fisher, which finally resulted in the capture of the fort 15 Jan. Among the Confederate defenders of Wilmington were several thousand soldiers commanded by Maj. Gen. BRAXTON BRAGG, but Bragg refused to commit his troops to the action, and they were withdrawn after the fall of FORT FISHER. On 23 Feb. 1865, Wilmington was surrendered to Maj. Gen. ALFRED H. TERRY by Mayor John Dawson. The loss of the port was a major blow to the South's ability to continue the war.   —NCD

Wilmington, N.C., engs. at. 12–22 Feb. 1865 Since the outbreak of the war WILMINGTON, N.C., had served the Confederate nation as an industrial center, a supply depot, and a haven for a highly productive fleet of BLOCKADE RUNNERS. "By late 1864," writes one historian, "Wilmington was in many respects the most important city in the Confederacy. Only RICHMOND was as vital to the South. . . ." However, after 15 Jan. 1865, when Federals under Maj. Gen. ALFRED H. TERRY and Rear Adm. DAVID D. PORTER captured FORT FISHER, guarding the city's ocean approach from the south, Wilmington's days were numbered.

With Fort Fisher gone, Gen. BRAXTON BRAGG, commanding troops outside the city, evacuated other fortifications at the mouth of the Cape Fear River, removing their garrisons to Fort Anderson, across the river from, and 6 mi northwest of, Terry's position. While the Federals seized the abandoned works and nearby points including the village of Smithville, they were unwilling to challenge Fort Anderson or the line of works directly above Fort Fisher, held by 6,600 troops under Maj. Gen. ROBERT F. HOKE. Reconnaissances had convinced Terry that Hoke's position was too formidable to assault unless the attackers were reinforced.

In the second week of February, reinforcements reached Terry: the XXIII Corps, up from Tennessee under Maj. Gen. JOHN M. SCHOFIELD. As senior officer, the latter took command of and reorganized the combined force of 12,000. On the 11th, Schofield led it up the beach against Hoke. The next day he attempted to turn the enemy's left and gain their rear with an amphibious movement up the Atlantic coast. The drive began well, with Terry's X Corps holding Hoke in place while the XXIII Corps division of Maj. Gen. JACOB D. COX marched toward Admiral Porter's waiting transports. By the 14th, however, poor weather and the quicksand-like terrain had slowed the movement enough to rob it of the element of surprise. Reluctantly, Schofield canceled it.

Planning anew, the Union leader decided to strike those

Confederates west of the Cape Fear, where navigable ground predominated. On the 16th he ferried Cox's troops across to Smithville, then sent them against Fort Anderson. While Porter's warships pounded the works, Cox—now reinforced by a X Corps division under Brig. Gen. ADELBERT AMES—made a wide detour to the west and closed in on the fort's rear. Detecting the move, the enemy garrison, under Brig. Gen. JOHNSON HAGOOD, evacuated before dawn 19 Feb.—barely in time to escape envelopment. Retreating to Town Creek, 8 mi to the north, Hagood's troops built a new defense line, but were pried loose by the Federals' relentless pressure. The next day, attempting a stand north of the creek, the Confederates again fled, following a brisk engagement that cost them 350 casualties against only 60-some for Cox.

Hagood's retreat doomed Wilmington. By the 21st, Cox was within reach of the city's southwest side, while Terry's corps, to which Ames's division had returned, stood poised to cooperate in a final push. That night Bragg diagnosed his situation as hopeless. He recalled Hoke's and Hagood's commands and withdrew them from the city under cover of darkness, while his rear guard destroyed military stores likely to fall into the hands of the invaders. Terry closely followed Hoke's withdrawal, and in the small hours of 22 Feb., as the last Confederates cleared the city, the X Corps entered it from the south, its bands playing what amounted to the funeral dirge of the Confederacy.   —EGL

Wilmot, David. USP b. Bethany, Pa., 20 Jan. 1814. Educated locally and at an academy in Aurora, N.Y., Wilmot studied law and in 1839 passed his bar examinations in Pennsylvania. Gradually his interests shifted from the law to politics. In 1844 he was elected to the first of 3 consecutive terms in the U.S. House of Representatives, first as a Jacksonian Democrat and, from 1848, as a Free-Soiler and Republican.

His greatest contribution to national politics was the Wilmot Proviso, which he presented to Congress in 1846, calling for slavery to be prohibited in any territory gained as fruits of the Mexican War. Passed by the House but voted down in the Senate, the proviso was finally passed 19 June 1862 to forbid SLAVERY in all U.S. territories. By then Wilmot had been out of Congress for a decade, having accepted a district judgeship in Pennsylvania.

Wilmot supported ABRAHAM LINCOLN in the 1860 election, turning down a cabinet appointment in favor of completing SIMON CAMERON's Senate term. Forced to resign by a Democratic majority in Pennsylvania's state legislature, Wilmot accepted a judgeship in the court of claims. He died at his home in Towanda, Pa., 16 Mar. 1868.   —PLF

Wilson, Claudius Charles. CSA b. Effingham Cty., Ga., 1 Oct. 1831. Graduating in 1851 from Emory College, Wilson read law, became a member of the Savannah bar, and 1859–60 was solicitor for the eastern circuit of his state. In late summer 1861 he joined Company I/25th Georgia Infantry and by September had become the regiment's colonel.

Until early in 1863, Wilson and his unit served at various points in the DEPARTMENT OF SOUTH CAROLINA, GEORGIA, AND FLORIDA, including several months in coastal garrisons. During the VICKSBURG CAMPAIGN, the 25th Georgia was sent to northern Mississippi but did not participate in the operations that led to the surrender of the Confederate stronghold. After the fall of Vicksburg, Wilson was transferred to his native state, where he remained for the Battle of CHICKAMAUGA, 19–20 Sept. 1863. In that struggle, he was placed in command of an infantry brigade in the reserve corps of Maj. Gen. W.H.T. WALKER, consisting of Wilson's own regiment, 2 others, and 2 battalions. Early on the 19th, a Union brigade drove a part of Brig. Gen. NATHAN B. FORREST's cavalry along the Confederate right. Wilson's and another infantry brigade rushed up to initiate the battle, keening the "Rebel yell."

LC

Under Wilson's guidance, the troops thrust the Federals backward and overran their artillery support. The reinforced enemy in turn pushed back Wilson, but his spirited counterassault had attracted favorable notice throughout the Army of Tennessee and helped him win the appointment of brigadier general as of 16 Nov.

He did not enjoy a chance to enlarge his reputation. On 27 Nov. 1863, while commanding his brigade near Chattanooga, Tenn., he died of camp fever. On 17 Feb. 1864, long after his burial at Savannah, he was posthumously confirmed a brigadier by the Confederate Senate.   —EGL

Wilson, Henry. USP b. Farmington, N.H., 16 Feb. 1812. Born Jeremiah Jones Colbath to an impoverished sawmill laborer, he legally changed his name to Henry Wilson after a 10-year indenture to a local farmer. In 1833 he apprenticed himself to a cobbler in Natick, Mass., to learn the trade. Self-educated except for a few terms in Massachusetts academies, Wilson built a profitable shoe-making factory in Natick.

His election to the state house of representatives in 1841 marked the beginning of a 30-year political career in which he championed abolitionism and the interests of the workingman. He renounced the Whigs in 1848 when that party failed to

LC

endorse the Wilmot Proviso, legislation that would have contained the expansion of SLAVERY, and led the antislavery delegates in withdrawing from the presidential convention to launch the FREE SOIL party. Until 1851 he edited the Boston Republican, a Free Soil newspaper.

Wilson joined the American (Know Nothing) party in 1854, and was elected to the Senate the next year to fill a vacancy. His alignment with the nativists drew sharp criticism, and he soon left the party, disillusioned by its failure to support an antislavery platform.

Joining the Republicans, Wilson campaigned for ABRAHAM LINCOLN in 1860. He argued against the CRITTENDEN COMPROMISE when the Southern states seceded following Lincoln's election and, as wartime chairman of the Senate Committee on Military Affairs, energetically framed and defended legislative mechanisms for organizing, enlisting, and provisioning a large army. The vigorous emancipationist also introduced many bills to free slaves in the border states before the 13TH AMENDMENT passed. Along with CHARLES SUMNER, Wilson became one of the most powerful of the RADICAL REPUBLICANS. As a result of his sincere concern for the future of freed blacks, he took a prominent role in establishing the FREEDMEN'S BUREAU Mar. 1865.

Wilson bitterly opposed ANDREW JOHNSON's attempts to achieve a moderate Reconstruction. Until he visited the devastated region, he did not understand the chaos in the postwar South or recognize the efforts of Southern leaders to deal with Radical Reconstruction. More sympathetic on his return to Washington, he supported Federal aid for education and homesteading in the South.

A pragmatic man sometimes criticized for his willingness to achieve his ends through coalition politics, Wilson always followed a course he believed would benefit the working class. Elected to the vice-presidency in 1872, he presided over the Senate until his death in office 22 Nov. 1875. He wrote several books during the last decade of his life. The best known, the 3-volume *History of the Rise and Fall of Slave Power in the United States,* was published 1872–77.   —PLF

Wilson, James Harrison. USA b. near Shawneetown, Ill., 2 Sept. 1837. In summer 1861 Wilson, an ambitious 2d lieutenant, left Fort Vancouver, Wash., eager to fight in the Civil War. Though he had graduated 6th in the West Point class of 1860, he was saddled with engineering and staff positions during the first few years of war.

Late in 1862 he was sent west to join the army of Maj. Gen. ULYSSES S. GRANT, forming a friendship with the general that first bore fruit when Wilson was promoted to staff lieutenant colonel and appointed inspector general of the ARMY OF THE TENNESSEE. Wilson was active throughout the VICKSBURG CAMPAIGN of 1863, received his pro-

USMHI

motion to brigadier general 30 Oct. 1863, and was with Grant during the battles that secured CHATTANOOGA in November. As soon as Grant, the new general-in-chief, came east, he offered Wilson command of the 3d Cavalry Division in the ARMY OF THE POTOMAC. Although he performed well with Maj. Gen. PHILIP H. SHERIDAN around Richmond, Wilson came close to disaster on his first independent raid June 1864 (*see* WILSON-KAUTZ RAID).

After leading his division in the Shenandoah Valley, he was transferred 30 Sept. to the command of Maj. Gen. WILLIAM T. SHERMAN's cavalry with the rank of brevet major general. Wilson began reorganizing the cavalry corps under Maj. Gen. GEORGE H. THOMAS at Nashville while Sherman set out for the sea. In December, at the Battle of Nashville (*see* FRANKLIN AND NASHVILLE CAMPAIGN), his troopers helped rout and pursue Gen. JOHN B. HOOD's army. For the next 2 months Wilson re-equipped his men, and 22 Mar. 1865 was ready to meet Lt. Gen. NATHAN B. FORREST in Alabama. Moving rapidly before Forrest could unite his command, Wilson's 13,500 men routed all resistance and pushed the Confederates back to Selma, which fell 2 Apr. For the first time in the war a Union general had outmaneuvered and outmarched Forrest (*see* WILSON'S RAID TO SELMA). Wilson's raid ended in Macon, Ga., 20 Apr., when he learned of the war's end. His troopers added to their commander's laurels when they captured JEFFERSON DAVIS 10 May. Wilson was advanced to major general 21 June 1865.

Resigning from his commission in 1870, he began a civilian career as an engineer and railroad executive. At the beginning of the Spanish-American War he returned to military service, remaining with the army until 1901. That year he was retired with the rank of brigadier general, Regular Army. He died at his home in Wilmington, Del., 23 Feb. 1925, one of the last surviving Union generals. —CMS

Wilson–Kautz Raid, Va. 22–30 June 1864 Following his unsuccessful attacks against Petersburg, 15–18 June 1864, Lt. Gen. ULYSSES S. GRANT sought to cut the city's supply lines. From Petersburg, 2 railroads ran southward and westward, hauling rations and matériel to Gen. ROBERT E. LEE's army from the Confederate interior. To strike them Grant called on young Brig. Gen. JAMES H. WILSON, who had led the 3d Cavalry Division/Army of the Potomac for only 2 months. For the raid Wilson was also given Brig. Gen. AUGUST V. KAUTZ's cavalry division of the ARMY OF THE JAMES, a total of 3,300 troopers, plus HORSE ARTILLERY and a supply train.

Heading south from Lee's Mill, 22 June, Wilson and Kautz ripped up miles of track on the Petersburg & Weldon Railroad, then marched west, striking the Southside line near Ford's Station, 14 mi southwest of Petersburg. Since most of Lee's horsemen had followed the cavalry of Maj. Gen. PHILIP H. SHERIDAN toward Lynchburg a few days before, the raiders met light opposition, damaging trackage, rolling stock, and depot facilities as far west as Burkeville Junction.

From Burkeville the Federals moved down a third railroad, the Richmond & Danville, before being halted on the 25th at the Staunton River Bridge near Roanoke Station by 900 Confederate Regulars and home guards. As pursuers gathered in their rear, the Federals fled east, returning to the Weldon line near Stony Creek Station on the 28th. There, and farther north at Reams' Station, they were battered by cavalry under the command of Maj. Gen. WADE HAMPTON, recently returned from chasing Sheridan, and by 3 infantry brigades under Brig. Gen. WILLIAM MAHONE.

Outnumbered and virtually surrounded, Wilson and Kautz abandoned their artillery, wagons, and wounded, and raced north and east toward Grant's headquarters, where their troops arrived in small detachments until 1 July. Their mission proved a failure: the 60 mi of track they had destroyed were repaired rapidly by Confederate labor gangs. —EGL

Wilson's Creek (Oak Hills, Springfield), Mo., Battle of. 10 Aug. 1861 Springfield, Mo., is located in the southeastern section of that state. In Aug. 1861 a newly formed Union army commanded by Brig. Gen. NATHANIEL LYON was concentrated in that city. A Confederate army, commanded by Brig. Gen. BEN MCCULLOCH, was advancing to attack Lyon at Springfield and by the night of 9 Aug. had camped alongside Wilson's Creek about 15 mi from the city. The attack was scheduled for the next day.

However, the Union forces delivered a surprise attack against the Confederate army at 5 a.m. on the 10th. Lyon's initial assault pushed Southern cavalry units commanded by

Col. James Cawthorn from Bloody Hill, a dominating piece of ground on the west side of the creek. Capt. James Totten's Company F of the 2d U.S. Artillery Battery played a significant role in the Union advance. Confederate infantry, commanded by Maj. Gen. STERLING PRICE, was rushed to the front and by 6:30 a.m. the situation was stabilized, with Union forces holding the crest and with Confederate troops positioned at the base of Bloody Hill.

Simultaneous with Lyon's attack, a Union column commanded by Col. FRANZ SIGEL assaulted the other end of the Confederate camp. Sigel also caught the Southerners unprepared and drove them toward their comrades who were engaging Lyon.

After the Union troops had reached the top of Bloody Hill, Lyon sent a detachment under Capt. Joseph B. Plummer across the creek (to the east side) in an effort to silence the Pulaski Arkansas Battery, commanded by Capt. William E. Woodruff, which was enfilading the Northern position. However, a Confederate column led by Brig. Gen. JAMES M. MCINTOSH halted Plummer and pushed him back. In his pursuit of Plummer, McIntosh in turn was halted by Federal artillery. The Southern troops later recrossed the creek at another point and aided in the fight against Sigel.

At approximately 7:30 a.m. a Confederate attack led by Brig. Gen. James H. McBride was launched against the Union right flank on Bloody Hill. The fighting was severe, with each side putting in reinforcements, but after a short while the Confederates withdrew to regroup.

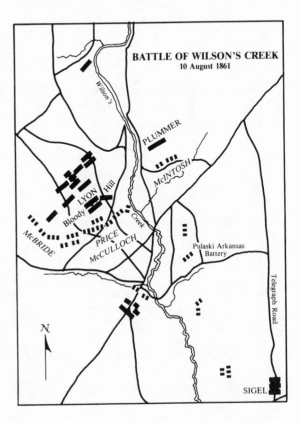

BATTLE OF WILSON'S CREEK
10 August 1861

Coincidental with the cessation of fighting on the hill, Sigel's force, which had advanced unmolested north on the Telegraph road, parallel to Wilson's Creek, was attacked by Confederate units commanded by McCulloch. Sigel was soon routed and driven in disorder from the field, the Confederates conducting a limited pursuit before returning to Bloody Hill.

The Southerners initiated another attempt to gain control of Bloody Hill at 9 a.m. However, Lyon hurried reinforcements to the front, halting the assault and, counterattacking, pushed the Confederates back. Lyon was killed during the fighting and command of the army devolved on Maj. SAMUEL D. STURGIS. As the Union forces were advancing, a Southern cavalry column composed of several units and commanded by Col. ELKANAH B. GREER, attacked their right flank. Caught by surprise, the Federal troops recovered quickly and, aided by artillery, routed Greer's force. However, the cavalry attack interrupted the Federal advance and afforded Price time to retreat and reorganize.

After a short respite, and after being reinforced by the units that had defeated Sigel, Price again sent his men forward. After an hour of combat, the Union line was unbroken and the Confederates withdrew at 11 a.m. At that time Sturgis was informed that his soldiers were exhausted and that the ammunition supply was low. Additionally, Sigel's failure to exert pressure on the Southern rear was an increasing matter of concern. Therefore, Sturgis ordered the army to withdraw toward Springfield. The Confederates learned of the movement when they moved forward for another attack. McCulloch and Price decided not to pursue Sturgis since their forces were disorganized and they too were low on ammunition.

The Union army had 5,500 effectives, of which 1,300 were casualties (24%), while the Confederates had approximately 10,000 effectives, of which 1,200 were casualties (12%).

—MMul

Wilson's Raid to Selma, Ala.

22 Mar.–2 Apr. 1865 Following its Dec. 1864 victory at Nashville, Maj. Gen. GEORGE H. THOMAS' Union command saw no active campaigning in Tennessee. That winter, while his infantry was dispersed to other fronts, Thomas' cavalry, under 28-year-old Brig. Gen. JAMES H. WILSON, gathered at Waterloo and Gravelly Springs, Ala., for a thrust into the Deep South. A brash and gifted soldier, protégé of both Thomas and Gen.-in-Chief ULYSSES S. GRANT, Wilson was originally ordered to make a diversion in favor of a larger force bound for Mobile. Eventually he won permission to conduct an independent campaign against Selma, Ala., one of the Confederacy's most vital munitions depots.

On 22 Mar., following 2 months of organizing and training, Wilson led 13,500 well-armed and -equipped troopers—the largest mounted force assembled during the war—south from Gravelly Springs toward the Black Warrior River. The corps moved along 3 divergent trails to facilitate mutual support and confuse enemy leaders. The latter included Lt. Gen. NATHAN B. FORREST, one of the South's ablest commanders, now in charge of all cavalry in Alabama, Mississippi, and eastern Louisiana.

Unimpressed by his adversary's reputation as the "Wizard of the Saddle," Wilson invited a showdown by a rapid advance into Forrest's bailiwick. He moved so nimbly that he eluded brigades of horsemen sent to slow his march and even dispatched a brigade under Brig. Gen. John T. Croxton on a side campaign against Tuscaloosa, drawing attention from the main raiding body. On 31 Mar. Wilson's advance drove a force

under Forrest from Montevallo, 40 mi above Selma. The next day, at EBENEZER CHURCH, 20 mi farther south, the Federals emerged victorious from a bloody saber-and-pistol duel against 2,000 cavalry and 6 cannon.

Besides drubbing the Confederates, Wilson gathered enough intelligence to plot Forrest's countermoves, then burned a strategic bridge near Centreville, thereby preventing reinforcements from reaching Selma. By the afternoon of the 2d, when it drew up outside Selma, Wilson's force had come 300 mi in 12 days.

—EGL

Winchester, Va., First Battle of.

25 May 1862 The First Battle of Winchester was the second Confederate victory in Maj. Gen. THOMAS J. "STONEWALL" JACKSON'S SHENANDOAH VALLEY CAMPAIGN, pitting his army of 15,000 men against that of Maj. Gen. NATHANIEL P. BANKS'S 20,000.

After his victory at MCDOWELL, 8 May, Jackson moved north down the valley toward Harrisonburg. He knew that Banks was building strong fortifications at Strasburg and that he had a strong outpost at Front Royal. In order to bypass Banks's works and force him to evacuate them, Jackson decided to attack Front Royal, approaching through the Luray Valley and using Massanutten Mountain as a screen.

On 23 May Jackson's troops scored an easy victory at FRONT ROYAL and forced Banks to move his troops north toward Winchester. At Newtown, 24 May, Jackson took Banks in the flank, capturing large numbers of supply wagons. His main worry, however, was that Banks would have time to fortify the hills southwest of Winchester and there make a stand. To prevent this, or at least to give Banks as little time as possible to prepare, Jackson force-marched his troops most of the night of 24–25 May.

On the morning of 25 May, Jackson sent against the hills the 1st (Stonewall) Brigade, under Brig. Gen. CHARLES S. WINDER, supported by the 2d Brigade under Col. John A. Campbell. The attacking troops found light resistance on the first ridge but Banks in force on the second. Confederate artillery was brought up, but it suffered heavily in a duel with Federal guns. Meanwhile, Maj. Gen. RICHARD S. EWELL'S division had opened the engagement on the Confederate right. Jackson ordered up Brig. Gen. RICHARD TAYLOR'S Louisiana brigade and placed them on the extreme left. When Taylor charged, the rest of the army followed. The Federals resisted stubbornly until they broke their formations, stampeded, then retreated northward, all the way to the Potomac. Jackson demonstrated near Harpers Ferry, then turned south.

—LDJ

Winchester, Va., Second Battle of.

14–15 June 1863 Gen. ROBERT E. LEE'S Army of Northern Virginia started marching westward from Fredericksburg, Va., 3 June 1863 on what would be the initial leg of the GETTYSBURG CAMPAIGN. During the next 10 days, the Confederate units, moving incrementally, advanced toward the Shenandoah Valley, the avenue of invasion selected by Lee. The vanguard of the army, Lt. Gen. RICHARD S. EWELL'S II Corps, reached Berryville, Va., in the Shenandoah, on the 13th. A dozen miles west of Berryville was Winchester, occupied by a Union garrison of 6,900 effectives under Maj. Gen. ROBERT H. MILROY.

Warned of the Confederate approach, Milroy had dismissed the intelligence, believing that Lee's troops could not evade the Union Army of the Potomac, which lay opposite Fredericksburg. Authorities in Washington, D.C., had strongly suggested

SECOND BATTLE OF WINCHESTER
14–15 June 1863

N

that Milroy retreat to Harpers Ferry, but the Union officer remained steadfast until it was too late. By the afternoon of the 14th, Ewell was closing on Winchester with 2 divisions while his third marched on Martinsburg, located north of Winchester and in Milroy's rear.

Ewell's men descended on Winchester from 3 directions—south, east, and west. While part of Maj. Gen. EDWARD JOHNSON's division demonstrated south and east of town, Ewell shifted the rest of his brigades, including Maj. Gen. JUBAL A. EARLY's division, to the west, where the main Federal works were located. About 6 p.m. Confederate artillery opened fire on Milroy's fortifications; 45 minutes later one of Early's brigades charged and overran an earthwork. Union counterattacks failed and, by nightfall, Milroy's command was facing possible encirclement. At 9 o'clock Milroy held a council of war and decided to retreat after destroying wagons and cannon.

The Union withdrawal began at 1 a.m. on the 15th. Anticipating such a movement, Ewell had ordered Johnson, with 3 brigades, to intercept it. Johnson's infantrymen struck the Union column at Stephenson's Depot, 4 mi north of Winchester, about 3:30 a.m. A hot skirmish ensued, but the Confederate numbers prevailed, engulfing the fleeing Northerners. Milroy, who escaped, suffered a near total defeat. Nearly 4,000 Federals were reported captured or missing while 95 were killed and 348 were wounded. Ewell's men also bagged 23 cannon, 300 wagons, large quantities of stores, and more than 300 horses. Southern losses amounted to 47 killed, 219 wounded, and 3 missing.

Demonstrating excellent tactical skill, Ewell cleared the

northern end of the Shenandoah Valley of Federals with this spectacular minor victory. On 15 June Maj. Gen. ROBERT E. RODES's division of the corps crossed the Potomac River, the first of a flood of Confederates. A court of inquiry exonerated Milroy of responsibility for the defeat.   —JDW

Winchester, Va., Third Battle of (Opequon Creek). 19 Sept. 1864 Just before daylight 19 Sept., a Federal cavalry division splashed across Opequon Creek east of Winchester. Behind the horsemen 35,000 of Maj. Gen. PHILIP H. SHERIDAN's Union infantry marched, advancing toward a piecemeal destruction of the scattered Confederate divisions of Lt. Gen. JUBAL A. EARLY's II Corps. But Sheridan blundered by deciding to funnel his command through a narrow, wooded canyon. The exasperatingly slow Federal advance lasted nearly 4 hours.

Shortly before noon, 3 Federal divisions of the VI and XIX corps finally charged Maj. Gen. STEPHEN D. RAMSEUR's Confederate division, driving the Southerners back. Sheridan's slow advance, however, had allowed Early to regroup his divisions, and now Maj. Gens. JOHN B. GORDON's and ROBERT E. RODES's veterans counterattacked. Gordon's fierce charge shredded the XIX Corps's ranks, nearly crumbling it entirely. Rodes was mortally wounded as his men surged into a wide gap between the 2 Union commands, rolling back the VI Corps's lines. Sheridan counterattacked with a Union reserve division that repulsed the Southerners and saved the Federal army from possible destruction.

While the 2 bloodied commands rested, Sheridan advanced his III Corps under Brig. Gen. GEORGE CROOK, whose lone division marched beyond Early's left flank. Shortly after 3 p.m. Crook charged, followed soon by 2 Union cavalry divisions advancing from the north. The Confederates, fighting stubbornly, shrank before the Union numbers and armament. Finally the Federal troopers charged in a serried assault, fragmenting the Confederate ranks. Sheridan's infantry renewed their attacks, and the Southerners retreated into the darkening shadows. For the first time, the Confederate II Corps had been driven from a battlefield.

Sheridan lost slightly more than 5,000 men, while Early's 12,000-man army had been reduced by more than 3,500 casualties. The undermanned Confederates fought tenaciously, but Sheridan's unbroken ranks of horsemen and waves of infantry doomed Early's army.   —JDW

Winder, Charles Sidney. CSA b. Talbot Cty., Md., 18 Oct. 1829. Graduating 22d in the West Point class of 1850, Winder served on garrison and frontier duty for the next decade. While en route to California in 1854, he displayed outstanding heroism when the troopship he was on was battered by a hurricane. His performance earned him promotion to captain, supposedly the youngest man of that rank in the army at the time. Resigning his commission 1 Apr. 1861, he entered Confederate service as a major of artillery. He participated in the bombardment of FORT SUMTER, S.C., and 8 July became colonel of the 6th South Carolina.

LC

On 7 Mar. 1862, to rank from the 1st, Winder was promoted to brigadier general and selected by Maj. Gen. THOMAS J. "STONEWALL" JACKSON to command the STONEWALL BRIGADE. Jackson's decision enraged both the officers and men of his old command. A strict disciplinarian, Winder enforced the rules, and the veterans despised him. The regimental commanders greeted him coldly, and the enlisted men hissed their new commander when he rode past the ranks. Some in the ranks threatened to kill him when an opportunity in battle offered. Winder, however, refused to bend.

He led them into battle for the first time during Jackson's 1862 SHENANDOAH VALLEY CAMPAIGN. Though his conduct did not gain the brigade's affection, it earned their grudging respect. On one occasion, when he stood up to Jackson, the brigade cheered him. During the SEVEN DAYS' CAMPAIGN, he directed his men with gallantry.

On 9 Aug. 1862, during the Battle of CEDAR MOUNTAIN, Winder was horribly mangled by an exploding shell. He died a few hours later on the field, his death lamented by Jackson and Gen. ROBERT E. LEE, but not by the Stonewall Brigade.

—JDW

Winder, John Henry. CSA b. Somerset Cty., Md., 21 Feb. 1800, Winder graduated from West Point in 1820, 11th in his class, with a commission as 2d lieutenant in the artillery. He served capably in the U.S. Army, and by 1860 was a regular major of artillery. Winder resigned his commission 27 Apr. 1861 and accepted a brigadier general's commission in the Confederate service 21 June.

With this rank came an assignment as provost marshal and prison commandant in Richmond. Assigned some of the most difficult and thankless tasks associated with the Confederate war effort, Winder was charged with responsibility for Federal prisoners of war and

LC

with the internal security of the Confederate capital. In carrying out his duties he received praise from his superiors and scorn from the public. What he most merited was sympathy.

Winder took his duties seriously and received severe criticism for his seemingly high-handed methods. Particularly odious were the civilian detectives whom he employed to enforce his regulations and issue passports at the capital. Some Union prisoners complained of poor treatment at Winder's hands, but others termed his administration fair-minded, and at least one carved a bone pipe as a present for the commandant.

In June 1864 Winder received orders placing him in charge of ANDERSONVILLE PRISON in Georgia, in July he was given command of all prison facilities in Alabama and Georgia, and in November he became commissary general of all prisons east of the Mississippi.

His abrupt manner and attention to rules and regulations, combined with the dwindling resources of the Confederacy, hampered him in these assignments. On 8 Feb. 1865, he died in Florence, S.C., principally of strain and fatigue.   —EMT

Winslow, John Ancrum. USN b. Wilmington, N.C., 19

Nov. 1811, Winslow moved to Massachusetts in 1825. On 1 Feb. 1827, he was appointed a midshipman from that state, was promoted to lieutenant in 1839, and to commander in 1855. In 1846 both Winslow and Lt. RAPHAEL SEMMES lost ships while blockading the Mexican coast; afterward the two became friends and messmates aboard the USS *Cumberland.*

When the Civil War began, Winslow was an inspector at the Boston Lighthouse District. He commanded the *BENTON* on the Mississippi River until Dec. 1861, when, after an injury, he was invalided home. By June 1862 he had recovered and was back on the Mississippi. Promotion to captain came a month later. Deeply religious and an uncompromising abolitionist, Winslow was an outspoken critic of the Lincoln administration for its failure to make the war into a crusade to end SLAVERY.

USMHI

Late in 1862 he was ordered to command the *KEARSARGE,* a third-class ship that ordinarily would not have warranted a commander of such high rank. Months of frustration and disappointment followed as Winslow searched for Confederate commerce destroyers from the Azores to the English Channel. At Brest, the CSS *FLORIDA* eluded him, and the CSS *RAPPAHANNOCK* was detained by France at Calais until war's end. Finally, 11 June 1864, while at Flushing, in the Netherlands, Winslow learned that the CSS *ALABAMA* was at Cherbourg. Arriving there 3 days later, he kept the *Kearsarge* outside French territorial waters while waiting for the *Alabama* to leave port. Believing that he could win a fight, Raphael Semmes, now a Confederate captain, brought the *Alabama* to sea 19 June. Winslow sank the vessel in just over an hour. The North gained a new hero, and Winslow's promotion to commodore was made retroactive to the date of the battle. Nevertheless, his victory was dampened by unproven rumors that he had purposely allowed Semmes to escape to England aboard the yacht *Deerhound.*

After returning to the U.S., Winslow was assigned shore duty. In Mar. 1865 he sat on the court-martial of Commodore THOMAS T. CRAVEN, who was found guilty of having failed to engage the formidable CSS *STONEWALL* off Spain. After the war Winslow briefly commanded the Gulf Squadron, then, following promotion to rear admiral in 1870, the Pacific Fleet. In 1872 he retired, but a special act of Congress kept his name on the active list. d. Boston, Mass., 29 Sept. 1873.

—NCD

Winston County, Ala. On 11 Jan. 1862, in Montgomery, Ala., all but 24 delegates to the secession convention signed the state's secession ordinance. The next day secessionists proposed a countermeasure allowing the 24 to acknowledge Alabama's secession without taking responsibility for it; all signed but 3 final hold-outs, including C. Christopher Sheats from Winston County.

After the ordinance passed, Sheats, champion of the county's cooperationist cause, continued to argue his point on the convention floor. A mob of citizens wildly celebrating Alabama's entry into the Confederacy dragged him from the hall and took him to a jail. Several days later, at the end of the convention, he was released.

In April, Winston County pro-Union citizens, angry about their state's secession and the detention of Sheats, met in Bill Looney's tavern along with Unionists from other northern Alabama, Georgia, Mississippi, and Tennessee counties. More than 2,500 conventioneers in their formal resolutions protested Southern nationalist WILLIAM LOWNDES YANCEY's accusations that they were traitors. At the same time, they agreed with Tenn. Sen. ANDREW JOHNSON, who contended that secession was illegal; disdained the Southern majority that had bolted from the Democratic Party, assuring ABRAHAM LINCOLN's election; and, finally, asked that the Confederacy and the Union both leave them unmolested, for they wanted no part of the war. The citizens declared that if a state could secede from the Federal Union, then a county could secede from a state. But their wish for neutrality was not to be honored by either side.

Although Winston County's mountainous terrain proved advantageous to neither army, both Confederates and Federals launched attacks against opposing factions in the region. While the Union troops scoured the area for Southern loyalists, Sheats and his constituency became targets for home-guard and PARTISAN RANGER units organized to rid the state of Unionists. Captives were given the choice between entering Confederate service and execution. Many chose the latter.

By summer 1862 public outrage in the county had reached such a point that several residents decided to join the Union army to oppose the Southern cause they hated. Under Col. ABEL D. STREIGHT they became the Federal 1st Alabama Cavalry. But in September the Federals left Alabama and the Confederates moved in again. By October Sheats was once more in jail in Montgomery, not to be released until 1864.

In 1863–64 returning Alabama Federals were outraged at what had been done in their absence: their homes had been burned, families murdered. These soldiers, along with disenchanted Confederate deserters and the Unionists of Winston and surrounding counties, formed a partisan army to retaliate against the Confederate intrusions. Their force was strong and sought revenge with nearly as much abandon as had the enemy, shooting Confederate recruiting officers and raiding Confederate Fort Mitchell. Even an invasion by 3 Confederate brigades May 1864 could not stop the Unionists. Alabama— and the entire Confederacy—was collapsing.

Although Winston County never seceded from Alabama, its citizens stood up for their beliefs throughout 4 years of war.
—FLS

wire entanglements. The Civil War witnessed the introduction of numerous tactical devices, one of which, further developed in later wars, was wire entanglements. Introduced by Federal soldiers, the entanglements usually consisted of telegraph wire stretched between stumps and trees, which served to trip or stall charging troops.

Apparently the initial use of such entanglements occurred at FORT SANDERS, in the KNOXVILLE CAMPAIGN, 29 Nov. 1863. The wire, however, hampered the attacking Southerners only slightly. The most celebrated use of the entanglements was 16 May 1864, when assaulting Confederate troops at DREWRY's BLUFF, Va., floundered in them. A Union officer reported that the Southerners were "being piled in heaps over the telegraph wire." A Confederate prisoner described the wire barrier as "a devilish contrivance which none but a Yankee could devise."

Maj. Gens. BENJAMIN F. BUTLER and WILLIAM F. SMITH claimed credit for the use of the "devilish contrivance."   —JDW

Wirz, Heinrich Hartmann. CSA b. Zurich, Switzerland, Nov. 1823. In 1865, in America, Wirz was to claim, "I am by profession a physician," but he had no medical training. His father, a tailor, had insisted he abandon his interest in medical study to enter business. In the late 1840s Wirz served a short prison term, but accounts fail to tell of his offense, except that it "had to do with money." In 1849 he sailed to America, where he worked in a factory in Lawrence, Mass. He was then employed as a doctor's assistant around Kentucky, but failed in efforts to set up a practice for himself. He drifted to Louisiana and was employed on a plantation as "Dr. Wirz."

In 1861 he enlisted in the 4th Louisiana Infantry, which soon saw duty in Virginia. On 31 May 1862, during the Battle of SEVEN PINES, Wirz, a sergeant, suffered an incurable wound to his right arm. He lost use of the arm and was in pain the few remaining years of his life. Promoted to captain, he was assigned to the staff of Brig. Gen. JOHN H. WINDER, who put him in command of the Richmond military prison. Called "Dutch Sergeant" by prisoners, he was said to be the "essence of authority," "a good fellow at times and a very bad one at other times," and "an infallible dog" who "thought himself omnipresent and omniscient."

In Dec. 1862 Wirz went to Europe on a mission for Pres. JEFFERSON DAVIS. He returned Feb. 1864 and in March was sent as commandant to the prison at ANDERSONVILLE, Ga. Conditions there were terrible almost beyond description, and in the North Wirz was considered to be the "monster . . . the fiend" responsible.

In May 1865 Wirz was sending the last prisoners north when Federal Capt. Henry E. Noyes arrested him. The captive protested that conditions at Andersonville were beyond his control and pleaded to be allowed to take his family to Europe; instead, he was taken to Washington and charged with "impairing the health and destroying the lives of prisoners." During his 3-month trial witnesses swore they had seen Wirz "strike, kick, and shoot prisoners in August 1864," a time during which the commandant was absent from the prison on sick leave. On 6 Nov. 1865, he was condemned to death.

Wirz remains a controversial Civil War figure. There is no question about the horrible suffering in Andersonville, and Wirz was certainly a harsh man, rough in manner and profane in speech. But his Confederate contemporaries insisted that he did the best job possible in one of the impoverished nation's most poorly equipped, scantily provisioned, and overcrowded prisons—a fact that has prompted many Civil War historians to claim that Wirz was a scapegoat and the victim of postwar hysteria.

Not long before he was taken into the yard at OLD CAPITOL PRISON to be hanged 10 Nov. 1865, a secret emissary from the War Department offered Wirz a reprieve in exchange for a statement that would convict Jefferson Davis of conspiracy to murder prisoners. Wirz calmly answered, "Jefferson Davis had no connection with me as to what was done at Andersonville." The condemned man said to the major directing his hanging, "I know what orders are, Major—I am being hung for obeying them."   —PR

Wisconsin. When the Civil War broke out, Wisconsin had existed as a state for only 12 years. Of a population of 775,-

881, 407,449 were male. In the first year of the war the state raised 11 regiments of infantry, 3 of which (the 2d, 6th, and 7th) formed the famed IRON BRIGADE OF THE WEST. Before the war was over it had supplied the Federal service with 52 regiments, plus cavalry, artillery, sharpshooters, 3 brigade bands, scouts, sailors, and black troops. It has been estimated that for every 9 persons living in the state, Wisconsin furnished 1 soldier. Of 91,379 men in the service (79,934 volunteers and 11,445 draftees and substitutes), approximately 11,583 died of battle wounds or disease. The 25th Infantry suffered the greatest loss with 460 men killed or dead of disease.

Wisconsin furnished the 3 colorful CUSHING brothers: WILLIAM B., who was responsible for the destruction of the Confederate ram *ALBEMARLE*; ALONZO B., an artillery captain at FIRST BULL RUN, CHANCELLORSVILLE, and GETTYSBURG, where he was killed when Maj. Gen. GEORGE E. PICKETT's men crossed the WHEATFIELD; and Howard B., who also served gallantly as an artillery officer. Also from the state came Brig. Gen. Lewis Cass Hunt; Col. Hans Christian Heg of the 15th, who was mortally wounded at CHICKAMAUGA; and Col. JOSEPH BAILEY of the 14th Cavalry, who helped free a Federal gunboat fleet trapped in low water on the Red River in 1864 (*see* RED RIVER CAMPAIGN).

Wisconsin regiments were part of Lt. Gen. ULYSSES S. GRANT's command; the 2d became part of Maj. Gen. IRVIN MCDOWELL's army and was under Maj. Gen. WILLIAM T. SHERMAN. In fact, Wisconsin men fought on the soil of every Southern state but Florida. Their performance prompted Sherman to say that he "estimated a Wisconsin regiment equal to an ordinary brigade." The 9th, however, had the dubious honor of having missed every major battle of the war, though it lost 191 men during its 3 years of service.

By 1862 Wisconsin was sending not only men to the Civil War battlefields but 17 million pounds of much-needed lead, wool for blankets and clothing, and foodstuffs from 2 million acres of cultivated farmland.   —AG

26th Wisconsin. Under Col. William H. Jacobs, the 26th Wisconsin was mustered into Federal service at Milwaukee, Wis., 17 Sept. 1862. Composed largely of German immigrants and Americans of German extraction, the unit traveled to Washington, D.C., after the ANTIETAM CAMPAIGN and joined the 2d Brigade/3d Division/XI Corps/Army of the Potomac. German immigrant Maj. Gen. CARL SCHURZ led its division; Col. WLADIMIR KRZYZANOWSKI, a native of Prussian-occupied Poland, led its brigade.

The 26th was held in reserve during the Battle of FREDERICKSBURG, suffered through BURNSIDE's "MUD MARCH," then engaged in heavy combat at CHANCELLORSVILLE and GETTYSBURG, losing in the former battle more than 11% of its men, and in the latter taking a loss in excess of 12% of its effective strength. Remaining under Krzyzanowski, it transferred to the west Sept. 1863, served in CHATTANOOGA campaigning under Capt. Frederick C. Winkler (later colonel of the regiment), then transferred into the 3d Brigade/3d Division/XX Corps Apr. 1864 for the ATLANTA CAMPAIGN. In the next year it fought in the Battles of RESACA, NEW HOPE CHURCH, KENNESAW MOUNTAIN, and PEACHTREE CREEK, and saw action at AVERASBOROUGH, N.C., and in the Battle of BENTONVILLE. At Peachtree Creek, the 26th won commendation for its capture of the flag of the 33d Mississippi. Earlier, in Eastern service, the unit had elicited praise from the colonel of the 2d Massachusetts, who called it "one of the finest military organizations in the service."

The 26th mustered out of volunteer service 17 June 1865. Of the 1,089 men in its original muster, it lost 683 to disease and wounds, deaths, and captures in combat.   —JES

36th Wisconsin. Although it did not take the field until May 1864, the 36th Wisconsin ranked 17th among Federal regiments in percentage of men killed in action. Organized at Camp Randall, in Madison, Wis., it was placed under Col. Frank Aretas Haskell, former aide to Brig. Gen. JOHN GIBBON and, subsequently, author of a classic account of the *Battle of Gettysburg*, first published in book form in 1908.

Under Haskell, the 36th left Wisconsin 10 May and a week later joined the ARMY OF THE POTOMAC around Spotsylvania Court House, Virginia. On the 19th it became a member of Gibbon's 2d Division/II Corps, and saw its first action a few days later along the NORTH ANNA RIVER, supporting batteries and sharpshooting at long range. Late on 26 May, 2 companies of the regiment captured a line of Confederate works, suffering slight loss.

Near Bethesda Church, 1 June, the regiment engaged in a demonstration to prevent Confederates from reinforcing other, more strategic parts of their line. Deserted by veteran outfits assigned to support them, 4 companies of the 36th doublequicked up to the enemy line, suffering almost 130 casualties under a murderous barrage. 2 days later, along the II Corps line at COLD HARBOR, the regiment joined in a general assault against Gen. ROBERT E. LEE's right flank. Leading its brigade, the 36th again absorbed heavy losses while moving over open ground. When the brigade leader fell dead, Colonel Haskell replaced him, only to take a bullet through the head. On Haskell's death, Lt. Col. John A. Savage extricated the outfit from danger.

Crossing the James River with the rest of the army, the 36th soon moved against the stronghold of Petersburg. As the unit attacked east of the city 18 June, Savage, now a colonel, took a mortal wound, Lt. Col. Harvey M. Brown was severely injured, and the regiment—the only participant in the charge to reach the enemy line—saw 119 others become casualties. After recovering, Brown commanded the remnant throughout the PETERSBURG CAMPAIGN, including 2 expeditions north of the James and the WELDON RAILROAD OPERATIONS. As of 26 Aug., only 3 officers and 45 men of the regiment could be accounted for. After taking part at BURGESS' MILL and HATCHER'S RUN and in the APPOMATTOX CAMPAIGN, the outfit reported having lost, during its term of service, 342 officers and men dead of wounds or disease out of an enrollment of 1,014.   —EGL

Wise, Henry Alexander. CSA b. Drummondtown, Va., 3 Dec. 1806, Wise enrolled in Washington College, Pa., where he graduated with honors in 1825. After attending law school for 2 years, he began a legal practice. Early in his political life, he developed a reputation as an outspoken orator and zealous advocate of Southern rights and the slave trade. His first major political triumph came in 1833 when he was elected to the U.S. House of Representatives as a member of the Jacksonian Democratic party. A vocal member of Congress until 1844, he became the U.S. minister to Brazil until 1847, then, returning to the U.S., participated in the Virginia constitutional convention. He served as Democratic governor of Virginia 1856–60, during John Brown's raid on Harpers Ferry, the final, most prominent act of his administration being the execution of Brown.

After Virginia seceded from the Union, and with war impending, Wise, despite his lack of military training, volunteered for military service. On 5 June 1861, he was appointed brigadier general of the Confederate army. However, he proved to be an unsuccessful military leader. His troops suffered defeats by Maj. Gen. JACOB D. COX in the Kanawha Valley and by Brig. Gen. AMBROSE E. BURNSIDE at Roanoke Island, N.C. For the remainder of the war he served

USMHI

in the coastal defenses of South Carolina and fought in the battles near Richmond, Petersburg, and Appomattox. Confederate Maj. Gen. FITZHUGH LEE epitomized Wise's aggressive determination when he reported that "the disheartening surrounding influences during the retreat to Appomattox had no effect upon Wise . . . his spirit was as unconquerable as four years before."

After the war Wise reopened his law office, never applying for the pardon that would have restored his U.S. citizenship. When he died in Richmond, 12 Sept. 1876, he was considered to be one of the last great Southern individualists.   —KAK

Wise's Forks, N.C., Battle of. 8–10 Mar. 1865   *See* KINSTON, N.C., BATTLE OF.

Withers, Jones Mitchell. CSA b. Madison Cty., Ala., 12 Jan. 1814, Withers graduated 44th in the West Point class of 1835. Brevetted a 2d lieutenant, he resigned his commission 5 Dec. 1835, studied law privately in Alabama, fought as a volunteer officer in the Creek Indian War of 1836, then passed the state bar. An attorney and cotton dealer at the start of the Mexican War, he secured a commission as lieutenant colonel of the 13th U.S. Infantry 3 Mar. 1847 and was promoted colonel of the 9th U.S. Infantry 13 Sept. He resigned his commission 23 May 1848, returned to the cotton business, won a term as a state legislator, and was elected mayor of Mobile, Ala., in 1858,

USMHI

serving until mustering in as colonel of the 3d Alabama in 1861.

Respected in his state, Withers won commission as brigadier general 10 July 1861, assignment to command all state forces 12 Sept., and was charged with the defense of the state's gulf coast 27 Jan. 1862. Withers maintained headquarters at Mobile, assumed command of the 2d Division/II Corps for the Battle of SHILOH, and so distinguished himself there that he won promotion to major general to date from 6 Apr. 1862. He next served with Gen. BRAXTON BRAGG in the autumn 1862 KENTUCKY CAMPAIGN, and, leading the 2d Division of Lt. Gen. LEONIDAS POLK's corps, was heavily engaged in the Battle of STONE'S RIVER. Losing 26% of his command in the first day of fighting there, when the Federal force resisted further attacks he wrote

a memorandum with Maj. Gen. BENJAMIN F. CHEATHAM requesting Bragg to call retreat. Endorsed by Polk, the memorandum fired controversy within the army. Withers maintained that he meant no personal disrespect to Bragg, and the issue was dropped.

While he was serving in TULLAHOMA operations, Withers' health began to fail. On 13 Aug. 1863, Maj. Gen. THOMAS C. HINDMAN took charge of his division. Withers went on recuperative leave, then assumed command of the District of North Alabama 6 Feb. 1864. On 27 July 1864, Sec. of War JAMES A. SEDDON appointed him commander of Alabama state reserve forces, charged with organizing for state defense boys and men under and over draft age. He maintained this office until the end of the war.

Withers returned to the cotton business after the war, won election as mayor of Mobile in 1867 and as Mobile city treasurer in 1878, and for a time edited the Mobile *Tribune*. In the 1880s he worked in Washington, D.C., as a claims agent, dying in Mobile 13 Mar. 1890.   —JES

Wittemyer, Annie Turner. nurse b. Sandy Springs, Ohio, 26 Aug. 1828, Turner received her education at a private seminary for girls in Ohio, marrying William Wittemyer shortly after graduating. In 1850 the couple and their 3 children moved to Keokuk, Iowa. By the time civil war began, her husband had died, leaving Wittemyer in comfortable circumstances. She organized a local soldiers' aid society and quickly became prominent coordinating relief efforts throughout the state. In Apr. 1862 she traveled to Savannah, Tenn., to nurse wounded from the battle at SHILOH, and that September was appointed state sanitary agent by the Iowa legislature, in recognition of her capable service. Until resigning the position 13 Jan. 1864, she was responsible for distributing goods and money raised for the benefit of sick and wounded Western troops. During this time she also worked as an agent for the U.S. CHRISTIAN COMMISSION.

Wittemyer was particularly active in the Federal hospitals at Vicksburg, and 5 July 1863, the day after the city was surrendered, she distributed a large store of supplies to Confederate hospitals for the relief of those wounded during the siege. In all, she dispensed goods and cash estimated at between $116,-000 and $136,000. During the latter months of war, she traveled east to nurse in the overcrowded Federal hospitals in Virginia. She is best known for developing a special hospital diet and a system for managing hospital kitchens.

After the war Wittemyer was prominent in the Anti-Saloon League and president of the Women's Christian Temperance Union 1874–79. In 1889 she established the Women's Relief Corps of the GRAND ARMY OF THE REPUBLIC, helped found the Kentucky Soldiers' Home, and is generally credited with securing the passage in 1892 of an act providing pensions for former army nurses. Among the first beneficiaries of the legislation was Wittemyer, to whom Congress awarded a monthly pension of $50.

Wittemyer published her memoirs in 1895 under the title *Under the Guns*. A balanced, objective account of her experience, it is one of the best books written by a Northern nurse. d. Saratoga, Pa., 2 Feb. 1900.   —PLF

Wofford, William Tatum. CSA b. Habersham Cty., Ga., 28 June 1824. Raised by his widowed mother, Wofford was educated in local schools, then studied law in Athens, opening

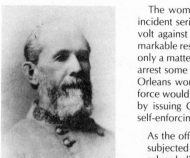

LC

a practice in Cassville. A captain of Georgia mounted volunteers during the Mexican War, he later farmed a large plantation, served in the Georgia legislature, edited the Cassville *Standard,* was a delegate to Southern commercial conventions, and as a member of the Georgia secession convention of 1861 assumed a Unionist stance.

When his state seceded, Wofford reluctantly, then wholeheartedly, followed it. Promoted colonel of infantry, he commanded the 18th Georgia in North Carolina and on the Virginia peninsula. Quickly selected for higher command, he guided HOOD'S TEXAS BRIGADE at SECOND BULL RUN, SOUTH MOUNTAIN, and ANTIETAM, being lauded for "gallant conduct" and "conspicuous bravery." His was a temporary command, and Wofford did not receive a brigade of his own till he replaced Brig. Gen. THOMAS R. R. COBB, killed at FREDERICKSBURG, in charge of 5 Georgia infantry units. On 17 Jan. 1863, Wofford himself became a brigadier general.

On 4 May he led his new command on the Confederate eastern flank at SALEM CHURCH, during the Battle of CHANCELLORSVILLE. 2 months later he was conspicuous at GETTYSBURG, driving Federals from the PEACH ORCHARD 2 July and fighting tenaciously in the WHEATFIELD on the 3d. On 7 July, during the Southern retreat from Pennsylvania, he served effectively at Downsville, Md., and again 3 days later near Williamsport. He remained successful on the battlefield in 1864 until falling wounded at the WILDERNESS and SPOTSYLVANIA. In the former battle, he suggested the route by which Lt. Gen. JAMES LONGSTREET's corps overwhelmed the Federal south flank 6 May 1864. On the first day at COLD HARBOR, Wofford's brigade was flanked and forced to give ground, but Wofford rebounded to fight ably at PETERSBURG under Gen. ROBERT E. LEE and at CEDAR CREEK under Lt. Gen. JUBAL A. EARLY.

In Jan. 1865 Wofford was sent to northern Georgia, where he helped feed a starving populace, broke up unauthorized military organizations, and restored civil law to disaffected regions. After being paroled in May, he was active in the law, railroading, and education. Though he refused a congressional seat in 1865 by RADICAL REPUBLICANS, he remained prominent in Georgia politics and was a member of the state constitutional convention of 1877. d. near Cass Station, Ga., 22 May 1884.   —EGL

"Woman's Order" (General Orders No. 28), New Orleans, La. 15 May 1862 One of the major problems confronted by Maj. Gen. BENJAMIN F. BUTLER on his occupation of New Orleans, Apr. 1862, was the abuse his soldiers endured from patriotic Confederate women. Bitterly resentful of the Union occupation, whenever any of Butler's men were present they would contemptuously gather in their skirts, cross streets, flee rooms, cast hateful glances, or make derisive comments. Some sang spirited renditions of "THE BONNIE BLUE FLAG" and other Confederate songs or spat on soldiers' uniforms, teaching their children to do the same. One woman emptied a chamber pot on Capt. DAVID G. FARRAGUT from her window shortly after the mayor surrendered the city to him.

The women hoped their actions would force a retaliatory incident serious enough to incite paroled Confederates to revolt against the occupation troops. Butler's men showed remarkable restraint against the insults, but he realized that it was only a matter of time until one of them, pressed too far, would arrest some female belligerent. Undoubtedly the men of New Orleans would attempt a rescue, and Butler feared his small force would be overcome. He dealt with the problem 15 May by issuing General Orders No. 28, carefully worded to be self-enforcing:

> As the officers and soldiers of the United States have been subjected to repeated insults from the women (calling themselves ladies) of New Orleans, in return for the most scrupulous noninterference and courtesy on our part, it is ordered that hereafter when any female shall, by word, gesture, or movement, insult or show contempt for any officer or soldier of the United States, she shall be regarded and held liable to be treated as a woman of the town plying her avocation.

Except for isolated incidents, the insults stopped abruptly when the women learned they would be treated as common whores for demeaning a man wearing a U.S. army uniform. A few who persisted were arrested and imprisoned on Ship Island, notably Mrs. Philip Philips, who was confined from 30 June until mid-September for laughing when the funeral procession of a Federal officer was passing her house.

Butler's "Woman's Order" provoked criticism throughout the Confederacy and in Europe from people who considered his proclamation an unpardonable affront to womanhood. In defense of the order he emphasized the restraint his soldiers had shown civilians in New Orleans, and many observers confirmed the generally respectful treatment accorded Confederates. Nevertheless, the infamous order excited indignation and personal animosity toward Butler. Many felt his nickname, "Beast" Butler, was deserved.   —PLF

Wood, John Taylor. CSN b. Fort Snelling, Iowa Territory, 13 Aug. 1830(?), Wood was the son of army surgeon Robert Crooke Wood, Sr. Choosing a naval career, the young officer graduated from the Annapolis Naval Academy 10 June 1853 and went to sea aboard the *Cumberland.* An instructor of gunnery tactics at the Academy in 1861, with strong family ties to the South (his mother was a Louisianan and a daughter of Zachary Taylor; his aunt had married JEFFERSON DAVIS), he resigned his commission 21 Apr. after Federal troops occupied Maryland. The Navy Department refused the resignation and dismissed him from the service. Fleeing in September to Richmond with his wife and daughter, he entered Confederate service and became one of the staunchest advocates of Southern independence.

His close relationship with Davis added weight to his professional achievement, and Wood emerged as one of the most influential men in the capital. Given rank as 2d lieutenant and sea duty aboard the CSS *VIRGINIA,* he fought in the first duel between IRONCLADS 8–9 Mar. 1862 (*see* HAMPTON ROADS, VA., BATTLE OF). After the *Virginia* was destroyed to prevent its capture, Wood led the crew to victory manning heavy gun emplacements at DREWRY'S BLUFF 15 May, thwarting Maj. Gen. GEORGE B. MCCLELLAN's best chance to take Richmond during the PENINSULA CAMPAIGN. Largely for his success at Drewry's Bluff, Davis promoted Wood to 1st lieutenant 29 Sept.

Believing naval successes could boost sagging public morale and induce Congress to vote more money for shipbuilding, in mid-1862 the resourceful Wood approached Sec. of the Navy STEPHEN R. MALLORY with a plan to strike Federal craft in a series of midnight naval raids. The attacks, dependent on surprise and speed, were carried out by a crew of 15 to 20 handpicked men in specially built shallow-draft boats light enough to be hauled overland in wagons and launched in small streams and inlets. The first raid against the transport schooner *Frances Elmore*, 7 Oct., marked the beginning of Wood's reputation as a coastal raider to be feared.

On 26 Jan. 1863, Davis appointed Wood his aide with rank as colonel of cavalry, making the officer liaison between the army and navy and one of the few men to hold dual rank in the Confederacy. His inspection tour of Southern ports and vessels that spring resulted in strengthened coastal and river defenses and in the establishment of a Provisional Navy as a means of promoting talented younger officers over veterans of the old navy reluctant to adapt to advances in naval warfare.

Back at sea in July, he raided into Chesapeake Bay, and Feb. 1864 received the THANKS OF CONGRESS (CONFEDERATE) for his capture the previous fall of the *Underwriter*, the largest Federal gunboat at New Berne, N.C. That July he put to sea aboard the *TALLAHASSEE*, a twin-screw-propeller converted BLOCKADE RUNNER and the fastest steamer afloat. Eluding Federal pursuers, in less than 3 weeks Wood terrorized the coast from New York to Maine, capturing or destroying 31 coastal and fishing craft. He was promoted to captain 10 Feb. 1865.

Wood was with Davis at St. Paul's Episcopal Church when the president learned of Gen. ROBERT E. LEE's retreat from PETERSBURG and accompanied Davis on his flight from Richmond. Captured with the presidential party near Irwinville, Ga., 10 May, he managed to escape by bribing a guard. Making his way to Madison, Fla., a refugee town for Confederates, he met Sec. of War JOHN C. BRECKINRIDGE. They and 4 other men traveled a perilous route to Fort Butler on the St. John's River, sailing from there 26 May in a captured lifeboat. They arrived at Cardenas Bay, Cuba, 11 June, having survived near-starvation, an encounter with pirates, and a violent storm in which Wood nearly lost his life.

Learning that Federal authorities had issued a warrant for his arrest, Wood arranged to meet his family in Canada, where they settled in the expatriate community in Halifax, Nova Scotia. There he established a profitable merchant commission house with former blockade runner John Wilkenson, remaining a devoted Confederate until his death in Halifax 19 July 1904.
—PLF

Wood, Sterling Alexander Martin. CSA b. Florence, Ala., 17 Mar. 1823, Wood received a Jesuit education, graduating from St. Joseph's College, Bardstown, Ky., in 1841. After reading law, he worked as an attorney in Murfreesboro, Tenn., established a practice in Florence, received appointment as solicitor for the 4th circuit court of Alabama in 1851, won a seat in the state legislature in 1857, and assumed the editorship of the Florence *Gazette* in 1860.

Wood joined the Florence Guards company as captain, then entered the 7th Alabama Infantry as colonel 18 May 1861. Posted to Gen. BRAXTON BRAGG's force at Pensacola, in August he expressed displeasure with his assignment, briefly led a punitive expedition against Tennessee loyalists in the Chattanooga area in November, returned to Florida, and received

a brigadier general's appointment 7 Jan. 1862. He joined Gen. ALBERT SIDNEY JOHNSTON's Kentucky force Feb. 1862, and, assigned command of the 3d Brigade/III Corps under Maj. Gen. WILLIAM J. HARDEE, endured severe combat on both days of the Battle of SHILOH.

That autumn, commanding the 4th Brigade, Maj. Gen. SIMON B. BUCKNER's division, he served at Munfordville and was wounded in the Battle of PERRYVILLE. Next commanding his 4th

LC

Brigade in Maj. Gen. PATRICK R. CLEBURNE's 2d Division/Hardee's Corps at the Battle of STONE'S RIVER, Wood won praise from superiors when, on the first day of battle, through an error in disposition and movement, Wood's 1,100 men found themselves briefly unsupported, far in the Confederate advance, and under heavy fire. Escaping annihilation, they were on rear echelon duty later that day.

Wood was next detached from his brigade, placed in command of the District of North Alabama, then rejoined his force 28 Mar. 1863. During the CHICKAMAUGA CAMPAIGN, he shared in the difficulties experienced by other commanders operating under Bragg, but in the Battle of CHICKAMAUGA he performed creditably. For unknown reasons, at CHATTANOOGA he resigned his commission 17 Oct. 1863 and returned to Alabama, taking up residence and a law practice in Tuscaloosa.

In postwar years Wood was an attorney for the Alabama Great Southern Railway, won election to a single term in the state legislature in 1882, and taught law at the University of Alabama 1889–90. d. Tuscaloosa, 26 Jan. 1891. —JES

Wood, Thomas John. USA b. Munfordville, Ky., 25 Sept. 1823. After receiving a rural education, Wood attended West Point, graduating 5th of 41 in the class of 1845. He served in the Mexican War and was later transferred to the cavalry, where he saw much action on the frontier.

At the beginning of the war, Wood spent time on recruitment duty in Indiana. On 11 Oct. 1861, he received a commission as brigadier general of volunteers. He first saw action at SHILOH, Tenn., leading the 6th Division in Maj. Gen. DON CARLOS BUELL's Army of the Ohio, then fought at the Battle of PERRYVILLE Oct. 1862 and was wounded 2 months later during the Battle of STONE'S RIVER, 31 Dec.

USMHI

On 19 Sept. 1863, Maj. Gen. WILLIAM S. ROSECRANS and Gen. BRAXTON BRAGG's ARMY OF TENNESSEE clashed along Chickamauga Creek, Tenn. Wood's division was stationed in the Union center. The next morning, Rosecrans received a false report that a gap existed between Wood and Maj. Gen. JOSEPH J. REYNOLDS' 4th Division. In fact, Brig. Gen. JOHN M. BRANNAN's 3d Division was positioned there, though it was somewhat concealed. Ordered by Rosecrans to close up "as fast as possible" on Reynolds, Wood protested, then dutifully moved his 2 brigades. A very real gap now existed in the Federal line. Quick to exploit the situation, Confederate Lt. Gen. JAMES LONGSTREET's 5 divisions sliced through the Federal center and came very close to destroying Rosecrans' army.

Later that month Wood and the ARMY OF THE CUMBERLAND were besieged in Chattanooga, Tenn., and on 25 Nov. his division participated in the successful assault on MISSIONARY RIDGE. After the CHATTANOOGA CAMPAIGN, Wood took part in Maj. Gen. WILLIAM T. SHERMAN's drive on ATLANTA, and was wounded during the Federal repulse at LOVEJOY'S STATION 2 Sept. 1864.

In December, Wood was placed in command of the IV Corps and sent to Nashville, Tenn., where he participated in the destruction of Gen. JOHN B. HOOD's Army of Tennessee (*see* FRANKLIN AND NASHVILLE CAMPAIGN). Wood was promoted to major general, Regular Army, 13 Mar. 1865, for his outstanding combat record. After the war he served in Reconstruction Mississippi, retiring from the army in 1868, due in part to his wounds. Wood died in Dayton, Ohio, 25 Feb. 1906 and was buried at West Point.   —MTC

Woods, Charles Robert.   USA b. Newark, Ohio, 19 Feb. 1827. Educated at home, Woods won appointment to West Point, graduated 20th in the class of 1852, and received a brevet to 2d lieutenant of infantry. He served in New York, Texas, Virginia, and Washington Territory through 1860.

Woods saw active service from the start of the Civil War until its conclusion. On recruiting duty in the East during the FORT SUMTER crisis, he received promotion to captain of Regulars 1 Apr. 1861 and command of troops on the failed *STAR OF THE WEST* expedition. As quartermaster with Brig. Gen. ROBERT PATTERSON, he marched in that officer's failed June and July

LC

Shenandoah Valley campaigning, went on recruiting duty in St. Louis, Mo., and won a volunteer commission as colonel of the 76th Ohio Infantry 13 Oct. 1861. With the 76th he campaigned in western Virginia through November, and fought at FORT DONELSON Feb. 1862 and at SHILOH 7 Apr. in the 3d Brigade of Brig. Gen. LEWIS WALLACE's 3d Division.

He next saw action at CHICKASAW BLUFFS and ARKANSAS POST, won command of the 2d Brigade/1st Division/XV Corps 22 May 1863 for the Siege of Vicksburg (*see* VICKSBURG CAMPAIGN, SECOND), then received promotion to brigadier general 4 Aug. 1863. Assuming command of the 1st Brigade/1st Division/XV Corps 13 Sept., he campaigned to CHATTANOOGA, won commendation for action there in November, briefly led the 1st Division Jan.–Feb. and July 1864, commanded the 3d Division/XVII Corps Aug.–Sept. 1864, then returned to command of the 1st Division/XV Corps.

From Chattanooga to the Battle of BENTONVILLE to the GRAND REVIEW in Washington, Woods served in every operation of the ARMY OF THE TENNESSEE and commanded the Union force in the only notable combat during the MARCH TO THE SEA, a fight at

Griswoldville, Ga., 22 Nov. 1864. Brevetted major general of volunteers to date from the Griswoldville engagement, he was brevetted brigadier and major general U.S.A. 13 Mar. 1865.

On occupation duty in the South, Woods mustered out of volunteer service July 1866 and won promotion to lieutenant colonel of Regulars commanding the 33d Infantry. He served on garrison duty until being retired in poor health in 1874 as colonel of the 2d Infantry. He returned to Newark, Ohio, and died on his nearby farm 26 Feb. 1885.   —JES

Wool, John Ellis.   USA b. Newburgh, N.Y., 29 Feb. 1784. Orphaned at age 4 on the upstate New York frontier, Wool received little formal education and few opportunities for advancement until the War of 1812 gave him the chance to distinguish himself as a soldier. He ended the war as lieutenant colonel of the 6th Infantry, and with the post of inspector general of the army. He retained that position until 1841, when he finally won promotion to brigadier general. He saw further action in the Mexican War, where he again distinguished himself as an administrator, and won a major general's brevet for his role at the Battle of Buena Vista. Afterward, he was as-

USMHI

signed to command the Eastern Military Division, 1848–53; the Department of the Pacific, 1854–57; and the Department of the East, 1857–61.

In 1861, Wool was the army's senior brigadier, and had every reason to expect that command of the Union forces would devolve upon him when the army's senior officer, Lt. Gen. WINFIELD SCOTT, retired. Instead, Wool was given command of the DEPARTMENT OF VIRGINIA, while GEORGE B. MCCLELLAN was promoted to major general over Wool's head and given overall command of the Union forces. However, Wool successfully prevented the Confederate capture of FORT MONROE, and by announcing that he would take no orders from McClellan, he managed to have the fort exempted from McClellan's jurisdiction. Wool seized this as an opportunity for advancement, and May 1862 directed his own independent occupation of Norfolk, Va. Although the operation resulted in Wool's promotion to full major general, McClellan demanded submission of Wool's department to his command to ensure the success of the PENINSULA CAMPAIGN. Lincoln conceded and removed Wool to command of the MIDDLE DEPARTMENT 1 June 1862.

In July 1862 Wool was given command of the VIII Corps, but was returned to departmental duties Jan. 1863 as commander of the Department of the East. In July 1863, he retired to Troy, N.Y., where he died 10 Nov. 1869.   —ACG

Worden, John Lorimer.   USN b. Westchester Cty., N.Y., 12 Mar. 1818, Worden began his naval career as a midshipman at age 15. Just before the outbreak of war, he served at sea, then in 1861 was sent on a secret mission to the USS *Sabine,* stationed off FORT PICKENS, Fla. After delivering a message to the squadron at Pensacola that called for the increased protection of the fort, he was arrested by the Confederates and imprisoned at Montgomery, Ala., for 7 months before being released.

LC

On 6 Mar. 1862, Worden headed for Hampton Roads in command of the *MONITOR*, an experimental IRONCLAD designed to protect the Northern seacoast BLOCKADE. He steamed into Hampton Roads 2 days later, after the CSS *VIRGINIA* had demolished the wooden frigates *Cumberland* and *Congress.* On the morning of 9 Mar. the famed Battle of HAMPTON ROADS ended. For 3 hours the ships exchanged shells. Worden, wounded and partially blinded, was forced to consign his command to his lieutenant, SAMUEL D. GREENE. After returning from a temporary withdrawal, Worden found that the disabled *Virginia* had retreated from the fight. The duel was considered a draw, but the Federal blockade was intact. Subsequently, Worden was given a vote of thanks by Congress (*see* THANKS OF CONGRESS, UNITED STATES) for his determined service and was eventually promoted to the rank of captain.

Early in 1863 he commanded the steam frigate *Montauk,* an ironclad, in the SOUTH ATLANTIC BLOCKADING SQUADRON in operations against Georgia's FORT MCALLISTER. On 28 Feb. his vessel destroyed the CSS *Nashville* and later that year was engaged in actions against Charleston (*see* CHARLESTON, S.C., DU PONT'S ATTACK ON).

Following the war, Worden served as superintendent of the Naval Academy at Annapolis 1869–74 and was promoted to rear admiral before his death in the District of Columbia, 18 Oct. 1897.   —KAK

Wright, Ambrose Ransom. CSA b. Louisville, Ga., 26 Apr. 1826. A lawyer by profession, Wright actively engaged in antebellum Georgia politics. A brother-in-law of Herschel V. Johnson, who was governor of Georgia and, later, a Confederate senator from the state, he was an unsuccessful Democratic candidate for the legislature and for Congress. When Georgia seceded, he served as a member of the commission that endeavored to persuade Maryland to embrace the Confederate cause.

LC

Wright received a commission as colonel of the 3d Georgia 18 May 1861, serving in North Carolina and Georgia until late spring 1862. On 3 June "Rans" Wright, as he was familiarly called, was promoted to brigadier general, transferred to the ARMY OF NORTHERN VIRGINIA, and assigned a brigade in Maj. Gen. BENJAMIN F. HUGER'S division. He led his brigade with distinction during the SEVEN DAYS' CAMPAIGN, his unit suffering heavy casualties at MALVERN HILL.

Wright then fought at SECOND BULL RUN, ANTIETAM (where he was wounded), FREDERICKSBURG, and CHANCELLORSVILLE. At

GETTYSBURG, 2 July 1863, his brigade of Georgians stormed across the valley between the 2 armies and made a temporary lodgment on CEMETERY RIDGE in the center of the Union line. The brigadier continued with the army until fall 1864, participating in the bloody engagements of the WILDERNESS, SPOTSYLVANIA, COLD HARBOR, and PETERSBURG. On 26 Nov. he was promoted to major general and assigned to Georgia, where he held command until the conclusion of hostilities.

After the war, Wright resumed his legal practice, and in 1866 acquired the Augusta *Chronicle and Sentinel.* An unsuccessful candidate for the 1871 Democratic nomination for the U.S. Senate, he was elected to the House of Representatives the next year. He died in Augusta, 21 Dec. 1872, before he could take his seat.   —JDW

Wright, George. USA b. Norwich, Vt., 21 Oct. 1803. Educated at the institution that became NORWICH UNIVERSITY, Wright entered West Point in 1818. 4 years later he graduated 24th in his 40-man class and became a subaltern in the 3d U.S. Infantry. After serving on the Canadian border and against the Seminoles in Florida, he entered the Mexican War as a captain in the 8th Infantry and won brevets for gallantry at Contreras, Churubusco, and Molino del Rey.

LC

In Mar. 1855 he became colonel of the 9th Infantry, stationed on the Pacific Coast, where he spent the remainder of his active career. Until 1857 Wright commanded the northern district of the DEPARTMENT OF THE PACIFIC, fighting Indian tribes such as the Spokanes, against whom he led a punitive expedition in the WASHINGTON TERRITORY.

In July 1860 the government honored his many abilities and long service by appointing him to command the DEPARTMENT OF OREGON, and Oct. 1861 the Department of the Pacific, headquartered in San Francisco. To qualify for the latter command, he was named a brigadier general of volunteers 28 Sept. 1861. Though California was far from the seat of war, and many of its troops had been sent to fight in the East, Wright was kept quite busy. As he informed the War Department early in 1862: "In this state we have peace but I cannot say that we are very quiet." For the next two and a half years he resisted Confederate incursions; built forts up and down the coast, drawing on a government appropriation of $300,000; and kept the French in upper Mexico from aiding the enemy. He also made treaties with numerous Indian nations and removed 1 tribe to reservation land on Santa Catalina Island. He protected settlers, the telegraph, and the Overland Mail, and supervised numerous expeditions, including that of Col. JAMES H. CARLETON, which reasserted Union authority in Arizona and NEW MEXICO TERRITORY in mid-1862.

Relieved from duty with the Army of the Pacific 1 July 1864, Wright remained in California as head of the department encompassing that state. The following summer he was assigned to command the newly formed Department of the Columbia, which embraced Oregon, Washington, and Idaho. En route to his new post, he died when the steamer *Brother Jonathan* struck a rock and went down off Crescent City, Calif., 30 July 1865. —EGL

Wright, Horatio Gouverneur. USA b. Clinton, Conn., 6 Mar. 1820, Wright graduated from West Point in 1841, ranking 2d in his class. Assigned to the Corps of Engineers, he assisted in the construction of fortifications and harbors and in teaching French and engineering at the Military Academy. A captain since 1855, he acted Apr. 1861 as chief engineer of the Federal expedition to destroy the Norfolk Navy Yard before it fell into Confederate hands. Captured in the abortive affair, he was soon released and served as chief engineer of Brig. Gen. SAMUEL P. HEINTZELMAN's division at FIRST BULL RUN. On 6 Aug. he was promoted to major and 16 Sept. was jumped to brigadier general.

USMHI

Wright then commanded a brigade in the Union operation against PORT ROYAL, S.C. In Apr. 1862 he assumed command of a division, which he led in the disastrous Union defeat at SECESSIONVILLE, S.C. The War Department then assigned him to command the DEPARTMENT OF THE OHIO, with headquarters at Cincinnati. He was promoted to major general, to rank from 18 July 1862, but, Mar. 1863, the Senate revoked the appointment. Wright held his departmental post until May 1863, when he assumed command of a division in Maj. Gen. JOHN SEDGWICK's VI Corps.

He led his new command at GETTYSBURG, RAPPAHANNOCK STATION, MINE RUN, and the WILDERNESS, and when Sedgwick died from a Confederate sharpshooter's bullet 9 May 1864, he replaced the popular corps commander and was promoted to major general, to rank from the 12th. He directed the VI Corps at COLD HARBOR and during the early phases of the PETERSBURG CAMPAIGN. In July the corps moved to the SHENANDOAH VALLEY, where it opposed Lt. Gen. JUBAL A. EARLY's Confederates. Wright conducted the pursuit after the Southerners abandoned their raid against Washington, D.C., and acted with deliberate caution. His corps then fought in Maj. Gen. PHILIP H. SHERIDAN's campaign against Early in the valley. On 19 Oct. 1864, at CEDAR CREEK, Early surprised the Federals, commanded by Wright in Sheridan's absence. Slightly wounded, Wright regrouped the broken troops, but it was Sheridan, just returned, who rallied them to victory. Wright and the corps subsequently went back to Petersburg and fought well until the war's end.

Reverting to the regular rank of lieutenant colonel, Wright commanded the DEPARTMENT OF TEXAS for a year. Returning to engineer duty, he was promoted to colonel in 1879 and that year was commissioned brigadier general and named chief engineer. He directed many projects, including the completion of the Washington Monument. He retired in 1884 on his 64th birthday, living in the nation's capital until his death there 2 July 1899. —JDW

Wright, Marcus Joseph. CSA b. Purdy, Tenn., 5 June 1831. Educated at a local academy, Wright studied law and settled in Memphis, serving as a clerk of the common-law and chancery court. Active for a number of years in the state militia, he was lieutenant colonel of the 154th Tennessee when the Civil War began. Renamed the 154th Senior Tennessee Infantry, the militia unit entered Confederate service, with Wright accepting a commission as lieutenant colonel.

LC

Acting as military governor of Columbus, Ky., until its evacuation by the Confederates, he then led the 154th at the Battle of BELMONT, Mo., 7 Nov. 1861, and fell wounded at SHILOH Apr. 1862. During the Southern invasion of Kentucky in September and October, he served on the staff of Maj. Gen. BENJAMIN F. CHEATHAM. Promoted to brigadier general 20 Dec. 1862, to rank from the 13th, Wright returned to line command with a brigade of Tennessee veterans, directing his soldiers in the CHICKAMAUGA and CHATTANOOGA campaigns in autumn 1863. During 1864 and 1865 he commanded successively the District of Atlanta, the garrison at Macon, Ga., and the District of North Mississippi and West Tennessee. He was paroled at Granada, Miss., 19 May 1865.

During the early postwar years, Wright resumed his legal practice in Memphis, then briefly acted as assistant purser of the U.S. Navy Yard until 1878, when the government selected him as agent for the collection of Confederate archives. From this date until his retirement June 1917, he devoted himself to the preservation of records pertaining to the war, and to writing books. He was one of the main compilers of the *WAR OF THE REBELLION OFFICIAL RECORDS OF THE UNION AND CONFEDERATE ARMIES,* the 128-volume work that is the primary source of the history of the conflict. In 1911 he published his valuable, though now outdated, *General Officers of the Confederate Army.* d. District of Columbia, 27 Dec. 1922. —JDW

Wyoming, USS. *See* SHIMONOSEKI, JAPAN, BATTLE OF.

Y

Yancey, William Lowndes. CSP b. "The Aviary," Warren Cty., Ga., 10 Aug. 1814. Yancey's widowed mother married an antislavery minister who settled the family in Troy, N.Y., in 1822. Educated in Northern schools, Yancey moved to Greenville, S.C., without completing his studies at Williams College in Massachusetts. He read law under an old friend of his father and edited the Unionist Greenville *Mountaineer* during the NULLIFICATION crisis. 3 years later he opened a law practice in Dallas Cty., Ala.

Yancey excelled as a public speaker, a talent he used to advantage in his political career. A Democrat elected to the Alabama state legislature in 1841 and again in 1843, he was sent by the party to the U.S. House of Representatives in 1844. 2 years later he resigned before his term expired, when his first debate, in which he demanded protection for slave property in the territories, ended in a duel with future Confederate Gen. THOMAS L. CLINGMAN. The quick-tempered STATES-RIGHTS advocate held no further elective office until voted into the Confederate Senate.

That the Southern states seceded to form an independent nation was to a great extent the result of Yancey's efforts to unite Southerners into a cohesive sectional party powerful enough to block antislavery legislation in Congress. His Alabama Platform, written in 1848, summarized the demands repeated by Southern Democrats, with increasing hostility, through the antebellum years: preservation of states rights, equal rights for all citizens in the territories, and the guarantee of property rights, including chattel slavery. He urged the organization of local Southern-rights associations to run states-rights candidates for political office, carried on an extensive correspondence with other secessionists anxious to promote disunion, and in 1858 formed the League of United Southerners, the most formal of his efforts to encourage SOUTHERN NATIONALISM. His position appealed to states-rights delegates who walked out of the Democratic national convention meeting in Charleston, S.C., in 1860. He led the faction that nominated JOHN C. BRECKINRIDGE, certain that splitting the Democratic vote would ensure the Republican victory necessary to push the South into withdrawing from the Union.

Once the Southern states began seceding in winter 1860–61, Yancey's radicalism had served its purpose. He wrote the Alabama ordinance of secession, but was not chosen to represent his state in the Provisional Confederate Congress meeting in Montgomery Feb. 1861, nor did the more conservative delegates there consider him for the Confederate presidency, as he hoped they might. In deference, JEFFERSON DAVIS appointed him a commissioner to Europe with instructions to secure recognition for the Confederacy, if necessary by threatening to withhold cotton from the world market (*see* COTTON DIPLOMACY). Unsuccessful, he resigned after a year abroad to take his seat in the Confederate Senate, 27 Mar. 1862.

In Congress Yancey became a leader of the opposition, trying to limit Davis' powers whenever they impinged on state sovereignty. But despite his appraisal of the president as a "conceited, wrong-headed, wranglesome, and obstinate" traitor, he urged his colleagues not to allow divisiveness to harm the war effort. He himself supported most of the administration's economic programs and the military draft, so long as it left to the states some control over CONSCRIPTION (*see also* CONGRESS, CONFEDERATE STATES).

Yancey, whose careful planning and persistence had prepared the public to embrace the idea of Southern nationhood, did not live to see the Confederacy defeated. In declining health for several years prior to the war, he died at his home in Montgomery, 27 July 1863. —PLF

Yates, Richard. war governor b. Warsaw, Ky., 18 Jan. 1815. Yates's family moved to Illinois when he was still a teenager. After graduating from Illinois College, he passed the bar in 1837 and entered politics. Elected to the Illinois house of representatives in 1842, Yates served there throughout most of the decade. In Mar. 1851, he won a seat in the U.S. House. Defeated for reelection 3 years later, he attended the 1860 Republican national convention in Chicago and supported ABRAHAM LINCOLN's bid for nomination. In the Illinois governor's race that year, he defeated Democrat James C. Allen.

At the outbreak of hostilities, the governor supported Lincoln's war measures. An excitable man, he viewed with considerable alarm Confederate incursions into Kentucky and Missouri, and stridently and repeatedly wired Washington, D.C., for help. Frequently the governor bypassed the War Department and made his pleas directly to Lincoln, much to the annoyance of other governors.

Antiwar sentiment was a problem during Yates's term. Although Illinois never had to draft men, since bounties drew enough recruits, Copperheads posed a definite threat to the war effort (*see* PEACE DEMOCRATS). The governor also had to contend with a Democratic legislature. To Yates, the Democratic legislature was the result of a Copperhead plot to take Illinois out of the war; consequently, he started to make arbitrary arrests of disloyal citizens. War-weariness and Yates's dictatorial actions led the Illinois house of representatives to pass a resolution demanding a national convention on reconciliation with the South. Alarmed, Yates prorogued the legislature, then ran the state for an entire year without a congress.

By Illinois law, a governor could not succeed himself; thus when Yates's term ended Jan. 1865, he ran for the U.S. Senate. Elected that year, he served until Mar. 1871 and, due to failing health, did not seek another term. Appointed a Federal commissioner of railroads, he died 27 Nov. 1873 while in St. Louis, Mo. He was buried in Jacksonville, Ill. —MTC

Yazoo Pass Expedition, Miss. Feb.–Mar. 1863 Following the unsuccessful FIRST VICKSBURG CAMPAIGN and the battle at CHICKASAW BLUFFS, Maj. Gen. U. S. GRANT encouraged more waterborne offensives. In June 1862 Federals from Baton Rouge, La., had traveled up the Mississippi River and begun doomed efforts to dig a canal through the Swampy Toe peninsula opposite Vicksburg. Had the canal been completed, Union war vessels could have used this route to stay out of the range of Vicksburg's cannon. On 22 Jan. 1863, Grant set troops of Maj. Gen. JOHN A. MCCLERNAND's command to work on a renewal of this project. A second canal was begun shortly thereafter by Maj. Gen. WILLIAM T. SHERMAN's men at Duckport, northwest of Vicksburg on the Mississippi's west bank, its objective roughly the same as the first. This canal would link inland bayous and bring Union boats from Duckport to a point 20 mi south of Vicksburg. Simultaneously with these projects, Maj. Gen. JAMES B. MCPHERSON led probes south from Lake Providence and Bayou Macon, La., looking for a bayou-and-lake route to Vicksburg's southern approaches. All these projects were to end late in March, prior to the SECOND VICKSBURG CAMPAIGN.

The Yazoo Pass Expedition was also conceived in January. Lt. Col. of Engineers JAMES H. WILSON received orders 29 Jan. 1863 to bring men and equipment from Helena, Ark., and open a levee sealing the Yazoo Pass, a natural inland water route connecting the Mississippi River and, moving east and south, Moon Lake and the Coldwater River. This passage would allow vessels to move from the Coldwater to the Tallahatchie and Yazoo rivers and permit the lengthy but safe passage of troops and gunboats to Vicksburg's northern approaches. Crossing from the Arkansas banks, on 2–3 Feb. Wilson had workmen cut into the levee, then blast a hole through. The natural flow of water enlarged the hole and allowed vessels to enter the pass by 7 Mar. Aware of the probability of this maneuver, Confederate Lt. Gen. JOHN C. PEMBERTON had ordered the pass blocked with obstructions before Wilson's project began. Subsequently, Wilson spent 8–10 Mar. clearing enormous trees and stumps from the waterway.

Following behind were 5,000 Federal troops, under Brig. Gen. Leonard F. Ross, aboard transports, the ironclads *Chillicothe* and *Baron De Kalb,* and several lighter combat vessels. A 22-boat flotilla, by 10 Mar. it had passed all obstructions and traveled south on the Tallahatchie to that river's confluence with the Yalobusha. These were the headwaters of the Yazoo. At this point, the Tallahatchie flowed east, joined the Yalobusha, then reached the Yazoo.

The neck of land between the Tallahatchie on the north and the Yazoo on the south was approximately 400 yd wide. Here Confederates built small Fort Pemberton. Commanded by Maj. Gen. WILLIAM WING LORING and holding fewer than 10 cannon, not all of which could be brought to bear on the flotilla, the fort held off the Federals. Under naval Lt. Cmdr. Watson

Smith, the *Chillicothe* and *Baron De Kalb* exchanged fire with the fort but, Wilson later claimed, would come no closer than 800 yd to it. Swamp, bayou, and positioning did not allow an assault by Ross's troops. Wilson erected a land battery northeast of the fort 12–13 Mar. Until the 20th efforts were made at artillery assault and infantry probes. An encounter 16 Mar. disabled the *Chillicothe.*

After a final failure on the 20th, the flotilla put about and headed for Moon Lake, effectively ending the Yazoo Pass Expedition. Met on the waterway 21 Mar. by Federal reinforcements under Brig. Gen. Isaac F. Quinby, Ross was persuaded to return to Fort Pemberton. 2 more unsuccessful artillery duels were fought 1 and 3 Apr. During this period Rear Adm. DAVID D. PORTER tried a second water route on his STEELE'S BAYOU EXPEDITION. —JES

Yellow Bayou (Bayou De Glaize; Norwood's Plantation; Old Oaks), La., eng. at. 18 May 1864 By the third week of May 1864, Union Maj. Gen. NATHANIEL P. BANKS's RED RIVER CAMPAIGN was nearing its conclusion. Undertaken 2 months earlier, the operation into western Louisiana had resulted in failure. The Federals had clashed with Maj. Gen. RICHARD TAYLOR's Confederates in 2 major engagements, at MANSFIELD, 8 Apr., and on the following day at Pleasant Hill. Though Banks won a tactical victory in the latter battle, he started a retreat toward Alexandria, which he reached on the 25th.

Taylor's Southerners harassed the retiring Federals, and 1–8 May the opponents engaged in a series of actions around Alexandria. The Confederates destroyed 5 Union boats of Rear Adm. DAVID D. PORTER's fleet, which was stranded above Alexandria because of low water in the Red River. Col. JOSEPH BAILEY, an engineer, in a remarkable feat, raised the river level by the ingenious use of wing dams. On 13 May Porter's fleet sailed downstream, and Banks abandoned Alexandria.

The Confederates once again pursued, and from the 14th through the 17th combat flared along the Union rear. By the latter date, the Federals had closed on the 600-yd-wide Atchafalaya River, which could shield Banks once he crossed it. But Taylor's troops had to be delayed until Bailey constructed a bridge. When Banks learned on the morning of 18 May that Taylor had closed on Yellow Bayou, he ordered Maj. Gen. ANDREW J. SMITH's division to stop Taylor's advance.

Smith's 3 brigades, numbering about 5,000, encountered a Southern skirmish line beyond the bayou, and the Federals shoved the Confederates rearward before coming up against Taylor's main line. The Southern commander counterattacked, hammering back the Union division. The Federals rallied and repulsed the Southerners. For the next 2 hours the action seesawed, with ground won, then lost, by each side. Finally, the underbrush caught fire, and both commands disengaged. Smith's men fought well, losing about 350 while inflicting 608 Confederate casualties.

The engagement at Yellow Bayou was the final action of the campaign. While Taylor and Smith fought, Bailey, using steamers, improvised a bridge. By 20 May Banks's army had crossed the river. Disgraced, Banks was soon relieved. Yellow Bayou, like the campaign, amounted to little. —JDW

Yellow Tavern, Va., Battle of. 11 May 1864 Maj. Gen. J.E.B. STUART's weary cavalrymen reached Yellow Tavern after 8 a.m. 11 May 1864. A weatherbeaten, abandoned stagecoach inn, Yellow Tavern lay 6 mi from Richmond on the Brook Turnpike and half a mile below the intersection of the Mountain and Telegraph roads. Heavily outnumbered, Stuart deployed his 2 brigades in a concave line to fire on the Mountain road, where Maj. Gen. PHILIP H. SHERIDAN's powerful command was advancing.

The Federal horsemen arrived before noon, their rear harassed throughout the morning by Stuart's 3d Brigade. Sheridan spent 2 hours deliberately deploying his 7 brigades and reconnoitering Stuart's position. Intent on destroying Stuart, Sheridan attacked with 4 brigades. For 2 hours the combat swirled across the grassy fields, which were dotted with small copses of trees. The Confederates stubbornly resisted in hand-to-hand fighting at critical points. About 4 o'clock Brig. Gen. GEORGE A. CUSTER's brigade charged the Confederate left just north of the tavern. The blue-coated troopers overran an artillery section, then recoiled before a mounted charge by the 1st Virginia, which Stuart had kept in reserve. The Confederate commander rode forward to the fence, encouraging his men, when a Michigan trooper fired a bullet into his chest. The Confederates rallied and restored their beleaguered lines.

Sheridan probed the Southern defenses for another hour, then withdrew down the Brook Turnpike toward Richmond. Stuart's action permitted Confederate authorities to man the capital's works and hasten forward reinforcements. Sheridan entered the outer works before steering eastward. The next day Stuart died peacefully in the capital he had so stoutly defended. The Battle of Yellow Tavern, a minor engagement, cost Lee his greatest cavalry officer.   —JDW

York, Zebulon. CSA b. Avon, Maine, 10 Oct. 1819, York, a Northerner by birth, became one of Louisiana's wealthiest antebellum planters. Educated at a seminary in Maine, he studied at Transylvania University in Kentucky before graduating as a lawyer from the University of Louisiana (now Tulane). He stayed in Louisiana, became a prominent attorney, and acquired a fortune as a planter. By 1861 he and his partner reputedly owned 6 plantations, 1,700 slaves, and paid the highest realty taxes in the state.

At the outbreak of the Civil War, York organized a company of the 14th Louisiana. Elected its major, he went with

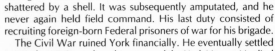
LC

the regiment to Virginia later in the year. In spring and summer 1862, York, now a lieutenant colonel, fought in the PENINSULA and SEVEN DAYS' campaigns, after which he was elected colonel, leading the 14th at SECOND BULL RUN, ANTIETAM, and FREDERICKSBURG. Assigned to recruiting duty in Louisiana early in 1863, he returned to the regiment to command it at the Battle of GETTYSBURG.

Continuing in regimental command during the Battles of the WILDERNESS and SPOTSYLVANIA, he was promoted to brigadier general, to rank from 31 May 1864, and given command of 2 ravaged brigades of Louisiana troops fused into one. He led his veterans during the Confederate raid on Washington, D.C., in July, being engaged at Monocacy, Md. On 19 Sept. 1864,

during the THIRD BATTLE OF WINCHESTER, York had his left arm shattered by a shell. It was subsequently amputated, and he never again held field command. His last duty consisted of recruiting foreign-born Federal prisoners of war for his brigade.

The Civil War ruined York financially. He eventually settled in Natchez, Miss., where he operated the York House. He died in Natchez 5 Aug. 1900.   —JDW

Yorktown, Va., Siege of. 5 Apr.–3 May 1862 Union Maj. Gen. GEORGE B. MCCLELLAN landed his 105,000-man army at FORT MONROE Mar. 1862, intending to conquer the Virginia peninsula immediately. In his path were only 10,000 Confederates, commanded by Maj. Gen. JOHN B. MAGRUDER, occupying a line across the tip of the peninsula between Yorktown and the Warwick River. Magruder moved his men from one point to another to create the impression of a troop strength greater than he had. To enhance the bluff, he even emplaced "QUAKER GUNS," logs painted black to resemble cannon. Yet Magruder was less than confident. "I have made my arrangements to fight with my small force," he wrote his superiors, "but without the slightest hope of success."

On the other side of the line, McClellan was impressed by Magruder's position. Confederate batteries at Gloucester Point on the York River hindered Union naval operations and prevented McClellan from transporting troops upriver beyond Yorktown. The ironclad CSS *VIRGINIA* sealed the James River. Probing the Yorktown line, McClellan's forces were surprised to find the Warwick River a significant stream. And units that struck Magruder's defenses nearer Yorktown later reported their strength.

McClellan therefore decided to undertake siege operations, bring up heavy artillery, and blast the Confederates out of their works. His course was cautious because he believed Magruder's bluff; he wrote that the Confederates had "probably not less than 100,000 men, and possibly more." His caution was also due to his pique at being denied use of Maj. Gen. IRVIN MCDOWELL's oversized corps to support his operations.

The siege lasted throughout April. During that time the Confederates assured themselves that McClellan was the primary threat to RICHMOND and reinforced Magruder with Gen. JOSEPH E. JOHNSTON's army. Then, 3 May, 3 days before McClellan's intended approach to Yorktown, Johnston's troops withdrew up the peninsula seeking more favorable circumstances in which to confront the Federals. The Federals surged forward in pursuit, and the Siege of Yorktown ended.
                                                                         —EMT

Young, John Russell. journalist b. Cty. Tyrone, Ireland, 20 Nov. 1840. Brought to Downingtown, Pa., in infancy, Young was reared there and in Philadelphia until orphaned in 1851. Relocating to an uncle's New Orleans, La., home, he finished his schooling there, returned to Philadelphia in 1856, worked as a proofreader, then joined the Philadelphia *Press* as a copy boy in 1857.

A protégé of John Forney, publisher of the *Press* and the Washington, D.C., *Chronicle,* Young was in the capital at the outset of the FIRST BULL RUN CAMPAIGN. His account of the battle, well-written but inaccurate, was one of the first to be read in the North. Young left the battlefield early, believing the Union victorious, and did not find out about the Federal rout until reaching Alexandria. Hastily rewriting his story, he sent it to Philadelphia in advance of several other accounts. For his speed and industry he was made editor of Forney's *Chronicle.*

Washington authorities arrested Young early in Mar. 1862 for inadvertently publishing troop movements, then released him to cover the PENINSULA CAMPAIGN. He came down with typhoid fever following the May Battle of WILLIAMSBURG, returned to Philadelphia, then assumed editorship of the *Press.* In Mar. and Apr. 1864 he resumed war reportage, covering Maj. Gen. NATHANIEL P. BANKS's RED RIVER CAMPAIGN while serving as the general's volunteer aide. The campaign was not as well reported as other campaigns, but Young's coverage stood out because of its partisanship. He believed Banks's defeat had been overblown and that Federal troops had acquitted themselves well, particularly at the Battle of MANSFIELD. Young left the *Press* early in 1865, and wrote public-relations and advertising material for financier JAY COOKE, promoting the sale of war loan bonds. Meanwhile, he published his own New York newspaper, *The Morning Post.* It failed the same year.

Young's postwar career was lengthy and distinguished. Managing editor of the NEW YORK *TRIBUNE* 1866–69, he published the New York *Standard* 1870–72, covered the Franco-Prussian War, served as a New York *Herald* European correspondent until 1877, accompanied ULYSSES S. GRANT on his world tour, then served as U.S. minister to China 1882–85. He returned to the *Herald,* writing in New York, London, and Paris, briefly retired to Philadelphia in 1890, held a vice-presidency with the Reading Railroad in 1892, and was appointed Librarian of Congress by Pres. WILLIAM MCKINLEY in 1897, the first librarian to preside over the building complex used today. d. District of Columbia, 17 Jan. 1899.   —JES

Young, Pierce Manning Butler. CSA b. Spartanburg, S.C., 15 Nov. 1836. Moving with his family to Cartersville, Ga., in 1839, Young entered Georgia Military Academy at age 15. There he displayed sufficient aptitude to win a West Point appointment. At the Military Academy he manifested courtliness, charm, and a fierce loyalty to his native South. This attitude prompted him to resign his cadetship Mar. 1861, 3 months before graduation.

Named a lieutenant of Georgia militia, Young soon entered the CONFEDERATE REGULAR ARMY. After weeks of staff duty under Brig. Gen. BRAXTON BRAGG at Pensacola, Fla., he went to Richmond, where in

USMHI

July he became adjutant of COBB'S LEGION. He so impressed his superior, Col. THOMAS R. R. COBB, that early in 1862 he became major in the legion's cavalry contingent.

After several bouts of illness, Young entered active campaigning and earned a reputation as one of the young stalwarts of Brig. Gen. WADE HAMPTON's cavalry brigade/Army of Northern Virginia. He was wounded at Burkittsville, Md., Aug. 1862, and took a second wound, in the chest, near Middletown, 13 Sept. Named colonel of the Cobb Legion cavalry 1 Nov. 1862, he won fame the following June when leading the right advance of Hampton's command at Second BRANDY STATION, charging up the northern slope of Fleetwood Heights and dispersing hordes of Union riders. He also fought staunchly

later in the GETTYSBURG CAMPAIGN, notably at Hunterstown, Pa., 2 July 1863.

Again wounded south of the Rappahannock River that August, on his recuperation he was assigned the cavalry brigade most recently led by Brig. Gen. M. CALBRAITH BUTLER. He was named a brigadier general 2 months later, to rank from 28 Sept. On 30 May 1864, he took another chest wound at Ashland, Va., but returned to action in time to join the HAMPTON-ROSSER CATTLE RAID that September. In November, Young went to Georgia to secure remounts and recruits and to help defend Augusta and SAVANNAH against Maj. Gen. WILLIAM T. SHERMAN's legions. He finished out the war as a major general and division leader under Hampton during the CAROLINAS CAMPAIGN.

In later life Young was a planter in Georgia, a 4-term member of the House of Representatives 1868–75, consul-general at St. Petersburg, Russia, 1885–87, and from 1893 until his death in New York City, 6 July 1896, U.S. minister to Guatemala and Honduras.   —EGL

Young, William Hugh. CSA b. Boonville, Mo., 1 Jan. 1838. Moving in his youth to Grayson Cty., Tex., Young attended college in that state as well as in Tennessee and Virginia. During the early months of the Civil War, he studied tactics at the military academy attached to the University of Virginia. In Sept. 1861 he returned to Texas, where he raised a company for Confederate service. His military education brought him a captain's commission in the state's 9th Infantry.

Assigned to the ARMY OF MISSISSIPPI, Young's outfit first saw action at SHILOH. There, as part of Brig. Gen. J. PATTON ANDERSON's brigade of Maj. Gen.

LC

BRAXTON BRAGG's corps, the 9th Texas was mowed down and put to flight by an Illinois artillery battery. After the engagement, Young succeeded to the command of the 9th, which fared much better in subsequent battles. His conspicuous leadership, however, made him an inviting target for Federal sharpshooters. As a result, while his troops acquired an enviable reputation, he collected a variety of wounds. At STONE'S RIVER, 31 Dec. 1862–2 Jan. 1863, the 9th served bravely against strong forces along the Union north flank. In action near the Round Forest, Young had 2 horses killed beneath him and received a minié bullet in the right shoulder. In 1863, during the VICKSBURG CAMPAIGN, the 9th Texas fought under Gen. JOSEPH E. JOHNSTON near Jackson, Miss., where Young was wounded in the right thigh. A few months later, he was shot through the left breast at CHICKAMAUGA, while serving in Bragg's ARMY OF TENNESSEE.

During the ATLANTA CAMPAIGN, Young's Texans formed part of Brig. Gen. MATTHEW D. ECTOR's brigade of Lt. Gen. LEONIDAS POLK's corps. At KENNESAW MOUNTAIN, 27 June 1864, while holding a position on the northern end of the Confederate line, Young took 2 more wounds, in the neck and jaw. Despite his afflictions, he replaced the more severely wounded Ector during the battle and was successful enough to be promoted to brigadier general 15 Aug. 2 months later, Young led his 4 Texas and 2 North Carolina regiments during Gen. JOHN B. HOOD's campaign against communications lines in northwestern Georgia. In the attack on ALLATOONA, 5 Oct., the general again fell, this time with a mangled ankle.

Captured at Allatoona, Young spent 4 months in Federal hospitals and another 5 in the prison camp on JOHNSON'S ISLAND, Ohio. After his release, he became a lawyer and real-estate operator in San Antonio, Tex., dying in that city 28 Nov. 1901. —EGL

Z

Zollicoffer, Felix Kirk. CSA b. Maury Cty., Tenn., 19 May 1812, Zollicoffer worked as a youth on the family plantation and attended Jackson College in Columbia, Tenn., for a year. At age 16 he entered the newspaper trade in Paris, Tenn., and within 2 years was a journeyman printer in Knoxville. In 1834 he became editor of the Columbia *Observer* and helped edit the *Southern Agriculturist* and the Huntsville, Ala., *Mercury*. Named state printer in 1835, he then served as a lieutenant in the Tennessee Volunteers during the Second Seminole War.

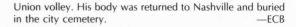

LC

By 1842 he was associate editor of the Nashville *Republican Banner,* a powerful Whig organ. He served as state adjutant general and comptroller 1846–49 and as a state senator 1849–52, but these offices did not reflect the significance of his political power. In 1850 he spearheaded the campaign that elected William B. Campbell governor. In 1852 he helped carry Tennessee for Whig presidential candidate Gen. WINFIELD SCOTT and secured his own election to the U.S. House of Representatives. During the campaign Zollicoffer fought a duel with the editor of the Nashville *Union.* He remained in Congress until 1859, when he declined to seek election to a fourth term. A champion of STATES RIGHTS, he worked in vain for peace in the sectional crisis, campaigned for John Bell for the presidency in 1860, and attended the WASHINGTON PEACE CONFERENCE in 1861.

When Tennessee seceded, Gov. ISHAM G. HARRIS made Zollicoffer a brigadier general of state troops. On 9 July 1861, he accepted a brigadier general's commission in the PROVISIONAL CONFEDERATE ARMY and was ordered to East Tennessee. In November he advanced into Kentucky and crossed the Cumberland River. There his small army was encamped, the river to its rear, when Maj. Gen. GEORGE B. CRITTENDEN, his immediate superior, arrived. With a Union force advancing on the poorly positioned command, on 19 Jan. 1862 the Confederates attacked the Federals at MILL SPRINGS. Extremely nearsighted and riding in the advance, Zollicoffer was killed by a Union volley. His body was returned to Nashville and buried in the city cemetery. —ECB

zouave. In the Crimean and the 1859 Franco-Austrian wars, the French Army Zouaves received notoriety for their bravery and, more so, for their strange, colorful uniforms. Officially organized in 1831 in Algeria and composed of tribesmen from Zouaoua, the zouaves eventually admitted Europeans into their ranks. Somewhat changed from the original, the zouave uniform that became famous throughout the world included white leggings, red baggy pants, a blue sash, a dark blue vest, a·red cape trimmed short, a dark blue jacket, and a blue tasseled red fez that for dress was wrapped with a green turban. However, in the summer and for drill, white trousers replaced the baggy pants.

The fame of the zouaves, a frequent subject of articles and illustrations in American newspapers and magazines, influenced the formation of similar units in the U.S. Probably the first of these American units, the U.S. Zouave Cadets, was organized in Chicago by ELMER E. ELLSWORTH, who also wrote a zouave drill manual. Later, in New York City, Ellsworth formed another zouave unit composed of firemen.

When the Civil War began, many of these American zouave units, which had originally been organized for drill competition, volunteered to fight. Ellworth's Fire Zouaves and (Rush C.) Hawkins' and (George) Duryea's Zouaves, all from New York, joined the Union army, which also included (John M.) Wallace's Zouaves of Indiana and the Salem Zouaves from Massachusetts. Perhaps the most famous zouave unit in the Confederate army was "WHEAT'S TIGERS." The Eufaula Zouaves of Alabama, the Chichester Zouaves of South Carolina, the Richmond Zouaves from Virginia, and the Maryland Guard Zouaves were only a few of the many zouave units in the Confederate army. Each of the American units, which varied in size from a company to a regiment, created its own distinctive uniform.

Contrary to popular belief, American zouave units did not discard their colorful uniforms, which made good targets, for others of less visibility. Continually receiving new recruits, zouave units fought bravely during the occupation of Alexandria in 1861, the Battle of PORT REPUBLIC, and in numerous other engagements throughout the war. —DEF